India

a Lonely Planet travel survival kit

Hugh Finlay
Tony Wheeler
Bryn Thomas
Michelle Coxall

Leanne Logan
Geert Cole
Prakash A Raj

India

6th edition

Published by
Lonely Planet Publications
Head Office: PO Box 617, Hawthorn, Vic 3122, Australia
Branches: 155 Filbert St, Suite 251, Oakland, CA 94607, USA
                10 Barley Mow Passage, Chiswick, London W4 4PH, UK
                71 bis rue du Cardinal Lemoine, 75005 Paris, France

Printed by
Colorcraft Ltd, Hong Kong

Photographs by

Chris Beall	Rob van Driesum	Sally Hone	Avinash Pasricha
Paul Beinssen	Greg Elms	Richard I'Anson	Peter Ryder
Sara-Jane Cleland	Hugh Finlay	Markus Lehtipuu	Bryn Thomas
Michelle Coxall	Greg Herriman	Leanne Logan	Tony Wheeler

Front cover: Pushkar, Rajasthan: holy city and host to one of India's great spectacles, the annual
Camel Fair (Sara-Jane Cleland).

First Published
October 1981

This Edition
January 1996

Although the authors and publisher have tried to make the information as
accurate as possible, they accept no responsibility for any loss, injury or
inconvenience sustained by any person using this book.

National Library of Australia Cataloguing in Publication Data

India.

   6th ed.
   Includes index.
   ISBN 0 86442 321 7.

   1. India – Guidebooks. I. Finlay, Hugh. (Series :
   Lonely Planet travel survival kit).

915.40452

Hugh Finlay

After an unsuccessful foray into academia in Melbourne, Hugh first hit the road in 1976, on a trail which eventually led him to Africa via Asia, Europe and the Middle East in the early '80s.

Since joining Lonely Planet in 1985, Hugh has co-authored with Geoff Crowther the LP travel survival kits to *Kenya*, *East Africa*, and *Morocco, Algeria & Tunisia*. Other LP books he is involved with include *Africa*, *Australia* and *Malaysia, Singapore & Brunei*.

Hugh currently lives in central Victoria with Linda and their two daughters, Ella and Vera, trying to juggle the demands – and pleasures! – of family life, restoring an old farmhouse, writing, raising sheep, gardening, and lengthy phone-calls from Lonely Planet editors!

Tony Wheeler

Tony was born in England but grew up in Pakistan, the Bahamas and the USA. He returned to England to do a degree in engineering at Warwick University, worked as an automotive design engineer, returned to university to complete an MBA in London, then dropped out on the Asian overland trail with his wife Maureen.

They've been travelling, writing and publishing guidebooks ever since, having set up Lonely Planet Publications in the mid-'70s. Travel for the Wheelers is considerably enlivened by their daughter Tashi and their son Kieran.

Bryn Thomas

Born in Zimbabwe, where he grew up on a farm, Bryn contracted an incurable case of wanderlust during camping holidays by the Indian Ocean in Mozambique.

An anthropology degree at Durham University in England earned him a job polishing the leaves of pot plants in London. He has also worked as a ski-lift operator in Colorado, encyclopaedia seller in South Dakota and English teacher in Cairo, Singapore and Tokyo. Travel on four continents has included a 2500-km cycling trip and five visits to India.

Bryn's first guide, the *Trans-Siberian Handbook*, was short-listed for the Thomas Cook Guidebook of the Year awards. He is also the co-author of the LP guide to *Britain*.

Michelle Coxall

Michelle trained as an editor with Lonely Planet before leaving to work in the Tibetan community in Northern India. She's currently living and writing in Greece, but dreams of India, where she plans to return when she has weaned herself off retsina.

Leanne Logan

Bitten by the travel bug before even reaching her teens, Leanne has long been lured by travel. She explored parts of her homeland as a reporter for several newspapers and Australian Associated Press after completing a journalism degree at the Queensland University of Technology. In 1987, she set off through Asia and the Middle East to London. She has been travelling ever since especially in Africa and India.

Geert Cole

When not running his stained-glass studio close to hometown Antwerp, Geert has been found sailing the Pacific, sorting Aussie sheep, and amongst other challenges, trekking through Alaska and diving tropical reefs. With each trip, an extra diary was put on the shelf and another job experience added to life's list.

A special spark of destiny saw Geert linked to companion Leanne, with whom he researched Lonely Planet's travel survival kits to *France* and *New Caledonia* and *Africa on a shoestring*.

Prakash A Raj
Prakash was born in Nepal and studied for two years in Varanasi where he learnt to speak fluent Hindi. He spent five years at university in the USA and a year in the Netherlands. He travelled extensively in Europe and returned to Nepal where he worked on the Kathmandu English-language daily as a journalist and also for the Nepalese government's planning agency. Prakash has also worked for the OECD in Paris, the UN secretariat in New York and is now working for the UNHCR in Asia. Prakash has written several books about Nepal and his life there in both English and Nepali.

From the Authors

Hugh Finlay As always with a project of this size, thanks are due to many people. To Rajendra Kumar in Delhi for all his help and information; to Sanjay Puri and Avnish Puri, also of Delhi; Chewang Sherpa in Darjeeling, for firing up the generator during the many power cuts so I could still run my computer; Sonam Bhutia in Gangtok for helping me penetrate the depths of Sikkimese bureaucracy and get a permit to visit Tsangu Lake; the staff of the various Government of India tourist offices in Bhubaneswar, Khajuraho, Patna and Delhi, who were helpful and resourceful given the limitations of the materials they have at hand; and to Jim & Lucy Amos for their updates to the Getting Around motorcycling section.

Thanks also to Andrea from our UK office and Bryn Thomas for providing info on flights from the UK to India, and checking all the relevant addresses.

Tony Wheeler I would like to once again thank our good friends Ashok and Lalita Khanna.

Bryn Thomas I would like to thank Anna Jacomb-Hood for reading through over 1000 readers' letters and typing out the relevant sections for checking in India. Thanks also to Johnnie and Nicola Loram for their collection of 'Letters Home', which made great reading on the flight out but which would probably put anyone off visiting the sub-continent.

Thanks to the numerous travellers I met along the way, for all their advice and suggestions. In Goa, Jo Highet and Willie Taylor for tips on out-of-the-way spots, John Barker, Catherine Farrell and Kathleen Clark, Maria Rego in Panaji, and Ben the German Biker.

In Rajasthan, thanks to Sheila Williams for her help in Udaipur, Rita Sharma and Rosh Sathananthan, Petri Hottola for information on Bharatpur, and Le Jen Chen for testing out elephant rides at Amber. I'd also like to thank Jatin Sarkar in Delhi, and Vinod Mahendru in Mandi.

In the Andamans, thanks to Syed Iqbal at the Govt of India Tourist Office in Port Blair, Shairal & Billa Jain from Delhi, Sam Cook, Pete Hopkins, Pedro Silvius, Zana Briski; and to diving buddies Sharon Heger, Erik Jensen, and Johnathan Wells.

Michelle Coxall I would like to thank Vyvyan Cayley, Nyalah Asantewa, Ken Brunn, and Helen Lawson-Williams from Australia for their friendship in Dharamsala; Nitin & Surabhi (Bhuj); Shah Mayank and the Malik family (Ahmedabad); and Richard Haycraft (Scotland) for his insights on the Aina Mahal, Bhuj.

Special thanks to Cathryn Collins, Theresa Dooley and my great mate and prolific correspondent, Therese Barnett.

Leanne Logan & Geert Cole We'd like to thank the staff of the following tourist organisations for their enthusiastic support. From the Government of India tourist office, thanks to Mr Arya and Ms Bhalla (Amsterdam), Meenakshi Mehta and Rajan (Bombay), Mr Rao (Bangalore) and Dr Poornima Sastry, Raji Muralidharan and the ever-obliging mine of information Venkatesh (Madras). Thanks also to Mr Premkumar from the Maharashtra Tourism Development Corporation (Bombay), to the staff of both the Andhra Pradesh Travel & Tourist Development Corporation (Hyderabad) and the Karnataka State Tourism Development Corporation (Bangalore) and to Air India.

In Pune, a special thanks to the indefatigable Sheetal Bhutada for her animated tours of the city and for the colourful Lord Ganesh, and to the Bhutada family as a whole for their gracious hospitality (especially at such short notice!).

Also, our appreciation to Ruth Rose at Kotagiri for her warm welcome; to K Suryanarayanam in Madras for resolutely helping to track down the lost luggage; to Kalsang Youdou at Kodaikanal for the invitation to her Tibetan refugee settlement; and the birdwatchers at Topslip. Back in Belgium, thanks again to Hugo de Craen from UFSIA University in Antwerp and, this time, to the two buddies Hamish & Sixy.

This Edition

For this sixth edition of *India*, Hugh Finlay coordinated the whole project. He also updated the introductory chapters, Delhi, Jammu & Kashmir, Uttar Pradesh, Bihar, Calcutta, West Bengal, Orissa, Sikkim, North-East Region and northern and eastern regions of Madhya Pradesh.

Tony Wheeler updated the Kerala chapter and the Mysore and Around Mysore sections of Karnataka.

Bryn Thomas updated the Punjab & Haryana, Himachal Pradesh, Agra and northern Uttar Pradesh, Rajasthan, Goa and the Andaman & Nicobar Islands.

Michelle Coxall updated Gujarat and western and central Madhya Pradesh.

Leanne Logan and Geert Cole covered Bombay, Maharashtra, Karnataka, Andhra Pradesh, Tamil Nadu and Madras.

This Book

When the first edition of this book emerged in 1981 it was the biggest, most complicated and most expensive project we'd tackled at Lonely Planet. It began with an exploratory trip to south India by Tony and Maureen to see what information would be needed. The following year Geoff Crowther, Prakash Raj, Tony and Maureen returned to India and spent a combined total of about a year of more-or-less nonstop travel. The second, third and fourth editions were researched by Tony, Prakash, Geoff and Hugh Finlay. The fifth edition was researched by Hugh, Tony, Geoff and Bryn Thomas.

The first edition exceeded all our hopes and expectations: it instantly became our best-selling guide. In the UK it won the Thomas Cook Guidebook of the Year award and in India it became the most popular guide to the country – a book used even by Indians to explore their own country. It has continued to be one of Lonely Planet's most popular and successful guides.

From the Publisher

This book was coordinated by Sharan Kaur. Miriam Cannell, David Collins, Paul Smitz, Jenny Missen, Kristin Odijk and Diana Saad assisted with the editing and proofing, Sharon Wertheim and Kerrie Williams did the indexing and Christine Niven did some last-minute checking of bits and pieces and wrote some of the captions.

Thanks to Gary Weare for supplying updated information for some of the trekking sections and to Ann Sorrel for updating the India by Bicycle section in the Getting Around chapter.

The colour section was put together by Hugh Finlay and edited by Janet Austin. The design and layout of the colour section was muddled through by Adam McCrow with lots of help and advice from Valerie Tellini, who has now gone 'slide projector' blind.

Adam developed insomnia and acute nicotine addiction while coordinating the mapping of this book. He was assisted, thankfully, by Sandra Smythe, Louise Keppie, Sally Woodward, Chris Lee-Ack and Chris Love. Adam was also responsible for the layout of this book. Adam procrastinated over the illustrations, while Tamsin Wilson, Trudi Canavan and Margaret Jung did a great job helping him out.

Thanks to Simon Bracken and Adam for

designing the cover, and to Dan Levin for adapting the climate charts.

Thanks to Greg Alford and Valerie for wading through and checking the final artwork, and last but not least thanks must also go to Sue Galley for her advice and moral support.

Thanks

All those involved in producing this book greatly appreciate the contributions of those travellers who put so much effort into writing and telling us of their experiences. Your names appear on page 1135.

Warning & Request

Things change – prices go up, schedules change, good places go bad and bad places go bankrupt – nothing stays the same. So if you find things better or worse, recently opened or long since closed, please write and tell us and help make the next edition better.

Your letters will be used to help update future editions and, where possible, important changes will also be included in a Stop Press section in reprints.

We greatly appreciate all information that is sent to us by travellers. Back at Lonely Planet we employ a hard-working readers' letters team to sort through the many letters we receive. The best ones will be rewarded with a free copy of the next edition or another Lonely Planet guide if you prefer. We give away lots of books, but, unfortunately, not every letter/postcard receives one.

Contents

Map Legend

BOUNDARIES

.... International Boundary
.... Disputed Boundary
.... Regional Boundary

ROUTES

.... Freeway
.... Highway
.... Major Road
.... Unsealed Road or Track
.... City Road
.... City Street
.... Railway
.... Underground Railway
.... Walking Track
.... Walking Tour
.... Ferry Route
.... Cable Car or Chairlift

AREA FEATURES

.... Park, Gardens
.... National Park
.... Built-Up Area
.... Pedestrian Mall
.... Market
.... Cemetery
.... Reef
.... Beach or Desert
.... Glacier

HYDROGRAPHIC FEATURES

.... Coastline
.... River, Creek
.... Intermittent River or Creek
.... Lake, Intermittent Lake
.... Canal
.... Swamp

SYMBOLS

✪ CAPITAL		National Capital
◉ Capital		Regional Capital
🏙 CITY		Major City
● City		City
● Town		Town
● Village		Village
■		Place to Stay
▼		Place to Eat
♒		Pub, Bar
✉	☎	Post Office, Telephone
❶	❸	Tourist Information, Bank
⊖	℗	Transport, Parking
🏛	☗	Museum, Youth Hostel
⌂	▲	Caravan Park, Camping Ground
✝	✚	Church, Cathedral
☾	✡	Mosque, Synagogue
☸	卍	Buddhist Temple, Hindu Temple

☯	⌾	Sikh Temple, Temple (Other)
✛	★	Hospital, Police Station
✈	✝	Airport, Airfield
✿	⚐	Gardens, Golf Course
✤	🐾	Shopping Centre, Zoo
←	A25	One Way Street, Route Number
	∴	Archaeological Site or Ruins
🏛	⚱	Palace, Monument
🏯	▣	Castle, Tomb
⌒	⌂	Cave, Hut or Chalet
▲	☀	Mountain or Hill, Lookout
🗼	⚓	Lighthouse, Shipwreck
)(	◎	Pass, Spring
		Ancient or City Wall
		Rapids, Waterfalls
		Cliff or Escarpment, Tunnel
		Railway Station

Note: not all symbols displayed above appear in this book

Introduction

India, it is often said, is not a country but a continent. From north to south and east to west, the people are different, the languages are different, the customs are different, the country is different.

There are few countries on earth with the enormous variety that India has to offer. It's a place that somehow gets into your blood. Love it or hate it you can never ignore India.

It's not an easy country to handle, and more than a few visitors are only too happy to finally get on an aircraft and fly away. Yet a year later they'll be hankering to get back.

It all comes back to that amazing variety – India is as vast as it is crowded, as luxurious as it is squalid. The plains are as flat and featureless as the Himalaya are high and spectacular, the food as terrible as it can be

India

0   300   600 km

The external boundaries of India on this map have not been authenticated and may not be correct.

magnificent, the transport as exhilarating as it can be boring and uncomfortable. Nothing is ever quite the way you expect it to be.

India is far from the easiest country in the world to travel around. It can be hard going, the poverty will get you down, Indian bureaucracy would try the patience of even a Hindu saint, and the most experienced travellers find themselves at the end of their tempers at some point in India. Yet it's all worth it.

Very briefly, India is a triangle with the top formed by the mighty Himalayan mountain chain. Here you will find the intriguing Tibetan region of Ladakh and the astonishingly beautiful Himalayan areas of Kashmir, Himachal Pradesh, the Garhwal of Uttar Pradesh and the Darjeeling and Sikkim regions. South of this is the flat Ganges basin with the colourful and comparatively affluent Punjab to the north-west, the capital city Delhi and important tourist attractions like Agra (with the Taj Mahal), Khajuraho, Varanasi and the holy Ganges. This plain reaches the sea at the northern end of the Bay of Bengal where you find teeming Calcutta, a city which seems to sum up all of India's enormous problems.

South of this northern plain the Deccan plateau rises. Here you will find cities that mirror the rise and fall of the Hindu and Muslim kingdoms, and the modern metropolis that their successors, the British, built at Bombay. India's story is one of many different kingdoms competing with each other, and this is never more clear than in places like Bijapur, Mandu, Golconda and other centres in central India. Finally, there is the steamy south where Muslim influence reached only fleetingly. Here Hinduism was least altered by outside influences and is at its most exuberant. The temple towns of the south are quite unlike those of the north and are superbly colourful.

Basically India is what you make of it and what you want it to be. If you want to see temples, there are temples in profusion with enough styles and types to confuse anybody. If it's history you want India has plenty of it; the forts, abandoned cities, ruins, battlefields and monuments all have their tales to tell. If you simply want to lie on the beach there are enough of those to satisfy the most avid sun worshipper. If walking and the open air is your thing then head for the trekking routes of the Himalaya, some of which are as wild and deserted as you could ask for. If you simply want to meet the real India you'll come face to face with it all the time – a trip on Indian trains and buses may not always be fun, but it certainly is an experience. India is not a place you simply and clinically 'see'; it's a total experience, an assault on the senses, a place you'll never forget.

LEANNE LOGAN

MICHELLE COXALL

LEANNE LOGAN

PAUL BEINSSEN

PAUL BEINSSEN

Many faces of India

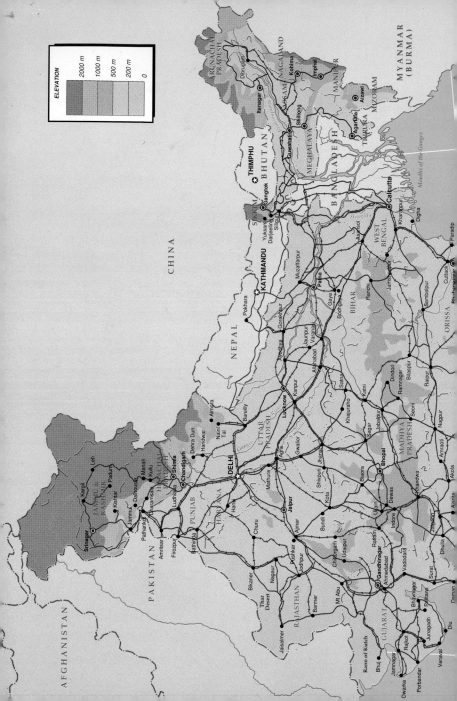

India

The external boundaries of India
on this map have not been authenticated
and may not be correct.

0   200   400 km

BAY OF BENGAL

ARABIAN SEA

INDIAN OCEAN

Lakshadweep Sea

Gulf of Mannar

Andaman Sea

ANDAMAN ISLANDS

Port Blair

NICOBAR ISLANDS

SRI LANKA

COLOMBO

Lakshadweep

MAHARASHTRA

KARNATAKA

ANDHRA PRADESH

TAMIL NADU

KERALA

GOA

Bombay
Kalyan
Pune
Mahabaleshwar
Parbhani
Nanded
Nizamabad
Sholapur
Bijapur
Hospet
Hyderabad
Warangal
Jagdalpur
Berhampur
Bheemunipatam
Visakhapatnam
Kakanda
Masulipatam
Vijayawada
Ongole
Nellore
Madras
Mahabalipuram
Pondicherry
Chidambaram
Chittoor
Nandi Hills
Bangalore
Tiruchirapalli
Rameswaram
Belgaum
Panaji
Mormugao
Gadag
Hubli
Jog Falls
Hassan
Mysore
Coimbatore
Madurai
Mangalore
Thalassery
Kozhikode
Kochi
Kollam
Thiruvananthapuram
Kovalam
Kanyakumari

Krishna

70°E   75°E   80°E   85°E   90°E

15°N   10°N   5°N

SALLY HONE

CHRIS BEALL

CHRIS BEALL

CHRIS BEALL

Top Left: Wankaner Palace, Gujarat.
Top Right: Tea plantation, Darjeeling, West Bengal.
Bottom Left: Do-Drul Chorten, Gangtok, Sikkim.
Bottom Right: Street vendor, Jaipur, Rajasthan.

Facts about the Country

India is one of the few countries in the world today in which the social and religious structures which define the nation's identity remain intact, and have continued to do so for at least 4000 years despite invasions, famines, religious persecutions, political upheavals and many other cataclysms. To describe it as a land of contrasts is to state the obvious. There are many countries which would qualify for such a description in terms of the different ethnic groups, languages, religions, geography and traditions which make up the whole, but few can match the vast scale and diversity to be found in India.

Change is inevitably taking place as modern technology reaches further and further into the fabric of society, yet essentially village India remains much the same as it has for thousands of years. So resilient are its social and religious institutions and, at the same time, so static, that it has either absorbed or thrown off all attempts to radically change or destroy them. Even in the fast-paced modern cities like Bombay, Bangalore and Delhi, what appears to be a complete change of attitude and lifestyle is only surface gloss. Underneath, the age-old verities, loyalties and obligations still rule people's lives.

There is possibly no other country where religion is so inextricably intertwined with every aspect of life. Coming to understand it can be a long process littered with pitfalls, particularly for those educated in the Western liberal tradition with its basis in logic. For those people, 'Indian logic' can often seem bizarre, convoluted and even exasperating. Yet, in its own way, it encompasses a unique cosmology which is both holistic and coherent as well as being fascinating.

It's well to remember that India was the birthplace of two of the world's great religions (Hinduism and Buddhism) and one of its smallest (Jainism). It's also home to one of the world's few remaining communities of Parsis, adherents of the faith of Zoroastrianism.

The modern state itself is a relatively recent creation born out of a people's desire to throw off the yoke of colonialism. Even the mightiest of India's ancient civilisations did not encompass all of modern India, and today it is still as much a country of diversities as of unities. You may hear it said that there are many Indias. In terms of ethnic origin, language and geographical location, that is undoubtedly true, and it sometimes bedevils efforts at creating a national consciousness. Yet it's worth remembering that for nearly 50 years, India has remained the world's largest democracy.

HISTORY
Indus Valley Civilisation

India's first major civilisation flourished for 1000 years from around 2500 BC along the Indus River valley in what is now Pakistan. Its great cities were Mohenjodaro and Harappa, where a civilisation of great complexity developed. The major city sites were only discovered during this century but other, lesser cities have been subsequently unearthed at sites like Lothal, near Ahmedabad in India.

The origins of Hinduism can be traced all the way back to this early civilisation. The society was ruled by priests rather than by kings, and it was they who interceded with the gods, dictated social modes and determined such issues as land tenure. Clay figurines have been found at these sites suggesting worship of a Mother Goddess (later personified as Kali) and a male, three-faced god sitting in the attitude of a yogi attended by four animals (the prehistoric Siva), as well as black stone pillars (phallic worship associated with Siva). Even at this time, certain animals were regarded as sacred; the most prominent being the humped bull (later, Siva's mount). The traditional Hindu fear of pollution and the need for ritual washing is also reflected in the intricate system of drains found at Harappa. There is even evidence of an organised system of garbage collection!

Comparatively little is known about the development and eventual demise of this civilisation. Their script has still not been deciphered, nor is it known why such an advanced civilisation collapsed so quickly following invasion by the Aryans.

Early Invasions & the Rise of Religions

The Aryan invaders swept south from central Asia between 1500 and 200 BC. They eventually controlled the whole of northern India as far as the Vindhya hills, and pushed the original inhabitants, the Dravidians, south. The invaders brought with them their nature gods, among whom the ones of fire and battle were predominant, as well as their cattle-raising and meat-eating traditions. Yet, even by the 8th century BC, the priestly caste had succeeded in reasserting its supremacy and the nature gods were displaced or absorbed into the concept of a universal soul (Brahman) to which the *aatman* (individual soul) was identical. These events are recorded in the literature of the time as the victory of Brahma over Indra (formerly the goddess of food and the law but later of thunder and battle). Indra supposedly led a bizarre double life, being a woman for one phase of the moon and then changing overnight into a man for the next phase. It was also during this period of transition (1500-1200 BC) that the Hindu sacred scriptures, the *Vedas*, were written.

The social order which reflected the assimilation of the Aryans and the supremacy of the priests became consolidated in the caste system, which survives to this day despite efforts by the central government to enhance the status of those at the bottom of the pile. Control over this social order was maintained by extremely strict rules designed to secure the position of the Brahmins (priests). Elaborate taboos were established concerning marriage, diet, travel, modes of eating and drinking and social intercourse. Within the system, each caste adopted its own unique set of rules with which to assert its superiority over those considered to be inferior. Anyone disregarding the rules would be outcast and driven away. Yet the priests could not have it all their own way. Despite the strictures concerning respect for the priests and for all animal life, the meat-eating traditions of the Aryans had to be accommodated. It's essentially from these times that the vague division between the meat-eating north and vegetarian south stems.

During the period when the Aryans were consolidating their hold on northern India, the heartland narrowly missed two other invasions from the West. The first was by the Persian king, Darius (521-486 BC), who annexed the Punjab and Sind but went no further. Alexander the Great reached India in his epic march from Greece in 326 BC, but his troops refused to march further than the Beas River, the easternmost extent of the Persian Empire he had conquered, and he turned back without extending his power into India itself. The most lasting reminder of his appearance in the East was the development of Gandharan art, that intriguing mixture of Grecian artistic ideals and the new religious beliefs of Buddhism.

Buddhism arose around 500 BC contemporaneously with Jainism and presented Brahmanical Hinduism with its greatest challenge. The appeal of both of these cosmologies was that they rejected the *Vedas* and condemned caste, though, unlike the Buddhists, the Jains never denied their Hindu heritage and their faith never extended beyond India.

Buddhism, however, drove a radical swathe through the spiritual and social body of Hinduism and enjoyed spectacular growth after Ashoka embraced the faith and declared it the state religion. Nevertheless, it gradually lost touch with the general population and faded as Hinduism underwent a revival between 200 and 800 AD, based on devotion to a personal god represented today by sects based on Rama and Krishna (*avataars*, or manifestations, of Vishnu). Yet such was the appeal of the greatest of India's spiritual teachers that the Buddha could not be side-

Krishna and Radha – erotic temple art

bureaucracy which kept tabs on everyone for the collection of taxes, tithes and agricultural produce. There were heavy penalties for those who evaded taxes and an extensive system of spies, but corruption was rife and life for the ordinary peasant remained unrelentingly harsh.

The empire reached its peak under Emperor Ashoka, who converted to Buddhism in 262 BC. He left pillars and rock-carved edicts which delineate the enormous span of his empire. Ashokan edicts and pillars can be seen in Delhi, Gujarat, Orissa, Sarnath in Uttar Pradesh, and at Sanchi in Madhya Pradesh.

Ashoka also sent missions abroad, and in Sri Lanka his name is revered because he sent his brother as a missionary to carry Buddhism to the island. The development of art and sculpture also flourished during his rule, and his standard, which topped many of his pillars, is now the seal of the modern state of India. Under Ashoka, the Mauryan Empire controlled more of India than probably any subsequent ruler prior to the Mughals or the British. Following his death, in 232 BC, the empire rapidly disintegrated and collapsed in 184 BC.

lined and forgotten. He was therefore incorporated into the Hindu pantheon as yet another of the avataars of Vishnu. It was a prime example of the way in which Hinduism has absorbed spiritual competitors and heretical ideologies.

The Mauryas & Ashoka

Two centuries before Alexander made his long march east, an Indian kingdom had started to develop in the north of India. It expanded into the vacuum created by Alexander's departure when Chandragupta Maurya's empire came to power in 321 BC. From its capital at the site of present-day Patna, the Mauryan Empire eventually spread across northern India. The Mauryas set up a rigid and well-organised empire with a huge standing army paid for directly by the emperor. They also developed an efficient

An Interlude, then the Guptas

A number of empires rose and fell following the collapse of the Mauryas. The successors to Alexander's kingdoms in the north-west expanded their power into the Punjab and this later developed into the Gandharan Kingdom. In the south-east and east, the Andhras or Telugus expanded inland from the coast, while the Mauryan Empire was replaced by the Sungas, who ruled from 184 to 70 BC. During this period, many Buddhist structures were completed and the great cave temples of central India were commenced. This was the period of the 'lesser vehicle' or Hinayana Buddhism, in which the Buddha could never be directly shown but was alluded to through symbols such as stupas, footprints, trees or elephants. Although this form of Buddhism probably continued until about 400 AD, it was already being supplanted by 100 AD by the 'greater vehicle' or Mahayana Buddhism.

In 319 AD, Chandragupta II founded the Gupta Empire, the first phase of which became known as the Imperial Guptas. His successors extended their power over northern India, first from Patna and later from other northern cities such as Ayodhya. The Imperial Guptas gave way to the later Guptas in 455 AD but the Gupta period continued to 606 AD. The arts flourished during this period, with some of the finest work being done at Ajanta, Ellora, Sanchi and Sarnath. Poetry and literature also experienced a golden age. Towards the end of the Gupta period, however, Buddhism and Jainism both began to decline and Hinduism began to rise in popularity once more.

The invasions of the White Huns signalled the end of this era of history, although the they were at first repelled by the Guptas. The Huns drove the Gandharas from the northwest region, close to Peshawar, into Kashmir. Subsequently, North India broke up into a number of separate Hindu kingdoms and was not really unified again until the coming of the Muslims.

Meanwhile in the South

In Indian history, events in one part of the country do not necessarily affect those in another. The kingdoms that rose and fell in the north of the country generally had no influence or connection with those in the south. While Buddhism and, to a lesser extent, Jainism were displacing Hinduism in the centre and north of India, Hinduism continued to flourish in the south.

The south's prosperity was based upon its long-established trading links with other civilisations. The Egyptians and, later, the Romans both traded by sea with the south of India. Strong links were also formed with parts of South-East Asia. For a time, Buddhism and, later, Hinduism flourished in the Indonesian islands, and the people of the region looked towards India as their cultural mentor. The *Ramayana*, that most famous of Hindu epics, is today told and retold in various forms in many South-East Asian

countries. Bali is the only Hindu stronghold in South-East Asia today and, though it's clearly recognisable as such, its isolation from the heartland of Hinduism has resulted in considerable modification of the faith.

Other outside influences which came to the south of India in this period included St Thomas the Apostle, who is said to have arrived in Kerala in 52 AD. To this day, there is a strong Christian influence in the region.

Great empires that rose in the south included the Cholas, Pandyas, Cheras, Chalukyas and Pallavas. The Chalukyas ruled mainly over the Deccan region of central India, although at times their power extended further north. With a capital at Badami in Karnataka, they ruled from 550 to 753 AD before falling to the Rashtrakutas. They rose again in 972 and continued their rule through to 1190. Further south, the Pallavas pioneered Dravidian architecture with its exuberant, almost baroque, style. They also carried Indian culture to Java in Indonesia, Thailand and Cambodia.

In 850 AD, the Cholas rose to power and gradually superseded the Pallavas. They too were great builders, as their temple at Thanjavur indicates. They also carried their power overseas and, under the reign of Raja Raja (985-1014 AD), controlled almost the whole of southern India, the Deccan, Sri Lanka, and parts of the Malay peninsula and the Sumatran-based Srivijaya Kingdom.

First Muslim Invasions

While the Hindu kingdoms ruled in the south and Buddhism was fading in the north, Muslim power was creeping towards India from the Middle East. Less than a century after the death of the Prophet Mohammed, there were Arab raids into the Sind and Gujarat.

Muslim power first made itself strongly felt on the subcontinent with the raids of Mahmud of Ghazni. Today, Ghazni is just a grubby little town between Kabul and Kandahar in Afghanistan, but from 1001 AD Mahmud conducted raids from here on an annual basis. His army descended upon India, destroying infidel temples and carrying off everything of value that could be moved. In 1033, after his death, one of his successors actually took Varanasi. The raids stopped in 1038 when the expansionist Seljuk Turks took Ghazni.

These early visits, however, were no more than banditry, and it was not until 1192 that Muslim power arrived on a permanent basis. In that year, Mohammed of Ghori, who had been expanding his powers across the Punjab, broke into India and took Ajmer. The following year, his general, Qutb-ud-din, took Varanasi and then Delhi. After Mohammed of Ghori was killed in 1206, Qutb-ud-din became the first of the Sultans of Delhi. Within 20 years, the Muslims had brought the whole of the Ganges basin under their control, but the Sultans of Delhi were never consistent in their powers. With each new ruler, the kingdom grew or shrank depending on personal abilities.

In 1297, Ala-ud-din Khilji pushed the borders south into Gujarat; his general subsequently moved further south, but could not maintain the extension. In 1338, Mohammed Tughlaq decided to move his capital south from Delhi to Daulatabad, near Aurangabad in Maharashtra, but having marched most of Delhi's population south, eventually had to return north. Soon after, the Bahmani Kingdom arose and the Delhi Sultanate began to retreat north, only to be further weakened when Timur (Tamerlane) made a devastating raid from Samarkand into India in 1398. From then on, the power of this Muslim kingdom steadily contracted, until it was supplanted by another Muslim kingdom, that of the Mughals.

The Muslims were a somewhat different breed of invader. Unlike previous arrivals, they retained their own identity, and the contempt which they heaped on their infidel subjects prevented their absorption into the prevailing Hindu religious and social systems. Nevertheless, Hinduism survived and Islam found India relatively infertile ground for conversion. By the 20th century, after 800 years of Muslim domination, only 25% of the population had converted to Islam.

The Muslims could not rule without Hindu assistance, so many Hindus were inducted into the bureaucracy. This resulted in the development of a common language, Urdu, which is a combination of Persian vocabulary and Hindi grammar using Perso-Arabic script. It remains the language of large parts of northern India and of Pakistan.

Meanwhile in the South (again)

Once again, events in the south of India took a different path to those in the north. Just as the Aryan invasions never reached the south, so the early Muslim invasions failed to permanently affect events there. Between 1000 and 1300 AD, the Hoysala Empire, which had centres at Belur, Halebid and Somnathpur, was at its peak. It eventually fell to a predatory raid by Mohammed Tughlaq in 1328, and then to the combined opposition of other Hindu kingdoms.

Two other great kingdoms developed in the north of modern-day Karnataka – one Muslim and one Hindu. The Hindu kingdom of Vijayanagar was founded in 1336. Its capital was at Hampi, and it was probably the strongest Hindu kingdom in India during the period that the Muslim Sultans of Delhi were dominating the north. At the same time, the Bahmani Muslim kingdom developed, but in 1489 it split into five separate kingdoms at Berar, Ahmednagar, Bijapur, Golconda and Ahmedabad. In 1520, Vijayanagar took Bijapur, but in 1565 the kingdom's Muslim opponents combined to destroy Vijayanagar in the epic Battle of Talikota. Later, the Bahmani kingdoms were to fall to the Mughals.

The Mughals

These larger-than-life individuals ushered in a golden age of building, arts and literature, and spread their control over India to an extent rivalled only by Ashoka and the British. Their rise to power was rapid but their decline was equally quick. There were only six great Mughals; after Aurangzeb, the rest were emperors in name only.

The Mughals did more than simply rule, however – they had a passion for building which resulted in some of the greatest buildings in India – Shah Jahan's magnificent Taj

Mahal ranks as one of the wonders of the world. Art and literature also flourished under the Mughals and the magnificence of their court stunned early European visitors.

The six great Mughals and their reigns were:

Babur	1527-1530
Humayun	1530-1556
Akbar	1556-1605
Jehangir	1605-1627
Shah Jahan	1627-1658
Aurangzeb	1658-1707

Babur, a descendant of both Timur and Genghis Khan, marched into the Punjab from his capital at Kabul in Afghanistan in 1525 to defeat the Sultan of Delhi at Panipat. This initial success did not totally destroy opposition to the Mughals, and in 1540 the Mughal Empire came to an abrupt but temporary end when Sher Shah defeated Humayun, the second great Mughal. For 15 years, Humayun lived in exile until he was able to return and regain his throne. By 1560, Akbar, his son and successor, who had come to the throne aged only 14, was able to claim effective and complete control of his empire.

The Mughal emperor Akbar ruled from 1556 to 1605, and was probably the greatest of the Mughal rulers, who dominated northern India for three centuries.

Akbar was probably the greatest of the Mughals, for he not only had the military ability required of a ruler in that time, but he was also a man of culture and wisdom with a sense of fairness. He saw, as previous Muslim rulers had not, that the number of Hindus in India was too great to subjugate. Instead, he integrated them into his empire and made use of many Hindu advisers, generals and administrators. Akbar also had a deep interest in religious matters, and spent many hours in discussion with religious experts of all persuasions, including Christians and Parsis. He eventually formulated a religion which combined the best points of all those he had studied.

Jehangir followed Akbar and maintained his father's tolerance of other religions but took advantage of the stability of the empire to spend most of his time in his beloved Kashmir, eventually dying while en route there. His tomb is at Lahore in Pakistan. Shah Jahan, however, who secured his position as emperor by executing all male collateral relatives, stuck much more to Agra and Delhi. During his reign, some of the most vivid and permanent reminders of the Mughals' glory were constructed. Best known, of course, is the Taj Mahal, but that was only one of Shah Jahan's many magnificent buildings. Indeed, some say that it was his passion for building that led to his downfall, and that his son, Aurangzeb, deposed him in part to put a halt to his architectural extravagances. Shah Jahan also ditched Akbar's policy of religious tolerance in favour of a return to Islam. Yet it was during his reign that the British were granted their trading post at Madras in 1639.

The last of the great Mughals, Aurangzeb, devoted his resources to extending the empire's boundaries, but it was the punitive taxes which he levied on his subjects to pay for his military exploits and his religious zealotry that eventually secured his downfall. It was also during his reign that the empire began to rot from the inside as luxury and easy living corroded the mettle and moral fibre of the nobles and military commanders. His austere and puritanical beliefs led him to destroy many Hindu temples and erect mosques on their sites, alienating the

Shah Jahan, who ruled from 1627 to 1658, had a passion for building, and was responsible for one of the most stunning buildings in the world – the Taj Mahal.

very people who were such an important part of his bureaucracy.

It didn't take long for revolts to break out on all sides and, with his death in 1707, the Mughal Empire's fortunes rapidly declined. There were Mughal 'emperors' right up to the time of the Indian Mutiny, when the British exiled the last one and executed his sons, but they were emperors without an empire. In sharp contrast to the magnificent tombs of his Mughal predecessors, Aurangzeb's tomb is a simple affair at Rauza, near Aurangabad.

The states which followed the Mughal Empire did, in some cases, manage to sustain themselves. In the south, the viceroyalty in Hyderabad became one of the British-tolerated princely states and lasted until Independence. The nawabs of Avadh in north India ruled eccentrically, flamboyantly and badly until 1856, when the British 'retired' the last nawab. In Bengal, the Mughals unwisely clashed with the British far earlier, and their rule was terminated by the Battle of Plassey in 1757.

The Rajputs & the Marathas

Mughal power was not replaced by another, greater power. It declined due to a number of factors and power passed to a number of other rulers.

Throughout the Muslim period in the north of India, there were still strong Hindu powers, most notably the Rajputs. Centred in Rajasthan, the Rajputs were a warrior caste with a strong and almost fanatical belief in the dictates of chivalry, both in battle and in the conduct of state affairs. Their place in Indian history is much like that of the knights of medieval Europe. The Rajputs opposed every foreign incursion into their territory, but were never united or sufficiently organised to be able to deal with superior forces on a long-term basis. Not only that, but when not battling foreign oppression they squandered their energies fighting each other. This eventually led to them becoming vassal states of the Mughal Empire, but their prowess in battle was well recognised, and some of the best military men in the emperors' armies were Rajputs.

The Marathas first rose to prominence with Shivaji who, between 1646 and 1680, performed feats of arms and heroism across central India. Tales of his larger-than-life exploits are still popular with wandering storytellers in small villages today. He is a particular hero in Maharashtra, where many of his wildest exploits took place, but is also revered for two other things: as a lower-caste Sudra, he showed that great leaders do not have to be Kshatriyas (soldiers or administrators), and he demonstrated great abilities in confronting the Mughals. At one time, Shivaji was captured by the Mughals and taken back to Agra but, naturally, he managed to escape and continue his adventures.

Shivaji's son was captured, blinded and executed by Aurangzeb. His grandson was not made of the same sturdy stuff, but the Maratha Empire continued under the Peshwas, hereditary government ministers who became the real rulers. They gradually took over more and more of the weakening Mughal Empire's powers, first by supplying troops and then by actually taking control of Mughal land.

When Nadir Shah from Persia sacked Delhi in 1739, the declining Mughals were weakened further. But the expansion of Maratha power came to an abrupt halt in 1761 at Panipat. There, where Babur had won the battle that established the Mughal Empire over 200 years earlier, the Marathas were defeated by Ahmad Shah Durani from Afghanistan. Though their expansion to the west halted, the Marathas consolidated their control over central India and the region known as Malwa. Soon, however, they were to fall to India's final imperial power, the British.

Expansion of British Power

The British were not the first European power to arrive in India, nor were they the last to leave – both those honours go to the Portuguese. In 1498, Vasco da Gama arrived on the coast of modern-day Kerala, having sailed around the Cape of Good Hope. Pioneering this route gave the Portuguese a century of uninterrupted monopoly over Indian and Far Eastern trade with Europe. In 1510, they captured Goa, the Indian enclave they controlled right through to 1961, 14 years after the British had left. So rich was Goa during its heyday that it was rated as the Lisbon of the East. In the long term, however, the Portuguese simply did not have the resources to hold onto a worldwide empire and they were quickly eclipsed when the British, French and Dutch arrived.

In 1612, the British made their first permanent inroad into India when they established a trading post at Surat in Gujarat. In 1600, Queen Elizabeth I had granted a charter to a London trading company giving it a monopoly on British trade with India. For 250 years, British power was exercised in India not by the government but by the East India Company which developed from this initial charter. British trading posts were established on the eastern coast at Madras in 1640, at Bombay in 1668 and at Calcutta in 1690.

The British and Portuguese were not the only Europeans in India. The Danes and Dutch also had trading posts, and in 1672 the French established themselves at Pondicherry, an enclave that they, like the Portuguese in Goa, would hold even after the British had departed.

The stage was set for over a century of rivalry between the British and French for control of Indian trade. In 1746, the French took Madras, only to hand it back in 1749. In subsequent years, there was to be much intrigue between the imperial powers. If the British were involved in a struggle with one local ruler, they could be certain the French would be backing him with arms, men or expertise. In 1756, Siraj-ud-daula, the Nawab of Bengal, attacked Calcutta and outraged Britain with the 'black hole of Calcutta' incident. A year later, Robert Clive retook Calcutta and in the Battle of Plassey defeated Siraj-ud-daula and his French supporters, thus not only extending British power but also curtailing French influence. The victory ushered in a long period of unbridled profiteering by members of the East India Company until its powers were taken over by the British Government in the 19th century.

India at this time was in a state of flux due to the power vacuum created by the disintegration of the Mughal Empire. The Marathas were the only real Indian power to step into this gap and they were more a collection of local kingdoms who sometimes cooperated, sometimes did not, than a power in their own right. In the south, where Mughal influence had never been great, the picture was confused by the strong British-French rivalry, as one ruler was played off against another.

This was never clearer than in the series of Mysore wars. In the 4th Mysore War (1789-99), that irritant to British power, Tipu Sultan, was killed at Srirangapatnam and British power took another step forward. The long-running British struggle with the Marathas was finally concluded in 1803, which left only the Punjab outside British control. Even that fell to the British in 1849 after the two Sikh wars.

It was during this time that the borders of Nepal were delineated, following a brief series of battles between the British and the Gurkhas in 1814. The Gurkhas were initially victorious but, two years later, were forced to sue for peace as the British marched on Kathmandu. As part of the price for peace, the Nepalese were forced to cede the provinces of Kumaon and Shimla, but mutual respect for each others' military prowess prevented Nepal's incorporation into the Indian Empire and led to the establishment of the Gurkha regiments of the British Army.

British India

By the early 19th century, India was effectively under British control. In part, this takeover had come about because of the vacuum left by the demise of the Mughals, but the British also followed the rules Akbar had laid down so successfully. To them, India was principally a place to make money, and the Indians' culture, beliefs and religions were left strictly alone. Indeed, it was said the British didn't give a damn what religious beliefs a person held so long as they made a good cup of tea. Furthermore, the British had a disciplined, efficient army and astute political advisers. They followed the policy of divide and rule with great success and negotiated distinctly one-sided treaties giving them the right to intervene in local states if they were inefficiently run; 'inefficient' could be, and was, defined as the British saw fit.

Even under the British, India remained a patchwork of states, many of them nominally independent but actually under strong British influence. This policy of maintaining 'princely states' governed by maharajas and nawabs (and a host of other titled rulers) continued right through to Independence and was to cause a number of problems at that time. The British interest in trade and profit resulted in expansion of iron and coal mining; the development of tea, coffee and cotton growing; the construction of the basis of today's vast Indian rail network; and the commencement of irrigation projects which have today revolutionised agriculture.

In the sphere of government and law, Britain gave India a well-developed and smoothly functioning government and civil service structure. The fearsome love of bureaucracy which India inherited from Britain may be a down side of that, but the country reached Independence with a better organised, more efficient and less corrupt administrative system than most ex-colonial countries.

There was, however, a price to pay: colonies are not established for altruistic reasons. Cheap textiles from Britain's new manufacturing industry flooded into India, crippling local cottage industries. On one hand, the British outlawed *sati*, the Hindu custom of burning the wife on her husband's funeral pyre, but on the other hand they encouraged the system of *zamindars*. These absentee landlords eased the burden of administrative and tax collection for the British, but contributed to an impoverished and landless peasantry in parts of India – a problem which in Bihar and West Bengal is still chronic today.

The British also established English as the local language of administration. While this may have been useful in a country with so many different languages, and still fulfils a very important function in nationwide communication today, it did keep the new rulers at arm's length from the Indians.

The Indian Mutiny

In 1857, less than half a century after Britain had taken firm control of India, the British had their first serious setback. To this day, the causes of the 'Indian Mutiny' are hard to unravel – it's even hard to define if it really was the 'War of Independence' by which it is sometimes referred to in India, or merely a mutiny. The causes were a run-down administration, the dismissal of local rulers, and a bullet lubricant. A rumour, quite possibly true, leaked out that a new type of bullet issued to the troops, many of whom were Muslim, was greased with pig fat. A similar rumour claimed that the bullets were actually greased with cow fat. Pigs, of course, are unclean to Muslims, and cows are holy to Hindus.

The British were slow to deny these rumours and even slower to prove that either they were incorrect or that changes had been made. The result was a loosely coordinated mutiny of the Indian battalions of the Bengal Army. Of the 74 battalions, seven (one of them Gurkhas) remained loyal, 20 were disarmed and the other 47 mutinied. The Mutiny broke out at Meerut, close to Delhi, and soon spread across north India. There were massacres and acts of senseless cruelty on both sides, long sieges and protracted struggles, but in the end the Mutiny died out rather than came to a conclusive finish. It never spread beyond the north of India, and although there were brilliant self-made leaders on the Indian side, there was never any real coordination or common aim.

Post-Mutiny

The British made two moves after the Mutiny. First, they wisely decided not to look for scapegoats or to exact official revenge, although revenge and looting had certainly taken place on an unofficial level. Second, the East India Company was wound up and administration of the country was belatedly handed over to the British government. The remainder of the century was the peak period for the empire on which 'the sun never set', and India was one of its brightest stars.

Two parallel developments during the latter part of the 19th century gradually paved the way for the independent India of today. First, the British slowly began to hand over power and bring more people into the decision-making processes. Democratic systems began to be implemented, although the British government retained overall control. In the civil service, higher and higher posts were opened up for Indians instead of being reserved for colonial administrators.

At the same time, Hinduism began to go through another of its periodic phases of resurgence and adjustment. During the Mughal and early British periods, it had gradually lost much of its mass appeal, if only because of the demise of its once-great Hindu kingdoms. It was clearly time to drag the religion back into the present and re-establish its relevance for the common people. The main protagonists in this revival were reformers like Ram Mohan Roy, Ramakrishna and Swami Vivekananda, who pushed through sweeping changes in Hindu society and paved the way for the Hindu beliefs of today. Other reformers, such as Sri Aurobindo, attempted to meld Hindu philosophy with the rapidly emerging precepts of modern science.

It was largely as a result of their efforts that hybrid spiritual groups based on Hinduism and a variety of pre-Christian Western mysticism also made their appearance in the early part of the 20th century. Societies like the Theosophical Society of Annie Besant and her guru, Krishnamurti, date from this period. Even Aleister Crowley owed a debt to these popularisers of Hindu philosophy and mysticism.

Road to Independence

Opposition to British rule began to increase at the turn of the century. The 'Congress', which had been established to give India a degree of self-rule, now began to push for the real thing. Outside the Congress, hot-blooded individuals pressed for independence by more violent means. Eventually, the British mapped out a path towards independence similar to that pursued in Canada and Australia. However, WW I shelved these plans and events in Turkey, a Muslim country, alienated many Indian Muslims. After the war, the struggle began again in earnest, and its new leader was Mahatma Gandhi.

In 1915, Mohandas Gandhi returned from South Africa, where he had practised as a lawyer and devoted himself to fighting the racial discrimination which the country's many Indian settlers had to face. In India, he soon turned his abilities to the question of independence, particularly after the infamous massacre at Amritsar in 1919 when a British army contingent opened fire on an unarmed crowd of protesters. Gandhi, who subsequently became known as the Mahatma, or 'great soul', adopted a policy of passive resistance, or *satyagraha*, to British rule.

The central pillar of his achievement was to broaden the scope of the independence struggle from the middle classes to

Mahatma Gandhi is often referred to as the 'Father of the Nation'. He spent many years campaigning against the British, his preferred action being *satyagraha* (passive resistance).

the peasants and villagers. He led movements against the iniquitous salt tax and boycotts of British textiles, and for his efforts was jailed on a number of occasions. Not everyone involved in the struggle agreed with or followed Gandhi's policy of noncooperation and nonviolence, yet the Congress Party and Mahatma Gandhi remained at the forefront of the push for independence.

By the time WW II was concluded, independence was inevitable. The war dealt a deathblow to colonialism and the myth of European superiority, and Britain no longer had the power or the desire to maintain a vast empire. Within India, however, a major problem had developed: the large Muslim minority had realised that an independent India would also be a Hindu-dominated India, and that despite Gandhi's fair-minded and even-handed approach, others in the Congress Party would not be so willing to share power.

Independence

The July 1945 Labour Party victory in the British elections brought a new breed of political leaders to power who realised that a solution to the Indian problem was imperative.

However, elections in India revealed an alarming growth of communalism. The country was divided along purely religious lines, with the Muslim League, led by Muhammad Ali Jinnah, speaking for the overwhelming majority of Muslims, and the Congress Party, led by Jawaharlal Nehru, representing the Hindu population. Mahatma Gandhi remained the father figure for Congress, but did not have an official role – and, as events were to prove, his political influence was slipping.

'I will have India divided, or India destroyed', were Jinnah's words. This uncompromising demand, Jinnah's egotistical bid for power over a separate nation, and Congress' desire for an independent greater-India proved to be the biggest stumbling blocks to the British granting independence. However, each passing day increased the prospects for intercommunal strife and bloodshed. In early 1946, a British mission failed to bring the two sides together and the country slid closer towards civil war. A 'Direct Action Day', called by the Muslim League in August 1946, led to the slaughter of Hindus in Calcutta, followed by reprisals against Muslims. Attempts to make the two sides see reason had no effect. In February 1947, the British government made a momentous decision: the current viceroy, Lord Wavell, would be replaced by Lord Louis Mountbatten and independence would come by June 1948.

The Punjab region of northern India was aleady in a state of chaos, and the Bengal region in the east was close to it. The new viceroy made a last-ditch attempt to convince the rival factions that a united India was a more sensible proposition, but they – Jinnah in particular – remained intransigent. The reluctant decision was then made to divide the country. Only Gandhi stood firmly against the division, preferring the possibility of a civil war to the chaos he so rightly expected.

Neatly slicing the country in two proved to be an impossible task. Although some areas were clearly Hindu or Muslim, others had evenly mixed populations or were isolated 'islands' of Muslims surrounded by Hindu regions. The impossibility of attempting to divide all the Muslims from all the Hindus is illustrated by the fact that, after Partition, India was still the third-largest Muslim country in the world – only Indonesia and Pakistan had greater Muslim populations. Even today, India has a Muslim population greater than any of the Arab countries, or Turkey or Iran.

Unfortunately, the two overwhelmingly Muslim regions were on opposite sides of the country – Pakistan would inevitably have an eastern and western half divided by a hostile India. The instability of this arrangement was self-evident, but it took 25 years before the predestined split came and East Pakistan became Bangladesh. On top of this, the Sikhs would also find their 'homeland' split in half.

Other problems showed up only after independence was achieved. Pakistan was painfully short of the administrators and clerical workers with which India was so well endowed because these were not traditionally Muslim occupations. Many other occupations, such as moneylending and the menial tasks performed by the untouchables, had also been purely Hindu callings.

Mountbatten decided to follow a breakneck pace to independence and announced that it would come on 14 August 1947. Historians have wondered ever since if much bloodshed might not have been averted if the impetuous and egotistical Mountbatten had not decided on such a hasty process.

Once the decision had been made to divide the country, there were countless administrative decisions to be made, the most important being the actual location of the dividing line. Since a locally adjudicated dividing line was certain to bring recriminations from either side, an independent British referee was given the odious task of drawing the line, knowing that its effects would be disastrous for countless people. The most difficult decisions had to be made in Bengal and the Punjab. In Bengal, Calcutta, with its Hindu majority, port facilities and jute mills, was divided from East Bengal, which had a Muslim majority, large-scale jute production, no mills and no port facilities.

The problem was far worse in the Punjab, where intercommunal antagonisms were already running at fever pitch. Punjab was one of the most fertile and affluent regions of the country, and had large percentages of Muslims (55%), Hindus (30%) and a substantial number of India's Sikhs. It was clear that the Punjab contained all the ingredients for an epic disaster but, with the announcement of the dividing line only days after Independence, the resulting bloodshed was even worse than expected. Huge exchanges of population took place as Muslims moved to Pakistan and Hindus and Sikhs to India.

The dividing line cut neatly between the Punjab's two major cities – Lahore and Amritsar. Prior to Independence, Lahore's total population of 1.2 million included approximately 500,000 Hindus and 100,000 Sikhs. When the dust had finally settled, Lahore had a Hindu and Sikh population of only 1000.

For months, the greatest exodus in human history took place east and west across the Punjab. Trains full of Muslims, fleeing westward, were held up and slaughtered by Hindu and Sikh mobs. Hindus and Sikhs fleeing to the east suffered the same fate. The army sent to maintain order proved totally inadequate and, at times, all too ready to join the partisan carnage. By the time the Punjab chaos had run its course, over 10 million people had changed sides and even the most conservative estimates calculate that 250,000 people had been slaughtered. The true figure may well have been over half a million. An additional million people changed sides in Bengal, mainly Hindus heading west since few Muslims migrated from West Bengal to East Pakistan.

The division of the Punjab was not to be the only excuse for carnage. Throughout the British era, India had retained many 'princely states', and incorporating these into independent India and Pakistan proved to be a considerable headache. Guarantees of a substantial measure of independence convinced most of them to opt for inclusion into the new countries, but at the time of Independence there were still three hold-outs.

One was Kashmir, a predominantly Muslim state with a Hindu maharaja. In October 1948, the maharaja had still not opted for India or Pakistan when a rag-tag Pathan (Pakistani) army crossed the border, intent on racing to Srinagar and annexing Kashmir without provoking a real India-Pakistan conflict. Unfortunately for the Pakistanis, the Pathans had been inspired to mount their invasion by the promise of plunder, and they did so much plundering on the way that India had time to rush troops to Srinagar and prevent the town's capture. The indecisive maharaja finally opted for India, provoking the first, although brief, India-Pakistan war.

The UN was eventually persuaded to step in and keep the two sides apart but the issue of Kashmir has remained a central cause for disagreement and conflict between the two countries ever since. With its overwhelming Muslim majority and its geographic links to Pakistan, many people were inclined to support Pakistan's claims to the region. But, by then, Kashmir had become a *cause célèbre* in the Congress Party and, despite a promised plebiscite, India has consistently evaded holding such a vote. To this day, India and Pakistan are divided in this region by a demarcation line (known as the Line of Actual Control) yet neither side agrees that this constitutes the official border.

The final stages of Independence had one last tragedy to be played out. On 30 January 1948, Gandhi, deeply disheartened by Partition and the subsequent bloodshed, was assassinated by a Hindu fanatic.

Independent India

Since Independence, India has made enormous strides and faced enormous problems. The mere fact that India has not, like so many Third World countries, succumbed to dictatorships, military rule or wholesale foreign invasion is a testament to the basic strength of the country's government and institutions. Economically, it has made major steps forward in improving agricultural output, and its industries have expanded to the stage where India is one of the world's top 10 industrial powers.

Jawaharlal Nehru, India's first prime minister, tried to follow a strict policy of nonalignment and was universally recognised as one of the major leaders of the Nonaligned Movement, along with Tito (of Yugoslavia) and Soekarno (of Indonesia). Yet, despite maintaining generally cordial relations with its former coloniser, and electing to join the Commonwealth, India moved towards the former USSR – partly because of conflicts with China and partly because of US support for arch-enemy Pakistan.

There were further clashes with Pakistan in 1965 and 1971, one over the intractable Kashmir dispute and the other over Bangladesh. A border war was also fought with China in 1962 in the North-East Frontier Agency (NEFA; now referred to as the

Jawaharlal Nehru, India's first prime minister, campaigned hard for Independence from Britain in the 1930s and 1940s.

North-Eastern Region) and Ladakh, which resulted in the loss of Aksai Chin (Ladakh) and smaller areas in the NEFA. India continues to dispute sovereignty over these areas.

These outside events drew attention away from India's often serious internal problems, especially the failure to address rapid population growth.

Indira's India

Politically, India's major problem since Independence has been the personality cult that has developed with its leaders. There have only been three real prime ministers of stature – Nehru, his daughter Indira Gandhi (no relation to Mahatma Gandhi) and her son Rajiv Gandhi. Having won elections in 1966, Indira Gandhi faced serious opposition and unrest in 1975, which she countered by declaring a state of emergency – a situation which in many other countries might quickly have become a dictatorship.

During the 'emergency', a mixed bag of good and bad policies were followed. Freed of many parliamentary constraints, Indira Gandhi was able to control inflation remarkably well, boost the economy and decisively increase efficiency. On the negative side, political opponents often found themselves behind bars, India's judicial system was turned into a puppet theatre, the press was fettered and there was more than a hint of personal aggrandisement, particularly in relation to her son, Sanjay Gandhi. His disastrous programme of forced sterilisations, in particular, caused much anger.

Despite murmurings of discontent, Indira Gandhi decided that the people were behind her and in 1977 called a general election. Sanjay had counselled against holding the election and his opinion proved to be a wise

Did You Know?

In a country as large and diverse as India, where the weird and the wonderful are even more weird and wonderful than anywhere else, it comes as no surprise that the country holds many world records – although some of them are of dubious worth!

Obviously with its vast population, a number of records relate to crowds and people: the largest recorded assembly of people was an estimated 15 million at the Kumbh Mela at Allahabad in 1989 – a similar number attended the funeral of the Tamil Nadu chief minister in 1969; the largest single employer in the world is Indian Railways with 1,624,121 people on the payroll; the South Point High School in Calcutta has the largest enrolment with 11,683 regular students; and, in the world's largest democracy, the 1989 Lok Sabha elections produced a few records when 304,126,600 people voted for the 291 parties contesting the 543 seats at over 593,000 polling stations across the country!

India also has its fair share of biggest, longest and highest: Hero Cycles in Punjab is the world's largest manufacturer: in 1989 it built no less than 2,936,073 clunkers; the longest railway platform in the world (833 metres) is at Kharagpur in West Bengal; the State Bank of India has the most branches, with 12,203 across the country; the wettest place on earth is also in India, at Cherrapunji in Meghalaya, which in a one-year period copped a massive 26.46 metres; and pop star Lata Mangeshkar holds the record for the greatest number of recordings, with over 30,000 songs recorded in 20 Indian languages.

The bizarre and downright silly? Yes, India has them too. Indians hold the records for nonstop talking (360 hours), balancing on one foot (34 hours), clapping (58 hours, nine minutes), nonstop chanting (11,100 days and still rising), continuous typewriting (123 hours), standing still (over 17 years!), crawling (1,400 km), nonstop solo singing (262 hours), whistling (45 hours, 20 minutes), and walking with a full milk-bottle balanced on the head (65 km).

India also has the tree with the largest canopy – a banyan tree in the Calcutta Botanical Gardens covers 1.2 hectares; the highest bridge in the world (5600 metres) is found on the Manali to Leh road; and, not surprisingly, the Howrah Bridge in Calcutta is the world's busiest – every day it carries almost 60,000 vehicles and innumerable pedestrians; while the Qutab Minar in Delhi, at 72.5 metres, is the tallest free-standing stone tower.

Indian disasters, both natural and otherwise, also feature in the record books. No-one could forget Bhopal, where 4000 people died and at least 200,000 others were injured, but in 1888, 246 people were killed in a hailstorm, while a dam which burst its banks in Gujarat killed at least 5000 in 1979.

Lastly, a record that's hardly likely to be challenged is that held by a Pune man who, in 1966, won a court case which had been filed by his ancestor 761 years earlier – the Indian bureaucracy in full swing! ■

Indira Gandhi, the country's first woman prime minister, is still held in extremely high esteem. Her house in Delhi where she was assassinated by one of her own bodyguards, is today a very popular museum.

one; Mrs Gandhi and her Congress Party were bundled out of power in favour of the hastily assembled Janata People's Party.

Janata, however, was a coalition formed with the sole purpose of defeating Indira Gandhi and her partially renamed Congress Party (Indira). Once it had won, it quickly became obvious that it had no other cohesive policies. Its leader, Morarji Desai, seemed more interested in protecting cows, banning alcohol and getting his daily glass of urine than coming to grips with the country's problems. With inflation soaring, unrest rising and the economy faltering, nobody was surprised when Janata fell apart in late 1979 and the 1980 election brought Indira Gandhi back to power with a larger majority than ever.

India in the 1980s

Mrs Gandhi's political touch seemed to have faded as she grappled unsuccessfully with communal unrest in several areas, violent attacks on untouchables, numerous cases of police brutality and corruption, and the upheavals in the north-east and the Punjab. Then her son and political heir, the none-too-popular Sanjay, was killed in a light aircraft accident, and in 1984 Mrs Gandhi herself was assassinated by her Sikh bodyguards, clearly in reprisal for her earlier, and somewhat ill-considered, decision to send in the Indian Army to flush out armed Sikh radicals from the Golden Temple in Amritsar.

The radicals were demanding a separate Sikh state, to be named Khalistan. Regardless of the viability of such a land-locked state adjacent to a hostile Pakistan and what would have been a none-too-friendly India, her decision to desecrate the Sikhs' holiest temple was a disaster which led to large-scale riots, big problems in the army (in which Sikhs form a significant part of the officer corps), and a seemingly intractable legacy of hate and distrust in the Punjab which has defied solution ever since.

Meanwhile, Mrs Gandhi's son, Rajiv, an Indian Airlines pilot until his younger brother's death, quickly become the next heir to the throne, and was soon swept into power with an overwhelming majority and enormous popular support.

Despite his former lack of interest in politics, Rajiv Gandhi brought new and pragmatic policies to the country. Foreign investment and the use of modern technology were encouraged, import restrictions eased and many new industries were set up. They undoubtedly benefited the middle classes and provided many jobs for those who had been displaced from the land and migrated to the cities in search of work, but whether these policies were necessarily in the long-term best interests of India is open to question. They certainly projected India into the 1990s, woke the country from its partially self-induced isolationism, and broke its protectionist stance to world trade, but they didn't stimulate the rural sector.

Furthermore, his administration continually failed to quell unrest in the Punjab or

Kashmir. It was also during his tenure in power that the Indian armed forces became bogged down in the turmoil in neighbouring Sri Lanka, caused by Tamil secessionists in that country demanding an independent state. Support for the Sri Lankan Tamils was clearly being supplied by their mainland brethren, and police activities in Tamil Nadu state aimed at rooting out sympathisers and curtailing the flow of arms and equipment made Rajiv a marked man.

There was also the Bofors scandal which dogged his administration. This concerned alleged bribes paid to various members of the government to secure a contract to supply a Swedish heavy artillery gun to the Indian army. It was even alleged that Rajiv, or at least his Italian-born wife, Sonia, were recipients of such bribes. The affair has never been satisfactorily exposed and has even threatened to bring down the current administration which is headed by Narasimha Rao. As recently as 1992, the Minister of External Affairs, Mahavsingh Solanski, was forced to resign following what appeared to be an attempt to induce Swiss lawyers to abandon their investigation of certain bank accounts in that country which were suspected of holding the alleged bribes. It's unlikely the truth will ever emerge but it smells badly of a determined cover-up by people in high places.

Following the November 1989 elections, Rajiv Gandhi's Congress(I) Party, although the largest single party in Parliament, was unable to form a government in its own right. As a result, a new National Front Government, made up of five parties, including the Hindu fundamentalist Bharatiya Janata Party (BJP), were to form the next government. Like the previous attempt to cobble together a government of national unity from minority parties with radically different viewpoints, it didn't last long and fresh elections had to be announced.

During the election campaign, disaster struck. While on a campaign tour of Tamil Nadu, Rajiv Gandhi, many of his aides and a number of bystanders were blown to bits by a bomb carried by a supporter of the Tamil Tigers (who was herself killed in the blast).

The assassination had clearly been planned in advance and a massive police crackdown subsequently resulted in a shoot-out with Tamil mainland leaders and the arrest of several others. Meanwhile, the septuagenarian Narasimha Rao assumed the leadership of the Congress(I) party and led it to victory at the polls. There were attempts, immediately after the assassination, to induce Rajiv's wife Sonia to assume the leadership but she made it clear she had little interest in doing so. However, more recently, her name has once again surfaced, and although she doesn't seem interested in the actual leadership of the Congress(I) (at this stage, at least), it is clear she is a powerful, behind-the-scenes influence.

India Today

Although no political heavyweight, Narasimha Rao has displayed remarkable savvy in surviving and deflecting the often acrimonious and sometimes scurrilous accusations of the opposition, particularly in respect of the Bofors affair. Nevertheless, it has become clear that he supported Rajiv's determination to drag India (kicking and screaming, if necessary) into the economic realities of the 1990s, particularly after the collapse of the USSR, India's long-term ally and aid supplier.

After years of languishing behind tariff barriers and a somewhat unrealistic currency exchange rate, the economy was given an enormous boost in 1992 when the finance minister, Manmohan Singh, made the momentous step of partially floating the rupee against a basket of 'hard' currencies and legalising the import of gold by non-resident Indians. He also announced a number of price hikes in unprofitable state-controlled industries – in particular, the railways. It certainly didn't endear him to lower-paid urban workers, especially commuters, but it definitely made black-marketeering, and the corruption associated with it, less attractive. Diplomatic initiatives were also launched with a view to improving relations with Western countries.

On the other hand, Rao inherited a number

of intractable problems which tested the mettle of his government. Although elections were finally held under difficult circumstances in the Punjab, and Congress(I) secured power at state level, the elections were boycotted by the Sikh opposition parties, and Khalistani militants threatened to shoot anyone who voted. The resulting turnout was extremely low, but the state government has established some degree of credibility, despite the limited franchise.

The Kashmir issue again moved onto centre stage during the early 1990s with demonstrations on both sides of the Line of Actual Control and an alarming increase in Jammu & Kashmir Liberation Front (JKLF) guerrilla activities in the Vale of Kashmir. Pakistan was almost certainly involved in encouraging, funding and supplying arms to the militants on the Indian side of the 'border' (which, of course, is denied) but reports suggest that the over-zealous activities of the Indian Army are also partially responsible for the upsurge in militancy. Mutual suspicions brought India and Pakistan to the brink of war yet again in early 1992. It was averted in the nick of time following a meeting between the leaders of the two countries in Switzerland and Pakistani Army intervention in preventing Kashmiri radicals from attempting to cross the Line of Actual Control.

Pakistan's support of the Kashmiri militants, both on its side of the 'border' (known as Azad Kashmir) and in the Vale itself, have rebounded By early 1992, Kashmiri militants and their supporters on both sides were demanding nothing short of independence from both India and Pakistan. This demand is anathema to both India and Pakistan but with the examples of the former USSR, Yugoslavia and Afghanistan, anything could happen.

Another problem which Rao faces is the long-running conflict in many of the states of the North-Eastern Region. For many years, a number of these states – particularly Nagaland and Assam – have been under central government control, though there have been periods when a state assembly was able to function. The biggest threat to the govern-ment is the United Liberation Front of Assam (ULFA), which accuses the government of exploiting the resources of Assam (particularly oil) while neglecting its development. Its guerrilla forces were able to restrict the movements of the armed forces for many years until a massive army operation ('Operation Rhino') in 1992 forced them to the negotiating table. The talks, however, were inconclusive and the conflict simmers on.

A resolution to the conflict in Nagaland is as far away as it ever was, and Arunachal Pradesh is set to become the new focus of problems in the north-east. In Arunachal Pradesh, the powerful student unions and the Congress(I) Chief Minister are demanding the expulsion of all 'foreigners', which basically refers to Bangladeshi immigrants, from India. This is despite the fact that many of the 'foreigners' have lived in India for 30 or more years, and were settled in India as refugees by the state government of Assam after their traditional areas in the then East Pakistan were flooded by a hydroelectric project. (At that time, Arunachal Pradesh was part of Assam, which was known as the North-East Frontier Agency.)

Other secessionist movements have surfaced in Bihar/West Bengal ('Jharkhand'); in the Darjeeling district of West Bengal ('Gorkhaland'); and most recently in the northern part of Uttar Pradesh ('Uttarakhand'), where there were violent clashes between protesters and police in 1994.

Bihar's problems stem from the British encouragement of the zamindar system. At one time, it may have been a convenient and efficient (though exploitative and iniquitous) way of collecting taxes and maintaining what the ruling powers decided was acceptable 'law and order', but it has been transformed into what is essentially an Indian Mafia. Just about everyone in this state, from politicians to police officers and bureaucrats, operates on bribes and, failing that, violence or murder. Anyone who is game enough to stick their neck out and criticise those with power, money or influence is on dangerous ground. This has been going on for years yet no-one at central

P V Narasimha Rao, India's current prime minister, has devoted much effort to freeing up the Indian economy.

government level has ever considered seriously addressing the problem.

In Uttar Pradesh, the problems stem from the official practice of reserving a large number of civil service posts for members of the so-called 'backward classes'.

Perhaps Rao's biggest headache though is the simmering issue of communalism – that potentially explosive conflict between different religious groups, particularly between Hindus and Muslims. 'Ayodhya' is the most recent call to arms. This small town in central Uttar Pradesh is revered by Hindus as the birthplace of Rama. There are many Hindu temples here, but during Mughal times, the emperors razed several temples and constructed mosques on their sites. It's claimed that one of these mosques, the Babri Masjid, stands on the site of what was previously the Rama Temple.

Fundamentalists among the Hindus agitated for the mosque to be demolished and a new Rama Temple to be built in its place. Just about everyone who stood to gain political capital out of this issue jumped into the fray, particularly the BJP (which controlled the UP state government) and its paramilitary organisation, the Rashtriya Swayamsevak Sangh (RSS). The BJP is staunchly Hindu

revivalist and it was quite clear that they were prepared to push this issue regardless of the outcome. As a consequence, hardly a day went by in 1992 without newspaper reports of confrontations or riots. Finally, in December 1992, the mosque was destroyed by Hindus, leading almost immediately to rioting and over 200 deaths.

During the following year, the BJP enjoyed tremendous support in the Hindu-dominated states of northern India. At one time, the BJP appeared poised to become the dominant political party of the 1990s. However, although the Ayodhya issue still smoulders, the BJP has largely failed to capitalise on the popularity it gained. In state elections in late 1993, it lost power in three of the four states in which it governed, and just scraped home in the fourth (Rajasthan) although at state elections in early '95 it managed to take power in Maharashtra, but only in a coalition with another fundamentalist party, the Shiv Sena. The Ayodhya issue is currently before the Uttar Pradesh High Court.

Religious violence has also been unleashed by the practice of reserving government jobs and university places for members of so-called 'backward' classes, which generally means lower caste Hindus. This policy has been used by all parties to buy huge blocs of votes, but it has also caused outbreaks of violence across the country, most recently in Uttar Pradesh, as students and other Hindus protest against it. This system also disaffects lower class Muslims because they don't qualify for places reserved for lower class Hindus.

The reservation practice has gone a long way to undoing much of the work done by people such as Mahatma Gandhi, who worked tirelessly to improve the lot of the socially disadvantaged; once again, caste has been brought to the fore. The only bright spot in this whole issue is that as economic liberalisation takes hold, the private sector will expand at the expense of the public sector, so these policies will apply to a rapidly shrinking proportion of the economy.

In late 1994, Rao's Congress(I) party was dealt a severe blow with election routs in the states of Andhra Pradesh (Rao's home state) and Karnataka (where the party's number of seats fell from 178 to just 35). It's hard to pinpoint the reasons for the voters' lack of confidence in the Congress(I), but there was definitely some backlash against on-going corruption scandals and perhaps against economic policies. Liberalisation has gained momentum, but the reduction of agricultural subsidies combined with high inflation

Gurus & Religion

Religion is of paramount importance in India, so it's no surprise that so many people embark on some sort of spiritual quest here. There are all sorts of ashrams and all manner of gurus.

Rishikesh, in Uttar Pradesh, has been a guru centre ever since the Beatles went there with the Maharishi Mahesh Yogi; it's still popular today. Vrindaban, near Mathura, between Delhi and Agra, is the centre for the Hare Krishna movement. Muktananda had his ashram at Ganeshpuri near Bombay. After his death, there was a bitter battle for the succession, though this has now been settled. The Theosophical Society and the Krishnamurti Foundation have their headquarters in Madras. Not far from there, in Pondicherry, is the ashram of Sri Aurobindo and its offshoot, Auroville. The Ramakrishna Mission has centres all over India, although Calcutta is its headquarters.

Sai Baba is at Puttaparthi near Bangalore, while Brahma Kumaris' Raja Yoga (Prajapita Brahma) is based in Mt Abu. One of the most famous centres is the Rajneesh ashram (now renamed the Osho ashram) at Pune. It still attracts devotees by the thousands. Since the death of Rajneesh, however, many former Rajneeshis have begun flocking to the ashram of Poonjaji at Lucknow. His rise to fame has been meteoric. Poonjaji is a disciple of Ramana Maharishi, whose ashram is at Tiruvannamalai in Tamil Nadu.

There are plenty of other centres, but one guru you won't find in India is the Divine Light Mission's Guru Maharaji. He's currently resident in the USA, and jets around the world to preside over festivals and gatherings.

At Bodhgaya in Bihar, there's been a lot of monastery-building activity. The Root Institute is a Western-run place offering courses in Buddhism and meditation that are attracting increasing numbers of travellers. The Dalai Lama spends a month here in winter, and other Tibetans stay for most of the winter – it's quite a 'scene'. And finally, with the Dalai Lama living in Dharamsala, where better to study Tibetan Buddhism?

Movement	Place	Page
various	Rishikesh (Uttar Pradesh)	381
Krishna Consciousness	Vrindaban (Uttar Pradesh)	368
Poonjaji	Lucknow (Uttar Pradesh)	401
Theosophical Society	Madras (Tamil Nadu)	1006
Krishnamurti Foundation	Madras (Tamil Nadu)	1006
Ramana Maharishi	Tiruvannamalai (Tamil Nadu)	1039
Ramakrishna	Calcutta (West Bengal)	469
Sri Aurobindo	Pondicherry (Tamil Nadu)	1040
Sai Baba	Puttaparthi (Andhra Pradesh)	958
Raja Yoga	Mt Abu (Rajasthan)	625
Osho	Pune (Maharashtra)	810
Tibetan Buddhism	Dharamsala (Himachal Pradesh)	278
Buddhism	Bodhgaya (Bihar)	450

Poonjaji

(currently around 11%) has made life even more difficult for millions of peasant farmers and labourers. Whatever the cause, it's an indication that Rao faces serious challenges in the next national election, due in the first half of 1996.

Despite all these problems, it's worth remembering that 50% of all the people in the world who live in democratic societies, live in India – and, as 1977 indicated, it's a democratic society with teeth. Furthermore, despite its population problems, rural poverty, corruption and political opportunism, India manages to feed its own people without importing food, can turn out hi-tech products with little outside assistance, has a free and highly critical press, and hassles by security and customs officials are either nonexistent or minimal. This is a lot more than you can say about many countries.

GEOGRAPHY

India has a total area of 3,287,263 sq km. The north of the country is decisively bordered by the long sweep of the Himalaya, the highest mountains on earth. They run from south-east to north-west, separating India from China. Bhutan in the east and Nepal in the centre actually lie along the Himalaya, as does Sikkim, Darjeeling, the northern part of Uttar Pradesh, Himachal Pradesh and Jammu & Kashmir.

The Himalaya are not a single mountain range but a series of ranges with beautiful valleys wedged between them. The Kullu Valley in Himachal Pradesh and the Vale of Kashmir in Jammu & Kashmir are both Himalayan valleys, as is the Kathmandu Valley in Nepal. Kanchenjunga (8598 metres) is the highest mountain in India, although until Sikkim (and Kanchenjunga) were absorbed into India that honour went to Nanda Devi (7817 metres). Beyond the Himalaya stretches the high, dry and barren Tibetan plateau; in Ladakh, a small part of this plateau actually lies within India's boundaries.

The final southern range of the Himalaya, the Siwalik Hills, ends abruptly in the great northern plains of India. In complete contrast to the soaring mountain peaks, the northern plain is oppressively flat and slopes so gradually that all the way from Delhi to the Bay of Bengal it drops only 200 metres. The mighty Ganges River, which has its source in the Himalaya, drains a large part of the northern plain and is the major river in India. The Brahmaputra, flowing from the northeast of the country, is the other major river of the north. In the north-west, the Indus River starts flowing through Ladakh in India but soon diverts into Pakistan to become that country's most important river.

South of the northern plains, the land rises up into the high plateau known as the Deccan. The Deccan plateau is bordered on both sides by ranges of hills which parallel the coast to the east and west. The Western Ghats are higher and have a wider coastal strip than the Eastern Ghats. The two ranges meet in the extreme south in the Nilgiri Hills. The southern hill stations are in these hills: Matheran and Mahabaleshwar, near Bombay in the Western Ghats; Ooty and Kodaikanal in the Nilgiri Hills. The major rivers of the south are the Godavari and the Krishna. Both rise on the eastern slope of the Western Ghats and flow across the Deccan into the sea on the eastern coast.

The north-eastern boundary of India is also defined by the foothills of the Himalaya, which separate the country from Myanmar (Burma). In this region, India bends almost entirely around Bangladesh, a low-lying country at the delta of the Ganges and Brahmaputra, and almost meets the sea on the eastern side.

On the western side, India is separated from Pakistan by three distinct regions. In the north, in the disputed area of Kashmir, the Himalaya forms the boundary between the two countries. The Himalaya drop down to the plains of the Punjab, which then merge into the Great Thar Desert in the western part of Rajasthan. This is an area of great natural beauty and extreme barrenness. Finally, the Indian state of Gujarat is separated from the Sind in Pakistan by the unusual marshland known as the Rann of Kutch. In the dry season, the Rann dries out, leaving isolated salt islands on an expansive plain; in the wet season, it floods to become a vast inland sea.

CLIMATE

India is so vast that the climatic conditions in the far north have little relation to that of the extreme south. While the heat is building up to breaking point on the plains, the people of Ladakh will still be waiting for the snow to melt on the high passes.

Basically, India has a three-season year – the hot, the wet and the cool. The best time to visit is during the winter (November through February), except for the northern Himalayan regions where late spring and summer (April through August) is the best time. See the climate charts in this section.

The Hot

The heat starts to build up on the northern plains of India from around February, and by April or May it becomes unbearable. In central India, temperatures of 45°C and above are commonplace – in the summer of 1994, Delhi had temperatures approaching 50°C! It's dry and dusty and everything is seen through a haze.

Later in May, the first signs of the monsoon are seen – high humidity, short rainstorms, violent electrical storms, and dust storms that turn day into night. The hot and humid weather towards the end of the hot season is like a hammer blow; you feel listless and tired and tempers are short.

The hot season is the time to leave the plains and retreat to the hills. Kashmir and the Kullu Valley come into their own, and the Himalayan hill stations and states such as Sikkim are at their best. The hill stations further south – Mt Abu in Rajasthan,

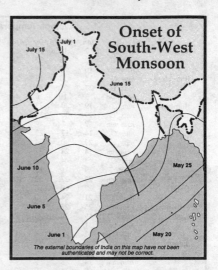

Onset of South-West Monsoon

July 1
July 15
June 15
June 10
May 25
June 5
June 1
May 20

The external boundaries of India on this map have not been authenticated and may not be correct.

Matheran in Maharashtra, Ooty and Kodaikanal in Tamil Nadu – are generally not high enough to be really cool but they are better than being at sea level. By early June, the snow on the passes into Ladakh melts and the roads reopen. This is the best trekking season in northern India.

The Wet

When the monsoon finally arrives, it doesn't just suddenly appear one day. After a period of advance warning, the rain comes in steadily, starting around 1 June in the extreme south and sweeping north to cover the whole country by early July. The monsoon doesn't really cool things off; at first you simply trade the hot, dry, dusty weather for hot, humid, muddy conditions. Even so, it's a great relief, not least for farmers who now have the busiest time of year ahead of them as they prepare their fields for planting. It doesn't rain solidly all day during the monsoon, but it certainly rains every day; the water tends to come down in buckets for a while and then the sun comes out and it's quite pleasant.

The usual monsoon comes from the south-west, but the south-eastern coast is affected

Seasons		
English	**Hindi**	**Period**
Spring	Vasanta	mid-March to mid-May
The Hot	Grishma	mid-May to mid-July
The Wet	Varsha	early-July to mid-September
Autumn	Sharada	mid-September to mid-November
Winter	Hemanta	mid-November to mid-January
The Cool	Shishira	mid-January to mid-March

Average Temperatures & Rainfall

		Jan	Feb	Mar	Apr	May	Jun	Jul	Aug	Sep	Oct	Nov	Dec
Agra	min °C	7	10	16	22	27	30	27	26	24	19	12	8
	max °C	22	26	32	38	42	41	35	33	33	33	30	24
	rain mm	16	9	11	5	10	60	210	263	152	24	2	4
Bangalore	min °C	15	17	19	21	21	20	19	19	19	19	17	15
	max °C	27	30	32	32	33	29	27	27	28	28	26	26
	rain mm	3	10	6	46	117	80	117	147	143	185	54	16
Bombay	min °C	19	20	23	25	27	26	25	25	25	25	23	21
	max °C	29	30	31	32	33	32	30	30	30	32	32	31
	rain mm	2	1	-	3	16	520	710	439	297	88	21	2
Calcutta	min °C	14	17	22	25	27	27	26	26	26	24	18	14
	max °C	27	30	34	36	36	34	32	32	32	32	30	27
	rain mm	14	24	27	43	121	259	301	306	290	160	35	3
Darjeeling	min °C	3	4	8	11	13	15	15	15	15	12	7	4
	max °C	9	11	15	18	19	19	20	20	20	19	15	12
	rain mm	22	27	52	109	187	522	713	573	419	116	14	5
Delhi	min °C	7	10	15	21	27	29	27	26	25	19	12	8
	max °C	21	24	30	36	41	40	35	34	34	33	30	23
	rain mm	25	22	17	7	8	65	211	173	150	31	1	5
Goa	min °C	19	20	23	25	27	25	24	24	24	23	22	21
	max °C	31	32	32	33	33	31	29	29	29	31	33	33
	rain mm	2	-	4	17	18	500	892	341	277	122	20	37
Jaipur	min °C	8	11	15	21	26	27	26	24	23	18	12	9
	max °C	22	25	31	37	41	39	34	32	33	33	29	24
	rain mm	14	8	9	4	10	54	193	239	90	19	3	4
Jaisalmer	min °C	8	11	17	21	26	27	27	26	25	20	13	9
	max °C	24	28	32	38	42	41	38	36	36	36	31	26
	rain mm	2	1	3	2	5	7	90	86	14	1	5	2
Jodhpur	min °C	9	12	17	22	27	29	27	25	24	20	14	11
	max °C	25	28	33	38	42	40	36	33	35	36	31	27
	rain mm	7	5	2	2	6	31	122	145	47	7	3	1
Kochi	min °C	23	24	26	26	26	24	24	24	24	24	24	24
	max °C	31	31	31	31	31	29	28	28	28	29	30	30
	rain mm	10	34	50	140	364	756	572	386	235	333	184	37
Leh	min °C	-14	-12	-6	-1	3	7	10	10	5	-1	-7	-11
	max °C	-3	1	6	12	17	21	25	24	21	14	8	2
	rain mm	12	9	12	7	7	4	16	20	12	7	3	8
Lucknow	min °C	9	11	16	22	27	28	27	26	23	20	13	9
	max °C	23	26	33	38	41	39	34	33	33	33	29	25
	rain mm	24	17	9	6	12	94	299	302	182	40	1	6
Madras	min °C	20	21	24	26	28	28	26	26	25	25	23	21
	max °C	29	31	33	35	38	37	35	35	34	32	29	28
	rain mm	24	7	15	25	52	53	84	124	118	267	309	139
Mysore	min °C	16	18	20	21	21	20	20	20	19	20	18	17
	max °C	28	31	34	34	33	29	27	28	29	28	27	27
	rain mm	3	6	12	68	156	61	72	80	116	180	67	15
Shimla	min °C	2	4	7	15	15	17	16	15	14	10	7	4
	max °C	9	10	14	19	23	24	21	20	20	18	15	11
	rain mm	66	50	61	38	54	147	420	385	195	45	7	24
Srinagar	min °C	-2	-1	4	7	11	14	18	18	13	6	0	-2
	max °C	4	8	13	19	25	29	31	30	28	23	16	9
	rain mm	73	72	100	78	63	30	61	63	32	29	18	36
Thiruvanan-thapuram	min °C	22	23	24	25	25	24	23	23	23	23	23	22
	max °C	31	32	33	32	32	29	29	29	30	30	30	31
	rain mm	20	20	44	122	249	331	215	164	123	271	207	73
Udaipur	min °C	8	10	15	20	25	25	24	23	22	19	11	8
	max °C	24	28	32	36	38	36	31	29	31	32	29	26
	rain mm	9	4	3	3	5	87	197	207	120	16	6	3
Udhagaman-dalam (Ooty)	min °C	5	6	8	10	11	11	11	11	10	10	8	6
	max °C	20	21	22	22	22	18	10	17	18	19	19	20
	rain mm	26	12	30	109	173	139	177	128	110	213	127	59
Varanasi	min °C	9	11	17	22	27	28	26	26	25	21	13	9
	max °C	23	27	33	39	41	39	33	32	32	32	29	25
	rain mm	23	8	14	1	8	102	346	240	261	38	15	2

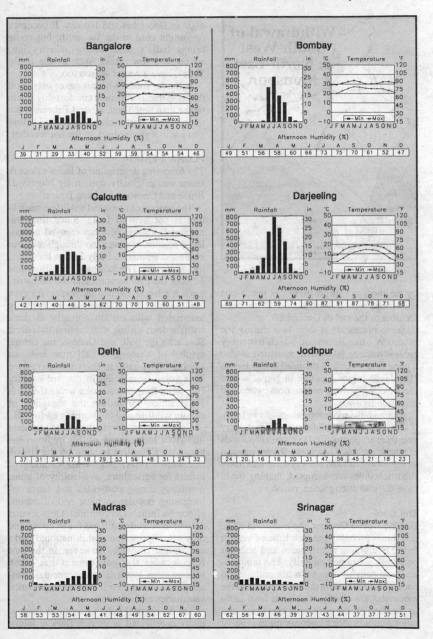

Bangalore

Rainfall (mm / in)
Temperature (°C / °F)
Min ─■─ Max ─+─
JFMAMJJASOND

Afternoon Humidity (%)

J	F	M	A	M	J	J	A	S	O	N	D
39	31	29	33	40	52	59	59	54	54	54	46

Bombay

Rainfall (mm / in)
Temperature (°C / °F)
Min ─■─ Max ─+─
JFMAMJJASOND

Afternoon Humidity (%)

J	F	M	A	M	J	J	A	S	O	N	D
49	51	56	58	60	66	73	75	70	61	52	47

Calcutta

Rainfall (mm / in)
Temperature (°C / °F)
Min ─■─ Max ─+─
JFMAMJJASOND

Afternoon Humidity (%)

J	F	M	A	M	J	J	A	S	O	N	D
42	41	40	46	54	62	70	70	70	60	51	48

Darjeeling

Rainfall (mm / in)
Temperature (°C / °F)
Min ─■─ Max ─+─
JFMAMJJASOND

Afternoon Humidity (%)

J	F	M	A	M	J	J	A	S	O	N	D
69	71	62	59	74	90	87	91	87	78	71	68

Delhi

Rainfall (mm / in)
Temperature (°C / °F)
Min ─■─ Max ─+─
JFMAMJJASOND

Afternoon Humidity (%)

J	F	M	A	M	J	J	A	S	O	N	D
37	31	24	17	18	29	53	56	48	31	24	32

Jodhpur

Rainfall (mm / in)
Temperature (°C / °F)
Min ─■─ Max ─+─
JFMAMJJASOND

Afternoon Humidity (%)

J	F	M	A	M	J	J	A	S	O	N	D
24	20	16	16	20	31	47	56	45	21	18	23

Madras

Rainfall (mm / in)
Temperature (°C / °F)
Min ─■─ Max ─+─
JFMAMJJASOND

Afternoon Humidity (%)

J	F	M	A	M	J	J	A	S	O	N	D
58	53	53	54	46	41	48	49	54	62	67	60

Srinagar

Rainfall (mm / in)
Temperature (°C / °F)
Min ─■─ Max ─+─
JFMAMJJASOND

Afternoon Humidity (%)

J	F	M	A	M	J	J	A	S	O	N	D
62	56	49	46	39	37	43	44	37	37	37	51

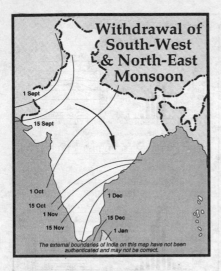

Withdrawal of South-West & North-East Monsoon

1 Sept
15 Sept
1 Oct
15 Oct
1 Nov
15 Nov
1 Dec
15 Dec
1 Jan

The external boundaries of India on this map have not been authenticated and may not be correct.

by the short and surprisingly wet north-east monsoon, which brings rain from mid-October to the end of December.

Some places are at their best during the monsoon – like Rajasthan, which has many palaces built on lakes. The monsoon is also a good time to trek in the north-west Indian Himalayan regions, unlike in Nepal where the trekking season commences when the monsoon finishes.

Although the monsoon brings life to India, it also brings its share of death. Almost every year there are destructive floods and thousands of people are made homeless. Rivers rise and sweep away road and railway lines and many flight schedules are disrupted, making travel more difficult during the monsoon.

The Cool

Finally, around October, the monsoon ends, and this is probably the best time of year in India. Everything is still green and lush but you don't get rained on daily. The temperatures are delightful, not too hot and not too cool. The air is clear in the Himalaya, and the mountains are clearly visible, at least early in the day. As the cool rolls on, Delhi and other northern cities become quite crisp at

night in December and January. It becomes downright cold in the far north, but snow brings India's small skiing industry into action so a few places, such as the Kullu Valley, have a winter season too.

In the far south, where it never gets cool, the temperatures become comfortably warm rather than hot. Then, around February, the temperatures start to climb again, and before you know it you're back in the hot weather.

FLORA & FAUNA

The following description of India's flora & fauna was originally written by Murray D Bruce and Constance S Leap Bruce.

The concept of forest and wildlife conservation is not new to India. Since time immemorial, wildlife here has enjoyed a privileged position of protection through religious ideals and sentiment. Early Indian literature, including the Hindu epics, the Buddhist Jatakas, the Panchatantra and the Jain strictures, teach nonviolence and respect for even lowly animal forms. Many of the gods are associated with certain animals: Brahma with the deer, Vishnu with the lion and cobra, Siva with the bull, and Ganesh, the eternal symbol of wisdom, is half man and half elephant. The earliest known conservation laws come from India in the 3rd century BC, when Emperor Ashoka wrote the Fifth Pillar Edict, forbidding the slaughter of certain wildlife and the burning of forests.

Unfortunately, during the recent turbulent history of India, much of this tradition has been lost. Extensive hunting by the British and Indian rajas, large-scale clearing of forests for agriculture, availability of guns, poaching, strong pesticides and the ever-increasing population have had disastrous effects on India's environment. Only around 10% of the country still has forest cover, and only 4% is protected within national parks and similar reserves. However, in the past few decades the government has taken serious steps towards environmental management and has established over 350 parks, sanctuaries and reserves.

The diversity of India's climate and topography is reflected in its rich flora & fauna.

India is renowned for its tigers, elephants and rhinoceroses, but these are just three of the more than 500 species of mammals living in the country. Conservation projects have been established to preserve them, but for some species, such as the Indian cheetah, protection has come too late – the Indian cheetah was last seen in 1948.

A variety of deer and antelope species can be seen, but these are now mostly confined to the protected areas because of competition with domestic animals and the effects of their diseases. They include graceful Indian gazelles (chinkaras); Indian antelopes (blackbucks); diminutive, four-horned antelopes (chowsinghas); large and ungainly looking blue bulls (nilgais); rare swamp deer (barasinghas); sambars, India's largest deer; beautiful spotted deer (chitals); the larger barking deer (muntjacs); and the tiny mouse deer (chevrotains).

Also seen are wild buffaloes, massive Indian bisons (gaurs), shaggy sloth bears, striped hyenas, wild pigs, jackals, Indian foxes, wolves, and Indian wild dogs (dhole), which resembles giant foxes but roam in packs in forests. Amongst the smaller mammals are mongooses, renowned as snake killers, and giant squirrels.

Cats include leopards, panthers, short-tailed jungle cats, and beautiful leopard cats. Various monkeys can be seen, with rhesus macaques, bonnet macaques (in the south only) and long-tailed common langurs the most likely.

India is blessed with over 2000 species and sub-species of birds. The diverse birdlife of the forests includes large hornbills, serpent eagles and fishing owls, as well as the elegant national bird, the peacock. Waterbirds, such as herons, ibises, storks, cranes, pelicans and others, are seen not only in parks but at numerous special waterbird sanctuaries. These sanctuaries contain large breeding colonies, and are of great importance for the countless numbers of migrating birds which visit India annually.

Among the other wildlife are over 500 species of reptiles and amphibians, including magnificent king cobras, pythons, croco-diles, large freshwater tortoises and monitor lizards. There are also 30,000 insect species, including large and colourful butterflies.

The vegetation, from dry desert scrub to alpine meadow, comprises some 15,000 species of plants recorded to date.

Many of the wildlife sanctuaries, and some national parks, have been established in the former private hunting reserves of the British and Indian aristocracy. Often, the parks are renowned for one particular creature, such as Asian lions in Gir, Indian rhinoceroses in Kaziranga, elephants in Periyar, and tigers in Kanha and Corbett; other areas have been established to preserve unique habitats such as lowland tropical rainforest or the mangrove forest of the Sunderbans.

Geographically, India is divided into three main regions, each with many subregions and distinctive altitudinal climatic variations. The important national parks, wildlife sanctuaries and reserves within these regions are listed below. These and other reserves are included in more detail in the relevant chapters.

National Parks & Wildlife Sanctuaries
National parks and other protected areas in India are administered at the state level and are often promoted as part of each state's tourist attractions. To encourage more visitors, accommodation, road systems, transport and other facilities continue to be developed and upgraded. Whenever possible, book in advance for transport and accommodation through the local tourist offices or state departments, and check if a permit is required, particularly in border areas. Various fees are charged for your visit (entrance, photography, etc) and these are usually included in advance arrangements. Meals may also be arranged when you book, but in some cases you must take your own food supplies and have it prepared for you.

Some parks offer modern-style guest houses with electricity, while in others only dak-style bungalows are available. Facilities usually include van and jeep rides, and at some parks you can take a boat trip to approach wildlife more discreetly. Watchtowers and hides are also often available, and provide good opportunities to observe and photograph wildlife close up.

Northern India This is a region of extremes, ranging from the snow-bound peaks and deep valleys of the Himalaya to flat plains and tropical lowlands.

Dachigam Wildlife Sanctuary (Kashmir) This sanctuary is in a very scenic valley with a large meandering river. The surrounding mountain slopes contain rare Kashmir stags (hangul), as well as black and brown bears. There are also musk deer, a small

species widely hunted for the male's musk gland, which is considered valuable in treating impotence and is exported to Europe's perfumeries. The instability in Kashmir in recent years has seriously endangered the wildlife of Dachigam. The sanctuary is 22 km by road from Srinagar, and is certainly worth a visit (if Kashmir is open). Best Time to Visit: June to July.

Valley of Flowers National Park (Uttar Pradesh) This 'garden on top of the world' is in the north of Uttar Pradesh near Badrinath, at an elevation of 3500 metres. When the famous Valley of Flowers is in bloom, it's an unforgettable experience. Unfortunately, the park has suffered intense tourist pressure and is periodically closed. Best Time to Visit: June to August.

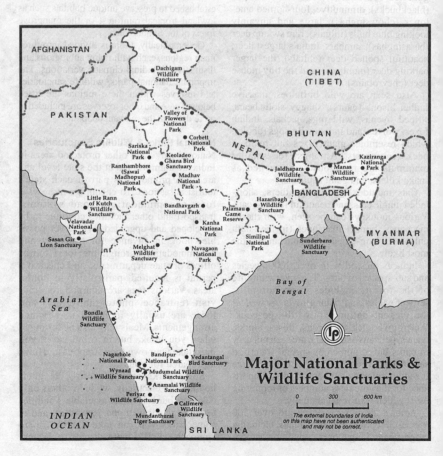

Gangetic Plain Some of the most famous parks in Asia are in this region. It contains the flat, alluvial plains of the Indus, Ganges and Brahmaputra rivers – an immense tract of level land stretching from the Arabian Sea to the Bay of Bengal and separating the Himalayan region from the southern peninsula. Climate varies greatly, from the arid, sandy deserts of Rajasthan and Gujarat, with temperatures up to 50°C, to the cool highlands of Assam, where annual rainfall can exceed 15 *metres* – allegedly the wettest place on earth.

Corbett National Park (Uttar Pradesh) This park is famous for its tigers, but it is not the best place to see these animals – Kanha in Madhya Pradesh and Ranthambhore in Rajasthan are both better.

Other wildlife includes chitals and hog deer, elephants, leopards, sloth bears and muntjacs. There are numerous watchtowers, but only daylight photography is allowed. The park has magnificent scenery, from sal forest (giant, teak-like hardwood trees) to extensive river plains. The Ramganga River offers tranquil settings and good fishing. It's a bit touristy, but worth a visit. Best Time to Visit: November to May.

Hazaribagh Wildlife Sanctuary (Bihar) This is an area of rolling, forested hills with large herds of deer, as well as tigers and leopards. Best Time to Visit: February to March.

Palamau Game Reserve (Bihar) Palamau is smaller than Hazaribagh but has good concentrations of wildlife, including tigers, leopards, elephants, gaurs, sambars, chitals, nilgais and muntjacs, as well as rhesus macaques, common langurs and (rarely) wolves. It is 150 km south of Ranchi, with bungalows at Betla. Best Time to Visit: February to March.

Sunderbans Wildlife Sanctuary (West Bengal) This reserve, south-east of Calcutta, protects the extensive mangrove forests of the Ganges Delta, which are an important haven for tigers. Unfortunately, there's no way you'll see a tiger here unless you're being eaten by one because the park guards are wary of savage cats and won't take you into the narrow channels.

Other wildlife includes fishing cats, which can be seen looking for fish at the water's edge, and great birdlife. The only access is by chartered boat. Best Time to Visit: February to March.

Jaldhapara Wildlife Sanctuary (West Bengal) The tropical forests extending from South-East Asia end around here, and if you don't go further east, this is your best chance to see Indian rhinoceroses, ele-

phants and other wildlife. The area protects 100 sq km of lush forest and grasslands, cut by the wide Torsa River. It is 224 km from Darjeeling, via Siliguri and Jalpaiguri (nearest railhead Hashimara). There's a rest house at Jaldhapara. Best Time to Visit: March to May.

Manas Wildlife Sanctuary (Assam) This lovely area bordering Bhutan is formed from the watershed of the Manas, Hakua and Beki rivers. The bungalows at Mothanguri, on the banks of the Manas, offer views of jungle-clad hills. Established trails enter nearby forests and follow the riverbanks. Try to arrange a boat cruise. Besides tigers, the grassland is home to wild buffaloes, elephants, sambars, swamp deer and other wildlife; rare and beautiful golden langurs may be seen on the Bhutan side of the Manas. Unfortunately, the park has been used in recent times as a refuge by Bodo rebels and much of the infrastructure has been damaged or destroyed. Best Time to Visit: January to March.

Kaziranga National Park (Assam) This is the most famous place to see one-horned Indian rhinoceroses, hunted almost to extinction as big game and for the Chinese apothecary trade. As an anti-poaching measure, plans were drawn up recently to translocate a number of animals to the Terai grasslands of Dudhwa National Park in Uttar Pradesh. However, this plan now seems to have been shelved, and the outlook for the rhino here is not good.

The park is dominated by tall (up to six metres) grasslands and *jheels* (swampy areas). The first sighting of a rhinoceros is always impressive; they can reach a height of over two metres and weigh more than two tonnes. Despite their appearance, rhinos are incredibly agile and fast. Spotting them in the tall grass may be difficult. Watch for egrets and other birds who use the rhino's armoured back as a perch, and listen for the 'churring' sound of a large animal moving through the grass. The best viewing areas are around the jheels, where the rhinoceros bathe. Best Time to Visit: February to March.

Sariska & Ranthambhore National Parks (Rajasthan) Both of these areas provide good opportunities to see the wildlife of the Indian plains. Sariska is notable for night viewing and its nilgai herds. Unfortunately, it has recently become the haunt of hordes of loud and insensitive tourists who seem to have little regard for the very thing they have come to the park to see. Illegal mining also poses a threat to the park.

Ranthambhore (or Sawai Madhopur) is smaller, which can make seeing animals easier, and it has a lake with crocodiles. However, it too is suffering because its reputation as a place to spot tigers has drawn ever increasing numbers of tourists. It's actually becoming more difficult to see tigers at Ranthambhore though; *BBC World* magazine (Jan/Feb '93) revealed that corrupt officials have allowed illegal poaching to rapidly deplete the tiger population. The sanctuary is on the Delhi to Bombay railway line, and is 160 km south of Jaipur by road. Best Time to Visit: February to June (Sariska); November to May (Ranthambhore).

Keoladeo Ghana Bird Sanctuary (Rajasthan)

This is the best known and most touristy bird sanctuary (usually just called Bharatpur). It features large numbers of breeding waterbirds and thousands of migrating birds from Siberia and China, including herons, storks, cranes and geese. The network of crossroads and tracks through the sanctuary can increase opportunities to see the birds, deer and other wildlife. It is also on the Delhi to Bombay railway line. Best Time to Visit: September to February.

Sasan Gir National Park (Gujarat)

This forested oasis in the desert is famous for the last surviving Asian lions (around 250 of them), but it also supports a variety of other wildlife, notably the chowsinghas and the crocodiles which live in Lake Kamaleshwar. The lake and other watering holes are good places to spot animals. The park is closed from mid-May to mid-October. Best Time to Visit: December to April.

Velavadar National Park (Gujarat)

This park, 65 km north of Bhavnagar, protects the rich grasslands in the delta region on the west side of the Gulf of Khambhat (Cambay). The main attraction is a large concentration of beautiful blackbucks. There is a park lodge for visitors. Best Time to Visit: October to June.

Little Rann of Kutch Wildlife Sanctuary (Gujarat)

This sanctuary was designated for the protection of the desert region of north-west Gujarat. A variety of desert life can be found here, notably the surviving herds of the Indian wild ass *(khur)*. Also in residence are wolves and caracal (a large, pale cat with tufted ears). Access is difficult, but can be arranged at Bhuj. Best Time to Visit: October to June.

Madhav National Park (Madhya Pradesh)

This picturesque park close to Gwalior has open forests surrounding a lake. There are good opportunities for photographing various deer, including chinkaras, chowsinghas and nilgais. It is also home to tigers and leopards. Best Time to Visit: February to May.

Kanha National Park (Madhya Pradesh)

Kanha is one of India's most spectacular and exciting parks for both variety and numbers of wildlife. Originally proposed to protect a unique type of swamp deer (barasinghas), it is also an important area for tigers,

---

Wildlife Problems

While India has made a laudable effort to protect its endangered species by establishing wildlife sanctuaries, greed and corruption are threatening to undermine the success of these endeavours. It is estimated that since 1990 over 20 tigers have been slaughtered at Ranthambhore (Rajasthan). After its skin is removed, the carcass is dumped to allow insects and scavengers to remove the flesh. The bones inevitably find their way to China, where they form the basis of 'tiger wine', believed to have healing properties. The penis is coveted for its alleged aphrodisiacal powers. The skin and claws can fetch up to US$6000 in Nepal.

National parks and sanctuaries are proving to be lucrative hunting grounds for poachers. Frequently, only main roads in parks are patrolled by often poorly paid guards, so poachers can trespass without fear of detection. In July 1992, Badia, one of Ranthambhore's more diligent and committed trackers, was brutally murdered – allegedly by poachers, who have still not been convicted. It is now suspected that gangs of poachers have moved their operations to Madhya Pradesh, where recently over 40 tigers are believed to have been killed. These tigers had become conditioned to humans on 'safaris', making them easy game for poachers. Efforts to protect tigers from this conditioning have been thwarted by local tour operators, who wish to protect their businesses.

Industry poses another threat to India's wildlife. Vast tracts of wilderness designated as 'protected areas' have been denotified to make way for mining ventures. The Indian Aluminium Company has requested a portion of the Radhnagari Bison Sanctuary to mine bauxite. One-third of the Melghat Wildlife Sanctuary in Maharashtra was requisitioned for the construction of a dam. Other impediments include: the focussing of attention on Project Tiger, which has led to the neglect of other pressing problems; the lack of Centre-state co-operation; inadequate staffing, funding and infrastructure; the use of some parks (such as Manas in Assam) as refuges by militants and other malcontents; and, most recently, the increased tourist traffic in ecologically fragile areas. This last problem has led to strong measures being taken at some parks in order to limit the number of human visitors: at Corbett, day visitors are banned from areas of the park; at Ranthambhore, a limit has been placed on the number of vehicles which can enter the park at any one time.

Without a concerted effort on the part of conservationists, and the requisite political will to effect meaningful conservationist policies, mausoleum-like museums will prove to be the final home of India's wildlife – and stuffed tigers and lions will be all that remains of India's once rich wildlife heritage. ■

chitals, blackbucks, gaurs, leopards and hyenas. The park is closed from 1 July to 31 October. Best Time to Visit: March and April, although wildlife can be seen throughout the season, from November to May.

Bandhavgarh National Park (Madhya Pradesh)

Bandhavgarh is smaller and less touristy than Kanha, has an impressive setting, and boasts an old fort on the cliffs above the plains. Although the park is not part of Project Tiger, tigers are occasionally seen. The park is closed from 1 July to 31 October. Best Time to Visit: November to April.

Similipal National Park (Orissa)

This reserve is a vast and beautiful area protecting India's largest region of sal forest. It has magnificent scenery and a variety of wildlife, including tigers (thought to number around 80), elephants, leopards, sambars, chitals, muntjacs and chevrotains. The park is closed from July to October. Best Time to Visit: November to June.

Southern India

The Deccan peninsula is a triangular plateau ranging in altitude from 300 to 900 metres. It is intersected with rivers, and scattered with peaks and hills, including the Western and Eastern Ghats. The Ghats form a natural barrier to the monsoons and have created areas of great humidity and rainfall on the Malabar Coast, and drier regions on the mountains' leeward sides.

Sanjay Gandhi National Park (Maharashtra)

This 104-sq-km park, formerly known as Borivli, protects an important and scenic area close to Bombay. Amongst the smaller types of wildlife to be seen are a variety of waterbirds. Best Time to Visit: October to June.

Taroba National Park (Maharashtra)

This is a large park featuring mixed teak forests and a lake. Night viewing offers good opportunities to see tigers, leopards, gaurs, nilgais, sambars and chitals. The park is 45 km from Chandrapur, south-west of Kanha National Park. You can arrange to stay in the park. Best Time to Visit: March to May.

Periyar Wildlife Sanctuary (Kerala)

Periyar is a large and scenic park comprises the watershed of a reservoir developed around a large, artificial lake. It is famous for its large elephant population, which can easily be seen by boat from the lake.

Other wildlife includes the gaurs, Indian wild dogs and nilgiri langurs, as well as otters, large tortoises and flights of hornbills. At the water's edge, you may see the flashing, brilliant hues of several kinds of kingfisher, perhaps even fishing owls. Best Time to Visit: February to May.

Jawahar National Park

There was a recent proposal to merge Bandipur and Nagarhole national parks (Karnataka), Mudumulai Wildlife Sanctuary (Tamil Nadu), and Wynaad Wildlife Sanctuary (Kerala). Situated at the junction of the Western Ghats, the Nilgiri Hills and the Deccan plateau, the merging of these contiguous areas would protect the largest elephant population in India and one of the most extensive forested areas in the south. The mixed, diverse forests harbour leopards, gaurs, sambars, chitals, muntjacs, chevrotains, bonnet macaques and giant squirrels.

The very rich birdlife includes many spectacular species such as hornbills, barbets, trogons, parakeets, racquet-tailed drongos and streamer-tailed Asian paradise flycatchers. The two most popular areas are Bandipur and Mudumulai. This area should not be missed if you visit the south. Best Time to Visit: January to June.

Vedantangal Bird Sanctuary (Tamil Nadu)

About 35 km south of Chengalpattu, this is one of the most spectacular breeding grounds for water birds in India. Cormorants, egrets, herons, storks, ibises, spoonbills, grebes and pelicans come here to breed and nest for about six months from October/November to March, depending on the monsoons. At the height of the breeding season (December and January), you can see up to 30,000 birds at once. Many other species of migratory birds also visit the sanctuary.

Calimere Wildlife Sanctuary (Tamil Nadu)

Also known as Kodikkarai, this coastal sanctuary is 90 km south-east of Thanjavur in a wetland area jutting into the Palk Strait, which separates India and Sri Lanka. It is noted for the vast flocks of migratory water fowl, especially flamingoes, which congregate here every winter. Blackbucks, spotted deer and wild pigs can also be seen. From April to June there's very little activity; the main rainy season is between October and December. Best Time to Visit: November to January.

Mundanthurai Tiger Sanctuary (Tamil Nadu)

Mundanthurai is in the mountains near the border with Kerala. It's principally a tiger sanctuary, though it's also noted for chitals, sambars and rare lion-tailed macaques. The main rainy season is between October and December. Tiger sightings are apparently extremely infrequent. Best Time to Visit: January to March, though it is open all year.

Anamalai Wildlife Sanctuary (Tamil Nadu)

This wildlife sanctuary is on the slopes of the Western Ghats along the border between Tamil Nadu and Kerala. Though recently renamed the Indira Gandhi

Wildlife Sanctuary, most people still refer to it by its original name. It covers almost 1000 sq km and is home to elephants, gaurs, tigers, panthers, spotted deer, wild boars, bears, porcupines and civet cats.

In the heart of this beautiful forested region is the Parambikulam Dam, which has formed an immense plain of water that spreads into Kerala.

GOVERNMENT

India has a parliamentary system of government with certain similarities to the US system. There are two houses – a lower house known as the Lok Sabha (House of the People) and an upper house known as the Rajya Sabha (Council of States).

The lower house has 544 members (excluding the Speaker), all but two elected on a population basis (proportional representation). Elections for the Lok Sabha are held every five years, unless the government calls an election earlier. All Indians over the age of 18 have the right to vote.

Of the 544 seats, 125 are reserved for the Scheduled Castes & Tribes (see the Population & People section later in this chapter for details on these people). The upper house has 245 members. The lower house can be dissolved but the upper house cannot.

There are also state governments with legislative assemblies known as Vidhan Sabha. The two national houses and the various state houses elect the Indian president, who is a figurehead – the prime minister wields the real power.

There is a strict division between the activities handled by the states and by the national government. The police force, education, agriculture and industry are reserved for the state governments. Certain other areas are jointly administered by the two levels of government.

The central government has the controversial right to assume power in any state if the situation in that state is deemed to be unmanageable. Known as President's Rule, it has been enforced in recent years, either because the law and order situation has got out of hand – notably in Punjab from 1985 to 1992, Kashmir in 1990 and in Assam in 1991 – or because there is a political stalemate – such as occurred in Goa, Tamil Nadu, Pondicherry, Haryana and Meghalaya in 1991, and Nagaland in 1992. Of these states, Kashmir, Meghalaya and Nagaland are still under central rule.

The current government, headed by P V Narasimha Rao, is a minority government, since Rao's Congress(I) party failed to win an absolute majority in the 1991 elections. As of early 1994, the party breakdown of the Lok Sabha seats is: Congress(I) 258, BJP 118, Janata Dal 39, CPI (M) 36, CPI 14, Independents & Others 79.

Despite some serious fluctuations in its popularity, the radical Hindu nationalist party, the BJP, has made great gains in the last couple of elections. It is the main opposition party and holds power in Gujarat. It also held Uttar Pradesh, Madhya Pradesh, Himachal Pradesh and Rajasthan until the destruction of the Babri Mosque in Ayodhya led to the dissolution of the government in those states. In the 1994-5 state elections, the BJP held Gujarat but failed to make any major gains.

National Emblem, Flag & Anthem

The national flag is known as the tricolour. It features three horizontal bands of colour – from top to bottom orange, white and dark green. The *chakhra* wheel in the centre of the flag is based on the design that appears on the famous Ashokan pillar at Sarnath.

The words of the national anthem are taken from a Hindi poem by Rabindranath Tagore. Tagore's English translation is as follows:

Thou art the ruler of the minds of all people,
Dispenser of India's destiny.
Thy name rouses the hearts of the Punjab,
Sind, Gujarat and Maratha.
Of the Dravid and Orissa and Bengal.
It echoes in the hills of the Vindhyas and Himalayas,
Mingles in the music of the Jamuna and the Ganges,
And is chanted by the waves of the Indian Sea.
They pray for the blessings and sing thy praise,
The saving of all people waits in thy hand,
Thou dispenser of India's destiny,
Victory, victory, victory to thee.

ECONOMY

Although India is a predominantly agricultural country, it has a large manufacturing base and is one of the world's major industrial powers. The economic reforms of the last few years are now enabling India to attract multinationals who want to tap into the huge Indian market.

Agriculture

The agriculture sector, for so long the mainstay of the Indian economy, now accounts for only about 20% of GDP, yet still employs over 50% of the population. For some years after Independence India depended on foreign aid to meet its food needs, but in the last 35 years food production has risen steadily, mainly due to an increase in irrigated areas and the widespread use of high-yield seeds, fertilisers and pesticides. The country has large grain stockpiles and is a net exporter of food grains.

The main crops are rice (annual yield of 75 million tonnes) and wheat (55 million tonnes), but it's the cash crops such as tea and coffee which are the export earners. India is the world's largest producer of tea, with an annual production of around 740 million kg, of which around 200 million tonnes is exported. Virtually all the Indian tea is grown in the states of Assam, West Bengal, Kerala and Tamil Nadu. India also holds around 30% of the world spice market, with exports of around 120,000 tonnes per year.

Other significant crops grown and used domestically are rubber, with an annual production of around 400,000 tonnes, and coconuts, with production running to almost one billion nuts annually.

Industry

For many years India's industrial sector was strictly controlled by the central government, but the level of central intervention has decreased markedly over the past decade. Since Narasimha Rao initiated sweeping economic reforms in mid-1991, foreign investment has poured in. During 1994, the international finance community 'discovered' India, and not only did investment in

Indian companies reach record levels, but many multinationals decided to set up shop in India to take advantage of the improved financial climate.

One reason for the eagerness of foreign companies to establish operations in India is to gain access to the 300 million Indians who have an annual income of more than US$700 and the 100 million who earn more than US$1400. Both these groups have high enough disposable incomes to purchase consumer goods.

In purely economic terms, the results of the reforms have been impressive, with economic growth reaching 5.5% in 1994-95, with record levels of exports and foreign exchange reserves. Predictably, the 40% of the population who live on or below the poverty line have been little affected, and inflation (currently running at 11%) is threatening to get out of control. Despite the existence of a large middle class, the national GNP per capita income is still only Rs 12,000 per annum, or around Rs 35 per day.

Although things are improving, most industries are still hopelessly inefficient, use outdated technology and equipment, produce inferior goods unsuitable for export, are often dangerous places to work, and are polluting the environment at an incredible rate. Virtually everything you come across in Indian shops is still made locally by Indian companies, which is quite an amazing achievement given that the country had very little industrial diversity at Independence.

Textiles account for around 25% of exports, but engineering goods, marine products, chemicals, and, increasingly, high-tech items such as computer software, are all important exports. The major import is oil and petroleum products, accounting for around 25% of imports.

POPULATION & PEOPLE

India has the second-largest population in the world, exceeded only by that of China. It had 439 million people in 1961, 547 million in 1971, 687 million in 1981, and 843 million in 1991. Estimates for 1995 put the figure at 930 million. Despite extensive birth control programmes, it is still growing far too rapidly for comfort – around 2% per year.

Yet, despite India's many large cities, the country is still overwhelmingly rural. It is estimated that about 280 million of the total population live in urban areas, but with increasing industrialisation the shift from village to city continues.

The Indian people are not a homogeneous group. It is quite easy to tell the difference between the shorter Bengalis of the east, the taller and lighter-skinned people of the centre and north, the Kashmiris with their distinctly central Asian appearance, the Tibetan people of Ladakh, Sikkim and the north of Himachal Pradesh, and the dark-skinned Tamils of the south. Despite these regional variations, the government has managed to successfully establish an 'Indian' ethos and national consciousness.

Although India is overwhelmingly Hindu, there are large minorities of other religions. These include around 105 million Muslims, making India one of the largest Muslim countries in the world, much larger than any of the Arab Middle East nations. Christians number about 22 million, Sikhs 18 million, Buddhists 6.6 million and Jains 4.5 million. About 7% of the population is classified as 'tribal'. They are found scattered throughout the country, although there are concentrations of them in the north-eastern corner of the country, as well as in Bihar, Orissa, Madhya Pradesh and Andhra Pradesh.

The literacy rate is 53% nationally, up from 44% in 1981. Men are generally more literate than women – 64% to 39% respectively. The literacy rate varies hugely from state to state – Kerala boasts 91% literacy, while in Bihar it's 38%. Amongst the Scheduled Castes & Tribes, the literacy rates are abysmal – 28% among men and 9% among women.

Birth Control

India had a birth control blitz in the early 1970s. Slogans and posters appeared all over the country, and the (in)famous 'transistor radio in exchange for sterilisation' campaign began. More sinister still was the brief campaign during the emergency era, when squads of sterilisers terrorised the country and people were afraid to go out after dark. This wayward campaign harmed India's birth control programme severely.

It wasn't until the mid-1980s that population control was once again a government priority – Rajiv Gandhi mounted an ambitious project, with the target of 1.3 billion Indians by the year 2050.

Although there has been some success at slowing the rate of increase, the picture is far from promising. Many experts feel that the solution to the population increase problem in India is to educate the women, particularly in the rural communities. Literate and educated women are much better equipped to understand the need for limiting the size of families and the population as a whole. Decreasing the mortality rate among small children is also seen as a significant factor in reducing the desire for large families. As long as children are seen as a source of security in old age, and while male heirs are so avidly desired, it is going to be difficult to successfully limit population growth.

Although educating women is an important part of the programme, the emphasis is once again on sterilisation, with women the main target. It seems men are unwilling to volunteer for a vasectomy. In regional areas, social workers are recruited to find 'volunteers' for the operation. As an incentive, they are paid a small fee for every person encouraged to go through with it. There is also a small financial incentive offered to people who undergo sterilisation.

Another part of the family planning drive involves widespread use of the media – particularly TV. The two-child family is portrayed as the ideal, and the use of contraceptives, especially condoms, is encouraged.

Castes

The caste system is one of India's more confusing mysteries – how it came about, how it has managed to survive for so long and how much harm it causes are all topics of discussion for visitors to India. Its origins are hazy, but it seems to have been developed

---

India's Million-Plus Cities

Nearly 30% of India's people live in urban areas and the country has more than 20 cities with populations of more than one million. In order, they are:

City	Million people
Bombay	14.5
Calcutta	12.0
Delhi	10.1
Madras	5.7
Hyderabad	4.7
Bangalore	4.5
Ahmedabad	3.6
Pune	2.7
Kanpur	2.3
Lucknow, Nagpur	1.8
Jaipur	1.7
Surat	1.6
Bhopal, Coimbatore, Indore, Madurai, Patna, Vadodara, Varanasi	1.2
Ludhiana, Visakhapatnam	1.1

---

by the Brahmins or priest class in order to maintain its superiority. Later, it was probably extended by the invading Aryans who felt themselves superior to the indigenous pre-Aryan Indians. Eventually, the caste system became formalised into four distinct classes, each with rules of conduct and behaviour.

At the top are the Brahmins who are the priests and the arbiters of what is right and wrong in matters of religion and caste. Next come the Kshatriyas, who are soldiers and administrators. The Vaisyas are the artisan and commercial class and, finally, the Sudras are the farmers and the peasant class. These four castes are said to have come from Brahma's mouth (Brahmins), arms (Kshatriyas), thighs (Vaisyas) and feet (Sudras).

Beneath the four main castes is a fifth group, the untouchables. These people, members of the so-called Scheduled Castes, literally have no caste. They perform the most menial and degrading jobs. At one time, if a high-caste Hindu used the same temple as an untouchable, was touched by one, or even had an untouchable's shadow cast across them, they were considered polluted and had to go through a rigorous series of rituals to be cleansed.

Today, the caste system has been weakened but it still has considerable power, particularly among less educated people. Gandhi put great effort into bringing the untouchables into society, including renaming them the 'Harijans' or 'Children of God'. Recently, the word Harijan has lost favour, and the use of it in official business has actually been banned in Madhya Pradesh. The term the members of these groups prefer is Dalit, meaning Oppressed or Downtrodden.

It must be remembered that being born into a certain caste does not limit you strictly to one occupation or position in life, just as being black in the USA does not mean you are poverty stricken and live in Harlem. Many Brahmins are poor peasants, for example, and hundreds of years ago the great Maratha leader Shivaji was a Sudra. None of the later Marathas, who controlled much of India after the demise of the Mughals, were Brahmins. Nevertheless, you can generalise that the better-off Indians will be of higher caste and that the 'sweeper' you see desultorily cleaning the toilet in your hotel will be a Dalit. In fact, when Indian Airlines appointed its first Dalit flight attendant, it was front-page news in Indian newspapers.

How can you tell which caste a Hindu belongs to? Well, if you know that their job is a menial one, such as cleaning streets, or in some way defiling, such as working with leather, they are a Dalit. But for most Hindus, you can't really tell which caste they belong to. However, if you see a man with his shirt off and he has the sacred thread looped round one shoulder, he belongs to one of the higher castes, but then Parsis also wear a sacred thread. The Sikhs, Muslims and Christians do not have caste.

In many ways, the caste system also functions as an enormous unofficial trade union, with strict rules to avoid demarcation disputes. Each caste has many subdivisions so that the servant who polishes the brass cannot, due to their caste, also polish silver. Many of the old caste rules have been considerably relaxed, although less educated or more isolated Hindus may still avoid having a lower-caste person prepare their food for fear of becoming polluted. Better educated people are demonstrably none too worried about shaking hands with a caste-less Westerner though! Nor does the thought of going overseas, and thus losing caste completely, carry much weight these days. Often, quite the opposite, particularly if they return with a degree from an overseas university.

The caste system still produces enormous burdens for India, however. During the last few years, there have been frequent outbreaks of violence towards members of the Scheduled Castes and so-called 'backward' classes ('tribals', and those who are poor or poorly educated for reasons other than caste). In an effort to improve the lot of these people, the government reserves huge numbers of public sector jobs, parliamentary seats and university places for them. With nearly 60% of the jobs reserved, many well-educated people are missing out on jobs which they would easily get on merit. In 1994, some state governments (such as Karnataka) raised the reservation level even higher in an effort to win mass support. In 1991, and again in 1994, there were serious protests against the raising of the quotas. These protests were most violent in Gujarat, Uttar Pradesh, Delhi and Haryana, and at least 100 people died or were seriously injured in self-immolation incidents in the 1991 protests.

Going far back into Western history, it's important to remember that the medieval ideal of heaven was developed in part to keep the peasants in their place – behave yourself, work hard, put up with your lot and you'll go to heaven. Probably caste developed in a similar fashion – your life may be pretty miserable but that's your *karma*; behave yourself and you may be born into a better one next time around.

Tribals

For most people, it comes as a surprise to learn that more than 50 million Indians belong to tribal communities distinct from the great mass of Hindu caste society. These Aadivasi, as they are known in India, have origins which precede the Vedic Aryans and the Dravidians of the south. For thousands of years they have lived more or less undisturbed in the hills and densely wooded regions which were regarded as unattractive by the peasantry of more dynamic populations. Many still speak tribal languages not understood by the politically dominant Hindus, and they follow archaic customs foreign to both Hindus and Muslims alike.

Although there was obviously some contact between the tribals and the Hindu villagers on the plains, this rarely led to friction since there was little or no competition for resources and land. All this changed dramatically when improved communications opened up previously inaccessible tribal areas, and rapid growth of the Indian population led to pressure on resources. In the space of just over 40 years, the vast majority of tribal people have been dispossessed of their ancestral land and turned into impoverished labourers exploited by all and sundry. The only region where this has not taken place and where tribals continue to manage their own affairs is in Arunachal Pradesh, in the extreme north-east of India. Only here can it be said that the tribes have benefited from contact with modern civilisation and are managing to hold their own.

Elsewhere in India, and especially in Madhya Pradesh, Andhra Pradesh, and Bihar, a shocking tale of exploitation, dispossession and widespread hunger has unfolded with the connivance and even encouragement of officialdom. It's a record which the government would prefer to forget about and which it vehemently denies. Instead, it points to the millions of rupees which it says have been sunk into schemes to improve the condition of the aborigines. Although some of this aid has got through, corruption has claimed much of it.

It's unlikely that any genuine effort will be made to improve the lot of the tribals in peninsular India, given the pressure for land. What is far more likely is that the erosion of their cultures and traditions will continue until they eventually 'disappear' as distinct tribes.

CULTURE
Women in Society
India is a country of great hardship, and the people who face the worst of it are generally the women. It is a cruel paradox that at a time when India's prime minister was arguably the world's most powerful woman, 75% of the country's women had little education, few rights, strenuous and poorly paid jobs, and little prospect of anything better.

Problems for Indian women begin at birth. Even now, boys are considered more desirable than girls because they offer parents security in old age – traditionally, the sons remain in their parents' house even after marriage. Girls are often seen as a burden on the family, not only because they leave the family when married, but also because an adequate dowry must be supplied. Consequently, girls may often be fed less if there is inadequate food, and their education is neglected. Such is the desire for boys that clinics in India used to advertise pregnancy testing to determine the sex of the foetus; in many instances, abortions were performed if it was female. Although such practices are now illegal, it is believed they still occur.

Arranged marriages are still the norm rather than the exception. A village girl may well find herself married off while still in her early teens to a man she has never met. She then goes to live in his village, where she is expected not only to do manual labour (at perhaps half the wages that a man would receive for the same work), but also raise children and keep house. This might involve a daily trek of several km to fetch water, as much again to gather firewood, and a similar amount again to gather fodder for domestic animals. She would have no property rights should her husband own land, and domestic violence is common; indeed, a man often feels it is his right to beat his wife. In many ways, her status is little better than that of a slave.

For the urban, middle-class woman, life is materially much more comfortable but pressures still exist. She is much more likely to be given an education, but only because this will make her marriage prospects better. Once married, she is still expected to be mother and home maker above all else. Like her village counterpart, if she fails to live up to expectations – even if it is just not being able to give her in-laws a grandson – the consequences can be dire, as the practice of 'bride burning' is not uncommon. On a daily basis, there are newspaper reports of women burning to death in kitchen fires, usually from 'spilt' kerosene. The majority of these cases, however, are either suicides – desperate women who could no longer cope with the pressure from their parents-in-law – or outright murders by in-laws who want their son to remarry someone they consider to be a better prospect.

A married woman faces even greater pressure if she wants to divorce her husband. Although the constitution allows for divorcees (and widows) to remarry, few are in a position to do this simply because they are considered outcasts from society – even her own family will turn their back on a woman who seeks divorce, and there is no social security net to provide for her. A marriage in India is not so much a union based on love between two individuals, but a social contract joining two people and their families. It is then the responsibility of the couple to make the marriage work, whatever the obstacles; if the marriage fails, both husband and wife are tainted, but the fall-out for the woman is far worse. Divorce rates are, not surprisingly, low.

While all this is the downside of being a woman in India, the picture is not all gloomy. In the past decade or so, the women's movement has had some successes in improving the status of women. Although the professions are still very much male dominated, women are making inroads – in 1993, the first women were inducted into the armed forces, and they account for around 10% of all parliamentarians. Two high-profile professional women of recent times are, of course, former Prime Minister Indira Gandhi, and Kiran Bedi, India's first female police officer, then deputy commissioner of police in Delhi and now head of Delhi's main prison, Tihar Jail.

For the village women, it's much more

difficult to get ahead, but groups such as SEWA (Self Employed Women's Association) in Ahmedabad have shown what can be achieved. Here, poor and/or low caste women, many of whom work only on the fringes of the economy, such as scavenging for waste-paper at the dump, have been organised into unions, giving them at least some lobbying power against discriminatory and exploitative work practices. SEWA has also set up a bank, giving many poor women their first access to a savings or lending body, since conventional banks were unwilling to deal with people of such limited means. (See the boxed SEWA section in the Gujarat chapter for more information about SEWA.)

Although attitudes towards women are slowly changing, it will be a long time before they gain even a measure of equality with men. For the moment, their power lies in their considerable influence over family affairs and so remains largely invisible.

Marriage

One place where the caste system is still well entrenched is the choosing of marriage partners. You only need to read a few of the 'matrimonial' advertisements which appear in many places, including the national Sunday newspapers (and even these days on the Internet!) to realise that marriage across the 'caste bar', even among wealthy, well-educated or higher caste people, is basically not on. The majority of marriages are still arranged by the parents, although 'love marriages' are becoming more common, particularly in urban centres.

When a couple are choosing a partner for their son or daughter, a number of factors are taken into consideration: caste of course is pre-eminent, but other considerations are beauty and physical flaws – the matrimonial ads can seem brutally frank in this regard – and a horoscope for the would-be partner is often called for. Many potential matches are rejected simply because the astrological signs are not propitious. The financial status of the prospective partner's family is also taken into account.

Another facet of marriage is the perni-

cious dowry. A dowry was originally a gift to the bride from her parents, so she would have something of her own and would in turn be able to provide a dowry to her own daughters. These days, however, the dowry is a matter of status for the bride's family – the bigger the dowry and grander the ceremony, the greater the prestige to the family.

Although the practice is officially outlawed, a dowry is still expected in the majority of marriages. For poorer families, the marriage can become a huge financial burden. Many families have to borrow money, either for their daughter's dowry or to stage a lavish ceremony and feast (or both), usually at outrageous rates of interest. The end result is that for the rest of their lives they are indebted to the feared moneylenders, or become bonded labourers.

The amount of an expected dowry varies, but it is never small. The main determining factor is the level of education and social standing of the young man; a dowry of at least US$20,000 would be expected from the family of a young woman hoping to marry a graduate of a foreign university, a doctor or other highly paid professional. A 'Green Card' (American residence card) is also highly desirable, and the holder of one can command a high price.

The official age for marriage is 18 years, but this is widely ignored – 8% of girls aged between 10 and 14 are married, and nearly 50% of females aged between 15 and 19 are married, although the average age for marriage is 18.3 for women and 23.3 for men. Virginity is also of vital importance, and it is often listed among the woman's attributes in the matrimonial columns.

Indian Clothing

Many travellers start wearing Indian clothes while in India – after all, much of it is a lot more appropriate to India's climate than jeans and T-shirts. The best known Indian clothing is the *sari*. It is also the one piece of clothing which is very difficult for Western women to wear properly. This supremely graceful attire is simply one length of material, a bit over a metre in width and five to nine metres long. It's worn without any pins, buttons or fastenings. The tightly fitted, short blouse worn under a sari is a *choli*. The final length of the sari, which is draped over the wearer's shoulder, is known as the *pallav* or *palloo*.

The sari is not the only women's costume in India. Kashmiri and Sikh women wear loose pyjama-like trousers. Over these trousers, known as *salwars*, they wear a long, loose tunic known as a *kameez*. This attire is comfortable and 'respectable'. A *churidhar* is similar to the salwar but tighter fitting. Over this goes a collarless or mandarin-collar *kurta* – an item of clothing worn by both men and women which is also popular in the West.

Although the overwhelming majority of Indian women wear traditional costume, many Indian men wear quite conventional Western clothing. Indeed, a large proportion of India's consumer advertising appears to be devoted to 'suitings & shirtings' – the material made for tailor-made, Western-style business suits and shirts. You can easily get a suit made to measure, although the styling is likely to be somewhat dated. The collarless jackets, known as 'Nehru jackets', are a popular buy among travellers. These khadi (homespun cloth) coats are best bought at the government khadi emporiums found in the major cities.

The traditional *lungi* originated in the south and today is worn by women as well as men. It's a short length of material worn rather like a sarong. The lungi can be rolled up but should be lowered when sitting down or when entering someone's home or a temple. A *dhoti* is like a longer lungi but with a length of material pulled up between the legs, effective but a long way from elegant! A dhoti is a more formal piece of attire than a lungi, however. Pyjama-like trousers, worn by country folk, are known as *lenga*. Striped pyjamas are casual and comfortable but they're looked upon as a labourer's outfit; not something to wear to a fancy restaurant or to somebody's home.

There are many religious and regional variations in costume, such as the brightly mirrored Rajasthani skirts and their equally colourful tie-dye materials. In Ladakh, the women wear superbly picturesque Tibetan costumes with high 'top hats'. The men wear long dressing-gown-like coats. Muslim women, of course, wear much more staid and all-covering attire than their Hindu sisters. More traditional Muslim women wear the all-enveloping, tent-like *burkha*.

Sport

India's national sport (obsession almost) is cricket. There's something about a game with as many idiosyncrasies and peculiarities as cricket which simply has to appeal to the Indian temperament. During the cricket season, if an international side is touring India and there is a Test match on, you'll see crowds outside the many shops which have a TV, and people walking down the street with a pocket radio pressed to their ear. Test matches with Pakistan have a particularly strong following as the rivalry is intense. One thing you can count on is that most Indians will know the names of the entire touring cricket team and, if you come from the same country but don't know their names, then you may well be regarded as mentally retarded. On the other hand, if you do have an interest in cricket, it can be a great way to start up conversations.

India is also one of the world leaders in hockey, and has several Olympic gold medals to its credit. Soccer has a keen following, particularly Calcutta.

LANGUAGE

There is no 'Indian' language, which is part of the reason why English is still widely spoken over 40 years after the British left India, and it's still the official language of the judiciary. There are a great number of local languages, and in many cases the state boundaries have been drawn on linguistic lines. In all, there are 18 languages officially recognised by the constitution, and these fall into two major groups: Indic, or Indo-Aryan, and Dravidian. Additionally, there are over 1600 minor languages and dialects listed in the 1991 census. The scope for misunderstanding can be easily appreciated!

The Indic languages are a branch of the Indo-European group of languages (of which English is also a member), and were the language of the central Asian peoples who invaded what is now India. The Dravidian languages are native to south India, although they have been influenced by Sanskrit and Hindi.

Most of the languages have their own script, and these are used along with English. In some states, such as Gujarat, you'll hardly see a word of English, whereas in Himachal Pradesh virtually everything is in English. For a sample of the different scripts, look at a Rs 5 or larger banknote where 13 languages are represented. From the top, they are: Assamese, Bengali, Gujarati, Kannada, Kashmiri, Malayalam, Hindi (Devanagari), Oriya, Punjabi, Rajasthani, Tamil, Telugu and Urdu.

Major efforts have been made to promote Hindi as the national language of India and to gradually phase out English. A stumbling block to this plan is that while Hindi is the predominant language in the north, it bears little relation to the Dravidian languages of the south; and in the south very few people speak Hindi. It is from the south, particularly the state of Tamil Nadu, that the most vocal opposition to the adoption of Hindi comes, along with the strongest support for the retention of English.

For many educated Indians, English is virtually their first language, and for the large number of Indians who speak more than one language, English is often their

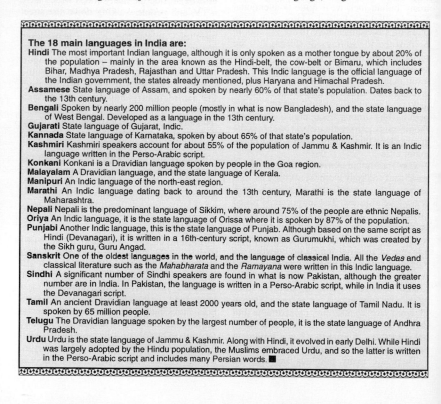

The 18 main languages in India are:

Hindi The most important Indian language, although it is only spoken as a mother tongue by about 20% of the population – mainly in the area known as the Hindi-belt, the cow-belt or Bimaru, which includes Bihar, Madhya Pradesh, Rajasthan and Uttar Pradesh. This Indic language is the official language of the Indian government, the states already mentioned, plus Haryana and Himachal Pradesh.

Assamese State language of Assam, and spoken by nearly 60% of that state's population. Dates back to the 13th century.

Bengali Spoken by nearly 200 million people (mostly in what is now Bangladesh), and the state language of West Bengal. Developed as a language in the 13th century.

Gujarati State language of Gujarat, Indic.

Kannada State language of Karnataka, spoken by about 65% of that state's population.

Kashmiri Kashmiri speakers account for about 55% of the population of Jammu & Kashmir. It is an Indic language written in the Perso-Arabic script.

Konkani Konkani is a Dravidian language spoken by people in the Goa region.

Malayalam A Dravidian language, and the state language of Kerala.

Manipuri An Indic language of the north-east region.

Marathi An Indic language dating back to around the 13th century, Marathi is the state language of Maharashtra.

Nepali Nepali is the predominant language of Sikkim, where around 75% of the people are ethnic Nepalis.

Oriya An Indic language, it is the state language of Orissa where it is spoken by 87% of the population.

Punjabi Another Indic language, this is the state language of Punjab. Although based on the same script as Hindi (Devanagari), it is written in a 16th-century script, known as Gurumukhi, which was created by the Sikh guru, Guru Angad.

Sanskrit One of the oldest languages in the world, and the language of classical India. All the *Vedas* and classical literature such as the *Mahabharata* and the *Ramayana* were written in this Indic language.

Sindhi A significant number of Sindhi speakers are found in what is now Pakistan, although the greater number are in India. In Pakistan, the language is written in a Perso-Arabic script, while in India it uses the Devanagari script.

Tamil An ancient Dravidian language at least 2000 years old, and the state language of Tamil Nadu. It is spoken by 65 million people.

Telugu The Dravidian language spoken by the largest number of people, it is the state language of Andhra Pradesh.

Urdu Urdu is the state language of Jammu & Kashmir. Along with Hindi, it evolved in early Delhi. While Hindi was largely adopted by the Hindu population, the Muslims embraced Urdu, and so the latter is written in the Perso-Arabic script and includes many Persian words. ■

second tongue. Thus it is very easy to get around India with English – after all, many Indians have to speak English to each other if they wish to communicate. Nevertheless, it's always nice to know at least a little of the local language.

Hindi
See Lonely Planet's *Hindi/Urdu Phrasebook* for a comprehensive list of Hindi words and phrases.

Hello/Goodbye.	*namaste*
Excuse me.	*maaf kijiyeh*
Please.	*meharbani seh*
Yes/No.	*haan/nahin*

big	*bherra*
small	*chhota*
today	*aaj*
day	*din*
night	*raat*
week	*haftah*
month	*mahina*
year	*saal*
medicine	*dava-ee*
ice	*baraf*
egg	*aanda*
fruit	*phal*
vegetables	*sabzi*
sugar	*chlnl*
butter	*makkhan*
rice	*chaaval*
water	*paani*
tea	*chai*
coffee	*kaafi*
milk	*dudh*

Do you speak English?	*kya aap angrezi samajhte hain?*
I don't understand.	*meri samajh men nahin aaya*
Where is a hotel?	*hotal kahan hai?*
How far is...?	*...kitni duur hai?*
How do I get to...?	*...kojane ke liyeh kaiseh jaana parega?*
How much?	*kitneh paiseh? kitneh hai?*

This is expensive.	*yeh bahut mehnga hai*
Show me the menu.	*mujheh minu dikhaiyeh*
The bill please.	*bill de dijiyeh*
What is your name?	*aapka shubh naam kya hai?*
What is the time?	*kitneh bajeh hain?*
How are you?	*aap kaiseh hain?*
Very well, thank you.	*bahut acha, shukriya*

Beware of *acha*, that all-purpose word for 'OK'. It can also mean 'OK, I understand what you mean, but it isn't OK'.

Tamil
Although Hindi is promoted as the 'official' language of India, it won't get you very far in the south, where Tamil reigns supreme (although English is also widely spoken). Tamil is a much more difficult language to master and the pronunciation is not easy.

Hello.	*vanakkam*
Goodbye.	*sendru varugiren*
Excuse me.	*mannithu kollungal*
Please.	*dhayavu seidhu*
Yes/No.	*aamam/illai*

big	*periyadhu*
small	*siriyadhu*
today	*indru*
day	*pagal*
night	*iravu/rathiri*
week	*vaaram*
month	*maadham*
year	*aandu*
medicine	*marundhu*
ice	*panikkatti*
egg	*muttai*
fruit	*pazhlam*
vegetables	*kaaikari*
sugar	*sarkarai/seeni*
butter	*vennai*
rice	*saadham/soru*
water	*thanner*
tea	*thenneer*
coffee	*kapi*
milk	*paal*

Do you speak English?	*neengal aangilam pesuveergala?*
I don't understand.	*yenakku puriyavillai.*
Where is there a hotel?	*hotel yenge irrukindradhu?*
How far is...?	*yevallavu dhooram...?*
How do I get to...?	*haan yeppadi selvadhu...?*
How much?	*yevvallvu?*
This is expensive.	*idhu vilai adhigam*
Show me the menu.	*saapatu patiyalai kamiungal*
The bill please.	*vilai rasidhai kodungal*
What is your name?	*ungal peyar yenna?*
What is the time?	*ippoludhu mani yevallavu?*
How are you?	*neengal nalama?*
Very well, thank you.	*nandri, nandraga irukkindren*

Numbers

Whereas we count in tens, hundreds, thousands, millions and billions, the Indian numbering system goes tens, hundreds, thousands, hundred thousands, ten millions. A hundred thousand is a *lakh,* and 10 million is a *crore.*

These two words are almost always used in place of their English equivalent. Thus you will see 10 lakh rather than one million and one crore rather than 10 million. Furthermore, the numerals are generally written that way too – thus three hundred thousand appears as 3,00,000 not 300,000, and ten million, five hundred thousand would appear numerically as 1,05,00,000 (one crore, five lakh) not 10,500,000. If you say something costs five crore or is worth 10 lakh, it always means 'of rupees'.

When counting from 10 to 100 in Hindi, there is no standard formula for compiling numbers – they are all different. Here we've just given you enough to go on with!

	Hindi	Tamil
1	*ek*	*onru*
2	*do*	*irandu*
3	*tin*	*moonru*
4	*char*	*naangu*
5	*panch*	*ainthu*
6	*chhe*	*aaru*
7	*saat*	*ezhu*
8	*aath*	*ettu*
9	*nau*	*onpathu*
10	*das*	*pathu*
11	*gyaranh*	*padhinondru*
12	*baranh*	*pannirendu*
13	*teranh*	*padhimundru*
14	*chodanh*	*padhinaangu*
15	*pandranh*	*padhinainthu*
16	*solanh*	*padhinaaru*
17	*staranh*	*padhinezhu*
18	*aatharanh*	*padhinettu*
19	*unnis*	*patthonpathu*
20	*bis*	*irubadhu*
21	*ikkis*	*irubadhiondru*
22	*bais*	*irubadhirandu*
23	*teis*	*irubadhimoonru*
24	*chobis*	*irubadhinaangu*
25	*pachis*	*irubadhiainthu*
26	*chhabis*	*irubadhiaaru*
27	*sattais*	*irubadhiezhu*
28	*athais*	*irubadhiettu*
29	*unnattis*	*irubadhionpathu*
30	*tis*	*muppathu*
35	*paintis*	*muppathiainthu*
40	*chalis*	*narpathu*
45	*paintalis*	*narpathiainthu*
50	*panchas*	*aimbathu*
55	*pachpan*	*aimbathiainthu*
60	*saath*	*arubathu*
65	*painsath*	*arubathiainthu*
70	*sattar*	*ezhbathu*
75	*pachhattar*	*ezhubathiainthu*
80	*assi*	*enbathu*
85	*pachasi*	*enabathiainthu*
90	*nabbe*	*thonooru*
95	*pachanabbe*	*thonootriainthu*
100	*so*	*nooru*
200	*do so*	*irunooru*
1000	*ek hazaar*	*aayiram*
2000	*do hazaar*	*irandaayiram*
100,000	*lakh*	*lacham*
10,000,000	*crore*	*kodi*

Sacred India

SACRED INDIA

India has a veritable kaleidoscope of religions. There is probably more diversity of religions and sects in India than anywhere else on earth. Apart from having nearly all the world's great religions represented, India was the birthplace of Hinduism and Buddhism, a vital supporter of Zoroastrianism (one of the world's oldest religions) and home to Jainism (an ancient religion unique to India).

Previous Page: Creative genius – Jain temple at Khajuraho. (photograph by Bryn Thomas)

Top: Worshippers pause before a shrine in a Madurai temple, Tamil Nadu.

Bottom: Women pray for their husbands' well-being during the Karwachot Festival, Varanasi, Uttar Pradesh.

SARA-JANE CLELAND

SARA-JANE CLELAND

HINDUISM

India's major religion, Hinduism, is practised by approximately 80% of the population – over 670 million people. Only in Nepal, the Indonesian island of Bali, the Indian Ocean island of Mauritius and possibly Fiji do Hindus also predominate, but in terms of numbers of adherents, it is the largest religion in Asia. It is one of the oldest extant religions, with firm roots extending back to beyond 1000 BC.

The Indus Valley civilisation developed a religion which bore a close relationship to Hinduism. Later, this religion was influenced by the combined religious practices of the southern Dravidians and the Aryan invaders who arrived in the north of India around 1500 BC. Around 1000 BC, the Vedic scriptures were introduced, providing the first loose framework for the religion.

Hinduism today has a number of holy books, the most important being the four *Vedas* (divine knowledge) which are the foundation of Hindu philosophy. The *Upanishads* are contained within the *Vedas* and delve into the metaphysical nature of the universe and soul. The *Mahabharata* (Great War of the Bharatas) is an epic poem containing over 220,000

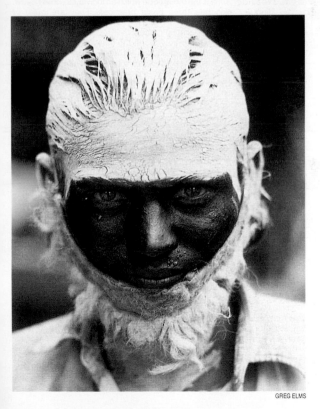

GREG ELMS

A Jaipur devotee as Hanuman, monkey god and Rama's faithful ally.

lines. It describes the battles between the Kauravas and Pandavas, who were descendants of the Lunar race. It also includes the story of Rama, and it is probable that the most famous Hindu epic, the *Ramayana*, was based on this. The *Ramayana* is highly revered by Hindus, perhaps because a verse in the introduction says 'He who reads and repeats this holy life-giving *Ramayana* is liberated from all his sins and exalted with all his posterity to the highest heaven'. The *Bhagavad Gita* is a famous episode of the *Mahabharata* where Krishna relates his philosophies to Arjuna.

Basically, the religion postulates that we will all go through a series of rebirths or reincarnations that eventually lead to *moksha*, the spiritual salvation which frees us all from the cycle of rebirths. With each rebirth we can move closer to or further from eventual *moksha*; the deciding factor is our karma, which is literally a law of cause and effect. Bad actions during our lives result in bad karma, which ends in a lower reincarnation. Conversely, if our deeds and actions have been good, we will reincarnate on a higher level and be a step closer to eventual freedom from rebirth.

Dharma, or the natural law, defines the total social, ethical and spiritual harmony of our lives. There are three categories of dharma, the first being the eternal harmony which involves the whole universe. The second category is the dharma that controls castes and the relations between castes. The third dharma is the moral code which an individual should follow.

The Hindu religion has three basic practices. They are *puja*, or worship, the cremation of the dead, and the rules and regulations of the caste system. There are four main castes: the Brahmin, or priest caste; the Kshatriyas, or soldiers and governors; the Vaisyas, or tradespeople and farmers; and the Sudras, or menial workers and artisans. These basic castes are then subdivided into a great number of lesser divisions. Beneath all the castes are the Dalits (formerly known as Harijans), or untouchables, the lowest class for whom all the most menial and degrading tasks are reserved.

Early-morning devotions at Varanasi.

PAUL BEINSSEN

Hinduism is not a proselytising religion since you cannot be converted. You're either born a Hindu or you are not; you can never become one. Similarly, you cannot change your caste – you're born into it and are stuck with it for the rest of that lifetime. Nevertheless, Hinduism has attracted many Westerners, and India's 'export gurus' are many and successful.

A guru is not so much a teacher as a spiritual guide, somebody who by example or simply by their presence indicates what path you should follow. In a spiritual search one always needs a guru.

Hindu Gods

Westerners have trouble understanding Hinduism principally because of its vast pantheon of gods. In fact you can look upon all these different gods simply as pictorial representations of the many attributes of one god. The one omnipresent god usually has three physical representations. Brahma is the creator, Vishnu is the preserver and Siva is the destroyer and reproducer. All three gods are usually shown with four arms, but Brahma has the added advantage of four heads to represent his all-seeing presence. The four *Vedas* are supposed to have emanated from his mouths.

Each god has an associated animal known as the 'vehicle' on which they ride, as well as a consort with certain attributes and abilities. Generally, each god also holds a symbol; you can often recognise which god is represented by the accompanying vehicle or symbol. Brahma's consort is Sarasvati, the goddess of learning. She rides upon a white swan and holds the stringed musical instrument known as a *veena*.

GREG ELMS

Left: Ganesh graces a Jaisalmer house, Rajasthan.

Bottom: Vishnu, the source of life.

Vishnu, the preserver, is usually shown in one of the physical forms in which he has visited earth. In all, Vishnu has paid nine visits and on his 10th he will be called Kalki, and will appear riding a white horse. On earlier visits he appeared in animal form, as in his boar or man-lion (Narsingh) incarnations, but on visit seven he appeared as Rama, regarded as the personification of the ideal man and the hero of the *Ramayana*. Rama also managed to provide a number of secondary gods, including his helpful ally Hanuman, the monkey god. Hanuman's faithful nature is symbolised in the representations of him often found guarding fort or palace entrances. Naturally, incarnations can also have consorts and Rama's companion was Sita.

On visit eight Vishnu came as Krishna, who was raised by peasants and thus became a great favourite of the working classes. Krishna is renowned for his exploits with the *gopis* or shepherdesses, and his consorts are Radha (the head of the gopis), Rukmani and Satyabhama. Krishna is often blue in colour and plays a flute. Vishnu's last incarnation was on visit nine, as the Buddha. This was probably a ploy to bring the Buddhist splinter group back into the Hindu fold.

GREG ELMS

When Vishnu appears as himself, rather than one of his incarnations, he sits on a couch made from the coils of à serpent and in his hands he holds two symbols, the conch shell and the discus. Vishnu's vehicle is the half-man half-eagle known as the Garuda. The Garuda is benevolent and has a deep dislike of snakes – Indonesia's national airline is named after the Garuda. Vishnu's consort is the beautiful Lakshmi (Laxmi), who came from the sea and is the goddess of wealth and prosperity.

CHRIS BEALL

Top: Colourful gods, goddesses, animals and mythical figures covering Madurai's Shree Meenakshi Temple draw pilgrims and tourists alike.

Middle: Garlanded with skulls and endowed with a taste for sacrifice, Kali is among the fiercest deities in the Hindu pantheon.

Bottom: Siva – destroyer and creator.

SALLY HONE

GREG ELMS

Siva's creative role is phallically symbolised by his representation as the frequently worshipped lingam. Siva rides on the bull Nandi and his matted hair is said to carry Ganga, the goddess of the river Ganges, in it. Siva lives in the Himalaya and devotes much of his time to smoking pot. He has the third eye in the middle of his forehead and carries a trident. Siva is also known as Nataraj, the cosmic dancer whose dance shook the cosmos and created the world. Siva's consort is Parvati, the beautiful. She, however, has a dark side when she appears as Durga, the terrible. In this role she holds weapons in her 10 hands and rides a tiger. As Kali, the fiercest of the gods, she demands sacrifices and wears a garland of skulls. Kali usually represents the destructive side of Siva's personality.

TONY WHEELER

HUGH FINLAY

TONY WHEELER

Far Left: Sacred symbols form a hilltop shrine in Gujarat.

Top: Nandi the bull in repose at Mysore, Karnataka.

Middle: Chamunda, manifestation of tiger-borne Durga.

Bottom: Elephant-headed Ganesh, popular god of prosperity and wisdom.

Siva and Parvati have two children. Ganesh is the elephant-headed god of prosperity and wisdom, and is probably the most popular of all the gods. Ganesh obtained his elephant head due to his father's notorious temper. Coming back from a long trip, Siva discovered Parvati in her room with a young man. Not pausing to think that their son might have grown up a little during his absence, Siva lopped his head off! He was then forced by Parvati to bring his son back to life but could only do so by giving him the head of the first living thing he saw – which happened to be an elephant. Ganesh's vehicle is a rat. Siva and Parvati's other son is Kartikkaya, the god of war.

A variety of lesser gods and goddesses also crowd the scene. Most temples are dedicated to one or other of the gods, but curiously there are very few Brahma temples – perhaps just one in all of India (at Pushkar in Rajasthan). Most Hindus profess to be either Vaishnavites (followers of Vishnu) or Shaivites (followers of Siva). The cow, of course, is the holy animal of Hinduism.

GREG ELMS

Sadhus

A sadhu is an individual on a spiritual search. They're an easily recognised group, usually wandering the countryside half-naked, smeared in dust with matted hair and beard; what few clothes they wear are usually saffron coloured.

Sadhus following Siva will sometimes carry his symbol, the trident. A sadhu is often someone who has decided that their business and family life have reached their natural conclusions and that it is time to throw everything temporal aside. They may previously have been the village postman or a businessperson.

Sadhus perform various feats of self-mortification and travel great distances around the country, occasionally coming together in great pilgrimages and other religious gatherings. Many sadhus are simply beggars following a more sophisticated approach to gathering in the paise, but others are completely genuine in their search.

MARKUS LEHTIPUU

This Page and Following Page: Saffron-robed or ash-smeared, with matted hair and begging bowl, the sadhu wanders, homeless, on a personal spiritual quest.

SARA-JANE CLELAND

RICHARD I'ANSON

SARA-JANE CLELAND

GREG ELMS

RICHARD I'ANSON

BRYN THOMAS

Hindu Weddings

Hindu weddings are usually colourful, lavish affairs. Vast sums are shelled out by the bride's father to put on a show worthy of both his own status and that of the bridegroom's family. The fact that he may not be in a position to stage such a grand event matters little.

In a typical ceremony, the two families – and all their assorted relatives – gather on an auspicious day and get stuck into the food and drink. The bride often remains out of sight in the house until the time of the ceremony. The groom *(barr)* arrives to much fanfare, having paraded through the streets, often on horseback, wearing a *sehra* (traditional garland). The parade is accompanied by a boisterous uniformed brass band (which usually pays small attention to minor details such as melody, harmony and rhythm), and the whole spectacle is lit by walking light poles – men carrying trees of sprouting fluorescent tubes, all wired together in a vast and dangerous clump of spaghetti leading to a generator carried at the rear of the procession on a truck or cycle-rickshaw. The parade itself is known as a *baraat*.

The wedding ceremony centres around the *havan*, or sacred fire, which the couple circle seven times after the priest has placed a *tika* on the forehead of each.

Wedding bells in Bangalore, Karnataka.

Top: The bride and groom must wait until a priest has placed tikas on their foreheads before circling the sacred fire.

Bottom Left: No wedding would be complete without a band.

Bottom Right: The groom rides out to meet his bride.

GREG ELMS

GREG ELMS

GREG ELMS

MICHELLE COXALL

MICHELLE COXALL

MICHELLE COXALL

MICHELLE COXALL

Facing Page: Swathed in red and gold, a wedding guest at McLeod Ganj in Himachal Pradesh watches the festivities. The bindi on her forehead signifies she is married.

Top Left: Unshaven and smeared in yellow paste, the bridegroom prepares to undergo ritual cleansing. He holds a crude bow in his right hand and in his left, an arrow. He wears a quiver on his back.

Top Right: Women and children crowd the family compound balcony to catch a glimpse of the groom's ritual cleansing.

Bottom: A guest displays an elaborate nose ring.

Tika

The *tika* is the forehead markings with which most adult Hindu (and sometimes Christian) women adorn themselves. On a man it is referred to as a *tilak,* although these days the word tika has become common for both sexes. The mark takes many forms, and can be applied either by the wearer or by a temple priest as a sign of blessing.

The markings are usually made from a red vermilion paste *(sindoor),* white sandalwood paste or ash *(vibhuti),* and can be used to denote sects. Although there's a multitude of marks, they can be roughly divided into two main groups: three horizontal bars indicate the person is a Shaivite (follower of Siva); vertical stripes indicate a Vaishnavite (follower of Vishnu). The central stroke on a Vaishnavite's forehead is usually red, representing the radiance of the goddess Lakshmi (the wife of Vishnu in his incarnation as Narayan).

The small circle which a married woman places on her forehead is known as a *bindi* ('zero'). These are usually bought ready-made from the market and have become almost a fashion accessory, with every imaginable shape and colour to match the occasion. You'll also come across a wide variety of used bindis stuck to the mirrors in hotel bathrooms!

The brightly coloured powders at this store in Mysore's Devarajan market are used to make distinctive forehead markings known as tikas.

GREG ELMS

SARA-JANE CLELAND

GREG ELMS

Top Left: A tika on a southern Indian woman. The mark can take many forms.

Top Right and Bottom Left: Tika powder comes in a variety of shades and colours.

Bottom Right: Swami Bambola of Varanasi.

GREG ELMS

GREG ELMS

Holy Cows

India has nearly 200 million cattle, which play a vitally important role in the rural economy – pulling the farmer's cart to market or ploughing the fields. Their religious protection probably first developed as a means of safe-guarding them during droughts or famine when they might have been killed off and subsequently been hard to replace. There is also some dairy production.

All dressed up...a cow in its best for the Pongal Festival, Mahabalipuram, Tamil Nadu.

GREG ELMS

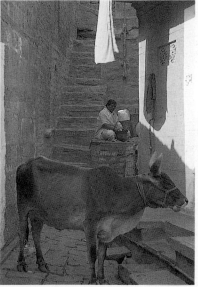

HUGH FINLAY

PAUL BEINSSEN

One of the most amazing sights in India, especially for the first-time visitor, is the number of cows which roam the streets of every town and city. They seem to be completely oblivious to the Tata bus bearing down on them at 100 miles an hour – I guess they've learnt that the driver will do anything to avoid a collision and the damage to their karma (let alone vehicle) that would accompany such an incident.

In the cities, cows also form an involuntary arm of the garbage-disposal department, and when not roaming the streets munching on cardboard, they can be seen rummaging through the concrete bins where waste vegetable matter is tipped.

PAUL BEINSSEN

Top Left and Right: In Rajasthan, cows wander freely through Jaisalmer's winding streets and shaded courtyards.

Bottom: A cow and her calf at rest in Varanasi.

PAUL BEINSSEN

Holy Hindu Cities

A handful of India's many holy cities are of particular holiness. Sites like Varanasi and Kanchipuram are famous, while others such as Dwarka are relatively unknown outside India. The cities are usually dedicated to Siva or Vishnu. They include Rameswaram and Kanyakumari in Tamil Nadu, Puri in Orissa and Badrinath and Haridwar in Uttar Pradesh. A pilgrimage to Badrinath, Puri, Rameswaram and Dwarka covers the four corners (north, east, south and west) of India.

PAUL BEINSSEN

HUGH FINLAY

Scenes from Varanasi

Facing Page: Boats glide by a sunken temple.

Far Left: A vendor proffers votive offerings on Dasaswamedh Ghat.

Right: The Ganges – elixir of life.

Bottom Left: Hindu devotee deep in contemplation.

Bottom Right: A dip in the Ganges.

CHRIS BEALL

SARA-JANE CLELAND

Hindu Festivals

Pongal This Tamil festival marks the end of the harvest season. It is observed on the first day of the Tamil month of Thai, which is in the middle of January. The festivities last four days and include such activities as the boiling-over of a pot of *pongal* (a mixture of rice, sugar, dhal and milk), symbolic of prosperity and abundance. On the third day, cattle are washed, decorated and even painted, and then fed the pongal. In Andhra Pradesh the festival is known as Makar Sankranti.

Vasant Panchami The most notable feature of this spring festival, held on the 5th of Magha (in January), is that many people wear yellow clothes. In some places, however, especially in West Bengal, Saraswati, the goddess of learning, is honoured. Books, musical instruments and other objects related to the arts and scholarship are placed in front of the goddess to receive her blessing.

Sivaratri Held in February/March, this day of fasting is dedicated to Lord Siva, who danced the *tandava* on this day. Temple processions are followed by the chanting of mantras and anointing of lingams.

GREG ELMS

Top: Madurai farmers give thanks for a good harvest at the Pongal Festival.

Bottom Left: Dancers sway to the beat of a drum.

Bottom Right: A woman puts the finishing touches to festive decorations.

GREG ELMS

GREG ELMS

PAUL BEINSSEN

SARA-JANE CLELAND

Top: Holi Festival revellers daubed with coloured water and powder at Hampi in Central Karnataka.

Bottom: A fire festival in honour of Rama's birthday, Rishikesh, Uttar Pradesh.

Holi This is one of the most exuberant Hindu festivals, with people marking the end of winter by throwing coloured water and powder *(gulal)* at one another. Unfortunately, in tourist places it is seen by some as an opportunity to take liberties with foreigners; don't wear good clothes on this day, and be prepared to duck. On the night before Holi, bonfires are built to symbolise the destruction of the evil demon Holika. Held in February/March, it's mainly a northern festival; in the south, where there is no real winter to end, it is not widespread.

In Maharashtra, this festival is known as Rangapanchami and is celebrated with dancing and singing.

Gangaur This Rajasthani festival honours Siva and Parvati. The Rajasthani women are at their most colourful, and can be seen dancing, praying and singing near any Siva idol. The festival is held in March.

Ramanavami In temples all over India the birth of Rama is celebrated on this day (in March/April). In the week leading up to Ramanavami, the *Ramayana* is widely read and performed.

Rath Yatra (Car Festival) Lord Jagannath's great temple chariot makes its stately journey from his temple in Puri, Orissa, during this festival (held in June/July). Similar but far more grandiose festivals take place in other locations, particularly in the Dravidian south. Lord Jagannath is one of Krishna's names, and the main procession in Puri celebrates Krishna's journey to Mathura to visit his aunt for a week! The images of his brother (Balarama) and sister (Subhadra) are also carried in the parade.

Teej Another Rajasthani festival, Teej celebrates the onset of the monsoon in June/July. Idols of the goddess Parvati are paraded through the streets, amid much singing and dancing.

Naag Panchami This festival is dedicated to Ananta, the serpent upon whose coils Vishnu rested between universes. Offerings are made to snake images, and snake charmers do a roaring trade. Snakes are supposed to have power over the monsoon rainfall and keep evil from homes. The festival is held in July/August.

Raksha Bandhan (Narial Purnima) On the full-moon day of the Hindu month of Sravana (July/August), girls fix amulets known as *rakhis* to their brothers' wrists to protect them in the coming year. The brothers reciprocate with gifts. Some people also worship the Vedic sea-god deity Varuna on this day. Coconuts are thrown into the sea.

GREG ELMS

Right: A stately elephant carries Teej celebrants through the streets of Jaipur in Rajasthan.

Below: Welcome relief from the heat, the arrival of the monsoon is celebrated in Jaisalmer during the Teej Festival.

GREG ELMS

Ganesh Chaturthi This festival, held on the fourth day of the Hindu month Bhadra (August/September), is dedicated to Ganesh. It is widely celebrated all over India, but with particular enthusiasm in Maharashtra: In every village, shrines are erected and a clay Ganesh idol is installed. Firecrackers explode at all hours, and each family buys a clay idol of Ganesh. On the day of the festival the idol is brought into the house, where it is kept and worshipped for a specified period before being ceremoniously immersed in a river, tank or the sea. As Ganesh is the god of wisdom and prosperity, Ganesh Chaturthi is considered to be the most auspicious day of the year. It is considered unlucky to look at the moon on this day.

Janmashtami The anniversary of Krishna's birth is celebrated with happy abandon – in tune with Krishna's own mischievous moods. Although it is a national holiday, Agra, Bombay and Mathura (his birthplace) are the main centres of celebration. Devotees fast all day until midnight, and the festival is held in August/September.

Shravan Purnima After a day-long fast, high-caste Hindus replace the sacred thread which they always wear looped over their left shoulder. This ceremony takes place in August/September.

HUGH FINLAY

Top: An image of Ganesh is carried through the streets of Badami, Northern Karnataka, during a special festival in his honour.

Bottom Left: Krishna's birthday celebrations in Delhi.

Bottom Right: Devotees splash a statue of Vasudeva, Krishna's father.

SALLY HONE

SALLY HONE

SARA-JANE CLELAND

Just before Diwali women pray for their husbands during the Karwachot Festival

Dussehra This is the most popular of all the Indian festivals and takes place over 10 days, beginning on the first day of the Hindu month of Asvina (September/October). It celebrates Durga's victory over the buffalo-headed demon Mahishasura. In many places it culminates with the burning of huge images of the demon king Ravana and his accomplices, symbolic of the triumph of good over evil. In Delhi it is known as Ram Lila (Life story of Rama), with fireworks and re-enactments of the *Ramayana*, while in Mysore and Ahmedabad there are great processions. In West Bengal the festival is known as Durga Puja and in Gujarat it's Navratri (Festival of Nine Nights). In Kullu, in the north, the festival takes place a little later than elsewhere. It is a delightful time when the Kullu Valley shows why it is known as the Valley of the Gods.

Diwali (or Deepavali) This is the happiest festival of the Hindu calendar, celebrated on the 15th day of Kartika (October/November). At night, countless oil lamps are lit to show Rama the way home from his period of exile. Today, the festival is also dedicated to Lakshmi (particularly in Bombay) and to Kali in Calcutta. In all, the festival lasts five days. On the first day, houses are thoroughly cleaned and doorsteps are decorated with intricate *rangolis* (chalk designs). Day two is dedicated to Krishna's victory over Narakasura, a legendary tyrant. In the south on this day, a pre-dawn oil bath is followed by the donning of new clothes. Day three is spent in worshipping Lakshmi, the goddess of fortune. Traditionally, this is the beginning of the new financial year for companies. Day four commemorates the visit of the friendly demon Bali whom Vishnu put in his place. On the fifth day men visit their sisters to have a tika put on their forehead.

Diwali has also become the Festival of Sweets, with families exchanging sweets at this time. This has become as much a part of the tradition as the lighting of oil lamps and firecrackers. Diwali is also celebrated by the Jains as their New Year's Day.

Govardhana Puja This festival is dedicated to that holiest of animals, the cow. It is held in October/November.

GREG ELMS

Top: Celebrating in Jaipur

Bottom Left: A family in West Bengal makes New Year offerings outside the Kilkat temple.

Bottom Right: Karwarchot Festival.

RICHARD I'ANSON

SARA-JANE CLELAND

CHRIS BEALL

BUDDHISM

Although there are only about 6.6 million Buddhists in India, the religion is of great importance because it had its birth here and there are many reminders of its historic role. Strictly speaking Buddhism is not a religion, since it is not centred on a god, but a system of philosophy and a code of morality.

Buddhism was founded in northern India in about 500 BC when Siddhartha Gautama, born a prince, achieved enlightenment. Gautama Buddha was not the first Buddha, but the fourth, and is not expected to be the last 'enlightened one'. Buddhists believe that the achievement of enlightenment is the goal of every being, so eventually we will all reach Buddhahood.

The Buddha never wrote down his dharma, or teachings, and a subsequent schism resulted in the development of two major Buddhist schools. The Theravada (Doctrine of the Elders), or Hinayana (Small

CHRIS BEALL

CHRIS BEALL

Facing Page: Monk and novice share a moment at a Sikkim monastery.

Top: A pilgrim spins prayer wheels at Rumtek Monastery in Sikkim.

Bottom: Monks debate at Tikse Monastery in Ladakh.

Vehicle), holds that the path to nirvana, the eventual aim of all Buddhists, is an individual pursuit. In contrast, the Mahayana (Large Vehicle) school holds that the combined belief of its followers will eventually be great enough to encompass all of humanity and bear it to salvation. The less austere and ascetic Mahayana school is considered by some to be a soft option. Today, it is chiefly practised in Vietnam, Japan and China, while the Hinayana school is followed in Sri Lanka, Myanmar (Burma), Cambodia and Thailand. There are other, sometimes more esoteric, divisions of Buddhism such as the Hindu-Tantric Buddhism of Tibet which you can see in Ladakh and other parts of north India.

The Buddha renounced his material life to search for enlightenment but, unlike other prophets, he found that starvation did not lead to discovery. Therefore, he developed his rule of the 'middle way': moderation in everything. The Buddha taught that all life is suffering but that suffering comes from our sensual desires and the illusion that they are important. By following the 'eight-fold path' these desires will be extinguished and a state of nirvana, where we are free from their delusions, will be reached. Following this process requires going through a series of rebirths until the goal is eventually reached and no more rebirths into the world of suffering are necessary. The path that takes you through this cycle of births is karma, but this is not simply fate. Karma is a law of cause and effect: your actions in one life determine the role you will play and what you will have to go through in your next life.

Top Right: Rebuilt in the 1960s following an earthquake, Rumtek features intricate, colourful murals.

Bottom Left: Deities preside over the monastery's entrance.

Bottom Right: In Darjeeling, novices at Dali Monastery study to become monks.

RICHARD I'ANSON

ROB VAN DRIESUM

RICHARD I'ANSON

BRYN THOMAS

BRYN THOMAS

BRYN THOMAS

RICHARD I'ANSON

In India, Buddhism developed rapidly when it was embraced by the great Emperor Ashoka. As his empire extended over much of India, so Buddhism was carried forth. He also sent out missions to other lands to preach the Buddha's word, and his own son is said to have carried Buddhism to Sri Lanka. Later, however, Buddhism began to contract in India because it had never really taken a hold on the great mass of people. As Hinduism revived, Buddhism in India was gradually reabsorbed into the older religion. Today, Hindus regard the Buddha as another incarnation of Vishnu.

At its peak, magnificent structures were erected wherever the religion held sway. The earlier Theravada form of Buddhism, however, did not believe in the representation of the Buddha in human form. His presence was always alluded to in Buddhist art or architecture through symbols such as the bo tree (under which he was sitting when he attained enlightenment), the elephant (which his mother saw in a dream before he was born) or the wheel of life. Today, however, even Theravada Buddhists produce Buddha images.

Top Left: This Japanese pagoda in Rajgir, Bihar, is one of many built in India by countries that have large Buddhist communities.

Top Right: Detail of the Buddha golden image brought to India from Japan.

Bottom Left: Mani stones such as this one in Manali, Himachal Pradesh, are inscribed with mantras by the faithful.

Bottom Right: Prayer flags flutter over a pass at Rajgir, Bihar.

Top Left: Tibetan paintings keep the pious company along a footpath at Dalhousie, Himachal Pradesh.

Top Right: A merchant caters to pilgrims who flock to Rewalsar Lake in Himachal Pradesh for the Tso-Pema Festival.

Bottom Left: Performing a gompa puja in Ladakh.

Bottom Right: By spinning this prayer wheel a pilgrim at Rewalsar Lake makes the word of Buddha fly on the wind.

HUGH FINLAY

HUGH FINLAY

RICHARD I'ANSON

HUGH FINLAY

Buddhist Festivals

Tso-Pema This is a pilgrimage festival to Rewalsar Lake in Himachal Pradesh. It is particularly important in the Year of the Monkey, which falls every 12 years (the next occurs in 2004). Literally thousands of Buddhists make the pilgrimage to the lake, and His Holiness the Dalai Lama leads prayers in the monastery, and then completes a circuit of the lake. It's a very colourful event.

Buddha Jayanti (Saga Dawa) This 'triple blessed festival' celebrates Buddha's birth, enlightenment and attainment of nirvana. Processions of monks carrying sacred scriptures pass through the streets of Gangtok (Sikkim) and other towns. The festival falls on the full moon of the fourth lunar month (late May or early June).

Drukpa Teshi This festival celebrates the first teaching given by the Buddha. It is held on the fourth day of the sixth month (August).

RICHARD I'ANSON

RICHARD I'ANSON   HUGH FINLAY

Top: Festivities at Khechepari Monastery, Sikkim.

Bottom Left: Hemis Festival, Ladakh. Elaborate masked dances and crowds of eager spectators.

Bottom Right: Street vendor, Tso-Pema Festival.

HUGH FINLAY

ISLAM

Muslims, followers of the Islamic religion, constitute India's largest religious minority. They number about 105 million in all, almost 10% of the country's population. This makes India one of the largest Islamic nations in the world. India has had two Muslim presidents and several cabinet and state chief ministers since Independence. Islam is the most recent and widespread of the Asian religions; it predominates from the Mediterranean across to India and is the major religion east of India in Bangladesh, Malaysia and Indonesia.

The religion's founder, the prophet Mohammed, was born in 570 AD at Mecca, now part of Saudi Arabia. His first revelation from Allah (God) occurred in 610, and this and later visions were compiled into the Muslim holy book, the Koran. As his purpose in life was revealed to him, Mohammed began to preach against the idolatry for which Mecca was then the centre. Muslims are strictly monotheistic and believe that to search for God through images is a sin. Muslim teachings correspond closely with the Old Testament of the Bible, and Moses and Jesus are both accepted as Muslim prophets, although Jesus is not believed to be the son of God.

Mohammed's attacks on idolatry and local businesses eventually caused him and his followers to be run out of town in 622. They fled to Medina, the 'city of the Prophet', and by 630 were strong enough to march back into Mecca and take over. Although Mohammed died in 632, most of Arabia had been converted to Islam within two decades.

Facing Page: A Muslim contemplates the Koran outside the Ahmed Shah Mosque in Ahmedabad, Gujarat.

Left: Morning prayers during the Muslim Baqr-id (Id-ul-Asha) Festival, Nizam-uddin village, Delhi.

SALLY HONE

SARA-JANE CLELAND

BRYN THOMAS

The Taj Mahal, Agra, built between 1631 and 1653 by Emperor Shah Jahan in memory of his wife Mumtaz. Graceful from any angle.

CHRIS BEALL

PETER RYDER

HUGH FINLAY

HUGH FINLAY

The Muslim faith was more than a religion; it called on its followers to spread the word. In the succeeding centuries Islam was to expand over three continents. The Arabs, who first propagated the faith, developed a reputation as being ruthless opponents but reasonable masters, so people often found it advisable to surrender to them. In this way, the Muslims swept aside the crumbling Byzantine Empire, whose people felt no desire to support their own distant Christian emperor.

Islam only travelled west for 100 years before being pushed back at Poitiers, France, in 732, but it continued east for centuries. It regenerated the Persian Empire, which was then declining from its protracted struggles with Byzantium, and in 711, the same year that the Arabs landed in Spain, they sent dhows up the Indus River into India. This was more a casual raid than a full-scale invasion, but in the 12th century all of north India fell into Muslim hands. Eventually, the Mughal Empire controlled most of the subcontinent. From here it was spread by Indian traders into South-East Asia.

At an early stage in its history, Islam suffered a fundamental split that remains to this day. The third caliph, successor to Mohammed, was murdered and followed by Ali, the Prophet's son-in-law, in 656. Ali was assassinated in 661 by the governor of Syria, who set himself up as caliph in preference to the descendants of Ali. Most Muslims today are Sunnites, followers of the succession from the caliph, while the others are Shias or Shi'ites who follow the descendants of Ali.

Converts to Islam have only to announce that 'There is no god but Allah and Mohammed is his prophet' to become Muslim. Friday is the Muslim holy day and the main mosque in each town is known as the Jama Masjid or Friday Mosque. One of the aims of every Muslim is to make the pilgrimage (hajj) to Mecca and become a hajji.

Top Left: Lattice-work graces the mid-18th century Safdarjang Tomb, Delhi.

Top Right: Semi-precious stones set in marble at the Taj Mahal.

Despite its initial vigour, Islam eventually became inert and unchanging, though it remains to be seen what effect the fundamentalism of recent years will have on the religion worldwide. In India itself, despite Islam's long period of control, it never managed to make great inroads into Hindu society and religion. Converts to Islam were principally from the lowest castes, with the result that at Partition Pakistan found itself with a shortage of the educated clerical workers and government officials with which India is so liberally endowed. However, the effects of Muslim influence in India are particularly visible in its architecture, art and food.

CHRIS BEALL

Sufism

Sufism is a branch of Islamic philosophy which has its basis in the belief that abstinence, self-denial and tolerance – even of other religions – are the route to union with God. This religious tolerance sets the Sufis very much apart from conventional Islamic thought, which has led to their persecution in some countries; in India, the sect appeals to members of all religions and is growing in popularity.

Sufis also believe that the achievement of a trance-like state of ecstasy brings the believer close to God, and to this end music and dance are used extensively. Qawwali music (rhymed, devotional Urdu couplets, usually with harmonium accompaniment) is still performed at the *dargahs* (shrine-tombs) of Sufi saints of the Chisti sect in India today. It is at such times that dervishes (Sufi holymen) become so entranced they go into a frenzied whirling.

Top: The tomb of Shaikh Salim Chishti inside Fatehpur Sikri's Dargah Mosque, Uttar Pradesh, is a place of pilgrimage for women wishing to bear children.

Bottom: Detail of the Quwwat-ul-Islam Mosque, Delhi's first.

HUGH FINLAY

Islamic Festivals

Ramadan The most important Muslim festival is this 30-day dawn-to-dusk fast. It was during this month that the prophet Mohammed received his revelation from Allah. Ramadan starts around 21 January 1996, 10 January 1997, 31 December 1997 and 20 December 1998.

Id-ul-Fitr This day celebrates the end of Ramadan.

Id-ul-Zuhara This festival commemorates Abraham's attempt to sacrifice his son. It is celebrated with prayers and feasts, and will be held in April in 1996 and 1997, and in March in 1998.

Muharram This 10-day festival commemorates the martyrdom of Mohammed's grandson, Imam Hussain, and will be held in May in 1996 and 1997, and in April in 1998.

Milad-un-Nabi The birth of Mohammed will be celebrated in the month of July in 1996-98.

Top: The tomb of Sufi saint, Shaikh Hazrat Nizam-ud-din Aulia, Delhi.

Bottom Left: Sweet sellers at the Muslim Baqr-id Festival, Nizamuddin village, Delhi.

Bottom Right: Sufi devotees at Shaikh Hazrat Nizam-ud-din Aulia's shrine.

HUGH FINLAY

SALLY HONE

HUGH FINLAY

SIKHISM

The Sikhs in India number 18 million and predominate in the Punjab, although they are found all over India. They are the most visible of the Indian religious groups because of the five symbols introduced by Guru Gobind Singh to help Sikh men easily recognise each other. They are known as the five *kakkars* and are: *kesh* – uncut hair (symbol of saintliness); *kangha* – the wooden or ivory comb (symbol of cleanliness); *kuccha* – shorts (symbol of alertness); *kara* – the steel bracelet (symbol of determination); and *kirpan* – the sword (for the defence of the weak). Because of their kesh, Sikh men wear their hair tied up in a bun and hidden by a turban. Wearing kuccha and carrying a kirpan came about because of the Sikhs' military tradition – they didn't want to be tripping over a long dhoti or be caught without a weapon. Normally the sword is simply represented by a tiny image set in the comb. The steel bracelet has a useful secondary function as a bottle opener. With his beard, turban and upright, military bearing, the 'noble' Sikh is hard to miss!

GREG ELMS

GREG ELMS

Facing Page: Sikh pilgrim at Amritsar in the Punjab.

Top: Amritsar is named after this pool surrounding the Golden Temple.

Bottom: The Golden Temple, the Sikhs' holiest shrine, silhouetted at sunset.

GREG ELMS

RICHARD I'ANSON

GREG ELMS

Inside the Golden Temple at Amritsar: prayers and pilgrims.

The Sikh religion was founded by Guru Nanak, who was born in 1469. It was originally intended to bring together the best of the Hindu and Islamic religions. Its basic tenets are similar to those of Hinduism, with the important modification that the Sikhs are opposed to caste distinctions and pilgrimages to rivers. They are not, however, opposed to pilgrimages to holy sites.

They worship at temples known as *gurdwaras*, baptise their children (when they are old enough to understand the religion) in a ceremony known as *pahul* and cremate their dead. The holy book of the Sikhs is the *Granth Sahib*, which contains the works of the 10 Sikh gurus together with Hindu and Muslim writings. The last guru died in 1708.

In the 16th century, Guru Gobind Singh introduced military overtones into the religion in an attempt to halt the persecution the Sikhs were then suffering. A brotherhood, known as the Khalsa, was formed, and entry into it was conditional on a person undergoing baptism *(amrit)*. From that time the majority of Sikhs have borne the surname Singh which means Lion (although just because a person has the surname Singh doesn't mean they are necessarily a Sikh; many Rajputs also have this surname).

Sikhs believe in one god and are opposed to idol worship. They practise tolerance and love of others, and their belief in hospitality extends to offering shelter to anyone who comes to their gurdwaras. Because of their get-on-with-it attitude to life they are one of the more affluent groups in Indian society. They have a well-known reputation for mechanical aptitude and specialise in handling machinery of every type, from jumbo jets to auto-rickshaws.

Off-limits to foreign visitors for many years, owing to the terrorist activities of extremist groups, the Punjab region of India is now peaceful once more.

Sikh Festivals

Baisakhi This festival commemorates the day on which Guru Gobind Singh founded the Khalsa. The *Granth Sahib* is read in its entirety at gurdwaras, and is then carried in a procession. Feasting and dancing follow in the evening. The festival is held in April/May.

Nanak Jayanti The birthday of Guru Nanak is celebrated with prayer readings and processions, particularly in Amritsar and Patna (April/May).

SALLY HONE

SALLY HONE

Top: Sikh women worship with song at a gurdwara.

Bottom: The Granth Sahib, the Sikhs' spiritual guide, Delhi.

BRYN THOMAS

JAINISM

The Jain religion is contemporaneous with Buddhism and bears many similarities to both it and Hinduism. It was founded around 500 BC by Mahavira, the 24th and last of the Jain prophets, known as *tirthankars* or Finders of the Path. The Jains now number only about 4.5 million but are found all over India, predominantly in the west and south-west. They tend to be commercially successful and have an influence disproportionate to their actual numbers.

The religion originally evolved as a reformist movement against the dominance of priests and the complicated rituals of Brahminism, and it rejected the caste system. Jains believe that the universe is infinite and was not created by a deity. They also believe in reincarnation and eventual spiritual salvation, or *moksha*, through following the path of the tirthankars. One factor in the search for salvation is *ahimsa*, or reverence for all life and the avoidance of injury to all living things. Due to this belief, Jains are strict vegetarians and some monks actually cover their mouths with a piece of cloth in order to avoid the risk of accidentally swallowing an insect.

Facing Page: Inside a Jain temple.

This Page: The Sravana-belagola shrine in Karnataka.

LEANNE LOGAN   HUGH FINLAY

Top: Jain temples at Khaju-raho in Madhya Pradesh.

Bottom: Jain Temple, Jai-salmer.

BRYN THOMAS

GREG ELMS

The Jains are divided into two sects, the white-robed Shvetambara and the Digambara. The Digambaras are the more austere sect; their name literally means Sky Clad since, as a sign of their contempt for material possessions, they do not even wear clothes. Not surprisingly, Digambaras are generally monks who are confined to a monastery! The famous Sravanabelagola shrine in Karnataka state, south India, is a Digambara temple.

The Jains constructed extraordinary temple complexes, notable for the large number of similar buildings clustered together in the one place. The temples also feature many columns, no two of which are ever identical. Their most spectacular 'temple city' is at Palitana in eastern Gujarat – a mountain-top fortress filled with hundreds of beautiful temples. Down south, Sravanabelagola in Karnataka, though only a village, is also a holy site.

Jain Festivals

Mahavir Jayanti The major Jain festival marks the birth of Mahavira, and is celebrated in March/April.

HUGH FINLAY

Top Left and Bottom Right: Detail inside the Dilwara group of Jain temples near Mt Abu in Rajasthan. It is here that marble carving reached unsurpassed heights.

Top Right: Restoration under way at a Jain temple in Amar Sagar, Rajasthan.

Bottom Left: Jain temple, Calcutta.

GREG HERRIMAN

RICHARD I'ANSON

HUGH FINLAY

ZOROASTRIANISM

This is one of the oldest religions on earth and was founded in Persia by the prophet Zarathustra (Zoroaster) in the 6th or 7th century BC. He was born in Mazar-i-Sharif in what is now Afghanistan. At one time, Zoroastrianism stretched all the way from India to the Mediterranean, but today it is found only around Shiraz in Iran, Karachi in Pakistan and Bombay in India. The followers of Zoroastrianism are known as Parsis because they originally fled to India to escape persecution in Persia.

Zoroastrianism was one of the first religions to postulate an omnipotent and invisible god. Their scripture is the *Zend-Avesta*, which describes the continual conflict between the forces of good and evil. Their god is Ahura Mazda, the god of light, who is symbolised by fire. Humanity ensures the victory of good over evil by following the principles of *humata* (good thoughts), *hukta* (good words) and *huvarshta* (good deeds).

Parsis worship in fire temples and wear a *sadra*, or sacred shirt, and a *kasti*, or sacred thread. Children first wear these sacred items in a ceremony known as Navjote. Flames burn eternally in their fire temples and are worshipped as a symbol of their god. Because Parsis believe in the purity of elements, they will not cremate or bury their dead since this might pollute the fire, earth, air or water. Instead, they leave the bodies in 'Towers of Silence' where they are soon cleaned off by vultures.

Although there are only about 85,000 Parsis, they are very successful in commerce and industry, and have become notable philanthropists. Parsis have influence far greater than their numbers would indicate, having acted as a channel of communication between India and Pakistan when the two countries were at loggerheads. Their numbers are gradually declining because of the strict requirements that a Parsi must only marry another Parsi. The offspring of mixed liaisons are not regarded as true Parsis.

CHRISTIANITY & JUDAISM

India has around 22 million Christians. There have been Christian communities in Kerala since the coming of Christianity to Europe (St Thomas the Apostle is supposed to have arrived here in 54 AD). The Portuguese, who unlike the English were as enthusiastic about spreading their brand of Christianity as making money from trade, left a large Christian community in Goa. Generally, however, Christianity has not been greatly successful in India, if success is counted in number of converts. The first round of Indian converts to Christianity were generally those from the ruling classes, and subsequently they were mainly from the lower castes. There are, however, two small states (Mizoram and Nagaland) where Christians form a majority of the population. A quarter of the population of Kerala and a third of Goa are also Christian. The Christian festivals of Good Friday and Christmas Day are both celebrated in India.

There are small Jewish communities in a number of cities, but the Jews of Kochi (Cochin) in Kerala are of special interest because a group claims to have arrived here in 587 BC.

The ornate interior of a Keralan church, South India.

TONY WHEELER

GREG ELMS

Top: Church of the Immaculate Conception, Goa. Roman Catholicism is a legacy of Portuguese rule.

Bottom from Left: A 16th-century synagogue in Jewtown, Cochin, Kerala; Shimla's Christ Church. Church of Saint Cajetan, Old Goa.

Back Page: Two girls pause before an image of Krishna, Lord of the Universe, at New Delhi's Jagannath Temple. During the annual Rath Yatra (Car Festival) held in Krishna's honour, giant vehicles are dragged from the temple and through the streets. The event attracts thousands of pilgrims to the Jagannath Temple in Puri, Orissa. (photograph by Sally Hone)

GREG ELMS

BRYN THOMAS

BRYN THOMAS

Facts for the Visitor

VISAS, PERMITS & EMBASSIES

Indian Visas

Virtually everybody needs a visa to visit India. The application is (in theory) straightforward and the visas are usually issued with a minimum of fuss.

Tourist visas come in a variety of flavours: 15-day, single or double-entry transit visas, valid for 30 days from date of issue; three-month, *non-extendable*, multiple-entry visas, valid for three months *from the date of first entry into India* (which must be within 30 days of date of issue); and six-month, multiple-entry visas valid for six months *from the date of issue of the visa*, not the date you enter India. For the latter, this means that if you enter India five months after the visa was issued, it will be valid only for one more month, not the full six months. If you enter India the day after it was issued, you can stay for the full six months. We get many letters from travellers who get caught out, thinking a six-month visa gives them a six-month stay in India. Only six-month visas are extendable.

The cost of the visa varies depending on your nationality. Currently Brits pay UK£3/13/26 for a 15-day/three-month/six-month visa, while Aussies pay A$17/40/70 for a 15-day/three-month/six-month visa. Most other nationalities are charged much the same.

In Pakistan The high commission in Islamabad is quite efficient, although if there is an Indian embassy in your home country they may have to fax there to check that you are not a thief, wanted by the police or in some other way undesirable. The process takes a few days, and of course you have to pay for the fax.

Indian Embassies

India's embassies and consulates include:

Australia
   3-5 Moonah Place, Yarralumla, ACT 2600 (☎ (06) 273-3999; fax 273-3328)
   153 Walker St, North Sydney, NSW 2060 (☎ (02) 9955-7055; fax 9929-6058)
   13 Munro St, Coburg, Melbourne, Vic 3058 (☎ (03) 9384-0141; fax 9384-1609)
   195 Adelaide Terrace, East Perth, WA 6004 (☎ (09) 221-1207; fax 221-1206)
Bangladesh
   120 Road 2, Dhanmodi Residential Area, Dhaka (☎ (02) 50-3606; fax 86-3662)
   1253/1256 O R Nizam Rd, Mehdi Bagh, Chittagong (☎ (031) 21-1007; fax 22-5178)
Belgium
   217 Chaussee de Vleurgat, 1050 Brussels (☎ (02) 640-9802; fax 648-9638)
Bhutan
   India House Estate, Thimpu, Bhutan (☎ (0975) 22-162; fax 23-195)
Canada
   10 Springfield Rd, Ottawa K1M 1C9 (☎ (613) 744-3751; fax 744-0913)
China
   1 Ri Tan Dong Lu, Beijing (☎ (01) 532-1908; fax 532-4684)
Denmark
   Vangehusvej 15, 2100 Copenhagen (☎ (045) 3118-2888; fax 3927-0218)
Egypt
   5 Aziz Ababa St, Zamalek, Cairo 11511 (☎ (02) 341-3051; fax 341-4038)
France
   15 Rue Alfred Dehodencq, 75016 Paris (☎ (01) 4050-7070; fax 4050-0996)
Germany
   Adenauerallee 262, 53113 Bonn 1 (☎ (0228) 54-050; fax 54-0514)
Israel
   4 Kaufman St, Sharbat House, Tel Aviv 68012 (☎ (03) 58-4585; fax 510-1434)
Italy
   Via XX Settembre 5, 00187 Rome (☎ (06) 488-4642; fax 481-9539)
Japan
   2-2-11 Kudan Minami, Chiyoda-ku, Tokyo 102 (☎ (03) 3262-2391; fax 3234-4866)
Jordan
   1st Circle, Jebel Amman, Amman (☎ (06) 62-2098; fax 65-9540)
Kenya
   Jeevan Bharati Bldg, Harambee Ave, Nairobi (☎ (02) 22-2566; fax 33-4167)

Korea
>37-3 Hannam-dong, Yongsan-ku, Seoul 140210 (☎ (02) 798-4257; fax 796-9534)

Malaysia
>2 Jalan Taman Dlita, 50480 Kuala Lumpur (☎ (03) 253-3504; fax 253-3507)

Myanmar (Burma)
>545-547 Merchant St, Yangon (Rangoon) (☎ (01) 82-550; fax 89-562)

Nepal
>Lainchaur, GPO Box 292, Kathmandu (☎ (071) 41-1940; fax 41-3132)

Netherlands
>Buitenrustweg 2, 252 KD, The Hague (☎ (070) 346-9771; fax 361-7072)

New Zealand
>180 Molesworth St, Wellington (☎ (04) 473-6390; fax 499-0665)

Pakistan
>G5 Diplomatic Enclave, Islamabad (☎ (051) 81-4371; fax 82-0742)
>India House, 3 Fatima Jinnah Rd, Karachi (☎ (021) 52-2275; fax 568-0929)

Russia
>6 Ulitsa Obukha, Moscow (☎ (095) 297-0820; fax 975-2337)

Singapore
>India House, 31 Grange Rd (☎ 737-6777; fax 732-6909)

South Africa
>Sanlam Centre, Johannesburg (☎ (011) 333-1525; fax 333-0690)

Sri Lanka
>36-38 Galla Rd, Colombo 3 (☎ (01) 421-605; fax 44-6403)

Sweden
>Adolf Fredriks Kyrkogata 12, 11183 Stockholm (☎ (08) 10-7008; fax 24-8505)

Switzerland
>Effingerstrasse 45, CH-3008 Berne (☎ (031) 382-3111; fax 382-2687)

Syria
>40/46 Adnan Malki St, Yassin, Damascus (☎ (011) 71-9581; fax 71-3294)

Tanzania
>NIC Investment House, Samora Ave, Dar es Salaam (☎ (051) 28-198; fax 46-747)

Thailand
>46 Soi 23 (Prasarnmitr), Sukhumvit Rd, Bangkok (☎ (02) 258-0300; fax 258-4627)
>113 Bumruangrat Rd, Chiang Mai 50000 (☎ (053) 24-3066; fax 24-7879)

UK
>India House, Aldwych, London WC2B 4NA (☎ (0171) 836-8484; fax 836-4331)
>8219 Augusta St, Birmingham B18 6DS (☎ (0121) 212-2782; fax 212-2786)

USA
>2107 Massachusetts Ave NW, Washington DC 20008 (☎ (202) 939-7000; fax 939-7027)
>3 East 64th St, Manhattan, New York, NY 10021-7097 (☎ (212) 879-7800; fax 988-6423)
>540 Arguello Blvd, San Francisco, CA 94118 (☎ (415) 668-0662; fax 668-2073)

Visa Extensions

Only six-month tourist visas are extendable. If you want to stay in India beyond the 180 days from the date of issue of your visa, *regardless of your date of entry into India*, you're going to have to try to extend your visa. Extensions are not given as a matter of routine. If you have already been in the country for six months, it can be difficult to get an extension, and then you may only be given a month. If you've been in India less than six months the chances are much better. A one-month extension costs anything from Rs 600 to Rs 800, and four photos are required.

If you stay beyond four months you are also supposed to get an income tax clearance before you leave. See the upcoming Tax Clearance Certificates section for details.

Foreigners' Registration Offices

Visa extensions and permits for Sikkim, the Andaman & Nicobar Islands and Lakshadweep are issued by the Foreigners' Registration Offices. The main offices include:

Bombay
>Special Branch II, Annexe 2, Office of the Commissioner of Police (Greater Bombay), Dadabhoy Naoroji Rd (☎ (022) 262-0446)

Calcutta
>237 Acharya J C Bose Rd (☎ (033) 247-3301)

Delhi
>1st floor, Hans Bhavan, Tilak Bridge (☎ (011) 331-9489)

Madras
>Shashtri Bhavan Annexe, 26 Haddows Rd (☎ (044) 827-8210)

Visas can also be extended in all state and district capitals at the office of the Superintendent of Police.

Tax Clearance Certificates

If you stay in India for more than 120 days

you need a 'tax clearance certificate' to leave the country. This supposedly proves that your time in India was financed with your own money, not by working in India or by selling things or playing the black market.

Basically all you have to do is find the Foreign Section of the Income Tax Department in Delhi, Calcutta, Madras or Bombay and turn up with your passport, visa extension form, any other similar paperwork and a handful of bank exchange receipts (to show you really have been changing foreign currency into rupees officially). You fill in a form and wait for anything from 10 minutes to a couple of hours. You're then given your tax clearance certificate and away you go. We've never yet heard from anyone who has actually been asked for this document on departure.

Special Permits

Even with a visa you are not allowed everywhere in India. Certain places require special additional permits. These are covered in the appropriate sections in the main text, but briefly they are:

Andaman Islands For those flying in, permits for a stay of up to 30 days are issued on arrival at the airport in Port Blair. If you're arriving by ship, you need a permit in advance; the shipping company won't let you buy a ticket without one. Permits are obtainable from an embassy or consulate abroad, from the Ministry of Home Affairs in Delhi, or from the Foreigners' Registration Offices in Madras or Calcutta.

Getting the permit in Delhi could take several days; in Calcutta or Madras it's generally a few hours. If you think there's a chance you might visit the Andamans on your Indian trip, get a permit when you get your Indian visa; it costs nothing and could save time later.

Bhutan Although Bhutan is an independent country, India has firm control over foreign policy and most other things. Applications to visit Bhutan must be made through the Director of Tourism, Ministry of Finance,

Tachichho Dzong, Thimpu, Bhutan; or through the Bhutan Foreign Mission (☎ (011) 60-9217), Chandra Gupta Marg, Delhi 110021, India; or through the Bhutanese mission in New York. And don't hold your breath – unless you have high-up Indian connections or a personal friend in the Bhutanese aristocracy, you needn't expect to get a permit. Very few permits are issued for overland travel. The only way around these restrictions is to book an organised tour, and these don't come cheap.

Lakshadweep A permit for these islands west and south-west of Kerala state is problematic. Only one island is currently open to foreigners. See the Lakshadweep section at the end of the Kerala chapter for full details.

North-Eastern Region Foreigners must have a permit for these remote north-eastern states, and you are restricted in where you may go. Furthermore, don't hold your breath when applying as they can take months to come through, if at all. It helps if you have a reference from an Indian who has political elbow.

Basically, the only states it's worth trying to get a permit for are Assam and Meghalaya. In theory it's possible to visit all the north-eastern states as long as you are part of a group of four. Permits allow for a maximum 10-day stay in each state. In practice things are, predictably, a lot different; you might get into Assam and Meghalaya, but getting permission to go any further is extremely difficult. This situation may change, especially with regard to Assam and Meghalaya, as the states want the permit restrictions lifted, and the central government is taking its time thinking about it.

Sikkim Permits are issued either while you wait or within two or three hours (depending on where you apply for them) – see the Sikkim chapter for full details.

Other Visas

If you're heading to other places near India the visa situation is as follows.

Myanmar (Burma) The embassy in Delhi is fast and efficient and issues four-week visas. There is *no* Burmese consulate in Calcutta, although there is one in Kathmandu and in Dhaka, Bangladesh.

Nepal The Nepalese Embassy in Delhi is on Barakhamba Rd, quite close to Connaught Place, not out at Chanakyapuri like most other embassies. It is open Monday to Friday from 10 am to 1 pm. Single-entry, 30-day visas take 24 hours and cost US$25 (payable in rupees). A 30-day visa is available on arrival in Nepal for US$25, and can be extended, but doing so involves rather a lot of form filling and queuing – it's better to have a visa in advance if possible.

There is also a consulate in Calcutta, and they issue visas on the spot. You'll need one passport photo and the rupee equivalent of US$25.

Sri Lanka Most Western nationalities do not need a visa to visit Sri Lanka, but there are diplomatic offices in Delhi, Bombay and Madras.

Thailand There are Thai embassies in Delhi and Calcutta. One-month visas cost about US$10 and are issued in 24 hours. They can be extended in Thailand. If you are flying into and out of Thailand and don't intend to stay more than 15 days, a visa is not required, but you cannot extend your period of stay.

Foreign Embassies in India
Most foreign diplomatic missions are in the nation's capital, Delhi, but there are also quite a few consulates in the other major cities of Bombay, Calcutta and Madras. See the relevant cities for listings.

DOCUMENTS
You must have a passport; it's the most basic travel document. In fact you should have your passport with you all the time. We had a letter from two Australians who spent four days in jail during the Pushkar cattle fair because they'd left their passports for safe-keeping in Jaipur. Two of the four days were spent while a friend returned to Jaipur and collected the passports for them! Another traveller who was comprehensively ripped off on a day trip to Gwalior had fortunately left his passport in Agra. The police, however, were more upset about the passport left behind than the theft! The fact that had he been carrying it with him, he would not now have it to show to the police, made no difference at all!

A health certificate, while not necessary in India, may well be required for onward travel. Student cards are virtually useless these days – many student concessions have either been eliminated or replaced by 'youth fares' or similar age concessions. Similarly, a Youth Hostel (Hostelling International – HI) card is not generally required for India's many hostels, but you do pay slightly less at official youth hostels with one.

There is not much opportunity to get behind the wheel in India, but if you do intend to drive then get an International Driving Permit from your local national motoring organisation. These days motor-cycles are more readily available for hire, particularly in Goa, and an International Permit is useful if you rent one. An International Permit can also be used for other identification purposes, such as plain old bicycle hire.

It's worth having a batch of passport photos for visa applications and other uses. If you run out, Indian photo studios will do excellent portraits at pleasantly low prices.

CUSTOMS
The usual duty-free regulations apply for India; that is, one bottle of whisky and 200 cigarettes.

You're allowed to bring in all sorts of Western technological wonders, but big items, such as video cameras, are likely to be entered on a 'Tourist Baggage Re-Export' form to ensure you take them out with you when you go. It's not necessary to declare still-cameras, even if you have more than one.

Note that if you are entering India from

Nepal you are not entitled to import anything free of duty.

MONEY

The rupee (Rs) is divided into 100 paise (p). There are coins of five, 10, 20, 25 and 50 paise, Rs 1, 2 and 5 (rare), and notes of Rs 1, 2, 5, 10, 20, 50, 100 and 500.

You are not allowed to bring Indian currency into the country or take it out of the country. You are allowed to bring in unlimited amounts of foreign currency or travellers' cheques, but you are supposed to declare anything over US$10,000 on arrival.

The rupee is a fully convertible currency, ie the rate is set by the market not the government. For this reason there's not much of a black market, although you can get a couple of rupees more for your dollars or pounds cash. In the major tourist centres you will have constant offers to change money. There's little risk involved although it is officially illegal; the major advantage is it's much quicker than changing at a bank. If you do decide to change on the black market, do it off the street rather than in the open. US$100 bills fetch the best rates.

In major cities you can change most foreign currencies or travellers' cheques – Australian dollars, Deutschmarks, yen or whatever – but out of town it's best to stick to US dollars or pounds sterling. Thomas Cook and American Express are both popular travellers' cheques, and these two companies have a number of branches in India.

Although it's usually not a problem to change travellers' cheques, it's best to stick to the well-known brands – American Express, Visa, Thomas Cook, Citibank and

Barclays – as more obscure ones may cause problems. It also happens occasionally that a bank won't accept a certain type of cheque – American Express, Visa and Citibank in particular – and for this reason it's worth carrying more than one flavour.

Outside the main cities the State Bank of India is usually the place to change money, although occasionally they'll direct you to another bank, such as the Bank of India, the Punjab National Bank or the Bank of Baroda.

Many people make the mistake of bringing too many small-denomination cheques. Unless you are moving rapidly from country to country you only need a handful of small denominations for end-of-stay conversions. In between, change as much as you feel happy carrying. This applies particularly in India where changing money can take time – especially in the smaller towns. You can also spend a lot of time finding a bank which will change money. The answer is to change money as infrequently as possible and to change it only in big banks in big cities.

Exchange Rates

A$1	=	Rs 22.86
C$1	=	Rs 22.90
DM1	=	Rs 22.61
FFr1	=	Rs 6.33
Jap ¥100	=	Rs 35.43
Nep Rs100	=	Rs 61.28
NZ$1	=	Rs 21.07
Sin$1	=	Rs 22.41
US$1	=	Rs 31.18
UK£1	=	Rs 50.02

Encashment Certificates

All money is supposed to be changed at official banks or moneychangers, and you are supposed to be given an encashment

---

Do You Want My Money Or Not?
A simple thing like changing money can often become farcical. In the major tourist centre of Varanasi, for example, the main branch of the State Bank of India accepts many different currencies in cash, but only pounds and dollars travellers' cheques. Some other State Bank of India branches accept only cash, others only travellers' cheques. At other banks, such as the Bank of Baroda or the State Bank of Benares, it's the same story, and the bank that handles credit card cash-advances won't have anything to do with changing cash *or* cheques, and *not one* of them will accept Australian dollars travellers' cheques! ■

Banknotes
Indian currency notes circulate far longer than in the West and the small notes in particular become very tatty – some should carry a government health warning! A note can have holes right through it (most do in fact, as they are bundled together with staples when new) and be quite acceptable but if it's slightly torn at the top or bottom on the crease line then it's no good and you'll have trouble spending it. Even a missing corner makes a bill unacceptable. The answer to this is to simply accept it philosophically or think of clever uses. Use it for tips or for official purposes. I'd love to pay the Rs 300 departure tax with 300 totally disreputable Rs 1 notes – although someone who did just that wrote to say he had some trouble getting them to accept it! Some banks have special counters where torn notes will be exchanged for good ones, but who wants to visit banks more than necessary? ■

certificate for each transaction. In practice, some people surreptitiously bring rupees into the country with them – they can be bought at a useful discount price in places like Singapore or Bangkok. Indian rupees can be brought in fairly openly from Nepal and again you can get a slightly better rate there.

Banks will usually give you an encashment certificate, but occasionally they don't bother. It is worth getting them, especially if you want to re-exchange excess rupees for hard currency when you depart India.

The other reason for saving encashment certificates is that if you stay in India longer than four months, you have to get an income tax clearance. This requires production of a handful of encashment certificates to prove you've been changing money all along and not doing anything naughty.

Credit Cards
Credit cards are widely accepted in India, particularly Diners Club, MasterCard, American Express and Visa.

With American Express, MasterCard or Visa cards you can use your card to obtain cash rupees. With Amex you can also get dollar or sterling travellers' cheques, or get cash rupees locally from an Amex office, but you must have a personal cheque to cover the amount, although counter cheques are available if you ask for them.

Transferring Money
Don't run out of money in India unless you have a credit card against which you can draw travellers' cheques or cash. Having money transferred through the banking system can be time-consuming. It's usually

straightforward if you use a foreign bank, Thomas Cook or American Express in one of the main cities; elsewhere it may take a fortnight and will be a hassle.

If you do have money sent to you in India, specify the bank, the branch and the address you want it sent to. Overseas banks with branches in India include Bank of America, HongKong Bank, Standard Chartered Bank, Banque Nationale de Paris, Citibank and, particularly, ANZ Grindlays, which has many branches in smaller cities as well as in the major cities.

Costs
It is virtually impossible to say what travelling around India will cost you. It depends on where you stay, what you eat, how you travel and how fast you travel. Two people travelling at exactly the same standard can spend vastly different amounts on a daily basis if one travels twice as fast as the other. A week lying on the beach at Goa watching the waves roll in brings daily costs down very rapidly.

Whatever budget you decide to travel on, you can be assured that you'll be getting a whole lot more for your money than in most other countries – it's fantastic value.

From top to bottom: if you stay in luxury hotels, fly everywhere, and see a lot of India in a very short trip, you can spend a lot of money. India has plenty of hotels at US$50 or more a day and some where a room can cost US$100 plus. At the other extreme, if you scrimp and save, stay in dormitories or the cheapest hotels, always travel 2nd class on trains, and learn to exist on dhal and rice, you can see India on less than US$7 a day.

Most travellers will probably be looking for something between these extremes. If so, you'll stay in reasonable hotels with the sort of standard provided by the tourist bungalows in many states – a clean but straightforward room with fan cooling and bathroom. You'll eat in regular restaurants but occasionally splash out on a fancy meal when you're in a big town. If you mix your travel, you'll try 2nd class most of the time, and opt for 1st class only if you're travelling on a long overnight trip; you'll take autorickshaws rather than always looking for a bus. In that case India could cost you something like US$15 to US$25 a day on average. It totally depends on what you're looking for.

As everywhere in Asia, you get pretty much what you pay for, and many times it's worth paying a little more for the experience. That old-fashioned Raj-style luxury is part of India's charm and sometimes it's foolish not to lay out the money and enjoy it.

Baksheesh

In most Asian countries tipping is virtually unknown, but India is an exception to that rule – although tipping has a rather different role in India than in the West. The term *baksheesh*, which encompasses tipping and a lot more besides, aptly describes the concept in India. You 'tip' not so much for good service, but to get things done.

Judicious baksheesh will open closed doors, find missing letters and perform other small miracles. Tipping is not necessary for taxis nor for cheaper restaurants, but if you're going to be using something repeatedly, an initial tip will ensure the standards are kept up – this may explain why the service is slower every time in your hotel restaurant for example. Keep things in perspective though. Demands for baksheesh can quickly become never-ending. Ask yourself if it's really necessary or desirable before shelling out.

In tourist restaurants or hotels, where service is usually tacked on in any case, the normal 10% figure usually applies. In smaller places, where tipping is optional, you need only tip a few rupees, not a percentage of the bill. Hotel porters usually get about Rs 1 per bag; other possible tipping levels are Rs 1 to Rs 2 for bike-watching, Rs 10 for train conductors or station porters performing miracles for you, and Rs 5 to Rs 15 for extra services from hotel staff.

Many Westerners find this aspect of Indian travel the most trying – the constant demands for baksheesh and the expectations that because you're a foreigner, you'll tip. However, from an Indian perspective, baksheesh is an integral part of the system – it wasn't invented simply to extract money from tourists. Take some time to observe how Indians (even those who are obviously not excessively wealthy) deal with baksheesh situations; they always give something, and it's expected and accepted by both sides.

Although you may not consider yourself well off, think of how an Indian who earns Rs 500 a month sees you. Foreigners who spend their whole time trying to fight the system, instead of rolling with it philosophically, inevitably find themselves constantly involved in vitriolic and unpleasant arguments with people over what is, in the end, a pittance. No-one would be naive enough to suggest that all demands for baksheesh are justified, or that the amount demanded is always reasonable, but if you can accept the fact that this is how things work here, and tip fairly, chances are you'll find that things are a whole lot easier.

Although most people think of baksheesh in terms of tipping, it also refers to giving alms to beggars. Wherever you turn in India you'll be confronted by beggars – many of them (often handicapped or hideously disfigured) genuinely in dire need, others, such as kids hassling for a rupee or a pen, obviously not.

All sorts of stories about beggars do the rounds of the travellers' hang-outs, many of them with little basis in fact. Stories such as rupee millionaire beggars, people (usually kids) being deliberately mutilated by their parents so they can beg, and a beggars' Mafia are all common.

It's a matter of personal choice how you approach the issue of beggars and baksheesh.

Dhobi-Wallahs

When you travel in India there's hardly any need for more than one change of clothes. Every day there will be a knock on your door and the laundry boy will collect all those dusty, sweaty clothes you wore yesterday, and every evening those same clothes will reappear – washed and ironed with more loving care than any washing-powder-ad mum ever lavished upon anything. And all for a few rupees per item. But what happened to your clothes between their departure and their like-new return?

Well, they certainly did not get anywhere near a washing machine. First of all they're collected and taken to the *dhobi ghat*. A ghat is a place with water, a dhobi-wallah is a washerperson, so the dhobi ghat is where the dhobi-wallahs ply their trade and wash clothes. In big cities, dhobi ghats will be huge places with hundreds of dhobi-wallahs doing their thing with thousands of articles of clothing.

Then the clothes are separated – all the white shirts are washed together, all the grey trousers, all the red skirts, all the blue jeans. By now, if this was the West, your clothes would either be hopelessly lost or you'd need a computer to keep track of them all. Your clothes are soaked in soapy water for a few hours, following which the dirt is literally beaten out of them. No multiprogrammed miracle of technology can wash as clean as a determined dhobi-wallah, although admittedly after a few visits to the Indian laundry your clothes do begin to look distinctly thinner. Buttons also tend to get shattered, so bring some spares. Zips sometimes fare likewise.

Once clean, the clothes are strung out on miles of clothesline to quickly dry in the Indian sun. They're then taken to the ironing sheds where hundreds of ironers wielding primitive irons press your jeans like they've never been pressed before. Not just your jeans – your socks, your T-shirts, even your underwear will come back with knife-edge creases. Then the Indian miracle takes place. Out of the thousands upon thousands of items washed that day, somehow your very own brown socks, blue jeans, yellow T-shirt and red underwear all find their way back together and head for your hotel room. A system of marking clothes, known only to the dhobis, is the real reason behind this feat. They say criminals have been tracked down simply by those telltale 'dhobi marks'. ∎

Some people feel it is best to give nothing to any beggar as it 'only encourages them' and to contribute by helping out at Mother Teresa's or similar; others give away loose change when they have it; unfortunately, others insulate themselves entirely and give nothing in any way. It's up to you.

Whether or not you decide to give to beggars on the street, the 'one pen, one pen' brigades should be firmly discouraged.

WHAT TO BRING

The usual travellers' rule applies – bring as little as possible. It's much better to have to get something you've left behind than find you have too much and need to get rid of it. In the south of India you can count on short-sleeves weather year-round, but in the north it gets cool enough to require a sweater or light jacket in the evenings during the winter. In the far north it will get down to freezing and you will need all the cold-weather gear you can muster.

Remember that clothes are easily and cheaply purchased in India. You can buy things off the peg or have clothes made to measure in the small tailor shops found throughout the country. In the big cities there are plenty of the Indian fashions so popular in the West, and the prices often approximate in rupees what they cost in dollars back home! One item of clothing to have made as soon as possible is a pair of lightweight pyjama-style trousers. You'll find them far cooler and more comfortable than jeans and they'll only cost a few dollars.

Modesty rates highly in India, as in most Asian countries. Although men – or women – wearing shorts is accepted as a Western eccentricity, they should at least be of a decent length. Wearing shorts or a T-shirt in a more formal situation is definitely impolite. A reasonable clothes list would include:

• underwear and swimming gear
• one pair of cotton trousers
• one pair of shorts
• one cotton skirt (women)
• a few T-shirts or short-sleeved cotton shirts
• sweater for cold nights
• one pair of sneakers or shoes plus socks
• sandals and/or thongs
• lightweight jacket or raincoat
• a set of 'dress up' clothes

Other useful items include washing gear, medical and sewing kits, sunglasses and a padlock. A length of clothesline and a handful of clothes pegs are also worth considering if you're going to do your own laundry. A number of travellers have suggested taking small gifts such as ballpoint pens (very popular), combs, sweets etc for people, especially children, who have been friendly or helpful. Another item to consider is an umbrella – invaluable in the monsoon. See the upcoming Miscellaneous Items section for more details.

Sleeping Bag

A sleeping bag can be a hassle to carry, but can serve as something to sleep in (and avoid unsavoury looking hotel bedding), a cushion on hard train seats, a seat for long waits on railway platforms or a bed top-cover (since cheaper hotels rarely give you one).

If you're trekking in the north then a sleeping bag will be an absolute necessity. Unlike in Nepal, it is not easy to hire trekking gear in India. A sheet sleeping bag, like those required by youth hostels in the West, can be very useful, particularly on overnight train trips or if you don't trust the hotel's sheets. Mosquito nets are also rare, so your own sheet or sheet sleeping bag will also help to keep mosquitoes at bay.

Some travellers find that a plastic sheet is useful for a number of reasons, including to bedbug-proof unhealthy looking beds. Others have recommended an inflatable pillow as a useful accessory. These are widely available for Rs 30.

Toilet Paper

Indian sewerage systems are generally overloaded enough without having to cope with toilet paper as well. However, if you can't adapt to the Indian method of a jug of water and your left hand, toilet paper is widely available throughout the country in all but the smallest towns. A receptacle is sometimes provided in toilets for used toilet paper.

Toiletries

Soap, toothpaste and other toiletries are readily available. A sink plug is worth having since few cheaper hotels have plugs. A nailbrush can be very useful. For women, tampons are available in most major places; sanitary pads are more widely available, however.

Men can safely leave their shaving gear at home. One of the pleasures of Indian travel is a shave in a barber shop every few days. With AIDS becoming more widespread in India, however, choose a barber's shop that looks clean, avoid roadside barbers, and make sure that a fresh blade is used. For just a few rupees you'll get the full treatment – lathering, followed by a shave, then the process is repeated, and finally there's the hot, damp towel and sometimes talcum powder. If you're not quick you'll find that before you know it you're also in for a scalp massage.

How to Carry It

Where to put all this gear? Well, for budget travellers the backpack is still the best carrying container. Many packs these days are lockable, otherwise you can make it a bit more thief-proof by sewing on tabs so you can padlock it shut. It's worth paying the money for a strong, good quality pack as it's much more likely to withstand the rigours of Indian travel.

An alternative is a large, soft, zip bag with a wide shoulder strap. This is obviously not an option if you plan to do any trekking. Suitcases are only for jet-setters!

Lots of plastic bags will keep your gear in some sort of order and will also be invaluable for keeping things dry should your pack get rained on.

Miscellaneous Items

It's amazing how many things you wish you had with you when you're in India. One of the most useful for budget travellers is a padlock. In fact a padlock is a virtual necessity. Most cheap hotels and quite a number of mid-range places have doors locked by a latch and padlock. You'll find having your own sturdy lock on the door instead of the flimsy thing the hotel supplies does wonders for your peace of mind. Other uses are legion. Many trains have loops under the berths which you can padlock luggage to, for example. It may not make it thief-proof, but it helps. You can buy a reasonable lock in India for Rs 25 to Rs 50.

A universal sink plug is also useful as sinks never have them. Ever tried to wash your underwear in a sink without a plug? A knife (preferably Swiss Army) finds a whole field of uses, in particular for peeling fruit. Some travellers rhapsodise about the usefulness of a miniature electric element to boil water in a cup. A sarong is a handy item. It can be used as a bed sheet, an item of clothing, an emergency towel, something to lie on at the beach, and a pillow on trains!

Insect repellent can also be extremely useful. Electric mosquito zappers are widely available. Power cuts are common in India ('load shedding' as it is euphemistically known) and there's little street lighting at night so a torch (flashlight) and candles can be useful. A mosquito net can be very useful, depending on where you're going and the season. A small rubber wedge door-stop was one suggestion; it helps keep doors both open and closed. Bring along your spectacle prescription if you're short-sighted. Should you lose or damage your glasses a new pair can be made very cheaply, competently (in the big cites, at least) and quickly. Earplugs are useful for light sleepers, and even heavier sleepers can have difficulty shutting out the din in some hotels.

Hot-weather survival requires another book of rules in India. First of all a sun hat is essential. Stepping out into the sun in the hot season is like using your head as a blacksmith's anvil. You don't just feel the sun, it reaches out and hits you. Secondly, a water bottle should always be by your side; and thirdly, if you're not drinking bottled water, have water purification tablets. You'll also need something with long sleeves, particularly if you're going to ride a bicycle very far. High-factor sun block cream is becoming more widely available, especially at beach resorts, but it's *expensive*!

TOURIST OFFICES
Local Tourist Offices
Within India the tourist office story is somewhat blurred by the overlap between the national and state tourist offices. As well as the national tourist office, each state maintains its own tourist office and this can lead to some confusion. In some cities the national office is much larger than the state one, or the state one is virtually nonexistent. Government of India offices include:

Agra
    191 The Mall (☎ (0562) 36-3377)
Aurangabad
    Krishna Vilas, Station Rd (☎ (02432) 31-217)
Bangalore
    Kentucky Fried Chicken Bldg, 48 Church St (☎ (080) 558-9517)
Bhubaneswar
    B21, B J B Nagar (☎ (0674) 41-2203)
Bombay
    123 Maharishi Karve Rd, Churchgate (☎ (022) 203-2932)
Calcutta
    Sandozi Bldg, 26 Himayat Nagar, Hyderabad (☎ (0842) 63-0037)
Delhi
    88 Janpath (☎ (011) 332-0005)
Jaipur
    Rajasthan State Hotel (☎ (0141) 37-2200)
Khajuraho
    Near Western Group Temples (☎ (076861) 2047)
Kochi (Cochin)
    Willingdon Island (☎ (0484) 66-8352)
Madras
    154 Anna Salai (☎ (044) 852-4295)
Panaji (Goa)
    Communidade Bldg, Church Square (☎ (0832) 43-412)
Patna
    Tourist Bhavan, Beer Chand Patel Path (☎ (0612) 22-6721)
Shillong
    Tirot Singh Syiem Rd, Police Bazaar (☎ (0364) 25-632)
Varanasi
    15B The Mall (☎ (0542) 43-744)

The state tourist offices vary widely in their efficiency and usefulness. Some of them are very good, some completely hopeless. In many states the tourism ministry also runs a chain of tourist bungalows which generally offer good accommodation at very reasonable prices. State tourist offices will usually be in the tourist bungalows (where there is one).

The confusion and overlap between the national and state tourist offices often causes wasteful duplication. Both offices produce a brochure on place A, neither produces anything on place B. More confusion arises with the division between the Government of India tourist office and the Indian Tourism Development Corporation (ITDC). The latter is more an actual 'doing' organisation than a 'telling' one. The ITDC will actually operate the tour bus on the tour for which the tourist office sells tickets. The ITDC also runs a series of hotels and travellers' lodges around the country under the Ashok name. States may also have a tourist transport operation equivalent to the national ITDC, so in some cities you can have a national and a state tourist operator as well as a national and a state tourist office!

Foreign Reps

The Government of India Department of Tourism maintains a string of tourist offices in other countries where you can get brochures, leaflets and some information about India. The tourist office leaflets and brochures are often very high in their informational quality and worth getting hold of. On the other hand, some of the foreign offices are not always as useful for obtaining information as those within the country. There are also smaller 'promotion offices' in Osaka (Japan) and in Dallas, Miami, San Francisco and Washington DC (USA).

Australia
   Level 1, 17 Castlereagh St, Sydney NSW 2000 (☎ (02) 9232-1600; fax 9223-3003)
Canada
   60 Bloor St West, Suite No 1003, Toronto, Ontario M4W 3B8 (☎ (416) 962-3787; fax 962-6279)
France
   8 Blvd de la Madeleine, 75009 Paris (☎ (01) 4265-8386; fax 4265-0116)
Germany
   Kaiserstrasse 77-III, D-6000 Frankfurt-am-Main-1 (☎ (069) 23-5423; fax 23-4724)

Italy
   Via Albricci 9, 20122 Milan (☎ (02) 80-4952; fax 7202-1681)
Japan
   Pearl Bldg, 9-18 Ginza, 7-Chome, Chuo ku, Tokyo 104 (☎ (03) 571-5062; fax 571-5235)
Malaysia
   Wisma HLA, Lot 203 Jalan Raja Chulan, 50200 Kuala Lumpur (☎ (03) 242-5285; fax 242-5301)
Netherlands
   Rokin 9-15, 1012 KK Amsterdam (☎ (020) 620-8991; fax 38-3059)
Singapore
   United House, 20 Kramat Lane, Singapore 0922 (☎ 235-3800; fax 235-8677)
Sweden
   Sveavagen 9-11, S-III 57, Stockholm 11157 (☎ (08) 21-5081; fax 21-0186)
Switzerland
   1-3 Rue de Chantepoulet, 1201 Geneva (☎ (022) 732-1813; fax 731-5660)
Thailand
   Kentucky Fried Chicken Bldg, 3rd floor, 62/5 Thaniya Rd, Bangkok 10500 (☎ (02) 235-2585)
UK
   7 Cork St, London W1X 2AB (☎ (0171) 437-3677; fax 494-1048)
USA
   30 Rockefeller Plaza, 15 North Mezzanine, New York NY 10112 (☎ (212) 586-4901; fax 582-3274)
   3550 Wilshire Blvd, Suite 204, Los Angeles CA 90010 (☎ (213) 380-8855; fax 380-6111)

BUSINESS HOURS

Indian shops, offices and post offices are not early starters. Generally shops are open Monday to Saturday from 10 am to 5 pm. Some government offices open on alternate Saturdays and some commercial offices are open on Saturday morning. Post offices are open weekdays from 10 am to 5 pm, and on Saturday morning. Main city offices may be open longer hours, such as 8 am to 6 pm in Delhi.

Banks are open for business on weekdays between 10 am and 2 pm. Shops and offices are usually closed on Sunday.

POST & TELECOMMUNICATIONS
Post

The Indian postal and poste restante services are generally excellent. Expected letters almost always are there and letters you send almost invariably reach their destination, although they take up to three weeks. American Express, in its major city locations, offers an alternative to the poste restante system.

Have letters addressed to you with your surname in capitals and, underlined, the poste restante, GPO, and the city in question. Many 'lost' letters are simply misfiled under given (Christian) names, so always check under both your names.

Holidays

Due to its religious and regional variations, India has a great number of holidays and festivals. Most of them follow the Indian lunar calendar and therefore change from year to year according to the Gregorian calendar, particularly the Muslim holidays and festivals, which are listed at the end of this section.

In the following lists, only national public holidays are given; there are many other local and regional events when holidays are only observed in a particular state. Only the religious festivals which have a designated public holiday are listed here, but these and all other religious festivals are described in more detail in the Sacred India colour section on page 57.

January

Republic Day Republic Day on 26 January celebrates the anniversary of India's establishment as a republic in 1950; there are activities in all the state capitals but most spectacularly in Delhi, where there is an enormously colourful military parade. As part of the Republic Day celebrations, three days later a *Beating of the Retreat* ceremony takes place outside Rashtrapati Bhavan, the residence of the Indian president, in Delhi.

February-March

Holi Hindu festival, when people mark the end of winter by throwing coloured water and powder at one another. In Maharashtra this festival is known as Rangapanchami and is celebrated with dancing and singing.

March-April

Mahavir Jayanti Jain festival marking the birth of Mahavira, the founder of Jainism.
Ramanavami The birth of Rama, an incarnation of Vishnu, is celebrated.
Good Friday This Christian holiday is also celebrated in India.

May-June

Buddha Jayanti The Buddha's birth, enlightenment and attainment of nirvana are all celebrated on this day.

August

Independence Day This holiday on 15 August celebrates the anniversary of India's independence from the UK in 1947. The prime minister delivers an address from the ramparts of Delhi's Red Fort.

August-September

Janmashtami The anniversary of Krishna's birth.

September-October

Dussehra This ten-day festival beginning on the first day of the Hindu month of Asvina celebrates Durga's victory over the buffalo-headed demon Mahishasura.
Gandhi Jayanti This is a solemn celebration of Gandhi's birthday on 2 October with prayer meetings at the Raj Ghat in Delhi where he was cremated.

October-November

Diwali (or *Deepavali*) Hindu festival celebrated on the 15th day of Kartika.
Govardhana Puja Hindu festival dedicated to that holiest of animals, the cow.

November-December

Nanak Jayanti The birthday of Guru Nanak, the founder of the Sikh religion.
Christmas Day Also a holiday in India.

Muslim Holidays

The dates of the Muslim festivals are not fixed, as they fall about 11 days earlier each year.

Id-ul-Fitr This festival celebrates the end of Ramadan, the Muslim month of fasting. Falls on 8 February 1997 and 29 January 1998.
Id-ul-Zuhara This festival commemorates Abraham's attempt to sacrifice his son. Falls on 20 April 1996, 9 April 1997 and 30 March 1998.
Muharram A 10-day festival commemorating the martyrdom of Mohammed's grandson, Imam Hussain. Falls on 19 May 1996, 9 May 1997 and 29 April 1998.
Milad-un-Nabi A festival celebrating the birth of Mohammed. Falls on 29 July 1996, 18 July 1997 and 7 July 1998.

You can often buy stamps at good hotels, saving a lot of queuing in crowded post offices.

Postal Rates Aerogrammes and postcards cost Rs 6.50, airmail letters Rs 12.

Posting Parcels Most people discover how to do this the hard way, in which case it'll take half a day. Go about it this way, which can still take up to an hour:

- Take the parcel to a tailor and tell him you'd like it stitched up in cheap linen. At some larger post offices this stitching service is offered either outside or inside the office. Negotiate the price first.
- Go to the post office with your parcel and ask for the necessary customs declaration forms. Fill them in and glue one to the parcel. The other will be stitched onto it. To avoid excise duty at the delivery end it's best to specify that the contents are a 'gift'. Be careful with how much you declare the contents to be worth. If you specify over Rs 1000, your parcel will not be accepted without a bank clearance certificate. You can imagine the hassles involved in getting one of these so always state the value as less than Rs 1000.
- Have the parcel weighed and franked at the parcel counter.

If you are just sending books or printed matter, these can go by bookpost, which is considerably cheaper than parcel post, but the package must be wrapped a certain way: make sure that the package can either be opened for inspection along the way, or else is just wrapped in brown paper or cardboard and tied with string, with the two ends exposed so that the contents are visible. No customs declaration form is necessary for such parcels.

Be cautious with places which offer to mail things to your home address after you have bought them. Government emporiums are usually OK, but although most people who buy things from other places get them eventually, some items never turn up (were they ever sent?) or what turns up isn't what they bought.

Sending parcels in the other direction (to you in India) is an extremely hit-and-miss affair. Don't count on anything bigger than a letter getting to you. And don't count on a letter getting to you if there's anything worthwhile inside it.

Telephone & Fax

The telephone system in India is generally very good. Most places are hooked up to the STD (long-distance)/ISD network, and so making local, interstate and international calls is simplicity itself from even the smallest town.

Everywhere you'll come across private 'STD/ISD' call booths with direct local, interstate and international dialling. These phones are usually found in shops or other businesses, but are well signposted with large 'STD/ISD' signs advertising the service. A digital meter lets you keep an eye on what the call is costing, and gives you a printout at the end. You then just pay the shopowner – quick, painless and a far cry from the not so distant past when a night spent at a telegraph office waiting for a line was not unusual. Direct international calls from these phones cost around Rs 70 per minute, depending on the country you are calling. The international access code from India is 00, so to ring Australia, for example, you dial 0061, followed by the Australian STD code and phone number.

Also available is the Home Country Direct service, which gives you access to the international operator in your home country. You can then make reverse charge (collect) or credit card calls, although this is not always easy, and beware in hotels of exorbitant con-

Indian Lunar Months & their Gregorian Equivalents	
Chaitra	March-April
Vaishaka	April-May
Jyaistha	May-June
Asadha	June-July
Sravana	July-August
Bhadra	August-September
Asvina	September-October
Kartika	October-November
Aghan	November-December
Pausa	December-January
Magha	January-February
Phalguna	February-March

nection charges on these sort of calls. You may also have trouble convincing the owner of the telephone you are using that they are not going to get charged for the call. The countries and numbers to dial are:

Country	Number
Australia	0006117
Canada	000167
Germany	0004917
Italy	0003917
Japan	0008117
Netherlands	0003117
New Zealand	0006417
Singapore	0006517
Spain	0003417
Taiwan	00088617
Thailand	0006617
UK	0004417
USA	000117

Many of the STD/ISD booths also have a fax machine for public use.

The Indian government has set up modern, 24-hour communications centres in the four main cities, and these can be handy. The government company which runs these centres is VSNL (Videsh Sanchar Nigam Ltd), and the addresses are:

Bombay
   Videsh Sanchar Bhavan, Mahatma Gandhi Rd, Bombay 400 001 (☎ (022) 262-4001; fax 262-4027)
Calcutta
   Poddar Court, 18 Ravindra Sarani, Calcutta 700 001 (☎ (033) 30-3266; fax 30-3218)

Delhi
   Videsh Sanchar Bhavan, Bangla Sahib Rd, Delhi 110001 (☎ (011) 374-6769; fax 374-6769)
Madras
   Videsh Sanchar Bhavan, 5 Swami Sivananda Salai, Madras 600 002 (☎ (044) 56-1994; fax 58-3838)

There are also similar government exchanges in some other state capitals but they are generally only open daily between 8 am and 8 pm (not 24 hours).fax services, see telephone & fax services

TIME
India is 5½ hours ahead of GMT/UTC, 4½ hours behind Australian Eastern Standard Time and 10½ hours ahead of American Eastern Standard Time. It is officially known as IST – Indian Standard Time, although many Indians prefer to think it stands for Indian Stretchable Time!

ELECTRICITY
The electric current is 230-240 V AC, 50 cycles. Electricity is widely available in India but breakdowns and blackouts ('load shedding') are endemic. Sockets are of a three round-pin variety, similar (but not identical) to European sockets. European round-pin plugs will go into the sockets, but as the pins on Indian plugs are somewhat thicker, the fit is loose and connection is not always guaranteed.

You can buy small immersion elements, perfect for boiling water for tea or coffee, for Rs 30. For about Rs 70 you can buy electric

---

Indian Standard Time

It is surprising in a country as vast as India that there is only one time zone. This is a leftover from the days of the British Raj. For the sake of simplicity, the British decided to have just the one time zone throughout the whole country.

The base point used was Allahabad in Uttar Pradesh. This is fine in most places, but it's a daylight nightmare if you live in the far east of the country. In summer in Assam or the Andaman Islands, for instance, sunrise is around 4 am, and it's dark by around 5 pm! This means that the average office worker who might start work at 10 am has already been up for half the day before they even get to work, and is ready for an afternoon nap!

The issue of splitting the country into two or more time zones has been raised in parliament recently, but it seems to have gone into the 'too hard' basket for the moment. This may not be such a bad thing – the scope for chaos is great enough as it is! ■

mosquito zappers. These are the type that take chemical tablets which melt and give off deadly vapours (deadly for the mosquito, that is). There are many different brands and they are widely available – they come with quaint names such as Good Knight.

BOOKS & MAPS

India is a great place for reading – there's plenty to read about, there's plenty of time to read on those never-ending bus or train trips, and when you get to the big cities you'll find plenty of bookshops where you can purchase the reading matter.

India is one of the world's largest publishers of books in English. After the USA and the UK, it's up there with Canada or Australia as a major English-language publisher. You'll find a great number of interesting books on India by Indian publishers, which are generally not available in the West.

Indian publishers also do cheap reprints of Western bestsellers at prices far below Western levels. A meaty Leon Uris or Arthur Hailey novel, ideal for an interminable train ride, will often cost less than US$3. Compare that with your local bookshop prices. The favourite Western author is probably P G Wodehouse – 'Jeeves must be considered another incarnation of Vishnu', was one explanation.

Recently published British and American books also reach Indian bookshops remarkably fast and with very low mark-ups. If a bestseller in Europe or America has major appeal for India they'll often rush out a paperback in India to forestall possible pirates. The novel *City of Joy* (a European bestseller about Calcutta) was out in paperback in India before the hardback had even reached Australia.

The suggested books that follow are only a few interesting ones that should be readily available. Of course there are many more now long out of print which you may still find in some shops. There are also many beautiful coffee-table books on India – ideal for whetting the appetite or for conjuring up the magic of India after your return. India has spawned an equally large number of cookery books – if you want to get into curry and all

those spices you'll have no trouble finding plenty of instructions. Indian art has also generated a great number of interesting books of all types. So, too, have politics, economics and environmental issues.

Novels

Plenty of authors have taken the opportunity of setting their novels in a country as colourful as India. Rudyard Kipling, with books like *Kim* and *Plain Tales from the Hills*, is the Victorian English interpreter of India *par excellence*. In *A Passage to India*, E M Forster perfectly captures that collision of incomprehension between the English and the Indians. A very readable book.

Much more recent but again following that curious question of why the English and Indians, so dissimilar in many ways, were so similar in others, is Ruth Prawer Jhabvala's *Heat & Dust*. The contemporary narrator of the tale also describes the backpacker's India in a flawless fashion. Other books by this author are equally impressive.

Probably the most widely acclaimed Indian novel in recent times was Salman Rushdie's *Midnight's Children*, which won the Booker Prize. It tells of the children who were born, like modern India itself, at the stroke of midnight on that August night in 1947 and how the life of one particular 'midnight's child' is inextricably intertwined with events in India itself. Rushdie's follow-up, *Shame*, was set in modern Pakistan. His sardonic treatment of the post-Independence rulers of India and Pakistan in these two novels upset quite a few over-inflated egos. His novel *The Satanic Verses* inflamed Muslim passions to the limit and resulted in Iran's now-deceased Ayatollah Khomeini pronouncing a death sentence on him. The book is banned in India.

Vikram Seth's epic novel about post-Independence India, *A Suitable Boy*, is set to become a classic. It is set in the newly independent India of the 1950s, and centres around a Hindu mother's search for a suitable husband for her daughter. It ranges far and wide and touches on most aspects of Indian culture, as well as important historical issues of the time, such as the abolition of the zamindar system, the fall-out from Partition, Hindu-Muslim conflict and general elections. It is well worth the effort – although at 1300-odd pages it is a bit of a monster to carry!

Paul Scott's *The Raj Quartet* and *Staying On* are other important novels set in India. The big 'bestseller' Indian novel of recent years was the monster tome *Far Pavilions* by M M Kaye. Women's magazine romance in some ways, but it has some interesting angles on India.

Nectar in a Sieve by Kamala Markandaya is an interesting account of a woman's life in rural India. See the Calcutta chapter for more on *City of Joy*, the 1986 bestseller in Europe and India which has been made into a popular film.

Kushwant Singh is one of India's most published contemporary authors and journalists, although he seems to have as many detractors as fans. One of his more recent offerings is simply titled *Delhi* (Penguin India, 1990). This novel spans a 600-year time frame and brings to life various periods in Delhi's history through the eyes of poets, princes and emperors. It is ingeniously spiced with short dividing chapters describing the author's peripatetic affair with a *hijda* (hermaphrodite) whore and his own age-induced and overindulgent activities which play havoc with his libido. As the author states: 'History provided me with the skeleton. I covered it with flesh and injected blood and a lot of seminal fluid into it'. A lively and essential read!

Kushwant Singh has also written the harrowing *Train to Pakistan* on the holocaust of Partition, the humorous *India – An Introduction*, and a collection of short stories, published in hardback, some of which are superb.

Also extremely well known and highly regarded are the books of R K Narayan. Many were set in the fictional town of Malgudi, and offer unique glimpses and insights into Indian village life. They're excellent reading. His most well-known works include: *Swami & His Friends, The Financial Expert, The Guide, Waiting for the Mahatma* and *Malgudi Days*.

If you prefer pulp in the form of Dallas-type financial double-dealing, adultery and sex in the boardroom amongst the Bombay stock market elite, try Shobha De's series of upmarket Mills & Boon novels. One of the most recent was *Sisters*.

General Interest

John Keay's *Into India* (John Murray, London, 1973) is a fine general introduction to travelling in India. One traveller's observations and perceptions of life in India today provide an illuminating idea of what it's really like.

Paul Theroux's best-selling railway odyssey *The Great Railway Bazaar* takes you up and down India by train (and across most of the rest of Asia) and turns the whole world into a railway carriage. Engrossing, like most such books, as much for its insights into the author as for those into the people he meets. *Slow Boats to China* by Gavin Young follows much the same path but this time by boat. *Slowly Down the Ganges* by Eric Newby is another boat-trip tale; this one borders, at times, on sheer masochism!

Karma Kola by Gita Mehta is accurately subtitled 'the marketing of the mystic east'. It amusingly and cynically describes the unavoidable and hilarious collision between India looking to the West for technology and modern methods, and the West descending upon India in search of wisdom and enlightenment.

India File by Trevor Fishlock (Indian paperback by Rupa, Delhi, 1984) is a very readable collection of articles on India by the *Times* correspondent. The chapter on sex in India is often hilarious. An updated second edition is available.

Delhi is also the subject of William Dalrymple's very readable *City of Djinns* (Flamingo, 1994). Subtitled A Year in Delhi, it delves into this city's fascinating – and in many respects largely overlooked – history. Dalrymple turns up a few surprises in his wanderings around Delhi, and the book is written in a light style which makes it accessible to even hardened non-history readers.

Ved Mehta has written a number of interesting personal views of India. *Walking the*

Indian Streets (Penguin paperback) is a slim and highly readable account of the culture shock he went through on returning to India after a long period abroad. *Portrait of India* is by the same author.

Ronald Segal's *The Crisis of India* (Penguin, London, 1965) is written by a South African Indian on the theme that spirituality is not always more important than a full stomach. *The Gunny Sack* by M G Vassanji explores a similar theme, this time from the point of view of a group of Gujarati families who migrated to East Africa in Raj times but retain their connections with India. It's a good read and has been dubbed 'Africa's answer to Midnight's Children' by certain literary critics.

Third Class Ticket by Hilary Ward is an interesting account of the culture shock experienced by a group of Bengali villagers as they explore the country for the first time. *Unveiling India* (Penguin) by Anees Jung is a contemporary documentary on women in India. *An Indian Attachment* by Sarah Lloyd is an interesting and surprisingly unsentimental account of an Englishwoman's life in small villages in Punjab and Uttar Pradesh.

For an assessment of the position of women in Indian society, it is well worth getting hold of *May You Be The Mother of One Hundred Sons* (Penguin, 1991) by Elisabeth Bumiller. The author spent 3½ years in India in the late 1980s and interviewed Indian women from all walks of life. Her book offers some excellent insights into the plight of women in general and rural women in particular, especially with regard to arranged marriages, dowry deaths, *sati* and female infanticide.

Chasing the Monsoon by Alexander Frater (Penguin India, 1990) is an Englishman's account of, as the title suggests, a journey north from Kovalam in Kerala all the way to one of the wettest places on earth (Cherrapunji in Meghalaya), all the while following the onset of the monsoon as it moves north across the country. It's a fascinating insight into the significance of the monsoon, and its effect on people.

Goddess in the Stones by Norman Lewis

is an interesting account of the author's travels through Bihar and the tribal villages of Orissa.

Finally, no survey of personal insights into India can ignore V S Naipaul's two controversial books *An Area of Darkness* and *India – A Wounded Civilisation*. Born in Trinidad but of Indian descent, Naipaul tells in the first book of how India, unseen and unvisited, haunted him and of the impact upon him when he eventually made the pilgrimage to the motherland. You may well find that much of this book rings very true with your own experiences while in India. In the second book he writes of India's unsuccessful search for a new purpose and meaning for its civilisation. His most recent book, *A Million Mutinies Now*, is also excellent.

History

If you want a thorough introduction to Indian history then look for the Pelican two-volume *A History of India*. In volume one Romila Thapar follows Indian history from 1000 BC to the coming of the Mughals in the 16th century. Volume two by Percival Spear follows the rise and fall of the Mughals through to India since Independence. At times both volumes are a little dry, but if you want a reasonably detailed history in a handy paperback format they're worth having. More cumbersome, but offering more detail, is the 900-page paperback *Oxford History of India* by Vincent Smith (OUP, Rs 140).

The Wonder that was India by A L Basham gives detailed descriptions of the Indian civilisations, origins of the caste system and social customs, and detailed information on Hinduism, Buddhism and other religions in India. It is also very informative about art and architecture. It has a wealth of background material on ancient India without being overly academic.

Christopher Hibbert's *The Great Mutiny – India 1857* (Penguin, London, 1980) is a single-volume description of the often lurid events of the Mutiny. This readable paperback is illustrated with contemporary photographs.

Plain Tales from the Raj, edited by Charles

Allen (Futura paperback, London, 1976), is the delightful book derived from the equally delightful series of radio programmes of the same name. It consists of a series of interviews with people who took part in British India on both sides of the table. Extremely readable and full of fascinating little insights into life during the Raj era.

British historian Bamber Gascoigne's *The Mughals* is an excellent combination of informed and interesting historical text and glossy pictures. It's well worth the Rs 500 price tag.

The Nehrus & the Gandhis (Picador, 1988) by Tariq Ali is a very readable account of the history of these families and hence of India this century.

Freedom at Midnight is one of India's best-selling books. Authors Larry Collins and Dominique Lapierre have written other equally popular modern histories, but you could hardly ask for a more enthralling series of events than those that led to India's independence in 1947. In India you can find *Freedom at Midnight* in a cheap Bell Books paperback (Vikas Publishing, Delhi, 1976).

Highness – the Maharajas of India by Ann Morrow (Grafton Books, 1986) provides an illuminating, if at times sycophantic, insight into the rarefied and extravagant lives of these Indian rulers during the days of the Raj and since Independence.

For a good insight into the country since Independence there is *From Raj to Rajiv – 40 Years of Indian Independence* (BBC Books UK, Universal Book Stall, Delhi, 1988). It is written by old India hand and former BBC correspondent Mark Tully, and Zareer Masani.

Two current-affairs books which are well worth reading are *Bhopal – the Lessons of a Tragedy* by Sanjoy Hazarika and *Riot after Riot – Reports on Caste & Communal Violence in India* by M J Akbar. Both are published by Penguin.

Finally, for those interested in the continuing and often shocking and sad story of India's treatment of its tribals, there is the scholarly *Tribes of India – the Struggle for Survival* by Christoph von Fürer-Haimendorf (Oxford University Press, 1982).

Autobiography of an Unknown Indian and *Thy Hand, Great Anarch!: India 1921-1952* are two autobiographical books by one of India's most prominent contemporary writers, Nirad Choudhuri. They are an excellent account of the history and culture of modern India.

Religion

If you want a better understanding of India's religions there are plenty of books available in India. The English series of Penguin paperbacks are amongst the best and are generally available in India. In particular, *Hinduism* by K M Sen (Penguin, London, 1961) is brief and to the point. If you want to read the Hindu holy books these are available in translations: *The Upanishads* (Penguin, London, 1965) and *The Bhagavad Gita* (Penguin, London, 1962). *Hindu Mythology*, edited by Wendy O'Flaherty (Penguin, London), is an interesting annotated collection of extracts from the Hindu holy books. Convenient if you don't want the whole thing.

A Classical Dictionary of Hindu Mythology & Religion by John Dowson (Rupa, Delhi, 1987) is an Indian paperback reprint of an old English hardback. As the name suggests, it is in dictionary form and is one of the best sources for unravelling who's who in Hinduism. There's also *Indian Mythology* by Jan Knappert (Harper Collins, Delhi, 1992), a paperback encyclopedia.

Penguin also has a translation of the Koran. To gain some insight into Buddhism, Guy Claxton's *The Heart of Buddhism* (Aquarian Press, London, 1992) is a good place to begin. *A Handbook of Living Religions* edited by John R Hinnewls (Pelican, London, 1985) provides a succinct and readable summary of all the various religions you will find in India, including Christianity and Judaism.

An excellent, detailed and dispassionate introduction to 16 of India's best known gurus and religious teachers is the recently published *Guru – the Search for Enlightenment* by John Mitchiner (Viking, 1991, Rs

150, available in India). It's essential reading for anyone interested in the relevance and contribution of Indian gurus to contemporary thought and experience.

Travel Guides

First published in 1859, the 22nd edition of *A Handbook for Travellers in India, Pakistan, Nepal, Bangladesh & Sri Lanka* (John Murray, London, 1975) is that rarest of animals, a Victorian travel guide. If you've got a deep interest in Indian architecture and can afford the somewhat hefty price, then take along a copy of this immensely detailed guidebook. Unfortunately its system of following 'routes', in the manner of all good Victorian guidebooks, makes it somewhat difficult to locate things, but the effort is worth it. Along the way you'll find a lot of places where the British army made gallant stands, and more than a few statues of Queen Victoria – most of which have been replaced by statues of Mahatma Gandhi.

For relatively cheap but excellently produced photo-essays of the subcontinent, try Insight Guides' *Rajasthan* and *India* by APA Productions. They're both done by a team of experienced writers, many of them Indian, and while the text and photographs are generally excellent, the 'Guide in Brief' section at the back is of extremely limited use. The Nelles Guides' *Northern India* and *Southern India* (Nelles Verlag, 1990) are similar general guides with good photographs and text but skimpy hard information.

There are a great number of regional and local guidebooks published in India. Many of them are excellent value and describe certain sites (the Ajanta and Ellora Caves or Sanchi for example) in much greater detail than is possible in this book. The guides produced by the Archaeological Survey of India are particularly good. Many of the other guides have a most amusing way with English. Another good guide, this time on the painted *havelis* (merchant's mansions) of a small region in Rajasthan, is *The Guide to Painted Towns of Shekhawati* by Ilay Cooper which comes complete with street maps. It's available in the bookshops of Jaipur.

Books on wildlife are difficult to get, but birdwatchers may find the *Collins Handguide to the Birds of the Indian Subcontinent* useful. It doesn't cover all the birds by any means but it does have the best illustrations and text, and if you're not a very serious birdwatcher you will probably find it useful. Visitors to Kashmir and Sikkim can use *Birds of Nepal*, which includes notes on these two regions. The Insight *Indian Wildlife* guide (APA, 1988) is available from major bookshops in India and is valuable if you're keenly interested in visiting national parks.

Railway buffs should enjoy *India by Rail* by Royston Ellis.

Other Lonely Planet Guides

It's pleasing to be able to claim that for more information on India's neighbours and for travel beyond India, most of the best guides come from Lonely Planet! If you're heading north to Nepal then look for *Nepal* for complete information on this Himalayan nation. If you're planning on trekking in Nepal or simply want more information on trekking in general, look for *Trekking in the Nepal Himalaya* and *Trekking in the Indian Himalaya*. Or you can cross right over the Himalaya with our *Tibet* and *Karakoram Highway*.

There are Lonely Planet guides for other Indian neighbours. *Pakistan* is our guide to the 'unknown land of the Indus'. We also have a guide to India's other Muslim neighbour: *Bangladesh*. *Myanmar* covers that unpredictable country. If you're travelling to Sri Lanka then you need *Sri Lanka*, or for a visit to the Maldives and other islands there is also Lonely Planet's *Maldives & Islands of the East Indian Ocean*. If it's further east you want then look for *South-East Asia*.

Finally, we have a city guide for *Delhi* and if you want more information on the north and east of India then look for our guide to the *Indian Himalaya*.

Also Recommended

Readers have recommended numerous other

Indian Maps

Getting maps of India 'right' is a real headache. In early 1995 imported atlases and copies of Encyclopaedia Britannica were banned in India because the Indian government didn't like the way they portrayed the country's borders. We have had the same problem with this book. The main problem is Kashmir where Pakistan claims they own the lot, India claims it owns the lot and the reality is there's a 'line of control' through the middle with Indian troops on one side and Pakistani troops on the other. Showing the actual line of control is not good enough, the whole lot has to be shown as part of India and even then a disclaimer has to added to the map, presumably in case the government decides their border extends even further.

We used to put 'Government of India Statement – The external boundaries of India are neither correct nor authenticated' but midway through the life of the last edition the government decided that this wasn't good enough. By saying it was a government statement perhaps it could be interpreted that only the government believed it! So we had to reprint books for the Indian market with a new disclaimer. The absurdity of these rules are indicated by history books with disclaimers about the borders of India tagged on to maps of India under the Emperor Ashoka two millenniums ago! Turn on the BBC satellite TV news and you'll see maps the government can't put statements on; it's said the politicians just have to close their eyes or switch off the TV. ■

books such as *Eating the Indian Air* by John Morris; *The Gorgeous East* by Rupert Croft-Cooke; *Delhi is Far Away* and *The Grand Trunk Road* by John Wiles; and books by Jan and Rumer Godden. *A Princess Remembers* by Gayatri Devi is useful if you're going to Jaipur. Irish wanderer Dervla Murphy heads south in her book *On a Shoestring to Coorg*.

There are some wonderful Indian comic books dealing with Hindu mythology and Indian history. *An Indian Summer* by James Cameron (Penguin) is an autobiographical account of independence and south India.

Phrasebooks

Lonely Planet has the sub-continent well covered, with phrasebooks for Hindi/Urdu, Bengali and Sinhalese.

There are many phrasebooks and teach-yourself books available in India if you want to learn more of a language.

Maps

Lonely Planet's *India Travel Atlas* breaks the country down into over 100 pages of maps, and so gives unequalled coverage. It is fully indexed and the book format means it is easy to refer to, especially on buses and trains. It gives you plenty of detail on small towns and villages to help speed along those long bus or train trips.

The Lascelles 1:4,000,000 map of *India, Pakistan, Nepal, Bangladesh & Sri Lanka* is probably the most useful general map of

India. Its biggest failing is that it does not always include places of great interest but small population – Khajuraho, for instance. The Bartholomews map is similar, and is widely available in India as well as overseas.

The Nelles Verlag series gives more detailed coverage, but you need to carry five maps to cover the whole country. They are excellent maps, but they're not widely available in India.

Locally, the Government Map Office produces a series of maps covering all of India. In Delhi their shambolic office is opposite the tourist office on Janpath. The maps are not all that useful since the government will not allow production of anything at a reasonable scale which shows India's sea or land borders, and many of them date back to the 1970s. They do, however, have some good city maps. It is illegal to take any Survey of India map of larger than 1:250,000 scale out of the country.

The Government of India tourist office has a number of excellent giveaway city maps and also a reasonable all-India map. State tourist offices do not have much in the way of maps, but the Himachal Pradesh office has three excellent trekking maps which cover the trekking routes in that state.

FILM
Indian Films

The Indian film industry is the largest in the world in purely volume terms – in 1992, a massive 836 films were registered for classification with the censorship board! There are more than 12,000 cinemas across the country, and at least five times as many 'video halls'. The vast proportion of what is produced are your average Bollywood 'masala movies' – cheap melodramas based on three vital ingredients: romance, violence and music. Most are dreadful, but it's cheap escapism for the masses, a chance to dream.

However, for all the dross churned out, India has produced some wonderful films from brilliant directors, foremost among them being Satyajit Ray. Ray first came onto the scene in the 1950s when his film *Pather Panchali* gained international recognition. For the next 40 years Ray turned out consistently excellent work, and in 1992, shortly before he died, he was awarded an Oscar, which was presented to him at his bedside in Calcutta where he was seriously ill. His best films include *Pather Panchali, Apur Sansar, Ashani Sanket* and *Jana Aranya*.

Shot on the streets of Bombay is the excellent film *Salaam Bombay* by Meera Nair. It concentrates on the plight of the street children in Bombay, and won the Golden Camera Prize at Cannes in 1989.

Other notable Indian directors include Mrinal Sen, Ritwik Ghatak, Shaji N Karuns, Adoor and Aravindan.

Foreign Films

A number of foreign films have been made about India over the years. Keep your eyes open for a showing of Louis Malle's two-part film *Phantom India*. Running to about seven hours in all, this is a fascinating in-depth look at contemporary India. At times it's very self-indulgent and is now somewhat dated, but as an overall view it can't be beaten – it has been banned in India. The Australian ABC TV has produced two excellent documentary series on India, one titled *Journey into India*, the other *Journey into the Himalayas*. Both of them, but particularly the former, are worth seeing if you get a chance.

Of course the epic *Gandhi* was a major film, spawning a host of new and reprinted books on the Mahatma. *Heat & Dust* has also been made into an excellent film, as has *A Passage to India* and *Far Pavilions*. The film version of Lapierre's *City of Joy* was filmed in Calcutta in 1992 at a purpose-built slum. Directed by Roland Joffe (of *The Killing Fields*) with the principal character played by Patrick Swayze, it attracted a lot of flak from the West Bengal government which felt it was yet another condescending look at India's poor, but the critics, in general, felt otherwise.

Bandit Queen

The real life story of Phoolan Devi, queen of the dacoits, is such an extravagant saga of violence, sex, chivalry and revenge that it belittles even the most far-fetched Bollywood epic. This outrageous tale begins in a remote village in Uttar Pradesh, reaches its climax in the deep ravines of the Chambal Valley in Madhya Pradesh, and has its epilogue in a modern flat in urban Delhi.

A low caste bride at the age of eleven to a thirty-four year old man, Phoolan Devi's life was a 15-year chronicle of rape and trauma at the hands of her husband, upper caste landowners, the police, and a gang of desperadoes (known as dacoits). Eventually turning into a dacoit leader herself, she earned notoriety by slaying 22 of her tormentors in a single encounter. Her exploits assumed mythical proportions as she terrorised the countryside leaving death in her wake.

Finally tracked to the ravines of the Chambal Valley, she surrendered at a televised public ceremony, placing her gun in front of an image of Mahatma Gandhi, the apostle of nonviolence, and Durga, the fierce goddess of strength and valour.

Following an 11-year incarceration, Phoolan's transformation to respectability is now complete. Ensconced in a Delhi apartment, she is now the darling of vote-hungry politicians and addresses rallies, sharing her thoughts on social and prison reforms. Front cover news, the topic of PhD dissertations, and the subject of the internationally acclaimed film, *Bandit Queen*, Phoolan Devi has a new role that combines national celebrity, Hindu mythology, politics and film stardom. Not bad for someone with 55 criminal cases pending against them.

Meera Govil

MEDIA
Newspapers & Magazines

A number of daily English-language newspapers are printed in India. All of them are of the heavy news variety; none of them are tabloids (although there are weekly English tabloids). English-language dailies include the *Times of India*, the *Hindustan Times*, the *Indian Express* and the *Statesman*; many feel the *Express* is the best of the bunch. The *Times* has its headquarters in Bombay and the *Statesman* in Calcutta, but there are many regional editions in both cases. The *Times of India* is the largest selling English daily, with a circulation of 643,000. (The highest seller of all is the Malayalam daily, *Malayala Manorama*, which sells 692,000 copies!)

International coverage is generally pretty good. When it comes to national news, especially politics and economics, the copy is invariably strewn with a plethora of acronyms and Indian words which have no English equivalent, the majority of which mean nothing to the uninitiated. One exception is the *Independent* which is published in Bombay and is an excellent quality broadsheet with good international coverage.

So far all the Indian print media is locally owned, although there's been much debate recently about the pros and cons of allowing foreign ownership. Predictably, Rupert Murdoch is one of a number of people itching to get a toehold in India.

There's an excellent variety of meaty weekly magazines which cover a whole range of issues in depth and make good reading on long train rides as well as giving you an insight into contemporary India. Possibly *Frontline* is the best of the lot, but *India Today, The Week, Sunday* and the *Illustrated Weekly of India* are also very good. They're all available at bookshops, especially those at major railway stations. As with daily newspapers, however, you won't find much international news in them. What you will find are stories and photographs which, though interesting and of major regional importance, would never make the pages of Western daily newspapers. They're also interesting for the different slant which they give to political and social issues of worldwide concern.

There are dozens of other Indian magazines written in English, although many are of very limited interest to Western visitors – it takes a long time to build up an interest in Indian movie stars and their fanzines. Indian women's magazines, so alike yet so unlike their Western counterparts, are definitely worth looking at – *Femina* is probably the most well known. There's even an Indian 'male interest' magazine called *Debonair* with some fairly tame photographs of glamorous Indian women in various states of undress.

In keeping with the Indian preoccupation with sport, there is an incredible proliferation of sports magazines, but apart from tennis and cricket, there is little about what's happening on the international scene.

Time and *Newsweek* are only available in the main cities, and anyway, once you've become used to Indian prices they seem very expensive! You can also find newspapers like the *Herald Tribune* and *Guardian* and magazines like *Der Spiegel* and its English, French and Italian clones in the major cities and at expensive hotels but, again, they're not cheap.

One thing you'll quickly find is that newspapers and magazines become public property on trains and buses. By your side you may have your virgin copy of a *Time* magazine on which you have lashed out to help pass the time on a long train journey, and are just waiting for the right moment to start reading it. If a fellow passenger spots it, you'll be expected to hand it over, and it will then circulate until you go and collect it. If this annoys you, keep any reading matter out of sight until you are ready to use it.

Radio & TV

The revolution in the TV network has been the introduction of satellite TV. It's amazing to see satellite dishes, even in the remotest villages. The result is that viewers can tune in to the BBC, and, broadcasting from Hong Kong, Murdoch's Star TV, Prime Sports and V (an MTV-type music channel). Z TV is a local Hindi cable channel. So now even the

Indians can keep up with what's happening on *Neighbours*!

The national broadcaster, Doordarshan, which prior to the coming of satellite TV used to plod along with dry, dull and generally dreadful programmes, has lifted its game and now offers some good viewing.

Most mid-range and all top-end hotels have a TV in every room with a choice of satellite or Doordarshan.

FILM & PHOTOGRAPHY

Colour print film is readily available in India, and developing and printing facilities are not hard to find in most cities. They're usually cheap and the quality is usually (but not always) good. Kodak 100 colour print film costs around Rs 140 for a roll of 36. Developing costs are around Rs 25, plus Rs 5 per photo for printing.

If you're taking slides bring the film with you, and bring plenty – India is a photogenic country. Colour slide film can really only be found in the major cities. Colour slides can be developed in major centres, and the quality is usually good. Fujichrome slide film costs around Rs 240 for 36 exposures. Developing costs about Rs 100 with paper mounts, or Rs 150 with plastic mounts.

Kodachrome or other 'includes developing' film will have to be sent overseas. It's up to you whether you send it straight back or carry it back with you at the end of your trip. Film manufacturers warn that once exposed, film should be developed as quickly as possible; in practice the film seems to last, even in India's summer heat, without deterioration for months. But, if that's how long you're going to be carrying exposed film, consult a specialist photography handbook about ways of enhancing preservation.

There are plenty of camera shops which should be able to make minor repairs should you have any mechanical problems.

Photography itself presents some special problems in India. In the dry season the hazy atmosphere makes it difficult to get sharp shots or to get much contrast between what you are photographing and the background. Everything looks washed out and flat even with a polarising filter. In the mountains you should allow for the extreme clarity of the air and light intensity, and take care not to overexpose your shots. In general, photography is best done in the early morning and late afternoon.

Be careful what you photograph. India is touchy about places of military importance – this can include railway stations, bridges, airports and any military installations. If in doubt, ask. In general most people are happy to be photographed, but care should be taken in pointing cameras at Muslim women. Again, if in doubt, ask.

HEALTH

Travel health depends on your predeparture preparations, your day-to-day health care while travelling and how you handle any medical problem or emergency that does develop. While the list of potential dangers can seem quite frightening, with a little luck, some basic precautions and adequate information few travellers experience more than upset stomachs.

Travel Health Guides

There are a number of books on travel health:

Good Views & Pictures

For those interested in getting a good view of a town or city, mosques are perfect. The Jama Masjid in Delhi is one example, but in smaller places it's free and the warmth of Indian hospitality will shine through. In the heart of old Ujjain, there is a large mosque. I went there just hoping to see the inside, but the friendly caretaker took me all the way to the top of the minaret and scolded me for not bringing my camera. The view was wonderful! This is not guaranteed to work for every mosque, but if you're interested in beautiful views and aerial photos, it never hurts to try.

Peter Christensen, Canada

Staying Healthy in Asia, Africa & Latin America, Dirk Schroeder, Moon Publications, 1994. Probably the best all-round guide to carry, as it's compact but very detailed and well organised.

Travellers' Health, Dr Richard Dawood, Oxford University Press, 1992. Comprehensive, easy to read, authoritative and also highly recommended, although it's rather large to lug around.

Where There is No Doctor, David Werner, Macmillan, 1994. A very detailed guide intended for someone, like a Peace Corps worker, going to work in an underdeveloped country, rather than for the average traveller.

Travel with Children, Maureen Wheeler, Lonely Planet Publications, 1995. Includes basic advice on travel health for younger children.

Predeparture Planning

Health Insurance A travel insurance policy to cover theft, loss and medical problems is a wise idea. There are a wide variety of policies and your travel agent will have recommendations. The international student travel policies handled by STA Travel or other student travel organisations are usually good value. Some policies offer lower and higher medical-expense options but the higher one is chiefly for countries like the USA which have extremely high medical costs. Check the small print:

• Some policies specifically exclude 'dangerous activities' which can include scuba diving, motorcycling, even trekking. If such activities are on your agenda you don't want that sort of policy. A locally acquired motor-cycle licence may not be valid under your policy.

• You may prefer a policy which pays doctors or hospitals direct rather than you having to pay on the spot and claim later. If you have to claim later make sure you keep all documentation. Some policies ask you to call back (reverse charges) to a centre in your home country where an immediate assessment of your problem is made.

• Check if the policy covers ambulances or an emergency flight home. If you have to stretch out you will need two seats and somebody has to pay for them!

Medical Kit A small, straightforward medical kit is a wise thing to carry. A kit should include:

• Aspirin or Panadol – for pain or fever.

• Antihistamine (such as Benadryl) – useful as a decongestant for colds and allergies, to ease the itch from insect bites or stings, and to help prevent motion sickness. Antihistamines may cause sedation and interact with alcohol so care should be taken when using them.

• Antibiotics – useful if you're travelling well off the beaten track, but they must be prescribed and you should carry the prescription with you. Some individuals are allergic to commonly prescribed antibiotics such as penicillin or sulpha drugs. It would be sensible to always carry this information when travelling.

• Kaolin preparation (Pepto-Bismol), Imodium or Lomotil – for stomach upsets.

• Rehydration mixture – for treatment of severe diarrhoea. This is particularly important if travelling with children, but is recommended for everyone.

• Antiseptic such as Betadine, which comes as impregnated swabs or ointment, and an antibiotic powder or similar 'dry' spray – for cuts and grazes.

• Calamine lotion – to ease irritation from bites or stings.

• Bandages and Band-aids – for minor injuries.

• Scissors, tweezers and a thermometer (note that mercury thermometers are prohibited by airlines).

• Insect repellent, sunscreen, suntan lotion, chap stick and water purification tablets.

• A couple of syringes, in case you need injections in a country with medical hygiene problems. Ask your doctor for a note explaining why they have been prescribed.

Ideally, antibiotics should be administered only under medical supervision and should never be taken indiscriminately. Take only the recommended dose at the prescribed intervals and continue using the antibiotic for the prescribed period, even if the illness seems to be cured earlier. Antibiotics are quite specific to the infections they can treat. Stop immediately if there are any serious reactions and don't use the antibiotic at all if you are unsure that you have the correct one.

In many countries, if a medicine is available at all it will generally be available over the counter and the price will be much cheaper than in the West. However, be careful if buying drugs in developing countries, particularly where the expiry date may have passed or correct storage conditions may not have been followed. Bogus drugs are common and it's possible that drugs which are no longer recommended, or have even been banned, in the West are still being dispensed in many Third World countries.

In many countries it may be a good idea to leave unwanted medicines, syringes etc with a local clinic, rather than carry them home.

Various so-called 'AIDS kits' are available in the UK and other Western countries, and these have all the gear necessary for blood transfusions and injections. If you are going to be in India for a long time and intend to get off the beaten track, they can be a good idea. In fact even in many places where there are plenty of tourists – such as Jaisalmer in Rajasthan – the medical facilities are extremely basic. Having your own sterile equipment could be worthwhile if you have an accident and are hospitalised. For such a kit to be useful for a blood transfusion, however, it needs to have the plastic tube which carries the blood from the bag or bottle, as well as the intravenous needle which actually goes into the arm – some kits have the latter but not the former.

Health Preparations Make sure you're healthy before you start travelling. If you are embarking on a long trip make sure your teeth are OK; there are lots of places where a visit to the dentist would be the last thing you'd want.

If you wear glasses take a spare pair and your prescription. Losing your glasses can be a real problem, although in many places you can get new spectacles made up quickly, cheaply and competently.

If you require a particular medication take an adequate supply, as it may not be available locally. Take the prescription or, better still, part of the packaging showing the generic rather than the brand name (which may not be locally available), as it will make getting replacements easier. It's a wise idea to have a legible prescription with you to show you legally use the medication–it's surprising how often over-the-counter drugs from one place are illegal without a prescription or even banned in another.

Immunisations Vaccinations provide protection against diseases you might meet along the way. For some countries no immunisations are necessary, but the further off the beaten track you go the more necessary it is to take precautions.

It is important to understand the distinction between vaccines recommended for travel in certain areas and those required by law. Essentially the number of vaccines subject to international health regulations has been dramatically reduced over the last 10 years. Currently yellow fever is the only vaccine subject to international health regulations. Vaccination as an entry requirement is usually only enforced when coming from an infected area.

Occasionally travellers face bureaucratic problems regarding cholera vaccine even though all countries have dropped it as a health requirement for travel. Under some situations it may be wise to have the vaccine despite its poor protection, eg for the trans-Africa traveller.

On the other hand a number of vaccines are recommended for travel in certain areas. These may not be required by law but are recommended for your own personal protection.

All vaccinations should be recorded on an International Health Certificate, which is available from your physician or government health department.

Plan ahead for getting your vaccinations: some of them require an initial shot followed by a booster, while some vaccinations should not be given together. It is recommended you seek medical advice at least six weeks prior to travel.

Most travellers from Western countries will have been immunised against various diseases during childhood but your doctor may still recommend booster shots against measles or polio, diseases still prevalent in many developing countries. The period of protection offered by vaccinations differs widely and some are contraindicated if you are pregnant.

In some countries immunisations are available from airport or government health centres. Travel agents or airline offices will tell you where. Vaccinations include:

Smallpox
Smallpox has now been wiped out worldwide, so immunisation is no longer necessary.
Cholera
Not required by law but occasionally travellers face bureaucratic problems on some border crossings. Protection is poor and it lasts only six months. It is contraindicated in pregnancy.
Tetanus & Diphtheria
Boosters are necessary every 10 years and protection is highly recommended.
Typhoid
Available either as an injection or oral capsules. Protection lasts from one to three years and is useful if you are travelling for long in rural, tropical areas. You may get some side effects such as pain at the injection site, fever, headache and a general unwell feeling. A new single-dose injectable vaccine, which appears to have few side effects, is now available but is more expensive. Side effects are unusual with the oral form but occasionally an individual will have stomach cramps.
Hepatitis A
The most common travel-acquired illness which can be prevented by vaccination. Protection can be provided in two ways – either with the antibody gammaglobulin or with a new vaccine called Havrix.

Havrix provides long term immunity (possibly more than 10 years) after an initial course of two injections and a booster at one year. It may be more expensive than gammaglobulin but certainly has many advantages, including length of protection and ease of administration. It is important to know that being a vaccine it will take about three weeks to provide satisfactory protection – hence the need for careful planning prior to travel.

Gammaglobulin is not a vaccination but a ready-made antibody which has proven very successful in reducing the chances of hepatitis infection. Because it may interfere with the development of immunity, it should not be given until at least 10 days after administration of the last vaccine needed; it should also be given as close as possible to departure because it is at its most effective in the first few weeks after administration and the effectiveness tapers off gradually between three and six months.
Yellow Fever
Protection lasts 10 years and is recommended where the disease is endemic, chiefly in Africa and South America. You usually have to go to a special yellow-fever vaccination centre. Vaccination is contraindicated during pregnancy but if you must travel to a high-risk area it is probably advisable.

Basic Rules

Care in what you eat and drink is the most important health rule; stomach upsets are the most likely travel health problem (between 30% and 50% of travellers in a two-week stay experience this) but the majority of these upsets will be relatively minor. Don't become paranoid; trying the local food is part of the experience of travel, after all.

Water The number one rule is *don't drink the water* and that includes ice. If you don't know for certain that the water is safe always assume the worst. Reputable brands of bottled water or soft drinks are generally fine, although in some places bottles refilled with tap water are not unknown. Only use water from containers with a serrated seal – not tops or corks. Take care with fruit juice, particularly if water may have been added. Milk should be treated with suspicion, as it is often unpasteurised. Boiled milk is fine if it is kept hygienically and yoghurt is always good. Tea or coffee should also be OK, since the water should have been boiled.

Water Purification The simplest way of purifying water is to boil it thoroughly. Vigorously boiling for five minutes should be satisfactory; however, at high altitude water boils at a lower temperature, so germs are less likely to be killed.

Simple filtering will not remove all dangerous organisms, so if you cannot boil water it should be treated chemically. Chlorine tablets (Puritabs, Steritabs or other brand names) will kill many but not all pathogens, including giardia and amoebic cysts. Iodine is very effective in purifying water and is available in tablet form (such as Potable Aqua), but follow the directions carefully and remember that too much iodine can be harmful.

If you can't find tablets, tincture of iodine (2%) or iodine crystals can be used. Four drops of tincture of iodine per litre or quart of clear water is the recommended dosage; the treated water should be left to stand for 20 to 30 minutes before drinking. Iodine crystals can also be used to purify water but this is a more complicated process, as you have to first prepare a saturated iodine solution. Iodine loses its effectiveness if exposed to air or damp so keep it in a tightly sealed container. Flavoured powder will disguise the taste of treated water and is a good idea if you are travelling with children.

Food There is an old colonial adage which says: 'If you can cook it, boil it or peel it you can eat it...otherwise forget it'. Salads and fruit should be washed with purified water or peeled where possible. Ice cream is usually OK if it is a reputable brand name, but beware of street vendors and of ice cream that has melted and been refrozen. Thoroughly cooked food is safest but not if it has been left to cool or if it has been reheated. Shellfish such as mussels, oysters and clams should be avoided as well as undercooked meat, particularly in the form of mince. Steaming does not make shellfish safe for eating.

If a place looks clean and well run and if the vendor also looks clean and healthy, then the food is probably safe. In general, places that are packed with travellers or locals will be fine, while empty restaurants are questionable. The food in busy restaurants is cooked and eaten quite quickly with little standing around and is probably not reheated.

Nutrition If your food is poor or limited in availability, if you're travelling hard and fast and therefore missing meals, or if you simply lose your appetite, you can soon start to lose weight and place your health at risk.

Make sure your diet is well balanced. Eggs, tofu, beans, lentils (dhal in India) and nuts are all safe ways to get protein. Fruit you can peel (bananas, oranges or mandarins for example) is always safe and a good source of vitamins. Try to eat plenty of grains (rice) and bread. Remember that although food is generally safer if it is cooked well, overcooked food loses much of its nutritional value. If your diet isn't well balanced or if your food intake is insufficient, it's a good idea to take vitamin and iron pills.

In hot climates make sure you drink enough – don't rely on feeling thirsty to indicate when you should drink. Not needing to urinate or very dark yellow urine is a danger sign. Always carry a water bottle with you on long trips. Excessive sweating can lead to loss of salt and therefore muscle cramping. Salt tablets are not a good idea as a preventative, but in places where salt is not used much adding salt to food can help.

Everyday Health Normal body temperature is 98.6°F or 37°C; more than 2°C higher indicates a 'high' fever. The normal adult pulse rate is 60 to 80 per minute (children 80 to 100, babies 100 to 140). You should know how to take a temperature and a pulse rate. As a general rule the pulse increases about 20 beats per minute for each °C rise in fever.

Respiration (breathing) rate is also an indicator of illness. Count the number of breaths per minute: between 12 and 20 is normal for adults and older children (up to 30 for younger children, 40 for babies). People with a high fever or serious respiratory illness (like pneumonia) breathe more quickly than normal. More than 40 shallow breaths a minute usually means pneumonia.

In Western countries with safe water and excellent human waste disposal systems we often take good health for granted. In years gone by, when public health facilities were not as good as they are today, certain rules attached to eating and drinking were observed, eg washing your hands before a meal. It is important for people travelling in areas of poor sanitation to be aware of this and adjust their own personal hygiene habits.

Clean your teeth with purified water rather than straight from the tap. Avoid climatic extremes: keep out of the sun when it's hot, dress warmly when it's cold. Avoid potential diseases by dressing sensibly. You can get worm infections through walking barefoot or dangerous coral cuts by walking over coral without shoes. You can avoid insect bites by covering bare skin when insects are around, by screening windows or beds and by using insect repellents. Seek local advice: and in situations where there is no information, discretion is the better part of valour.

Medical Problems & Treatment

Potential medical problems can be broken down into several areas. Firstly there are the problems caused by extremes of temperature, altitude or motion. Then there are diseases and illnesses caused through poor environmental sanitation, insect bites or stings, and animal or human contact. Simple cuts, bites and scratches can also cause problems.

Self-diagnosis and treatment can be risky, so wherever possible seek qualified help. Although we do give drug dosages in this section, they are for emergency use only. Medical advice should be sought where possible before administering any drugs.

An embassy or consulate can usually recommend a good place to go for such advice. So can five-star hotels, although they often recommend doctors with five-star prices. (This is when that medical insurance really comes in useful!) In some places standards of medical attention are so low that for some ailments the best advice is to get on a plane and go somewhere else.

Environmental Hazards

Sunburn In the tropics, the desert or at high altitude you can get sunburnt surprisingly quickly, even through cloud. Use a sunscreen and take extra care to cover areas which don't normally see sun – eg your feet. A hat provides added protection, and you should also use zinc cream or some other barrier cream for your nose and lips. Calamine lotion is good for mild sunburn.

Prickly Heat Prickly heat is an itchy rash caused by excessive perspiration trapped under the skin. It usually strikes people who have just arrived in a hot climate and whose pores have not yet opened sufficiently to cope with greater sweating. Keeping cool but bathing often, using a mild talcum powder or even resorting to air-conditioning may help until you acclimatise.

Heat Exhaustion Dehydration or salt deficiency can cause heat exhaustion. Take time to acclimatise to high temperatures and make

sure you get sufficient liquids. Wear loose clothing and a broad-brimmed hat. Do not do anything too physically demanding.

Salt deficiency is characterised by fatigue, lethargy, headaches, giddiness and muscle cramps and in this case salt tablets may help. Vomiting or diarrhoea can deplete your liquid and salt levels. Anhydrotic heat exhaustion, caused by an inability to sweat, is quite rare. Unlike the other forms of heat exhaustion it is likely to strike people who have been in a hot climate for some time, rather than newcomers.

Heat Stroke This serious, sometimes fatal, condition can occur if the body's heat-regulating mechanism breaks down and the body temperature rises to dangerous levels. Long, continuous periods of exposure to high temperatures can leave you vulnerable to heat stroke. You should avoid excessive alcohol or strenuous activity when you first arrive in a hot climate.

The symptoms are feeling unwell, not sweating very much or at all and a high body temperature (39°C to 41°C). Where sweating has ceased the skin becomes flushed and red. Severe, throbbing headaches and lack of coordination will also occur, and the sufferer may be confused or aggressive. Eventually the victim will become delirious or convulse. Hospitalisation is essential, but meanwhile get victims out of the sun, remove their clothing, cover them with a wet sheet or towel and then fan continually.

Fungal Infections Fungal infections, which occur with greater frequency in hot weather, are most likely to occur on the scalp, between the toes or fingers (athlete's foot), in the groin (jock itch or crotch rot) and on the body (ringworm). You get ringworm (which is a fungal infection, not a worm) from infected animals or by walking on damp areas, like shower floors.

To prevent fungal infections wear loose, comfortable clothes, avoid artificial fibres, wash frequently and dry carefully. If you do get an infection, wash the infected area daily with a disinfectant or medicated soap and water, and rinse and dry well. Apply an anti-fungal powder like the widely available Tinaderm. Try to expose the infected area to air or sunlight as much as possible and wash all towels and underwear in hot water as well as changing them often.

Cold Too much cold is just as dangerous as too much heat, particularly if it leads to hypothermia. If you are trekking at high altitudes or simply taking a long bus trip over mountains, particularly at night, be prepared.

Hypothermia occurs when the body loses heat faster than it can produce it and the core temperature of the body falls. It is surprisingly easy to progress from very cold to dangerously cold due to a combination of wind, wet clothing, fatigue and hunger, even if the air temperature is above freezing. It is best to dress in layers; silk, wool and some of the new artificial fibres are all good insulating materials. A hat is important, as a lot of heat is lost through the head. A strong, waterproof outer layer is essential, as keeping dry is vital. Carry basic supplies, including food containing simple sugars to generate heat quickly and lots of fluid to drink. A space blanket is something all travellers in cold environments should carry.

Symptoms of hypothermia are exhaustion, numb skin (particularly toes and fingers), shivering, slurred speech, irrational or violent behaviour, lethargy, stumbling, dizzy spells, muscle cramps and violent bursts of energy. Irrationality may take the form of sufferers claiming they are warm and trying to take off their clothes.

To treat mild hypothermia, first get the person out of the wind and/or rain, remove their clothing if it's wet and replace it with dry, warm clothing. Give them hot liquids – not alcohol – and some high-kilojoule, easily digestible food. Do not rub victims, instead allow them to slowly warm themselves. This should be enough to treat the early stages of hypothermia. The early recognition and treatment of mild hypothermia is the only way to prevent severe hypothermia, which is a critical condition.

Altitude Sickness Acute Mountain Sickness or AMS occurs at high altitude and can be fatal. The lack of oxygen at high altitudes affects most people to some extent.

A number of measures can be adopted to prevent acute mountain sickness:

- Ascend slowly – have frequent rest days, spending two to three nights at each rise of 1,000 metres. If you reach a high altitude by trekking, acclimatisation takes place gradually and you are less likely to be affected than if you fly direct.
- Drink extra fluids. The mountain air is dry and cold and moisture is lost as you breathe.
- Eat light, high-carbohydrate meals for more energy.
- Avoid alcohol as it may increase the risk of dehydration.
- Avoid sedatives.

Even with acclimatisation you may still have trouble adjusting. Breathlessness; a dry, irritative cough (which may progress to the production of pink, frothy sputum); severe headache; loss of appetite; nausea; and sometimes vomiting are all danger signs. Increasing tiredness, confusion, and lack of coordination and balance are real danger signs. Any of these symptoms individually, even just a persistent headache, can be a warning. Mild altitude sickness will generally abate after a day or so but if the symptoms persist, or become worse, the only treatment is to descend – even 500 metres can help.

There is no hard and fast rule as to how high is too high: AMS has been fatal at altitudes of 3000 metres, although 3500 to 4500 metres is the usual range. It is always wise to sleep at a lower altitude than the greatest height reached during the day.

Motion Sickness Eating lightly before and during a trip will reduce the chances of motion sickness. If you are prone to motion sickness try to find a place that minimises disturbance – near the wing on aircraft, close to midships on boats, near the centre on buses. Fresh air usually helps; reading and cigarette smoke don't. Commercial motion-sickness preparations, which can cause drowsiness, have to be taken before the trip commences; when you're feeling sick it's too late. Ginger is a natural preventative and is available in capsule form.

Jet Lag Jet lag is experienced when a person travels by air across more than three time zones (each time zone usually represents a one-hour time difference). It occurs because many of the functions of the human body (such as temperature, pulse rate and emptying of the bladder and bowels) are regulated by internal 24-hour cycles called circadian rhythms. When we travel long distances rapidly, our bodies take time to adjust to the 'new time' of our destination, and we may experience fatigue, disorientation, insomnia, anxiety, impaired concentration and loss of appetite. These effects will usually be gone within three days of arrival, but there are ways of minimising the impact of jet lag:

- Rest for a couple of days prior to departure; try to avoid late nights and last-minute dashes for travellers' cheques, passport etc.
- Try to select flight schedules that minimise sleep deprivation; arriving late in the day means you can go to sleep soon after you arrive. For very long flights, try to organise a stopover.
- Avoid excessive eating (which bloats the stomach) and alcohol (which causes dehydration) during the flight. Instead, drink plenty of non-carbonated, non-alcoholic drinks such as fruit juice or water.
- Avoid smoking, as this reduces the amount of oxygen in the aeroplane cabin even further and causes greater fatigue.
- Make yourself comfortable by wearing loose-fitting clothes and perhaps bringing an eye mask and ear plugs to help you sleep.

Infectious Diseases
Diarrhoea A change of water, food or climate can all cause the runs; diarrhoea caused by contaminated food or water is more serious. Despite all your precautions you may still have a mild bout of travellers' diarrhoea but a few rushed toilet trips with no other symptoms is not indicative of a serious problem. Moderate diarrhoea, involving half-a-dozen loose movements in a day, is more of a nuisance.

Dehydration is the main danger with any diarrhoea, particularly for children where dehydration can occur quite quickly. Fluid replacement remains the mainstay of management. Weak black tea with a little sugar, soda water, or soft drinks allowed to go flat and diluted 50% with water are all good. With severe diarrhoea a rehydrating solution is necessary to replace minerals and salts. Commercially available ORS (oral rehydration salts) are very useful; add the contents of one sachet to a litre of boiled or bottled water. In an emergency you can make up a solution of eight teaspoons of sugar to a litre of boiled water and provide salted cracker biscuits at the same time. You should stick to a bland diet as you recover.

Lomotil or Imodium can be used to bring relief from the symptoms, although they do not actually cure the problem. Only use these drugs if absolutely necessary – eg if you *must* travel. For children Imodium is preferable, but under all circumstances fluid replacement is the most important thing to remember. Do not use these drugs if the person has a high fever or is severely dehydrated.

In certain situations antibiotics may be indicated:

- Watery diarrhoea with blood and mucous. (Gut-paralysing drugs like Imodium or Lomotil should be avoided in this situation.)
- Watery diarrhoea with fever and lethargy.
- Persistent diarrhoea for more than five days.
- Severe diarrhoea, if it is logistically difficult to stay in one place.

The recommended drugs (adults only) would be either norfloxacin 400 mg twice daily for three days or ciprofloxacin 500 mg twice daily for three days.

The drug bismuth subsalicylate has also been used successfully. It is not available in Australia. The dosage for adults is two tablets or 30ml and for children it is one tablet or 10ml. This dose can be repeated every 30 minutes to one hour, with no more than eight doses in a 24-hour period.

The drug of choice in children would be co-trimoxazole (Bactrim, Septrin, Resprim) with dosage dependent on weight. A three-day course is also given.

Ampicillin has been recommended in the past and may still be an alternative.

Giardiasis The parasite causing this intestinal disorder is present in contaminated water. The symptoms are stomach cramps, nausea, a bloated stomach, watery, foul-smelling diarrhoea and frequent gas. Giardiasis can appear several weeks after you have been exposed to the parasite. The symptoms may disappear for a few days and then return; this can go on for several weeks. Tinidazole, known as Fasigyn, or metronidazole (Flagyl) are the recommended drugs for treatment. Either can be used in a single treatment dose. Antibiotics are of no use.

Dysentery This serious illness is caused by contaminated food or water and is characterised by severe diarrhoea, often with blood or mucus in the stool. There are two kinds of dysentery. Bacillary dysentery is characterised by a high fever and rapid onset; headache, vomiting and stomach pains are also symptoms. It generally does not last longer than a week, but it is highly contagious.

Amoebic dysentery is often more gradual in the onset of symptoms, with cramping abdominal pain and vomiting less likely; fever may not be present. It is not a self-limiting disease: it will persist until treated and can recur and cause long-term health problems.

A stool test is necessary to diagnose which kind of dysentery you have, so you should seek medical help urgently. In case of an emergency the drugs norfloxacin or ciprofloxacin can be used as presumptive treatment for bacillary dysentery, and metronidazole (Flagyl) for amoebic dysentery.

For bacillary dysentery, norfloxacin 400 mg twice daily for seven days or ciprofloxacin 500 mg twice daily for seven days are the recommended dosages.

If you're unable to find either of these drugs then a useful alternative is co-trimoxazole 160/800 mg (Bactrim, Septrin, Resprim) twice daily for seven days. This is a sulpha drug and must not be used by people with a known sulpha allergy.

In the case of children the drug co-trimoxazole is a reasonable first-line treatment. For amoebic dysentery, the recommended adult dosage of metronidazole (Flagyl) is one 750-mg to 800-mg capsule three times daily for five days. Children aged between eight and 12 years should have half the adult dose; the dosage for younger children is one-third the adult dose.

An alternative to Flagyl is Fasigyn, taken as a two gram daily dose for three days. Alcohol must be avoided during treatment and for 48 hours afterwards.

Cholera Cholera vaccination is not very effective. The bacteria responsible for this disease are waterborne, so attention to the rules of eating and drinking should protect the traveller.

Outbreaks of cholera are generally widely reported, so you can avoid such problem areas. The disease is characterised by a sudden onset of acute diarrhoea with 'rice water' stools, vomiting, muscular cramps, and extreme weakness. You need medical help – but treat for dehydration, which can be extreme, and if there is an appreciable delay in getting to hospital then begin taking tetracycline. The adult dose is 250 mg four times daily. It is not recommended for children aged eight years or under nor for pregnant women. An alternative drug is Ampicillin. Remember that while antibiotics might kill the bacteria, it is a toxin produced by the bacteria which causes the massive fluid loss. Fluid replacement is by far the most important aspect of treatment.

Viral Gastroenteritis This is caused not by bacteria but, as the name suggests, by a virus. It is characterised by stomach cramps, diarrhoea, and sometimes by vomiting and/or a slight fever. All you can do is rest and drink lots of fluids.

Hepatitis Hepatitis is a general term for inflammation of the liver. There are many causes of this condition: drugs, alcohol and infections are but a few.

The discovery of new strains has led to a virtual alphabet soup, with hepatitis A, B, C, D, E and a rumoured G. These letters identify specific agents that cause viral hepatitis. Viral hepatitis is an infection of the liver, which can lead to jaundice (yellow skin), fever, lethargy and digestive problems. It can have no symptoms at all, with the infected person not knowing that they have the disease. Travellers shouldn't be too paranoid about this apparent proliferation of hepatitis strains; hep C, D, E and G are fairly rare (so far) and following the same precautions as for A and B should be all that's necessary to avoid them.

Viral hepatitis can be divided into two groups on the basis of how it is spread. The first route of transmission is via contaminated food and water, and the second route is via blood and bodily fluids. The following types of hepatitis are spread by contaminated food and water:

Hepatitis A This is a very common disease in most countries, especially those with poor standards of sanitation. Most people in developing countries are infected as children; they often don't develop symptoms, but do develop life-long immunity. The disease poses a real threat to the traveller, as people are unlikely to have been exposed to hepatitis A in developed countries.

The symptoms are fever, chills, headache, fatigue, feelings of weakness and aches and pains, followed by loss of appetite, nausea, vomiting, abdominal pain, dark urine, light coloured faeces, jaundiced skin and the whites of the eyes may turn yellow. In some cases you may feel unwell, tired, have no appetite, experience aches and pains and be jaundiced. You should seek medical advice, but in general there is not much you can do apart from resting, drinking lots of fluids, eating lightly and avoiding fatty foods. People who have had hepatitis must forego alcohol for six months after the illness, as hepatitis attacks the liver and it needs that amount of time to recover. •

The routes of transmission are via contaminated water, shellfish contaminated by sewerage, or foodstuffs sold by food handlers with poor standards of hygiene.

Taking care with what you eat and drink can go a long way towards preventing this disease. But this is a very infectious virus, so if there is any risk of exposure, additional cover is highly recommended. This cover comes in two forms: Gammaglobulin and Havrix. Gammaglobulin is an injection where you are given the antibodies for hepatitis A, which provide immunity for a limited time. Havrix is a vaccine, where you develop your own antibodies, which gives lasting immunity.

Hepatitis E This is a very recently discovered virus, of which little is yet known. It appears to be rather common in developing countries, generally causing mild hepatitis, although it can be very serious in pregnant women.

Care with water supplies is the only current prevention, as there are no specific vaccines for this type of hepatitis. At present it doesn't appear to be too great a risk for travellers.

The following strains are spread by contact with blood and bodily fluids:

Hepatitis B This is also a very common disease, with almost 300 million chronic carriers in the world. Hepatitis B, which used to be called serum hepatitis, is spread through contact with infected blood, blood products or bodily fluids, for example through sexual contact, unsterilised needles and blood transfusions. Other risk situations include having a shave or tattoo in a local shop, or having your ears pierced. The symptoms of type B are much the same as type A except that they are more severe and may lead to irreparable liver damage or even liver cancer.

Although there is no treatment for hepatitis B, a cheap and effective vaccine is available; the only problem is that for long-lasting cover you need a six-month course. The immunisation schedule requires two injections at least a month apart followed by a third dose five months after the second. Persons who should receive a hepatitis B vaccination include anyone who anticipates contact with blood or other bodily secretions, either as a health-care worker or through sexual contact with the local population, particularly those who intend to stay in the country for a long period of time.

Hepatitis C This is another recently defined virus. It is a concern because it seems to lead to liver disease more rapidly than hepatitis B.

The virus is spread by contact with blood – usually via contaminated transfusions or shared needles. Avoiding these is the only means of prevention, as there is no available vaccine.

Hepatitis D Often referred to as the 'Delta' virus, this infection only occurs in chronic carriers of hepatitis B. It is transmitted by blood and bodily fluids. Again there is no vaccine for this virus, so avoidance is the best prevention. The risk to travellers is certainly limited.

Typhoid Typhoid fever is another gut infection that travels the faecal-oral route – ie contaminated water and food are responsible. Vaccination against typhoid is not totally effective and it is one of the most dangerous infections, so medical help must be sought.

In its early stages typhoid resembles many other illnesses: sufferers may feel like they have a bad cold or flu on the way, as early symptoms are a headache, a sore throat, and a fever which rises a little each day until it is around 40°C or more. The victim's pulse is often slow relative to the degree of fever present and gets slower as the fever rises – unlike a normal fever where the pulse increases. There may also be vomiting, diarrhoea or constipation.

In the second week the high fever and slow pulse continue and a few pink spots may appear on the body; trembling, delirium, weakness, weight loss and dehydration are other symptoms. If there are no further complications, the fever and other symptoms will slowly diminish during the third week. However you must get medical help before this because pneumonia (acute infection of the lungs) or peritonitis (perforated bowel) are common complications, and because typhoid is very infectious.

The fever should be treated by keeping the victim cool and dehydration should also be watched for.

The drug of choice is ciprofloxacin at a dose of one gram daily for 14 days. It is quite expensive and may not be available. The alternative, chloramphenicol, has been the mainstay of treatment for many years. In many countries it is still the recommended antibiotic but there are fewer side affects with Ampicillin. The adult dosage is two 250-mg capsules, four times a day. Children aged between eight and 12 years should have half the adult dose; younger children should have one-third the adult dose.

People who are allergic to penicillin should not be given Ampicillin.

Plague There was an outbreak of pneumonic plague in 1994 in Surat, Gujarat, although the risk to travellers is tiny.

Meningococcal Meningitis This disease is found in Nepal, although it could possibly be caught in India too.

Trekkers to rural areas should be particularly careful, as the disease is spread by close contact with people who carry it in their throats and noses, spread it through coughs and sneezes and may not be aware that they are carriers. Lodges in the hills where travellers spend the night are prime spots for the spread of infection.

This very serious disease attacks the brain and can be fatal. A scattered, blotchy rash, fever, severe headache, sensitivity to light and neck stiffness which prevents forward bending of the head are the first symptoms. Death can occur within a few hours, so immediate treatment is important.

Treatment is large doses of penicillin given intravenously, or, if that is not possible, intramuscularly (ie in the buttocks). Vaccination offers good protection for over a year, but you should also check for reports of current epidemics.

Tuberculosis (TB) Although this disease is widespread in many developing countries, it is not a serious risk to travellers. Young children are more susceptible than adults and vaccination is a sensible precaution for children under 12 travelling in endemic areas. TB is commonly spread by coughing or by unpasteurised dairy products from infected cows. Milk that has been boiled is safe to drink; the souring of milk to make yoghurt or cheese also kills the bacilli.

Diphtheria Diphtheria can be a skin infection or a more dangerous throat infection. It is spread by contaminated dust contacting the skin or by the inhalation of infected cough or sneeze droplets. Frequent washing and keeping the skin dry will help prevent skin infection. A vaccination is available to prevent the throat infection.

Sexually Transmitted Diseases Sexual contact with an infected sexual partner spreads these diseases. While abstinence is the only 100% preventative, using condoms is also effective. Gonorrhoea and syphilis are the most common of these diseases; sores, blisters or rashes around the genitals, discharges or pain when urinating are common symptoms. Symptoms may be less marked or not observed at all in women. Syphilis symptoms eventually disappear completely but the disease continues and can cause severe problems in later years. The treatment of gonorrhoea and syphilis is by antibiotics.

There are numerous other sexually transmitted diseases, for most of which effective treatment is available. However, there is no cure for herpes and there is also currently no cure for AIDS (Acquired Immune Deficiency Syndrome).

HIV/AIDS HIV, the Human Immunodeficiency Virus, may develop into AIDS. HIV is a major problem in many countries. Any exposure to blood, blood products or bodily fluids may put the individual at risk. In many developing countries transmission is predominantly through heterosexual sexual activity. This is quite different from industrialised countries where transmission is mostly through contact between homosexual or bisexual males, or via contaminated needles shared by IV drug users. Apart from abstinence, the most effective preventative is always to practise safe sex using condoms. It is impossible to detect the HIV-positive status of an otherwise healthy-looking person without a blood test.

HIV/AIDS can also be spread through infected blood transfusions; most developing countries cannot afford to screen blood for transfusions. It can also be spread by dirty needles – vaccinations, acupuncture, tattooing and ear or nose piercing can potentially be as dangerous as intravenous drug use if the equipment is not clean. If you do need an injection, ask to see the syringe unwrapped in front of you, or better still, take a needle and syringe pack with you overseas – it is a cheap insurance package against infection with HIV.

Fear of HIV infection should never preclude treatment for serious medical conditions. Although there may be a risk of infection, it is very small indeed.

The AIDS situation in India is quite serious; an article in *Navbharat Times* a few years ago estimated that 30% of the 100,000 prostitutes in Bombay are HIV positive. Further, a random survey of truck drivers revealed that 25% were HIV positive and most did not know anything about AIDS.

Worms These parasites are most common in rural, tropical areas and a stool test when you return home is not a bad idea. They can be present on unwashed vegetables or in undercooked meat and you can pick them up through your skin by walking in bare feet. Infestations may not show up for some time, and although they are generally not serious, if left untreated they can cause severe health problems. A stool test is necessary to pinpoint the problem and medication is often available over the counter.

Tetanus This potentially fatal disease is found in undeveloped tropical areas. It is difficult to treat but is preventable with immunisation. Tetanus occurs when a wound becomes infected by a germ which lives in the faeces of animals or people, so clean all cuts, punctures or animal bites. Tetanus is also known as lockjaw, and the first symptom may be discomfort in swallowing, or stiffening of the jaw and neck; this is followed by painful convulsions of the jaw and whole body.

Rabies Rabies is found in many countries and is caused by a bite or scratch by an infected animal. Dogs are noted carriers as are monkeys and cats. Any bite, scratch or even lick from a warm-blooded, furry animal should be cleaned immediately and thoroughly. Scrub with soap and running water, and then clean with an alcohol solution. If there is any possibility that the animal is infected medical help should be sought immediately. Even if the animal is not rabid, all bites should be treated seriously as they can become infected or can result in tetanus. A rabies vaccination is now available and should be considered if you are in a high-risk category – eg if you intend to explore caves (bat bites can be dangerous) or work with animals.

Insect-Borne Diseases

Malaria This serious disease is spread by mosquito bites.

If you are travelling in endemic areas, which in India is everywhere except the Himalayan region, it is extremely important to take malarial prophylactics. Symptoms include headaches, fever, chills and sweating which may subside and recur. Without treatment malaria can develop more serious, potentially fatal effects.

Antimalarial drugs do not prevent you from being infected but kill the parasites during a stage in their development.

There are a number of different types of malaria. The one of most concern is falciparum malaria. This is responsible for the very serious cerebral malaria. Falciparum is the predominant form in many malaria-prone areas of the world, including Africa, South-East Asia and Papua New Guinea. Contrary to popular belief cerebral malaria is not a new strain.

The problem in recent years has been the emergence of increasing resistance to commonly used antimalarials like chloroquine, maloprim and proguanil. Newer drugs such as mefloquine (Lariam) and doxycycline (Vibramycin, Doryx) are often recommended for chloroquine and multidrug-resistant areas. Expert advice should be sought, as there are many factors to consider when deciding on the type of antimalarial medication, including the area to be visited, the risk of exposure to malaria-carrying mosquitoes, your current medical condition, and your age and pregnancy status. It is also important to discuss the side-effect profile of the medication, so you can work out some level of risk versus benefit ratio. It is also very important to be sure of the correct dosage of the medication prescribed to you. Some people have inadvertently taken weekly medication (chloroquine) on a daily basis, with disastrous effects. While discussing dosages for prevention of malaria, it is often advisable to include the dosages required for treatment, especially if your trip is through a high-risk area that would isolate you from medical care.

The main messages are:

- Primary prevention must always be in the form of mosquito-avoidance measures. The mosquitoes that transmit malaria bite from dusk to dawn and during this period travellers are advised to:
  – wear light coloured clothing
  – wear long pants and long sleeved shirts
  – use mosquito repellents containing the compound DEET on exposed areas (overuse of DEET may be harmful, especially to children, but its use is considered preferable to being bitten by disease-transmitting mosquitoes)
  – avoid highly scented perfumes or aftershave
  – use a mosquito net – it may be worth taking your own
- While no antimalarial is 100% effective, taking the most appropriate drug significantly reduces the risk of contracting the disease.

- No one should ever die from malaria. It can be diagnosed by a simple blood test. Symptoms range from fever, chills and sweating, headache and abdominal pains to a vague feeling of ill-health, so seek examination immediately if there is any suggestion of malaria.

Contrary to popular belief, once a traveller contracts malaria he/she does not have it for life. One of the parasites may lie dormant in the liver but this can also be eradicated using a specific medication. Malaria is curable, as long as the traveller seeks medical help when symptoms occur.

Dengue Fever There is no prophylactic available for this mosquito-spread disease; the main preventative measure is to avoid mosquito bites. A sudden onset of fever, headaches and severe joint and muscle pains are the first signs before a rash starts on the trunk of the body and spreads to the limbs and face. After a further few days, the fever will subside and recovery will begin. Serious complications are not common but full recovery can take up to a month or more.

Typhus Typhus is spread by ticks, mites or lice. It begins as a bad cold, followed by a fever, chills, headache, muscle pains and a body rash. There is often a large painful sore at the site of the bite and nearby lymph nodes are swollen and painful.

Seek local advice on areas where ticks pose a danger and always check your skin carefully for ticks after walking in a danger area. A strong insect repellent can help, and serious walkers in tick areas should consider having their boots and trousers impregnated with benzyl benzoate and dibutylphthalate.

Japanese Encephalitis This viral infection of the brain is transmitted by mosquitoes. Vaccination is recommended for those intending to spend some time in a rural-risk area. The risk to travellers is tiny.

Cuts, Bites & Stings
Cuts & Scratches Skin punctures can easily become infected in hot climates and may be difficult to heal. Treat any cut with an anti-

septic such as Betadine. Where possible avoid bandages and Band-aids, which can keep wounds wet. Coral cuts are notoriously slow to heal, as the coral injects a weak venom into the wound. Avoid coral cuts by wearing shoes when walking on reefs, and clean any cut thoroughly with sodium peroxide if available.

Bites & Stings Bee and wasp stings are usually painful rather than dangerous. Calamine lotion will give relief and ice packs will reduce the pain and swelling. There are some spiders with dangerous bites but antivenenes are usually available. Again, local advice is the best suggestion.

Snakes To minimise your chances of being bitten always wear boots, socks and long trousers when walking through undergrowth where snakes may be present. Don't put your hands into holes and crevices, and be careful when collecting firewood.

Snake bites do not cause instantaneous death and antivenenes are usually available. Keep the victim calm and still, wrap the bitten limb tightly, as you would for a sprained ankle, and then attach a splint to immobilise it. Then seek medical help, if possible with the dead snake for identification. Don't attempt to catch the snake if there is even a remote possibility of being bitten again. Tourniquets and sucking out the poison are now comprehensively discredited.

Bedbugs & Lice Bedbugs live in various places, but particularly in dirty mattresses and bedding. Spots of blood on bedclothes or on the wall around the bed can be read as a suggestion to find another hotel. Bedbugs leave itchy bites in neat rows. Calamine lotion may help.

All lice cause itching and discomfort. They make themselves at home in your hair (head lice), your clothing (body lice) or in your pubic hair (crabs). You catch lice through direct contact with infected people or by sharing combs, clothing and the like. Powder or shampoo treatment will kill the lice and infected clothing should then be washed in very hot water.

Leeches & Ticks Leeches may be present in damp rainforest conditions; they attach themselves to your skin to suck your blood. Trekkers often get them on their legs or in their boots. Salt or a lighted cigarette end will make them fall off. Do not pull them off, as the bite is then more likely to become infected. An insect repellent may keep them away. Vaseline, alcohol or oil will persuade a tick to let go. You should always check your body if you have been walking through a tick-infested area, as they can spread typhus.

Women's Health

Gynaecological Problems Poor diet, lowered resistance due to the use of antibiotics for stomach upsets and even contraceptive pills can lead to vaginal infections when travelling in hot climates. Keeping the genital area clean, and wearing skirts or loose-fitting trousers and cotton underwear will help to prevent infections.

Yeast infections, characterised by a rash, itch and discharge, can be treated with a vinegar or lemon-juice douche, or with yoghurt. Nystatin suppositories are the usual medical prescription. Trichomoniasis is a more serious infection; symptoms are a discharge and a burning sensation when urinating. Male sexual partners must also be treated, and if a vinegar-water douche is not effective medical attention should be sought. Metronidazole (Flagyl) is the prescribed drug.

Pregnancy Most miscarriages occur during the first three months of pregnancy, so this is the most risky time to travel as far as your own health is concerned. Miscarriage is not uncommon, and can occasionally lead to severe bleeding. The last three months should also be spent within reasonable distance of good medical care. A baby born as early as 24 weeks stands a chance of survival, but only in a good modern hospital. Pregnant women should avoid all unnecessary medication, but vaccinations and malarial prophylactics should still be taken where possible. Additional care should be taken to prevent illness and particular atten-

tion should be paid to diet and nutrition. Alcohol and nicotine, for example, should be avoided.

Women travellers often find that their periods become irregular or even cease while they're on the road. Remember that a missed period in these circumstances doesn't necessarily indicate pregnancy. There are health posts or Family Planning clinics in many urban centres in developing countries, where you can seek advice and have a urine test to determine whether or not you are pregnant.

Hospitals

Although India does have a few excellent hospitals such as the Christian Medical College Hospital in Vellore, Tamil Nadu, the Breach Candy Hospital in Bombay and the All India Institute of Medical Sciences in Delhi, most Indian cities do not have the quality of medical care available in the West. Usually hospitals run by Western missionaries have better facilities than government hospitals where long waiting lines are common. Unless you have something very unusual, these Christian-run hospitals are the best places to head for in an emergency.

India also has many qualified doctors with their own private clinics which can be quite good and, in some cases, as good as anything available anywhere in the world. The usual fee for a clinic visit is about Rs 80; Rs 200 for a specialist. Home calls usually cost about Rs 100.

WOMEN TRAVELLERS

Foreign women travelling in India have always been viewed by Indian men as free and easy, based largely on what they believed to be true from watching cheap Western soapies. Women have been hassled, stared at, spied on in hotel rooms, and often groped, although the situation was rarely threatening.

Recently, however, the situation has become more difficult for women travellers, mainly because the 'sexual revolution' which swept the West 25 years ago has now hit India. Movies and magazines are much more explicit, and the widespread billboard advertisements for condoms often quote passages from the Kama Sutra and depict naked or semi-naked women and men. The message getting through to the middle-class Indian male is that sex before and outside of marriage is less of a taboo than in the past, and so foreign women are seen as even more free and easy than ever before.

Close attention to standards of dress will go a long way to minimising problems for female travellers. The light cotton drawstring skirts that many foreign women pick up in India are really sari petticoats and to wear them in the street is rather like going out half dressed. Ways of blending into the Indian background include avoiding sleeveless blouses, skirts that are too short and, of course, the bra-less look. Remember that *lungis* are the only acceptable wear for women in the state of Kerala.

Getting stared at is something which you'll have to get used to. Don't return male stares, as this will be considered a come-on; just ignore them. Dark glasses can help. Other harassment likely to be encountered includes obscene comments, touching-up and jeering, particularly by groups of youths.

Getting involved in inane conversations with men is also considered a turn-on. Keep discussions down to a necessary minimum unless you're interested in getting hassled. If you get the uncomfortable feeling he's encroaching on your space, the chances are that he is. A firm request to keep away is usually enough. Firmly return any errant limbs, put some item of luggage in between you and if all else fails, find a new spot. You're also within your rights to tell him to shove off!

When travelling on buses and trains in the south (particularly in rural Tamil Nadu), women may find men reluctant to sit next to them. Even if you offer the neighbouring seat to a man standing in the crowded aisle, it's likely that he'll shake his head and mumble something about 'getting off at the next stop'. The fact that the next stop is two hours down the track is inconsequential. Likewise, Indian women from rural areas will often stand rather than sit next to a man.

It must be said that the further you get from the heavily touristed areas, the fewer problems you'll encounter. The south is also generally more relaxed than the north.

Being a woman also has some advantages. There is often a special ladies' queue for train tickets or even a ladies' quota and ladies' compartments. One woman wrote that these ladies' carriages were often nearly empty – another said that they were full of screaming children. Special ladies' facilities are also sometimes found in cinemas and other places.

DANGERS & ANNOYANCES
Theft

Having things stolen is a problem in India, not so much because it's a theft-prone country – it isn't – but because you can become involved in a lot of hassles getting the items replaced. If your passport is stolen you may have a long trip back to an embassy to replace it. Travellers' cheques may be replaceable if stolen, but, of course, it's best to avoid theft in the first place. Always lock your room, preferably with your own padlock in cheaper hotels. Lock it at night as well; countless people have had things stolen from their rooms when they've actually been in them.

Never leave those most important valuables (passport, tickets, health certificates, money, travellers' cheques) in your room; they should be with you at all times. Either have a stout leather passport wallet on your belt, or a passport pouch under your shirt, or simply extra internal pockets in your clothing. On trains at night keep your gear near you; padlocking a bag to a luggage rack can be useful, and some of the newer trains have loops under the seats which you can chain things to. Never walk around with valuables casually slung over your shoulder. Take extra care in crowded public transport. In Bombay, for example, pickpockets are adept at the 'razor on the back pocket or shoulder bag' technique.

Thieves are particularly prevalent on train routes where there are lots of tourists. The Delhi to Agra *Shatabdi Express* service is notorious; and Delhi to Jaipur, Varanasi to Calcutta, Delhi to Bombay, Jodhpur to Jaisalmer and Agra to Varanasi are other routes to take care on. Train departure time, when the confusion and crowds are at their worst, is the time to be most careful. Just as the train is about to leave, you are distracted by someone, while his or her accomplice is stealing your bag from by your feet. Airports are another place to be careful, especially when international arrivals take place in the middle of the night, when you are unlikely to be at your most alert.

From time to time there are also drugging episodes. Travellers meet somebody on a train or bus or in a town, start talking and are then offered a cup of tea or something similar. Hours later they'd wake up with a headache and all their gear gone. The tea was full of sleeping pills. Don't accept drinks or food from strangers no matter how friendly they seem, particularly if you're on your own.

Beware also of your fellow travellers. Unhappily there are more than a few backpackers who make the money go further by helping themselves to other peoples'. At places like Goa be very careful with things on the beach – while you're in the water your camera or money can walk away very fast.

Remember that backpacks are very easy to rifle through. Don't leave valuables in them, especially during flights. Remember also that something may be of little or no value to a thief, but to lose it would be a real heartbreak to you – like film. Finally, a good travel insurance policy helps.

If you do have something stolen, you're going to have to report it to the police. You'll also need a statement proving you have done so if you want to claim on insurance. Unfortunately the police are generally less than helpful, and at times are downright unhelpful, unsympathetic and even disbelieving, implying that you are making a false claim in order to defraud your insurance company. It's also tempting to think that in some cases the police are actually operating in collusion with the thieves.

Insurance companies, despite their rosy promises of full protection and speedy settlement of claims, are just as disbelieving as the Indian police and will often attempt every devious trick in the book to avoid paying out on a baggage claim.

Stolen Travellers' Cheques If you're unlucky enough to have things stolen, some precautions can ease the pain. All travellers' cheques are replaceable but this does you little immediate good if you have to go home and apply to your bank. What you want is instant replacement. Furthermore, what do you do if you lose your cheques and money and have a day or more to travel to the replacement office? The answer is to keep an emergency cash-stash in a totally separate place. In that same place you should keep a record of the cheque serial numbers, proof of purchase slips and your passport number.

American Express make considerable noise about 'instant replacement' of their cheques but a lot of people find out, to their cost, that without a number of precautions 'instantly' can take longer than you think. If you don't have the receipt you were given when you bought the cheques, rapid replacement will be difficult. Obviously the receipt should be kept separate from the cheques, and a photocopy in yet another location doesn't hurt either. Chances are you'll be able to get a limited amount of funds on the spot, and the rest will be available when the bank has verified your initial purchase of the cheques. American Express have a 24-hour number in Delhi (☎ (011) 687-5050) which you must ring within 24 hours of the theft.

One traveller wrote that his travellers' cheques were stolen and he didn't discover the loss for a month. They had been left in his hotel room and the thief (presumably from the hotel) had neatly removed a few cheques from the centre of the cheque pouch. Explaining that sort of theft is really difficult and, of course, the thief has had plenty of time to dispose of them.

Drugs
For a long time India was a place where you could indulge in all sorts of illegal drugs

(mostly grass and hashish) with relative ease – they were cheap, readily available and the risks were minimal. These days things have changed. Although dope is still widely available, the risks have certainly increased – currently there are a number of foreigners languishing in jail in Goa awaiting trial. Many claim they are innocent and that the drugs (in most cases an insignificant amount) were planted on them.

Nevertheless, in the Indian justice system it seems the burden of proof is on the accused, and proving one's innocence is virtually impossible. The police forces are often corrupt and will pay 'witnesses' to give evidence. If convicted on a drugs-related charge, sentences are long (*minimum* of 10 years), even for minor offences, and there is no remission or parole.

So, if you partake in drugs, be aware of the risks.

VOLUNTARY WORK

Numerous charities and international aid agencies have branches in India and, although they're mostly staffed by locals, there are some opportunities for foreigners. Though it may be possible to find temporary volunteer work when you are in India, you'll probably be of more use to the charity concerned if you write in advance and, if they need you, stay for long enough to be of help. A week on a hospital ward may go a little way towards salving your own conscience but you may actually do not much more than get in the way of the people who work there long-term.

Some areas of voluntary work seem to be more attractive to volunteers than others. One traveller commented that there was no difficulty getting foreign volunteers to help with the babies in the orphanage where he was working but few came forward to work with the severely mentally handicapped adults.

For information on specific charities in India contact the main branches in your own country. For long-term posts, the following organisations may be able to help or offer advice and further contacts:

Voluntary Service Overseas (VSO)
    317 Putney Bridge Rd, London SW15 2PN, UK
    (☎ (0181) 780-2266; fax 780-1326)
International Voluntary Service (IVS)
    St John's Church Centre, Edinburgh EH2 4BJ,
    UK (☎ (0131) 226-6722)
Co-Ordinating Committee for International Voluntary Service
    c/o UNESCO, 1 rue Miollis, F-75015 Paris,
    France (☎ (01) 4568-2731)
Peace Corps of the USA
    1990 K St NW, Washington DC 20526, USA
    (☎ (202) 606-3970; fax (202) 606-3110)
Council of International Programs (CIP)
    1101 Wilson Blvd Ste 1708, Arlington VA 22209,
    USA (☎ (703) 527-1160)
Australian Volunteers Abroad: Overseas Service Bureau Programme
    PO Box 350, Fitzroy Vic 3065, Australia (☎ (03)
    9279-1788; fax (03) 9416-1619)

The Mahabodhi International Meditation Centre (PO Box 22, Leh, Ladakh, 194 101 Jammu & Kashmir state, India), which operates a residential school for poor children, requires volunteers to assist with teaching and secretarial work. Contact the centre at the above address, or through their head office: 14 Kalidas Rd, Gandhinagar, Bangalore, 560 009 (☎ (0812) 26-0684; fax 26-0292).

Mother Teresa's Missionaries of Charity headquarters, the 'Mother House', is at 54A Lower Circular Rd in Calcutta. For information about volunteering, contact the London branch: International Committee of Co-Workers (☎ (0181) 574-1892), Missionaries of Charity, 41 Villiers Rd, Southall, Middlesex, UK.

HIGHLIGHTS

India can offer almost anything you want, whether it's beaches, forts, amazing travel experiences, fantastic spectacles or even a search for yourself. Listed here are just a few of those possibilities and where to start looking.

Beaches

People generally don't come all the way to India just to laze on a beach – but there are some superb beaches if you're in that mood. On the west coast, at the southern end of

Kerala, there's Kovalam; further north, Goa has a whole collection of beautiful beaches complete with soft white sand, gentle lapping waves and swaying palms. If you find it a little overcommercialised these days then head for the tiny ex-Portuguese island of Diu off the southern coast of Saurashtra (Gujarat).

Over on the east coast you could try the beach at Mahabalipuram in Tamil Nadu. From the Shore Temple the beaches stretch north towards Madras and there are some fine places to stay. In Orissa the beach at Gopalpur-on-Sea is clean and quiet.

While they're not easily accessible, some of the beaches in the Andamans are straight out of a holiday brochure for the Caribbean – white coral sand, gin-clear water and multicoloured fish and coral.

Beach	State	Page
Kovalam	Kerala	999
-	Goa	840
Diu	Gujarat	685
Mahabalipuram	Tamil Nadu	1033
Konark	Orissa	532
Gopalpur-on-Sea	Orissa	535
-	Andaman Islands	1095

Faded Touches of the Raj

Although the British left India almost 50 years ago, there are many places where you'd hardly know it. Of course much of India's government system, bureaucracy, communications, sports (the Indians are crazy over cricket) and media are British to the core, but you'll also find the British touch in more unusual, enjoyable and amusing ways.

Could anything be more British than the Dal Lake houseboats, all chintz and overstuffed armchairs? Or the Residency at Lucknow where with stiff upper lip the British held out against the mutineers in 1857. Or relax in true British style for afternoon tea at Glenary's Tea Rooms in Darjeeling and later retire for a preprandial cocktail in front of the open fire in the lounge of the Windamere Hotel to await the gong which summons you to dinner. Or stay in fading Edwardian splendour at the Hotel Metropole in Mysore, or the twee Home Counties rural atmosphere of the Woodlands Hotel

in Udhagamandalam (Ooty). Even better is the Fernhill Palace Hotel, also in Ooty.

The Tollygunge Club in Calcutta is run by a Brit and is also a great place to stay.

Other particularly British institutions include Victoria Terminus railway station in Bombay, and the Lutyens-designed secretariat buildings in Delhi. The Naini Tal Boat Club is an old British club with a lakeside ballroom which was once the preserve of only true-blue Brits (the famous British hunter, Jim Corbett, having been born in Naini Tal, was refused membership). The Gymkhana Club in Darjeeling still has its original snooker tables, Raj ghosts and cobwebs. Perhaps more nostalgic than all these is St Paul's Cathedral (Calcutta), which is stuffed with memorials to the Brits who didn't make it home, plus a Burne-Jones stained-glass window.

Sight	Place	State	Page
Victoria Memorial	Calcutta	West Bengal	464
Tollygunge Club	Calcutta	West Bengal	474
St Paul's Cathedral	Calcutta	West Bengal	465
Glenary's Tea Rooms	Darjeeling	West Bengal	505
Windamere Hotel	Darjeeling	West Bengal	504
Gymkhana Club	Darjeeling	West Bengal	501
Mysore Palace	Mysore	Karnataka	899
Hotel Metropole	Mysore	Karnataka	902
Lalitha Palace	Mysore	Karnataka	904
Fernhill Palace	Udhagamandalam	Tamil Nadu	1089
Woodlands Hotel	Udhagamandalam	Tamil Nadu	1089
Houseboats	Dal Lake	Kashmir	318
Hotel Brijraj Bhawan	Kota	Rajasthan	604
Victoria Terminus	Bombay	Maharashtra	794
Secretariat Buildings	Delhi		221
The Residency	Lucknow	Uttar Pradesh	404
Naini Tal Boat Club	Naini Tal	Uttar Pradesh	388

Freak Centres

India has been the ultimate goal of the on-the-road hippie dream for years and somehow the 1960s still continues in India's kind climate. Goa has always been a great freak centre. The beaches are an attraction at any time of the year and every full moon is the occasion for a great gathering of the clans – but Christmas is Goa's peak period when half the freaks in India seem to flock to its beaches. There are occasional 'purges' of the Goan beaches which shouldn't worry most people, but the purist die-hards have decided this is too uncool and have moved to more remote locations.

Hill Stations

Although they may take the credit for having popularised the concept of the hill station, the British cannot claim to have invented it. Back in Mughal times the emperors were retreating into the Himalaya to avoid the searing heat of mid-summer on the plains. Their favourite spot was Kashmir.

In the 19th century, British troops exploring the country discovered that the incidence of disease was much lower in the cooler hills. In 1819 a hospital was opened in Shimla and the first hill station was established. As the British presence in India grew, other hill stations were built and it became the custom to despatch women and children to them for the summer months. They eventually developed into temporary capitals, with all the machinery of government decamping to the hills in the summer. Darjeeling was Calcutta's summer capital, and Delhi's was Shimla.

The cooler climate was certainly healthier but it seemed to infect most foreign residents with severe cases of nostalgia and they soon made their hill stations into little corners of England, building bungalows with names like 'Earl's Court', 'Windamere' and 'Windsor Cottage'. During the summer season they were great social centres with balls, theatrical performances and an endless round of dinner parties. The main thoroughfare was almost always known as The Mall and closed to all but pedestrians – as long as they were not Indian.

Today, most hill stations have become holiday resorts for middle-class Indian tourists, often on their honeymoon. Although they are dilapidated shadows of the preserves of the elite which they once were, they're nonetheless great fun to visit. The journey there is usually interesting in itself – often by narrow-gauge railway (up to Shimla, Darjeeling or Matheran, for example). Some hill stations are built around a lake, as at Naini Tal and Kodaikanal, and most have superb views and good walks along the surrounding ridges. ■

Further south at Kovalam the fine beaches attract a steady clientele. The holy lake of Pushkar in Rajasthan has a smaller, semi-permanent freak population. The technicolour Tibetan outlook on life (they've got a way with hotels and restaurants too) works well in Kathmandu so why not in India – you'll find Dharamsala and Manali, both in Himachal Pradesh, also have longer-term populations of visitors. Hampi, capital of the Vijayanagar kingdom, has only a small number of visitors but is definitely on the circuit. Finally, Puri (Orissa) and Mahabalipuram (Tamil Nadu) both have temples and beaches, a sure-fire combination.

Centre	State	Page
-	Goa	837
Pushkar	Rajasthan	595
Kovalam	Kerala	999
Dharamsala	Himachal Pradesh	278
Manali	Himachal Pradesh	294
Hampi	Karnataka	922
Puri	Orissa	524
Mahabalipuram	Tamil Nadu	1033

Colourful Events

India is a country of festivals and there are a number of places and times that are not to be missed. They start with the Republic Day Festival in Delhi each January – elephants, a procession and military might with Indian princely splendour.

Also early in the year is the Desert Festival in Jaisalmer, Rajasthan.

In June/July the great Car Festival (Rath Yatra) in Puri is another superb spectacle as the gigantic temple car of Lord Jagannath makes its annual journey, pulled by thousands of eager devotees.

In Kerala, one of the big events of the year is the Nehru Cup Snake Boat Races on the backwaters at Alappuzha (Alleppey) which takes place on the second Saturday of August.

September/October is the time to head for the hills to see the delightful Festival of the Gods in Kullu. This is part of the Dussehra Festival, which is at its most spectacular in Mysore. November is the time for the huge and colourful Camel Festival at Pushkar in Rajasthan. Finally, at Christmas where else is there to be in India than Goa?

For more information on festivals, see the Holidays section earlier and the Sacred India colour section on page 57.

Festival	Place	Page
Republic Day Festival	Delhi	116
Desert Festival	Jaisalmer (Rajasthan)	643
Car Festival	Puri (Orissa)	524
Snake Boat Races	Alappuzha (Kerala)	985
Dussehra	Mysore (Karnataka)	901
Festival of the Gods	Kullu (Himachal Pradesh)	289
Camel Fair	Pushkar (Rajasthan)	595
Christmas	Goa	840

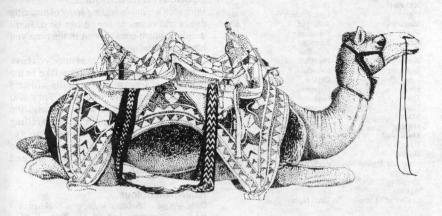

Camel at Pushkar Camel Fair, Rajasthan. Camels are still an important mode of transport in the largely desert state of Rajasthan. Camel safaris are a very popular activity among visitors to Jaisalmer in the west of the state.

Deserted Cities

There are a number of places in crowded India where great cities of the past have been deserted. Fatehpur Sikri, near Agra, is the most famous since Akbar founded, built and left this impressive centre in less than 20 years. Hampi, the centre of the Vijayanagar Empire, is equally impressive. Not too far from there are the ancient centres of Aihole and Badami. Some of the great forts that follow are also deserted cities.

Site	State	Page
Fatehpur Sikri	Uttar Pradesh	362
Hampi	Karnataka	922
Aihole & Badami	Karnataka	930

Great Forts

India has more than its share of great forts – many of them now deserted – to tell of its tumultuous history. The Red Fort in Delhi is one of the most impressive, but Agra Fort is an equally massive reminder of Mughal power at its height. A short distance south is the huge, impregnable-looking Gwalior Fort. The Rajputs could build forts like nobody else and they've got them in all shapes and sizes and with every imaginable tale to tell. Chittorgarh Fort is tragic, Bundi and Kota forts are whimsical, Jodhpur Fort is huge and high, Amber Fort simply beautiful, and Jaisalmer the essence of romance.

Way out west in Gujarat, there are the impressive forts of Junagadh and Bhuj built by the princely rulers of Saurashtra.

Further south there's Mandu, another fort impressive in its size and architecture but with a tragic tale to tell. Further south again at Daulatabad it's a tale of power, ambition and not all that much sense with another immense fort which was built and soon deserted. Important forts in the south include Bijapur and Golconda.

Naturally the European invaders had their forts too. You can see Portuguese forts in Goa, Bassein, Daman and Diu, the last being the most impressive. The British also built their share: Fort St George in Madras is open to the public and has a fascinating museum. Those built by the French, Dutch and Danes are, regrettably, largely in ruins.

Where Gandhi Went

Following the success of the film *Gandhi* you might be interested in making a Gandhi trek round India, starting at Porbandar where he was born and Rajkot where he spent the early years of his life. After his period in South Africa he returned to India and stayed in Bombay, a city he visited on numerous occasions. The massacre of 2000 peaceful protesters, one of the seminal events in the march to Independence, took place in Amritsar. For many years Gandhi had his ashram at Sabarmati, across the river from Ahmedabad. In the 1930s Gandhi established the Sevagram Ashram in Wardha, and spent more than 15 years there. Today it is a museum.

The British interned him in the Aga Khan's Palace in Pune. Finally he was assassinated in the garden of the wealthy Birla family in Delhi and his cremation took place at Raj Ghat. His ashes were scattered in the Narmada River at Jabalpur in Madhya Pradesh.

SUGGESTED ITINERARIES

With such a mind-boggling array of amazing things and places to see, it can be difficult deciding which ones to visit in the time you have available.

The following itineraries assume you have a month to spend in India. They take in the highlights of a region and hopefully will help you make the most of your time. They also assume that you don't want to spend the greater part of your time actually travelling between places – many first-time visitors to India make the mistake of trying to see too much in too short a period of time, and end up tired and frustrated.

Rajasthani Colour

Delhi – Agra – Bharatpur – Jaipur – Shekhawati – Bikaner – Jaisalmer – Jodhpur – Pushkar – Bundi – Chittorgarh – Udaipur – Aurangabad (Ajanta and Ellora caves) – Bombay.

This route gives you a taste of just about everything – Mughal architecture, including, of course, the Taj Mahal, wildlife, the desert, Hindu temples, hippie hang-outs, Rajput exuberance, unusual Islamic architecture and the superb Buddhist paintings and sculptures of the Ajanta and Ellora caves. Bombay and Delhi are both cities where you could happily spend a week, although a couple of days in each is usually all there's time for. Travel is by bus and train, except for the Udaipur to Aurangabad leg which can be flown.

Mughals, Jains & the Portuguese – India West

Delhi – Agra – Jaipur – Pushkar – Jodhpur – Ranakhpur – Udaipur – Bhuj – Rajkot – Junagadh – Sasan Gir – Diu – Palitana – Ahmedabad – Bombay.

Gujarat offers the chance to get off the well-beaten tourist circuit and is well worth any time spent there. The route takes in not only Rajasthan but also the best of what Gujarat has to offer – the tribal cultures of the Rann of Kutch in the far west of the state, the fortified town of Junagadh with some fine buildings, a history as long as your arm and the magnificent Jain temples atop Girnar

Hill, Sasan Gir – the last home of the Asian lion, Diu – the old Portuguese enclave with its beaches, Palitana – another town with hills and Jain temples, and Ahmedabad – the busy city which has, among other things, the Gandhi Ashram. Travel is by bus and train.

Hindu & Mughal Heartlands

Delhi – Jaipur – Agra – Varanasi – Khajuraho – Jhansi – Sanchi – Mandu – Aurangabad – Bombay.

Madhya Pradesh is another state that is largely untouristed but has enough places of interest to make a visit worthwhile. The Hindu temples at Khajuraho are of course the big attraction, but Sanchi and Mandu between them have fine examples of Buddhist, Hindu and Afghan architecture.

Varanasi, one of the holiest places in the country, Agra, with the incomparable Taj Mahal, and the caves of Ajanta and Ellora are other attractions on this route.

Hill Stations & the Himalaya

Delhi – Dalhousie – Dharamsala – Shimla – Manali – Leh – (Srinagar) – Delhi.

Travel in this part of the country is generally by bus and, because of the terrain, is slow. This is a good route to follow if you're in India during the summer, when the heat on the plains becomes unbearable, and in fact the road from Manali to Leh is only open for a couple of months a year when the snow melts.

The hill stations of Shimla and Dalhousie hark back to an era that is rapidly being consigned to history; Dharamsala is a fascinating cultural centre, being the home of the exiled Tibetan leader His Holiness the Dalai Lama; Manali in the Kullu Valley is simply one of the most beautiful places in the country, while the two-day bus trip from there to Leh, high on the Tibetan Plateau, is incredibly rough but equally memorable – it's one of the highest motorable roads in the world. Leh is the capital of Ladakh and centre for another unique Himalayan culture. If troubled Kashmir has once again become stable, a visit to Srinagar and the houseboats

on Dal Lake is mandatory; otherwise there are direct flights from Leh back to Delhi.

Trekkers and adventure seekers are well catered for at various places on this route. From Manali there are literally dozens of treks, ranging from a couple of days to a couple of weeks, into places such as the remote Zanskar Valley. Leh, too, is a centre for trekkers, and the Markha Valley is a popular trip. Trekking agencies in both Manali and Leh can arrange everything, or you can strike out on your own.

Palaces, Temples & Holy Cities

Delhi – Jaipur – Agra – Jhansi – Khajuraho – Jabalpur – Kanha – Varanasi – Calcutta.

Starting from Delhi, this route gives you a taste of Rajasthan and includes the Taj Mahal. Jhansi is the station for the bus journey to the famous temples of Khajuraho, but it's worth stopping at Orchha, 18 km from Jhansi, to see this well-preserved old city of palaces and temples. From Khajuraho, a three-hour bus journey brings you to Satna for trains to Jabalpur. A boat trip through the Marble Rocks is the main attraction here. Next stop is Kanha National Park where the chances of seeing a tiger are good, and then it's back to Jabalpur to pick up a train to the holy city of Varanasi. There are direct trains from here to Calcutta, one of the most fascinating cities in the country.

Flight-Pass Route

Delhi – Agra – Khajuraho – Varanasi – Bhubaneswar – Calcutta – Andaman & Nicobar Islands – Darjeeling (Bagdogra) – Delhi.

With a US$500 flight pass, distance becomes no object and you can visit as many places as you like, within three weeks. This suggested itinerary links a number of the more exotic and distant places as well as 'musts' like the Taj. From Delhi fly to Agra, on to Khajuraho the next day and continue to Varanasi two days later. Next stop is the temple city of Bhubaneswar before taking the flight to Calcutta. An early-morning departure brings you to Port Blair, the capital of the

Andaman & Nicobar Islands, for four or five days at this rarely visited tropical paradise. On the day you leave, you may have watched the sun rise over the ocean but you'll see it set over the Himalaya in Darjeeling, after a change of planes in Calcutta.

Temples & Ancient Monuments – Central & South India

Madras – Kanchipuram – Mahabalipuram – Pondicherry – Kumbakonam – Thanjavur – Tiruchirappalli – Madurai – Kodaikanal – Udhagamandalam (Ooty) – Mysore – Bangalore – Belur/Halebid/Sravanabelagola – Hampi – Badami – Bijapur – Bombay.

This route takes in a small slice of modern India plus a popular travellers' beach resort, a glimpse of ex-French India along with Auroville, and several days in the mountains bordering Tamil Nadu and Kerala. Transport is by train and bus plus the use of a one-day tourist development corporation bus ex-Mysore or ex-Bangalore to the temple towns of Belur, Halebid and Sravanabelagola.

Temples & Beaches – South India

Madras – Mahabalipuram – Pondicherry – Thanjavur – Tiruchirappalli – Madurai – Kanyakumari – Thiruvananthapuram – Kovalam Beach – Kollam – Alappuzha – Kochi – Bangalore & Mysore – Hampi – Bijapur – Bombay.

This route, a variation of the above, gives you a much broader perspective of southern India and takes you through the tropical paradise of Kerala with its beaches, backwaters, Kathakali dance-dramas and historical Indo-European associations. Yet it also includes some of the major temple complexes of Tamil Nadu, the palaces of Mysore, the Vijayanagar ruins of Hampi and the Muslim splendour of Bijapur. Transport is by train, bus and boat. If time is getting short by the time you reach Bangalore, flights are available from there to Bombay.

ACCOMMODATION

India has a very wide range of accommodation possibilities apart from straightforward hotels.

Youth Hostels

Indian youth hostels (HI – Hostelling International) are generally very cheap and sometimes in excellent condition with superb facilities. They are, however, often some distance from the town centres. You are not usually required to be a YHA (HI) member (as in other countries) to use the hostels, although your YHA/HI card will generally get you a lower rate. The charge is typically Rs 15 for members, Rs 20 for non-members. Nor do the usual rules about arrival and departure times, lights-out or not using the hostel during the day apply. A list of official hostels includes:

Delhi
    Youth Hostel, 5 Nyaya Marg, Chanakyapuri (☎ (011) 301-6285)
Goa
    Youth Hostel, Panaji (☎ 45-433)
Gujarat
    Youth Hostel, Sector 16, Gandhinagar (☎ (02712) 22-364)
Himachal Pradesh
    Youth Hostel, Bus Stand, Dalhousie
Jammu & Kashmir
    Patnitop Youth Hostel, c/o Tourist Office, Kud
Maharashtra
    Youth Hostel, Padampura, Station Rd, Aurangabad (☎ (02432) 29-801)
Orissa
    Youth Hostel, Sea Beach, Puri (☎ (06752) 22-42424)
Rajasthan
    Youth Hostel, SMS Stadium, Bhagwandas Rd, Jaipur (☎ 67-576)
Tamil Nadu
    Youth Hostel, Indira Nagar, Madras (☎ (044) 41-2882)
    Youth Hostel, Solaithandam Kuppam, Pondicherry
Uttar Pradesh
    Youth Hostel, Malli Tal near Ardwell Camp, The Mall, Naini Tal (☎ (05942) 2513)
    Mahatma Gandhi Rd, Agra
West Bengal
    Darjeeling Youth Hostel, 16 Dr Zakir Hussain Rd, Darjeeling (☎ (0354) 2290)

There are also some state government youth hostels. In Tamil Nadu, for example, there are state hostels in Mahabalipuram, Madras, Rameswaram, Kanyakumari, Kodaikanal, Mudumalai and Ooty.

Government Accommodation

Back in the days of the British Raj, a whole string of government-run accommodation units were set up with labels like Rest Houses, Dak Bungalows, Circuit Houses, PWD (Public Works Department) Bungalows, Forest Rest Houses and so on. Today most of these are reserved for government officials, although in some places they may still be available for tourists, if there is room. In an approximate pecking order the dak bungalows are the most basic; they often have no electricity and only essential equipment in out-of-the-way places. Rest houses are next up and at the top of the tree comes the circuit houses, which are strictly for travelling VIPs.

Tourist Bungalows

Usually run by the state government, tourist bungalows often serve as replacements for the older government-run accommodation units. Tourist bungalows are generally excellent value, although they vary enormously in facilities and level of service offered.

They often have dorm beds as well as rooms – typical prices are around Rs 30 to Rs 40 for a dorm bed, and Rs 100 to Rs 250 for a double room. The rooms have a fan, two beds and bathroom; more expensive air-con

Great Places to Stay

India has some superb hotels – it's also got a large number of bug-infested filthy dumps and a fair number of 'international class' hotels which are mediocre in standards and service but decidedly 1st class in price. But it's hard to think of a more enchanting hotel than the Lake Palace in Udaipur – it's far more than merely a palace; elegant, whimsical and romantic are all labels that can be applied to it. In fact all over Rajasthan there are palaces and forts owned by the former rulers of the princely states – or their nobles – and many of these have been turned into hotels and are excellent places to stay. Samode, Bharatpur, Mandawa, Jodhpur, Bikaner, Mt Abu and Jaipur all have palace-hotels.

In Kashmir (assuming it's safe), staying on a houseboat is one of the main reasons for going there; they come in all price ranges, from the rock-bottom 'doonga boats' to 'five-star' luxury complete with TV.

In Bombay the elegant Taj Mahal Intercontinental Hotel is probably the best in India – even if you don't stay there its air-conditioned lounge and strategic location are a magnet for everyone from backpackers on up.

Further south in the ex-princely state of Mysore (now Karnataka), are the Hotel Metropole and the Ashok Radisson Lalitha Palace Hotel at Mysore city. In Udhagamandalam, there's the Fernhill Palace Hotel.

There are some very fine tourist bungalows, run by the state government tourist offices, scattered around India. They're often in fine locations and usually great value.

Backpackers' favourites include the wonderful old Broadlands in Madras and the equally well-kept Z Hotel in Puri. In Kochi (Cochin) the Bolgatty Palace Hotel is an old Dutch Palace built in 1744 and later a British Residency – now a relatively cheap hotel. The Hotel Sheesh Mahal, in a wing of the Jehangir Mahal palace in Orchha, is definitely worth a visit.

The Tollygunge Club in Calcutta is still run by a Brit and is an amazing place to stay. The clubhouse was once the mansion at the centre of a large indigo plantation, now a championship golfcourse. Sitting by the swimming pool here, with a cold beer or an excellent club sandwich, it's hard to believe you're still in Calcutta. Tolly (as it's affectionately called) is now the playground of the city's elite.

Hotel	Place	Page
Lake Palace Hotel	Udaipur (Rajasthan)	620
Houseboats	Dal Lake (Kashmir)	318
Taj Mahal Intercontinental	Bombay (Maharashtra)	788
Broadlands Hotel	Madras (Tamil Nadu)	1016
Fernhill Palace Hotel	Udhagamandalam (Tamil Nadu)	1089
Hotel Metropole	Mysore (Karnataka)	904
Lalitha Palace Hotel	Mysore (Karnataka)	904
Z Hotel	Puri (Orissa)	529
Bolgatty Palace Hotel	Kochi (Cochin; Kerala)	972
Sheesh Mahal	Orchha (Madhya Pradesh)	725
Bikaner House (Palace Hotel)	Mt Abu (Rajasthan)	631
Tollygunge Club	Calcutta (West Bengal)	474

rooms are often also available. Generally there's a restaurant or 'dining hall' and often a bar. Particularly good tourist bungalows can be found in Tamil Nadu (where they are known as Hotel Tamil Nadu), in Karnataka (Hotel Mayura) and in Rajasthan, although almost every state has some towns where the tourist bungalow is definitely the best place to stay. Their biggest drawback is that, in common with state-run companies virtually anywhere, the staff may be less than 100% motivated – in some cases they are down-right lazy and rude – and maintenance is not what it might be.

In tourist bungalows, as in many other government-run institutions in India, such as the railways, you will find a curiously Indian institution: the 'complaints book'. In this you can write your complaints and periodically someone higher up the chain of command comes along, reads the terrible tales and the tourist bungalow manager gets his knuckles rapped. In disputes or other arguments, calling for the complaints book is the angry customer's best weapon; it's the one thing which minions seem to be genuinely afraid of. In many places the complaints book can provide interesting and amusing reading.

Railway Retiring Rooms

These are just like regular hotels or dormitories except they are at the railway stations. To stay here you are generally supposed to have a railway ticket or Indrail Pass. The rooms are, of course, extremely convenient if you have an early train departure, although they can be noisy if it is a busy station. They are often very cheap and in some places they are also excellent value. Some stations have retiring rooms of definite Raj pretensions, with huge rooms and enough furniture to do up a flat or apartment back home. They are usually excellent value, if a little institutional in feel, and are let on a 24-hour basis. The main problem is getting a bed, as they are very popular and often full.

Railway Waiting Rooms

For emergency accommodation when all else fails or when you just need a few hours rest before your train departs at 2 am, waiting rooms are a free place to rest your weary head. The trick is to rest it in the (usually empty) 1st-class waiting room and not the crowded 2nd-class one. Officially you need a 1st-class ticket to be allowed to use the 1st-class room and its superior facilities. In practice, luck, a 2nd-class Indrail Pass or simply your foreign appearance may work. In some places your ticket will be checked.

Cheap Hotels

There are cheap hotels all over India, ranging from filthy, uninhabitable dives (but with prices at rock bottom) up to quite reasonable places in both standards and prices. Ceiling fans, mosquito nets on the beds, private toilets and bathrooms are all possibilities, even in rooms which cost Rs 120 or less per night for a double.

Throughout India hotels are defined as 'Western' or 'Indian'. The differentiation is basically meaningless, although expensive hotels are always Western, cheap ones Indian. 'Indian' hotels will be more simply and economically furnished but the acid test is the toilet. 'Western' hotels have a sit-up-style toilet; 'Indian' ones usually (but not always) have the traditional Asian squat style. You can find modern, well-equipped, clean places with Indian toilets and dirty, dismal dumps with Western toilets. Some places even have the weird hybrid toilet, which is basically a Western toilet with foot-pads on the edge of the bowl!

Although prices are generally quoted in this book for singles and doubles, most hotels will put an extra bed in a room to make a triple for about an extra 25%. In some smaller hotels it's often possible to bargain a little if you really want to. On the other hand these places will often put their prices up if there's a shortage of accommodation.

Many hotels, and not only the cheap ones, operate on a 24-hour system. This can be convenient if you check in at 8 pm, as it gives you until 8 pm the following day to check out. Conversely, if you arrive at 8 am one day it can be a nuisance to have to be on the streets again by 8 am the next day. There are, however, considerable regional variations. Some hotels maintain a noon checkout; hill stations often operate on a 9 am (or even 7 am!) checkout. Make sure you know the checkout time at your hotel. Some hotels will offer a half-day rate if you want to stay a few extra hours.

Expensive Hotels

You won't find 'international standard' hotels throughout India. The big, air-conditioned, swimming-pool places are generally confined to the major tourist centres and the large cities. There are a number of big hotel chains in India. The Taj Group has some of India's flashiest hotels, including the luxurious Taj Mahal Intercontinental in Bombay, the romantic Rambagh Palace in Jaipur and the Lake Palace in Udaipur. Other interesting hotels are the Taj Coromandel in Madras, the Fort Aguada Beach Resort in Goa, and the Malabar Hotel in Kochi (Cochin). The Oberoi chain is, of course, well known outside India as well as within. Clarks is a small chain with popular hotels in Varanasi and Agra, amongst other places. The Welcomgroup (affiliated with Sheraton), the Ritz chain, the Casino chain and the Air India-associated Centaur hotels are other chains.

Other chains include the government-operated ITDC group which usually append the name 'Ashok' to their hotels. There's an Ashok hotel in virtually every town in India, so that test isn't foolproof, but the ITDC places include a number of smaller (but higher-standard) units in places like Sanchi or Konark where accommodation possibilities are limited. The ITDC has been under attack in India for some time about its overall inefficient operation, financial losses and poor standards in its hotels. Privatisation was mooted at one stage as a way of raising capital and improving service, but this is still yet to happen and standards remain unchanged.

Most expensive hotels operate on a noon checkout basis.

You may be able to negotiate a discount on air-con rooms in December and January since air-con often isn't necessary then.

Home Stays

Staying with an Indian family can be a real education. It's a change from dealing strictly with tourist-oriented people, and the differences and curiosities of everyday Indian life can be very interesting.

Home-stay accommodation is organised on an official basis in Rajasthan, and then only in the cities of Jaipur, Jodhpur and Udaipur. The cost is anything from Rs 150 upwards, depending on the level of facilities offered. The tourist offices in the three cities have comprehensive lists of the families offering this service. It's known as the Paying Guest Scheme and is administered by the Rajasthan Tourism Development Corporation. In Madras and Bombay it is known as Paying Guest Accommodation.

Other Possibilities

There are YMCAs and YWCAs in many of the big cities – some of these are modern, well equipped and cost about the same as a mid-range hotel (but are still good value). There are also a few Salvation Army Hostels – in particular in Bombay, Calcutta and Madras. There are a few camping places around India, but travellers with their own vehicles can almost always find hotels with gardens where they can park and camp.

Free accommodation is available at some Sikh temples where there is a tradition of hospitality to visitors. It can be interesting to try one, but please don't abuse this hospitality and spoil it for other travellers.

At many pilgrimage sites there are *dharamsalas* and *choultries*, places which offer accommodation to pilgrims, and travellers are often welcome to use these. This particularly applies at isolated sites like Ranakhpur in Rajasthan. The drawback here (especially with Jain choultries) is that no leather articles are allowed inside.

Taxes & Service Charges

Most state governments impose a variety of taxes on hotel accommodation (and restaurants). At most rock-bottom hotels you won't have to pay any taxes. Once you get into the top end of budget places, and certainly for mid-range accommodation, you will have to pay something. As a general rule, you can assume that room rates over about Rs 250 will attract a 10% (sometimes just 5%) tax. Most mid-range and all luxury hotels attract a 10% loading.

Another common tax, which is additional to the above, is a service charge which is pegged at 10%. In some hotels, this is only levied on food, room service and use of telephones, not on the accommodation costs. At others, it's levied on the total bill. If you're trying to keep costs down, don't sign up meals or room service to your room bill and keep telephone use to a minimum if you know that service charge is levied on the total bill.

Rates quoted in this book are the basic rate only unless otherwise indicated. Taxes and service charges are extra.

Seasonal Variations

In popular tourist places (hill stations, beaches and the Delhi-Agra-Rajasthan triangle), hoteliers crank up their prices in the high season by a factor of two to three times the low-season price.

The definition of the high and low seasons obviously varies depending on location. For the beaches and the Delhi-Agra-Rajasthan triangle it's basically a month before and two months after Christmas. In the hill stations and Kashmir, it's usually April to July when the lowlands are unbearably hot. In some locations and at some hotels, there are even higher rates for the brief Christmas/New Year period, or during major festivals such as Diwali and Dussehra.

Conversely, in the low season(s), prices at even normally expensive hotels can be surprisingly reasonable.

Touts

Hordes of accommodation touts operate in many towns in India – Agra, Jaipur and Varanasi in particular – and at any international airport terminal. Very often they are the rickshaw-wallahs who meet you at the bus or railway station. The technique is simple – they take you to hotel A and rake off a commission for taking you there rather than to hotel B. The problem with this procedure is that you may well end up not at the place you want to go to but at the place that pays the best commission. Some very good cheap hotels simply refuse to pay the touts and you'll then hear lots of stories about the hotel you want being 'full', 'closed for repairs', 'no good any more' or even 'flooded'. Nine chances out of 10 they will be just that – stories.

Touts do have a use though – if you arrive in a town when some big festival is on, or during peak season, finding a place to stay can be very difficult. Hop in a rickshaw, tell the driver in what price range you want a hotel, and off you go. The driver will know which places have rooms available and unless the search is a long one you shouldn't have to pay the driver too much. Remember that he will be getting a commission from the hotel too.

FOOD

Despite the very fine meals that can be prepared in India, you'll often find food a great disappointment. In many smaller centres there is not a wide choice and you'll get bored with rice, mushy vegetables and dhal. When you're in larger cities where the food can be excellent, take advantage of it.

Contrary to popular belief, not all Hindus are officially vegetarians. Strict vegetarianism is confined more to the south, which has not had the meat-eating influence of the Aryan and later Muslim invasions, and also to the Gujarati community. For those who do eat meat, it is not always a pleasure to do so in India – the quality tends to be low (most chickens give the impression that they died from starvation) and the hygiene is not all that it might be. Beef, from the holy cow, is strictly taboo of course – and leads to interesting Indian dishes like the mutton-burger. Where steak is available, it's usually buffalo and found only in Muslim restaurants. Pork is equally taboo to the Muslims and is generally only available in areas where there are significant Christian communities (such as Goa), or among the Tibetans in Himachal Pradesh and Sikkim. If you're a non-vegetarian you'll end up eating a lot more vegetarian food in India.

Although you could travel throughout India and not eat a single curry, Indian interpretations of Western cuisine can be pretty horrific; in smaller places it's usually best to stick to Indian food.

Meals served on trains are usually palatable and reasonably cheap. At most stops you will be besieged by food and drink sellers. Even in the middle of the night that raucous cry of 'Chai! Chai!' or 'Ah, coffeecoffeecoffee!' will inevitably break into your sleep. The sheer bedlam of an Indian station when a train is in is a part of India you never forget.

If, after some time in India, you do find the food is getting you down physically or psychologically, there are a couple of escapes. It is very easy for budget travellers to lose weight in India and feel lethargic and drained of energy. The answer is to increase your protein intake – eat more eggs, which are readily available. It also helps to eat more fruit and nuts, so buy bananas, mandarin oranges or peanuts, all easily found at stations or in the markets. Many travellers carry multi-vitamins with them. Another answer, if you're travelling on a budget, is to occasionally splash out on a meal in a fancy hotel or restaurant – compared to what you have been paying it may seem amazingly expensive, but try translating the price into what it would cost at home.

There are considerable regional variations from north to south, partly because of climatic conditions and partly because of historical influences. In the north, as already mentioned, much more meat is eaten and the cooking is often 'Mughal style' (often spelt 'Mughlai') which bears a closer relationship to food of the Middle East and central Asia. The emphasis is more on spices and less on chilli. In the north, grains and breads are eaten far more than rice.

In the south more rice is eaten, there is more vegetarian food, and the curries tend to be hotter – sometimes very hot. Another feature of southern vegetarian food is that you do not use eating utensils; food is always eaten with fingers (of the right hand only). Scooping up food that way takes a little practice but you soon become quite adept at it. It is said that eating this way allows you to get the 'feel' of the food, as important to south Indian cuisine as the aroma or arrangement are to other cooking styles. It also offers the added protection that you never need worry if the eating utensils have been properly washed.

In the most basic Indian restaurants and eating places, known as *dhabas* or *bhojanalyas*, the cooking is usually done right out the front so you can see exactly what is going on and how it is done. Vegetables will be on the simmer all day and tend to be overcooked and mushy to Western tastes. In these basic places *dhal* (curried lentil gravy) is usually free but you pay for *chapatis, parathas, puris* or rice. Vegetable preparations, dhal and a few chapatis make a passable meal for around Rs 15. If you order half-plates of the various dishes brewing out the front you get half the quantity at half the price and get a little more variety. With chutneys and a small plate of onions, which come free, you can put together a reasonable vegetarian meal for Rs 30, or non-vegetarian for Rs 40. In railway station restaurants and other cheaper restaurants always check the prices and add up your bill. If it's incorrect, query it.

At the other end of the price scale there are many restaurants in India's five-star hotels that border on the luxurious and by Western standards are absurdly cheap. Paying US$10 to US$15 for a meal in India seems exorbitant after you've been there for a while, but check what a meal in your friendly local Hilton would cost you. Many of the international-standard hotels, like the Malabar Hotel in Kochi (Cochin), the Taj Mahal Intercontinental in Bombay, the Connemara in Madras and the Umaid Bhawan Palace in Jodhpur offer all-you-can-eat buffet deals. One place to which *every* traveller goes for a splurge is the Lake Palace in Udaipur where, for around US$10, you can treat yourself to a range of dishes in one of India's most luxurious settings – including a dance show and the boat fare. For budget travellers it makes a very pleasant change from dhal and rice.

Finally, a couple of hints on how to cope with curry. After a while in India you'll get used to even the fiercest curries and will find Western food surprisingly bland. If, however, you do find your mouth is on fire don't reach for water; in emergencies that hardly helps at all. Curd *(dahin,* yoghurt) or fruit do the job much more efficiently.

Curry & Spice

Believe it or not, there is no such thing as 'curry' in India. It's an English invention, an all-purpose term to cover the whole range of Indian food spicing. *Carhi,* incidentally, is a Gujarati dish, but never ask for it in Kumaon where it's a very rude word!

Although all Indian food is certainly not curry, this is the basis of Indian cuisine. Curry doesn't have to be hot enough to blow your head off, although it can if it's made that way. Curry most definitely is not something found in a packet of curry powder. Indian cooks have about 25 spices on their regular list and it is from these that they produce the curry flavour. Normally the spices are freshly ground in a mortar and pestle known as a *sil-vatta.* Spices are usually blended in certain combinations to produce *masalas* (mixes). *Garam masala* ('hot mix'), for example, is a combination of cloves, cinnamon, cardamom, coriander, cumin and peppercorns.

Popular spices include saffron, an expensive flavouring produced from the stamens of certain crocus flowers. This is used to give rice that yellow colouring and delicate fragrance. (It's an excellent buy in India, where a one-gram packet costs around Rs 35 – you'll pay about 10 times more at home.) Turmeric also has a colouring property, acts as a preservative and has a distinctive smell and taste. Chillies are ground, dried or added whole to supply the heat. They come in red and green varieties but the green ones are the

hottest. Ginger is supposed to be good for the digestion, while many masalas contain coriander because it is said to cool the body. Strong and sweet cardamom are used in many desserts and in rich meat dishes. Other popular spices and flavourings include nutmeg, poppy seeds, caraway seeds, fenugreek, mace, garlic, cloves, bay leaves and curry leaves.

Breads & Grains

Rice is, of course, the basic Indian staple, but although it is eaten throughout the country, it's all-important only in the south. The best Indian rice, it is generally agreed, is found in the north where Basmati rice grows in the Dehra Dun Valley. It has long grains, is yellowish and has a slightly sweetish or *'bas'* smell. In the north (where wheat is the staple) rice is supplemented by a whole range of breads known as *rotis* or *chapatis.* In the Punjab a roti is called *phulka/fulka.* Western-style white sliced bread is widely available, and it's generally pretty good.

Indian breads are varied but always delicious. Simplest is the chapati/roti, which is simply a mixture of flour and water cooked on a hotplate known as a *tawa.* Direct heat blows them up but how well that works depends on the gluten content of the wheat. A *paratha* is also cooked on the hotplate but ghee is used and the bread is rolled in a different way. There are also parathas that have been stuffed with peas or potato. Deep-fried bread which puffs up is known as a *puri* in the north and a *luchi* in the east. Bake the bread in a clay (tandoori) oven and you have *naan.* However you make them, Indian breads taste great. Use your chapati or paratha to mop or scoop up your curry.

Found all over India, but originating from the south, are *dosas.* These are basically paper-thin pancakes made from lentil and rice flour. Curried vegetables wrapped inside a dosa makes it a *masala dosa* – a terrific snack meal. An *idli* is a kind of south Indian rice dumpling, often served with a spicy curd sauce *(dahin idli)* or with spiced lentils and chutney. They're a popular breakfast dish in the south. *Papadams* are crispy deep-fried lentil-flour wafers often served with *thalis* or other meals. An *uttapam* is like a dosa.

Outside the Delhi Jama Masjid, you may see 'big' chapatis known as *rumali roti* (handkerchief bread). Note that Hindus use their tawa concavely, Muslims convexly!

Basic Dishes

Curries can be vegetable, meat (usually chicken or lamb) or fish, but they are always fried in ghee (clarified butter) or vegetable oil. North or south they will be accompanied by rice, but in the north you can also choose from the range of breads.

There are a number of dishes which aren't really curries but are close enough to them for Western tastes. *Vindaloos* have a vinegar marinade and tend to be hotter than most curries. Pork vindaloo is a favourite dish in Goa. *Kormas*, on the other hand, are rich, substantial dishes prepared by braising. There are both meat and vegetable kormas. *Navratan korma* is a very tasty dish using nuts, while a *malai kofta* is a rich, cream-based dish. *Dopiaza* literally means 'two onions' and is a type of korma which uses onions at two stages in its preparation.

Probably the most basic of Indian dishes is dhal. Dhal is almost always there, whether as an accompaniment to a curry or as a very basic meal in itself with chapatis or rice. In the very small rural towns dhal and rice is just about all there is on the menu. The favourite dhal of Bengal and Gujarat is yellow *arhar*, whereas in Punjab it is *black urad*. The common green lentils are called *moong*; *rajmaa* (kidney beans) is the Heinz 57 varieties of dhal!

Other basic dishes include *mattar panir* – peas and cheese in gravy; *saag gosht* – spinach and meat; *aalu dum* – potato curry; *palak panir* – spinach and cheese; and *aalu chhole* – diced potatoes and spicy-sour chickpeas. Some other vegetables include *paat gobi* (cabbage), *phuul gobi* (cauliflower), *baingan* (eggplant or brinjal) and *mattar* (peas).

Indian Menus

One of the delights of Indian menus is their amazing English. Start the morning, for example, with corn flaks, also useful for shooting down enemy aircraft. Or perhaps corn flex – Indian corn flakes are often so soggy they'll do just that.

Even before your corn-whatever you should have some tea, and what a variety of types of tea India can offer. You can try bed tea, milk tea, light tea, ready tea, mixed tea, tray tea, plain tea, half set tea and even (of course) full set tea. Eggs also offer unlimited possibilities: half-fried eggs, pouch eggs (or egg pooch), bolid eggs, scimbled eggs, skamal and egg tost, sliced omelettes, skerem boil eggs (interesting combination there), bread omelt, or simply aggs. Finally, you could finish off breakfast with that popular Scottish dish – pordge, or maybe porch with hunney.

Soup before a meal – how about French onion soap, or that old favourite crap soup? Or Scotch brath, mughutoni, or perhaps start with a parn coactale. Follow that up with some amazing interpretations of Western dishes, like the restaurant that not only had Napoleon spaghetti but also Stalin spaghetti! Perhaps a seezling plator or vegetable augrotten sounds more like it? Or simply a light meal – well, why not have a sandwitch or a vegetable pup? Feeling strong – then try a carate salad, or a vegetable cutlass.

Chickens come in for some pretty amazing treatment too, with chicken buls, bum chicken, chicken cripes, chicken manure, chicken merrylens and possibly the all-time classic: chicken katan blueinside chess – no, I don't have any idea what it is either!

If you want a drink how about orange squish or that popular Indian soft drink Thumps Up.

Chinese dishes offer a whole new range of possibilities, including mashrooms and bamboo sooghts, spring rolos, American chopsy, vege chapsey, Chinies snakes, vegetable chop off, vegetable nuddles, plane fried rice and park fried rice.

Finally for dessert you could try apple pai, apple filter, sweet pannking with hanni or banana panecake, or treat yourself to leeches & cream, or even semenolina pudding!

Travellers have sent in lots more menu suggestions since the first edition of this book, like tired fruit juice (tinned you know), plane tost (the stuff they serve on Indian Airlines?), omlet & began, two eggs any shape, loose curds, curds bath, tomatoe stuff, scram bled eggs, chicken poodle soup, screambled eggs, banana frilters, pain-apple cream and chocolet padding. Or something even Colonel Sanders hasn't thought of yet – fried children. ■

Tandoori & Biryani

Tandoori food is a northern speciality and refers to the clay oven in which the food is cooked after first being marinated in a complex mix of herbs and yoghurt. Tandoori chicken is a favourite. This food is not as hot as curry dishes and usually tastes terrific.

Biryani (again chicken is a popular biryani dish) is another northern Mughal dish. The meat is mixed with a deliciously flavoured, orange-coloured rice which is sometimes spiced with nuts or dried fruit. A Kashmiri biryani is basically fruit salad with rice.

A *pulao* is flavoured rice often with pulses and with or without meat. You will also find it in other Asian countries further west. Those who have the idea that Indian food is always curry and always fiery hot will be surprised by tandoori and biryani dishes.

Regional Specialities

Rogan josh is straightforward lamb curry, always popular in the north and in Kashmir where it originated. *Gushtaba*, pounded and spiced meatballs cooked in a yoghurt sauce, is another Kashmiri speciality. Still in the north, *chicken makhanwala* is a rich dish cooked in a butter sauce.

Many coastal areas have excellent seafood, including Bombay where the *pomfret*, a flounder-like fish, is popular; so is Bombay duck, which is not a duck at all but another fish dish. *Dhansaak* is a Parsi speciality found in Bombay – lamb or chicken cooked with curried lentils and steamed rice. Further south, Goa has excellent fish and prawns; in Kerala, Kochi (Cochin) is famous for its prawns.

Another indication of the influence of central Asian cooking styles on north Indian food is the popularity of kababs. You'll find them all across north India with a number of local variations and specialities. The two basic forms are *seekh* (skewered) or *shami* (wrapped). In Calcutta *kati kababs* are a local favourite. Another Bengali dish is *dahin maach* – curried fish in yoghurt sauce, flavoured with ginger and turmeric. Further south in Hyderabad you could try *haleen*, pounded wheat with a lightly spiced mutton gravy.

Lucknow is famous for its wide range of kebabs and for *dum pukht* – the 'art' of steam pressure cooking, in which meat and vegetables are cooked in a sealed clay pot.

Side Dishes

Indian food generally has a number of side dishes to go with the main meal. Probably the most popular is *dahin* – curd or yoghurt. It has the useful ability of instantly cooling a fiery curry – either blend it into the curry or, if it's too late, you can administer it straight to your mouth. Curd is often used in the cooking or as a dessert and appears in the popular drink *lassi*. *Raita* is another popular side dish consisting of curd mixed with cooked or raw vegetables, particularly cucumber (similar to Greek *tzatziki)* or tomato.

No-Name Confusion

A really good place to eat, so we were told, was the tea house near the end of the street. Apparently it had no name but we'd recognise it by the tables in the garden. Sure enough, we found it and sat down in the well-tended garden. Service obviously wasn't a strong point at this restaurant as there was no-one about. Eventually a man appeared and asked us (rather curtly, we thought) what we wanted. We ordered dhal, chapatis and omelettes and he was gone for a very long time. When he came out again I said we had a train to catch so could he please hurry up. Without a reply he served the food and stomped off inside. Finishing the meal (which was none too good) I asked for the bill and he said 'Rs 100' which was rather high. I told him so and he took a deep breath, as if trying to keep his temper, and said: 'Sir, you are a very rude man! You enter my house, ask for food, complain about the delay when I have to send out my bearer to fetch it and then tell me I am robbing you!'

The restaurant, of course, was further down the street!

Chris Jenney, UK

An Interesting Breakfast
Arriving after midnight, we found the railway retiring rooms full, so we laid out our sleeping-bags on the deserted platform. It had been a long, hard journey and we fell asleep immediately. We woke to find the station crowded and a waiter standing over us enquiring as to what we'd like for breakfast. We said we'd come to the refreshment room in a few minutes, but no, he insisted that we stay put and he'd bring us breakfast in bed. Ten minutes later he reappeared with trays laden with cornflakes, eggs, toast and coffee and stood by as we breakfasted under the feet of the early-morning commuters!

A brilliant start to the day apart from the fact that the cornflakes had been fried in ghee!

Chris Jenney, UK

Sabzi is curried vegetables, and *baingan bharta* is a puréed eggplant dish. *Mulliga-tawny* is a soup-like dish which is really just a milder, more liquid curry. It's a dish adopted into the English menu by the Raj. Chutney is pickled fruit or vegetables and is the standard relish for a curry.

Thalis

A *thali* is the all-purpose Indian dish. Although it is basically a product of south India, you will find restaurants serving thalis or 'plate meals' (veg or non-veg) all over India. Often the sign will simply announce 'Meals'. In addition, there are regional variations like the particularly sumptuous and sweet Gujarati thalis.

The name is taken from the 'thali' dish in which the meal is served. This consists of a metal plate with a number of small metal bowls known as *katoris* on it. Sometimes the small bowls will be replaced by simple indentations in the plate; in more basic places the 'plate' will be a big, fresh banana leaf. A thali consists of a variety of curry vegetable dishes, relishes, a couple of papadams, puris or chapatis and a mountain of rice. A fancy thali may have a *pataa*, a rolled leaf stuffed with fruit and nuts. There'll probably be a bowl of curd and possibly even a small dessert or paan.

Thalis are consistently tasty and good food value, but they have two other unbeatable plus points for the budget traveller – they're cheap and they're usually 100% filling. Thalis can be as little as Rs 8 and will rarely cost much more than Rs 30 at the very most, though Gujarati thalis are the exception and you'll consistently be paying Rs 35 to Rs 40 for these at reasonable restaurants. Most are 100% filling because they're normally 'all you can eat'. When your plate starts to look empty they come round, add another mountain of rice and refill the katoris. Thalis are eaten with fingers, although you may get a spoon for the curd or dhal. Always wash your hands before you eat one – a sink or other place to wash your hands is provided in a thali restaurant.

Snacks

Samosas are curried vegetables fried in a pastry triangle. They are very tasty and are found all over India. *Bhujias* or *pakoras* are bite-size pieces of vegetable dipped in chickpea flour batter and deep-fried. Along with samosas they're the most popular snack food in the country.

Bhelpuri is a popular Bombay snack peddled across the city, and always found in holiday resort towns around the country. *Channa* is spiced chick-peas *(gram)* served with small puris. *Sambhar* is a soup-like lentil and vegetable dish with a sour tamarind flavour. *Chaat* is the general term for snacks, while *namkin* is the name for the various spiced nibbles that are sold prepackaged – although one waiter I encountered referred to them as 'bitings'.

Western Food

Sometimes Indian food simply becomes too much and you want to escape to something familiar and reassuring. The Indian-food blues are particularly prone to hit at breakfast time – somehow idlis never really feel like a breakfast. Fortunately that's the meal where you'll find an approximation to the West most easily obtained. All those wonderful Indian varieties of eggs can be had – half-fried, omelettes, you name it.

Toast and jam can almost always be found, and very often you can get cornflakes and hot milk, although Indian cornflakes would definitely be rejects from Mr Kellogg's production line. The Scots must have visited India too, because porridge is often on the breakfast menu and is usually good.

That peculiar Raj-era term for a midmorning snack still lives – tiffin. Today tiffin means any sort of light meal or snack. One Western dish which Indians seem to have come 100% to terms with is chips (French fries). Unfortunately ordering chips is very much a hit and miss affair – sometimes they're excellent, and at other times truly dreadful. Some Indian cooks call potato chips 'Chinese potatoes', and 'finger chips' is also quite common.

Other Cuisines

Other Asian foods, apart from Indian, are often available. There's still a small Chinese population in India, particularly in Calcutta and Bombay. You can find Chinese food in the larger cities, and Bombay and Bangalore in particular have excellent Chinese food.

Elsewhere, Chinese food (or Indian interpretations of it) features on most menus in mid-range or better restaurants. The results are highly unpredictable, but the food is usually rather bland and stodgy.

In the north, where many Tibetans settled following the Chinese invasion of Tibet, you'll find Tibetan restaurants in places like Darjeeling, Dharamsala, Gangtok, Kalimpong and Manali.

In the big 'gateway' cities, and other large cities like Bangalore, restaurants featuring other cuisines, such as French, Thai, Japanese or Italian, are becoming more common. They are usually confined to the luxury hotels, and are therefore priced accordingly.

Desserts & Sweets

Indians have quite a sweet tooth and an amazing selection of desserts and sweets to satisfy it. The desserts are basically rice or milk-based, and consist of various interest-ing things in sweet syrup or else sweet pastries. Most are horrendously sweet.

Kulfi is a delicious pistachio-flavoured sweet similar to ice cream and is widely available. You can, of course, also get Western-style ice cream all over India. The major brands, such as Vadelal, Go Cool, Kwality and Havmor, are safe and very good. *Ras gullas* are another very popular Indian dessert; they're sweet little balls of cream cheese flavoured with rose water.

Gulaab jamuns are a typical example of the small 'things' in syrup – they're fried and made from thickened boiled-down milk (known as *khoya*) and flavoured with cardamom and rose water. *Jalebis*, the orange-coloured squiggles with syrup inside, are made of flour coloured/flavoured with saffron. *Ladu* are yellow coloured balls made from chickpea flour.

Barfi is also made from khoya and is available in flavours like coconut, pistachio, chocolate or almond. *Sandesh* is another milk sweet; it's a particular favourite in Calcutta. Payasam is a sweet southern drink made from coconut milk, mango pulp, cashews and spices. *Gajar ka halwa* is a translucent, vividly coloured sweet made from carrot, sweet spices and milk

Many of the Indian sweets are covered in a thin layer of silver, as are some of the desserts. It's just that, silver beaten paper-thin. Don't peel it off, it's quite edible. There are countless sweet shops with their goodies all lined up in glass showcases. Prices vary

A Bengali sweet maker

from Rs 40 to Rs 60 for a kg but you can order 50 or 100 grams at a time or simply ask for a couple of pieces. These shops often sell curd, as well as sweet curd which makes a very pleasant dessert. Sweets include all sorts of unidentifiable goodies; try them and see.

Fruit

If your sweet tooth simply isn't sweet enough to cope with too many Indian desserts, you'll be able to fall back on India's wide variety of fruit. It varies all the way from tropical delights in the south to apples, apricots and other temperate-region fruits in the north. Some local specialities include cherries and strawberries in Kashmir, and apricots in Ladakh and Himachal Pradesh. Apples are found all over this north-western region but particularly in the Kullu Valley of Himachal Pradesh.

Melons are widespread in India, particularly watermelons, which are a fine thirst quencher when you're unsure about the water and fed up with soft drinks. Try to get the first slice before the flies discover it. Green coconuts are even better and there are coconut stalls on many city street corners, especially in the south. When you've drunk the milk the stall-holder will split the coconut open and cut you a slice from the outer shell with which to scoop the flesh out.

Mangoes are delicious and are widespread in summer. Bananas are also found virtually all over India, particularly in the south; pineapples are found in West Bengal and Kerala as well as elsewhere. You don't see oranges all over the place (lots in Kerala and throughout the Ganges plain though), but tangerines are widespread in central India, particularly during the hot season. You can go through an awful lot of them in a day.

Cooking Back Home

There are all sorts of books about Indian cooking should you want to continue after you leave India. *Indian Cookery* by Dharamjit Singh (Penguin, London, 1970) is a useful paperback introduction to the art. Premila Lal is one of the country's leading cookery writers, and her books are widely

available. The problem is that ingredients are only given their local name, which makes many of the recipes impractical or impossible if you don't know exactly what is being called for. Charmaine Solomon's *Asian Cookbook* (Summit Books) is an excellent source, and includes not only Indian but also other Asian cuisines.

Paan

An Indian meal should properly be finished with *paan* – the name given to the collection of spices and condiments chewed with betel nut. Found throughout eastern Asia, betel is a mildly intoxicating and addictive nut, but by itself it is quite inedible. After a meal you chew paan as a mild digestive.

Paan sellers have a whole collection of little trays, boxes and containers in which they mix either *saadha* 'plain' or *mithaa* 'sweet' paans. The ingredients may include, apart from the betel nut itself, lime paste (the ash not the fruit), the powder known as *catachu*, various spices and even a dash of opium in a pricey paan. The whole concoction is folded up in a piece of edible leaf which you pop in your mouth and chew. When finished you spit the leftovers out and add another red blotch to the pavement. Over a long period of time, indulgence in paan will turn your teeth red-black and even addict you to the betel nut. Trying one occasionally won't do you any harm.

DRINKS
Non-Alcoholic Drinks

Tea & Coffee Surprisingly, tea is not the all-purpose and all-important drink in India that it is in Iran and Afghanistan. What's worse, the Indians, for all the tea they grow, make some of the most hideously over-sweetened, murkily-milky excuses for that fine beverage that you'll ever see. Still, many travellers like it and it is cheap. At railway stations it is often served in small clay pots, which you then smash on the ground when empty.

Better tea can be obtained if you ask for 'tray tea', which gives you the tea, the milk and the sugar separately and allows you to combine them as you see fit. Unless you

Paan-Wallahs

In India, as the red-stained walls and floors bear witness, the chewing of paan is something of a national obsession. Even the smallest village will have a paan-wallah, sitting cross-legged in front of a pile of paan leaves and tins of ingredients in a shop which is often not much more than a niche in a wall.

Although most paans cost around Rs 1 there are rumours of paan-wallahs who have become millionaires. In spite of reduced sales after the introduction of factory-prepared packets of paan masala, with low overheads and high turnover, the owners of some paan shops are undoubtedly very wealthy. At Prince Pan Centre, in Daryaganj in Delhi, the city's rich will pay up to Rs 100 for the best preparation.

Apart from the usual ingredients of lime, betel nut and catachu, every paan-wallah has his or her secret recipe which may include tobacco, flower essences or even silver and gold leaf. Amongst the numerous varieties of paan is one subtly named *palang tor* ('bed breaker') that is sometimes given to the groom on his wedding night. Thought to contain rhino-horn and other traditional aphrodisiacs, its ingredients are more usually cocaine or opium, resulting in a performance that is likely to be an illusion to the groom and a disappointment to the bride. ∎

specify otherwise, tea is 'mixed tea' or 'milk tea', which means it has been made by putting cold water, milk, sugar and tea into one pot and bringing the whole concoction to the boil, then letting it stew for a long time. The result can be imagined.

Tea is more popular in the north, while in the south coffee, which is generally good, is the number one drink. It's almost impossible to get a decent cup of coffee in the north. Even in an expensive restaurant instant coffee is almost always used. The branches of the Indian Coffee House are one of the few places with decent coffee.

Water In the big cities, the water is chlorinated and safe to drink, although if you've just arrived in India, the change from what you are used to drinking is in itself enough to bring on a mild dose of the shits.

Outside the cities you're on your own. Some travellers drink the water everywhere and never get sick, others are more careful and still get hit with a bug. Basically, you should not drink the water in small towns unless you know it has been boiled, and definitely avoid the street vendors' carts everywhere. Even in the better class of hotel and restaurant, the water is usually only filtered and not boiled. The local water filters remove solids and do nothing towards removing any bacteria. Water is generally safer in the dry season than in the monsoon when it really can be dangerous.

Water-purifying tablets are available from pharmacies and camping shops in the West, but not in India. Most tablets, such as Puritabs, do not remove amoebic cysts (hepatitis, giardiasis, amoebic dysentery) but are sufficient to make tap water safe. Iodine solution or, more conveniently, tablets such as those made by Coghlans in the USA, do remove these amoebas and are necessary if you are trekking and will be drinking stream water. Either way, the purified water tastes pretty much like swimming-pool water!

Mineral Water Most travellers to India these days avoid tap water altogether and stick to mineral water. It is available virtually everywhere, and comes in one-litre plastic bottles. The price ranges from Rs 12 to Rs 30, with Rs 18 being about the average. Brand names include Bisleri, India King, Officer's Choice, Honeydew and Aqua Safe.

Virtually all the so-called mineral water available is actually treated tap water. A recent reliable survey found that 65% of the available mineral waters were less than totally pure, and in some cases were worse than what comes out of the tap! Generally, though, if you stick to bottled water, any gut problems you might have will be from other sources – food, dirty utensils, dirty hands, etc. (See under Basic Rules in the Health section earlier.).

Soft Drinks Soft drinks are a safe substitute for water although they tend to have a high sugar content. Coca-Cola got the boot from India a number of years back for not cooperating with the government, but both they and Pepsi Cola are back with a vengeance. There are many similar indigenous brands with names like Campa Cola, Thums Up, Limca, Gold Spot or Double Seven. They are reasonably priced at around Rs 7 for a 250-ml bottle (more in restaurants). They're also sickly sweet.

Juices & Other Drinks One very pleasant escape from the sickly sweet soft drinks is apple juice, sold for Rs 4 per glass from the Himachal fruit stands found at many railway stations. Also good are the small cardboard boxes of various fruit juices. For Rs 6 these are excellent, if a little sweet.

Coconut milk, straight from the young green coconut, is a popular drink, especially in the south. Another alternative to soft drinks is soda water – Bisleri, Spencer's and other brands are widely available. Not only does it come in a larger bottle, but it is also cheaper – generally around Rs 3.50. With soda water you can get excellent, and safe, lemon squash sodas.

Falooda is a popular drink made with milk, nuts, cream and vermicelli strands. Finally there's lassi, that oh so cool, refreshing and delicious iced curd (yoghurt) drink.

Alcohol
Alcohol is relatively expensive – a bottle of Indian beer can cost anything from Rs 23 up to Rs 160 in a flash hotel; Rs 40 to Rs 60 is the usual price range. In some states (like Goa, Sikkim and Pondicherry) it is very cheap, and in some very expensive. Indian beers have delightful names like Golden Eagle, Rosy Pelican, Cannon Extra Strong, Bullet, Black Label, Knock Out, Turbo, Kingfisher, Guru or Punjab. They're not too bad if you can find them cold, but most tend to be insipid. Avoid over-indulgence or you'll wake up late in the morning feeling thoroughly disoriented with a thumping headache to boot. Preservatives (sulphur dioxide in the main) are lavishly used to combat the effects of climate on 'quality'.

Beer and other Indian interpretations of Western alcoholic drinks are known as IMFL – Indian Made Foreign Liquor. They include imitations of Scotch and brandy under a plethora of different brand names. The taste varies from hospital disinfectant to passable imitation Scotch. Always buy the best brand.

With the continuing freeing up of the economy, it is likely that in the near future well-known foreign brands of beer and spirits will be available.

Beer

India's climate being what it is, there are few travellers who don't relish a wee drop of the amber nectar at the end of a hot, dusty day or as an accompaniment to the setting sun at a beach cafe. There are a plethora of different brands, some of which are only brewed locally and others on a national basis.

In terms of taste, consistent quality, popularity and availability nationwide, the top five bottled beers would be Kingfisher, UB Export Lager, Kalyani Black Label, Black Knight and London Pilsner, which average around 5% v/v. There are others which are usually only available locally but which are just as good such as Goa Pilsner Dry, Hamburg Pils, Khajuraho and Haywards. Draught beer (usually Kingfisher or London Pilsner) is also becoming more common in the big cities. Occasionally you'll come across obscure local brands, and these vary from quite OK to totally undrinkable – 'like the dregs after a party, minus the cigarette butts' was one assessment.

Beers which purport to be strong or even super strong (around 8% v/v) with dangerous names like Bullet, Hit and Knock Out are definitely in the 'hangovers installed and serviced' category and should be imbibed in moderation.

Since most beers are lagers, they should always be drunk as cold as possible. This is often not a fact appreciated by bar owners, so feel the bottle first before allowing the waiter to pop the top. Some beers, especially the stronger varieties, are totally unpalatable served in any way other than ice-cold.

Beer and other alcoholic drinks have always been regarded in India as luxury items and are frowned on by the Hindu and Muslim elites alike. As a result, they're heavily taxed by most state governments (except Pondicherry, Sikkim and Goa) making the price of a bottle of beer three to four times the price of a thali meal.

Despite this disparity, brewing is a growth industry and bars proliferate, except in Gujarat and Andhra Pradesh states where prohibition is in force. Prohibition was a common feature in many states during the 1960s and its legacy survives (especially in Tamil Nadu) in the form of 'permit rooms' which are so dark you can't even see the drink in front of you. The overall impression is that you ought not to be involved in such nefarious activities as drinking beer. Other states have a much more enlightened attitude so bars are well lit, there's contemporary music playing and they're often the centre of social activity. They do, however, maintain licenced hours – commonly 11 am to 3 pm and 5 to 11 pm unless you're also eating.

Neither Pondicherry, Sikkim nor Goa have ever suffered from the approbation of rabid prohibitionists and it's there you'll find not only the cheapest beers (as low as Rs 18) but there are also no licenced hours – only the barperson's willingness to stay awake.

The majority of non-vegetarian restaurants these days also serve alcoholic drinks but you will never find them in vegetarian restaurants – they remain the preserve of those who eschew such impurities. ■

Local drinks are known as Country Liquor and include *toddy*, a mildly alcoholic extract from the coconut palm flower, and *feni*, a distilled liquor produced from fermented cashew nuts or from coconuts. The two varieties taste quite different.

Arak is what the peasants (and bus drivers' best boys) drink to get blotto. It's a clear, distilled rice liquor and it creeps up on you without warning. Treat with caution and only ever drink it from a bottle produced in a government-controlled distillery. *Never, ever* drink it otherwise – hundreds of people die or are blinded every year in India as a result of drinking *arak* produced in illicit stills. You can assume it contains methyl alcohol (wood alcohol).

The only states in India which are 'dry' are Gujarat and Andhra Pradesh. You cannot buy beer or any other liquor for love nor money, except at the most expensive hotels and even then you'll have to consume it in your room. Bars don't exist.

THINGS TO BUY

India is packed with beautiful things to buy – you could easily load yourself up to the eyeballs with goodies you pick up around the country. The cardinal rule when purchasing handicrafts is to bargain and bargain hard. You can get a good idea of what is reasonable in quality and price by visiting the various state emporiums, particularly in Delhi, and the Central Cottage Industries Emporiums which can be found in Delhi, Calcutta, Bombay, Madras, Bangalore and Hyderabad. You can inspect items at these places from all over the country. Because prices are fixed, you will get an idea of how hard to bargain when you purchase similar items from regular dealers.

As with handicrafts in any country, don't buy until you have developed a little understanding and appreciation. Rushing in and buying the first thing you see will inevitably lead to later disappointment and a considerably reduced stash of travellers' cheques.

Be careful when buying items which include delivery to your home country. You may well be given assurances that the price includes home delivery and all customs and handling charges. Inevitably this is not the case, and you may find yourself having to collect the item yourself from your country's main port or airport, pay customs charges (which could be as much as 20% of the item's value) and handling charges levied by the airline or shipping company (up to 10% of the value). If you can't collect the item promptly, or get someone to do it on your behalf, exorbitant storage charges may also be charged.

Carpets

It may not surprise you that India produces and exports more hand-crafted carpets than Iran, but it probably is more of a surprise that some of them are of virtually equal quality. In Kashmir, where India's best carpets are produced, the carpet-making techniques and styles were brought from Persia even before the Mughal era. The art flourished under the Mughals and today Kashmir is packed with small carpet producers. There are many carpet dealers in Delhi, Bombay, Calcutta, Madras and even Kovalam, as well as in Kashmir. Persian motifs have been much embellished on Kashmiri carpets, which come in a variety of sizes – three by five feet, four by six feet and so on. They are either made of pure wool, wool with a small percentage of silk to give a sheen (known as silk touch) or pure silk. The latter are more for decoration than hard wear. Expect to pay

---

A Warning!

In touristy places, particularly places like Agra, Jaipur, Varanasi, Delhi and Calcutta, take extreme care with the commission merchants – these guys hang around waiting to pick you up and cart you off to their favourite dealers where whatever you pay will have a hefty margin built into it to pay their commission. Stories about 'my family's place', 'my brother's shop' and 'special deal at my friend's place' are just stories and nothing more.

Whatever you might be told, if you are taken by a rickshaw driver or tout to a place, be it a hotel, craft shop, market or even restaurant, the price you pay will be inflated. This can be by as much as 50%, so try to visit these places on your own. And don't underestimate the persistence of these guys. I heard of one desperately ill traveller who virtually collapsed into a cycle rickshaw in Agra and asked to be taken to a doctor – he ended up at a marble workshop, and the rickshaw driver insisted that, yes, indeed a doctor did work there! The high-pressure sales techniques of both the runners and the owners is the best in the world. Should you get up and leave without buying anything, the feigned anger is just that. Next time you turn up (alone), it will be all smiles – and the prices will have dropped dramatically.

Another trap which many foreigners fall into occurs when buying with a credit card. You may well be told that if you buy the goods, the merchant won't forward the credit slip for payment until you have received the goods, even if it is in three months time – this is total bullshit. No trader will be sending you as much as a postcard until he or she has received the money, in full, for the goods you are buying. What you'll find in fact is that within 48 hours of you signing the credit slip, the merchant has telexed the bank in Delhi and the money will have been credited to his or her account.

Also beware of any shop which takes your credit card out the back and comes back with the slip for you to sign. It has occurred that, while out of sight, the vendor will imprint a few more forms, forge your signature, and you'll be billed for items you haven't purchased. Get them to fill out the slip right in front of you.

If you believe any stories about buying anything in India to sell at a profit elsewhere, you'll simply be proving (once again) that old adage about separating fools from their money! Precious stones and carpets are favourites for this game. Merchants will tell you that you can sell the items in Australia, Europe or the USA for several times the purchase price, and will even give you the (often imaginary!) addresses of dealers who will buy them. You'll also be shown written statements, supposedly from other travellers, documenting the money they have supposedly made – it's all a scam. The stones or carpets you buy will be worth only a fraction of what you pay. Don't let greed cloud your judgement. It seems that with every edition of this book we make the warnings longer and more explicit, and yet we still get a steady trickle of letters from people with tales of woe, and they usually concern scams we specifically warn about!

While it is certainly a minority of traders who are actually involved in dishonest schemes, virtually all are involved in the commission racket, so you need to shop with care – take your time, be firm and bargain hard. Good luck! ■

Child Labour & the 'Smiling Carpet'.

In India hundreds of thousands of children, mostly poor and virtually all uneducated, work in factories across the country. This is despite the Child Labour Prohibition & Regulation Act of 1986, which prohibits the employment of children below the age of 14 in hazardous industries.

The carpet-weaving industry employs an estimated 300,000 children, mostly in Uttar Pradesh state. The children are in demand because their small, nimble fingers are ideal for intricate weaving work, and of course being young, they get minimal wages. The conditions the children work under are generally atrocious – up to 16-hour working days, poor lighting and dangerous workplaces are all par for the course.

In an effort to combat this exploitation of children, in 1992 the UN childrens' fund (UNICEF), the Indo-German Export Promotion Council (IGEP) and a group of nongovernment organisations came up with the 'Smiling Carpet' label – a label which was to be attached to any carpet produced without child labour. Also throwing its weight behind the project was the South Asian Coalition Against Child Servitude (SACACS). These bodies lobbied to ban the export of Indian child-made carpets.

Predictably, there has been opposition to the new label from the carpet manufacturers/exporters and the government, who say there are insufficient controls within the industry to allow for detailed inspection and therefore legitimate labels. Nevertheless, the movement has the support of German carpet importers, who are paying 1% more for their carpets and using this extra money to establish a fund to aid the child workers.

Despite the opposition, the scheme is gaining credibility and increasing numbers of manufacturers are getting involved. While it is obviously not going to put an end to child labour, the 'Smiling Carpet' label is a major achievement. ∎

from Rs 5000 for a good quality four-by-six carpet and don't be surprised if the price is more than twice as high.

Other carpet-making areas include Badhoi and Mirzapur in Uttar Pradesh or Warangal and Eluru in Andhra Pradesh. In Kashmir and Rajasthan, the coarsely woven woollen *numdas* are made. These are more primitive and folksy than the fine carpets. Around the Himalaya and Uttar Pradesh *dhurries*, flat-weave cotton warp-and-weft rugs are woven. In Kashmir *gabbas* are appliqué-like rugs. The many Tibetan refugees in India have brought their craft of making superbly colourful Tibetan rugs with them. A three-by-five Tibetan rug will be less than Rs 1000. Two of the best places to buy them are Darjeeling and Gangtok.

Unless you're an expert it is best to have expert advice or buy from a reputable dealer if you're spending large amounts of money on carpets. Check prices back home too; many Western carpet dealers sell at prices you would have difficulty matching even at the source.

Papier Mâché

This is probably the most characteristic Kashmiri craft. The basic papier-mâché article is made in a mould, then painted and polished in successive layers until the final intricate design is produced. Prices depend upon the complexity and quality of the painted design and the amount of gold leaf used. Items include bowls, cups, containers, jewel boxes, letter holders, tables, lamps, coasters, trays and so on. A cheap bowl might cost only Rs 25, a large, well-made item might approach Rs 1000.

Pottery

In Rajasthan interesting white-glazed pottery is made with hand-painted blue-flower designs – it's attractively simple. Terracotta images of the gods and children's toys are made in Bihar.

Metalwork

Copper and brass items are popular throughout India. Candle holders, trays, bowls, tankards and ashtrays are made in Bombay and other centres. In Rajasthan and Uttar Pradesh the brass is inlaid with exquisite designs in red, green and blue enamel. *Bidri* is a craft of north-eastern Karnataka and Andhra Pradesh, where silver is inlaid into gunmetal (for more details see the Bidriware of Bidar boxed section at the end of the Karnataka chapter). Hookah pipes, lamp bases and jewellery boxes are made in this manner.

Jewellery

Many Indian women put most of their wealth into jewellery, so it is no wonder that so much of it is available. For Western tastes the heavy folk-art jewellery of Rajasthan has particular appeal. You'll find it all over the country, but particularly in Rajasthan. In the north you'll also find Tibetan jewellery, even chunkier and more folk-like than the Rajasthani variety.

If, on the other hand, you're looking for fine jewellery as opposed to folk jewellery, you may well find, as most of those who are *au fait* with *haute couture* do, that much of what is produced in India is way over the top. They simply don't know when to stop and certainly have no concept of elegant simplicity.

Leatherwork

Of course Indian leatherwork is not made from cow-hide but from buffalo-hide, camel, goat or some other substitute. *Chappals*, those basic sandals found all over India, are the most popular purchase. In craft shops in Delhi you can find well-made leather bags, handbags and other items. Kashmiri leather shoes and boots, often of quite good quality, are widely found, along with coats and jackets of often abysmally low quality.

Kanpur in Uttar Pradesh is the country's major city for leatherwork.

Textiles

This is still India's major industry and 40% of the total production is at the village level where it is known as *khadi*. There are government khadi emporiums (known as Khadi Gramodyog) around the country, and these are good places to buy handmade items of homespun cloth, such as the popular 'Nehru jackets' and the *kurta pajama*. Bedspreads, tablecloths, cushion covers or material for clothes are other popular khadi purchases.

There is an amazing variety of cloth styles, types and techniques around the country. In Gujarat and Rajasthan heavy material is embroidered with tiny mirrors and beads to produce the mirror-work used in everything from dresses to stuffed toys to wall hangings.

Tie-dye work is also popular in Rajasthan and Kerala.

In Kashmir embroidered materials are made into shirts and dresses. Fine shawls and scarves of pashmina goats' wool are popular purchases in the Kullu Valley. Phulkari bedspreads or wall hangings come from the Punjab. Another place which is famous for its stunning embroidery work is Barmer, close to the Pakistani border and south-west of Jaisalmer in Rajasthan. Batik is a fairly recent introduction from Indonesia but already widespread; kalamkari cloth from Andhra Pradesh and Gujarat is an associated but far older craft.

Silks & Saris

Silk is cheap and the quality is often excellent. The 'silk capital' these days is Kanchipuram in Tamil Nadu, although Varanasi is also popular, especially for silk saris.

If you are buying a silk sari, it helps to know a bit about both the silk and the sari. Saris are 5½ metres long, unless they have an attached blouse (*choli*), in which case they are six metres. Sari silk is graded and sold by weight – in grams per metres. Soft plain silk up to 60 grams per metre costs Rs 3.20 per gram; chiffon silk of 20 grams per metre is Rs 4.50 per gram, but you'll be lucky to find a sari of printed chiffon for less than Rs 600. A thin Kanchipuram silk sari weighs around 400 grams, a heavy sari around 600 grams. Pure gold jerri silk (the only one that doesn't blacken with time) costs Rs 12.50 per gram. A half-inch gold border weighs around 25 grams and is worth around Rs 320; a one-inch band, which weighs 35 grams, will cost about Rs 450. This must be added to the price of the silk.

Bronze Figures

In the south, delightful small images of the gods are made by the age-old lost-wax process. A wax figure is made, a mould is formed around it and the wax is melted and poured out. The molten metal is poured in and when it's solidified the mould is broken open. Figures of Siva as dancing Nataraj are amongst the most popular.

Woodcarving

In the south, images of the gods are also carved out of sandalwood. Rosewood is used to carve animals – elephants in particular. Carved wooden furniture and other household items, either in natural finish or lacquered, are also made in various locations. In Kashmir intricately carved wooden screens, tables, jewellery boxes, trays and the like are carved from Indian walnut. They follow a similar pattern to that seen on the decorative trim of houseboats. Old temple carvings can be delightful.

Paintings

Reproductions of the beautiful old miniatures are painted in many places, but beware of paintings claimed to be antique – it's highly unlikely that they are. Also note that quality can vary widely; low prices often mean low quality, and if you buy before you've had a chance to look at a lot of miniatures and develop some appreciation you'll inevitably find you bought unwisely. Udaipur (Rajasthan) has some good shops specialising in modern reproductions.

In Kerala, and, to a lesser extent, Tamil Nadu, you'll come across beautiful and incredibly vibrant miniature paintings on leaf skeletons enclosed on a printed card depicting domestic and rural scenes as well as gods and goddesses. They're a superb buy at between Rs 10 and Rs 20 depending on quality and how many you buy. Kovalam beach is the prime place to find them, though they're also marketed around Mahabalipuram (Tamil Nadu) these days.

Antiques

Articles over 100 years old are not allowed to be exported from India without an export clearance certificate. If you have doubts about any item and think it could be defined as an antique, you can check with:

Bombay
    Superintending Archaeologist, Antiquities, Archaeological Survey of India, Sion Fort

Calcutta
    Superintending Archaeologist, Eastern Circle, Archaeological Survey of India, Narayani Bldg, Brabourne Rd
Delhi
    Director, Antiquities, Archaeological Survey of India, Janpath
Kashmir (Srinagar)
    Superintending Archaeologist, Frontier Circle, Archaeological Survey of India, Minto Bridge
Madras
    Superintending Archaeologist, Southern Circle, Archaeological Survey of India, Fort St George

Other Things to Buy

Marble inlay pieces from Agra are pleasant reminders of the beauty of the Taj. They come as either simple little pieces or larger items like jewellery boxes. Appliqué work is popular in many places, such as Orissa.

Indian musical instruments always have an attraction for travellers, although you don't see nearly as many backpackers lugging sitars or tablas around as you did 15 years ago. A more portable Indian music buy might be records or tapes. Certain Indian streets in major cities now resemble Taipei, Bangkok, Bali and Singapore in having street stalls and shops offering the full range of contemporary, '80s, '70s and even '60s Western music, though they're often pirated and on inferior tapes. You're looking at around Rs 50 per tape.

At the many Bata shoe shops in India, Western-style shoes are cheap and reasonably well made. The best quality men's shoes are about Rs 1000, far less than shoes of similar quality in London or New York.

THINGS TO SELL

All sorts of Western technological items are good things to sell in India, but cameras, tape recorders and VCRs are as dead as a dodo in terms of making profit. The market is flooded with them. In any case, VCRs might well be entered into your passport to ensure they leave the country with you. But there's always a good market, particularly in Calcutta, Delhi and Madras, for your bottle of duty-free whisky.

Getting There & Away

AIR
Buying a Plane Ticket

Your plane ticket will probably be the single most expensive item in your budget, and buying it can be an intimidating business. There is likely to be a multitude of airlines and travel agents hoping to separate you from your money, and it is always worth putting aside a few hours to research the current state of the market. Start early: some of the cheapest tickets have to be bought months in advance, and some popular flights sell out early. Talk to other recent travellers – they may be able to stop you making some of the same old mistakes. Look at the ads in newspapers and magazines, consult reference books and watch for special offers. Then phone around travel agents for bargains. (Airlines can supply information on routes and timetables; however, except at times of inter-airline war, they do not supply the cheapest tickets.) Find out the fare, the route, the duration of the journey and any restrictions on the ticket. (See Restrictions in the Air Travel Glossary in this chapter.) Then sit back and decide which is best for you.

You may discover that those impossibly cheap flights are 'fully booked, but we have another one that costs a bit more...' Or the flight is on an airline notorious for its poor safety standards and leaves you in the world's least favourite airport in mid-journey for 14 hours. Or they claim only to have the last two seats available for that country for the whole of July, which they will hold for you for a maximum of two hours. Don't panic – keep ringing around.

Use the fares quoted in this book as a guide only. They are approximate and based on the rates advertised by travel agents at the time of going to press. Quoted air fares do not necessarily constitute a recommendation for the carrier.

If you are travelling from the UK or the USA, you will probably find that the cheapest flights are being advertised by obscure bucket shops whose names haven't yet reached the telephone directory. Many such firms are honest and solvent, but there are a few rogues who will take your money and disappear, to reopen elsewhere a month or two later under a new name. If you feel suspicious about a firm, don't give them all the money at once – leave a deposit of 20% or so and pay the balance when you get the ticket. If they insist on cash in advance, go somewhere else. And once you have the ticket, ring the airline to confirm that you are actually booked on the flight.

You may decide to pay more than the rock-bottom fare by opting for the safety of a better-known travel agent. Firms such as STA, who have offices worldwide, Council Travel in the USA or Travel CUTS in Canada are not going to disappear overnight, leaving you clutching a receipt for a nonexistent ticket, but they do offer good prices to most destinations.

Warning

The information in this chapter is particularly vulnerable to change: prices for international travel are volatile, routes are introduced and cancelled, schedules change, special deals come and go, and rules and visa requirements are amended. Airlines and governments seem to take a perverse pleasure in making price structures and regulations as complicated as possible. You should check directly with the airline or a travel agent to make sure you understand how a fare (and ticket you may buy) works. In addition, the travel industry is highly competitive and there are many lurks and perks.

The upshot of this is that you should get opinions, quotes and advice from as many airlines and travel agents as possible before you part with your hard-earned cash. The details given in this chapter should be regarded as pointers and are not a substitute for your own careful, up-to-date research. ■

Once you have your ticket, write its number down, together with the flight number and other details, and keep the information somewhere separate. If the ticket is lost or stolen, this will help you get a replacement.

It's sensible to buy travel insurance as early as possible. If you buy it the week before you fly, you may find, for example, that you're not covered for delays to your flight caused by industrial action.

Air Travellers with Special Needs

If you have special needs of any sort – you've broken a leg, you're vegetarian, travelling in a wheelchair, taking the baby, terrified of flying – you should let the airline know as soon as possible so that they can make arrangements accordingly. You should remind them when you reconfirm your booking (at least 72 hours before departure) and again when you check in at the airport. It may also be worth ringing around the airlines before you make your booking to find out how they can handle your particular needs.

Airports and airlines can be surprisingly helpful, but they do need advance warning. Most international airports will provide escorts from check-in desk to plane where needed, and there should be ramps, lifts, accessible toilets and reachable phones. Aircraft toilets, on the other hand, are likely to present a problem; travellers should discuss this with the airline at an early stage and, if necessary, with their doctor.

Guide dogs for the blind will often have to travel in a specially pressurised baggage compartment with other animals, away from their owner, though smaller guide dogs may be admitted to the cabin. All guide dogs will be subject to the same quarantine laws (six months in isolation etc) as any other animal when entering or returning to countries currently free of rabies such as Britain or Australia. Deaf travellers can ask for airport and in-flight announcements to be written down for them.

Children under two travel for 10% of the standard fare (or free, on some airlines), as long as they don't occupy a seat. They don't get a baggage allowance either. Bassinettes should be provided by the airline if requested in advance; these will take a child weighing up to about 10 kg. Children between two and 12 can usually occupy a seat for half to two-thirds of the full fare, and do get a baggage allowance. Strollers can often be taken as hand luggage.

Round-the-World Fares

Round-the-World (RTW) fares are very competitive and are a popular way to travel to India. Basically there are two types – airline tickets and agent tickets. An airline RTW ticket usually means two or more airlines have joined together to market a ticket which takes you round the world on their combined routes. Within certain limitations of time and number of stopovers you can fly pretty well anywhere you choose using their combined routes so long as you keep moving in the same direction.

Compared to the full-fare tickets, which permit you to go anywhere you choose on any IATA airline so long as you do not exceed the 'maximum permitted mileage', these tickets are much less flexible. But they are also much cheaper.

Quite a few of these combined-airline RTW tickets go through India, including ones in combination with Air India which will allow you to make several stopovers within India. RTW tickets typically cost around A$1950 to A$2400, UK£560 to UK£940 and US$1250 to US$2500.

The other type of RTW ticket, the agent ticket, is a combination of cheap fares strung together by an enterprising travel agent. These can be cheaper than an airline RTW ticket but the choice of routes may not be so wide.

Cheap Tickets in India

Although you can get cheap tickets in Bombay and Calcutta, it is in Delhi that the real wheeling and dealing goes on. There are a number of 'bucket shops' around Connaught Place, but enquire with other travellers about their current trustworthiness.

Fares from Delhi to various European capitals cost around Rs 5000 to Rs 7000, a bit less from Bombay. The cheapest flights to Europe are with airlines like Aeroflot, LOT, Kuwait Airways, Syrian Arab Airways or Iraqi Airways. Delhi-Hong Kong-San Francisco costs around US$600.

Although Delhi is the best place for cheap tickets, many flights between Europe and South-East Asia or Australia pass through Bombay; it's also the place for flights to East Africa. Furthermore, if you're heading east from India to Bangladesh, Myanmar (Burma) or Thailand you'll probably find much better prices in Calcutta than in Delhi, even though there are fewer agents.

To/From Africa

There are plenty of flights between East Africa and Bombay due to the large Indian population in Kenya. Typical fares from Bombay to Nairobi are around US$440 return with either Ethiopian Airlines, Kenya Airways, Air India or Pakistan International Airlines (PIA, via Karachi).

Aeroflot operates a service between Delhi and Cairo (via Moscow).

To/From Australia & New Zealand

Advance-purchase return fares from the east coast of Australia to India range from A$1250 to A$1500 depending on the season and the destination in India. Fares are slightly cheaper to Madras and Calcutta than to Bombay or Delhi. From Australia fares are cheaper from Darwin or Perth than from the east coast. The low travel period is from March to September; peak is from October to February.

Tickets from Australia to London or other European capitals with an Indian stopover range from A$1200 to A$1350 one way and A$2000 to A$2500 return, again, depending on the season.

Return advance-purchase fares from New Zealand to India range from NZ$1799 to NZ$1889 depending on the season.

STA and Flight Centres International are major dealers in cheap airfares in both Australia and New Zealand. Check the travel agents' ads in the Yellow Pages and ring around.

To/From Bangladesh

Bangladesh Biman and Indian Airlines fly from Calcutta to Dhaka (US$32) and Chittagong (US$40) in Bangladesh. Many people use Biman from Calcutta through to Bangkok – partly because they're cheap and partly because they fly through Yangon (Rangoon) in Myanmar (Burma). Biman should put you up overnight in Dhaka on this route but be careful – it appears they will only do so if your ticket is specifically endorsed that you are entitled to a room. If not, tough luck – you can either camp out overnight in the hot transit lounge or make your way into Dhaka on your own, pay for transport and accommodation, and get hit for departure tax the next day.

To/From Europe

Fares from continental Europe are mostly far more expensive than from London; see the To/From the UK section for comparison. At the rates listed below it's obviously much cheaper to go to London and buy a flight ticket from there.

From Amsterdam to Delhi/Bombay, return excursion fares are about DFL2400 (UK£900). To Calcutta, expect to pay around DFL2665 (UK£1000).

From Paris to Bombay/Delhi, return excursion fares range upwards from FFr7880 (UK£980; about one-third the standard return economy fare).

From Frankfurt to Bombay/Delhi, return excursion fares are around DM1950 (UK£820).

To/From Malaysia

Not many travellers fly between Malaysia and India because it is so much cheaper from Thailand, but there are flights between Penang or Kuala Lumpur and Madras. You can generally pick up one-way tickets for the Malaysian Airline System (MAS) flight from Penang travel agents for around RM$780, which is rather cheaper than the regular fare. Other fares include Kuala

Lumpur-Bombay for RM$700 one way and RM$1275 return, and Kuala Lumpur-Delhi for RM$700 one way and RM$1070 return.

To/From the Maldives

Thiruvananthapuram (Trivandrum)-Malé costs US$63. This is cheaper than flying to the Maldives from Colombo in Sri Lanka.

To/From Myanmar (Burma)

There are no land crossing points between Myanmar and India (or between Myanmar and any other country), so if you want to visit Myanmar your only choice is to fly there. Myanma Airways flies Calcutta-Yangon (Rangoon); Bangladesh Biman flies Dhaka-Yangon.

If you are coming from Bangkok via Myanmar, the one-way Bangkok-Yangon-Calcutta fare is around US$240 with Thai, or US$225 on Myanma Airways.

To/From Nepal

Royal Nepal Airlines Corporation (RNAC)

Air Travel Glossary

Apex Apex, or 'advance purchase excursion' is a discounted ticket which must be paid for in advance. There are penalties if you wish to change it.

Baggage Allowance This will be written on your ticket: usually one 20 kg item to go in the hold, plus one item of hand luggage.

Bucket Shop An unbonded travel agency specialising in discounted airline tickets.

Bumped Just because you have a confirmed seat doesn't mean you're going to get on the plane – see Overbooking.

Cancellation Penalties If you have to cancel or change an Apex ticket there are often heavy penalties involved, insurance can sometimes be taken out against these penalties. Some airlines impose penalties on regular tickets as well, particularly against 'no show' passengers.

Check In Airlines ask you to check in a certain time ahead of the flight departure (usually 1½ hours on international flights). If you fail to check in on time and the flight is overbooked the airline can cancel your booking and give your seat to somebody else.

Confirmation Having a ticket written out with the flight and date you want doesn't mean you have a seat until the agent has checked with the airline that your status is 'OK' or confirmed. Meanwhile you could just be 'on request'.

Discounted Tickets There are two types of discounted fares – officially discounted (see Promotional Fares) and unofficially discounted. The lowest prices often impose drawbacks like flying with unpopular airlines, inconvenient schedules, or unpleasant routes and connections. A discounted ticket can save you other things than money – you may be able to pay Apex prices without the associated Apex advance booking and other requirements. Discounted tickets only exist where there is fierce competition.

Full Fares Airlines traditionally offer first class (coded F), business class (coded J) and economy class (coded Y) tickets. These days there are so many promotional and discounted fares available from the regular economy class that few passengers pay full economy fare.

Lost Tickets If you lose your airline ticket an airline will usually treat it like a travellers' cheque and, after inquiries, issue you with another one. Legally, however, an airline is entitled to treat it like cash and if you lose it then it's gone forever. Take good care of your tickets.

No Shows No shows are passengers who fail to show up for their flight, sometimes due to unexpected delays or disasters, sometimes due to simply forgetting, sometimes because they made more than one booking and didn't bother to cancel the one they didn't want. Full fare passengers who fail to turn up are sometimes entitled to travel on a later flight. The rest of us are penalised (see Cancellation Penalties).

On Request An unconfirmed booking for a flight, see Confirmation.

and Indian Airlines share routes between India and Kathmandu. Both airlines give a 25% discount to those under 30 years of age on flights between Kathmandu and India; no student card is needed.

Delhi is the main departure point for flights between India and Kathmandu. The daily one-hour Delhi to Kathmandu flight costs US$142.

Other cities in India with direct air connections with Kathmandu are Bombay (US$257), Calcutta (US$96) and Varanasi (US$71). The flight from Varanasi is the last leg of the popular Delhi-Agra-Khajuraho-Varanasi-Kathmandu tourist flight.

If you want to see the mountains as you fly into Kathmandu from Delhi or Varanasi, you must sit on the left side.

To/From Pakistan

Pakistan International Airlines (PIA) and Air India operate flights from Karachi to Delhi for US$75 and Lahore to Delhi for about US$140. Flights are also available between Karachi and Bombay.

Open Jaws A return ticket where you fly out to one place but return from another. If available this can save you backtracking to your arrival point.

Overbooking Airlines hate to fly empty seats and since every flight has some passengers who fail to show up (see No Shows) airlines often book more passengers than they have seats. Usually the excess passengers balance those who fail to show up but occasionally somebody gets bumped. If this happens guess who it is most likely to be? The passengers who check in late.

Promotional Fares Officially discounted fares like Apex fares which are available from travel agents or direct from the airline.

Reconfirmation At least 72 hours prior to departure time of an onward or return flight you must contact the airline and 'reconfirm' that you intend to be on the flight. If you don't do this the airline can delete your name from the passenger list and you could lose your seat. You don't have to reconfirm the first flight on your itinerary or if your stopover is less than 72 hours. It doesn't hurt to reconfirm more than once.

Restrictions Discounted tickets often have various restrictions on them – advance purchase is the most usual one (see Apex). Others are restrictions on the minimum and maximum period you must be away, such as a minimum of 14 days or a maximum of one year. See Cancellation Penalties.

Standby A discounted ticket where you only fly if there is a seat free at the last moment. Standby fares are usually only available on domestic routes.

Tickets Out An entry requirement for many countries is that you have an onward or return ticket. In other words, a ticket out of the country. If you're not sure what you intend to do next, the easiest solution is to buy the cheapest onward ticket to a neighbouring country or a ticket from a reliable airline which can later be refunded if you do not use it.

Transferred Tickets Airline tickets cannot be transferred from one person to another. Travellers sometimes try to sell the return half of their ticket, but officials can ask you to prove that you are the person named on the ticket. This is unlikely to happen on domestic flights, on an international flight tickets may be compared with passports.

Travel Agencies Travel agencies vary widely and you should ensure you use one that suits your needs. Some simply handle tours while full-service agencies handle everything from tours and tickets to car rental and hotel bookings. A good one will do all these things and can save you a lot of money but if all you want is a ticket at the lowest possible price, then you really need an agency specialising in discounted tickets. A discounted ticket agency, however, may not be useful for other things, like hotel bookings.

Travel Periods Some officially discounted fares, Apex fares in particular, vary with the time of year. There is often a low (off-peak) season and a high (peak) season. Sometimes there's an intermediate or shoulder season as well. At peak times, when everyone wants to fly, not only will the officially discounted fares be higher but so will unofficially discounted fares or there may simply be no discounted tickets available. Usually the fare depends on your outward flight – if you depart in the high season and return in the low season, you pay the high-season fare. ∎

To/From Singapore
Singapore is a great cheap-ticket centre and you can pick up Singapore-Delhi tickets for about S$900 return.

To/From Sri Lanka
Few travellers continue to Sri Lanka from India due to the level of unrest in the north of that unhappy country. In addition, because the ferry service is out of operation flying is now the only way to get there.

There are flights to and from Colombo (the capital of Sri Lanka) and Bombay, Madras, Tiruchirappalli or Thiruvananthapuram (Trivandrum). Flights are most frequent on the Madras-Colombo route.

To/From Thailand
Bangkok is the most popular departure point from South-East Asia into Asia proper because of the cheap flights from there to Calcutta, Yangon (Rangoon) in Myanmar (Burma), Dhaka in Bangladesh or Kathmandu in Nepal. The popular Bangkok-Kathmandu flight is about US$220 one way and US$400 return. You can make a stopover in Myanmar on this route and do a circuit of that fascinating country. Bangkok-Calcutta via Myanmar is about US$270 one way.

To/From the UK
Various excursion fares are available from London to India, but you can get better prices through London's many cheap-ticket specialists. Check the travel page ads in the *Times, Business Traveller* and the weekly 'what's on' magazines *City Limits* and *Time Out*; or check give-away papers like *TNT*. Two reliable London shops are Trailfinders, 194 High Street Kensington, London W8 7RG (☎ (0171) 938-3939), or 46 Earls Court Rd, London W8 (☎ (0171) 938-3366); and STA, 74 Old Brompton Rd, London SW7 (☎ (0171) 937-9962), or 117 Euston Rd, London NW1. Also worth trying are Quest Worldwide (☎ (0181) 547-3322) at 29 Castle St, Kingston, Surrey KT11ST, and Bridge the World (☎ (0171) 911-0900) at 1-3 Ferdinand St, Camden Town, London NW1.

From London to Delhi, fares range from around UK£300/342 one way/return in the low season, or UK£409/493 one way/return in the high season – cheaper short-term fares are also available. The cheapest fares are usually with Middle Eastern or Eastern European airlines. You'll also find very competitive air fares to the subcontinent with Bangladesh Biman or Air Lanka. Thai International always seems to have competitive fares despite its high standards.

Some travel companies offer packages to Goa at competitive rates which include accommodation, breakfast, transfers and an Indrail Pass – check with travel agents and travel page ads in newspapers and magazines. From November 1995 there will also be packages including charter flights between London and Agra.

If you want to stop in India en route to Australia expect to pay around UK£500 to UK£600. You might find fares via Karachi (Pakistan) or Colombo (Sri Lanka) slightly cheaper than fares via India.

Most British travel agents are registered with the Association of British Travel Agents (ABTA). If you have paid for your flight to an ABTA-registered agent who then goes out of business, ABTA will guarantee a refund or an alternative. Unregistered bucket shops are riskier but are also sometimes cheaper.

To/From the USA & Canada
The cheapest return air fares from the US west coast to India are around US$1350. Another way of getting there is to fly to Hong Kong and get a ticket from there. Tickets to Hong Kong cost about US$430 one way and around US$725 return from San Francisco or Los Angeles; in Hong Kong you can find one-way tickets to Bombay for US$300 depending on the carrier. Alternatively, you can fly to Singapore for around US$595/US$845 one way/return, or to Bangkok for US$470/US$760 one way/return.

From the east coast you can find return tickets to Bombay or Delhi for around US$950. The cheapest one-way tickets will be around US$660. An alternative way of getting to India from New York is to fly to London and buy a cheap fare from there.

Check the Sunday travel sections of papers like the *New York Times, San Francisco Chronicle/Examiner* or *Los Angeles Times* for cheap fares. Good budget travel agents include the student travel chains STA or CIEE. The magazine *Travel Unlimited* (PO Box 1058, Allston, Mass 02134) publishes details of the cheapest air fares and courier possibilities for destinations all over the world from the USA.

Fares from Canada are similar to the USA fares. From Vancouver the route is like that from the US west coast, with the option of going via Hong Kong. From Toronto it is easier to travel via London.

The *Toronto Globe & Mail* and the *Vancouver Sun* carry travel agents' ads. The magazine *Great Expeditions* (PO Box 8000-411, Abbotsford BC V2S 6H1) is useful.

LAND

Drivers of cars and riders of motorbikes will need the vehicle's registration papers, liability insurance and an international drivers' permit in addition to their domestic licence. Beware: there are two kinds of international permit, one of which is needed mostly for former British colonies. You will also need a *carnet de passage en douane*, which is effectively a passport for the vehicle, and acts as a temporary waiver of import duty. The carnet may also need to have listed any more-expensive spares that you're planning to carry with you, such as a gearbox. This is necessary when travelling in many countries in Asia, and is designed to prevent car import rackets. Contact your local automobile association for details about all documentation.

Liability insurance is not available in advance for many out-of-the-way countries, but has to be bought when crossing the border. The cost and quality of such local insurance varies wildly, and you will find in some countries that you are effectively travelling uninsured.

Anyone who is planning to take their own vehicle with them needs to check in advance what spares and petrol are likely to be available. Lead-free fuel is not available in India, and neither is every little part for your car.

Cycling is a cheap, convenient, healthy, environmentally sound and above all fun way of travelling. One note of caution: before you leave home, go over your bike with a fine-toothed comb and fill your repair kit with every imaginable spare. As with cars and motorbikes, you won't necessarily be able to buy that crucial gizmo for your machine when it breaks down somewhere in the back of beyond as the sun sets.

Bicycles can travel by air. You *can* take them to pieces and put them in a bike bag or box, but it's much easier simply to wheel your bike to the check-in desk, where it should be treated as a piece of baggage. You may have to remove the pedals and turn the handlebars sideways so that it takes up less space in the aircraft's hold; check all this with the airline well in advance, preferably before you pay for your ticket.

For more details on driving your own vehicle in India, see the Driving section in the Getting Around chapter.

To/From Bangladesh

Unfortunately most land entry and exit points are closed, so the choice is much more limited than a glance at the map would indicate. You do not need an exit permit to leave Bangladesh on the Calcutta route; you may need one on the Darjeeling route.

Calcutta to Dhaka The Calcutta to Dhaka route is the one used by the majority of land travellers. Stage one is a train from Calcutta (Sealdah) to Bangaon (Rs 13, 2½ hours), the town closest to the border. From Bangaon it's about 10 km (Rs 10, 20 minutes) by cycle-rickshaw to the border at Haridaspur on the Indian side, or Rs 50 by auto-rickshaw. It's possible to change money at Bangaon, and the rate is better than at the border.

Crossing the border takes an hour or so with the usual form filling and stamping. From the border it's about 10 minutes by rickshaw (Tk 5) to Benapole on the Bangladesh side. If you leave Calcutta in the early afternoon you should be in Benopol (the Bangladeshi border town) in time for the bus departures between 6 and 8.30 pm. There are no buses in the daytime between the border and Benopol.

Alternatively, you can take a Coaster (minibus) from Benapole to Jessore (Tk 12), from where you can proceed to Dhaka. The last 'direct' buses from Jessore leave around 1 pm.

From Benopol it's an eight or nine-hour bus trip to Dhaka, a distance of 291 km. The first leg of the trip, to Jessore, takes about 1½ hours; then it's an hour to a small ferry crossing. It only takes about 10 minutes to cross the river but the waiting, loading and unloading will occupy an hour or two. Another 1½ hours takes you to a larger ferry crossing at Aricha. Getting across the river takes a couple of hours; going to Dhaka this ferry takes about half an hour longer as the crossing is upstream. Finally, it's another 1½ hours to Dhaka.

Coming from Dhaka it's wise to book your seat on the bus at least a day in advance. The buses that operate overnight between Dhaka and the border are direct. Buses only depart from 8 to 11 pm; they reach Benapole at dawn.

From Darjeeling From Darjeeling to Siliguri, you can take the fast buses (three hours) or the slower but more picturesque toy train (about 10 hours). If you take the train, it is more convenient to get off at New Jalpaiguri than at the other two stations in Siliguri.

The trip from New Jalpaiguri to Haldibari (the Indian border checkpoint) takes two hours and costs Rs 9 by train, but you have a little travelling yet before you reach Bangladesh. It's a seven-km walk along the disused railway line from Haldibari to the Bangladesh border point at Chiliharti! 'It's here you discover how much excess baggage you're carrying', wrote one traveller. You should be able to arrange for a rickshaw to carry you the first few km to the Bangladeshi border, however.

There's a railway station at Chiliharti from where you can set off into Bangladesh. Bring some takas (the currency of Bangladesh) in with you. This is officially illegal but chang-

ing money in Chiliharti is virtually impossible. You should be able to change some at Haldibari.

To/From Europe

The classic way of getting to India has always been overland. Sadly, the events in the Middle East and Afghanistan have turned the cross-Asian flow into a trickle. Afghanistan is still off-limits but the trip through Turkey, Iran and into Pakistan is straightforward.

The Asia overland trip is certainly not the breeze it once was, but it is definitely possible. Many travellers combine travel to the subcontinent with the Middle East by flying from India or Pakistan to Amman in Jordan or one of the Gulf states. A number of the London-based overland companies operate their bus or truck trips across Asia on a regular basis. Check with Exodus (☎ (0181) 675-5550), 9 Weir Rd, London SW18 0LT, UK; Encounter Overland (☎ (0171) 370-6951), 267 Old Brompton Rd, London SW5 9LA, UK; or Top Deck Travel (☎ (0171) 370-4555) for more information.

For more detail on the Asian overland route see the Lonely Planet guides to Pakistan, Iran and Turkey.

To/From Nepal

There are direct buses from Delhi to Kathmandu, but these generally get bad reports from travellers. It's cheaper and more satisfactory to organise this trip yourself.

For more details of the land routes into Nepal see the Uttar Pradesh, Bihar and West Bengal sections in this book. The most popular routes are from Raxaul (near Muzaffarpur), Sunauli (near Gorakhpur), and Kakarbhitta (near Siliguri). If you are heading straight to Nepal from Delhi or elsewhere in western India then the Gorakhpur to Sunauli route is the most convenient. From Calcutta, Patna or most of eastern India, Raxaul to Birganj is the best entry point. From Darjeeling it's easiest to go to Kakarbhitta.

To give an idea of costs, a 2nd-class rail ticket from Delhi to Gorakhpur costs US$6 and buses from Gorakhpur to the border and then on to Kathmandu cost another US$6.

There are other roads into Nepal from northern Bihar to the east of Birganj but they are rarely used by travellers, and a couple of them are closed. One such is the crossing between Jogbani (near Purnia) and Biratnagar. Additionally, the narrow-gauge railway from Jaynagar (near Darbhanga) which crosses the border to Janakpur (an attractive Nepalese city famous as the birthplace of Sita) is also closed.

It is also possible to cross the border at Nepalganj, Dhangadi and Mahendrenagar in the far west of Nepal. The entry at Mahendrenagar, just over the border from the northern Uttar Pradesh village of Banbassa, is the most interesting possibility. It may take a while for things to start operating smoothly, but when they do, this will present an interesting alternative route to/from Delhi. If the Mahendra Highway is completed by now (in theory it should be, but don't count on it) the route will be open all year; otherwise it is a dry season-only proposition, and strictly for the hardy. It takes 12 hours on the Delhi-Mahendrenagar route, nine hours for Mahendrenagar-Nepalganj, and 16 hours for Nepalganj-Kathmandu. See under Banbassa in the Uttar Pradesh chapter for more details on this route.

To/From Pakistan

At present, due to the continuing unstable political situation between India and Pakistan, there's only one border crossing open.

Lahore to Amritsar The crossing at Attari is open daily to all traffic. It may be worth checking the situation in the Punjab with the Home Ministry in Delhi or the Indian High Commission in Islamabad, Pakistan, before you travel, as this could change if there's major problems either side of the border.

For the Lahore (Pakistan) to Amritsar (India) train you have to buy one ticket from Lahore to Attari, the Indian border town, and another from Attari to Amritsar. The train departs Lahore daily at 11.30 am and arrives in Amritsar at 3 pm after a couple of hours at

the border passing through immigration and customs. Going the other way, you leave Amritsar at 9.30 am and arrive in Lahore at 1.35 pm. Pakistan immigration and customs are handled at Lahore station. Sometimes, however, border delays can make the trip much longer.

From Amritsar you cannot buy a ticket until the morning of departure and there are no seat reservations – arrive early and push. Moneychangers offer good rates for Pakistan rupees on the platform. Travellers have reported that whichever direction you're travelling, the exchange rate between Indian and Pakistan rupees is more advantageous to you on the Pakistan side of the border, but you can change Indian rupees to Pakistani rupees or vice versa at Wagah (the Pakistani border town) and in Amritsar – no matter what the Pakistanis may tell you!

Few travellers use the road link between India and Pakistan. It's mainly of interest to people with vehicles or those on overland buses. By public transport the trip from Lahore entails taking a bus to the border at Wagah between Lahore and Amritsar, walking across the border and then taking another bus or taxi into Amritsar.

From Lahore, buses and minibuses depart from near the general bus station on Badami Bagh. The border opens at 9.15 am and closes at 3.30 pm. If you're stuck on the Pakistan side you can stay at the *PTDC Motel*, where there are dorm beds and double rooms.

To/From South-East Asia

In contrast to the difficulties of travelling overland in central Asia, the South-East Asian overland trip is still wide open and as popular as ever. From Australia the first step is to Indonesia – Timor, Bali or Jakarta. Although most people fly from an east-coast city or from Perth to Bali, there are also flights from Darwin and from Port Hedland in the north of Western Australia. The shortest route is the flight between Darwin and Kupang on the Indonesian island of Timor.

From Bali you head north through Java to Jakarta, from where you either travel by ship or fly to Singapore or continue north through Sumatra and then cross to Penang in Malaysia. After travelling around Malaysia you can fly from Penang to Madras in India or, more popularly, continue north to Thailand and eventually fly out from Bangkok to India, perhaps with a stopover in Myanmar (Burma). Unfortunately, crossing by land from Myanmar to India (or indeed to any other country) is forbidden by the Myanmar government.

An interesting alternative route is to travel from Australia to Papua New Guinea and from there cross to Irian Jaya; then to Sulawesi in Indonesia. There are all sorts of travel variations possible in South-East Asia; the region is a delight to travel through, it's good value for money, the food is generally excellent and healthy, and all in all it's an area of the world not to be missed. For full details see the Lonely Planet guide *South-East Asia*.

SEA

The ferry service from Rameswaram in southern India to Talaimannar in Sri Lanka has been suspended for some years due to the unrest in Sri Lanka. This was a favourite route for shipping arms and equipment to the Tamil guerrilla forces in the north of the country.

The shipping services between Africa and India only carry freight (including vehicles), not passengers.

The service between Penang and Madras also ceased some years ago.

TOURS

There are numerous foreign eco-travel and adventure travel companies which can provide unusual and interesting trips in addition to companies that provide more standard tours. There are too many to include them all; check newspapers and travel magazines for advertisements, and journals such as *Earth Journal* (USA) for listings. Companies that organise tours to various parts of India include the following:

Australasia
New Experience Holidays
   3/131 Keen St, Lismore, NSW 2480, Australia (☎ toll-free 1-800-067-2218; fax (066) 22-2267)
Peregrine Adventures
   258 Lonsdale St, Melbourne 3000, Australia (☎ (03) 663 8611). Also offices in Sydney, Brisbane, Adelaide, Perth and Hobart.
Venturetreks
   164 Parnell Rd (PO Box 37610), Parnell, Auckland, New Zealand (☎ (09) 379-9855; fax (09) 377-0320)
World Expeditions
   3rd Floor, 441 Kent St, Sydney, NSW 2000, Australia (☎ (02) 9264-3366; fax (02) 9261-1974)
   1st Floor, 393 Little Bourke St, Melbourne, Vic 3000, Australia (☎ (03) 670-8400; fax (03) 670-7474)
Destinations
   2nd Floor, Premier Bldg (near Queen and Durham St East) Auckland, New Zealand (☎ (09) 309 0464)
UK
Encounter Overland
   267 Old Brompton Rd, London SW5 9JA (☎ (0171) 370-6845)
Exodus Expeditions
   9 Weir Rd, London SW12 OLT (☎ (0181) 673-0859)
Imaginative Traveller (international reservation office)
   14 Barley Mow Passage, Chiswick, London W4 4PH, UK (☎ (081) 742 3113; fax (081) 742 3046
USA
Adventure Center
   1311 63rd St, Suite 200, Emeryville, CA 94608 (☎ (800) 227-8747)
All Adventure Travel, Inc.
   PO Box 4307, Boulder, CO 80306 (☎ (303) 440-7924)
Asian Pacific Adventures
   826 S. Sierra Bonita Ave, Los Angeles, CA 90036 (☎ (800) 825-1680)
Inner Asia Expeditions
   2627 Lombard St, San Francisco, CA 94123 (☎ (415) 922-0448; fax (415) 346-5535)

DEPARTURE TAX

For flights to neighbouring countries (Pakistan, Sri Lanka, Bangladesh, Nepal) the departure tax is Rs 100, but to other countries it's Rs 300.

This airport tax applies to everybody, even to babies who do not occupy a seat – in most countries airport tax applies only to seat occupants or adults. The method of collecting the tax varies but generally you have to pay it before you check in, so look out for an airport tax counter as you enter the check-in area.

INSURANCE

Regardless of how you plan to travel to India, it's worth taking out travel insurance. Work out what you need. You may not want to insure that grotty old army surplus backpack – but everyone should be covered for the worst possible case: an accident, for example, that will require hospital treatment and a flight home. It's a good idea to make a copy of your policy, in case the original is lost. If you are planning to travel for a long time, the insurance may seem very expensive – but if you can't afford it, you certainly won't be able to afford to deal with a medical emergency overseas.

Getting Around

AIR

India's major domestic airline, the government-run Indian Airlines, flies extensively throughout the nation and into neighbouring countries. The country's international carrier, Air India, also operates domestic services, principally on the Bombay-Delhi, Bombay-Calcutta, Delhi-Calcutta and Bombay-Madras routes.

For many years, Vayudoot, also a government-owned concern, was the only other operator, and it functioned mainly as a feeder airline, servicing smaller airports, especially in the north-east states.

With this cosy government duopoly in place, there was little incentive for either airline to pay much heed to that nuisance known as the customer. In-flight service was lousy, the food barely edible, delays and cancellations frequent, reservations difficult to make at the best of times and refund conditions punitive. It all made air travel within India rather a fraught affair.

Fortunately this dismal state has radically changed in the last few years as the Indian skies have, to a large degree, been deregulated. At least half a dozen new airlines, known as Air Taxi Operators (ATOs), have started services, and while they currently only serve larger centres, new routes are constantly being added as the ATOs lease more aircraft and settle in.

Not only has the introduction of ATOs given the air traveller a choice of airlines on many routes, it has also forced Indian Airlines to pull its finger out in a major way in an effort to compete. The result is that the overall standard of service has improved greatly, despite many pilot defections to the ATOs, lured by lucrative salaries, although the airline continues to lose money by the crore. The ATOs, on the other hand, are laughing all the way to the bank. Vayudoot seems to have gone the way of the dinosaur, with staff and aircraft being largely absorbed into Indian Airlines.

The ATOs currently flying are: East West, which gets some of its staff on secondment from Malaysian Airlines; ModiLuft, which

---

Indian Airlines' Office Addresses

(Distance from the office to the airport in brackets)

Agartala (12 km)
  Khosh Mahal Bldg, Central Rd (☎ (0381) 5470)
Agra (7 km)
  Hotel Clarks Shiraz, 54 Taj Rd
  (☎ (0562) 36-0948)
Ahmedabad (10 km)
  Airlines House, Lal Darwaja
  (☎ 140, (079) 35-3333)
Allahabad (12 km)
  Tourist Bungalow, MG Rd (☎ (0532) 60-2832)
Amritsar (11 km)
  48 The Mall (☎ (0183) 64-433)
Aurangabad (10 km)
  Dr Rajendra Prasad Marg (☎ (02432) 24-864)
Bagdogra (14 km)
  Hotel Sinclairs, Mallaguri, Siliguri
  (☎ (03556) 20-692)
Bangalore (13 km)
  Housing Board Bldg, Kempegowda Rd
  (☎ (080) 221-1914)
Bhavnagar (8 km)
  Diwanpara Rd (☎ (0278) 26-503)
Bhopal (11 km)
  Bhadbhada Rd, TT Nagar (☎ (0755) 55-0480)
Bhubaneswar (4 km)
  Unit 1, Raj Path, Bapuji Nagar
  (☎ (0674) 40-0533)
Bhuj (6 km)
  Outside Waniawad Gate, Station Rd
  (☎ (0735) 21-433)
Bombay (26 km)
  Army & Navy Bldg, M G Rd
  (☎ (022) 287-6161, 202-3031)
Calcutta (16 km)
  Airlines House, 39 Chittaranjan Ave
  (☎ (033) 26-3390, 26-4433)
Chandigarh (11 km)
  SCO-186-187-188 Sector 17C
  (☎ (0172) 54-4034)
Chittagong, Bangladesh (23 km)
  Hotel Agrabad (☎ 50-2814)
Coimbatore (12 km)
  Civil Aerodrome, Peelamedy (☎ (0422) 21-2743)
Colombo, Sri Lanka (32 km)
  95 Sir Baron Jayatilaka Mawatha
  (☎ 32-3136)
Darjeeling
  Bellevue Hotel, Chowrasta (☎ (0354) 2355)

is linked with Germany's Lufthansa; Sahara Indian Airlines; Archana Airways; Jagson Airlines; NEPC and Jet Airways.

Booking Flights

Indian Airlines has computerised booking at all but the smallest offices, so getting flight information and reservations is relatively simple – it's just getting to the head of the queue that takes the time. Nevertheless, all flights are still heavily booked and you need to plan as far in advance as possible.

Delhi (16 km)
   Malhotra Bldg, Connaught Place (☎ (011) 331-0517)
   PTI Building, Snsad Marg (☎ 371-9168)
   Domestic Terminal (24 hours) (☎ 140, 141, 144)
Dhaka, Bangladesh (17 km)
   Sharif Mansion, Motijheel (☎ 50-3693)
Dibrugarh (16 km)
   CIWTC Bungalow, Assam Medical College Rd (☎ (0373) 20-114)
Dimapur (3 km)
   Dimapur-Imphal Rd (☎ (03862) 20-875)
Gangtok
   Tibet Rd (☎ (03592) 23-099)
Goa (30 km)
   Dempo Building, D Bandodkar Marg, Panaji (☎ (0832) 22-4067)
Guwahati (23 km)
   Paltan Bazar (☎ (0361) 56-4420)
Gwalior (12 km)
   Tansen Marg, Barrar (☎ (0751) 28-533)
Hyderabad (16 km)
   Secretariat Rd (☎ (0842) 24-3333, 23-6902)
Imphal (8 km)
   Mahatma Gandhi Rd (☎ (03852) 22-0999)
Indore (9 km)
   Dr R S Bhandari Marg (☎ (0731) 43-1595)
Jaipur (13 km)
   Tonk Rd (☎ (0141) 51-4407)
Jammu (6 km)
   Tourist Reception Centre, Veer Marg (☎ (0191) 54-2735)
Jamnagar (10 km)
   Indra Mahal, Bhind Bhanjan Rd (☎ (0288) 78-569)
Jodhpur (5 km)
   Airport Rd (☎ (0291) 36-757)
Jorhat (7 km)
   Tarajan Rd, Garhali (☎ (0376) 32-0011)
Karachi, Pakistan (19 km)
   Hotel Inter-Continental (c/o PIA) (☎ 568-1577)
Kathmandu, Nepal (6 km)
   26 Durbar Marg (☎ 41-9649)
Khajuraho (5 km)
   Khajuraho Hotel (☎ (076861) 2035)
Kochi (Cochin) (6 km)
   Durbar Hall Rd, Ernakulam (☎ (0484) 37-0242)
Kozikhode (Calicut)
   Eroth Centre, Bank Rd (☎ (0495) 65-482)
Leh (8 km)
   Ibex Guest House (☎ (01982) 2276)
Lucknow (14 km)
   Clarks Avadh, 5 Mahatma Gandhi Marg (☎ (0522) 24-0927)

Madras (18 km)
   19 Marshalls Rd, Egmore (☎ (044) 825-1677, 141, 827-7888)
Madurai (12 km)
   Pandyan House, 7A West Veli St (☎ (0452) 37-234)
Malé, Maldives (5 km)
   Beach Hotel (☎ 32-3003)
Mangalore (20 km)
   Hathill Rd, Lalbagh (☎ (0824) 41-4300)
Mysore
   Hotel Mayura Hoysala, 2 Jhansi Lakshmi Bai Rd (☎ (0821)51-6943)
Nagpur (11 km)
   242A Manohar Niwas, Rabindranath Tagore Rd, Civil Lines (☎ (0712) 53-3962)
Patna (8 km)
   South Gandhi Maidan (☎ (0612) 22-6433)
Port Blair (3 km)
   Tagore Marg (☎ (03192) 21-108)
Pune (10 km)
   39 Dr Ambedkar Rd (☎ (0212) 65-9939, 140)
Raipur (16 km)
   LIC Bldg (☎ (0771) 52-6707)
Rajkot (4 km)
   Angel Chamber, Station Rd (☎ (0281) 27-916)
Ranchi (13 km)
   Welfare Centre, Main Rd (☎ (0651) 30-2481)
Silchar (26 km)
   Red Cross Rd (☎ (03842) 20-072)
Srinagar (14 km)
   Air Cargo Complex Bldg, Shervani Marg (☎ (0194) 76-868)
Tezpur (16 km)
   Jankin Rd (☎ (03804) 20-083)
Thiruvananthapuram (Trivandrum) (6 km)
   Mascot Hill Bldg, Museum Rd (☎ (0471) 43-6870)
Tiruchirappalli (8 km)
   Southern Railway Employees Co-op Credit Society Bldg, Dindigul Rd (☎ (0431) 42-233)
Tirupathi (15 km)
   Hotel Vishnupriya, Ranigunta Rd (☎ 22-349)
Udaipur (24 km)
   LIC Bldg, outside Delhi Gate (☎ (0294) 41-0999)
Vadodara (Baroda) (6 km)
   University Rd, Fateh Ganj (☎ (0265) 32-8596)
Varanasi (22 km)
   Mint House Motel, Vadunath Marg, Cantonment (☎ (0542) 43-746)
Visakhapatnam (16 km)
   Jeevan Prakash, LIC Bldg Complex (☎ (0891) 46-503)

The private operators are all reasonably efficient, and most have computerised booking.

Tickets

All Indian Airline tickets must be paid for with foreign currency or by credit card, or rupees backed up by encashment certificates. Change, where appropriate, is given in rupees.

Infants up to two years old travel at 10% of the adult fare, but only one infant can travel at this fare per adult. Children two to 12 years old travel at 50% fare. There is no

---

Private Airline Domestic Operators

Ahmedabad
    Damania Airways ☎ 30-5747
    East West ☎ 42-3311, 42-3312
    Jet Airways ☎ 46-7886, 46-2839
    ModiLuft ☎ 46-6228
Aurangabad
    East West ☎ 24-307, 29-990
Bangalore
    Damania ☎ 558-8866, 558-8736
    East West ☎ 58-6874, 58-6894
    Jet Airways ☎ 558-8354, 558-6095
    ModiLuft ☎ 558-2199, 558-2202
    NEPC ☎ 558-7322
    Sahara ☎ 558-6976, 558-3917
Bhavnagar
    East West ☎ 29-244
Bombay
    Damania ☎ 610-2545, 610-4676
    East West ☎ 643-6678, 644-1880
    Jet Airways ☎ 285-5788, 285-5789
    ModiLuft ☎ 363-5085, 363-1921
    NEPC ☎ 611-5144
    Sahara ☎ 283-2446, 873-8825
Calcutta
    Damania ☎ 475-7090, 475-7396
    East West ☎ 29-1469, 29-1463
    ModiLuft ☎ 29-6257, 29-8437
Kochi (Cochin)
    East West ☎ 36-3542, 36-9592
    Jet Airways ☎ 36-9423, 36-9582
    ModiLuft ☎ 37-0015
    NEPC ☎ 36-7720
Coimbatore
    Damania ☎ 57-6898
    East West ☎ 21-0285
    Jet Airways ☎ 21-2036
    NEPC ☎ 21-6741
Delhi
    Archana ☎ 682-9323, 329-5126 ext 2354
    Damania ☎ 688-1122, 688-8951
    East West ☎ 372-1510, 332-0222
    Jet Airways ☎ 372-4727, 372-4729
    Sahara ☎ 332-6851, 335-2771
    ModiLuft ☎ 643-0689, 63-1128
    Jagson ☎ 372-1593
Diu
    East West ☎ 2180
Goa
    Damania ☎ 22-0192, 22-2791

East West ☎ 22-4108, 22-4723
Jet Airways ☎ 22-4471, 22-1476
ModiLuft ☎ 22-7577
Hyderabad
    East West ☎ 81-3566
    Jet Airways ☎ 23-1263
    ModiLuft ☎ 24-3783
Jaipur
    East West ☎ 51-6809
Jaisalmer
    Jagson Airlines ☎ 52-392
Jodhpur
    East West ☎ 37-516
    Jagson Airlines ☎ 44-010, extn 360
Kozhikode (Calicut)
    East West ☎ 64-883
    Jet Airways ☎ 35-6052
Madras
    Damania Airways ☎ 828-0610
    East West ☎ 827-7007, 826-6669
    Jet Airways ☎ 825-7914, 825-9817
    ModiLuft ☎ 826-0048
    NEPC ☎ 434-4259
Madurai
    East West ☎ 24-995
    NEPC Airlines ☎ 24-520
Mangalore
    East West ☎ 44-0541, 44-0105
    Jet Airways ☎ 44-0694, 44-0794
    NEPC ☎ 45-6659
Pune
    Damania ☎ 64-0815
    East West ☎ 66-5862
    NEPC ☎ 64-7441
Rajkot
    East West ☎ 40-422
Thiruvananthapuram (Trivandrum)
    East West ☎ 43-8288
    NEPC ☎ 44-1005
Udaipur
    ModiLuft ☎ 65-5281
    East West ☎ 71-757, 77-569
Vadodara (Baroda)
    East West ☎ 33-0009, 33-2628
    Jet Airways ☎ 33-7051, 33-7052
    NEPC Airways ☎ 33-7899
Visakhapatnam
    East West ☎ 64-119)
    NEPC ☎ 57-4151

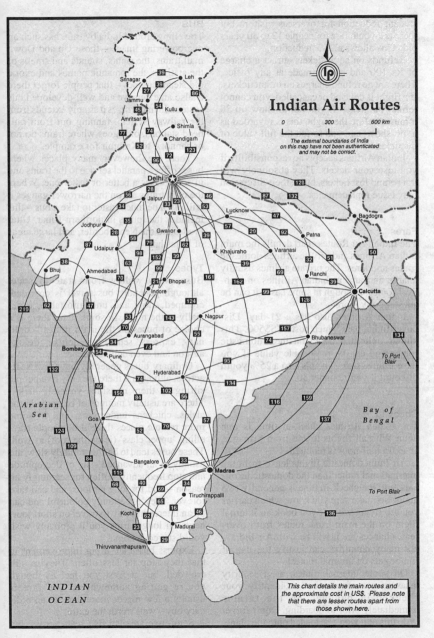

Indian Air Routes

0   300   600 km

The external boundaries of India
on this map have not been authenticated
and may not be correct.

Srinagar
Leh 39
Jammu 27 39
Kullu 86
Amritsar 45 54
Shimla
Chandigarh
77 74 123
52 72
96
Delhi
120
28 87 132
Jaipur 56 46
34 33 23 Lucknow
Agra 53 47 Bagdogra
Jodhpur 35 57 29 92 Patna
Udaipur 58 79 Gwalior 39 Varanasi 50
87 26 98 152 Khajuraho 32 51
38 63 99 39 69 Ranchi
Bhuj 70 21 Bhopal 162 99 39
Ahmedabad Indore 161 124 Calcutta
219 62 47 53 143 Nagpur 128
70 157 134
Bombay 34 Aurangabad 55 74 Bhubaneswar
54 Pune 73 95
132 Hyderabad 134
46 74 116 159
150 84 102 56 137
Goa 52 57
124 79
109 Bangalore 33
84 Madras
115 To Port
68 40 Blair
Kochi 69 34 Tiruchirappalli
62 65 16
23 Madurai 46 136 To Port Blair
Thiruvananthapuram 29

*Arabian
Sea*

*Bay of
Bengal*

*INDIAN
OCEAN*

This chart details the main routes and
the approximate cost in US$. Please note
that there are lesser routes apart from
those shown here.

student reduction for overseas visitors but there is a youth fare for people 12 to 30 years old. This allows a 25% reduction.

Refunds on adult tickets attract a charge of Rs 100 and can be made at any office. There are no refund charges on infant tickets. If a flight is delayed or cancelled, you cannot refund the ticket. If you fail to show up 30 minutes before the flight, this is regarded as a 'no-show' and you forfeit the full value of the ticket.

Indian Airlines accepts no responsibility if you lose your tickets. They absolutely will not refund lost tickets, but at their discretion may issue replacements.

Fares

The Indian Air Routes chart details the main Indian Airlines and private airlines domestic routes and fares. The private airlines usually charge the same as Indian Airlines on identical routes, although in some cases it can be substantially more.

Indian Airlines also has a 21-day 'Discover India' pass which costs US$500. This allows unlimited travel on their domestic routes and can be reasonable value if you have limited time. There's also a 25% youth discount if you're under 30.

Check In

The Indian Airlines check-in time is one hour. With all flights to and from Srinagar, an extra half-hour is required.

Air India domestic flights leave from the international rather than the domestic terminals, and the check-in time is generally two hours, so make sure you know which carrier you are flying with. If you book an internal flight on the main trunk routes from overseas, chances are it will be with Air India – not many countries can justify the use of Jumbo jets on internal routes!

On some internal routes, as a security measure you are required to identify your checked-in baggage on the tarmac immediately prior to boarding. Don't forget to do this or it won't be loaded onto the plane.

BUS

Travelling around India by train has such an overpowering image – those Up and Down mail trains, the sights, sounds and smells of the stations, the romantic names and exotic old steam engines – that people forget there is also an extensive and well-developed bus system. In many cases it simply extends from the railway system, fanning out from railhead stations, or it goes where trains do not or cannot – to Kashmir for example.

There are, however, many places where buses offer a parallel service to the trains and in some cases a better or faster one. Where the only trains are on the narrower gauges it will often be much faster to take a bus – this includes the routes in northern Bihar, Uttar Pradesh to the Nepal border, and large areas of Rajasthan.

Types

Buses vary widely from state to state, although generally bus travel is crowded, cramped, slow and uncomfortable, especially in the north. In some states there is a choice of buses on the main routes – ordinary, express, semi-luxe, deluxe, deluxe air-con and even deluxe sleeper!

Ordinary buses generally have five seats across, although if there are only five people sitting in them consider yourself lucky! There are usually mounds of baggage in the aisles, chickens under seats and in some more remote places there'll be people travelling 'upper class' (ie on the roof) as well. These buses tend to be frustratingly slow, are usually in an advanced state of decrepitude and stop frequently – often for seemingly no reason – and for long periods, and can take forever. They're certainly colourful and can be an interesting way to travel on short journeys; on longer trips you'll probably wish you'd stayed at home.

Express buses are a big improvement in that they stop far less often. They're still crowded, but at least you feel as though you're getting somewhere. The fare is usually a few rupees more than on an ordinary bus – well worth the extra.

Semi-luxe are also five seats across, but

In rural areas bus travel is often crowded and uncomfortable, simply because there are too few buses to cope with demand. Passengers on this bus in Rajasthan cling to every available space.

they have more padding and 'luxuries' such as tinted windows, and the buses stop infrequently. The fare is about 20% more than the ordinary fare, which discourages many of the locals who can only afford the cheapest mode of travel. The big difference between deluxe and semi-luxe is that deluxe buses have only four seats across and these will usually recline.

There is generally a state-operated bus company in each state, and in most places this is backed up by privately operated buses – although they may only operate on certain routes. Unlike state-operated bus companies, private operators are keen to maximise profits and therefore maintenance is less and speed more – a dangerous combination.

Despite the extra speed buses often offer, they become uncomfortable sooner than trains. If it's a long trip, particularly overnight, it's better opting for a train if there's a choice.

The thing that foreigners find hardest to cope with on the buses is the music. The Hindi pop music is usually played at maximum volume and seems to screech on and on without end. Requests to turn it down are usually greeted with amusement and complete disbelief. Just as bad are the video

machines found on many deluxe buses. These generally screen macho garbage, also at full volume, for hours on end. If you're travelling overnight by bus, try to avoid video coaches.

Getting a Seat

If there are two of you, work out a bus boarding plan where one of you can guard the gear while the other storms the bus in search of a seat. The other accepted method is to pass a newspaper or article of clothing through the open window and place it on an empty seat, or ask a passenger to do it for you. Having made your 'reservation' you can then board the bus after things have simmered down. This method rarely fails.

The big advantage of buses over trains is that they go more frequently and getting one involves comparatively little predeparture hassle. You can, however, often make advance reservations for a small additional fee, but this usually only applies to express, semi-luxe and deluxe services. Private buses should always be booked in advance.

At many bus stations there is a separate women's queue. You may not notice this because the relevant sign (where it exists at all) will not be in English and there may not be any women queuing. Usually the same ticket window will handle the male and the female queue, taking turn about. What this means is that women can usually go straight up to the front of the queue (ie straight up beside the front of the male queue) and get almost immediate service.

Baggage

Baggage is generally carried for free on the roof so it's an idea to take a few precautions. Make sure it's tied on properly and that nobody dumps a tin trunk on top of your (relatively) fragile backpack. At times a tarpaulin will be tied across the baggage – make sure it covers your gear adequately.

Theft is sometimes a problem so keep an eye on your bags at chai stops. Having a large, heavy-duty bag into which your pack will fit can be a good idea, not only for bus travel but also for air travel.

If someone carries your bag onto the roof, expect to pay a few rupees for the service.

Toilet Stops

On long-distance bus trips, chai stops can be far too frequent or, conversely, agonisingly infrequent. Long-distance trips can be a real hassle for women travellers – toilet facilities are generally inadequate to say the least.

TRAIN

The Indian Railways system is the world's fourth-largest with a route length of over 60,000 km. Every single day over 7,000 passenger trains run, carrying over 10.5 million passengers and connecting 7100 stations. It's also the world's largest single employer with a shade over 1.6 million employees!

The first step in coming to grips with Indian Railways is to get a timetable. *Trains at a Glance* (Rs 10) is a handy, 100-page guide covering all the main routes and trains. It is usually available at major railway stations, and sometimes on newsstands in the larger cities. If you can't find it, a regional timetable provides much the same information, including the more local train services and a pink section with timetables for the major mail and express trains (the fast ones) throughout the country. Unfortunately, these are also often unavailable!

There is also the 300-page *Indian Bradshaw* (Rs 50) which covers every train service throughout the country. It's more detailed than most people need and it can be frustratingly difficult to find things, but for serious exploring it's invaluable. Published monthly, it's not widely available but you can usually find it on the bookstalls at major city railway stations. Thomas Cook's *Overseas Timetable* has good train timetables for India, although it's not available in India.

The timetables indicate the km distance between major stations and a table in front shows the fares for distances from one km to 5000 km for the various train types. With this information it is very easy to calculate the fare between any two stations. Unless otherwise indicated, the fares quoted in this guide are based on the faster ('express' rather than 'passenger') trains.

The Konkan Railway

The British may have scratched a spiderweb of railway lines across the map of India but they left one blank space: the Konkan coast from Bombay down through Maharashtra to Goa and on through Karnataka to Mangalore, just north of the border with Kerala. Hills, ravines, rivers, floodplains and swamps made railway construction an intimidating prospect and as a result connections down the coast have always been slow going and hard work. This will all change when the 760-km Konkan Railway opens, optimistically by 1996 for freight services only, with passenger services following once these are established. The Rs 20 billion project is the biggest railway construction in South Asia this century and a formidable engineering undertaking with 140 major rivers to cross, nearly 2000 bridges in all and over 10% of the total distance made up of either bridges or tunnels. It will also be the fastest railway line in India, capable of handling trains travelling at up to 160 km/h. When the line opens rail travel time between Bombay and Goa will be cut from 20 hours to 10 and from Bombay to Mangalore from 44 hours to 18. ∎

Gricing

For some travellers, India's rail system is more than just public transport: with its large number of working steam engines, train fanatics (otherwise known as gricers) find India irresistible.

Since the first railways appeared in India in the 19th century, locomotives of various designs have been imported from the UK and the USA, and of course a large number were actually built in India, initially using imported technology and designs.

Fortunately examples of most major designs have been preserved in the Rail Transport Museum in Delhi. Locomotives from all three gauges (broad, metre and narrow) have been beautifully restored, many in their original railway company colours. Amongst those on show is the oldest surviving engine in India, built in 1855, and a diminutive two-foot-gauge loco from Darjeeling, making a stark contrast beside a 234-ton Beyer Garratt locomotive.

The remaining 3000 or so broad-gauge steam locomotives in India are of only two basic and rather austere designs. The more attractive of the two is the distinctive semi-streamlined WP class introduced in 1947. The engines of the WG class were originally built for heavy freight traffic, but as most of these duties are now worked by diesel and electric traction, the WGs have been allotted such menial tasks as shunting, local freight and slow passenger trains. There's plenty of room on the footplate of these broad-gauge giants and many of the crew are not averse to having you aboard; it's always worth asking.

The mainstays of the metre-gauge system are the post-war YP (passenger) and YG (freight) designs which are found everywhere. A large number were built in India, the last YG being made in 1972. A handful of the attractive YD and YB classes have managed to survive. The YDs still slog their way up the ghats east of Goa on local passenger trains, while the last few YBs are found on the Western Railway in Gujarat.

Other curiosities are the narrow-gauge lines: the rack railway to Ooty, which uses Swiss engines; the Darjeeling Himalayan Railway, arguably the most famous and most spectacular steam railway in the world; and the lines from Kalka to Shimla and from Neral (near Bombay) to Matheran. With the exception of the Darjeeling line, all these routes are now worked by diesels.

Although steam locomotives will be around in India well past the year 2000, the variety and colour that remain will certainly have disappeared before then. But before you point that camera, a word of warning. Indian authorities can go overboard when it comes to railway security, so try to ensure that no police or other officials are around.

Mark Carter

A factor to consider with Indian trains is that getting there may not always be half the fun but it is certainly 90% of the experience. Indian rail travel is unlike any other sort of travel in any other place on earth. At times it can be uncomfortable or incredibly frustrating (since the trains are not exactly fast) but an experience it certainly is. Money aside, if you simply want to get from A to B, fly. If getting from A to B is as much a part of India as what you see at both ends, then take the train.

During and shortly after the monsoon, rail services can be drastically affected by floods and high rivers, particularly in low-lying areas along the Ganges basin or where major rivers reach the sea, such as the coastal region of Andhra Pradesh.

Classes

There are generally two classes – 1st and 2nd – but there are a number of subtle variations on this basic distinction. For a start there is 1st class and 1st-class air-con. The air-con carriages only operate on the major trains and routes. The fare for 1st-class air-con is more than double normal 1st class. A slightly cheaper air-con alternative is the air-con two-tier sleeper, which costs about 25% more than 1st class. These carriages are a lot more common than 1st-class air-con, but are still only found on the major routes.

Between 1st and 2nd class there are two more air-con options: the air-con three-tier sleeper and air-con chair car. The former has three levels of berths rather than two, while the latter, as the name suggests, consists of carriages with aircraft-type layback seats. Once again, these carriages are only found on the major routes, and the latter only on day trains. The cost of air-con three-tier is about 70% of the 1st-class fare; air-con chair is about 55% of the 1st-class fare.

Types

What you want is a mail or express train. What you do not want is a passenger train. No Indian train travels very fast, but at least the mail and express trains keep travelling

Runaway Luggage

I was taking the Jaipur to Jodhpur express, minding my own business in a 1st-class compartment occupied by a very pleasant Indian family. My backpack was padlocked and chained to the compartment's parcel shelf; for the first (and last!) time I'd taken my moneybelt off and put it in the locked pack because I was feeling rather hot and sweaty wearing it across the desert (the number of times I pulled out damp Rs 100 notes!). In true Indian fashion, the train stopped from time to time for anything from two to 20 minutes, to be besieged by hordes of chai, cold drink and snack sellers.

Halfway into the journey, I found my stocks of mineral water were low. Concerned about dehydration, I decided to replenish my supply at the next station. The Indian family assured me that it was to be a five to 10-minute stop, so I hopped off the train in search of mineral water. There was nothing for sale on the platform so I ran out of the station and tried a few stalls. I was greeted with blank stares which, I guess, meant: 'There's a tap over there – why do you want to pay for water in a bottle?' Little English was spoken and in the end, I settled for two cartons of mango fruit drink.

I'd been gone for about four minutes when I sprinted back to the station to find – you guessed it – only a stretch of empty track where my train should have been. I don't think I will ever forget the overwhelming sense of blind panic and desperation that came over me. This would have been bad enough in England...but in India! It was my worst nightmare realised, almost everything I had was on that train: backpack, clothes, camera, film, medical supplies, most of my money, and my moneybelt which had my passport and travellers' cheques. I was left with only the clothes I wore and around Rs 100 in change...oh, and two cartons of mango juice.

I raced madly up the platform, shouting at people and asking them where the train had gone. There was no sign of it along the track, and the vague wave one guy gave in the direction of the empty stretch of line confirmed that it had left without me.

After sprinting back to the stationmaster's office, I breathlessly tried to explain what had happened, only to find that he too spoke very little English and insisted that I write down whatever I wanted to say. It was the most frustrating half-hour of my life – playing with a pen and paper as my luggage steamed ever further into the dry, distant desert.

By this time I was really starting to lose my cool, and in true Indian fashion, the station staff seemed unperturbed by the whole scenario. I wandered around the office muttering a stream of invectives, thumping the walls and kicking the furniture in an effort not to go totally bananas – much to the amusement of a band of locals pressing at the door. In the middle of this desperate situation, the line that came flooding into my

more of the time. Passenger trains spend a lot of time at a lot of stations and are subject to interminable delays, which quickly becomes very boring unless you have a keen interest in small-town stations. According to figures published by Indian Railways, express/mail trains average 47.1 km/h, passenger trains 27.2 km/h – just in case you had any ideas about going places in a hurry! Passenger trains are usually 2nd class only; 2nd-class fares on passenger trains are less than on a mail or express train over the same route.

Air-con 'superfast' express services operate on certain main routes, and because of tighter scheduling and fewer stops they are much faster. A separate fare structure applies to them as meals are included (except on the Delhi to Bangalore and Madras *Rajdhani* services). These trains are the *Rajdhani Express*, which operates between Delhi and Bombay, Bangalore, Madras and Calcutta, and the *Shatabdi Express*, with sep-arate services connecting Delhi with Chandigarh/Kalka, Bhopal, Jaipur, Dehra Dun and Lucknow; Madras with Mysore; and Bombay with Ahmedabad. The *Rajdhani* and *Shatabdi* services are claimed to average around 130 km/h.

Gauge

There are three gauge types in India: broad, metre and narrow, and what you want nearly as much as a mail or express train is broad gauge. In broad gauge the rails are 1.676 metres apart; metre gauge is, as it says, one metre wide; narrow gauge is either 0.762 metres (two feet six inches) or 0.610 metres (two feet).

Broad gauge has a major advantage – it is much faster. It also gives a smoother ride. The carriages are much the same between broad gauge and metre gauge, but on narrow gauge they are much, much narrower and the accommodation very cramped. In areas

head was one from an English TV comedy, spoken by a hotel proprietor trying frantically to communicate with his Spanish waiter: 'Please try and understand before one of us dies!'

Several pieces of paper later, it became apparent that all I could hope for was that my luggage would be unloaded at Degana (a name eternally etched in my memory!), the next station about 45 km away and the last stop before Jodhpur. A hesitant call was duly put through to Degana, but it was hardly a confidence-inspiring effort. The line appeared to keep going dead and the phone was one of those 'wind-up' affairs! After an agonising half-hour wait, Degana replied confirming that my luggage was there.

Still not convinced that the luggage was safe, I decided to head off to Degana by road to collect my luggage rather than wait for it to return on the next train. There then followed a couple of sprints between the jeep taxi rank and the station in an effort to arrange the trip as quickly as possible; in the end I was stung Rs 250 for the two-hour journey. They're not daft, they know when there's a panic on.

By this time I had my fan club, a group of 30 or so locals, following my every move, anxious to see what this eccentric Westerner would do next – more running around, more shouting and waving or more furniture thumping. They weren't disappointed as I made my way back to the mango juice stall and tried to explain I wanted 20 cartons to last me across the desert. The stallkeeper was amazed, and the locals loved the finale to the saga as the Western visitor leaped into a taxi jeep with two bulging carrier bags full of mango juice cartons. (I've gone off mango juice now.)

The ride seemed like an eternity, yet when I reached Degana all my luggage was there – intact! Not only had they removed it from the train (cutting the chain that secured the pack to the train in the process) but they'd taken all the contents out of the unlocked side and top pockets of the pack and put them into bags sealed with wax, to ensure that nobody could interfere with them. Everything had been carefully logged and held secure in a locked cupboard till I arrived – it was an amazing feat of organisation. I was given something to eat and drink – the station superintendent had a meal brought from his own home. I was given a chit stating what had happened and that I was to be allowed to continue my journey to Jodhpur on a different train but using the same ticket. I was safely deposited on the night train which arrived in Jodhpur at 5 am the next day. Was it all a dream I wondered when I woke up.

I offered the Degana crew some money for their trouble but they refused and insisted that all I should do is take some group photos and send them copies. I reckon they deserve medals – well done India!

Two important lessons I learnt from this experience were: never let go of the most important possessions – passport and money; and never lose sight of the train you are travelling in when stopped at a station. Both are painfully obvious 'golden rules' but it took my escapade to hammer them home to me. I'm left in no doubt that I was extraordinarily fortunate to get away with it all.

François Baker, UK

where there are no broad-gauge lines it may be worth taking a bus, which will often be faster then the metre-gauge trains. These areas include much of Rajasthan and the northern Bihar and Uttar Pradesh areas towards the Nepal border.

Life on Board

It's India for real on board the trains. In 2nd class, unreserved travel can be a nightmare since the trains are often hopelessly crowded, and not only with people – Indians seem unable to travel without the kitchen sink and everything that goes with it. Combined with the crowds, the noise and the confusion there's the discomfort. Fans and lights have a habit of failing at prolonged stops when there's no air moving through the carriage, and toilets can get a bit rough towards the end of a long journey. Worst of all are the stops. Trains seem to stop often, interminably and for no apparent reason.

Often it's because somebody has pulled the emergency stop cable because they are close to home – well, so it's said; some people deny this. Still, it's all part of life on the rails.

In 2nd-class reserved it's a great deal better since, in theory, only four people share each bench but there's inevitably the fifth, and sometimes even the sixth, person who gets the others to bunch up so they can get at least part of their bum on the seat. This normally doesn't happen at night or in 1st class, where there are either two or four people to a compartment, and the compartment doors are lockable.

Costs

Fares operate on a distance basis. The timetables indicate the distance in km between the stations and from this it is simple to calculate the cost between any two stations. If you have a ticket for at least 400 km you can break your journey at the rate of one day per 200 km so long as you travel at least 300 km on the first sector. This can save a lot of hassle buying tickets and also, of course, results in a small saving.

The Indian Rail Fares table below indicates fares for set distances.

Reservations

The cost of reservations is nominal – it's the time it takes which hurts, although even this is generally not too bad as computerised reservation becomes more widespread. At the moment it is limited to the major towns and cities only.

In Delhi, Bombay, Calcutta and Madras there are special tourist booking facilities at the main booking offices. These are for any foreign tourists and they make life much easier. The people at these offices are generally very knowledgeable (although you will be surprised how often you find other railway booking clerks who really know their stuff). They will often give you excellent advice and suggest connections and routes which can save you a lot of time and effort.

At other major stations with computerised reservation offices, such as Ahmedabad and Jaipur, one ticket window will deal with foreign tourists and other minorities (such as 'Freedom Fighters'!). These windows are generally queue-free, so check to see if one exists.

Reservations can be made up to six months in advance and the longer in advance you make them the better. Your reservation ticket will indicate which carriage and berth you have, and when the train arrives you will find a sheet of paper fixed to each carriage listing passenger names beside their appropriate berth number. Usually this information is also posted on notice boards on the platform. It is Indian rail efficiency at its best.

As at many bus stations, there are separate women's queues, usually with a sign saying 'Ladies' Queue'. Usually the same ticket window handles the male and female queue, taking one at a time. This means that women can go to the front of the queue, next to the first male at the window, and get almost immediate service.

Reservation costs are Rs 25 in air-con 1st class, Rs 15 in 1st class and air-con chair class, Rs 10 in a 2nd-class three-tier sleeper, and Rs 5 in 2nd-class sitting. There are very rarely any 2nd-class sitting compartments with reservations. There are also some superfast express trains that require a supplementary charge.

If the train you want is fully booked, it's often possible to get an RAC (Reservation Against Cancellation) ticket. This entitles you to board the train and have seating accommodation. Once the train is under way, the TTE (Travelling Ticket Examiner) will find a berth for you, but it may take an hour or more. This is different from a wait-listed ticket, as the latter does not give you the right to actually board the train (should you be so cheeky you can be 'detrained and fined'). The hassle with RAC tickets is that you will probably get split up if there are two or more of you.

			Indian Rail Fares			
Distance (km)	1st-class (air-con)	1st class	Air-con chair	2nd-class express, sleeper	2nd-class express, seat	2nd-class passenger
50	Rs 186	Rs 75	Rs 57	Rs 62	Rs 17	Rs 9
100	Rs 298	Rs 114	Rs 77	Rs 62	Rs 26	Rs 14
200	Rs 450	Rs 183	Rs 123	Rs 62	Rs 49	Rs 26
300	Rs 629	Rs 255	Rs 173	Rs 85	Rs 68	Rs 36
400	Rs 805	Rs 326	Rs 210	Rs 107	Rs 85	Rs 43
500	Rs 951	Rs 382	Rs 250	Rs 128	Rs 102	Rs 50
1000	Rs 1415	Rs 624	Rs 381	Rs 208	Rs 166	Rs 72
1500	Rs 1913	Rs 837	Rs 509	Rs 259	Rs 207	Rs 89
2000	Rs 2378	Rs 1040	Rs 618	Rs 294	Rs 235	Rs 106

If you've not had time to get a reservation or been unable to get one, it's worth just getting on the train in any reserved carriage. Although there's the risk of a small fine for 'ticketless travel', most TTEs are sympathetic. If there are spare berths/seats they'll allot you one, and charge the normal fare plus reservation fee. If all the berths/seats are already reserved you'll simply be banished to the crush and confusion in the unreserved carriages. This trick only works well for day travel. At night sleepers are generally booked out well in advance so if you can't get one (or an RAC ticket) then sitting up in 2nd class is your only choice.

If you plan your trip well ahead, you can avoid all the hassles by booking in advance from abroad. A good Indian travel agent will book and obtain tickets in advance and have them ready for you on arrival. As an alternative to buying tickets as you go along, it's possible to buy a ticket from A to Z with all the stops along the way prebooked. It might take a bit of time sitting down and working it out at the start, but if your time is limited and you can fix your schedule rigidly, this can be a good way to go.

Refunds

Booked tickets are refundable but cancellation fees apply. If you present the ticket more than one day in advance, a fee of Rs 10 to Rs 30 applies, depending on the class. Up to four hours before you lose 25% of the ticket value; within four hours before departure and up to three to 12 hours after departure (depending on the distance of the ticketed journey) you lose 50%. Any later than that and you can keep the ticket as a souvenir.

Tickets for unreserved travel can be refunded up to three hours after the departure of the train, and the only penalty is a Rs 2 per passenger fee.

When presenting your ticket for a refund, you are officially entitled to go straight to the head of the queue (where there isn't a dedicated window for refunds), the rationale being that the berth/seat you are surrendering may be just the one required by the next person in the queue.

Sleepers

There are 2nd-class and 1st-class sleepers, although by Western standards even 1st class is not luxurious. Bedding is available, but only on certain 1st class and air-con two-tier services, and then only if arranged when booking your ticket. First-class sleepers are generally private compartments with two or four berths in them, sometimes with a toilet as well. Usually the sleeping berths fold up to make a sitting compartment during the day. First-class air-con sleepers are more luxurious, and much more expensive, than regular 1st-class sleepers.

Ticket to Bangalore, Please
Scene: At the Goa Railway booking office.

'I'd like a ticket to Bangalore please.'
I am sorry, sir, you cannot. Train is cancelled.'
'Oh, I see. Well, tomorrow will do.'
'No, sir, you cannot. Train is cancelled permanently.'
'Permanently? You mean there is no service to Bangalore from here?'
'No, sir. Government has cancelled this. From November already.'
'Of course. Silly me for not knowing. Well, can I get to Mysore from here?'
'Yes, sir! But not today, only tomorrow.'
'Tomorrow will be fine. Second class please. How much is that?'
'Ninety-two rupees, sir. Here is your ticket. Your train leaves at 7 am, and journey time is 20 hours including a one-hour stop in Bangalore to change trains.'
Aaargh!

Nick Ferris, Australia

Second-class sleepers are known as three-tier. They are arranged in doorless sections each of six berths. During the day the middle berth is lowered to make seats for six or eight. At night they are folded into position, everybody has to bed down at the same time, and a TTE ensures that nobody without a reservation gets into the carriage. Broadgauge, three-tier sleeping carriages also have a row of narrow two-tier (upper and lower) berths along one side. These are not only narrower than the 'inside' berths, but are about 20 cm shorter, so that for the average person stretching right out is not possible. When reserving 2nd-class berths, always write 'inside' on the 'Accommodation Preference' section of the booking form. Sleeping berths are only available between 9 pm and 6 am.

For any sleeper reservation you should try to book at least several days ahead. There is usually a board in each station indicating what is available or how long before the next free berth/seat comes up on the various routes. At the major city stations this is usually computerised and TV screens give a continuous read-out. Once you've selected a particular train and date, you must fill in a reservation form. Do this before you get to the front of the queue. The forms are usually found in boxes around the reservation hall. The demand for 1st-class sleepers is generally far less than for 2nd class.

At most major city stations there's usually a separate section or counter(s) in the booking hall (often called 'Tourist Cell'!) which deals with the tourist quota. Only foreigners and nonresident Indians are allowed to use this facility. Here you can make your reservations in relative comfort away from the madding crowds *but* you must pay in foreign currency (cash or travellers' cheques in US dollars or pounds sterling only) or with rupees backed up by exchange certificates, and any change will be given in rupees.

Lastly, when deciding which train to take along any route, you may come up against that major source of bewilderment – the Indian custom of naming a train without

indicating where it goes. On the timetable or state-of-reservation board at a station you could, for example, see the *Brindavan Express* or the *Cholan Express* etc. But where do they go to? It might be the train you want, but it might not. This is where your *Trains at a Glance* or *Indian Bradshaw* comes in. If you don't have one, you'll have to ask – and that's going to soak up time. Tourist offices can usually help by suggesting the best trains but there isn't always a tourist office. It's something you'll just have to come to terms with.

Getting a Space Despite Everything

If you want a sleeper and there are none left then it's time to try and break into the quotas. Ask the stationmaster, often a helpful man who speaks English, if there is a tourist quota, station quota or if there is a VIP quota. The latter is often a good last bet because VIPs rarely turn up to use their quotas.

If all that fails then you're going to be travelling unreserved and that can be no fun at all. To ease the pain get yourself some expert help. For, say, Rs 10 baksheesh you can get a porter who will absolutely ensure you get a seat if it's humanly possible. If it's a train starting from your station, the key to success is to be on the train before it arrives at the departure platform. Your porter will do just that so when it rolls up you simply stroll on board and take the seat he has warmed for you. If it's a through train then it can be a real free-for-all, and you can be certain he'll be better at it than you are – he'll also not be encumbered with baggage or backpacks.

Women can ask about the Ladies' Compartments which many trains have and are often a refuge from the crowds in other compartments.

Left Luggage

Most stations have a left-luggage facility, quaintly called a Cloak Room, where backpacks can be left for Rs 2 per day. This is a very useful facility if you're visiting (but not staying in) a town, or if you want to find a place to stay, unencumbered by gear. The regulations state that any luggage left in a

Cloak Room must be locked, although this is not strictly enforced.

Special Trains

A special 'Palace on Wheels' makes a regular circuit around Rajasthan – you not only travel by train, you stay in the 'fit for a maharaja' carriages. See the Rajasthan chapter for more details.

The English organisation Butterfield's Indian Railway Tours operates regular train tours of India using a special carriage in which you travel, eat and sleep. The carriage is hooked on to regular trains and is left on the sidings of various towns you visit. The accommodation facilities are basic but you cover a lot of India and using the railway in this way brings you into much closer contact with the people than you'd get on a usual package tour staying in upmarket hotels. Tours from 16 to 29 days are available, and prices start from UK£845. For more information contact Butterfield's Railway Tours (☎ (01262) 47-0230) Burton Fleming, Driffield, Humberside YO25 0PQ, England, UK. Butterfield's can also be contacted through the Madras Hotel, Connaught Circus, Delhi.

Indrail Passes

Indrail passes permit unlimited travel on Indian trains for the period of their validity, but they are expensive and, overall, probably not worth the expense. In purely dollar terms, to get the full value out of any of the passes you need to travel around 300 km per day; with the speed of Indian trains that's at least six hours travelling!

Although the pass covers the cost of reservations, it doesn't get you to the front of the queue, so is of little help there. Nor does the pass give you any advantage when it comes to trying to get a berth or seat on a fully booked train; you join the waitlist like anybody else. The only occasion when it's going to save you time is if you want to travel unreserved on a train, when you can simply hop on without queuing for a ticket. As these journeys are likely to be far fewer and shorter than those when you want to have a reserved berth, it's not much of a gain.

The average visitor to India might cover around 3000 km in a month by rail. An air-con Indrail Pass for this would cost US$500; to buy the tickets as you go along would cost around US$100 to US$160, depending on the number and length of the individual journeys; even if you did twice as many km, you still wouldn't even come close to getting your money's worth. It's the same story with the other class passes: using the example above, a 2nd-class, one-month Indrail Pass would cost US$110, the individual tickets US$12 to US$25. See the Indian Rail Fares table for the cost of Indrail passes.

Children aged five to 12 years pay half-fare. Indrail passes can be bought overseas through some travel agents or in India at certain major railway offices. Payment in India can be made only in either US dollars or pounds sterling, cash or travellers' cheques, or in rupees backed up with exchange certificates. Second-class passes are not available outside India. Indrail passes cover all reservation and berth costs at night, and they can be extended if you wish to keep on travelling. The main offices in India which handle Indrail passes are:

Bombay
    Railway Tourist Guide, Western Railway, Churchgate
    Railway Tourist Guide, Central Railway, Victoria Terminus
Calcutta
    Railway Tourist Guide, Eastern Railway, Fairlie Place
    Central Reservation Office, South-Eastern Railway, Esplanade Mansion
Delhi
    Railway Tourist Guide, New Delhi Railway Station
Madras
    Central Reservation Office, Southern Railway, Madras Central

They are also available from central reservation offices at Secunderabad-Hyderabad, Rameswaram, Bangalore, Vasco da Gama, Gorakhpur (Indian rupees only), Jaipur and

Thiruvananthapuram (Trivandrum), as well as at certain 'recognised tourist agencies'.

S&K Enterprises Ltd (☎ (0181) 903-3411) is a UK company which specialises in Indrail passes. They sell the passes and can make reservations if given at least one month's notice. Their address is: 103 Wembley Park Drive, Wembley, Middlesex, HA9 8HG, UK. Second/1st-class passes cost from £49/90 for seven days up to £145/320 for 90 days.

DRIVING

Few people bring their own vehicles to India. If you do decide to bring a car or motorcycle to India it must be brought in under a carnet, a customs document guaranteeing its removal at the end of your stay. Failing to do so will be very expensive.

Rental

Self-drive car rental in India is not widespread, but it is possible. Both Budget and Hertz maintain offices in the major cities (Bangalore, Bombay, Delhi, Faridabad, Goa, Hyderabad, Jaipur, Madras and Pune).

If you don't feel confident about driving on Indian roads, or if self-drive rental is unavailable, it is easy to hire a car and driver, either from the local state tourist authority or privately through your hotel. By Western standards the cost is quite low, certainly cheaper than a rent-a-car (without driver) in the West. Almost any local taxi will quite happily set off on a long-distance trip in India; even trips lasting several days do not (so it seems) even require a phone call home to tell the wife to keep dinner warm. Enquiring at a taxi rank is the easiest way to find a car – you can also ask your hotel to book one for you although this will cost slightly more.

Trips are either 'one-way', in which case they cost Rs 6 per km, or a 'running trip', which costs Rs 3 per km. This is because the one-way fare is costed on the basis of returning empty to the starting point. A running trip means a minimum of 200 km a day, so if you take a car for four days it's going to cost at least Rs 2400 (800 km at Rs 3 per km). If you're going to drive 200 km from A to B on day one, spend two days in B, then drive 200 km back to A on day four, it's exactly the same cost to take a taxi each way as to take one taxi and have the driver wait for you for two days. And they will wait, your driver will stretch himself out on the back seat and be ready to go when you turn up for the return trip.

Long-distance car hire with driver is becoming an increasingly popular way of getting around parts of India. Spread amongst say four people, it's not overly expensive and you have the flexibility to go where you want when you want.

Some Indian Rules of the Road

Drive on the Left Theoretically vehicles keep to the left in India – as in Japan, Britain or Australia. In practice most vehicles keep to the middle of the road on the basis that there are fewer potholes in the middle than on the sides. When any other vehicle is encountered the lesser vehicle should cower to the side. Misunderstandings as to status can have unfortunate consequences.

Overtaking In India it is not necessary to ascertain that there is space to complete the overtaking manoeuvre before pulling out. Overtaking can be attempted on blind corners, on the way up steep hills or in the face of oncoming traffic. Smaller vehicles unexpectedly encountered in mid-manoeuvre can be expected to swerve apologetically out of the way. If a larger vehicle is encountered it is to be hoped that the overtakee will slow, pull off or otherwise make room for the overtaker.

Use of Horn Although vehicles can be driven with bald tyres or nonexistent brakes, it is imperative that the horn be in superb working order. Surveys during the research for this edition revealed that the average driver uses the horn 10 to 20 times per km, so a 100-km trip can involve 2000 blasts of the horn. In any case the horn should be checked for its continued loud operation at least every 100 metres. Signs prohibiting use of horns are not to be taken seriously. ■

Self-drive costs around Rs 500 per 24 hours (150 km minimum) plus Rs 4 per extra km. Fuel is extra, and a deposit of Rs 1000 is payable (returnable if there's no damage whatsoever to the car – a scratch constitutes 'damage').

All the above price examples assume you'll be driving an Ambassador. The rates for hiring a Maruti are slightly less.

Buying a Car or Motorcycle

Buying a car is naturally expensive in India and not worth the effort unless you intend to stay for months. Buying a motorcycle, on the other hand, is becoming more popular with long-stays. See the Two-Wheeled Experiences section that follows for a detailed discussion on motorcycles.

Road Conditions

Because of the extreme congestion in the cities and the narrow bumpy roads in the country, driving is often a slow, stop-start process – hard on you, the car and fuel economy. Service is so-so in India, parts and tyres not always easy to obtain, though there are plenty of puncture-repair places. All in all driving is no great pleasure except in rural areas where there's little traffic.

Road Safety

In India there are 155 road deaths daily – 56,000 or so a year – which is an astonishing total in relation to the number of vehicles on the road. In the USA, for instance, there are 43,000 road fatalities per year, but it also has more than 20 times the number of vehicles.

The reasons for the high death rate in India are numerous and many of them fairly obvious – starting with the congestion on the roads and the equal congestion in vehicles. When a bus runs off the road there are plenty of people stuffed inside to get injured, and it's unlikely too many of them will be able to escape in a hurry. One newspaper article stated that 'most accidents are caused by brake failure or the steering wheel getting free'!

Many of those killed are pedestrians involved in hit-and-run accidents. The propensity to disappear after the incident is not wholly surprising – lynch mobs can assemble remarkably quickly, even when the driver is not at fault!

Most accidents are caused by trucks, for on Indian roads might is right and trucks are the biggest, heaviest and mightiest. You either get out of their way or get run down. As with so many Indian vehicles they're likely to be grossly overloaded and not in the best of condition. Trucks are actually licensed and taxed to carry a load 25% more than the maximum recommended by the manufacturer. It's staggering to see the number of truck wrecks by the sides of the national highways, and these aren't old accidents, but ones which have obviously happened in the last 24 hours or so – if they haven't been killed, quite often the driver and crew will be sitting around, wondering what to do next.

The karma theory of driving also helps to push up the statistics – it's not so much the vehicle which collides with you as the events of your previous life which caused the accident.

If you are driving yourself, you need to be extremely vigilant at all times. At night there are unilluminated cars and ox carts, and in the daytime there are fearless bicycle riders and hordes of pedestrians. Day and night there are the crazy truck drivers to contend with. Indeed, at night, it's best to avoid driving at all along any major trunk route unless you're prepared to get off the road completely every time a truck is coming in the opposite direction! The other thing you have to contend with at night is the eccentric way in which headlights are used – a combination of full beam and totally off (dipped beams are virtually unheard of). A loud horn definitely helps since the normal driving technique is to put your hand firmly on the horn, close your eyes and plough through regardless. Vehicles always have the right of way over pedestrians and bigger vehicles always have the right of way over smaller ones.

Indian Vehicles

The Indian vehicle manufacturing industry has gone through an explosion in the last

Getting There is Half the Fun

A lot of travel in India can be indescribably dull, boring and uncomfortable. Trains take forever, buses fall apart and shake your fillings loose, even Indian Airlines sometimes manages to make your delay time far longer than your flying time.

Despite the hassles there are a fair number of trips where getting there is definitely half the fun. Trains, of course, are the key to Indian travel and elsewhere in this book you'll find a section on India's unique and wonderful old steam trains. The narrow-gauge line to Darjeeling, which winds back and forth on its long climb up to the hill station, is the last remaining steam-powered line and the trip up (or down) is half the fun of visiting Darjeeling. Other 'toy trains' include the run up to Matheran, just a couple of hours outside Bombay; the 'rack train' which makes the climb to Ooty from Mettupalayam in Tamil Nadu; and the narrow-gauge line which connects the hill station of Shimla (Himachal Pradesh) with Kalka on the plains.

Then there is the delightful backwater trip through the waterways of Kerala between Kollam (Quilon) and Alappuzha (Alleppey) – not only is the trip fascinating, it's absurdly cheap.

Indian buses are generally a refined form of torture but the two-day trip between Manali in Himachal Pradesh and Leh in Ladakh is too good to miss. The bus route from Darjeeling or Kalimpong to Gangtok in Sikkim is pretty good too, as is the climb up to Kodaikanal from Madurai in Tamil Nadu. Finally, there could hardly be a more spectacular flight in the world than the Srinagar to Leh route, which crosses the full width (and height!) of the Himalaya.

Trip	State	Page
Siliguri to Darjeeling (toy train)	West Bengal	507
Neral to Matheran (toy train)	Maharashtra	805
Mettupalayam to Udhagamandalam (rack train)	Tamil Nadu	1090
Kalka to Shimla (toy train)	Himachal Pradesh	274
Alappuzha to Kollam (backwater trip)	Kerala	987
Manali to Leh (bus or jeep)	Himachal Pradesh/Jammu & Kashmir	338
Darjeeling to Gangtok (bus or jeep)	West Bengal/Sikkim	506
Madurai to Kodaikanal (bus)	Tamil Nadu	1069
Srinagar to Leh (air)	Jammu & Kashmir	337

decade, and the number of cars and motorcycles on the road has increased dramatically. The old totally Indian Hindustan Ambassador, a copy of an early 1950s British Morris Oxford, is still the everyday vehicle on the Indian roads but there are now several more modern ones. These include licence-manufactured Rover 2000s (for the Indian executive), Datsun-engined Fiat 124s and a version of the British Vauxhall – but the big story is the Maruti.

The Maruti is a locally assembled Japanese Suzuki minicar or minivan, put together in the abortive Sanjay Gandhi 'people's car' factory near Delhi. They've swept the country and you now see them everywhere in surprisingly large numbers. Whether they will have the endurance of the old rock-solid (and rock-heavy), fuel-guzzling Ambassador is a different question.

Marutis start at around Rs 180,000 new. Ambassadors (now with safety belts!) start from around Rs 280,000. More expensive versions now have Isuzu engines and five-speed gearboxes. The new, vaguely Mercedes-looking Tata station wagon costs over Rs 400,000.

India's truck and bus industry was always a more important business, with companies like Tata and Ashok Leyland turning out sturdy trucks which you see all over India, and also in a number of other developing countries. Here too there has been a Japanese onslaught; modern Japanese trucks have appeared. All Japanese vehicle builders in India must have at least 50% Indian ownership. The name thus becomes an Indo-Japanese hybrid, so you get Maruti-Suzuki, Hindustan-Isuzu, Allwyn-Nissan, Swaraj-Mazda and Honda-Kinetic.

The active motorcycle and motor scooter industry has also experienced rapid growth. The motorcycles include the splendid Enfield India – a replica of the old British single-cylinder 350cc Royal Enfield Bullet of the 1950s. Enthusiasts for the old British singles will be delighted to see these modern-day vintage bikes still being made. Motor scooters include Indian versions of both the Italian Lambretta and the Vespa. When production ceased in Italy, India bought the manufacturing plant from them lock, stock and barrel.

There is a variety of mopeds but the assembly of small Honda, Suzuki and Yamaha motorcycles is widespread and they are becoming as familiar a sight on the roads of India as in South-East Asia. The arrival of Japanese manufacturing companies in India has provided some insightful culture clashes. A *Time* magazine article some years ago noted that Honda had found it impossible to instil the Japanese-style team spirit at the Hero-Honda plant near Delhi. Workers didn't mind rubbing shoulders with the management – but not with the Dalits (untouchables), please. And despite having quality inspectors, unknown in Japanese plants where everybody is a quality inspector, the rejection rate at the end of the assembly line was 30% against 3% in Japan.

TWO-WHEELED EXPERIENCES

The following descriptions outline two different ways of travelling independently in India. The motorcycle section is based largely on information originally contributed by intrepid Britons Ken Twyford and Gerald Smewing, while updates from Jim & Lucy Amos, while the cycling information from Ann Sorrel includes updates from various travellers.

India by Motorcycle

Travelling around India by motorcycle has become increasingly popular in recent years, and it certainly has its attractions – motoring along the backroads through small untouristed villages, picnics in the wilds, the freedom to go when and where you like – making it the ideal way to get to grips with the vastness that is India. You'll still get a sore bum, have difficult and frustrating conversations, get fed up with asking directions and receiving misleading answers, and get frequently lost, but you'll also have a wide range of adventures not available to the visitor who relies on public transport.

What to Bring An International Driving Licence is not mandatory, but is handy to have.

Helmets should definitely be brought with you. Although Indian helmets are cheap, it is often hard to find one that fits well, and the quality is suspect. You are not required by law to wear a helmet. If required, leathers, gloves, boots, waterproofs and other protective gear should also be brought from your home country.

A few small bags will be a lot easier to carry than one large rucksack.

Which Bike? The big decision to make is whether to buy new or secondhand. Obviously cost is the main factor, but remember that with a new bike you are less likely to get ripped off as the price is fixed, the cost will include free servicing and you know it will be reliable. Old bikes are obviously cheaper and you don't have to be a registered resident foreign national, but you are far more open to getting ripped off, either by paying too much or getting a dud bike.

Everyone is likely to have their own preferences, and so there is no one bike which suits everybody. However, here is a rundown of what's readily available:

Mopeds These come with or without gears. As they are only 50cc capacity, they are really only useful around towns or for short distances.

Scooters There are the older design Bajaj and Vespa scooters, or the more modern Japanese designs by Honda-Kinetic and others. The older ones are 150cc while the Honda is 100cc and has no gears.

Scooters are inherently unstable creatures, largely due to the high centre of gravity and small wheels. On rough roads they're positively lethal.

On the plus side, they are economical to buy and run, are easy to ride, have a good resale value, and most have built-in lockable storage.

100cc Motorcycles This is the area with the greatest choice. The four main Japanese companies – Honda, Suzuki, Kawasaki and Yamaha – all have 100cc, two-stroke machines, while Honda and Kawasaki also have four-stroke models.

There's little to differentiate between these bikes; all are lightweight, easy to ride, very economical and reliable, with good resale value. They are suitable for intercity travel on reasonable roads, but they should not be laden down with too much gear. Spares and servicing are readily available. The cost of a new bike of this type is about Rs 32,000, plus the costs of getting it on the road.

Another competitor in this market is the Rajdoot 175 XLT, based on a very old Polish model. It lacks power but is a cheap option, costing around Rs 6000 to Rs 10,000 less than the Japanese bikes.

The Enfield Fury is a modern machine with front disc brake. It's very unpopular, has a poor gearbox, spares are hard to come by and the resale value is low – avoid.

Bigger Bikes The Yezdi 250 Classic is a cheap and basic bike. It's a rugged machine, and one which you often see in rural areas.

The Enfield Bullet is the classic machine and is the one most favoured among foreigners. Attractions are the traditional design, thumping engine sound, and the price, which is not much more than the new 100cc Japanese bikes. It's a wonderfully durable bike, is easy to maintain, economical to run, but mechanically they're a bit 'hit and miss', largely because of poorly engineered parts and inferior materials – valves and tappets are the main problem areas. Another drawback is the lack of an effective front brake – the small drum brake is a joke, totally inadequate for what is quite a heavy machine. The Bullet is also available in a 500cc single-cylinder version. It has a functional front brake and has 12-volt electrics which are superior to the 350's 6-volt. If you opt for a

350cc, consider paying the Rs 4000 extra to have the 500cc front wheel fitted.

If you are buying a new Enfield with the intention of shipping it back home, it's definitely worth opting for the 500cc as it has features – such as folding rear foot-rest and longer exhaust pipe – which most other countries would require. The emission control regulations in some places, such as California, are so strict that there is no way these bikes would be legal. You may be able to get around this by buying an older bike, as the regulations often only apply to new machines. Make sure you check all this out before you go lashing out on a new Enfield, only to find it unregisterable at home. The price is around Rs 40,000, or Rs 45,000 for the 500cc model.

The Rajdoot 350 is an imported Yamaha 350cc. It's well engineered, fast and has good brakes. Disadvantages are that it's relatively uneconomical to run, and spares are hard to come by. These bikes are also showing their age badly as they haven't been made for some years now. They cost around Rs 12,000 to Rs 15,000.

Buying & Selling India does not have used-vehicle dealers, motorcycle magazines or weekend newspapers with pages of motorcycle classified advertisements. To purchase a secondhand machine one simply needs to enquire. A good place to start is with mechanics. They are likely to know somebody who is selling a bike.

To buy a new bike, you'll have to have a local address and be a resident foreign national. However, unless the dealer you are buying from is totally devoid of imagination and contacts, this presents few problems. When buying secondhand, all you need to do is give an address.

New bikes are generally purchased through a showroom. When buying secondhand it is best to engage the services of an 'autoconsultant'. These people act as go-betweens to bring buyers and sellers together. They will usually be able to show you a number of machines to suit your price bracket. These agents can be found by enquiring, or may sometimes advertise on their shop fronts.

For around Rs 500, which usually covers a bribe to officials, they will assist you in transferring the ownership papers through the bureaucracy. Without their help this could take a couple of weeks.

The overall appearance of the bike doesn't seem to affect the price greatly. Dents and scratches don't reduce the cost much, and added extras don't increase it by much.

When the time comes to sell the bike, don't appear too anxious to get rid of it, don't hang around in one town too long as word gets around the autoconsultants and the offers will get smaller as the days go by. If you get a reasonable offer, grab it. Regardless of which bike it is, you'll be told it's the 'least popular in India' and other such tales.

Ownership Papers A needless hint perhaps, but do not part with your money until you have the ownership papers, receipt and affidavit signed by a magistrate authorising the owner (as recorded in the ownership papers) to sell the machine. Not to mention the keys to the bike and the bike itself!

Each state has a different set of ownership transfer formalities. Get assistance from the agent you're buying the machine through or from one of the many 'attorneys' hanging around under tin roofs by the Motor Vehicles Office. They will charge you a fee of up to Rs 300, which will consist largely of a bribe to expedite matters.

Alternatively you could go to one of the many typing clerk services and request them to type out the necessary forms, handling the matter cheaply yourself – but with no guarantee of a quick result.

Check that your name has been recorded in the ownership book and stamped and signed by the department head. If you intend to sell your motorcycle in another state then you will need a 'No Objections Certificate'. This confirms your ownership and is issued by the Motor Vehicles Department in the state of purchase, so get it immediately when transferring ownership papers to your name. The standard form can be typed up for a few

rupees, or more speedily and expensively through one of the many attorneys. This document is vital if you are going to sell the bike in another state.

Other Formalities As in most countries it is compulsory to have third-party insurance. The New India Assurance Company or the National Insurance Company are just two of a number of companies who can provide it. The cost for fully comprehensive insurance is Rs 720 for 12 months, and this also covers you in Nepal.

Road tax is paid when the bike is bought new. This is valid for the life of the machine and is transferred to the new owner when the bike changes hands.

Helmets Good-quality helmets are available in the big cities for Rs 500 to Rs 600. The cheaper ones should be avoided as they don't come up to standard.

On the Road It must be said that, given the general road conditions, motorcycling is a reasonably hazardous endeavour, and one best undertaken by experienced riders only – you don't want to discover on the Grand Trunk Road with a lunatic in a Tata truck bearing down on you that you don't know how to take evasive action! The hazards to be encountered range from families of pigs crossing the road to broken-down vehicles, left where they stopped, even if that is in the middle of the road.

Route-finding can be very tricky. It's certainly much easier to jump on a bus and leave the navigating to someone who knows the way. The directions people give you can be very interesting. It is invariably a 'straight road', although if pressed the person might also reveal that the said straight road actually involves taking two right turns, three left turns and the odd fork or two. People generally seem to discount the fact that although the road appears to go straight across an intersection, and all the traffic is turning right, MG Rd in fact turns left. Pronunciation can also cause problems, particularly in country areas.

On the whole people are very welcoming, and curious about how you are coping with the traffic conditions.

Parking the bike and getting things stolen from it seems not to be a problem. The biggest annoyance is that people seem to treat parked motorcycles as public utilities – handy for sitting on, using the mirror to do the hair, fiddling with the switches – but they don't deliberately do any damage. You'll just have to turn all the switches off and readjust the mirrors when you get back on!

Run-ins with the law are not a major problem. The best policy is to give a smile and a friendly wave to any police officers, even if you are doing the opposite of what is signalled.

In the event of an accident, call the police straight away, and don't move anything until the police have seen exactly where and how everything ended up. One foreigner reported spending three days in jail on suspicion of being involved in an accident, when all he'd done was taken a child to hospital from the scene of an accident.

Don't try to cover too much territory in one day. As such a high level of concentration is needed to survive, long days are tiring and dangerous. On the busy national highways expect to average 50 km/h without stops; on smaller roads, where driving conditions are worse, 10 km/h is not an unrealistic average. On the whole you can expect to cover between 100 km and 150 km in a day on good roads.

Night driving should be avoided at all costs. If you think driving in daylight is difficult enough, imagine what it's like at night when there's the added hazard of half the vehicles being inadequately lit (or not lit at all), not to mention the breakdowns in the middle of the road.

Putting the bike on a train for really long hauls can be a convenient option. You'll pay about as much as the 2nd-class passenger fare for the bike. It can be wrapped in straw for protection if you like, and this is done at the parcels office at the station, which is also where you pay for the bike. The petrol tank must be empty, and there should be a tag in an obvious place detailing name, destination, passport number and train details.

Repairs & Maintenance Anyone who can handle a screwdriver and spanner in India can be called a mechanic, or *mistri*, so be careful. If you have any mechanical knowledge it may be better to buy your own tools and learn how to do your own repairs. This will save a lot of arguments over prices. If you are getting repairs done by someone, don't leave the premises while the work is being done or you may find that good parts have been ripped off your bike and replaced with bodgy old ones.

Original spare parts bought from an 'Authorised Dealer' can be rather expensive compared to the copies available from your spare-parts wallah.

If you buy an older machine you would do well to check and tighten all nuts and bolts every few days. Indian roads and engine vibration tend to work things loose and constant checking could save you rupees and trouble. Check the engine and gearbox oil level regularly. With the quality of oil it is advisable to change it and clean the oil filter every couple of thousand km.

Punctures Chances are you'll be requiring the services of a puncture-wallah at least once a week. They are found everywhere, often in the most surprising places, but it's advisable to at least have tools sufficient to remove your own wheel and take it to the puncture-wallah (*punkucha wallah* in Hindi).

Given the hassles of constant flat tyres, it's worth lashing out on new tyres if you buy a secondhand bike with worn tyres. A new rear tyre for an Enfield costs around Rs 500.

Fuel Petrol is expensive relative to the West and when compared to the cost of living in India – Rs 18 per litre – but diesel is much cheaper at around Rs 7.50 per litre. Petrol is usually readily available in all larger towns and along the main roads so there is no need to carry spare fuel.

Should you run out, try flagging down a

passing car (not a truck or bus since they use diesel) and beg for some. Most Indians are willing to let you have some if you have a hose or syphon and a container. Alternatively, hitch a truck ride to the nearest petrol station.

Organised Motorcycle Tours A couple of operators run motorcycle tours through India. Mad Dogs & Englishmen (in the UK phone ☎ (0207) 55349 from May to November and ☎ (0904) 48-9522 from December to April) operate two-week tours of south India riding 350cc Enfield India motorcycles. The trips cost £895 for the rider and £455 for a passenger and include use of the motorcycle plus all fuel used, accommodation and breakfast each day. A support vehicle follows with a spare motorcycle, just in case anything goes wrong.

Classic Bike Adventure (☎ (030) 782-3315; fax 7879-2720), Haupstrasse 5, D 10827, Berlin, Germany, organise bike tours on well-maintained Enfields with full insurance. Tours last two to three weeks and cover Rajasthan, the Himalaya between Kullu-Manali and Gangotri, and the south from Goa. Costs are from DM2800 to DM3820. See the Getting Around section in the Goa chapter for more information.

India by Bicycle
Every day millions of Indians pedal along the country's roads. If they can do it so can you. India offers an immense array of challenges for a long-distance bike tourer. There are high-altitude passes and rocky dirt tracks; smooth-surfaced, well-graded highways with roadside restaurants and lodges; coastal routes through coconut palms; and winding country roads through coffee plantations. There are city streets with all manner of animal and human-powered carts and vehicles and the spectacular Asian bazaars. Hills, plains, plateaus, deserts – you name it, India's got it!

Nevertheless, long-distance cycling is not for the faint of heart or weak of knee. You'll need physical endurance to cope with the roads and the climate, plus you'll face cultural challenges which I call 'the people factor'.

Further Information Before you set out, read some books on bicycle touring such as the Sierra Club's *The Bike Touring Manual* by Rob van de Plas (Bicycle Books, 1993). Cycling magazines provide useful information including listings for bicycle tour operators and the addresses of spare-parts suppliers. They're also good places to look for a riding companion.

For a real feel of the adventure of bike touring in strange places read Dervla Murphy's classic *Full Tilt – From Ireland to India on a Bike*, now available in paperback, or Lloyd Sumner's *The Long Ride* and *Riding the Mountains Down* (subtitled 'A Journey by Bicycle to Kathmandu'), by Bettina Selby (Unwin Publications, 1984).

The International Bicycle Fund (IBT; ☎ (206) 628-9314), 4887 Columbia Drive South, Seattle, Washington 98108-1919, USA, has two publications which may help you prepare for your cycling adventure. These are *Selecting and Preparing a Bike for Travel in Remote Areas* and *Flying With Your Bike*. Each is US$2 plus postage and handling (in the USA: US$1 for first item and US$0.50 for each additional item; other countries: US$2 for first item and US$1 for each additional item).

The IBT are also happy to help prospective long-distance cyclists with information and advice.

Using Your Own Bike If you are planning to tour India by bicycle you will have to decide whether to use a lightweight touring bicycle or a mountain bike. If you are going to keep to sealed roads and already have a touring bike, by all means consider bringing it. Mountain bikes, however, are especially suited to countries such as India. Their smaller sturdier construction makes them more manoeuvrable, less prone to damage, and allows you to tackle rocky, muddy roads unsuitable for lighter machines.

I travelled 22,000 miles in South Asia by bicycle in 1982-83. I wish I had a mountain bike then. I couldn't venture down the Kargil-Padum (Ladakh) road, nor could I avail myself of all sorts of opportunities for single-track riding.

A friend later went with a mountain bike and pedalled to Everest Base Camp. While I discourage mountain biking on foot trails because of environmental degradation, a mountain bike lets you move off paved roads and onto less-used routes, confident that the machine will withstand the rougher terrain.

Ann Sorrel

Bringing your own bicycle does have disadvantages. Your machine is likely to be a real curiosity and subject to much pushing, pulling and probing. If you can't tolerate people touching your bicycle, don't bring it to India.

Spare Parts If you bring a bicycle to India, prepare for the contingencies of part replacement or repair. Bring spare tyres, tubes, patch kits, chassis, cables, freewheels and spokes. Ensure you have a working knowledge of your machine. Bring all necessary tools with you as well as a compact bike manual with diagrams in case the worst happens and you need to fix a rear derailleur or some other strategic part. Indian mechanics can work wonders and illustrations help overcome the language barrier.

Most of all, be ready to make do and improvise.

Roads don't have paved shoulders and are very dusty, so keep your chain lubricated.

Although India is officially metricated, tools and bike parts follow 'standard' or 'imperial' measurements. Don't expect to find tyres for 700cc rims, although 27 x 1¼ tyres are produced in India by Dunlop and Sawney. Some mountain bike tyres are available but the quality is dubious. Indian bicycle pumps cater to a tube valve different from the Presta and Schraeder valves commonly used in the West. If you're travelling with Presta valves (most high-pressure 27 x 1¼ tubes) bring a Schraeder (car type) adaptor. In India you can buy a local pump adaptor, which means you'll have an adaptor on your adaptor. Bring your own pump as well; most Indian pumps require two or three people to get air down the leaky cable.

In major cities Japanese tyres and parts (derailleurs, freewheels, chains) are available, but pricey – although so is postage, and transit time can be considerable. If you receive bike parts from abroad beware of exorbitant customs charges. Say you want the goods as 'in transit' to avoid these charges. They may list the parts in your passport!

There are a number of shops where you may locate parts. Try Metre Cycle, Kalba Devi Rd, Bombay, or its branch in Thiruvananthapuram (Trivandrum); the cycle bazaar in the old city around Esplanade Rd, Delhi; Popular Cycle Importing Company on Popham's Broadway, Madras; and Nundy & Company, Bentinck St, Calcutta. Alternatively, take your bicycle to a cycle market and ask around – someone will know which shop is likely to have things for your 'special' cycle. Beware of Taiwanese imitations and do watch out for tyres which may have been sitting collecting dust for years.

Luggage Your cycle luggage should be as strong, durable and waterproof as possible. I don't recommend a set with lots of zippers, as this makes pilfering easier. As you'll be frequently detatching luggage when taking your bike to your room, a set designed for easy removal from the racks is a must: the fewer items, the better. *(Never leave your cycle in the lobby or outside your hotel – take it to bed with you!)*

Bike luggage that can easily be reassembled into a backpack is also available, just the thing when you want to park your bike and go by train or foot.

Theft If you're using an imported bike, try to avoid losing your pump (and the water bottle from your frame) – their novelty makes them particularly attractive to thieves. Don't leave anything on your bike that can easily be removed when it's unattended.

Don't be paranoid about theft – outside the major cities it would be well-nigh impossible for a thief to resell your bike as it would stand out too much. And not many folk understand quick-release levers on wheels. Your bike is probably safer in India than in Western cities.

Buying a Bike in India Finding an Indian bike is no problem: every town will have at least a couple of cycle shops. Shop around for prices and remember to bargain. Try to get a few extras – bell, stand, spare tube – thrown in. There are many brands of Indian clunkers – Hero, Atlas, BSA, Raleigh, Bajaj, Avon – but they all follow the same basic, sturdy design. A few mountain-bike lookalikes have recently come on the market, but they have no gears. Raleigh is considered the finest quality, followed by BSA which has a big line of models including some sporty jobs. Hero and Atlas both claim to be the biggest seller. Look for the cheapest or the one with the snazziest plate label.

Once you've decided on a bike you have a choice of luggage carriers – mostly the rat-trap type varying only in size, price and strength. There's a wide range of saddles available but all are equally bum-breaking. A stand is certainly a useful addition and a bell or airhorn is a necessity. An advantage of buying a new bike is that the brakes actually work. Centre-pull and side-pull brakes are also available but at extra cost and may actually make the bike more difficult to sell. The average Indian will prefer the standard model.

Sportier 'mountain bike' styles with straight handlebars are popular in urban areas. It is also possible to find in big cities and touristy areas used touring bikes left by travellers. Also check with diplomatic community members for bikes.

Spare Parts As there are so many repair 'shops' (some consist of a pump, a box of tools, a tube of rubber solution and a water pan under a tree) there is no need to carry spare parts, especially as you'll only own the bike for a few weeks or months. Just take a roll of tube-patch rubber, a tube of Dunlop patch glue, two tyre irons and the wonderful 'universal' Indian bike spanner, which fits all

the nuts. There are plenty of puncture-wallahs in all towns and villages who will patch tubes for a couple of rupees, so chances are you won't have to fix a puncture yourself anyway. Besides, Indian tyres are pretty heavy duty, so with luck you won't get a flat.

Selling It Reselling the bike is no problem. Ask the proprietor of your lodge if they know anyone who is interested in buying a bike. Negotiate a price and do the deal personally or through the hotel. Most people will be only too willing to help you. Count on losing a couple of hundred rupees or about 30%, depending on local prices. Retail bike stores are not usually interested in buying or selling secondhand bikes. A better bet would be a bike-hire shop, which may be interested in expanding its fleet.

On the Road The 'people factor' makes a bike ride in India rewarding and frustrating. Those with Indian bikes are less likely to be 'mobbed' by curious onlookers. A tea stop with an imported bike can attract a crowd of 50 men and boys eagerly commenting on the bike's operation – one points to the water-bottle saying 'petrol', another twists the shifter lever saying 'clutch', another squeezes a tyre saying 'tubeless' or 'airless', yet others nod knowingly as 'gear system', 'automatic' and 'racing bike' are mouthed. In some areas you'll even get 'disco bike'!

The worst scenario is stopping on a city street for a banana, looking up as you are pushing off to find rickshaws, cyclists and pedestrians all blocking your way! At times the crowd may be unruly – schoolboys especially. If the mob is too big, call over a lathi-wielding policeman. The boys will scatter pronto! Sometimes hostile boys throw rocks. The best advice is to keep pedalling; don't turn around or stop, and don't leave your bike and chase them as this will only incite them further. Appeal to adults to discipline them. Children, especially boys seven to 13 years old, are unruly and dangerous in crowds. Avoid riding past a boys' school at recess.

Routes You can go anywhere on a bike that you would on trains and buses with the added pleasure of seeing all the places in between.

Try to avoid the major highways up north like the NH1 through Haryana, and the NH2 – the Grand Trunk Road between Delhi and Calcutta. They're plagued by speeding buses and trucks. Other national highways can be pleasant – often lonely country roads well marked with a stone every km. A basic knowledge of Hindi will help you to translate the signs, although at least one marker in five will be in English.

Another option is to follow canal and river paths. It's also possible in some areas to bike along railway tracks on maintenance roads. Do make enquiries before venturing off road.

I once travelled most of a day before discovering the reason I had not encountered any pedestrian traffic: a major railway bridge was down and no ferry in service to ford the raging waters!

Ann Sorrel

If mountain bicycling is your goal and you're concerned about the situation in Kashmir give serious consideration to Himachel Pradesh as well as the hill stations of South India.

Crossing international borders with a bicycle is relatively uncomplicated. India has border crossings with Pakistan, Nepal, Bangladesh and Sri Lanka (ferry). Unlike a car or motorcycle, papers need not be presented. Do not be surprised, however, if the bike is thoroughly inspected for contraband!

Distances If you've never before cycled long distances, start with 20 to 40 km a day and increase this as you gain stamina and confidence. Cycling long distances is 80% determination and 20% perspiration. Don't be ashamed to get off and push the bike up steep hills. For an eight-hour pedal a serious cyclist and interested tourist will average 125 to 150 km a day on undulating plains, or 80 to 100 km in mountainous areas.

Accommodation There's no need to bring a tent. Inexpensive lodges are widely available, and a tent pitched by the road would merely draw crowds. There's also no need to bring a stove and cooking kit (unless you cannot tolerate Indian food), as there are plenty of tea stalls and restaurants (called 'hotels'). When you want to eat, ask for a 'hotel'. When you want a room ask for a 'lodge'. On major highways stop at *dhabas*, the Indian version of a truck stop. The one with the most trucks parked in front generally has the best food (or serves alcohol). Dhabas have *charpoys* (string beds) to serve as tables and seats or as beds for weary cyclists. You should keep your cycle next to you throughout the night. There will be no bathroom or toilet facilities but plenty of road noise. Dhabas are not recommended for single women riders.

This is the best part of travelling on a bike – finding places to stay between the cities or important tourist places.

Directions Asking directions can be a real frustration. Approach people who look like they can speak English and aren't in a hurry. Always ask three or four different people just to be certain, using traffic police only as a last resort. Try to be patient; be careful about 'left' and 'right' and be prepared for instructions like 'go straight and turn here and there'.

Transporting your Bike Sometimes you may want to quit pedalling. For sports bikes, air travel is easy. With luck airline staff may not be familiar with procedures, so use this to your advantage. Tell them the bike doesn't need to be dismantled and that you've never had to pay for it. Remove all luggage and accessories and let the tyres down a bit.

Bus travel with a bike varies from state to state. Generally it goes for free on the roof. If it's a sports bike stress that it's lightweight. Secure it well to the roof rack, check it's in a place where it won't get damaged and take all your luggage inside.

Train travel is more complex – pedal up to the railway station, buy a ticket and explain you want to book a cycle for the journey.

You'll be directed to the luggage offices (or officer) where a triplicate form is prepared. Note down your bike's serial number and provide a good description of it. Again leave only the bike, not luggage or accessories. Your bike gets decorated with one copy of the form, usually pasted on the seat, you get another, and God only knows what happens to the third. Produce your copy of the form to claim the bicycle from the luggage van at your destination. If you change trains en route, *personally* ensure the cycle changes too!

Final Words Just how unusual is a cycle tourist in India? I'd venture to guess that currently 2000 foreign cyclists tour for a month or more each year somewhere on the subcontinent. That number appears to be growing rapidly. Perhaps 5000 Indians tour as well – mostly young men and college students. 'Kashmir to Kanyakumari' or a pilgrimage to holy places are their most common goals.

If you're a serious cyclist or amateur racer and want to contact counterparts while in India there's the Cycle Federation of India; contact the Secretary, Yamun Velodrome, New Delhi. Last words of advice – make sure your rubber solution is gooey, all your winds are tailwinds and that you go straight and turn here and there.

HITCHING

Hitching is not a realistic option. There are not that many private cars streaking across India so you are likely to be onboard trucks. You are then stuck with the old quandaries of: 'Do they understand what I am doing?'; 'Should I be paying for this?'; 'Will the driver expect to be paid?'; 'Will they be unhappy if I don't offer to pay?'; 'Will they be unhappy if I offer or will they simply want too much?'. But it is possible.

However, it is a very bad idea for women to hitch. Remember India is a developing country with a patriarchal society far less sympathetic to rape victims than the West, and that's saying something. A woman in the cabin of a truck on a lonely road is perhaps tempting fate.

BOAT

Apart from ferries across rivers (of which there are many) the only real boating possibilities are the trips through the backwaters of Kerala – not to be missed (see the Kerala chapter for more details) and the new ferry between Bombay and Goa.

The Bombay to Goa ferry service is operated by Damania Shipping. The modern, 400-seat, air-con 'jetfoil' leaves Bombay daily at 7 am, arriving in Panaji at 2 pm. On the return leg it leaves Panaji at 3 pm, arriving in Bombay between 10.15 and 10.45 pm. The fare is US$35/50 in economy/business class, and the fare includes a snack, a meal, refreshments and 'infoil' entertainment, which consists of recent-release Hollywood (not Bollywood!) films. Children under two pay 10%; children above two pay full fare. For bookings contact the Damania Shipping ferry terminal in Panaji (☎ (0832) 22-8711) or Bombay (☎ (022) 610-2525; fax 610-4219), or any of the Damania Airways regional offices.

The only other ferries connecting coastal ports are those from Calcutta and Madras to the Andaman Islands, and even these aren't all that regular. See Getting There & Away in the Port Blair section of the Andaman & Nicobar Islands chapter.

LOCAL TRANSPORT

Although there are comprehensive local bus networks in most major towns, unless you have time to familiarise yourself with the routes you're better off sticking to taxis, auto-rickshaws, cycle-rickshaws and hiring bicycles. The buses are often so hopelessly overcrowded that you can only really use them if you get on at the starting point – and get off at the terminus!

A basic ground rule applies to any form of transport where the fare is not ticketed or fixed (unlike a bus or train), or metered – agree on the fare beforehand. If you fail to do that you can expect enormous arguments and hassles when you get to your destination.

And agree on the fare clearly – if there is more than one of you make sure it covers all of you. If you have baggage make sure there are no extra charges, or you may be asked for more at the end of the trip. If a driver refuses to use the meter, or insists on an extortionate rate, simply walk away – if he really wants the job the price will drop. If you can't agree on a reasonable fare, find another driver.

To/From the Airport

There are official buses, operated by the government, Indian Airlines or some local cooperative, to most airports in India. Where there aren't any, there will be taxis or auto-rickshaws. There are even some airports close enough to town to get to by cycle-rickshaw.

When arriving at an airport anywhere in India, make an effort to find out if there's a prepaid taxi booth inside the arrival hall. If there is, pay for one there. If you don't do this and simply walk outside to negotiate your own price, you'll invariably pay more. Taxi drivers are notorious for refusing to use the meter (where fitted) outside airport terminals.

Taxi

There are taxis in most towns in India, and most of them (certainly in the major cities) are metered. Getting a metered fare is rather a different situation. First of all the meter may be 'broken'. Threatening to get another taxi will usually fix it immediately, except during rush hours.

Secondly the meter will almost certainly be out of date. Fares are adjusted upwards so much faster and more frequently than meters are recalibrated that drivers almost always have 'fare adjustment cards' indicating what you should pay compared to what the meter indicates. This is, of course, wide open to abuse. You have no idea if you're being shown the right card or if the taxi's meter has actually been recalibrated and you're being shown the card anyway. In states where the numbers are written differently (such as Gujarat) it's not much use asking for the chart if you can't read it!

The only answer to all this is to try and get an idea of what the fare should be before departure (ask information desks at the airport or your hotel). You'll soon begin to develop a feel for what the meter says, what the cards say and what the two together should indicate.

Auto-Rickshaw

An auto-rickshaw is a noisy three-wheel device powered by a two-stroke motorcycle engine with a driver up front and seats for two (or sometimes more) passengers behind. They don't have doors (except in Goa) and have just a canvas top. They are also known as scooters or autos.

Although they are all made by Bajaj, it's amazing how the designs differ from town to town. Design seems to be unique to a particular town: in Chittorgarh in Rajasthan, for example, the auto-rickshaws are fitted with an extra seat facing backwards, and so they can carry four people (although they'll often carry eight or more!).

They're generally about half the price of a taxi, usually metered and follow the same ground rules as taxis.

Because of their size, auto-rickshaws are often faster than taxis for short trips and their drivers are decidedly nuttier – hair-raising near-misses are guaranteed and glancing-blow collisions are not infrequent; thrill-seekers will love it!

In busy towns you'll find that, when stopped at traffic lights, the height you are sitting at is the same as most bus and truck exhaust pipes – copping dirty great lungfuls of diesel fumes is part of the fun of auto-rickshaw travel. Also their small wheel size and rock-hard suspension makes them supremely uncomfortable; even the slightest bump will have you instantly airborne. The speed humps and huge potholes found everywhere are the bane of the rickshaw traveller – pity the poor drivers.

Tempo

Somewhat like a large auto-rickshaw, these ungainly looking three-wheel devices operate rather like minibuses or share-taxis along fixed routes. Unless you are spending large amounts of time in one city, it is generally impractical to try to find out what the routes are. You'll find it much easier and more convenient to go by auto-rickshaw.

Cycle-Rickshaw

This is effectively a three-wheeler bicycle with a seat for two passengers behind the rider. Although they no longer operate in most of the big cities except in the old part of Delhi and parts of Calcutta, you will find them in all the smaller cities and towns, where they're the basic means of transport.

Fares must always be agreed on in advance. Avoid situations where the driver says something like: 'As you like'. He's punting on the fact that you are not well acquainted with correct fares and will overpay. Invariably no matter what you pay in situations like this, it will be deemed too little and an unpleasant situation often develops. This is especially the case in heavily touristed places, such as Agra and Jaipur. Always settle the price beforehand.

In the well-touristed places the riders are as talkative and opinionated as any New York cabby.

It's quite feasible to hire a rickshaw-wallah by time, not just for a straight trip. Hiring one for a day or even several days can make good sense.

Hassling over the fares is the biggest difficulty of cycle-rickshaw travel. They'll often go all out for a fare higher than it would cost you by taxi or auto-rickshaw. Nor does actually agreeing on a fare always make a difference; there is a greater possibility of a post-travel fare disagreement when you travel by cycle-rickshaw than by taxi or auto-rickshaw – metered or not.

Other Transport

In some places, tongas (horse-drawn two-wheelers) and victorias (horse-drawn carriages) still operate. Calcutta has an extensive tramway network and India's first underground railway. Bombay, Delhi and Madras have suburban trains.

Once upon a time there used to be people-drawn rickshaws but today these only exist in parts of Calcutta.

Bicycle

India is a country of bicycles – it's an ideal way of getting around the sights in a city or

Cycle-rickshaws are a common form of transport in Indian towns and cities. A lucky rickshaw-wallah may get the contract to take school children to and from school, and thereby have at least a certain amount of guaranteed daily income.

even for making longer trips – see the section on touring India by bicycle earlier in this chapter. Even in the smallest of towns there will be a shop which rents bicycles. They charge from around Rs 3 to Rs 5 per hour or Rs 10 to Rs 15 per day. In tourist areas (such as hill stations) and places where foreigners are common (like Pondicherry) you'll pay about double the normal rate. In some places they may be unwilling to hire to you since you are a stranger, but you can generally get around this by offering some sort of ID card as security, or by paying a deposit – usually Rs 300 to Rs 500.

If you should be so unfortunate as to get a puncture, you'll soon spot men sitting under trees with puncture-repair outfits at the ready – it'll cost just a couple of rupees to fix it.

If you're travelling with small children and would like to use bikes a lot, consider getting a bicycle seat made. If you find a shop making cane furniture they'll quickly make up a child's bicycle seat from a sketch. Get it made to fit on a standard-size rear carrier and it can be securely attached with a few lengths of cord.

TOURS

At almost any place of tourist interest in India, and quite a few places where there's not much tourist interest, there will be tours operated either by the Government of India tourist office, the state tourist office or the local transport company – sometimes by all three. These tours are usually excellent value, particularly in cities or places where the tourist sights are widespread. You probably could not even get around the sights in Delhi on public transport as cheaply as you could on a half or full-day tour.

These tours are not strictly for Western tourists; you will almost always find yourself far outnumbered by local tourists, and in many places just a little off the beaten track you will often be the only Westerner on the bus. Despite this the tours are usually conducted in English – which is possibly the only common language for the middle-class Indian tourists in any case. These tours are an excellent place to meet Indians.

The big drawback is that many of them try to cram far too much into too short a period of time. A one-day tour which whisks you from Madras to Kanchipuram, Tirukalikundram, Mahabalipuram and back to Madras is not going to give you time for more than the most fleeting glimpse. If a tour looks too hectic, you're better off doing it yourself at a more appropriate pace or taking the tour simply to find out to which places you want to devote more time.

Delhi

Delhi is the capital of India and its third-largest city. The city actually consists of two parts. Old Delhi was the capital of Muslim India between the 17th and 19th centuries. In Old Delhi you will find many mosques, monuments and forts relating to India's Muslim history. The other Delhi is New Delhi, the imperial city created as the capital of India by the British. It is a spacious, open city and contains many embassies and government buildings.

In addition to its historic interest and role as the government centre, Delhi is a major travel gateway. It is one of India's busiest entrance points for overseas airlines, the hub of the north Indian travel network, and is on the overland route across Asia. The city of Delhi covers most of the Delhi Union Territory, which is a federal district similar to Washington DC, Canberra or Brasilia.

Not many travellers have a lot of good things to say about Delhi, but it has a long and fascinating history, there are plenty of interesting things to see, and it's an easy place to get things done. If you're arriving in India for the first time it's also probably the easiest of the four main 'gateway' cities in which to get acquainted with – and adjust to – India.

HISTORY

Delhi has not always been the capital of India but it has played an important role in Indian history. The settlement of Indraprastha, which featured in the epic *Mahabharata* over 3000 years ago, was located approximately on the site of present-day Delhi. Over 2000 years ago, Pataliputra (near modern-day Patna) was the capital of Emperor Ashoka's kingdom. More recently, the Mughal emperors made Agra the capital through the 16th and 17th centuries. Under the British, Calcutta was the capital until the construction of New Delhi in 1911. Of course, it is only comparatively recently that India as we know it has been unified as one

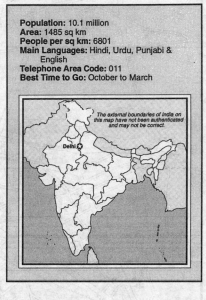

Population: 10.1 million
Area: 1485 sq km
People per sq km: 6801
Main Languages: Hindi, Urdu, Punjabi & English
Telephone Area Code: 011
Best Time to Go: October to March

The external boundaries of India on this map have not been authenticated and may not be correct.

Delhi

country. Even at the height of their power the Mughals did not control the south of India, for example. But Delhi has always been an important city or a capital of the northern region of the subcontinent.

There have been at least eight cities around modern Delhi. The first four were to the south around the area where the Qutab Minar stands. The earliest known Delhi was called Indraprastha and was centred near present-day Purana Qila. At the beginning of the 12th century the last Hindu kingdom of Delhi was ruled by the Tomara and Chauthan dynasties and was also near the Qutab Minar and Suran Kund, now in Haryana.

This city was followed by Siri, constructed by Ala-ud-din near present-day Hauz Khas in the 12th century. The third Delhi was Tughlaqabad, now entirely in ruins, which stood 10 km south-east of the Qutab Minar. The fourth Delhi dates from

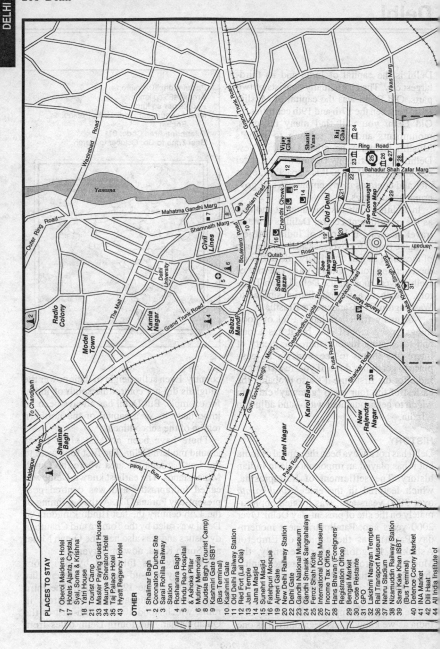

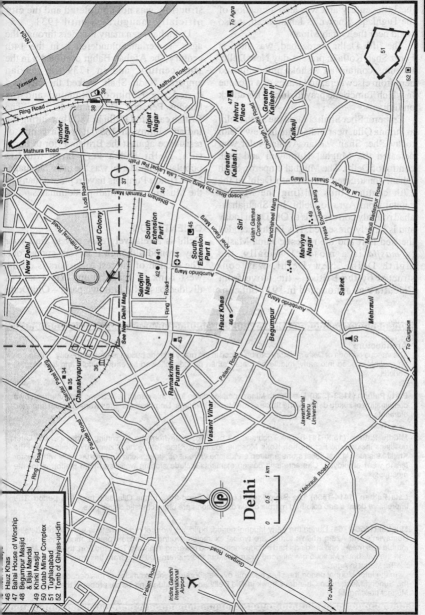

Delhi

0   0.5   1 km

To Agra

Yamuna

Ring Road

Sunder
Nagar

Mathura Road

Mathura Road

New Delhi

Lodi Road

Lodi Colony

Panchkuin Road

See New Delhi Map

Chanakyapuri

Sardar Patel Marg

Pandara Road

Ring Road

Vasant Vihar

Palam Road

Ramakrishna
Puram

Sarojini
Nagar

Ring Road

South
Extension
Part I

South
Extension
Part II

Lala Lajpat Rai Path

Bhisham Pitamah Marg

Lajpat
Nagar

Greater
Kailash I

Greater
Kailash II

Nehru
Place

Chirag Delhi Road

Kalkaji

Josep Broz Tito Marg

Lal Bahadur Shastri Marg

Siri

Khel Gaon Marg

Aurobindo Marg

Aurobindo Marg

Hauz Khas

Begumpur

Palam Road

Asian Games
Complex

Panchsheel Marg

Press Enclave Marg

Mehrauli Badarpur Road

Malviya
Nagar

Saket

Mehrauli

Jawaharlal
Nehru
University

Mehrauli Road

To Gurgaon

To Jaipur

Gurgaon Road

Indira Gandhi
International
Airport

47
39
38
37
40
45
41
44
42
46
43
34
35
36
48
49
50
51
52

46 Hauz Khas
47 Bahai House of Worship
48 Begumpur Masjid
   & Bijai Mandal
49 Khirki Masjid
50 Qutab Minar Complex
51 Tughlaqabad
52 Tomb of Ghiyas-ud-din

DELHI

the 14th century and was also a creation of the Tughlaqs. Known as Jahanpanah, it also stood near the Qutab Minar.

The fifth Delhi, Ferozabad, was sited at Feroz Shah Kotla in present-day New Delhi. Its ruins contain an Ashoka pillar, moved here from elsewhere, and traces of a mosque in which Tamerlane prayed during his attack on India.

Emperor Sher Shah created the sixth Delhi at Purana Qila, near India Gate in New Delhi today. Sher Shah was an Afghan ruler who defeated the Mughal Humayun and took control of Delhi. The Mughal emperor, Shah Jahan, constructed the seventh Delhi in the 17th century, thus shifting the Mughal capital from Agra to Delhi; his Shahjahanabad roughly corresponds to Old Delhi today and is largely preserved. His Delhi included the Red Fort and the majestic Jama Masjid (a *masjid* is a mosque). Finally, the eighth Delhi, New Delhi, was constructed by the British – the move from Calcutta was announced in 1911 but con-

struction was not completed and the city officially inaugurated until 1931.

Delhi has seen many invaders through the ages. Tamerlane plundered it in the 14th century; the Afghan Babur occupied it in the 16th century, and in 1739 the Persian emperor, Nadir Shah, sacked the city and carted the Kohinoor Diamond and the famous Peacock Throne off to Iran. The British captured Delhi in 1803 but during the Indian Mutiny of 1857 it was a centre of resistance against the British. Prior to Partition, Delhi had a very large Muslim population and Urdu was the main language. Now Hindu Punjabis have replaced many of the Muslims, and Hindi predominates.

ORIENTATION

Delhi is a relatively easy city to find your way around although it is very spread out. The section of interest to visitors is on the west bank of the Yamuna River and is divided basically into two parts – Old Delhi

Architecture

The various periods of Delhi's history can be traced in the many historic buildings around the city. These can be roughly divided into early, middle and late-Pathan periods followed by early, middle and late-Mughal periods.

Early Pathan (1193-1320) The Qutab Minar complex dates from this period, which was characterised by a combination of Hindu designs and those of the Muslim invaders. Domes and arches were the chief imported elements.

Middle Pathan (1320-1414) The Tughlaqabad buildings date from the beginning of this period. Later buildings include the Feroz Shah Kotla Mosque, the Hauz Khas Tomb, the Nizamuddin Mosque and the Khirki Mosque. At first, local stone and red sandstone were used; later, stone and mortar walls with plaster facing were employed. Characteristic design elements include sloping walls and high platforms for the mosques.

Late Pathan (1414-1556) The Sayyid and Lodi tombs and the Purana Qila date from this period. The impressive domes and coloured marble or tile decorations are characteristic of this time.

Mughal (1556-1754) During the early Mughal period, buildings were of red sandstone with marble details; Humayun's and Azam Khan's tombs are typical examples. During the middle period, much more use of marble was made, and buildings had bulbous domes and towering minarets. The Red Fort, the Jama Masjid and the Fatehpuri Mosque are all good examples, but the supreme building from this period is, of course, the Taj Mahal in Agra.

In the later Mughal period the style became over-elaborate; good examples of this decadent period are the Sunehri Mosque on Chandni Chowk in Old Delhi and the Safdarjang Tomb, probably the last notable Mughal building. ■

and New Delhi. Desh Bandhu Gupta Rd and Asaf Ali Rd mark the boundary between the tightly packed streets of the old city and the spacious, planned areas of the new capital.

Old Delhi is the 17th-century walled city of Shahjahanabad with city gates, narrow alleys, the enormous Red Fort and Jama Masjid, temples, mosques, bazaars and the famous street known as Chandni Chowk. Here you will find the Delhi railway station and, a little further north, the main interstate bus station near Kashmir Gate. Near New Delhi railway station, and acting as a sort of 'buffer zone' between the old and new cities, is Paharganj. This has become the budget travellers' hangout, and there are many popular cheap hotels and restaurants in this area.

New Delhi is a planned city of wide, tree-lined streets, parks and fountains. It can be further subdivided into the business and residential areas around Connaught Place and the government areas around Rajpath to the south. At the east end of Rajpath is the India Gate memorial and at the west end is Rashtrapati Bhavan, the residence of the Indian president.

The hub of New Delhi is the great circle of Connaught Place and the streets that radiate from it. Here you will find most of the airline offices, banks, travel agents, the various state tourist offices and the national one, more budget accommodation and several of the big hotels. The Regal Cinema, at the south side of the circle, and the Plaza Cinema, at the north, are two important Connaught Place landmarks and are very useful for telling taxi or auto-rickshaw drivers where you want to go.

Janpath, running off Connaught Place to the south, is one of the most important streets, with the Government of India tourist office, the Student Travel Information Centre in the Imperial Hotel and a number of other useful addresses.

South of the New Delhi government areas are Delhi's more expensive residential areas with names like Defence Colony, South Extension, Lodi Colony, Greater Kailash and Vasant Vihar. The Indira Gandhi International Airport is to the south-west of the city, and about halfway between the airport and Connaught Place is Chanakya-puri, the diplomatic enclave. Most of Delhi's embassies are concentrated in this modern area and there are several major hotels here.

The 200-page *A to Z Road Guide for Delhi* includes 60 area maps, and is a good reference if you are venturing further into the Delhi environs. It's available at most larger bookstores or at the Delhi Tourism Development Corporation.

INFORMATION
Tourist Offices

The Government of India tourist office (☎ 332-0005) at 88 Janpath is open Monday to Friday from 9 am to 6 pm and Saturday from 9 am to 2 pm; closed Sunday. The office has a lot of information and brochures on destinations all over India, but none of it is on display – you have to know what you want and ask for it. They have a good giveaway map of Delhi and New Delhi, and can also assist you in finding accommodation.

In the arrivals hall at the international airport terminal there is a tourist counter (☎ 32-9117) open around the clock. Here, too, they can help you find accommodation although, like many other Indian tourist offices, they may tell you the hotel you choose is 'full' and steer you somewhere else when actually your selected hotel is not full at all.

There is also a Delhi Tourism Corporation office (☎ 331-3637) in N Block, Connaught Place. They also have counters at New Delhi (☎ 35-0574), Old Delhi (☎ 251-1083) and Nizamuddin (☎ 61-1712) railway stations, as well as at the Interstate bus station (☎ 251-2181) at Kashmir Gate.

Most of the state governments have information centres in Delhi, and the offices for Assam (☎ 38-5897), Bihar (☎ 37-0147), Gujarat (☎ 34-3173), Karnataka (☎ 34-3862), Maharashtra (☎ 34-5332), Manipur

(☎ 34-4026), Orissa (☎ 34-4580), Tamil Nadu (☎ 34-4651), Uttar Pradesh (☎ 332-2251) and West Bengal (☎ 34-3825) are all on Baba Kharak Singh Marg, which runs off Connaught Place.

The offices for Haryana (☎ 332-4911), Himachal Pradesh (☎ 332-5320) and Rajasthan (☎ 332-2332) are in the Chandralok Building at 36 Janpath.

Jammu & Kashmir (☎ 332-5373), Kerala (☎ 331-6541), Madhya Pradesh (☎ 332-1187) and Punjab (☎ 332-3055) have their offices in the Kanishka Shopping Centre between the Yatri Niwas and Kanishka hotels.

Others include: Andaman & Nicobar Islands (☎ 38-7015), F-105 Curzon Rd Hostel, Kasturba Gandhi Marg; Goa, Daman & Diu (☎ 462-9968), 18 Amrita Shergil Marg; Meghalaya, 9 Aurangzeb Rd (☎ 301-4417); and Sikkim (☎ 301-3026), at Sikkim Bhavan, Chanakyapuri.

A monthly publication called *Genesis*, available for Rs 12 from many hotels and bookstands, gives information on what's happening in Delhi each month. *Delhi Diary* (Rs 6) is a similar booklet. *First City* is a monthly society magazine which gives some useless gossip on what the city's social set are up to, but it also has good listings of cultural events. It's available from newsstands for Rs 15.

Warning Steer clear of the dozen or so 'tourist information centres' across the road from New Delhi railway station. None of them are tourist offices as such, despite bold claims to the contrary; they are simply travel agents, and many are simply out to fleece unsuspecting visitors – both foreign and Indian.

If you are going to make a booking at the foreign tourist booking office at the station you may well be approached by touts from these shops who will insist the office you want is closed and try to steer you to the shonky travel agents and rake off a commission. Don't be tempted by offers of cheap bus fares or hotels.

Money
The major offices of all the Indian and foreign banks operating in India can be found in Delhi. As usual, some branches will change travellers' cheques, some won't. If you need to change money outside regular banking hours, the Central Bank has a 24-hour branch at the Ashok Hotel in Chanakyapuri, but it doesn't accept all currencies.

American Express (☎ 332-4119; fax 332-1706) has its office in A Block, Connaught Place, and although it's usually crowded, service is very fast. You don't have to have Amex cheques to change money here. It's open every day from 9 am to 7 pm. If you want to replace stolen or lost American Express travellers' cheques, you need a photocopy of the police report and one photo, as well as the proof-of-purchase slip and the numbers of the missing cheques. If you don't have the latter they will insist on telexing the place where you bought them before reissuing. If you've had the lot stolen, Amex are empowered to give you limited funds while all this is going on. For lost or stolen cheques, they have a 24-hour number (☎ 687-5050) which you should contact as soon as possible.

Other banks include:

ANZ Grindlays
    E Block, Connaught Place (☎ 331-9643)
Bank of America
    15 Barakhamba Rd (☎ 372-2332)
Banque Nationale de Paris
    15 Barakhamba Rd (☎ 331-3883)
Citibank
    Jeevan Bharati Building, Connaught Place (☎ 371-2484)
Hongkong Bank
    28 Kasturba Gandhi Marg (☎ 331-4355)
Standard Chartered Bank
    17 Sansad Marg (☎ 31-0195)
Thomas Cook
    Imperial Hotel, Janpath (☎ 332-7135; fax 371-5685)

Post & Telecommunications
There is a small post office in A Block at Connaught Place but the GPO is on the roundabout on Baba Kharak Singh Marg

(Radial No 2), half a km south-west of Connaught Place. Poste restante mail can be collected nearby from the Foreign Post Office on Market Rd (officially renamed Bhai Vir Singh Marg). The poste restante office is around the back and up the stairs, and is open weekdays from 9 am to 5 pm. Poste restante mail addressed simply to 'Delhi' will end up at the inconveniently situated Old Delhi post office, so ask your correspondents to specify 'New Delhi'. Some people also send mail to the tourist office on Janpath or the Student Travel Information Centre. Of course, American Express have their clients' mail service.

There are plenty of the usual private STD/ISD call offices dotted around, or there's the 24-hour, government-run VSNL communication office on Bangla Sahib Rd. This place also deals with credit card and reverse charge (collect) calls via the Home Country Direct service, or you can use any telephone which has an STD facility.

Foreign Embassies

Some of the foreign missions in Delhi include:

Afghanistan
5/50F Shantipath, Chanakyapuri (☎ 60-3331; fax 687-5439)

Australia
1/50G Shantipath, Chanakyapuri (☎ 688-8232; fax 688-5088)

Bangladesh
56 Ring Rd, Lajpat Nagar III (☎ 683-4668; fax 683-9237)

Belgium
50N Shantipath, Chanakyapuri (☎ 687-6500; fax 688-5821)

Bhutan
Chandragupta Marg, Chanakyapuri (☎ 60-9217; fax 687-6710)

Canada
7/8 Shantipath, Chanakyapuri (☎ 687-6500; fax 687-6579)

China
50D Shantipath, Chanakyapuri (☎ 60-0328; fax 688-5486)

Denmark
11 Aurangzeb Rd (☎ 301-0900; fax 301-0961)

France
2/50E Shantipath, Chanakyapuri (☎ 60-4004; fax 687-2305)

Germany
6/50G Shantipath, Chanakyapuri (☎ 60-4861; fax 687-3117)

Indonesia
50A Chanakyapuri (☎ 60-2352; fax 60-4865)

Iran
5 Barakhamba Rd (☎ 332-9600; fax 332-5493)

Iraq
169 Jor Bagh Rd (☎ 461-8011; fax 462-0996)

Ireland
13 Jor Bagh Rd (☎ 461-7435; fax 469-7053)

Israel
15th floor, Gopaldas Varma Bhavan, 28 Barakhamba Rd (☎ 375-5389; fax 371-6798)

Italy
50E Chandragupta Marg, Chanakyapuri (☎ 60-0071; fax 687-3889)

Japan
4-5/50G Shantipath, Chanakyapuri (☎ 687-6581)

Kenya
66 Vasant Marg, Vasant Vihar (☎ 687-6540; fax 687-6550)

Malaysia
50M Satya Marg, Chanakyapuri (☎ 60-1297; fax 688-1538)

Myanmar (Burma)
3/50F Nyaya Marg, Chanakyapuri (☎ 60-0251; fax 687-7942)

Nepal
Barakhamba Rd (☎ 332-8191; fax 332-6857)

Netherlands
6/50F Shantipath, Chanakyapuri (☎ 688-4951; fax 688-4856)

New Zealand
50N Nyaya Marg, Chanakyapuri (☎ 688-3170; fax 687-2317)

Pakistan
2/50G Shantipath, Chanakyapuri (☎ 60-0603; fax 687-2339)

Russia
Shantipath, Chanakyapuri (☎ 60-6026; fax 687-6823)

Singapore
E6 Chandragupta Marg, Chanakyapuri (☎ 688-5659; fax 688-6798)

Spain
12 Prithviraj Rd (☎ 379-2085; fax 379-3375)

Sri Lanka
27 Kautilya Marg, Chanakyapuri (☎ 301-0201; fax 301-5295)

Sweden
Nyaya Marg, Chanakyapuri (☎ 60-4961; fax 688-5401)

Syria
28 Vasant Marg, Vasant Vihar (☎ 67-0233)

Thailand
56N Nyaya Marg, Chanakyapuri (☎ 60-5679)

UK
    50 Shantipath, Chanakyapuri (☎ 687-2161; fax 687-2882)
USA
    Shantipath, Chanakyapuri (☎ 60-0651)

See under Visas in the Facts for the Visitor chapter for more details on obtaining visas in Delhi for other countries.

Visa Extensions & Other Permits

Hans Bhavan, near the Tilak Bridge railway station, is where you'll find the Foreigners' Registration Office (☎ 331-9489). Come here to get permits for restricted areas such as Assam. It's as chaotic and confused as ever with no organisation or plan, but surprisingly, with a little push and shove, you can get permits issued remarkably quickly. Four photos are required for permits; a photographer outside the building will do them on the spot for a small fee. The office is open weekdays from 9.30 am to 1.30 pm and 2 to 4 pm.

The Foreigners' Registration Office can issue 15-day visa extensions if you just need a few extra days before you leave the country. To apply for a longer visa extension, first you have to collect a form from the Ministry of Home Affairs at Khan Market which is then taken to the Foreigners' Registration Office (about a Rs 15 rickshaw ride away). You can usually get 15 days free, but a one-month extension costs Rs 800 (four photos required). When (and if) the extension is authorised, the authorisation has to be taken *back* to the Home Office, where the actual visa extension is issued. Also, it is extremely difficult to get an extension on a six-month visa; currently, very few extensions are being issued at all. If you need a tax clearance certificate before departure, the Foreign Section of the Income Tax Department (☎ 331-7826) is around the corner from Hans Bhavan in the Central Revenue Building on Vikas Marg. Bring exchange certificates with you, though it's quite likely nobody will ask for your clearance certificate when you leave the country. The office is closed from 1 to 2 pm.

Export of any object over 100 years old requires a permit. If in doubt, contact the Director, Antiquities, Archaeological Survey of India, Janpath (☎ 301-7220).

Libraries & Cultural Centres

The American Center (☎ 331-6841) is at 24 Kasturba Gandhi Marg and is open from 9.30 am to 6 pm. It has an extensive range of books. The British Council Library (☎ 371-0111) is at 17 Kasturba Gandhi Marg and is open Tuesday to Saturday from 10 am to 6 pm. It's much better than the US equivalent but officially you have to join to get in. Other cultural centres include: Alliance Francaise (☎ 644-0128), D-13 South Extension Part II; Italy (☎ 644-9193), Golf Links Rd; Japan (☎ 332-9803), 32 Ferozshah Rd; and Russia (☎ 332-9102), 24 Ferozshah Rd.

Sapru House on Barakhamba Rd is an institution devoted to the study of people of the world and has a good library. The India International Centre (☎ 61-9431), beside the Lodi Tombs, has lectures each week on art, economics and other contemporary issues by Indian and foreign experts.

Sangeet Natak Akademi (☎ 38-7248) at 35 Ferozshah Rd is the main performing arts centre and has substantial archive material.

Travel Agencies

In the Imperial Hotel, the Student Travel Information Centre (☎ 332-7582) is used by many travellers and is the place to renew or obtain student cards, although their tickets are not usually as cheap as elsewhere. Aerotrek Travels (☎ 371-5966) in the Mercantile Building in E Block is reportedly reliable. Some of the ticket discounters around Connaught Place are real fly-by-night operations, so take care.

Outbound Travel (☎ 60-3902) at B-2/50 Safdarjang Enclave has been recommended as a reliable place to organise travel within India.

There are also a couple of agencies catering to budget travellers in Paharganj, and you'll be approached on the streets or in cafes.

For more upmarket travel arrangements, both within India and for foreign travel, there are a number of places, mostly around Connaught Place. These include: Cox & Kings (☎ 332-0067), Sita World Travels (☎ 331-1133) and the Travel Corporation of India (☎ 331-2570).

Bookshops
There are a number of excellent bookshops around Connaught Place – a good place to look for interesting Indian books or to stock up with hefty paperbacks to while away those long train rides. Some of the better shops include: the New Book Depot at 18 B Block, Connaught Place; the English Book Depot; the Piccadilly Book Store, 64 Shankar Market, the Oxford Book Shop in N Block, Connaught Place; and Bookworm at 29B Radial Rd No 4, Connaught Place. Prabhu Book Service in Hauz Khas Village has an interesting selection of secondhand and rare books.

There are plenty of pavement stalls at various places around Connaught Place, with the major concentration on Sansad Marg, near the Kwality Restaurant. They have a good range of cheap paperbacks, and will often buy them back from you if they are returned in a reasonable condition.

Film & Photography
The Delhi Photo Company, at 78 Janpath close to the tourist office, processes both print and slide film quickly, cheaply and competently.

Medical Services
If you need medical attention in Delhi, the East West Medical Centre (☎ 69-9229, 62-3738), 38 Golf Links Rd, has been recommended by many travellers, diplomats and other expatriates. It's well equipped and the staff know what they're doing. Charges are high by Indian standards, but if you want good treatment...

For 24-hour emergency service, try the All India Institute of Medical Sciences (☎ 66-1123) at Ansari Nagar. Other reliable places include the Dr Ram Manohar Lohia Hospital (☎ 331-1621), Baba Kharak Singh Marg;

and the Ashlok Hospital (☎ 60-8407) at 25A Block AB, Safdarjang Enclave.

Ambulance service is available by phoning 102.

Other Shops
If you are in the market for a new Enfield motorcycle, try Essaar on Jhandi Walan Extension, Karol Bagh. For second-hand bikes and parts, try Inder Motors (☎ 572-8579) or Madaan Motors, also in Karol Bagh.

OLD DELHI
The old walled city of Shahjahanabad stands to the west of the Red Fort and was at one time surrounded by a sturdy defensive wall, only fragments of which now exist. The **Kashmir Gate**, at the northern end of the walled city, was the scene of desperate fighting when the British retook Delhi during the Mutiny. West of here, near Sabzi Mandi, is the British-erected **Mutiny Memorial** to the soldiers who lost their lives during the uprising. Near the monument is an **Ashoka pillar**, and like the one in Feroz Shah Kotla, it was brought here by Feroz Shah Tughlaq.

Chandni Chowk
The main street of Old Delhi is the colourful shopping bazaar known as Chandni Chowk. It's hopelessly congested day and night, a very sharp contrast to the open, spacious streets of New Delhi. At the east (Red Fort) end of Chandni Chowk, and north of the Jama Masjid, there is a **Jain temple** with a small marble courtyard surrounded by a colonnade. Next to the *kotwali* (old police station) is the **Sunehri Masjid**. In 1739, Nadir Shah, the Persian invader who carried off the Peacock Throne when he sacked Delhi, stood on the roof of this mosque and watched while his soldiers conducted a bloody massacre of the Delhi inhabitants.

The west end of Chandni Chowk is marked by the **Fatehpuri Mosque** which was erected in 1650 by one of Shah Jahan's wives.

Red Fort
The red sandstone walls of Lal Qila, the Red

Fort, extend for two km and vary in height from 18 metres on the river side to 33 metres on the city side. Shah Jahan started construction of the massive fort in 1638 and it was completed in 1648. He never completely moved his capital from Agra to his new city of Shahjahanabad in Delhi because he was deposed and imprisoned in Agra Fort by his son Aurangzeb.

The Red Fort dates from the very peak of Mughal power. When the emperor rode out on elephant-back into the streets of Old Delhi it was a display of pomp and power at its most magnificent. The Mughal reign from Delhi was a short one, however. Aurangzeb was the first and last great Mughal emperor to rule from here.

Today, the fort is typically Indian with would-be guides leaping forth to offer their services as soon as you enter. It's still a calm haven of peace if you've just left the frantic streets of Old Delhi, however. The city noise and confusion are light years away from the fort gardens and pavilions. The Yamuna River used to flow right by the eastern edge of the fort, and filled the 10-metre-deep moat. These days the river is over one km to the east and the moat remains empty. Entry to the fort is Rs 0.50; free on Friday.

Lahore Gate The main gate to the fort takes its name from the fact that it faces towards Lahore, now in Pakistan. If one spot could be said to be the emotional and symbolic heart of the modern Indian nation, the Lahore Gate of the Red Fort is probably it. During the struggle for independence, one of the nationalists' declarations was that they would see the Indian flag flying over the Red Fort in Delhi. After independence, many important political speeches were given by Nehru and Indira Gandhi to the crowds amassed on the *maidan* (open place or square) outside, and on Independence Day (15 August) each year, the prime minister addresses a huge crowd.

You enter the fort here and immediately find yourself in a vaulted arcade, the Chatta Chowk (Covered Bazaar). The shops in this arcade used to sell the upmarket items that the royal household might fancy – silks, jewellery, gold. These days they cater to the tourist trade and the quality of the goods is certainly a little less, although some still carry a royal price tag! This arcade of shops was also known as the Meena Bazaar, the shopping centre for ladies of the court. On Thursdays the gates of the fort were closed to men; only women were allowed inside the citadel.

The arcade leads to the Naubat Khana, or Drum House, where musicians used to play for the emperor, and the arrival of princes and royalty was heralded from here. The open courtyard beyond it formerly had galleries along either side, but these were removed by the British Army when the fort was used as their headquarters. Other reminders of the British presence are the huge, monumentally ugly, three-storey barrack blocks which lie to the north of this courtyard.

Diwan-i-Am The Hall of Public Audiences was where the emperor would sit to hear complaints or disputes from his subjects. His alcove in the wall was marble-panelled and set with precious stones, many of which were looted following the Mutiny. This elegant hall was restored as a result of a directive by Lord Curzon, the viceroy of India between 1898 and 1905.

Diwan-i-Khas The Hall of Private Audiences, built of white marble, was the luxurious chamber where the emperor would hold private meetings. Centrepiece of the hall (until Nadir Shah carted it off to Iran in 1739) was the magnificent Peacock Throne. The solid gold throne had figures of peacocks standing behind it, their beautiful colours resulting from countless inlaid precious stones. Between them was the figure of a parrot carved out of a single emerald.

This masterpiece in precious metals, sapphires, rubies, emeralds and pearls was broken up, and the so-called Peacock Throne displayed in Tehran simply utilises various bits of the original. The marble pedestal on which the throne used to sit remains in place.

In 1760, the Marathas also removed the silver ceiling from the hall, so today it is a pale shadow of its former glory. Inscribed on the walls of the Diwan-i-Khas is that famous Persian couplet:

If there is a paradise on earth
it is this, it is this, it is this.

Royal Baths Next to the Diwan-i-Khas are the *hammams* or baths – three large rooms surmounted by domes, with a fountain in the centre – one of which was set up as a sauna! The floors used to be inlaid with *pietra dura* work, and the rooms were illuminated through panels of coloured glass in the roof. The baths are closed to the public.

Shahi Burj This modest, three-storey octagonal tower at the north-eastern edge of the fort was once Shah Jahan's private working area. From here water used to flow south through the Royal Baths, the Diwan-i-Khas, the Khas Mahal and the Rang Mahal. Like the baths, the tower is closed to the public.

Moti Masjid Built in 1659 by Aurangzeb for his own personal use, the small and totally enclosed Pearl Mosque, made of marble, is next to the baths. One curious feature of the mosque is that its outer walls are oriented exactly to be in symmetry with the rest of the fort, while the inner walls are slightly askew, so that the mosque has the correct orientation with Mecca.

Other Features The **Khas Mahal**, south of the Diwan-i-Khas, was the emperor's private palace, divided into rooms for worship, sleeping and living.

The **Rang Mahal** or Palace of Colour, further south again, took its name from the painted interior, which is now gone. This was once the residence of the emperor's chief wife, and is where he ate. On the floor in the centre is a beautifully carved marble lotus, and the water flowing along the channel from the Shahi Burj used to end up here. Originally there was a fountain made of ivory in the centre.

There is a small Museum of Archaeology in the **Mumtaz Mahal**, still further south along the eastern wall. It's well worth a look, although most visitors seem to rush through the Red Fort, bypassing the museum.

The **Delhi Gate** to the south of the fort led to the Jama Masjid.

Gardens Between all the exquisite buildings were highly formal *charbagh* gardens, complete with fountains, pools and small pavilions. While the general outline and some of the pavilions are still in place, the gardens are not what they once were.

Sound & Light Show Each evening an interesting sound & light show re-creates events of India's history, particularly those connected with the Red Fort. There are shows in English and Hindi, and tickets (Rs 20) are available from the fort. The English sessions are at 7.30 pm from November through January, 8.30 pm from February to April and September-October, and at 9 pm from May to August. It's well worth making the effort to see this show, but make sure you are well equipped with mosquito repellent.

Jama Masjid

The great mosque of Old Delhi is both the largest in India and the final architectural extravagance of Shah Jahan. Commenced in 1644, the mosque was not completed until 1658. It has three great gateways, four angle towers and two minarets standing 40 metres high and constructed of alternating vertical strips of red sandstone and white marble.

Broad flights of steps lead up to the imposing gateways. The eastern gateway was originally only opened for the emperor, and is now only open on Fridays and Muslim festival days. The general public can enter by either the north or south gate (Rs 15). Shoes should be removed and those people considered unsuitably dressed (bare legs for either men or women) can hire robes at the northern gate.

The courtyard of the mosque has a capacity of 25,000 people. For Rs 5 it's possible to climb the southern minaret, and the views in all directions are superb – Old Delhi, the Red Fort and the polluting factories beyond it across the river, and New Delhi to the south. You can also see one of the features that the architect Lutyens incorporated into his design of New Delhi – the Jama Masjid, Connaught Place and Sansad Bhavan (Parliament House) are in a direct line. There's also a fine view of the Red Fort from the east side of the mosque.

There's a Rs 15 fee to take a camera inside the mosque, and another Rs 15 to take it up the minaret.

Coronation Durbar Site

This is a must for incurable raj fans looking for their fix of nostalgia. It's north of Old Delhi and is best reached by auto-rickshaw. In a desolate field stands a lone obelisk and it was on this site in 1877 and 1903 that the durbars were enacted.

It was also here in 1911 that King George V was declared emperor of India. If you look closely you can still see the old boy – a statue of him rises ghost-like out of the bushes nearby, where it was unceremoniously dumped after being removed from the canopy midway along Rajpath, between India Gate and Rashtrapati Bhavan. (The place where it was taken from remains empty, supposedly signifying the freedom of India, although a bronze statue of Gandhi was due to be installed in 1995.)

Further inspection reveals other imperial dignitaries languishing in the scrub. These days this historic bit of spare ground is used for backyard cricket matches and is a place for young men to teach their girlfriends how to ride the family scooter.

FEROZ SHAH KOTLA

Erected by Feroz Shah Tughlaq in 1354, the ruins of Ferozabad, the fifth city of Delhi, can be found at Feroz Shah Kotla, just off Bahadur Shah Zafur Marg between the old and new Delhis. In the fortress-palace is a 13-metre-high sandstone Ashoka pillar inscribed with Ashoka's edicts (and a later inscription). The remains of an old mosque and a fine well can also be seen in the area,

but most of the ruins of Ferozabad were used for the construction of later cities.

RAJ GHAT

North-east of Feroz Shah Kotla, on the banks of the Yamuna, a simple square platform of black marble marks the spot where Mahatma Gandhi was cremated following his assassination in 1948. A commemorative ceremony takes place each Friday, the day he was killed.

Jawaharlal Nehru, the first Indian prime minister, was cremated just to the north at Shanti Vana (Forest of Peace) in 1964. His daughter, Indira Gandhi, who was killed in 1984, and grandsons Sanjay (1980) and Rajiv (1991) were also cremated in this vicinity.

The Raj Ghat area is now a beautiful park, complete with labelled trees planted by a mixed bag of notables including Queen Elizabeth II, Gough Whitlam, Dwight Eisenhower and Ho Chi Minh!

NEW DELHI
Connaught Place

Located at the northern end of New Delhi, Connaught Place is the business and tourist centre. It's a vast traffic circle with an architecturally uniform series of colonnaded buildings around the edge – mainly devoted to shops, banks, restaurants, airline offices and the like. It's spacious but busy, and you're continually approached by people willing to provide you with everything imaginable, from an airline ticket for Timbuktu to having your fortune read.

Jantar Mantar

Only a short stroll down Sansad Marg (Parliament St) from Connaught Place, this strange collection of salmon-coloured structures is one of Maharaja Jai Singh II's observatories. The ruler from Jaipur constructed this observatory in 1725 and it is dominated by a huge sundial known as the Prince of Dials. Other instruments plot the course of heavenly bodies and predict eclipses.

Lakshmi Narayan Temple
Situated due west of Connaught Place, this garish modern temple was erected by the industrialist B D Birla in 1938. It's dedicated to Lakshmi, the goddess of prosperity and good fortune, and is commonly known as Birla Mandir.

Rajpath
The Kingsway is another focus of Lutyens' New Delhi. It is immensely broad and is flanked on either side by ornamental ponds. The Republic Day parade is held here every January 26, and millions of people gather to enjoy the spectacle.

At the eastern end of Rajpath lies the India Gate, while at the western end lies Rashtrapati Bhavan, now the president's residence, but built originally for the viceroy. It is flanked by the two large Secretariat buildings, and these three buildings sit upon a small rise, known as Raisina Hill.

India Gate
This 42-metre-high stone arch of triumph stands at the eastern end of the Rajpath. It bears the name of 85,000 Indian Army soldiers who died in the campaigns of WW I, the North-West Frontier operations of the same time and the 1919 Afghan fiasco.

Secretariat Buildings
The north and south Secretariat buildings lie either side of Rajpath on Raisina Hill. These imposing buildings, topped with *chhatris* (small domes), now house the ministries of Finance and External Affairs respectively.

Rashtrapati Bhavan
The official residence of the President of India stands at the opposite end of the Rajpath from India Gate. Completed in 1929, the palace-like building is a blend of Mughal and Western architectural styles, the most obvious Indian feature being the huge copper dome. To the west of the building is a Mughal garden which occupies 130 hectares, and this is open to the public in February.

Prior to Independence this was the viceroy's residence. At the time of Mountbatten, India's last viceroy, the number of servants needed to maintain the 340 rooms and its extensive gardens was enormous. There were 418 gardeners alone, 50 of them boys whose sole job was to chase away birds!

Sansad Bhavan
Although another large and imposing building, Sansad Bhavan, the Indian parliament building, stands almost hidden and virtually unnoticed at the end of Sansad Marg, or Parliament St, just north of Rajpath. The building is a circular colonnaded structure 171 metres in diameter. Its relative physical insignificance in the grand scheme of New Delhi shows how the focus of power has shifted from the viceroy's residence, which was given pride of place during the time of the British Raj when New Delhi was conceived.

Permits to visit the parliament and sit in the public gallery are available from the reception office on Raisina Rd, but you'll need a letter of introduction from your embassy.

The Battle of the Gradient
The rise known as Raisina Hill, and the approach road up to it (or, more precisely, the angle of the approach road up to it), were the cause of a trivial yet major dispute, known as the 'battle of the gradient', between Delhi's designer, Lutyens, and his colleague, Herbert Baker. While Baker was charged with designing the Secretariat and parliament buildings, Lutyens made himself responsible for the viceregal residence and the India Gate. It was Lutyens' intention that the residence should be slightly higher than the Secretariats and visible from a greater distance. Baker wanted all three buildings on the same level, so that the viceroy's residence would majestically come into view as one approached it up the rise. After numerous discussions, and referral to successive viceroys, Baker won, and the two men refused to talk to one another for some years. ■

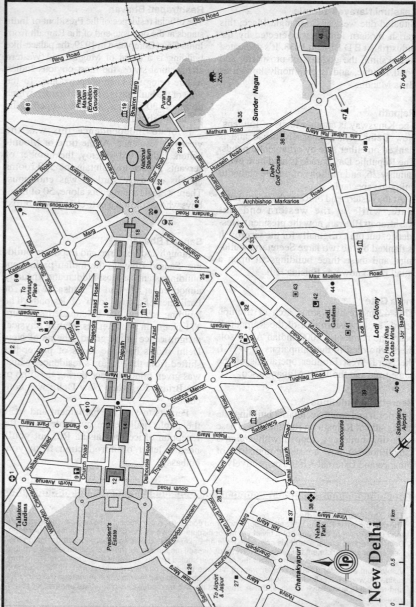

Zoo

Ring Road

Ring Road

Ring Road

Pragati Maidan (Exhibition Grounds)

Purana Qila

Bhairon Marg

Mathura Road

To Agra

Sunder Nagar

Mathura Road

Lala Lajpat Rai Marg

Lodi Road

Delhi Golf Course

Archbishop Markarios Road

National Stadium

Sher Shah Road

Purana Qila Road

Dr Zakir Hussein Road

Subramania Bharti Marg

Tilak Marg

Bhagwandas Road

Copernicus Marg

Pandara Road

Max Mueller Road

Lodi Road

Lodi Gardens

Annie Shaprji Marg

Lodi Colony

Jor Bagh Road

To Hauz Khas & Qutab Minar

Kasturba Gandhi Marg

Feroz Shah Road

Shahjahan Road

Janpath

Janpath

Janpath

To Connaught Place

Aurangzeb Road

Prithviraj Road

Rajaji Marg

Dr Rajendra Prasad Road

Ashoka Road

Aurobindo Marg

Max Mueller Road

Rajpath

Maulena Azad Road

Ashoka Road

Ashoka Road

Kamal Ataturk Road

Tughlaq Road

Krishna Menon Marg

Rajaji Marg

Dupleix Marg

Safdarjang Road

Ashoka Road

Pandit Pant Marg

Talkatora Road

Willingdon Crescent

North Avenue

Church Road

Dalhousie Road

Tyagraj Marg

Mutri Marg

South Road

Kamal Ataturk Road

Safdarjang Airport

Racecourse

President's Estate

Willingdon Crescent

Talkatora Gardens

Teen Murti Road

Nili Marg

Vinay Marg

Nehru Park

Shantipath

Kautilya Marg

Panchsheel Marg

Balar Marg

Safdar

To Airport & Jaipur

Chanakyapuri

New Delhi

0   0.5   1 km

PLACES TO STAY		9	Church of the Redemption	24	Pandara Market
2	YWCA International Guest House	10	Sansad Bhavan (Parliament House)	28	Nehru Museum
3	Ashok Yatri Niwas Hotel	12	Rashtrapati Bhavan	29	Indira Gandhi Memorial Museum
4	Janpath Hotel	13	Secretariat (North Block)	30	Gandhi Smriti
5	Kanishka Hotel	14	Secretariat (South Block)	32	Israeli Embassy
11	Le Meridien Hotel	15	Vijay Chowk	33	Khan Market
25	Taj Hotel	16	Indira Gandhi National Centre for the Arts	35	Sunder Nagar Market
26	Diplomat Hotel			38	Santushti Shopping Centre
27	Vishwa Yuvak Kendra	17	National Museum	39	Safdarjang Tomb
31	Claridges Hotel	18	India Gate	40	Indian Airlines (24 hours)
34	Ambassador Hotel	19	Crafts Museum	41	Mohammed Shah's Tomb
36	Oberoi Hotel	20	Childrens Park		
37	Ashok Hotel	21	Bikaner House (Deluxe buses to Jaipur)	42	Bara Gumbad & Mosque
46	Lodhi Hotel			43	Sikander Lodi's Tomb
		22	National Gallery of Modern Art	44	India International Centre
OTHER				45	Tibet House
1	Ram Manohar Lohia Hospital	23	Sher Shah's Gate & Khairul Manzil Masjid	47	Hazrat Nizamuddin Aulia
6	Max Mueller Bhavan			48	Humayun's Tomb
7	Rabindra Bhavan				
8	Appu Ghar				

MUSEUMS & GALLERIES
National Museum
Located on Janpath just south of Rajpath, the National Museum has a good collection of Indian bronzes, terracotta and wood sculptures dating back to the Mauryan period (2nd-3rd century BC), exhibits from the Vijayanagar period in south India, miniature and mural paintings, and costumes of the various tribal peoples. The museum is definitely worth visiting and is open Tuesday to Sunday from 10 am to 5 pm. Admission is Rs 0.50. There are film shows most days of the week.

Right next door is the Archaeological Survey of India office. Publications available here cover all the main sites in India. Many of these are not available at the particular sites themselves.

National Gallery of Modern Art
This gallery stands near India Gate at the eastern end of Rajpath, and was formerly the Delhi residence of the Maharaja of Jaipur. It houses an excellent collection of works by both Indian and colonial artists.

It is open daily from 10 am to 5 pm; admission is free.

Nehru Museum
Located on Teen Murti Rd near Chanakyapuri, the residence of the first Indian prime minister, Teen Murti Bhavan, has been converted into a museum. Photographs and newspaper clippings on display give a fascinating insight into the history of the independence movement.

During the tourist season there is a sound & light show about his life and the independence movement. The museum is open Tuesday to Sunday from 10 am to 5 pm. Admission is free.

Rail Transport Museum
This museum at Chanakyapuri will be of great interest to anyone who becomes fascinated by India's exotic collection of railway engines. The exhibit includes an 1855 steam engine, still in working order, and a large number of oddities such as the skull of an elephant that charged a mail train in 1894, and lost. See the boxed Gricing section in the Getting Around chapter for more details.

DELHI

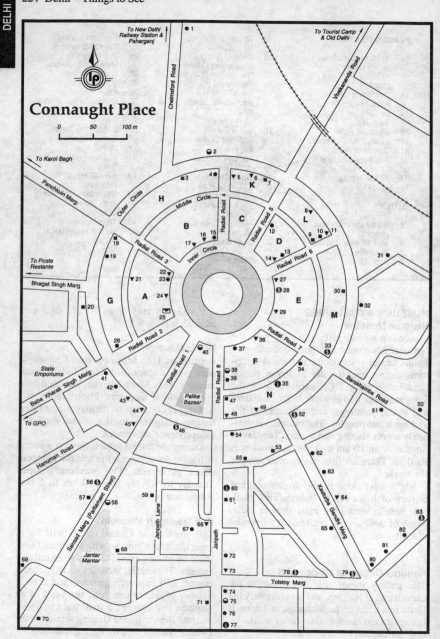

Connaught Place

To New Delhi
Railway Station &
Paharganj

To Tourist Camp
& Old Delhi

Vivekananda Road

Chelmsford Road

0   50   100 m

To Karol Bagh

Panchkuin Marg

To Poste
Restante

Bhagat Singh Marg

State
Emporiums

Baba Kharak Singh Marg

To GPO

Hanuman Road

Outer Circle

Middle Circle

Inner Circle

Radial Road 3

Radial Road 2

Radial Road 1

Radial Road 4

Radial Road 5

Radial Road 6

Radial Road 7

Radial Road 8

Barakhamba Road

Kasturba Gandhi Marg

Sansad Marg (Parliament Street)

Janpath Lane

Janpath

Tolstoy Marg

Palika
Bazaar

Jantar
Mantar

H

B

A

G

K

C

D

E

M

F

N

L

1

2

3   4

5   6   7

8

9 10 11

12

13

14

15
16

17

18

19

20

21

22

23

24

25

26

27

28

29

30

31

32

33

34

35

36

37

38

39

40

41

42

43

44

45

46

47

48

49

50

51

52

53

54

55

56

57

58

59

60

61

62

63

64

65

66

67

68

69

70

71

72

73

74

75

76

77

78

79

80

81

82

83

The museum is open Tuesday to Sunday from 9.30 am to 5 pm and there's a small admission fee.

Tibet House

This small museum has a fascinating collection of ceremonial items brought out of Tibet when the Dalai Lama fled following the Chinese occupation. Downstairs is a shop selling a wide range of Tibetan handicrafts.

There are often lecture/discussion sessions. The museum is in the Institutional Area, Lodi Rd, and hours are Monday to Saturday from 10 am to 1 pm and 2 to 5 pm. Admission is free.

International Dolls Museum

This museum in Nehru House on Bahadur Shah Zafar Marg displays 6000 dolls from 85 countries. Over a third of them are from

PLACES TO STAY		43	Gaylord	42	Regal Cinema
		44	El Arab Restaurant	46	Citibank & Air India
3	Hotel 55	45	Kwality Restaurant	50	East-West Airlines &
7	York Hotel	48	Wimpy		Emirates Air
9	Jukaso Inn	49	Shangri-la Chinese	51	Budget Rent-a-Car
10	Nirula's Hotel		Restaurant	52	Hongkong Bank
13	Hotel Palace Heights	64	Parikrama	54	Oxford Bookshop
18	Hotel Marina		Restaurant	56	Standard Chartered
20	Alka Hotel	66	Bankura Café		Bank
30	Hotel Bright &	73	Sona Rupa	58	Bus 433 to Bahai
	Andhra Bank		Restaurant &		Temple & Bus 620
47	Hotel Metro		Royal Nepal		to Youth Hostel &
53	Sunny Guest House		Airlines		Chanakyapuri
55	Ringo Guest House			60	Government of India
57	Park Hotel	OTHER			Tourist Office &
59	Mrs Colaco's Guest				Delhi Photo
	House	1	Railway Booking		Company
61	Janpath Guest House		Office	62	Pakistan
68	Mr SC Jain's Guest	2	Bus 620 to Youth		International
	House		Hostel &		Airlines
69	YMCA Tourist Hotel		Chanakyapuri	63	American Center
70	YWCA International	4	Plaza Cinema	65	British Council
	Guest House	12	Odeon Cinema	67	Map Sales Office
71	Imperial Hotel,	15	Bookworm	72	Lufthansa
	Thomas Cook &	19	Singapore Airlines &	74	Central Cottage
	Student Travel		Gulf Air		Industries
	Information Centre	23	American Express		Emporium
		25	Post Office	75	Bus 505 to Qutab
PLACES TO EAT		26	Malaysian & Royal		Minar
			Jordanian Airlines,	76	Japan Airlines
5	Chinar Restaurant		El Al & Lot	77	Haryana, Himachal
6	Palki Chinese	28	ANZ Grindlays Bank		Pradesh,
	Restaurant	31	Shankar Market		Rajasthan, Uttar
8	Delhi Durbar & Minar	32	Super Bazaar		Pradesh & West
	Restaurants	33	Bank of Baroda		Bengal Tourist
11	Nirula's Restaurants	34	Aeroflot		Offices
14	Embassy Restaurant	35	Delhi Tourism	78	Deutsche Bank
16	Zen Restaurant &		Corporation Office	79	Credit Lyonnaise
	Café 100	37	Cathay Pacific Airlines	80	Thai International
17	Volga Restaurant	38	EATS Bus & Vayudoot		Airways
21	Fa Yian Restaurant	39	Indian Airlines	81	KLM
22	Wenger's	40	Motorcycle	82	ModiLuft
24	El Rodeo Restaurant		Rickshaws to Old	83	Bank of America,
27	Kovil		Delhi		Banque Nationale
29	United Coffee House	41	Khadi Gramodyog		de Paris & Saudia
36	The Host		Bhavan		Airlines

India and one exhibit comprises 500 dolls in the costumes worn all over the country. The museum is open Tuesday to Sunday from 10 am to 5.30 pm.

Crafts Museum

Located in the Aditi Pavilion at the Pragati Maidan Exhibition Grounds, Mathura Rd, this museum contains a collection of traditional Indian crafts in textiles, metal, wood and ceramics. The museum is part of a 'village life' complex where you can visit rural India without ever leaving Delhi. Opening hours are daily from 9.30 am to 4.30 pm. Admission is free.

Gandhi Darshan

At Raj Ghat is the Gandhi Darshan, a display of paintings and photos about the Mahatma's life and deeds. The Gandhi Smarak Sangrahalaya, also at Raj Ghat, has displays of some of Gandhi's personal possessions.

Indira Gandhi Memorial Museum

The former residence of Indira Gandhi at

Miniature painting:
tranquil scenes from times past

1 Safdarjang Rd has also been converted into a museum. On show are some of her personal effects, including the sari (complete with blood stains) she was wearing at the time of her assassination. Striking a somewhat macabre note is the crystal plaque in the garden, flanked constantly by two soldiers, which protects a few brown spots of Mrs Gandhi's blood on the spot where she actually fell after being shot by two of her Sikh bodyguards in December 1984.

Other Museums

The **Museum of Natural History** is opposite the Nepalese Embassy on Barakhamba Rd. Fronted by a large model dinosaur, it has a collection of fossils, stuffed animals and birds, and a 'hands on' discovery room for children. It's open Tuesday to Sunday from 10 am to 5 pm.

There is a **National Philatelic Museum** hidden in the post office at Dak Bhavan, Sardar Patel Chowk on Sansad Marg (Parliament St). It's closed on Saturday and Sunday. At Indira Gandhi International Airport there is an **Air Force Museum**, open daily except Tuesday from 10 am to 1.30 pm.

PURANA QILA

Just south-east of India Gate and north of Humayun's Tomb and the Nizamuddin railway station is the old fort, Purana Qila. This is the supposed site of Indraprastha, the original city of Delhi. The Afghan ruler, Sher Shah, who briefly interrupted the Mughal Empire by defeating Humayun, completed the fort during his reign from 1538-45, before Humayun regained control of India. The fort has massive walls and three large gateways.

Entering from the south gate you'll see the small octagonal red sandstone tower, the Sher Mandal, later used by Humayun as a library. It was while descending the stairs of this tower one day in 1556 that he slipped, fell and received injuries from which he later died. Just beyond it is the Qila-i-Kuhran Mosque, or Mosque of Sher Shah, which, unlike the fort itself, is in a fairly reasonable condition.

There's a small archaeological museum just inside the main gate, and there are good views of New Delhi from atop the gate.

ZOO

The Delhi Zoo, on the south side of the Purana Qila, is not terribly good. The cages are poorly labelled and in winter many of the animals are kept inside. There are a number of white tigers though. The zoo is open daily except Friday, in summer from 8 am to 6 pm and in winter from 9 am to 5 pm. Entry is Rs 0.50.

HUMAYUN'S TOMB

Built in the mid-16th century by Haji Begum, senior wife of Humayun, the second Mughal emperor, this is an early example of Mughal architecture. The elements in its design – a squat building, lighted by high arched entrances, topped by a bulbous dome and surrounded by formal gardens – were to be refined over the years to the magnificence of the Taj Mahal in Agra. This earlier tomb is thus of great interest for its relation to the later Taj. Humayun's wife is also buried in the red-and-white sandstone, black-and-yellow marble tomb.

Other tombs in the garden include that of Humayun's barber and the Tomb of Isa Khan, a good example of Lodi architecture. Entry to Humayun's Tomb is Rs 0.50, except on Friday when it is free. An excellent view can be obtained over the surrounding country from the terraces of the tomb.

NIZAMUDDIN

Across the road from Humayun's Tomb is the shrine of the Muslim Sufi saint, Nizam-ud-din Chishti, who died in 1325 aged 92. His shrine, with its large tank, is one of several interesting tombs here. The construction of Nizam-ud-din's tank caused a dispute between the saint and the constructor of Tughlaqabad, further to the south of Delhi (see Tughlaqabad in the upcoming Greater Delhi section for details).

Other tombs include the later grave of Jahanara, the daughter of Shah Jahan, who stayed with her father during his imprison-ment by Aurangzeb in Agra's Red Fort. Amir Khusru, a renowned Urdu poet, also has his tomb here as does Atgah Khan, a favourite of Humayun and his son Akbar. Atgah Khan was murdered by Adham Khan in Agra. In turn Akbar had Adham Khan terminated and his grave is near the Qutab Minar.

It's worth visiting the shrine at around sunset on Thursdays, as it is a popular time for worship, and *qawwali* singers start performing after the evening prayers.

LODI GARDENS

About three km to the west of Humayun's tomb and adjoining the India International Centre are the Lodi Gardens. In these well-kept gardens are the tombs of the Sayyid and Lodi rulers. Mohammed Shah's Tomb (1450) was a prototype for the later Mughal-style tomb of Humayun, a design which would eventually develop into the Taj Mahal. Other tombs include those of his predecessor Mubarak Shah (1433), Ibrahim Lodi (1526) and Sikander Lodi (1517). The Bara Gumbad Mosque is a fine example of its type of plaster decoration.

SAFDARJANG TOMB

Beside the small Safdarjang airport, where Indira Gandhi's son Sanjay was killed in a light plane accident in 1980, is the Safdar-jang Tomb. It was built in 1753-54 by the Nawab of Avadh for his father, Safdarjang, and is one of the last examples of Mughal architecture before the final remnants of the great empire collapsed. The tomb stands on a high terrace in an extensive garden. Entry is Rs 0.50; free on Friday.

HAUZ KHAS

Situated midway between Safdarjang and the Qutab Minar, this area was once the reservoir for the second city of Delhi, Siri, which lies slightly to the east. Interesting sights here include Feroz Shah's Tomb (1398) and the remains of an ancient college. It was around this area that Timur defeated the forces of Mohammed Shah Tughlaq in 1398.

Also part of the old city of Siri is the Moth

ki Masjid, which lies some distance to the east of Hauz Khas. It is said to be the finest in the Lodi style.

BAHAI TEMPLE
Lying to the east of Siri is this building shaped like a lotus flower. Built between 1980 and 1986, it is set amongst pools and gardens, and adherents of any faith are free to visit the temple and pray or meditate silently according to their own religion. It looks particularly spectacular at dusk when it is floodlit. The temple is open to visitors from April to September, daily except Monday from 9 am to 7 pm, and October to March from 9.30 am to 5.30 pm.

Getting There & Away
Bus No 433 from opposite the Park Hotel on Sansad Marg near Connaught Place will bring you very close to the temple.

SWIMMING POOLS
The New Delhi Municipal Corporation has its pool at Nehru Park, near the Ashok Hotel in Chanakyapuri.

Most of the deluxe hotels have pools, and many allow non-guest use – for a fee, which can be anything from Rs 150 up to Rs 550! In the winter months many hotel pools are closed, which is hardly surprising given the weather. The pool at the Sheraton is heated and open year-round, but to hotel guests only.

ORGANISED TOURS
Delhi is very spread out, so taking a city tour makes a lot of sense. Even by public transport, getting from, say, the Red Fort to the Qutab Minar is comparatively expensive.

Two major organisations arrange Delhi tours – beware of agents offering cut-price (and sometimes inferior) tours. The ITDC, operating under the name Ashok Travels & Tours (☎ 332-2336), has tours which include guides and a luxury coach. Their office is in L Block, Connaught Place, but you can book at the tourist office on Janpath or at the major hotels. Delhi Tourism (☎ 331-4229), a branch of the city government, arranges

similar tours and their office is in N Block, Middle Circle.

A 4½-hour morning tour of New Delhi costs Rs 70 with ITDC. Starting at 8.30 am, the tour includes the Qutab Minar, Humayun's Tomb, India Gate, the Jantar Mantar and the Lakshmi Narayan Temple. The afternoon Old Delhi tour for Rs 60 starts at 2.15 pm and covers the Red Fort, Jama Masjid, Raj Ghat, Shanti Vana and Feroz Shah Kotla. If you take both tours on the same day it costs Rs 120.

'Delhi by Evening' is a Delhi Tourism tour which takes in a number of sights, including the sound & light show at the Red Fort, but a minimum of 10 people is required.

Tours further afield include ITDC day tours to Agra for Rs 400.

PLACES TO STAY
Places to Stay – bottom end
Delhi is certainly no bargain when it comes to cheap hotels. You can easily pay Rs 120 for the most basic single room – a price that elsewhere in India will generally get you a reasonable double room with bath.

There are basically two areas for cheap accommodation in Delhi. The first is around Janpath at the southern side of Connaught Place in New Delhi. The second area, which is cheaper, more popular and has a greater range of places than Connaught Place, is Paharganj near New Delhi railway station – this is about midway between Old Delhi and New Delhi.

There are also a number of rock-bottom hotels in Old Delhi itself. They're colourful but generally noisy and too far away from New Delhi's agents, offices, airlines and other facilities for most travellers, especially given Delhi's difficult public transport situation.

Camping If you want to camp there are several possibilities in Delhi. The *Tourist Camp* (☎ 327-2898) is one of the cheapest places to stay and is surprisingly popular. It's some distance from Connaught Place but is well served by buses. Most of the overland operators arrange accommodation here and it's also the starting point for the direct buses to Kathmandu. Run by retired Indian Army officers, the camp is actually in Old Delhi, near Delhi Gate on Jawaharlal Nehru Marg, across from the J P Narayan Hospital (Irwin Hospital), only two km from Connaught Place. You can camp with your own tent (Rs 25), or there are basic rooms with shared bathrooms for Rs 90/130. They're nothing flash, but OK; this place generally gets good recommendations from travellers. There's a restaurant and a left-luggage room where you can leave your accumulated junk while you explore elsewhere.

There is a second camping site, the *Qudsia Gardens Tourist Camp* (☎ 252-3121), right across the road from the Interstate bus station. Camping here costs Rs 30 per person, or there are ordinary rooms for Rs 80/100, and deluxe doubles for Rs 150. It's convenient for an early-morning bus departure, but little else.

Connaught Place & Janpath Area There are several cheap lodges or guest houses near the Government of India tourist office. They're often small and cramped but you meet lots of fellow travellers; they're also conveniently central and there are often dormitories for shoestring travellers. Since many of these places are so popular, you may find that your first choice is full. If that's the case simply stay at one of the others until a room becomes available – it's unlikely you'll have to wait more than a day.

One of the most well-known places to stay is the *Ringo Guest House* (☎ 331-0605) at 17 Scindia House, down a small side street near the tourist office. This place has been a travellers' institution for many years, and it has its fair share of detractors as well as fans. Nevertheless, it is still popular. Beds in crowded, 14-bed dorms are Rs 60; rooms with common bath are Rs 160/180 and with private bath it's Rs 210/260. You can also sleep on a *charpoy* (Indian rope bed) on the roof for Rs 50. The rooms are very small but it's clean enough and the showers and toilets are well maintained. Meals are available in the rooftop courtyard, although at a higher

price than in the nearby restaurants. You can also store luggage for a hefty Rs 7 per item per day.

A place with similar prices is the *Sunny Guest House* (☎ 331-2909) at 152 Scindia House, a few doors further along the same side street. Dorm beds are Rs 60 and singles/doubles with common bath range from Rs 90/170 to Rs 120/250. Again, the rooms are small but the place has a sort of shabby charm, and this, along with the location, are what attract so many people. The left-luggage facility is also Rs 7 per item per day.

On the west side of Janpath along Janpath Lane are a couple of places which have been minor legends among travellers for well over a decade now. *Mrs Colaco's* (☎ 332-8758) at No 3 is the first one you'll come to. A charpoy in the reasonably roomy dormitory costs Rs 55, and there are good doubles for Rs 135 with common bath. There's a safe deposit for valuables, a laundry service and baggage storage. Round the corner, *Mr S C Jain's Guest House*, at 7 Pratap Singh Building also on Janpath Lane, is yet another legend. Extremely plain rooms with common bath cost Rs 150 to Rs 170, depending on the size. The big advantage of both these places is that they are in a quiet residential area.

Across on the north side of Connaught Place is the *Hotel Bright* (☎ 332-0444), 85 M Block Connaught Circus, opposite the Super Bazaar. There's definitely nothing bright about this place, but it's not too bad. The dark and somewhat grotty rooms cost Rs 250/300 with attached bath, but the ones facing the road can be noisy.

The *Hotel Palace Heights* (☎ 332-1419) in D Block, Connaught Place, is a moderately priced place close to Nirula's. It's on the 3rd floor of an office building and has a huge verandah overlooking Connaught Place – great for breakfast or afternoon tea. Although the facilities are fairly primitive, it's a relaxed place with a small-town atmosphere. Rooms cost Rs 175/285 with air-cooler but common bath, or there are air-con doubles with bath for Rs 480.

The ITDC *Ashok Yatri Niwas* (☎ 332-4511) is just a 10-minute walk from Connaught Place on Ashoka Rd at the intersection with Janpath. This huge (556 rooms) government-run hotel is a managerial disaster – it's been setting the standard for lousy service for some years now; if your sanity is precious, don't even think about staying here. Simple matters such as checking in and out can easily take half an hour, the service is terrible – surly at best – the whole place is poorly maintained, bed linen is often threadbare, you may have to beg for a blanket and the lifts are hopelessly unreliable. The only saving grace is the views from the upper floor rooms – it's just a pity you can barely see through the filthy windows! All this can be yours for just Rs 250/350. Maximum stay is seven days, but anyone who lasts that long deserves a medal – and a professional assessment of their sanity!

Paharganj Area Directly opposite New Delhi railway station is the start of Main Bazaar, a narrow road which stretches due west for about a km. Because of its proximity to the station it has become a major accommodation centre for Indians and foreigners alike, and these days also seems to be a magnet for Russians on shopping sprees. It has also become a crowded and bustling market selling virtually anything you'd care to name – from incense to washing machines. Because it's so busy, walking along Main Bazaar at any time requires patience. There are any number of cheap hotels along this road, offering varying degrees of comfort and quality.

As you walk up Main Bazaar from the station, one of the first places you come to is the *Hotel Kanishta* (☎ 52-5365). It's not one of the more popular places as it's very close to the station and the accompanying noise of Qutab Rd, nor is it great value. Air-cooled rooms with bath, TV and balcony cost Rs 300, and hot water is available by the bucket.

The next place is the *Kailash Guest House* (☎ 777-4993) at No 4469. It's a modern, clean and quite friendly place, although many of the rooms face inwards and tend to

be a bit stuffy; those with windows are fine. It's good value at Rs 75/125 with common bath, and Rs 150 for a double with attached bath. Hot water is available free by the bucket. The *Kiran Guest House* (☎ 52-6104) next door is virtually an identical twin to the Kailash, and prices are similar at Rs 85/150 with attached bath.

A little further along on the right is the *Bright Guest House* (☎ 752-5852) at No 1089-90. It's one of the cheapest places in Paharganj, and one of the best for the money. Clean rooms around a small courtyard cost Rs 70/80 with common bath, Rs 100 for a double with bath or air-cooler, and Rs 130 with both.

Down a narrow alley to the right, not far beyond the Bright Guest House, is the very popular *Hotel Namaskar* (☎ 752-1234, 752-2233), at 917 Chandiwalan. This is a very friendly place run by two brothers, and they go out of their way to make sure you are comfortable. All rooms have windows and attached bath, and there's a geyser on each floor so there's plenty of hot water for your buckets. There's filtered, cooled drinking water available, and luggage is stored free of charge for guests. It's not the cheapest place, but is well worth the extra. Rooms cost Rs 150/200, and there are also rooms with three (Rs 300) and four (Rs 400) beds. There's also a couple of air-con rooms at Rs 400. It's an excellent place, and they can also arrange cheap bus tickets, and car hire for trips further afield.

Moving further west along Main Bazaar, the next place is the funky old *Camran Lodge* (☎ 52-6053) at No 1116, which touts itself as a 'Trusted lodging house for distinguished people'. It's in an old building which is a bit of maze. The rooms are small and shabby, but cheap at Rs 60/100 with common bath, Rs 125 for a double with bath attached. Hot water by the bucket is free.

The *Hotel Vivek* (☎ 777-7062) at No 1534-50 is a very popular place, partly because of the restaurant on the ground floor. The rooms are pretty standard – smallish – as are the prices at Rs 80/100 with common bath, and with attached bath for Rs 110/180.

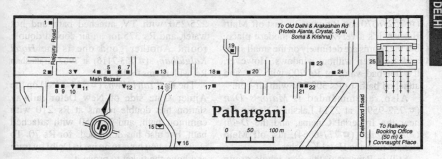

There are also air-con rooms for Rs 275/325 with bath.

The *Ankush Guest House* (☎ 751-9000) at No 1558 is another place popular with travellers. There are single rooms with common bath at Rs 60, or doubles/triples with attached bath for Rs 120/150.

The popular *Hotel Vishal* (☎ 753-2079), a little further along, is similar, and has two good restaurants on the ground floor. Rooms cost Rs 120/160.

The *Hare Krishna Guest House*, next to the Vishal, is another place worth checking out. It has good, clean rooms for Rs 125, and there are good views from the roof.

Also here is the *Anoop Hotel* (☎ 73-5219) at No 1566. It's quite modern and clean, and is excellent value for money. The rooms, which have attached bath and hot water, are a decent size and are marble-lined, which makes them cool, although a bit tomb-like. They're well worth the Rs 160/200 cost. The biggest attraction of this place, however, is the rooftop terrace and snack bar. Checkout is based on the 24-hour system.

On Main Bazaar near Rajguru Rd is the *Sapna Hotel* (☎ 52-4066), very basic and a bit tatty around the edges, but habitable and cheap at Rs 60/80 with common bath, and Rs 100 for a double with attached bath. Next door is the *Hotel Satyam* (☎ 73-1155), which is certainly a step up the scale, with clean rooms for Rs 150/200 with attached bath and hot water. The front rooms can be noisy, but that's true of all the places along Main Bazaar.

At the very top of the range is the *Metropolis Tourist Home* (☎ 753-5766) at 1634

Main Bazaar. This place offers dorm beds with lockers in air-cooled, four-bed rooms for Rs 100, or there are doubles for Rs 350 with attached bath, or Rs 700 with air-con.

Also in this range is the *Hotel Kelson*

PLACES TO STAY

1	Hotel Kelson
2	Metropolis Tourist Home
4	Hotel Vishal & Hare Krishna Guest House
5	Anoop Hotel
6	Ankush Guest House
7	Hotel Vivek
8	Hotel Satyam
9	Sapna Hotel
11	Kesri Hotel & Mehta Electricals (Bicycle Hire)
13	Hotel Payal
17	Hotel Relaxo
18	Camran Lodge
19	Hotel Namaskar
20	Bright Guest House
21	Kiran Guest House
22	Kailash Guest House
23	Delhi Guest House
24	Hotel Kanishta

PLACES TO EAT

3	Madaan Cafe
4	Appetite Restaurant & Lords Cafe
10	Khosla Cafe
12	Diamond Cafe
16	Golden Cafe

OTHER

14	Vegetable Market
15	Paharganj Post Office
25	New Delhi Railway Station

(☎ 752-7070) on Rajguru Rd, just off Main Bazaar. It's a very clean and modern place, but the rooms are definitely on the small side, and are often without windows. However, it's not bad value at Rs 200 with TV and attached bath, or Rs 300/350 with air-con.

Also recommended is *Major's Den* (☎ 752-9599) at 2314 Lakshmi Narain St, near the Imperial Cinema, and the *Delhi Guest House* (☎ 777-6864), just off Main Bazaar near the Hotel Kanishta.

Still in Paharganj, there's a whole group of places on Arakashan Rd, which is just to the north of New Delhi railway station, past the Desh Bandhu Gupta Rd flyover (see the New Delhi map). These are definitely at the top end of the budget category, and charge from Rs 165, but they are all modern and pretty well equipped.

Pick of the bunch here is the friendly *Hotel Ajanta* (☎ 752-0925) at 36 Arakashan Rd. This clean and modern place is popular with travellers looking for a modicum of comfort and prepared to pay a bit above rock bottom. All rooms have attached bath with hot water, and the deluxe rooms have colour TV and phone with ISD facility. The charge is Rs 165/245 for rooms with common bath, Rs 355/445 for deluxe, and Rs 595 for deluxe air-con. This hotel also has a taxi available for various trips, such as to the airport.

A few doors along from the Ajanta is the *Hotel Crystal* (☎ 753-1639) at 8501 Arakashan Rd (I defy you to find the logic in the numbering system!). The rooms are quite good, and it's a bit cheaper than the Ajanta, charging Rs 245/325 with attached bath, and Rs 50 extra with TV. Almost next door is the *Hotel Syal* (☎ 51-0091) at 43 Arakashan Rd. It is similar to the Crystal, although none of the rooms have air-cooling or air-con, which is a major inconvenience in summer.

The *Hotel Soma* (☎ 752-1002), close by at 33 Arakashan Rd, boasts a 'gay atmosphere'. The clean and modern rooms are a good size, and cost Rs 200/250, or Rs 250/300 with air-cooler and Rs 350/400 with air-con. Also in this area is the *Krishna Hotel* (☎ 751-0252) at 45 Arakashan Rd. This place offers standard facilities for Rs

225/250 with TV, attached bath and hot water, and Rs 375 for an air-cooled double room. Another good one is the *Hotel Kalgidhar* (☎ 753-7116) at 7967 Arakashan Rd, with rooms for Rs 150.

The *Rail Yatri Niwas* (☎ 331-3484) on the Ajmer Gate side of New Delhi railway station has double rooms at Rs 210 with common bath, and Rs 250 with attached bath, but also has dorm beds for Rs 70. To stay there you have to arrive in Delhi by train and have the ticket to prove it.

Old Delhi There's a group of hotels around the south-western corner of the Jama Masjid, and many more along Matya Mahal, the road which runs due south of the same mosque.

One of the best places is the *Hotel New City Palace* (☎ 327-9548) right behind the mosque. The front rooms have windows but also get the early morning call from the mosque. The hotel boasts it's a 'home for palatial comfort', which is perhaps overstating things a bit, but it is clean, modern and the management friendly. Double rooms with attached bath with hot water cost Rs 200; with air-con it's Rs 300.

Also good, and perhaps a bit quieter, is the *Hotel Bombay Orient* (☎ 328-6253) on Matya Mahal, not far from the southern gate of the Jama Masjid. It's also clean and well-kept, and singles/doubles with common bath are Rs 75/150, doubles with attached bath Rs 200, or with air-con Rs 300.

At the west end of Chandni Chowk, around the Fatehpuri Mosque, there are a few basic hotels. These places are fine if you like the hustle and bustle, and don't mind being away from the business centre of Connaught Place.

The *Bharat Hotel* (☎ 23-5326) is on the opposite side of the road from the eastern gate of the mosque. It's an old rambling place with a few small courtyards and quite a bit of atmosphere. The rooms are a bit gloomy, and the 25-watt bulbs used to illuminate them certainly don't help. Nevertheless, it's cheap and cheerful, with rooms for Rs 80/120.

Just across the road from the southern gate of the Fatehpuri Mosque is the *Star Guest House* at 186 Katra Baryan. It's a more modern place than the Bharat, and is tolerably grubby. Rooms cost Rs 80/140 with common bath.

Other Areas Out at Chanakyapuri is the *Vishwa Yuvak Kendra* or *International Youth Centre* (☎ 301-3631) on Circular Rd. The rooms are very good but not all that cheap at Rs 341, but this does include breakfast. There's also a dormitory with beds at Rs 50. There's a cafeteria with good food at low prices, and lousy service. It's not a bad place to stay if you don't mind the 20-minute bus trip or shorter auto-rickshaw ride from Connaught Place. To get there take a No 620 bus from the Plaza Cinema in Connaught Place and get off near the Indonesian Embassy, or take a No 662 from the (Old) Delhi railway station and get off at the Ashok Hotel. It's right behind the Chinese Embassy and near the Chanakyapuri police station.

There is also a *youth hostel* (☎ 301-6285) in Chanakyapuri, at 5 Nyaya Marg. Dorm beds cost Rs 25, including breakfast. With the inconvenient location, and the fact that this place takes members only, it's a fairly unattractive proposition.

If all else fails there are railway *retiring rooms* at both railway stations (Old Delhi and New Delhi), with prices for both 24-hour and 12-hour periods. At the (Old) Delhi railway station the charges are Rs 25 for a dorm bed, and Rs 100 for a double room. As you can imagine, these are noisy places and you deserve a medal if you can actually manage to get some sleep. At New Delhi the cost is Rs 150/250, or Rs 210/500 with air-con, all with common bath.

There are *retiring rooms* at both the domestic (Terminal I: ☎ 329-5126) and international (Terminal II: ☎ 545-2011) sections of the airport. You can use them if you have a confirmed departure within 24 hours of your arrival by plane, but you'll need to ring in advance as demand far outstrips supply. They cost Rs 175/250 for an air-con single/double at Terminal II; and Rs 80 for an air-con dorm bed and Rs 175/250 for an air-con double at Terminal I. The tourist information officer at the desk at the airport may insist that the retiring rooms are 'full'

and try to direct you to a hotel from which the officer gets commission.

Places to Stay – middle
The Ys There are three YMCA or YWCA places, all of which take either sex. The *YMCA Tourist Hotel* (☎ 31-1915) is on Jai Singh Rd and opposite the Jantar Mantar. It's not bad value with rooms having hot and cold water, and there are gardens, a swimming pool, lounge and a restaurant with Western, Indian and Mughlai cuisine. Despite what the touts may tell you if you arrive in Delhi late at night, the hotel is open 24 hours, and credit cards are accepted. The rooms cost Rs 250/425 with common bath, and Rs 460/765 with air-con and attached bath. There's also a temporary membership charge of Rs 10, valid for one month.

The *YWCA International Guest House* (☎ 31-1561) at 10 Sansad Marg (Parliament St) has singles/doubles for Rs 300/500 (plus 10% service charge), and all rooms have bath and air-con. It's conveniently located near Connaught Place and has a restaurant, where a set breakfast costs Rs 45.

There's a second, lesser known YWCA, the *YWCA Blue Triangle Family Hostel* (☎ 31-0133), on Ashoka Rd just off Sansad Marg (Parliament St). It's clean, well run and has a restaurant. Rates, including breakfast, are Rs 405/740 with air-con and bathrooms. There's also a small temporary membership fee and a 5% service charge. This place is only about a 10-minute walk from the heart of Connaught Place.

Connaught Place & Janpath Area There are several mid-range hotels around Janpath and Connaught Place. The *Janpath Guest House* (☎ 332-1935) is a few doors down from the tourist office at 82-84 Janpath. It's popular with travellers, reasonably well kept and clean, and the staff are friendly; the rooms, though, are claustrophobically small and most don't have a window to talk of. Singles/doubles with air-cooling cost Rs 220/250, Rs 400/450 with air-con.

The *Hotel 55* (☎ 332-1244; fax 332-0769)

at 55 H Block Connaught Circus is well designed with air-con throughout. Rooms with balcony and bath are Rs 475/675, but the place suffers from indifferent service. The *Alka Hotel* (☎ 34-4328; fax 373-2796) is also centrally located at 16 P Block Connaught Circus and has air-con singles/doubles for Rs 850/1050. As is typical of many places in this area, most of the rooms don't have windows. The *Hotel Metro* (☎ 331-3856) on N Block is better than initial impressions might indicate, with rooms at similar prices.

The *York Hotel* (☎ 332-3769) in K Block is clean but fairly characterless, and the rooms cost Rs 800/1200. In L Block, the more modern *Jukaso Inn* (☎ 332-9694) has very small rooms, although at least most of them have windows. The charge here is Rs 750/1000.

Other Areas There are two excellent private guest houses to the west of Connaught Place. The small inconvenience of being further from the heart of things is compensated for by the friendly and relaxed atmosphere you find at these places.

The first is the family-run *Master Paying Guest House* (☎ 574-1089) at R-500 New Rajendra Nagar, a Rs 20 auto-rickshaw ride from Connaught Place. This small and friendly place is in a quiet residential area and the owner has worked hard to create a home-like atmosphere. It has large, airy and beautifully furnished doubles from Rs 250 to Rs 550, and there's a 25% discount during summer. Good meals are available, there's a pleasant rooftop terrace, and car hire for extended trips can also be arranged.

The second place is *Yatri House* (☎ 752-5563) at 3/4 Rani Jhansi Rd, which is opposite the junction of Panchkuin Marg (Radial No 3) and Mandir Marg, about one km west of Connaught Place. It's calm, secure and moderately priced, and there are trees, a lawn and a small courtyard at the back. The good-sized rooms, all with attached bath, are kept spotlessly clean and are good value at Rs 550/650 for a single/double, or Rs 700 with air-con. The owner is very friendly and helpful, there's

car hire available for sightseeing trips, and air tickets can be arranged. Advance bookings are advisable during the high season.

The *Hotel Ashoka Palace* (☎ 67-7308) is the cheapest hotel near the airport (three km from the domestic terminal, 13 km from the international). It's definitely nothing special, but you may be directed here from the airport by the tourist information desk or the taxi wallahs – the commission system is alive and well! For a shabby room with threadbare carpet and minimal facilities you'll be hit for Rs 850.

The *B-57 Inn* (☎ 469-4239) is at (you guessed it) B-57 South Extension Part I, 200 metres north of the Ring Road. Carpeted, air-cooled singles/doubles with colour TV, direct-dial ISD phone and attached bath cost Rs 495/595, or with air-con it's Rs 595/695, plus 10% tax. South Indian meals and snacks are available.

Places to Stay – top end
Many of the 'tourist class' hotels are at Chanakyapuri, the main location of the foreign embassies. This is about midway between the airport and the New Delhi city centre. There are, however, more places around the centre as well.

Moderately priced top-end hotels include *Nirula's Hotel* (☎ 332-2419; fax 332-4669) on L Block, Connaught Place, right beside the Nirula restaurants and snack bars. Singles/doubles range from Rs 850/1050 in this small but good standard hotel. Advance bookings are advisable.

The *Hotel Marina* (☎ 332-4658; fax 332-3138) on the outer circle of Connaught Place in G Block is surprisingly good inside; the outside is drab. The rooms, mostly with windows, are Rs 1015/1450 including breakfast, although the service tends to be abrupt.

Four-Star Unless otherwise stated, these four-star places do not have a swimming pool:

Ambassador Hotel (☎ 463-2600; fax 463-2254) is a small hotel at Sujan Singh Park, a short distance south of India Gate. There are just 75 rooms, costing from Rs 1075/1500. It has a noted vegetarian restaurant, coffee shop, bar and in-house astrologer(!), and major credit cards are accepted.

Connaught Hotel (☎ 34-4225; fax 31-0757) is due west of Connaught Place, on Bhagat Singh Marg. It offers restaurants, 24-hour room service and car rental. Rooms cost from Rs 1300/1800 with breakfast.

Diplomat Hotel (☎ 301-0204; fax 301-8605), 9 Sardar Patel Marg, south-east of Rashtrapati Bhavan, is a smaller place with just 25 rooms, a restaurant and bar. All rooms have colour TV, phone and attached bath. The charge is Rs 1090/1550.

Hotel Hans Plaza (☎ 331-6861), Tolstoy Marg, is conveniently central and pretty good value. Rooms are Rs 1200/1800.

Hotel Janpath (☎ 332-0070; fax 36-0233) is run by the ITDC with typically indifferent service. This large hotel has a good position on Janpath. Rooms start at Rs 1100/1500.

Hotel Kanishka (☎ 332-4422; fax 332-4242) is another ITDC hotel. It's next to the disastrous Hotel Ashok Yatri Niwas, and fortunately is much better run. It is one of the few places in this class to have a swimming pool. The room rate is Rs 1200/1800. It's popular with Russians in Delhi buying up on cheap goods.

Oberoi Maidens Hotel (☎ 252-5464; fax 292-9800), 7 Sham Nath Marg, is inconveniently located north of Old Delhi, but the building itself is a verandahed colonial relic and is very pleasant, as is the large garden. It also has a swimming pool. Rooms start at Rs 1200/1800.

Five-Star If you're looking for a little more luxury, try one of the following hotels:

Claridges Hotel (☎ 301-0211; fax 301-0625) at 12 Aurangzeb Rd is south of Rajpath in New Delhi. It's a very comfortable, older place, with four restaurants, a swimming pool and a travel agency. Singles/doubles start from Rs 3000.

Imperial Hotel (☎ 332-5332; fax 332-4542) is conveniently situated on Janpath near the centre of the city. It's a pleasantly old-fashioned hotel with a big garden, and is surprisingly quiet given its central location. It's one of the cheaper top-end places, and represents good value for money at Rs 2150/2300.

Park Hotel (☎ 373-2477; fax 35-2025) on Sansad Marg (Parliament St) is in a very central location only a block from Connaught Place. This hotel has a swimming pool, bookshop, and a business centre. Rooms are Rs 2800/3100.

Five-Star Deluxe Delhi's top-of-the-range hotels include:

Ashok Hotel (☎ 60-0121; fax 687-3216), 50B Chanakyapuri, is the 571-room flagship of the ITDC

hotel fleet. It offers everything from restaurants, coffee shops, bars, discos, a travel agent, post office, bank, conference rooms and swimming pool to full air-conditioning, a baby-sitting service and evening music recitals. Singles/doubles cost from Rs 2700/2900.

Centaur Hotel (☎ 545-2223; fax 545-2256) is on Gurgaon Rd, about two km from the international airport, and about five km from the domestic terminal. It's a big modern hotel with 376 rooms, swimming pool, health club, tennis courts, putting green, and a children's park. It also offers weekend package deals pitched at Delhites who want to escape from the city for a weekend; however, with the bleak expanses of flat land all around it's hardly paradise, and the roar of planes overhead at all hours certainly doesn't add to the ambience. It is, however, the closest hotel to the airport. Room rates are reasonable at Rs 1700/1900.

Holiday Inn Crowne Plaza (☎ 332-0101; fax 332-5335) is a modern 500-room hotel which is very centrally located just off Barakhamba Rd, south-east of Connaught Place. It boasts every conceivable mod con, including an open-air swimming pool on a 3rd-floor terrace, and it also has a floor of nonsmoking rooms. Standard singles/doubles cost Rs 4200/4500, and there are more expensive suites available.

Hyatt Regency (☎ 688-1234; fax 688-6833), with 523 rooms, is in the south of New Delhi, between Hauz Khas and Chanakyapuri. Facilities include a fitness centre, in-house movies, restaurants, bar and coffee shop. For all this you pay Rs 4750 for a double room.

Hotel Le Meridien (☎ 371-0101; fax 371-4545) is another very modern place. This 358-room hotel has a swimming pool, restaurants and 24-hour room service. The rates are Rs 4200/4500 for standard singles/doubles.

Hotel Oberoi New Delhi (☎ 436-3030; fax 436-0484) is south of New Delhi near the Purana Qila. This 290-room hotel is one of the best value luxury places. Services include a 24-hour business centre, travel desk, swimming pool and secretarial services. Rooms cost from Rs 3850.

Hotel Maurya Sheraton (☎ 301-0101; fax 301-0908) is between Connaught Place and Chanakyapuri on Sardar Patel Marg, the road to the airport. Apart from a high level of comfort, the hotel boasts two excellent restaurants, a solar-heated swimming pool (the only one in Delhi) and a disco. It has 500 rooms costing from Rs 5000/5800 up to Rs 8000/8500.

Taj Mahal Hotel (☎ 301-6162; fax 301-7299), at 1 Man Singh Rd, is a luxurious place that is fairly central but quiet. It has all the usual facilities including a swimming pool, photographer, restaurants and coffee shop, and even has telephones in the bathrooms! Singles/doubles start from Rs 3750/4050. The French restaurant here is expensive but excellent.

DELHI

PLACES TO EAT

Delhi has an excellent array of places to eat – from a dhaba house with dishes for less than Rs 10 up to top-of-the-range restaurants where a meal for two can easily top Rs 2500!

Janpath & Connaught Place Area

There are many Indian-style fast-food places in this area. Their plus point is that they have good food at reasonable prices and are clean and healthy. A minus point for some of them is they have no place to sit – it's stand, eat and run. They serve Indian food (from samosas to dosas) and Western food (burgers to sandwiches). Ice-cream parlours have also hit Delhi with a vengeance.

Nirula's is probably the most popular and long running of these fast-food places and does a wide variety of light snacks, both Indian and Western. They've also got good cold drinks, milk shakes and ice cream, or they will pack you a lunch box – ideal to take on train trips. The ice-cream parlour is amazingly busy, and is open from 10 am to midnight. The main Nirula's is on L Block on the outer circle, and there are various other outlets dotted throughout suburban Delhi. Next door to Nirula's snack bar is an ice-cream parlour on one side and pizzas on the other. Above the ice-cream parlour is the fourth part of Nirula's, a sit-down restaurant called *Pot Pourri*, which used to be something of a travellers' Mecca but these days seems to be living off its reputation. The smorgasbord salad bar is still good value at Rs 72, but other dishes are not so good, and the air-con is feeble. It's a good place for breakfast, which is served from 7.30 am. Also upstairs at Nirula's is the *Chinese Room*, with Chinese dishes in the Rs 100 to Rs 150 range, and a very congenial, if somewhat smoky, bar.

The *Embassy* restaurant on D Block has excellent veg and non-veg food including korma and biryani. It's not too expensive and is popular among office workers.

On Janpath at N Block, opposite the underground bazaar, there is a small string of fast-food places. At the outer end is a branch of the British *Wimpy* hamburger chain. Until MacDonalds is up and running in Delhi, this is the closest you're going to get to a Big Mac (100% lamb!) in India. The burgers are fair imitations but, again, if you're used to Indian prices, spending Rs 60 on a burger and a shake seems like reckless extravagance.

In the same lane as the Ringo and Sunny guest houses, there are a number of basic eateries. *Don't Pass Me By* is a popular little place which caters to international tastes. Other places close by include the *Anand, New Light, Kalpana, Swaram* and *Vikram* restaurants.

Other places around Connaught Place include *Kovil* in E Block with very good south Indian vegetarian food, and the *United Coffee House*, also on E Block, a pleasantly relaxed and popular place. The *Sona Rupa Restaurant* on Janpath does good south Indian vegetarian food and has a bizarre self-service system. Also on Janpath is the *Bankura Cafe*. It makes a welcome retreat from the heat, and is popular with office workers at lunchtime.

The fresh milk is excellent at *Keventers*, the small milk bar on the corner of Connaught Place and Radial Rd No 3, round the corner from American Express. If you just want a cheap soft drink and somewhere cool to drink it, descend into the air-conditioned underground Palika Bazaar between Janpath and Sansad Marg (Parliament St) at Connaught Place.

Moving up a price category, there are several restaurants worth considering on Sansad Marg and by the Regal Cinema. The *Kwality Restaurant* on Sansad Marg is spotlessly clean and very efficient but the food is only average. The menu is the almost standard non-vegetarian menu you'll find at restaurants all over India. Main courses are mainly in the Rs 40 to Rs 70 range. This is also a good place for non-Indian food if you want a break; you can have breakfast here for Rs 45.

The *El Arab Restaurant*, right on the corner of Sansad Marg and the outer circle of Connaught Place, has an interesting Middle Eastern menu with most dishes in the Rs 55 to Rs 80 bracket, and a good buffet for

Rs 110. Downstairs here is the more expensive *Cellar*. Round the corner is the even more expensive *Gaylord* with big mirrors, chandeliers and excellent Indian food. Also on Connaught Place you can find good vegetarian food at the *Volga Restaurant*; it's a little expensive but it's air-conditioned, and the food and service are excellent.

Another restaurant on Connaught Place is *The Host*, which serves excellent Indian and Chinese food. It's extremely popular with well-heeled Indians, but it ain't cheap – it wouldn't be hard to spend Rs 600 here on a meal and drinks for two!

The *Cafe 100* on B Block is one of the newest places around, and has good snacks and ice creams. There's also a good buffet for Rs 105. This place is set to give Nirula's a real shock.

The *Zen Restaurant*, also on B Block, is another new place. Its focus is Chinese and Japanese food, its target well-stuffed wallets.

On A Block near American Express is the *El Rodeo* restaurant serving good Mexican food; it's worth visiting just for the sight of waiters in cowboy suits! Main dishes are around Rs 70 to Rs 100, but well worth the money.

Located near the Bengali Market at the traffic circle where Tansen Marg meets Babar Rd, the neat and clean *Nathu's* is a good place for sweets or for a meal of the snacks known as chat. You could try cholaphatura (puffed rotis with a lentil dip), tikkas (fried stuffed potatoes), papri chat (sweet/hot wafers), or golguppas (hollow puffs you break open and use as a scoop for a peppery liquid accompaniment).

For Chinese food there's the excellent *Fa Yian* on A Block, Middle Circle. It's owned and run by Chinese, the prices are very reasonable and the air-con positively Arctic. Main dishes are in the Rs 50 to Rs 90 range. Another Chinese option is the *Palki* restaurant on K Block outer circle. The Rs 101 buffet lunch here is good value.

For an interesting dining experience there's the *Parikrama* revolving restaurant on Kasturba Gandhi Marg. Unlike in many places of this ilk where the first-class views

are perhaps supposed to distract you from decidedly second-class food, the fare here is excellent, and it's moderately priced. A full rotation takes around 1½ hours – time enough for a leisurely three courses. It's open daily for lunch and dinner, and for drinks from 3 to 7 pm.

Finally, there's one Delhi food place that should not be forgotten. *Wenger's* on Connaught Place is a cake shop with an awesome range of little cakes which they'll put in a cardboard box and tie up with a bow so you can self-consciously carry them back to your hotel room for private consumption.

Paharganj Area

In keeping with its role as a travellers' centre, Main Bazaar in Paharganj has a handful of cheap restaurants which cater almost exclusively to foreign travellers. They are all up towards the western end of Main Bazaar. The *Diamond Cafe* and *Lords Cafe* in the Hotel Vishal both have extensive menus and cheap food. The garlic steaks in Lords Cafe are pretty good, while the Diamond Cafe has a menu full of tortured English. The rooftop *Leema* restaurant in the Hotel Vivek is a popular place.

Next door to Lords Cafe and still in the Hotel Vishal building is the *Appetite Restaurant*. This place has similar food to the others, but is a bit more upmarket with some more sophisticated dishes. The pizzas here are popular, but what is even more popular is the fact that this place has cable TV, and international sports broadcasts, especially cricket, draw big audiences.

Further along Main Bazaar are some very basic eating stalls with tables on the footpath. These are a popular place for chai, and for the really impecunious they offer cheap snack food.

Lastly there's the air-con *Metropolis Restaurant*, in the hotel of the same name just past Rajguru Rd. The food here is definitely more expensive than the other Main Bazaar cheapies, but it's worth the extra.

Old Delhi

In Old Delhi there are many places to eat at

the west end of Chandni Chowk. The *Inderpuri Restaurant* has a good selection of vegetarian dishes, and *Giani* has good masala dosas. *Ghantewala*, near the Siganj Gurdwara on Chandni Chowk, is reputed to have some of the best Indian sweets in Delhi. The stalls along the road in front of the Jama Masjid are very cheap. In the Interstate bus station the *ISBT Workers' Canteen* has good food at low prices, and Delhi Tourism's *Nagrik Restaurant* is also here.

At the other end of the price scale there are two well-known tandoori restaurants in Old Delhi. The *Tandoor* at the Hotel President on Asaf Ali Rd near the tourist camp is an excellent place with the usual two-waiters-per-diner service and a sitar playing in the background. The tandoori kitchen can be seen through a glass panel.

Close by in the same street is the Hotel Broadway with its *Chor Bazaar (Thieves' Market)* restaurant. They've certainly put some effort into decorating this place with an eclectic mix of bits and pieces collected from various markets – a four-poster bed, an old sports car (now used as a salad bar) and an old cello. The food is good, although not outstanding, and main dishes range from Rs 60 to Rs 150.

Lying round the corner on Netaji Subhash Marg in Darayaganj, the famous old *Moti Mahal Restaurant* is noted for its tandoori dishes including murga musalam. Quantities are large and there's live *qawwali* singing nightly except Tuesdays.

South Delhi

There are a few good eating options in the area south of Connaught Place, but you'll need a taxi or transport to get to most of them. In the swish Santushti shopping centre (see the Things to Buy section) in Chanakyapuri, the *Basil & Thyme* restaurant is Delhi's place to be 'seen' – the swish of expensive silk sarees and glitter of gold jewellery, high prices, excellent service and good food.

Defence Colony is one of the upmarket residential suburbs in south Delhi. The *market* here draws middle-class Delhi-wallahs and their families in numbers in the

evenings, especially on weekends. *Colonel's Kababz* is a very popular stand-up kebab, tandoori and seafood place, although most diners remain in their cars and are served by scurrying waiters! The *Sagar* restaurant here offers what is reckoned to be the best south Indian food in Delhi, and on weekends the queue to get in can be 20 metres long!

At Hauz Khas is the Village Bistro, a restaurant complex incorporating a number of eating places, including *Al Capone* (Italian and Continental), *Darbar*, *Mohalla*, *Great Wall of China* (Chinese), *Golconda Terrace* (spicy Andhra Pradesh dishes and good views). Other Hauz Khas restaurants include *Sukhotthai* (Thai), *Tandoori Nights* and *Duke's Place*, which is a pleasant Italian place with live jazz some nights.

International Hotels

Many Delhi residents reckon that the best food in the capital is at the large five-star hotels. At the Maurya Sheraton the *Bukhara* is widely regarded as the city's best restaurant. It has many Central Asian specialities, including tandoori cooking and dishes from the Peshawar region in north-west Pakistan. This is a place for big meat eaters and you can expect to pay around Rs 200 to Rs 350 for a main course. Another restaurant here is the *Dum Phukt*, named after a cuisine first invented by the *nawabs* of Avadh (Lucknow) around 300 years ago. It involves the dishes being covered by a pastry cap when cooked, so the food is steamed as much as anything else. It's quite distinctive and absolutely superb, and you'd be looking at around Rs 500 for two, plus drinks. The *Shatranj* cafe here does a good-value buffet lunch, and the featured cuisine changes daily.

Claridges Hotel has a few unusual theme restaurants: the *Dhaba* offers 'rugged roadside' cuisine, and is set up like a typical roadside cafe; the *Jade Garden* serves Chinese food in a bamboo grove setting; *Pickwicks* offers Western food, and the decor is 19th-century England; while *Corbetts* gets its inspiration from Jim Corbett of man-eating tiger fame, and so has a hunting camp theme, complete with recorded jungle sounds. As might be expected, meat features prominently on the menu. All restaurants are moderately priced.

The *House of Ming* at the Taj Mahal Hotel is a popular Sichuan Chinese restaurant. Also at the Taj Mahal is the *Haveli* restaurant which serves an excellent range of dishes, and there's live music and dancing from 8.30 pm. The Hyatt also has a Sichuan Chinese restaurant, the *Pearls*.

The Hotel Oberoi has the *Baan Thai* for superb Thai food; nearly as good is the *Orchid* in the Holiday Inn Crowne Plaza.

The *Park Hotel* on Sansad Marg has a good buffet breakfast at Rs 125, and diabolically bad service.

Several cheaper hotels have noted vegetarian restaurants. Thalis at *Dasaprakash* in the Ambassador Hotel are good value. The Lodhi Hotel, in south Delhi, is noted for the vegetarian thalis at its *Woodlands Restaurant*. The old *Imperial Hotel* is great for an alfresco breakfast in the pleasant garden.

For Japanese food, try the *Osaka Restaurant* in Hauz Khas, or the *Fujiya Restaurant* at 12/48 Malcha Marg in Chanakyapuri.

ENTERTAINMENT

Delhi's strict licensing laws certainly don't help its nightlife scene. Bars and discos are basically limited to the five-star hotels. The *Jazz Bar* at the Maurya Sheraton is very good, with live jazz each evening, but drinks are expensive; beers are Rs 170! The discos at these hotels are quite exclusive and entry is usually restricted to members and hotel guests; couples and women stand a better chance of being admitted than unaccompanied men.

Indian dances are held each evening at 7 pm at the *Parsi Anjuman Hall* on Bahadur Zafar Marg, opposite Ambedkar Stadium. Phone ☎ 331-7831 for details. The *India International Centre* (☎ 461-9431) at 40 Max Mueller Marg is another regular classical dance venue.

For films there are a number of cinemas around Connaught Place, but the fare is typically Hindi mass-appeal movies. For something a little more cerebral, the *British*

Council (☎ 371-0111) on Kasturba Gandhi Marg often screens good foreign films, and the other cultural centres are also worth trying.

THINGS TO BUY

Good buys include silk products, precious stones, leather and woodwork, but the most important thing about Delhi is that you can find almost anything from anywhere in India. If this is your first stop in India, and you intend to buy something while you are here, then it's a chance to compare what is available from all over the country. If this is your last stop and there was something you missed elsewhere in your travels, Delhi provides a chance to find it.

Two good places to start are in New Delhi, near Connaught Place. The Central Cottage Industries Emporium is on Janpath. In this building you will find items from all over India, generally of good quality and reasonably priced. Whether it's woodcarvings, brasswork, paintings, clothes, textiles or furniture, you'll find it here. Along Baba Kharak Singh Marg, two streets round from Janpath, are the various state emporiums run by the state governments. Each of them display and sell handicrafts from their state. There are many other shops around Connaught Place and Janpath. By the Imperial Hotel are a number of stalls and small shops run by Tibetan refugees and rapacious Kashmiris selling carpets, jewellery and many (often instant) antiques.

In Old Delhi, Chandni Chowk is the famous shopping street. Here you will find carpets and jewellery but you have to search the convoluted back alleys. In the narrow street called Cariba Kalan, perfumes are made as well.

Main Bazaar in Paharganj has a good range. You can find an interesting variety of perfumes, oils, soaps and incense at two places (both signposted), one near the Hotel Vivek and another near the Camran Lodge. Monday is the official weekly holiday for the shops in Main Bazaar, and many are closed on that day, although a surprising number

DELHI

remain open seven days a week. Sunday is a very busy day in Paharganj.

In recent years the Karol Bagh Market, two km west of Connaught Place along Panchkuin Marg (Radial Rd No 3), has become even more popular than Connaught Place or Main Bazaar.

Just south of the Purana Qila, beside Dr Zakir Hussain Rd and across from the Hotel Oberoi New Delhi, is the Sunder Nagar Market, a collection of shops selling antiques and brassware. The prices may be high but you'll find fascinating and high-quality arte-facts. Shops in the major international hotels often have high-quality items, at equally high prices.

Opposite the Ashok Hotel in Chanakya-puri is the Santushti shopping arcade, which is just inside the gate of the New Wellington airforce camp! There's a string of small upmarket boutiques here with a good range of crafts and high prices to match.

Hauz Khas Village in south Delhi has become a very interesting little shopping enclave.

GETTING THERE & AWAY

Delhi is a major international gateway to India; for details on arriving from overseas see the introductory Getting There & Away chapter. At certain times of the year interna-tional flights out of Delhi can be heavily booked so it's wise to make reservations as early as possible. This particularly applies to some of the heavily discounted airlines out of Europe – check and double-check your reservations and make sure you reconfirm your flight.

Delhi is also a major centre for domestic travel, with extensive bus, rail and air con-nections.

Air

The domestic terminal (Terminal I of the Indira Gandhi International Airport) is seven km from the centre, and the newer international terminal (Terminal II) is a further nine km.

If you're arriving at New Delhi Airport from overseas, there's 24-hour State Bank of India and Thomas Cook foreign-exchange counters in the arrivals hall, after you go through customs and immigration. Once you've left the arrivals hall you won't be allowed back in. The service is fast and efficient.

Many international flights to Delhi arrive and depart at terrible hours of the morning. Take special care if this is your first foray into India and you arrive exhausted and jet-lagged. If you're leaving Delhi in the early hours of the morning, book a taxi the after-noon before. They'll be hard to find in the night. See Other Areas in the Places to Stay – bottom end section in this chapter for infor-mation about the retiring rooms at the airport.

When leaving Delhi with Air India (domes-tic or international flights) all baggage must be X-rayed and sealed, so do this at the machine just inside the departure hall before you queue to check in. For international flights the departure tax (Rs 300) must be paid at the State Bank counter in the depar-tures hall, also before check-in.

Facilities at the international terminal include a dreadful snack bar, bookshop and bank. Once inside the departure lounge there are a few duty-free shops with the usual inflated prices, and another terrible snack bar where you have the privilege of paying in US dollars. There's also the Ashok Restaurant, with possibly some of the worst food in the country.

Delhi Transport Corporation buses connect the two terminals for Rs 10. There is also the free IAAI bus between the two terminals. The EATS bus (see the Getting Around section later) will also transport you between the two terminals.

Indian Airlines Indian Airlines has a number of offices. The Malhotra Building office (☎ 331-0517) in F Block, Connaught Place, is probably the most convenient. It is, however, fairly busy at most times. It's open daily except Saturday from 10 am to 5 pm.

There's another office in the PTI Building (☎ 371-9168) on Sansad Marg, open daily except Sunday from 10 am to 5 pm.

At the old Safdarjang airport, there's a

24-hour office (☎ 141), and this can be a very quick place to make bookings.

Business-class passengers can check in by telephone on ☎ 329-5166. For prerecorded flight information, ring ☎ 142.

Indian Airlines flights depart from Delhi to all the major Indian centres. Check-in at the airport is 75 minutes before departure. Note that if you have just arrived and have an onward connection to another city in India, it may be with Air India, the country's international carrier, rather than the domestic carrier, Indian Airlines. If that is the case, you must check in at the international terminal (Terminal II) rather than the domestic terminal. India must be one of the few countries in the world where they can fill 747s on domestic routes!

Indian Airlines & Private Airline Flights from Delhi

Destination	Time (hours)	IC	JA	D2	9W	AL	4S	S2	M9	Fare (US$)
Agra	0.40	1d	-	-	-	-	-	-	-	23
Ahmedabad	1.25	2d	-	-	-	-	-	-	4w	79
Amritsar	1.00	3w	-	-	-	-	-	-	-	52
Aurangabad	3.30	5w	-	-	-	-	-	-	-	99
Bagdodgra	1.55	4w	-	-	-	-	-	-	-	128
Bangalore	2.40	4w	-	-	-	-	1d	1d	1d	161
Bhopal	2.00	1d	-	-	-	6w	-	-		110
Bhubaneshwar	3.00	1d	-	-	-	-	-	-	-	128
Bombay	1.50	7d	-	2d	4d	-	1d	1d	2d	115
Calcutta	2.05	3d	-	-	-	-	6w	-	2d	132
Chandigarh	1.00	-	6w	-	-	5w	-	-		72
Goa	2.00	6w	-	-	-	-	-	-	3w	150
Guwahati	2.25	1d	-	-	-	-	-	-	-	149
Gwalior	0.50	2w	-	-	-	-	-	-	-	33
Hyderabad	2.00	2d	-	-	-	-	-	-	6w	124
Indore	2.15	5w	-	-	-	-	-	-	-	78
Jaipur	0.40	2d	-	-	-	-	-	-	-	28
Jammu	1.10	1d	-	-	-	-	-	-	3w	74
Jodhpur	1.55	5w	-	-	-	-	-	-	-	56
Kanpur	1.20	-	6w	-	-	-	-	-	-	82
Khajuraho	2.00	1d	-	-	-	-	-	-	1d	53
Kochi (Cochin)	4.05	6w	-	-	-	-	-	-	-	200
Kulu	1.30	-	6w	-	-	2d	-	-	-	123
Leh	1.15	6w	-	-	-	-	-	-	-	86
Lucknow	0.50	1d	-	-	-	-	-	5w	-	46
Ludhiana	1.05	-	6w	-	-	6w	-	-	-	96
Madras	2.30	2d	-	6w	-	-	-	-	6w	162
Nagpur	1.25	4w	-	-	-	-	-	-	-	87
Patna	1.25	1d	-	-	-	-	-	-	-	87
Pune	2.00	1d	-	-	-	-	-	-	-	130
Raipur	1.40	6w	-	-	-	-	-	-	-	114
Ranchi	2.55	1d	-	-	-	-	-	-	-	111
Shimla	1.10	-	-	-	-	1d	-	-	-	96
Srinagar	1.15	2d	-	-	-	-	-	-	-	77
Thiruvananthapuram (Trivandrum)	5.10	6w	-	-	-	-	-	-	-	219
Udaipur	1.55	10w	-	-	-	-	-	-	-	58
Vadodara	2.45	1d	-	-	-	-	-	-	-	88
Varanasi	1.15	11w	-	-	-	-	-	-	3w	74

*Airline abbreviation codes:

IC – Indian Airlines	9W – Jet Airways	S2 – Sahara Indian Airlines
JA – Jagson Airlines	AL – Archana Airways	M9 – ModiLuft
D2 – Damania Airlines	4S – East West	

See the table on page 241 for details of flights from Delhi.

Other Domestic Airlines As well as the offices listed below, all the private airlines also have offices at the airport's domestic terminal. There are currently no Vayudoot flights operating.

Archana Airways
    41A Friends Colony East, Mathura Rd (☎ 684-7760)
Damania Airways
    UG 26A Somdutt Chambers, 5 Bhikaji Cama Place (☎ 688-1122)
East-West Airlines
    DCM Bldg, Barakhamba Rd (☎ 375-5167)
Jagson Airlines
    12E Vandana Bldg, 11 Tolstoy Marg (☎ 372-1593)
Jet Airways
    3E Hanslaya Bldg, Barakhamba Rd (☎ 372-4727)
ModiLuft
    Vandana Bldg, Tolstoy Marg (☎ 371-9347)
NEPC Airlines
    G39 4th floor, Pawan House, Connaught Place (☎ 332-2525)
Sahara Indian Airlines
    Ambadeep Bldg, Kasturba Gandhi Marg (☎ 332-6851)
Vayudoot
    Malhotra Bldg, F Block, Connaught Place (☎ 331-2587)

International Airlines International airlines that fly to Delhi include the following:

Aeroflot
    Cozy Travels, BMC House, 1st floor, 1N Connaught Place (☎ 331-2916)
Air France
    7 Atma Ram Mansion, Connaught Circus (☎ 331-0407)
Air India
    Jeevan Bharati Bldg, Connaught Place (☎ 331-1225)
Air Lanka
    Student Travel Information Centre, Imperial Hotel, Janpath (☎ 332-4789)
Alitalia
    19 Kasturba Gandhi Marg (☎ 331-1019)
British Airways
    DLF Bldg, Sansad Marg (Parliament St) (☎ 332-7428)

Gulf Air
    G Block, Connaught Place (☎ 332-2018)
Iran Air
    Ashok Hotel, Chanakyapuri (☎ 60-4397)
Iraqi Airways
    Ansal Bhawan (☎ 331-8632)
Japan Airlines
    Chandralok Bldg, 36 Janpath (☎ 332-3409)
KLM
    Tolstoy Marg (☎ 331-5841)
Lot Polish Airlines
    G Block, Connaught Place (☎ 332-4308)
Lufthansa
    56 Janpath (☎ 332-3206)
Malaysia Airlines
    G Block, Connaught Place (☎ 332-5786)
Pakistan International Airlines (PIA)
    Kailash Bldg, 26 Kasturba Gandhi Marg (☎ 331-6121)
Royal Nepal Airlines
    44 Janpath (☎ 332-0817)
SAS
    B Block, Connaught Place (☎ 332-7503)
Singapore Airlines
    Marina Arcade, G11 Connaught Place (☎ 332-6373)
Syrian Arab Airlines
    GSA Delhi Express Travels, 13/90 Connaught Place (☎ 34-3218)
Thai International Airways
    Amba Deep Bldg, Kasturba Gandhi Marg (☎ 332-3608)

International Flights The only international route served by Indian Airlines from Delhi is the daily flight to Kathmandu (US$142).

Bus
The main bus station is the Interstate Bus Terminal (ISBT) at Kashmir Gate, north of the (Old) Delhi railway station. It has 24-hour left-luggage facilities, a State Bank of India branch, post office, pharmacy, and Delhi Transport's Nagrik Restaurant. City buses depart from here to locations all around Delhi (☎ 252-3145). State government bus companies operating from here are:

Delhi Transport Corporation (☎ 251-8836) – bookings from 8 am to 8 pm.
Haryana Government Roadways (☎ 252-1262) – bookings from 6.15 am to 12.30 pm and 2 to 9.30 pm. Reservations can also be made at the Haryana Emporium from 10 am to 5 pm.
Himachal Pradesh Roadways (☎ 251-6725) – bookings from 7 am to 7 pm.

Punjab Roadways (☎ 251-7842) – bookings from 8 am to 8 pm.

Rajasthan Roadways (☎ 252-2246) – bookings from 7 am to 9 pm. Bookings can also be made at Bikaner House (☎ 38-3469) just south of Rajpath from 6 am to 7 pm.

Uttar Pradesh Roadways (☎ 251-8709) – bookings from 6 am to 9.30 pm.

Buses popular with travellers include the frequent and fast service to Jaipur for Rs 70. Deluxe buses for Jaipur leave from Bikaner House, take five hours and cost Rs 122, or Rs 210 for the less frequent air-con services.

For the five-hour trip to Chandigarh, from where you can take a bus or the narrow-gauge train up to Shimla, the regular buses cost Rs 70. There are deluxe buses for Rs 100. You can also get buses direct to Shimla (10 hours) for Rs 90; Dharamsala (13 hours) for Rs 165, or Rs 240 deluxe; and there's a daily deluxe service to Manali (16 hours) for Rs 285. To northern Uttar Pradesh buses cost Rs 60 for Haridwar or Rs 64 for Dehra Dun.

Other destinations served by bus from Delhi include Bharatpur, Bikaner, Jammu, Lucknow, Mussoorie, Naini Tal and Srinagar (Rs 350, 24 hours).

There's also the new Sarai Kale Khan ISBT, close to Nizamuddin railway station. There are buses from here to Agra (Rs 49 ordinary, Rs 56 express, Rs 71 deluxe and Rs 55 video) from 6 am to midnight, Mathura and Vrindaban (Rs 35/41 ordinary/express), Gwalior (Rs 81/90) and Bharatpur. There's a city bus link between this station and Kashmir Gate ISBT.

To Kathmandu Around Paharganj and the other travellers' hangouts you'll probably see posters advertising direct buses to Kathmandu – these take around 36 hours. Most travellers seem to find that it's cheaper, more comfortable and better value to do the trip by train to Gorakhpur (Uttar Pradesh), and then take buses from there.

A number of travellers have also entered Nepal at the border crossing just east of the northern Uttar Pradesh village of Banbassa. There are daily buses to this village from

New Delhi. See the Uttar Pradesh chapter for more details.

Train

Delhi is an important rail centre and an excellent place to make bookings. There is a special foreign tourist booking office upstairs in New Delhi railway station. It is open Monday to Saturday from 7.30 am to 5 pm. This is the place to go if you want a tourist-quota allocation, are the holder of an Indrail Pass or want to buy an Indrail Pass. It gets very busy and crowded, and it can take up to an hour to get served. If you make bookings here tickets must be paid for in foreign currency (US dollars and pounds sterling only, and your change will be given in rupees), or with rupees backed up by bank exchange certificates.

The main ticket office is on Chelmsford Rd, between New Delhi railway station and Connaught Place. This place is well organised, but incredibly busy. Take a numbered ticket from the counter as you enter the building, and then wait at the allotted window. Even with 50 computerised terminals, it can take up to an hour to get served. It's best to arrive first thing in the morning, or when it reopens after lunch. The office is open Monday to Saturday from 7.45 am to 1.50 pm and 2 to 9 pm. On Sunday it's open until 1.50 pm only.

Remember that there are two main stations in Delhi – Delhi railway station in Old Delhi, and New Delhi railway station at Paharganj. New Delhi is much closer to Connaught Place, and if you're departing from the Old Delhi railway station you should allow adequate time to wind your way through the traffic snarls of Old Delhi. Between the Old Delhi and New Delhi stations you can take the No 6 bus for just Rs 1. There's also the Nizamuddin railway station south of the New Delhi area where some trains start or finish. It's worth getting off here if you are staying in Chanakyapuri or elsewhere south of Connaught Place.

Recently trains between Delhi and Jaipur, Jodhpur and Udaipur have been operating to and from Sarai Rohilla station rather than

Major Trains from Delhi

Destination	Train Name & Number	Departure time *	Distance (km)	Duration (hours)	Fare (Rs) (2nd/1st)
Agra	2180 Taj Exp	7.15 am ND	199	4.35	62/183
	2002 Shatabdi Exp**	6.15 am ND		1.55	235/470
Bangalore	2430 Rajdhani Exp**	9.30 am HN Sat	2444	35	800/1000
	2628 Karnataka Exp	9.15 pm ND		41	349/1162
Bombay	2952 Rajdhani Exp**	4.05 pm ND	1384	17	840/1370
	1038 Punjab Mail	6 am ND		26	264/877
Calcutta	2302 Rajdhani Exp**	5.15 pm ND	1441	18	705/865
	2304 Poorva Exp	4.30 pm ND		24	259/837
Gorakhpur	2554 Vaishali Exp	7.45 pm ND	758	13	177/530
Jaipur	2901 Pink City Exp	6 am SR	308	6	90/262
	Shatabdi Exp **	5.50 am ND		4.25	300/600
Jammu Tawi	4645 Shalimar Exp	4.10 pm ND	585	14	147/436
Lucknow	4230 Lucknow Mail	10 pm ND	487	9.15	130/387
	2004 Shatabdi Exp **	6.20 am ND		6.25	385/770
Madras	2622 Tamil Nadu Exp	10.30 pm ND	2194	33.20	308/1122
Shimla	4095 Himalayan Queen	6.10 am ND	364	11	103/303
Udaipur	2901 Pink City Exp	6 am SR	739	13.30	172/521
Varanasi	2382 Poorva Exp	4.30 pm ND	764	12.20	179/541

*Abbreviations for train stations: ND – New Delhi, OD – Old Delhi, HN – Hazrat Nizamuddin, SR – Sarai Rohilla
** Air-con only; fare includes meals and drinks.

Old Delhi – it's about 3.5 km north-west of Connaught Place on Guru Govind Singh Marg. They may still be, so check when you book your ticket. The exception is the new *Shatabdi Express* to Jaipur, which operates from New Delhi.

GETTING AROUND

Delhi is large and the buses get hopelessly crowded. The alternative is a taxi, auto-rickshaw or bicycle.

To/From the Airport

Although there are a number of options, airport-to-city transport is not as straightforward as it should be, due to predatory taxi and auto-rickshaw drivers who prey on the unwary – usually first-time visitors.

Bus The Ex-Servicemen's Air Link Transport Service (EATS) (☎ 331-6530) has a regular bus service between the airport (both terminals) and Connaught Place. The fare is Rs 25 and they will drop you off or pick you up at most of the major hotels en route if you ask – although this doesn't include Pahar-

ganj. In Connaught place the service leaves from the Vayudoot office on Janpath, opposite the underground Palika Bazaar, between 4 am and 11.30 pm.

When leaving the international terminal, the counter for the EATS bus is just to the right as you exit the building. This is probably the best, although not the quickest, way into the city if you arrive late at night (see the warning about pre-paid taxis in the Taxi section that follows).

Once at Connaught Place, however, there are sometimes shonky auto-rickshaw drivers around who have a scam set up. You are taken into a side street where a bogus policeman – complete with uniform and *lathi* (stick) – stops the vehicle due to supposed 'Hindu-Muslim problem' at Paharganj or wherever you happen to be going. You'll then end up at a hotel of their choice (usually in Karol Bagh), and pay way over the top, and from there may be talked into getting out of Delhi as quick as possible, usually in chartered transport at exorbitant rates.

There is also a regular Delhi Transport Corporation bus service that runs from the airport to New Delhi railway station and the Interstate bus station; it costs Rs 20 and there is a Rs 5 charge for luggage. At New Delhi railway station it uses the Ajmer Gate (east) side. There is also a public bus service to the airport (No 780) from the Super Bazaar at Connaught Place, but it can get very crowded.

Taxi Just outside the international terminal is a pre-paid taxi booth, and a taxi to the centre costs Rs 280 when booked here. However, recently we've had reports from a number of travellers who have been given the run around by the pre-paid taxis in the middle of the night; they get taken to a hotel, told it's full, then on to another hotel (often in Karol Bagh) and intimidated into staying there at vastly inflated prices (up to US$150). This seems to happen only once the driver has established that the person hasn't been to India before, and only in the middle of the night when it's difficult to get your bearings and there are few other vehicles about.

Bear in mind that if you do head into the centre late at night, the bulk of the budget hotels will be closed (and firmly locked) from around midnight until at least 6 am, so unless you have arranged a late arrival in advance, you're options are limited. If you do take a taxi from the airport late at night, before getting into the vehicle make an obvious point of noting down the registration number. Once under way, don't believe *any* stories about hotels being full, or 'Hindu-Muslim problem' where you want to go or any other bullshit; if the driver is not prepared to go where *you* want to go, find another taxi.

Given the above-mentioned problems with getting yourself from the airport to a hotel in the centre in the middle of the night, if this is your first trip to India it is probably best to wait in the terminal building until daylight when there is much less risk of getting led astray and your surroundings are far less intimidating.

At the domestic terminal, the taxi booking desk is just inside the terminal and charges Rs 98 to Connaught Place, plus Rs 2 per bag.

The taxi-wallahs outside will try for much more.

A taxi from Connaught Place to the international terminal costs around Rs 150.

Bus

Avoid buses during the rush hours as the situation is hopeless. Whenever possible try to board (and leave) at a starting or finishing point, such as the Regal and Plaza cinemas in Connaught Place, as there is more chance of a seat and less chance of being trampled. There are some seats reserved for women on the left-hand side of the bus. The Delhi Transport Corporation runs some buses, others are privately owned, but they all operate along the same set routes.

Useful buses include bus No 505 to the Qutab Minar from the Super Bazaar, or from Janpath opposite the Imperial Hotel. Bus No 101 runs between the Kasmir Gate Interstate bus station and Connaught Place. Bus Nos 620 and 630 will take you between Connaught Place (from outside the Jantar Mantar) and Chanakyapuri. Bus Nos 101, 104 and 139 run between the Regal Cinema bus stand and the Red Fort. A short bus ride (like Connaught Place to Red Fort) is only about Rs 1.

Taxi & Auto-Rickshaw

All taxis and auto-rickshaws are metered but the meters are invariably out of date, allegedly 'not working' or the drivers will simply refuse to use them. It matters not a jot that they are legally required to do so. A threat to report them to the police results in little more than considerable mirth, so you should negotiate a price before you set out. Naturally, this will always be more than it should be. There are exceptions; occasionally a driver will reset the meter without even a word from you. At places like New Delhi railway station or the airport, where there are always plenty of police hanging around, you can generally rely on the meter being used because it's too easy to report a driver. Trips during the rush hour or middle-of-the-night journeys to the airport are the times when meters are least likely to be used.

At the end of a metered journey you will have to pay according to a scale of revised charges or simply a flat percentage increase. Some drivers display these cards in the cab, others consign them to the oily-rag compartment, still others feed them to the cows. So if you do come across a legible copy it's worth noting down a few of the conversions, paying what you think is the right price and leaving it at that. You may rest assured that no-one is going to be out of pocket, except yourself, despite hurt or angry protestations to the contrary.

Connaught Place to the Red Fort should cost around Rs 35 by taxi or Rs 20 by auto-rickshaw, depending on the traffic. From 11 pm to 5 am there is a 20% surcharge for auto-rickshaws and 25% in taxis.

There are also unusual six-seater motorcycle rickshaws running fixed routes at fixed prices. From Connaught Place their starting point is Palika Bazaar and drivers chop their way through the traffic as far as the fountain in Chandni Chowk via the Red Fort in Old Delhi. They cost Rs 2 per person and are good value, especially during rush hours.

Bicycle & Cycle-Rickshaw
As is so often the case, the bicycle is an excellent way of getting around, especially in New Delhi where the roads are wide, in good condition and, by Indian standards, are uncrowded. At the large traffic roundabouts you need to take a deep breath and plunge in, but otherwise the traffic is pretty orderly. All the sites of New Delhi are easily reached by bicycle, and even the Qutab Minar and the sites to the south are accessible if you don't mind a bit of exercise, although attempting this in summer might be a bit ambitious.

What is surprising is that there are so few places to hire bikes. In Paharganj, the only place seems to be Mehta Electricals in Main Bazaar next to the Kesri Hotel, near Rajguru Rd. The bikes are old but well maintained, and cost Rs 20 per day, with a Rs 400 deposit. As with many shops in Main Bazaar, this place is closed on Monday.

Cycle-rickshaws are banned from the Connaught Place area and New Delhi itself, but they can be handy for travelling between the northern edge of Connaught Place and Paharganj, and around Old Delhi.

Greater Delhi

KHIRKI MASJID & JAHANPANAH
This interesting mosque with its four open courts dates from 1380. The nearby village of Khirki also takes its name from the mosque.

Close to the mosque are remains of the fourth city of Delhi, Jahanpanah, including the high Bijai Mandal platform and the Begumpur Mosque with its multiplicity of domes.

TUGHLAQABAD
The massively strong walls of Tughlaqabad, the third city of Delhi, are east of the Qutab Minar. The walled city and fort with its 13 gateways was built by Ghiyas-ud-din Tughlaq and its construction involved a legendary quarrel with the saint Nizam-ud-din. When the Tughlaq ruler took the workers whom Nizam-ud-din wanted for work on his shrine, the saint cursed the king with the warning that his city would be inhabited only by Gujars (shepherds). Today that is indeed the situation.

The dispute between king and saint did not end with curse and countercurse. When the king prepared to take vengeance on the saint, Nizam-ud-din calmly told his followers (in a saying that is still current in India today): 'Delhi is a long way off'. Indeed it was, for the king was murdered on his way from Delhi in 1325.

The fort walls are constructed of massive blocks and outside the south wall of the city is an artificial lake with the king's tomb in its centre. A long causeway connects the tomb to the fort, both of which have walls that slope inward.

Getting There & Away
The easiest way to visit Tughlaqabad is to

combine it with a visit to the Qutab Minar, and catch a bus from there.

QUTAB MINAR COMPLEX

The buildings in this complex, 15 km south of Delhi, date from the onset of Muslim rule in India and are fine examples of early-Afghan architecture. The Qutab Minar itself is a soaring tower of victory which was started in 1193, immediately after the defeat of the last Hindu kingdom in Delhi. It is nearly 73 metres high and tapers from a 15-metre-diameter base to just 2.5 metres at the top.

The tower has five distinct storeys, each marked by a projecting balcony. The first three storeys are made of red sandstone, the fourth and fifth of marble and sandstone. Although Qutab-ud-din began construction of the tower, he only got to the first storey. His successors completed it and, in 1368, Feroz Shah Tughlaq rebuilt the top storeys and added a cupola. An earthquake brought the cupola down in 1803 and an Englishman replaced it with another in 1829. However, that dome was deemed inappropriate and was removed some years later.

Today, this impressively ornate tower has a slight tilt, but otherwise has worn the centuries remarkably well. The tower is closed to visitors, and has been for some years after a stampede during a school trip led to a number of deaths.

Quwwat-ul-Islam Masjid

At the foot of the Qutab Minar stands the first mosque to be built in India, the Might of Islam Mosque. Qutab-ud-din began construction of the mosque in 1193, but it has had a number of additions and extensions over the centuries. The original mosque was built on the foundations of a Hindu temple, and an inscription over the east gate states that it was built with materials obtained from demolishing '27 idolatrous temples'. Many of the elements in the mosque's construction indicate their Hindu or Jain origins.

Altamish, Qutab-ud-din's son-in-law, surrounded the original small mosque with a cloistered court in 1210-20. Ala-ud-din added a court to the east and the magnificent Alai Darwaza gateway in 1300.

Iron Pillar This seven-metre-high pillar stands in the courtyard of the mosque and has been there since long before the mosque's construction. A six-line Sanskrit inscription indicates that it was initially erected outside a Vishnu temple, possibly in Bihar, and was raised in memory of the Gupta King Chandragupta Vikramaditya, who ruled from 375 to 413.

What the inscription does not tell is how it was made, for the iron in the pillar is of quite exceptional purity. Scientists have never discovered how this iron, which is of such purity that it has not rusted after 2000 years, could be cast with the technology of the time. It is said that if you can encircle the pillar with your hands whilst standing with your back to it, your wish will be fulfilled.

Alai Minar

At the same time Ala-ud-din made his additions to the mosque, he also conceived a far more ambitious construction programme. He would build a second tower of victory,

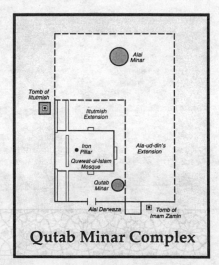

Qutab Minar Complex

exactly like the Qutab Minar, except it would be twice as high! When he died the tower had reached 27 metres and no-one was willing to continue his overambitious project. The uncompleted tower stands to the north of the Qutab Minar and the mosque.

Other Features
Ala-ud-din's Alai Darwaza gateway is the main entrance to the whole complex. It was built of red sandstone in 1310 and stands just south-west of the Qutab Minar. The tomb of Imam Zamin stands beside the gateway, while the tomb of Altamish, who died in 1235, is by the north-west corner of the mosque.

A short distance west of the enclosure, in Mehrauli village, is the Tomb of Adham Khan who, amongst other things, according to legend drove the beautiful Hindu singer Rupmati to suicide following the capture of Mandu (see Mandu in the Madhya Pradesh chapter). When Akbar became displeased with him he ended up being heaved off a terrace in the Agra Fort.

There are some summer palaces in the area and also the tombs of the last kings of Delhi, who succeeded the last Mughals. An empty space between two of the tombs was intended for the last king of Delhi, who died in exile in Rangoon, Burma (Myanmar), in 1862, following his implication in the 1857 Indian Mutiny.

Getting There & Away
You can get out to the Qutab Minar on a No 505 bus from the Ajmer Gate side of New Delhi railway station, or from Janpath, opposite the Janpath Hotel.

Punjab & Haryana

The Punjab was probably the part of India which suffered the most destruction and damage at the time of Partition, yet today it is far and away the most affluent state in India. No natural resource or advantage gave the Punjabis this enviable position; it was sheer hard work.

Prior to Partition the Punjab extended across both sides of what is now the India-Pakistan border, and its capital Lahore is now the capital of the Pakistani state of Punjab. The population of the Punjab was split into a Muslim region and a Sikh and Hindu region by the grim logic of Partition that sliced the region in two. As millions of Sikhs and Hindus fled eastward and equal numbers of Muslims fled west, there were innumerable atrocities and killings on both sides.

More recently Sikh political demands racked the state. In 1984, extremists occupied the Golden Temple in Amritsar and were only finally evicted after a bloody battle with the Indian army. The terrorist activities of the five extremist groups continued into the early 1990s, putting Punjab firmly off-limits to travellers. Support for these groups has dwindled, things are quiet now, and it's safe to visit the area once more.

The major city in the Punjab is Amritsar, the holy city of the Sikhs, but it is so close to the Pakistani border that it was thought wise to build a safer capital further within India. At first Shimla, the old imperial summer capital, served as capital, but Chandigarh, a new planned city, was conceived and built in the 1950s to serve as the capital of the new Punjab.

In 1966, however, the Punjab was to undergo another split. This time it was divided into the predominantly Sikh and Punjabi-speaking state of Punjab and the state of Haryana. At the same time some of the northern parts of the Punjab were hived off to Himachal Pradesh. Chandigarh, on the

Punjab
    Population: 21.6 million
    Area: 50,362 sq km
    Capital: Chandigarh
    People per sq km: 433
    Main Language: Punjabi
    Literacy Rate: 57%
    Best Time to Go: October to March

Haryana
    Population: 18 million
    Area: 44,212 sq km
    Capital: Chandigarh
    People per sq km: 407
    Main Language: Hindi
    Literacy Rate: 55%
    Best Time to Go: October to March

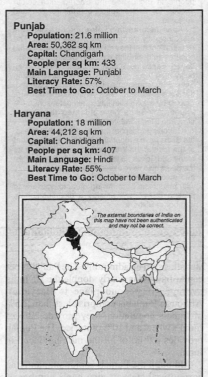

The external boundaries of India on this map have not been authenticated and may not be correct.

border of Punjab and Haryana, remained the capital of both states until 1986 when it was announced that it would be handed over to Punjab in an attempt to placate the Sikhs. However, with the continued violence in Punjab this didn't take place, although eventually it will. In the meantime, Chandigarh remains the capital of the two states, yet is administered as a Union Territory from Delhi.

At the time of Partition the Punjab was devastated but the Sikhs' no-nonsense approach to life has won for it a position that

249

The Sikhs

The Sikhs are the reason for the Punjab's success story and they're amongst the most interesting people in India. See the Sacred India colour section for a description of their religion and customs.

Apart from anything else, the Sikhs are the most instantly recognisable people in India. The requirement that they do not cut their hair *(kesha)* ensures that all Sikh men are bearded and turbaned. For some reason they all seem to be big, bulky men too – you rarely see a weedy-looking Sikh. Sikh women also have a unique costume, the *salwar-kameez*: wide pyjama-style trousers topped by a long shirt which almost reaches the knees. All Sikhs have adopted the Rajput surname Singh, meaning Lion.

Curiously, despite their undoubted success, the Sikhs have a reputation in India rather like that of the Irish in the West and the Indians have as many Sikh jokes as the West has Irish jokes. Yet the Sikhs also have a reputation for great dexterity and mechanical ability and in India any activity with machines, from driving an auto-rickshaw to piloting a 747, will employ a disproportionate number of Sikhs. ■

statistics sum up admirably. The Punjab's per capita income is nearly double the all-India average (in second place is Haryana). Although Punjabis comprise less than 2.5% of India's population, they provide 22% of India's wheat and 10% of its rice. The Punjab provides a third of all the milk produced in India.

Although the Punjab is predominantly an agricultural state, it also has a number of thriving industries including Hero Bicycles at Ludhiana – India's (and the world's) biggest bicycle manufacturer. The Punjabis also have the highest consumption of alcohol in India – the iron bangle *(karra)*, which all Sikh men must wear, is an ideal instrument for taking the caps off beer bottles!

From the traveller's point of view, the area has just one attraction – the beautiful Golden Temple in Amritsar. Apart from this the states are mainly places of transit for travellers on their way to the Himachal hill stations, Pakistan, and, if things have quietened down there, Kashmir.

Haryana

The state of Haryana has one of the most successful tourist departments in India, which is interesting when you consider that the state has virtually no tourist attractions. What the clever Haryanans have done is take advantage of their geographical location. If you're going from Delhi to almost any major attraction in the north of India – Jaipur, Agra, Kashmir, Amritsar – you go through Haryana. So they've built a series of 'service centres' along the main roads – the sort of motel-restaurant-service station complexes that are quite common in the West, but are all too rare in India. They are all named after birds found in Haryana and are clean, well kept and, if you're after a place to stay, make travelling through Haryana a pleasure. Typically the complexes may have a camping site, camper huts (usually around Rs 200) and rooms (in the Rs 300 to Rs 400 range if they have air-con, cheaper without). Some

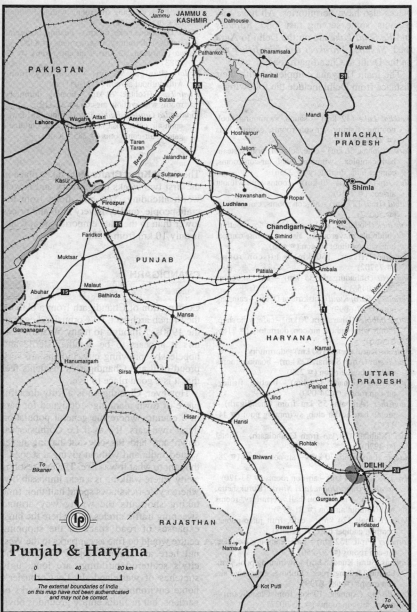

Punjab & Haryana

0   40   80 km

The external boundaries of India
on this map have not been authenticated
and may not be correct.

places also have dormitories. All have restaurants, some serving fast food. *Rajhans* and *Badkhal Lake* are on the Delhi to Agra road. *Skylark, Parakeet* and *Kingfisher* are on the Delhi to Chandigarh road.

The main Haryana complexes with their distance from Delhi include the following:

Badkhal Lake (32 km) – sauna, swimming pool, boating, fishing, air-con rooms, camper huts (☎ 21-8731)

Barbet (Sohna, 56 km) – cafe, sulphur springs, steam bath complex, swimming pool, air-con rooms, camper huts, dormitory (☎ 2256)

Blue Jay (Samalkha, 70 km) – rooms with/without air-con (☎ 2110)

Bulbul (Jind, 127 km) – air-con rooms, camper huts (☎ 56087)

Dabchick (Hodal, 92 km) – elephant rides, boating, children's playgrounds, air-con rooms, camper huts with/without air-con (☎ 626)

Flamingo (Hissar, 160 km) – air-con rooms (☎ 75702)

Gauriyya (Bahadurgarh, 35 km) – air-con rooms (☎ 81-0455)

Hermitage Suraj Kund (outskirts of Delhi) – camping huts (☎ 27-6099)

Jungle Babbler (Dharuhera, 70 km) – cafe, wine shop, rooms with/without air-con, dormitory (☎ 2186, Rewari)

Jyotisar (Kurukshetra, 160 km) – dormitory

Kala Teetar (Abub Shehar, 325 km) – boating, rooms with/without air-con (☎ 239)

Karna Lake (Uchana, 124 km) – boating, fishing, air-con rooms (☎ 24-099)

Kingfisher (Ambala, 55 km from Chandigarh) – motel, bar, health club, swimming pool (☎ 44-3732)

Koel (Kaithal, 123 km from Chandigarh) – motel (☎ 4270)

Magpie (Faridabad, 30 km) – air-con rooms (☎ 28-8083)

Myna (Rohtak, 74 km) – air-con rooms (☎ 33-120)

Neelkanth Krishna Dham Yatri Niwas (Kurukshetra, 154 km) – meditation hall, dormitory, rooms with/without air-con (☎ 31-615)

Oasis (Karnal, 124 km) – cafe, fruit juice corner, boating, camper huts (☎ 24-264)

Parakeet (Pipli, 152 km) – cafe, camping facilities, air-con rooms (☎ 30-250)

Rajhans (Suraj Kund, 8 km) – swimming pool, gym, boating, fishing, rock climbing, expensive air-con rooms (☎ 681-0799)

Red Bishop (Ambala, 10 km from Chandigarh) – motel, air-con rooms (☎ 56-0027)

Rosy Pelican (Sultanpur, 46 km) – bird-watching facilities, camping site, rooms with and without air-con (☎ 85-242)

Saras (Damdama Lake, 64 km) – boating, hovercraft (really!), dormitory, air-con rooms (☎ 8352)

Shama (Gurgaon, 32 km) – air-con rooms (☎ 32-0683)

Skylark (Panipat, 92 km) – dormitory, rooms with/without air-con (☎ 21-051)

Tilyar Lake (Rohtak, 70 km) – boating, dormitory, rooms with/without air-con (☎ 33-119)

Yadavindra Gardens Budgerigar (Pinjore, 281 km) – open-air cafe, dosa shop, mini-zoo, children's games, air-con rooms (☎ 2855, Kalka)

The **Suraj Kund Crafts Mela** takes place in the first two weeks of February and is well worth attending. You buy direct from the craftspeople, quality is very high and prices lower than in the state emporia. Suraj Kund is only 10 km from Delhi.

CHANDIGARH

Population: 600,000
Telephone Area Code: 0172

Construction of Chandigarh from a plan by the French architect, Le Corbusier, began in the 1950s. Although to many Western visitors it appears to be a rather sterile and hopelessly sprawling city, Indians are very proud of it and Chandigarh's residents feel that it is a good place to live.

However, Chandigarh is a truly dreadful piece of town planning – designed for cars in a country where the general population don't own cars. It's as if Le Corbusier sat down and laid the city out having never visited India and without giving a second's thought to what it was like. The end result is a city where walking is a near impossibility, where cycle-rickshaws spend half their time taking shortcuts the wrong way around sweeping traffic circles, and where the huge expanses of road space in the shopping centre would be fine as car parks in the West but here are simply empty. Between the city's scattered buildings are long, ugly stretches of wasteland. In Le Corbusier's home environment they might be parks or gardens, but in India empty ground is obviously doomed.

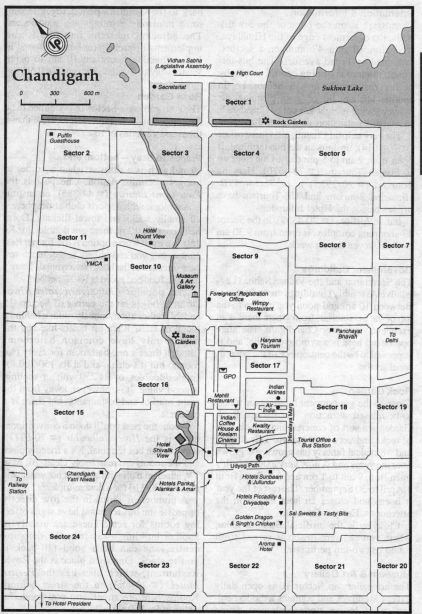

Chandigarh

0   300   600 m

Vidhan Sabha
(Legislative Assembly)

● High Court

● Secretariat

Sukhna Lake

Sector 1

✿ Rock Garden

■ Puffin
Guesthouse

Sector 2

Sector 3

Sector 4

Sector 5

Sector 11

Hotel
Mount View

Sector 8

Sector 7

■ YMCA

Sector 10

Museum
& Art
Gallery ⋔

Sector 9

Foreigners' Registration
Office ●

Wimpy
Restaurant ▼

✿ Rose
Garden

Haryana
ℹ Tourism

■ Panchayat
Bhavah

To
Delhi

✉ GPO

Sector 17

Sector 16

Mehfil
Restaurant ▼

Indian
Airlines ●

Air
India ●

Sector 18

Sector 19

Sector 15

Hotel
Shivalik View ◆

Indian
Coffee
House &
Keelam
Cinema

Kwality
Restaurant ▼

Himalaya Marg

Tourist Office &
Bus Station

Udyog Path

ℹ

To
Railway
Station

■ Chandigarh
Yatri Niwas

Hotels Pankaj,
Alankar & Amar

Hotels Sunbeam
& Jullundur

Hotels Piccadilly &
Divyadeep

■ Sai Sweets & Tasty Bite

Golden Dragon
& Singh's Chicken ▼

Sector 24

■ Aroma
Hotel

Sector 23

Sector 22

Sector 21

Sector 20

To Hotel President

Orientation & Information

Chandigarh is on the edge of the Siwalik Hills, the outermost edge of the Himalaya. It is divided into 47 numbered sectors, separated by broad avenues. The bus terminal, modern shopping centre, and many of the restaurants are in Sector 17. In another brilliant bit of town planning, the railway station is eight km out of Chandigarh, so buses are much more convenient than trains.

The very helpful Chandigarh tourist office (☎ 70-4614), upstairs in the bus terminal, is open from 9 am to 5 pm daily. One floor up is Punjab Tourism (☎ 70-4570). Haryana Tourism (☎ 70-2955) is in Sector 17B. Himachal Tourism and UP Tourism have offices beside the Hotel Jullundur.

Indian Airlines (☎ 70-4539), in the Sector 17 shopping complex, is open from 9.30 am to 7 pm, seven days a week.

Government Buildings

The Secretariat and the Vidhan Sabha (Legislative Assembly) buildings are in Sector 1. Between 10 am and noon you can go to the top of the Secretariat, from where there is an excellent view over Chandigarh. The huge open hand here is a symbol of unity, and is supposed to be the centrepiece of the government sector.

Rock Garden

Close to the government buildings is a not-to-be-missed attraction, the bizarre Rock Garden – a sort of concrete maze with a lot of rocks and very little garden. This strange and whimsical fantasy has grown and grown over the years and is now very extensive. It's open from 9 am to 1 pm and 3 to 7 pm from 1 April to 30 September. The rest of the year it opens and closes an hour earlier in the afternoons. Entry is Rs 0.50.

Close by is the artificial **Sukhna Lake**, where you can rent rowboats or just stroll round its two-km perimeter.

Museum & Art Gallery

The art gallery in Sector 10 is open daily except Mondays and contains a modest collection of Indian stone sculptures dating back to the Gandhara period, together with some miniature paintings and modern art. The adjacent museum has fossils and implements of prehistoric humans found in India. Opening hours are 10 am to 5 pm Wednesday to Sunday. Entry is Rs 0.50.

Rose Garden

The rose garden in Sector 16 is claimed to be the biggest in Asia and contains more than a thousand varieties of roses.

Places to Stay – bottom end

Chandigarh is a disaster when it comes to budget accommodation. Cheapest is the *Panchayat Bhavan* (☎ 44-385), an institutional block with a sports club atmosphere – all smelly socks and towel-flicking. Dorm beds cost Rs 12 or there are doubles for Rs 150. An even worse option is the *Tourist Rest House*, but you're unlikely to get much rest here since it's at the busy bus terminal. There's just one four-bed room at Rs 12 per bed.

The popular *Chandigarh Yatri Niwas* (☎ 54-5904) is on the corner of Sectors 15 and 24, rather anonymously hidden behind a block of flats. It's a bit hostel-like and the rooms only have common bathrooms (though there's one bathroom for every two rooms) but it's clean, and at Rs 150/200 for singles/doubles, or Rs 250 with air-cooling, is good value. It is, however, away from the main market and restaurants; but there is a cafeteria.

About the best you'll do in a conventional hotel is the *Hotel Jullundur* (☎ 70-6777), opposite the bus terminal. It's a friendly place and the rooms are reasonably clean. All have TV, attached bath with constant hot water, and cost Rs 230/310 for a double/triple.

A number of shops in the row directly opposite the bus terminal have signs offering rooms for rent. These are usually in another building away from the shopping centre, and can be a good fall-back if you're stuck. One such place is the Royal Restaurant, which also has the *Peeush Motel* (☎ 20-683) in the street behind. Rooms here are small, and not wonderful value at Rs 250 for a double.

Places to Stay – middle

About 500 metres north-west of the bus terminal there are three bottom to middle-range hotels side by side in Sector 22. Best value here is the *Amar* (☎ 70-3608), which charges Rs 250 for doubles (Rs 350 with air-con) and has a good restaurant. There's also the *Alankar* (☎ 70-8801), with doubles from Rs 300, and the *Hotel Pankaj* (☎ 70-7906), the pick of the bunch, with comfortable rooms at Rs 295/325.

On the southern edge of Sector 22, the *Hotel Divyadeep* (☎ 70-5191) on Himalaya Marg has rooms at Rs 120/150, or Rs 170/200 for air-cooling and Rs 220/270 with air-con. Just past the traffic lights, about 10 minutes' walk from the bus terminal, is the long-running *Aroma Hotel* (☎ 70-0045). Room rates range from Rs 300 for an ordinary double to Rs 695/795 for an air-con suite. The place is clean and well kept and there's a restaurant and coffee shop.

Haryana Tourism's *Puffin Guest House* (☎ 54-0321) is a long way from anywhere in Sector 2. There are air-con rooms from Rs 250/350.

Places to Stay – top end

Closest to the bus terminal is the *Hotel Sunbeam* (☎ 70-8107) with air-con rooms costing Rs 650/850. Nearby on Himalaya Marg in Sector 22 is the *Hotel Piccadilly* (☎ 70-7571) which charges Rs 495/627 for singles/doubles and is popular with business-people.

The *Hotel Shivalik View* (☎ 70-4497) is a large modern place centrally located in Sector 17. Rooms cost Rs 700/850.

Set in peaceful gardens in Sector 10, the *Hotel Mount View* (☎ 54-7882; fax 54-7120) is Chandigarh's top hotel. There are 61 air-con rooms at Rs 1000/1400 for a single/double, a restaurant and coffee shop, swimming pool and health club.

Places to Eat

While Chandigarh may be lacking in budget hotels and tourist sights, it certainly has plenty of places to eat. In the row of shops on Udyog Path opposite the bus terminal there are a number of cheap restaurants serving standard Indian food. These include the *Royal, Vince* and *Punjab* restaurants.

Around the corner on Himalaya Marg *Singh's Chicken* has a good range of chicken dishes. Close by is the *Golden Dragon* Chinese restaurant, cheaper than it looks and the food is good. Also here is *Tasty Bite*, a very ritzy takeaway place with decent burgers and south Indian snacks. The *Bhoj Restaurant* at the Hotel Divyadeep serves slightly expensive vegetarian food in glossy surroundings.

If you're staying in the Panchayat Bhavan there's *Chopstix 2*, a Chinese place across the road. North in Sector 9 is a newly opened branch of *Wimpy*, the British hamburger chain that lives up to its name.

There are lots of places to eat in the Sector 17 shopping centre. Fast-food outlets include *Hot Millions* (near Air India) with burgers from Rs 21 to Rs 38, pizzas from Rs 32 and wide-screen satellite TV to watch as you eat. Also here are two outlets of the *Indian Coffee House*.

In the same area are Chandigarh's top two restaurants, *Ghazal* and, in the same street, *Mehfil*. Both are expensive with main dishes at around Rs 80, served in plush surroundings. Menus are the standard mix of Continental, Chinese and Indian. The Ghazal also has a pub that serves draught beer. The Mehfil also has home delivery (☎ 70-3539).

Things to Buy

Woollen sweaters and shawls from the Punjab are good buys, especially in the Government Emporium. The Sector 17 shopping centre is probably the most extensive in India.

Getting There & Away

Air Jagson Airlines stops in Chandigarh on its Delhi-Kullu flight, and Rajair may also touch down here when its Bombay-Kullu service begins.

Bus Chandigarh has a huge and noisy bus terminal. For the five-hour trip to Delhi there are nearly 200 buses every day, at all hours of the day and night. Ordinary buses cost Rs

58, deluxe buses are Rs 118 and air-con buses cost Rs 175. There are deluxe buses to numerous destinations including Shimla (Rs 86, five hours), Kullu (Rs 112, eight hours), Manali (Rs 132, 10 hours), Dharamsala (10 hours), Amritsar (six hours) and Jaipur.

Train Buses are more convenient than trains to or from Chandigarh; if you prefer to travel by train, however, reservations can be made at the office (☎ 70-4382) upstairs in the bus terminal. It's open from 8 am to 8 pm.

It is 245 km from Delhi to Chandigarh and the twice-daily *Shatabdi Express* does the journey in just three hours. The fare is Rs 250 in a chair car, and Rs 500 in 1st class; this includes a meal.

Kalka is just 25 km up the line, and from there it takes nearly six hours to reach Shimla on the narrow-gauge mountain railway.

Getting Around
To/From the Airport The airport is 11 km to the south of Sector 17 and it's Rs 120 by taxi or Rs 44 by auto-rickshaw.

Local Transport Chandigarh is much too spread out to get around on foot. The extensive bus network is the cheapest way of getting around. Bus No 1 runs by the Aroma Hotel as far as the government buildings in Sector 1, and bus No 37 runs to the railway station from the bus terminal.

Cycle-rickshaws operate on the normal bargaining basis but Chandigarh is a bit big even for them. If you're planning a longer trip across the city consider taking an auto-rickshaw, of which there aren't so many. There is a prepaid auto-rickshaw stand behind the bus terminal. A sign lists all the set fares, but rickshaw-wallahs may offer lower rates when business is slack. From the railway station to the bus terminal should cost around Rs 30.

Bicycle is the best form of transport, but they're hard to find; ask at your hotel.

AROUND CHANDIGARH
Pinjore
The **Yadavindra Gardens** at Pinjore were designed by Fidai Khan, Aurangzeb's foster brother, who also designed the Badshahi Mosque in Lahore, Pakistan. Situated 20 km from Chandigarh, near Kalka, the gardens include the Rajasthani Mughal-style **Shish Mahal** palace. Below it is the Rang Mahal and the cubical Jal Mahal. There is an otter house, and other animals can be seen in the mini-zoo near the gardens. The fountains only operate on weekends.

Haryana Tourism's *Yadavindra Gardens Budgerigar Motel* (☎ (01733) 2855) has air-con rooms from Rs 350. There are hourly buses from Chandigarh which stop by the entrance to the gardens.

CHANDIGARH TO DELHI
There are many places of interest along the 260-km route from Chandigarh to Delhi. The road, part of the Grand Trunk Road, is one of the busiest in India.

Karnal & Kurukshetra
Events in the *Mahabharata* are supposed to have occurred in Karnal, 118 km from Delhi, and also at the tank of Kurukshetra, a little further north. It was at Karnal that Nadir Shah, the Persian who took the Peacock Throne from Delhi, defeated the Mughal emperor, Mohammed Shah, in 1739.

The Kurukshetra **tank** has attracted as many as a million pilgrims during eclipses, as at these times the water in the tank is said to contain water from every other sacred tank in India. Thus its cleansing ability during the eclipse is unsurpassed. Kurukshetra also has an interesting small mosque, the **Lal Masjid**, and a finely designed **tomb**.

Gharaunda
The gateways of an old Mughal *serai* (rest house) stand to the west of this village, 102 km north of Delhi. Shah Jahan built *kos minars* (milestones) along the road from Delhi to Lahore and serais at longer intervals. Most of the kos minars still stand but there is little left of the various serais.

HUGH FINLAY

HUGH FINLAY

Delhi

Top: Humayun's Tomb, built of sandstone and marble by his wife, and a precursor to the Taj Mahal in Agra.

Bottom: Courtyard of the Jama Masjid, India's largest mosque, built by Shah Jahan in 1644.

SALLY HONE

CHRIS BEALL

BRYN THOMAS

Punjab & Haryana
Top Left: The Golden Temple, Amritsar.
Top Right: Domes of the Golden Temple.
Bottom: Flower sellers in Amritsar.

Panipat

Panipat, 92 km north of Delhi, is reputed to be one of the most fly-infested places in India – due, it is said, to a Muslim saint buried here. He is supposed to have totally rid Panipat of flies, but when the people complained that he had done too good a job he gave them all the flies back, multiplied by a thousand.

It is also the site of three great battles, although there is little reminder of these today. In 1526, Babur defeated Ibrahim Lodi, king of Delhi, at Panipat and thus founded the Mughal Empire in India. In 1556, Akbar defeated the Pathans at this same site. Finally in 1761, the Marathas, who had succeeded the Mughals, were defeated here by the Afghan forces of Ahmad Shah Durani.

SULTANPUR

There are many birds, including flamingoes, at this bird sanctuary 46 km south-west of Delhi. September to March is the best time to visit, and you can stay at the *Rosy Pelican* (✆ 85-242) complex. To get there take a blue Haryana bus from Delhi to Gurgaon, and then take a Chandu bus (three times a day) to Sultanpur.

DELHI TO SIRSA

This route takes you north-west through Haryana towards the Punjab and Pakistan, south of the Delhi to Amritsar route. From Delhi the railway line runs through **Rohtak**, 70 km north-west of Delhi, which was once a border town between the Sikhs' and Marathas' regions, and the subject of frequent clashes.

Hansi, north-west of Rohtak, was where Colonel Skinner died. (Skinner's Horse, the private cavalry regiment he founded in the 1790s, was responsible for the conquest of large areas of northern India for the East India Company.) **Sirsa**, 90 km further north-west, is an ancient city but little remains apart from the city walls.

Punjab

AMRITSAR

Population: 760,000
Telephone Area Code: 0183

Founded in 1577 by Ram Das, the fourth guru of the Sikhs, Amritsar is both the centre of the Sikh religion and the major city of Punjab state. The name means Pool of Nectar, referring to the sacred tank around which the Sikhs' Golden Temple is built. Although Amritsar itself is just another dusty Indian city, the Golden Temple is an exceptionally beautiful and peaceful place. It's well worth a visit, and since it's close to the only border crossing open between India and Pakistan, all overlanders pass through Amritsar.

The original site for the city was granted by the Mughal emperor, Akbar, but in 1761 Ahmad Shah Durani sacked the town and destroyed the temple. It was rebuilt in 1764, and in 1802 was roofed over with copper-gilded plates by Ranjit Singh and became known as 'the Golden Temple'. During the turmoil of the Partition of India in 1948, Amritsar was a flash point for the terrible events that shook the Punjab.

During unrest in the Punjab during the early '80s the Golden Temple was occupied by Sikh extremists who were finally evicted by the Indian army in 1984 with much bloodshed. This action was a contributing factor to Indira Gandhi's subsequent assassination. The temple was again occupied by extremists in 1986. The damage wrought on the Golden Temple by the tanks of the Indian army has now been repaired, and things are quiet again.

The Sikhs are justifiably proud of their capital city and the Golden Temple, and travellers have commented on their friendliness and helpfulness.

Orientation & Information

The old city is south-east of the main railway station and is surrounded by a circular road which used to contain the massive city walls. There are 18 gates still in existence but only

the north gate, facing the Ram Bagh gardens, is original. The Golden Temple and the narrow alleys of the bazaar area are in the old city.

The more modern part of Amritsar is north-east of the railway station, where you will also find the beautiful gardens known as Ram Bagh, Mall Rd and 'posh' Lawrence St. The bus terminal is two km east of the railway station on the road to Delhi.

The tourist office (☎ 23-1452) is in the former youth hostel, now occupied by the army, one km east of the bus terminal. It has very little information and is closed at weekends. Marijuana plants thrive in the surrounding ditches, as they do all over this area.

Telephone numbers in Amritsar are in the process of being changed. If you have difficulty in getting through to any of the numbers listed, phone ☎ 55-0197 for the new number.

Golden Temple

The holiest shrine of the Sikh religion, also known as the Hari Mandir, is in the centre of the old part of town. The temple itself is surrounded by the pool which gave the town its name, and is reached by a causeway. Open to all, it's a beautiful place, especially early in the morning. However, at the weekends it can get quite crowded.

Restoration work to repair the damage done when the Indian army stormed the Golden Temple in 1984 has largely been completed, although bullet holes are still visible in some buildings. The small rooms around the pool and those in the basement have been sealed, along with other hiding places favoured by the extremists.

Pilgrims and visitors to the Golden Temple must remove their shoes and cover their heads before entering the precincts. No smoking is allowed; photography is permitted from the Parikrama, the marble walkway that surrounds the sacred pool. An English-speaking guide is available at the information office near the clock tower which marks the temple's main entrance. The information office has a number of interesting publications including one eclectic booklet entitled *Human Hair – Factory of Vital Energy*!

Hari Mandir Standing in the middle of the sacred pool, the Golden Temple is a two-storey marble structure reached by a causeway known as the Gurus' Bridge. The lower parts of the marble walls are decorated with inlaid flower and animal motifs in the *pietra dura* style of the Taj Mahal. Once inside the temple, pilgrims offer sweet doughy *prasaad* to the attendants who take half to distribute to everyone as they leave the temple.

The architecture of the Golden Temple is a blend of Hindu and Muslim styles. The golden dome (said to be gilded with 100 kg of pure gold) is supposed to represent an inverted lotus flower. It is inverted, turning back to the earth, to symbolise the Sikhs' concern with the problems of this world. The dome is currently being re-covered in gold donated by Birmingham's Sikh community.

Granth Sahib Four priests at key positions around the temple keep up a continuous reading in Punjabi from the Sikhs' holy book that is broadcast by loudspeaker. The origi-

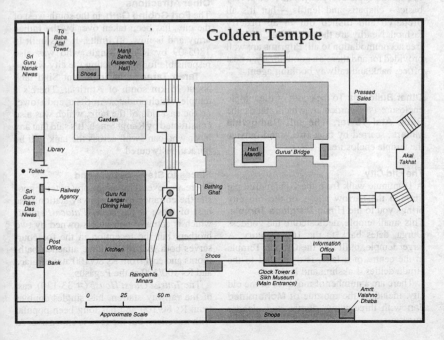

nal copy of the Granth Sahib is kept under a pink shroud in the Golden Temple during the day and at around 10 pm each evening is ceremoniously returned to the Akal Takhat (Sikh Parliament) building. The morning processional ceremony takes place at 4 am in summer, 5 am in winter.

Sikh Museum The Central Sikh Museum is upstairs in the clock tower and comprises a gallery of paintings telling the story of the Sikhs and their martyrs.

Akal Takhat The Shiromani Gurdwara Parbandhak Committee, or Sikh Parliament, traditionally meets in this building, which is why it was a target for the Indian army in 1984. It has since been completely rebuilt.

Guru Ka Langar & Gurdwaras All Sikh temples have a community kitchen and in this one volunteers prepare free meals for up to 30,000 people every day. The food is very basic – chapatis and lentils – but it's all prepared and dished out in an orderly fashion. Nearby are the gurdwaras, offering free accommodation to all. Pilgrims are well provided for and there's a good library, a post office, bank and railway booking agent.

Other Buildings To the south of the temple enclosure is a garden in which stands the **Baba Atal Tower**. The tall **Ramgarhia Minars**, scarred by tank fire, stand outside the temple enclosure.

The Old City

A 15-minute walk from the Golden Temple through the narrow alleys of the old city brings you to the Hindu **Durgiana Temple**. This small temple, dedicated to the goddess Durga, dates back to the 16th century. A larger temple, built like the Golden Temple in the centre of a lake, is dedicated to the Hindu deities, Lakshmi and Narayan.

There are a number of mosques in the old city, including the mosque of **Mohammed Jan** with three white domes and slender minarets.

Jallianwala Bagh

This park is just five minutes' walk from the Golden Temple and commemorates the 2000 Indians who were killed or wounded at this site, shot indiscriminately by the British in 1919. This was one of the major events in India's struggle for independence and was movingly re-created in the film *Gandhi*.

The story of this appalling massacre is told in the Martyrs' Gallery. A section of wall with bullet marks still visible is preserved, and the well into which some people jumped to escape can still be seen.

Ram Bagh

This beautiful garden is in the new part of town and has a museum in the small palace built by the Sikh Maharaja Ranjit Singh. The museum contains weapons dating back to Mughal times and some portraits of the ruling houses of the Punjab. It's closed on Wednesday.

Other Attractions

The **Fort Gobind Garh**, in the south-west of the city, has been taken over by the Indian army and is now off limits. It was built in 1805-09 by Ranjit Singh, who was also responsible for constructing the city walls.

Taren Taran is an important Sikh tank about 25 km south of Amritsar. There's a temple, which predates Amritsar, and a tower on the east side of the tank, which was also constructed by Ranjit Singh. It's said that any leper who can swim across the tank will be miraculously cured.

Places to Stay – bottom end

There are several rather grubby hotels opposite the entrance to the railway station. The best of these is the *Hotel Palace-Pegasus* which is actually two hotels owned by two brothers but the reception in the forecourt serves both. All rooms have attached bathrooms and cost from Rs 80/100 at the Palace and Rs 100/120 at the Pegasus.

The *Tourist Guest House* (☎ 33-130), east of the railway station, has singles/doubles from Rs 80/100 and has long been popular with travellers, but the food is expensive. At the front there are also clean doubles with attached bath for Rs 150 and air-con rooms for Rs 250. Sadly, the friendly old colonel who ran the place and in his time helped many travellers newly arrived from Pakistan to buy Enfields, died in 1994. Watch out for touts at the station who will direct you to the inferior *Hotel Tourist Bureau*, just outside the north entrance of the station.

Near the Golden Temple, the *Hotel Sita Niwas* has a range of doubles from Rs 100 (common bath) to Rs 150 (with bath and air-cooling). Bucket hot water costs Rs 4. While it's not a bad place to stay, it's built around a courtyard and can be a little noisy.

Hospitality to pilgrims is part of the Sikh faith, and the most interesting place to stay in Amritsar is at the Golden Temple itself. However, if you do stay here it is imperative that you respect the fact that this is a holy place – smoking, alcohol, drugs and any public display of familiarity between the sexes is grossly insulting to the Sikhs. The gurdwaras *(Sri Guru Ram Das Niwas* and *Sri Guru Nanak Niwas)* are staffed by volunteers. Accommodation is free but you must pay a deposit of Rs 50 (returnable on departure) and you can stay for up to three days. There's a large dorm, bedding is provided and the toilets and shower block are in the centre of the courtyard. There's no pressure from any of the staff but a donation is expected – and you shouldn't forget to make one. Doubles with attached bath are sometimes available for foreigners in the Sri Guru Nanak Niwas, for a charge of Rs 15. Nearby, a new guest house, the *Sri Guru Hargobind Niwas*, with 125 doubles with attached bath, is under construction.

Places to Stay – middle

The *Hotel Airlines* (☎ 64-848), Cooper Rd, is near the railway station and a reasonable place to stay. Rooms are a bit tatty and they range from Rs 193/250 (ordinary) to Rs 440/550 (air-con), and there's one single at Rs 165. All have attached bathroom and there's a pleasant sun terrace and restaurant. The friendly *Grand Hotel* (☎ 62-977), near the Hotel Palace-Pegasus opposite the

railway station, is not such good value, although all rooms have satellite TV, and are set around a small garden. They charge Rs 225/300 for ordinary singles/doubles, more for air-con rooms.

On Mall Rd, in the new area of the city and about one km from the railway station, you'll find the pleasant *Hotel Blue Moon* (☎ 20-416) with double rooms at Rs 200/250.

The best place in this price range, *Mrs Bhandari's Guest House* (☎ 22-2390), at 10 The Cantonment, is a delightful place to stay, and popular with overlanders. Rooms are Rs 500, Rs 600 with air-con, and some of these have four beds. There are also singles for Rs 400. The charming Mrs Bhandari has now retired and the place is efficiently run by her two daughters. Nothing seems to have changed, the kitchen ('Commando Bridge') is still spotless and the bedrooms stuck in a now very fashionable '50s time warp. Meals are available – breakfast is Rs 75, lunch and dinner Rs 150. The guest house is set in a large peaceful garden with a swimming pool (open May to August) and resident cow. Camping charges are Rs 70 per person.

Places to Stay – top end

Punjab Tourism's centrally air-conditioned *Amritsar International Hotel* (☎ 31-991) is a modern building near the bus terminal. Rooms cost from Rs 400/450. The *Hotel Ritz* (☎ 22-6606), at 45 Mall Rd, has overpriced air-con rooms at Rs 700/950. There's also a gym and swimming pool that non-guests can use for Rs 50.

The top hotel is the *Mohan International Hotel* (☎ 22-7801; fax 22-6520), on Albert Rd, with rooms from Rs 725/1000 with bathtubs in the attached bathrooms. It has air-con, a swimming pool (Rs 50 for non-guests) and a good restaurant.

Places to Eat

It's interesting to join the pilgrims for a basic meal at the *Guru ka Langar* at the Golden Temple; there's no charge but you should make a donation when you eat here. Opposite the clock tower entrance to the temple are a number of cheap dhabas. *Amrit Vaishno*

Dhaba (at the end of the group, opposite the information office) does good chana bhatura (spiced chickpeas with fried Indian bread) for Rs 6.

Near the Ram Bagh on Mall Rd is a clutch of mid-range restaurants. Main dishes at the *Kwality Restaurant* are around Rs 60; cheaper snacks are available at *South Land*, which has masala dosas for Rs 12, and at nearby *Salads Plus*. Opposite Ram Bagh is *Sindhi Coffee House* which offers full meals at prices similar to Kwality's, and snacks such as French toast with cheese (Rs 21).

Amritsar also has a number of cheaper and locally popular places such as *Kasar de Dhawa* near the Durgiana Temple and the telephone exchange in the old city. Parathas and other vegetarian dishes are the speciality here, and you can eat well for around Rs 25.

British home cooking is available at *Mrs Bhandari's Guest House* – Rs 150 for a non-veg lunch or dinner. Non-guests should book in advance.

Things to Buy

Woollen blankets, shawls and sweaters are supposed to be cheaper in Amritsar than in other places in India, as they are locally manufactured. Katra Jaimal Singh, near the telephone exchange in the old city, is a good shopping area.

Getting There & Away

Air The Indian Airlines office (☎ 22-5321) is just north of Mall Rd at 367 Green Ave. Amritsar is linked by a thrice-weekly Indian Airlines flight to Delhi (US$52) and Srinagar (US$45). Modiluft (☎ 22-6606) has two flights a week to Bombay (US$152) via Delhi. Archana (☎ 65-150) has three flights a week to Delhi.

Bus The bus journey to Delhi (Rs 111, 10 hours) is less comfortable than going by train. There are also early-morning buses to Dehra Dun (Rs 108, 10 hours), Shimla (Rs 104, 10 hours), Dalhousie and Dharamsala.

There are frequent buses to Pathankot (Rs 28, three hours), Chandigarh (Rs 42, six

hours) and Jammu (Rs 46, five hours) for Srinagar. There are privately operated buses to Jammu or Chandigarh (Rs 160) but these do not go from the bus terminal. Tickets must be bought in advance from the agents near the railway station.

Getting to Rajasthan from Amritsar can be a pain unless you go via Delhi. It's possible to get a direct bus as far as Ganganagar (just over the Rajasthan border); the journey takes around 10 hours.

Train There are direct rail links to Delhi (447 km, Rs 94/352 in 2nd/1st class) in eight to 10 hours, but the daily *Shatabdi Express* does the journey in just over seven hours. Tickets are Rs 370/740 in chair car/1st class. The *Amritsar-Howrah Mail* links Amritsar with Lucknow (850 km, 17 hours), Varanasi (1251 km, 23 hours) and Calcutta (1829 km, 38 hours).

To/From Pakistan The rail crossing point is at Attari, 26 km from Amritsar, and the *4607 Indo-Pak Express* leaves Amritsar daily at 9.30 am, reaching Lahore in Pakistan at 1.35 pm. However, it can be delayed for hours at the border. In the other direction, the train doesn't always stop in Amritsar.

The road crossing at Wagah, 32 km from Amritsar, is quicker. The border is open from 9 am to 4 pm daily and there are frequent buses from Amritsar (Rs 9, one hour). Taxis cost Rs 200 to Rs 300. Punjab Tourism operates the *Neem Chameli Tourist Complex* at Wagah, with dorm beds and cheap doubles.

See the introductory Getting There & Away chapter for further details.

Getting Around

The airport is 15 km from the city centre. An auto-rickshaw should cost around Rs 50, a taxi Rs 80 but you'll probably have to pay two or three times this amount.

Auto-rickshaws charge Rs 20 from the station to the Golden Temple. The same trip on a cycle-rickshaw will cost Rs 10.

PATHANKOT

Population: 160,000
Telephone Area Code: 0186

The town of Pathankot in the extreme north of the Punjab, 107 km from Amritsar, is important to travellers purely as a crossroad. It's the gateway to the Himachal Pradesh hill stations of Dalhousie and Dharamsala, and on the route to Jammu and Srinagar. Otherwise it's a dull little place, although there's the picturesque **Shahpur Kandi Fort** about 13 km north of the town on the River Ravi.

Places to Stay

Turn right outside the railway station for the *Hotel Tourist* (☎ 20-660), a basic place with rooms from Rs 50/125 with attached bath, and a reasonable restaurant. The nearby *Hotel Green* is similar.

By the post office is the *Hotel Airlines* (☎ 20-505), a clean but slightly gloomy hotel with rooms from Rs 100/150, all with TV and attached bath.

Getting There & Away

The dusty bus stand and the railway station are only 300 metres apart, on opposite sides of the road. There are buses to Dalhousie (Rs 34, four hours), Dharamsala (Rs 35, 4½ hours), Chamba (Rs 49, 5½ hours), and Jammu. You can also get taxis for these longer trips next to the bus stand; to either Dalhousie or Dharamsala it's two hours and Rs 660, try for a reduction if things are quiet.

PATIALA

Population: 290,000

Located a little south of the road and railway lines from Delhi to Amritsar, Patiala was once the capital of an independent Sikh state.

There is a museum in the Motibagh Palace of the maharaja in the Baradari Gardens.

SIRHIND

Population: 33,500

This was once a very important town and the capital of the Pathan Sur dynasty. In 1555, Humayun defeated Sikander Shah here and a year later his son, Akbar, completed the destruction of the Sur dynasty at Panipat. From then until 1709 Sirhind was a rich Mughal city, but clashes between the declining Mughal and rising Sikh powers led to the city's sacking in 1709 and complete destruction in 1763.

The Pathan-style **tomb of Mir Miran** and the later Mughal **tomb of Pirbandi** Nakshwala, both ornamented with blue tiles, are worth seeing. The **Salabat Beg Haveli** is probably the largest private home remaining from the Mughal period. South-east of the city is an important Mughal serai.

LUDHIANA

Population: 1.1 million
Telephone Area Code: 0161

The textile centre of India, Ludhiana was the site of a great battle in the First Sikh War. Hero Bicycles, the world's largest manufacturer, with a production of nearly three million bikes annually, is based here.

There's little here to see; but if you're sick, the Christian Medical College Hospital (affiliated with the hospital of the same name in Vellore in Tamil Nadu) is a good place to head for. Established in 1895, it was the first school of medicine in Asia.

The PTDC *Amaltas Hotel* (☎ 51-500) has a cheap dormitory and reasonably priced rooms, some with air-con. The *Hotel City*

Patiala Maharajas

Patiala's maharajas were a colourful bunch and several saucy tales exist about their flamboyant lifestyles. Maharaja Bhupinder Singh is said to have had 365 wives, one for each night of the year. Every evening, the same number of oil lamps, each with the name of one of his wives inscribed upon it, would be placed around the bathing pool. The wife whose name was on the first lamp to go out would be the one who spent the night with him. The maharaja had one night off every leap year – and is said to have suffered from severe back problems in later life. ■

Heart (☎ 40-0240), a short walk from the railway station and just beyond the clock tower, is one of the top places here. Rooms cost Rs 600/900. It also has a good restaurant and bar.

JALANDHAR

Population: 560,000
Telephone Area Code: 0181

Only 80 km south-east of Amritsar, this was once the capital of an ancient Hindu kingdom. It survived a sacking by Mahmud of Ghazni nearly a thousand years ago and later became an important Mughal city. The town has a large serai built in 1857.

Not far from the bus stand, the *Skylark Hotel* (☎ 76-981) has good rooms from Rs 220/295. Other places include the *Plaza*

Hotel (☎ 75-886), which is cheaper; and the three-star *Kamal Palace Hotel* (☎ 58-462), in Civil Lines, with air-con rooms for Rs 650/900.

SOUTH-WEST PUNJAB

The railway line from Sirsa (Haryana) to Firozpur stops at **Bathinda**, which was an important town of the Pathan Sur dynasty.

Faridkot, 350 km north-west of Delhi and close to the Pakistan border, was once the capital of a Sikh state of the same name and has a 700-year-old fort.

Firozpur, almost on the border, is 382 km north-west of Delhi; prior to Partition, the railway line continued to Lahore, now in Pakistan.

Himachal Pradesh

The state of Himachal Pradesh came into being in its present form with the partition of the Punjab into Punjab and Haryana in 1966. Himachal Pradesh is essentially a mountain state – it takes in the transition zone from the plains to the high Himalaya and, in the trans-Himalayan region of Lahaul and Spiti, actually crosses that mighty barrier to the Tibetan plateau. It's a delightful state for visitors, particularly during the hot season when people flock to its hill stations to escape the searing heat of the plains.

High points for the visitor include Shimla, the 'summer capital' of British India and still one of India's most important hill stations. The Kullu Valley is very beautiful – a lush, green valley with the sparkling Beas River running through it and the snowcapped Himalayan peaks forming the background. From Manali the trip along the spectacular mountain road to Leh is breathtaking, and it takes you across the second-highest vehicular pass in the world – only open for a few brief months each year. Since 1992 the eastern valleys of Lahaul, Spiti and Kinnaur have been open to foreigners holding Inner Line Permits (see those sections for details), and these are now only necessary for the Tibetan border areas of Spiti and Kinnaur. The people in these bleak high-altitude regions practise Tibetan Buddhism; it's a fascinating area to visit. Then there's Dharamsala, home-in-exile for the Dalai Lama, and a host of other hill stations, lakes, walks and mountains.

Trekking & Mountaineering

See Lonely Planet's *Trekking in the Indian Himalaya* by Garry Weare for more information on trekking in this region. The Himachal Pradesh tourist office has a brochure on trekking which briefly details a number of treks in the state. They also have three excellent large-scale maps of Himachal Pradesh, which are invaluable for trekkers.

The trekking season here runs from mid-

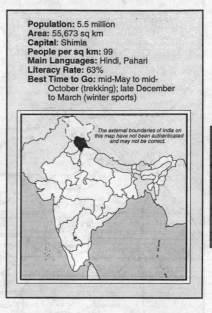

Population: 5.5 million
Area: 55,673 sq km
Capital: Shimla
People per sq km: 99
Main Languages: Hindi, Pahari
Literacy Rate: 63%
Best Time to Go: mid-May to mid-October (trekking); late December to March (winter sports)

The external boundaries of India on this map have not been authenticated and may not be correct.

May to mid-October. In Manali there is a Department of Mountaineering & Allied Sports which can advise you on trekking and mountaineering possibilities in the state. Dharamsala also has a Mountaineering Institute, and from here it's possible to take organised climbs. For more serious mountaineering, the Indian Mountaineering Foundation in Delhi is the place to go for information. Unlike in Nepal, no trekking permits are necessary in Himachal Pradesh.

Equipment and provisions will depend very much on where you trek. In the lower country in the Kullu or Kangra valleys, or around Shimla, there are many rest houses and villages. On the other hand, in Lahaul, Spiti and Kinnaur the population is much less dense and conditions are more severe. You will need to be better equipped in terms of cold-weather gear, food and provisions.

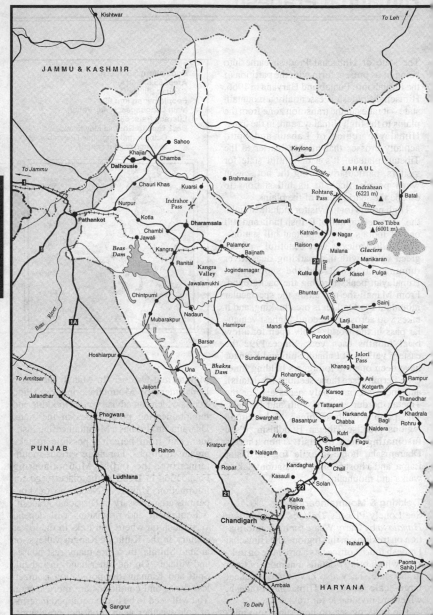

JAMMU & KASHMIR

CHINA (TIBET)

SPITI

Kibar

Kaza

Dankhar   Tabo

KINNAUR   Puh

Moorang

Nachar   Kalpa
Sarahan Tapri   Kinnaur
      Sangla   ▲ Kailash
              (6050 m)

UTTAR PRADESH

Himachal Pradesh

0   30   60 km

The external boundaries of India
on this map have not been authenticated
and may not be correct.

Some of the better known treks are detailed in the appropriate sections. There are many Forest Rest Houses, Public Works Department (PWD) Rest Houses and other semi-official accommodation possibilities along the Himachal Pradesh trekking routes. Enquire at local tourist offices about using these places before setting off.

The *Trekking Guide* published by the Himachal Pradesh Tourism Development Corporation (HPTDC) lists 136 mountains over 5000 metres high. The majority of them are unclimbed, most not even named. It's virgin territory for mountaineers.

Skiing
Manali is becoming a popular place to ski, particularly now that Gulmarg in Kashmir is virtually off limits. **Solang Nullah** is the area's winter ski capital, with 2.5 km of runs, while in the warmer months it is possible to ski on the slopes of the Rohtang Pass. If you've got US$600 to burn you can rent a helicopter in Manali and ski in virgin snow.

Narkanda, 60 km north of Shimla, is also popular. It lies at 3143 metres and so gets a good coverage of snow for a few months of the year. The season runs from late December until the end of March. (See the Narkanda section later in this chapter for more details.) The road from Shimla remains open most of the time, so access isn't a problem. There's a range of slopes, one with a T-bar.

Kufri is much closer to Shimla, but snow coverage is unreliable and the slopes here are mainly suited to beginners.

Wildlife
There are fishing possibilities in many places in Himachal Pradesh and a number of trout hatcheries have been established. The various local tourist offices can advise you on where to fish and how to obtain fishing licences.

Some of the state's deer, antelope, mountain goats and sheep are now rather rare. Himalayan black bears and brown bears are found in many parts of the state; the black bear is fairly common but the brown bear is usually found only at higher elevations. Wild boar are found at lower elevations in certain districts.

Snow leopards are now very rare and only found at high elevations in the most remote parts of the state. Panthers and leopards are, however, still found in many forested regions. Himachal Pradesh has numerous kinds of pheasants and partridges, and many mountain birds.

Temples

Although Himachal Pradesh does not have any particularly renowned temples, it does have many interesting and architecturally diverse ones. In the Kangra and Chamba valleys there are several 8th to 10th-century temples in the Indo-Aryan *sikhara* (curved spire) style. Pagoda-style temples with multi-tiered roofs are found in the Kullu Valley. There are many temples of purely local design, often with interesting wood-carvings, particularly in the Chamba region.

In the south of the state there are numerous temples with elements of Mughal and Sikh design, while in several locations there are cave temples. Finally, the Tibetans, who came to the state following the Chinese invasion of their country, have built colourful *gompas* (monasteries) and temples. The people of Lahaul and Spiti in the north of the state are also of Tibetan extraction and have many interesting gompas. Tabo Gompa, dating from 996 AD, is the oldest in the region and one of the most important Tibetan Buddhist monasteries in the world. It contains superb wall paintings.

Things to Buy

The Kullu Valley is full of spinners and weavers, mostly men, and their fine shawls are very popular. The cheapest ones are made from imported Australian wool. The shawls made from the hair of the pashmina goat are the finest. Fine-quality scarves made from Angora rabbit hair are also relatively inexpensive.

Chamba is well known for its leather *chappals* (sandals).

In the high Himalaya, soft, fleecy blankets

known as *gudmas* are woven, as well as traditional rugs and *numdas* (Rajasthani rugs). In the bazaars you can find locally made jewellery and metalwork. Tibetan handicrafts include coral jewellery, carpets and religious paraphernalia.

Getting Around

Apart from two railway lines, which are both narrow gauge and hence have more tourist appeal than practical travel significance, getting around Himachal Pradesh means taking a bus – unless you can afford a taxi. The two trains run from Kalka (just north of Chandigarh) to Shimla, and from Pathankot in Punjab along the Kangra Valley to Jogindarnagar.

Himachal Pradesh buses are generally the Indian norm – slow, crowded, uncomfortable and tiring. The mountainous terrain means that if you can manage to average 20 km/h on a bus trip, you're doing well. Taxis are readily available but taxi unions are rapacious and travelling this way is more expensive than in many other parts of India. One way you can make a saving is to find a taxi on a return trip – in that case you can often knock the price down a bit. Ask the people running your hotel.

The HPTDC has a number of deluxe tourist bus services. They often operate overnight but usually only in the high seasons or on demand.

SHIMLA

Population: 119,000
Telephone Area Code: 0177

In the days before Independence, Shimla was the most important British hill station, and in the hot season became the 'summer capital' of India. Shimla was first 'discovered' by the British in 1819, but it was not until 1822 that the first permanent house was erected and not until many years later that Shimla became the summer capital.

As the heat built up on the plains each year, first the women, then the men (or at least those who could escape) made their way to the cool mountain air of Shimla. The high-flown social life here in the summer

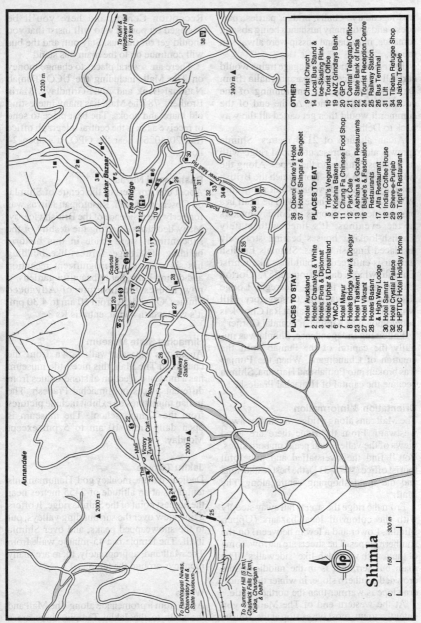

PLACES TO STAY

1 Hotel Auckland
2 Hotels Chanakya & White
3 Hotels Flora & Diplomat
4 Hotels Uphar & Dreamland
6 YMCA
7 Hotel Mayur
8 Hotels Bridge View & Doegar
23 Hotel Tashkent
27 Hotel Vikrant
28 Hotels Basant
    & High Way Lodge
30 Hotel Samrat
32 Hotel Crystal Palace
35 HPTDC Hotel Holiday Home

PLACES TO EAT

5 Tripti's Vegetarian
10 Krishna Bakers
11 Chung Fa Chinese Food Shop
12 Park Cafe
13 Ashiana & Goofa Restaurants
16 Baljee's & Fascination
    Restaurants
17 Alfa Restaurant
18 Indian Coffee House
29 Shere-e-Punjab
33 Tripti's Restaurant

36 Oberoi Clarke's Hotel
37 Hotels Shingar & Sangeet

OTHER

9 Christ Church
14 Local Bus Stand &
    Ice-Skating Rink
15 Tourist Office
19 ANZ Grindlays Bank
20 GPO
21 Central Telegraph Office
22 State Bank of India
24 Tourist Reception Centre
25 Railway Station
26 Bus Terminal
31 Lift
34 Tibetan Refugee Shop
38 Jakhu Temple

Shimla

To Kufri &
Wildflower Hall
(13 km)

▲ 2200 m

▲ 2400 m

Lakkar Bazaar

The Ridge

Lower Mall Rd

Cart Road

Scandal
Corner

Annandale

▲ 2000 m

▲ 2000 m

Railway
Station

The
Victory
Tunnel

Cant Road

The Mall

To Rashtrapati Niwas,
Observatory Hill &
State Museum

To Summer Hill (5 km),
Chadwick Falls (7 km),
Kalka, Chandigarh
& Delhi

0   150   300 m

was legendary – balls, bridge, parties, parades – and with many husbands being absent, romance, intrigue and gossip were always in the air.

Every summer huge baggage trains would cart all the necessary paraphernalia from Delhi so that the efficient running of the country could continue. At the end of the summer it would then get carted all the way back to Delhi.

At an altitude of 2130 metres, Shimla sprawls along a crescent-shaped ridge with its suburbs clinging to the slopes. Along the ridge runs The Mall – from which the British not only banned all vehicles but also, until WW I, all Indians. These days The Mall is a busy scene with throngs of holiday-makers in the evenings. It's lined with stately English-looking houses bearing strangely displaced English names. Shimla's English flavour is enforced by buildings like Christ Church which dates from 1857, Gorton Castle, and the former Viceregal Lodge (Rashtrapati Niwas) on Observatory Hill which dates from 1888. Lajpat Rai Chowk is better known as Kipling's 'Scandal Corner'.

Following Independence, Shimla was initially the capital of the Punjab until the creation of Chandigarh. When the Punjab was broken into Punjab and Haryana, Shimla became the capital of Himachal Pradesh.

Orientation & Information

The Mall runs along a ridge which dips away westward. From the ridge there are good views of the valleys and peaks on both sides. You'll find the overstaffed and unhelpful tourist office (☎ 78-311), the best restaurants and the main shopping centre along The Mall.

From the ridge the streets fall away steeply with the colourful local bazaars (Upper, Middle, Lower and a few in between) on the southern slopes. The streets are narrow, some of them with verandah-like 'sidewalks'. The main bus terminal is in the middle of the crowded southern slope. In winter the southern slope is warmer than the northern side.

At the western end of The Mall as you enter the town, most buses stop at the Tourist Reception Centre, and here you'll be besieged by porters who will insist that you should get off the bus. Stay put, and the bus will continue on to the main bus stand.

There are several places to change money on The Mall, including the UCO, Punjab National Bank and ANZ Grindlays. Maria Brothers, 78 The Mall, has many interesting old maps and books. The best place to send or receive a fax is the central telegraph office (fax 20-4026), near the GPO. It's open 24 hours.

Rashtrapati Niwas

About one km west of the centre of Shimla, on Observatory Hill, Rashtrapati Niwas was formerly the residence of the British viceroy. Many decisions affecting the destiny of the subcontinent were made in this historic building. The huge, fortress-like building has six storeys and magnificent reception and dining halls. Set in beautiful gardens, it now houses the Institute of Advanced Studies. Open daily from 10 am to 4.30 pm, it's well worth a visit; entry is Rs 3.

Himachal State Museum

An hour's pleasant walk down from the church on The Mall, this nice little museum has a modest collection of stone statues from different places in Himachal Pradesh. The Indian miniatures on exhibit include pictures from the Kangra school. The museum is open daily from 10 am to 5 pm except Monday.

Jakhu Temple

Dedicated to the monkey god, Hanuman, this temple is at an altitude of 2455 metres near the highest point of the Shimla ridge. It offers a fine view over the surrounding valleys, out to the snowcapped peaks, and over Shimla itself. The temple is a 45-minute walk from The Mall and, appropriately, there are many monkeys around the temple.

Walks

Apart from a promenade along The Mall and the walk to the Jakhu Temple, there are a great number of interesting walks around Shimla. The network of motorable roads offers access to other scenic spots.

Summer Hill (1983 metres) is five km away on the Shimla to Kalka railway line and has pleasant, shady walks.

Chadwick Falls (1586 metres) are 67 metres high but are only really worth visiting during the monsoon, between July and October. The falls are seven km from Shimla and reached via Summer Hill.

Prospect Hill (2145 metres) is five km west from Shimla and a 15-minute climb from Boileauganj. The hill is a popular picnic spot with fine views over the surrounding country and a temple of Kamna Devia.

Sankat Mochan (1875 metres) has a Hanuman Temple and a fine view of Shimla, and can be reached on foot or by car (seven km from Shimla).

Tara Devi (1851 metres) is a hilltop temple seven km from Shimla by rail or car. There's a *PWD Rest House* (☎ 3675) there.

Wildflower Hall (2593 metres), 13 km from Shimla on the road to Kufri, was the former residence of Indian commander-in-chief Lord Kitchener. The present huge mansion, surrounded by pine trees, was not the actual one built for Kitchener. Damaged by fire in 1994, it's now being rebuilt as a luxury hotel. There's a fine view back to Shimla and out to mountain peaks in the Pir Panjal and Badrinath ranges. Before the fire, Himachal Tourism (HPTDC) ran the place as a hotel. In the grounds, the *Wildflower Hall Cottages* were the only part of the complex to escape the flames and can be rented for Rs 975.

Snow cover at **Kufri** (2501 metres) has been so unreliable in recent years that Himachal Tourism has plans to suspend its operations there. This is no bad thing since ski-hire charges were twice what they are at more distant Narkanda. But, if there is snow, the slopes are still great for sliding down – all you need is a strong plastic bag.

Mashobra (2149 metres) is a picnic spot with pleasant forest walks 14 km from Shimla and accessible by car.

Other Activities

In winter there's ice skating on the rink on the north side of the ridge, just down below ANZ Grindlays Bank.

On The Mall, in the area of the Indian Coffee House, there're at least two billiards halls where, for a few rupees, you can have a game on a full-sized table.

Organised Tours

Local tours, which operate more frequently in the summer season, cost Rs 100, last from 10 am to 5 pm, and are booked from the tourist office on The Mall. Longer tours (Rs 110) include the 64-km trip out to the skiing centre of Narkanda where there is a very fine panoramic view of the Himalaya.

The YMCA (☎ 72-375; fax 21-1016) organises treks in Himachal Pradesh for Rs 700 to Rs 800 per person per day. Their four-day Jalori Pass trek is popular with people heading for the Kullu Valley. They will also organise jeep safaris around Kinnaur, Spiti and Lahaul. For groups of two to five persons they charge US$89 for the eight-day trip; advance notice of at least a month is required.

Places to Stay

Accommodation in Shimla is expensive, particularly during the peak seasons of mid-April to mid-July, mid-September to the end of October, and mid-December to early January. During these times it can be difficult to find a room so book in advance. It's not a good time to be here from mid-July to mid-September as it's very wet. Prices given below are for doubles (singles are rare here) during the low season. Rates double during the high season.

Places to Stay – bottom end

The very clean and quiet *YMCA* (☎ 72-375; fax 21-1016) is by far the best value in the high season, when it's virtually full all the time – book in advance. Rooms cost Rs 90/130/200 for a single/double/triple with common bath and hot water, and there's one double with attached bath for Rs 150. There's also a Rs 40 temporary membership charge per person, but breakfast is included. Since the rate is the same throughout the year, this place is less of a bargain in the low season, but still a pleasant place to stay. Filling thali meals are available for Rs 30 for vegetarian dishes, and Rs 45 for non-veg. A late-night coffee shop with satellite TV and an entrance charge of Rs 25 is planned. The views from the terrace are terrific, and activities such as billiards and table tennis are offered. See Organised Tours earlier for the YMCA's trek and jeep safari programme. The path up to the YMCA heads off between the Hotel Mayur and the Ritz Cinema. The touts at the bus and railway stations will spin the usual stories about the YMCA being closed, full, far away, flooded, etc.

The *Hotel Tashkent*, virtually above the Victory Tunnel and about a 10-minute walk from the centre, has rather basic rooms with bath for Rs 80/100. Also on this side of the ridge, and an easy walk from the bus terminal, is the more upmarket *Hotel Vikrant* with rooms from Rs 100 with common bath, Rs 150 with attached bath.

The *Hotel Basant* (☎ 78-381) is a well-run, friendly place and excellent value. Singles with common bath cost Rs 66; singles/doubles with attached bath from Rs 83/110. Hot water comes by the bucket, at Rs 5. This hotel is on Cart Rd, east of the bus terminal and a steep climb down from The Mall. Right in front is the more expensive *Hotel High Way Lodge* (☎ 20-2008), with rooms with attached bath and constant hot water for Rs 200.

Above The Mall, on the north side of the ridge, there are several hotels that have to keep their prices low in the off season because they're quite a trek from the bus terminal. The best of this bunch is the *Hotel Uphar* (☎ 77-670), which is clean and friendly. Rooms with attached bath and constant hot water cost Rs 100/150, and Rs 200 with a view – a good deal in a town where good deals are as scarce as hens' teeth.

The nearby *Hotel Dreamland* (☎ 77-377) is not quite so good, but still cheap for Shimla. Rates here are Rs 95/120 for a room with attached bath and free bucket hot water.

They also have rooms with bath and constant hot water for Rs 150. The *Hotel Ashoka*, across the road, is similarly priced. Next door is the *Hotel Shimla View* (☎ 20-3244) with four rooms with common bath for Rs 75 and one with an attached bath for Rs 125.

On the next road down the slope is the *Hotel Flora* (☎ 78-027). Rather run-down, it's an older place with an amazingly unimaginative design that does nothing to take advantage of the spectacular views. Rooms are from Rs 70/130 with attached bath and hot water.

Places to Stay – middle

The majority of Shimla's hotels are in this range, but they're only good value in the off season.

On the north side of the ridge is Lakkar Bazaar, where there are several good places. Best is the new *Hotel Chanakya* (☎ 21-1232), which is clean and comfortable with rooms from Rs 150 with attached bath. Just a few doors away is the *Hotel Diplomat* (☎ 72-001), which has rooms from Rs 170, or Rs 220 with a view; all rooms have attached bath. The nearby *Hotel White* (☎ 5276) is also good but doesn't give off-season discounts. Rooms are Rs 330/380, all with attached bath and constant hot water.

Also on this same street is the *Hotel Auckland* (☎ 72-621). It's a very pleasant place, and is about as far away from The Mall as it's convenient to be. There are rooms from around Rs 180.

On the south side of the ridge there's a whole group of places at the lower (eastern) end of The Mall, near the passenger lift. The large *Hotel Bridge View* (☎ 78-537) looks attractive and there are good views from here, but the management is far from friendly. Rooms are Rs 300, with attached bath. Above the Bridge View is the much better *Doegar Hotel* (☎ 21-1927) with rooms from Rs 150 with attached bath and satellite TV (black & white only in the cheaper rooms).

The *Hotel Samrat* (☎ 78-572) has a range of rooms, many of them small and with no view. These are the cheapest at Rs 260, while bigger rooms with a view cost Rs 348. At the bottom of the lift from the Samrat is the *Hotel Crystal Palace* (☎ 77-588). It's better value at Rs 230 for rooms at the back, and Rs 260 with a view.

There are two good places across from the Oberoi Clarke's, at the eastern end of The Mall. The *Hotel Shingar* (☎ 72-881) has rooms with attached bath, constant hot water and satellite TV for Rs 250, Rs 300 with a view. It's well run and good value. Nearby is the *Hotel Sangeet* (☎ 20-2506), another good clean place that's excellent value in the off season. Rooms are Rs 175 with bath, constant hot water and black & white TV. The best rooms here cost Rs 300, and also have a view.

The HPTDC *Hotel Holiday Home* (☎ 21-2890) is further along the lower road, about 10 minutes' walk downhill from the centre, and is a friendly, well-run place. There's a bar and coffee shop, and the more expensive rooms have satellite TV. The cost is Rs 400 for an ordinary double, up to Rs 975 for a deluxe room. Rates are the same year-round.

Places to Stay – top end

Without doubt the most pleasant top-end place is the *Woodville Palace Resort* (☎ 72-763), 1.5 km past the Oberoi Clarke's. This ivy-covered building was constructed in 1938 by Raja Rana Sir Bhagat Chandra, the ruler of Jubbal princely state, and is currently owned by his grandson. It's only a small place, but it has a very pleasant garden, and activities such as table tennis and billiards are available. Double rooms are Rs 1120, suites cost Rs 1600, and during the high season prices rise by around 25%.

Back towards the centre of town is the Tudor-style *Oberoi Clarke's Hotel* (☎ 21-2991; fax 21-1321), one of Shimla's earliest hotels. The facilities are what you'd expect for US$52/106, and there's no increase in the high season.

Places to Eat

Curiously, Shimla is not as well endowed with restaurants as other hill stations – it's a long way behind Darjeeling for example. All the better known restaurants are along The Mall.

One of the most popular restaurants is *Baljee's*, and it's usually packed solid in the evenings. It has the standard Indian non-veg menu, uninspiring decor, reasonable food, and very attentive service. Prices are on the high side: main dishes are Rs 50 to Rs 70. Upstairs is an associated restaurant known as *Fascination*, similarly priced and just as popular.

Further down The Mall, the *Alfa Restaurant* also has the standard non-veg menu, and it's as pricey as Baljee's. Just beyond the Alfa is a branch of the *Indian Coffee House* with south Indian food and snacks at reasonable prices. The milk coffee here is excellent. Nearby is *The Devicos*, a clean new place that does good fast food and also has a bar.

The state tourism department has two restaurants at the main square on the ridge, close to the tourist office. The ritzier *Ashiana Restaurant* is supposed to be a cut above the *Goofa* below it. Prices are much the same in both restaurants.

Just below The Mall is the *Park Cafe*. This place does the best pizzas in Shimla – and makes them with real mozzarella cheese. Their special pizza costs Rs 40, plain cheese and tomato is Rs 22. They also do an excellent cappuccino, good banana yoghurt, shakes and fresh fruit juice. There's quite a good tape selection, too.

The best place for non-veg tandoori dishes is the *Shere-e-Punjab*, on Lower Mall Rd. Cheaper than Baljee's, it's very popular with local people.

There are two branches of *Tripti's*, a small south Indian vegetarian restaurant and takeaway in Lakkar Bazaar, and a larger veg and non-veg restaurant near Oberoi Clarke's. Neither is cheap but the quality of the food is very good and both places are well run. The main restaurant is currently being rebuilt but should reopen soon.

As you move down into the bazaar area the prices also start to descend. Right at the bottom end of the scale are a couple of basic, one-person Chinese eating places, serving good food. Best is the *Chung Fa Chinese*

Food Shop, on Middle Bazaar, just down the steps, behind 62 The Mall. It's run by a Cantonese-speaking Bengali. The other place is *Kwon Tung Aunty's Chinese Food Shop* at 44/31 Middle Bazaar. To find it take the steps down next to Baljee's on The Mall, and it's signposted along the first lane to the right.

Between these two Chinese places is the *Malook Restaurant*, run by a very friendly Sikh. It's a bit more expensive and offers Chinese and Tibetan dishes.

For a splurge, the *Oberoi Clarke's* is recommended. There's a fixed-menu lunch and dinner (Rs 162), and a buffet for the same price in the season. A carafe of Australian red wine costs Rs 300.

Finally, there are several good bakeries along The Mall and Lower Mall Rd. *Baljee's* has a bakery counter at the front. *Krishna Bakers*, along the eastern end of The Mall, does good chicken or vegie burgers, cakes and pastries.

Things to Buy
Shimla's not a great place for souvenirs although there are lots of shops flogging things to the tourists, mainly woodcarvings and shawls. One place worth checking out is the Tibetan Refugee Shop, between the lift and Oberoi Clarke's. As well as weavings, bags and clothes they have a good selection of earrings and other jewellery.

Getting There & Away
Air On Tuesday and Thursday Jagson Airlines flies Delhi-Shimla-Kullu-Gaggal and return. Shimla to Delhi is US$82, Shimla to Kullu costs US$49. Archana and KCV fly between Shimla and Delhi on Monday, Wednesday and Friday.

Bus All deluxe buses should be booked from the tourist office in The Mall.

A variety of buses run between Shimla and Delhi (Rs 204 in a deluxe bus, 10 hours). There are frequent departures from Chandigarh (Rs 43/86 ordinary/deluxe, five hours).

There are buses north from Shimla to

other hill stations in Himachal Pradesh such as Dharamsala or the Kullu Valley. From Shimla to Manali costs Rs 115/200 ordinary/deluxe and takes 11 hours. To Dharamsala costs Rs 88 and takes 10 hours. To Mandi it's about six hours for Rs 60. Dehra Dun is a weary nine-hour trip for Rs 88/114 in ordinary/semideluxe.

Train The railway reservation office at the station has quotas on all the trains from both Shimla and the broad-gauge line from Kalka.

The journey to Shimla by rail involves a change from broad gauge to narrow gauge at Kalka, a little north of Chandigarh. The narrow-gauge trip to Shimla takes nearly six hours. It is great fun as the little train winds its way around the mountains, although in summer it can get uncomfortably hot and crowded. If you're travelling from Shimla to Chandigarh, you can catch the train for the three-hour journey to Solan, than take a bus to Chandigarh from there.

There are three classes – 2nd class uses old coaches with wooden seats; chair car is modern and comfortable; but 1st class is definitely the way to travel this line, if you can afford it. By train all the way from Delhi it's 364 km at a cost of Rs 82/303 in 2nd/1st class. If you want to do the whole trip by train in daylight, the *Himalayan Queen* leaves New Delhi at 6.10 am, and (with connections) you arrive in Shimla at 5.05 pm. In the opposite direction the 10.15 am departure from Shimla also connects with the *Himalayan Queen*, which arrives back in New Delhi at 9.40 pm.

Taxi The taxi union has 'set' fares to the following places: the airport (Rs 300), Kalka (Rs 550), Chandigarh (Rs 750), Kullu (Rs 1500) and Delhi (Rs 2200). It's always worth trying to bargain these prices down a bit.

Getting Around
Local bus services operate from the Cart Rd bus stand on the north side of the ridge. It's just below the ice-skating rink, on the path which leads off The Mall from beside ANZ Grindlays Bank.

Half a km to the east of the main bus stand, a two-part 'tourist lift' takes you up to The Mall for Rs 2. It saves a long and tedious climb and it's the only lift I've ever seen with a fire to keep the operator warm!

AROUND SHIMLA

Craignano

At 2279 metres and 16 km from Shimla, Craignano, with its hilltop *Municipal Rest House*, is only three km from Mashobra. Contact the Water Works Engineer in Shimla (☎ 72-815) for bookings.

Chail

This was once the summer capital of the princely state of Patalia. Today the old palace is a luxurious hotel. Chail is 45 km by bus from Shimla via Kufri, or you can reach it via Kandaghat on the Shimla to Kalka road or narrow-gauge railway line.

Chail, at an altitude of 2250 metres, is built on three hills, one of which is topped by the Chail Palace, and one by the ancient Sikh temple. Chail also boasts a temple of quite another religion – cricket. Here you will find the highest cricket pitch in the world!

In the *Chail Palace Hotel* (☎ (01792) 8337) there are rooms from Rs 500 but the 'maharaja' and 'maharani' suites are Rs 2000 and Rs 2375. The *Himneel Hotel* charges Rs 400, and there are also a number of local hotels.

Solan

This dreary town is between Kalka and Shimla, on both the railway line and the road. It's best known as the home of Golden Eagle beer; the Mohan Meakin brewery is about four km from town along the road to Shimla, and tours can be arranged on request.

Kasauli

This pleasant little hill station at 1927 metres is only a short distance north of Kalka. It's an interesting 15-km trek from Kalka to Kasauli, or you can get there from Dharampur, which is on the narrow-gauge railway.

Only four km from Kasauli is **Monkey Point**, a picnic spot and lookout with a very fine view over the plains to the south and to the mountains in the north. **Sabathu**, 38 km from Kasauli, has a 19th-century Gurkha-built fortress.

Places to Stay & Eat There is a *PWD Rest House* with rooms for Rs 40, and a number of private guest houses such as the *Alasia, Morris* and *Kalyan* with doubles from Rs 150 to Rs 250 in the off season. HPTDC's *Hotel Ros Common* (☎ 01793) 2005) has rooms from Rs 300 to Rs 750. In Dharampur the simple *Mazdoor Dhaba* restaurant near the station has good (and cheap) vegetarian meals and a dormitory upstairs.

Kalka

The narrow-gauge railway line from Kalka to Shimla was built between 1903 and 1904. Although going by road is cheaper and quicker, the train trip is more fun. Fares for 2nd/chair car/1st class are Rs 36/127/184.

Five km south-west of Kalka, on the Chandigarh road, are the attractive Yadavindra Gardens in Pinjore (see the Punjab & Haryana chapter).

Naldera

At 2044 metres, Naldera is 23 km from Shimla and has a golf course (supposedly the oldest in the country) and cafeteria. There's cheap accommodation at the *Golf Club* (under Rs 100) and the *Hotel Golf Glade* (doubles for Rs 400).

Chabba

This *Rest House*, 35 km from Shimla, is a pleasant five-km walk from Basantpur, on the road to Tattapani. For reservations contact the Electricity Engineer in Shimla.

Tattapani

There's a direct bus (Rs 15) to these popular sulphur hot springs (655 metres), 51 km from Shimla. Doubles in the small *Tourist Bungalow* are Rs 100 to Rs 200; dorm beds are Rs 30.

Fagu

Fagu, at 2510 metres, has very fine views. It's 22 km from Shimla, and receives a lot of snow in winter. This town also has a potato research centre (!). The *Hotel Peach Blossom* (☎ Shimla 28-5522) has doubles from Rs 275.

Narkanda

At 3143 metres, 64 km from Shimla, this is a popular spot for viewing the Himalaya, particularly from the 3300-metre Hattu peak. Narkanda has recently been developed as a skiing centre. The season lasts from late December to early March, there's a 600-metre slope and a 110-metre ski lift. Ski and boot hire costs around Rs 150 for a full day. Himachal Tourism runs ski courses here from 10 January each year.

From Narkanda you can make trips to **Bagi** and **Khadrala**, which are on the road leading to the Tibetan border. Alternatively, you can visit the apple-growing area at **Thanedhar** or continue to the Kullu Valley via Luhri. There are *Rest Houses* in Bagi, Khadrala and Thanedhar.

Places to Stay The HPTDC *Hotel Himview* (☎ 8430) has doubles from Rs 200 and, at the High Altitude Trekking-cum-Skiing Centre, dorm beds for Rs 30. Reservations are made through the tourist office in Shimla. There's also a *PWD Rest House*, with rooms for under Rs 100.

Rohru

Situated 129 km from Shimla, this is the site for the annual Rohru Fair which takes place over two days in April. The temple of Devta Shikri is the centre for this colourful fair. The Pabar River, which runs through Rohru, is noted for its trout; there's a trout hatchery 13 km upstream at **Chirgaon**.

Haktoti, a little before Rohru, has an interesting ancient Hindu temple dedicated to the goddess Durga. The temple contains a metre-high image of the eight-armed goddess, made of copper and bronze.

There's a *PWD Rest House* in Rohru, a small *Forest Rest House* (booked in Rohru)

at Chirgaon and *log cabins* (booked through the tourist office in Shimla) at **Seema**, two km upstream towards Chirgaon.

SOUTH HIMACHAL
Paonta Sahib

Situated on the Yamuna River, on the border with Uttar Pradesh, Paonta Sahib is a transit point for travellers coming from the hill stations of northern Uttar Pradesh.

Paonta Sahib is linked with Gobind Singh, the 10th Sikh guru who lived here. At **Bhangani**, 23 km away, he achieved a great military victory when his forces defeated the combined might of 22 hill-country kingdoms. His weapons are displayed in the town and his gurdwara still overlooks the river.

HPTDC's *Hotel Yamuna* (☎ 2341) has doubles from Rs 200. There are also local hotels.

By the lake at **Renuka**, 25 km north-west of Paonta Sahib, a major Hindu fair and festival is held each November beside Parshuram Tal. There's a small zoo and a wildlife sanctuary with deer and many water birds.

Nahan

At 932 metres, Nahan is in the Siwalik Hills, where the climb to the Himalayan heights commences. There are a number of interesting walks around the town, including the trek to **Choordhar** (3647 metres) from where there are fine views of the plains to the south and the Sutlej River.

Saketi, 14 km south of Nahan, has a fossil park with life-sized fibreglass models of prehistoric animals whose fossilised skeletons were unearthed here.

There's a *PWD Rest House* in Nahan, and a number of local hotels.

MANDI

Population: 25,000
Telephone Area Code: 01905

Formerly an important junction on the salt route to Tibet, Mandi is the gateway to the Kullu Valley. From here you climb up the narrow, spectacular gorge of the Beas River and emerge from this grey and barren stretch into the green and inviting Kullu Valley. At an altitude of only 760 metres, temperatures are higher here and Mandi mainly serves as a travel crossroads as its name, which means 'market', might suggest.

Mandi's biggest attraction is the **Sivarati Festival**, held in February/March. This is one of the most interesting festivals in Himachal Pradesh. It lasts for a week and deities from all over Mandi district are brought here. Large numbers of people have *darshan* (viewing of a deity) at the Bhutnath Temple.

Places to Stay & Eat

A path behind the bus stand leads up to the HPTDC *Hotel Mandav* (☎ 22-123), across the river from the main part of the town. In the old annexe there are rooms for Rs 150/200 with attached bath and constant hot water. There are smarter doubles in the main building from Rs 350 with satellite TV. The restaurant here is not bad.

On the other side of the river there are a number of cheap hotels. About the best of them is the *Hotel Standard*, on the main square, which charges Rs 65 for a double with attached bath.

Across the square is the rambling *Raj Mahal* (☎ 22-401), a strange old place with a shrine in the garden; it has plenty of atmosphere if nothing else. Rooms start at Rs 97/125 with bath, or Rs 200/275 for larger rooms. The Copacabana Bar here is a popular place, and very good food is served in the open-air restaurant.

The top hotel in town is the new *Hotel Mayfair* (☎ 22-570) with doubles from Rs 330 with TV, attached bath and constant hot water. It's also on the main square, and there's a rooftop restaurant.

Getting There & Away

Mandi is 202 km north of Chandigarh and 110 km south of Manali. Dharamsala is 150 km to the north-west on the road to Pathankot.

There are five buses to Dharamsala daily (six hours, Rs 50), to Kullu (three hours) and Manali (five hours) they leave hourly, and there are also departures to Shimla and Pathankot.

REWALSAR LAKE

The Rewalsar Lake, a pilgrimage centre for Hindus, Buddhists and Sikhs, is high up in the hills 24 km south-east of Mandi. There is a mountain cave-refuge near here. The small lake is revered by Tibetan Buddhists and every year, shortly after the New Year (sometime in March), many make a pilgrimage here, especially those from Dharamsala.

The festival, known as **Tso-Pema**, is particularly important in the Year of the Monkey, which falls every 12 years. At this time there are literally thousands of people here, and the Dalai Lama gives *puja* (prayers) in the monastery, and then does a circuit around the lake. It's a very colourful event, and will next be held in 2004.

The HPTDC *Tourist Inn* has dorm beds for Rs 45, doubles with common bath for Rs 150 and doubles with attached bath for Rs 200 to Rs 300. There are also a number of local hotels, such as the *Lomush, Lake View* and *Shimla*. There are buses every half hour from Mandi (Rs 8, one hour).

KANGRA VALLEY

The beautiful Kangra Valley starts near Mandi, runs north, then bends west and extends to Shahpur near Pathankot. To the north the valley is flanked by the Dhauladhar mountain range, to the side of which Dharamsala clings. There are a number of places of interest along the valley, including the popular hill station of Dharamsala.

The main Pathankot to Mandi road runs through the Kangra Valley and there is a narrow-gauge railway line from Pathankot as far as Jogindarnagar. The Kangra school of painting developed in this valley.

Baijnath

Only 16 km from Palampur, the small town of Baijnath is an important pilgrimage place due to its very old Siva temple. The temple is said to date from 804 AD. There is a *PWD Rest House* in Baijnath.

Palampur

A pleasant little town surrounded by tea plantations, Palampur is 35 km from

Dharamsala and stands at 1260 metres. The main road runs right through Palampur and there are some pleasant walks around the town. A four-day trek takes you from Palampur to Holi via the Waru Pass.

Places to Stay & Eat The HPTDC *Hotel T-Bud* is about a km from the bus stand and has rooms from Rs 400. Meals are available. For something cheaper try the *Silver Oaks Motel*, 2.5 km from the bus stand, which has great views; or the more basic *Hotel Sawney*, near the bus stand.

The *Joy Restaurant*, in the main bazaar, serves good cheap meals. The HPTDC *Neugal Cafe* is 1.5 km from the Hotel T-Bud.

Kangra

There is little to see in this ancient town, 18 km almost directly south of Dharamsala, but at one time it was a place of considerable importance. The famous temple of Bajreshwari Devi was of such legendary wealth that every invader worth their salt took time to sack it. Mahmud of Ghazni carted off a fabulous fortune in gold, silver and jewels in 1009. In 1360 it was plundered once again by Tughlaq but it was still able to recover and, in Jehangir's reign, was paved in plates of pure silver.

The disastrous earthquake which shook the valley in 1905 destroyed the temple, which has since been rebuilt. Kangra also has a ruined fort on a ridge overlooking the Baner and Manjhi rivers. It too was sacked by Mahmud, captured by Jehangir in 1620 and severely damaged in the 1905 quake.

Kangra has several basic places to stay along the road that runs from the bus stand to the main part of the town, and a *PWD Rest House*.

Jawalamukhi

In the Beas Valley, 34 km south of Kangra, the temple of Jawalamukhi is famous for its eternally burning flame. It's the most popular pilgrimage site in Himachal Pradesh.

The HPTDC *Hotel Jawalaji* (☎ 2281) has doubles from Rs 300 up to Rs 600 with air-con; and there's a Rs 45 dorm. There's also a *PWD Rest House*. **Nadaun**, south of

Jawalamukhi on the Beas River, has another *Rest House*.

Masrur

Three km from Haripur, and about 15 km south-west of Kangra, Masrur has 15 richly carved rock-cut temples in the Indo-Aryan style. They are partly ruined but still show their relationship to the better known and much larger temples at Ellora in Maharashtra.

Nurpur

Only 24 km from Pathankot on the Mandi to Pathankot road, this town was named by Jehangir, after his wife, Nurjahan. Nurpur Fort is now in ruins but still has some finely carved reliefs. A ruined Krishna Temple, also finely carved, stands within the fort. Nurpur has a *PWD Rest House*.

DHARAMSALA

Population: 18,500
Telephone Area Code: 01892

Following the Chinese invasion of Tibet, it was to Dharamsala that the Dalai Lama and his followers fled, and this hill station is now best known as the seat of Tibet's government-in-exile and the temporary home of His Holiness. It's a popular destination for travellers, particularly in March, when the Dalai Lama gives public lectures. Throughout his more than 30 years of exile, for religious as well as practical reasons, the Dalai Lama has worked for a peaceful settlement with China, which is in line with his pacifist approach to all personal and political conflicts in the world. In 1989, he was awarded the Nobel Peace Prize, presented to him not only for his spiritual activities but for his struggle for the liberation of Tibet.

The sad truth about the Tibetan problem is that the world seems to be less interested now than it was in the days when the planet was threatened by the spectre of communism. In fact, if India had not been engaged in a war with China when the Tibetan refugees began pouring into the country, it's debatable whether they would have allowed these people to settle here.

For the serious student of Tibetan culture there's the monastery up at McLeod Ganj and the school of Tibetan studies and its library, one of the best in the world for studying Tibet and its culture, about midway between McLeod Ganj and the lower town.

For the not-so-serious, McLeod Ganj is a small hippie centre with lots of Tibetan-run hotels and restaurants, all the menu favourites, low prices, crowds of Western travellers – almost another Kathmandu in fact. McLeod Ganj is full of colour and energy: there's a small temple with a giant prayer wheel in the middle of the main street; yappy little Tibetan terriers scoot around everywhere; and strings of multicoloured Tibetan prayer flags wave in the breeze.

Orientation
The town is actually in two completely separate parts. Dharamsala is the lower section; a three-km walk (10 km by road) away and 500 metres above it is the higher settlement, McLeod Ganj, which the Tibetans have made their home.

Information
Tourist Office The tourist office (☎ 23-107) is in the lower town close to the bus stand and the Dhauladhar Hotel. Jagson Airlines (☎ 4328) is below the tourist office. In the main street of McLeod Ganj are a couple of travel agents who can arrange all sorts of tickets.

Money For moneychanging there are branches of the State Bank of India in both McLeod Ganj and Dharamsala.

Tibetan Welfare Office Opposite the Koko Nor Hotel in McLeod Ganj, this office appreciates gifts of clothes and blankets for newly arrived refugees.

Bookshops In McLeod Ganj, the Tibetan Charitable Trust has a small handicraft shop and bookshop. It's a good place for books about Tibetan Buddhism. The Tibetan Bookshop & Information Centre is on the same street and has some disturbing photos of what the Chinese are up to in Lhasa. For a bit of lighter reading material, try the Bookworm shop near the State Bank of India.

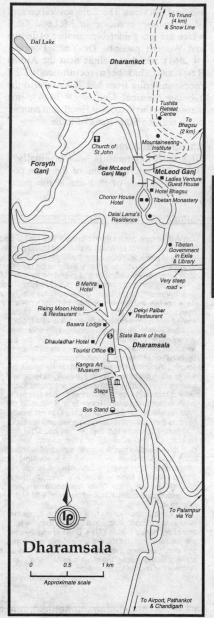

Dharamsala

HIMACHAL PRADESH

Medical Services There are several centres of alternative medicine in McLeod Ganj which get a considerable number of Indian and Western patients. Dr Yeshi Dhonder (☎ 2461), who has a clinic near the Aroma Restaurant, has been recommended by people suffering from MS. There's also the Tibetan Medical Centre (☎ 2484), just across from the Koko Nor Hotel; and another clinic near the State Bank of India.

Church of St John
Of course Dharamsala was originally a British hill resort and one of the most poignant memorials of that era is the pretty Church of St John in the Wilderness. It is only a short distance below McLeod Ganj and has beautiful stained-glass windows. Here Lord Elgin, Viceroy of India, was buried in 1863.

Kangra Art Museum
This museum is in Dharamsala, down the road from the tourist office. It houses miniature paintings from the famous Kangra school of art, which flourished in the Kangra Valley in the 17th century. It's open Tuesday to Saturday from 10 am to 5 pm.

Meditation Courses
His Holiness the Dalai Lama gives teachings

An Audience with His Holiness the Dalai Lama

The Dalai Lama is so much in demand that a private audience at his residence in Dharamsala is now very difficult to arrange. You can try, however, by contacting his private office in McLeod Ganj at least four months in advance. You're much more likely to be able to meet him face to face by attending a public audience. Contact his private office to find out when the next public audience is being held.

Meeting this 14th incarnation of Chenresig, Tibetan Buddhism's deity of Universal Compassion, is no ordinary event. Not so much because of his title, nor even because of the high degree of reverence in which he is held by the Tibetan people; but more because of how it feels to be in his company. As an American friend put it: 'When you look at him, he is the size of a normal human being; but when you look away; you realise that his presence is filling the whole room'.

After waiting, strangely nervous, in the anteroom, we were ushered into his reception room for our audience with His Holiness, which seemed to speed by in a flash. However, several strong impressions remain, including the way in which he gives his whole attention to questions. He really listens, and pauses before replying, to give consideration to the subject matter. He responds rather than reacts to the issue under discussion. There is a wisdom in his thinking which comes through clearly in his words, filled as they are with common sense and realism.

I remember his direct and friendly gaze, his firm handshake, and a sense of compassion almost palpable. He also has a superb sense of humour, often remarked upon by those who meet him. He laughs often and easily – and what a laugh! He throws back his head to release a deep, thorough chuckle which rises from his abdomen and expresses pure mirth. It is kind laughter, and highly infectious.

As our audience came to a close, he accompanied us to the door. With each of us in turn, he took one of our hands in both of his. Bowing slightly over the joined hands, he looked up into our faces and beamed. Following this farewell, we seemed to be walking inches above the streets of McLeod Ganj. And we just couldn't stop smiling.

Vyvyan Cayley

His Holiness the Dalai Lama, leader of the Tibetan people.

every year for 10 days following the Tibetan New Year in March, and this is obviously a popular time to be in Dharamsala. As there are so many Westerners in town at this time, it's also a busy time for meditation courses. At the library in McLeod Ganj they have courses for beginners, as well as Tibetan language courses; the teachers are all Tibetans.

The Tushita Retreat Centre (☎ 4366; fax 23-374) has facilities for a retreat, and also has Buddhism courses. The monks here are either Tibetan or Western. Even if you don't stay at the centre it is possible to attend some of the courses. Course fees are Rs 80 per day, plus Rs 75 for meals. Live-in accommodation is available for Rs 33 in a dorm, or Rs 55/90 with common bathroom and Rs 65 for a single with attached bathroom. Couples are assigned separate rooms.

There are also many courses offered by individual monks who live in monasteries.

Walks

There are many fine walks and even finer views around Dharamsala. The sheer rock wall of Dhauladhar rises behind McLeod Ganj and seems just an arm's length away from the lower road.

Interesting walks from McLeod Ganj include the two-km stroll to **Bhagsu** where there is an old temple, a spring, slate quarries and a small waterfall. It's a popular picnic spot and you can continue on beyond here on the ascent to the snow line. **Dal Lake** is a bit brown and dull; it's about three km from McLeod Ganj, just beyond the Tibetan Children's Village School. A similar distance from McLeod Ganj takes you to the popular picnic spot at **Dharamkot** where you'll also enjoy a very fine view.

An eight-km trek from McLeod Ganj will bring you to **Triund** (2827 metres) at the foot of Dhauladhar. It's another five km to the snow line at **Ilaqa**. There is a *Forest Rest House* here for overnight accommodation.

The Mountaineering Institute, half a km north of McLeod Ganj, runs eight to 10-day high-altitude treks from April to December. A minimum of 10 people is required, and the cost is Rs 1500 to Rs 2000 per person all-inclusive. Rock-climbing training is also available on application. If you want to organise your own trek, guides and porters can be hired from the institute, as can tents and sleeping bags. A useful guide book, *Treks & Passes of Dhauladhar & Pir Panjal*, is also for sale.

Places to Stay

Dharamsala Dharamsala has two accommodation areas – the lower part of town and McLeod Ganj, the upper part. The accommodation in the lower part is generally poor, and there's little reason to stay there.

The best of the cheapies is the *Basera Lodge*, by the entrance to the Dhauladhar Hotel. It's clean and airy with doubles with attached bath for Rs 75. There's also the extremely laid-back and rather basic *Rising Moon Hotel & Restaurant* with dorm beds and rooms for around Rs 50, some with bathroom.

Dharamsala's only attempt at a deluxe hotel is the HPTDC *Dhauladhar Hotel* (☎ 2107) with rooms from Rs 337/400. There's a restaurant and a pleasant sun terrace – ideal for sipping a beer at sunset while you look out over the plains below.

McLeod Ganj Most Western visitors stay 500 metres (and 10 km by road) above the main part of town at McLeod Ganj. Here the Tibetan community have set up a whole series of hotels and restaurants. McLeod Ganj is very popular and many places are often full, especially in March.

In the north of the settlement is a group of three hotels with good views. At the top of a long flight of stairs is the *Paljor Gakyil Guest House* (☎ 22-571, but no reservations are possible). This immaculate place is run by a friendly Tibetan couple who have lived in Europe for some years and speak French, German and English. The rooms are good value at Rs 110 for a double with bath, or Rs 220 with carpet, constant hot water and a wonderful view. They also have a few dorm beds for Rs 24.

Nearby is the *Kalsang Guest House* (☎ 22-609), a larger place with rooms with common bath for Rs 45/75, and doubles with

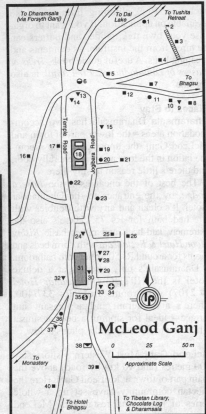

McLeod Ganj

attached bath and hot water from Rs 135 to Rs 250. Down by the road is the small, similarly priced *Seven Hills Lodge* (☎ 22-580).

There are several hotels along the Bhagsu road which runs east from the bus stop. The long-running *Hotel Tibet* (☎ 22-587), once a popular cheapie, has now been spruced up and given a major price hike. Comfortable rooms with attached bath and TV cost Rs 350 to Rs 500. Across the road is the *Lhasa Guest House*, which has rooms with common bath for Rs 65, and for Rs 175 with attached bath.

Further along the Bhagsu road, the *Koko Nor Hotel* has rooms for Rs 50 to Rs 100.

The *Green Hotel* is a popular cheapie and has rooms for Rs 35/60 with common bath, and Rs 100 with attached bath. On Jogibara Rd in the heart of town there's quite a few more places, including the *Shangrila Guest House* and the very basic *Hotel Snow Palace*.

Further along, and down a narrow lane off

to the left, are two very popular guest houses. The *Drepung Loseling Guest House* (☎ 23-187) is owned and run by the Drepung Monastery in Karnataka. The rooms are some of the best in Dharamsala, all are doubles with attached bath, and they cost Rs 125 with cold water, Rs 165 with hot water, and Rs 220 for the best rooms with a view. There's also a dorm for Rs 25.

Nearby is another excellent choice, the *Tibetan Ashoka Guest House* (☎ 22-763). The rooms are very clean and cost Rs 45/55 with common bath, and Rs 165 to Rs 205 for a double with attached bath. Since it's on the edge of the settlement there are pleasant views over the fields.

On Temple Rd the *Kailash Hotel* is very basic, while the *Om Hotel* on the next level down is so popular it often has a waiting list during peak times, although it's hard to see exactly why. Rooms here cost Rs 35/70 with common bath.

Ladies Venture Guest House is a smart new place a short walk along the road to the library. Spotlessly clean and with very friendly management, it has singles/doubles for Rs 125/175 with bath shared between two rooms, and rooms with attached bath for Rs 150/250. On the way to this place is the cheaper *Kalsang Tsomo International Guest House*, also run by very friendly people, and with rooms from Rs 90 with common bath, Rs 150 with attached bath.

In the southern part of town, precariously balanced on a spur which juts out towards the plains, are three ugly upmarket hotels. The swanky *Surya Resorts* charges Rs 890/1080, the *Hotel Natraj* (☎ 22-529) has rooms from Rs 400, and the *Hotel Him Queen* is similarly priced. In the same area is the unremarkable HPTDC *Hotel Bhagsu* (☎ 3191) with rooms from Rs 400 to Rs 1200.

Better top-end options include *Chonor House* (☎ 22-006; fax 22-010), near the monastery and south of McLeod Ganj. There are five doubles with attached bath for Rs 800, and six singles with bath shared between two rooms for Rs 600. Run by the Tibetan Department of Religion & Culture,

it's furnished by craftspeople from Norbu Linka, the new Japanese-sponsored monastery.

About one km north of the bus stand, along the road towards Dal Lake, is *Glenmore Cottages* (☎ 4410; fax 23-374), with comfortable accommodation in five peacefully located cottages from US$35/45.

Elsewhere It's possible to stay in some of the other villages around Dharamsala. Bhagsu is a 20-minute walk from McLeod Ganj bus stand and there are several small hotels there. *Sunil Lodge* charges just Rs 30/45 for a room with common bath; there are also lodges with rooms with attached bath and hot water.

An even more peaceful alternative is the village of Dharamkot, a 50-minute walk from McLeod Ganj. Small guest houses here offer accommodation with and without attached bath for Rs 30 to Rs 100 per day.

Places to Eat

For those heartily sick of dhal and rice, the restaurants in McLeod Ganj offer a wide range of Tibetan/Chinese dishes plus Western travellers' favourites such as banana pancakes. Overall, food here is a pleasant change from the Indian norm.

For Tibetan food, the rooftop *Tsongkha Restaurant*, run by recent arrivals from Tibet, is excellent. It's all vegetarian, and their tofu vegetarian dishes are particularly recommended (rice, vegetables and fried tofu costs Rs 27), and they also do good momos. Service is a little erratic, though.

Another good place is the small *Yak Restaurant*, run by a charming family. Large batches of delicious momos are freshly made each morning so you don't have to wait long to get served. Vegetarian or mutton momos in soup cost Rs 14.

Patronised by Richard Gere when he's in town, the *Cafe Shambala* does the best approximations of Western dishes. It's best known for its 'farmer's breakfast' (Rs 18), a filling mixture of eggs, potato and vegetable. There are eight varieties of pancakes, from apple to cheese.

There's basic Tibetan fare at the *Gakyi Restaurant*, better known for its muesli (Rs 25). In this same area are the *Snowland, Tibet Memory* and *Aroma*. Tibet Memory shows recently released videos (Rs 5) each evening.

Right on the corner by the bus stop is the *McLLo Restaurant*. This place is definitely a cut above the average but it's not cheap. The atmosphere and the views are good and the limited menu features Western snacks and a few Indian dishes. The best place for Indian food, however, is the *Ashoka Restaurant*, although service is very slow here.

Also in this area is the *Shangri La*, which apart from the usual Chinese and Tibetan dishes, has superb banana cake, lemon curd cake and apple pie. The *Om Hotel* is another popular place with a nice sun terrace.

The best cakes in McLeod Ganj come from *Chocolate Log*, beside the road to the library. As well as chocolate cake and rum balls, they also do excellent breakfasts and quiches for lunch. They're closed in the evenings and on Mondays.

Down in Dharamsala the *Dhauladhar Hotel* has a good restaurant; food is also available at the *Rising Moon Hotel* and there are numerous cheap dhabas.

Entertainment

The three most popular places for a drink are *McLLo Restaurant*, *Friend's Corner* next door, and the dingy bar at the *Hotel Tibet*.

Getting There & Away

Air On Tuesday and Thursday, Jagson Airlines flies to Delhi (US$100) and Kullu (US$49) from Kangra Airport at Gaggal, 15 km from Dharamsala.

Bus The main bus stand is in Dharamsala, about 300 metres below the tourist office. All long-distance buses leave from here; most of the buses from McLeod Ganj only ferry passengers to the Dharamsala bus stand. The first bus down to Dharamsala from McLeod Ganj is at 4 am.

You can also make train reservations at the railway booking office in the bus stand,

although they have a quota of only two reservations per day per train.

There are about four buses a day to Shimla and Delhi, and just one or two to other destinations. Approximate distances, journey times and fares on ordinary buses from Dharamsala are:

Destination	Distance	Time (hrs)	Fare
Manali	253 km	12½	Rs 114
Kullu	214 km	10	Rs 95
Shimla	317 km	10	Rs 88
Chandigarh	248 km	9	Rs 75
Pathankot	90 km	3½	Rs 35
Delhi	526 km	13	Rs 125

Getting Around

It's about 10 km from the lower part to McLeod Ganj – a 45-minute ride for Rs 4. There are buses every hour, or plenty of Maruti van-taxis which do the trip for Rs 60. Walking down via the library takes about 40 minutes.

TREKS FROM DHARAMSALA

The trek over the Indrahar Pass is one of many that can be completed over the Dhauladhar range. However no trek over the Dhauladhar is easy and this one is no exception. Compared to the treks in Kashmir or in the nearby Kullu Valley this trek is demanding and a local guide or porters should be hired from McLeod Ganj. Allow up to Rs 200 per day.

The trek over the Indrahar Pass goes from McLeod Ganj to **Triund** (three to four hours) where there is a *Rest House*. From Triund it is a further stage to Lahesh Cave (four to five hours) and the base of the pass. There is demanding ascent over boulders to the **Indrahar Pass** (4350 metres) from where there are uninterrupted views towards the Indian plains. There follows a steep descent to the camp at Chatru Parao (six to seven hours) before continuing to the village of Kuarsi (five to six hours). It is a further stage to Machhetar (six hours) and a five-hour bus ride to Chamba.

DALHOUSIE

Population: 9800
Telephone Area Code: 018982

Sprawling over and around five hills at around 2000 metres, Dalhousie was, in the British era, a sort of 'second string' hill station, mainly used by people who lived in Lahore. It was a place frequented by those who could not aspire to Shimla. The town was founded by Lord Dalhousie, and has some pleasant walks.

Orientation & Information

Dalhousie is very spread out; most of the

shops are clustered around Gandhi Chowk, while the 'town' – if Dalhousie can be called such a thing – is crowded down the hillside close to Subhash Chowk, a steep uphill climb from the bus stand. The houses almost rest on top of one another.

The tourist office (☎ 2136) is on the top floor of the building by the bus stand. You can change money at the Punjab National Bank by the Aroma-n-Claire Hotel.

Things to See & Do

Today Dalhousie has a busy population of

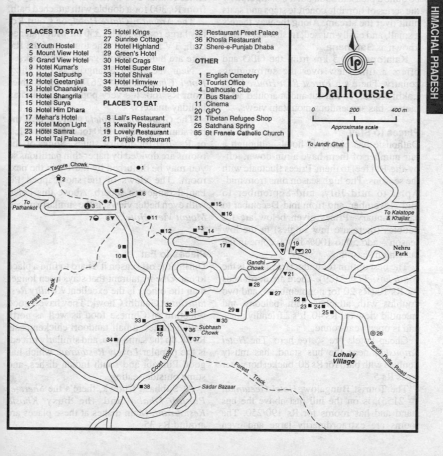

Tibetan refugees – if you take the footpath from Subhash Chowk to Gandhi (GPO) Chowk, you'll pass brightly painted **low-relief pictures** the Tibetans have carved into the rocks. Near Gandhi Chowk there's a good Tibetan refugee handicrafts shop with carpets featuring unusual rabbit and elephant designs.

With its dense forest, old British houses and colourful Tibetans, Dalhousie can be a good place to spend some time, although very few travellers pass through here. About two km from Gandhi Chowk along Ajit Singh Rd, **Panch Pulla** (Five Bridges) could be quite a pleasant spot, but it's disfigured by the series of horrible concrete steps and seats built over the stream. Along the way there's a small, and easily missed, freshwater spring known as **Satdhana**.

Kalatope is 8.5 km from the GPO and offers a fine view over the surrounding country. There's a *Forest Rest House* here. **Lakhi Mandi**, 15 km out and at around 3000 metres, has stupendous mountain views.

Places to Stay

Dalhousie has plenty of hotels, although a fair number of them have a run-down, left-by-the-Raj feel to them. Prices fluctuate with the seasons. The high season runs from mid-April to mid-July, mid-September to mid-November, and from mid-December to early January. Prices given below are for doubles (there are few singles) in the low season – add 50 to 100% if you come in the busy high season.

The best option for budget travellers is the *youth hostel* (☎ 2189). There are dorm beds for Rs 10 (Rs 20 for nonmembers), and two doubles with attached bath, balcony and splendid view for Rs 40. It's a friendly place and is open year-round.

Cheap hotels are scarce here. The *Hotel Satpushp*, near the bus stand, has musty doubles with bath for Rs 80; bucket hot water costs Rs 5.

The Tourist Bungalow, *Hotel Geetanjali* (☎ 2155), is on the hill just above the bus stand and has rooms for Rs 190/250. The rooms are extraordinarily large and even

contain separate living rooms. It's a friendly place and there are good views.

The *Hotel Shivali* (☎ 2229), by Subhash Chowk, has rooms with attached bath, constant hot water, TV and even a small kitchen area, for Rs 150. Other places in this price range are along Panch Pulla Rd and include the *Hotel Moon Light* (☎ 5239) and *Hotel Kings* (☎ 2450).

The *Hotel Shangrila* (☎ 2314) is an old house which has been converted. It is within walking distance of Gandhi Chowk and has very good views. Doubles cost Rs 240, all with TV and hot water. Near the bus stand, *Hotel Kumar's* is a modern place charging from Rs 300 for a double with attached bath.

The *Aroma-n-Claire Hotel*, on Court Rd, has large rooms for Rs 350 all with attached bath, TV and fridge. The touches of the Raj here are hidden behind garish paintwork.

Near the Hotel Shangrila is the glitzy *Hotel Chaanakya* (☎ 2670), with doubles from Rs 760. It's very popular with Indian holiday-makers.

The *Grand View Hotel* (☎ 2123) near the bus stand charges Rs 500 for deluxe doubles, or Rs 700 for luxury suites. Some of the rooms are divided by paper-thin partitions so you may be disturbed by the TV in the next room. The views of the snowcapped Pir Panjal range are superb. Above this hotel, with even better views, is the similarly priced *Mount View Hotel*.

Places to Eat

During the off season it's hard to find a place to eat. One restaurant that stays open longer than the others is the excellent *Kwality Restaurant* in Gandhi Chowk. They have a good selection of Chinese food as well as north Indian dishes; a half tandoori chicken costs Rs 38. In the same area, and similarly priced, is the popular *Lovely Restaurant* which has good Punjabi and south Indian dishes, and some outside seating.

At Subhash Chowk, there's the *Shere-e-Punjab Dhaba* and the busy *Khosla Restaurant*. Main dishes at these places are around Rs 35.

Getting There & Away

Pathankot, 80 km away, is the usual departure point for buses to Dalhousie. The trip takes about four hours and costs Rs 34.

There are also direct buses to Amritsar, Jammu, Dharamsala (10 hours) and Shimla (16 hours). For Shimla and Dharamsala it's far quicker to catch a bus back to Pathankot, and take another from there. For Chamba there are four buses daily doing the two-hour trip (Rs 18).

Taxis between Dalhousie and Pathankot cost Rs 620 and take two hours.

KHAJIAR

This grassy 'marg' is 22 km from Dalhousie, and you can get here by bus or on foot, a day's walk. Over a km long and nearly a km wide, it is ringed by pine trees with a lake in the middle. There's a golf course here and a golden-domed temple. The woodcarvings in the temple are very impressive and date back to the 14th century.

The Tourist Bungalow, *Hotel Deodar*, has dorm beds at Rs 45 and doubles from Rs 350. Other alternatives are the *youth hostel* and the *PWD Rest House*.

CHAMBA

Population: 18,400
Telephone Area Code: 018992

Situated 56 km from Dalhousie, beyond Khajiar, Chamba is at 926 metres – quite a bit lower than Dalhousie, so it's warmer in the summer. Perched on a ledge high above the River Ravi, it has often been compared to a medieval Italian village and is famed for its temples, many of them within walking distance of the town centre.

For 1000 years prior to Independence, Chamba was the headquarters of a district of the same name, which included Dalhousie, and was ruled by a single dynasty of maharajas. There are many reminders of this period, including the palace (now a hotel) and the museum.

The town is a centre for the Gaddis, traditional shepherds who move their flocks up to the alpine pastures during the summer and

descend to Kangra, Mandi and Bilaspur in the winter. The Gaddis live only on the high range which divides Chamba from Kangra.

Chamba has a grassy promenade known as the *chaugan* – it's only 75 metres wide and less than a km long. The village is a busy trading centre for villagers from the surrounding hills and each year it's the site for the Minjar Festival in August, with a colourful procession and busy crowds of Gaddi, Churachi, Bhatti and Gujjar people. An image of Lord Raghuvira leads the procession and other gods and goddesses follow in palanquins.

Temples

The hilltop **Chamundra Temple** gives an excellent view of Chamba with its slate-roof houses (some of them up to 300 years old), the River Ravi and the surrounding countryside. It's a steep half-hour climb.

Next to the maharaja's palace is the temple complex of **Lakshmi Narayan** which contains six temples, three dedicated to Siva and three to Vishnu, the oldest dating back to the 10th century, the newest to 1828. The sikhara-style **Hariraya Temple** is also dedicated to Vishnu.

Bhuri Singh Museum

Chamba also has the Bhuri Singh Museum, which has an interesting collection relating to the art and culture of this region – particularly the miniature paintings of the Basohli and Kangra schools. It is open from 10 am to 5 pm daily except Sunday. The Rang Mahal palace in the upper part of town was badly damaged by fire, but some of its murals are now in the museum.

Places to Stay & Eat

The HPTDC has two Tourist Bungalows: the *Hotel Champak* (☎ 2774) with doubles from Rs 100, dorm beds at Rs 45; and the more upmarket *Hotel Iravati* (☎ 2671) with rooms from Rs 300 to Rs 500. The *Hotel Akhand Chandi* (☎ 6363) on College Rd has air-con rooms at Rs 300. For something cheaper try the *Janta Hotel*.

Meals are available in the *Ravi View Cafe* and the *Hotel Iravati*. Despite its grotty appearance, the *Gupta Dhaba*, opposite RK Tailors near the GPO, has excellent food. The *Olive Green Restaurant* on Temple Rd, is also recommended. At the *Khalsa Tea Stall* you can get toast with real Chamba butter.

Getting There & Away

Taxis and jeeps can be hired in Dalhousie but they're expensive at Rs 550 return. The local bus is Rs 18 and takes two hours, or you can walk there in two days, resting overnight in Khajiar. Buses from Pathankot take five hours and leave every two hours.

From Chamba trekkers can make an interesting, but hard-going, trek through Brahmaur and Triund to Dharamsala. Or via Tisa you can trek all the way into Lahaul or Kashmir.

TREKS FROM BRAHMAUR

A number of interesting treks can be made from Brahmaur, 65 km from Chamba. These include the 35-km trek to **Manimahesh Lake** (3950 metres) at the base of the sacred Manimahesh Kalias. Thousands of pilgrims undertake this trek in August/September each year and complete the trek in three stages.

Alternatively there are treks over the Pir Panjal range to the Chandra Valley and Lahaul. The most popular crosses the Kugti Pass. Porters can be hired from Brahmaur for which you should budget Rs 200 per day.

The first stage of the approach follows the Budhil River to the village of Kugti. The trail then ascends above the conifer forest to a grazing meadow before crossing a large moraine field to the base of the pass. It's then a short steep climb to the top. The route follows the migration of the Gaddi shepherds taking their huge flocks to the grazing pastures in Lahaul. On the far side of the pass allow one intermediary camp before descending to the road in the Chandra Valley and the daily bus service to Manali.

See Lonely Planet's *Trekking in the Indian Himalaya* for a full description of this trek.

Kullu Valley

The fertile Kullu Valley rises northward from Mandi at 760 metres to the Rohtang Pass at 3978 metres, the gateway to Lahaul and Spiti. In the south the valley is little more than a narrow, precipitous gorge, with the Beas River (pronounced 'bee-ahs') sometimes a sheer 300 metres below the narrow road.

Further up, the valley widens and its main part is 80 km long, though rarely more than a couple of km wide. Here there are stone-fruit and apple orchards, rice fields and wheat fields along the valley floor and lower slopes, and deodar forests higher up the slopes, with snow-crowned rocky peaks towering behind. The main towns, Kullu and Manali, are in this fertile section of the valley.

The people of the Kullu Valley are friendly, devout, hard-working and relatively prosperous. The men wear the distinctive Kullu cap, a pillbox with a flap around the front in which they may stick flowers. The women wear lots of silver jewellery and long garments of homespun wool secured with great silver pins; they are rarely without a large conical basket on their backs, filled with fodder, firewood or even a goat kid.

The other people of the valley are the nomads (Gaddis) who take their flocks of black sheep and white goats up to the mountain pastures in the early summer and retreat before the winter snows. You don't really know what wool smells like until you've travelled in a bus overcrowded with rain-soaked villagers.

The valley also has many Tibetan refugees, some running restaurants and hotels in Manali, but many others in camps near the rivers. The Tibetans are great traders – you'll find them in all the bazaars – but many also work in road gangs, whole families toiling together.

The Kullu Valley was always a popular place, but it managed to retain a very peace-

Painting, Sculpture & Architecture

Indian art and sculpture is basically religious in its themes and developments, and its appreciation requires at least some knowledge of the country's Buddhist and Hindu background.

Buddhist Influence

The earliest Indian artefacts (mainly small items of sculpture) were those found in the Indus Valley cities in modern-day Pakistan. It was not until the Mauryan era (4th to 2nd centuries BC) that India's first major artistic period flowered. This classical school of Buddhist art reached its peak during the reign of Ashoka (died 238 BC), and its superb sculpture can be seen at its best at Sanchi.

Close to Peshawar, in today's Pakistan, the Gandharan period combined Buddhism with a strong Greek influence from the descendants of Alexander the Great's invading army. During this period, the Buddha began to be represented directly in human form rather than by symbols such as the footprint or stupa.

Meanwhile, another school was developing at Mathura, between Agra and Delhi. Here, the Buddhist influence was beginning to be altered by the revival of Brahmanism, the forerunner of Hinduism. It was in this school that the tradition of sculpturing *yakshis*, those well-endowed heavenly damsels, began.

During the Gupta period (320-600), Indian art experienced a golden age, and the Buddha images developed their present-day form – even today in Buddhist countries the representations of the Buddha's attitudes, clothing and hand positions have scarcely altered. However, this period saw the end of Buddhist art in India, as Hinduism began to reassert itself and a strongly Hindu tradition was developing in the south. Both schools of art produced metal-cast sculptures using the now lost wax method, as well as larger sculptures in stone.

Left: Statue of Buddha, Gangtok, Sikkim.

Right: Temple detail, Hoysaleswara Temple, Halebid, Karnataka. The temple's sculpture is an outstanding example of Hoysala art.

CHRIS BEALL

LEANNE LOGAN

GLENN BEANLAND

GLENN BEANLAND

GLENN BEANLAND

Top Left: Brass dancing Ganesh figure.

Top Right: Wooden baby Krishna floating in a lotus leaf, South India.

Bottom Left: Wooden Rajasthani musicians.

Bottom Right: Silver trinket catching the afternoon sunlight, Patwon ki Haveli, Jaisalmer, Rajasthan.

HUGH FINLAY

Hindu Influence

The following 1000 years saw a slow but steady development through to the exuberant medieval period of Indian Hindu art. This development can be studied at the caves of Ajanta and Ellora, where there are some of the oldest wall paintings in India, and the sculpture can be traced from the older, stiff and unmoving Buddhist sculptures through to the dynamic and dramatic Hindu figures.

These figures reached their culmination in the period when sculpture became an integral part of architecture – it is impossible to tell where building ends and sculpture begins. Some of the finest examples from this era can be seen in the Hoysala temples of Karnataka, the elaborate Sun Temple at Konark and the Chandelas' temples at Khajuraho. The architecture competes valiantly with the artwork, which manages to combine high quality with quite awesome quantity. An interesting common element is the highly detailed erotic scenes. The heavenly maidens of an earlier period have blossomed into positions and possibilities that leave little to the imagination. Art of this period was not purely a representation of gods and goddesses. Every aspect of human life appeared in the sculptures, and it's pretty obvious that sex was considered a fairly important aspect of daily life!

MARKUS LEHTIPUU

BRYN THOMAS

BRYN THOMAS

Top (left & right) & Bottom Right: Stone sculptures from the temples of Khajuraho. These themes are drawn from the Kama Sutra as well as aspects of Indian life a thousand years ago.

Middle Right: Detail from an episode of the Buddha's life. The scene is carved onto a pillar of the Great Stupa, Sanchi.

Bottom Left: Carvings on an ancient Durga temple, near Udaipur.

HUGH FINLAY

HUGH FINLAY

Mughal Influence

At first, the arrival of the Muslims and their intolerance of other religions and 'idols' caused enormous damage to India's artistic relics. The early invaders' art was chiefly confined to painting, but the Mughal era saw Indian art experience yet another golden age. The best known of the art forms they encouraged was the painting of miniatures. These delightfully detailed and brightly coloured paintings showed the events and activities of the Mughals in their magnificent palaces. Other paintings included portraits and studies of wildlife and plants.

At the same time, there was a massive revival of folk art; some of these developments embraced the Mughal miniature concepts but combined them with Indian religious arts. The popular Rajasthan or Mewar schools often included scenes from Krishna's life and escapades – Krishna is usually painted blue. Interestingly, this school followed the Persian-influenced Mughal school in its miniaturised and highly detailed approach, but made no use of the Persian-developed sense of perspective. As a result, the works are generally almost two-dimensional.

HUGH FINLAY

TONY WHEELER

HUGH FINLAY

Top: Detail of a mural found inside the Goenka Haveli, Fatehpur, Shekhawati, Rajasthan.

Bottom Left: Indian miniature painting.

Bottom Right: Design on a house interior, Shilpgram, Udaipur, Rajasthan.

ful and unhurried atmosphere. With the troubles in Kashmir, however, the valley in general and Manali in particular, have largely replaced Kashmir as the place to go to see the snow. The result is that it is going ahead at an enormous rate – the Manali area now has over 400 hotels, compared with less than 50 eight years ago, and more are appearing each month. Unfortunately the expansion seems to be largely unplanned, and so the landscape is changing rapidly, often for the worse as more and more insensitively designed buildings get thrown up. One can only wonder just what will happen to all the hotels when and if the problems in Kashmir are resolved.

KULLU

Population: 15,500
Telephone Area Code: 01902

At an altitude of 1200 metres, Kullu is the district headquarters of the valley but it is not the main tourist centre; that honour goes to Manali. Nevertheless there are a number of interesting things to see around Kullu, and some fine walks.

The town, which sprawls on the western bank of the Beas, is dominated by the grassy *maidans* (open areas) on the southern side of town. They're the site for Kullu's fairs and festivals, in particular the colourful Dussehra Festival, from which the Kullu Valley gained the name Valley of the Gods.

Orientation & Information

The helpful tourist office (☎ 2349) is by the maidan at the southern end of town. It's open daily from 9 am to 7 pm in summer, and from 10 am to 5 pm in winter. There's also an information counter at the airport.

There's a bus and taxi stand on the opposite side of the maidan, and all the HPTDC accommodation units, several of the hotels, the State Bank of India, and the Deputy Commissioner's office are around the maidan. The main bus stand is by the river in the northern area of town.

Temples

In the north of the town, and dedicated to the

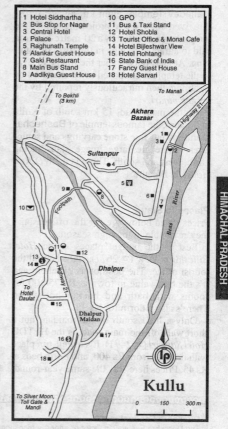

1 Hotel Siddhartha	10 GPO
2 Bus Stop for Nagar	11 Bus & Taxi Stand
3 Central Hotel	12 Hotel Shobla
4 Palace	13 Tourist Office & Monal Cafe
5 Raghunath Temple	14 Hotel Bijleshwar View
6 Alankar Guest House	15 Hotel Rohtang
7 Gaki Restaurant	16 State Bank of India
8 Main Bus Stand	17 Fancy Guest House
9 Aadikya Guest House	18 Hotel Sarvari

Kullu

principal god in the valley, is the **Raghunath Temple**. Although it's the most important temple in the area, it's not terribly interesting and is only open from 5 pm.

Three km from Kullu, in the village of Bhekhli, is **Jagannathi Devi Temple**. It's a stiff climb, but from the temple there are fine views over the town. Take the path off the main road to Akhara Bazaar after crossing the Sarawai bridge.

Four km along the Kullu to Manali road is the **Vaishno Devi Temple**, a small cave with an image of the goddess Vaishno.

A jeep track links Kullu with **Bijli**

Mahadev Temple, eight km away. Across the river, high on a projecting bluff, the temple is surmounted by a 20-metre-high rod said to attract blessings in the form of lightning. At least once a year the image of Siva in the temple is supposed to be shattered by lightning, then miraculously repaired by the temple *pujari*.

On the main road, 15 km south of Kullu in Bajaura, the famous temple of **Basheshar Mahadev** has fine stone carvings and sculptures. There are large image slabs facing north, west and south. There is a *PWD Rest House* in Bajaura.

Places to Stay

Prices given below are for the off season – they're double in the high season.

Best of the budget places is the *Hotel Bijleshwar View* (☎ 2677), right behind the tourist office. The position is excellent and it's the best value in town at Rs 75/100 for rooms with bath and bucket hot water. There's also a dorm for Rs 35.

Only a little south of the maidan, but a short walk off the main road, is the HPTDC *Hotel Sarvari* (☎ 2471). It's a well-run place with doubles from Rs 400, and dorm beds at Rs 45. Prices here stay the same year-round.

Also beside the maidan, the *Hotel Rohtang* is better value at Rs 185. Up the road behind the maidan, the *Hotel Daulat* (☎ 2358) has rooms with balcony for Rs 200.

Across the other side of the maidan, towards the river, is the cheap and basic *Fancy Guest House* (☎ 2681), although there's certainly nothing fancy about the place. It's good value, at Rs 125 for a room with attached bath and constant hot water.

On the path which connects the northern and southern parts of town is the *Aadikya Guest House*, right by the footbridge. The roar of the river can be amazingly loud at times, so it's a bit like trying to sleep beside an aeroplane! It's Rs 175 for a double with TV, attached bath and hot water.

There are other rock-bottom places at the Manali end of town, such as the *Kullu Valley Lodge* or the *Central Hotel*, both with singles with common bath for Rs 35, and doubles with attached bath for Rs 75.

The best place in this area is the new *Hotel Siddhartha* (☎ 4243), which is well run with clean doubles with attached bath and constant hot water for Rs 175. It's good value.

Back in the centre of town is the *Hotel Shobla* (☎ 2800), a new place by the river with overpriced rooms for Rs 385. Finally, the HPTDC *Silver Moon* (☎ 2488) is to the

---

Dussehra Festival

The Dussehra Festival, in October after the monsoons, is celebrated all over India but most particularly in Kullu. The festival starts on the 10th day of the rising moon, known as Vijay Dashmi, and continues for seven days. Dussehra celebrates Rama's victory over the demon king Ravana but in Kullu the festival does not include the burning of Ravana and his brothers, as it does in other places around India.

Kullu's festival is a great gathering of the gods from temples all around the valley. Approximately 200 gods are brought from their temples to pay homage to Raghunathji, the paramount Kullu god, at Kullu's Raghunathpura temple. The festival cannot commence until the powerful goddess Hadimba, tutelary deity of the Kullu rajas, arrives from Manali. Like the other gods she is pulled in her own temple car, or *rath*, and Hadimba likes speed so she has to be pulled as fast as possible. She not only arrives before all the other gods but also leaves before them. Another curiosity is that the Jamlu god from Malana comes to the festival but does not take part – this god stays on the opposite side of the river from the Dhalpur maidan.

The Raghunathji rath is brought down, decked with garlands and surrounded by the other important gods. Priests and the descendants of Kullu's rajas circle the rath before it is pulled to the other side of the maidan. There is great competition to aid in pulling the car since this is a very auspicious thing to do.

The procession with the cars and bands takes place on the evening of the first day of the festival. During the following days and nights there are dances, music, a market and festivities far into the night. On the penultimate day the gods assemble for the *devta darbar* with Raghunathji, and on the final day the temple car is taken to the river bank where a small heap of grass is burnt to symbolise Ravana's destruction. Raghunathji is carried back to his main temple in a wooden palanquin. ∎

left of the road just as you enter town from the south. It has six double rooms at Rs 600 (year-round).

Places to Eat

The *Hotel Sarvari* has the usual sort of dining hall. By the tourist office there's the HPTDC's *Monal Cafe* with good light meals and snacks. Nearby is *Hotstuff Fast Food* a popular place serving foot-longs (filled rolls) for Rs 25 to Rs 45, burgers, and ice cream as well as more substantial meals.

For ultra-basic Tibetan food, try the *Gaki Restaurant* near the main bus stand. It only has momos and thukpa (Tibetan soup), and no English is spoken, but it's very cheap.

Getting There & Away

Air The airport is at Bhuntar, 10 km south of Kullu. On Tuesday and Thursday, Jagson Airlines (☎ 65-286) flies from Kullu to Delhi (US\$123), Shimla (US\$49) and Dharamsala (Gaggal, US\$49).

Archana Airways (☎ 65-630) has at least one flight a day to Delhi. Rajair has daily flights to Bombay via Chandigarh. KCV flies to Delhi and Amritsar. Contact Aggrawal Travels (☎ 65-220), by the bus stand in Bhuntar, for more information about these two new airlines.

Bus & Taxi There are direct buses to Kullu from Dharamsala, Shimla (235 km), Chandigarh (270 km) or Delhi (512 km). The Kullu to Chandigarh buses do not go via Shimla. All these direct buses continue to Manali, 42 km further north.

A direct bus from Delhi takes 14 hours. Regular express buses cost Rs 180, but there are various classes right up to a superdeluxe bus which costs Rs 310.

Buses run regularly along the main road from Kullu to Manali (Rs 15, 1¾ hours). There are fewer buses on the eastern side of the Beas River and the trip can take a long time, up to two hours from Manali to Nagar alone. Add another 1½ hours from Nagar to Kullu. The combined fare is not much different from the direct one.

Cars can get to Nagar by crossing the river

at Patlikuhl near Katrain – the bridge is very narrow. Or you can get off the Kullu to Manali bus there and walk up. It's six km up to the castle by road but much less on foot, although the path is very steep.

Plenty of taxis make the trip up from the plains, but count on around Rs 1700 or more for Shimla or Chandigarh to Kullu or Manali. A taxi from Kullu to Manali costs Rs 400.

AROUND KULLU

You can make some interesting excursions from Kullu Valley to the adjoining valleys. See also Treks from Manali & the Kullu Valley later in this chapter.

Parbatti Valley

The Parbatti Valley runs north-east from Bhuntar, which is south of Kullu. You can travel up the valley by bus. Manikaran is built near sulphur hot springs and it's interesting to watch the locals cook their food in the pools of hot water at the Sikh temple. There are also hot baths (separate baths for men and women) at the temple and, of course, free accommodation. Hot water is nice to have in Manikaran because the sides of the valley are very steep, and not much sun gets in. It's said that Siva sat and meditated for 2000 years at **Khir Ganga**, a 30-km walk from Manikaran.

There are a lot of French and Italian hippies in the area. There's great trekking and wonderful scenery here.

Places to Stay The HPTDC *Hotel Parvati* (☎ 235) has 10 doubles at Rs 300. Rooms in shops or houses are easily available if you ask around. The *Padha Family House*, near the bridge, is an excellent place where quite a few travellers stay. There are big, clean rooms for around Rs 100, and there's a private sulphur rock-bath indoors. You can get food, and expensive, though lovely, wild honey.

In the local chai shops try *kheerh*, the delicious rice dessert made with milk, sugar, fresh coconut and sultanas.

Getting There & Away Buses from Kullu to Bhuntar take 1½ hours and cost about Rs 6.

Bhuntar to Manikaran is another 1½ hours for about the same price.

Sainj Valley

The area from Aut to Sainj is not as beautiful as the other valleys but it has a charm of its own. It's also very rarely visited by travellers so the locals are friendly. There is no accommodation as such, but rooms are easily available if you ask around. A bus from Bhuntar to Aut takes an hour and costs Rs 6.

KULLU TO MANALI

There are a number of interesting things to see along the 42-km road between Kullu and Manali. There are actually two Kullu-to-Manali roads; the direct road runs along the west bank of the Beas, while the much rougher and more winding east-bank road is not so regularly used, but does take you via Nagar with its delightful castle.

Raison

Only eight km from Kullu there's a camping place on the grassy meadow beside the river. It's a good base for treks in the vicinity. There are 14 *Tourist Huts* at the site with doubles at Rs 150, which can be booked through the Kullu tourist office.

Katrain

At about the midpoint on the Kullu to Manali road, this is the widest point in the Kullu Valley and is overlooked by the 3325-metre Baragarh peak. Two km up the road on the left side is a trout hatchery.

Places to Stay There's a small *Rest House* and a pleasant HPTDC Tourist Bungalow known as the *Hotel Apple Blossom* with doubles at Rs 200, and a five-bed dorm for Rs 45 per bed. It's an interesting alternative to staying in Kullu or Manali. There's also the very expensive riverside *Span Resort* (☎ 83140), which costs Rs 3950 for doubles with all meals.

Nagar

High above Katrain, on the east bank of the river, is Nagar with its stunning Castle Hotel.

Transport to the castle is a little problematical but the effort is worthwhile.

Nagar Castle At one time Nagar was the capital of the Kullu Valley and the castle was the raja's headquarters. Around 1660 Sultanpur, now known as Kullu, became the new capital. The quaint old fort is built around a courtyard with verandahs right around the outside and absolutely stupendous views over the valley. Inside the courtyard is a small temple containing a slab of stone with an intriguing legend about how it was carried there by wild beasts.

Temples There are a number of interesting temples around the castle. The grey sandstone Siva **Temple of Gauri Shankar** is at the foot of the small bazaar below the castle and dates from the 11th or 12th century. Almost opposite the front of the castle is the curious little **Chatar Bhuj Temple** to Vishnu. Higher up the hill is the pagoda-like **Tripura Sundri Devi Temple** and higher still, on the ridge above Nagar, the **Murlidhar Krishna Temple**.

Roerich Gallery Also up the hill above the castle is the Roerich Gallery, a fine old house displaying the artwork of both Professor Nicholas Roerich, who died in 1947, and his son, Svetoslav Roerich, who died in Bangalore in 1993. Its location is delightful and the views over the valley are very fine.

Places to Stay The reputedly haunted HPTDC *Castle Hotel* (☎ 16) has a good range of accommodation but is so popular you often need to book in advance; the Kullu tourist office can make reservations. There are 10 dorm beds for Rs 45, four double rooms with common bath for Rs 125 and seven larger doubles with bath from Rs 250 to Rs 400, plus a three-bed room for Rs 200.

The friendly *Poonam Mountain Lodge & Restaurant* (☎ 12) is opposite Nagar Castle near the post office. The owner is extremely helpful and can arrange trekking. The rooms are very large, and cost around Rs 200. Meals and picnic lunches are available.

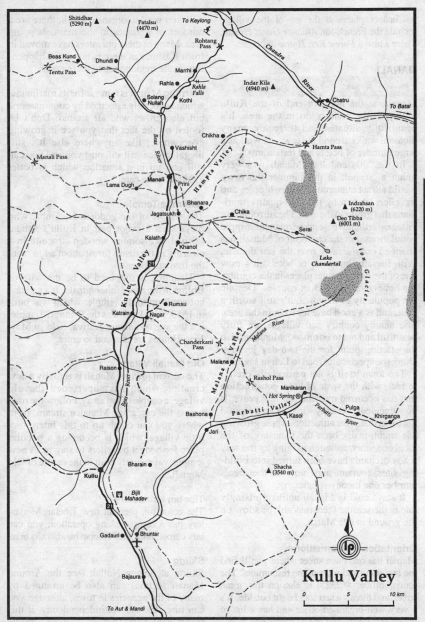

Kullu Valley

Shitidhar (5290 m) ▲
Patalsu (4470 m) ▲
To Keylong
Rohtang Pass
Chandra River
Beas Kund
Dhundi
Tentu Pass
Marrhi
Indar Kila (4940 m) ▲
Chatru
To Batal
Rahla
Rahla Falls
Hamta Pass
Solang Nullah
Kothi
Chikha
Hamta Valley
Vashisht
Manali Pass
Manali
Prini
Lama Dugh
Bhanara
Indrahsan (6220 m) ▲
Chika
Deo Tibba (6001 m) ▲
Jagatsukh
Kalath
Serai
Khanol
Lake Chandartal
Dudjon Glacier
Kullu Valley
21
Rumsu
Katrain
Nagar
Chanderkani Pass
Malana Valley
Malana River
Malana
Rashol Pass
Manikaran
Hot Spring
Pulga
Raison
Bashona
Parbatti Valley
Kasol
Parbatti River
Khirganga
Jari
Bharain
Shacha (3540 m) ▲
Kullu
21
Bijli Mahadev
Gadauri
Bhuntar
Bajaura
To Aut & Mandi

0   5   10 km

Cheaper places at the top of the village include the French-run *Alliance Guest House*. There's also a *Forest Rest House* in Nagar.

MANALI

Population: 4000
Telephone Area Code: 01901

Manali, at the northern end of the Kullu Valley, is the main resort in the area. It's beautifully situated and there are many pleasant walks around the town, as well as a large number of hotels and restaurants.

In the '70s and '80s Manali was very much a 'scene'. In the summer the town would attract numerous Western hippies and travellers, drawn by the high-quality marijuana that grows in the area. The surrounding villages still have semi-permanent hippie populations, but the character of Manali has changed considerably over the last decade. With literally hundreds of hotels, it's now one of the most popular places in the country for honeymooning Indian couples. Despite the popularity of the town, it's still worth a visit, and is a good base for treks in the area. The nearby country and villages are truly beautiful and not to be missed. Manali is also the starting point for the two-day journey along the spectacular road to Leh in Ladakh.

The town itself is not particularly pretty; in fact, with the spate of hotel construction that has occurred over the last few years, is now decidedly scrappy – it's the area around the town that is the attraction. Apple growing has traditionally been the mainstay of the local economy, although judging by the way many orchards have been turned into building sites, tourism must now be the area's number one money-spinner.

It stays cold in Manali until surprisingly late in the season; there may still be snow on the ground in late March.

Orientation & Information

Manali has one main street where you'll find the bus stand and most of the restaurants. The tourist office (☎ 2325) is also on this main street, and there's a taxi stand right outside. It's a very well-organised office and has a list of hotels and tariffs, and of taxi routes and fares.

If you want to organise a trek, there are a number of agencies in the main shopping area. Many of these operators have moved in from Kashmir as there is not much happening on the trekking scene there now.

Warning Manali is famous for its marijuana, which is not only esteemed by connoisseurs, but also grows wild all around. Don't be fooled by the fact that you see it growing everywhere; like anywhere else it's still illegal, police will still bust you and you can still end up in a situation which is better avoided. Take care.

Hadimba Temple

The temple of the goddess Hadimba, who plays such a major part in Kullu's annual festival, is a sombre wooden structure in a clearing in the dense forest about a km from the tourist office.

Hadimba is supposed to be the wife of Bhima in the epic *Mahabharata*. It's a pleasant stroll up to the temple, which was built in 1553. Also known as the Dhungri Temple, it's the site of a major festival held in May. Non-Hindus are allowed to enter.

Old Manali Village

The current town of Manali is actually a new creation which has superseded the old village, a couple of km away. Follow the road across the cascading Manalsu stream, from where you can climb up to this interesting little village, which is becoming a popular place for budget travellers to stay in. A new temple was recently built in the centre of Old Manali.

Tibetan Monastery

The colourful, pleasant new Tibetan Monastery has a carpet-making operation; you can buy carpets and other Tibetan handicrafts here.

Skiing

Skiing at Solang Nullah (see the Around Manali section) can also be arranged by many of the agencies in town, although you can hire skis and ski independently at this resort. For US$600 per day it's even possible

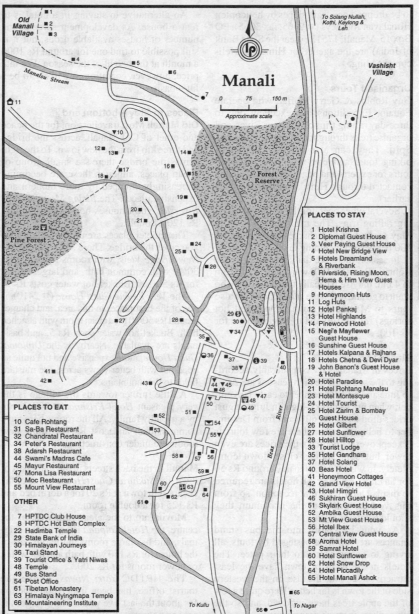

Manali

0   75   150 m

Approximate scale

Old Manali Village

Manalsu Stream

Pine Forest

Forest Reserve

To Solang Nullah, Kothi, Keylong & Leh

Vashisht Village

Beas River

To Kullu

To Nagar

HIMACHAL PRADESH

PLACES TO STAY

1 Hotel Krishna
2 Diplomat Guest House
3 Veer Paying Guest House
4 Hotel New Bridge View
5 Hotels Dreamland & Riverbank
6 Riverside, Rising Moon, Hema & Him View Guest Houses
9 Honeymoon Huts
11 Log Huts
12 Hotel Pankaj
13 Hotel Highlands
14 Pinewood Hotel
15 Negi's Mayflower Guest House
16 Sunshine Guest House
17 Hotels Kalpana & Rajhans
18 Hotels Chetna & Devi Dyar
19 John Banon's Guest House & Hotel
20 Hotel Paradise
21 Hotel Rohtang Manalsu
23 Hotel Montesque
24 Hotel Tourist
25 Hotel Zarim & Bombay Guest House
26 Hotel Gilbert
27 Hotel Sunflower
28 Hotel Hilltop
33 Tourist Lodge
35 Hotel Gandhara
37 Hotel Solang
40 Beas Hotel
41 Honeymoon Cottages
42 Grand View Hotel
43 Hotel Himgiri
46 Sukhiran Guest House
51 Skylark Guest House
52 Ambika Guest House
53 Mt View Guest House
56 Hotel Ibex
57 Central View Guest House
58 Aroma Hotel
59 Samrat Hotel
60 Hotel Sunflower
62 Hotel Snow Drop
64 Hotel Piccadily
65 Hotel Manali Ashok

PLACES TO EAT

10 Cafe Rohtang
31 Sa-Ba Restaurant
32 Chandratal Restaurant
34 Peter's Restaurant
38 Adarsh Restaurant
44 Swami's Madras Cafe
45 Mayur Restaurant
50 Mona Lisa Restaurant
55 Moc Restaurant
     Mount View Restaurant

OTHER

7 HPTDC Club House
8 HPTDC Hot Bath Complex
22 Hadimba Temple
29 State Bank of India
36 Himalayan Journeys
     Taxi Stand
39 Tourist Office & Yatri Niwas
48 Temple
54 Bus Stand
     Post Office
61 Tibetan Monastery
63 Himalaya Nyingmapa Temple
66 Mountaineering Institute

to be dropped on virgin slopes by helicopter. Himalayan Journeys (☎ 2365; fax 3065), PO Box 15, Manali, 175131 (near the State Bank of India) are the agents for Himachal Helicopter Skiing.

Organised Tours

Guy Robins & Gerry Moffat, who operate Equator Expeditions, run excellent one to three-day rafting trips on the Beas River, and organise treks throughout the area, including Spiti. They can also arrange mountain-biking tours and day trips, and kayaking tours for experts and beginners. They can be contacted through Himalayan Journeys (see earlier).

Several other operators have started offering rafting trips. The main season is from May to August and charges are around Rs 600 per person including lunch.

In season there are daily bus tours to the Rohtang Pass (Rs 100) which last from 9 am to 4 pm; they're basically for the locals who want to go and touch the snow. There are also tours to Manikaran (Sikh temple and hot springs) for Rs 140 and to Nagar Castle for Rs 100.

Places to Stay

Prices in Manali vary considerably according to the season. The high seasons are April to June and mid-September to early November, when prices go sky-high. In July/August prices drop by about 60% and from December to February, when there are few tourists (except over Christmas), the prices are even lower but some hotels close down completely. In winter expect to pay around Rs 50 for an electric heater. All hotels are required to display a tariff card at reception, so from this you can find out the maximum they should be charging.

As your bus pulls into the bus stand chances are you'll be besieged by touts, all trying to entice you into their place. The hotels in the heart of town have the least attractive location, the rise on the western side of the town is far better. Here quite a few of the apple trees have survived, and so the atmosphere is much more rustic.

An alternative to staying in a hotel is to rent a house. As development spreads, the number of houses available drops, but it is still possible to find one for around Rs 1000 a month at the height of the season. For that price, however, conditions are likely to be a little basic.

Places to Stay – bottom end

Old Manali Most travellers opt for the peace and quiet of Old Manali, across the bridge and three km from the new town. To the right across the bridge there's a small group of cheap places, although these are becoming increasingly cramped by more modern and expensive places. The *Rising Moon* and the *Riverside* guest houses both charge around Rs 120 a double.

The quieter places are up to the left after you cross the bridge. There's the basic *Hotel New Bridge View*, with rooms from just Rs 30/40 with common bath, and larger rooms for Rs 50/100. Bucket hot water costs Rs 3.

The *Veer Paying Guest House* (☎ 2410), is one of the best places in this area, and charges around Rs 50/70 for a clean room with attached bath. Bucket hot water costs Rs 5, and basic meals are available. Nearby is the *Diplomat Guest House*, more expensive and not quite so good but with better views across the mustard fields to the mountains.

A little further towards the village is the very pleasant *Hotel Krishna* (☎ 3071), run by a friendly family. All the rooms here have common bath and cost Rs 50. Some new rooms are under construction.

Manali In the back streets in the main part of town, the *Sukhiran Guest House* is one of the cheapest in town at Rs 20 for a dorm bed and Rs 125 for a double room.

Moving up to the area north-west of the centre, the *Hotel Kalpana* is one of the originals, and has large rooms in the old part of the house for Rs 150 with bath and hot water, or newer rooms for Rs 200.

The HPTDC *Yatri Niwas*, above the tourist office, has been under construction for about the last five years. They've got the roof on now so it should be opening soon and promises dorm beds for around Rs 45 and some double rooms. Another possibility, although a pretty uninteresting one, is the HPTDC *Beas Hotel* by the riverside, with double rooms from Rs 200.

Places to Stay – middle

The main concentration of places is in the streets between the main road and the rise. Here virtually every building is a hotel, so if you want to stay in this area it's just a matter of finding one to suit. They all have the tariff displayed, and charge around Rs 300 to Rs 400 in the season, dropping to Rs 100 to Rs 200 at other times. Places in this area include the *Rock Sea, Diamond, Skylark, Chelsea, Karma, Shiwalik, Raj Palace, Hill View, Mona Lisa* and *Park View*. There are many others.

The HPTDC *Hotel Rohtang Manalsu* (☎ 2332) is not a bad option and there are decent views across the valley. Double rooms cost Rs 300 to Rs 500 and there are four-bed rooms for Rs 350.

Once again, the best places are out of the centre of town. The *Hotel Tourist* (☎ 2297) is a quiet and pleasant place, just off the road to Old Manali. All rooms have a small balcony with a view, TV, attached bath and hot water. At Rs 400 these are good value for expensive Manali; the off-season rate is Rs 200.

Further along this road is one of Manali's oldest places, *John Banon's Guest House* – not to be confused with the modern resort of the same name nearby. It's a very nice old Raj building with good facilities, and it's good value at Rs 225/450. There's only one single, and some of the doubles are in the less attractive new building. Surprisingly this place doesn't offer discounts.

The *Sunshine Guest House* (☎ 2320), a little further on, is also in an older building and is run by friendly people. The rooms are spacious, there's a lawn for relaxing on and the views aren't bad either. Cost for all this is Rs 275 to Rs 500 for a double with attached bath.

Higher up the hill is another Manali oldie, the *Hotel Highlands*. Rooms in this atmo-

spheric place go for Rs 350 to Rs 500. The *Hotel Pankaj* (☎ 2444) next door has similar prices but lacks appeal.

Near the Highlands a footpath leads to the Hadimba Temple, and there are several places along here. One of the best is the bright and airy *Hotel Chetna*, with uninterrupted views of the pine forest, as well as over the town. There are rooms from Rs 400 with TV, bath and hot water, but it's closed during the off season.

Places to Stay – top end

The top hotel here is the *Holiday Inn* (☎ 2262; fax 3312), three km south of the centre on the left bank of the river. Packages including all meals range from Rs 2800 to Rs 5000 per day for a double room and there's a 30% off-season discount. This hotel has all the amenities you'd expect for the price.

Dominating the western ridge above the town is the *Hotel Shingar Regency* (☎ 2252), with doubles from Rs 1390, while on the left bank of the river, about 1.5 km from town, is the expanded ITDC *Hotel Manali Ashok* (☎ 2331). Doubles here range from Rs 700 to Rs 1000, with a sitting room and fine views of the snow-capped peaks around Manali. There's a 40% off-season discount.

The HPTDC has self-contained *Log Huts*, up the road past the Cafe Rohtang; these cost Rs 2500 to Rs 3500. In town the *Hotel Piccadily* (☎ 2114) and the *Hotel Ibex* (☎ 2440) are both on the main street, just south of the shopping centre. The Piccadily charges Rs 500/1200 for a single/double and the Ibex is a little cheaper.

Places to Eat

Manali is remarkably well endowed with places to eat. On the main street the *Mount View Restaurant* has good food and, in winter, it's pleasantly warm from the stove in the middle of the room. The food is mainly Chinese and Tibetan – the thalumein soup is excellent – and there's good music to eat by. Down a side street nearby is the *Mayur Restaurant* (☎ 2448) which is so popular with travellers that you may need to reserve a

HIMACHAL PRADESH

table in the evening. Tandoori trout machhali costs Rs 35 and is a good choice.

The smaller *Mona Lisa* is another busy place. Once again, the food and music are both good, and the fresh trout is very popular. The *Chinese Room* near the post office serves good Chinese, Indian and Continental food.

In the same area there's *Swami's Madras Cafe*, a pure veg place serving thalis for Rs 30. Across the street from the Sukhiran Guest House, *Moc Restaurant* has chicken momos for Rs 30, Singapore noodles for Rs 34, and chicken sukiyaki at Rs 55. It's a good place.

If you want to get a taste of the old Manali, visit *Peter's*, tucked away near the State Bank of India. It's still a popular (if slightly grubby) place, especially with those looking for goodies to take trekking – home-made jams, peanut butter, wholewheat bread and muesli are all tried and tested. Cheddar cheese costs Rs 70 for 100 g. 'Please Don't Use Drug Here – Go Forest' says the sign. Not like the old days.

For those on a short shoestring, there are a number of basic dhaba places on the main street opposite the tourist office. One which seems to have a bit more variety than the others is the *Kamal*.

There are several options near Old Manali, including the *Ish Cafe* by the river, and *Shiva Garden Cafe*. The *German Bakery* sells good cinnamon rolls for Rs 12, brown bread for Rs 18 and not terribly authentic croissants for Rs 6.

Getting There & Away
Bus The bus terminal is well organised and the ticket office is computerised. There are deluxe buses daily to Delhi and Shimla, and semideluxe buses to Shimla and Dharamsala. Demand for all these buses is heavy in summer, so make a reservation as far in advance as possible. Deluxe buses are booked, and leave from, the tourist office, while semideluxe are handled from the bus terminal itself. In the off season both the deluxe and semideluxe services are subject to demand, although there's a better chance of the semideluxe running.

Deluxe bus fares are Rs 400 (Rs 600 aircon) to Delhi (16 hours), and Rs 200 to Shimla. The semideluxe fares are Rs 130 to Shimla (10 hours) or Dharamsala (12½ hours).

Ordinary buses run to many destinations including Shimla (Rs 115), Dharamsala (Rs 114), Mandi (Rs 37), Chandigarh (Rs 117), Amritsar (Rs 184), Jammu (Rs 175) and Delhi (Rs 190).

There are many buses to Kullu (Rs 15), a few of which travel via the left bank of the Beas River. For Keylong there are buses hourly in summer. The trip takes six hours and costs Rs 30.

To/From Leh For the two-day trip to Leh, there's a choice of buses. Most comfortable are the HPTDC's luxury coaches. Tickets must be bought in advance from the tourist office and cost Rs 700, or Rs 1000 including the night at their deluxe camp. At the bus stand you can book HPSRTC's ordinary bus for Rs 460. If there's a J&KSRTC bus at the station you can buy a ticket from the driver. These last two buses are equally ramshackle – take whichever one is leaving earlier or you'll have a very long second day. There are also several private buses on this route; tickets are sold by the travel agents around town.

Avoid the seats at the back of any of the buses as the road is very bumpy – so bumpy in fact that we actually hit the roof at one point! When the route is open (July to mid-September) there's usually one or more buses every day. See the Leh section in the Jammu & Kashmir chapter for more information about this route.

Taxi Typical fares are Rs 400 to Kullu, Rs 1900 to Shimla and Rs 10,000 to Leh, but these are negotiable if you approach the driver direct.

AROUND MANALI
Vashisht
Vashisht is a picturesque little place, clinging to the steep hillside about three km out of Manali. On foot the distance is a bit shorter

since you can follow paths up the hillside, whereas cars have to wind up the road.

On the way up to the village you'll come upon the HPTDC Vashisht Hot Bath Complex, where a natural sulphur spring is piped into a modern bathhouse. It's open from 7 am to 7 pm. The cost for a 30-minute soak is Rs 40 for the ordinary baths (you can fit two people in these) or Rs 80 for the larger baths. If you've suffered a long, rough bus trip from Leh there's no better way to soak away the strain. The public hot baths are at the top of the road by the temple and there are separate tanks for men and women.

Places to Stay Vashisht is a centre for Manali's longer term Western residents and there are numerous basic guest houses here, offering rooms from Rs 35 to Rs 70 with discounts for longer stays. One of the best is the *Dharma Guest House* with doubles for around Rs 70 and some rooms with three beds. Follow the path up from the public hot baths to reach it. Down by the road the *Janata* and *Sonam* guest houses are cheaper. The *Dolnath Guest House* is on the square and has a range of rooms from Rs 60.

The *Hotel Bhrigu* has doubles from Rs 300 (around Rs 100 off season) with attached bathrooms and superb views. Right at the top of the price range is the *Ambassador Resort* with doubles from Rs 2100 and heli-skiing and white-water rafting on offer. There's a 30% off-season discount.

Places to Eat The *Cafe Vashisht*, at the HPTDC hot baths, is very well run and serves drinks, snacks and more substantial meals. On the village square there's the *Tibetan Cafe* with a good cake shop beside it. The *Hari Om Cafe Bijurah* here is also popular and does a range of snacks including masala dosas.

The *Freedom Cafe* is very laid-back and has a good range of food. There are no set prices – just put what you think is about right in the box on the way out. The *Snack & Bite* is a similar place.

Solang Nullah
Himachal Pradesh's best ski slopes are at Solang Nullah, 14 km north-west of Manali in the Solang Valley. There are 2.5 km of runs, with black, red and blue routes. Facilities are currently limited to a 300-metre ski lift operated by the Mountaineering & Allied Sports Institute. Ski hire is available for Rs 120 to Rs 150 per day. February is the best month to ski; it's bitterly cold in January.

There are three possibilities for ski courses. HPTDC (book through the tourist office in Manali) runs seven-day packages for Rs 3200 with accommodation in the Hotel Rohtang Manaslu in Manali. If the road gets snowed in, which it often does, you'll spend most of the day getting to Solang Nullah, and only a few hours on the slopes. The 17-day course offered by the Mountaineering & Allied Sports Institute in Manali costs US$170 for foreigners, and the main advantage is that only people on this course are allowed to use the lift. A significant minus point is that the size of the classes is very large – up to 25 students.

The third option is the course offered by the North Face Ski School (book through Hotel Rohtang Inn in Manali), a private operation managed by Jagdish Lal, the national ski coach of India. His seven-day course costs Rs 2450 including ski hire, tuition, accommodation and food; it's been recommended as the best deal by several travellers. The school is presently installing a portable ski lift.

Places to Stay & Eat The small *Friendship Hotel* has doubles for around Rs 150, with attached bath and wood-burning heater. Buckets of hot water and wood for the heater are provided; meals can be arranged for around Rs 25 for lunch or dinner. The *Raju Paying Guest House* is similarly priced.

Jagatsukh
About 12 km north of Nagar and six km south of Manali on the left-bank road, Jagatsukh was the capital of Kullu state until it was supplanted by Nagar. There are some very old temples in the village, particularly

the sikhara-style Siva temple. **Shooru** village nearby has the old and historically interesting Devi Sharvali Temple.

Kothi

Kothi is a pretty little village, 12 km from Manali on the Keylong road.

There are very fine views from Kothi, and the Beas River flows through a very deep and narrow gorge at this point. The trip to Rahla Falls, 16 km away, is another popular excursion.

Places to Stay The *Rest House* is a popular stopover for trekkers heading for the Rohtang Pass. It's surrounded by glaciers and mountains, two old tea stalls and nothing else. Doubles have a bathroom, two big beds, carpets and a balcony. The food is good and the place is quiet.

TREKS FROM MANALI & THE KULLU VALLEY

Treks from Manali & the Kullu Valleyhere are a number of interesting trekking possibilities out of Manali or from the nearby villages of Jagatsukh or Nagar, or from Manikaran in the Parbatti Valley.

There are several agencies in Manali that can assist with the hiring of staff. However it is advisable to bring a sleeping bag and tent with you as most of the gear in Manali is of poor quality or is only for hire by those on an organised trek. Porters can be hired for Rs 150 per day plus return.

Malana Valley

It is less than 30 km from Katrain, on the Kullu to Manali road, across the Chanderkani Pass to the interesting Malana Valley. The pass is at less than 3600 metres and is open from March to December. Malana can also be reached from the Parbatti Valley – either from Manikaran over the 3150-metre Rashol Pass or from Jari. Jari is connected with the Kullu Valley by a jeep track and is only 12 km from Malana.

There are about 500 people in Malana and they speak a peculiar dialect with strong Tibetan elements. It's an isolated village with

its own system of government and a caste structure so rigid that it's forbidden for visitors to touch either the people or any of their possessions. It's very important to respect this custom; wait at the edge of the village for an invitation to enter.

The 6000-metre peak of Deo Tibba overlooks Malana and from the top of the Chanderkani Pass you can see snowcapped peaks on the border of Spiti to the east. Starting from Nagar, it is possible to climb up to the pass summit and return to Nagar on the same day – but it is fairly hard-going.

Local legends relate that when Jamlu, the main deity of Malana, first came there, he bore a casket containing all the other Kullu gods. At the top of the pass he opened the casket and the breeze carried the gods to their present homes, all over the valley.

At the time of the Dussehra Festival in Kullu, Jamlu plays a special part. He is a very powerful god with something of the demon in him. He does not have a temple image so, unlike the other Kullu gods, has no temple car to be carried in. Nor does he openly show his allegiance to Raghunathji, the paramount Kullu god, as do the other Kullu gods. At the time of the festival Jamlu goes down to Kullu but stays on the east side of the river, from where he watches the proceedings.

Every few years a major festival is held for Jamlu in the month of Bhadon. In the temple at Malana there is a silver elephant with a gold figure on its back which is said to have been a gift from Emperor Akbar.

Hampta Pass & Chandratal

The trek over the Hampta Pass to Lahaul is one of the most popular in Himachal Pradesh. It can also be extended to Chandratal and the Baralacha La before either returning to Manali or continuing by road to Leh and the Indus Valley.

The trek commences at Prini village which is four km down the Kullu Valley from Manali. The first few km of the trek are uphill to the village of Sythen (three to four hours) before entering the Hampta Valley. The next two stages are to Chikha (three to four hours) and to Bera-ka-kera (three to four hours). Hampta Pass (4270 metres) is crossed en route to Siliguri (seven hours). From the pass the peaks of Deo Tibba (6001 metres) and Indrahsan (6221 metres) can be appreciated. The descent to the Chandra Valley and the settlement at Chatru takes about three hours.

From Chatru there is the choice of returning by bus to Manali or continuing up the valley to Chandratal and the Baralacha La.

The two stages from Chatru to Batal follow the Manali to Spiti road, stopping at Chota Dara. From Batal the trek diverts from the road with a long stage to Chandratal; a beautiful lake with views to the Mulkila range. From this camp the Baralacha La can be reached in two or three stages. However care should be taken on a number of the river crossings. The Gaddi shepherds should be able to assist with advice and directions.

From the Baralacha La there are regular truck convoys stopping overnight at either Sarchu or Pang and reaching Leh the following day. See Lonely Planet's *Trekking in the Indian Himalaya* for more details.

Base of Deo Tibba

This delightful trek to the base of Deo Tibba (6001 metres) can be undertaken in five stages. The trek commences from the village of Jagatsukh and winds through a series of villages to the grazing pastures at Khanol (two to three hours). From here there is a steady climb (steep in places) to the Gujjar shepherd camp at Chika (four to five hours). The stage between Chika and the high camp at Serai (four to five hours) is covered in wildflowers in July and August while the hanging glaciers beneath Deo Tibba form a backdrop at the head of the valley. From the Gaddi shepherd camp at Serai a day trek can be made to the moraine below Deo Tibba (seven hours return). The final stage back to Jagatsukh can be completed with time to catch the bus back to Manali the same day.

Nagar to Malana & the Pin Parbatti Valley

This trek commences from Nagar village and is a long and steady climb (in two stages) towards the Chanderkani Pass (3650 metres). The first stage is to Rumsu village (two to three hours) and the second stage takes five to six hours. From the pass there are views across to the upper Kullu Valley and to many of the peaks at the head of the Bara Shingri Glacier. The descent to Malana (six hours) is very steep, even for the sure-footed. (See the earlier Parbatti Valley section under Around Manali for more information about this interesting village.) After camping outside the village there is a further stage to the Pin Parbatti Valley (four to five hours) and the road at Jari. Here, there are buses back to the Kullu Valley and Manali.

Parbatti Valley

The Parbatti Valley provides a number of trekking options including a challenging trek over the Pin Parbatti Pass to Spiti. There is also a shorter trek from the roadhead at Manikaran to the hot springs at Khir Ganga.

From Manikaran the well-defined trail leads to the village of Pulga (four to five hours). The next stage continues on up the Parbatti Valley to the hot springs at Khir Ganga. Here there are a number of teahouses to spend the night before returning directly to Manikaran in one long stage.

If you're trekking further up the valley, a tent and good sleeping bag are necessary. The trail follows the Parbatti Valley to the famous Pandu bridge, a natural rock bridge over the Parbatti River. It is a further stage across the rich alpine pastures to Mantakal Lake crossing the extensive moraine and boulder fields to the base of the Pin Parbatti Pass. The pass itself is at the head of a small snow field and there are magnificent views of the main Himalaya range, while to the north is the stark Zanskar range. Once over the pass it is two stages to the village of Sangam where there is a daily bus service to Kasa, the headquarters of Spiti. See Lonely Planet's *Trekking in the Indian Himalaya* for a more detailed description.

Lahaul, Spiti & Kinnaur

Fifty-one km north of Manali, the road to Leh crosses the Rohtang Pass and enters the Tibetan regions of Lahaul and Spiti, which are quite unlike the Kullu Valley. The Rohtang Pass has the same 'gateway' nature as the Zoji La between Kashmir and Ladakh. The region is bound by Ladakh to the north, Tibet to the east, and Kullu to the south-east. South of Spiti is Kinnaur, accessible from Shimla.

Much of this area is open only during the short summer season when the snow on the passes melts.

Inner Line Permits

Inner Line Permits are not necessary for travel to Spiti and you are now permitted to go as far down valley as Tabo. A permit is only necessary if travelling from Spiti to northern Kinnaur and this is not granted unless you are in group of at least four persons on an itinerary arranged through an authorised travel agent.

Inner Line Permits are available from the Senior District Magistrate (SDM) in Keylong or Rekong Peo, or from the Deputy Commissioner in Kullu or Shimla and also from the Ministry of Home Affairs in Delhi. Three photographs are required. As restrictions are further eased it's likely that individuals may be granted permits too.

Trekking

There are many trekking possibilities in this area, a popular one being the trek from Darcha to Padam via the Shingo La (5090 metres). From Padam, the headquarters of the Zanskar region, there are regular buses to Kargil on the Leh to Srinagar road. See Lonely Planet's *Trekking in the Indian Himalaya* for more information.

Jeep Safaris

With a permit it's now possible to make a complete circuit of the area from Shimla through Saharan, Rekong Peo, Akpa,

Nachar, Sumdo, Tabo, Kaza, Kibar, Kunzam, Chandratal, Batal, Chatru to Manali and the Kullu Valley. Several travel agencies in Shimla and Manali offer jeep safaris covering this 10-day route. Shimla's YMCA (see Shimla) offers a tour that is good value.

Climate

As in Ladakh, little rain gets over the high Himalayan barrier so Lahaul and Spiti are dry and, for the most part, barren. Kinnaur is a transition zone between the forested valleys of the west and the bleak dry Tibetan region of the east.

The air is sharp and clear and the warm summer days are followed by cold, crisp nights. Beware of the burning power of the sun in this region – you can get burnt very quickly even on cool days. The heavy winter snow from September to May closes the passes except for a few months of each year.

Culture

The people of Lahaul, Spiti and Kinnaur follow a Tibetan form of Tantric Buddhism with a panoply of demons, saints and followers. The monasteries, known as gompas, are colourful places where the monks or lamas lead lives ordered by complicated regulations and rituals. There are many similarities between these people and the Ladakhis, further north. The people of Spiti are almost all Buddhists of Tibetan ancestry, but Lahaul and Kinnaur are split roughly 50:50 between Buddhists and Hindus.

ROHTANG PASS

The 3978-metre Rohtang Pass is the only access into Lahaul and is open only from June to September each year, although trekkers can cross the pass a little before it opens for vehicles. During the short season it's open, there are regular buses from Manali to Keylong. The weather can change very quickly up here and before the road was built many travellers never made it over the pass (the word *rohtang* means 'pile of dead bodies' in Tibetan!).

The tourist office in Manali operates a

daily Rs 100 bus up to the pass, mainly for tourists to 'see the snow'. It's a spectacular trip.

KEYLONG

Keylong is the main town in the Lahaul and Spiti region; there are a number of interesting monasteries within easy reach of this oasis-like town. The old Kharding Monastery, formerly the capital of Lahaul, overlooks Keylong, only 3.5 km away. Other monasteries include Shashur (three km), Tayal (six km) and Guru Ghantal (11 km).

Places to Stay & Eat

The HPTDC *Tourist Bungalow* has just three doubles at Rs 200, and dorm beds for Rs 45, but during the summer season they set up tents which cost Rs 125 for two people. There is also a *PWD Rest House*. The *Lamayuru* serves up good food and music in a pleasant atmosphere, although the cheap rooms are dark and dirty.

There are several other basic places to stay here.

Getting There & Away

Between Manali and Keylong there are buses hourly from 5 am in summer. The trip takes six hours and costs Rs 30. You can also pick up ordinary buses from here on Monday, Wednesday and Friday for the two-day trip to Leh but at present the more comfortable HPTDC buses run only from Manali. As the route becomes more popular it's likely that more buses will be laid on and it may also be possible to get a seat in a jeep. See the Leh section in the Jammu & Kashmir chapter for more information about this route.

AROUND KEYLONG

A short distance before Keylong on the Manali to Keylong road, is **Gondhla** with its eight-storey castle of the Thakur of Gondhla and an historically significant gompa. You can trek back to Gondhla from Keylong, cutting across the loop the road makes. Between Gondhla and Keylong is **Tandi**,

where the Chandrabagha or Chenab River meets the road.

Following the Chenab Valley to the north-west towards Kilar will bring you to **Triloknath** with its white-marble, six-armed image of Avalokitesvara. Close by is the village of **Udaipur**, with a finely carved wooden temple from the 10th or 11th century which is dedicated to Mrikula Devi.

SPITI VALLEY

The 4500-metre **Kunzam Pass** connects the Lahaul and Spiti valleys. Although the pass may be open by mid-May, a safer date is mid-June. Outside the brief summer season, Spiti is closed to the outside world.

A road now runs from Kaza, the principal Spiti village, south-east through Samdoh to meet the Hindustan to Tibet road in Kinnaur. There are few settlements in this barren, high region.

Kaza

Kaza (or Kaja) is the main village in Spiti. It's not of great interest in itself but there are good treks in the area and several gompas worth visiting.

Kee Gompa, a picturesque collection of Tibetan-style buildings set on a small hill, is the largest in Spiti. Along the road it's 14 km from Kaza, but the best way to get here is on foot, a 10-km hike along the path. A monk will show you around this monastery which houses a priceless collection of ancient thangkas.

Fifteen km north-west of Kaza is **Kibar** (or Kyipur), which at 4205 metres is reputed to be the highest village in the world.

Places to Stay There's a *Rest House* and, in the old part of the town, several cheap lodges catering to travellers.

Getting There & Away Two hundred km from Manali, there's just one bus a day to Kaza via Keylong. The bus trip from Keylong takes eight hours.

Infrequent local buses link Kaza with Kee Gompa and Kibar.

Tabo

One of the most important gompas, not just in Spiti but in the whole of the Tibetan Buddhist world, is at Tabo.

Tabo was founded in 996 AD by Rinchen Zangpo, who brought artists from Kashmir to decorate the gompa. Their beautiful work can still be seen here. There are eight temples in the monastery complex, some dating from the 10th century. There's also a modern gompa and painting school founded by the Dalai Lama.

Places to Stay There's a *Rest House* and a few rooms at the monastery. Leave a donation if you stay there.

Getting There & Away There are infrequent buses to Kaza. Most foreigners visit Tabo on an organised jeep safari from Manali or Shimla.

KINNAUR REGION

Lying on an ancient trade route to Tibet that follows the valley of the Sutlej River, much of this border area is now open to foreigners. There are some fascinating treks in the Kinnaur region but you need to be self-sufficient since there are few places to stay.

Rampur

Rampur, 140 km from Shimla, beyond Narkanda, is the gateway to the region. It's the site for a major trade fair in the second week of November each year, and was once a major centre for trade between India and Tibet. There are direct buses from Shimla to Rampur, which has a *PWD Rest House* and a few cheap hotels.

Sarahan

The last village in the district before entering Kinnaur, Sarahan is spectacularly located above the Sutlej River. It was the summer capital of the local Bhushar rajas and is now best known for its hill architecture. The Bhimakali Temple with its two wooden pagodas is a remarkable sight, a curious blend of Buddhist and Hindu styles. Until the early 19th century, this was the scene of

human sacrifices. The blood still flows during Dussehra but no longer from human victims.

An easy five-day walk takes you from Sarahan along the old Hindustan to Tibet road through the scenic Sutlej Valley. Along the route there are *Rest Houses* at Chaura, Tranda, Paunda and Nechar. From Wangtu you can catch a bus to Shimla or Kalpa.

Places to Stay The HPTDC *Hotel Srikhand* (☎ 234) is a modern building with dorm beds for Rs 45, one double at Rs 150, and a range of other rooms from Rs 250 to Rs 500. It's also possible to stay at the Bhimakali Temple.

Getting There & Away Sarahan is 180 km from Shimla, and the Kinnaur region (see separate section). There are direct buses to Jeori, which is 19 km from Ghart, the village just below Sarahan. There are only a couple of buses (late afternoon) from Jeori to Ghart, but you can walk this in a couple of hours up the path that takes a short cut between the two villages.

Nachar

This picturesque village is, like Sarahan, on the Hindustan to Tibet road which has been replaced by the new road nearby. There's a *Rest House* in the orchards.

Tapri & Choltu

Only 15 km further up the valley from Nachar, three roads meet at this scenic spot. One is the main road continuing up the valley to Kalpa. The second is the old road, also continuing to Kalpa via Rogi. The third is a small road which crosses the river and passes through Choltu and Kilba to the Sangla Valley. Choltu has a pleasant *Rest House*.

Sangla

The main village in the Sangla Valley is 18 km from Karcham, on the Hindustan to Tibet road, and can be reached by jeep or on foot. It's a good base for trekking and there's a comfortable *Rest House*.

Rekong Peo

This uninspiring collection of buildings forms the district headquarters of Kinnaur, three km above the main road. Inner Line Permits are available from the District Magistrate, and you can hire porters and buy trekking supplies here. You can walk up to Kalpa from here in about an hour.

Rekong Peo has a *Rest House* and a few cheap hotels. There are six buses a day to Shimla and the journey takes up to 10 hours.

Kalpa

Formerly known as Chini, when it was the main town in Kinnaur, Kalpa is dramatically located close to the foot of 6050-metre-high Kinnaur Kailash. This is the legendary winter home of Siva; during the winter the god is said to retire to his Himalayan home here and indulge his passion for hashish. In the month of Magha (January/February) the gods of Kinnaur supposedly meet here for an annual conference with Siva.

Kalpa has a *Rest House* and it's also possible to stay with villagers.

North Kinnaur

An Inner Line Permit is required to visit this remote region, geographically part of Tibet. From Kalpa you can continue on the northern side of the river to Puh and Namgia, close to the Tibetan border. Only 14 km from Kalpa, the tiny village of **Pangli** has a small *Rest House* and a fine view of Kinnaur Kailash. **Rarang**, eight km further on, is another centre for trade to Tibet.

The spectacular pilgrimage trekking route around Kinnaur Kailash takes at least five days, and you'll also need to allow time to acclimatise before crossing the Charang La. A tent is necessary since the only accommodation is the *Rest House* at Chitkul. The route starts at Morang (reached by bus from Rekong Peo) and continues through Thangi, Rahtak, over the 5265-metre Charang La, through Chitkul, and down to Sangla following the Baspar Valley to Karcham.

HIMACHAL PRADESH

Jammu & Kashmir

The state of Jammu & Kashmir, J&K for short, is a region of widely varying people and geography. In the south, Jammu is a transition zone from the Indian plains to the Himalaya. Correctly, the rest of the state is Kashmir but in practice this title is reserved for the beautiful Vale of Kashmir, a large Himalayan valley in the north of the state. Here the people are predominantly Muslim and in many ways look towards Pakistan and central Asia rather than towards India.

Finally, to the north-east is the remote Tibetan plateau region known as Ladakh, primarily Buddhist and Tibetan in its culture and a very clear contrast to the rest of Kashmir, indeed to the rest of India. Sandwiched between the Kashmir and Ladakh regions is a long narrow valley known as Zanskar. This valley is even more isolated than Ladakh although, with the improvement of the road into the valley, the number of visitors has soared in recent years and things are changing rapidly.

The political violence in the Kashmir Valley since the late 1980s has discouraged most travellers from visiting what was once one of India's most popular tourist regions. A spell on a houseboat on Dal Lake has always been one of India's real treats and Kashmir also offers some delightful trekking opportunities and unsurpassed scenery. Before 1990 over 600,000 Indian tourists and 60,000 foreign visitors were visiting Srinagar each year but this has now been reduced to virtually nil. The Kashmiris say that the Government of India is trying to dissuade tourists from visiting the area in order to starve the local tourist industry of earnings. The actions of a few militant Kashmiris in the past have not been helpful, though. In the last five years a number of foreigners have been abducted and released, while a few have actually died.

J&K Tourism insists that whatever the future may bring for Kashmir, tourism will still be of vital importance to the local

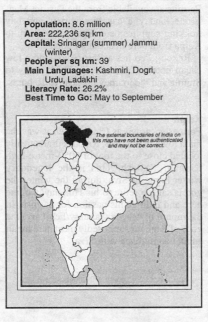

Population: 8.6 million
Area: 222,236 sq km
Capital: Srinagar (summer) Jammu (winter)
People per sq km: 39
Main Languages: Kashmiri, Dogri, Urdu, Ladakhi
Literacy Rate: 26.2%
Best Time to Go: May to September

The external boundaries of India on this map have not been authenticated and may not be correct.

economy, so terrorist attacks and kidnappings will not be targeted on tourists. There's still a steady trickle of hardy travellers visiting Kashmir, but as your movement is restricted to certain areas of Srinagar there seems little point. Before visiting Srinagar and the Kashmir Valley check the current situation with your embassy and talk to recently returned travellers.

Ladakh, on the other hand, is far removed from the troubles and has greatly benefited from the slump in tourism to the west of the state. A regular bus service runs between Leh and Manali in Himachal Pradesh, a spectacular two-day trip over the world's second-highest motorable road. Ladakh offers a chance to study a region which, in today's world, is probably even more Tibetan than Tibet.

No special permits are required to visit Kashmir or Ladakh, but your movements are restricted in that you are not allowed to approach within a certain distance of the border. In Ladakh this means you are not allowed more than 1.6 km north of the Srinagar to Leh road without permission. In the Kashmir Valley all foreigners are required to register their arrival. In Srinagar this is done at the airport or can be handled by your houseboat owner if you come by bus.

Mid-May to mid-July, the hot season in the plains, is when people head for the hills. The roads will usually be open between Srinagar and Ladakh by early June and this is the best trekking time. August is the high season in Ladakh; book planes well in advance if you plan to arrive then. Skiing used to be from mid-January to mid-March near Gulmarg, but is not possible at present.

Warning

Security in this region is very tight. Srinagar town is potentially dangerous, and Jammu has suffered several bomb blasts, with serious loss of life. Most alarming for travellers is that foreigners are being targeted by insurgent groups. In mid-1995, five trekkers

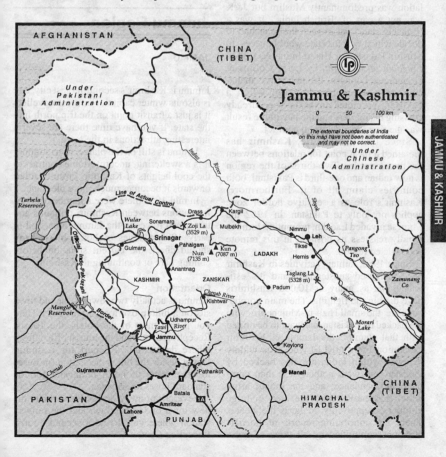

JAMMU & KASHMIR

were kidnapped – one of the group, a young Norwegian, was executed. Lonely Planet advises that travellers do *not* visit the western part of Jammu & Kashmir state, especially Jammu, Srinagar, the Kashmir Valley and the Zanskar Valley. See also the Warning in the Zanskar section.

History

Jammu & Kashmir has always been a centre of conflict for independent India. When India and Pakistan became independent, there was much controversy over which country the region should go to. The population was predominantly Muslim but J&K was not a part of 'British India'. It was a 'princely state' and as such the ruler had to decide which way his state would move – to Muslim Pakistan or Hindu India. As told in *Freedom at Midnight*, by Larry Collins & Dominique Lapierre, the indecisive maharaja only made his decision when a Pakistani-prompted invasion was already crossing his borders and the inevitable result was the first Indo-Pakistani conflict.

Since that first battle, Kashmir has remained a flash point for relations between the two countries. Two-thirds of the region is now Indian and one-third is Pakistani; both countries claim all of it. Furthermore, Kashmir's role as a sensitive border zone applies not only to Pakistan. In 1962 the Chinese invaded Ladakh, prompting India to rapidly reassess its position in this remote and isolated region.

Since 1988, militant activities in Kashmir have increased substantially and it's estimated that as many as 10,000 Kashmiris have died in the fighting. The main combatants are: the small Hizb-ul-Mujahedin, who are backed by Pakistan and want to be united with that country; the Jammu & Kashmir Liberation Front (JKLF) who, it is widely believed within India, are also backed by Pakistan and want nothing less than complete independence; and the Indian army which has moved into the area in large numbers, supposedly to keep the peace. There are continuing reports of horrific atrocities committed by all three of these groups and in spite of talks between India and Pakistan it is unlikely that the situation will improve in the near future.

In 1990 the government of Kashmir was dissolved and the state placed under direct rule from Delhi (President's Rule). In an effort to restore confidence and, it was hoped, something approaching normalcy, the central government rather optimistically scheduled state elections for September 1994. However, these elections were not held and the ongoing problems here continue to make Kashmir India's most troubled state.

Jammu Region

JAMMU

Population: 257,000
Telephone Area Code: 0191

Jammu is Kashmir's second-largest city, and is also its winter capital. For most travellers it is just a transit point on the trip north into the state. If you have time there are several interesting attractions in the town.

Jammu is still on the plains, so in summer it is a sweltering, uncomfortable contrast to the cool heights of Kashmir. From October onwards it becomes much more pleasant.

In mid-1992 there were a number of confrontations between Kashmiri militants and the armed forces in the Jammu area, and in early 1995 a series of bomb blasts. You should check the current situation before coming here or continuing to Kashmir.

Orientation

Jammu is actually two towns – the old town sits on a hilltop overlooking the river. Here you'll find most of the hotels, the Tourist Reception Centre and the tourist office, from where deluxe buses depart for Kashmir. Down beside the hill is the station for buses to other parts of north India and for the standard buses to Srinagar.

Several km away across the river is the new town of Jammu Tawi and the railway station where you'll find a second Tourist Reception Centre.

If you're en route to Srinagar and arrive in Jammu by train (as most people do), then you have two choices: you can keep going straight through to Srinagar or stay overnight in Jammu.

If you choose the first option you have to take one of the buses which wait at the railway station for the arrival of the trains. If these buses don't leave Jammu early enough they stop for the night at Banihal, just below the Jawarhar Tunnel, and continue on to Srinagar the following day. Following the political problems in Kashmir the tunnel is closed at night. Accommodation in Banihal is usually in the *Tourist Lodge* and is very basic.

The second choice is to stay overnight in Jammu and take a bus to Srinagar the first thing next day. These early buses complete the journey to Srinagar in one day. If you decide to stay overnight then it's important first to find yourself a room and then book a ticket on the bus.

Information
The J&K tourist office (☎ 548-172) is at the Tourist Reception Centre on Vir Marg. They have very little general information, but may have some good information about trekking routes in the Patnitop and Bhadarwah areas. Trekking gear can be hired from the Tourist Reception Centre at the station in Jammu Tawi.

Raghunath & Rambireswar Temples
The Raghunath Temple is in the centre of the city, only a short stroll from the Tourist Reception Centre. This large temple complex was built in 1835 but is not especially interesting, although it makes a good sunset silhouette. The Rambireswar Temple, also centrally located, is dedicated to Siva and dates from 1883.

Dogra Art Gallery
The Dogra Art Gallery, in the Gandhi Bhavan near the new Secretariat, has an

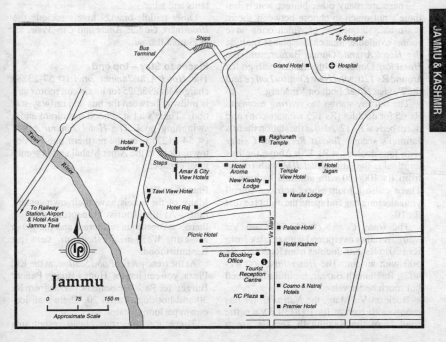

Jammu

0   75   150 m

Approximate Scale

Bus Terminal

Steps

To Srinagar

Grand Hotel   ✚ Hospital

Tawi River

Hotel Broadway

Steps

Raghunath Temple

Amar & City View Hotels

Hotel Aroma

New Kwality Lodge

Temple View Hotel

Hotel Jagan

Tawi View Hotel

Narula Lodge

Hotel Raj

To Railway Station, Airport & Hotel Asia Jammu Tawi

Picnic Hotel

Vir Marg

Palace Hotel

Hotel Kashmir

Bus Booking Office

ℹ Tourist Reception Centre

Cosmo & Natraj Hotels

KC Plaza

Premier Hotel

JAMMU & KASHMIR

important collection of miniature paintings including many from the locally renowned Basohli and Kangra schools. The gallery is open from 7.30 am to 1 pm in summer and from 11 am to 5 pm in winter but is closed on Monday; admission is free.

Amar Mahal

On the northern outskirts of town, just off the Srinagar road, is the Amar Mahal palace, a curious example of French architecture. The palace **museum** has a family portrait gallery and another important collection of paintings.

Places to Stay – bottom end

At the bottom end of the market, the popular *Tawi View Hotel* (☎ 547-301), Maheshi Gate, is the best of the bunch at Rs 70/90 for singles/doubles with bath. There's a restaurant here. Another simple place is the *Hotel Kashmir*, Vir Marg, with singles/doubles at Rs 80/100, or Rs 100/130 with attached bath.

There are many other budget hotels but there's not much to choose between them; it's usually a question of which ones have rooms available. Reasonable places include the *Hotel Aroma*, Gumat Bazaar, and the *Hotel Raj*. Doubles with attached bath go for around Rs 120 at the *New Kwality Lodge* and the *Palace Hotel*, both on Vir Marg.

The railway station has *retiring rooms* at Rs 65 for doubles (Rs 125 with air-con) and dorm beds at Rs 12. Also at the station there's Jammu's second *Tourist Reception Centre* with four doubles at Rs 120. Above the bus terminal is the basic *Hotel JDA* with rooms from Rs 100/130 with attached bathroom. There's also a room where you can unroll your sleeping bag and spend the night for just Rs 10.

The *Hotel Cosmo* (☎ 547-561), on Vir Marg, is rather overpriced with singles from Rs 120 to Rs 200, doubles from Rs 200 or Rs 500 with air-con. The *Hotel Jagan* (☎ 42-402), Raghunath Bazaar, is similarly priced but much better value.

Back on Vir Marg, the *Natraj Hotel* has rooms with bath at Rs 100/130. Down the road from the Raghunath Temple are a number of other bottom and middle-range hotels.

Places to Stay – middle

The large *Tourist Reception Centre* (☎ 54-9554) has doubles with attached bathroom for Rs 150, or Rs 250 with air-cooling, Rs 300 with air-con. Nearby is the spotless *Narula Lodge* with just five rooms for Rs 150/250. Guests have their own bathrooms but these are not attached to the rooms.

Near the Hotel Raj and beside the Jewel Cinema, *Hotel Jewel's* (☎ 54-7630) is a good clean place with air-cooled rooms for Rs 250/310 and air-con rooms for Rs 350/410. All rooms have attached bathroom and cable TV. There's a fast-food restaurant downstairs.

On Vir Marg, the *Premier Hotel* (☎ 54-3234) is not quite so good with ordinary rooms at Rs 265/335 or Rs 300/370 for air-cooled rooms, Rs 410/500 with air-con. Rooms have TV and there are two restaurants and a bar.

Other middle-bracket hotels include the *Broadway, Gagan, Amar* and *City View*, all in Gumat Bazaar.

Places to Stay – top end

The *Hotel Asia Jammu Tawi* (☎ 57-2328) charges Rs 895/995 for its air-con rooms and is midway between the bus and railway stations. There's a bar, a good restaurant and a swimming pool. The *Hotel Jammu Ashok* (☎ 54-3127) is on the northern outskirts of town, close to the Amar Mahal and is somewhat cheaper.

Places to Eat

Many of the hotels have their own restaurants. At the Tourist Reception Centre, there's a vegetarian restaurant and the plush air-con *Wazman Restaurant* serving Kashmiri food.

At the trendy *KC's Food Station*, at the KC Plaza, you can have a 'Huggy Buggy Paneer Burger' for Rs 20, reasonable pizzas from Rs 30 and hot dogs for Rs 20. There's an ice-cream parlour upstairs.

There are numerous cheap restaurants

along Vir Marg and towards the bus terminal. At the railway *refreshment room* a vegetarian thali is Rs 12.

The air-con restaurant at the *Cosmo Hotel* is better than the accommodation – good for a cold beer and a pleasant meal in cool surroundings. Main dishes are around Rs 60. A few doors down, the *Premier* has Chinese and Kashmiri food and is similarly priced.

Getting There & Away

Air The Indian Airlines office (☎ 54-2735) is at the Tourist Reception Centre.

Indian Airlines has daily flights to Delhi (US$74) and Srinagar (US$27), and a weekly (Saturday) flight to Leh (US$39).

Bus Srinagar buses depart from various locations: superfast mini-coaches, A-class and deluxe go from the Tourist Reception Centre; B-class leave from the bus terminal; and private buses depart from various parts of the city. Buses also leave from the railway station where they meet arriving trains – thus you can take the overnight *4645 Shalimar Express* from Delhi and catch a bus as soon as you arrive at around 6.15 am. Buses normally depart between 6 and 7 am in order to reach Srinagar by nightfall. It is vital to book your bus ticket as soon as you arrive.

Jammu to Srinagar bus fares are Rs 94 for A-class, Rs 130 superdeluxe and Rs 210 for the mini-coaches. The journey takes 10 to 12 hours on most of the buses and under 10 hours on the mini-coaches.

Southbound, there are frequent buses from Jammu to Delhi (14 hours), Amritsar (five hours), Pathankot (three hours) and other cities. Pathankot is the departure point for Dharamsala, Dalhousie and the other Himachal Pradesh hill stations.

Train The *4645 Shalimar Express* leaves Delhi at 4.10 pm and arrives in Jammu at 6.15 am. This is the only train that arrives early enough to link up with the early buses to Srinagar. The fare for the 585-km trip from Delhi is Rs 147 in 2nd class, Rs 436 in 1st. There are also direct rail links with

Madras, Bombay, Calcutta, Varanasi and Gorakhpur.

Taxi As a faster alternative to the buses, you could take a share taxi to Srinagar, from outside the railway station in Jammu. Seats cost around three times the deluxe bus fare and they depart as soon as they've collected five passengers.

Getting Around

The airport is seven km out of town, and is serviced by auto-rickshaws and taxis.

Jammu has metered taxis, auto-rickshaws, a minibus service and a tempo service between a number of points.

JAMMU TO SRINAGAR

Although most people simply head straight through from Jammu to Srinagar, there are a few places of interest between the two centres. Some can also be reached using Jammu as a base. Prior to the completion of the Jawarhar Tunnel into the Kashmir Valley, the trip from Jammu took two days with an overnight stop at Batote.

Akhnoor

The Chenab River meets the plains here, 32 km north-west of Jammu. This used to be the route to Srinagar in the Mughal era. Jehangir, who died en route to Kashmir, was temporarily buried at Chingas.

Surinsar & Mansar Lakes

East of Jammu, these lakes are picturesque and the scene for an annual festival at Mansar.

Vaishno Devi

This important cave temple is dedicated to the three mother goddesses of Hinduism. Thousands of pilgrims visit the cave each year after making a steep 12-km climb from the roadhead at Katra or taking a shorter and easier climb from a new road.

Riasi

Near this town, 20 km beyond Katra, is the ruined **fort** of General Zorawar Singh, renowned for his clashes with the Chinese

JAMMU & KASHMIR

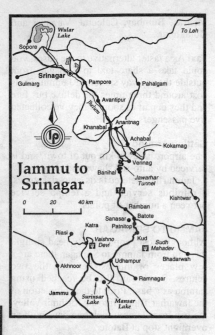

Jammu to Srinagar

over Ladakh. Nearby is a **gurdwara** with some interesting old frescoes and another important **cave temple**.

Ramnagar
The Palace of Colours has many beautiful Pahari-style wall paintings. Buses run here from Jammu or Udhampur. Krimchi, 10 km from Udhampur, has Hindu **temples** with fine carvings and sculptures.

Kud
This is a popular lunch stop at 1738 metres on the Jammu to Srinagar route. It's also popular in its own right as a hill resort and has a *tourist bungalow*. There's a well-known **mountain spring**, Swamai Ki Bauli, 1.5 km from the road.

Patnitop
At 2024 metres, this popular hill station has many pleasant walks. Patnitop is intended to be the nucleus of tourist developments in this area, and there are *Tourist Huts*, a *Tourist Rest House* and a *youth hostel*.

Paragliding courses are run here; they must be arranged through the Tourist Reception Centre in Jammu.

Batote
Only 12 km from Kud, and connected to Patnitop and Kud by a number of footpaths, this hill resort at 1560 metres was the overnight stop between Jammu and Srinagar before the tunnel was opened. There is a *Tourist Bungalow*, *Tourist Huts* and several private hotels. As in Kud, there is a **spring** close to the village – Amrit Chasma is only 2.5 km away.

Sudh Mahadev
Many pilgrims visit the Siva temple here during the annual July/August **Asad Purnima** festival which features three days of music, singing and dancing.

Five km from Sudh Mahadev is **Man Talai**, where some archaeological discoveries have been made. An eight-km walking or jeep track leads to Sudh Mahadev from Kud or Patnitop.

Sanasar
At 2079 metres, this beautiful valley is a centre for the Gujjar shepherds each summer. There is a *Tourist Bungalow*, tourist huts and several private hotels.

Bhadarwah
Every two years a procession of pilgrims walks from this beautiful high-altitude valley to the 4400-metre-high **Kaplash Lake**. A week later the three-day **Mela Patt** festival takes place in Bhadarwah. There is a *Tourist Rest House* in this scenic location.

Kishtwar
Well off the Jammu to Srinagar road there is a trekking route from Kishtwar to Srinagar. You can also trek from Kishtwar into Zanskar. There are many waterfalls around Kishtwar, and 19 km from the town is the pilgrimage site of **Sarthal Devi**.

Jawarhar Tunnel

During the winter months, Srinagar was often completely cut off from the rest of India before this tunnel was completed. The 2.5-km-long tunnel is 200 km from Jammu and 93 km from Srinagar and has two separate passages. It's extremely rough and damp inside.

From Banihal, 17 km before the tunnel, you are already entering the Kashmiri region and people speak Kashmiri as well as Dogri. As soon as you emerge from the tunnel you are in the green, lush Vale of Kashmir.

Kashmir Valley

This is one of the most beautiful regions of India but over the last five years or so it has been racked by political violence. See the warnings at the beginning of this chapter before venturing up here.

The Mughal rulers of India were always happy to retreat from the heat of the plains to the cool green heights of Kashmir, and indeed Jehangir's last words, when he died en route to the 'happy valley', were a simple request for 'only Kashmir'. The Mughals developed their formal garden-style art to its greatest heights in Kashmir, and some of their gardens are beautifully kept even to this day.

One of Kashmir's greatest attractions is undoubtedly the Dal Lake houseboats. During the Raj period Kashmir's ruler would not permit the British (who were as fond of Kashmir's cool climate as the Mughals) to own land here. So they adopted the superbly British solution of building houseboats – each one a little bit of England, afloat on Dal Lake. A visit to Kashmir, it is often said, is not complete until you have stayed on a houseboat.

Of course Srinagar, Dal Lake and houseboats are not all there is to Kashmir. Around the edges of the valley are Kashmir's delightful hill stations. Places like Pahalgam and Gulmarg are pleasant in their own right and also good bases for trekking trips.

SRINAGAR

Population: 725,000
Telephone Area Code: 0194

The summer capital of Kashmir stands on Dal Lake and the Jhelum River, and is the transport hub for the valley as well as a departure point for trips to Ladakh.

Srinagar is a crowded, colourful city with a distinctly Central Asian flavour. Indeed the people look different from those in the rest of India; and when you head south from Srinagar it is always referred to as 'returning to India'.

Srinagar now has the feel of an occupied city and there's often a curfew after dark. There are roadblocks everywhere and soldiers in bunkers on all street corners. Most of the fighting takes place in the old city, usually during the night. This part of town looks like Beirut at the height of the troubles and should be avoided if you value your life. Information below on the sights within the old city is included in the hope that the situation may improve. At present, the safest areas are the lakes, and the houseboat owners are the best sources of information for which places in Srinagar to avoid. Be sure to take their advice.

Orientation

Srinagar is initially a little confusing because Dal Lake, so much a part of the city, is such a strange lake. It's actually three lakes, separated by dykes or 'floating gardens', and at times it's hard to tell where lake ends and land begins.

On the lake there are houseboats that are firmly attached to the bottom, and houses that look like they could float away. Most of the houseboats are at the southern end of the lake, although you will also find them on the Jhelum River and north on Nagin Lake. The Jhelum River makes a loop around the main part of town, and a canal connecting the river with Dal Lake converts that part of town into an island. Along the south of this 'island' is the Bund, a popular walk where you will find the GPO and the handicrafts centre. The large Tourist Reception Centre is just north of the Bund.

JAMMU & KASHMIR

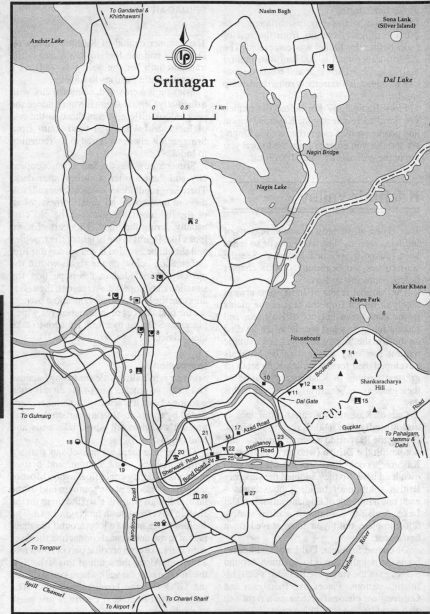

JAMMU & KASHMIR

Srinagar

To Gandarbal &
Khirbhawani

Nasim Bagh

Sona Lank
(Silver Island)

Anchar Lake

Dal Lake

0   0.5   1 km

Nagin Bridge

Nagin Lake

Kotar Khana

Nehru Park

Houseboats

Shankaracharya
Hill

Dal Gate

Boulevard

Gupkar

Road

To Pahalgam,
Jammu &
Delhi

To Gulmarg

To Tengpur

To Airport

To Charari Sharif

Azad Road

Residency
Road

Sherwani Road

Bund Road

Aerodrome
Road

Spill Channel

Jhelum River

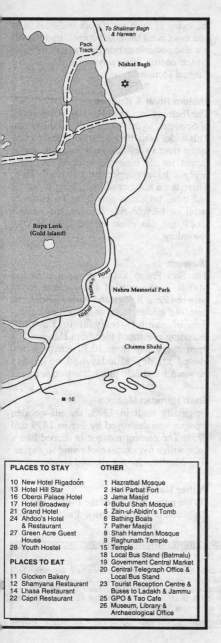

There are many restaurants, shops, travel agents and hotels in the island part of town. The more modern part of Srinagar stretches away south of the Jhelum River while the older parts of town are north and north-west of here.

The Boulevard, running alongside Dal Lake, is an important address in Srinagar with the *shikara* ghats providing access to the houseboats, hotels, restaurants and shops along the way. Other main roads are Residency Rd, linking the Tourist Reception Centre with the downtown area, and Polo View Rd, lined with handicraft shops and travel agencies.

Information

Tourist Office The J&K Department of Tourism office (☎ 77-305) is at the Tourist Reception Centre, which is a large complex housing (among other things) the various tourist departments and Indian Airlines. It's also the departure and arrival point for Jammu and Leh buses. In recent times it has been partly occupied by the Indian army but the tourist counter, railway agency and bus booking offices were still operating.

Post & Telecommunications The heavily barricaded GPO is on the Bund and is open from 10 am to 1 pm and 1.30 to 3 pm Monday to Saturday, closed Sunday.

Parcels are normally sent from the Air Cargo Complex on Residency Rd, near the Tourist Reception Centre and across from the Cafe de Linz. However, to avoid the risk of incendiary devices hidden in parcels nothing larger than a letter may now be sent from Srinagar.

The central telegraph office is on Hotel (Maulana Azad) Rd.

Visa Extensions The Foreigners' Registration Office is next to the park with the Government Handicrafts Emporium near the Bund.

Bookshops The best bookshops are the Kashmir Bookshop and the Hind Bookshop,

PLACES TO STAY	OTHER
10 New Hotel Rigadoon	1 Hazratbal Mosque
13 Hotel Hill Star	2 Hari Parbat Fort
16 Oberoi Palace Hotel	3 Jama Masjid
17 Hotel Broadway	4 Bulbul Shah Mosque
21 Grand Hotel	5 Zain-ul-Abidin's Tomb
24 Ahdoo's Hotel	6 Bathing Boats
& Restaurant	7 Pather Masjid
27 Green Acre Guest	8 Shah Hamdan Mosque
House	9 Raghunath Temple
28 Youth Hostel	15 Temple
	18 Local Bus Stand (Batmalu)
PLACES TO EAT	19 Government Central Market
	20 Central Telegraph Office &
11 Glocken Bakery	Local Bus Stand
12 Shamyana Restaurant	23 Tourist Reception Centre &
14 Lhasa Restaurant	Buses to Ladakh & Jammu
22 Capri Restaurant	25 GPO & Tao Cafe
	26 Museum, Library &
	Archaeological Office

JAMMU & KASHMIR

across from each other on Sherwani Rd (the continuation of Residency Rd) downtown.

Dal Lake

Much of Dal Lake is a maze of intricate waterways rather than a simple body of open water. The lake is divided into Gagribal, Lokut Dal and Bod Dal by a series of causeways. Dal Gate, at the city end of the lake, controls the flow of the lake water into the Jhelum River canal.

Within the lake are two islands which are popular picnic spots. **Sona Lank** (Silver Island) is at the northern end of the lake while **Rupa Lank** (Gold Island) is to the south. Both are also known as Char Chinar because they each have four *chinar* trees on them. There's a third island, Nehru Park, at the end of the main stretch of the lakeside Boulevard, but it is a miserable affair. East of Nehru Park a long causeway juts out into the lake towards **Kotar Khana**, the House of Pigeons, which was once a royal summer house.

The waters of Dal Lake are amazingly clear, considering what must be poured into them, not only from the houseboats but from the city and outlying areas too. There is no real sewage disposal system and, despite what you may be told, all the waste from the houseboats goes straight into the lake.

Whether you're just lazing on your houseboat balcony watching the shikaras glide by, or visiting the Mughal gardens around the lake, there's plenty to see and do. A shikara circuit of the lake is an experience not to be missed. A leisurely cruise around will take all day, including visits to the Mughal gardens, and cost about Rs 100 for the day or Rs 20 per hour. There's hardly a more leisurely and pleasurable way of getting into

the swing of Srinagar. If your budget is tight you can circuit the lake yourself by bicycle. It's also possible to ride right across the lake on the central causeway – see the Getting Around section.

Jhelum River & Bridges

The Jhelum flows from Verinag, 80 km south of Srinagar, to the Wular Lake to the north. This wide, swift-flowing, muddy and picturesque river sweeps through Srinagar, and is famed for its nine old bridges, but new bridges have popped up between them. There are a number of interesting mosques and other buildings near it, and a leisurely stroll or bicycle ride through the narrow lanes that run close to the river is very rewarding.

Museum

The Shri Pratap Singh Museum is in Lal Mandi, just south of the Jhelum River between Zero Bridge and Amira Kadal, the first 'old' bridge. It has an interesting collection of exhibits relevant to Kashmir, including illustrated tiles from Harwan. It's open every day from 10.30 am to 4 pm, closed all day Monday and on Friday between 1 and 2.30 pm; admission is free.

Shah Hamdan Mosque

Originally built in 1395, the all-wooden mosque was destroyed by fire in 1479 and 1731. The present mosque is shaped like a cube with a pyramidal roof rising to a spire. Non-Muslims are not allowed inside.

Pather Masjid

On the opposite bank of the Jhelum River is the unused and run-down Pather Masjid.

Complaints

J&K was the first Indian state to instigate legislation to protect tourists from being ripped off. According to the 1978 Act, tourists may report any person found 'cheating, touting or obstructing in allowing free choice for shopping or stay or travel arrangements'. The offender is liable to be blacklisted, fined up to Rs 1000 or imprisoned for up to three months! It may be enough just to threaten someone with the Act. If this doesn't work go to the Deputy Director of Tourism in the Tourist Reception Centre. ■

This fine stone mosque was built by Nur Jahan in 1623.

Tomb of Zain-ul-Abidin

Back on the east bank between the Zaina Kadal and Ali Kadal bridges is the slightly decrepit tomb of King Zain-ul-Abidin, the highly regarded son of Sultan Sikander. Built on the foundations of an earlier temple, the tomb shows a clear Persian influence in its domed construction and glazed tiles.

Jama Masjid

This impressive wooden mosque is notable for the 300-plus pillars supporting the roof, each made of a single deodar tree trunk. The present mosque, with its green and peaceful inner courtyard, was rebuilt to the original design after a fire in 1674.

The mosque has had a chequered history: first built in 1385 by Sultan Sikander, it was enlarged by Zain-ul-Abidin in 1402 and then destroyed by fire in 1479. Rebuilt in 1503, it was destroyed by another fire during Jehangir's reign. Again it was rebuilt only to burn down once more before its most recent rebuilding.

Shankaracharya Hill

Rising up behind The Boulevard beside Dal Lake, this hill was once known as Takht-i-Sulaiman, the Throne of Solomon. A temple is said to have first been built here by Ashoka's son around 200 BC, but the present **Hindu temple** dates from Jehangir's time. It's a pleasant stroll to the top, from where you have a fine view over Dal Lake. The Srinagar TV tower is also here. There's a road right to the top.

Mughal Gardens

Chasma Shahi (nine km from Srinagar) Smallest of the Mughal gardens at Srinagar, the Chasma Shahi are well up the hillside, above the Nehru Memorial Park. The gardens were laid out in 1632 but have been recently extended. These are the only gardens with an admission charge.

Pari Mahal (10 km) Just above the Chasma Shahi is this fine old Sufi college. The ruined, arched terraces have recently been turned into a very pleasant and well-kept garden with fine views over Dal Lake. From the Pari Mahal you can descend straight down the hill to the road that runs back to the Oberoi Palace Hotel.

Nishat Bagh (11 km) Sandwiched between the lake and the mountains, the Nishat gardens have a superb view across the lake to the Pir Panjal mountains. Designed in 1633 by Nur Jahan's brother Asaf Khan, these are the largest of the Mughal gardens and follow the traditional pattern of a central channel running down a series of terraces.

Shalimar Bagh (15 km) Set some distance back from the lake but reached by a small canal, the Shalimar gardens were built for Nur Jahan, 'light of the world', by her husband Jehangir in 1616. During the Mughal period the topmost of the four terraces was reserved for the emperor and the ladies of the court.

Since the curfew began, the nightly son et lumiére (sound & light show) that used to be put on in these beautiful gardens during the tourist season (May to September) has been suspended.

Nasim Bagh (eight km) Just beyond the Hazratbal Mosque, these gardens were built by Akbar in 1586 and are the oldest of Kashmir's Mughal gardens. Today, they are used by an engineering college and not maintained as gardens. Before the political troubles it was possible to camp in these gardens with prior permission from the Tourist Reception Centre.

Hazratbal Mosque

This shiny, modern mosque is on the northwest shore of Dal Lake. The mosque enshrines a hair of the prophet, but to non-believers it is most interesting for its stunningly beautiful setting on the shores of the lake with snowcapped peaks as a backdrop. In 1994 it was the scene of a violent siege when the Indian army flushed out a number of militants who had taken refuge in the mosque.

Nagin Lake
The Jewel in the Ring is held to be the most beautiful of the Dal lakes and is ringed by trees. There are a number of houseboats on this quieter, cleaner lake – ideal if you want to get away from it all.

Hari Parbat Fort
Clearly visible on top of the Sharika hill, to the west of Dal Lake, this fort was originally built between 1592 and 1598 during the rule of Akbar, but most of the present construction dates from the 18th century. Visits were only possible with written permission from the Archaeology Department but since the army has moved into the fort, this is unlikely to be granted. At the southern gate there is a shrine to the sixth Sikh guru.

Pandrethan Temple
This small but beautifully proportioned Siva temple dates from 900 AD and is in the military cantonment area on the Jammu road out of Srinagar.

Organised Tours
Since travel around Kashmir is severely restricted all tours have been suspended. J&K Road Transport Corporation (J&KRTC) used to operate tours to Pahalgam, Daksum, Gulmarg, Aharbal, Verinag, Wular Lake, Yusmarg, Sonamarg and the Mughal gardens with departures from the Tourist Reception Centre. Private bus companies, particularly the KMDA (Kashmir Motor Drivers' Association), also had several tours. No doubt these will be resumed when the political situation improves.

Places to Stay
The houseboats are the prime attraction of a stay in Srinagar and with so few tourists visiting Kashmir there are remarkable bargains to be found. There are also plenty of hotels but only a very few are open, many having been commandeered as barracks for the Indian army. The rest remain closed since

their Kashmiri owners would rather they remained empty than occupied by the 'Indian invaders'.

Houseboats There is no greater escape from the noise and hassle of Srinagar, a typically noisy Asian city, than the superbly relaxing houseboats. As soon as you get out on the lake traffic, pollution and hassles fade away. The houseboats are grouped in three areas, Dal Lake, the more peaceful Nagin Lake and the banks of the Jhelum River (mainly cheaper houseboats).

Opposite the Tourist Reception Centre is the Houseboat Owners' Association hut which is where the tourist office will direct you for accommodation. However there is no reason why you shouldn't just go out to the lake and look around for yourself. Booking through the tourist centre only means you get less choice in the matter and pay a higher price. It's now very much a buyer's market and you can afford to be choosy and bargain hard.

Srinagar is, however, notorious for its houseboat touts. They'll grab you at the airport, hassle you as you walk through town, and even try to snare you in Jammu or Delhi! Don't consider any houseboat until you've actually been out and looked at it for yourself. It may sound terrific on paper but turn out to be a miserable dump overdue for downgrading to a lower category, or it might be a fine place in a terrible location. Despite this advice, it's amazing the number of letters we've had from people who committed themselves to a particular boat without seeing it and ended up regretting it.

Basically most houseboats are the same. There's a small verandah at one end where you can sit and watch the world pass by, and behind this is a living room, usually furnished in British 1930s style. Then there is a dining room and beyond that two or three bedrooms, each with a bathroom. Officially, houseboats come in five categories, each with an officially approved price for singles/doubles, with and without meals. There are different charges for children or for renting an entire boat.

Houseboat	Full Board	Lodging Only
Deluxe or 5-star	Rs 500/700	Rs 350/450
A-class	Rs 275/400	Rs 190/275
B-class	Rs 200/350	Rs 140/230
C-class	Rs 150/275	Rs 100/200
D-class*	Rs 100/150	Rs 75/100

* doonga boats

In practice these 'official prices' were always a bit meaningless and with most of the boats now standing empty you can negotiate substantial discounts. You should be able to get around 50% off the price of the cheaper boats and discounts of up to 75% on the more expensive ones.

There is a wide variance between boats. A good C-class boat can be better than a poor A-class boat. Also, most houseboats are managed in groups of three or more. You can be sure the food is not going to differ much from the best boat in the group to the worst.

To find a houseboat, go down to the shikara ghats along the lakeside and announce that you want one. Either there will be somebody there with a boat available or you can hire a kid with a shikara to paddle you around the boats to ask. Check if shikara trips to shore are included; they should be. Pin down as many details as possible. Check what breakfast is going to be, for example – exactly how many eggs? Check if they'll supply a bucket of hot water for washing each morning – Kashmir can be chilly. If you decide to miss a meal (eg lunch) each day, then that can generally be negotiated into a lower price.

It's virtually impossible to recommend a particular boat; there are about 1000 of them, they all only have a few rooms and there are so many variable factors. A pleasant shikara man, who runs you back and forth between boat and shore, makes tea, supplies hot water and so on, can make a nondescript boat into a pleasant one. A pleasant boat can be ruined by a poor cook. Or simply having some pleasant fellow houseboaters to chat with in the evening can make all the difference. Even on the best boats the food can get rather monotonous, but there are plenty of 'supermarket' boats cruising by if you need

soft drinks, chocolate, toilet paper, hashish or any other of life's necessities.

A peaceful life out on the lake depends, to some extent, on avoiding the attentions of the vendors who continually paddle by. If you don't want to spend your whole time going through everything from woodcarvings to carpets and embroidery to papier-mâché, it's necessary to be very firm and decisive with these people. You can always retreat from the houseboat verandah to the more secluded roof, but why should you have to? Equally important is the attitude of the houseboat owners who rake off a handy little commission from everything that gets sold on their houseboat. On some houseboats you may actually find that the service, food or general attitude take a disastrous dip if you don't spend, spend, spend. The only answer to this policy is to move to a better houseboat, where the owners have more respect for their guests' comfort.

Hotels Currently almost all the hotels in Srinagar are closed. Exceptions are the *Grand Hotel* on Residency Rd, with doubles with attached bath from Rs 100, and *Ahdoo's Hotel* (☎ 72-593) which is almost opposite. Rooms here are Rs 350/500 with attached baths and TV and there's an excellent restaurant in the hotel.

Places to Eat
Probably because so many people eat on board their houseboats, Srinagar is not a very exciting place for eating out.

The *Tao Cafe* on Residency Rd, by the turn-off to the GPO, has a lovely garden which makes a nice place to chat or write postcards while you wait for your order. The food is mainly Chinese and generally good. The nearby *Cafe de Linz* is cheaper. As in all the restaurants, you can get excellent Kashmiri tea here.

On The Boulevard there's the *Shamyana Restaurant* which does surprisingly good pizza and excellent garlic bread. The tiny *Alka Salka* on Residency Rd across from Polo View Rd serves very good Chinese and Indian food but it's quite expensive.

Ahdoo's, in the hotel of the same name on Residency Rd, has long been one of Srinagar's best places for Kashmiri food and Indian specialities, and there's a good bakery downstairs.

The *Mughal Darbar* is another of Srinagar's better places for Kashmiri and Indian food. This is despite its often filthy appearance, its scruffy and inefficient waiters and the loud and overbearing locals. It's adjacent to the Suffering Moses store and across from the polo field on Residency Rd.

The *Lhasa Restaurant* serves good Chinese-Tibetan style food. It's near Dal Lake, just off The Boulevard. J&K Tourism runs the plush *Nun Kun* Chinese restaurant by Dal Lake.

The *Glocken Bakery* near Dal Gate is popular. It's run by a German-Kashmiri couple and has apple pie, delicious walnut honey cake, brown bread and chocolate cake. There are a few tables to sit at and they also serve hot and cold drinks. *Sultan Bakery* has excellent gingernut biscuits, apple pie and cheesecake. Stock up with goodies before heading to Leh.

Things to Buy

Kashmir is famous for its many handicrafts, and selling them is an activity pursued with amazing energy. You can visit workshops to see many of them being made. Popular buys include carpets, papier-mâché articles, leather and furs, woodcarvings, shawls and embroidery, tailor-made clothing, pleasantly coarse-knitted sweaters and cardigans, expensive spice saffron and many other items.

There is a whole string of government handicraft emporiums scattered around Srinagar, but the main one is housed in the fine old British Residency building by the Bund. The flashiest shops are along The Boulevard by Dal Lake. The Bund also has some interesting shops, including Suffering Moses with high-quality goods. On Polo View Rd there's the elderly and engaging Cheerful Chippendale. Shikaras patrol Dal Lake like sharks, loaded down with goodies.

Kashmir is also famous for its high-quality honey, which goes very well with the Middle Eastern-style bread available in Leh. It's quite expensive and you should try before you buy since sugar is occasionally substituted. The best shop is the Oriental Apiary, midway between Dal Gate and Nagin Lake, where there's a wide range of honeys including lotus blossom, saffron and even marijuana flower honey!

Getting There & Away

Air The Indian Airlines office (☎ 77-370) is at the Tourist Reception Centre and is open from 10 am to 4 pm.

Indian Airlines has twice-daily flights to Delhi (US$77) and Jammu (US$27), three flights a week to Amritsar (US$45) and a weekly flight (Sunday) to Leh (US$39).

Security at the airport is *very* tight so don't carry anything you shouldn't have on you (ie hash). You must arrive two hours before the flight and no hand luggage is allowed. Even cameras must be consigned to the hold.

Bus The routes between Jammu and Leh are reserved for the Jammu & Kashmir Road Transport Corporation buses which go from the Tourist Reception Centre. For Jammu, A-class buses leave at 7.30 am; B-class buses go from the Lal Chowk bus stand.

For Leh, J&KRTC buses leave from the Tourist Reception Centre at 8 am. They cost Rs 195 for A-class, Rs 280 for superdeluxe. Buses to Kargil cost Rs 100 for A-class, Rs 150 for superdeluxe. Also from the Tourist Reception Centre there's a daily bus to Delhi for Rs 300. The journey is supposed to take 24 hours but can take up to 36.

If the buses around the Kashmir Valley are running, they go from the Batmalu bus stand, which has two sections: buses to Pahalgam, Sonamarg and the Mughal gardens depart from the Eastern bus stand; buses to Gulmarg, Tangmarg and Wular Lake leave from the Western bus stand.

Train There's no railway line to Srinagar (although one is under construction), but train reservations can be made at the railway booking office at the Tourist Reception

BRYN THOMAS

CHRIS BEALL

CHRIS BEALL

Jammu & Kashmir
   Top Left: Dal Lake shikaras, Srinagar.
Top Right: Old man, Srinagar.
   Bottom: Srinagar market.

BRYN THOMAS

BRYN THOMAS

HUGH FINLAY

PETER RYDER

A	
B	C
	D

Jammu & Kashmir
A: Leh Palace with the Leh and Tsemo gompas above it.
B: Stupa, Leh.
C: Dal Lake, Srinagar.
D: Nagin Lake, Srinagar.

Centre for train departures from Jammu. However, their quota is just two 2nd-class berths per train to Delhi, Bombay, Madras, Calcutta and Gorakhpur.

Taxi For those with thick wallets, taxis are available for long-distance trips such as Jammu or Kargil (Rs 1500 for the whole vehicle or Rs 300 per seat) and Leh (Rs 500 for the whole vehicle). You can also arrange day trips to Gulmarg and Pahalgam.

Getting Around
To/From the Airport From Srinagar Airport, which is about 13 km out of the city, the airport bus runs only occasionally so you may have to take a taxi. The rate is posted outside the airport and is currently Rs 100 but the drivers will try for Rs 150. They will also attempt to steer you into the hands of the Houseboat Owners' Association. If that's not what you want insist they take you right to the lake.

Bus Take a No 12 bus to Nagin Lake or the Hazratbal Mosque.

Taxi & Auto-Rickshaw There are stands for these at the Tourist Reception Centre and other strategic locations in town. Srinagar's auto-rickshaw-wallahs are extremely reluctant to use their meters so you'll have to bargain hard. You should pay about Rs 5 from the Tourist Reception Centre to Dal Gate, Rs 10 from the bus stand at Batmalu to the Tourist Reception Centre. For longer trips the official fares are all posted by the stands.

Bicycle Cycling is an extremely pleasant way of getting around, especially as the valley is fairly flat. You can hire bikes for Rs 15 per day and there are several stores along The Boulevard close to Dal Gate. Following are some suggested trips but check with your houseboat owner that these areas are currently safe to visit.

Around Dal Lake – an all-day trip going by the Mughal gardens. It's particularly pleasant around the north of the lake where the villages are still relatively untouched.
Across Dal lake – you can ride across the lake on the causeway, a nice trip since there are no traffic problems and there is plenty of opportunity to observe lake life without being in a boat.
Nagin Lake – you can ride out to the Hazratbal Mosque via Nagin Lake and then make a complete loop around the lake on the way back. This trip can easily be combined with a trip along the Jhelum, taking in the various mosques close to the river. The streets here are very narrow so vehicles keep away and bike riding is pleasant.

Shikara Shikaras are the graceful, long boats which crowd the Srinagar lakes. They're used for getting back and forth from the houseboats or for longer tours. Officially there is a standard fare for every trip around the lake and these are prominently posted at the main landings (ghats); in practice the fares can be quite variable. To be shuttled across to your houseboat should cost Rs 3 in a covered ('full spring seats') shikara, but the kids who are always out for a little money will happily paddle you across for Rs 1 in a basic, open shikara. If the curfew is still in operation no-one is allowed out after dark and near this time getting back to your houseboat at a reasonable price may require a little ingenuity!

Try paddling a shikara yourself sometime – it's nowhere near as easy as it looks. You'll spend lots of time going round in circles.

AROUND SRINAGAR
There are a number of interesting places in the Kashmir Valley for day trips from Srinagar, and several popular hill stations which serve as good bases for short or long treks into the surrounding mountains. Pahalgam and Gulmarg are the two main Kashmiri hill resorts. However travel around the valley is currently restricted and you are likely to be stopped and searched at the numerous roadblocks. Seek local advice before setting off from Srinagar.

Harwan
At the northern end of Dal Lake, archaeolo-

gists have discovered unusual ornamented tiles near Harwan. The tiles are believed to have been from a 3rd-century Buddhist monastery which was built on the site, and examples of them can be seen in the Srinagar museum. The water supply for Srinagar is pumped from here and piped along the causeway across the lake.

Sangam

Sangam, 35 km north-east of Srinagar, is a centre for the production of (would you believe) cricket bats. They're lined up by the road in their thousands.

Verinag

Verinag is in the extreme south of the Kashmir Valley. The **spring** here is said to be the actual source of the Jhelum River. Jehangir built an octagonal stone basin at the spring in 1612 and Shah Jahan laid out a garden around it in 1620.

SRINAGAR TO PAHALGAM

The route to Pahalgam passes through some interesting places including, if you take the bus tour to Pahalgam, enough Mughal gardens to leave you botanically saturated. Only 16 km south-east of Srinagar is **Pampore**, centre of Kashmir's saffron industry. Saffron is highly prized for its flavouring and colouring properties and is consequently rather expensive.

At **Avantipur** are two ruined **Hindu temples**, built between 855 and 883 AD. The Avantiswami Temple, the larger of the two, is dedicated to Vishnu and still has some fine relief sculptures and columns of an almost Grecian appearance. The smaller temple, dedicated to Siva, is about one km before the main temple and close to the main road.

At **Anantnag** the road forks, and the Pahalgam road turns north. Just beyond the Pahalgam turn-off is **Achabal**, a Mughal garden laid out in 1620 by Shah Jahan's daughter, Jahanara. This carefully designed garden was said to be a favourite retreat of Nur Jahan. **Kokarnag**, further on, is certain to give you garden overload but is famous for its rose gardens. Back on the Pahalgam

route, **Mattan** has a fish-filled spring which is an important pilgrimage spot. Above Mattan on a plateau is the huge ruined temple of **Martland**.

PAHALGAM

Pahalgam is about 95 km from Srinagar, and at 2130 metres the night-time temperatures here are warmer than in Gulmarg, which is higher up.

The beautiful Lidder River flows right through the town, which is at the junction of the Sheshnag and Lidder rivers and is surrounded by soaring, fir-covered mountains with snowcapped peaks rising behind them.

There are many short walks from Pahalgam and it is an ideal base for longer treks to Kolahoi Glacier or Amarnath Cave – see Treks in Kashmir later in this chapter. Pahalgam is also famous for its many shepherds. They're a common sight, driving their flocks of sheep along the paths all around town.

Although trekkers are still visiting this region, most of the hotels and restaurants are closed. Bus services are suspended but it is possible to reach Pahalgam by taxi from Srinagar.

Information

The rather useless tourist office is just around the corner from the bus stop. There is a bank and a post office open in the tourist season.

Fishing permits have to be obtained in Srinagar. Trekking supplies can be obtained here, although they are cheaper to buy in Srinagar.

Pahalgam Walks

Mamaleswara Only a km or so downstream and on the opposite bank of the Lidder, this small Siva temple with its square stone tank is thought to date back to the 12th century.

Baisaran There are excellent views over the town and the Lidder Valley from this meadow, five km from Pahalgam. A further 11 km takes you to the **Tulian Lake** at 3353 metres. It is covered with ice for much of the year.

Aru The pleasant little village of Aru makes a very interesting day walk, following the Lidder River for 11 km upstream. Unfortunately, the main track on the left bank also takes cars, although there is a less used (and more difficult) track on the right bank. This is actually the first stage of the Kolahoi Glacier trek.

Places to Stay
Before the political troubles began most travellers stayed in the lodges on the western bank. The hotels on the main street of Pahalgam catered mainly to Indian tourists.

The other lodges were not as good. The best among them was probably the *Brown Palace*, although it is a long way from town. Another option was the *Windrush House*. The government *Tourist Bungalow* and the adjacent *Tourist Huts* would also be worth checking out.

The *Hotel Kolahoi Kabin*, between the two rivers, was not bad but the other places,

including the *White House* and *Bentes Lodge*, were a lot more decrepit.

Just outside Pahalgam on the Amarnath route the *Yog Niketan* ashram was an interesting place to stay. It offered yoga and meditation courses.

The *Pahalgam Hotel* was the top hotel with all the facilities you'd expect in the Rs 600/800 price range, including heated swimming pool, sauna and massage. The *Woodstock Hotel* (☎ 27) next door was somewhat cheaper.

In Aru, the *Milkyway Guest House & Restaurant* has been recommended. Rooms cost Rs 30 to Rs 40.

Places to Eat
At last report, places to eat were restricted to *dhabas* (hole-in-the-wall restaurants or snack bars). Previously, people staying on the west bank area used to eat in this area too. In the main street on the west bank, the *Lhasa Restaurant* was not as good as its namesake in Srinagar. The *Pahalgam Hotel* did expensive set meals.

Getting There & Away
When they're operating, local buses from Srinagar to Pahalgam take 2½ to four hours. There were also more expensive tour buses operated by J&KRTC. Taxis cost about Rs 600 return.

Ponies can easily be hired in Pahalgam for trekking trips. The fixed costs to popular destinations are clearly posted, although they're basically bargaining guidelines.

GULMARG
The large meadow of Gulmarg is 52 km south-west of Srinagar at 2730 metres. The name means Meadow of Flowers and in spring it's just that. This is also an excellent trekking base. In winter it used to be India's premier skiing resort, until the activities of the militants frightened off the tourists. The skiing equipment available was fairly good and the costs very low. The area was also wonderful for ski-touring although very little cross-country equipment was available.

Gulmarg can get pretty cold at times, even

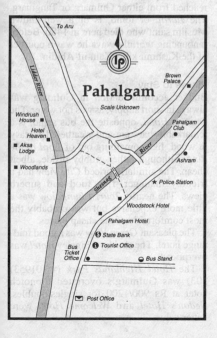

To Aru

Lidder River

Pahalgam

Scale Unknown

Brown Palace

Windrush House
Hotel Heaven
■ *Aksa Lodge*
■ *Woodlands*

Sheshnag
River

Pahalgam Club

● *Ashram*

★ *Police Station*

Woodstock Hotel
Pahalgam Hotel
● State Bank
● Tourist Office
Bus Ticket Office
● Bus Stand

✉ *Post Office*

JAMMU & KASHMIR

compared to Pahalgam, so come prepared with plenty of warm clothes. In 1995, the hotels and ski-lifts here remained closed. The following information is included in the hope that the situation may improve.

Information

The tourist office, in the valley bottom about half a km beyond the golf course, is the green-blue building complex with three patches of new wooden roof.

Skiing

There is one chairlift, one T-bar, four pomas and a cable car to the top of Mt Apharwat. The slopes vary from beginner to intermediate and equipment could be hired cheaply. All lifts operated from 10 am to 5 pm, closing for one hour at lunch. Limited amounts of cross-country equipment were available from S D Singh, Hut 209A.

Gulmarg Walks

Outer Circular Walk A circular road, 11 km in length, runs right round Gulmarg through pleasant pine forests with excellent views over the Kashmir Valley. Nanga Parbat is visible to the north, and Haramukh and Sunset peaks are visible to the south-east.

Khilanmarg This smaller valley is about a six-km walk from the Gulmarg bus stop and car park. The meadow, carpeted with flowers in the spring, is the site for Gulmarg's winter ski runs and offers a fine view of the surrounding peaks and the Kashmir Valley. During the early spring, as the snow melts, it can be a very muddy hour's climb up the hill.

Alpather Beyond Khilanmarg, 13 km from Gulmarg at the foot of the 4511-metre Apharwat peak, this lake is frozen until mid-June, and even later in the year you can see lumps of ice floating in its cold waters. The walk from Gulmarg follows a well-graded pony track over the 3810-metre Apharwat Ridge, separating the lake from Khilanmarg, and proceeds up the valley to the lake at 3843 metres.

Ningle Nallah Flowing from the melting snow and ice on Apharwat peak and Alpather Lake, this pretty mountain stream is 10 km from Gulmarg. The stream continues down into the valley below and joins the Jhelum River near Sopore. The walking path crosses the Ningle Nallah by a bridge and continues on to the **Lienmarg**, another grassy meadow and a good spot for camping.

Ferozpore Nallah Reached from the Tangmarg road, or from the outer circular walk, this mountain stream meets the Bahan River at a popular picnic spot known as **Waters Meet**. The stream is reputed to be particularly good for trout fishing; it's about five km from Gulmarg. You can continue on from here to **Tosamaidan**, a three-day, 50-km walk to one of Kashmir's most beautiful meadows.

Ziarat of Baba Reshi This Muslim shrine is on the slopes below Gulmarg and can be reached from either Gulmarg or Tangmarg. The *ziarat*, or tomb, is of a well-known Muslim saint who died here in 1480. Before renouncing worldly ways he was a courtier of the Kashmir king, Zain-ul-Abidin.

Places to Stay

Budget accommodation in Gulmarg was always in short supply, as was hot water. The *Tourists Hotel*, opposite the bus stand, is a remarkably baroque and weathered fantasy in wood, like something out of *Lord of the Rings* although rather grubby inside, albeit cheap. The similarly priced *City View* had a friendly manager, fine food and superb views. The nearby *Tourist Bungalow* was a little more expensive but was probably the most comfortable of the cheap places.

The pleasant *Green View* was a good mid-range hotel. The shabby *Kingsley Hotel* was overpriced.

The *Hotel Highlands Park* (☎ (01953) 203) was Gulmarg's overrated topnotch hotel at Rs 900/1200 for singles/doubles. *Nedou's Hotel* and *Welcome Hotel* were better value.

Places to Eat
As has been the case in Pahalgam, dhabas have recently been the only option as far as food goes.

Getting There & Away
There used to be a variety of buses running from Srinagar to Gulmarg, many of them on day tours. These tours enabled only a few hours at the hill resort, just long enough for one of the shorter day walks.

In 1995 it was only possible to get a bus from Srinagar as far as Tangmarg, seven km in distance and 500 metres in altitude below Gulmarg. The last stretch must be completed on foot or by pony. The winding road from Tangmarg to Gulmarg is 13 km in length, nearly twice as far as the more direct pony track.

SOUTH OF SRINAGAR
Interesting places in the south-west of the Kashmir Valley include **Yusmarg**, reputed to have the best spring flowers in Kashmir, and a good base for treks further afield. **Chari Sharif** is on the road to Yusmarg and has the shrine, or ziarat, of Kashmir's patron saint. **Aharbal** was a popular resting place for the Mughal emperors when they made the long trip north from Delhi.

SINDH VALLEY
This is a scenic area north of Srinagar through which the road to Ladakh passes. The Zoji La pass marks the boundary from the Sindh Valley into Ladakh. From Srinagar you pass the **Dachigam Wildlife Reserve**, once a royal game park; you need a signed permit from the Srinagar tourist office to enter the reserve.

Anchar Lake, rarely visited, is close to Srinagar and has a wide variety of water birds. There is a Mughal garden built by Nur Jahan at **Manasbal Lake**. The Jhelum River flows into **Wular Lake**, one of the largest freshwater lakes in India.

Sonamarg, at 2740 metres, is the last major town before Ladakh and an excellent base for trekking. Its name means Meadow of Gold, which could derive from the spring flowers or from the strategic trading position

it once enjoyed. There are *Tourist Huts*, a *Tourist Rest House* and some small hotels here.

The tiny village of **Baltal** is the last place in Kashmir, right at the foot of the Zoji La. When conditions are favourable you can walk to the **Amarnath Cave** from here. The Zoji La is the watershed between Kashmir and Ladakh – on one side you have the green, lush scenery of Kashmir while on the other side everything is barren and dry.

TREKS IN KASHMIR
There are various treks both within Kashmir and from Kashmir to Ladakh. Access to some of the treks described in this section may be restricted by the activities of militants or the army. Check the current situation in Srinagar. The short Pahalgam to Kolahoi Glacier trek is the most popular and even in 1994 there were travellers doing this trek. The Pahalgam to Amarnath Cave trek is well known for the annual pilgrimage that is still undertaken by many thousands of Hindus during the July/August full moon.

Porters in Kashmir are used less frequently than they are in Nepal; ponies carry the gear. Since 1990 most of the local trekking agencies have either closed down or relocated to Delhi. As an alternative, some houseboat owners can organise treks for you, although you would be well advised to check out exactly what you are paying for before you part with your money. Typical daily charges vary considerably, from as little as US$5 per day to over US$50 per day, depending on the length of the trek, the number of people and your bargaining skills. Some travellers were organising things themselves, renting a horseman and pony for around Rs 100 a day in Pahalgam for the Kolahoi Glacier trek.

Acute Mountain Sickness (AMS) is a factor that needs to be considered on all treks that go above 3000 metres. Refer to this book's comprehensive health section for more details.

Maps included in this chapter are guides only. Accurate topographical maps should be obtained if you are planning to trek in Jammu & Kashmir.

For more detailed trekking information
and itineraries, see the Lonely Planet guide
Trekking in the Indian Himalaya.

Pahalgam to Kolahoi Glacier

This is a short, popular trek from Pahalgam
to the glacier and return. You may need to
take a tent although some of the lodges at
Pahalgam, Aru and Lidderwat are open from
June until September.

The first stage from Pahalgam takes you
to the village of Aru along the bank of the
West Lidder River. There are a number of
lodges at Aru.

The second stage takes you to Lidderwat
where there is a *Government Rest House* and
the *Paradise Lodge*. There is a very pleasant
campsite situated on a meadow above the
confluence of the river coming from the
Kolahoi Glacier and the river coming down
from Tarsar.

On the third stage you trek up to the glacier
that flows from Mt Kolahoi (5485 metres).
It's a hard stage and an early start is essential
as the peak is often clouded over by midmorning. The final stage can see you back in
Pahalgam in a few hours with time to catch
the bus back to Srinagar the same day.

Stage 1	Pahalgam to Aru (2-3 hrs)
Stage 2	Aru to Lidderwat (3 hrs)
Stage 3	Lidderwat to Kolahoi Glacier & return (8-9 hrs)
Stage 4	Lidderwat to Pahalgam (4-5 hrs)

Pahalgam to Sumbal via Sonamous Pass

This trek is an extension of the Kolahoi
Glacier trek. The first two stages to Lidderwat are the same as the above trek. It is also
recommended to trek to the Kolahoi Glacier
before continuing to Tarsar. The fourth stage
follows the trail to Seikwas before continuing to Tarsar and returning the following day.
From Seikwas it is a gradual ascent to the
Sonamous Pass (3960 metres) before a steep
descent to the Gujar shepherd camp at
Sonamous.

The final stage involves a descent which
is steep in places to the Sindh Valley and the

village of Sumbal. From here there are
regular buses back to Srinagar or on to
Sonamarg.

Stage 1	Pahalgam to Aru (2-3 hrs)
Stage 2	Aru to Lidderwat (3 hrs)
Stage 3	Lidderwat to Kolahoi Glacier & return (8-9 hrs)
Stage 4	Lidderwat to Seikwas (4-5 hrs)
Stage 5	Seikwas to Tarsar & return (6-7 hrs)
Stage 6	Seikwas to Sonamous via Sonamous Pass (5-6 hrs)
Stage 7	Sonamous to Sumbal (4 hrs)

Pahalgam to Amarnath Cave

On the full moon in the month of
July/August, thousands of Hindu pilgrims
make the *yatra* (pilgrimage) to the Amarnath
cave where a natural ice lingam, the symbol
of Siva, reaches its greatest size. Although at
the time of the yatra it's less a trek than a long
queue, the spirit of the pilgrimage is unforgettable.

The first stage out of Pahalgam follows a
jeep track to Chandanwadi. The following
stage is harder with a long and (in places)
steep ascent to the sacred Sheshnag Lake.
The third stage crosses the Mahagunas Pass
(4270 metres) before a gradual descent to the
camp at Panchtarni and the trek to the cave.

Many of the pilgrims trek to the cave
during the full moon night. It's an eerie experience sharing a trail with the steady flow of
pilgrims making their way slowly up to the
huge limestone cave. Some years the ice
lingam does not form. This is taken as a most
inauspicious sign and means that the most
devout pilgrims (and trekkers!) will have to
return the following year.

After paying their respects in the cave,
most pilgrims return via Panchtarni to
Sheshnag the same day, reaching Pahalgam
the following day.

Stage 1	Pahalgam to Chandanwadi (4-5 hrs)
Stage 2	Chandanwadi to Sheshnag (5-6 hrs)
Stage 3	Sheshnag to Panchtarni via the Mahagunas Pass (5-6 hrs)
Stage 4	Panchtarni to Amarnath Cave & return (5-6 hrs)
Stage 5	Panchtarni to Sheshnag (4-5 hrs)
Stage 6	Sheshnag to Pahalgam (6-7 hrs)

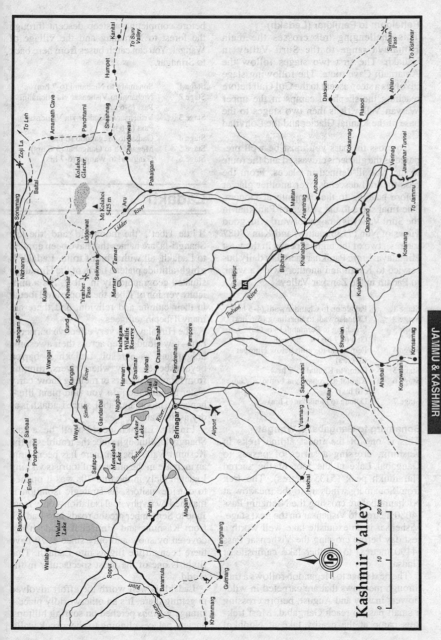

Kashmir Valley

JAMMU & KASHMIR

Pahalgam to Panikhar (Ladakh)

This challenging trek crosses the main Himalaya range to the Suru Valley in Ladakh. The first two stages follow the Amarnath Cave route. The following stage involves a steep ascent to the Gul Gali before reaching the shepherd camps in the upper Warvan Valley. It is then two stages to the base of the Kanital Glacier and the Lonvilad Gali.

To cross the pass you must be well prepared as the glacier is crevassed and the route to the pass ill-defined in places. From the pass the trail descends over another glacier before heading to the campsite at Donara. The final stage to the village of Panikhar in the Suru Valley is straightforward with good views of Nun (7135 metres) and Kun (7087 metres), two of the highest peaks in the west Himalaya. From Panikhar there is a daily bus service to Kargil and another twice a week to Padam in the Zanskar Valley.

Stage 1	Pahalgam to Chandanwadi (4-5 hrs)
Stage 2	Chandanwadi to Sheshnag (5-6 hrs)
Stage 3	Sheshnag to Permandal via Gul Gali (6-7 hrs)
Stage 4	Permandal to camp below Humpet (6-7 hrs)
Stage 5	Camp to Kanital (6-7 hrs)
Stage 6	Kanital to Donara via Lonvilad Gali (10 hrs)
Stage 7	Donara to Panikhar (3 hrs)

Sonamarg to Gangabal & Wangat

This is one of the finest alpine treks in Kashmir, crossing a series of passes to Gangabal Lake at the foot of the sacred Haramukh peak (5135 metres). The trek from Sonamarg winds up to the meadow at Nichanni before crossing the Nichanni Pass (4080 metres) to Vishensar on the next stage. Vishensar is an exquisite lake well worth a rest day before crossing the Vishensar Pass (4190 metres) to another lake campsite at Gadsar.

The next stage to Megandob follows a trail through meadows that are carpeted in wildflowers in July and August, before crossing a small pass to reach Gangabal. Most trekkers camp at the nearby lake at Nudhkol

before completing a steep descent through the forest to Narannag and the village of Wangat. You can catch buses from here back to Srinagar.

Stage 1	Sonamarg to Nichanni (6-7 hrs)
Stage 2	Nichanni to Vishensar via Nichanni Pass (5-6 hrs)
Stage 3	Vishensar to Gadsar via Vishensar Pass (5-6 hrs)
Stage 4	Gadsar to Megandob (6 hrs)
Stage 5	Megandob to Gangabal (5-6 hrs)
Stage 6	Gangabal to Wangat (6-7 hrs)

Ladakh

'Little Tibet', 'the moonland' and 'the last Shangri-la' are names that have been applied to Ladakh, all with a bit of truth. Ladakh is a high-altitude plateau north of the Himalaya situated geographically in Tibet. It's a miniature version of Tibet, the people are Tibetan in their culture and religion, and there are many Tibetan refugees.

The Himalaya is a very effective barrier to rain – few clouds creep across their awesome height and as a result Ladakh is barren beyond belief. Only where rivers, running from faraway glaciers or melting snow, carry water to habitation do you find plant life – hence the moonland label, since Ladakh is as dry as the Sahara.

Finally, Ladakh could well be a last Shangri-la, although since the troubles in the Kashmir Valley began there has been quite an increase in the number of tourists visiting Ladakh. Only in the mid-70s was it opened to outside visitors. Its strategic isolation is matched by its physical isolation – only from June to September are the roads into Ladakh from Kashmir and Himachal Pradesh not covered by snow and only since 1979 have there been airline flights into Ladakh. That flight is one of the most spectacular in the world.

Ladakh is well worth the effort involved in getting there. It's an otherworldly place – strange *gompas* perched on soaring hilltops, ancient palaces clinging to sheer rock walls, and shattered-looking landscapes splashed with small but brilliant patches of green. But most of all there are the delightful Ladakhis, friendly as only Tibetan people can be and immensely colourful.

Religion
At Kargil, on the Srinagar to Leh road, the Islamic influence dies out and you are in a Buddhist region. The people follow Tibetan Tantric Buddhism which has much emphasis on magic and demons. All around Ladakh are gompas, the Buddhist monasteries. They're fascinating to visit, although they have become very commercially minded since Ladakh's tourist boom commenced. There's a good side to this though. Prior to tourism the gompas were gradually becoming more and more neglected. Today many of them are being refurbished and repaired with the profits from visiting Westerners. The monks are happy to have visitors wander around the gompas, sit in on the ceremonies, try the unusual butter tea (bring your own cup) and take photographs.

Information
A sleeping bag is very useful in Ladakh even if you're not trekking or camping. The nights can get very cold and visiting many of the gompas by public transport will require an overnight stop. Be prepared for dramatic temperature changes and for the extreme burning power of the sun in Ladakh's thin air (Leh is at 3505 metres). A cloud across the sun will change the air temperature from T-shirt to sweater level in seconds. Without a hat and/or sunscreen you'll have sunburn and a peeling nose in hours.

Acclimatise to Ladakh's altitude slowly – don't go scrambling up mountainsides as soon as you arrive. A spell in Kashmir is a good halfway acclimatisation, but people who fly straight from Delhi to Ladakh may feel very uncomfortable for a few days.

Outside Leh it is not easy to change money and in the tourist season there is often a severe shortage of small change. One very important word to learn for Ladakh is the all-purpose and frequently used greeting 'Jullay'. Finally, remember that this is a sensitive border region disputed by India, Pakistan and China. You are not allowed more than 1.6 km north of the Srinagar to Leh road without permission.

If you visit Ladakh in winter be prepared for the fact that many gompas are only open to visitors in the summer months.

Permits Three regions of Ladakh were opened up to foreigners in 1994. These are: the Dahanu area, north of the Kargil to Leh road at Kahlsi; the Nubra Valley; and Pangong Tso (Lake Pangong). For all places you have to be officially part of a group of four people and permits are issued at the police station in Leh.

SRINAGAR TO LEH
It's 434 km from Srinagar to Leh and the road is surfaced most of the way. It follows the Indus River for much of the distance. Buses run along this road daily during the summer season (see Getting There & Away for Leh) and take two days with an overnight stop at Kargil. With the military roadblocks and numerous passport checks these are currently two very long days. Sonamarg is the last major town in the Vale of Kashmir, shortly before you climb over the Zoji La (3529 metres) and enter the Ladakh region.

There is accommodation of some form or other at Drass, Kargil, Mulbekh, Bodh Kharbu, Lamayuru, Khalsi, Nurla, Saspul and Nimmu.

Zoji La
This is one of the few unsurfaced stretches on the route. It's also the first pass to snow over in winter and the last to be cleared in summer. At 3529 metres it's not, however, the highest pass along the route. The other passes get less snow because they are across the Himalaya and in the mountain rain shadow.

The road up the pass is breathtaking, even more so than the road up the much higher Taglang La (5328 metres) on the Leh to Manali road. The road clings to the edge of sheer drops and there are times when you'll wonder if you were sane to make this trip!

Drass

This is the first village after the pass and the place from where road crews clear the road up to the pass for the start of the summer season. In winter, Drass is noted for its heavy snowfalls and extreme cold.

The buses stop here and tourists have to register their names and passport numbers.

Kargil

Telephone Area Code: 01985

Once an important trading post, Kargil is now simply an overnight halt on the way to Leh or the point where you turn south for the Zanskar Valley. The people of Kargil are chiefly Muslim and noted for their extreme orthodoxy. Already you are in a region where irrigation is vitally important.

Places to Stay On the main street, the *Popular Chacha, De Lux, New Light, Puril, Punjab Janta* and *Argalia* provide rock-bottom accommodation at around Rs 60 a bed. The *Naktul View*, between the main street and the truck park, and the *Crown* on the other side of the truck park, are of a better standard. The *International* is overpriced at Rs 100 a double.

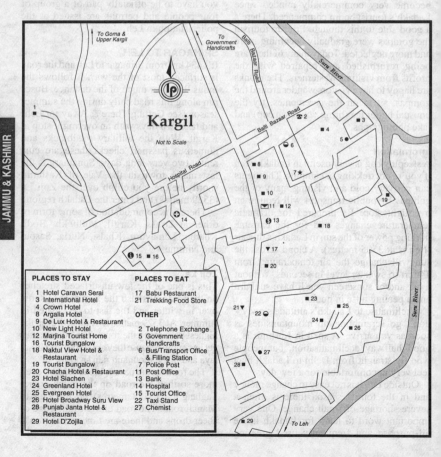

Kargil

Not to Scale

To Goma & Upper Kargil

To Government Handicrafts

Balti Bazaar Road

Suru River

Hospital Road

To Leh

PLACES TO STAY	
1	Hotel Caravan Serai
3	International Hotel
4	Crown Hotel
8	Argalia Hotel
9	De Lux Hotel & Restaurant
10	New Light Hotel
12	Marjina Tourist Home
16	Tourist Bungalow
18	Naktul View Hotel & Restaurant
19	Tourist Bungalow
20	Chacha Hotel & Restaurant
23	Hotel Siachen
24	Greenland Hotel
25	Evergreen Hotel
26	Hotel Broadway Suru View
28	Punjab Janta Hotel & Restaurant
29	Hotel D'Zojila

PLACES TO EAT	
17	Babu Restaurant
21	Trekking Food Store

OTHER	
2	Telephone Exchange
5	Government Handicrafts
6	Bus/Transport Office & Filling Station
7	Police Post
11	Post Office
13	Bank
14	Hospital
15	Tourist Office
22	Taxi Stand
27	Chemist

The *Marjina Tourist Home* has a range of rooms of varying degrees of cleanliness. They ask what they think you'll pay (as do most of the hotel owners here) but you should be able to get a clean double with attached bathroom for around Rs 130. The *Greenland Hotel* is similarly priced as is the *Tourist Bungalow*, which used to be the best deal in town.

Top-end accommodation includes the *Caravan Serai*, *Siachen* (☎ 221), *Broadway Suru View* and the *D'Zojila*. At the Siachen, rooms cost Rs 300/450, and are good value.

Places to Eat The food is little better than the accommodation but with buses arriving late at night and leaving at the crack of dawn, it's unlikely you'll get much of a chance to sample Kargil cuisine. The *Naktul* is easily the best in town and provides Chinese dishes. Otherwise the *Marjina Tourist Home* leads the pack, with the *Babu* and *New Light* taking the overflow and those fooled by the rash promises of French, Italian, German, Chinese and Tibetan cuisine.

Getting There & Away As well as the daily buses to Leh and Srinagar, there are daily services to Mulbekh, Drass and Panikhar, and twice-daily services to Sauku and Trespone.

The Zanskar bus service is a lot less reliable. Basically a bus leaves for Padum twice a week, although the frequency decreases at either end of the summer. Check with the Tourist Reception Centre, and consider hitching with a private truck (around Rs 100). Jeep hire to Padum will set you back about Rs 5000.

Shergol

Between Kargil and Shergol you cross the dividing line between the Muslim and Buddhist areas. The small village of Shergol has a tiny **gompa** perched halfway up the eastern slope of the mountain.

Mulbekh

There are two gompas on the hillside above the village of Mulbekh. As in other villages, it is wise to enquire if the gompa is open before making the ascent. If not, somebody from the village may have keys and will accompany you to the gompas.

Just beyond Mulbekh is a huge **Chamba statue**, an image of a future Buddha, cut into the rock face beside the road. It's one of the most interesting stops along the road to Leh. Those with time to spare can make a short trek from Mulbekh to the village of **Gel**.

Lamayuru

From Mulbekh the road crosses the 3718-metre Namika La, passes through the large military encampment of Bodh Kharbu and then crosses the 4094-metre Fatu La, the highest pass on the route.

Lamayuru is the first of the typical Ladakhi gompas perched on a hilltop with its village at the foot of the hill. In its heyday the **gompa** had five buildings and as many as 400 monks, but today there is only one building, tended by 20 or 30 monks.

Rizong

On beyond Khalsi, and a few km off the road, is the **nunnery of Julichen** and the **monastery** of Rizong. If you stay here overnight men must stay in the monastery, women in the nunnery.

Alchi

Near Saspul, this gompa is unusual in that it is built on lowland, not perched on a hilltop. It is noted for its massive **Buddha statues** and lavish woodcarvings and the only examples of Kashmiri-style wall paintings in the area. There are many *chortens* (stupas) around the village.

There are two hotels here with basic rooms around Rs 120 for doubles and some dormitory accommodation. There's also a pleasant little hotel in Saspul; it makes a good base for visiting Rizong, Alchi and Lekir.

Lekir & Basgo

Shortly after Saspul a steep road turns off to the Lekir Gompa, which also has a monastery school. Closer to Leh there is a badly damaged **fort** at Basgo. The Basgo Gompa has interesting **Buddha figures**, although its wall paintings have suffered much water damage.

LEH

Population: 24,500
Telephone Area Code: 01982

Centuries ago this was an important stop on the old caravan silk route from China. Today it's merely a military base and tourist centre, but wandering the winding back streets of the town is still fascinating. It's about 10 km northeast of the Indus River in a fertile side valley.

Orientation

Leh is small enough to make finding your way around very easy. There's one main street with the Leh Palace rising up at the end of it. The bus stand and jeep halt is on the southern or airport side of town. The airport, with its steeply sloping runway, is several km out of town near the Spitok Gompa.

Information

The tourist office (☎ 2497) is inconveniently located in the Tourist Reception Centre, on the road to the airport. It has very little information but is a good place to rent trekking gear. They have surprisingly high-quality tents for Rs 20 per day (Rs 100 per week) as well as jackets (Rs 16 per day) and boots (Rs 20 per day). Trekking equipment can also be rented from the Nezer View Guest House for similar prices.

The Ladakh Ecological Development Group (LEDeG) has a solar demonstration house and a good library on Ladakh. Pick up a copy of their leaflet with important guidelines for tourists in Ladakh. Shorts and bare shoulders, as well as public displays of affection, are not the cultural norm here. It's a sad fact that in recent years visitors have been acting with decreasing sensitivity towards the local people.

A convenient place for STD/ISD calls is the private communications office, Gypsy's World (opposite the Hotel Yak Tail), where you can make international calls without waiting but at great expense.

Artou Bookshop has the best selection of books on Ladakh and also sells novels and postcards.

If you're feeling the effects of the altitude (3505 metres) and your symptoms do not subside (or get worse) after 36 hours, phone 2560 for medical help. The clinic is staffed 24 hours.

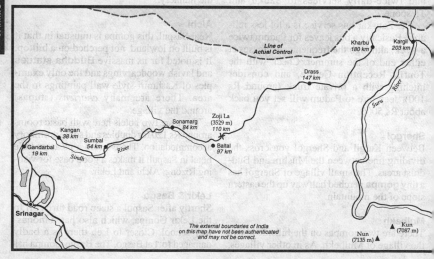

Leh Palace

Looking for all the world like a miniature version of the Potala in Lhasa, Tibet, the palace was built in the 16th century. It is now deserted and badly damaged, a legacy of Ladakh's wars with Kashmir in the last century.

The main reason for making the climb up to the palace is for the superb views from the roof. The Zanskar mountains, across the Indus River, look close enough to touch. The palace was sold to the Archaeological Survey of India by the Ladakhi royal family (who now reside at nearby Stok) and an ambitious renovation project is underway. Try to get a monk to unlock the preserved, but now unused, central prayer room; it's dusty and spooky, with huge masks looming out of the dark. There's a Rs 5 entry charge and you should watch out for the holes in the floor.

Leh & Tsemo Gompas

The Leh Gompa stands high above the palace and houses manuscripts and paintings. The Red (Tsemo) Gompa, built in 1430, contains a fine three-storey-high seated Buddha image. It's open from 7 to 9 am. The gompa above the Leh and Tsemo gompas is in a very ruined condition but the views down on Leh are superb.

Sankar Gompa

It's an easy stroll to the Sankar Gompa, a couple of km north of the town centre. This interesting little gompa is only open from 7 to 10 am and from 5 to 7 pm, and there's a Rs 10 entry fee. The gompa has electric lighting so an evening visit is worthwhile. Upstairs is an impressive representation of Avalokitesvara complete with 1000 arms and 1000 heads.

Ecological Development Centre

Next door to the Tsemo-La Hotel is the headquarters of the Ladakh Ecological Development Group (LEDeG), which initiates and promotes 'a development strategy for Ladakh that is carefully tailored to its environment, available resources and culture'. This includes solar energy, environmental and health education, strengthening the traditional system of organic farming and publishing books in the local language. Visitors are welcome to hear what LEDeG is all about, and to use the library and the restaurant.

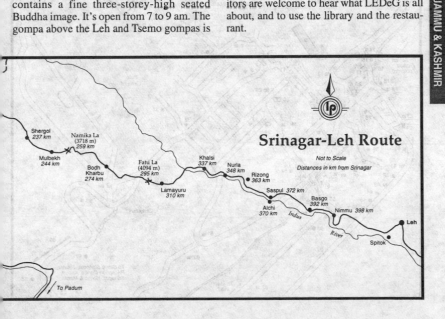

Srinagar-Leh Route

Not to Scale
Distances in km from Srinagar

Shergol 237 km
Namika La (3718 m) 259 km
Mulbekh 244 km
Bodh Kharbu 274 km
Fatu La (4094 m) 295 km
Lamayuru 310 km
Khalsi 337 km
Nurla 348 km
Rizong 363 km
Saspul 372 km
Alchi 370 km
Basgo 392 km
Nimmu 398 km
Indus River
Leh
Spitok

To Padum

At 3 pm on Monday, Wednesday and Friday the video *Ancient Futures – Learning from Ladakh* is shown. It's well worth seeing but the voice of Helena Norberg-Hodge, who started the Ladakh project and appears in the video, bears a chilling resemblance to that of a recent British prime minister!

Students' Educational & Cultural Movement of Ladakh (SECMOL)

This movement organises cultural shows to promote traditional art forms. You can meet Ladakhi students and help them practise their English at the meetings held here on Monday and Thursday at 4 pm. SECMOL can also arrange for you to stay with a Ladakhi family.

Meditation

The Mahabodi Society (opposite Hotel Ri-Rab) has a daily group meditation session at 5 pm and sometimes runs meditation courses at Choglamsar.

Places to Stay

There's an amazing number of hotels and guest houses in Ladakh, many of which are only open during the tourist season. Prices

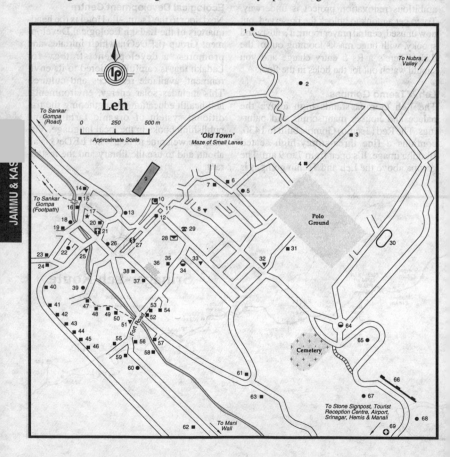

Leh

are variable – soaring in the peak season, plummeting at other times. Prices quoted here are for the high season. The cheaper guest houses are usually rooms rented out in private homes. Many of the older places still have a traditional Ladakhi stove in the kitchen.

Places to Stay – bottom end

The long-established *Old Ladakh Guest House* has rooms with common bathroom for Rs 60/80 and doubles with attached bath from Rs 120. Other good places in this area with similarly priced rooms include the *Shalimar Guest House*, a clean friendly place and the nearby *Tak Guest House* which is also popular. The larger *Palace View Kiddar* is much the same. More central and better is the friendly *Khan Manzil Guest House*.

Also away from the more touristy areas of Leh, the *Namgyal Hotel* is popular with budget travellers. Doubles are from Rs 50 or Rs 70 for the upstairs rooms, all with common bath. Beside the archery stadium, *Firdous Hotel* is a friendly little place with doubles for Rs 80 or Rs 120 with attached bath.

In the northern part of the town, the *Hotel Shangrila* is a very pleasant place run by a helpful family. Rooms are Rs 60/100, all with common bath but hot water is supplied free of charge. The *Antelope Guest House* is another clean and friendly place with great views up to Leh Palace. They have some small singles at Rs 60 and doubles for Rs 140 or Rs 200 with attached bathroom. The nearby *Hotel Himalaya* is rather run down, with doubles from Rs 120 or Rs 180 with bath.

The *Hotel Tse Mo View* (just north of the Hotel Himalaya) is in a very quiet location (follow the signs through the fields) with

PLACES TO STAY					
		48	Ti-Sei Guest House	5	Delite Cinema
		49	Dehlux Hotel		(No Sign)
3	Namgyal Hotel	50	Bimla Guest House	9	Palace
4	Palace View Hotel	52	Hotel Yak Tall	10	Mosque
6	Old Ladakh Guest	53	Dreamland Hotel &	11	Small Plaza
	House		Restaurant	13	Syed Ali Shah's Post-
7	Tak Guest House	54	Khangri Hotel & Res-		cards
12	Hilltop Hotel &		taurant	17	Police Station
	Restaurant	55	Lung-Se-Jung Hotel	18	Ecological
14	Antelope Guest	56	Hotel Rockland		Development
	House	57	Hotel Choskor		Centre
15	Hotel Himalaya	58	Padma Guest House	21	Moravian Church
16	Hotel Shangrila	59	Hotels Lha-Ri-Mo &	22	Circuit House
19	Tsemo-La Hotel		K-Sar	26	Artou Bookshop
20	Khan Manzil Guest	61	Dragon Hotel & Nezer	27	State Bank
	House		View Guest House	28	Post Office
23	Two Star Guest	62	Mandala Hotel	29	Telegraph Office
	House	63	Hotel Hills View	30	National Archery
24	Rainbow Guest House				Stadium
31	Palace View	**PLACES TO EAT**		34	Taxi Stand
	iddar Hotel			36	Vegetable Market
35	Hotel Ibex	8	Chang Pubs	39	SECMOL
37	Hotel Galdan	25	Mentakling	60	Indian Airlines
	Continental		Restaurant	64	Bus Station
38	Hotel Lingzi	32	Burman Restaurant	65	Large Chorten
40	Eagle Guest House	33	La Montessori	66	Mani Wall
41	Tsavo Guest House		Restaurant	67	Handicraft Training
42	Hotel Omasila	51	German Bakery		Centre
43	Otsal Guest House		Restaurant	68	Radio Station
44	Asia Guest House			69	Hospital
45	Larchang Guest	**OTHER**			
	House				
46	Hotel Ri-Rab	1	Leh & Tsemo Gompas		
47	Indus Guest House	2	Buddha Picture		

rooms with attached bath for Rs 100/150. Follow the path towards Sankar Gompa to reach the spotless *Hotel Kailash*, surrounded by a walled garden and fields. Doubles are from Rs 130, all with common bathroom.

Along the path from the German Bakery Restaurant is a group of popular places which have lovely gardens and great views. The friendly *Bimla* (☎ 3854) is at the top of this price bracket, charging Rs 100/180 for rooms with common bath, Rs 180/240 with bath. The *Indus* has singles/doubles for Rs 80/120 or Rs 180 for a double with an attached bathroom and solar-heated water. The *Dehlux* is similarly priced, as is the last in the row, the *Ti-sei* with a nice garden and a traditional Ladakhi kitchen.

Up past the Tsemo-La Hotel, the *Karzoo Guest House* has doubles from Rs 80. The nearby *Two Star Guest House* is another favourite, with doubles from Rs 100 and dorm beds for Rs 40. Further along this road is the *Mansoor Guest House* with a friendly family atmosphere and rooms from Rs 60. To the south of the road is the *Rainbow Guest House*, which is good value at Rs 50/60 for rooms with common bath.

Changspa village is about 10 minutes' walk from Leh and is a good place to escape the noise. The *Eagle Guest House* has double rooms for Rs 70/100. The *Tsavo* is very basic but is an authentic Ladakhi home and has doubles from Rs 60. The *Otsal, Asia* and *Larchang* have rooms for Rs 60/80 and the *Greenland Guest House* opposite is a little cheaper. The *Rinchens Guest House* further down this road has clean rooms for Rs 70 a double or Rs 170 with attached bath. A further 10 minutes' walk away is the popular *Oriental Guest House* which has doubles from Rs 70 and is run by a very friendly family.

South of the centre of Leh are two recommended places. The *Padma Guest House* is very clean and has a pleasant garden. Rooms are Rs 80/100 for singles/doubles or Rs 150/240 with attached bath. They do a good Ladakhi dinner here for Rs 30. The *Nezer View Guest House* has rooms from Rs 60/80, Rs 150 with attached bath. The guy who runs it is very helpful and also rents out trekking equipment.

Places to Stay – middle

The recently renovated *Yasmin Guest House* (opposite Hotel Rockwood) has doubles with attached bath for Rs 280. The *Hotel Choskor* (☎ 3626) has doubles with attached baths for Rs 180. The *Hotel Rockwood* charges Rs 280 for doubles with attached bath and the *Hotel Bijoo* (☎ 2331) near the Hotel Choskor has singles/doubles for Rs 300/400, all with attached bath.

The *Lung-Se-Jung* down past the Dreamland Restaurant is popular, if only because of the reliable evening supply of hot water. Rooms cost Rs 200/300. The *Ibex* is similarly priced. Below the main town, the *Dragon Hotel* has nice surroundings and better rooms for the same price. Nearby is the *Hotel Hills View*, with rooms for Rs 100/150 with common bath or Rs 250 for a double with attached bath. The *Hotel Horzay* is nearby with doubles for Rs 400.

The *Siachen Hotel* has rooms from Rs 300/400 with attached bathrooms but has nothing to recommend it other than being right beside the bus stand.

Places to Stay – top end

With singles/doubles at around Rs 600/800 including meals, Leh's top-end places include the *Tsemo-La* (☎ 2281), the central *Khangri* (☎ 2251), the *Lha-ri-Mo* (☎ 2377) and the *K-Sar* (☎ 2548) next door, the *Mandala* further down the road, the *Hotel Galdan Continental* (☎ 2373) in the town centre, and the *Shambala* (☎ 2267) out of town towards the edge of the valley.

The *Hotel Omasila* (☎ 2319) has an attractive garden and is in a peaceful location. Without meals, doubles are Rs 650.

Places to Eat

The centrally located *Dreamland Restaurant* has good food at reasonable prices. The Tibetan specialities and noodle dishes are a pleasant change from rice and more rice. They also make nice jasmine tea. This is a Leh favourite which has been able to outlast any of the competition. The basic *Tashi Tibetan Restaurant* has managed to maintain its reputation for great, cheap, nourishing food. It's on Fort Rd near the German Bakery.

La Montessori serves up big portions of very tasty Chinese, Tibetan and some Western favourites and is popular with local monks. The *Tibetan Friends Corner Restaurant*, near the taxi stand, is another established favourite. Although most of the dishes are Tibetan and very good, it has the reputation for producing the best French fries in Ladakh.

The open-air *Mentokling Restaurant* is a good place to go in the evening. They serve up interesting versions of hummus, felafel, cakes, pies and generally unusual dishes for this part of the world. There's a bar and good music. The *Mona Lisa* (near the Ecological Development Centre) is a similar place with tables in the garden and it gets quite lively in the evening. There's also a bar here and as well as the usual drinks it serves (expensive) chang. It's much cheaper in the unofficial (illegal) chang pubs behind the main street.

The *Ecological Development Centre* offers good coffee, herbal tea, walnut cookies and cakes. Service is rather slow but the boiled potatoes and fried spinach with garlic are very good. They do a special Ladakhi dinner (which must be ordered in advance) for Rs 80. It's all cooked by solar power and cake is only included in the menu if the sun's been shining all day.

The *German Bakery Restaurant* (near the Hotel Yak Tail) is a great place for a cup of coffee and a cream cheese and tomato sandwich. Other popular items on the menu include carrot juice, cinnamon rolls and pizza. They also have a shop near the vegetable market where you can buy excellent trekking bread that keeps fresh for several days, and they will make up packed lunches for long bus trips. Lastly, there's good fresh bread in the early mornings from the bakery stalls in the street behind the mosque. This Middle Eastern-style bread is excellent with honey – bring some honey from Srinagar.

Entertainment

The Cultural & Traditional Society (CATS) puts on a cultural show each evening opposite the Hotel Yak Tail. It's a bit touristy but the performers take it very seriously, sometimes rehearsing late into the night.

Things to Buy

After a number of greedy tourists spirited important antiquities out of Ladakh, the government sensibly clamped down on the sale of important older items. You must be able to prove that anything you buy is less than 100 years old. Baggage is checked on departure from Leh Airport.

Things you might buy include *chang* (Tibetan rice beer) and tea vessels, cups and butter churns, knitted carpets with Tibetan motifs, Tibetan jewellery or, for just a few rupees, a simple prayer flag. Prices in Ladakh are generally quite high – you might find exactly the same Tibetan-inspired item on sale at far lower prices in Kashmir, Dharamsala or Nepal.

Syed Ali Shah's postcard shop is well worth a visit. What the elderly proprietor sells is not actually postcards but a range of photographs he's taken himself over the years. They cost from Rs 10 to over Rs 100.

Getting There & Away

Air Indian Airlines has four flights weekly from Delhi (US$86), and one service a week each to Srinagar (Sunday, US$39), Jammu (Saturday, US$39) and Chandigarh (Friday, US$54). The flight from Srinagar is very short (30 minutes) and extremely spectacular (you cross right over the Himalaya) but also very problematic.

Flights can only be made into Leh in the morning and only when weather conditions are good. If there's a possibility that conditions could deteriorate after arrival in Leh and the aircraft cannot leave, the flight will be cancelled. The end result is a lot of cancellations, a lot of flights that actually leave Srinagar but are not able to land at Leh (since conditions can change very rapidly) and a lot of frustrated passengers.

At difficult times of the year, such as when

the season is about to start but the roads are still closed, the flights can be heavily overbooked. The answer is to book well ahead but be prepared for disappointment. If you can't get a booking in economy it's worth trying for 1st class, as it's only about 10% more expensive. If you're unable to get on a flight from Srinagar ask your houseboat owner for help – every Kashmiri has 'connections'.

The Indian Airlines office (☎ 2276) is near the Hotel Lha-ri-Mo, not far from the centre of town.

Bus There are two overland routes into Leh: the road from Srinagar, and the road (opened in 1991) from Manali in Himachal Pradesh.

A complication when trying to leave Leh for Srinagar or Manali is that you may not be able to buy tickets on the local buses until the evening before departure, because buses may not turn up from either of these places. Thus you can't be certain you will be leaving until the last moment. These two routes are very heavily booked in both directions at the height of the season (August). You have to book days ahead.

To/From Srinagar The Srinagar to Leh road should be open from the beginning of June to October, but in practice the opening date can be variable – sometimes mid-May, sometimes mid-June. The trip takes two days, about 12 hours travel on each day. The overnight halt is made at Kargil. There is a variety of bus classes with fares from around Rs 120 to Rs 250. Jeeps, which take up to six passengers, cost around Rs 5000 but will permit additional stops and diversions along the interesting route.

Before the Srinagar to Leh road officially opens it's possible to cross the Zoji La on foot or by pony, although if there is still a lot of snow the Beacon Patrol will only let you through if you're properly equipped. The pass is cleared of snow before the road is repaired and ready for vehicles, and there is usually transport running along the roads on both sides of the pass before the through buses start to operate. Locals cross the pass

regularly on foot in the pre-season so it is easy to tag along with a larger group or find a guide. But it can be hard work!

To/From Manali The Manali to Leh road is open for a shorter period, usually from July to mid-September, but again the opening and closing dates can be variable. At present the most comfortable bus is the one operated by Himachal Tourism from their office opposite the Dreamland Hotel. Since the road goes up to 5328 metres at its highest point most people suffer the effects of the altitude (headaches, nausea) unless they have spent time acclimatising in Leh. If you plan to fly one way, then fly into Leh and take the bus out since the altitude gain on the bus journey will not be so great as doing the journey in the other direction.

Tickets to Manali on Himachal Tourism's deluxe bus cost Rs 700 and go on sale from 9 am on the day before the bus departs. No advance booking is possible and in the high season you may need to join the queue several hours early. The bus leaves at 6 am and the journey takes two days with an overnight stop at Sarchu. Himachal Tourism has dormitory accommodation here in tents for the outrageously high price of Rs 80. The alternative to this bus is the less comfortable local buses which run from Leh bus terminal for Rs 400, departing at 4 am. An even cheaper option is to hitch a lift in a truck, which costs around Rs 150. At the other end of the scale, a jeep will set you back around Rs 10,000. There are also several private buses on this route; enquire at travel agents around town.

Getting Around
To/From the Airport The bus service from Leh to the airport costs Rs 5 but it doesn't run regularly; a jeep or taxi costs Rs 65.

Bus The enquiry office (☎ 2285) is in the dirty stone building with green windows on the north side of the bus terminal.

There's a reasonably extensive network around Leh of both state road transport and private buses. Destinations served include:

Choglamsar, Chushot, Hemis, Khalsi, Matho, Phyang, Sabu, Sakti, Saspul, Shey, Spitok, Stok and Tikse.

There are buses to Alchi on Wednesday and Sunday at 8.30 am. You can walk to Saspul (two km from Alchi) to catch a bus back to Leh. There are also buses to further afield. The enquiry office at the bus terminal has the full details. Services are much less frequent in winter.

Jeep & Taxi Jeeps can also be hired and, although not cheap, for a group of people they can be a good alternative to the crowds and delays of the buses. The fares are set by the Taxi Drivers' Union for certain popular routes. A return trip to Spitok with an hour at the gompa costs Rs 160. A six-hour return trip from Leh covering Shey, Tikse and Hemis costs Rs 650, with an hour's wait at each monastery. Other destinations served by taxi include Manali, Srinagar, Kargil and Leh Airport. Check the current charges at the taxi union office at the taxi stand and try to negotiate a lower price directly with the drivers.

AROUND LEH
Rafting
Several agencies in Leh run white-water rafting trips on the Indus River. Prices are around Rs 700 per person for a day trip. Indus Himalaya (near the Hotel Yak Tail) and Highland Adventures are two companies that have been recommended.

Spitok Gompa
On a hilltop above the Indus and beside the end of the airport runway, the Spitok Gompa is 10 km from Leh. The temple (Gonkhang) is about 1000 years old. There's an entry fee of Rs 13 and there are fine views over the Indus from the gompa. The walk out here from Leh is uninteresting as it's straight through the large army camp – 'rather like walking round Aldershot', remarked one reader!

Phyang
About 24 km from Leh, on the road back towards Srinagar, the gompa has 50 monks

and the entry fee is Rs 10. There is an interesting little village below the gompa.

Beacon Highway & Nubra Valley
The beautiful Nubra Valley is one of the most recently opened areas of Ladakh. It was once on the trading route which connected eastern Tibet with Turkistan via the Karakoram Pass. Nubra was an important staging post as the area is well cultivated and so fruits and grains were relatively easy to procure.

The villagers in the valley (90% Buddhist, 10% Muslim) still practise polyandry, where three brothers might share the one wife.

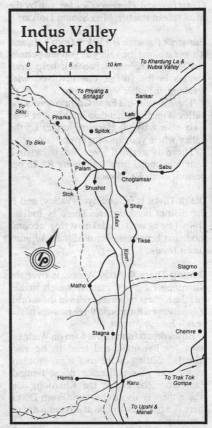

Indus Valley Near Leh

0   5   10 km

To Khardung La & Nubra Valley

To Phyang & Srinagar

Sankar

To Skiu

Pharka

Leh

Spitok

To Skiu

Palam

Sabu

Choglamsar

Stok

Shushot

Shey

Indus River

Tikse

Stagmo

Matho

Stagna

Chemre

Hemis

Karu

To Trak Tok Gompa

To Upshi & Manali

Permits Most people visit on a package deal organised by one or other of the travel agents in Leh, as you have to be part of a group of four. Foreigners are allowed to go as far as Panamik, and Diskit in the Shyok Valley.

Permits must be obtained first in Leh at the District Directorate. The noticeboard at the German Bakery is a good place to look for fellow travellers if you need to make up a group.

Somoor The 150-year-old Samling Gompa here is interesting, and you can sleep here overnight if you want to attend the morning puja at 4 am. Otherwise there's the *Ibex Guest House & Camping Garden*, run by the local school teacher, Miss Sonam Dolkar.

Panamik Panamik is 150 km from Leh, and it's as far along the valley as you are permitted to go. There are two self-help craft centres in the village, one involved with weaving, the other woodcarving.

The 250-year-old **Ensa Gompa** across the valley is much further than it looks – at least a six-hour walk via Hargam, further up the valley where you cross the river.

There is a small *guest house* with a camping ground here. Rooms are Rs 25 per person, meals Rs 25 each.

Diskit Diskit is in the Shyok Valley, and is the district headquarters. There is Indian-style (as against Ladakhi-style) accommodation here in the form of the *Shapnam Guest House*.

Getting There & Away Access is over the Khardong La (5606 metres) which makes this the highest motorable road in the world. It is only open for around three months of the year – June to August.

Buses depart from Leh at 6 am on Wednesdays for Panamik, and tend to be *very* crowded. Sitting on the roof is no problem as long as your policeman doesn't mind. Passes are checked at the Khardong La, where there is also a chai tent. From Diskit there is a bus back to Leh at around 6 am on Saturday.

In the valley itself there is a bus from Panamik to Diskit on Thursday and Sunday at around 11 am, and from Somoor to Diskit on Wednesdays at 8 am. The other option is to hitch rides with the military.

Choglamsar

The **Tibetan refugee camp** at Choglamsar has become an important centre for the study of Tibetan literature and history, and Buddhist philosophy. Don't indulge the kids who demand 'bonbons' – it turns them into beggars.

The impressive temporary residence of the Dalai Lama stands near the river. Nearby, a bridge crosses the Indus to Stok and a rougher road to Hemis.

The Mahabodi Society runs **meditation courses** at Rde-wa Chan near Choglamsar. You can get more information from their centre in Leh.

Shey

This was the old summer palace of the kings of Ladakh and was built about 560 years ago. It's now in ruins but the palace gompa has a 12-metre-high seated **Buddha image**. The entry fee is Rs 10 and the gompa is open from 7 to 9 am and 5 to 6 pm. At other times ask for the monk, Tashi, in the village below; he will know where to find the key.

Tikse Gompa

The Tikse Gompa, 17 km from Leh, is visible from Shey. Its new-found tourist wealth is being put to good use in extensive restoration work. The monastery is very picturesque and superbly sited on a hilltop overlooking the village and the Indus. Beside the car park is the small **Zan-La Temple**.

The gompa has an important collection of Tibetan-style books in its library and some excellent artwork. This is a good place to watch the religious ceremonies either around 6.30 am or noon. They are preceded by long mournful sounds from horns on the roof. Entry fee is Rs 15.

You can get good doubles at the *Skalzang Chamba Hotel*. There are no dorm beds or singles here.

Karu

The road to Manali climbs out of the Indus Valley after this village. Twenty minutes beyond Karu there is a stop at the police checkpoint at Upshi. There are a number of tea shops here.

Hemis Gompa

Hemis Gompa, one of the largest and most important gompas in Ladakh, is 45 km from Leh on the western side of the Indus. It's easy to get there by car or jeep, but on public transport you will have to spend the night at the monastery as it is not easy to bus out there from Leh, walk the six km up from the river to the gompa, see it, walk back down and get back to Leh in one day.

The Hemis Gompa is famous for its **Hemis Festival**, which usually falls in the second half of June or in early July. This is one of the largest and most spectacular of the gompa festivals and at one time was virtually the only one which took place in the summer tourist season. The business-minded monks at some other gompas are now switching their festivals to more lucrative dates. The festival takes two days and features elaborate mask dances and crowds of eager spectators.

The gompa has an excellent library, well-preserved wall paintings and good Buddha figures. Entry is Rs 15.

If instead of turning right at Karu to climb up to Hemis you turn left, you reach the **Chemre Gompa**, five km off the road, and the **Trak Tok Gompa**, 10 km further on. Both lie in the restricted zone but tourists are allowed to visit them.

Places to Stay At Hemis there's a *Rest House & Restaurant* with rather dirty dorm beds. You'll find cheaper and much cleaner rooms in local homes. The *Parachute Restaurant*, next to the bus stand, has good food.

Matho

The west-bank road on the Indus is not in as good condition as the more frequently used east-bank road, but you can return from Hemis on it and there are several interesting places to visit. Matho is in a side valley five

km from Stagna, and in an important festival at the **gompa** here the monks are possessed by spirits and go into a trance. **Stagna**, on the west-bank road, has a gompa too.

Stok

Close to the Choglamsar bridge, a road turns off the west-bank road to the palace of Stok. The last king of Ladakh died in 1974 but his widow, the Rani of Stok, still lives in the 200-year-old **palace**. It is expected that her eldest son will become king when he reaches an auspicious age. You can only enter the **museum** here, which costs Rs 20 and is open from 7 am to 7 pm.

Pharka Gompa

This small cave gompa is almost directly opposite the Spitok Gompa on the Stok side of the Indus. You can reach it by crossing the Choglamsar bridge or the bridge near Spitok, but the last few km must be made on foot.

LEH TO MANALI

This road was opened to foreigners only in 1989 and has rapidly become a popular way

Hemis Festival: masked dancer

into and out of Leh. It's the world's second-highest motorable road, reaching an elevation of 5328 metres at Taglang La. Buses run along this route during the summer season (see the Getting There & Away sections for Leh and Manali). Since only about half of the total distance of 485 km between Leh and Manali is paved it can be a rough journey, especially if you're in the back of the bus.

Taglang La
A rough road leads to this pass, at 5328 metres, the highest on the road. There's a little **temple** here and you can get a free cup of tea at the government tea shop. The two other structures up here are clearly labelled: 'Gents Urinal' and 'Ladies Urinal'! There are superb views back down the valley.

Pang Camp
A number of restaurants in tents have been set up by the river and most buses stop here for lunch. A plate of rice, dhal and veg costs about Rs 20. A bottle of mineral water costs twice what it does in Leh or Manali. About an hour from here is the J&K *Tourist Camp*, also by the river.

Lachlung La
At 5065 metres, this is the second-highest pass on the Leh to Manali road.

Sarchu
Sarchu is just over the state line into Himachal Pradesh, and most buses stop at Himachal Tourism's *Tourist Camp* here. It's ridiculously overpriced at Rs 80 for a dorm bed in a tent. Vegetarian thalis are Rs 30. No receipts are issued for anything so it's obvious where the money is going. Although the driver will try to dissuade you, you can demand to sleep on the bus if you wish. Alternatively, 100 metres away back in J&K is another restaurant tent where you can get cheaper food and they may even let you unroll your sleeping bag in a corner.

Bharatpur City
Once a settlement for the labourers who built

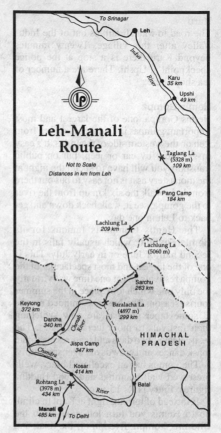

Leh-Manali Route

Not to Scale
Distances in km from Leh

To Srinagar
Leh
Karu 35 km
Upshi 49 km
Taglang La (5328 m) 109 km
Pang Camp 184 km
Lachlung La 209 km
Lachlung La (5060 m)
Sarchu 263 km
Keylong 372 km
Baralacha La (4897 m) 299 km
Darcha 340 km
Chenab River
Jispa Camp 347 km
Kosar 414 km
Rohtang La (3978 m) 434 km
Chandra
Batal
River
HIMACHAL PRADESH
Manali 485 km To Delhi

this road, just two restaurant tents are all that is left of this self-styled 'metropolis'. The *Dhaba Himalaya* is the better of the two.

Baralacha La
It's only a short climb to this 4883-metre pass. About an hour further on you reach the police checkpoint at Patsio.

Darcha
There are half a dozen small restaurants in this small community by the Chenab River. Shortly after Darcha you pass through Jispa, where there is a large army camp.

Keylong to Manali

Keylong is the first town of any size on the journey from Leh to Manali, and the administrative capital of Lahaul and Spiti in which several interesting treks can be made. See the Himachal Pradesh section for more details. After a lunch stop at **Kosar**, where there's an impressive waterfall, you cross the Rohtang La (3978 metres) and descend to Manali.

TREKS IN LADAKH

Treks out of Leh and the Indus Valley can be organised by one of the local agents in Leh with prices between Rs 500 to Rs 1000 per day. You would, however, be advised to bring your own sleeping bag and tent with you. If making your own arrangements, it is possible to organise a horseman at one of the trekking-off points. However, this can take time and you should allow at least a day or two before setting off. Budget for Rs 200 and upwards per horse per day.

The trek from Spitok, just below Leh, to the Markha Valley and Hemis Monastery is the most popular trek in Ladakh. The trek from Lamayuru to Alchi is more demanding and requires a local guide on some sections where the trail is not well defined. Altitude is a very important consideration on these treks with many of the passes in the vicinity of 5000 metres. As an alternative, the trek from Likir Monastery to Temisgam is a trek over relatively low passes and can be completed throughout the year.

Spitok to Markha Valley & Hemis

The trek from Spitok Monastery up the Jingchen Valley avoids crossing any passes on the first two stages. However, at least one rest day should be included before crossing the Ganda La (4920 metres). From the pass it is a steady descent to the Markha Valley and the village of Skiu. Trekking up the valley it is one stage to Markha village, a substantial place with a small monastery, before ascending to the yak grazing pastures at Nimaling. Above the camp is the impressive peak of Kangyaze (6400 metres). The Kongmaru La (5030 metres) is the highest pass on the trek and affords great views south

to the Zanskar range and north to the Ladakh range. After crossing the pass there is one further campsite at the village of Chogdo before reaching Hemis Monastery and the bus back to Leh.

Stage 1	Spitok to Rumbak (6-7 hrs)
Stage 2	Rumbak to Yurutse (3-4 hrs)
Stage 3	Yurutse to Skiu via the Ganda La (7-8 hrs)
Stage 4	Skiu to Markha (7-8 hrs)
Stage 5	Markha to Nimaling (7-8 hrs)
Stage 6	Nimaling to Chogdo via Kongmaru La (7-8 hrs)
Stage 7	Chogdo to Hemis (4-5 hrs)

Lamayuru to Alchi

This trek is often undertaken by travellers coming from Srinagar or Kargil en route to Leh. At Lamayuru there are a number of lodges that can assist with horsemen before trekking over a small pass, the Prinkiti La, to the monastery at Wanla.

From Wanla allow a further two stages before crossing the Konze La (4940 metres) to the village at Sumdo. From here the trail to the village of Sumdochoon at the base of the Stakspi La is not well defined. The views from the Stakspi La (4970 metres) are worth the effort, with a rewarding panorama of the Ladakh and Karakoram ranges, before a long descent to Alchi Monastery and transport to Leh.

Stage 1	Lamayuru to Wanla (3 hrs)
Stage 2	Wanla to Phanjila (4 hrs)
Stage 3	Phanjila to base of Konze La (5 hrs)
Stage 4	Camp to Sumdo via Konze La (5-6 hrs)
Stage 5	Sumdo to Sumdochoon (5 hrs)
Stage 6	Sumdochoon to Alchi via Stakspi La (8 hrs)

Likir to Temisgam

This trek can be completed in a day if you are fit! From Likir Monastery the trail crosses a small pass to the village of Yantang, a short distance from Rizdong Monastery. The next stage leads to the village of Hemis-Shukpachu. It is a further short stage over two minor passes to Temisgam, where there is a daily bus back to Leh.

Stage 1	Likir to Yantang (4-5 hrs)
Stage 2	Yangtang to Hemis-Shukpachu (3 hrs)
Stage 3	Hemis-Shukpachu to Temisgam (3-4 hrs)

Zanskar

The long, narrow Zanskar Valley was opened even more recently than Ladakh. A jeep road reaches all the way from Kargil to Padum, the capital, and although it is not open all the time, it has opened up the area.

For the moment at least, it remains an area for trekking, and some of them are definitely hard going. You can make a number of interesting ones either down the valley or out of it to Ladakh, Kashmir or Himachal Pradesh.

Warning
Unfortunately, in mid-1995 a Zanskar liberation movement emerged and placed a ban on foreign travellers. We advise that you check locally before entering Zanskar.

PADUM
The 'capital' of Zanskar has a population of around 1000, of whom about 300 are Sunni Muslims. It's on the southern part of a wide fertile plain where two rivers join to form the Zanskar River.

There is a tourist bureau where you can arrange accommodation and the hire of horses. On arrival in Padum you must register with the Tourism Department.

Places to Stay
There's a limited choice of a few basic hotels, and rooms in private houses. The *Shapodok-la*, in the centre of town, has cheap dorm beds. The *Haftal View* and *Ibex* hotels have rooms from Rs 50 to Rs 80 but the similarly priced *Chora-la* is probably the best of the bunch. The *Tourist Bungalow* is more expensive but has doubles with attached bath.

AROUND PADUM
Zangla & Karsha Gompa
This is an interesting four-day trek around Padum. The first day takes you to **Thonde**

on the riverbank with a monastery high above it. Since horses cannot cross the rope bridge from Padum, this is the first place on this side of the river where they can be hired for treks further afield.

The second day takes you from Thonde to **Zangla**, where the king of Zanskar has his castle. On day three you backtrack towards Thonde, cross the river and continue to **Karsha**, the most important gompa in Zanskar. On the final day you can cross the river by ferry or continue down to the wooden Tungri Bridge and double back to Padum.

Tungri-Zongkhul Gompa Round Trip
This four-day trek around Padum takes you to the Sani and Zongkhul gompas by following the route up towards the Muni La, then cutting across to the base of the Umasi La.

TREKS IN ZANSKAR
Trekking in the Zanskar can be difficult and you should be equipped for every eventuality. You should bring most of your supplies with you. There are a number of agencies in Leh that can organise things for you for between Rs 500 to Rs 1000 per day but their equipment – sleeping bags, down jackets and tents – is not of a very high quality.

While a number of the treks out of Padam, the administrative centre of the Zanskar, follow routes through villages where there are teahouses-cum-lodges, lodgings cannot be guaranteed and some of the stages require an overnight camp. It is therefore advisable that you bring all your own gear and be self-sufficient for the trek.

Horses can be hired out of Padam for around Rs 200 per day.

Padam to Darcha
This is one of the most popular treks out of the Zanskar Valley. The trek can be completed in a week. It follows a well-defined route up the Tsarap Valley for the first three stages before diverting to Phugtal Monastery, one of the oldest monasteries in the Zanskar region.

From Phugtal the trek continues through a number of villages to Kargyak, the highest settlement in this part of the Zanskar. From Kargyak it is a further stage to the base of the Shingo La (5090 metres). The pass crossing over the main Himalaya is completed in one stage before the final stage to the village of Darcha.

From Darcha it is possible to either get a lift in a truck to the Indus Valley and Leh, or to catch the daily bus service to Manali in the Kullu Valley.

Stage 1	Padam to Mune (6 hrs)
Stage 2	Mune to Purne (8 hrs)
Stage 3	Purne to Phugtal Monastery & Testa (6 hrs)
Stage 4	Testa to Kargyak (7 hrs)
Stage 5	Kargyak to Lakong (6-7 hrs)
Stage 6	Lakong to Rumjak via the Shingo La (6-7 hrs)
Stage 7	Rumjak to Darcha (6-7 hrs)

Padam to Lamayuru

This trek crosses a number of high passes in the vicinity of 5000 metres in order to reach Lamayuru Monastery. As with the trek over the Shingo La, trekkers must be fully equipped as there are a number of stages where there is neither food nor overnight shelter.

The trek commences at Padam or at the nearby Karsha Monastery, the largest in the Zanskar region. The trek follows the true left bank of the Zanskar River for two stages before diverting towards the Hanuma La (4950 metres) and Lingshet Monastery. From here it is a single stage to the base of the Singge La (5050 metres), the highest pass on this trek. It is not a difficult pass crossing and the descent to the village of Photaksar can easily be completed in one stage.

From Photaksar the trail climbs to the summit of the Sisir La (4850 metres) to the village of Honupatta. Two further stages complete the trek to Lamayuru Monastery and the Leh to Srinagar highway, where it is possible to get a lift by bus or truck to Leh.

Stage 1	Padam to Karsha (3 hrs)
Stage 2	Karsha to Pishu (4-5 hrs)
Stage 3	Pishu to Hanumil (4-5 hrs)

Stage 4	Hanumil to Snertse (5 hrs)
Stage 5	Snertse to Lingshet via the Hanuma La (5-6 hrs)
Stage 6	Lingshet to base of Singge La (5 to 6 hrs)
Stage 7	Singge La to Photaksar (5-6 hrs)
Stage 8	Photaksar to Honupatta via the Sisir La (6 hrs)
Stage 9	Honupatta to Wanla (5 hrs)
Stage 10	Wanla to Lamayuru (3-4 hrs)

Padam to Kishtwar

This challenging trek over the main Himalaya range at the Umasi La takes a minimum of a week and should only be attempted by well-prepared parties. Horses cannot cross the Umasi La so porters from Sani Monastery close to Padam are often hired. The going rate is up to Rs 2000 per porter to the village of Suncham on the far side of the pass. Thereon the porters return to the Zanskar and you are then left with hiring whatever horses or mules are available.

From Padam the route heads up the Zanskar Valley past Tungri village to Zongkul Monastery. It is a further stage to the base of the Umasi La. The actual route to the pass is not well defined and a local guide is essential. The climb to the pass crosses a series of glaciers and is very steep just below the summit. From the pass (5340 metres) there are panoramic views of the inner Himalaya. Beyond the pass there is a large rock overhang where the porters insist on sheltering overnight before a long descent to the village of Suncham. It is then recommended to allow two stages from here to the village of Atholi.

From Atholi you can catch the bus to Kishtwar or head up the Chandra Valley by three trek stages to the village of Kilar and the newly constructed road to the Kullu Valley and Manali.

Stage 1	Padam to Zongkul Monastery (6-7 hrs)
Stage 2	Zongkul to base of Umasi La (6-7 hrs)
Stage 3	Cross Umasi la to Camp (7 hrs)
Stage 4	Camp to Suncham (8 hrs)
Stage 5	Suncham to Marchel (3 hrs)
Stage 6	Marchel to Atholi (8 hrs)

Uttar Pradesh

In terms of population Uttar Pradesh is the largest state in India – it's staggering to think that if it were a country in its own right, it would rank among the 10 biggest in the world! It is also one of the great historical and religious centres of India. The Ganges River, which forms the backbone of Uttar Pradesh, is the holy river of Hinduism, and there are several important pilgrimage towns along it. The main ones are Rishikesh and Haridwar, where the river emerges from the Himalaya and starts across the plains, but there's also Varanasi, the most holy city of all. Buddhism also has its great shrine in the state, for it was at Sarnath, just outside Varanasi, that the Buddha first preached his message of the middle way.

Geographically and socially the state varies greatly. Most of it consists of the vast Ganges plain, an area of awesome flatness which often suffers dramatic floods during the monsoon. The people of this area are predominantly poorly educated farmers who scratch a bare existence from the overcrowded land, and the region is often referred to as the cow belt or the Hindi belt. By contrast, the north-west corner of the state is a part of the soaring Himalaya, with excellent treks, beautiful scenery and some of India's highest mountains.

In recent times the state has also become the focus for the right-wing Hindu party, the BJP. The dispute at Ayodhya over the construction of a Hindu temple on the site of an ancient mosque, known as the Ranajanambhumi issue, brought the state to flash point on several occasions in 1992. It also led to riots and killings in other parts of India. The issue remains unresolved thus far; in late 1994 the central government referred the issue to the Supreme Court. It asked the court to rule whether or not there had been a Hindu shrine on the site prior to the existence of the now-demolished mosque, therefore taking that sensitive ruling out of the government's hands. The court refused to get dragged into

Population: 152.7 million
Area: 294,411 sq km
Capital: Lucknow
People per sq km: 518
Main Language: Hindi
Literacy Rate: 41.7%
Best Time to Go: October to March

The external boundaries of India on this map have not been authenticated and may not be correct.

the mire, and so now the issue is back with the central government.

History

Over 2000 years ago the state was part of Ashoka's great Buddhist empire. More recently it was part of the Mughal Empire, and for some years Agra was its capital. Today, of course, Agra is famed for that most perfect of Mughal masterpieces, the Taj Mahal. More recently still, it was in Uttar Pradesh that the Mutiny broke out in 1857 (at Meerut) and some of its most dramatic (Lucknow) and unfortunate (Kanpur) events took place.

The state was first known as United Province when Agra was merged with Avadh after the British took over, but was renamed Uttar Pradesh (Northern State) after Independence.

Uttar Pradesh has produced seven of the

nine Indian prime ministers since Independence in 1947 – Jawaharlal Nehru, Lal Bahadur Shastri, Indira Gandhi, Charan Singh, Rajiv Gandhi, VP Singh and Chandrasekhar.

Agra Region

AGRA

Population: 1,050,500
Telephone Area Code: 0562

At the time of the Mughals, in the 16th and 17th centuries, Agra was the capital of India, and its superb monuments date from that era. Agra has a magnificent fort and the building which many people come to India solely to see – the Taj Mahal.

Situated on the banks of the Yamuna River, Agra, with its crowded alleys and predatory rickshaw riders, is much like any other north Indian city, once you're away from its imposing Mughal monuments. It's possible to take a day trip to Agra from Delhi (there's an excellent train service making this eminently practicable); however, Agra is worth more than a day's visit, particularly if you intend to visit, as you certainly should,

the deserted city of Fatehpur Sikri. In any case, the Taj certainly deserves more than just a single visit if you want to appreciate how its appearance changes under different lights.

History

Agra became the capital of Sikandar Lodi in 1501, but was soon passed on to the Mughals, and both Babur and Humayun made some early Mughal constructions here. It was under Akbar that Agra first aspired to its heights of magnificence. From 1570 to 1585 he ruled from nearby Fatehpur Sikri. When he abandoned that city he moved to Lahore (now in Pakistan), but returned to Agra in 1599 and remained there until his death in 1605.

Jehangir, with his passion for Kashmir, did not spend a great deal of time in the city; Shah Jahan is the name inevitably connected with Agra. He built the Jama Masjid, most of the palace buildings inside the Agra Fort and, of course, the Taj Mahal. In 1638 a new capital – complete with a Red Fort and Jama Masjid – were started in Delhi and the capital was moved there in 1648.

In 1761, Agra fell to the Jats who did much

Commissions, Touts & Rip-Offs

Of all the cities in India, Agra is the city most seriously entangled in the nefarious activity of giving commission – it seems virtually everyone is into it. From the minute you step off the train or bus, there'll be a rickshaw driver wanting to take you to a hotel, handicraft shop or on a sightseeing tour. Some visitors find that all this rather mars their visit to Agra but the persistence and tenacity of these touts is understandable – the commission they get from the handicraft shops can be as much as 20%.

If you escape the rickshaw drivers the next approach will probably be from a well-dressed young man, complete with cool sunglasses, on a moped, who insists he is a student (often from Punjab) and is interested in learning about your country as a place of study. Well, no genuine Indian student has the sort of funds necessary to be turned out in the manner that these blokes are, and so it can be assumed that they, too, are simply commission agents. An invitation to visit their home inevitably leads straight to a craft shop of some kind (usually belonging to an 'uncle' or 'brother'), where you will be pressured to buy at highly inflated prices. If when first approached you are cool and show a reluctance to talk, they'll try to hang the old guilt trip on you with comments such as: 'Don't you like to talk to Indians?'.

If you're shopping for carpets in Agra, watch out for the current scam. This involves you agreeing to help the carpet shop import some extra carpets for their 'agent' in your country, for a profit. You pay with a credit card but are 'protected' from this being presented to the credit card company by an official-looking form you sign guaranteeing that you won't be billed until the carpets are received. Back home, however, you're landed with high import duties for four or five carpets, the credit card company bills you not just for the one you bought but for them all – and does the 'agent' show up?

See the boxed Warning section under Things to Buy in the Facts for the Visitor chapter for more details. ■

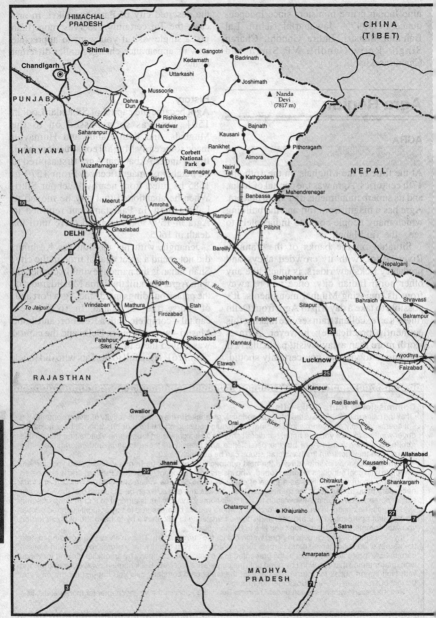

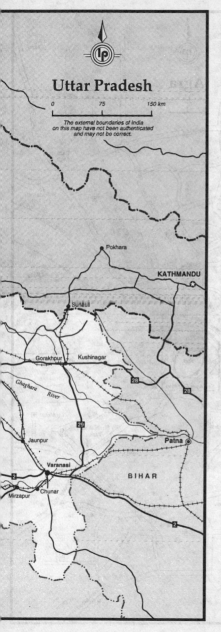

Uttar Pradesh

0   75   150 km

The external boundaries of India
on this map have not been authenticated
and may not be correct.

Pokhara

KATHMANDU

Sunauli

Gorakhpur   Kushinagar

Ghaghara River

28

28

29

Jaunpur

Patna

Varanasi

BIHAR

Mirzapur   Chunar

2

2

damage to the city and its monuments, even going so far as to pillage the Taj Mahal. In turn, it was taken by the Marathas in 1770 and went through several more changes before the British took control in 1803. There was much fighting around the fort during the Mutiny in 1857.

Orientation

Agra is on the west bank of the Yamuna River, 204 km south of Delhi. The old part of the town, where you'll find the main marketplace in a narrow street (Kinari Bazaar), is north of the fort. The cantonment area to the south is the modern part of town, known as Sadar Bazaar. On The Mall are the tourist office, GPO and poste restante. In this area you will also find handicraft shops, restaurants and many moderately priced hotels.

There are some lower priced hotels and the UP Tourist Bungalow near the Raja Mandi railway station, but this area is rather inconveniently located. It's far from the Taj and the main hotel and restaurant area. Immediately south of the Taj in an area known as Taj Ganj is a tightly packed area of narrow alleys where you can find some popular rock-bottom hotels. It's a pleasant walk along the riverside between the Taj and the fort. The 'tourist class' hotels are mainly in the spacious areas of Taj Ganj, south of the Taj itself.

Agra's main railway station is Agra Cantonment; trains from New Delhi station arrive here. The main bus terminal for cities in Rajasthan, Delhi and for Fatehpur Sikri is Idgah. Buses going to Mathura leave from Agra Fort bus terminal. Agra Airport is seven km out of town.

Information

Tourist Offices The Government of India tourist office (☎ 36-3377) is at 191 The Mall. It's open from 9 am to 5.30 pm weekdays and 9 am to 1 pm Saturday; closed Sunday. The UP tourist office (☎ 36-0517) is on Taj Rd, near the Clarks Shiraz Hotel. There's also a tourist information counter at the railway station.

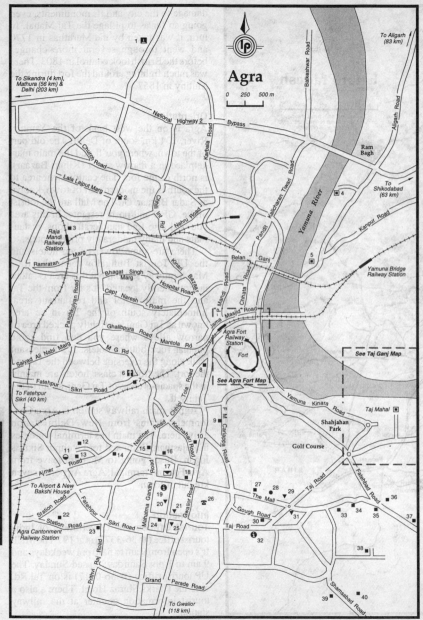

Agra

0   250   500 m

To Aligarh
(83 km)

To Sikandra (4 km),
Mathura (56 km) &
Delhi (203 km)

National Highway 2

Bypass

Karbala Road

Kalicharan Tiwari Road

Balkeshwar Road

Aligarh Road

Ram
Bagh

Yamuna River

To
Shikodabad
(63 km)

Church Road

Lala Lajput Marg

Chin Int Rd

Nehru Road

Pandit

Ganj

Kanpur Road

Raja
Mandi
Railway
Station

Ramratan   Marg

Bhagat   Singh
Marg

Capt   Naresh
Road

Kinari
Bazaar

Belan

Yamuna Bridge
Railway Station

Panokhuyian Road

Hospital Road

Ghalibpura Road

Mantola Rd

M G Rd

Chhata Road

P Mandi Road

Jama Masjid Road

Agra Fort
Railway
Station

Fort

See Taj Ganj Map

Saiyad Ali Nabi Marg

Fatehpur   Sikri   Road

To Fatehpur
Sikri (40 km)

See Agra Fort Map

Yamuna Kinara Road

Taj Mahal

Shahjahan
Park

Nannar Road

Chhipi Tola Road

Kachahri Road

F M Cariappa Road

Golf Course

Ajmer

To Airport & New
Bakshi House

Fatehpur

Station Road

Station Road

Agra Cantonment
Railway Station

Sikri Road

Mahatma Gandhi Road

Gwalior Road

Taj Road

Gough Road

The Mall

Fatehbad Road

Prithvi Raj Road

Grand   Parade Road

Taj Road

Shamsabad Road

To Gwalior
(118 km)

PLACES TO STAY				
		27	Hotel Akbar Inn	25	Park & Lakshmi Vilas
2	Youth Hostel	30	Clarks Shiraz Hotel		Restaurants
3	Tourist Bungalow	33	Hotels Amar &	29.	Sonar Restaurant
7	Kapoor Tourist Rest		Mumtaz	31	Only Restaurant
	House	34	Paradise Guest		
8	Tourist Guest House		House	**OTHER**	
	& Agra Fort Bus	35	Taj View Hotel &		
	Terminal		Mayur Tourist	1	Dayal Bagh Temple
9	Agra & Akbar Hotels		Complex	4	Chini Ka Rauza
10	Tourist Rest House &	36	Mughal Sheraton	5	Itimad-ud-daulah
	Priya Restaurants		Hotel	6	Central Methodist
12	Hotel Rose	37	Novotel Agra		Church
13	Hotel Sheetal	38	Upadyay's Mumtaz	11	Idgah Bus Terminal
14	Deepak Lodge		Guest House	17	GPO
15	Lauries Hotel	39	Highway Inn	19	Government of India
16	Major Bakshi's Tourist	40	Hotel Safari		Tourist Office
	Home			26	Telegraph Office
18	Agra Ashok Hotel	**PLACES TO EAT**		28	Archaeological
22	Hotel Vijay				Survey of India
23	Grand Hotel	20	Zorba the Buddha	30	Indian Airlines Office
24	Hotel Jaiwal &		Restaurant	32	UP Tourist Office
	Kwality Restaurant	21	Prakash Restaurant		

Post The post office is on The Mall, opposite the tourist office. Poste restante is very inefficient here with many letters sorted incorrectly; it may take some baksheesh to get to look through all the letters.

Bookshops The Modern Book Depot, near Kwality Restaurant, has a good selection of general books, including travel guides. They also sell cards and stationery.

Taj Mahal
If there's a building which represents a country – like the Eiffel Tower for France, the Sydney Opera House for Australia – then it has to be the Taj Mahal for India.

This most famous Mughal monument was constructed by Emperor Shah Jahan in memory of his wife Mumtaz Mahal, Chosen of the Palace. It has been described as the most extravagant monument ever built for love, for the emperor was heartbroken when Mumtaz, to whom he had been married for 17 years, died in 1631 in childbirth, after producing 14 children.

Construction of the Taj began in the same year and was not completed until 1653. Workers were recruited not only from all over India but also from central Asia, and in total 20,000 people worked on the building. Experts were even brought from as far away as Europe – the Frenchman Austin of Bordeaux and the Italian Veroneo of Venice had a hand in its decoration. The main architect was Isa Khan, who came from Shiraz in Iran.

The most unusual (but almost certainly apocryphal) story about the Taj is that there might well have been two of them. Shah Jahan, it is said, intended to build a second Taj as his own tomb in black marble, a negative image of the white Taj of Mumtaz Mahal. Before he could embark on this second masterpiece he was deposed by his son, Aurangzeb. Shah Jahan spent the rest of his life imprisoned in the Agra Fort, looking out along the river to the final resting place of his wife.

The Taj is definitely worth more than a single visit as its character changes with the differing lights during the day. Dawn is a magical time, and it's virtually deserted. Fridays tend to be impossibly crowded and noisy – not very conducive to calm enjoyment of this most serene of buildings.

The main entrance to the Taj is on the western side, open from 6 to 8 am, 8.30 am to 4 pm and 5 to 7 pm. Entry costs Rs 100 for the early morning and evening opening times, Rs 10.50 during the day. You can also enter through the south and east gates, but they're open only between 8.30 am and 5 pm. There's no entry charge on Fridays.

The high red sandstone **entrance gateway** is inscribed with verses from the Koran in Arabic, but these days you only exit through here. The entrance is now through a small door to the right of the gate, where everyone has to undergo a security check. The policy on cameras – how close you can photograph the Taj and whether or not there's a charge – varies from year to year. If you are carrying a video camera (permit currently Rs 25), photography is only allowed from inside the main gate; once you have shot from there the camera must be deposited in one of the lockers at the desk inside the main gate.

Paths leading from the gate to the Taj are divided by a long **watercourse** in which the Taj is beautifully reflected. The ornamental gardens through which the paths lead are set out along the classical Mughal *charbagh* lines – a square quartered by watercourses. In spring the flowerbeds by the paths are a profusion of colour. To the west is a small **museum** (open Saturday to Thursday, 10 am to 5 pm, free admission) housing original architectural drawings of the Taj, arms, min-

Taj patterns

iatures and some examples of celadon plates, said to split into pieces or change colour if the food served on them contained poison.

The Taj Mahal itself stands on a raised marble platform on the northern edge of the ornamental gardens. Tall, purely decorative white **minarets** grace each corner of the

---

Taj Pollution Alert

Scientists fear that after centuries of undiminished glory the Taj may soon be irreparably damaged by the city's severe air pollution problem. From the Red Fort, a distance of only two km, it is often almost impossible to see the Taj through the cloud of smoke, smog and haze which envelops it.

The Mathura oil refinery, less than 50 km upstream from the Taj, dumps a tonne of sulphur dioxide into the atmosphere every day. To add to that, there are more than 150 registered iron foundries in the vicinity. The UP government insists that all is fine, but the amount of suspended particles in the air is more than five times what the government itself says is the maximum the Taj can sustain without being damaged. A band of cleaners scrubs at the yellowing marble with chemicals, and some slabs have been so badly damaged they've had to be replaced. Not that people haven't damaged the Taj in the past – in 1764 silver doors fitted to the entrance gate were ripped off and carted away, and raiders have also made off with the gold sheets that once lined the subterranean vault.

Environmentalists finally managed to get a hearing in the Supreme Court, who ordered that the state government tackle the problem immediately. New industries within a 50-km radius of the Taj have been banned; but many existing operations remain. In 1994 an article in the British press suggesting that the world's most beautiful building should be put under international control caused a flood of indignant letters in Indian newspapers.

Indian environmentalists have now launched a petition to save the Taj, aiming to collect a million signatures demanding tougher action. Ideas for limiting pollution in the vicinity include the banning of vehicles of all types within a three km radius of the Taj; visitors would arrive only by cycle-rickshaw or tonga. By refusing to take auto-rickshaws or taxis to visit the Taj, this is one idea that tourists can put into immediate effect. ■

platform – as the Taj Mahal is not a mosque, nobody is called to prayer from them. Twin red sandstone buildings frame the building when viewed from the river; the building on the west side is a mosque, the identical one on the east side is purely for symmetry. It cannot be used as a mosque as it faces the wrong direction.

The central Taj structure has four small domes surrounding the huge, bulbous, central dome. The **tombs** of Mumtaz Mahal and Shah Jahan are in a basement room. Above them in the main chamber are false tombs, a common practice in mausoleums of this type. Light is admitted into the central chamber by finely cut marble screens. The echo in this high chamber, under the soaring marble dome, is superb and there is always somebody there to demonstrate it.

Although the Taj is amazingly graceful from almost any angle, it's the close-up detail which is really astounding. Semiprecious stones are inlaid into the marble in beautiful patterns and with superb craft in a process known as *pietra dura*. The precision and care which went into the Taj Mahal's design and construction is just as impressive whether you view it from across the river or from arm's length.

Agra Fort

Construction of the massive Agra Fort was begun by Emperor Akbar in 1565, and additions were made up until the time of his grandson, Shah Jahan. While in Akbar's time the fort was principally a military structure, by Shah Jahan's time it had become partially a palace. A visit to the fort is an Agra 'must' since so many of the events which led to the construction of the Taj took place here.

There are many fascinating buildings within the massive walls which stretch for 2.5 km, surrounded by a moat over 10 metres wide. Inside, the fort is really a city within a city. Not all of the buildings are open to visitors, and Shah Jahan's beautiful marble Moti Masjid (known as the Pearl Mosque for its perfect proportions) is, unfortunately, closed.

The fort is on the banks of the Yamuna

River and the Amar Singh Gate to the south is the only entry point. It's open from sunrise to sunset and admission is Rs 10.50 except on Fridays when there's no charge.

Diwan-i-Am The Hall of Public Audiences was also built by Shah Jahan and replaced an earlier wooden structure. Shah Jahan's predecessors had a hand in the hall's construction, but the throne room, with its typical inlaid marble work, indisputably bears Shah Jahan's influence. Here he sat to meet officials or listen to petitioners. Beside the Diwan-i-Am is the small **Nagina Masjid** or Gem Mosque and the Ladies' Bazaar where merchants came to display and sell goods to the ladies of the Mughal court.

Diwan-i-Khas The Hall of Private Audiences was also built by Shah Jahan between 1636 and 1637. Here the emperor would meet important dignitaries or foreign ambassadors. The hall consists of two rooms

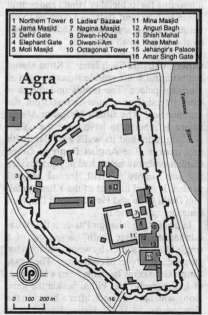

1	Northern Tower	6	Ladies' Bazaar	11	Mina Masjid
2	Jama Masjid	7	Nagina Masjid	12	Anguri Bagh
3	Delhi Gate	8	Diwan-i-Khas	13	Shish Mahal
4	Elephant Gate	9	Diwan-i-Am	14	Khas Mahal
5	Moti Masjid	10	Octagonal Tower	15	Jehangir's Palace
				16	Amar Singh Gate

Agra Fort

UTTAR PRADESH

connected by three arches. The famous Peacock Throne was kept here before being moved to Delhi by Aurangzeb. It was later carted off to Iran and its remains are now in Tehran.

Octagonal Tower The Musamman Burj, or Octagonal Tower, stands close to the Diwan-i-Khas and the small, private Mina Masjid. Also known as the Saman Burj, this tower was built by Shah Jahan for Mumtaz Mahal and is another of his finely designed buildings. It was here, with its views along the Yamuna to the Taj, that Shah Jahan died in 1666, after seven years' imprisonment. Unfortunately the tower has been much damaged over the years.

Jehangir's Palace Akbar is believed to have built this palace, the largest private residence in the fort, for his son. This was one of the first constructions demonstrating the fort's changing emphasis from military to luxurious living quarters. The palace is also interesting for its blend of Hindu and central Asian architectural styles – a contrast to the unique Mughal style which had developed by the time of Shah Jahan.

Other Buildings Shah Jahan's **Khas Mahal** is a beautiful white marble structure used as a private palace. The rooms underneath it were intended as a cool retreat from the summer heat. The **Shish Mahal** or Mirror Palace is reputed to have been the harem dressing room and its walls are inlaid with tiny mirrors. The **Anguri Bagh** or Grape Garden probably never had any grapevines but was simply a small, formal Mughal garden. It stood in front of the Khas Mahal. The **Delhi Gate** and **Hathi Pol**, or Elephant Gate, are now closed.

In front of the Jehangir Palace is the **Hauz-i-Jehangri**, a huge 'bath' carved out of a single block of stone – by whom and for what purpose is a subject of conjecture. The **Amar Singh Gate** takes its name from a Maharaja of Jodhpur who was killed beside the gate, along with his followers, after a brawl in the Diwan-i-Am in 1644! Justice tended to be

summary in those days; there is a shaft leading down to the river into which those who made themselves unpopular with the great Mughals could be hurled without further ado.

Jama Masjid
Across the railway tracks from the Delhi Gate of Agra Fort, the Jama Masjid was built by Shah Jahan in 1648. An inscription over the main gate indicates that it was built in the name of Jahanara, Shah Jahan's daughter, who was imprisoned with Shah Jahan by Aurangzeb. Large though it is, the mosque is not as impressive as Shah Jahan's Jama Masjid in Delhi.

Itimad-ud-daulah
There are several interesting sights on the opposite bank of the Yamuna and north of the fort. You cross the river on a narrow two-level bridge carrying pedestrians, bicycles, rickshaws and bullock carts.

The first place of interest is the exquisite Itimad-ud-daulah – the tomb of Mirza Ghiyas Beg. This Persian gentleman was Jehangir's *wazir*, or chief minister, and his beautiful daughter later married the emperor. She then became known as Nur Jahan, the Light of the World, and her niece was Mumtaz Mahal, Chosen of the Palace. The tomb was constructed by Nur Jahan between 1622 and 1628 and is very similar to the tomb she constructed for her husband, Jehangir, near Lahore in Pakistan.

The tomb is of particular interest since many of its design elements foreshadow the Taj, construction of which started only a few years later. The Itimad-ud-daulah was the first Mughal structure totally built from marble and the first to make extensive use of pietra dura, the inlay work of marble which is so characteristic of the Taj. The mausoleum is small and squat compared to the soaring Taj, but the smaller, more human scale somehow makes it attractive, and the beautifully patterned surface of the tomb is superb. Extremely fine marble latticework passages admit light to the interior. It's well worth a visit.

The Itimad-ud-daulah is open from sunrise to sunset and admission is Rs 5.50; free on Fridays. The tomb is often referred to locally as the 'baby Taj', although the comparison is largely inappropriate.

Chini Ka Rauza
The China Tomb is one km north of the Itimad-ud-daulah. The squat, square tomb, surmounted by a single huge dome, was constructed by Afzal Khan, who died at Lahore in 1639. He was a high official in the court of Shah Jahan. The exterior was covered in brightly coloured enamelled tiles and the whole building clearly displayed its Persian influence. Today it is much decayed and neglected, and the remaining tile work only hints at the building's former glory.

Ram Bagh
Laid out in 1528 by Babur, first of the Mughal emperors, this is the earliest Mughal garden. It is said that Babur was temporarily buried here before being permanently interred at Kabul in Afghanistan. The Ram Bagh is two km north of the Chini Ka Rauza on the riverside and is open from sunrise to sunset; admission is free. It's rather overgrown and neglected.

Dayal Bagh Temple
In Dayal Bagh, the white marble *samadhi* (or temple) of the Radah Soami religion is currently under construction. It was started in 1904 and is not expected to be completed until sometime next century. You can see pietra dura inlaid marblework actually being worked on. Although the building is architecturally nothing remarkable (some would go so far as to call it gaudy, disproportioned and somewhat ugly), the level of artisanship has to be admired.

Dayal Bagh can be reached by bus or bicycle.

Akbar's Mausoleum
At Sikandra, 10 km north-west of Agra, the tomb of Akbar lies in the centre of a large peaceful garden. Akbar started its construction himself but it was completed by his son,

Jehangir, who significantly modified the original plans, which accounts for the somewhat cluttered architectural lines of the tomb.

The building has three-storey minarets at each corner and is built of red sandstone inlaid with white marble polygonal patterns. Four red sandstone gates lead to the tomb complex: one is Muslim, one Hindu, one Christian, and one is Akbar's patent mixture. Like Humayun's Tomb in Delhi, it is an interesting place to study the gradual evolution in design that culminated in the Taj Mahal. Akbar's mausoleum is open from sunrise to sunset and entry is Rs 5.50, except on Fridays when it is free. A permit for a video camera costs Rs 25; still cameras are free.

Sikandra is named after Sultan Sikandar Lodi, the Delhi ruler who held power from 1488 to 1517, immediately preceding the rise of Mughal power on the subcontinent. The **Baradi Palace**, in the mausoleum gardens, was built by Sikandar Lodi. Across the road from the mausoleum is the **Delhi Gate**. Between Sikandra and Agra are several tombs and two *kos minars*, or milestones.

From Agra Cantonment railway station auto-rickshaws charge Rs 90 for the return trip with two hours at Sikandra. You can also get there on a cycle-rickshaw.

Other Attractions
The **Kinari Bazaar**, or old marketplace, is a fascinating area to wander around. It's in the old part of Agra, near the fort, and the narrow alleys of the market start near the Jama Masjid. There are several market areas, or *mandis*, in Agra with names left over from the Mughal days, although they bear no relation to what is sold there today. The **Loha Mandi** (Iron Market) and **Sabji Mandi** (Vegetable Market) are still used, but the **Nai Ki Mandi** (Barber's Market) is now famous for textiles. In the **Malka Bazaar** women beckon to passing men from the upstairs balconies.

Swimming
Some of the larger hotels allow non-guests

to use their pools, for a fee of course. Cheapest is the Lauries Hotel, which charges Rs 50. It's Rs 80 at the Hotel Amar, Rs 100 at the Agra Ashok, Rs 200 at the Clarks Shiraz, and a dip at the Sheraton will set you back Rs 300.

Organised Tours

If you're just day-tripping from Delhi, tours commence from Agra Cantonment railway station and tickets are sometimes sold on the *Taj Express* or *Shatabdi Express* trains. The tours start when the trains arrive (10 am for the *Taj Express*, 8.30 am for the *Shatabdi*). They last all day and include visits to the Taj, the fort and Fatehpur Sikri. Tickets cost Rs 100.

In Agra itself, you can book the tours (and get picked up) from the tourist office in The Mall, or from the tourist information counter at Agra Cantonment railway station.

Places to Stay – bottom end

The two main areas for cheap accommodation are the Taj Ganj tangle of narrow streets directly south of the Taj, and the Sadar area, close to Agra Cantonment railway station, the tourist office and the GPO, and only a short rickshaw ride from the Taj.

Taj Ganj Area Many of the hotels in this area boast of Taj views, but often it's just wishful thinking. Only two have a truly uninterrupted view from their rooftops, and the better of them is the relatively new *Hotel Kamal* (☎ 36-0926). There are singles with common bath for Rs 50, and doubles/triples with attached bath from Rs 80/100. The rooms are clean but a little dark. From the sitting area on the roof, however, there's a superb view of the Taj. Since this place gives commissions to rickshaw-wallahs they may try to charge you a higher price.

The other place with a real Taj view is the *Shanti Lodge* (☎ 36-1644). It's been getting mixed reports lately but the view from the rooftop restaurant is still as wonderful as it's always been. Rooms are Rs 60/80 for singles/doubles with common bath, Rs 80/100 with attached bath; if you stay for a

while you may be able to get a cheaper deal. Some rooms are definitely better than others, so try to look at more than one. Checkout is at 10 am.

Another good hotel is the *Hotel Siddhartha* (☎ 26-4711), not far from the western gate. It's a clean place run by very friendly Sikhs, and has a pleasant garden courtyard. Rooms range from Rs 60/80 to Rs 80/175, all with attached bathroom (bucket hot water in the cheaper rooms). There are limited views from the roof. Nearby, the *Hotel Host* is a little cheaper, and has its own bike hire for Rs 10 per day.

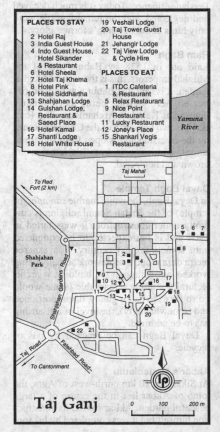

PLACES TO STAY	19 Veshali Lodge
	20 Taj Tower Guest
2 Hotel Raj	House
3 India Guest House	21 Jehangir Lodge
4 Indo Guest House,	22 Taj View Lodge
Hotel Sikander	& Cycle Hire
& Restaurant	
6 Hotel Sheela	PLACES TO EAT
7 Hotel Taj Khema	
8 Hotel Pink	1 ITDC Cafeteria
10 Hotel Siddhartha	& Restaurant
13 Shahjahan Lodge	5 Relax Restaurant
14 Gulshan Lodge,	9 Nice Point
Restaurant &	Restaurant
Saeed Place	11 Lucky Restaurant
16 Hotel Kamal	12 Joney's Place
17 Shanti Lodge	15 Shankari Vegis
18 Hotel White House	Restaurant

Yamuna River

Taj Mahal

To Red Fort (2 km)

Shahjahan Park

Shahjahan Gardens Road

Taj Road

To Cantonment

Fatehbad Road

Taj Ganj

0   100   200 m

By the eastern gate, the friendly *Hotel Pink* (☎ 36-0677) is indeed pink, and set around a small courtyard draped in crimson bougainvillea. All rooms have attached baths and range from Rs 40/70 with a bucket shower, to Rs 120/150 for a double/triple with running hot water. Also in this area is the recently renovated *Veshali Lodge* (☎ 26-9673). Airy rooms lead off a verandah and cost Rs 50 for a double, Rs 60/80 with attached bathroom and Rs 100 for the double with a bathtub.

On the road leading from the eastern gate is the *Hotel Sheela* (☎ 36-1794). The large garden is the best thing about this place. The cheapest rooms are grotty doubles for Rs 80; there are also rooms at Rs 100/150 with attached bath and bucket hot water, and over-priced deluxe doubles for Rs 250. A little further along the same road is UP Tourism's *Hotel Taj Khema* (☎ 36-0140). There are rooms with common bath for Rs 100/125, but the semideluxe rooms with attached bath and water heater are much better value at Rs 150/175. There are excellent views of the Taj from the artificial hill in the garden – non-guests are charged Rs 10 to see it. You can camp here for Rs 25.

There are several options along South Gate. The long-running *India Guest House* is a small, family-run place with just a few spartan rooms for Rs 30/45 with common bath, or there's one rooftop room with a view for Rs 60. Across the road, the *Indo Guest House* is similarly priced and also has some rooms for Rs 40/60 with attached bath. It's run by a very friendly family who supply free tea and don't try to sell you things. Next door is the *Hotel Sikander*, also in this price range and with a roof terrace. A few doors down, the *Hotel Noorjahan* is marginally cheaper.

The best hotel in this area is the new *Hotel Raj*, 2/26 South Gate, with a wide range of rooms from dorm beds at Rs 40 and rooms with common bath from Rs 50/100. Better value are the ordinary rooms with attached bath (and hot water geysers) for Rs 125/150. There are air-cooled rooms with satellite TV for Rs 150/200 and air-con rooms with TV

and bathtub for Rs 250/300. It's all spotlessly clean and sparkling – but for how long?

The *Shahjahan Lodge* is run by a friendly Muslim man, and is in a good spot in the heart of Taj Ganj. Rooms cost Rs 30/40 with shared bathroom, Rs 60 and Rs 80 for doubles with attached bath and hot water, and there's one large four-bed room, complete with bath (and tub) for Rs 210. Nearby is the *Gulshan Lodge*, which is a bit gloomy but for Rs 30/40 with common bath it's as cheap as you'll find. There are also some doubles with attached bath for Rs 60.

A short distance east is the *Hotel White House*, a clean place with rooms for Rs 60/80 with attached bathroom, and cheaper rooms with common bath. There's a rooftop restaurant but no Taj views. Nearby, the *Taj Tower Guest House* has some nice rooms at Rs 25/40 for singles/doubles with common bath or Rs 50 for a double with attached bathroom.

Not far from the traffic roundabout is the *Taj View Lodge*. The name is hardly justified but from the double bed in the cosy little room on the rooftop (Rs 20) you can just glimpse tiny bits of the Taj through the trees. Further into Taj Ganj is the *Jehangir Lodge*. It's a bit rough around the edges but is otherwise OK, and the price is right – Rs 20 for a bed in a three-bed dorm, Rs 30/40 for a single/double, Rs 50 for a double with attached bath.

South of Taj Ganj There's been a mini building boom in the area south of Taj Ganj and there are several reasonable hotels at the top of this price range, as well as numerous mid-range places. The *Paradise Guest House* (☎ 36-9199) hardly lives up to its name, but one advantage of this place is that it has a generator – Agra has chronic power problems, with blackouts virtually every night. Rooms cost Rs 120/150 with attached bath. South of here is the popular *Hotel Safari* (☎ 36-0013) on Shamsabad Rd. It's clean and good value at Rs 75/120 with air-cooling and hot-water bath. There are also rooms with three and four beds for Rs

150 and Rs 175 respectively. Meals are available, and the Taj is visible from the rooftop.

Nearby is the *Highway Inn* (☎ 36-0458), which is popular with overlanders for its camping facilities – Rs 60 for two people and a tent. Rooms are Rs 150/250 with bath, Rs 100/150 without.

On a quiet residential street just to the east of this area is the very pleasant *Upadhyay's Mumtaz Guest House* (☎ 36-0865), 3/7 Vibhav Nagar. Rooms with attached bath are Rs 75/150, or Rs 200 for a deluxe double with bathtub. There's a small garden and sun terrace on the roof.

Sadar The popular and long-running *Tourist Rest House* (☎ 36-3961) is on Kachahari Rd, not far from The Mall. Set around a small garden, it's managed by two helpful brothers who will even make train reservations for you. This pleasant though rather dog-eared hotel has a variety of rooms with and without bath, ranging from Rs 55/65 for the most basic rooms. They don't need to give commissions so rickshaws may be unwilling to take you there, and will instead take you to a couple of other places purporting to be the Tourist Rest House. One such place is the *Kapoor Tourist Rest House*, a real dive on a busy intersection on Fatehpur Sikri Rd, right beside the railway track. Another pretender is the so-called *Tourist Rest House*, near the Agra Fort bus terminal.

Down the scale a bit is the friendly *Deepak Lodge* at 178 Ajmer Rd. The rooms are somewhat small and dark, and the 'attached bath' is virtually part of the room. All this is yours for Rs 60/80.

Midway between Sadar and Taj Ganj is the *Hotel Akbar Inn* (☎ 36-3212), as distinct from the Hotel Akbar (mentioned later in this section). It has a convenient location right on The Mall, and the large peaceful garden and lawn are added bonuses. The small rooms in the separate wing are cheap at Rs 30/45, while those in the main building are very good value at Rs 80/100 with attached bath. You can camp here for Rs 15; and there's also a restaurant.

On Field Marshal Cariappa Rd, in a spacious residential area closer to the Taj and just a few minutes' walk from the fort, there are a couple of good places. The friendly *Agra Hotel* (☎ 36-3331) would be the perfect setting for a novel; it's a large crumbling old place that people either love or hate. There's a good range of rooms from Rs 110/150, all with attached baths, and some with the most amazing antediluvian plumbing. A double air-con suite costs Rs 450. There are views of the Taj from the garden. Right next door is the *Hotel Akbar* (☎ 36-3312), which is a little cheaper and also has a pleasant garden.

Major Bakshi's Tourist Home (☎ 36-3829) has been popular for many years – even Julie Christie has stayed here. The rooms are comfortable and well furnished, and are quite good at Rs 150/250 with attached bath and hot water. It's peaceful and efficiently run.

'Situated in the heart of the poshed centre', the main shopping and restaurant area, is the *Hotel Jaiwal* (☎ 36-3716). Rooms are varied but there are some quite good ones at the back for Rs 200/300 including attached bathroom (with tub), and air-cooling.

Elsewhere The *youth hostel* is in the north of the city on M G Rd. It's certainly cheap at Rs 12 (Rs 22 for nonmembers), but the location is such a detraction that you'd need a pretty good reason to stay here. The UP *Tourist Bungalow* (☎ 35-0120), with rooms from Rs 150/175, is also in this part of the city.

If you need to be near the Idgah bus terminal, the *Hotel Sakura* has rooms with attached bath from Rs 100/150. Private buses for Rajasthan leave from right outside, and next door is the similarly priced *Hotel Sheetal*. Much better than these, however, is the *Hotel Rose* (☎ 36-7562) at 21 Old Idgah Colony, just off Ajmer Rd. There are dorm beds for Rs 35, and rooms from Rs 60/80 to Rs 225/300, all with attached bath.

If you're looking for a place near Agra Cantonment railway station there are several options along Station Rd. The *Hotel Vijay* is the best of these, with doubles for Rs 150.

Places to Stay – middle

The *New Bakshi House* (☎ 36-8159) is a very pleasant upmarket guest house at 5 Laxman Nagar, between the railway station and the airport. The owner is the son of the late Major Bakshi whose guest house is in the Sadar area. Comfortable rooms in this well-equipped and clean place range from Rs 400/500 to Rs 650. The food is excellent and they can also arrange to pick you up from the station or airport. They're often booked up so you need to ring in advance.

One of the nicest places in this range is the elderly *Lauries Hotel* (☎ 36-4536) in the Sadar area. The management and staff are very pleasant and claim that this was where the Queen stayed on a visit to India in 1963. You'd hardly believe it, it's certainly not by royal appointment now – the rooms are a tad shabby but the ones at the back are OK. They cost Rs 325/450 and discounts may be given in the off season. It has a peaceful garden, a swimming pool (not always full) and camping is possible at Rs 30 per person, including access to a hot shower.

The main group of middle and top-end places is in the area south of Taj Ganj, about 1.5 km from the Taj itself. The *Mayur Tourist Complex* (☎ 36-0302) is one of these places, and has very pleasant cottages arranged around a lawn and swimming pool. The cottages cost Rs 400/550 with air-cooling, Rs 500/750 with air-con and Rs 700/950 for air-con deluxe cottages. It's very well run and the food is good.

The *Grand Hotel* (☎ 36-4014) is a reasonable place with a pleasant garden, near the railway station in the cantonment area. Rooms are Rs 430/530, or Rs 630/720 with air-con. Meals are available for Rs 50 for breakfast, or Rs 100 for lunch or dinner.

The *Hotel Amar* (☎ 36-0695) has a popular swimming pool, jacuzzi and sauna. Room rates are Rs 700/900 with air-con. At the top of this price range is the *Hotel Mumtaz* (☎ 36-1771) under renovation in an attempt to raise itself from three to five-star status. Standard rooms are Rs 1100/1500.

Places to Stay – top end

Agra's five-star hotels are generally in the open area south of the Taj. The Clarks Shiraz, Agra Ashok and Novotel are all in the same price range.

The *Clarks Shiraz Hotel* (☎ 36-1421; fax 36-1620) is a long-standing Agra landmark and is one of the better expensive hotels. It's fully air-conditioned, has a swimming pool and singles/doubles cost Rs 1195/2380. The Indian Airlines office is also here.

The *Agra Ashok Hotel* (☎ 36-1223; fax 36-1428), despite being part of the Indian Tourism Development Corporation (ITDC) chain, is well managed and a pleasant place to stay. Room rates are Rs 1195/2000 for singles/doubles. The new *Novotel Agra* (☎ 36-8282), Fatehbad Rd, is a low-rise Mughal-style hotel built around a lawn and swimming pool. Rooms are US$38/75.

The five-star hotel with Taj views from most of its rooms is the *Taj View Hotel* (☎ 36-1171; fax 36-1179). It charges US$135/145 for a room where you can admire the Taj from the comfort of your bed. Standard rooms (no view) are US$110/125.

Agra's top hotel is the *Mughal Sheraton* (☎ 36-1701; fax 36-1730) on Fatehbad Rd. It's a very elegant place, with thick creepers cascading down the brickwork of the fort-like architecture. Facilities include everything you'd expect in a five-star deluxe hotel – plus camel or elephant rides and an in-house astrologer. The rooms, which cost from US$165/180, are all very well appointed but only the more expensive ones give you a Taj view. For US$275, in the Mughal Chamber Exclusive, you and your loved one can recline on silk cushions before a picture window and contemplate the immortal view.

Places to Eat

Taj Ganj Area In the Taj Ganj area there are several places catering to travellers. Food tends to be mainly vegetarian here and hygiene is not always quite what it might be.

UTTAR F

The tiny *Joney's Place* is one of the area's longest running places, although its 'Yum Yum Food' is nothing great. It is, however, a good meeting place. The *Shankari Vegis Restaurant* is a bit better and equally popular. Main dishes are Rs 20 to Rs 30 and there's a pleasant sitting area on the roof. It also has books, magazines and games you can use – and they let you choose the music.

On the same square as Joney's, the small *Gulshan Lodge Restaurant* is good for a snack. Next door is *Saeed Place* which includes a range of Israeli food on its have-a-go-at everything menu. Hummus and salad is Rs 15. Further along this street is the *Lucky Restaurant* which claims that its food is so good you'll get your money back if you don't agree. For one reader the main attraction here was not the food but the owner – 'the spitting image of a younger Richard Gere'!

Honey's Restaurant, near Shanti Lodge, is a small place that's good value – a set breakfast with tomato, eggs, porridge and coffee costs Rs 20. The popular little *Sikander Restaurant* has good food, reasonable prices and a varied menu, although the servings are small. Nearby, the *Hotel Noorjahan* does a good buffalo steak and chips.

The ITDC *Cafeteria & Restaurant* just outside the west gate to the Taj has fine Indian and Western food, but it's not cheap and the waiters expect high tips. The *Nice Point Restaurant* near the west gate also has good travellers' food. At the east gate the *Relax Restaurant* does excellent real coffee and desserts; and there's a pleasant rooftop sitting area.

The *Only Restaurant* is an outdoor place by the roundabout on Taj Rd. It has a good reputation for the quality of its ingredients and claims to have a different chef for each of its cuisines – Indian, Chinese and Continental. Nearby is the equally good *Sonar Restaurant*, set in a garden with tables inside and out. There's excellent Mughlai food here.

The *Tourist Rest House* in the Sadar area is a pleasant place to eat. The tables are outside and at night the candles are a nice touch. The *Priya*, nearby, advertises 'Delicious Meals & Joy Forever' and manages to come close to the first part of its promise, at least.

There's a bunch of mid-range restaurants at the western end of Taj Rd. The excellent *Kwality Restaurant* is air-conditioned and certainly one of the best restaurants in Agra. Main dishes are from Rs 50 and Rs 7 buys you a chocolate éclair from the bakery. Opposite is *Hot Bite*, which is good but more expensive.

The *Park Restaurant* is an open-air place just along from the Kwality, and it serves south Indian and Chinese dishes. Nearby is the *Lakshmi Vilas*, a vegetarian restaurant highly recommended for its cheap south Indian food. There are 22 varieties of dosa; a thali is Rs 20.

Zorba the Buddha is an interesting Osho-run vegetarian restaurant. There are stars on the ceiling, clouds on the wall, it's spotlessly clean and the food is excellent. Muesli with fruit, nuts and curd is Rs 20, a lassi is Rs 14. In the same block of shops is the *Savitri Restaurant*, which specialises in barbecue kebabs and chicken tikka; and on the opposite side of the road, is the *Chung Wah* Chinese restaurant – good value.

The deluxe hotels have excellent food – for a major splurge *Clarks Shiraz* is worth considering. Main dishes here are around Rs 150 and it's Rs 125 for a beer; their lunchtime buffet (Rs 300) is very good.

Agra has a local speciality, the ultra-sweet candied melon called *peitha*.

Things to Buy

Agra is well known for leather goods, jewellery and marble items inlaid like the pietra dura work on the Taj. The Sadar and Taj Ganj areas are the main tourist shopping centres, although the prices here are likely to be more expensive. Around Pratapur, in the old part of Agra, there are many jewellery shops, but precious stones are cheaper in Jaipur.

About one km along the road running from the east gate of the Taj is Shilpgram, a crafts village and open-air emporium. At festival times there are live performances by dancers and musicians; the rest of the time there are displays of crafts from all over the country. Prices are certainly on the high side, but the quality is good and the range hard to beat.

Getting There & Away

Air The Indian Airlines office (☎ 36-0948) is at the Clarks Shiraz Hotel. It is open daily from 10 am to 1 pm and from 2 to 5 pm.

Agra is on the popular daily tourist route from Delhi to Agra, Khajuraho, Varanasi and return. It's only a 40-minute flight from Delhi to Agra. Fares from Agra are: Delhi US$23, Khajuraho US$39, and Varanasi US$57.

Bus Most buses leave from the Idgah bus terminal. Buses between Delhi and Agra operate about every hour and cost Rs 49; deluxe buses cost Rs 56, and superdeluxe are Rs 60; the trip takes about five hours. From Delhi buses leave from Sarai Kale Khan, the new bus terminal in the south of the city by Nizamuddin railway station.

There are deluxe buses between Agra and Jaipur every half an hour for Rs 76; there are also air-con buses for Rs 106. They leave from a small booth right outside the Hotel Sheetal on Ajmer Rd, very close to the Idgah bus terminal.

There's an early-morning bus to Khajuraho at 5 am. The fare is Rs 84 and the journey takes 10 to 12 hours. It's better to take the *Shatabdi Express* train to Jhansi (two hours), from where it's six hours by bus to Khajuraho.

Train The tourist-quota allotment here is not great, so getting a booking, especially to Varanasi, can be difficult. Try to plan as far in advance as possible.

Agra is on the main Delhi to Bombay broad-gauge railway line, so there are plenty of trains coming through. Agra is 200 km from Delhi and 1344 km from Bombay. The fastest train between Delhi and Agra is the daily air-con *Shatabdi Express*, which does the trip in a shade under two hours. It leaves Delhi at 6.15 am, returning from Agra at 8.15 pm, and so is ideal for day-tripping. The fare is Rs 235 in a chair car, or Rs 470 1st class, and this includes meals.

There is also the daily *Taj Express* to and from Delhi, but this is slower and gives you less time in Agra. Take great care at New Delhi station; pickpockets, muggers and others are very aware that this is a popular tourist route and they work overtime at parting unwary visitors from their valuables.

To Bombay the journey takes 29 hours at a cost of Rs 198/776 in 2nd/1st class. There are also direct trains to Goa, Madras and Thiruvananthapuram (Trivandrum). If you're heading north towards the Himalaya there are trains through Agra which continue straight through Delhi – you don't have to stop and get more tickets.

The line between Agra and stations in Rajasthan is currently undergoing conversion from metre gauge to broad gauge, and services are reduced. The evening service to Jaipur (2nd class only) is still running. By the time you read this there should be more trains running; and journey times should be shorter. Previously, trains left only from

---

An Experience

Full moon in Agra and what else could we do but make the recommended pilgrimage to the Taj. Finding transport was no problem with all the rickshaw-wallahs shouting 'Tajtajtaj' at every tourist on the street. Negotiating a price, we hopped in and set off. After a while we stopped and the driver shouted something to a passer-by. We turned round and disappeared down smaller and smaller side streets as we became more and more worried. Surely the driver couldn't not know the way to India's top tourist destination, so were we about to be mugged? A few minutes later the rickshaw came to a halt. The driver got out slowly and looked into the back. Clutching his hands to his head he said: 'I am sorry – I have lost Taj'!

We ended the journey on foot – about five minutes walk!

Chris Jenney, UK

Agra Fort station and the daily *Agra-Jaipur Express* did the 208-km trip in five hours for Rs 53/189 in 2nd/1st class, passing through Bharatpur. There should be daily broad-gauge connections with Ajmer and Jodhpur.

Getting Around

To/From the Airport Agra's airport is seven km from the centre of town. Taxis charge around Rs 90 and auto-rickshaws Rs 50.

Taxi & Auto-Rickshaw There are set fares from the cantonment railway station. Auto-rickshaws charge Rs 15 to any hotel, Rs 45 to the fort and back with a couple of hours at the fort, and Rs 250 for a full day's sightseeing. A taxi to any hotel is Rs 60. For the Taj, a cycle-rickshaw is the most environmentally friendly form of transport.

Cycle-Rickshaw & Bicycle Agra is very spread out so walking is really not on – even if you could. It's virtually impossible to walk because Agra's hordes of cycle-rickshaw wallahs pursue would-be pedestrians with unbelievable energy and persuasive ability. Beware of rickshaw-wallahs who take you from A to B via a few marble shops, jewellery shops and so on – just great when you want to catch a train, and it can also work out very expensive!

A simple solution to Agra's transport problem is to hire a rickshaw for the day. You can easily negotiate a full-day rate (Rs 60 to Rs 100) for which your rickshaw-wallah will not only take you everywhere, but will wait outside while you sightsee or even have a meal. How much you pay depends on your bargaining ability but never get in a rickshaw here without first establishing a price. Being told you can pay 'as you like' does not mean that.

Agra is so touristy that many rickshaw-wallahs speak fine English and, like Western cabbies, are great sources of amusing information – like how much they can screw out of fat-cat tourists for a little pedal down to the Taj and back to the air-con hotel. Around Rs 10 should take you from pretty well anywhere in Agra to anywhere else, but the rickshaw drivers will try for much more.

If, however, you really don't want to be pedalled around, Agra is sufficiently traffic-free to make pedalling yourself an easy proposition. There are plenty of bicycle-rental places around. The cost is typically Rs 3 per hour and Rs 15 per day.

FATEHPUR SIKRI

Population: 27,500
Telephone Area Code: 05619

Between 1570 and 1585, during the reign of Emperor Akbar, the capital of the Mughal Empire was situated here, 40 km west of Agra. Then, as suddenly and dramatically as this new city had been built, it was abandoned, mainly due, it is thought, to difficulties with the water supply. Today it's a perfectly preserved example of a Mughal city at the height of the empire's splendour – an attraction no visitor to Agra should miss.

Legend says that Akbar was without a male heir and made a pilgrimage to this spot to see the saint Shaikh Salim Chishti. The saint foretold the birth of Akbar's son, the future emperor, Jehangir, and in gratitude Akbar named his son Salim. Furthermore, Akbar transferred his capital to Sikri and built a new and splendid city.

Although a Muslim, Akbar was known to be very tolerant towards other religions, and he spent much time discussing and studying them in Fatehpur Sikri. He also developed a new religion called Deen Ilahi which attempted to synthesise elements from all the major religions. Akbar's famous courtiers, such as Bibal, Raja Todarmal and Abu Fazal, had their houses near his palace in the city.

Most people visit Fatehpur Sikri as a day trip from Agra, but it can be a pleasant place to stay. Spending the night here would allow you to watch the impressive sunset over the ruins. The best place is from the top of the city walls, a two-km walk to the south.

Orientation & Information

The deserted city lies along the top of a ridge while the modern village, with its bus stand

and railway station, is down the ridge's southern side.

Fatehpur Sikri is open from sunrise to sunset and entry is Rs 0.50; free on Fridays. There's no charge for a camera unless it's a video (Rs 25). Note that the Jama Masjid and the tomb of Shaikh Salim Chishti are outside the city enclosure; there's no entry fee to visit them.

As Fatehpur Sikri is one of the most perfectly preserved 'ghost towns' imaginable, you may well decide it is worthwhile hiring a guide. Around the ticket office, licensed guides are available; the official charge is set at Rs 48 but if business is slack they ask only about half that. At the Buland Darwaza, the gateway to the mosque and shrine, unlicensed guides will try to lure you into hiring them for around Rs 10 to Rs 20.

Day-trippers in search of toilets or a place to leave their luggage, should head for the Maurya Rest House. They charge Rs 2 for left luggage.

Jama Masjid (Dargah Mosque)

Fatehpur Sikri's mosque is said to be a copy of the mosque at Mecca, and is a beautiful building containing elements of Persian and Hindu design.

The main entrance is through the 54-metre-high **Buland Darwaza**, the Gate of Victory, constructed to commemorate Akbar's victory in Gujarat. This impressive gateway is reached by an equally impressive flight of steps. A Koranic inscription inside the archway includes the useful thought: 'The world is a bridge, pass over it but build no house upon it. He who hopes for an hour may hope for eternity'. A large colony of bees has established itself at this gateway but apart from raining little yellow stains on passers-by below they seem to leave visitors alone. Just outside the gateway is a deep well and, when there is a sufficient number of tourists assembled, local daredevils leap from the top of the entrance into the water.

The eastern gate of the mosque is known

Fatehpur Sikri

0   150   300 m

Nagar Village

To Bharatpur

Sikri Village

Lal Darwaza

To Agra

Tansen Mahal

Wire Fence

Agra Gate

Archaeological Survey Rest House

Diwan-i-Khas

Diwan-i-Am

Naubat Khana

Hiran Minar (Deer Minaret)

Ankh Micholi

Panch Mahal

Karawan Serai

Birbal Bhavan

Palace of the Christian Wife

Palace of Jodh Bai

Gulistan Tourist Complex

Shaikh Salim Chishti's Tomb

Ticket Office & Entrance

Jama Masjid

Shahi Darwaza

Buland Darwaza

Kallu Hotel

Maurya Rest House

Bus Station

Gate & Clock Tower

Shree Tourist Guest House

Railway Station

Fatehpur Sikri

UTTAR PRADESH

as the **Shahi Darwaza** (King's Gate), and was the one formerly used by Akbar.

In the northern part of the courtyard is the superb white marble *dargah* or **tomb of Shaikh Salim Chishti**, built in 1570. Just as Akbar came to the saint four centuries ago looking for a son, childless women visit his tomb today. The carved marble lattice screens *(jalis)* are probably the finest examples of such work you'll see anywhere in the country.

The saint's grandson, Islam Khan, also has his tomb within the courtyard. Abul Fazi and Faizi, adviser and poet to Akbar, had their homes just outside the mosque.

Palace of Jodh Bai

North-east of the mosque is the ticket office and entrance to the old city. The first building inside the gate is the Palace of Jodh Bai, named after Jehangir's mother, who was the daughter of the Maharaja of Amber, and was also a Hindu.

Here again the architecture is a blend of styles with Hindu columns and Muslim cupolas. The **Hawa Mahal** (Palace of the Winds) is a projecting room with walls made entirely of stone latticework. The ladies of the court probably sat in here to keep a quiet eye on events below.

Birbal Bhavan

Built either by or for Raja Birbal, Akbar's favourite courtier, this small palace is extremely elegant in its design and execution. Victor Hugo, the 19th-century French author, commented that it was either a very small palace or a very large jewellery box. Birbal, who was a Hindu and noted for his wit and wisdom, unfortunately proved to be a hopeless soldier and lost his life, and most of his army, near Peshawar in 1586. Enormous stables adjoin the Jodh Bai Palace, with nearly 200 enclosures for horses and camels. Some stone rings for the halters are still in place.

Karawan Serai & Hiran Minar

The Karawan Serai or Caravanserai was a large courtyard surrounded by the hostels used by visiting merchants. The Hiran Minar (Deer Minaret), which is actually outside the fort grounds, is said to have been erected over the grave of Akbar's favourite elephant. Stone elephant tusks protrude from the 21-metre-high tower from which Akbar is said to have shot at deer and other game which were driven in front of him. The flat expanse of land stretching away from the tower was once a lake which even today occasionally floods.

Palace of the Christian Wife

Close to the Jodh Bai Palace, this house was used by Akbar's Goan Christian wife, Maryam, and at one time was gilded throughout – giving it the name the Golden House.

Panch Mahal

This amusing little five-storey palace was probably once used by the ladies of the court

Intricate wall carvings inside the palace complex of the Mughal ruler Akbar in Fatehpur Sikri.

and originally had stone screens on the sides. These have now been removed, making the open colonnades inside visible. Each of the five storeys is stepped back from the previous one until at the top there is only a tiny kiosk, its dome supported by four columns. The lower floor has 56 columns, no two of which are exactly alike.

Ankh Micholi
The name of this building translates as something like 'hide and seek', and the emperor is supposed to have amused himself by playing that game with ladies of the harem! It is more likely that the building was used for storing records, although it has some curious struts with stone monsters carved into them. By one corner is a small canopied enclosure where Akbar's Hindu guru may have sat to instruct him.

Diwan-i-Khas
The exterior of the Hall of Private Audiences is plain, but its interior design is unique. A stone column in the centre of the building supports a flat-topped 'throne'. From the four corners of the room stone bridges lead across to this throne. Akbar spent much time here with scholars of many different religious persuasions, discussing and debating.

Diwan-i-Am
Just inside the gates at the north-east end of the deserted city is the Hall of Public Audiences. This consists of a large open courtyard surrounded by cloisters. Beside the Diwan-i-Am is the **Pachisi Courtyard**, set out like a gigantic game board. It is said that Akbar played the game pachisi here, using slave girls as the pieces.

Other Monuments
Musicians would play from the **Naubat Khana**, at one time the main entrance to the city, as processions passed by beneath. The entrance road then ran between the mint and the treasury before reaching the Diwan-i-Am. The **Khwabgah**, in front of the Daftar Khana, or record office, was Akbar's own sleeping quarters. Beside the Khwabgah is

the tiny but elaborately carved **Rumi Sultana** or Turkish Queen's House. Near the Karawan Serai, badly defaced elephants still guard the **Hathi Pol**, or Elephant Gate.

Outside the Jama Masjid are the remains of the small stone-cutters' mosque. Shaikh Salim Chishti's cave was supposedly at this site and the mosque predates Akbar's imperial city. There is also a **Hakim's House** (Doctor's House), and a fine **hammam**, or Turkish bath, beside it.

Places to Stay & Eat
The cheapest place to stay is the *Archaeological Survey Rest House*. At only Rs 9 it's great value but bookings must be made in advance at the Archaeological Survey of India, 22 The Mall, Agra.

Just below the Buland Darwaza is the *Maurya Rest House* (☎ 2348), the most pleasant of the budget hotels in the village. There are basic singles/doubles for Rs 40/60 with common bath, and from Rs 60/80 with attached bath, Rs 80/120 for the bigger rooms. It's run by a very friendly and helpful family and there's a good vegetarian restaurant in the shady courtyard. Two of the brothers play the sitar and tabla and there are occasional impromptu concerts in the evening. Down the hill by the bazaar is the *Shree Tourist Guest House* (☎ 2276), clean and similarly priced. The *Kallu Hotel* is a very basic restaurant charging Rs 15 for a thali.

At the top of the scale is the UPSTDC *Gulistan Tourist Complex* (☎ 2490), about half a km back along the main road. The design is sympathetic to the local surroundings, and the facilities reasonable. The rooms are large and cost Rs 200/250, or Rs 350/425 with air-con, but during the tourist season they charge the higher price for all rooms. A dormitory is advertised at Rs 15 per bed, but it's definitely an afterthought, and after three years they still haven't even bothered to put any beds in it! The complex also houses a restaurant and a bar.

Fatehpur Sikri is famous for *khataie*, the biscuits you'll see piled high in the bazaar.

UTTAR PRADESH

Getting There & Away

The tour buses only stop for an hour or so at Fatehpur Sikri. If you want to spend longer (which is recommended) it is worth taking a bus from Agra's Idgah bus terminal (Rs 10, one hour). You can spend a day in Fatehpur Sikri and continue on to Bharatpur (Rs 7, 45 minutes) in the evening. The train service used to be slow and infrequent but should have improved with the line's conversion to broad gauge.

MATHURA

Population: 256,000
Telephone Area Code: 0565

This area, popularly known as Brij Bhoomi, is a major pilgrimage place for Hindus – there are literally thousands of temples here. Krishna, the popular incarnation of Vishnu, is believed to have been born in Mathura and the area is closely linked with many episodes in his early life. Nearby is Vrindaban where Krishna 'sported' with his *gopis* (milkmaids) and where the Hare Krishnas have their headquarters.

The tourist office is at the old bus stand in Mathura and guided tours covering the main Krishna sites are sometimes available, departing at 6.30 am. Most temples are closed between about 11 am and 4 pm, siesta time for the deities and their attendants.

History

Mathura (Muttra) is an ancient cultural and religious centre. The Buddhist monasteries here received considerable patronage from Ashoka, and Mathura was mentioned by Ptolemy and by the Chinese visitors Fa Hian (who visited India in 401-410 AD) and Hiuen Tsang (634 AD). By then the population of the 20 monasteries had dropped from 3000 to 2000 as Buddhism began to give way to Hinduism here.

In 1017, Mahmud of Ghazni arrived on his rape, burn and pillage trip from Afghanistan, damaging the Hindu and remaining Buddhist shrines. Sikandar Lodi continued the destruction in 1500 and the fanatical Aurangzeb flattened the Kesava Deo Temple, which had been built on the site of one of the most important Buddhist monasteries, and built a mosque in its place.

Shri Krishna Janmbhoomi

Amongst the foundations of the Kesava Deo Temple is a small room made up to look like a prison cell. Here pilgrims file past the stone slab onto which Krishna is said to have been born, 3500 years ago. He was obliged to make his entry into the world in these undignified surroundings as his parents had been imprisoned by the tyrannical King Kansa. Aurangzeb's mosque rises above the site and there's a more recent Hindu temple beside it. Following the clashes between Hindus and Muslims in Ayodhya there's now a heavy military presence.

Two hundred metres from the Shri Krishna Janmbhoomi there's an alternative birthplace, and nearby is the **Potara-Kund**, where baby Krishna's nappies (diapers) are supposed to have been washed.

Along the Yamuna River

The 300-metre-wide Yamuna River, which flows through Mathura, is lined with ghats. **Vishram Ghat** is the most important bathing ghat and is where Krishna is said to have rested after killing King Kansa. Boats take pilgrims out for short river trips; large turtles are often seen in the water here.

The **Sati Burj**, beside Vishram Ghat, is a four-storey tower built by the son of Behari Mal of Jaipur in 1570 to commemorate his mother's *sati*. Aurangzeb knocked down the upper storeys, but they have since been rebuilt.

The ruined fort, **Kans Qila**, on the riverbank was built by Raja Man Singh of Amber; Jai Singh of Jaipur built one of his observatories here, but it has since disappeared.

Set back from the river in the main part of the town are the **Jama Masjid**, which was built by Abo-in Nabir Khan in 1661, and the **Dwarkadheesh Temple**. Built in 1814 by Seth Gokuldass of Gwalior, this is Mathura's main temple and is dedicated (surprise, surprise) to Krishna.

Archaeological Museum

The Archaeological Museum is worth a visit for its large collection of examples of the Mathura school of ancient Indian sculpture. This includes the famous, and impressive, 5th-century standing Buddha found here. There are many other sculptures, terracotta work, coins and bronze objects and there's a pleasant garden. It's open daily (except Monday) from 10.30 am to 4.30 pm (7.30 am to 12.30 pm from 16 April to 30 June). Admission is free.

Gita Mandir

This modern temple was funded by the Birla family (the wealthy industrialists). Pilgrims stop off on their way to Vrindaban to see the Gita Stambh, a pillar on which the whole of the *Bhagavad Gita* is carved.

Places to Stay & Eat

The most interesting cheap place is the *International Guest House* right beside Shri Krishna Janmbhoomi. It's excellent value with singles/doubles for as little as Rs 20/30 and there are doubles with attached bathrooms for Rs 60, or Rs 85 with air-coolers. The soldiers are not welcome here – 'No Arms & Ammunition' reads the sign by the entrance. There's a good vegetarian restaurant (a thali is just Rs 11) and a garden.

The *Hotel Agra* (☎ 403318) is highly recommended and in a pleasant location overlooking the river on Bengali Ghat. There are singles with common bath for Rs 75, doubles with attached bath from Rs 200, and also a few air-con rooms. It's a clean place run by a friendly family.

The *Hotel Nepal* (☎ 40-4308), Delhi Rd, is convenient, being right opposite the new bus stand. Rooms are set around a courtyard and range from Rs 100/150 for a single/double to Rs 400 for an air-con double. All have attached bathrooms, and there's a cheap restaurant. The *Kwality Hotel*, near the old bus stand, is a little cheaper but noisy. The restaurant's not bad, though nothing to do with the Kwality chain. There's a *Tourist*

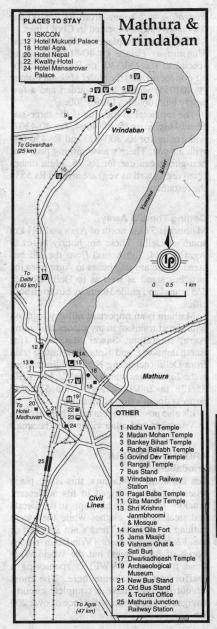

PLACES TO STAY

9 ISKCON
12 Hotel Mukund Palace
18 Hotel Agra
20 Hotel Nepal
22 Kwality Hotel
24 Hotel Mansarovar Palace

Mathura & Vrindaban

To Goverdhan (25 km)

Vrindaban

Yamuna River

To Delhi (140 km)

0   0.5   1 km

Mathura

To Hotel Madhuvan

Civil Lines

To Agra (47 km)

OTHER

1 Nidhi Van Temple
2 Madan Mohan Temple
3 Bankey Bihari Temple
4 Radha Ballabh Temple
5 Govind Dev Temple
6 Rangaji Temple
7 Bus Stand
8 Vrindaban Railway Station
10 Pagal Baba Temple
11 Gita Mandir Temple
13 Shri Krishna Janmbhoomi & Mosque
14 Kans Qila Fort
15 Jama Masjid
16 Vishram Ghat & Sati Burj
17 Dwarkadheesh Temple
19 Archaeological Museum
21 New Bus Stand
23 Old Bus Stand & Tourist Office
25 Mathura Junction Railway Station

UTTAR PRADESH

Bungalow with rooms from Rs 75/100 but it's inconveniently located in Civil Lines.

More upmarket places include the *Hotel Mansarovar Palace* (☎ 40-8686), nothing special at Rs 230/330, or Rs 375/475 for air-con rooms, and the *Hotel Mukund Palace* (☎ 404055) with a large garden and a few newly built doubles for Rs 300.

The top hotel in the area is the three-star *Hotel Madhuvan* (☎ 40-4064; fax 40-4307) with rooms for Rs 300/400 and Rs 450/600 with air-con. There's a swimming pool that non-guests can use for Rs 75. Main dishes (non-veg as well as veg) are around Rs 55 in the restaurant.

Getting There & Away

Mathura is 57 km north of Agra and 141 km south of Delhi. There are hourly buses to Agra (Rs 14, 1½ hours) from the old bus stand. There are also buses to Agra from the new bus stand as well as to Delhi (Rs 35, 3½ hours) and guided tours by bus from both cities.

Mathura is an important railway junction with direct trains to many places, including Agra, Bharatpur, Sawai Madhopur (for Ranthambhore), and Kota. The fastest train from Delhi (departing Nizamuddin station) is the *Taj Express* which takes 1¾ hours (Rs 35/138 in 2nd/1st class) – the *Shatabdi Express* doesn't stop at Mathura.

It's also possible to rent bikes here to cycle to Vrindaban and other villages in the area.

AROUND MATHURA
Vrindaban

Ten km north of Mathura, this is the place where Krishna indulged in his adolescent pranks – flirting with his gopis in the forests and stealing their clothes while they were bathing in the river. There's not a lot left of the 12 famous forests (Vrindaban means Forest of Basil Trees) but the World Wide Fund for Nature (WWF) is sponsoring a reafforestation scheme here. The most devout pilgrims make a complete circumnavigation of the area, a distance of over 200 km.

The large red **Govind Dev Temple** is the most impressive building in the area. The name means Divine Cowherd – in other words Krishna. Shoes must, of course, be left outside but it's well worth picking your way through the bat droppings to see the vaulted ceiling in this cathedral-like building. Architecturally it's one of the most advanced Hindu temples in northern India and was built in 1590 by Raja Man Singh of Jaipur. It was originally seven storeys high but Aurangzeb lopped off the top four floors.

The **Rangaji Temple** dates from 1851 and is an incredible mixture of architectural styles including a soaring south Indian *gopuram* (gate) and an Italianate colonnade. At the entrance are two amusing electronic puppet shows telling the stories of the *Ramayana* and the *Mahabharata* – it's Rs 1 to have the power switched on. Around the back there's a weed-choked tank and a garden. Non-Hindus are not allowed in the middle enclosure of the temple, where there is a 15-metre gold-plated pillar.

There are 4000 other temples in Vrindaban including the popular **Bankey Bihari**, **Radha Ballabh** (built in 1626), **Madan Mohan**, the 10-storey **Pagal Baba**, and the **Nidhi Van** – where some of the monkeys are said to have learnt to steal cameras, only returning them in exchange for food!

The International Society of Krishna Consciousness (ISKCON) has its Indian base in Vrindaban (☎ (0565) 442478). By the **Krishna Balaram Temple** here an impressive marble memorial temple is nearing completion for their founder Swami Prabhupada, who died in 1977. Some of the most skilled masons in the country have been working on it since then. The Swami's rooms have been turned into a museum where you can see hallowed objects including the last piece of soap he used, his bottle of Listerine mouthwash, and the British Airways complimentary slippers from his UK trip. Every year several hundred Westerners attend courses and seminars here on everything from astrology to ayurvedic medicine. Phone the society for details.

Places to Stay & Eat The *ISKCON Guest House* (☎ 44-2591) has a range of good rooms where you may stay for a donation – Rs 125 is the minimum suggested. If you plan to stay it might be worth phoning in advance as they are often full; a new guest house is planned. It's also possible to stay in some of the ashrams in Vrindaban.

The restaurant at the ISKCON Guest House is the best place to eat in Vrindaban (pure veg, of course) and serves fruit juices, milk shakes and thalis (Rs 25 to Rs 35).

Getting There & Away From Mathura there are tempos (Rs 3) from Shri Krishna Janmbhoomi and from the railway station. Tongas charge Rs 35; auto-rickshaws cost around Rs 50. There are three steam trains a day on the metre-gauge run to Vrindaban (Rs 4 in 2nd), leaving Mathura at 6.55 am, 2.55 and 6.50 pm, and leaving Vrindaban at 7.55 am, 4 and 8.05 pm.

Gokul & Mahaban
Sixteen km south-east of Mathura, Gokul is where Krishna was secretly raised. Hordes of pilgrims flock here during his birthday festival each July/August. There's a very basic *Tourist Bungalow* with doubles for Rs 60.

Mahaban, 18 km north of Mathura, is another place from the Krishna legend, where he also spent some of his youth.

Barsana & Goverdhan
Krishna's consort, Radha, was from Barsana, 50 km from Mathura. This is an interesting area to be during the festival of Holi when the women of Barsana attack the men of nearby Nandgaon with coloured water. There's a *Tourist Bungalow* with beds in the dorm for Rs 10, and doubles for Rs 100.

At Goverdhan, 26 km from Mathura, Krishna is said to have protected the inhabitants from Indra's wrath (rain) by holding the hilltops, neatly balanced on top of his finger, over the town for seven days.

Northern Uttar Pradesh

Uttarakhand, the Land of the North, is the name given to the northern part of Uttar Pradesh. It's an area of hills, mountains and lakes; the western half is known as the Garhwal region and the eastern part is the Kumaon.

There are some popular hill stations here, including Naini Tal and Mussoorie, and many trekking routes – most of them little known and even less used. As Indo-Chinese relations improve, sensitive border areas previously closed to foreign trekkers and mountaineers are opening up. In the summer pilgrims walk to the source of the holy Ganges near Gangotri, not far from the border with China. Gangotri is one of the four main Himalayan *yatra* (pilgrimage) destinations, the others being Badrinath, Kedarnath and Yamunotri – collectively known as the Char Dham. More accessible pilgrimage centres include Haridwar and Rishikesh, where the Ganges leaves the Himalaya and joins the plains for its long trip to the sea.

For several years there's been local agitation to make Uttarakhand a separate state. In September 1994 violence erupted in the usually sedate hill station of Mussoorie. The police opened fire killing seven protesters and injuring many more. The following month, in Muzaffarnagar, police gunned down 12 unarmed protesters who were on their way to a Uttarakhand rally in Delhi. The curfews in Mussoorie, Naini Tal and Haldwani have been lifted, the tourists have returned and things appear to be back to normal for the moment. Uttarakhand as a separate state is an unlikely prospect since the Delhi administration would not want to set a precedent. A separate administrative hill council for Uttarakhand would be a practical alternative.

It's possible to enter Nepal from the northern Uttar Pradesh region. See under Banbassa at the end of this section for more details.

Northern Uttar Pradesh

The external boundaries of India on this map have not been authenticated and may not be correct.

0   20   40 km

Information

UP Tourism has two regional subsidiaries in this area, Garhwal Mandal Vikas Nigam (GMVN) and Kumaon Mandal Vikas Nigam (KMVN). GMVN has offices in Dehra Dun, Mussoorie and Rishikesh; KMVN is based in Naini Tal. Both have smaller offices, usually in the numerous tourist rest houses they operate.

UP Tourism recently published a set of three maps (Rs 20 each) of the northern part of this area, in their *Trekking Map Series*. They're quite well produced but at a scale of 1:250,000 they're not trekking maps.

MEERUT

Population: 932,000
Telephone Area Code: 0121

Only 70 km north-east of Delhi, this was the place where the 1857 Mutiny first broke out, when Meerut was the largest garrison in northern India. There's little to remember that event by today – just the cemetery near St John's Church, which also has the grave of General Ochterlony, whose monument dominates the Maidan in Calcutta. The Suraj Khund is the most interesting Hindu temple in Meerut and there's a Mughal mausoleum, the Shahpir, near the old Shahpir Gate.

Meerut is a green revolution boom town

and the new-found wealth, indicated by the many well-stocked stores, has led to inter-communal tensions.

Sardhana, 18 km north of Meerut, is the palace of Begum Samru. She was converted to Roman Catholicism and built the basilica here in 1809, which has an altar of white Jaipur marble. The begum's tomb can be found in the basilica.

There are several hotels in Meerut; the best is the *Hotel Shaleen* and there's also the cheaper *Anand Hotel* – both in the Begum Bridge area. The *Hotel Navin Deluxe* (☎ 54-0125), Abu Lane, charges Rs 350/550 for an air-con single/double, Rs 150/250 for an ordinary room.

SAHARANPUR
Population: 411,000

Situated 178 km north of Delhi, the industrial city of Saharanpur is a major railway junction. The large botanical gardens, known as the Company Bagh, are over 175 years old.

DEHRA DUN
Population: 404,000
Telephone Area Code: 0135

Also spelt Dehra Doon, this pleasant town is situated in a valley in the Siwaliks, the foot-hills of the Himalaya. The hill station Mussoorie can be seen, 34 km away, on the high mountain range above Dehra Dun.

Dehra Dun is at the centre of a forest area and the impressive Forest Research Institute is here. Apart from this there's not much else of interest. The town is a major academic and research centre and the Indian Military Academy and the Survey of India (which sells large-scale maps of many Indian cities) are both based here. There are also several prestigious boarding schools including the Doon School, India's most exclusive private school, which numbers Rajiv Gandhi among its ex-pupils.

Orientation
The clock tower is the hub of the town and most of the budget hotels are near it or close to the railway station. The top-end hotels are all in the area known as Astley Hall, north of the clock tower. The main market is Paltan Bazaar and one of the main items sold here is high quality basmati rice, for which the region is famous.

Information
The UP tourist office (☎ 23-217) is in the Hotel Drona close to the bus stands and the railway station. On Rajpur Rd the GMVN tourist office (☎ 26-817) specifically covers the Garhwal region and pilgrimages (yatras) to the holy places north of here. Trek Himalaya (☎ 23-005), 16 Tagore Villa, is a private company which organises treks in the area. (See the Trekking in Garhwal & Kumaon section later for more information.)

Dehra Dun's numerous educational establishments mean that it has several excellent bookshops. The English Book Depot beside Kumar Restaurant, and Natraj Booksellers by the Motel Himshri nearby, both have a wide range of titles.

Forest Research Institute
Established by the British earlier this century the FRI is now reputedly one of the finest institutes of forest sciences in the world. It's set in large botanical gardens, with the Himalaya providing a spectacular backdrop.

In the six galleries of the extensive museum, exhibits are laid out in glass cases with Victorian attention to detail. They include examples of wood types, before and after models for social forestry programmes, a furniture gallery, stuffed examples of forest dwellers (from bugs and pests to tigers), and a cross section of a deodar (Himalayan cedar) which is over 700 years old.

The institute is open Monday to Friday from 10 am to 5 pm and there's no admission charge. To get there take a six-seater tempo (known here as a Vikram) from the clock tower to the institute gates.

Other Things to See
At the **Wadia Institute of Himalayan Geology** there's a museum containing rock samples, semiprecious stones and fossils. It's open Monday to Friday from 10 am to 5 pm.

UTTAR PRADESH

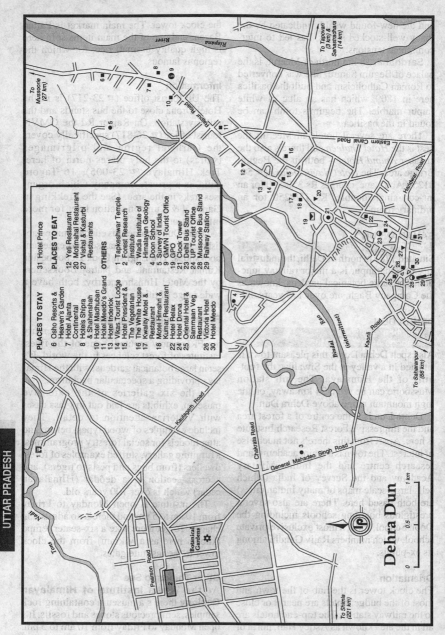

PLACES TO STAY
6 Osho Resorts & Heaven's Garden
7 Hotel Ajanta Continental
8 Hotels Shipra & Shahenshah
10 Hotel Madhuban
11 Hotel Meedo's Grand
13 Hotel Inderlok
14 Vikas Tourist Lodge
15 Hotel President & The Vegetarian
16 The White House Restaurant
17 Kwality Motel & Restaurant
18 Motel Himshri & Kumar Restaurant
22 Hotel Relax
24 Hotel Drona
25 Oriental Hotel & Samman Veg Restaurant
26 Victoria Hotel
30 Hotel Meedo
31 Hotel Prince

PLACES TO EAT
12 Yeti Restaurant
20 Motimahal Restaurant
27 Vishal & Kasturbi Restaurants

OTHERS
1 Tapkeshwar Temple
2 Forest Research Institute
3 Wadia Institute of Himalayan Geology
4 Doon School
5 Survey of India
9 GMVN Tourist Office
19 GPO
21 Clock Tower
23 Delhi Bus Stand
24 UP Tourist Office
28 Mussoorie Bus Stand
29 Railway Station

UTTAR PRADESH

Dehra Dun

The main temple is **Tapkeshwar Temple**, dedicated to Siva. It's beside a stream, which (when there's water in it) is directed to flow onto the lingam. A large fair is held here on Sivaratri day (usually in March).

Other places to visit include the **Lakshman Sidh Temple**; the village of **Sahastradhara** (14 km from Dehra Dun) with cold sulphur springs and a Tourist Rest House; the **Robbers' Cave**, a popular picnic spot just beyond Anarwala village; and **Tapovan** where there is an ashram.

Places to Stay – bottom end

The *Oriental Hotel* (☎ 62-448), an old place in the bazaar, is run by a friendly Sikh family and it's good value at Rs 55/90 for singles/doubles with attached bathroom. They're renovating some of the rooms and also building a restaurant. Also near the station, rooms at the *Victoria Hotel* are built around a courtyard and at Rs 80/130 with basic attached bathrooms they're not a bargain. North of the clock tower, the *Vikas Tourist Lodge* is a bit better with rooms at Rs 60/120.

Set in a large garden in Astley Hall, away from the busy and polluted market area, *The White House* (☎ 26-594) is a recommended place. There are a couple of singles and doubles at Rs 98/135, four doubles at Rs 160 and two suites at Rs 190. It's popular and is often full.

The *Hotel Meedo* ('Famous for Hospitality, Comfort and Glamour') has good rooms at the back for Rs 100/175 with attached baths and little balconies. These rooms are quieter than the front rooms above the rather sleazy bar. (Don't confuse this place with the top-end Hotel Meedo's Grand.)

Another reasonable place in the station area is the *Hotel Prince* (☎ 62-7070) where rooms cost Rs 115/165 with attached baths. There are dorm beds for Rs 30 and doubles for Rs 100 at the railway *retiring rooms*.

The large *Hotel Drona* (☎ 24-371) is run by UP Tourism's local branch GMVN. Prices have shot up and it boasts dorm beds with lockers for Rs 60, and rooms with attached bathrooms and hot water from Rs 200/250 to Rs 425/550 with air-con.

Places to Stay – middle & top end

The *Hotel Relax* (☎ 27-776), 7 Court Rd, has good rooms from Rs 275/425. Most of the other middle and top-end places are in the north of the town, along Rajpur Rd. The *Kwality Motel* (☎ 27-001) is reasonable at Rs 190/325 for ordinary rooms, Rs 360/410 for air-con. The *Motel Himshri* (☎ 23-880) is similarly priced.

Rooms at *Hotel Meedo's Grand* (☎ 27-171) range from Rs 300/400 to Rs 450/600. The *Hotel President* (☎ 27-386; fax 28-210) has singles/doubles for Rs 500/650 with air-con. The *Hotel Shipra* (☎ 24-611) charges Rs 500/700 for air-con rooms. From November to February they chop 40% off their prices, making it the best value of any hotel in this range.

At the northern end of Rajpur Rd is a bizarre establishment, *Osho Resorts* (☎ 29-544), that describes itself as a 'retreat with a waterfall'. It's part of the Bhagwan Rajneesh organisation, and videos of the late guru's lectures are piped into all rooms. The rooms themselves are hardly a snip at Rs 390/490, and the Buddha Cottage at Rs 590 for two turns out to be an overpriced porta-cabin. The restaurant is good, however, and there's even a meditation centre.

Also along Rajpur Rd, there are several top-end hotels, all with air-con rooms from about Rs 600/800. They include the glitzy *Shahenshah* (☎ 28-508; fax 22-731), the *Inderlok* (☎ 28-113) and the *Hotel Ajanta Continental* (☎ 29-595; fax 27-722) which is the best of them and has a swimming pool. In spite of dropping its rates over the last few years, the *Hotel Madhuban* (☎ 24-094; fax 23-181) is still overpriced at Rs 1100/1350.

Places to Eat

'Purity of mind follows purity of diet' is the motto of the *Kumar* – the best vegetarian restaurant in town. Their naan bread is excellent – amongst the best you'll taste anywhere. Main dishes are between Rs 20 and Rs 35 and in winter they have the sweet

UTTAR PRADESH

gajar ka halwa, made from carrot, spices and milk.

In the station area the *Sammaan Veg Restaurant* by the Oriental Hotel is a clean place serving good thalis. Two other popular thali restaurants are the *Vishal* and the *Kasturbi* but they're rather more basic. At all these places you can have *kheerh* (rice pudding) after your thali.

There's a popular *Kwality* branch – often crowded with rich kids from Dehra Dun's expensive schools. *The Vegetarian*, near the Hotel President, serves good milk shakes and masala dosas. The *Yeti Restaurant* has Chinese food, including hot Sichuan dishes for around Rs 50.

Osho Resort's *Heaven's Garden* is a good place that also serves non-veg dishes; there are some tables in the garden. There's good Indian non-veg food at the *Motimahal Restaurant* with main dishes at around Rs 45. The nearby *Sind-Hyderabad Restaurant* and *Punjab* are slightly cheaper, and right outside is the *A-One Grill* with tandoori chicken and kebabs to take away. The *Trishna Bar* in the Hotel Drona is a good place for a beer (Rs 45) with Star TV to watch, but the hotel's restaurant is expensive.

Dehra Dun has several good bakeries and sweet shops. The *Standard Confectioners* near the Hotel President have delicious home-made toffees. The *Grand Bakers* in Paltan Bazaar has a large selection of bread, snacks and excellent macaroons. There are several good Indian sweet shops by the clock tower.

Getting There & Away
Air Jolly Grant Airport is 24 km from the city. It's not currently served by any airline and unlikely that any operator will be interested in the routing since the start of the high-speed *Shatabdi* train service from Delhi in 1995.

Bus The Mussoorie bus stand, by the railway station, is for destinations in the hills. There are frequent departures to Mussoorie (Rs 13, 1½ hours) and shared taxis (Rs 40 a seat) also leave from here. Other buses go to Naini

Tal (Rs 106, 11 hours), Uttarkashi (Rs 74, seven hours) and Tehri (Rs 45, four hours).

The Delhi bus stand, beside the Hotel Drona, serves destinations on the plains: Delhi (Rs 68, six hours), Haridwar (Rs 14, two hours), Rishikesh (Rs 10.50, 1½ hours), Lucknow (Rs 141, 14 hours) and Shimla (Rs 88 to Rs 114, nine hours).

Train Dehra Dun is the terminus of the Northern Railway. The fastest train is the *Shatabdi Express* which runs daily except Wednesday leaving New Delhi at 6 am and reaching Dehra Dun at 11.45 am, stopping only at Saharanpur and Haridwar along the way. For the return journey it departs at 4.20 pm and reaches the capital at 10.05 pm. Tickets cost Rs 300/600 in chair car/1st class.

On regular services the 320-km Delhi-Haridwar-Dehra Dun trip costs Rs 74/275 in 2nd/1st class. It takes 9½ hours, which is longer than the bus, but can be more relaxing. The *Mussoorie Express* is the overnight service to Delhi. The *Doon Express* is the overnight train to Lucknow (545 km, Rs 109/408 in 2nd/1st class); and there are also services to Calcutta, Varanasi and Bombay.

Getting Around
Six-seater tempos (Vikrams) pollute the city but are a cheap way to get around. They run on fixed routes charging, for example, Rs 2 from the station to the clock tower. For this distance an auto-rickshaw would charge about Rs 10.

MUSSOORIE
Population: 32,000
Telephone Area Code: 0135

At an altitude of 2000 metres and 34 km beyond Dehra Dun, Mussoorie has been a popular hill station since it was 'discovered' in 1823 by a Captain Young. There are over 100 hotels jostling for the views across the Dun Valley to accommodate the hordes of tourists from Delhi in the hot season. It can be quite peaceful in the off season and there are good walks along the mountain ridges.

UTTAR PRADESH

Orientation & Information

The Mall connects Gandhi Chowk with Kulri Bazaar, two km away. Buses from Dehra Dun go to Library (Gandhi Chowk) or Picture Palace (Kulri Bazaar), but not both, so make sure you get the one you want since The Mall is closed to traffic during the high season. There's a good UP tourist office (☎ 63-2863) on The Mall (its sign defaced by a Uttarakhand supporter to read 'UK Tourism').

Trek Himalaya (behind the tourist office) organises treks and rafting expeditions.

Things to See & Do

A ropeway (Rs 15 return, open 9 am to 7 pm daily) runs up to **Gun Hill**. For the early-morning views of the Himalaya including Bandar Punch (6315 metres), you have to walk up. At the top, photo agencies will dress you up in sequined Garhwal national dress in which you can have your photo taken for Rs 10.

The walks around Mussoorie offer great views. **Camel's Back Road** was built as a promenade and passes a rock formation that looks like a camel – hence the name. You can rent ponies (Rs 60) or rickshaws (pulled by two rickshaw-wallahs and often pushed by a third) for Rs 60. Another good walk takes you down to Happy Valley and the **Tibetan Refugee Centre** where there's a temple and a small shop selling hand-knitted sweaters. An enjoyable longer walk (five km) takes you through Landour Bazaar to **Childers Lodge** (Lal Tibba), the highest point in Mussoorie, and Sisters' Bazaar.

If you don't want to walk, you can rent fairly new 100cc motorcycles from 'Bertz'. They can also supply crash helmets and insurance.

GMVN (which has a booth at the Library bus stand) runs tours to **Kempty Falls** (Rs 25) and **Dhanolti** (Rs 75) where there are good Himalayan views.

Other suggestions for passing the time here include a visit to the astrologer, going to a movie at the Picture Palace (Rs 12), video games (Rs 1) at numerous arcades along The Mall, billiards at Hotel Clarks (Rs 50), joining the library (Rs 25) or roller skating (Rs 30) on the wooden floor of The Rink, the largest in the country.

Places to Stay – bottom end

With so many hotels competing for customers, prices vary enormously according to the season. Rates given here are for the off season (November to March) but you may be able to negotiate a further reduction at this time. Note that some hotels are closed in January and February. Prices rise by up to 300% in the summer. Most places have only double rooms with attached bathrooms and checkout time is usually 10 am. Porters from either bus stand to any hotel expect Rs 16.

Kulri Bazaar With northern views, the *Hotel Broadway* was a small English guest house run by a Miss Lee until 1954. It's still a good clean place, resistant to change (no Star TV here), and popular with Western travellers. The helpful manager, Mr Malik, has doubles from Rs 90 and a few singles for Rs 40.

With rooms from Rs 75, some with a sitting room, the *New Bharat Hotel*, below The Mall, is a creaky old building run by an equally creaky old caretaker who's very helpful. He's a keen gardener and the place is filled with flourishing potted plants. This hotel may be closed in January and February, though.

Basic doubles at the old *Hotel Regal* are Rs 75. The large *Hotel Hill Queen*, under the ropeway, is good value with rooms from Rs 50 to Rs 150.

The small *Hotel Valley View* (☎ 63-2324) is an excellent place set in a small garden above The Mall, with clean rooms from Rs 100/150 for a single/double, and a good restaurant. There's a sunny terrace beside the hotel.

The *Hotel Sunny Cot* (☎ 63-2789) is a relatively new hotel with good doubles from Rs 150. Next door, the *Hotel Mussoorie International* (☎ 63-2943) charges from Rs 200.

Library Area Right opposite the library, the *Hotel Imperial* is a rickety place with rooms from Rs 60. The small *Hotel Kanak* (☎ 63-2351) has better rooms with attached bath for Rs 75. The Sikh-run *Hotel India* is recommended, with great views to the north and good rooms from Rs 80 – but prices may rise as this place is upgraded. The similarly priced *Hotel Eagle* is nearby.

High above The Mall is the *Hotel Prince*, a large old building with superb views from the terrace. Big tatty rooms are Rs 100/150 for a single/double.

The well-kept *Hotel Vikram* has some nice doubles with balconies from Rs 175, and there's a great view over the Dun Valley from the double bed in room 25.

The *Hotel Paramount* (☎ 63-2352) is a friendly place on The Mall with good doubles from Rs 200. The *Hotel Vishnu Palace* (☎ 63-2932) is similarly priced. The *Hotel Upstairs & Downstairs* (☎ 63-2020), above the Whispering Windows Restaurant, has rooms from Rs 175 to Rs 275.

On The Mall, rooms are Rs 200 at *Hakman's Grand Hotel*, a large run-down place full of Raj-reject furniture and with a cash register still calibrated in annas.

GMVN's *Hotel Garhwal Terrace* (☎ 63-

2682) has had a lick of paint and a major price hike. Who would pay Rs 60 for a bed in a dorm? Doubles are Rs 400 with attached bathroom, and satellite TV.

Landour Bazaar Out of the tourist area past the clock tower in Landour Bazaar is the basic *Hotel Nishima* (☎ 63-2227) with doubles for Rs 60.

Places to Stay – middle & top end
Kulri Bazaar The large and characterless *Hotel Shipra* (☎ 63-2662) has rooms from Rs 300 to Rs 850; and the pleasant *Hotel Filigree* (☎ 63-2380) with northern views from the roof terrace offers doubles from Rs 350.

The *Hotel Nand Villa* (☎ 63-2088) is a good place with doubles from Rs 225 to Rs 550. It's in a peaceful location, and some rooms have their own terrace.

The top hotel in this area is the new *Claridges Connaught Castle* (☎ 63-2210) with rooms from Rs 1200.

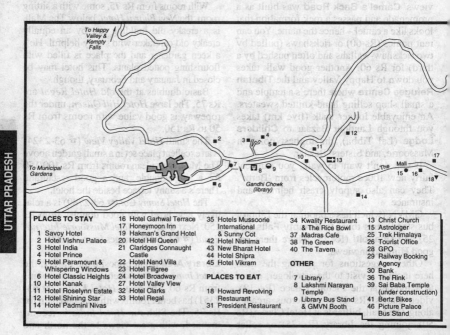

PLACES TO STAY			
1 Savoy Hotel	16 Hotel Garhwal Terrace	35 Hotels Mussoorie	34 Kwality Restaurant
2 Hotel Vishnu Palace	17 Honeymoon Inn	International	& The Rice Bowl
3 Hotel India	19 Hakman's Grand Hotel	& Sunny Cot	37 Madras Cafe
4 Hotel Prince	20 Hotel Hill Queen	42 Hotel Nishima	38 The Green
5 Hotel Paramount &	21 Claridges Connaught	43 New Bharat Hotel	40 The Tavern
Whispering Windows	Castle	44 Hotel Shipra	
6 Hotel Classic Heights	22 Hotel Nand Villa	45 Hotel Vikram	**OTHER**
10 Hotel Kanak	23 Hotel Filigree		
11 Hotel Roselynn Estate	24 Hotel Broadway	**PLACES TO EAT**	7 Library
12 Hotel Shining Star	32 Hotel Clarks		8 Lakshmi Narayan
14 Hotel Padmini Nivas	33 Hotel Regal	18 Howard Revolving	Temple
		Restaurant	9 Library Bus Stand
		31 President Restaurant	& GMVN Booth

13 Christ Church	
15 Astrologer	
25 Trek Himalaya	
26 Tourist Office	
28 GPO	
29 Railway Booking	
Agency	
30 Bank	
36 The Rink	
39 Sai Baba Temple	
(under construction)	
41 Bertz Bikes	
46 Picture Palace	
Bus Stand	

UTTAR PRADESH

Library Area The *Hotel Classic Heights* (☎ 63-2514), near the library, has a range of rooms from Rs 495/795. The *Hotel Roselynn Estate* (☎ 63-2201) is a friendly place charging Rs 400 for a double room, Rs 500 for a suite.

For a special occasion you could try the *Honeymoon Inn* (☎ 63-2378) which charges Rs 490 for a double bed and giant-size bathtub (bring your own plug). However, the schizophrenic decor doesn't encourage romance. Much better is the *Hotel Shining Star* (☎ 63-2500) with big double beds, satellite TV and sauna for Rs 775.

The *Hotel Padmini Nivas* (☎ 63-1093) once belonged to the Maharaja of Rajpipla but this English-style villa is now a small hotel, one of the few here that combines character with comfort. Room rates range from Rs 400 to Rs 1000. Room 10 has a great view over the Dun Valley.

Built in 1890, the *Savoy Hotel* (☎ 63-2010) is the largest place in Mussoorie.

There's a huge ballroom (complete with band in the high season), tennis, squash courts and a beer garden. The touches of the Raj are very faded here including peeling gloss paint and moth-eaten deer heads. Rooms are overpriced at Rs 895/1435.

Sisters' Bazaar Beyond Landour Bazaar, and four km from Mussoorie, the *Hotel Dev Dar Woods* (☎ 63-2644) is in a lofty wooded location by Sisters' Bazaar. Popular with foreigners working at the nearby language school, it's an interesting place to stay. Quoted rates are Rs 400/550 for a single/double including breakfast but there are discounts for stays of more than a few days, and all meals can be provided.

Places to Eat

In Kulri, the *Madras Cafe* has good south Indian food and 24 varieties of dosa from Rs 10 to Rs 30. *The Green* nearby is the best vegetarian place in town. The *President Res-*

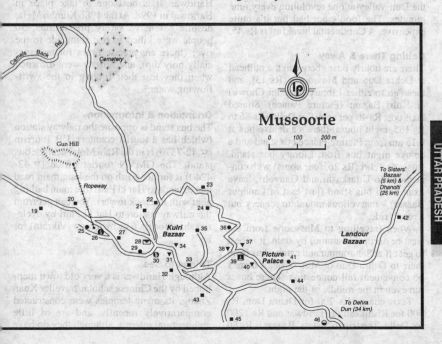

taurant is a very good non-veg place with a nice sitting area outside. Nearby, the *Rice Bowl* serves cheap Tibetan and Chinese dishes; and the *Tavern* has been recommended for its Chinese food.

There's a *Kwality* branch with the usual menu and Star TV to watch as you eat. At GMVN's *Garhwal Terrace* the food is nothing special but there are good views from the restaurant. On the terrace outside is an excellent fresh juice stand.

Places for snacks include the sweet shop *Luxmi Misthan Bhandar* near the library, the ice-cream parlour at *Whispering Windows*, *Le Chef*, which is close to the bank, for fast food and takeaway pizzas, and *Chit Chat* nearby. If you get to Sisters' Bazaar, A Prakash & Co is a long-established grocery store that produces superb cheddar cheese (Rs 150 per kg), peanut butter, jams and chutneys.

For a novel dining experience try the *Howard Revolving Restaurant* and admire the Dun Valley at one revolution every nine minutes. The food's not bad but it's quite expensive. A Continental breakfast is Rs 45.

Getting There & Away
There are hourly buses between the railhead at Dehra Dun and Mussoorie (Rs 13), and these go to either Library (Gandhi Chowk) or Kulri Bazaar (Picture Palace). Shared taxis cost Rs 40 per seat. For Delhi (Rs 86 to Rs 135, eight hours) there's a deluxe bus at 9.15 am from Picture Palace bus stand and a deluxe night bus from Library bus stand. Buses to Tehri (Rs 26, four hours) with connections to Uttarkashi and Gangotri, leave from Tehri bus stand (just east of Landour Bazaar) – marvellous mountain scenery but a rough ride.

When travelling to Mussoorie from the west or north (ie Jammu) by train, it is best to get off at Saharanpur and catch a bus from there to Dehra Dun or Mussoorie, if there's no convenient rail connection. These buses run even in the middle of the night.

Taxis charge Rs 200 for Dehra Dun, Rs 500 for Rishikesh or Haridwar and Rs 1200 for Delhi. The trip to Sisters' Bazaar is Rs 80 one way or Rs 100 return with a half-hour wait at the viewpoint.

With at least 24 hours' notice, rail tickets can be arranged through the Northern Railway booking agency (☎ 63-2846).

HARIDWAR
Population: 208,000
Telephone Area Code: 0133

Haridwar's propitious location at the point where the Ganges emerges from the high Himalaya to begin its slow progress across the plains makes it a particularly holy place. There are many ashrams here but you may find Rishikesh (24 km to the north) more pleasant, especially if you wish to study Hinduism. Haridwar means Gateway to the Gods, but despite its sanctity it's really just another noisy Indian town.

Every 12 years the Kumbh Mela attracts millions of pilgrims who bathe here. Kumbh Mela takes place every three years, consecutively at Allahabad, Nasik, Ujjain and then Haridwar. It is next due to take place in Haridwar in 1998. At the 1986 Kumbh Mela, despite extensive safety precautions, 50 people were killed in one stampede to the river (there are precise times for an especially holy dip), and dozens were drowned when they lost their footing in the swift-flowing water.

Orientation & Information
The bus stand is opposite the railway station (which has a tourist counter). UP Tourism (☎ 42-7370) is in the Rahi Motel near the bus stand. The GMVN tourist office (☎ 42-4240) is further north on the long main road that extends to Har ki Pairi (the main bathing ghat with its clock tower). You can get from the railway station to Har ki Pairi by cycle-rickshaw for Rs 6 or by tempo (Vikram) for Rs 3.

Things to See
Although Haridwar is a very old town mentioned by the Chinese scholar/traveller Xuan Zhang, its many temples were constructed comparatively recently, and are of little architectural interest, although they do have

many idols and illustrated scenes from the Hindu epics.

The main ghat, **Har ki Pairi**, is supposed to be at the precise spot where the Ganges leaves the mountains and enters the plains. Consequently the river's power to wash away sins at this spot is superlative and the seal of sanctity is a footprint Vishnu left in a stone here. Each evening at sunset priests perform the Ganga Aarti, or river worship, ceremony here. Non-Hindus can watch only from the bridge on the other side of the river.

It's worth taking the chairlift (Rs 10 return) to the **Mansa Devi Temple** on the hill above the city. The lift is not exactly state of the art, but it's well maintained. It's open from 8 am to noon and 2 to 5 pm. Vendors sell colourfully packaged *prasaad* of coconuts, marigolds and other offerings to take up to the goddess. Mansa is one of the forms of Shakti Durga and, as the signs inform you, is not keen on photographers.

The **Daksha Mahadev Temple** is another important temple. Daksha, the father of Sati (Siva's first wife) performed a sacrifice here but neglected to invite Siva. Sati was so angry at this snub to her husband that she managed to spontaneously self-immolate!

Other temples and buildings of lesser interest include the **Bhimgoda Tank** (said to have been formed by a blow of Bhima's knee – Bhima is the brother of Hanuman), **Sapt Rishi Ashram**, and the **Parmath Ashram** which has fine images of the goddess Durga. These ashrams lie five km from the centre on the road to Rishikesh. A little further out is the recently constructed **Bharat Mata Temple**, looking like an apartment block with a central dome. It's seven storeys high and there's a lift to the top for lazy pilgrims. **Chandi Devi** and a number of other temples in the hills are reached by a four-km walk to the south-east.

Places to Stay

Due to the close proximity of Haridwar to

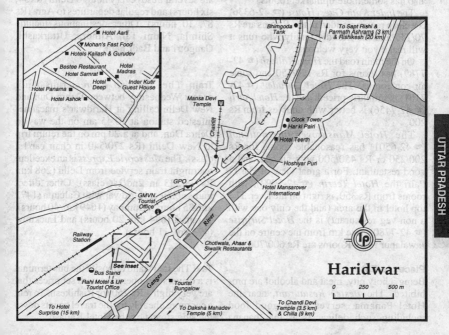

Rishikesh, it's easy to stay in the latter and day trip to Haridwar. However, if you want to stay in Haridwar, the *Tourist Bungalow* (☎ 42-6379) has singles/doubles from Rs 175/200 and there's a Rs 40 dorm. It's pleasantly situated in a peaceful location right on the river, outside the main part of town. Very close to the bus and railway stations there's UP Tourism's new *Rahi Motel* (☎ 42-6430); prices are the same as for the Tourist Bungalow but there's no dorm.

The *Hotel Madras* has basic singles/doubles/triples for Rs 40/75/90 with common bathrooms. There's a reasonable south Indian restaurant downstairs. The *Hotel Samrat* across the road is similarly priced, and the *Hotel Deep* (☎ 42-7609) has rooms from Rs 50/80 or Rs 110/150 with attached bathroom. In the next street are two similar hotels, the *Hotel Panama* and the *Hotel Ashok* ('A Best Northern Hotel'!). They're both good value with rooms with attached bathrooms for Rs 55/75. The Ashok also has some more upmarket rooms.

The *Inder Kutir Guest House* (☎ 42-6336) is a clean recommended place. Rooms are Rs 70/140 and the friendly family who runs it will make you very welcome.

On the main road the *Hotel Kailash* (☎ 42-7789) has rooms for Rs 120/150 and some air-con rooms. The *Hotel Gurudev* (☎ 42-7101) is similarly priced; and the *Hotel Aarti* (☎ 42-7456) is better with doubles from Rs 200.

The *Hotel Mansarover International* (☎ 42-6501) has reasonable rooms for Rs 200/250 or Rs 450/500 with air-con, and a good restaurant. For a great view of Har ki Pairi the *Hotel Teerth* (☎ 42-7092), with rooms from Rs 350, is right on the river. The top hotel in the area (and the only one with a non-veg restaurant) is the *Hotel Surprise* (☎ 42-7780), five km from the centre on the Jawalapur road. Rooms are Rs 600/700.

Places to Eat

Being a holy city, meat and alcohol are prohibited. The *Bestee Restaurant*, near the Hotel Panama, serves quite good food including such delicacies as the 'banana filter' (Rs 15). Nearby, *Mohan's Fast Food* produces cheese burgers and pizzas from a microwave oven.

There are three good restaurants across the road from the GMVN tourist office. *Chotiwala* does full thalis for Rs 20 to Rs 35 and Chinese and south Indian dishes. (There are several other places around town with the same name). The *Siwalik* has a wider menu and the *Ahaar* is also very good. Main dishes are from Rs 25 to Rs 35.

The cheaper *Hoshiyar Puri* has been serving thalis for over 50 years and is very popular. The restaurant in the *Hotel Mansarover International* is good. Carnivores should head for the *Hotel Surprise*.

Getting There & Away

Bus There are frequent buses for the 45-minute trip to Rishikesh (Rs 7) and hourly buses to Dehra Dun (Rs 14, two hours) where there are connections to Mussoorie. There are several buses every hour to Delhi (Rs 54, six hours) and regular departures to Agra (Rs 87, 10 hours). Other destinations include Shimla, Naini Tal, Almora, Uttarkashi, Gangotri and Badrinath.

Train The *Shatabdi Express* runs daily except Wednesday between Dehra Dun and New Delhi calling at Haridwar's macaque-infested station at 10.45 am on the way to Dehra Dun, and at 5.20 pm on the return trip to New Delhi (Rs 270/540 in chair car/1st class). The *Mussoorie Express* is an excellent overnight train service from Delhi (268 km, Rs 78/233 in 2nd/1st class). Other direct trains connect Haridwar with Calcutta (1472 km, 35 hours), Bombay (1649 km, 40 hours), Varanasi (894 km, 20 hours) and Lucknow (493 km, 11 hours).

Taxi The taxi stand opposite the bus terminal is a drivers' co-operative with set prices that are very high – Rs 250 for Rishikesh. To rent a car more cheaply try the travel agents down the side streets by the Hotel Kailash.

UTTAR PRADESH

RAJAJI NATIONAL PARK

This attractive park is best known for its herds of wild elephant, numbering around 150 in all. Unfortunately their future is in question since human competition for land has severed their traditional migration route, which once stretched from here to the area now part of Corbett National Park to the east. Plans for a 'migration corridor' would involve moving several villages and have become bogged down in the usual bureaucracy.

As well as elephants, the park contains some rarely seen tigers and leopards, chital, sambars, wild boars and sloth bears. It's not as impressive as Corbett but worth a visit if you're spending some time in the area.

Open from mid-November to mid-June, there are eight entry gates. Ramgarh is 14 km from Dehra Dun; Ranipur, Motichur and Chilla each nine km from Haridwar; and Kunnao is six km from Rishikesh. Entry fees and regulations are as for Corbett (see later in this section).

There are buses from Haridwar to Chilla, where there's a *Tourist Rest House* with dorm beds for Rs 40 and doubles for Rs 200. There are elephant rides (Rs 50) into the park from Chilla. Accommodation is available at the 10 *Forest Rest Houses* (Rs 100 to Rs 300 per suite) dotted around the park. Bookings should be made at the Rajaji National Park office, 5/1 Ansari Marg, Dehra Dun (☎ 23-794).

RISHIKESH

Population: 78,000
Telephone Area Code: 01364

In spite of its claim to being the 'Yoga Capital of the World' Rishikesh is a quieter and more easy-going place than Haridwar. Surrounded by hills on three sides, it lies at 356 metres. The holy Ganges (almost clear here) flows through the town and, as in Haridwar, there are many ashrams along its sandy banks. This is an excellent place to stay and study yoga, meditation and other aspects of Hinduism.

Back in the '60s Rishikesh gained instant – and fleeting – fame as the place where the Beatles (or, as the UP Tourism brochure calls them, 'the Beatless'!) came to be with their guru, the Maharishi Mahesh Yogi. Rishikesh is also the starting point for trips to Himalayan pilgrimage centres like Badrinath, Kedarnath and Gangotri.

Orientation & Information

The helpful tourist office (☎ 30-209) is on Railway Station Rd. GMVN (☎ 30-372), which runs buses and tours to the pilgrimage centres north of here, is near the Tourist Complex, in the area known as Muni-ki-Reti.

Most of the ashrams are in the northern part of the town on either side of the Ganges, connected by two bridges: the Shivanand Jhula and the Lakshman Jhula. For Rs 2.50 you can also cross by boat (particularly auspicious).

Things to See

Triveni Ghat is an interesting place to be at dawn, when people make offerings of milk to the river and feed the surprisingly large fish. After sunset, priests set floating lamps on the water in the Ganga Aarti (river worship) ceremony. Nearby is the **Bharat Mandir**, the oldest temple here.

The suspension bridge, **Lakshman Jhula**, was built in 1929 to replace a rope bridge. This is where Rama's brother Lakshmana is said to have crossed the river on a jute rope, and the old **Lakshman Temple** is on the west bank. Across the river are some turreted architectural oddities including the 13-storey **Kailashanand Mission Ashram** – there's a good view from the top. It's a pleasant two-km walk along this east bank to the Shivanand Jhula.

Pilgrims take Ganga water to offer at **Neel Kanth Mahadev**, a four-hour walk from Lakshman Jhula on the east bank. There are fine views on the way up to the temple at 1700 metres but take something to drink and start early as it can get very hot. It's now possible to make the journey by bus.

There are also great views from **Kunjapuri**, in the hills north of Rishikesh. It's a three-km walk from Hindola Khal (45

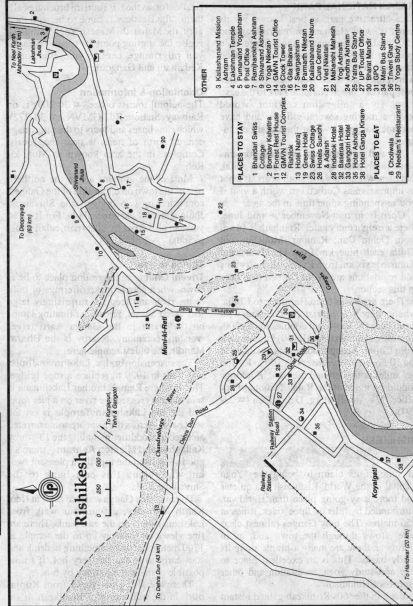

Rishikesh

UTTAR PRADESH

OTHER
3 Kailashanand Mission Ashram
4 Lakshman Temple
5 Purnanand Yogashram
6 Post Office
7 Ramjharokha Ashram
9 Shivanand Ashram
10 Yoga Niketan
14 GMVN Tourist Office
15 Clock Tower
16 Gita Bhavan
17 Swargashram
18 Parmarth Niketan
20 Kailashanand Nature Cure Centre
21 Ved Niketan
22 Maharishi Mahesh Yogi Ashram
24 Andhra Ashram
25 Yatra Bus Stand
27 UP Tourist Office
30 Bharat Mandir
31 GPO
34 Main Bus Stand
36 Triveni Ghat
37 Yoga Study Centre

PLACES TO STAY
1 Bhandari Swiss Cottage
2 Bombay Kshettra
11 Forest Rest House
12 GMVN Tourist Complex Rishilok
13 Hotel Natraj
19 Green Hotel
23 Swiss Cottage
26 Hotels Suruchi & Adarsh
28 Inderlok Hotel
32 Baseraa Hotel
33 Gangotri Hotel
35 Hotel Ashoka
38 Hotel Ganga Kinare

PLACES TO EAT
8 Choltiwala
29 Neelam's Restaurant

To Neel Kanth Mahadev (12 km)

Lakshman Jhula

To Deoprayag (63 km)

Shivanand Jhula

Ganges River

Lakshman Jhula Road

Muni-ki-Reti

Chandrabhaga River

Dehra Dun Road

To Kunjapuri, Tehri & Gangotri

Railway Station Road

Railway Station

To Dehra Dun (43 km)

Ghat Road

Koyalgati

To Haridwar (20 km)

0   250   500 m

minutes by bus from Rishikesh) which all buses to Tehri pass through.

Organised Tours

Among the 10 packages organised by GMVN (mainly in the summer season) is a 12-day bus trip covering the Char Dham (Yamunotri, Gangotri, Kedarnath and Badrinath) for Rs 3025.

A number of travel agents in the Ghat Rd area organise river rafting trips from Shivpuri, 15 km upstream. Near the GMVN tourist office in Muni-ki-Reti, Apex Adventure Tours (☎ 31-503) offers rafting for Rs 580 per person for a minimum of two people. They also organise pricey trekking packages.

Places to Stay

If you're not staying at an ashram, there's a good range of other accommodation here.

GMVN's Tourist Bungalow, *Tourist Complex Rishilok* (☎ 30-373), is pleasantly situated close to the ashrams. It's clean if a bit run-down but has doubles from Rs 100

and rooms with attached bathrooms from Rs 170/220. There's a reasonably priced dining hall and a peaceful garden to relax in.

For long-term residents, the *Swiss Cottage* has been popular for years. Rooms are basic and you'll pay between Rs 25 and Rs 40 a night. Across the river, near the Lakshman Jhula, there's the similarly basic *Bombay Kshettra* with rooms for Rs 40/80 with common bathroom. The *Green Hotel* (☎ 31-242) has excellent rooms for Rs 50/90 with attached bathrooms and some air-cooled doubles for Rs 200. There's a restaurant serving good food, lassis and milkshakes but Star TV doesn't seem quite right here.

There are classes in yoga and dance at the *Omkarananda Ganga Sadan*, a guest house that's more like an ashram, near Shivanand Jhula. Rooms are Rs 40 and classes cost around Rs 50 per hour. In a more peaceful location in the countryside about 1.5 km from Lakshman Jhula is the *Bhandari Swiss Cottage*, with rooms from Rs 50 (common bath). Nearby is the more upmarket *High Bank Peasant's Cottage* (☎ 32-732) charging Rs 200

Staying at an Ashram

Studying aspects of Hinduism has, naturally, become somewhat commercialised at Rishikesh. However, once you've found a place to suit your needs, spending some time here can be a fulfilling experience. There are many ashrams to choose from; only a few are listed below. Most charge between Rs 40 and Rs 80 per day for a basic room; some also include three meals in this price. It's worth first talking to other travellers and going to a few classes at different ashrams to find a guru who gets through to you.

Many ashrams post up a 'code of conduct' advising you to bath daily, avoid unnecessary chatting, and abstain from eggs, meat, fish, liquor, onions, garlic, tobacco and pan. Notices also state that women are not allowed into temples or the courtyard when having *masik dharma* (menstruating). Helpful hints for the practice of yoga include such tips as: 'Those who are suffering from pus in the ear or displacement of the retina should avoid topsy turvy poses'.

Yoga Niketan (☎ 30-227) is located in a peaceful spot high above the main road in Muni-ki-Reti. It has been recommended by several travellers for the serious study of yoga but you must stay for a minimum of 15 days. The charge of Rs 80 per day covers all meals and the basic courses but many people opt for the additional courses which cost extra.

Ved Niketan is a popular ashram with over 100 rooms arranged around a large courtyard. Rooms are Rs 30, or Rs 40 with attached bathroom; meals are Rs 14. It's a very relaxed place and you don't have to join the yoga class (5.30 am) or the evening lectures. Courses cost Rs 300 for a week, Rs 1000 for a month.

Shivanand Ashram (The Divine Life Society), founded by Swami Shivanand, is a well-known ashram and the society has branches in many countries. You can stay for short-term study or for longer three-month courses, although to do this you need to contact them two months in advance (fax 31-190). Or simply drop by for the daily lectures at 10 am and 5 pm.

The **Yoga Study Centre** (☎ 31-196), at Koyalgati, runs three-week courses for beginners, intermediate and advanced students. Payment is by donation and accommodation can be arranged.

Maharishi Mahesh Yogi's **Transcendental Meditation Centre** was the Oberoi of ashrams, charging similar prices, but it's temporarily closed. It was never the kind of place at which you could just turn up. Write in advance to Maharishi Mahesh Yogi Ashram, Rishikesh, 249201 UP. ■

to Rs 300 for doubles with attached bath. There are good views from these two places.

If you need to be near the bus stands, the best place is the *Hotel Ashoka* (☎ 30-715), which has clean rooms for Rs 55 or Rs 65 with attached bathroom, and a helpful manager. By the Yatra bus stand, the *Hotel Adarsh* (☎ 31-301) charges Rs 25 in the dorm, Rs 100 for a double. The more upmarket *Hotel Suruchi* (☎ 30-356) nearby is a very nice place run by a desperately enthusiastic manager. Rooms are from Rs 175/250 with attached bathrooms.

In the town centre, the *Baseraa Hotel* (☎ 30-767), close to Triveni Ghat, has good rooms from Rs 150/200, and in the same area is the similarly priced, once-glitzy *Gangotri Hotel*. Opposite is the *Inderlok Hotel* (☎ 30-555) whose resident yoga teacher gives free lessons on the rooftop lawn if you stay. Rooms range from Rs 300/400 to Rs 500/600 with air-con and bathtub.

The well-located *Hotel Ganga Kinare* (☎ 30-566) is right on the river and has a private ghat, but rooms are overpriced at Rs 840/940, and US$15 for a 20-minute boat ride must be the biggest rip-off in the area. The *Hotel Natraj* (☎ 31-099) has rooms at Rs 625/875 and a swimming pool and sauna that non-guests can use for Rs 150.

Places to Eat

Meat and alcohol are prohibited in this holy town. The most famous restaurant is *Chotiwala* ('Two children or one adult can eat in a thali, Rs 20') just across the Shivanand Jhula. Next door is the equally good *Luxmi Hotel*. On the other side of the river near the boat landing, the *Madras Restaurant* does good masala dosas but wouldn't win any awards for cleanliness. Opposite the Bombay Kshettra, *Ganga Darshan Restaurant* has good coffee, thalis and masala dosas. There are a couple of tables outside by the river.

In the main part of town *Neelam's* is very popular with travellers for its sandwiches, soups and pasta dishes. The *Daana Paani*, the restaurant at the Baseraa Hotel, is good for Indian food.

Getting There & Away

A small branch railway line runs from Haridwar up to Rishikesh but the buses are more convenient. From the main bus stand there are four buses an hour to Haridwar (Rs 7, 45 minutes) from 4 am to 10 pm. There are taxis to Dehra Dun for Rs 250 and buses for Rs 10.50 (1½ hours) with connections to Mussoorie. There are hourly buses to Delhi (Rs 61 to Rs 75, 6½ hours), an early-morning bus to Ramnagar (for Corbett; Rs 60, six hours) and Naini Tal (Rs 100, 10 hours). Buses leave at 5.30 am and 10.30 pm for Shimla (Rs 80, 11 hours).

From the Yatra bus stand there are hourly departures to Uttarkashi (Rs 60, 10 hours), Tehri (Rs 42, four hours) and also buses to Gangotri (Rs 114, 12 hours), Badrinath (Rs 117, 12 hours), Kedarnath (Rs 86, 10 hours), Govind Ghat (Rs 107, 12 hours) and Gopeswar (Rs 83, nine hours), with numerous buses during the summer Yatra season.

Getting Around

Tempos (Vikrams) run from Ghat Rd junction up to Shivanand Jhula (Rs 3) and Lakshman Jhula (Rs 5). On the east bank of the river, a seat in a jeep between Lakshman Jhula and Shivanand Jhula costs Rs 3.

UTTARKASHI DISTRICT

This northern district of Uttarakhand is best known for the two major pilgrimage centres: Gangotri, near the source of the Ganges; and Yamunotri by the source of the Yamuna. The region hit the world news in October 1991 when a powerful earthquake caused US$130 million of damage; 800 people died and 2000 were injured.

Uttarkashi

Uttarkashi, 155 km from Rishikesh, is the administrative headquarters of the district. Several trekking companies operate from here and the town is also the base for the Nehru Institute of Mountaineering, which operates climbing courses and also organises treks. Accommodation in Uttarkashi includes GMVN's *Tourist Rest House* (☎ 171) which charges from Rs 120 to Rs

400 for doubles and Rs 60 for dorm beds at the height of the summer season. There are numerous other places to stay.

Yamunotri

Yamunotri is the source of the Yamuna River – it emerges from a frozen lake of ice and glaciers on the Kalinda Parvat at an altitude of 4421 metres. The temple of the goddess Yamunotri is on the left bank of the river and, just below it, there are several hot springs. Buses go as far as Hanumanchatti from Mussoorie or Rishikesh. From Hanumanchatti to Yamunotri takes five to six hours but there's a *Tourist Rest House* just past the halfway point, at Jankichatti. You can also stay at Yamunotri in the *dharamsalas*. Pilgrims cook their food in the boiling water of the hot springs.

For more information on treks in this region see Trekking in Garhwal & Kumaon at the end of that section.

CORBETT NATIONAL PARK

Telephone Area Code: 05945

Established in 1936 as India's first national park, Corbett is famous for its wide variety of wildlife and its beautiful location in the foothills of the Himalaya by the Ramganga River. With the recent inclusion of the Sonanadi wildlife sanctuary to the west, Corbett has grown from 520 to 1318 sq km. It may seem incongruous for a national park to be named after a famous British hunter – Jim Corbett is best known for his book *The Man-Eaters of Kumaon*, and was greatly revered by local people for shooting tigers that had developed a liking for human flesh. However, he was instrumental in setting up the reserve and eventually shot more wildlife with his camera than with his gun.

Seeing a tiger here is dependent on chance, since baiting has been discontinued and there is no tiger tracking (unlike at Kanha in Madhya Pradesh). However, your best chance is if you come late in the season (April to mid-June) and stay for several days.

More commonly seen wildlife includes the wild elephant, langur monkey (black face, long tail), rhesus macaque, peacock, and several types of deer including chital

(spotted deer), sambars, hog deer and barking deer. There are also crocodiles, the odd-looking gavial or gharial (a thin-snouted, fish-eating crocodile often spotted from High Bank), monitor lizards, wild boars and jackals. Leopards (referred to as panthers in India) are occasionally seen.

Corbett is also a bird-watcher's paradise, and since the creation of the Kalagarh Dam on the Ramganga River, large numbers of waterfowl have been attracted here.

Orientation & Information

Corbett is open from mid-November to mid-June but you should avoid the crowded weekends. The gates are closed at sunset and no night driving is allowed. Dhikala is the main accommodation centre in the park, 51 km from Ramnagar (the nearest railhead). Outside Corbett there are some expensive resorts and a few hotels in Ramnagar.

Permits for an overnight stay in the park have to be obtained from the park reception centre at Ramnagar (☎ 85-489) where accommodation is booked. It's open daily from 8 am to 1 pm and 3 to 5 pm. It's also possible to book some accommodation through UP Tourism in Delhi (☎ (011) 332-2251), and the three rooms at Khinanauli (Rs 600) must be booked through the Forest Office in Lucknow (☎ (0522) 246-140). Some travellers have reported that they've arrived at Ramnagar to be told that accommodation in Dhikala is booked out for up to five days ahead. If this is the case, rather than waiting in Ramnagar, make a booking and head for the nearby hill stations of Naini Tal or Ranikhet.

Day visitors are not allowed to enter from Dhangarhi Gate or to visit Dhikala. To visit Bijrani you must first get permits from Ramnagar; only 100 permits are granted each day and no advance reservation is possible.

Charges given in this section are for foreign nationals; Indians are charged about two-thirds less. At the park gates you must pay an entry fee of Rs 100 for a stay of up to three days, then Rs 15 per day. It costs Rs 50 for a camera permit, Rs 500 for a video or movie camera. To take a car into the park costs Rs 100, plus another Rs 100 for a guide (compulsory).

At Dhikala there's a library and interesting wildlife films are shown there (free) in the evenings. The elephant rides at sunrise and sunset are not to be missed and cost Rs 50 for about two hours. During the day you can sit in one of the observation posts to watch for animals.

At Bijrani there's an interpretation centre and restaurant. It's sometimes possible to get elephant rides from here. There's a bank for foreign exchange in Ramnagar.

Places to Stay & Eat

Dhikala There's a wide range of accommodation but the prices charged for foreigners mean that it's not good value. There's a very basic dormitory (like three-tier sleepers on the trains!) for Rs 50 in the *Log Huts* but it's better to go for the triples (Rs 240) in the *Tourist Hutment*. An extra charge (Rs 25) is made for mattresses and sheets in all these

places. More comfortable doubles at Rs 450 are in the cabins; rooms in the *Forest Rest Houses* cost Rs 600. There are two restaurants, one run by KMVN and the other a private operation.

With your own transport and food, you can also stay in *Forest Rest Houses* at Sarapduli, Bijrani, or Gairal for Rs 450; Khinanauli for Rs 600; and any of the other Forest Rest Houses (see the Corbett National Park map) for Rs 150. Don't forget to get a 'clearance certificate' at Dhikala before you leave the park.

Ramnagar Note that if you use Ramnagar as a base you'll have to rent a jeep here and you won't be able to go out on elephant rides in the centre of the park, as day visits to Dhikala are not allowed.

There's a good *Tourist Bungalow* (☎ 85-225), next to the reception centre. It has doubles for Rs 100 and dormitory beds for Rs 30. Down the side street off the main

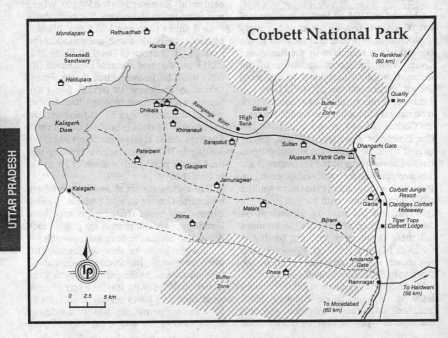

Corbett National Park

Mondiapani
Rathuadhab
Kanda
Sonanadi Sanctuary
Haldupara
Dhikala
Ramganga River
Gairal
High Bank
Buffer Zone
To Ranikhet (60 km)
Quality Inn
Kalagarh Dam
Khinanauli
Paterpani
Sarapduli
Sultan
Dhangarhi Gate
Museum & Yatrik Cafe
Gaujpani
Kalagarh
Jamunagwar
Malani
Jhirna
Bijrani
Kosi River
Corbett Jungle Resort
Garjia
Claridges Corbett Hideaway
Tiger Tops Corbett Lodge
Amdanda Gate
Buffer Zone
Dhela
Ramnagar
To Haldwani (56 km)
To Moradabad (80 km)

0   2.5   5 km

Project Tiger

By 1973, India's tiger population had fallen to around 1800. The demands of Chinese folk medicine, which regards the bones and flesh of the animal as having powerful medicinal qualities, placed a high price on the tiger. As well as the threat from poachers, tiger habitat was rapidly dwindling as India's population spiralled. In order to save the animal from extinction Project Tiger was launched with the assistance of the World Wide Fund for Nature (WWF). Corbett was the first Project Tiger reserve, and there are now 19 reserves in this conservation scheme.

Numbers appeared to grow and by the late 1980s the project was being lauded and the tiger population estimated at around 4000 – a considerable success story. But in the 1990s the Chinese market in tiger bones continued to thrive, sightings of tiger in India's national parks were becoming rarer and experts began questioning the methods used for estimating tiger numbers. Officials in India claim that pug marks are like human fingerprints: no two are the same. Prints are, however, rarely clear enough to be told apart and this may be part of the reason for numbers having been exaggerated over the years. It's just as likely that the numbers have been deliberately inflated to hide the large-scale poaching that has been going on, often (as in the case of Ranthambhore in Rajasthan) involving government officials.

The poaching trade is extremely lucrative and a complete tiger can fetch around US$6000 in China. In an attempt to stem the trade, Traffic India was set up. Much of the trade passes through Delhi and the Tibetan camps near the city; the bones are smuggled into China via the old trade routes through Tibet. Between 1990 and 1993 it's estimated that poachers killed as many as 1000 animals.

No-one knows exactly how many tigers remain in India; the figure is now somewhere between 2000 and 3000, 80 to 90 of them in Corbett National Park. ∎

---

drag, the *Hotel Everest* has rooms with bathrooms for Rs 60/80. Rooms at the *Hotel Govind* are a little cheaper but not so clean. This place does, however, have a good restaurant – excellent fruit lassis for Rs 16, and the malai kofta (Rs 20) and mutton curry (Rs 26) are also good. The manager is very helpful but don't believe the sign that says 'Alcoholic Drinks Strictly Prohibited'!

Other Places There are some upmarket resorts, but they're outside the park. The *Quality Inn Corbett Jungle Resort* (☎ 85-230) has attractive cottages high above the river for Rs 925 (including meals) and offers elephant rides and excursions into Corbett.

The *Corbett Riverside Resort* (☎ 85-961) has some pleasant rooms in a peaceful loca-

tion close to the river. They charge Rs 1200 per person including meals. The *Claridges Corbett Hideaway* (☎ 85-959) is more upmarket with accommodation in attractive ochre cottages set in an orchard of mango trees. Double rooms cost Rs 3000; meals are Rs 175.

Tiger Tops Corbett Lodge (☎ (011) 644-4016) is a very luxurious place with prices to match – US$120 per person. There are elephant rides, jeep trips and a swimming pool. Despite the name it's not part of the company that operates the resort in Chitwan (Nepal).

Getting There & Away

Ramnagar is connected by train with Moradabad and by bus with Delhi (Rs 68, six hours), Lucknow, Naini Tal and Ranikhet. The bus terminal is near the reception centre and the hotels; the railway station is 1.5 km south.

UTTAR PRADESH

A bus runs from Ramnagar to Dhikala (Rs 20, two hours) at 3.30 pm, returning from Dhikala at 9 am the next day. The airport at Pantnagar is 110 km away – too far to be of any use. There are also three-day package tours operated by UP Tourism (Rs 1600) and others from Delhi.

Getting Around
Apart from the daily bus service to Dhikala the only form of transport available there is elephants. Jeeps can usually only be rented at Ramnagar (Rs 6 per km).

KATHGODAM & HALDWANI
These two towns, six km apart, form an important travel junction for travellers to Naini Tal and most of the hill stations in the Kumaon region. Kathgodam is the railhead and there are evening trains to Lucknow, Agra and Jodhpur. There are retiring rooms, a good refreshment room and a tourist office. Bookings can be made in the out-agencies in many hill stations.

There's supposed to be a connecting bus to Naini Tal but if the train is late you'll miss it. If you're coming up to this area it may be better to get off the train at Haldwani, where there's a big bus terminal.

NAINI TAL
Population: 34,000
Telephone Area Code: 05942

At 1938 metres in the Kumaon Hills, this attractive hill station was once the summer capital of Uttar Pradesh. The hotels and villas of this popular resort are set around the peaceful Naini lake or *tal*, hence the name.

Naini Tal is very much a green and pleasant land that immediately appealed to the homesick Brits, who were reminded of the Cumbrian Lake District. It was discovered by a Mr Barron and he had his yacht carried up here in 1840. The Naini Tal Boat Club, whose wooden clubhouse still graces the edge of the lake, became the fashionable focus of the community. Disaster struck on 16 September 1880 when a major landslip occurred, burying 151 people in the Assem-bly Halls area and creating the recreation ground now known as the Flats.

This is certainly one of the most pleasant hill stations to visit and there are many interesting walks through the forests to points with superb views of the Himalaya.

The high season, when Naini Tal is packed and hotel prices double or triple, corresponds to school holidays. Avoid Christmas and the New Year, mid-April to mid-July and mid-September to early November.

Orientation & Information
The two bazaars, Tallital and Mallital, are at either end of the lake, connected by The Mall. A toll keeps most motorised traffic off this road during the high season.

There's a UP tourist office (☎ 2337) and a travel company (Parvat Tours) run by its local subsidiary, KMVN (☎ 2543). The bus stand (☎ 2641) and railway booking agency (☎ 2518) are in Tallital.

The Naini Tal Mountaineering Club (☎ 2051) runs courses and can give advice on treks and expeditions in the area. The Modern Book Shop, below the Alps Hotel, has a good range of titles.

Naini Lake
This attractive lake is said to be one of the emerald green eyes of Siva's wife, Sati. She had jumped into a sacrificial bonfire and as her mourning husband dragged her charred remains across the country, various appendages dropped off. India is now littered with places 'formed' by parts of her body. Her eye falling here makes this a holy spot and the popular **Naina Devi Temple** is by the northern end of the lake. Nearby is a small Tibetan market.

You can rent rowing boats and pedal boats for around Rs 30 per hour from a number of places along The Mall. The Naini Tal Boat Club has a few yachts for Rs 50 per hour and you may be able to persuade them to waive the temporary membership fee (Rs 300 for three days) if you don't want to use the clubhouse facilities (bar, restaurant, ballroom and library). The club is less exclusive than it was. When Jim Corbett lived here he was refused membership because he'd been born in India, and hence was not a pukkah sahib.

St John's Church

Built in 1847, soon after the British arrived, this church contains a brass memorial to the victims of the famous landslip. The few bodies that could be uncovered from the rubble were buried in the graveyard here.

Snow View

A chairlift (ropeway) takes you up to this popular viewpoint at 2270 metres. The lift is open from 10 am to 4 pm and costs Rs 20 (one way). It's a pleasant walk down past the Tibetan gompa. The Rs 30 return ticket gives you only one hour at the top and a set time for your return. A sign says: 'Don't be panicy in case of power failure'!

At the top there are powerful binoculars (Rs 2) for a close-up view of Nanda Devi (7817 metres), which was, as the old brass plate here tells you, 'the highest mountain in the British Empire'. Nanda Devi is India's highest peak until Sikkim (and thus Kanchenjunga) was absorbed into the country. You can be dressed in Kumaon national costume and have your photo taken for Rs 15, with a spectacular Himalayan backdrop.

Walks

There are several other good walks in the area, with views of the snowcapped mountains to the north. China Peak, also known as Naini Peak is the highest point in the area (2610 metres) and can be reached either from Snow View or from Mallital (five km). Climb up in the early morning when the views are clearer.

A four-km walk to the west of the lake brings you to Dorothy's Seat (2292 metres) where a Mr Kellet built a seat in memory of his wife, killed in a plane crash. Laria Kanta is a peak at 2480 metres on the opposite side of the lake and Deopatta (2435 metres) is west of Mallital.

Hanumangarh & Observatory

There are good views and spectacular sunsets over the plains from this Hanuman temple, three km south of Tallital. Just over one km further on is the state observatory, which is sometimes open at weekends. Check with the tourist office.

Other Activities

If you don't feel like walking you can rent ponies (which are well looked after) to climb to any of the viewpoints. Expect to pay around Rs 30 per hour, or Rs 50 for China Peak (3½ hours). You can play billiards for Rs 30 per hour at Naini Billiards or rent fishing gear at the lake at Bhim Tal, an over-rated excursion spot 23 km from Naini Tal.

Organised Tours

KMVN's Parvat Tours (☎ 2656) operates tours to the nearby lakes (Sat Tal and Bhim Tal) and to places further north, like Kausani and Ranikhet. In the summer they offer a six-day pilgrimage to Badrinath and Kedarnath. Along The Mall there are lots of private travel agents offering similar tours and selling bus tickets to Delhi. They have day trips to Corbett National Park for Rs 120. A taxi to the national park would charge Rs 1000 for up to five people.

Places to Stay – bottom end

There are over 100 places to stay. Off-season rates are given here but you may be able to get a further discount. It's worth paying a bit more for a room with a view over the lake and you often get a better deal for a more expensive room in a cheaper hotel, than for a cheap room in an upmarket place.

KMVN's *Tourist Rest House* (☎ 2570) in Tallital has dormitory accommodation (Rs 25) in eight-bed rooms, with lots of hot water, and doubles from Rs 150. Similarly priced, the other *Tourist Rest House* (☎ 2400) is away from the lake on the road to Delhi – not a great location. The *Hotel Himalaya*, high above the bus terminal, has some tiny singles for Rs 40 and some nice doubles (with attached bathrooms) facing the lake for Rs 150.

UTTAR PRADESH

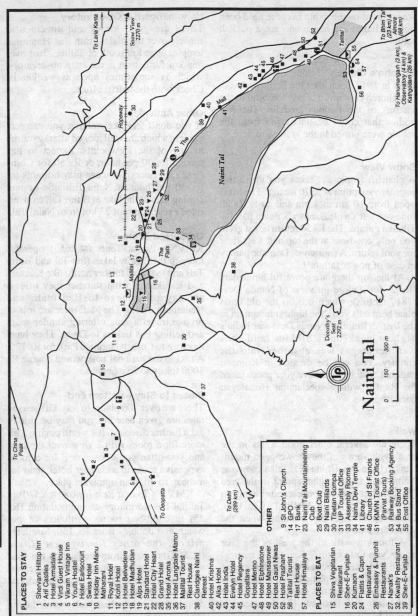

Naini Tal

To Laria Kanta

Snow View 2270 m

Ropeway

To China Peak

Mall

Naini Tal

The Mall

The Flats

Tallital

To Bhim Tal (23 km) & Bhowali (68 km)

To Hanumangarh (3 km), Observatory (4 km) & Kathgodam (35 km)

To Deopatta

To Delhi (289 km)

Dorothy's Seat 2292 m

0   150   300 m

PLACES TO STAY

1   Shervani Hilltop Inn
2   Arif Castles
3   Hotel Armadale
4   Virdi Guest House
5   Vikram Vintage Inn
6   Youth Hostel
7   Hotel Earlscourt
8   Swiss Hotel
10   Holiday Inn Manu Maharani
11   Royal Hotel
12   Kohli Hotel
13   Hotel Belvedere
18   Hotel Madhuban
19   Alps Hotel
21   Standard Hotel
22   Hotel City Heart
28   Grand Hotel
35   Hotel Aroma
36   Hotel Langdale Manor
37   Mallital Tourist Rest House
38   Claridges Naini Retreat
40   Hotel Krishna
42   Alka Hotel
43   Hotel India
44   Evelyn Hotel
45   Hotel Regency Gopattara
47   Hotel Merino
48   Hotel Elphinstone
49   Hotel Mansarover
50   Hotel Gauri Niwas
52   Hotel Prashant
56   Talital Tourist Rest House
57   Hotel Himalaya

PLACES TO EAT

15   Shiva Vegetarian Restaurant
16   Sher-E-Punjab
24   Kumaon
24   Flatis & Capri
26   Embassy & Purohit Restaurants
32   Nanak's
32   Kwality Restaurant
39   Sher-E-Punjab

OTHER

9   St John's Church
14   GPO
17   Bank
23   Naini Tal Mountaineering Club
25   Boat Club
29   Naini Billiards
30   Tibetan Gompa
31   UP Tourist Office
33   Assembly Rooms
34   Naina Devi Temple
41   Library
46   Church of St Francis
51   KMVN Tourist Office (Parvat Tours)
53   Railway Booking Agency
54   Bus Stand
55   Post Office

Behind the big Hotel Mansarover, the *Hotel Gauri Niwas* has some good-value rooms with attached bathrooms for Rs 50. Nearby, the *Hotel Punjab* is not so good and the *Lake View* has rooms from Rs 80. On The Mall the *Hotel Merino*, with doubles from Rs 80, is an old place worth checking out.

The *Hotel Prashant* (☎ 2345) is popular with foreigners and has rooms with attached bathrooms from Rs 100 to Rs 300 and good views from the balconies. The *Hotel Regency Gopaltara* is similarly priced. The *Hotel Krishna* (☎ 2662) has some good-value rooms from Rs 100, with bathroom and satellite TV. There are some better rooms above for Rs 350.

Opposite the Naini Tal Mountaineering Club, the *Hotel City Heart* (☎ 2228) is another good choice with doubles from Rs 90 and hot-water geysers in all rooms.

Further along The Mall are some cheaper places. The *Alps Hotel* is a creaky old place with vast rooms for Rs 80 – the front rooms have a balcony. The owner is an interesting guy and this is a pleasant place to stay. The *Standard Hotel* has some singles with common bath for Rs 50 and doubles with attached bathroom from Rs 110. Behind it is the *Hotel Madhuban* which has some doubles with attached bathrooms from Rs 75 and is very good value. Next door the *Hotel Basera* is similarly priced.

In Mallital the *Kohli Hotel* (☎ 3368) is an excellent, clean guest house, run by a friendly Sikh, with doubles from Rs 80 to Rs 150 (with satellite TV). There are great views from the rooms upstairs and a newly constructed roof terrace.

The *youth hostel* (☎ 2513) has dorm beds for Rs 12 (members) or Rs 22 (nonmembers) and there are also two doubles. It's a well-run place in a peaceful location, a 25-minute walk from Mallital Bazaar. The set meals for Rs 10 are great value and you can get information on the Pindari Glacier trek here. Nearby is the *Virdi Guest House*, which is run by a Sikh piano tuner. Rooms here with common bathroom are Rs 60.

Places to Stay – middle & top end

The *Evelyn Hotel* (☎ 2457) has doubles from Rs 250 to Rs 350, a pleasant terrace overlooking the lake and a good restaurant. On The Mall there are doubles from Rs 250 at the large *Alka Hotel* (☎ 2220).

The *Grand Hotel* (☎ 2406) is one of the oldest places here with rooms from Rs 550. The best rooms are upstairs, with views over the lake. It's much better than the other Raj leftover, the *Royal Hotel* (☎ 3007), which is vast and dilapidated, with disinterested staff, and bizarre sculptures in the garden. Even at Rs 300 in the off season it's hardly a bargain.

Most of the other up-market places are above Mallital and they operate a free jeep service down to The Mall. The *Swiss Hotel* (☎ 3013) has large, high-ceilinged rooms for Rs 550 but good discounts are available when business is slack. Nearby is the *Hotel Earlscourt* (☎ 3381) which was once an English family house. The shelves are lined with the books they left behind – edifying publications like 'A Handbook for Girl Guides' and 'Hymns Ancient & Modern'. Rooms with bathrooms are Rs 700 and there's a pricey restaurant.

Further up is the resort hotel *Arif Castles* (☎ 2801) with rooms for Rs 950, and above it the *Shervani Hilltop Inn* (☎ 3128) which has a pleasant garden and is good value at Rs 595 for a double.

The *Hotel Belvedere* (☎ 2082) is an old whitewashed maharaja's palace which is rather run-down, with moth-eaten tiger skins on the walls, but it has a certain character to it, and there are good views. The suites for Rs 680 are good, there are some cheaper rooms, and the manager is very helpful and friendly.

The *Vikram Vintage Inn* (☎ 2877) is a solid plush hotel with double rooms for Rs 920. The *Claridges Naini Retreat* (☎ 2105) is in a secluded spot above Mallital. Only a few rooms have views of the lake but there's a nice garden. Rooms are Rs 1765 including breakfast and one other meal. At the top of the pile is the *Holiday Inn Manu Maharani* (☎ 2531; fax 2228), with good lake views and all mod cons. Doubles cost from Rs 1200; at the height of the season they are Rs 2400 including meals.

Places to Eat
For a cheap snack, there's *The Dhaba*, a stall outside the Standard Hotel serving great masala dosas for Rs 10. In Mallital Bazaar there's the *Sher-E-Punjab* and the *Shiva*, a well-known place with good vegetarian thalis for Rs 20.

Along The Mall there's quite a range of places to choose from. The *Kumaon* does vegetarian food and has video games but the best vegetarian food is at the *Purohit Restaurant*, next to Embassy Restaurant. The *Capri Restaurant* is quite good and main dishes are around Rs 50. *Flattis* is another popular place, and it's a bit cheaper. *Sakley's Restaurant* by the Alps Hotel has a bakery attached and some good pastries. At the other end of The Mall is another branch of *Sher-E-Punjab*, and the *Ahaar Vihar Restaurant* which has been recommended for its Gujarati food. By the Hotel Merino is the *Tandoor Restaurant*.

The best place for pizzas, hamburgers and ice cream is *Nanak's* but it's also expensive and trendy. The *Kwality Restaurant* has a great location right on the water, and its Indian food is excellent. Main dishes are Rs 40 to Rs 65. The *Embassy Restaurant* is more expensive but has a good reputation.

For a special occasion, the restaurants at the *Holiday Inn* are good. If there are tour groups staying they often put on a buffet dinner for Rs 150.

Getting There & Away
The nearest airport is Pantnagar, 71 km away, but it's not currently served by any scheduled flights.

Kathgodam (35 km south) is the nearest railway station, and the railway booking agency in Naini Tal has a quota for trains to Agra, Lucknow, Jodhpur and Calcutta. There are shared taxis to Kathgodam and Haldwani for Rs 25, and buses (Rs 14.50, 1½ hours) every 30 minutes. Morning and evening buses take nine hours to Delhi (Rs 75) and private operators run video coaches and air-con buses (Rs 175).

Other bus destinations include Bhim Tal (Rs 8.50, one hour), Ramnagar (Rs 29.50,

3½ hours), Almora (Rs 26, three hours), Ranikhet (Rs 25, three hours), Kausani (Rs 45, five hours), Pithoragarh (Rs 70, nine hours), Bareilly (Rs 39, five hours), Haridwar (Rs 90, nine hours), Rishikesh (Rs 100, 10 hours) and Dehra Dun (Rs 106, 10½ hours). There's one early-morning bus to Song (for the Pindari Glacier trek).

Getting Around
Getting up and down The Mall is no problem as there are speedy cycle-rickshaws charging a fixed Rs 3 between Tallital and Mallital. If you can't find an empty one you may need to join the queue at either end of The Mall for a few minutes.

RANIKHET
Telephone Area Code: 05966
North of Naini Tal and at an altitude of 1829 metres, this peaceful hill station offers excellent views of the snowcapped Himalaya including Nanda Devi (7817 metres). It's an important army town and the headquarters of the Kumaon Regiment. There are a couple of churches that have been converted into tweed and shawl mills with hand-operated looms.

Not yet developed as a tourist centre, Ranikhet is a delightful place to spend some time. There are several good walks – to **Jhula Devi Temple** (one km south of West View Hotel) and the orchards at **Chaubatia** (three km further on), and there's even a golf course with a 300-km panoramic view of the Himalaya!

The tourist office (☎ 2227) is by the UP Roadways bus stand.

Places to Stay & Eat
There are several hotels in the bazaar area between the bus stands. The *Hotel Raj Deep* is the best of the cheap places, with doubles for Rs 45, or Rs 125 with bathroom, and a vegetarian restaurant. The *Alka Hotel* has doubles from Rs 150 and a pleasant balcony with mountain views. The *Hotel Tribhuwan* has a range of rooms in three buildings – doubles with balconies from Rs 100 and more expensive rooms in the house below.

Rooms at the *Moon Hotel* are overpriced

1 Hotel Tribhuwan
2 KMOU Bus Stand
3 Alka Hotel
4 Moon Hotel
5 Hotel Raj Deep
6 Parwati Inn
7 UP Roadways
   Bus Stand
8 Tourist Office
9 Shawl & Tweed
   Factory
10 KRC Woollens
11 Catholic Church
12 GPO
13 Kumaon Lodge
   (Officers' Mess)
14 Hotel Meghdoot
15 Norton's Hotel
16 Tourist Rest House
17 West View Hotel

Ranikhet

0   250   500 m

To Jhula Devi
Temple (1 km)
& Chaubatia

To Naini
Tal

region, Kathgodam is the nearest railhead.
There are buses to Kathgodam (Rs 32, four
hours), Naini Tal (Rs 25, three hours),
Almora (Rs 22, three hours), Kausani (Rs 26,
3½ hours), Ramnagar (Rs 37, five hours),
Delhi (Rs 106 to Rs 132, 12 hours) as well
as to Lucknow, Haridwar and Badrinath.
Buses depart from the UP Roadways and the
KMOU bus stands.

ALMORA

Population: 29,000
Telephone Area Code: 05962

This picturesque hill station, at an altitude of
1650 metres, is one of the few not created by
the British. Some 400 years ago it was the
capital of the Chand rajas of Kumaon.

Almora is larger than Ranikhet and
Kausani, there's an interesting bazaar, good
views of the mountains and great
walks. The eight-km walk up to the **Kasar
Devi Temple** is recommended – this is where
Swami Vivekananda came to meditate. The
area has the reputation of being something of
a 'power centre' and some travellers rent
houses and stay for months. Attractions for
tourists include the Himalaya Woollen Mills
above the Holiday Home, and the town
museum. The clock tower was built in 1842
and carries the motto 'Work as if thou hadst
to live for aye, Worship as if thou wert to die
today'. There's a Siva shrine in the room
below it.

Beside the Savoy Hotel is a small tourist
office (☎ 22-180). High Adventure (☎ 23-
445) can organise treks in the area.

Places to Stay & Eat

There are several hotels in the bazaar including the very basic *Tourist Cottage*, by the
Glory Restaurant, with rooms from Rs 50.
The *Hotel Pawan*, further up the street, is
much cleaner with singles/doubles from Rs
83/131 with attached bathrooms, and billiards upstairs. Best is the large *Hotel
Shikhar* (☎ 22-395) with a wide range of
good rooms from Rs 80 to Rs 500. The
restaurant is also good, with main dishes
from Rs 30 to 40. Nearby is the recom-

at Rs 150/250 but the restaurant is quite good
(main dishes cost from Rs 35 to Rs 50). The
Parwati Inn, once quite impressive, has
rapidly deteriorated and, at Rs 175 for the
cheapest rooms, is also overpriced.

The other places to stay are about four km
from the bazaar in a peaceful wooded location. The *Hotel Meghdoot* (☎ 2475) charges
Rs 200 for a large clean double, and has a
good restaurant. Nearby *Norton's Hotel*
(☎ 2377) is a Raj leftover with doubles from
Rs 150 to Rs 250. It's closed between December and March. The *Tourist Rest House*
(☎ 2297) is a good place with rooms at Rs 150
(with kitchens) and dorm beds at Rs 20.

The *West End Hotel* (☎ 2261) is another
former Raj establishment. For Rs 325/525
there are large rooms with panelled ceilings
and fireplaces; and in the afternoon there's
tea and croquet on the lawn.

Getting There & Away

As with the other hill stations in the Kumaon

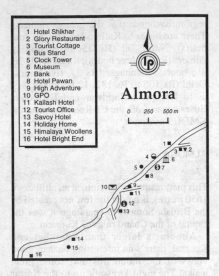

1 Hotel Shikhar
2 Glory Restaurant
3 Tourist Cottage
4 Bus Stand
5 Clock Tower
6 Museum
7 Bank
8 Hotel Pawan
9 High Adventure
10 GPO
11 Kailash Hotel
12 Tourist Office
13 Savoy Hotel
14 Holiday Home
15 Himalaya Woollens
16 Hotel Bright End

Almora

0   250   500 m

mended *Glory Restaurant* for vegetarian food.

Many people prefer the hotels outside the bazaar as they're more peaceful. The *Kailash Hotel* ('Junction of East and West Managed by House Wives') is an interesting place. 'You have to stay here to figure out what's going on', said one reader, and most travellers who do seem to enjoy the eccentricities of this guest house and its elderly proprietor, Mr Shah. Mrs Shah's cooking is good and her herbal teas excellent. There are rooms from Rs 50 although, as the sign above the door says, 'The Kingdom of Heaven is not a Place but a State of Mind'. In the same area is the *Savoy Hotel* with rooms from Rs 100 with attached bath.

At KMVN's Tourist Bungalow *Holiday Home* (☎ 22-250) the doubles at Rs 100 are good value, with a hot water geyser in each attached bathroom. There's a Rs 25 dorm, and twin-bed cottages with good views are available for Rs 175. If the nearby *Hotel Bright End* reopens it might be worth checking out.

Getting There & Away
There are buses to Delhi (Rs 111 to Rs 139,

12 hours), Naini Tal (Rs 26, three hours), Kausani (Rs 20, two hours), Ranikhet (Rs 22, three hours), Pithoragarh (Rs 40, seven hours), Song (Rs 45, five hours) for the Pindari Glacier trek, and Banbassa (Rs 68, seven hours) on the border with Nepal.

AROUND ALMORA
Katarmal & Jageshwar
There are a number of ancient temple sites in the area. At Katarmal (17 km from Almora) is the 800-year-old Sun Temple. A much larger group, dating back to the 7th century AD, is 34 km away at Jageshwar in an attractive valley of deodars. There's a *Tourist Rest House* (Rs 100 for doubles) and a small museum at Jageshwar.

PITHORAGARH
Population: 30,000
Situated at 1815 metres, Pithoragarh is the main town of a region that borders both Tibet and Nepal. It sits in a small valley that has been called 'Little Kashmir' and there are a number of picturesque walks in the area. You can climb up to **Chandak** (seven km) for a view of the Pithoragarh Valley.

There's a KMVN *Tourist Rest House* here, with doubles from Rs 50, and several other hotels. There are buses to Almora, Naini Tal, Haldwani, Delhi and Tanakpur (the railhead, 158 km south).

KAUSANI
Telephone Area Code: 059628
For an even closer view of the Himalaya, Kausani, 53 km north of Almora, is the place to head for. At 1890 metres, it's a peaceful village that is perfect for quiet contemplation. Gandhi stayed at the Anasakti Ashram in 1929 and was inspired by the superb Himalayan panorama, and the Hindi poet laureate Sumitra Nandan Pant grew up here.

Among the numerous hikes in the area, the 14-km walk to the 12th-century temples at **Baijnath** is definitely worth it. Don't follow the road, as it's six km further, but ask for the path through the forest.

Places to Stay & Eat

The best views are from the places up the ridge from the bus stop. You can stay at *Anasakti Ashram* (Gandhi Ashram) for Rs 50 and it has a good library that is open to all, and an indicator on the terrace that's useful for mountain identification. Nearby is the upmarket *Krishna Mountain View* (☎ 4108) with doubles for Rs 450 and a 40% off-season discount. The *Hotel Prashant* next door is much cheaper with basic singles from Rs 50; and a good four-bed room with mountain views and attached bathroom for Rs 300. The *Amar Holiday Home* and the *Hotel Jeetu* beside the Hotel Prashant are similarly priced.

Cheaper places on the other side of the ridge include the *New Pines Hotel* and the *Old Pines Hotel*, with doubles for Rs 50. Below the TV mast, the *Hill Queen Restaurant* is a recommended place to eat.

The KMVN *Tourist Rest House* (☎ 4106) is a couple of km beyond the village. It's very good value and has doubles from Rs 75 with great views, balconies and hot water, as well as some cottages for Rs 175 and dorm beds for Rs 20.

Getting There & Away

Kathgodam is the nearest railhead and there are buses from Kausani to Almora (Rs 20, two hours), Ranikhet (Rs 26, 3½ hours) and Naini Tal (Rs 45, five hours).

OTHER TOWNS
Bareilly
Population: 669,000

The former capital of the region known as Rohilkand, Bareilly came under British control when the Rohillas, an Afghan tribe, became too involved with the Marathas and the Nawab of Avadh.

Banbassa

Banbassa is the closest Indian village to the Nepalese border post of Mahendrenagar, and it's possible to enter Nepal at this point. There are daily buses from Delhi (12 hours) and Banbassa is also connected by rail to

Bareilly. From Almora there's a daily bus leaving at 7.30 am (Rs 68, seven hours).

From Banbassa, you can catch a rickshaw (20 minutes) to the border and across to Mahendrenagar. There are direct night buses from Mahendrenagar to Kathmandu, but they take a gruelling 25 hours. The country-side is beautiful and fascinating, so it's much better to travel during the day and to break the journey at Nepalganj. If you can't get a direct bus for the nine-hour trip from Mahendrenagar to Nepalganj, take a bus to Ataria (at the junction for Dhangadhi) and from there to Nepalganj. There are plenty of buses from Nepalganj to Kathmandu (day and night journeys, 16 hours) and to Pokhara (night, 15 hours).

Rampur
Population: 267,000

In this former Rohilla state capital, the state library has a collection of old manuscripts and miniatures (some of great importance) housed in a fine building in the old fort. There's a large Jama Masjid nearby and interesting bazaars around the walls of the palace.

TREKKING IN GARHWAL & KUMAON

The whole of the Himalayan region of northern Uttar Pradesh has traditionally been referred to as the Garhwal Himal by Western trekkers and expeditions. This is something of a misnomer since Garhwal is only the western part (Kumaon is the eastern part) of this region.

Although only a handful of trekkers visit this region there are some superb trekking opportunities. Treks that follow the outer rim of the Nanda Devi Sanctuary are well worth noting including the Kuari Pass trek out of Joshimath, the trek to Rup Kund beneath Trisul (7120 metres), trekking to the Pindari Glacier to the south of the sanctuary and the recently opened Milam Glacier trek to the east of Nanda Devi (7817 metres), India's second-highest peak. It is important to note, however, that trekking in the Nanda Devi Sanctuary is still banned by the Indian government and at present there are no plans to lift this restriction.

There are also treks in the vicinity of many of the important pilgrimage sites, such as Badrinath, Yamunotri, Kedarnath, Gangotri (near the source of the Ganges) and Hem Kund close to the Valley of the Flowers.

The best time to trek in Garhwal and Kumaon is either in the pre-monsoon period from mid-May to the end of June, or from mid-September to mid-October during the post-monsoon period. In July and August the region is subject to the monsoon rains. It is however the best time to appreciate the wildflowers in the high-altitude *bugyals* (meadows) including the Valley of the Flowers.

UP Tourism's two regional subsidiaries, Garhwal Mandal Vikas Nigam (GMVN) and Kumaon Mandal Vikas Nigam (KMVN) have some information on trekking in these areas and can also organise guided treks which include most of the routes described here. For three to five people, GMVN's Rishikesh office quotes Rs 1325 per person per day including food, transport and porters. If you are trekking independently you can also rent equipment from them – sleeping bag (Rs 12), tent (Rs 35) – in Rishikesh, Uttarkashi, Joshimath, Gangotri and a number of other hill offices. Since supplies may be limited at some of the smaller branches it is advisable to rent in Rishikesh. Arranged through GMVN, porters cost Rs 350 for high-altitude treks and Rs 150 for standard treks.

Following a thaw in Indo-Chinese relations some of the hitherto closed areas, including the Milam Glacier, are now open to trekkers. Permission must be obtained in advance from the Ministry of Home Affairs, the UP government, District Magistrate or the Indo-Tibet Border Police. At present the regulations stipulate that you must be part of a group of at least four persons and your arrangements have to be made through a recognised travel agency.

The mountaineering schools in Naini Tal and Rishikesh (near the GMVN tourist office) can also help with information. You should also refer to the Lonely Planet guide *Trekking in the Indian Himalaya*.

Har-Ki-Dun Valley

The trek up the beautiful Har-Ki-Dun Valley can be undertaken from April to November. No high passes are crossed. Accommodation is available in PWD *Rest Houses* along the way and some food can be purchased in the villages. From Mussoorie take the bus to **Sankri** where you commence the trek.

Stage 1	Sankri to Taluka by jeep or 3-hour trek
Stage 2	Taluka to Osla (5-hour trek)
Stage 3	Osla to Har-Ki-Dun (4-hour trek)
Stage 4	Har-Ki-Dun to Taluka (7-hour trek)
Stage 5	Taluka to Sankri by jeep or 3-hour trek

During July and August it would be possible to cross from Har-Ki-Dun Valley to Yamunotri via the Majhakanda Pass. The trail starts at Osla and since it's sometimes difficult to follow, it's advisable to hire a guide there. Osla to Yamunotri takes three to four days.

Dodi Tal

From Uttarkashi, take the bus to the roadhead at Kalyani from where you trek to the Forest Rest House at **Agoda** the same day. The following day you reach Dodi Tal (3310 metres) where there is another Forest Rest House. The lake (filled with trout) is set in a forest of oak, pine, deodar and rhododendron. From Dodi Tal it is possible to extend the trek by traversing the Sonpara Pass (3950 metres) that leads to Hanumanchatti near to Yamunotri, where there are buses to Mussoorie and Rishikesh.

Stage 1	Kalyani to Agoda (3-hour trek)
Stage 2	Agoda to Dodi Tal (5-hour trek)
Stage 3	Dodi Tal/Sonpara Pass/alpine camp (6-hour trek)
Stage 4	Alpine camp to Hanumanchatti (6-hour trek)

Gangotri & Gaumukh

The popular pilgrimage destination of Gangotri can be reached from Rishikesh by bus via Tehri and Uttarkashi, a 10 to 12-hour journey. There are also some buses from Mussoorie. The trek to the source of the holy Ganges starts from the tiny village of

Gangotri (3140 metres). The temple of the goddess Ganga is on the right bank of the Bhagirathi River, which eventually becomes the holy Ganges. Gaumukh, the actual source of the river, is at the base of the Bhagirathi peaks.

At 4225 metres, the Gangotri Glacier is nearly 24 km long and two to four km wide. The glacier has gradually retreated over the centuries, but during the Vedic period it is believed to have extended as far as Gangotri.

At **Bhujbasa** there's a *Tourist Bungalow* and restaurant. During the high season they charge Rs 60 for a bed in the tents, Rs 75 in the dorm, and Rs 200 for a double. During the monsoon period from July to mid-September the rates drop to Rs 48, Rs 60 and Rs 160 respectively. From here it takes about an hour to reach Gaumukh and it's worth continuing for a further four hours to the camp at **Tapovan** where you gain excellent views of Bhagirathi Parbat (6856 metres), Shivling (6543 metres) and Sudarshan (6507 metres) across the valley.

Stage 1	Gangotri to Chibasa (4-hour trek)	
Stage 2	Chibasa to Gaumukh (4-hour trek)	
Stage 3	Gaumukh to Tapovan (4-hour trek)	
Stage 4	Tapovan to Chibasa (4 to 5-hour trek)	
Stage 5	Chibasa to Gangotri (3-hour trek)	

From Gangotri it's also possible to trek up to **Kedar Tal**. Although this takes only two days, acclimatisation is necessary as this glacial lake is at 4500 metres.

Kedarnath

Like Badrinath, this is an important Hindu pilgrimage centre. The temple of Kedar (Siva) is surrounded by snowcapped peaks, and is said to date back to the 8th century.

To get to Kedarnath you can either make the short, direct trek from **Sonprayag**, 205 km north-east of Rishikesh, or you can follow the longer and more arduous yatra (pilgrimage) route from Gangotri. Along the way you pass through beautiful scenery and many colourful mountain villages. The trek starts from Malla, 20 km beyond Uttarkashi towards Gangotri.

Day 1	Malla to Belak Khal	15 km
Day 2	Belak Khal to Budakedar	14 km
Day 3	Budakedar to Ghuttu	16 km*
Day 4	Ghuttu to Panwali Khanta	12 km
Day 5	Panwali Khanta to Maggu	8 km
Day 6	Maggu to Sonprayag	9 km
Day 7	Sonprayag to Kedarnath	20 km**
Day 8	Kedarnath to Sonprayag	20 km**

* It's possible to set out from Tehri, getting a bus from there to Ghuttu (three hours), which will shorten the trek by three days.

** Taxis are available for the five km between Sonprayag and Gaurikund, on the route to Kedarnath.

Badrinath, Valley of Flowers & Hem Kund

The beautiful Valley of Flowers National Park and the holy Hem Kund lake can be reached from Govind Ghat. In addition, you can visit the pilgrimage centre of Badrinath on the same trip. From Rishikesh it is 252 km (10 hours) by bus to Joshimath, where there's a *Tourist Bungalow* and hotels, and a further 44 km to Badrinath. You then have to backtrack 30 km to **Govind Ghat** for the start of the trek. From June to September the trail up to Hem Kund Sahib is crowded with Sikh pilgrims.

Surrounded by snowcapped peaks, Badrinath, just a short distance from the Tibetan border, has been a Hindu pilgrimage centre since time immemorial. There are many temples, ashrams and dharamsalas here, attracting crowds of pilgrims. The most important temple, on the left bank of the Alakananda, shows clear Buddhist influence in its architecture, indicating that in an earlier period this must also have been a Buddhist centre. The temple is open between May and October and there is a *Tourist Bungalow* here.

The mountaineer Frank Smythe is believed to be the 'discoverer' of the Valley of Flowers. Between mid-June and mid-September the valley is an enchanting sight with a dazzling array of wildflowers. As a backdrop, snow-clad mountains stand in bold relief against the skyline. The valley is nearly 10 km long and two km wide, and is divided by the Pushpawati Stream, into which several tiny streams and waterfalls merge. The valley has suffered from large numbers of trekkers and shepherds in the past and was recently turned into a national park. The current stipulation allows trekkers to camp or stay at the Tourist Rest House at **Ghangaria** (seven hours from Govind Ghat) and take day walks into the valley. No overnight camping is permitted.

From Ghangaria, you can follow the Laxma Ganga to the lake of Hem Kund – quite a steep climb (eight hours return). In the Sikh holy book, the *Granth Sahib*, the Sikh Guru Gobind Singh recounts that in a previous life he had meditated on the shores of a lake surrounded by seven snowcapped mountains. Hem Kund Sahib, Sikh pilgrims have decided, is that holy lake, and so you'll see them plunging into the icy waters!

Pindari Glacier

The Pindari Glacier is the most easily accessible in the region, flowing from Nanda Kot (6861 metres) and Nanda Khat (6611 metres) on the southern rim of the Nanda Devi Sanctuary. The glacier, three km long and nearly half a km wide, is at an altitude of 3350 metres.

This popular trek passes pine forests, fern glades and tumbling waterfalls. From mid-May to mid-June there are many wildflowers, while from mid-September to mid-October the air is exceptionally clear.

From Naini Tal there's an early-morning bus to **Song**, a km or so before Loarkhet. If you are not camping you should book your rest house accommodation at the Tourist Rest House in Bageshwar (☎ 2234), which is about 30 km before Song. You can stay the night at Bageshwar or there's alternative accommodation in Bharari (15 km further on), and you can catch a bus or jeep the next day from either place to Song.

The trek from Song through Loarkhet and up to the Dhakuri Pass is a long, hard uphill slog. Nevertheless it is a fine walk with wonderful scenery. A km or two over the pass is the *Tourist Rest House*. There is an excellent view of the glacier from **Purkiya**, where some trekkers stop. The walk from Purkiya to the Pindari Glacier and

back takes about six hours. On the return trek you can travel by road from Baijnath to Rishikesh or return via Almora to Naini Tal.

Dorm beds (Rs 25) are available at the KMVN *Tourist Rest Houses* at Loarkhet, Dhakuri, Khati, Dwali and Purkiya and there are also *PWD Bungalows* at all these places as well as at Kapkot but they tend to fill up relatively early in the day. At **Khati** there is also the small *Himalayan Hotel* (with restaurant).

Khatling Glacier

The Khatling Glacier is a lateral glacier from the centre of which the Bhilangana River emerges. The summer rains turn the flat land on the glacial moraines into excellent pasture, which makes for ideal camping sites. Around Khatling Glacier are the snow-capped peaks of the Jogin ground (6466 metres), spectacular Sphetic Prishtwan (6905 metres), Kirti Stambh (6402 metres) and Barte Kanta (6579 metres).

Ghuttu, the starting point of the trek, is three hours by bus from Tehri which is five hours from Rishikesh. There are hotels at Ghamsali and at Ghuttu, a *Forest Rest House* at Buranschauri (above Reeh) and at Gangi you can stay in the school shelter.

Day 1	Rishikesh/Tehri/Ghamsali	99 km*
Day 2	Ghamsali/Ghuttu/Reeh	40 km**
Day 3	Reeh to Gangi	10 km
Day 4	Gangi to Khansoli	15 km
Day 5	Khansoli to Khatling	11 km
Day 6	Khatling to Naumuthi	9 km
Day 7	Naumuthi to Kalyani	12 km
Day 8	Kalyani to Reeh	15 km
Day 9	Reeh/Ghuttu/Ghamsali	40 km**
Day 10	Ghamsali/Tehri/Rishikesh	99 km*

* by bus
** 30 km by bus

Nanda Devi Sanctuary

Some of the most outstanding peaks in the central Himalaya are clustered between the glaciers of Gangotri and Milam. Nanda Devi, with its camel-humped summit, is the most important peak at 7871 metres. The Nanda Devi Sanctuary is surrounded by almost 70 white peaks which form a natural fortress, enclosing an area of 640 sq km. It's dotted with meadows and waterfalls and is the base camp for mountaineering attempts on Nanda Devi.

Unfortunately, this national park is currently closed to trekkers and it is not known when (or even if) it will reopen. Contact KMVN for more information.

Kuari Pass – the Curzon Trail

The route from Joshimath to the Kuari Pass is also known as the Curzon Trail – named after Lord Curzon, an enthusiastic Himalayan hiker. However, this is a bit of a misnomer since the Curzon party did not actually cross the Kuari Pass, abandoning their attempt after being attacked by wild bees.

There are two approaches to the pass. The most established trail leads from the village of Tapovan while the other meanders through the meadows from Auli, a small village above Joshimath. Nonetheless the Auli route is preferable for the bird's-eye view up the Rishi Ganga into the Nanda Devi Sanctuary.

On the approach to Kuari Pass the summit of Dunagiri (7066 metres) features prominently on the north rim of the Nanda Devi Sanctuary while Chaukhamba (7138 metres) and the rest of the impressive Chaukhamba range can be seen above Joshimath. To gain the best views of Nanda Devi (7817 metres) requires a day's walk along the ridge above the pass.

From the Kuari Pass it is a steep descent to the meadow at Dakwani before continuing to the shepherd camp at Sutoli. From there the trail crosses forested ridges and passes small villages high above the Birthi Ganga to the village of **Ramni**. From here it is a further stage down to the roadhead at Ghat where jeeps and buses complete the 30 km to Nandprayag on the Joshimath to Rishikesh road.

Stage 1	Auli to Chitragandta (6 to 7 hours)
Stage 2	Chitragandta to base of Kuari Pass (3 to 4 hours)
Stage 3	Camp to Sutoli (4 to 5 hours)
Stage 4	Sutoli to Ghangri (5 hours)
Stage 5	Ghangri to Ramni (5 to 6 hours)
Stage 6	Ramni to Ghat (3 to 4 hours)

Rup Kund

At an altitude of 4778 metres and set beneath the towering summit of Trisul (7120 metres), Rup Kund is sometimes referred to as the 'mystery lake' on account of the skeletons of humans found there. Every 12 years, thousands of devout pilgrims make an arduous trek when following the Raj Jay Yatra from Nauti village, near Karnaprayag. The pilgrims are said to be led by a four-horned ram which takes them from here to Rup Kund. A golden idol of the goddess Nanda Devi is carried by the pilgrims in a silver palanquin.

The small market town of Gwalden is 78 km from Almora or 131 km from Naini Tal and there are bus connections to Tharali. From Tharali there is a daily bus or jeep to Mandoli.

The first stage of the trek is to **Wan** (four to five hours) where there is a *Forest Rest House*. From here there is a steep climb to the camp at **Badni Bugyal** (five hours). The views from this alpine camp are among the finest in the west Himalaya. To the east are the peaks beyond Joshimath, while to the south-east the main Himalaya range extends as far as the eye can see towards the western Garhwal. To the south the foothills descend to the Indian plains, while to the north Trisul provides an impressive backdrop.

It's a further four to five-hour walk to the camp at **Bhogabasa** and from there Rup Kund can be reached with time to return to Badni Bugyal the same day. From Badni Bugyal there is a short cut back to the trail between Lohajang and Wan and the route back to Mandoli.

Extensions to this route include a challenging trek over the Jyuri Gali to Hom Kund. Alternatively the trek can be extended from Wan by two stages to Ramni and on to the Kuari Pass and Joshimath.

SKIING IN UTTAR PRADESH
Auli

This skiing resort, the best equipped in the country, boasts five-km-long slopes which drop from an altitude of 3049 metres to 2519 metres. Prospective travellers in the cable car will be reassured to learn from the glossy

Auli ski resort brochure that it incorporates 'remote controlled hydrauwlic and pneumetic braking system...electronic circuitry with telemetry and storm warning devices to minimise human error'. There's also a 500-metre ski lift.

Open from January to March, Auli is 15 km from Joshimath. GMVN operates the resort and has *Tourist Rest Houses* at Joshimath (☎ (01389) 2118) and Auli (☎ (013712) 2226). Skis and boots can be hired here (Rs 100 per day) and seven or 14-day ski courses are offered for Rs 1600/2800.

Central Uttar Pradesh

ALIGARH
Population: 528,000

Formerly known as Koil, this was the site of an important fort as far back as 1194. During the upheavals following the death of Aurangzeb and the collapse of the Mughal Empire, the region was fought for by the Afghans, Jats, Marathas and Rohillas – first one coming out on top, then another. Renamed Aligarh (High Fort) in 1776, it fell to the British in 1803, despite French support for its ruler Scindia. The **fort** is three km north of the town, and in its present form dates from 1524.

Aligarh is best known today for the **Aligarh Muslim University** where the 'seeds of Pakistan were sown'. Muslim students come here not just from India but from all over the Islamic world.

ETAWAH

This town rose to some importance during the Mughal period, only to go through the usual series of rapid changes during the turmoil that followed the Mughals. The **Jama Masjid** shows similarities to the mosques of Jaunpur, and there are **bathing ghats** on the riverbank, below the ruined fort.

KANNAUJ

Only a few dismal ruins indicate that this was once a mighty Hindu city, the capital of the region in the 7th century (AD). It quickly fell into disrepair after Mahmud of Ghazni's raids. This was where Humayun was defeated by Sher Shah in 1540, forcing him to temporarily flee India. There's not much to see now – just an archaeological museum, a mosque and the ruins of the fort.

KANPUR
Population: 2,320,000
Telephone Area Code: 0512

Although Lucknow is the capital of Uttar Pradesh, Kanpur (79 km south west) is the largest city in the state. A major business and industrial centre on the Ganges, it attracts very few tourists.

During the 1857 Mutiny, some of the more tragic events took place here when the city was known as Cawnpore, the headquarters of a large Indian garrison. General Sir Hugh Wheeler defended a part of the cantonment for most of the month of June but, with supplies virtually exhausted and having suffered considerable losses, he surrendered to Nana Sahib, only to be massacred with most of his party at Sati Chaura Ghat. Over 100 women and children were taken hostage and imprisoned in a small room. Just before relief arrived on 17th July, they were murdered and the dismembered bodies thrown down a well.

General Neill, their avenger, behaved just as sadistically as Nana Sahib. Some of the mutineers he captured were made to drink the English blood that still lay in a deep pool in the murder chamber, before they were executed. Others suffered what must have been regarded as a far worse fate for a Hindu or Muslim – being force-fed beef or pork.

Things to See

The site of **General Wheeler's entrenchment**, two km from the station, can be visited. Nearby is **All Souls' Memorial Church**, completed in 1875, which has some rather moving reminders of the tragic events of the Mutiny. There are also several temples, none of them very old, the most interesting being **JK Glass Temple**. This is actually made of white marble but has some unusual glass statues. Kanpur also has a large zoo.

The main shopping centre, **Navin Market**, is famous for its locally produced cotton goods. The main leather market is on Matson Rd and articles such as bags and shoes are very cheap.

Places to Stay & Eat

Kanpur has a large range of accommodation mainly centred along The Mall and around the railway station. The *Hotel Ganges* (☎ 35-2962), with a good vegetarian restaurant, is a cheap place near the station, and has rooms from Rs 200.

The *Yatrik Hotel* (☎ 26-0373), which has singles/doubles for Rs 100/150 and air-con rooms for 225/275 is also near the station. On Civil Lines the small but popular *Attic* has similarly priced, air-con rooms.

Middle-range hotels include the *Geet Hotel* (☎ 21-1024) and the *Hotel Gaurav* (☎ 26-9599), both on The Mall, and the *Hotel Swagat* (☎ 24-1923) with air-con rooms for Rs 250/320 at 80 Feet Road. The *Grand Trunk Hotel* on Grand Trunk Road is more expensive.

The best hotel in town is the *Hotel Meghdoot* (☎ 31-1999; fax 31-0209) on The Mall with air-con singles/doubles for Rs 700/900 and three expensive restaurants, which local people rate as the best place for Mughlai cuisine.

Getting There & Away

Kanpur is on the main Delhi to Calcutta railway line and less than five hours from Delhi on the *Shatabdi* or *Rajdhani Express* (air-con chair car is the cheapest ticket on both these trains, at Rs 365 and Rs 375 respectively). Other expresses take five to six hours from Delhi to Kanpur (435 km, Rs 118/352 in 2nd/1st class).

There are also direct rail links to Calcutta (16 to 25 hours, 1007 km), Bombay (24 hours, 1342 km), Agra (six hours, 254 km), Allahabad (3½ hours, 192 km) and Varanasi

(five hours, 329 km). By train, Lucknow takes 1½ hours on the *Shatabdi* (Rs 120 in air-con chair class), or just over two hours by ordinary express (Rs 22 in 2nd class) and there's also a frequent bus service.

JHANSI

Situated at the neck of a 'peninsula' of Uttar Pradesh which is almost entirely surrounded by Madhya Pradesh, Jhansi is a major transport hub for the north of that state. As it is also the most popular transit point for Khajuraho, we have included Jhansi in the Madhya Pradesh chapter. For details, see the Northern Madhya Pradesh section of that chapter.

LUCKNOW

Population: 1,800,000
Telephone Area Code: 0522

The capital of Uttar Pradesh, Lucknow rose to prominence as the capital city of the nawabs of Avadh. These ultimately decadent Muslim rulers controlled a region of north-central India for about a century after the decline of the Mughal Empire, and most of the interesting monuments in Lucknow date from this period. The nawabs were:

Burhan-ul-mulk	1724-39
Safdar Jang	1739-53
Shuja-ud-Daula	1753-75
Asaf-ud-Daula	1775-97
Sa'adat Ali Khan	1798-1814
Ghazi-ud-din Haidar	1814-27
Nasir-ud-din Haidar	1827-37
Mohammad Ali Shah	1837-42
Amjad Ali Shah	1842-47
Wajid Ali Shah	1847-56

It was not until Asaf-ud-Daula that the capital of Avadh was moved to Lucknow from Faizabad. Safdar Jang lived in and ruled from Delhi and his tomb is a familiar landmark near Delhi's Safdarjang Airport. After Sa'adat Ali Khan the rest of the Avadh nawabs were uniformly hopeless at running affairs of state. Wajid Ali Shah was so extravagant and indolent that to this day his name is regarded by many in India as synonymous with lavishness. However the nawabs were

UTTAR PRADESH

great patrons of the arts, especially dance and music, and Lucknow's reputation as a city of culture and gracious living stems from this time.

In 1856 the British annexed Avadh, exiling the incompetent Wajid Ali Shah to a palace in Calcutta with an annual pension of UK£120,000. Satyajit Ray's 1977 film *The Chess Players* was based on these events. It was not a box-office success, suggesting as it did that Indians had themselves to blame for the British move. The annexation was one of the sparks that in 1857 lit the Indian Mutiny (or Uprising, as Indians understandably prefer to call it). Lucknow became the scene for some of the most dramatic events of the Mutiny, as the British residents held out in the Residency for 87 harrowing days, only to be besieged again for a further two months after being relieved.

The huge crumbling mausoleums of the nawabs and the pock-marked ruins of the Residency make Lucknow an interesting place to visit. However, it's not really on the tourist trail which makes a stay even more worthwhile. It's recently become popular with Western followers of the octogenarian guru, Poonjaji, who spends some of the year here. If you're interested, contact the Carlton Hotel to see if he's in town.

Orientation

Lucknow is rather spread out and there is quite a distance between the various places of interest. The historic monuments are mainly in the north-eastern part of the old city around the Chowk area. The main shopping area, with its narrow alleys, is Aminabad, while the modern area with wide avenues and large shops is the fashionable Hazratganj.

Information

Tourist information is available at the Hotel Gomti from UP Tours which runs the half-day sightseeing tour (Rs 60, departing 8.30 am). The tourist office (☎ 24-6205) is hidden down an alley opposite the Hotel Kohinoor at 10/4 Station Rd and there's a branch in the main railway station building.

There's a British library (☎ 24-2144) in the Mayfair Building in Hazratganj. The Universal Bookseller at 82 Hazratganj is an excellent bookshop as is the British Bookshop opposite. Ram Advani's bookshop, next to the Mayfair Cinema on Hazratganj, is another good one.

Bara Imambara

The Bara or Great Imambara (an *imambara* is the tomb of a Shi'ite Muslim holy man) was built in 1784 by Asaf-ud-Daula as a famine-relief project. The central hall of the Imambara, 50 metres long and 15 metres high, is one of the largest vaulted galleries in the world. An external stairway leads to an upper floor laid out as an amazing labyrinth known as the *bhulbhulaiya*, where a guide may be useful. From the top there's a fine view over the city and the Aurangzeb Mosque. Entry is Rs 5 and includes a visit to the ancient well *(baoli)* and to Rumi Darwaza.

There's a mosque with two tall minarets in the courtyard of the Imambara but non-Muslims are not allowed in. To the right of this, in a row of cloisters, is the baoli, the 'bottomless' well. The Imambara is open from 6 am to 5 pm.

Rumi (Roomi) Darwaza

Beside the Bara Imambara and also built by Asaf-ud-Daula, this huge and finely designed *darwaza* (gate) is a replica of one in Istanbul. 'Rumi' (relating to Rome) is the term Muslims applied to Istanbul when it was still Byzantium, the capital of the eastern Roman Empire.

Lakshman Tila

This high ground on the right bank of the River Gomti was the original site of the town which became known as Lucknau in the 15th century. Aurangzeb's Mosque now stands on this site.

Hussainabad Imambara

Also known as the Chhota, or Small Imambara, this was built by Muhammad Ali Shah in 1837 to serve as his own mausoleum. Thousands of labourers worked on the

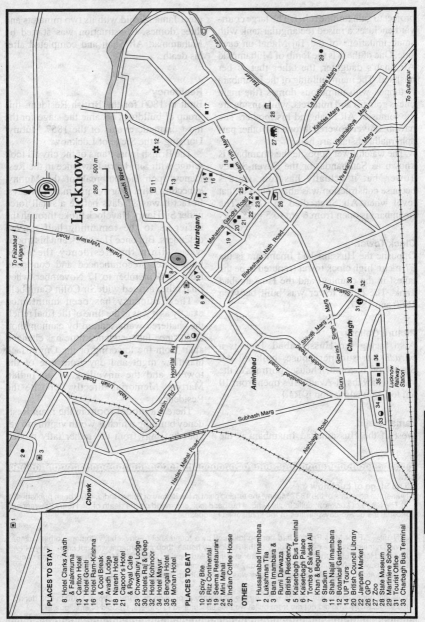

Lucknow

0 250 500 m

Gomti River

To Faizabad
& Aligani

Chowk

Aminabad

Hazratganj

Charbagh

Lucknow
Railway
Station

Vishwa Vidyalaya Road

Nabi Ullah Road

J. Narain Rd

Hospital Rd

Subhash Marg

Nadan Mahal Road

Aishbagh Road

Mahatma Gandhi Road

Bisheshwar Nath Road

Buddha Road

Shivaji Marg

Govind Singh Marg

Guru

Station Rd

Ram Tirth Marg

Kalidas Marg

Vikramadhya Marg

La Martiniere Marg

Vivekanand Marg

Central Jhulel

To Sultanpur

PLACES TO STAY

8 Hotel Clarks Avadh
 & Falakmuna
12 Carlton Hotel
14 Hotel Gomti
16 Hotel Ram-Krishna
 & Cool Break
17 Avadh Lodge
18 Naresh Hotel
21 Capoor's Hotel
 & Royal Cafe
23 Chowdhury Lodge
30 Hotels Raj & Deep
32 Hotel Kohinoor
34 Hotel Mayur
35 Bengali Hotel
36 Mohan Hotel

PLACES TO EAT

10 Spicy Bite
15 Ritz Continental
19 Seema Restaurant
24 Mini Mahal
25 Indian Coffee House

OTHER

1 Hussainabad Imambara
2 Lakshman Tila
3 Bara Imambara &
 Rumi Darwaza
4 British Residency
5 Kaiserbagh Bus Terminal
6 Kaiserbagh Palace
7 Tombs of Sa'adat Ali
 Khan & Begum
9 Stadium
11 Shah Najaf Imambara
13 Botanical Gardens
14 UP Tours
20 British Council Library
22 Janpath Market
26 GPO
27 Zoo
28 State Museum
29 Martinière School
31 Tourist Office
33 Charbagh Bus Terminal

UTTAR PRADESH

project to gain famine relief. The large court-yard encloses a raised rectangular tank with small imitations of the Taj Mahal on each side. One of them is the tomb of Muhammad Ali Shah's daughter, the other that of her husband. The main building of the Imambara is topped with numerous domes (the main one is golden) and minarets, while inside are the tombs of Ali Shah and his mother. The nawab's silver-covered throne and other par-aphernalia of state are here.

The watchtower opposite the Imambara is known as Satkhanda, or the Seven-Storey Tower, but it actually has four storeys because construction was abandoned at that level when Ali Shah died in 1840. The Imambara is open from 6 am to 5 pm.

Clock Tower
Opposite the Hussainabad Imambara is the 67-metre-high clock tower (reputed to be the tallest in the country) and the Hussainabad Tank. The clock tower was built between 1880 and 1887.

Picture Gallery
Also facing the Hussainabad Tank is a *baradari* or summer house, built by Ali Shah. Now restored, it houses portraits of the various nawabs of Avadh. It's open from 10 am to 5 pm; admission is Rs 1.

Jama Masjid
West of the Hussainabad Imambara is the great Jama Masjid with its two minarets and three domes. Construction was started by Muhammad Ali Shah and completed after his death.

Residency
Built in 1800 for the British Resident, this group of buildings became the stage for the most dramatic events of the 1857 Mutiny/Uprising – the Siege of Lucknow.

The British inhabitants of the city all took refuge with Sir Henry Lawrence in the Res-idency upon the outbreak of the Mutiny, expecting relief to arrive in a matter of days. In fact it was 87 days before a small force under Sir Henry Havelock broke through the besiegers to the remaining half-starved defenders. But once Havelock and his troops were within the Residency the siege immediately recommenced and continued from 25 September to 17 November, when final relief arrived with Sir Colin Campbell.

The Residency has been maintained exactly as it was at the time of the final relief, the shattered walls scarred by cannon shot. Even since Independence little has changed apart from the lowering of the Union Jack that flew night and day from one of the towers, and the unveiling of an Indian Martyrs' Memorial directly opposite the Residency.

There's a **model room** in the main Resi-dency building which is worth visiting to get your bearings from the rather tatty model.

The Siege of Lucknow
Numerous accounts of the 1857 Mutiny, the turning point in the history of British India, have been published. In *The Siege of Lucknow*, Julia Inglis (whose husband took command on the death of Sir Henry Lawrence) records the day-to-day activities of the imprisoned Europeans:

July 1st – ...Poor Miss Palmer had her leg taken off by a round shot to-day, she, with some other ladies, having remained in the second storey of the Residency house, though warned it was not safe... July 4th – Poor Sir Henry (Lawrence) died to-day, after suffering fearful pain... July 8th – Mr Polehampton, one of our chaplains, was shot through the body to-day whilst shaving... October 1st – I was with Mrs Couper nearly all day, watching her baby dying...My baby was ill today. Sharp musketry firing at 10 am.

With stiff upper lip the Europeans watched the Residency population drop from almost 3000 to 980 during the siege. Many who did not die from bullet wounds succumbed to cholera, typhoid or smallpox. ■

Downstairs you can see the cellars where many of the women and children lived throughout the siege. The **cemetery** at the nearby ruined church has the graves of 2000 men, women and children, including that of Sir Henry Lawrence, 'who tried to do his duty' (according to the famous inscription on his weathered gravestone).

The whole place would make an excellent film set and indeed during the winter months there's supposed to be a sound & light show here. There are no set opening hours for the Residency but the model room is open only from 9 am to 5.30 pm. Admission is free to the Residency gardens, Rs 1 to the model room, except on Fridays when it's free.

Shah Najaf Imambara

Opposite the Carlton Hotel, this mausoleum takes its name from Najaf, the town 190 km south-west of Baghdad in Iraq where Hazrat Ali, the Shi'ite Muslim leader, is buried. The Imambara is the tomb of Ghazi-ud-din Haidar Khan, who died in 1827. His wives are also buried here. This was the scene of desperate fighting in November 1857 during the second relief of Lucknow.

The domed exterior is comparatively plain, but inside are chandeliers and it's said that at one time the dome was covered with gold. The building is used to store *tazia*, elaborate creations of wood, bamboo and silver paper which are carried through the streets at Muharram, the festival which commemorates the martyrdom of Mohammed's grandson, Iman Hussain. They are usually models of the Kerbala in Iraq. Many precious items from the mausoleum were looted following the Mutiny. The Imambara is open from 8 am to 5 pm.

Martiniere School

Outside the town is this strange school built by the Frenchman Major-General Claude Martin. Taken prisoner at Pondicherry in 1761, he joined the East India Company's army, then in 1776 entered service with the Nawab of Avadh, while at the same time maintaining his East India Company connections. He quickly made a substantial fortune

from his dual occupations of soldier and businessman, and started to build a palatial home which he named Constantia.

Martin designed much of the building himself, and his architectural abilities were, to say the least, a little mixed – Gothic gargoyles were piled merrily atop Corinthian columns to produce a finished product which a British marquess sarcastically pronounced was inspired by a wedding cake. Martin died in 1800 before his stately home could be completed, but left the money and directions that it should become a school. He now keeps watch from his tomb in the basement.

'Kim', the boy hero of Kipling's story of the same name, went to school here, and there are similar establishments, also financed from Martin's fortune, in Calcutta and Lyon, France. The school can be visited but you should get permission from the Principal first. It's still run like a British private school – the boys sing hymns in chapel every morning even though, a teacher reported with almost a tinge of regret, 'very few of them are Christians'.

Other Attractions

The **Kaiserbagh Palace** was built for Nawab Wajid Ali Shah in 1850. Nearby, are the stone **tombs** of Sa'adat Ali and his wife. There is also a summer house in the well-kept garden. The **State Museum** (open 10.30 am to 4.30 pm, closed on Monday) is in the Banarsi Bagh. The **zoo**, founded in 1921, is also here and has a large collection of snakes. It is open from 5 am to 7 pm.

Sikandarbagh, the scene of pitched battles in November 1857, is now the home of the **National Botanical Research Institute**. The excellent botanical gardens are open from 6 am to 5 pm. General Havelock, who led the first relief of Lucknow, has his grave and memorial in the **Alambagh**, three km south of the railway station.

Nadan Mahal is the tomb of the first governor of Avadh appointed by Akbar, and it is one of the earliest buildings in Lucknow, dating from around 1600. Other buildings nearby include the small **Sola Khamba Pavilion** and the **tomb of Ibrahim Chisti**.

UTTAR PRADESH

Festivals

Local people say that these days it is only during the **Lucknow Festival** in February that something of the old Mughal-era returns. There are processions, plays, *kathak* dancing, *ghazal* and sitar recitals as well as kite-flying and cock-fighting during the 10-day festival of nostalgia.

Lucknow is a good place to see the **Shi'ite Muharram** celebrations (dates vary from year to year; see the boxed Holidays section in the Facts for the Visitor chapter and Sacred India colour section on page 57) since it has been the principal Indian Shi'ite city since the nawabs arrived. The other major Muslim cities like Delhi and Agra are mainly Sunnite. The activity during Muharram, which centres on the Bara Imambara, can get very hectic as penitents scourge themselves with whips; keep a low profile.

Places to Stay – bottom end

Don't get caught out by the 24-hour checkout which most Lucknow hotels operate.

Best value in the railway station area has to be the *retiring rooms* at Rs 25 for a dorm bed or doubles from Rs 50 to Rs 150 with air-con. There are numerous hotels in the vicinity but many are noisy and overpriced. The *Bengali Hotel* (☎ 55-819), has very basic singles/doubles at Rs 90/140 with bath.

There are clean dorm beds for Rs 40 in the expensive-looking *Mohan Hotel* (☎ 54-216) and there's also an air-cooled dorm here (Rs 50 per bed). This hotel has a wide range of accommodation and prices. On the roof the singles/doubles at Rs 80/140 may not seem great value with no bathroom attached but they're clean and quiet, and are arranged around a courtyard.

Along the road between the station and Hazratganj there's the *Deep Hotel* (☎ 23-6521) with rooms from Rs 140/180 with attached bath to Rs 280/360 with air-con, but it's on a very noisy stretch of road. Nearby, the *Hotel Raj* has a similar range of rooms that cost a few rupees more.

Most travellers head for the Hazratganj area. *Chowdhury Lodge* down a little alley opposite the GPO is a popular place with singles from Rs 55 (Rs 90 with bath), doubles with bathroom from Rs 130, or with air-coolers for Rs 150/190. The rooms are OK and there's an annexe nearby.

There are several places along Ram Tirth Marg, a lane which runs through a pleasant market area. The *Pal Hotel* has a friendly manager and the rooms are good value at Rs 80/100 with attached bathroom. Also in Hazratganj, there's the *Hotel Ram-Krishna* (☎ 23-2653) with air-cooled rooms from Rs 125/170, and a good restaurant.

The *Avadh Lodge* (☎ 28-2861) at 1 Ram Mohan Rai Marg is a great old place with vast, tatty rooms and marble floors. Unfortunately the previous owner was a pretty good shot and large quantities of the local fauna, including the now rare gharial (fish-eating crocodile), decorate the walls. It's an interesting place to stay in a quiet area and rooms cost Rs 150/180 to Rs 280/375 (with air-con). The rooms vary widely, so ask to see more than one before deciding. Tempos run from the station to Sikhandarbagh which is a short walk away.

Centrally located on Hazratganj, *Capoor's* (☎ 24-3958; fax 23-4023) is a long-established hotel with good air-cooled rooms with attached bath and TV for Rs 180/250 – it's good value.

Places to Stay – middle & top end

In the Hazratganj area near the Hotel Gomti is the *Carlton Hotel* (☎ 24-4021; fax 24-9793) which was once a palace and is still an impressive building with a musty air of decaying elegance. The large gardens around the hotel make this a wonderfully relaxing place to stay. Rooms cost from Rs 350/450 to Rs 500/850 (with air-con). It's popular with Westerners and often full.

UP Tourism's big *Hotel Gomti* (☎ 23-4708) is rather shabby, and indifferently run. Rooms are Rs 250/275 to Rs 550/650 (with air-con). A bed in the air-cooled dorm costs Rs 45.

The *Hotel Kohinoor* (☎ 23-2715) is a modern place one km from the railway station and charges Rs 450/650 for air-con singles/doubles.

Lucknow Cuisine

The refined palates of the nawabs have left Lucknow with a reputation for rich Mughlai cuisine. The city is famous for its wide range of kebabs and for *dum pukht* – the 'art' of steam pressure cooking, in which meat and vegetables are cooked in a sealed clay pot. Huge paper-thin chapatis *(rumali roti)* are served in many small Muslim restaurants in the old city. They arrive folded up and should be eaten with a goat or lamb curry like bhuna ghosht or roghan josh. *Kulfi falooda*, ice cream with cornflour noodles, is a popular dessert, and there are several places in Aminabad that serve it. The sweet orange-coloured rice dish known as *zarda* is also popular. In the hot months of May and June, Lucknow has some of the world's finest mangoes, particularly the wonderful *dashhari* variety grown in the village of Malihabad, west of the city. ■

The *Hotel Clarks Avadh* (☎ 24-0131; fax 23-6507) may look like an apartment block but it's Lucknow's best hotel. It's the only real 'international' standard hotel in fact, but service and facilities don't match the prices and there's no pool. Singles/doubles start at Rs 1195/2000.

Places to Eat

The *refreshment room* in Lucknow Junction station is good value and there are also numerous cheap places to eat in the alleys across the road.

In Hazratganj there's a fair selection of places. The *Indian Coffee House* is where the local intelligentsia used to meet over a coffee and snack – the masala dosas are good. There are several Chinese restaurants in Hazratganj including the *Hong Kong Restaurant* where the food is not bad. Near the Hotel Ram-Krishna is the *Ritz Continental*, a trendy vegetarian restaurant serving pizza (Rs 30 to Rs 50), masala dosas and sweets. Just round the corner is the *Cool Break*, a small, air-con fast-food place which is currently very popular.

In the Hotel Elora is *Seema Restaurant* which serves good food at reasonable prices – main dishes are around Rs 20. The *Royal Cafe* in Capoor's Hotel is slightly more expensive but the food is also good. Close by is the *Mini Mahal*, a popular place for ice creams and snacks, and there's a Chinese restaurant upstairs.

Spicy Bite, in the Tulsi Theatre Building, is rated very highly by locals. It offers pizzas (Rs 30), burgers and Chinese food (main dishes Rs 50) and a wide range of ice creams.

The *Baker's Hat* bakery here does good biscuits and cakes.

At the *Carlton Hotel* there's an all-you-can-eat buffet dinner for Rs 160, and this is served on the very pleasant front lawn. It's just a pity there's not enough light to see what you're eating.

For a special occasion the *Falaknuma*, in Hotel Clarks Avadh, would be the best place to try Lucknow cuisine. Main dishes are Rs 100 to Rs 140, the food is good and there are great views across the city.

Entertainment

In winter there are often excellent classical music performances and dances at the Rabindralaya auditorium, in a garden down Vidhan Sabha Marg towards the new city from Charbagh bus terminal. The Mayfair Cinema often shows English-language movies.

Things to Buy

The bazaars of Aminabad and Chowk are fascinating places to wander through, even if you're not buying. Down the narrow lanes of Aminabad you can buy *attar* – perfume made in the traditional way from essential oils which are mixed with flower fragrances. In Chowk, Nakkhas is the bird-sellers' district. Pigeon-keeping and cock-fighting have been popular since the time of the nawabs.

Several states have their government emporia in Hazratganj. The Gangotri government emporium is a good place for local handicrafts including the hand-woven embroidered cloth known as *chikan* for which Lucknow is famous. It's made into saris for women and kurtas for men. Prices are lower in Aminabad, but you have to bargain.

Getting There & Away
Air The Indian Airlines office (☎ 24-0927) is at the Hotel Clarks Avadh. There are daily connections to Delhi (US$46) and three flights a week to Patna (US$49), Calcutta (US$92) and four times weekly to Bombay (US$152) on Indian Airlines.

Sahara India Airlines connects Lucknow with Delhi on weekdays (US$46).

Bus There are two bus terminals: Charbagh near the railway station, and Kaiserbagh. You should check which bus terminal your bus leaves from as this is subject to change.

Currently from Charbagh there are several buses an hour to Kanpur (Rs 20, two hours), regular departures to Allahabad (Rs 50, six hours), early-morning buses to Varanasi (Rs 72, nine hours) and evening departures for Agra (Rs 80, 10 hours).

From Kaiserbagh there are buses to Delhi from 9 am to 10 pm (Rs 130, 12 hours); Gorakhpur (Rs 64, seven hours), Sunauli (Rs 80, 11 hours) and Faizabad (Rs 35, three hours) from 4 am to 10.30 pm.

To/From Nepal From the border at Sunauli, where you enter Nepal, it's an 11-hour, Rs 80 bus ride to Lucknow.

Train The two main stations are side by side in Charbagh: Lucknow and the mainly metre-gauge Lucknow Junction. Few trains stop at the third station, Lucknow City.

On the *Shatabdi Express*, Lucknow is only 6½ hours from Delhi (Rs 385 in air-con chair class) and 1½ hours (Rs 120) from Kanpur. Other express trains take eight to nine hours to Delhi (507 km, Rs 130/387 in 2nd/1st class), five to six hours to Gorakhpur (276 km, Rs 65/240 in 2nd/1st class, with services on broad gauge and metre gauge), 27 hours to Bombay (1414 km, Rs 259/837), 23 hours to Calcutta (979 km, Rs 208/614), 22 hours to New Jalpaiguri (for Darjeeling; 1121 km, Rs 230/714), 4½ hours to Allahabad (129

km, Rs 34/131) and three hours to Faizabad (106 km, Rs 62/122).

Varanasi is 4½ hours away on the *Himgiri Express* (three times a week), five to six hours on other expresses (301 km, Rs 90/262 in 2nd/1st). There are overnight trains to Agra (486 km, Rs 127/382 in 2nd/1st class), Dehra Dun (545 km, stopping at Haridwar) and Kathgodam (399 km) for Naini Tal.

Getting Around
To/From the Airport Amausi Airport is 15 km out of Lucknow and there's an airport bus (Rs 20) which leaves the Hotel Clarks Avadh to connect with flights. To check departure times, telephone the airport (☎ 24-4030).

Local Transport Tempos are more convenient than the buses and run along fixed routes connecting the railway station (Charbagh) with the GPO (Hazratganj), Sikandarbagh (for the botanical gardens), Kaiserbagh (for the other bus terminal) and Chowk (for the imambaras). Most journeys cost around Rs 3. There are plenty of cycle-rickshaws (but no auto-rickshaws) which charge local people around Rs 5 for the four km between the station and Hazratganj. A cycle-rickshaw for a day's sightseeing costs around Rs 80 and you can also tour the historic areas of Lucknow by tonga.

ALLAHABAD
Population: 945,000
Telephone Area Code: 0532

The city of Allahabad is 135 km west of Varanasi at the confluence of two of India's most important rivers – the Ganges and the Yamuna (Jumna). This meeting point of the rivers, the *sangam*, is believed to have great soul-cleansing powers and is a major pilgrimage site. It is even more holy because the invisible Saraswati River is supposed to join the Ganges and the Yamuna at this point. Every 12 years the Kumbh Mela, the world's largest pilgrimage gathering, draws millions for a holy dip here.

Allahabad also has an historic fort built by Akbar which overlooks the confluence of the rivers and contains an Ashoka pillar. The Nehru family home, Anand Bhavan, is in Allahabad and is worth a visit. Not many foreign visitors pause in this peaceful city, but it can be an interesting and worthwhile stop.

History
Built on a very ancient site, Allahabad was known in Aryan times as Prayag, and Brahma himself is said to have performed a sacrifice here. The Chinese pilgrim Hiuen Tsang described visiting the city in 634 AD, and it acquired its present name in 1584, under Akbar. Later Allahabad was taken by the Marathas, sacked by the Pathans and finally ceded to the British in 1801 by the Nawab of Avadh.

It was in Allahabad that the East India Company officially handed over control of India to the British government in 1858, following the Mutiny. The city was a centre of the Indian National Congress and at the conference here in 1920, Mahatma Gandhi proposed his programme of nonviolent aggression to achieve independence.

Orientation & Information
Allahabad is less congested and more modern than its sister city, touristy Varanasi. Civil Lines, with its modern shopping centre (and numerous bookshops), has broad tree-lined avenues and the main bus terminal. The older part of town is near the Yamuna River. The hub of the older part of the city is known as Chowk, and this is also the location of the main produce market, Loknath.

The tourist office (☎ 60-1873) is at the Tourist Bungalow on Mahatma Gandhi Rd.

Indian Airlines has an office here (☎ 60-2832) but is not currently operating flights from Allahabad.

Sangam
At this point the shallow, muddy Ganges (about two km wide here) meets the clearer, deeper, green Yamuna. During the month of Magha (mid-January to mid-February) hundreds of thousands of pilgrims come to bathe at this holy confluence for the festival known as the **Magh Mela**. Astrologers calculate the holiest time to enter the water and draw up a 'Holy Dip Schedule'. The most propitious time of all happens only every 12 years when the massive **Kumbh Mela** takes place. There's a half-Mela (Ardh Mela) every six years.

A huge temporary township springs up on the vacant land on the Allahabad side of the river and elaborate precautions have to be taken for the pilgrims' safety – in the early '50s, 350 people were killed in a stampede to the water (an incident recreated in Vikram Seth's epic novel, *A Suitable Boy*).

Sunrise and sunset can be spectacular here. Boats out to the confluence are a bit of a tourist trap and what you pay very much depends on how many other people are around. Right by the fort you should be able to get a boat for about Rs 6; from Saraswati Ghat further up the Yamuna it should be around Rs 20.

Fort
Built by Akbar in 1583, the fort, which stands at the confluence on the Yamuna side,

Kumbh Mela
Aeons ago the gods and demons, who were constantly at odds, fought a great battle for a *kumbh* or pitcher. Apparently whoever drunk the contents of this pitcher would be ensured immortality. They had combined forces to raise the pitcher from the bottom of the ocean, but once it was safely in their hands Vishnu grabbed it and ran. After a struggle lasting 12 days the gods eventually defeated the demons and drank the nectar – it's a favourite scene in illustrations of Hindu mythology. During the fight for the pitcher's possession four drops of nectar spilt on the earth, at Allahabad, Haridwar, Nasik and Ujjain. The mela is held every three years, rotating among the four cities. Thus each has its own mela every 12 years (for a god's day is a human's year).

Holiest of these four sacred sites is Allahabad where the Kumbh Mela returns in 2001. ■

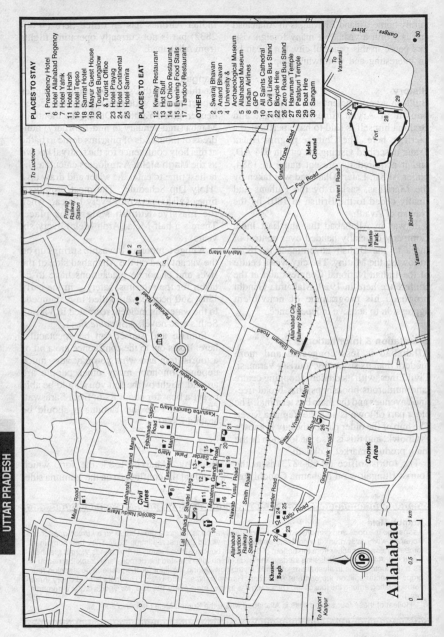

UTTAR PRADESH

PLACES TO STAY

1 Presidency Hotel
6 Hotel Allahabad Regency
7 Hotel Yatrik
11 Hotel Harsh
16 Hotel Tepso
18 Samrat Hotel
19 Mayur Guest House
20 Tourist Bungalow
& Tourist Office
23 Hotel Prayag
24 Hotel Continental
25 Hotel Samira

PLACES TO EAT

12 Kwality Restaurant
13 Hot Stuff
14 El Chico Restaurant
15 Evening Food Stalls
17 Tandoor Restaurant

OTHER

2 Swaraj Bhavan
3 Anand Bhavan
4 University &
Allahabad Museum
5 Archaeological Museum
8 Indian Airlines
9 GPO
10 All Saints Cathedral
21 Civil Lines Bus Stand
22 Bicycle Hire
26 Zero Road Bus Stand
27 Hanuman Temple
28 Patalpuri Temple
29 Boat Hire
30 Sangam

To Lucknow

To Varanasi

Ganges River

Fort

Yamuna River

Minto Park

Mela Ground

Grand Trunk Road

Fort Road

Triveni Marg

Prayag Railway Station

Malviya Marg

Panralal Road

Allahabad City Railway Station

Lal Sharam Road

Kamla Nehru Marg

Kasturba Gandhi Marg

Sapru Marg

Tehbahadur Road

Patel Marg

Tashkent Marg

Sardar Marg

Mahatma Gandhi Road

Nawab Yusuf Road

Smith Road

Leader Road

Dr Katju Road

Swami Vivekanand Marg

Zero Road

Grand Trunk Road

Chowk Area

Maharshi Dayanand Marg

Muir Road

Civil Lines

Lal Bahadur Shastri Marg

Sarojini Naidu Marg

Allahabad Junction Railway Station

Khusru Bagh

To Airport & Kanpur

Allahabad

0   0.5   1 km

has massive walls and pillars and three magnificent gateways flanked by high towers. It is made from huge bricks and is at its most impressive when viewed from the river.

The fort is in the hands of the army so prior permission is required for a visit. Officially, passes can be obtained from the Defence Ministry Security Officer but the amount of patience required to get a permit is out of all proportion to the sights to be seen.

Apart from one Mughal building the only item of antiquity inside the walls is an **Ashoka pillar** dating from 232 BC, with an inscription eulogising the victories of Samudragupta, plus the usual edicts.

Patalpuri Temple & Undying Tree A small door in the east wall of the fort near the river leads to the one area in the fort you can go without permission – the underground Patalpuri Temple and the 'Undying Banyan Tree'. Also known as Akshai Veta, this tree is mentioned by Hiuen Tsang, who tells of pilgrims sacrificing their lives by leaping to their deaths from it in order to seek salvation. This would be difficult now as there's not much of it left.

Hanuman Temple This popular temple, open to non-Hindus, is unusual because of the reclining position of Hanuman, in contrast to the usual standing position. It is said that every year during the floods the Ganges rises high enough to touch the feet of the sleeping Hanuman before it starts receding.

Anand Bhavan
This shrine to the Nehru family must be the best kept museum in the country, which indicates the high regard in which this famous dynasty is held in India. The family home was donated to the Indian government by Indira Gandhi in 1970. The exhibits in the house show how this well-off family became involved in the struggle for Indian independence and later produced four generations of astute politicians – Motilal Nehru, Jawaharlal Nehru, Indira Gandhi and Rajiv Gandhi.

Visitors and pilgrims walk around the verandahs of the two-storey mansion looking through glass panels into the rooms. You can see Nehru's bedroom and study, the room where Mahatma Gandhi used to stay during his visits and Indira Gandhi's room, as well as many personal items connected with the Nehru family. Opening hours are from 9.30 am to 5 pm; closed Mondays. There's a Rs 2 charge to go upstairs.

In the well-manicured gardens is an outbuilding housing a pictorial display of Jawaharlal Nehru's life, with pictures of him with everyone from JFK to Ho Chi Minh. Also in the gardens is a **planetarium**, built in 1979. Several shows take place here each day. Tickets are Rs 4 and the programme lasts about an hour.

Next door is **Swaraj Bhavan**, where Motilal Nehru lived until 1930. Today it houses the Jawaharlal Nehru Trust and a children's school for creative art. Indira Gandhi was born in this building, and this room is open to the public.

Khusru Bagh
This peaceful garden, close to the railway station, contains the tomb of Prince Khusru, son of Jehangir, who was executed by his own father. Nearby is the unoccupied tomb intended for his sister and the tomb of his Rajput mother who was said to have poisoned herself in despair at Khusru's opposition to his father.

All Saints Cathedral
This cathedral was designed more than a century ago by Sir William Emerson, the architect of the Victoria Memorial in Calcutta. The polished brass memorial plaques make interesting reading and show that even for the sons and daughters of the Raj, life was not all chukkas of polo and pink gins. The inscriptions morbidly record the causes of death: 'died of blood poisoning', 'accidentally killed', 'died of cholera', 'died in a polo accident' and probably even more likely today: 'died in a motor accident on the road to Naini Tal'. There are some attractive stained-glass windows and services in English on Sundays.

UTTAR PRADESH

Allahabad Museum

Set in a peaceful park, this large museum has galleries devoted to local archaeological finds (terracotta figures, stone sculptures and fossils), natural history and also exhibits donated by the Nehru family. Part of the museum is an art gallery with a fine collection of Rajasthani miniatures and paintings by the artist Professor Nicholas Roerich. The museum is open from 10.30 am to 4.30 pm and is closed Mondays. Admission is Rs 1.

Other Attractions

The **Bharadwaja** Ashram is mentioned in the *Ramayana* and the Allahabad University now occupies its site. The **Archaeological Museum** in the university has numerous artefacts from Kausambi. Opposite the university is the house where Rudyard Kipling lived, but it isn't open to the public.

In **Minto Park** a memorial marks the spot where Lord Canning read out the declaration by which Britain took over control of India from the East India Company in 1858. The **Nag Basuki Temple** is mentioned in the Puranas and is on the banks of the Ganges, north of the railway bridge.

Places to Stay – bottom end

There are hotels around the Leader Rd area and north of the railway line in Civil Lines, the more peaceful area to stay in.

Set back from M G Rd the *Hotel Tepso* (☎ 62-3635) has rooms for Rs 120/165, but it's not great value and the radical green wallpaper is a bit over the top.

Better is the *Mayur Guest House* (☎ 62-4855), just off M G Rd. The rooms are small but comfortable, and have attached bath with hot water (soap and towel provided) and TV, and there's a newspaper under your door in the morning. The charge is Rs 110 for a double, or Rs 175 with air-cooling.

The UP *Tourist Bungalow* (☎ 60-1441) is at 35 Mahatma Gandhi Rd and is probably the best value for money in Allahabad but it can be noisy if your room is overlooking the adjacent bus terminal. Rooms cost Rs 150/175 to Rs 350/400 (including air-con). It's a clean place set in a well-kept garden. A

cycle-rickshaw from Allahabad City railway station costs about Rs 5.

Barnett's Hotel has been renamed the *Hotel Harsh* (☎ 62-2197). This was obviously once a very comfortable place, although poor Mr Barnett is probably turning in his grave at the dilapidated condition of his old hotel. Rooms in this wedding cake of a place certainly don't lack space or character, but they are poor value at Rs 113/141 with attached bathroom.

There are several cheap places south of Allahabad Junction railway station. The *Hotel Prayag* (☎ 60-4430) is a modern block with a wide range of accommodation from Rs 50/70 for singles/doubles with common bathroom to Rs 80/100 for rooms with attached bath. Doubles with air-cooling cost Rs 150 and Rs 400 with air-con.

In the next street, opposite the mosque, is the *Hotel Continental* (☎ 65-2629), with rooms from Rs 90/100 with attached bathrooms, Rs 140/160 with air-cooling and Rs 250/300 with air-con. Further down this street is the smaller *Hotel Samira* (☎ 55-058) with rooms from Rs 40/80 with bath, and Rs 60/95 with air-cooling.

There are numerous other places to stay in this price bracket along Leader Rd.

At the railway station there are *retiring rooms* and dormitories.

Places to Stay – middle & top end

Near the junction of Mahatma Gandhi Rd and Sardar Patel Marg, the *Samrat Hotel* (☎ 60-4888; fax 60-4987) has rooms from Rs 300/500, or Rs 400/600 with air-con, but not all rooms have windows.

Two-star is the best you can get in Allahabad and the *Presidency Hotel* (☎ 62-3308) is in a quiet residential area north of Civil Lines. Singles/doubles (all air-con) cost Rs 450/525 and the bathrooms have bathtubs. There's a pool, but like the one at the Regency, it's not used during the winter.

The *Hotel Allahabad Regency* (☎ 60-1519) is also two-star and charges Rs 475/600 for singles/doubles with air-con. There's a very pleasant garden and a pool.

Nearby on Sardar Patel Marg, the *Hotel*

Yatrik (☎ 60-1713) is of a similar standard, although the plastic fold-up chairs in the lobby are a bit tacky. Rooms cost Rs 400/450 without air-con, Rs 560/750 with air-con. They boast of a 'Lush Green Lawn with Garden to Relax'.

Places to Eat

Outdoor eating is all the rage in Allahabad. In the evenings along M G Rd in Civil Lines, many semipermanent stalls set up tables on the footpath, and it's a popular and cheap area to eat. The *Chicken King* stall has excellent tandoori chicken. Next door is the *Spicy Bite*, which has a wide range of dishes. Another place is the *Little Hut*, which is right next door to the clothes stall called Hippo Garments!

Most of the hotels have restaurants. At the *Tourist Bungalow* you can get a vegetarian thali or a Western breakfast, and there's the standard non-veg menu as well.

There are several snack bars. The bright young things in Allahabad hang out in *Hot Stuff*, an ice-cream parlour and fast-food place where pizzas are Rs 32. The *Kwality Restaurant* is also good for snacks. Burgers are Rs 16 and there's a great range of ice creams including the 'Killer Driller' for Rs 28.

Sweet shops are also popular here, and *Kamdhenu Sweets* (near the Hotel Tepso) is a clean place to try them.

The two best restaurants in the city are the *Tandoor*, with good service and excellent Indian food (main dishes Rs 35 to Rs 50, but no beer), and *El Chico* which is a little more expensive and does good Chinese. There's a pastry shop at El Chico.

There are also many restaurants in the crowded streets of the old town on the southern side of the railway tracks, plus many small dhaba places close to the station along Dr Katiu Rd.

Getting There & Away

Allahabad is a good place from which to travel to Khajuraho. If you spend the night in Allahabad you can catch a morning train to Satna (the *Bhagalpur Kurla Express*

leaves at 8.20 am), from where buses go to Khajuraho (four hours). There are also buses to Satna from Allahabad but they take several hours longer than express trains.

Bus From Civil Lines bus stand, beside the Tourist Bungalow, there are regular buses to Varanasi (Rs 31.50, 3½ hours), Faizabad (Rs 41, 4½ hours), Gorakhpur (Rs 71, eight hours) via Jaunpur, and Sunauli (Rs 77, 12 hours) for Nepal. At 3 pm there's a deluxe bus to Lucknow (Rs 50, six hours) plus numerous others throughout the day.

Train The main station is Allahabad Junction in the central part of the city. The journey to Varanasi takes three to four hours (137 km, Rs 36/140 in 2nd/1st). Direct expresses take 10 hours to Delhi (627 km, Rs 155/364), 15 hours to Calcutta (814 km, Rs 185/582), 24 hours to Bombay (1373 km, Rs 250/797), 3½ hours to Lucknow (129 km, Rs 34/131) and four hours to Satna (180 km, Rs 47/168) for Khajuraho.

Getting Around

Use the back exit at Allahabad Junction station for Civil Lines. There are plenty of cycle and auto-rickshaws. It's Rs 12 for the six km to the Sangam in a cycle-rickshaw.

Renting a bicycle for the day is probably the best bet. There's a shop on Dr Katju Rd just outside the railway station which rents them for Rs 15 per day.

AROUND ALLAHABAD

Bhita

Excavations at this site, 18 km south of Allahabad, by the Yamuna River, have revealed the remains of an ancient fortified city. Layers of occupation dating from the Gupta period (320-455 AD) back to the Mauryan period (321-184 BC) and even earlier have been uncovered. There's a museum with stone and metal seals, coins and terracotta statues.

Garwha

The ruined temples in this walled enclosure are about 50 km from Allahabad. Garwha is eight km from Shankargarh and the last three km have to be completed on foot.

The major temple has 16 beautifully carved stone pillars, and inscriptions reveal that the temples date back to the Gupta period at the very least. Some of the better sculptures from Garwha are now shown in the State Museum in Lucknow.

Kausambi

This ancient Buddhist centre, once known as Kosam, is 63 km from Allahabad. At one time it was the capital of King Udaya, a contemporary of the Buddha. There's a huge **fortress** near the village, and the broken remains of an **Ashoka pillar**, minus any pre-Gupta period inscriptions, can be seen inside the fort. Many of the archaeological finds here are on display in the museum at Allahabad University. A bus runs from Allahabad to Serai Akil which is 15 km from Kausambi.

Chitrakut

It was here that Brahma, Vishnu and Siva are believed to have been 'born' and taken on their incarnations, which makes this town a popular Hindu pilgrimage place. **Bathing ghats** line the Mandakini River and there are over 30 temples in the town. It's on the banks of the Mandakini River by the border with Uttar Pradesh, and is 195 km from Khajuraho and 132 km from Allahabad.

Both MP Tourism and UP Tourism have *Tourist Bungalows* here, and there are a number of other cheap hotels and basic restaurants.

SHRAVASTI

The extensive ruins of this ancient city and Jetavana monastery are here, near the villages of Saheth-Maheth. It was at Shravasti that the Buddha performed the miracle of sitting on a 1000-petalled lotus and multiplying himself a million times, fire and water emanating from his body. Ashoka was among the early pilgrims and left a couple of pillars to commemorate his visit.

The site can be reached from Gonda on the Gorakhpur-Naugarh-Gonda metre-gauge loop. The nearest station is Gainjahwa and the nearest large town is 20 km away at Balrampur.

FAIZABAD

Population: 195,000
Telephone Area Code: 0527

Faizabad was once the capital of Avadh but rapidly declined after the death of Bahu Begum. Her mausoleum is said to be the finest of its type in Uttar Pradesh. Her husband, Nawab Shujaddaula, who preceded her as ruler, also has a fine mausoleum. There are three large mosques in the market (chowk) area and pleasant gardens in Guptar Park, where the temple from which Rama is supposed to have disappeared stands.

Places to Stay

Down side streets off the chowk area are three cheap places, but they can be difficult to find. The *Hotel Priya* (painted green with its name in Hindi) has singles/doubles for Rs 40/50 with bath. The *Hotel Amber* run by a friendly Sikh is similarly priced and has a good restaurant. Opposite, the *Hotel Abha* has good air-cooled rooms with hot water and TV for Rs 100/120, and a dingy restaurant with poor service.

The hotels in the Civil Lines area, which is also where the bus and railway station are located, is about 1.5 km west of the chowk. Rooms in the *Hotel Shan-e-Awadh* (☎ 81-3586) range from Rs 95/120 to Rs 295/350 with air-con. It's a good, clean hotel and even in the cheap rooms soap and towel are provided.

The *Hotel Tirupati* (☎ 81-3231) next door is more expensive, and has rooms from Rs 145/195 to Rs 295/350 with air-con, and there's a good restaurant, the *Thripur*. Avoid the front rooms as both these places are right on the main Lucknow to Gorakhpur road.

Getting There & Away

Faizabad is three hours by train from either Varanasi or Lucknow. There are numerous buses for Allahabad (Rs 45, five hours), Lucknow (Rs 35, three hours), Gorakhpur (Rs 45, three hours) and one direct early-morning bus to Sunauli (for Nepal) for Rs 45. For Ayodhya there are many buses and tempos (Rs 3) from the main road near the chowk.

AYODHYA

Population: 45,000
Telephone Area Code: 05278

Only six km from Faizabad, Ayodhya is one of Hinduism's seven holy cities (the others being Dwarka, Haridwar, Varanasi, Mathura, Ujjain, and Kanchipuram), and is a popular pilgrimage place. It's connected with many events in the *Ramayana* (including the birth of Rama), and has been very much in the news since 1990 on account of the 'temple-mosque' dispute.

It's a small and interesting town which sees few foreigners, but keep an ear on the latest developments in the temple-mosque saga. If there is any rioting give Ayodhya a wide berth.

Babri Masjid – Ram Janam Bhumi

The **Babri Masjid** was originally constructed on the site of Rama's birth by the Mughals in the 15th century, but it was eventually closed to Muslims by the civil authorities, although limited Hindu *puja* was permitted inside.

In 1990, plans by the Hindus to build a temple to Rama (the Ram Mandir) in its place led to outbreaks of violence between Hindus and Muslims here, and temples were damaged in the riots. A fragile court order called for the maintenance of the status quo and armed guards attempted to keep the two communities from each others' throats.

In late 1992, however, gangs of Hindus moved in and destroyed the mosque, erecting a small Hindu shrine in its place (known as **Ram Janam Bhumi**). This caused rioting and many deaths in various places in India and unrest in neighbouring Muslim countries. The central government enacted legislation which allowed it to take over ownership of 96 acres of land, including temple site.

Since then the government has sat on the fence, knowing that any decision it makes could result in a repeat of the riots. It has

promised to build a temple on the site, but only if it is decided that a temple existed here before the Mughal mosque (as is claimed by militant Hindus). In late 1994 the Indian High Court refused to adjudicate on the issue, claiming it was outside its purview. The matter currently rests with the Allahabad High Court.

The issue – and the tensions it has generated – is really just smouldering below the surface, and violence could erupt if a court or other ruling is seen by either community as unjust. A peaceful solution to this problem is one of the major tasks currently facing the Narasimha Rao government, and – not surprisingly – it seems unwilling to make a decision one way or the other.

There is a massive security presence at the temple/mosque site – this is, after all, the country's most volatile potential flash point. About 100 metres before the temple, you come to the first of at least six military/police checkpoints, and at each you'll be given a body search. Bags (and even your pocket contents!) have to be deposited at the main security point, where you are also likely to be politely questioned by plain-clothes police. Once through here you enter a narrow caged path (lined on the outside by armed men and women of the police Rapid Action Force) which takes you across the foundations of the old mosque, past the shrine and back to the main security checkpoint. It's all very orderly, and very secure.

The entrance to the site is along the road next to the Hanuman temple (see the following section), off the main road – just follow the steady stream of pilgrims.

Other Temples

The **Hanumangadhi** (dedicated to Hanuman) is another major temple in Ayodhya. It was built within the thick white walls of the fortress and there are good views from the ramparts. There's also the **Kanak Mandir** (built by the Maharaja of Tikamgadh last century) and a ghat; the town is on the Gogra (Ghaghara) River.

There are over 100 other temples in Ayodhya, many open to non-Hindus.

Places to Stay

Since Faizabad, with a larger range of accommodation, is so close it's easy to make a day trip from there. In Ayodhya, the Tourist Bungalow *Pathik Niwas Saket* (and tourist office) is next to the railway station. There's a pleasant dorm with beds (and lockers) for Rs 20 and singles/doubles from Rs 80/100 to Rs 275/350 for air-con. As this is a holy city, the restaurant serves only vegetarian food.

Getting There & Away

There are regular tempos and buses from Faizabad for Rs 3.

Varanasi Region

VARANASI

Population: 1,200,000
Telephone Area Code: 0542

Varanasi, the 'eternal city', is one of the most important pilgrimage sites in India and also a major tourist attraction. Situated on the banks of the sacred Ganges, Varanasi has been a centre of learning and civilisation for over 2000 years. It was at Sarnath only 10 km away that the Buddha first preached his message of enlightenment, 25 centuries ago. Later the city became a great Hindu centre, but was looted a number of times by Muslim invaders from the 11th century on. These destructive visits climaxed with that of the Mughal emperor, Aurangzeb, who destroyed almost all of the temples and converted the most famous one into a mosque.

Varanasi has also been known as Kashi and Benares, but its present name is a restoration of an ancient name meaning the city between two rivers – the Varuna and Asi. For the pious Hindu the city has always had a special place. Besides being a pilgrimage centre, it is considered an auspicious place to die, ensuring an instant route to heaven. To this day Varanasi is a centre of learning, especially for Sanskrit scholars, and students flock here from all over India. Ironically it is in the centre of one of the most underdeveloped areas of India – a largely agrarian and overpopulated area that has changed little since Independence.

On the other hand Varanasi has become a symbol of the Hindu renaissance and has a special role in the development of Hindi – the national language of India. The well-known novelist Prem Chand and the literary figure Bharatendu Harischand have played their parts in this development. Tulsi Das, the famous poet who wrote the Hindi version of the *Ramayana* known as the *Ram Charit Manas*, also lived in this city for many years.

Orientation

The old city of Varanasi is situated along the west bank of the Ganges and extends back from the riverbank ghats in a winding collection of narrow alleys. They're too narrow for anything but walking, and tall houses overhang the picturesque, though hardly clean, lanes. It's a fascinating area to wander around. The town extends from Raj Ghat, near the bridge, to Asi Ghat, near the university. Areas known as Chowk, Lahurabir and Godaulia (also spelt Godowlia and Gadaulia) are just outside the old city area along the river.

One of the best ways to get oriented in Varanasi is to remember the positions of the ghats, particularly important ones like Dasaswamedh Ghat. The big 'international hotels' and the national tourist office are in the cantonment area north of the Varanasi Junction railway station. The TV tower is the most obvious landmark there. The broad, tree-lined avenues of the cantonment are a great contrast to the crowds of people, bicycles and rickshaws in the old part of town.

Information

Tourist Office The most helpful place for information is the Government of India tourist office (☎ 43-744), at 15B The Mall in the cantonment. It is open weekdays from 9 am to 5.30 pm, and Saturdays from 9 am to 1 pm. The UP tourist office (☎ 43-413) is in the Tourist Bungalow and the staff are amazingly unhelpful. There's also a tourist kiosk at Varanasi Junction railway station.

BRYN THOMAS

BRYN THOMAS

PAUL BEINSSEN

PAUL BEINSSEN

Uttar Pradesh
    Top Left: Buland Darwaza, Fatehpur Sikri.
    Top Right: Palace of Jodh Bai, Fatehpur Sikri.
    Bottom Left: Pilgrims, Fatehpur Sikri.
Bottom Right: Street scene, Fatehpur Sikri.

PAUL BEINSSEN

PAUL BEINSSEN

CHRIS BEALL

Varanasi
Top: Old server of the English Raj.
Middle: Morning boat.
Bottom: Bathing ghats.

Money There are many places to change money including a bank in the international section at the airport. The State Bank of India has branches in some of the cantonment hotels. If you're staying near Dasaswamedh Ghat the closest bank to change at is the State Bank of Benares (see map). Don't bother trying to change Australian dollar travellers' cheques in Varanasi – no bank accepts them.

Post & Telecommunications The Varanasi GPO is a good place to send parcels from, as there are tailors' stalls for wrapping and sealing right outside.

Newspapers & Magazines The *Pioneer* is an informative local English-language newspaper. *Benares: City of Light* by Diana Eck (Princeton University Press) is a good guide to the city, with information on each ghat and temple and a good introduction to Hinduism.

Ghats

Varanasi's principal attraction is the long string of bathing ghats which line the west bank of the Ganges. Ghats are the steps which lead down to the river, and where, at the two 'burning ghats', bodies are cremated. The best time to visit the ghats is at dawn when pilgrims take their morning dip – the city is coming alive, the light is magical and Varanasi is an exotic place.

There are over 100 ghats in all; Dasaswamedh Ghat is probably the most convenient starting point. A trip from there to Manikarnika Ghat makes an interesting short introduction to the river and will cost Rs 25 an hour (with bargaining) if you hire a boat. There are plenty of boat operators by the river waiting for tourists to appear.

Look out for the people on the ghats – the women bathing discreetly in their saris, the young men going through contortionist yoga exercises, the Brahmin priests offering blessings (for a price) and the ever-present beggars giving others an opportunity to do their karma some good. Look for the lingams which mark each ghat, for Varanasi is the city of Siva. Look for the buildings and temples

An early morning dip in the holy Ganges River is part of a daily ritual for millions of Hindus.

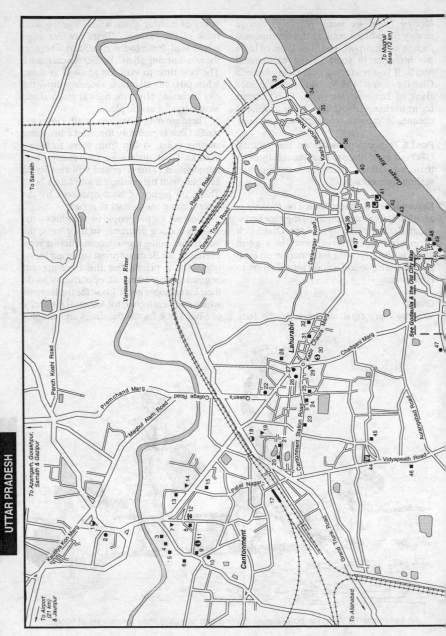

See Godaulia & the Old City Map

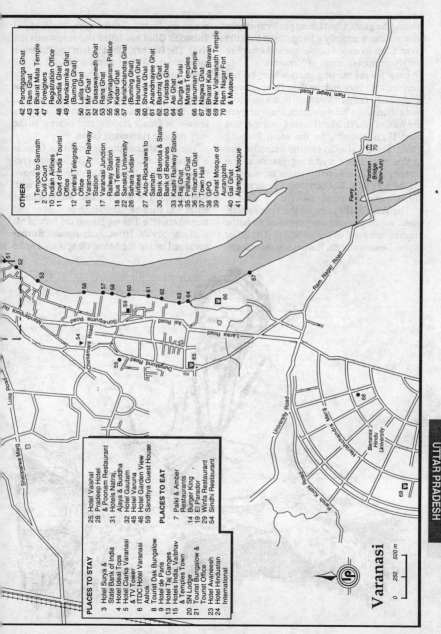

OTHER

1	Tempos to Sarnath
2	Civil Court
10	Indian Airlines
11	Govt of India Tourist Office
12	Central Telegraph Office
16	Varanasi City Railway Station
17	Varanasi Junction Railway Station
18	Bus Terminal
22	Sanskrit University
26	Sahara Indian Airlines
27	Auto-Rickshaws to Sarnath
30	Bank of Baroda & State Bank of Benares
33	Kashi Railway Station
34	Raj Ghat
35	Prahlad Ghat
36	Trilochan Ghat
37	Town Hall
38	GPO
39	Great Mosque of Aurangzeb
40	Gai Ghat
41	Alamgir Mosque
42	Panchganga Ghat
43	Ram Ghat
44	Bharat Mata Temple
47	Foreigners Registration Office
48	Scindia Ghat
49	Manikarnika Ghat (Burning Ghat)
50	Lalita Ghat
51	Mir Ghat
52	Dasaswamedh Ghat
53	Rana Ghat
55	Vijaynagaram Palace
56	Kedar Ghat
57	Harishchandra Ghat (Burning Ghat)
58	Hanuman Ghat
60	Shivala Ghat
61	Anandmayee Ghat
62	Bachraj Ghat
63	Tulsidas Ghat
64	Asi Ghat
65	Durga & Tulsi Manas Temples
66	Hanuman Temple
67	Nagwa Ghat
68	Bharat Kala Bhavan
69	New Vishwanath Temple
70	Ram Nagar Fort & Museum

PLACES TO STAY

3	Hotel Surya & State Bank of India
4	Hotel Ideal Tops
5	Hotel Clarks Varanasi & TV Tower
6	ITDC Hotel Varanasi Ashok
8	Tourist Dak Bungalow
9	Hotel de Paris
13	Hotel Taj Ganges
15	Hotels India, Vaibhav & Temples Town
20	SN Lodge
21	Tourist Bungalow & Tourist Office
23	Hotel Avaneesh
24	Hotel Hindustan International
25	Hotel Vaishal
28	Pradeep Hotel & Poonam Restaurant
31	Hotels Natraj, Ajaya & Buddha
32	Hotel Gautam
45	Hotel Varuna
46	Hotel Garden View
59	Sandhya Guest House

PLACES TO EAT

7	Palki & Amber Restaurants
14	Burger King
19	El Parador
29	Winfa Restaurant
54	Sindhi Restaurant

Varanasi

0   250   500 m

around the ghats, often tilting precariously or in some cases actually sliding down into the river. Each monsoon causes great damage to the riverbank buildings of Varanasi.

Look for the burning ghats where bodies are cremated after making their final journey to the holy Ganges swathed in white cloth and carried on a bamboo stretcher – or even the roof of a taxi. Manikarnika and the less used Harishchandra are the main burning ghats. There's also an electric crematorium at this ghat. Don't try taking photos at the burning ghats, especially when cremations are taking place. Just carrying a camera can sometimes cause problems here.

The **Asi Ghat** is one of the five special ghats which pilgrims are supposed to bathe from in order and on the same day. The order is Asi, Dasaswamedh, Barnasangam, Panch-ganga and finally Manikarnika. Much of the **Tulsidas Ghat** has fallen down towards the river. The **Bachraj Ghat** is Jain and there are three riverbank Jain temples. Many of the ghats are owned by maharajas or other princely rulers, such as the very fine **Shivala Ghat** owned by the Maharaja of Varanasi. The **Dandi Ghat** is the ghat of ascetics known as Dandi Panths, and nearby is the very popular **Hanuman Ghat**.

The **Harishchandra** or Smashan Ghat is a secondary burning ghat. Bodies are cremated by outcasts known as *chandal*. Above the **Kedar Ghat** is a shrine popular with Bengalis and south Indians. **Mansarowar Ghat** was built by Man Singh of Amber and named after the Tibetan lake at the foot of Mt Kailash, Siva's Himalayan home. **Someswar** or Lord of the Moon Ghat is said to be

A Sadhu

able to heal diseases. The **Munshi Ghat** is very picturesque, while **Ahalya Bai's Ghat** is named after the Maratha woman ruler of Indore.

The **Dasaswamedh Ghat**'s name indicates that Brahma sacrificed (*medh*) 10 (*das*) horses (*aswa*) here. It's one of the most important ghats and is conveniently central. Note its statues and the shrine of Sitala, goddess of smallpox.

Raja Man Singh's **Man Mandir Ghat** was built in 1600 but was poorly restored in the last century. The northern corner of the ghat has a fine stone balcony. Raja Jai Singh of Jaipur also erected one of his unusual observatories on this ghat in 1710. It is not as fine as the Jai Singh observatories in Delhi or Jaipur, but its setting is unique. There are good views from the top but you should watch out for the monkeys which can be aggressive.

The **Mir Ghat** leads to the Nepalese Temple with its erotic sculptures. Between here and the Jalsain Ghat is the Golden Temple (see separate section) which stands back from the river. The **Jalsain Ghat**, where cremations take place, virtually adjoins one of the most sacred of the ghats, the **Manikarnika Ghat**. Above the steps is a tank known as the Manikarnika Well; Parvati is said to have dropped her earring here and Siva dug the tank out to recover it, filling the depression with his sweat! The **Charand-paduka**, a slab of stone between the well and the ghat, bears footprints made by Vishnu. Privileged VIPs are allowed to be cremated at the Charandpaduka. There is also a temple dedicated to Ganesh on the ghat.

Dattatreya Ghat bears the footprint of the Brahmin saint of that name in a small temple nearby. **Scindia Ghat** was originally built in 1830 but was so huge and magnificent that it collapsed into the river and had to be rebuilt. The **Ram Ghat** was built by the Raja of Jaipur. The **Panch-ganga Ghat**, as its name indicates, is where five rivers are supposed to meet. Above the ghat is Aurangzeb's smaller mosque, also known as the Alamgir Mosque, built over a Vishnu temple. The **Gai Ghat** has a figure of

a cow made of stone upon it. The **Trilochan Ghat** has two turrets emerging from the river, and water between them is especially holy. **Raj Ghat** was the ferry pier until the road and rail bridge was completed here.

Golden Temple
Dedicated to Vishveswara (Vishwanath), Siva as Lord of the Universe, the Golden Temple is across the road from its original position. Aurangzeb destroyed the original temple and built a mosque over it – traces of the earlier 1600 temple can be seen behind his mosque.

The present temple was built in 1776 by Ahalya Bai of Indore, and the gold plating (three-quarters of a ton of it!) on the towers was provided by Maharaja Ranjit Singh of Lahore. Next to the temple is the **Gyan Kupor Well** (Well of Knowledge). Much esteemed by the faithful, this well is said to contain the Siva lingam removed from the original temple and hidden to protect it from Aurangzeb. Non-Hindus are not allowed into the temple but can view it from upstairs in a house across the street – soldiers sit downstairs. Be discreet if taking photos from here as the soldiers sometimes disapprove.

Near the temple, which is interesting to visit in the evening, are narrow alleys filled with many shops.

Great Mosque of Aurangzeb
Constructed using columns from the Biseswar Temple razed by Aurangzeb, this great mosque has minarets towering 71 metres above the Ganges. Armed guards protect the mosque as the Indian government wants to ensure there are no problems between Hindus and Muslims.

Durga Temple
The Durga Temple is commonly known as the Monkey Temple due to the many monkeys that have made it their home. It was built in the 18th century by a Bengali maha-rani and is stained red with ochre. The small temple is built in north Indian Nagara style with a multi-tiered *sikhara*.

Durga is the 'terrible' form of Siva's

consort Parvati, so at festivals there are often sacrifices of goats. Although this is one of the best known temples in Varanasi, it is, like some other Hindu temples, closed to non-believers. However, you can look down inside the temple from a walkway at the top. Beware of the monkeys here who are daring and vicious – they'll snatch glasses off your face, and even scratch or bite if you get too close.

Next to the temple is a tank with stagnant water where, as usual, pilgrims bathe.

Tulsi Manas Temple

Next to the Durga Temple is this modern marble sikhara-style temple. Built in 1964, the walls of the temple are engraved with verses and scenes from the *Ram Charit Manas*, the Hindi version of the *Ramayana*. This tells of the history and deeds of Rama, an incarnation of Vishnu. Its medieval author, Tulsi Das, lived here while writing it and died in 1623.

On the 2nd floor you can watch the production of moving and performing statues and scenes from Hindu mythology. If you are at all familiar with figures from the *Ramayana* or *Mahabharata*, you will find a visit here very enjoyable. Non-Hindus are allowed into this temple.

Benares Hindu University

A further 20-minute walk from the Durga Temple, or a short rickshaw ride, is the Benares Hindu University (BHU), constructed at the beginning of the century. The large university covers an area of five sq km, and you can get there by bus from Godaulia or by a rickshaw for Rs 6.

The university was founded by Pandit Malaviya as a centre of education in Indian art, culture and music, and for the study of Sanskrit. The Bharat Kala Bhavan at the university has a fine collection of miniature paintings and also sculptures from the 1st to 15th centuries. In a room upstairs there are some old photographs and a map of Varanasi. It's open from 11 am to 4 pm (8 am to 12.30 pm in May and June) and is closed on Sundays.

New Vishwanath Temple

It's about a 30-minute walk from the gates of the university to the new Vishwanath Temple which was planned by Pandit Malaviya and built by the wealthy Birla family of industrialists. A great nationalist, Pandit Malaviya wished to see Hinduism revived without its caste distinctions and prejudices – accordingly this temple, unlike so many in Varanasi, is open to all, irrespective of caste or religion. The interior has a Siva lingam and verses from Hindu scriptures inscribed on the walls. The temple is supposed to be a replica of the original Vishwanath Temple, destroyed by Aurangzeb.

Alamgir Mosque

Locally known as Beni Madhav Ka Darera, this was originally a Vishnu temple erected by the Maratha chieftain Beni Madhav Rao Scindia. Aurangzeb destroyed it and erected the mosque in its place, but it is a curious Hindu/Muslim mixture with the bottom part entirely Hindu.

Bharat Mata Temple

Dedicated to 'Mother India', this temple has a marble relief map of India instead of the usual images of gods and goddesses. It gives an excellent impression of the high isolation of the Tibetan plateau. The temple was opened by Mahatma Gandhi, and non-Hindus are allowed inside.

Ram Nagar Fort & Museum

On the other side of the river, this 17th-century fort is the home of the Maharaja of Benares. There are tours to the fort or you can catch a ferry across the river to get to it. The interesting museum contains old silver and brocade palanquins for the ladies of the court, elephant howdahs made of silver, old brocades, a replica of the royal bed and an armoury of swords and old guns. The fort is open from 9 am to noon and 2 to 5 pm; entry to the museum is Rs 1.50.

Activities

Swimming If you're staying in one of Varanasi's cheaper hotels and could do with a swim, the following hotels permit non-guests to use their pools: Hotel Hindustan International (Rs 100), Hotel Varanasi Ashok (Rs 75), and the Hotel Clarks Varanasi (Rs 100).

Yoga If you're interested in studying yoga, pay a visit to the Malaviya Bhavan at the university. They offer courses in yoga and also in Hindu philosophy.

There are also many private teachers and organisations offering courses. Some of these cost virtually nothing, and others are quite expensive. You could try the Yoga Clinic at D 16/19 Man Mandir (near Man Mandir Ghat) where Yogi Prakash Shankar Vyas runs a seven-day course in the principles of yoga.

River Trips Many people prefer to do things themselves, and if the ITDC tours aren't operating (see next section) you have no choice but to do this. Organising a boat for sunrise over the ghats is easy and rickshaw-wallahs are keen to get a pre-dawn rendezvous arranged for the trip down to the river. Get them to take you to a large ghat such as Dasaswamedh, since there will be a number of boats to choose from. Travellers have reported being taken to smaller ghats where there was only one boat, placing them in a poor bargaining position. Aim to pay around Rs 25 per hour.

Organised Tours
The Varanasi tours operated by ITDC have been discontinued, supposedly temporarily; check at either of the tourist offices. The morning tour took you down the Ganges by the ghats, around the various temples and out to the university; the afternoon tour to Sarnath and to the Ram Nagar Fort.

Places to Stay
There are three main accommodation areas in Varanasi. The spacious cantonment area is north of the railway tracks, and most of the hotels on the broad avenues in this peaceful area are mostly upmarket and have pleasant gardens. The newer part of the city is south

of the railway station and also near the bus terminal. However, the true atmosphere of this ancient holy city lies in the crowded, confused but colourful area by the river. These old city places are the cheapest you'll find, and staying close to the river has the advantage of being cooler during the hot season, and you can go down to the ghats at any time.

Wherever you stay in Varanasi, watch out for the rickshaw-wallahs who are heavily into hotel commissions. Suggest a hotel and if it doesn't give a commission you'll probably be told that it's 'closed', 'full up', or 'burnt down', or there's been 'Hindu-Muslim problem' in the area. Hotels by the river may even be 'flooded'! For places in this old city area it's better to ask the rickshaw-wallah for Dasaswamedh Ghat and walk to the hotel from there.

Places to Stay – bottom end & middle
Railway Station Area There are several cheap rooms down the road opposite Varanasi Junction station. The *Hotel Glory* ((☎ 46-812) has rooms for Rs 60/90 with attached bathrooms. The *Hotel Amar* (☎ 43-509) has rooms for Rs 50/80 or Rs 80/100 with attached bathroom; the *Hotel Raj Kamal* and *Hotel Diwan* are slightly cheaper. All are fairly characterless and unattractive.

The *Tourist Bungalow* (☎ 43-413) is quite popular since it has a pleasant garden and is within easy walking distance of the bus and railway stations. Recently, prices have risen substantially (standards haven't) and it's not such great value. There are dorm beds for Rs 20, singles/doubles for Rs 100/125 with attached bath, Rs 150/200 with air-cooler and Rs 275/350 with air-con. The staff here have a well-earned reputation for being less than helpful, as does the UP tourist office here.

Just outside the Tourist Bungalow is the *Hotel Relax* (☎ 43-503), which is cheaper at Rs 60/90 with common bath, Rs 75/125 with attached bath and Rs 125/175 with air-con. Like the other hotels in the area, it does good business when the Tourist Bungalow is full.

Beside the El Parador Restaurant is the

recently renovated *Hotel Sandona*. It has good singles/doubles/triples with attached bathroom from Rs 80/120.

There are a number of hotels between the railway station and the bus terminal which can be noisy. The *Nar Indra* (☎ 43-586) has rooms for Rs 125/155 or Rs 300/350 with air-con.

In the *retiring rooms* at Varanasi Junction station there are doubles for Rs 50 and Rs 75 (with air-con) or dorm beds for Rs 15.

Cantonment Area In this area, on the north side of Varanasi Junction station, hotels are mainly at the top of the price scale but there are a few cheaper places. The *Tourist Dak Bungalow* (☎ 42-182) on The Mall is very popular with overlanders and has a nice garden. You can camp for Rs 20, but the rooms are overpriced at Rs 100/250. There's also a reasonable restaurant here.

The *Hotel Surya* (☎ 38-5930), just behind the Hotel Clarks Varanasi, is a recommended place with a garden that's great for relaxing in. It also has a good Chinese restaurant. All rooms have attached bathrooms. There are some singles/doubles for Rs 75/90 and air-con rooms for Rs 275/300.

On Patel Nagar, the street that runs up from the station, there's another group of hotels. Cheapest here is the *Hotel Temples Town* (☎ 46-582), although the rooms lack outward-facing windows. The cost is Rs 90/130 with attached bathroom.

Next door is the smart *Hotel Vaibhav* (☎ 46-466), which has very comfortable rooms at Rs 200/250, or with air-con at Rs 375/450. All rooms have carpet and TV, and attached bathrooms with hot water and bathtubs. It's a friendly, clean and well-run place.

Next door again is the *Hotel India* (☎ 43-309). It's similar to the Vaibhav, with rooms at Rs 175/250, or Rs 300/400 with air-con. Rooms in the new extension may be more expensive. The hotel has its own restaurant and bar.

Lahurabir Area Hotels in Lahurabir, between the station and Godaulia, are mainly in the middle price bracket. An exception is

the *Hotel Vaishal* (☎ 56-577) which is a big, characterless place with singles/doubles/triples for 60/100/150 with attached bathroom (bucket hot water).

The *Hotel Natraj* (☎ 43-652) has rooms for Rs 70/90 with attached bathroom, Rs 20 more with air-cooling. Next door the *Hotel Ajaya* (☎ 43-707) is slightly better and marginally more expensive at Rs 80/100, or with air-cooling at Rs 130/150. Checkout is based on the 24-hour system.

The best choice in this area, however, is the *Hotel Buddha* (☎ 43-686), behind the Hotel Ajaya. It is a nice old building with high ceilings and a verandah. The rooms are spartan but very spacious, and although they lack windows, the high ceilings help to keep the temperature down. The staff are friendly and helpful, and the food, served on the verandah, is pretty good. Rooms with attached bath cost Rs 100 to Rs 160, all with attached bath.

The two-star *Pradeep Hotel* (☎ 44-963), also in Lahurabir, has good rooms from Rs 200/250 (Rs 350/400 with air-con) and the Poonam Restaurant here is very good.

Another good place is the *Hotel Gautam* (☎ 46-329), around the corner from the Hotel Natraj, with clean rooms from Rs 200/250, or Rs 350/400 with air-con.

Back on Station Rd, the *Hotel Avaneesh* (☎ 54-178) is a modern place with comfortable but smallish rooms from Rs 375/450 with air-con.

West of Lahurabir, halfway between Varanasi Junction station and the ghats, in a quiet area is the *Hotel Varuna* (☎ 54-524). It's a friendly place where good singles/doubles with attached bath are Rs 100/200, or Rs 375/450 with air-con. It's very easy to find by rickshaw as this place is into the commission racket in a big way.

The *Hotel Garden View* (☎ 36-0859) is about one km away on the noisy Vidyapeeth Rd. The garden is tiny and the rooms not great value at Rs 50/100 without attached bathroom but they have some better air-cooled doubles for Rs 130/150.

The *Hotel Siddharth* (☎ 54-161; fax 35-2301) is a new place a little closer towards

Luxa Rd. The rooms are well furnished and cost Rs 200/275, or Rs 325/400 with air-con.

East of Lahurabir near the GPO at Maidagin is the *Hotel Barahdari* (☎ 33-0346), well run by an aristocratic Jain family. It's right in the middle of the town and there are air-cooled rooms for Rs 165/190 or Rs 275/330 with air-con, a good vegetarian restaurant and a garden.

Godaulia The hotels around the Dasaswamedh Ghat Rd area tend to be a bit more spacious but rather less interesting than those right in the old city. There are a few cheap places such as the *Hotel Binod*, the *Palace Hotel*, and the nearby *Hotel Samman* (☎ 32-2241) which is the best of these similarly priced hotels with rooms from Rs 60/100 with attached bath, Rs 90/120 with air-cooler and Rs 250 for an air-con double. The *Banaras Lodge* and *Tripti Hotel* also have cheaper rooms without bathrooms.

The *Hotel Ganges* (☎ 32-1097) is a big place with a friendly manager and rooms from Rs 100/150 to Rs 250/300 with air-con and 'Video-Vision'.

Opposite Aces Restaurant is the *Seema Hotel* (☎ 35-2785), which has clean rooms for Rs 175/200 and hot-water heaters in the attached bathrooms. Air-con rooms cost Rs 350/400. Avoid the front rooms as this road is busy and noisy.

A number of places around here won't let you stay because they don't have 'C' forms for foreigner registration. *Dasaswamedh Lodge* is one place, the *Madras Hotel* another. Perhaps it's just as well since the sign for this last place advises you to 'Stay and Die in Varanasi'!

Old City & Ghats Area This is the place to look for rock-bottom hotels. The streets here are very narrow; you even have to abandon cycle-rickshaws and make your way down the convoluted alleys on foot. There are a number of good lodges right on the river with superb views along the ghats. They all have roof terraces for relaxing on and in some you can watch the sunrise without even getting out of bed!

A popular place, especially amongst Japanese travellers, is the *Vishnu Rest House* (no phone), right on the river. It has singles/doubles with common bathroom for Rs 40/60, or Rs 60/80 with attached bath. Virtually next door is the *Kumiko House Pension* with similar prices, run by a friendly Japanese woman and her Indian husband.

In the north of this area, right above Scindia Ghat (beside Manikarnika Ghat), the *Scindhia Guest House* (☎ 32-0319) is an excellent choice. It's small, clean and well run by a helpful manager. Doubles (no singles) are Rs 80, or Rs 100 with attached bath. The food here is a bit pricey but there are superb views along the river.

Between the Scindhia Guest House and the Dasaswamedh Ghat is the well-signposted *Shanti Guest House* (☎ 32-2568). It's a very friendly and popular place, with a rooftop restaurant (open 24 hours) offering fine views of the river. There's a variety of rooms, although few have outward-facing windows. The cheapest are Rs 30/50 with common bath, and there are a few doubles with attached bath for Rs 90.

Also here is the *Alaknanda Guest House*, which has rooms with attached bath at Rs 40/75, or there are doubles with a river view for Rs 100.

Many travellers prefer the places down the alleys set back from the ghats. The *Yogi Lodge* (☎ 32-2588) has long been a favourite with budget travellers and it's efficiently run by a friendly family. Dorm beds are Rs 20, and rooms are Rs 50/75 but they're quite small. There's a travellers' notice board, hot showers and a good restaurant. Its success has spawned the Jogi Lodge, the Old Yogi Lodge, Gold Yogi Lodge, New Yogi Lodge and Yogi Guest House, some of which are inferior copies offering commissions to rickshaw-wallahs – be warned. The *Old Yogi Lodge* (☎ 35-0141), while still cashing in on the Yogi name, is a reasonable place nonetheless. Near the Yogi Lodge is *Golden Lodge* which is slightly cheaper and has a good roof terrace.

The *Sri Venkateshwar Lodge* (☎ 32-2357), beside the small blue temple, is a good place with singles/doubles for Rs 40/70 with common bath and some larger rooms with attached bathrooms. The management is helpful and not overly keen on noxious substances.

The *Trimurti Guest House* (☎ 32-3554) is good value (although some of the rooms are a little cell-like) and has a popular restaurant. Dorm beds are Rs 20, rooms cost from Rs 30/45 upwards, some have attached baths and air-cooling, and there are great views from the roof over the Golden Temple.

Further back from the river, the *Om House Lodge* (☎ 32-2728), in the Bansphatak area

of the old city, is extremely cheap with rooms with common bath at Rs 35/50. It's popular with travellers and the owner gives yoga lessons. You have to wander down a maze of winding lanes to find it, but it's pleasantly quiet.

Away to the south of this area in a quiet location by the Shivala post office is the *Sandhya Guest House* (☎ 31-0644). It's run by a friendly, helpful manager and has a good restaurant on the roof with home-made soups and brown bread. There are dorm beds for Rs 20, rooms for Rs 50/75 or Rs 60/90 with attached bathrooms and it's only a few minutes from Shivala Ghat.

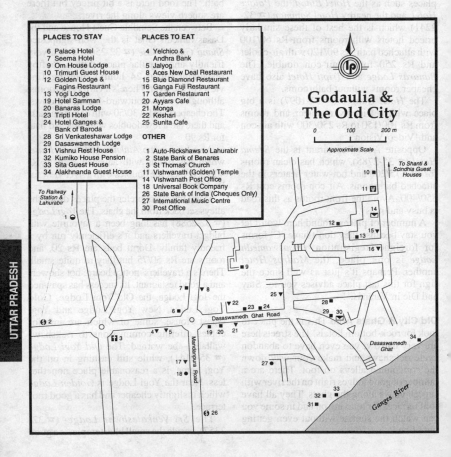

PLACES TO STAY

6 Palace Hotel
7 Seema Hotel
9 Om House Lodge
10 Trimurti Guest House
12 Golden Lodge & Fagins Restaurant
13 Yogi Lodge
19 Hotel Samman
20 Banaras Lodge
23 Tripti Hotel
24 Hotel Ganges & Bank of Baroda
28 Sri Venkateshawar Lodge
29 Dasaswamedh Lodge
31 Vishnu Rest House
32 Kumiko House Pension
33 Sita Guest House
34 Alakhnanda Guest House

PLACES TO EAT

4 Yelchico & Andhra Bank
8 Jalyog
15 Aces New Deal Restaurant
15 Blue Diamond Restaurant
16 Ganga Fuji Restaurant
17 Garden Restaurant
20 Ayyars Cafe
21 Monga
22 Keshari
25 Sunita Cafe

OTHER

1 Auto-Rickshaws to Lahurabir
2 State Bank of Benares
3 St Thomas' Church
11 Vishwanath (Golden) Temple
14 Vishwanath Post Office
18 Universal Book Company
26 State Bank of India (Cheques Only)
27 International Music Centre
30 Post Office

Godaulia & The Old City

0   100   200 m

Approximate Scale

To Railway Station & Lahurabir

To Shanti & Scindhia Guest Houses

Dasaswamedh Ghat Road

Mandapura Road

Dasaswamedh Ghat

Ganges River

Places to Stay – top end

The *Hotel de Paris* (☎ 46-601) occupies a large rambling building of whitewashed arches set in a spacious garden. It's got a certain run-down style but probably doesn't deserve its three stars. Singles/doubles are Rs 550/760 with air-con. Meals are available for Rs 105 for breakfast, or Rs 165 for lunch or dinner. Visa, Amex and Diners credit cards are accepted.

The four-star *Hotel Hindustan International* (☎ 57-075; fax 35-2374) is a modern concrete block in the centre of the city with air-con rooms at Rs 1150/2000 and bathrooms with tubs. There's also a swimming pool. It's probably better value than the four-star *Hotel Varanasi Ashok* (☎ 46-020; fax 34-8089), next to Clarks in the cantonment area, which has rooms for Rs 1195/2000. However the Ashok is in a quieter location with a better garden, and it too has a pool.

The *Hotel Clarks Varanasi* (☎ 34-8501; fax 34-8186) is the oldest hotel here, dating back to the British era but there's now a large modern extension. Air-con singles/doubles cost Rs 1195/2250, and there's a swimming pool. It's considered the best place in town and is more popular than the equally upmarket *Hotel Taj Ganges* (☎ 34-8301; fax 32-2067) which has air-con rooms from US$75/90.

Right next door to the Hotel Clarks is the new *Hotel Ideal Tops* (☎ 34-8091; fax 34-8685) which offers well-appointed air-con rooms for US$28/35.

Places to Eat
Railway Station & Lahurabir Areas

Varanasi's railway station *restaurant* is the best value place in this area. Their breakfasts are particularly good as is their 'pot tea'. There's a restaurant at the *Tourist Bungalow* where the food is reasonable but overpriced. Just outside is the *Mandarin Chinese Restaurant*, which is cheaper although the food is only vaguely Chinese. Around the corner, the small *Most Welcome Restaurant* is OK.

The *Winfa Restaurant* in Lahurabir, behind the cinema, is the best Chinese restaurant here, with dishes from Rs 15 to Rs 40. In the Pradeep Hotel, the *Poonam Restaurant* does excellent Indian food. Main dishes are around Rs 40 and service is good. They even have the bizarre Mughlai dessert called shahi tukra which will appeal to fans of bread-and-butter pudding – it's basically fried bread cooked in cream, with nuts.

However the best place to eat in this area, whether for a cappuccino or a splurge, is *El Parador*. It serves great soups and salads, fettuccine, enchiladas, stews, crepes, chocolate cake and all the things you'd expect from a restaurant in Kathmandu rather than Varanasi. It's quite an expensive place with main dishes around Rs 70, but well worth it and very popular. They also do set brunches of waffles, pancakes, hash browns and cereal for Rs 40.

The food served at the *Hotel Buddha* is pretty good, and there are a couple of basic dhaba-type places in the street behind if you want cheap Indian food.

Cantonment Area The *Tourist Dak Bungalow* is about the cheapest place in the cantonment, although the food is not all that wonderful. Good Chinese food is available at the *Hotel Surya*, with main dishes around Rs 35.

The *Palki Restaurant* in the Vaibhav Hotel and the *Amber Restaurant*, next door in the India Hotel, are both quite decent places. For a quick snack, *Burger King*, near the Taj Ganges Hotel is a reasonable place offering vegetable burgers, among other things.

If you want to dine in style in the cantonment, there's the *Hotel Clarks* and the *Hotel Taj Ganges*.

Godaulia & the Old City Many of the lodges here offer room service, with vegetarian thalis ranging in price from Rs 15 to Rs 30. There are a number of places in Godaulia for breakfast and snacks including the *Aces New Deal Restaurant*, popular with travellers for many years. The menu is extremely varied, as are the reports about the food. It's still popular and you can sit outside in the small courtyard, although it's not exactly romantic.

For an Indian-style breakfast of puris and

vegetables, known as kachauri, go to *Jalyog*, by the main square in Godaulia. The restaurant's name is mainly in Hindi with just small writing in English but as it was established nearly 100 years ago everyone knows it. There are good samosas here too.

The best vegetarian restaurant in the area is *Keshari* down a small alley off Dasaswamedh Ghat Rd. The place is very clean and main dishes are around Rs 20. Another popular place is the basement restaurant *Yelchico*, which serves veg and non-veg food. It has the standard Indian-Chinese-Continental menu with main dishes at Rs 30 to Rs 45 and is one of the few restaurants around the old city where you can get a beer (Rs 40). *Monga* is a subterranean Chinese restaurant with similar prices, and *Ayyars Cafe* has good masala dosas and other light meals.

The outdoor *Garden Restaurant* is a very pleasant little place with a menu catering to foreigners. The small terrace is ringed by numerous pot plants, and is in the shade in the afternoons. The food is cheap and nicely presented.

The small *Fagins Restaurant*, on the ground floor of the Golden Lodge, is not a bad place, although you may well be thinking about your own cremation by the time the food arrives.

The *Ganga Fuji* and the *Blue Diamond* restaurants, not far from the Golden Temple both serve pretty decent food, and boast live classical Indian music in the evenings.

The restaurants in the *Trimurti Guest House*, *Yogi Lodge* and the *Shanti Guest House* are all popular with travellers. Near the Sri Venkateshwar Lodge is the *Sunita Cafe* which has good masala dosas for Rs 8.

In Bhelupura, near the Lalita Cinema, the *Sindhi Restaurant* does excellent vegetarian food. Rickshaw-wallahs all know the cinema but not the restaurant.

Varanasi is well known for its sweets, and *Madhur Jalpan Grih*, on the same side of the street as the cinema in Godaulia, is an excellent place to try them. The city is also known for its high-quality paan. For greater highs the government *bhang* shop is on the way to the well-signposted Shanti Guest House.

Entertainment
Varanasi is not renowned for its nightlife. About the only choice, other than the cinemas showing the usual Bollywood junk, are the twice-weekly classical music recitals, held at the *International Music Centre*, near Dasaswamedh Ghat.

Things to Buy
Varanasi is famous all over India for silk brocades and beautiful Benares saris. However, there are lots of rip-off merchants and commission people at work. Invitations to 'come to my home for tea' will inevitably mean to somebody's silk showroom, where you will be pressured into buying things. If you're 'only looking' they may even try to charge you for tea and electricity! Beware of anyone in your hotel (including the manager) who offers to take you to a cheap place. You'll be quoted at least 30% more for goods as commission has to be paid.

There's a market near the GPO called Golghar where the makers of silk brocades sell directly to the shops in the area. You can get cheaper silk brocade in this area than in the big stores, but you must be careful about the quality. Mixtures of silk and cotton can look very like pure silk to the untrained eye. The big shops selling silk brocades are all in the chowk area of the old city. There's a fixed-price Cottage Industries Emporium in the cantonment but since it's opposite the Hotel Taj Ganges the prices aren't fixed at the bottom end of the market.

The same care is necessary with sitars – yes, Ravi Shankar does live here (when he's not on tour in the West), but don't believe that every sitar maker is his personal friend! A place which has been recommended is the Triveni Music Centre, at 19/3 Kewalgali Lane near Dasaswamedh Ghat. You may well see posters up advertising music recitals at this place.

Getting There & Away
Air The Indian Airlines office (☎ 43-746) is in the cantonment near the Hotel de Paris. Office hours are 10 am to 1.15 pm, and 2 to 5 pm. ModiLuft (☎ 46-477) has its office in

Major Trains from Varanasi

Destination	Train number & name	Departure time *	Distance (km)	Duration (hours)	Fare (Rs) (2nd/1st)
Bombay	1066 *Ratnagiri Exp*	5.45 pm V	1509	30	262/847
	1028 *Dadar Exp*	10.50 am V		33	
Calcutta	2382 *Poorva Exp*	6.15 am MS	661	10	159/481
	3010 *Doon Exp*	4.15 pm V	578	15	143/430
Gaya	2382 *Poorva Exp*	6.15 am MS	204	2.40	52/189
Gorakhpur	5104 *Gorakhpur Exp*	5.30 am V	231	4.40	57/208
Lucknow	4227 *Varuna Exp*	5.15 am V	302	4.45	90/262
Madras	6040 *Ganga Kaveri Exp*	5.45 pm V	2144	41	305/1101
Delhi	2301 *Rajdhani Exp***	12.40 am MS	764	14.05	510/635
	2381 *A/C Exp****	8 pm V	792	12.05	428/777
	4057 *Kashi Vishwanath Exp*	2 pm V		16.40	180/552
New Jalpaiguri	5622 *NE Exp*	6 pm MS	848	15.30	188/553
Patna	3040 *Janata Exp*	11.50 am MS	228	5	56/205
Puri	2802 *Purushotam Exp*	10.30 am MS	1044	21	215/642
Satna	4248 *Kurla Exp*	11.30 pm V	316	7	93/267

* Abbreviations for train stations: V – Varanasi Junction, MS – Mughalserai
** Air-con only; fare includes meals and drinks
*** Air-con only

the Vaibhav Hotel. Sahara India Airlines (☎ 44-853) is close to the main roundabout in Lahurabir.

Varanasi is on several Indian Airlines routes including the popular daily tourist shuttle Delhi-Agra-Khajuraho-Varanasi and back. ModiLuft also flies this route on a daily basis. To Delhi it costs US$74, Agra US$57 and Khajuraho US$39. There are also four Indian Airlines flights a week to Lucknow (US$29), Bombay (US$148) and Bhubaneswar (US$69) plus a daily flight to Kathmandu (US$71).

Bus From the bus terminal opposite the main (Varanasi Junction) railway station there are frequent departures to Jaunpur (Rs 16, two hours), Allahabad (Rs 31.50, 3½ hours), Lucknow (Rs 72, nine hours), Faizabad (Rs 51, seven hours) and Gorakhpur (Rs 56, 6½ hours). There are deluxe buses to Sunauli (Rs 100, nine hours) at 7 am, and 6 and 7 pm, and ordinary buses (Rs 81) at 5 and 6 am, and 8 pm.

No buses run direct to Khajuraho so take the train to Satna and a bus from there. The bus trip takes three to four hours.

Train Varanasi Junction (also known as Varanasi Cantonment) is the main station. There is a separate computerised booking office to the left of the main building. It is open Monday to Saturday from 8 am to 8 pm, and on Sunday from 8 am to 2 pm.

There are not many trains running directly between here and Delhi or Calcutta but most Delhi to Calcutta trains do pass through Mughalserai, 12 km south of Varanasi. This is a nightmarish 45-minute ride by bus (Rs 3), tempo (Rs 10) or auto-rickshaw (Rs 40) along a horrendously congested stretch of the Grand Trunk Road. The only reasonable accommodation in Mughalserai is the railway retiring rooms (Rs 60 for a good double) – the hotels opposite are fleapits.

To/From Nepal A bus may be better than the metre-gauge trains from here to the border. There are morning and evening government buses (Rs 81 ordinary, Rs 100 deluxe) to Sunauli (the border post) which go via Gorakhpur and take around nine hours.

Private companies operate buses to the Nepalese border and on to Kathmandu and Pokhara. They charge Rs 250 to Kathmandu or Pokhara which includes spartan accommodation at Sunauli. Alternatively, you can take one of their deluxe buses as far as the border for Rs 150 (or a much cheaper ordinary bus) and another bus from the border to Kathmandu or Pokhara for the Nepalese equivalent of Indian Rs 70. This gives you a choice of bus within Nepal and also of accommodation at Sunauli.

Getting Around
To/From the Airport Babatpur Airport is 22 km from the city and a bus runs from the Vaibhav Hotel in the cantonment at 10.30 am and 2.30 pm via the cantonment hotels for Rs 25. Telephone ☎ 46-477 for reservations. Auto-rickshaws charge Rs 80 and taxis around Rs 140.

Bus Godaulia is the midtown bus stop, just an easy walk from the ghats. Lanka is the bus stop closest to Benares Hindu University. Between the railway station and Godaulia a bus costs around Rs 1, but unless you can get on at the starting point Varanasi buses tend to be very crowded.

Auto-Rickshaw & Tempo These operate on a shared basis with fixed prices (Rs 1 to Rs 3) along set routes. Once the driver realises you're not going to rent the whole rickshaw, these can be the best way to get around the city cheaply, although not with a lot of luggage as they're very cramped.

From the stand outside the north entrance of the station it's Rs 1 to the cantonment TV tower or Rs 2 to the Civil Court (for auto-rickshaws to Sarnath). There's a stand outside the south entrance of the station for destinations including Lahurabir, the Civil Court and Godaulia (Rs 3).

Cycle-Rickshaw & Bicycle The main problem with cycle-rickshaws in Varanasi is the rickshaw-wallahs, who can be a major pain. A trip between the railway station and Godaulia, near Dasaswamedh Ghat, should be about Rs 10 but you'll probably have to pay twice that. The quoted 'two rupees anywhere' fare only applies if you let them take you to one of their 'cheap' hotels where

their commission is included in the room price.

There are several places to rent bicycles around Lanka; all-day rates are about Rs 15.

SARNATH
Only 10 km north-east of Varanasi is Sarnath, one of the major Buddhist centres. Having achieved enlightenment at Bodhgaya, the Buddha came to Sarnath to preach his message of the middle way to nirvana. Later, Ashoka, the great Buddhist emperor, erected magnificent stupas and monasteries here.

Sarnath was at its peak when the indefatigable Chinese traveller Fa Xien visited the site early in the 5th century AD. In 640 AD when Xuan Zhang, another Chinese traveller, made his call Sarnath had 1500 priests, a stupa nearly 100 metres high, Ashoka's mighty stone pillar and many other wonders. The city was known as the Deer Park, after the Buddha's famous first sermon, The Sermon in the Deer Park.

Soon after, Buddhism went into decline and after the Muslim invaders destroyed and desecrated the city's buildings, Sarnath was little more than a shell. It was not until 1836 when British archaeologists started excavations that Sarnath regained some of its past glory.

It's an interesting place to spend an afternoon but is quite touristy. Although you can stay in some of the monasteries here, if you're interested in studying Buddhism you'd probably be better off going to Bodhgaya or Dharamsala.

Dhamekh Stupa
This 34-metre-high stupa dominates the site and is believed to mark the spot where the Buddha preached his famous sermon. In its present form it dates from around 500 AD but was probably rebuilt a number of times. The geometrical and floral patterns on the stupa are typical of the Gupta period, but excavations have revealed brickwork from the Mauryan period around 200 BC.

Originally there was a second stupa,

Dharmarajika Stupa, but this was reduced to rubble by 19th-century treasure seekers.

Main Shrine & Ashoka Pillar

Ashoka is said to have meditated in the building known as the 'main shrine'. The foundations are all that can now be seen and to the north of it are the extensive ruins of the monasteries.

Standing in front of the main shrine are the remains of Ashoka's pillar. At one time this stood over 20 metres high, but the capital is now in the Sarnath Archaeological Museum. An edict issued by Ashoka is engraved on the remaining portion of the column and below this are representations of a lion, elephant, horse and bull. The lion is supposed to represent bravery, the elephant symbolises the dream Buddha's mother had before his birth, and the horse recalls that Buddha left his home on horseback in search of enlightenment.

Archaeological Museum

The main attraction at this excellent archaeological museum is the superb capital from the Ashokan pillar. It has the Ashokan symbol of four back-to-back lions which has been adopted as the state emblem of modern India. Other finds from the site include many figures and sculptures from the various periods of Sarnath – Mauryan, Kushana, Gupta and later. Among them is the earliest Buddha image found at Sarnath, Buddha figures in various positions dating back to the 5th and 6th centuries, and many images of Hindu gods such as Saraswati, Ganesh and Vishnu from the 9th to 12th centuries. The museum is open from 10 am to 5 pm daily, but is closed on Fridays. Entry is Rs 0.50, and there is a booklet available for Rs 3 at the counter.

Mulgandha Kuti Vihar

This modern Mahabodhi Society temple has a series of frescoes by the Japanese artist Kosetsu Nosi in the interior. A bo tree growing here was transplanted in 1931 from the tree in Anuradhapura, Sri Lanka, which in turn is said to be an offspring of the

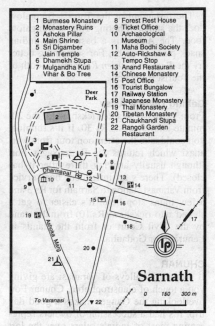

1 Burmese Monastery
2 Monastery Ruins
3 Ashoka Pillar
4 Main Shrine
5 Sri Digamber Jain Temple
6 Dhamekh Stupa
7 Mulgandha Kuti Vihar & Bo Tree
8 Forest Rest House
9 Ticket Office
10 Archaeological Museum
11 Maha Bodhi Society
12 Auto-Rickshaw & Tempo Stop
13 Anand Restaurant
14 Chinese Monastery
15 Post Office
16 Tourist Bungalow
17 Railway Station
18 Japanese Monastery
19 Thai Monastery
20 Tibetan Monastery
21 Chaukhandi Stupa
22 Rangoli Garden Restaurant

Sarnath

original tree under which the Buddha attained enlightenment. There's a group of statues here showing the Buddha giving his first sermon to his five disciples.

Other Temples & Deer Park

You can visit the modern temples in the Thai, Chinese, Tibetan, Burmese and Japanese *viharas* monasteries.

North of the Mulgandha Kuti Vihar is the deer park. This is now a mini-zoo with a few unhappy-looking deer foraging in the dust, and some large displays of Indian birds and waterfowl.

Places to Stay & Eat

The *Tourist Bungalow* has singles/doubles from Rs 62/75 to Rs 132/155, all with attached bathroom. There's also a very basic dorm at Rs 20 per bed. You can stay in some of the monasteries for a donation. The Burmese Vihara has 14 rooms, some with attached bathrooms, set around a peaceful courtyard.

UTTAR PRADESH

The restaurant at the Tourist Bungalow does the standard boring Tourist Bungalow food. The *Anand* is a basic south Indian snack place close by. For something better try the *Rangoli Garden Restaurant* south of the Tourist Bungalow.

Getting There & Away
From Varanasi, an auto-rickshaw for the 20-minute journey costs Rs 30. If it's running, you could take the afternoon tour from Varanasi which returns via Ram Nagar Fort (though usually arriving there after it has closed). There's an infrequent bus service from Varanasi station to Sarnath for Rs 3 and a few trains stop here. It's easier to get a shared auto-rickshaw (Rs 10) from the stand by the Civil Court or from the stands in Lahurabir or Godaulia.

CHUNAR
If the narrow alleys of Varanasi are giving you a touch of claustrophobia, Chunar Fort overlooking the Ganges makes a good day trip. It's had a succession of owners representing most of India's rulers over the last 500 years. Sher Shah took it from Humayun in 1540, Akbar recaptured it for the Mughals in 1575 and in the mid-18th century it passed to the nawabs of Avadh. They were shortly followed by the British, whose gravestones here make interesting reading. Chunar is 36 km from Varanasi and can be reached by bus.

JAUNPUR
Population: 150,000
Telephone Area Code: 05452
This town sees very few travellers but is of great interest to architectural historians for its mosques, built in a unique style that is part Hindu and Jain, and part Islamic.

Founded by Feroz Shah Tughlaq in 1360 on an ancient site, Jaunpur became the capital of the independent Muslim Sharqui kingdom. The most impressive mosques were constructed between 1394 and 1478. They were built on the ruins of Hindu, Buddhist and Jain temples, shrines and monasteries and are notable for their odd mixture of architectural styles, their two-storey

arcades and large gateways, and for their unusual minarets. Jaunpur was sacked by Sikandar Lodi, who left only the mosques undamaged, and the Mughals took over in 1530.

Most of the mosques and the railway station are in the older part of the town north of the Gomti River. They are spread out over two or three sq km and although you can walk to them a cycle-rickshaw can be useful, and the wallahs can also act as guides.

The **Atala Masjid**, built in 1408 on the site of a Hindu temple dedicated to Atala Devi, is one km from the station near the GPO. Continue 500 metres south of here and you come to **Jaunpur Fort** (built by Feroz Shah in 1360) and the stone **Akbari Bridge** constructed between 1564 and 1568. The largest of the mosques is the impressive **Jama Masjid** built between 1438 and 1478, one km north of the bridge. Other places to see include the Jhanjhri Masjid, the tombs of the Shaqui sultans, the Char Ungli Masjid and the Lal Darwaza Masjid.

Places to Stay & Eat
Jaunpur has a few very basic hotels and no fancy restaurants. Near the fort there's the *Hotel Gomti*, with doubles for Rs 80. Foreigners can also stay at the *Marwari Dharamsala* in the same area.

Getting There & Away
Varanasi is 58 km away, a journey of two hours by train (Rs 20) or bus (Rs 13).

Eastern Uttar Pradesh

GORAKHPUR
Population: 540,000
Telephone Area Code: 0551
This is a city that most travellers (on their way to Kathmandu or Pokhara from Delhi or Varanasi) are happy to quickly pass through, spending a night here only if necessary. Apart from the Gorakhnath Temple which you pass on the road to Nepal, there's not a lot to see. And even if there were, the plagues

of flies and mosquitoes early and late in the season would not encourage long stays.

Named after the sage Yogi Gorakhnath, Gorakhpur is in the centre of a rich agricultural area which has nevertheless remained very undeveloped. The city is also a centre for the printing and publishing of Hindu religious literature, and the well-known Geeta Press is here.

Information
There are tourist offices at the railway station and on Park Rd (☎ 33-5450) on the way to the city centre. If you have just come from Nepal, Indrail Passes can be bought at the railway station, although they only accept Indian rupees backed by exchange certificates.

If you are heading for Nepal, watch out for the ticket touts who home in like vultures as you get off the bus or train here. Their through tickets to Nepal by bus cost about 50% more than doing it yourself and are not always reliable, and they charge hefty commissions on rail tickets. However they may be useful during the high season when things are booked up, and they're also able to change Nepalese rupees.

Places to Stay
If you're catching the 5 am bus to Sunauli (at the border) then the hotels opposite the railway station are the most convenient, but they're certainly nothing special and this area is very noisy. The *Hotel Raj* has unappealing single/doubles with attached bath for Rs 60/100. The *Hotel Gupta & Tourist Lodge* (☎ 33-7899) is no better, and has rooms with common bath for Rs 50/80 or Rs 70/100 with attached bath.

Much better is the *Standard Hotel* (☎ 33-6439), with singles/doubles with attached bathrooms for Rs 70/125 and they've got the mosquito problem under control with netting on the windows. Unfortunately this makes it rather hot from late March onwards.

Also good is the *Hotel Elora* (☎ 33-0647). The rooms at the back have balconies overlooking a large playing field, and are also insulated from the noise. The cost is Rs 75/115 with attached bath and TV. There are also air-con rooms for Rs 225/300.

The *Hotel Siddhartha* (☎ 33-4976) has some air-con rooms for Rs 250/300 as well as small rooms without air-con for Rs 75/110/145. At the railway station there are *retiring rooms* for Rs 65/100, air-con deluxe doubles for Rs 125/220 and dorm beds for Rs 30.

In the centre of the city there's the *Hotel Yark-Inn* (☎ 33-8233) with rooms from Rs 70/125 with attached bath to air-con doubles for Rs 300. The similarly priced *Hotel Ambar* (☎ 33-8331) is close by.

The *Hotel Marina* (☎ 33-7630) is a good place with rooms from Rs 125/160 with attached bath and TV, air-cooled doubles for Rs 175 and air-con doubles for Rs 275. It's directly behind the *Hotel President* (☎ 33-7654), which is more expensive but the rooms are much the same. Ordinary rooms here are Rs 200, while rooms with air-con and TV are Rs 400. There are no single rooms.

Places to Eat
Around the railway station there are plenty of places to eat and the *refreshment room* in the station itself has good-value vegetarian meals.

In the city centre there's a much better range including the *Ganesh Restaurant* (good masala dosas) and *Bobi's* at the Ambar Hotel, which has a full menu (veg and nonveg) as well as an ice-cream parlour.

Slightly more expensive but probably the best place to eat in Gorakhpur is the *Queen's Restaurant* in the Hotel President. It has good service, powerful air-conditioning and the added advantage of staying open until around midnight.

Getting There & Away
Bus There are regular departures for the border at Sunauli (Rs 25, three hours) between 5 am and 8 pm from the bus stand near the railway station. You'll need to take the 5 am bus from Gorakhpur to be sure of catching a day bus from the border to Kathmandu or Pokhara. There are also private buses from the road in front of the railway station.

UTTAR PRADESH

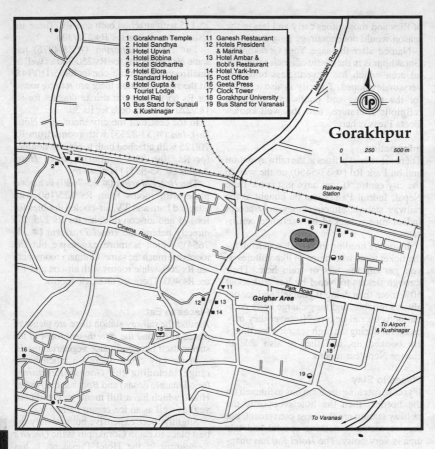

1	Gorakhnath Temple	11	Ganesh Restaurant
2	Hotel Sandhya	12	Hotels President
3	Hotel Upvan		& Marina
4	Hotel Bobina	13	Hotel Ambar &
5	Hotel Siddhartha		Bobi's Restaurant
6	Hotel Elora	14	Hotel Yark-Inn
7	Standard Hotel	15	Post Office
8	Hotel Gupta &	16	Geeta Press
	Tourist Lodge	17	Clock Tower
9	Hotel Raj	18	Gorakhpur University
10	Bus Stand for Sunauli	19	Bus Stand for Varanasi
	& Kushinagar		

Gorakhpur

Travel agents offer through tickets to Kathmandu (Rs 150) or Pokhara (Rs 140) but doing it yourself is not only cheaper and more reliable, it also gives you a choice of bus at the border. Even with 'through' tickets you have to change buses at the border.

Buses to Varanasi (Rs 56, 6½ hours) depart from the Katchari bus terminal which is a Rs 4 rickshaw ride from the city centre.

There are also regular buses to Lucknow (Rs 64) and Faizabad (Rs 45) as well as Kanpur and Patna. Buses to Kushinagar (Rs 14, 1½ hours) depart from the bus stand near the railway station.

Train Gorakhpur is the headquarters of the North Eastern Railway and is an important junction. There are evening departures for Delhi (783 km, 14½ hours, Rs 180/552 in 2nd/1st class) via Lucknow (276 km, 5½ hours, Rs 65/240). There's an early-morning departure for Bombay (1690 km, 35 hours, Rs 273/921) and six daily departures for Varanasi (231 km, five hours, Rs 57/208).

There are also metre-gauge trains to Nautanwa for Nepal, but as this is about eight km short of the border at Sunauli, the buses are more convenient.

UTTAR PRADESH

KUSHINAGAR

It's here that the Buddha is reputed to have breathed his last words, 'Decay is inherent in all component things' and expired. Pilgrims now come in large numbers to see the remains of his brick cremation stupa, the large, reclining Buddha figure in the Mahaparinirvana Temple, the modern Indo/Japan/Sri Lanka Buddhist Centre and the monasteries.

Places to Stay

For a small donation it's possible to stay in some of the monasteries. *Pathik Nivas*, the UP Tourist Bungalow, has singles/doubles for Rs 150/200, air-con rooms and a restaurant. There's also the ITDC Ashok *Traveller's Lodge*.

Getting There & Away

Kushinagar is 55 km east of Gorakhpur and there are frequent bus services (Rs 14, 1½ hours).

SUNAULI

Telephone Area Code: 05523

Right on the border with Nepal this sleepy village is just a bus stop, a couple of hotels, a few shops and the border post (open 24 hours). There's a much greater range of facilities on the Nepalese side. Whichever side you are staying, you are free to wander back and forth between the two without going through any formalities. Doing this carrying a backpack, however, is likely to attract attention.

The Nepalese border post is actually called Belhiya but everyone also refers to it as Sunauli. Nepalese visas are available here for US$25.

The easy-to-miss Indian immigration checkpoint is by the Sanju Lodge, about 200 metres from the border post.

There's a branch of the State Bank of India in Sunauli, but it is overrun, understaffed and open limited hours. If you have only travellers' cheques and it's outside regular banking hours (ie, 10 am to 2 pm weekdays), there's no alternative but to change with one of the numerous moneychangers on the Nepalese side. Their rates are competitive.

Places to Stay & Eat

The UP *Hotel Niranjana* (☎ 4901) is a clean and friendly although somewhat moth-eaten place 700 metres from the border. It's good value with singles/doubles with attached bath for Rs 75/100 and some air-cooled rooms for Rs 125/150. The restaurant serves standard, unexciting Tourist Bungalow food.

Closer to the border post is the dumpy *Sanju Lodge* (dorm beds Rs 25). On the Nepalese side there are several good cheap hotels.

Getting There & Away

The Sunauli bus stand is on the edge of the town, not more than one km from the border post, although the rickshaw-wallahs insist it's anything up to four km.

From Sunauli there are direct buses to Varanasi (Rs 81 to Rs 100, nine hours) in the early morning and early evening, and to Allahabad (Rs 77, 12 hours) and Lucknow (Rs 80, 11 hours).

Buses to Gorakhpur (Rs 25, three hours) depart every half hour from 5 am to 7 pm. Be wary of touts offering onward combined bus/rail tickets since these are not 100% reliable. They're easy enough to arrange yourself at Gorakhpur railway station.

To/From Nepal There are numerous private buses from the Nepalese side of the border to Kathmandu leaving hourly between 4.30 and 9 am (and sometimes additional buses at 10 and 11 am).

The night buses leave between 4.30 and 8 pm but of course on these you miss the great views on the journey. Buses take 10 to 12 hours and cost Nepalese Rs (NRs) 97 for the day buses, NRs 118 at night. You can pay for these tickets (and in fact anything else on the Nepalese side) with Indian rupees.

There is a bus booking office at the bus stand, and you should get a ticket in advance. It only sells tickets on the day of departure; for morning bus bookings it opens at 3 am.

The government 'Saja' buses are faster but

leave from Bhairawa, four km from Sunauli, at 6.30 and 7.30 am, then at 6.30 and 7.30 pm. They're very popular and booking is essential (NRs 97 from the kiosk opposite the Hotel Yeti in Bhairawa).

From Sunauli there are also morning and evening buses to Pokhara, which take nine to 10 hours and cost NRs 87 by day and NRs 95 at night.

For Lumbini (the birthplace of the Buddha) there are numerous buses from Bhairawa for the 22-km journey.

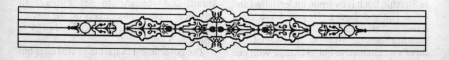

Bihar

Passing along the Ganges in the area that is now Bihar, the Buddha prophesied that a great city would arise here, but added that it would be always in danger from 'feud and fire and flood'. Over 250 years later, in the 3rd century BC, the mighty Ashoka was ruling from Pataliputra, now Patna. It's difficult to imagine that this city, the capital of one of the most backward and depressed states in the country, was once the capital of the greatest empire in India.

The name 'Bihar' is derived from 'Vihara' meaning monastery. Bihar was a great religious centre for Jains, Hindus and, most importantly, Buddhists. It was at Bodhgaya that the Buddha sat under the bo tree and attained enlightenment, and a descendant of that original tree still flourishes today. Nearby Nalanda was a world-famous Buddhist university in the 5th century AD, while Rajgir was associated with both the Buddha and the Jain apostle Mahavira.

Today the Buddha's predictions continue to come true. The rivers periodically flood causing disastrous problems for Bihar's dense population, which scratches a bare living from the soil. Per capita income is low yet the Chotanagpur plateau in the south produces 40% of India's mineral wealth. Bihar's literacy rate is one of the lowest in the country, the state is considered to have the most widespread corruption and the state government is chronically short of money ('funds crunch'). Civil servants and teachers get paid only every now and then – a recent newspaper article reported that a government department was putting off 80 staff due to lack of funds, but the staff were staying on because there was no money to pay them out! 'Feud and fire' take the form of outbreaks of inter-caste warfare and violence – dacoity is still widespread in Bihar.

Few travellers spend much time here, most just passing through Patna on their way to Calcutta or Kathmandu. However, Bodhgaya is an excellent place to study

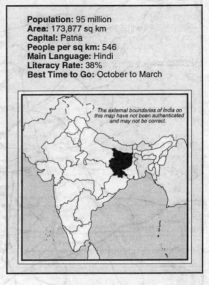

Population: 95 million
Area: 173,877 sq km
Capital: Patna
People per sq km: 546
Main Language: Hindi
Literacy Rate: 38%
Best Time to Go: October to March

The external boundaries of India on this map have not been authenticated and may not be correct.

Buddhism, and Rajgir, Nalanda and Sasaram are interesting places that are not on the tourist trail.

PATNA

Population: 1.2 million
Telephone Area Code: 0612

As you would expect of one of India's poorest and most densely populated states, Bihar's capital is noisy, crowded, polluted and typically chaotic. It sprawls along the southern bank of the Ganges, which at this point is very wide; between Varanasi and Patna, it is joined by three major tributaries and triples in width. The Mahatma Gandhi Seti, one of the longest bridges in the world at 7.5 km, crosses the Ganges here.

History

Ajatasatru shifted the capital of the Magadha Empire from Rajgir early in the 5th century

BIHAR

437

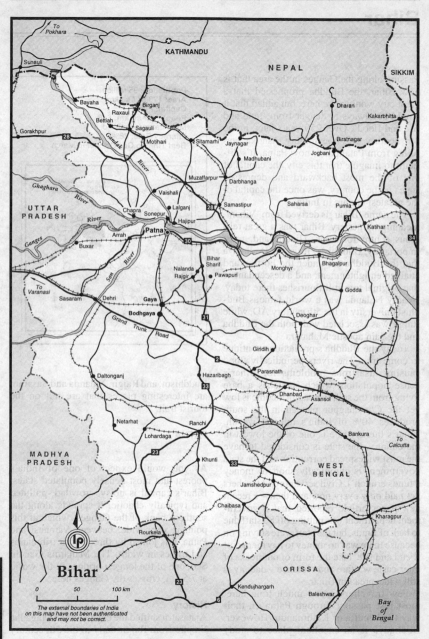

To Pokhara

Sunauli

KATHMANDU

NEPAL

SIKKIM

Dharan

Kakarbhitta

Bayaha

Raxaul

Bettiah

Birganj

Gorakhpur

28

Sagauli

Motihari

Sitamarhi

Jaynagar

Biratnagar

Jogbani

Madhubani

Muzaffarpur

Darbhanga

Vaishali

Ghaghara River

UTTAR
PRADESH

Chapra

Sonepur

Lalganj

Samastipur

Saharsa

Purnia

31

28

Hajipur

Patna

Katihar

34

Arrah

30

Buxar

Ganges

Son River

Bihar
Sharif

Monghyr

Bhagalpur

Nalanda

Rajgir

Pawapuri

To
Varanasi

Sasaram

Dehri

Gaya

31

Godda

Deoghar

Bodhgaya

Grand Trunk Road

Giridih

2

Daltonganj

Hazaribagh

Parasnath

33

Dhanbad

Asansol

Netarhat

Ranchi

Bankura

To
Calcutta

Lohardaga

23

Khunti

33

WEST
BENGAL

MADHYA
PRADESH

Jamshedpur

Chaibasa

Kharagpur

Rourkela

23

Kendujhargarh

6

ORISSA

Baleshwar

Bay
of
Bengal

Bihar

0   50   100 km

The external boundaries of India
on this map have not been authenticated
and may not be correct.

BIHAR

BC, fulfilling the Buddha's prophecy for a great city here. The remains of his ancient city of Pataliputra can still be seen at the site in Kumrahar, a southern district of Patna. This was the capital of a huge empire spanning a large part of ancient India with Chandragupta Maurya and Ashoka among the emperors who ruled from here. For almost 1000 years Pataliputra was one of the most important cities on the subcontinent.

Renamed Azimabad, the city regained its political importance in the mid-16th century AD when Sher Shah, after defeating Humayun, made it his capital. It passed to the British in 1764 after the Battle of Buxar.

Orientation

The city stretches along the southern bank of the Ganges for about 15 km. The hotels, main railway station and airport are all in the western half of Patna, known as Bankipur, while the older and more traditional area is to the east, in Patna City. The 'hub' of the new Patna is at Gandhi Maidan. The main market area is Ashok Raj Path, which starts from Gandhi Maidan.

Two important roads near the railway station, Fraser and Exhibition Rds, have officially had their names changed to Muzharul Haque Path and Braj Kishore Path respectively, but everyone still uses the old names. On the other hand, Gardiner Rd is now referred to as Birchand Patel Path.

Information

The state tourist office (☎ 22-5295, but currently disconnected due to lack of funds!) is on Fraser Rd; the entrance is through the Chef Restaurant entrance. There are also counters at the railway station and the airport – but don't expect much from any of them. There's also a Government of India tourist office (☎ 22-6721), inconveniently located south of the railway line.

There are a couple of reasonable bookshops along Fraser Rd and a British Library (☎ 22-4198) on Bank Rd near the Bishuram Bhavan by Gandhi Maidan.

Golghar

Overlooking the maidan, this huge, beehive-shaped building was constructed in 1786 as a granary to store surpluses against possible famines. It was built by Captain John Garstin at the instigation of the British administrator, Warren Hastings, and although the Bihar government is making use of it now, it has hardly ever been filled. Standing about 25 metres high with steps winding around the outside to the top, the Golghar provides a fine view over the town and the Ganges.

Patna Museum

This excellent, albeit somewhat dog-eared, museum contains metal and stone sculptures dating back to the Maurya (3rd century BC) and Gupta (4th to 7th centuries AD) periods, terracotta figures and archaeological finds from sites in Bihar such as Nalanda. To the right as you walk in is the world's longest fossilised tree – 16 metres of it, 200 million years old. Stuffed wildlife includes the usual (tiger, deer, crocodile) and the unusual (a kid with three ears and eight legs). Upstairs are Chinese and Tibetan paintings and *thankas* (Tibetan cloth paintings). The museum is open from 10 am to 4.30 pm; closed on Mondays. Entry costs Rs 0.50.

Kumrahar Excavations

The remains of Pataliputra, the ancient capital of Ajatasatru (491-459 BC), Chandragupta (321-297 BC) and Ashoka (274-237 BC), have been uncovered in Kumrahar, south of Patna. The main points of interest are the assembly hall (a few large pillars are all that remain) dating back to the Mauryan period, and the foundations of the brick Buddhist monastery known as Anand Bihar. There's a small display of some of the clay figures and wooden beams discovered here.

The Kumrahar excavations are fairly esoteric, however, and are likely to attract only those with a keen interest in archaeology and India's ancient history. They are set in a pleasant park open daily (except Monday) from 9 am to 5 pm; entry costs Rs 0.50. Shared auto-rickshaws between Patna Junction railway station and Gulzarbagh pass right by here and cost Rs 3.

Har Mandir

At the eastern end of the city, in the Chowk area of old Patna, stands one of the holiest Sikh shrines. Built of white marble by Ranjit Singh, it marks the place where Gobind Singh, the 10th and last of the Sikh gurus, was born in 1660.

Not only must you go barefoot within the temple precincts, but your head must be covered. They lend cloths for this purpose at the entrance.

Qila House (Jalan Museum)

Built on the foundations of Sher Shah's fort, Qila House contains an impressive private collection of antiques, including a dinner-service that once belonged to George III, Marie Antoinette's Svres porcelain, Napoleon's four-poster bed, Chinese jade and Mughal silver filigree. Phone ☎ 64-2354 for permission to visit.

Khuda Baksh Oriental Library

Founded in 1900, this library has a renowned collection of rare Arabic and Persian manu-scripts, Mughal and Rajput paintings, and

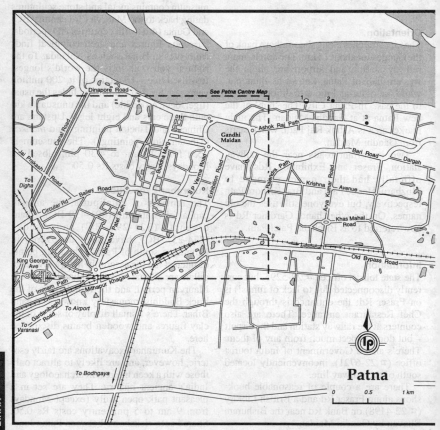

Patna

0   0.5   1 km

oddities like the Koran inscribed in a book only 25 mm wide. The library also contains the only books to survive the sacking of the Moorish University of Cordoba in Spain.

Other Attractions

Non-Hindus are welcome at the modern **Mahavir Mandir**, dedicated to the popular god, Hanuman. At night this place is lit up in garish pink and green neon – you can't possibly miss it as you leave the main railway station.

The heavy, domed **Sher Shahi**, built by the Afghan ruler Sher Shah in 1545, is the oldest mosque in Patna. Other mosques include the squat **Pathar ki Masjid** and the riverbank **Madrassa**.

Gulzarbagh, to the east of the city, was the site of the East India Company's **opium warehouse**. The building is currently occupied by a Bihar state government printing works.

Organised Tours

The state tourist office operates a day trip which includes Patna, Rajgir, Nalanda and Pawapuri. It runs on Saturday and Sunday, and the cost is Rs 100. For departure times,

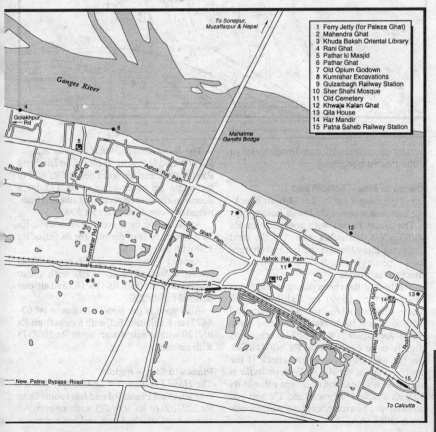

1 Ferry Jetty (for Paleza Ghat)
2 Mahendra Ghat
3 Khuda Baksh Oriental Library
4 Rani Ghat
5 Pathar ki Masjid
6 Pathar Ghat
7 Old Opium Godown
8 Kumrahar Excavations
9 Gulzarbagh Railway Station
10 Sher Shahi Mosque
11 Old Cemetery
12 Khwaje Kalan Ghat
13 Qila House
14 Har Mandir
15 Patna Saheb Railway Station

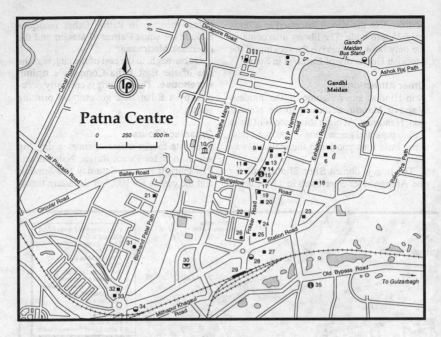

Patna Centre

0   250   500 m

contact the tourist office or Hotel Kautilya Vihar (tourist bungalow).

Places to Stay – bottom end
Don't get caught out by the 24-hour check-out time that many of the hotels here apply.

The *Hotel Parker* with rooms from Rs 40/50 is OK but rather dark. On the next block, the *Ruby Hotel* is spartan and charges Rs 40 for singles, Rs 50/70 for rooms with attached bathrooms.

The best of the cheap places is the *Hotel Shyama* (☎ 65-5539) on Exhibition Rd, where singles/doubles/triples with attached bathrooms cost Rs 40/60/85. Close by is the *Hotel Rajkumar* (☎ 65-5011) which is slightly more expensive at Rs 60/100/130. On the way there you could check if the double room at the *AA of Eastern India* is available. It's clean and excellent value at Rs 50 with attached bathroom and TV and you don't have to be a member of the Automobile Association (AA).

The *Hotel Kautilya Vihar (Tourist Bungalow)* (☎ 22-5411) is in 'R-block' on Birchand Patel Path. There are dorm beds at Rs 60 but the rooms are better value at Rs 175 for a double, with water heaters in the attached bathrooms. Air-con doubles are Rs 300.

At the station there are *retiring rooms*; Rs 30 for dorm beds or doubles for Rs 90, or Rs 150 with air-con.

Another good place is the small *Hotel Sheodar Sadan* (☎ 22-7210) with clean singles/doubles from Rs 115/145 and air-con doubles for Rs 250.

Also good is the *Hotel Chaitanya* (☎ 65-8473) on Exhibition Rd, with rooms from Rs 95/120 with attached bath, up to Rs 300/375 with air-con.

Places to Stay – middle
The *Hotel President* (☎ 22-0600) is down a side street off Fraser Rd and has rooms from Rs 225/260 or Rs 400/475 with air-con. All rooms have attached bath and hot water.

PLACES TO STAY

3	Maurya Patna Hotel
5	Hotel Shyama
6	Hotel Rajkumar
7	Ruby Hotel
8	Hotel Sheodar Sadan
9	Hotel Parker
11	Hotel President
13	Rajasthan Hotel
16	Hotel Rajdhani
17	AA of Eastern India
18	Republic Hotel
19	Hotel Dai Ichi
20	Samrat International Hotel
21	Hotel Pataliputra Ashok
22	Hotel Satkar International
23	Hotel Chaitanya
25	Hotel Mayur & Mamta Restaurant
27	Hotel Anand Lok
32	Hotel Kautilya Vihar (Tourist Bungalow)
33	Hotel Chanakya

PLACES TO EAT

12	Jal Annapurna Restaurant
14	Ashoka Restaurant
24	Mayfair Ice-Cream Parlour

OTHER

1	British Library
2	Golghar
4	Indian Airlines
10	Patna Museum
15	Government of Bihar Tourist Office
26	Jail
28	Auto-Rickshaw Stand (for Gulzarbagh)
29	Patna Junction Railway Station
30	GPO
31	Water Tower
34	Main Bus Terminal
35	Government of India Tourist Office

The *Hotel Samrat International* (☎ 22-0560, fax 22-6386) on Fraser Rd is a good mid-range hotel, with single/doubles from Rs 350/450, or with air-con at Rs 600/700; it boasts the first solar hot-water system in the state.

Also on Fraser Rd is the *Rajasthan Hotel* (☎ 22-5102), which charges Rs 240/300 for single/doubles, or Rs 350 with air-con, although at these prices you'd expect hot

water to be supplied. Not far away is the *Satkar International Hotel* (☎ 22-0551, fax 22-0556), where rooms cost Rs 275/375, or there are deluxe rooms for Rs 450/550. This is one of the few places with a noon check-out.

Places to Stay – top end
The *Hotel Chanakya* (☎ 22-3141, fax 22-0598), near the tourist bungalow, is a centrally air-conditioned three-star place that charges Rs 850/1000 for singles/doubles, or there are suites for Rs 1195.

Overlooking Gandhi Maidan, the *Welcomgroup Maurya Patna* (☎ 22-2060, fax 22-2069) is Patna's top hotel and has the usual mod cons, including a pool. Rooms cost from Rs 1150/1350. The *Hotel Pataliputra Ashok* (☎ 22-6270) is better value at Rs 1050/1300.

Places to Eat
Patna has plenty of places to eat, many of which are along Fraser Rd not far from the railway station. The *Mayfair Ice-cream Parlour* is a clean and popular place with good masala dosas and other snacks, as well as 16-odd ice-cream flavours. The nearby *Mamta Restaurant* has main dishes for Rs 30 and beer is available for Rs 38. Further up Fraser Rd, the *Ashoka Restaurant* is rather dark but the non-vegetarian food (Chinese, tandoori) is good.

Not far from the Ashoka, the *Rajasthan Hotel* has the best vegetarian restaurant in the city. It's not cheap but the food is excellent and they have a good range of ice creams. The *Jai Annapurna Restaurant* does good chicken kebabs and has a takeaway service. In the same area is the *Bansi Vihar Restaurant*, which specialises in south Indian food.

Getting There & Away
Air Indian Airlines (☎ 22-6433) has daily flights between Patna and Delhi (US$87), Calcutta (US$51) and Ranchi (US$32). Three flights a week connect Patna with Lucknow (US$47).

Bus The main bus terminal is at Harding Park, just west of Patna Junction railway station. It's a large place with departure gates spread out along the road. Buses for Siliguri (Rs 101 to Rs 112, 12 hours), Gaya (Rs 20, three hours), Rajgir (Rs 20, three hours), Ranchi (Rs 75, eight hours) and Sasaram (Rs 35, 4½ hours) go from Gate 7. Buses for Raxaul (Rs 50, five hours) on the Nepalese border go from Gate 6, via Muzaffarpur.

The Gandhi Maidan bus stand is used by government buses to many places in Bihar. There are night buses to Ranchi and also a deluxe bus to Siliguri (Rs 115, departing at 7.30 pm). There's also a deluxe night bus to Raxaul (Rs 55, seven hours).

Train Patna Junction is the main railway station. The fastest trains on the Calcutta to Delhi line take 12 hours to Delhi (992 km, Rs 208/624 in 2nd/1st) and 5½ hours to Calcutta (545 km, Rs 139/415 in 2nd/1st). There are a number of direct trains daily to Varanasi (228 km, five hours); Gaya (92 km, two hours); Ranchi (591 km, 10 hours); Bombay and a weekly service to Madras.

If you're heading to Darjeeling or the north-east region, the fast *North East Express* from Delhi leaves Patna at 9.15 pm, arriving in New Jalpaiguri at 9.25 am. From Patna to New Jappaiguri it's 636 km and Rs 155/464 in 2nd/1st class.

To/From Nepal There are no direct trains from Patna to the border town of Raxaul (you have to change at Muzaffarpur) so the buses are faster. From the main bus terminal, there are departures at 6.30 am, and 12.30, 2.20 and 10 pm, and other departures from the government bus stand. Buses take five hours and cost Rs 50.

It's also possible to buy through-tickets to Kathmandu from a number of operators, including the Rajasthan Hotel. They offer a bus to Raxaul, a rickshaw for the border crossing and a voucher for a Nepalese bus on to Kathmandu for Rs 280 with an overnight stay in a hotel at Raxaul. It's just as easy to do it yourself which not only gives you a choice of bus from the border, but is also cheaper.

Getting Around
To/From the Airport There's no bus service but the airport is so close you can get there by cycle-rickshaw for Rs 15. Taxis charge about Rs 70.

Auto-Rickshaw Shared auto-rickshaws shuttle back and forth between the main Patna Junction railway station and Gulzarbagh for Rs 5 per person. The other main route is from the Patna Junction railway station to Gandhi Maidan bus stand it costs Rs 3.

PATNA TO NEPAL
Sonepur
A month-long cattle fair is held in October-November at Sonepur, 25 km north of Patna. It takes place around the full moon at Kartika Purnima, the most auspicious time to bathe at the confluence of the Ganges and the Gandak here. This is probably the largest animal fair in Asia and not only cattle but all types of animals are traded here. At the Haathi Bazaar, elephants change hands for anything from Rs 10,000 to Rs 100,000, depending on age and condition. If you'd like to purchase an alternative form of transport, Mark Shand's *Travels on my Elephant* is essential reading for the modern mahout.

Vaishali
As long ago as the 6th century BC, Vaishali was the capital of a republic. It's the birthplace of Mahavira, one of the Jain tirthankars, and was where the Buddha preached his last sermon. There's very little to see – an **Ashoka pillar** (with its lion capital intact), a couple of dilapidated **stupas** (one contains an eighth of the Buddha's ashes) and a small **museum**. There are guided tours from Patna or buses from Lalganj and Muzaffarpur. There's a *tourist bungalow* at Vaishali.

Muzaffarpur
Population: 264,000

Apart from being a bus-changing point on the way to the Nepal border, Muzaffarpur is of limited interest. This is a poverty-stricken, agriculturally backward area. There are a number of places to stay, including the *Hotel*

Deepak with reasonable food and very spartan rooms. The *Hotel Elite*, near the railway station on Saraiya Gunj, is more expensive.

Motihari & Raxaul

North of Muzaffarpur, the area becomes even poorer. Motihari, where George Orwell was born, is a small provincial town which is also the district headquarters. Raxaul is right on the border and is virtually a twin town with Birganj, just across the border in Nepal. Both towns are crowded and dirty. Cycle-rickshaws take 30 minutes (Rs 18) to get from the border (open 4 am to 10 pm) to the bus stand in Birganj. Nepalese visas are available at the border for US$25.

Places to Stay This is not a place to stick around. There are rooms at the *Hotel Kaveri* in Raxaul for Rs 40/60. The *Hotel Ajanta* is better. It's down a side road near the bus stand and charges Rs 40/70 for a room with common bath. Alternatively, you can cross the border and stay in equally unattractive Birganj.

Getting There & Away There are several buses a day from Raxaul to Patna (Rs 50, five hours) and more to Muzaffarpur. Beware of touts selling combined bus/train tickets as it's much more reliable to organise things yourself.

From Birganj there are morning and evening buses to Kathmandu taking around 12 hours (Nepalese Rs 110) or Pokhara (Nepalese Rs 100, 10 hours). To Kathmandu most buses take the much longer road via Narayanghat and Mugling, rather than the dramatically scenic Tribhuvan Highway via Naubise.

Warning Immigration procedures can be somewhat unorthodox at Birganj. Officials there have been known to demand the US$25 visa fee (if you don't already have a Nepalese visa) in US dollars cash *only*. They may not accept any other currency – Nepalese rupees and Indian rupees included – so be prepared for this.

PATNA TO VARANASI
Sasaram

It's worth stopping off here between Varanasi and Gaya or Patna to see the impressive **mausoleum of Sher Shah** who died in 1545. Built of red sandstone in the middle of

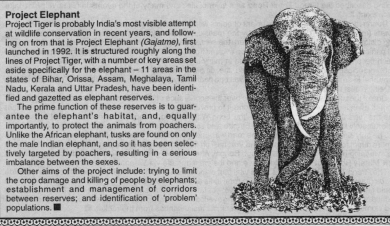

Project Elephant

Project Tiger is probably India's most visible attempt at wildlife conservation in recent years, and following on from that is Project Elephant *(Gajatme)*, first launched in 1992. It is structured roughly along the lines of Project Tiger, with a number of key areas set aside specifically for the elephant – 11 areas in the states of Bihar, Orissa, Assam, Meghalaya, Tamil Nadu, Kerala and Uttar Pradesh, have been identified and gazetted as elephant reserves.

The prime function of these reserves is to guarantee the elephant's habitat, and, equally importantly, to protect the animals from poachers. Unlike the African elephant, tusks are found on only the male Indian elephant, and so it has been selectively targeted by poachers, resulting in a serious imbalance between the sexes.

Other aims of the project include: trying to limit the crop damage and killing of people by elephants; establishment and management of corridors between reserves; and identification of 'problem' populations. ■

a large artificial pond, it's particularly striking in the warm light of sunset. The 46-metre dome has a 22-metre span, which is four metres wider than the Taj Mahal's dome.

Sasaram is on the Grand Trunk Road, the famous Indian highway that was built by Sher Shah in the mid-16th century. The narrow streets of this small town are interesting to wander round. There's also the **tomb of Hassan Khan** (Sher Shah's father) and several other Muslim monuments.

There are more Muslim tombs at **Maner**. At **Dehri**, 17 km from Sasaram, the railway and the Grand Trunk Road cross the River Son on a three-km bridge. The hill fort of **Rohtas** is 38 km from here.

Places to Stay & Eat The best place to stay is the friendly *Tourist Lodge* which is a 15-minute walk from the station. Turn left onto the Grand Trunk Road outside the railway station and it's by the second petrol station. Doubles are Rs 50, or Rs 60 with attached bathrooms and Rs 75 with air-cooler. The *Ruchi Restaurant* is a good place to eat.

Getting There & Away There are frequent buses for Patna (Rs 35, 4½ hours). For Varanasi and Gaya it's better to take a train as buses start at Dehri, 17 km away, and few stop here.

PATNA TO GAYA
Nalanda
Founded in the 5th century BC, Nalanda was one of the world's great universities and an important Buddhist centre until it was sacked by the Afghans in the 12th century. When the Chinese scholar and traveller Xuan Zhang was here in the early 7th century AD, there were 10,000 monks and students in residence.

The brick-built remains are extensive and include the **Great Stupa**, with steps, terraces and a few intact votive stupas around it, and the monks' cells. There's an interesting **archaeological museum** (Rs 0.50; closed on Friday) housing the Nalanda University seal, sculptures and other remains found on the site. Pilgrims venerate the Buddha figures in spite of signs saying 'Do not offer

The Grand Trunk Road
India's Grand Trunk Road (GTR) runs the breadth of the country, from the Pakistan border near Amritsar to Calcutta. It has been in existence for many centuries, and is by far the busiest road in the country. Rudyard Kipling described the Grand Trunk Road as a 'river of life', and many of the events in his novel, *Kim*, take place along it.

During the time of Ashoka's rule, pillars of edicts were placed along the road. In Mughal times it was *kos minars* (milestones) which were placed by the roadside, as the royal *kos* was the base unit for measuring long distances. Also of great importance were the *serais* (rest houses), established by many rulers over time but particularly during the Mughal era. These evolved from basically postal relay stations into establishments which became the focal point for commerce in many areas, and housed government officials; some were more grandiose constructions which even the emperor himself used when he passed through. The Nurmahal-ki-serai on the outskirts of Agra was one particularly grand serai, as was the serai of Begum Sahib in Delhi, eldest daughter of Shah Jahan.

One of the rulers with greatest influence over the appearance of the GTR was the emperor Jehangir, who planted avenues of trees *(khayabans)* along it to provide shade for travellers along the route. So pleasant was the road that it became known as 'the Long Walk' among European travellers in the 17th century. Unfortunately the decline of the Mughal Empire also saw a decline in the trees, as maintenance ceased.

The only significant realignment of the road was under the British, when the East India Company sought a more direct route between Calcutta and Varanasi on the mid-Ganges Plain; prior to that the road followed the sweeping bend of the Ganges through Bengal. After the realignment in 1781 the British renamed it the New Military Road, but this fell into disuse and the present route via Varanasi was completed in 1838.

The Grand Trunk Road today is still a vital part of the Indian road network. If you were to sit at a roadside *dhaba* (basic truckers' cafe) somewhere in rural India and observe the passing parade for a day or two, you would get a vivid picture of Indians on the move – oil tankers from Assam, Tata trucks from Punjab, barefoot sadhus on a Ganga pilgrimage, farmers steering overloaded ox-carts, wayward cows, schoolkids on bicycles and women on foot. You'd probably also suffer industrial deafness from the racket. ■

anything to the objects in the museum'! Buy a guidebook at the booking office for Rs 3.

The newest building here is the **Hiuen Tsang Memorial Hall**, built as a Peace Pagoda by the Chinese. Xuan Zhang spent five years here as both student and teacher.

There's also an international centre for the study of Buddhism, established in 1951. There are Burmese, Japanese and Jain dharamsalas at Nalanda as well as a PWD *rest house*.

Getting There & Away Shared Trekkers (jeeps) cost Rs 3 from Rajgir to Nalanda village, and from there it's Rs 2 for the 10-minute ride on a shared tonga to the university site. Take another jeep (Rs 3) from Nalanda village to Bihar Sharif for buses to Patna (Rs 18, 2½ hours).

Rajgir

Telephone Area Code: 06119

This was the capital of the Magadha Empire until Ajatasatru moved to Pataliputra (Patna) in the 5th century BC. Today, Rajgir is a minor Indian holiday centre. In winter, visitors are drawn by the hot springs and the healthy climate of this hilly region, 19 km south of Nalanda.

Rajgir is an important Buddhist pilgrimage site since the Buddha spent 12 years here, and the first Buddhist council after the Buddha attained nirvana was held here. It's also an important place for Jains, as the Mahavir spent some time in Rajgir and the hills are topped with Digambara shrines. A mention in the *Mahabharata* also ensures a good supply of Hindu pilgrims.

Orientation & Information The main road passes about half a km west of the town. On it are the railway station and bus stand, and there are a number of hotels in this area.

There's a tourist office by the hot springs, which are about one km south of town along the main road.

Things to See Most people rent a tonga for half a day to see the sites as they're spread out over several km. This costs about Rs 50,

but, with the brutal way these horses are treated, do them a favour and take a taxi, although this will cost more.

Main sites include parts of the ruined city, caves and places associated with Ajatasatru and his father Bhimbisara, whom he imprisoned and murdered. The pink building by the crowded hot springs is the **Lakshmi Narayan Temple**. There are separate bathing areas for men and women, and you'll be pestered for baksheesh by the temple 'priest' if he shows you around the baths ('just a small donation, Rs 100 or Rs 200'!). On the other hand, the tourist police will show you around, then wave goodbye rather than hold out a hand for a tip.

There's also a Burmese temple, an interesting **Jain exhibition** (Rs 5), a modern Japanese temple and on the top of Ratnagiri Hill, three km south of the hot springs, the **Japanese Shanti Stupa**, reached by a chairlift (Rs 8 return; 8.15 am to 1 pm and 1.30 to 5 pm daily).

Places to Stay & Eat Accommodation prices vary widely depending on the season. High season is mid-September to mid-November.

One of the cheaper places is the *Hotel Anand*, near the bus stand. Gloomy rooms downstairs cost Rs 75, or much better rooms upstairs are Rs 100, all with attached bath. The hotel serves basic vegetarian meals for Rs 18.

The *Hotel Siddharth*, south of town near the hot springs, is set within a pleasant walled courtyard. Rooms are Rs 70/125 with attached bathrooms.

The *Hotel Rajgir* (☎ 5266) has a pleasant garden and the rooms are OK at Rs 75/165 with attached bathrooms. *Triptee's Hotel* has some good double rooms with balconies for Rs 200. Non-veg meals are available for Rs 20.

The *Hotel Gautam Vihar* (Tourist Bungalow No 1) is on the main road, five minutes' walk from both the bus and railway stations. Dorm beds are Rs 45, but the rooms are overpriced at Rs 175, or Rs 275 with air-con.

The off-season prices are much more realistic – Rs 25, Rs 90 and Rs 175 respectively.

The top hotel here is the Japanese-designed *Hotel Centaur Hokke* (☎ 5245), signposted three km west of the hot springs. It's a very pleasant hotel with both Japanese and Western-style rooms, at US$68/106, or with meals for US$103/186. The restaurant here is moderately expensive, and serves Indian and Japanese food. If you are staying elsewhere and want to eat here, you'll have to hire a cycle-rickshaw or tonga to take you there, and wait while you eat to take you back again.

Getting There & Away Rajgir is on a branch line with daily trains to Patna but the buses are faster (Rs 20, three hours). There are also buses to Gaya (Rs 13, two hours) and Pawapuri. For Nalanda take a shared jeep for Rs 3.

Pawapuri

Mahavira, the final tirthankar and founder of Jainism, died and was cremated here in about 500 BC. It is said that the demand for his sacred ashes was so great that a large amount of soil was removed around the funeral pyre, creating the lotus-filled tank. A marble temple, the **Jalmandir**, was later built in the middle of the tank and is now a major pilgrimage spot for Jains. You can get here by bus from Rajgir or Bihar Sharif.

GAYA

Population: 323,000
Telephone Area Code: 0631

Gaya is about 100 km south of Patna. Just as nearby Bodhgaya is a major centre for Buddhist pilgrims, Gaya is a centre for Hindu pilgrims. Vishnu is said to have given Gaya the power to absolve sinners. Pilgrims offer *pindas* (funeral cakes) at the ghats along the river here, and perform a lengthy circuit of the holy places around Gaya, to free their ancestors from bondage to the earth.

If you're on your way to Bodhgaya but only reach Gaya after dark, spend the night here – there have been a number of night-time muggings on the Gaya to Bodhgaya road. There are also reports of pilgrims being 'befriended' at the station, drugged with cups of tea and robbed.

There's a tourist office at the railway station.

Vishnupad Temple

In the crowded central part of the old town, this sikhara-style temple was constructed in 1787 by Queen Ahalya Bai of Indore on the banks of the River Falgu. Inside the temple the 40-cm-long 'footprint' of Vishnu is imprinted in solid rock and surrounded by a silver-plated basin, although non-Hindus are not allowed to enter.

During the monsoon, the river carries a great deal of water but it dries up completely in winter. You can see cremations taking place on the river banks.

Other Attractions

A flight of 1000 stone steps leads to the top of the **Brahmajuni Hill**, one km south-west of the Vishnupad Temple. There's a good view over the town from the top. Gaya has a small **archaeological museum** (closed on Monday), near the tank.

A **temple of Surya**, the sun god, stands 20 km to the north at Deo. The **Barabar Caves**, dating back to 200 BC, are 36 km north of Gaya. These are the 'Marabar' caves of E M Forster's *A Passage to India*. Two of the caves contain inscriptions from Ashoka himself. To get there take the train to Bela, a tonga from there for 10 km and it's then a five-km walk to the two groups of caves.

Places to Stay & Eat

There are railway *retiring rooms* with a Rs 20 dorm and doubles at Rs 70 or Rs 125 with air-con. There are many other places to stay around the station, most of them spartan but OK for a short pause.

The *Paul Rest House* (☎ 29-282), set back from the road, is quiet and cheap, with rooms with bathroom for Rs 50/90. The *Shanti Rest House* and the *Madras Hotel* are similar places. The *Hotel Siddharth* is a friendly place with dorm beds for Rs 25, or basic singles/doubles with common bath for Rs 40/60.

Dance

Classical Indian dancing relates back to the Hindu god Siva's role as Nataraj, Lord of the Dance. Lord Siva's first wife was Sati and when her father, who disliked Siva, insulted him Sati committed suicide in a sacrifice by fire that later took her name. Outraged, Siva killed his father-in-law and danced the *tandava* – the Dance of Destruction. Later, Sati reincarnated as Parvati, married Siva again and danced the *lasya*. Thus, the tandava became the male form of dance, the *lasya* the female form. Dancing was a part of the religious temple rituals and the dancers were known as *devadasis*. Their dances retold stories from the *Ramayana* or the *Mahabharata*.

Although temple dancing is no longer practised, classical Indian dancing is still based on its Hindu roots. Indian dance is divided into *nritta*, the rhythmic elements; *nritya*, the combination of rhythm with expression; and *natya*, the dramatic element. Nritya is usually expressed through eye, hand and facial movements and with nritta makes up the usual dance programmes. To appreciate natya, or dance drama, you have to understand and appreciate the Hindu legends and mythology.

Classical dance is divided into four basic forms known as Bharath Natyam, Kathakali, Manipuri and Kathak. Bharath Natyam is further subdivided into three other classical forms, and is one of the most popular dances. It originated in the great temples of the south and usually tells of events in Krishna's life. Bharath Natyam dancers are usually women and, like the sculptures they take their positions from, always dance with bent knees, never standing upright, and use a huge repertoire of hand movements. Orissi, Mohini Attam and Kuchipudi are variations of Bharath Natyam which take their names from the places where they originated.

LEANNE LOGAN

Left: The celebrated Bharath Natyam dancer, Meenakshi Seshadri.

Right: Performance of the traditional dance forms of Bharath Natyam, Pune Festival, Maharashtra.

LEANNE LOGAN

Kathakali, the second major dance form, originated in Kerala and is exclusively danced by men. It tells of epic battles of gods and demons and is as dynamic and dramatic as Bharath Natyam is austere and expressive. Kathakali dancing is noted for the elaborate make-up and painted masks which the dancers wear. They even use special eye drops to turn their eyes a bloodshot red!

As the name indicates, Manipuri dances come from the Manipur region in the north-east. These are folk dances and the message is made through body and arm movements. The women dancers wear hooped skirts and conical caps which are extremely picturesque.

The final classical dance type is Kathak, which originated in the north and at first was very similar to the Bharatha Natyam school. Persian and Muslim influences later altered the dance from a temple ritual to a courtly entertainment. The dances are performed straight-legged and there are intricately choreographed foot movements to be followed. The ankle bells which dancers wear must be adeptly controlled and the costumes and themes are often similar to those in Mughal miniature paintings.

There are many opportunities to see classical Indian dancing while you are in India. The major hotels often put on performances to which outsiders as well as hotel guests are welcome.

Left Top & Bottom: Kathakali dancers in preparation for traditional dances.

Right: The elaborate make-up and costume of a Kathakali dancer.

GREG ELMS

GREG ELMS

GREG ELMS

Music

Indian music is most unlike the Western concept of music, and is very difficult for a Westerner to appreciate without a lengthy introduction and much time spent in listening. Music plays an important role in the Hindu religion, and is linked to the god Siva. It can also be a mystical experience, akin to yoga.

The two main forms of Indian music are the southern Carnatic (folk) and the northern Hindustani Vedic (religious) traditions. The basic difficulty is that there is no harmony in the Western sense. The music has two basic elements, the *tala* and the raga. Tala is the rhythm and is characterised by the number of beats. *Teental* is a tala of 16 beats. The audience follows the tala by clapping at the appropriate beat, which in teental is at one, five and 13. There is no clap at the beat of nine since that is the *khali* or 'empty section' indicated by a wave of the hand.

The raga provides the melody; just as there are a number of basic talas so there are many set ragas. The classical Indian music group consists of three musicians who provide the drone, the melody and the rhythm – in other words a background drone, a tala and a raga. The musicians are basically soloists – the concept of an orchestra of Indian musicians is impossible since there is not the harmony that a Western orchestra provides – each musician selects their own tala and raga. The players then zoom off in their chosen directions, as dictated by the tala and the raga selected, and, to the audience's delight, meet every once in a while before again diverging.

Top: Musicians at the Pongal religious festival, Madurai.

Bottom left: Rajasthani folk dancers, Shilpgram.

Bottom right: Indian band, Fatehpur Sikri.

GREG ELMS

HUGH FINLAY

PAUL BEINSSEN

Yehudi Menuhin, who has devoted much time and energy to understanding Indian music, suggests that it is much like Indian society: a group of individuals not working together but every once in a while meeting at some common point. Western music is analogous to Western democratic societies: a group of individuals (the orchestra) who each surrender part of their freedom to the harmony of the whole.

Although Indian religious music has one of the longest continuous histories of any musical form, the music had never, until quite recently, been recorded in any written notation. Furthermore, within the basic framework set by the tala and the raga, the musicians improvise – providing variations on the basic melody and rhythm.

Best known of the Indian instruments are the sitar and the tabla. The sitar is the large stringed instrument popularised by Ravi Shankar in the West – and which more than a few Westerners have discovered is notoriously difficult to tune. This is the instrument with which the soloist plays the raga. Other stringed instruments are the sarod (which is plucked) or the sarangi (which is played with a bow). The tabla, a twin drum rather like a Western bongo, provides the tala. The drone, which runs on two basic notes, is provided by the oboe-like *shehnai* or the *tampura*.

Top: Tampura. (photograph by Glenn Beanland)

Bottom left: Tabla.

Bottom right: A young boy beats a tabla under the watchful eye of a male relative at an Indian wedding.

GLENN BEANLAND

MICHELLE COXALL

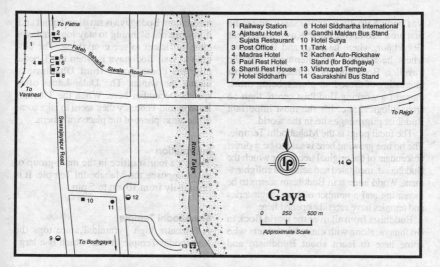

1	Railway Station	8	Hotel Siddhartha International
2	Ajatsatu Hotel &	9	Gandhi Maidan Bus Stand
	Sujata Restaurant	10	Hotel Surya
3	Post Office	11	Tank
4	Madras Hotel	12	Kacheri Auto-Rickshaw
5	Paul Rest Hotel		Stand (for Bodhgaya)
6	Shanti Rest House	13	Vishnupad Temple
7	Hotel Siddharth	14	Gaurakshini Bus Stand

Gaya

0   250   500 m

Approximate Scale

The *Ajatsatu Hotel* (☎ 21-514) is opposite the railway station and boasts 'best lodging with appropriated rooms'. It has reasonable doubles with attached bathrooms for Rs 150, or Rs 350 with air-con. The hotel's *Sujata Restaurant* is quite good (main dishes cost Rs 25).

Of a similar standard is the *Hotel Surya* (☎ 24-004), a newish place a Rs 4 cycle-rickshaw ride from the railway station, with doubles for Rs 125 with attached bathrooms, or Rs 175 with water heaters and TV.

The top hotel in town is the *Hotel Siddhartha International* (☎ 21-254) which caters to upmarket pilgrims. Rooms cost US$17/22, or US$23/28 with air-con. There's a good non-vegetarian restaurant with main dishes around Rs 35.

All over Bihar you will see stalls selling the popular puff-pastry sweet known as khaja, which originated in a village between Gaya and Rajgir. Catch them as they come out of the oil – the flies are as partial to them as the Biharis are.

Getting There & Away

Buses to Patna (Rs 20, three hours) and Ranchi (Rs 45, seven hours) leave from the Gandhi Maidan bus stand. Buses to Rajgir (Rs 13, two hours) leave from the Gaurakshini bus stand which is across the river.

Gaya is on the main Delhi to Calcutta line and there are direct trains to Delhi, Calcutta, Varanasi, Puri and Patna.

The auto-rickshaws from the railway station cost Rs 80 for the 14-km trip to Bodhgaya but they'll try for twice as much. From the Kacheri auto-rickshaw stand, which is a 25-minute walk from the station, it's Rs 4 for a seat, plus Rs 2 for a rucksack. Watch your head on the low roof in the back, though, or you'll attain a state of unconsciousness before you reach Bodhgaya!

Getting Around

It's Rs 5 by cycle-rickshaw to the Kacheri auto-rickshaw stand (for Bodhgaya) or to the Gaurakshini bus stand (for Rajgir) from the railway station.

BODHGAYA

Population: 24,000
Telephone Area Code: 0631

The four most holy places associated with the Buddha are Lumbini, in Nepal, where he was born; Sarnath, near Varanasi, where he first preached his message; Kushinagar, near Gorakhpur, where he died; and Bodhgaya, where he attained enlightenment. For the traveller, Bodhgaya is probably the most interesting of these four places, being much more of a working Buddhist centre than an archaeological site. It's the most important Buddhist pilgrimage site in the world.

The focal point is the Mahabodhi Temple. The bo tree growing here is said to be a direct descendant of the original tree under which the Buddha sat, meditated and achieved enlightenment. World interest in Buddhism seems to be increasing and a number of new monasteries and temples have recently opened here.

Buddhists from all over the world flock to Bodhgaya, along with many Westerners who come here to learn about Buddhism and meditation. Bodhgaya is small and quiet and, if you are not planning to stay long, a day is quite sufficient to see everything. The best time to visit Bodhgaya is when the Tibetan pilgrims come down from Dharamsala, during the winter. The Dalai Lama often spends December here. When the Tibetans leave in mid-February they seem to take some of the atmosphere of the place with them.

Information

There's a tourist office in the main group of shops opposite the Mahabodhi Temple. It is open daily from 10 am to 5 pm.

Mahabodhi Temple

A 50-metre high pyramidal spire tops the Mahabodhi Temple, inside which is a large

---

Life of the Buddha

Legend tells that the birth of the prince of the Sakya clan who was to become the Buddha was attended by great portents and prophesies. He was named Siddhartha ('one whose aim is accomplished') because at his birth (in about 560 BC in Lumbini, now in Nepal) a soothsayer predicted that he would attain a position of immense power, either as a secular ruler or as a religious leader. Further predictions warned that if he ever laid eyes on the sufferings of the world he would have no choice but to follow the latter course and give up his family's kingdom.

His father, the king, anxious that this shouldn't happen, ensured that he was surrounded with youth, beauty and good health. He grew up happily, got married and had a son. As he grew older, however, the soothsayer's prediction came true. Outside the palace, amongst his father's subjects, he was confronted by the spectres of old age, sickness and death. Observing a wandering ascetic, and impressed by his tranquil countenance, he resolved to give up his privileged life in a search for absolute truth.

Subjecting himself to the most extreme deprivations, he spent nearly six years as an ascetic. He is said to have lived on just one grain of rice a day, fasting until he could feel his backbone when he clasped his stomach. He is also reputed to have spent long periods sitting on thorn bushes and sleeping amongst rotting corpses.

Barely alive and staggering along beside a river near Bodhgaya one day, he fainted and fell into the water. Coming to, he decided that such mortifica-

gilded image of the Buddha. The temple is said to stand on the site of a temple erected by Ashoka in the 3rd century BC. Although the current temple was restored in the 11th century, and again in 1882, it is said to be basically the same as the one standing here in the 7th century. The stone railing around the temple, parts of which still stand, was originally thought to date from Ashoka's time but is now considered to be from the Sunga period around 184-172 BC. The carved and sculptured railing has been restored, although parts of it now stand in the museum in Calcutta and in the Victoria & Albert Museum in London. Stone stupas, erected by visiting pilgrims, dot the temple courtyard. Entry to the temple grounds costs Rs 1, plus Rs 10 for a camera, and the temple is closed between noon and 2 pm.

Bodhi Tree

A sapling from the original bo tree under which the Buddha sat was carried to Sri Lanka by Sanghamitta (the Emperor Ashoka's daughter) when Ashoka took Buddhism to that island. That tree now flourishes at Anuradhapura in Sri Lanka and, in turn, a cutting from it was carried back to Bodhgaya when the original tree here died. A red sandstone slab under the tree is said to be the Vajrasan, or diamond throne, on which the Buddha sat.

Monasteries

Most countries with a large Buddhist population have a temple or monastery here, usually built in a representative architectural style. Thus the Thai temple looks very much like the colourful *wats* you see in Thailand. The Tibetan temple and monastery was built

tions were counterproductive to his quest, and indulged in a restorative meal. After his meal he settled down beneath a bodhi tree to meditate.

While meditating, he came to the realisation that the human lot is one of an endless cycle of birth and death to which people are bound because of human desire. He realised that he had been unable to achieve enlightenment as an ascetic because he desired it and sought it so actively. Now that he had ceased to desire he became enlightened and could attain nirvana (escape from the cycle of birth and death into a state of perfect bliss).

The Buddha summarised his teachings into the Four Noble Truths:

1) Existence comprises conflict, dissatisfaction, sorrow and suffering;
2) This state is caused by selfish desire;
3) It is possible to escape from this and attain nirvana;
4) The key to achieving this is to follow the Eight-Fold Path.

Eight-Fold Path
- Right Understanding (uninhibited by superstition or delusion);
- Right Thought (as befits human consciousness and intelligence);
- Right Speech (honest and compassionate);
- Right Action (peaceful and honest);
- Right Mode of Living (without causing harm to other living creatures);
- Right Endeavour (self-discipline and control);
- Right Mindfulness (having an alert and contemplative mind);
- Right Concentration (deep contemplation on the realities of life).

The Buddha first enunciated the Eight-Fold Path to five ascetics, former companions on his pilgrimage, at present-day Sarnath. This first sermon was known as the Dhammacakkappavattana-sutta ('Setting in Motion the Wheel of Truth'). He maintained that it is inappropriate to follow two extremes, that is, self-indulgence and self-mortification. By avoiding these two extremes the Buddha had discovered the 'Middle Path'.

The Buddha died in Kushinagar (near Gorakhpur) in about 480 BC, reputedly after eating poisonous mushrooms.

The tenets encompassed in the Four Noble Truths and the Eight-Fold Path, transmitted orally by disciples of the Buddha after his death, form the basis of the philosophy of Buddhism today. ■

in 1934 and contains a large prayer wheel. The Tibetans have two other places here, the Sakya monastery and the Karma Temple.

The Burmese, who led the campaign to restore the Mahabodhi Temple in the 19th century, built their present monastery in 1936. The Japanese temple (Indosan Nipponji) has a very beautiful image of the Buddha brought from Japan and across the road is the Daijokyo Temple. There are also Chinese, Sri Lankan, Bhutanese and Vietnamese monasteries. The Tai Bodhi Kham monastery is being built by Buddhist tribes from Assam and Arunachal Pradesh. Laos is

also working on a monastery. The newest is the Nepalese Tamang monastery, opened in 1992.

Other Attractions
The **archaeological museum** (open 10 am to 5 pm daily except Friday) has a small collection of Buddha figures and pillars found in the area. The Hindu Shankaracharya Math has a **temple**, and a sculpture gallery is due to open there. Across the river are the Dungeshwari and Suraya temples.

The 25-metre **Great Buddha Statue** in the Japanese Kamakura style was unveiled

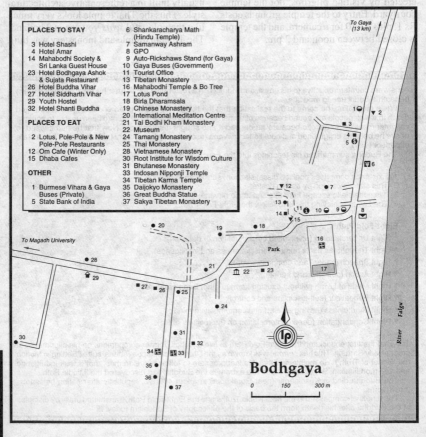

PLACES TO STAY

3 Hotel Shashi
4 Hotel Amar
14 Mahabodhi Society & Sri Lanka Guest House
23 Hotel Bodhgaya Ashok & Sujata Restaurant
26 Hotel Buddha Vihar
27 Hotel Siddharth Vihar
29 Youth Hostel
32 Hotel Shanti Buddha

PLACES TO EAT

2 Lotus, Pole-Pole & New Pole-Pole Restaurants
12 Om Cafe (Winter Only)
15 Dhaba Cafes

OTHER

1 Burmese Vihara & Gaya Buses (Private)
5 State Bank of India
6 Shankaracharya Math (Hindu Temple)
7 Samanway Ashram
8 GPO
9 Auto-Rickshaws Stand (for Gaya)
10 Gaya Buses (Government)
11 Tourist Office
13 Tibetan Monastery
16 Mahabodhi Temple & Bo Tree
17 Lotus Pond
18 Birla Dharamsala
19 Chinese Monastery
20 International Meditation Centre
21 Tai Bodhi Kham Monastery
22 Museum
24 Tamang Monastery
25 Thai Monastery
28 Vietnamese Monastery
30 Root Institute for Wisdom Culture
31 Bhutanese Monastery
33 Indosan Nipponji Temple
34 Tibetan Karma Temple
35 Daijokyo Monastery
36 Great Buddha Statue
37 Sakya Tibetan Monastery

To Gaya (13 km)

To Magadh University

Park

River Falgu

Bodhgaya

0   150   300 m

by the Dalai Lama in 1989. There's a plan to build a much bigger Maitreya Buddha statue in Bodhgaya as a symbol of world peace.

Meditation Courses

Courses and retreats take place in the winter, mainly from November to early February.

Some of the most accessible courses are run by the Root Institute for Wisdom Culture (☎ 81-714), set in a peaceful location on the edge of Bodhgaya. They run basic five-day meditation courses and hold retreats. Travellers who have spent some time here all seem impressed, not only with the courses but by the way the Institute is working to put something back into the local community with health, agricultural and educational projects.

Courses are also run by the International Meditation Centre (☎ 81-734) near Magadh University (five km from Bodhgaya) and at their new centre (☎ 81-707) near the Thai Temple. The annual insight meditation (Vipassana) and spiritual enquiry retreats take place from 7 to 17 January, 17 to 19 January, and 29 January to 5 February at the Thai Monastery. Led since 1975 by Christopher Titmuss, the retreats have spaces for 125 people, and the all-inclusive cost is US$50. Write in advance to Gaia House (☎ (01803) 81-3188), Wodland Rd, Denbury, Nr Newton Abbot, Devon TQ12 6DY, UK or (from 15 October) Thomas Jost, Thai Monastery, Bodhgaya. Meditation courses are also offered at the Burmese and Tibetan monasteries. Some courses are advertised on the noticeboard in the (seasonal) Om Cafe.

If you're interested in working on social development projects in the area, contact the Samanway Ashram.

Places to Stay – bottom end

The Tourist Bungalows (No 1 and No 2) are next door to each other and have been given more imaginative names: the *Hotel Buddha Vihar* has only dormitory accommodation at Rs 35 a bed. *Hotel Siddharth Vihar*, next door, has doubles with attached bathrooms for Rs 200, and air-con rooms for Rs 275. There's also dorm beds for Rs 45.

The *Sri Lanka Guest House* run by the Mahabodhi Society charges Rs 100 for a double and is a popular and well-run place. On the road to Gaya, there are some basic little hotels like the *Amar* and the *Shashi*, with doubles for around Rs 75.

If you're planning a longer stay and/or don't mind roughing it a little, it's possible to stay at the monasteries. The Burmese monastery, which has a peaceful garden, is particularly popular with Westerners for its study courses. The rooms are extremely basic and you're expected to make a donation of Rs 10 per night. Dignified conduct is expected but unfortunately some travellers have abused the monastery's hospitality by smoking or breaking the rules in other ways.

Western visitors have also made themselves unpopular at the Japanese monastery and they may not be keen to let you in. It's clean and comfortable but packed out with Japanese tour groups during the season.

Pilgrims can stay at most of the monasteries although some have better facilities than others. The Bhutanese monastery is a good place and rooms without bath cost between Rs 30 and Rs 50. The Tibetan monastery is somewhat more spartan and cheaper.

Other places to try include the Sakya Tibetan monastery, and the Thai and Nepalese monasteries.

Places to Stay – middle

The new *Hotel Shanti Buddha* (☎ 81-785) has comfortable rooms, but it's hard to see how they justify the prices – Rs 350/450 for singles/doubles with attached bath, and Rs 700/850 with air-con. It's wildly overpriced. Next door another mid-range place, under construction at the time of writing, should have opened by now.

Places to Stay – top end

The ITDC *Hotel Bodhgaya Ashok* (☎ 22-708) has singles/doubles at Rs 800/1200, or Rs 1195/1800 with air-con. Prices and charges are reduced in the April to September off-season.

BIHAR

Places to Eat

The standard of food here is pretty low out of season and surprisingly high during the winter, when the pilgrims arrive. The *Mahabodi Canteen* at the Sri Lanka Guest House is a reliable place serving quite reasonable Chinese food.

The *Siva Hotel*, near the tourist office, tries to cater to Western tastes, with mixed results.

The best places are tent-restaurants opposite the Burmese Vihar. Here the *Lotus Pole-Pole*, the *New Pole-Pole* and the *Gautam* restaurants all have varied menus, good tape collections and are popular.

There are also several restaurants, such as the *Om Cafe*, run by Tibetans behind the Tibetan monastery. These restaurants operate in tents and only during the December to February season.

The *Sujata Restaurant* at the Hotel Bodhgaya Ashok is expensive and not very popular.

Getting There & Away

Bodhgaya is 13 km from Gaya and share auto-rickshaws shuttle back and forth. They're phenomenally overloaded, carrying three passengers on each side on benches in the back, one squeezed between them at the front, and another standing up at the very back. Then the driver up the front sits on a plank with two people see-sawing on each side of him, and for good measure there may be one or two on the roof! A total of up to 15 people (plus children, animals, goods, etc) travel on a vehicle intended for three! The fare is Rs 4 (or Rs 80 to rent the whole auto-rickshaw).

There are frequent buses, and these are also very crowded. Private buses (Rs 3) leave from outside the Burmese Vihar, government buses (Rs 2) from near the tourist office.

SOUTHERN BIHAR
Ranchi

Telephone Area Code: 0651

At 652 metres, Ranchi doesn't really deserve its title of hill station, especially since it has now lost most of its tree-cover. In British times it was Bihar's summer capital, with a reputation as a health resort. The Kanke hospital for the mentally handicapped is the best known in the country and was formerly a stop on the local tourist office's city tour.

One of the most interesting things to see here is the **Jagannath Temple**, a small version of the great Jagannath Temple at Puri, which celebrates its own, smaller festival of the cars. It's six km south-west of Ranchi and visitors are welcome.

There are a number of hills on the edges of Ranchi for sunset views over the rocky landscape. There's also a Tribal Research Institute with a **museum** here.

Places to Stay & Eat There are numerous hotels around the bus stand. The best small place is the friendly *Hotel Konark* with clean singles/doubles at Rs 80/100 with attached bathrooms and a good restaurant. Another good place is the *Hotel Paradise* at Rs 50/70.

The *Hotel Yuvraj* (☎ 30-0403), 'a house of respectable living', is 15 minutes from the station with rooms from Rs 175/300. Nearby, the centrally air-conditioned *Hotel Yuvraj Palace* (☎ 30-0805) has rooms from Rs 700/900. This is Ranchi's best hotel.

Getting There & Away Ranchi has good air, bus and train connections. The railway station is 500 metres from the bus stand. There are buses to Gaya (Rs 45, seven hours), Hazaribagh (Rs 20, three hours) and Netarhat (Rs 24, four hours). A through bus to Puri takes 15 hours.

Hazaribagh

This pleasant leafy town lies 107 km north of Ranchi, at an altitude of 615 metres. About the only reason for coming here would be to visit **Hazaribagh National Park**, 19 km to the north. You can stay in the park at the *Tourist Lodge* or *Forest Rest House*. In Hazaribagh, the *Hotel Upkar* (☎ (06546) 2246) is the best hotel and good value with singles/doubles for Rs 90/120.

The railway station, Hazaribagh Rd, is 67 km away. There are private minibuses for

Gaya (Rs 24, four hours) from outside the bus terminal.

Parasnath

Just inside the Bihar state boundary from West Bengal, and only a little north of the Grand Trunk Road, Parasnath is the major Jain pilgrimage centre in the east of India. Like so many other pilgrimage centres, it's perched on top of a steep hill and is reached by a stiff climb on foot. Rich Calcuttan Jain pilgrims are carried up in palanquins by porters.

The 24 temples, representing the Jain tirthankars, stand at an altitude of 1366 metres. Parasnath, the 23rd tirthankar, achieved nirvana at this spot 100 years after his birth in Varanasi.

Calcutta

Densely populated and polluted, Calcutta is often an ugly and desperate place that to many people sums up the worst of India, yet it's also one of the country's more fascinating centres and has some scenes of rare beauty. Certainly the people are a friendly bunch and Bengali humour is renowned throughout India.

Don't let the squalor of first impressions put you off this city. There are a lot of jewels to be discovered and they're not far from the surface. However, Calcutta is not a good introduction to India and is best visited after you've had a chance to get used to some of the country's extremes.

Economically Calcutta is suffering: the port has been silting up, making navigation from Calcutta down to the sea steadily more difficult and limiting the size of ships that can use the port. The Farakka Barrage (250 km north of Calcutta), designed to improve the river flow through the city, has been the subject of considerable dispute between India and Bangladesh because it will also affect the flow of the Ganges through Bangladesh.

Furthermore, Calcutta has been plagued by chronic labour unrest resulting in a decline of its productive capacity. Hindustan Motors is just one of the several major industries that have given up on the city and have transferred their operations to other states. The situation is summed up in the city's hopeless power-generation system. Electrical power in Calcutta has become so on-again off-again that virtually every hotel, restaurant, shop or small business has to have some sort of standby power generator or battery lighting system. The workers are blamed, the technicians are blamed, the power plants are blamed, the coal miners are blamed, even Indian railways are blamed for not delivering the coal on time, but it's widely pointed out that Bombay, for example, certainly doesn't suffer the frequency and extent of power cuts that are a way of life in Calcutta.

Population: 12 million
Main Language: Bengali
Telephone Area Code: 033
Best Time to Go: November to March

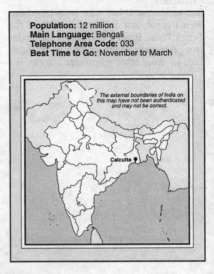

The external boundaries of India on this map have not been authenticated and may not be correct.

Calcutta

The Marxist government of West Bengal has come in for much criticism over the chaos currently existing in Calcutta but, as it is also pointed out, their apparent neglect and mismanagement of the city is combined with a considerable improvement in the rural environment. Threats of flood or famine in the countryside no longer send hordes of refugees streaming into the city as in the past.

Despite all these problems Calcutta is a city with a soul, and one which many residents are inordinately fond of. The Bengalis, so ready to raise arms against the British in the struggle for independence, are also the poets and artists of India. The contrast between the Bombay and Calcutta movie industries more or less sums it up. While Bombay, the Hollywood of India (known locally as Bollywood), churns out movies of amazing tinsel banality, the smaller number of movie makers in Calcutta make non-commercial gems that stand up to anything produced for sophisticated Western audiences.

The city's soul shows in other ways, too, and amongst the squalor and confusion Calcutta has places of sheer magic: flower sellers beside the misty, ethereal Hooghly River; the majestic sweep of the Maidan; the arrogant bulk of the Victoria Memorial; the superb collection of archaeological treasures exhibited in the Indian Museum. They're all part of this amazing city, as are massive Marxist and trade union rallies which can block traffic in the city centre for hours at a time. There's never a dull moment!

History

Calcutta isn't an ancient city like Delhi with its impressive relics of the past. In fact, it's largely a British creation which dates back only some 300 years and was the capital of British India until the beginning of this century.

In 1686, the British abandoned Hooghly, their trading post 38 km up the Hooghly River from present-day Calcutta, and moved downriver to three small villages – Sutanati, Govindpur and Kalikata. Calcutta takes its name from the last of those three tiny settlements. Job Charnock, an English merchant who later married a Brahmin's widow whom he dissuaded from becoming a sati, was the leader of the British merchants who made this move. At first the post was not a great success and was abandoned on a number of occasions, but in 1696 a fort was laid out near present-day BBD Bagh (Dalhousie Square) and in 1698, Aurangzeb's grandson gave the British official permission to occupy the villages.

Calcutta then grew steadily until 1756, when Siraj-ud-daula, the Nawab of Murshidabad, attacked the town. Most of the British inhabitants escaped, but those captured were packed into an underground cellar where, during the night, most of them suffocated in what became known as 'the black hole of Calcutta'.

Early in 1757, the British, under Clive of India, retook Calcutta and made peace with the nawab. Later the same year, however, Siraj-ud-daula sided with the French and was defeated at the Battle of Plassey, a turning point in British-Indian history. A much stronger fort was built in Calcutta and the town became the capital of British India.

Much of Calcutta's most enduring development took place between 1780 and 1820. Later in the 19th century, Bengal became an important centre in the struggle for Indian independence, and this was a major reason for the decision to transfer the capital to Delhi in 1911. Loss of political power did not alter Calcutta's economic control, and the city continued to prosper until after WW II.

Partition affected Calcutta more than any other major Indian city. Bengal and the Punjab were the two areas of India with mixed Hindu and Muslim populations and the dividing line was drawn through them. The result in Bengal was that Calcutta, the jute-producing and export centre of India, became a city without a hinterland; while across the border in East Pakistan (Bangladesh today), the jute (a plant fibre used in making sacking and mats) was grown without anywhere to process or export it. Furthermore, West Bengal and Calcutta were disrupted by tens of thousands of refugees fleeing from East Bengal, although fortunately without the communal violence and bloodshed that Partition brought to the Punjab.

The massive influx of refugees, combined with India's own postwar population explosion, led to Calcutta becoming an international urban horror story. The mere name was enough to conjure up visions of squalor, starvation, disease and death. The work of Mother Teresa's Calcutta mission also focused worldwide attention on Calcutta's festering problems. In 1971, the India-Pakistan conflict and the creation of Bangladesh led to another flood of refugees, and Calcutta's already chaotic condition further deteriorated. The problem of having too many mouths to feed will undoubtedly get worse since the birth rate has been rising, not falling, over the last 10 years. Calcutta has the largest population, after Bombay, of any Indian city.

Orientation

Calcutta sprawls north-south along the eastern bank of the Hooghly River, which

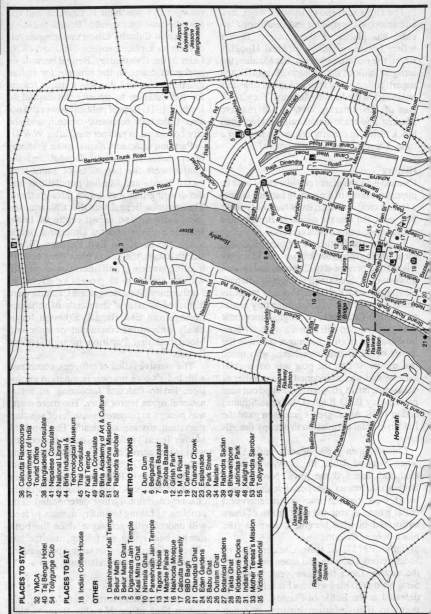

To Airport,
Darjeeling &
Jessore
(Bangladesh)

Barrackpore Trunk Road

Kosipore Road

Dum Dum Road

Raja Manindra Rd

Belgachia Rd

Cossipore Road

Canal Circular Road

Raja Dinendra Road

Canal East Road

Canal West Road

Chandra

Acharya Prafulla

Bagh Bazaar

Bose Ave

Aurobindo Sarani

Vivekananda Rd

Ram Mohan Sarani

Raja

Bidhan Sisu (Uday Saran)

Bidhan Sarani

D D Kharna Road

J Mohan Ave

Rabindra Sarani

K C Sen St

College

Chittaranjan

Hooghy River

Girish Ghosh Road

Nasalagore Rd

J N Mukherji Rd

B K Paul Ave

Tagore St

Cotton St

M Gandhi Rd

Howrah Bridge

Strand Road South

Netaji Subhash Road

Benlick Road

Srl Aurobindo Road

Kings Road

Dr A Dutta Rd

School Rd

Howrah Railway Station

Tikiapara Railway Station

Grand Trunk Road

Howrah

Nesai Subhash Road

Panchanantala Road

Chapur Road

Beillios Road

Desnagar Railway Station

Ramjatala Railway Station

PLACES TO STAY
32 YMCA
40 Taj Bengal Hotel
54 Tollygunge Club

PLACES TO EAT
18 Indian Coffee House

OTHER
1 Dakshineswar Kali Temple
2 Belur Math
3 Belur Math Ghat
5 Digambara Jain Temple
8 Kasi Mitra Ghat
10 Nimtala Ghat
11 Pareshnath Jain Temple
13 Tagore House
14 Marble Palace
16 Nakhoda Mosque
17 Calcutta University
20 BBD Bagh
24 Eden Gardens
25 Babu Ghat
26 Outram Ghat
27 Botanical Gardens
28 Takta Ghat
29 Kidderpore Docks
31 Indian Museum
33 Mother Teresa's Mission
35 Victoria Memorial

36 Calcutta Racecourse
37 Government of India Tourist Office
38 Bangladeshi Consulate
41 Nepalese Consulate
42 National Library
44 Birla Industrial & Technological Museum
45 Kali Temple
47 Thai Consulate
49 Italian Consulate
50 Birla Academy of Art & Culture
51 Ramakrishna Mission
52 Rabindra Sarobar

METRO STATIONS
4 Dum Dum
6 Belgachia
7 Shyam Bazaar
9 Shoba Bazaar
12 Girish Park
15 M G Road
19 Central
22 Chandni Chowk
23 Esplanade
30 Park Street
39 Rabindra Sadan
43 Bhawanipore
46 Jatindas Park
48 Kalighat
53 Rabindra Sarobar
55 Tollygunge

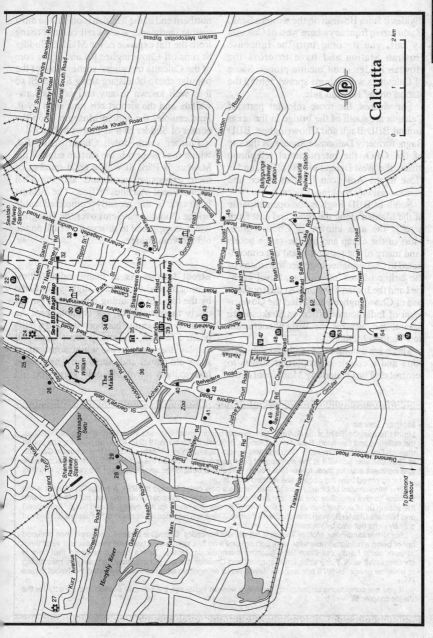

Calcutta

divides it from Howrah on the western bank. If you arrive from anywhere west of Calcutta by rail, you'll come into the immense Howrah Station and have to cross the Howrah Bridge into Calcutta proper. Some of Calcutta's worst slums sprawl behind the station on the Howrah side.

For visitors, the more relevant parts of Calcutta are south of the bridge in the areas around BBD Bagh and Chowringhee. BBD Bagh, formerly Dalhousie Square, is the site of the GPO, the international telephone office, the West Bengal tourist office, and is close to the American Express office and various railway booking offices.

South of BBD Bagh is the open expanse of the Maidan along the river, and east from here is the area known as Chowringhee. Most of the cheap and middle-range hotels (and many of the top-end ones) are concentrated in Chowringhee together with many of the airline offices, restaurants, travel agencies and the Indian Museum. At the southern end of Chowringhee you'll find the Government of India tourist office on Shakespeare Sarani, and, nearby, the Birla Planetarium and Victoria Memorial.

There are a number of landmarks in Calcutta and a couple of important streets to remember. The Ochterlony Monument at the northern end of the Maidan is one of the most visible landmarks – it's a tall column rising from the flat expanse of the Maidan. Sudder St runs off Chowringhee Rd and is the core of the Calcutta travellers' scene. Most of the popular cheap hotels are along Sudder St so it is well known to any taxi or rickshaw-wallah, and the airport bus runs right by it. Furthermore, the Indian Museum is on the corner of Sudder St and Chowringhee Rd.

Further south down Chowringhee Rd, which runs alongside the eastern edge of the Maidan, is Park St with a great number of more expensive restaurants and the Thai International Airlines office. The newest landmark is the recently completed cable bridge (Vidyasagar Setu) over the Hooghly, which is supposed to relieve the crush on the old Howrah Bridge.

Street Names As in many Indian cities, getting around Calcutta is slightly confused by the habit of renaming city streets, particularly those with Raj-era connotations. As usual this renaming has been done in a half-hearted fashion, and many street signs still display the old names, while some maps show old names and others show new ones; taxi-wallahs inevitably only know the old

---

Mother Teresa

Mother Teresa, the 'Saint of the Gutters', has come to epitomise selflessness in her dedication to the destitute, the suffering and the dying. Born Agnes Gonxha Bojaxhiu in Serbia in 1910 to Albanian parents, she joined the Irish Order of Loreto nuns in 1929 and was sent to Darjeeling as a teacher. Moving to a school in Calcutta in 1937 she was horrified at the numbers of poor people left to die on the streets of the city because there was nowhere else for them to go. She began to feel that behind the secure walls of the nunnery she was too far removed from the people she wanted to help.

The Missionaries of Charity was Mother Teresa's new order, formed in 1950. Amongst their vows is the promise 'to give wholehearted and free service to the poorest of the poor'. This vow was put into action with the setting up of several homes including Nirmal Hriday (the home for the dying), Shanti Nagar (for lepers) and Nirmala Shishu Bhavan (the children's home). There are now homes in many other places, staffed not only by nuns but also by volunteers or co-workers.

For all her saintliness, Mother Teresa is not without her critics. Germaine Greer, for example, has accused her of being a religious imperialist, although anyone who has spent some time with the nuns and seen them at work could hardly call them Bible-bashing evangelicals. Mother Teresa herself has said that hers is contemplative work. Her inspiration is spiritual and Christian but it is put into practice mainly by ministering to physical needs. In 1979 her work achieved world recognition when she was awarded the Nobel Peace Prize.

If you are considering undertaking voluntary work in India, see the relevant section in the Facts for the Visitor chapter. ■

Calcutta's Renamed Roads

Old Name	New Name
Ballygunge Store Rd	Gurusday Rd
Bowbazar St	Bepin Behary Ganguly
Buckland Rd	Bankim Ch Rd
Chowringhee Rd	Jawaharlal Nehru Rd
Harrington St	Ho Chi Minh Sarani
Harrison Rd	Mahatma Gandhi Rd
Kyd St	Dr M Ishaque Rd
Lansdowne Rd	Sarat Bose Rd
Lower Chitpur Rd	Rabindra Sarani
Lower Circular Rd	Acharya Jagadish Chandra Bose Rd
Machuabazar St	Madan Mohan St & Keshab Sen St
Mirzapore St	Suryya Sen St
Theatre Rd	Shakespeare Sarani
Wellesley St	Rafi Ahmed Kidwai Rd
Wellington St	Nirmal Chunder St

names. It's going to be a long time before Chowringhee Rd becomes Jawaharlal Nehru Rd! There's a certain irony that the street the US Consulate is on was renamed Ho Chi Minh Sarani!

Information

Tourist Offices The Government of India tourist office (☎ 242-1402, 242-3521) is at 4 Shakespeare Sarani and is very helpful. They can give you (somewhat dated) computerised printouts of any destination in India.

The West Bengal tourist office (☎ 248-8271) is at 3/2 BBD Bagh – the opposite side to the post office. It is open Monday to Saturday from 7 am to 1.30 pm and 2.15 to 6 pm, and on Sunday and holidays from 7 am to 12.30 pm. Both the state (☎ 552-9611, ext 440) and national tourist offices (☎ 552-9611, ext 444) have counters at the airport and West Bengal has an office at Howrah Station (☎ 660-2518; open daily 7 am to 1 pm).

Most other states have tourist offices here including the more obscure North-Eastern Region states, Sikkim and the Andaman & Nicobar Islands. They are as follows:

Andaman & Nicobar Islands
  3A Auckland Place (☎ 247-5084)
Arunachal Pradesh
  4B Chowringhee Place (☎ 248-6500)
Assam
  8 Russell St (☎ 29-8335)
Bihar
  26B Camac St (☎ 247-0821)
Madhya Pradesh
  Chitrakoot Bldg, 6th floor, 230A AJC Bose Rd (☎ 247-8543)
Manipur
  25 Asutosh Shastri Rd (☎ 350-4412)
Meghalaya
  9 Russell St (☎ 29-0797)
Mizoram
  24 Old Ballygunge Rd (☎ 475-7034)
Nagaland
  11 Shakespeare Sarani (☎ 242-5269)
Orissa
  55 Lenin Sarani (☎ 244-3653)
Sikkim
  5/2 Russell St (☎ 244-6717)
Tripura
  1 Pretoria St (☎ 242-5701)

To find out exactly what's happening on the cultural front, get hold of a free copy of the leaflet *Calcutta This Fortnight* from any tourist office.

Money American Express (☎ 248-4464, fax 248-8096) is at 21 Old Court House St. The Thomas Cook office (☎ 247-4560, fax 247-5854) is in the Chitrakoot Building, 230 AJC Bose Rd.

On Chowringhee Rd there are branches of the State Bank of India and ANZ Grindlays (beside Maidan metro station). ANZ Grindlays has another branch on Shakespeare Sarani. The Banque National de Paris has a branch at BBD Bagh, next to the West Bengal tourist office. Next door again, in the crumbling Stephen Building, is RN Dutt, a licensed private moneychanger who deals with just about any currency you can think of. On Sudder St there's at least one licensed moneychanger.

The State Bank of India has a 24-hour counter in the new terminal building at the airport.

Post & Telecommunications The large

Calcutta GPO is on BBD Bagh and has an efficient poste restante and a philatelic bureau for stamp collectors. The New Market post office is far more conveniently located if you're staying in the Sudder St area. The Park St post office is useful if you're staying in that area and more reliable for posting parcels than the GPO. There are people here who will handle the whole process for you (prices negotiable) and even the officials are friendly and helpful.

The Telephone Bhavan is also on BBD Bagh, while the Central Telegraph Office is at 8 Red Cross Place. There are lots of places to make international calls and faxes from, most with 'computerised' meters. American citizens only can make collect calls to the USA from the US Consulate.

International telephone calls are no problem but it takes several attempts to get through on a local call. When you eventually succeed, you invariably find that the number has been changed, although now that most numbers have seven digits, this problem should ease.

Foreign Consulates Some of the useful addresses in Calcutta include:

Bangladesh
    9 Circus Ave (☎ 247-5208)
Bhutan
    48 Tivoli Court, Pramothesh Barua Sarani (☎ 241-301)
Russia
    31 Shakespeare Sarani (☎ 247-2006)
Denmark
    3 N S Rd (☎ 248-7478)
France
    26 Park St (☎ 29-0978), inside the courtyard on the right-hand side of Alliance Franaise
Germany
    1 Hastings Park Rd (☎ 479-1141)
Italy
    3 Raja Santosh Rd (☎ 479-2426)
Japan
    12 Pretoria St (☎ 242-2241)
Nepal
    19 Sterndale Rd (☎ 479-1003)
Thailand
    18B Mandeville Gardens (☎ 76-0836)
UK
    1 Ho Chi Minh Sarani (☎ 242-5171)

USA
    5/1 Ho Chi Minh Sarani (☎ 242-3611)

The Nepalese Embassy is open from 9.30 am to 12.30 pm and 1.30 to 4.30 pm, and visas are issued while you wait.

The nearest Myanmar (Burmese) consulates are in Dhaka, Kathmandu and Delhi. For visas to Bangladesh, travellers have to go to Delhi even though there's an embassy here.

Those requiring Thai visas also have a problem as the Thai Consulate is hard to find. It's probably best to take a taxi, though the No 102 bus will get you close to it. It's near South Point School (not South Point High School) and closes at noon.

Visa Extensions & Permits The Foreigners' Registration Office (☎ 247-3301) is at 237 AJC Bose Rd. Visa exten- sions and permits for the Andaman Islands are issued here, although the latter are only required if you are arriving by boat. If you are flying to the Andamans, a permit can be obtained on arrival in Port Blair. Tax clearance certificates are available from Room 11, 4th floor, Income Tax Building, Bentinck St.

Travel Agencies If you're looking for cheap airline tickets, various places advertise their services around Sudder St. Pan Asian Tours, a tiny office on the 2nd floor at 20 Mirza Ghalib St (Free School St), seem to know what they're on about and have been recommended.

Books & Bookshops Geoffrey Moorhouse's classic 1971 study *Calcutta* is available as a Penguin paperback. More recently, V S Naipaul has some interesting chapters on Calcutta in his *India – A Million Mutinies Now*. Dominique Lapierre's *City of Joy* has become *de rigeur* reading among travellers to Calcutta and is available in paperback at almost every bookshop (pirated or otherwise). It's dangerous to criticise this book given the guru-like status that many readers accord him, but many parts of the book seem a little fanciful though otherwise interesting. What it certainly has done is to put the Anand Nagar slums in Howrah onto the tourist circuit, but we have a nagging feeling that this is pure voyeurism. When the book was filmed in 1991 a brand new slum was specially built as the set.

The main bookshop area is along College St, opposite the university. In the same building as the Indian Coffee House here, Rupa has a good range including its own publications. Newman's, the publishers of the Bradshaw railway timetable, run one of Calcutta's oldest bookshops, in the same block as the Great Eastern Hotel.

The Cambridge Book & Stationery Company at 20D Park St is a good small bookshop. Further down Park St towards Chowringhee Rd, the Oxford Book Shop is larger and also has some specialised stock. The Bookmark, upstairs at 56D Mirza Ghalib St, has a good general selection of books. Classic Books, at 10 Middleton Row, has a wide variety of both Indian and Western books, and the owner, Bharat, is also a mine of information. Booklands is a small bookstall at the eastern end of Sudder St.

At the end of January a large book fair is held on the Maidan.

Camera Repairs & Musical Instruments A recommended place for camera repairs is Camera Craft, Park Centre, 24 Park St, on the 1st floor. Mr Choudhury here is a helpful, honest guy. Best place for strings, tunings, repairs and negotiable prices on musical instruments is Braganza & Co at 2A Marquis St. The character who runs it really knows his instruments. Another good place is J Reynold & Co, 15 Free School St, where there's a great selection of instruments.

Medical Services Two places which have been recommended are: Dr Paes at Vital Medical Services (☎ 242-5664), 6 Ho Chi Minh Sarani. Opening hours are between 8 and 10 am.

The Wockhardt Medical Centre (☎ 475-4046) has also been recommended. It is at 2/7 Sarat Bose (Lansdowne) Rd, and hours are 10 am to noon. Alternatively, medical queries should be directed to any of the large hospitals.

Indian Museum

Conveniently situated on the corner of Sudder St and Chowringhee Rd, the Indian Museum was built in 1875. It's certainly the largest and probably the best museum in India, and one of the best in Asia. Unfortunately, it appears to have been starved of funds in recent years and many of the exhibits are literally falling apart. Some of the display cases are so dusty you can hardly see into them and Calcutta's power cuts don't help. Its widely varied collection includes oddities such as a whole roomful of meteorites. Other exhibits include the usual fossils, stuffed animals, skeletons and so on. There are a number of unique fossil skeletons of prehistoric animals, among them giant crocodiles and an amazingly big tortoise.

The art collection has many fine pieces from Orissan and other temples, and superb examples of Buddhist Gandharan art – an interesting meeting point between Greek artistry and Buddhist ideals centred around the North-West Frontier Province, now in Pakistan, that produced Buddha images and other sculptures of great beauty.

The museum is open from 10 am to 5 pm daily except Monday. Between December and February it closes half an hour earlier. Entry fee is Rs 1 except on Friday when it is free.

Maidan & Fort William

After the events of 1756, the British decided there would be no repetition of the attack on the city and set out to replace the original Fort William, in the Maidan, with a massive and impregnable new fort. First they cleared out the inhabitants of the village of Govindpur and in 1758 laid the foundations of a fort which, when completed in 1781, would cost them the awesome total, for those days, of 2 million. Around the fort a huge expanse of jungle was cut down to give the cannons a clear line of fire but, as usually happens, the fort has never fired a shot in anger.

The fort is still in use today and visitors

Calcutta Mounted Police
Every day at around 5 am, 25 officers of the Calcutta Mounted Police force mount up at the stables in Chowringhee and head off around Calcutta's 25-sq-km Maidan for the first of the day's half dozen or so sorties – a practice which has been going on for the last 150 years.

The force was first formed in the 1840s, and their role then was to carry communications between the city's administrators and the port's harbourmaster. At that time the force consisted of just one senior officer and two juniors. As the city grew, however, the force was enlarged, and its duties increased to include the patrolling of the city's Maidan, which was notorious as the hang-out of undesirables – thieves, muggers and prostitutes all frequented it. The force was gradually expanded to its present number of 98 horses, 105 men and as many syces.

In the early days all officers of the Mounted Police were British; only after independence was the first non-British officer appointed (an Anglo-Indian). The ranks were recruited from Uttar Pradesh, Kashmir and Rajasthan.

These days the main role of the force is to keep the city's football fans in order. A big match may draw a crowd of 90,000 excited fans to the Maidan, and outbreaks of violence are not uncommon; other duties include forming the guard of honour for visiting dignitaries.

The horses themselves are all bred in India specifically for the force, and cost around Rs 30,000 apiece. In the past, when cash was less of a worry, they were imported direct from Australia. ■

are only allowed inside with special permission (rarely granted). Even the trenches and deep fortifications surrounding the fort's massive walls seem to be out of bounds.

The area cleared around Fort William became the Maidan, the 'lungs' of modern Calcutta. This huge green expanse stretches three km north to south and is over a km wide. It is bound by Strand Rd along the river to the west and by Chowringhee Rd, lined with shops, offices, hotels and eating places, to the east. The stream known as Tolly's Nullah forms its southern boundary, and here you will find a racecourse and the Victoria Memorial. In the north-west corner of the Maidan is Eden Gardens, while Raj Bhavan overlooks it from the north.

Within the gardens are cricket and football fields, tennis courts, ponds, trees and Calcutta's latest attraction, the musical fountains. Cows graze, political discussions are held, people stroll across the grounds or come for early morning yoga sessions. And of course the place is used, like any area of open land in India, as a public toilet.

Ochterlony Monument Now officially renamed the Shahid (Martyr's) Minar, this 48-metre-high column towers over the northern end of the Maidan. It was erected in 1828 and named after Sir David Ochterlony, credited with winning the Nepal War (1814-

16). The column is a curious combination of Turkish, Egyptian and Syrian architectural elements.

There's a fine view from the top of the column, but permission to ascend (not granted for the first and last week of each month) must be obtained from the Deputy Commissioner of Police, Police headquarters, Lal Bazaar St. It's only open Monday to Friday and you should simply ask for a 'monument pass' at the Assistant Commissioner's office on the 2nd floor.

Eden Gardens In the north-west corner of the Maidan are the small and pleasantly laid-out Eden Gardens. A tiny Burmese pagoda was brought here from Prome, Myanmar (Burma) in 1856; it's set in a small lake and is extraordinarily picturesque. The gardens were named after the sister of Lord Auckland, the former governor general. The Calcutta Cricket Ground (Ranji Stadium), where international Test and one-day matches are held, is also within the gardens.

Near the gardens is a pleasant walk along the banks of the Hooghly River. Ferries run across the river from several ghats and there are plenty of boat operators around offering to take you out on the water for half an hour.

Victoria Memorial At the southern end of the Maidan stands the Victoria Memorial, the most solid reminder of British Calcutta – in fact probably the most solid reminder of the Raj to be found in India. The Victoria Memorial is a huge white-marble museum, a strange combination of classical European architecture with Mughal influences or, as some have put it, an unhappy British attempt to build a better Taj Mahal.

The idea behind the memorial was conceived by Lord Curzon, and the money for its construction was raised from 'voluntary contributions by the princes and peoples of India'. The Prince of Wales (later King George V) laid the foundation stone in 1906 and it was opened by another Prince of Wales (later the Duke of Windsor) in 1921.

Whether you're interested in the British Raj period or not, the memorial is an attraction not to be missed. It tells the story of the British Empire in India at its peak, just when it was about to begin its downhill slide. The imposing statue of Queen Victoria, at her bulky and least amused best, fronts the memorial and sets the mood for all the displays inside.

Inside you'll find portraits, statues and busts of almost all the main participants in British-Indian history. Scenes from military conflicts and events of the Mutiny are illustrated. There are some superb watercolours of Indian landscapes and buildings made by travelling Victorian artists. A Calcutta exhibit includes many early pictures of the city and a model of Fort William. Of course there are many fine Indian and Persian miniatures and rare manuscripts and books. Queen Victoria appears again inside, much younger and slimmer than her statue outside. There's also a piano she played as a young girl and other memorabilia. A huge painting depicts King Edward VII entering Jaipur in a regal procession in 1876. French guns captured at the Battle of Plassey are on exhibit along with the black stone throne of the nawab whom Clive defeated. To top it all off, there is a good view over the Maidan from the balcony above the entrance.

The booklet *A Brief Guide to the Victoria Memorial* is available in the building. The memorial is open from 10 am to 3.30 pm in winter, an hour later in summer. It is closed on Mondays, and entry costs Rs 2. The Sound & Light show is worth going to; the English-language programme starts at 8.15 pm, daily except Mondays. Tickets are Rs 5 and Rs 10.

St Paul's Cathedral
Built between 1839 and 1847, St Paul's Cathedral is one of the most important churches in India. It stands just to the east of the Victoria Memorial at the southern end of the Maidan. The steeple fell during an earthquake in 1897 and, following further damage in a 1934 quake, was redesigned and rebuilt. Inside, the memorials are interesting and there's some impressive stained glass, including the great west window by Sir Edward Burne-Jones. It's open to visitors from 9 am to noon, and from 3 to 6 pm. Sunday services are at 7.30 and 8.30 am, and 6 pm.

Birla Planetarium
This planetarium, near the Government of India tourist office, is one of the largest in the world. For Rs 8 you'll get a much better view of the stars in here than in the polluted atmosphere outside. There are shows in English every day, but as times vary, check in advance. Beware of pickpockets, especially in the queue outside.

Nehru Children's Museum
This small museum, conveniently situated at 94/1 Chowringhee Rd, is worth visiting for its models depicting the Hindu epics, the *Ramayana* and the *Mahabharata*. It's open from 11.30 am to 8.30 pm daily except Monday; admission is Rs 2, shows are Rs 10.

Kali Temple
Rebuilt in 1809 on the site of a much older temple, Kalighat (as it is also known) is the actual temple from which Kalikata (anglicised to Calcutta) takes its name. According to legend, when Siva's wife's corpse was cut up, one of her fingers fell here. Since then it has been an important pilgrimage site.

Kali represents the destructive side of Siva's consort and demands daily sacrifices. In the mornings goats have their throats slit here to satisfy the goddess' bloodlust. During the day many poor people come here for a free feed. This is an extremely busy temple (and one of the grubbiest), and you'll be latched on to by temple 'priests' who will whisk you around and then ask for a donation of Rs 100 for a 'small bag of rice'!

Mother Teresa's Hospital for the Dying Destitute is right next door to the temple and you are welcome to visit.

The temple is about two km directly south of St Paul's Cathedral and is easily accessible by metro.

Zoo & Horticultural Gardens

South of the Maidan, Calcutta's 16-hectare zoo was opened in 1875. Some of the animals are displayed in near natural environments, others in the pitiful conditions characteristic of Third World zoos. It's open from sunrise to sunset; admission is Rs 1.50.

Just south of the zoo on Alipore Rd are the pleasant and quiet horticultural gardens. They're open from 8 am to 5 pm; admission is Rs 1.

Howrah Bridge

Until 1943, the Hooghly River was crossed by a pontoon bridge which had to be opened to let river traffic through. There was considerable opposition to construction of a bridge due to fears that it would affect the river currents and cause silting problems. This problem was eventually avoided by building a bridge that crosses the river in a single 450-metre span with no pylons at all within the river.

The cantilevered bridge, also known as Rabindra Setu, is similar in size to the Sydney Harbour Bridge but carries a flow of traffic which Sydney could never dream of – with a daily stream of nearly 60,000 vehicles, and pedestrians too numerous to count, it is the busiest bridge in the world. It's intriguing to stand at one end of the bridge at morning rush hour and watch the procession of double-decker buses come across.

They heel over like yachts in a heavy wind due to the weight of passengers hanging onto the sides. In between are lumbering bullock carts, hordes of bicycles and even the odd car. During the morning and evening rush hours it can take 45 minutes to get across. The ferries running from below Howrah Station are a more convenient way to cross the river and give you a good view of the bridge.

The second bridge, Vidyasagar Setu, two km downriver, was an on-off project for 22 years but was finally completed in 1992. The problem now is that the approach roads to it are too narrow to handle the amount of traffic that uses the bridge, and there are no funds left for further development.

BBD Bagh (Dalhousie Square)

When Calcutta was the administrative centre for British India, BBD Bagh was the centre of power. On the north side of the square stands the huge Writers' Building which dates from 1880. In those days clerical workers were known as 'writers' and the East India Company's 'writers' have been replaced by modern-day ones employed by the West Bengal state government. That's where all the quintuplicate forms, carbon copies and red ink come from. Also on BBD Bagh is a rather more useful place, the Calcutta GPO, and on the eastern side of the square is the West Bengal tourist office.

Until it was abandoned in 1757, the original Fort William used to stand on the site of the present-day post office. It stretched from there down to the river, which has also changed its course since that time. Brass markers by the GPO indicate where the fort walls used to be. Calcutta's famous black hole actually stood at the north-east corner of the post office, but since Independence, all indications of its position have been removed. The black hole was actually a tiny guardroom in the fort and, according to the British version of the story, 146 people were forced into it on that fateful night when the city fell to Siraj-ud-daula. Next morning only 23 were still alive.

However, historians now suggest that the

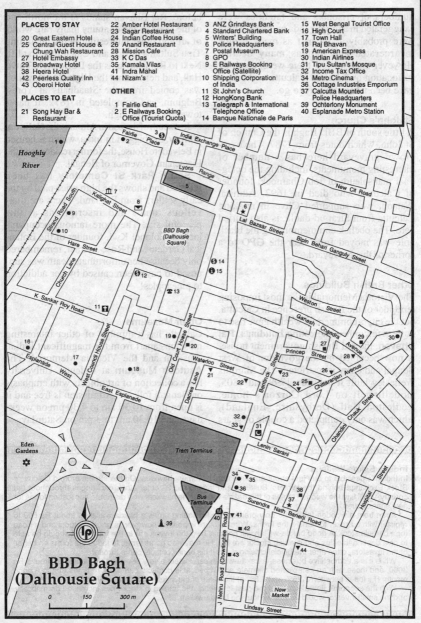

PLACES TO STAY
20 Great Eastern Hotel
25 Central Guest House & Chung Wah Restaurant
27 Hotel Embassy
29 Broadway Hotel
38 Heera Hotel
42 Peerless Quality Inn
43 Oberoi Hotel

PLACES TO EAT
21 Song Hay Bar & Restaurant
22 Amber Hotel Restaurant
23 Sagar Restaurant
24 Indian Coffee House
26 Anand Restaurant
28 Mission Cafe
33 K C Das
35 Kamala Vilas
41 Indra Mahal
44 Nizam's

OTHER
1 Fairlie Ghat
2 E Railways Booking Office (Tourist Quota)
3 ANZ Grindlays Bank
4 Standard Chartered Bank
5 Writers' Building
6 Police Headquarters
7 Postal Museum
8 GPO
9 E Railways Booking Office (Satellite)
10 Shipping Corporation of India
11 St John's Church
12 HongKong Bank
13 Telegraph & International Telephone Office
14 Banque Nationale de Paris
15 West Bengal Tourist Office
16 High Court
17 Town Hall
18 Raj Bhavan
19 American Express
30 Indian Airlines
31 Tipu Sultan's Mosque
32 Income Tax Office
34 Metro Cinema
36 Cottage Industries Emporium
37 Calcutta Mounted Police Headquarters
39 Ochterlony Monument
40 Esplanade Metro Station

BBD Bagh (Dalhousie Square)

0   150   300 m

numbers of prisoners and fatalities were exaggerated in a propaganda exercise. There were probably about half as many people incarcerated and half as many deaths. However many or few there were, death by suffocation on a humid Calcutta night must have been a horrific way to go.

St John's Church

A little south of BBD Bagh is the Church of St John, which dates from 1787. The overgrown graveyard here has a number of interesting monuments, including the octagonal mausoleum of Job Charnock, founder of Calcutta, who died in 1692. Admiral Watson, who supported Clive in retaking Calcutta from Siraj-ud-daula, is also buried here. The obelisk commemorating the black hole was moved from near the GPO to a corner of this graveyard.

Other British Buildings

The Victoria Memorial is the most imposing reminder of the British presence in Calcutta, but the city's commercial wealth gave rise to quite a few other interesting buildings. **Raj Bhavan**, the old British government house, is now occupied by the governor of West Bengal and entry is restricted. The Marquis Wellesley built it between 1799 and 1805, modelling it on Lord Curzon's home, Kedleston Hall (Derbyshire, England), which was only completed a couple of years before. Raj Bhavan stands at the north end of the Maidan and contains many rare works of art and other interesting items, including Tipu Sultan's throne and Calcutta's first lift. Next to Raj Bhavan is the Doric-style **Town Hall**, and next to that the **High Court**, which was copied from the Staadhaus at Ypres, Belgium, and completed in 1872. It has a tower 55 metres high.

Just south of the zoo in Alipur is the **National Library**, the biggest in India, which is housed in Belvedere House, the former residence of the Lieutenant-Governor of Bengal.

South Park St Cemetery has been restored and shows the high price paid by the early settlers from England. There are marvellous tombs and inscriptions at this peaceful site. The more famous occupants include Colonel Kyd, founder of the Botanical Gardens, and Rose Aylmer, remembered only because her unfortunate death was supposed to have been caused by her addiction to pineapples!

Other Museums

Calcutta has a number of other interesting museums apart from the magnificent Indian Museum and the Victoria Memorial. The **Asutosh Museum** at Calcutta University has a collection of art objects with emphasis on Bengali folk art. Admission is free and it is open from 10.30 am to 4.30 pm on weekdays, and 10.30 am to 3 pm on Saturday.

India's *Bakda*-Wallahs

In India it's possible to buy just about anything from pavement hawkers. On the streets around Calcutta's Stock Exchange behind the Writers' Building, and indeed the 22 other stock exchanges throughout the country, you'll find the wooden tables of the *bakda*-wallahs, the hawkers who distribute application forms for new share issues.

Apart from a wooden table, the only prerequisite for setting up as a bakda-wallah is about Rs 600 to register with a broker to handle the forms. What is more important, however, is good contacts and a nose for a bargain stock. A good bakda-wallah will not only help the investor fill in the forms, but should be able to give dependable tips about which stocks are hot. He may also go as far as to lodge the forms on behalf of the investors, often after the official closing dates if his bank contacts come through.

While it is a competitive business, a bakda-wallah can expect a very tidy monthly income of around Rs 3000, and those with an established clientele and impeccable contacts can earn 10 times that in a good month. His fee is between 1.25% and 1.8% of the value of the shares sold through him.

With the economic liberalisation of the past few years, the trading in stocks has increased dramatically, and the small investor would be lost without the bakda-wallah. ■

At 19A Gurusday Rd is the **Birla Industrial & Technological Museum**, open from 10 am to 5 pm daily. Admission is Rs 1. Those philanthropic (and very wealthy) Birlas have also provided the **Birla Academy of Art & Culture** at 109 Southern Ave, open from 4 to 8 pm daily except Monday; admission is Rs 1. It has a good collection of sculpture and modern art. They have also built a huge Birla temple, just around the corner from the Industrial & Technological Museum.

The **Academy of Fine Arts**, on Cathedral Rd beside the cathedral in Chowringhee, has a permanent exhibition and runs an artists' studio. There are cultural shows in the evening. The academy is open from 3 to 8 pm daily except Monday. Entry is Rs 1.

On Muktaram Babu St, a narrow lane in north Calcutta, is the **Marble Palace**, a private mansion housing an incongruous collection of statues and paintings, including works of Rubens and Sir Joshua Reynolds. It's open from 10 am to 4 pm except Monday and Thursday, and entry is free with a permit from the Government of India tourist office. Nearby is the rambling old **Tagore House**, a centre for Indian dance, drama, music and other arts. This is the birthplace of Rabindranath Tagore, India's greatest modern poet, and his final resting place. It's just off Rabindra Sarani and is open from 10 am to 5 pm weekdays, to 2 pm on Saturday and is closed on Sunday.

Next door to the GPO there's a small **postal museum**.

Pareshnath Jain Temple
This temple, in the north-east of the city, was built in 1867 and dedicated to Sheetalnathji, the 10th of the 24 Jain tirthankars. The temple is an ornate mass of mirrors, coloured stones and glass mosaics. It overlooks a garden, and is open from 6 am to noon and 3 to 7 pm daily.

Nakhoda Mosque
North of BBD Bagh is Calcutta's principal Muslim place of worship. Built in 1926, the huge Nakhoda Mosque is said to accommodate 10,000 people and was modelled on Akbar's tomb at Sikandra near Agra. The red sandstone mosque has two 46-metre-high minarets and a brightly painted onion-shaped dome. Outside the mosque you can buy attar, perfume made from essential oils and flower fragrances (not Sundays).

Belur Math
North of the city, on the west bank of the Hooghly River, is the headquarters of the Ramakrishna Mission, Belur Math. Ramakrishna, an Indian philosopher, preached the unity of all religions. He died in 1886, and his follower Swami Vivekananda founded the Ramakrishna Mission in 1897. There are now branches all over India. Belur Math, the movement's international headquarters, was founded in 1899. It is supposed to represent a church, a mosque and a temple, depending on how you look at it. Belur Math is open from 6.30 to 11 am and from 3.30 to 7 pm daily, and admission is free.

Dakshineswar Kali Temple
Across the river from Belur Math is this Kali temple where Ramakrishna was a priest, and where he reached his spiritual vision of the unity of all religions. The temple was built in 1847 and is surrounded by 12 other temples, dedicated to Siva.

Rabindra Sarobar & Ramakrishna Mission
Rabindra Sarobar, in the south of the city, is a park and picnic spot with a central lake. Beside the park is the Ramakrishna Mission Institute of Culture, which has a library, reading rooms and lecture halls.

Botanical Gardens
On the west bank of the Hooghly River, 10 km south of Howrah, are the extensive Botanical Gardens. They stretch for over a km along the riverfront and occupy 109 hectares. The gardens were originally founded in 1786 and initially administered by Colonel Kyd. It was from these gardens that the tea now grown in Assam and Darjeeling was first developed.

The gardens' prime attraction is the 200-year-old banyan tree, claimed to have the second largest canopy in the world (the largest is in Andhra Pradesh). It covers an area of ground nearly 400 metres in circumference and continues to flourish despite having its central trunk removed in 1925, because of fungus damage. The cool and tropical tall-palm house in the centre of the gardens is also well worth a visit.

The gardens are at Sibpur over the Howrah Bridge and 19 km from Chowringhee on a No 55 or 56 bus. However it's much more pleasant to go by ferry and there are frequent departures from Chandpal and Babu Ghats (Rs 1.50). The gardens are open from sunrise to sunset, and although they tend to be very crowded on Sundays, on other days they are peaceful and make a pleasant escape from the hassles and crowds of Calcutta. Take something to drink as the cafes in the gardens are often closed during the week.

Organised Tours
The Government of India tourist office (☎ 242-1402) at 4 Shakespeare Sarani has a full-day tour for Rs 50, departing daily (except Monday) from their office at 8 am. It covers Belur Math, Dakshineswar Temple, the Jain temple, the Victoria Memorial, the Indian Museum, the Academy of Fine Arts, Jawaharlal Sishu Bhavan and the zoo.

The West Bengal tourist office (☎ 248-8271) at 3/2 BBD Bagh has a similar tour for Rs 50 or a second tour takes a slightly different route cramming in even more for Rs 60. Museums are closed on Mondays. One of the problems with sightseeing in Calcutta is that an awful lot of time is spent just sitting in traffic jams.

Bus tours are also conducted for the various festivals and pujas around the state – consult *Calcutta This Fortnight* or a tourist office for details. West Bengal Tourism operates weekly trips to the Sunderbans Wildlife Sanctuary from October to March. See the Sunderbans section in the West Bengal chapter for more information.

Places to Stay – bottom end
Calcutta suffers from a shortage of good cheap places to stay. Budget travellers' accommodation is centred on Sudder St, running off Chowringhee Rd beside the Indian Museum. Aim to arrive in Calcutta before mid-day or you may have great difficulty in finding a cheap bed.

Chowringhee At 2 Sudder St the popular *Salvation Army Red Shield Guest House* (☎ 245-0599) has dorm beds at Rs 20 to Rs 30 and private double rooms at Rs 150. The more expensive rooms have a bath. Although the water supply is decidedly erratic, the guest house is clean and well kept, and great value if you can get in. Much of the accommodation here is taken by volunteers working for Mother Teresa.

Further down Sudder St is the equally popular *Hotel Maria* (☎ 245-0860) with dorm beds for Rs 40, some on the roof. They also have singles/doubles with Rs 80/150 with common bathroom, and Rs 100/150 with bath. They claim to have a strict no drugs, no alcohol policy.

Around the corner down Stuart Lane you'll find two of Calcutta's most popular budget establishments – the *Modern Lodge* (☎ 244-4960) at No 1, and the *Hotel Paragon* (☎ 244-2445) opposite at No 2. The Paragon has dorm beds at Rs 40 (downstairs) and Rs 45 (upstairs), tiny singles/doubles with common bath for Rs 80/100 and doubles with bath from Rs 150. There's a pleasant courtyard upstairs but the ground-floor rooms are rather gloomy. Baggage lockers and meals are available. The Modern Lodge is similar but a bit cheaper, and there are also four-bed rooms and dorms. All the rooms have a fan, and the food is reasonable. The rooftop area is a popular meeting place in the evening, and tea and soft drinks are available.

The *Hotel Hilson* (☎ 244-5283) at 4 Sudder St has clean singles with common bath for Rs 70, doubles with bath from Rs 150 and some triples at Rs 200. The *Shilton Hotel* (☎ 245-1512) further down Sudder St has singles/doubles with attached bathrooms for Rs 150/220.

The Sikh-run *Times Guest House* is a friendly place near the Blue Sky Cafe. It has an eight-bed dorm for Rs 40 per bed and three doubles with attached bathrooms for Rs 150. The *Tourist Inn* is fairly clean with rooms with common bath for Rs 50/100 and a four-bed room with attached bath for Rs 200.

Opposite is the *Hotel Diplomat* (☎ 244-2145) with dark rooms from Rs 60/100 with common bath.

Around the corner from Sudder St, at 20 Mirza Ghalib St (Free School St), is the popular *Centrepoint Guest House* (☎ 244-3928). This friendly place has a range of accommodation from Rs 125/150 for rooms with attached bath. There are also some air-con rooms for Rs 260/325 and there's a travel agent here.

Down Chowringhee Lane there's the *Hotel Palace* (☎ 244-6214), which has rooms for Rs 100/150 with attached bath, or Rs 125/200 with TV, and the *Capital Guest House* (☎ 245-0598) which has similar rooms for Rs 100/160, and more expensive air-con rooms. Neither of them is anything special, nor is the *Timestar Hotel* (☎ 245-0028) on the next lane over, although it's a bit cheaper at Rs 85/140 for attached rooms.

Also south of Sudder St, there are two hotels right opposite each other along Dr M Ishaque Rd. The first is the *East End Hotel* (☎ 29-8921), an old, well-maintained place run by friendly people. It has singles/doubles with attached bath for Rs 180/280. The *Neelam Hotel* (☎ 29-2582) is better value with singles/doubles for Rs 100/225.

Nearby is the *Classic Hotel* (☎ 29-7390), down an alley off Mirza Ghalib St, which has singles with common bath for Rs 100 and doubles with bath for Rs 185, and with air-con for Rs 375. Hot water is available free by the bucket.

The Ys Calcutta has a collection of Ys but they're often full. The *YMCA* (☎ 244-3814) at 42 Surendra Nath Banerji Rd has singles/doubles for Rs 50 and a dorm for Rs

20 plus Rs 15 for temporary membership. The *YMCA* (☎ 249-2192) at 25 Chowringhee Rd is a big, gloomy building which is popular with Indian businesspeople. All accommodation includes early-morning tea, breakfast and dinner; the rooms have attached baths. There are dorm beds for Rs 160 (in three, four and six-bed rooms), singles/doubles for Rs 270/370 or Rs 500/650 with air-con. They've got some excellent full-size snooker and billiard tables in the lounge and, if you're discreet, it's possible to use them without being a resident.

The *YWCA* (☎ 29-7033), 1 Middleton Row, is for women and couples only. It's a grand old place; airy, spotless and with a beautiful tennis court. It's good value at Rs 250/400 with common bath and all meals, but with attached bath it's a bit much at Rs 500/600 and all meals.

Other Places The *youth hostel* (☎ 667-2869) is at 10 Dr J B Ananda Dutta Lane in Howrah. It's small and a bit run down but OK; take a No 52 or 58 bus from Howrah railway station to Shamasri Cinema, or a No 63 bus to Khirertala. Dorm beds are Rs 15.

Howrah railway station has *retiring rooms* – four doubles with attached bathrooms for Rs 70. Next door is the *Railway Yatri Nivas* (☎ 660-1742) with dorm beds for Rs 75 and doubles with attached bathrooms for Rs 250, or Rs 390 with air-con. You can only stay here with a train ticket for 200 km or more, and then only for one night. There are also *retiring rooms* at Sealdah.

Finally, Calcutta Airport has *rest rooms* if you're in transit, with dorm beds for Rs 40 and air-con singles/doubles for Rs 125/190. Check at the reservations desk at the terminal.

Places to Stay – middle
BBD Bagh The *Central Guest House* (☎ 27-4876) is a recommended hotel that's good value with clean singles/doubles for Rs 150/200 or Rs 300 for air-con. All rooms have attached bathrooms. The hotel fronts

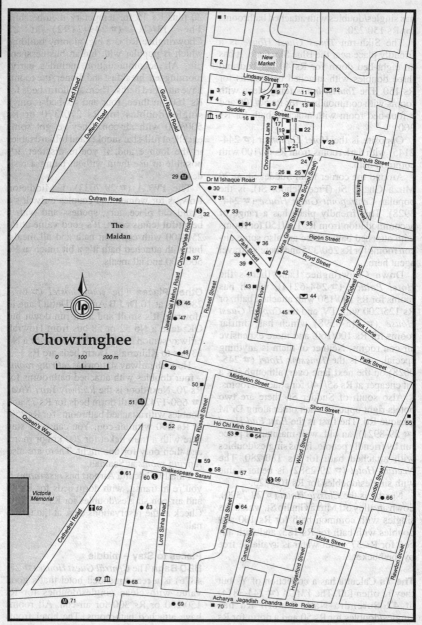

Chowringhee

The Maidan

Victoria
Memorial

0   100   200 m

PLACES TO STAY

1 Oberoi Grand Hotel
3 YMCA
6 Lytton Hotel
8 Fairlawn Hotel
9 Gujral Guesthouse &
   City Express
   Supermarket
10 CKT Inn
13 Centrepoint Guest
   House
14 Astoria Hotel
16 Salvation Army Guest
   House
18 Hotel Maria
19 Hotel Paragon
20 Timestar Hotel
22 Modern Lodge
26 Neelam Hotel
27 East End Hotel
28 Classic Hotel
34 Park Hotel & Kwality
   Restaurant
43 YWCA
50 Old Kenilworth Hotel
55 Hotel Rutt Deen
57 Astor Hotel
59 New Kenilworth Hotel
70 Hotel Hindustan
   International

PLACES TO EAT

2 Hindustan Restaurant
4 Zaranj Restaurant
5 Khalsa Restaurant

7 Oasis Restaurant
11 Kathleen's Restaurant
   & Bakery
17 Blue Sky Cafe
21 Abdul Khalique Hotel
23 Gypsy Fast Food
24 Hong Kong
   Restaurant
25 Cafe 48 & Off cum
   On Rambo Bar
31 Peijing Restaurant
33 Gulnar Restaurant
35 Gupta Restaurant
36 Oasis, Moulin Rouge,
   Starlit Garden, Bar
   BQ & Blue Fox
38 Magnolia Bar
40 Mocambo Restaurant
45 Waldorf & Litle
   Bangkok
   Restaurants

OTHER

12 New Market Post
   Office
15 Indian Museum
30 Bangladesh Biman
   Airlines &
   Lufthansa
32 Standard Chartered
   Bank & ANZ
   Grindlays Bank
37 Japan Airlines
39 Singapore Airlines
41 Thai International,

Flury's, Peter Cat
   & Silver Grill
42 French Consulate &
   Golden Dragon
44 Park St Post Office
46 State Bank of India
47 American Center
48 British Airways,
   RNAC, Air France,
   Citibank & ANZ
   Grindlays Bank
49 KLM & Cathay Pacific
52 British High
   Commission
53 US Consulate
54 Vital Medical Services
56 ANZ Grindlays Bank
58 British Council
60 Government of India
   Tourist Office
61 Birla Planetarium
62 St Paul's Cathedral
63 Air India
64 Japanese Consulate
65 ISKCON
66 Russian Consulate
67 Nehru Children's
   Museum
68 Aeroflot
69 Foreigners'
   Registration Office

METRO STATIONS

29 Park St
51 Maidan
71 Rabindra Sadan

onto Chittaranjan Ave but the entrance is round the back at 18 Prafulla Sarkar St.

Nearby on Princep St is the old *Hotel Embassy* (☎ 27-9040) with singles/doubles for Rs 175/250 including attached bath, TV and phone. Air-con doubles cost Rs 400. One block east is the *Broadway Hotel* (☎ 26-3930), which has a range of rooms from Rs 140 for a single with common bathroom to singles/doubles/triples for Rs 200/290/360 with attached bath, TV and phone. It's popular and often full.

Chowringhee In the Sudder St area the *Gujral Guest House* (☎ 244-0620) is a small clean guest house with rooms at Rs 140/350 with attached bath and air-con doubles at Rs 450. On the floor above is the *Lindsay Guest*

House (☎ 244-1039) with air-con rooms at Rs 350/450. Their other place, the *Hotel Lindsay* (☎ 244-1374, fax 245-0310), at 8A Lindsay St, is better and worth the climb or lift ride to the 6th floor. Rooms are Rs 350/450, or Rs 575/750 with air-con.

At 12A Lindsay St is the *CKT Inn* (☎ 244-8246). It's a small friendly place with rooms for Rs 488/610 but this includes all taxes and service charge. The rooms are air-con and have TVs and attached bathrooms. It's often full.

The recently renovated *Hotel Plaza* (☎ 244-6411) at 10 Sudder St has good rooms for Rs 250/350 with attached bath, or Rs 350/450 with air-con, all including a continental breakfast.

The *Astoria Hotel* (☎ 244-9679), 6/2

CALCUTTA

Sudder St, offers only air-con rooms which are rather overpriced at Rs 450/550 plus taxes. All the rooms have a bath, colour TV and telephone.

The *Heera Hotel* (☎ 248-0663) at 28 Grant St, just north of New Market, is a modern place with carpeted rooms with attached bath for Rs 250/300, or with air-con Rs 490/550.

The classic old *Great Eastern Hotel* (☎ 248-2311, fax 248-0289), 1-3 Old Court House St (south of BBD Bagh), is a rambling place that's distinctly tatty round the edges. This huge, Raj-style hotel with some 200 rooms is often full by late morning. There are singles/doubles from Rs 400/500 or Rs 870/1200 with air-con. There are a number of restaurants and a coffee shop with the peculiar name, 'Dragon in Sherry's'.

Places to Stay – top end

For an idea of how the other half lived and played in the days of the Raj, the *Tollygunge Club* (☎ 473-4741, fax 473-1903), set in 44 hectares on the southern edge of Calcutta, is a wonderfully relaxing place to stay. It's run by an Englishman, Bob Wright, along the exclusive lines set down almost 100 years ago. The elegant clubhouse was once the mansion at the centre of a large indigo plantation, now a championship golf course. Sitting by the swimming pool here, with a cold beer or an excellent club sandwich, it's hard to believe you're still in Calcutta.

Tolly (as it's affectionately called) is now the playground of the city's elite. As well as an indoor and an outdoor pool, there are grass and clay tennis courts, two squash courts, a croquet lawn, billiards, badminton and table tennis, as well as a stable full of ponies. As a foreign visitor, so long as you telephone, fax, or write in advance (120 Deshapran Sasmal Rd, Calcutta 700033), you may stay here and are given temporary membership allowing you to use the facilities. Guests are expected to be reasonably tidy but jackets and ties are not necessary.

The cheapest rooms are in 'Hastings' and these cost Rs 600/650, with air-con and attached baths. The cottages ('Grandstand')

cost Rs 1300/1400 and have small sitting areas overlooking the golf course. Rooms in Tolly Towers or Tolly Terrace are similarly priced. There are no additional taxes. The club is a 10-minute walk from Tollygunge metro station.

The *Fairlawn Hotel* (☎ 245-1510, fax 244-1835), 13A Sudder St, is a piece of Calcutta where the Raj still lives, albeit in a decidedly eccentric manner which you may find quaintly amusing or downright irritating. Edmund Smith and his Armenian wife, Violet, the couple who still run the hotel more than 45 years after Independence, look like they've been time-warped from Brighton in the 1950s.

Most of the rooms are air-conditioned and have TV and phone, but the bathrooms are a bit on the primitive side and the hot water is sporadic. The doubles at US$50 are much better value than the singles at US$35, as the latter seem to be an afterthought. This is expensive, but it does include three meals (variable Western food), plus afternoon tea in the garden. Service can be abrupt to the point of rudeness, which many people find off-putting. Bed & breakfast costs US$25/35, and a 20% discount is offered from April to September. The hotel has its own well and water filtration equipment.

The *'Old' Kenilworth Hotel (Purdy's Inn)* (☎ 242-5325), 7 Little Russell St in Chowringhee, is an ageing place full of character. It's run by long-time Calcutta resident, Mrs Joyce Purdy. It is not connected with the New Kenilworth Hotel, and is an old colonial-style house in its own grounds. Some people enjoy the character of the place and its somewhat eccentric proprietor, others complain that it's overpriced and the service lacking. Large doubles are Rs 750, or Rs 1000 with air-con. All the rooms have a bath, meals are available and there's a refrigerator for guests' use.

As far as modern places go, the centrally air-con *Lytton Hotel* (☎ 249-1872, fax 249-1747), 14 Sudder St, is a good choice. Singles/doubles are US$30/38 with attached bathroom and TV. There's a laundry service, restaurant, bar, money-changing facilities and a small bookshop/newsagency. It's a popular place so get there early in the day if possible.

The three-star *Hotel Rutt Deen* (☎ 247-5240, fax 247-5210), 21B Loudon St, is also good. It has singles/doubles from Rs 650/750 with air-con.

The *Astor Hotel* (☎ 242-9957), 15 Shakespeare Sarani, is in a good location and has singles/doubles from Rs 600/800 with air-con, TV and attached bath. The hotel has a very pleasant garden and there are daily barbecues.

The *New Kenilworth Hotel* (☎ 242-3403, fax 242-5136), 1-2 Little Russell St, has old and new wings. Air-con rooms are US$36/45, definitely overpriced for rooms in the old wing. All rooms have a fridge, TV and attached bath.

The four-star *Quality Inn* (☎ 243-0222, fax 29-3381), very conveniently located just off Chowringhee Rd, is a new place with good rooms at Rs 1065/1400.

The *ITDC Airport Ashok* (☎ 552-9111, fax 552-9137), at the airport, is modern and convenient for passengers in transit. Singles/doubles with air-con cost Rs 1600/1850. It has all the facilities you would expect of a five-star hotel.

Going up in price, the *Park Hotel* (☎ 29-7336, fax 29-7343), at 17 Park St, is another modern hotel; it costs Rs 2300/2500 for air-con singles/doubles, and there's a restaurant, bar and pool. More expensive again is the 212-room *Hotel Hindustan International* (☎ 247-2394, fax 247-2824) at 235/1 AJC Bose Rd, with rooms at Rs 2500/2800.

The *Oberoi Grand Hotel* (☎ 29-2323, fax 29-1217), 15 Chowringhee Rd, is pretty plain externally but very grand inside. Rooms start at US$170/190. There are four restaurants, and beneath the palm trees in the central courtyard there's a swimming pool. The Oberoi Grand has long been acknowledged as Calcutta's best hotel and the jewel in the Oberoi crown.

Providing stiff competition for the Oberoi Grand, the plush *Taj Bengal* (☎ 248-3939, fax 248-1766) is at the southern end of the Maidan. It has all the mod cons you'd expect,

and an opulent atrium with a waterfall. Singles/doubles are Rs 3350/3650, with more expensive suites. There are four restaurants, a nightclub, swimming pool and health club.

Places to Eat

Cheap Finding good food at reasonable prices is no problem in the Chowringhee/Sudder St area and everyone seems to have their own favourite place. *Blue Sky Cafe*, halfway down Sudder St, is always packed with travellers and does excellent breakfasts and snacks. They have good curd with fruit, milk shakes, fresh juice, great porridge and a range of burgers and snacks. It's a good place to start the day. At the *Delhi Durbar*, nearby on Chowringhee Lane, there are pizzas from Rs 25 and boiled potatoes with cheese for Rs 20.

The other places less geared to the Western traveller are cheaper. Just south of Sudder St is the *Abdul Khalique Hotel* where you can get a delicious egg-roll (wrapped in newspaper) for Rs 3 and a cup of tea for Rs 1. The Sikh-run *Khalsa Restaurant*, across from the Salvation Army Guest House and down the street a few doors, has been popular with both locals and travellers for many years. The *Taj Continental*, opposite the entrance to Stuart Lane, is another good cheap place.

On nearby Mirza Ghalib St there are several other places. The *Shamiana Bar & Restaurant* is clean and offers Indian and Chinese food; close by and similar is *Gypsy Fast Food*. Opposite the Shamiana Restaurant the *Mughal Durbar* gets mixed reports. The nearby *Cafe 48* has good veg thalis.

For good bread and takeaway snacks there's the *Hare Krishna Bakery* on the corner of Middleton and Russell Sts. Go early for the excellent brown bread. Nearer Sudder St is *Kathleen's Bakery* which has greater variety. This is where the Calcuttans who can afford to eat cake indulge themselves.

In the New Market on Lindsay St there are also good cake shops including *Nahoum*, a third-generation Jewish bakery in Frow.

Also within reach of the Sudder St area is *Nizam's*, around the corner from the Elite Cinema. It's very popular among Calcuttans for mutton and chicken rolls, kebabs and Muslim food.

If you're staying near Chittaranjan Ave, the *Mission Cafe* is a good choice with masala dosa for Rs 10 and espresso coffee for Rs 4. In the same area is the *Chung Wah Chinese Restaurant*. It looks like something out of Shanghai in the 1930s and you can sit in private wooden booths. Beer is Rs 40 and main dishes are around Rs 35; their Rs 50 set lunch is good value. Nearby is the air-con *Anand Restaurant*, probably the best vegetarian restaurant in the city. It's a smart place and main dishes are around Rs 25. There's a wide range of dosas and you can finish with an ice cream followed by coconut paan, wrapped in leaves specially brought in from Tamil Nadu.

Back in the Sudder St area, *Kathleen's Restaurant*, beside the bakery, is a good place for a full meal. They do good tandoori food, and most main courses are around Rs 35. A beer is Rs 40 here and there's a wide range of ice creams including a hot fudge sundae for Rs 25. Along the street opposite the Salvation Army Guest House, the *Oasis Restaurant* offers a similar menu. It's not bad and slightly cheaper than Kathleen's. South along Mirza Ghalib St is the *Gupta Restaurant*.

For reasonable Chinese food, try the *How Hua* on Mirza Ghalib St; they've even got northern Chinese dishes such as jiaozi, which is a bit like Tibetan momo. Other similar Chinese restaurants are the *Hong Kong Restaurant* and the *Golden Dragon Restaurant*, both on Mirza Ghalib St. Calcuttans say the place to go for really good cheap Chinese food is the Tangra area, and they recommend the *Tangra Chinese Restaurant*. It's in the west of the city and you'll need a taxi to get there.

On Middleton Row, near the YWCA, *Peter Cat* has excellent kebabs, and a good bar.

A Calcutta institution is the *Indian Coffee House*, near Calcutta University, for years the meeting place of the city's intellectuals. Nowadays it's mostly younger undergraduates who congregate beneath the faded portrait of Rabindranath Tagore in this large cafe. Nevertheless it's a good place to meet people and is convenient for a coffee and snack if you've been looking round the many bookshops in this area. There's a much more central branch on Chittaranjan Ave, and a sign warns that the management 'reserves the right to maintain the dignity of the coffee shop'.

The Bengali sweet tooth is legendary and *Indra Mahal* is a great place to try Bengali sweets. It's on Chowringhee Rd just up from the Grand Hotel; they also serve chat and other snacks. Bengali specialities are Mughal paratha and misthi dhoi (curd sweetened with jaggery). Another famous sweet shop is *K C Das*, on Lenin Sarani near the corner of Bentinck St.

Curiously, it's hard to find real Bengali food in Calcutta unless you dine at a Bengali's home. Just about the only restaurant specialising in this cuisine is *Suruchi*, on Elliot Rd, by the Mallik Bazaar bus stop.

For good, no-frills south Indian vegetarian food there's *Kamala Vilas*, in a small side street off Chowringhee Rd, near the Metro Cinema.

More Expensive Right in the centre of town at 11 Waterloo St (the narrow street that runs by the Great Eastern Hotel) is the *Amber Hotel*. The food is excellent and the place is often voted by residents of Calcutta as the best place to eat in the city. Prices are very reasonable, with most dishes around Rs 40 and the tandoori items are very good. Beer is around Rs 40 and there's a range of ice creams. Across the road is the *West End Takeaway* and nearby is the *Sagar*, both part of the same group.

Most of the other upmarket restaurants are on Park St though there are one or two cheap places amongst them. There are a whole stack of restaurants to choose from, some with very un-Calcutta names like *Blue Fox* and *Moulin Rouge*! The *Oasis Restaurant* does an excellent fish & chips with vegetables for Rs 50. The *Silver Grill* and *Bar B Q* are both good Chinese restaurants on Park St.

One of the cheapest is the *Kwality* at 17 Park St, beside the Park Hotel. It has a small menu with main dishes around Rs 30 but is a good place to eat. Nearby is the similar *Tandoor* but the *Gulnar Restaurant* next to the Park Hotel is better. The food is excellent but quite expensive and you'll have to pay a surcharge if, as is usual, there's a band playing. It's very popular with relatively affluent local people. The restaurant is open from 5.30 to 11.30 pm and is licensed (last drinks 11 pm).

Flury's, also on Park St, is the place for tea and cakes, the *Magnolia Bar* is good for ice cream.

The *Astor Hotel*, on Shakespeare Sarani, has a very pleasant garden that's good for a relaxing drink (beers are Rs 40) or a barbecue (daily between 6 and 11 pm). On Saturday evenings there's live music here.

At the *Fairlawn Hotel* on Sudder St the food is English-style, and non-residents can eat here. The set lunches and dinners can be

fun and are certainly different, announced by a gong and served in impatient style by uniformed waiters. You sit where you're told, but at least can help yourself. Check the day's menu (posted at reception) before you decide to eat here. The food varies but is generally OK and, at Rs 85 for lunch and Rs 95 for dinner, very good value. The garden in front of the hotel is an excellent place for afternoon tea or a beer (Rs 40) in the evening, although the mosquitoes are very friendly, and the drinks dry up at 8 pm *sharp*.

Also in Sudder St is the opulent *Zaranj Restaurant*, with a waterfall flowing through its middle. It's as expensive as its decor with most dishes around Rs 80, but is packed with rich Calcuttans who say it's worth it. If money is no object you could also try the restaurants at the Oberoi Grand and the Taj Bengal. The *Ming Court* at the Oberoi Grand has excellent Chinese food but a three-course meal including beer and taxes will set you back Rs 500!

Entertainment

Calcutta is famous for its culture – film,

Children in Calcutta: a city with soul

poetry, music, art and dance all have their devotees here. Programmes are listed in the daily newspapers or in the leaflet *Calcutta This Fortnight*, available free from the tourist offices.

There are dances held at the Oberoi Grand Hotel on Chowringhee Rd every night at 6.30 pm. Even though there's no charge, the audience is sometimes extremely small and it's worth going to.

A dance-drama performance, Bengali poetry reading or a similar event takes place on most nights at the Rabindra Sadan (☎ 247-9936) on Cathedral Rd. Foreign films and retrospectives are shown at the Nandan complex nearby.

The Calcutta Film Association, next to the Birla Planetarium on Chowringhee Rd, has regular screenings of English-language movies, as does the American Center (6 pm Friday).

Bars & Discos In the Sudder St area, the *Sun Set Bar* at the Lytton Hotel is a good place for a drink. This bar is popular with travellers, young expatriate workers and local young people involved on the fringes of the tourist trade. It's a friendly place and they have a good music system. Similar is the open-air bar in the forecourt of the *Fairlawn Hotel* where there's always an interesting crowd. There are plenty of other, much more basic, bars, some with bizarre names like *Off cum On Rambo Bar*! (Mirza Ghalib St).

Quite a few of the larger hotels have discos which go on until early morning. The best of them is probably the *Pink Elephant* at the Oberoi Grand Hotel but you have to be invited by a member or resident.

Thursday is a 'dry' day in Calcutta and the only places where you can get alcoholic drinks are in the four and five-star hotels, although some places seem to disregard this ruling. Several of the licensed restaurants are closed on Thursday.

Things to Buy
Calcutta has the usual government emporiums and quite a good Central Cottage Industries Emporium at 7 Chowringhee Rd.

There are numerous interesting shops along Chowringhee Rd selling everything from carpets to handicrafts. The shops along the entrance arcade to the Oberoi Grand Hotel are particularly interesting. There's also an amazing variety of pavement vendors selling everything imaginable.

Amid this mêlée are many runners from other shops, particularly the New Market, looking for customers. Naturally, 'their' shop is only 'just round the corner', yet rarely is this true. If you follow them, it's going to take up quite a bit of your time and the prices of the goods which you're invited to examine will be relatively high. After all, it's a long way back and a lot of wasted time for them to find another punter.

New Market, formerly Hogg Market, is Calcutta's premier place for bargain shopping despite part of it being burnt out in late 1985. Here you can find a little of almost everything, and it is always worth an hour or so wandering around. A particular bargain, if you're flying straight home from Calcutta, is caneware. This is ridiculously cheap compared to prices in the West and, of course, is very light if rather bulky.

New Market is the place to sell things too. Whisky, cigarettes and watches are in demand but the prices offered for optical and electronic goods are nothing to write home about. Smuggled electronic goods are also bought and sold at the market in Kidderpore. There's another good street market (mainly clothes) along Lenin Sarani in the evenings.

Between Sudder St and New Market is an expensive air-con market. In the basement is City Express Supermarket offering fully computerised checkout and at least one supermarket helper per customer, some even involved in product promotion!

Down Sudder St or in the lanes off there, those in search of highs derived from the plant kingdom are attended to by touts offering a range of services. Discretion is the key word.

Getting There & Away
Air Most airline offices are around Chowringhee. Indian Airlines is on Chittaranjan

Ave, and they also have an office in the Great Eastern Hotel. Other airline offices are:

Aeroflot
  58 Chowringhee Rd (☎ 242-9831)
Air France
  41 Chowringhee Rd (☎ 29-0011)
Air India
  50 Chowringhee Rd (☎ 242-2356)
Bangladesh Biman
  1 Park St (☎ 29-3709)
British Airways
  41 Chowringhee Rd (☎ 29-3453)
Cathay Pacific
  1 Middleton St (☎ 403-2112)
Damania Airways
  (☎ 475-5660)
East West Airlines
  (☎ 29-0667)
Indian Airlines
  39 Chittaranjan Ave (☎ 26-3390, 26-4433)
JAL
  35A Chowringhee Rd (☎ 29-8370)
KLM
  1 Middleton St (☎ 247-4593)
Lufthansa
  30A/B Chowringhee Rd (☎ 29-9365)

ModiLuft
  2 Russell St (☎ 29-6257, 29-8437)
Royal Nepal Airlines (RNAC)
  41 Chowringhee Rd (☎ 29-3949)
Sahara India Airlines
  101 Mangal Jyoti Apartments, 227/2 AJC Bose
  Rd (☎ 247-2795)
SAS
  18G Park St (☎ 74-7622)
Singapore Airlines
  18G Park St (☎ 29-9293)
Swissair
  46C Chowringhee Rd (☎ 242-4643)
Thai International
  18G Park St (☎ 29-9846)
Vayudoot
  29B Shakespeare Sarani (☎ 247-7062)

Calcutta is a good place for competitive air fares to other parts of Asia. You can expect to pick up tickets to Bangkok for around Rs 6000 and to Kathmandu for around US$95 – payable in Indian rupees. Flights are usually with Air India, Indian Airlines, Thai International, Royal Nepal Airlines or Bangladesh Biman.

Airline Flights from Calcutta

Destination	Time (hours)						Fare (US$)
		IC	D2	9W	4S	M9	
Agartala	0.5	1d	-	-	-	-	34
Bagdogra	0.5	3w	-	-	-	-	50
Bangalore	2.2	1d	-	-	-	-	159
Bhubaneswar	0.5	5w	-	-	-	-	41
Bombay	2.3	2d	2d	2d	-	-	157
Delhi	2.0	3d	-	-	6w	2d	132
Dibrugarh	1.3	6w	-	-	-	-	74
Dimapur	2.1	2w	-	-	-	-	69
Guwahati	1.1	4d	-	-	6w	-	46
Hyderabad	2.0	6w	-	-	-	-	134
Imphal	2.1	1d	-	-	-	-	58
Lucknow	2.2	3w	-	-	-	-	92
Madras	2.0	2d	-	-	-	-	137
Patna	0.5	6w	-	-	-	-	51
Port Blair	2.0	3w	-	-	-	-	134
Ranchi	0.5	3w	-	-	-	-	39

* Airline abbreviation codes:
IC – Indian Airlines   9W – Jet Airways   M9 – ModiLuft
D2 – Damania Airways   4S – East West

Frequency & Airline* (d-daily, w-weekly)

CALCUTTA

Calcutta's Indian Airlines office (☎ 26-3390) is fully computerised and it's a breeze buying tickets. It's open from 9 am to 9 pm seven days a week. There's a tourist counter which rarely has anyone waiting in front of it so it's very quick. Even refunds or a change of flight date are no hassle.

As well as its domestic routes (see Airline Flights table), Indian Airlines also flies four international routes; to Dhaka (five times weekly, US$43), Chittagong (weekly, US$55), Bangkok (four times weekly, US$170) and Kathmandu (three times weekly, US$96).

Bus Bus services from Calcutta are not as good an alternative as they are from a number of other Indian cities. It's generally better to travel from Calcutta by train, although there are several useful bus routes to other towns in West Bengal.

Buses generally depart from the bus stand area at the northern end of the Maidan, near Chowringhee Rd, but there are a number of private companies which have their own stands. Buses to and from the south generally use the bus stand near Fort William.

The only buses which travellers use with any regularity are those from Calcutta to Siliguri and New Jalpaiguri (for Darjeeling). The 'Rocket Service' (!) costs Rs 135 and leaves Calcutta at 8 pm, arriving next morning. It's much rougher than going by train.

Train Calcutta has two major railway stations, both of them frenetic. Howrah, on the west bank of the Hooghly River, handles most trains into the city, but if you're going north to Darjeeling or the north-east region then the trains leave from Sealdah station on the east side of the Hooghly. Beware of pickpockets and people of similar inclination at both stations. At Howrah station, platforms 1 to 14 are in the old main building, platforms 15 and above are in the new annexe next door.

The tourist railway booking office is on the 1st floor at 6 Fairlie Place near BBD Bagh. It's fully computerised and has a tourist quota but can be very crowded with foreigners. It's open Monday to Saturday from 9 am to 1 pm and 1.30 to 4 pm, and on Sunday between 9 am and 2 pm. They'll even handle bookings for trains that don't start or finish in Calcutta, but only if you have an Indrail pass. If you don't, go to the other booking office nearby, at 14 Strand Rd, which has a satellite link. Here you can buy advance tickets on routes into and out of Delhi, Madras and Bombay (get a form and join the correct queue). Bookings can be made up to 60 days before departure for all trains apart from the *Shatabdi Express*, for which bookings are only open within 15 days of departure.

Both these places attract long queues and the staff at Fairlie Place office demand to see

Major Trains from Calcutta					
Destination	*Train number & name*	*Departure time* *	*Distance (km)*	*Duration (hours)*	*Fare (Rs) (2nd/1st)*
Bombay VT	2860 *Gitanjali Exp*	12.30 pm H	1960	33	294/1040
Madras	2841 *Coromandel Exp*	2.10 pm H	1663	27.30	273/921
Delhi	2305 *Rajdhani Exp***	1.45 pm H	1441	18	705/865
	2303 *Poorva Exp*	9.15 am H		24	259/837
New Jalpaiguri	3142 *Darjeeling Mail*	7.15 pm S	586	11.45	147/436
Patna	2303 *Poorva Exp*	9.15 am H	545	8	139/415
	3005 *Amritsar Mail*	7.20 pm H	9.4	9.40	
Puri	8007 *Puri Exp*	10.15 pm H	500	10	128/382
Varanasi	2381 *Poorva Exp*	9.15 am H	678	10.30	159/487

* Abbreviations for train stations: H – Howrah, S – Sealdah
** Air-con only; fare includes meals and drinks.

BRYN THOMAS

BRYN THOMAS

BRYN THOMAS

Calcutta
Top: Howrah Bridge.
Bottom Left: Street band.
Bottom Right: Rickshaw.

RICHARD I'ANSON

Away from the crowds, Calcutta.

exchange certificates if you pay in rupees. There are other computerised booking offices which may be better for advance tickets out of Calcutta. The office at Tollygunge metro station is easy to get to and never seems to be very busy.

If you've just flown into Calcutta, it might be worth checking the rail reservation desk at the airport as they have an air-travellers' quota (!) for same-day or next-day travel on the main expresses.

Boat See the Andaman & Nicobar Islands chapter for details on the shipping services from Calcutta.

Getting Around

To/From the Airport An airport bus costing Rs 17 runs past the Indian Airlines office and down Chowringhee Rd past Sudder St on its way in from the airport. On the way out to the airport it departs from the Indian Airlines office at 5.30, 7.15, 9.45 and 11.15 am, and 3.15 and 5.30 pm, and takes under an hour. There's also a public minibus (No S10) from BBD Bagh to the airport for Rs 5.

If you want to take a taxi from the airport, it's cheaper to go to the prepaid kiosk where you'll be assigned one. It costs Rs 80 to Sudder St or the Oberoi Grand. In the opposite direction expect to pay at least an extra 25% or more. All the same, shared between four people, that's about as cheap as the airport bus.

Incidentally, Calcutta's airport takes its name, Dum Dum Airport, from the fact that this was the site of the Dum Dum Barracks, where the explosive dumdum bullet, banned after the Boer War, was once made.

Bus Calcutta's bus system is hopelessly crowded. It's an edifying sight to watch the double-decker buses come across Howrah Bridge during the rush hour. Fares are from Rs 0.70. Take a No 5 or 6 bus between Howrah station and Sudder St; ask for the Indian Museum. There is a secondary private minibus service, which is rather faster and slightly more expensive, with fares a few paise more. You need to be a midget to ride in these buses though.

The second Howrah Bridge is now complete, and has reduced congestion on the original and made it easier to get across the river. Beware of pickpockets on any of Calcutta's public transport.

Tram Calcutta has a public tram service but the amazingly dilapidated trams are like sardine tins. They may be pollution-free but since they're a major cause of the traffic jams, there's talk of abolishing them. Fares start at Rs 0.70 and they're least crowded on Sundays. Take a No 12A from Howrah station to the Indian Museum.

Metro India's first underground railway system is being built at minimum cost and in maximum time almost totally by hand. The soggy soil makes digging holes by hand no fun at all, and after each monsoon it takes half the time to the next monsoon simply to drain out what has already been dug. Nevertheless, the northern and southern sectors are open, and by the time you read this the whole system may be finished. It's the current southern sector, from Chandni Chowk to Tollygunge station, that is of more use to visitors and there's a station near Sudder St. After using surface transport, you're in a different world down here. It's clean, efficient and almost a tourist attraction in itself. Movies are shown on platform TVs and the stations are air-conditioned and well decorated. (Rabindra Sadan has Tagore's poems on the walls.) Trains run from 8.15 am to 8.30 pm, Monday to Saturday and from 3 to 8.30 pm on Sunday. Tickets cost from Rs 1.

Taxi Calcutta's taxi drivers are renowned not only for their passion for strikes, which in turn cause the buses to be even worse than usual, but also for their belligerent refusal to use the meter. Officially, the fare starts at Rs 6 and goes up by Rs 0.50 increments, but that's all in theory. In practice you have to agree on a price before setting off and that will always be more than it should cost. Occasionally you will find a driver willing to use the meter; the final cost is the meter reading plus 50%, as the meters are, predictably, out of date.

At Howrah station there's a pre-paid taxi rank outside, and from here it will cost you Rs 22 to Sudder St, although it can take 15 minutes or more to get to the front of the queue. If you want to avoid the queue, other sharks will offer to take you for Rs 40.

Rickshaw Calcutta is the last bastion of the human-powered rickshaw, apart from at resorts like Mussoorie where they're just for the tourists. Calcutta's rickshaw-wallahs would not accept the new-fangled cycle-rickshaws when they were introduced elsewhere in India. After all, who could afford a bicycle? Most can't even afford their rickshaw and have to rent it from someone who takes the lion's share of the fares.

You may find it morally unacceptable to have a man pulling you around in a carriage – and these men are usually very thin, unhealthy and die early – but Calcutta's citizens are quite happy to use them. The only compensation is that they wouldn't have a job if people didn't use them and, as a tourist, you naturally pay more than local people.

These sort of rickshaws only exist in small parts of central Calcutta, though. They are restricted to the small roads, which are often very congested, and much of the time it's quicker to walk. Across the river in Howrah or in other Calcutta suburbs, there are cycle-rickshaws.

Ferry The ferries can be a quicker and a more pleasant way to get across the river than the congested Howrah Bridge. From Howrah to Chandpal Ghat or Fairlie Ghat there are several crossings an hour between 8.30 am and 8 pm. Ferries to the Botanical Gardens go from Chandpal Ghat or Babu Ghat. The fares are minimal.

West Bengal

At the time of Partition, Bengal was split into East and West Bengal. East Bengal became the eastern wing of Pakistan and later, with the disintegration of that country, Bangladesh. West Bengal became a state of India with Calcutta as its capital. The state is long and narrow, running from the delta of the Ganges River system at the Bay of Bengal in the south to the heights of the Himalaya at Darjeeling in the north.

There is not a great deal of interest in the state apart from these two extremes – Calcutta, with its bewildering maelstrom of noise, culture, confusion and squalor at one end; and Darjeeling, serene and peaceful, at the other. This serenity was interrupted for a while in the 1980s when Gurkha agitators resorted to violence in their bid for a separate Gurkha state in the north.

Outside these two centres the intrepid traveller will find a number of places to consider visiting, either south of Calcutta on the Bay of Bengal or north along the route to Darjeeling. Few foreign tourists visit the ruined mosques of Malda, the palaces of Murshidabad, the temples of Vishnupur or the Sunderbans Wildlife Sanctuary. If you do, the friendly Bengalis will make you feel all the more welcome for being an exception to the rule.

History

Referred to as Vanga in the *Mahabharata*, this area has a long history that predates the Aryan invasions of India. It was part of the Mauryan Empire in the 3rd century before being overrun by the Guptas. For three centuries from around 800 AD, the Pala dynasty controlled a large area based on Bengal and including parts of Orissa, Bihar and modern Bangladesh.

Bengal was brought under Muslim control by Qutb-ud-din, first of the sultans of Delhi, at the end of the 12th century. Following the death of Aurangzeb in 1707, Bengal became an independent Muslim state.

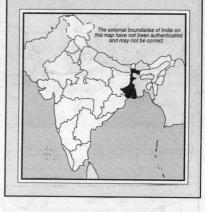

Population: 75 million
Area: 87,853 sq km
Capital: Calcutta
Main Language: Bengali
People per sq km: 854
Literacy Rate: 58%
Best Time to Go: October to March

The external boundaries of India on this map have not been authenticated and may not be correct.

Britain had established a trading post in Calcutta in 1698 which quickly prospered. Sensing rich pickings, Siraj-ud-daula, the Nawab of Bengal, came down from his capital at Murshidabad and easily took Calcutta in 1756. Clive defeated him the following year at the Battle of Plassey, helped by the treachery of Siraj-ud-daula's uncle, Mir Jafar, who commanded the greater part of the nawab's army. He was rewarded by succeeding his nephew as nawab but after the Battle of Buxar in 1764, the British took full control of Bengal. For entertaining background reading on this period as seen through the eyes of a modern-day traveller, Peter Holt's book, *In Clive's Footsteps*, is recommended. The author is the five-times removed great grandson of Clive.

Permits

Permission is necessary if you wish to visit

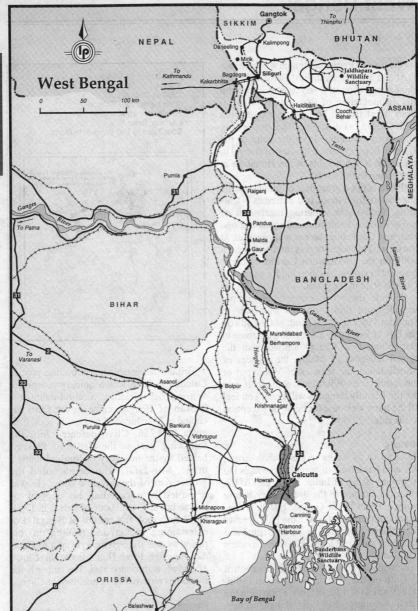

West Bengal

0   50   100 km

To Thimphu

SIKKIM

Gangtok

NEPAL

BHUTAN

Darjeeling   Kalimpong

Mirik

To Kathmandu

Bagdogra   Siliguri

Kakarbhitta

Jaldhapara Wildlife Sanctuary

Haldibari   Cooch Behar

ASSAM

Teesta

MEGHALAYA

Purnia

Raiganj

Ganges River

To Patna

Pandua

Malda
Gaur

BANGLADESH

Jamuna River

BIHAR

Ganges River

Murshidabad
Berhampore

Hooghly River

To Varanasi

Asanol   Bolpur

Krishnanagar

Purulia   Bankura

Vishnupur

Calcutta

Howrah

Midnapore

Kharagpur

Canning

Diamond Harbour

Sunderbans Wildlife Sanctuary

ORISSA

Baleshwar

Bay of Bengal

the Sunderbans Wildlife Sanctuary. For Sajnekhali and the Project Tiger areas, permits are available free of charge, while you wait (and wait...) at the Forest Department (G Block, 6th floor) in the Writers' Building, Calcutta. You must bring your passport. For other areas in the Sunderbans go to the Divisional Forest Officer (☎ 245-1037), 24 Parganas, 35 Gopalnagar Rd, Calcutta.

SOUTH OF CALCUTTA
Down the Hooghly
The Hooghly River is a very difficult river to navigate due to the constantly shifting shoals and sandbanks. Hooghly River pilots have to continuously stay in touch with the river to keep track of the frequent changes in its course. When the Howrah Bridge was constructed it was feared that it would cause severe alterations to the river's flow patterns. The tide rises and falls 3.5 metres at Calcutta and there is a bore, which reaches two metres in height, at the time of the rising tide. Because of these navigational difficulties and the silting up of the Hooghly, Calcutta is losing its importance as a port.

Falta, 43 km downriver, was the site of a Dutch factory. The British retreated here in 1756 when Calcutta was captured by Siraj-ud-daula. It was also from here that Clive recaptured Calcutta. Just below Falta the Damodar River joins the Hooghly. The Rupnarain River also joins the Hooghly nearby and a little up this river is **Tamluk**, which was an important Buddhist centre over 1000 years ago. The James & Mary Shoal, the most dangerous on the Hooghly, is just above the point where the Rupnarain River enters. It takes its name from a ship which was wrecked here in 1694.

Diamond Harbour
A resort 51 km south of Calcutta by road, Diamond Harbour is at the point where the Hooghly turns south and flows into the open sea. It can be reached by bus or train from Calcutta. Launches run from here to Sagar Island.

Accommodation in the *Sagarika Tourist*

Lodge can be booked through West Bengal Tourism in Calcutta.

Haldia
The new port of Haldia is 96 km south of Calcutta, on the west bank of the Hooghly. The port was constructed to try to regain the shipping lost from Calcutta's silting problems. There are regular buses between Calcutta and Haldia.

Sagar Island (Sagardwip)
At the mouth of the Hooghly, this island is considered to be the point where the Ganges joins the sea, and a great three-day bathing festival takes place here in mid-January. A lighthouse marks the south-west tip of the island but navigation is still difficult for a further 65 km south.

Digha
Close to the border with Orissa, 185 km south-west of Calcutta on the Bay of Bengal, Digha is another self-styled 'Brighton of the East'. The beach is seven km long and very wide but if a beach holiday is what you want, carry on south to Puri or Gopalpur-on-Sea.

There are daily buses between Calcutta and Digha (Rs 30, six hours) departing Calcutta from 6.15 am. The Chandaneshwar Siva Temple is just across the border in Orissa, eight km from Digha.

Places to Stay There's a *Tourist Lodge* with rooms and meals at reasonable prices. Digha has a wide range of other accommodation, including new and old *Tourist Cottages* and a *youth hostel*, with dorm beds at Rs 20 (Rs 10 for members). The *Hotel Sea Hawk* has a range of rooms, with or without air-con.

Bakkali
Also known as Fraserganj, this is another beach resort, 132 km from Calcutta, on the east side of the Hooghly. Accommodation here is also reserved through West Bengal Tourism. From here you can get boats to the small island of Jambu Dwip to the south-west.

WEST BENGAL

Sunderbans Wildlife Sanctuary

The innumerable mouths of the Ganges form the world's largest delta, and part of this vast mangrove swamp is a 2585-sq-km wildlife reserve that extends into Bangladesh. It's designated a World Heritage Site and as part of Project Tiger has one of the largest tiger populations of any of the Indian parks. Tourist agencies capitalise on this fact but few visitors get even a glimpse of one of the 269 well-hidden tigers.

You wouldn't want to get too close to these animals. Partial to a little human flesh, they kill about 20 people each year, lying in wait beside the narrow channels that crisscross the estuarine forest. Fishermen and honey collectors have now taken to wearing masks, painted with human faces, on the back of their heads since a tiger is less likely to attack you if it thinks you're watching it.

An entry in the visitors' book at Sajnekhali seems to sum up the feelings of many visitors to the Sunderbans: 'Who came here but here is not see tiger, his visited is not success'. However, the area has other attractions and you may see some wildlife, mainly spotted deer, wild pigs and monkeys. The journey here, by local boats and cycle-rickshaws through small traditional Bengali villages, can be fun. The whole area is wonderfully peaceful after frenetic Calcutta, and is teeming with birdlife.

There's a heron sanctuary (best between July and September) near Sajnekhali. At the Sajnekhali visitor's centre there's a crocodile enclosure, shark pond, turtle hatchery and an interesting Mangrove Interpretation Centre. From here boats are available for excursions through the mangroves; it's around Rs 400 for the whole day, or Rs 300 for a four-hour trip, and you need a guide and boat permits. There are watchtowers here and at several other points around the park. In the south of the Sunderbans are two other sanctuaries at **Lothian** and **Halliday** islands, reached from Namkhana (three hours by bus from Calcutta).

Permission is required to visit the Sunderbans; see the permits section at the beginning of this chapter. There's a small

entry fee to visit the reserve, payable at Sajnekhali.

Places to Stay The *Sundar Chital Tourist Lodge* at Sajnekhali charges Rs 75 for a double with attached bathroom, and there's a basic restaurant here. The signs say 'Movement prohibited after evening' and mean it. In 1991 a couple of tigers jumped over the fence and spent the night sniffing at the doors of the rooms where the tourists were sleeping!

Getting There & Away From October to

March, West Bengal Tourism organises weekly boat tours, including food and accommodation (on board or in the Tourist Lodge). A two-day trip with boat/lodge accommodation costs Rs 500/580, or Rs 810/1000 for a three-day trip. They have offices opposite the railway station in Canning, and if you just arrived early on a Sunday morning during the season you could probably join a tour without booking.

Travelling independently is rather more complex. From Calcutta it's quickest to get a bus to Sonakhali/Basunti (Rs 15, three hours) from Babu Ghat. Alternatively you can take the train to Canning (Rs 10, 1¼ hours), then cross the river to Dok Kart opposite (Rs 1) by *bodbooti* (small overcrowded ferry) and go overland to Sonakhali by shared auto-rickshaw (Rs 6) or bus (Rs 3, 50 minutes). If you go via Canning you may be able to get a ride directly to Sajnekhali with one of the tour boats.

Continuing from Sonakhali/Basunti the next step is a boat to Gosava (Rs 5, 1¼ hours). From there get a cycle-rickshaw (no seats, just a wooden platform!) for the 40-minute ride to Pakhirala (Rs 15) for a boat across the river to Sajnekhali. There's also a direct boat (Rs 5) leaving Gosava at 1 pm to reach Sajnekhali at 3.30 pm. In the morning it departs from Sajnekhali at 8.30 am for Gosava.

A private boat to Sajnekhali costs Rs 500 from Canning or Rs 300 from Sonakhali/Basunti.

NORTH OF CALCUTTA
Serampore & Barrackpore
Twenty-five km from Calcutta on the Hooghly River, Serampore was a Danish centre until their holdings in India were transferred to the East India Company in 1845. The old **Danish church** and **cemetery** still stand. The missionaries Ward, Marshman and Carey operated from here in the early 1800s.

Across the river is Barrackpore. A few dilapidated buildings are all that are left of the East India Company's cantonment here.

There are also some gardens and a memorial to Gandhi by the river.

Mahesh, three km from Serampore, has a large and very old Jagannath temple. In June/July of each year the Mahesh Yatra (Car Festival) takes place here. It is second in size only to the great Car Festival of Jagannath at Puri, Orissa.

Chandernagore
Also known as Chandarnagar, this was one of the French enclaves in India which were handed over at the same time as Pondicherry in 1951. Situated on the banks of the Hooghly, 39 km north of Calcutta, are several crumbling buildings dating from the French era. The first French settlers arrived here in 1673 and the place later became an important trading post, although it was taken by the British during conflicts with the French.

Hooghly & Satgaon
The historic town of Hooghly is 41 km north of Calcutta and very close to two other interesting sites – Chinsura and Bandel. Hooghly was an important trading port long before Calcutta rose to prominence. In 1537 the Portuguese set up a factory here; before that time Satgaon, 10 km further north, had been the main port of Bengal but was abandoned because of the river silting up. There are still a few traces of Satgaon's former grandeur, including a ruined **mosque**.

The Portuguese were kicked out of Hooghly in 1632 by Shah Jahan, after a lengthy siege, but were allowed to return a year later. The British East India Company also established a factory here in 1651. The **imambara**, built in 1836, with its gateway flanked by lofty minarets, is the main sight. Across the road is an older imambara, dating from 1776-7.

Chinsura
Only a km or so south of Hooghly, Chinsura was exchanged by the Dutch for the British-held Indonesian island of Sumatra in 1825. There is a fort and the Dutch **cemetery**, with many old tombs, a km to the west.

WEST BENGAL

Bandel

A couple of km north of Hooghly, and 43 km from Calcutta, Bandel is the site of a Portuguese **church** and monastery which were built here in 1599. Destroyed by Shah Jahan in 1640, they were later rebuilt.

To get there, take the train to Naihati and then the hourly shuttle service across the river.

Bansberia

A further four km north of Bandel, Bansberia has the **Vasudev Temple**, with interesting terracotta wall carvings, and the Hanseswari Temple.

Vishnupur

Also spelt Bishnupur, this interesting town of terracotta temples is a famous cultural centre. It flourished as the capital of the Malla kings from the 16th to the early 19th centuries. The Mallas were great patrons of the arts.

Since there is no stone in the area, the traditional building material for important buildings was brick. The facades of the dozen or so **temples** here are covered with ornate terracotta tiles depicting lively scenes from the Hindu epics. The main temples to see are the highly decorated Jor Bangla, the large Madan Mohan, the pyramidal Ras Mancha and the Shyam Rai, built in 1643.

Vishnupur is in Bankura district, famous for its pottery (particularly the stylised Bankura horse) and silk. In the markets here you can also find metalwork, tussar silk and Baluchari saris, *ganjifa* (circular playing cards for a game long forgotten) and conch shell jewellery. In August, the Jhapan Festival draws snake charmers to honour the goddess Manasa who is central to the cult of snake worship.

Places to Stay Accommodation is very limited. There's the good *Tourist Lodge*, with dorm beds for Rs 25 and singles/doubles for Rs 100/150 with attached bathroom, or Rs 250 for an air-con double. It's about three km from the railway station. Cheaper hotels include the *Lali Hotel* and *Bharat Boarding*.

Getting There & Away There are buses from Calcutta (Rs 25, 4½ hours). The *Purulia Express*, from Howrah, is the fastest train, taking 3½ hours.

Jairambati & Kamarpukur

Ramakrishna was born in Kamarpukur, 143 km north-west of Calcutta, and there is a Ramakrishna Mission ashram here. Ramakrishna was a 19th-century Hindu saint who did much to rejuvenate Hinduism when it was going through a period of decline during the British rule. Jairambati, five km away, is another important point for Ramakrishna devotees.

Shantiniketan

The Visvabharati University is at Shantiniketan, three km from Bolpur. The brilliant and prolific poet, writer and nationalist Rabindranath Tagore (1861-1941) founded a school here in 1901. It later developed into a university with emphasis on humanity's relation with nature – many classes are conducted in the open air. Tagore went on to win the Nobel Prize in 1913 and is credited with introducing India's historical and cultural greatness to the modern world. In 1915 Tagore was awarded a knighthood by the British but he surrendered it in 1919 as a protest against the Amritsar massacre.

There are colleges of science, teacher training, Hindi, Sino-Indian studies, arts and crafts, and music and dance. It's difficult to get the real atmosphere of the place if you're not studying here but there are a number of things to visit. There's a **museum** and **art gallery** within the Uttarayan complex where Tagore lived. They are open from 10.30 am to 1 pm and 2 to 4.30 pm Thursday to Monday, mornings only on Tuesday. The university is open to visitors in the afternoons (mornings only on Tuesday and during vacations) but closed on Wednesday, the day the university was founded.

Four km away is **Sriniketan**, started as a project to revitalise traditional crafts, such as *kantha* embroidery, weaving, batik and pottery.

Places to Stay The university's *International Guest House* has cheap accommodation and meals. *Shantiniketan Tourist Lodge* is run by West Bengal Tourism and is a good place with singles/doubles for Rs 100/150 or Rs 275 for an air-con double.

There are several other places, including the three-star *Mayurakshi Hotel* (☎ 52-958) and university guest houses. At Bolpur railway station there are *retiring rooms*.

Getting There & Away The *Shantiniketan Express* leaves Howrah daily at 9.55 am, reaching Bolpur at 12.25 pm. It departs from Bolpur at 1 pm for Howrah. For Darjeeling, there is the nightly *Darjeeling Mail* at 10.30 pm, which connects with the toy train at New Jalpaiguri. Many other trains stop here.

Nabadwip

Also known as Nadia, the last Hindu king of Bengal, Lakshman Sen, moved his capital here from Gaur. It's an ancient centre of Sanskrit culture, 114 km north of Calcutta. There are many temples at this important pilgrimage centre.

Mayapur

Across the river from Nabadwip, this is a centre for the ISKCON (Hare Krishna) movement. There's a large new temple and gardens, and accommodation is available in the *ISKCON Guest House*. A bus tour is run from Calcutta on Sunday (daily during the winter). Details are available from ISKCON (☎ 247-6075) at 3C Albert Rd, Calcutta.

Plassey (Palashi)

In 1757 Clive defeated Siraj-ud-daula and his French supporters here, a turning point in British influence in India. Plassey, or Palashi as it's now known, is 172 km north of Calcutta. There's nothing to see here apart from the 15-metre memorial a couple of km west of the village.

Berhampore

Eleven km south of Murshidabad is this large town, a notable centre for silk production. The Government Silk Research Centre is

interesting to visit. In the old bazaar area of Khagra, in the northern part of Berhampore, the dilapidated mansions of European traders are quietly subsiding into the river.

Places to Stay & Eat The *Tourist Lodge* is good value and the best place to eat. Doubles are Rs 125 with attached bathroom, four-bed rooms are Rs 160 and there are also air-con rooms for Rs 275. It's about 15 minutes from Berhampore Court railway station by cycle-rickshaw and close to the bus stand.

At the railway station *retiring rooms* there's a four-bed dorm.

Getting There & Away On this branch line between Sealdah and Lalgola, there are several trains a day from Calcutta (186 km, four to six hours). There's a bus from Calcutta (Rs 30, five hours) leaving at 6.45 am, and other buses to Malda (Rs 20, 3½ hours), Bolpur (Rs 18, four hours) and Siliguri (Rs 70, seven hours).

Across the river is Khagraghat Rd station which is on the Howrah to Azimganj line.

Murshidabad

Population: 33,000

When Siraj-ud-daula was Nawab of Bengal, this was his capital, and it was here that he was assassinated after the defeat at Plassey. Murshidabad was also the major trading town between inland India and the port of Calcutta, 221 km south. Today it's a quiet town on the banks of the Bhagirathi River; a chance to see typical rural Bengali life.

Cycle-rickshaw wallahs offer you guided tours of all the sites for Rs 40 for a half day. This is a good idea as everything's fairly spread out. The main attraction is the **Hazarduari**, the classical-style Palace of a Thousand Doors built for the nawabs in 1837. In the recently renovated throne room a vast chandelier, presented by Queen Victoria, is suspended above the nawab's silver throne. There are portraits of British dignitaries, an ivory sofa, ivory palanquins and silver sedan chairs. In the armoury downstairs is a cannon used at Plassey. It's open from 10 am to 4.30 pm daily except Friday; entry is Rs 0.50.

Across the grass from the palace is the rapidly deteriorating **Great Imambara**. Murshid Quli Khan, who moved the capital here in 1705, is buried beside the impressive ruins of the **Katra Mosque**. Siraj-ud-daula was assassinated at the **Nimak Haram Deohri** (Traitor's Gate). The Jain **Parswanath Temple** is at Kathgola, and south of the railway station there's the **Moti Jhil**, or Pearl Lake, a fine place to view the sunset. It's worth taking a boat across the river to visit Siraj's **tomb** at Khusbagh, the Garden of Happiness. There are a number of other interesting buildings and ruins.

Places to Stay Accommodation here is very basic and rather overpriced, apart from the *retiring rooms* at the railway station which cost Rs 25 for a double with attached bathroom. The *Hotel Anurag* overlooking the palace has grubby singles/doubles for Rs 60/80 but they may try for more. The *Hotel Historical* has a room for Rs 70 or you can sleep on the roof.

The *Hotel Omrao* is the best (but nothing special), with singles for Rs 60 and doubles with attached bathroom for Rs 120. There's a reasonable restaurant here.

The *Tourist Lodge* in Berhampore is cleaner and much better value than most of these, but it's 11 km away by bus or train.

Getting There & Away Murshidabad is also on the Sealdah to Lalgola line and there are several trains daily from Calcutta (197 km, four to six hours). For long-distance buses you must go to Berhampore.

Malda
On the route to Darjeeling, 349 km north of Calcutta, Malda is the base for visiting the ruins of the cities of Gaur and Pandua, although it's probably more famous now for its large Fajli mangoes. There's a small museum in Malda.

English Bazaar, also transliterated as Ingraj Bazar, is now a suburb of Malda. An English factory was established here in 1771.

Old Malda is nearby, at the junction of the Kalindi and Mahananda rivers. It was once an important port for the former Muslim capital of Pandua.

Places to Stay & Eat Set around a garden of monster dahlias, the *Malda Tourist Lodge* is a reasonable place charging Rs 60 for an economy double room, Rs 90/120 for singles/doubles with attached bathroom and Rs 275 for an air-con double. The tourist bureau is here and a rickshaw from the railway station costs Rs 5. Also OK and similarly priced are the *Hotel Samrat*, opposite, and the *Hotel Natraj*, on the road to the bus stand.

There are also *retiring rooms* and a good *refreshment room* at the railway station.

The top hotel is the *Hotel Purbanchal*, with rooms from Rs 100/125 to Rs 300/375 with air-con, but it's 20 minutes from the station by rickshaw.

Getting There & Away Situated on the main railway line, Malda is directly connected to Calcutta (344 km, seven hours) and New Jalpaiguri (233 km, five hours). There are buses to Siliguri (Rs 40, six hours) for Darjeeling, Berhampore (Rs 20, three hours) Murshidabad and Calcutta (Rs 50, eight hours).

Gaur
Twelve km south of Malda and right on the border with Bangladesh, Gaur was first the capital of the Buddhist Palas, then the Hindu Senas and finally the Muslim nawabs. The ruins of the extensive fortifications and several large mosques are all that remain. (There are also some ruins on the other side of the ill-defined border.) Most impressive are the **Bara Sona Mosque** and the nearby brick **Dakhil Darwajah** built in 1425. **Qadam Rasul Mosque** enshrines a footprint of the Mohammed but it looks as if he was wearing thongs when he made it! Fath Khan's tomb is nearby and a sign informs you that he 'vomited blood and died on this spot'. There are still some colourful enamelled tiles on the **Gumti Gate** and **Lattan**

Mosque but few left on the **Firoz Minar**, although you can climb this tower for a good view.

Getting There & Away The monuments are very spread out and not all easy to find. Determined cycle-rickshaw wallahs offer half-day trips from Malda for anything up to Rs 100. Taxis cost Rs 250 and also include Pandua.

Pandua

Gaur once alternated with Pandua as the seat of power. The main place of interest is the vast **Adina Mosque**, built by Sikander Shah in the 14th century. Built over a Hindu temple, traces of which are still evident, it was one of the largest mosques in India but is now in ruins. Nearby is the **Eklakhi mausoleum**, so-called because it cost Rs 1 lakh to build. There are also several smaller mosques. The dusty deer park, 2.5 km across the highway in the 'forest', is not worth going to.

Getting There & Away Pandua is on the main highway (NH34), 18 km north of Malda, and there are many buses that can drop you here. The main sites are at Adina, two km north of the village of Pandua, and right by the highway.

SILIGURI & NEW JALPAIGURI

Population: 249,000
Telephone Area Code: 0353

This crowded, sprawling, noisy place is the departure point for visits to Darjeeling, Kalimpong, Sikkim or the North-East states. Siliguri is a real boom town as the major trade centre for the north-east, Darjeeling, Sikkim and eastern Nepal, so it's packed with trucks and buses and is not a pleasant place to stay for a moment more than necessary. New Jalpaiguri (known throughout the district as NJP), the main railway junction, is eight km south of Siliguri, though there's effectively no break in the urban sprawl between the two places.

Twelve km west of Siliguri is Bagdogra, the airport serving this northern region.

Orientation & Information

Siliguri is very confusing at first, especially if you arrive at night. It's essentially just one north-south main road. New Jalpaiguri (NJP) is the main railway junction, nothing more. The distance is about five km from there to Siliguri Town railway station and another three or four km on to Siliguri Junction railway station. You can catch the toy train to Darjeeling from any of these three stations. The new bus terminal, Tenzing Norgay Central, is beside Siliguri Junction station.

There's a tourist information centre (☎ 21-632) in the centre of town and counters at the New Jalpaiguri and Siliguri Junction stations.

There's a useful railway booking office in the centre of town covering trains from all three stations here. Indian Airlines (☎ 20-692) have their office at Hotel Sinclairs.

Permits for Sikkim are available from the SNT bus stand, opposite the main bus terminal.

Places to Stay

If you arrive in Siliguri too late to continue straight on to Darjeeling, there are over 40 hotels to choose from. There are good *retiring rooms* at NJP railway station but they're often full.

Just past the Siliguri Town station and to the left is the popular *Rajasthan Guest House* (☎ 21-815). It's a friendly place with dorm beds for Rs 30 and a range of singles/doubles from Rs 60/90 upwards and a triple for Rs 150 with bathroom. It's a fairly modern hotel and the vegetarian restaurant, though dark, is very good.

Continuing north along Hill Cart Rd, you come to two similar places, right beside each other and much in competition. The *Venus Hotel* (☎ 25-035) has clean rooms from Rs 40/80 with common bath and Rs 60/100 with attached bath. Next door is the *Hotel Natraj* (☎ 26-561), with rooms at Rs 70/100 with attached bath.

North past the grubby *Airview Hotel* you cross the bridge and come to a group of reasonable places. West Bengal Tourism's

WEST BENGAL

To Darjeeling

To Bagdogra
Airport &
Calcutta

Siliguri Junction
Railway Station

Tenzing Norgay Road

Hill Cart Road

Siliguri

0   0.5   1 km

Approximate Scale

To
Kalimpong

Hospital Road

Siliguri Town
Railway Station

To Calcutta &
New Delhi

New Jalpaiguri (NJP)
Railway Station

To North East

1	Hotel Sinclairs
2	Hotel Sharda
3	Mainak Tourist Lodge & Indian Airlines
4	Bus Terminal
5	Mountview Hotel
6	Shere Punjab Hotel & Restaurant
7	Siliguri Lodge
8	SNT (Sikkim) Bus Stand
9	Siliguri Tourist Lodge
10	Airview Hotel
11	Taxi Stand
12	West Bengal Tourist Office
13	Ranjit & Amber Restaurants
14	Rajasthan Guest House
15	Venus & Nataraj Hotels
16	Railway Booking Office
17	GPO
18	Holydon Hotel & Miami Restaurant

Siliguri Tourist Lodge (☎ 21-018), near the bus terminal, has only dorm beds for Rs 42, or you can just take a shower for Rs 10. The road noise here is horrendous. The *Shere Punjab Hotel & Restaurant*, also opposite the bus terminal, is one of a number of places here. It charges Rs 70/120 for rooms with common bath.

A better bet is the *Siliguri Lodge* as it's set back from the road and so is less affected by the noise. Rooms cost Rs 75/110 with common bath, Rs 140 for a double with attached bath, and a bed in the four-bed dorm costs Rs 40.

Further along is the larger *Mainak Tourist Lodge* (☎ 20-986), also run by West Bengal Tourism. Although not particularly old this place is a bit rough around the edges. Rooms are Rs 225/300 or Rs 400/550 with air-con, and the hotel is set in a nice garden. Nearby is the modern *Hotel Sharda*, with singles/doubles for Rs 100/150, including attached bathrooms.

The best hotel here is the three-star *Hotel Sinclairs* (☎ 22-674), but it's quite a distance from the railway station. Singles/doubles cost US$15/17 or US$21/27 with air-con, plus taxes. All rooms have attached bathrooms with hot water. The hotel has a good restaurant, bar, foreign-exchange facilities and a swimming pool.

The only place within walking distance of New Jalpaiguri railway station is the new *Hotel Holydon* (☎ 23-558), about 10 minutes' walk towards Siliguri. Rooms here are Rs 150 for a double with attached bath.

Places to Eat
There are several places to eat along Hill Cart Rd, including the *Amber Bar & Restaurant* and *Ranjit South Indian Restaurant*. For Punjabi food, there's the *Shere Punjab Hotel & Restaurant*. You can get a beer at all of these places as well. There's a good vegetarian restaurant at the *Rajasthan Guest House*, and the food at *Hotel Sinclairs* is pricey but recommended.

The *Miami Restaurant* is next to the Hotel Holydon near NJP station, and is good if you want a decent meal while waiting for a train. There's a basic vegetarian 'refreshment room' upstairs at the station itself.

Getting There & Away

Air Bagdogra Airport is 12 km west of Siliguri. There are three flights a week to Calcutta (US$50), and four weekly each to Delhi (US$128) and Guwahati (US$30).

Bus State Transport Corporation (STC) buses leave from the Tenzing Norgay Central bus terminal, private buses from just outside. There are day and overnight services between Siliguri and Calcutta (Rs 135, 12 hours), although the train is more comfortable. Reservations can be made in Darjeeling.

Other destinations to the south include Malda (Rs 40, six hours), Berhampore (Rs 70, seven hours) and Patna (Rs 112, 12 hours).

From Bagdogra Airport there's a direct bus for Darjeeling (Rs 55, 3½ hours) connecting with flights. Ask at the West Bengal tourist office at the airport as taxi drivers try to convince you this doesn't exist. Even the cheapest buses to Darjeeling (Rs 40, 3½ hours) are much faster than the toy train. From Siliguri, there are several buses an hour from 6 am to 5 pm. Direct buses connect Siliguri with Kalimpong (Rs 25, three hours).

Sikkim Nationalised Transport (SNT) runs hourly buses to Gangtok (Rs 50, five hours) between 7 am and 4 pm from its depot on Hill Cart Rd, opposite the main bus terminal.

The buses between Darjeeling and Kathmandu also run through Siliguri and regardless of which company you go with you'll have to change buses here. For further details see the Darjeeling section later in this chapter.

Train From Calcutta, trains go from Sealdah to New Jalpaiguri or Siliguri, where you take a bus (or the toy train if it's running) up to the hill station. The *Darjeeling Mail* leaves Sealdah at 7.15 pm for the 12-hour trip to New Jalpaiguri (566 km, Rs 143/430 in 2nd/1st class).

The *NE Express* is the fastest train between New Jalpaiguri and New Delhi (1628 km, 33 hours). It also goes by Mughalserai (847 km, 19 hours) near Varanasi, and Patna (636 km, 16 hours). This train also links New Jalpaiguri with Guwahati (423 km, 8½ hours).

If the toy train from Siliguri/New Jalpaiguri to Darjeeling is running, it's possible to buy through tickets to Darjeeling all the way from your point of origin. For details on the toy train see under Getting There & Away in the Darjeeling section.

Taxi Share taxis run between Siliguri and Darjeeling for Rs 100, leaving when there are five passengers.

Share taxis between Bagdogra and Darjeeling cost Rs 120 per person and leave when there are five people on board. They take 3½ hours. You can also get taxis from Bagdogra to Kalimpong and Gangtok. A taxi into Siliguri costs Rs 50.

Getting Around

A cycle-rickshaw from NJP railway station to Siliguri Junction is about Rs 15 and takes half an hour. Buses run this route for Rs 2, and a taxi charges Rs 30.

MIRIK

Being promoted as a 'new' hill station, Mirik is about 50 km from both Siliguri and Darjeeling at an altitude of 1767 metres. The lake is the main attraction here and there's a 3.5-km path around it. Mirik is surrounded by tea estates, orange orchards and cardamom plantations.

Accommodation is available at the *Tourist Lodge*, with dorm beds for Rs 25 and doubles for Rs 300 in cottages. Cheaper places include the *Chandrama Lodge*, with doubles from Rs 85, and the *Parijat Lodge*, with doubles from Rs 150. Buses run to Darjeeling, Kurseong and Siliguri for Rs 15.

KURSEONG

Kurseong is about halfway between Siliguri on the plains and Darjeeling. If you want to stay overnight there's the *Tourist Lodge*, with doubles for Rs 200, or the much cheaper *Jeet Hotel*.

DARJEELING

Population: 80,000
Telephone Area Code: 0354

Straddling a ridge at 2134 metres and surrounded by tea plantations on all sides, Darjeeling has been a very popular hill station since the British established it as an R&R centre for their troops in the mid-1800s. These days people come here to escape from the heat, humidity and hassle of the north Indian plain. You get an indication of how popular Darjeeling is from the 60 or so hotels recognised by the tourist office and the scores of others which don't come up to its requirements. Here you will find yourself surrounded by mountain people from all over the eastern Himalaya who have come to work, to trade or – in the case of the Tibetans – as refugees.

Outside of the monsoon season (June to September), the views over the mountains to the snowy peaks of Kanchenjunga and down to the swollen rivers in the valleys are magnificent. Darjeeling is a fascinating place where you can see Buddhist monasteries, visit a tea plantation and see how the tea is processed, go for a ride on the chairlift, spend days hunting for bargains in colourful markets and handicraft shops, or go trekking to high-altitude spots near the border with Sikkim.

Like many places in the Himalaya, half the fun is in getting there and Darjeeling has the unique attraction of its famous toy train. This miniature train loops and switchbacks its way up the steep mountainsides from New Jalpaiguri to Darjeeling.

History

Until the beginning of the 18th century the whole of the area between the present borders of Sikkim and the plains of Bengal, including Darjeeling and Kalimpong, belonged to the rajas of Sikkim. In 1706 they lost Kalimpong to the Bhutanese, and control of the remainder was wrested from them by the Gurkhas who invaded Sikkim in 1780, following consolidation of the latter's rule in Nepal.

These annexations by the Gurkhas, however, brought them into conflict with the British East India Company. A series of wars were fought between the two parties, eventually leading to the defeat of the Gurkhas and the ceding of all the land they had taken from the Sikkimese to the East India Company. Part of this territory was restored to the rajas of Sikkim and the country's sovereignty guaranteed by the British in return for British control over any disputes which arose with neighbouring states.

One such dispute in 1828 led to the dispatch of two British officers to this area, and it was during their fact-finding tour that they spent some time at Darjeeling (then called Dorje Ling – Place of the Thunderbolt – after the lama who founded the monastery which once stood on Observatory Hill). The officers were quick to appreciate Darjeeling's value as a site for a sanatorium and hill station, and as the key to a pass into Nepal and Tibet. The officers' observations were reported to the authorities in Calcutta and a pretext was eventually found to pressure the raja into granting the site to the British in return for an annual stipend of Rs 3000 (raised to Rs 6000 in 1846).

This transfer, however, rankled with the Tibetans who regarded Sikkim as a vassal state. Darjeeling's rapid development as a trading centre and tea-growing area in a key position along the trade route leading from Sikkim to the plains of India began to make a considerable impact on the fortunes of the lamas and leading merchants of Sikkim. Tensions arose, and in 1849 two British travellers Sir Joseph Hooker and Dr Campbell, who were visiting Sikkim with the permission of the raja and the British government, were arrested. Various demands were made as a condition of their release, but the Sikkimese eventually released both prisoners unconditionally about a month later.

In reprisal for the arrests, however, the British annexed the whole of the land between the present borders of Sikkim and the Bengal plains, and withdrew the annual Rs 6000 stipend from the raja. The latter was restored to his son, raised to Rs 9000 in 1868 and raised again to Rs 12,000 in 1874.

These annexations brought about a significant change in Darjeeling's status. Previously it had been an enclave within Sikkimese territory and to reach it the British had to pass through a country ruled by an independent raja. After the takeover, Darjeeling became contiguous with British territory further south and Sikkim was cut off from access to the plains except through British territory. This was eventually to lead to the invasion of Sikkim by the Tibetans and the British military expedition to Lhasa.

When the British first arrived in Darjeeling it was almost completely forested and virtually uninhabited, though it had once been a sizeable village before the wars with Bhutan and Nepal. Development was rapid and by 1840 a road had been constructed, numerous houses and a sanatorium built and a hotel opened. By 1857 Darjeeling had a population of some 10,000.

Most of the population increase was due to the recruitment of Nepalese labourers to work the tea plantations established in the early 1840s by the British. Even today, the vast majority of people speak Nepali as a first language and the name Darjeeling continues to be synonymous with tea.

The immigration of Nepali-speaking peoples, mainly Gurkhas, into the mountainous areas of West Bengal, eventually lead to political problems in the mid-1980s. Resentment had been growing among the Gurkhas over what they felt was discrimination against them by the government of West Bengal. Even their language was one of those not recognised by the Indian constitution and, that being so, government jobs were only open to those who could speak Bengali.

The tensions finally came to a head in widespread riots throughout the hill country which continued for some two years, and in which hundreds of people lost their lives and thousands were made homeless. Tourism came to a grinding halt, the toy train was put out of action and the Indian army was sent in to maintain some semblance of order. The riots were orchestrated by the Gurkha National Liberation Front (GNLF), led by Subash Ghising, which demanded a separate state to be known as Gurkhaland. The Communist Party of India (Marxist) were also responsible for a good deal of the violence since they were afraid of losing the support that they had once enjoyed among the hill peoples.

A compromise was eventually hammered out in late 1988 whereby the Darjeeling Gorkha Hill Council was to be given a large measure of autonomy from the state government and fresh elections to the council were to be held in December of that year. These resulted in the GNLF gaining 26 of the 28 seats in the hill council. Darjeeling remains part of West Bengal but with greater control over its own affairs as a Nepali-language administrative unit within it.

Climate

For mountain views, the best time to visit Darjeeling is from mid-September to mid-December, although it gets pretty cold by December. The season resumes around mid-March and continues to mid-June but as the haze builds up the views become less clear. During the monsoon months (June to September), clouds obscure the mountains and the rain is often so heavy that whole sections of the road from the plains are washed away, though the town is rarely cut off for more than a few days at a time.

Average temperatures range from 8.5°C to 15°C in summer and from 1.5°C to 6°C in winter. It can get very cold indeed in winter, a real surprise if you've just come from Calcutta. If you go there during the monsoon, an umbrella – available cheaply in the market – is essential.

People

Although the Buddhists, with their monasteries at Ghoom and Darjeeling, are perhaps the most conspicuous religious group, they

WEST BENGAL

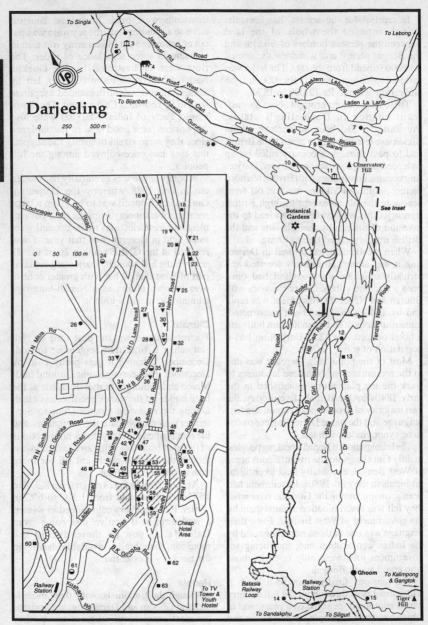

Darjeeling

WEST BENGAL

PLACES TO STAY

8	Tourist Lodge, Gymkhana Club & St Andrew's Church
13	Youth Hostel
16	New Elgin Hotel
17	Hotel Alice Villa
18	Windamere Hotel
20	Pineridge Hotel
22	Bellevue Hotel, Tourist Office & Indian Airlines
23	Main Bellevue Hotel
27	Central Hotel
28	Hotels Chanakya & Mahakal
32	Darjeeling Club
39	Hotel Tshering Denzongpa
46	Hotel Apsara
49	Hotels Valentino, Continental & Daffodil
50	Rockville Hotel
51	Hotels Purnima & Broadway
53	Hotel Prestige
54	Timber Lodge & Washington Restaurant
55	Hotel Tara
57	Hotel Chancellor
58	Hotel Pagoda
59	Shamrock Hotel
60	Hotels Kadambari & Nirvana
62	Hotel Sinclairs
63	Everest Luxury Hotel

PLACES TO EAT

19	Amigos & Oxford Bookshop
21	Star Dust Restaurant
25	Shangri La Restaurant
29	Glenary's
30	Hasty Tasty
31	Kev's (Keventer's Snack Bar)
33	New Sathi Restaurant
34	Kim Fung Chinese Restaurant
36	Dafey Munal Restaurant
37	Dekevas Restaurant
38	New Dish Restaurant
42	Park Restaurant
43	Himalayan Restaurant
52	Tibetan Restaurants

OTHER

1	Ropeway Station
2	Snow Leopards
3	Himalayan Mountaineering Institute & Museums
4	Zoo
5	Tibetan Refugee Centre
6	Raj Bhavan
7	Bhutia Busty Monastery
9	Happy Valley Tea Estate
10	District Commissioner's Office
11	Natural History Museum
12	TV Tower
14	Ghoom Monastery
15	Monastery
24	Buses, Jeeps & Taxis to Kalimpong & Siliguri
26	Market
35	Taxi Stand
40	ANZ Grindlays Bank
41	Foreigners' Registration Office
44	Buses to Gangtok (Sikkim Nationalised Transport)
45	GPO
47	State Bank of India
48	Telegraph Office
56	Joey's Pub
61	Taxis to Ghoom

constitute only a minority of the population – about 14%. The majority of the inhabitants are Hindus, reflecting their origins in the northern Indian states and Nepal. Christians and Muslims comprise little more than 3% each of the district's total population, though there are numerous churches scattered around Darjeeling dating mostly from the British period.

Orientation

Darjeeling sprawls over a west-facing ridge, spilling down the hillside in a complicated series of interconnecting roads and flights of steps. Hill Cart Rd has been renamed Tenzing Norgay Rd (even though there's already another road by the same name in Darjeeling) but the old name seems to stick. It's the main road through the lower part of the town, and the railway station and the bus and taxi stand are all on it. The most important route connecting this road with Chowrasta (the town square) at the top of the ridge is Laden La and Nehru Rds. The youth hostel is further back up the ridge, virtually at the high point.

Along these two roads are a fair number of budget hotels and cheap restaurants, the GPO, the bus terminals for Sikkim and Kathmandu, the Foreigners' Registration Office, the State Bank of India, curio shops and photographic supply shops. At the Chowrasta end of Nehru Rd and on Gandhi Rd above Laden La Rd are many of the mid-range hotels and restaurants. The bulk of the top-range hotels are clustered around Observatory Hill beyond Chowrasta. There are others along Dr Zakir Hussain Rd and AJC Bose Rd.

Information

Tourist Office The tourist office (☎ 54-050) is below the Bellevue Hotel, Chowrasta. They are helpful and have reasonably up-to-date pamphlets and a map of Darjeeling for Rs 5. They run a bus to Bagdogra Airport for Rs 55, which leaves from opposite the Hotel Alice Villa just below Chowrasta. Buy tickets in advance. The office is open from 10 am to 4.30 pm daily except Sunday, but these hours are quite flexible.

Money The State Bank of India on Laden La Rd is the usual place to change money but there's also a branch of ANZ Grindlays very close by.

Post & Telecommunications The GPO is on Laden La Rd and the telegraph office is on Gandhi Rd.

Permits The Foreigners' Registration Office is on Laden La Rd. To get a 15-day permit for Sikkim you must first visit the Deputy Commissioner's Office, otherwise known as the DM (District Magistrate). Then get an endorsement from the Foreigners' Registration Office and return to the DM to collect your permit. The DM's office is open for permit applications on weekdays from 11 am to 1 pm and 2 to 4 pm. The whole process takes about an hour. If you want to enter western Sikkim direct from Darjeeling, rather than first going to Gangtok, make sure that Naya Bazar is one of the places listed on the permit.

Bookshops The Oxford Book & Stationery Company on Chowrasta is the best bookshop here.

Trekking Equipment Trekking gear can be hired from the youth hostel, but you must leave a deposit to cover the value of the articles you borrow (deposits returnable, less hire charges, on return of the equipment). Typical charges per day are: sleeping bag Rs 5, rucksack Rs 5, boots Rs 7, jacket Rs 5 and two-person tent Rs 25. The hostel keeps an interesting book in which trekkers write comments about the routes.

Darjeeling Gorkha Hill Council Tourism also rents out gear for similar prices – contact the tourist office. There are a number of trekking agencies, including Trek Mate on Nehru Rd and U-Trek on N B Singh Rd, which have been recommended. Their gear is more expensive but some of it is good quality.

Tiger Hill

The highest spot in the area at 2590 metres, Tiger Hill is near Ghoom, about 11 km from Darjeeling. The hill is famous for its magnificent dawn views over Kanchenjunga and other eastern Himalayan peaks. On a clear day even Mt Everest is visible.

Every day a large convoy of battered Land Rovers leaves Darjeeling at 4.30 am, which means that in the smaller lodges you get woken up at this time every day, whether you like it or not. A seat costs Rs 40 for the return trip. It can be very cold and very crowded at the top but coffee is available. There's a view tower and entry costs Rs 2 for the top or Rs 7 for the warmer VIP lounge. Halfway down the hill a temple priest causes a massive traffic jam by anointing the steering wheel of each vehicle for the return trip!

Many take the jeep one way (Rs 30), and then walk back, a very pleasant two-hour trip.

Senchal Lake

Close to Tiger Hill is Senchal Lake, which supplies Darjeeling with its domestic water. It's a particularly scenic area and popular as a picnic spot with Indian holiday-makers.

Kanchenjunga

At 8598 metres this is the world's third-highest mountain. From Darjeeling, the best uninterrupted views are to be had from Bhan Bhakta Sarani. From Chowrasta, take the road to the right-hand side of the Windamere Hotel and continue about 300 metres.

Ghoom Monastery

This is probably the most famous monastery

in Darjeeling and is about eight km south of town, just below Hill Cart Rd and the railway station near Ghoom. It enshrines an image of the Maitreya Buddha (the coming Buddha). Foreigners are allowed to enter the shrine and take photographs. A small donation is customary and the monks are very friendly.

There is another **monastery** nearby in Ghoom, and half an hour (by bus) further down the road to Siliguri is **Sonada**, with a large and interesting monastery of the Kagyupa sect.

Aloobari Monastery

Nearer Darjeeling, on Tenzing Norgay Rd, this monastery welcomes visitors. The monks often sell Tibetan and Sikkimese handicrafts and religious objects (usually hand bells). If the monastery is closed ask at the cottage next door and they'll let you in.

Observatory Hill

Situated above the Windamere Hotel, this viewpoint is sacred to both Hindus and Buddhists. There's a Kali shrine here and the multicoloured prayer flags double as trapezes for the monkeys. Watch out for them as they can be aggressive.

Bhutia Busty Monastery

Not far from Chowrasta is this colourful monastery, with Kanchenjunga providing a spectacular backdrop. Originally a branch of the Nygmapa sect's Phodang Monastery in Sikkim, it was transferred to Darjeeling in 1879. The shrine here originally stood on Observatory Hill. There's an old library of Buddhist texts upstairs.

Dhirdham Temple

The most conspicuous Hindu temple in Darjeeling, this is just below the railway station and is modelled on the famous Pashupatinath Temple in Kathmandu.

Natural History Museum

Established in 1903, a comprehensive but dusty collection of Himalayan and Bengali fauna is packed into this interesting museum. Amongst the 4300 specimens is the estuarine crocodile, the animal responsible for the greatest loss of human life in Asia. The museum is open daily from 10 am to 4 pm, but closes early on Wednesday at 1 pm. Entry is Rs 1.

Zoological Park

Conditions for some of the animals here are barely tolerable, made worse by the fact that they have no escape from the Indian male tourists who show off by teasing them mercilessly. The zoo houses India's only collection of Siberian tigers, and some rare species, such as the red panda. It's open daily from 8 am to 4 pm; entry is Rs 1.

Himalayan Mountaineering Institute (HMI) & Museums

Entered through the zoo, on Jawahar Rd West about two km from the town, the HMI runs courses to train mountaineers. There are a couple of interesting museums here. The **Mountaineering Museum** contains a collection of historic mountaineering equipment, specimens of Himalayan flora and fauna (though not one of the abominable snowman!) and a relief model of the Himalaya. The **Everest Museum** next door traces the history of attempts on the great peak.

Sherpa Tenzing Norgay, who conquered Everest with Edmund Hillary in 1953, lived in Darjeeling and was the director of the institute for many years. He died in 1986 and his statue now stands beside his cremation spot just above the institute.

There are film shows at the institute and for Rs 1 (minimum 10 people) you can view Kanchenjunga close up through a Zeiss telescope given to a Nepalese maharaja by Adolf Hitler.

The institute is open from 9 am to 1 pm and 2 to 4.30 pm, and entry costs Rs 0.50. There's a reasonable vegetarian restaurant by Sherpa Tenzing's statue.

Snow Leopard Breeding Programme

In contrast to the animals in the rest of the zoo the snow leopards are kept in a large separate enclosure on the way to the ropeway. These rare animals are reputedly less keen to breed in captivity than the panda (whose disinterest in sex is legendary) but they've had some success here. Much credit must be given to the devoted attentions of Kiran Moktan, who runs the programme and spends his days with the leopards. He welcomes interested visitors between 9 and 11 am and 2 to 4 pm, but you should not make too much noise. Ask to see his drawings as he's an accomplished artist.

Passenger Ropeway

At North Point, about three km from town, this was the first passenger ropeway (cable-car) to be constructed in India. It is five km long and connects Darjeeling with Singla Bazaar on the Little Ranjit River at the bottom of the valley. However, the power problems in Darjeeling have meant that for some years only the first two km of the route has been operational. A return trip (including insurance and a very necessary standby generator!) is Rs 30 and takes about an hour. Cars go half-hourly from 8 am to 3.30 pm but it's closed on Sunday and holidays. You can phone to check it's running (☎ 2731). It's a popular trip and you need to book in advance, and this can only be done in person, not on the phone.

Botanical Gardens

Below the bus and taxi stand near the market, these gardens contain a representative collection of Himalayan plants, flowers and orchids. The hothouses are well worth a visit. The gardens are open between 6 am and 5 pm; entrance is free.

Tibetan Refugee Self-Help Centre

A 20 to 30-minute walk from Chowrasta brings you down to this Tibetan centre. It was established in October 1959 to help rehabilitate Tibetan refugees who fled from Tibet with the Dalai Lama following the Chinese invasion. Religious importance is attached to this place, as the 13th Dalai Lama (the present is the 14th) stayed here during his visit to India in 1919-22. The centre produces superb carpets, woollens, wood-

The beautiful but threatened snow leopard

carvings and leatherwork, and has various Tibetan curios for sale (coins, banknotes, jewellery etc).

You can wander at leisure through the workshops and watch the work in progress. The weaving and dyeing shops and the woodcarving shop are particularly interesting, and the people who work there are very friendly. Their prices, however, are on a par with those in the curio shops of Chowrasta and Nehru Rd. It's an interesting place to visit even apart from the workshops, and the views are magnificent.

Tea Plantations

Tea is, of course, Darjeeling's most famous export. From its 78 gardens, employing over 40,000 people, it produces the bulk of West

Bengal's crop, which is almost a quarter of India's total.

The most convenient plantation to visit is the Happy Valley Tea Estate, only two km from the centre of town, where tea is still produced by the 'orthodox' method as opposed to the 'Curling, Tearing and Crushing' (CTC) method adopted on the plains. However, it's only worth going when plucking is in progress (April to November) because it's only then that the processing takes place. It's open daily from 8 am to noon and 1 and 4.30 pm, except on Monday and Sunday afternoon. An employee might latch on to you, whisk you around the factory and then demand some outrageous sum for his trouble; Rs 10 per person is not inappropriate.

If you're buying tea, First Flush Super Fine Tippy Golden Flowery Orange Pekoe I is the top quality. The price varies tremendously; at Chowrasta you'll pay anything from Rs 600 to Rs 1600 per kg! The way to test the tea is to take a small handful in your closed fist, breath firmly on it through your fingers and then open your hand and smell the aromas which are released from the tea by your warm breath. At least it will look like you know what you're doing even if you don't have a clue! Avoid the tea in fancy boxes or packaging as this is all blended and comes from Calcutta.

Gymkhana Club

Membership of the Darjeeling Gymkhana Club costs just Rs 15 per day but the activities here are not equestrian. The word gymkhana is actually derived from the Hindi *gendkhana* (ball house). Ball games on offer here include tennis (mornings only, Rs 5 racquet hire), squash, badminton, table tennis and billiards, and roller-skating is also available.

The club must have been magnificent when it was the playground of the Raj; these days it's semi-derelict. Any old members would be horrified to see it's current condition. In the billiard room extension, donated by the Maharaja of Cooch Behar in 1918, there's now a poster of Marilyn Monroe!

Other Activities

Beware of the pony-wallahs who congregate in Chowrasta. They'll come along with you

---

Producing the World's Best Tea

Tea from some of the estates in the Darjeeling area is very high quality, attracting the highest prices at auction. Although the climatic conditions are just right for producing fine tea bushes, the final result is dependent on a complex drying process.

After picking, the fresh green leaves are placed 15 to 25 cm deep in a 'withering trough' where the moisture content is reduced from between 70% and 80% to between 30% and 40% using high-velocity fans. When this is complete the withered leaves are rolled and pressed to break the cell walls and express their juices onto the surface of the leaves. Normally two rollings at different pressures are undertaken, and in between rolls the leaves are sifted to separate the coarse from the fine. Next the leaves, coated with their juices, are allowed to ferment on racks in a high-humidity room, a process which develops their characteristic aroma and flavour. This fermentation must be controlled carefully since either over or under-fermentation will ruin the tea.

The process is stopped by passing the fermenting leaves through a dry air chamber at 115°C to 120°C on a conveyer belt to further reduce the moisture content to around 2% or 3%. The last process is the sorting of the tea into grades. In order of value they are: Golden Flowery Orange Pekoe (unbroken leaves), Golden Broken Orange Pekoe, Orange Fannings and Dust (the latter three consisting of broken leaves).

In the last few years, tea estates have employed modern agricultural practices to maintain and improve their viability. They were one of the first agricultural enterprises to use clonal plants in their replanting schemes, though very little of this has been done and most of the tea trees are at least 100 years old and nearing the end of their useful or even natural lives. The ageing plants and deteriorating soil causes grave concern since tea is not only a major export item but also provides much employment in the area.

Although the auction prices for the lower qualities of tea are often disappointing for producers, the top qualities continue to achieve record prices. At an auction in 1991, tea from the Castleton Estate in Darjeeling went to a Japanese bidder for Rs 6010 (US$275) per kg – a world record! ■

as a guide and at the end you'll find you're paying for a second pony and for their guiding time! The usual charge is around Rs 25 an hour, but make sure of the price first.

The video craze has hit India everywhere, particularly in Darjeeling and some other hill stations. Lots of places have set themselves up as mini-cinemas; a blackboard outside indicates what's showing. Often it's Western films that would have had trouble getting by the censor in the old days.

Language Courses
Three-month courses in Tibetan language are offered by the Manjushree Centre of Tibetan Culture at 8 Burdwan Rd.

Organised Tours
In the season (mid-September to mid-December), the tourist office offers a sunrise trip to Tiger Hill which leaves daily at 4.30 am. Tickets are Rs 40 and must be booked in advance. Most people go with the independent operators who charge a little less, and some send a runner to your hotel to make sure you get up! Depending on demand, the tourist office also organises a local sightseeing tour, a trip to Mirik and a two-day tour to Kalimpong and Gangtok.

There are numerous travel agents and tour operators. Juniper Tours & Travels (☎ 2625), near the clock tower on Laden La Rd, seems to be reliable and also organises trips to Gangtok. Also recommended is Himalayan Adventures, near the Tshering Denzongpa Hotel.

Places to Stay
There are a great number of places to stay in Darjeeling. Those that follow are only a limited selection. Prices vary widely with the season; as far as possible those listed are for the high season (15 March to 15 July and 15 September to 15 November). In the low season, prices drop by 50% to 75% and discounts are open to negotiation.

Darjeeling suffers from chronic power and water shortages. Many hotels have back-up generators, many don't.

Places to Stay – bottom end
For cheap accommodation and the best views in Darjeeling, many travellers head for the area around the youth hostel and TV tower. It's about 20 minutes from the railway station; you simply walk straight up the hill, the operative word here being *up*!

The *youth hostel* (☎ 2290), above Dr Zakir Hussain Rd right on the top of the ridge, used to be very popular with budget travellers. Unfortunately, it's now pretty run-down, and being on the top of the ridge the cold wind whistles through the spartan dorms. However, the people who run it are very friendly and informative about trekking in this region, and the views up here are great. With dorm beds at Rs 25 for nonmembers (Rs 20 for members) it still attracts a few hardy and impecunious souls.

If you don't fancy the hostel, right opposite is the popular *Triveni Guest House*, well run by a friendly family. There are dorm beds for Rs 25 and doubles for Rs 60 with common bathroom. There's a good restaurant here, and hot water is available by the bucket. In this same area is the recommended *Aliment Restaurant & Hotel*, a great restaurant with a few clean rooms at Rs 40/60. The friendly manager just can't do enough for you.

From the TV tower, the road over the ridge brings you to the popular *Hotel Tower View*. Dorm beds are Rs 30, doubles with common bath Rs 60 and with attached bath Rs 80. There's hot showers in the morning, and a cosy restaurant. The sunrise views from this place are excellent, the only disadvantage being that it's on the shaded side of the ridge.

Just beyond the post office there is a whole cluster of cheap hotels either on Laden La Rd or on the alleys and steps running off it. Take the stone steps uphill just beyond the post office and on the left is the popular *Hotel Prestige* (☎ 2699). It offers clean, smallish rooms with bathroom and gas water heater for Rs 80/120, or from Rs 120/150 with views. Heaters are available on request (for an extra charge), the staff are very friendly and there are good views.

If you turn right just before the Prestige

you reach the very popular *Shamrock Hotel* (☎ 3378). The upstairs rooms are more expensive (Rs 120 for a double) than the downstairs ones, but this Tibetan-run place is very friendly and well kept, and there is a fire at night in winter. There's supposedly hot water in the communal shower, but this is at best a trickle. Large vegetarian meals are available for Rs 25 if you order in advance. Watch out for the low ceilings!

The smarter-looking *Hotel Pagoda* next door has good-sized rooms with polished floors at Rs 40/80 with common bath, or Rs 150 for a double with attached bath. Hot water comes by the bucket.

At the top of the steps and left a few metres along Nehru Rd is the *Hotel Springburn* (☎ 2054), which is OK for a short stay. Nearby is the *Hotel Tara*, similarly tatty and more expensive but run by friendly Tibetans.

Going up in price a little, there's another collection of hotels above the taxi stand on Nehru Rd, including the *Hotel Crystal, Holiday Home, Kundus, Shree Anapurna* and the *Capital*, which has doubles from Rs 150. There's not too much to choose between them and they're all similar in price but the views from the front rooms are definitely superior to those from the hotels further down the hill off Laden La Rd.

Further up the hill from this cluster on Rockville Rd is another group of Indian holiday hotels which includes the *Purnima, Broadway, La Bella, Ashoka, Rockville, Continental* and *Daffodil*. The *Hotel Purnima* (☎ 3110), for example, charges Rs 300 for a double. The rooms have a bathroom and hot water by the bucket, and the hotel has its own restaurant. There are no singles. The *Rockville* (☎ 2513) has some nice doubles from Rs 330, or Rs 440 with hot water. Off-season discount is 30%.

Further along Nehru Rd is the *Everest Luxury Hotel*. It's anything but luxurious though it does have good views. Large, basic rooms are good value at Rs 80/150 with attached bath and hot water by the bucket.

Places to Stay – middle

An old favourite in this price bracket is the excellent *Bellevue Hotel* (☎ 2221), right on Chowrasta. It's very well kept and run by a friendly Tibetan family. There are no singles but a variety of doubles and triples are available at Rs 350 to Rs 550, all with bathroom and hot water. Room 49 has the best views and also has a separate sitting room. The hotel has its own cafe for snacks and breakfast, overlooking Chowrasta. Heaters have been installed in most rooms and the sitting room, a must in the cold season.

Independently run by a member of the same Tibetan family is the confusingly named *Main Bellevue Hotel* (☎ 54-178), just above the other Bellevue. It's quieter and in an old building. Doubles with attached bathrooms with hot water geyser are Rs 550 (a bargain at Rs 200 off season).

Back down Nehru Rd there's a couple of restaurants which also have a few rooms. The *Shangri La* (☎ 54-149) has good doubles at Rs 650, with nice views and log fires in the bedrooms.

An excellent place in this range is the very friendly, Sherpa-run *Hotel Tshering Denzongpa* (☎ 3412), on JP Sharma Rd, about five minutes' walk from the bus stand and midway between it and The Mall. Standard double rooms with attached bath and bucket hot water on request cost Rs 200 (Rs 80 off season), while deluxe rooms with carpet, TV, attached bath and hot water in the mornings cost Rs 400 to Rs 600 (Rs 200 to Rs 300 off season). There are good views from the upper floor.

Dekevas Restaurant runs the *Hotel Dekeling* (☎ 54-149). It's another friendly Tibetan place, with rooms ranging from Rs 300 to Rs 500, most with views, and all with bathroom and hot water. It's good value

Opposite the Bellevue is the large *Pineridge Hotel* (☎ 54-074), with spacious doubles for Rs 425 and triples for Rs 550. All rooms have attached bathrooms and hot water. Deluxe double rooms with TV cost Rs 550. Off-season rates are Rs 250, and Rs 325 deluxe.

The *Hotel Alice Villa* (☎ 54-181) offers singles/doubles for Rs 480/680, including breakfast and dinner. Outside the main season you can get a double room without meals here for as little as Rs 200. A few of the rooms have fireplaces and there's a modern extension.

West Bengal Tourism's *Tourist Lodge* (☎ 54-411) is quite some way from the centre past Loreto College and next to the Gymkhana Club. Singles/doubles with attached bathroom are Rs 520/785 which includes breakfast and dinner. There are no reductions if you don't want to eat here. The rooms are OK and there are good views from the garden but it's nothing special. Off-season rates are 25% less.

Run by a Calcutta-based Chinese family, the *Hotel Valentino* (☎ 2228), on Rockville Rd, offers some of the best views in Darjeeling. Doubles here are Rs 700, including early-morning tea and breakfast. All rooms have a TV, bathroom, hot water and optional heating. The hotel has its own bar and Chinese restaurant (one of the best in town). Discounts of 40% are offered in the off season.

Down the hill towards the market, the *Central Hotel* (☎ 2033), Robertson Rd, has singles/doubles for Rs 750/1050. With meals the rate is Rs 1000/1500. Rooms have a bathroom and hot water, and the doubles also have a sitting room with a fireplace. The hotel has its own bar and a restaurant with good Indian food.

The *Darjeeling Club* (☎ 54-348) above Nehru Rd was the Tea Planters' Club in the days of the Raj. You can get a room here for Rs 400/500 or Rs 600/700 for a deluxe suite with a fire in the bedroom (buckets of coal are Rs 50). The upstairs suites are very pleasant but the cheaper rooms downstairs are dark, overpriced and not recommended. There's a billiard room, a musty library, plenty of memorabilia and lots of nice sitting areas. The restaurant is only for residents, and meals cost Rs 40 for breakfast, Rs 60 to Rs 80 for lunch or dinner. There's a temporary membership charge of Rs 25 per day, and rates are discounted by up to 40% in the off season.

Places to Stay – top end

The *Windamere Hotel* (☎ 54-041), on the

slopes of Observatory Hill, is the best place to stay in Darjeeling. It's one of the oldest established hotels and a gem of a leftover from the Raj. Set in beautifully maintained gardens, it consists of a main block with detached cottages and dining room, and is for all lovers of nostalgia. The hotel, owned since the 1920s by Mrs Tenduf-La, a Tibetan lady now in her 80s, describes its attitude to hotel management as defying 'fashion and the cramping dictates of an amusement industry which sees personalised service as an obsolete indulgence'. The service is indeed excellent and the hotel is also characterised by its policy of deliberately side-stepping modern indulgences like TVs and central heating. There are, however, fires in almost every room and hot water bottles should you require them. There's a library and a bar, and a string quartet entertains you in the drawing room, and a pianist during dinner. A discreet notice in the lounge asks visitors not to 'lie supine on the hearth or sleep behind the settees, lest unintended offence be given to others'. Rooms cost US$59/89 for a single/double, and suites are US$98. The prices include all meals, which are excellent.

The recently refurbished *Hotel Sinclairs* (☎ 3431) at 18/1 Nehru Rd has excellent views. Singles/doubles cost Rs 1050/1900, including dinner and breakfast. All the rooms have bathroom, hot water and central heating. There's a restaurant and bar, and the hotel has its own generator.

Along the road opposite the GPO is the flashy *Hotel Chancellor* (☎ 2956), a concrete block with singles/doubles for Rs 1005/1410 with attached bathrooms. Breakfast is included and the staff is friendly. The off-season discount is only 15%.

A popular place is the *New Elgin Hotel* (☎ 2182), off Robertson Rd, which is a delightful old place with a resident labrador and pictures of the queen on the walls. The staff are friendly, and singles/doubles cost Rs 1600/1800 with all meals. All rooms are heated and have attached bath, hot water and colour TV. It also has a popular bar, restaurant and garden/patio.

Places to Eat

If you're staying at the youth hostel or the Triveni and don't want to make the trek into town, the restaurant at *Triveni Guest House* is very clean and has good food. The *Aliment Hotel* close by also has a restaurant, and the *Ratna Restaurant* is also worth a try.

There are numerous cheap restaurants along Laden La Rd all clustered together between the State Bank of India and the post office. Several of them are Tibetan-run while the remainder offer Indian cuisine of various sorts. Most of them are pretty basic and could use a good scrub down. They include the *Golden Dragon, Vineet, Utsang, Potala, Lotus, Lhasa, Penang, Soatlee* and *Washington*. Also in this area is the new *Park Restaurant*, which is a step up the scale, and has good food and music.

Opposite the Hotel Capital is the *Dafey Munal Restaurant* which offers 'chocolate pudding with fire'!

A popular place for breakfast and great views is the terrace at *Kev's* (Keventer's Snack Bar). They've got ham, bacon, sausages and cheese. Bacon or sausages and eggs cost Rs 25; service can be tediously slow and hygiene is not what it might be.

Across the road, on Nehru Rd overlooking the small square, is the *Dekevas Restaurant*. It's a neat, clean, shiny little place with good pizzas for up to Rs 22. They have other food in the same price bracket and also do breakfasts. It's as popular with travellers as Kev's.

A short walk up the hill brings you to *Glenary's*, an excellent place with a definite ghost-of-the-Raj air to it. Tea time here is still an occasion that calls for freshly starched table linen. Prices are very reasonable and Darjeeling tea is Rs 15 per pot. You can also have full meals here (main dishes are Rs 25 to Rs 35) but the restaurant closes at 7.30 pm. It's licensed and beer is Rs 40, sweet red Golconda wine is Rs 10 a glass. Downstairs is the bakery where, if you arrive early enough, you can get excellent brown bread. Their doughnuts (Rs 6) are legendary and they have a range of cakes (cherry, Madeira, Dundee) from Rs 30. You can also buy Kalimpong cheese here.

Nearby is the *Shangri La Restaurant* which offers Indian and Chinese food. Main dishes are between Rs 25 and Rs 50, and the restaurant has a log fire on winter evenings.

Hasty Tasty is a flash, new fast-food place which offers good vegetarian food and a range of ice creams

On Chowrasta itself, the *Star Dust Restaurant* is an open-air restaurant offering south Indian vegetarian snacks. It's a good place to sit and watch the activity on the square, and there are masala dosas for Rs 11 and espresso coffee for Rs 5. Also on Chowrasta is *Amigos*, another fast-food place serving burgers and pizzas.

The best Chinese food is at the *New Embassy Chinese Restaurant* in the Hotel Valentino. Main dishes are Rs 35 to Rs 50, and they don't let anyone in after 7 pm. Better value for an evening out is the *New Elgin Hotel*, where set dinners are Rs 75. The food is good and the daily menu features such eclectic dishes as cream of cherry soup (delicious)! For cheaper Chinese food there's the little *Kim Fung Restaurant* on NB Singh Rd, which also serves tofu dishes on Thursday.

For a real splurge you can't beat dinner at the *Windamere Hotel* but, if you are a non-guest, you must book in advance since they usually cater only for their guests. It's a set menu which costs Rs 310. Here you are served a full Western meal, such as roast chicken, followed by a full-on Indian meal of curry, rice and chapatis! A pianist plays during dinner and afterwards you can retire to the drawing room for a brandy by the fire.

Things to Buy

Curio Shops The majority of these are on Chowrasta and along Nehru Rd. All things Himalayan are sold here – thankas, brass statues, religious objects, jewellery, wood-carvings, woven fabrics, carpets etc – but if you're looking for bargains you have to shop judiciously and be prepared to spend plenty of time looking. Thankas in particular are nowhere near the quality of 10 years ago. They may look impressive at first sight, but on closer inspection you will find that little care has been taken over the finer detail. The brocade surroundings (said to originate from China) are often of much finer quality.

If you're looking for bronze statues, the real goodies are kept under the counter and cost in multiples of US$100! You have to indicate that you are not interested in the mass-produced stuff on display before they get the better ones out.

Woodcarvings tend to be excellent value for money. Most of the shops accept international credit cards. There is also a market off Hill Cart Rd next to the bus and taxi stands. Here you can find excellent and relatively cheap patterned woollen sweaters. If you need an umbrella these can be bought here cheaply. Made out of bamboo, they are collectors' items themselves!

For Tibetan carpets, the cheapest place in the area is at Hayden Hall, opposite the State Bank of India on Laden La Rd. It's a women's co-operative, excellent value and well worth checking out.

West Bengal's Manjusha Emporium, on Nehru Rd, is a fixed-price shop selling Himalayan handicrafts, silk and handloomed products. About two km from town on the way to Ghoom is the Ava Art Gallery, featuring embroidered pictures done by the owner. Entry is Rs 0.25 and the pictures are for sale.

Getting There & Away

Air The nearest airport is 90 km away at Bagdogra, down on the plains near Siliguri. See under Getting There & Away in the Siliguri section earlier in this chapter for details.

Indian Airlines (☎ 2355) is in the Bellevue Hotel at Chowrasta and is open Monday to Saturday from 10 am to 1 pm and 2 to 4 pm. On Sunday it is open until 1 pm. The airport bus (Rs 55) departs from opposite the Hotel Alice Villa.

Bus Most of the buses from Darjeeling depart from the Bazaar bus stand (Hill Cart Rd). Most jeeps and taxis depart from the taxi stand, at the intersection of Robertson and Laden La Rds. There are many different companies operating buses, jeeps and taxis.

Buses to Calcutta, Kathmandu and other points further afield generally go through Siliguri.

To/From New Jalpaiguri/Siliguri There are numerous buses, jeeps and taxis in either direction daily between 6 am and 10 pm. The journey takes 3½ to 4½ hours by express bus or jeep (sometimes less) and costs Rs 40. A share taxi costs Rs 70 per person.

To/From Bagdogra West Bengal Tourism buses connect with the arrival of flights from Calcutta and Delhi. The fare from Bagdogra to Darjeeling is Rs 55 and the journey takes 3½ hours, including a 15-minute stop at Kurseong for refreshments. Buses from Darjeeling to Bagdogra depart from opposite the Hotel Alice Villa and must be booked in advance at the tourist office.

To/From Kalimpong Jeeps and buses make this 2½-hour trip regularly between 7.30 am and 3 pm. Jeeps cost Rs 50 per person for a front seat, Rs 35 in the back. These are so much more convenient than the buses that they're worth the extra expense. All vehicles for Kalimpong leave from the Bazaar bus stand.

To/From Sikkim If you don't want to go by taxi or jeep to Gangtok, there is the Sikkim Nationalised Transport (SNT), which has its Darjeeling office in the first building below the GPO on Laden La Rd. There is one minibus daily (Rs 60, seven hours,) in either direction (1 pm from Darjeeling), and as there are few seats available, early booking is essential. Private buses also operate from the bus stand, or there are frequent jeeps for Rs 80.

If you want to head straight for western Sikkim, there are regular jeeps from 8.30 am to Jorethang (Rs 40, 1½ hours), from where there is transport on to Gezing.

To/From Kathmandu There are a number of companies which offer daily buses between Darjeeling and Kathmandu (Rs 275), but none of them actually have a direct service;

you have to change buses at Siliguri. The usual arrangement is that the agents will sell you a ticket as far as Siliguri (Rs 40) but guarantee you a seat on the connecting bus with the same agency (for which you pay a further Rs 235 on average). You arrive at the border around 3 pm (Kakarbhitta is the name of the town on the Nepalese side), leave again around 4 pm and arrive in Kathmandu around 9 or 10 am the next day.

Most travellers prefer to do the trip independently, though it involves four changes – bus from Darjeeling to Siliguri (Rs 40), bus (Rs 5) or jeep (Rs 15) from Siliguri to Panitanki on the border, rickshaw across the border to Kakarbhitta (Rs 5), and bus from Kakarbhitta to Kathmandu (Nepalese Rs 250). This is cheaper than the package deal, and you get a choice of buses from the border, plus you have the option of travelling during the day and overnighting along the way. There are day buses from Kakarbhitta that go to a number of other towns on the Terai (Nepalese plains), including Janakpur (NRs 100), and night buses direct to Pokhara (NRs 250).

A more comfortable alternative is to take a flight from the border (the airstrip is Bhadrapur) to Kathmandu with Everest Air or Royal Nepal (US$99).

There is no Nepalese consulate in Darjeeling; the nearest one is in Calcutta, but visas are available at the border for US$25 (which must be paid in cash), and these can be extended in Kathmandu.

Once in Nepal, buses travel west as far as Narayanghat on the Mahendra Highway, skirting the foothills and passing a number of interesting places and sights on the Terai; from Narayanghat the road climbs through the Siwalik Hills to Mugling and the Trisuli River valley, where you double back towards Kathmandu. If it isn't too hot, consider travelling by day, so you can see the sights and stop in Janakpur and/or the Royal Chitwan National Park.

Avalanches and floods can sometimes delay the bus. One traveller was held up for three days. The road is in very poor condition in the vicinity of the Kosi Barrage and there's another very bad section on the Prithvi Highway (the Pokhara to Kathmandu road) between Mugling and Kathmandu. Many travellers consider it one of the roughest bus journeys on the subcontinent!

To/From Other Places Deluxe buses are also available to Calcutta, Patna, Guwahati, Shillong, Silchar and Agartala.

Train New Jalpaiguri/Siliguri is the railhead for all trains other than the narrow-gauge toy train. See under Getting There & Away in the Siliguri section earlier in this chapter for train details to or from Calcutta and other centres. If the toy train is operating, you can make reservations at the Darjeeling railway station for major trains out of New Jalpaiguri.

Although a bus or taxi is the fastest means of getting from New Jalpaiguri or Siliguri to Darjeeling, the most interesting way of doing this last stage of the journey is to take the toy train at least part of the way; the whole trip from Siliguri takes up to 10 hours.

Toy Train The journey to Darjeeling from New Jalpaiguri or Siliguri on the famous miniature railway is a superb experience which shouldn't be missed.

The train runs daily, although services during the monsoon are often disrupted due to the track being washed away. The train leaves Siliguri at 9 am, arriving in Darjeeling at 5.30 pm. An additional service leaves Siliguri at 7.15 am during the season. The cost is Rs 153/19 in 1st/2nd class. It's a slow but interesting trip, although the black soot belched out by the little steam engine soon gets annoying, and the carriages are extremely cramped, especially when there's a dozen hefty foreigners complete with backpacks! The best bet is to take the train only as far as Kurseong (Rs 33/9, five hours), and from there take a bus (Rs 10) or a seat in a jeep (Rs 30) for the 1½-hour run to Darjeeling. This also gets you into Darjeeling before dark.

WEST BENGAL

TREKKING IN THE DARJEELING REGION

The best months to trek in this region are April, May, October and November. There may be occasional showers during April and May but, in a way, this is the best time to go as many shrubs are in flower, particularly the rhododendrons. There may be occasional rains during the first half of October if the monsoon is prolonged. November is generally dry, and visibility is excellent during the first half of December, though it's usually cold by then. After the middle of December there are occasional snowfalls.

When planning what clothes to take, bear in mind that you will be passing through valley bottoms as low as 300 metres and over mountain ridges as high as 4000 metres, so you'll need clothing for low, tropical climates and high mountain passes. No matter what time of year you go, it's a good idea to take a light raincoat which can be folded up and put inside your rucksack since the weather can be unpredictable, particularly at high altitudes. Another tip is to wear one thin pair of socks within a thicker pair and you'll get fewer blisters.

Acute Mountain Sickness (AMS) can occur at high altitudes. See the Health section in the Facts for the Visitor chapter for more details.

For the following Sandakphu/Phalut trek, you don't need to bring much with you as there's accommodation along the way. Most places have quilts but in the high season it might be worth bringing your own sleeping bag in case there's not enough bedding to go round.

Although you can get basic meals along the way everyone recommends bringing along some snacks like nuts, biscuits, raisins and chocolate. You'll need a water bottle – even a plastic mineral water bottle will do – as there are some stretches where there's no water or places to eat.

Guides and porters are not necessary but can be arranged through the youth hostel or the trekking agencies. A porter would cost about Rs 80 per day, a guide Rs 150 per day. If you don't take a guide, you should ask directions at every opportunity as the path is not always clear.

Note Before leaving Darjeeling you're advised to browse through the Darjeeling Youth Hostel's book in which trekkers write their comments about the routes.

Sandakphu/Phalut Trek

This trek to the Himalayan viewpoint at Phalut (3600 metres) is the most popular trek in the area. It involves a short bus trip from Darjeeling to Manaybhanjang, from where you walk steadily towards the mountains via Sandakphu. Here you can turn back or continue to Phalut and walk down to Rimbik for a bus to Darjeeling. The trek can be done in the opposite direction but you'll spend more time walking with your back to the mountains.

There's a rough jeep track from Manaybhanjang through Sandakphu but it's not used much. If you prefer, Rs 2500 will get you a return trip from Darjeeling to Sandakphu by Land Rover.

Day 1: Darjeeling to Jaubari (8 to 9 hours)

From Darjeeling take the 7 am bus to Manaybhanjang (Rs 15, 1½ hours). The first 30-minute walk out of Manaybhanjang is steep but after about 3½ hours you reach Meghma, a good place for lunch. Jaubari, about three hours further on, is the night halt, or there's also a lodge in Tunling, just before Jaubari.

Jaubari is just inside Nepal but there's no border post. There are three places to stay here: the *Everest Lodge*, the *Indira Lodge* and *Teacher's Lodge*. They are all fairly similar and charge Rs 25 per bed but in the quieter season they take it in turns to open. You can get food and even beer here.

Day 2: Jaubari to Sandakphu (5 to 6 hours)

There are good views for most of the second day. Start with a half-hour descent to Gairibas then climb up to Kalipokhari, where there's a restaurant and a hotel. This is about 3½ hours from Jaubari. A further three hours takes you through Bikhay Bhanjang to Sandakphu; the last few km are steep. There are two *PWD Bungalows* here with beds for Rs 20 and a *Trekkers' Hut* also for Rs 20. Be careful with the drinking water here as the source is not very clean.

Day 3: Sandakphu to Molley (4 to 5 hours)

Between Sandakphu and Sabarkum, a four to five-hour walk, there is nowhere to get food or water so you must bring both with you. For lodging, you have to go down to Molley, less than half an hour's walk. The place to stay here is *Didi's* – it has good food and a warm fire.

Day 4: Molley to Gorkhey (5 to 6 hours)
Go back up to Sabarkum, from where it's a two-hour walk to Phalut. There are superb views of Kanchenjunga from here and, if it's clear, you should also be able to make out Everest in the centre of the group of mountains to the north-west. There's a very basic *Trekkers' Hut* but no mattresses or bedding. From Phalut it's an easy three hours down to Gorkhey for a night halt. There's a Darjeeling Gorkha Hill Council *Trekkers' Hut*, with beds for Rs 20, and also private houses where you can stay.

Day 5: Gorkhey to Rimbik (6 to 7 hours)
A 2½-hour walk through the forest brings you to Raman, where there's the friendly *Sherpa Hotel*, a nice place to stay. From here it's a level 3½-hour stroll through a number of small villages to Rimbik. There are only two hotels to choose from, and both are good. The *Shiva Pradhan Hotel*, with hot water and beer, operates a 'pay what you think it's all worth' system that seems to work. The *Sherpa Hotel* is also popular and has a 'great family atmosphere'.

Day 6: Rimbik to Darjeeling
You can catch the early-morning bus from here to Darjeeling (Rs 25, five hours). Alternatively, you can walk on for 5½ hours to Bijanbari where buses also run to Darjeeling.

Short Cuts If you don't have time for a six-day trek, there are a number of short cuts you can take. You can go just as far as Sandakphu where there are also good views. Sandakphu is actually slightly higher than Phalut, although further back from the mountains. From here you can backtrack to Bikhay Bhanjang and cut straight across to Rimbik in five to six hours for a bus to Darjeeling. Bear in mind that there's no water or food on this stretch.

The other shortcut is between Molley and Raman, which takes a day. It may be easier, however, to take this path as far as the village of Siri Kola (five hours), and then the next day will be an easy walk to Rimbik. There is a fairly new *Trekkers' Hut* in Siri Kola.

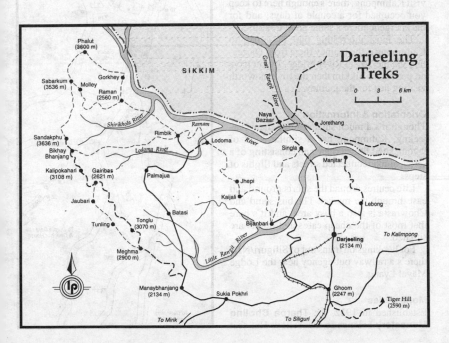

KALIMPONG

Population: 45,000
Telephone Area Code: 03552

Kalimpong is a bustling and rapidly expanding, though still relatively small, bazaar town
set amongst the rolling foothills and deep
valleys of the Himalaya at an altitude of 1250
metres. It was once part of the lands belonging to the rajas of Sikkim, until the beginning
of the 18th century when it was taken from
them by the Bhutanese. In the 19th century
it passed into the hands of the British and
thus became part of West Bengal. It became
a centre for Scottish missionary activity in
the late 19th century, and Dr Graham's
orphanage and school is still running today.

Kalimpong's attractions include three
monasteries, a couple of solidly built
churches, an excellent private library for the
study of Tibetan and Himalayan language
and culture, a sericulture centre, orchid nurseries and the fine views over the surrounding
countryside. Although not many travellers
visit Kalimpong, there's enough here to keep
you occupied for a couple of days, and for
the energetic there's some good trekking.

The most interesting part of a trip to
Kalimpong is the journey there from Darjeeling via the Teesta River bridge. If you have
no permit for Sikkim then the town is worth
visiting just for the journey.

Orientation & Information

Though it's a much smaller town than Darjeeling, Kalimpong has a similar kind of
layout, straddling a ridge and consisting of a
series of interconnected streets and flights of
steps.

Life centres around the sports ground and
east through the market. The bus stand and
Chowrasta is also a busy area, and it's here
that most of the cheap cafes and hotels are
situated.

For bookings on trains out of Siliguri/NJP,
there's a railway out-agency near the Lodge
Mayal Lyang.

Monasteries

Established in 1922, the **Tharpa Choling
Monastery** belongs to the Yellow Hat sect

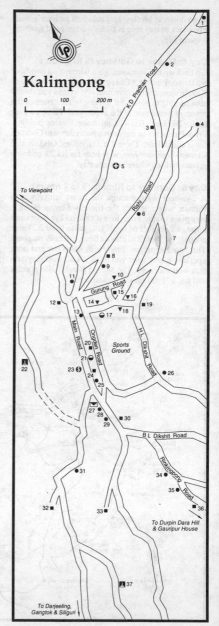
Kalimpong

PLACES TO STAY

3	Deki Lodge
8	Mayal Lyang Lodge
12	Gompu's Hotel & Restaurant
15	Janakee & Cozy Nook Lodges
19	Crown Lodge
20	Sherpa Lodge
24	Tripti Hotel
30	Hotel Silver Oaks
32	Shangri La Tourist Lodge
33	Himalayan Hotel
36	Park Hotel

PLACES TO EAT

10	TT Restaurant
14	Mandarin Restaurant
16	Punjab Lodge
18	Kalsang Restaurant

OTHER

1	Dr Graham's Homes
2	Tharpa Choling Monastery
4	Thongsa Gompa
5	Hospital
6	Kanchan Cinema
7	Market
9	Railway Booking Office
11	Arts & Crafts Co-Op
13	SNT (Sikkim) Bus Office
17	Bus & Jeep Stand
21	Mintri Transport
22	Thakur Baru Temple
23	Bank
25	Kalimtrek
26	Hill Crafts Institute
27	GPO
28	Foreigners' Registration Office
29	Town Hall
31	Cinema
34	Nature Interpretation Centre
35	Rishi Bankim Park
37	Kali Mandir Temple

(Geluk-pa) of Tibetan Buddhism, founded in Tibet in the 14th century and to which the Dalai Lama belongs. It's a 40-minute walk (uphill) from town; take the path to the right off K D Pradhan Rd, just before the Milk Collection and Extension Wing Building.

Lower down the hill, the **Thongsa Gompa**, or Bhutanese Monastery, is the oldest monastery in the area and was founded in 1692. The present building is a little more recent since the original was destroyed by the Gurkhas in their rampage across Sikkim before the arrival of the British.

Zong Dog Palri Fo-Brang Monastery, five km south of the town centre at the end of the ridge, was built in the mid-1970s at Durpin Dara Hill and was consecrated by the Dalai Lama. There are good mountain views from Durpin Dara Hill. This area is a big military camp, although you are free to walk or drive through it.

Flower Nurseries
Kalimpong is an important orchid-growing area and flowers are exported from here to many cities in northern India. The Sri Ganesh Moni Pradhan Nursery and the Udai Mani Pradhan Nursery are among the most important in the area. The Standard and the Universal Nurseries also specialise in cacti. There's a flower festival in Kalimpong in October.

Sericulture Centre
The sericulture centre, where silkworms are bred and silk is produced, is on the road to Darjeeling and can be visited. Nearby is the Swiss Welfare Dairy, established by a Swiss missionary and the source of the delicious hard cheese you can buy here and in Darjeeling.

Nature Interpretation Centre
This centre, on Rinkingpong Rd, is run by the Soil Conservation Division of the Ministry of Environment & Forests. It consists of a number of nicely put together dioramas which depict the effects of human activity on the environment. While it's not wildly exciting, it's good to see public awareness displays such as this being set up. The centre is open daily, except Thursday, from 10 am to 1.30 pm and 2 to 4 pm.

Arts & Crafts
Market days are Wednesday and Saturday, and the market is definitely worth visiting, especially if you want to meet and talk with local people, but it's otherwise overrated. It's certainly not a replica of Kathmandu and there's not much for sale here that you can't

find in either Darjeeling or Gangtok, though antique (or imitation antique) Tibetan jewellery may be somewhat cheaper here.

Kalimpong tapestry bags and purses, copperware, scrolls and paintings from Dr Graham's Homes are sold at the Kalimpong Arts & Crafts Co-Operative. The homes were originally built in 1900 as a residential public school by the missionary Dr Graham. It was set on 50 acres of land and was virtually self-sufficient, with poultry and other farm animals. These days it's a large private school.

Rabindranath Tagore spent his summers here and started Chitrabhanu, a home for destitute women, at Gauripur House. Crafts produced here are also for sale.

Places to Stay – bottom end

There are a number of very basic places around the bus stand. The *Lodge Himalshree* (☎ 55-070) is a small family place on the 3rd floor of a building on Ongden Rd. The owner is friendly and helpful, and there are singles/doubles for Rs 60/120, all with common bathroom. The *Punjab Lodge* cannot be described as spotless and has rooms with common bathroom for Rs 50/100. The *Cozy Nook Lodge* (☎ 55-541) is better, and costs Rs 150 for a double with bath. Hot water is not available.

The *Janakee Lodge* (☎ 55-479) close by is a good place with doubles from Rs 100/120 with common/attached bathroom. Hot water is available in the mornings.

Probably the most popular hotel with travellers is the *Deki Lodge* (☎ 55-095), about 10 minutes' walk north of the bus stand. It's run by very friendly and helpful Tibetans, and they can offer good suggestions about things to do in the Kalimpong area. Rooms cost Rs 70/150 with attached bath, or there are some cheaper rooms in a basic timber outbuilding for Rs 60/100 with common bath. There's a nice little garden out the back, hot water is free by the bucket, and cheap meals are available if ordered in advance.

Gompu's Hotel (☎ 55-818) on Chowrasta is also run by a friendly Tibetan family. There are good singles/doubles for Rs 100/200

with attached bath. There's a good restaurant downstairs. The *Lodge Mayal Lyang* (☎ 55-333) is much the same at Rs 200 for a double with attached bath, but there are no singles and no reduction for single occupancy.

The *Sherpa Lodge* (☎ 55-572) overlooks the sports ground and is reasonable value at Rs 150/250 for rooms with attached bathroom. It's run by very pleasant people, and hot water is available by the bucket.

Away from this area on the road down to the Teesta Bridge is another quite good place – West Bengal Tourism's *Shangri-La Tourist Lodge* (☎ 55-230). It's a clean, old wooden place and offers single/double rooms with bathroom for Rs 150/200. The staff are pleasant and meals are available. The hotel isn't signposted so, if walking out of Kalimpong, watch for a cinema on the left-hand side and then take the small road downhill on the right-hand side shortly afterwards.

The *Crown Lodge* (☎ 55-546) is a few metres down a side street off H L Dikshit Rd. It's quiet, spacious and clean, and has singles/doubles from Rs 180/320 with attached bathroom (hot showers in the mornings), TV in the double rooms – and bed tea at 6.30 am, like it or not! The staff are friendly but the hotel has no restaurant.

The *Hilltop Tourist Cottage* (☎ 55-654) is about two km from the town centre, signposted off Rinkingpong Rd. This place, also run by West Bengal Tourism, is a somewhat spartan and cavernous old timber building, but pleasant nonetheless. Rooms cost Rs 150/325 with attached bath and hot water by the bucket. Meals are available.

Places to Stay – middle

The few mid-range places are all out of the town centre to the south, along Rinkingpong Rd. Pick of the bunch is the *Park Hotel* (☎ 55-304; fax 55-982), about one km from the bus stand. The main part of the hotel is a very pleasant, turn-of-the-century colonial bungalow with polished wooden floors and timber-lined ceilings. The rooms are good value at Rs 450/600 with attached bath, hot water and TV, and those at the front have excellent views. There are also rooms for the same price in the new block at the rear, and although comfortable, they are far less attractive. The hotel has its own bar and restaurant.

West Bengal Tourism has two places further out along the same road. They are also in old colonial bungalows, and have nice gardens and views, but can be a hassle to get to without your own transport. The *Tashiding Tourist Lodge* (☎ 55-929) is three km from the bus stand, and has spacious rooms for Rs 535/713 – the tariff includes dinner and breakfast. One km further along is the nicer of the two places, the *Kalimpong Tourist Lodge (Morgan House)* (☎ 55-384). Prices are the same as the Tashiding.

Places to Stay – top end

If you have the money, there's no better place to stay in Kalimpong than the beautiful old, stone *Himalayan Hotel* (☎ 55-248; fax 55-122), on the right-hand side about 300 metres up the hill past the post office. It is the former home of a British trade agent with Tibet named David MacDonald, who wrote *20 Years in Tibet* and *Land of the Lamas*. The hotel is surrounded by superb gardens looking across to the snow-covered peaks of Kanchenjunga. The hotel is still in the MacDonald family, now run by Tim and Neelam MacDonald, and although the staff are the same, many of the valuable antiques which gave the place its character, including priceless thankas, were stolen some years ago. However, it's still a great place to stay. The management is friendly and helpful, suggesting interesting walks in the neighbourhood and arranging picnics and bird-watching trips. Singles/doubles are Rs 700/1000, or Rs 1000/1600 with all meals, plus 10% tax. Tibetan food is available and is very good. Log fires in the rooms cost Rs 60.

By contrast, there is the *Hotel Silver Oaks* (☎ 55-260; fax 55-368) on Upper Cart Rd, about 100 metres uphill from the post office. It's not a patch on the Himalayan Hotel and is somewhat devoid of life but is very pleasant and does have good views. It's pretty expensive at Rs 1600/1800 for singles/doubles.

Meals are available for Rs 75 for breakfast, and Rs 125 for lunch or dinner.

Places to Eat

The *Kalsang Restaurant* is a cosy little Tibetan place, tucked away down a few steps opposite the Usha Restaurant near the bus stand. The food is cheap and tasty, and the people here are very friendly.

The *TT Restaurant* is a good Chinese/Tibetan place where you can have gyathuk, which is like thukpa (noodle soup), for Rs 15 or sweet and sour pork for Rs 25.

Gompu's Restaurant, Chowrasta, is a pleasant restaurant with friendly staff and is highly recommended by local people and travellers alike. They serve Tibetan, Indian and Chinese food, and Western breakfasts. Roast chicken and chips is Rs 35, a plate of momos Rs 10.

For Chinese food, there's the *Mandarin Restaurant* opposite the bus stand. Another good Chinese restaurant is the *Lee Restaurant* at the Lodge Mayal Lyang.

The *Pure Veg Punjab Restaurant*, below the Lodge Cozy Nook, is a good clean place serving straightforward Indian food. It's popular, and one of the few restaurants open later than 7.30 pm. For a cheap simple meal, the *Usha Restaurant*, a tiny and very friendly chai shop between the Crown Lodge and the bus stand, is worth trying. For standard Indian food you could try one of the restaurants along the main street, such as the restaurant at the *Tripti Hotel*.

If you give staff a bit of notice you can eat at the *Himalayan Hotel*, where European, Indian and Tibetan food is available. However, the atmosphere and surroundings far surpasses the quality of the food. Lunch or dinner costs Rs 120, breakfast Rs 80.

Getting There & Away

Bus & Jeep There are frequent jeeps (Rs 35 for a back seat, Rs 50 for the front) and a few taxis in either direction for the three-hour trip to Darjeeling. The buses are so much less frequent, slower and more uncomfortable that it's hardly worth the small cost saving.

All the transport, other than the taxis, leaves from the Bazaar bus stand.

Buses for Siliguri cost Rs 27 for the three-hour trip and should be booked in advance from one of the offices around the bus stand. The road to Siliguri follows the Teesta River after the bridge, so it's much cheaper and quicker than going via Darjeeling. The views are magnificent.

To Gangtok, Sikkim Nationalised Transport (SNT) has two buses daily, at 8.30 am and 1.15 pm, and these should be booked in advance at the SNT office on Ongden Rd at the bus stand. The trip takes four hours and costs Rs 30. There are also private buses and jeeps on this route.

Mintri Transport operates one bus daily to Siliguri and Bagdogra Airport at 7.15 am from their office (which is also the Indian Airlines office; ☎ 55-241) on Main Rd. The trip takes about three hours and costs Rs 75. Mintri Transport can also book flights (including tickets on Royal Nepal Airlines).

Train The nearest station is Siliguri/New Jalpaiguri. There is an out-agency booking office near the Mayal Lyang Lodge, and they have a small quota of berths on trains originating from or passing through New Jalpaiguri. The office is open daily from 10 am to 1 pm and 4 to 5 pm.

AROUND KALIMPONG

There are a number of things worth visiting in the surrounding area. **Lava**, about 30 km to the east, is a small village with a small monastery, which belongs to the same order as the one at Rumtek (Sikkim). Tuesday is market day, and a good time to visit.

There's a *Forest Rest House* here if you want to stay overnight (book ahead at the Forest Department office in Kalimpong), and buses and jeeps run regularly from Kalimpong.

Kaffer is another small village east of Kalimpong, and it also has a *Forest Rest House*.

Thrill seekers should head for the **Samco Ropeway**, a chairlift installed by the Swedish as part of an aid programme to help villagers cross the Teesta River. If the idea of dangling from a piece of wire 30 metres above the water doesn't entice, give this a miss – it's definitely not for vertigo sufferers or heart patients! The ropeway is on the main Siliguri to Gangtok road, at a place known locally as 27th Mile. Catch any Siliguri bus from Kalimpong.

All these places listed can be visited in one hit on a four-day trek from Kalimpong. There are a couple of travel agencies in Kalimpong which can organise this; ask at the Deki Lodge for more details.

Orissa

The tropical state of Orissa lies along the eastern seaboard of India, south of Bengal. Its main attractions are the temples of the capital Bhubaneswar, the long sandy beach at Puri and the great Sun Temple at Konark. These three sites make a convenient and compact triangle, and Bhubaneswar is on the main Calcutta to Madras railway route.

Orissa is predominantly rural, with fertile green coastal plains rising to the hills of the Eastern Ghats. The majority of the population live on or below the poverty line with annual per capita income one of the lowest in the country. Largely based on agriculture, Orissa's economy is often destabilised by natural disasters, including flooding, drought, cyclone or tornado. However, flooding in the Mahanadi delta, which used to occur regularly, has been much reduced by the building of the Hirakud Dam. The state is mineral rich and is a big exporter of iron ore, with a large factory at Rourkela.

Few visitors venture outside the Bhubaneswar-Puri-Konark triangle and although travel off the beaten track in Orissa is often rough, with few tourist facilities, it can be an interesting and rewarding experience. The Oriyas, 25% of whom are indigenous tribal peoples, are particularly friendly and hospitable.

Population: 33.5 million
Area: 155,707 sq km
Capital: Bhubaneswar
People per sq km: 225
Main Language: Oriya
Literacy Rate: 48.7%
Best Time to Go: November to March

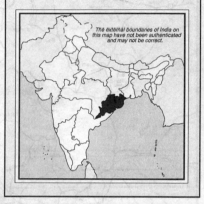

The external boundaries of India on this map have not been authenticated and may not be correct.

ORISSA

History

Orissa's hazy past focuses with the reign of Kalinga. In 260 BC he was defeated by Ashoka, the great Indian emperor, near modern Bhubaneswar. The bloody battle left Ashoka with such a bitter taste that he converted to Buddhism and spread that gentle

---

Orissan Temple Architecture

Orissan temples – whether the mighty Lingaraj in Bhubaneswar, the Jagannath in Puri, the Sun Temple at Konark or the many smaller temples – all follow a similar pattern. Basically there are two structures – the *jagamohan*, or entrance porch, and the *deul* where the image of the temple deity is kept and above which the temple tower rises. The design is complicated in larger temples by the addition of other entrance halls in front of the jagamohan. These are the *bhoga-mandapa* (hall of offering) and the *natamandir* (dancing hall).

The whole structure may be enclosed by an outer wall and within the enclosure there may be smaller, subsidiary temples and shrines. The most notable aspects of the temple design are the soaring tower and the intricate carvings that cover every surface. These may be figures of gods, men and women, plants and trees, flowers, animals and every other aspect of everyday life, but to many visitors it is the erotic carvings which create the greatest interest. They reach their artistic and explicit peak at Konark, where the close-up detail is every bit as interesting as the temple's sheer size. ∎

ORISSA

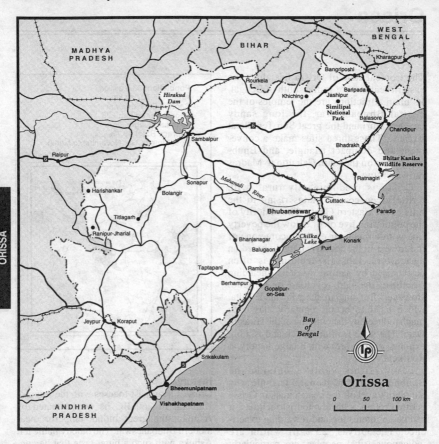

religion far and wide. Buddhism soon declined in Orissa, however, and Jainism held sway until Buddhism reasserted itself in the 2nd century AD.

By the 7th century AD, Hinduism had, in turn, supplanted Buddhism and Orissa's golden age began. Under the Kesari and Ganga kings the Orissan culture flourished and countless temples from that classical period still stand today. The Oriyas managed to defy the Muslim rulers in Delhi until the region finally fell to the Mughals during the 16th century. Many of Bhubaneswar's temples were destroyed at that time.

Things to Buy

Orissa has a very wide and distinctive range of handicrafts. Best known is probably the appliqué work of Pipli. Brightly coloured patches of fabric, cut into animal and flower shapes, are sewn onto bed covers, cushions and beach umbrellas. The village of Raghurajpur is famous for its *patachitra*, paintings on specially prepared cloth. Cuttack is known for its silver filigree jewellery.

Numerous types of Orissan handloomed fabrics are produced. Sambalpur is the centre of the area specialising in tie-dye and *ikat* fabrics. The complex ikat process involves tie-dying the thread before it is woven. This produces cloth with a slightly 'blurred' pattern which is particularly attractive. At Puri you can buy strange little carved wooden replicas of Lord Jagannath and his brother and sister. At Balasore, lacquered children's toys are manufactured.

BHUBANESWAR

Population: 444,000
Telephone Area Code: 0674

Although it was only in 1950 that the state capital was moved from overcrowded Cuttack to Bhubaneswar, the town's history goes back over 2000 years, as excavations at Sisuphal Garh, the remains of a ruined city, have shown. Beside the site of the capital of ancient Kalinga, Bhubaneswar is known as Temple Town and Cathedral City on account of its many temples in the extravagant Orissan style. They date from the 8th to the 13th century AD and it is said that at one time the Bindu Sagar tank had over 7000 temples around it.

Today, the tour guides tell you that there are only 500 but even this seems like a bit of an exaggeration. Only about a dozen are of real interest, including the great Lingaraj Temple. It's one of the most important temples in India, but unfortunately is closed to non-Hindus.

During the last week of January the Tribal Festival is held here with dances, handicrafts and folk art on display.

Orientation & Information

A sprawling, rapidly expanding town, Bhubaneswar is divided by the railway line which runs roughly north-south through the

ORISSA

Orissan Tribal People

Orissa has no less than 62 distinct tribal groups of aboriginal people who inhabited this region prior to the Aryan invasion of India. Officially known as 'tribals' they constitute more than a quarter of the state's population and live mainly in the hilly areas outside the small coastal plain. Many have adopted the ways of the invader and, as far as the foreign visitor is concerned, may not seem to look or dress very differently to the average Aryan Orissan – though an anthropologist or a caste-conscious Indian would hardly agree. Others, such as the Bonda, who wear very little, are more obviously different.

Kondhs The most numerous of the tribals are the 950,000 Kondhs. They still practise colourful ceremonies, although animal sacrifices have been substituted for the human ones which the British took so much trouble to stop – particularly around Russelkonda (Bhanjanagar).

Juang The Juang number only around 30,000 and live in thatched huts decorated with white wall paintings. Their small villages are mainly in the central districts of Dhenkanal and Keonjhar to the north.

Santal There are about 500,000 Santal, living in the northern Mayurbhanj and Balasore districts, particularly around Baripada and Khiching. Their marriage system is interesting in that it involves several different methods for a woman to get her man, including *nir balak bapla* or 'marriage by intrusion'. Unable to hook him by any other method, she can just move in and if he and his parents can't get her out after a week or so, he must marry her!

Saoras This tribe, numbering over 300,000, is divided into nine subdivisions. Now partially assimilated into the Indian community they are spread over a wide area in the central and southern districts. They speak an Austro-Asiatic language of the Munda family. The Lanjia Saoras of Ganjam and Koraput districts are still fairly traditional and are polygamous.

Bonda The Bonda, known as the 'naked people', are renowned for their wild ways and for the dormitories where young men and women are encouraged to meet for night-time fun and frolics. Only about 5000 Bonda remain, in the Bonda Hills of Koraput district. Women wear only a strip of cloth around their middle, long rows of beads and heavy metal neckbands.

Other major tribes are the Parajas, the colourful Godabas and the Koyas. Permission from the Orissa Home Ministry is needed to visit tribal villages, except for those along the main highways. ■

middle of it. The bus terminal is five km away on the western edge of town – further out from the centre than the airport. The temples are mainly in the south-east and the closest hotel to them, the Panthanivas Tourist Bungalow, is within walking distance.

The tourist offices all seem very helpful. Orissa Tourism (☎ 50-099) is down the lane by the Panthanivas Tourist Bungalow and has branches at the airport and the railway station (open 24 hours). There's also a Government of India tourist office (☎ 41-2203) not far from the Tourist Bungalow.

Lingaraj Mandir

Surrounded by a high wall, the great temple of Bhubaneswar is off limits to all non-Hindus. Although the British Raj respected this ruling, it did not deter them from building a viewing platform beside the northern wall. It was put up for the visit of Lord Curzon and is still used by tourists today. You'll be asked for a donation at the platform and shown a book to 'prove' that some people give over Rs 1000. How much you give is up to you but just a few rupees is more than enough. In fact, you're now approached at many temples in Bhubaneswar with such persistence, you wonder whether these people really are the 'temple priests' they say they are.

The temple is dedicated to Tribhuvaneswar, or Lord of the Three Worlds, also known as Bhubaneswar. In its present form it dates from 1090-1104, although parts of it are over 1400 years old. The granite block which represents Tribhuvaneswar is said to be bathed daily with water, milk and bhang. The temple compound is about 150 metres square and is dominated by the 40-metre-high temple tower.

From the viewing platform of the ornately carved tower you can easily see the lions crushing elephants, which are said to be a representation of the re-emergence of Hinduism over Buddhism. More than 50 smaller temples and shrines crowd the enclosure. In the north-east corner, a smaller temple to Parvati is of particular interest.

There is also an annual chariot festival in the temple in April.

Bindu Sagar

The Ocean Drop Tank (Bindu Sagar), just north of the great temple, is said to contain water from every holy stream, pool and tank

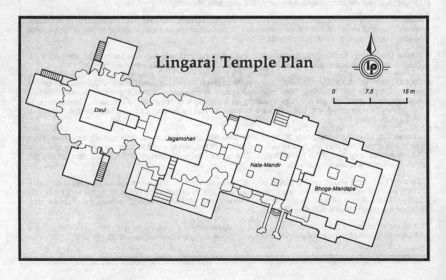

Lingaraj Temple Plan

Deul

Jagamohan

Nata-Mandir

Bhoga-Mandapa

0   7.5   15 m

in India. Consequently, when it comes to washing away sin this is the tank that washes cleanest. There are a number of temples and shrines scattered around the tank, several with towers in imitation of the ones at the Lingaraj Temple. In the centre of the tank is a water pavilion where, once a year, the Lingaraj Temple's deity is brought to be ritually bathed.

Vaital Mandir

Close to the Bindu Sagar, this temple has a double-storey 'wagon roof', an influence from Buddhist cave architecture. It dates from the 8th century and was a centre of Tantric worship, the presiding deity being Chamunda (Kali). She can be seen in the dingy interior, although her necklace of skulls and the corpse she's sitting on are usually hidden beneath her temple robes.

Parsurameswar Mandir

Close to the main Bhubaneswar to Puri road, on the same side as the Lingaraj Temple, the Grove of the Perfect Beings is a cluster of about 20 smaller temples, including some of the most important in Bhubaneswar. The best preserved of the early temples is the Parsurameswar, a Siva temple built about 650 AD. It has interesting and lively bas-reliefs of elephant and horse processions, lattice windows, Siva images and a temple 'priest' who won't leave you alone unless he considers your donation suitably generous.

Mukteswar, Siddheswar & Kedargauri Temples

Not far from the Parsurameswar is the small 10th-century Mukteswar Mandir, one of the most ornate temples in Bhubaneswar. The finely detailed carvings show a mixture of Buddhist, Jain and Hindu styles but unfortunately some of the figures have been defaced. The carvings of dwarfs are particularly striking.

In front of the temple is a beautiful arched *torana* (architrave) showing clear Buddhist influence. The large green temple tank makes a perfect swimming pool for local children.

The later Siddheswar Mandir is in the same compound. Although plainer than the Mukteswar, it has a fine standing Ganesh figure.

Also by the road, across the path from the Mukteswar, the Kedargauri Mandir is one of the older temples at Bhubaneswar, although it has been substantially rebuilt.

Outside the Mukteswar compound there are chai shops and curio sellers.

Raj Rani Mandir

This interesting temple is surrounded by well-maintained gardens. It's one of the latest of the Bhubaneswar temples and is famous for its ornate *deul* (sanctuary), decorated with some of the most impressive Orissan temple sculptures. Around the compass points are statues of the eight *dikpalas* (temple guardians), who protect the temple, two for each side. Between them, nymphs, embracing couples, elephants and lions fill the niches and decorate the pillars. As it's no longer used for worship you are free to wander at will.

Brahmeswar Mandir

About a km east of the main road, the Brahmeswar Temple stands in a courtyard flanked by four smaller structures. It's notable for its very finely detailed sculptures with erotic and sometimes amusing elements. The temple dates from the 9th century.

Other Temples

There are two other temples near the Brahmeswar which are not of such great interest. The **Bhaskareswar Mandir** has an unusual stepped design in order to accommodate the unusually large three-metre lingam it once contained. About 300 metres east along the same road is the **Megheswar Mandir**, in a courtyard beside a tank.

North of the Bindu Sagar, the **Lakshamaneswar Mandir** is a very plain temple. Dating from the 7th century, it is one of the earliest specimens of Orissan architecture and acts as a gateway to the city.

ORISSA

ORISSA

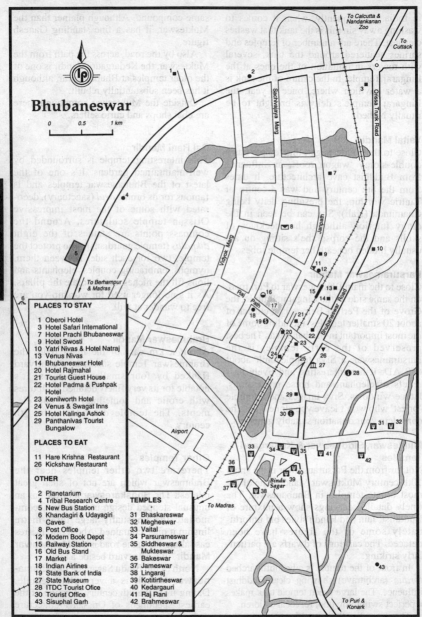

Bhubaneswar

0   0.5   1 km

PLACES TO STAY

1 Oberoi Hotel
3 Hotel Safari International
7 Hotel Prachi Bhubaneswar
9 Hotel Swosti
10 Yatri Nivas & Hotel Natraj
13 Venus Nivas
14 Bhubaneswar Hotel
20 Hotel Rajmahal
21 Tourist Guest House
22 Hotel Padma & Pushpak
    Hotel
23 Kenilworth Hotel
24 Venus & Swagat Inns
25 Hotel Kalinga Ashok
29 Panthanivas Tourist
    Bungalow

PLACES TO EAT

11 Hare Krishna Restaurant
26 Kickshaw Restaurant

OTHER

2 Planetarium
4 Tribal Research Centre
5 New Bus Station
6 Khandagiri & Udayagiri
   Caves
8 Post Office
15 Railway Station
16 Modern Book Depot
17 Old Bus Stand
17 Market
18 Indian Airlines
19 State Bank of India
27 State Museum
28 ITDC Tourist Ofice
30 Tourist Office
43 Sisuphal Garh

TEMPLES

31 Bhaskareswar
32 Megheswar
33 Vaital
34 Parsurameswar
35 Siddheswar &
    Mukteswar
36 Bakeswar
37 Jameswar
38 Lingaraj
39 Kotitirtheswar
40 Kedargauri
41 Raj Rani
42 Brahmeswar

To Calcutta &
Nandankanan
Zoo

To
Cuttack

Orissa Trunk Road

Sachivalya Marg

Janpath

Vidyok Marg

Raj
Path

To Berhampur
& Madras

Bhubaneswar Road

Airport

To Madras

Bindu
Sagar

To Puri &
Konark

State Museum

The museum is opposite the Hotel Kalinga Ashok and has an interesting collection focusing on Orissan history, culture and architecture and the various Orissan tribes. The museum is open from 10 am to 5 pm daily, except Monday. Entry is Rs 2.

Tribal Research Centre (Museum of Man)

Although this is primarily an anthropological research centre, visitors are welcome. There's an interesting outdoor display of reconstructed houses of Orissan tribal people, including the Santal, Juang, Gadaba, Saora and Kondh. Admission is free, and it's open daily from 10 am to 5 pm except Sunday. Buses between the new bus terminal and the centre of town pass right by the museum.

Other Attractions

The partly excavated ruins at **Sisuphal Garh** are thought to be the remains of an Ashokan city. In the north of the city, the **botanical gardens** and regional plant reserve have a large collection of plants, including many cacti. A recent attraction is the city's **planetarium**, where there are shows at 3 and 4.30 pm daily except Monday; tickets cost Rs 5.

Organised Tours

During the high season, various tours operate from the Panthanivas Tourist Bungalow (☎ 55-515). If you really want to you can cover Orissa's main tourist sites (conveniently located in the Bhubaneswar/Puri/Konark triangle) in one long 12-hour tour for Rs 75 (Rs 100 by air-con bus). By taxi this tour would cost upwards of Rs 500. Travellers complain that the tours that include Nandankanan zoological park spend too long there and not long enough at the caves and temples.

Places to Stay – bottom end

Budget accommodation is available in Bhubaneswar municipality's *Yatri Nivas*, although the location is inconvenient. It's a friendly place, very much like a youth hostel,

and has beds for Rs 15 in 18-bed dorms or Rs 20 in three or five-bed rooms. There's a cheap restaurant here. In the railway *retiring rooms* there are dorm beds for Rs 15 and doubles for Rs 80, or Rs 150 with air-con.

The *Hotel Bhagat Niwas* (☎ 41-1545) is a recommended place that's good value, with single/double rooms with attached bathroom from Rs 50/80. There's also air-cooled rooms for Rs 100/150. It's clean and friendly. Close by is the *Hotel Pushpak* (☎ 50-896), which is also cheap at Rs 70 for a double, or Rs 200 with air-cooling.

The *Hotel Gajapati* (☎ 51-893) opposite the Kenilworth Hotel has basic rooms from Rs 50/65 with attached bathrooms, as well as more expensive rooms. It's OK, if a little gloomy.

The *Venus Inn* (☎ 40-1738) has singles/doubles for Rs 75/90 and a good south Indian restaurant downstairs. Nearby, the *Swagat Inn* (☎ 40-8486) has rooms for Rs 90/100, air-con doubles for Rs 300 and a fast-food restaurant. Both these places are fine but could be a bit noisy as they back onto the railway track.

Also on the eastern side of the railway station is the popular *Bhubaneswar Hotel* (☎ 51-977), which has singles/doubles with attached bathrooms for Rs 80/125, or rooms with air-con for Rs 350. There's also a restaurant here.

Places to Stay – middle

The *Panthanivas Tourist Bungalow* (☎ 54-515) is popular even though it's relatively poor value. On the plus side, it's close to the temples and has comfortable rooms. Doubles are Rs 175, or Rs 350 with air-con, and all rooms have attached bathrooms and hot-water heaters. The 8 am checkout is less than generous.

The *Tourist Guest House* (☎ 40-0857) is a small place popular with foreigners. It's clean and comfortable with rooms for Rs 150/200 with attached bathrooms. However, you may have to ask for clean sheets, which is a bit rough when you're paying this sort of money. Meals are available.

The modern *Hotel Siddhartha* (☎ 54-842)

has rooms from Rs 290/390 or Rs 425/525 with air-con, and 24-hour checkout.

Places to Stay – top end

With a good reproduction of a Konark chariot wheel outside it, the *Kenilworth Hotel* (☎ 41-1723; fax 45-6147) is recommended for its position and facilities. Air-con rooms are Rs 775/900. There's a swimming pool here that non-guests can use for Rs 100 (closed between noon and 4 pm), a pastry shop, bookshop and resident masseur.

The air-conditioned *Hotel Prachi* (☎ 40-2366; fax 40-3287) is also a good place with rooms at Rs 700/800. Facilities include the 'Wim Bul Don' (a tennis court!) and a pool that non-guests can use for Rs 100.

The *Hotel Swosti* (☎ 40-4178; fax 40-7524), on Janpath not far from the railway station, is a good three-star hotel with rooms from Rs 700/800.

Not far from the Tourist Bungalow is the ITDC *Hotel Kalinga Ashok* (☎ 53-318), almost opposite the museum. This place is modern, air-conditioned, and has a good restaurant and bar. Singles/doubles cost from Rs 500/700 in the old block and from Rs 650/850 in the new block.

At the top of the pile is the impressive *Oberoi Hotel* (☎ 56-116; fax 56-269) on the outskirts of town. Mimicking Orissan temple layout and design, it charges US$38/70 for rooms and has all mod cons, including swimming pool, health club, floodlit tennis courts and jogging track.

Places to Eat

The *Modern South Indian Hotel*, behind the Hotel Rajmahal and under the Hotel Chand, is a good place for a cheap meal. It's one of many south Indian places around the junction of Raj Path and Janpath.

The best vegetarian eatery in Bhubaneswar is the *Hare Krishna Restaurant*, run by the organisation itself. It's a smart place with powerful air-con and excellent, though pricey, food. Expect to pay around Rs 100 per person.

The *Hotel Chancellor*, on Raj Path near

the railway flyover, is an excellent little place serving good veg and non-veg food.

Over the flyover and around the corner is the *Kickshaw Restaurant*, which has a basic menu of Indian food, and the usual Indian interpretation of Chinese dishes.

The *Sarigam Restaurant* at the Panthanivas Tourist Bungalow is a vegetarian restaurant, with thalis for Rs 18. The menu states: 'We serve with smile', but this doesn't always happen. The waiters neither speak nor read English,

A recommended place for an evening out during the dry season is the *Kenilworth Hotel*. It has a barbecue on the roof terrace and the food is excellent. Food from its *Sangam* restaurant can be served out here, too. The restaurant at the *Hotel Swosti* is also worth trying.

There are plenty of vegetarian meal places around the Lingaraj Temple if you are down that way at lunchtime.

Things to Buy

Orissan handicrafts, including appliqué and ikat work, can be bought at the new market off Raj Path. There are a number of shops, including the Orissa State Handloom Co-operative or Utkalika.

There's also the Orissa State Handicrafts Emporium, not far from the temples.

Getting There & Away

Air Indian Airlines (☎ 40-0533) has five flights a week between Bhubaneswar and Calcutta (US$41), and daily flights to Delhi (US$128). There are two flights a week to Madras (US$116), and three to Nagpur (US$74) and Hyderabad (US$106). There are also four flights a week from Varanasi to Bhubaneswar (US$69), but nothing in the opposite direction.

Bus The impressive bus terminal (which looks more like an airport terminal) is on the main highway to Calcutta, five km north of the town centre. Buses to Cuttack, Puri and Konark still stop at the old bus stand, which is much more conveniently located in the centre of town. You can also pick up the Puri and Konark buses from the old bus stand on Raj Path, right near the railway flyover. The trip to Puri takes a little over an hour and costs Rs 10. If it's not possible to get a direct bus to Konark, all Puri buses go through Pipli, where the Konark road branches off. It is then possible to catch another bus from there to Konark.

From the new (main) bus terminal there are numerous departures to Calcutta (Rs 85, overnight), Cuttack (Rs 10, one hour) and Berhampur (Rs 35, five hours). Private video coaches are faster and run to most popular places, including Berhampur (Rs 50, four hours), Baripada (Rs 60, seven hours) and Sambalpur (Rs 60, overnight).

Train Bhubaneswar is on the main Calcutta to Madras railway line, so there are plenty of trains to those places. Many services from the north terminate at Puri. The crack *Rajdhani Express* departs from Calcutta at 10.45 am and arrives in Bhubaneswar just over seven hours later. The fare for the 437-km journey is Rs 412 in air-con chair car. This train leaves Bhubaneswar at 8.50 am for the return journey to Calcutta and goes on to Delhi (2077 km, 24 hours).

There are also direct rail connections to Berhampur (166 km, 2½ hours), Madras (1226 km, 20 hours), Varanasi (998 km, 21 hours) and Agra (1874 km, 39 hours).

Getting Around

The airport is very close to the town. There's no bus service and a taxi costs Rs 45 to the Tourist Bungalow or Rs 80 to the Oberoi. A cycle-rickshaw costs only Rs 15 but you may have to walk the last km between the entrance of the airport and the terminal.

Between the new bus terminal and the town centre you're up for Rs 25 by auto-rickshaw, or there are city buses to the old bus stand for Rs 1.

Cycle-rickshaws offer 'five temple' tours for around Rs 30 that cover the main temples; shorter journeys are around Rs 5.

Taxis have set rates which are available from the tourist office, although they may be unwilling to drive you for those rates.

AROUND BHUBANESWAR
Udayagiri & Khandagiri Caves

A couple of km south of the new bus terminal in Bhubaneswar, these two hills facing each other across the road are riddled with caves, some of them ornately carved. Most are thought to have been chiselled out for Jain ascetics in the first century BC.

On the right of the road, **Udayagiri**, or Sunrise Hill, has the more interesting caves, which are scattered at various levels up the hill; all are numbered. At the base of the hill, around to the right, is the two-storey Rani ka Naur or Queen's Palace Cave (cave 1). Both levels have eight entrances and the cave is extensively carved.

Return to the road via the Chota Hathi Gumpha (cave 3), with its carvings of elephants coming out from behind a tree. The Jaya Vijaya Cave (5) is again double-storey and a bo tree is carved in the central compartment. Back at the entrance, ascend the hill to cave 9, the Swargapuri, and cave 14, the Hathi Gumpha or Elephant Cave. The latter is plain but an inscription relates in 117 lines the exploits of its builder, King Kharaveli of Kalinga, who ruled from 168 to 153 BC.

Circle around the hill to the right, to the single-storey Ganesh Gumpha (10), which is almost directly above the Rani ka Naur. The carvings here tell the same tale as in the lower level cave but are better drawn. Retrace your steps to Cave 14, then on to the Pavana Gumpha or Cave of Purification and the small Sarpa Gumpha or Serpent Cave, where the tiny door is surmounted by a three-headed cobra.

Only 15 or so metres from this is the Bagh Gumpha (12) or Tiger Cave, entered through the mouth of the beast. The hill is topped by the foundations of some long-gone building. The oldest of these various caves date back to the 2nd century BC. Some are of Jain origin.

Across the road, **Khandagiri** is equally interesting, and there is a fine view back over Bhubaneswar from its summit. You can see the airport, the tower of the Lingaraj Temple rising behind it and, further away, the Dhauli Stupa. The steep path divides about a third

ORISSA

of the way up the hill. The right path goes to the Ananta Cave (3), with carved figures of athletes, women, elephants and geese carrying flowers. The right path also leads to a series of Jain temples, and at the top of the hill is an 18th-century Jain temple.

The caves are open from 8 am to 6 pm. There's a government restaurant here and lots of chai shops.

Getting There & Away Only a few buses go specifically to the caves, but there are plenty which pass the nearby junction, the main Calcutta to Madras highway. It's about Rs 1 from town, or you can get there by auto-rickshaw for about Rs 25.

Dhauli
Around 260 BC, King Ashoka had his famous edicts carved onto a large rock, halfway up the hill here at Dhauli, eight km south of Bhubaneswar, just off the Puri road. After murdering large numbers of his family to gain power, then hundreds of thousands on the battlefield as he enlarged his empire, Ashoka finally 'saw the light' after his bloody victory at nearby Kalinga and converted to Buddhism.

Given his past record, Ashoka was wise to choose a pen name for these edicts, referring to himself as King Piyadasi (meaning He Who Looks on Everything with Kindness). In the edicts he tells his subjects, 'Meritorious is abstention from killing living creatures, meritorious is abstention from reviling the unorthodox...'

At the top of the hill is a dazzling white Peace Pagoda built by the Japanese in the 1970s, with older Buddha figures set into the modern structure.

You can get to the place where you turn off the main road on any Puri or Konark bus for Rs 2, and from there it's a three-km walk to Dhauli.

Nandankanan Zoo
Famous for its white tigers (see the section on Bandhavgarh in the Madhya Pradesh chapter), this zoo is 25 km north of Bhubaneswar. There are also lion and tiger

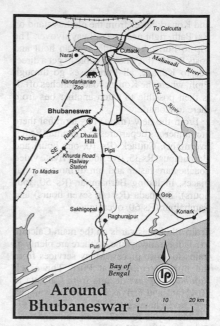

safaris in 'armoured buses', elephant rides and boating on the lake.

It's open daily from 7 am to 6 pm except Monday in summer, and from 7.30 am to 5 pm in winter. The nearest railway station is Barang, a couple of km from the zoo, or there are state transport buses from the bus stand in Bhubaneswar.

PURI
Population: 135,000
Telephone Area Code: 06752

The seaside resort of Puri, 60 km from Bhubaneswar, is one of the four *dhams* (holiest Hindu pilgrimage places in India). Religious life in the city revolves around the great Jagannath Temple and its famous Rath Yatra, or Car Festival. It is thought that Puri was the hiding place for the Buddha tooth of Kandy before it was spirited away to Sri Lanka. There are similarities between the Rath Yatra and the annual Kandy procession.

Puri's other great attraction is its long

sandy beach that draws large numbers of Western travellers and Indians, especially during the October to January high season. Parts of the beachfront are getting quite built up but it can still be a relaxing place to spend a few days. Many Indian companies and government departments have vacation homes here but the town is mostly visited by Bengali holiday-makers.

Orientation & Information

Grand Rd, a wide highway built to accommodate the hundreds of thousands of pilgrims who come to Puri for the Rath Yatra festival, runs from the Jagannath Temple to the Gundicha Mandir. The bus stand is at the eastern end of this road. Most of the hotels are along the seafront but there are two distinct beach areas – Indians to the west, foreign travellers to the east.

The tourist office (☎ 22-664) is on Station Rd and there's a counter (open 24 hours) at the railway station (☎ 23-536). Both are of very limited use.

The State Bank of India offers the usual slow service for foreign exchange. It is also open on Sunday between 11.30 am and 1.30 pm. The Punjab Bank by the Holiday Resort is more convenient and much quieter. The Andhra Bank near the post office handles Visa cash advances. No bank in Puri will change Australian dollar travellers' cheques.

The Loknath Bookshop on CT Rd is a good place to rent or buy second-hand books, and they also stock some interesting and unusual postcards.

Warning A number of swimmers have come to grief in Puri's treacherous surf – see under Beach later in this section.

Jagannath Temple

The temple of Jagannath, Lord of the Universe and an incarnation of Vishnu, is unfortunately closed to non-Hindus. As at the Lingaraj Temple in Bhubaneswar, non-believers have to be content with looking over the wall, this time from the roof of the library opposite, but you won't see much inside the temple. An additional platform on the roof was built for the viceroy's visit in 1939. The library is open from 9 am to noon and from 4 to 8 pm; a donation is required. Watch out for the monkeys. There's a good collection of ancient palm-leaf manuscripts in the library and another 'donation' is required if you wish to take a look.

The temple makes Puri one of the four dhams, cardinal centres of pilgrimage (the others being Dwarka in the west, Badrinath in the north and Rameswaram in the south). Its considerable popularity amongst Hindus is also partly due to the lack of caste distinctions – all are welcome before Lord Jagannath. Well, almost all – Indira Gandhi was barred from entering as she had married a non-Hindu.

The temple was built in its present form in 1198 and is protected by two surrounding walls. The outer enclosure is nearly square, measuring almost 200 metres on each side. The walls of the enclosure are six metres high. Inside, a second wall encloses the actual temple. The conical tower of the temple is 58 metres high and is topped by the flag and wheel of Vishnu, visible from far out to sea.

In front of the main entrance is a beautiful pillar, topped by an image of the Garuda, which originally stood in front of the temple at Konark. The main entrance is known as the Lion Gate due to the two stone lions guarding the entrance, and it is also the gate used in the chariot procession. The southern, eastern and northern gates are guarded by statues of men on horseback, tigers and elephants respectively.

In the central jagamohan, pilgrims can see the images of Lord Jagannath, his brother Balbhadra and sister Subhadra. Non-Hindus are not, of course, able to see them but the many shop stalls along the road outside the temple sell small wooden replicas. The curious images are carved from tree trunks, in a childlike caricature of a human face. The brothers have arms but the smaller Subhadra does not. All three are garlanded and dressed for ceremonies and the various seasons.

The temple employs 6000 men to perform the temple functions and the complicated

ORISSA

ORISSA

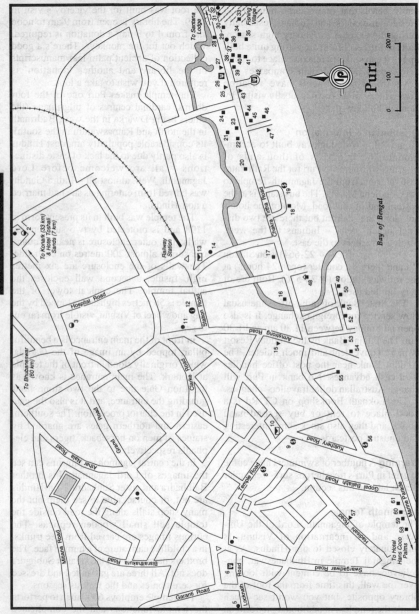

Puri

0   100   200 m

Bay of Bengal

To Santana
Lodge

Fishing
Village

To Konark (33 km)
& Hotel Toshali
Sands (7 km)

Railway
Station

To Bhubaneswar
(60 km)

Hospital Road

Station Road

Armstrong Road

Clarke Road

Grand Road

Athar Nala Road

Millana Road

Bisrainakura Road

Swargadwar Road

Garanti Road

Locknath
Road

Hadsun Road

Temple Road

Kutchery Road

Gopal Ballabh Road

Marine Parade

To Hotel
Hans Coco
Palms

Chakra Tirtha Road

PLACES TO STAY				
16	Hotel Sealand	46	Hotel Shankar International	
17	South-Eastern Railway Hotel	48	Youth Hostel	
18	Hotel Holiday Resort	49	Hotel Samudra	
20	Bay View Hotel	50	Hotel Vijoya International	
21	Hotel Dreamland	51	Mayfair Beach Resort	
22	Hotel Love & Life	52	Hotel Repose	
23	Hotel Gandhara	53	Panthanivas Tourist Bungalow	
24	Hotel Sea 'n Sand	54	Hotel Golden Palace	
28	Hotel Sri Balaji	55	Hotel Nilachal Ashok	
30	Satya Lodge	58	Panthabhavan	
33	Sagar Saikate	59	Sea View Hotel	
34	Hotels Beach Hut, Sapphire & International	60	Victoria Club	
35	Pink House	61	Puri Hotel	
36	Nundy Cottage			
37	Hotel Derby	**PLACES TO EAT**		
38	Z Hotel	15	Lee Garden Restaurant	
39	Travellers' Inn	25	Harry's Cafe	
40	Hotel Nilambu	27	Mickey Mouse Restaurant	
41	Leo Castle	31	Raju's Restaurant	
44	Holiday Inn & Tribe Tours	43	Peace Restaurant	
45	Sea Foam Hotel	47	Sambhoo Restaurant	

OTHER		
57	Chung Wah Restaurant	
1	Gundicha Mandir	
2	Bus Station	
3	Bhubaneswar Bus Stand	
4	Govt Bhang Shop	
5	Govt Bhang Shop	
6	Jagannath Temple	
7	Library	
8	Allahabad Bank	
9	Andhra Bank	
10	GPO	
11	Govt Bhang Shop	
12	Tourist Office	
13	Post Office	
14	Liquor Shop	
19	Punjab National Bank	
26	Temple	
29	Loknath Bookshop	
32	Govt Bhang Shop	
42	Temple	
56	State Bank of India	

ORISSA

rituals involved in caring for the gods. It has been estimated that in all, 20,000 people are dependent on Jagannath, and the god's immediate attendants are divided into 36 orders and 97 classes!

Gundicha Mandir
The Garden House, in which the images of the gods reside for seven days each year, is off limits to non-Hindus. The walls enclose a garden where the temple is built. It's also known as the Aunt's House. Puri has a number of other temples, but most of these are off limits to non-Hindus.

Beach
Puri has a stretch of white sand from where Indian pilgrims bathe in their customary fully attired manner. Don't come here expecting a tropical paradise, however. The beach is very wide and exposed, and there's not a scrap of shade to be found.

Orissan fishermen, wearing conical straw hats, guide bathers out through the surf. They're unlikely to be much help should trouble arise, as one traveller reported, wit-

nessing a rescue attempt: 'To our amazement the lifeguards turned back having done only 10 yards and the swimmer (or non-swimmer) disappeared for good. Too late for anyone else to go by then. The victim was a young man of 19'. Another traveller reported two drownings in three days. The currents can be treacherous so don't go out of your depth unless you're a very strong swimmer.

Past the travellers' beach to the east is the local fishing village.

For swimming, avoid the area opposite the youth hostel unless the sewage outlet here has been closed. As with all beaches, this one doubles as a public lavatory, automatically flushed twice daily by the sea. Around the fishing village is the worst part and it really can stink here in the afternoon when the catch is being gutted on the beach. The cleanest area is just a 15-minute walk to the east, past the fishing village where the empty beach extends for miles.

Organised Tours
Tours operate out of Puri daily, except Monday, to Konark, Pipli, Dhauli, Bhubaneswar and

Fishing

Many of the fishing families at Puri come from Andhra Pradesh. It's worth getting up before sunrise to watch them head out to sea. For a little baksheesh they'll take you with them and one traveller said, 'It was the highlight of my trip witnessing the dawn over the sea and fishing boats'. The crude construction of the boats is unusual – they're made of solid tree trunks and are enormously heavy. Buoyancy is achieved purely from the bulk of the wood. They're made in two or three pieces, split longitudinally and bound together. When not in use they're untied and the pieces laid out on the beach to dry. ■

the Udayagiri and Khandagiri caves. They depart at 6.30 am from the Panthabhavan, and return at 6.30 pm. The cost is Rs 70. On Monday, Wednesday and Friday there's a tour to Chilka Lake for Rs 80. There are a number of private operators running similarly priced tours. Tribe Tours (☎ 24-233) can organise a car and interpreter for visits to tribal areas in the south of Orissa.

Places to Stay

Most of the budget hotels popular with travellers are at the eastern end of the beach towards the fishing village, along or off Chakra Tirtha Rd (CT Rd to the rickshaw-wallahs). In the centre are most of the middle-range and top-end hotels, but the disadvantage of staying in this area is that there's nowhere to eat apart from the hotels themselves. At the western end is a mixture of middle-range and budget hotels – the former catering mainly to holidaying Calcutta-wallahs and families, the latter to Indian pilgrims.

Prices below are for the high season (October to January) but you should be able to negotiate some healthy discounts outside this period, especially at the mid-price places. Because most people arrive in Puri on overnight trains, checkout times can be as early as 7 am in some hotels!

Places to Stay – bottom end

The characterless *youth hostel* (☎ 22-424) has separate 10-bed dormitory accommodation for men and women at Rs 20 per bed, Rs 10 if you're a HI member. The management is not particularly friendly and the 10 pm curfew is a drag. The restaurant is recommended for its excellent Orissan-style thalis.

In an old English villa, the scruffy *Bay View Hotel* is quiet and pleasant, with rooms from Rs 50 to Rs 100 (most with attached bathrooms) and a nice verandah for sitting out on.

The *Hotel Dreamland* is a small, recommended place with singles/doubles for Rs 40/50 and a friendly manager. It's set back from the road in a secluded garden. Nearby, there's the modern, Japanese-run *Hotel Ghandara* (☎ 24-117), with dorm beds for Rs 30 and rooms from Rs 80/100 with bath.

The popular *Hotel Shankar International* (☎ 23-637) is a good beachfront hotel, with doubles from Rs 120 up to Rs 250 for a double with a sea-facing balcony. There's a walled garden and good food at the restaurant here.

By the Holiday Inn, the *Hotel Tanuja* has basic doubles from Rs 75, and a pleasant garden atmosphere. Nearby, the *Hotel Sea 'n Sand* is a clean place with doubles with attached bathroom for Rs 80. The *Z Hotel* (that's Zed not Zee!) (☎ 22-554) is an excellent place and popular with travellers, although it's not that cheap these days. Formerly the palace of a very minor maharaja, it's an old, rambling building with large, airy rooms, many of them facing the sea. The management is friendly and easy-going, the hotel peaceful and the restaurant serves good seafood. Singles/doubles with common bath cost Rs 75/150, while huge rooms with attached bath and balcony are Rs 250. There's a nice roof terrace for sunbathing.

The basic *Travellers' Inn* (☎ 23-592) is beside the Z, and has singles/doubles from Rs 40/75 with common bathroom. There are several other similar places towards the beach here, including the *Hotel Derby, Nundy Cottage, Hotel Nilambu* and *Leo Castle*.

The *Pink House* is a popular place right on the beach. Basic rooms are Rs 40/80, and there's a good restaurant. Just behind the Pink House is the *Sapphire International*, with double rooms at Rs 150 with attached bath. In this same area is the *Hotel Beach Hut*, which is similar and has a roof terrace. These places right on the beach are, obviously, convenient for the beach but there's not a scrap of shade here and it seems a bit desolate.

Back across the road, the family-run *Hotel Sri Balajee* is a good choice, set in an enclosed garden. They charge Rs 30/50 for rooms with common bath, and Rs 70 for a double with bath. Each room has its own little verandah with table and chairs, not unlike an Indonesian losmen.

Right opposite is the ugly *Hotel Akash International* (☎ 24-204), which has small doubles with attached bath for Rs 75. They claim the rooms face the sea, which is being a little liberal with the truth, and besides, the windows are too dirty to see out of anyway!

Sagar Saikate looks like a small yellow castle and was a fortified English villa, right on the beach. It has a great roof area that is perfect for undisturbed sunbathing and big, high-ceiling rooms. Rooms start at Rs 30/40 with common bath.

Deep into the fishing village, set back from the sea, is the *Santana Lodge*. It's a recommended place run by a very friendly and helpful manager. Singles/doubles are Rs 40/60 with common bath. They have some doubles with attached bathroom for Rs 75, and there's a nice roof terrace. It's an Rs 10 cycle-rickshaw ride from the railway station. The area is known as Pentakota; the rickshaw-wallah may not know the hotel.

At the other end of the beach, along Marine Parade, there are many, many other hotels patronised almost exclusively by Indian pilgrims. The *Sea View Hotel* (☎ 23-417) is rather run-down, with doubles from Rs 100. The *Victoria Club* (☎ 22-005) is better and has doubles from Rs 120. The *Puri Hotel* (☎ 22-114), with singles/doubles from Rs 110/150 upwards, claims to be Orissa's biggest and is very popular with middle-class Indians. They also have a free minibus which can pick you up from the railway station in the mornings, and it's one of the few places with 24-hour checkout.

Places to Stay – middle & top end

The *Panthanivas Tourist Bungalow* (☎ 22-562) is a reasonable place, with doubles with attached bathroom for Rs 160 and air-con rooms for Rs 300. Some rooms in the new building have excellent views of the sea. It's

ORISSA

Rath Yatra (Car Festival)

One of India's greatest annual events takes place in Puri each June or July when the fantastic festival of the cars sets forth from the Jagannath Temple. It commemorates the journey of Krishna from Gokul to Mathura. The images of Jagannath, his brother and his sister are brought out from the temple and dragged in huge 'cars', known as *raths*, down the wide Grand Rd to the Gundicha Mandir (Garden House), over a km away.

The main car of Jagannath stands 14 metres high, over 10 metres square and rides on 16 wheels, each over two metres in diameter. It is from these colossal cars that our word 'juggernaut' is derived and, in centuries past, devotees were known to have thrown themselves beneath the wheels of the juggernaut in order to die in the god's sight. To haul the cars takes over 4000 professional car-pullers, all employees of the temple. Hundreds of thousands of pilgrims (and tourists) flock from all over India to witness this stupendous scene. The huge and unwieldy cars take an enormous effort to pull, are virtually impossible to turn and, once moving, are nearly unstoppable.

Once they reach the other end of the road the gods take a week-long summer break, then they are reloaded onto the cars and trucked back to the Jagannath Temple, in a virtual repeat of the previous week's procession. Following the festival the cars are broken up and used for firewood in the communal kitchens inside the temple, or for funeral-pyre fuel. New cars are constructed each year. At intervals of eight, 11 or 19 years (or combinations of those numbers depending on various astrological occurrences), the gods themselves are also disposed of and new images made. In the past 150 years there have been new images in 1863, 1893, 1931, 1950, 1969 and 1977. The old ones are buried at a site near the northern gate. ∎

fairly well kept, conveniently located and has a reasonable dining hall. In contrast, Orissa Tourism's other hotel, the *Pantha-bhavan*, on Marine Parade, is a gloomy converted palace with doubles with attached bath for Rs 160.

The friendly *Hotel Golden Palace* (☎ 23-192) is in a good spot right on the beach, with doubles on the ground floor for Rs 180, and doubles upstairs with balconies from Rs 250. There's a beachside restaurant here.

There are several hotels along the beach from the Panthanivas Tourist Bungalow. The *Hotel Repose* (☎ 23-376) charges Rs 275 for sea-facing doubles, Rs 400 with air-con. The *Hotel Vijoya International* (☎ 22-702) is a modern block with double rooms at Rs 300, or Rs 500 with air-con. The smaller *Hotel Samudra* (☎ 22-705) almost next door is the best of this group. It's right on the beach; most rooms have a balcony facing the sea and cost from Rs 160/200 on the ground floor and Rs 280/350 upstairs. Beware of the 7 am checkout time!

Back on Chakra Tirtha Rd, the *Hotel Sealand* (☎ 23-185) is a group of rather cramped cottages for Rs 275 or Rs 350 with air-con. At the eastern end of this road is the relatively new and immaculately clean *Holiday Inn* (☎ 23-782), which has good doubles with attached bathrooms from Rs 200, or Rs 250 for doubles upstairs with a sea view.

Set back from the beach also on the Chakra Tirth Rd is the delightfully old-world *South-Eastern Railway Hotel* (☎ 22-063), also still referred to as 'the BNR' (Bengal Nagpur Railway, as it was once known). Ordinary singles/doubles, including breakfast, cost Rs 332/474. These rooms have more character than the modern air-con rooms at Rs 387/524. The hotel has a pleasant lounge, bar, dining room, billiards room and an immaculate stretch of lawn. Non-guests can eat here with advance notice; lunch or dinner costs Rs 90 and the set meals are good. It also offers 24-hour checkout.

You can't miss the ugly bulk of the *Hotel Holiday Resort* (☎ 22-440), which has double rooms with balconies overlooking the sea for

Rs 370/450 and air-con cottages for Rs 650. If you stay here you'll feel more as if you are on the Spanish Costa Brava than in India.

The new *Mayfair Beach Resort* (☎ 24-041) is well located, and a lot of thought has gone into the design and layout. Comfortable air-con rooms with their own terrace cost US$40 a single or double. This place also has the only swimming pool in Puri, which non-guests can use for Rs 100.

The *Hotel Nilachal Ashok* (☎ 23-639) is a pleasant place, but has a poor reputation. It's set back from the beach and air-con rooms are Rs 450/700.

At the far western end of the beach is the excellent *Hans Coco Palms* (☎ 22-638), with air-con rooms for Rs 450/800. This is a modern, well-run hotel in a private beach-front location. There's a good restaurant.

The *Hotel Toshali Sands* (☎ 22-888) is a very secluded 'ethnic village resort', seven km from Puri on the road to Konark. Doubles in the cottages cost Rs 850. It's a three-km walk through the Balukhand Forest and Turtle Reserve to the beach but the hotel does have a swimming pool which non-guests can use for Rs 100. The food here is very good, although it's not cheap.

Places to Eat

You can get some excellent seafood here – good tuna steaks and occasionally even lobster. Some of the restaurants along the travellers' end of the beach manage passable cakes and pies – and do an interesting line in apple pies with a special extra ingredient! Quite a few places close during the off-season.

As at Kovalam, Mahaballipuram, Goa and other places where travellers congregate, Puri has a number of restaurants which cater almost exclusively to travellers. They all serve much the same food – poor imitations of Western dishes – and service is typically very slow. The *Peace Restaurant, Harry's, Brady, Mickey Mouse* and *Xanadu* are all in a group near the Zed Hotel, and all have their admirers and detractors.

Similar places are *Raju's Restaurant*, a cheap gathering place on the edge of the fishing village, and, right on the beach, the *Pink House* serves the usual travellers' fare.

There are some good restaurants in the budget hotels. The best of them is at the *Z Hotel*, but with most main dishes around Rs 25, a meal can be relatively pricey. The Hotel Shankar's *Om Restaurant* also does quite good food.

There are a number of small cafes at the western end of the beach. In the old town there are countless vegetarian places, like the *New Raj Restaurant* on Grand Rd, five minutes from the Jagannath Temple. Down the road beside the Puri Hotel there's a Chinese restaurant, the *Chung Wah*, and another, the *Lee Garden* on Armstrong Rd.

For an evening out, the set dinner at the *South-Eastern Railway Hotel* can be good, authentically Raj (often including puddings like trifle) and served in style by attentive uniformed waiters. It costs Rs 90 for four courses plus coffee, and it's best to make a reservation. The restaurant at the *Mayfair Beach Resort* is good but expensive. Alternatively, the restaurants at the *Hans Coco Palms* and the *Toshali Sands* are both very good, but are really only convenient if you are staying there.

Things to Buy

Being a holy place, Puri is one of those delightfully eccentric Indian towns where the use of ganja is not only legal, the government very thoughtfully provides for smokers' requisites at special bhang shops. Ganja is available here at Rs 50 a *tola* but quality is reportedly not as good as in Kerala.

You'll come across quite a few craft and salespeople offering fabric, bead and bamboo work. Some of it is well worth a second look. Prices are negotiable, as always with this sort of thing. There are also plenty of people trying to sell snake and animal skins in such numbers that one dreads to think what is happening to the wildlife in the Orissan forests.

On Temple Rd and Swargadwar Rd there are numerous places selling Orissan hand-woven ikat cloth. Some of this material is very attractive, and you can buy it in lengths, or there are some ready-made garments.

Getting There & Away

Bus Puri's bus stand is beside the Gundicha Mandir, though some of the private buses depart from around the nearby junction of Grand and Hospital Rds. Take one of the minibuses for the trip to Bhubaneswar (Rs 10, one hour) as they're much quicker than the big buses.

Between 6 am and 4.30 pm there are frequent departures for Konark (Rs 7, one hour), early morning services for Berhampur (Rs 40, 5½ hours) and Taptapani (Rs 53, eight hours), night departures for Sambalpur (Rs 60, nine hours) and an overnight bus to Calcutta, but the trains are more comfortable for this route.

Train There are two overnight trains each way between Puri and Calcutta (500 km, Rs 128/382 in 2nd/1st class) and a daily morning departure to Delhi (2140 km, 32 hours). There are several trains between Puri and Bhubaneswar (Rs 9, two hours) but the buses are quicker.

If you're travelling to or from Madras and railway stations in the south it's not necessary to go via Bhubaneswar. Khurda Road, 44 km from Puri, is a convenient junction that all trains pass through. The *Coromandel Express* passes through at 10 pm, arriving in Madras (1207 km away) at 5.30 pm the following day.

The railway booking office is computerised and is open from 8 am to noon and 12.30 to 3 pm. It's advisable to book ahead during the pilgrim season when trains to Madras and Calcutta are often booked out five to 10 days ahead.

Getting Around

A cycle-rickshaw from the bus stand to the hotels along the beach is around Rs 10. Buses shuttle between the Jagannath Temple and the bus stand and between the railway station and the bus stand for Rs 1.

The best way to get around is by bicycle and there are several places at the travellers'

ORISSA

end of the beach where you can rent one for around Rs 15 per day. You can even try out an Enfield India from Tribe Tours for Rs 350 per day, or they have a Vespa scooter for Rs 300. You need to book and pay for these a day in advance, and the money is non-refundable should you change your mind.

AROUND PURI
Raghurajpur
Famous for its patachitra painting, this artists' village, 10 km from Puri, makes an interesting excursion. The paintings are done on specially prepared cotton cloth which is coated with a mixture of gum and chalk and polished, before natural colours are applied.

The best way to get to the village is by taxi or bicycle as it's 1.5 km off the main road. From Puri, take the Bhubaneswar road for nine km, almost to Chandapur. Turn right before the bridge, cross the railway line, then follow the right fork through the coconut plantation for a km until you come to Raghurajpur.

Pipli
Twenty-three km from Puri, at the junction where the Konark road branches from the Bhubaneswar to Puri road, this small village is notable for its appliqué craft. The colourful materials are used to make temple umbrellas and wall hangings.

KONARK
Population: 12,000

The great temple of Konark (also known as Konarak) is three km from the coast, 36 km from Puri and 64 km from Bhubaneswar. The site consists of little more than the temple and a handful of shops, stalls and places to stay. Although most people make a day trip to Konark from Puri or Bhubaneswar, it's a wonderfully peaceful place to spend a few days, and the temple has even more atmosphere once the day-trippers have all gone home. However, there isn't a lot of accommodation here – yet. Several of the major hotel chains want to turn Konark into a new beach resort but planning permission for their hotels has so far been withheld on envi-

ronmental grounds. Konark is protected as a UNESCO World Heritage Site.

If you come to Konark for the day you can take an early morning bus from Puri and a late bus back (or on to Bhubaneswar) in the afternoon, which will give you plenty of time to have a look at the temple.

An open-air theatre has been built near the temple and the Konark Dance Festival is staged here in November. There's a smaller festival in February.

There's a tourist office in the Yatri Nivas.

Sun Temple
Konark was constructed in the mid-13th century, but remarkably little is known about its early history. It's thought to have been built by the Orissan king Narashimhadev I, to celebrate his military victory over the Muslims. It is believed to have fallen into disuse in the early 17th century after being desecrated by one of Jehangir's envoys. Until the early 1900s it was simply an interesting ruin of impressive size.

Then in 1904 debris and sand were cleared from around the temple base and the sheer magnitude of its architect's imagination was revealed. The entire temple was conceived as a chariot for the sun god, Surya. Around the base of the temple are 24 gigantic carved stone wheels. Seven mighty stone horses haul at the temple and the immense structure is covered with carvings, sculptures, figures and bas-reliefs. It is not known if the construction of the temple was ever completed. If the tower was completed it would have soared to 70 metres and archaeologists wonder if the sandy foundations could have supported such a structure. Part of the tower was still standing in 1837 but by 1869 had collapsed. Today the temple's interior has been filled in to support the ruins.

The main entrance, from the Tourist Bungalow side, is guarded by two stone lions crushing elephants. Steps rise to the main entrance, flanked by straining horses. The jagamohan still stands, but the deul behind it has collapsed. The three impressive chlorite images of Surya have been restored to their positions, aligned to catch the sun at dawn,

ORISSA

Konark Sun Temple: a temple to the sun built in the form of a procession chariot

noon and sunset. Between the main steps up to the jagamohan and the entrance enclosure is an intricately carved dancing hall. To the north is a group of elephants and to the south a group of horses rearing and trampling men.

At the western end of the temple, the rubble from the collapsed deul has been cleared allowing visitors to climb right down into the sanctuary. The image of the deity that was here is thought to have been moved to the Jagannath Temple in Puri in the 17th century.

Around the base of the temple and up the walls and roof is a continuous procession of carvings. Many are in the erotic style for which Konark, like Khajuraho, is famous. These erotic images of entwined couples, or solitary exhibitionists, can be minute images on the spoke of a temple wheel or life-size figures higher up the walls.

Originally nearer the coast (the sea has receded), Konark was visible from far out at sea and was known as the Black Pagoda by sailors, in contrast to the whitewashed

temples of Puri. It was said to contain a great mass of magnetic iron which would draw unwary ships to the shore.

It's worth hiring a guide for an hour (about Rs 25) as they can show you interesting features and sculptures – such as the dancer with high-heeled shoes, giraffes and even a man treating himself for venereal disease! – which you would otherwise probably overlook. Just be sure that your guide is registered and wears his badge; unlicensed guides abound but are unreliable.

If you are here in the evening, the temple looks particularly impressive as it's illuminated between 6 and 9 pm.

Nine Planets' Shrine

The six-metre chlorite slab, once the architrave above the main entrance of the jagamohan, is now the centrepiece of a small shrine just outside the temple walls. The carved seated figures represent Surya (the sun), Chandra (the moon), Mars, Mercury, Jupiter, Venus, Saturn, Rahu and Ketu.

ORISSA

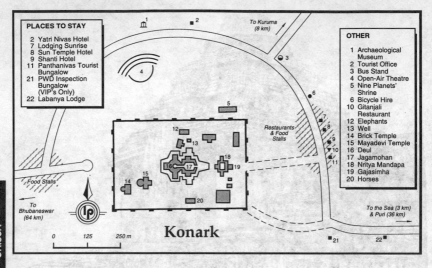

PLACES TO STAY
2 Yatri Nivas Hotel
7 Lodging Sunrise
8 Sun Temple Hotel
9 Shanti Hotel
11 Panthanivas Tourist
   Bungalow
21 PWD Inspection
   Bungalow
   (VIP's Only)
22 Labanya Lodge

OTHER
1 Archaeological
   Museum
2 Tourist Office
3 Bus Stand
4 Open-Air Theatre
5 Nine Planets'
   Shrine
6 Bicycle Hire
10 Gitanjali
   Restaurant
12 Elephants
13 Well
14 Brick Temple
15 Mayadevi Temple
16 Deul
17 Jagamohan
18 Nritya Mandapa
19 Gajasimha
20 Horses

To Kuruma (8 km)
Restaurants & Food Stalls
Food Stalls
To Bhubaneswar (64 km)
To the Sea (3 km) & Puri (36 km)

0   125   250 m

Konark

Archaeological Museum

Outside the temple enclosure is a museum (open from 10 am to 5 pm, closed Friday) containing many sculptures and carvings found during the temple excavation. Some of the small pieces (the statue of Agni, the fire god for example) are particularly good. For more information, the Archaeological Survey of India's *Sun Temple – Konark* is on sale here but not at the temple itself.

Konark Beach

The sea is three km from the temple; you can walk there or hire a bicycle (Rs 15 per day) or take a cycle-rickshaw. This part of the beach is much cleaner than at Puri, but beware of the strong current. It's also much quieter than Puri but if there are any children about you're likely to attract their attention, since not many foreigners swim here. With miles of open sand, you can of course always move along the beach a bit. A number of chai shops sell drinks and snacks here.

Places to Stay & Eat

The cheapest accommodation is around the bus stand and is fairly basic. *Lodging Sunrise*

has doubles for Rs 40 with common bathroom, and the nearby *Banita Lodge* has rooms with attached bath.

In a quiet location, the *Labanya Lodge* is a good, friendly place popular with travellers. Doubles are Rs 60, or Rs 75 upstairs, and there's a nice roof terrace for sunbathing. You can get meals here.

The government-run *Yatri Nivas* is excellent value at Rs 60 for a double with attached bathroom, but the restaurant is best avoided.

The *Panthanivas Tourist Bungalow* (☎ 8831) is opposite the temple's main entrance. Doubles with bathroom are Rs 80 and Rs 110. It's well kept and pleasantly located. Many people taking day trips from Puri use the Bungalow's *Gitanjali Restaurant* for meals; the food is OK, but the service can be slow.

Sun Temple Hotel is only a restaurant but is a recommended place to eat. There are numerous chai-shops outside the temple entrance – the *Shanti Hotel* has cold beer and good food. There are also a few chai shops down by the beach.

Getting There & Away

Dilapidated buses and overcrowded minibuses run along the coastal road between Puri and Konark (Rs 7, one hour). Some people even cycle the 36 km from Puri and stay the night at Konark. Although it's a good flat road, make sure the bicycle you hire is in reasonable condition because there are few repair shops along the way.

There are buses fairly regularly to Bhubaneswar, including at least one express bus, usually at 10 am. The fare is Rs 10 and the trip takes around 1½ hours on the express tourist bus, longer on a stop/start local service.

CHILKA LAKE
South-west of Puri, Chilka Lake is dotted with islands and is noted for the many migratory birds which flock to the nesting sanctuary here in winter (December to January). The shallow lake is about 70 km long and averages 15 km wide, and is supposedly one of the largest brackish-water lakes in the country. It's separated from the sea only by a narrow sand bar. The railway line and the main road run along the inland edge of the lake. It's a peaceful enough place but probably of greatest interest to ornithologists. Environmental and human problems – such as siltation and commercial prawn fishing – are threatening this important wetland.

Places to Stay
Orissa Tourism is developing a resort on the lake at Satapada, about 50 km from Puri, where a *Tourist Bungalow* is being built.

There are private hotels at Balugaon, which has a railway station and bus stand. Six km south at Barkul, Orissa Tourism has a *Tourist Bungalow* (☎ 488), with doubles for Rs 195 or Rs 300 for air-con rooms. There are launches for hire here, from Rs 150 per hour for a seven-seater, and kayaks for Rs 40 per hour. The hotel is rather run-down – even more so since being damaged by a bomb which some guests were apparently putting together in their bedroom when it accidentally went off!

The *Tourist Bungalow* (☎ 346) at Rambha, 130 km from Bhubaneswar, is far more pleasantly located and is a friendly place to stay. Doubles with attached bathrooms, and balconies overlooking the lake are Rs 120 or Rs 250 with air-con. There's a good restaurant which sometimes serves crab and prawns from the lake. A launch is available for hire here or the fishermen will take you out for Rs 50 per hour.

GOPALPUR-ON-SEA
The sea is clean and there's an excellent beach at this popular but decaying little seaside resort, 18 km south-east of Berhampur.

Places to Stay
Prices vary according to season and demand, and you should be able to get a 50% discount on the high-season (October to January) prices given below if there aren't many people about.

By the lighthouse, the *youth hostel* is rather run-down but has beds for Rs 10. Nearby is the friendly *Holiday Inn Lodge*, with singles/doubles for Rs 90/120 with attached bathroom.

The *Hotel Kalinga* is a recommended place, right by the sea, with good singles/doubles for Rs 120/180 or Rs 205 for a four-bed room, all with attached bathrooms. It's well run and there's a restaurant here. The *Hotel Holiday Home* opposite is overpriced.

Two cheaper places are the *Hotel Rosalin* and *Wroxham House*, which is an old bungalow at the far end of Beach Rd. The *Hotel Sea Breeze* has doubles for Rs 150 as well as some cheaper rooms, and it's beside the beach.

The *Motel Mermaid* on Beach Rd is flashy, clean and modern, with rooms from Rs 280/400 but this includes all meals.

At the top end there is the 21-room *Oberoi Palm Beach Hotel* (☎ (0681281) 21), with rooms from US$53/106, including all meals. It's a luxurious low-key retreat in a coconut grove right by the sea.

Getting There & Away
The only buses from Gopalpur are to

ORISSA

Berhampur (Rs 4, 45 minutes) which is on the main Calcutta-Madras railway line. A cycle-rickshaw for the three km between the railway station and the Berhampur bus stand costs Rs 8. From the bus stand there are regular departures to Bhubaneswar (Rs 30, five hours), overnight buses to Jeypur in the south for Rs 80 and regular buses to Taptapani (Rs 9, two hours).

TAPTAPANI

Apart from the small hot springs in this peaceful place in the hills west of Gopalpur, there's not much else to see, and it's really not worth a day trip. However, it would make a great winter splurge if you booked one of the two rooms at the *Panthanivas Tourist Bungalow* (☎ Podamari 431), which have hot spring water channelled directly to the vast tubs (accommodating several people) in their Roman-style bathrooms. Double rooms cost Rs 250 and there are also ordinary rooms for Rs 150, with ordinary bathrooms.

Near **Chandragiri**, 36 km away, there's a Tibetan refugee community and a temple. The Tibetans support themselves by weaving carpets, which you can buy here.

CUTTACK

Population: 474,000
Telephone Area Code: 0671

Only 35 km north of Bhubaneswar, on the banks of the Mahanadi and Kathajuri rivers, Cuttack was the capital of Orissa until 1950. Today it's a chaotic and largely uninteresting place.

Only a gateway and the moat remain of the 14th-century Barabati Fort. The stone retaining wall on the Kathajuri River, which protects the city from seasonal floods, dates from the 11th century. The Kadam Rasul is a Muslim shrine which contains the Prophet's footprint and has become a place of pilgrimage for Hindus as well as Muslims.

Paradip, 90 km east of Cuttack, is a major port and minor beach resort.

Places to Stay

The *Panthanivas Tourist Bungalow* (☎ 23-867) in Buxi Bazaar has singles/doubles for Rs 100/130 or Rs 250/275 with air-con. The *Hotel Neeladri* (☎ 23-831) has singles/doubles from Rs 100/150, and the *Hotel Ashoka* (☎ 25-708) offers rooms for Rs 240/280 or Rs 320/370 with air-con. The *Hotel Akbari Continental* (☎ 25-242) has air-con rooms for Rs 400/525, and there is also a restaurant. There are a number of other small hotels, but if you wish to visit Cuttack it is probably easier to take a day trip from Bhubaneswar.

LALITGIRI, UDAIGIRI & RATNAGIRI

Buddhist relics and ruins can be found at these three hilltop complexes, north-east of Cuttack and about 100 km from Bhubaneswar.

At Lalitgiri, a gold casket was discovered, thought to contain relics of the Buddha, and excavations are continuing. In the village here artisans make replicas of stone sculptures. Eight km away is Udaigiri with another monastery complex and a brick stupa.

The Ratnagiri site, five km beyond Udaigiri, has the most interesting and extensive ruins and is well worth a visit. The two large monasteries here flourished from the 6th to the 12th centuries AD. There are beautifully carved doorways, a large stupa and enormous Buddha figures.

BHITAR KANIKA WILDLIFE SANCTUARY

This sanctuary on the coast between Paradip and Chandipur was proclaimed largely to protect the nesting habitat of the 300,000-odd olive ridley marine turtles which come to the mouth of the Brahmani River here each winter to nest.

As yet there is little in the way of facilities, but it may become a national park, and a park headquarters and accommodation centre is planned at Chandbali, which is accessed from the main highway at Bhadrakh.

BALASORE & CHANDIPUR

Balasore is the first major town on the railway line from Calcutta in north Orissa. It was once an important trading centre with Dutch, Danish, English and French factories.

In 1634 it had the first British East India Company factory in Bengal. **Remina**, eight km away, has the Gopinath Temple, an important pilgrimage centre.

Chandipur, 16 km away on the coast, is a beach resort where the beach extends five km at low tide and the sea can be very shallow. There are several buses a day from Balasore.

Places to Stay

The Municipal Tourist Bungalow in Balasore, known as *Deepak Lodging*, is pleasant and reasonably priced. Walk from the railway station to the main road, turn left and it's on the right-hand side, two blocks from the corner and across the street from the cinema. There are a few small hotels, such as the *Hotel Sagarika* or the *Hotel Moonlight*.

In Chandipur there's a good *Panthanivas Tourist Bungalow* (☎ (06785) 2251), with dorm beds for Rs 40, doubles for Rs 195 or Rs 305 with air-con, and cheaper private accommodation.

SIMILIPAL NATIONAL PARK

In the north-east of the state, 250 km from Calcutta and 320 km from Bhubaneswar, this park covers 2750 sq km and is part of Project Tiger. There are tigers (thought to number around 80), elephants and several types of deer among the many species here. The scenery is beautiful and varied with hills, waterfalls and undisturbed forest in which the extensive wildlife manages to remain well hidden. The park is closed from July to October.

Tourist facilities are not well developed and you must bring money and food, and arrange your own transport. The entrances to the park are on the western side at Jashipur, or more conveniently at Baripada. Your first stop has to be the Similipal park office (☎ 06792) 2773) at Baripada, to book your accommodation. Doubles at the six *Forest Rest Houses* dotted round the park cost Rs 100 for a double. The one at Barheipani is recommended as it's near a 450-metre waterfall. About 10 km inside the park (35 km from Baripada) is the *Aranya Niwas Tourist*

Lodge at Lulung. Double rooms cost Rs 300, or there's cheaper dorm accommodation.

Jashipur is accessible by bus (or train and bus via Bangriposhi) from Baripada. Mr Roy charges Rs 50 for a double at his *Tourist Lodge* in Jashipur and you can arrange a jeep here (Rs 3.50 per km).

For touring within the park, jeeps cost Rs 1000 to Rs 1400 from Baripada, depending on where you go, and this can be shared among up to five people.

SAMBALPUR

Population: 208,000
Telephone Area Code: 0663

In the west on the border with Madhya Pradesh is the large town of Sambalpur. It's the heart of an ikat weaving district, although there doesn't appear to be any on sale in the town itself. This area is right off the beaten tourist path, and you'll be something of a local attraction.

The town is promoted as a holiday destination by the Orissa Tourism Development Corporation largely, it seems, on account of the 24-km-long **Hirakud Dam**, built to control monsoon floods in the Mahanadi delta around Bhubaneswar.

Sonapur, 80 km south, is another textile centre, and there are Tantric temples here.

The Orissa Tourist Development Corporation (OTDC) maintains tourist offices at the railway station and the Panthanivas Tourist Bungalow.

Places to Stay & Eat

For basic accommodation there's the *Indhrapuri Guest House* (☎ 21-712), right by the bus stand. It has small rooms from Rs 30/50. The *Rani Lodge*, about five minutes' walk away on the main street, is another basic place.

Also close to the bus stand is the *Hotel Uphar* (☎ 21-558), a good place with basic rooms with attached bath for Rs 175/225, although a 20% discount seems to be standard. There are more expensive rooms at Rs 225/275 with air-cooler and TV, and Rs 375/425 for air-con and colour TV. The restaurant here is not great.

ORISSA

On top of a small hill at the end of the main street is the OTDC *Panthanivas Tourist Bungalow* (☎ 21-482). It's not brilliantly run or maintained, but there are good views from some rooms. The cost is Rs 110 for a double with attached bath, and Rs 220 with air-con.

The *Central Hotel*, opposite the Indhrapuri Guest House, is a good place for cheap meals. For something a little more salubrious, try the restaurant in the Hotel Uphar Palace, on the main street.

Getting There & Away
Bus The bus stand is in the centre of town. There are three buses daily for Puri (Rs 60, nine hours), but these leave in the afternoon and so arrive quite late. It's better to catch an earlier bus for Cuttack (5.30 or 8.30 am, Rs 53, 6½ hours) and another from there to Puri.

On the main street outside the bus stand there are plenty of private companies with deluxe video coaches (night only) for Puri, Bhubaneswar and Raipur. The state bus company also has a deluxe night bus to Bhubaneswar (Rs 60). Book in advance at the bus stand.

Train The railway station is about three km

from the town centre, a rip-off Rs 30 by auto-rickshaw. There are direct trains to Bilaspur, Jhansi, Calcutta, Bhubaneswar (17 hours, via Vizianagram in Andhra Pradesh), Delhi and Madras.

OTHER ATTRACTIONS
In the north of Orissa, 50 km from Jashipur, **Khiching** was once an ancient capital and has a number of interesting temples (some in ruins) and a small museum. Further inland is the important industrial city of **Rourkela**, which has a major steel plant. A little northwest of Cuttack is the Siva temple of **Kapilas**.

Bronze-casting is done in the **Bolangir** area. **Harishankar**, west of Bolangir, has a number of temples and a waterfall. The twin villages of **Ranipur-Jharial** are 30 km from Titlagarh and are noted for the extensive collection of temples on a rock outcrop. They include a circular 64-*yogini* temple, similar to the one at Khajuraho.

Gupteswar Cave is 85 km west of Koraput. This is in Orissa's large southern district which is inhabited by several tribal peoples, including the Bonda.

Sikkim

Until 1975, Sikkim, or New House, was an independent kingdom, albeit under a treaty which allowed the Indian government to control Sikkim's foreign affairs and defence. However, following a period of political crises and riots in the capital, Gangtok, India annexed the country and Sikkim became the 22nd Indian state. The move sparked widespread criticism, but tensions have now cooled. The central government has been spending relatively large sums of money to subsidise Sikkim's road building, electrification, water supply and agricultural and industrial development.

Much of this activity was no doubt motivated by India's fear of Chinese military designs on the Himalayan region. Even today, there's still a lot of military activity along the route from Siliguri to Gangtok.

For many years, Sikkim was regarded as one of the last Himalayan 'Shangri-las' because of its remoteness, spectacular mountain terrain, varied flora and fauna and ancient Buddhist monasteries. It was never easy to visit and, even now, you need a special permit to enter, though this is easy to obtain (see the Permits section later in this chapter). All the same, access to the eastern part of Sikkim along the Tibetan border remains highly restricted, and trekking to the base of Kanchenjunga has to be organised through a recognised travel agency.

Compared with other parts of the country, tourism in Sikkim is in its infancy. In 1993 only 7000 foreigners and 70,000 Indians visited the state.

History

The country was originally home to the Lepchas, a tribal people thought to have migrated from the hills of Assam around the 13th century. The Lepchas were pacifist forest foragers and small-crop cultivators who worshipped nature spirits. They still constitute some 18% of the total population of Sikkim, though their ability to lead their

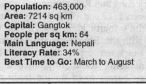

Population: 463,000
Area: 7214 sq km
Capital: Gangtok
People per sq km: 64
Main Language: Nepali
Literacy Rate: 34%
Best Time to Go: March to August

The external boundaries of India on this map have not been authenticated and may not be correct.

traditional lifestyle has been severely limited by emigration from Tibet and, more recently, from Nepal.

The Tibetans started to immigrate into Sikkim during the 15th and 16th centuries to escape religious strife between various Lamaist sects. In Tibet itself, the Yellow Hat sect, or Geluk-pa (to which the Dalai Lama belongs), gradually gained the upper hand. In Sikkim, however, the Red Hat sect, or Nyingma-pa, remained in control and was the official state religion until the country became a part of India. In the face of the waves of Tibetan immigrants, the Lepchas retreated to the more remote regions. A blood brotherhood was eventually forged between their leader, Thekong Tek, and the Bhutias leader, Khye-Bumsa, and spiritual and temporal authority was imposed on the anarchistic Lepchas.

In 1641, the Dalai Lama in Lhasa appointed Penchoo Namgyal the first king of Sikkim. At that time, the country included the area encompassed by the present state as well as part of eastern Nepal, the Chumbi Valley (Tibet), Ha Valley (Bhutan) and the Terai foothills down to the plains of India, including Darjeeling and Kalimpong.

Between 1717 and 1734, during the reign of Sikkim's fourth king, a series of wars fought with the Bhutanese resulted in the loss of much territory in the southern foothills, including Kalimpong, then a very important bazaar town on the trade route between Tibet and India. More territory was lost after 1780 following the Gurkha invasion from Nepal, though the invaders were eventually checked by a Chinese army with Bhutanese and Lepcha assistance. Unable to advance into Tibet, the Gurkhas turned south where they came into conflict with the British East India Company. The wars between the two parties ended in the treaty of 1817 which delineated the borders of Nepal. The Gurkhas also ceded to the British all the Sikkimese territory they had taken; a substantial part was returned to the raja of Sikkim in return for British control of all disputes between Sikkim and its neighbours. The country thus became a buffer state between Nepal, Tibet and Bhutan.

In 1835, the British, seeking a hill station as a rest and recreation centre for their troops and officials, persuaded the raja to cede the Darjeeling area in return for an annual stipend. The Tibetans objected to this transfer of territory. They continued to regard Sikkim as a vassal state, and Darjeeling's rapid growth as a trade centre had begun to make a considerable impact on the fortunes of Sikkim's leading lamas and merchants.

Tensions rose and, in 1849, a high-ranking British official and a botanist, who were exploring the Lachen region with the permission of both the Sikkimese raja and the British government, were arrested. Although the two prisoners were unconditionally released a month later following threats of intervention, the British annexed the entire area between the present Sikkimese border and the Indian plains and withdrew the raja's stipend (the stipend was eventually restored to his son).

Further British interference in the affairs of this area led to the declaration of a protectorate over Sikkim in 1861 and the delineation of its borders. The Tibetans, however, continued to regard these actions as illegal and, in 1886, invaded Sikkim to reassert their authority. The attack was repulsed by the British, who sent a punitive military expedition to Lhasa in 1888 in retaliation. The powers of the Sikkimese raja were further reduced and high-handed treatment by British officials prompted him to flee to Lhasa in 1892, though he was eventually persuaded to return.

Keen to develop Sikkim, the British encouraged emigration from Nepal, as they had done in Darjeeling, and a considerable amount of land was brought under rice and cardamom cultivation. This influx of labour continued until the 1960s and, as a result, the Nepalese now make up approximately 75% of the population of Sikkim. The subject of immigration became a topic of heated debate in the late '60s and the raja was constrained to prohibit further immigration. New laws regarding the rights of citizenship were designed to placate those of non-Nepalese origin, but they served to inflame the opposition parties.

There was also a great deal of grass-roots support for a more popular form of government than Sikkim's *chogyal*. The British treaties with Sikkim had passed to India at independence and the Indian government had no wish to be seen propping up the regime of an autocratic raja while doing their best to sweep away the last traces of princely rule in India itself. However, the chogyal resisted demands for a change in the method of government until the demonstrations threatened to get out of control and he was eventually forced to ask India to take over the country's administration.

In a 1975 referendum, 97% of the electorate voted for union with India. Despite significant international resentment at the time, the political situation has cooled down and Sikkim is now governed by its own democratic congress with representatives in the central government in Delhi.

The current population of Sikkim is approximately 18% Lepcha and 75% Nepalese; the other 7% are Bhutias and Indians from various northern states. About 60% of the population is Hindu and 28% is Buddhist, although the two religions exist, as in many parts of Nepal, in a syncretic form. The ancient Buddhist monasteries, of which there are a great many, are one of the principal attractions of a visit to Sikkim.

Permits

Permits for Sikkim can be obtained either while you wait or within a few hours. You will need your passport and one photo; there's no charge. The permitted length of stay in Sikkim is 15 days, and one 15-day extension is currently allowable, although this could change.

The places you are allowed to visit with a 'standard' permit are Gangtok, Rumtek, Phodang, Pemayangtse area (including Tashiding, Yuksam and Lake Khechepari) and Naya Bazar.

If you are part of a group of four or more, permits can be obtained in Gangtok to visit Tsangu Lake, in eastern Sikkim not far from the Tibetan border, and Yumthang, in north-

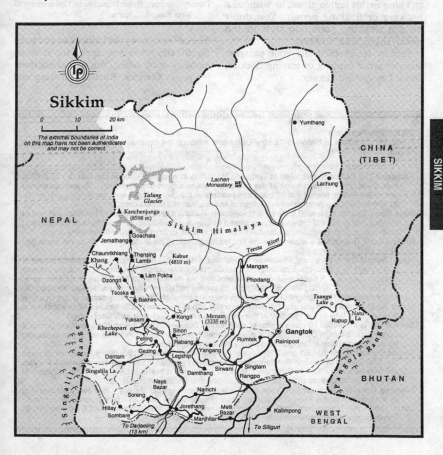

ern Sikkim. These permits are in addition to the permit needed to enter Sikkim in the first place.

Trekking permits are obligatory for those wishing to trek in the Dzongri region. These are also in addition to the normal permit and are issued at the permit office in Gangtok (next to the tourist office). To get one, you must be part of a group of at least four people and have made a booking for a trek with a recognised travel agent. The government will arrange for a liaison officer/guide to accompany you. You cannot simply go trekking in this region alone, or without a booking or trekking permit. You don't need a trekking permit to trek in the Pemayangtse area, however.

Permits are checked and your passport stamped when entering or leaving Sikkim, and at Legship and Yuksam.

Permits are best obtained in India itself from any of the following places:

Any regional Foreigners' Registration Office (Delhi, Bombay, Calcutta, Madras)
Immigration offices at Delhi, Bombay, Calcutta or Madras airports
Resident Commissioner, Government of Sikkim, 14 Panchsheel Marg, Chanakyapuri, Delhi (☎ (011) 301-5346)
Sikkim Tourist Information Centre, SNT Bus Compound, Siliguri, West Bengal (☎ (0353) 24-602)
Assistant Resident Commissioner, Government of Sikkim, 4C Poonam, 5 Russell St, Calcutta (☎ (033) 29-7516)
Deputy Commissioner, Darjeeling, West Bengal
Deputy Secretary, Home Department, Government of West Bengal, Calcutta

You can also have your Indian visa endorsed for Sikkim when you apply for it at an embassy or consulate. You should ask them to specify Gangtok, Rumtek, Phodang and

---

Sikkimese Festivals

The focus of festivals in Sikkim is Tibetan Buddhism, although the Lepchas and Nepalese Hindus also celebrate certain events.

Bhumchu This festival is celebrated at Tashiding Monastery in western Sikkim on the 15th day of the first month (March). The head monk at the monastery opens a glass box containing 300-year-old sacred water. This is then poured into 21 cups and prophesies are divined about what the coming year holds. At Khechepari Lake people make offerings of flowers, fruit and butter lamps.

Saga Dawa This 'triple blessed festival' is to celebrate Buddha's birth, attainment of Buddhahood and of nirvana. Processions of monks carrying sacred scriptures proceed through the streets of Gangtok and other towns. Saga Dawa falls on the full-moon of the fourth lunar month (late May or early June).

Drukpa Teshi This festival is to celebrate the first teaching given by the Buddha. It is held on the fourth day of the sixth month (August).

Pang Lhabsol This is a uniquely Sikkimese festival as it is devoted to Kanchenjunga, the guardian deity of Sikkim, and to Yabdu, the 'supreme commander' of Kanchenjunga. The festival is celebrated with dramatic dances, with Kanchenjunga represented by a red mask ringed by five human skulls, and Yabdu by a black mask. Dancing warriors, replete in Sikkimese battledress with helmets, shields and swords, also participate. The highlight of the dance is the entrance of Mahakala (the protector of the Dharma, or Buddhist path), who instructs Kanchenjunga and Yabdu to ensure that Sikkim remains peaceful and prosperous. It falls on the 15th day of the seventh month (late August or early September).

Dasain This is the Nepali Hindus version of north Indian Dussehra, Delhi's Ram Lila and West Bengal's Durga Puja. It falls in October, and is also the main holiday period. At this time accommodation and transport, particularly in Gangtok and Darjeeling, are in high demand.

Kagyat Dance Held on the 28th and 29th days of the 12th month (February), this dance festival symbolises the destruction of evil forces. The dances are performed by monks in the monastery courtyard. Prayers are held before the dance. The main centre for the dance is the Tsuk-La-Khang (Royal Chapel) in Gangtok, but dances are also held at Pemayangste and Phodang monasteries.

Loosong This is the Sikkimese New Year, and it falls in the last week of February. It is known as Namsoong by the Lepchas, and is also called Sonam Losar (Farmers' New Year), as it falls around harvest time.

Losar This is the Tibetan New Year, and two days prior to it, dances are performed by the monks at Pemayangste and Rumtek monasteries. It falls in early March. ■

Pemayangtse, which they are authorised to issue.

You are only allowed one 15-day permit and one extension for Sikkim per year. It's virtually impossible to get around this as your permit and passport are checked and stamped both on the way in and on the way out, so there's a record of your visit.

If you're on your way to Sikkim by train from Calcutta, you'll find a Foreigners' Registration Office on the platform at New Jalpaiguri station, Siliguri (West Bengal). In theory, you're supposed to present your passport here but they don't stamp it so you can give it a miss. This office is a legacy of the days when a permit was required to visit Darjeeling/Kalimpong and should have been closed down a long time ago. Retrenchment of staff at redundant offices is obviously not a West Bengal government priority.

Gangtok

Population: 82,000
Telephone Area Code: 03592

Gangtok, the capital of Sikkim, occupies the west side of a long ridge flanking the Ranipul River. The scenery is spectacular and there are excellent views of the entire Kanchenjunga range from many points in the vicinity. Many people expect Sikkim to be a smaller version of Kathmandu. It's not, but it is an interesting and pleasant place to stay and people here are exceptionally friendly. Gangtok only became the capital in the mid-1800s (previous capitals were at Yuksam and Rabdantse) and the town has undergone rapid modernisation in recent years.

Gangtok has also become something of a hill station resort for holidaying Bengalis – the large number of sweet shops on M G Marg is testament to that. The influx peaks during the 10-day Durga Puja holiday period in October, when Bengalis descend (ascend, perhaps?) en masse from the plains. It's a good time to give Gangtok a miss as prices rise – especially for accommodation and

local transport – and finding a room at *any* price can be a major headache.

Orientation

To the north is Raj Bhavan, the former British and later Indian Residency. Above this is Siniolchu Lodge, Enchey Monastery and the telecommunications tower. The palace of the former chogyal and the impressive Royal Chapel (the Tsuk-La-Khang) are lower down along the ridge. Nearby is the huge Tashiling, or Secretariat complex, and, below it, the newly built Legislative Assembly, both executed in a traditional architectural style.

On a continuation of this ridge but much lower is the Institute of Tibetology, an orchid sanctuary and, not far beyond the institute, a large *chorten* (Tibetan stupa) and adjoining monastery.

All the main facilities – hotels, cafes, bazaars, bus stand, post office, tourist information centre and the Foreigners' Registration Office – are either on, or very near, the main Darjeeling road (Highway 31A).

Information

Tourist Office The tourist office is open Monday to Saturday from 8 am to 4 pm.

The office for trekking permits, for permits to visit north Sikkim or Tsangu Lake or for permit extensions is in the same building as the tourist office. It is open on weekdays from 10 am to 4 pm.

The Foreigners' Registration Office is open Monday to Friday from 10 am to 1 pm.

Money The State Bank of India, opposite the tourist office, is very helpful and efficient, as is the State Bank of Sikkim at the junction of the National Highway and Paljor Stadium Rd. Be warned that none of the banks will accept Visa travellers' cheques, no matter what the currency.

Post & Telecommunications The post office is open for mail Monday to Saturday and every day for long-distance/IDD telephone calls.

SIKKIM

Bookshops & Newspapers There are very few bookshops in Gangtok. The best is General Stores, M G Marg, diagonally opposite the tourist office. National daily newspapers are available here but are always a day old.

Tsuk-La-Khang

The Royal Chapel is the Buddhists' principal place of worship and assembly and the repository of a large collection of scriptures. It's a beautiful and impressive building, and its interior is covered with murals. Lavishly decorated altars hold images of the Buddha, bodhisattvas and Tantric deities, and there are also a great many fine woodcarvings. Unfortunately, the only time it's open to visitors is during the Tibetan New Year celebration when the famous Black Hat dance portraying the triumph of good over evil is performed.

Namgyal Institute of Tibetology

Established in 1958 and built in traditional style, this unique institute promotes research of the language and traditions of Tibet, as well as of Mahayana Buddhism. It has one of the world's largest collection of books and rare manuscripts on the subject of Mahayana Buddhism, many religious works of art and a collection of astonishingly beautiful and incredibly finely executed silk-embroidered *thankas* (cloth paintings). It also has a number of religious art and craft works, as well as books, for sale. The institute is open Monday to Saturday from 10 am to 4 pm; entrance is Rs 2.

Chorten & Monastery

The gold apex of a huge white chorten, located about 500 metres beyond the institute, is visible from many points in Gangtok and is surrounded by prayer flags attached to bamboo poles. Next to it is a monastery for young lamas with a shrine containing huge images of Guru Padmasambhava, the Indian teacher of Buddhism in Tibet, and his manifestation, Guru Snang-Sid Zilzon. As at other Buddhist monasteries, the chorten is surrounded by prayer wheels.

Orchid Sanctuaries

Surrounding the institute and itself enclosed by a peaceful forest is the **Orchid Sanctuary**, where you can see many of the 454 species of orchid found in Sikkim. The best times to visit are April to May and July to August.

There is another, much larger, orchid sanctuary, off the main road to Rangpo alongside the Teesti River, called the **Orchidarium**, which is accessible by public bus. It's also usually included on tours to the Rumtek Monastery.

Up on top of the ridge, next to White Hall, there's a **Flower Exhibition Centre**, but it's not always open.

Institute of Cottage Industries

High up on the main road above the town, the Cottage Industries Emporium specialises in producing handwoven carpets, blankets,

Buddhist image in Rumtek Monastery

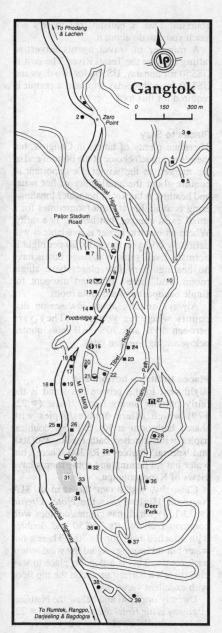

Gangtok

To Phodang & Lachen

0   150   300 m

Zero Point

National Highway

Paljor Stadium Road

Footbridge

Tibet Road

M G Marg

Bhanu Path

National Highway

Deer Park

To Rumtek, Rangpo, Darjeeling & Bagdogra

SIKKIM

PLACES TO STAY

1	PWD Bungalow
4	Siniolchu Lodge
7	Nor-Khill Hotel
9	Hotel Chumila
11	Hotel Norbu Gang
13	Hotel Tibet
14	Hotel Mayur
17	Green Hotel
18	Sunny Guest House & Private Bus Stand
23	Hotel Lhakpa
24	Modern Central Lodge
25	Hotel Shere-e-Punjab
26	Hotel Orchid
32	Sunshine Lodge & Hotel Hillview
33	Hotel Tashi Delek
34	Hotel Laden La
36	Pine Ridge Hotel

PLACES TO EAT

20	House of Bamboo

OTHER

2	Cottage Industries Emporium
3	Telecommunications Tower
5	Enchey Monastery
6	Stadium
8	SNT Bus Stand
10	Ridge Park & Flower Exhibition Centre
12	GPO
15	State Bank of India
16	Tourist Office & Blue Sheep Restaurant
19	Tashila Tourist Travels
21	Jeep Stand
22	Indian Airlines
27	Palace
28	Tsuk-La-Khang (Royal Chapel)
29	Foreigners' Registration Office
30	Share Jeeps to Rumtek
31	Lall Market
35	Secretariat Complex
37	Legislative Assembly
38	Namgyal Institute of Tibetology & Orchid Sanctuary
39	Chorten & Monastery

shawls, Lepcha weaves, patterned decorative paper and 'Choktse' tables, exquisitely carved in relief. It's open daily (except Sunday and every second Saturday) from 9 am to 12.30 pm and 1 to 3.30 pm.

Deer Park

This popular viewpoint is on the edge of the ridge next to the Secretariat building. In it, as you might expect, are deer and a replica of the Buddha image at Sarnath in Uttar Pradesh, as well as a caged bear, which anyone with only a vague sympathy for the Animal Liberation movement would want to see released. The current obsession with human rights obviously does not extend to animal rights in this place.

Enchey Monastery

Located above Siniolchu Lodge, about three km from the centre of town, the 200-year-old Enchey Monastery is well worth a visit, particularly if you're in Gangtok when religious dances are performed in January (18th and 19th days of 12th lunar month). It's a relatively small place and doesn't compare with the other larger monasteries in Sikkim, but it does sit on a spectacular ridge overlooking Gangtok, and there are views across to Kanchenjunga.

Lall Market

If you've been to markets in Kathmandu or Darjeeling, this one may come as a disappointment due to its limited range of craft shops, but the vegetable market is certainly colourful and there's plenty of activity.

Organised Tours

This section should perhaps be called Disorganised Tours, as the tours operated by the Department of Tourism seem to be very much a hit and miss affair. There are supposedly daily tours which include Tashi Viewpoint, the Deer Park, Enchey Monastery, the Royal Chapel, the Secretariat, the Cottage Industries Emporium, the Institute of Tibetology and the nearby chorten and orchid sanctuary, Rumtek Monastery and the Orchidarium. Enquire at the tourist office.

Sikkim Tourism also supposedly offers tours to Tsangu Lake, but the bus is invariably unavailable or fully booked by travel agents. If you can get on, the cost is Rs 130. The local travel agents also run tours to Tsangu, but they have clubbed together and all charge foreigners US$12. They insist that this is the figure set by the Department of

Tourism. This is bullshit, but there's not much you can do about it.

A number of travel agents advertise rafting trips on the Teesti River. The cost is US$50 for one day, US$60 for two days and US$70 for a three-day trip, and a permit is required for this too!

Places to Stay

There are plenty of hotels in Gangtok, but there's not much choice at the bottom end of the market. In the winter it's important to enquire about the availability of hot water and heating. A bucket of hot water for showering is available at most (sometimes for a small extra charge), but heating is a rarity. Where an electric heater is available it will definitely cost you more (Rs 30 per night is normal). Even some mid-range hotels have no heating. Very few places have single rooms, and there's often no discount for single occupancy of a double room.

Always enquire about low-season discounts wherever you stay. They vary between 15% and 30%. All rates quoted below are high-season rates.

Places to Stay – bottom end

Right next to the private bus stand is the fairly popular *Sunny Guest House* (☎ 22-179) which offers doubles/triples with shared bathroom at Rs 150/250, doubles/triples with attached bath for Rs 250/300, and 'special' doubles at Rs 300. There's hot water but no heating and some rooms have views of Kanchenjunga.

Close by, just down the road at 31A National Highway, is the *Hotel Orchid* (☎ 23-151) which has singles/doubles with common bath for Rs 75/150 and doubles with attached bath for Rs 300. There's hot water but no heating. Avoid the windowless back rooms. This is a popular place to stay plus there's a bar/restaurant on the top floor with excellent views.

Directly opposite and below the National Highway is the *Hotel Shere-e-Punjab* (☎ 22-823), which costs Rs 60/100 for a single/double with common bath and Rs 150 for a double with attached bath. It's not bad value, but the staff are indifferent. Hot water is available by the bucket.

Right in the thick of things on M G Marg is the *Green Hotel* (☎ 23-354). It's a long-time favourite but there are no views and no heating. Singles/doubles with attached bath are Rs 150/250 or Rs 250/350 with geyser (water heater). On the ground floor there's a popular bar and restaurant. Bucket hot water is available in the rooms which have no geyser.

There are a number of other places along this same road, including the *Glacier Guest House*, the *Karma Hotel*, *Sunshine Lodge*, *Crown Lodge* and *Hotel Hillview*. They're all similarly priced but most are featureless concrete boxes with no views and no hot water or heating.

Down in Lall Market, the *Hotel Laden La* is pleasant and there are good views over the market from the front rooms. The cost is Rs 80/100 with common bath and Rs 120/150 with attached bath, but there's no hot water.

Above M G Marg, along Tibet Rd, are a number of modern upper-range budget hotels. These are generally much better value and you can often get a room with a view of Kanchenjunga.

Excellent value and very popular is the *Modern Central Lodge* (☎ 23-417), run by two young Sikkimese brothers who are very friendly and helpful. It's excellent value at Rs 120/140 for a single/double room with toilet but common bath, or Rs 250 for doubles with attached bath with geyser. The common showers have hot water around the clock. Cheap, tasty food is available in the restaurant/bar (which also has a good sound system) and there's even a snooker hall! They also run the new *Pine Ridge Hotel*, near the Legislative Assembly building. Prices and facilities are the same, and it too is a good place to stay.

Almost next door to the Modern Central is the *Hotel Lhakpa* (☎ 23-002) which isn't as popular but is probably just as good. It has doubles/triples with common bath for Rs 80/120 as well as doubles/triples with attached bath and hot water for Rs 230/250. There's bucket hot water for the common baths. The hotel also has its own restaurant and bar.

Along Paljor Stadium Rd below the GPO are another cluster of budget hotels. They include the *Hotel Chumila* (☎ 23-361), a small place with singles/doubles with attached bath for Rs 150/200. Like the Modern Central Lodge, this is run by a very friendly and helpful young Sikkimese man. The single rooms are very pokey, others much better. The bar/restaurant here turns out cheap, tasty food.

Below the Chumila along the same road are other budget hotels – the *Hotel Orient*, *Hotel Sikkim* (very basic), *Hotel Lhakhar* and *Hotel Mount View*.

Very cheap but a long way out from the centre and a strenuous hike uphill is the *Siniolchu Lodge* (☎ 22-074), just below the entrance to Enchey Monastery. The lodge is run by Sikkim Tourism and has possibly the best views in town. Self-contained 'economy' singles/doubles are Rs 70/100, and it's Rs 10/150 plus 10% tax for 'deluxe' rooms (with their own water heater). There's no heating. Although it's good value, unless you have your own transport it's a long slog up the hill from the centre of town. Taxis cost Rs 15.

Places to Stay – middle

The best hotel by far in this range is the three-star *Hotel Tibet* (☎ 22-523), Paljor Stadium Rd, next door to the GPO. Done out in traditional Tibetan style, it's very pleasant and comfortable. On the top floor is the residence of the Dalai Lama's Sikkim representative. Standard singles/doubles are Rs 413/550 and deluxe singles/doubles Rs 503/670, plus there are more expensive suites. All the rooms have hot water and TV, and heating is available. The views of Kanchenjunga from the back rooms are excellent. There's a bar and restaurant serving excellent Tibetan, Chinese, Indian and Continental dishes and credit cards are accepted. A discount of up to 30% applies in the low season.

SIKKIM

Close to the Hotel Tibet above at the junction of National Highway and Paljor Stadium Rd is the *Hotel Mayur* (☎ 22-825), another of the hotels run by Sikkim Tourism. Standard singles/doubles are Rs 200/250, deluxe singles/doubles Rs 325/400, and superdeluxe singles/doubles Rs 400/475, excluding 10% service charges. All the rooms are self-contained with hot water. There's a bar and restaurant, and car-parking facilities are also available.

Close by is the *Hotel Norbu Gang* (☎ 22-237), also on Paljor Stadium Rd. It's comfortable and good value at Rs 315/425 for singles/doubles including 'bed tea'. Superdeluxe rooms are available for Rs 400/500.

Places to Stay – top end

The best and most convenient hotel in this range is the *Hotel Tashi Delek* (☎ 22-038), M G Marg, which, like the Hotel Tibet, is done out in traditional decor. The staff are very friendly and eager to please and there are great views from the roof garden/restaurant (Sikkimese, Chinese, Continental and tandoori cuisine). There's also a bar. Singles/doubles are Rs 1150/1700 and there are double suites for Rs 2000, with an additional 10% service charge. These rates include all meals and afternoon tea. Credit cards are accepted.

Further afield, the *Nor-Khill Hotel* (☎ 23-187), just off the bottom of Paljor Stadium Rd and above the actual stadium, isn't such good value though it is spacious, and is cheaper in the low season. Like the Tashi Delek, you can only take a room with full board (American plan). Singles/doubles are Rs 1800/2200 and suites are Rs 2600, all with an additional 10% service charge. There's a bar and restaurant (Indian, Chinese, tandoori and Continental cuisine).

Places to Eat

Most of the hotels in Gangtok have their own restaurants and some of them are very good. Those at the *Hotel Orchid, Green Hotel* and *Modern Central Lodge* are popular with budget travellers. All offer cheap, tasty and filling meals in a variety of cuisines – usually Tibetan, Chinese and Indian – plus most can usually rustle up what would pass for a Western-style breakfast (eggs, toast and the like).

Other than hotel restaurants, an excellent cheap place to eat which is popular with both local people and travellers is the *House of Bamboo*, on M G Marg opposite the Green Hotel. The restaurant offers tasty Tibetan and Chinese dishes and is a cosy place to be on a cold day. As with most Sikkimese restaurants, there's an attached bar.

Slightly more formal is the *Blue Sheep*, also on M G Marg next to the tourist office and run by Sikkim Tourism. The speciality here is sizzlers but they also do Sikkimese and Chinese dishes. The food is reasonably priced, but nothing special. This place only seems to be open at lunchtimes.

Further afield, try the *Snow Lion Restaurant* in the Hotel Tibet. The setting is elegant and the food inexpensive. They do good sizzlers and other Continental dishes, as well as Tibetan, Chinese, Mughlai and even some Japanese food.

Top of the line is a meal at the *Blue Poppy* in the Hotel Tashi Delek. A Chinese and Indian buffet dinner is Rs 160 plus 10%.

Try *thungba* from a chang shop in the market – a large bamboo mug full of millet to which you add hot water to get fresh chang.

Entertainment

Gangtok is essentially early-to-bed territory, though there are cinemas. There are also numerous bars, most attached to restaurants. Drinkers will find the price of beer and spirits in Sikkim refreshingly cheap after West Bengal. Note that full-moon and new-moon days are 'dry' days throughout the state.

Things to Buy

There are shops all over town selling Tibetan handicrafts. A good shop is Charitrust, in the Hotel Tibet. As the name suggests, this is a nonprofit shop, with all proceeds going to needy Tibetans.

Getting There & Away

Air Indian Airlines (☎ 23-099) has an agency on Tibet Rd. It has a computer link, but the nearest airport is at Bagdogra near Siliguri.

Interstate Buses Sikkim Nationalised Transport (SNT) is the main bus operator to Gangtok and they have plenty of services. Buses should be booked in advance at the SNT bus stand as far ahead as possible, especially during the Durga Puja holiday period. The booking office is open from 9 am to noon and 1 to 2 pm.

To West Bengal there are daily buses to Siliguri (Rs 50, five hours), Kalimpong (Rs 27, three hours), Darjeeling (Rs 60, seven hours) and Bagdogra (Rs 50, 4½ hours).

In addition to the SNT buses, there are private buses which run from Gangtok to Siliguri, Darjeeling and Kalimpong. To Siliguri there are at least 10 buses daily (mostly in the afternoon), and to Darjeeling and Kalimpong at least two daily. They cost much the same as the SNT buses, and should also be booked in advance at the private bus stand.

All the private buses depart from and arrive at the private bus stand adjacent to the Sunny Guest House in Gangtok.

Local Buses & Jeeps There are plenty of domestic bus routes within Sikkim operated by SNT but, due to permit restrictions, only some of these are of interest to travellers. The main jeep stand is just above M G Marg in the centre of town.

To get to Phodang Monastery (38 km from Gangtok) you need to take a bus going to Mangan or Singhik. They depart Gangtok daily at 8 am, 1.30 and 4 pm and take about two hours to Phodang and five hours to Mangan. It's better to set out from Gangtok early, in which case you should take the 6.30 am share jeep from the jeep stand. The fare is Rs 25 (Rs 50 for a front seat).

To Rumtek there is a daily bus from Gangtok at 4.30 pm which returns at 8 am the next day (Rs 7, one hour). It obviously means you have to stay overnight in Rumtek.

The alternative is the share jeeps (Rs 25) which leave from outside Lall Market.

To Jorethang (for Darjeeling) there are two buses daily from Gangtok, at 8 am and 3 pm.

To Gezing (for Pemayangtse, Dzongri or Tashiding in western Sikkim) there are daily buses from Gangtok at 7 am and 1 pm which take six hours and cost Rs 35. This service is heavily subscribed and advance booking is essential.

From the jeep stand there are departures for, among other places, Gezing (Rs 70), Jorethang and Mangan (for Phodang). For Siliguri (Rs 80) and Kalimpong (Rs 75) share jeeps leave from the private bus stand throughout the day.

Train The nearest railheads are at Siliguri/ New Jalpaiguri and Darjeeling.

There is a railway booking office at the SNT bus stand which is open Monday to Saturday from 9.30 to 11 am and 1.30 to 2.30 pm. You can make reservations here for trains passing through or originating from Siliguri/New Jalpaiguri.

Getting Around

All the taxis are new or near-new Maruti vans. Rs 15 will get you just about anywhere around town. To Rumtek you're looking at about Rs 250 return, including about an hour at the monastery. If you want to spend longer there, make sure the driver is well aware of this.

AROUND GANGTOK
Rumtek Monastery

Rumtek, on the other side of the Ranipul Valley, is visible from Gangtok though it's 24 km away by road. The monastery is the seat of the Gyalwa Karmapa, the head of the Kagyu-pa order of Tibetan Buddhism. The order was founded in the 11th century by Lama Marpa, the disciple of the Indian guru Naropa, and later split into several subsects, the most important of which are Druk-pa, Kagyu-pa and Karma-pa. The teachings of the sect are communicated to the disciples orally.

The main monastery is a recent structure,

built by the Gyalwa Karmapa in strict accordance with the traditional designs of his monastery in Tibet. Visitors are welcome and there's no objection to your sitting in on the prayer and chanting sessions. They'll even bring you a cup of salted butter tea when it's served to the monks. Mural work here is exquisite and a visit is a must if you're interested in the Tibetan style of religious painting.

The main *chaam*, or religious dance, known as Tse Chu, is performed on the 10th day of the fifth lunar month (July), and depicts events in Guru Rimpoche's life. Another chaam, presenting the battle between good and evil, takes place two days before Tibetan New Year.

Most activity takes place in the late afternoon. At other times you may well find the main door locked, in which case it's a matter of asking around for someone to open it up for you, which they are quite happy to do.

If you follow the tarmac road for two or three km beyond Rumtek, through a gate off to the left you'll find another interesting, but smaller, monastery which was restored in 1983. Opposite is an old and run-down monastery with leather prayer wheels.

Places to Stay & Eat

The *Sangay Hotel*, 100 metres down the motor road from the monastery, is a friendly little place. It's basic but clean, and blankets are provided. Rooms cost Rs 50/60 with common bath, and hot water is available by the bucket. The restaurant here has a pretty limited menu, but there are great views across the valley to Gangtok.

The alternative to the hotels is to find a room with one of the villagers.

The new *Shambala Hotel*, not far from the main gate, may be open by now. By the looks of what is being built, it will be a mid-range hotel.

Getting There & Away

There are buses and share jeeps from Gangtok or you can take a taxi. See the Gangtok section for details.

If you feel like a bit of exercise, it's a very pleasant 12-km walk (downhill!) to the National Highway, from where it's easy to

Sikkimese woman

get a ride for the 12 km (uphill!) trip to Gangtok.

Phodang & Labrang Monasteries

Phodang Monastery, some 38 km north of Gangtok along a winding and somewhat tortuous but largely tarmac road, is much smaller and less ornate than Rumtek but it doesn't have the tourist hordes that Rumtek attracts. Here you can feel the timelessness of a part of Sikkim which tourists rarely visit. The monastery sits high up above the main road to Mangan and there are tremendous views down into the valley below.

Phodang is a fairly recent structure and there are far fewer monks here than at Rumtek, but they're very friendly and will take you around and explain the salient features of the monastery. The back room behind the altar has perhaps the most striking murals and was succinctly described by one of the authors' travelling companions as 'an acid-head's nightmare'! Executed largely in black, it depicts various demonic deities dismembering miscreants in the bowels of hell. Leave a donation.

Labrang Monastery is some two km further uphill from Phodang and is a much older structure. You need to set out early from Gangtok if you want to visit both monasteries and return the same day, as the last transport back to Gangtok passes through Phodang at about 3 pm.

Places to Stay & Eat Phodang village is about two km past the turn-off to the monasteries. The *Yak & Yeti Hotel* has single rooms with common bath for Rs 50, or doubles with attached bath for Rs 100. Hot water is free by the bucket.

Close by is the newer *Hotel Northway*, with rooms at Rs 50/80.

Both hotels have restaurants, and there are a couple of other basic eating places in between the two.

Getting There & Away See the Gangtok section for details of local buses and taxis to Phodang.

Tsangu Lake

Tsangu Lake (also spelt Tsongo and Changu) lies at 3750 metres, 34 km east of Gangtok and just eight km from the Tibetan border. The two-hour trip there from Gangtok offers spectacular views, although the destination itself is nothing special. It is very popular among holidaying Indians.

The problem with visiting Tsangu is that foreigners need a special permit to do so, and these are only issued if you are part of a group of four, or if you go on the Sikkim Tourism bus. It's another bit of useless bureaucracy which, together with the US$12 which the travel agents charge foreigners, makes the whole exercise hardly worth the effort. If you can get on the Sikkim Tourism trip, the cost is Rs 130 per person.

If you still want to go, you need photocopies of your passport data page, Indian visa and Sikkim permit, and one photo. These you take to the permit office at the tourist office, and fill in a form. The permit may be issued on the spot, but usually takes a day, and

you need to have a confirmed booking with a travel agent before they'll entertain you.

Western Sikkim

This area of Sikkim is attracting more and more visitors. Its main attractions, other than trekking up to Dzongri at the base of Kanchenjunga, are the two old monasteries of Pemayangtse and Tashiding, and trekking in the Pemayangtse area.

PEMAYANGTSE MONASTERY

Standing at a height of 2085 metres and surrounded on two sides by snowcapped mountains, Pemayangtse (Perfect Sublime Lotus) is one of the state's oldest and most important monasteries. It was founded in 1705 but was badly damaged in the earthquakes of 1913 and 1960. It has been reconstructed several times and belongs to the Tantric Nyingma-pa sect, which was established by the Indian teacher Padmasambhava in the 8th century. All the sect's monasteries are characterised by a prominent image of this teacher, together with two female consorts, and this monastery is the head of all others in Sikkim. The sect followers wear red caps.

The monastery is a three-storey structure filled with wall paintings and sculptures including *Zandog-palri*, a seven-tiered painted wooden model of the abode of Guru Rimpoche, complete with rainbows, angels and the whole panoply of Buddhas and bodhisattvas on the third floor. The model was built single-handedly by the late Dungzin Rinpoche in five years.

In February each year the chaam, or religious dance, is performed by the monks. The exact dates are the 28th and 29th days of the 12th lunar month.

Pemayangtse is about six km uphill from Gezing on the Pelling road, two km before Pelling. The SNT buses between Gezing and Pelling pass by the turn-off for Pemayangtse, from where it's just a few minutes' walk.

Places to Stay & Eat

Just off the approach to the monastery is the *Hotel Mt Pandim* (☎ (03593) 756), run by Sikkim Tourism and known to the locals as the 'Tourist Lodge'. Standard singles/doubles with attached bath cost Rs 275/375 or Rs 300/525 for deluxe rooms with a view of Kanchenjunga, all plus 10% service charge. Meals are available for guests, and cost Rs 40 for breakfast, and at lunch or dinner there's the choice of vegetarian (Rs 55), non-veg (Rs 65) or Chinese food (Rs 60). If the hotel is not full, non-guests can eat dinner here, but you must book by 4 pm.

Right next door to the Mt Pandim is a *PWD Rest House* which has huge rooms and great views but you won't be able to stay there, even if it's empty, unless you have made a booking in Gangtok.

PELLING

Pelling is a pleasant little town perched high on a ridge. There are great views north to Kanchenjunga and to the south when the weather is clear.

Most travellers to western Sikkim use Pelling as their base. It offers the best budget accommodation and you can store gear while you trek.

The town has a post office, and a branch of the State Bank of India, where you can change cash and travellers' cheques (not Visa or Citibank, and only US dollars and pounds sterling).

If you intend to trek from Pelling, bring some supplies (fruit, nuts etc) from Gangtok or Darjeeling to supplement the ubiquitous dhal-bhat – there's not much for sale in Pelling apart from biscuits and soap!

Things to See

As well as a visit to **Pemayangtse Monastery**, 2.5 km away, there are a number of other attractions in the vicinity worth checking out. Most of them involve a bit of walking, but it's excellent walking territory around here – despite the leeches!

The **Sangachoeling Monastery** predates Pemayangtse by some 10 years and is the second-oldest in Sikkim. Like Pemayangtse,

the interior walls are highly decorated with paintings. It's about a 45-minute walk west from Pelling along a well-defined track through the forest.

Further afield are the **Sangay Waterfalls**, 10 km from Pelling along the road to Dentam.

Places to Stay & Eat

The *Hotel Garuda* (☎ (03593) 614) is right at the town's intersection, where the buses stop. It's a friendly, if somewhat dis-organised place, and is a good spot to meet other travellers. There's excellent trekking information available, both on the wall and in a trekkers' comments book. You can also store excess gear here while you trek. Dorm beds cost Rs 30, or there are single/double rooms for Rs 50/80. Bucket hot water is available on request. The food here is filling, but varies from bland to almost inedible. Beer is cheap at Rs 22.

Close by is the *Hotel Kabur*. It lacks the atmosphere of the Garuda, but is still quite OK. Dorm beds are Rs 30, doubles are Rs 75 (no single tariff). There's also a restaurant here.

Between these two budget hotels is Pelling's newest place, the mid-range *Sikkim Tourist Centre* (☎ (03593) 855). The rooms (all doubles) have attached bath with hot water and cost from Rs 250, to Rs 300 with a view.

Getting There & Away

Although a number of buses pass through Pelling, the choice is far greater from Gezing. It's about an hour's steep downhill walk to Gezing, via the obvious shortcuts.

From Pelling there are buses to Dentam, Gezing (Rs 4), Rimbi, Jorethang (Rs 20) and Khechepari Lake.

There's one jeep which does a daily run to Gangtok at 6 am (Rs 90). Tickets should be booked the day before at the paan stall between the Sikkim Tourist Centre and the Hotel Garuda.

GEZING

Gezing is the administrative centre for western Sikkim. There's not much to see, apart from the lively Friday market in the town square, and little reason to stay, unless you want to catch an early-morning bus or jeep to Gangtok.

Places to Stay & Eat

There are half a dozen hotels around the town square; most are pretty basic. The *Hotel Bamboo House* has basic wooden double and triple rooms for Rs 25 per person. It's OK for a night and, like the other places, has a restaurant serving Tibetan food and beer.

A better place is the *Hotel Kanchenjunga* (☎ (03593) 755). It's a more substantial place with good double rooms at Rs 60 with common bath.

There's also a *PWD Rest House* but, as at Pemayangtse, you can't stay there unless you make a prior reservation in Gangtok.

The restaurants of the hotels *Shambala* and *No Name* are both good.

Getting There & Away

There are SNT buses from Gezing to Gangtok (8 am and 1 pm, Rs 35), Jorethang (10 and 11 am, and 1 and 4 pm, Rs 15), Pelling (1 pm, Rs 4), Yuksam (2 pm, Rs 17) via Tashiding (Rs 11) and Legship (Rs 6), Siliguri (7 am, Rs 40) and Dentam. Tickets should be bought an hour in advance; demand can be heavy.

Private jeeps also run to Gangtok (7 and 11 am, and 12.30 pm).

A taxi up to Pelling costs Rs 200.

KHECHEPARI LAKE

Pronounced 'catch a perry', and sometimes spelt Khecheopalri or Khechupherei, Khechepari is a common destination for trekkers. This sacred lake lies in a depression surrounded by prayer flags and forested hills. Resist the temptation to swim as it's a holy place.

By road the lake is about 27 km from Pelling; the walking trail is shorter but much steeper.

Places to Stay & Eat

The *Trekkers Hut* here is pretty rough, but the only alternative (and only if you have a sleeping bag) is to doss down in one of the teahouses. These basic places serve noodles, eggs, dhal bhat and hot raksi.

Getting There & Away

There is one bus daily to Gezing via Pelling. The road to Yuksam is currently being upgraded. If the work has been completed there may be buses to Yuksam.

YUKSAM

Yuksam (also spelt Yoksum and Yuksom), 35 km by road from Pemayangtse, is the furthest north you can get by road in Western Sikkim. It's just a sleepy hamlet but is the trailhead for those intending to trek to Dzongri.

The **Dubdu Monastery**, an hour's walk uphill from Yuksam, was the first capital of Sikkim, and was where the first monarch of Sikkim was crowned in 1641. It's worth a visit.

Places to Stay & Eat

Near the police post is the *Dzongrila Hotel*, with basic beds for Rs 25 as well as good food, beer and tongba (unfiltered chhang). It's run by a friendly, English-speaking family. Across the street is the large *Demazong Hotel*, which is a bit more sophisticated.

The *Trekkers' Hut* has beds, blankets and electricity but the caretaker tends to keep the inside toilets locked due to complications with the water system. There is, however, water outside and a row of toilets in a separate building. Beds cost Rs 25 per night and you can camp here on a large grassy area. Meals are not provided; you must bring your own or eat elsewhere.

The best place to stay is the beautiful *Forest Rest House No 1*, up a hill just before you get to the police post, but you must make a booking for it in Gangtok at the Forest Department.

The *Arpan Restaurant*, downhill past the secondary school, is another possibility for food if you're staying at the Trekkers' Hut.

Getting There & Away

There is one bus daily (in the morning) to Gezing (Rs 17) via Tashiding and Legship.

SIKKIM

TASHIDING
The friendly little town of Tashiding is becoming popular with trekkers and is worth a day or two of your time.

Tashiding Monastery
Founded around 1716, Tashiding Monastery is another of the more remote monasteries in western Sikkim. It is perched atop an almost conical hill between the Ranjit and Ratong rivers, and is a 45-minute slog on foot from Tashiding village. Only Pemayangtse Monastery is more sacred in Sikkim. The Bumchu festival is held here in March. (See the boxed section on Sikkimese Festivals at the start of this chapter for details.)

Places to Stay & Eat
The *Blue Bird Hotel* is a welcoming little place, and the dhal-bhat served up here gets rave reviews from hungry trekkers.

Getting There & Away
There is one bus daily to Yuksam (3 pm), and in the morning it passes through at 8 am on the return journey to Legship and Gezing (Rs 11).

Trekking in Sikkim

Yuksam to Dzongri
The most popular trek in Sikkim is from Yuksam to Dzongri. To undertake this trek you must organise arrangements through a recognised travel agency in Gangtok. They usually charge from US$40 per person per day. What they provide on the trek will depend on your negotiating skills. Most do not have good sleeping bags or tents and tend to schedule their stages to stay in the state government huts that have been constructed on the trek. Whatever the option it is imperative not to trek too high too quickly, in particular to Dzongri at 4550 metres.

From Yuksam the trail follows the Rathong Valley through unspoilt forests to the small Lepcha settlement at Bakhim. From Bakhim there is a steep ascent to the village of Tsoska, where a coupe of lodges provide overnight accommodation. Above Tsoska the trail enters magnificent rhododendron forests to an intermediary camp at Pethang. A tent must be carried for this stage. It is a further stage to Dzongri where you gain excellent views of Kanchenjunga (8586 metres) and many other impressive peaks on the Singali Ridge, which marks the border between Sikkim and Nepal.

As an alternative to returning direct from Dzongri to Yuksam, many trekkers opt to continue across the grazing pastures to the Prek Valley and the camp at Thansing. From here there are impressive views of the east ridge of Kanchenjunga before returning through pristine rhododendron forests to Pethang and the main trail back to Tsoska and Yuksam.

Stage 1	Yuksam to Bakhim (5-6 hrs)
Stage 2	Bakhim to Pethang (4-5 hrs)
Stage 3	Pethang to Dzongri (2-3 hrs)
Stage 4	Dzongri to Thansing (4 hrs)
Stage 5	Thansing to Tsoska (6-7 hrs)
Stage 6	Tsoska to Yuksam (5-6 hrs)

North-Eastern Region

The north-eastern region is the most varied and at the same time the least visited part of India. Before Independence the whole region was known as Assam Province, but it was finally split into five separate states and two Union Territories – Mizoram and Arunachal Pradesh.

In many ways the north-east is unlike the rest of India. It is the country's chief tribal area, with a great number of tribes speaking many different languages and dialects – in Arunachal Pradesh alone over 50 distinct languages are spoken! These tribal people have many similarities to the hill tribes, who live across an arc that stretches from the eastern end of the Himalaya through Myanmar (Burma) and Thailand into Laos. Also, the north-east has a high percentage of Christians, particularly in the more isolated areas where the population is predominantly hill tribespeople.

For a number of reasons India has always been touchy about the north-east, and a visit to the region can involve a bureaucratic nightmare for foreigners. For a start the north-east is a sensitive border zone where India meets Bhutan, China, Myanmar and Bangladesh. Equally important, the region is remote – only the narrow Siliguri corridor connects it to the rest of India, and before Independence the usual route to Assam would have been through Bangladesh. Today, it involves making a long loop north and then east by metre-gauge rail. Roads have been improved dramatically but there are still very few of them compared with the rest of India.

Until the early 1980s, permits for foreigners wishing to visit Assam and Meghalaya were relatively easy to procure, at least for specific tourist attractions, but the other states were, to all intents and purposes, off limits. Only with friends in high places and cast-iron references was it possible to get a permit for the more remote states and, even then, your movements would be carefully monitored.

Assam
Population: 24,100,000
Area: 78,000 sq km
Capital: Guwahati

Manipur
Population: 2,010,000
Area: 22,300 sq km
Capital: Imphal

Meghalaya
Population: 2,030,000
Area: 22,400 sq km
Capital: Shillong

Nagaland
Population: 1,500,000
Area: 17,000 sq km
Capital: Kohima

Tripura
Population: 3,070,000
Area: 10,400 sq km
Capital: Agartala

Arunachal Pradesh
Population: 981,000
Area: 84,000 sq km
Capital: Itanagar

Mizoram
Population: 793,000
Area: 21,000 sq km
Capital: Aizawl

The external boundaries of India on this map have not been authenticated and may not be correct.

By the mid-1980s, however, a dark cloud had descended over the north-east. A whole series of strikes and riots followed each other in quick succession which, in turn, led to widespread violence and terrorism. This put the whole area firmly off limits to outsiders. There were a number of reasons for this unrest, including a feeling of central government neglect (poor transport links and lack of infrastructure development were the main complaints). This feeling strengthened as oil prices rose since Assam has a substantial part of India's small but important oil reserves.

Very little of this oil wealth found its way back to improve Assam's industrial development, and the whole region remained overwhelmingly agricultural.

But economic neglect and exploitation was only a minor issue. The main issue was about the inflow of 'foreigners' into the region. Military repression and economic stagnation, combined with high birth rates in Bangladesh, pushed thousands of Bangladeshis over the lightly policed borders into the north-east region. The influx was so great that, in some cases, it threatened to outnumber the indigenous population, and demands for the Bangladeshis' repatriation became more and more strident. Such wholesale repatriation would have presented the central government with an extremely difficult problem since few of the 'foreigners' carried identification papers making it almost impossible to decide which of them had arrived recently and which had lived in the region for generations – legally or otherwise.

Lack of action in addressing the indigenous population's grievances, however, proved catastrophic. In 1983, wholesale massacres of 'foreigners' began to take place and photographs of their bodies floating down various tributaries of the Ganges and Brahmaputra rivers appeared in the world's press. The killings eventually subsided and events in the north-east were soon relegated to the back pages as a result of the greater unrest in the Punjab. Yet little had actually changed.

Then came the formation of the United Liberation Front of Assam (ULFA) pledged to the independence of Assam through armed struggle. Its military wing enjoyed a great deal of initial success and kept the Indian army on the run for many years, operating from bases deep in the jungle and from Bangladesh. Unwilling to countenance the loss of Assam, the Indian government was finally forced to mount a series of massive military operations to flush out the guerrillas, the latest, codenamed Operation Rhino, in 1991. With the movement almost crushed and its leaders in hiding in Bangladesh, the state governor, Saikia, punted on a reconciliation by offering talks with the rebels on the basis of a ceasefire and the rebels laying down their arms.

The talks duly took place in Guwahati but it soon became apparent that not all of the ULFA's leaders were in favour of talks. Those who were in favour of continued armed struggle not only refused to attend but issued statements condemning those who agreed to the talks. It was also alleged that the ceasefire was conveniently used to give the recalcitrant rebels time to regroup and rearm. At the time of writing, little progress appears to have been made.

As if the trouble in Assam was not enough, the central government also had to contend with political and military agitation in Nagaland and Manipur at a time when they felt things in those states were under reasonable control. Nagaland has proved to be an intractable problem virtually since Independence, although it appeared that progress was being made in 1991 until the governor precipitously dissolved the state assembly and put the state back under President's rule. Manipur's complaints were more benign, amounting to not much more than a demand that Manipuri be added to the constitution as one of the official languages of India.

The states bordering Myanmar (Burma) were further hit with problems in 1991 following the Myanmar army's massive drive against the Muslim inhabitants in the country's north-west. As a result, tens of thousands of refugees fled over the border into Mizoram, Manipur and Nagaland. Feeding and sheltering these refugees has been a major burden on the Indian government and, although an agreement was signed between the Indian and Myanmar governments in early 1992 to allow the refugees to return, trust is an elusive commodity. Most of the refugees believe they will be shot if they return and few are keen to do so.

With all this violence and upheaval taking place in India's north-east states, it's not surprising that the central government is extremely reluctant to allow foreigners into this area of India. This is in contrast to the attitude of the state governments, who would prefer the region to be more accessible.

Permits

In theory, foreigners can obtain Restricted Area Permits for Assam, Meghalaya, Manipur and Tripura. (Indians require permits for Arunachal Pradesh, Nagaland and Manipur, which in effect means that those states are off-limits for foreigners.) In practice, however, the whole process is set up to make it as difficult as possible to get a permit, and therefore few people currently bother. It's quite possible that the central government may relax travel restrictions for foreigners visiting the north-east states, so check at least one source on arrival.

Currently permits for foreigners are valid for 10 days in one state, and you need separate permits for each state you intend to visit! As the permits only allow foreigners to fly in to Guwahati (Assam), it's pointless therefore to have a permit for say, Meghalaya, if you can't get one for Assam. It's official Indian obstruction and obfuscation at its best!

If your patience knows no bounds and you want to try your luck, permits can be applied for at any overseas Indian consular office, or in India at the Foreigners' Registration Office, Hans Bhavan (near Tilak Bridge), Bahadur Shah, Zafar Marg, New Delhi

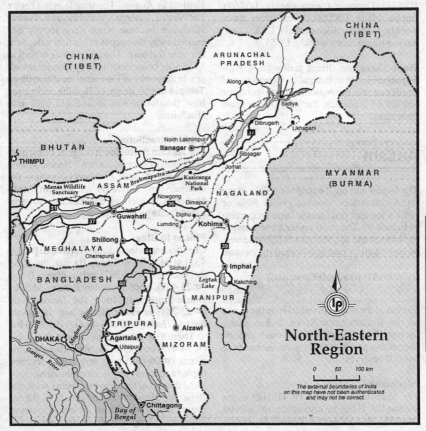

North-Eastern Region

The external boundaries of India
on this map have not been authenticated
and may not be correct.

110002. For Assam you can also try at the Trade Adviser, Government of Assam, 8 Russell St, Calcutta 700071. Permits for Meghalaya can be applied for at the Meghalaya Information Centre in Calcutta, which is next to the Assam office at 9 Russell St. For the other states try the relevant tourist offices in Calcutta (see that chapter for addresses).

Getting There & Away

Air Indian Airlines flies from Calcutta to Guwahati three times daily for US$46. Other regional flights from Calcutta include: Agartala (daily, US$34), Dibrugarh (daily, US$74), Dimapur (twice weekly, US$69), Imphal (daily, US$58), Jorhat (three times weekly, US$69), Silchar (daily, US$52) and Tezpur (three times weekly, US$57).

Train There are direct trains from New Jalpaiguri in West Bengal to Guwahati and further on into the region, but foreigners are limited to accessing the area by air from Guwahati.

Assam

The largest and most easily accessible of the north-east states, Assam grows 60% of India's tea and produces a large proportion of India's oil. The main visitor attractions are the Manas and Kaziranga wildlife reserves, home of India's rare one-horned rhinoceros.

GUWAHATI (Gauhati/Gawahati)

Population: 632,000
Telephone Area Code: 0361

Capital of the state, Guwahati is on the banks of the Brahmaputra River. It has many ancient Hindu temples but its main importance is as a gateway to the north-east and the wildlife reserves.

Information

The state tourist office (☎ 47-012) is on Station Rd. There are also offices in Calcutta (☎ (033) 39-8331), at 8 Russell St; and in

Delhi (☎ (011) 34-3961), at Kharak Sing Marg.

Temples

The **Umananda Temple** is a Siva temple on Peacock Island in the middle of the river. There's a pleasant ferry across the river. The **Navagrah Temple** is the Temple of the Nine Planets. In ancient times this was a centre for the study of astrology. It is on Chitrachal Hill, near the city.

Guwahati's best known temple is the **Kamakshya Temple** on Nilachal Hill, 10 km from the city. It attracts pilgrims from all over India, especially during the Ambuchi Festival in August. The temple is the centre for Shakti (energy) worship and Tantric Hinduism because when Siva sorrowfully carried away the corpse of his first wife, Sati, her *yoni* fell here. The temple was rebuilt in 1665 after being destroyed by Muslim invaders. In the centre of Guwahati the **Janardhan Temple** has an image of Buddha, indicating how Buddhism was assimilated back into Hinduism.

Other Attractions

The **Assam State Zoo** has tigers, lions, panthers and, of course, Assam's famous rhinos – plus the African two-horned variety for comparison. There is an **Assam State Museum** as well as the **Assam Government Cottage Industries Museum**.

Places to Stay

Cheaper hotels include the *Hotel Alka* (☎ 43-437) at M S Rd in Fancy Bazaar, the *Hotel Ambassador* (☎ 25-587) and the *Happy Lodge* (☎ 23-409), both in Paltan Bazaar. Middle-range hotels include the *Nova Hotel* (☎ 23-258) in Fancy Bazaar and the *North-Eastern Hotel* (☎ 25-314) on G N Bordoloi Rd.

There's a government *tourist bungalow* (☎ 24-475) on Station Rd, and railway retiring rooms (☎ 26-688) with very cheap doubles, triples and dormitory accommodation.

At the top of the Guwahati price scale, the *Belle Vue Hotel* (☎ 28-291) on M G Rd has rooms with and without air-con. However, it's quite a long way from the centre. The

Hotel Nandan (☎ 32-681) on G S Rd is comparable at Rs 320/450 for an air-con single/double, and is more conveniently located.

Top of the range is the *Dynasty Hotel* (☎ 35-610, fax 44-813) on S S Rd with air-con rooms from Rs 550/750. The ITDC *Brahmaputra Ashok* (☎ 33-233) on M G Rd has rooms from Rs 700/900.

Getting There & Away

Air See Getting There & Away in the introductory section to this chapter for details about flights from Calcutta to Guwahati and other centres in the North-Eastern Region.

Train The most convenient points from which to get to Guwahati are Calcutta and New Jalpaiguri.

From Calcutta (Howrah), it's 993 km and about 24 hours to Guwahati on the *Kamrup Express* or 22 hours on the *Kanchenjunga Express* (to/from Sealdah) at a cost of Rs 208/624 in 2nd/1st class. These trains pass through New Jalpaiguri station at 7 am and 6.10 pm respectively. There is also the *North East Express* which comes from New Delhi

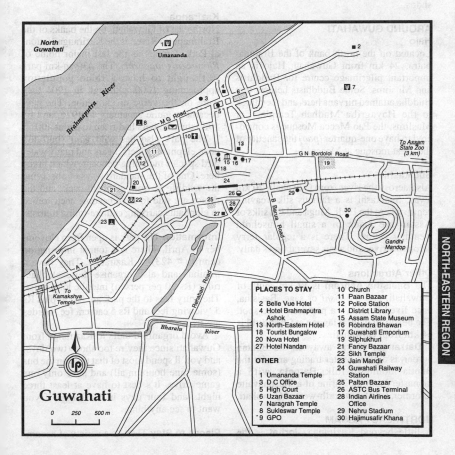

Guwahati

0   250   500 m

PLACES TO STAY		10	Church
2	Belle Vue Hotel	11	Paan Bazaar
4	Hotel Brahmaputra	12	Police Station
	Ashok	14	District Library
13	North-Eastern Hotel	15	Assam State Museum
18	Tourist Bungalow	16	Robindra Bhawan
20	Nova Hotel	17	Guwahati Emporium
27	Hotel Nandan	19	Silphukhuri
		21	Fancy Bazaar
OTHER		22	Sikh Temple
		23	Jain Mandir
1	Umananda Temple	24	Guwahati Railway
3	D C Office		Station
5	High Court	25	Paltan Bazaar
6	Uzan Bazaar	26	ASTC Bus Terminal
7	Naragrah Temple	28	Indian Airlines
8	Sukleswar Temple		Office
9	GPO	29	Nehru Stadium
		30	Hajimusafir Khana

and passes through New Jalpaiguri at 9.25 am. The 422-km journey from here to Guwahati takes about eight hours and costs Rs 114/347 in 2nd/1st class.

If you're going further east than Guwahati, you must change here from broad gauge to metre gauge. There's a good network of metre-gauge lines to all the major centres of population in the north-east but as the area is essentially off limits to foreigners, there's little point in providing details. For further information, the best reference is *Newman's Indian Bradshaw* published monthly for Rs 50. It's sporadically available at most bookshops.

AROUND GUWAHATI
Hajo
Located on the north bank of the Brahmaputra, 24 km from Guwahati, Hajo is an important pilgrimage centre for Buddhists and Muslims. Some Buddhists believe that Buddha attained nirvana here, and they flock to the Hayagriba Madhab Temple. For Muslims, the Pao Mecca Mosque is considered to have one-quarter *(pao)* the sanctity of the great mosque at Mecca.

Sualkashi
Also across the river from Guwahati, 20 km away, Sualkashi is a famous silk-weaving centre where the Endi, Muga and Pat silks of Assam are made in a small household weaving centre. There is a regular ferry across the river and a bus several times daily.

Other Attractions
The **Basistha Ashram** is 12 km south of Guwahati, and the *rishi* or sage, Basistha, once lived here. It's a popular picnic spot. The beautiful natural lagoon at **Chandubi** is 64 km from Guwahati.

Darranga, 80 km away on the Bhutan border, is a great winter trading area for the Bhutia mountain folk. **Barpeta**, with a monastery and the shrine of a Vaishnavaite reformer, is 145 km north-west of Guwahati.

NORTH-EAST ASSAM
A little beyond Kaziranga, **Jorhat** is the gateway to the north-east of Assam. **Sibsagar**, 55 km away, has the huge Jay Sagar Tank and many temples in the environs; it was the old capital of the Ahom kingdom. There's a small *tourist bungalow* by the tank.

WILDLIFE PARKS
Assam is famous for its rare one-horned Great Indian Rhinoceros – when Marco Polo saw it he thought he had found the legendary unicorn! Kaziranga and Manas are the two well-known parks in Assam. There are smaller parks at Orang and Sonai.

Kaziranga
North-east of Guwahati, on the banks of the Brahmaputra River, is the Kaziranga National Park, famous as the last major home of *Rhinoceros unicornis*. The 430-sq-km park is thought to have a rhino population approaching 1000, although in 1904 they were on the verge of extinction. The park became a game sanctuary in 1926, and by 1966 the numbers had risen to about 400.

The park also has wild *gaur* (buffalo), deer, elephants, tigers, bears and many water bird species including pelicans, which breed here. One of the standard ways of observing the wildlife is from elephant-back, and the rhinos are said to have become accustomed to elephants carrying camera-toting tourists.

Information The park is open from November to April. There is a tourist information centre (☎ 423) at Kaziranga. They have a minibus and also organise those elephant rides (Rs 50 per person) into the long grass. The entry fees to the park are Rs 50 plus Rs 5 'viewing fee' and Rs 5 camera fee. Guides are free.

Avoid organised tours to Kaziranga from Guwahati since they're too short (two days) and you'll spend most of that time on the bus (some nine hours in all) and have only one game drive. It's best to have at least three nights and four days in Kaziranga if you want to see anything.

Places to Stay There is a variety of accommodation around the park, including *Forest Inspection Bungalows* at Beguri (no bedding or mosquito nets), Arimarh (no electricity) and Kohora. Or there is a *Soil Conservation Inspection Bungalow*, a *PWD Inspection Bungalow* and two *tourist bungalows*. Bungalow No 1 (Bonani) has rooms for around Rs 200/300 and Bungalow No 2 (Kunjaban) has rooms for Rs 150 and dormitory accommodation. Air-con at either costs an additional Rs 100.

At the top of the price scale there is the *Aranya Lodge*, which has rooms without air-con for Rs 300/400, Rs 100 more with air-con, including taxes. It's a good place to stay and is well run. The lodge provides a jeep and driver and the forest department provides a guide.

Another good place is the *Wild Grass Resort* (☎ (037762) 81437).

Getting There & Away Calcutta to Jorhat flights land 84 km from the park. Furketing is the most convenient railway station, 72 km away; from here buses and jeeps run to Kaziranga. Guwahati is 233 km away on Highway 37. There are state transport buses from Guwahati.

Manas

In the foothills of the Himalaya, north-west of Guwahati, Manas Wildlife Sanctuary is on the Bhutan border. Three rivers run through the sanctuary, which has abundant bird and animal life. The rare pygmy hog and the golden langur (monkey) are amongst the notable animals here, although you may also see rhinos.

The park has been closed for some years due to the Bodo rebels, who frequently shelter in the park to evade the authorities. It may re-open in the future, but even in late 1994 the Bodo rebels were active so don't hold your breath.

Information Manas is best from January to March, although there is excellent fishing from November to December. **Mothangiri** is the main town in the park but the tourist information centre (☎ 49) is on Barpeta Rd. Entry and camera charges are the same as Kaziranga. Boats can be hired for excursions or fishing trips on the Manas River.

Places to Stay The *Manas Tourist Lodge* has a range of rooms which are all relatively cheap or you can camp if you have a tent. The *Forest Bungalow* doesn't have electricity but it is cheaper, and includes bedding and mosquito nets. There is a *rest house* at the Barpeta Rd tourist centre.

Getting There & Away Guwahati, 176 km away, has the nearest airport. Barpeta Rd, 40 km from Mothangiri, is the nearest railway station. Transport from Barpeta Rd to Mothangiri must be arranged in advance.

Meghalaya

Created in 1971, this state is the home for Khasia, Jantia and Garo tribespeople. The hill station of Shillong is the state capital while Cherrapunji, 58 km away, was until recently said to be the wettest place on earth, with an average annual rainfall of 1150 cm, nearly 40 feet! In one year 26.46 metres of rain fell. (Nearby Mawsynram recently

NORTH-EASTERN REGION

took the title from Cherrapunji.) It's no wonder Meghalaya means Abode of Clouds.

Other places of interest around the state include **Jakrem** with its hot springs, Kayllang Rock at **Mairang**, Mawjymbuin Cave at **Mawsynram** and **Umiam Lake**.

SHILLONG

Population: 245,000

Telephone Area Code: 0634

This pleasant hill station, standing at 1496 metres, is renowned for its climate and breathtaking views; it's even had the label 'Scotland of the East' applied to it! Around town you can pass the time observing the tiny red-light district behind the Delhi Hotel, as there's not a lot to do apart from pass through.

The people around Shillong, the Khasias, have a matrilineal social organisation, passing down property and wealth through the female rather than the male line.

Information

Police Bazaar has a Government of Meghalaya tourist office (☎ 22-6054) on Tirot Singh Syiem Rd and a Government of India tourist office (☎ 25-632) on G S Rd. The GPO is also on G S Rd.

Things to See

The **State Museum** covers the flora, fauna, culture and anthropology of the state. The town has a number of parks and gardens. The **Crinoline Waterfalls** are near Lady Hydari Park, and there are various other waterfalls around Shillong. The town takes its name from the 1960-metre-high **Shillong Peak**, from which there are fine views. It's 10 km from the centre.

The Anglican graveyard and **All Saints' Cathedral** may be of interest to fans of the Raj; the gravestones have inscriptions such as 'killed in the great earthquake' or 'murdered by headhunters'. If it's locked, get the key from the adjoining gatekeeper's house.

Places to Stay & Eat

There's a good *tourist bungalow* near the polo grounds with rooms and dormitory accommodation. There are many other middle-priced hotels around, and cheap accommodation can be found in the Police Bazaar near the tourist office. There's good food at the *Lhasa Restaurant*, and there are several other restaurants around town.

The *Hotel Centre Point* (☎ 22-5210, fax 22-7222) in the town centre has good singles/doubles with attached bath for Rs 300/360. The *Hotel Pinewood Ashok* (☎ 23-116) is Shillong's Raj-era hotel, though it's hardly up to the normal standard of the Ashok group of hotels. Rooms cost Rs 450/675. Cheaper is the modern *Hotel Alpine Continental* (☎ 22-5361) with rooms from Rs 200/250.

Getting There & Away

A good road runs the 100 km from Guwahati in Assam to Shillong. Cherrapunji is 58 km south of Shillong, and there are daily buses; if it's not raining the views from here over Bangladesh are superb. Permission is required from the Commissioner of Police to visit the area.

Coming from Bangladesh, you cross the border (if it's open) at Dawki, from where it's a 1.5-km walk to the town, and then a 3½-hour trip to Shillong.

Other States & Territories

All of these are essentially off limits to foreigners so the following information is for interest only.

The only railway to these states and territories terminates at Ledo, but the roads have been improved. Indian Airlines operates a number of services to the region from Calcutta.

ARUNACHAL PRADESH

The furthest north-east of the region, this Union Territory was known as the North-East Frontier Agency under the British.

Arunachal Pradesh borders with Bhutan, China and Myanmar (Burma) and is a mountainous, remote and predominantly tribal area. The old 'Stillwell Road' used to run from Ledo in the south of Arunachal Pradesh to Myitkyinya in the north-east of Myanmar. Built in 1944 by General 'Vinegar Joe' Stillwell, it must rate as one of the most expensive roads in the world. The 430 km cost US$137 million way back then, and after opening for just a few months it has hardly been used since. All road routes into Myanmar are closed.

NAGALAND

South of Arunachal Pradesh and north of Manipur, the remote and hilly state of Nagaland is bordered by Myanmar. **Kohima**, the capital of Nagaland, was the furthest point Japanese troops advanced into India during WW II. Your chances of getting a permit are better if you state that you want to visit the war cemetery.

MANIPUR

South of Nagaland and north of Mizoram, Manipur also borders with Myanmar. The state is inhabited by over two dozen different tribes, many of them Christians. It is famous for its Manipuri dances and handloomed textiles.

The capital, **Imphal** (population 145,000), is surrounded by wooded hills and lakes and has the golden Shri Govindaji Temple. During WW II a road was built from Imphal to Tamu on the Myanmar border but, as with the Stillwell Road further north, this route into Myanmar is also closed.

MIZORAM

This finger-like extension in the extreme south-east of the region pokes between Myanmar and Bangladesh. The name means Hill People's Land – from Mizo, Man of the Hill, and Ram, Land. It's a picturesque place where the population is both predominantly tribal and overwhelmingly Christian.

TRIPURA

The tiny state of Tripura is almost totally surrounded by Bangladesh. It's a lush, wooded region with many beautiful waterfalls. **Agartala** is the capital; near it is the lake palace of Nirmahal. Here, too, the population is largely tribal.

NORTH-EASTERN REGION

Rajasthan

Rajasthan, the Land of the Kings, is India at its exotic and colourful best. It is the home of the Rajputs, a group of warrior clans who have controlled this part of India for 1000 years according to a code of chivalry and honour akin to that of the medieval European knights. While temporary alliances and marriages of convenience were the order of the day, pride and independence were always paramount. The Rajputs were therefore never able to present a united front against a common aggressor. Indeed, much of their energy was spent squabbling amongst themselves and the resultant weakness eventually led to their becoming vassal states of the Mughal Empire. Nevertheless, the Rajputs' bravery and sense of honour were unparalleled.

Rajput warriors would fight on against all odds and, when no hope was left, chivalry demanded that *jauhar* be declared. In this grim ritual, the women and children committed suicide by immolating themselves on a huge funeral pyre, while the men donned saffron robes and rode out to meet the enemy and certain death. In some of the larger battles, tens of thousands of Rajput warriors lost their lives in this way. Three times in Chittorgarh's long history, the women consigned themselves to the flames while the men rode out to their martyrdom. The same tragic fate befell many other fortresses around the state. It's hardly surprising that Akbar persuaded Rajputs to lead his army, nor that subsequent Mughal emperors had such difficulty controlling this part of their empire.

With the decline of the Mughal Empire, the Rajputs gradually clawed back their independence through a series of spectacular victories but, by then, a new force had appeared on the scene in the form of the British. As the Raj inexorably expanded, most Rajput states signed articles of alliance with the British which allowed them to continue as independent states, each with its own maharaja (or similarly titled leader), subject

Population: 54.4 million
Area: 342,239 sq km
Capital: Jaipur
People per sq km: 142
Main Languages: Rajasthani & Hindi
Literacy Rate: 38.8%
Best Time to Go: mid-October to mid-March

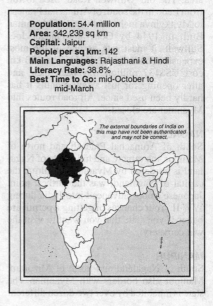

The external boundaries of India on this map have not been authenticated and may not be correct.

to certain political and economic constraints. The British, after all, were not there for humanitarian reasons, but to establish an empire and gain a controlling interest in the economy of the subcontinent in the same way as the Mughals had done.

These alliances proved to be the beginning of the end for the Rajput rulers. Indulgence and extravagance soon replaced chivalry and honour so that, by the early 1900s, many of the maharajas spent most of their time travelling the world with a vast army of wives, concubines and retainers, playing polo, racing horses, gambling and occupying whole floors of the most expensive hotels in Europe and America. While it suited the British to indulge them in this respect, their profligate waste of the resources of Rajputana (the land of the Rajputs) was socially and educationally disastrous. When India gained its independence, Rajasthan had one of the subcontinent's lowest life expectancy and literacy rates.

At Independence, India's ruling Congress Party was forced to make a deal with the nominally independent Rajput states in order to secure their agreement to join the new India. The rulers were allowed to keep their titles, their property holdings were secured and they were paid an annual stipend commensurate with their status. It couldn't last forever, given India's socialist persuasion, and the crunch came in the early 1970s when Indira Gandhi abolished both the titles and the stipends and severely sequestered their property rights.

While some of the rulers have survived this by turning their forts into museums and their palaces into luxury hotels, many have fallen by the wayside, unable to cope with the financial and managerial demands of the late 20th century.

Although the fortunes of its former rulers may be in tatters, the culture of Rajasthan, with its battle-scarred forts, its palaces of amazing luxury and whimsical charm, its riotous colours and even its romantic sense of pride and honour, is still very much alive.

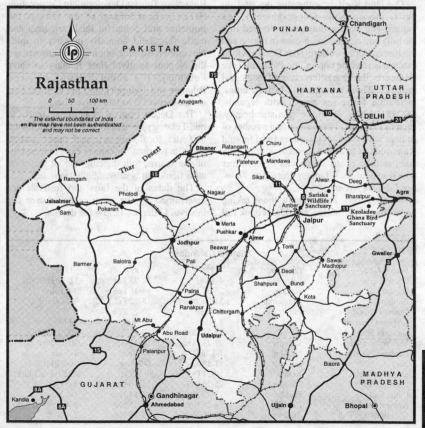

It is certainly part of India, yet is visibly unique. That visibility extends from the huge pastel-coloured turbans and soup-strainer moustaches sported by the men and the bright mirrored skirts and chunky silver jewellery of the women, to the manner in which these people deal with you. In some parts of India, you can never be sure that agreements will be kept. There are always exceptions, of course, but an agreement struck in Rajasthan is generally solid. Tourism has obviously made inroads here, but it will be a long time before it corrupts the traditional sense of honesty or destroys the cultural vitality of these people.

The land itself is somewhat dry and, in parts, inhospitable. Geographically, it's varied. The state is diagonally divided into the hilly and rugged south-eastern region and the barren north-western Thar Desert, which extends across the border into Pakistan. Like all deserts, the Thar offers oases of magic and romance. There are plenty of historic cities, incredible fortresses awash with legends, and rare gems of impressionistic beauty, such as Udaipur. There are also a number of centres which attract travellers from far and wide, such as peaceful Pushkar with its holy lake, and the exotic desert city of Jaisalmer which resembles a fantasy from *The Thousand & One Nights.*

No-one visits Rajasthan without taking home superb memories, an address book full of friends and, often, a bundle of embroidery and jewellery.

Festivals

Rajasthan has all the usual Hindu and Muslim festivals, some celebrated with special local fervour, as well as a number of festivals of its own. The spring festival of Gangaur (late March to early April) is particularly important, as is Teej (early to late August) which welcomes the monsoon. The state is at its most beautiful when the monsoon rains fill the many lakes and tanks.

Rajasthan also has many fairs, some traditional and others the creation of the Rajasthan Tourist Development Corporation (RTDC). Best known of the fairs is the immense and colourful Pushkar camel and cattle fair, held annually in early to mid-November. Similar, but less well known, are the Nagaur Festival (late January to early February; it's about halfway between Bikaner and Jodhpur), and the Kolayat Fair at Bikaner (mid to late November).

The Desert Festival at Jaisalmer (early to mid-February) is a modern creation designed to foster local folk arts and music and to promote tourism. It features camel races, tug-of-war teams, folk dancing and all the usual attractions, but is substantially overrated.

The dates of the fairs and festivals are determined by the lunar calendar. See the Festival Calendar below for details.

Festival Calendar

Festival	Location	1996	1997	1998
Camel Festival	Bikaner	4-5 Jan	22-23 Jan	11-12 Jan
Nagaur Fair	Nagaur	26-30 Jan	13-16 Feb	3-6 Feb
Baneshwar Fair	Dungarpur	31 Jan to 3 Feb	18-22 Feb	7-11 Feb
Desert Festival	Jaisalmer	2-4 Feb	20-22 Feb	9-11 Feb
Elephant Festival	Jaipur	4 Mar	23 Mar	12 Mar
Gangaur Festival	Jaipur	22-23 Mar	10-11 Apr	30-31 Mar
Mewar Festival	Udaipur	22-23 Mar	10-11 Apr	30-31 Mar
Summer Festival	Mt Abu	1-3 Jun	1-3 Jun	1-3 Jun
Teej	Jaipur	17-18 Aug	6-7 Aug	26-27 Jul
Dussehra Mela	Kota	19-21 Oct	9-11 Oct	29 Sept to 1 Oct
Marwar Festival	Jodhpur	25-26 Oct	15-16 Oct	4-5 Oct
Cattle Fair	Pushkar	22-25 Nov	11-14 Nov	1-4 Nov
Kolayat Festival	Bikaner	24-26 Nov	13-15 Nov	2-4 Nov
Chandrabhaga Fair	Jhalawar	24-26 Nov	13-15 Nov	2-4 Nov

RAJASTHAN

Art & Architecture

Rajasthan has a school of miniature painting, the style deriving from the Mughal but with some clear differences – in particular, the palace and hunting scenes are complemented by religious themes, relating especially to the Krishna legends. This art carried through to the elegant palaces built by the Rajputs when they were freed from confrontation with the Mughals. Many, such as Bundi, are liberally covered with colourful frescoes.

Most of Rajasthan's early architecture was damaged or destroyed by the first waves of Muslim invaders. Fragments remaining from that period include the Adhai-din-ka-jhonpra Mosque in Ajmer, which is basically a converted Hindu temple of great elegance, and the ruined temples at Osian, near Jodhpur. There are many buildings dating from the 10th to 15th centuries, including the superb Jain temples at Ranakpur, Mt Abu and Jaisalmer. Most of the great forts date, in their present form, from the Mughal period.

Accommodation

Palaces, Forts & Castles Rajasthan is famous for its delightful palace hotels. In these harder times, many of Rajasthan's maharajas have had to turn their palaces into hotels to make ends meet. The most famous are the super-luxurious Rambagh Palace in Jaipur, the Lake Palace Hotel and Shiv Niwas Palace in Udaipur, and the Umaid Bhawan Palace in Jodhpur.

You don't have to spend a fortune to stay in a palace – there are plenty of smaller ones which are more moderately priced. Many of these are known as Heritage Hotels, and they include *havelis* (traditional mansions built around a courtyard), forts and hunting lodges. Tourist offices have a brochure listing Heritage Hotels.

Tourist Bungalows On a more day-to-day level, the RTDC operates a series of Tourist Bungalows in almost every large town. A few years ago they were very often the best value in town, but their prices are no longer the bargain they once were. In addition, the fabric and services have been allowed to deteriorate. However, they usually have a restaurant and bar and, for real shoestringers, frequently offer dormitory accommodation. The local tourist office is often found in the Tourist Bungalow.

Home-Stay Accommodation Staying with an Indian family can be a real education. It's a change from dealing strictly with tourist-oriented people, and the differences and curiosities of everyday Indian life can be very interesting.

Rajasthan's home-stay programme operates in Jaipur, Jodhpur, Udaipur, Jaisalmer, Bikaner, Ajmer and Pushkar. The cost is anything from Rs 50 per day upwards, depending on the level of facilities offered, but most places charge Rs 100 to Rs 200. Meals are available with prior notice. The scheme is administered by the RTDC and tourist offices have comprehensive lists of the families offering the service. Since there appears to be only a handful of these lists in circulation you must visit a tourist office to make a booking.

Getting Around

Bus Rajasthan has an extensive and reasonably good state bus system. On most sectors there is a choice of ordinary and express buses. You're advised to stick to expresses since the ordinary buses stop frequently, make a lot of detours off the main route and take a long time to get anywhere.

If you're taking a bus from a major bus stand, it's worth buying a ticket from the ticket office rather than on board the bus. It guarantees (or at least comes closer to guaranteeing) a seat, and you're also certain of getting on the right bus since the ticket clerk writes the bus registration number on your ticket. This can be an important consideration because timetables at bus stations are invariably in Hindi.

A number of private bus companies run luxury buses between the major population centres and many travellers prefer these to the state buses. Fares are higher than those on the state system but the buses are faster, more comfortable and don't take standing

RAJASTHAN

passengers. Their only drawback is that some are equipped with that curse known as the video cassette recorder. As elsewhere in India, this is always played at full volume. Try to choose a bus without one of these infernal machines.

Train Travelling by train in Rajasthan was always a slow process because much of the track was metre gauge, narrower than the broad gauge as used in the rest of the country. As part of the national 'uni-gauge' drive, some of the lines have now been converted and most of the rest will be upgraded by 1998. This means that you're likely to find some parts of the rail system in Rajasthan out of action during your visit.

There are now fast broad-gauge connections between Delhi and Jaipur, Jaipur and Jodhpur, Jodhpur and Jaisalmer, and Jaipur/Jodhpur and Bikaner. The line from Jaipur to Ahmedabad should have been converted by mid-1996. Udaipur is unlikely to be broad gauge before 1997.

The RTDC *Palace on Wheels* is a special tourist train service which operates weekly tours of Rajasthan, departing from Delhi every Wednesday from September to April. The itinerary takes in Jaipur, Chittorgarh, Udaipur, Ranthambhore National Park, Jaisalmer, Jodhpur, Bharatpur and Agra. It's a hell of a lot of ground to cover in a week, but most of the travelling is done at night. In 1995 the carriages were converted to run on broad gauge, but since Udaipur is still metre gauge, the three-hour journey between Chittorgarh and Udaipur is made by bus.

Originally, this train used carriages which once belonged to various maharajas, but these became so ancient that newer carriages were refurbished to look like the originals. They were also fitted with air-conditioning. The result is a very luxurious mobile hotel, and it can be a memorable way to travel if you have limited time and limitless resources.

The cost includes tours, entry fees, accommodation on the train plus all meals. Rates

---

Tribal People of Rajasthan

The main tribes of Rajasthan are the Bhils and the Minas, who were the original inhabitants of the area now called Rajasthan, but who were forced into the Aravalli ranges by the Aryan invasion. The war-like invaders fitted into the Kshatriya caste, which was later divided into 36 Rajput clans.

Smaller tribes include the Sahariyas, Damariyas, Garasias, and the Gaduliya Lohars. The tribal people of Rajasthan now constitute around 12% of the state's population.

Bhils The Bhils are an important tribal group and traditionally inhabited the south-eastern corner of the state – the area around Udaipur, Chittorgarh and Dungarpur – although the largest concentrations of them are found in neighbouring Madhya Pradesh.

Legend has it that the Bhils were fine archers, and Bhil bowmen are mentioned in both the *Mahabharata* and the *Ramayana*. They were highly regarded as warriors, and the Rajput rulers relied on them heavily to thwart the invading Marathas and Mughals. The British even formed a Mewar Bhil Corps in the 1820s in recognition of their martial tradition.

Although originally food gatherers, the Bhils these days have taken up small-scale agriculture, or have abandoned the land altogether and taken up city residence and employment. The literacy rate of the Bhils, particularly the women, is amongst the lowest of any group in the country (7%) which has made them prime targets for exploitation and bonded labour.

The Baneshwar Festival is a Bhil festival held near Dungarpur in February each year, and large numbers of Bhils gather for four days of singing, dancing and worship. Holi is another important time for the Bhils.

Witchcraft, magic and superstition are deeply rooted aspects of Bhil culture.

Minas The Minas are the largest tribal group in the state, and are also the most widely spread, being found throughout Shekhawati and eastern Rajasthan. Originally they were a ruling tribe, but their downfall was a long drawn-out affair. It began with the Rajputs and was complete when the British government declared them a criminal tribe, mainly to stop them trying to regain their territory from the Rajputs. Their culture was totally destroyed and they have been given protection as a Scheduled Tribe.

per person per day are US$240 for triple occupancy, US$300 in a double, and US$425 for single occupancy. It's a very popular service and bookings must be made in advance at the RTDC Central Reservation Office in Delhi (☎ (011) 38-1884; fax 38-2823).

Eastern Rajasthan

JAIPUR

Population: 1.7 million
Telephone Area Code: 0141

The capital city of the state of Rajasthan is popularly known as the 'pink city' because of the pink paint applied to the buildings in its old walled city. (In Rajput culture, pink was traditionally a colour associated with hospitality.) In contrast to the cities on the Ganges plain, Jaipur has broad avenues and a remarkable harmony. The city sits on a dry lake bed in a wild and somewhat arid landscape, surrounded by barren hills surmount-ed by fortresses and crenellated walls. Jaipur long ago outstripped the confines of its city wall yet retains a less crowded and more relaxed atmosphere than its large size and population might suggest.

History

The city owes its name, its foundation and its careful planning to the great warrior-astronomer Maharaja Jai Singh II (1699-1744). His predecessors had enjoyed good relations with the Mughals and Jai Singh was careful to cultivate this alliance.

In 1727, with Mughal power on the wane, Jai Singh decided the time was ripe to move down from his somewhat cramped hillside fortress at nearby Amber to a new site on the plains. He laid out the city, with its surrounding walls and six rectangular blocks, according to principles of town planning set down in the *Shilpa-Shastra*, an ancient Hindu treatise on architecture. In 1728, he built the remarkable observatory which is still one of Jaipur's main attractions.

With the withdrawal of the Criminal Tribes Act, the Minas took to agriculture. As is the case with the Bhils, the literacy rate amongst the Minas is very low (8.3%).

The Minas are Siva worshippers, and one of their main deities is Sheetla Mata, the goddess of smallpox! Marriage is generally within the tribe. This is arranged by the parents and most marriages take place when the children are quite young.

Gaduliya Lohars The Gaduliya Lohars were originally a martial Rajput tribe, but these days are nomadic blacksmiths. Their traditional territory was Mawar (Udaipur) and they fought with the maharaja against the Mughals. With typical Rajput chivalry, they made a vow to the maharana that they would only enter his fort at Chittorgarh after he had overcome the Mughals. As he died without achieving this, the clan was forced to become nomadic. When Nehru was in power he led a group of Gaduliya Lohars into Chittorgarh fort, with the hope that they would then resettle in their former lands, but they preferred to remain nomadic.

Garasias The Garasias are a small Rajput tribe found in the Abu Road area of southern Rajasthan. It is thought that they intermingled with the Bhils to some extent, which is supported by the fact that bows and arrows are widely used.

The marriage ceremony is curious in that the couple elope, and a sum of money is paid to the father of the bride. If the marriage fails, the bride returns home, with a small sum of money to give to the father. Widows are not entitled to a share of their husband's property, and so generally remarry.

Sahariyas The Sahariyas are thought to be of Bhil origin, and inhabit the areas of Kota, Dungarpur and Sawai Madhopur in the south-east of the state. They are one of the least educated tribes in the country and, as unskilled labourers, have been cruelly exploited.

As all members of the clan are considered to be related, marriages are arranged outside the tribe. Their food and worship traditions are closely related to Hindu customs. ■

RAJASTHAN

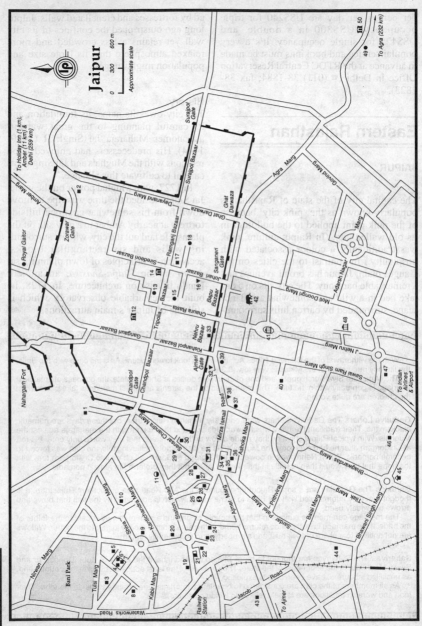

Jaipur

To Holiday Inn (1 km);
Amber (11 km) &
Delhi (259 km)

Amber Marg

Royal Gaitor

Nahargarh Fort

Bani Park

Niwan Marg

Tulsi Marg

Kabir Marg

Station Road

Kanchande Marg

Shiva Marg

Watermorks Road

Railway Station

Jacob Road

To Ajmer

Ajmer Marg

Sardar Patel Marg

Ashoka Marg

Mirza Ismail Road

Bhagwandas Marg

Tilak Marg

Bajaj Marg

Bhawani Singh Marg

Prithviraj Marg

Sansar Chandra Marg

Chandpol Gate

Chandpol Bazaar

Kishanpol Bazaar

Gangauri Bazaar

Tripolia Bazaar

Chaura Rasta

Nehru Bazaar

Bapu Bazaar

Johari Bazaar

Sireideon Bazaar

Ajmeri Gate

Sanganeri Gate

Ramganj Bazaar

Dayanand Marg

Suraipol Bazaar

Ghat Darwaza

Suraipol Gate

Ghat Darwaza

Zorawar Gate

Agra Marg

Govind Marg

Adarsh Nagar Marg

Moti Doongri Marg

J Nehru Marg

Sawai Ram Singh Marg

To Indian
Airlines
& Airport

To Agra (232 km)

Approximate scale

0   300   600 m

PLACES TO STAY		24	Hotel Gangaur Tourist Bungalow	34	Handi Restaurant
1	Hotels Bissau Palace & Khetri	26	Atithi Guest House	38	Niro's Restaurant
2	Samode Haveli Hotel	27	Neelam Hotel	**OTHER**	
3	Hotel Megh Niwas	28	Mansingh Hotel		
4	Madhuban Guest House	30	Hotel Arya Niwas	11	Bus Terminal
5	Umaid Bhawan Guest House	33	Hotel Sweet Dream	12	City Palace & Museum
		35	Jaipur Tourist Hotel	13	Jantar Mantar Observatory & Tripolia Gate
6	Marudhara Hotel	36	Evergreen Guest House		
7	Pipalda House	40	Hotel Diggi Palace	14	Hawa Mahal
8	Shapura House	43	Jai Mahal Palace Hotel	15	Gopalji ka Rasta
9	Hotel Jaipur Ashok			18	Haldion ka Rasta
10	Jaipur Inn	44	Rajmahal Palace Hotel	25	Thomas Cook
17	Hotel Kailash			31	GPO
19	Hotel Swagatam Tourist Bungalow	45	Youth Hostel	37	Raj Mandir Cinema
		46	Rambagh Palace Hotel	39	Rajasthali Emporium & Rajasthan Handloom House
20	Hotel Teej Tourist Bungalow	47	Narain Niwas Palace Hotel		
21	Hotel Rajputana Sheraton			41	Central Museum
		PLACES TO EAT		42	Zoo
22	Hotel Kaiser-I-Hind			48	Museum of Indology
23	Hotel Khasa Kothi & Government of India Tourist Office	16	LMB Restaurant	49	Vidyadharji ka Bagh
		29	Golden Sand Restaurant	50	Sisodia Rani Palace & Gardens
		32	Indian Coffee House		

Orientation

The walled 'pink city' is in the north-east of Jaipur, while the new parts have spread to the south and west. The city's main tourist attractions are in the old part of town. The principal shopping centre in the old city is Johari Bazaar, the jewellers' market. Unlike other shopping centres in narrow alleys in India and elsewhere in Asia, this one is broad and open. All seven gates into the old city remain but, unfortunately, much of the wall itself has been torn down for building material. There is now a preservation order on the remainder.

There are three main interconnecting roads in the new part of town – Mirza Ismail Rd (M I Rd), Station Rd and Sansar Chandra Marg. Along or just off these roads are most of the budget and mid-range hotels and restaurants, the railway station, the bus terminal, the GPO, many of the banks and the modern shopping centre.

Information

Tourist Offices The main tourist office (☎ 31-5714) is on platform No 1 at the railway station. The people here are very helpful and offer a range of literature. It's open daily from 6 am to 8 pm. There's also a window at platform 2 at the bus terminal, open daily except Sunday from 10 am to 5 pm.

The Government of India tourist office (☎ 37-2200) is in the Hotel Khasa Kothi and, although it has the usual range of glossy leaflets, there's little other information, so it's of limited use. It's open Monday to Friday from 9 am to 6 pm, and Saturday from 9 am to 1 pm.

Money The State Bank of India has a very quick and efficient foreign exchange counter on the 1st floor of its branch in M I Rd at the Sanganeri Gate. It's open six days a week.

Jaipur also has a number of bank branches which open later than the usual hours, such as the 'evening branch' of the State Bank of Bikaner & Jaipur opposite the GPO. It is open only from 2 to 6 pm and will change travellers' cheques.

Thomas Cook (☎ 36-0940) is on the 1st

floor in Jaipur Towers on M I Rd. It's open daily except Sunday from 9.30 am to 6 pm.

Post & Telecommunications The GPO is pretty efficient. There's a man who sets up shop in the entrance every day from 10 am to 4.30 pm and sews up parcels, sealing them with wax. He has supplies of cloth for this purpose and his prices are very reasonable.

There are numerous fax agencies in the city; and even one at the railway station, on platform No 1.

Bookshops There's an excellent range of English-language hardbacks and paperbacks as well as magazines and guidebooks at Books Corner, near Niro's Restaurant. The bookshop at the Rambagh Palace Hotel also has a good choice. A smaller but thoughtfully chosen selection can be found at the Hotel Arya Niwas.

Old City

The old city is partially encircled by a crenellated wall with seven gates – the major gates are Chandpol, Ajmeri and Sanganeri. Broad avenues, over 30 metres wide, divide the pink city into neat rectangles.

It's an extremely colourful city and, in the evening light, the pink and orange buildings have a magical glow which is complemented by the brightly clothed Rajasthanis. Cameldrawn carts are a characteristic of Jaipur's passing street scene, along with the ubiquitous Ambassador taxis and the more modern Maruti vans and cars, all jostling for space with the innumerable tempos, bicycles, autorickshaws and pedestrians.

The major landmark in this part of town is the Iswari Minar Swarga Sul, the Minaret Piercing Heaven, near the Tripolia Gate, which was built to overlook the city.

The main bazaars in the old city are Johari Bazaar (for jewellery and saris), Tripolia Bazaar (for brassware, carvings and lacquerware), Bapu Bazaar (for perfumes and textiles) and Chandpol Bazaar (for modern trinkets and bangles).

Hawa Mahal

Built in 1799, the Hawa Mahal, or Palace of the Winds, is one of Jaipur's major landmarks, although it is actually little more than a facade. This five-storey building, which looks out over the main street of the old city, is a stunning example of Rajput artistry with its pink, semioctagonal and delicately honeycombed sandstone windows. It was originally built to enable ladies of the royal household to watch the everyday life and processions of the city. You can climb to the top of the Hawa Mahal for an excellent view over the city. The palace was built by Maharaja Sawaj Pratap Singh and is part of the City Palace complex. There's a small archaeological museum on the same site.

Entrance to the Hawa Mahal is from the rear of the building. To get there, go back to the intersection on your left as you face the Hawa Mahal, turn right and then take the first right again through an archway. It's signposted and open daily from 9 am to 4.30 pm. There's an entry fee of Rs 2 – plus a whopping Rs 50 if you want to use a camera.

City Palace

In the heart of the old city, the City Palace occupies a large area divided into a series of courtyards, gardens and buildings. The outer wall was built by Jai Singh but other additions are much more recent, some dating to the start of this century. Today, the palace is a blend of Rajasthani and Mughal architecture. The former maharaja still lives in part of the palace.

The seven-storey Chandra Mahal is the centre of the palace and commands fine views over the gardens and the city. The ground and 1st floor of the Chandra Mahal form the **Maharaja Sawai Man Singh II Museum**. The apartments are maintained in luxurious order and the museum has an extensive collection of art, carpets, enamelware and old weapons. The paintings include miniatures of the Rajasthani, Mughal and Persian schools. The armoury has a collection of guns and swords dating back to the 15th century, as well as many of the ingenious and tricky weapons for which the warrior Rajputs were famous. The textile section contains dresses and costumes of the former maharajas and maharanis of Jaipur.

Other points of interest in the palace include the **Diwan-i-Am**, or Hall of Public Audiences, with its intricate decorations and manuscripts in Persian and Sanskrit, and the **Diwan-i-Khas**, or Hall of Private Audiences, with a marble-paved gallery. There is also a clock tower and the newer **Mubarak Mahal**.

Outside the buildings, you can see a large silver vessel which a former maharaja used to take drinking water with him to England. Being a devout Hindu, he could not drink the English water! The palace and museum are open daily, except on public holidays, between 9.30 am and 4.45 pm. Entry is Rs 30, plus Rs 50 if you wish to take photos with a still camera; Rs 100 for a video.

Jantar Mantar

Adjacent to the entrance to the City Palace is the Jantar Mantar, or observatory, begun by Jai Singh in 1728. Jai Singh's passion for

astronomy was even more notable than his prowess as a warrior and, before commencing construction, he sent scholars abroad to study foreign observatories. The Jaipur observatory is the largest and the best preserved of the five he built, and was restored in 1901. Others are in Delhi (the oldest, dating from 1724), Varanasi and Ujjain. The fifth, the Muttra observatory, has now disappeared.

At first glance, Jantar Mantar appears to be just a curious collection of sculptures but, in fact, each construction has a specific purpose, such as measuring the positions of stars, altitudes and azimuths, or calculating eclipses. The most striking instrument is the sundial with its 30-metre-high gnomon. The shadow this casts moves up to four metres an hour. Admission to the observatory is Rs 4; free on Monday. Hours are 9 am to 4.30 pm. Photography is discouraged by the usual Rs 50 fee.

Those interested in the theory behind the construction of these monumental instruments should buy a copy of *A Guide to the Jaipur Astronomical Observatory* by B L Dhama, which can be purchased on site.

Central Museum

This dusty collection is housed in the architecturally impressive Albert Hall in the Ram Niwas Gardens, south of the old city. The upper floor contains portraits of the Jaipur maharajas and many other miniatures and artwork. The ground floor has a collection of costumes and woodwork from different parts of Rajasthan and a description of the people and life in the rural areas of the state. The collection, which was started in 1833, is also notable for its brassware, jewellery and pottery. Entry to the museum is Rs 3, free on Monday. It is open daily (except Friday) from 10 am to 4.30 pm. No photography is allowed.

Royalty at play: ivory door panel
(18th century)

Other Attractions

The Ram Niwas Gardens also has a **zoo** with unhappy-looking animals and a small crocodile breeding farm. Jaipur has a modern **art gallery** in the 'theatre' near the zoo. To visit it you need to make enquiries as it's normally locked. **Kripal Kumbh**, B18/A Shiva Marg, where Jaipur's famous blue pottery is made, can also be visited.

The **Museum of Indology** is an odd private collection of folk art objects and other bits and pieces of interest – there's everything from a map of India painted on a rice grain, to manuscripts (one written by Aurangzeb), jewellery, fossils, coins, old currency notes, clocks, watches and much more. The museum is in fact in a private house (although the living quarters seem to have been swallowed up by the collection), and is signposted off Nehru Marg, south of the Central Museum. The owner now obviously intends to make some money out of his collection – the entry fee has risen steeply and some of the exhibits are offered for sale. It's open daily from 10 am to 5 pm. Entry is Rs 30.

Finally, if you go to only one Hindi movie while you're in India, see it at the **Raj Mandir**. This opulent and extremely well-kept cinema is a Jaipur tourist attraction in its own right and is always full, despite its immense size.

Organised Tours

Jaipur City The RTDC offers half-day and full-day bus tours of Jaipur and Amber. They visit the Hawa Mahal, Amber Fort, Jantar Mantar, City Palace and Central Museum (except Friday), and include the inevitable stop at a craftshop. Here, the processes of production are explained and you'll be persuaded to buy something. You may also be taken to the new Laxmi Narayan Temple in the hope that you'll contribute to construction costs.

The half-day tours are a little rushed but otherwise OK. If possible, take a full-day tour. Times are 8 am to 1 pm, 11.30 am to 4.30 pm and 1.30 to 6.30 pm. The full-day tours are from 9 am to 6 pm, including a lunch break at Nahagarh Fort. Half-day tours cost Rs 50, full-day tours Rs 80. They all depart from the railway station, but you can arrange to be collected from any of the RTDC hotels.

Those who want to spend more time at places in the old town than tours allow should hire an auto-rickshaw, walk, or use a bicycle.

Other Tours On Saturday and Sunday there are full-day tours to Nahargarh Fort for Rs 80, run by RTDC.

Leaving at 6 pm most evenings, there are also RTDC tours (including veg dinner) to Nahargarh Fort (Rs 75) and Chokhi Dhani (Rs 100). Check in advance to make sure these are operating.

Festivals

Jaipur's elephant festival is held in early to mid-March (depending on the lunar calendar) and is actually part of the Holi Festival. For the exact dates, see the festival calendar at the start of this chapter.

Places to Stay

Getting to the hotel of your choice in Jaipur can be a problem. Auto-rickshaw drivers besiege every traveller who arrives by train (less so if you come by bus). If you don't want to go to a hotel of their choice, they'll either refuse to take you at all or they'll demand at least double the normal fare. If you do go to the hotel of their choice, you'll pay through the nose for accommodation because the manager will be paying them a commission of at least 30% of what you are charged for a bed (and the charge won't go down for subsequent nights).

Many hotel owners cooperate with this 'mafia' but others refuse. It's very easy to find out which hotels don't cooperate – the auto-rickshaw drivers will either refuse to take you there or demand extortionate rates for transport. It's invariably cheaper and generally more satisfactory in the long run to pay double the normal fare to be taken to the hotel of your choice. If you want to stay at a mid-range hotel, you'll be charged double fare anyway because you can obviously afford it.

Most hotels will give discounts of 25% to 40% in the low season (April to September).

Places to Stay – bottom end

One of the most popular of Jaipur's budget hotels is the *Jaipur Inn* (☎ 31-6157) in Bani Park, about a km west of Chandpol Gate. It's clean, well run, helpful and friendly. It has a kitchen for guests to use or you can arrange to have meals prepared. Large dormitories cost Rs 40 per person and there's a range of rooms from Rs 80 for a single or double or Rs 120 for some slightly larger rooms. Their most expensive rooms are Rs 250/300. You can even camp on the lawn (Rs 25) if you have your own tent.

The ever-expanding *Evergreen Guest House* (☎ 36-3446), off M I Rd opposite the GPO, is another popular option. Formerly a small guest house, it's now a large hotel, complete with restaurant and buildings of various vintages arranged around a cramped garden courtyard. Because of its size the personal touch has been lost, but it's still a good place to meet other travellers. All rooms are doubles with attached bath and range from Rs 70 to Rs 120 with bucket hot water (Rs 5), and Rs 150 to Rs 250 with constant hot water; there's a dorm for Rs 50. The more expensive rooms have air-cooling and there's also a small swimming pool. If you find the Evergreen too much of a scene, check out the new *Hotel Pink Sun* by the entrance. Rooms here are Rs 120/150 with attached bath; and they have a few singles with common bath for Rs 60.

One of the most pleasant places to stay is the *Hotel Diggi Palace* (☎ 37-3091), just off Sawai Ram Singh Marg, less than a km south of Ajmeri Gate. The building is the former palace of the *thakur* (similar to a lord or baron) of Diggi, and has a huge lawn area which gives the place a very spacious and peaceful ambience. The part which has been turned into a hotel is basically the old servant's quarters, but it's quite comfortable and the facilities are good. There's a range of rooms starting at Rs 100/150, and some very nice small suites at Rs 350/400. Good meals are available.

Dating from 1882, the *Hotel Kaiser-I-Hind* (☎ 31-0195), near the station, is certainly an interesting place to stay with large dusty rooms for Rs 100/150 and vast bathrooms attached. The manager claims that this was Jaipur's first hotel. Mark Twain stayed in room No 6, Henry Ford was another guest, and Mussolini's brother-in-law was kept here as a prisoner of war. If it's all true they wouldn't recognise the place now.

Few foreigners stay at the inconveniently located 64-bed *youth hostel* (☎ 37-5455). There are tightly packed dorm beds (Rs 10 for members) as well as two double rooms for Rs 50. Another cheap option is the railway *retiring rooms* with dorm beds for Rs 30, rooms with common bath for Rs 40/80, or Rs 60/100/120 for singles/doubles/triples with attached bath.

Other cheapies include the *Marudhara Hotel*, D250 Bani Park, with singles with common bath for Rs 50, and rooms with attached bath for Rs 80/125. Nearby, and opposite the bank, *Pipalda House* (☎ 32-1912) is better with doubles with common bath for Rs 100, or Rs 200 with bath attached.

There are few places to stay within the old city. Cheapest is the *Hotel Kailash* (☎ 56-5372), across the road from the Jama Masjid. Rooms range from Rs 135/160 to Rs 245/295 all with attached bath. To the south in Nehru Bazaar is *Hotel Sweet Dream* with reasonable rooms from Rs 150/200 with bath. Checkout is 24 hours, and there's a good vegetarian restaurant on the roof.

Behind the Neelam Hotel is *Karni Niwas* (☎ 36-5433), a friendly place with rooms from Rs 175/200 with attached bath and constant hot water. They also have more expensive rooms, some with their own balconies.

At the top of this range there are four excellent places, two near M I Rd and two in Bani Park. Close to the centre is the deservedly popular *Hotel Arya Niwas* (☎ 37-2456; fax 36-4376), just off Sansar Chandra Rd. It has spotlessly clean, pleasantly furnished and decorated rooms, ranging in price from Rs 150/250 up to Rs 350/450 for deluxe rooms. All rooms have attached baths and, in the winter months, hot water. The hotel restaurant serves tasty vegetarian food at very reasonable prices. Also available are money exchange facilities, a travel agency, parking area, bicycle hire (Rs 20), a pleasant front lawn with tables and chairs and a small bookshop. For a beer, cross the road to the Hotel Mangal.

Equally good as the Arya Niwas, and with a beautiful home atmosphere, is the smaller *Atithi Guest House* (☎ 37-8679), 1 Park House Scheme, Motilal Atal Rd, between M I Rd and Station Rd. Run by the Shukla family, it's superbly maintained, squeaky clean, very friendly and it offers excellent meals. There are ordinary rooms from Rs 225/250, deluxe rooms for Rs 325/350. All rooms have air-cooling, and attached bath with hot water. The family here are very keen to please and nothing is too much trouble.

In the peaceful residential district of Bani Park is the very pleasant *Madhuban* (☎ 31-9033). This small, family-run place is well run and has a nice garden and lawn area. The air-cooled rooms all have attached bath and cost Rs 200/250, or Rs 350/400 for a large room. There are also some plush deluxe rooms with air-con for Rs 500/550. It's a very relaxing place to stay.

In the same area is *Shapura House* (☎ 31-2293), D257 Devi Marg (off Jai Singh Highway). All rooms have air-cooling and attached bath; doubles range from Rs 200 to Rs 395. They operate camel safaris and also have a horse-drawn carriage for sightseeing around Jaipur (Rs 1000 for two!).

RTDC Places Tourist accommodation places in Jaipur include two bottom-end places and one with a cheap dormitory.

The *Hotel Swagatam Tourist Bungalow* (☎ 31-0595) near the railway station is the best value, although it has something of an institutional feel to it. Dorm beds are Rs 40, singles/doubles with attached bath and constant hot water are Rs 100/150, and deluxe rooms cost Rs 200/300. Although it's close to the station it's reasonably quiet and there's a pleasant lawn.

The *Jaipur Tourist Hotel* (☎ 36-0238) is housed in the rambling former Secretariat building off M I Rd. It's shabby and in need

of renovation, but reasonable value. Dorm beds are Rs 40, single/double rooms are Rs 100/150, deluxe rooms with air-cooling are Rs 175/250; all rooms have attached bath and hot water.

Although it's a mid-range place, the *Hotel Teej Tourist Bungalow* also has dorm beds for Rs 40. See the mid-range accommodation section for full details.

Places to Stay – middle
The *Hotel Megh Niwas* (☎ 32-2661; fax 32-1018), C9 Jai Singh Highway, is in Bani Park. It has the homely atmosphere of a large guest house and is very well run and an excellent place to stay. Rooms cost Rs 400/500 with air-cooling, Rs 500/600 with air-con or Rs 850 for a suite. There's a peaceful garden and swimming pool. Meals cost Rs 60 for breakfast, Rs 110 for lunch or dinner. Also in Bani Park is the new *Umaid Bhawan Guest House* (☎ 31-6184), D1-2A. Doubles with attached bath range from Rs 250 to Rs 600; it's also very well run, spotlessly clean and there's a small garden.

Right in the heart of the old city is the *LMB Hotel* (☎ 56-5844) in Johari Bazaar. Although it's probably better known for its restaurant, the hotel does have reasonable rooms, and the location is hard to beat. All rooms have air-con, TV, fridge and attached bath with tub, and cost Rs 625/825.

Along Banasthli Marg, which connects the bus terminal on Station Rd with Sansar Chandra Rd, are a number of modern mid-range hotels including the *Hotel Archana, Hotel Kumar, Hotel Shalimar, Hotel Gauray, Hotel Goyal, Hotel Kohinoor, Hotel Purohit* and the *Hotel Sagar*. In the same area is the *Neelam Hotel*. They all offer much the same facilities and are similarly priced – expect to pay upwards of Rs 300/400.

The *Hotel Bissau Palace* (☎ 31-7628) is full of old-world charm and is surrounded by its own well-maintained gardens. The rooms, however, vary greatly; some are very pleasant while others are definitely not as good. Prices have risen dramatically and it now costs Rs 495/660 for air-cooled rooms.

PAUL BEINSSEN

PAUL BEINSSEN

PAUL BEINSSEN

Rajasthan, Pushkar Camel Fair
Top: Rajasthani men with their camels.
Bottom Left: Camel sellers.
Bottom Right: Snake charmer.

RICHARD I'ANSON

Tribal women at the Pushkar Camel Fair, Rajasthan.

The hotel has a restaurant, swimming pool (not always filled), tennis court and library. The approach to this place is along one of the dirtiest streets in the city.

The *Hotel Khasa Kothi* (☎ 37-5151) was a former minor palace and, before that, the state hotel. Although it's in need of a major revamp, the huge gardens and lawns are quiet and relaxing. Huge rooms, all with air-cooling and attached bath, range from Rs 570/680 up to Rs 1500. Facilities include a swimming pool, money exchange, the Government of India tourist office, a bar and restaurant.

The *Narain Niwas Palace Hotel* (☎ 56-3448) is a very interesting and peaceful place to stay. In the south of the city, it's yet another former palace, surrounded by the obligatory large garden. The four suites (Rs 1150) are huge and filled with ancient furniture and fittings; some even have four-poster beds. There's an annex, modern but decorated in style with wall paintings. Rooms here are Rs 650/865. Meals are available at Rs 70/140/140 for breakfast/lunch/dinner. The owners also operate the similarly priced *Royal Castle Kanota*, 15 km from Jaipur on the Agra road.

RTDC Places The RTDC *Hotel Teej Tourist Bungalow* (☎ 37-4373) is at Bani Park Circle, within walking distance of both the bus and railway stations. Air-cooled rooms cost Rs 250/350, air-con rooms are Rs 400/550. All the rooms have bath and hot water, and there's a bar and restaurant.

The RTDC *Hotel Gangaur Tourist Bungalow* (☎ 37-1641) is just off Sansar Chandra Rd. It's seems to be better maintained than the average RTDC place. Deluxe singles/doubles cost Rs 200/250, air-cooled rooms are Rs 300/350 and air-con rooms are Rs 400/500, all with bath and hot water. It's a bit noisy but there's a pleasant sunny courtyard, a restaurant, 24-hour coffee shop and bar.

Places to Stay – top end
The superb *Samode Haveli* (☎ & fax 42-407) is in the north-east corner of the old city. This

200-year-old building was once the town house of the *rawal* (nobleman) of Samode, who was also prime minister of Jaipur. It has a beautiful open terrace area, a stunning painted dining room, and a couple of amazing suites – one totally covered with original mirrorwork, the other one painted. The charge is Rs 1000/1200 for ordinary rooms, or Rs 1100/1800 for the suites. It's the perfect film set, and was, in fact, a location for the movie *Far Pavilions*. The Samode Haveli is a delightful place to stay, much better than some of the more expensive places below.

The *Rambagh Palace* (☎ 38-1919; fax 38-1098) is one of India's most prestigious and romantic hotels, offering the elegance of cool white marble, endless terraces overlooking manicured lawns, fountains and browsing peacocks. Formerly the palace of the maharaja of Jaipur, it's now operated by the Taj Group. It's an impressive place to stay by any standards, although some find the sumptuousness overdone – the dining room decor is likely to induce indigestion. The cheapest singles/doubles are US$140/160, but they are poor value. The luxury rooms, at US$275, are much more sumptuous and spacious – if you're going to splurge, take one of these. Prices go right up to US$625 for the royal suites. However, it's important to note that, even within the same price category, some rooms are much nicer than others. Try to see more than one. From May to July prices of the cheaper rooms drop by around 40%. If you can't afford to stay here, at least come for an evening drink at the terrace bar.

Only a little more modest, and also part of the Taj Group, is the very pleasant *Jai Mahal Palace Hotel* (☎ 37-1616; fax 36-5237) on the corner of Jacob Rd and Ajmer Marg, south of the railway station. This building also used to belong to the maharaja of Jaipur, and has rooms ranging from US$115/135 all the way up to US$425 for luxury suites. From May to September the cheapest rooms are a bargain US$38/55. There's a swimming pool, coffee lounge, bar and a restaurant serving Indian and Western food.

Smallest of the Taj Group's hotels in Jaipur, the *Rajmahal Palace* (☎ 52-1757) on Sardar Patel Marg in the south of the city is yet another former important building, this time the former British Residency. It is by no means as luxurious as the previous two, but it still offers top of the range facilities, such as a swimming pool and a quality restaurant. It's a much more personal place as it has just 13 rooms and suites, and these cost US$65/85 (US$38/55 from May to September), or US$250 for the suites. The huge forecourt is used for wedding receptions.

The *Rajputana Sheraton* (☎ 36-0011; fax 36-7848), Palace Rd, is within walking distance of the railway station in the centre of town. It's a modern five-star deluxe hotel, tastefully designed and built around a swimming pool. Rooms range from US$125/140 right up to US$700.

The *Hotel Clarks Amer* (☎ 55-0616), Jawaharlal Nehru Marg, is less expensive at Rs 1195/2380, but about 10 km south of the centre of town. It is air-conditioned, and has a pool, 24-hour coffee shop, sauna and a restaurant.

There are several other modern, upmarket hotels. The new *Holiday Inn* (☎ 45-897) is in bleak surroundings just north of the old city on Amber Rd. Clean and comfortable rooms cost from Rs 1800/2000. The *Mansingh Hotel* (☎ 37-8771), off Sansar Chandra Rd in the centre of town, has rooms from Rs 1195/2390, and a swimming pool. The ITDC *Hotel Jaipur Ashok* (☎ 32-0091), Jai Singh Circle, Bani Park, is one of those hotels which was fine when it first opened but has been on the decline ever since. Rooms are Rs 1195/1750, and there's a pool that non-guests can use for Rs 100.

Places to Eat

Two restaurants stand out above the others in Jaipur. The best place for non-veg food is *Niro's* on M I Rd, popular with Indians and Westerners alike. It's so popular, in fact, that you may have to wait for a table; since service is fast you don't usually have to wait long. Main dishes range from Rs 70 to Rs 100 and ingredients are of a high quality.

They offer Indian, Chinese and Continental dishes.

For food which 'promotes longevity, intelligence, vigour, health and cheerfulness', head for *LMB* (Laxmi Mishthan Bhandar) in Johari Bazaar, near the centre of the old city. This is the city's best vegetarian restaurant; it also has amazingly pristine '50s 'hip' decor – definitely worth seeing. Main dishes range from Rs 35 to Rs 50. A dessert speciality is LMB kulfi, including dry fruits, saffron and cottage cheese. Out the front, a snack counter serves good snacks and excellent ice cream and offers a wide range of Indian sweets.

Near Niro's are two more good vegetarian places. *Natraj Restaurant* is also famous for its sweets and namkin, and further up M I Rd, *Chanakya Restaurant* is more expensive. A veg steak sizzler (totally veg) is Rs 80; but most other main dishes are around Rs 40.

In the same area, opposite the GPO, is the *Handi Restaurant*, which has excellent barbecue chicken and kebabs in the evening, although it is open at lunchtimes as well. It's tucked away at the back of the Maya Mansions building. Don't confuse this place with the Bamboo Hut Handi Restaurant (in the grounds of the Jaipur Tourist Hotel) which is not as good.

For really cheap food in the same area, you could try one of the cheap eating houses, known as *bhojnalyas*, on the other side of the road, just along from the post office. There are plenty of similar places right outside the railway station, and on Station Rd, not far from the bus terminal, is the very popular *Shree Shanker Bhojnalya*, for cheap bottomless thalis.

If you are suffering withdrawal symptoms from lack of a decent cup of coffee, head for the *Indian Coffee House* on M I Rd. It's one of the chain found all over the country, and here too the waiters are all trussed up in cummerbunds and turbans. It's a good place for snacks, breakfast and, of course, coffee. It's tucked away off the street, in a narrow arcade next to Snowhite Drycleaners.

Near the Arya Niwas, the *Golden Sand Restaurant* has quite good non-veg food at prices that are similar to Niro's. For Chinese food there's the *Golden Dragon Chinese Restaurant* down the side street next to Niro's. It's nothing flash but the prices are reasonable and the food tasty.

Local licensing laws mean that only hotels can serve alcohol. This piece of legislation has been skillfully circumvented by some restaurants and beer may be served in glasses shrouded in paper napkins – or even served in a teapot and drunk out of cups. 'Special Tea', they call it!

For a splurge, you couldn't find more opulent surroundings that the dining room at the *Rambagh Palace*, although the food gets mixed reports. Main dishes are around Rs 140, jumbo tandoori prawns are Rs 325.

Things to Buy

Jaipur is well known for precious stones, which seem cheaper here than elsewhere in India, and is even better known for semi-precious stones. For precious stones, find a narrow alley called Haldion ka Rasta off Johari Bazaar (near the Hawa Mahal). Semi-precious stones are sold in another alley, called the Gopalji ka Rasta, on the opposite side of the street. There are many shops here which offer bargain prices, but you do need to know your gems.

Shops around the City Palace and Hawa Mahal are likely to be more expensive, although they do have many interesting items including miniatures and clothes. Marble statues, jewellery and textile prints are other Jaipur specialities. The Rajasthali government emporium in M I Rd is reasonably priced; it has a branch in Amber as well as a workshop/sales outlet en route where RTDC tour buses stop.

Jaipur's salespeople are hard-working and very persuasive, so take care. Most rickshaw-wallahs are heavily into the commission business and you can be sure that they'll be getting a large cut from any shop they take you to. Many unwary visitors get talked into buying things for resale at inflated prices. Beware of these 'buy now to sell at a profit later' scams – see the warning under Things to Buy in the Facts for the Visitor chapter for more details.

For fixed-price *khadi* (homespun cloth)

Embroidery: a popular souvenir

and cotton, there are two good places to try. For khadi, the Khadi Gramodyog shops are the best bet. These government-run shops have a wide range and everything is hand-made. There's one just inside Sanganeri Gate in Bapu Bazaar, and another at the Panchbatti intersection. For cotton there's the Rajasthan Handloom House on M I Rd, next to the Rajasthali Emporium.

Getting There & Away

Air The Indian Airlines office (☎ 51-4407) in Jaipur is on Tonk Rd. The Air India office (☎ 36-5559) is in Rattan Mansion on M I Rd. Numerous international airlines have offices in Jaipur Towers on M I Rd.

Indian Airlines (IA) flies Delhi-Jaipur (US$28) at least daily, and all flights continue to Bombay, via any one or all of Jodhpur (US$34), Udaipur (US$35) and Aurangabad (US$79). There's also a direct flight to and from Bombay (US$98) three times weekly. For the same prices as IA, ModiLuft has daily flights to Delhi, Udaipur,

Bombay and Cochin (US$186). Jagsan Airlines flies between Delhi, Jaipur and Kota (US$44) three times weekly. East West Airlines has flights between Bombay, Jodhpur and Jaipur five times a week.

Bus Buses to all Rajasthan's main population centres and to Delhi and Agra are operated by the Rajasthan State Transport Corporation (RSTC) from the bus terminal. Some services are deluxe (essentially nonstop). The deluxe buses all leave from platform No 3, which is tucked away in the right-hand rear corner of the bus terminal yard. These buses should be booked in advance, and the booking office, open from 8 am to 10 pm, is also at platform 3.

State transport deluxe buses depart every 15 minutes for Delhi (Rs 125, 5½ hours). There are also ordinary buses for Rs 68 and air-con coaches for Rs 215. There are frequent departures for the five-hour trip to Agra (Rs 72 deluxe, Rs 101 air-con). Deluxe buses run eight times a day to Ajmer (Rs 38, 2½ hours). Six deluxe buses per day take seven hours to reach Jodhpur and cost Rs 101. To Udaipur, there are four deluxe buses daily; they take about 10 hours and cost Rs 120. There are also six buses daily to Kota (Rs 77, five hours). For Jaisalmer there's an ordinary bus (Rs 155, 15 hours) leaving at 5 am, and also a faster night bus (Rs 190, 13 hours) leaving around 9 pm.

A number of private companies cover the same routes, and also offer services to Ahmedabad, other cities in Gujarat and Bombay. These companies have their own depots, but the most useful collection is opposite the Neelam Hotel on Motilal Atal Rd, just off M I Rd. The buses are not as frequent as those operated by the RSTC and often travel at night. Avoid video buses unless you want a thumping headache the next morning.

Train Many of the lines into Jaipur have been converted to broad gauge. As other parts of the state's railway are converted expect disruptions to services.

The computerised railway reservation office, at the station entrance, is open Monday to Saturday from 8 am to 8 pm, and Sunday from 8 am to 2 pm. Join the queue for 'Freedom Fighters & Foreign Tourists'. For metre-gauge trains the booking office is on platform No 6.

There's a swift *Shatabdi Express* service leaving New Delhi station at 5.50 am, reaching Jaipur at 10.15 am, and then departing at 5.50 pm to reach New Delhi at 10.15 pm. It runs daily except Thursday and tickets cost Rs 300/600 for chair car/1st class. There's also a new *Intercity* service on the same route, leaving daily from Jaipur at 5.30 am.

Since schedules will be changing as broad-gauge conversion proceeds you need to enquire about trains such as the *Pink City Express* which used to leave Old Delhi at 6 am for Jaipur, and the overnight *Ahmedabad Mail* and *Chetak Express*. The 308-km journey costs Rs 72/262 in 2nd/1st class.

The daily superfast express between Jaipur and Agra (the *Jaipur-Agra Fort Express*) takes under five hours. It leaves Jaipur at 6.10 am and Agra at 5 pm, and reservations should be made one day in advance. Fares for the 208-km journey are Rs 53/189 in 2nd/1st class. There are plenty of express trains to Ajmer, Abu Road and Ahmedabad.

For Jodhpur, there's the *Intercity* service leaving Jodhpur at 5.30 am, arriving in Jaipur at 10.30 am, departing at 5.30 pm and reaching Jodhpur again at 10.30 pm. Fares for the 318-km trip are Rs 86 in 2nd class, Rs 211 in chair car.

To Udaipur, there's the metre-gauge *Garib Nawar Express* that leaves Jaipur at 12.15 pm, arriving in Udaipur at 10.30 pm. The 431-km journey costs Rs 94/352 in 2nd/1st class.

There are also daily connections with Sawai Madhopur (3½ hours) and Bikaner (519 km, 10 hours).

Getting Around

To/From the Airport The airport is 15 km out of town. The airport bus costs Rs 20; a taxi costs about Rs 120.

Local Transport Jaipur has taxis (unmetered), auto-rickshaws and a city bus service, which also operates to Amber. A cycle-rickshaw from the station to the Jaipur Inn or Arya Niwas Hotel should cost about Rs 6, and from the station to Johari Bazaar, Rs 12, or Rs 12 and Rs 18 for an auto-rickshaw on these trips. However, if you're going to a hotel with your baggage and the hotel doesn't pay the driver's commission, you'll be extremely lucky to get a ride for these prices. In such cases, expect to pay two to three times the usual price. If they quote you the normal fare to a hotel whose rates you don't know, it probably means they're guaranteed an especially big commission at your expense.

Bicycles can be hired from several of the budget hotels, as well as from the Arya Niwas Hotel, at Rs 20 per day.

AROUND JAIPUR

There are several attractions around Jaipur, including some on the road between Jaipur and Amber. Jaipur tours usually stop at some of these sites on the way to or from Amber.

Amber

Situated about 11 km out of Jaipur on the Delhi to Jaipur road, Amber was once the ancient capital of Jaipur state. Construction of the fortress-palace was begun in 1592 by Raja Man Singh, the Rajput commander of Akbar's army. It was later extended and completed by the Jai Singhs before the move to Jaipur on the plains below. The fort is a superb example of Rajput architecture, stunningly situated on a hillside and overlooking a lake which reflects its terraces and ramparts.

You can climb up to the fort from the road in 10 minutes, and cold drinks are available within the palace if the climb is a hot one. A seat in a jeep up to the fort costs Rs 15. Riding up on elephants is popular, though daylight robbery at Rs 250 per elephant one way (each can carry up to four people). A quick ride around the palace courtyard costs about Rs 20.

An imposing stairway leads to the **Diwan-i-Am**, or Hall of Public Audiences, with a double row of columns and latticed galleries above. Steps to the right lead to the small **Kali Temple**. There is also the white marble **Sila Devi Temple**.

The maharaja's apartments are on the higher terrace – you enter through a gateway decorated with mosaics and sculptures. The **Jai Mandir**, or Hall of Victory, is noted for its inlaid panels and glittering mirror ceiling. Regrettably, much of this was allowed to deteriorate during the '70s and '80s but restoration work proceeds. Opposite the Jai Mandir is the **Sukh Niwas**, or Hall of Pleasure, with an ivory-inlaid sandalwood door, and a channel running right through the room which once carried cooling water. From the Jai Mandir you can enjoy the fine views from the palace ramparts over the lake below.

Amber palace is open from 9 am to 4.30 pm and entry costs Rs 4. Photographers are hit with the usual steep Rs 50 charge (Rs 100 for a video).

Getting There & Away A bus to Amber from the Hawa Mahal in Jaipur costs Rs 2.50. The trip takes under half an hour and buses depart every few minutes.

Galtor

The **cenotaphs** of the royal family are at Gaitor, 6.5 km from Jaipur on the road to Amber. The white marble cenotaph of Maharaja Jai Singh II is the most impressive and is decorated with carved peacocks. Next to it is the cenotaph of his son.

Opposite the cenotaphs is the **Jal Mahal** (Water Palace) in the middle of a lake and reached by a causeway. Or at least it was in the middle of a lake; the water is now all but squeezed out by the insidious weed, water hyacinth. There is another Royal Gaitor just outside the Jaipur city walls.

Tiger Fort

The Nahargarh Fort overlooks the city from a sheer ridge to the north, and is floodlit at night. The fort was built in 1734 and extended in 1868. An eight-km road runs up through the hills from Jaipur, and the fort can be reached along a zigzagging two-km path.

The views fully justify the effort, and the entry fee is only Rs 2.

There's a small restaurant on the top, and this is a great place to come at sunset. You can even stay here, although there's only one double room (Rs 250) which must be booked at the tourist office in Jaipur.

Jaigarh Fort

The imposing Jaigarh Fort, built in 1726 by Jai Singh, was only opened to the public in mid-1983. It's within walking distance of Amber and offers a great view over the plains from the Diwa Burj watchtower. The fort, with its water reservoirs, residential areas, puppet theatre and the cannon, Jaya Vana, is open from 9 am to 4.30 pm.

Samode

The small village of Samode is nestled amongst rugged hills about 50 km north of Jaipur, via Chomu. The only reason to visit it is if you can afford to stay in the beautiful **Samode Palace** (although strictly speaking it's not actually a palace, as it wasn't owned by a ruler but by one of his noblemen). Like the Samode Haveli in Jaipur, this building was owned by the rawal of Samode. It's a beautiful building built on three levels, each with its own courtyard. The highlight of the building is the absolutely exquisite Diwan-i-Khas, which is covered with completely original painting and mirrorwork, and is probably the finest example of its kind in the country. Unfortunately the palace is open only to guests, and public transport (overloaded jeeps from Chomu) is infrequent and risky.

To stay in the palace (☎ (01423) 4114; fax 4123) will cost you Rs 1195/1800, or there are suites for Rs 2200. Breakfast is available for Rs 130, while lunch and dinner are Rs 225. There's also luxurious tented accommodation three km away at *Samode Bagh*. Bookings can be made through the Samode Haveli in Jaipur.

Galta

The temple of the sun god at Galta is 100 metres above the city to the east, a 2.5-km climb from the Surajpol. A deep temple-filled gorge stands behind the temple and there are fine views over the surrounding plain.

Sisodia Rani Palace & Gardens

Six km from the city on the Agra road and surrounded by terraced gardens, this palace was built for Maharaja Jai Singh's second wife, the Sisodia princess. The outer walls are decorated with murals depicting hunting scenes and the Krishna legend.

Vidyadharji ka Bagh

Nestled in a narrow valley, this beautiful garden was built in honour of Jai Singh's chief architect and town planner, Vidyadhar.

Balaji

The Hindu exorcism temple of Balaji is about 1.5 km off the Jaipur to Agra road, about 1½ hours by bus from Bharatpur. The exorcisms are sometimes very violent and those being exorcised don't hesitate to discuss their experiences. Buses leave for Balaji from the bus station in Delhi.

Sanganer

The small town of Sanganer is 16 km south of Jaipur and is entered through the ruins of two *tripolias*, or triple gateways. In addition to its ruined palace, Sanganer has a group of Jain temples with fine carvings to which entry is restricted. The town is noted for handmade paper and block printing.

BHARATPUR

Telephone Area Code: 05644

A must for those with an interest in ornithology, Bharatpur is famous for its World Heritage-listed bird sanctuary, the Keoladeo Ghana National Park. The best time to visit the sanctuary is from October to February when many migratory birds can be seen, though population densities differ from year to year.

In the 17th and 18th centuries, the town was an important Jat stronghold. Before the arrival of the Rajputs, the Jats inhabited this area and were able to retain a high degree of autonomy, both because of their prowess in battle and because of their chiefs' marriage alliances with Rajput nobility. They successfully opposed the Mughals on more than one occasion and their fort at Bharatpur, constructed in the 18th century, withstood an attack by the British in 1805 and a long siege in 1825. This siege eventually led to the signing of the first treaty of friendship between the Indian states of north-west India and the East India Company.

The town itself, which was once surrounded by an 11-km-long wall (now demolished), is of little interest. Bring insect repellent with you as mosquitoes can be a problem.

Information

The tourist office (☎ 22-545) is at the Hotel Saras. A guidebook including a map is available at the park entrance. It contains a short history of the park and a seemingly endless list of bird species, but is otherwise of little help to anyone without an understanding of ornithology.

You can change travellers' cheques at the State Bank of Bikaner & Jaipur or at the Ashok Forest Lodge.

Keoladeo Ghana National Park

No less than 415 kinds of birds have been

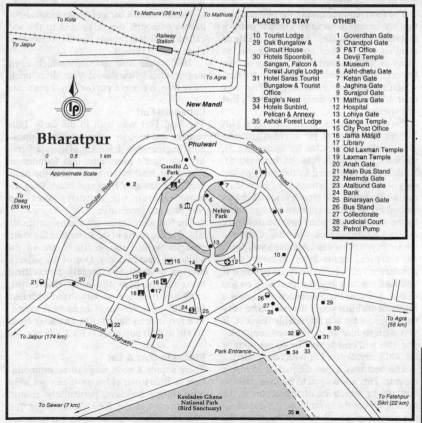

Bharatpur

0   0.5   1 km
Approximate Scale

PLACES TO STAY		OTHER	
10	Tourist Lodge	1	Goverdhan Gate
29	Dak Bungalow & Circuit House	2	Chandpol Gate
30	Hotels Spoonbill, Sangam, Falcon & Forest Jungle Lodge	3	P&T Office
		4	Deviji Temple
		5	Museum
		6	Asht-dhatu Gate
31	Hotel Saras Tourist Bungalow & Tourist Office	7	Ketan Gate
		8	Jaghina Gate
		9	Surajpol Gate
33	Eagle's Nest	11	Mathura Gate
34	Hotels Sunbird, Pelican & Annexy	12	Hospital
		13	Lohiya Gate
35	Ashok Forest Lodge	14	Ganga Temple
		15	City Post Office
		16	Jama Masjid
		17	Library
		18	Old Laxman Temple
		19	Laxman Temple
		20	Anah Gate
		21	Main Bus Stand
		22	Neemda Gate
		23	Atalbund Gate
		24	Bank
		25	Binarayan Gate
		26	Bus Stand
		27	Collectorate
		28	Judicial Court
		32	Petrol Pump

recorded at the Keoladeo sanctuary, 117 of which migrate from as far away as Siberia and China. The sanctuary was formerly a vast semi-arid region, filling during the monsoon season only to rapidly dry up afterwards. To prevent this, the maharaja of Bharatpur diverted water from a nearby irrigation canal and, within a few years, birds began to settle in vast numbers. Naturally, his primary concern was not the environment but, rather, his desire to take guests on shooting sprees. A 'bag' of over 4000 birds per day was not unusual. The carnage continued until shooting was banned in 1964 and, today, some 80 types of ducks are among the species which nest in the sanctuary.

The food requirements of the bird population can be enormous and it's hard to believe that these shallow lakes would be capable of meeting it – yet they do. For example, as many as 3000 painted storks nesting in a sq km need about three tonnes of fish every day, which amounts to over 90 tonnes of fish over their 40-day nesting period – and that's just one species.

Entry costs Rs 25, plus Rs 10 for a still camera and Rs 100 for a video camera. There's also an entry fee for cycles (Rs 3), scooters (Rs 10) and cycle-rickshaws (Rs 5). Vehicles are prohibited in the park, so the only way of getting around is by bicycle or cycle-rickshaw. Only those cycle-rickshaws authorised by the government (recognisable by the yellow plate bolted onto the front) are allowed inside the park – beware of anyone who tells you otherwise! Although you don't pay entry fees for the drivers of these cycle-rickshaws, you'll be up for Rs 25 per hour if you take one and they'll expect a tip on top of that. Some of the drivers actually know a lot about the birds you'll see and can be very helpful, so a tip is a reasonable request. If you wish to hire an experienced ornithologist, this will cost around Rs 40 per hour or Rs 300 a day. Sohan Lal is recommended.

The best way to see the park is to hire a bicycle. This allows you to easily avoid the bottlenecks which inevitably occur at the nesting sites of the larger birds. It's just about the only way you'll be able to watch the numerous kingfishers at close quarters – noise or human activity frightens them away. You can also avoid clocking up a large bill with a rickshaw driver. Some of the hotels rent bicycles; otherwise, they can be hired from near the Hotel Saras, but these are not cheap at Rs 30 per day. If you plan to visit the sanctuary at dawn (one of the best times to see the birds), you'll have to hire your bicycle the day before. The southern reaches of the park are virtually devoid of *humanus touristicus* and so are much better than the northern part for serious bird-watching.

Boats can be hired from the ticket checkpoint for Rs 60 per day. They are a very good way of getting close to the wildlife in this park.

There's a snack bar and drinks kiosk about halfway through the park, next to the so-called Keoladeo Temple (hardly a temple – more a small shrine).

This is one bird sanctuary which even non-ornithologists should visit. It is open daily from 6 am to 6 pm (exit by 7 pm).

Lohagarh Fort

The Iron Fort was built in the early 18th century and took its name from its supposedly impregnable defences. Maharaja Suraj Mal, the fort's constructor and founder of Bharatpur, built two towers within the ramparts, the Jawahar Burj and Fateh Burj, to commemorate his victories over the Mughals and the British.

The fort occupies the entire small artificial island in the centre of the town, and the three palaces within its precincts are in an advanced state of decay. One of the palaces houses a small and largely unexciting museum; perhaps the most interesting exhibit is the huge *punkah* (hand-operated fan) still in place in one of the upstairs rooms. The fort is open Saturday to Thursday from 10 am to 4.30 pm; entry is Rs 2.

Places to Stay & Eat

There's quite a good range of accommodation in Bharatpur, although it can get very busy during holidays, particularly around Christmas and the New Year. Since the railway station is about seven km from the park, it's best to stay somewhere between Mathura Gate and the park entrance.

A place that's popular with travellers is the friendly little *Tourist Lodge* (☎ 23-742), near Mathura Gate. There are singles/doubles with common bath for Rs 40/60, or from Rs 50/70 with bath attached. Hot water is by the bucket, and there's a restaurant. Bikes can be rented for Rs 30, binoculars for Rs 30. The *Shagun Tourist Home*, inside Mathura Gate, is run by a friendly guy who charges Rs 60 for double rooms.

There's a line of places between the main road and the park entrance. The RTDC *Hotel Saras Tourist Bungalow* (☎ 23-700) is right by the road and so cops a fair amount of traffic noise. It's also unfriendly and badly maintained – not a great choice. Dorm beds are Rs 40, singles/doubles range from Rs 200/250 to Rs 450/550 with air-con. There's a restaurant and bar. Directly opposite is the *Hotel Eagle's Nest* with 12 rooms, ridiculously overpriced at Rs 450/600. Not surprisingly it's often empty; you should be able to bargain these prices down by around 40%.

Further along the road is the *Hotel Sunbird*, but the four rooms in this popular little place fill up quickly. They are clean with attached bath and constant hot water and cost Rs 200/250. Nearby is the *Hotel Pelican*, run by the same people as the Tourist Lodge. There are basic rooms with common bath for Rs 50/75, or for Rs 125/150 with attached bath and hot water. It's also a good place to rent bikes.

Next is the *Annexy*, with rooms from Rs 50/80 with common bath, and more expensive rooms with attached bath. The outdoor restaurant here is an excellent place to eat, and the staff are very friendly. In the eucalyptus grove beside the Annexy is the *Keoladeo Resort*, a tented camp for Rs 40/60. Cover yourself from head to toe in mosquito repellent if you're going to stay here.

Just behind the Hotel Saras is the *Spoonbill Hotel & Restaurant*. There are just two rooms, both with bathroom attached. They charge Rs 100 downstairs, Rs 200 for the larger one upstairs. Good meals are available and they rent bikes for Rs 20. Further along

this road are: the *Forest Jungle Lodge*, with new rooms from Rs 100 with attached bath; the *Hotel Sangam*, where rooms cost Rs 175/250; and the similarly priced *Hotel Falcon*.

You have to pay for the privilege of staying in the national park itself. The ITDC *Ashok Forest Lodge* (☎ 22-722) is about one km beyond the entrance gate. It's a very pleasant hotel but not cheap at Rs 1195/2000 from October to April or Rs 900/1200 for the rest of the year. Meals are available (buffet lunch or dinner costs Rs 275) and there's also a bar.

All the other hotels are much closer to the railway station. They also seem to pay the rickshaw drivers commission, so you pay more. These hotels include the *Hotel Alora* (☎ 22-616), Kumher Gate; the *Hotel Avadh* (☎ 22-462), Kumher Gate; the *Hotel Tourist Complex*; the *Hotel Nannd* (☎ 23-119); and the *Hotel Kohinoor* (☎ 23-733). The *Park Palace Hotel* (☎ 23-222) near Kumher Gate is a good, clean and friendly place, charging around Rs 250 for a double with bath.

Getting There & Away

Bus Bharatpur is on the Agra to Jaipur road, just two hours by bus from Agra or an hour from Fatehpur Sikri – buses cost about Rs 7. The Fatehpur Sikri buses pass the front door of the Hotel Saras Tourist Bungalow and will stop there if you ask.

Buses from Jaipur take about 4½ hours and the fare is Rs 40. However, as the RSTC seems to select their most decrepit buses for this run, the train is preferable.

Train Bharatpur is on the Delhi to Bombay broad-gauge line as well as the Delhi-Agra-Jaipur-Ahmedabad metre-gauge line, ensuring a good choice of trains. Be certain that the one you choose is going to stop at Bharatpur – not all trains do. The line between Jaipur and Agra is currently being converted to broad gauge so you may find it closed. The 188-km journey from Jaipur costs Rs 48/178 in 2nd/1st class.

Getting Around

You can use tongas, auto-rickshaws and cycle-rickshaws to get around town, and the state tourist office has a minibus (see the tourist officer). You can hire bicycles for Rs 20 to Rs 30 a day.

DEEG

Population: 38,000

Very few travellers ever make it to Deeg, about 36 km north of Bharatpur. This is unfortunate because this small town with its massive fortifications, stunningly beautiful palace and busy market is much more interesting than Bharatpur itself. It's an easy day trip from Bharatpur, Agra or Mathura.

Built by Suraj Mal in the mid-18th century, Deeg was formerly the second capital of Bharatpur state and the site of a famous battle in which the maharaja's forces successfully withstood a combined Mughal and Maratha army of some 80,000 men. Eight years later, the maharaja even had the temerity to attack the Red Fort in Delhi! The booty he carried off included an entire marble building which can still be seen.

Gopal Bhavan

Suraj Mal's palace, Gopal Bhavan, has to be one of India's most beautiful and delicately proportioned buildings. It's also in an excellent state of repair and, as it was used by the maharajas until the early 1970s, most of the rooms still contain their original furnishings.

Built in a combination of Rajput and Mughal architectural styles, the palace fronts onto a tank, the Gopal Sagar, and is flanked by two exquisite pavilions which were designed to resemble pleasure barges. The tank and palace are surrounded by well-maintained gardens which also contain the Keshav Bhavan, or Summer Pavilion, with its hundreds of fountains, many of which are still functional though only turned on for local festivals.

The palace is open daily from 8 am to noon and 1 to 7 pm; admission is free. Deeg's massive walls (up to 28 metres high) and 12 bastions, some with their cannons still in place, are also worth exploring.

As Deeg is essentially an agricultural town and few visitors ever come here with the intention of stopping overnight, the choice of accommodation is very limited. The *Deeg Dak Bungalow* is a possibility, with beds for around Rs 20.

SARISKA TIGER RESERVE & NATIONAL PARK

Situated 107 km from Jaipur and 200 km from Delhi, the sanctuary is in a wooded valley surrounded by barren mountains. It covers 800 sq km (including a core area of 498 sq km) and has blue bulls, sambar, spotted deer, wild boar and, above all, tigers. Project Tiger (see the boxed section in the Uttar Pradesh chapter for more information) has been in charge of the sanctuary since 1979.

As at Ranthambhore National Park, also in Rajasthan, this park contains ruined temples as well as a fort, pavilions and a palace (now a hotel) built by the maharajas of Alwar, the former owners of this area. The sanctuary can be visited year-round, except during July/August when the animals move to higher ground, but the best time is between November and June.

You'll see most wildlife in the evening, though tiger sightings are becoming more common during the day. The best way to see game is to book a 'hide' overlooking one of the waterholes. Take along food, drink and a sleeping bag (mattresses are provided).

Places to Stay

Most travellers stay at the RTDC *Hotel Tiger Den* (☎ (0144) 41-342). It is very good, but somewhat expensive at Rs 200/250 for ordinary singles/doubles, Rs 300/400 with air-cooling and Rs 500/550 with air-con, though they do have a Rs 40 dormitory. The hotel has a bar and restaurant. There's also a very pleasant *Forest Rest House* where rooms cost Rs 200.

The *Hotel Sariska Palace* (☎ (0144) 41-322), at the park entrance, is the imposing former hunting lodge of the maharajas of Alwar. Rooms are US$35/46 with air-con;

all rooms have heating in winter and attached bathrooms with constant hot water. There's a bar and restaurant so, even if you don't stay here, it warrants a visit.

Getting There & Away
Sariska is 35 km from Alwar, which is a convenient town from which to approach the sanctuary. There are direct buses to Alwar from Delhi (170 km) and Jaipur (146 km). Though some people attempt to visit Sariska on a day trip from Jaipur, this option is expensive and largely a waste of time.

ALWAR
Population: 235,000
Telephone Area Code: 0144

Alwar was once an important Rajput state, which emerged in the 18th century under Pratap Singh, who pushed back the rulers of Jaipur to the south and the Jats of Bharatpur to the east, and who successfully resisted the Marathas. It was one of the first Rajput states to ally itself with the fledgling British Empire, though British interference in Alwar's internal affairs meant that this partnership was not always amicable.

There is a tourist office (☎ 21-868) near the Purjan Vihar Garden.

Bala Quila
This huge fort, with its five km of ramparts, stands 300 metres above the city. Predating the time of Pratap Singh, it's one of very few forts in Rajasthan constructed before the rise of the Mughals. Unfortunately, because the fort now houses a radio transmitter station, it can only be visited with special permission.

Palace Complex
Below the fort sprawls the huge city palace complex, its massive gates and tank lined by a beautifully symmetrical chain of *ghats* and pavilions. Today, most of the complex is occupied by government offices, but there is a museum (closed on Friday) housed in the former City Palace. Examples of miniature writing, miniature paintings of the Bundi school and ivory, sandalwood and jade *objets d'art* are among the museum's unusual exhibits.

Places to Stay & Eat
If you're in the area, the RTDC *Hotel Lake Castle* (☎ 22-991) at Siliserh is an ideal place to unwind, though it is some 20 km from Alwar. It is a former palace, built by Vinay Singh, Alwar's third ruler, and overlooks a lake. As palaces go, it's also relatively cheap at Rs 200/250 for ordinary singles/doubles, with more expensive air-cooled rooms for Rs 250/350 or with air-con for Rs 500/600, and there's a Rs 40 dormitory. It also has a bar and restaurant.

In Alwar itself there is a variety of cheaper hotels, including the *Alka Hotel* (☎ 22-796) and the *Ashoka Hotel* (☎ 22-027). Near the railway station, the *Aravali Hotel* has a good range of accommodation from dorm beds to air-con rooms, and there's a good restaurant. The railway station also has *retiring rooms*. RTDC's *Hotel Meenal* (☎ 22-852) is a mid-range place, charging from Rs 250/300 for deluxe rooms.

About 50 km north of Alwar, and 122 km from Delhi, is the *Neemrana Fort Palace* (☎ (01494) 6005; fax (011) 462-1112), the impressive fortified palace of the Rajput king Prithviraj Chaudan III. Dating from the 15th century, rooms cost Rs 800/1000 and meals are available. There are superb views from the fort and good walks in the area.

Getting There & Away
There are frequent buses to Bharatpur and Deeg, and also to Jaipur and Delhi; there are also rail links with Jaipur and Delhi.

SHEKHAWATI
The semi-desert Shekhawati region lies in the triangular area between Delhi, Jaipur and Bikaner. Starting around the 14th century, a number of Muslim clans moved into the area and the towns which developed in the region became important trading posts on the caravan routes emanating from the ports of Gujarat.

The merchants prospered and in later years, encouraged by the British, established themselves as traders across the country. Some of India's richest industrialists of the

RAJASTHAN

20th century, such as the Birlas, were originally Marwars (as the people from Shekhawati came to be known).

Although the towns have long since lost any importance they may once have had, what they have not lost is the amazing painted havelis (houses) built by the merchants for their families, who had stayed behind in their home towns. Most of the buildings date from the 18th century to early this century, and such is their splendour that the area has been dubbed by some as the 'open-air gallery of Rajasthan'. There is also the obligatory (for Rajasthan) forts, a couple of minor castles, distinctive wells, stepwells, *chhatris*, and a handful of mosques.

The major towns of interest in the region are Fatehpur, Mandawa, Ramgarh and Jhunjhunu, although virtually every town has at least a few surviving havelis.

The tourist boom has still not caught up with Shekhawati, but with so much to see, and some interesting places to stay, it's an area well worth exploring for a few days. The best plan is to just wander at random through these small, dusty towns. There's no chance of getting lost, and there are surprises around every corner.

Guidebooks

For a full rundown of the history, people, towns and buildings of the area, it's well worth investing in a copy of *The Guide to the Painted Towns of Shekhawati* (Ilay Cooper). Unfortunately, the cheap edition is difficult to find and the new full-colour edition is expensive at Rs 450. The book gives excellent details of the buildings of interest in each town, along with fine sketch maps of the larger towns in the area.

Tourist offices have a free colour brochure with details of the main Shekhawati towns.

Getting There & Away

Access to the region is easiest from Jaipur or

Havelis

With large amounts of money coming from trade, the merchants of Shekhawati were keen to build mansions on a grand scale. The popular design was a building which, from the outside, was relatively unremarkable, the focus being the one or more internal courtyards. This served the purposes of security and privacy for the women, as well as offering some relief from the fierce heat which grips the area in summer. The plain exteriors also made the houses easily defendable.

The main entrance is usually a large wooden gate leading into a small courtyard, which in turn leads into another larger courtyard. The largest mansions had as many as four courtyards and were up to six storeys high.

Having built a house of grand proportions, the families then had them decorated with murals, and it is these murals which are the major attraction today. The major themes found are Hindu mythology, history (both old and contemporary), folk tales, eroticism (many now defaced or destroyed), and – one of the most interesting – foreigners and their modern inventions such as trains, planes, telephones, record players and bicycles. Animals and landscapes are also popular.

It is thought that the complex and sophisticated murals on the interiors of the buildings were executed by specialist painters from outside the area, while the more crude exterior ones were done by the local masons, after they had finished building the haveli. Originally the colours used in the murals were all ochre-based, but in the 1860s artificial pigments were introduced from Germany. The predominant colours are blue and maroon, but other colours such as yellow, green and indigo are also featured.

Most of the havelis these days are not inhabited by the owners, who find that the small rural towns in outback Rajasthan have little appeal. Many are occupied just by a single *chowkidar* (caretaker), while others may be home to a local family. None are open as museums or for display, and consequently many are either totally or partially locked. While the locals seem fairly tolerant of strangers wandering into their front courtyard, be aware that these are private places, so tact and discretion should be used – don't just blunder in as though you own the place. Local custom dictates that shoes should be removed when entering the inner courtyard of the haveli.

One unfortunate aspect of the tourist trade is also beginning to manifest itself here – the desire for antiques. A couple of towns have antique shops chock a block full of items ripped from the havelis – particularly doors and window frames, but anything that can be carted away is fair game. ■

Bikaner. The towns of Sikar and Fatehpur are on the main Jaipur to Bikaner road and are served by many buses. From Jaipur the bus takes four hours to Fatehpur at a cost of Rs 40, five hours to Jhunjhunu for Rs 48.

Churu is on the main Delhi to Bikaner railway line, while Sikar, Nawalgarh and Jhunjhunu have one slow daily rail link with Jaipur.

Getting Around

The Shekhawati region is crisscrossed by narrow bitumen roads, and all towns are well served by buses, either STC or private ones, although using these buses can be very time consuming. The local services to the smaller towns can get very crowded and riding 'upper class' (on the roof!) is quite acceptable – and usually necessary.

If you have a group of four or five people, it is worth hiring a taxi for the day to take you around the area. It's easy to arrange in the towns which have accommodation, although finding a driver who speaks English is more of a problem. The rate for a diesel Ambassador is Rs 3 per km; the driver will expect lunch or a tip. In Sikar, there's a taxi rank opposite the petrol station not far from the railway station.

Fatehpur

Fatehpur, just off the main Bikaner to Jaipur road, is easily accessible. It also has a reasonable RTDC Tourist Bungalow, and is fairly central, making it a good place to base yourself for further explorations.

The town was established in 1451 as a capital for Muslim nawabs, but it was taken by the Shekhawat Rajputs in the 18th century.

One of the main points of interest is the **Goenka Haveli**, which, although still lived in, is in a semi-derelict state. Built in 1860, it has just a single courtyard, and the main feature is the painted room upstairs, which features mirrorwork and some fine murals. A tip is usually expected by the man living here, especially if you want to take pictures.

There's the remains of a huge **17th-century step-well** in the middle of town opposite the cinema. Unfortunately it is half-full with rubbish, and at least one building has collapsed into it. Before long it will be beyond restoration.

Places to Stay The RTDC *Hotel Haveli Tourist Bungalow* (☎ (01571) 20-293) is on the southern edge of town, about one km from the bus stand. It's currently a very pleasant and comfortable place to stay – but it'll no doubt deteriorate as it gets older, like most RTDC places. Dorm beds are Rs 30, or there are large single/double rooms for Rs 100/150, or Rs 150/250 with air-cooling, and Rs 300/400 with air-con. Good meals are available and transport to other villages can be arranged. Also in Fatehpur, not far from the bus stand, is the very basic *Hotel Shanti Lodge*.

Mandawa

The compact and busy little market town of Mandawa was settled in the 18th century, and was fortified by the dominant merchant families. Today it has some of the finest painted havelis in the region, and is a perfect place for wandering at random.

The **fort**, dating back to 1760, dominates the town and now houses a comfortable mid-range hotel. Of the havelis, the **Bansidhar Newatia Haveli** (built around 1910) has some curious paintings on its outer eastern wall – a boy using a telephone, and other 20th-century inventions such as an aeroplane and a car. The haveli is in the main street, almost opposite the lane which leads to the fort. The **Gulab Rai Ladia Haveli** (1870) is one of the finest in the region, and has some superb murals. In the forecourt there's a very low-key souvenir stall, selling, among other things, the previously mentioned guidebook to the region. This haveli is a few minutes' walk from the main street, south and east of the fort – just ask. Other buildings worth seeking out are the **Harlalka well**, in the western part of town, and the **Majisa ka Kuan well**, north of the central bazaar.

Places to Stay The *Hotel Castle Mandawa* (☎ (0519289) 524; fax (0141) 38-2214) is wildly atmospheric. The rooms have been tastefully modernised, while the medieval feel of the place has remained undiminished. It's a wonderful place to stay if you can afford the price of Rs 900/1000 for singles/doubles with attached bathrooms. There are also suites for Rs 1195 and some of the rooms have balconies with superb views over the town – highly recommended.

There are a few other alternatives, but two of them are inconveniently located well out of the town centre – the *Thar Hotel* and the *Desert Resort*, both on the road to Mukundgarh. The Desert Resort is actually part of the Mandawa Castle operation, and costs Rs 750/800 for air-con rooms.

The *Hotel Rath Mandawa* is on the northern edge of town and charges around Rs 400 for a comfortable double.

Dundlod

Dundlod is a tiny town right in the heart of the Shekhawati region. Although it has little of interest, the **fort** here dates back to 1750, though much of it is more recent. It is owned by a direct descendent of the rawal who built the place. The Diwan-i-Khas audience hall is still in very good condition.

Places to Stay The fort, known as *Dera Dundlod Kila* (☎ (0141) 36-6276), is more a fortress than a palace, but offers comfortable accommodation for Rs 750/850 with attached bath and hot water. There are also suites for Rs 1100. Meals cost Rs 75/150/170 for breakfast/lunch/dinner.

Nawalgarh

The main building in this town is also the **fort**, founded in 1837 but today largely disfigured by modern accretions. It houses government offices and a branch of the Bank of Baroda. One of the main havelis is the **Anand Lal Paddar Haveli**, built in the 1920s. Today it houses a school, but has many fine paintings; also worth a look is the **Kulwal Haveli**.

Places to Stay & Eat The *Hotel Natraj* is in the Sabzi Mandi, right outside the entrance to the fort. It is a very primitive Indian hotel, with just a couple of rooms for Rs 30/50 with common bath. It also has a restaurant serving extremely basic meals.

In an entirely different category, and a much more pleasant alternative, is the *Roop Niwas Palace* (☎ (01594) 22008). Right on the eastern edge of town, about one km from the fort, it was formerly the country house of the rawal of Nawalgarh and has a pleasant garden setting. The quaintly furnished rooms cost Rs 700/900; meals are Rs 80 for breakfast, and Rs 160/180 for lunch/dinner. Excursions on horses or camels are available.

Jhunjhunu

Jhunjhunu is one of the largest towns of Shekhawati and is the current district headquarters. It has some of the region's most beautiful buildings and should not be missed. Jhunjhunu has a few hotels, a bank and the only tourist office in the region – at the Shiv Shekhawati Hotel. It is also on the bus and railway routes, so it has good connections with other parts of the state.

The town was founded by the Kaimkhani nawabs in the middle of the 15th century, and remained under their control until it was taken by the Rajput ruler Sardul Singh in 1730.

It was in Jhunjhunu that the British based their Shekhawati Brigade, a troop raised locally in the 1830s to try to halt the activities of the *dacoits* (bandits), who were largely local petty rulers who had decided it was easier to become wealthy by pinching other peoples' money than by earning their own.

The main item of interest here is the **Khetri Mahal**, a fine minor palace dating back to around 1760. It has very elegant lines and is architecturally the most sophisticated building in the region, although it's not in the greatest condition. The **Sri Bihariji Temple** is from a similar period and contains some fine murals, although these too have suffered over the years. The **Modi Haveli** and **Tibrewala Haveli**, both in the main bazaar, are covered with murals, and the latter is particularly interesting. The town also has a number of chhatris and wells.

Places to Stay Jhunjhunu has the widest range of accommodation of any of the Shekhawati towns. The bus stand is one km south of the centre, and close to it are a number of hotels. The best of these is the *Hotel Sangam* with singles/doubles with attached bath for Rs 150/250, and a few singles with common bath for Rs 40. Opposite is the *Hotel Khilhari* where rooms with attached bath are Rs 60/100.

A far better bet is the *Hotel Shiv Shekhawati* (☎ (01592) 32-651; fax 32-603), in a quieter area on the eastern edge of town, but still close to the centre. Rooms cost Rs 100/150 with common bath and air-cooling, Rs 350/400 with air-cooling and attached bath, and Rs 400/500 with air-con. Meals are available (Rs 35/70/90) and there's also a bar. There are free pick-ups from the bus and railway stations, and the owner is very knowledgeable about the Shekhawati area.

About one km away is the *Hotel Jamuna Resort*, part of the Shiv Shekhawati. As well as a swimming pool (which non-guests can use for Rs 50), there are three double rooms for Rs 400/450, traditionally decorated with mirrorwork.

Ramgarh

The town of Ramgarh was founded by the powerful Poddar merchant family in 1791, after they had left the village of Churu following a disagreement with the thakur. It had its heyday in the mid-19th century and was one of the richest towns of the area. As a result, today it has probably the greatest concentration of painted havelis anywhere – it's a fascinating place to wander around.

The **Poddar chhatris** near the bus stand, and the **Poddar havelis** near the Churu Gate (northern) are all fine examples. Down the side street next to the well near the northern gate is one of the antique shops which makes its living from pieces ripped out of the buildings in the area.

Lachhmangarh

Dominating this town are the smooth walls of the **fort**, as simply designed as the cooling towers of a power station. It's now deserted but there are superb views down to the town which was laid out, like Jaipur, along a grid pattern. There are several interesting buildings, the largest being the **Char Chowk Haveli**.

AJMER

Population: 447,000
Telephone Area Code: 0145

South-west of Jaipur is Ajmer, a green oasis on the shore of the Ana Sagar, hemmed in by barren hills. Historically, Ajmer always had great strategic importance and was sacked by Mahmud of Ghazni on one of his periodic forays from Afghanistan. Later, it became a favourite residence of the great Mughals. One of the first contacts between the Mughals and the British occurred in Ajmer when Sir Thomas Roe met with Jehangir here in 1616.

The city was subsequently taken by the Scindias and, in 1818, it was handed over to the British, becoming one of the few places in Rajasthan controlled directly by the British rather than being part of a princely state. Ajmer is a major centre for Muslim pilgrims during the fast of Ramadan but, although it has some superb examples of early Muslim architecture, a fort overlooking the town and a lively bazaar, Ajmer is just a stepping stone to nearby Pushkar for most travellers.

Orientation & Information

The bus stand is close to the Tourist Bungalow on the Jaipur side of town. The railway station and most of the hotels are on the other side of town.

The tourist office (☎ 52-426) is in the Khadim Tourist Bungalow and has a good range of literature. The tourist officer, Mr Hazarilal Sharma, is very keen to help – he's one of those rare tourist officers who takes an active interest in his job. There's also a tourist information counter at the railway station.

Ana Sagar

This artificial lake was created in the 12th century by damming the River Luni. On its bank is a fine park, the **Dault Bagh**, containing a series of marble pavilions erected in 1637 by Shah Jahan. It's popular for an evening stroll.

The lake tends to dry up if the monsoon is poor, so the city's water supply is taken from **Foy Sagar**, three km further up the valley. There are good views from the hill beside the Dault Bagh.

Dargah

Situated at the foot of a barren hill in the old part of town, this is one of India's most important places for Muslim pilgrims. The Dargah is the tomb of a Sufi saint, Khwaja Muin-ud-din Chishti, who came to Ajmer from Persia in 1192. Construction of the shrine was completed by Humayun and the gate was added by the Nizam of Hyderabad. Akbar used to make the pilgrimage to the Dargah from Agra once a year.

As you enter the courtyard, removing your shoes at the gateway, a mosque constructed by Akbar is on the right. The large iron cauldrons are for offerings which are customarily shared by families involved in the shrine's upkeep. In an inner court, there is another mosque built by Shah Jahan. Constructed of white marble, it has 11 arches and a Persian inscription running the full length of the building.

The saint's tomb is in the centre of the second court. It has a marble dome and the actual tomb inside is surrounded by a silver platform. The horseshoes nailed to the shrine doors are offerings from successful horse dealers! Beware of 'guides' hassling for donations around the Dargah using the standard fake donation books – all the donations registered in these books are over Rs 100!

The tomb attracts hundreds of thousands of pilgrims every year on the anniversary of the saint's death, the Urs, in the seventh month of the lunar calendar (May/June). It's an interesting festival that's worth attending if you're in the area. As well as the pilgrims, sufis from all over India converge on Ajmer. You may even get to see a whirling dervish.

Adhai-din-ka-jhonpra & Taragarh

Beyond the Dargah, on the very outskirts of town, are the ruins of this mosque. According to legend, its construction, in 1153, took 2½ days, as its name indicates. It was built as a Jain college but in 1198 Muhammad Ghori took Ajmer and converted the building into a mosque by adding a seven-arched wall in front of the pillared hall.

Although the mosque is now in need of repair, it is a particularly fine piece of architecture – the pillars are all different and the arched 'screen', with its damaged minarets, is noteworthy.

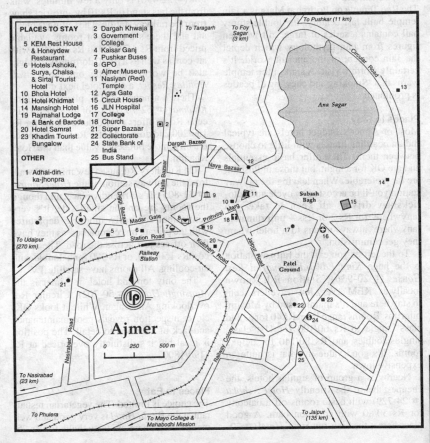

PLACES TO STAY
5 KEM Rest House & Honeydew Restaurant
6 Hotels Ashoka, Surya, Chalsa & Sirtaj Tourist Hotel
10 Bhola Hotel
13 Hotel Khidmat
14 Mansingh Hotel
19 Rajmahal Lodge & Bank of Baroda
20 Hotel Samrat
23 Khadim Tourist Bungalow

OTHER
1 Adhai-din-ka-jhonpra
2 Dargah Khwaja
3 Government College
4 Kaisar Ganj
7 Pushkar Buses
8 GPO
9 Ajmer Museum
11 Nasiyan (Red) Temple
12 Agra Gate
15 Circuit House
16 JLN Hospital
17 College
18 Church
21 Super Bazaar
22 Collectorate
24 State Bank of India
25 Bus Stand

Ajmer

0   250   500 m

Three km and a steep 1½-hour climb beyond the mosque, the Taragarh, or Star Fort, commands an excellent view over the city. The fort was the site of much military activity during Mughal times and was later used as a sanatorium by the British.

Akbar's Palace

Back in the city, near the railway station, this imposing fort was built by Akbar in 1570 and today houses the Ajmer Museum, which is really not worth the bother. It is closed on Friday and charges a small admission fee.

Nasiyan Temple

The Red Temple on Prithviraj Marg is a Jain temple built last century. Its double-storey hall contains a series of large, gilt wooden figures from Jain mythology which depict the Jain concept of the ancient world. It's certainly worth a visit. A sign in the temple warns that 'Smoking and chewing of beatles is prohibited'.

Places to Stay

Most of Ajmer's budget hotels are typical Indian boarding houses with little to choose between them. They offer basic essentials and are OK for a night, but those in Pushkar are far preferable. When leaving the railway station you'll be accosted by cycle and auto-rickshaw drivers all keen to take you 'anywhere' for Rs 2 or less – unfortunately 'anywhere' always means to a hotel where they get commission.

To the left as you exit the railway station is the huge *King Edward Memorial Rest House* (☎ 20-936), Station Rd, known locally as 'KEM'. Very few travellers seem to stay here and it's mainly used by Muslim pilgrims. Rooms range from Rs 40 for a '2nd class' single to Rs 60/100 for '1st class' singles/doubles and Rs 80/140 for deluxe rooms. It's good value in what is quite an expensive town.

Nearby is a group of similar hotels, the cheapest being the friendly *Hotel Ashoka* (☎ 24-729) with basic rooms off a balcony for Rs 50/80 with common bath. A good place here is the Sikh-run *Sirtaj Hotel* (☎ 20-096) with rooms around a courtyard. They cost Rs 80/150 with bathroom attached, and there's also a restaurant serving Punjabi food.

There are more budget hotels along Prithviraj Marg, between the GPO and the Red Temple. Opposite the church at Agra Gate, is the *Bhola Hotel* (☎ 23-844) with singles/doubles for Rs 75/125 with bath. Hot water comes from the geyser outside the room, but there's no shortage. It's a reasonable place although it can get a bit noisy here. The vegetarian restaurant is excellent.

The RTDC *Hotel Khadim Tourist Bungalow* (☎ 52-490) is only a few minutes' walk from the bus stand or Rs 10 by auto-rickshaw from the railway station. The setting is pleasant and there's a range of rooms available priced from Rs 150/200 to Rs 300/400 with air-con, as well as a Rs 40 dormitory. It might also be worth checking out the *Aravali Holiday Resort*, a new hotel next door.

There's a newer RTDC place, the *Hotel Khidmat* (☎ 52-705), east of the lake on Circular Rd. It offers only deluxe rooms for Rs 150/200 and dorm beds for Rs 40. This place is a bit remote but better value than the Hotel Khadim.

On Kutchery Rd, just a few minutes' walk from the railway station, is the *Hotel Samrat* (☎ 31-805). It's a friendly place, and though the rooms are on the small side, it's very convenient for early morning departures with the private bus companies, as they have their offices just across the road. The rooms cost Rs 150/250, or Rs 300 for a double with air-cooling. All rooms have satellite TV.

The only top-end hotel in Ajmer is the *Mansingh Hotel* (☎ 50-702), Circular Rd, overlooking Ana Sagar. While it looks OK, closer inspection reveals poor maintenance and lack of attention to detail. The position is ideal but it's distinctly overpriced at Rs 1190/1800.

Places to Eat

The choice is limited. The vegetarian restaurant at the *Bhola Hotel* is very good and well maintained. There are tasty thalis for Rs 25, and a good range of other dishes and ice cream.

The *Honeydew Restaurant* near the KEM Rest House has veg and non-veg dishes and is also good. The restaurant has a tandoor oven and also does pizzas and espresso coffee. Main dishes are around Rs 35; there's seating indoors and outdoors.

The top restaurant in town is the *Sheesh Mahal*, at the Mansingh Hotel. It's an expensive place, though, with main dishes ranging from Rs 65 to Rs 95.

Getting There & Away

Bus There are buses from Jaipur to Ajmer every 15 minutes, some nonstop. The trip costs Rs 40 and takes 2½ hours. From Delhi, 20 buses run daily in either direction at a cost of Rs 110.

Deluxe state transport buses also go to Jodhpur (Rs 62, 4½ hours, 210 km), Udaipur (Rs 86, 303 km via Chittorgarh), Chittorgarh (Rs 48, 190 km), Kota (Rs 53 to Rs 62, 200 km via Bundi), Ranakpur (Rs 70, 237 km), Bharatpur (Rs 80, 305 km) and Bikaner (Rs 84, 277 km). In addition, buses leave for Agra (Rs 85, 385 km) each morning at 7.30, 9 and 11.30 am and for Jaisalmer (Rs 125, 490 km) daily at 7.45 am. There are also regular buses to Kota and Bundi.

Also available are private deluxe buses to Ahmedabad, Udaipur, Jodhpur, Jaipur, Mt Abu, Jaisalmer, Bikaner, Delhi and Bombay. Most of the companies have offices on Kutchery Rd. If you book your ticket to one of these destinations through an agency in Pushkar, they will provide a free jeep transfer to Ajmer to commence your journey.

Train Ajmer is on the Delhi-Jaipur-Marwar-Ahmedabad line and most trains stop at Ajmer. The 135-km journey from Jaipur costs Rs 35/138 in 2nd/1st class. The *Pink City Express* takes about the same time as the buses to cover the distance. To Udaipur the fastest express takes 7½ hours.

Getting Around

Ajmer is a relatively small town and easy enough to get around on foot, but there are plenty of auto and cycle-rickshaws.

PUSHKAR

Population: 12,000
Telephone Area Code: 014581

Like Goa or Dharamsala, the mellow, quiet and interesting little town of Pushkar is one of those travellers' centres where people go for a little respite from the hardships of life on the Indian road. It's only 11 km from Ajmer but separated from it by Nag Pahar, the Snake Mountain, and is situated right on the edge of the desert.

The town clings to the side of the small but beautiful Pushkar Lake with its many bathing ghats and temples. For Hindus, Pushkar is a very important pilgrimage centre. Unfortunately, after a poor monsoon the lake doesn't get refilled and can be almost empty. This is a great pity, as it is a big factor in the town's appeal.

Pushkar is also world-famous for the huge Camel Fair which takes place here each October/November. At this time, the town is thronged with tribal people from all over Rajasthan, pilgrims from all over India and film-makers and tourists from all over the world. If you're anywhere within striking distance at the time, it's an event not to be missed. Camel rides, however, are available year-round from a number of operators around the town. Camel safaris lasting several days are also possible.

Being a holy place, alcohol, meat and even eggs are banned.

Camel Fair

The exact date on which the Camel Fair is held depends on the lunar calendar but, in Hindu chronology, it falls on the full moon of Kartik Purnima. Each year, up to 200,000 people flock to Pushkar for the Camel Fair, bringing with them some 50,000 camels and cattle for several days of pilgrimage, horse dealing, camel racing and colourful festivities.

The Rajasthan tourist office has promoted the fair as an international attraction by adding Rajasthan dance programmes and

RAJASTHAN

other cultural events, and by putting up a huge tent city for the Indian and foreign visitors. It's one of India's biggest and most colourful festivals. In 1995 it's from 4 to 7 November, in 1996 it's 22 to 25 November, in 1997 it's 11 to 14 November, and in 1998 it's 1 to 4 November.

Temples

Pushkar boasts temples, though few are as ancient as you might expect at such an important pilgrimage site since many were destroyed by Aurangzeb and subsequently rebuilt. The most famous is what is said to be the only **temple** in India dedicated to Brahma. It's marked by a red spire, and over the entrance gateway is the *hans*, or goose symbol, of Brahma, who is said to have personally chosen Pushkar as its site. The **Rangji Temple** is also important.

The one-hour trek up to the **hilltop temple** overlooking the lake is best made early in the morning; the view is magnificent.

Ghats

Numerous ghats run down to the lake, and pilgrims are constantly bathing in the lake's holy waters. If you wish to join them, do it with respect – remove your shoes, don't smoke and don't take photographs. This is not Varanasi and the pilgrims here can be very touchy about insensitive intrusions by non-Hindus.

Places to Stay

Pushkar is such a small but popular town that it can be difficult to find accommodation, especially if you arrive late in the day. Most of the available hotels are very basic, and rooms have just a bed, common bathroom facilities and no hot water. Many have only *charpoys* (string beds) with no mattress or sheets. On the other hand, they're generally clean and freshly whitewashed. You should ask to see a few rooms before deciding as many have a cell-like atmosphere due to the small or nonexistent windows. Mosquitoes come with most rooms, so bring insect repellent.

The most popular place to stay is the *Hotel Pushkar Palace* (☎ 3401; fax 2226), an upmarket hotel that also has 14 budget rooms at Rs 60/100 with common bath. These are very small but in a superb position right by the lake. Smart rooms with attached bath and hot water range from Rs 250/350 for a single/double to Rs 650/750 for air-con rooms. There's a nice lawn and an excellent, though pricey, restaurant.

Next to the Pushkar Palace, but approached from a different entrance, is the RTDC *Hotel Sarovar Tourist Bungalow* (☎ 2040), set in its own spacious grounds at the far end of the lake and with a restaurant. It's better value than the Tourist Bungalow in Ajmer, and has ordinary singles/doubles for Rs 75/100 with common bath, Rs 100/150 with attached bath, and air-cooled deluxe rooms for Rs 200/250. Part of this hotel was once a small palace belonging to the maharaja of Jaipur.

Other hotels in this area include the *V K Tourist Palace* (☎ 2174), a popular cheapie with rooms from Rs 40/60 with common bath, Rs 70/100 with attached bath. This place has a good rooftop restaurant. The *Krishna Guest House* and the *Om Hotel*, both nearby, are similarly priced.

Pushkar Passports

You can tell a traveller who's been to the ghats in Pushkar by the red ribbon (the 'Pushkar Passport') tied round their wrist. Getting one can be an expensive procedure if you allow yourself to be talked into a more generous donation than you might otherwise have wanted to give. Priests, some genuine, some not, will approach you near the ghats and offer to do a puja. At some point during the prayers they'll ask you to tell Brahma how much you're going to give him, Rs 100 to Rs 300 being the suggested figure. Don't fall for this emotional blackmail – if you want to give just a few rupees, that's fine, although the 'priest' will tell you it's not enough and doesn't even cover the cost of his 'materials'. ■

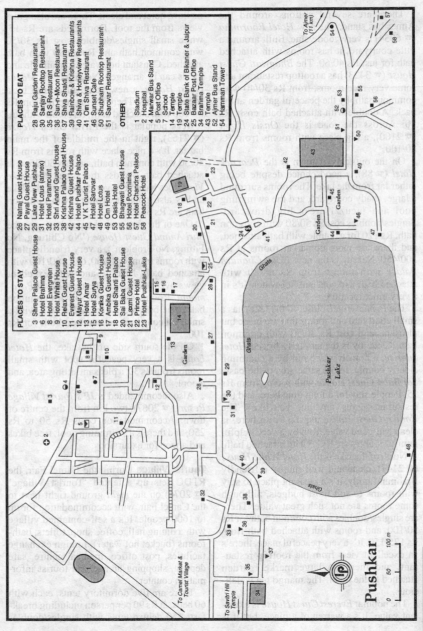

PLACES TO STAY

3 Shree Palace Guest House
6 Hotel Brahma
8 Hotel Evergreen
9 Hotel White House
10 Relax Guest House
11 Everest Guest House
12 Mayur Guest House
13 Hotel Amar
15 Hotel Surya
16 Korika Guest House
17 Ambika Guest House
18 Hotel Shanti Palace
20 Sai Baba Guest House
21 Laxmi Guest House
22 Prince Hotel
23 Hotel Pushkar-Lake

26 Natraj Guest House
27 Payal Guest House
29 Lake View Pushkar
31 Hotel Lotus (annex)
32 Hotel Paramount
33 Shri Anand Guest House
38 Krishna Palace Guest House
42 Krishna Guest House
44 Hotel Pushkar Palace
45 V K Tourist Palace
47 Hotel Sarovar
48 Hotel Lotus
49 Om Hotel
53 Oasis Hotel
55 Bhagwati Guest House
56 Hotel Poornima
57 Hotel Chandra Palace
58 Peacock Hotel

PLACES TO EAT

28 Raju Garden Restaurant
30 Sanjay Rooftop Restaurant
35 R S Restaurant
36 Sun-n-Moon Restaurant
37 Shiva Shakti Restaurant
39 Rainbow & Krishna Restaurants
40 Shiva & Honeyview Restaurants
41 Om Shiva Restaurant
46 Sunset Cafe
50 Shubham Rooftop Restaurant
51 Sarovar Restaurant

OTHER

1 Stadium
2 Hospital
4 Marwar Bus Stand
5 Post Office
7 School
14 Temple
19 Temple
24 State Bank of Bikaner & Jaipur
25 Bazaar Post Office
34 Brahma Temple
43 Temple
52 Ajmer Bus Stand
54 Hamman Tower

To Ajmer (11 km)

Pushkar Lake

Garden

Garden

Garden

Ghats

Ghats

Ghats

To Camel Market & Tourist Village

To Savitri Hill Temple

Pushkar

0   50   100 m

RAJASTHAN

There are several options around the Ajmer bus stand. The new *Hotel Poornima* (☎ 6054) is very good value. Built around a little courtyard, it has rooms with attached bath for just Rs 40/60. The *Bhagwati Guest House* (☎ 3423) has a rooftop restaurant and some very nice rooms, from Rs 30/40 with common bath, by the peaceful garden at the back. A double with attached bath costs Rs 80. Across the road is the *Oasis Hotel* (☎ 2100), a big place with rooms from Rs 80/100.

On the outskirts of town is the *Peacock Hotel* (☎ 88), a good choice despite being rather far from the lake. The rooms surround a large, shady courtyard, and the swimming pool and jacuzzi are a big drawcard. Singles/doubles cost Rs 50/80 with common bath, Rs 120 for a double with bath attached, and there are more upmarket rooms at Rs 300/450. Nearby is the new *Hotel Chandra Palace* with rooms from Rs 60/80 with attached bath and constant hot water. It's in a very quiet location.

The *Prince Hotel*, closer to the lake, has a small courtyard and rooms that are basic but pleasant, and cost Rs 30/50 with common bath. Close by is the similarly priced *Hotel Sunrise*, a homely place run by a charming elderly couple. In the same area is the basic *Sai Baba Guest House* with rooms from Rs 25. People stay for a long time here, and the restaurant serves 'anything you like'! The *Konika Guest House*, not far from here, is clean and good value. Run by a very helpful family, doubles are Rs 75 with attached bath.

North of the lake is the *Hotel White House* (☎ 2147), clean and well run by a friendly Brahmin family. It's a pleasant place to stay with rooms to suit most budgets, although some rooms are not such great value. There are singles/doubles with common bath for Rs 50/100, and rooms with attached bath from Rs 125/150. It's a very peaceful place, there's an excellent view from the rooftop restaurant, and there's a large market garden attached to the hotel. The mango tea is delicious.

The popular *Everest Guest House* is excellent value. It's a warren of a place, but it is mellow, quiet and clean. There are also great views from the roof. Dorm beds are Rs 15, while small singles/doubles cost Rs 30/50 with common bath and Rs 60/80 with bath attached. Constant hot water is available and meals can be arranged. Nearby is the *Mayur Guest House*, a new small place run by a friendly family. There are big rooms from Rs 80/100 with attached bath, Rs 30/50 without.

Very popular is the *Payal Guest House* (☎ 2163), right in the middle of the main bazaar. It's a nice place with rooms from Rs 30/50 with common bath, and Rs 60/75 with attached bath. Across the street, the *Lake View* does have very good views of the lake and is also popular. Rooms with common bath are Rs 35/70.

One of the first guest houses here was the *Shri Anand Guest House* ('No Chitting, No Fitting, No Problem'), a very friendly place with rooms from Rs 40/60, or Rs 80/100 with attached bath. Nearby, and with excellent views over the lake, is the new *Hotel Paramount*. Rooms are Rs 30/50 with common bath. The best room here is No 107, with a small balcony and an attached bath for Rs 100.

On the south side of the lake, the *Hotel Lotus* is a very peaceful spot with small rooms from Rs 30, a pleasant sitting area, and a pool.

Also recommended is *JP's Tourist Village Resort* (☎ 2067), two km from the centre of town. Accommodation costs Rs 50 to Rs 250, and there's a swimming pool, free bikes and a jeep for excursions.

Tourist Village During the Camel Fair, the RTDC sets up a tented 'Tourist Village' (☎ 2074) on the *mela* ground right next to the Camel Fair, with accommodation for up to 1600 people. It's a self-contained village with a dining hall, coffee shop, toilets, bathrooms (bucket hot water), foreign exchange facilities, post office, medical centre, safe deposit, shopping arcade and tourist information counter.

There are five dormitory tents, each with 60 beds, at Rs 90 per person including breakfast, 150 deluxe tents with singles/doubles for Rs 900/1200 including all meals. There are also 20 huts which cost Rs 1400/1800 including meals. These huts are in fact open all year round, and are available for Rs 150/200 when the cattle fair is not on.

Demand for tent accommodation can be high so, if you want to be sure of a bed, contact the General Manager (☎ Jaipur 31-0586 or 31-9531; fax 31-6045), RTDC, Hotel Swagatam Campus, Nr Railway Station, Jaipur, well in advance. Full payment must be received 45 days in advance if you want to be sure of accommodation.

Places to Eat

As a travellers' Mecca, Pushkar is one of those towns in which everyone has a favourite restaurant, and there's plenty to choose from. Strict vegetarianism that forbids even eggs rather limits the range of ingredients but the cooks make up for this with imagination. You can even get an eggless omelette in some places!

Buffet meals seem to have taken off here in a big way, with many places offering all-you-can-eat meals for Rs 20 to Rs 25 – breakfast, lunch or dinner. The *Shiva Restaurant* on the western edge of the lake was the original buffet specialist, but these days the *Om Shiva* (with the 'Om' written in Hindi to try and cash in on the original Shiva Restaurant's popularity), near the State Bank, is better. The rooftop restaurant at the *V K Tourist Palace* also does a good buffet. These meals are good value, especially at breakfast, but for lunch and dinner the selection can be a bit boring. Breakfast consists of cornflakes, porridge, curd, brown toast, banana, butter & jam, and tea/coffee, and usually goes until around 11 am. It's safest to eat buffet meals at the busiest places where the food is more likely to be freshly cooked for each meal, rather than reheated.

There are several pleasant garden restaurants in Pushkar. The *Sun-n-Moon* has tables arranged around a bo tree, and has a range of Western dishes such as pizzas and apple pie. *Raju Garden Restaurant* has oven-baked pizza for Rs 30 and enough jars of Marmite to last well into the next century.

The best buffet is at the *Hotel Pushkar Palace*. It costs Rs 60 and the menu is posted up each evening. The *Sunset Cafe*, nearby, is popular, especially at sunset, and they have a good selection of breads, croissants, cinnamon rolls and sandwiches. The fruit juices are also very good, although the service is erratic, and it is indeed pleasant to sit by the lake shore.

Things to Buy

Pushkar has a wide selection of handicraft shops all along the main bazaar and is especially good for embroidered fabrics such as wall hangings, bed covers, cushion covers and shoulder bags. A lot of what is stocked here actually comes from the Barmer district south of Jaisalmer and other tribal areas of Rajasthan. There's something to suit all tastes and pockets though you'll have to haggle over prices. The shopkeepers here have been exposed to tourists with plenty of money and not much time, so there's the usual nonsense about 'last price' quotes which aren't negotiable. Take your time and visit a few shops. In between these shops are the inevitable clothing shops catering to styles which were in vogue in Goa and Kathmandu at the end of the '60s. You may find occasional timeless items, but most of it is pretty clichéd.

Woman playing a veena

RAJASTHAN

The music shops (selling tapes and records), on the other hand, are well worth a visit if you're interested in picking up some examples of traditional or contemporary classical Indian music. The shops here don't seem to stock the usual banal current film-score rages.

There are a number of bookshops in the main bazaar selling secondhand novels in various languages, and they'll buy them back for 50% of what you pay.

Getting There & Away
Buses depart Ajmer frequently from the stop near the railway station for the Rs 4 trip (although it's only Rs 3 when going *from* Pushkar *to* Ajmer – because of the road toll). It's a spectacular climb up and over the hills – if you can see out of the window.

It is possible to continue straight on from Pushkar to Jodhpur without having to back-track to Ajmer, but the buses go there via Merta and can take eight hours. It's much faster to go to Ajmer and take the 4½-hour express bus.

There are a couple of agents in Pushkar offering tickets for private buses to various destinations. These buses all leave from Ajmer, but the agents provide you with free transport to Ajmer in time for the departures. See the Ajmer section for destinations.

RANTHAMBHORE NATIONAL PARK
Situated near the town of Sawai Madhopur, midway between Bharatpur and Kota, Ranthambhore National Park is one of the prime examples of Project Tiger's conservation efforts in Rajasthan. Sadly, it also demonstrates that programme's overall failure; for it was in this park that government officials were implicated in the poaching of tigers for the Chinese folk medicine trade. Experts reckon that the tiger population here may now be as low as 15, although the official figure is 22 – down from 44 a few years back. There's still a reasonable chance of seeing one, but you should plan on two or three safaris. Other game, especially the larger and smaller herbivores, are more numerous. Even if you don't see a

tiger, it's worth the effort for the scenery alone: in India it's not often you get the chance to visit such a large area of virgin bush, and the contrast with the often denuded land elsewhere is stark.

The park itself covers some 400 sq km and its scenery is very beautiful. A system of lakes and rivers is hemmed in by steep high crags and, on top of one of these, is the extensive and well-preserved fortress of Ranthambhore, built in the 10th century. The fort is definitely worth visiting and there are superb views over the park from the ramparts. The lower lying ground alternates between open bushland and fairly dense forest and is peppered with ruined pavilions, chhatris and 'hides' – the area was formerly a hunting preserve of the maharajas.

A good network of four gravel tracks crisscrosses the park and safaris are undertaken in open-sided jeeps driven by a ranger. If you've ever been on safari in Africa, you might think this is an unduly risky venture but the tigers appear unconcerned by jeep loads of garrulous tourists touting cameras only metres away from where they're lying. No-one has been mauled or eaten – yet!

The best time to visit the park is between October and April, and the park is actually closed during the monsoon from 1 June to 1 October. Early morning and late afternoon are the best times to view game.

Orientation & Information
There's a tourist office (☎ 20208) in the Project Tiger office in Sawai Madhopur. It is tucked away half a km south of the railway station. Just follow the tracks south from the station, through the overpass, and the office is on the left, just before the cinema, which is on the other side of the tracks.

The number of vehicles allowed into the park is strictly controlled. There are four trails within the park, and on each safari two or three jeeps take each trail. There are also large trucks (also open-topped), seating 22 people, but they're limited to only two of the trails.

It's 10 km from Sawai Madhopur to the first park gate, where you pay the entry fees, and a further three km to the main gate and the Jogi Mahal. The accommodation is strung out all the way along the road from the town to the park. Advance booking is essential during the busy Christmas and New Year periods.

If you are taking photos, it's worthwhile bringing some 400 or 800 ASA film, as the undergrowth is dense and surprisingly dark.

There's a Rs 25 entry fee to the park, plus Rs 10 for a camera. You'll also have to pay the entry fee of Rs 75 per vehicle. A guide costs Rs 55; Shahid Ali is a young guide who's good at spotting wildlife.

Places to Stay

There's some basic accommodation in the town itself, while the better places are along the park road. When stepping off the train you'll be besieged by touts trying to drum up business. Don't be intimidated into staying somewhere you don't want to. Many of the hotels quote high prices but they can usually be bargained down if things are quiet.

The railway *retiring rooms* are set back from the tracks and so quieter than most. There are big doubles with attached bath for Rs 85, and dorm beds for Rs 30. About half a km from the railway station, right in the town, is the *Hotel Swagat* (☎ 2601). It's pretty basic, but reasonable for what it offers, at Rs 40/60 or Rs 80 for a double with attached bath. The *Hotel Vishal*, in the same street, is similar.

Moving out of town along the road to the park, the first place is *The Cave* (one km from town), which is a tented camp of a dozen or so large tents, each fitted with a bathroom (!), supplied with bucket hot water. It's ridiculously overpriced at Rs 450/600, and if the tents are empty (they often are), you should be able to bargain them down to around Rs 150.

Next up is the Taj Group's *Sawai Madhopur Lodge* (☎ 20-541; one km), formerly belonging to the maharaja of Jaipur. It is suitably luxurious, and has a bar, restaurant, pool and beautiful garden. Rooms are US$64/120 and there's also distinctly upmarket tented accommodation for US$60/90. Meals cost Rs 150 for lunch, Rs 180 for dinner, and the food is very good.

Another 500 metres brings you to the small and very pleasant *Ankur Resort* (1.5 km. This is a clean and modern place with good-sized rooms, all with bath attached. The price is Rs 350/450, but if it's not full you shouldn't need to pay more than half this price. Very similar in price and facilities is the *Anurag Resort* (☎ 20451), a further 500 metres towards the park (two km from town); it also has a dorm (Rs 50) and accepts campers.

Next is the first of the RTDC places, the *Kamdhenu Tourist Bungalow* (☎ 20-334; three km). It's a fairly modern and characterless building, offering unremarkable accommodation. The price is Rs 30 for dorm beds, Rs 250/300 for single/double rooms with attached bath, or Rs 300/350 with air-cooling. Meals are available; thalis cost Rs 50. There's a newly opened RTDC *Tourist Hotel* about two km further along the road. It has eight rooms for Rs 325/400, and a good restaurant.

Stunningly sited on the hillside to the right of the road, the *Castle Jhoomar Baori* (☎ 20-495; five km, then two km off the road) is a former royal hunting lodge. It's also operated by RTDC, but reasonably well run for a change. The 11 rooms are comfortable, spacious and well furnished, and have modern toilet and bathroom facilities with hot water. There's also a beautiful lounge as well as open rooftop areas. The ordinary air-cooled rooms cost Rs 325/400, but there's also a 'panther suite' for Rs 500/600 and a 'tiger suite' for Rs 600/750.

Other options include the *Hotel Tiger Moon* (☎ Bombay (022) 640-6399), a resort at the end of the road, with bungalows (US$50/76) built around a swimming pool; and the overpriced *Hammir Wildlife Resort*, at Rs 585/890, near the Tourist Bungalow.

Unfortunately, owing to the activities of the poachers, the wonderful Jogi Mahal, a former hunting lodge in an idyllic location by the lake, and the only place to stay within the park, is closed. It might be worth finding out if it has been reopened.

Getting There & Away

Sawai Madhopur is on the main Delhi to

Bombay broad-gauge railway line and, as most trains stop here, there's a wide range to choose from. The 108-km trip to Kota takes two hours and 10 minutes and costs Rs 29/122 in 2nd/1st class, while to Agra Fort it's 226 km, a trip which takes eight hours and costs Rs 56/205.

Sawai Madhopur is also the junction of the metre-gauge spur to Jaipur and Bikaner, but this may soon be converted to broad gauge. Three trains a day travel this line in either direction. The 130-km trip to Jaipur takes around three hours and costs Rs 34/131.

Getting Around

Excursions into the park must be booked at room No 2 at the Project Tiger office (☎ 20-223), and jeeps can currently only be booked with them. A seat in the truck (Canter) costs Rs 60, and you can arrange to be picked up if your hotel is on the road between the town and the park. Jeeps cost Rs 500 per trip and this can be shared by up to six people, although four is preferable. This includes all km charges, so staying further from the park entrance isn't going to cost more. Safari times are 6.30 to 10 am, and 2.30 to 5 pm (one hour later in summer).

You can hire bikes for Rs 10 per day at the shops just outside the main entrance to the railway station.

DHOLPUR

Although the town of Dholpur is in Rajasthan, this place can be more easily accessed from Madhya Pradesh. Hence, details are given in that chapter.

Southern Rajasthan

KOTA

Population: 596,000
Telephone Area Code: 0744

Following the Rajput conquest of this area of Rajasthan in the 12th century, Bundi was chosen as the capital with Kota as the land grant of the ruler's eldest son. This situation continued until 1624 when Kota became a

separate state, remaining so until it was integrated into Rajasthan following independence.

Building of the city began in 1264 following the defeat of the Bhil chieftains but Kota didn't reach its present size until well into the 17th century when Rao Madho Singh, a son of the ruler of Bundi, was made ruler of Kota by the Mughal emperor, Jehangir. Subsequent rulers have all added to the fortress and palaces which stand here today.

Today, Kota serves as an army headquarters. It's also Rajasthan's industrial centre (mainly chemicals), powered by the hydroelectric plants on the Chambal River – the only permanent river in the state – and the nearby atomic plant, which made headlines in 1992 when it was revealed that levels of radioactivity in the area were way above 'safe' levels. Very few tourists visit Kota, which is surprising because the fortress and part of the palace complex are open to the public and the Rao Madho Singh Museum has to be one of the best in Rajasthan.

Orientation & Information

Kota is strung out along the east bank of the Chambal River. The railway station is well to the north; the Tourist Bungalow, a number of other hotels and the bus stand are in the middle; and Chambal Gardens, the fort and the Kota Barrage are to the south.

The tourist office (☎ 27-695) is at the Tourist Bungalow. The staff here are keen and a range of leaflets is available. It's open Monday to Saturday from 8 am to 6 pm.

You can change money at the State Bank of India, near the Hotel Marudhar on Chawni Circle, or at the State Bank of Bikaner & Jaipur in the Instrumentation Colony several km to the south. The Hotel Brijraj Bhawan will change cheques for guests.

City Palace & Fort

Standing beside the Kota Barrage, overlooking the Chambal River, the City Palace and Fort is one of the largest such complexes in Rajasthan. Some of its buildings are now occupied by schools but most of the complex is open to the public. Entry is from the south side through the **Naya Darwaza**, or New Gate.

The **Rao Madho Singh Museum**, in the City Palace, is superb. It's on the right-hand side of the complex's huge central courtyard and is entered through a gateway topped by rampant elephants like those at the Bundi Fort. Inside, you'll find displays of weapons, clothing and some of the best preserved murals in the state. Indeed, everything about this former palace is colourful. The museum is open daily, except Friday, from 11 am to 5 pm. Foreigners are charged Rs 25, plus Rs 25 for a camera.

After visiting the museum, it's worth wandering around the rest of the complex just to appreciate how magnificent this place must have been in its heyday. Unfortunately, a lot of it is falling into disrepair and the gardens are no more, but there are some excellent views over the old city, the river and the huge industrial complex with its enormous twin chimneys across the river.

Jagmandir

Between the City Palace and the Tourist Bungalow is the picturesque artificial tank of Kishore Sagar, constructed in 1346. Right in

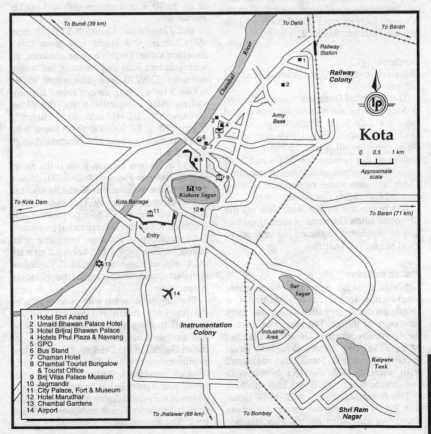

1 Hotel Shri Anand
2 Umaid Bhawan Palace Hotel
3 Hotel Brijraj Bhawan Palace
4 Hotels Phul Plaza & Navrang
5 GPO
6 Bus Stand
7 Chaman Hotel
8 Chambal Tourist Bungalow
   & Tourist Office
9 Brij Vilas Palace Museum
10 Jagmandir
11 City Palace, Fort & Museum
12 Hotel Marudhar
13 Chambal Gardens
14 Airport

Kota

0   0.5   1 km

Approximate scale

To Bundi (39 km)
To Dehli
To Baran
Railway Station
Railway Colony
Chambal River
Army Base
To Kota Dam
Kota Barrage
Kishore Sagar
Entry
To Baran (71 km)
Sur Sagar
Instrumentation Colony
Industrial Area
Raipura Tank
To Jhalawar (88 km)
To Bombay
Shri Ram Nagar

the middle of the tank, on a small island, is the enchanting little palace of Jagmandir. Built in 1740 by one of the maharanis of Kota, it's best seen early in the morning but is exquisite at any time of day. It's not currently open to the public but you could get a close look by renting one of the RTDC paddle boats (Rs 20) to get out there.

Brij Vilas Palace Museum

The government museum is in this small plain palace near the Kishore Sagar. It has a collection of stone idols and other such fragments, mainly from the archaeological sites at Baroli and Jhalawar. Neither the museum nor the palace are of great interest, though. It's open daily except Friday between 10 am and 4.30 pm; entry is Rs 2.

Gardens

There are several well-maintained, peaceful gardens in Kota.

The **Chambal Gardens**, south of the fort at Amar Niwas, are popular for picnics and there's a cafe here. The centrepiece is a murky pond well stocked with crocodiles. Once common all along the river, by the middle of this century crocodiles had been virtually exterminated through hunting. There are also some rare gharial – thin-snouted fish-eating crocodiles.

Just beside the Tourist Bungalow are the **Chhattar Bilas Gardens**, a curious collection of somewhat neglected but impressive royal tombs, or chhatris.

Places to Stay

Although there are a number of reasonable hotels close to the railway station, few people choose to stay such a long way from the centre of things. The best place here is the 'genteelly situated' *Hotel Shri Anand* (☎ 21-773), 100 metres along the street opposite the station. Small clean rooms, all with satellite TV, cost Rs 50/80 with common bath, Rs 80/110 with bath attached.

The *Hotel Marudhar* (☎ 26-186), Jhalawar Rd, is between the fort and Kishore Sagar. An air-cooled double with attached

bath and black & white TV costs Rs 165; an extra Rs 35 gets you colour TV. Air-con rooms cost Rs 300/350. There are several other similarly priced hotels in this area.

The RTDC *Hotel Chambal Tourist Bungalow* (☎ 26-527) is near Kishore Sagar, set in scrubby gardens. The mosquitoes at this place are tenacious, but this is a problem common to all hotels here. Air-cooled rooms cost Rs 200/250 or Rs 350/400 for air-con. It's not great value but all rooms have attached bath with constant hot water. For something cheaper, try the *Chaman Hotel* (☎ 23-377), closer to the bus stand, on Station Rd. It's grubby but undeniably cheap at Rs 30/40 with common bath and bucket showers.

The *Hotel Phul Plaza* (☎ 22-614), near the Chaman, is a bright new place that's excellent value. There's a range of rooms, all with attached bath and constant hot water, from Rs 220/270 with air-cooling to Rs 600/675 for a deluxe air-con room. It's providing stiff competition for the *Hotel Navrang* (☎ 23-294), next door, currently overpriced at Rs 300/400 for a room with attached bath – clean and pleasant though this place is.

By far the best hotel in Kota is the *Hotel Brijraj Bhawan Palace* (☎ 25-203), once a palace of the maharaos of Kota and also the former British Residency. This superb hotel sits on an elevated site overlooking the Chambal River and is surrounded by beautifully maintained gardens, complete with peacocks. Everything has been left exactly as it was in those unhurried days before socialist India swept aside the princely states.

The lounge is awash with photographs of the former maharao and his son (now a general) shaking hands with everyone who was anyone during the '50s and '60s, from Indira Gandhi to J G Diefenbaker (Canadian prime minister) and Giscard d'Estaing (French president). There are more antelopes' and tigers' heads brooding over the diners in the period dining hall than there are live animals in Ranthambhore National Park. The rooms, better described as suites, are furnished with armchairs, a writing table and enormous beds, and have verandahs on which you could stage a June Ball.

Prices for all this are a bargain at Rs 500/925, or Rs 675/1250 including meals. Since there's only one single and five doubles, you should try to make reservations in advance.

The Welcomgroup is converting the *Umaid Bhawan Palace* (☎ 23-003), in the north of the town, into an upmarket hotel.

Places to Eat

Virtually all the cheap restaurants are up by the railway station; there are very few around the Tourist Bungalow or the bus stand.

On the footpath outside the GPO, many omelette stalls set up in the early evening, and this can be a cheap way to eat. There's a good vegetarian restaurant at the *Hotel Phul Plaza*, and the *Hotel Navrang* offers quite reasonable food – main dishes (non-veg) are Rs 35 to Rs 45.

If you're staying at the *Hotel Brijraj Bhawan*, you'd be mad to eat anywhere else – it's certainly an experience. Unfortunately, the dining room is not open to non-guests.

Getting There & Away

Air Jagson Airlines has flights to Jaipur (US$44) on Monday, Wednesday and Friday. You can make reservations through several travel agents here including Goodluck Travels (☎ 22-269).

Bus There are bus connections to Bundi, Ajmer, Chittorgarh (six hours), Jaipur, Udaipur and other centres in Rajasthan. If you're heading into Madhya Pradesh, several buses a day go to such places as Gwalior, Ujjain and Indore. None of the timetables at the bus stand are in English.

Buses leave for Bundi every hour, usually on the half hour, from around 6.30 am to 10.30 pm. The fare for the 50-minute journey is Rs 10. Tickets should be bought from window No 1 at the bus stand.

Train Kota is on the main broad-gauge Bombay to Delhi line via Sawai Madhopur,

so there are plenty of trains to choose from. For Sawai Madhopur, the 108-km journey takes a bit over two hours at a cost of Rs 29/122 in 2nd/1st class. To Agra Fort it's 343 km at a cost of Rs 77/291 in 2nd/1st class. There's a broad-gauge line linking Kota with Chittorgarh via Bundi. The daily train departs at 7.30 am.

Getting Around

Minibuses link the railway station and bus stand (Rs 1.50). An auto-rickshaw should cost Rs 12 for this journey, although naturally you'll be asked for more.

AROUND KOTA
Baroli

One of Rajasthan's oldest temple complexes is at Baroli, 56 km from Kota on the way to Pratap Sagar. Many of the temples were vandalised by Muslim armies but much remains and it warrants a visit. Many of the sculptures from these **9th-century temples** are displayed in the government museum in Kota. There are hourly buses from Kota.

Jhalawar

Situated 87 km south of Kota, at the centre of an opium-producing region, Jhalawar was the capital of a small princely state created in 1838. The **Jhanan Khas**, part of the palace, can be visited; it's decorated with murals and glass-work paintings. There's also a small **museum**.

There's an annual tourist festival in February/March. In October/November the Chandrabhaga cattle fair is held on the banks of this river, just outside Jhalara-Patan (see next section). During the fair, on the last day of Kartika, thousands of devotees take a holy dip.

Accommodation is limited; the best option is the RTDC *Hotel Chandrawati* (☎ (07432) 30-015). There are dorm beds for Rs 40, ordinary rooms for Rs 100/125 and deluxe rooms for Rs 200/250, all with attached bath. The tourist office is here.

There are hourly buses from Kota and the journey takes 2½ hours.

Jhalara-Patan

At Jhalara-Patan, seven km north of Jhalawar on the Kota road, are the ruins of a huge 10th-century Surya (the sun god), **temple** containing magnificent sculptures as well as one of the best preserved idols of Surya in the whole of India.

Gagron Fortress

While you're in this area, you should also take a look at the Gagron Fortress, 10 km from Jhalawar. Very few tourists even suspect its existence, and if you like to explore in peace and quiet this place is perfect. Though perhaps not as famous as others like Chittorgarh, Jodhpur and Jaisalmer, the huge fort occupies a prominent place in the annals of Rajput chivalry and has been fought over for centuries.

The fort is close to (and visible from) the road between Kota and Ujjain and Indore. There are local buses from Jhalawar.

BUNDI

Population: 72,000
Telephone Area Code: 0747

Bundi, only 39 km north-west of Kota, was the capital of a major princely state during the heyday of the Rajputs. Although its importance dwindled with the rise of Kota during Mughal times, it maintained its independence until its incorporation into the state of Rajasthan in 1947. Kota itself was part of Bundi until its separation in 1624 at the instigation of the Mughal emperor, Jehangir.

Today, Bundi is a picturesque little town whose medieval atmosphere more or less remains. It's also well off the beaten track, so there are very few tourists here. The town's Rajput legacy is well preserved in the shape of the massive Taragarh Fort, which broods over the town in the narrow valley below, and the huge palace which stands beneath it. In this palace are found the famous Bundi murals – similar to those in the Rao Madho Singh Museum in Kota.

Many people visit Bundi on a day trip from Kota, but it's worth spending the night here. There's a small, helpful tourist office

(π 22-697) in the grounds of the Circuit House.

Taragarh Fort

The Star Fort was built in 1354. It is reached by a steep road leading up the hillside to its enormous gateway, topped by rampant elephants. Inside are huge reservoirs carved out of solid rock and the Bhim Burj, the largest of the battlements, on which is mounted a famous cannon. Views over the town and surrounding countryside are excellent. It's just a pity that the national broadcaster, Doordarshan, decided to build a huge concrete transmission tower right next to the fort – it's a real eyesore.

Palace

The palace itself is reached from the north-western end of the bazaar, through a huge wooden gateway and up a steep cobbled ramp. Only two parts of the outer perimeter of the palace, known variously as the Chitra Mahal and Ummed Mahal, are generally open to the public. Some of the famous Bundi **murals** can be seen on the upper level. Photography is prohibited.

The rest of the palace, which houses the bulk of the absolutely superb Bundi murals, can only be visited with special permission. It was closed to the public, mainly because of a dispute between the current maharaja and his sister. It seems that the maharaja sold all of the family properties (Taragarh Fort, this palace and the Phool Sagar Palace) to the Oberoi hotel chain, but his sister is now claiming her share of the proceeds. Until the dispute is settled (if it is in fact settled), it seems likely the palace will remain closed. What is more, maintenance seems to be non-existent and the palace is already rapidly deteriorating, which is tragic.

Nawal Sagar

Visible from the fort is the square artificial lake of Nawal Sagar. In the centre is a temple to Varuna, the Aryan god of water.

Baoris

Bundi has a couple of beautiful *baoris* (step-

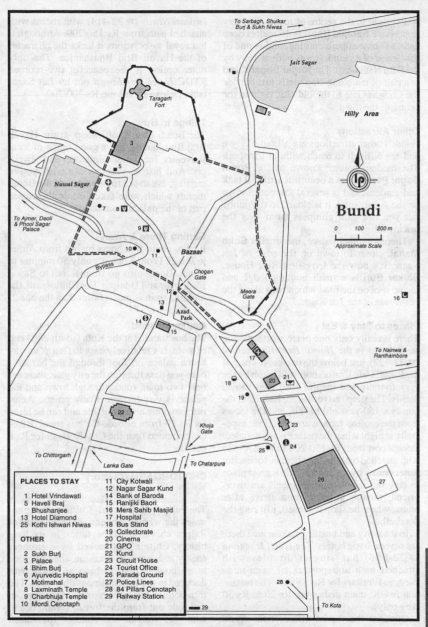

To Sarbagh, Shuikar Burj & Sukh Niwas

Jait Sagar

Hilly Area

Taragarh Fort

Nawal Sagar

To Ajmer, Deoli & Phool Sagar Palace

Bazaar

Bypass

Chogan Gate

Meera Gate

Bundi

0   100   200 m

Approximate Scale

To Nainwa & Ranthambore

Azad Park

Khoja Gate

To Chittorgarh

Lanka Gate

To Chatarpura

To Kota

RAJASTHAN

PLACES TO STAY
1 Hotel Vrindawati
5 Haveli Braj Bhushanjee
13 Hotel Diamond
25 Kothi Ishwari Niwas

OTHER
2 Sukh Burj
3 Palace
4 Bhim Burj
6 Ayurvedic Hospital
7 Motimahal
8 Laxminath Temple
9 Charbhuja Temple
10 Mordi Cenotaph
11 City Kotwali
12 Nagar Sagar Kund
14 Bank of Baroda
15 Ranijiki Baori
16 Mera Sahib Masjid
17 Hospital
18 Bus Stand
19 Collectorate
20 Cinema
21 GPO
22 Kund
23 Circuit House
24 Tourist Office
26 Parade Ground
27 Police Lines
28 84 Pillars Cenotaph
29 Railway Station

wells) right in the centre of town. The very impressive **Ranijiki Baori** is 46 metres deep and has some superb carving, and is one of the largest of its kind. It was built in 1699 by the Rani Nathavatji. The **Nagar Sagar Kund** is a pair of matching step-wells just outside the Chogan Gate to the old city, right in the centre of the town.

Other Attractions

Bundi's other attractions are all out of town and are difficult to reach without transport. The modern palace, known as the **Phool Sagar Palace**, has a beautiful artificial tank and gardens, and is several km out of town on the Ajmer road. It is closed to the public but you can gain glimpses from over the brick wall.

There's another palace, the smaller **Sukh Mahal**, closer to town on the edge of Jait Sagar. It's now the Irrigation Rest House. **Shikar Burj** is a small hunting lodge and picnic spot on the road which runs along the north side of the Jait Sagar.

Places to Stay & Eat

There is really only one place worth staying at, and that is the *Haveli Braj Bhushanjee* (☎ 32-322), just below the palace. It's part of the Bundi Cafe Crafts shop, and is run by the very friendly and helpful Braj Bhushanjee family. The shop and rooms are housed in the family's 150-year-old haveli, and the views from the rooftop terrace are excellent, especially at night when the palace is illuminated. Rooms cost from Rs 150/200 to Rs 250/325 with attached bath; in the cheaper rooms hot water comes by the bucket. It's a great place to stay but the vegetarian meals are overpriced, though good. If you arrive after hours, when the shop is closed, just ring the doorbell.

In the noisy and bustling bazaar area there are several basic hotels. The *Hotel Diamond* (☎ 22-656) has singles/doubles with attached bath and posters of semi-nude Western filmstars for Rs 50/100. The restaurant is OK; main dishes are Rs 20 to Rs 30 (veg only).

Opposite the tourist office is the *Kothi*

Ishwari Niwas (☎ 32-414) with rooms with attached bath from Rs 150/200. Although it has royal associations it lacks the character of the Haveli Braj Bhushanjee. The only other option is the peaceful two-roomed RTDC *Hotel Vrindawati* out by Jait Sagar tank. Deluxe rooms are Rs 200/300.

Things to Buy

The Bundi Cafe Crafts shop, at the Haveli Braj Bhushanjee, has a good range of local souvenirs, including miniatures and jewellery. And just so you can see what you're missing, ask to see their photos of the Bundi murals which were taken inside the closed part of the palace – amazing!

Getting There & Away

It takes about five hours by bus from Ajmer to Bundi. From Kota, it's only 50 minutes to Bundi. Buses also go from Bundi to Sawai Madhopur and Udaipur. For Chittorgarh, the morning train is much faster than the bus.

Getting Around

The bus stand is at the Kota (south-east) end of town. It's relatively easy to find your way to the palace on foot through the bazaar – once you pass through the city gate, there are only two main roads through town and the palace is visible from many points. Autorickshaws are also available and can be hired for Rs 10 from outside the bus stand. Bikes can be rented near the City Kotwali for Rs 8 per day.

CHITTORGARH (Chittor)
Population: 79,000
Telephone Area Code: 01472

The hilltop fortress of Chittorgarh epitomises the whole romantic, doomed ideal of Rajput chivalry. Three times in its long history, Chittor was sacked by a stronger enemy and, on each occasion, the end came in textbook Rajput fashion as jauhar was declared in the face of impossible odds. The men donned the saffron robes of martyrdom and rode out from the fort to certain death, while the women and children immolated

Flower Garlands

Flower garlands *(mala)* are widely used by people of many faiths – they are offered to both people and gods as a sign of respect. At a wedding, cars are often completely covered in garlands, and a groom may be presented with a garland of rupee notes *(noton ki mala)*. After a wedding, the bride places a flower garland of honour *(jaimala)* around her husband's neck.

The two most common flowers used in garlands are white jasmine and the orange marigold, and you'll often come across a garland-maker *(malakar)* squatting on the pavement patiently threading the flowers.

GREG ELMS

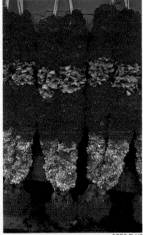

GREG ELMS

LEANNE LOGAN

Top left: Mysore flower market.

Top right: Flower garlands, Mysore.

Bottom: Flower vendors arranging their stall, Tamil Nadu.

Street Vendors

One of the most interesting aspects of travel in India is the wide variety of goods and services offered by pavement vendors – everything from stocks and shares to a replacement tooth! The ones you'll see most often are the shoe-repair wallahs and pavement barbers, whose tools of the trade may be nothing more than a razor, scissors and the all-important mirror for customers to admire themselves in.

The pavement dentist may have an impressive display of dentures and teeth – and an array of implements straight out of the Middle Ages. Ear-cleaners also ply their trade on the streets, and are easily recognised by their small red turbans, into which they stick their various picks and prods.

Then there are the unemployed who sell various items on commission from shops. You might see a boy trying to sell half a dozen pairs of black socks, another with pens, padlocks or cheap and nasty plastic toys. It's hard to see how some of them make any money at all; the commission on a Rs 2 plastic comb can't be worth a lot, and how many can you sell in a day anyway?

In the hot season, the men with their large metal water carts do a good trade at 25 paise a glass, as do the ice-cream sellers with their decorated white carts. It's probably best to avoid the water carts, and only buy well-known brands of ice cream, such as Kwality, Havmore and Milkfood.

Top: Glass bangles, worn by most Indian women, for sale, Delhi.

Middle: Roadside stall selling Rajasthani puppets.

Bottom Left: Shoe-repair wallah, Ahmedabad, Gujarat.

Bottom Right: Tourists check out souvenirs along Jan-path, Delhi.

Food Markets

Some of the most colourful scenes you'll see in India are the food markets that you'll come across in every city and town. Many of these are weekly events, with people coming in from the surrounding districts to buy and sell produce. Others may be just a collection of fruit and vegetable sellers who set up at a particular spot each day. The larger cities usually have purpose-built markets.

With vegetarianism being so widespread, most markets are devoted purely to fruit, vegetables, herbs and spices. Markets selling meat, poultry or fish are kept apart and are often found in the Muslim part of town.

Top Left: Vegetable vendor at Crawford Market, Bombay, Maharashtra.

Top Right: Roadside spices, Mysore.

Bottom Right: Street vendor making samosas.

Bottom Left: Samples of goods at the Old Delhi wholesale spice market.

LEANNE LOGAN

GREG ELMS

HUGH FINLAY

BRYN THOMAS

Henna Markings

Marking the hands and feet with henna, a plant extract, is a popular practice in many places, but especially in Rajasthan. When mixed with water, the green powder forms a reddish dye, which is then used to paint intricate patterns on the skin. This is usually done using thin plastic stencils bought cheaply in the bazaar, although there are still people who make a living from painting the designs freehand. Once applied, the dye can't be washed off, but gradually fades after about 10 days.

The Urdu word 'henna' comes from Arabic; Hindi speakers generally use the word *mehndi*, which is also used to describe the pre-marriage ceremony when henna patterns are drawn on the bride's hands and feet.

AVINASH PASRICHA

Henna painting being applied by a roadside vendor.

AVINASH PASRICHA

AVINASH PASRICHA

themselves on a huge funeral pyre. Honour was always more important than death.

Despite the fort's impressive location and colourful history, Chittor is well and truly off the main tourist circuit and sees surprisingly few visitors. It's well worth the detour.

History

Chittor's first defeat occurred in 1303 when Ala-ud-din Khilji, the Pathan King of Delhi, besieged the fort in order to capture the beautiful Padmini, wife of the Rana's uncle, Bhim Singh. When defeat was inevitable the Rajput noblewomen, including Padmini, committed sati and Bhim Singh led the orange-clad noblemen out to their deaths.

In 1535 it was Bahadur Shah, the sultan of Gujarat, who besieged the fort and, once again, the medieval dictates of chivalry determined the outcome. This time, the carnage was immense. It is said that 13,000 Rajput women and 32,000 Rajput warriors died following the declaration of jauhar.

The final sack of Chittor came just 33 years later, in 1568, when the Mughal emperor, Akbar, took the town. Once again, the fort was defended heroically but, once again, the odds were overwhelming and the women performed sati, the fort gates were flung open and 8000 orange-robed warriors rode out to their deaths. On this occasion, Maharana Udai Singh fled to Udaipur where he re-established his capital. In 1616, Jehangir returned Chittor to the Rajputs but there was no attempt at resettlement.

Orientation & Information

The fort stands on a 280-hectare site on top of a 180-metre-high hill, which rises abruptly from the surrounding plain. Until 1568, the town of Chittor was also on the hilltop within the fort walls but today's modern town, known as Lower Town, sprawls to the west of the hill. A river separates it from the bus stand, railway line and the rest of the town.

The new Tourist Reception Centre (☎ 41-089) is in the RTDC Janta Avas Grah, near the railway station. It's open Monday to Saturday from 10 am to 5 pm.

Fort

Bhim, one of the Pandava heroes of the *Mahabharata*, is credited with the fort's original construction. All of Chittor's attractions are within the fort. A zigzag ascent of over one km leads through seven gateways to the main gate on the western side, the Ram Pol.

On the climb, you pass two chhatris, memorials marking spots where Jaimal and Kalla, heroes of the 1568 siege, fell during the struggle against Akbar. Another chhatri, further up the hill, marks the spot where Patta fell. The main gate on the eastern side of the fort is the Suraj Pol. Within the fort, a circular road runs around the ruins and there's a deer park at the southern end.

Today, the fort of Chittor is a virtually deserted ruin, but impressive reminders of its grandeur still stand. The main sites can all be seen in half a day (assuming you're not walking) but, if you like the atmosphere of ancient sites, then it's worth spending longer as this is a very mellow place and there are no hassles whatsoever.

Rana Kumbha Palace Entering the fort and turning right, you come almost immediately to the ruins of this palace. It contains elephant and horse stables and a Siva temple. One of the jauhars is said to have taken place in a vaulted cellar. Across from the palace is the archaeological office and museum, and the treasury building or Nau Lakha Bhandar.

Fateh Prakash Palace Just beyond the Rana Kumbha Palace, this palace is much more modern (Maharana Fateh Singh died in 1930). It houses a small and poorly lit **museum**, and the rest of the building is closed. The museum is open daily except Friday from 10 am to 4 pm. Entry costs Rs 2.

Tower of Victory Continuing anticlockwise around the fort, you come to the Jaya Stambh, or Tower of Victory. Erected by Rana Kumbha to commemorate his victory over Mahmud Khilji of Malwa in 1440, the tower was constructed between 1458 and

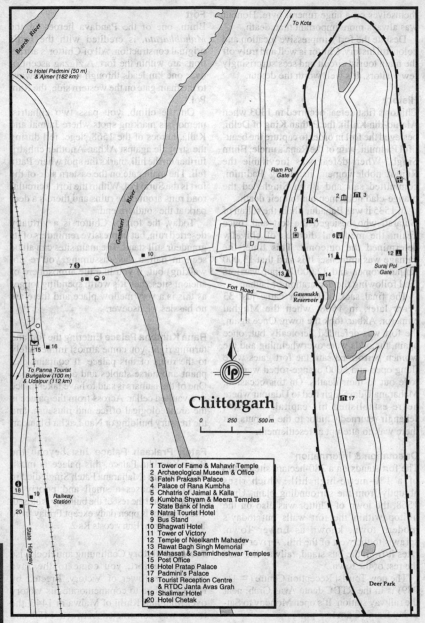

Chittorgarh

0   250   500 m

1 Tower of Fame & Mahavir Temple
2 Archaeological Museum & Office
3 Fateh Prakash Palace
4 Palace of Rana Kumbha
5 Chhatris of Jaimal & Kalla
6 Kumbha Shyam & Meera Temples
7 State Bank of India
8 Natraj Tourist Hotel
9 Bus Stand
10 Bhagwati Hotel
11 Tower of Victory
12 Temple of Neelkanth Mahadev
13 Rawat Bagh Singh Memorial
14 Mahasati & Sammidheshwar Temples
15 Post Office
16 Hotel Pratap Palace
17 Padmini's Palace
18 Tourist Reception Centre
   & RTDC Janta Avas Grah
19 Shalimar Hotel
20 Hotel Chetak

To Kota

Ram Pol
Gate

Suraj Pol
Gate

Fort Road

Gaumukh
Reservoir

Deer Park

To Hotel Padmini (50 m)
& Ajmer (182 km)

Beach River

Gambhieri River

To Panna Tourist
Bungalow (100 m)
& Udaipur (112 km)

Railway
Station

State Highway

RAJASTHAN

1468. It rises 37 metres in nine storeys and you can climb the narrow stairs to the top. Entry is Rs 0.50; free on Friday. Watch your head on the lintels!

Hindu sculptures adorn the outside of the tower, but the dome was damaged by lightning and repaired during the last century. Close to the tower is the Mahasati, an area where the ranas were cremated during Chittorgarh's period as the Mewar capital. There are many sati stones here. The **Sammidheshwar Temple** stands in the same area.

Gaumukh Reservoir Walk down beyond the temple and, at the very edge of the cliff, you'll see this deep tank. A spring feeds the tank from a carved cow's mouth in the cliffside – from which the reservoir got its name. The opening here leads to the cave in which Padmini and her compatriots are said to have committed jauhar.

Padmini's Palace Continuing south, you come to Padmini's Palace, built beside a large pool with a pavilion in its centre. Legends relate that, as Padmini stood in this pavilion, Ala-ud-din was permitted to see her reflection in a mirror in the palace. This glimpse was the spark that convinced him to destroy Chittor in order to possess her.

The bronze gates in this pavilion were carried off by Akbar and can now be seen in the fort at Agra. Continuing round the circular road, you pass the deer park, the Bhimlat Tank, the Suraj Pol gate and the Neelkanth Mahadev Jain temple, before reaching the Tower of Fame.

Tower of Fame Chittor's other famous tower, the Kirti Stambha, or Tower of Fame, is older (probably built around the 12th century) and smaller (22 metres high) than the Tower of Victory. Built by a Jain merchant, it is dedicated to Adinath, first Jain tirthankar, and is decorated with naked figures of the various tirthankars, thus indicating that it is a Digambara, or 'sky clad', monument. A narrow stairway leads through the seven storeys to the top.

Other Buildings Close to the Fateh Prakash Palace is the **Meera Temple**, built during the reign of Rana Kumbha in the ornate Indo-Aryan style and associated with the mystic-poetess Meerabai. The larger temple in this same compound is the **Kumbha Shyam Temple**, or Temple of Vriji. The Jain (but Hindu-influenced) **Singa Chowri Temple** is nearby.

Across from Padmini's Palace is the **Kalika Mata Temple**, an 8th-century Surya temple. It was later converted to a temple to the goddess Kali. At the northern tip of the fort is another gate, the **Lokhota Bari**, while at the southern end is a small opening from which criminals and traitors were hurled into the abyss.

Places to Stay & Eat

Accommodation possibilities in Chittor are limited. At the railway station, *retiring rooms* cost Rs 55 for an ordinary double or Rs 170 for the air-con room. The revamped RTDC *Janta Avas Grah*, above the Tourist Reception Centre near the railway station, should now be open. There's a small amount of budget accommodation here.

There are several other places around the station. The *Shalimar Hotel* (☎ 40-842) has rooms for Rs 60/80 with common bath, Rs 80/100 with bath attached. The *Hotel Chetak* (☎ 41-588), nearby, is better, with rooms from Rs 150/225 – hot water only in the mornings. This hotel has a good restaurant, however.

By the bus stand there's the very basic *Natraj Tourist Hotel*. Rooms cost Rs 25/35, Rs 50/75 with bath; but you'll probably have to get them to change the sheets. The *Bhagwati Hotel*, just over the river, is better but a bit more expensive.

Closer to the town centre is the fairly modern RTDC *Hotel Panna Tourist Bungalow* (☎ 41-238). There's a dusty dorm for Rs 40 per bed, ordinary rooms with cold water in the attached bathrooms for Rs 80/125, better rooms for Rs 170/250 with constant hot water, and air-con rooms for Rs 350/450. The hotel has a bar and surprisingly good meals are available in the restaurant. A whole roast chicken costs Rs 100, and there are set meals for Rs 67 (veg) and Rs 83 (non-veg).

The *Hotel Pratap Palace* (☎ 40-099; fax 41-042), between the bus stand and the Panna Tourist Bungalow, is more upmarket. Clean and airy air-cooled rooms here cost Rs 225/275 with attached bath, or Rs 325/375 with air-con. The restaurant is good and there's some seating outside. A half chicken tandoori costs Rs 50; set meals are Rs 110.

In a peaceful location by the Bearch River is the overpriced *Hotel Padmini* (☎ 41-718) with rooms at Rs 550/650. The vegetarian restaurant is recommended, however. Main dishes are just Rs 10 to Rs 20.

Getting There & Away

Chittor is on the main bus and rail routes. By road, it's 182 km from Ajmer, 158 km from Bundi and 112 km from Udaipur. There are frequent connections to both places, and all the Kota buses go via Bundi (a slow 4½-hour trip).

It's possible to take an early bus from Udaipur to Chittorgarh (Rs 34, two hours), spend about three hours visiting the fort (by auto-rickshaw or tonga), and then take a late afternoon bus to Ajmer, but this is definitely pushing it.

Chittorgarh also has rail links with Ahmedabad, Udaipur, Ajmer, Jaipur and Delhi. The broad-gauge line to Kota and Bundi would be convenient, except that the only passenger train on this route leaves Chittor at 2.50 pm, reaching Bundi at 6 pm and Kota at 7.15 pm.

Getting Around

It's six km from the railway station to the fort, less from the bus stand, and seven km around the fort itself, not including the long southern loop out to the deer park. Auto-rickshaws charge around Rs 80 from either the bus or railway station, and this includes waiting time at the various sites. Bicycles can also be rented near the railway station to visit the fort but, as Indian bicycles never have gears, you'll have to push the machine to the top. Still, they're great on the top and for the journey back down.

AROUND CHITTORGARH
Bijaipur

The 16th-century palace in this village, 40 km south of Chittor, is now a delightful hotel, the *Castle Bijaipur*. Rooms in this peaceful palace cost Rs 415/525 for singles/doubles, and meals are available – the set dinner is Rs 120. The owner, Rao Narendra Singh, is a keen horseman and can organise a variety of horse safaris. They're not cheap – from around Rs 2600 per person, full board. Village safaris by jeep cost around Rs 300. Bookings for the hotel should be made through the Hotel Pratap Palace in Chittor.

Menal & Bijolia

Lying on the Bundi to Chittorgarh road, 48 km from Bundi, Menal is a complex of Siva temples built during the Gupta period.

Bijolia, 16 km from Menal, was once a group of 100 temples. Today, only three are left standing, one of which has a huge figure of Ganesh.

Mandalgarh

A detour between Menal and Bijolia takes you to Mandalgarh. It is the third fort of Mewar built by Rana Kumbha – the others are the great fort of Chittorgarh and the fort at Kumbhalgarh.

Nagri

One of the oldest towns in Rajasthan, Nagri is 14 km north of Chittor. Hindu and Buddhist remains from the Mauryan to the Gupta period have been found here.

Jagat

At this small town, 20 km south of the road between Udaipur and Chittorgarh, is a small 10th-century **Durga temple**. There are some fine carvings, including a couple of small erotic carvings, which has inspired some people to call the town the Khajuraho of Rajasthan, which is total nonsense.

UDAIPUR

Population: 342,500
Telephone Area Code: 0294

Possibly no city in Rajasthan is quite as romantic as Udaipur, even though the state is replete with fantastic hilltop fortresses, exotic fairytale palaces and gripping legends of medieval chivalry and heroism. The French Impressionist painters, let alone the Brothers Grimm, would have loved this place and it's not without justification that Udaipur has been called the 'Venice of the East'. Jaisalmer is certainly the 'Beau Geste' of the desert and Udaipur is the 'Versailles'.

Founded in 1568 by Maharana Udai Singh following the final sacking of Chittorgarh by the Mughal emperor, Akbar, Udaipur rivals any of the world-famous creations of the Mughals with its Rajput love of the whimsical and its superbly crafted elegance. The Lake Palace is certainly the best late example of this unique cultural explosion, but Udaipur is full of palaces, temples and havelis ranging from the modest to the extravagant. It's also proud of its heritage as a centre for the performing arts, painting and crafts. And, since water is relatively plentiful in this part of the state (in between the periodic droughts), there are plenty of parks and gardens, many of which line the lake shores.

Until recent times, the higher uninhabited parts of the city were covered in forests but, as elsewhere in India, most of these have inevitably been turned into firewood. There is, however, a movement afoot to reverse this process. The city was once surrounded by a wall and, although the gates and much of the wall over the higher crags remain, a great deal of it has disappeared. It's sad that this fate should have befallen such a historic place but the essence remains.

In common with all Indian cities, Udaipur's urban and industrial sprawl goes beyond the city's original boundaries and pollution of various kinds can be discouraging. This will be your first impression of Udaipur if you arrive at the railway or bus stations. Ignore it and head for the old city where a different world is waiting for you.

Orientation & Information

The old city, bound by the remains of a city wall, is on the east side of Lake Pichola. The railway and bus stations are both just outside the city wall to the south-east.

The Tourist Reception Centre (☎ 41-1535) and the Tourist Bungalow are also outside the city wall, to the north-east and only a km or so from the bus stand. The office is open Monday to Saturday from 10 am to 1.30 pm and 2 to 5 pm. There are also tourist information counters at the railway station and airport.

The GPO is directly north of the old city, behind the movie theatre at Chetak Circle, but poste restante is at the post office at the junction of Hospital Rd and the road north from Delhi Gate, close to the Tourist Bungalow. It's efficient and the staff are friendly and helpful.

Lake Pichola

The beautiful Lake Pichola was enlarged by Maharana Udai Singh after he founded the city. He built a masonry dam, known as the Badi Pol, and the lake is now four km in length and three km wide. Nevertheless, it remains fairly shallow and can actually dry up in severe droughts. At these times, you can walk to the island palaces from the shore. Fortunately, this doesn't happen often. The City Palace extends a considerable distance along the east bank of the lake. South of the palace, a pleasant garden runs down to the lake. North of the palace, you can wander along the lake, where there are some interesting bathing and *dhobi* (laundry) ghats.

Out in the lake are two islands – Jagniwas and Jagmandir. Boat rides, which leave regularly from the City Palace jetty (known as Bansi Ghat), are pleasant but expensive at Rs 45 for half an hour, Rs 90 for an hour. The popular sunset cruise is Rs 110.

Jagniwas Island (Lake Palace Hotel)

Jagniwas, the Lake Palace island, is about 1.5 hectares in size. The palace was built by Maharana Jagat Singh II in 1754 and covers the whole island. Today, it has been converted into the ultimate in luxury hotels, with

RAJASTHAN

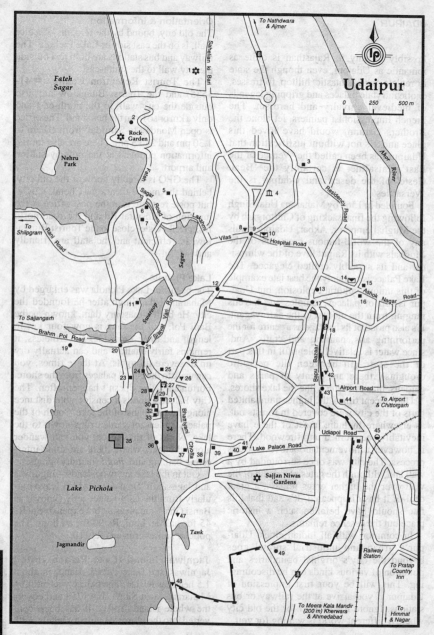

Udaipur

0   250   500 m

Fateh Sagar

Nehru Park

Rock Garden

To Nathdwara & Ajmer

To Shilpgram

To Sajjangarh

Brahm Pol Road

To Pratap Country Inn

To Airport & Chittorgarh

To Meera Kala Mandir
(200 m) Kherwara
& Ahmedabad

To Himmat & Nagar

Lake Pichola

Jagmandir

Sajjan Niwas Gardens

Lake Palace Road

Udaipol Road

Airport Road

Bapu Bazaar

Hospital Road

Residency Road

Ashok Nagar Road

Ahar River

Railway Station

Tank

Bhatiyani Chotta

Suarcop

Sihgal Vati Rd

Lakshmi

Fateh Sagar Road

Rani Road

Sahelian ki Bari

Sajjan Vilas

PLACES TO STAY				
		31	Centre View Guest	47 Cafe Hill Park
3	Mewar Inn		House	48 Jai Burj Cafe
5	Hotels Laxmi Vilas	32	Hotel Sai-Niwas &	
	Palace & Anand		Shiva Guest House	**OTHER**
	Bhawan	33	Lake Corner Soni	
6	Gulab Niwas		Paying Guest	1 Saheliyon ki Bari
7	Hotel Hilltop Palace		House	2 Moti Magri Hill
11	Hotel Natural	35	Jagniwas (Lake	4 Bhartiya Lok Kala
15	Kajri Tourist		Palace Hotel)	Museum
	Bungalow	37	Hotel Raj Palace	9 Chetak Circle
16	Prince & Alka Hotels	38	Rang Niwas Palace	10 GPO
23	Lake Pichola & Lake		Hotel	12 Hathi Gate
	Shore Hotels	39	Ranjit Niwas Hotel	13 Indian Airlines
24	Jheel Guest House	40	Hotel Mahendra	14 Poste Restante
25	Badi Haveli &		Prakash	15 Tourist Office
	Anjani Guest	41	Haveli Hotel	17 Delhi Gate
	House	44	Hotel Apsara	18 Bank of Baroda
28	Lalghat & Evergreen	46	Hotel Welcome	19 Brahm Gate
	Guest Houses			20 Amba Gate
29	Lake Ghat & Ratan	**PLACES TO EAT**		21 Chand Gate
	Palace Guest			22 Clock Tower
	Houses	8	Berry's Restaurant	27 Jagdish Temple
30	Jagat Niwas Palace	26	Mayur Cafe	34 City Palace
	Hotel &	28	Natural View	36 Bansi Ghat
	Rainbow Guest		Restaurant	43 Suraj Gate
	House	42	Park View	45 Bus Stand
			Restaurant	49 Kishan Gate

courtyards, fountains, gardens and a swimming pool. It's a magical place but casual visitors are discouraged. It used to be possible to visit the palace for afternoon tea but now non-guests can only come over for lunch or dinner – and then only if the hotel is not full, which it often is. Hotel launches cross to the island from the City Palace jetty.

Jagmandir Island The other island palace, Jagmandir, was commenced by Maharana Karan Singh, but takes its name from Maharana Jagat Singh (1628-52) who made a number of additions to it. It is said that the Mughal emperor, Shah Jahan, derived some of his ideas for the Taj Mahal from this palace after staying here in 1623-24 while leading a revolt against his father, Jehangir. The view across the lake from the southern end, with the city and its great palace rising up behind the island palaces, is a scene of rare beauty.

City Palace & Museums
The huge City Palace, towering over the lake, is the largest palace complex in Rajasthan. Actually a conglomeration of buildings added by various maharanas, the palace manages to retain a surprising uniformity of design. Building was started by Maharana Udai Singh, the city's founder. The palace is surmounted by balconies, towers and cupolas and there are fine views over the lake and the city from the upper terraces.

The palace is entered from the northern end through the Bari Pol of 1600 and the Tripolia Gate of 1725, with its eight carved marble arches. It was once a custom for maharanas to be weighed under the gate and their weight in gold or silver distributed to the populace.

The main part of the palace is now preserved as a museum with a large and varied, although somewhat run-down, collection. The museum includes the Mor Chowk with its beautiful mosaics of peacocks, the favourite Rajasthani bird. The Manak (or Ruby) Mahal has glass and porcelain figures while Krishna Vilas has a remarkable collection of miniatures. In the Bari Mahal, there is a fine

RAJASTHAN

central garden. More paintings can be seen in the Zanana Mahal. The Moti Mahal has beautiful mirrorwork and the Chini Mahal is covered in ornamental tiles.

Enter the **City Palace Museum** through the Ganesh Deori which leads to the Rai Angam, or Royal Courtyard. The museum is open from 9.30 am to 4.30 pm and entry is Rs 30, plus Rs 30 for a camera. A guide (Rs 45) is worthwhile. There's also a **government museum** (Rs 2) within the palace complex. Exhibits include a stuffed kangaroo, a scarcely recognisable ostrich and Siamese-twin deer.

The other part of the palace is up against the lake shore and, like the Lake Palace, it has been converted into a luxury hotel – two, in fact, known as the Shiv Niwas Palace and the Fateh Prakash Palace hotels.

Jagdish Temple

Located only 150 metres north of the entrance to the City Palace, this fine Indo-Aryan temple was built by Maharana Jagat Singh in 1651 and enshrines a black stone image of Vishnu as Jagannath, Lord of the Universe. A brass image of the Garuda is in a shrine in front of the temple and the steps up to the temple are flanked by elephants.

Bagore ki Haveli

This 18th-century house is on the lake shore, below the Jagdish Temple. It was built by a nobleman, and was once used as a royal guest house. It is one of the finest examples of its type, and now houses the Western Zone Cultural Centre. The labyrinthine haveli houses a graphics studio, **art gallery** (which occasionally has exhibitions by local artists), and some fine coloured glass and inlay work. It is open daily from 9.30 am to 6 pm, and entry is Rs 20.

Fateh Sagar

North of Lake Pichola, this lake is overlooked by a number of hills and parks. It was originally built in 1678 by Maharana Jai Singh but, after heavy rains destroyed the dam, it was reconstructed by Maharana Fateh Singh. A pleasant lakeside drive winds along the east bank of the lake. In the middle of the lake is Nehru Park, a popular garden island with a boat-shaped cafe. You can get there by boat from near the bottom of Moti Magri Hill for Rs 6 return. Pedal boats (Rs 20) are also available.

Pratap Samak

Atop the Moti Magri, or Pearl Hill, overlooking Fateh Sagar, is a **statue** of the Rajput hero Maharana Pratap, who frequently defied the Mughals. The path to the top traverses elegant **gardens**, including a Japanese rock garden. The park is open from 9 am to 6 pm and there's a small admission fee.

Bhartiya Lok Kala Museum

The interesting collection exhibited by this small museum and foundation for the preservation of folk arts includes dresses, dolls, masks, musical instruments, paintings and – the high point of the exhibits – puppets. The museum is open daily from 9 am to 6 pm and admission costs Rs 7. Regular puppet shows are held daily from 6 to 7 pm. Call ☎ 52-4296 for details.

Saheliyon ki Bari

The Saheliyon ki Bari, or Garden of the Maids of Honour, is in the north of the city. This small ornamental garden, with its fountains, kiosks, marble elephants and delightful lotus pool, is open from 9 am to 6 pm. Entry is Rs 2. They sometimes ask for Rs 5 to turn the fountains on; a camera fee of Rs 10 is charged.

Shilpgram

Shilpgram, a crafts village three km west of Fateh Sagar, was inaugurated by Rajiv Gandhi in 1989. It's an interesting place with traditional houses from four states – Rajasthan, Gujarat, Goa and Maharashtra – and there are daily demonstrations by musicians, dancers, or artisans from the various states. Although it's much more animated during festival times (check with the Tourist Reception Centre for details), there's usually something happening.

The site covers 80 hectares but most buildings are in a fairly compact area. It's open daily from 9.30 am to 4.30 pm, and is well worth a visit; entry is Rs 10.

The open-air *Shilpi Restaurant* next to the site serves very good Indian and Chinese food, and snacks. It also has a swimming pool (Rs 75), open from 10 am to 4 pm. There's no public transport to Shilpgram, so you'll have to rent a bicycle, or take an auto-rickshaw or taxi.

Ahar Museum

Three km east of Udaipur are the remains of an ancient city. Here, you'll find a small museum and the cenotaphs of the maharanas of Mewar.

Other Attractions

Patel or Sukhadia Circle is north of the city. The huge **fountain** in the centre is illuminated at night. **Sajjan Niwas Gardens** have pleasant lawns, a zoo and a children's train (if it's operating). Beside it is the Rose Garden, or **Gulab Bagh**. Don't confuse the **Nehru Park** opposite Bapu Bazaar with the island park of the same name in Fateh Sagar. The city park has some strange topiary work, a giant cement teapot and children's slides incorporating an elephant and a camel.

On the distant mountain range, the gleaming white edifice visible from the city is the former maharaja's **Monsoon Palace**. Now deserted, the views from the top are incomparable. The round trip takes about three hours.

Organised Tours

A five-hour tour starts at the Tourist Bungalow at 8 am each day. It costs Rs 30 and takes in all the main city sights. An afternoon tour (2 to 7 pm) goes out to Eklingi, Haldighati and Nathdwara and costs Rs 70.

There are also day trips with lunch included to Chittorgarh (Rs 170) and, for Rs 165, to Kumbhalgarh, Ranakpur and Ghanerao, but these don't go every day.

Places to Stay

Home-Stays Udaipur pioneered the paying guest scheme in Rajasthan, and there are now over 130 families participating. Expect to pay Rs 100 to Rs 300, depending on the level of comfort and facilities you want. The Tourist Reception Centre has a list detailing all the places and the services offered.

Places to Stay – bottom end

There are four main clusters of budget hotels in Udaipur, but those around the Jagdish Temple are definitely preferable to the others. Next best are those between the City Palace and the bus stand, along Lake Palace Rd and Bhattiyani Chotta. The third cluster is along the main road between the bus stand and the Delhi Gate. This is a very noisy and polluted road and you have to be desperate or totally lacking in imagination to stay here. The last cluster is around the Tourist Bungalow and, although it's better than staying on the main road, it's somewhat inconvenient.

Watch out for checkout times which vary greatly in Udaipur; and note that many places slap a 10% service charge on the room rates they advertise.

Jagdish Temple Area You'll pay more for a hotel in this area, but there is no traffic noise, most places have fantastic views over the lake, and the central location is ideal. As it's the most popular area to stay in, you get a lot of the 'yes have a look change money buy something' from the touts and shopowners, but this is not Agra.

The *Badi Haveli* (☎ 52-3500) is a popular place run by a hospitable family. This little labyrinth has narrow staircases, terraces, a courtyard and two rooftops with superb views over the lake and old city. The 10 rooms (two with attached bath) are all different and range from Rs 80/120 with common bath to Rs 180 for the best room at the top.

The long-running *Lalghat Guest House* (☎ 52-5301) is another travellers' favourite. Right by the lake, it has a large courtyard with tables and chairs, rooftop areas with excellent views over the water and a back terrace which overlooks the ghats. A variety of rooms are available, ranging from dorm beds for Rs 40, small rooms for Rs 75/100, larger rooms for Rs 150, or Rs 200 with attached bath, and for Rs 250 you also get a lake view. All the rooms have fans and mosquito nets. There are facilities for self-caterers, and a shop. It's certainly not the cheapest, but it's clean and well run.

Next door is the small *Evergreen Guest House* (☎ 52-7823) with just seven rooms around a small courtyard, soft beds and the Restaurant Natural View on the roof. The management is friendly and helpful, and hot water is available by the bucket at no extra charge. Rooms cost Rs 50/80 with common bath, or Rs 80/100 with attached bath. The nearby *Rainbow Guest House* is similarly priced.

Across the road from the Lalghat, the *Lake Ghat Guest House* is also popular. Again, there's a wide range of accommodation, although none of the rooms here have a view. Singles/doubles without bath cost Rs 60/80 and doubles with bath go for Rs 100 to Rs 150. While some of the cheaper rooms are very dark and cell-like, there's a good restaurant and terrace area and the management are friendly.

Behind the Lake Ghat Guest House is the *Centre View Guest House* (☎ 52-0039) with just a few rooms, all with common bath, for Rs 30/50. There are no views but the family who run it are very friendly. Another cheapie in the same area is the *Shri Karni Guest House*.

Towards Nav Ghat is the peaceful *Lake Corner Soni Paying Guest House*, with clean basic rooms set around a courtyard. Charges are Rs 60/80 for rooms with common bath, Rs 100 for a double with bath attached. Meals are available, there are superb views from the roof and it's run by a charming elderly couple. Nearby is the similarly priced *Shiva Guest House*.

Close to the Badi Haveli is the *Anjani Hotel* (☎ 52-7670). It's a modern place with a range of rooms from Rs 80 for a double; many have a lake view.

The *Jheel Guest House* (☎ 28-321) is right at the bottom of the hill, by the ghat. It is housed in an old haveli and has a good deal of character and charm. Doubles cost Rs 100 with common bath, or Rs 200 in a larger

room with bath attached and a view. There are cheaper rooms in the annex across the road.

If you want to escape the bustle and the touts, try the *Lake Shore Hotel*, next to the Lake Pichola Hotel, across the Chand Pol bridge, about a 10-minute walk from the Jagdish Temple. This place has just a few rooms, and a fine terrace with views back across to Lal Ghat. It's fairly basic, but very peaceful. Rooms range from Rs 80 to Rs 225; most have a lake view.

Further away, and even more peaceful, is the funky *Hotel Natural* (☎ 52-7879). It's right by the water and a delightful place to stay. The rooms are basic but clean and many are decorated with wall paintings. They cost Rs 40/80 with common bath, Rs 75/120 with bath attached. There's excellent food in the rooftop restaurant and, for Rs 20, they'll even bake you a cake.

Lake Palace Rd Area There are numerous places in this area. The *Haveli Hotel* (☎ 52-8294) is a small hotel with a little garden. Rooms are comfortable and range from Rs 80 to Rs 200, all with attached bath. Further along Lake Palace Rd is the *Hotel Mahendra Prakash* (☎ 52-9370), a modern building with rooms arranged around a courtyard. There are doubles from Rs 50 with common bath, from Rs 100 with attached bath and Rs 200 gets you a large double with bath and constant hot water.

The *Ranjit Niwas Hotel* (☎ 52-5774) is a small, family-run guest house in quite a good location. It's a very pleasant place to stay. Dorm beds cost Rs 30, while single/double rooms with common bath are Rs 100, or Rs 150 with bath attached. There's a discount if you stay for three days or more. Meals are available and there's a small garden courtyard.

Tourist Bungalow Area Like many of the RTDC operations, the *Hotel Kajri Tourist Bungalow* (☎ 41-0501), at the traffic circle on Ashoka Rd, has seen better days. With so many more interesting and better-located hotels in Udaipur, there's little reason to stay here. There are dorm beds for Rs 40, and rooms from Rs 150/200 to Rs 400/500.

Across the road are some cheaper places. The *Prince Hotel* (☎ 41-4355) offers ordinary rooms for Rs 60/80 and doubles with TV, attached bath and constant hot water for Rs 100. The *Alka Hotel* (☎ 41-4611) is a very large place with singles/doubles from Rs 70/120 to Rs 120/200. The more expensive rooms are air-cooled and have constant hot water. Reasonably priced vegetarian meals are served. The nearby *Ashok Hotel* is very similar in price and standard.

Bus Stand Area For those who don't mind the noise and pollution of the main road, there are a number of choices. Best of the group is the *Hotel Apsara* (☎ 52-3400), a huge place set back from the road. The rooms front onto an internal courtyard making them relatively quiet. There are dorm beds for Rs 35 and singles/doubles for Rs 75/100 to Rs 250. The more expensive rooms have constant hot water and air-con.

There are several hotels opposite the bus stand. The best of these is the *Hotel Welcome* (☎ 52-5375), with rooms with attached bath and satellite TV from Rs 95/125.

Elsewhere The only other budget option in town is the *Mewar Inn* (☎ 52-2090). Although it slags off at this book in its leaflet, it's a cheap and friendly place well away from the centre. The rickshaw drivers hate the place, and you'll have difficulty persuading one to take you there. Basic but clean rooms go for just Rs 28/37, bigger rooms cost Rs 59 to Rs 79, there are dorm beds for Rs 12, and a discount is given to YHA members. There's a vegetarian restaurant; and new rooms are under construction. The slightly inconvenient location is no great disadvantage as there are bicycles for hire (Rs 8).

There's also an interesting place at Titadha village, seven to eight km outside Udaipur – the *Pratap Country Inn*. Comfortable accommodation is in double rooms with attached bathrooms, ranging from Rs 200 to Rs 600. Set in beautiful surroundings, it's a straightforward place with a very relaxed atmosphere. Horse riding is available and they also organise longer safaris – from Rs 600 to Rs 1800 per person per day, depending on the level of luxury you choose. There's currently no phone here. It's simplest just to take an auto-rickshaw from Udaipur (Rs 30) to check the place out. City buses and tempos run from Bapu Bazaar to Titadha, from where it's a 500-metre walk. Alternatively, you could ride out here on a bike.

Places to Stay – middle
Right on the lake shore in the Lal Ghat area is the delightful *Jagat Niwas Palace Hotel* (☎ 52-9728), a converted haveli. There are cool white courtyards, marble floors and a very pleasant open-air restaurant with superb views across to the Lake Palace. Rooms with common bath range from Rs 150 to Rs 300; with attached bath they cost from Rs 450 to Rs 750.

The *Rang Niwas Palace Hotel* (☎ 52-3891), Lake Palace Rd, is one of the best mid-range options. Set in peaceful gardens, with a newly constructed marble swimming pool, it's a very relaxed hotel and an interesting place to stay. There's accommodation in the old building, formerly a palace, and also comfortable rooms in the tastefully designed new building. There are just five beds in the dorm – Rs 30 each and shared with the ping-pong table. Rooms with common bath start at Rs 150/200, and cost from Rs 250/350 to Rs 400/500 with bathroom attached. It's all very clean and well run, and there's a good vegetarian restaurant.

Also highly recommended is the *Hotel Sai-Niwas* (☎ 52-4909), just down the hill towards the ghat from the City Palace entrance. The rooms (all doubles) are imaginatively decorated, and the more expensive ones have balconies with a lake view. The cost is Rs 350 to Rs 600, all with attached bath and hot water.

Very good value is the new *Ratan Palace Guest House* (☎ 52-7935), near the Sai-Niwas. Spotlessly clean and with really comfortable beds, rooms cost from Rs 250 to Rs 400 for a double. There are lake views from the terrace and excellent food is available.

Midway along Bhattiyani Chotta down from the Jagdish Temple, is the *Hotel Raj Palace* (☎ 52-3092), currently being renovated and extended. Much of the new extension has taken up the old garden, but there's still an open-air restaurant with views of the city side of the City Palace. It's a friendly place with rooms from Rs 100/150 to Rs 250/500 – all with attached bath.

There are other options away from this area. The *Gulab Niwas* (☎ 52-3644) is a small guest house in an attractive old lodge near Fateh Sagar Lake. There are air-cooled rooms with attached bath from Rs 300/375 and a pleasant garden to relax in. Not far away along Rani Rd is the *Hotel Lakend* (☎ 52-3841) with rooms for Rs 500/700. There's a swimming pool, bar, restaurant and a garden running down to the Fateh Sagar.

Places to Stay – top end

Without a doubt, the best of the lower priced top-range hotels is the *Lake Pichola Hotel* (☎ 52-9387), Chand Pol, which looks out across to the ghats, the Jagdish Temple and the northern end of the City Palace. It's a modern building in the traditional style, and is very well maintained and managed. All rooms have air-con, telephone, carpet and bath with constant hot water, and are excellent value at Rs 575/600. There's a money-exchange facility, bar and restaurant.

Between Pichola and Fateh Sagar lakes, up on the hill, are two upper-notch hotels, side by side. The ITDC *Laxmi Vilas Palace Hotel* (☎ 52-9711) is a four-star place where air-con rooms cost Rs 1500/2300. There's a swimming pool, bar and restaurant. Next door is the smaller *Hotel Anand Bhawan* (☎ 52-3247). It's excellent value with air-con rooms with bath and constant hot water for Rs 450/550. The restaurant serves veg and non-veg food.

The *Hotel Hilltop Palace* (☎ 52-8764) is a modern hotel atop another hill in the same area. Rooms start at Rs 700/900 but this place is rather lacking in character.

About three km out of town on the

Ahmedabad road is the four-star *Shikarbadi Hotel* (☎ 58-3200) where air-con singles/doubles cost US$30/45. It's a small but pleasant hotel set in beautiful grounds with swimming pool, lawns and a small lake. It has a deer park and a stud farm – horse and elephant rides are available.

At the very top end of the scale are two of India's most luxurious hotels, facing each other across Lake Pichola. The incomparable *Lake Palace Hotel* (☎ 52-7961; fax 52-7974) is on the smaller of the lake's two islands. It's the very image of what a maharaja's palace should be like and most people with sufficient money to spend would not pass up an opportunity to stay here. It offers every conceivable comfort, including a mango tree-shaded swimming pool. The cheapest rooms are US$140/165, but with a lake view you'll pay US$170/190, while suites cost US$220 to US$550. Needless to say, you need to book well in advance.

The equally luxurious *Shiv Niwas Palace Hotel* (☎ 52-8410; fax 52-8006) forms part of the City Palace complex. It's a good deal cheaper at US$55 for standard air-con rooms, with suites ranging from US$150 to US$350. There's heavy demand for rooms here, too. In the same complex, the intimate *Hotel Fateh Prakash Palace* (☎ 52-8410) has just eight similarly priced rooms, and most of them overlook the lake. If you can't get into the Lake Palace, this is a good alternative. This hotel doesn't have its own dining room, so guests have to cross the courtyard and use the one in the Shiv Niwas.

Places to Eat

There's quite a reasonable range of restaurants in Udaipur, from rooftop cafes catering to travellers in the Lal Ghat area to excellent restaurants at the top hotels.

The little *Mayur Cafe*, by the Jagdish Temple, has long been popular, serving good south Indian dishes as well as Western alternatives such as spaghetti with cheese (Rs 22) and apple pie (Rs 20). This was one of the first places to start a nightly showing of the video *Octopussy* – partly filmed in Udaipur. Several other restaurants now try to attract customers with this James Bond movie to watch as you eat.

Above the Evergreen Guest House, the rooftop *Restaurant Natural View* serves pizzas from Rs 25, baked potatoes from Rs 20 and has a good range of Chinese dishes. One of their specialities is delicious local cheese flavoured with garlic. Other popular places in this area include the *Gokul Restaurant*, the *Four Seasons Restaurant*, and the *Relish Roof Top Restaurant*.

Just round the corner from the Rang Niwas Palace Hotel, facing the City Palace, the *Roof Garden Cafe* has the appearance of a Hanging Gardens of Babylon. The food here is slightly expensive but there's a good menu and live folk music several nights per week. The *Mayur Roof Top Restaurant*, in the same area, has reasonable food and also sometimes screens *Octopussy*.

There are several places to eat around the Hotel Natural, a 15-minute walk from the Jagdish Temple, on the other side of the northern arm of Lake Pichola. Food at the rooftop restaurant at the *Hotel Natural* is good – vegetarian, and they sometimes have homemade cakes. Next door is the *Natural Attic*. The extensive menu features Mexican, Chinese, Western, Indian and Tibetan dishes, and there's a free puppet show most evenings at 7.30 pm. Their branch in Lal Ghat is not as good.

South of the Sajjan Niwas Gardens, on the hill overlooking Lake Pichola, is the *Cafe Hill Park*, worth a visit just for the views. They offer moderately priced south Indian dishes and snacks.

For excellent north Indian food, go to the *Park View*. It's opposite the park in the main part of town but there's absolutely no view. Prices are reasonable – a half chicken tandoori costs Rs 38 – and it's often packed with middle-class Indian families. *Berry's Restaurant* on Chetak Circle is more expensive but also good. Opposite is a branch of *Kwality* which offers the usual selection.

For a minor splurge the restaurant at the *Jagat Niwas* is recommended, and the position – right above the water and overlooking the Lake Palace – is superb. Western non-veg

dishes are expensive (around Rs 85) but Indian food is cheaper. The *Shiv Niwas Palace Hotel* is more expensive but an excellent place for a special meal. Their Indian food is best, and they do great mango and strawberry ice cream.

The ultimate dining experience is, of course, at the *Lake Palace Hotel*. While the food gets mixed reports, and the dining room is not the most impressive room in the palace, it's nevertheless well worth it just to see this beautiful hotel. There's live sitar music to accompany the buffet dinner, service is attentive, and after your meal you can take a drink in the bar and watch the folk dances. There's no guarantee that you'll be able to get in, though, since it's only possible to eat here when the hotel is not full. Reservations are almost always necessary, and reasonably tidy dress is expected. The buffet dinner (7.30 to 10.30 pm) costs Rs 450, and there's also a buffet lunch for Rs 365 (12.30 to 2.30 pm). Charges include the boat crossing.

Entertainment

From August to April there are Rajasthani folk dance and music performances daily (except Sunday) at 7 pm at the Meera Kala Mandir (☎ 52-3976), Sector 11, Hiran Magari, near the Pars Theatre. They cost Rs 30 per head and are well worth attending. You can expect to see not only a whole range of tribal dances, but also some more spectacular acts which involve balancing numerous pots on top of the head while dancing on broken glass or unsheathed sabres. An autorickshaw to the auditorium from the City Palace area costs around Rs 20.

Things to Buy

Udaipur has countless small shops and many interesting local crafts, particularly miniature paintings in the Rajput-Mughal style. There's a good cluster of these shops on Lake Palace Rd, next to the Rang Niwas Palace Hotel, and others around the Jagdish Temple.

Getting There & Away

Air Indian Airlines has at least one flight a

day to Delhi (US$58), Jaipur (US$35), and Bombay (US$70), and flights five times a week to Jodhpur (US$28) and Aurangabad (US$63). The direct flight between Udaipur and Aurangabad can save a great deal of bus or train time. The office (☎ 41-0999) at Delhi Gate is open every day from 10 am to 1 pm and 2 to 5 pm.

ModiLuft (☎ 65-5281) has daily flights to Bombay (US$70), Goa (US$104), Delhi (US $58), Jaipur (US$35) and Kochi (US$161).

Bus Frequent RSTC buses run from Udaipur to other regional centres, as well as to Delhi and Ahmedabad. If you use these buses, make sure you take an express bus since the ordinary buses take forever, make innumerable detours to various towns off the main route and can be very uncomfortable. For long-distance travel, it's best to use private buses.

Destinations served by express buses include Jaipur (Rs 106, nine hours, nine daily), Ajmer (Rs 75, eight hours, 11 daily), Kota/Bundi (Rs 86, six hours, six daily), Jodhpur (Rs 70, eight to 10 hours) via either Ranakpur (four hours, six daily) or Nathdwara (two daily) and Chittorgarh (Rs 34, three hours, five daily). Express and deluxe buses should be booked in advance.

There are quite a few private bus companies which operate to such places as Ahmedabad (Rs 70, six hours), Vadodara (Rs 120, eight hours), Bombay (Rs 180, 16 hours), Delhi (Rs 140, 14 hours), Indore (Rs 110, 10 hours), Jaipur (Rs 70, nine hours), Jodhpur (Rs 60, nine hours), Kota (Rs 60, six hours) and Mt Abu (Rs 60, five hours). Most have their offices along the main road from the bus stand to Delhi Gate (Khangipir Rd). Book at least one day in advance.

Train Lines into Udaipur are currently metre gauge only. As the city is not high on the list for conversion to broad gauge, rail travel to and from Udaipur is likely to become less convenient as other places in Rajasthan are linked to the wider gauge.

The best train between Delhi and Udaipur is the *Pink City/Garib Nawaz Express* which covers the 739 km in 15½ hours, and goes via Jaipur, Ajmer and Chittorgarh. It currently leaves Delhi's Sarai Rohilla station daily except Sunday (daily except Saturday in the other direction), but you may need to change trains at Rewari (83 km from Delhi) since the Delhi end of this metre-gauge route is being converted to broad gauge. Fares for the trip are Rs 137/521 in 2nd/1st class. This train operates during the day, and so reaches its destination in the late evening. If you'd rather do the journey overnight and arrive at a more civilised hour, the *Chetak Express* does the trip, but it takes 20 hours.

There's currently still a metre-gauge link between Udaipur and Jodhpur (221 km).

Taxi If you want to rent a taxi to tour this area of Rajasthan the drivers will show you a list of 'official' rates to places like Mt Abu and Jodhpur. Shop around – you can often get a better price from travel companies. One place that seems to be reliable and reasonably priced is Voice of Travel & Trade (☎ 52-3036), 16 Lake Palace Rd, near the Rang Niwas Palace Hotel.

Getting Around
To/From the Airport The airport is 25 km from the city. There's no airport bus; a taxi costs around Rs 120.

Local Transport Udaipur has a reasonably good city bus service. Auto-rickshaws and taxis are unmetered so you need to agree on a fare before setting off. The standard fare for tourists anywhere within the city appears to be Rs 15, and you'll be very lucky to get it for less since there are too many well-heeled tourists around who pay the first price asked.

The commission system is in place with a vengeance, and so rickshaw drivers will try to take you to a place of their choice rather than yours, especially if you want to go to the Lal Ghat area. If that's the case, just ask for the Jagdish Temple, as all the guest houses in that area are within easy walking distance of the temple.

Udaipur is small enough and vehicle traffic slow enough to make getting around on a bicycle quite enjoyable. You can hire bicycles all over town for around Rs 3 an hour or Rs 15 per day. Rates tend to be higher at the places right by the tourist hotels.

AROUND UDAIPUR
Eklingi & Nagada
The interesting little village of Eklingi, with a number of ancient **temples**, is only 22 km and a short bus ride north of Udaipur. The Siva temple in the village itself was originally built in 734, although its present form dates from the rule of Maharana Raimal between 1473 and 1509. The walled complex includes an elaborately pillared hall under a large pyramidal roof and features a four-faced Siva image of black marble. The temple is open at rather odd hours – 5 to 7 am, 10 am to 1 pm and 5 to 7 pm.

At Nagada, about a km off the road and a km before Eklingi, are three old temples. The Jain temple of **Adbudji** is essentially ruined, but its architecture is interesting and it's very old. The nearby **Sas Bahu**, or Mother and Daughter-in-Law, group has very fine and intricate architecture and carvings, including some erotic figures. You can reach these temples most conveniently by hiring a bicycle in Eklingi itself.

Getting There & Away Buses run from Udaipur to Eklingi every hour from 5 am onwards. There's a small guest house in the village if you want to stay overnight.

Haldighati
This site, 40 km from Udaipur, is where Maharana Pratap valiantly defied the superior Mughal forces of Akbar in 1576. The site is a battlefield and the only thing to see is the chhatri to the warrior's horse, Chetak, a few km away.

The RTDC *Motel Haldighati* has just one room, which costs Rs 75/100, or there are dorm beds for Rs 40. Reasonable meals are available on request.

An RSTC bus to Haldighati leaves Udai-

pur daily at 9 am; private buses depart between 11.30 am and 12.30 pm.

Nathdwara
The important 18th-century Vishnu temple of **Sri Nathji** stands here, 48 km from Udaipur, and it's an important shrine for Vaishnavite devotees. The black stone Vishnu image was brought here from Mathura in 1669 to protect it from Aurangzeb's destructive impulses. According to legend, when an attempt was later made to move the image, the getaway vehicle, a wagon, sank into the ground up to the axles,

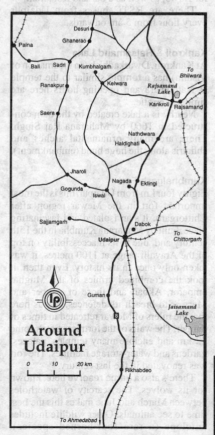

Around Udaipur

0   10   20 km

indicating that the image preferred to stay where it was!

Attendants treat the image like a delicate child, getting it up in the morning, washing it, putting its clothes on, offering it specially prepared meals, putting it down to sleep etc. It's a very popular pilgrimage site, and the temple opens and closes around the image's daily routine. It gets very crowded around 4.30 to 5 pm when Vishnu gets up after a siesta.

The RTDC *Hotel Gokul Tourist Bungalow* (☎ (02953) 2685) offers an air-cooled four-bed room for Rs 200, air-con doubles for Rs 200/250, and there's a dormitory with beds for Rs 40, as well as a bar and restaurant.

There are RSTC buses from Udaipur every hour from 5 am onwards.

Kankroli & Rajsamand Lake

At Kankroli, Dwarkadhish (an incarnation of Vishnu) has a **temple** similar to the temple at Nathdwara and opening hours here are similarly erratic.

Nearby is a lake created by the dam constructed in 1660 by Maharana Raj Singh. There are many ornamental arches and chhatris along the huge bund (embankment).

Kumbhalgarh Fort

Eighty four km from Udaipur, this is the most important fort in the Mewar region after Chittorgarh. It's an isolated and fascinating place, built by Maharana Kumbha in the 15th century and, due to its inaccessibility on top of the Aravalli range at 1100 metres, it was taken only once in its history. Even then, it took the combined armies of the Mughal emperor, Akbar, and those of Amber and Marwar to breach its defences. It was here that the rulers of Mewar retreated in times of danger. The walls of the fortress stretch some 12 km and enclose many temples, palaces, gardens and water-storage facilities. The fort was renovated in the last century.

There's also a **game reserve** here, known for its wolves. The scarcity of waterholes between March and June makes this the best time to see animals. Other wildlife includes antelope (a rare four-horned species),

leopard and bear, and it's a good area for walking.

There's a *PWD Rest House*, or the upmarket *Aodhi Hotel* (☎ Kelwara 222), where double rooms cost Rs 900. Alternatively you could stay in Ghanerao or Ranakpur.

There are four RSTC buses a day from Udaipur (Rs 15, three hours), but not all leave from the bus stand – some go from Chetak Circle. Private buses are also available. From where the bus drops you, it's a pleasant two to three km walk to the fort. If you want to hire a jeep, it's a good idea to come here as part of a small group and share the cost.

Ranakpur

One of the biggest and most important Jain temples in India, the extremely beautiful Ranakpur complex is well worth seeing. Sixty km from Udaipur, it lies in a remote and peaceful valley of the Aravalli range.

The main temple is the **Chaumukha Temple**, or Four-Faced Temple, dedicated to Adinath. Built in 1439, this huge, beautifully crafted and well-kept marble temple has 29 halls supported by 1444 pillars, no two alike. Within the complex are two other Jain temples to Neminath and Parasnath and, a little distance away, a Sun Temple. One km from the main complex is the Amba Mata Temple.

The temple is open to non-Jains from noon to 5 pm. Shoes and all leather articles must be left at the entrance. There's a Rs 20 camera charge.

Places to Stay & Eat Staying overnight at Ranakpur breaks up the long trip between Udaipur and Jodhpur.

The poorly run RTDC *Hotel Shilpi Tourist Bungalow* (☎ Ranakpur 26) has singles/doubles for Rs 125/150, air-cooled rooms for Rs 200/250, and dorm beds for Rs 40. Overpriced thalis are available in the dining room. The dhaba at the bus stand is far better value and has tasty veg dishes with rice and chapattis.

For a donation, you can stay at the *dharamsala* within the temple complex. If you arrive at a meal time, you can get a good thali in the dining hall, just inside the main entrance to the complex on your left, again for a small donation.

Four km from Ranakpur is the *Maharani Bagh Orchard Retreat* (bookings through Umaid Bhawan Palace in Jodhpur). It offers comfortable accommodation in 11 cottage rooms for Rs 675/975, with bathrooms attached. Meals are available; lunch or dinner cost Rs 190.

Getting There & Away Ranakpur is 39 km from Palna (or Falna) Junction on the Ajmer to Mt Abu rail and road routes. From Udaipur (Rs 21, 3½ to 4½ hours), there are five RSTC express buses per day, leaving in the morning. Although it's just possible to travel through from Ranakpur to Jodhpur or Mt Abu on the same day, it's hardly worth it since you'll arrive well after dark. It's better to stay for the night and continue on the next day. There's also a daily bus from Mt Abu which terminates at Sadri, only seven km from Ranakpur.

Ghanerao

The attractive town of Ghanerao can make a good base for explorations of the various attractions around Udaipur. The Ghanerao Royal Castle's helpful owners can arrange a trek from Ghanerao to Kumbhalgarh with an overnight stay at their hunting lodge, Bagha ka Bagh, en route. They offer very expensive horse safaris (at over US$100 per day!) or reasonably priced excursions by jeep.

Situated about a km out of town, the *Ghanerao Royal Castle* (☎ (02934) 7335) is a red sandstone castle with 20 well-kept rooms for Rs 650/900. Meals are available.

Jaisamand Lake

Located 48 km south-west of Udaipur, this stunningly sited artificial lake, created by damming the Gomti River, was built by Maharana Jai Singh in the 17th century. There are beautiful marble chhatris around the embankment, each with an elephant in front. The summer palaces of the Udaipur queens are also here and a wildlife sanctuary is nearby.

There's a *Tourist Bungalow* on the shores of the lake. The new *Jaisamand Island Resort* (☎ (02906) 2222) is a modern hotel in an isolated position 20 minutes by boat across the lake. Rooms are around Rs 1000/1500, all with views over the water.

Hourly RSTC buses from Udaipur run from 5.30 am onwards.

MT ABU

Population: 17,000
Telephone Area Code: 02974

Rajasthan's only hill station sprawls along a 1200-metre-high plateau in the south of the state, close to the Gujarati border. It's a pleasant hot-season retreat from the plains for both Rajasthan and Gujarat, but you won't find many Western travellers here – apart from those who come to study at the Brahma Kumaris Spiritual University. The predominantly Indian visitors include many honeymooners. Mt Abu's pace is easy-going and relaxed.

Mt Abu has more to attract visitors than just its cooler climate – it has a number of important temples, particularly the superb Dilwara group of Jain temples, five km away. Also, like some other hill stations in India, it has its own lake.

Orientation & Information

Mt Abu is on a hilly plateau about 22 km long by six km wide, 27 km from the nearest railway station, Abu Road. The main part of the town extends along the road in from Abu Road, down to Nakki Lake.

The tourist office (☎ 3151) is opposite the bus stand and is open from 8 am to 1.30 pm and 2 to 5 pm. The GPO is on Raj Bhavan Rd, opposite the art gallery and museum. Several banks and a number of top-end hotels will change money.

Telephone numbers in Mt Abu may have changed by now. If you can't get through you may need to prefix the old number with 2.

Nakki Lake

Virtually in the centre of Mt Abu, the small lake takes its name from the legend that it was scooped out by a god, using only his nails, or *nakk*. It's a short and easy stroll around the lake – look for the strange **rock formations**. The best known, Toad Rock, looks just like a toad about to hop into the lake. Others, like Nun Rock, Nandi Rock or Camel Rock, require more imagination. The 14th-century **Raghunath Temple** stands beside the lake.

You can hire your own boat (Rs 20), or be rowed (Rs 4 per person).

Viewpoints

Of the various viewpoints around town, **Sunset Point** is the most popular. Hordes stroll out here every evening to catch the setting sun, the food stalls and all the usual entertainments. Other popular spots include **Honeymoon Point**, which also offers a view of the sunset, **The Crags** and **Robert's Spur**. You can follow the white arrows along a rather overgrown path up to the summit of **Shanti Shikhar**, west of Adhar Devi Temple, where there are superb panoramic views. It's not advisable to come up here alone, though.

For a good view over the lake the best point is probably the terrace of the maharaja of Jaipur's former **summer palace**. No-one

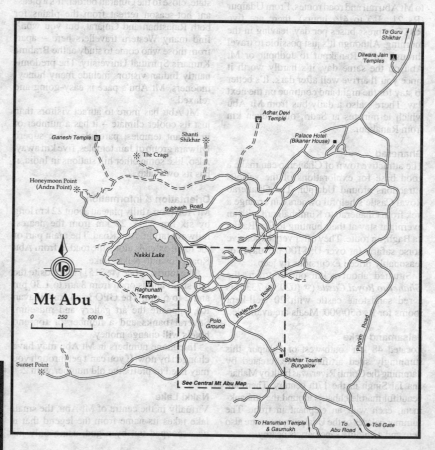

Mt Abu

0   250   500 m

seems to mind if you climb up here for the view and a photo.

Museum & Art Gallery

Although it's not very interesting, the museum, opposite the GPO, does have some items from archaeological excavations which date from the 8th to 12th centuries, as well as Jain bronzes, carvings, brasswork and local textiles. 'Art gallery' is hardly an accurate description of the collection of half a dozen pictures. The museum, on Raj Bhavan Rd, is open daily except Friday from 10 am to 4.30 pm, and admission is free. There is also a **Rajasthan Emporium** back towards the market.

Adhar Devi Temple

Three km out of the town, 200 steep steps lead to this Durga temple built in a natural cleft in the rock. You have to stoop to get through the low entrance to the temple. There are good views over Mt Abu from up here.

Brahma Kumaris Spiritual University & Museum

The Brahma Kumaris teach that all religions lead to God and so are equally valid, and the principles of each should be studied. The sect's stated aim is the establishment of universal peace through 'the impartation of spiritual knowledge and training of easy raja yoga meditation'. There are over 4000 branches in 60 countries around the world and followers come to Mt Abu to attend courses at the sect's spiritual university. To attend one of these residential courses you need to contact your local branch and arrange things in advance. You can, however, arrange for someone here to give you an introductory course (seven lessons) while you're in Mt Abu; this would take a minimum of three days. There's no charge – the organisation is entirely supported by donations.

There's a museum (free) in the town outlining the sect's teachings and offering meditation sessions. It's open daily from 8 am to 8 pm.

Dilwara Temples

These Jain temples are Mt Abu's main attraction and amongst the finest examples of Jain architecture in India. The complex includes two temples in which the art of carving marble reached unsurpassed heights.

The older of the temples is the **Vimal Vasahi**, built in 1031 and dedicated to the first tirthankar, Adinath. The central shrine has an image of Adinath, while around the courtyard are 52 identical cells, each with a Buddha-like cross-legged image. Forty-eight elegantly carved pillars form the entrance to the courtyard. In front of the temple stands the **House of Elephants** with figures of elephants marching in procession to the temple entrance.

The later **Tejpal Temple** is dedicated to Neminath, the 22nd tirthankar, and was built in 1230 by the brothers Tejpal and Vastupal. Like Vimal, they were ministers in the government of the ruler of Gujarat. Although the Tejpal Temple is important as an extremely old and complete example of a Jain temple, its most notable feature is the fantastic intricacy and delicacy of the marble carving. The carving is so fine that, in places, the marble becomes almost transparent. In particular,

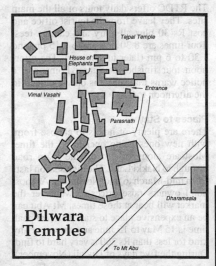

Dilwara Temples

the lotus flower which hangs from the centre of the dome is an incredible piece of work. It's difficult to believe that this huge lace-like filigree actually started as a solid block of marble. The temple employs several full-time stone carvers to maintain and restore the work. There are three other temples in the enclosure, but they all pale beside the Tejpal and Vimal Vasahi.

The complex is open from noon to 6 pm. Photography is not allowed, and bags are thoroughly searched to prevent cameras being taken in. As at other Jain temples, all articles of leather (belts as well as shoes) have to be left at the entrance. You must also observe a number of other regulations which include 'no smoking, no chewing, no drinking, no umbrellas, no transistor or tape recorders and no videos', and there's a dire warning for women: 'Entry of ladies in monthly course is strictly prohibited. Any lady in monthly course if enters any of the temples she may suffer'.

You can stroll out to Dilwara from the town in less than an hour, or take a share taxi for Rs 2 from opposite the Madras Cafe in the centre of town.

Organised Tours

The RTDC offers daily tours of all the main sites. They leave from the tourist office and cost Rs 30 plus all entry and camera fees. Tour times are 8.30 or 9 am to 1.15 pm and 1.30 to 6 pm (later in summer). The afternoon tour finishes at Sunset Point, and a notice warns that sunset is only included in the afternoon tour!

Places to Stay

There are plenty of hotels to choose from, with new ones being opened all the time. Most are along or just off the main road through to Nakki Lake. The high season lasts from mid-March to mid-November. As most hotel owners raise prices to whatever the market will bear at those times, Mt Abu can be an expensive place to stay. The real peak time is 15 May to 15 June and a room of any kind for less than Rs 200 is very hard to find. During the five days of Diwali (November),

rooms are virtually unobtainable without advance booking. Avoid the place at this time.

In the low season (with the exception of Christmas and New Year), discounts of up to 50% are available and mid-range accommodation can be an absolute bargain. Most places are definitely open to a bit of bargaining, and the rates get cheaper the longer you stay. The hotels usually have a 9 am checkout time.

At all times of the year there are plenty of touts working the bus and taxi stands. In the low season you can safely ignore them; at peak times they can save you a lot of legwork as they'll know exactly where the last available room is.

Places to Stay – bottom end

The popular *Hotel Lake View* (☎ 3659) overlooks picturesque Nakki Lake but, although the views are certainly good, it's really only an average hotel. In winter, there are singles with common bath from Rs 80, doubles with bath attached from Rs 100 to Rs 350. The minimum summer rate is Rs 200. Hot water is available between 6 and 11 am, and there's a pleasant terrace.

Close by and better value is the *Hotel Panghat* (☎ 3386). There are rooms with a lake view, attached bathroom and TV for Rs 70, as well as a range of other rooms, some with common bath. Hot water is available from 7 to 9 am. Also in this lakeside area is the similarly priced *Hotel Nakki Vihar* (☎ 3481). Some rooms have a lake view.

A recommended place is the *Shree Ganesh Hotel* (☎ 3591), up the hill towards the old summer palace. The location is certainly quiet and the owner is very friendly and helpful. The rooms are clean and well kept, although some lack windows, and there are good views from the rooftop terrace. As this place is a little further from the centre of things, the high-season rates tend to be a little more sensible than elsewhere, and bargaining is possible. Low-season rates are around Rs 60 for a double with bath.

About the cheapest place to stay is the tiny and very basic *Hotel Suryodaya*, opposite the polo ground. There are just a few doubles

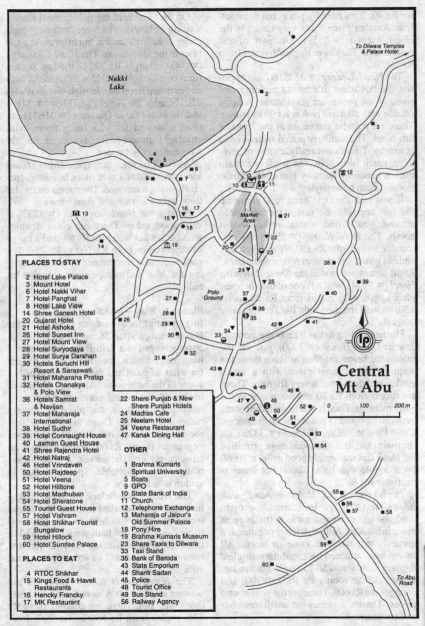

Central Mt Abu

0   100   200 m

PLACES TO STAY

2 Hotel Lake Palace
3 Mount Hotel
6 Hotel Nakki Vihar
7 Hotel Panghat
8 Hotel Lake View
14 Shree Ganesh Hotel
20 Gujarat Hotel
21 Hotel Ashoka
26 Hotel Sunset Inn
27 Hotel Mount View
28 Hotel Suryodaya
29 Hotel Surya Darshan
30 Hotels Suruchi Hill
    Resort & Saraswati
31 Hotel Maharana Pratap
32 Hotels Chanakya
    & Polo View
36 Hotels Samrat
    & Navijan
37 Hotel Maharaja
    International
38 Hotel Sudhir
39 Hotel Connaught House
40 Laxman Guest House
41 Shree Rajendra Hotel
42 Hotel Natraj
46 Hotel Vrindavan
50 Hotel Rajdeep
51 Hotel Veena
52 Hotel Hilltone
53 Hotel Madhuban
54 Hotel Sheratone
55 Tourist Guest House
57 Hotel Vishram
58 Hotel Shikhar Tourist
    Bungalow
59 Hotel Hillock
60 Hotel Sunrise Palace

PLACES TO EAT

4 RTDC Shikhar
15 Kings Food & Haveli
    Restaurants
16 Hencky Francky
17 MK Restaurant

22 Shere Punjab & New
    Shere Punjab Hotels
24 Madras Cafe
25 Neelam Hotel
34 Veena Restaurant
47 Kanak Dining Hall

OTHER

1 Brahma Kumaris
   Spiritual University
5 Boats
9 GPO
10 State Bank of India
11 Church
12 Telephone Exchange
13 Maharaja of Jaipur's
    Old Summer Palace
18 Pony Hire
19 Brahma Kumaris Museum
23 Share Taxis to Dilwara
33 Taxi Stand
35 Bank of Baroda
43 State Emporium
44 Shanti Sadan
45 Police
48 Tourist Office
49 Bus Stand
56 Railway Agency

Nakki
Lake

To Dilwara Temples
& Palace Hotel

Market
Area

Polo
Ground

To Abu
Road

RAJASTHAN

for Rs 40. It's a friendly place, but not spotless. Another place that's very cheap is the *Hotel Ashoka* (☎ 3559), just east of the market area. They have singles/doubles from Rs 40/60.

The *Hotel Rajdeep* (☎ 3525) is right opposite the bus stand. It's an old building and some of the rooms are good value. A large double with attached bath is Rs 60 in winter. There's a popular restaurant at the front of this hotel. The similarly priced *Hotel Veena* is nearby. There's not really a view of anything much from here, and while the main road is generally quiet by Indian standards, the noise can be annoying.

If you take the right-hand fork going up the hill opposite the taxi stand and polo ground, you'll find several other budget hotels. The *Hotel Natraj* (☎ 3532) has reasonable rooms from Rs 150, all with balcony and hot water, and cheaper rooms at the back. Right across the road is the *Shree Rajendra Hotel* (☎ 3174), which is one of the cheapest places here, with rooms from Rs 50 to Rs 250, all with attached bath. Bucket hot water costs Rs 2.

Further still from the lake is the popular *Tourist Guest House* (☎ 3200), just off the main road below the Tourist Bungalow. It's a quiet and pleasant place with a small garden and the owner is very friendly. There are rooms from Rs 80 and hot water in the early morning. Food is available in the rooms between 6.30 and 11 pm at reasonable prices. Close by is the *Hotel Vishram* (☎ 3323), on the main road. It is somewhat more primitive but clean and reasonably good value at Rs 60 for a double with bath. Bucket hot water is available for Rs 2.

The 80-room RTDC *Hotel Shikhar Tourist Bungalow* (☎ 3129), back from the main road and up a steepish path, is the biggest place in Mt Abu. Although fairly popular, it's certainly not the best value in town. All rooms have attached bath; ordinary singles/doubles cost Rs 125/175 (with bucket hot water), deluxe rooms are Rs 250/300, and cottages are Rs 600. These are the year-round prices. There's a somewhat indifferent bar and a restaurant.

On the far side of the polo ground there's a string of hotels, which are definitely mid-range in the high season, but offer quite good rates in the low season. The *Hotel Chanakya* (☎ 3438) charges Rs 225 in the low season for a comfortable double with attached bath and constant hot water. In high season it's Rs 450. Nearby, the *Hotel Polo View* (☎ 3487) and the *Hotel Surya Darshan* (☎ 3165) both charge around Rs 125 for a room with attached bath and bucket hot water, Rs 200 with constant hot water.

Also in this price range, the *Hotel Mount View* (☎ 3320) is a nice older building, currently being renovated. The rooms on the 1st floor have a terrace and good views.

Nearby, the *Hotel Saraswati* (☎ 3237) is very good value. There are clean doubles with bucket hot water for Rs 60, and a range of other rooms from Rs 100 to Rs 250. It's well run and a recommended place to stay, but the lilac and orange paint job is a bit radical.

Places to Stay – middle
In a peaceful location along the road to the Dilwara temples, the *Mount Hotel* (☎ 3150) once belonged to a British army officer and has changed little since those days, except for a lick of paint and the installation of hot water in the bathrooms. Although it's full of old-world charm and surrounded by well-maintained gardens, the place is homely rather than grand. There are only a few rooms, and these cost Rs 200/300. Good vegetarian meals (Rs 60) are available with advance notice. The owner, a keen horseman, is very hospitable. Spots, the dog, is said to be a labrador.

The *Hotel Lake Palace* (☎ 3254) makes the most of its excellent location just across from the water with high prices. Doubles/triples with attached bath are Rs 550/650 in the high season; bargain hard in the low season and you should be able to get at least 30% off these prices.

The *Hotel Sunset Inn* (☎ 3194) on the western edge of Mt Abu is a modern hotel that's well run. There are doubles from Rs 475, triples from Rs 550 and a 30% low-season discount. Nearby is the *Hotel Savera Palace* (☎ 3354), similarly priced but not as good. At the bottom end of the polo ground is the *Hotel Suruchi Hill Resort* (☎ 3577). Doubles here cost Rs 690 in the high season, and there's a 50% low-season discount. At the end of this road is the *Hotel Maharana Pratap* (☎ 3667), a smart new place with rooms from Rs 500.

There are numerous other hotels in this price bracket. The *Hotel Vrindavan* (☎ 3147) is a very pleasant place near the bus stand with rooms from Rs 350 with TV and attached bath. In the same area, at around Rs 500 for a double, are the *Hotel Sheratone* (☎ 3544), with large airy rooms, and the *Hotel Madhuban* (☎ 3122).

The *Hotel Samrat* (☎ 3153) and *Hotel Navijan* (☎ 3173), on the main street, are basically the same hotel although they appear to be separate. Off-season rates in the Samrat are from Rs 215 for a double with bath and hot water; the Navijan is a little cheaper. Prices double in the high season. The *Hotel Maharaja International* (☎ 3161), directly opposite, is a little more upmarket.

Places to Stay – top end
The delightful *Palace Hotel (Bikaner House)* (☎ 3121; fax 3674) is a worthwhile treat but is usually heavily booked in the high season. The hotel was once the summer residence of the maharaja of Bikaner and is now managed by the maharaja's very amiable and helpful son-in-law. The building itself is not the most attractive of palaces, but the 34 rooms are very comfortable, each with separate sleeping and living areas, and there are four magnificent suites. The hotel is in a beautiful location near the Dilwara temples and has well laid-out gardens, a private lake, two tennis courts and pony rides by arrangement. The cost is a very reasonable Rs 750/900 all year round, and excellent meals are available at Rs 150 for veg and Rs 180 for non-veg.

Those looking for the fading splendour of the Raj should seriously consider staying at the *Hotel Connaught House* (☎ 3439), which belongs to the former maharaja of Jodhpur. This beautiful old place is set in extensive gardens and its somewhat gloomy and claustrophobic interior features numerous period photographs of members of the Indian aristocracy and polo-playing British officers. As well as rooms in the old building there's also a new wing of bright and airy rooms. Singles/doubles with attached bath and constant hot water are Rs 800/1150. There are low-season discounts on rooms in the new building. Meals are available but should be ordered in advance.

At the southern end of Mt Abu is the *Hotel Sunrise Palace* (☎ 3214), yet another former summer residence of a Rajput maharaja (this time the maharaja of Bharatpur). Although it lacks the style of the above two places, it's a very quiet and comfortable hotel with fabulous views. The rooms are well furnished and have attached bath, TV and phone, and range in price from Rs 500 to Rs 950. Capacious suites with views cost Rs 950, and there is a 30% discount in the low season.

If you want a modern hotel, the *Hotel Hilltone* (☎ 3112) is centrally located and is a good choice. Within the complex there's a swimming pool, restaurant, bar, sauna and bookshop. Singles/doubles cost Rs 600/850; there's a 20% to 30% discount in the low season. Near the Tourist Bungalow, the *Hotel Hillock* (☎ 3467) is a flash place – large, spotlessly clean and well decorated. Its year-round tariff is Rs 890 to Rs 1190 plus taxes.

Places to Eat
Near the bus stand, the *Kanak Dining Hall* is a good place to eat. It's very clean and offers excellent south Indian vegetarian dishes and tasty lunchtime thalis for Rs 30, making this a popular place at that time.

Further uphill, next to the junction at the bottom end of the polo ground, are several more restaurants. The *Veena Restaurant* has very good Gujarati thalis for Rs 25, among the best in town, and with plenty of refills. It's open from 11 am to 2.30 pm, and 7 to 9.30 pm. The nearby *Shanti Restaurant* is particularly recommended for its breakfasts.

In the bazaar area, there's strong competition between the *Shere Punjab Hotel* and the *New Shere Punjab Hotel*. The former has an

RAJASTHAN

excellent reputation; the latter is a bit cheaper. Both serve tandoori dishes, veg and non-veg; each pours scorn on the other's catering abilities.

The *Madras Cafe*, also in this area, is pure veg. There's some outdoor seating and the menu includes pizzas (Rs 18) and vegie burgers (Rs 15). It's a reasonable place. Nearby, the *Neelam Hotel* does non-veg as well as veg dishes.

At the top of the road leading down to the lake there's a cluster of restaurants. The *MK Restaurant* has been popular for a number of years for its ice cream and thalis. Around the corner on the opposite side of the road, *Kings Food* has the usual have-a-go-at-anything menu and a good fresh juice stand. Behind it is the *Haveli Punjabi*, a pure veg restaurant. The amazingly named *Hencky Francky* is a fast-food place offering pizzas, burgers, and south Indian food. From here down to the lake are a number of small snack places. On the lake itself there's a large dilapidated concrete 'boat' restaurant, the RTDC *Shikhar*, a teashop that's closed in the low season.

For a splurge, go to a hotel restaurant. To eat at Bikaner House, where the set meals (Rs 150 for lunch, Rs 180 for dinner) are excellent, you need to reserve in advance.

Things to Buy

The Rajasthan Emporium is on Raj Bhavan Rd and there are quite a few shops on the road down to the lakefront. Jewellery shops have a good selection. As in most of India, jewellery is usually sold by weight.

Getting There & Away

As you enter Mt Abu, there's a toll gate where bus and car passengers are charged Rs 5, plus Rs 5 for a car.

Bus From 6 am onwards, regular buses make the 27-km climb from Abu Road up to Mt Abu (Rs 10, one hour). Some RSTC buses go all the way to Mt Abu, while others terminate at Abu Road, so make sure you get the one you want.

The bus schedule from Mt Abu is exten-
sive and, to many destinations, you will find a direct bus faster and more convenient than going down to Abu Road and waiting for a train. To Udaipur, STC buses take seven hours at a cost of Rs 50. To Ajmer (Rs 131, eight hours) and Jaipur (Rs 159, 11 hours) there's one departure daily. For Ahmedabad there are many departures and the journey takes seven hours.

Private buses are more expensive but definitely preferable to state transport buses and there's plenty of choice. There are seemingly many companies with offices on the main street, but most are just ticketing agents; Shobha is one that operates its own buses. Buses to Udaipur take 4½ hours and cost Rs 65. Other destinations served include Ahmedabad, Ajmer and Jaipur.

Train Abu Road, the railhead for Mt Abu, is on the (by now broad-gauge) line between Delhi and Ahmedabad via Jaipur and Ajmer.

In Mt Abu there's a railway agency at the HP service station near the Tourist Bungalow, and it has quotas on most of the express trains out of Abu Road. It is open daily from 9 am to 1 pm and 2 to 4 pm (only until noon on Sunday).

There's a variety of trains; the best is the daily superfast Delhi to Ahmedabad *Ashram Express*. Fares for the five-hour, 187-km journey from Ahmedabad are Rs 48/178 in 2nd/1st class. The 440-km journey from Jaipur takes eight hours and costs Rs 94/352 in 2nd/1st class.

Direct trains also run from Abu Road to Ajmer, Jodhpur and Agra. For Bhuj and the rest of the Kathiawar peninsula in Gujarat, change trains at Palanpur, 53 km south of Abu Road.

Taxi A taxi, which you can share with up to five people, costs Rs 130 from Abu Road. A two-day trip by car from Udaipur should cost around Rs 1400. The journey takes a minimum of four hours, partly along a rough road, so the day trips advertised in Udaipur are not a good idea.

Getting Around

Buses from the bus stand go to the various sites in Mt Abu, but it takes a little planning to get out and back without too much hanging around. Some buses go just to Dilwara, while others will take you out to Achalgarh, so you'll need to decide which place to visit first, depending on the schedule. For Dilwara it's easier to take a share taxi, and these leave when full from opposite the Madras Cafe in the centre of town; the fare is Rs 2.

There are plenty of taxis with posted fares to anywhere you care to mention.

AROUND MT ABU
Achalgarh

The Siva temple of **Achaleshwar Mahandeva**, 11 km north of Mt Abu, has a number of interesting features, including a toe of Siva, a brass Nandi and, where the Siva lingam would normally be, a deep hole said to extend all the way to the underworld.

Outside, by the car park, is a tank beside which stand three stone buffaloes and the figure of a king shooting them with a bow and arrows. A legend states that the tank was once filled with ghee, but demons in the form of buffaloes came down and drank each night – until the king shot them. A path leads up the hillside to a group of colourful **Jain temples** with fine views out over the plains.

Guru Shikhar

At the end of the plateau, 15 km from Mt Abu, is Guru Shikhar, the highest point in Rajasthan at 1721 metres. A road goes almost all the way to the summit. At the top is the **Atri Rishi Temple**, complete with a priest and good views all around.

Below the temple is a cafe selling soft drinks and snacks.

Gaumukh Temple

Down on the Abu Road side of Mt Abu, a small stream flows from the mouth of a marble cow, giving the shrine its name. There is also a marble figure of the bull Nandi, Siva's vehicle. The tank here, Agni Kund, is said to be the site of the sacrificial

fire, made by the sage Vasishta, from which four of the great Rajput clans were born. An image of Vasishta is flanked by figures of Rama and Krishna.

ABU ROAD

This station down on the plains is the rail junction for Mt Abu. The railway station and bus stand are right next to each other on the edge of town. Although there are RSTC buses from Abu Road to other cities such as Jodhpur, Ajmer, Jaipur, Udaipur and Ahmedabad, there's little point in catching them here as they're all available from Mt Abu itself. Buses operated by private companies also run from Mt Abu.

In the main market area, the *Bhagwati Guest House* is only five minutes' walk from the railway station. It has cheap rooms and dorm beds. It's OK for one night and there are other simple places around. The railway station has *retiring rooms*.

Western Rajasthan

JODHPUR

Population: 720,600
Telephone Area Code: 0291

Jodhpur stands at the edge of the Thar Desert and is the largest city in Rajasthan after Jaipur. The city is totally dominated by a massive fort, topping a sheer rocky hill which rises right in the middle of the town. Jodhpur was founded in 1459 by Rao Jodha, a chief of the Rajput clan known as the Rathores. His descendants ruled not only Jodhpur, but also other Rajput princely states. The Rathore kingdom was once known as Marwar, the Land of Death.

The old city of Jodhpur is surrounded by a 10-km-long wall, built about a century after the city was founded. From the fort, you can clearly see where the old city ends and the new begins. It's fascinating to wander around the jumble of winding streets in the old city, out of which eight gates lead. It's one of India's more interesting cities and, yes, it was from here that those baggy-tight

RAJASTHAN

horse-riding trousers, jodhpurs, took their name. Today, you're more likely to see them worn in Saurashtra in Gujarat than here.

Part of the film *Rudyard Kipling's Jungle Book*, starring Sam Neill and John Cleese, was recently shot in Jodhpur.

Orientation

The tourist office, railway stations and bus terminal are all outside the old city. High Court Rd runs from the Raika Bagh railway station, directly across from the bus terminal, past the Umaid Gardens, the Tourist Bunga-low and tourist office, and round beside the city wall towards the main station and the GPO. Most trains from the east stop at the Raika Bagh station before the main station – handy if you want to stay at the hotels on the eastern side of town.

Information

The tourist office (☎ 45-083) is at the Tourist Bungalow and is open Monday to Saturday from 9 am to 6 pm, and on Sunday from 9 to 11 am. There's also a useful International Tourists Bureau at the railway station (see the Getting There & Away section).

Although there are lots of STD places, there currently seems to be only one phone/fax agency in Jodhpur – the Hello Hut in the forecourt of the main railway station. This place has to be seen to be believed. Built around a tree that's fenced in and contains an aviary full of songbirds are a series of luxu-rious telephone booths with easy-chairs and tables; one even has a bed in it in case you'd like to make your call in a horizontal posi-tion!

Meherangarh Fort

Still run by the former maharaja of Jodhpur, the Majestic Fort is just that. Sprawled across the 125-metre-high hill, this is the most impressive and formidable fort in fort-studded Rajasthan. A winding road leads up to the entrance from the city below. The first gate is still scarred by cannon ball hits, indi-cating that this was a fort which earned its keep. The gates include the **Jayapol**, built by Maharaja Man Singh in 1806 following his

victory over the armies of Jaipur and Bikaner, and the **Fatehpol**, or Victory Gate, erected by Maharaja Ajit Singh to commem-orate his defeat of the Mughals.

The final gate is the **Lahapol**, or Iron Gate, beside which there are 15 hand prints, the sati marks of Maharaja Man Singh's widows who threw themselves upon his funeral pyre in 1843. They still attract devo-tional attention and are usually covered in red powder.

Inside the fort, there is a whole series of courtyards and palaces. The **palace apart-ments** have evocative names like the Moti Mahal, or Pearl Palace, the Sukh Mahal, or Pleasure Palace and the Phool Mahal, or Flower Palace. They house a fantastic collec-tion of the trappings of Indian royalty, including an amazing collection of elephant *howdahs* (used when the maharajas rode their elephants in glittering procession through their capitals), miniature paintings of a variety of schools, superb folk music instruments and the inevitable Rajput armoury, palanquins, furniture and cos-tumes. In one room, there's even an exhibit of rocking cradles. Finally, there's an enor-mous, luxurious and stunningly beautiful tent, originally made for the Mughal emper-ors but carried off as booty by the Rajputs following one of their many battles. The palace apartments are beautifully decorated and painted and have delicately carved lat-ticework windows of red sandstone. It's one of the best palace museums in Rajasthan.

At the southern end of the fort, old cannons look out from the ramparts over the sheer drop to the old town beneath. There's no guard rail and you can clearly hear voices and city sounds carried up by the air currents from the houses far below. The views from these ramparts are nothing less than magical. From here, you can also see the many houses painted blue to distinguish them as those of Brahmins. The **Chamunda Temple**, dedi-cated to Durga, stands at this end of the fort.

The fort is open from 9 am to 5 pm and admission is Rs 35; there's no charge if you only want to visit the ramparts. There's an additional charge of Rs 50 to use a camera.

The fee includes a guided tour by the unenthusiastic liveried attendants, but they generally expect a small tip at the end. A group of musicians usually sits outside the cafe near the museum entrance and strike up a merry Rajasthani number to herald your arrival – it helps set the mood for a visit to this superb fort and they, too, appreciate a tip.

Jaswant Thanda
This white marble memorial to Maharaja Jaswant Singh II is a short distance from the fort, just off the fort road. The cenotaph, built in 1899, was followed by the royal crematorium and three later cenotaphs which stand nearby. Inside are portraits of the various Jodhpur rulers.

Clock Tower & Markets
The clock tower is a popular landmark in the old city. The colourful Sardar Market is close to the tower, and narrow alleys lead from here to bazaars selling textiles, silver and handicrafts.

Umaid Gardens & Museum
The Tourist Bungalow is on the edge of the Umaid Gardens, which contain the government museum, the library and a zoo. The museum has a small and fairly uninteresting collection. There are lots of badly moth-eaten stuffed animals, including a number of almost featherless desert birds in two glass cases. The military section includes cumbersome wooden biplane models and an extraordinary brass battleship. Open daily except Friday, from 10 am to 4.30 pm, the admission is Rs 2. You can safely skip it.

Umaid Bhawan Palace & Museum
Constructed of marble and red sandstone, this immense palace is also known as the Chhittar Palace because of the local Chhittar sandstone used. Begun in 1928, it was designed by the president of the British Royal Institute of Architects for Maharaja Umaid Singh, and took 15 years to build.

Probably the most surprising thing about this grandiose palace is that it was built so close to Independence. It seems to have escaped the attention of the maharaja and his British advisers that the upheavals of Independence were just around the corner, and that maharajas, princely states and the grand extravagances common to this class would soon be a thing of the past. Such considerations, however, seem rarely to have impinged on the consciences of rulers anywhere in the world. It has been suggested that the palace was built as some sort of royal job-creation programme; but the fact that the project did provide employment for several thousand local people during a time of severe drought is probably coincidental.

Maharaja Umaid Singh died in 1947, four years after the palace was completed; his successor still lives in part of the building. The rest has been turned into a hotel – and what a hotel! While it lacks the charm of Udaipur's palace hotels, it certainly makes up for it in spacious grandeur. Few who could afford it would miss the chance of staying here and the hotel corridors echo with languages from around the world. Unfortunately, the palace is not open to non-guests, unless you want to pay the visiting fee of Rs 330, although this is deductible from any food or drink you might purchase.

There's an excellent museum here. On display is an amazing array of items belonging to the maharaja – model aeroplanes, weapons, antique clocks and fob watches, priceless crockery, and hunting trophies – and there's even a private cinema! It's well worth a look, and is open daily from 10 am to 5 pm; entry is Rs 10 and tickets are sold in the gate house.

Organised Tours & Village Safaris
The RTDC operates daily tours of Jodhpur from 9 am to 1 pm and 2 to 6 pm. These take in all the main sites including the Umaid Bhawan Palace, Meherangarh Fort, Jaswant Thanda, Mandore Gardens and the museum. The tours start from the Tourist Bungalow and cost Rs 50.

Maharaja Swaroop Singh, who owns the Ajit Bhawan Palace Hotel, runs 'village safaris' which are an ideal way to get out into the villages and see a bit of the local way of life – something that is not always easy to do in India. You visit villages of the Bishnoi, a people whose belief in the sanctity of the environment and the need to protect trees and animals dates from the 15th century but seems very modern today. The cost is Rs 400 for a half-day tour, including lunch, but as the trips don't run unless there are at least four people, ring in advance (☎ 37-410).

A private tour guide, the 62-year-old Mr N L Tak (☎ 30-637), has been recommended for day tours to Bishnoi villages. It costs around Rs 700 for up to five people and the trips last all day.

Places to Stay – bottom end

The cheapest place to stay is the new *Sun City Youth Hostel* (☎ 20-150), by the Indian Airlines office. A bed in a clean dorm costs Rs 20 for members, Rs 40 for nonmembers, and large lockers are provided. There are also some doubles with attached bath for Rs 80. It's built around a sunny courtyard.

The *retiring rooms* at the recently renovated railway station are another good budget option. They charge Rs 40 for a dormitory bed, and Rs 90 for a double, and all accommodation is air-cooled.

There's not a great deal of other cheap

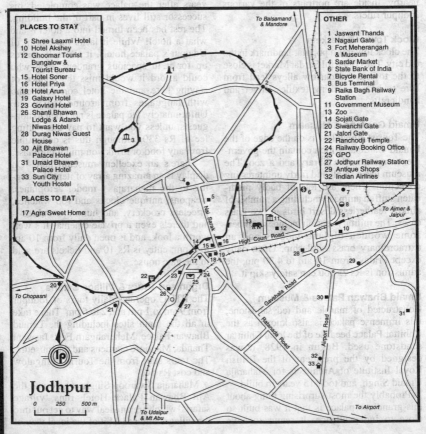

PLACES TO STAY

5 Shree Laaxmi Hotel
10 Hotel Akshey
12 Ghoomar Tourist Bungalow & Tourist Bureau
15 Hotel Soner
16 Hotel Priya
18 Hotel Arun
19 Galaxy Hotel
23 Govind Hotel
26 Shanti Bhawan Lodge & Adarsh Niwas Hotel
28 Durag Niwas Guest House
30 Ajit Bhawan Palace Hotel
31 Umaid Bhawan Palace Hotel
33 Sun City Youth Hostel

PLACES TO EAT

17 Agra Sweet Home

OTHER

1 Jaswant Thanda
2 Nagauri Gate
3 Fort Meherangarh & Museum
4 Sardar Market
6 State Bank of India
7 Bicycle Rental
8 Bus Terminal
9 Raika Bagh Railway Station
11 Government Museum
13 Zoo
14 Sojati Gate
20 Siwanchi Gate
21 Jalori Gate
22 Ranchodji Temple
24 Railway Booking Office
25 GPO
27 Jodhpur Railway Station
29 Antique Shops
32 Indian Airlines

To Balsamand & Mandore

To Ajmer & Jaipur

Nai Sarak

High Court Road

Gaushala Road

Ratanada Road

Airport Road

To Chopasni

To Udaipur & Mt Abu

To Airport

Jodhpur

0   250   500 m

RAJASTHAN

accommodation in Jodhpur and, unfortunately, the main budget hotel area around the railway station is extremely noisy, chock-a-block full of vehicles, dusty and polluted. The *Shanti Bhawan Lodge* (☎ 21-689), just up the road opposite the station, has 74 rooms and operates a 24-hour checkout. Singles/doubles with common bath cost Rs 50/75, rooms with attached bath and air-cooling are Rs 75/130. It's difficult to believe this place was once the home of the prime minister of the former princely state of Jodhpur! Next door, the *Charli Bikaner Lodge* (☎ 23-985) is similarly priced but very scruffy.

Opposite the post office, the *Govind Hotel* (☎ 22-758) is the best of the budget hotels, and there's a rooftop restaurant with superb views of the fort. There are dorm beds for Rs 35, rooms with common bath for Rs 50/75 and with bath attached for Rs 95/125. The enthusiastic manager still hasn't got over his visit from the film crew of *The Jungle Book*, and may wish to show you his photos. Similarly priced hotels in this area include the *Hotel Soner* (☎ 25-732), the *Galaxy Hotel* (☎ 20-796), and the *Hotel Arun* (☎ 20-238) – the best of these last three.

The *Durag Niwas Guest House* (☎ 24-990) is a small place run by a friendly family with clean rooms at around Rs 150 for a double. There's safe parking for bikes; excursions to Bishnoi villages and meals are also available. A filling dinner costs Rs 60 but they tend to cater for Western palates so if you like your spices Indian-hot let them know.

The *Hotel Ghoomar Tourist Bungalow* (☎ 44-010) is on noisy High Court Rd. There are ordinary singles/doubles for Rs 150/200, air-cooled rooms for Rs 300/350 and air-con rooms for Rs 400/500. Dorm beds cost Rs 40. There's a bar and restaurant here, as well as the tourist office.

Home-stay accommodation, from Rs 125 to Rs 300, can be arranged through the tourist office.

Places to Stay – middle

At the bottom end of this bracket is the modern and well-maintained *Hotel Akshey* (☎ 37-327), just behind Raika Bagh Palace railway station, and just five minutes' walk from the bus terminal. Ordinary rooms are Rs 100/150, air-cooled rooms cost Rs 200/250 and there are air-con rooms for Rs 350/400. All rooms have satellite TV, attached bath and hot water. It's a good place.

If you want to be close to the railway station the *Adarsh Niwas Hotel* (☎ 26-936) is very convenient. The plain rooms have TV, phone and attached bath with hot water, and cost Rs 350/400 with air-cooling, and Rs 500/600 with air-con.

Moving up the scale there's the delightful *Ajit Bhawan Palace Hotel* (☎ 37-410; fax 37-774) on Airport Rd, a very popular place to stay and great for a small splurge. The rooms actually consist of a series of 20 modern stone cottages arranged around a relaxing garden with fish-stocked pools. All the cottages are furnished in their own whimsical style but they're all equipped with very clean, modern bathrooms. It's a whole world away from the noise and pollution around the railway station. The cottages cost Rs 895/995, or there are suites for Rs 1195 in the main building. The buffet meals here are excellent.

The new *Raj Baseera* (☎ 31-973), out of town towards the airport on Residency Rd, has copied the theme of the Ajit Bhawan with cottages built round a central building. Doubles are around Rs 800 and there's a swimming pool.

Places to Stay – top end

Jodhpur's finest hotel is the *Umaid Bhawan Palace* (☎ 33-316; fax 35-373), the residence of the former maharaja of Jodhpur. As the sales blurb says, 'To create luxury we did not change history'. They are not wrong! This has to be one of the world's most incredible hotels. It has everything from an indoor swimming pool to golf, badminton, tennis and croquet facilities, a billiard room, endless manicured lawns, bars, a vast dining hall, countless tigers' heads hanging from the walls and every conceivable service. Armies of cleaners keep every square inch squeaky clean and there are fine views across to the fort. This place used to be an amazing bargain – just US$35 for a double in 1990. Rooms are now US$145/160, and suites range from US$275 to US$850 per night. If you can possibly afford it, opt for a suite, as the cheaper rooms are modern and while they are very comfortable and offer all the mod cons, they are hardly palatial.

The only other hotel in this category is the *Hotel Ratanada Polo Palace* (☎ 31-910; fax 33-118), on Residency Rd, some distance out towards the airport. At Rs 2000/2500 for an air-con single/double it's overpriced, but there's a 30% low-season discount.

Places to Eat

While you're in Jodhpur, try makhania lassi, a delicious saffron-flavoured variety of that most refreshing of drinks. The *Agra Sweet Home* opposite the Sojati Gate is so popular that in summer they claim to sell over 1500 glasses a day. Other popular dessert specialities in Jodhpur include mawa ladoo and the baklava-like mawa kachori. Dhood fini is a cereal dish consisting of fine threads of wheat in a bowl with milk and sugar.

Surprisingly, one of the best places to eat is the veg/non-veg *refreshment room* on the 1st floor of the railway station. It's a cool and quiet haven, and the food is cheap and quite good. A veg thali is Rs 13, finger chips cost Rs 5. This place is thronged with travellers each evening, most of them catching the night train to Jaisalmer. It's open from 7 am to 10 pm.

The *Mid Town Restaurant*, in the Shanti Bhawan Lodge opposite the station, is another place popular with travellers waiting for a train. Their vegie burgers (Rs 16) are excellent, and the lassis enormous. The *Kalinga Restaurant* in the Adarsh Niwas Hotel next door has excellent non-veg food, although it's not all that cheap at around Rs 30 to Rs 45 for veg dishes and Rs 55 to Rs 75 for non-veg dishes.

The rooftop *Fort View Restaurant* at the Govind Hotel is a good veg place that certainly does have an excellent view of the fort.

A veg pizza is Rs 26, and their masala milk is worth trying.

There are essentially only two places to go for a splurge and you should make sure that you go to one or the other whilst you're in Jodhpur, if only for the experience and the live music and dance which each present. The cheaper of the two is the *Ajit Bhawan Palace Hotel*, where a buffet dinner in the main courtyard costs Rs 186, including tax. Although there are only a few dishes to choose from, the food is excellent. Rajasthani folk music and dancing is put on every evening between 6 and 8 pm and a skeleton band continues until late. Non-guests should book in advance, though it's not always necessary.

The more expensive of the two is the *Umaid Bhawan Palace*. A meal here is better described as a memorable banquet because it's served in the largest of the palace's halls and is accompanied by a live sitar, sarod and tabla recital. The food is superb, the range of dishes endless, and it all costs Rs 530. Advance booking is not necessary as a rule, but it's a good idea to check beforehand in the high season.

Things to Buy

The usual Rajasthani handicrafts are available here, but Jodhpur specialises in antiques. The greatest concentration of antique shops is along the road connecting the Ajit Bhawan with the Umaid Bhawan and the well-known Abani Handicrafts is next to the Tourist Bungalow. However, the existence of these shops is well known to Western antique dealers who come here with wallets stuffed with plastic cards. As a result, you'll be hard-pressed to find any bargains, though this is no reflection on the generally excellent quality of the goods available.

Certain restrictions apply to the export of Indian items over 100 years old – see the section under Things to Buy in the Facts for the Visitor chapter for more details.

Getting There & Away

Air Indian Airlines (☎ 28-600) has flights five times a week to Delhi (US$56), Jaipur

(US$34), Udaipur (US$28) and Bombay (US$87). Their office (☎ 36-757) is south of the centre on Airport Rd; open daily from 10 am to 1.15 pm and 2 to 4.30 pm.

Jagson Airlines (☎ 44-010, ext 360) is in the Tourist Bungalow. They have flights to/from Jaisalmer (US$70) and Delhi (US$94) on Tuesday, Thursday and Saturday. East West (☎ 37-516) flies to Jaipur (US$34) and Bombay (US$98) daily except Monday and Saturday.

Bus RSTC buses and private luxury buses connect Jodhpur with other cities and places of interest in Rajasthan. The private companies sell tickets opposite the main railway station.

The best bus to Jaisalmer is the daily superdeluxe which departs from the Ghoomar Tourist Bungalow at 6 am and arrives in Jaisalmer five hours later. The fare is Rs 80. The cheaper buses from the State Roadways bus stand take up to eight hours. There are more private buses to Jaisalmer during the low-season months than during the season.

Buses to Udaipur (Rs 83/69 for deluxe/express) take eight to 10 hours – much faster than the train. The six-hour trip across the desert to Bikaner costs Rs 66. There are hourly buses to Jaipur (Rs 101, seven hours) and Ajmer (Rs 60, 4½ hours). Buses for Mt Abu (Rs 80, six hours) leave in the early morning and early evening; some go only as far as Abu Road.

Train The booking office is on Station Rd, between the railway station and Sojati Gate. Demand for tickets is heavy, so come here soon after you arrive, especially if you want to catch the night train to Jaisalmer on the same evening. There's a tourist quota and the office is open Monday to Saturday from 8 am to 8 pm, and to 1.45 pm on Sunday.

At the recently modernised station building, an International Tourists Bureau has been set up to provide help for foreign railway passengers. It makes an excellent base if you just want to visit Jodhpur for the day and catch the night train to Jaisalmer, as

there are comfortable armchairs, and a shower and toilet. Unattended luggage must be deposited in the railway station cloak room, however.

Many people take the night train to Jaisalmer; so many, in fact, that it became a happy hunting ground for petty thieves and other characters of dubious ilk. In the high season, all foreigners are booked into the same carriages, and each carriage has a policeman stationed on it for the first part of the journey. There are both overnight and day trains to Jaisalmer (Rs 67/255 in 2nd/1st class) and the line was recently converted to broad gauge so the 295-km journey should now take only around seven hours.

There are superfast expresses between Delhi and Jodhpur (11 hours) and Ahmedabad and Jodhpur (eight hours). Fares for the 626-km trip from Delhi are Rs 124/459 in 2nd/1st class. There's also a daily train to Agra Fort, but the 439-km journey takes around 20 hours and can get horrendously crowded.

Not many people make the trip from Delhi straight through; most take the train from Jaipur, now connected to Jodhpur on broad gauge. The fastest service is the daily 2435/6 *Intercity* which leaves Jaipur at 5.30 pm, reaching Jodhpur five hours later. In the other direction it leaves Jodhpur at 5.30 am. Tickets cost Rs 297/540 in chair car/1st class. Slower trains do this 318-km trip in around seven hours for Rs 74/267 in 2nd/1st class.

To Udaipur there are day and night trains which take 10½ hours to cover the 221 km at a cost of Rs 56/205 in 2nd/1st class. Three trains a day link Jodhpur with Barmer in the west of the state, a 113-km journey that takes 5½ hours and costs Rs 30/122 in 2nd/1st class.

Getting Around
To/From the Airport The airport is only five km from the centre. It costs about Rs 30 in an auto-rickshaw and Rs 70 in a taxi, less when coming from the city to the airport.

Taxi & Auto-Rickshaw Jodhpur has unmetered taxis and allegedly metered auto-rickshaws as well as tongas. Auto-rickshaw drivers are rapacious, but most journeys should cost no more than Rs 10. You'd have difficulty getting through the narrow lanes of the old city in anything wider than an auto-rickshaw.

If you want to rent a car and driver, Solanki Travels (☎ 39-572), near the Shanti Bhawan Lodge, seems to be reliable.

Bicycle Jodhpur is a good place to explore by bicycle. They can be rented from several places, including one next to the Charli Bikaner Lodge.

AROUND JODHPUR
Maha Mandir & Balsamand Lake

Two km north-east of the city is the Maha Mandir (Great Temple). It's built around a 100-pillared Siva temple but is not of great interest. Five km further north is Balsamand Lake, a popular excursion spot. A palace, built in 1936, stands by the lake.

West of Jodhpur, the larger Pratap Sagar and Kailana Sagar (where there is also a garden) provide the city's water supply.

Mandore

Situated nine km to the north of Jodhpur, Mandore was the capital of Marwar prior to the foundation of Jodhpur. Today, its extensive gardens with high rock terraces make it a popular local attraction. The gardens also contain the cenotaphs of Jodhpur rulers, including Maharaja Jaswant Singh and, largest and finest of all, the soaring temple-shaped memorial to Maharaja Ajit Singh.

The Hall of Heroes contains 15 figures carved out of a rock wall. The brightly painted figures represent Hindu deities or local heroes on horseback. The Shrine of 33 Crore (330 million) Gods is painted with figures of deities and spirits. Regular buses run to Mandore from Jodhpur.

Rohet

In this village, 40 km south of Jodhpur, the (former local ruler) has converted his 350-year-old house into an excellent heritage hotel. Rooms at *Rohet Garh* (☎ (02932) 66-

231) cost around Rs 800. The place seems to attract travel writers; Bruce Chatwin wrote *The Songlines* here and William Dalrymple began *City of Djinns* in the same room – No 14.

Osian

The ancient Thar Desert town of Osian, 65 km north of Jodhpur, was a great trading centre between the 8th and 12th centuries when it was dominated by the Jains. Today, it's a desert oasis with numerous peacocks. The wealth of Osian's medieval inhabitants allowed them to build lavish and beautifully sculptured temples, most of which have withstood the ravages of time. The largest of the 16 Jain and Brahmanical temples is dedicated to Mahavira, the last of the Jain tirthankars. The sculptural detail on the Osian temples rivals that of the Hoysala temples of Karnataka and the Sun Temple of Konark in Orissa; so, if you have the time, make the effort to visit this place.

About six buses a day make the two-hour trip from Jodhpur.

Nagaur

Nagaur, north-east of Jodhpur, has a historic fort and palace and also sports a smaller version of Pushkar's cattle and camel fair. The week-long **fair** takes place in late January or early February and attracts thousands of rural people from far and wide. As at Pushkar, the fair includes camel races and various cultural entertainment programmes. There is very little in the way of accommodation here, however.

Sardar Samand Lake

The route to this wildlife centre, south-east of Jodhpur, passes through a number of colourful villages. There's upmarket accommodation at the maharaja's stylish art-deco summer palace, the *Sardasamand Lake Resort*. Rooms, which should be booked through the Umaid Bhawan Palace in Jodhpur, cost a mere Rs 1190/2390. Lunch or dinner are Rs 350, and there's a lakeside swimming pool.

Dhawa, or Doli, is another wildlife sanc-

CHRIS BEALL

PAUL BEINSSEN

BRYN THOMAS

PAUL BEINSSEN

HUGH FINLAY

A
B	C	D
E

Rajasthan
A: The Jal Mahal Palace, near Jaipur.
B: Jodhpur fortress.
C: Surya Pol, Jaisalmer Fort, Jaisalmer.

D: Beggars outside the Hawa Mahal, Jaipur.
E: City Palace, seen from Lake Pichol, Udaipur.

BRYN THOMAS

VALERIE TELLINI

HUGH FINLAY

Rajasthan

Top: Jaisalmer Fort.
Middle: Detail of Jain sculptures at the Dilwara Temples, Mt Abu.
Bottom: A stand-off in the streets of Jaisalmer.

tuary with many antelope, 45 km from Jodhpur on the road to Barmer.

JAISALMER

Population: 43,400
Telephone Area Code: 02992

Nothing else in India is remotely similar to Jaisalmer. Jodhpur certainly has one of the country's most spectacular fortress-palace complexes, and both Chittorgarh and Kumbhalgarh far surpass Jaisalmer in fame and sheer size. Yet this desert fortress is straight out of the *Tales of the Arabian Nights* and you could easily be forgiven for imagining that you'd somehow been transported back to medieval Afghanistan. This magic, incomparably romantic and totally unspoiled city has been dubbed the 'Golden City' because of the colour imparted to its stone ramparts by the setting sun. Jaisalmer is all of this and much more besides. No-one who makes the effort to get to this remote outpost leaves disappointed.

Centuries ago, Jaisalmer's strategic position on the camel train routes between India and central Asia brought it great wealth. The merchants and townspeople built magnificent houses and mansions, all exquisitely carved from wood and from golden-yellow sandstone. These havelis can be found elsewhere in Rajasthan but nowhere are they quite as exotic as in Jaisalmer. Even the humblest shops and houses display something of the Rajput love of the decorative arts in its most whimsical form. It's likely to remain that way for a long time to come, too, since the city planners are keen to ensure that all new buildings blend in with the old.

The rise of shipping trade and the port of Bombay saw the decline of Jaisalmer. At Independence, Partition and the cutting of the trade routes through to Pakistan seemingly sealed the town's fate, and water shortages could have pronounced the death sentence. However, the 1965 and 1971 Indo-Pakistan wars revealed Jaisalmer's strategic importance, and the Rajasthan Canal, to the north, is beginning to restore life to the desert. Paved roads and a railway, recently converted from metre to broad gauge, link Jaisalmer to the rest of Rajasthan. There are flights to Delhi and Jodhpur several times a week.

Today, tourism rivals the military base as the pillar of the city's economy. The presence of the Border Security Force hardly impinges at all on the life of the old city and only the occasional sound of war planes landing or taking off in the distance ever disturbs the tranquillity of this desert gem.

It has not always been so peaceful, of course, since fortresses have rarely been constructed for aesthetic reasons and medieval desert chieftains were not known for their pacific temperaments. Chivalric rivalry and ferocity between the various Rajput clans were the order of the day and the Bhatti Rajputs of Jaisalmer were regarded as a formidable force throughout the region. While Jaisalmer largely escaped direct conquest by the Muslim rulers of Delhi, it did experience its share of sieges and sackings with the inevitable jauhar being declared in the face of inevitable defeat. There is perhaps no Rajasthani city in which you can more easily conjure up the spirit of those times.

Orientation & Information

Finding your way around Jaisalmer is not really necessary – it's a place to simply wander around and get lost. The streets within the old city walls are a tangled maze, but it's small enough not to matter. You simply head off in what seems like the right direction and you'll get somewhere eventually.

The old city was once completely surrounded by an extensive wall, much of which has sadly been torn down for building material in recent years. Much remains, however, including the city gates and, inside them, the massive fort which rises above the city and is the essence of Jaisalmer. The fort itself is a warren of narrow, paved streets complete with Jain temples and the old palace of the former ruler, still flying his standard.

The central market area is directly below the hill, while the banks, the new palace and several other shops and offices are near the Amar Sagar Gate to the west. Continue outside the walled city in this direction and you'll soon come to the Tourist Bungalow, which also houses the tourist office (☎ 52-406) – open Monday to Saturday from 8 am to noon and 3 to 6 pm.

The State Bank of India, below Skyroom Restaurant, is the best place to change travellers' cheques. This can also be done at the Bank of Baroda, nearby, which does cash advances on Visa cards, too.

The hospital here is a nightmare – it's dirty, overcrowded, there's often no running water and the staff are overworked. Avoid it if at all possible.

Fort

Built in 1156 by Rawal Jaisal, the fort crowns the 80-metre-high Trikuta Hill. About a quarter of the old city's population resides within the fort walls, which have 99 bastions around their circumference. It's fascinating to wander around this place. Nothing has changed here for centuries and if ever an effort were made to pack as many houses, temples and palaces into the smallest possible area, this would be the result. It's honeycombed with narrow, winding lanes, all of them paved in stone and with a remarkably efficient drainage system which keeps them free of excrement and effluent. It's also quiet – vehicles are not allowed up here and even building materials have to be carried up by camel cart. The fort walls provide superb views over the old city and surrounding desert. Strolling around the outer fort ramparts at sunset is a popular activity, but be warned that the entire outer rampart is used as a public toilet, so watch your step!

The fort is entered through a forbidding series of massive gates leading to a large courtyard. The former maharaja's seven-storey palace fronts onto this. The square was formerly used to review troops, hear petitions and present extravagant entertainment for important visitors. Part of the palace is open to the public, but there's little to see inside, although one room has some beautiful murals. Opening hours are 8 am to 1 pm and 3 to 5 pm; entry is Rs 5.

Jain Temples

Within the fort walls are a group of beautifully carved Jain temples built between the 12th and 15th centuries. They are dedicated to Rikhabdevji and Sambhavanthji.

The Gyan Bhandar, a library containing some extremely old manuscripts, is also in the temple complex. The temples are only open in the morning until noon and the library only opens between 10 and 11 am. A Rs 15 charge is payable if you want to take pictures. There are also Siva and Ganesh temples within the fort.

Havelis

The beautiful mansions built by the wealthy merchants of Jaisalmer are known as havelis, and several of these fine sandstone buildings are still in beautiful condition.

There are no entry fees to most of the havelis, but some people are keen to get you to buy stone carvings and the like – there's some beautiful material to choose from. The havelis are open between 10.30 am and 5 pm.

Patwon ki Haveli This most elaborate and magnificent of all the Jaisalmer havelis stands in a narrow lane. It's divided into five apartments, two owned by the Archaeological Survey of India, two by families who operate craftshops here, and one still lived in that is closed to the public. There are murals on some of the inside walls and a fine view from the roof.

Salim Singh ki Haveli This haveli was built about 300 years ago and part of it is still occupied. Salim Singh was the prime minister when Jaisalmer was the capital of a princely state, and his mansion has a beautifully arched roof with superb carved brackets in the form of peacocks. The mansion is just below the hill and, it is said, once had two additional wooden storeys in an attempt to make it as high as the maharaja's palace. The maharaja had the upper storeys of the prime minister's haveli torn down! There's a Rs 10 entry charge at this haveli.

RAJASTHAN

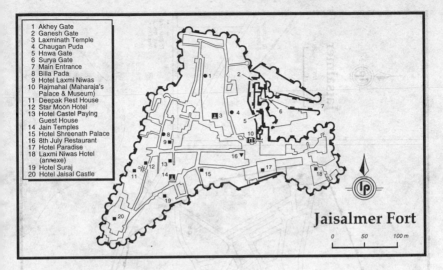

1 Akhey Gate
2 Ganesh Gate
3 Laxminath Temple
4 Chaugan Puda
5 Hawa Gate
6 Surya Gate
7 Main Entrance
8 Billa Pada
9 Hotel Laxmi Niwas
10 Rajmahal (Maharaja's Palace & Museum)
11 Deepak Rest House
12 Star Moon Hotel
13 Hotel Castel Paying Guest House
14 Jain Temples
15 Hotel Shreenath Palace
16 8th July Restaurant
17 Hotel Paradise
18 Laxmi Niwas Hotel (annexe)
19 Hotel Suraj
20 Hotel Jaisal Castle

Jaisalmer Fort

0   50   100 m

Nathmal ki Haveli This late 19th-century haveli was also a prime minister's house. The left and right wings of the building were carved by brothers and are very similar, but not identical. Yellow sandstone elephants guard the building, and even the front door is a work of art.

Gadi Sagar Tank & Museum

This tank, south of the city walls, was once the water supply of the city and there are many small temples and shrines around it. A wide variety of water birds flock here in winter.

The beautiful gateway which arches across the road down to the tank is said to have been built by a famous prostitute. When she offered to pay to have this gateway constructed, the maharaja refused permission on the grounds that he would have to pass under it on going down to the tank, and he felt that this would be unseemly. While he was away, she built the gate anyway, adding a Krishna temple on top so the king could not tear it down.

The small museum here has displays of folk art. Open daily from 10 am to 5.30 pm, it's considerably more interesting than the

dusty town museum by the Tourist Bungalow.

Organised Tours

Few travellers visit Jaisalmer without taking a camel safari into the desert. For details, see the comments under Places to Stay (below), and the information in the boxed section on Camel Safaris later in this chapter.

The tourist office offers a city sightseeing tour (Rs 40) from 9 am to noon, and a sunset tour to the Sam sand dunes (Rs 70). A minimum of four people is required for each tour.

Festivals

The annual Desert Festival is supposed to have camel races and dances, folk music, desert ballads and puppeteers, but it seems to have quickly become a purely commercial tourist trap. The RTDC sets up a special 'Tourist Village' at this time, similar to the one in Pushkar. The festival takes place between late January and mid-February; see the start of this chapter for the exact dates.

Places to Stay

Jaisalmer is a very popular place, and many

RAJASTHAN

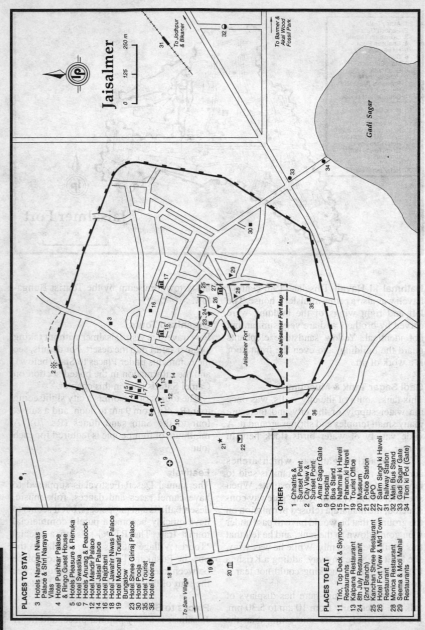

Jaisalmer

0   125   250 m

PLACES TO STAY

3 Hotels Narayan Niwas
   Palace & Shri Narayan
   Vilas
4 Hotel Pushkar Palace
   & Ringo Guest House
5 Hotels Pleasure & Renuka
6 Hotel Swastika
7 Hotels Anurag & Peacock
12 Hotel Mandir Palace
14 Hotel Jaisal Palace
16 Hotel Rajdhani
18 Hotel Jawahir Niwas Palace
19 Hotel Moomal Tourist
   Bungalow
23 Hotel Shree Giriraj Palace
30 Hotel Pooja
35 Hotel Tourist
36 Hotel Neeraj

PLACES TO EAT

11 Trio, Top Deck & Skyroom
   Restaurants
13 Kalpana Restaurant
24 8th July Restaurant
   (2nd Branch)
25 Kanchan Shree Restaurant
26 Hotel Fort View & Mid Town
   Restaurant
29 Monica Restaurant
   Seema & Moti Mahal
   Restaurants

OTHER

1 Chhatris &
   Sunset Point
2 City View &
   Sunset Point
8 Amar Sagar Gate
9 Hospital
10 Bus Stand
15 Nathmal ki Haveli
17 Patwon ki Haveli
19 Tourist Office
20 Museum
21 Police Station
22 GPO
27 Salim Singh ki Haveli
31 Railway Station
32 Main Bus Stand
33 Gadi Sagar Gate
34 Tilon ki Pol (Gate)

To Jodhpur & Bikaner

To Barmer &
Akal Wood
Fossil Park

Gadi Sagar

Jaisalmer Fort

See Jaisalmer Fort Map

To Sam Village

hotels, both cheap and not so cheap, have sprung up to meet the demand. More than anywhere else, the thing you'll notice on arrival, whether by bus or train, is the number of touts who swarm around, trying to grab the new arrivals. Unfortunately, some of them are less than honest about the service they provide – don't believe *anyone* who offers to take you 'anywhere you like' for Rs 2, and take with a grain of salt claims that the hotel you want to stay in is 'full', 'closed', 'no good anymore' or has suffered some other inglorious fate. They'll only lead you to a succession of hotels, where of course they get commission if you stay. If, after being carted from one hotel to another, you still insist on staying where *you* want and not where *they* want, you'll be dropped unceremoniously outside the main fort gate, from where you'll have to walk to the hotel of your choice. If you have made no decision about where to stay and just want a lift into the centre, then these people may be of use, but just be prepared for the roundabout tour and pressure to stay in a particular place.

Many of the popular budget hotels send their own vehicles to meet the bus or train. They display their own sign and offer free transport; otherwise you can take an auto-rickshaw. The touting situation has reached such dramatic proportions that the district magistrate has set up a Tourist Protection Squad. The aim of this squad is to keep the touts at a distance, so that travellers can at least gather their wits and baggage in peace before running the gauntlet. Their aims are very laudable – it's just a pity they are totally ineffective; the cynical might even say they work in collusion with the touts.

Unfortunately, quite a few of the cheap places are really into the high-pressure selling of camel safaris. Some places can get quite ugly if you book a safari through someone else. Not only will they refuse to hold your baggage, but in many cases they'll actually evict you from the hotel!

Staying at one of the hotels within the fort itself is the most imaginative choice, but don't take this to imply that there aren't equally good hotels outside the fort walls.

Jaisalmer is also one of those places where travellers fervently defend their choice of hotel over all others, so this selection will undoubtedly create controversy.

As is so often the case in Rajasthani towns, if there's a festival on, prices skyrocket and accommodation of any kind can be hard to get.

Places to Stay – bottom end

Town Area There's a good choice of budget hotels along the two streets that run parallel to each other north of the Trio Restaurant.

Down the first of these streets, the *Ringo Guest House* (☎ 53-027) has rooms with common bath from Rs 10 – providing you take their safari. There are two excellent doubles on the roof for Rs 70, including attached bathrooms with tub and geyser. Opposite is the *Hotel Peacock* (☎ 53-287), a basic place with dorm beds for Rs 10 and rooms with common bath for Rs 25/35. Also in this street is the *Hotel Anurag* with rooms from Rs 60/80, less if you sign up for their safari. The *Hotel Pushkar Palace* has doubles with attached bath for Rs 70, and cheaper rooms with common bath.

Along the next street is the deservedly popular *Hotel Swastika* (☎ 52-483). It's clean, well run, the staff is friendly and there are great views from the roof. Dorm beds are Rs 30, singles/doubles cost Rs 60/90 and rooms with bath are Rs 100 to Rs 120. Bucket hot water is available and there's free tea in the morning. A reasonable alternative is the *Hotel Pleasure* (☎ 52-323), further up the street. It's very small and exceptionally clean, but the rooms are small and many have no windows. The charge is Rs 40/50, all with common bath.

The *Hotel Renuka* (☎ 52-757), nearby, is a clean airy place but not particularly friendly. Like the Swastika, it has great rooftop views. There are dorm beds at Rs 20, singles/doubles from Rs 40/50 with common bath, and Rs 60/80 to Rs 80/100 with bath attached.

Across the other side of the old town is another group of budget hotels, close to the entrance to the fort. The *Hotel Fort View*

(☎ 52-214) is popular, mainly because of the fine views from the roof and some rooms. There are dorm beds for Rs 15, singles/doubles from Rs 44/55 and bucket hot water is available. There's also a couple of rooms with fort view and geyser, and these cost Rs 150/200 for a double/triple. The restaurant is reasonable and overlooks the small square below and the fort. You can change money, and arrange air, rail and bus tickets here. The *Hotel Flamingo* next door has just a few cheap rooms. It's very basic but popular.

Also in this area is the *Hotel Shree Giriraj Palace* (☎ 52-268). It's a friendly place with a range of clean rooms from Rs 40/60 with common bath to Rs 50/75 with attached bath or Rs 150 for a large double. Dorm beds are Rs 20, and there's a rooftop restaurant.

· The *Hotel Pooja* (☎ 52-608) is a small and friendly place, not far from Gadi Sagar Pol. It's in an old haveli, and rooms are Rs 40/60 with common bath, or there are more expensive rooms with attached bath.

In the south of the town, rather out on a limb, is a group of very cheap hotels. The *Hotel Tourist* (☎ 52-484) is a basic place run by an extremely friendly family, and they claim that this was the first hotel in Jaisalmer. At Rs 30/50 for rooms with attached bath the price can't be beaten. Opposite is the *Hotel Padam Niwas* (☎ 53-330), with rooms from Rs 20/25 with common bath. There are several other cheapies in this area.

At the top of this bracket is the modern *Hotel Rajdhani* (☎ 52-746), not far from the Patwon ki Haveli. The rooms all have attached baths with showers and hot water from (tiny) water heaters, for Rs 100/125. It's clean, comfortable and well run. There's a rooftop vegetarian restaurant with excellent views across to the fort. Opposite is the *Hotel Jag Palace* (☎ 52-746), a new hotel with overpriced rooms for Rs 150/300 with attached bath. It's worth trying to bargain them down a little.

Fort Area The *Deepak Rest House* (☎ 52-665) has long been popular, and deservedly so. It's actually part of the fort wall and offers stunning views from its rooftop. There are 14 rooms, six with bath and eight with common bath. Room No 9 (Rs 150) is the best one since it has its own balcony (the top of one of the bastions). Next best is room No 8 (Rs 100). Other doubles are upwards of Rs 50; Rs 80/100 for a single/double with attached bath. There are also singles for Rs 30 and a dorm for Rs 15, or you can sleep on the roof for Rs 10. The cheaper rooms are somewhat cell-like and have no views. Hot water is available round the clock at no extra charge.

Even cheaper is the newly opened *Star Moon Hotel* (☎ 52-910), next door. There are rooms with common bath for Rs 20/40; the best room is No 11, which has an attached bathroom and desert views for Rs 100. It's a friendly little place.

Of a similar standard to these two, and equally hard to find, is the *Hotel Laxmi Niwas* (☎ 52-758). If anything it's even smaller, and rooms cost Rs 40/60 with common bath, Rs 125 with attached bath, or you can sleep on the roof for Rs 20. It's a great place to stay with plenty of atmosphere, and is often full. They also have an annex above their tour office on the other side of the fort. Rooms in this modern building are Rs 150/200 with attached bath.

The *Hotel Paradise* (☎ 52-674) is a very popular place. You'll see it on the far side of the main square from the palace as you come through the last gate into the fort. It's a kind of haveli, with 18 rooms arranged around a leafy courtyard and excellent views from the roof. It has only a few cheap rooms from Rs 40/80 with common bath; rooms with attached bath range from Rs 200 to Rs 450, depending on size and views. You can sleep on the roof for Rs 20.

The *Hotel Castel Paying Guest House* (☎ 52-988) has just four double rooms ranging from Rs 100 to Rs 250. It's fairly basic but the family who run it are very friendly.

Places to Stay – middle
Town Area Near the Amar Sagar Gate is the *Hotel Jaisal Palace* (☎ 52-717), a good place that's clean and efficiently run. All

rooms have attached bath with shower and water heater and most cost Rs 390/440. There's one small room (No 107) for Rs 300/350. On the rooftop is a shady restaurant that serves excellent vegetarian food, and there are wonderful views of the fort.

The RTDC *Hotel Moomal Tourist Bunga-low* (☎ 52-392) is reasonable value, although it's out of the walled city. In the grounds there are thatched huts for Rs 150/200 with attached bathrooms (Rs 200/250 for larger huts). In the main building, dorm beds cost Rs 40, while ordinary single/double rooms are Rs 200/250, air-cooled rooms are Rs 300/400 and rooms with air-con go for Rs 500/550. Off-season rates are offered between April and August. There's a reasonable restaurant, a bar that gets quite lively at times, and a beer shop.

There are several other hotels in this category but they're even further away from the centre than the Tourist Bungalow. The characterless *Hotel Neeraj* (☎ 52-442) offers overpriced singles/doubles with bath and hot water for Rs 550/850.

Fort Area The charming *Hotel Suraj* (☎ 53-023) is near the Jain temple. The five suites in this atmospheric old haveli are decorated with wall paintings, and the attached bathrooms are hidden away down passages and through decorated archways. The room at the front is particularly recommended. Accommodation ranges from Rs 250 to Rs 450 and good vegetarian meals are available for Rs 40/65 for lunch/dinner. The owners live on the ground floor and are most helpful and friendly.

Nearby is another haveli still lived in by the owners, the *Hotel Shreenath Palace* (☎ 52-907). Don't expect too many modern facilities here, as this place is totally authentic. Rooms cost Rs 250/300 with common bath and bucket shower, and breakfast is available. It's a very pleasant place to stay.

Places to Stay – top end
The *Hotel Jaisal Castle* (☎ 52-362) is a restored haveli in the south-west corner of the fort. Its biggest attraction is its position

high on the ramparts looking out over the desert. Tastefully decorated rooms with attached bathrooms cost Rs 500/650. Some rooms are definitely better than others – the one on the top floor has big picture windows and superb views. The only flaw with this place seems to be the staff. Some guests find them friendly and helpful enough, others, particularly those who don't arrange a camel safari through the hotel, say their attitude varies from bored indifference to outright surliness. In the high season there are Rajasthani barbecues (Rs 300) in the courtyard. The hotel is not well signposted, but entry is through a large wooden doorway in front of a small courtyard at the far side of the fort.

The *Jawahar Niwas Palace* (☎ 52-208) is an impressive sandstone palace belonging to the maharaja, standing in its own sandy grounds near the Tourist Bungalow. It's around 100 years old, intricately decorated outside but with plainly furnished rooms and a billiard table covered in pigeon droppings. The large air-cooled rooms are Rs 700/800 for a single/double with attached bath, but these prices are likely to rise when the place is renovated.

The older royal palace, the *Mandir Palace* (☎ 52-788), is just inside the town walls. It's a beautiful building and now partly converted into a hotel. The rooms are large and decorated with coloured tiles; they cost Rs 650/750 with attached bath. The smaller doubles downstairs for Rs 400 are dark, stuffy and not recommended. Room service is from the nearby Trio Restaurant. Like the Jawahar Niwas this place is very high on atmosphere but rather low on luxury.

The well-run *Narayan Niwas Palace* (☎ 52-408) is a much slicker operation than the above three places. Recently extended, it's a modern hotel, not a palace, but it's been well designed to simulate the atmosphere of a Rajput ruler's desert camp. The pleasant rooms surround a grassy courtyard and the place is festooned with local crafts and *objets d'art*. Prices have been rising fast here and it's certainly no bargain – rooms cost Rs 1075/1375, or Rs 1175/1475 with air-con.

Meals are available and local musicians play in the courtyard while dinner (Rs 220) is served.

Next door, the much smaller *Shri Narayan Vilas* (☎ 52-283) is an older hotel that has tried to capture the same atmosphere with mixed success. It is, however, a pleasant place to stay and significantly cheaper at Rs 475/600 for a room with attached bath and tub. There are a few smaller rooms with showers attached for Rs 300/450. The rooms vary widely – try to see at least a couple before deciding.

Places to Eat

Like all travellers' centres, Jaisalmer sports a clutch of budget restaurants/juice bars which seem to attract their own cliques of long-time stayers. All the usual travellers' favourites are offered – muesli, pancakes, spaghetti, juices and lassis – and most places do a pretty good job. Hygiene is not always what it might be, though, and prices have risen in line with tourist numbers.

The *8th July Restaurant* is the best place to eat within the fort. Above the square, it's an excellent place to sit and watch the world go by. It's vegetarian only and the menu is not very extensive but what there is is good. A 'foot long' with cheese and tomato is Rs 27, pizzas are around Rs 30, and baked beans with cheese, onions and mashed potato is Rs 32. There's another branch outside the fort but it's not as good and only open at the height of the season.

There's a clutch of rooftop restaurants by the first fort gate. The thalis at the *Monica Restaurant* are excellent, and it's very popular in the early morning and evening. For a meal with a view of something different, try the *Natraj Restaurant*, just down the hill from the Monica. The open-air top floor has an excellent view of the upper part of the Salim Singh ki Haveli next door, and away to the south of town. The Natraj is a little more upmarket than the average places, but the food is good and the prices still reasonable. The *Seema Restaurant* nearby is cheaper and offers 'Green Peace Masala' on its menu!

Also near the fort gate, the *Mid Town*

Restaurant has great rooftop views, particularly in the early morning. A Rajasthani thali is Rs 40. Next door is the restaurant on the top floor of the *Hotel Fort View*.

In a small lane behind the Fort View is the *Kanchan Shree Restaurant*, which is very popular for its 18 varieties of lassi – the chocolate banana ones (Rs 10) are positively addictive! They also do lassis with ice cream (Rs 17) and sell home-made peanut butter. Rather more potent lassis are offered outside the government bhang shop – Rs 12 for medium strength, Rs 16 for something with more of a kick.

Down near the Amar Sagar Gate there are several good restaurants. The *Trio* is one of Jaisalmer's longest running; the food is tasty and well presented but prices are very high. A half chicken tandoori is Rs 80, spaghetti bolognese is Rs 45. Musicians play in the evenings, and the restaurant has its own generator for when the power fails – which is often in this desert town. At the end of the meal you'll be presented with a comments card, which the waiter will help you to fill in. Dare to write anything derogatory and your card will be torn up after you've left the restaurant! Close by is the *Skyroom Restaurant*, only a few rupees cheaper and on the top floor of an old haveli, above the State Bank of India.

The best value in this area is the popular *Kalpana Restaurant*, much cheaper and with a good range of dishes. *Top Deck* nearby is also recommended. A half chicken tandoori is Rs 45, veg dishes range from Rs 20 to Rs 35.

Things to Buy

Jaisalmer is famous for embroidery, Rajasthani mirrorwork, rugs, blankets, old stonework and antiques. Tie-dye and other fabrics are made at the Kadi Bundar, north of the city. One traveller reports that you should watch out for silver items bought in Jaisalmer as the metal may be adulterated with bronze.

Getting There & Away

Air Jagson Airlines (☎ 52-392) has an office at the Tourist Bungalow and flies between

Jaisalmer and Delhi (US$152) via Jodhpur (US$70) on Tuesday, Thursday and Saturday.

Bus The main bus terminal is some distance from the centre of town, near the railway station. Fortunately, all buses start from the traffic roundabout just outside Amar Sagar Gate, and then call at the main station. Reservations are only needed on the night buses, and these should be made at the main bus terminal.

There are eight daily STC buses on the route to Jodhpur, the deluxe one leaving at 5 pm. For Bikaner (Rs 85, eight hours) there are departures at 6 (deluxe) and 11 am, and 8 and 9.30 pm.

Every day there are five RSTC buses each way between Jaisalmer and Barmer (Rs 35, 3½ hours). There are also buses to Udaipur (Rs 150, 14 hours).

Train At the railway station there's an International Tourists Bureau, similar to the one at Jodhpur. It has comfortable armchairs, and a toilet and shower for use by rail patrons. The reservations office at the station is only open from 8 to 11 am, 2 to 4 pm and in the chaotic period just before departure.

There's a day and a night train in either direction between Jodhpur and Jaisalmer. The 295-km trip takes around nine hours and costs Rs 67/255 in 2nd/1st class.

Getting Around

Unmetered taxis, auto-rickshaws and jeeps are available. From the railway station, expect to pay Rs 15 to the old town, a little more to the Tourist Bungalow.

Quite a few of the hotels provide their own transport from the station, which is free if you're going to stay there. Those hotels which own jeeps generally also hire them out for visits to the surrounding area. A visit to the sand dunes at Sam, for instance, is Rs 70 per person.

The best way to get quickly around Jaisalmer itself is to hire a bicycle. There are a number of hire places, including one in Gandhi Chowk just inside Amar Sagar Gate, and another just outside the main gate of the fort.

AROUND JAISALMER

There are some fascinating places to see in the area around Jaisalmer, although it soon fades out into a barren sand-duned desert which stretches across the lonely border into Pakistan.

Due to the troubles in Punjab and alleged arms smuggling across the border from Pakistan, most of Rajasthan west of National Highway No 15 is a restricted area. Special permission is required from the Collector's office in Jaisalmer if you want to go there, and this is only issued in exceptional circumstances. The only places exempted are Amar Sagar, Bada Bagh, Lodhruva, Kuldhara, Akal, Sam, Ramkunda, Khuri and Mool Sagar.

Bada Bagh & Cenotaphs

Only a km or so north of Jaisalmer, Bada Bagh is a fertile oasis with a huge old dam. Much of the city's fruit and vegetables are grown here and carried into the town each day by colourfully dressed women.

Above the gardens are royal cenotaphs with beautifully carved ceilings and equestrian statues of former rulers. In the early evening, this is a popular place to watch the setting sun turn Jaisalmer a beautiful golden brown.

Amar Sagar

North-west of Jaisalmer, this once pleasant formal garden has now fallen into ruins. The lake here dries up several months into the dry season.

A beautifully carved **Jain temple** is being painstakingly restored by craftspeople brought in from Agra. Commenced in the late '70s, this monumental task is still continuing.

Lodhruva

Further out beyond Amar Sagar, 15 km from Jaisalmer, are the deserted ruins of this town which was the ancient capital before the move to Jaisalmer. The **Jain temples**, rebuilt in the late '70s, are the only reminders of the city's former magnificence. The temples have ornate carved arches at the entrance and a **Kalputra**, the Divine Tree, within. In the temple is a hole from which a snake is said to emerge every evening to drink an offering of milk. Only the 'lucky' can see it.

At the same time that they rebuilt the temples, Jain benefactors had the road out from Jaisalmer sealed, but it deteriorates into a desert track immediately beyond Lodhruva.

Mool Sagar
Situated nine km directly west of Jaisalmer, this is another pleasant, small garden and tank. It belongs to the maharaja of Jaisalmer.

Sam
A desert national park has been established in the Thar Desert near Sam village. One of the most popular excursions is to the sand dunes on the edge of the park, 42 km from Jaisalmer. This is the nearest real Sahara-like desert to Jaisalmer. It's best to be here at sunrise or sunset, and many camel safaris spend a night at the dunes. Just before sunset jeep loads of trippers arrive from Jaisalmer to be chased across the sands by persistent camel owners offering short rides.

There's only one bus a day between Jaisalmer and Sam so if you're only coming for the sunset you'll need to take a tour (Rs 70). It's well worth camping out on the dunes but you'll need a thick sleeping bag and blankets as it gets very cold. The only place to stay is the RTDC *Motel Sam Dhani* with eight rooms for Rs 150/200, and dorm beds for Rs 40. Book in advance at the Tourist Bungalow in Jaisalmer.

Khuri
Khuri is a village 40 km south-west of Jaisal-

Camel Safaris
The most interesting means of exploring the desert around Jaisalmer is on a camel safari and virtually everyone who comes here goes on one of them. October to February is the best time for a safari.

Competition between safari organisers is cut-throat and standards vary considerably. This has resulted in many complaints when promises have been made and not kept. Touts will begin to hassle you even before you get off the bus or train; and, at the budget end of the market, hotel rooms can be as little as Rs 10 – providing you take the hotel's safari. Try to talk to other travellers for feedback on who is currently offering good, reliable and honest service, and don't be pressured by agents who tell you that if you don't go on the trip leaving tomorrow there won't be another until next week. Naturally, they all offer *the best* safari and spare no invective in pouring scorn on their rivals.

The truth is more mundane. None of the hotels have their own camels – these are all independently owned – so the hoteliers and the travel agents are just go-betweens, though the hotels often organise the food and drink supplies. You need to consider a few things before jumping at what appears to be a bargain. Hotel owners typically pay the camel drivers around Rs 80 per camel per day to hire them, so, if you're offered a safari at Rs 120 per day, this leaves only a small margin for food and the agent's profit. It's obvious that you can't possibly expect three reasonable meals a day on these margins, but this is frequently what is promised. As a result, a lot of travellers feel they've been ripped-off when the food isn't what was offered. It's a moot point which of the parties ought to shoulder the responsibility for this – is it the agents who make impossible promises or the travellers who have unrealistic expectations?

The realistic minimum price for a basic safari is Rs 150 to Rs 200 per person per day. For this you can expect a breakfast of porridge, tea and toast, and lunch and dinner of rice, dhal and chapatis – pretty unexciting stuff. Blankets are also supplied. For Rs 250 you should also get fruit, and some relief from the rice-dhal-chapati tedium. You must bring your own mineral water. Of course you can pay still more for greater levels of comfort – tents, stretcher beds, better food, beer etc.

Two camel safari agents that are not linked to any hotels have been recommended. Sahara Travels (☎ 52-609), by the fort gate, is run by Mr Bissa, alias Mr Desert. If you think you've seen his face before it's because he's India's Marlboro Man – the model in the Jaisalmer cigarette ads. His basic tours cost Rs 250 a day for two to four days, or Rs 350 with a greater range of meals. Tented safaris start at Rs 500. Thar Safari Excursion Agent (☎ 52-722; fax 53-214), by the Trio Restaurant, organises deluxe safaris for Rs 550 including tents, a guide and mineral water. For Rs 400 the food is the same but you sleep out under the stars and no guide is included.

However much you decide to spend, make sure you know exactly what is being provided and make sure

mer, out in the desert, in the touchy area near the Pakistan border. It's a delightfully peaceful place with houses of mud and straw decorated like the patterns on Persian carpets.

As it's right on the 40-km limit from Jaisalmer, permits must be obtained from the Chief Magistrate's office, opposite the hospital, before setting out.

Accommodation is limited – try Mr Singh, who also organises camel safaris. *Mama's Guest House* is good but overpriced. Nice rooms in the cottages are Rs 300 with shared bath; vegetarian meals cost Rs 150.

There are infrequent buses between Jaisalmer and Khuri, and the trip takes 2½ hours.

Akal Wood Fossil Park

Three km off the road to Barmer, at a point 14 km from Jaisalmer, are the fossilised remains of a 180-million-year-old forest. To the untrained eye it's not particularly interesting.

POKARAN

At the junction of the Jaisalmer, Jodhpur and Bikaner roads, 110 km from Jaisalmer, is the site of another magnificent Rajasthan fortress. The sandstone fort rises from the desert and shelters a tangle of narrow streets lined by balconied houses decorated with parrots, elephants and Rajasthan's inevitable peacocks.

The RTDC *Motel Midway Pokran* (☎ (029942) 2275) is on the edge of town. It has just two rooms with attached bath for Rs 200/300, and meals are available. Far better is the more upmarket *Hotel Pokaran*, within the fort itself.

BARMER

Barmer is a centre for woodcarving, carpets,

---

it's there before you leave Jaisalmer. You should also make sure you know where they're going to take you. Attempting to get a refund on your return for services not provided is a waste of time.

Most safaris last three to four days and, if you want to get to the most interesting places, this is a bare minimum. Bring something very comfortable to sit on – many travellers neglect to do this and come back with very sore legs and/or backsides! A wide-brimmed hat (or Rajput-style turban), sun cream and a personal water bottle are also essential. It gets very cold at night so if you have a sleeping bag bring it along even if you're told that lots of blankets will be supplied.

If you're on your own it's worth getting a group of at least four people together before looking for a safari. Organisers will make up groups but four days is a long time to spend with people you might not get on with.

The usual circuit takes in such places as Amar Sagar, Lodruva, Mool Sagar, Bada Bagh and Sam, as well as various abandoned villages along the way. Usually it's one person per camel, but check this when booking. The reins are fastened to the camel's nose peg, so the animals are easily steered. At resting points, the camels are completely unsaddled and hobbled. They limp away to browse on nearby shrubs while the cameleers brew sweet chai or prepare food. The whole crew rests in the shade of thorn trees by a tank or well.

It's a great way to see the desert, which is surprisingly well populated and sprinkled with ruins. You constantly come across tiny fields of millet, girls picking berries or boys herding flocks of sheep or goats. The latter are always fitted with tinkling neck bells and, in the desert silence, it's music to the ears. Camping out at night in the Sam sand dunes, huddling around a tiny fire beneath the stars and listening to the camel drivers' yarns can be quite romantic. The camel drivers will expect a tip or gift at the end of the trip. Don't neglect to do this.

Take care of your possessions, particularly on the return journey. A current scam involves the drivers suggesting that you walk to some nearby ruins while they stay with the camels and keep an eye on your bags. The police station in Jaisalmer receives numerous reports of items missing from luggage but seems unwilling to help.

If you don't have the time, money or inclination to do an extended safari, there are any number of shorter options available. One currently in favour is a 2½-day trip which involves transport out to Sam by jeep, the return journey being made by camel. The cost of a trip like this is around Rs 550 per person. For those with even less time, a one-day, half-jeep/half-camel safari costs around Rs 250 per person. On any of these trips which include jeep transport try to establish how many people will be in the group, and therefore how crowded the jeep will be. I've seen jeeps heading out of Jaisalmer loaded to the eyeballs with 10 travellers, a driver, a couple of camel drivers, *plus* bedding and provisions for all these people! Five travellers plus drivers and gear is a safer and more comfortable number. ■

embroidery, block printing and other handicrafts and its products are famous throughout Rajasthan. Otherwise, this desert town, 153 km from Jaisalmer and 220 km from Jodhpur, isn't very exciting. There's no fortress here and the most interesting part is probably the journey to Barmer through small villages, their mud-walled houses decorated with the characteristic geometrical designs of each different village. It might be worth coming for the cattle fair, held at Tilwara nearby over a fortnight in March/April. There's also the Barmer Thar Festival organised by the tourist office (☎ (02982) 20-168) in early March.

There's hardly anywhere to stay here. Try the basic *Agra Rest House* or the *Krishna Hotel*, both near the railway station.

A couple of buses a day run between Barmer and Jaisalmer (Rs 35, 3½ hours), and south to Palanpur in Gujarat. Barmer is also connected to Jodhpur by metre-gauge railway. Although the line continues on to the Pakistani border, there are no through trains to that country and, in any case, foreigners are not allowed to cross the border at this point.

BIKANER

Population: 461,500
Telephone Area Code: 0151

This desert town in the north of the state was founded in 1488 by Rao Bikaji, a descendant of the founder of Jodhpur, Jodhaji. Like many others in Rajasthan, the old city is surrounded by a high crenellated wall and, like Jaisalmer, it was once an important staging post on the great caravan trade routes. The Gang Canal, built between 1925 and 1927, irrigates a large area of previously arid land around Bikaner.

Although it's less impressive than Jaisalmer, Bikaner is still an interesting place to visit, but not many travellers stop here. There's a superb large fort, a government camel breeding farm just outside the town (see the start of this chapter for the dates of the town's Camel Festival), and 30 km to the south is the Karni Mata Temple where thousands of holy rats are worshipped.

Orientation & Information

The old city is encircled by a seven-km-long city wall with five entrance gates, constructed in the 18th century. The fort and palace, built of the same reddish-pink sandstone as Jaipur's famous buildings, are outside the city walls.

The tourist office (☎ 27-445), in Junagarh Fort, is open daily except Sunday from 10 am to 5 pm.

It's possible to organise camel safaris from Bikaner. Desert Tours, behind the GPO, is one operator.

A torch/flashlight is essential for an overnight stay here as there are frequent power cuts.

Junagarh Fort

Constructed between 1588 and 1593 by Raja Rai Singh, a general in the army of the Mughal emperor, Akbar, the fort has a 986-metre-long wall with 37 bastions and two entrances. The Suraj Pol, or Sun Gate, is the main entrance to the fort. The palaces within the fort are on the southern side and make a picturesque ensemble of courtyards, balconies, kiosks, towers and windows. A major feature of this fort and its palaces is the superb quality of the stone carving – it rivals the best anywhere in the world.

Among the places of interest are the **Chandra Mahal**, or Moon Palace, with paintings, mirrors and carved marble panels. The **Phool Mahal**, or Flower Palace, is also decorated with glass and mirrors. The **Karn Mahal** was built to commemorate a notable victory over the Mughal Aurangzeb.

Other palaces include the Rang Mahal, Bijai Mahal and Anup Mahal. The contents include the usual Rajput weapon collection, not to mention the decaying pieces of a couple of old WW I biplanes. The Durga Niwas is a beautifully painted courtyard while the Ganga Niwas, another large courtyard, has a finely carved red sandstone front. Har Mandir is the royal temple, dedicated to Siva.

The fort is open daily except Friday from 10 am to 4.30 pm. Entry is Rs 20 for foreigners and there's a Rs 25 camera charge. A guide is included in this price but a little baksheesh is required to see all the rooms.

Lalgarh Palace

Three km north of the city centre, this red sandstone palace was built by Maharaja Ganga Singh (1881-1942) in memory of his father Maharaja Lal Singh. Although it's a grand building with overhanging balconies and delicate latticework, it's not the most beautiful of Rajasthani royal residences.

The **Shri Sadul Museum** covers the entire first floor of the palace. A fawning brochure describes the contents as 'some gorgious paintings and other rare artefacts that reveal these maharaja's appreciation and profound interest for art skill and brilliance'. But the museum is worth seeing, and houses an incredible array of photos, and an extraordinary collection of the former maharaja's personal possessions – golf clubs, camera, clothes, books, passport, glasses, earplugs and electric toothbrush! There's also the usual exhibition of Indian wildlife, shot and stuffed.

The Bikaner royal family still lives in part of the palace, while the rest has been turned into a luxury hotel. The museum is open from 10 am to 5 pm; entry is Rs 25 (Rs 10 for a camera), and you'll need to take an auto-rickshaw from the centre of town (Rs 15 each way).

Other Attractions

The narrow odoriferous streets of the old city conceal a number of old havelis and a couple of notable **Jain temples**. Built by two brothers, the Bhandeshwar and Sandeshwar temples date from the 14th century. Unlike most other Jain temples in Rajasthan they are decorated inside with colourful wall paintings.

The **Ganga Golden Jubilee Museum** contains a collection of sculpture, terracotta ware, coins, paintings and arms. It's open daily except Friday from 10 am to 5 pm; entry is Rs 2.

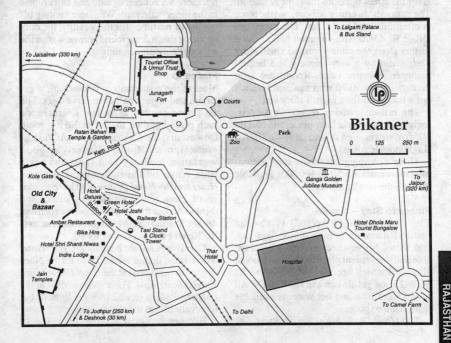

Places to Stay – bottom end

There are numerous budget options near the railway station. Station Rd is an amazingly busy thoroughfare so the noise level in any room fronting it can be diabolical – choose carefully. The *Green Hotel* (☎ 23-396) has singles/doubles with common bath for Rs 45/70, and rooms with satellite TV and attached bath for Rs 75/100. The *Hotel Deluxe* (☎ 23-292) next door is similar in price and standards but has a quieter annex around the corner. Beside this annex is the *Hotel Akashdeep* (☎ 26-024), a fairly typical grubby flophouse. There are rooms with common bath for Rs 30/45, or with attached bath for Rs 50/75. Most of these places charge Rs 3 for a bucket of hot water.

Best of these cheapies is the *Hotel Amit* (☎ 28-064), down the side street by the Green Hotel. Clean rooms with attached bath cost Rs 70/125. They also have cheaper doubles for Rs 80.

The *Hotel Shri Shanti Niwas* (☎ 25-025) is up the street opposite the railway station. The manager's a crusty old guy, and the place is often full later in the day. The rooms are OK at Rs 45/70 with common bath. A little further along the same street, the small *Indre Lodge*, run by a very friendly and helpful manager, is better value. Rooms are a bit dark, but at Rs 50/70 with attached bath it's not a bad place for a night's stopover.

The railway *retiring rooms* are surprisingly quiet for such a busy place, and cost Rs 30 for dorm beds, and Rs 40/80 for single/double rooms.

There's paying guest (home-stay) accommodation from Rs 50 to Rs 300, available through the tourist office.

Places to Stay – middle

The *Hotel Joshi* (☎ 61-162) is also on Station Rd near the railway station. Well run, and with 24-hour checkout, it's a comfortable and convenient place to stay. Air-cooled singles/doubles are Rs 185/225; for Rs 350/425 you get air-con and satellite TV. All rooms have bath and hot water is available from 6 am to noon.

The *Hotel Dhola Maru Tourist Bungalow*

(☎ 28-621) is pleasantly quiet but rather run-down. It's on Pooran Singh Circle, about one km from the centre of the city. Dorm beds are Rs 40, ordinary rooms Rs 100/150, air-cooled rooms Rs 200/250, and it's Rs 350/400 for air-con. There's a beer shop, bar and restaurant.

The *Thar Hotel* (☎ 27-180) is on the left-hand side of Hospital Rd on the way to the Tourist Bungalow. Rooms with bath and constant hot water are rather overpriced at Rs 350/470. There's a discount of 20% between April and August. The hotel's restaurant is quite good, and serves non-veg as well as veg dishes.

Places to Stay – top end

Well-appointed rooms at the *Lalgarh Palace Hotel* (☎ 61-963; fax 23-293), part of the maharaja's modern palace, are US$42/85 for a single/double including breakfast. There's a restaurant and the buffet lunch costs Rs 275, dinner is Rs 325. Between 7.30 and 8.30 pm there's a concert of sitar and tabla music in the inner courtyard. With tiger hunting off the list of pastimes for the wealthy, the only shooting that's done round here now is on the adjacent clay pigeon range.

Places to Eat

Most of the restaurants in Bikaner are vegetarian, and some don't even serve eggs. The 1st-floor restaurant at the *Hotel Joshi* is one such place but their thalis (Rs 30) are good. Downstairs, the *Chhotu Motu Joshi Restaurant* (sign in Hindi) also serves good vegetarian food, icy cold lassis and has a wide range of Indian sweets. The *Green Hotel* and the *Hotel Deluxe* both have similar small, clean restaurants serving snacks and drinks. Across the road is the more expensive *Amber Restaurant*. A tandoori cheese naan is Rs 20, an espresso coffee Rs 10.

Carnivores should head for the *Thar Hotel* where main dishes are Rs 30 to Rs 40. Non-veg is also available at the *Hotel Dhola Maru Tourist Bungalow*. For a splurge, dine at the *Lalgarh Palace* (Rs 325 for the buffet), but reservations are usually necessary.

Bikaner is noted for the spicy snacks

known as namkin, sold in the shops along Station Rd, among other places.

Things to Buy

On the right-hand side as you enter the fort, by the tourist office, is an excellent craft shop, run by the Urmul Trust. Items sold here are of high quality and made by people from surrounding villages. Proceeds go directly to improve health and education projects in these villages. You can browse here without the usual constant hassles to buy.

Getting There & Away

The airport is 15 km from the centre but not currently served by any airline.

Bus The bus stand is three km north of the city centre, right opposite the Lalgarh Palace. There are at least two RSTC buses daily between Bikaner and Jaisalmer (Rs 85, eight hours). Private companies also operate on this route.

To Jaipur (Rs 85, seven hours) there are at least six buses daily, including one deluxe bus at 9.30 pm. Overnight private buses leave from outside the Green Hotel (where tickets should be bought in advance).

The Jaipur buses go via the Shekhawati town of Fatehpur (Rs 48, 4½ hours). Other places served by bus from Bikaner include Udaipur (Rs 144, 13 hours), Ajmer (Rs 72, seven hours), Agra and Delhi.

Train The computerised booking office, open daily from 8 am to 8 pm (until 2 pm on Sunday), is in the building to the right as you approach the station.

Bikaner is now connected to Jodhpur and Jaipur by broad-gauge lines. Services on the 463-km metre-gauge trip to Delhi (Rs 99/367 in 2nd/1st class, 11 hours), currently leaving twice daily – morning and evening – in each direction, may be disrupted as gauge conversion proceeds; you may need to change trains at Rewari, 83 km from Delhi.

Getting Around

Auto-rickshaws are unmetered; they charge Rs 15 for the trip between the bus and railway stations. Bikaner also has tongas and there are bicycle-hire places along Station Rd.

AROUND BIKANER
Bhand Sagar Temple

The 16th-century Jain temple to the 23rd tirthankar, Parasvanath, is the most important of the complex. Others include the **Chintamani Temple** of 1505 and the **Adinath Temple**. There is a fine view of the city wall and surrounding countryside from the park behind the temple.

Devi Kund

Eight km east of Bikaner, this is the site of the royal chhatris (cenotaphs) of many of the Bika dynasty rulers. The white marble chhatri of Maharaja Surat Singh is among the most imposing.

Camel Breeding Farm

This government-managed camel breeding station, eight km from Bikaner, is probably unique in Asia. There are hundreds of camels here and it's a great sight in the late afternoon as the camels come back from grazing. The British army had a camel corps drawn from Bikaner during WW I.

The farm is open afternoons only and rides are available. Half the auto-rickshaw and taxi drivers in Bikaner appear to be on the lookout for tourists to take out there, but you need to bargain hard with them. For the round trip including a half-hour wait at the farm, you'll have to pay around Rs 40 for an auto-rickshaw, Rs 100 for a taxi.

Gajner Wildlife Sanctuary

The lake and forested hills of this reserve, 32 km from Bikaner on the Jaisalmer road, are inhabited by wildfowl and a number of deer and antelope. Imperial sand grouse migrate here in winter.

The old royal summer palace, on the banks of the lake, is now the *Gajner Palace Hotel*. Rooms in this upmarket hotel start at US$30 and can be booked through the Lalgarh Palace Hotel in Bikaner.

Deshnok

Following the highly publicised 1994 outbreak of plague in India, state governments have been attempting to reduce rat populations with heavy use of pesticides. Of course, this being India, not all rats are on the death list. The thousands that inhabit the **Karni Mata Temple** in Deshnok are future incarnations of mystics and sadhus, so pest control here would be sacrilege.

A visit to this fascinating temple, dedicated to Karni Mata, an incarnation of Durga, is not for the squeamish. Once you've admired the huge silver gates and marble carvings donated by Maharaja Ganga Singh, you plunge into the sea of swarming rodents, hoping that some will scamper over your feet – most auspicious. Little boys pick them up by their tails and let them perch on your shoulders. Devotees buy prasad to offer to the rats, finishing off anything they may leave. Eating prasad that has been salivated over by these holy rats brings even greater good fortune, but is not recommended for wimpish Western constitutions. Tetracycline courses are available from chemists in Bikaner.

There's a Rs 10 camera charge at the temple.

Places to Stay The RTDC *Yatri Niwas* (☎ (0151) 65-332) has deluxe rooms for Rs 130/150 and dorm beds for Rs 35.

Getting There & Away Deshnok is 30 km from Bikaner along the Jodhpur road. There are hourly buses from Bikaner for Rs 9. Taxi drivers don't seem keen to make this trip. You'll have to bargain hard for the round-trip charge of Rs 150; make sure this includes at least an hour at the temple.

Gujarat

The west coast state of Gujarat is not one of India's busiest tourist destinations and although it is quite easy to slot Gujarat in between Bombay and the cities of Rajasthan, few people pause to explore this interesting state.

Gujarat has a long and varied history and a great number of interesting places to visit. If you want to go beyond history into the realm of legend, then the Temple of Somnath was actually there to witness the creation of the universe! Along the south coast are the sites where many of the great events in Krishna's life took place.

On firmer historic footing, Lothal was the site of a Harappan or Indus Valley civilisation over 4000 years ago. The main sites of this very ancient culture are now in Pakistan, but it is thought that Lothal may have survived the great cities of the Sindh by as much as 500 years. Gujarat also featured in the exploits of the great Buddhist emperor, Ashoka, and one of his rock edicts can be seen near Junagadh.

Later, Gujarat suffered Muslim incursions from Mahmud of Ghazni and subsequent Mughal rulers, and was a battlefield between the Mughals and the Marathas. It was also an early point of contact with the West and the

Population: 44.5 million
Area: 196,024 sq km
Capital: Gandhinagar
People per sq km: 227
Main Language: Gujarati
Literacy Rate: 61.29%
Best Time to Go: October to March

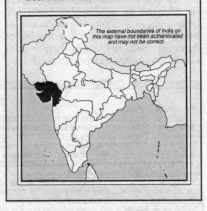

The external boundaries of India on this map have not been authenticated and may not be correct.

first British commercial outpost was established at Surat. Daman and Diu survived as Portuguese enclaves within the borders of Gujarat until 1961. Gujarat also had close

---

Gujarati Food

The strict vegetarianism of the Jains has contributed to Gujarat's distinctive regional cuisine. Throughout the state, you'll find the Gujarati version of the thali – it's the traditional all-you-can-eat vegetarian meal with an even greater variety of dishes than usual. It can, however, be overpoweringly sweet.

Popular dishes include *kadhi*, a savoury curry of yoghurt, fried puffs and finely chopped vegetables. *Undhyoo* is a winter speciality of potatoes, sweet potatoes, broad beans and aubergines roasted in an earthenware pot which is buried upside down (undhyoo) and a fire built on top. In Surat, the local variation of this dish is more spicy and curry hot. *Sev ganthia*, a crunchy fried chickpea-flour snack, is available from *farsan* stalls.

In winter, try Surat's *paunk*, a curious combination of roasted cereals; or *jowar*, garlic chutney and sugar. Then there's *khaman dhokla*, a salty, steamed chickpea flour cake, and *doodhpak*, a thick, sweetened, milk-based dessert with nuts. *Srikhand* is a dessert made from yoghurt and spiced with saffron, cardamom, nuts and candied fruit. *Gharis* are rich sweets made of milk, clarified butter and dried fruits – another Surat speciality. In summer, *aamb rasis* is a popular mango drink.

The Gujaratis make superb ice cream, available throughout western India under the brand name of Vadilal. It comes in about 20 flavours, some of which are seasonal. ■

ties with the life of the father of modern India, Mahatma Gandhi. It was in Gujarat that Mahatma Gandhi, the father of modern India, was born and spent his early years, and it was to Ahmedabad, the main city of Gujarat, that he returned to wage his long struggle with the British for independence.

Gujarat has always been a centre for the Gujarat, and some of its most interesting sights are Jain temple centres like those at Palitana, and at Girnar Hill, near Junagadh. The Jains are an influential and energetic group and, as a result, Gujarat is one of India's wealthier states with a number of important industries, particularly textiles and electronics, and has the dubious distinc-

tion of having the largest petrochemical complex in the country. Apart from its Jain temples, Gujarat's major attractions include the last Asian lions, in the Gir Forest, and the fascinating Indo-Saracenic architecture of Ahmedabad. The colourful tribal villages of Kutch are well worth the effort of making your way out to this barren region. For more hedonistic pleasures, there are the pristine beaches at Diu, off Gujarat's southern coast, and at Mandvi, 60 km south-west of Bhuj, in Kutch.

Geographically, Gujarat can be divided into three areas. The eastern (mainland) region includes the major cities of Ahmedabad, Surat and Vadodara (Baroda). The Gulf

Festivals & Fairs

Gujarat has many fairs in its temple towns and small villages. They offer a chance to see religious festivals and celebrations and, in the villages, also provide an opportunity to see the finest examples of local handicrafts. The village of Ambaji, 177 km north of Ahmedabad, celebrates four major festivals each year. The Bhavnath Fair, held at the foot of Girnar Hill near Junagadh in the month of Magha (January/February), is a fine opportunity to hear local folk music and see folk dances.

In the week preceding Holi (February/March), the tribal Adivasi people have a major festival in the forested region called The Dangs, east of Surat near the Maharashtra border – it's known as the Dang Durbar. Krishna's birthday falls in August and his temple at Dwarka is the place to be for the celebration of the Janmashtami Festival held in his honour on this day. Along the coast at Madhavpur near Porbandar, the Madhavrai Fair is held in the month of Chaitra (March/April) to celebrate Krishna's elopement with Rukmini. In the same month, a major festival takes place at the foot of Pavagadh Hill at Champaner, near Vadodara, honouring the goddess Mahakali.

Somnath has a large fair at the full moon of Kartika Purnima in November/December. An important festival is held in honour of Siva, the three-eyed one, or Trinetreshwar, in the month of Bhadra (August/September) in Tarnetar village – you'll see colourful local tribal costumes here.

Bhuj in Kutch hosts the annual Rann Festival in February/March. There're craft demonstrations, cultural programmes and tours to places of interest in the region.

Gujarat has a busy calendar of events. Some of the main ones include:

January
Makar Sankranti This end-of-winter festival is celebrated with kite-flying contests, and Ahmedabad hosts an international contest.

January/February
Muharram Tazias, large replicas of the tombs of two Muslim martyrs, are paraded in the evening, particularly in Surat, Junagadh and Ahmedabad.

September/October
Navaratri Nine nights of music and dancing celebrate this festival of the mother goddess, Amba. The Dandiya Ras, which Krishna danced with his *gopis* (milkmaids), is featured. Other folk dances, such as the Gujarati Ras Garba, are also performed. Vadodara (Baroda) is a good place to be during Navaratri as many cultural events are organised at this time.

October
Dussehra The 10th day of Navaratri culminates in the celebration of Rama's victory over the evil Ravana in the *Ramayana*.

October/November
Sharad Purnima Song and dance celebrate the end of the monsoon on the night of the full moon in the month of Kartika. ∎

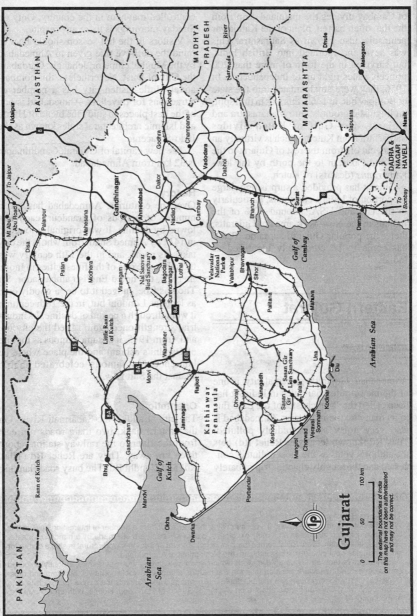

Gujarat

The external boundaries of India
on this map have not been authenticated
and may not be correct.

of Cambay divides the mainland strip from the flat, often barren, plain of the Kathiawar peninsula, also known as Saurashtra. This was never incorporated into British India, but survived in the form of more than 200 princely states right up to Independence. In 1956, they were amalgamated into the state of Bombay but, in 1960, this was in turn split, on linguistic grounds, into Maharashtra and Gujarat. The Gulf of Kutch divides Saurashtra from Kutch, which is virtually an island, cut off from the rest of Gujarat to the east and Pakistan to the north by the low-lying *ranns* (deserts) of Kutch.

Gujarat has provided a surprisingly large proportion of India's emigrants, particularly to the UK and USA. Around 40% of the Indians in the New York area are Gujaratis; there, the popular Gujarati surname 'Patel' has come to be commonly identified as Indian.

Eastern Gujarat

AHMEDABAD

Population: 3,600,000
Telephone Area Code: 079

Ahmedabad, Gujarat's principal city, is one of the major industrial cities in India. It has been called the 'Manchester of the East' due to its many textile industries. Ahmedabad is also very noisy and incredibly polluted; Tilak Rd (known locally as Relief Rd) gets the author's votes as the most polluted, congested and thoroughly chaotic strip of barely controlled mayhem in the country. Only on Sunday mornings is there any respite.

Visitors in the hot season should bear in mind the derisive title given to Ahmedabad by the Mughal emperor, Jehangir: Gardabad, the City of Dust. Nevertheless, this comparatively little-visited city has a number of attractions for travellers. Ahmedabad is one of the best places to study the blend of Hindu and Islamic architectural styles known as the Indo-Saracenic.

The new capital of Gujarat, Gandhinagar, is 32 km from Ahmedabad.

History
Over the centuries, Ahmedabad has had a number of periods of grandeur, each followed by decline. It was originally founded in 1411 by Ahmed Shah, from whom the city takes its name, and in the 17th century was thought to be one of the finest cities in India. In 1615, the noted English ambassador, Sir Thomas Roe, judged it to be 'a goodly city, as large as London' but, in the 18th century, it went through a period of decline. Its industrial strength once again raised the city up, and, from 1915, it became famous as the site of Gandhi's ashram and the place where he launched his famous celebrated march against the Salt Law.

Orientation
The city straddles the Sabarmati River. On the eastern bank, two main roads run east from the river to the railway station, about three km away. They are Relief Rd (Tilak Rd) and Gandhi Rd. The busy road flanking

---

Things to Buy

With its busy modern textile works, it's not surprising that Gujarat offers a number of interesting buys in this line. Extremely fine, and often extremely expensive, patola silk saris are still made by a handful of master craftspeople in Patan. From Surat comes the *zari*, or gold-thread embroidery work. Surat is also a centre for silk saris. Less opulent, but still beautiful, are the block prints of Ahmedabad.

Jamnagar is famous for its tie-dye work, which you'll see throughout Saurashtra. Brightly coloured embroideries and beadwork are also found in Saurashtra, along with woollen shawls, blankets and rugs. Brass-covered wooden chests are manufactured in Bhavnagar, and Kutch is the centre for exquisite, fine embroidery. Most Gujarati handicrafts are on display at Gurjari or Handloom House, both on Ashram Rd, Ahmedabad. ■

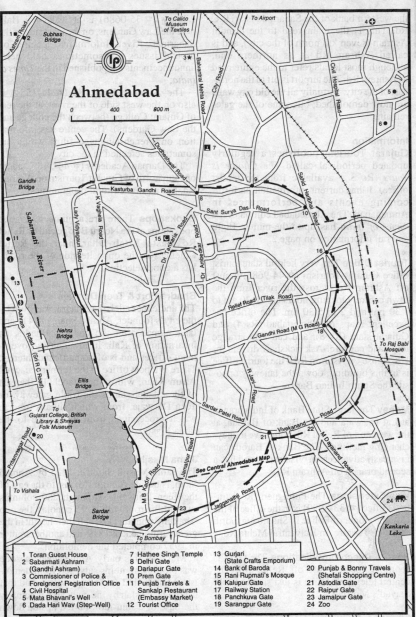

Ahmedabad

0   400   800 m

To Calico
Museum
of Textiles

To Airport

Ashram Road

Subhas
Bridge

Bahramrai Mehta Road

City Road

Civil Hospital Road

Dudheshwar Road

Gandhi
Bridge

Kasturba Gandhi Road

Sant Surya Das Road

Sahid Haribhai Road

Sabarmati River

K Vaghela Road

Lady Vidyagaun Road

Dr Tankaria Road

Dr Ambekar Road

Relief Road   (Tilak Road)

Gandhi Road (M G Road)

To Raj Babi
Mosque

Nehru
Bridge

Ashram Road (Sri R C Road)

Ellis
Bridge

R Jani Road

Sardar Patel Road

Vivekanand Road

M Dayanand Road

To
Gujarat College, British
Library & Shreyas
Folk Museum

Pritamnagar Road

Jamalpur Road

M B Kadri Road

Jaggannathji Road

See Central Ahmedabad Map

To Vishala

Sardar
Bridge

To Bombay

Kankaria
Lake

1 Toran Guest House	7 Hathee Singh Temple	13 Gurjari
2 Sabarmati Ashram	8 Delhi Gate	(State Crafts Emporium)
(Gandhi Ashram)	9 Dariapur Gate	14 Bank of Baroda
3 Commissioner of Police &	10 Prem Gate	15 Rani Rupmati's Mosque
Foreigners' Registration Office	11 Punjab Travels &	16 Kalupur Gate
4 Civil Hospital	Sankalp Restaurant	17 Railway Station
5 Mata Bhavani's Well	(Embassy Market)	18 Panchkuva Gate
6 Dada Hari Wav (Step-Well)	12 Tourist Office	19 Sarangpur Gate

20 Punjab & Bonny Travels	
(Shefali Shopping Centre)	
21 Astodia Gate	
22 Raipur Gate	
23 Jamalpur Gate	
24 Zoo	

the western bank of the Sabarmati is Sri R C Rd. This is the main road to the Gandhi Ashram (seven km north of the city), and is called Ashram Rd at its northern end, although most locals refer to the entire road as Ashram Rd. The airport is off to the north-east of the city. Virtually all the old city walls are now demolished, but some of the gates remain.

Information
Gujarat Tourism publishes a regularly updated periodical called *The Choice is Yours* (Rs 3 – available from the tourist office). It has current information on forth-coming events and performances in Ahmedabad. The Ahmedabad edition of the *Times of India* has up-to-the-minute flight and rail information on page 2.

Tourist Office The very helpful state tourist office Gujarat Tourism (☎ 44-9683) is just off Ashram Rd, across the river from the town centre. Opening hours are 10.30 am to 1.30 pm and 2 to 5.30 pm. The office has excellent maps of Ahmedabad (Rs 4) and Gujarat state (Rs 8), and can also arrange tours and car hire. Ask rickshaw drivers for HK House on Ashram Rd – the tourist office is in this building, down the laneway oppo-site the South Indian Bank.

Money The large State Bank of India branch at Lal Darwaja and the Bank of Baroda, at the west end of Relief Rd, both have money-changing facilities. The Bank of Baroda can give cash advances on Visa cards, and has a second branch on Ashram Rd.

Visa Extensions The Foreigners' Registra-tion Office (☎ 33-3999) is in the office of the Commissioner of Police in Shahibaug, north of the city centre on Balvantrai Mehta Rd.

Post & Telecommunications The GPO is centrally located just off Relief Rd. The central telegraph office is just south of Sidi Saiyad's Mosque.

Libraries & Cultural Centres The British

Library (☎ 35-0686) is at Kakabhai Hall, near the Law Gardens, on the west side of the Sabarmati River. Informative lectures on topical issues are sometimes held here; announcements are published in the *Times of India*.

The Alliance Francaise (☎ 44-1551) is also on the west side of the river, at the rear of Gujarat College (between the college and the Law Gardens). The centre has informa-tion on French-language films which are sometimes screened in the city.

The Darpan Academy (☎ 44-5189), about one km north of Gujarat Tourism on Ashram Rd, has regular cultural programmes.

Bookshops There are a number of good bookshops at the Nehru Bridge end of Relief Rd. Sastu Kitab Dhar, near the Relief Cinema (on the opposite side of the road), has a good selection.

Bhadra Fort & Teen Darwaja
The ancient citadel, the Bhadra, was built by the city's founder, Ahmed Shah, in 1411 and later named after the goddess Bhadra, an incarnation of Kali. It now houses govern-ment offices and is of no particular interest. There is a post office in the former Palace of Azam Khan, within the citadel. To the east of the citadel stands the triple gateway, or Teen Darwaja, from which sultans used to watch processions from the palace to the Jama Masjid.

Jama Masjid
The Jama Masjid, built in 1423 by Ahmed Shah, is beside Gandhi Rd, just to the east of the Teen Darwaja. Although 260 columns support the roof with its 15 cupolas, the two 'shaking' minarets lost half their height in the great earthquake of 1819, and another tremor in 1957 completed the demolition.

Much of this early Ahmedabad mosque was built using items salvaged from demol-ished Hindu and Jain temples. It is said that a large black slab by the main arch is actually the base of a Jain idol, buried upside down for the Muslim faithful to tread on.

Tombs of Ahmed Shah & his Queens

The tomb of Ahmed Shah, with its perforated stone windows, stands just outside the east gate of the Jama Masjid. His son and grandson, who did not long survive him, also have their cenotaphs in this tomb. Women are not allowed into the central chamber. Across the street on a raised platform is the tomb of his queens – it's now really a market and in very poor shape compared to Ahmed Shah's tomb.

Sidi Saiyad's Mosque

This small mosque, which once formed part of the city wall, is close to the river end of Relief Rd. It was constructed by Sidi Saiyad, a slave of Ahmed Shah, and is noted for its beautiful carved stone windows, depicting the intricate intertwining of the branches of a tree.

Ahmed Shah's Mosque

Dating from 1414, this was one of the earliest mosques in the city and was probably built on the site of a Hindu temple, using parts of that temple in its construction. It is to the south-west of the Bhadra. The front of the mosque is now a garden.

Rani Rupmati's Mosque

A little north of the city centre, Rani Rupmati's Mosque was built between 1430 and 1440 and named after the sultan's Hindu wife. The minarets were partially brought down by the disastrous earthquake of 1819. Note particularly the way the dome is elevated to allow light in around its base. As with so many of Ahmedabad's early mosques, this one displays elements of both Hindu and Islamic design.

Rani Sipri's Mosque

This small mosque is also known as the Masjid-e-Nagira, or Jewel of a Mosque, because of its extremely graceful and well-executed design. Its slender minarets again

'Marble trees' weave delicate patterns at Sidi Saiyad's Mosque

GUJARAT

blend Hindu and Islamic styles. The mosque is said to have been commissioned in 1514 by a wife of Sultan Mahmud Begada after he executed their son for some minor misdemeanour, and she is in fact buried here. It's to the south-east of the city centre.

Sidi Bashir's Mosque & Shaking Minarets

Just south of the railway station, outside the Sarangpur Gate, the Sidi Bashir Mosque is famed for its shaking minarets, or jhulta minars. When one minaret is shaken, the other rocks in sympathy. This is said to be a protection against earthquake damage. It's a fairly fanciful proposition, and one which you'll be unable to verify, unless of course you happen to be on the spot during an earthquake.

Raj Babi Mosque

The Raj Babi Mosque, south-east of the railway station in the suburb of Gomtipur, also had shaking minarets, one of which was partially dismantled by an inquisitive Englishman in an unsuccessful attempt to find out how it worked. It's worth a visit but, once again, you're specifically prohibited from shaking the remaining minaret.

A little to the north of the railway station, other minarets are all that remain of a mosque which was destroyed in a battle between the Mughals and Marathas in 1753.

Hathee Singh Temple

Just outside the Delhi Gate, to the north of the old city, this temple, as with so many Jain temples, is made of white marble. Built in 1848, it is dedicated to Dharamanath, the 15th Jain *tirthankar* (teacher).

Step-Wells

Dada Hari Wav Step-wells *(wavs* or *baolis)* are strange constructions, unique to northern India, and this is one of the best. The curious well, built in 1501 by one of the women of Sultan Begara's harem, has a series of steps leading down to lower and lower platforms, eventually terminating in a small octagonal well. The depths of the well are cool, even

on the hottest day, and it must once have been quite beautiful. Today, it is completely neglected and often bone dry, but it's a fascinatingly eerie place with galleries above the well and a small portico at ground level.

The best time to visit and/or photograph the well is between 10 and 11 am; at other times, the sun is in the wrong place and doesn't penetrate to the various levels. There's no entry or camera fee. Behind the well is the equally neglected mosque and *rauza* (tomb) of Dada Hari. The mosque has a tree motif like the one on the windows of Sidi Saiyad's Mosque.

Mata Bhavani's Well This well is a couple of hundred metres north of Dada Hari's. Ask children to show you the way. Thought to be several hundred years older, it is much less ornate and is now used as a crude Hindu temple.

Kankaria Lake

South-east of the city, this artificial lake, complete with an island summer palace, was constructed in 1451 and has 34 sides, each 60 metres long. Once frequented by Emperor Jehangir and Empress Nur Jahan, it is now a local picnic spot. The huge **zoo** and children's park by the lake are outstanding, and the Ghattamendal pavilion in the centre houses an **aquarium**. To get there, take bus No 32, 42, 60, 152 or 153 from the Lal Darwaja bus stand (Rs 2).

Other Mosques & Temples

It's very easy to get bored with mosques in Ahmedabad. If your enthusiasm for them is limited, don't go further than Sidi Saiyad's Mosque and the Jama Masjid. If you have real endurance, you could continue to **Dastur Khan's Mosque** near the Rani Sipri Mosque. Or there're also the mosques of Haibat Khan, Saiyad Alam, Shuja'at Khan, Shaikh Hasan Muhammed Chisti and Muhafiz Khan.

Then, for a complete change, you could plunge into the narrow streets of the old part of town and seek out the brightly painted **Swami Narayan Temple**. Enclosed in a large courtyard, it dates from 1850. To the south of this Hindu temple are the nine tombs known as the Nau Gaz Pir, or Nine Yard Saints.

Other Attractions

In many streets, there are Jain bird-feeding places known as *parabdis*. Children catch and release pigeons for the fun of it. The older parts of the city are divided into totally separate areas known as *pols*. It's easy to get lost. The pleasant **Victoria Gardens** are at the east end of the Ellis Bridge.

Unlike so many other large cities, Ahmedabad has little evidence of the British period. The chief landmarks of the era are the tall smokestacks that ring this industrial city. On the sandy banks of the Sabarmati River, traditional block-printed fabrics are still stretched out to dry, despite the city's 70-plus large textile mills. The river dries to a mere trickle in the hot season.

Other places of interest in and around town include the ruined **tomb of Darya Khan**, north-west of the Hathee Singh Temple. Built in 1453, the tomb has a particularly large dome. Nearby is the **Chhota Shahi Bagh**, across the railway line. Ladies of the harem used to live in the *chhota* (small) garden. In Saraspur, east of the railway line, the **Temple of Chintaman** is a Jain temple originally constructed in 1638 and converted into a mosque by Aurangzeb.

Museums

The excellent **Callco Museum of Textiles** exhibits antique and modern textiles including rare tapestries, wall hangings and costumes. Also on display are old weaving machines. The museum is in Sarabhai House, a former *haveli* (mansion), in the Shahi Bagh Gardens. Admission is free, but you can only enter on a guided tour. Tours depart at 10.15 am and 2.45 pm, and the museum is closed on Wednesday. To get there, take bus No 101, 102, 103 or 105 (Rs 3) out through the Delhi Gate.

The **N C Mehta Museum of Miniatures** at Sanskar Kendra, Paldi, has excellent examples of the various schools of Indian

miniature painting. It is open from 9 to 11 am and 4 to 7 pm daily, except Mondays. The building was designed by Le Corbusier, who also had a hand in the new capital of Gandhinagar.

The **Shreyas Folk Museum** (closed Wednesday), about 2½ km west of the Sabarmati in the suburb of Ambavadi, displays the folk arts & crafts of Gujarat. It's open from 9 am to noon, and 3 to 5 pm. To get there, take bus No 34, 34/5 or 200 (Rs 3). There're also the **National Institute of Design**, the **Tribal Research & Training Institute Museum**, on Ashram Rd, and a **Philatelic Museum**.

The **Institute of Indology** on the university campus has an important collection of illustrated manuscripts and miniatures and one of the finest collections relating to Jainism in India. It is only open in the afternoons from around 3 pm.

Sabarmati Ashram

Seven km from the centre of town, on the west bank of the Sabarmati River, this was Gandhi's headquarters during the long struggle for Indian independence. His ashram was founded in 1915 and still makes handicrafts, handmade paper and spinning wheels. Gandhi's spartan living quarters are preserved as a small museum and there is a pictorial record of the major events in his life. There's also a bookshop selling books by and about the Mahatma.

The ashram is open from 8.30 am to 6.30 pm (till 7 pm between April and September). Admission is free. At 8.30 pm on Sunday, Tuesday, Thursday and Friday evenings there is a sound & light show in English for Rs 5. Bus No 81, 83/1 or 84/1 (Rs 2.50) will take you there. An auto-rickshaw will cost about Rs 20 with serious bargaining.

Organised Tours

The municipal corporation runs tours from the local bus stand (Lal Darwaja) which depart daily at 9.30 am and 2 pm. They take four hours, and commentaries are given in English (Rs 30).

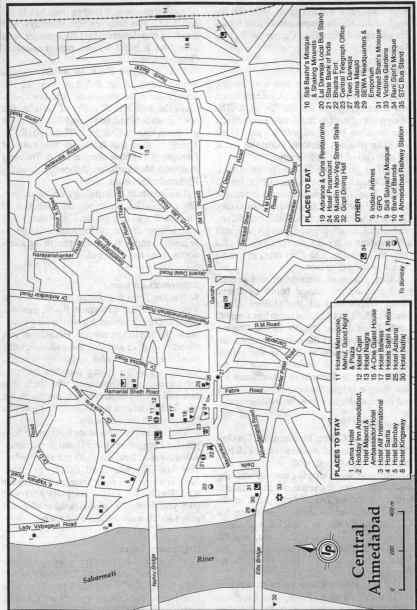

Central Ahmedabad

Places to Stay – bottom end

Most of the cheap hotels are scattered along or close to Relief Rd and around the railway station. The real cheapies are opposite the railway station, but most are assailed by Ahmedabad's horrendous noise and air pollution and are probably best avoided unless you have a very early morning departure. The area around Sidi Saiyad's Mosque at the western end of Relief Rd is better, although it's still far from serene.

The very basic *A-One Guest House* (☎ 34-9823) is opposite the railway station. The single/double rooms with attached bathroom (from Rs 120/180) are quite OK, but the singles with common bathroom (Rs 70) are dingy. Dorm beds (men only) are Rs 30.

Just off Relief Rd is the *Hotel Naigra* (☎ 38-4977) with fairly quiet, though small, rooms for Rs 60 with common bathroom, or from Rs 115/175 with attached bathroom.

The friendly *Hotel Natraj* (☎ 35-0048), near the Lal Darwaja local bus stand, has good-sized rooms with attached bathroom for Rs 75/130 (cold water only, but free bucket hot water on request). Ask for a room facing the pleasant gardens of Ahmed Shah's Mosque. Make sure rickshaw drivers don't take you to the upmarket Hotel Nataraj, on the west side of the Sabarmati River; your best bet is to ask to be taken to Lal Darwaja bus stand, and ask a local to direct your driver from there.

Another good choice is the *Hotel Plaza* (☎ 35-3397) in a very quiet lane behind the Hotel Capri. There's a range of comfortable rooms from Rs 70 to Rs 130, all with bathroom (cold water only; bucket hot water Rs 2).

The *Hotel Ashiana* (☎ 35-1114), on the same street as the GPO but on the south side of Relief Rd, has spartan, cell-like singles/doubles with common bathroom for Rs 80/100, or with attached bathroom (cold water only), Rs 90/110. Checkout is 24 hours.

Down a quiet lane opposite the Advance Cinema is the *Hotel Relax* (☎ 35-4301). Tiny singles/doubles cost Rs 80/120, or there are slightly larger rooms for Rs 100/120, or with air-con, Rs 160/200. Rooms are dark but clean.

Just to the north of Sidi Saiyad's Mosque is the *Hotel Bombay* (☎ 35-1746). It's on the 3rd floor of the KB Commercial Centre, and is not very obvious from street level. Claustrophobic windowless singles with common bath cost Rs 65, or Rs 100 with a shower but no toilet. More commodious singles/doubles with bathroom (hot water) cost Rs 150/200, and checkout is 24 hours.

Places to Stay – middle

The *Hotel Sahil* (☎ 35-3265), opposite the Advance Cinema, has small but clean rooms for Rs 190/230, or Rs 235/275 with colour TV. Air-con rooms are from Rs 290/330. This place prides itself on its 'Zero bacteria drinking water'.

The friendly *Hotel Balwas* (☎ 35-1135), around the corner on Relief Rd, has clean rooms from Rs 180/230, or Rs 250/300 with air-con, all with hot and cold water. Meals can be brought up to your room from the hotel's restaurant.

Only a few doors from the GPO, the *Hotel Kingsway* (☎ 30-1215) has very well appointed rooms with running hot and cold water from Rs 275/400 to Rs 400/525.

Almost at the western end of Relief Rd, down a side alley opposite Electric House and close to the Hotel Capri, is a cluster of mid-range hotels. The *Hotel Metropole* (☎ 35-4988) has very small singles/doubles for Rs 150/300, but the sheets look like they could do with a good scrubbing. Air-con rooms cost Rs 325/400. The nearby *Hotel Mehul* (☎ 35-2862) has rooms with attached bathroom (hot water) for Rs 130/170. Rooms are large and clean, although a little shabby.

Also in this group is the three-star *Hotel Good Night* (☎ 35-1997). Rooms with direct-dial telephone and Star TV cost Rs 200/250, or Rs 275/325 with air-con. Room service is available from the hotel's Food Inn restaurant.

The *Hotel Capri* (☎ 35-4643) has quite good, although not cheap, rooms for Rs 310/360, or Rs 350/410 with air-con. Checkout is 24 hours.

The brand new *Hotel Sarita* (☎ 32-1260) is in a quiet area close to the Indian Airlines office. Clean, modern rooms cost Rs 225/275, or Rs 300/350 with air-con.

The *Ambassador Hotel* (☎ 35-3244) on Lady Vidyagauri Rd, which runs parallel to the eastern bank of the Sabarmati River, has rooms from Rs 200/275, to Rs 300/375 with air-con. However, the Ambassador is looking a little shabby compared to some of the new mid to top-range hotels which have sprung up along this road.

The *Hotel Alif International* (☎ 35-9440) is a fairly new place with rooms starting at Rs 265/305, or Rs 310/430 with air-con. The hotel reception can arrange sightseeing tours around the city, and there's a good restaurant.

The modern, government-run *Toran Guest House* (☎ 48-3742) is close to the river, right across the road from the Gandhi Ashram. Doubles/triples cost Rs 350/400, or Rs 550/650 with air-con (no single rate). Checkout is 9 am.

Places to Stay – top end

For pure luxury, you won't beat the spectacular *Holiday Inn Ahmedabad* (☎ 35-0105; fax 35-9501), on Lady Vidyagauri Rd. Sumptuous rooms start at Rs 1050/1250, up to Rs 2600 for a suite, and the tariff includes a buffet breakfast. Decadent touches include 24-hour room service, an indoor swimming pool, jacuzzi, sauna, 24-hour coffee shop and two restaurants (one with an indoor waterfall). Checkout is an ungenerous 9 am.

The four-star *Cama Hotel* (☎ 30-5281; fax 30-5285), further north along Lady Vidyagauri Rd, is another luxury option, with a very good restaurant, a coffee shop, pool and bookshop. Rooms cost Rs 1190/1400, and, as with the Holiday Inn, checkout is 9 am.

The *Hotel Mascot* (☎ 35-9547) is a brand new hotel with air-con rooms from Rs 600/800 and a courtesy airport service. It is less ostentatious than its grand neighbours, but is beautifully appointed. Checkout is noon.

Places to Eat

Ahmedabad is a good place to sample a Gujarati thali. One of the best thali specialists is the *Gopi Dining Hall*, just off the west end of Ellis Bridge, near V S Hospital. A full all-you-can-eat Gujarati thali is Rs 28 (lunch) or Rs 35 (dinner).

The *Advance Restaurant*, opposite the cinema of the same name, and the *Cona Restaurant*, a few doors down, open early and are good places for breakfast.

At the bottom end of the scale there's excellent Muslim (non-veg) street food available near Teen Darwaja on Bhathiyar Gali, a small street which runs parallel to Gandhi Rd, around the corner from the Hotel Ashiana. Each evening stalls are set up, and for around Rs 20 you can get a good feed. There're meat and fish dishes to choose from as well as vegetarian items. To get to this area, you'll have to walk through the live poultry market, where prospective chicken dishes are blissfully unaware of the fate whch lies just a few metres away.

Also close to Teen Darwaja, the *Hotel Paramount* has Continental, Chinese and Indian cuisine, and you can dine in private curtained booths, with a massive crystal chandelier swinging overhead! A full butter chicken is Rs 60.

For a splurge, head for the restaurants at the Holiday Inn and Cama hotels. The Cama's *Cactus Restaurant* has live music on Monday and Thursday nights, or you can throw yourself over the restaurant's namesake when you see the bill after dining at the Holiday Inn's *Waterfall* restaurant.

On the other side of the river, the air-con *Sankalp Restaurant*, off Ashram Rd near Dinesh Hall in the Embassy Market area, is definitely worth at least one visit. This restaurant boasts the longest dosas in India – eight feet (2.4 metres) long! (Rs 301). The Rs 25 south Indian thalis also make a very pleasant change from the sweet Gujarati cuisine. The restaurant is very close to Gujarat Tourism.

For an interesting night out try *Vishalla* (☎ 40-3357), a rural complex on the southern edge of town in Vasana which evokes the atmosphere of a Gujarat village. Here, you'll dine in Indian fashion, seated on the floor, while watching puppet shows. It's not cheap, but the food is excellent. Lunch runs from 11 am to 1 pm, and dinner from 8 to 11 pm.

Things to Buy

On Ashram Rd, just to the south of the tourist office, is the Gujarat state crafts emporium, called Gurjari. For hand-printed fabrics and other textiles, the Self-Employed Women's Association or SEWA (see the boxed section on SEWA) has two retail outlets: shop 21/22, Goyal Towers, near Jahnvi Restaurant, University Rd, on the western side of the Sabarmati, and at the eastern end of Ellis Bridge, opposite the Victoria Gardens. The headquarters is adjacent to this shop, and visitors are welcome.

Getting There & Away

Air The Indian Airlines office (☎ 35-3333) is on Relief Rd, close to the Nehru Bridge, on the right-hand side coming from the railway station.

Air India (☎ 42-5622) is in Premchand House, near the High Court building on Ashram Rd, west of the river. Ahmedabad has an international airport and there are direct flights with Air India to the UK and the USA.

Indian Airlines flies from Bombay to Ahmedabad at least once a day (US$47), and there are twice-daily direct flights to Delhi (US$79). Other destinations are Vadodara (daily, US$15), Bangalore (four times weekly, US$132) and Madras (three times weekly, US$143). Twice weekly, flights to Bombay have connections through to Goa (US$93).

Jet Airways (☎ 46-7886), near the income tax office (about one km north of Gujarat Tourism), has flights twice daily to Bombay (US$47). ModiLuft has three flights a week to Delhi. The agent is Zen Travels (☎ 46-6228), near the stadium.

Bus Buses to Gandhinagar (Rs 5) depart every five minutes from Lal Darwaja or from one of the numerous stops on Ashram Rd.

Plenty of buses operate around Gujarat and to neighbouring states. The Gujarat State Transport Corporation (STC) buses are almost all standard-issue, battered meat wagons, but they're usually not too crowded and they run to schedule.

If you're travelling long-distance, private minibuses are a more expensive but much quicker alternative. Punjab Travels (☎ 44-9777), Embassy Market, near Dinesh Hall, just off Ashram Rd and only five minutes'

SEWA

The Self-Employed Women's Association, more commonly known by its acronym, SEWA, comprises over 54,000 members, and is Gujarat's single largest union. Established in 1972, SEWA identifies three types of self-employed workers: hawkers and vendors, who sell their wares from carts, baskets or small shops; home-based workers such as weavers, potters and bidi rollers; and manual labourers and service providers such as agricultural labourers, contract labourers, construction workers, and laundry and domestic workers. More than 93% of all workers in India fall into one of these categories, and women constitute over half of these workers. However, SEWA recognises that frequently this 'work' is not considered to be 'employment', and the actual number of women workers is not known.

Adhering to a Gandhian philosophy of change through non-violent means, SEWA embodies three movements: the labour movement; the co-operative movement; and the Women's Movement. The aim of the organisation is to enable women to actively participate in the mainstream economy and to attain empowerment through financial autonomy. Self-employment is the keystone of the organisation and SEWA aims to assist its members by raising the profile of women in the social and political arenas. SEWA assists self-employed workers to organise into unions and cooperatives, so that ultimately they can control the fruits of their own labours. Policies and programmes are implemented in an endeavour to reflect the experience, needs and realities of the self-employed.

The two main goals of the movement are full employment and self-reliance, and the fulfilment of these goals is based on policies which focus on areas such as health and child care, literacy, appropriate housing and self-sufficiency. ∎

walk from Gujarat Tourism, has a number of intercity services, including: Ajmer and Jaipur at 5.30 pm (10 hours, Rs 120, and 12 hours, Rs 140); Bhavnagar at 7 and 11.30 am and 6 pm (four hours, Rs 50); Bombay at 8.15 pm (15 to 17 hours, Rs 130); Bhuj at 9 pm (seven hours, Rs 80); Indore at 8.30 pm (10 to 11 hours, Rs 130); Junagadh at 9.30 pm (seven hours, Rs 70); Mt Abu at 10 pm (seven hours, Rs 80); Rajkot at 7 am (four hours, Rs 50); Udaipur at 9.30 pm (seven hours, Rs 70); and Veraval and Somnath at 9.30 pm (six hours, Rs 70).

Punjab has another office in the Shefali Shopping Centre, 2.5 km to the south on Pritamnagar Rd, the southern extension of Ashram Rd. Note that buses to Bhavnagar and Rajkot leave from this office; all of Punjab's other buses depart from Embassy Market.

Another private bus company with numerous intercity services is Bonny Travels (☎ 79-265), also at the Shefali Shopping Centre.

Train There is a computerised booking office to the left as you exit the main terminal. It's open Monday to Saturday from 8 am to 8 pm, and on Sunday from 8 am to 2 pm. Window No 12 handles the foreign tourist quota, and booking is a breeze.

Getting Around
To/From the Airport An auto-rickshaw to the airport will cost at least Rs 80. A much cheaper option is a local bus from Lal Darwaja (bus No 103 or 105, Rs 3.50).

Local Transport Ahmedabad is well on the way to displacing Lagos as the world's craziest city as far as traffic is concerned. Venturing out in an auto-rickshaw is a nerve-shattering experience not to be undertaken lightly. Most drivers are willing to use the meter, but at the end of the journey may ask for something ridiculous. Ask to see the fare adjustment card; however, this is entirely in Gujarati, so you'll need to learn the Gujarati numbers to make any sense of it.

The local bus stand is known as Lal Darwaja, and is on the east side of the river, between Nehru and Ellis bridges. The routes, destinations and fares are all posted in Gujarati.

AROUND AHMEDABAD
Sarkhej
The suburb of Sarkhej, eight km south-west of Ahmedabad, is noted for its elegant group of buildings, including the **Mausoleum of Azam & Mu'assam**, built in 1457 by the brothers who were responsible for Sarkhej's architecture. The architecture here is interesting because the style is almost purely Hindu, with little of the Saracenic influence so evident in Ahmedabad.

As you enter Sarkhej, you pass the **Mausoleum of Mahmud Begara** and, beside the tank and connected to his tomb, that of his queen, Rajabai (1461). Also by the tank is the **tomb of Ahmad Khattu Ganj Buksh**, a renowned Muslim saint and spiritual adviser to Ahmed Shah. The saint is said to have died in 1445 at the age of 111. Next to this is the

Major Trains from Ahmedabad					
Destination	**Train Name & Number**	**Departure Time**	**Distance (km)**	**Duration (hours)**	**Fare (US$) (2nd/1st)**
Bhavnagar	9810 *Shetrunji Exp*	5.10 pm	299	5.30	68/255
Bhuj	9031 *Kutch Exp*	1.55 am	359	8.35	99/296
Bombay	2934 *Karnarvati Exp*	5.10 am	492	7.35	102/382
	9102 *Gujarat Mail*	10.10 pm		8.35	128/382
Jaipur	9904 *Delhi Exp Mail*	6 pm	626	16.25	155/459
Jodhpur	2908 *Surya Nagri Exp*	9.30 pm	455	8.30	122/360
Delhi	2474 *Sarvodaya Exp*	12.05 pm	1097	16.35	214/634
	2906 *Ashram Exp*	5 pm	934	17.10	202/593
Rajkot	9005 *Saurashtra Mail*	5.45 am	246	4.40	57/219

fine mosque. Like the other buildings, it is notable for the complete absence of arches, a usual feature of Muslim architecture. The palace, with pavilions and a harem, is also around the tank.

The Dutch established a factory in Sarkhej in 1620 to process the indigo grown here.

Batwa

Ten km south-east of Ahmedabad, the suburb of Batwa has tombs of a noted Muslim saint (himself the son of another saint) and the saint's son. Batwa also has an important mosque.

Adalaj Wav

Nineteen km north of Ahmedabad, Adalaj Wav is one of the finest of the Gujarati step-wells, or baolis, with carvings depicting intricate motifs of flowers and birds. It was built by Queen Rudabai in 1499 and provided a cool and secluded retreat during the hot summer months. STC buses run here regularly.

Cambay

The old seaport of Ahmedabad is 92 km to the south, at the northern end of the Gulf of Cambay. At the height of Muslim power in Gujarat, the entire region was known as Cambay and, when the first ambassadors arrived from England in 1583, they bore letters from Queen Elizabeth addressed to Akbar, the 'King of Cambay'. Dutch and Portuguese factories were established in the port before the British arrived, but the rise of Surat eclipsed Cambay and, when its port silted up, the city's decline was inevitable.

From Ahmedabad, it's a three-hour bus trip from the STC bus stand to Cambay (Rs 23).

Nal Sarovar Bird Sanctuary

Between November and February, this 116-sq-km lake, 60 km south-west of Ahmedabad, is home to vast flocks of indigenous and migratory birds. Ducks, geese, pelicans and flamingoes are best seen early in the morning and in the evening. The sanctuary is best visited as a day excursion by taxi, as buses are infrequent and there is no convenient accommodation. Desert Coursers (☎ (079) 44-5068), a family-run Ahmedabad tour outfit, takes personalised day tours to the sanctuary. Prices cost Rs 1200 per person, including lunch, and a courtesy service is provided to and from Ahmedabad Airport and railway station.

You can hire a boat on Nal Sarovar with someone to punt you to the areas where the flamingoes and pelicans are; but please avoid going too close and try to restrain the boatman from scaring the birds, as this causes them to fly away. One of the main reasons for the decline in population of some birds is excessive human disturbance. If possible, avoid weekends and holidays when it gets quite crowded.

Krys Kazmierczak, UK

Lothal

About 85 km south-west of Ahmedabad, towards Bhavnagar, this important archaeological site was discovered in 1954. The city which stood here 4500 years ago was clearly related to the Indus Valley cities of Mohenjodaro and Harappa, both in Pakistan. It has the same neatly laid-out street pattern, the same carefully assembled brickwork and the same scientific drainage system.

The name Lothal actually means Mound of the Dead in Gujarati, as does Mohenjodaro in Sindhi. Excavations have revealed a dockyard – at its peak, this was probably one of the most important ports on the subcontinent. Seals discovered at the site suggest that trade may have been conducted with the civilisations of Mesopotamia, Egypt and Persia.

There is an **archaeological museum** at the site.

Places to Stay The *Toran Holiday Home* has three double rooms from Rs 80 to Rs 100, and dorm beds for Rs 30. Checkout time here is 9 am.

Seven km from the archaeological site is the grand *Utelia Palace* by the Bhugavo River. Rooms cost Rs 550/650, and breakfast is available for Rs 75, and lunch or dinner for Rs 150. Trips to local villages, Nal Sarovar and Velavadar National Park can all be arranged.

Getting There & Away Lothal is a day trip from Ahmedabad. You can reach it by rail, disembarking at Bhurkhi on the Ahmedabad to Bhavnagar railway line, from where you can take a bus. Alternatively, take a bus to Bagodara (two hours, Rs 20), from where you can get local transport for the seven km to the site.

Modhera

The beautiful and partially ruined Sun Temple of Modhera was built by King Bhimdev I (1026-27) and bears some resemblance to the later, and far better known, Sun Temple of Konark in the state of Orissa, which it predates by some 200 years. Like that temple, it was designed so that the dawn sun shone on the image of Surya, the sun god, at the time of the equinoxes. The main hall and shrine are reached through a pillared porch and the temple exterior is intricately and delicately carved. As with the Temple of Somnath, this fine temple was ruined by Mahmud of Ghazni. The temple is open from 8 am to 6 pm daily.

Places to Stay There is a *PWD Rest House* but foreigners find it difficult to get a bed here for the night. The *Tilla Panchayat Rest House* near the Sun Temple has doubles for Rs 50 and Rs 60.

Getting There & Away Modhera is 102 km north-west of Ahmedabad. There are direct buses (3½ hours, Rs 30), or you can take the train to Mahesana and then catch a bus for the 26-km trip to Modhera.

Unjha & Sidhpur

A little north of Mahesana and a base for those visiting the Modhera Temple, the town of Unjha is interesting for the marriage customs of the Kadwakanbis who live in this region. Marriages occur only once every 11 years and, on that day, every unmarried girl over 40 days old must be wed. If no husband can be found, a proxy wedding takes place

and the bride immediately becomes a 'widow'. She later remarries when a suitable husband shows up. There are a number of private guest houses at Unjha.

About 10 km north of Unjha is Sidhpur where you'll find the very fragmented ruins of an ancient temple. This region was an important centre for growing opium poppies.

Patan

About 130 km north-west of Ahmedabad, this was an ancient Hindu capital before being sacked by Mahmud of Ghazni in 1024. Now a pale shadow of its former self, it still has over 100 **Jain temples** and is famous for the manufacture of beautifully designed patola **silk saris**. There's also a renovated **step-well** here.

Places to Stay The only place to stay is the *Hotel Neerav*, about 500 metres from the bus stand, next to Kohinoor Talkies. Double rooms cost Rs 100.

Getting There & Away Patan is 25 km north-west of the Mahesana railway station, which also serves as a departure point for Modhera. Buses from Ahmedabad take 3½ hours and cost Rs 40.

Little Rann of Kutch

The Little Rann of Kutch, the barren expanse of 'desert' (actually salt plains) which divides Gujarat's western region of Kutch from the rest of Gujarat, is the home of the last remaining population of *khur* (Asiatic wild ass) in India.

The Rann can be treacherously difficult to explore as the desert consists of salt deposited at a time when the area formed part of the delta of the River Indus. This means that rain can quickly turn parts of the desert into a sea of mud, and what to the untrained eye looks like solid ground may in fact be a thin crust of dry silt with soft mud underneath. Hence it is essential to have someone along who is familiar with local conditions.
Krys Kazmierczak, UK

The small town of **Zainabad**, 105 km north-west of Ahmedabad, is very close to the Little Rann of Kutch. Desert Coursers

☎ (0272) 44-5068) is a tour company which organises safari and cultural tours on the Rann.

Dasada is a small town 10 km east of Zainabad. The Fatima Manzil Castle here is an old 17th-century bastion combining British and Nawabi architecture. Meals are served in the main hall, while the old dungeons have beds for a cool lie down. Jeep expeditions into the Rann can be organised. Accommodation is at *Camp Zainabad* (☎ (02757) 3322) in *koba*, traditional thatched-roofed huts (with attached bathrooms!) at Rs 450 per person, including a four-hour jeep safari, or Rs 850 with unlimited safaris. The self-contained huts are basic but comfortable and have been hand-painted by local Bajania people. The camp is run by the Malik family, who operate Desert Coursers.

Getting There & Away From Ahmedabad, take a bus to Dasada, 12 km north-east of Zainabad (two hours, Rs 23). From here there are local buses to Zainabad. There are also direct buses from Rajkot. Alternatively, taxis which take up to four people can be arranged through Desert Coursers for Rs 3 per km.

GANDHINAGAR
Population: 132,000
Telephone Area Code: 02712 outside of Ahmedabad (dial 92 from Ahmedabad)

Although Ahmedabad initially became the capital of Gujarat state when the old state of Bombay was split into Maharashtra and Gujarat in 1960, a new capital was planned 32 km north-east on the west bank of the Sabarmati River. Named Gandhinagar after Mahatma Gandhi, who was born in Gujarat, it is India's second planned city after Chandigarh and, like that city, is laid out in numbered sectors, and is equally dull. Construction of the city commenced in 1965 and the secretariat was moved there in 1970.

Places to Stay
Gandhinagar has an excellent *youth hostel* (☎ 22-364) in sector 16 which charges Rs 20

for a bed. In sector 11, there is the *Panthik Ashram* government rest house. For more upmarket accommodation, the *Hotel Haveli* (☎ 23-905) in sector 11 charges Rs 250/400 for standard rooms, or Rs 500/700 with air-con.

Getting There & Away
Buses from Ahmedabad cost Rs 5. They leave from Lal Darwaja, or from one of the numerous stops along Ashram Rd.

VADODARA (Baroda)
Population: 1,200,000
Telephone Area Code: 0265

Baroda was the capital of the princely Gaekwad state prior to Independence. Present-day Vadodara is a pleasant, medium-sized city with some interesting museums and art galleries and a fine park. The city's well-known Fine Arts College attracts students from around the country and abroad. It's a good place for a short pause.

Orientation & Information
The railway station, bus stand and a cluster of cheaper hotels are all on the west side of the Vishwarmurti River, which disects the city. The tourist office is on the upper floor of a building opposite the railway station. Tilak Rd runs straight out from the station, across the river by the Sayaji Bagh park and into the main part of town. The State Bank of India, near the Kirti Mandir, is open from 11 am to 3 pm Monday to Friday, and 11 am to 1 pm Saturday.

Sayaji Bagh & Vadodara Museum
This extensive park, encircled by a mini-railway, is a popular spot for an evening stroll. Within the park is the Vadodara Museum & Art Gallery, open from 9.30 am to 4.45 pm daily, except Saturday when it opens at 10 am. The museum has various exhibits, while the gallery has Mughal miniatures and a collection of European masters. Also within the park grounds is a **planetarium**, where demonstrations are given each evening (in English), and there is also a small **zoo**.

GUJARAT

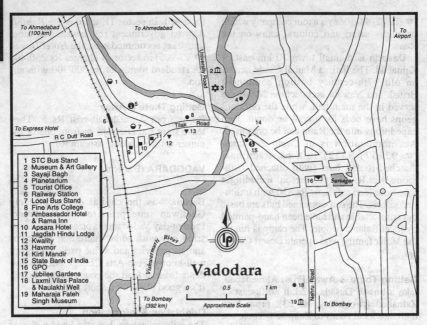

1 STC Bus Stand
2 Museum & Art Gallery
3 Sayaji Bagh
4 Planetarium
5 Tourist Office
6 Railway Station
7 Local Bus Stand
8 Fine Arts College
9 Ambassador Hotel
  & Rama Inn
10 Apsara Hotel
11 Jagdish Hindu Lodge
12 Kwality
13 Havmor
14 Kirti Mandir
15 State Bank of India
16 GPO
17 Jubilee Gardens
18 Laxmi Vilas Palace
   & Naulakhi Well
19 Maharaja Fateh
   Singh Museum

Vadodara

Maharaja Fateh Singh Museum

A little south of the centre, this royal art
collection includes European works by
Raphael, Titian and Murillo and examples of
Greco-Roman, Chinese and Japanese art, as
well as Indian exhibits. The museum is in the
palace grounds and is open from 9 am to
noon and 3 to 6 pm between July and March,
4 to 7 pm from April to June. It is closed on
Monday.

Other Attractions

The **Laxmi Vilas Palace** has a large collection
of armour and sculptures but is not normally
open to the public. The **Naulakhi Well**, a fine
baoli, is 50 metres north of the palace.

Places to Stay – bottom end

If you head straight out from the railway
station and take the third road on the right,
you'll find the *Jagdish Hindu Lodge*, with
gloomy and basic rooms arranged around a
courtyard. Doubles with attached bathroom

cost Rs 60. In the same street, and a notch up
the scale, is the *Hotel Vikram* (☎ 32-7737),
which has rooms from Rs 70 per person with
attached bathroom.

In the next street back towards the station
is the pleasant and well-kept *Apsara Hotel*
(☎ 32-8251), with comfortable rooms at Rs
100/140 with bathroom.

Places to Stay – middle

Across the road from the Apsara and a little
further down is the big *Ambassador Hotel*
(☎ 32-7653), with large, quiet rooms from
Rs 165/275, or Rs 335/385 with air-con.
Right next to the Ambassador is the *Rama
Inn* (☎ 33-0131), which boasts a swimming
pool and two restaurants (veg and non-veg).
Rooms start at Rs 350/500, or Rs 575/800
with air-con.

The *Hotel Surya* (☎ 33-6500), opposite
the Ambassador Hotel, is a little cheaper at
Rs 325/450, or Rs 550/750 with air-con, but
is older and has less in the way of facilities.

The *Express Hotel* (☎ 33-7001) on R C Dutt Rd, about one km west of the railway station, has air-con rooms at Rs 750/1000. There's a 24-hour coffee shop as well as a restaurant which offers a variety of cuisines.

Places to Eat
Along the main road from the station towards the gardens and the river, there's a reasonable *Kwality* and a *Havmor*. Expect to pay at least Rs 50 for a meal at either place. The railway station also has a good restaurant.

Getting There & Away
Air The Indian Airlines office (☎ 32-8596) is on University Rd, Fateh Ganj. There are flights from Vadodara to Bombay (US$39), Delhi (US$88) and Ahmedabad (US$15). NEPC Airlines (☎ 33-7899) has an office in the Express Hotel, and has daily flights to both Bombay and Ahmedabad.

Bus The long-distance bus stand is 500 metres north of the railway station, and there are STC buses to many destinations in Gujarat, western Madhya Pradesh and northern Maharashtra. Buses to Ahmedabad leave at least every 30 minutes (2½ hours, Rs 27).

The private companies all have their offices in the vicinity of the bus stand.

Train Vadodara is 100 km south of Ahmedabad by rail and 392 km north of Bombay. As it's on the main Bombay to Ahmedabad railway line, there are plenty of trains to choose from. Rail fares to Bombay cost Rs 85/326 (2nd/1st class) on the daytime services, or Rs 107/326 for a sleeper (six hours). Fares to Ahmedabad cost Rs 27/114 (two hours).

Between Vadodara and Ahmedabad you pass through **Anand**, noted for its dairy produce. At the station, hordes of vendors selling bottles of cold milk often besiege passing trains.

AROUND VADODARA
Champaner
This city, 47 km north-east of Vadodara, was taken by Sultan Mahmud Begara in 1484, and he renamed it Muhammadabad. The **Jama Masjid** here is one of the finest mosques in Gujarat and is similar in style to the Jama Masjid of Ahmedabad.

The **Hill of Pavagadh**, with its ruined fort, rises beside Champaner in three stages. In 1553, the Mughals, led by Humayun himself, scaled the fort walls using iron spikes driven into the rocks, and captured both the fort and its city. Parts of the massive fort walls still stand. According to Hindu legend, the hill is actually a chunk of the Himalayan mountainside which the monkey god Hanuman carted off to Lanka in an episode of the *Ramayana*, hence the name Pavagadh, which means Quarter of a Hill.

Places to Stay The state tourist organisation runs the *Hotel Champaner* (☎ 641). Dorm beds cost Rs 30 per person and singles/doubles are Rs 150/250. Checkout time is 11 am.

Getting There & Away Buses from Vadodara take one hour and cost Rs 10.

Dabhoi Fort
The 13th-century fort of Dabhoi is 29 km south-east of Vadodara. A fine example of Hindu military architecture, it is notable for the design of its four gateways – particularly the Hira, or Diamond Gate.

Dakor
Equidistant from Vadodara and Ahmedabad, the Temple of Ranchodrai in Dakor is sacred to Krishna and is a major centre for the Sharad Purnima festival in October or November.

Buses from Ahmedabad take 2½ hours and cost Rs 23.

BHARUCH (Broach)
Population: 149,000

This very old town was mentioned in historical records nearly 2000 years ago. In the 17th century, English and Dutch factories were established here. The **fort** overlooks the wide Narmada River from a hilltop and,

Sardar Sarovar Dam Project

The Narmada River has featured in the news both locally and internationally as a large dam, the Sardar Sarovar, is being constructed upstream of Bharuch near the village of Manibeli. This is part of a hugely extravagant US$6 billion project in the Narmada Valley to provide massive amounts of irrigation water and electricity. The Sardar Sarovar dam is only a part of the entire project, which, if ever completed, will include 30 mega-dams, 135 medium dams and 3000 small dams.

The aim is laudable, but it's hard to see how the immediate disruption it causes will be effectively managed – the conservation lobby estimates that more than 100,000 people will need to be relocated as a result of the dam, a further 200,000 will be affected by associated canal and dam works, and the homes of at least one million people will be submerged. Leading lobbyists have undertaken hunger strikes in protest at the dislocation of the inhabitants in the region, and to draw attention to the environmental problems it is envisaged the construction of this huge dam will cause. ■

located at its base, is the **Jama Masjid**, constructed from a Jain temple. On the riverbank, outside the city to the east, is the **Temple of Bhrigu Rishi**, from which the city took its name, Bhrigukachba, later shortened to Bharuch.

It is possible to stay at the *dharamsala* at the Kabirvad Temple (by donation) in the town of Suklatirth, about 20 km from Bharuch. The nearby island of Kabirwad, in the river, features a gigantic banyan tree which covers a hectare.

AROUND BHARUCH
Rajpipla

This small town on the Narmada River is not far from the Sardar Sarovar dam project. There are bathing ghats on the river, and close by is the magnificent Raj-era Rajpipla Palace, which offers accommodation at Rs 250/350 to Rs 350/450, and meals are available. The owners can arrange camel rides and trips to tribal villages.

SURAT

Population: 1,630,000
Telephone Area Code: 0261

Surat stands on the banks of the River Tapti and was once one of western India's major ports and trading towns. Two hundred years ago, it had a bigger population than it does today and was far more important than Bombay. Parsis first settled in Surat in the 12th century; they had earlier been centred 100 km south in Sanjan, where they had fled from Persia five centuries before. In 1573,

the city fell to Akbar after a prolonged siege. It then became an important Mughal trading port and also the point of departure for Mecca-bound Muslim pilgrims.

Surat soon became a wealthy city. In 1612, the British established a trading factory there, followed by the Dutch in 1616 and the French in 1664. Portuguese power on the west coast had been severely curtailed by a crushing naval defeat at the hands of the British. In 1664, Mughal power and prestige suffered a severe blow when the Maratha leader, Shivaji, sacked the town. In a classic display of the British stiff upper lip, Sir George Oxenden sent a message to Shivaji from the strongly defended English factory, saying that he should 'save the labour of his servants running to and fro on messages and come himself with all his army'. Perhaps Shivaji took the implied threat seriously, because the English factory was not attacked.

Although the English factory later transferred its 'presidency' to Bombay, Surat continued to prosper. A dock was built in 1720, followed by two British shipyards. By 1759, when the British took virtually full control over the city, Mughal power was long past its prime and, by 1800, the city was in British hands. Surat is no longer of any importance as a port, but it is a major industrial centre, especially for the manufacture of textiles and chemicals, and the processing and finishing of diamonds. The city is probably best known these days, however, as the site of an outbreak of pneumonic plague in 1994 (see the boxed Plague section).

Despite its industrial importance, the city is of little interest to travellers, except those with a fascination for urban decay, noise and pollution. If Ahmedabad is bad in this respect, Surat is horrific. Avoid it like the plague!

Orientation & Information
Surat is bordered on one side by the Tapti River, and on the other by a brick wall. This wall was once an eight-km-long mud wall, but after the city was sacked by Shivaji, it was reconstructed in brick. The railway station, with many cheaper hotels in its immediate vicinity, is connected to the old fort beside the river by one of Surat's few wide roads.

Castle
Built in 1546, the castle is on the riverbank, beside the Tapti Bridge. Since most of it has been given over to offices it is no longer of great interest, but there is a good view over the city and river from its bastions. To get there, ask for the Tapti Bridge.

Factories
Without a guide, you would have difficulty finding the remains of the factories and, in any case, there is little to indicate their former importance. They are near the IP Mission High School. The English factory is about midway between the castle and the Kataragama Gate, out of the old city. Not too far away, standing close to the river, are the remains of the Portuguese factory, French Lodge and Persian factory. From the river-

bank, you can see the Tapti Bridge to your left and across the river to your right is the mosque-studded suburb of Rander. There's a small temple by the river which is dedicated to Hanuman.

Cemeteries
The now very run-down, overgrown and neglected **English cemetery** is just beyond the Kataragama Gate, to the right of the main road. As you enter the cemetery, the huge mausoleum to the right is that of Sir George Oxenden, who died in 1669. Another large tomb next to it is said to be that of Gerald Aungier, the next president of the English factory. The imposing mausoleums are in a sorry state.

Backtrack towards the city and, about 500 metres after the Kataragama Gate and some 100 metres off the road to the left (to the right if you are coming from the centre), you'll find the **Dutch cemetery**. The massive mausoleum of Baron Adriaan van Reede, who died in 1691, was once decorated with frescoes and woodcarvings. Adjoining the Dutch cemetery is the **Armenian cemetery**.

Other Attractions
Surat has a number of mosques and Jain, Hindu and Parsi temples. Nearby **Rander**, five km across the Hope Bridge, was built on the site of a very ancient Hindu city which had been taken by the Muslims in 1225. **Swally** (Suvali) was the old port for Surat, 19 km to the west. It was off Swally, in 1615, that Portuguese colonial aspirations in India were ended by the British navy.

The Plague
In October 1994, Surat gained international notoriety when pneumonic plague, closely related to the dreaded bubonic plague, broke out in the city. The 'plague' caused a mass exodus of frightened inhabitants, some fairly extreme responses within India and positively hysterical coverage in the Western media. The whole outbreak did massive damage to India's tourist trade as foreigners stayed away in droves, even though the risk of infection was small. What the outbreak did highlight was the governments' (both local and central) lack of preparedness for an outbreak such as this – it was a number of days before the city was actually sealed off, by which time hundreds of thousands of people had fled the city. Once emergency measures were finally in place the outbreak was brought under control with relatively little loss of life – 54 deaths were directly attributed to the disease. ■

GUJARAT

Places to Stay – bottom end

There are lots of hotels near the railway station but none stand out. In the rock-bottom bracket, the *Rupali Hotel* has dorm beds for Rs 30, doubles with bathroom for Rs 95 and singles with common bathroom for Rs 50. Facilities are basic.

On the street facing the station, the *Simla Guest House* (☎ 31-782) is slightly better but still unremarkable. It has doubles with bathroom for Rs 140 and singles/doubles with common bathroom for Rs 60/90.

Good value at the top end of this category is the *Sarvajanik Hotel* (☎ 42-6159). It offers singles for Rs 100 to Rs 150 and doubles for Rs 200.

Places to Stay – middle

The large *Central Hotel* (☎ 42-5325), close to the railway station, has rooms from Rs 375, or air-con rooms for Rs 425/525.

The nearby *Hotel Yuvrav* (☎ 53-621) is a good middle-range place with two vegetarian restaurants. All rooms have air-con and cost Rs 490/590.

Places to Stay – top end

Surat's best hotel is the *Hotel Rama Regency* (☎ 66-6565; fax 66-7294) near Bharti Park in Athwa Lines, five km from the central city area. Air-con rooms with plenty of buttons and switches are a whopping Rs 1420/2320. The hotel has a number of facilities, including a swimming pool, health club and two restaurants.

Places to Eat

Close to the railway station and next to the Central Hotel, the *Gaurav Restaurant* offers excellent and very cheap south Indian dishes. It's clean, popular and highly recommended. For a more substantial meal, try the *Hotel Ashoka*, next to the Simla Guest House.

Getting There & Away

Surat is on the main Bombay to Ahmedabad railway line. The 263-km trip to Bombay takes between 4½ and 6½ hours and costs Rs 62/233, or Rs 77/233 for a sleeping berth.

To Ahmedabad, the 229-km trip takes from 3½ to 4½ hours and costs Rs 56/205.

AROUND SURAT

There are a number of beaches near Surat. Only 16 km away, **Dumas** is a popular health resort. **Hajira** is 28 km from the city and **Ubhrat** is 42 km out, while **Tithal** is 108 km away and only five km from Valsad on the Bombay to Vadodara train line.

Twenty-nine km south of Surat, **Navsari** has been a headquarters for the Parsi community since the earliest days of their settlement in India. **Udvada**, only 10 km north of Vapi, the station for Daman, has the oldest Parsi sacred fire in India. It is said that the fire was brought from Persia to Diu, on the opposite coast of the Gulf of Cambay, in 700 AD. **Sanjan**, in the extreme south of the state, is the small port where the Parsis first landed. A pillar marks the spot.

Places to Stay

State-run *Holiday Homes* abound in this area. Hajira has one, with cottages for Rs 300 and double rooms for Rs 200, as does Ubhrat, where double rooms cost from Rs 100 to Rs 500, and dorm beds are Rs 30.

There's another one at Tithal (☎ (02632) 2731), where bungalows cost Rs 500 and single/double rooms Rs 150/200.

DAMAN

Population: 62,100 (Daman Town: 26,900)
Telephone Area Code: 02636

Right in the south of Gujarat, the 56-sq-km enclave of Daman was, along with Diu, taken from the Portuguese at the same time as Goa. For a time, Daman and Diu were governed from Goa but both now constitute the Union Territory of Daman & Diu, which is governed from Delhi.

Daman's main role now seems to be as a place to buy alcohol, since the surrounding state of Gujarat is completely 'dry'. The streets of Daman are lined with bars selling beer, 'Finest Scotch Whisky – Made in India' and various other spirits such as *feni* (distilled from fermented cashew nuts or coconuts).

The Portuguese seized Daman in 1531 and were officially ceded the region by Bahadur Shah, the last major Gujarati sultan, in 1559. There is still a lingering Portuguese flavour to the town, with its fine old forts and a number of churches, but it is definitely not a smaller version of Goa. The town is divided by the Damao Ganga River. The northern section is known as Nani Daman, or Little Daman, and contains the hotels, restaurants, bars and so on. In the southern part, known as Moti Daman, or Big Daman, government buildings and churches are enclosed within an imposing wall.

Like Goa, Daman is beside the sea but its beaches bear no relation to the glowing, golden stretches of sand further south. Daman's beaches are grey, drab, dirty and dismal and function as local latrines.

Information
The main post office is south of the river in Moti Daman, but there's a more convenient branch near the Hotel Sun n Sea in Nani Daman.

Churches
The **Se Cathedral** in the Moti Daman fort

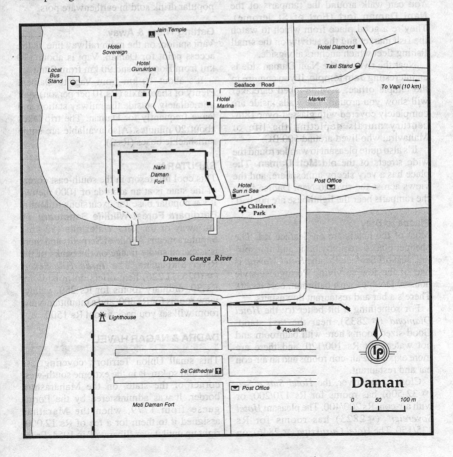

dates from the 17th century and is totally Iberian. It has recently been renovated and newly painted, and looks quite impressive. The **Church of Our Lady of the Rosary** has ancient Portuguese tombstones set into its cool, damp floor. The altar is a masterpiece of intricately carved, gold-painted wood. Light filters through the dusty windows, illuminating wooden panels painted with scenes of Christ and the apostles. The church is not always open; check with the vicar of the Se Cathedral for the key.

Other Attractions

You can walk around the ramparts of the **Nani Daman fort** (Fort of St Jerome). They're a good place from which to watch the fish market and the activity on the small fishing fleet which anchors alongside.

Near the river on the Nani Daman side is an interesting **Jain temple**. If you enquire in the temple office, a white-robed caretaker will show you around. The walls inside are completely covered with glassed-over 18th-century murals depicting the life of Mahavira, who lived around 500 BC.

It's also quite pleasant to wander round the wide streets of the old **Moti Daman**. The place has a very sleepy atmosphere, and the views across the river to Nani Daman from the ramparts near the lighthouse are not bad.

Places to Stay

Most of the hotels are on Seaface Rd. The cheaper places are pretty basic and uninspiring. Just off Seaface Rd, the *Hotel Marina* is one of the few surviving Portuguese-style houses. Doubles with bathroom cost Rs 80. There's a bar and restaurant downstairs.

For something a bit better try the *Hotel Diamond* (☎ 2835), near the taxi stand. Good-sized rooms here with bathroom and hot water cost Rs 100/120, and there are more expensive air-con rooms and an air-con bar and restaurant.

Close to the river, the *Hotel Sun n Sea* (☎ 32-506) has rooms for Rs 170/200, or with air-con, Rs 200/400. The pleasant *Hotel Sovereign* (☎ 2823) has rooms for Rs 135/150. The *Hotel Gurukripa* (☎ 2846), on

Seaface Rd, has air-con rooms for Rs 300/350.

Places to Eat

The air-con restaurant at the *Hotel Gurukripa* has veg and non-veg dishes and the food is very good, if a little spicy. Most dishes are around Rs 45. A Kingfisher will set you back Rs 25 at any of Daman's numerous bars.

In February, Daman is noted for *papri*, boiled and salted sweet peas served wrapped in newspaper. Crabs and lobsters are in season in October. *Tari* palm wine is a popular drink sold in earthenware pots.

Getting There & Away

Vapi station, on the main railway line, is the access point for Daman. Vapi is about 170 km from Bombay and 90 km from Surat.

It's about 10 km from Vapi to Daman. Plenty of share taxis (Rs 10 per person) wait immediately outside the railway station and leave frequently for Daman. The trip takes about 20 minutes. Also available are some ramshackle buses (Rs 2).

SAPUTARA

This cool hill resort in the south-east corner of the state is at an altitude of 1000 metres. It's a popular base for excursions to **Mahal Bardipara Forest Wildlife Sanctuary**, 60 km away or the **Gira Waterfalls** (52 km). Saputara means Abode of Serpents and there is a sacred snake image on the banks of the River Sarpagana. The *Toran Hill Resort* (☎ (02631) 226) here offers dorm beds for Rs 30, ordinary rooms for Rs 250, valley-view rooms for Rs 300, and a mountain-view room will set you back a cool Rs 1500.

DADRA & NAGAR HAVELI

Population: 157,000

This small Union Territory, covering less than 500 sq km, is in the extreme south-west corner of the state, on the Maharashtra border. It was administered by the Portuguese from 1779, when the Marathas assigned it to them for a fee of Rs 12,000, right up until it was 'liberated' in 1954. From then until 1961 the territory was directly administered by the people – probably the only place in the country where this had happened. It is now governed by an administrator appointed by the government in Delhi.

Saurashtra

The often bleak plains of Saurashtra on the Kathiawar peninsula are inhabited by friendly but reserved people. Those in the country are distinctively dressed – the men wear white turbans, pleated jackets (short-waisted and long-sleeved) and jodhpurs (baggy seat and drainpipe legs) and often sport golden stud earrings. The women are nearly as colourful as the women of Rajasthan and wear embroidered backless cholis, which are known by various names but most commonly the *kanjeri*.

The peninsula took its name from the Kathi tribespeople who used to roam the area at night stealing whatever was not locked into the many village forts, or *kots*. Around Kathiawar, you may notice long lines of memorial stones known as *palias* – men are usually depicted riding on large horses while women ride on wheels, showing that they were in carriages.

Although somewhat off the main tourist routes, Saurashtra is a pleasant area to travel around with very interesting – sometimes spectacular – temple sites and cities to explore, not to mention some beautiful beaches and the Sasan Gir Lion Sanctuary.

The network of metre-gauge railway lines is extensive but the trains are very slow and most people choose buses.

BHAVNAGAR

Population: 437,000
Telephone Area Code: 0278

Founded as a port in 1743, Bhavnagar is still an important trading post for the cotton goods manufactured in Gujarat. The Bhavnagar lock gate keeps ships afloat in the city's port at low tide. On the surface, Bhavnagar isn't the most interesting place to visit and few travellers get here. It does, however, have a beautiful old bazaar area with overhanging wooden balconies, thousands of little shops, lots of local colour and not a tourist in sight.

Orientation & Information

Bhavnagar is a sprawling city with distinctly separate old and new sections. The bus stand is in the new part of town and the railway station is at the far end of the old town around 2½ km away. To complicate matters, private bus companies usually have their own depots which are sometimes a long way from the bus stand.

There are no cheap hotels around the bus stand so, if you're on a budget, take an auto-rickshaw into the old town. Even there, the choice is very limited.

Takhteshwar Temple

This temple sits on the highest hillock in Bhavnagar. The views over the city and out into the Gulf of Cambay are excellent but the temple itself is of minor interest.

Alang

On the coast between Bhavnagar and Talaja is Alang, India's largest ship-breaking site. Here supertankers, container ships, warships and other vessels are dismantled – literally by hand – by 20,000 workers day and night.

It's no problem to watch, but if you want to take photos, permission must be obtained from the Port Officer (☎ 29-3020), Gujarat Maritime Board, New Port Bhavnagar 5.

Despite the Taj Mahal, all the palaces and temples, this was the most impressive sight we saw on our trip. It's difficult to reach by bus, so take a taxi for the day from Bhavnagar (Rs 350).

Thomas Tolk & Hilke Rensing, Germany

GUJARAT

Places to Stay – bottom end

The only cheap hotels in Bhavnagar are in the old bazaar area and there's very little choice. Perhaps the best value is offered by the *Shital Guest House* (☎ 28-360), Amba Chowk, Mali Tekra, right in the middle of the bazaar area. It's clean and the manager speaks English, but beware of the precipitous, almost vertical staircase here! Singles/doubles with common bathroom cost Rs 40/60, or with bathroom, Rs 45/70. Ask for a room with a balcony; the other rooms are very dark.

Not far from the Shital is the *Vrindavan Hotel* (☎ 27-391). It's well signposted but the entrance can still be quite difficult to find. Entry is through an archway and across a courtyard; the steps leading to the reception area are directly opposite the archway. This huge, rambling old place has basic but clean singles/doubles with bathroom for Rs 60/120, or with common bathroom, Rs 50/80. Dorm beds cost Rs 35.

Going up in price, the extremely pleasant *Hotel Mini* (☎ 24-415), Station Rd, is about two minutes' walk from the railway station. It's very clean and quiet, and has singles for Rs 70 (hot water in buckets) and singles/doubles from Rs 90/100 to Rs 125/150. The staff are very friendly and there's a dining hall. Checkout is 24 hours.

Places to Stay – middle

The cheapest rooms at the *Hotel Apollo* (☎ 25-249), directly opposite the bus stand, cost Rs 250/350, or with air-con, Rs 350/430. There are money-changing facilities and the hotel has a non-veg restaurant.

Down the road a little from the taxi stand are two modern middle-range hotels. The *Bluehill Hotel* (☎ 26-951) is very well appointed, and has rooms with air-con from Rs 390/550. There are two restaurants, 24-hour room service, and the hotel will exchange travellers' cheques for both guests and non-guests. The *Jubilee Hotel* (☎ 20-

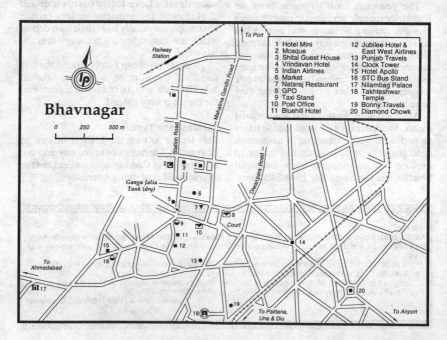

Bhavnagar

0   250   500 m

To Port

1 Hotel Mini
2 Mosque
3 Shital Guest House
4 Vrindavan Hotel
5 Indian Airlines
6 Market
7 Nataraj Restaurant
8 GPO
9 Taxi Stand
10 Post Office
11 Bluehill Hotel
12 Jubilee Hotel &
   East West Airlines
13 Punjab Travels
14 Clock Tower
15 Hotel Apollo
16 STC Bus Stand
17 Nilambag Palace
18 Takhteshwar
   Temple
19 Bonny Travels
20 Diamond Chowk

Railway Station

Mahatma Gandhi Road

Station Road

Diwanpara Road

Ganga Jalia Tank (dry)

Court

To Ahmedabad

To Palitana, Una & Diu

To Airport

045) next door offers similar facilities, and has rooms for Rs 300, or with air-con, from Rs 375/525, all including breakfast. Check-out is noon.

If you can afford it, the most interesting place to stay is the *Nilambag Palace* (☎ 24-340), west of the bus stand on the Ahmedabad road. As its name suggests, the Nilambag is a former maharaja's palace, and it's wildly ostentatious, with rich wood panelling and countless original oil paintings. Rooms are huge and cost Rs 1150/1500, or Rs 3000 for the Maharaja's suite, which has a separate entertaining area. There's also a magnificent swimming pool on the hotel grounds (guests only).

Places to Eat

The *Nataraj Restaurant* has average food and a two-page menu of ice-cream goodies. Look for the Vadilal Ice Cream sign on the east side of the Ganga Jalia. This place opens late, so is not a good option for breakfast. Prices at the *Apollo*, *Bluehill* and *Jubilee* hotels are all pretty reasonable and the food is good.

For more regal dining, the dining hall at the *Nilambag Palace* is open to non-guests, and is surprisingly reasonably priced (chicken Mughlai is Rs 45).

Getting There & Away

Air The Indian Airlines office (☎ 26-503) is on the west side of the Ganga Jalia. There are four flights a week to Bombay (US$35). East West Airlines (☎ 29-244) is in the Jubilee Hotel, and flies to Bombay three times weekly (US$40).

Bus State transport buses connect Bhavnagar with Ahmedabad and other centres in the region. For Una (and Diu) there are departures almost every hour from 5.30 am. The trip takes five hours and costs Rs 47. To Palitana there are departures every hour from 5 am for the 1½-hour journey (Rs 14). The timetable at the state bus stand in Bhavnagar is entirely in Gujarati.

The main private bus company is Punjab Travels (☎ 24-582), opposite the Galaxy

Cinema, near the municipal office. It has buses to Ahmedabad every 30 minutes (Rs 50). Bonny Travels (☎ 29-178) has departures for Ahmedabad at 6.30 and 7 am, noon and 4 and 6 pm (Rs 50). They also have an overnight service to Diu departing at midnight (six hours, Rs 50). The office is in the Madhav Darshan Complex, a huge aqua-coloured architectural nightmare near the Takhteshwar Temple. Bonny's sign is in Hindi.

Train Bhavnagar is 299 km by rail from Ahmedabad. The trip takes about 5½ hours and costs Rs 68/255 in 2nd/1st class. There's one direct train daily, departing Bhavnagar at 5.30 am. To Palitana there are three steam trains daily at 6.15 am, 2.45 and 6.45 pm. They cover the 51 km in a dazzling two hours (Rs 9).

Getting Around

A rickshaw to the airport costs about Rs 40.

AROUND BHAVNAGAR
Valabhipur

About 42 km north-west of Bhavnagar, this ancient city was once the capital of this part of India. Extensive ruins have been located and archaeological finds are exhibited in a museum, but there's little to see apart from scattered stones.

PALITANA

Situated 51 km south-west of Bhavnagar, the town of Palitana is little more than a gateway to **Shatrunjaya**, the Place of Victory. The 600-metre ascent from the base of the hill to the summit is a walk of some two km, up more than 3000 steps. Over a period of 900 years, 863 temples have been built here. The hilltop is dedicated entirely to the gods; at dusk, even the priests depart from the temples, leaving them deserted.

Almost all the temples are Jain and this hill, one of Jainism's holiest pilgrimage places, is another illustration of their belief that merit is derived from constructing temples. The hilltops are bounded by sturdy

684 Gujarat – Saurashtra – Palitana

walls and the temples are grouped into nine enclosures or *tunks* – each with a central major temple and many minor ones clustered around. Some of the earliest temples here were built in the 11th century but were destroyed by the Muslims in the 14th and 15th centuries, so the current temples date from the 16th century onwards.

The hilltop affords a very fine view in all directions; on a clear day you can see the Gulf of Cambay beyond Bhavnagar. The most notable of the temples is dedicated to **Shri Adishwara**, the first Jain tirthankar. Note the frieze of dragons around this temple. Adjacent is the Muslim shrine of **Angar Pir**. Women who want to have children make offerings of miniature cradles at this shrine.

Built in 1618 by a wealthy Jain merchant, the **Chaumukh**, or Four-Faced shrine, has images of Adinath facing out in the four cardinal directions. Other important temples are those to Kumar Pal, Sampriti Raj and Vimal Shah.

The temples are open from 6 am to 6 pm. A photography permit can be purchased for Rs 15 at the main entrance on top of the hill. (There are two entrances – the main one is reached by taking the left-hand fork as you near the top and the other by the right-hand fork.) Shoes should be removed at the entrance to the compound, and leather items, including belts and bags, are not supposed to be brought onto the site.

A horse cart to the base of the hill costs Rs 20, or you can walk the three km from the village in about 30 minutes. The heat can be extreme by late morning, so it's a good idea to get an early start for the ascent. Water (although not bottled water) can be purchased at intervals, and you can buy very good, refreshing curd in pottery bowls just outside the temple compound for Rs 10. At a moderate pace, the ascent will take about 1½ hours. You can be carried up the hill in a *dooli* swing chair for Rs 100, as do quite a few affluent and obese pilgrims – the most conspicuous sight on first entering the temple compound is that of exhausted dooli bearers resting in the shade.

Places to Stay

Palitana has scores of dharamsalas (pilgrims' rest houses) but, unless you're a Jain, you're unlikely to be allowed to stay at any of them. The *Hotel Sumeru* (☎ 2327) on Station Rd is a Gujarat Tourism enterprise which has rooms for Rs 250/300, or Rs 375/400 with air-con. Dorm beds are Rs 30, and there's a vegetarian restaurant.

The *Hotel Shravak* (☎ 2428), opposite the bus stand, has single rooms with common bath for Rs 75 or singles/doubles/triples with bathroom for Rs 100/175/250 (free bucket hot water). Dorm beds (men only) cost Rs 25, and checkout is 24 hours.

Places to Eat

The *Hotel Sumeru* has a reasonable restaurant with Gujarati thalis as well as Punjabi food. Down the alley towards the cinema, beside the Shravak, the *Jaruti Restaurant*, a wildly busy 24-hour snack place, offers puris, sabzi, curd, roasted peppers and ganthia (varieties of fried dough). A very good all-you-can-eat thali here is Rs 14. There's a *Havmor* ice-cream parlour on the right as you approach the base of Shatrunjaya.

Getting There & Away

Bus If you're coming from the north, plenty of STC buses make the 1½-hour trip from Bhavnagar. The fare is Rs 10.50, or Rs 14 for the 'express' service. There are regular departures for Ahmedabad (five hours, Rs 50).

There is a direct bus to Una for Diu at 1 pm (five hours, Rs 31), or via Mahuva at 7 am (five hours, Rs 30). Whether you travel direct or via Mahuva, this is a trip from hell, along corrugated village roads in dilapidated old rattletraps.

Train Express trains make the trip from Ahmedabad in nine to 11 hours with a change at Sihor shortly before Palitana. A passenger service departs Palitana at 8.45 am (Rs 35), or there's an overnight express service departing at 8.30 pm (Rs 60/240).

Local trains between Bhavnagar and Palitana take about two hours (Rs 9).

DIU

Population: 39,500 (Diu Town: 22,900)
Telephone Area Code: 028758

This was the first landing point for the Parsis when they fled from Persia, although they stayed only three years. Like Daman and Goa, Diu was a Portuguese colony until it was taken over by India in 1961. Along with Daman, it is still governed from Delhi as a Union Territory rather than as part of Gujarat. The former colony includes the island of Diu itself, about 13 km long by three km wide, separated from the coast by a narrow channel. There are also two tiny mainland enclaves. One of these, on which the village of Ghoghla stands, is the entry point to Diu if you arrive through the town of Una.

Diu's crowning glory is the huge fort, a sight which justifies the long trip here. The northern side of the island, facing Gujarat, is tidal marsh and saltpans while the southern coast alternates between limestone cliffs, rocky coves and sandy beaches. The somewhat windswept and arid island is riddled with quarries from which the Portuguese removed vast quantities of limestone to construct their huge fort, city walls, monuments and buildings.

The rocky or sandy interior reaches a maximum height of just 29 metres, so agriculture is limited although there are extensive stands of coconut and other palms. Branching palms (*Hyphaene* species) are very much a feature of the island and were originally introduced from Africa by the Portuguese.

History

These days, it's hard to understand why the Portuguese should have been interested in capturing and fortifying such an apparently unimportant and isolated outpost but, between 14th and 16th centuries, Diu was an important trading post and naval base from which the Ottoman Turks controlled the shipping routes in the northern part of the Arabian Sea.

After an unsuccessful attempt to capture the island in 1531, during which Bahadur Shah, the Sultan of Gujarat, was assisted by the Turkish navy, the Portuguese finally secured control in 1535 by taking advantage

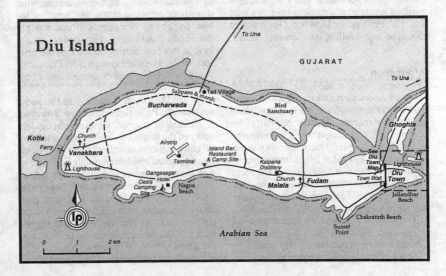

Diu Island

of a quarrel between the sultan and the Mughal emperor, Humayun. Humayun had defeated Bahadur Shah the previous year and had forced him into exile in Malwa, but while he was distracted by clashes with the Afghan Sher Khan, Bahadur was able to return.

With pressure still being exerted by both the Portuguese and the Mughals, Bahadur concluded a peace treaty with the Portuguese, effectively giving them control over the port at Diu. The treaty was soon cast to the wind and, although both Bahadur Shah and his successor, Sultan Mahmud III, attempted to contest the issue, the peace treaty which was eventually signed in 1539 ceded the island of Diu and the mainland enclave of Ghoghla to the Portuguese. Soon after the signing of this treaty, the Portuguese began constructing their fortress.

The Indian government appears to have an official policy of playing down the Portuguese era. Seven Rajput soldiers (six of them Singhs) and a few civilians were killed in Operation Vijay, which ended Portuguese rule. After the Indian Air Force unnecessarily bombed the airstrip and terminal, near Nagoa, it remained derelict until the late 1980s. The old church in Diu Fort was also bombed and is now a roofless ruin. It's said that the Portuguese blew up Government House to stop it falling into 'enemy' hands.

Information

The tourist office (☎ 2653) is on Bunder Rd, the main road which runs through Diu Town parallel to the waterfront. It's in the building on the waterfront, directly opposite the customs office. Unfortunately it has no maps of Diu Town, so you'll have to resign yourself to getting lost in the labyrinthine streets.

The State Bank of Saurashtra is the most efficient place to change travellers' cheques. The main post office is on the town square, and there's another post office at Ghoghla.

The Jethibai bus stand, for intercity buses, is just over the bridge which joins Diu to Ghoghla, and just outside the city walls.

Diu Festival is held every May, and features various cultural activities, including Portuguese and Gujarati dances.

Diu Town

The island's main industry would have to be fishing, followed by booze and salt. A distillery at Malala produces rum from sugar cane grown on the mainland. The town boasts quite a few bars where visitors from the 'dry' mainland can enjoy a beer (or stronger IMFL – 'Indian Made Foreign Liquor').

The town is sandwiched between the massive fort to the east and a huge city wall to the west. The main **gateway** in the wall has some nice carvings of lions, angels and a priest, while just inside the gate is a miniature chapel with an icon, dating from 1702.

Diu Town has three churches, although only one is fulfilling its original function. (It's said that there are now only 15 Christian families left on the whole island.) Access to **St Paul's** is through the adjacent school ground. This wonderful old church is suffering serious neglect, with beautiful old paintings slowly disintegrating, but it is still a peaceful and evocative place. Nearby is St Thomas', which now houses the **Diu Museum**. There's an interesting collection of Catholic statues, including a somewhat disturbing prostrate statue of Christ on his bier, flanked by two angels. If you thought the Hindu pantheon was confusing, take a look at this bewildering collection of Christian saints. The third church is St Francis of Assisi, which has been converted into a hospital.

Unlike Daman, the buildings in Diu show a significant Portuguese influence. The town is a maze of narrow, winding streets and many of the houses are well ornamented and brightly painted. Further away from this tightly packed residential quarter, the streets turn into meandering and often leafy lanes.

At the back of the town square, there's also a tiny but interesting bazaar. In a small park on the esplanade, between the square and the police station, the **Marwar Memorial**, topped by a griffin, commemorates the liberation of the island from the Portuguese. You could be excused for failing to see **Diu Aquarium** on your right on the road to the fort. It's a tiny tank containing about six gold-fish-sized specimens.

Fort Completed in 1541, the massive Portuguese fort with its double moat (one tidal) must once have been virtually impregnable, but sea erosion and neglect are leading to a slow but inevitable collapse. Piles of cannon balls litter the place and the ramparts have a superb array of cannons, many old yet in good condition. Legible script on one says it

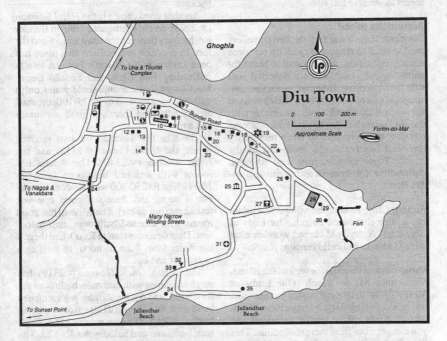

Diu Town

PLACES TO STAY		OTHER		15	Vegetable Market
12	Hotel Prince	1	Petrol Pump	18	Manisha Electronics (Moped Hire)
14	Nilesh Guest House	2	Jethibai Bus Stand	19	Public Gardens
16	Hotels Alishan & Apana	3	Local Bus Stand	21	Collectorate
17	Hotel Sanman	4	Oceanic Travels (East West Airlines)	22	Police
20	Hotel Mozambique	5	Post Office	24	Jampa Gate
23	Hotel Samrat	6	Town Square	25	Diu Museum (St Thomas' Church)
29	PWD Rest House	7	Tourist Office	26	Aquarium
33	Tourist Cottages	8	Goa Travels	27	St Paul's Church
		9	Chandani Bike Hire	28	School
PLACES TO EAT		10	Bazaar	30	Deer Park
32	Jay Shankar Restaurant	11	State Bank of Saurashtra & RR Travels	31	St Francis of Assisi (Hospital)
		13	Fish Market	34	Summer House
				35	Circuit House

was built in 1624 by Don Diego de Silva Conde de Porta Legre in the reign of Don Philippe, Rex d'Espana.

Since the fort also serves as the island's jail, it closes at 5 pm each day. Entry is free. Signs prohibit photography but no-one seems to observe this rule.

Around the Island

Beaches Temple and fort-satiated travellers used to head to **Nagoa** to catch up on some serious relaxation, and it's still a beautiful palm-fringed beach, largely deserted and safe for swimming. However, since the construction of a new road which stretches from the south of Diu Town's wall, joining up with the old Fudam Rd after about two km, access has now been provided to Diu's previously unvisited beaches in the south-east of the island. These include, from east to west, **Jallandhar**, **Chakratirth** and stunning **Sunset Point**.

Fudam Close to Diu, the village of Fudam has a huge abandoned church, Our Lady of Remedies. A large old carved wooden altar with Madonna and child remains inside.

Vanakbara At the extreme west of the island, Vanakbara has a church (Our Lady of Mercy), fort, lighthouse, small bazaar, post office and fishing fleet. A ferry crosses from here to Kotla village on the mainland and you can get a bus from there to Kodinar. This little fishing village is definitely worth a visit – wander through the town to the port area where you can see the locals mending nets and repairing their colourful fishing boats.

Places to Stay

Many of the guest houses in Diu offer quite a good discount in the off season. Prices below are for the peak season, which runs roughly from October to June.

Diu Town Many budget travellers stay at the *Hotel Mozambique* (☎ 2223), an old Portuguese-style house facing the vegetable market. Doubles/triples with common bathroom cost Rs 60/90, or with attached bathroom, Rs 80/120. There's also a 'VIP' suite, with two double beds (including a four-poster) for Rs 200. All rooms have access to balconies with magnificent views out over the channel between Diu Town and Ghoghla, and free hot water is available in buckets.

Another good choice is the *Hotel Sanman* (☎ 2273), an old Portuguese villa on Bunder Rd, halfway between the town square and the fort. In previous incarnations this place has been known as the Baron's Inn, the totally misleading Fun Club, and Pensão Beira-Mar! Large, basic rooms (cold water only) with good sea views cost Rs 75/100, the staff are friendly, and there's a good restaurant and bar.

Close to the Sanman are two modern hotels, the *Hotel Apana* (☎ 2112) and the *Hotel Alishan* (☎ 2340). The Apana has rooms with attached bathroom from Rs 100/125, or Rs 250/300 with air-con. Check-out is noon, and there's a good non-veg restaurant (but no bar). The Alishan has good rooms with attached bathroom, and balconies. Double rooms start at Rs 60, and there's hot water from 7 am to noon, as well as a restaurant and bar.

The *Nilesh Guest House* (☎ 2319) has singles/doubles with common bathroom for Rs 60/100, and doubles/triples with attached bathroom for Rs 120/180. Hot water in buckets is Rs 5. The new annexe has doubles with bathroom and balcony for Rs 120. The floral curtains may make you feel like you're back at grandma's, but rooms are clean and the manager is very friendly. The restaurant here gets good reports from travellers.

Clean, modern rooms are available at the *Hotel Prince* (☎ 2265), close to the fish market. Standard rooms are Rs 175, deluxe rooms are Rs 225 (no single rates), and there's 24-hour hot water. The 'sea views' are mere glimpses, however. Breakfast is available, and there's a beer bar, but no dining room.

The *Hotel Samrat* (☎ 2354), a couple of blocks back from the main square, has rooms from Rs 250, or Rs 450 with air-con, and there are two four-bed dorms for Rs 50 per person. Discounts and single-occupancy rates are offered in the off season. Rooms are well appointed, all with balconies, and room service is available. There's a good restaurant and bar here. If the kitchen is not busy, the chef will cook fish bought by guests at the fish market for about Rs 15 to Rs 20 per person.

The *PWD Rest House* (☎ 2476), close to the fort, has rooms from Rs 100, or Rs 300 with air-con (no single rates). Most rooms have balconies, and there are good views out over the channel and the fort. There's a small deer park behind the guest house.

Jallandhar Beach Just out of Diu Town, in a magnificent location opposite Jallandhar Beach and about one km from the fort, are the *Tourist Cottages* (☎ 2654). Clean and spacious cottages with double or twin beds cost Rs 200, or Rs 350 with air-con. There are also four-person rooms (the second double bed is in a loft) for Rs 350. All rooms have sea views, and there's an excellent non-veg restaurant and bar (non-guests welcome). If you don't mind being a little way out of town, this is a wonderfully laid-back place, and is the closest accommodation to Sunset Point.

Mansukhlal Motichand (☎ 2424), the maestro from Jay Shankar's (see Places to Eat), should have his budget guest house up and running by now. The guest house is at the same location as the restaurant.

Nagoa Beach As it is forbidden to rent local cottages or freelance camp, accommodation is limited and the following are currently the only available options.

The *Oasis Camping Site* next to the Gangasagar Hotel has tents for Rs 175 with light and fan, and there's a bar and restaurant. The site is only established between October and late June. Enquire at the tourist office (☎ 2653) in Diu Town.

The *Island Bar & Restaurant* (no phone), on the Diu Town to Nagoa Beach road, has tents with light, fan and bed for Rs 100 per person. This site is set up from October to December. The restaurant is open all year.

The *Gangasagar Hotel* (☎ 2249) is the only hotel at Nagoa Beach. Very small rooms cost Rs 75/100. Double rooms have a toilet, but no shower. This place is very regimented: meals are at set times, and if you are hungry outside these times, bad luck! Checkout is a very ungenerous 8 am.

Ghoghla In the village of Ghoghla on the mainland part of Diu is the *Tourist Complex* (☎ 2212). This is the first building in Diu after you come through the barrier which marks the border with Gujarat. Although relatively new, this place is already looking a little shabby. Doubles cost Rs 175, or with air-con, Rs 350. Dorm beds are Rs 75. There's a pleasant restaurant and bar, looking out over the sea.

Places to Eat
A number of hotels and guest houses have quite good restaurants, but dining in Diu will never be the same since the arrival on the scene of *Jay Shankar Restaurant*, a cafe on Jallandhar Beach. The family of Mansukhlal Motichand manage to prepare the most exquisite (and cheap) dishes in their tiny kitchen. The food is excellent, and the Motichand family are very friendly hosts. The restaurant is not licensed, but abstention is a small price to pay for what may prove to be a culinary highlight of travel in Gujarat.

The restaurants at the *Hotel Samrat* and *Nitesh Guest House* are very good, as is that at the *Tourist Cottages* on Jallandhar Beach. Many bars offer basic staples, such as dhal and rice. The restaurant on tiny Fortim-do-Mar, the little fortified island just to the north of the main town fort, should have been completed by now.

Beer and drinks are exceedingly cheap (Rs 18 for a Kingfisher). The bar at the *Hotel Mozambique* has private drinking booths where shady deals can be consummated over a bottle of IMFL.

Food at Nagoa Beach is a problem; basically you need to bring it with you – there are no cafes at the beach. If you're lucky, the bar at the *Gangasagar Hotel* might rustle up an omelette or toast at a pinch. The bar is

GUJARAT

open to non-guests. The *Manali* snack bar at Sunset Point has drinks and hot and cold snacks during the tourist season only.

Getting There & Away

Air East West Airlines has three flights a week to Bombay (US$57). The East West agent is Oceanic Travels (☎ 2180), on the town square near the post office.

Bus Una is the access point for Diu, and there are direct buses to there from Bhavnagar, Palitana, Veraval and Talaja. Once in Una, you have to get yourself the 10 or so km to Ghoghla and Diu. Buses depart every 30 minutes from Una bus stand between 6.30 am and 8.15 am (Rs 6). There's a passport check at the Diu border. From Una, if you don't want to wait for a bus, walk the one km from the bus stand to Tower Chowk (ask directions), from where crowded share rickshaws take you to Ghoghla (Rs 5), and another share rickshaw on to Diu costs Rs 2. An auto-rickshaw from Una costs about Rs 50.

There are a number of Gujarat STC buses which actually run all the way to Diu from places such as Veraval and Bhavnagar.

A quicker and more comfortable option to the STC buses are the private minibuses. RR Travels (☎ 2329), next to the State Bank of Saurashtra, has an overnight service to Ahmedabad departing Diu at 7 pm (10½ hours, Rs 85). There are departures almost every 30 minutes between 6 am and 8 pm to Veraval (2½ hours, Rs 25), Junagadh (four hours, Rs 40) and Rajkot (seven hours, Rs 60). To Porbandar, buses depart at 6 and 8 am, and 1 pm (five hours, Rs 55), and to Bombay, there's a bus at 10 am (22 hours, Rs 200). Bookings should be made preferably 24 hours in advance. RR departures prior to 8 am leave from their office; after 8 am, buses depart from the new Jethibai bus stand. Goa Travels (☎ 2191), on the town square, also has a service to Bombay, departing at 10.30 am.

Train Delwada, between Una and Ghoghla and only about eight km from Diu, is the nearest railhead. A share auto-rickshaw from there to Ghoghla costs about Rs 3. There's a direct train at 6 am from Delwada to Veraval, arriving at 10.30 am, or at 1 pm, there's a service via Talala, reaching Veraval at 5 pm (96 km, Rs 27/114). There is also a daily service to Junagadh (164 km, 6½ hours, Rs 43/159) via Sasan Gir.

Getting Around

Auto-rickshaw drivers will demand Rs 50 to Una, but you may be able to bargain this down. Rs 5 gets you anywhere within the town of Diu itself. To Nagoa Beach, expect to pay Rs 25, and to Sunset Point, Rs 15. Share rickshaws to Ghoghla cost Rs 2 per person.

Cycling is a good way to get around Diu Town, although it can be a long, hot haul out to Nagoa or further afield to Vanakbara. Chandani Bike Hire at the back of the town square has bikes for Rs 20 per day. For more mobility with less effort, Manisha Electronics, next to the Hotel Sanman, rents out mopeds for Rs 120 per day plus fuel, or Rs 630 per week (discounted in the off season). Some of these old rattletraps have been known to break down, stranding riders in far-flung corners of the island – check the bike over carefully before heading off. You can also rent bicycles here.

Local buses from Diu Town to Nagoa Beach and Vanakbara leave from the bus stand opposite the petrol pump on Bunder Rd at 7 and 11 am, and 4 pm. From Nagoa, they depart for Diu Town from near the police post at 1, 5.30 and 7 pm (Rs 1.50).

VERAVAL

Population: 105,000
Telephone Area Code: 02876

On the south coast of Saurashtra is Veraval, which was the major seaport for Mecca pilgrims before the rise of Surat. It still has some importance as one of India's major fishing ports (over 1000 boats work from here), and as the base for a visit to Somnath Temple, five km south of the town.

Wooden dhows of all sizes, from fishing dinghies right up to ocean-going vessels, are still built totally by hand. The largest dhows still make the journey from here to Dubai and other Middle Eastern destinations, and you may well see some of them loading or discharging cargo.

It's well worth a wander around the **port**, although photography is supposedly prohibited. If you're on a bicycle heading for Somnath, you can take a shortcut right through the port area. Apart from the port, there's not a lot to see in Veraval, despite its size.

Information

Be warned that no bank here will change travellers' cheques. The State Bank of India near the railway station will change cash, however.

Places to Stay

One of the best places to stay is the *Hotel Satkar* (☎ 20-120), close to the bus stand. Rooms are from Rs 75/125, or Rs 250/350

with air-con. All rooms have attached bathroom with hot water (mornings only), and the staff are very friendly and helpful. The 'dining room' here is actually two tables set up in a bedroom! Checkout is 10 am.

The nearby *Hotel Kasturi* (☎ 20-248) has spacious rooms from Rs 80/150, or Rs 225/260 with air-con. There's hot and cold water in the attached bathrooms, and checkout is at 10 am.

The *Toran Tourist Bungalow* (☎ 20-488), College Rd, is a huge old place in an inconvenient location. It looks derelict, and has an atmosphere similar to the Addams Family home. Dusty rooms cost Rs 150/200 with ceiling fan. This place is somewhat redeemed by the views from some rooms of the nearby old nawab's palace (now a college). Checkout is 9 am, and there is no dining hall.

There are *retiring rooms* at the railway station (dorm beds Rs 30; singles/doubles Rs 50/60), and the slightly dingy *Chandrani*

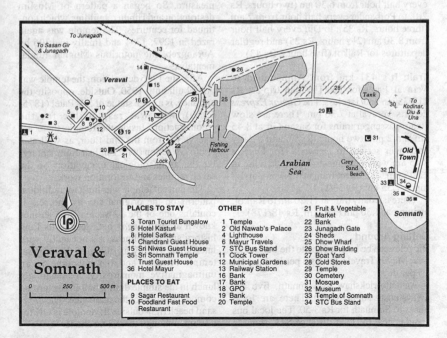

Veraval & Somnath

0   250   500 m

PLACES TO STAY	OTHER	21 Fruit & Vegetable Market
3 Toran Tourist Bungalow	1 Temple	22 Bank
5 Hotel Kasturi	2 Old Nawab's Palace	23 Junagadh Gate
8 Hotel Satkar	4 Lighthouse	24 Sheds
14 Chandrani Guest House	6 Mayur Travels	25 Dhow Wharf
15 Sri Niwas Guest House	7 STC Bus Stand	26 Dhow Building
35 Sri Somnath Temple	11 Clock Tower	27 Boat Yard
Trust Guest House	12 Municipal Gardens	28 Cold Stores
36 Hotel Mayur	13 Railway Station	29 Temple
	16 Bank	30 Cemetery
PLACES TO EAT	17 Bank	31 Mosque
	18 GPO	32 Museum
9 Sagar Restaurant	19 Bank	33 Temple of Somnath
10 Foodland Fast Food Restaurant	20 Temple	34 STC Bus Stand

Guest House (☎ 20-356) is nearby, with very basic, but adequate doubles for Rs 50. Close to the Chandrani is the *Sri Niwas Guest House* (☎ 20-138), which has tiny singles with common bath for Rs 30, and singles/doubles with bathroom for Rs 40/60 (cold water only).

Places to Eat

The *Sagar Restaurant* is a pleasant air-con vegetarian restaurant about five minutes' walk from the bus stand towards the clock tower. Diagonally opposite is the *Foodland Fast Food Restaurant*.

Getting There & Away

Bus Daily buses run from the bus stand to Diu, Kodinar, Porbandar, Junagadh, Rajkot and Bhavnagar. There are regular departures for Sasan Gir (1½ hours, Rs 12). Mayur Travels (☎ 21-602), opposite the bus stand, is the agent for the private bus companies. There are daily departures for Junagadh every half hour from 6.30 am (two hours, Rs 20); to Porbandar every half hour from 7 am (three hours, Rs 35); to Diu every half hour from 8.30 am (2½ hours, Rs 25) and regular departures for Rajkot (five hours, Rs 43).

Train It's 431 km from Ahmedabad to Veraval. Fares for the 11½-hour trip are Rs 118/352 in 2nd/1st class. The *Girnar Express* departs Veraval at 7.30 pm. There are slow steam passenger trains for Sasan Gir at 8.45 am and 2 pm (two hours, Rs 9), and a daily passenger service to Delwada (for Diu) at 8.45 am with a change at Talala, arriving at 12.45 pm, or a direct train at 3.30 pm, arriving at 7.35 pm (Rs 33/114).

There is a daily train at 11.20 am to Rajkot, arriving at 4.30 pm (186 km, Rs 48/178).

Getting Around

Bicycles can be hired opposite the bus stand, near Mayur Travels, for Rs 2 per hour, or Rs 15 per day.

An auto-rickshaw to Somnath, five km away, costs about Rs 20. There are local buses to Somnath for Rs 3.50. The local bus stand is near the long-distance STC stand.

SOMNATH
Temple of Somnath

This temple, at Somnath Patan near Veraval and about 80 km from Junagadh, has an extremely chequered past. Its earliest history fades into legend – it is said to have been originally built out of gold by Somraj, the moon god, only to be rebuilt by Rawana in silver, then by Krishna in wood and Bhimdev in stone. A description of the temple by Al Biruni, an Arab traveller, was so glowing that it prompted a visit in 1024 by a most unwelcome tourist – Mahmud of Ghazni. At that time, the temple was so wealthy that it had 300 musicians, 500 dancing girls and even 300 barbers just to shave the heads of visiting pilgrims.

Mahmud of Ghazni, whose raids on the riches of India were to gain him quite a reputation, descended on Somnath from his Afghan kingdom and, after a two-day battle, took the town and the temple. Having looted its fabulous wealth, he destroyed it for good measure. So began a pattern of Muslim destruction and Hindu rebuilding which continued for centuries. The temple was again razed in 1297, 1394 and finally in 1706 by Aurangzeb, the notorious Mughal fundamentalist.

After the 1706 demolition, the temple was not rebuilt until 1950. Outside, opposite the entrance, is a large statue of S V Patel (1875-1950), who was responsible for the reconstruction. Inside the temple there are fine views from the 2nd floor, as well as a photo collection (with English commentary) on the archaeological excavation of the seven temples and restoration work.

The current temple was built to traditional patterns on the original site by the sea. It contains one of the 12 sacred Siva shrines known as *jyoti lingas* but, despite its long history and its holiness, it's not really very interesting. Hardly anything of the original temple remains and the new one is an unimaginative monstrosity. You can get lunch in the simple dining hall in the temple compound, north of the main gate. The grey-sand beach right outside the temple is OK for a swim, although there's no shade.

Museum

Down the lane from the temple is a museum, open from 9 am to noon and 3 to 6 pm, closed Wednesdays, holidays and every 2nd and 4th Saturday. Admission is Rs 0.50. Remains of the old temple can be seen here as a jumble of old carved stones littering a courtyard. There are pottery shards, a seashell collection and a (strange) glass case of water bottles containing samples from the Danube, Nile, St Lawrence, Tigris, River Plate and even the Australian Murray, as well as seawater from Hobart and New Zealand.

Other Sites

The town of Somnath Patan is entered from Veraval by the **Junagadh Gate**. This very ancient triple gate was the one which Mahmud finally broke through to take the town. Close to the second gate is an old **mosque** dating from Mahmud's time. The **Jama Masjid**, reached through the town's busy **bazaar**, was constructed using parts of a Hindu temple and has interesting bo tree carvings at all four corners. It is now a museum with a collection from many of these temples.

About a km before the Junagadh Gate, coming from Veraval, the finely carved **Mai Puri** was once a Temple of the Sun. This Hindu temple was converted into a mosque during Mahmud's time and is surrounded by thousands of tombs and palias (memorial stones). Two old tombs are close by and, on the shore, the **Bhidiyo Pagoda** probably dates from the 14th century.

To the east of the town is the **Bhalka Tirth** where Krishna was mistaken for a deer and wounded by an arrow while sleeping in a deerskin. The legendary spot is at the confluence of three rivers. You get to it through the small *sangam* (confluence gate), which is simply known as the Nana, or Small Gate. North of this sacred spot is the **Suraj Mandir**, or Temple of the Sun, which Mahmud also had a go at knocking down. This very old temple, with a frieze of lions with elephant trunks around its walls, probably dates from the same time as the original Somnath Temple. Back inside the small gate is a

temple which Ahalya Bai of Indore built as a replacement for the Somnath Temple.

Places to Stay

Directly opposite the bus stand, the *Sri Somnath Temple Trust* has a vast guest house. The rooms are a bit dingy but, at Rs 40/60 for a double/triple, they're good value. Just down the road (heading away from the temple) the *Hotel Mayur* (☎ 20-286) has doubles with hot and cold water for Rs 100.

CHORWAD

The summer palace of the Junagadh nawabs, situated at the popular beach resort of Chorwad 20 km from Veraval (70 km from Junagadh), was converted by the Gujarat State Tourism Department into the beautiful *Palace Beach Resort* (☎ (0287688) 557). The hotel is surrounded by well-tended gardens and overlooks the sea. Doubles in the detached cottages cost Rs 375, and in the main palace building, they range from Rs 200 to Rs 500. All meals have to be ordered in advance.

SASAN GIR LION SANCTUARY

The last home of the Asiatic lion (*Panthera leo lersica*) is 59 km from Junagadh via Visavadar. The sanctuary, which covers 1400 sq km, was set up to protect the lion and its habitat, and in this respect has been a success: since 1980 numbers have increased from less than 200 to an estimated 250. However, while the lions have been the winners, the local herders (the *maaldharis*) have lost valuable grazing land for their cattle. Although the lions seem remarkably tame, in recent years they have reportedly been wandering further afield, well outside the limits of the sanctuary, in search of easy game – namely calves – which in earlier times was found within the park itself. The problem is compounded by the declining areas of forest outside the sanctuary, forcing villagers to forage for fuel within the sanctuary precincts, reducing the habitat of the lions.

The best time to visit the sanctuary is from December to April, and it is closed completely from 16 June to 15 October. If there has been a heavy monsoon, the sanctuary may open later.

Apart from the lions there are over 30 species of other mammals, including bears, hyenas, foxes and a number of species of deer and antelope. The deer include the largest Indian antelope (the nilgai), the graceful chinkara gazelle, the chousingha and the barking deer. You may also see parrots, peacocks and monkeys.

The lions themselves are elusive but you'd be unlucky not to see at least one on a safari, although it would be safer to allow for a couple of trips if you're determined to see one. Morning safaris are generally a better bet than those in the afternoons. Unfortunately the local guides are poorly trained and speak little English.

Whatever else you do, take a jeep and not a minibus. While the latter stick to the main tracks, the jeeps can take the small trails where you're much more likely to come across lions. (This doesn't apply to the Gir Interpretation Zone – see later in this section.)

Before you can go on safari, you must get a permit. These are issued on the spot at the Sinh Sadan Forest Lodge office and cost Rs 15 per person (valid for three days) plus Rs 7.50 for a still camera. Jeeps cost Rs 6 per km and can take up to six people. There are three main tracks in the park, so you will cover 25 to 35 km, depending on the track your jeep is assigned to. The guide's fee is set at Rs 7.50 (total, not per person), for the first three hours, and Rs 4 per hour thereafter, but expect to get hassled for a tip – if your guide's been keen and searched hard then a tip is certainly justified, otherwise it's up to you. Jeeps are available from the lodge office every day between 7 and 11 am and 3 and 6.30 pm during winter (October to February) and from 6.30 am during summer (March to June).

Twelve km from Sasan is the **Gir Interpretation Zone**, at Devalia, within the sanctuary precincts. The 4.12-sq-km zone has a cross-section of the wildlife in Gir. No private vehicles are permitted in the zone; jeep hire (which includes waiting time while visitors are taking their tour) costs about Rs 150 from Sasan village. The cost to enter the zone, including a minibus mini-safari, permit and guide, is Rs 70.

There are 25 species of reptiles in the sanctuary. A **crocodile-rearing centre** has been established next to Sihn Sadan Lodge, where hatchlings are reared and then released into their natural habitat.

Places to Stay & Eat

There are two places to stay at Sasan Gir village. About a 10-minute walk from the railway station is the *Sinh Sadan Forest Lodge* (☎ 40). It is a very pleasant place to stay, with rooms set around a quiet green garden. A very aged and faded film about the park is screened here every evening at 7 pm. Good singles/doubles with mosquito nets and baths cost from Rs 100/150, or Rs 400/450 with air-con. Whilst advance booking is generally not necessary, the period between Christmas and New Year can be packed out. There's a restaurant (guests only) which serves thalis (Rs 25) or a non-veg dinner (Rs 90), but you need to order in advance.

Gujarat Tourism's *Lion Safari Lodge* (☎ 21) is down by the river, about 200 metres from the Sinh Sadan, surrounded by well-maintained gardens. Singles/doubles cost Rs 250/350, and dorm beds are Rs 30; there are no air-con rooms. The non-vegetarian *Safari Restaurant* here is open to non-guests, but meals must be ordered in advance. You can also get snacks at the shacks opposite the Sinh Sadan Lodge.

Getting There & Away

STC buses between Junagadh and Veraval travel via Sasan Gir numerous times throughout the day. The 45-km trip to Veraval takes 1½ hours (Rs 12). To Junagadh, the 59-km trip takes around two hours (Rs 13, or Rs 19 'express'). Slow steam trains run to Veraval (two hours, Rs 9) twice daily, to Delwada (for Diu) once daily at 8.30 am, and to Junagadh once a day (2½ hours, Rs 13).

JUNAGADH

Population: 181,000
Telephone Area Code: 0285

Junagadh is an interesting town situated right at the base of the temple-studded Girnar Hill, and is also the departure point for visits to the Gir Forest. This friendly and unspoilt town has some very exotic old buildings, most in a state of disrepair, and is a fascinating place to explore, but very few tourists come here.

The city takes its name from the fort which enclosed the old city. Dating from 250 BC, the Ashokan edicts near the town testify to the great antiquity of this site. At the time of Partition, the Nawab of Junagadh opted to take his tiny state into Pakistan. However, the inhabitants were predominantly Hindu and the nawab soon found himself in exile, perhaps explaining the sorry state of his former palace and fort.

Information

The best source of information is the Hotel Relief, the city's unofficial tourist centre. The Bank of Baroda, opposite the central post office, has money-changing facilities.

Junagadh's GPO is inconveniently located south of the city centre at Gandhigram. There's a branch in a small street just off M G Rd near the local bus stand. The telegraph office is on Jhalorapa Rd, near Ajanta Talkies.

Uparkot

This very old fort, from which the city derives its name (*jirna* means old), stands on the eastern side of Junagadh and has been rebuilt and extended many times over the centuries. In places, the walls are 20 metres high and an ornate triple gateway forms the entrance to the fort. It's said that the fort was once besieged, unsuccessfully, for a full 12 years. In all, it was besieged 16 times. It is also said that the fort was abandoned from the 7th to 10th centuries and, when rediscovered, it was completely overgrown by jungle. The plateau-like area formed by the top of the old fort is covered in lantana scrub. Entry is Rs 1.

The **Jama Masjid**, the mosque inside the fort, was built from a demolished Hindu temple. Other points of interest include the **tomb of Nuri Shah** and two fine baolis (step-wells) known as the **Adi Chadi** and the **Naughan**. The Adi Chadi is named after two of the slave girls who fetched water from it. The Naughan is reached by a magnificent circular staircase.

Cut into the hillside close to the mosque are some ancient **Buddhist caves** which are thought to be at least 1500 years old. These eerie double-storey caves have six pillars with very fine carvings. The soft rock on which Junagadh is built encouraged the construction of caves and wells, and there are other caves in Junagadh, including some thought to date back to the time of Ashoka.

Mahabat Maqbara

This stunning mausoleum of one of the nawabs of Junagadh is resplendent with silver doors and intricate architecture, including minarets encircled by spiralling stairways. The mausoleum is generally locked but you may be able to obtain the keys from the adjacent mosque.

Darbar Hall Museum

This museum has the usual display of weapons and armour from the days of the nawabs, together with their collections of silver chains and chandeliers, settees and thrones, howdahs and palanquins, and a few cushions and gowns, as well as a huge carpet which was woven in Junagadh's jail. There's a portrait gallery of the nawabs and local petty princes, including photos of the last nawab with his various beloved dogs.

It's open from 9 am to 12.15 pm and 3 to 6 pm daily except Wednesday, the 2nd and 4th Saturday of every month and all public holidays (Rs 0.50).

Ashokan Edicts

On the way to the Girnar Hill temples, you pass a huge boulder on which Emperor Ashoka inscribed 14 edicts in around 250 BC. His inscription is in the Pali script. Later Sanskrit inscriptions were added around 150

AD by Rudradama and in about 450 AD by Skandagupta, the last emperor of the Mauryas. The 14 edicts are moral lectures, while the other inscriptions refer mainly to recurring floods destroying the embankments of a nearby lake, the Sudershan, which no longer exists. The boulder is actually housed in a small roadside building, on the right if you're heading towards Girnar.

Girnar Hill

The 600-metre climb up 10,000 stone steps to the summit of Girnar is best made early in the morning, preferably at dawn. The steps are well built and maintained and were constructed between 1889 and 1908 from the proceeds of a lottery. The start of the climb is in a scrubby teak forest, a km or two beyond the Damodar Kund, and the road actually takes you to around step No 3000 – which leaves you with only 7000 to the top!

There are frequent refreshment stalls on the 2½-hour ascent. These stalls also sell chalk, so you can graffiti your name onto the rocks beside the path. If you really can't face the walk, doolis (rope chairs) carried by porters can be hired; for these you pay by weight so, before setting off, you have to suffer the indignity of being weighed on a huge beam scale, just like a sack of grain. From the summit, the views are superb.

Like Palitana, the temple-topped hill is of great significance to the Jains. The sacred tank of **Damodar Kund** marks the start of the climb to the temples. The path ascends through a wood to the marble temples near the summit. Five of them are Jain temples, including the largest and oldest – the 12th-century **Temple of Neminath**, the 22nd Jain tirthankar. There is a large black image of Neminath in the central shrine and many smaller images around the temple.

The nearby triple **Temple of Mallinath**, the 9th tirthankar, was erected in 1177 by two brothers. During festivals, this temple is a favourite gathering place for sadhus and a great fair is held here during the Kartika Purnima festival in November or December. On top of the peak is the **Temple of Amba Mata**, where newlyweds are supposed to worship at the shrine of the goddess in order to ensure a happy marriage.

A No 3 or 4 bus from the stand opposite the central post office will take you to Girnar Taleti at the base of the hill. Buses run about once an hour from 6 am, cost Rs 2 and go by the Ashoka edicts. An auto-rickshaw from town costs Rs 20.

Other Attractions

If you are unable to visit the Gir Forest, Junagadh's **zoo** at Sakar Bagh, 3.5 km from the centre of town on the Rajkot road, has Gir lions. The zoo was set up by the nawab in 1863 specifically to save the lion from extinction and is surprisingly good with lions, tigers and leopards being the main attractions. The zoo is open from 9 am to 6 pm, and costs Rs 2. There is also a fine local **museum** at the zoo with paintings, manuscripts, archaeological finds and various other exhibits including a natural history section. It's open daily, except on Wednesday and the 2nd and 4th Saturday of each month, from 9 am to noon and 3 to 6 pm. Take a No 6 bus (Rs 2), or walk there by the old Majevadi Gate on your right.

The **Ayurvedic College** at Sadarbag on the western edge of town is housed in one of the former nawab's palaces, and has a small museum devoted to ayurvedic medicine. The staff are knowledgeable and it's a good place to obtain information on this ancient form of traditional medicine.

Other old buildings include the gate opposite the railway station on Dhal Rd, the clock tower near the central post office and the building opposite the Darbar Hall.

Places to Stay

Many travellers head for the *Hotel Relief* (☎ 20-280) on Dhal Rd (the road leading to the fort), where singles with common bathroom cost Rs 75, or with toilet only, Rs 100. Doubles cost Rs 100 and Rs 150 respectively, and air-con rooms are Rs 300/400. The manager, Mr Sorathia, is a good source of information about local points of interest. The restaurant was closed at the time of

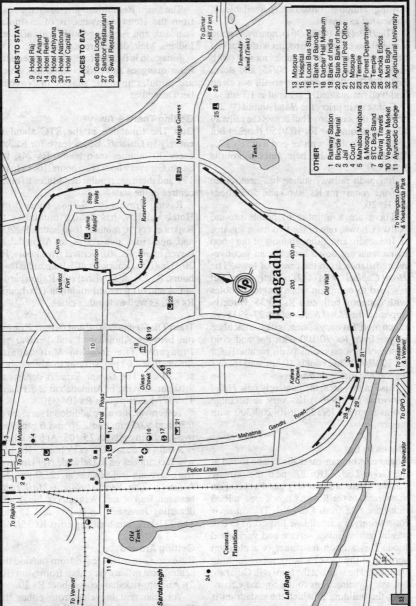

PLACES TO STAY
9 Hotel Raj
12 Hotel Anand
14 Hotel Relief
29 Hotel Ashiyana
30 Hotel National
31 Hotel Capital

PLACES TO EAT
6 Geeta Lodge
27 Santoor Restaurant
28 Swati Restaurant

OTHER
1 Railway Station
2 Bicycle Rental
3 Jail
4 Court
5 Mahabat Maqbara & Mosque
7 Forest Department
8 STC Bus Stand
10 Ravirai Travels
11 Ayurvedic College
13 Mosque
15 Hospital
16 Local Bus Stand
17 Bank of Baroda
18 Darbar Hall Museum
19 Bank of India
20 State Bank of India
21 Central Post Office
22 Mosque
23 Temple
24 Forest Department
25 Temple
26 Ashoka Edicts
32 Moti Bagh
33 Agricultural University

Junagadh

GUJARAT

writing, although breakfast is available, if somewhat expensive.

The *Hotel Raj* (☎ 23-961), nearby, is good value. It has clean single rooms with attached bathroom for Rs 50, double rooms (with single occupancy) for Rs 60/75, and dorm beds for Rs 20. Rooms are small, but clean and well maintained. Checkout is 10 am.

Going up in price, the *Hotel Anand* (☎ 22-657), on the same road but across the railway line, has rooms for Rs 100/150 (bucket hot water), or doubles with air-con from Rs 275. Breakfast is available here, and checkout is 9 am.

Junagadh railway station has neat, clean *retiring rooms* for Rs 30/60 and dorm beds for Rs 20.

There are a number of hotels around Kalwa Chowk, one of the two main squares in Junagadh, and although most of the good restaurants are down here, it's an inconvenient distance from the centre of town. The *Hotel Capital* (☎ 21-442) is pretty grim, but it's hard to complain when singles/doubles with common bath cost Rs 20/35. Directly opposite, the *Hotel National* (☎ 27-891) is a much more savoury option, with immaculate rooms from Rs 70/100 with hot and cold water, or air-con rooms (with bathtub!) for Rs 200/300. Checkout is 10 am, and there's a good restaurant downstairs.

Also in this area, the relatively new *Hotel Ashiyana* (☎ 20-706) has very respectable rooms from Rs 75/125, or Rs 200/300 with air-con.

Places to Eat

Cheap all-you-can-eat thalis can be found at the *Geeta Lodge* (Rs 20), near the railway station. There are two very good vegetarian restaurants in the Kalwa Chowk area, a Rs 5 rickshaw ride from Dhal Rd. The *Santoor Restaurant*, in a small lane just off M G Rd, has incredibly quick service and very good food. This air-con restaurant is a pleasant surprise at the top of a fairly seedy-looking staircase. The sign out the front is in Gujarati, but ask for directions to the Snehal Chambers, the building in which the restaurant is located.

The *Swati Restaurant*, just down the road from the Hotel Ashiyana, is of a similar standard, and is very popular with affluent Indians. Main dishes are around Rs 35.

Junagadh is famous for its fruit, especially kesar mangoes and *chiku* (sapodilla) which are popular in milk shakes in November/December.

Getting There & Away

Bus The timetable at the STC stand is entirely in Gujarati. Buses leave for Rajkot every 30 minutes (two hours, Rs 24), for Sasan Gir every hour (two hours, Rs 13 to Rs 19), and there are regular departures to other centres in the state.

Raviraj Travels (☎ 26-988), beneath the Hotel Vaibhav, has deluxe minibuses to Rajkot every 10 minutes (two hours, Rs 20), and numerous departures to Ahmedabad (seven hours, Rs 70), Veraval (two hours, Rs 20), Una (four hours, Rs 40), Porbandar (two hours, Rs 25), and to Bhuj (via Rajkot) at 11 am, 4 and 10 pm, and midnight (six hours, Rs 80), as well as to other cities.

Train The *Somnath Mail* and *Girnar Express* run between Ahmedabad and Veraval via Junagadh. The *Somnath Mail* departs Junagadh at 7.03 pm, arriving in Ahmedabad at 4.20 am. The *Girnar Express* departs at 9.10 pm, arriving in Ahmedabad at 6.10 am. The 377-km-trip costs Rs 104/310.

To Veraval, there are additional services at 6.30 and 9.05 am, and 2.30 and 6 pm. The two-hour trip costs Rs 25/105. At 6 am there is a train to Sasan Gir (2½ hours, Rs 13), which continues on to Delwada (for Una and Diu), arriving in Delwada at 12.30 pm (Rs 43/101). The *Veraval-Rajkot Mail* runs between Rajkot and Veraval via Junagadh, departing Junagadh for Rajkot at 1.15 pm. The 131-km, four-hour trip costs Rs 35/138.

Getting Around

Buses to Girnar Hill leave from outside the central post office every hour from 6 am (Rs 2). An auto-rickshaw costs about Rs 20.

You can rent bicycles from either the Hotel Relief or the small yellow shack near the railway station (Rs 2 per hour, Rs 20 per day). Junagadh's taxis seem to be mostly 1940s vintage Ford Plymouths, and there're dozens of them; probably the greatest concentration of working examples anywhere in the world – it would certainly bring a smile to old Henry Ford's face!

Most auto-rickshaw trips around town will cost no more than Rs 5.

PORBANDAR

Population: 174,000
Telephone Area Code: 0286

On the south-east coast, about midway between Veraval and Dwarka, modern-day Porbandar is chiefly noted as the birthplace of Mahatma Gandhi. In ancient times, the city was called Sudamapuri after Sudama, a compatriot of Krishna, and there was once a flourishing trade from here to Africa and the Persian Gulf. The Africa connection is apparent in the number of Indianised Blacks, called Siddis, who form a virtually separate caste of Dalits.

Porbandar has several large cement and chemical factories and a textile mill. Dhows are still built here and fish-drying is an important activity, lending a certain aroma to the town!

Swimming at Chowpatty Beach is not recommended. This beach is used as a local toilet and there is a factory drain outlet by the Hazur Palace. Swimming is said to be OK a few km down the coast towards Veraval.

Information

The Bank of Baroda, beneath the Hotel Flamingo, and the State Bank of India, opposite, both have money-changing facilities.

Kirti Mandir

The Kirti Mandir, Gandhi's birthplace, houses one of India's many collections of Gandhian memorabilia. A swastika on the floor in a small room marks the actual spot! There is also an exhibit of photographs, some with English captions, and a small bookshop.

Nehru Planetarium & Bharat Mandir

Across the muddy creek, which is spanned

by the Jynbeeli (once Jubilee) Bridge, are the Nehru Planetarium and the Bharat Mandir. Flocks of flamingoes are an unexpected sight along the creek. Men and women enter the planetarium from the verandah by separate doors whose panels celebrate Indian nonalignment, showing Shastri with Kosygin on one side and Nehru with JFK on the other! The planetarium has afternoon sessions in Gujarati.

The large Bharat Mandir hall is in a charming irrigated garden opposite the planetarium. On the floor inside is a huge relief map of India and the building's pillars are brilliantly painted with bas-reliefs of over 100 religious figures and legendary persons from Hindu epics.

Places to Stay

The *Nilam Guest House* (☎ 20-503) has dusty rooms from Rs 50 with cold water (bucket hot water is free), and dorm beds for Rs 20. All the windows face into the hall, so rooms are quite dark. Checkout is 24 hours.

The *Rajkamal Guest House* (☎ 20-374) on M G Rd is very cheap at Rs 19/34 with attached bathroom (cold water), and is no worse than any of the other bottom-end places.

Up the scale a bit is the *Hotel Flamingo* (☎ 23-123), also on M G Rd. It's a friendly place run by a helpful Indian who used to reside in the UK. Doubles cost Rs 200, or with air-con, from Rs 350. Some of the rooms have no external windows, so although they're quite big, they could be a little claustrophobic. There's a dining hall here.

Of a similar standard is the *Hotel Sheetal* (☎ 41-821), opposite the GPO. All rooms have hot and cold water, and are quite well appointed. Prices start at Rs 150 for a double (no single rates).

The *Vaibhav Guest House* (☎ 22-001) is a relatively new place close to the Flamingo. Small rooms cost Rs 100/160, or from Rs 300/350 with air-con. The sign out the front is in Gujarati.

Very close to the railway station, the *Shree Kandhlikrupa Guest House* (☎ 22-655) is

GUJARAT

very good value, with spotless rooms without air-con for Rs 50/75, all with hot and cold water. Checkout is a generous 24 hours.

The *New Oceanic Hotel* (☎ 20-217) is a small villa on Chowpatty Beach. Its air-con rooms cost Rs 400/600 for doubles/triples, but strangely, although the sea is only a stone's throw away, only one room has a sea view! There's a non-veg restaurant here. Non-guests are welcome, but you need to order 45 minutes in advance.

Places to Eat

The *Aardash* has good, basic vegetarian

food. For dining in more salubrious surroundings, the *Swagat Restaurant* is probably the best restaurant in town, and it's not unduly expensive. At sunset the usual snack-food places set up along the sea wall. The *Marine Restaurant* here is a basic snack bar.

Getting There & Away

Air East West has three flights a week to Bombay; NEPC Airlines has four flights weekly. Flights with both airlines cost US$70. Bookings can be made with Bhutiya Travels (☎ 41-889).

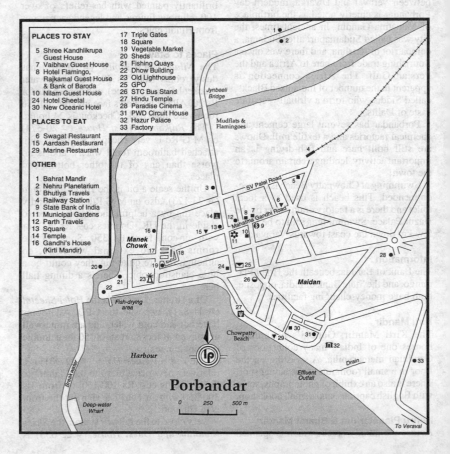

PLACES TO STAY
5 Shree Kandhlikrupa Guest House
7 Vaibhav Guest House
8 Hotel Flamingo, Rajkamal Guest House & Bank of Baroda
10 Nilam Guest House
24 Hotel Sheetal
30 New Oceanic Hotel

PLACES TO EAT
6 Swagat Restaurant
15 Aardash Restaurant
29 Marine Restaurant

OTHER
1 Bahrat Mandir
2 Nehru Planetarium
3 Bhutiya Travels
4 Railway Station
9 State Bank of India
12 Municipal Gardens
12 Parth Travels
13 Square
14 Temple
16 Gandhi's House (Kirti Mandir)

17 Triple Gates
18 Square
19 Vegetable Market
20 Sheds
21 Fishing Quays
22 Dhow Building
23 Old Lighthouse
25 GPO
26 STC Bus Stand
27 Hindu Temple
28 Paradise Cinema
31 PWD Circuit House
32 Hazur Palace
33 Factory

Jynbeeli Bridge

Mudflats & Flamingoes

SV Patel Road

Mahatma Gandhi Road

Manek Chowk

Maidan

Fish-drying area

Chowpatty Beach

Harbour

Deep-water Wharf

Effluent Outfall

Drain

Porbandar

0   250   500 m

To Veraval

Bus The STC bus stand is a 15-minute walk from M G Rd. There are regular services to Dwarka, Jamnagar, Veraval and Rajkot. The private bus companies have their offices on M G Rd, in the vicinity of the Hotel Flamingo. They only have signs in Gujarati so you'll need to enlist some local help to find the one you want. The main companies are Jay, Eagle, Raviraj and Parth. Parth Travels (☎ 22-140) has services to Jamnagar (2½ hours, Rs 35), Dwarka (two hours, Rs 25), Veraval (three hours, Rs 35), Rajkot (3½ hours, Rs 50), Diu (five hours, Rs 55) and Junagadh (two hours, Rs 25).

Train Porbandar is the terminus of a railway line; the main service is the *Saurashtra Express* to and from Bombay via Rajkot (4½ hours, Rs 56/205) and Ahmedabad (10 hours, Rs 124/367). The 959-km 23-hour trip to Bombay costs Rs 203/604.

Getting Around

An auto-rickshaw to the airport costs Rs 25.

DWARKA

Population: 30,500
Telephone Area Code: 02892

On the extreme western tip of the Kathiawar peninsula, Dwarka is one of the four most holy Hindu pilgrimage sites in India and is closely related to the Krishna legend. It was here that Krishna set up his capital after fleeing from Mathura. Dwarkanath, the name of the main temple here, is dedicated to Krishna.

The temple is only open to Hindus (though one visitor reported that you can sign a form and go in), but the exterior, with its tall five-storey spire supported by 60 columns, is far more interesting than the interior. Archaeological excavations have revealed five earlier cities at the site, all now submerged. Dwarka is the site of the important Janmashtami Festival which falls in August or September.

Dwarka's **lighthouse** is open to the public between 4.30 and 6 pm, and affords an excellent panoramic view from the top (Rs 1).

A little north of Dwarka, a ferry crosses from Okha to the **Island of Bet**, where Vishnu is said to have slain a demon. There are modern Krishna temples on the island.

A traveller advises to beware of the unfriendly dogs on this island.

Places to Stay & Eat

The State-run *Toran Tourist Dormitory* (☎ 313) has dorm beds for Rs 30 and doubles for Rs 200. The *Satnam Wadi Guest House* has very basic, but clean rooms for Rs 80/100. The *Meera Hotel*, on the main approach road, has rooms for Rs 40/60, and the dining room here has a good thali for Rs 14. The *Natraj Hotel* also has a good, although slightly more expensive thali for Rs 25.

Getting There & Away

There is a railway line between Dwarka and Jamnagar, 132 km away (Rs 35/138), and there are trains to Bombay (945 km, Rs 202/593) via Rajkot (207 km, Rs 53/189) and Ahmedabad (453 km, Rs 122/360).

STC buses run to all points in Saurashtra, and to Ahmedabad.

JAMNAGAR

Population: 396,000
Telephone Area Code: 0288

Prior to independence, the princely state of Jamnagar was ruled by the Jadeja Rajputs. The city was built around the small Ranmal Lake, in the centre of which is a small palace, reached by a causeway.

This bustling city has a long history of pearl fishing and a local variety of tie-dyeing, but today is more well known for having the only ayurvedic university in India and a temple listed in the *Guinness Book of Records*!

The old part of town has a number of interesting and impressive old buildings, such as the Mandvi Tower, and is very colourful and vibrant. The centre of the old town is known as Darbar Gadh, a semicircular gathering place where the former Maharaja of Nawanagar used to hold public audiences.

GUJARAT

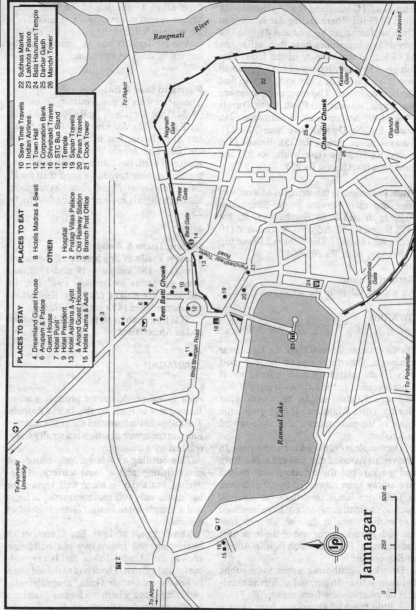

Rangmati River

To Kalavad

To Rajkot

Kalawat Gate

Ghachi Gate

Chandni Chowk

Nagnath Gate

Three Gate

Bedi Gate

Pancheshwar Road

Khambhalia Gate

Teen Batti Chowk

Bhid Bhanjan Road

Ranmal Lake

To Porbandar

To Ayurvedic University

To Airport

Jamnagar

0   250   500 m

PLACES TO STAY
4 Dreamland Guest House
6 Arupam & Palace
  Guest House
7 Hotel Punit
9 Hotel President
13 Hotel Ashiana & Jyoti
  & Anand Guest Houses
15 Hotels Kama & Aarti

PLACES TO EAT
8 Hotels Madras & Swati

OTHER
1 Hospital
2 Pratap Vilas Palace
3 Old Railway Station
5 Branch Post Office
10 Save Time Travels
11 Indian Airlines
12 Town Hall
14 Corporation Bank
16 Shivshakti Travels
17 STC Bus Stand
18 Temple
19 Sapan Travels
20 Pavan Travels
21 Clock Tower
22 Subhas Market
23 Lakhota Palace
24 Bala Hanuman Temple
25 Darbar Gadh
26 Mandvi Tower

Orientation & Information

The state bus stand and the new railway station are several km apart and both are a long way from the centre of the city, so you'll need to take an auto-rickshaw. Most of the best-avoided bottom-end guest houses are near the old railway station, in Teen Batti Chowk. There are a couple of more commodious cheap places near Bedi Gate.

English-language dailies can be found at the newsstand near the Hotel Swati restaurant.

The Corporation Bank, just inside the Bedi Gate, exchanges travellers' cheques on weekdays between 11 am and 3 pm. It can be quite time-consuming, but the staff are friendly. You may have to remind them to give you an exchange certificate.

Lakhota Palace

This diminutive palace once belonged to the Maharaja of Nawanagar. Today it houses a small museum with displays from archaeological sites in the area. The **museum** is reached by a short causeway from the northern side of the lake, and is open from 10.30 am to 1 pm and 3 to 5.30 pm daily except Wednesday (entry Rs 0.50).

Bala Hanuman Temple

The Bala Hanuman Temple is on the southeastern side of Ranmal Lake, and here, 24 hours a day since 1 August 1964, there's been continuous chanting of the invocation 'Shri Ram, Jai Ram, Jai Jai Ram'. This devotion has earned the temple a place in the *Guinness Book of Records*. Early evening is a particularly good time to visit as it's fairly animated then. In fact this whole area on the southeastern edge of the lake becomes very lively around sunset when people come to promenade, and the usual chai and kulfi stalls set up and ply their trade.

Cremation Park

You don't require a morbid disposition to visit Jamnagar's cremation park, 10 minutes' north of the city centre by auto-rickshaw. There are statues of saints and deities, as well as scenes from the *Ramayana*. This is a

fascinating place to visit, and the atmosphere is anything but depressing.

Places to Stay

At the bottom end of the market, Jamnagar offers some of the worst hotels in the whole of India and you'd be well advised to give these disgusting dosshouses a miss. They're mostly clustered around the old railway station in Teen Batti Chowk, and include the *Anupam* and *Palace* guest houses, with rooms for Rs 20/60 and Rs 35/45 respectively. The *Dreamland Guest House* (☎ 70-436) is a better bet in this area, with clean rooms (cold water only) for Rs 75. It's set back from the road, so is reasonably quiet.

The modern and clean *Hotel Punit* (☎ 70-559) is a notch up the scale, although the rooms facing the road can be hellishly noisy. Singles/doubles at this place go for Rs 150/190, or with air-con it's Rs 400 for a double.

The centrally located *Hotel Ashiana* (☎ 77-421), a vast, rambling place on the top floor of the New Super Market complex, is overpriced with doubles from Rs 100. Evidently they have spent so much money on the enormous flashing neon sign on top of the building that they have had to increase their room rates. If you are not prepared to pay these prices, they'll send you down to the grimy *Anand Guest House* in the same building, with seedy rooms for Rs 55 with cold water. There's a vegetarian restaurant in the Ashiana.

On the floor below the Ashiana is the *Jyoti Guest House* (☎ 71-155), which has good-sized doubles for Rs 75 and free bucket hot water. Checkout is 24 hours.

The *Hotel Kama* (☎ 77-778) is right opposite the bus stand, on the 4th floor of a modern high-rise building. There's a good range of rooms, from Rs 75/135 with bathroom, up to huge deluxe air-con suites for Rs 400/500. In the same building, on the 3rd floor, is the *Hotel Aarti* (☎ 78-220). Clean and comfortable rooms with bathroom are from Rs 100/120 (all non air-con).

Jamnagar's best hotel is the modern *Hotel President* (☎ 70-516), Teen Batti Chowk, right in the centre of town. Singles/doubles cost Rs 220/320, or Rs 400/500 with air-con, all with bathroom and constant hot water. The hotel has a restaurant, money-changing facilities and also accepts credit cards.

Places to Eat

For snack food in the evening try the various stalls that set up near the Bala Hanuman Temple. In the centre of town, in the Teen Batti Chowk area, there are plenty of reasonable eating places. The *Hotel Swati* is a vegetarian place with an extensive range of south Indian, Jain and Punjabi dishes. The nearby *Madras Hotel* specialises in Punjabi cuisine. For a splurge, the *7 Seas Restaurant* at the Hotel President offers reasonable veg and non-veg food and is far from being expensive, with non-veg dishes from Rs 35.

Around Mandvi Tower in the heart of the old town there's an extraordinary array of 'sweetmeat' shops selling a wide variety of sweet and sticky creations. *H J Vyas* is famous for its gooey confections.

Getting There & Away

Air The efficient Indian Airlines office (☎ 78-569) on Bhid Bhanjan Rd is open from 10 am to 4.30 pm (closed for lunch from 1 to 1.45 pm). Indian Airlines has four flights a week to Bombay (US$52). Bookings can also be made with Save Time Travels (☎ 71-739), between Bedi Gate and the town hall.

Bus There are STC buses to Rajkot every 30 minutes or less, and other departures to Dwarka, Porbandar, Bhuj, Junagadh and Ahmedabad.

Rather than compete with each other, the private bus companies have complicated bus bookings for travellers by each operating services to different destinations. Sapan Travels (☎ 71-646), just off Pancheshwar Tower Rd, books buses to Rajkot (5.30 am, 2.30 and 10 pm; two hours, Rs 25) and to Ahmedabad (six hours, Rs 70). Pavan Travels (☎ 72-002), on the same road, also has departures to Ahmedabad, as well as to Bombay at 3 pm (20 hours, Rs 200) and to Dwarka at 6 am (2½ hours, Rs 35).

Shivshakti Travels (☎ 70-091), in the basement of the building opposite the bus stand, has departures almost every 15 minutes to Rajkot, as well as services to Junagadh (three hours, Rs 30); Porbandar (2½ hours, Rs 35); and twice-daily departures to Bhuj at 2 and 10 pm (six hours, Rs 70).

Train There are direct trains from Bombay and Ahmedabad via Rajkot. The fare for the 321-km trip to Ahmedabad is Rs 93/275 for a 2nd/1st-class sleeper, or Rs 74/275 on the daytime service. The 813-km trip to Bombay costs Rs 185/552.

To Dwarka, the 132-km journey takes three hours by express train, or a tedious 5½ hours on the daily 'fast passenger' service (Rs 35).

Getting Around

There is no minibus service to the airport, which is a long way out. Auto-rickshaw drivers demand Rs 25. A rickshaw from the bus stand to the Bedi Gate area costs about Rs 7. To the new railway station, about four km north of the city centre, expect to pay about Rs 15.

RAJKOT

Population: 707,000
Telephone Area Code: 0281

This pleasant town was once the capital of the princely state of Saurashtra and is also a former British government headquarters. Mahatma Gandhi spent the early years of his life here while his father was the chief minister, or Diwan, to the Raja of Saurashtra. The Gandhi family home, the Kaba Gandhi no Delo, now houses a permanent exhibition of Gandhi items.

The Rajkumar College dates back to the second half of last century and is regarded as one of the best private schools in the country. It was originally one of five schools set up by the British for the education of the sons of the princely State rulers (*rajkumar* means prince).

Information

Rajkot has a very efficient tourist office

(☎ 34-507), but it's hidden away behind the old State Bank of Saurashtra building on Jawahar Rd, almost opposite the Galaxy Hotel. It's open weekdays and the 1st and 3rd Saturday of the month, from 10.30 am to 6 pm (closed for lunch from 1.30 to 2 pm).

The State Bank of India, to the north of the Jubilee Gardens and on the opposite side of the road, has money-changing facilities. Entry is at the rear of the building.

Watson Museum

The Watson Museum & Library in the Jubilee Gardens commemorates Colonel

John Watson, Political Agent from 1886-89. The entrance is flanked by two imperial lions and among the exhibits are copies of artefacts from Mohenjodaro, 13th-century carvings, silverware, natural history exhibits and textiles as well as dioramas of local tribal costumes and housing styles.

Perhaps the most startling piece is a huge marble statue of Queen Victoria seated on a throne and decidedly not amused – hardly surprising, given that she has to endure the indignity of a brass crown and thumblessly hold an orb and sceptre. The museum is open from 9 am to 5.30 pm (closed between 12.30

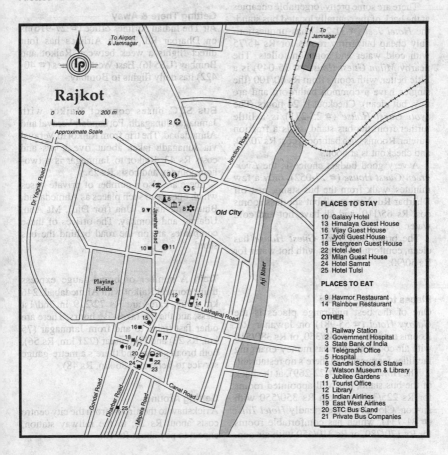

Rajkot

0   100   200 m
Approximate Scale

Old City

Playing Fields

To Airport & Jamnagar

To Jamnagar

PLACES TO STAY

10 Galaxy Hotel
13 Himalaya Guest House
16 Vijay Guest House
17 Jyoti Guest House
18 Evergreen Guest House
22 Hotel Jeel
23 Milan Guest House
24 Hotel Samrat
25 Hotel Tulsi

PLACES TO EAT

9   Havmor Restaurant
14 Rainbow Restaurant

OTHER

1   Railway Station
2   Government Hospital
3   State Bank of India
4   Telegraph Office
5   Hospital
6   Gandhi School & Statue
7   Watson Museum & Library
8   Jubilee Gardens
11 Tourist Office
12 Library
15 Indian Airlines
19 East West Airlines
20 STC Bus S.and
21 Private Bus Companies

GUJARAT

and 1.30 pm), daily except Wednesday. Entry is Rs 0.50.

Places to Stay – bottom end

On Lakhajiraj Rd, the road leading into the heart of the bazaar area, are a number of hotels. The *Himalaya Guest House* (☎ 22-880) is a huge place with basic rooms with bathroom for Rs 50/100 (hot water in buckets). Doubles are very spacious, but the singles are a little dark and pokey. The entrance to this place is right inside the shopping complex over which it stands.

There are some pretty forgettable cheapies at the back of the centrally located bus stand: the *Hotel Jeel* (☎ 31-244) has unquestionably cheap but grimy rooms for Rs 45/75 with cold water and common toilets. The nearby *Milan Guest House* (☎ 35-049) is a little better, with rooms from Rs 60/100 (the singles have a common bathroom and are tiny, but clean). Checkout is 24 hours. The *Jyoti Guest House* (☎ 25-271) is a little further from the bus stand, so is a fraction quieter. Rooms with bathroom cost Rs 70/80, and checkout is at noon.

A very good budget choice is the *Evergreen Guest House* (☎ 27-052), only a few minutes' walk from the bus stand, just off Dharbar Rd. Very small but spotless rooms cost Rs 65/110, and all have hot and cold water.

The brand new *Vijay Guest House* has clean, comfortable rooms with hot water for Rs 50/90.

Places to Stay – middle

One of the best mid-range places is the *Galaxy Hotel* (☎ 55-981) on Jawahar Rd. Rooms cost from Rs 240/360, or Rs 380/510 with air-con. The hotel has money-changing facilities for guests, but there's no restaurant.

The *Hotel Samrat* (☎ 22-269), at the back of the bus stand, has well-appointed rooms for Rs 225/310, or from Rs 350/550 with air-con. Close by is the friendly *Hotel Tulsi* (☎ 31-731), which has comfortable rooms for Rs 170/280, or Rs 310/450 with air-con.

Places to Eat

There's good, cheap south Indian food at the *Rainbow Restaurant* near the Himalaya Guest House. There's an air-con section upstairs. This place has an impressive selection of ice cream with some very imaginative names: see if you can resist 'Thrice Blessed' or 'Nuts in Love'!

The better class *Havmor*, up near the Jubilee Gardens, serves Indian, Chinese and Western food, and the *Samkarand* at the Hotel Samrat is a good, reasonably priced restaurant.

Getting There & Away

Air The Indian Airlines office (☎ 27-916) is on Dharbar Rd. Indian Airlines has four direct flights a week between Rajkot and Bombay (US$46). East West Airlines (☎ 40-422) has daily flights to Bombay.

Bus STC buses connect Rajkot with Jamnagar, Junagadh, Porbandar, Veraval and Ahmedabad. The trip from Rajkot to Veraval via Junagadh takes about five hours and costs Rs 43. Rajkot to Jamnagar is a two-hour journey and costs Rs 25.

There are also a number of private buses which operate to such places as Ahmedabad, Bhuj, Bhavnagar, Una (for Diu), Mt Abu, Udaipur and Bombay. The offices of these companies are on the road behind the bus stand.

Train A number of broad-gauge express trains connect Rajkot with Ahmedabad, 246 km away. Fares are Rs 72/219 in 2nd/1st class, and the trip takes 5½ hours. There are other fast trains to and from Jamnagar (75 km, Rs 23) and Porbandar (221 km, Rs 56), both broad gauge, and there's a metre-gauge service to Veraval (186 km, Rs 48).

Getting Around

A rickshaw to the airport from the city centre costs about Rs 20; to the railway station, expect to pay about Rs 10.

AROUND RAJKOT
Wankaner
Like so many Indian palaces, the palace at Wankaner (☎ (02828) 20-000), about 38 km from Rajkot, has been put to good use as a place to stay. The difference between this place and the palace hotels of Rajasthan is that here guests are accommodated by the royal family, and the place is more a private guest house than a hotel. It was built in 1907 and is an amazing Greco-Roman Gothic Indo Scottish baronial extravagance trapped in a 80-year-old time warp.

As the royal family still live in the palace, guests are accommodated a couple of km away in a building known as the *Oasis House*, a wonderful Art Deco building built in the 1930s, complete with indoor swimming pool. While hardly palatial, the rooms are very comfortable and spacious, and meals are taken at the palace with the family. Rooms cost Rs 1100 per person, including meals.

There are regular buses to Rajkot every half hour, and Wankaner Junction is on the main railway line to Ahmedabad (204 km, Rs 67/189).

Surendranagar (Wadhwan)
This town on the route from Ahmedabad to Rajkot features the very old **Temple of Ranik Devi**, who became involved in a dispute between local rulers Sidh Raja (who planned to marry her) and Rao Khengar (who carried her off and did marry her). When Sidh Raja defeated Rao Khengar, Ranik Devi chose *sati* over dishonour and Sidh Raja built the temple as her memorial.

Tarnetar
Every year in the month of Bhadra (around September), the Trineteshwar Temple at Tarnetar, 65 km north-east of Rajkot, hosts the colourful three-day **Tarnetar Fair**. The fair is most well known for the different *shhatris* (umbrellas) made specifically for the occasion, and as an opportunity to procure a spouse – one of the main functions of the fair is to enable villages from the Bharwad community to form matrimonial alliances.

Prospective candidates are appropriately bedecked in their finery, making this fair an extraordinarily colourful spectacle.

According to legend, Arjuna once danced at this site, and the River Ganges flows into the tank here once a year.

Gondal
On the Rajkot to Porbandar road, south of Rajkot on the River Gondali, is the town of Gondal. Once the centre of a former prosperous princely state, it still has some impressive buildings. The Naulakaha Darbargadh palace (named after the nine lakhs it cost to build) is well worth a look, as is *Riverside Palace*, where you can stay for Rs 1500 including all meals, or Rs 2500 including meals and local sightseeing. The present royal family still has the Maharaja's collection of 30 or so vintage cars, and in the palace railway yard are two dilapidated royal rail carriages.

Kutch (Kachchh)

The westernmost part of Gujarat is virtually an island; indeed, during the monsoon period from May onwards, it really is an island. The Gulf of Kutch divides Kutch from the Kathiawar peninsula while to the north, Kutch is separated from the Sind region of Pakistan by the Great Rann of Kutch.

The salt in the soil makes this low-lying marsh area almost completely barren. Only on scattered 'islands' which rise above the salt level is there vegetation. During the dry season, the Rann is a vast expanse of hard, dried mud. Then, with the start of the monsoon in May, it is flooded first by sea water, then by the fresh water from rivers as they fill. Kutch is also separated from the rest of Gujarat to the east by the Little Rann of Kutch.

During the winter, the Gulf of Kutch is a breeding ground for flamingoes and pelicans. The Asiatic wild ass lives in the Little Rann of Kutch and part of the area has been

GUJARAT

declared a sanctuary for this rare animal. Very few tourists visit this part of India.

BHUJ

Population: 119,000
Telephone Area Code: 02832

Bhuj, the major town of Kutch, is an old walled city – in the past the city gates were locked each night from dusk to dawn. You can lose yourself for hours in the maze-like streets and alleyways of this town. There are walls within walls, crenellated gateways, old palaces with intricately carved wooden pavilions, and brightly decorated Hindu temples.

Bhuj resembles much of India before the tourist invasion, and you're much more likely to come across that disarming hospitality which was once the hallmark of rural India.

Unfortunately if there has been no monsoon, the picturesque lake remains dry.

Information

The tourist office (☎ 20-004), housed in the Aina Mahal, is staffed by the very helpful Mr P J Jethi, who is a mine of information on anything to do with Bhuj and Kutch. It is possible to arrange a guide (Rs 300 per day) through the tourist office. Ask Mr Jethi for details. The office is open daily except Saturday from 9 am to noon, and 3 to 6 pm.

Changing money in Bhuj is a big problem. The only bank which offers money-changing facilities is the State Bank of India on Station Rd; however, it *only* changes Thomas Cook travellers' cheques (weekdays, from noon to 3 pm). The Hotel Prince will change travellers' cheques for their guests.

If you feel the need for a refreshing dip, there's a swimming pool at the Lakeview Restaurant, at the south end of the lake. It's sparkling clean, and is open to the public from 7 to 10 am, and 2.45 to 5.45 pm (Rs 10 for 45 minutes).

The GPO is about a five-minute auto-rickshaw ride from the bus stand. There is a branch in Dharbar Gadh, in the walled city.

Permits To visit the villages north of Kutch,

including Khavda, Bhirandiara and Dumaro, permission is required from the District Collector. First you need to present yourself (in person) at the District Superintendent of Police (DSP) office, where you have to complete a form advising which villages you wish to visit, dates, your passport details, etc. You then take this form to the District Collector's office (about five minutes' walk; open weekdays, 10.30 am to 5.30 pm, closed for lunch between 1 and 2 pm), where the form will be authorised and signed. The whole procedure should take no more than 1½ hours, and there is no fee.

Aina Mahal (Old Palace)

Maharao Lakhpatji's old palace, built in traditional Kutchi style, is in a small fortified courtyard in the old part of the city. It's a beautifully presented museum and is one of the highlights of a visit to Bhuj. The entrance to the palace houses the tourist office, and this is also the site of the **Maharao Sinh Madansinhji Museum**, which has a varied collection of paintings, photos and embroideries. There's a 15-metre long scroll depicting the Royal Procession of the Maharao Shri Pragmalji Bahadur (1838-75). Check out the expression on the last blue-turbanned figure on this epic painting – he looks quite peeved at having to ignobly bring up the rear of the procession!

The real attraction here, though, is the **Hall of Mirrors**, created by the master artisan, Ram Singh Malam, under the patronage of his poet-ruler, Maharao Shri Lakhpatji around the middle of the 18th century. A blend of Indian and European artistry (Ram Singh acquired his skills in Europe), the walls of the great hall are of white marble covered by mirrors separated by gilded ornaments, lighting being provided by elaborate candelabra, with shades of Venetian glass. The most remarkable feature, however, is a **pleasure pool**, in the middle of which rises a square platform where the maharao composed his poems and gave full encouragement to the classical arts of dancing girls, bards and musicians.

This palace is well worth half a day, and

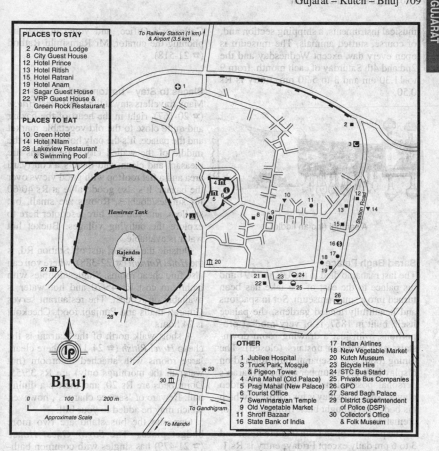

PLACES TO STAY

2 Annapurna Lodge
8 City Guest House
12 Hotel Prince
13 Hotel Ritish
15 Hotel Ratrani
19 Hotel Anam
21 Sagar Guest House
22 VRP Guest House &
 Green Rock Restaurant

PLACES TO EAT

10 Green Hotel
14 Hotel Nilam
28 Lakeview Restaurant
 & Swimming Pool

Hamirsar Tank

Rajendra
Park

Bhuj

0   100   200 m

Approximate Scale

To Railway Station (1 km)
& Airport (3.5 km)

Station Road

To Gandhigram

To Mandvi

OTHER

1 Jubilee Hospital
3 Truck Park, Mosque
 & Pigeon Tower
4 Aina Mahal (Old Palace)
5 Prag Mahal (New Palace)
6 Tourist Office
7 Swaminarayan Temple
9 Old Vegetable Market
11 Shroff Bazaar
16 State Bank of India

17 Indian Airlines
18 New Vegetable Market
20 Kutch Museum
23 Bicycle Hire
24 STC Bus Stand
25 Private Bus Companies
26 GPO
27 Sarad Bagh Palace
29 District Superintendent
 of Police (DSP)
30 Collector's Office
 & Folk Museum

is open from 9 am to noon and 3 to 6 pm;
closed on Saturdays. Entry is Rs 3.

Prag Mahal (New Palace)
Across the courtyard from the Aina Mahal is
the new palace, an ornate Italianate marble
and sandstone building which was constructed in the latter part of the 19th century.
Parts of it are now used for government
offices but the vast and amazingly kitsch
Darbar Hall and the **clock tower** are open to
the public. High up on the walls of this
unfurnished hall are portraits of past
maharaos, while down below is the usual

mausoleum of big game driven to the verge
of extinction by egotism and pompous stu-
pidity. Entry is Rs 4.

Kutch Museum
The Kutch Museum was originally known as
the Fergusson Museum after its founder, Sir
James Fergusson, a governor of Bombay
under the British Raj. Built in 1877, it's the
oldest museum in Gujarat and has an excellent collection. The well-maintained exhibits
(labelled in English and Gujarati) include a
picture gallery, an anthropological section,
archaeological finds, textiles, weapons,

musical instruments, a shipping section and, of course, stuffed animals. The museum is open every day, except Wednesday and the 2nd and 4th Saturday of each month, from 9 to 11.30 am and 3 to 5.30 pm. Entry is Rs 0.50.

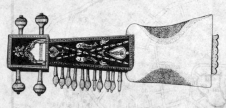

A sarangi (Indian fiddle)

Sarad Bagh Palace

The last maharao died in the UK in 1991 and his palace to the east of the lake has been turned into a small museum. Set in spacious and beautifully tended gardens, the palace itself, built in 1867, is of very modest proportions, with just a drawing room downstairs and bedroom upstairs (closed). The dining room is in a separate building and on display here are a number of the maharao's personal possessions, including his video player. Also on display is his coffin, in which his body was brought back from the UK for cremation!

The palace is open from 9 am to noon and 3 to 6 pm daily except Friday; entry is Rs 1.

Other Attractions

A huge old wall stretches around the hills overlooking the city. Unfortunately, you cannot explore as this is all a restricted military area.

The very colourful and richly decorated **Swaminarayan Temple** is near the Aina Mahal. It's open to the public from 7 to 11 am and 4 to 7 pm.

The **Bhartiya Sanscruti Darshan Kutch** (Folk Museum) houses an interesting private collection of beautiful textiles and artefacts, and also has reconstructions of typical village habitats. The museum is close to the Collector's Office, and you can visit by phoning the curator, Mr Ramsinjhi Rathod (☎ 21-518).

Places to Stay – bottom end

Many travellers stay at the *City Guest House* (☎ 20-167), right in the heart of the bazaar and quite close to the old vegetable market and the palace. It's the only hotel right in the middle of the walled city. The rooms are pleasant and clean, and there's a courtyard area and a flat rooftop with good views over the bazaar. It's also good value at Rs 40/60 for singles/doubles. Rooms are small, but spotless, and you can hire a scooter here to explore the outlying villages. Bucket hot water is available.

Outside the bazaar, just off Station Rd, is the *Hotel Ratrani* (☎ 22-388), where you can also find cheap rooms. Singles/doubles with bathroom cost Rs 45/70 and hot water is available on request. The restaurant serves Gujarati thalis and Punjabi food. Checkout is 24 hours.

A short walk north of the Ratrani is the cheap *Hotel Ritish* (☎ 24-117) where clean, large rooms with attached bathroom (hot water in the mornings only) are Rs 35/55. Dorm beds are Rs 20, and there's a dining hall. Beware of 'service charges', however, which may be added to your bill.

Opposite the bus stand are two more budget places. The *Sagar Guest House* (☎ 21-479) has singles with common bathroom for Rs 30, and rooms with attached bathroom for Rs 50/70/100. There's a dorm (10 beds) for Rs 20 per person. The rooms are right above the street, so could be noisy. Around the corner, the *VRP Guest House* (☎ 21-388) has rooms with attached bathroom for Rs 55/80. This place is clean, quiet, and the rooms are quite sizeable. Checkout is 24 hours. The hotel sign is in Gujarati.

Up near the truck park is the very friendly *Annapurna Lodge* (☎ 20-831). Very cheap rooms with common bathroom are Rs 35/50, or with attached bathroom, Rs 45/60. This is not exactly the quietest area in town, but this place is quite good value.

Places to Stay – middle

The good value *Hotel Anam* (☎ 21-390), on Station Rd, has a range of spotless rooms, all with bathroom and constant hot water, for Rs 130/250, or Rs 380/500 with air-con.

The *Hotel Prince* (☎ 20-370), also on Station Rd, is equally good but a bit pricey. Singles/doubles cost Rs 225/275, or Rs 450/550 with air-con, and a good non-veg restaurant. There are money-changing facilities for guests. Checkout is at noon.

Places to Eat

You can get an excellent cheap breakfast (omelette and toast plus tea or coffee) from the *Omlet Center*, in the line of shops outside the bus stand.

The restaurant at the *Hotel Anam* and the *Green Rock* restaurant in the same building as the VRP Lodge are both excellent places for an all-you-can-eat Gujarati thali.

The *Hotel Prince* has both veg and non-veg dishes, and is quite reasonably priced. Opposite the Prince, the *Hotel Nilam* is an excellent vegetarian restaurant, specialising in Punjabi and Chinese cuisine.

The nearest restaurant to the City Guest House is the *Green Hotel*, down a small alley opposite the old vegetable market. It offers cheap vegetarian meals and snacks.

Things to Buy

If you are genuinely interested in the embroidery from villages in the Kutch region, get in touch with Mr A A Wazir (☎ 24-187, or contact the tourist office). He has a priceless collection of over 3000 pieces, many of them very old, which he has gathered over the last 20 years or so. Some pieces are for sale (with prices starting at around Rs 200 and peaking at Rs 20,000).

The Uday Store, in the Shroff Bazaar, has ready-made fabric and old embroidery.

Getting There & Away

Air The Indian Airlines office (☎ 21-433) is open daily from 11 am to 1 pm and 1.45 to 6 pm. There are four flights weekly to Bombay (US$62). As the Indian Air Force has a base at the airport, there is tight security there.

Bus The private bus companies have their offices in the bus stand area, and have services to Rajkot (six hours, Rs 60), Bombay (18 hours, Rs 250), Ahmedabad (seven hours, Rs 80 for a seat, or Rs 100 for a berth – yes, sleeper coaches!), and other areas in Gujarat. Patel Tours, Sahjanand Tours and M K Tours can all book sleeper coaches.

STC buses run to Jaisalmer in Rajasthan via Rathapur and Tarada (15 hours, Rs 163). For other places in Rajasthan, such as Abu Rd, Ajmer and Jaipur, you'll need to get a bus to Palanpur, and a second bus from there.

There are regular departures to the villages of Kutch; see under Around Bhuj for details.

Train New Bhuj railway station is one km north of town along a very rough little back road from the north gate of the old town. It is possible to travel to Ahmedabad via Palanpur (491 km, 16 hours, Rs 128/382), but it's quicker to get a train or bus to Gandhidham to connect with the overnight *Gandhidham-Kutch Express* (300 km, seven hours). The total rail fare ex Bhuj is Rs 99/296.

To book a ticket, it is not necessary to go out to the railway station. For Rs 15, Hemal Travels (☎ 22-491), near the bus stand, will make the necessary reservations.

Share Taxi A share taxi to Mandvi is Rs 20. They leave from the STC stand.

Getting Around

An auto-rickshaw to the railway station costs Rs 15, and to the airport, at least Rs 25. From Darbar Gadh to the bus stand shouldn't cost more than Rs 6.

There are places renting bicycles along the road outside the bus stand. Scooters such as Vespas and Honda Heroes can be hired from the City Guest House or from the scooter hire shop close to the bus stand. However, they're not cheap, at Rs 200 per day, though you may be able to negotiate a discount for a longer rental.

GUJARAT

AROUND BHUJ
Gandhidham
Population: 113,000
Telephone Area Code: 02836

The new town of Gandhidham, near Kandala, was established to take refugees from the Sind following Partition. The town has nothing of interest, but if you are stuck here for a night, there's the *Hotel Natraj* (☎ 21-955), opposite the bus stand, with rooms from Rs 120/160, and the *Hotel Gokul* (☎ 20-068), with rooms from Rs 180/250, about 300 metres away.

The bus stand is about 200 metres diagonally to your right when leaving the railway station. Buses to Bhuj leave every 30 minutes (1½ hours, Rs 15).

Kutch Villages

The villages of the Kutch region each specialise in a different form of handicraft, and it would be easy to spend a week visiting some of them using Bhuj as a base. Due to their proximity to the Pakistan border, to visit the villages north of Bhuj you will require a permit signed by the Bhuj District Collector. See under Bhuj for details.

Some of the more important villages, and the crafts they specialise in include Bhujjodi (wool and cotton weaving), Padhar and Dhaneti (Ahir embroidery), Dhamanka (block printing), Lilpur (embroidery) and Anjar (nut-crackers, block printing and tie-dyeing).

Dholavira is a little village on a small 'island' north-east of Bhuj. Here archaeologists have unearthed a city belonging to the Harappan (Indus Valley) civilisation.

For more information on the area, contact Mr Jethi, the supervisor of the Bhuj tourist office.

Places to Stay Accommodation in the villages is predictably limited. Lilpur has a *Gandhi Ashram*, where you can stay for around Rs 60 per night including meals. Anjar village also has a couple of basic guest houses.

Getting There & Away There are buses to Anjar every 30 minutes from the bus stand in Bhuj. To Lilpur, there is one direct bus at 6.30 am, or you can take one of the many buses to Rapar and get another bus from there. Alternatively, ask the driver on the bus to Rapar to drop you off at the turn-off to Lilpur, and walk the three km to the village.

Than Monastery

About 60 km from Bhuj, at the base of the Dhinodar Hill, a good area for trekking, is the Than Monastery. Visitors are welcome, and accommodation and meals are provided

---

Vernu

In Vernu, a tiny village with only 600 inhabitants on the southern edge of the Great Rann of Kutch, a self-imposed state of perpetual mourning has become a way of life. The villagers have been in mourning for over 250 years – ever since Venu Parmar, a Rajput chieftain, died fighting to protect the village from cattle thieves. In this village, cattle are not decorated, and festivals are conducted without the usual elaborate decorative touches such as garlands which make these events so colourful in other villages in this region. Even marriages are celebrated in distant villages, so as not to instil this sombre village with a spirit of gaiety or revelry. To do so would be to show disrespect to the soul of the brave Venu.

A temple in the village dedicated to the chieftain is believed to bring death to those who sleep in it. The untimely demise of Captain James McMurdo, the first British resident of Kutch, who failed to heed local advice – only to be found dead in the temple the next morning – confirms the villagers' belief in its fatal powers.

Venu was the younger brother of the Thakur of Muli, ruler of a princely state in Saurashtra. Learning of the plight of a group of villagers 70 km distant who had been the victims of repeated acts of cattle theft by local dacoits (bandits or robbers), Venu valiantly went to their aid, and the battle which ensued, and in which Venu lost his life, is today the site of the village which bears his name ('Vernu' is a corruption of the warrior's name). According to legend, the indefatigable Venu lost his head at the site on which the temple dedicated to him stands today, but his body continued fighting until it dropped, four km distant! ■

Dharamanath

Indian saints and sadhus are renowned for the lengths to which they will go in their quests to attain spiritual salvation. From standing on nails to sealing themselves in caves for decades, acts of self-mortification seem limited only by the practitioner's imagination.

One of these spiritual warriors was Dharamanath, who journeyed to Kutch to find a tranquil spot in which to practise penance. He settled himself under a tree near Raipur and, whilst focussing on matters spiritual, depended on the people of Raipur to attend to his material needs. However, the Raipurians were not exactly forthcoming so, in a fit of rage, Dharamanath invoked a curse upon them. The city became desolate and its inhabitants hastily removed themselves to Mandvi. Dharamanath, overcome by remorse, resolved to climb the highest hill he could find, there to engage in a penance commensurate with his vengeful act. After being rejected by two hills, which refused to carry the burden of his guilt, he climbed *backwards* up a third hill – Dhinodar – and there proceeded to stand on his head – for 12 years. The gods, concerned at this excess, pleaded with Dharamanath to cease his penance. Dharamanath acceded – on condition that wherever his gaze fell, that region should become barren. Casting his gaze before him, the seas receded, leaving a barren, desolate wasteland – the Great Rann of Kutch.

On the highest peak of Dhinodar, a small shrine dedicated to Dharamanath contains a red besmeared stone, which allegedly bore the head of the inverted ascetic during his extraordinary act of penance. ■

at the *dharamsala* (by donation). Permission is required from the District Collector in Bhuj to visit this area. To get there, take a bus to Nakatrana, west of Bhuj, and then another bus to Than. You will have to walk the last three km to the monastery, which is at the end of the road.

MANDVI

Population: 39,600
Telephone Area Code: 02834

Sixty km south-west of Bhuj, Mandvi is being promoted as a beach resort, and locals reckon its beaches are comparable with the best of those at Diu. It was once a walled port town famous for shipbuilding.

Places to Stay & Eat

The *Government Guest House* is two km out of town and costs Rs 100 for a double. More basic accommodation is available at either the *Vinayak Guest House* (Rs 30), or the *Shital Guest House* (Rs 50). The *Vijay Villas Palace* (☎ 20-043), about eight km from Mandvi and 10 minutes from a good beach, has five large, clean double rooms for Rs

250. A thali is served at dinner (order in advance), for Rs 40.

Zorba the Buddha, in the heart of the city, also has good thalis.

Getting There & Away

Buses leave for Mandvi from the bus stand in Bhuj every 30 minutes. A share taxi from the bus stand to Mandvi costs Rs 20.

A hovercraft service has been slated between Mandvi and Dwarka, on the western tip of the Kathiawar peninsula. If this service does get up and running, it will reduce the 11-hour trip by road to a speedy 2½-hour crossing.

LITTLE RANN OF KUTCH

Access to the Little Rann of Kutch, home of the last remaining population of khur (Asiatic wild ass) in India, is possible from either Bhuj or Ahmedabad. As a number of tours depart from Ahmedabad to this region, information has been included in the Around Ahmedabad section of this chapter. Contact the Forest Office (☎ (02832) 22-753) in Bhuj to arrange trips to the Little Rann from Bhuj.

Madhya Pradesh

Madhya Pradesh is India's largest state and the geographical heartland of the country. Most of the state is a high plateau and in summer it can be very dry and hot. Virtually all phases of Indian history have left their mark on Madhya Pradesh, historically known as Malwa. There are still many pre-Aryan Gond and Bhil tribal people in the state, but Madhya Pradesh is overwhelmingly Indo-Aryan with the majority of the people speaking Hindi and following Hinduism.

Some of Madhya Pradesh's attractions are remote and isolated: Khajuraho, in the north of the state, is a long way from anywhere and most easily visited when travelling between Agra and Varanasi; Jabalpur, with its marble rocks, is in the centre of the state; Kanha National Park, famous for its tigers, is 170 km south-east of Jabalpur.

Most of the state's other attractions are on or near the main Delhi to Bombay railway line. From Agra, just outside the state to the north, you can head south through Gwalior (with its magnificent fort), Sanchi, Bhopal, Ujjain, Indore and Mandu. From there you can head west to Gujarat or south to the Ajanta and Ellora caves in Maharashtra.

Madhya Pradesh constitutes part of what is known as the Hindi belt, a region of northern India inhabited predominantly by Hindus. Politically it is dominated, not surprisingly, by the Hindu fundamentalist BJP. State elections were held in late 1993, after the state assembly was dissolved by the

Population: 73 million
Area: 443,446 sq km
Capital: Bhopal
People per sq km: 165
Main Language: Hindi
Literacy Rate: 43%
Best Time to Go: September to February

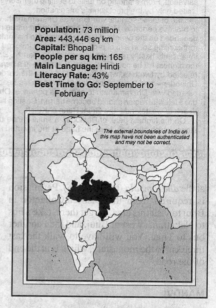

The external boundaries of India on this map have not been authenticated and may not be correct.

central government following the demolition of the disputed mosque at Ayodyha. While the BJP was returned to power, the Congress Party managed to gain some ground.

History

The history of Madhya Pradesh goes back to the time of Ashoka, the great Buddhist

---

Diwali Celebrations in Madhya Pradesh

In the village of Kanasia I witnessed Diwali. There was a parade in which at least 90% of the village of 5000 was either a participant or spectator. The village cows were decorated in the most outrageous splendour conceivable – you think Cher is gaudy? They were painted, wore garlands of flowers and enough tinsel to make a closer look necessary to confirm it was a cow. It was the closest thing I saw to a Christmas tree. There were cow-dung sculptures of the mountain that Lord Krishna raised with his finger and, strangest of all was the ritual to re-enact the battle in which cows fought for Lord Krishna.

Peter Christensen, Canada

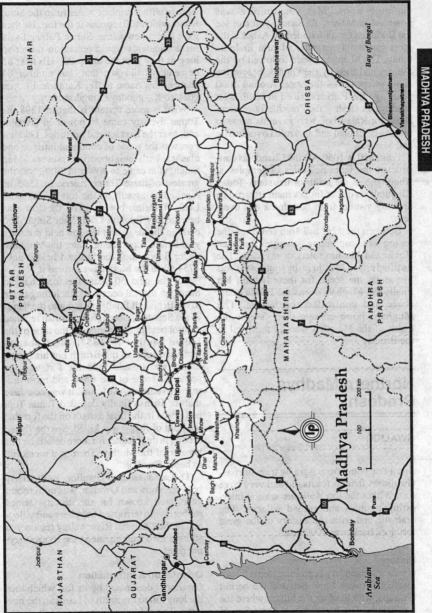

MADHYA PRADESH

Madhya Pradesh

emperor whose Mauryan Empire was powerful in Malwa. At Sanchi you can see the Buddhist centre founded by Ashoka, the most important reminder of him in India today. The Mauryans were followed by the Sungas and then by the Guptas, before the Huns swept across the state. Around 1000 years ago the Parmaras ruled in south-west Madhya Pradesh – they're chiefly remembered for Raja Bhoj, who gave his name to the city of Bhopal and also ruled over Indore and Mandu.

From 950 to 1050 AD the Chandelas constructed the fantastic series of temples at Khajuraho in the north of the state. Today Khajuraho is one of India's main attractions, drawing visitors from both India and overseas.

Between the 12th and 16th centuries, the region saw continuing struggles between Hindu and Muslim rulers or invaders. The fortified city of Mandu in the south-west was frequently the scene for these battles, but finally the Mughals overcame Hindu resistance and controlled the region. The Mughals, however, met their fate at the hands of the Marathas who, in turn, fell to the British.

Northern Madhya Pradesh

GWALIOR

Population: 780,000
Telephone Area Code: 0751

Just a few hours from Agra by train or road, Gwalior is famous for its old and very large fort. Within the fort walls are several interesting temples and ruined palaces. The dramatic and colourful history of the great fort goes back over 1000 years.

History

Gwalior's legendary beginning stems from a meeting between Suraj Sen and the hermit Gwalipa, who lived on the hilltop where the fort stands. The hermit cured Suraj Sen of leprosy with a drink of water from the Suraj Kund, which still remains in the fort. He then gave him a new name, Suhan Pal, and said his descendants would remain in power so long as they kept the name Pal. His next 83 descendants did just that, but number 84 changed his name to Tej Karan and – you guessed it – goodbye kingdom.

What is more certain is that in 1398 the Tomar dynasty came to power in Gwalior and, over the next several centuries, Gwalior Fort was the scene of continual intrigue and clashes with neighbouring powers. Man Singh, who came to power in 1486, was the greatest of these Tomar rulers. In 1505 he repelled an assault on the fort by Sikandar Lodi of Delhi, but in 1516 the fort was besieged by Ibrahim Lodi. Man Singh died early in the siege, but his son held out for a year before capitulating. Later the Mughals, under Babur, took the fort and held it until 1754 when the Marathas captured it.

For the next 50 years the fort changed hands on several occasions, including twice to the British. It finally passed into the hands of the Scindias, although the British retained control behind the scenes. At the time of the Indian Mutiny in 1857, the maharaja remained loyal to the British but his troops didn't, and in mid-1858 the fort was the scene for some of the final, and most dramatic, events of the Mutiny. It was near here that the British finally defeated Tantia Topi and it was in the final assault on the fort that the Rani of Jhansi was killed. See the Jhansi section in this chapter for more details on this heroine of the Mutiny. There is a memorial to her in Gwalior.

The area around Gwalior, particularly between Agra and Gwalior, was until recent years well known for the dacoits (armed robbers) who terrorised travellers and villagers. In the Chambal River valley region you still see men walking along the roads carrying rifles.

Orientation & Information

Gwalior is dominated by its fort which tops the long hill to the north of Lashkar, the new town. The old town clings to the hill, north-east of the fort. The main market area, the Jayaji Chowk, is Lashkar's hub. Gwalior is a big place and everything is very spread out.

The tourist office (☎ 34-2606) is in the Hotel Tansen, about half a km south-east of the railway station.

Fort

Rising 100 metres above the town, the fort hill is about three km in length. Its width varies from nearly a km to less than 200 metres. The walls, which encircle almost the entire hilltop, are 10 metres high and imposingly solid. Beneath them, the hill face

is a sheer drop away to the plains. On a clear day the view from the fort walls is superb: over old Gwalior at the north-eastern end and far across the plains.

You can approach the fort from the south or the north-east. The north-eastern path starts from the archaeological museum and follows a wide, winding slope to the doors of the Man Singh Palace (Man Mandir). The southern entrance (Urbai Gate) is a long, gradual ascent by road, passing cliff-face Jain sculptures.

The climb can be sweaty work in the hot season. A taxi or auto-rickshaw up the

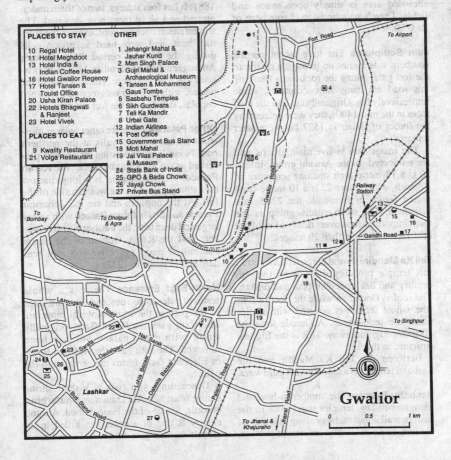

PLACES TO STAY
10 Regal Hotel
11 Hotel Meghdoot
13 Hotel India & Indian Coffee House
16 Hotel Gwalior Regency
17 Hotel Tansen & Touist Office
20 Usha Kiran Palace
22 Hotels Bhagwati & Ranjeet
23 Hotel Vivek

PLACES TO EAT
9 Kwality Restaurant
21 Volga Restaurant

OTHER
1 Jehangir Mahal & Jauhar Kund
2 Man Singh Palace
3 Gujri Mahal & Archaeological Museum
4 Tansen & Mohammed Gaus Tombs
5 Sasbahu Temples
6 Sikh Gurdwara
7 Teli Ka Mandir
8 Urbai Gate
12 Indian Airlines
14 Post Office
15 Government Bus Stand
18 Moti Mahal
19 Jai Vilas Palace & Museum
24 State Bank of India
25 GPO & Bada Chowk
26 Jayaji Chowk
27 Private Bus Stand

Gwalior

0   0.5   1 km

MADHYA PRADESH

southern road is probably the easiest way in. You can then walk down from the palace to the museum when you've looked around the fort. If you're walking both ways then it's better to go the other way: in at the north-east and out at the south. No refreshments are available in the fort, so come prepared in summer.

Check at the gates to see if the sound & light show is operating, as it's worth a look. Indian megastar Amitabh Bachchan is the narrator.

There are several things to see in and around the fort, although most of the enclosed area is simply open space and fields. There's an admission charge here of Rs 0.20.

Jain Sculptures The long ascent on the southern side climbs up through a ravine to the fort gate. Along the rock faces flanking this road are many Jain sculptures, some impressively big. Originally cut into the cliff faces in the mid-1400s, they were defaced by the forces of Babur in 1527 but were later repaired.

The images are in five main groups and are numbered. In the Arwahi group, image 20 is a 17-metre-high standing sculpture of Adinath, while image 22 is a 10-metre-high seated figure of Nemnath, the 22nd Jain tirthankar. The south-eastern group is the most important and covers nearly a km of the cliff face with more than 20 images.

Teli Ka Mandir Beyond the Suraj Kund tank, this temple probably dates from the 9th century and has a peculiar plan and design. The roof is Dravidian while the decorations (the whole temple is covered with sculptures) are Indo-Aryan. A Garuda tops the 10-metre-high doorway. This is the highest structure in the fort.

Between the Teli Ka Mandir and the Sasbahu temples is a modern Sikh gurdwara.

Sasbahu Temples The 'mother-in-law' and 'daughter-in-law' temples stand close to the eastern wall about midway along that side of the fort. The two temples are similar in style,

and date from the 9th to 11th centuries. The larger temple has an ornately carved base and figures of Vishnu over the entrances, and four huge pillars carry the heavy roof.

Man Singh Palace The palace, a delightfully whimsical building, is also known as the Chit Mandir or Painted Palace because of the tiled and painted decorations of ducks, elephants and peacocks. Painted blue, with hints of green and gold, it still looks very good today.

The palace was built by Man Singh between 1486 and 1516, and was repaired in 1881. It has four storeys, two of them underground and all of them now deserted. The subterranean ones are cool, even in the summer heat, and were used as prison cells during the Mughal period. The Emperor Aurangzeb had his brother Murad imprisoned and executed here. The east face of the palace, with its six towers topped by domed cupolas, stands over the fort entrance path.

Other Palaces There are other palaces clustered within the fort walls at the northern end. None is as interesting or as well preserved as the Man Singh Palace. The **Karan Palace**, or Kirti Mandir, is a long, narrow two-storey palace on the western side of the fort. At the northern end are the **Jehangir Palace** and **Shah Jahan Palace** with a very large and deep tank, the **Jauhar Kund**. It was here that the Rajput women of the harem committed mass *sati* after the raja was defeated in battle in 1232.

North-East Entrance There is a whole series of gates as you descend the worn steps of the path to the archaeological museum. The sixth gate, the **Hawa Gate**, originally stood within the palace but has been removed. The fifth gate, the **Hathiya Paur**, or Elephant Gate, forms the entrance to the palace.

Descending, you pass a Vishnu shrine dating from 876 AD known as **Chatarbhuj Mandir**, Shrine of the Four-Armed. A tomb nearby is that of a nobleman killed in an assault on this gate in 1518. From here a series of steps lead to some rock-cut Jain and Hindu **sculptures** at the north-east of the fort. They are not as impressive as the sculptures on the southern side.

The interesting fourth gate was built in the 1400s and named after the elephant-headed god, Ganesh. There is a small pigeon house or **Kabutar Khana** here, as well as a small four-pillared **Hindu temple** to the hermit Gwalipa, after whom the fort and town were named.

The third gate dates from the same period as the Gujri Mahal and is known as the **Badalgarh**, after Badal Singh, Man Singh's uncle, or as the Hindola Gate after a swing, or *hindol*, which used to stand here. The second gate, the Bansur, or Archer's Gate, has disappeared. The first gate is the **Alamgiri Gate**, dating from 1660. It was named after Aurangzeb, who took the title of Governor of Alamgiri in this region.

Archaeological Museum The museum is within the Gujri Mahal palace. Built in the 15th century by Man Singh for his favourite queen, Mrignayni, the palace is now rather deteriorated. There's a large collection of Hindu and Jain sculptures and copies of the Bagh Caves' frescoes. It's open from 10 am to 5 pm daily except Monday; admission is Rs 2 plus Rs 2 for a camera.

Jai Vilas Palace & Museum
Located in the new town, which actually dates from 1809, this was the palace of the Scindia family. Although the current maharaja still lives in the palace, a large part of it is now a museum. It's full of the bizarre items Hollywood maharajas are supposed to collect, such as Belgian cut-glass furniture (including a rocking chair), and what looks like half the tiger population of India, all shot, stuffed and moth-eaten. Modes of transport range from a Rolls Royce on rails to a German bubble car. Then there's a little room full of erotica, including a life-sized marble statue of Leda having her way with a swan. But the *pièce de résistance* is a model railway that carried brandy and cigars around the dining table after dinner.

The main durbar hall is quite impressive. The gold paint used around the room is said to weigh 58 kg, and the two giant chandeliers are incredible; they each hold 248 candles, are 12.5 metres high and weigh 3.5 tonnes apiece, so heavy that elephants were suspended from the ceiling to check that it could take the weight.

If you go there by auto-rickshaw, get dropped off at the museum, not at the palace entrance as the two are far apart. The museum is open daily, except Monday, from 10 am to 5 pm; entry is Rs 30 and photography is prohibited.

Old Town
The old town of Gwalior lies to the north and north-east of the fort hill. The 1661 **Jama Masjid** is a fine old building, constructed of sandstone quarried from the fort hill. On the eastern side of town is the fine **tomb of Mohammed Gaus**, a Muslim saint who played a key role in Babur's acquisition of the fort. It has hexagonal towers at its four corners, and a dome which was once covered with glazed blue tiles. It's a very good example of early Mughal architecture.

Close to the large tomb is the smaller **tomb of Tansen**, a singer much admired by Akbar. Chewing the leaves of the tamarind tree near his grave is supposed to do wonders for your voice, although some years ago some enthusiasts got somewhat carried away and ate the whole tree – roots and all! It is a place of pilgrimage for musicians during December/January. To find it, follow the Fort Rd from the north-eastern gate for about 15 minutes and turn right onto a small road.

The **Moti Mahal** is an imposing edifice. It was formerly a palace, but these days it's government offices.

Places to Stay – bottom end
The cheapest good places are near Bada Chowk in Lashkar, several km from the station. The *Hotel Bhagwati* on Nai Sarak is excellent value with rooms with attached bathroom for Rs 35/60 and good views of the fort from the terrace, but no English is

spoken here. Next door the *Ranjeet Hotel* has rooms with common bathroom for Rs 50/80.

The *Regal Hotel* has little to offer apart from the great fort views from its roof terrace. There's a range of rooms from Rs 75/100 with common bathroom to doubles with bathroom and air-cooler for Rs 200 and some air-con rooms. The restaurant is reasonable and you can get a beer here.

A better bet perhaps is the *Hotel Vivek* (☎ 27-016), near Bada Chowk. Air-cooled rooms with attached bath cost Rs 100/150, or with air-con Rs 300/350.

The best of the places near the station is the *Hotel India* (☎ 34-1983) which has singles/doubles with attached bath from Rs 85/120. Air-coolers are available for Rs 30, or there are air-con rooms for Rs 270/320. It's run by the Indian Coffee Workers' Cooperative whose coffee houses you see in many Indian towns. There's one here too, staffed as usual by waiters in starched fan-shaped headgear.

Places to Stay – middle & top end
Beside the Indian Airlines office, the *Hotel Meghdoot* (☎ 32-6148) is a gloomy place with scruffy air-cooled rooms from Rs 200/250 and some air-con rooms at Rs 300/350, all with attached bath and TV.

MP Tourism's *Hotel Tansen* (☎ 34-0370) is pleasantly situated in a shady area about one km from the station. It's not bad value at Rs 225/275 for air-cooled singles/doubles, or Rs 440/490 with air-con.

The centrally air-conditioned *Hotel Gwalior Regency* (☎ 34-0670) has rooms for Rs 300/400. Non-guests can use the health club and jacuzzi for Rs 100 and the swimming pool for Rs 25.

Gwalior's top hotel is the *Usha Kiran Palace* (☎ 32-3213). Set in a garden behind the Jai Vilas Palace, it was (as the name suggests) once a palace. It's not cheap at Rs 1000/1700, but it's cool and quiet.

Places to Eat
The *Indian Coffee House* at the Hotel India is a good cheap place with masala dosas for Rs 6 and other vegetarian snacks.

For a cheap vegetarian thali (Rs 13), the *refreshment room* at the railway station is OK, and you may well be asked to sign the visitors' book!

Near the Usha Kiran Palace is the *Volga Restaurant*. There's nothing Russian about it, but very good Indian food is served. Main dishes are around Rs 35. The restaurant at the *Usha Kiran Palace* is expensive (main dishes are Rs 60 to Rs 90) but the Indian dishes here are good.

Getting There & Away
Air Indian Airlines (☎ 28-533) has a twice-weekly flight from Delhi (US$33) through Gwalior to Bhopal (US$39), Indore (US$55) and Bombay (US$103) which also returns from Bombay through the same cities.

Bus From the government bus stand there are regular services to Agra (Rs 30, three hours), Jhansi (Rs 28, three hours), Shivpuri (Rs 30, three hours) and Ujjain, Indore, Bhopal and Jabalpur. There's one bus in the morning to Khajuraho (Rs 65, nine hours). There are also departures from the private bus stand in Lashkar.

Train Gwalior is on the main Delhi to Bombay railway line with connections to most places. The superfast *Shatabdi Express* links Gwalior with Delhi (3¼ hours, Rs 300/600 in 2nd/1st class), Agra (1¼ hours, Rs 140/280), Jhansi (one hour, Rs 130/260) and Bhopal (4½ hours, Rs 325/650). If you've got the money but not the time you could use this reliable service for a day trip to Gwalior from Agra.

On other express trains it's five hours to Delhi (317 km, Rs 74/267 in 2nd/1st), two hours to Agra (118 km, Rs 30/126), 12 hours to Indore (652 km, Rs 158/473) and 24 hours to Bombay (1225 km, Rs 237/757).

Getting Around
To/From the Airport To or from the airport taxis charge at least Rs 120; auto-rickshaws are cheaper.

Auto-Rickshaw & Tempo Auto-rickshaw

drivers use their meters without too much persuading. The tempos are good and run fixed routes around the city; the fare is Rs 3 from the railway station to Bada Chowk, the main square in Lashkar.

AROUND GWALIOR
Shivpuri
The old summer capital of the Scindias was at Shivpuri, 114 km south-west of Gwalior and 94 km west of Jhansi. Set in formal gardens, the **chhatris** (tombs) are the main attraction here. With Mughal pavilions and *sikhara* spires these beautiful memorials to the Scindia rulers are inlaid in *pietra dura* style, like the Taj Mahal. The chhatri of Madho Rao Scindia faces his mother's chhatri across the tank.

Nearby is **Madhav National Park**, essentially a deer park. On the edge of the park is the Sakhya Sagar lake. Swimming from the old boat club pier here might not be wise as there are crocodiles in the lake.

The road from Gwalior passes through **Narwar**, with its large old fort.

Places to Stay MP Tourism's *Chinkara Motel* (☎ (07492) 2297) in Shivpuri has singles/doubles at Rs 180/240. On the main road right in the middle of town, the *Harish Lodge* has cheaper rooms and a restaurant. The *Tourist Village* (☎ (07492) 2600) is near Bhadaiya Kund and has comfortable rooms in attractive cottages for Rs 250/350, more with air-con.

Towards Agra
Between Gwalior and Agra, actually in a part of Rajasthan that separates Madhya Pradesh and Uttar Pradesh, is **Dholpur**. It was near here that Aurangzeb's sons fought a pitched battle to determine who would succeed him as emperor of the rapidly declining Mughal Empire. The Shergarh Fort in Dholpur is very old and is now in ruins.

Near Bari is the **Khanpur Mahal**, a pavilioned palace built for Shah Jahan but never occupied.

Towards Jhansi
To the east of the railway line, 61 km south of Gwalior towards Jhansi, a large group of white **Jain temples** is scattered along a hill. They're one of those strange, dream-like apparitions that so often seem simply to materialise in India. Sonagir is the nearest railway station.

Only 26 km north of Jhansi is **Datia**, with the deserted seven-storey palace of Raj Bir Singh Deo. It's an impressive building, and some of the rooms still contain murals. It's worth the short bus trip from Jhansi. The town is surrounded by a stone wall and the palace is to the west.

CHANDERI
At the time of Mandu's greatest power, Chanderi was an important place, as indicated by the many ruined palaces, serais, mosques and tombs – all in a Pathan style similar to Mandu. The **Koshak Mahal** is a ruined Muslim palace which is still being maintained.

Today the town is chiefly known for its gold brocades and saris. Chanderi is 33 km west of Lalitpur, which is 90 km south of Jhansi on the main railway line. Accommodation in the town includes a *Circuit House* and the *Rest House* near the bus stand.

JHANSI
Population: 409,000
Telephone Area Code: 0517

Jhansi, situated 101 km south of Gwalior, is actually just across the border in Uttar Pradesh, but for convenience we've included it here. Although Jhansi has played a colourful role in Indian history, most visitors to the town today go there simply because it's a convenient transit point for Khajuraho. This is the closest the Delhi to Bombay railway line runs to Khajuraho, and there are good connections with Delhi and Agra; it's 5½ hours by bus from Jhansi to Khajuraho.

History
In the 18th century, Jhansi became an important centre, eclipsing Orchha 18 km to the south, but in 1803 the British East India Company got a foot in the door and gradually

MADHYA PRADESH

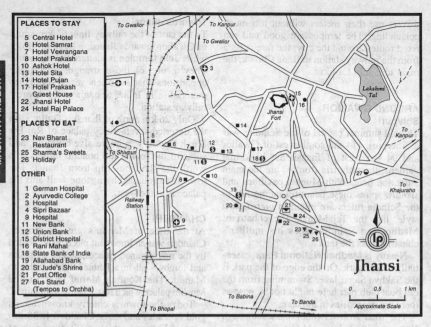

PLACES TO STAY
5 Central Hotel
6 Hotel Samrat
7 Hotel Veerangana
8 Hotel Prakash
10 Ashok Hotel
13 Hotel Sita
14 Hotel Pujan
17 Hotel Prakash
    Guest House
22 Jhansi Hotel
24 Hotel Raj Palace

PLACES TO EAT
23 Nav Bharat
    Restaurant
25 Sharma's Sweets
26 Holiday

OTHER
1 German Hospital
2 Ayurvedic College
3 Hospital
4 Sipri Bazaar
9 Hospital
11 New Bank
12 Union Bank
15 District Hospital
16 Rani Mahal
18 State Bank of India
19 Allahabad Bank
20 St Jude's Shrine
21 Post Office
27 Bus Stand
    (Tempos to Orchha)

To Gwalior
To Kanpur
To Gwalior
Lakshmi Tal
Jhansi Fort
To Kanpur
To Shivpuri
To Khajuraho
Railway Station
To Bhopal
To Babina
To Banda

Jhansi

0   0.5   1 km
Approximate Scale

assumed control over the state. The last of a string of none-too-competent rajas died without a son in 1853 and the British, who had recently passed a neat little law allowing them to take over any princely state under their patronage when the ruler died without a male heir, pensioned the rani off and took full control.

Orientation & Information
The old city is behind the fort, which is two km from the railway station. The town is quite spread out so you'll need to use auto-rickshaws to get around.

The Uttar Pradesh and Madhya Pradesh state governments have tourist booths at the railway station, although neither of them is particularly good. There's also a UP tourist office at the Hotel Veerangana, but it's often closed.

Jhansi Fort & Museum
Once used by the Indian army, the fort can

now be visited. It was built in 1613 by Maharaja Bir Singh Deo of Orchha. The British ceded the fort to the Maharaja of Scindia in 1858, but later exchanged it for Gwalior in 1866. There's nothing much to see, apart from the excellent views from the ramparts. Watch out for the band of aggressive monkeys by the temples here. It's open from 6 am to 5 pm daily, and entry is Rs 0.25.

Just below the walls as you approach the fort is a bizarre blood-and-guts diorama (a 'life-like picturisation', according to the sign) depicting the battle where the Rani of Jhansi died.

Also below the fort is the government museum, which houses a small collection of 9th to 12th-century sculpture. It's open from 10.30 am to 4.30 pm in winter; 7.30 am to 12.30 pm in summer.

Places to Stay & Eat
There are dorm beds for Rs 20 in the railway *retiring rooms* and doubles cost Rs 80 or

Rs 160 with air-con. The *refreshment room* is excellent value.

UP Tourism's *Hotel Veerangana* (☎ 44-2402) also has dorm beds (Rs 20) and singles/doubles from Rs 75/100 up to Rs 250/300 with air-con. Though a bit run-down it's a large place and has a good restaurant. It's a Rs 10 auto-rickshaw ride, or 15-minute walk, from the railway station.

The *Central Hotel* (☎ 44-0509) has a range of basic singles/doubles from Rs 44/50 without bathroom to Rs 77/110 with attached bathroom. The rooms on the terrace upstairs are nicer than the dark cells downstairs. The *Hotel Shipra* nearby, furnished with Raj jumble including metal bedsteads and wooden hat stands, is cheaper but far from spotless.

The new *Hotel Samrat* (☎ 44-4943) is much better with air-cooled rooms from Rs 75/110 with attached bathrooms and 24-hour checkout. It's good value.

Also good is the bright and airy *Hotel Prakash Guest House* (☎ 44-3133). Air-cooled doubles with attached bath, TV and phone cost Rs 150, or Rs 275 with air-con.

The friendly *Jhansi Hotel* (☎ 44-1360) is one of the best in town. It was a hotel in British times and touches of the Raj are still evident. The heads of animals shot in the area line the verandah walls and in the hot season the old method of cooling is still used here: *tatties* (large grass mats) are hung over the front of the hotel, kept damp to lower the air temperature as the water evaporates in the sun. Air-cooled doubles are Rs 310 and some air-con rooms are also available at Rs 350/450. There's a good restaurant and bar.

Nearby is the modern *Hotel Raj Palace* (☎ 44-2554) with air-cooled rooms from Rs 170/200, or with air-con Rs 275/325. The hotel features '24 hours lightning service and Posh Location'. It's a good clean place, though it lacks the atmosphere of the Jhansi Hotel.

If you like your creature comforts, head for the clean and well-maintained three-star *Hotel Sita* (☎ 44-2956). All rooms have carpet, TV and phone, and cost Rs 325/400 with air-cooling, Rs 475/525 with air-con. It also has a good bar and restaurant.

Places to Eat

Most of the hotels have restaurants. Near the Jhansi Hotel the *Nav Bharat Restaurant* and the *Holiday* both serve good food, and there're a number of good ice-cream parlours here too.

Getting There & Away

Bus Buses to Khajuraho (Rs 43, 5½ hours) leave from the railway station at 6, 7 and 11 am (Shatabdi Link). There are later buses from the bus stand at 11.45 am and 1 pm. Also from the bus stand there are buses to many other places including Gwalior (Rs 28, three hours), Shivpuri (Rs 28, three hours) and Datia (Rs 8, one hour). For Orchha, the tempos from here are better. They cost only Rs 5 for the 40-minute journey and leave when full.

Train Jhansi is on the main Delhi-Agra-Bhopal-Bombay railway line and therefore has good rail connections. Tickets on the crack *Shatabdi Express* cost Rs 350/700 for Delhi, Rs 195/390 for Agra, Rs 130/260 for Gwalior and Rs 280/560 for Bhopal. It

---

Rani of Jhansi

The Rani of Jhansi was unhappy about being forcibly retired by the British in 1853, so when the Indian Mutiny burst into flame four years later, she was in the forefront of the rebellion at Jhansi. The British contingent in Jhansi were all massacred, but the following year the rebel forces were still quarrelling amongst themselves and the British retook Jhansi. The rani fled to Gwalior and, in a valiant last stand, she rode out against the British, disguised as a man, and was killed. She has since become a heroine of the Indian independence movement, a sort of central Indian Joan of Arc. ■

departs at 10.47 am for Bhopal and 5.47 pm for Delhi.

Other expresses connect Jhansi with Delhi (414 km, Rs 113/338 in 2nd/1st), Agra (215 km, three hours, Rs 54/199), Gwalior (97 km, 1½ hours, Rs 27/114), Bhopal (291 km, 4½ hours, Rs 84/255), Indore (555 km, 10 hours, Rs 139/415) and Bombay (1158 km, 21 hours, Rs 230/714). There are also direct trains from Jhansi to Bangalore, Lucknow, Madras, Pune and Varanasi.

Getting Around

The forecourt outside the railway station is filled with predatory auto-rickshaw drivers. They charge around Rs 10 for the trip to the bus stand; there are also tempos for Rs 2.

ORCHHA

Once the capital city of the Bundelas, Orchha is now just a village, set amongst a complex of well-preserved palaces and temples. It's definitely worth a visit. Tour groups do it in a couple of hours but it's a wonderfully relaxing place to stay, and you can even get a room in part of the palace here.

Orchha was founded in 1531 and remained the capital of a powerful Rajput kingdom until 1783 when nearby Tikamgadh became the new capital. Bir Singh Deo ruled from Orchha between 1605 and 1627 and built the Jhansi Fort. A favourite of the Mughal Prince Salim, he feuded with Akbar and in 1602 narrowly escaped the emperor's displeasure; his kingdom was all but ruined by Akbar's forces. Then in 1605 Prince Salim became Emperor Jehangir, and for the next 22 years Bir Singh was a powerful figure. In 1627, Shah Jahan became emperor and Bir Singh once again found himself out of favour; his attempt at revolt was put down by 13-year-old Aurangzeb.

Orchha's golden age was during the first half of the 17th century. When Jehangir visited the city in 1606, a special palace, the Jehangir Mahal, was built for him. Later, both Shah Jahan and Aurangzeb raided the city.

If you're wondering what all the numbers and arrows painted on the palace floors are, they're for the 1½-hour Walkman tour! Go-ahead MP Tourism has Walkmans that can be rented for Rs 25 (with Rs 500 deposit) from the Hotel Sheesh Mahal. In spite of – or perhaps because of – the breathless enthusiasm of the narrator, the recording really brings the empty palaces to life.

Palaces

The **Jehangir Mahal** is of impressive size and there are good views of the countryside from the upper levels. There's a small archaeological museum on the ground floor. Cameras attract a Rs 2 charge, and video cameras are not allowed. The **Raj Mahal** nearby has superb murals but you may need to find the attendant to unlock some of the rooms. Below the Jehangir Mahal is the smaller **Raj Praveen Mahal**, a palace built near a garden. The *hammam* (baths) and camel stables are nearby.

Dinman Hardaul's Palace is also interesting, as is his story. The son of Bir Singh Deo, he committed suicide to 'prove his innocence' over an affair with his brother's wife, and has achieved the status of a local god through his martyrdom.

Temples

Orchha's impressive temples date back to the 17th century. They're still in use today and are visited regularly by thousands of devotees. In the centre of the modern village is the **Ram Raja Temple** with its soaring spires. Originally a palace, it was turned into a temple when an image of Rama, temporarily installed, proved impossible to move. It now seems to have somehow made its way into the nearby **Chaturbhuj Temple** where it is hidden behind silver doors. The **Lakshmi Narayan Temple** is worth the walk for its well-preserved murals.

Other Attractions

The walled **Phool Bagh** gardens, a cool summer retreat, are also worth visiting. Other places to see include the dilapidated **Sundar Mahal** and the **chhatris** (memorials) to Orchha's rulers, down by the Betwa River.

Places to Stay & Eat

The *Hotel Mansarover*, right in the centre of the village and run by the Special Area Development Authority (SADA), has clean rooms for Rs 50/75 with common bathroom (with a big marble tub but only cold water). SADA also runs the rooftop *Betwa Tarang* restaurant nearby.

MP Tourism runs the very pleasant *Betwa Cottages*, half a km from the village by the Betwa River. The cottages are set in a spacious, well-tended although shadeless garden, and there are good views to the palace and the river. The cost is Rs 225/275 with air-cooling and Rs 400/450 with air-con.

The most romantic place to stay in Madhya Pradesh must be the *Hotel Sheesh Mahal* (✆ 224), in a wing of the Jehangir Mahal. Run by the MPTDC, there's one single for Rs 100, six singles/doubles for Rs 170/200 and an air-con suite for Rs 550/600. The best rooms are No 1 (the air-con suite) and No 2 below it. Both have great views, even from the toilet! There's a good restaurant here and it's a friendly place.

Getting There & Away

There are regular buses and tempos (Rs 5) from the Jhansi bus stand for the 18-km journey to Orchha.

KHAJURAHO

Population: 7200
Telephone Area Code: 076861

Close behind the Taj and up there with Varanasi, Jaipur and Delhi, the temples of Khajuraho are one of India's major attractions. Once a great Chandela capital, Khajuraho is now just a quiet village of just over 7000 people. In spite of all the tourist attention it's still a very mellow place to spend a few days.

The temples are superb examples of Indo-Aryan architecture, but it's the decorations with which they are so liberally embellished that has made Khajuraho famous. Around the temples are bands of exceedingly fine and artistic stonework. The sculptors have shown many aspects of Indian life 1000

years ago – gods and goddesses, warriors and musicians, real and mythological animals.

But two elements appear over and over again and in greater detail than anything else – women and sex. Stone figures of *apsaras* or 'celestial maidens' appear on every temple. They pout and pose for all the world like pin-up models posing for the camera. In between are the *mithuna*, erotic figures, running through a whole Kamasutra of positions and possibilities.

These temples were built during the Chandela period, a dynasty which survived for five centuries before falling to the Mughal onslaught. Khajuraho's temples almost all date from one century-long burst of creative genius from 950 to 1050 AD. Almost as intriguing as the sheer beauty and size of the temples is the question of why and how they were built here. Khajuraho is a long way from anywhere and was probably just as far off the beaten track 1000 years ago as it is today. There is nothing of great interest or beauty to recommend it as a building site, there is no great population centre here and during the hot season Khajuraho is very hot, dry, dusty and uncomfortable.

Having chosen such a strange site, how did the Chandelas manage to recruit the labour to turn their awesome dreams into stone? To build so many temples of such monumental size in just 100 years must have required a huge amount of human labour. Whatever their reasons, we can be thankful they built Khajuraho where they did, because its very remoteness helped preserve it from the desecration Muslim invaders were only too ready to inflict on 'idolatrous' temples elsewhere in India.

Large numbers of visitors come to Khajuraho in March for the dance festival. This lasts 10 days and draws some of the best classical dancers in the country who perform by the western enclosure, with the floodlit temples providing a spectacular backdrop.

Orientation

The modern village of Khajuraho is a cluster of hotels, restaurants, shops and stalls near the western group of temples. A km or so east

MADHYA PRADESH

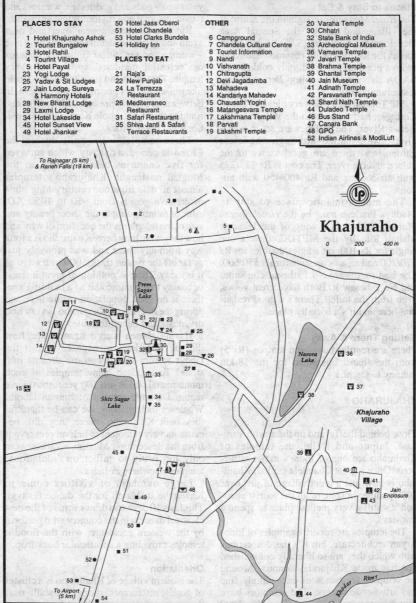

PLACES TO STAY
1 Hotel Khajuraho Ashok
2 Tourist Bungalow
3 Hotel Rahil
4 Tourint Village
5 Hotel Payal
23 Yogi Lodge
25 Yadav & Sit Lodges
27 Jain Lodge, Sureya
    & Harmony Hotels
28 New Bharat Lodge
29 Laxmi Lodge
34 Hotel Lakeside
45 Hotel Sunset View
49 Hotel Jhankar
50 Hotel Jass Oberoi
51 Hotel Chandela
53 Hotel Clarks Bundela
54 Holiday Inn

PLACES TO EAT
21 Raja's
22 New Punjab
24 La Terrezza
    Restaurant
26 Mediterraneo
    Restaurant
31 Safari Restaurant
35 Shiva Janti & Safari
    Terrace Restaurants

OTHER
6 Campground
7 Chandela Cultural Centre
8 Tourist Information
9 Nandi
10 Vishvanath
11 Chitragupta
12 Devi Jagadamba
13 Mahadeva
14 Kandariya Mahadev
15 Chausath Yogini
16 Matangesvara Temple
17 Lakshmana Temple
18 Parvati
19 Lakshmi Temple
20 Varaha Temple
30 Chhatri
32 State Bank of India
33 Archeological Museum
36 Vamana Temple
37 Javari Temple
38 Brahma Temple
39 Ghantai Temple
40 Jain Museum
41 Adinath Temple
42 Parsvanath Temple
43 Shanti Nath Temple
44 Duladeo Temple
46 Bus Stand
47 Canara Bank
48 GPO
52 Indian Airlines & ModiLuft

Khajuraho

0   200   400 m

To Rajnagar (5 km)
& Raneh Falls (19 km)

Prem
Sagar
Lake

Ship Sagar
Lake

Narora
Lake

Khajuraho
Village

Jain
Enclosure

To Airport
(5 km)

Kholar River

of the bus stand is the old village of Khajuraho. Around it are the temples of the eastern group and to the south are two further groups of temples.

Information

Tourist Offices The helpful Government of India tourist office (☎ 2047) is in the modern village of Khajuraho. There is also an office at the airport.

MP Tourism has a small stall at the bus stand, but the main office is hidden away at the Tourist Bungalow. This office is a classic example of paid idleness; four guys sit here, in a location where they're almost guaranteed of not being troubled by bothersome tourists, reading the paper and waiting for the next pay packet.

Money As well as the usual opening hours, the State Bank of India is also open for foreign currency transactions between 4 and 5 pm Monday to Friday and 2.30 to 3.30 pm on Saturday. (The chhatri behind the bank is a memorial to Maharaja Pratap Singh Ju Deo.)

If you are carrying only Australian dollars, head for the Canara Bank down behind the bus stand. It's much less busy than the State Bank of India anyway.

Post & Telecommunications Until the Khajuraho exchange is upgraded there is a real shortage of international lines – just five for the whole town – so making calls can be a problem. There's a small STD/ISD call office by the Jati Shankar restaurant opposite the State Bank of India. The Hotel Chandela currently has the only fax machine in town. Non-guests are welcome to use it, although a charge is made for the service.

Western Group of Temples

The main temples are in the western group, conveniently close to the tourist part of Khajuraho. Most are contained within a fenced enclosure which is very well maintained as a park. The enclosure is open from

---

Khajuraho's Erotica

The most frequently asked question by visitors to Khajuraho is why all the sex? One theory has it that the erotic posturing was a kind of Kamasutra in stone, a how-to-do-it manual for adolescent Brahmin boys growing up segregated from the world in special temple schools. Another claims that the figures were thought to prevent the temples being struck by lightning, by appeasing the rain god Indra. This old lecher is supposedly a keen voyeur who wouldn't want the source of his pleasure damaged.

Rather more convincing is the explanation that these are Tantric images. According to this cult, gratification of the baser instincts is one way to blot out the evils of the world and achieve final deliverance. *Bhoga* (physical enjoyment) and *yoga* (spiritual exercise) are seen as equally valid in this quest for nirvana.

Probably the most accurate theory is that the Khajuraho sculptors were simply representing life as it was viewed by their society, unhampered by Old Testament morality. In spite of the fact that modern visitors are drawn as much for reasons of prurience as for cultural appreciation, this is not pornography. Although there are certainly large numbers of erotic images here, many other day-to-day scenes are also shown. The carvings should be seen as a joyous celebration of all aspects of life. ∎

sunrise to sunset and entry is Rs 0.50. This includes entry to the archaeological museum across the road, so don't lose your ticket. Admission is free on Fridays. Just inside the enclosure you can buy an excellent Archaeological Survey of India guidebook to Khajuraho for Rs 5.

The temples are described here in a clockwise direction.

Lakshmi & Varaha Facing the large Lakshmana Temple are these two small shrines. The Varaha Temple, dedicated to Vishnu's boar incarnation or Varaha *avatar*, actually faces the Matangesvara Temple. Inside this small, open shrine is a huge, solid and intricately carved figure of the boar incarnation, dating from around 900 AD.

Lakshmana The large Lakshmana Temple is dedicated to Vishnu, although in design it is similar to the Kandariya Mahadev and Vishvanath temples. It is one of the earliest of the western enclosure temples, dating from around 930 to 950 AD, and is also one of the best preserved, with a full five-part

---

Temple Terminology

The Khajuraho temples follow a fairly consistent design pattern unique to Khajuraho. Understanding the architectural conventions and some of the terms will help you enjoy the temples more. Basically all the temples follow a five-part or three-part layout.

You enter the temples through an entrance porch, known as the *ardhamandapa*. Behind this is the hall or *mandapa*. This leads into the main hall, or *mahamandapa*, supported with pillars and with a corridor around it. A vestibule or *antarala* then leads into the *garbhagriha*, the inner sanctum, where the image of the god to which the temple is dedicated is displayed. An enclosed corridor, the *pradakshina*, runs around this sanctum. The simpler three-part temples don't have a mandapa or pradakshina, but otherwise follow the same plan as the five-part temples.

Externally the temples consist of successive waves of higher and higher towers culminating in the soaring sikhara (spire), which tops the sanctum. While the lower towers, over the mandapa or mahamandapa, may be pyramid-shaped, the sikhara is taller and curvilinear. The ornate, even baroque, design of all these vertical elements is balanced by an equally ornate horizontal element from the bands of sculptures that run around the temples. Although the sculptures are superbly developed in their own right, they are also a carefully integrated part of the overall design – not some tacked-on afterthought.

The interiors of the temples are as ornate as the exteriors. The whole temple sits upon a high terrace, known as the *adisthana*. Unlike temples in most other parts of India, these had no enclosing wall but often had four smaller shrines at the corners of the terrace; many of them have now disappeared. The finely carved entrance gate to the temple is a *torana*, and the lesser towers around the main sikhara are known as *urusringas*.

The temples are almost all aligned east to west, with the entrance facing east. Some of the earliest temples were made of granite, or granite and sandstone, but all the ones from the classic period of Khajuraho's history are made completely of sandstone. At that time there was no mortar, so the blocks were fitted together. The sculptures and statues play such an important part in the total design that many have their own terminology:

apsara – heavenly nymph, beautiful dancing woman.

mithuna – Khajuraho's most famous image, the sensuously carved, erotic figures which have been shocking people from Victorian archaeologists to busloads of blue-rinse tourists.

nayika – it's really impossible to tell a nayika from a surasundari, since the only difference is that the surasundari is supposed to be a heavenly creature while a nayika is human.

salabhanjika – female figure with tree, which together act as supporting brackets in the inner chambers of the temple. Apsaras also perform this bracket function.

sardula – a mythical beast, part lion, part some other animal or even human. Sardulas usually carry armed men on their backs, and can be seen on many of the temples. They all look like lions but the faces are often different. They may be demons or *asuras*.

surasundari – when a surasundari is dancing she is an apsara. Otherwise she attends the gods and goddesses by carrying flowers, water, ornaments, mirrors or other offerings. She also engages in everyday activities like washing her hair, applying make-up, taking a thorn out of her foot, fondling herself, playing with pets and babies, writing letters, playing musical instruments or posing seductively. ∎

floor plan and four subsidiary shrines. Around the temple are two bands of sculpture instead of the usual three; the lower one has fine figures of apsaras and some erotic scenes. Inside are excellent examples of apsaras acting as supporting brackets.

On the subsidiary shrine at the south-west corner you can make out an architect working with his students – it is thought this may be the temple's designer including himself in the grand plan. Around the base of the temple is a continuous frieze with scenes of battles, hunting and processions. The first metre or two of the frieze consists of a highly energetic orgy, including one gentleman proving that a horse can be a person's best friend, while a stunned group of women look away in shock.

The temple platform gives you a good view of the Matangesvara Temple (see later in this section). It's outside the western enclosure and the only temple in this area that is still in use today.

Kandariya Mahadev The first of the temples on the common platform at the back of the western enclosure is the one temple to see in Khajuraho above all others. The Kandariya Mahadev is not only the largest of the temples, it is also artistically and architecturally the most perfect. Built between 1025 and 1050, it represents Chandella art at its finest. Although the four subsidiary shrines which once stood around the main temple have long disappeared, the central shrine is in superb condition and shows the typical five-part design of Khajuraho temples.

The main spire is 31 metres high, and the temple is lavishly carved. The English archaeologist Cunningham counted 226 statues inside the temple and a further 646 outside – 872 in total with most of them nearly a metre in height. The statues are carved around the temple in three bands and include gods, goddesses, beautiful women, musicians and, of course, some of the famed erotic groups. The mithuna on the Kandariya Mahadev include some of the most energetic eroticism to be seen at Khajuraho.

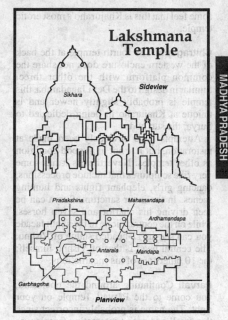

Lakshmana Temple

Sideview

Sikhara

Planview

Pradakshina   Mahamandapa
                          Ardhamandapa
        Antarala   Mandapa
Garbhagriha

Mahadeva This small and mainly ruined temple stands on the same base as the Kandariya Mahadev and the Devi Jagadamba. Although small and insignificant compared to its mighty neighbours, it houses one of Khajuraho's best sculptures – a fine *sardula* figure (see the boxed section on Temple Terminology), caressing a lion.

Devi Jagadamba The third temple on the common platform is slightly older than the Kandariya Mahadev and of a simpler, three-part design. It was probably originally dedicated to Vishnu, but later changed to Parvati and then Kali. Some students believe it may still be a Parvati temple and that the Kali image (or Jagadamba) is actually an image of Parvati, painted black. The sculptures around the temple are again in three bands. Many of the two lower band images are of Vishnu with sardulas in the inner recesses. But on the third and uppermost band the mithuna again come out to play, and some feel that this is Khajuraho's most erotic temple.

Chitragupta The fourth temple at the back of the western enclosure does not share the common platform with the other three. Similar in design to the Devi Jagadamba, this temple is probably slightly newer and is unique at Khajuraho in being dedicated to Surya, the sun god.

Attempts have obviously been made at restoration, but it is not in as good condition as other temples. Nevertheless it has some very fine sculptures that include processions, dancing girls, elephant fights and hunting scenes. In the inner sanctum, Surya can be seen driving his chariot and seven horses, while on the central niche in the south facade you can see an 11-headed statue of Vishnu. The central head is that of Vishnu himself; the 10 others are of his incarnations.

Parvati Continuing around the enclosure, you come to the Parvati Temple on your right. The name is probably incorrect since this small and not so interesting temple was originally dedicated to Vishnu and now has an image of Ganga riding on the back of a crocodile.

Vishvanath Temple & Nandi Believed to have been built in 1002, this temple has the complete five-part design of the larger Kandariya Mahadev Temple, but two of its four subsidiary shrines still stand. That it is a Siva shrine is made very clear by the large image of his vehicle, the bull Nandi, which faces the temple from the other end of the common platform. Steps lead up to this high terrace, flanked by lions on the northern side and elephants on the southern side.

The sculptures around the temple include the usual Khajuraho scenes, but the sculptures of women are particularly notable here. They write letters, fondle a baby, play music and, perhaps more so than at any other temple, languish in provocative poses.

Matangesvara Temple Standing next to the Lakshmana Temple, this temple is not within the fenced enclosure because it is still in everyday use, unlike all the other old Khajuraho temples. It may be the plainest temple here (suggesting that it was one of the first built) but inside it sports a polished lingam, 2.5 metres high.

Early in the morning, flower-sellers do a brisk trade in garlands for the statue of Ganesh outside. People drape them round the elephant-headed statue, say a prayer and as they walk away the flower-sellers whip them off to resell!

Chausath Yogini Standing beyond the tank, some distance from the other western group temples, this ruined temple is probably the oldest at Khajuraho, dating from 900 AD or earlier. It is also the only temple constructed entirely of granite and the only one not aligned east to west. Chausath means 64 – the temple once had 64 cells for figures of the 64 yoginis who attended the goddess Kali. A 65th cell sheltered Kali herself.

A further half km west is the **Lalguan Mahadev Temple**, a small, ruined shrine dedicated to Siva and constructed of granite and sandstone.

Archaeological Museum

Close to the western enclosure, this museum has a fine collection of statues and sculptures rescued from around Khajuraho. It's small and worth a visit but the attendants tend to hassle you for baksheesh. There's a wonderful dancing Ganesh figure in the entrance gallery. Admission is included in the western enclosure entrance fee and the museum is open from 10 am to 5 pm but is closed on Friday.

Opposite the museum, in the Archaeological Survey of India's compound beside the Matangesvara Temple, there are many more rescued sculptures – but this area is off limits.

Eastern Group of Temples

The eastern group of temples can be sub-divided into two groups. The first is made up of interesting Jain temples in the walled enclosure. The other four temples are scattered through the old village of Khajuraho (as distinct from the modern village near the western temples).

Jain Museum Outside the Jain enclosure is this recently constructed circular gallery, filled with statues of the 24 tirthankars. It's open every day from 7 am to 6 pm and entry is Rs 1.

Parsvanath The largest of the Jain temples in the walled enclosure is also one of the finest at Khajuraho. Although it does not approach the western enclosure temples in size, and does not attempt to compete in the sexual activity stakes, it is notable for the exceptional skill and precision of its construction, and for the beauty of its sculptures. Some of the best known figures at Khajuraho can be seen here, including the classic figure of a woman removing a thorn from her foot and another of a woman applying eye make-up. Although it was originally dedicated to Adinath, an image of Parsvanath was substituted about a century ago and the temple takes its name from this newer image.

Adinath Adjacent to the Parsvanath Temple, the smaller Adinath has been partially restored over the centuries. It has fine carvings on its three bands of sculptures and, like the Parsvanath, is very similar to the Hindu temples of Khajuraho. Only the striking black image in the inner sanctum indicates that it is Jain rather than Hindu.

Shanti Nath This temple is a relatively modern one built about a century ago, but it contains many components from older temples around Khajuraho. The 4½-metre-high statue of Adinath is said to have been sculptured in 1028. A triple-padlocked metal chest beside it is labelled 'secret donation box'. Groups of Digambara Jain pilgrims occasionally stay at the dharamsala here, their nakedness causing raised eyebrows amongst package tourists.

Ghantai Walking from the eastern Jain temple group towards Khajuraho village, you come to this small, ruined Jain temple.

Only its pillared shell remains, but it is interesting for the delicate columns with their bell-and-chain decoration and for the figure of a Jain goddess astride a Garuda which marks the entrance.

Javari Walk through the village, a typical small Indian settlement, to this temple. Dating from around 1075 to 1100 AD, it is dedicated to Vishnu and is a particularly fine example of Khajuraho architecture on a small scale. The exterior has more of Khajuraho's maidens.

Vamana About 200 metres north of the Javari Temple, this temple is dedicated to Vamana, the dwarf incarnation of Vishnu. Slightly older than the Javari Temple, the Vamana Temple stands out in a field all by itself. It's notable for the relatively simple design of its sikhara. The bands of sculpture around the temples are, as usual, very fine with numerous 'celestial maidens' adopting interesting poses.

Brahma & Hanuman Turning back (west) towards the modern village, you pass this granite and sandstone temple, one of the oldest at Khajuraho. It was actually dedicated to Vishnu and the definition of it as a Brahma temple is incorrect.

Taking the road directly from the modern village to the Jain enclosure, you pass a Hanuman Temple containing a large image of the monkey god. This 2½-metre statue has on it the oldest inscription here – 922 AD.

Southern Group of Temples

There are only two temples in the southern group, one of which is several km south of the river.

Duladeo A dirt track runs to this isolated temple, about a km south of the Jain enclosure. This is the latest temple at Khajuraho, and experts say that at this time the skill of Khajuraho's temple builders had passed its peak and the sculptures are more 'wooden' and 'stereotyped' than on earlier temples. Nevertheless, it's a fine and graceful temple with figures of women in a variety of pin-up poses and a number of mithuna couples.

Chaturbhuja South of the river, about three km from the village and a healthy hike down a dirt road, this ruined temple has a fine three-metre-high image of Vishnu.

Organised Tours

There are currently no guided tours operated by the tourist office, although they are planning to reintroduce them. Licensed private guides are available for hire, charging around Rs 80 for a half day. If you want a taxi this would be a further Rs 150.

Places to Stay – bottom end

MP Tourism has quite a few hotels here and they're good value at the height of the season but overpriced at other times when private hotels reduce their prices. If there aren't many people here it's worth trying to get a reduction wherever you decide to stay. On arrival at the bus stand you'll be besieged by plenty of the usual rickshaw-wallahs offering Rs 2 rides – these are commission agents and you'll find hotel bargaining difficult if they take you to a hotel. Get them to drop you near the hotel of your choice.

The cheapest places are in the centre of the new village, close to the western group of temples. The *New Bharat Lodge* and *Laxmi Lodge* are side-by-side and are very similar, very basic and not too clean. Singles/doubles with attached bathroom are around Rs 40/50. Nearby are two more cheap lodges, in the same price range, the *Yadav* and the *Sita Lodge*. The Yadav Lodge is the best of this group.

The *Yogi Lodge* (☎ 2158) is the best of the cheapies, with singles/doubles with attached bathroom from around Rs 50/70. The rooms are arranged around a small courtyard.

In a very quiet location on the way to the Jain temples, the *Hotel Plaza* is newly built with doubles with attached bathrooms from Rs 50.

An old favourite with travellers is the *Jain Lodge* (☎ 2052), which has a range of rooms from Rs 50/70 upwards, including air-cooled and air-con rooms. There's a good vegetarian

restaurant here. Next door the *Hotel Surya* (☎ 2145) is a step up the scale with a small garden and good rooms with attached bathroom for Rs 80/100, or Rs 150 with air-cooler. The upstairs rooms at the back (Rs 200) have a balcony and views over the fields.

Right beside the Surya is the *Hotel Harmony* (☎ 2135), which also claims to be 'the only hotel with a garden in the city'. Comfortable rooms with attached bath are Rs 150 and there's a vegetarian restaurant. The small walled garden is immaculate.

To the north of the modern village of Khajuraho are a number of hotels run by MP Tourism. The *Tourist Village* (☎ 2128) is in a very peaceful location and the manager is friendly and helpful. It's a somewhat shabby collection of cottages (watch your head on the low doorways), decorated with local carpets and furnishings. Singles/doubles with attached bathroom cost Rs 110/150 and there's an open-air restaurant. The *Hotel Rahil* (☎ 2062) is a large concrete block nearby with an institutional feel to it. The dorms are small and clean with beds for Rs 30 and there are rooms with attached bathrooms and hot water for Rs 130/150.

The aging *Tourist Bungalow* (☎ 2064) is a popular, conveniently located place. Spacious singles/doubles with attached bathroom cost Rs 175/225 and there's a restaurant here.

The *Hotel Sunset View* (☎ 2077) has a wide range of accommodation including dorm beds at Rs 20 and doubles with attached bathrooms from Rs 60 to Rs 240. Clean and modern with a nice garden, it's a reasonable place to stay. Be careful buying jewellery from its craft shop, though. It's on the main road from the airport, just before the town.

The *Hotel Lakeside* (☎ 2120) has very clean rooms set around a courtyard, right in the middle of the new village. Singles/doubles with attached bathroom cost from Rs 150/200.

Places to Stay – middle

Also run by the state tourism organisation,

the *Hotel Payal* (☎ 2076) is a modern place with a garden and spacious singles/doubles for Rs 200/250 or Rs 400/450 with air-con. It's clean, well kept and there's an information booth. Good food is available in the restaurant although the service is very slow.

MP Tourism's flagship here is the *Hotel Jhankar* (☎ 2063). Rooms are well decorated and also cost Rs 200/250 or Rs 400/450 for air-con, all with attached bathrooms and hot-water heaters. The restaurant is not that great and there's no beer.

Places to Stay – top end
The Indian Tourism Development Corporation (ITDC) *Hotel Khajuraho Ashok* (☎ 2024), a short walk north of the modern village, is poor value compared to the other top-end offerings. At Rs 900/1100 it's way overpriced. Service is slow in the overpriced restaurant. You can, however, use the swimming pool for Rs 50 as a non-guest.

The *Hotel Chandela* (☎ 2054; fax 2095), south of the modern village, is one of a group of deluxe hotels in this area. Air-con rooms cost US$39/75, with comfortable beds, and bathtubs in the attached bathrooms. Diversions for when guests are 'templed out' include tennis, yoga, archery, croquet and badminton. Non-guests can use the swimming pool for Rs 100 or have a massage at the health club, also for Rs 100. There's a good bookshop and two excellent restaurants.

Another good choice is the *Hotel Jass Oberoi* (☎ 2085) nearby. The prices are very reasonable at US$38/70, and the hotel has facilities similar to the Chandela. The pool here is not open to non-guests.

The *Hotel Clarks Bundela* (☎ 2366), south of the Hotel Chandela, is one of two excellent new upmarket places to open in Khajuraho in 1994. It is good value at US$35/50, and also has a swimming pool.

The second new arrival is the *Holiday Inn* (☎ 2178), also south of the Hotel Chandela. The rooms are very tastefully furnished and the staff helpful. In keeping with the other places in this category, it has a pool, bar and at least one restaurant.

Places to Eat
For a cheap meal the vegetarian *Jati Shankar*, in a lane opposite the State Bank of India, does an excellent vegetarian thali for Rs 15. It's much better value than the *Madras Coffee House* which is nearby, where the South Indian thali is overpriced at Rs 50, but they have an extensive menu and plenty of other cheap dishes. If you're game you can try 'Porch with Hunney'.

Raja's Cafe has been here for years and so has the Swiss woman who runs it. The large shady tree in the restaurant's courtyard is a popular gathering spot and there are good views over the temples from the terrace above. The quality of food here is variable and the service generally lacking. It seems to survive largely on reputation these days, although the Swiss rostis (Rs 35) remain popular.

The *New Punjab Restaurant* is cheaper and also has a nice terrace with umbrellas and views of the temples. The *La Terrazza* next door is, not surprisingly, an Italian outdoor restaurant. Apparently it has pretty decent food, although it was not open when we last visited.

Prominent signs around town advertise the *Mediterraneo* restaurant on Jain Temples Rd, opposite the Hotel Surya. The food is quite good and reasonably priced, although I'm dubious about their claim to having an Italian chef. The pizzas are just glorified chapatis; the pasta dishes are better.

The *Safari Terrace Restaurant* and the *Shiva Janti Restaurant* are similar places with reasonable food. Both have terraces and overlook the small Shiv Sagar. It's a good place to be in the early evening as the sun sets over the lake.

The top-end hotels all have good restaurants, but don't expect to get out of it cheaply – count on at least Rs 150 per person, plus drinks.

Getting There & Away
Getting to Khajuraho can be a major pain. It's really on the way from nowhere to nowhere, and is not near any railway station. Although many travellers slot it in between

Varanasi and Agra, it involves quite a lot of slow bus travel over small country roads to cover not particularly great distances. Flying is a good alternative.

Air Indian Airlines (☎ 2035) have a daily Delhi-Agra-Khajuraho-Varanasi flight that returns by the same route to Delhi. It's probably the most popular tourist flight in India and can often be booked solid for days by tour groups. Hopefully the ModiLuft flights, which started in late 1994, will have taken some of the pressure off.

If you've got one of those middle-of-the-night international flights out of Delhi don't rely on flying in from Khajuraho the day before. However, problems with flights from here may lessen when the new runway beacons are installed and when Indian Airlines finally gets a computer link.

Indian Airlines' prices from Khajuraho are: Agra US$39, Delhi US$53 and Varanasi US$39. ModiLuft has daily flights to Delhi (US$53) and Varanasi (US$39).

The Indian Airlines office (☎ 2035) and the ModiLuft office are both next door to the Clarks Bundela Hotel.

Bus & Train From the west there are bus services from Agra (Rs 83, 12 hours), Gwalior (Rs 65, nine hours) and Jhansi (Rs 43, 5½ hours). Jhansi is the nearest approach to Khajuraho on the main Delhi to Bombay railway line, and there are half a dozen buses a day on this popular route. You can also go by train from Jhansi to Mahoba, 60 km north of Khajuraho (Rs 15, 2½ hours), and then catch a bus on to Khajuraho. The problem here is that there aren't many trains along this line, which connects Jhansi with Varanasi.

There is no direct route to Varanasi from Khajuraho. Satna (Rs 23, four hours from Khajuraho) is the nearest reliable railhead for travellers from Varanasi and the east. It's on the Bombay to Allahabad line and so there are plenty of connections. There are five buses daily from Satna to Khajuraho. However, it may not be possible to get from Varanasi to Khajuraho in one day as there are generally no buses from Satna after about 1

pm. The best bet is to take the overnight *Varanasi Kurla Express* from Varanasi at 11.30 pm, which gets you into Satna at 6.30 am.

You can also get to Khajuraho from Varanasi via Mahoba, as described above from Jhansi.

There's a 7.30 am daily bus to Jabalpur (Rs 65, 11 hours) but it is more comfortable to take a train from Satna.

Getting Around

To/From the Airport There's an Indian Airlines airport bus; taxis charge Rs 70 for this short journey. If there aren't too many tourists about, you should be able to get a cycle-rickshaw to the airport for about Rs 30.

Local Transport The best way to get around Khajuraho is by bicycle, since it's all flat and pleasantly traffic-free. Bicycles cost Rs 15 per day from several places in the new village. Cycle-rickshaws are a rip-off. This is hardly surprising with rich tourists willing to pay Rs 30 for the trip from the Hotel Chandela to the western temples!

It's a long walk to the eastern group of temples. If you're planning to take a cycle-rickshaw it's best to arrange a number of stops, including the southern temples and waiting time.

AROUND KHAJURAHO
Dhubela

In the old fort in this town, 64 km from Khajuraho along the road to Jhansi, there's a small **museum**. Exhibits include Shakti cult sculptures, weapons, clothes and other personal belongings of the Bundela kings.

Panna National Park

The road to Satna passes through this recently created park, lying along the River Ken, 32 km from Khajuraho. It contains large areas of unspoilt forest and a variety of wildlife. There are tigers here but you'd be very lucky to see one. The numerous waterfalls in this area are popular picnic spots. Day trips often also take in a visit to the **diamond mines** at Majhgawan, the **Rajgarh Palace** and the **temples** of Panna town, 48 km from Khajuraho.

The park is open year-round, but the best time to visit is in the cooler months; in summer the heat can take on furnace-like proportions.

Access to the park is from the village of Madla, 22 km from Khajuraho, and accommodation is available in the *Forest Rest House*.

Ajaigarh & Kalinjar Forts

At Ajaigarh, 80 km from Khajuraho, is the large isolated hilltop fort, designed to protect the local population during attacks and sieges. It was built by the Chandellas when their influence in the area was on the decline. Kalinjar Fort, 25 km north (just inside Uttar Pradesh) is much older, built during the Gupta period and mentioned by Ptolemy in the 2nd century AD.

SATNA

Telephone Area Code: 07672

You may find it convenient or necessary to stay overnight here on your way to or from Khajuraho. The tourist office is at the railway station.

Places to Stay & Eat

The *Hotel India* is a good place near the bus stand. Singles/doubles are Rs 75/125 with attached bathroom and downstairs there's an excellent, cheap vegetarian restaurant. It's part of the Indian Coffee House chain. Nearby the *Hotel Star* has rooms for Rs 60/90 and the *Hotel Glory* has singles for Rs 50 but they're both very basic.

The *Hotel Park* is in a slightly quieter location, with clean singles/doubles for Rs 65/90, air-cooled doubles for Rs 160, and air-con rooms. It's 1.5 km from the railway station and there's a vegetarian restaurant here.

MP Tourism's *Hotel Barhut* (☎ 5471) is the revamped Tourist Bungalow. It's a good clean place with singles/doubles at Rs 175/225 or Rs 250/300 with air-con. There's a restaurant and the bathroom here gives you

the choice of urinal, Indian squat lavatory or Western throne – all in the one room!

Getting There & Away

There are about five buses to Khajuraho (Rs 23, four hours) between 6 am 1 pm, and a morning bus to Tala (Rs 28, four hours) for Bandhavgarh National Park.

The railway station and the bus stand are about two km apart and cycle-rickshaws charge Rs 5, although you'll probably have to pay double that. There are direct trains from Satna to Varanasi (316 km, Rs 93/267 in 2nd/1st class) taking eight hours and other direct expresses connect with Allahabad (180 km, four hours), Calcutta, Bombay and Madras.

Central Madhya Pradesh

SANCHI

Telephone Area Code: 07592

Beside the main railway line, 46 km north of Bhopal, a hill rises from the plain. It's topped by some of the oldest and most interesting Buddhist structures in India. Although this site had no direct connection with the life of Buddha, it was the great Emperor Ashoka, Buddhism's most famous convert, who built the first stupas here in the 3rd century BC, and a great number of stupas and other religious structures were added over the succeeding centuries.

As Buddhism was gradually absorbed back into Hinduism in its land of origin, the site decayed and was eventually completely forgotten. In 1818 a British officer rediscovered the site, but in the following years amateur archaeologists and greedy treasure hunters did immense damage to Sanchi before a proper restoration was first commenced in 1881. Finally, between 1912 and 1919, the structures were carefully repaired and restored to their present condition by Sir John Marshall.

Despite the damage which was wrought after its rediscovery, Sanchi is a very special place and is not to be missed if you're anywhere within striking distance. The site is one of the most evocative in India, and Sanchi is a good base for a number of interesting bicycle excursions.

Orientation & Information

Sanchi is little more than a small village at the foot of the hill on which the site is located. The site is open daily from dawn to dusk and tickets are available from the kiosk outside the museum. Entry costs Rs 0.50 (free on Fridays) which covers both the site and the museum. It's worth buying a copy of the *Sanchi* guidebook (Rs 4) from the museum, published by the Archaeological Survey of India. There's also a museum guidebook (Rs 3.75) on sale here.

At the crossroads the Mrignayni Emporium sells local handicrafts including batik bed covers for Rs 110 and bell-metal figures. It's sometimes possible to visit the silkworm farm (Sericulture Centre). Ask at the MP Travellers' Lodge next door.

The quickest way up to the site is via the stone steps off to the right of the tarmac road. There's a drink stall by the modern *vihara* (monastery) on Sanchi hill, and Buddhist publications are for sale in the vihara. Following is a brief description of the buildings at the site; the *Sanchi* guidebook describes all these buildings, and many others, in much greater detail.

Archaeological Museum

This museum has a small collection of sculpture from the site. The most interesting pieces are the lion capital from the Ashoka pillar, a *yakshi* (maiden) hanging from a mango tree and a beautiful Buddha figure in red sandstone. It's open from 10 am to 5 pm daily except Friday.

Great Stupa

Stupa 1, as it is listed on the site, is the main structure on the hill. Originally constructed by Ashoka in the 3rd century BC, it was later enlarged and the original brick stupa enclosed within a stone one. In its present form it stands 16 metres high and 37 metres in diameter. A railing encircles the stupa and

there are four entrances through magnificently carved gateways, or *toranas*. These toranas are the finest works of art at Sanchi and amongst the finest examples of Buddhist art in India.

Toranas The four gateways were erected around 35 BC and had all fallen down at the time of the stupa's restoration. The scenes carved onto the pillars and their triple architraves are mainly tales from the Jatakas, the episodes of the Buddha's various lives. At this stage in Buddhist art the Buddha was never represented directly – his presence was always alluded to through symbols. The lotus stands for his birth, the bo tree represents his enlightenment, the wheel his teachings and the footprint and throne symbolise his presence. Even a stupa itself is a symbol of the Buddha.

Walk around the stupa clockwise, as one should around all Buddhist monuments.

Northern Gateway The northern gateway, topped by a broken wheel of law, is the best preserved of the gateways. It shows many scenes from the Buddha's life, both in his last incarnation and in earlier lives. Scenes include a monkey offering a bowl of honey to the Buddha, whose presence is indicated by a bo tree. In another panel he ascends a road into the air (again represented by a bo tree) in the 'miracle of Sravasti'. This is just one of several miraculous feats he performs on the northern gateway – all of which leave his spectators stunned. Elephants, facing in four directions, support the architraves above the columns, while horses with riders and more elephants fill the gaps between the architraves.

Eastern Gateway One pillar on this gateway includes scenes of the Buddha's entry to nirvana. Across the front of the middle architrave is the 'great departure', where the Buddha (symbolised by a riderless horse) renounces the sensual life and sets out to find enlightenment. Maya's dream of an elephant standing on the moon, which she had when she conceived the Buddha, is also shown on one of the columns. The figure of a yakshi, hanging out from one of the architraves, is one of the best known images of Sanchi.

Southern Gateway The oldest of the gateways, this includes scenes of the Buddha's birth and also events from Ashoka's life as a Buddhist. At the rear of the top architrave there is another representation of the great departure. As on the western gateway, the tale of the Chhaddanta Jataka features on this gateway.

Western Gateway The western gateway, with the architraves supported by dwarfs, has some of the most interesting scenes at the site. The rear face of one of the pillars shows the Buddha undergoing the temptation of Mara, while demons flee and angels cheer his resistance. Mara also tempts on the back of the lowest architrave. The top front architrave shows the Buddha in seven different incarnations, but since he could not, at the time, be represented directly, he appears three times as a stupa and four times as a tree. His six incarnations prior to the seventh, Gautama Buddha, are known as the Manushi Buddhas.

The colourful events of the Chhaddanta Jataka are related on the front face of the bottom architrave. In this tale the Buddha, in a lower incarnation, took the form of a six-tusked elephant, but one of his two wives became jealous; she managed to reincarnate as a queen and then arranged to have the six-tusked elephant hunted and killed. The sight of his tusks, sawn off by the hunter, was sufficient for the queen to die of remorse! Pot-bellied dwarfs support the architraves on this gateway.

Other Stupas

There are many other stupas on the hill, some of them tiny votive ones less than a metre high. They date from the 3rd century AD. Eight were built by Ashoka but only three remain, including the great stupa. **Stupa 2**, one of the most interesting of the lesser stupas, is halfway down the hill to the west.

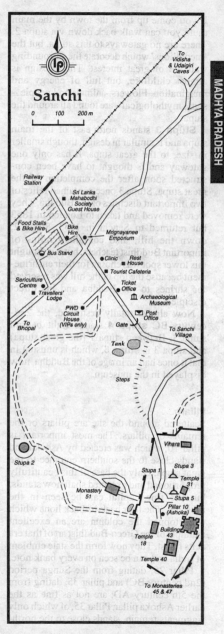

Sanchi

0   100   200 m

Railway Station

Sri Lanka
Mahabodhi
Society
Guest House

Food Stalls
& Bike Hire

Bike
Hire

Mrignayanee
Emporium

Bus Stand

Clinic

Rest
House

Tourist Cafeteria

Sericulture
Centre

Ticket
Office

Archaeological
Museum

Travellers'
Lodge

PWD
Circuit
House
(VIPs only)

Post
Office

To
Bhopal

Gate

To Sanchi
Village

Tank

Steps

To
Vidisha &
Udaigiri
Caves

Vihara

Stupa 2

Stupa 3

Stupa 1

Temple
31

Monastery
51

Stupa 5

Pillar 10
(Ashoka)

Building
43

Temple
18

Temple 40

To Monasteries
45 & 47

If you come up from the town by the main route you can walk back down via stupa 2. There are no gateways to this stupa, but the 'medallions' which decorate the surrounding wall are of great interest. Their design is almost childlike, but full of energy and imagination. Flowers, animals and people – some mythological – are found all around the stupa.

Stupa 3 stands north-east of the main stupa and is similar in design, though smaller in size, to the great stupa. It has only one gateway and is thought to have been constructed soon after the completion of the great stupa. Stupa 3 once contained relics of two important disciples of the Buddha. They were removed and taken to London in 1853 but returned to Sanchi in 1953. Stupa 2, down the hill, also contained relics of important Buddhist teachers, but it is thought this lower spot was chosen for their enshrinement because the top of the hill was reserved for shrines to the Buddha and his direct disciples.

Now almost totally destroyed, the 2nd-century-BC **stupa 4** stands right behind stupa 3. Between stupa 1 (the great stupa) and stupa 3 is **stupa 5**, which is unusual in that it once had an image of the Buddha, now displayed in the museum.

Pillars

Scattered around the site are pillars or the remains of pillars. The most important is pillar 10, which was erected by Ashoka and stands close to the southern entrance to the great stupa. Only the base of this beautifully proportioned and executed shaft now stands, but the fine capital can be seen in the museum. The four back-to-back lions which once topped the column are an excellent example of the Greco-Buddhist art of that era at its finest. They now form the state emblem of India and can be seen on every bank note.

Pillar 25, dating from the Sunga period (2nd century BC) and pillar 35, dating from the 5th century AD, are not as fine as the earlier Ashoka pillar. Pillar 35, of which only fragments remain, stands close to the north-

ern gateway of the great stupa; again, the capital figure is in the museum.

Temples

Immediately south of stupa 1 is **temple 18**, a *chaitya* which, in style, is remarkably similar to classical Greek-columned buildings. It dates from around the 7th century AD but traces of earlier wooden buildings have been discovered beneath it. Beside this temple is the small **temple 17**, also Greek-like in style. The large **temple 40**, slightly south-east of these two temples, in part dates back to the Ashokan period.

Temple 31, built originally during the 6th or 7th centuries but reconstructed during either the 10th or 11th centuries, is adjacent to stupa 5. This flat-roofed rectangular temple contains a well-executed image of the Buddha. This appears to have been moved here from another temple during the reconstruction of Temple 31, as it does not exactly fit the pedestal on which it is mounted.

Monasteries

The earliest monasteries on the site were made of wood and have long since disappeared. The usual plan is of a central courtyard surrounded by monastic cells. **Monasteries 45 and 47** stand on the higher, eastern edge of the hilltop. They date from the later period of building at Sanchi, a time of transition from Buddhism to Hinduism, and show strong Hindu elements in their design. There is a good view of the village of Sanchi below and Vidisha in the distance from this side of the hill.

Monastery 51 is partway down the hill on the western side toward stupa 2. Close to it is the **'great bowl'** in which food and offerings were placed for distribution to the monks. It was carved out of a huge boulder. The modern **vihara** (monastery) on the hill was constructed to house the returned relics from stupa 3. The design is a poor shadow of the former artistry of Sanchi.

Places to Stay

It's possible to take in all that Sanchi has to offer in just two or three hours – less if you're pushed for time – so few people stay overnight. However, this is such a peaceful place that it's really worth spending the night here. Electricity cuts are frequent, so if you are planning to stay overnight, bring a torch (flashlight).

The best budget option in Sanchi is the clean, if somewhat spartan, *Sri Lanka Mahabodhi Society Guest House*. Rooms are in a tranquil garden setting and cost Rs 35/40 without/with attached bath (cold water only). Ask around for the very friendly caretaker if it looks closed.

The railway *retiring rooms* are clean and spacious, and cost Rs 60 per bed for the first 24 hours, Rs 90 thereafter.

The creaky Gothic-looking *Rest House* has only two rooms, which are fairly basic, although not exactly cheap. They cost Rs 80 per person, but this includes breakfast and dinner. Visiting officials have priority on rooms. If there's no-one around, ask at the house across the courtyard.

In front of the Rest House is MP Tourism's *Tourist Cafeteria* (☎ 81-243) which offers very clean rooms for Rs 175/225. Rooms have ceiling fans, and there's a (hefty) Rs 75 surcharge to use the air-cooler. As the name suggests, snacks are available here and non-guests are welcome.

On the main road to Bhopal about 250 metres from the crossroads is MP Tourism's other place, the *Travellers' Lodge* (☎ 81-223). All rooms have attached bathrooms and cost Rs 225/275. There is also a restaurant here.

Places to Eat

The best food is from the spotlessly clean *Tourist Cafeteria* and the dishes are also good value at Rs 15 to Rs 20. The food in the *Travellers' Lodge* is also good but slightly more expensive. Apart from these two places there's the cluster of food stalls at the bus stand.

Getting There & Away

Bus Local buses connect Bhopal with Sanchi (and other towns and villages in the area) about every hour from dawn to dusk,

but there are two possible routes. The longer route goes via Raisen (see Around Sanchi), takes three hours for the 68-km trip and costs Rs 12. The shorter route follows the railway line to Bhopal, takes 1¼ hours and costs Rs 10.

To Vidisha, buses depart from the Sanchi bus stand about every 30 minutes, and cost Rs 4.

Train Sanchi is on the main Delhi to Bombay railway line only 46 km north of Bhopal. However, officially, it is not possible to purchase a ticket on an express train service for this short trip. A passenger service departs Bhopal at 9.50 am and takes up to two hours. At Sanchi, the less pedantic railway clerks will sell tickets on any service back to Bhopal. The fare is Rs 9/16 passenger/express. To Bhopal there's an express train at 5.30 pm (40 minutes), and a passenger service at 4.30 pm (1½ to two hours).

Getting Around

In Sanchi itself everything's within easy walking distance. For excursions to places nearby like Vidisha (10 km) and the Udaigiri caves (14 km) you can rent bikes in Sanchi for Rs 2 per hour.

AROUND SANCHI

In the immediate vicinity of Sanchi there are more Buddhist sites, although none are of the scale or as well preserved as those at Sanchi. Most are within cycling distance. **Sonari**, 10 km south-west of Sanchi, has eight stupas, two of them important. At **Satdhara**, west of Sanchi on the bank of the Beas River, there are two stupas, one 30 metres in diameter. Another eight km southeast is **Andher**, where there are three small but well-preserved stupas. These stupas were all discovered in 1851, after the discovery of Sanchi.

Vidisha

Population: 103,000

Vidisha was important in Ashoka's time and it was from here that his wife came. Then it was known as Besnagar and was the largest town in the area. The ruins of the 2nd-

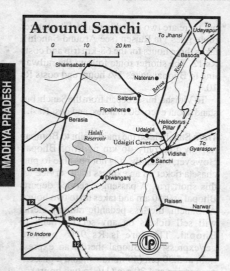

Around Sanchi

century BC Brahmanical shrine here show traces of lime mortar – the earliest use of cement in India. Finds from the site are displayed in the museum near the railway station.

From the 6th century AD the city was deserted for three centuries. It was renamed Bhilsa by the Muslims who built the now-ruined Bija Mandal, a mosque constructed from the remains of Hindu temples. From Sanchi you can reach Vidisha by bike (see Udaigiri below for directions), train (Rs 10, 8.30 and 10.40 am, and 4 pm) or bus (Rs 4, every 30 minutes).

Heliodorus Pillar

Between Vidisha and Udaigiri, one km north of the Udaigiri caves turn-off, is this inscribed pillar, known locally as the Khamb Baba pillar. It was erected in about 140 BC by Heliodorus, a Greek ambassador to the city from Taxila (now in Pakistan). The pillar celebrates his conversion to Hinduism. It's dedicated to Vishnu and worshipped by local fishers.

Udaigiri Caves

Cut into the sandstone hill, five km from Vidisha, are about 20 Gupta cave shrines dating from 320 to 606 AD; two are Jain, the

other 18 Hindu. In cave 5 there is a superb image of Vishnu in his boar incarnation. Cave 7 was cut out for the personal use of King Chandragupta II. Cave 20 is particularly interesting with detailed Jain carvings. On the top of the hill are the ruins of a 6th-century Gupta temple.

Getting There & Away From Bhopal take a Sanchi bus or train to Vidisha, and from there take a tonga or auto-rickshaw to the caves (Rs 40 to Rs 50 including waiting time, with serious bargaining). To reach the caves by bike from Sanchi, cycle towards Vidisha until you cross the river (six km). One km further on turn left (or carry straight on if you want to visit Vidisha first). After three km you'll reach a junction in the colourful bazaar – turn left again. One km further is another left turn. Take this road for the caves (3.5 km) or continue for one km for the Heliodorus Pillar.

Raisen

On the road to Bhopal, 23 km south of Sanchi, the huge and colourful hilltop fort of Raisen has temples, cannons, three palaces, 40 wells and a large tank. This Malwa fort was built around 1200 AD and although initially the centre of an independent kingdom, it later came under the control of Mandu. There are also ancient paintings in the caves in this area.

Gyaraspur

There are tanks, temples and a fort dating from the 9th and 10th centuries AD at this town, 51 km north-east of Sanchi. The town's name is derived from the big fair which used to be held here in the 11th month, sometimes known as Gyaras.

Udayapur

Udayapur is 90 km north of Sanchi. The large **Neelkantheswara Temple** here is thought to have been built in 1059 AD. It's profusely and very finely carved with four prominent decorated bands around the sikhara. The temple is aligned so that the first rays of the morning sun shine on the Siva lingam in the sanctum. It's a particularly fine example of Indo-Aryan architecture and is reached via the railway station at Bareth, which is seven km away.

BHOPAL

Population: 1,179,000
Telephone Area Code: 0755

The capital of Madhya Pradesh, Bhopal was built on the site of the 11th-century city of Bhojapal. It was founded by the legendary Raja Bhoj who is credited with having constructed the lakes around which the city is built. The present city was laid out by the Afghan chief Dost Mohammed Khan who was in charge of Bhopal during Aurangzeb's reign, but took advantage of the confusion following Aurangzeb's death in 1707 to carve out his own small kingdom.

Today, Bhopal presents a multifaceted profile. There's the old city with its crowded marketplaces, huge old mosques, and the palaces of the former begums who ruled over the city from 1819 to 1926. To the north sprawl the huge industrial suburbs and the slums which these developments inevitably give rise to. The new city with its broad avenues, sleek high-rise offices and leafy residential areas lies to the west. In the centre of Bhopal are two lakes which, while providing recreational facilities, are also the source of its plagues of mosquitoes.

The city is also famous as the site of the world's worst industrial disaster. See the boxed section below on the Bhopal disaster.

Orientation

Both the railway station and bus stand are within easy walking distance of the main

The Bhopal Disaster – A Decade Later

On the night of 3 December 1984, 15 tonnes of deadly methyl icocyanate, a toxic gas used in the manufacture of pesticides by Union Carbide, a US-based multinational company, leaked out over the city of Bhopal. Carried by the wind, this deadly gas soon enveloped the sleeping city.

Unable to understand the sense of suffocation that overwhelmed them, the barely awake residents of Bhopal ran into the streets, falling by the roadside as they succumbed to the toxic gas. The majority of the immediate victims were children, women, elderly people and the disabled, who couldn't outdistance the spreading fumes.

The Union Carbide plant was located only a short distance from the railway station, and this heavily populated area, inhabited predominantly by the poor and homeless, was the worst affected.

Panic and chaos ensued; officials intent on saving the lives of themselves and their families headed, literally, for the hills, leaving the bulk of the population to fend for themselves. Exact figures of those who perished in the disaster, or whose health was permanently destroyed, may never be known; local residents claim that the figures quoted by government officials are grossly unrepresentative. To date, the official death toll stands at an estimated 6000 people, and it is believed over half a million people have had their health destroyed for the rest of their lives.

A report prepared by a team of international medical experts which was released on the 10th anniversary of the disaster has found that 'a substantial proportion of Bhopal's population' is suffering from 'genuine long-term morbidity', with victims exhibiting symptoms disturbingly similar to those suffered by AIDS victims – a gas-induced breakdown of the immune system resulting in susceptibility to tuberculosis and respiratory problems.

The Indian government demanded US$3 billion in compensation, but was persuaded to accept US$470 million or have the case drawn out for at least a decade. All criminal charges were dropped, Union Carbide renounced any liability for the accident, and the money was paid to the government. It was not until seven years after the disaster and after another 2000 people had died that a tiny portion of this money began to trickle through to the victims. So far US$90 million has been paid out to about one tenth of the almost 700,000 claimants. At this rate, it will take until the year 2007 before all victims have received recompense – by which time, many will have died.

Today Bhopal is a pleasant, cosmopolitan city, and residents are understandably reluctant to talk about the horror which suddenly enveloped their lives over 10 years ago. Outside the now-closed factory, which lies just north of Hamidia Rd, a memorial statue to the dead is the only testimony to the tragedy of Bhopal.

Union Carbide is a profitable business once more, and batteries produced by this company are available throughout the country. Read the small print when buying batteries in India. ∎

MADHYA PRADESH

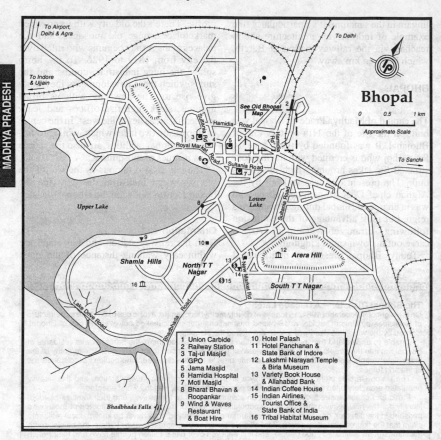

Bhopal

0   0.5   1 km
Approximate Scale

To Airport,
Delhi & Agra

To Indore
& Ujjain

To Delhi

To Sanchi

Hamidia Road

Sultania Road

Hamidia Road

See Old Bhopal
Map

Royal Market

Sultania Road

Upper Lake

Lower
Lake

Shamla Hills

North T T
Nagar

Arera Hill

South T T Nagar

New Market Rd

Lake Drive Road

Bhadbhada Road

Bhadbhada Falls

1 Union Carbide
2 Railway Station
3 Taj-ul Masjid
4 GPO
5 Jama Masjid
6 Hamidia Hospital
7 Moti Masjid
8 Bharat Bhavan &
   Roopankar
9 Wind & Waves
   Restaurant
   & Boat Hire
10 Hotel Palash
11 Hotel Panchanan &
    State Bank of Indore
12 Lakshmi Narayan Temple
    & Birla Museum
13 Variety Book House
    & Allahabad Bank
14 Indian Coffee House
15 Indian Airlines,
    Tourist Office &
    State Bank of India
16 Tribal Habitat Museum

hotel area along Hamidia Rd. When arriving by train, you need to leave the station by platform No 4 or 5 to reach Hamidia Rd.

The new part of the city, which encompasses T T Nagar, site of most of the major banks, the tourist office and Indian Airlines, is a long way from either of the transport terminals so you'll have to take an auto-rickshaw or taxi. Old and New Bhopal are effectively separated by the Upper and Lower lakes.

Information

There are helpful and efficient tourist infor-mation counters at both the railway station and airport. The headquarters of MP Tourism (☎ 55-4340) is in the Gangotri Complex, 4th floor, T T Nagar, in the new town. MP Tourism can book MP hotels and guest houses throughout the state. Five days advance booking is required. They can also arrange car hire (including driver) for Rs 4.50 per km. There's a 24-hour left-luggage facility at the railway station.

Shops in New Bhopal close on Mondays, and in Old Bhopal, on Sundays. Businesses such as airlines, banks, etc, close at noon on Saturday and all day Sunday.

Money The Indian Overseas Bank, Old Bhopal, may be able to cash travellers' cheques. Otherwise you'll have to head over to T T Nagar, where the State Bank of India (near the Rangmahal Talkies cinema, close to the tourist office), the State Bank of Indore (beneath the Hotel Panchanan) or the Allahabad Bank, Bhadbhada Rd, will do the requisite. All banks change money between 10.30 am and 2.30 pm only.

Post & Telecommunications The GPO and telegraph office are on Sultania Rd, Old Bhopal, near the Taj-ul-Masjid. Post restante letters are only held for two weeks, and letters should be marked 'Bhopal GPO', or they will be directed to the central post office in T T Nagar.

Cultural Centres The Alliance Française (☎ 56-6596) is in Arera Colony. Officially services are for members only, but French visitors may be able to peruse French newspapers and journals. Ring first.

Bookshops Bhadbhada Rd, between the Hotel Panchanan and MP Tourism in T T Nagar, has a couple of bookshops with a small English-language range. Variety Book House probably has the best selection, but it's not extensive.

Taj-ul-Masjid
Commenced by Shah Jahan Begum, but never really completed, the Taj-ul-Masjid is one of the largest mosques in India. It's a huge pink mosque with two massive white-domed minarets and three white domes over the main building. The entrance to the mosque is not on Sultania Rd, despite the huge staircase here; it's around the corner on busy Royal Market Rd.

Other Mosques
The **Jama Masjid**, built in 1837 by Qudsia Begum, is surrounded by the bazaar and has very squat minarets. The **Moti Masjid** was built by Qudsia Begum's daughter, Sikander

Jahan Begum, in 1860. Similar in style to the Jama Masjid in Delhi, it is a smaller mosque with two dark-red minarets crowned by golden spikes.

Lakes
The larger Upper Lake covers six sq km and a bridge separates it from the Lower Lake. MP Tourism has a veritable flotilla of boats available for hire on the Upper Lake, including rowboats (Rs 30 for 30 minutes), pedal boats (Rs 60 per hour), sailboats (Rs 50 per hour) and motorboats (Rs 10 per person for 10 minutes). The booking office is at the bottom of the driveway leading to the Wind & Waves Restaurant.

Hindu ascetic or sadhu on a personal spiritual quest.

MADHYA PRADESH

Lakshmi Narayan Temple & Birla Museum

There are good views over the lakes to the old town from the Lakshmi Narayan Temple, also known as the Birla Mandir. Beside it on Arera Hill is an excellent museum, containing a small but very selective collection of local sculptures dating mainly from the Paramana period. The stone sculptures are mainly of Vishnu, Siva and their respective consorts and incarnations. There's also a small selection of terracotta exhibits from Kausambi and a reconstruction of the Zoo Rock Shelter from Bhimbetka. The museum is open daily (except Monday) from 9 am to noon, and 2 to 6 pm; entry is Rs 2.

Bharat Bhavan

Bharat Bhavan is a complex for the verbal, visual and performing arts, designed by the well-known architect Charles Correa and opened in 1982. It's now regarded as one of the most important centres in the country for the preservation of traditional folk art. As well as the workshops and theatres here, there's the **Roopankar**, the impressive art gallery that 'shows you what is sadly missing from the folk art churned out for tourists', as one reader put it. Bharat Bhavan is in the Shamla Hills and is open from 2 to 8 pm, daily except Monday; admission is Rs 1.

Tribal Habitat Museum (Museum of Man)

This interesting open-air exhibition of tribal buildings from all over India is at Rashtriya Manav Sangrahalaya in the Shamla Hills, on a 40-hectare site overlooking the Upper Lake. Ancient rock-art shelters are encompassed within the exhibit area. There are craft and pottery demonstrations, and film shows on Saturdays at 4 pm (one hour). Entry to the exhibit and admission to the film are free. The display is open from 10 am to 6 pm (closed public holidays and Mondays).

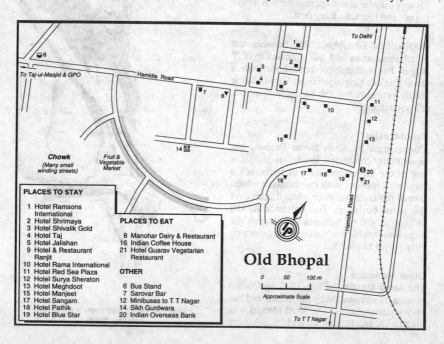

Old Bhopal

0   50   100 m

Approximate Scale

PLACES TO STAY

1 Hotel Ramsons International
2 Hotel Shrimaya
3 Hotel Shivalik Gold
4 Hotel Taj
5 Hotel Jalishan
9 Hotel & Restaurant Ranjit
10 Hotel Rama International
11 Hotel Red Sea Plaza
12 Hotel Surya Sheraton
13 Hotel Meghdoot
15 Hotel Manjeet
17 Hotel Sangam
18 Hotel Pathik
19 Hotel Blue Star

PLACES TO EAT

8 Manohar Dairy & Restaurant
16 Indian Coffee House
21 Hotel Guarav Vegetarian Restaurant

OTHER

6 Bus Stand
7 Sarovar Bar
12 Minibuses to T T Nagar
14 Sikh Gurdwara
20 Indian Overseas Bank

To Delhi

To Taj-ul-Masjid & GPO

Hamidia Road

Chowk (Many small winding streets)

Fruit & Vegetable Market

Hamidia Road

To T T Nagar

Places to Stay – bottom end

It can be difficult to find cheap accommodation in Bhopal, as many hotels and guest houses do not have 'C' forms for foreigner registration. All of the following places have telephones in the rooms and attached bathrooms, and most have TVs.

The best value moderately priced hotel is the *Hotel Ranjit* (☎ 75-211), which has very clean singles/doubles for Rs 80/100, and there's an excellent restaurant downstairs. The similarly priced *Hotel Rama International* nearby is not quite as good value. Rooms are spacious, if a little shabby, and the staff have a habit of barging in unannounced. Singles/doubles here are Rs 80/120, or Rs 200/255 with air-con.

The *Hotel Meghdoot* (☎ 51-1375) has rooms from Rs 65/85 to Rs 100/125, all with attached bathroom. The rooms open onto the stairwell, so could be noisy.

The *Hotel Sangam* (☎ 54-2382) has basic but clean rooms from Rs 90/110 to Rs 150/180. This place is set back from the main drag, so guests are spared the cacophony of Hamidia Rd. Close by, the *Hotel Manjeet* (☎ 76-168) has singles without air-con from Rs 110 to Rs 125, and doubles without air-con from Rs 135 to Rs 185.

The *Hotel Red Sea Plaza* (☎ 75-551) looms over the main Hamidia Rd junction. Singles/doubles are Rs 90/130, or Rs 300/350 with air-con. A deposit of Rs 300 is demanded on check-in!

The *Hotel Jalishan* (☎ 75-778) is centrally located on Hamidia Rd and has basic singles/doubles from Rs 80/150, or for Rs 250/300 with air-con. Checkout is 24 hours after arrival.

There is a vast selection of seedy flophouses in the chowk area, but they don't have the requisite 'C' form, so will not take foreigners.

Places to Stay – middle

The *retiring rooms* at the railway station are all air-con and cost Rs 200 for a single or double (there are no dormitory beds). There's a good choice of mid-range hotels available in the city. Most have a very wide range of rooms from basic doubles to air-cooled and air-con rooms.

The *Hotel Taj* (☎ 53-3162) has well-appointed rooms for Rs 100/130, or Rs 300/400 with air-con. There's an à la carte restaurant, but no bar. Behind the Taj, the *Hotel Shivalik Gold* (☎ 76-000) is slightly more expensive at Rs 150/200 or Rs 450/525 with air-con. Rooms are comfortable and spotless.

Also in this cluster of mid-range hotels on the north side of Hamidia Rd is the *Hotel Shrimaya* (☎ 75-454), where rooms are Rs 125/175, or Rs 275/300 with air-con. At the back of this hotel alley is the *Hotel Ramsons International* (☎ 75-298). Ramsons is looking a little gloomy and cavernous compared to its modern neighbours, but the rooms are large and quiet, and not bad value at Rs 145/220, or Rs 275/365 with air-con. Checkout is 24 hours.

A few doors down from the Hotel Red Sea Plaza is the *Hotel Surya Sheraton* (☎ 72-218), where standard singles/doubles are Rs 150/200, and deluxe rooms with air-con are Rs 450/500.

The *Hotel Pathik* (☎ 77-251) is in a quiet area and has clean, straightforward rooms for Rs 135/175, or Rs 345/395 with air-con. Rooms at the nearby *Hotel Blue Star* (☎ 75-526) are good value at Rs 110/130, or Rs 185/225 with air-con.

If you have business in the T T Nagar area, MP Tourism's *Hotel Palash* (☎ 55-3006) is conveniently located close to Bhadbhada Rd. Rooms are not cheap, however, at Rs 250/300 to Rs 440/490.

Places to Stay – top end

The three-star *Residency* (☎ 55-6002), Zone 1, M P Nagar, is the only hotel in Bhopal with a swimming pool. Standard rooms are Rs 600/800 and deluxe rooms are Rs 750/950. Close by is the *Amer Palace Hotel* (☎ 55-7127), which is a little cheaper with standard rooms for Rs 500/650 and deluxe rooms for Rs 575/700.

The *Hotel Lake View Ashok* (☎ 54-1600; fax 54-1606) is a well-appointed hotel in the Shamla Hills with an excellent restaurant.

All rooms have private balconies, and there are good views over the lake. Comfortable singles/doubles are Rs 750/950.

The *Jehan Numa Palace* (☎ 54-0100; fax 54-0720), only a stone's throw away, was formerly a palace, built in the late 19th century. Rooms are from Rs 750/900 and there's a restaurant and bar.

Places to Eat

The cheapest places to eat are the street stalls surrounding the bus and railway stations. The ubiquitous *Indian Coffee House* is another good cheap place; there are outlets in both Old and New Bhopal.

Many of the hotels around Hamidia Rd have good restaurants/bars. The one at the *Hotel Ranjit* has an excellent (and well-deserved) reputation. Most dishes are around Rs 35, and ice-cold beer is Rs 38.

Good vegetarian food can be found at the *Hotel Guarav*, also in Old Bhopal, but they don't serve alcohol.

The *Manohar Dairy & Restaurant* (sign in Hindi), Hamidia Rd, has lots of gooey favourites such as gulab jamun (Rs 7.50), as well as an astonishing variety of ice cream. Dosas and idlis are also available. This place is very popular with locals.

The *Sarovar Bar* above the Hotel Rajdoot serves beer, cocktails and snacks, but it has a pretty seedy ambience.

For a splurge, try the *Shahnama* restaurant at the Jehan Numa Palace. It's not cheap, with main dishes from Rs 80 to Rs 110, but the food is excellent.

At the boat-hire office on the Upper Lake is MP Tourism's (fairly ordinary) *Wind & Waves Restaurant*, which serves snacks only.

Things to Buy

Bhopal's two main shopping areas are the New Market area, in New Bhopal, and the old market area, or Chowk, in Old Bhopal. Whilst similar items can be found in both markets, prices are much more reasonable in the Chowk, and the labyrinthine streets and alleys here make this a fascinating area to wander around – but count on getting totally lost! Here you'll find fine gold and silver jewellery, beautifully woven saris and hand-embroidered applique skirts at reasonable prices.

'Mrignayni' is the registered trade name for MP state handicraft merchandise – many retail shops carry Mrignayni line.

Getting There & Away

Air Indian Airlines (☎ 55-0480) has five flights weekly to Bombay (US$70), Indore (US$21) and Delhi (US$62), and twice weekly to Gwalior (US$39). The office is in T T Nagar, adjacent to MP Tourism.

Bus There are numerous daily buses to Sanchi (Rs 10, 1¼ hours; via Raisen, Rs 12); Vidisha (Rs 17, 2¼ hours); Indore (Rs 36, 5½ hours, or express, Rs 55, 4½ hours); Ujjain (Rs 48, four hours); and Jabalpur (Rs 77, 10 to 11 hours). There are no direct services to Mandu; first you have to travel to Indore, from where regular buses depart for Mandu (5½ hours, Rs 19).

There's an overnight service to Khajuraho departing at 10.30 pm (Rs 85, 12 hours), but it's better to go by train to Jhansi or Satna and connect by bus from there.

A new computerised reservation system should now be up and running, so bus bookings should be a breeze.

MP Tourism operates an impressive air-con bus to Indore (Rs 150, four to five hours). It departs from the railway station at 2.30 pm after having collected passengers off the *Shatabdi Express* from Delhi.

Train There is a new, efficient air-con reservation hall on the left as you exit the main terminal, and a separate counter for the *Shatabdi Express* within the railway terminal.

Bhopal is on one of the two main Delhi to Bombay railway lines. At present it's the terminus of the daily *Shatabdi Express*, which leaves New Delhi station at 6.15 am reaching Bhopal at 2 pm, returning to New Delhi after a stop here of 40 minutes. Cheapest fares from Bhopal are Rs 280 for Jhansi (three hours), Rs 325 for Gwalior (4¼ hours), Rs 380 for Agra (5½ hours) and Rs 495 for New Delhi (7¾ hours).

Other express trains connect Bhopal with Delhi (705 km, 10 to 12 hours, Rs 168/499 in 2nd/1st class), Bombay (837 km, 12 to 15 hours, Rs 188/553), Agra (506 km, 8½ hours, Rs 130/387), Gwalior (388 km, 6½ hours, Rs 105/320) and Jhansi (291 km, 4½ hours, Rs 67/255). Sanchi is only 46 km north of Bhopal, but officially it is not possible to purchase a ticket on an express train. See the Sanchi section for more details.

For Khajuraho, travel to Jhansi and take a bus from there.

Getting Around
To/From the Airport Taxis are available at the airport, which is about 10 km from Old Bhopal. The official rate is Rs 4.50 per km. A rickshaw to the city costs about Rs 30.

Local Transport Auto-rickshaw drivers almost always use their meters, except at night when you'll have to negotiate the fare. Minibuses for T T Nagar depart about every two minutes from in front of the Hotel Surya Sheraton. The fare is Rs 2. A rickshaw costs about Rs 20.

AROUND BHOPAL
Bhojpur
The legendary Raja Bhoj (1010-53) not only built the lakes at Bhopal but also built another one, estimated at 400 sq km, in Bhojpur, 28 km south-east of the state capital. History records that the lake was held back by massive earthen dams faced on both sides with huge blocks of sandstone set without mortar. Unfortunately, the lake no longer exists having been destroyed by Hoshang Shah, the ruler of Mandu, in a fit of destructive passion in the early 15th century. It's said that the lake took three years to empty and that the climate of the area was radically affected by the loss of this enormous body of water.

What does survive here is the huge, partially completed, **Bhojeshwar Temple** which originally overlooked the lake. Dedicated to Siva, it has some very unusual

design features and sports a lingam 2.3 metres high by 5.3 metres in circumference. The earthen rampart used to raise stones for the construction of the dome still remains. Nearby is another incomplete monolithic temple, this time a **Jain shrine** containing a colossal statue of Mahavira over six metres in height. Though a long way from rivalling the 17-metre-high statue of Gomateshvara at Sravanabelagola in Karnataka, this has to be one of the largest Jain statues in India.

Bhimbetka
Like the Aboriginal rock paintings in the outback of Australia, the cave paintings of the Bushmen in the Kalahari Desert in Africa or the Palaeolithic Lascaux caves of France, the Bhimbetka caves are a must. Amongst forests of teak and sal in the craggy cliffs of an almost African setting 45 km south of Bhopal, some 1000 rock shelters have been discovered. Almost half contain ancient paintings depicting the life and times of the different people who lived here.

Because of the natural red and white pigments which the painters used, the colours have been remarkably well preserved and it's obvious in certain caves that the same surface has been used by different people at different times. There's everything from figures of wild buffalo (gaur), rhinoceros, bears and tigers to hunting scenes, initiation ceremonies, childbirth, communal dancing and drinking scenes, religious rites and burials.

The extent and archaeological importance of the site was only recently realised and dating is still not complete. The oldest paintings are believed to be up to 12,000 years old whereas some of the crude, geometric figures probably date from as recently as the medieval period.

The caves are not difficult to find; a path connects the 15 that the local guide will show you. The **Zoo Rock Shelter** is one of the first you come to, famous for its variety of animal paintings. There's nothing here other than the caves so bring something to drink.

Getting There & Away From Bhopal, 45 km

away, take a Hoshangabad bus (Rs 13) via Obaidullaganj, 50 minutes south of Bhopal. (It may be necessary to change buses at Obaidullaganj.) Get off the Hoshangabad bus 6.5 km after Obaidullaganj by the sign pointing right with '3.2' and some Hindi on it. Follow this sign, crossing the railway track for the 3.2-km walk to the hills in front of you. To get back you can flag down a truck on the main road. A taxi for the trip from Bhopal costs about Rs 450 return.

Other Places
Neori, only six km from Bhopal, has an 11th-century Siva temple and is a popular picnic spot. **Islampur**, 11 km from Bhopal on the Berasia Rd, was built by Dost Mohammed Khan and has a hilltop palace and garden. At **Ashapuri**, six km north of Bhopal, there are ruined temples and Jain palaces with statues scattered on the ground. **Chiklod**, 45 km out, has a palace in a peaceful sylvan setting.

PACHMARHI
Population: 13,800
Telephone Area Code: 07578

Madhya Pradesh's peaceful hill station stands at an altitude of 1067 metres, and is 210 km south-east of Bhopal. It was 'discovered' by a Captain Forsyth who realised the potential of the saucer-shaped valley as a health resort in 1857, when he first saw it from the viewpoint that now bears his name.

Although it's nothing like a Himalayan hill station, Pachmarhi is a very attractive place rarely visited by foreign tourists. The area draws quite a few artists; Ravi Shankar has a music school here. Gurus occasionally hold retreats up here and up to 100,000 sadhus and tribals attend the **Sivaratri** celebrations (February/March) at Mahadeo Temple.

There are fine views out over the surrounding red sandstone hills, pools and waterfalls to bathe in, ancient **cave paintings** and some interesting walks through the sal forests. A recommended long day walk is to the hilltop shrine of **Chauragarh**, four km from Mahadeo. You can see the cave paintings

at Mahadeo on the way. There's a golf course, a couple of churches and if you don't feel like walking, bicycles can be rented from the shop near the New Hotel or in the bazaar.

Places to Stay & Eat
Almost all the accommodation in Pachmarhi is run by MP Tourism. The *New Hotel* (☎ 2017), however, is a large, recommended place operated by the Public Works Department (PWD). It's clean and good value with doubles from Rs 75 to Rs 175 and some cottages. There's a reasonable restaurant with main dishes at around Rs 35.

If you want something cheaper try the *Youth Centre* which has a large open hall with 50 beds at Rs 30 each. The other cheap place is the friendly *Holiday Homes* although it's not in such a good location as the New Hotel. Singles and doubles are Rs 125, plus Rs 50 for each extra person. Rooms have a small courtyard and attached bathrooms. Hot water comes in buckets.

The *Nilamber Cottages* are an excellent choice. They're right beside the TV relay centre on the top of a hill so the views are great. Doubles with attached bathroom with water heater are Rs 155. The *Panchvati Huts & Cottages* below the hill are not such good value with singles/doubles from Rs 200/250 but the good *China Bowl* restaurant is here. The *SADA Nandan Van* cottages are better value at Rs 150 a double.

The top hotel is the *Satpura Retreat* (☎ 2097), a former English bungalow with a large verandah around it, comfortable rooms and vast bathrooms. It's in a very quiet location along the Mahadeo road. Rooms are from Rs 275/325, or Rs 550/600 with aircon. *Amaltas* (☎ 2098) was also a Raj bungalow and has rooms for Rs 225/275 with attached bathrooms but no air-con.

Getting There and Away
From the bus stand near the bazaar in Pachmarhi there's one early-morning bus to Bhopal (Rs 50, five hours) and departures every couple of hours to Pipariya (Rs 15, 1½ hours). Jeeps also ply this route for

Rs 40 per person or Rs 250 for the whole jeep. Signs by the winding road warn drivers that 'Overtakers provide job for undertakers'!

PIPARIYA
Telephone Area Code: 07576

Pipariya is the nearest road/rail junction to Pachmarhi, 47 km away. It's on the railway line that runs from Bombay to Jabalpur. Opposite the railway station, there's an excellent little MP Tourism *Tourist Motel* (☎ 22-299) with doubles at Rs 100 and a restaurant.

A bus from Bhopal costs Rs 36 and takes six hours.

Western Madhya Pradesh

UJJAIN
Population: 407,000
Telephone Area Code: 0734

Only 56 km from Indore, ancient Ujjain is one of India's holiest cities for Hindus. It gets its sanctity from a mythological tale about the churning of the oceans by the gods and demons in search of the nectar of immortality. When the coveted vessel of nectar was finally found there followed a mad scramble across the skies with the demons pursuing the gods in an attempt to take the nectar from them. Four drops were spilt and they fell at Haridwar, Nasik, Ujjain and Prayag (Allahabad). As a result, Ujjain is one of the sites of the Kumbh Mela which takes place here every 12 years. The 1992 Kumbh Mela drew millions (literally!) to bathe here in the River Shipra.

Despite its relative obscurity today, Ujjain ranks equal as a great religious centre with such places as Varanasi, Gaya and Kanchipuram. Non-Hindus, however, may well find it a relatively uninteresting city as there's not much going on here most of the year.

History
On an ancient trade route, Ujjain has a distinguished history whose origins are lost in the mists of time. It was an important city under Ashoka's father, when it was known as Avantika. Later it was so attractive to Chandragupta II (380-414 AD) that he ruled from here rather than from his actual capital, Pataliputra. It was at his court that Kalidasa, one of Hinduism's most revered poets, wrote the *Meghdoot*, with its famous lyrical description of the city and its people.

With the passing of the Guptas and the rise of the Parmaras, Ujjain became the centre of much turmoil in the struggle for control of the Malwa region. The last of the Paramaras, Siladitya, was captured by the Muslim sultans of Mandu, and Ujjain thus passed into the hands of Mughal vassals.

Muslim rule was sometimes violent, sometimes benign. An invasion by Altamish in 1234 resulted in the wholesale desecration of many temples but that was halted during the reign of Baz Bahadur of Mandu. Bahadur himself was eventually overthrown by the Mughal emperor, Akbar. Later on, under Aurangzeb, grants were provided to fund temple reconstruction.

Following the demise of the Mughals, Maharaja Jai Singh (of Jaipur fame) became the governor of Malwa and during his rule the observatory and several new temples were constructed at Ujjain. With his passing, Ujjain experienced another period of turmoil at the hands of the Marathas until it was finally taken by the Scindias in 1750. When the Scindia capital was moved to Gwalior in 1810, Ujjain's commercial importance declined rapidly.

Orientation & Information
The railway line divides the city: the old section, including the bazaar and most of the temples and ghats, are to the north-west of the city, and the new section is on the south-east side. The majority of hotels are in front of the railway station. Tourist information is available at the Hotel Shipra.

Temples
Mahakaleshwar Temple The most important temple in Ujjain, the Mahakaleshwar Temple is dedicated to Siva. The temple

enshrines one of India's 12 *jyoti lingam* – lingam believed to derive currents of power *(shakti)* from within themselves as opposed to lingam ritually invested with *mantra-shakti* by the priests.

The myth of the jyoti lingam (the lingam of light) stems from a long dispute for primacy between Brahma and Vishnu. During this dispute, according to legend, the earth split apart to reveal an incandescent column of light. To find the source of this column, Vishnu became a boar and burrowed underground while Brahma took to the skies in the form of an eagle. After 1000 years of fruitless searching, Siva emerged from the lingam of light and both Brahma and Vishnu acknowledged that it was he who was the greatest of the gods.

The temple was destroyed by Altamish of Delhi in 1235 but restored by the Scindias in the 19th century.

Bade Ganeshji Ka Mandir Above the tank near the Mahakaleshwar Temple, the large ornate statue of Ganesh here makes this temple a popular pilgrimage spot.

Harsiddhi Temple Built during the Maratha period, this temple enshrines a famous image of the goddess Annapurna. The two large pillars adorned with lamps were a special feature of Maratha art and are spectacular when lit at Navratri (Dussehra) in September/October. (See the Sacred India colour section on page 57 for more information about this festival.)

Gopal Mandir The marble-spired Gopal Mandir was constructed by the queen of Maharaja Daulat Rao Scindia in the 19th century and is an excellent example of Maratha architecture.

The silver-plated doors of the sanctum have quite a history. They were originally taken from the temple at Somnath in Gujarat to Ghazni in Afghanistan and then to Lahore

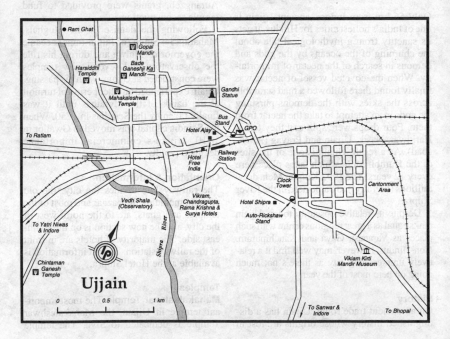

Ujjain

0   0.5   1 km

by Mahmud Shah Abdati. From there they were rescued by Mahadji Scindia and shortly afterwards installed in the temple. This is a very large temple but is easy to miss as it's buried in the bazaar.

Chintaman Ganesh Temple On the opposite bank of the River Shipra, this temple is believed to be of considerable antiquity. The artistically carved pillars of the assembly hall date back to the Paramara period.

Ghats
Since most of the temples are of relatively recent construction you may find more of interest on the ghats. The largest of these is Ram Ghat, fairly close to the Harsiddhi Temple. The others are some considerable distance north of the centre.

Vedh Shala (Observatory)
Since the 4th century BC, Ujjain has been India's Greenwich (as far as Indian geographers were concerned), with the first meridian of longitude passing through it. With modern calculations, the Tropic of Cancer is now actually just to the north. Maharaja Jai Singh built one of his quirky observatories here between 1725 and 1730 AD. This one is smaller than those in Jaipur or Delhi but it's still in use and quite interesting. The very enthusiastic curator will demonstrate the function of the exhibits, but his English is a little hard to follow. Astrologers can purchase the complete year's astronomical ephemeris in both English and Hindi at the observatory for Rs 13.

Kaliadeh Palace
On an island in the River Shipra, eight km north of town is the water palace of the Mandu sultans, constructed in 1458. River water is diverted over stone screens in the palace, and the bridge to the island uses carvings from the sun temple which once stood here. The central dome of the palace is a good example of Persian architecture.

With the downfall of Mandu, the palace gradually fell into ruin but was restored, along with the nearby sun temple, by Madhav Rao Scindia in 1920.

Places to Stay
There's quite a range of accommodation right opposite the railway station. Even the cheapest rooms seem to have attached bathrooms. At the bottom of the pile is the *Hotel Vikram* (☎ 25-780) with singles/doubles from Rs 50/75. However, the rooms are tiny and dirty. Next door the *Hotel Surya* (☎ 25-747) is a better bet, with rooms for Rs 55/65, or Rs 70/80 with TV. Hot water is available in buckets (Rs 4).

The *Hotel Rama Krishna* (☎ 25-912) and the *Hotel Chandragupta* (☎ 25-500) are nearby, both quite good and in close competition with each other. Rooms at the Rama Krishna range from Rs 35/45 (pokey, and no bathroom) to Rs 125/150 with TV. Some rooms have no external windows, and are a little stuffy. The Chandragupta is not a bad choice, despite its manic, Fawlty Towers atmosphere. Rooms range from Rs 70/90 to Rs 125/150, and bucket hot water is free. The cheaper rooms are a little dingy, but OK. Checkout is 24 hours.

One of the best budget choices is the *Hotel Ajay* (☎ 50-856). It's around the corner from the railway station road where the bulk of the other cheapies are located, and is good value at Rs 60/75 (cold water only) to Rs 75/100 (with hot water). There are also air-cooled rooms for Rs 105/150 with TV.

The *Hotel Free India* (☎ 55-457) is the large building opposite the Rama Krishna. The sign is in Hindi. Comfortable, large rooms with hot and cold water range from Rs 125 to Rs 175 (no single rate). There's a restaurant here.

Railway *retiring rooms* are Rs 70, or Rs 155 with air-con. Dorm beds are Rs 30.

MP Tourism's *Yatri Niwas* (☎ 51-498) is inconveniently located two km from the city centre, and has only two rooms. Dorm beds cost Rs 30 and singles/doubles are 125/150.

The top hotel is MP Tourism's *Hotel Shipra* (☎ 51-495), down a quiet road in a very pleasant setting. There's an impressive marble foyer, and the rooms are well appointed. Rooms range from Rs 250/275, to Rs 440/490 with air-con. The restaurant here is quite good, and there's a bar. To get to the Shipra from the railway station, exit at platform 7.

Places to Eat

There are a number of places to eat opposite the station. The *Chanakya Restaurant*, next to the Hotel Chandragupta, serves excellent vegetarian food and beer for Rs 35. Don't mistake the 'uroinal' here for the 'toilat'! The *Sudama Restaurant* next door has good vegetarian dishes for under Rs 20.

The *Nauratna Restaurant* in the Hotel Shipra is not bad, although the size of the servings is a little modest, and beer is expensive at Rs 45.

Getting There & Away

Bus There are frequent daily buses to Indore (Rs 14, 56 km, 1½ hours) which are generally faster than the train, and to Bhopal (Rs 48, four hours). There are currently no direct services to Mandu; all buses go via Indore. A few buses connect Ujjain with Kota in Rajasthan (256 km, Rs 60).

Train The overnight *Malwa Express* is the fastest link with Delhi. It takes 17½ hours to New Delhi (885 km, Rs 192/569 in 2nd/1st), via Bhopal (184 km, four hours, Rs 47/175), Jhansi (475 km, nine hours, Rs 125/374), Gwalior (572 km, 10½ hours, Rs 143/430) and Agra (690 km, 13 hours, Rs 160/492).

The *Narmada Express* connects Ujjain with Indore (2¼ hours, Rs 24/63) and, heading east, Bhopal (184 km, five hours, Rs 47/175), Jabalpur (540 km, 12½ hours, Rs 137/408) and Bilaspur (929 km, 25 hours, Rs 200/588).

The *Awantika Express* is the only direct service to Bombay, leaving at 9 pm. The fare for the 639-km journey is Rs 155/464. Alternatively, you can catch the 2.20 pm passenger train to Nagda (1½ hours, Rs 9), to connect with the *Frontier Mail* which departs at 6.15 pm, arriving in Bombay at 7 am (Rs 163/492).

The *Bhopal-Rajkot Express* to Ahmeda-bad departs at 11.15 pm and arrives in Ahmedabad at 8.15 am (Rs 132/375).

There is an efficient reservation hall to the left as you leave the station.

Getting Around

Many of Ujjain's sights are a long way from the centre of town so you'll probably find yourself using quite a few auto-rickshaws. Concerned at the reputation that Ujjain's rapacious rickshaw drivers had earned, the municipal authorities have instituted a registration system at both the bus and railway stations. Drivers have to register the journey and fare with the police to ensure that tourists aren't ripped off!

INDORE

Population: 1,220,000
Telephone Area Code: 0731

Indore is not of great interest, but it makes a good departure point for visiting Mandu. The city is a major textile-producing centre and at Pithampur, 35 km away, Hindustan Motors, Kinetic Honda, Bajaj Tempo and Eischer all have factories. Indians call Pithampur the Detroit of India, and Indore is its gateway.

The Khan and Sarasvati rivers run through Indore. Although it is on an ancient pilgrimage route to Ujjain, nothing much happened here until the 18th century. From 1733, it was ruled by the Holkar dynasty who were firm supporters of the British, even during the Mutiny.

Orientation

The older part of town is on the western side of the railway line, the newer part on the east. If arriving by train, leave the station by platform No 1 for the east side of town and by platform No 4 for the west side.

The railway station and main bus terminal (Sarwate) are close together but are separated by a complicated flyover system. Not surprisingly a number of holes have appeared in the fence between the two and people just march straight through.

Information

The tourist office (☎ 38-888) is by the Tourist Bungalow at the back of the R N Tagore Natya Griha Hall, R N Tagore Rd. You can make enquiries about tours to Mandu here. The office is open from 10 am to 5.30 pm (closed Sundays). There are sometimes exhibitions held at the magnificent Gandhi Hall (town hall). It's open to visitors daily from 10 am to 5 pm.

Travellers' cheques can be changed at the State Bank of India (main branch) near the GPO, or the more centrally located branch on Yeshwant Niwas Rd.

The central telegraph office is behind the Regal Cinema, Nehru Park. It's open 24 hours, and fax/telex facilities are available between 7 am and 8 pm.

Rupayana, beneath the Central Hotel, is a very good bookshop, and there's also quite a good selection at Badshah Book Shop, further down M G Rd.

Rajwada

In the old part of town, the multistorey gateway of the Rajwada or Old Palace looks out onto the palm-lined main square in the crowded streets of the Kajuri Bazaar. A

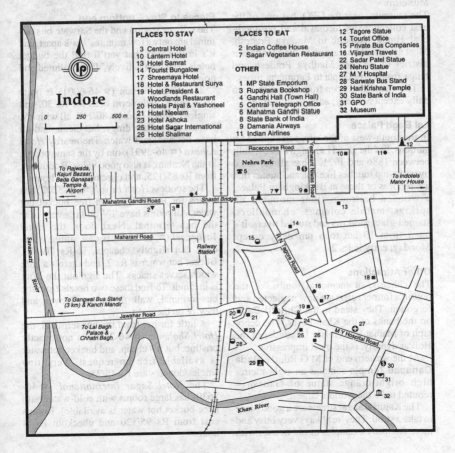

Indore

0   250   500 m

PLACES TO STAY
3 Central Hotel
10 Lantern Hotel
13 Hotel Samrat
14 Tourist Bungalow
17 Shreemaya Hotel
18 Hotel & Restaurant Surya
19 Hotel President & Woodlands Restaurant
20 Hotels Payal & Yashoneel
21 Hotel Neelam
23 Hotel Ashoka
25 Hotel Sagar International
26 Hotel Shalimar

PLACES TO EAT
2 Indian Coffee House
7 Sagar Vegetarian Restaurant

OTHER
1 MP State Emporium
3 Rupayana Bookshop
4 Gandhi Hall (Town Hall)
5 Central Telegraph Office
6 Mahatma Gandhi Statue
8 State Bank of India
9 Damania Airways
11 Indian Airlines

12 Tagore Statue
14 Tourist Office
15 Private Bus Companies
16 Vijayant Travels
22 Sadar Patel Statue
24 Nehru Statue
27 M Y Hospital
28 Sarwate Bus Stand
29 Hari Krishna Temple
30 State Bank of India
31 GPO
32 Museum

To Rajwada, Kajuri Bazaar, Bada Ganapati Temple & Airport

Mahatma Gandhi Road

Maharani Road

Sarasvati River

River

To Gangwal Bus Stand (3 km) & Kanch Mandir

To Lal Bagh Palace & Chhatri Bagh

Jawahar Road

Shastri Bridge

Railway Station

Racecourse Road

Nehru Park

Yeshwant Niwas Road

R N Tagore Road

M Y Hospital Road

To Indotels Manor House

Khan River

mixture of French, Mughal and Maratha styles, the palace has been up in flames three times in its 200-year history. After the serious 1984 conflagration it's now not much more than a façade.

Kanch Mandir

On Jawahar Rd, not far from the Rajwada, is the Kanch Mandir or Seth Hukanchand Temple. This Jain temple is very plain externally, but inside is completely mirrored with pictures of sinners being tortured in the afterlife.

Museum

The museum, near the GPO, has one of the best collections of medieval and pre-medieval Hindu sculpture in Madhya Pradesh. Most are from Hinglajgarh in the Mandasaur district of western Madhya Pradesh and range from early Gupta to Paramana times.

The museum is open from 10 am to 5 pm daily except Monday; admission is free.

Lal Bagh Palace

In the south-west of the city, surrounded by gardens, lies the grand Lal Bagh Palace, built between 1886 and 1921. It has all the usual over-the-top touches like entrance gates that are replicas of those at Buckingham Palace, a wooden ballroom floor mounted on springs, marble columns, chandeliers, stained-glass windows and stuffed tigers. It's open from 10 am to 6 pm daily except Monday; entry is Rs 2.

Other Attractions

The chhatris, or memorial tombs, of the region's former rulers are now neglected and forgotten. They stand in the **Chhatri Bagh** on the banks of the Khan River. The cenotaph of Malhar Rao Holkar I, founder of the Holkar dynasty, is the most impressive.

At the western end of M G Rd, the **Bada Ganapati Temple** contains an eight-metre-high bright-orange statue of Ganesh – reputed to be the world's largest.

The **Kajuri Bazaar** streets are a good place to take a stroll. They're always very busy and there are many examples of old houses with picturesque overhanging verandahs. Unfortunately, these are disappearing fast as concrete rapidly replaces wood.

Organised Tours

Several private bus companies offer guided tours to Mandu, usually only at the weekends. If this is what you're looking for, one company to try is Trimurti Tours & Travel (☎ (0731) 37-403), near the Shastri Bridge in Indore. They have a full-day Sunday tour departing at 8 am for Rs 60. MP Tourism also operates a Sunday day tour for Rs 100.

Places to Stay – bottom end

The railway station and the Sarwate bus terminal are only a few minutes' walk apart, and it's in this area that you'll find the budget hotels. The area is lively, dirty, polluted and noisy.

The *Hotel Neelam* (☎ 46-6001) is quite good value, with dorm beds for Rs 30, and singles/doubles from Rs 80/110, all with TV. Rooms are a little dingy, but clean, and all have hot and cold water. The nearby *Hotel Ashoka* (☎ 46-5991), run by the same people as the Neelam, is also good value. Rooms are from Rs 85/125, and checkout is 24 hours.

The spotless *Hotel Payal* (☎ 46-3202) has rooms for Rs 90/125 with free bucket hot water. All rooms have TV, and it's very near the bus terminal. Next door, the *Hotel Yashoneel* (☎ 46-5286) is of a similar standard, but slightly cheaper, at Rs 70/110. Bucket hot water is Rs 2, and there's a cafe which serves snacks. The sign out the front is in Hindi. To find these two hotels from the bus terminal, walk under the flyover, and they're on the right.

A little further from the bus terminal, the *Hotel Shalimar* (☎ 46-2581) is not exactly pristine, but it's cheap, and bucket hot water is available free on request. Very tiny singles/doubles are Rs 45/75.

The *Hotel Sagar International* (☎ 46-2630) has large rooms with cold-water bath (free bucket hot water is available). Rooms cost from Rs 95/120 and checkout is 24 hours.

Places to Stay – middle

The *Tourist Bungalow* (☎ 38-888), on R N Tagore Rd, is at the back of the Tagore Natya Griha Hall. Rooms are Rs 200/250, and all have air-con.

The *Lantern Hotel* (☎ 39-426) is in a very quiet, tree-lined area, but this place is ramshackle and dilapidated. Massive rooms with enormous bathrooms are Rs 110/135, or Rs 175/250 with air-con.

The *Hotel Samrat* (☎ 43-3890) is a large modern place with comfortable rooms with TV from Rs 200/250, or Rs 300/350 with air-con. There's a very good restaurant and bar, and checkout is 24 hours. Another good choice is the *Hotel Surya* (☎ 43-1155), which has standard rooms for Rs 225/325 and air-con rooms for Rs 300/400. The restaurant here is also very popular. All rooms have a balcony.

Rooms at the popular *Central Hotel* (☎ 53-8547) are huge, with separate sitting areas. Singles/doubles are Rs 150/200, or Rs 250/300 with air-con.

The *Shreemaya Hotel* (☎ 43-1941), opposite the more conspicuous Hotel President, has comfortable rooms from Rs 250/350, and will exchange travellers' cheques for guests.

The *Hotel President* (☎ 43-3156; fax 32-230) boasts a health club and sauna for guests. Well-appointed rooms are Rs 375/525, or Rs 475/625 with air-con. Checkout is 9 am.

The top hotel is the *Indotels Manor House* (☎ 53-7301; fax 39-2250), a four-star place with all the usual mod cons. Rooms cost from Rs 430/550 to Rs 1500/1700 (for the Maharaja suite), and there's a good restaurant.

Places to Eat

There are several good places offering standard Indian fare close to the bus stand. The *Sagar Vegetarian Restaurant*, M G Rd, is nothing flash, but has good cheap food and is popular with locals. Main dishes are between Rs 15 and Rs 30. The *Indian Coffee House* is always a good, cheap choice.

There's a branch on M G Rd, near the Central Hotel.

Most of the hotels have restaurants and bars. The *Woodlands Restaurant* at the Hotel President is an excellent choice, and meals are very reasonably priced. The chef's special biryani (Rs 30) is a technicolour architectural extravaganza which has to be seen to be believed. The trick is getting it to your table before the elaborate edifice collapses.

The restaurant at the *Hotel Surya* is a great place for a splurge. Main (non-veg) dishes are around Rs 60 and beer costs Rs 45. In the Surya Bar you can enjoy 'silent lights, sound of sips, soft & sweet heart music' and 'testy meals'.

Indore is famous for its variety of *namkin* – 'Prakash' brand is the best. If you're here during one of the festivals watch out for the *bhang gota* – samosas with added spice!

Things to Buy

The Kajuri Bazaar is only one of a number of colourful and lively bazaars in the vicinity of the Rajwada, specialising in gold and silverwork, cloth, leather work and traditional garments.

Getting There & Away

Air Indore Airport is nine km from the city. Indian Airlines (☎ 43-1595) has daily flights to Bombay (US$53), and five flights a week to Delhi (US$78), via Bhopal (US$21) and Gwalior (US$55).

Damania Airways (☎ 43-3922) has daily flights to Bombay (Rs 1757).

Bus There are frequent departures from the Sarwate bus terminal to Ujjain (Rs 14, 1½ hours). For Mandu, there is only one direct bus, departing at 3.20 pm (Rs 19, 4½ hours). However, it takes approximately the same amount of time to take a bus to Dhar (Rs 14) and another to Mandu from there (Rs 9). From Sarwate station there are buses to Dhar at 5, 6 7, 8 and 9 am. From Gangwal bus stand, about three km west along Jawahar Rd, there are departures to Dhar every 30 minutes.

From the Sarwate bus stand there are two services to Aurangabad (for the Ajanta and Ellora caves): a morning service via Ajanta which departs at 5 am and an evening service via Ellora which leaves at 9 pm. Both services take about 15 hours. Indore to Ajanta is Rs 75 (12 hours) and to Ellora, Rs 120 (12 hours; the Ellora service is a 'luxury' service).

Buses to Bhopal depart every 30 minutes (4½ to 5½ hours, Rs 36 to Rs 55). To Udaipur buses leave every evening at 7 pm (12 hours, Rs 90).

There are a number of private bus companies between the bus and railway stations and R N Tagore Rd. Destinations include Bombay (Rs 200), Pune (Rs 200), Nagpur (Rs 160), Jaipur (Rs 150), and Gwalior, Aurangabad and Ahmedabad (all Rs 130).

MP Tourism has a luxury service to Bhopal. It departs from the MP office at 8 am, takes four to five hours, and costs a hefty Rs 150!

Train Indore is connected to the main broad-gauge lines between Delhi and Bombay by tracks from Nagda via Ujjain in the west and Bhopal in the east. The daily *Malwa Express* leaves Indore at 3 pm for New Delhi (969 km, 19 hours, Rs 205/606 in 2nd/1st), via Ujjain (1½ hours, Rs 24), Bhopal (264 km, 5½ hours, Rs 62/223), Jhansi (555 km, 10½ hours, Rs 139/415), Gwalior (652 km, 12½ hours, Rs 158/473) and Agra (770 km, 14 hours, Rs 177/536).

The other broad-gauge line runs from Indore to Bilaspur via Ujjain, Bhopal and Jabalpur. The *Narmada Express* reaches Jabalpur (600 km, 14½ hours, Rs 147/436) at dawn.

There is also a metre-gauge line through Indore. Services on this line run from Jaipur in Rajasthan (610 km, 16 hours, Rs 150/444 2nd/1st class) via Indore south-east to Khandwa, Nizamabad and Secunderabad (787 km, 24 hours, Rs 179/541).

Getting Around
To/From the Airport The airport is nine km from the city. There's no airport bus; auto-

rickshaws charge Rs 50 and taxis at least Rs 100.

Local Transport There are plenty of taxis, auto-rickshaws and tempos in Indore. The auto-rickshaws are cheap (most journeys are around Rs 5) and drivers will generally use their meters. Tempos operate along set routes and cost Rs 2 from point to point. The main stands are in front of the railway station and at Gandhi Hall.

AROUND INDORE
Omkareshwar
This island at the confluence of the Narmada and Kaveri rivers has drawn Hindu pilgrims for centuries on account of its jyoti lingam, one of the 12 throughout India, at the Siva **Temple of Shri Omkar Mandhata**. (For an explanation of the myth of the jyoti lingam refer to the Mahakaleshwar Temple section under Ujjain earlier in this chapter.)

The temple is constructed from local soft stone which has enabled its artisans to achieve a rare degree of detailed work, particularly in the friezes on the upper parts of the structure.

There are other temples on this island including the **Siddhnath**, a good example of early medieval Brahminic architecture, and a cluster of other Hindu and Jain temples. Though damaged by Muslim invaders in the time of Mahmud of Ghazni (11th century), these temples and those on the nearby river-banks remain essentially intact. The island temples present a very picturesque sight and are well worth visiting.

Places to Stay There are many *dharamsalas* offering basic accommodation at Omkareshwar, and also the *Holkar Guest House* at Omkareshwar Mandir, but they're mainly for Hindu pilgrims.

Getting There & Away Omkareshwar Road, on the Ratlam-Indore-Khandwa line, is the nearest railway station. Omkareshwar itself is 12 km from here by road. There are regular local buses to Omkareshwar from Indore (68 km, Rs 15), Ujjain (124 km, Rs 27) and Khandwa (68 km, Rs 15).

Maheshwar

Maheshwar was once an important cultural and political centre at the dawn of Hindu civilisation and was mentioned in the *Ramayana* and *Mahabharata* under its former name of Mahishmati. It languished in obscurity for many centuries after that until revived by the Holkar queen, Rani Ahilyabai of Indore, in the late 18th century. It's from these times that most of the temples and the fort complex of this riverside town date.

The principal sights are the **fort** which is now a museum displaying heirlooms and relics of the Holkar dynasty (open to the public), the three **ghats** lining the banks of the Narmada River, and the many-tiered **temples** distinguished by their overhanging balconies and intricately worked doorways.

Maheshwar saris are famous throughout the country for their unique weave and beautifully complex patterns.

Places to Stay There is a *Government Rest House*, the *Ahilya Trust Guest House* and a number of basic *dharamsalas*.

Getting There & Away Maheshwar is best reached by road as the nearest railhead is 39 km away. Local buses run here on a regular basis from Barwaha (30 km, Rs 8) and Dhar (70 km, Rs 16) both of which, in turn, can be reached by local bus from Indore (46 km and 56 km respectively; Rs 12).

Maheshwar is often included on bus tours from Indore to Mandu.

Dhar

Founded by Raja Bhoj, the legendary founder of Bhopal and Mandu, this was the capital of Malwa until Mandu rose to power. There are good views from the ramparts of Dhar's well-preserved **fort**. Dhar also has the large stone **Bhojashala Mosque** with ancient Sanskrit inscriptions, and the adjoining **tomb** of the Muslim saint Kamal Maula.

Dhar is best visited en route to or from Mandu, 33 km away.

MANDU

Telephone Area Code: 07292

The extensive and now mainly deserted hilltop fort of Mandu is one of the most interesting sights in central India. It's on an isolated outcrop separated from the tableland to the north by a deep and wide valley, over which a natural causeway runs to the main city gate. To the south of Mandu the land drops steeply away to the plain far below and the view is superb. Deep ravines cut into the sides of the 20-sq-km plateau occupied by the fort.

Although it's possible to make a day trip from Indore, it's really worth spending the night here, although accommodation is limited. If you're visiting at the height of the season it might be a good idea to phone and book a room in advance. In the winter, Mandu is quite popular with foreign visitors (mainly French and Italian tour groups) but the local tourist season is during the monsoon, when the place turns green and the buildings are mirrored in the lakes.

Entry to Mandu costs Rs 1 per person, although if you arrive by bus, this is included in the fare. There are soft drink and fruit stalls at most of the major sites.

History

Mandu, known as the 'city of joy', has had a chequered and varied history. Founded as a fortress and retreat in the 10th century by Raja Bhoj (see the Bhopal section earlier), it was conquered by the Muslim rulers of Delhi in 1304. When the Mughals invaded and took Delhi in 1401, the Afghan Dilawar Khan, Governor of Malwa, set up his own little kingdom and Mandu embarked on its golden age. Even after it was added to the Mughal Empire by Akbar, it retained a considerable degree of independence, until the declining Mughals lost control of it to the Marathas. The capital of Malwa was then shifted back to Dhar, and Mandu became a ghost town. For a ghost town, however, it's remarkably grandiose and impressive, and has one of the best collections of Afghan architecture to be seen in India.

Although Dilawar Khan first established

MADHYA PRADESH

Mandu as an independent kingdom, it was his son, Hoshang Shah, who shifted the capital from Dhar to Mandu and raised it to its greatest splendour.

Hoshang's son ruled for only a year before being poisoned by Mahmud Shah, who became king himself and ruled for 33 years. During his reign Mandu was in frequent and often bitter dispute with neighbouring powers.

In 1469, Mahmud Shah's son, Ghiyas-ud-din, ascended the throne and spent the next 31 years devoting himself to women and song, before being poisoned at the age of 80 by his son, Nasir-ud-din. The son lived only another 10 years before dying, some say of guilt. In turn his son, Mahmud, had an unhappy reign during which his underlings, like Gada Shah and Darya Khan, often had more influence than he did. Finally, in 1526, Bahadur Shah of Gujarat conquered Mandu.

In 1534 Humayun, the Mughal, defeated Bahadur Shah, but as soon as Humayun turned his back an officer of the former dynasty took over. Several more changes of fortune eventually led to Baz Bahadur taking power in 1554. In 1561 he fled from Mandu rather than face Akbar's advancing troops, and Mandu's period of independence ended. Although the Mughals maintained the fort for a time and even added some new minor buildings, its period of grandeur was over.

Orientation & Information

The buildings of Mandu can be divided into three groups. When you enter through the north gate of the fort, a road branching off to the west leads to the group of buildings known as the Royal Enclave. (For some mysterious reason, the gate providing access to the Royal Enclave from the north is sometimes locked during the daytime. If you approach this gate from within the enclave, it is not necessary to retrace your steps back to the village: if you pass through the tiny archway on your left, you can scramble around to the other side of the gate and continue on to the village.)

If you continue straight on from the entrance you'll pass the Traveller's Lodge and come to the small village which is the only inhabited part of Mandu today. The buildings here are known as the village group. Continuing on, you'll eventually reach the Rewa Kund group at the extreme south of the fort.

You can get a copy of the Archaeological Survey of India's excellent guidebook *Mandu* for Rs 4.25 from the Taveli Mahal in the Royal Enclave. There are many other buildings in Mandu apart from those we've described here.

The nearest bank for cashing travellers' cheques is in Indore.

Royal Enclave Buildings

Jahaz Mahal The Ship Palace is probably the most famous building in Mandu. It really is shiplike, being far longer (110 metres) than it is wide (15 metres), and the illusion is completed by the two lakes that flank it to the east and west.

It was built by Ghiyas-ud-din, son of Mahmud Shah for his harem, reputed to number more than 15,000 maidens. The Jahaz Mahal with its lookouts, arches, cool rooms and beautiful pool was their magnificent playground, but the only sighs you'll hear today are those of the wind whistling through the empty ruins.

Taveli Mahal Just south of the Jahaz Mahal this palace is now the Archaeological Survey of India's Rest House. There is a small museum here, open daily from 9.30 am to 5.30 pm (entry free). Exhibits include fragments of utensils and vessels found at the site, and some stone images.

Hindola Mahal Just north of Ghiyas' stately pleasure dome, this churchlike hall is known as the Swing Palace because the inward slope of the walls is supposed to create the impression that the walls are swaying. The wide, sloping ramp at the northern end of the building is said to have been built to enable the ruler to be conveyed upstairs by elephant.

Champa Baoli To the west of the first two

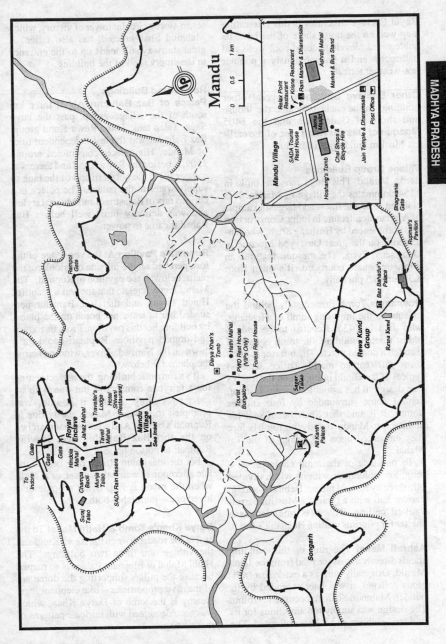

Mandu

0 0.5 1 km

Mandu Village

Ashrafi Mahal
Market & Bus Stand
Relax Point Restaurant
Krisne Restaurant
Ram Mandir & Dharamsala
SADA Tourist Rest House
Jama Masjid
Jain Temple & Dharamsala
Post Office
Hoshang's Tomb
Chai Shops & Bicycle Hire
Bhagwania Gate
Rupmati's Pavilion

Rampol Gate

Baz Bahadur's Palace

Darya Khan's Tomb
Hathi Mahal
PWD Rest House (VIPs Only)
Forest Rest House

Rewa Kund Group
Rewa Kund

Sagar Talao

Tourist Bungalow

To Indore
Gate
Gate
Royal Enclave
Jahaz Mahal
Hindola Mahal
Taveli Mahal
Hotel Shivani (Restaurant)
Traveller's Lodge
Champa Baoli
Munja Talao
Suraj Talao
SADA Rain Besera

Mandu Village
See Inset

Nil Kanth Palace

Songarh

MADHYA PRADESH

MADHYA PRADESH

Royal Enclave structures is this interesting step-well on the north shore of the lake. Its subterranean levels featured cool wells and bathrooms and it was obviously a popular hot-weather retreat.

Other Enclave Buildings Several other buildings in the enclave include the 'house and shop' of Gada Shah and the 1405 **Mosque of Dilawar Khan**, one of the earliest Muslim buildings in Mandu.

Village Group Buildings

Jama Masjid This huge mosque built in 1454 dominates the village of Mandu. It is claimed to be the finest and largest example of Afghan architecture in India. Construction was commenced by Hoshang Shah, who patterned it on the great Omayyed Mosque in Damascus, Syria. The mosque features an 80-metre-square courtyard. It's open from 8.30 am to 5 pm daily.

Hoshang's Tomb Immediately behind the mosque is the imposing tomb of Hoshang, who died in 1435. Reputed to be India's oldest marble building, the tomb is entered through a domed porch. The interior is lit by stone *jali* (carved marble lattice screens) typical of the Hindu influence on the tomb's fine design. It has a double arch and a squat, central dome surrounded by four smaller domes. It is said that Shah Jahan sent his architects to Mandu to study this tomb before they embarked upon the design of the Taj Mahal.

To one side of the tomb enclosure is a long, low colonnade with its width divided into three by rows of pillars. Behind is a long, narrow hall with a typically Muslim barrel-vaulted ceiling. This was intended as a shelter for pilgrims visiting Hoshang's tomb.

Ashrafi Mahal The ruin of this building stands directly across the road from the Jama Masjid. Originally built as a *madrassa* (religious college), it was later extended by its builder, Mahmud Shah, to become his tomb. The design was simply too ambitious for its builders' abilities and it later collapsed. The

seven-storey circular tower of victory, which Mahmud Shah erected, has also fallen. A great stairway still leads up to the entrance to the empty shell of the building.

Rewa Kund Buildings

Palace of Baz Bahadur About three km south of the village group, past the large Sagar Talao tank, is the Rewa Kund group. Baz Bahadur was the last independent ruler of Mandu. His palace, constructed around 1509, is beside the Rewa Kund and there was a water lift at the northern end of the tank to supply water to the palace. The palace is a curious mix of Rajasthani and Mughal styles, and was actually built well before Baz Bahadur came to power.

Rupmati's Pavilion At the very edge of the fort, perched on the hillside overlooking the plains below, is the pavilion of Rupmati. The Malwa legends relate that she was a beautiful Hindu singer, and that Baz Bahadur persuaded her to leave her home on the plains by building her this pavilion. From its terrace and domed pavilions Rupmati could gaze down on the Narmada River, winding across the plains far below.

It's a romantic building, the perfect setting for a fairytale romance – but one with an unhappy ending. Akbar, it is said, was prompted to conquer Mandu partly due to Rupmati's beauty. And when Akbar marched on the fort Baz Bahadur fled, leaving Rupmati to poison herself.

For the maximum effect come here in the late afternoon to watch the sunset, or at night when the moon is full. Bring a bottle or a loved one – preferably both.

Darya Khan's Tomb & Hathi Mahal To the east of the road, between the Rewa Kund and the village, are these two buildings. The Hathi Mahal or Elephant Palace is so named because the pillars supporting the dome are of massive proportions – like elephant legs. Nearby is the tomb of Darya Khan, which was once decorated with intricate patterns of mosaic tiles.

Nil Kanth Palace This palace, at the end of one of the ravines which cuts into the fort, is actually below the level of the hilltop and is reached by a flight of steps down the hillside. At one time it was a Siva shrine, as the name – God with the Blue Throat – suggests. Under the Mughals it became a pleasant water palace with a cascade running down the middle. Though once one of Emperor Jehangir's favourite retreats, it has once again become a Siva temple and a playground for monkeys.

At the top of the steps, villagers sell the seeds of the baobab tree; Mandu is one of the few places in India where the baobab is found. It's not difficult to miss – it's the tubby grey tree that looks as if it has been planted upside down with its roots in the air.

Organised Tours

Tours to Mandu are run from Indore. See Organised Tours under Indore earlier in this chapter for details.

Places to Stay & Eat

Right opposite the Jama Masjid, the Special Area Development Authority (SADA) has some basic but adequate rooms in its *Tourist Rest House*. The rooms have attached bathrooms (hot water in buckets) and cost only Rs 30 a double but they insist you deposit Rs 50 in case of 'dammige'. The second SADA place is called *Rain Besera*. Double rooms with cold-water bath are Rs 200, although bucket hot water is provided for Rs 4. Whilst rooms are large and clean, this place is not great value, and it's hard to find. To get here, head towards the Royal Enclave from the village, past Hoshang's tomb, and take the turn-off to the left opposite the pink, rectangular building on your right, just past the SADA office. It's about five minutes' walk up a dirt track.

The most romantic place to stay is actually in one of the old buildings in the Royal Enclave. The *Archaeological Survey Rest House* (☎ 63-225) is in the Taveli Mahal and there are two rooms here (Rs 50/100) with massive bathrooms complete with bathtub and hot-water heater. There's also a dining

hall for guests only (a thali costs Rs 22). However, they're often booked up – ring from the village before you walk out there with a fully laden pack. The only problem with this place is it's about 15 minutes' walk from the bus stand, which is a hassle if you have an early-morning departure, but it really is in an incredibly beautiful, tranquil setting, and is great value.

The *PWD Rest House* is reserved for visiting VIPs. You can only stay in the *Forest Rest House* if you reserve at the Forest Department in Dhar (☎ 22-232).

The other accommodation listed in this section is run by MP Tourism and should be booked at the tourist office in Indore (☎ (0731) 38-888) if you want to be sure of a bed.

The *Traveller's Lodge* (☎ 63-221) has rooms at Rs 225/275 with bathroom and hot water, but there's a Rs 50 charge to use the air-cooler. Non-guests are welcome at the non-vegetarian restaurant, which has quite an extensive menu.

The *Tourist Bungalow/Cottages* (☎ 63-235) is a series of cottages in a very pleasant location overlooking a lake. Rooms with attached bathroom cost Rs 225/275, or Rs 440/490 with air-con. Dinner is served in the outdoor restaurant between 7 and 10 pm, and breakfast from 7 to 10 am, and non-guests are welcome.

If you are really stuck for accommodation, try the *Jain Dharamsala* at the Jain Temple, or the *Ram Dharamsala* at Ram Mandir.

Cheap vegetarian food is available at the *Relax Point* and *Krisne* restaurants, both at the main intersection in the village. Further north, back towards the Traveller's Lodge, is the Hotel Shivani, also with good, reasonably priced veg food.

Getting There & Away

There are numerous buses from Mandu to Dhar (Rs 9, 1½ hours) from 5.30 am to 6 pm and lots of buses from there on to Indore (three hours, Rs 14). There's a direct bus to Indore which departs at 7.25 am and travels via Mhow (4½ hours, Rs 19), but the time difference between travelling direct or changing buses at Dhar is negligible.

For Bhopal, take the 5.30 am bus to Indore where you can connect with a bus to Bhopal; however, this service will not connect with MP Tourism's deluxe coach to Bhopal. There are no direct buses from Mandu to Ujjain – they all travel via Indore. The buses stop near the Jama Masjid.

The alternative to the erratic tours is to get a group together and hire a car. Taxis charge Rs 700 for the return journey from Indore plus Rs 250 for an overnight stay. They can be found outside the railway station or near the tourist office. MP Tourism has some cars but even their cheapest Ambassador costs more than a taxi.

Getting Around

You can hire bikes from the shop on the south side of the Jama Masjid for Rs 20 a day or Rs 2 an hour. This is a great way to get around as the sights are quite far apart, and the terrain is relatively flat. On the other hand, this is a fine area for walking and it's pleasantly unpopulated.

There is one auto-rickshaw and three tempos here, and they hang around the bus stand. They'll try to sting you for Rs 130 for a three to four-hour tour of Mandu's sights. It costs Rs 10 from the village to Rupmati's Pavilion or, for sole use, Rs 50 return.

BAGH CAVES

The Bagh Caves are seven km from the village of Bagh and three km off the main road. Bagh is about 50 km west of Mandu, on the road between Indore and Vadodara in Gujarat. The Buddhist caves date from 400 to 700 AD and all are in very bad shape. Cave-ins, smoke and water damage have reduced them to such poor condition that restoration work is barely worthwhile. Compared to the caves of Ajanta or Ellora, the Bagh Caves are hardly worth the considerable effort of getting to them. There's a *PWD Dak Bungalow* there.

RATLAM & MANDSAUR

The railway line passes through Ratlam,

capital of a former princely state whose ruler died in one of those tragically heroic Rajput battles against the might of the Mughals.

At Mandsaur, north of Ratlam, a number of interesting archaeological finds were made in a field three km from the town. Some of them are displayed in the museum at Indore. Two 14-metre-high sandstone **pillars** are on the site, and an inscription commemorates the victory of a Malwa king over the Huns in 528 AD. In the **fort** are some fine pieces from the Gupta period.

Eastern Madhya Pradesh

JABALPUR

Population: 983,000
Telephone Area Code: 0761

Almost due south of Khajuraho and east of Bhopal, the large city of Jabalpur is principally famous today for the gorge on the Narmada River known as the Marble Rocks. It's also the departure point for a visit to the national parks of Kanha (175 km away) and Bandhavgarh (197 km).

Today Jabalpur is a major administrative and educational centre and the army headquarters for the states of Orissa and Madhya Pradesh. It also has an unusual number of Christian schools, colleges and churches scattered throughout the cantonment area and, judging from the names on the houses, a large community of Goans.

History

The original settlement in this area was ancient Tripuri and the rulers of this city, the Hayahaya, are mentioned in the *Mahabharata*. It passed successively into Mauryan and then Gupta control until, in 875 AD, it was taken by the Kalchuri rulers. In the 13th century it was overrun by the Gonds and by the early 16th century it had become the powerful state of Gondwana.

Though besieged by Mughal armies from time to time, Gondwana survived until 1789 when it was conquered by the Marathas. Their rule was unpopular, due largely to the increased activities of the thuggees who were ritual murderers and bandits. The Maratha were defeated in 1817 and the thuggees subdued by the British who developed the town in the mid-19th century.

Information

The tourist office (☎ 32-2111) is at the railway station, and is open daily from 10 am to 5 pm, except Sunday and the second and third Saturday of the month. They have the usual range of leaflets and can book MP

Tourism accommodation for you at Kanha National Park a minimum of four days in advance, but they require a 50% deposit.

Money can be changed at the main branch of the State Bank of India and at Jackson's Hotel, where there's also a post office.

Bazaar

The old bazaar area of Jabalpur is huge and full of typically Indian smells, sights, sounds and goods for sale. Put aside a whole morning or afternoon to stroll through it. You'll be lucky to see another tourist though you may well meet quite a few students from

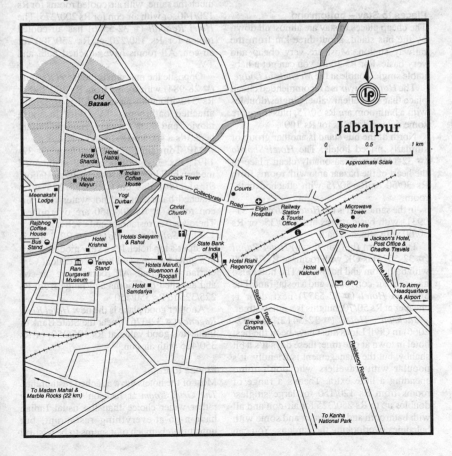

Jabalpur

To Madan Mahal & Marble Rocks (22 km)

To Kanha National Park

To Army Headquarters & Airport

East Africa. There're currently around 150 of them studying at the university here.

The **Rani Durgavati Museum**, south of the bazaar, is also worth a visit. It's open from 10 am to 5 pm daily except Mondays.

Madan Mahal
This Gond fortress, built in 1116 AD, is on the route to the Marble Rocks, perched on top of a huge boulder. The Gonds, who worshipped snakes, lived in this region even before the Aryans arrived, and maintained their independence right up until Mughal times.

Places to Stay – bottom end
The cheap places to stay are almost all down by the bus stand, about three km from the railway station. Most are very cheap and very basic. For Rs 30/50 you can get a habitable single/double at the *Meenakshi Lodge*.

The *Hotel Mayur* is a recommended cheap place that's excellent value. Singles/doubles with a bathroom are Rs 50/75, plus there are some deluxe doubles for Rs 100.

North of the bus stand is another group of similarly priced hotels. The *Hotel Sharda* (☎ 32-1119) is a reasonably clean place in the heart of the bazaar area with rooms from Rs 30/50 or Rs 50/75 with attached bathroom.

In the same area is the *Hotel Natraj* (☎ 31-0931) with basic rooms at Rs 30/35, or Rs 50/60 with attached bath.

The modern (but run-down) *Hotel Rahul* (☎ 32-5525) is OK with rooms at Rs 75/100 with bathroom and hot water. The hotel also has some air-con rooms and a restaurant. The *Swayam Hotel* (☎ 32-5377) next door is cheaper at Rs 50/70, but this is a noisy street.

Jackson's Hotel (☎ 32-3412; fax 32-2066) in Civil Lines must have been the best hotel in town at one time; these days it's a bit shabby, but the management is friendly. It's popular with travellers who don't mind spending a little extra. There's a range of rooms from Rs 120/150 for large singles/doubles up to Rs 250/325 for air-con and all with bathroom and hot water, and some with balconies overlooking the gardens. You can

change travellers' cheques, and excess baggage can be left here safely while you visit Kanha National Park.

There's also *retiring rooms* at the railway station, and these cost Rs 35 for a dorm bed, Rs 45 for a bed in a double room, and Rs 75 in an air-con double.

Places to Stay – middle & top end
There are three good mid-range modern hotels close to each other. The *Hotel Maruti* (☎ 32-4677) has a good range of rooms from Rs 100/130 to Rs 205/250 with air-con. The *Hotel Bluemoon* (☎ 25-146) next door is much the same, with air-cooled rooms for Rs 120/140, or with air-con for Rs 200/275. The *Hotel Roopali* (☎ 32-5566) has air-cooled rooms for Rs 180/220 or Rs 250/300 for air-con. All rooms have attached bath and TV.

Opposite the museum is the *Hotel Krishna* (☎ 28-984) with rooms from Rs 200/280 or Rs 340/400 with air-con. All rooms have attached bathrooms, TVs with in-house movies and there's a very good restaurant here. It's a good place to stay.

MP Tourism's *Hotel Kalchuri* (☎ 32-1491; fax 32-1490) is a well-maintained modern building close to the railway station. Singles/doubles cost Rs 225/275 with attached bathroom and hot water. The air-con rooms at Rs 400/450 are overpriced. There's a bar, restaurant and even a gym.

The *Samdariya Hotel* (☎ 22-150) is Jabalpur's top hotel. It's a very modern place in a quiet location and has an excellent vegetarian restaurant. All rooms have air-con and attached bathrooms and range from Rs 225/325 to Rs 350/450.

Another good place is the new *Hotel Rishi Regency* (☎ 32-3261), near the State Bank of India. It's good value at Rs 195/250, or Rs 350/425 with air-con.

Places to Eat
Most of the hotels have attached restaurants. *The Grub Room* at Jackson's Hotel has a rather wider choice than the usual Indian have-a-go-at-everything restaurant, but unfortunately much of it seems to be wishful

thinking. The food is good, however, and there's cold beer.

The *Haveli* restaurant in the Hotel Krishna is another good place, though a little more expensive.

Also worth a try is the restaurant in the MPTDC's *Hotel Kalchuri*. They do a pretty reasonable fish & chips for Rs 30.

The *Woodlands Restaurant* at the Samdariya is recommended and across the road there's the *Avtar Restaurant* which is quite expensive.

For a snack there's the *Rajbhog Coffee House*, by the bus stand; the waiters have fan-shaped headgear and cummerbunds, and you are given a newspaper to read when you sit down. The *Indian Coffee House* is similar.

Main dishes at the popular *Yogi Durbar* are in the Rs 25 to Rs 50 range. They also serve ice creams.

Getting There & Away
Bus There are buses to Jabalpur from Allahabad, Khajuraho, Varanasi, Bhopal, Nagpur and other main centres. For overnight bus journeys private buses are better. Madhya Pradesh state transport buses are mostly in an advanced state of decay.

For Kanha National Park there are state transport buses to Kisli (Rs 40, 6½ hours) at 7 am and 11 am, and Mukki (Rs 50, 7½ hours) at 9 am (the Malakhand bus). The Kisli buses only run when the park is open (November to June).

There's one bus a day to Khajuraho (Rs 65, 11 hours) leaving at 9 am but it's more comfortable to take the train to Satna from where there are regular buses to Khajuraho (Rs 23, four hours).

Train There are direct connections between Jabalpur and Satna (189 km, Rs 48/178 in 2nd/1st class) in three hours, Varanasi (505 km, Rs 130/387) in 13 hours and Bhopal (336 km, Rs 95/282) in 7½ hours.

If you're heading for the Ajanta and Ellora caves, catch a train on the Bombay line to Bhusaval (all the trains stop here) and take another train to Jalgaon. There are buses to the caves from there.

Getting Around
Local Transport Be careful with Jabalpur auto-rickshaw drivers; they can be rapacious, so always agree on a fare first. You probably don't need one if you arrive by train and are staying at Jackson's or the Kalchuri. If arriving by bus, most of the budget and mid-range hotels are within 10 minutes' walk of the city bus stand. Cycle-rickshaw-wallahs are almost as bad.

If you want to rent a bicycle there are several places where you can do this between Jackson's and the Hotel Kalchuri as well as across the other side of the railway tracks.

AROUND JABALPUR
Marble Rocks
Known locally as Bhedaghat, this gorge on the Narmada River is 22 km from Jabalpur. The gleaming white and pink cliffs rise sheer from the clear water and are a very impressive sight, especially by moonlight. However it's been heavily promoted by MP Tourism and views on this tourist spot vary from 'truly spectacular' to 'a total bust'. It really all depends on when you come. Steer clear of the place at weekends and on the night of the full moon as it's packed with local tourists.

The best way to see the km-long gorge is by shared rowboat – Rs 5 per person or Rs 75 for the whole boat. These go all day every day from November to July from the jetty at the bottom of the gorge.

The cliffs at the foot of the gorge are floodlit at night. At the head of the gorge is the **Dhuandhar** or Smoke Cascade. All around the falls are hundreds of stalls selling marble carvings, much of it fairly clichéd but you can find some nice pieces if you shop around and bargain hard. Above the lower end of the gorge, a flight of over 100 stone steps leads to the **Chausath Yogini** or Madanpur Temple. The circular temple has damaged images of the 64 yoginis, or attendants of the goddess Kali.

Places to Stay & Eat Marble Rocks is a very mellow place to stay and the best accommodation is at MP Tourism's *Motel Marble*

Rocks (☎ (0761) 83-424), which overlooks the foot of the gorge and has an excellent restaurant. The motel is a comfortable ex-colonial bungalow and has only four rooms, for Rs 200/250 a single/double with bathroom, so it's best to book in advance. There are plenty of cheap cafes in the village.

In the village itself there's a couple of basic lodgings.

Getting There & Away Tempos run to the Marble Rocks from the city tempo stand near the museum in Jabalpur for Rs 7. Ask for the Tourist Motel, otherwise you'll end up at the head of the gorge, which is about a km further on.

An alternative way to get there is to hire a bicycle for the 22-km trip. The road is busy but mostly flat with plenty of stalls to stop at along the way. Follow the road for Nagpur out of Jabalpur, then take the right fork below the Jain temples high on the hill. After about 15 km turn left at the crossroads following the 'Bhedaghat 5 km' sign.

Narsinghpur
Narsinghpur (84 km west of Jabalpur) is just a sleepy provincial town but worth visiting if you're interested in following the Sleeman trail (see the Thugs boxed section below). There's a fascinating account of Sleeman's anti-thug detective work in Sir Francis Tuker's *The Yellow Scarf*, and the novel *The Deceivers* by John Masters was based on Sleeman and the Thugs.

You can visit **Narsingh Mandir**, an old temple with a honeycomb of underground tunnels beneath it. The caretaker will take you down to show the room where Sleeman cornered some of the thuggee leaders.

Places to Stay Accommodation is available at the *Gunawat Inn*, which has doubles at Rs 100 and is near the station. Or else try *Nira Farm Guest House* (☎ (07792) 238). Here, Mrs Nagu has just one basic double at Rs 100 and this must be arranged in advance. You can write to Mrs Prem Nagu at Nira Farm, Narsinghpur, Madhya Pradesh, or telephone. She's an excellent cook and her husband, a retired colonel, is particularly knowledgeable about Sleeman as well as about places in the nearby Satpura Hills.

KANHA NATIONAL PARK
Kanha, 175 km south-east of Jabalpur, is one of India's largest national parks covering 1945 sq km including a 'core zone' of 940 sq km. The setting for Kipling's *Jungle Book*, it's a beautiful area of forest and lightly wooded grassland with many rivers and streams, and it supports an excellent variety of wildlife. It is also part of Project Tiger, one of India's most important conservation efforts. A scandal within this project, though, means tiger numbers may be decreasing. (See the boxed section on Project Tiger in the Uttar Pradesh chapter.)

Wildlife was first given limited protection here as early as 1933 but it wasn't until 1955 that the area was declared a national park. Additions to the park were made in 1962 and 1970. Kanha is a good example of what can be achieved under a determined policy of wildlife management: between 1973 and 1988 the tiger population increased from 43 to over 100, leopards from 30 to 62, chital (spotted deer) from 9000 to over 17,000, sambar from 1058 to 1853 and barasinga from 118 to 547. In spite of a serious outbreak of rinderpest in 1976, the numbers of gaur (Indian bison) rose from 559 to 671.

Thugs
It was from Narsinghpur in the early 19th century that Colonel Sleeman waged his war against the bizarre Hindu *thuggee* cult that, over the centuries, probably claimed as many as a million lives. It was largely due to his efforts that thuggee (from which the word 'thug' is derived) was wiped out. For years its followers had roamed the main highways of India engaging in ritual murders, strangling their victims with a yellow silk scarf in order to please the bloodthirsty goddess Kali. ■

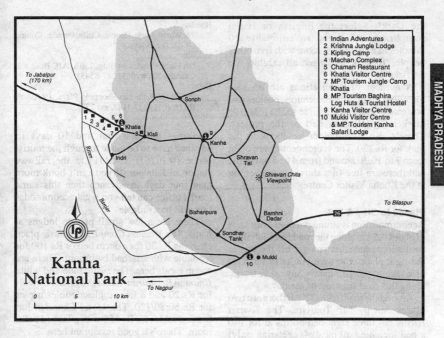

1 Indian Adventures
2 Krishna Jungle Lodge
3 Kipling Camp
4 Machan Complex
5 Chaman Restaurant
6 Khatia Visitor Centre
7 MP Tourism Jungle Camp
    Khatia
8 MP Tourism Baghira
    Log Huts & Tourist Hostel
9 Kanha Visitor Centre
10 Mukki Visitor Centre
    & MP Tourism Kanha
    Safari Lodge

Kanha National Park

MADHYA PRADESH

The park is very well organised and a popular place to visit. There's a good chance of sighting tiger, gaur and many herbivores.

Excursions into the park are made in the early morning and evening; no night driving is allowed. Between 1 July and 31 October, Kanha is completely closed owing to the monsoons. Although the wildlife can be seen throughout the season, sightings increase as the weather gets hotter in March and April and the animals move out of the tree cover in search of water. The hottest months are May and June when the temperature can reach 42°C in the afternoons. December and January are the coldest months and, although it's warm enough to do without a sweater during the day, as soon as the sun sets the temperature quickly plunges to zero and below. Excursions into the park can be very cold so bring plenty of warm clothes.

There are no facilities for changing travellers' cheques here. The nearest places to do this are at Mandla and Jabalpur. There's

a telephone and small shop at Kisli but no petrol – the pump here has been dry for years. Make sure you bring enough film. It needs to be fast film (400 ASA or higher) because of the low light of the early morning and evening excursions.

The local market at **Sarekha** on Fridays draws the colourful Baiga tribal people and is worth going to.

There's a small fee for entry to the park.

Visitor Centres

In a joint project with the US National Park Service and the Indian Centre for Environment Education, three visitor centres have been set up. The interpretative displays in these centres at Khatia and Mukki gates and at Kanha itself are of a very high standard and well worth looking round. The Kanha display is the most impressive with five galleries and a research hall. As well as displays of the animals and the environment, there's a novel sound & light show 'Encounters in the Dark'. Select the English or Hindi soundtrack and spend an enjoyable 20 minutes in a small dark room with five other people, 'there is no danger, all exhibits are artificial'!

A number of publications are on sale including informative brochures, posters and postcards, and a small guide to the roadside markers installed as part of the project. There's also a full-colour handbook to the park for Rs 120. The visitor centres are open from 7 to 10.30 am and from 4 to 6 pm daily, and there are free film shows each evening at the Khatia Visitor Centre.

Places to Stay & Eat

Accommodation is strung out over a distance of about 6.5 km along the road from Jabalpur so it's important that you get off the bus at the right place otherwise you're in for a lot of walking – there's hardly any other traffic along this road for most of the day.

Around the main gate at Kisli there are two places run by MP Tourism. The *Tourist Hostel* has three eight-bed dorms at Rs 140 a bed including all meals (vegetarian only) and hot showers. It's clean and a much better deal than the nearby *Baghira Log Huts* where air-cooled rooms are Rs 300/350. There's a restaurant here with main dishes around Rs 25, and cold beer.

Three km back towards Jabalpur is the Khatia Gate where MP Tourism's *Jungle Camp Khatia* has 18 rooms with attached bathroom at Rs 100/200 including vegetarian thali meals. There's a nice thatched sitting area. This is probably a better place to be than at Kisli, since there are more jeeps here and in the evenings you can go to the film shows at the Khatia Visitor Centre.

It's advisable to book these places in advance, though not essential if you're happy with a dorm bed. Bookings more than 10 days in advance have to be made at one of the following MP State Tourism offices and a 50% deposit is required:

Bhopal
4th Floor, Gangotri, T T Nagar (☎ (0755) 55-4340)

Bombay
74 World Trade Centre, Cuffe Parade, Colaba (☎ (022) 218-4860)
Calcutta
6th Floor, Chitrakoot Bldg, 230A, AJC Bose Rd, Calcutta 20 (☎ (033) 247-8543)
Delhi
2nd Floor, Kanishka Shopping Plaza, 19 Ashok Rd (☎ (011) 332-1187, ext 277).

Bookings between four and 10 days in advance have to be made through the tourist office (☎ (0761) 32-2111) at the railway station in Jabalpur. If you can't book more than four days in advance then this same tourist office can tell you what accommodation will be available.

There are a few small private lodges at Katia. The *Machan Complex* is a basic place charging Rs 30 for a dorm bed or Rs 100 for a double with attached bathroom. There are cheap meals here. The rustic blue and white *Chaman Restaurant* has set vegetarian meals for Rs 20 and a few singles/doubles/triples for Rs 50/80/120. The *Motel Chandan* has better doubles for Rs 150 with attached bathroom. There's a good restaurant here.

Of the privately run accommodation, the furthest from Kisli is *Indian Adventures*, next to the ford across the river on the way in from Jabalpur. It has double chalets with bathrooms and an attractive open dining area with a fireplace. The staff are friendly and keen, and it's a good place to stay if there are other people there, but if you find yourself on your own, it can be quite lonely and isolated. It's also expensive at Rs 1000 per person per day including all meals and transport into and around the park (two game drives per day), except for the elephant rides which are extra. Their Maruti jeep is quiet and comfortable and they don't skimp on time. Bookings should be made through Indian Adventures (☎ Bombay 640-6399), 257 S V Road, Bandra, Bombay 400050, at least 10 days in advance. Bookings less than 10 days in advance can be made through Chadha Travels (☎ (0761) 32-2178), Jackson's Hotel, Civil Lines, Jabalpur.

Nearby, the new *Krishna Jungle Lodge*, should be finished by now. It's likely to be

Madhya Pradesh
   Top: Statue outside Gujri Mahal, Gwalior.
Bottom: Inside the Jama Masjid, Mandu.

Madhya Pradesh

A: Sanchi.
B: Jahaz Mahal, Mandu.
C: Detail of carvings at Sanchi.

D: Jama Masjid from Ashrafi Mahal, Mandu.
E: Udaigiri Caves, near Sanchi.

very similar in price to Indian Adventures. Contact the Hotel Krishna in Jabalpur (☎ (0761) 28-984) for details.

Kipling Camp is the best place to stay at Kanha. Staffed by enthusiastic Brits and operated on the lines of an English house party, it's run by Bob Wright, who can be contacted through the Tollygunge Club (☎ (033) 473-3306; fax 473-1903) 120 D P Sasmal Rd, Calcutta 700 033. It's far from cheap at Rs 2200 per day, but prices include all meals, excursions into the park in open Land Rovers, guides, etc. It's also the home of Tara, the central character in Mark Shand's book *Travels on My Elephant*. She takes guests for rides in the surrounding forest and you can even join her for her daily bath in the river. Kipling Camp is open from 1 November to early May and all bookings must be made in advance. Arrangements can be made to meet you in Jabalpur (3½ hours by car), Bilaspur (6½ hours) or Nagpur (6½ hours). If you come via Nagpur you could break your journey at Kawardha Palace (see the Kawardha section later).

Finally, there's MP Tourism's *Kanha Safari Lodge* at Mukki on the other side of the park from Kisli, where there's also a visitor centre. Singles/doubles cost Rs 250/300 or Rs 400/450 with air-con and there's a bar and restaurant. It's in a pleasant location and is hardly ever full so is a good place to try if you can't get accommodation at Kisli. However, Mukki isn't easy to get to without your own transport. Bookings can be made in the same way as for the MP Tourism accommodation at Kisli.

Getting There & Away

There are direct state transport buses from the city bus stand in Jabalpur to Kisli Gate twice daily at 7 am (six hours) and 11 am (seven hours) which cost Rs 40. Tickets go on sale about 15 minutes before departure. In the opposite direction, the buses depart from Kisli at around 8 am and noon but the early bus can be late starting in winter. These are ramshackle old buses and crowded as far as Mandla though there are generally spare seats after that. Don't bring too much

baggage as there's hardly anywhere to put it. On the Kisli to Jabalpur run you may have to change buses at Mandla.

The nearest railway station to Kisli is 1½ hours by bus at Chiraidongri. It's reached on a slow journey by narrow-gauge trains that will appeal to rail enthusiasts, via Nainpur from either Jabalpur or Gondia (between Nagpur and Raipur).

Getting Around

Jeeps are for hire at both Khatia and Kisli Gates and the cost is calculated on a per-km basis. Expect to pay around Rs 400 (which can be shared by up to six people), plus a small hourly charge for a compulsory guide. Park entry fees are extra. Park gates are open from sunrise to noon and 3 pm to sunset from 1 November to 15 February; sunrise to noon and 4 pm to sunset from 16 February to 30 April, and sunrise to 11 am and 5 pm to sunset from 1 May to 30 June. An average distance covered on a morning excursion would be 60 km; less in the afternoon. At the height of the season there may not be enough jeeps to go round so book as soon as you arrive. As in other Indian national parks, drivers tend to drive too fast and not wait around long enough for game to appear. If you think they're being impatient, tell them to slow down. And stay in the jeep if it breaks down...

One evening we were travelling around the park in our rather old jeep when it decided to break down on us. After much fiddling around with the engine our driver decided that the only thing for us to do was to walk back to Kisli, a mere 15 km! So we gingerly jumped out of the back of the jeep and started to walk. Fifteen minutes earlier we had been searching for tigers. Now we hoped they weren't searching for us.

Relief was on everyone's face when another jeep picked us up after three km or so. Of course our jeep turned up again next morning at 6.30 am, the starter motor 'fixed'. However, yesterday's guide refused to go out with us again!

Linda & Paul Careling, Australia

Elephant Elephants are available for hire for Rs 50 per person per hour. They used to be used for game-viewing safaris but it seems this practice has now ceased; check on arrival at the park.

BANDHAVGARH NATIONAL PARK

This national park is 197 km north-east of Jabalpur in the Vindhyan mountain range. It's not part of Project Tiger but tigers are occasionally seen here, more frequently late in the season. There are 25 tigers in the 'core' area of 105 sq km but a buffer zone of 343 sq km has recently been added, along with another 25 tigers.

Bandhavgarh's setting is impressive. It's named after the ancient fort built on some 800-metre-high cliffs. There's a temple at the fort which can be visited by jeep and below it are numerous rock-cut cave shrines.

The core area of the park is fairly small with a fragile ecology but it supports such animals as nilgai, wild boar, jackal, gaur, sambar and porcupine as well as many species of birds. The ramparts of the fort provide a home for vultures, blue rock thrushes and crag martins.

Like Kanha, the park is closed for the middle part of the day, and completely from 1 July to 31 October. There's a small entry fee, and jeeps and guides can be hired.

Places to Stay & Eat

There's a small range of accommodation just outside the park gate in the village of Tala, where there are also several cheap places to eat.

The cheapest accommodation is at the ornate-looking Tiger Lodge, at Rs 80 a double with fan. The *Hotel Baghela* looks better and is

worth checking out, if it's open. The *Nature Resort* might be fun – it advertises 'lunch-time games for everyone' and charges Rs 60 for a bed in a tent and has some rooms at Rs 280 for a double.

MP Tourism's *White Tiger Forest Lodge* (☎ 308) is a good place, overlooking the river where the elephants bathe. Singles/doubles with attached bathroom cost Rs 250/300 or Rs 400/450 with air-con. The food is good and the waiters and manager all very friendly. Advance booking is advisable. Phone the lodge directly if you're booking less than five days in advance, otherwise see the MP Tourism contact addresses in the Kanha section.

You can also stay in the former palace of the Maharaja of Rewa here, the *Bandhavgarh Jungle Camp*. It's an expensive place at more than Rs 1000 but this includes all food and visits to the park. The address for bookings is 1/1 Rani Jhansi Rd, Delhi 110 055 (☎ (011) 52-3057).

Getting There & Away

Umaria, on the Katni to Bilaspur railway line, is the nearest railhead, 32 km away. Local buses are available from there to Tala (Rs 10, one hour). From Satna there's a morning bus to Tala which takes around four hours via Amarpatam.

MANDLA & RAMNAGAR

Mandla is about 100 km south-east of Jabalpur on the road to Kanha. Here there is a **fort** on a loop of the Narmada River built so that the river protects it on three sides

---

White Tigers

The famous white tiger of Rewa was discovered as a cub near Bandhavgarh in 1951. He was named Mohun and as his mother had been shot he was reared by hand. Mated with one of his daughters in 1958, a litter of white cubs was produced and Mohun's numerous descendants can now be seen in several zoos around the world. The interesting thing about these white tigers is that although they have a white coat, they are not albinos. Their eyes are blue, rather than pink and with their dark stripes they are the result of a recessive gene. Inbreeding has led to their decline and the world population of white tigers has dropped from over 100 to about 20. The original white tiger can still be seen today – Mohun's stuffed body is in the Maharaja of Rewa's palace, now a hotel in Tala. ■

while a ditch protects it on the fourth. Built in the late 1600s, the fort is now subsiding into the jungle although some of the towers still stand.

About 15 km away is Ramnagar with its ruined three-storey **palace** overlooking the Narmada. This palace, and the fort at Mandla, were both built by Gond kings, retreating south before the advance of Mughal power. Also near Mandla is a stretch of the Narmada where many temples dot the riverbank.

BHORAMDEO & KAWARDHA
At Bhoramdeo, 125 km east of Kisli (Kanha) is a small but interesting 11th-century **Siva temple** built in the style of the temples of Khajuraho. Carvings cover virtually every external surface with deities indulging in the usual range of activities including the familiar sexual acrobatics. Unlike most of the Khajuraho temples, this one's still very much in use today. A cobra lives in the temple and is fed by the priests. A few km away there are two other temples, the **Mandwa Mahal** and the **Madanmanjari Mahal** which date from the same time.

Twenty km south of Bhoramdeo, well off the tourist trail, the Maharaja of Kawardha has opened part of his palace to guests. The *Palace Kawardha* (☎ 07741) 32404) is a delightfully peaceful place and you're made to feel very welcome here. As far as palaces go it's neither enormous nor particularly old (it was built in 1939) but it does have the touches you'd expect in a maharaja's palace – Italian marble floors, stuffed tigers and ancient English bathroom fittings. If you can afford to stay here it's an experience not to be missed. It costs Rs 2438/3900 per person (with reductions for stays of more than one night). The price includes all meals (taken with the charming ex-maharaja and his family) and outings in the jeep – to the

temples or into the hills. Open from 1 October to 30 April, reservations must be made in advance. Write to Margaret Watts-Carter, Palace Kawardha, Kawardha, District Rajnandgaon, Madhya Pradesh 491 995.

BILASPUR
Population: 258,900
Telephone Area Code: 07752

Bilaspur is a bustling city in the far east of Madhya Pradesh. It's the headquarters of the South-Eastern Railways, and while it has no 'attractions' to speak of, you may find it convenient to stop here if heading from Kanha National Park to Puri in Orissa.

The region is a major rice-growing area, and after the monsoon is very green. The town of **Ratanpur**, 25 km north, has a ruined fort and a number of small, artificial lakes, all made by the region's former Rajput rulers. There are plenty of local buses from Bilaspur (Rs 7, 45 minutes).

Places to Stay & Eat
The *Natraj Hotel* near the bus stand is well located on the main street, and has rooms from Rs 75.

Also on the main street is the *Hotel Chandrika* (☎ 5088), which has singles/doubles for Rs 80/120 with attached bath, Rs 225/275 with TV and air-cooler, and Rs 350/400 with air-con. It also has a good bar and restaurant.

Getting There & Away
The bus stand is in the centre of town, and there are departures for Kawardha, Nagpur, Raipur and Mukki (for Kanha National Park).

The railway station is two km from the town centre. Bilaspur has rail connections with Jabalpur, Raipur, Bhopal, Puri, Calcutta and Delhi.

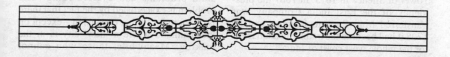

Bombay

Bombay is the capital of Maharashtra and the economic powerhouse of India. The fastest moving, most affluent and most industrialised city in India, it also has the country's busiest international airport and seaport, handling nearly 50% of the total foreign trade. It's the stronghold of Indian free enterprise and a major manufacturing centre for everything from cars and bicycles to pharmaceuticals and petrochemicals. Bombay is the centre for India's important textile industry as well as the financial centre and an important base for overseas companies. Nariman Point, with India's tallest buildings, is rapidly becoming a mini-Manhattan, and land prices throughout the city continue to soar. Yet once upon a time Bombay was nothing more than a group of low-lying, swampy and malarial mud flats, passed on to the British by its Portuguese occupiers as a wedding dowry!

History

When the Portuguese arrived on the scene Bombay consisted of seven islands occupied by fisherfolk known as Kolis. In 1534 the seven islands, from Colava in the south to Mahim in the north, were ceded to Portugal by the Sultan of Gujarat in the Treaty of Bassein. The Portuguese did little with them and the major island of the group, Mumba-devi, was part of the dowry when Catherine of Braganza married England's Charles II in 1661. In 1665 the British government took possession of all seven islands and in 1668 leased them to the East India Company for an annual UK£10 in gold.

Soon, Bombay started to develop as an important trading port. One of the first signs of this was the arrival of the Parsis, who settled in Bombay in 1670 and built their first Tower of Silence in 1675. In 1687 the presidency of the East India Company was transferred from Surat to Bombay and by 1708 it had become the trading headquarters for the whole west coast of India.

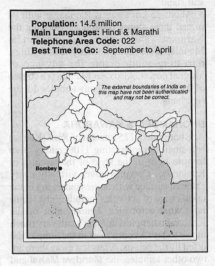

Population: 14.5 million
Main Languages: Hindi & Marathi
Telephone Area Code: 022
Best Time to Go: September to April

The external boundaries of India on this map have not been authenticated and may not be correct.

Bombay

Although Bombay grew steadily for the next century, it was around the mid-1800s that its development was most dynamic. The first railway was laid out of Bombay in 1854. Then the American Civil War provided Bombay's young cotton and textile industries with an enormous boost as supplies of cotton from the USA dried up. A major land-reclamation project in 1862 joined the original seven islands into a single land mass and a year later the governor, Sir Bartle Frere, dismantled the old fort walls, sparking a major building boom.

During this century Bombay has further reinforced its position as the major commercial, industrial, financial, trading and film centre of India. Its role as an economic magnet – the Indian city with streets paved with gold – has also contributed to enormous slum problems and overcrowding. The problem is exacerbated by the fact that there is no room for further expansion – except on the mainland where a 'new' city is in the making. Meanwhile, those who cannot afford the commuter fares from the mainland into the city continue to flock to and eke out a living on the peninsula itself in some of the worst slums in Asia.

Despite this, Bombay is a lively city, full of interest in its own right and is also, for many people, the gateway to India. It has its Beverly Hills, its Bronx, its super-rich and abject poor, its Victorian monuments and Buddhist relics, mega-congestion, gleaming high-rises and cardboard shanty towns, pollution you've never seen the like of and opulence fit for a Mughal emperor. It's India in an oyster.

Orientation

Bombay is an island connected by bridges to the mainland. Low, swampy areas indicate where it was once divided into several islands. The principal part of the city is concentrated at the southern end of the island. Sahar International Airport is 30 km north of the city centre.

There are three main railway stations in the city centre. Churchgate and Victoria Terminus (VT) are central, but Bombay Central is some distance out.

Orientation in Bombay is relatively simple. The southern promontory is Colaba Causeway and the northern end of this peninsula is known as Colaba. Most of the cheap hotels and restaurants, together with a number of Bombay's topnotch establishments, are here. The city's two main landmarks, the Gateway of India and the Taj Mahal Hotel, are also at Colaba.

Directly north of Colaba is the area known as Bombay Fort, since the old fort was once

here. Most of the impressive buildings from Bombay's golden period (1860-1900) are here, together with the GPO, offices, banks, tourist office and two of the main railway stations.

To the west of the fort is Back Bay, the city's beach, around which sweeps Marine Drive. At the southern end of this drive is Nariman Point, the modern business centre of Bombay with its international-class hotels, skyscrapers, airline offices, consulates and banks. The other end of the drive is Malabar Hill, a classy residential area.

Information

Tourist Offices The Government of India tourist office (☎ 203-2932; fax 201-4496) is at 123 Maharshi Karve Rd, Churchgate, directly across from Churchgate station. It's open Monday to Friday from 8.30 am to 6 pm, and Saturday and public holidays from 8.30 am to 2 pm; it's closed Sunday. This main office has a comprehensive leaflet and brochure collection and is one of the most helpful and efficient offices in the country. They also have a counter (☎ 832-5331) at the international airport (open 24 hours) and one at the domestic terminal (☎ 614-9200) which is open until the last flight.

The Maharashtra Tourism Development Corporation (MTDC) is also a very good source for information about Bombay and the state in general. Its head office (☎ 202-4482; fax 202-4521) is at Express Towers (9th floor), Nariman Point. Not far from here is their branch office (☎ 202-6713; fax 285-2182) at CDO Hutments, Madame Cama Rd, where bookings can be made for Bombay

---

Bombay Street Names

Bombay has had lots of official road name changes over the years and, while some of the new names are completely ignored, others are gradually coming to the fore. For example, Colaba Causeway is now called Shahid Bhagat Singh Rd and Marine Drive is Netaji Subhashchandra Bose Rd (though no-one uses these names). Churchgate St is now known as Veer Nariman Rd, Wodehouse Rd is N Parekh Marg, Wellingdon Circle is Dr S P Mukherjee Chowk, Rampart Row is K Dubash Marg and Martyr's Square is Hutatma Chowk. You might find it useful to pick up the MTDC's free Bombay tourist map which lists all the important name changes. ■

BOMBAY

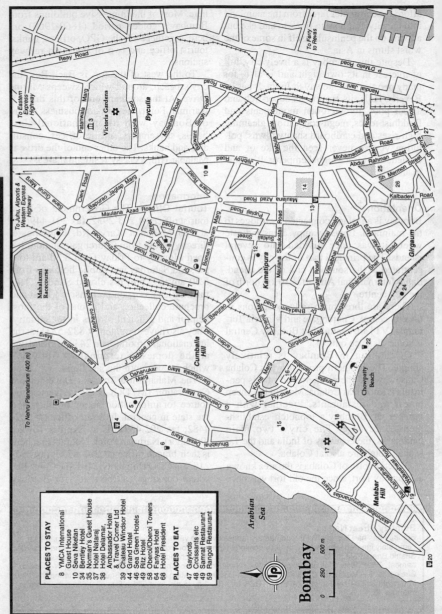

PLACES TO STAY

8   YMCA International
    Guest House
10 Seva Niketan
34 Bentley Hotel
35 Norman's Guest House
37 Hotel Nataraj
38 Hotel Delamar,
    Ambassador Hotel
    & Travel Corner Ltd
39 Chateau Windsor Hotel
44 Grand Hotel
46 Sea Green Hotels
49 Ritz Hotel
58 Oberoi/Oberoi Towers
64 Fariyas Hotel
68 Hotel President

PLACES TO EAT

47 Gaylords
48 Croissants etc
49 Samrat Restaurant
59 Rangoli Restaurant

Bombay

0   250   500 m

Arabian
Sea

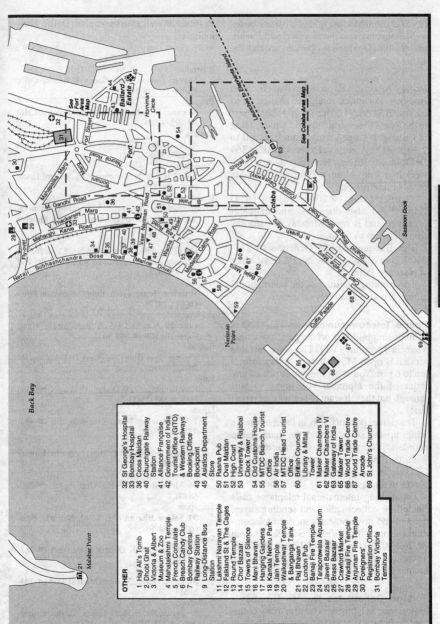

BOMBAY

OTHER

1 Haji Ali's Tomb
2 Dhobi Ghat
3 Victoria & Albert Museum & Zoo
4 Mahalakshmi Temple
5 French Consulate
6 Breach Candy Club
7 Bombay Central Railway Station
9 Long-Distance Bus Station
11 Lakshmi Narayan Temple
12 Falkland St & The Cages
13 Round Temple
14 Chor Bazaar
15 Towers of Silence
16 Mani Bhavan
17 Hanging Gardens
18 Kamala Nehru Park
19 Jain Temple
20 Walkeshwar Temple & Banganga Tank
21 Raj Bhavan
22 London Pub
23 Banaji Fire Temple
24 Taraporewala Aquarium
25 Javeri Bazaar
26 Brass Bazaar
27 Crawford Market
28 Wadiaji Fire Temple
29 Anjuman Fire Temple
30 Foreigners' Registration Office
31 Bombay Victoria Terminus
32 St George's Hospital
33 Bombay Hospital
36 Cross Maidan
40 Churchgate Railway Station
41 Alliance Française
42 Government of India Tourist Office (GITO) & Western Railways Booking Office
43 Bookpoint
45 Asiatics Department Store
50 Rasna Pub
51 Oval Maidan
52 High Court
53 University & Rajabai Clock Tower
54 Old Customs House
55 MTDC Branch Tourist Office
56 Air India
57 MTDC Head Tourist Office
60 British Council Library & Mittal Tower
61 Maker Chambers IV
62 Maker Chambers VI
63 Gateway of India
65 Maker Tower
66 World Trade Centre
67 World Trade Centre Arcade
69 St John's Church

city and suburban tours, long-distance buses to Mahabaleshwar, Aurangabad and Panaji, and for hotels which it operates around the state.

Money American Express has two offices in Bombay. For quick foreign exchange go to its Travel Services office (☎ 204-8291) next to the Regal Cinema at Shivaji Maharaj Marg at Colaba. It's open daily from 9.30 am to 7.30 pm. The American Express Bank, at 364 Dr D Naoroji Rd near Flora Fountain, is open weekdays from 11 am to 3 pm and Saturday from 11 am to 1 pm.

Thomas Cook (☎ 204-8556) on Dr D Naoroji Rd also does fast and efficient exchange and is open Monday to Saturday from 9.30 am to 6 pm.

The Banque Société Générale (☎ 287-0909) is in Maker Chambers IV, Bajaj Marg at Nariman Point.

The banking facilities at the international airport are also relatively efficient.

Post & Telecommunications The GPO is an imposing building off Nagar Chowk near Victoria Terminus (VT). The poste restante service is open Monday to Saturday from 9 am to 6 pm. You'll get the whole pile of any letter of the alphabet you name to sort through but they'll want to see your passport first.

The parcel post office is in the mezzanine wing, up the stairs behind the main stamp counters. It's open Monday to Saturday from 9 am to 7 pm. On the footpath outside the GPO there are people who will wrap your parcel in the required way.

For making international telephone calls (including collect calls) and sending faxes, head to the government's modern telecommunications office, Videsh Sanchar Bhavan (☎ 262-4020; fax 262-4027), on M G Rd. There are also plenty of ISD/STD booths around the city.

Foreign Consulates Due to Bombay's importance as a business centre, many countries maintain diplomatic representation in

Bombay as well as in the capital, Delhi. They include:

Australia
    Maker Towers (16th floor), E Block, Cuffe Parade (☎ 218-1071)
Belgium
    Morena, 11 B Dahanukar Marg, Cumballa Hill (☎ 492-9202)
Canada
    41/42 Maker Chambers VI, Nariman Point (☎ 287-6028)
Denmark
    L & T House, N Morarjee Marg, Ballard Estate (☎ 261-8181)
Egypt
    101 Beh Hur Apartment, 32 Narayan Dabholkar Rd, off Lakshmibai Jagmohandas Marg, Malabar Hill (☎ 367-6386)
France
    Data Prasad Bldg (2nd floor), N G Cross Rd, off G Deshmukh Marg (Peddar Rd), Cumballa Hill (☎ 495-0918)
Germany
    Hoechst House (10th floor), Nariman Point (☎ 283-2422)
Indonesia
    Lincoln Annex, 19 S K Barodawala Marg, Cumballa Hill (☎ 386-8678)
Ireland
    Thomas Cook Bldg (2nd floor), Dr D Naoroji Rd (☎ 285-0330)
Italy
    Kanchanjunga, 72 G Deshmukh Marg, Cumballa Hill (☎ 387-2341)
Japan
    1 B Dahanukar Marg, Cumballa Hill (☎ 493-4310)
Mauritius
    Dhanraj Mahal (3rd floor), Apollo Bunder (☎ 202-7244)
Netherlands
    16 Maharshi Karve Rd, Churchgate (☎ 206-6840)
Singapore
    94 Sakhar Bhavan (9th floor), Nariman Point (☎ 204-3209)
Spain
    Ador House, 6 K Dubash Marg, Fort (☎ 287-4797)
Sri Lanka
    Sri Lanka House, 34 Homi Modi St, Fort (☎ 204-5861)
Sweden
    85 Sayani Rd, Subhash Gupta Bhavan, Prabhadevi (☎ 436-0493)

Switzerland
Manek Mahal (7th floor), 90 Veer Nariman Rd, Fort (☎ 204-3550)

Thailand
Krishna Bagh (2nd floor), 43 Bhulabhai Desai Marg, Cumballa Hill (☎ 363-1404)

UK
Maker Chambers IV (1st floor), 222 Jamnalal Bajaj Marg, Nariman Point (☎ 283-3602; fax 202-7940)

USA
Lincoln House, 78 Bhulabhai Desai Marg, Cumballa Hill (☎ 363-3611, 822-3611)

Visa Extensions The Foreigners' Registration Office (☎ 262-0446) on Dr D Naoroji Rd near the Police Commissioner's Office handles visa extensions (up to the maximum stay of six months). Extensions cost Rs 625 and take at least one day to be processed; you'll need four passport photos.

Libraries & Cultural Centres The British Council Library (☎ 22-3530) is at Mittal Tower A Wing (1st floor), Nariman Point. Although it is ostensibly for members only, it's possible to get in to read the British newspapers. It is open Tuesday to Friday

from 10 am to 5.45 pm and Saturday from 9 am to 4.45 pm.

The Alliance Française (☎ 203-6187) is opposite the American Center at Theosophy Hall, 40 New Marine Lines. It's open weekdays from 10 am to 5.30 pm and Saturday until 1 pm. Visitors are welcome to browse through the French newspapers.

Travel Agencies For personal service and discounted tickets you won't find much better than Transway International (☎ 262-6066; fax 262-3518) at Pantaky House, 8 Maruti Cross Lane (off Maruti St), Fort, Bombay 400001. This small agency offers all sorts of assistance to travellers including a mail pick-up service and city information. It's on the 3rd floor of a decrepit building and can be a challenge to find but the service is worth the hunt.

Space Travels (☎ 266-3397) also gives very good service and is at Nanabhoy Mansion, Sir P Mehta Rd. Travel Corner Ltd (☎ 204-2882), Veer Nariman Rd (down an alley next to Hotel Delamar), is another

---

Bombay – the Riots and the Bombs

Ever since the Indian Mutiny of 1857, Bombay has basked in the image of being a 'safe' place, far from the religious zealots and insurrections of the north. But recent events have severely tarnished this patina, forcing Bombayites to admit that, these days, their city is as much a seething cauldron of communalism and a target for terrorism as any of its northern counterparts.

Insiders have always known that corruption here is rife and that politics is dictated along communal lines. The (Indian) mafia – or the *dons* as they are commonly known – rule here and many of the city's politicians work in close association with them. Those that have gotten out of line, such as three businessmen involved in recent land deals, are dead. The sectarian propaganda of the militant Hindu political party the Shiv Sena has also attracted a growing audience in recent times, especially among the lower ranks of the Bombay police.

And so the stage was set for the violence that engulfed the city following the destruction of the Babri Masjid at Ayodhya in Uttar Pradesh by Hindu fanatics in late 1992. More than 600 people were killed in the city in orgies of looting, murder and arson that broke out immediately after the mosque was torn down, and then again exactly one month later. On both occasions, the victims were mainly Muslims. In the first riot, many were killed by the police; in the subsequent violence, Shiv Sena gangs were largely blamed.

The metropolis had barely recovered from the riots when, on 12 March 1993, 13 bombs ripped through the heart of the city, killing 250 people. The first blast demolished the stock exchange while following explosions claimed the Air India Building, three top-end hotels near the airport and other commercial establishments. No-one claimed responsibility, but many Indian politicians blamed Pakistan believing that the bombs had been planted as punishment for the many Muslim deaths during the riots.

Over a year later, 189 people, including Bombay film star Sanjay Dutt (known locally as India's Sylvester Stallone), were charged with involvement in the bombings. However, 45 of those charged have 'absconded', and it remains to be seen whether the real criminals behind the blasts have been caught. With 3700 witnesses to be called and a 10,000-page charge list, the authorities will be busy until close to the end of the century just conducting the hearings. ■

reliable agency. Both Thomas Cook and American Express also have helpful travel shops.

Curiously enough, despite the great number of airlines flying through Bombay it is not as good a centre for cheap tickets as Delhi.

Bookshops & Publications The Nalanda Bookshop in the Taj Hotel is excellent. Other good bookshops are: Strand Bookstall, just off Sir P Mehta Rd, Fort, and Bookpoint on R Kamani Marg in Ballard Estate.

There are also many street bookstalls under the arcades along Dr D Naoroji Rd and along the southern section of M G Rd.

City of Gold, the Biography of Bombay is a good book to read about the city. *The Bombay Guide* is a boring 100-page booklet that's free from the Government of India tourist office.

Medical Services In an emergency, phone 102 for an ambulance. Two of the most central hospitals are St George's Hospital (☎ 262-0301) on P D'Mello Rd just east of VT, and the Bombay Hospital (☎ 286-3343) on V Thackersey Marg.

Gateway of India
In the days when most visitors came to India by ship and when Bombay was India's principal port, this was indeed the 'gateway' to India. Today it's merely Bombay's foremost landmark. The gateway was conceived following the visit of King George V in 1911 and officially opened in 1924. Architecturally it is a conventional Arch of Triumph, with elements in its design derived from the Muslim styles of 16th-century Gujarat. It is built of yellow basalt and stands on the Apollo Bunder, a popular Bombay meeting place in the evenings.

The Taj Mahal Intercontinental Hotel overlooks the Apollo Bunder and launches run from here across to Elephanta Island. Close to the gateway are statues of Swami Vivekananda and of the Maratha leader Shivaji astride his horse.

Colaba Causeway
With their cheap hotels and restaurants, the streets behind the Taj Mahal Hotel are the travellers' centre of Bombay. Colaba Causeway, now renamed Shahid Bhagat Singh Rd, extends to the end of the Colaba promontory, the southern end of Bombay Island. Sassoon Dock is always interesting to visit around dawn, when the fishing boats come in and unload their catch in a colourful scene of intense activity. There's an old lighthouse at the end of the promontory, although the lighthouse used today is further south on a rocky island.

St John's Church
This church, also known as the Afghan Church, is near the end of Colaba Causeway. It was built in 1847 and is dedicated to the soldiers who fell in the Sind campaign of 1838 and the First Afghan War of 1843.

Prince of Wales Museum
Beside Wellingdon Circle, close to the Colaba hotel enclave, is the Prince of Wales Museum, built to commemorate King George V's first visit to India in 1905 while he was still Prince of Wales. The first part of the museum was opened in 1923. It was designed in the Indo-Saracenic style and has sections for art and paintings, archaeology and natural history. Among the more interesting items is a very fine collection of miniature paintings, bas-reliefs from the Elephanta Caves and Buddha images. Put aside at least half a day to explore this fascinating place.

The museum is open daily except Monday from 10.15 am to 6 pm and entry is Rs 3 (children Rs 1).

Jehangir Art Gallery
Within the compound of the museum stands Bombay's principal art gallery. There are often special exhibitions of modern Indian art here. You'll also find public phones, public toilets and a good cafe. The gallery is open daily from 11 am to 7 pm.

University & High Court

Along B Patel Marg, overlooking Oval Maidan, there are several imposing public buildings erected during Bombay's period of great growth under the British. The university is in 14th to 15th-century Gothic style and is dominated by the 80-metre Rajabai Tower. This impressive clock tower rises above the university library.

Statues of Justice and Mercy top the huge High Court building beyond the university. It was built in Early English style and completed in 1878.

Madura's graceful standing Buddha

Flora Fountain

This is the business centre of Bombay, around which many of the major banks and business offices are centred. The fountain stands on Martyr's Square, officially renamed Hutatma Chowk, at the heart of a busy five-point intersection. It was erected in 1869 in honour of Sir Bartle Frere who was governor of Bombay from 1862-67, during which time Bombay experienced its most dramatic growth due to the worldwide cotton shortage caused by the American Civil War.

Horniman Circle

Several interesting old Bombay buildings stand close to Horniman Circle. If you're walking from the GPO back to Colaba some time, it's worth pausing to have a glance at some of these buildings.

St Thomas' Cathedral, begun by Gerald Aungier in 1672 but not formally opened until 1718, contains several interesting memorials. The old **Mint** was completed in 1829 and has an Ionic facade. It was built on land reclaimed in 1823 and adjoins the town hall. Behind the town hall stand the remains of the old **Bombay Castle**.

Opened in 1833, the **town hall** still houses the library of the Royal Asiatic Society. Ascend the imposing steps at the front of the town hall and have a short wander inside. You'll see statues of a number of the government officials and wealthy benefactors of Bombay's golden period, including Sir Bartle Frere and Sir Jamsetjee Jijibhoy. Continuing on, you pass the old **Customs House** built in 1720. The old Bombay dockyards are behind this building.

Marine Drive

Now officially renamed Netaji Subhashchandra Bose Rd, Marine Drive is built on land reclaimed in 1920. It runs along the shoreline of Back Bay, starting at Nariman Point and sweeping around by Chowpatty Beach and up to Malabar Hill. The road is backed with high residential buildings and is one of Bombay's most popular promenades.

BOMBAY

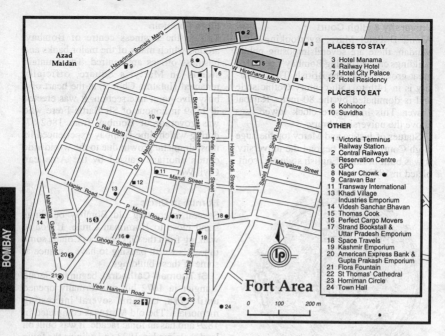

PLACES TO STAY
3 Hotel Manama
4 Railway Hotel
7 Hotel City Palace
12 Hotel Residency

PLACES TO EAT
6 Kohinoor
10 Suvidha

OTHER
1 Victoria Terminus
  Railway Station
2 Central Railways
  Reservation Centre
5 GPO
8 Nagar Chowk
9 Caravan Bar
11 Transway International
13 Khadi Village
  Industries Emporium
14 Videsh Sanchar Bhavan
15 Thomas Cook
16 Perfect Cargo Movers
17 Strand Bookstall &
  Uttar Pradesh Emporium
18 Space Travels
19 Kashmir Emporium
20 American Express Bank &
  Gupta Prakash Emporium
21 Flora Fountain
22 St Thomas' Cathedral
23 Horniman Circle
24 Town Hall

Fort Area

0   100   200 m

Taraporewala Aquarium

Constructed in 1951, the aquarium on Marine Drive has both freshwater and saltwater fish. It's open Tuesday to Saturday from 10 am to 7 pm and Sunday from 10 am to 8 pm, and admission is Rs 3 (children Rs 1.50).

Also along Marine Drive, before the aquarium, is a series of cricket pitches where in summer there always seem to be games underway.

Chowpatty Beach

Bombay's famous beach attracts few bathers and even fewer sunbathers – neither activity has much of a following in India, and in any case the water is none too healthy. Chowpatty has plenty of other activities though. It's one of those typical Indian slices of life where anything and everything can happen, and does. Sand-castle sculptors make elaborate figures in the sand, contortionists go through equally extravagant contortions and

family groups stroll around. In between there are kiosks selling Bombay's popular snack, *bhelpuri*, and *kulfi* (ice cream). Donkeys and ponies are available for children's rides.

Malabar Hill

At the end of Back Bay, Marine Drive climbs up to Malabar Hill. This is an expensive residential area, for not only is it a little cooler than the sea-level parts of the city, but there are fine views over Back Bay and Chowpatty Beach and right across to the central business district. At the end of the promontory is **Raj Bhavan**, the old British government headquarters and now the governor's residence.

Close by is the temple of **Walkeshwar**, the Sand Lord, an important Hindu pilgrimage site. According to the *Ramayana*, Rama rested here on his way from Ayodhya to Lanka to rescue Sita. He constructed a lingam of sand at the site. The original temple was built about 1000 years ago but was reconstructed in 1715.

Just below the temple is the **Banganga Tank** which was built on the spot where water flowed out after Rama shot a *bana* (arrow) into the ground.

Jain Temple

This marble temple on Malabar Hill was built in 1904 and is dedicated to the first Jain *tirthankar*, Adinath. It's typical of modern Jain temples in its gaudy, mirrored style. The walls are decorated with pictures of incidents in the lives of the tirthankars. The overriding sound inside is of temple priests counting money from the huge donation boxes.

Hanging Gardens

On top of Malabar Hill, these gardens were laid out in 1881 and are correctly known as the Pherozeshah Mehta Gardens. They take their popular name from the fact that they are built on top of a series of reservoirs that supply water to Bombay. The formally laid-out gardens have a notable collection of hedges shaped like animals and there are good views over the city.

Kamala Nehru Park

Directly across the road from the Hanging Gardens, this park is predominantly a children's park though it offers superb views over Bombay. It was laid out in 1952 and was named after Nehru's wife.

Towers of Silence

Beside the Hanging Gardens, but carefully shielded from viewers, are the Parsi Towers of Silence. The Parsis hold fire, earth and water as sacred and thus, if at all possible, they will not cremate or bury their dead. Instead the bodies are laid out within the towers to be picked clean by vultures (if there are any vultures in Bombay; maybe they're crows).

Elaborate precautions are taken to keep ghoulish sightseers from observing the towers, despite which a *Time-Life* book on Bombay provided a bird's-eye view of one of them. Parsi power in Bombay is suffi-ciently strong that the book was black-ink censored. Tour guides, always fond of a tall story for tourists, like to tell you that the reason the Hanging Garden reservoirs were covered over was that the vultures had an unpleasant habit of dropping the odd bit in the water supply.

Mahalakshmi Temple

Descending from Malabar Hill and continuing north around the coastline, you come to the Mahalakshmi Temple, the oldest in Bombay and, appropriately for this city of business and money, dedicated to the goddess of wealth. The images of the goddess and her two sisters were said to have been found in the sea.

Near here is the **Mahalakshmi Racecourse**, said to be the finest in India, where horse races are held each Sunday from December to May. The road along the seashore by the racecourse was once known as the Hornby Vellard, and was constructed in the 18th century to reclaim the swampland on which the course is now constructed.

Haji Ali's Tomb

This tomb and mosque are devoted to a Muslim saint who drowned here. The buildings are reached by a long causeway which can only be crossed at low tide. Here a scene of typical Indian ingenuity and resourcefulness takes place. Hundreds of beggars line the length of the causeway waiting for the regular stream of pilgrims. At the start of the causeway is a small group of moneychangers who, for a few paise commission, will change a Rs 1 or Rs 2 coin into lots of smaller denominations. Thus a pilgrim can do his/her soul the maximum amount of good for the minimum expenditure.

No doubt at the ebb tide the mendicants can change their low-value paise coins into something a little more manageable, thus giving the moneychangers their small change for the next low tide and no doubt providing them with another commission rake-off.

Mani Bhavan

At 19 Labernam Rd, near August Kranti Maidan, is the building where Mahatma Gandhi stayed during his visits to Bombay from 1917-34. Today it has a pictorial exhibit of incidents in Gandhi's life and contains a library of books by or about the Mahatma. It is open daily except Monday from 9.30 am to 6 pm; entry is Rs 3.

Victoria Gardens

These gardens, north of the city centre, contain Bombay's **zoo** and the **Victoria & Albert Museum**, and have been renamed the Veermata Jijabai Bhonsle Udyan. The museum has some interesting exhibits relating to old Bombay. Just outside the museum building is the large stone elephant removed from Elephanta Island in 1864, and after which the island was named.

The museum (☎ 872-7131) is open from 10.30 am to 5 pm, the zoo from sunrise to sunset. Both are closed on Wednesday and charge Rs 0.50 admission.

Juhu

Close to Bombay's airports, Juhu is 18 km north of the city centre. It's the nearest beach to the city and has quite a collection of upper-notch hotels, but it's no place for a swim as the water is filthy.

On weekdays it is fairly quiet, but on weekends and in the late afternoons there are camel and donkey rides, dancing monkeys, acrobats and every other type of Indian beach entertainment including thieves and hustlers. In recent years, unsuccessful attempts have been made to ban camel rides due to concern about their mistreatment. The camels, brought from Rajasthan or Gujarat, are abandoned once the monsoon arrives and must fend for themselves until the beach trade picks up again.

Bollywood & the Movies

Quickly, what are the biggest film-producing city and country in the world? Hollywood and the USA? Wrong twice – Bombay and India! The Indians turn out more than 600 full-length feature films a year and, of these, nearly half are made in Bombay. Calcutta makes some arty, intellectual films; Madras some family comedies or musicals; but for extravaganzas, action dramas, the 'starcast' A features, it's Bombay – or Bollywood – all the way.

Bombay films are known as 'masala movies' as they always have a bit of everything – drama, action, suspense, music, dancing and romance – all mixed together into one outrageous blend. They are down-to-earth entertainment: escapism and nothing more. After all, life for a lot of Indians is not all that much fun and Bombay film-makers are not trying to produce something for a sophisticated audience.

To many Westerners, masala movies are unadulterated rubbish. Fight scenes, in particular, are unbelievably unconvincing – two men will beat the daylights out of each other for up to five minutes without sustaining a single cut or bruise or shedding a drop of blood. Even a knockout is rare. Romance scenes are sickly sweet and unashamedly male chauvinist. Everyone lives happily ever after and, naturally, no-one ever has sex. Perish the thought!

The songs written for the movies are pure bubble gum and rely heavily on electronic effects. The leading lady (or her ghost singer) is *always* a soprano permanently hovering around top C and the leading man *always* a tenor with tight pants. It's guaranteed to make you reach for the earplugs.

Fortunately, India does have some good directors who make films with an international appeal so it's worth looking out for them.

A glance at the film billboards or movie magazines gives you the impression that Indian film actors are a band of escapees from weight-watchers. Well, there's no glamour in being thin in India; it's the well-padded look which appeals. It's amusing to see how this works on Western films – familiar European and American film stars become remarkably rotund when they're repainted for the Indian posters.

Nor are Indian films made one at a time as in the West. A big star could be involved in a number of films simultaneously – shooting a day on one, a week on another, a morning on a third. This involves phenomenal scheduling problems and also means that Indian films generally take a long time to make.

Bombay has about a dozen studios but visiting one of them is not easy. You must first get the manager's permission and that's not usually forthcoming. The closest to the city centre is Mehboob Film Studio(☎ 642-8045) at Hill Rd in Bandra. You could also try Natraj Studios (☎ 834-2371), Western Express Highway, Andheri East, or the biggest studio, Filmistan Studios (☎ 840-1533), Goregaon Rd, way to the north. ■

Festivals

Elephanta Festival
This two-day classical dance and music event is run under the auspices of the MTDC and is held in February on Elephanta Island.

Banganga Festival
Another of the MTDC's two-day music festivals, this one is held in January at the Banganga tank on Malabar Hill.

Ganesh Chaturthi
This is a famous Hindu festival (August/September) which climaxes with the large images of the elephant-headed god being immersed in the sea off Chowpatty Beach. ■

From Santa Cruz station you can get there on a No 231 bus.

Other Attractions

The **Nehru Planetarium** (☎ 492-8086) is on Dr Annie Besant Rd at Worli near the Haji Ali Tomb. There are one-hour shows in English daily except Monday at 3 and 6 pm. Admission is Rs 8.

Falkland St in the Kamatipura district to the north-west of Chor Bazaar is the centre for Bombay's notorious red-light district known as **The Cages**. The women and young teenagers who work here, many of them as forced labour, stand behind metal-barred doors, hence the name. A No 130 bus from the Prince of Wales Museum or Victoria Terminus passes through this depressing area.

Bombay's municipal laundry, or **dhobi ghat**, is close to Mahalakshmi railway station, the next station north of Bombay Central on the suburban line. Some 5000 men use the rows of open-air troughs and tanks here to wash (or rather beat) the thousands of kg of clothing brought from all around the city every day. Each cement trough is rented for Rs 100 per month, including water, and is shared by several *dhobi-wallahs*, most of whom start work before sunrise and finish their last load by about 3 pm. From Mahalakshmi station, just walk up onto the overhead bridge to get a view.

Organised Tours

Daily tours of Bombay are operated by the Maharashtra Tourist Development Corporation though, as elsewhere, they're a breathless rush-around. Tours generally last from 2 to 6 pm; the cost is Rs 55.

The MTDC also has a suburban tour which operates from 9.15 am to 6.15 pm and costs Rs 90. This goes to the Kanheri Caves, Juhu Beach and other fascinating places such as the airport.

Of more interest to travellers are the four-hour daily launch tours to Elephanta Island (for details see the upcoming Around Bombay section).

The MTDC also offers rushed tours to such places as Mahabaleshwar or Aurangabad/Ajanta/Ellora, but these tours need a minimum of 10 people and they are suspended during the monsoon.

Places to Stay

Bombay is India's most expensive city for accommodation. Not only that, but it's a magnet for Middle East and Gulf Arabs who come here for holidays, shopping expeditions and business. They invariably bring with them their entire entourage. Not all of these visitors are super-rich oil sheikhs who can afford to stay in the Taj Mahal Intercontinental, so the pressure for accommodation – even at the bottom end of the market – is intense.

There is no guarantee that you will be able to find a room in your preferred price range, at least for the first night and especially if you arrive late in the day. You may have to initially settle for something considerably more expensive until you've had time to walk

BOMBAY

around unencumbered with baggage. The standard of accommodation, too, at the bottom end of the market is often poor in comparison with elsewhere in India. Many Bombay hotels have a noon checkout; at some it's 10 am.

Taxi drivers are fond of telling new arrivals that the hotel of their choice is 'full' and suggesting somewhere else. This will inevitably be an expensive hotel (they often have a sticker for the hotel they suggest on their dashboard). It's a safe bet they pick up a commission for introducing a guest but this isn't always the case. What definitely is the case is that they haven't a clue whether a hotel is full or not. No taxi driver in Bombay routinely checks hotels for occupancy levels nor do they have mobile phones. If you want to go to a specific hotel, insist on going there first.

A new accommodation option is the home-stay (or 'paying guest scheme' as it's known here). The Government of India tourist office can give you a list of the 44 private homes participating in Bombay and elsewhere in Maharashtra. Room rates range from Rs 250 to Rs 3000. In Bombay, the Pradhan family are centrally located, welcoming and highly recommended.

Places to Stay – bottom end

Like other Indian cities, Bombay has its share of YMCAs and YWCAs. Although very good value for money, they're invariably full. The most popular is the *YWCA International Centre* (☎ 202-0445), in Colaba at 18 Madame Cama Rd. It takes both women and men and offers half board for Rs 300/585 including tax plus a Rs 30 membership charge (valid for one month). The rooms have attached bathrooms. It's sometimes booked out up to three months in advance and reservations are taken only between 9 am and 4 pm daily (except Sunday).

The *YMCA International Guest House* (☎ 307-0601) is at 18 YMCA Rd near Bombay Central. The rooms are well kept and the charges are much the same as for the YWCA, however this place is a long way from downtown Bombay.

For men only there is good dormitory accommodation for Rs 40 or triple rooms at Rs 50 per person at *Seva Niketan* (☎ 309-2934) on J Jijibhoy Rd, near Byculla railway station on the suburban line from Victoria Terminus.

The *retiring rooms* at the domestic airport are reserved for transit passengers and cost Rs 160/320 for a single/double. Ask at the airport manager's office.

Finally, both Bombay Central and VT have *retiring rooms*. At Central doubles cost Rs 200, or Rs 350 with air-con. At VT they range from Rs 90 to Rs 200 per bed, depending on the number of beds in the room.

Colaba The majority of the budget hotels are in Colaba directly behind the Taj Mahal Intercontinental.

The cheapest place is the *Salvation Army Red Shield Hostel* (☎ 24-1824), at 30 Mereweather Rd. It's a very popular place, with dorm beds (and breakfast) for Rs 70 or full board for Rs 100. There are also big doubles at Rs 300 and family rooms at Rs 125 (per person) with full board, but you must share the communal bathrooms and the facilities are sometimes not all that clean. Safe-deposit lockers can be hired. During busy periods, checkout time is 9 am and the maximum length of stay is one week.

Close by is the old *Carlton Hotel* (☎ 202-0642) at 12 Mereweather Rd. It's decidedly semi-derelict and only for those inured to rock-bottom Indian conditions. Prices for the older rooms with common showers and toilets are Rs 150 for a single and between Rs 220 to Rs 250 a double (depending on the size of the room and whether you want a window), including taxes. There are also three new rooms, all with attached bathroom, but they are small and overpriced at Rs 750/900 for a triple/quad.

Much better in terms of maintenance and the fabric of the building is the *Hotel Prosser's* (☎ 24-1715), on the corner of Henry Rd and P J Ramchandani Marg, which has 15 small hardboard partitioned singles/doubles with shared bath for Rs 200/300 including tax.

Away from this immediate area, but within easy walking distance, is the very popular 3rd-floor *Hotel Lawrence* (☎ 24-3618), Rope Walk Lane, off K Dubash Marg at the back of the Prince of Wales Museum. It's often full since it only has nine rooms, but it's excellent value at Rs 100/200 for singles/doubles with common bath including taxes. Some of the rooms have balconies.

Back in Colaba, there's the friendly *Bentley's Hotel* (☎ 24-1733; fax 287-1846), 17 Oliver Rd, which offers singles/doubles for Rs 240/460 including breakfast and tax. Double rooms with attached bath and colour TV cost Rs 600. The nearby *Hotel Kishan* (☎ 283-3886), Walton Rd, has simple rooms with attached bath for Rs 260/360. Also good is the small, friendly *Hotel Volga II* (☎ 287-3436), Navraji Rd, above street level and next door to the Leopold Cafe & Bar. Doubles/triples without bath cost Rs 300/350 while doubles with bath go for Rs 350. There are three clean shared bathrooms.

Cheaper but basic is the *Apollo Guest House* (☎ 204-5540), Mathuradas Estate Building (1st floor) on Colaba Causeway, which has small, clean singles/doubles with shared bathroom for Rs 180/260 including

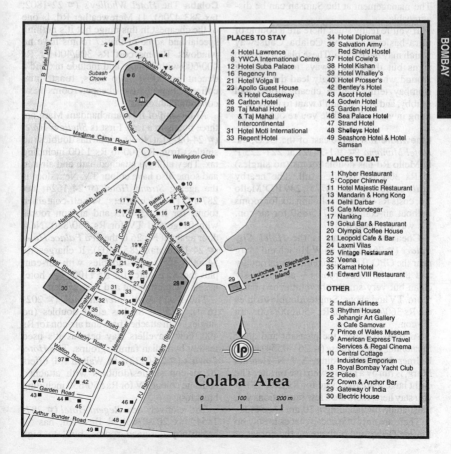

PLACES TO STAY

4 Hotel Lawrence
8 YWCA International Centre
12 Hotel Suba Palace
16 Regency Inn
21 Hotel Volga II
23 Apollo Guest House
   & Hotel Causeway
26 Carlton Hotel
28 Taj Mahal Hotel
   & Taj Mahal
   Intercontinental
31 Hotel Moti International
33 Regent Hotel
34 Hotel Diplomat
36 Salvation Army
   Red Shield Hostel
37 Hotel Cowie's
38 Hotel Kishan
39 Hotel Whalley's
40 Hotel Prosser's
42 Bentley's Hotel
43 Ascot Hotel
44 Godwin Hotel
45 Garden Hotel
46 Sea Palace Hotel
47 Strand Hotel
48 Shelleys Hotel
49 Seashore Hotel & Hotel
   Samsan

PLACES TO EAT

1 Khyber Restaurant
5 Copper Chimney
11 Hotel Majestic Restaurant
13 Mandarin & Hong Kong
14 Delhi Darbar
15 Cafe Mondegar
17 Nanking
19 Gokul Bar & Restaurant
20 Olympia Coffee House
21 Leopold Cafe & Bar
24 Laxmi Vilas
25 Vintage Restaurant
32 Veena
35 Kamat Hotel
41 Edward VIII Restaurant

OTHER

2 Indian Airlines
3 Rhythm House
6 Jehangir Art Gallery
   & Cafe Samovar
7 Prince of Wales Museum
9 American Express Travel
   Services & Regal Cinema
10 Central Cottage
   Industries Emporium
18 Royal Bombay Yacht Club
22 Police
27 Crown & Anchor Bar
29 Gateway of India
30 Electric House

Colaba Area

0   100   200 m

BOMBAY

tax. Don't confuse this place with the hotel of the same name on Garden Rd. On the 3rd floor of the same building, the new *Hotel Causeway* (☎ 202-0833) has decent-sized doubles (no singles) all with TV, attached bathroom and a hybrid toilet. Rooms cost Rs 500, or Rs 600 with air-con.

There's a whole collection of small hotels on various floors along the noisy and somewhat sleazy Arthur Bunder Rd. The *Seashore Hotel* and the *Hotel Samsan* (☎ 287-3240) at Kamal Mansion are both fairly clean and have decent-sized rooms for around Rs 300, although you'll be lucky to get a window. The management at the Samsan can be disagreeable.

If you're really stuck there are a couple of ultra-basic places on Colaba Causeway which may have room. These places have no signs but there are always touts hanging around who will willingly lead the way. In Bombay terms they're cheap, airless and grubby, and you wouldn't want to leave anything in your room while you're out.

Elsewhere Just to the east of the GPO, the *Hotel Manama* (☎ 261-3412) at 221-225 P D'Mello Rd has double rooms (no singles) at Rs 300 and is often full. The nearby *Railway Hotel* (☎ 262-0775), 249 P D'Mello Rd, costs Rs 495/605 including tax for rooms without air-con, or Rs 715/880 for air-con. It's way overpriced.

Cheaper and better is the *Hotel City Palace* (☎ 261-5515) on W Hirachand Marg near the GPO. The management are friendly and the refurbished rooms – all spotlessly clean but very small – have attached bathroom, TV and phone. Singles/doubles/triples are Rs 360/450/550, or Rs 450/600/700 with air-con.

At Ballard Estate, the pleasant and quiet *Fernandez Guest House* (☎ 261-0554) in the Balmer Lawrie Building, 5 J N Heredia Marg, is run by a family who live on site. The eight large, bare rooms go for Rs 200/400. If you stay here, there are a few regulations you must abide by including a 10 am checkout.

There are only two cheap places to stay on Marine Drive, and both are on the corner of D Rd. The first is the *Bentley Hotel* (☎ 203-1244) on the 3rd floor (there's no lift) of the Krishna Mahal Building, which offers B&B for Rs 275/300 in rooms with common bath. Some of the rooms are very small. Opposite is *Norman's Guest House* (☎ 203-4234) which has clean and simple rooms with attached bath for Rs 385/495 including tax.

Places to Stay – middle

Many of the middle-bracket hotels are in the Colaba area, though there is another, slightly more expensive cluster along Marine Drive.

Colaba The *Hotel Whalley's* (☎ 22-1802; fax 283-4206), 41 Mereweather Rd, is one of the cheapest in this range but it's nothing special and some of the 27 rooms have no windows. Rooms cost Rs 300/400 or Rs 400/600 with air-con, and include tax and a decent breakfast (two eggs, toast, jam, coffee). Some of the cheaper rooms have common bathrooms.

At the end of P J Ramchandani Marg are three hotels in a row. First is *Shelleys Hotel* (☎ 24-0229) at No 30, which has doubles (no singles) from Rs 700 to Rs 1400 including tax. They all have attached bath and air-con and some also have colour TV. Next door is the ageing *Strand Hotel* (☎ 24-1624; fax 287-1441) which offers 34 self-contained rooms for Rs 530/715 and air-con rooms with fridge and TV for Rs 750/880. Next door again at No 26 is the *Sea Palace Hotel* (☎ 24-1828; fax 285-4403). It charges Rs 545/850 for singles/doubles with air-con, plus there are suites for Rs 1100. The hotel has its own restaurant and roof garden.

The *Hotel Moti International* (☎ 202-1654), 10 Best St, has eight doubles (no singles) with attached bath and air-con for Rs 400. Few travellers stay here as it's used mainly by Indian family groups. The *Hotel Cowie's* (☎ 24-0232), 15 Walton Rd, offers 20 air-con singles/doubles with attached bath and colour TV for Rs 550/650 including breakfast.

The relatively new *Regent Hotel* (☎ 287-1854; fax 202-0363), 8 Best Rd, has 50 beautifully designed rooms, built to high standards. Air-con singles/doubles with TV and fridge cost Rs 720/1090 including taxes. The staff are friendly and eager to please. Round the corner from here behind the Taj is the *Hotel Diplomat* (☎ 202-1661) at 24-26 Mereweather Rd. It's popular with businesspeople and often full. Air-con rooms with TV and fridge go for Rs 700/900, or Rs 900/1100 for deluxe rooms. There's a bar and restaurant.

Behind the Regal Cinema, the run-down *Regency Inn* (☎ 202-0292; fax 287-3371), 18 Lansdowne House, Mahakavi Bhushan Marg, has doubles from Rs 400 to Rs 850. All are air-conditioned but musty. The refurbished *Hotel Suba Palace* (☎ 202-0636) on Battery St has clean, spacious rooms with TV, fridge, air-con and fan. Regular doubles go for Rs 860 and superior singles/doubles are Rs 700/960.

Up in price again there are three long-established hotels on Garden Rd but they're not great value. The *Ascot Hotel* (☎ 24-0020; fax 204-6449) at 38 Garden Rd has singles/doubles for Rs 925/1090 including breakfast; the *Godwin Hotel* (☎ 287-2050; fax 287-1592) at No 41 charges Rs 1150/1400 and has a rooftop restaurant and bar; and the *Garden Hotel* (☎ 24-1476; fax 287-1592) at No 42 offers rooms for Rs 800/1000. At all these places, rooms have air-con, TV and attached bath.

Fort Area One of the few options here, and an excellent one at that, is the friendly *Hotel Residency* (☎ 262-5525) on the corner of Dr D Naoroji Rd and Gunbow St (R S Marg). This fully air-con hotel is in the heart of the downtown bustle, yet it manages to be discreet, quiet and sensibly priced. The immaculate rooms are small but stylishly furnished and have TV. Singles/doubles cost Rs 600/650 including tax.

At the top end of this category is the elegant *Grand Hotel* (☎ 261-8211; fax 262-6581), 17 Sprott Rd, Ballard Estate. It's a large place with friendly staff and very popular with business people. Air-con rooms with marbled bathrooms, traditionally designed furniture, TV and small balcony

cost Rs 1045/1210 including tax. There's a restaurant, coffee shop and bar.

Marine Drive The two cheapest places are the *Sea Green Hotel* (☎ 22-2294), 145 Marine Drive, and the adjacent *Sea Green South Hotel* (☎ 22-1613). They both charge Rs 725/850 for air-con rooms with attached bath. Checkout time for advance reservations is 8 am (unusual in Bombay).

Nearby at 141 Marine Drive is the old *Hotel Delamar* (☎ 204-2848) which offers air-con rooms with shared bath for Rs 625/962, or Rs 687/1017 with private bathroom, including taxes. All the rooms have colour TV.

Close by is the popular *Chateau Windsor Hotel* (☎ 204-3376; fax 285-1415), 86 Veer Nariman Rd, which has a huge selection of rooms varying greatly in size. Some of the windowless little boxes are poor value so don't take a room until you've seen it (and if you take the elevator to do so, make sure you obey the sign: 'Servants are not allowed to make use of lift unless accompanied by children')! Singles go for Rs 550 up to Rs 950. Doubles are Rs 700 (shared bath), or Rs 900 to Rs 1100 (attached bath). There are also triples and quads for Rs 1100 to Rs 1400 with attached bath. All the higher priced rooms have air-con and all rooms have a colour TV.

Airport There are a number of hotels in the suburb of Vile Parle (pronounced 'Veelay Parlay') close to the domestic terminal. The *Hotel Aircraft International* (☎ 612-3667) at 179 Dayaldas Rd has ordinary/deluxe rooms at Rs 470/500 and superdeluxe rooms at Rs 580. Moving up in price, the *Hotel Airport International* (☎ 612-2883) and the *Hotel Avion* (☎ 611-3220), both on Nehru Rd, have rooms for Rs 700/900. Off Nehru Rd, close to the five-star Sun-n-Sand Hotel, is the *Hotel Transit* (☎ 610-5812) which has rooms including breakfast at Rs 1060/1450 and suites for Rs 1500. The hotel has its own bar and restaurant.

Juhu The *Kings Hotel* (☎ 614-9775) at 5

Juhu Tara Rd, opposite the local church, provides air-con rooms for Rs 575/650 including tax. The *Sea Side Hotel* (☎ 620-0293), 39/2 Juhu Beach, has air-con rooms with attached bath for Rs 650/750.

Places to Stay – top end

Hotels in this category, like many of those in the mid-range, invariably have both state and central government taxes imposed on room tariffs. In this range they can amount to as much as 40%, though 20% is more common.

Colaba One of the cheapest in this range is the *Fariyas Hotel* (☎ 204-2911; fax 283-4992), two streets south of Arthur Bunder Rd. The rooms are very pleasant, it's fully air-conditioned and the staff are friendly. Singles/doubles are Rs 1100/1900 plus there are more expensive suites. There's a swimming pool, a bar and a good restaurant.

At the other end of Colaba is the *Taj Mahal Hotel & Taj Mahal Intercontinental* (☎ 202-3366; fax 287-2711), Apollo Bunder, reputedly the best hotel in India, though that's a moot point these days. Certainly the affluence ostentatiously paraded in the Taj is amazing. BMWs and Mercedes Benz vie for space in front of the main entrance while Gulf Arab sheikhs in gleaming white gowns glide across the immense, deliciously cool, marble-floored foyer. If you don't look mega-rich here you don't exist, though that doesn't prevent you from entering. The Taj, after all, does have one of the best bookshops in Bombay. It also has the best public toilets (though you're expected to tip the man who keeps them clean).

All of the 650 rooms are luxuriously appointed and range from US$155/170 for a standard room in the Intercontinental section to US$195/215 in the old wing. Also in the old wing are various suites ranging from 'Executive' at US$400 to 'Presidential' at US$825. The hotel has every conceivable facility including four restaurants, three bars, coffee shop, disco (guests only) and swimming pool.

Nariman Point & Marine Drive The *Ritz*

Hotel (☎ 285-0500; fax 285-0494), 5 J Tata Rd, Churchgate, is one of the older top-end establishments with the usual range of facilities but no swimming pool. It has rooms for Rs 2620/3272 and suites for Rs 3930 to Rs 4585 (including tax), and is centrally air-conditioned.

More modern is the *Ambassador Hotel* (☎ 204-1131), Veer Nariman Rd, Churchgate, where the cheapest singles/doubles are Rs 1980/2300. More expensive rooms cost Rs 2500/3000; suites start from Rs 3000. There's a bar and revolving rooftop restaurant but no swimming pool.

In the same price bracket is the somewhat featureless (from the outside) *Hotel Nataraj* (☎ 204-4161; fax 204-3864), 135 Marine Drive, which has rooms for Rs 2070/3000 plus suites for Rs 4140 including taxes. The hotel has a limited range of facilities and is used mainly for conferences and banquets. The nightclub here is for members only.

Competing with the Taj for pride of place as Bombay's most opulent hotel is the huge and thoroughly modern Oberoi/Oberoi Towers on Marine Drive. The *Oberoi* (☎ 202-5757; fax 204-1505) offers singes/doubles without a sea view for US$235/260, or US$270/300 with a view. Suites range from US$500 to the prestigious Kohinoor suite at US$1500. The adjoining and slightly older *Oberoi Towers* (☎ 202-4343; fax 204-3282) has singles/doubles at US$190/215 plus there are a range of suites from US$395 to US$700. The enormous atrium at the Oberoi Towers, around which there's a shopping complex on two floors, is beautifully designed and well worth seeing even if you're not staying at the hotel. It's also deliciously cool! Combined, the hotels have a plethora of facilities including two swimming pools, four restaurants, a bar with superb views over the bay and dancing every evening from 6.30 pm, as well as a disco.

In the diplomatic/business enclave of Cuffe Parade is the *Hotel President* (☎ 215-0808; fax 215-1201), 90 Cuffe Parade, which has standard rooms at US$160/175, superior rooms at US$175/190, and suites for US$290. The hotel has a swimming pool, bookshop and banqueting halls and is used mainly by businesspeople and expatriates on long-term contracts.

Airport There are a number of hotels out by the airport but there are few incentives, besides a quick getaway, to stay in this area.

Right outside the domestic terminal is the *Centaur Hotel* (☎ 611-6660; fax 611-3535), a large circular hotel with all the usual five-star amenities including a swimming pool, three restaurants and a bar. Rooms cost Rs 3000/3300, and there are suites at Rs 3600 to Rs 9000.

There are several other hotels very close by, either beside the Centaur or just across the road. They're all air-con and offer good facilities. The *Kamat's Plaza* (☎ 612-3390; fax 610-7974) at 70-C Nehru Rd, Vile Parle, has rooms for Rs 1200/1650 and a swimming pool.

One kilometre from the international terminal, the five-star *Leela Kempinski* (☎ 836-3636; fax 836-0606)) has singles/doubles for US$225/245 and suites for US$375. It has a swimming pool, four restaurants, two bars and a range of sports facilities.

Juhu There are a lot of hotels along Juhu Beach but it's hard to think of a good reason to stay there. Don't even consider swimming at Juhu – one look at the untreated sewage which slithers sluggishly out to sea from the vast slum encampments from Dadar to Juhu will convince you. The beach is also a favourite patch for thieves.

Most of the top-end hotels located here have free courtesy buses to and from both Sahar and Santa Cruz airports.

The four-star *Hotel Sands* (☎ 620-4511), 39/2 Juhu Beach, has rooms for Rs 1100/1500 and suites at Rs 2200. It has a restaurant and bar but no swimming pool.

Close by is the *Hotel Horizon* (☎ 611-7979), 37 Juhu Beach, with rooms for Rs 2000 to Rs 2500 (single or double) and suites for Rs 3000 to Rs 7000. It has a swimming pool, restaurants, bar and disco but the whole place is starting to flake around the edges. Next door is the five-star *Sun-n-Sand Hotel* (☎ 620-1811; fax 620-2170), 39 Juhu Beach,

which has singles/doubles at Rs 2000/2500 and suites for Rs 2500 to Rs 3000. There's a swimming pool, health club, restaurant and bar. Similar is the *Hotel Sea Princess* (☎ 611-7600; fax 611-3973), Juhu Beach, another five-star hotel, with rooms at Rs 2000/2400 plus 'executive' rooms for Rs 4800. It too has a swimming pool, restaurant and bar.

Up in price again, the *Ramada Inn Palm Grove* (☎ 611-2323; fax 611-3682), Juhu Beach, has rooms for Rs 2400/2900 plus suites for Rs 5500. More expensive still is the *Holiday Inn* (☎ 620-4444; fax 630-4452), Balraj Sahani Marg, Juhu Beach, which has rooms for US$145 (single or double) and suites for US$210. This has even more facilities than the Ramada including two swimming pools, garden barbecue, restaurants, pub and shopping arcade.

The five-star deluxe *Centaur Hotel Juhu Beach* (☎ 611-3090; fax 611-6343), Juhu Tara Rd, is an enormous place but it's past its prime. It has rooms for Rs 3000/3500 and suites for Rs 6000 to Rs 9000 and a full range of amenities. There's also an Air India and Indian Airlines reservation counter here.

Places to Eat
The accommodation shortage certainly doesn't spill over into restaurants. Bombay probably has the best selection of restaurants of any major Indian city and a meal in a better-class restaurant can be one of India's bargains.

Places to Eat – Cheap
Colaba The *Leopold Cafe & Bar* on Colaba Causeway is one of Bombay's legends. It's very popular at all meal times and is also good for a cold beer (draught or bottled) while watching the street life through the open doors. The clientele is a mix of travellers, Bombay yuppies and expats, though you may even see Gulf Arabs having a surreptitious beer! It has an extensive vegetarian and non-veg menu but, because of its popularity, it's overpriced and you may be given the nudge to leave as soon as you're finished.

More popular amongst travellers and young Bombayites these days is the nearby *Cafe Mondegar*. This place has a jukebox, colourful mural-coated walls, beer, Western and Indian food and a really happening young crowd, all crammed into a rather confined area. Across the road, the *Hotel Majestic* is a big vegetarian plate-meal specialist; it's Rs 16 for a thali. There are also non-veg dishes.

Directly across from the Leopold, the *Olympia Coffee House* is a traditional old coffee bar with wonderful, mirrored decor and marble-topped tables.

The *Cafe Samovar* in the Jehangir Art Gallery is pleasant for a cold drink or a quick snack (closed on Sunday). On Navroji Furounji Rd, *Laxmi Vilas* has excellent thalis and lassis. *Veena* on Colaba Causeway is more expensive but tasty, costing around Rs 40 for two. A couple of doors down, the *Kamat Hotel* has superb vegetarian food and it's air-conditioned upstairs.

At the top of Garden Rd, next to the garage, the *Edward VIII Restaurant* is a well-kept little place with healthy fruit juices. The *Gokul Bar & Restaurant* on Tulloch Rd is mainly a drinking den but it also serves tasty, cheap food – the fried fish is excellent.

Colaba is renowned for fine prawns and seafood. You can get fish & chips in quite a few places around here, as well as over on Marine Drive right beside the aquarium! Ultra-cheap street-food vendors set up on Tulloch Rd each evening – it's a very animated area.

Elsewhere There's a couple of places to go if you want a meal, a snack or just a drink while you read the mail you've just picked up from the GPO. *Kohinoor* is virtually opposite the GPO and is a quaint little place with friendly old waiters. At 204 Dr D Naoroji Rd, back towards Colaba from the GPO, the *Suvidha* restaurant in the National Insurance Building has excellent vegetarian food although it's crowded at lunchtime.

Bombay also has its own string of fast-food places called *Open House*. They serve burgers and pizzas; the closest one to the centre is on Veer Nariman Rd near the Churchgate footbridge. Close to here, on the corner of Veer Nariman and J Tata roads, is *Croissants etc*, a brand new snack bar designed for those who enjoy eating pastries and made-to-order savoury croissants while they stand beneath overhead TVs blaring with music videos.

Bhelpuri is a Bombay speciality – a tasty

Dhaba Lunches

Mr Bombay business-wallah sets off from home, boards his train or bus and heads into the city every morning – just like his office-worker counterpart in the West. Just like many of his overseas office-wallah brothers and sisters, he'd like to take his lunch with him and eat in the office. But an Indian lunch isn't as simple as a couple of sandwiches and an apple. A cut lunch could never satisfy an Indian – there has to be curry and rice and parathas and spices and a lot of things that take a lot of time to prepare and would hardly slip into a brown paper bag in the briefcase.

Naturally there's a supremely complex, yet smoothly working, Indian solution to this problem – it's called the *dhaba* lunch system. After he's left for work, his wife – or the cook or bearer – sets to and fixes his lunch. When it's prepared it's packed into a multi-compartment metal container about 15 cm in diameter and 30 cm high. On the lid there's a mysterious colour-coded notation. The container is then carried down to a street corner pick-up point where it meets up with lots of other lunch containers. From the pick-up point they're conveyed to the nearest train station where they're transported to the appropriate city station.

In the city they're broken down to their separate destinations, and between 11 and 12 in the morning thousands upon thousands of individually coded lunches pour out of Victoria Terminus, Churchgate, Bombay Central and other stations. On the heads of porters, carried in carts, slung from long poles, tied on bicycle handlebars, those lunch containers then scatter out across the city. Most of the dhaba-wallahs involved in this long chain of events are illiterate, but by some miracle of Indian efficiency, when Mr Business-Wallah opens his office door at lunchtime there will be his lunch by the door. Every day, without fail, they never lose a lunch. ∎

snack of crisp noodles, spiced vegetables and other mysterious ingredients available for a few rupees. It's available from stalls all over town, but particularly on Chowpatty Beach.

Places to Eat – More Expensive

Colaba The Taj Mahal Hotel has a whole range of restaurants, bars and snack bars. The *Apollo Bar/Rooftop Rendezvous* on the roof of the Intercontinental section caters for Western tastes and has fine views. The lunchtime buffet here costs Rs 350 but the choice is limited, the food leaves much to be desired and the waiters can be downright off-hand. Also, beers here are mega-expensive. If that's what you primarily want, take one in the much cheaper *Harbour Bar* (Rs 72 for a draught or Rs 82 for a bottle). For coffee and snacks, the *Shamiana* is the place to head for. The *Tanjore* is probably the best place for a splash-out meal – it has traditional Indian food accompanied by sitar music, and classical Indian dancing in the evenings. It also offers thalis. Formal dress is required in all the Taj's restaurants in the evening but smart casual wear is acceptable at lunchtimes.

Just across from the Jehangir Art Gallery, the *Copper Chimney* at 18 K Dubash Marg offers north Indian and Mughlai dishes and is a good place to eat. It's a minor splurge at about Rs 75 for a meal. The nearby *Khyber Restaurant* at 145 M G Rd is also highly recommended. You'll be looking at about Rs 100 for a Punjabi meal in this cavernous place.

The air-con *Delhi Darbar* on Colaba Causeway has an extensive menu and is a good place to try the Parsi dish dhaansak. They have very good milk shakes and ice cream (try the pista kulfi). The relatively new *Vintage Restaurant* at 4 Mandlik Rd is a classy restaurant in a refurbished colonial house and serves delicious Indian and Continental food. You can try pomfret here for Rs 150; most meals range from Rs 120 to Rs 150.

Three Chinese restaurants on Shivaji Maharaj Marg rival each other for 'the best Chinese in India' award. There's the *Nanking* and, directly across the road, the *Mandarin*, which is marginally more expensive, or the adjacent *Hong Kong* which serves excellent Szechuan food.

Nariman Point & Marine Drive Much better than the Taj for a lunchtime buffet splurge is the *Polynesian* restaurant at the Oberoi Towers Hotel which costs Rs 344 for a splendid array of Indian, Oriental and Continental dishes. The waiters can be no less off-hand than at the Taj but the food here is excellent. If this is a bit above your price range, the *Rangoli Restaurant* in the Performing Arts Complex at Nariman Point has a buffet lunch which is fantastic value at Rs 175.

Another place where gourmands can indulge is the revolving rooftop restaurant at the *Ambassador Hotel*. The *Kabab Corner* in the Hotel Nataraj on Marine Drive has excellent food and a sitar player in the evenings.

The air-conditioned *Samrat Restaurant* on J Tata Rd just south of the Ritz Hotel at Churchgate is an immensely popular pure veg restaurant. For Rs 61, you'll get a superb thali which includes all-you-can-eat puris, chapatis, farsan (savoury fried snacks) and bhakri (wheat biscuits) as well as all the other accompaniments. You can also try the local apéritif known as jal jeera – 'very popular but it smells like rotten eggs and is very salty' according to one unimpressed drinker. Thankfully, beers are also available.

One of the city's trendiest places is *Gaylords* on Veer Nariman Rd. This large terrace cafe is seemingly straight out of Paris and has good Western and Indian cuisine in the Rs 80 to Rs 100 bracket. Beers cost Rs 65 for a bottle or Rs 35 for draught and the terrace is great for watching the district's urbane streetlife.

Entertainment

To find out what's happening on the classical dance, music and drama scenes, pick up the free, fortnightly brochure available at the Government of India tourist office.

For a day of relaxation away from the hassle of the streets, try the *Breach Candy Club* (☎ 367-4381), 66 Bhulabhai Desai

Marg (Wanden Rd), on the shoreline out near Cumballa Hill. This exclusive swimming and volleyball club charges Rs 200 per day for nonmembers or Rs 300 on weekends. There are two swimming pools, a bar and snack bar, all set in tropical gardens. It's popular with expatriates.

If you get tired of sitting over cold Kingfisher beers at the *Leopold Bar & Cafe* (or pushed to leave), there are a few other places in Colaba that are worth giving a go, such as the back room (or the mezzanine floor – mind your head!) of the *Gokul Bar & Restaurant*. It's just round the corner on Tulloch Rd and the beers are cheaper than at Leopold. Also, they have an excellent collection of tapes. *Cafe Mondegar* on Colaba Causeway is also popular for a beer but the music here gets pretty loud. *Fariyas Hotel* just off Arthur Bunder Rd also has a trendy watering hole.

Further afield, the *London Pub* at Chowpatty Beach, *Rasna* near Churchgate station and the *Caravan Bar* on Hazarimal Somani Marg near VT are also worth trying.

The upstairs section of the *Crown & Anchor Bar* on the corner of Mandlik Rd and Mereweather Rd is Colaba's answer to Bangkok's Patpong Rd girlie bars though, naturally, here it's pure silk saris instead of mini-bikinis. It's a pick-up joint but there's no pressure and decorum is the name of the game. You'll probably be the only non-Indian there unless you go along with a friend. It costs Rs 85 for a bottle of beer here and it's usually packed out every night.

Most of Bombay's discos are located in the five-star hotels and entry is generally reserved for members who have paid extortionate fees. The *Cellar Disco* at the Oberoi is the only one open to nonmembers but even then it's couples only. It starts at 10 pm.

Things to Buy

Bombay has a number of intriguing markets and some feel it's much better for shopping than Delhi. Chor Bazaar is Bombay's 'thieves' market'. It's south of Maulana Shaukatali Rd (Grant Rd) and here you'll find a phenomenal collection of 'antiques', jewellery, wooden items, leather and general

bric-a-brac. Mutton St, in Chor Bazaar, has a particularly interesting collection of shops for miscellaneous 'junk'. Shops are generally open from 10 am but are closed on Friday. The shopkeepers here really know the value of their stuff but it's still possible to pick up some interesting items.

Crawford Market, officially renamed Mahatma Phule Market, is the centre for flowers, fruit, vegetables, meat and fish in Bombay. This is the place to look for Bombay's two famous fish – the pomfret and the 'Bombay duck'. The market building was constructed in 1867 and is one of the most colourful and photogenic places in Bombay. Nearby is Javeri Bazaar, the jewellery centre off Mumbadevi Rd. There is some fantastic stuff here, especially silver belts and old statues and charms. Nearby is the brass bazaar on Kalbadevi Rd.

There are all sorts of places selling handicrafts, artefacts, antiques and art around the Colaba area. Shops in the Taj Hotel specialise in high quality – and high prices. Check the Jehangir Gallery by the Prince of Wales Museum too, as well as the excellent Central Cottage Industries Emporium at Apollo Bunder. The street stalls along Colaba Causeway are good places to buy incredibly cheap 'export reject' clothes.

One of the best places in Bombay to buy silver and gold (or at least have a look at what you can't afford) is at Gupta Prakash Emporium, next to the American Express Bank (not the Travel Service) at Flora Fountain. Nearby, the Khadi Village Industries Emporium at 286 Dr D Naoroji Rd has bits and pieces from all over India.

Those searching for a good selection of Indian music tapes must try Rhythm House at 40 K Dubash Marg in the Colaba area or, less preferably, the Asiatics Department Store facing Churchgate station.

Mereweather Rd at the back of the Taj Hotel is the centre for Kashmiri carpets and there's a superb choice but, as you might imagine from the location, prices are high. Make sure you check out the Jammu & Kashmir emporium first before buying from any of these shops.

If Bombay is your last (or only) stop, you can also pick up souvenirs from all over the country from the various state government emporiums. In the World Trade Centre Arcade near Cuffe Parade are the Madhya Pradesh, Himachal Pradesh, Maharashtra and Jammu & Kashmir emporiums. The Uttar Pradesh emporium, as well as Kashmir's second outlet, are on Sir P Mehta Rd in the Fort area.

For shipping things out of India, the best people to see are Perfect Cargo Movers (☎ 287-3935), 56 Abdullabmia Currimjee Building (4th floor), Jamabhoomi Marg, Fort. They're extremely reliable and recommended.

Getting There & Away

Air Bombay is the main international gateway to India, with far more flights than Delhi, Calcutta or Madras. It also has the busiest network of domestic flights. The international terminal (Sahar) is about four km away from the domestic terminal (Santa Cruz). They are 30 km and 26 km respectively from Nariman Point in downtown Bombay.

Facilities at Sahar include a 24-hour State Bank foreign exchange counter, counters of the national (Government of India) and state (MTDC) tourist organisations, car rental kiosks, and a cafe and snack bar. The duty-free shop inside the departure lounge area has inflated prices and will accept only US dollars.

For all international flights the departure tax is Rs 300 and must be paid at the counter opposite the check-in desks before you check in.

Most international airline offices in Bombay are in the Nariman Point area between Maharshi Karve Rd and Marine Drive. Air India is at the junction of Madame Cama Rd and Marine Drive – airport buses also depart from here.

Indian Airlines, which flies both nationally and on local international routes, moved its office to the Army & Navy Building on M G Rd just north of Colaba after the Air India Building was bombed in 1993. There

is talk of them moving back to the Air India Building – ask around before you go. Indian Airlines also has a reservations desk at both the Taj Mahal and Centaur Juhu Beach hotels.

Domestic Airlines Addresses of domestic carriers that service Bombay include:

Damania Airways
    17 Nehru Rd, Vakola, Santa Cruz (☎ 610-2545)
East West Airlines
    'Sophia', 18 New Kantwadi Rd, off Perry Cross Rd, Bandra (☎ 643-6678)
Indian Airlines
    Army & Navy Bldg, M G Rd (☎ 202-3031, 287-6161)
Jet Airways
    Amarchand Mansion, Madame Cama Rd (☎ 285-5788)
Modiluft
    Akash Ganga (2nd floor), 89 Bhulabhai Desai Marg, Cumballa Hill (☎ 363-1921)
NEPC Airlines
    Hotel Bawa International, Nehru Rd, Vile Parle (☎ 611-5144)
Sahara Indian Airlines
    (☎ 283-2446)

Domestic Flights from Bombay See the Domestic Flights table on page 795 for fares from Bombay.

International Airlines Addresses of international airlines with offices in Bombay include:

Aeroflot
    241/242 Nirmal, Nariman Point (☎ 22-1682)
Air Canada
    Amarchand Mansion B1, Madame Cama Rd (☎ 202-1111)
Air France
    Maker Chambers VI (1st floor), Nariman Point (☎ 202-4818)
Air India
    Air India Bldg, Nariman Point (☎ 202-4142)
Air Lanka
    Mittal Towers (C Wing), Nariman Point (☎ 22-3299)
Air Mauritius
    Air India Bldg (ground floor), Nariman Point (☎ 202-8474)

BOMBAY

Alitalia
  Industrial Assurance Bldg, Veer Nariman Rd, Churchgate (☎ 22-2144)
Biman Bangladesh Airlines
  199 J Tata Rd, Churchgate (☎ 22-4659)
British Airways
  Valcan Insurance Bldg, 202B Veer Nariman Rd, Churchgate (☎ 22-0888)
Cathay Pacific Airways
  Taj Mahal Hotel, Apollo Bunder, Colaba (☎ 202-9112)
Egypt Air
  Oriental House, 7 J Tata Rd, Churchgate (☎ 22-1415)
Ethiopian Airways
  Taj Mahal Hotel, Apollo Bunder, Colaba (☎ 202-8787)
Gulf Air
  Maker Chambers V, Nariman Point (☎ 202-4065)
Iraqi Airways
  Mayfair Bldg, 79 Veer Nariman Rd (☎ 22-1399)
Japan Air Lines
  2 Raheja Centre (ground floor), Nariman Point (☎ 287-4936)
Kenya Airways
  Airlines Hotel, 199 J Tata Rd, Churchgate (☎ 22-0064)
KLM
  Khaitan Bhavan, 198 J Tata Rd, Churchgate (☎ 283-3338)
Kuwait Airlines
  2A Stadium House, 86 Veer Nariman Rd, Churchgate (☎ 204-5351)
LOT (Polish Airways)
  6 Maker Arcade, Cuffe Parade (☎ 218-5494)
Lufthansa
  Express Towers (4th floor), Nariman Point (☎ 202-3430)
Malaysian Airlines
  GSA Stic Travels & Tours, 6 Maker Arcade, Cuffe Parade (☎ 218-1431)
Pakistan International Airlines
  7 Brabourne Stadium, Veer Nariman Rd, Churchgate (☎ 202-1598)
Qantas
  42 Sakhar Bhavan, Nariman Point (☎ 202-9297)
SAS
  Podar House, 10 Marine Drive (☎ 202-7083)
Singapore Airlines
  Taj Mahal Hotel, Apollo Bunder (☎ 287-0986)
Swissair
  Maker Chambers VI, 220 Nariman Point (☎ 287-2210)
Thai Airways International
  Podar House, 10 Marine Drive (☎ 202-3284)
Zambia Airways
  207 Maker Chambers V, Nariman Point (☎ 202-6942)

Bus Long-distance buses depart from the state road transport terminal opposite Bombay Central railway station. It's fairly chaotic and there are almost no signs or information available in English.

The state bus companies of Maharashtra, Goa, Gujarat, Karnataka and Madhya Pradesh all have offices here and bookings can be made (☎ 307-4272) between 8 am and 8.30 pm. There is computerised advance booking available for journeys by deluxe buses.

The MTDC operates daily deluxe buses to Mahabaleshwar (Rs 180, seven hours) at 6.30 am except during the monsoon, and to Aurangabad (Rs 165, 12 hours) at 7.45 pm, as well as other places. These are better than a lot of other deluxe buses as they are not the dreaded video coaches and the drivers don't seem to have the suicide wish that is common among Indian bus drivers. Bookings should be made in advance at the MTDC's office on Madame Cama Rd. The departure point for these buses varies so check when you book your ticket.

Train Two railway systems operate out of Bombay. Central Railways handles services to the east and south, plus a few trains to the north. The reservation centre (☎ 261-7575) behind VT is fully computerised and air-conditioned. Ticket window No 22 on the ground floor has a 'foreign tourist guide' specifically for dealing with foreigners and this is where you buy Indrail Passes as well as getting tourist-quota tickets (the latter are available one day before departure only). Window No 22 is open Monday to Saturday from 9 am to 1 pm and 1.30 to 4 pm (on Sundays, Window No 21 deals with tourist quotas and is open from 8 am to 2 pm).

The other railway system is Western Railways, which has services to the north from Churchgate and Central stations. Bookings can be made at the Western Railways booking office (☎ 203-8016, extension 4577) next to the Government of India tourist office opposite Churchgate, Monday to Saturday between 8 am and 8 pm (Sunday until 2 pm). Tourist-quota tickets are issued

BOMBAY

from here, but only between 9.30 am and 4.30 pm (Saturday from 9.30 am to 2.30 pm; closed Sunday). They can be paid in foreign currency, or in rupees if you can show a recent encashment certificate. Indrail Passes can also be purchased from here. If you get into any difficulties, ask for Mr Singh – he's a mine of invaluable information.

Just to confuse the issue, there are a few Central Railways trains which depart from Dadar station, further north of Bombay Central (but they can still be booked at Bombay Central). They include the *Chennai Express* and the *Dadar Express*, the two fastest trains to Madras.

To Ahmedabad, the *Shatabdi Express*

BOMBAY

Domestic Flights from Bombay

Destination	Time (hours)	IC	4S	M9	D2	9W	D5	S2	Fare (US$)
				Frequency & Airline*					
				(d-daily, w-weekly)					
Ahmedabad	1.00	3d	-	-	6w	2d	1d	-	47
Aurangabad	0.45	5w	4w	-	-	-	-	-	38
Bangalore	1.30	3d	-	-	2d	2d	3w	-	88
Baroda	1.15	-	1d	-	-	-	1d	-	45
Belgaum	1.30	-	3w	-	-	-	-	-	74
Bhavnagar	0.45	4w	3w	-	-	-	-	-	38
Bhopal	2.15	1d	-	-	-	-	-	-	70
Calcutta	2.15	2d	-	-	2d	2d	-	-	157
Coimbatore	1.45	5w	1d	-	1d	1d	-	-	94
Delhi	2.00	7d	1d	2d	2d	4d	-	2d	115
Diu	1.00	-	3w	-	-	-	-	-	57
Goa	1.00	1d	1d	-	2d	2d	-	-	46
Gwalior	3.30	1d	-	-	-	-	-	-	103
Hubli	1.30	-	-	-	-	-	3w	-	100
Hyderabad	1.10	2d	1d	-	-	6w	-	-	74
Indore	1.00	1d	-	-	6w	-	-	-	53
Jaipur	1.30	2d	5w	-	-	-	-	-	98
Jamnagar	1.00	4w	-	-	-	-	3w	-	52
Jodhpur	1.30	5w	5w	-	-	-	-	-	87
Kochi (Cochin)	1.45	1d	2d	-	-	1d	-	-	109
Kozhikode (Calicut)	1.30	1d	1d	-	-	1d	-	-	98
Lucknow	3.45	3w	-	-	-	-	-	5w	152
Madras	1.45	2d	2d	-	1d	2d	3w	-	110
Madurai	1.45	3w	1d	-	-	-	-	-	115
Mangalore	1.15	1d	1d	-	-	1d	-	-	75
Nagpur	1.15	1d	6w	-	-	-	-	-	73
Porbandar	2.15	-	3w	-	-	-	2w	-	70
Pune	0.35	-	3d	-	-	-	1-2d	-	54
Rajkot	0.50	4w	1d	-	-	-	-	-	46
Surat	1.00	-	-	-	-	-	3w	-	50
Trivandrum	2.00	1d	1d	-	-	-	-	-	124
Udaipur	1.15	1d	-	-	-	-	-	-	70
Vadodora	1.00	1d	-	-	-	-	-	-	39
Varanasi	2.00	3w	-	3w	-	-	-	-	148
Visakhapatnam	2.45	-	1d	-	-	-	-	-	132

*Airline abbreviation codes:
IC – Indian Airlines   D2 – Damania   S2 – Sahara India Airlines
4S – East West   9W – Jet Airways
M9 – ModiLuft   D5 – NEPC

departs from Bombay Central at 6.25 am.
The fare is Rs 380/760 in an air-con
chair/sleeper and includes snacks and drinking water. The 492-km trip takes 6½ hours.
The *Karnavati Express* to Ahmedabad
leaves every Wednesday at 1.40 pm and
arrives eight hours later, in time for the night
train connection (11 pm) to Udaipur.

The *Rajdhani Express* to Delhi costs Rs
840 in an air-con three-tier sleeper, or Rs
1370 in an air-con 1st-class sleeper. The fare
include drinks, dinner and breakfast. This
train leaves from Bombay Central at 5.40 pm
and the trip takes 17 hours.

In the past, travellers heading to Goa from
Bombay faced an arduous 20-hour train
journey via Miraj. By the time you read this,
that situation should hopefully have
changed thanks to the new Konkan railway
line which is being built along the coast
from Bombay to Mangalore in southern
Karnataka. (See the boxed section in the
Getting Around chapter for more details.)
This 740-km line will cut the travel time
from Bombay to Goa to about 10 hours.
You'll need to check with Central Railways to find out what train services are
now operating to Goa.

See the table below for a selection of trains
from Bombay.

Boat Damania Shipping (an affiliate of
Damania Airways) runs a new ferry between
Bombay and Goa. The modern, 400-seat,
air-con 'jetfoil' leaves Bombay's Baucha
Chakka ferry wharf daily at 7 am, arriving in
Panaji at 2 pm. On the return leg it leaves
Panaji at 3 pm, arriving in Bombay between
10.15 and 10.45 pm. The fare is US$35/50
in economy/club class, and the fare includes
a snack, a meal, refreshments and 'infoil'
entertainment, which consists of recent-
release Hollywood (not Bollywood!) films.
Children under two pay 10%; children above
two pay full fare. For bookings contact the
Damania ferry terminal (☎ 610-2525; fax
610-4219) or any of the regional Damania
Airways offices.

The Shipping Corporation of India (☎ 22-
2101) is at Apujay House, 4th floor, D Wacha
Rd, Churchgate.

Getting Around
To/From the Airport The airport bus service
operates between the Air India Building at
Nariman Point and Santa Cruz (domestic)
and Sahar (international) airports. The
journey to Santa Cruz takes about one hour
and costs Rs 36. To Sahar it takes about
1½ hours and is Rs 44. Baggage costs Rs 7
per piece. From Nariman Point, departures

Major Trains from Bombay

Destination	Train Name & number	Departure time	Distance (km)	Duration (hours)	Fare (Rs) (2nd/1st)
Ahmedabad	Gujarat Mail 9101	9.25 pm BC*	492	9.00	128/382
	Gujarat Exp 9011	5.45 am BC		9.20	
Aurangabad	Devagiri Exp 1003	10.30 pm VT	375	9.30	140/430
	Tapovan Exp 7517	6.10 am VT		7.20	
Bangalore	Udyan Exp 6529	7.55 am VT	1211	24.00	245/738
Calcutta	Gitanjali Exp 2859	6.05 am VT	1960	33.00	294/1040
	Howrah Mail 8001	8.16 pm VT		36.00	
Delhi	Rajdhani Exp 2951	4.55 pm BC	1384	17.00	840/1370
	Paschim Exp 2925	11.45 am BC		23.00	250/797
Madras	Chennai Exp 6063	7.50 pm D	1279	24.00	249/772
Pune	Deccan Queen 2123	5.10 pm VT	191	3.30	58/209
	Deccan Exp 1007	6.40 am VT		4.30	
Thiruvananthapuram	Trivandrum Exp 6331	12.15 pm VT	2062	42.20	302/1081
Varanasi	(Ratnagiri Exp 1065)	5.05 am VT	1509	27.00	264/877

*Abbreviation for train station: VT = Victoria Terminus; BC = Bombay Central; D = Dadar Station

are at 4, 5 and 8.15 am, then hourly until 2.15 pm, and then at 3.45, 5.30, 7, 8, 9, 11 pm and 12.30 am. It would be wise to check these departure times as they're subject to change. In peak hour the trip through Bombay's horribly congested streets can take well over two hours so don't cut things too fine. From the airports, there are departures hourly except between 1 and 4 am.

Tickets for the buses are bought either on the buses themselves, at the Air India Building or at the terminals. Buses between the domestic and international terminals depart every 30 minutes and are free if you can show a ticket for a connecting flight, otherwise they cost Rs 15.

For those die-hards determined to get there on the cheap regardless of inconvenience, it is possible to get from Sahar Airport to central Bombay for less than Rs 20. First, take the airport bus from the international to the domestic terminal, then an ordinary bus to Vile Parle (No 321), followed by a suburban train to Churchgate. If you're carrying more than a toothbrush, avoid doing anything as defiant as this in rush hours.

A taxi to the domestic airport on the meter costs about Rs 150 from Colaba and Rs 60 from Juhu, but they generally ask for more (Rs 170 and Rs 70 respectively). It's a bit further to the international airport. During rush hours you won't find anyone who's prepared to use the meter, so expect to pay even more.

From the international airport there's a prepaid taxi booth where you pay a set fare: Rs 93 to Juhu, Rs 113 to Dadar, Rs 138 to Bombay Central railway station and Rs 187 to Churchgate, VT or Colaba. You are assigned to a taxi, you give the driver your slip and there's no further fuss. You do, however, pay a bit more than the meter fare.

Bus Bombay has one of the best public bus systems of any major Indian city. However, it's gradually being crippled by the city's unbelievable congestion and traffic jams. There are lots of well-kept red double-decker buses, with fares beginning from Rs 1.50, but they invariably take a long time to go a relatively short distance. They're also very crowded, especially during rush hours, and Bombay's pickpockets are notoriously adept. Take care.

The buses are operated by Bombay Electric Supply & Transport (BEST) and have separate route maps for their extensive city and suburban services. From VT take a No 1, 6 Ltd, 21 Ltd, 22 Ltd or 124 to Electric House, a useful landmark in Colaba. From Bombay Central take No 43, 70 or 124. Ltd means 'limited stops' and you'll pay a couple of rupees more if you use these faster buses.

Train Bombay has an extensive system of suburban electric trains, and it's virtually the only place in India where it's worth taking trains for intracity travel. But *avoid* rush hours when they are so crowded that you have to start making your way towards the door at least three stops before you want to get out to have any chance of getting off, *and* you need to know which side the platform will be on – be prepared! First class is only marginally less crowded.

The main suburban route of interest to travellers is Churchgate to Bombay Central and Dadar, with many other stops in between. There's a train every two to five minutes in either direction between 4.30 am and 10.30 pm. The fare between Churchgate and Bombay Central is Rs 2/25 in 2nd/1st class. If you arrive at Bombay Central on the main railway system, your ticket covers you for the journey from there to the more convenient Churchgate station.

Taxi Bombay has a huge fleet of metered black-and-yellow taxis but, unlike most other Indian cities, there are no auto-rickshaws (except in the outer suburbs). You'll often have to try a few taxis before you find one willing to go where you want, especially during peak periods. As usual, the meters are out of date so you pay according to a fare conversion card which all drivers carry, regardless of how reluctant they are to pull them out when they'd prefer to tell you the first figure that comes into their head.

Drivers will usually use the meters from

dawn until late evening, but after midnight you'll probably have to negotiate a price.

AROUND BOMBAY
Elephanta Island

The island of Elephanta is about 10 km north-east of Apollo Bunder and is Bombay's major tourist attraction due to its four rock-cut temples. They are thought to have been cut out between 450 and 750, and at that time the island was known as Gharapuri, the Fortress City. When the Portuguese arrived they renamed it Elephanta after the large stone elephant near the landing place. This figure collapsed in 1814 and the remaining pieces were removed to the Victoria Gardens in Bombay in 1864 and reassembled in 1912.

Unfortunately the Portuguese took their traditional disdain for other religions to its usual lengths at Elephanta, and did considerable damage to the sculptures. Although some people feel that Elephanta is not as impressive as the rock-cut temples of Ellora, the size, beauty and power of the sculptures are without equal.

The caves are reached by a stairway up the hillside from the ferry landing. Palanquins are available for anybody in need of being carried up. There is one main cave with a number of large sculpted panels, all relating to Siva, and a separate lingam shrine.

The most famous of the panels includes one of Maheshmurti (Trimurti), or the three-headed Siva, where he also takes the role of Brahma, the creator, and Vishnu, the preserver. In other panels Siva appears as Ardhanari, where he unites both sexes in one body.

There are figures of Siva and his wife Parvati and of their marriage. In another panel Siva dances the Tandava, the dance that shakes the world. Parvati and their son, Ganesh, look on a little astonished. One of the best panels is that of Ravana shaking Kailasa. The demon king of Lanka decided to carry Siva and his companions off by the simple expedient of removing their Himalayan home, the mountain Kailasa. Parvati became panic-stricken at his energetic

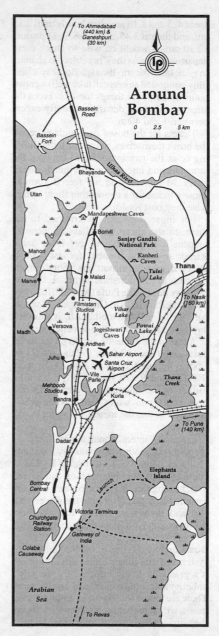

attempts to jerk the mountain free, but Siva calmly pushed the mountain back down with one toe, trapping Ravana beneath it for 10,000 years.

Getting There & Away Launches depart from Apollo Bunder by the Gateway of India. The ordinary boats cost Rs 35 return (children Rs 20) and the luxury launches including a tour guide are Rs 50 (children Rs 30). A good guide (and there are some excellent ones) can considerably increase your understanding and enjoyment – one tubby little gentleman with glasses even demonstrates how Siva danced the Tandava!

Both types of launch leave every hour from 9 am to 2.15 pm and return after four hours. The voyage takes an hour. During the monsoon, the ordinary boats are suspended. For any enquiries phone ☎ 202-6364.

A new alternative to the launches is the catamaran which leaves daily from Apollo Bunder at 10 am and returns at 2 pm. The voyage takes 45 minutes and the fare is Rs 100. For catamaran enquiries phone ☎ 287-5473.

Elephanta gets very crowded on weekends.

Sanjay Gandhi National Park
This national park, formerly called the Borivli National Park, is on Bombay's northern outskirts near the suburb of Borivli and covers 104 sq km of forest and hills.

The park is best known for the **Kanheri Caves** about 42 km from Bombay. These 109 caves line the side of a rocky ravine and were used by Buddhist monks during the 2nd to 9th centuries as *viharas* (monasteries) and *chaityas* or temples. Although there are many of them, most are little more than holes in the rock and only a handful are of real interest. The most important is cave 3, the Great Chaitya Cave, which has a long colonnade of pillars around the *dagoba* at the back of the cave. Further up the ravine are some good views out to the sea.

There is also a **Lion Safari Park**, open daily except Monday (Tuesday if Monday is a public holiday) from 9 am to 5 pm. Trips are made through the park in a 'safari vehicle' (ie minibus). Entry is Rs 10.

Other features are lakes Vihar, Tulsi and Powai, which act as reservoirs for much of Bombay's water supply, and a huge outdoor movie lot near the park entrance which has a fort frontage partly constructed from old oil drums.

Getting There & Away Take the train from Churchgate to Borivli station (40 minutes) and then a taxi or auto-rickshaw for the seven km or so to the Kanheri caves. On Sundays and public holidays there is a city bus service from Borivli station to the caves. Kanheri can also be visited (quickly) on the regular MTDC suburban tours.

Mandapeshwar & Jogeshwari Caves
There are a few Hindu caves, one of which was converted into a Portuguese church, near Borivli. The Jogeshwari Caves are near Andheri station.

Beaches
Bombay's best known beach, Juhu, is too close to the city and not sanitary enough for a pleasant swim, but there are some remote beaches on the island. **Manori beach** is about 40 km out of the city. You can get to it via the station at Malad, 32 km out. There's an interesting fishing village and an old Portuguese church nearby.

A nice place to stay near the village of Manori is the *Manoribel Hotel* (☎ 283-3918) which has cottages with two/four beds for Rs 545/1090 and double rooms for Rs 330, or there's the cheaper *Hotel Dominica* (☎ 45-7635). To get there, take the suburban electric train from Churchgate to Malad, then a bus (No 272) to Marve ferry, cross on the ferry and walk to the Manoribel. The walk to the beach is a little over a km.

Other beaches around Bombay include **Madh**, 45 km out and reached via Malad. **Versova** is 29 km from the city, reached via Andheri station, but it is very dirty.

Bassein
Just across the river which separates the

mainland from Bombay island is Bassein, which was a Portuguese fortified city from 1534 to 1739. The Portuguese took Bassein at the same time as Daman, further north in Gujarat. They built a fort containing a city of such pomp and splendour that it came to be known as the Court of the North. Only the Hidalgos or aristocracy were permitted to live within the fort walls, and by the end of the 17th century there were 300 Portuguese and 400 Indian-Christian families here, with a cathedral, five convents and 13 churches.

Then in 1739 the Marathas besieged the city and the Portuguese surrendered after three months of appalling losses. Today the city walls are still standing and you'll see the ruins of some of the churches and the Cathedral of St Joseph.

Bassein is 11 km from the Bassein Road (Vasai Road in Marathi) railway station.

Ganeshpuri Ashram

This ashram, also known as Gurudev Siddha Peeth, is about 90 km north-east of Bombay between the tranquil villages of Ganeshpuri, Vajreshwari and Akoli. Founded in 1949 by Bhagwan Nityananda, the ashram grew under the auspices of his disciple, Muktananda, who expounded Nityananda's teachings on Siddha Yoga. After his death in

1982, Muktananda was succeeded by Swami Chidvilasananda.

The hilly area surrounding Ganeshpuri is known for its hot springs and the **Vajreshwari Temple** which was built on the ruins of a Portuguese fort.

Gurudev Siddha Peeth is a Gurukula (school of the Guru) that requires a three-month advance application process for a minimum stay of one month or more. The easiest way to get there is to take a train from Churchgate to Bassein Road (Vasai Road in Marathi) railway station, from where you can get buses to Ganeshpuri (30 km).

Chaul

Located south of Bombay, this was another Portuguese settlement, although not as important as Bassein. The Portuguese took it in 1522 and lost it to the Marathas at the same time as Bassein. There are a few remains and old ruined churches within the Portuguese fortifications. Looking across to the Portuguese fort from the other side of the river is the hilltop Muslim Korlai Fort.

Ferries run to Revas from the New Ferry Wharf, a 1½-hour trip. From there you've got a 30-km bus trip to Chaul. It's possible to continue on from here by road to Murud-Janjira, Mahabaleshwar, or to join the Bombay to Pune road.

LEANNE LOGAN

LEANNE LOGAN

LEANNE LOGAN

Bombay
Top: On the road in Bombay.
Bottom Left: Weighing them up, Crawford Market.
Bottom Right: Traditional transport – a bullock cart.

Maharashtra

Top: Part of the mighty Kailasa Temple, Ellora.
Bottom: Sculptures inside the Indra Sabha cave temple, Ellora.

Maharashtra

The state of Maharashtra is one of the largest in India, both in terms of population and in area. Its booming capital, Bombay, makes it not only one of the most important states economically, but also a major gateway for overseas visitors. From Bombay you can head off into India in a number of directions, but most travellers will either be going south to Goa, south-east to Pune (Poona) with its famous ashram, or north-east to the amazing cave temples of Ajanta and Ellora.

Most of the state stands on the high Deccan plateau which stretches east some 800 km from the Western Ghats. Historically this was the main centre for the Maratha Empire, which defied the Mughals for so long, and which, under the fearless rule of Shivaji, carved out a large part of central India as its domain. Maharashtra's many inland and coastal forts are a legacy of Shivaji and, to a lesser extent, the Portuguese.

The Western Ghats run parallel to the coast for the full length of the state and are dotted with small, inviting hill stations such as Matheran and Mahabaleshwar. The ghats divide the Deccan from the relatively undeveloped Konkan coast where you'll find deserted beaches, abandoned forts and iso-

Population: 87 million
Area: 307,690 sq km
Capital: Bombay
People per sq km: 282
Main Language: Marathi
Literacy Rate: 63%
Best Time to Go: September to April (coast); September to mid-June (hill stations)

The external boundaries of India on this map have not been authenticated and may not be correct.

lated fishing communities. Unlike Goa to the south, this coastal strip has been largely overlooked by tourism, though this may

Cave Architecture

Maharashtra's famous rock-cut caves have several distinct design elements. The Buddhist caves, which are generally the older ones, are either *chaityas* (temples) or *viharas* (monasteries). Chaityas are usually deep and narrow with a stupa at the end of the cave. There may be a row of columns down both sides of the cave and around the stupa.

The viharas are usually not as deep and narrow as the chaitya caves. They were normally intended as living and sleeping quarters for the monks and often have rows of cells along both sides. In the back there is a small shrine room, usually containing an image of the Buddha. At Ajanta, the cliff face into which the caves are cut is very steep and there is often a small verandah or entrance porch in front of the main cave. At Ellora the rock face is more sloping and the verandah or porch element generally becomes a separate courtyard.

The cave temples reach their peak of complexity and design in the Hindu caves at Ellora, and particularly in the magnificent Kailasa Temple. Here they can hardly be called caves, for the whole enclosure is open to the sky. In design they are much like other temples of that era – except that instead of being built up from the bottom they were cut down from the top. They are an imitation of the conventional architecture of that period. ■

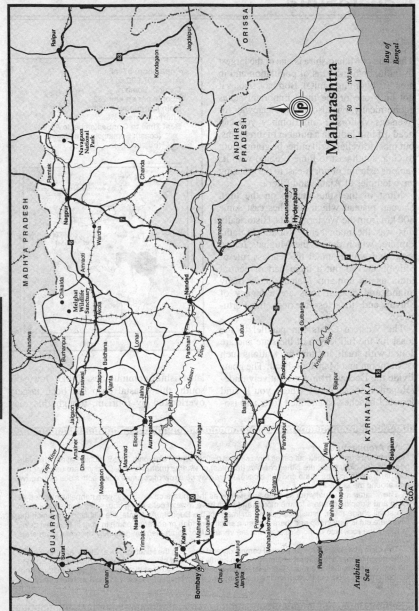

change in the foreseeable future with the opening of the new Konkan Railway connecting Bombay to Goa, Karnataka and Kerala (see the boxed section in the Getting Around chapter for details).

In September 1993, the Deccan region of Latur, in the state's far east, was struck by a powerful earthquake measuring 6.2 on the Richter scale. More than 10,000 people died in what was India's worst natural disaster in over half a century.

Bombay Area

MATHERAN

Population: 5200
Telephone Area Code: 021483

Matheran is the nearest hill station to Bombay. The name means Jungle Topped or Wooded Head, which is just what it is – an undulating hilltop cloaked in shady trees. It became a popular hill station during the days of the Raj as the abundant shade and altitude (800 metres) made it slightly cooler than the capital. Hugh Malet is credited with its 'discovery' in 1850.

Quite uniquely, Matheran is free of all forms of motor vehicles, making it an unbelievably tranquil respite after the congestion of Bombay. It is ringed by many km of walking tracks, which lead to lookouts that drop sheer to the plains. On a clear day the views are fantastic and it's possible to see, and supposedly even hear, Bombay from Porcupine or Louisa Point.

On weekends, Matheran is the hangout of trendy young day-trippers from Bombay who come equipped with ghetto blasters and whisky – say goodbye to the peaceful atmosphere! In April and May and the Diwali Festival in November you won't find accommodation unless you've made a reservation well in advance. They are good times to avoid Matheran anyway. (Complete dates for the high season in Matheran are November to January and mid-April to mid-June.) During the monsoon season (mid-June to early-October) Matheran virtually closes up.

Very few hotels and restaurants remain open, and the dirt walking trails and roads become very muddy. On the plus side, there are very few people around, and the hotels that remain open reduce their tariffs significantly.

Getting to Matheran is half the fun; from Neral Junction you take a tiny narrow-gauge toy train up the 21-km route to the hill station. It's a two-hour ascent as the train winds its way up the steep slopes and, at one point, passes through 'one kiss tunnel'. Alternatively, you can take a taxi or minibus from Neral which is much quicker (half an hour). However, as cars are prohibited in Matheran, you will then face a 40-minute walk into Matheran or you'll have to hire a horse or cycle-rickshaw. Only the toy train goes right into the centre of town.

Information
Entry to Matheran costs Rs 7 (Rs 2 for children). Coming by train, you pay this leaving the station. By road, you pay at the taxi stand.

The tourist office kiosk, opposite the station, is open daily and has maps of Matheran but not much else.

None of the paths around town are lit at night – a torch may come in handy. Also, if you buy bananas in the market, watch out for the monkeys.

Walks & Views
Porcupine Point is a good place for catching the sunset, but Panorama Point, at the extreme north, is said to have the finest views. The western side, from Porcupine to Louisa Point, is known as Cathedral Rocks, and Neral can be seen far below, straddling the central railway line. At the south, near One Tree Hill, is a trail down to the valley below known as Shivaji's Ladder, so called because the Maratha leader is said to have used it.

Places to Stay
Matheran is very spread out and much of the accommodation (and some of the best of it) is a 20-minute walk from the railway station. Many of the so-called 'resort' hotels offer

only full-board rates. As with most hill stations, it's important to know the checkout time since it can be as early as 7 am.

Places to Stay – bottom end

Budget accommodation is limited. Most of it is along M G Marg and the road above it running parallel. The staff at quite a few places don't speak English.

One of the cheapest places is *Khan's Cosmopolitan Hotel* (☎ 240) on M G Marg, a rather primitive rambling place, but well run and with a range of rooms. Doubles (no singles) with common bath are Rs 80/225 in the low/high season. English is spoken and there's a restaurant.

Better is the welcoming Christian-run *Hope Hall Hotel* (☎ 253), M G Marg, which is basic and offers lodging only at Rs 110/175 a double in low/high season. There are no singles. The bathrooms are newly tiled, the rooms spotlessly clean and the people who run it extremely affable.

Also relatively cheap but very inconvenient for the centre of town is the Maharashtra Tourism Development Corporation (MTDC) *Tourist Camp* (☎ 277), next to the taxi park, which has dorm beds for Rs 40 and doubles from Rs 150 to Rs 450. There are also larger cottages. It has a restaurant and beer is available.

Places to Stay – middle

The *Sayeban Lodge* (☎ 519), at the back of Khan's, has doubles at Rs 350. It's clean and tidy and all the rooms have attached bath and fan, but no English is spoken and food is not available.

Close by is the *Royal Hotel Matheran* (☎ 247), a two-star, garishly coloured 'resort' which is popular with Indian families. In the high season, rooms with full board cost Rs 760 for two people and air-con rooms with TV and full board are Rs 800 for two. In the low season it costs Rs 200 to Rs 250 per person. There's a bar and children's park and a vegetarian restaurant.

Better is the relaxed and friendly *Gujarat Bhavan Hotel* (☎ 278), another 'resort' hotel which offers regular/deluxe rooms at Rs

200/275 per person and cottages for Rs 350 a person, all with full board. In the peak season, prices are Rs 125 higher. Pure veg food is served.

The brand new *Red Wood Resort* (☎ 201), opposite the police station, has characterless rooms at Rs 350/700 for a single/double, or Rs 500/850 with air-con.

Places to Stay – top end

Room rates in the following top-end hotels include full board, unless stated otherwise.

The tranquil *Rugby Hotel* (☎ 291), on Vithalrao Kotwal Marg above the township, is one of Matheran's older and more charming establishments. Doubles range from Rs 961 to Rs 1047, including taxes. Air-con doubles are Rs 1160, and there are more expensive suites at Rs 1221. Checkout here is 8 am.

The *Regal Hotel* (☎ 243) offers regular/ superdeluxe rooms at Rs 900/1400. In the off season, prices are halved. There are also more expensive suites and air-con rooms. It's a big place with Western disco music blaring all day. Further up the same road is the *Brightlands Resort* (☎ 244), another lively place with a token swimming pool and disco nights. Rooms start at Rs 698 per person, or Rs 898 with air-con. In the low season, rooms are rented on a lodging-only basis (ie, no meals).

The amiable *Lord's Central Hotel* (☎ 228) on M G Marg is Matheran's most remarkable hotel. It has fading touches of the Raj and is the *only* hotel with views over the precipice. It's clean and quiet and there's a bar and restaurant. Doubles (no singles) are Rs 450 per person in the regular rooms, or Rs 750 in the 'valley view' rooms and there are more expensive suites. In the low season, they offer deals such as two nights (lodging only) for Rs 375/750 per person in the regular/ valley view rooms, or two nights accommodation plus all meals for Rs 1000/1375. Meals (Indian and Western) here are excellent.

Also recommended is the *Hotel Alexander* (☎ 290), a pleasant place in the midst of the forest at the southern end of town. It's ideal if you want to be away from the crowds.

Places to Eat

The trouble with Matheran for budget travellers is that most hotels cater for their own guests. This means there's little incentive for the few restaurants that are not part of a hotel to turn out decent food, as there's barely any competition. In any case, they really only have a market for breakfast and lunch, when the day-trippers are in town. In other words, don't expect too much. Better still, arrange a deal with one of the hotels (especially Lord's) and eat there if you're not on full board.

There is a string of snack-style eating places along M G Marg as well as a couple of basic restaurants such as the *Shangrila* and *Satyavijay*.

Matheran is famed for its honey and for *chikki*, a toffee-like confection made of gur sugar and nuts which is sold at many shops.

Getting There & Away

Train From Bombay, only a few of the Pune expresses stop at Neral Junction so make sure you take one which does. They include

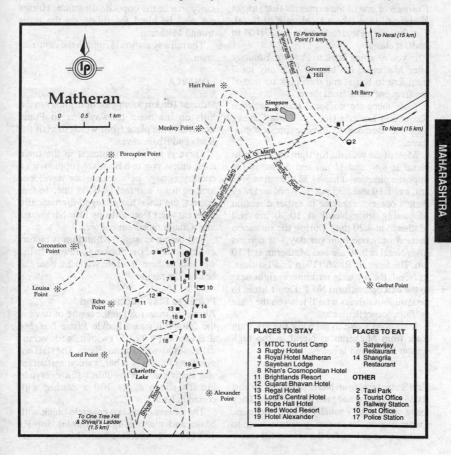

Matheran

PLACES TO STAY	PLACES TO EAT
1 MTDC Tourist Camp	9 Satyavijay
3 Rugby Hotel	Restaurant
4 Royal Hotel Matheran	14 Shangrila
7 Sayeban Lodge	Restaurant
8 Khan's Cosmopolitan Hotel	
11 Brightlands Resort	OTHER
12 Gujarat Bhavan Hotel	
13 Regal Hotel	2 Taxi Park
15 Lord's Central Hotel	5 Tourist Office
16 Hope Hall Hotel	6 Railway Station
18 Red Wood Resort	10 Post Office
19 Hotel Alexander	17 Police Station

MAHARASHTRA

the *Deccan Express* (at 6.40 am from Bombay VT) and the *Miraj Express* (at 8.45 am from Bombay VT). On the other hand, most (but not all) expresses from Bombay stop at Karjat further down the line from Neral. From here you can backtrack using local trains (which are frequent) to Neral. Alternatively, take a local Karjat train from Bombay VT to Neral (they all stop at Neral). The most convenient local trains are at 7.21 am and 1.42 pm from Bombay.

From Pune, it's the same story – either take one of the few express trains to Bombay that stop at Neral (such as the *Sahyadri Express)* or one of the expresses that stop at Karjat and then take a local train to Neral. The fare from Pune to Neral is Rs 27/104 in 2nd/1st class.

If you're going back to Pune or Bombay after Matheran, it's best to take any local train first to Karjat and then pick up one of the frequent trains from there.

Note there are no local trains between Karjat and Lonavla (for the Karla Caves), only the Bombay to Pune expresses stop there.

Most of the year, the toy train departs from Neral at 8.40 and 11 am and 5 pm; in the opposite direction it leaves Matheran at 5.45 am, and 1.10 and 2.35 pm. In April and May there's one extra service in either direction (departing from Neral at 10.20 am and Matheran at 4.20 pm). During the monsoon there is only one train per day – it departs from Neral at 8.40 am and Matheran at 1.10 pm. The fares are Rs 26/119 in 2nd/1st class. In Neral, the toy train terminus is right next to the exit on platform No 1. Don't listen to taxi/minibus drivers who'll tell you the train is 'full', 'cancelled', etc.

It's a wise move to prebook the toy train back from Matheran to Neral in the high season as demand is heavy.

Taxi Share taxis from Neral to Matheran cost Rs 35 per person and take half an hour. They leave when full – usually four passengers. Depending on the season, you may have to wait an hour or two for the taxi to fill up.

The shortest route to Bombay (100 km) is via Panvel; Pune is 140 km away.

Getting Around

Horses and cycle-rickshaws – one man pulls, two push (or hold it back on the descents) – are the only transport options in Matheran. Taxis and minibuses stop 2.5 km, or about 35 to 40 minutes' walk, from the centre. From here, you can either walk (quickest along the railway line), hire a horse (Rs 40) or a cycle-rickshaw (Rs 100) into the centre. It's quicker to walk into the centre than it is to hire a cycle-rickshaw but this isn't necessarily true in the opposite direction. Horses can also be hired for riding on the trails around Matheran.

The railway station is right in the centre of town.

LONAVLA

Telephone Area Code: 021147

Situated 106 km south-east of Bombay in the hills on the main railway line to Pune, Lonavla is the place from which to visit the Karla and Bhaja caves.

There is nothing of interest in the town itself unless you're a Bombay yuppie with a country cottage or a real estate developer looking for a contract to build one. In that respect, the town has changed dramatically in recent years from a sleepy little backwater into a major development area.

Just before Lonavla, **Khandala** is picturesquely situated overlooking a ravine. In the wet season there is a fine waterfall near the head of the ravine.

Places to Stay – bottom end

Above the main road in the centre of town is the delightfully ramshackle *Pitale Lodging & Boarding* (☎ 72-657) with its wide verandahs and old-world atmosphere. The staff are genial and there is a bar, garden restaurant and shady trees. It wouldn't suit everyone but it's cheap at Rs 100 a double with common bath.

The *Janata Hotel* is a concrete block with basic and clean singles/doubles for Rs 100/120 with attached bath. Not far from here is the *Matruchhaya Lodge* (☎ 72-875), an old-style house in quiet surroundings which is often full. It costs Rs 150/200 with attached bath.

Going up a bit in price is the friendly *Hotel Swiss Cottage* (☎ 72-561) which is clean and tidy and has dorm beds for Rs 75, singles/ doubles for Rs 150/300 and suites (four beds) for Rs 450. There's a 30% discount on these rates from Monday to Thursday, or if you stay a minimum of one week. They also offer full board for an extra Rs 100 a person. It's certainly *not* a 'Swiss cottage', but it is in a quiet and shady location and is definitely recommended.

Also hard to beat is the *Hotel Chandralok* (☎ 72-294), an excellent place with keen, friendly staff and superb, reasonably priced all-you-can-eat vegetarian Gujarati thalis for Rs 35 (Rs 45 for 'special thalis'). They have singles/doubles for Rs 150/225 including tax (Rs 60 per extra person). All the rooms have attached bath with hot water 24 hours a day.

On the same road is the *Adarsh Hotel* (☎ 72-353) which backs onto the bus stand, so avoid the rooms on that side. 'Economy' doubles are Rs 150, 'luxury' doubles go for Rs 350 to Rs 500, and there are also air-con suites for Rs 600.

Opposite the Janata Hotel is the large *N T Shalini Health Home* (☎ 72-784) which, according to its blurb, is 'run on a non-commercial basis'. Rooms with attached bath cost Rs 130 and meals are available for Rs 20.

Places to Stay – middle & top-end

The well-appointed *Hotel Dhiraj* (☎ 73-600) on the busy main road has doubles for Rs 450 or Rs 600 with air-con, plus there are deluxe doubles for Rs 750. They also offer a discount (25%) from Monday until Thursday. There's a car park, bar and restaurant.

Tucked away down a quiet leafy lane is the *Hotel Star Regency* (☎ 73-331), Justice Telang Rd, which has double rooms (no singles) from Rs 550 to Rs 760, as well as deluxe rooms for Rs 890.

About one km south of the railway lines is the *Ryewood Retreat* (☎ 72-060), which consists of a series of very spacious and comfortable cottages with all amenities. It costs Rs 600 for doubles and Rs 1200 for a duplex villa.

Top of the line is the *Fariyas Holiday Resort* (☎ 73-852; fax 2080), 8 Frichley Hill, on the western outskirts of town. It has all the facilities you'd expect including an indoor swimming pool. Singles/doubles cost Rs 1090/1590 plus there are suites for Rs 2950.

Places to Eat

The best places to eat are mostly the restaurants at the hotels mentioned above. Otherwise, try the *Lonavla Restaurant* on the main road which offers Sindhi-Punjabi veg and non-veg food as well as tandoori dishes. Close by is the *Mehfil Bar & Restaurant*, attached to the side of the noisy Hotel Gurukripa, which is slightly more expensive.

As in Matheran, the local speciality is chikki, a kind of nutty toffee.

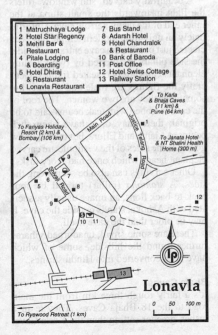

1 Matruchhaya Lodge
2 Hotel Star Regency
3 Mehfil Bar & Restaurant
4 Pitale Lodging & Boarding
5 Hotel Dhiraj & Restaurant
6 Lonavla Restaurant
7 Bus Stand
8 Adarsh Hotel
9 Hotel Chandralok & Restaurant
10 Bank of Baroda
11 Post Office
12 Hotel Swiss Cottage
13 Railway Station

To Karla & Bhaja Caves (11 km) & Pune (64 km)

To Fariyas Holiday Resort (2 km) & Bombay (106 km)

To Janata Hotel & NT Shalini Health Home (300 m)

Main Road

Justice Telang Road

Dhval Road

Lonavla

0   50   100 m

To Ryewood Retreat (1 km)

MAHARASHTRA

Getting There & Away

Lonavla is on the main Bombay to Pune road and railway line so there are plenty of trains and buses to/from both cities.

Bus The timetable at Lonavla bus stand is in Marathi except for the buses to Dadar (a suburb of Bombay). Most of the state transport corporation (MSRTC) buses are pretty rough and ready and, as they take up to four hours to get to Bombay, you'd be better off using the trains.

Train All express trains between Bombay and Pune stop at Lonavla. The trip to Bombay (128 km, three hours) costs Rs 34/131 in 2nd/1st class. To Pune (64 km) there are express trains (one hour) and hourly shuttle trains (two hours) and the fare is Rs 22/82 in 2nd/1st class.

Getting Around

According to the timetable, local buses are supposed to run about a dozen times a day between Lonavla and Karla and to the Rajmachi Fort. In reality they run far less frequently and are chock-full when they do arrive.

Auto-rickshaws are plentiful and the price usually includes waiting time at the sites. Lonavla to Karla costs Rs 120 one way or Rs 150 return; if you include Bhaja Cave as well it is Rs 200. In the monsoon, the road to Bhaja is closed to vehicles at the Malavli railway crossing.

If you don't mind doing some walking, you can get around comfortably in a day for about Rs 15. First, catch the 9 am bus from Lonavla to Karla Cave, then walk to Bhaja (five km, 1½ hours), walk back to Malavli railway station (three km, one hour) and catch a local train back to Lonavla.

KARLA & BHAJA CAVES

These superb rock-cut Buddhist caves are among the oldest in India and date from the time when the Hinayana Buddhism style of rock temple was at its height in terms of design purity.

The Karla Cave is about 11 km from

Lonavla, about 1.5 km off the main road. The Bhaja Caves are about three km off the other side of the main road across the railway tracks. If you plan on walking to the latter, take a local train from Lonavla to Malavli first.

It is possible to visit the caves in a day trip from either Bombay or Pune if you don't mind rushing and hiring an auto-rickshaw from Lonavla for the day. By all accounts you should avoid going to Karla Cave at weekends or on public holidays, when it is invaded by the picnic mobs from Bombay and Pune. Bhaja is too far from the main road for this to happen on the same scale, but it does get its fair share too.

Karla Cave

It's a steep 500-metre climb up the hillside to Karla Cave. The cave temple is Hinayana Buddhist and was completed around 80 BC. It is one of the best preserved chaityas of its type in India.

A beautifully carved 'sun window' filters the light in towards the small stupa at the inner end of the deep, narrow cave. Unfortunately an ugly little modern temple has been erected just outside the cave entrance. Inside, the side pillars are topped by two kneeling elephants carrying two seated figures. Generally the figures are male and female, but sometimes they are two women. The roof of the cave is ribbed with teak beams said to be original; there may once have been such beams at Ajanta and Ellora, but they are now gone. On the sides of the vestibule are carved elephant heads which once had ivory tusks.

Other carvings can also be seen along the sides. A *stambha* (pillar) topped by four back-to-back lions, an image usually associated with Ashoka, stands outside the cave. It may be older than the cave itself.

There are some small, unadorned viharas further round the hillside, some of which have been converted into Hindu shrines.

Bhaja Caves

It's a fairly rough three km from the main road to the 18 Bhaja Caves. They're in a lusher, greener setting than the Karla Cave,

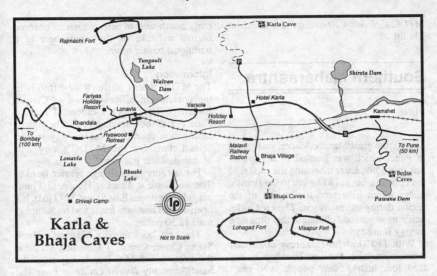

Karla & Bhaja Caves

and are thought to date from around 200 BC. Ten of these caves are viharas, while cave 12 is a chaitya, similar in style to the Karla Cave and the most important. About 50 metres past this is a strange group of 14 stupas, five inside and nine outside the cave. The last cave on the south side has some fine sculptures.

A few minutes' walk past the last cave is a beautiful waterfall which, during the monsoon and shortly afterwards, has enough water for a good swim. From the waterfall you can see some old forts.

Other Caves & Forts

Further along the line, six km south-east of Kamshet station, are the **Bedsa Caves**. They are thought to be more recent than the better executed Karla Cave. At one time the roof of the main cave was probably painted.

There are a number of old forts in the vicinity including the hilltop **Lohagad Fort**, which was taken twice by Shivaji, and **Visapur Fort**, both above the Bhaja Caves.

Places to Stay & Eat

Although most people stay at Lonavla, it is possible to stay closer to Karla Cave at the

MTDC's *Holiday Resort* (☎ 82-230). It's just off the Bombay to Pune road near the turn-off to the caves and has double rooms at Rs 175 and Rs 200 plus suites and cottages (all of which sleep four people) for Rs 325 to Rs 400. Some have air-con. There's a bar and a good restaurant.

Getting There & Away

See the previous Lonavla section for details on getting to the caves.

MURUD-JANJIRA

On the coast about 160 km due south of Bombay, the majestic island fortress of Murud-Janjira was the 16th-century capital of the Siddis of Janjira, descendants of sailor/traders from the Horn of Africa. It is without doubt one of Maharashtra's most commanding coastal forts, stretched along an island a short distance from the tranquil fishing town of Murud and only accessible by local sailing boat. The fort's 12-metre-high walls made it impregnable to everyone, even the Marathas – Shivaji tried to conquer it by sea and his son, Sambhaji, attempted to tunnel to it!

Accommodation is available at the

MAHARASHTRA

MTDC's *Holiday Resort* on the beach at Murud.

Southern Maharashtra

PUNE

Population: 2.7 million
Telephone Area Code: 0212

Shivaji, the great Maratha leader, was raised in Pune, which was granted to his grandfather in 1599. Later it became the capital of the Peshwas, but in 1817 went to the British, under whom it became the capital of the region during the monsoon. The city had a rather more pleasant climate at that time than muggy Bombay.

With fast (but full) express commuter trains connecting Pune to Bombay in less than four hours, many people who can't afford the sky-high prices of accommodation in Bombay actually commute daily between the two cities. As a result, the big-city influence has rubbed off on Pune, and fashion shops and fast-food outlets are constantly springing up. Pune itself boasts a prestigious university, and it is also a major industrial centre (chemicals, pharmaceuticals, steel and plastics).

For many Western visitors, the city's major attraction is the Osho Commune International, better known as the ashram of Bhagwan Rajneesh. Most Indians will assume that you're in Pune for just that and the ashram is so well known that it was formerly even included on the city bus tour, where, in a superb reversal of roles, Indians flocked to view Westerners.

Orientation

The city is at the confluence of the Mutha and Mula rivers. The majority of hotels and restaurants are concentrated near the railway station, though there are a few close to the main bus terminal, Swargate, way to the south near Nehru Stadium.

Mahatma Gandhi Rd (M G Rd) is the city's main street and is lined with trendy clothing shops, banks, hotels and restau-

rants. South-west of here, the streets become narrow and take on the atmosphere of a traditional bazaar-town.

Information

The MTDC tourist office (☎ 62-8169) is in the government offices known as Central Buildings. They stock a colourful map of Pune (Rs 5) but nothing else. The tourist information counter at the railway station sells tickets for the MTDC's city and Mahabaleshwar bus tours.

For fast foreign exchange service head to Thomas Cook at Thacker House, G Thimmaya Rd (between East St and M G Rd). It's open normal business hours and on Saturday until 12.30 pm.

The best bookshop is Manney's Book Seller, Clover Centre, 7 Moledina Rd (near the junction with M G Rd). It may stock the handy, monthly *Tourist Guide of Pune* (Rs 15).

The GPO on Connaught Rd is open Monday to Saturday from 10 am to 6 pm.

Osho Commune International

Bhagwan Rajneesh's famous ashram, renamed Osho Commune International several years ago, is at 17 Koregaon Park in a leafy northern suburb of Pune. More a New Age resort than a humble ashram, it has continued to prosper since the Bhagwan's death in 1990 and still attracts thousands of devotees each year. Facilities include a swimming pool, sauna, tennis and basketball courts, massage and beauty parlour, bistro, bookshop and a new five-hectare Zen garden, known as Osho Teerth, complete with a trickling stream. The commune's 'Multiversity' runs a plethora of (expensive) courses in traditional meditation as well as New Age techniques. For example, there's the School of Centering, the Academy of Healing Arts, and the Osho School of Mysticism. There are also cheaper weekend meditation camps.

Those wishing to stay at the commune must prove HIV-negative to the on-the-spot test given at the centre. You must also arrange your own accommodation. Casual

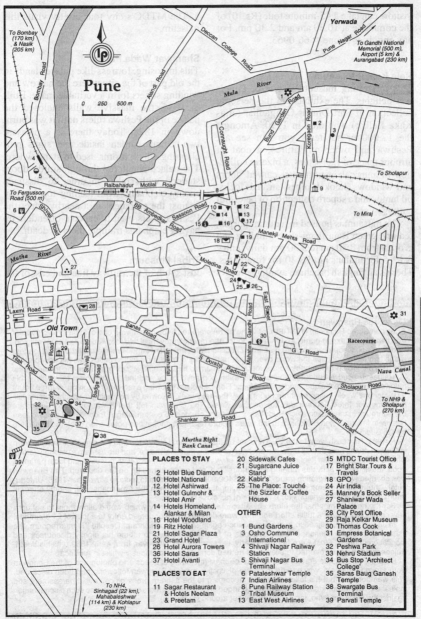

Pune

0   250   500 m

MAHARASHTRA

PLACES TO STAY

2   Hotel Blue Diamond
10 Hotel National
12 Hotel Ashirwad
13 Hotel Gulmohr &
    Hotel Amir
14 Hotels Homeland,
    Alankar & Milan
16 Hotel Woodland
19 Ritz Hotel
21 Hotel Sagar Plaza
23 Grand Hotel
26 Hotel Aurora Towers
36 Hotel Saras
37 Hotel Avanti

PLACES TO EAT

11 Sagar Restaurant
    & Hotels Neelam
    & Preetam

20 Sidewalk Cafes
21 Sugarcane Juice
    Stand
22 Kabir's
25 The Place: Touché
    the Sizzler & Coffee
    House

OTHER

1   Bund Gardens
3   Osho Commune
    International
4   Shivaji Nagar Railway
    Station
5   Shivaji Nagar Bus
    Terminal
6   Pataleshwar Temple
7   Indian Airlines
8   Pune Railway Station
9   Tribal Museum
13 East West Airlines

15 MTDC Tourist Office
17 Bright Star Tours &
    Travels
18 GPO
24 Air India
25 Manney's Book Seller
27 Shaniwar Wada
    Palace
28 City Post Office
29 Raja Kelkar Museum
30 Thomas Cook
31 Empress Botanical
    Gardens
32 Peshwa Park
33 Nehru Stadium
34 Bus Stop 'Architect
    College'
35 Saras Baug Ganesh
    Temple
38 Swargate Bus
    Terminal
39 Parvati Temple

visitors can take a 45-minute tour (Rs 10) of the commune at 10.30 am and 2.30 pm. For any enquiries phone ☎ 66-0963.

Raja Kelkar Museum

This interesting museum is one of Pune's real delights. The exhibits are the personal collection of Shri Dinkar Gangadhar (alias Kaka Kelkar) who died in 1990. Amongst the 17,000 or so items you can see are Peshwa and other miniatures, a coat of armour made of fish scales, a bizarre collection of musical instruments, carved doors and windows, hookah pipes, strange locks, oil lamps and a superb collection of betel-nut cutters.

The museum is housed in a quaint purple, red and green Rajasthani-style building and is open from 8.30 am to 5.30 pm daily; entry is Rs 5 for Indians but Rs 30 for foreigners. There's an English brochure available for Rs 5. The MTDC's city tour briefly visits this museum.

Shaniwar Wada Palace

This imposing, fortress-like palace stands in the old part of the city where the narrow and winding streets form a veritable maze. Built in 1736, the massive walls enclosed the palace of the Peshwa rulers until it was burnt down in 1828. Today there is a pleasant two-hectare garden inside and signs proclaiming which rooms used to stand where. The palace is entered through sturdy doors studded with spikes in order to dissuade enemy elephants from leaning too heavily against the entrance! In a nearby street the Peshwa rulers used to execute offenders by having elephants trample them to death.

Tribal Museum

Just south of the railway line and east of the

Osho, the Bhagwan

Bhagwan Shree Rajneesh (1931-90), or Osho as he preferred to be called, was one of India's most popular and flamboyant 'export gurus' and, without doubt, the most controversial. He followed no particular religion, tradition or philosophy and his often acerbic criticism and dismissal of various religious and political leaders made him many enemies the world over. What particularly outraged his Indian critics was his advocacy of sex as a path to enlightenment, an approach which earned him the epithet 'sex guru' from the Indian press.

Rajneesh used a curious blend of Californian pop psychology and Indian mysticism to motivate his followers. His last technique, tagged The Mystic Rose, involved following a regime of laughing for three hours a day for one week, crying for three hours a day the next week, followed by becoming a 'watcher on the hill' (ie sitting) for three hours a day for another week. The Bhagwan felt that it was 'the most important breakthrough in meditation since Buddha's *vipassana*, created 25 centuries ago'. Indeed, he began to lean heavily in favour of Zen Buddhism in the years before his death and, at one point, even declared himself to be the Buddha.

In 1981, Rajneesh went to the USA and set up the agricultural commune and ashram of Rajneeshpuram in Oregon. It was here that he drew the attention of the international media, and the ashram's notoriety (along with its highly publicised fleet of Rolls Royces) grew and grew. Eventually, with rumours and local paranoia about the ashram's activities running wild, the military and police turned up on the doorstep. The Bhagwan was charged with immigration fraud, fined US$400,000, and deported to India in November 1985. Unfortunately, the Indian government was no more sympathetic to him than the Americans and, shortly after his return, refused visa extensions for a number of his close followers.

For the next six months, the hierarchy attempted to find a country which would allow them to set up a new community. It was a futile effort and they were deported from or denied entry to a total of 21 countries!

In January 1987, Rajneesh took up residence again at the Pune ashram. Despite the interregnum, the ashram once more flourished and thousands of foreigners flocked to attend his nightly discourses and meditation courses. Most were from Germany, Italy and Japan. However, from early 1989 until his death, Rajneesh once again reverted to silence as he had done so once previously whilst in America.

Before his death, the orange clothes and the *mala* (the string of beads and photograph of the Bhagwan worn around the neck), which used to be the distinctive mark of Bhagwan followers, had been discarded. This was done so that his followers could, according to the ashram press office, 'avoid harassment and molestation by the authorities'. Times have changed and these days there seems to be no such discrimination against the followers (who, incidentally, now get around in maroon). ■

railway station, this excellent museum (☎ 66-9471) documents the cultures of Maharashtran tribal communities, particularly those from the Sahyadri and Gondwana regions. It is open weekdays from 10 am to 5 pm. City bus tours do not call here.

Temples & Gardens

The **Empress Botanical Gardens** have fine tropical trees and a small zoo nearby. The moated **Saras Baug Ganesh Temple** is in Peshwa Park. The **Bund Gardens**, on the banks of the river, are a popular place for an evening stroll. The bridge here crosses the river to Yerwada and the Gandhi National Memorial (formerly the Aga Khan's palace). The **Parvati Temple** is on the outskirts of the town on a hilltop. There's a good view from the top, where the last Peshwa ruler is said to have stood and watched whilst his troops suffered defeat at the hands of the British at Kirkee.

The rock-cut **Pataleshwar Temple**, a small 8th-century temple similar in style to the much grander rock temples of Ellora, is fairly central and dedicated to Siva. The story goes that it was excavated in one night. In front of the excavation is a circular *mandapam*.

Gandhi National Memorial

Across the river in Yerwada is this fine memorial set in 6.5 hectares of gardens. It was the Aga Khan's palace until 1956 after which it became a school. In 1969 it was donated to India.

At one time Mahatma Gandhi and other leaders of India's independence movement were interned here for two years. Some of the scenes from the movie *Gandhi* were shot in this building. Kasturba Gandhi, the Mahatma's wife, died here while interned and her ashes are kept in a memorial tomb in the gardens.

It is open from 9 am to 5.45 pm daily; entry is Rs 2. The city tour stops here for half an hour or so (too short if you want to read the blurbs which accompany the photographs).

Organised Tours

Four-hour bus tours of Pune leave from the railway station at 8 am and 2 pm daily and cost Rs 40. They cover all the main sights in a breathless rush. Book at the MTDC kiosk in the station's main hall.

The MTDC also offers day trips to Mahabaleshwar which start at 7.30 am and return at 10 pm. The cost is Rs 150. Naturally, you spend most of the day on the bus.

Festivals

While **Ganesh Chaturthi** is celebrated all over India, the festival is most extravagant at Bombay and, in more recent years, at Pune. Traditionally a household affair, it was converted into a public celebration a century ago when the freedom fighter, Lokmanya Tilak, used to unite the masses for the freedom struggle. Ganesh, or Ganpati as he's often affectionately called, is after all the remover of obstacles.

Kasturba & Mohandas Gandhi

Ganesh Mandals

'You must see them *all!*' our excited young guide, Sheetal, said as she led us through the dark, narrow backstreets of Pune to an area where the biggest and most opulent mandals had been erected. This was the third consecutive night she had made such a tour – the first with her mother, the second with friends – and yet her fervour, together with that of all those on the streets, was almost tangible.

The source of their excitement was the mandals – elaborately decorated statues of the elephant-headed god, Ganesh, which had been set up to celebrate the Ganesh Chaturthi Festival. More than 1000 mandals dotted the city, and many of them were immense. In some cases, purpose-built platforms occupied entire street corners (sometimes blocking the whole street), and were illuminated with the best that Indian electronics can muster. Each mandal had a theme – either traditional or contemporary. Thus, one minute you could be looking at a majestic Ganesh seated in a regal parlour with peacocks and his devoted mother, Parvati, by his side; the next minute, there's 'Ganesh in Jurassic Park'! Another favourite with Pune's young things was 'Disco Ganesh' – a sound & light show to beat all others.

We didn't see all the mandals that night, but by the time all these images were immersed in the river, Sheetal and many other Pune-ites probably had. ■

At the end of the 11-day festival, plaster and clay images of Ganesh, some of them six metres high, are taken from homes and street *mandals* (see the boxed section) and carried in huge processions to be immersed in water. In Bombay this is done at Chowpatty Beach, in Pune down by the river.

Pune's procession is the climax of an illustrious programme of events – classical dance and music concerts, folk dance, a village festival including bullock cart races and wrestling – which is organised by the MTDC. The opening ceremony, televised live on Doordarshan and attended by the Indian vice-president, features some of the country's best musicians and dancers.

In 1996, the festival will be held from 16 to 26 September, in 1997 from 6 to 15 September, and from 26 August to 5 September in 1998.

Places to Stay – bottom end

Most of the cheapies close to the railway station are fleapits but there are some in the area known as Wilson Gardens, directly opposite the station and behind the National Hotel, which are OK. There are good *retiring rooms* at the railway station.

The *Hotel Homeland* (☎ 62-7158), Wilson Gardens, is a big old house, newly painted in fresh pastel colours and run by a very sociable young guy. Clean singles cost Rs 170 and Rs 185, and doubles are Rs 220 to Rs 235, all with attached bath. There are also small horrible dorm beds for Rs 40. Hot water runs from 7 to 9.30 am. This place may also have a restaurant by now.

Also in Wilson Gardens are the cheaper *Hotel Alankar* (☎ 62-2024) with singles/doubles/triples at Rs 100/125/150 with attached bath, and *Hotel Milan* (☎ 62-0484) which has singles for Rs 70/110 with common/attached bath, and doubles for Rs 100/165.

The *Hotel National* (☎ 62-5054), 14 Sassoon Rd, opposite the railway station, is a beautiful, old mansion with verandahs and high ceilings (though some of the rooms have no windows). It's a popular place to stay, cordial, and the best choice in this range. In the main house there are singles with common bath for Rs 77 and singles/doubles/triples/quads with attached bath for Rs 150/223/270/320. In addition to these there is a row of cottages at the back which are simple but clean and peaceful and cost Rs 135/175 for a single/double. Breakfast is available if ordered in advance and there's hot water from 6 am to noon.

Further afield on Connaught Rd is the *Ritz Hotel* (☎ 62-2533), an old-fashioned wooden house with a mellow atmosphere. The rooms are large and clean though a little tatty and cost Rs 85/140. There's hot water in the morning only. The vegetarian restaurant here serves meals 'with or without chillies'!

Down on M G Rd, the *Grand Hotel* (☎ 66-8723) is another crumbling old place in its own grounds. Singles (airless cabins with no windows) cost Rs 55 with common bath. The double rooms with attached bath are better and go for Rs 130. The hotel has its own bar, patio and restaurant.

If you want to be near Swargate bus terminal for an early-morning getaway, the MTDC's *Hotel Saras* (☎ 43-0499) has decent singles/doubles starting at Rs 175/200. The hotel is attached to the Nehru Stadium and, from the terrace of its trendy restaurant, you can watch the occasional cricket match.

Places to Stay – middle

At the bottom of this category is the *Hotel Gulmohr* (☎ 62-2773), 15 A/1 Connaught Rd, within easy walking distance of the railway station. It has singles/doubles from Rs 165/245 and doubles with air-con for Rs 395. Some rooms have a small balcony. There's hot water 24 hours a day, and a bar.

Closer to the station is the *Hotel Ashirwad* (☎ 62-8585), 16 Connaught Rd, which offers spacious rooms with balcony for Rs 320/400 to Rs 350/450 without air-con and Rs 450/600 with air-con. There's a restaurant with good vegetarian food but no bar. Next door, the *Hotel Amir* (☎ 62-1840) at No 15 has a much greater range of facilities including a bar, restaurants (veg and non-veg), coffee shop and a dreary shopping arcade. It has 'budget' rooms for Rs 300/350, 'first-class' air-con rooms for Rs 500/600, and 'deluxe' rooms for Rs 550/650. The staff are friendly and helpful but the rooms are dark and run-down.

Not far from here is the huge *Hotel Woodland* (☎ 62-6161), off Sadhu Vaswani Circle, which has a range of singles/doubles from Rs 300/350 (regular) to Rs 450/500 (regular air-con) and Rs 500/600 (deluxe air-con) as well as suites. The rooms are good and well maintained but there's no bar or restaurant.

Close to Swargate bus terminal, the *Hotel Avanti* (☎ 44-5975) has clean, airy singles/doubles and hot water for Rs 200/350.

Places to Stay – top end

Pune has no shortage of four and five-star hotels.

The *Hotel Sagar Plaza* (☎ 62-2622; fax 62-2633), 1 Bund Garden Rd, off Moledina Rd, is relatively new and deliciously cool in summer. Air-con rooms cost Rs 900/1075 plus there are deluxe doubles for Rs 1395. Facilities include a bar, coffee shop, speciality restaurant, small swimming pool and bookshop.

The huge *Hotel Aurora Towers* (☎ 64-1818; fax 64-1826), 9 Moledina Rd at the junction of M G Rd, is also fully air-conditioned and has standard singles/doubles at Rs 875/1075 and deluxe doubles at Rs 1150. There are also more expensive suites. Facilities include a shopping arcade, parking, rooftop swimming pool, bar, two restaurants (Indian, Continental and Chinese) and a popular coffee shop.

Top of the line are the five-star *Hotel Executive Asoka* (☎ 57-391; fax 32-3228) at 5 University Rd and the *Hotel Blue Diamond* (☎ 66-3775; fax 64-6101), 11 Koregaon Rd.

Places to Eat

On the corner of Station and Connaught Rds, the *Sagar Restaurant* is a big, clean place serving vegetarian 'special meals' for Rs 25 as well as a long list of other dishes. You can get toast and tea here in the morning. Next door, in the large Hotel Metro Building, the *Hotel Neelam* and the *Hotel Preetam* are more intimate and offer reasonably priced veg and non-veg Indian and part-Western dishes. The Preetam also serves cold beers.

A good place to go in the evening for a cheap meal and to mix with the bright young things of Pune is the street opposite the GPO. A whole string of makeshift cafes here have tables and chairs strewn along the pavement and offer a variety of food and cold drinks. Another area that's popular with Pune's university crowd is Fergusson Rd. However, it's a few km west of the railway station so you'll need an auto-rickshaw. The restaurants here are generally cheaper than their inner-city counterparts and come highly recommended. Try the *Savoy* at 1199/B Fergusson Rd, or the nearby *Savera* or *Shabree*.

For something of a splurge, there are two excellent places opposite each other on Moledina Rd. On the north side is the part open-air *Kabir's* at No 6 which offers Indian, Mughlai and tandoori dishes. You'll be looking at about Rs 40 to Rs 50 to eat here. Opposite but more expensive is *The Place: Touché the Sizzler*, a two-tier indoor restaurant which specialises in sizzlers but also offers Indian, tandoori and continental dishes. The food is excellent and the service fast. Both restaurants have cold beers.

Also on Moledina Rd is the *Coffee House*, a trendy hangout and definitely the place to be seen.

The drink stand next to Hotel Sagar Plaza is a life-saver on hot days; Rs 1.50 for a big glass of freshly pressed sugar-cane juice.

Getting There & Away

Air The Indian Airlines office (☎ 65-9939, or 141) is inconveniently located at 39 Dr Ambedkar Rd, the main road to Bombay. NEPC Airlines' contact number is 64-7441. East West Airlines (☎ 66-5862) is next to the Hotel Amir. Air India (☎ 64-0932) is on Moledina Rd.

Indian Airlines has daily flights to Delhi (US$130), and three flights weekly to Bangalore (US$91) and Madras (US$102). East West has three flights a day to Bombay (US$54), while NEPC has flights to Bangalore (US$90), Madras (US$105) and Goa (US$85) three times a week, and twice-daily flights to Bombay (US$60).

Bus Pune has three bus terminals: the

Railway terminal for points south including Goa, Belgaum (341 km), Kolhapur, Mahabaleshwar and Panchgani; the Shivaji Nagar terminal for points north and north-east – Ahmednagar, Aurangabad (Rs 100, six hours, 238 km), Lonavla (64 km) and Nasik (209 km); and the Swargate terminal for Sinhagad (24 km), Bangalore, Mangalore and Bombay (Rs 50, five hours, 170 km).

MTDC (the state tourist office) operates deluxe buses to Mahabaleshwar (Rs 150, 117 km). Reservations can be made at the tourist information counter at the railway station.

The MSRTC buses tend to be pretty rough and ready and most travellers prefer to use the railway system. If you don't want to do this, there are plenty of private deluxe buses to most nearby centres but beware of going through agents (especially those advertising their services around the railway station) as you'll end up paying up to 50% commission and find yourself dumped on a regular MSRTC bus. Try Bright Star Tours & Travels (☎ 62-9666), 13 Connaught Rd (the office is not signposted – it's inside the petrol station), which has luxury buses daily to Ahmedabad, Aurangabad, Bangalore, Goa, Hubli/Belgaum, Hyderabad, Nagpur and Sholapur.

Train Pune is one of the Deccan's most important railway stations and all express and mail trains stop here. The computerised booking hall is to the left of the station as you face the entrance.

The *Deccan Queen* and *Pragati Express* are fast commuter trains to Bombay and are heavily subscribed, so book well in advance.

Train Services from Pune					
Destination	*Train number & name*	*Departure time*	*Distance (km)*	*Duration (hours)*	*Fare (Rs) (2nd/1st)*
Bangalore	6529 *Udyan Exp*	12.20 pm	1019	20	214/634
Bombay VT	2124 *Deccan Queen*	7.15 am	191	3.25	58/209
	2126 *Pragati Exp*	7.30 am		3.35	
Hyderabad	7031 *Hyderabad Exp*	5.15 pm	600	13.15	150/444
Madras	6063 *Chennai Exp*	11.55 pm	1088	20	219/668
	6511 *Dadar Madras Exp*	6.40 pm		22	
Delhi	1077 *Jhelum Exp*	5.35 pm	1595	27.45	264/877

Other express and mail trains to Bombay take four to five hours.

If you're heading for Matheran, the only express train which stops at Neral is the *Sahyadri Express* which leaves at 7.35 am. See the Matheran section for further details.

For a selection of major trains from Pune, see the Train Services table.

Taxi Long-distance share taxis (four passengers) also connect Pune and Bombay. They leave from the taxi stand in front of the railway station and cost Rs 155 per person for the four-hour trip.

Getting Around
To/From the Airport The airport is eight km north-east of the city. Indian Airlines operates an airport bus which departs from Hotel Amir and costs Rs 18 one way. An auto-rickshaw will cost Rs 25; a taxi Rs 40.

Bus The local buses are relatively uncrowded. The bus you are most likely to use is the No 4, which runs from the Railway bus terminal to Swargate via the Shivaji Nagar terminal. The Marathi number '4' looks like an '8' with a gap at the top.

Bicycle This is a good place to get around by bicycle (except at rush hours when it's bedlam). They can be rented from the stall near the entrance to the Hotel National.

AROUND PUNE
Sinhagad
Sinhagad, the Lion Fort, is 24 km south-west of Pune and makes an excellent day trip from Pune. It was the scene of another of Shivaji's daring exploits.

In 1670 Shivaji's general, Tanaji Malusre, led a force of men who scaled the steep hillside in the dark and defeated the unprepared forces of Bijapur. Legends about this dramatic attack relate that the Maratha forces used trained lizards to carry ropes up the hillside! There are monuments at the spot where Tanaji died, and also at the place where he lost his left hand before his death. The fort stands on top of a steep hill near a

telecommunications mast and, although the fort is largely ruined, there are a number of old bungalows up here, including one where Gandhi met with the freedom fighter, Tilak, in 1915.

A motorable road winds up to the fort, but if you come by local bus, it's a sweaty 1½ to two-hour climb to the top, where you'll find a tea stall and cool drinks. It's a good idea to bring water and food with you. *Lassiwallahs* are positioned at various intervals on the trail up, but give them a miss unless you feel the need for some exotic stomach germs.

Getting There & Away The Pune city bus No 50 runs frequently to Sinhagad village (from where you must walk) from 5.25 am until evening. It leaves from the bus stop 'Architect College' opposite Nehru Stadium and the trip (Rs 5) takes 45 minutes.

MAHABALESHWAR
Population: 11,500
Telephone Area Code: 02168

This popular hill station was the summer capital of the Bombay presidency during the days of the Raj. It has pleasant walks and good lookouts (the sea is visible on a clear day), and the area has interesting historical connections with Shivaji. The station was founded in 1828 by Sir John Malcolm.

As with most hill stations, Mahabaleshwar closes up tight for the monsoon season (mid-June to mid-September). Local buildings are clad with *kulum* grass to stop them being damaged by the torrential rain – an unbelievable six *metres* (around 235 inches) of rain falls during this time.

The small Venna Lake, about four km from Mahabaleshwar, has boating and fishing facilities. In the village of Old Mahabaleshwar there are three old temples, although they are badly ruined. The Krishnabai, or Panchganga (Five Streams), Temple is said to contain the springs of the Krishna, Venna and Koyana rivers.

The local specialities – strawberry and raspberry jam – are good, particularly if you can find some toast.

MAHARASHTRA

Information

Arriving by car or bus, you must pay a 'municipal tax' of Rs 5 to the officials on the roadside as you enter town. Private vehicles must also pay a Rs 2 per day parking fee.

Walks & Views

Elphinstone, Babington, Bombay and Kate's Point all offer fine views from this wooded plateau to the plains below. Arthur's Seat, 12 km from Mahabaleshwar, looks out over a sheer drop of 600 metres to the Konkan coastal strip. There are pleasant waterfalls such as Chinaman's Falls (2.5 km), Dhobi (three km) and Lingmala (six km). Most of the walking trails are well signposted, although the moss growing over the signs can make them difficult to read!

Organised Tours

In the high season, the MTDC organises tours (minimum of 10 people) of Mahabaleshwar, Pratapgarh Fort or Panchgani. Each tour costs Rs 35 per person and can be booked at the MTDC's Holiday Resort.

Places to Stay

Mahabaleshwar has plenty of hotels but most are closed during the monsoon. The cheaper lodges are in the town centre in the bazaar area, but even these are not cheap by local standards. Prices go up during the high season (generally from November to January and mid-April to mid-June).

The *Hotel Saraswati* on Mari Peth has singles/doubles with hot water for Rs 60/80 in the off season. Doubles jump to Rs 250 in the high season. The *Poonam Hotel* (☎ 60-291) is also in the bazaar but it's not cheap at Rs 500 for a double. Other cheaper lodges near the centre include the *Vyankatesh* (☎ 60-397), *Samartha* (☎ 60-416), and the *Ajantha* (☎ 60-272), all on Mosque St.

The *Ripon Hotel* (☎ 60-257) is a 20-minute walk from the bus stand. It is run by an elderly, amicable gentleman and there are fine views over the lake. Rooms cost Rs 300/500 per person in the low/high season (closed during the monsoon).

The MTDC's *Holiday Resort* (☎ 60-318),

about two km from the centre, has a variety of accommodation including dorm beds for Rs 50 per person, good doubles at Rs 150 to Rs 225, and cottages and suites (three to four people) for Rs 300 to Rs 500. A taxi from the bus stand to here costs Rs 20 one way.

More expensive hotels include the *Dreamland Hotel* (☎ 60-228), *Regal Hotel* (☎ 60-001), *Dina Hotel* (☎ 60-246) and *Fredrick Hotel* (☎ 60-240). These places generally quote all-inclusive prices in the range of Rs 1000 to Rs 1500 per person.

Places to Eat

As most of the hotels have their own restaurants, there are few independent places to eat. The *Veena Restaurant* at the Holiday Resort does good non-veg dishes at reasonable prices and beers are available. The army of young waiters here are extra keen.

The *Shere Punjab* at the Poonam Hotel also has good non-veg food. Next door and more popular is *Nukkad*. During the monsoon these two are about the only places open. Five minutes' walk from Shere Punjab, at the far end of the same road, is the *Imperial Stores* which does take-away toasted sandwiches, burgers and other small snacks.

Getting There & Away

Mahabaleshwar is 117 km south-west of Pune via Panchgani. The closest railway station is Satara Road, about 15 km north-east of the town of Satara.

There are daily buses to Kolhapur (Rs 30, five hours), Satara (Rs 18, two hours), Pune (Rs 20, 3½ hours) and Panchgani (Rs 4). There's an MTDC luxury bus daily (except during the monsoon) to/from Bombay (it leaves at 6.30 am from Bombay and at 3 pm from Mahabaleshwar) which takes seven hours and costs Rs 180. The MTDC also operates deluxe buses to Pune for Rs 150 but they're hardly worth the extra.

Getting Around

Mahabaleshwar has no auto-rickshaws but a few old Dodge limousines are still used as taxis and will take you around the main viewpoints or to Panchgani.

AROUND MAHABALESHWAR
Panchgani

Panchgani (Five Hills) is 19 km east of Mahabaleshwar and, at 1334 metres, is just 38 metres lower. It's also a popular hill station, splendidly located, but overshadowed by its better known neighbour. On the way up to Panchgani from Pune you pass through Wai, a site featured in the *Mahabharata*.

As in Mahabaleshwar, there are various hotels. Cheaper places include the *Prospect Hotel* (☎ 40-263), *Hotel Western* (☎ 40-288) and the *Malas Guest House* (☎ 40-321). The most expensive is the *Aman Hotel* (☎ 40-211) with rooms from Rs 550/850 in the low/high season. The *Hotel Five Hills* (☎ 40-301) has singles/doubles for Rs 350/450 and its *Silver Oaks Restaurant* is reasonably priced and serves excellent food.

Pratapgarh & Raigad Forts

Built in 1656, Pratapgarh Fort is about 24 km west of Mahabaleshwar and is connected with one of the more notable feats in Shivaji's dramatic life (see the 'Pratapgarh Protagonists' boxed section for more details).

Raigad Fort, 80 km north-west of Mahabaleshwar, was the Maratha capital for six years before Shivaji's death. The MTDC has plans to open accommodation here.

SATARA
Population: 105,000

On the main road from Pune to Belgaum and Goa, but 15 km off the railway line from Satara Road, this town houses a number of relics of the Maratha leader Shivaji. A building near the new palace contains his sword, the coat he wore when he met Afzal Khan and the *waghnakh* with which he killed him. The **Shivaji Maharaj Museum** is opposite the bus terminal.

The fort of **Wasota** stands in the south of the town – it has had a colourful and bloody history, including being captured from the Marathas in 1699 by the forces of Aurangzeb, only to be recaptured in 1705 by means of a Brahmin who befriended the fort's defenders, then let in a band of Marathas.

KOLHAPUR
Population: 458,000
Telephone Area Code: 0231

This was once the capital of an important Maratha state. One of Kolhapur's maharajas died in Florence, Italy, and was cremated on the banks of the Arno where his *chhatri* (cenotaph) now stands. The last maharaja, Major General His Highness Shahaji Chhatrapati II, died in 1983.

There's little of interest in the town itself, although the palace is worth a visit if you're passing through and Lake Rankala, five km from the railway station, offers some respite from the city bustle.

The MTDC tourist office, next to the Tourist Hotel, is open weekdays from 10 am to 6 pm and weekends from 8.30 am to noon and 4 to 6 pm.

Maharaja's Palace

The maharaja's 'new' palace, completed in 1881, was designed by Charles Mant, the

MAHARASHTRA

Pratapgarh Protagonists

Outnumbered by the forces of Bijapur, Shivaji arranged to meet with the opposing General Afzal Khan. Neither was supposed to carry any weapon or wear armour; but neither, it turned out, could be trusted.

When they met, Afzal Khan pulled out a dagger and stabbed Shivaji, but the Maratha leader had worn a shirt of mail under his white robe and concealed in his left hand was a *waghnakh*, a deadly set of 'tiger's claws'. This nasty weapon consisted of a series of rings to which long, sharpened metal claws were attached. Shivaji drove these claws into Khan and disembowelled him. Today a tomb marks where their encounter took place, and a tower was erected over the Khan's head. There is a statue of Shivaji in the ruined Pratapgarh Fort. ■

architect who fashioned the Indo-Saracenic style of colonial architecture. The palace contains the **Shahaji Chhatrapati Museum** – a weird and wonderful array of the old maharaja's possessions including his clothes, old hunt photos and the memorial silver spade used by the maharaja to 'turn the first sod of the Kolhapur State Railway' in 1888. There's even his Prince Shiraji Pig-Sticking Trophy. The gun and sword collection is comprehensive, and the ashtrays and coffee tables made from tigers' and elephants' feet, not to mention the lamp stands from ostrich legs, are unbelievably gross.

Only a few rooms are open to the public and there are officious men employed to make sure you don't wander off. The palace is a few km north of the centre. Rent a bicycle, or take an auto-rickshaw (Rs 5), but make sure you ask for the 'new palace' or you may end up at the Shalini Palace Hotel by the lake.

Places to Stay

The main hotel and restaurant area is around the square opposite the bus stand, five minutes' walk from the centre of town and the railway station, where there are *retiring rooms*.

The cheapest place here is the *Hotel Anand Malhar* (☎ 65-5091) which charges Rs 55/80 for a single/double without bath or Rs 100 for a double with bath. It also has a good restaurant. There is no English signpost for this place – you'll find it between the Sahyadri and Maharaja hotels.

The *Hotel Sahyadri* (☎ 65-0939) is of a similar standard but gets a bit noisy and is more expensive at Rs 110/140. The *Hotel Maharaja* (☎ 65-0829) is marginally better at Rs 95/155.

Just round the corner from these three is the friendly and clean *Hotel Girish* (☎ 65-2846). It has good rooms all with TV, phone and piped music (mercifully there's a switch to kill it) for Rs 110/130. There's also a restaurant and a bar.

At the top of the scale and very good value is the *Shalini Palace Hotel* (☎ 20-401), an old summer palace by Lake Rankala, five km from the bus stand or railway station. It dates back to the 1930s only but has plenty of regal grandeur. Simple singles/doubles cost Rs 250/325. Air-con rooms go for Rs 400/550 to Rs 425/650. The more expensive rooms have a lake view and there's also a 'maharaja' suite for Rs 1200.

Places to Eat

The restaurants are also concentrated around the square. The *Subraya Restaurant*, opposite Hotel Sahyadri, has north Indian veg and non-veg dishes, and sound thalis.

In the evening dozens of snack stalls are set up in the street to the right of the bus stand (as you leave it). They whip up great omelettes and other goodies – it's a very economical and interesting place to eat.

Getting There & Away

Bus The bus stand is not too chaotic but, as usual, there's nothing written in English. For buses originating in Kolhapur it is possible to book 24 hours in advance between 8 am and noon and 2 and 4.30 pm.

There are daily departures for Satara, Bijapur, Mahabaleshwar, Pune, Ratnagiri and Belgaum.

Train The railway station is close to the centre of town. The broad-gauge line connects Kolhapur via Miraj with Pune (eight hours) and Bombay (13 hours) – take the daily *Koyna Express* or the overnight *Mahalaxmi Express*. The *Maharashtra Express* zigzags 1220 km through the state to Nagpur.

The line through from Miraj to Goa should have been upgraded to broad-gauge by now, in which case services should be available (they were suspended during the conversion), but it's probably quicker to go via the new Konkan Railway which runs along the coast. Check at the station to ascertain current details.

AROUND KOLHAPUR
Panhala

Panhala is a little-visited hill station (altitude

975 metres) 18 km north-west of Kohlapur. There is a fort with a long and convoluted history; it was originally the stronghold of Raja Bhoj II in 1192. The Pawala Caves are nearby, plus a couple of Buddhist cave temples.

RATNAGIRI

Ratnagiri, on the coast 135 km from Kolhapur, was the place where Thibaw, the last Burmese king, was interned by the British from 1886 until his death in 1916.

SHOLAPUR (Solarpur)

Telephone Area Code: 0217

This busy town north of Bijapur (in neighbouring Karnataka) is a prominent industrial and trading centre. It's perhaps best known for handloom products and the boldly designed bed sheets, known as Sholapur Chadders, that are made here. With some time to spare, check out the superbly decorated municipal offices and the fort near the city wall.

Sholapur is on the broad-gauge line from Bombay to Hyderabad or Bangalore. You'll also pass through here if you're travelling by train north or south to/from Bijapur or Badami and, depending on the state of the booking on the broad-gauge system, may have to stay the night.

Places to Stay & Eat The few *retiring rooms* at the railway station cost Rs 100 for a double.

There are two good places about 400 metres from the railway station in a quiet residential area known as Railway Lines. The *Hotel Rajdhani* (☎ 23-295) has singles/doubles starting at Rs 80/105. Just down the road, the *Hotel Vikram Palace* (☎ 28-935) offers rooms for Rs 146/186 and has a non-veg restaurant. Between these two there is a restaurant/bar called the *King of Kings*. To get to this area, turn left out of the station, continue for about 200 metres and then turn right down a tree-lined lane.

Otherwise, for comfort, stay at the three-star *Hotel Pratham* (☎ 29-581; fax 28-724), 560/61 South Sadar Bazaar, 1.25 km from

the railway station just off the road to Bijapur. It's excellent value at Rs 275 a double or Rs 400 with air-con. There are also more expensive deluxe rooms and suites. The hotel has its own veg and non-veg restaurants (very tasty food) and a bar.

Northern Maharashtra

AHMEDNAGAR

Population: 245,000
Telephone Area Code: 0241

On the road between Pune (120 km away) and Aurangabad, Ahmednagar has had a colourful history. It was here that Emperor Aurangzeb died in 1707, aged 97. The town's imposing fort was erected in 1550, and at one time Nehru was imprisoned here by the British.

There are various hotels, including the *Hotel Natraj* (☎ 26-576) on the Aurangabad Rd and the *Hotel Sanket* (☎ 28-701) on Tilak Rd which has singles/doubles for Rs 200/250 or Rs 300/350 with air-con.

NASIK

Population: 795,000
Telephone Area Code: 0253

This interesting town with its 200 temples and picturesque bathing ghats stands on the Godavari River, one of the holiest rivers of the Deccan. Like Ujjain (in neighbouring Madhya Pradesh) and Allahabad and Haridwar (in Uttar Pradesh), Nasik is the site for the triennial Kumbh Mela, a huge Hindu gathering which takes place here every 12 years.

The town itself is actually about eight km north-west of the railway station, Nasik Road, which is 187 km from Bombay.

Temples & Caves

Nasik's riverbanks are lined with steps above which stand temples and shrines. Although there are no particularly notable temples in Nasik, the **Sundar Narayan Temple**, to the west of the city, is worth seeing.

Other points of interest include the **Sita**

MAHARASHTRA

Gupta Cave from which, according to the *Ramayana*, Sita, the deity of agriculture and wife of Rama, was supposed to have been carried off to the island of Lanka by the evil king Ravana. Near the cave, in its grove of large banyan trees, is the fine house of the Panchavati family. Also nearby is the Temple of **Kala Rama**, or Black Rama, in a 96-arched enclosure. The **Kapaleswar Temple** upstream is said to be the oldest in the town.

Kumbh Mela

The Kumbh Mela alternates between Allahabad, Nasik, Ujjain and Haridwar every three years. *Kumbh* means Pot, and in Hindu mythology, four drops of the nectar of immortality fell to earth, one in each of these places. For more details about this extraordinary pilgrimage, see the section under Allahabad in the Uttar Pradesh chapter.

Places to Stay & Eat

Unless you're here at Kumbh Mela time, there is no shortage of accommodation. A good place is the *Hotel Siddharth* (☎ 64-288) on the Pune Rd, about two km from the roundabout. Large, well-kept singles/doubles are Rs 115/150 or Rs 225/250 with air-con. The hotel has an uninviting restaurant but also a very enticing lawn where, at night, you can dine by lamplight or simply relax with a beer.

Somewhat more expensive are the *Hotel Samrat* (☎ 77-211), near the central bus stand on the old Agra Rd which offers rooms without/with air-con for Rs 320/475. Its restaurant serves good Gujarati thalis and there's a bar. The *Green View Hotel* (☎ 72-231), 1363 M I Trimbak Rd, about two km from the centre of town is surrounded by a garden.

More expensive is the central *Hotel Panchavati* (☎ 75-771), 430 Vakilwadi, which offers rooms without air-con for Rs 295/480 or Rs 460/660 with air-con. There are also cheaper rooms in its annex. Similarly priced is *Wasan's Inn* (☎ 70-202) on the old Agra Rd. Both have their own restaurant.

Across the road from the Hotel Siddharth is the brand new *Woodlands Restaurant*. This place looks expensive but it's actually sensibly priced, the south Indian meals are superbly presented and the service is impeccable. Alcohol is not served.

Getting There & Away

Local buses and auto-rickshaws ply between the Nasik Road railway station and the town centre. The fastest train to Bombay VT is the very popular *Panchvati Express* which does the trip in 3½ hours and leaves at 7.09 am.

There are frequent buses to Bombay but they're slower than the slowest trains as they get caught up in Bombay's traffic chaos. Try to get on one of the faster luxury buses which should get you to Bombay in 4½ hours. Frequent buses also go to Aurangabad (200 km, five hours) and Pune (209 km, five hours).

AROUND NASIK
Pandu Lena

About eight km south of Nasik, close to the Bombay road, are these 24 Hinayana Buddhist caves. They date from around the 1st century BC to the 2nd AD. The most interesting caves are Nos 3, 10, 18 and 20. Cave 3 is a large vihara with some interesting sculptures. Cave 10 is also a vihara and almost identical in design to cave 3, although it is much older and finer in its detail. It is thought to be nearly as old as the Karla Cave near Lonavla. Cave 18 is a chaitya cave believed to date from the same time as the Karla Cave. It too is well sculpted and its elaborate facade is particularly noteworthy. Cave 20 is another large vihara.

Trimbak

High on a steep hill above Trimbak, 33 km west of Nasik, the source of the Godavari River dribbles into a bathing tank whose waters are reputed to wash away sins. From this tiny start the Godavari eventually flows down to the Bay of Bengal, clear across India.

AURANGABAD

Population: 650,000
Telephone Area Code: 02432

Aurangabad has a number of attractions and could easily stand on its own were it not overshadowed by the famous Ellora and Ajanta caves nearby. The city is named after Aurangzeb, but earlier in its history it was known as Khadke.

Aurangabad is northern Maharashtra's largest city though, in comparison to other Deccan towns, it is remarkably uncrowded and quiet except for the occasional political rally.

Orientation

The railway station, tourist office and a variety of cheaper hotels and restaurants are clustered in the south of the town. There's a fairly open gap from here to the bus stand 1.5 km to the north. North-east of here is the crowded old town with its narrow streets and distinct Muslim quarter. The mid-range hotels are between the bus stand and railway station while the top-end places are dotted around town.

Information

The very helpful Government of India tourist office (☎ 31-217) on Station Rd (West) has a decent range of brochures and will try to answer almost any query. It's open from 8.30 am to 6 pm on weekdays and until 11.30 am on Saturday. The state tourist office (☎ 31-513) in the MTDC Holiday Resort, Station Rd (East), is open from 7 am to 7 pm but is not as useful.

Poste restante can be collected from the GPO at Juna Bazaar Monday to Saturday from 10 am to 5 pm.

Bibi-ka-Maqbara

This poor-man's Taj Mahal was built in 1679 by Aurangzeb's son for Rabia-ud-Darani, Aurangzeb's wife. It's a cheap imitation in both design and execution – somehow it simply looks awkward and uncomfortable compared to the sophisticated balance of the Taj; and where the Taj has gleaming marble, this tomb has flaking paint. Nevertheless it's an interesting building and the only example of Mughal architecture on the Deccan plateau.

It stands to the north of the city, and on the main gate an inscription reveals that it cost precisely Rs 665,283 and 7 annas to build. It's open from about 7 am to 10 pm and admission is Rs 0.50.

Panchakki

This water mill takes its name from the mill which once ground grain for pilgrims. In 1624 a Sufi saint and spiritual guide to Aurangzeb was buried here, and the pleasant garden with its series of fish-filled tanks serves as his memorial. It's a cool, relaxing and serene place, although some travellers have thought it nothing more than 'an unremarkable pair of murky pools'. The stream sometimes runs dry prior to the monsoons. Admission is Rs 1.

Aurangabad Caves

Although they're easily overlooked in favour of the Ajanta and Ellora caves, Aurangabad has its own group of caves a couple of km north of the Bibi-ka-Maqbara. They were carved out of the hillside around the 6th or 7th century AD. The 10 caves are all Buddhist; caves 1 to 5 are in the western group and caves 6 to 10 are about a km away in the eastern group. Other caves further east are little more than natural ones.

Western Group All the caves are viharas, except for cave 4. This is a chaitya with a ridged roof like the Karla Cave near Lonavla and is fronted by a stupa, now partially collapsed. Cave 3 is square and is supported by 12 highly ornate columns. It has an interesting series of sculptures depicting scenes from one of the Jatakas.

Eastern Group Cave 6 is fairly intact and the sculptures of women are notable for their exotic hairdos and ornamentation. There is a large Buddha figure here and Ganesh also makes an appearance. Cave 7 is the most interesting of the Aurangabad caves, particularly (as in the other caves) for the figures and sculptures – the figures of women, scant-

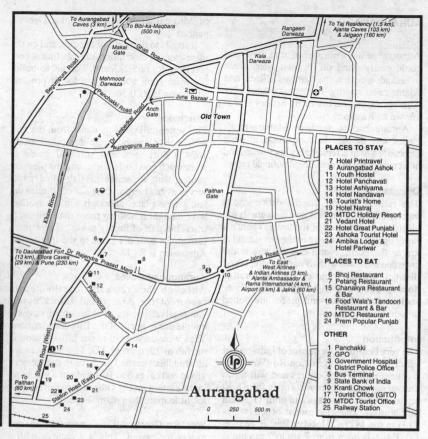

To Aurangabad Caves (3 km)
To Bibi-ka-Maqbara (500 m)
Makai Gate
Ghati Road
Mehmood Darwaza
Panchakki Road
Anch Gate
Begumpura Road
Dr Ambedkar Road
Aurangpura Road
Kham River
Rangeen Darwaza
Kala Darwaza
Juna Bazaar
Old Town
Paithan Gate
To Taj Residency (1.5 km), Ajanta Caves (103 km) & Jalgaon (160 km)
To Daulatabad Fort (13 km), Ellora Caves (29 km) & Pune (230 km)
Dr Rajendra Prasad Marg
Padampura Road
Jalna Road
To East West Airlines & Indian Airlines (3 km), Ajanta Ambassador & Rama International (4 km), Airport (8 km) & Jalna (60 km)
Station Road (West)
Station Road (East)
To Paithan (60 km)

Aurangabad

0   250   500 m

PLACES TO STAY

7   Hotel Printravel
8   Aurangabad Ashok
11 Youth Hostel
12 Hotel Panchavati
13 Hotel Ashiyama
14 Hotel Nandavan
18 Tourist's Home
19 Hotel Natraj
20 MTDC Holiday Resort
21 Vedant Hotel
22 Hotel Great Punjabi
23 Ashoka Tourist Hotel
24 Ambika Lodge & Hotel Pariwar

PLACES TO EAT

6   Bhoj Restaurant
7   Petang Restaurant
15 Chanakya Restaurant & Bar
16 Food Wala's Tandoori Restaurant & Bar
20 MTDC Restaurant
24 Prem Popular Punjab

OTHER

1   Panchakki
2   GPO
3   Government Hospital
4   District Police Office
5   Bus Terminal
9   State Bank of India
10 Kranti Chowk
17 Tourist Office (GITO)
20 MTDC Tourist Office
25 Railway Station

ily clad but ornately bejewelled, are very well done.

To the left of Cave 7 a huge figure of a Bodhisattva prays for deliverance from eight fears which are illustrated as fire, the sword of the enemy, chains, shipwreck, lions, snakes, mad elephants and a demon (representing death).

You can walk up to the caves from the Bibi-ka-Maqbara or take an auto-rickshaw up to the eastern group. From this group you can walk back down the road to the western group and then cut straight back across country to the Bibi-ka-Maqbara. If you take

an auto-rickshaw agree on a price first and make sure it includes waiting time.

Organised Tours

There are various tours from Aurangabad to the Ajanta and Ellora caves, Daulatabad Fort and the sights of Aurangabad but they're rushed affairs.

The MTDC operates a daily tour to the Ajanta Caves for Rs 120 which begins at 8 am and finishes at 5.30 pm, and to the Ellora Caves for Rs 85 which starts at 9.30 am and finishes at 5.30 pm. The Ellora tours include Daulatabad and the sites of Aurangabad (except the Aurangabad Caves) – way too much for one day. The tours start from the MTDC Holiday Resort but also pick up from the major hotels.

The MSRTC also runs special daily 'tourist buses' to Ellora (Rs 43) and Ajanta (Rs 100), both leaving at 8 am from the main bus stand.

Places to Stay – bottom end

There are *retiring . rooms* at the railway station.

Many of Aurangabad's cheaper hotels are close to the railway station. There's another batch of cheapies opposite the bus stand but this is a very noisy area and not recommended.

The excellent *youth hostel* (☎ 29-801) is midway between the bus terminal and the railway station. There are 37 dorm beds at Rs 27 each (Rs 17 for YHA members) and double rooms for Rs 70. There's also one family room for three people at Rs 105. The place is spotlessly clean, it has hot and cold water, and all meals are available. Check-in times are 7 to 11 am and 4 to 8 pm; checkout time is 9 am. There's also a 10 pm curfew. The people who run this place are very amiable.

There's a string of cheap and basic places near the station with double rooms from Rs 50 to Rs 70. They're all of a similar standard and include the *Ambika Lodge* (very run-down and worst of the lot), the *Hotel Pariwar* and the better *Ashoka Tourist Hotel* where rooms go from Rs 75 to Rs 100.

Better value are the two hotels on Station Rd (West). *Hotel Natraj* (☎ 24-260) is a typical Indian boarding house run by two affable old men and has singles/doubles at Rs 60/70 with bathroom. The *Tourist's Home* (☎ 24-212) next door is more of a backpackers' haunt and has basic but very clean rooms all with bathroom. Singles range from Rs 40 to Rs 65, doubles go for Rs 60 to Rs 90. Hot water is available for Rs 2 a bucket.

Next to the youth hostel is the *Hotel Panchavati* (☎ 25-204) which has singles/doubles at Rs 65/100 with attached bath, and hot water in the mornings. It's basic but the

staff are amicable and the hotel has a good restaurant and bar.

Going up in price, the *Hotel Printravel* (☎ 29-707) south of the bus terminal has singles/doubles for Rs 90/160, each with bath and hot water (6 to 9 am). Some also have large terraces and there's a popular restaurant. Also good is the new *Hotel Ashiyama* (☎ 29-322), just off Station Rd (West), which offers clean singles/doubles from Rs 100/150. All the rooms have attached bathrooms and there's constant hot water.

Places to Stay – middle

Heading north along Station Rd (East) there are several good hotels. First up is the new *Hotel Great Punjabi* (☎ 25-598), a huge place with a travel counter and room service (but no restaurant). Singles/doubles cost Rs 175/200, or Rs 300/350 with air-con.

Next up, the MTDC's *Holiday Resort* (☎ 34-259) is set in its own shady grounds and has four-bed rooms with communal bathroom for Rs 175, doubles with bathroom are Rs 200, or Rs 350 with air-con. Mosquito nets are provided and there's a very pleasant garden plus a restaurant and bar.

Lastly there's the *Hotel Nandavan* (☎ 23-311), about one km from the railway station, which is very good value at Rs 137/176 for singles/doubles with attached bathroom and hot water. The hotel has a small terrace restaurant and a bar.

Places to Stay – top end

Cheapest in this range is the two-star *Aurangabad Ashok* (☎ 20-520; fax 313-328), Dr Rajendra Prasad Marg, which has air-con rooms for Rs 800/1100. It's reasonable value and has all the usual amenities including a swimming pool, restaurant (Indian and Continental), bar and currency exchange.

Also in the heart of town is the new Quality Inn *Vedant Hotel* (☎ 33-844) on Station Rd (East). This modern, multistorey hotel has two restaurants, a bar and pool. Singles/doubles cost Rs 1195/1400 including breakfast.

Out near the airport at Chikal Thana there

are two five-star hotels, the *Ajanta Ambassador* (☎ 82-215; fax 84-367) and the *Welcomgroup Rama International* (☎ 84-441; fax 83-468). They both have it all – swimming pool, bar, restaurants and shopping arcades. The Ambassador is the cheaper of the two, with prices starting from Rs 1200/1800.

Better than either of these, especially for value for money, is the gleaming new *Taj Residency* (☎ 20-411), a few km from the town centre on the road to Ajanta. The hotel sweeps around an immaculate garden and swimming pool, and has an entrance almost as grand as the Taj itself. Well-appointed singles/doubles start at Rs 1195/1550.

Places to Eat

There's a string of rock-bottom restaurants along Station Rd (East). None of them stand out as deserving particular mention but the food is usually OK and cheap. The *Prem Popular Punjab* opposite Hotel Great Punjabi must set a record for the number of switches on the panel above the cashier.

More expensive but excellent vegetarian food can be found at *Bhoj*, Dr Ambedkar Rd, a popular 2nd-floor restaurant; its south Indian food is very tasty. The nearby *Petang Restaurant* at Hotel Printravel does a superb Rs 28 thali. You can wash it down with a mild beer (nothing 'strong' is available); this place stays open until quite late.

The MTDC's *Holiday Resort* has a garden which, in the evening, is pleasant for a beer but the food here is average. Further up Station Rd (East), the *Food Wala's Tandoori Restaurant & Bar* offers what its name implies. Meals here are worth the mild splurge. A little further up the road is another splurge tandoori place, the *Chanakya Restaurant & Bar*.

Getting There & Away

The cave groups at Ajanta and Ellora are off the railway lines and are usually approached from either Aurangabad (Ellora 30 km, Ajanta 106 km) or from Jalgaon (Ajanta 60 km). Jalgaon is on the main broad-gauge line from Bombay to Allahabad. Aurangabad is

off the main line, however, there are still direct trains from Bombay or Hyderabad.

Air The airport is about 10 km east of town on the Jalna road. En route you'll find the Indian Airlines office (☎ 24-864) and, almost opposite, the office of East West Airlines (☎ 29-990).

Indian Airlines flies daily (except Monday and Friday) to Bombay (US$34) and onto Udaipur (US$63), Jaipur (US$79) and Delhi (US$99). These flights can be booked up several days in advance. East West has daily flights to Bombay (US$34).

Bus There are ordinary MSRTC buses from Aurangabad to Pune (Rs 100, six hours, 225 km), Nasik (five hours), Indore and Bombay (388 km via Manmad, 400 km via Pune). The MSRTC and MTDC also offer luxury overnight buses to Bombay (Rs 165, 12 hours).

To Ellora & Ajanta Caves Unless you're planning on doing a day tour from Aurangabad to Ajanta, you'll probably find it more convenient to actually stay at Ajanta.

There are local buses to Ellora (Rs 8, every half hour), Ajanta (Rs 30, 2½ hours, four per day), and to Jalgaon (Rs 43, 4½ hours, hourly).

Not all the Aurangabad to Jalgaon buses go up to the end of the turn-off where the Ajanta Caves are situated, so if it's the caves you specifically want and not Fardapur (the nearest village on the main road), make sure you get on the right bus. Otherwise you'll have to walk the four km from the turn-off to the caves.

Train Aurangabad is not on one of the main lines and has only sporadic services. There are two direct trains daily to/from Bombay (375 km) but they're often heavily booked. The 7518 *Tapovan Express* departs at 3.20 pm and costs Rs 88/199 in 2nd/1st class but it gets you into Bombay VT at 11 pm. The overnight 1004 *Devagiri Express* departs from Aurangabad at 7.25 pm and arrives at Bombay at 5 am. It costs Rs 140/430 in 2nd/1st class. Coming from Bombay, the same train leaves at 10.30 pm and arrives at Aurangabad at 7 am.

Alternatively, you can get a bus or a local train to the nearest mainline station, Manmad, 113 km north-west of Aurangabad, from where there are more frequent express trains to Bombay.

When heading directly to the Ajanta Caves from Bombay, it's best to get an express to Jalgaon and then a local bus to the caves, though this is still quite a gruelling days' travel (for details see the Jalgaon section).

To Hyderabad (Secunderabad), the daily *Devagiri Express* departs from Aurangabad

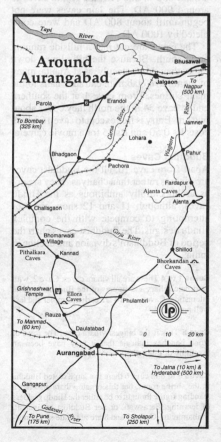

at 7.20 am. The journey takes 14 hours and costs Rs 124/624 in 2nd/1st class.

Getting Around

Almost all the Aurangabad auto-rickshaw-wallahs use their meters so you shouldn't have any problems with overpricing. You can hire a bicycle from stalls near the bus stand and, as the town is not too hilly nor busy, it's quite a good way to get around.

DAULATABAD

Halfway between Aurangabad (13 km) and the Ellora Caves is the magnificent hilltop fortress of Daulatabad. The **fort** is surrounded by five km of sturdy walls, while the central bastion tops a 200-metre-high hill, which was originally known as Devagiri, the Hill of the Gods. In the 14th century it was renamed Daulatabad, the City of Fortune, by Mohammed Tughlaq. This somewhat unbalanced Sultan of Delhi conceived the crazy plan of not only building himself a new capital here, but marching the entire population of Delhi 1100 km south to populate it. His unhappy subjects proceeded to drop dead like flies on this forced march, and 17 years later he turned round and marched them all back to Delhi. The fort remained.

It's worth making the climb to the top for the superb views over the surrounding country. Along the way you'll pass through a complicated and ingenious series of defences, including multiple doorways to prevent elephant charges, and spike-studded doors just in case. A magnificent tower of victory, the **Chand Minar**, built in 1435, soars 60 metres high. The Qutab Minar in Delhi, five metres higher, is the only loftier victory tower in India. On the other side of the entrance path is a mosque built from the remains of a Jain temple.

Higher up is the blue-tiled **Chini Mahal** where the last king of Golconda was imprisoned for 13 years until his death. Finally you climb the central fort to a huge six-metre **cannon**, cast from five different metals and engraved with Aurangzeb's name. The final ascent to the top goes through a pitch black, spiralling tunnel down which the fort's defenders could hurl burning coals at any invaders. Of course, your guide may tell you, the fort was once successfully conquered despite these elaborate precautions – by the simple expedient of bribing the guard at the gate.

If you take one of the MTDC bus tours to Daulatabad and Ellora you won't have time to climb to the summit.

RAUZA

Also known as Khuldabad, the Heavenly Abode, this walled town is only three km from Ellora. It is the Karbala or holy shrine of Deccan Muslims. A number of historical figures are buried here, including Aurangzeb, the last great Mughal emperor. Aurangzeb built the crenellated wall around the town, which was once an important centre although today it is little more than a sleepy village.

The emperor's final resting place is a simple affair of bare earth in a courtyard of the **Alamgir Dargah** at the centre of the town. Aurangzeb's pious austerity extended even to his own tomb, for he stipulated that his mausoleum should be paid for with money he earned himself by copying out the Koran. Within the building there is also supposed to be a robe worn by the Prophet Mohammed; it is only shown to the faithful once each year. Another shrine across the road from the Alamgir Dargah is said to contain hairs of the Prophet's beard and lumps of silver from a tree of solid silver, which miraculously grew at this site after a saint's death.

ELLORA CAVES

The caves of Ellora are about 30 km from Aurangabad. Whereas the Ajanta Caves are noted for their paintings, here it's the sculpture that is remarkable. The *pièce de résistance* is the Kailasa Temple (cave 16) which, for three days in March, is the venue of the annual Ellora Dance & Music Festival.

Chronologically, the Ellora Caves start where the Ajanta Caves finish – it's thought that the builders of Ajanta moved to here when they suddenly ceased construction at

their earlier site. The Ellora Caves are not all Buddhist like those of Ajanta; the earliest are, but during this time Buddhism was declining in India and a later series of Hindu and Jain cave temples were added.

In all there are 34 caves at Ellora: 12 Buddhist, 17 Hindu and five Jain. Although the temples are numbered consecutively and the various religious groups do not overlap, the caves are not arranged chronologically. It is thought that construction of the Hindu caves commenced before the Buddhist caves were completed, for example. Roughly, the Buddhist caves are thought to date from around 600 to 800 AD, the Hindu caves to around 900 AD. The Jain caves were not begun until about 800 AD and were completed by 1000 AD.

The caves are cut into a hillside running north-south. Because the hill slopes down rather than drops steeply, as at Ajanta, many of them have elaborate entrance halls to the main shrines. From cave 1 at the southern end to cave 34 in the north they cover about two km. Entry is free except to cave 16 which costs Rs 0.50 and Rs 25 for a movie camera.

Buddhist Caves

Apart from cave 10, all the Buddhist caves are viharas rather than chaityas. They are not as architecturally ambitious as the Hindu caves, although 11 and 12 show signs of attempting to compete with the complex Hindu designs. The Buddhist caves chart the period of Buddhism's division and decline in India.

Caves 1 to 4 These are all vihara caves. Cave 2, with its ornate pillars and figures of the Buddha, is quite interesting. Caves 3 and 4 are earlier, simpler and less well preserved.

Cave 5 This is the biggest vihara cave. The rows of stone benches indicate that it may have been an assembly or dining hall.

Caves 6 to 8 In cave 6 there is a large seated Buddha in the shrine room, but this ornate vihara also has a standing figure thought to be either the Hindu goddess of learning, Saraswati, or her Buddhist equivalent, Mahamayuri. Caves 7 and 8 are not quite so interesting.

Cave 10 The Viswakarma or Carpenter's Cave is the only chaitya cave in the Buddhist group. It takes its name from the ribs carved into the roof, in imitation of wooden beams. The temple is entered by steps to a courtyard, followed by further steps to the main temple. A finely carved horseshoe window lets light in and a huge seated Buddha figure fronts the nine-metre-high stupa.

Cave 11 The Do Thal (Two-Storey) Cave is also entered by a courtyard. Curiously, it actually has three storeys but the third was not discovered until 1876. Construction of the middle floor was never completed.

Cave 12 The Teen Thal (Three-Storey) Cave is entered through a courtyard. It contains a very large seated Buddha and a number of other figures. The walls are carved with relief pictures, as in the Hindu caves.

Hindu Caves

The Hindu caves are the most dramatic and impressive of the Ellora cave temples. In size, design and energy they are in a totally different league from the Buddhist or Jain caves. If calm contemplation describes the Buddhist caves, then dynamic energy is the description for the Hindu caves. The sheer size of the Kailasa Temple is overwhelming. It covers twice the area of the Parthenon in Athens and is 1½ times as high. Remember that this whole gigantic structure was cut out of solid rock. It has been estimated that carving out the Kailasa entailed removing 200,000 tonnes of rock! It is, without doubt, one of the wonders of the world.

All these temples were cut from the top down, so that it was never necessary to use any scaffolding – their builders started with the roof and moved down to the floor. It's worth contemplating the skill and planning that must have gone into such a process – there was no way of adding a panel or a pillar if things didn't work out as expected.

Cave 14 The first Hindu cave, cave 13, is not impressive, but cave 14, the Rava Kakhai, sets the scene for the others. Like them it is dedicated to Siva, who appears in many of the carvings. You can see Siva dancing the Tandava, a victory dance over the demon Mahisa, or playing chess with his wife Parvati, or defeating the buffalo demon. Parvati also appears in the form of Durga. Vishnu makes several appearances

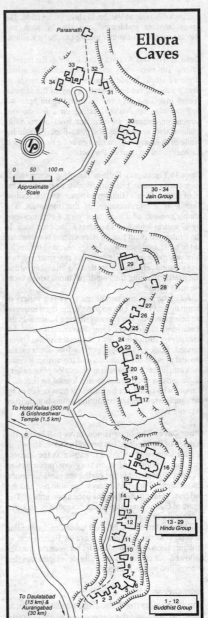

Ellora Caves

Parasnath

30 - 34
Jain Group

13 - 29
Hindu Group

To Hotel Kailas (500 m)
& Grishneshwar
Temple (1.5 km)

1 - 12
Buddhist Group

To Daulatabad
(15 km) &
Aurangabad
(30 km)

0   50   100 m

Approximate
Scale

MAHARASHTRA

too, including one as Varaha, his boar incarnation. The seven 'mother goddesses' can also be seen, and Ravana makes yet another attempt to shake Kailasa.

Cave 15 The Das Avatara Cave is one of the finest at Ellora. The two-storey temple is reached by a long flight of steps. Inside there is a modern image of Siva's vehicle, the bull Nandi. Many of the familiar scenes involving Siva can be found again here, but you can also see Vishnu resting on a five-hooded serpent or rescuing an elephant from a crocodile. Vishnu also appears as the man-lion, Narasimha, while Siva emerges from his symbolic lingam and in another panel he marries Parvati.

Cave 16 The mighty Kailasa Temple is where Indian rock-cut temple architecture reaches its peak. Kailasa is, of course, Siva's Himalayan home, and the Kailasa Temple is a representation of that mountain. The temple consists of a huge courtyard, 81 metres long by 47 metres wide and 33 metres high at the back. In the centre, the main temple rises up and is connected to the outer enclosure by a bridge. Around the enclosure are galleries, while towards the front are two large stone elephants with two massive stone 'flagstaffs' flanking the Nandi pavilion, which faces the main shrine.

As in the previous two caves, there is a variety of dramatic and finely carved panels, the most impressive being the image of Ravana shaking Kailasa. In the *Ramayana* the demon king Ravana flaunted his strength by lifting up Siva's mountain home. Unimpressed, Lord Siva simply put his foot down on the top and pressed the mountain and the upstart Ravana back into place. Vishnu also appears along one gallery as Narasimha once again; in this legend he defeats a demon, who could not be killed by man or beast, by the simple expedient of becoming a man-lion, neither man nor beast.

Other Caves The other Hindu caves pall beside the majesty of the Kailasa, but several of them are worth at least some study. Cave 21, known as the Rames-vara, has a number of interesting interpretations of scenes also depicted in the earlier temples. Siva once again marries Parvati and plays dice with her, and the goddesses Ganga and Yamuna once again appear. The figure of Ganga, standing on her crocodile or *makara*, is particularly notable.

The very large cave 29, the Dumar Lena, is similar in design to the Elephanta Cave at Bombay. It is thought to be a transitional model between the simpler hollowed-out caves and the fully developed temples exemplified by the Kailasa.

Jain Caves

The Jain caves mark the final phase of Ellora. They do not have the drama and high-voltage energy of the best Hindu temples nor are they as ambitious in size, but they balance this with their exceptionally detailed work. There are only five Jain temples, and they're one km north of the last Hindu temple (cave 29) at the end of the bitumen road.

Cave 30 The Chota Kailasa or Little Kailasa is a poor imitation of the great Kailasa Temple and was never completed. It stands by itself some distance from the other Jain temples, which are all clustered closely together.

Cave 32 The Indra Sabha (Assembly Hall of Indra) is the finest of the Jain temples. The ground-floor plan is similar to that of the Kailasa, but the upstairs area, reached by a stairway, is as ornate and richly decorated as downstairs is plain. There are images of the Jain tirthankars Parasnath and Gomateshvara, the latter surrounded by vegetation and wildlife. Inside the shrine is a seated figure of Mahavira, the 24th and last tirthankar, and founder of the Jain religion. Traces of paintings can still be seen on the roof of the temple.

Other Caves Cave 31 is really an extension of 32. Cave 33, the Jagannath Sabha, is similar in plan to 32 and has some particularly well-preserved sculptures. The final temple, the small cave 34, also has interesting sculptures. On the hilltop over the Jain temples a five-metre-high image of Parasnath looks down on Ellora. An enclosure was built around it a couple of hundred years ago.

Grishneshwar

Close to the Ellora Caves in the village of Verul, this 18th-century Siva temple has one of the 12 *jyoti lingams* (important shrines to Siva) in India, so it's an important place of pilgrimage for Hindus.

Places to Stay & Eat

The only place to stay in Ellora is the very pleasant *Hotel Kailas* (☎ (02347) 41063) close to the caves which offers a variety of accommodation. Attractive rooms with attached bath in individual cottages range from Rs 300 to Rs 700. The more expensive rooms have air-con and a view of the caves. There's also a cheaper section called Natraj which is simply a block of four basic double rooms. They all have a fan and bath and cost Rs 100 each. The restaurant at the hotel has both Indian and Chinese fare between Rs 25 and Rs 50, and is cheaper than the MTDC'S nearby restaurant which is intended for tour groups. On the road you'll also find a few little food stalls such as *Milan* and *Modern*.

Getting There & Away
See the Aurangabad section for details.

AJANTA CAVES
The Buddhist caves of Ajanta predate those of Ellora, so if you want to see the caves in chronological order you should visit these first. Unlike the Ellora Caves, which are easily visited using Aurangabad as a base, it's much easier to stay near the Ajanta Caves rather than make a day trip to them. And, whereas the Ellora Caves are masterpieces of sculpture, at Ajanta it's the magnificent paintings for which the caves are famous.

After their abandonment with the move to Ellora and the decline of Buddhism, the Ajanta Caves were gradually forgotten and their rediscovery was dramatic. In 1819 a British hunting party stumbled upon them, and their remote beauty was soon unveiled. Their isolation had contributed to the fine state of preservation in which some of the paintings remain to this day. The 29 caves are cut into the steep face of a deep rock gorge in the Waghore River. From the opposite side of the ravine there's a fine view of the caves. They date from around 200 BC to 650 AD and do not follow a chronological order; the oldest are mainly in the middle and the newer ones are close to each end.

Five of the caves are chaityas while the other 24 are viharas. Caves 8, 9, 10, 12 and 13 are the older Hinayana caves, while the others are Mahayana. In the simpler, more austere Hinayana school the Buddha was never represented directly – his presence was always alluded to by a symbol such as the footprint or wheel of law.

Although the Ajanta paintings are particularly notable, there are many interesting sculptures here as well. Many of the caves are dark, and without a light the paintings are hard to see – it's worth paying for a lighting ticket which will ensure that the cave guards turn the lights on for you. Or you could try

tagging along with a tour party, although normally the doors are shut after each party enters a cave.

The caves are open daily from 9 am to 5.30 pm. Entry costs Rs 0.50 plus Rs 5 for the lighting fee.

If at all possible, avoid coming here at weekends or on public holidays when Ajanta seems to attract half the population of India. The Calcutta rush hour has nothing on this place at those times – hardly the contemplative atmosphere which its monks and builders had in mind!

Cave 1
This vihara cave is one of the most recent and also most fully developed of the Ajanta Caves. A verandah at the front leads to a large square hall which has elaborate sculptures and paintings and a huge Buddha statue.

Amongst the interesting sculptures is one of four deer sharing a common head. There are many paintings of women, some remarkably similar to the paintings at Sigiriya in Sri Lanka. Notable paintings include those of the 'black princess' and the 'dying princess'. Other paintings include scenes from the Jatakas, and portraits of the Bodhisattvas (near-Buddhas) Padmapani (holding a lotus flower) and Vajrapani.

Cave 2
Also a more recent vihara cave, this one has important paintings too, although unfortunately some are damaged. As well as murals, there are paintings on the ceiling. The scenes include a number of Jatakas and events connected with the Buddha's birth, including his mother's dream of the six-tusked elephant which heralded the Buddha's conception.

Cave 4
This is the largest vihara cave at Ajanta and is supported by 28 pillars. Although it was never completed, the cave has some fine sculptures, including scenes of people fleeing from the 'eight great dangers' to the protection of the Buddha's disciple Avalokitesvara. One of the great dangers is an angry-looking elephant in pursuit of a man and woman. Caves 3 and 5 were never completed.

Cave 6
This vihara cave is the only two-storey one at Ajanta, but parts of the lower storey have collapsed. Inside is a seated Buddha figure with an intricately carved door to the shrine. Upstairs the hall is surrounded by cells with fine paintings on the doorways.

Caves 7 & 8

Cave 7 is of unusual design in that the verandah does not lead into a hall with cells down the sides and a shrine room at the rear. Here there are porches before the verandah, which leads directly to the four cells and the elaborately sculpted shrine. Cave 8 was never finished and now houses the generating equipment that lights the caves.

Cave 9

This is a chaitya cave and one of the earliest at Ajanta. Although it dates from the Hinayana period, two Buddha figures flanking the entrance door were probably later Mahayana additions. Similarly, the paintings inside, which are not in excellent condition, show signs of having been refurbished. Columns run down both sides of the cave and around the three-metre-high dagoba at the far end. At the front there is a horseshoe-shaped window above the entrance, and the vaulted roof has traces of wooden ribs.

Cave 10

This is thought to be the oldest cave and was the one first spotted by the British soldiers who rediscovered Ajanta. It is the largest chaitya cave and is similar in design to cave 9. The facade has collapsed and the paintings inside have been damaged, in some cases by graffiti dating from soon after the caves' rediscovery.

Caves 11 to 14

Caves 11, 12 and 13 are not of great interest – they are all relatively early, either Hinayana or early

Mahayana. Cave 14 is an uncompleted vihara, standing above cave 13, which is an early Mahayana vihara.

Cave 16

Some of Ajanta's finest paintings can be seen in this, one of the later vihara caves. It is thought that cave 16 may have been the original entrance to the entire complex, and there is a very fine view of the river from the front of the cave. Best known of the paintings here is the 'dying princess'. Sundari, wife of the Buddha's half-brother Nanda, is said to have expired at the hard news that her husband was renouncing the material life (and her) in order to become a monk. This is one of the finest paintings at Ajanta. Nanda features in several other paintings, including one of his conversion by the Buddha.

Cave 17

This is the cave with the finest paintings at Ajanta. Not only are they in the best condition, they are also the most numerous and varied. They include beautiful women flying overhead on the roof while carved dwarfs support the pillars. A popular scene shows a woman, surrounded by attendants, applying make-up. In one there is a royal procession, while in another a couple engage in a little private lovemaking. In yet another panel the Buddha returns from his enlightenment to his own home to beg from his wife and astonished son.

A detailed panel tells the story of Prince Simhala's expedition to Sri Lanka. With his 500 companions he is shipwrecked on an island where ogresses appear as

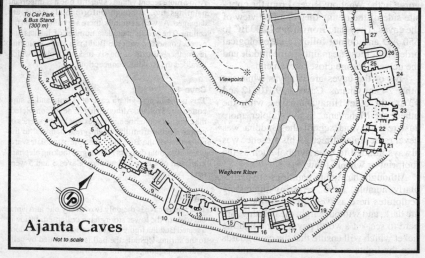

Ajanta Caves

Not to scale

To Car Park & Bus Stand (300 m)

Viewpoint

Waghore River

beautiful women, only to seize and devour their victims. Simhala escapes on a flying horse and returns to conquer the island.

Cave 19

The facade of this chaitya cave is remarkably detailed and includes an impressive horseshoe-shaped window as its dominant feature. Two very fine standing Buddha figures flank the entrance. Inside this excellent specimen of a chaitya cave is a tall dagoba with a figure of the Buddha on the front.

There are also some fine sculptures and paintings, but one of the most important is outside the cave to the west, where there is an image of the Naga king with seven cobra hoods arrayed around his head. His wife, hooded by a single cobra, is seated beside him.

Caves 20 to 25

These caves are either incomplete or not of great interest, although cave 24 would have been the largest vihara at Ajanta, if finished. You can see how the caves were constructed from this example – long galleries were cut into the rock, and then the rock between them was broken through.

Cave 26

The fourth chaitya cave's facade has fallen and almost every trace of its paintings has disappeared. Nevertheless there are some very fine sculptures remaining. On the left wall is a huge figure of the 'reclining Buddha', lying back as he prepares to enter nirvana. Other scenes include a lengthy depiction of the Buddha's temptation by Mara. In one scene Mara attacks the Buddha with demons, and then his beautiful daughters tempt him with more sensual delights. However, the Buddha's resistance is too strong, and the final scene shows a glum and dejected-looking Mara having failed to deflect the Buddha from the straight and narrow.

Caves 27 to 29

Cave 27 is virtually a vihara connected to the cave 26 chaitya. There's a great pond in a box canyon 200 metres upstream from the cave. Caves 28 and 29 are higher up the cliff face and relatively hard to get to.

Places to Stay & Eat

The five-roomed MTDC *Travellers' Lodge* (☎ 426) is right by the entrance to the caves. The rooms cost Rs 100/150 and share common bathroom facilities. Checkout time is 9 am. The restaurant here is half-decent and the food reasonably good.

Fifth-century Sri Lankan paintings are of similar style to those in Ajanta

Most people stay at Fardapur, five km from the caves, where there is the good MTDC *Holiday Resort* (☎ (026353) 430). Large, clean rooms along a pleasant verandah cost Rs 200/325 for a single/double with hot shower. Each room has two beds, clean sheets and a fan. You can also sleep in a dorm bed here for Rs 15. The attached *Vihara Restaurant* has thalis and non-veg food but it's all very ordinary. There are also cold beers. If you intend dining in the evening, it's wise to let them know in advance or they might close up early.

The only other place in Fardapur is the *Hotel Kanhayyakuni* about 700 metres from the Holiday Resort on the way to the caves. It has 12 very basic rooms built around an overgrown courtyard. Singles/doubles with attached bathroom and bucket showers cost Rs 40/95. The veg restaurant here has a classic misspelt menu, the most notable items being 'Tarkish' and 'Rashian' salads. In 'all, this is one of those places on the downhill path to Indian hotel oblivion.

There are a number of shacks along the main road where you can have *chai* and snacks but nothing that you could vaguely call a meal.

MAHARASHT

Getting There & Away

For information on buses from Aurangabad or Jalgaon, see those sections.

The caves are four km off the main Aurangabad to Jalgaon road, and Fardapur is one km further down the main road towards Jalgaon. There are regular buses between Fardapur and the Ajanta Caves which cost Rs 2.50. Not all buses travelling along the main road call at the caves – make sure you get on the right one otherwise you'll have to walk the four km.

There's a 'cloakroom' at the Ajanta Caves where you can leave gear, so it is possible to arrive on a morning bus from Jalgaon, look around the caves, and continue to Aurangabad in the evening, or vice versa.

JALGAON

Telephone Area Code: 0257

Jalgaon is on the main railway line from Bombay to the country's north-east. It can make a convenient overnight stop en route to the Ajanta caves, 60 km to the south.

Places to Stay

The *PWD Rest House* (☎ 29-702), just behind the Hotel Tourist Resort, has rooms for Rs 75 per person but it's often full. The three railway *retiring rooms* are good value at Rs 50/150 per person without/with air-con.

A good choice is the *Hotel Plaza Station* (☎ 24-854), about 100 metres up from the railway station on the left-hand side. It has spotless singles/doubles with white tiled floors, attached bath and TV for Rs 100/125.

The *Hotel Morako* (☎ 26-621) and the nearby friendly *Hotel Tourist Resort* (☎ 25-192) are further up the same road and then to the right at Nehru Chowk, in all about 300 metres from the railway station. Both these places have singles/doubles for about Rs 125/150 and deluxe rooms for Rs 210/230, and both have a restaurant.

Getting There & Away

Several trains between Bombay and Delhi or Calcutta stop briefly in Jalgaon. The trip to Bombay (eight hours, 420 km) costs Rs 113/338 in 2nd/1st class.

From Jalgaon there are frequent buses to Fardapur (Rs 15, 1½ hours), some of which go on to the Ajanta Caves and then continue to Aurangabad. The bus stand in Jalgaon is a long way from the railway station so you'll need to take a tonga or auto-rickshaw between the two.

LONAR METEORITE CRATER

At the small village of Lonar, three hours by bus north-east of Jalna or 4½ hours south-east of Ajanta, is this huge and impressive meteorite crater. Believed to be about 40,000 years old, it's two km in diameter and several hundred metres deep, with a shallow lake at the bottom. A plaque on the rim near the town states that this is 'the only natural hyper-velocity impact crater in basaltic rock in the world'.

There are several **Hindu temples** on the crater floor, and langur monkeys, peacocks and gazelles inhabit the bushes by the lake. The crater is only about five minutes' walk from the bus stand – ask for Lonar Tank.

It's possible to visit Lonar in a day en route between Fardapur and Aurangabad, but this would be rushing things.

There is a basic hotel by the bus stand in Lonar, and others in Buldhana, three hours to the north. The *MTDC Hotel* at the rim of the crater, about one km from the village, has two 'suites' for Rs 100.

From Lonar there are buses to Buldhana from where it's easy to catch a bus for the bumpy 1½-hour journey to Fardapur. Heading south from Lonar there are direct buses to Jalna, from where there are trains and buses to Aurangabad, a total of about five hours.

AKOLA & AMRAOTI

These two towns are between Jalgaon and Nagpur. Amraoti (Amravati) has the biggest cotton market in India and is the site of the old Amba temple near the walled city. The town has a famous sports college which has old-fashioned wrestling pits.

Either town can also make a good starting

point to get to the **Melghat Wildlife Sanctuary**, Maharashtra's only real tiger reserve (sightings very rare), and the little visited hill station of **Chikalda** (Chikhaldara), both in the lush Gawilgarh Hills about 100 km to the north near the border with Madhya Pradesh.

At Akola, the *Hotel Rama Krisha* (☎ 26-607) at Tower Chowk has singles/doubles from Rs 75/200 plus an air-con restaurant and a good snack bar. Across the vacant block is the cheaper *Hotel Neeta*. In Amraoti, try the *Maharaja Guest House*.

NAGPUR

Population: 1.0 million
Telephone Area Code: 0712

Situated on the River Nag, from which the town takes its name, Nagpur is the orange-growing capital of India. It was once the capital of the central province, but was later incorporated into Maharashtra. Long ago it was a centre for the aboriginal Gond tribes who remained in power until the early 18th century. Many Gonds still live in this region. Later it went through a series of changes before eventually falling to the British.

On 18 October each year the town is host to many Buddhists who come to celebrate the anniversary of Dr Ambedkar's conversion to Buddhism in 1956. Dr Ambedkar, a low-caste Hindu, was an important figure during the fight for independence, and was Law Minister and leader of the Scheduled castes. An estimated 200,000 low-caste Hindus followed him in converting to Buddhism.

Places to Stay

Among the centrally located cheaper places is the *Hotel Shyam* (☎ 52-4073) on Pandit Malaviya Rd, with rooms at Rs 120/180. The hotel has a good rooftop restaurant with a multi-cuisine menu and a bar. Similar is the *Hotel Jagsons* (☎ 48-611), 30 Back Central Ave, which has a variety of rooms including some with air-con, and there's a restaurant and bar. All the rooms have a TV. Cheaper, as far as rooms without air-con are concerned, is the *Hotel Blue Diamond* (☎ 72-7461) at 113 Dosar Chowk near Cent-

ral Ave, which has rooms for Rs 55/90 to Rs 80/140, or Rs 180/250 with air-con. It's close to the railway station and has a restaurant and bar.

More expensive is the *Rawell Continental* (☎ 52-3845), 7 Dhantoli, Wardha Rd, which is centrally air-con and has rooms for Rs 450/600 and suites for Rs 750.

The *Hotel Centre Point* (☎ 52-3093; fax 52-3093), 24 Central Bazaar Rd, Ramdaspeth, is about four km from the railway station. It has air-con rooms at Rs 425 for singles, Rs 650 to Rs 800 for doubles, and from Rs 900 for suites. There's a swimming pool, restaurant and bar. The city's top hotel, the new *Jagsons Regency* (☎ 52-8111; fax 52-4524), opposite the airport, is slightly more expensive.

Getting There & Away

Indian Airlines (☎ 53-3962) flies daily to Bombay (US$73) and three times a week to Hyderabad (US$61). East West Airlines also flies daily (except Sunday) to Bombay (US$68).

Nagpur Junction railway station and the main MSRTC bus terminal are roughly two km apart. Buses for Madhya Pradesh operate from a stand less than a km due south of the railway station. There are trains to Bangalore, Bombay, Calcutta, Delhi and Hyderabad, among other places.

RAMTEK

About 40 km north-east of Nagpur, Ramtek has a number of picturesque 600-year-old **temples** surmounting the Hill of Rama. In summer this is one of the hottest places in India. The old British cantonment of Kemtee is nearby, and a **memorial** to the Sanskrit dramatist Kalidasa is just along the road from the tourist bungalow, which has a spectacular view of the town.

SEVAGRAM

About 76 km south-west of Nagpur and eight km from Wardha station, is Sevagram, the Village of Service, where Gandhi established his ashram in 1933. For the 15 years from

MAHARASHTRA

then until India achieved independence, this was in some ways the alternative capital of India.

The Centre of Science for Villages (Magan Sangrahalaya) is a **museum** intended to explain and develop Gandhi's ideals of village-level economics. The huts of his ashram are still preserved in Sevagram and there is a photo exhibit of events in the Mahatma's life at Mahadev Bhavan, beside the Sevagram hospital.

Only three km from Sevagram is the **ashram of Vinoba Bhave**, Gandhi's follower who walked throughout India persuading rich landlords to hand over tracts of land for redistribution to the landless and poor.

NAVAGAON NATIONAL PARK

This wildlife sanctuary, about 140 km east of Nagpur, is home to small numbers of tiger, leopard, sloth bear and a variety of other animals. It's largely deciduous forest with dense bamboo groves in between hilly terrain. The **Salim Ali Bird Sanctuary** has been established around a lake within the park and, in winter, many migratory birds nest here. In summer the lake is a motorboat playground!

Accommodation in the park is available at the MTDC's attractive 'tree-top' retreats as well as in cottages and dorms. The Forestry Department also maintains basic lodges.

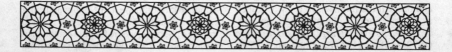

Goa

The former Portuguese enclave of Goa, one of India's gems, has enjoyed a prominent place in the travellers' lexicon for many years. The main reason for this is its magnificent palm-fringed beaches and renowned 'travellers' scene'. Yet it offers much more than just the hedonism of sun, sand and sea. Goa has a character quite distinct from the rest of India. Despite more than three decades of 'liberation' from Portuguese colonial rule, Roman Catholicism remains a major religion in Goa, skirts far outnumber saris, and the people display an easy-going tropical indulgence, humour and civility which you'll find hard to beat, even in Kerala.

Gleaming, whitewashed churches with Portuguese-style facades pepper the hillsides. There are paddy fields, dense coconut palm groves, and crumbling forts guarding rocky capes and estuaries. Markets are lively, colourful affairs, and siesta is widely observed during the hot afternoon hours. Carnival explodes onto the streets for four riotous days and nights prior to Lent. Not only that, but there seems to be a total lack of the excessive shyness which Hindu women display towards men, and there are very good reasons for that. One of them relates to the Goan property laws which ensure that a married woman is entitled to 50% of the couple's estate – a far cry from what applies in the rest of India.

Goa has one of the highest literacy rates,

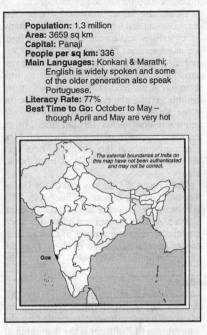

Population: 1.3 million
Area: 3659 sq km
Capital: Panaji
People per sq km: 336
Main Languages: Konkani & Marathi; English is widely spoken and some of the older generation also speak Portuguese.
Literacy Rate: 77%
Best Time to Go: October to May – though April and May are very hot

The external boundaries of India on this map have not been authenticated and may not be correct.

Goa

and boasts the third-highest GNP, in the country. Farming, fishing, tourism and iron-ore mining form the basis of the economy, although the latter two sources of income are sometimes incompatible with the former.

Water Conservation

Take great care to use water as sparingly as possible because Goa's supplies are severely limited. Tourism in general has placed a heavy strain on the state's water resources, but the upmarket hotels carry most of the blame. In some areas, guests languish beside Olympic-sized swimming pools while just outside the gates the water supply to the locals is limited to a few hours a day. Some of the bigger hotels have drilled deep tube wells to syphon off their own supplies, but the effect has been to lower the water table in the area. Wells have dried up in some villages and been polluted with salt water in others.

Don't leave taps running. Even if your hotel has a bathtub in the bathroom, use the shower instead, or, best of all, use a bucket of water. If you're selecting a package tour or choosing an upmarket hotel to stay at, consider whether you want to condone the use of a swimming pool in such circumstances. Who needs a pool anyway when the Arabian Sea is just a short walk away? ∎

Mining has caused damage to paddy fields, and the five-star tourist resorts, with their swimming pools, have placed a heavy strain on water supplies needed by farmers.

Goans are better informed about their environment and what threatens it than many other Indians, and are more prepared to fight for its protection. The Konkan Railway Corporation, currently constructing a major railway line along the west coast to link Bombay with Mangalore, has had more trouble getting planning permission for the route through the tiny state of Goa than anywhere else on the 760-km line. For an excellent overview of the current state of the Goan environment, buy a copy of *Fish Curry & Rice* (Rs 200), available at most bookshops.

Until recently, Goa was part of the Union Territory of Goa, Daman & Diu, but in 1987 it became the 25th state of the Indian Union. Daman & Diu remain a Union Territory, despite having the governor of Goa as lieutenant governor, and are dealt with in the Gujarat chapter of this book.

History

Goa's history stretches back to the 3rd century BC when it formed part of the Mauryan Empire. It was later ruled by the Satavahanas of Kolhapur at the beginning of the Christian era and eventually passed to the Chalukyans of Badami, who controlled it from 580 to 750 AD. Over the next few centuries it was ruled successively by the Shilharas, the Kadambas and the Chalukyans of Kalyani.

Goa fell to the Muslims for the first time in 1312, but the invaders were forced to evacuate it in 1370 by Harihara I of the Vijayanagar Empire, whose capital was at Hampi in present-day Karnataka state. The Vijayanagar rulers held on to Goa for nearly 100 years, and its harbours became important landing places for ships carrying Arabian horses to Hampi to strengthen the Vijayanagar cavalry.

In 1469, Goa was conquered by the Bahmani Sultans of Gulbarga. When this dynasty broke up, the area passed to the Adil Shahis of Bijapur, who made Goa Velha their second capital. The present Secretariat building in Panaji is the former palace of Adil Shah, and it was later taken over by the Portuguese viceroys as their official residence.

The Portuguese arrived in Goa in 1510 under the command of Alfonso de Albuquerque. They had unsuccessfully tried to establish a base further south, but were opposed by the Zamorin of Calicut and faced stiff competition from the Turks, who controlled the trade routes across the Indian Ocean at the time.

Blessed as it is by natural harbours and wide rivers, Goa was the ideal base for the seafaring Portuguese, who were intent on controlling the spice route from the East. They were also possessed with the strong desire to spread Christianity. Jesuit missionaries led by St Francis Xavier arrived in 1542. For a while, Portuguese control was limited to a small area around Old Goa, but by the middle of the 16th century it had expanded to include the provinces of Bardez and Salcete.

The eventual ousting of the Turks and the fortunes made from the spice trade led to Goa's golden age. The colony became the viceregal seat of the Portuguese Empire of the east, which included various East African port cities, East Timor and Macau. Decline set in, however, due to competition from the British, French and Dutch in the 17th century, combined with Portugal's inability to adequately service its far-flung empire.

Goa reached its present size in the 18th century after a series of annexations. In 1763, the provinces of Ponda, Sanguem, Quepem and Canacona were added, followed by Pednem, Bicholim and Satari in 1788.

The Marathas nearly vanquished the Portuguese in the late 18th century and there was a brief occupation by the British during the Napoleonic Wars in Europe. But it was not until 1961, when they were ejected by India, that the Portuguese finally disappeared from the subcontinent. The enclaves of Daman and Diu were also taken over at the same time.

GOA

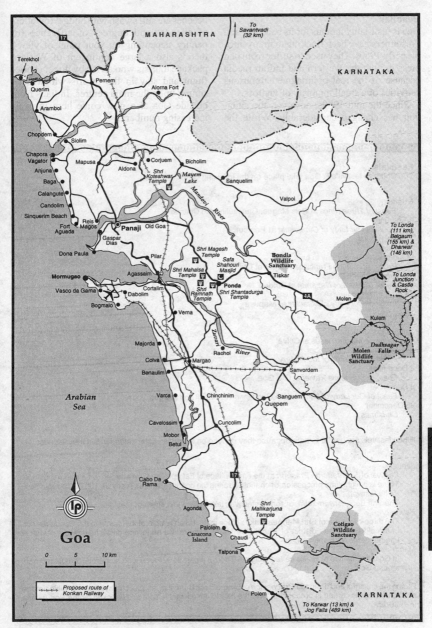

MAHARASHTRA

To Savantvadi
(32 km)

KARNATAKA

17

Terekhol
Querim
Arambol
Pernem
Alorna Fort
Chopdem
Siolim
Corjuem
Bicholim
Chapora
Vagator
Mapusa
Aldona
Shri
Koteshwar
Temple
Mayem
Lake
Banquelim
Anjuna
Baga
Calangute
Candolim
Sinquerim Beach
Fort
Aguada
Reis
Magos
Panaji
Old Goa
Valpoli
To Londa
(111 km),
Belgaum
(155 km) &
Dharwar
(146 km)
Gaspar
Dias
Dona Paula
Pilar
Shri Magesh
Temple
Safa
Shahouri
Masjid
**Bondla
Wildlife
Sanctuary**
Tiskar
To Londa
Junction
& Castle
Rock
Shri Mahalsa
Temple
Shri
Ramnath
Temple
Ponda
Shri Shantadurga
Temple
4A
Molen
Mormugao
Agassaim
Cortalim
Vasco da Gama
Dabolim
Bogmalo
Verna
Kulem
*Dudhsagar
Falls*
**Molen
Wildlife
Sanctuary**
Majorda
Colva
Benaulim
Margao
Rachol
River
Sanvordem
Varca
Chinchinim
Sanguem
Quepem
*Arabian
Sea*
Cavelossim
Mobor
Betul
Cuncolim
Cabo Da
Rama
17
Agonda
Shri
Mallikarjuna
Temple
Palolem
Canacona
Island
Chaudi
*Cotigao
Wildlife
Sanctuary*
Talpona

Goa

0   5   10 km

Polem

KARNATAKA

To Karwar (13 km) &
Jog Falls (489 km)

Proposed route of
Konkan Railway

GOA

Mandovi River
Zuari River

Beaches

Goa is justifiably famous for its beaches, and Westerners have been flocking to them since the early 1960s. They used to suffer from bad press in both the Western and Indian media because of the real or imagined nefarious activities of a small minority of visitors.

Since the mid-1980s, however, the situation has changed considerably. While the beaches are still awash with budget travellers of all ages and degrees of affluence (or penury, depending on your point of view), there's also a large contingent of Western package tourists who arrive by direct charter flight and stay in the resorts which have sprung up in the main centres. Indians from outside Goa also now come here in ever-increasing numbers.

Festivals

The Christian festivals in Goa take place on the following dates:

6 January
  Feast of Three Kings at Reis Magos, Cansaulim and Chandor
2 February
  Feast of Our Lady of Candelaria at Pomburpa
February/March
  Carnival
Monday after 5th Sunday in Lent
  Procession of the Franciscan Order at Old Goa
1st Sunday after Easter
  Feast of Jesus of Nazareth at Siridao
16 days after Easter
  Feast of Our Lady of Miracles at Mapusa
24 August
  Festival of Novidades
1st fortnight of October
  Fama de Menino Jesus at Colva
3rd Wednesday of November
  Feast of Our Lady of the Rosary
3 December
  Feast of St Francis Xavier at Old Goa
8 December
  Feast of Our Lady of Immaculate Conception at Panaji and Margao
25 December
  Christmas

Hindu festivals are harder to date because they depend on the Indian lunar calendar, but they include:

January
  Festival of Shantadurga Prasann at the small village of Fatorpa, south of Margao in Quepem province. There is a night-time procession of chariots bearing the goddess, and as many as 100,000 people flock to the festival.
  The Shri Bodgeshwar zatra, or temple festival, takes place just south of Mapusa.
February
  The three-day zatra of Shri Mangesh takes place in the lavish temple of that name in the Ponda district. In the old Fontainhas district of Panaji, the Maruti zatra draws huge and colourful crowds. Maruti is another name for Hanuman.
March
  In Goa, the festival of Holi is called Shigmo. There's a parade in Panaji and numerous temple festivals around Goa.

During the colourful and dramatic Procession of Umbrellas at Cuncolim, south of Margao, a solid silver image of Shantadurga is carried in procession over the hills to the original temple site wrecked by the Portuguese in 1580. ■

Theft

The growth of tourism in Goa has resulted in an increase in petty crime. Never leave valuables on the beach while you swim, and don't leave them in hotel rooms. Upmarket hotels have safety deposit boxes, which you should use. Alternatively, most banks have safety deposit boxes you can rent by the week or month. ∎

The only problem is deciding which beach to head for. Much depends on how long you intend to stay. Renting a room at a hotel is an expensive way of staying long term and most budget travellers prefer either to rent a simple room at one of the beach cafes or to rent a private house on a monthly basis (shared, if desired, with a group of friends). Rooms and houses can be found at all the main centres, but there's heavy demand for the latter in the winter (high) season, so it might take you several days to track one down. In the meantime, stay at a cafe or hotel and do a lot of asking around.

There's a wide range of accommodation at Colva, Benaulim, Calangute and Baga. Places to stay are generally more basic at Anjuna, Vagator and Chapora, which is where travellers tend to congregate. It's at these latter beaches that the full-moon parties are held. If you fancy somewhere that's less of a scene, Benaulim is an excellent choice. There's good accommodation and the beach is relatively peaceful.

All these beaches are touristed, so if you want something quieter, you'll have to look further afield. Arambol (or Harmal as it's spelt on some maps), near the northern tip of Goa, is one such place. Betul, south of Colva, and Palolem, even further south, are two others. The 'freaks' have gone over the border into Karnataka – though a few still hang on at Arambol.

The Aguada, Bogmalo, Varca and Cavelossim beaches are essentially for affluent tourists staying at beach resorts.

Nudism & Local Sensibilities

Despite the visible Catholic presence, Goa is predominantly a Hindu state (only 38% of Goans are Christian). So you should never make the mistake of thinking that because Goa is so welcoming, friendly and liberal, that you're at liberty to disregard local sensibilities. Too many people did that in the late 1960s and '70s by nude bathing, and Goa became (in)famous for it.

Away from the main tourist beaches, there are still places where you can lie around in your birthday suit, but don't do it where families bathe. Probably no-one will bother you (that's Goa), but remember that it's merely tolerated.

Ganja

In an effort to sanitise Goa for the package tourism market, there has recently been a spate of police crackdowns on drug users. Most of the 160 inmates in Aguada jail, 12 of them foreigners, are there on drug-related offences. One traveller wrote from the police lock-up in Mapusa to say that in Goa you can no longer expect to get off by paying a little baksheesh if you're caught. He was being held for possession of 15 grams of charas (hashish).

Despite all this, the dreaded weed is still available in Goa (it's usually from Kerala). Travellers who have come from Kashmir or the Kullu Valley may offer you resin but the quality varies. Read the warning in the Facts for the Visitor chapter.

Accommodation

Accommodation prices in Goa are based on high, middle and low seasons. This generally won't affect you much if you stay in budget accommodation, but certainly will if you stay in middle or top-range hotels. The high season covers the period from mid-December to late January, the middle (shoulder) period from October to mid-December and February to June, and the low season from July to September. Prices quoted

GOA

Goan Food & Drink

Although food in Goa is much like food anywhere else in India, there are several local specialities, including the popular pork vindaloo. Other pork specialities include the Goan sausage, or *chourisso*, and the pig's liver dish known as *sarpotel*. *Xacutí* is a chicken or meat dish; *Bangra* is Goan mackerel; *Sanna* are rice 'cupcakes' soaked in palm toddy before cooking; *dodol* and *bebinca* are special Christmas sweets; and *Moira kela* are cooking plantains (banana-like fruit) from Moira village in Bardez. The plaintains were probably introduced from Africa and can be found in the vegetable market in Panaji close to Indian Airlines.

Although the ready availability (and low price) of commercially produced alcohol contrasts markedly with most other parts of India, the Goans also brew their own local varieties. Most common of these is *feni*, a spirit made from coconut or cashews. A bottle bought from a liquor shop costs only slightly more than a bottle of beer bought at a restaurant. Reasonably palatable wines are also being turned out. The dry white is not bad; the red is basically a port. As always, the quality depends on the price you pay. ∎

in this chapter are the high-season rates. If you're in Goa during the rest of the year, then count on discounts of about 25% in the middle season and up to 60% in the low season.

At all times of year, there's a 5% luxury tax on rooms over Rs 100, 10% on rooms over Rs 500, and 15% for those over Rs 800. Prices quoted here do not include this tax.

Another thing to bear in mind is checkout times, which vary considerably and have no relation to the type of hotel you are staying in. Checkout times can be as early as 8 am or as late as noon; while in other establishments, you get to rent the room on a 24-hour basis. Watch this carefully, otherwise you could end up paying an extra 50% of the daily rate for overstaying a few hours. You'll come across this elsewhere in India, but in Goa disorder seems to rule.

Getting There & Away

Air Goa's international airport, Dabolim, is 29 km from Panaji, on the coast near Vasco da Gama. Most of India's domestic airlines operate services here, as well as several charter companies which fly into Goa direct from the UK and Germany,

Flights between Goa and Bombay are most numerous. Best for value and punctuality are the daily flights on ModiLuft and East West Airlines (both US$46), but Indian Airlines also has a daily service at this price. Jet Airways (US$57) flies daily except Sunday. Damania's daily flight costs US$65. Indian Airlines, Jet and ModiLuft offer seats

in executive class for about 20% extra – worth considering only if all seats in economy class are booked out.

Services to and from Delhi are daily on ModiLuft (US$150), and daily except Sunday on Indian Airlines (US$150).

ModiLuft has a daily connection from Udaipur to Goa (US$104) via Bombay. Indian Airlines has links daily except Sunday between Goa and Kochi (Cochin) (US$68) and Thiruvananthapuram (Trivandrum) (US$84), as well as flights three times a week to Bangalore (US$52) and Madras (US$79). On Tuesday, Thursday and Saturday, NEPC Airlines has flights in both directions linking Goa with Madras (US$100), Bangalore (US$70) and Pune (US$85).

Bus See the Getting There & Away section under Panaji for details of long-distance bus travel.

Train Goa's rail links with the rest of the country are presently being disrupted by two major engineering projects. The first, the conversion of the lines from metre to broad gauge, should be completed by early 1996.

The second project is much more ambitious – the building of an entirely new 760-km line, the Konkan Railway. It runs from Mangalore, along the coast through Goa, to Bombay. This is not easy terrain for railway construction; more than 10% of the line runs through tunnels, and 145 bridges needed to be built. Freight services should commence some time in 1996. Once these are established, they will be followed by passenger services. The estimated journey time from Bombay to the new station east of Panaji is just 10 hours.

At present, Goa has just one metre-gauge connection with Karnataka, so for long-haul journeys (especially from Bombay) the catamaran and the buses are faster. Trains run on broad gauge from Bombay and Hubli as far as Londa, 135 km from the railhead in Goa at Vasco da Gama. Goa's other main station is at Margao.

While conversion is underway, you're likely to find services between Londa and Vasco cancelled along part or all of this route. Buses run between Londa and Panaji; there are also buses to Panaji from Miraj, 188 km north of Londa, on the railway line to Bombay. A combination of train from Bombay to Miraj or Londa, and bus from either of these places into Goa is probably best; it's currently quicker than taking the train the whole way, and more comfortable than taking the bus the whole way.

If trains are running, seats and sleepers can be booked at Vasco da Gama, Margao or the railway out-agency at counter No 5 in the Panaji bus terminal – except for Indrail Pass holders who must book at Vasco da Gama (there's a special tourist quota allocated to them at this station). The out-agency is open from 10 am to 1 pm and 2 to 4.30 pm daily except Sundays.

Trains to Bangalore take about 20 hours. Fares for the 689-km trip are Rs 128/492 in 2nd/1st class, with some through carriages to Mysore. The 769-km trip to Bombay takes 24 hours. The fare is Rs 141/536 in 2nd/1st class. Now that the section between Miraj and Londa has been converted to broad gauge, most trains should run straight through to Londa. Getting to Delhi from Goa takes about 44 hours and the fare for the 2400-km trip is Rs 258/1200.

If you are heading for inland Karnataka – Hampi, Bijapur or Badami – there are two through carriages on the 7805 *Gomantak Passenger* (departing Vasco da Gama at 9 pm), which get detached at Londa and hook up with the 7838 *Miraj Link Express* to Hubli (arriving at 6.50 am). Hubli is a major railway junction with express trains to Bangalore, and passenger trains to Hospet (for the Vijayanagar ruins at Hampi), Badami and Bijapur.

Boat Until it ceased operating in the mid-1980s, the ship from Bombay to Goa was the best way to arrive. It was cheap and comfortable – even if you had to spend the night under the stars on deck in your sleeping bag. After years of speculation about when the service would restart, a flashy new catamaran service came into operation in November 1994. Run by Damania Shipping, it sails daily from October to May, leaving Bombay at 7 am and reaching Panaji at 2 pm. It departs again at 3 pm and docks in Bombay at 10 pm. Bookings can be made through any of the company's airline offices or at the Damania ferry terminals in Bombay (☎ (022) 610-2525) and Panaji (☎ (0832) 22-8711).

It's an impressive service, but since the boat is a brand new Norwegian-designed, Singapore-built vessel, tickets are nowhere near as cheap as they used to be. At US$35, economy class is only US$11 cheaper than flying; Club Class is US$50. It's certainly more comfortable than going by plane but, apart from the half-hour cruise up the Mandovi River, the trip is really about as interesting as flying. Once out at sea, the catamaran is obliged to stay at least 15 km from the coast to avoid fishing fleets, so there's nothing to see. If you're doing the journey from Panaji to Bombay, make sure you book a hotel in advance. Otherwise, since you arrive so late, you'll have to rely on the crooked taxi operators to find a room.

Taxi If the flights and catamaran from Bombay are full and you don't fancy a bus, you might consider a taxi. It takes 14 hours to drive the 600 km, but this can be done over two days. You'll have to pay for the taxi's return trip, so the cost will be between Rs 5000 and Rs 6000. Shop around for the taxi that offers you the lowest rate per km.

GOA

Getting Around

Bus The state-run Kadamba bus company is the main operator, although there are also many private companies. Buses are cheap and run to just about everywhere. Services are frequent and destinations at the bus stands are in English, so there are no worries about finding the bus you want. Pay your fare on the bus.

The only trouble is that the conductors have the same mentality as sardine-can manufacturers. If you want a seat, get on at a bus stand, otherwise you'll have to join the crush. The good news, on the other hand, is that Goans have a very mellow attitude to being packed into a tin can. There's no crazy panic and no-one will try to claw you out of the way in their manic attempt to board a bus. Seated passengers may even offer to take your bags if you're standing. The buses are, however, fairly slow because they make frequent stops.

Motorcycle Taxi Goa is the one place in India where motorcycles are a licensed form of taxi. If you don't mind travelling this way, they are much cheaper than other transport if you are travelling alone, and backpacks are no problem. Licensed motorcycles have a yellow front mudguard and are found in large numbers throughout the state.

Car Rental Self-drive car rental is available in Goa, although it's expensive. Several companies have counters at the airport. Budget (☎ (0832) 21-7063) charges from Rs 4000 for a week (unlimited km) for a small Maruti-Suzuki. Wheels/Hertz (☎ (0832) 22-4304) is also worth trying. It's usually cheaper to rent a car and driver for a specific trip. Wheels charges Rs 370 for a four-hour excursion of 50 km.

Motorcycle Rental Hiring a motorcycle in Goa is easy, and many long-term travellers do just that. The machines available are old Enfields (which often need loving care on the spark plugs), Indian-made Rajdoots (which one of the authors of this book asserts, from experience, are the worst in the world) and more modern Yamaha 100s and gearless Kinetic Honda scooters. Obviously what you pay for – with certain exceptions – is what you get, but on a daily basis you're looking at Rs 130 to Rs 200 for the smaller bikes; Rs 300 for an Enfield (or around Rs 900 for a week). Some places need your passport and a sizeable deposit before they'll let you go; others just want to know where you're staying.

While most bikes will have some sort of insurance, if you're involved in an accident you'll probably be required to pay for the damage to the rental bike, at the very least. Classic Bike Adventure (☎ & fax 27-6124), Villa Theresa, Candolim, rents well-maintained Enfields with full insurance for around Rs 2000 to Rs 3000 per week, depending on the season. See the Getting Around chapter for details of their bike tours and their address in Germany.

You should be aware that India has one of the worst records for road accidents in the world. Although Goan lanes are probably a little safer than the Grand Trunk Road, inexperienced, helmetless, foreigners on motorcycles are extremely vulnerable. Each season, more than a few tourists travel home in a box via the state mortuary in Panaji. Never forget that the Highway Code in India can be reduced to one essential truth – 'might is right'. On a motorcycle, you're pretty low on the hierarchy. Also make sure that the machine that you rent is in a reasonable state of repair, and watch out for pedestrians and animals on the roads. Goan pigs have an annoying habit of suddenly dashing out of the bushes and across the road when you're least expecting them.

Make sure that you carry the necessary paperwork (licence, registration and insurance) at all times because licence checks on foreigners by the police are a lucrative source of baksheesh for them. They may try for anything up to Rs 1000, but can usually be bargained down. Places to avoid are the towns, particularly Panaji, and Anjuna on market day (Wednesday).

If you're in the market for a new or used

motorcycle, try Auto Guides on Dr Dada Vaidya Rd, near the Hotel Samrat, in Panaji. A new Enfield will set you back Rs 42,000, but they can arrange to ship it home for you.

Bicycle There are plenty of places to hire bicycles in all the major towns and beaches in Goa. Charges are Rs 3 per hour or around Rs 20 for a full day. On the more touristy beaches, Calangute for example, some rental places try to charge twice this.

Boat One of the joys of travelling around Goa are the ferries which cross the many rivers in this small state. Almost without exception, they are combined passenger/car ferries. The main ferries are:

Siolim to Chopdem – you'll need to take this ferry for Arambol and places to the north. Services run at least every half hour for the 10-minute journey. Tickets cost Rs 0.75 for passengers; Rs 1.50 for motorcycles.
Querim to Terekhol – this ferry accesses Terekhol Fort, in the far north of the state. Services run approximately every half hour.
Dona Paula to Mormugao – this ferry runs between September and May only. There are regular crossings but they are infrequent and, at certain times of the day, you could find yourself waiting about two hours. The crossing takes 30 to 45 minutes; buses wait on either side for the arrival of boats. This is a passenger ferry only, but it's a pleasant way of getting from Panaji to Vasco da Gama. It stops running around 5 pm.
Old Goa to Piedade – ferries go every half hour.
Other Ferries – these include: Panaji to Betim; Aldona to Corjuem; Colvale to Macasana; Pomburpa to Chorao; and Ribander to Chorao. There are also launches from the central jetty in Panaji to Aldona (once daily), Britona (twice daily), Naroa (twice daily) and Verem.

North Goa

Goa comprises just two districts: North and South Goa. North Goa contains the state capital, Panaji; the former capital of Old Goa, with its interesting churches and cathedrals; and a string of beaches that runs right up the coast to Maharashtra. These range from the developed places like Calangute, Baga and Candolim, to beaches such as Anjuna, Chapora and Vagator, which attract a colourful crowd of long-term residents and travellers. It's in these latter three places that those famed midnight raves take place on full-moon nights. Arambol, in the far north, is rather quieter.

PANAJI (Panjim)
Population: 90,500
Telephone Area Code: 0832

Panaji is one of India's smallest and most pleasant state capitals. Built on the south bank of the wide Mandovi River, it officially became the capital of Goa in 1843, though the Portuguese viceroys shifted their Residence from the outskirts of Old Goa to the former palace of Adil Shah in Panaji as early as 1759.

While most people pass through Panaji on their way to the beaches or to Old Goa (nine km to the east), the town is well worth a visit for its own sake. The atmosphere is easy-going and the people are very friendly. In the oldest part of the town, the Portuguese heritage has survived remarkably well; there are narrow winding streets, old houses with overhanging balconies and red-tiled roofs, whitewashed churches and numerous small bars and cafes. Portuguese signs are still visible over many premises.

Information
Tourist Offices The tourist office (☎ 45-715) is in the government-run Tourist Home between the bus terminal and Ourem River (it's signposted). The staff here are very keen and their information is reliable, but it's closed at weekends. Excellent maps of Goa and Panaji are available for Rs 7. There's also a useful tourist counter and railway out-agency at the bus terminal. It's open Monday to Saturday from 10 am to 1 pm and from 2 to 4.30 pm. A third counter, at the airport, is open for incoming flights.

There's a Government of India tourist office (☎ 43-412) in the Communidade Building, Church Square. Also on this square is the Karnataka state tourist office (☎ 22-4110).

Money Banking hours are short at the State Bank of India – 10 am to 1 pm (noon on Saturday). Thomas Cook and Wall Street Finance are both open 9.30 am to 6 pm Monday to Saturday.

Post & Telecommunications The poste restante at the GPO is efficient. They give you the whole pile to sort through yourself and willingly check other pigeon holes if expected letters are not arriving. It's open from 9.30 am to 1 pm and 2 to 5.30 pm, Monday to Saturday.

International telephone calls are handled at the 24-hour central telegraph office, but it is quicker and only marginally more expensive to use one of the many private STD/ISD booths around town.

Visa Extensions & Tax Clearance Visa extensions are not granted as a matter of course in Panaji. The more respectable you look, the more your application is likely to be viewed favourably. If you're unsuccessful here, Bombay and Bangalore are the nearest alternatives. The Foreigners' Registration Office is in the centre of Panaji and is open from 9.30 am to 1 pm, Monday to Friday.

If you've stayed in India so long that you need a tax clearance certificate before you depart, the Taxation Department is in the Shanta Building at the end of Emidio Gracia Rd.

Travel Agencies Reasonably efficient travel agencies include Aero Mundial (☎ 44-831) at the Hotel Mandovi; Georgeson & Georgeson (☎ 43-742) opposite the GPO (1st floor); and MGM International Travels (☎ 45-150), Mamai Camotin Building (with branches at Calangute and Anjuna). If you have to reconfirm international flights, check if Air India will do it first. Some travel agents charge heavily for this service.

Bookshops & Libraries The Mandovi and Fidalgo hotels have good bookshops which stock international magazines

Three local English-language newspapers are published in Panaji. The 'establishment' paper is the *Navhind Times*, and the 'independent' papers are the *Herald* and the *Gomantok Times*.

The Alliance Francaise de Goa (☎ 22-3274), above the town in Altinho, is open Monday to Friday, 9.30 am to 1 pm and 3.30 to 6.30 pm. It has a small library and shows videos of classic French films (usually on Thursday at 6 pm). Three-month temporary membership costs Rs 150.

Medical Services If you're unlucky enough to be injured in a motorcycle accident, the best bone specialist in Goa is Dr Bale (no phone), who runs a 24-hour X-ray clinic at Porvorim, four km north of Panaji on the NH17 road to Mapusa. It may also be necessary to have a brain scan, and the only brain scanner in the state is in Vasco da Gama, 30 km from Panaji, at the Salgonkar Medical Research Centre (☎ (0834) 51-2524). There's currently nowhere to treat spinal injuries in Goa.

Things to See

The old district, **Fontainhas**, is to the west of the Ourem River. It's an interesting area to walk around, with narrow streets, tiled buildings with overhanging balconies and an atmosphere more reminiscent of the Mediterranean than of India. There are numerous little bars rarely visited by foreigners. Even if you don't stay there, the Panjim Inn is a beautiful, old building that's worth a visit.

At the centre of Fontainhas, the **Chapel of St Sebastian** stands at the end of a picturesque street. Although it dates only from the 1880s, it contains a number of interesting features – in particular a striking crucifix which originally stood in the Palace of the Inquisition in Old Goa.

The **Church of the Immaculate Conception** is Panaji's main place of worship, and it stands above the square in the main part of town, reached by several intersecting flights of stairs. The original construction was consecrated in 1541. Panaji was the first port of call for voyages from Lisbon, so Portuguese sailors would visit this church to give thanks for a safe crossing before continuing to Old Goa.

The **Secretariat** is the other building of interest in Panaji. Dating from the 16th century, it was originally Adil Shah's palace. In 1759, it became the viceroy's official Residence. In case you're wondering what the bizarre statue of a man apparently about to strangle a woman by the Secretariat building represents, this is Abbé Faria, a famous hypnotist and his assistant. Born in Candolim in 1756, he emigrated to France, where he became a celebrated hypnotic medium.

Other things to see in Panaji include a small, dusty **museum** (open Monday to Friday), and the modern **Mahalaxmi Temple**.

Organised Tours

Tours of Goa are offered by Goa Tourism (book at the tourist office or at the Panaji bus terminal) and by private agencies. The tours aren't very good because they pack too much into a short day, so you end up seeing very little. The beach tours are only for voyeurs hoping to catch a glimpse of Western bodies.

The North Goa tour visits Panaji, Datta Mandir, Mayem Lake, Mapusa, Vagator, Anjuna, Calangute and Fort Aguada. The South Goa tours take in Miramar, Dona Paula, Pilar Seminary, Marmugao, Vasco da Gama, Colva, Margao, Shantadurga Temple, Mangesh Temple and Old Goa. The tours cost Rs 60 (or Rs 80 for air-con buses) and depart daily at 9.30 am, returning to Panaji at 6 pm. The beach tour is Rs 50, lasts from 3 to 7 pm, and covers Calangute, Anjuna and Vagator. The Bondla Wildlife Sanctuary tour costs Rs 70 and departs daily at 9.30 am, returning at 5 pm.

There are also daily half-hour river cruises along the Mandovi River at 6 pm (Sunset Cruise) and 7.15 pm (Sundown Cruise) which cost Rs 55. They're good value and include a cultural programme of Goan folk songs and dances. Drinks and snacks are available. On full-moon nights, there are two-hour cruises from 8.30 pm for Rs 100;

dinner is available. Make sure you board the government-operated *Santa Monica*, which leaves from the former Bombay steamer jetty by the customs office. The other boats, in front of the Tourist Hostel, are privately owned; departures are more random, and rates a little higher.

Places to Stay

Note that throughout this chapter, unless otherwise stated, prices given are for the high season (mid-December to late January). For the shoulder season, prices drop by around 25% in the middle and top-end price ranges.

Whenever there is a religious festival in Goa – especially the festival of St Francis Xavier (several days on either side of 3 December) – it can be difficult to find accommodation in Panaji, especially at the small, inexpensive lodges. There is no accommodation at Old Goa.

Places to Stay – bottom end

Travellers looking for dormitory accommodation have a couple of options. The *Patto Tourist Home* (☎ 47-972), in a complex which includes the tourist office, is by the river, between the bus terminal and town centre. It's quite popular with Westerners and Indians alike, and costs Rs 40 per bed in the high season, Rs 30 in the low season. It has a restaurant and bar. The *Youth Hostel* (☎ 22-5433) is at Miramar, three km west of Panaji, in a shady she-oak garden by the water. The drawbacks are the institutional air and the distance from the centre of Panaji. Dorm beds cost Rs 15 (Rs 25 for non-members) and there's a solitary double room with bathroom for Rs 66.

In the old part of town, in the narrow streets running parallel to the Ourem River, there are several good, cheap places to stay. *Udipi Boarding & Lodging* and the *Elite Boarding & Lodging* are similar places with rooms for Rs 80/100 with common bathroom and Rs 100/125 with private bathroom. There's also one double room at the *Hotel Venite* restaurant for Rs 125.

On the hillside overlooking the Elite is the

similarly priced *Casa Pinho*, a large, old house with basic, dingy but relatively clean rooms. Across the road is the much better, but more expensive, *Hotel Embassy* (☎ 22-6019). It costs Rs 250 for a good, clean double, and there are geysers in the attached bathrooms.

The *Republica Hotel* (☎ 22-4630), on José Falcão Rd, at the back of the Secretariat, is an old place with fine views of the Mandovi River. It's slowly being done up and all rooms have attached bath. They charge Rs 150/200 for singles/doubles. The *Palace Hotel* next door is for emergencies

only. There are grubby cells for Rs 25/50, or rooms for Rs 100 with attached bath, but the atmosphere is gloomy and the very active Pentecostal church in one wing of the hotel will be an attraction to few.

Just up the road from the Republica, at the back of the Tourist Hostel, is the very popular *Mandovi Pearl Guest House* (☎ 22-3928), but as it has only four rooms, it's often full. Some rooms have attached bath and they range from Rs 150 for a single to Rs 200 for a triple.

There are a number of other places in Fontainhas. Prominent among them is the

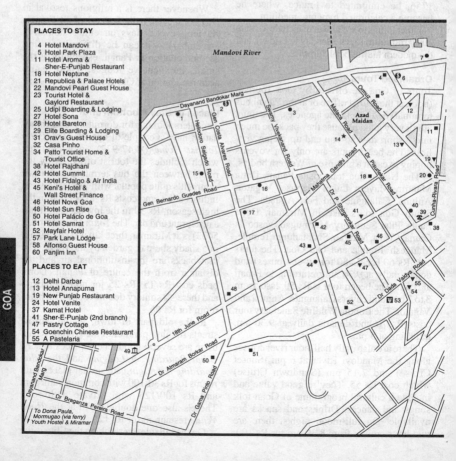

PLACES TO STAY

4 Hotel Mandovi
5 Hotel Park Plaza
11 Hotel Aroma &
   Sher-E-Punjab Restaurant
18 Hotel Neptune
21 Republica & Palace Hotels
22 Mandovi Pearl Guest House
23 Tourist Hotel &
   Gaylord Restaurant
25 Udipi Boarding & Lodging
27 Hotel Sona
28 Hotel Bareton
29 Elite Boarding & Lodging
31 Orav's Guest House
32 Casa Pinho
34 Patto Tourist Home &
   Tourist Office
38 Hotel Rajdhani
42 Hotel Summit
43 Hotel Fidalgo & Air India
45 Keni's Hotel &
   Wall Street Finance
46 Hotel Nova Goa
48 Hotel Sun Rise
50 Hotel Palácio de Goa
51 Hotel Samrat
52 Mayfair Hotel
57 Park Lane Lodge
58 Alfonso Guest House
60 Panjim Inn

PLACES TO EAT

12 Delhi Darbar
13 Hotel Annapurna
19 New Punjab Restaurant
24 Hotel Venite
37 Kamat Hotel
41 Sher-E-Punjab (2nd branch)
47 Pastry Cottage
54 Goenchin Chinese Restaurant
55 A Pastelaria

Mandovi River

Dayanand Bandokar Marg
Heliodoro Salgado Road
Gen Costa Alvares Road
Swami Vivekanand Road
Ormuz Road
Malaca Road
Azad Maidan
Mahatma Gandhi Road
Dr Pissurlekar Road
Cunha-Rivara Road
Gen Bernardo Guedes Road
Dr P. Shirgaonkar Road
Dr Dada Vaidya Road
18th June Road
Dr Atmaram Borkar Road
Dr Gama Pinto Road
Dayanand Bandokar Marg
Dr Braganza Pereira Road

To Dona Paula,
Mormugao (via ferry)
Youth Hostel & Miramar

GOA

family-run *Park Lane Lodge* (☎ 22-0238), an old Portuguese house that has a variety of good clean rooms and a very pleasant relaxed atmosphere. The price of a double with attached bath ranges from Rs 180 to Rs 300 during high season, and drops to Rs 120 in the low season. They also have some small triples with common bath, which they may let as singles. Also recommended is the nearby *Alfonso Guest House* (☎ 22-2359), in the same street as the St Sebastian Chapel. Spotlessly clean singles/doubles with attached bath cost Rs 250/300.

Lacking the character of these last two

places, but also good, is *Orav's Guest House* (☎ 22-6128), 31 January Rd. It is very clean and well run. Doubles with attached bath are Rs 250, and the front rooms have little balconies.

In the new part of town is the *Hotel Neptune* (☎ 47-727), Malaca Rd, which offers doubles at Rs 175, or Rs 275 with air-con. All the rooms have bathrooms and hot water, and there's a restaurant and bar.

Places to Stay – middle

A major price hike has meant that the *Tourist Hotel* (☎ 22-7103) is not the bargain it once

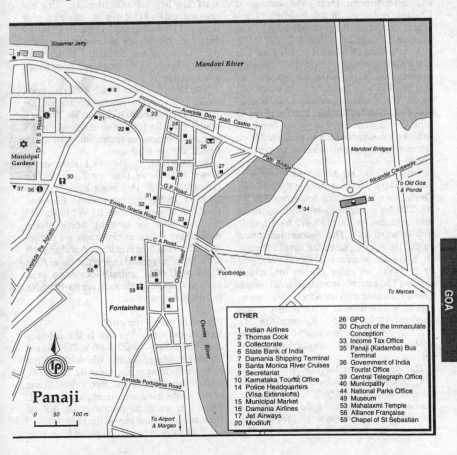

OTHER
1 Indian Airlines
2 Thomas Cook
3 Collectorate
6 State Bank of India
7 Damania Shipping Terminal
8 Santa Monica River Cruises
9 Secretariat
10 Karnataka Tourist Office
14 Police Headquarters (Visa Extensions)
15 Municipal Market
16 Damania Airlines
17 Jet Airways
20 Modiluft

26 GPO
30 Church of the Immaculate Conception
33 Income Tax Office
35 Panaji (Kadamba) Bus Terminal
36 Government of India Tourist Office
39 Central Telegraph Office
40 Municipality
44 National Parks Office
49 Museum
53 Mahalaxmi Temple
56 Alliance Française
59 Chapel of St Sebastian

Panaji

0   50   100 m

GOA

was, but it remains popular. It charges Rs 250/330 for doubles/triples, Rs 370 for an air-con room. Prices drop by only about Rs 50 in the low season. Front rooms overlook the river but tend to be noisy, so try to get a back room. There's a terrace restaurant, bar, bookshop and a handicraft shop on the ground floor.

The *Hotel Samrat* (☎ 44-546), Dr Dada Vaidya Rd, is a good choice, although high-season prices run from October through January. It charges Rs 250/350 for singles/doubles, Rs 400/450 for triples/four-bed rooms. Rooms are clean and all have attached bathrooms. There's a bar and a good Chinese restaurant in the building. Travellers' cheques can be changed here, and most credit cards are accepted.

Keni's Hotel (☎ 22-4581), 18th June Rd, is also quite popular with travellers. Singles/doubles cost Rs 200/300; air-con doubles cost Rs 450 with bathroom, hot water and colour TV. The hotel includes a bar, restaurant and shopping arcade. Keni's Hotel is actually classified as a three-star hotel, so don't be too surprised if you're quoted high prices when the rooms without air-con are full.

Fronting onto the Municipal Gardens is the modern *Hotel Aroma* (☎ 22-8308), Cunha Rivara Rd, which has rooms for Rs 200/250 for a single/double with common bathroom, and Rs 350 to Rs 475 for a double with attached bath. The tandoori restaurant on the 1st floor is one of the best in Panaji. Of a similar standard is the *Hotel Sona* (☎ 22-3488), on noisy Ourem Rd, which costs Rs 250 a double (no singles). All rooms have a bathroom with hot water in the mornings only. Much better is the nearby *Hotel Bareton* (☎ 22-6405). Rooms are Rs 175/375 with bathrooms attached and there is 24-hour hot water. Checkout time is 8.30 am.

The very pleasant *Mayfair Hotel* (☎ 46-174), Dr Dada Vaidya Rd, charges Rs 320 for a double with attached bath. In the shoulder season, these rooms are good value at Rs 240; they also let them as singles for Rs 180. There's a bar and a good restaurant. The

Hotel Summit (☎ 22-6734), Menezes Braganza Rd, is similar but more expensive at Rs 360 for a double with bathroom, and Rs 460 for an air-con double; all rooms have their own bathroom with hot and cold water 24 hours a day. Also worth considering is the similarly priced *Hotel Sun Rise* (☎ 22-0221), 18 June Rd, although it's often booked out by Indian business-wallahs.

By far the best place to stay in this price range is the *Panjim Inn* (☎ 22-6523) – a beautiful 300-year-old mansion with a large 1st-floor verandah and leafy garden. Run by a Tibetan family, it's a popular place and the staff are helpful and friendly. Singles/doubles cost Rs 315/410 with bathroom, plus around 12% between 21 December and 10 January. Try to see a couple of rooms because some are definitely better than others. There's a TV lounge, and good meals are available for guests.

The *Hotel Rajdhani* (☎ 22-5362) is a good clean place, right in the centre on Dr Atmaram Borkar Rd. It charges Rs 395 for a double (plus Rs 100 for air-con) and there's a popular vegetarian restaurant downstairs. Checkout time is 10 am.

Bombay glitz meets old Lisboa at the *Hotel Palácio de Goa* (☎ 22-4289), Dr Gama Pinto Rd. This place even boasts a Toshiba Technology Automatic Elevator. Double rooms range from Rs 495 to Rs 525 (Rs 100 more for air-con). Some of the rooms have balconies, and there's a restaurant. Checkout time is at 8 am. Another hotel at the top of this price range is the *Hotel Park Plaza* (☎ 42-601), centrally located on Azad Maidan. The cheapest rooms are Rs 495/650, but it's not great value.

Places to Stay – top end

Best of the top-end places is the colonial *Hotel Mandovi* (☎ 22-4405), Dayamond Bandokar Marg. Rooms overlooking the river are the most expensive at Rs 950/1500, while those at the rear cost Rs 650/900. Some of the rooms have been recently renovated. There's an excellent restaurant on the 1st floor and a pleasant bar on the balcony.

Of the modern hotels, the *Hotel Nova Goa*

(☎ 22-6231), Dr Atmaram Borkar Rd, is the best. Rooms cost Rs 800/1200 for a single/ double. There are also more expensive suites, and a shaded swimming pool. The *Hotel Fidalgo* (☎ 22-5061), 18th June Rd, also has a swimming pool. Rooms cost Rs 700/995.

Places to Eat

There's no shortage of good places to eat in Panaji. The *Hotel Venite*, 31 January Rd, has long been popular with travellers, although prices have risen considerably over the last few years. This attractive, old place has polished wooden floors, flower-decked balconies overlooking the street and bags of atmosphere. The Goan and seafood cuisine is very good, the servings are generous and all the food is fresh. Meals generally take a while to arrive, but the tape selection is good so waiting is not a chore. Fish curry rice is Rs 65, pepper steak Rs 55, hot garlic prawns Rs 110, and apple pie Rs 15. It's also a great spot for a cold beer or two during siesta. The Venite is open for breakfast, lunch and dinner daily except Sunday.

Udipi Boarding & Lodging, one street east of the Venite, also has a 1st-floor restaurant with a balcony overlooking the street. It's cheaper but less popular than the Venite, and has only basic dishes. Another very cheap place is the vegetarian *Hotel Annapurna*, a clean restaurant around the back of the Hotel Aroma. Barefoot waiters serve excellent 'special thalis' for Rs 19, and there are dosas from Rs 8.

Upstairs at the Tourist Hotel is the *Gaylord Restaurant*, which has a pleasant verandah overlooking the Mandovi River. It's a good place for breakfast, the food is reasonable and it's used by many travellers, though the lunch and dinner servings (especially of seafood) are very small.

On the south side of the Municipal Gardens is the *Kamat Hotel*, part of the excellent chain of vegetarian restaurants. Diagonally opposite is the popular *New Punjab Restaurant*, which offers good, cheap Punjabi food and more expensive tandoori specials. It's closed on Saturday.

The best tandoori in town, however, is the *Sher-E-Punjab* at the Hotel Aroma. Recently renovated, it serves excellent northern Indian food for around Rs 55. Also very good is the *Delhi Darbar* on M G Rd, though it's a little more expensive. It's one of the most popular restaurants in town and often fully booked in the later part of the evening. There's more north Indian food at the other branch of the *Sher-E-Punjab*, on 18th June Rd. Although it has a more extensive menu, it's not quite as good as the above two places.

There are two Chinese restaurants. The *Goenchin* (☎ 47-614), just off Dr Dada Vaidya Rd, is an excellent place but it's definitely a splurge. It's open from 12.30 to 3 pm and 7.30 to 11 pm daily. Prawns in hot garlic sauce are Rs 80. Anything on the menu marked with a red pepper means it will be very hot. Cheaper than the Goenchin, and also good, is the *Chunghwa* in the Hotel Samrat. Main dishes are from Rs 45 to Rs 65. It's run by a Chinese family.

The best restaurant for Goan food and seafood is the *Riorico* at the Hotel Mandovi. Here you can try caldo verde (potato soup with spinach, Rs 30), fish or prawn balchão (cooked in a rich, spicy tomato sauce, Rs 70), peixe caldeirada (fish and potato stew with wine, Rs 90), and round the meal off with bebinca, (the rich Goan sweet made from egg yolk and coconut, Rs 32).

For fruit juices, *Juicy Corner*, opposite the Secretariat, is a very popular place with travellers. There are several pastry shops in Panaji: the best is probably the *Pastry Cottage*, near the Hotel Nova Goa. Also good is *A Pastelaria* near the Goenchin Chinese restaurant.

Getting There & Away

Air Indian Airlines (☎ 22-4067) is at Dempo Building, D Bandodkar Marg, on the riverfront. It's open from 10 am to 1 pm and 2 to 4.30 pm. Air India (☎ 22-5172) and East West Airlines (☎ 22-4108) are at the Fidalgo Hotel on 18th June Rd. Other airlines with offices in Panaji include ModiLuft (☎ 22-7577), Dr Atmaram Bokar Rd; Jet Airways (22-4471), Rizvi Chambers, Caetano Albu-

GOA

querque Rd; and Damania Airlines (☎ 22-0192), Liv In Apartments, Bernard Guedes Rd. Until NEPC Airlines establishes a branch here, they can be contacted through local travel agents.

See the Getting There & Away section at the beginning of this chapter for flights to Goa's Dabolim Airport, which is 29 km from Panaji.

Bus Many private companies offer luxury/deluxe, superdeluxe and superdeluxe video buses to Bombay, Bangalore, Pune and Mangalore from Panaji and Margao daily. The buses generally depart at night but if you have any designs on sleeping, avoid the video buses. Most of the companies have offices in Panaji, Mapusa and Margao.

The state-operated Kadamba buses are pretty good, and the booking office at the bus terminal is open daily from 9 am to 1 pm and 2 to 5 pm. Reservations (Rs 2) can be made up to 30 days in advance.

The trip to Bombay is supposed to take 14 hours but can take up to 18. The cheapest fare for a luxury coach is Rs 219; air-con luxury is Rs 270. Most buses leave between 3 and 4 pm. Private operators have offices outside the entrance to the bus terminal, and their air-suspension coaches are the most comfortable (and expensive) way to do this trip. Paulo Holiday Makers (☎ 43-736) has a daily overnight coach to Bombay, for Rs 450.

From the bus terminal, there are also services to Miraj (a railway junction on the broad-gauge line to Bombay); Londa (where you can get a direct railway connection to Mysore every day), Hubli (another railway junction on the main Bombay to Bangalore line, where you can also get trains to Gadag for both Bijapur and Badami, and Hospet and Hampi) and Belgaum. The bus to Hubli (Rs 36, seven hours) leaves at 7 am. From Hubli to Hospet is another 4½ hours.

There are daily buses to Mysore, which take 16 hours. Mangalore is an 11-hour trip for Rs 113 in a Kadamba luxury bus. Other buses include those to Pune (Rs 176) and Bangalore (Rs 168). There are five Kadamba

buses daily to Karwar, the first major town across the southern border with Karnataka.

Boat See the Getting There & Away section at the start of this chapter for details of the daily catamaran service to and from Bombay.

Getting Around
To/From the Airport Kadamba operates infrequent buses (Rs 20) from the Indian Airlines office in Panaji to Dabolim Airport near Vasco da Gama. Most of the private airlines also operate airport buses. A taxi costs about Rs 275 and takes about 40 minutes. You can share this with up to five people. Many of the upmarket hotels have a free bus service; some will also take non-guests for around Rs 40.

The cheapest way from the airport into Panaji or Vasco is to take a motorcycle taxi from the airport to the main road (Rs 6) and then take a local bus to Panaji (Rs 5) or Vasco.

Bus Some of the more popular routes from Panaji include:

Vasco da Gama & Mormugao – there are two ways of getting there. You can either go via the ferry from Dona Paula to Mormugao, or by road via Agassaim and Cortalim. Unless you know there will be a ferry waiting for you on arrival at Dona Paula, the route via Agassaim and Cortalim is the quicker of the two. Either way, it costs Rs 5 and takes about one hour

Margao – you can get to Margao either via Agassaim and Cortalim or via Ponda. The former is the more direct route and takes about 1½ hours at a cost of Rs 5.50. Via Ponda, it takes about an hour longer and costs Rs 6.

Old Goa – take one of the frequent buses going straight to Old Goa or any bus going to Ponda. The journey costs Rs 2 and takes 25 minutes.

Calangute – there are frequent services throughout the day and evening. The journey takes about 35 minutes and costs Rs 2.50.

Mapusa – Buses cost Rs 2 and take about 25 minutes. Mapusa is pronounced 'Mapsa', and this is what the conductors shout. Change at Mapusa for Chapora.

Taxis & Auto-Rickshaws Taxis and auto-rickshaws are metered, but getting the drivers to use the meters is extremely difficult. Negotiate the fare before heading off.

Typical taxi fares from Panaji include: Calangute, Rs 100; Colva, Rs 280; and Dabolim Airport, Rs 275 (negotiable).

Other Transport See the Getting Around section at the start of this chapter for information on bike and motorcycle hire, and travel by boat within Goa.

AROUND PANAJI

Three km west of Panaji is **Miramar**, Panaji's nearest beach, but it's neither particularly attractive nor a good place to swim. There's plenty of accommodation, including the youth hostel (see Places to Stay above), should you decide to stay.

Four km further along this road is **Dona Paula**, a small town, with several resort complexes, that has grown up around a fishing village. The *Dona Paula Beach Resort* (☎ 47-955), across the narrow peninsula from the harbour, is not bad and has a small, private beach. Doubles with attached bath are Rs 475. The upmarket *Cidade de Goa*

(☎ 22-1301), by Vaniguinim Beach, has all the five-star trimmings. Rooms are US$70.

Frequent buses to Miramar and Dona Paula leave from the Kadamba bus terminal.

OLD GOA

Nine km east of Panaji, half a dozen imposing churches and cathedrals (amongst the largest in Asia) are all that remains of the Portuguese capital that was once said to rival Lisbon in magnificence. Some of the old buildings have become museums maintained by the Archaeological Survey of India – a maintenance very necessary because if the lime plaster which protects the laterite structure is not renewed frequently, the monsoons will reduce the buildings to ruin.

History

Even before the arrival of the Portuguese, Old Goa was a thriving and prosperous city, and the second capital of the Adil Shahi dynasty of Bijapur. At that time, it was a fortress surrounded by walls, towers and a moat, and contained temples, mosques and the large palace of Adil Shah. Today, none of

The Incorrupt Body of St Francis Xavier

Goa's patron saint, Francis Xavier, had spent 10 years as a tireless missionary in South-East Asia when he died on 2 December 1552, but it was through his death that his greatest power in the region was released.

He died on the island of Sancian, off the coast of China. His servant is said to have emptied four sacks of quicklime into his coffin to consume his flesh in case the order came to return the remains to Goa. Two months later, the body was transferred to Malacca, where it was observed to be still in perfect condition – refusing to rot despite the quicklime. The following year, it was returned to Goa, where the people were declaring the preservation a miracle.

The Church was slower to acknowledge it, requiring a medical examination to establish that the body had not been embalmed. This was performed, in 1556, by the viceroy's physician, who declared that all internal organs were still intact and that no preservative agents had been used. He noticed a small wound in the chest and asked two Jesuits to put their fingers into it. He noted, 'When they withdrew them, they were covered with blood which I smelt and found to be absolutely untainted'.

In comparison to 16th and 17th-century church bureaucracy, modern Indian bureaucracy seems positively streamlined, for it was not until 1622 that canonisation took place. By then, holy relic hunters had started work on the 'incorrupt body'. In 1614, the right arm was removed and divided between Jesuits in Japan and Rome, and by 1636, parts of one shoulder blade and all the internal organs had been scattered through South-East Asia. By the end of the 17th century, the body was in an advanced state of desiccation, and the miracle appeared to be over. The Jesuits decided to enclose the corpse in a glass coffin out of view, and it was not until the mid-19th century that the current cycle of 10-yearly expositions began. During the 54 days of the 1994-5 exposition over a million pilgrims filed past the ghoulish remains.

The next exposition is not until November 2004 but if you're anywhere in the area on 3 December the annual celebration of the saint's day is well worth attending. ■

GOA

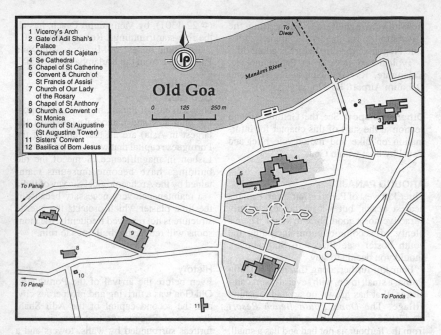

1 Viceroy's Arch
2 Gate of Adil Shah's Palace
3 Church of St Cajetan
4 Se Cathedral
5 Chapel of St Catherine
6 Convent & Church of St Francis of Assisi
7 Church of Our Lady of the Rosary
8 Chapel of St Anthony
9 Church & Convent of St Monica
10 Church of St Augustine (St Augustine Tower)
11 Sisters' Convent
12 Basilica of Bom Jesus

Old Goa

0   125   250 m

To Diwar

Mandovi River

To Panaji

To Panaji

To Ponda

these structures remain except for a fragment of the gateway to the palace.

Under the Portuguese, the city grew rapidly in size and splendour, despite an epidemic in 1543 which wiped out a large percentage of the population. Many huge churches, monasteries and convents were erected by the various religious orders which came to Goa under royal mandates. The Franciscans were the first to arrive.

Old Goa's splendour was short-lived, however, because by the end of the 16th century, Portuguese supremacy on the seas had been replaced by that of the British, Dutch and French. The city's decline was accelerated by the activities of the Inquisition and a devastating epidemic which struck in 1635. Indeed, if it had not been for the treaty between the British and the Portuguese, it is probable that Goa would either have passed to the Dutch or been absorbed into British India.

The city muddled on into the early 19th century as the administrative capital of Portugal's eastern empire. In 1843, the capital was shifted to Panaji.

Information

The Archaeological Survey of India publishes *Old Goa* by S Rajagopalan (New Delhi 1975), an excellent booklet about the monuments. It's available from the Archaeological Museum in Old Goa.

Se Cathedral

The largest of the churches in Old Goa, Se Cathedral was begun in 1562 during the reign of King Dom Sebastião (1557-78). It was substantially completed by 1619, though the altars were not finished until 1652. The cathedral was built for the Dominicans and paid for by the royal treasury out of the proceeds of the sale of crown property.

The building is Portuguese-Gothic in style with a Tuscan exterior and Corinthian interior. There were originally two towers, one on either side of the facade, but one collapsed in 1776. The remaining tower houses a famous bell, one of the largest in Goa, often called the Golden Bell because of its rich sound. The main altar is dedicated to St Catherine of Alexandria, and old paintings on either side of it depict scenes from her life and martyrdom.

Convent & Church of St Francis of Assisi

This is one of the most interesting buildings in Old Goa. It contains gilded and carved woodwork, old murals depicting scenes from the life of St Francis, and a floor substantially made of carved gravestones – complete with family coats of arms dating back to the early 1500s. The church was built by eight Franciscan friars who arrived here in 1517 and constructed a small chapel consisting of three altars and a choir. This was later pulled down and the present building was constructed on the same spot in 1661.

The convent at the back of this church is now the **archaeological museum** (open Saturday to Thursday, 10 am to 5 pm; free entry). It houses many portraits of the Portuguese viceroys, most of them inexpertly touched up; fragments of sculpture from Hindu temple sites in Goa, which show Chalukyan and Hoysala influences; stone Vetal images from the animist cult which flourished in this part of India centuries ago; and a model of a Portuguese caravel, minus the rigging.

Basilica of Bom Jesus

The Basilica of Bom Jesus is famous throughout the Roman Catholic world. It contains the tomb and mortal remains of St Francis Xavier who, in 1541, was given the task of spreading Christianity among the subjects of the Portuguese colonies in the east. A former pupil of St Ignatius Loyola, the founder of the Jesuit Order, St Francis Xavier's missionary voyages became legendary and, considering the state of transport at the time, they *were* nothing short of miraculous.

See the boxed section on St Francis Xavier for details on the remarkable manner in which he attained his saintly status.

Apart from the richly gilded altars, the interior of the church is remarkable for its simplicity. This is the only church which is not plastered on the outside (although it was originally). Construction began in 1594 and the church was completed in 1605. The centre of interest inside the church is, of course, the Tomb of St Francis. The construction of the tomb was underwritten by the Duke of Tuscany and executed by the Florentine sculptor Giovanni Batista Foggini. It took 10 years to build and was completed in 1698. The remains of the body are housed in a silver casket, which at one time was covered in jewels. On the walls surrounding it are murals depicting scenes from the saint's journeys, and one of his death on Sancian Island.

The **Professed House**, next door to the basilica, is a two-storey laterite building covered with lime plaster. It was completed in 1585, despite much opposition to the Jesuits. Part of the building burned down in 1633 and was partially rebuilt in 1783. There's a modern **art gallery** attached to the basilica.

Church of St Cajetan

Modelled on the original design of St Peter's in Rome, this church was built by Italian

Se Cathedral, Old Goa (16th century)

GOA

friars of the Order of Theatines, who were sent by Pope Urban III to preach Christianity in the kingdom of Golconda (near Hyderabad). The friars were not permitted to work in Golconda, so settled at Old Goa in 1640. The construction of the church began in 1655. Historically, it's of much less interest than the other churches.

Church of St Augustine Ruins

All that is really left of this church is the enormous 46-metre-high tower which served as a belfry and formed part of the facade of the church. The few other remnants are choked with creepers and weeds, and access is difficult. The church was constructed in 1602 by Augustinian friars who arrived at Old Goa in 1587.

It was abandoned in 1835 due to the repressive policies of the Portuguese government, which resulted in the eviction of many religious orders from Goa. The church fell into neglect and the vault collapsed in 1842. In 1931, the facade and half the tower fell down, followed by more sections in 1938.

Church & Convent of St Monica

This huge, three-storey, laterite building was commenced in 1606 and completed in 1627, only to burn down nine years later. Reconstruction started the following year, and it's from this time that the buildings date. Once known as the Royal Monastery, due to the royal patronage which it enjoyed, the building is now used by the Mater Dei Institute as a nunnery and was inaugurated in 1964. Visitors are allowed inside if they are reasonably dressed. There are fading murals on the inside of the western walls.

Other Buildings

Other monuments of minor interest in Old Goa are the Viceroy's Arch, Gate of Adil Shah's Palace, Chapel of St Anthony, Chapel of St Catherine, and the Church of Our Lady of the Rosary.

Getting There & Away

If you're a lover of old buildings and exotic ruins, you'll need the best part of a day to wander around Old Goa. Otherwise, a morning or an afternoon will be sufficient.

There are frequent buses to Old Goa from the bus stand at Panaji; buses from Panaji to Ponda also pass through Old Goa. The trip takes 25 minutes and costs Rs 2. There are also occasional boat tours from Panaji (ask at the kiosks near the steamer jetty).

MAPUSA

Population: 33,500
Telephone Area Code: 0832

Mapusa (pronounced locally as 'Mapsa') is the main centre of population in the northern provinces of Goa and the main town for supplies if you are staying either at Anjuna or Chapora. If you're staying at Calangute, Baga or Candolim, you have a choice of Panaji or Mapusa as a service centre.

There's not much to see in Mapusa, though the Friday market is worth a visit. You may, however, need to stay here overnight if you're catching a bus to Bombay the following day – there's no need to go to Panaji for long-distance buses.

Damania Airways/Shipping (☎ 26-2694) has an office in the Tourist Hotel and runs buses to the airport (Rs 40). The tourist office is also here.

Places to Stay & Eat

Accommodation at the nearby beaches of Anjuna, Vagator and Chapora is far preferable to what's on offer in Mapusa. The *Sirsat Lodge* (☎ 26-2419) is a basic place with doubles with common bath for Rs 65. The *Hotel Trishul* (☎ 26-2700) has doubles with attached bath for Rs 120, plus a range of other rooms.

The *Hotel Vilena* (☎ 26-3115) is a good, clean place with doubles at Rs 140 or Rs 200 with attached bath (and water heater). The popular *Tourist Hotel* (☎ 26-2794), on the roundabout at the entrance to Mapusa, has a good range of rooms from Rs 130/150. There are also rooms with four/six beds for Rs 200/260. Hot water is available by the bucket, except in the air-con doubles (Rs 270), which have water heaters. There's a

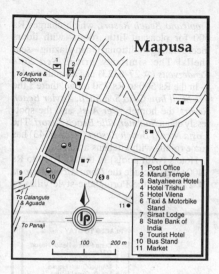

Mapusa

To Anjuna & Chapora

To Calangute & Aguada

To Panaji

0   100   200 m

1   Post Office
2   Maruti Temple
3   Satyaheera Hotel
4   Hotel Trishul
5   Hotel Vilena
6   Taxi & Motorbike
    Stand
7   Sirsat Lodge
8   State Bank of
    India
9   Tourist Hotel
10 Bus Stand
11 Market

reasonable restaurant with main dishes at around Rs 35; beer is Rs 30.

The *Satyaheera Hotel* (☎ 26-2849), near the Maruti Temple, is about the best Mapusa has to offer. Doubles range from Rs 150 to Rs 350 (air-con and TV), all with bathroom attached. Mapusa's top restaurant, the *Ruchira*, is on the top floor. Main dishes are Rs 30 to Rs 45 but 'Choice of Music Cannot be Obliged'!

Getting There & Away

From the bus stand, there are buses to Bombay (Rs 168 for semideluxe, Rs 215 for deluxe). Private operators have kiosks by the taxi and motorcycle stand. The most luxurious coach is the Aerowheels overnight air-con service to Bombay, leaving at 3.30 pm. There are individual headsets, an onboard toilet, free meals and soft drinks. Tickets cost Rs 500.

There are frequent bus departures for Panaji (Rs 2.50, 25 minutes), and buses at least hourly to Calangute (Rs 2.50), Anjuna (Rs 2.50, Rs 3.50 on Wednesdays – market day). Other buses go to Margao (Rs 7), Chapora and Candolim. A motorcycle to Anjuna or Calangute costs Rs 30 and takes about 15 minutes. Taxis charge around Rs 60.

FORT AGUADA & CANDOLIM

Telephone Area Code: 0832

The beaches of North Goa extend from Fort Aguada in an almost uninterrupted 30 km sandy stretch to the border with Maharashtra. Sinquerim, the beach below the fort, and Candolim are popular with package tourists, but independent travellers can also find accommodation here. These beaches tend to be quieter than Calangute, particularly at weekends. There are some pleasant places to stay, although there's nowhere for those on a very tight budget.

Guarding the mouth of the Mandovi River, **Fort Aguada** was built by the Portuguese in 1612. It's worth visiting the moated ruins on the hilltop for the views, which are particularly good from the old lighthouse. You can also visit the dungeons. There's no entry charge but the caretaker expects a hefty tip. Nearby, the new **lighthouse** can be visited from 4 to 5.30 pm (Rs 1); but no photography is allowed from it.

To the east is **Aguada Jail**; most inmates (12 of them Westerners) are in on drug charges. They're only allowed one visit a month, so although they usually appreciate visits from other foreigners, you need to make sure you won't be denying them the visit of someone they're expecting. You'll also need to contact your embassy for a list of names.

Places to Stay

Moving south from Calangute, the hotels become progressively more expensive. Prices listed below are for doubles with attached bathrooms in the high season. Some of these hotels are taken over entirely by package groups during this period.

There's a clutch of places ranging from Rs 250 to Rs 350 in an excellent position very close to the beach. These include the *Dona Florina Beach Resort*, *D'Mello's* (rooms with balconies upstairs) and *Shanu Holiday Home*. There are even sea views from some of these places.

Next is a group of guest houses used by the cheaper end of the package market, with doubles around Rs 350 – *Coqueiral Holiday*

GOA

Home (☎ 27-6070), *Silver Sands Holiday Village*, *Holiday Beach Resort* (☎ 27-6088), *Alexandra Tourist Centre* (☎ 27-6250), *Monte Villa* and *Sand Pebbles* (☎ 27-6136).

Cheaper places in this area, with doubles around Rs 250, include *Manuel Guest House*, and the friendly *Lobo's Guest House*. The *Pretty Petal Guest House* (☎ 27-6184) is particularly recommended; doubles are from Rs 250 and some come with a fridge. *Ave Maria* (☎ 27-7336) is good value at Rs 175/275 for a single/double. The cheapest place in the area is *Ti Bhat* at Rs 150.

More upmarket hotels include the *Tropicano Beach Resort*, which charges Rs 500 for pleasant little rooms with doors incorporating traditional Goan glazing – seashells! The similarly priced *Sea Side Rendezvous* (☎ 27-6323) has a small pool.

In the Rs 500 to Rs 750 range, there's the *Sea Shell Inn*, *Casa Sea Shell*, *Xavier Beach Resort*, the homely *Per Avel*, and the spotlessly clean *Summer Ville Beach Resort*. The *Costa Nicola Beach Resort* (☎ 27-6343) has some rooms with kitchens attached.

Hotels (with pools) in the Rs 1000 to Rs 1400 range include the *Dona Alcina Resorts* (☎ 27-6266), the Portuguese-style villas of

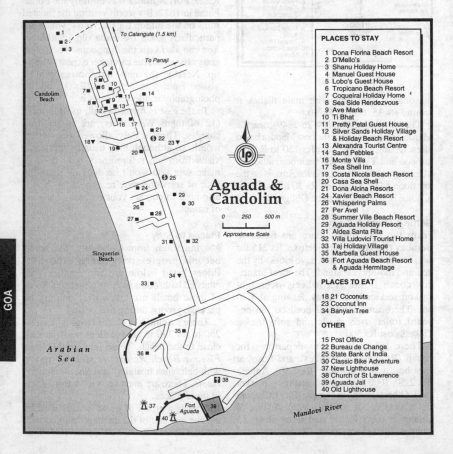

PLACES TO STAY

1 Dona Florina Beach Resort
2 D'Mello's
3 Shanu Holiday Home
4 Manuel Guest House
5 Lobo's Guest House
6 Tropicano Beach Resort
7 Coqueiral Holiday Home
8 Sea Side Rendezvous
9 Ave Maria
10 Ti Bhat
11 Pretty Petal Guest House
12 Silver Sands Holiday Village & Holiday Beach Resort
13 Alexandra Tourist Centre
14 Sand Pebbles
16 Monte Villa
17 Sea Shell Inn
19 Costa Nicola Beach Resort
20 Casa Sea Shell
21 Dona Alcina Resorts
24 Xavier Beach Resort
26 Whispering Palms
27 Per Avel
28 Summer Ville Beach Resort
29 Aguada Holiday Resort
31 Aldea Santa Rita
32 Villa Ludovici Tourist Home
33 Taj Holiday Village
35 Marbella Guest House
36 Fort Aguada Beach Resort & Aguada Hermitage

PLACES TO EAT

18 21 Coconuts
23 Coconut Inn
34 Banyan Tree

OTHER

15 Post Office
22 Bureau de Change
25 State Bank of India
30 Classic Bike Adventure
37 New Lighthouse
38 Church of St Lawrence
39 Aguada Jail
40 Old Lighthouse

To Calangute (1.5 km)
To Panaji
Candolim Beach
Aguada & Candolim
0   250   500 m
Approximate Scale
Sinquerim Beach
Arabian Sea
Fort Aguada
Mandovi River

GOA

the *Aldea Santa Rita* (☎ 27-7447), and the *Aguada Holiday Resort* (☎ 27-6071). The *Whispering Palms* (☎ 27-6141) has a very large pool but rooms here are Rs 3000.

Among all this concrete, only two places have managed to preserve something of their colonial heritage. The owner of the *Villa Ludovici Tourist Home* is holding out against the developers, and this is a very pleasant place to stay. She charges Rs 400 with breakfast for two, Rs 250 in the shoulder season.

Much more upmarket is the *Marbella Guest House* (fax 27-6308), a beautifully restored Portuguese villa hidden away down a quiet lane behind the Fort Aguada Beach Resort. Partly foreign-owned, there are six airy rooms, each superbly decorated in a different style. All rooms have a bathroom attached (one has a sunken marble tub) and the whole place is spotlessly clean. Rooms range from Rs 1200 to Rs 2200 (Rs 1080 to Rs 1980 in the shoulder season) and this includes all taxes. It's highly recommended, but in the high season you'll need to book in advance.

Beside Sinquerim Beach, to the south of Candolim, is a complex of three five-star deluxe hotels owned by the Taj Group (☎ 27-6201; fax 27-6044). The beachside *Taj Holiday Village* charges US$175 and has a water-sports centre. Within the outer walls of the old fort, the *Fort Aguada Beach Resort* has rooms for US$185. Above it are the luxurious villas of the *Aguada Hermitage*, which have northern views and are priced at US$400. If you're planning to stay here, check that they've managed to remove the oil tanker which ran aground in late 1994 right in front of the hotel. Luckily, oil spillage was minimal.

Places to Eat

Most of the hotels have restaurants attached. The pick of the beach huts, by a very long margin, is the partly Swiss-run *21 Coconuts*. It's not cheap – breakfast costs Rs 70, main dishes at lunch are Rs 95 (Rs 45 for the salad bar) – but everything tastes as it should, and the coffee is excellent. Open daily until

sunset, they even have a shower for customers to use.

The open-air *Coconut Inn* is a popular place in the evening, particularly amongst package groups. On Thursday, there's a seafood barbecue and a dance band for Rs 195 per person. One of the best restaurants in the area is the *Banyan Tree*, in the grounds of the Taj Holiday Village. It's an open-sided affair serving excellent Thai and Chinese cuisine. Main dishes range from Rs 100 to Rs 200.

Getting There & Away

Buses run from Panaji to Sinquerim (14 km) and continue north to Calangute. A taxi from the airport costs Rs 350.

CALANGUTE & BAGA

Telephone Area Code: 0832

Seemingly not all that long ago, Calangute was the beach all self-respecting hippies headed for, especially around Christmas when psychedelic hell broke loose and the beach was littered with more budding rock stars than most people have hot dinners. If you enjoyed taking part in those mass pujas, with their endless half-baked discussions about 'when the revolution comes' and 'the vibes, maaan', then this was just the ticket. You could frolic around with not a stitch on, be ever so cool and liberated, and completely disregard the feelings of the local inhabitants. You could get totally out of your head every minute of the night and day on every conceivable variety of ganja from Timor to Tenochtitlan, exhibit the most bizarre behaviour, babble an endless stream of drivel and bore everybody shitless. Naturally, John Lennon or The Who were always about to turn up and give a free concert. Ah, Woodstock! Where did you go?

Calangute's heyday as the Mecca of all expatriate hippies has passed. The local people, who used to rent out rooms in their houses for a pittance, have moved on to more profitable things, and Calangute has undergone a metamorphosis to become the centre of Goa's rapidly expanding package tourist market. The hotels and guest houses now

GOA

stretch almost without a break from Calangute to Baga.

Calangute isn't one of the best Goan beaches: there are hardly any palms gracing the shoreline, some of the sand is contaminated with red soil and the beach drops pretty rapidly into the sea. There is, however, plenty going on, and people who find Colva too quiet may find Calangute more to their liking. However, the beach at Baga is better and the landscape is more interesting.

Information

Shyam Bookshop offers a great range of books in many languages. You can buy, sell or exchange here.

The Kerkar Art Complex in South Calangute is well worth a visit. There's a gallery with paintings on sale by local artists and concerts of Indian classical music and dance on Tuesday and Saturday at 6.30 pm. Tickets are Rs 150.

Faxes can be sent and received at Telelink (fax 27-6124), near the petrol station. Damania Airways/Shipping has an office at the Calangute Tourist Resort.

Places to Stay

Prices quoted here are for a double room with attached bathroom during the high season. Note that single rooms are rare in this area.

Calangute In the centre of Calangute, there are a number of popular budget options. The large *Angela P Fernandes Guest House* offers doubles for Rs 150 (Rs 95 outside the Christmas/New Year period). There are also cheaper rooms with common bath. It's good value, a popular place to stay, the rooms have fans and the staff are very friendly. If it's full, there are several other places nearby. The *Conria Beach Resort* and the *Calangute Paradise* have rooms at Rs 150 to Rs 200.

The *Hotel Souza Lobo* has a great location right on the beach and offers clean, basic rooms for Rs 200. Unfortunately, the rooms don't have windows and the verandah is taken up by the restaurant. Hot water is available only between 3 and 6 pm when the restaurant is closed. Hidden away amongst the souvenir shops is *Fellah's Guest House*, a very basic place charging Rs 150 for a double with attached bath.

In the Rs 200 to Rs 250 bracket, the best place in Calangute is the *Hotel A Canôa* (☎ 27-6082), which has some nice rooms with sea views, but it's often full. Back from the beach are the ordinary *Alfa Guest House* (☎ 27-7358) and the very pleasant *Victor Guest House*.

Near Angela P Fernandes is the popular *Coco Banana*. Rooms in this mid-range establishment surround a quiet courtyard and are very clean. The beds are comfortable, fans are provided and the staff are friendly and helpful. Prices are in the Rs 350 to Rs 450 range. The *Sea Pearl Guest House* next door is cheaper.

The ugly, government-owned *Calangute Tourist Resort* (☎ 27-6009) dominates the beach. The cottages constructed as an extension are rather more attractively designed. From October to June, rooms cost Rs 180 for a single, Rs 220 a double and Rs 330 a triple, all with bathroom and fan. Between 15 June and 30 September they cost Rs 120, Rs 180 and Rs 250 respectively. There's also a dormitory for Rs 40 (Rs 30 low season). A restaurant forms part of the complex.

Meena's Lodge, nearby, is cheap at Rs 125, but tends to be noisy. Three doors down is the unremarkable *Falcon Resort* (☎ 27-7363), which charges Rs 200. Just north of the Tourist Resort is another group of small hotels very close to the beach. Rates at *La Bamba* and *Hotel O'Camarao* are from Rs 150 to Rs 200.

Also in this area is the attractively designed *Varma's Beach Resort* (☎ 27-6077). It's clean and friendly, and has its own bar and restaurant (guests only). The rooms surround a leafy courtyard. Doubles cost Rs 550 to Rs 850 with bathroom, air-con and your own small verandah with table and chairs. The hotel is closed from June to September.

At the start of the Calangute to Baga road are a couple of small places. *Rodrigues Cottages* has a few rooms at Rs 100 with attached bath. *Albenjoh* (☎ 27-6422) is a very good choice, with rooms from Rs 150

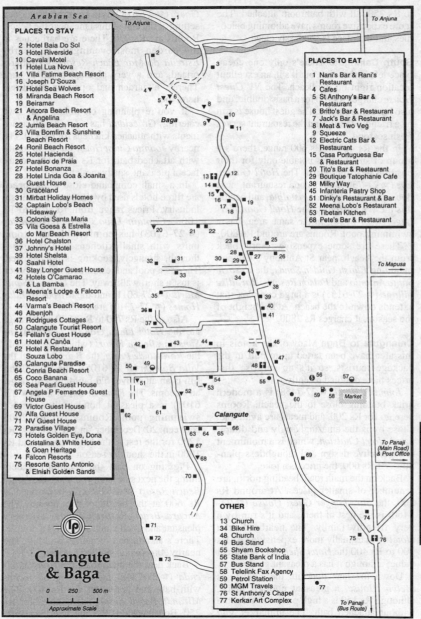

Arabian Sea

To Anjuna

Baga

To Anjuna

To Mapusa

To Panaji
(Main Road)
& Post Office

GOA

Market

To Panaji
(Bus Route)

PLACES TO STAY

2 Hotel Baia Do Sol
3 Hotel Riverside
10 Cavala Motel
11 Hotel Lua Nova
14 Villa Fatima Beach Resort
16 Joseph D'Souza
17 Hotel Sea Wolves
18 Miranda Beach Resort
19 Beiramar
21 Ancora Beach Resort
& Angelina
22 Jumla Beach Resort
23 Villa Bomfim & Sunshine
Beach Resort
24 Ronil Beach Resort
25 Hotel Hacienda
26 Paraíso de Praia
27 Hotel Bonanza
28 Hotel Linda Goa & Joanita
Guest House
30 Graceland
31 Mirbat Holiday Homes
32 Captain Lobo's Beach
Hideaway
33 Colonia Santa Maria
35 Vila Goesa & Estrella
do Mar Beach Resort
36 Hotel Chalston
37 Johnny's Hotel
39 Hotel Shelsta
40 Saahil Hotel
41 Stay Longer Guest House
42 Hotels O'Camarao
& La Bamba
43 Meena's Lodge & Falcon
Resort
44 Varma's Beach Resort
46 Albenjoh
47 Rodrigues Cottages
50 Calangute Tourist Resort
54 Fellah's Guest House
61 Hotel A Canôa
62 Hotel & Restautant
Souza Lobo
63 Calangute Paradise
64 Conria Beach Resort
65 Coco Banana
66 Sea Pearl Guest House
67 Angela P Fernandes Guest
House
69 Victor Guest House
70 Alfa Guest House
71 NV Guest House
72 Paradise Village
73 Hotels Golden Eye, Dona
Cristalina & White House
& Goan Heritage
74 Falcon Resorts
75 Resorte Santo Antonio
& Elnish Golden Sands

PLACES TO EAT

1 Nani's Bar & Rani's
Restaurant
4 Cafes
5 St Anthony's Bar &
Restaurant
6 Britto's Bar & Restaurant
7 Jack's Bar & Restaurant
8 Meat & Two Veg
9 Squeeze
12 Electric Cats Bar &
Restaurant
15 Casa Portuguesa Bar
& Restaurant
28 Tito's Bar & Restaurant
29 Boutique Tatophanie Cafe
38 Milky Way
45 Infanteria Pastry Shop
51 Dinky's Restaurant & Bar
52 Meena Lobo's Restaurant
53 Tibetan Kitchen
68 Pete's Bar & Restaurant

OTHER

13 Church
34 Bike Hire
48 Church
49 Bus Stand
55 Shyam Bookshop
56 State Bank of India
57 Bus Stand
58 Telelink Fax Agency
59 Petrol Station
60 MGM Travels
76 St Anthony's Chapel
77 Kerkar Art Complex

Calangute

**Calangute
& Baga**

0   250   500 m

Approximate Scale

to Rs 250, all with bathroom attached. The more expensive rooms have adjoining balconies and the place is spotlessly clean.

South Calangute There's only one cheap place left in this area, but it's in an excellent location right on the beach. The *NV Guest House* charges Rs 100 for a basic double, and also has some singles. The guest house is run by a friendly family and the restaurant serves fresh seafood.

In the Rs 400 to Rs 600 range, there's a group of small hotels notable only for their position near the beach. The *Hotel Golden Eye* (☎ 27-7308) has a good restaurant, next door is the *Hotel Dona Cristalina*, and beside it is the *White House*. The *Hotel Goan Heritage* (☎ 27-6120), in the same area, has a swimming pool. Rooms are around Rs 800.

There are some expensive resorts back from the beach, near St Anthony's Chapel, including *Elnish Golden Sands*, the *Resorte Santo Antonio* and *Falcon Resorts*. *Paradise Village* (☎ 27-6155) is a large complex that extends down to the beach. At the height of the season, it charges Rs 2800.

Calangute to Baga Many of the hotels in this area have been tarted up to pull in the package tourists, so it's no surprise that prices have doubled recently.

Johnny's Hotel (☎ 27-7458) is a modern brick building close to the beach. Rooms here go for Rs 200, and meals are available. Close by is the amazingly ugly and dilapidated *Hotel Chalston*, which is a monument to insensitive design and thoughtless planning. At Rs 600, the price is a joke.

Back on the main road, heading north, are a number of smaller places. At around Rs 200, the *Stay Longer Guest House* (☎ 27-7460) is the best of them, and it's run by a very friendly family. The nearby *Saahil Hotel* is marginally more expensive. At Rs 300 to Rs 400 the *Hotel Shelsta* is not great value, although it has a pleasant garden.

Down the lane opposite the Shelsta is *Melvin House*, a pleasant enough place, although Rs 150 is a high price for a double without attached bath. The upmarket *Vila Goesa* (☎ 27-6182) is in an attractive garden setting at the end of this lane, near the beach. Rooms are Rs 950. There are barbecues in the garden most evenings. The nearby *Estrella do Mar Beach Resort* is similarly priced, and a very pleasant place to stay. There's a garden and open-air restaurant here, too.

If you're planning on doing your own catering, *Graceland* has a few small apartments with attached kitchens for Rs 350. The nearby *Joanita Guest House* has good rooms with attached bath for Rs 250. The rooms face a pleasant, shady garden.

In a small compound close to the beach are three hotels used by the package tourism industry. Prices range from Rs 700 to Rs 1000. *Captain Lobo's Beach Hideaway* (☎ 27-6103) has comfortable two-room units with small kitchens and fridges – though, strangely, cooking is not allowed. There's a pool and restaurant, and the beach is just a short walk away. The *Colonia Santa Maria* (☎ 27-6011) and the *Mirbat Holiday Homes* (☎ 27-7310) are similar.

Also in the Rs 700 to Rs 1000 price range are the *Hotel Linda Goa* (☎ 27-6066), the *Sunshine Beach Resort* (which has a pool), the *Paraiso de Praia*, the *Beiramar* and the *Villa Bomfim* (☎ 27-6105). The Villa Bomfim is an attractive, old building with large, airy rooms. The *Ronil Beach Resort* (☎ 27-6101) is a pleasant hotel built around a swimming pool. Rooms cost Rs 2000 between 20 December and 8 January, Rs 1200 for the rest of the high season, and Rs 1000 in the shoulder season.

Pressing on past the Kashmiri traders lining the next side lane, you reach the *Jumla Beach Resort* (☎ 27-6102) – overpriced at Rs 600 at the height of the season. The *Ancora Beach Resort Cottages* are very pleasant and good value at Rs 180 a double. There's an attached restaurant and bar. The nearby *Angelina* is similarly priced.

Back near the main road, the *Hotel Hacienda* (☎ 27-7348) has some good rooms with bath and hot water for Rs 400. The *Miranda Beach Resort* has doubles for Rs 250. Better value is the characterless *Hotel*

Sea Wolves next door, where doubles with attached bath cost Rs 150.

Baga The *Villa Fatima Beach Resort* (☎ 27-6059), set back from the road amid the coconut palm groves, is a good choice. It's a somewhat grandiose name for what is essentially a three-storey building attached to a private house, but it's a very popular place to stay, especially long term, and the family who run it are pleasant. Double rooms with attached bath cost from Rs 150, doubles with hot water cost Rs 350. There's a restaurant and TV area, and you can rent a safety deposit box for Rs 50. It's often full in the high season.

In the old villa by the Casa Portuguesa Restaurant, *Joseph D'Souza* offers basic rooms at around Rs 100. There are larger rooms with attached bathrooms for Rs 150 to Rs 200 across the road.

There is a cluster of restaurants on the main road in the centre of Baga. Jack's, Britto's and St Anthony's are the places to ask around for a room or for a house to rent. There are also a number of houses and cottages for rent across the river, but they're often occupied by long-term visitors.

As for hotel accommodation, there's little choice. At around Rs 400, there's the *Hotel Riverside* (☎ 27-6062), which has pleasant rooms in a quiet area; and the newer, similarly priced *Hotel Lua Nova*, whose rooms look out over rice fields. More expensive is the two-star *Hotel Baia do Sol* (☎ 27-5207), a modern hotel set in an attractive flower garden. Doubles are around Rs 700, and the hotel has its own restaurant and bar. The *Cavala Motel* (☎ 27-6090), used by package groups, offers doubles with verandah and bathroom for around Rs 600.

Across the river, *Nani's Bar & Rani's Restaurant* (☎ 27-6313) has a few basic doubles with common bath for Rs 80; Rs 200 with attached bath. This pleasant place is popular and getting a room can be difficult at times. To reach it, you cross over to the northern side of the river by an extraordinary bridge which has to be seen to be believed. Somebody was evidently given an unlimited

amount of concrete and told to construct the ugliest and most extravagant bridge they could imagine. The result was a covered footbridge that could survive a direct nuclear hit.

Places to Eat

There are any number of small restaurants all the way from Calangute village to the beach, especially around the bus stand, and also on the beach at Baga. As you might expect, seafood features prominently on the menus.

The place to start the day is the *Infanteria Pastry Shop*, an excellent place for a croissant and coffee. There's also a good range of bread and cakes, and a few full meals.

One of the best places to eat is the *Hotel Souza Lobo*, which is a perfect place to watch the sunset or relax in the early afternoon (though it closes between 3 and 6 pm for the benefit of hotel residents). Service is off-hand but the food is very good. Pepper steak is Rs 40, whole grilled kingfish Rs 100, and tiger prawns Rs 225. It's also popular with the local feline population.

Another good place to eat or sit around with a few cold beers is *Pete's Bar & Restaurant*, beside the Angela P Fernandes Guest House. It's much more of a travellers' place than the Souza Lobo.

The *Tibetan Kitchen* offers momos and other Tibetan food in a relaxed setting, with magazines and board games available to encourage long stays. It's a good place to meet other travellers. For very cheap Chinese food, try the *China Town* by Meena's Lodge.

Mr Cater's, on the terrace in front of the Calangute Beach Resort, is the place for north Indian and tandoori dishes, and it's very reasonably priced. The *Oceanic Restaurant*, near the State Bank of India, does good seafood. Tandoori shark is Rs 65, most other main dishes are between Rs 50 and Rs 60.

Along the road to Baga, there's the popular *Boutique-Tatophanie Cafe*, a slick, German-run place selling designer clothes and serving treats such as apple pie, chocolate cake and filter coffee. Another good place is the *Milky Way*, which serves ice creams, milkshakes and a range of snacks. Honey nut yoghurt with papaya is Rs 15.

Vila Goesa has an open-air restaurant and a pub. There are live bands twice a week in the high season.

One of the most popular restaurants in this area is *Tito's Bar & Restaurant*, in an excellent setting by the beach. It's the only nightspot to speak of, and it boasts a high-powered sound system and dance floor. Prices are double what you'd pay in other restaurants in Calangute and Baga; main dishes are Rs 75 to Rs 150, and the cheapest beer is Rs 35.

Further along the main road to Baga is the *Casa Portuguesa Bar & Restaurant*. This is a good place for a minor splurge thanks to its old-world charm and pleasant setting among the coconut palms.

In Baga itself, the best place is *Squeeze* – although it doesn't look much from the outside. Within this grass shack, however, they whistle up superb home-made pasta, excellent coffee, and there's a good range of fresh juices and cocktails. Homesick Brits can catch the football results over shepherd's pie or meat balls at *Meat & Two Veg* nearby.

At the end of the road, take your pick of the open-air restaurants – *Jack's, Britto's* or *St Anthony's*. They're all popular and offer the same sort of fare at a similar price – Western breakfasts, seafood, fruit juices, beer and other drinks.

For a very mellow afternoon or a night out, try *Nani's & Rani's Bar & Restaurant*. The food is good and the atmosphere relaxed. There are several other places springing up on this side of the river.

Things to Buy

Calangute and Baga have been swamped by Kashmiri traders eager to cash in on the tourist boom. Their incessant hassling and pressure-selling can become tedious. There is, however, a good range of things to buy – Kashmiri carpets, embroideries, and papier-mâché boxes, as well as genuine and reproduction Tibetan and Rajasthani crafts. Interesting jewellery, bangles and other ethnic trinkets (usually Tibetan, Kashmiri and Indian tribal in origin) are available.

Most things are well made but nothing is cheap. If you're going to buy, bargain very hard and don't be afraid to offer a price far below the first price suggested.

Getting There & Away

There are frequent buses to Panaji (Rs 2.50, 35 minutes) and Mapusa from Calangute.

Taxis are also available and worth the extra cost if you have a small group and want to save time. Panaji to Calangute or Baga costs Rs 100 and takes about 20 minutes.

On Wednesday, boats leave regularly from Baga Beach for the Anjuna flea market.

Getting Around

Most of the buses between Panaji and this area terminate at Calangute; few continue on to Baga. Bicycles can be hired at many places in Calangute and Baga at the usual rates – Rs 3 per hour or Rs 20 for a full day, though many places ask up to Rs 40 per day. Motorcycles are also available for hire (see the Getting Around section at the start of this chapter) and touts cruise up and down looking for customers for the bike they're riding.

ANJUNA

Telephone Area Code: 0832

Famous throughout Goa for its Wednesday flea market, this is the beach that everyone went to when Calangute had been filmed, recorded, reported and talked about into the sand. There's a weird and wonderful collection of overlanders, monks, defiant ex-hippies, gentle lunatics, artists, artisans, seers, searchers and peripatetic expatriates who normally wouldn't be seen out of the organic confines of their health-food emporia in San Francisco or London.

There's no point in trying to define what Anjuna is or what it's like – it's many different things to many different people. The only way to find out is to stay here for a while and make some friends. Full moon, when the parties take place, is a particularly good time to be here.

Vagator Beach, Goa.

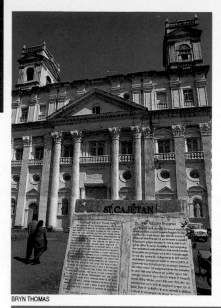
BRYN THOMAS

BRYN THOMAS

BRYN THOMAS

Goa
Top Left: Church of St Cajetan, Old Goa.
Top Right: Anjuna flea market.
Bottom: Fishing boat, Palolen Beach.

Unlike Calangute, the place has retained its charm and there's no package tourism. Nude bathing, on the other hand, is very much on the decline, as are the once freely available drugs. Local outrage and official concern about the excesses of a certain minority has led to periodic clampdowns and an exodus to more remote beaches like Arambol to the north and Gokarn, over the border in Karnataka, to the south.

Information

You can have mail sent to Anjuna post office. Halfway between Nelson's Bar and the beach is a branch of MGM Travels, where you can make bookings and get flights confirmed.

The retail needs of the expatriate community are served by the Oxford Stores (open daily from 8 am to 8.30 pm). You can get everything from a loaf of bread to a Christmas turkey (Rs 700), and they even have a cabinet of 'exotic' goodies – Vegemite,

Heinz baked beans, etc. You can change money here and at several other places around the village, but the bank only does cash advances on a Visa card. The nearest bank for foreign exchange is in Vagator.

Take great care of your possessions in Anjuna, particularly on party nights, as theft is a big problem. The bank has safety deposit boxes which you can use. You should also take care not to waste water because there's an acute shortage, especially late in the season.

Places to Stay

Several guest houses have sprung up over the past few years but this is still a beach where the majority of the foreign population stays on a long-term basis.

It isn't easy to find a place to stay between November and March. Most of the available houses are rented for six months or a year by people who come back again and again. If you want to stay here, you may have to make do with a very primitive shack to start with.

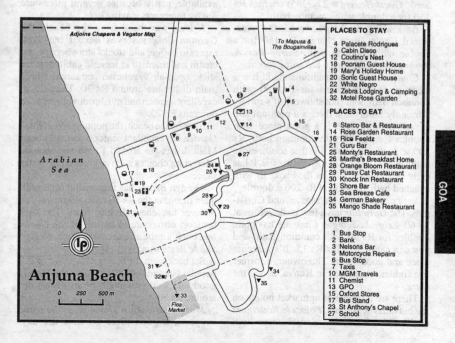

Anjuna Beach

0   250   500 m

Adjoins Chapora & Vagator Map

To Mapusa &
The Bougainvillea

Arabian
Sea

Flea
Market

GOA

PLACES TO STAY
4 Palacete Rodrigues
9 Cabin Disco
12 Coutino's Nest
18 Poonam Guest House
19 Mary's Holiday Home
20 Sonic Guest House
22 White Negro
24 Zebra Lodging & Camping
32 Motel Rose Garden

PLACES TO EAT
8 Starco Bar & Restaurant
14 Rose Garden Restaurant
16 Rice Feeldz
21 Guru Bar
25 Monty's Restaurant
26 Martha's Breakfast Home
28 Orange Bloom Restaurant
29 Pussy Cat Restaurant
30 Knock Inn Restaurant
31 Shore Bar
33 Sea Breeze Cafe
34 German Bakery
35 Mango Shade Restaurant

OTHER
1 Bus Stop
2 Bank
3 Nelsons Bar
5 Motorcycle Repairs
6 Bus Stop
7 Taxis
10 MGM Travels
11 Chemist
13 GPO
15 Oxford Stores
17 Bus Stand
23 St Anthony's Chapel
27 School

Anjuna Flea Market

The Wednesday flea market at Anjuna is a major attraction for people from all the Goan beaches. It's a wonderful blend of Tibetan and Kashmiri traders, colourful Gujarati tribal women and blissed-out '60s-style hippies. It's quite a scene. Whatever you need, from a used paperback to a new swimsuit, you'll find it here – though you have to bargain hard to get a reasonable deal. There's also lots of good Indian and Western food. Traditional-style fishing boats are available for transport to the market from Baga Beach – you'll see notices advertising this in Baga's restaurants. ■

Quite a few places have 'Rooms to Let' signs displayed, so head for these initially.

Accommodation prices given here are for the mid-December to late January high season. In November and February, they drop by about 30% to 50%.

There are several places by the bus park. *Poonam Guest House* (☎ 27-3247) is quite an attractive place, built around a garden. Rooms are basic but expensive at Rs 250 for a double with attached bath. The price drops to Rs 100 in November or February. Nearby, *Mary's Holiday Home* is similarly priced. *Sonic Guest House* (☎ 27-3285) charges Rs 150 for a double with common bath.

Back along the Mapusa road, the over-priced *Cabin Disco* charges Rs 150 for a double with common bath. *Starco Bar & Restaurant,* nearby, also has some rooms.

Coutino's Nest is recommended. It's a clean place with rooms for Rs 100 with common bathroom (hot shower). It's run by a friendly family and there's a pleasant sun terrace. *White Negro* is a good place with doubles for Rs 100 with common bath; Rs 200 with attached bath. Further south, close to the beach, is the *Motel Rose Garden*. It has eight reasonable rooms at the back, all with attached bath, for around Rs 200 a double.

Very cheap places are rare around Christmas. The *Guru Bar* has a few basic rooms at Rs 60. *Zebra Lodging & Camping* has plain doubles for Rs 70 with common bath, and you can camp here for Rs 15. It's a secure place and good value. The owner, a former fire fighter, once lived in Kenya, hence the name.

There are a couple of upmarket hotels on the outskirts of Anjuna. *Palacete Rodrigues* (☎ 27-4304) is an old colonial house built around a courtyard. Doubles are Rs 400 and suites Rs 550. It's quite a pleasant place. *The Bougainvillea* (☎ 27-3271; fax 27-4370) is much swankier, and partly foreign-owned. There's a swimming pool lined with black marble, a large garden, a bar and barbecue, and live music on Saturday evenings. Well-appointed rooms are Rs 600/1000 to Rs 800/1200 for a single/double.

Places to Eat

Anjuna has the usual beachside cafes, but there's some refreshingly different food available, partly because several places are run by foreigners staying here.

A long way back from the beach, the *German Bakery* serves herbal teas and espresso coffee, and stocks strawberries and cream and tiramisu in its cold cabinet. It's a slick, open-air vegetarian restaurant where main dishes are around Rs 30. They do an excellent spinach and mushroom burger with hummus Rs 20.

Back on the beach, the popular *Motel Rose Garden* has excellent seafood and cold beer. Main dishes are around Rs 40 and include interesting choices such as chicken in oyster sauce.

The *Sea Breeze* has reasonable food with main dishes in the Rs 30 to Rs 40 range. *Joe Banana* has cheap Indian food. The best tandoori dishes are to be had at the *Knock Inn,* but it's quite an expensive place. *Mango Shade Restaurant* is cheaper.

Set back from the beach, *White Negro* is a popular bar and restaurant where the food is good and well-presented. Main dishes are around Rs 50.

Martha's Breakfast Home is, as the name suggests, a good place to start the day.

There's good coffee and pancakes. At the *Pussy Cat*, nearby, there's lassi and ice cream and you can sometimes get strawberries. *Rice Feeldz*, south of Oxford Stores, should now be open. Homemade tofu was promised.

Entertainment

For most people, the evening begins with several beers on the steps of the *Shore Bar*, watching the sun go down. It can get very crowded, particularly after the flea market, and the powerful sound system keeps people here until long after dark. The *Guru Bar* is another popular drinking spot.

The famous parties are usually held on full-moon nights, particularly over Christmas and the New Year, but there's also often something going on after the flea market. If there's nothing happening, the *Primrose Cafe* in Vagator stays open late and is a popular place to move on to. If there's a party in the area, they'll probably know about it. The motorcycle taxi-wallahs are also good sources of information.

Getting There & Away

There are buses every hour or so to Anjuna and Chapora from Mapusa. They can be very crowded, so it's usually a lot easier, and certainly quicker, to take a motorcycle (Rs 30 to Rs 40, about 15 minutes) or to get a group together and hire a taxi.

Licence and insurance checks on foreigners who rent motorcycles are becoming more common, particularly on market day. See the warning under the Getting Around section at the beginning of this chapter for more details.

CHAPORA & VAGATOR

Telephone Area Code: 0832

This is one of the most beautiful and interesting parts of Goa's coastline, and a good deal more attractive than Anjuna for either a short or a long stay. Much of the inhabited area nestles under a canopy of dense coconut palms, and Chapora village is dominated by a rocky hill on top of which sits an old Portuguese fort. The fort is fairly well preserved and worth a visit; the views from its ramparts are excellent.

Secluded, sandy coves are found all the way around the northern side of this rocky outcrop, though Vagator's main beaches face west towards the Indian Ocean. Little Vagator, the beach to the south, is very popular with travellers and lots of people staying in Calangute and Baga come up here for the day.

Many Westerners stay here on a long-term basis but it's not a tourist ghetto. The local people remain friendly and, since the houses available for rent are widely scattered and there are several beaches and coves to choose from, it's really only on Little Vagator that you see large groups of travellers together in one place. However, although there's still no package tourism, the place is starting to change. The Vagator Beach Resort has been tarted up and you can even purchase a time-share here! Vagator is a major stop on the bus tours of North Goa, so for a few hours each day the nearest parts of the beach to the bus stop are flooded with day-trippers.

Places to Stay

Most people who come here stay for a long time. Initially, you'll have to take whatever is available and ask around, or stay at Calangute or Baga and 'commute' until you've found something. It helps if you get here before the real height of the season – try September and October when there are only a few people about and places have 'Rooms to Let' signs out.

Wherever you decide to live, make sure you have a torch (flashlight) handy. There are no street lights, and finding your way along the paths through coconut palms late at night when there's no full moon is a devil of a job. Houses for rent cost anything from Rs 500 to Rs 2000 a month depending on their size, location and the length of the rental period. If you're only going to be here for the month over Christmas, you may have to pay two or three times the usual rate – presuming you can find a place to stay, that is.

For short term accommodation, there are several guest houses and small hotels. In

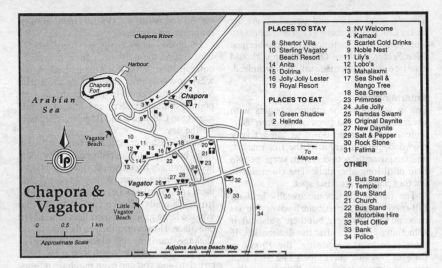

PLACES TO STAY
8 Shertor Villa
10 Sterling Vagator Beach Resort
14 Anita
15 Dolrina
16 Jolly Jolly Lester
19 Royal Resort

PLACES TO EAT
1 Green Shadow
2 Helinda

3 NV Welcome
4 Kamaxi
5 Scarlet Cold Drinks
9 Noble Nest
11 Lily's
12 Lobo's
13 Mahalaxmi
17 Sea Shell & Mango Tree
18 Sea Green
23 Primrose
24 Julie Jolly
25 Ramdas Swami
26 Original Daynite
27 New Daynite
29 Salt & Pepper
30 Rock Stone
31 Fatima

OTHER
6 Bus Stand
7 Temple
20 Bus Stand
21 Church
22 Bus Stand
28 Motorbike Hire
32 Post Office
33 Bank
34 Police

Chapora & Vagator

Chapora River

Harbour

Chapora Fort

Arabian Sea

Vagator Beach

Chapora

Vagator

Little Vagator Beach

To Mapusa

0   0.5   1 km
Approximate Scale

Adjoins Anjuna Beach Map

Vagator, the *Dolrina Guest House* has a good range of rooms and is run by a very friendly family. Singles/doubles with common bath are Rs 120/170; Rs 200 to Rs 250 for doubles with attached bath. The *Anita Lodge*, nearby, is a little cheaper, but in December they may rent the whole place out – Rs 3500 between six people for the month. In the same area, *Jolly Jolly Lester* has six good doubles with attached bath at Rs 250. You can also ask for rooms at *Lobo's* and *Lily's* restaurants.

In Chapora, *Shertor Villa* is OK. It has 12 rooms and charges Rs 70 for a double with common bath. Ask at the restaurants for rooms in villagers' houses. For short term accommodation, prices start from around Rs 35 for a very basic room.

The *Royal Resort* (☎ 27-4365) is one of those classic Indian places that deteriorates fast from the moment it opens. They charge an extortionate Rs 900 for a double for the Christmas peak; Rs 450 for the rest of the high season. There's a pool non-guests can use for Rs 25.

Much more attractive is the *Sterling Vagator Beach Resort* (☎ 27-3277), on the beach of the same name. The resort, in palm-shaded grounds, comprises a main block

containing the restaurant, bar and reception area, and two types of cottages. It's a friendly place and, as beach resorts go in Goa, quite good. Over Christmas, ordinary/air-con cottages cost Rs 1208/1725; Rs 715/1208 for the rest of the high season. For Rs 40,000 you can buy a time-share with Sterling Resorts and spend a week here each year for the next 99 years!

Places to Eat

There are numerous restaurants along the main street of Chapora village. For excellent ice cream and fruit salad, *Scarlet Cold Drinks* can't be beaten – but there's only one table. *Green Shadow* is good for tandoori dishes (around Rs 30). *Helinda*, next door, also has a good reputation. At *NV Welcome* there's a wide selection of seafood – kingfish, pomfret, tiger prawns, crabs, and (sometimes) lobster. *Kamaxi* is a little cheaper, and *Noble Nest* is also popular.

Just above Vagator Beach, there's a clutch of small restaurants including *Lily's*, *Lobo's* and *Mahalaxmi*. *Jolly Jolly Lester* is a friendly place with a good range of travellers' fare. Further east along this road, *Sea Green* does excellent Chinese food that's good value. Chilli fried prawns are Rs 35. *Mango Tree* also does tasty Chinese food.

To the south, and parallel to this road, is another group of restaurants. *Salt & Pepper* offers fried mussels with chips and salad for Rs 40. *Fatima's* has Kentucky chicken for Rs 50 and strawberries and cream for Rs 35.

The place to go at night is the *Primrose Cafe*, which stays open late and has a great sound system.

Getting There & Away

There are fairly frequent buses to Chapora from Mapusa throughout the day for Rs 2. A bus to Vagator is almost as convenient. There are also occasional direct buses from Panaji which follow the coast instead of going via Mapusa. The bus stand is near the road junction in Chapora village. It's often easier and much quicker to rent a motorcycle from Mapusa or to get a group together and hire a taxi.

ARAMBOL (Harmal)

Some years ago, when the screws were tightened at Anjuna in an attempt to control what local people regarded as the more outrageous activities (nudism and drug use) of a certain section of the travelling community, the diehards cast around for a more 'sympathetic' beach. Arambol, north of Chapora, was one of those which they chose.

Initially, only those willing to put up with very primitive conditions and a total lack of facilities came here. That has changed but development has so far been minimal, although there is talk of a golf course and resort being built here.

The seashore is beautiful and the village quiet and friendly, with just a few hundred locals, mostly fishing people, and a couple of hundred Western residents in the November to February high season.

Buses from Mapusa stop at the modern part of Arambol, on the main road, where there's a church, a few shops, but no bank. From here, a side road leads one km down to the village, and the beach is about 500 metres further on. This main beach is a good place to swim but to the north are several much

more attractive bays – follow the path over the headland. There are some new chalets on the hillside of the first bay. Behind the second bay is a small fresh water pool that's very pleasant to lie about in. You can give yourself a mudbath with the mud that lines the bottom of this pool, said to be very good for the skin; and there's a hot spring nearby.

Places to Stay & Eat

The most pleasant accommodation is in the little chalets on the next bay north. They're basic – outside toilets and water from a spring – but the sea views are superb. It costs Rs 70 to Rs 100 for a room.

About 500 metres back from the beach, *Ganesh Stores* has several double rooms at Rs 150 with attached bath; Rs 100 without. *Mrs Naik Home*, on the road to the beach, has doubles with attached bath for Rs 200.

Long-term residents rent rooms from the villagers, which range from Rs 30 to Rs 70, depending on facilities and the season. The most basic places are often no more than four walls and a roof. You can rent mattresses, cookers and all the rest from the shops at the village.

There are about 10 bars lining the main beach, the most interesting of them being *Jah Kingdom*, which specialises in Ethiopian and Jamaican food – and music. Steak is Rs 35, custard pie Rs 20. Set back from the beach, the *Garden of Meals* is open every evening and usually has a set special: fettuccine on Tuesday; couscous on Friday.

Getting There & Away

There are buses from Mapusa to Arambol every couple of hours which take three hours. Alternatively, get a group together and hire a taxi. Remember that if you do this, you'll have to pay the fare both ways since the driver is unlikely to be able to pick up passengers for the return journey. A taxi from Vagator costs around Rs 50.

Cars and motorcycles can use the ferry between Siolem and Chopdem, which runs every 30 minutes between 6 am and 10 pm.

There are boats every Wednesday to the Anjuna flea market.

TEREKHOL FORT

At Terekhol, on the north bank of the river of the same name, there's a small Portuguese fort with a little church (usually locked) within its walls. Formerly a cheap tourist guest house, the *Hotel Tirakhol Fort Heritage* (☎ Panaji 22-0705; fax Panaji 28-3326) has been privatised and revamped, and prices have increased dramatically. It's still a popular place to stay but not great value. The honeymoon suite is best, with superb views south along the sandy coast. The bathroom is intended for lovers (there's a circular tub) but not the bedroom (separate beds!). All this is yours for Rs 1750. There are other rooms with attached shower for Rs 1045, but the cheapest cell-like rooms downstairs are distinctly overpriced at Rs 500.

The fort makes a good outing on a motorcycle, and you could stop for a swim on deserted Querim Beach, but there's very little to see at the fort itself apart from the views.

There are occasional buses from Mapusa or Pernem to Querim, on the south bank of the river, opposite Terekhol, and also between Arambol and Querim. The ferry between Querim and Terekhol runs every half hour between 6 am and 10 pm. A taxi between the airport and Terekhol costs around Rs 600.

South Goa

Although the beaches of the southern district of Goa include travellers' centres like Colva and Benaulim, and a sprinkling of upmarket resort complexes, there's generally less tourist development here than in the north.

Margao is both the capital of the region and the transport hub. Goa's Dabolim Airport is near Vasco da Gama, which is also the state's railhead.

VASCO DA GAMA

Telephone Area Code: 0834

Close to Mormugao Harbour and three km from Dabolim Airport, Vasco da Gama is the terminus of the railway line to Goa – though a few local trains continue to the harbour. If you arrive in Goa by train, you can get off at Margao to reach Colva Beach; if you fly in, it's possible to arrive too late to get much further than Vasco unless you're prepared to take a taxi. Fortunately, there are several hotels in this unexciting town.

Places to Stay

The most pleasant budget option is *Twiga Lodge* (☎ 51-2682), near the bus stand. It's an old Portuguese house run by Tony and Iva Pereira, who worked in Nairobi for a while (twiga is Swahili for giraffe). There is just one single and four doubles for Rs 40/60, and they tend to fill up quickly.

At the western end of town is the recommended *Hotel Annapurna* (☎ 51-3715), Dattatria Deshpande Rd, which offers singles/doubles for Rs 95/135 with bathrooms attached. Good vegetarian food is served in the restaurant. Just opposite is the *Hotel Westend* (☎ 51-1576) which has double rooms at Rs 135.

Another good choice is the centrally located *Tourist Hotel* (☎ 51-3119), run by the Goa Tourist Development Corporation. Singles/doubles cost Rs 130/150 in the high season; Rs 100/120 in the low season. There are also rooms with four beds for Rs 200; Rs 180 in the low season.

The *Hotel Gladstone* (☎ 51-3966), on the eastern side of the old bus stand, is OK. Singles/doubles are Rs 120/160, or Rs 180/220 with air-con. The nearby *Hotel Urvashi* (☎ 51-0273) is also reasonable, with rooms for Rs 95/125 with common bath; Rs 125/180 with bath attached.

The Citadel (☎ 51-2097), near the Tourist Hotel, is more upmarket. Each room has a TV and an attached bathroom with water heater. They charge Rs 315/325, or Rs 360/400 for air-con rooms. The top place in town is the *Hotel La Paz Gardens* (☎ 51-2121; fax 51-3302), where air-con rooms cost Rs 600/700.

Less than one km from the airport is the *Hotel Airport* (☎ 51-2165). Plain rooms cost Rs 200/300 or Rs 350/550 with air-con.

GOA

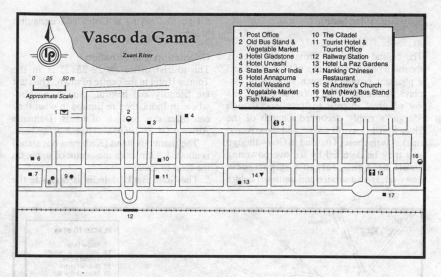

Vasco da Gama

Zuari River

0   25   50 m

Approximate Scale

1 Post Office
2 Old Bus Stand &
   Vegetable Market
3 Hotel Gladstone
4 Hotel Urvashi
5 State Bank of India
6 Hotel Annapurna
7 Hotel Westend
8 Vegetable Market
9 Fish Market
10 The Citadel
11 Tourist Hotel &
   Tourist Office
12 Railway Station
13 Hotel La Paz Gardens
14 Nanking Chinese
   Restaurant
15 St Andrew's Church
16 Main (New) Bus Stand
17 Twiga Lodge

Places to Eat

The *Nanking Chinese Restaurant*, three blocks east of the railway station, is a friendly place with good food. Szechuan chicken is Rs 32. On the corner of this street is a fast-food joint, the *Goodland*, serving pizzas for Rs 25, sausage rolls and ice cream. There's also a more expensive Chinese restaurant, the *Sweet N Sour*, in the Hotel La Paz Gardens. Main dishes here are around Rs 50.

The vegetarian restaurant at the *Hotel Annapurna* is a good, cheap option, with thalis for Rs 12. As a fall back, there's the typically uninspiring service and menu at the restaurant in the *Tourist Hotel*.

Getting There & Away

The new bus stand is on the eastern edge of town, although a few buses still start from the old bus stand in the centre. You can catch deluxe buses from the new bus stand to Bombay (Rs 227, 15 hours) and Bangalore (Rs 180, 12 hours), and there are frequent buses to Margao (Rs 5, one hour) and Panaji (Rs 5, one hour). Change at Panaji for Mapusa and the beaches of North Goa. Long-distance private buses can be booked at the kiosks outside the railway station.

See Getting There & Away at the start of this chapter for information about trains from Vasco.

A taxi to the airport costs Rs 40.

BOGMALO

Eight km from Vasco, and only four km from the airport, is Bogmalo Beach. It's a small, sandy cove dominated by the five-star Oberoi hotel, which evaded the restriction requiring all hotels to be built at least 500 metres from the beach. There's little here apart from the resort hotel and a couple of smaller places to stay, the reasonably pleasant beach, several expensive beach cafes, and the small village of Bogmalo.

Rooms at the *Oberoi Bogmalo Beach Resort* (☎ 51-3291; fax 51-2510) cost US$110/120; there's a pool and all the usual trimmings you'd expect in a hotel of this calibre. In the village, not far from the beach, there's the *Petite Guest House* (☎ 51-0122); a double with attached bath is around Rs 300. A 15-minute walk northeast along the road to the airport is *Vinny's Holiday Resort* (☎ 51-0174), where an air-con double costs Rs 880. The resort has a shuttle bus to the beach and the airport, and you can use the facilities at the Oberoi.

GOA

MARGAO (Madgaon)

Population: 77,000
Telephone Area Code: 0834

The capital of Salcete province, Margao is the main population centre of South Goa and a pleasant provincial town which still displays reminders of its Portuguese past. It's not of great interest to travellers, though Margao's richly decorated Church of the Holy Spirit is worth a visit, and the covered market is the best of its kind in Goa – though you may be deterred by the overpowering smell of fish. Margao's importance, however, is as a service and transport centre

for people staying at Colva and Benaulim beaches.

Orientation & Information

The tourist office (☎ 22-2513) is in the Tourist Hotel in the centre of town. The staff are friendly and helpful, though, as elsewhere in India, they're limited in what they can offer due to lack of funds. Damania Airways (☎ 22-1966) also has an office here.

The main bus stand (Kadamba bus stand) is about 1.5 km from the centre of town, on the road to Panaji.

The State Bank of India is opposite the

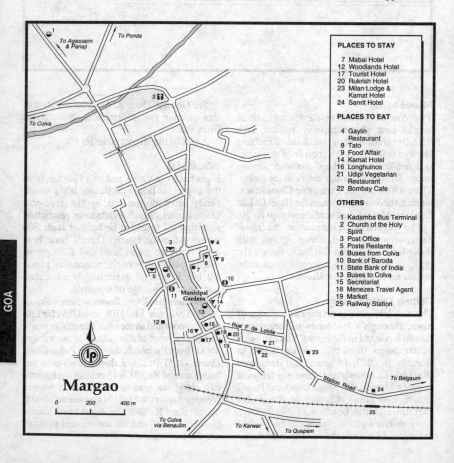

PLACES TO STAY

7   Mabai Hotel
12 Woodlands Hotel
17 Tourist Hotel
20 Rukrish Hotel
23 Milan Lodge &
    Kamat Hotel
24 Sanrit Hotel

PLACES TO EAT

4   Gaylin
    Restaurant
8   Tato
9   Food Affair
14 Kamat Hotel
16 Longhuinos
21 Udipi Vegetarian
    Restaurant
22 Bombay Cafe

OTHERS

1   Kadamba Bus Terminal
2   Church of the Holy
    Spirit
3   Post Office
5   Poste Restante
6   Buses from Colva
10 Bank of Baroda
11 State Bank of India
13 Buses to Colva
15 Secretariat
18 Menezes Travel Agent
19 Market
25 Railway Station

Margao

0   200   400 m

Municipal Gardens. You can change money at several hotels in Colva, but at 3% to 5% below the official rate.

Menezes, behind the Secretariat, is an Indian Airlines agent, but you'll get things done faster if you go direct to the office in Panaji.

The GPO is on the north side of the Municipal Gardens, but the poste restante (open only from 8.30 to 10.30 am and 3 to 4.30 pm) has its own office, 300 metres south-west of the GPO.

Places to Stay

Most of the cheapies are strung out along Station Rd between the Municipal Gardens and the railway station. The friendly *Rukrish Hotel* (☎ 22-1709) is probably the best of the bunch. It has good, clean singles with small balconies overlooking the street for Rs 60, or doubles with bathroom for Rs 120. The rooms are rented on a 24-hour basis.

The *railway retiring rooms* are Rs 65 for a double or Rs 15 per bed in a very basic dorm. Across the road is the *Sanrit Hotel*, where singles/doubles are Rs 45/80 without bath. All of these places fill up early. Between the station and the centre, the *Milan Lodge* (☎ 22-2715) is better value, with rooms for Rs 45/65 or Rs 50/75 with attached bath. Checkout time is at 5.30 pm – useful if you're catching an evening train.

Near the market in the middle of town, the government-run *Tourist Hotel* (☎ 22-1966) has singles/doubles for Rs 130/150 (Rs 30 less in the low season). It's of a similar standard to the Tourist Hotel in Panaji.

The *Mabai Hotel* (☎ 22-1653) is conveniently located at the northern end of the Municipal Gardens. There are singles/doubles for Rs 150/200; Rs 200/250 with air-con. The rooms are large and airy, although the front rooms tend to be noisy. There's also a restaurant, bar and roof garden.

Probably the best place to stay in Margao is the quiet *Woodlands Hotel* (☎ 22-1121), Miguel Loyola Furtado Rd, which has friendly staff and its own bar and restaurant. There's a wide range of rooms from basic singles/doubles for Rs 150/180 to air-con suites with TV at Rs 400.

Places to Eat

The *Kamat Hotel*, beside the Municipal Gardens, is part of the chain found throughout south India. It offers cheap, no-frills meals for Rs 15 and south Indian snack food. There's a second branch by the Milan Lodge. The *Bombay Cafe* is another popular place; the *Udipi Vegetarian Restaurant* opposite is also good. The best vegetarian restaurant in Margao, however, is *Tato*, east of the Municipal Gardens. A thali costs Rs 19, and the place is very clean.

Directly opposite the tourist office, the charming *Longuinhos* does pastries, sweets and serves very good meals. Tandoori pomfret is Rs 60. The restaurant at the *Woodlands Hotel* is extremely good value – fish curry rice is Rs 17.

Food Affair is a subterranean restaurant near Tato that has tasty northern Indian food and attentive service. Main dishes are Rs 50 to Rs 60. Nearby is an excellent Chinese restaurant, the *Gaylin*. There's a large room upstairs and a smaller air-con dining-room below. It's very popular, particularly at lunchtime. Main dishes are Rs 40 to Rs 60.

Getting There & Away

Bus From the Kadamba bus stand, buses leave at around 3 pm for Bombay (Rs 227 for a luxury bus, 16 hours). There are two buses in the morning for Hubli (Rs 37, six hours), and three buses for Belgaum (Rs 29, five hours) and Mangalore (Rs 105, 10 hours).

Margao has good connections with beaches and other towns in Goa:

Colva Beach – from the Municipal Gardens, buses run to Colva via Benaulim approximately every hour. The first bus from Margao leaves at about 7.30 am and the last at 8 pm. The fare is Rs 2.50 and the journey takes 20 minutes.

Panaji – buses depart from the Kadamba bus stand approximately every half hour from dawn to 8 pm, take about 1½ hours and cost Rs 5.50. It's a picturesque journey, if you get a seat, because there are many old, whitewashed churches and monasteries to be seen en route. The alternative route taken by some buses is via Ponda, and this takes at least an hour longer (Rs 6). Damania runs a deluxe bus (Rs 50!) to Panaji leaving the Tourist Hotel at noon to connect with its catamaran to Bombay.

Other Buses – you can find buses to most towns in Goa from the Kadamba bus stand in Margao. Timetables are approximate (the buses leave when full) but they're fairly frequent to the major population centres. To the smaller towns, such as Betul, south of Colva, they're much less frequent, so it's best to make enquiries at the bus stand in advance. Get there early if you want a seat.

Train See the Getting There & Away section at the start of this chapter for train information. Bookings for all classes can be made at Margao station, *except* for Indrail Pass holders who must go to Vasco da Gama to make bookings.

Taxi To get to Colva, you can take a motor-cycle for around Rs 20 (no objection to backpacks), auto-rickshaw (around Rs 30) or taxi (around Rs 55).

AROUND MARGAO
Rachol Seminary & Church
Six km from Margao, near the village of Raia, is the Rachol Seminary and Church. The **Museum of Christian Art** was opened here recently, partly funded by the Gulbenkian Foundation. The interesting displays include textiles, some of the silver once used in the churches of Old Goa, a magnificent 17th-century, silver monstrance in the shape of a swan, and a mobile mass kit (complete with candlesticks) – standard issue for missionaries out in the jungle. The museum is open daily from 9.30 am to 12.30 pm and 2.30 to 5 pm; entrance is Rs 5. There's a glossy catalogue for Rs 375.

The church dates from 1610 and the seminary has interesting architecture, a decaying library and paintings of Christian characters done in Indian styles. This is not a tourist site, so you should ask before wandering around.

There are buses from Margao, but make sure you get on one to Rachol Seminary not Illa de Rachol.

Menezes Briganza House
Twenty km east of Margao, in the village of Chandor, there are several interesting colonial mansions. One of the grandest, the Menezes Briganza House, is open to the public. The family has lived here since the 17th century and the rooms are furnished with antiques, hung with chandeliers, and the windows are glazed with stained glass. There's a ballroom, and even a baroque private chapel. For information on the erratic opening hours, contact the tourist office in Margao. There are frequent buses to Chandor from Margao.

Christ Ashram
To the east of the Margao to Cortalim road, near the village of Nuvem, is the Christ Ashram exorcism centre. It has been condemned by Catholic authorities because the trappings are Catholic but the ambience is definitely Hindu.

COLVA & BENAULIM
Telephone Area Code: 0834

The most beautiful stretches of white sand in Goa extend sun-drenched and palm-fringed for km after km all the way from Majorda, through Colva, Benaulim, Varca and Cavelossim, down to the point at Mobor.

Twenty years ago, precious little disturbed Colva, except the local fishing people who pulled their catch in by hand each morning, and a few of the more intrepid hippies who had forsaken the obligatory sex, drugs and rock & roll of Calangute for the soothing tranquillity of this paradise. Since there were only two cottages for rent and one restaurant (Vincy's), most people stayed either on the beach itself or in palm-leaf shelters, which they took over from departing travellers or constructed themselves.

Those days are gone forever. Even in days of yore, the property speculators and developers had begun to sniff around in search of a fast rupee. Today, you can see the results of their efforts – air-con resort complexes, close-packed ranks of tourist cottages, discos, trinket stalls and cold-drink stands. Between the bus park and beach, the small stream now runs black with pollution. You'll be lucky if you see an angler around the main area and most fishermen now have motorised trawlers which stand anchored in a line offshore. Likewise, you won't come across anyone sleeping out on the beach these days or throwing up a palm-leaf shelter.

It's only fair to point out that this development is contained within relatively small areas. The dozen or so resort complexes which have sprung up along this 30-km coastline are, for the most part, widely spaced and self-contained. Colva itself has suffered, but much of the development here is in the small area around the end of the road from Margao – it's simplicity itself to get away from it. Walk two km in either direction, and you'll get close to what it used to be like before the cement mixers began chugging away. Despite this, the area has a long way to go before it gets as developed as Calangute, or a lot of other beaches I could think of around the world.

Information

The nearest post office is in Colva village, where letters can be sent poste restante. There's no bank in Colva, but the larger hotels change travellers' cheques (at lower rates than the banks). The nearest banks are in Benaulim village, where the Bank of Baroda handles Visa card cash advances only, and Margao.

You can send and receive faxes from the booth outside the Tourist Complex.

Places to Stay

It's possible to rent houses long term in Colva and Benaulim, just ask around in the restaurants and shops. Most houses are a 20-minute walk from the beach. Prices vary enormously, depending on location, the size of the house and the season, but you can expect to pay anything from around Rs 800 a month to well over Rs 2000 – double the price over Christmas. Between November and March, competition for houses is stiff, so get there before then if possible.

Colva There's a wide choice of short-term accommodation in Colva. At the cheaper end of the market are the places strung out along the roads behind the beach, north of the main area.

Rodrickson Cottages are set back from the beach, but are very good value at Rs 60/80 for basic rooms with a shower and toilet behind a partition within the room.

The long-running *Hotel Tourist Nest* is a rambling, old Portuguese house that's similarly good value. Doubles are Rs 70 with common bath, or Rs 100 with attached bathroom. Just around the corner is the friendly *La Village*, a family-run place with six rooms at Rs 65 for a double with common bathroom. The *Garden Cottages* close by are similar.

Fishermen's Cottages is one of the closest places to the beach. There's a few rooms at Rs 100 for a double with bathroom, though it's not the cleanest place in Colva. In the same area is the *Lucky Star Restaurant*, which has sea-facing, double rooms with attached bath for Rs 150, plus some cheaper rooms.

There are several places right in the thick of things on the main street. The *Vailankanni Cottages* are very popular with travellers, mainly because of the friendly atmosphere. Rooms here cost from Rs 90 to Rs 150 for a double with attached bathroom, and there are good meals and snacks available.

A little closer to the beach is the *Blue Diamond Cottages*. This is an older place which offers good, clean rooms for Rs 175 with attached bathroom. *Jymi's Cottages* is run by a friendly family and is very close to the beach just south of the main drag. The rooms are pretty basic and cost Rs 130.

Goa Tourism's *Tourist Complex* (or Tourist Cottages) (☎ 22-2287) consists of a two-storey terrace of rooms facing the sea (each with its own balcony), a separate block of cottages, a restaurant, bar, reception area and garden. The rooms cost Rs 220 a double with fan and bathroom, or Rs 380 with air-con. There's also a dormitory for Rs 40 per bed. The staff are friendly and the hotel is quite pleasant but it's not great value.

The *Hotel Colmar* (☎ 22-1253) is much better and has rooms for all budgets. There are singles/doubles with common bath for Rs 75/100, Rs 150/200 with bath attached. There are also some cottages (Rs 350 to Rs 700). The hotel has its own restaurant, bar

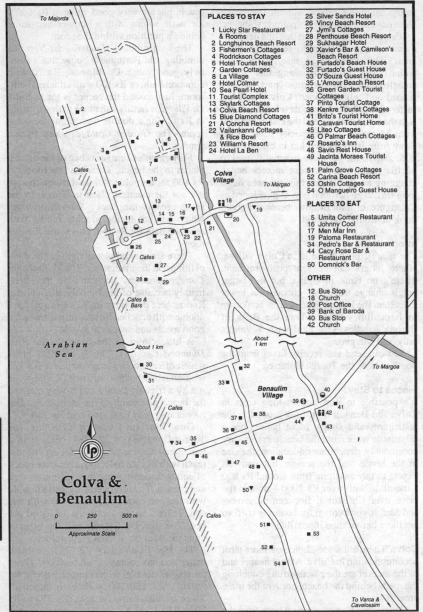

PLACES TO STAY

1 Lucky Star Restaurant & Rooms
2 Longhuinos Beach Resort
3 Fishermen's Cottages
4 Rodrickson Cottages
6 Hotel Tourist Nest
7 Garden Cottages
8 La Village
9 Hotel Colmar
10 Sea Pearl Hotel
11 Tourist Complex
13 Skylark Cottages
14 Colva Beach Resort
15 Blue Diamond Cottages
21 A Concha Resort
22 Vailankanni Cottages & Rice Bowl
23 William's Resort
24 Hotel La Ben
25 Silver Sands Hotel
26 Vincy Beach Resort
27 Jymi's Cottages
28 Penthouse Beach Resort
29 Sukhsagar Hotel
30 Xavier's Bar & Camilson's Beach Resort
31 Furtado's Beach House
32 Furtado's Guest House
33 D'Souza Guest House
35 L'Amour Beach Resort
36 Green Garden Tourist Cottages
37 Pinto Tourist Cottage
38 Kenkre Tourist Home
41 Brito's Tourist Home
43 Caravan Tourist Home
45 Liteo Cottages
46 O Palmar Beach Cottages
47 Rosario's Inn
48 Savio Rest House
49 Jacinta Moraes Tourist House
51 Palm Grove Cottages
52 Carina Beach Resort
53 Oshin Cottages
54 O Mangueiro Guest House

PLACES TO EAT

5 Umita Corner Restaurant
16 Johnny Cool
17 Men Mar Inn
19 Paloma Restaurant
34 Pedro's Bar & Restaurant
44 Cacy Rose Bar & Restaurant
50 Domnick's Bar

OTHER

12 Bus Stop
18 Church
20 Post Office
39 Bank of Baroda
40 Bus Stop
42 Church

To Majorda

Colva Village

To Margao

Arabian Sea

About 1 km

About 1 km

Cafes

Cafes

Cafes & Bars

Cafes

Benaulim Village

To Margoa

Cafes

Cafes

Colva & Benaulim

0   250   500 m

Approximate Scale

GOA

To Varca & Cavelossim

and money exchange facilities, and is used by overland tour groups.

Another good choice is the new *Sea Pearl Hotel*. The rooms are all spotlessly clean doubles with attached bath, and the rate is Rs 210. The staff are very friendly and helpful, and the restaurant is popular for its Western food.

The *Sukhsagar Hotel* (☎ 22-0224) is a reasonable place with doubles for Rs 240; Rs 380 with air-con. All rooms have bathrooms with individual water heaters. The *Hotel La Ben* (☎ 22-2009) is a fairly characterless new building on the main road. The unremarkable rooms are comfortable and good value at Rs 220 for a double with bathroom. There's a rooftop restaurant and bar.

The *Skylark Cottages* (☎ 22-3669) costs Rs 200 for a double with bathroom, or Rs 400 with air-con. The rooms are clean and it's good value.

The *Vincy Beach Resort* (☎ 22-2276), once the only bar/restaurant in the area, has been through many changes. The original Indo-Portuguese structure has sadly long since disappeared and Vincy's has joined the 20th century with a vengeance. It now offers plain double rooms with attached bathroom (and individual water heaters) for Rs 250. There's a restaurant on the ground floor, and although it has no atmosphere, the food is good.

Further away from the beach is the *Colva Beach Resort* (☎ 22-1975), which has doubles for Rs 375 and air-con doubles for Rs 500. More expensive, but definitely superior, is *William's Resort* (☎ 22-1077), which costs Rs 550 for a double; Rs 770 with air-con. There's a restaurant but the food is mediocre and the service slow; most people eat out. *A Concha Resort* (☎ 22-3593) is a long way back from the beach, near the church, but has good, clean rooms for Rs 460, and an excellent Chinese restaurant.

In the centre of Colva are two hotels with swimming pools, the *Silver Sands Hotel* (☎ 22-1645) and the *Penthouse Beach Resort* (☎ 22-1030). At the Silver Sands, doubles cost from Rs 795 (Rs 1000 over Christmas). As well as the pool, it boasts a health club, water sports, indoor games facilities, an excellent bar and restaurant, live bands in the high season, a travel counter and money exchange facilities. The Penthouse Beach Resort consists of a complex of Portuguese-style cottages built around a pool. Facilities and prices are similar to the Silver Sands.

The most pleasant hotel in this price range is *Longhuinos Beach Resort* (☎ 22-2918), which is in an excellent location near the beach. The rooms are simply furnished but most have balconies and face the sea. Rates are Rs 600/660 for a single/double with attached bath and hot water. There's a small garden with direct access to the beach.

Majorda There are several resort complexes north of Colva, along Majorda Beach. They include the *Majorda Beach Resort* (☎ 22-0025), which has 120 rooms costing Rs 2395 each; and the new *Regency Travelodge Resort* (☎ 25-4180), which has well-appointed rooms for Rs 2400 (Rs 5000 over Christmas).

A more interesting, though less luxurious, alternative would be to rent all or part of *Old Comfort* (☎ 25-4225; fax 22-0139), a 300-year-old Portuguese bungalow that's been partly renovated. Set back from the beach in a peaceful orchard, the five rooms range from Rs 350 to Rs 800 (Rs 250 to Rs 600 in the low season). There's a kitchen for guests or meals can be supplied.

Benaulim If you hanker after the more tranquil parts of this coastline, then Benaulim Beach, less than two km south of Colva, is the place to head for.

There are a few places right on the beach. *Furtado's Beach House* has four rooms with attached bath, each costing Rs 125. *Xavier's Bar*, nearby, has similar rooms, also at Rs 125. *Camilson's Beach Resort* has a few doubles at Rs 150, but most rooms here are around Rs 500.

L'Amour Beach Resort (☎ 22-3270) has reasonable rooms with attached bath, but prices have shot up recently and now range between Rs 250 and Rs 400. Most of the

GOA

rooms are cottages, and are aligned so that they catch the sea breezes. Opposite are the *O Palmar Beach Cottages* (☎ 22-3278), which are better value at Rs 189 with fan and bathroom. Neither of these places has much in the way of shade, but they're both very close to the beach and are often full in the high season.

Most of the other places are scattered around the village of Benaulim, about one km back from the beach, where accommodation is cheaper. *Rosario's Inn* is a pleasant place, run by a charming family, which has rooms with a verandah and attached bathroom for Rs 90. There are also cheaper rooms with common bath. In the same area is *Savio Rest House,* which charges just Rs 40 for a room with common bath; Rs 60 with attached bath. *Jacinta Moraes Tourist House*, nearby, has good doubles at Rs 80 with bath.

Also centrally located, *Green Garden Tourist Cottages* has two basic rooms for Rs 45/60 a single/double. *Kenkre Tourist Cottages*, nearby, is excellent value at Rs 60 for a double with attached bath. *Liteo Cottages* offers good doubles with attached bath for Rs 150.

A short distance north along one of the roads to Colva is the *D'Souza Guest House*. This is a small, excellent, upmarket guest house in a Goan bungalow with an extensive garden. Spotlessly clean rooms at this friendly, family-run place cost Rs 120 or Rs 175 with bath attached. They even accept credit cards! Also on this road is the *Pinto Tourist Cottage*, which has clean doubles for Rs 70 with attached bath.

Further south is *Palm Grove Cottages* (☎ 22-2533), which is an excellent place to stay. Set in a very peaceful garden, back from the beach, it has small rooms with attached bathroom for between Rs 125 and Rs 160, and larger rooms for Rs 175. Comfortable rooms in the new building cost Rs 225 to Rs 400 with bathroom and hot water, or Rs 500 with air-con. The staff are most helpful and good meals are available in the shady, garden restaurant.

South of this area, *O Mangueiro Guest House* has five doubles and a single that people often rent long term. Charges vary from Rs 40 to Rs 100. There's a kitchen and common bathroom. *Oshin Cottages* are in a very peaceful area, set back from the road. There are 12 doubles, all with attached bath, for Rs 150.

The top hotel in Benaulim is the small *Carina Beach Resort*, a low-key affair with a garden and swimming pool. Rooms are not great value at Rs 800, but they have a few cheaper rooms without attached bath.

The area around the second crossroads back from the beach is known as Maria Hall. The old *Caravan Tourist Home* (☎ 22-5679) here has a beautifully furnished sitting room, although the bedrooms are far more basic. Still, it's a pleasant place to stay, and singles/doubles are Rs 70/80. Right next door is the similarly priced *Priti Kunj Tourist Home*. On the Margao road nearby is *Brito's Tourist Home*. It's a fairly featureless place but is friendly and good value at Rs 70. You'll find the owner in the small general store attached.

Places to Eat

Colva The most popular places to eat (and drink) around Colva are the string of open-air, wooden restaurants which line the beach either side of where the road ends. They're all individually owned and, because of the competition, the standard of food is pretty high. Seafood is, of course, *de rigueur* and the restaurants are well tuned in to what travellers like for breakfast. Virtually all of them have a sound system but the variety and quality of the tapes they play varies enormously. Cold beer and spirits are available at all of them.

It would be unfair to single out individual restaurants for special mention since every traveller has their favourite place and this often depends on the particular crowd which congregates there. This naturally changes constantly, but if a restaurant is full, this tends to be a fairly good indication that the food is good.

Further back from the beach, along the back road, are a number of popular places. They include the *Men Mar Inn*, a laid-back place with a book exchange and cheap food. Main dishes are around Rs 25. *Umita Corner Restaurant* offers spaghetti with chicken for Rs 20. The improbably named *Johnny Cool* and the *Rice Bowl* are both popular.

For Western food, the new *Sea Pearl* is excellent and the kitchen must be one of the cleanest in India. Steak & chips is Rs 25, fresh juice Rs 15, and fish curry rice Rs 15.

The restaurant at the *Vincy Beach Resort* still dishes up some reasonable food, although service and atmosphere leave a lot to be desired. The *Hotel Colmar* has a restaurant with a good reputation. The *Silver Star Restaurant*, at the Tourist Complex, has barbecues on the lawn, and they have a good variety of Indian curries and seafood.

Near the roundabout is a group of shops and souvenir stalls, with several cheap, open-air restaurants among them. The best is *Pasta Hut* which delivers surprisingly good pasta in a range of sauces. The location beside the polluted stream isn't great, though. The late night action is centred on this area. *Pitstop* stays open until the last customer leaves; *Splash* has a dance floor by the beach and *Castaway* has a restaurant and disco (Rs 75) that has to be seen to be believed. There are lasers and UV tubes, and the DJ operates from an old Mini!

For a splurge, choose between *Longuinhos Beach Resort*, *Silver Sands Hotel* and *Penthouse Beach Resort*. The cuisine and service at these places is what you would expect from upmarket hotels and they all offer Goan, Indian and Continental dishes. Both the Silver Sands and the Penthouse have live bands during the high season and dinner is often an 'all you can eat' smorgasbord for a set price.

Benaulim Near the beach, the *L'Amour Beach Resort* produces excellent tandoori food, but you should check your bill carefully because there have been several complaints of overcharging. *Pedro's Bar & Restaurant* is a mellow place which has been popular for years, although it's somewhat *passé* these days.

There are several cafes and restaurants right on the beach in this area. Some of them do all-you-can-eat buffet dinners for Rs 70. *Domnick's Bar*, where the locals come to drink, is set back from the beach

The *Cacy Rose Bar & Restaurant* in Benaulim village is popular, and a good place to ask around for accommodation.

There's a good restaurant in the garden at *Palm Grove Cottages*. The nearby *Carina Beach Resort* is also a reasonable place to eat.

Getting There & Away

Buses run from Colva to Margao about every hour (Rs 25, 20 minutes). The first bus from Colva departs around 7.30 am and the last one back leaves about 8 pm. Buses from Margao to Benaulim are also frequent; some of them continue south to Varca and Cavelossim.

A taxi from Colva to Margao costs around Rs 50. Colva to Dabolim Airport costs Rs 190, and to Panaji Rs 220. All fares are negotiable. If you like the wind in your hair, the easiest way to get between Margao and Colva is to take a motorcycle taxi. The standard fare is Rs 20. Backpacks are no problem.

Domnick's and Johncey's both organise boat trips down the coast to Palolem for Rs 225, meals included.

Getting Around

There are plenty of places that rent motorcycles and bicycles in both Colva and Benaulim. For motorcycles, count on Rs 130 to Rs 200 a day (Rs 300 for an Enfield). For bicycles, the usual charge is Rs 3 an hour or Rs 20 for a full day. Some places charge more, so you'll have to negotiate. At low tide, you can ride 15 km along the beach to Mobor, at the southern end. It's possible to get a boat across the estuary to Betul and then cycle back via Margao.

You will see signs advertising buses to the weekly flea market at Anjuna Beach in many of the beach restaurants and at some of the hotels in Colva and Benaulim. If you're not planning on staying at any of the northern beaches, then it's worth making the day trip. The cost is Rs 75, and it will take the best

GOA

part of a day, but it's worth it because tackling this trip by public transport involves umpteen bus changes and a lot of messing about. It's also possible to hire one of the wooden ex-fishing boats to take you there, but get a group together because they're relatively expensive.

VARCA & CAVELOSSIM

Telephone Area Code: 0834

The 10-km strip of pristine beach south of Benaulim has become Goa's resort beach, with at least half a dozen hotels of varying degrees of luxury. As far as resorts go, some of them are quite good, and they are certainly isolated from anything which might disturb the peace. Access to the resorts is along the main road south from Benaulim. Prices given below are for the high season, which for these resort hotels tends to be from October to April. Over the Christmas peak (21 December to 10 January), prices rise by about 40%; during the rest of the year they drop by about 40%.

Varca

Varca is five km south of Benaulim, and the first resort you come to is the peaceful *Resorte de Goa* (☎ 24-5066; fax 24-5310). It's a reasonably small place with rooms and villas set around a swimming pool. The beach is a short walk away and very quiet. The cheapest rooms are Rs 1250 but the villas at Rs 1450 are nicest.

Half a km further on is the *Goa Renaissance Resort* (☎ 24-5200; fax 24-5225), a true five-star establishment. All rooms have a balcony facing the sea, there's a pool, beachside bar, and even a six-hole golf course. There's a couple of restaurants to choose from, and water sports are available. Rooms cost from US$135 during high season (US$170 in February).

Cavelossim

Cavelossim, seven km further south, is more developed. Several hotels are currently being built, and there's even a time-share resort under construction.

The cheapest place is *Gaffino's Beach*

Resort (☎ 24-6385), a guest house with rooms for Rs 300/350 (Rs 250/275 outside the peak period). It's a good, clean place and perfect if all you want to do is get away from India and rub shoulders with the package tourists. The restaurant is very popular with people staying at the more expensive hotels nearby; main dishes are Rs 60 to Rs 100.

Nearby is the *Dona Sylvia* (☎ 24-6321; fax 24-6320), which has a pool and is popular with package groups. Rooms cost Rs 2700 to Rs 3200 (Rs 4100 over Christmas). The *Old Anchor Resort* (☎ 24-6337; fax 24-6336) is 500 metres beyond. It's an older place with a reception area in an odd building that's supposed to resemble a Portuguese ship. There's a pool here too. Rooms are Rs 1150/2100 for a single/double; some could do with a lick of paint. Best of this group is the *Holiday Inn Resort* (☎ 24-6303; fax 24-6333) which has rooms arranged around a pool, just back from the beach. They cost Rs 1190/2150 for a single/double.

The road ends at Mobor, near the mouth of a small estuary and the grounds of the five-star deluxe *Leela Beach Resort* (☎ 24-6363; fax 24-6352). This imaginatively designed complex is built around an artificial lagoon. The main building is very airy and catches the sea breezes. Rooms cost from US$225 and leisure facilities include tennis and squash courts, gym, pool and health spa, plus a full range of water sports. The beach is particularly good here, with palm trees providing much-needed shade.

OTHER BEACHES

Opposite the narrow peninsula occupied by the Leela Beach Resort is the fishing village of **Betul**, reached either by boat or by bus from Margao (Rs 4, 45 minutes) via Chinchinim or Cuncolim. North of the village, near the harbour, is the peaceful *Oceanic Tourist Hotel* (☎ (0834) 22-1860). It's a small, popular place run by friendly staff. Double rooms with attached bath cost from Rs 125. It takes about an hour to walk to Betul Beach from the hotel, so it's better to take a boat across the estuary to Mobor.

There's currently nowhere to stay at

Agonda, a little village by an empty two-km stretch of sand in southern Goa. The road to Agonda winds over hills, past the old Portuguese fort of Cabo de Rama. On the edge of the village stands the shell of a resort hotel – a project that was abandoned before the building was completed.

In the far south of Goa, at **Palolem**, is an impossibly beautiful palm-fringed cove of white sand that is becoming a popular spot for day-trippers from Colva and Cavelossim. There's only one hotel to stay in at Palolem, although it's possible to rent rooms in villagers' houses by asking at the restaurants lining the beach. The *Palolem Beach Resort* (☎ (0834) 64-3054) is a low-key affair with basic doubles at Rs 150, and tents (better, since they catch the breeze) for Rs 90. Security seems to be pretty good, and there's a good restaurant.

There are only two buses a day from Margao to Palolem, but frequent services from Margao to Chaudi (Rs 7). You need to get off at the Palolem junction, 1.5 km before Chaudi. It's then a two-km ride in an autorickshaw (Rs 20); motorcycles charge Rs 15.

A couple of km south of Palolem is **Rajbag**, an exposed but isolated stretch of sand. There's only one hotel, the *Molyma Hotel* (☎ (0834) 64-3028), Kindlebaga, Canacona. It's in a plantation of cashew trees, a long way back from the beach. The hotel is good value at Rs 125/175 for a single/double with attached bath, but you really need your own transport to stay here.

PONDA

Although the central, inland town of Ponda is of no great interest, it does boast an old mosque and, in the surrounding area, numerous unique Hindu temples. There are regular buses from Panaji and Margao, but to get to the temples it's best to have your own transport.

When the Portuguese arrived in Goa, they destroyed every temple and mosque they could lay their hands on. As a result, temples in Goa are generally set back from the coast and comparatively new, although some date back about 400 years. The temples near Ponda have been rebuilt from originals destroyed by the Portuguese, and their lamp towers are a distinctive Goan feature.

Five of Goa's most important Hindu temples are close to Ponda, on the inland route between Panaji and Margao. The Siva temple of **Shri Mangesh** is at Priol-Ponda Taluka, about 22 km from Panaji. This tiny, 18th-century, hilltop temple, with its white tower, is a local landmark. Less than two km further down the road is **Shri Mahalsa**, a Vishnu temple.

About five km from Ponda are **Shri Ramnath** and **Shri Nagesh**, and nearby is the **Shri Shantadurga Temple**. Dedicated to Shantadurga, the goddess of peace, the latter sports a very unusual, almost pagoda-like structure with a roof made of long slabs of stone. Further south are the temples of **Shri Chandreshwar**, west of Quepem; the **Shantadurga**, east of Betul; and the **Shri Mallikarjuna**, east of Chauri.

The oldest mosque remaining in Goa is the **Safa Shahouri Masjid** at Ponda, built by Ali Adilshah in 1560. It once matched the mosques at Bijapur in size and quality, but was allowed to decay during the Portuguese period. Little remained of its former grandeur by the time the Portuguese left but the Archaeological Survey of India has now undertaken its restoration using local artisans.

BONDLA WILDLIFE SANCTUARY

Up in the lush foothills of the Western Ghats, Bondla is a good place to see sambar and wild boar. It's the smallest of the Goan wildlife sanctuaries (eight sq km) but the easiest one to reach. It's 52 km from Panaji and 38 km from Margao.

There is a botanical garden, fenced deer park and a zoo which is better than most, with reasonably spacious enclosures. The zoo was originally established to house orphaned animals, but these days is also a breeding colony for the larger species of deer.

Bookings for accommodation should be made in advance at the office of the Department of Forestry, directly opposite the Air India office, and beside the Hotel Fidalgo, in

GOA

Panaji. The accommodation is in chalets, which are very good value at under Rs 50, but they often get booked out. It may be easier to get a room on Thursdays, when the park is closed. This may not sound such a smart idea, but it's a very pleasant place to stay, and you're right at the sanctuary gates when they open at 9 am on Friday.

To get to Bondla, take a bus to Ponda, and then hire a taxi to the park (Rs 160). Alternatively, take the Molen bus as far as Tiskar, and catch a motorcycle taxi to the park (Rs 50). There is a minibus to get around the park, but it's easier (and quieter) to walk. The minibus is essentially for the deer park, which opens for an hour or so at 4 pm.

DUDHSAGAR FALLS

On the eastern border with Karnataka are Goa's most impressive waterfalls. They're particularly impressive if you're coming in by train soon after the monsoon, because the line crosses a bridge by the falls and the train often stops to let passengers get a good view.

If the trains are running, Dudhsagar is a two-hour trip from Margao or 50 minutes from Kulem station. You can catch a morning train up and spend several hours at the falls – there are pools to swim in – before taking an afternoon train back. Timetables may change while the line is being upgraded.

MOLEN & COTIGAO WILDLIFE SANCTUARIES

These wildlife sanctuaries are larger than Bondla but you will need your own transport to get to them. There's a treetop watchtower in Cotigao but the animals manage to remain well hidden, so you won't see a lot.

Accommodation is available at Molen in the *Tourist Resort* (☎ 5238). Doubles cost Rs 120, and meals are available for those who book in advance. There's no accommodation in the Cotigao sanctuary, although you can stay in the *Forest Rest House*, nearby, if you get permission from the Department of Forestry, opposite the Air India office in Panaji.

Karnataka

The state of Karnataka, formerly known as Mysore, is a state of strong contrasts, with the modern, industrialised city of Bangalore at one extreme and expanses of rural farming areas at the other. Karnataka also has some of the most interesting historic architecture in India, and a varied and tumultuous history.

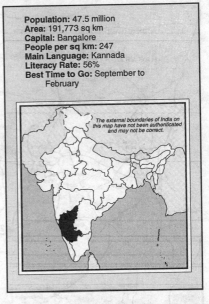

Population: 47.5 million
Area: 191,773 sq km
Capital: Bangalore
People per sq km: 247
Main Language: Kannada
Literacy Rate: 56%
Best Time to Go: September to February

The external boundaries of India on this map have not been authenticated and may not be correct.

History

It was to Sravanabelagola, Karnataka, in the 3rd century BC that Chandragupta Maurya, India's first great emperor, retreated after he had renounced worldly ways and embraced Jainism. Many centuries later, the mighty 17-metre-high statue of Gomateshvara, which celebrated its 1000th anniversary in 1981, was erected at Sravanabelagola. Fifteen hundred years ago at Badami, in the north of the state, the Chalukyans built some of the earliest Hindu temples in India. All later south Indian temple architecture stems from the Chalukyan designs at Badami, and the Pallavas at Kanchipuram and Mahabalipuram in Tamil Nadu.

Other important Indian dynasties, such as the Cholas and the Gangas, have also played their part in Karnataka's history, but it was the Hoysalas, who ruled between the 11th and 14th centuries, who left the most vivid evidence of their presence. The beautiful Hoysala temples at Somnathpur, Belur and Halebid are gems of Indian architecture with intricate and detailed sculptures rivalling anything to be found at Khajuraho (Madhya Pradesh) or Konark (Orissa).

In 1327, Hindu Halebid fell to the Muslim army of Mohammed bin Tughlaq but his triumph was brief and in 1346 Halebid was annexed by the Hindu kingdom of Vijayanagar, founded in 1336 with its capital at Hampi. Hampi is one of the most beautiful, extensive and fascinating of India's ruined kingdoms. Vijayanagar reached its peak in the early 1550s, but in 1565 it fell to the Deccan sultans and Bijapur became the most important city of the region. Today, Bijapur is just a small city surrounded by an imposing wall and packed with a fascinating collection of mosques and other reminders of its glorious past.

Following the demise of Vijayanagar, the Wodeyars of Mysore gradually grew in importance and, over a short period of time, established their own rule over a large part of southern India which included all of the old Mysore state and parts of Tamil Nadu. Their capital was at Srirangapatnam. Their power remained more or less unchallenged until 1761 when Hyder Ali (one of their generals) rose to great strength and deposed them. These were the years of bitter rivalry between the British and French for control of the Carnatic, and Hyder Ali, followed by his son, Tipu Sultan, were assisted by the French in consolidating their hold over the area in return for assistance in fighting the British.

KARNATAKA

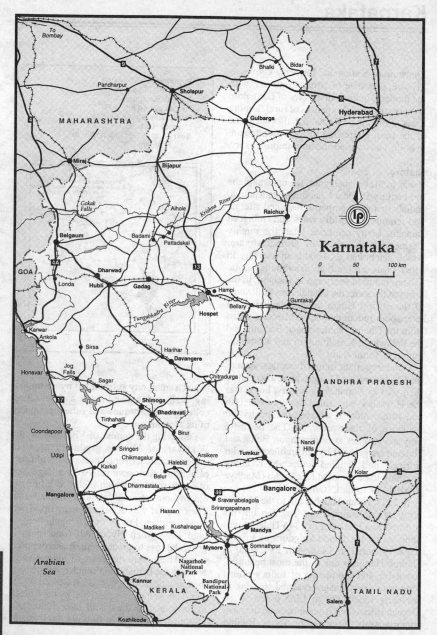

To Bombay

Pandharpur

Bhalki Bidar

Sholapur

MAHARASHTRA

Gulbarga

Hyderabad

Miraj

Bijapur

Gokak Falls

Aihole Krishna River

Raichur

Belgaum

Badami

Pattadakal

GOA

Dharwad

Londa Hubli Gadag

Hampi

Karwar

Tungabhadra River

Bellary Guntakal

Ankola

Hospet

Sirsa

Harihar

Honavar

Jog Falls

Davangere

Sagar

Chitradurga

ANDHRA PRADESH

Shimoga

Tirthahalli

Bhadravati

Coondapoor

Birur

Udipi

Sringeri Chikmagalur

Arsikere

Nandi Hills

Karkal

Tumkur

Halebid

Belur

Kolar

Dharmastala

Bangalore

Mangalore

Sravanabelagola

Srirangapatnam

Hassan

Madikeri Kushalnagar

Mandya

Mysore Somnathpur

Arabian Sea

Nagarhole National Park

Kannur

Bandipur National Park

KERALA

TAMIL NADU

Salem

Kozhikode

Karnataka

0   50   100 km

In 1799, however, the British finally defeated Tipu Sultan (who himself was killed in the battle), annexed a part of his kingdom, and placed the Hindu Wodeyars back on the throne of Mysore.

The Wodeyars continued to rule Mysore state until Independence when they were pensioned off, yet they were enlightened and progressive rulers and so popular with their subjects that the maharaja became the first governor of the post-Independence state. The maharaja remains very popular in Mysore city itself but, since Indira Gandhi rescinded the pensions of all India's princes in the 1970s, the Wodeyars fell on hard times. While they did convert many of their palaces and hunting lodges into hotels in the 1970s, the capital for maintenance, as well as managerial acumen, were obviously lacking. Since then, most have been franchised out to international hotel chains and relaunched as superdeluxe hotels. Meanwhile the erstwhile maharaja continues to live in the vast palace complex in Mysore, itself open to the public.

Under Nehru's premiership, vast irrigation schemes and dams to supply them were initiated in Karnataka state and most have now been completed. But since the dams tap two of the major rivers which flow into Tamil Nadu, in particular, the Cauvery (Kaveri), the state governments of Karnataka and Tamil Nadu are currently in bitter dispute over water rights. A compromise is proving hard to find. Perhaps more serious, though, is the deforestation over major areas of central and northern Karnataka. You can travel for hours by train in this area yet rarely see a single tree. As a result, soil erosion is a major problem and should the monsoons

ever fail, it would be a disaster for the people in the rural villages.

Southern Karnataka

BANGALORE

Population: 4.5 million
Telephone Area Code: 080

Though a modern, bustling city and an important industrial centre, Bangalore remains one of India's most pleasant cities. The central area is studded with beautifully laid out parks and gardens, wide tree-lined avenues, imposing buildings and lively bazaars. Situated 1000 metres above sea level and with a very pleasant climate, it's a city where people from all over India and abroad have come to look for work, business opportunities and higher education. It's to Bangalore that many of the multinationals establishing themselves in India are attracted. It is said that Bangalore is the fastest growing city in Asia, and is definitely India's yuppie heaven.

The pace of life, like the intellectual and political climate, is brisk, and hardly a day goes by without some new controversy boiling over across the front pages of its daily newspapers or onto the streets. It is also one of India's most progressive and liberal cities as far as social attitudes go. However, linguistic chauvinism is strong, as was demonstrated in October 1994 when 23 people were killed during riots in the city triggered by a proposal to broadcast 10 minutes of news each day in Urdu on Doordarshan. The city's important industries include machine tools, aircraft, electronics and computers.

Railway Conversion
As this book was being researched, sections of the state's railway lines were undergoing conversion from metre to broad gauge and services in some areas had been cancelled. This has meant major disruption around Hubli, the state's northern rail junction, as the lines between Hubli and Miraj (in neighbouring Maharashtra) and Hubli-Harihar were closed (though they were due to reopen in mid-1995). Also, there were no trains from Bangalore all the way to Goa – at last notice, you could get as far as Hubli from where you had to take a bus. You'll need to check which lines are now operating. ■

There's a wide range of hotels, restaurants, films and other cultural activities, excellent bookshops and craft shops.

History

Now the capital of Karnataka state, Bangalore was founded by Kempegowda in the early 16th century and became an important fortress city under Hyder Ali and Tipu Sultan two centuries later, though little remains from this period except the Lalbagh Botanical Gardens.

Orientation

Arrivals and departures in Bangalore revolve around Kempegowda Circle and in the narrow, busy streets of Gandhi Nagar and Chickpet adjacent to the bus stands and the City railway station. This is where you will find one of the main shopping areas, many of the cinemas and the cheaper hotels. It's a very busy area at lunchtime and in the evening, when workers spill out of their offices and into the numerous coffee shops, bars and restaurants and form long queues outside the cinemas.

On the other hand, the main centre of activity, particularly for the more affluent and the student population, is about four km from the railway station in the area bounded by Mahatma Gandhi Rd (M G Rd), Brigade Rd and Residency Rd east of Cubbon Park. It's here you'll find the more expensive hotels and restaurants, bars, travel agencies, airline offices, tourist information centres, bookshops and craft shops.

Bangalore's few remaining historical relics are all south of the City Market – some of them a considerable way to the south – in the old part of the city. Here there are narrow, winding streets, an endless variety of small cottage industries and manufacturing concerns, old temples, bullock carts and tea shops.

If you are in Bangalore for less than 24 hours, it's probably more convenient to stay close to the station. Otherwise it's well worth spending a little more and staying in the M G Rd area.

Information

Tourist Offices The Government of India tourist office (☎ 558-5917), in the KFC Building at 48 Church St, has friendly staff and a lot of material to give away. It is open weekdays from 10 am to 6 pm and Saturday from 9 am to 1 pm.

The Karnataka State Tourism Development Corporation (KSTDC) has its head office (☎ 221-2901) in Mitra Towers (2nd floor) at 10/4 Kasturba Rd, Queen's Circle. It is open from 10 am to 5.30 pm daily except Sunday. Also, there are counters at Badami House (☎ 221-5869; fax 223-8016), Narasimharaja Square, the City railway station (☎ 287-0068, open 6.30 am to 8.30 pm) and the airport (☎ 526-8012, open 6.30 am to 8.30 pm).

The handy what's-on guide, *Bangalore This Fortnight*, can be picked up (free) from many hotels.

Money Thomas Cook (☎ 558-6742) at 55 M G Rd is the best place for speedy foreign exchange. It's open Monday to Saturday from 9.30 am to 6 pm.

Post & Telecommunications The GPO on Cubbon St is open Monday to Saturday from 8 am to 6.30 pm and Sunday from 10.30 am to 1 pm. The efficient poste restante service is open Monday to Saturday from 10.30 am to 4 pm.

From the modern telecom office next to the GPO you can send international faxes and make phone calls 24 hours a day.

Visa Extensions These are issued without fuss in 24 hours (sometimes even the same day or same morning) at the office of the Commissioner of Police (☎ 226-6242 ext 513) on Infantry Rd, a 10-minute walk from the GPO. It is open Monday to Saturday from 10 am to 5.30 pm.

Libraries & Cultural Centres The British Library on St Mark's Rd has lots of British newspapers and magazines, and they don't seem to mind if you rest awhile and catch up

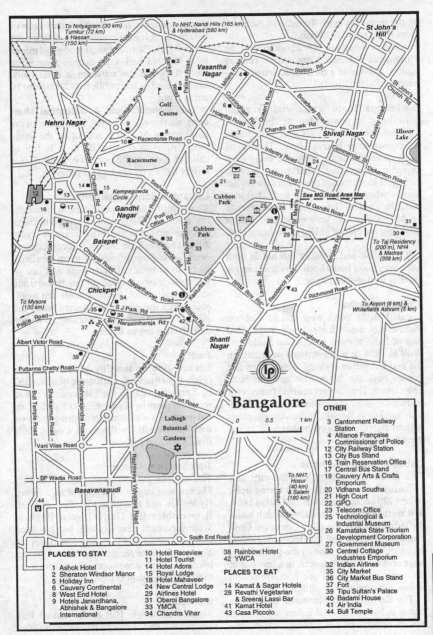

To Nrityagram (30 km)
Tumkur (72 km)
& Hassan
(150 km)

To NH7, Nandi Hills (165 km)
& Hyderabad (580 km)

St John's Hill'

Seshadripuram Road

Sampige Rd

Sankey Road

Palace Road

Station Rd

Vasantha Nagar

Millers Road

Queen's Road

Broadway Road

St John's Church Rd

Cavalry Road

Kumara Krupa Road

Golf Course

Cunningham Rd

Hospital Road

Chandni Chowk Rd

Shivaji Nagar

Ulsoor Lake

Subedar

Nehru Nagar

Racecourse Road

Infantry Road

Commercial St

Dickenson Road

Racecourse

Charan Rd

Kempegowda Circle

Seshadri Road

Post Office Rd

Cubbon Park

Cubbon Road

M Gandhi Road

St John's Church Rd

See MG Road Area Map

To Taj Residency
(200 m), NH4
& Madras
(359 km)

Gandhi Nagar

Balepet

Palace Road

Kempegowda Rd

Nrupathunga Rd

Cubbon Park

Grant Rd

St Mark's Rd

Brigade Rd

Residency Road

Richmond Road

Langford Road

To Airport (6 km) &
Whitefields Ashram (5 km)

Chickpet

Bhavani Road

Chickpet Road

Nagartharpet Road

S J Park Rd

Sri Narasimharaja Rd

Kasturba Rd

RRM Roy Rd

Lavelle St

Mission Rd

To Mysore
(130 km)

Police Road

Avenue Rd

Albert Victor Road

Puttanna Chetty Road

Jayachamaraya Road

Lalbagh Rd

Kengal Hanumanthiah Rd

Shanti Nagar

Bull Temple Road

Shankarmutt Road

Krishnarajendra Road

Vani Vilas Road

Lalbagh Fort Road

Bangalore

0   0.5   1 km

BP Wadia Road

Basavanagudi

Rashtreeya Vidyalaya Road

Hosur Rd

Lalbagh Botanical Gardens

South End Road

To NH7,
Hosur
(40 km)
& Salem
(180 km)

OTHER

3 Cantonment Railway Station
4 Alliance Française
7 Commissioner of Police
12 City Railway Station
13 City Bus Stand
16 Train Reservation Office
17 Central Bus Stand
19 Cauvery Arts & Crafts Emporium
20 Vidhana Soudha
21 High Court
22 GPO
23 Telecom Office
25 Technological & Industrial Museum
26 Karnataka State Tourism Development Corporation
27 Government Museum
30 Central Cottage Industries Emporium
32 Indian Airlines
35 City Market
36 City Market Bus Stand
37 Fort
39 Tipu Sultan's Palace
40 Badami House
41 Air India
44 Bull Temple

PLACES TO STAY

1 Ashok Hotel
2 Sheraton Windsor Manor
5 Holiday Inn
6 Cauvery Continental
8 West End Hotel
9 Hotels Janardhana, Abhishek & Bangalore International
10 Hotel Raceview
11 Hotel Tourist
14 Hotel Adora
15 Royal Lodge
18 Hotel Mahaveer
24 New Central Lodge
29 Airlines Hotel
31 Oberoi Bangalore
33 YMCA
34 Chandra Vihar
38 Rainbow Hotel
42 YWCA

PLACES TO EAT

14 Kamat & Sagar Hotels
28 Revathi Vegetarian & Sreeraj Lassi Bar
41 Kamat Hotel
43 Casa Piccolo

KARNATAKA

on the news. It's open Tuesday to Saturday from 10.30 am to 6.30 pm.

Alliance Française (☎ 226-8762) is on Thimmaiah Rd near Cantonment railway station and holds exhibitions, music evenings and video nights.

Bookshops There are several excellent bookshops in town. One of the best is Premier Bookshop, 46/1 Church St, round the corner from Berrys Hotel. There's no place quite like this – books on every conceivable subject are piled from floor to ceiling. It looks totally chaotic but the owner knows where everything is and, if it's in print, he's got it. Gangaram's Book Bureau on M G Rd is also very good, and almost next door is a branch of Higginbothams at 68 M G Rd.

The Ashok and Holiday Inn hotels both have very good bookshops. Fountainhead is another well-stocked store.

Vidhana Soudha

Located at the north-west end of Cubbon Park, this is one of Bangalore's, and indeed one of India's, most spectacular buildings. Built in 1954, it is constructed of granite in the neo-Dravidian style of architecture and houses both the Secretariat and the State Legislature. The Cabinet room is famous for its massive door made of pure sandalwood. The building is floodlit on Sunday evenings and on public holidays, however, it is not open to the public.

Cubbon Park & Museums

One of the main 'lungs' of the city, this beautiful shady park, full of flowering trees, covers 120 hectares and was laid out in 1864. In it are the red Gothic buildings which house the Public Library, the High Court, the Government Museum and the Technological & Industrial Museum. Also in the gardens is a huge **children's park** where, in a reversal of the usual roles, adults are not allowed in unless accompanied by children.

The **Government Museum**, one of the oldest in India, was established in 1886 and houses collections on geology, art, numismatics and relics from Mohenjodaro (one of the cradles of Indian civilisation, dating back 5000 years). There are also some good pieces from Halebid and Vijayanagar. Admission costs Rs 1 and the museum is open daily, except Monday and public holidays, from 10 am to 5 pm.

The **Technological & Industrial Museum**, also on Kasturba Rd, is adjacent to the Government Museum and open the same times. Admission costs Rs 4. It is full of children pressing the buttons of exhibits that reflect India's technological progress.

Lalbagh Botanical Gardens

This beautiful and popular park in the southern suburbs of Bangalore covers 96 hectares and was laid out in the 18th century by Hyder Ali and his son Tipu Sultan. It contains many centuries-old trees (most of them labelled), lakes, lotus ponds, flower beds and one of India's largest collections of rare tropical and subtropical plants. Refreshments are available within the park, and selected seeds and plants are sold here each morning. It's open daily from 8 am to 8 pm.

Fort

Located close to the City Market, this was originally a mud-brick structure built in 1537 by Kempegowda. In the 18th century it was rebuilt in stone by Hyder Ali and Tipu Sultan, but much of it was destroyed during the wars with the British. In theory, it's open daily from 8 am to 6 pm.

Tipu Sultan's Palace

This wooden palace, south-west of the City Market, was begun by Tipu Sultan's father, Hyder Ali, and completed by Tipu in 1791. It resembles the Daria Daulat Bagh at Srirangapatnam near Mysore, but has been sadly neglected and is falling into disrepair. You may find the temple next to it of greater interest. The palace is open daily from 8 am to 6 pm; admission is free.

Bull Temple

Situated on Bugle Hill at the end of Bull Temple Rd, this is one of Bangalore's oldest temples. Built by Kempegowda in the Dravidian style in the 16th century, it contains a huge monolith of Nandi similar to the one on Chamundi Hill, Mysore. Non-Hindus are allowed to enter and the priests are friendly. You will be offered jasmine flowers and are expected to leave a small donation.

Other Attractions

The remains of the four **watchtowers** built by Kempegowda are about 400 metres west of the Bull Temple and worth a visit if you're in the area. **Ulsoor Lake**, north-east of Cubbon Park, has boating facilities and a dirty swimming pool.

Organised Tours

The KSTDC offers tours which can be booked in any of their offices. They all start at Badami House and include, among many others:

City Sightseeing Tour
This five-hour tour is run twice daily at 7.30 am and 2 pm. The places visited are Tipu Sultan's Palace, Bull Temple, Lalbagh Botanical Gardens, Ulsoor Lake, Vidhana Soudha and the Government Museum. The tours cost Rs 65 and about half of the time is spent at government-owned emporiums that sell silks and handicrafts.

Srirangapatnam, Mysore & Brindavan Gardens
This daily tour (7.15 am to 11 pm) includes visits to Ranganathaswamy Temple, Gumbaz and Daria Daulat Bagh at Srirangapatnam, and St Philomena's Cathedral, Chamundi Hill, the palace, art gallery, zoo and Cauvery Arts & Crafts Emporium at Mysore. The tour costs Rs 150 including all entrance fees.

Belur, Halebid & Sravanabelagola
Daily tours (7.15 am to 10 pm) cost Rs 200. This is a good tour to take if you don't want to go to the trouble of visiting these places independently using local transport.

Hampi & Tungabhadra Dam
This is a weekend tour which departs on Friday at 9 pm and returns to Bangalore at 10 pm on Sunday. It includes visits to Mantralaya (the village associated with the Hindu saint, Raghavendra Swami), Tungabhadra Dam and Hampi. Overnight accommodation is at the *Hotel Mayura Vijayanagar* at Tungabhadra Dam. The cost of the tour is Rs 400, including accommodation.

Nandi Hills
Tours to this hill station (8.30 am to 6 pm), north of Bangalore, are conducted three times a week. The Rs 70 fare includes a vegetarian lunch.

Places to Stay – bottom end

Bus Stand Area Just east of the bus terminals are a dozen or more hotels and lodges to suit most budgets. One of the cheapest and oldest is the *Royal Lodge* (☎ 226-6951) at 251 Subedar Chatram Rd. It has clean singles with common bath for Rs 60 and doubles with attached bathroom from Rs 100. There's hot water in the mornings. Almost opposite, the *Hotel Adora* (☎ 287-2280) at No 47 has decent rooms for Rs 90/150.

A little further afield is the *Hotel Tourist* (☎ 226-2381), Racecourse Rd, which is good value at Rs 50/90 with attached bathroom, and hot water in the mornings.

At the top end of this range is the *Janardhana Hotel* (☎ 226-4444) across the road from the Bangalore International at High Grounds. It has spacious rooms with balconies, attached bathrooms and 24-hour hot water for Rs 130/180 and deluxe doubles at Rs 250.

Also very good and closer to the bus stands is the refurbished *Hotel Mahaveer* (☎ 287-3670; fax 226-9843) on the corner of Bhashyam Rd. Modern, clean but small rooms with attached bathroom (hot water from 6 to 8 am) cost Rs 120/170; credit cards are accepted.

There are *retiring rooms* at City railway station though they are often full by the afternoon. Dorm beds cost Rs 60 and doubles are Rs 150 to Rs 250.

M G Rd Area Budget accommodation is limited in this area but there are a few good places. The *New Central Lodge* (☎ 559-2395), 56 Infantry Rd, is a clean and popular place. Singles/doubles cost Rs 70/160 with common bath, or Rs 150/220 with private bathroom and there's hot water from 6 to 9 am. Cheaper is the *Hotel Imperial* (☎ 558-5473), 95 Residency Rd, with clean, airy rooms with attached bath for Rs 90/165.

One of the best budget options is the *Airlines Hotel* (☎ 221-3783) at 4 Madras Bank

Rd. This place is set back from the road in its own leafy grounds and is certainly not your typical no-frills Indian lodge. It has a range of facilities including a garden restaurant complete with drive-in service, supermarket, bakery and even an 'Asian Detective Agency'! All rooms join a verandah and newspapers are slid under the door each morning. The hotel's only drawback is the water – both hot and cold tend to run from 6 am to noon but after that it's bucket service only. Singles/doubles with attached bathroom cost Rs 140/195.

At the top end of this category is the *Brindavan Hotel* (☎ 558-4000), 108 M G Rd, which has ordinary singles/doubles at Rs 150/225, deluxe doubles for Rs 350, and air-con rooms at Rs 425. The hotel is set back from the road so it doesn't suffer too much from the traffic noise but it's often full.

City Market Area This is the place to stay if you want to be right in the thick of things.

It's the area of Bangalore with the noise, bustle and local atmosphere, and is a 25-minute walk from the railway station.

The *Rainbow Hotel* (☎ 60-2235), on Sri Narasimharaja Rd opposite the City Market bus stand and the big white mosque, is OK value at Rs 70/95 for singles/doubles. The *Chandra Vihar* (☎ 222-4146) on Avenue Rd charges Rs 80/140 for singles/doubles but they're not as good.

The *YWCA* (☎ 223-8574) at II Cross, CSI Compound, a quiet backstreet one block off Mission Rd, takes men and women and you don't have to be a member to stay here. B&B costs Rs 125 per person. Up on Cubbon Park, the men-only *YMCA* (☎ 221-1848) at Nirupathunga Rd has singles/doubles at Rs 90/150. However, it's heavily subscribed and you must be a member to stay here (annual membership costs Rs 250; there's no temporary rate).

Places to Stay – middle
Most of the hotels in this price range are in

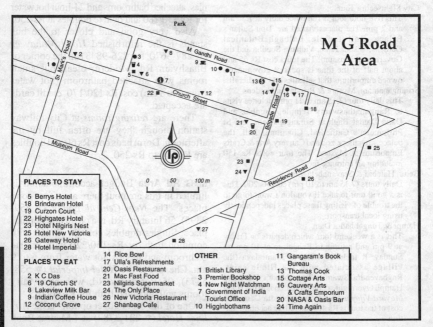

PLACES TO STAY
5 Berrys Hotel
18 Brindavan Hotel
19 Curzon Court
22 Highgates Hotel
23 Hotel Nilgiris Nest
25 Hotel New Victoria
26 Gateway Hotel
28 Hotel Imperial

PLACES TO EAT
2 K C Das
6 '19 Church St'
8 Lakeview Milk Bar
9 Indian Coffee House
12 Coconut Grove
14 Rice Bowl
17 Ulla's Refreshments
20 Oasis Restaurant
21 Mac Fast Food
23 Nilgiris Supermarket
24 The Only Place
26 New Victoria Restaurant
27 Shanbag Cafe

OTHER
1 British Library
3 Premier Bookshop
4 New Night Watchman
7 Government of India Tourist Office
10 Higginbothams
11 Gangaram's Book Bureau
13 Thomas Cook
15 Cottage Arts
16 Cauvery Arts & Crafts Emporium
20 NASA & Oasis Bar
24 Time Again

the M G Rd area but there are a few near the racecourse not too far from the City railway station and bus stands.

Racecourse Area The *Hotel Raceview* (☎ 220-3401) at 25 Racecourse Rd has doubles (no singles) for Rs 300, or Rs 350 with air-con. Keen punters may be interested to know that some of the more expensive rooms have a good view of the racetrack.

Nearby, the *Hotel Bangalore International* (☎ 226-8011), 2A/2B Crescent Rd, High Grounds, has ordinary singles/doubles for Rs 280/330. Air-con rooms start at Rs 350/410. All the rooms have a small terrace and colour TV plus there's a restaurant and bar with a live band every evening. This place is old but slowly being renovated. Immediately opposite, the *Hotel Abhishek* (☎ 226-2713) is newer and has rooms for Rs 450/510, or Rs 540/600 with air-con. There are two vegetarian restaurants and a bar.

M G Rd Area For a touch of class and old-world charm head to the *Hotel New Victoria* (☎ 558-4076; fax 558-4945), 47 Residency Rd. This long-established hotel, set in grounds filled with huge shady trees, is a popular place to stay but there are not many rooms so you need to make an advance reservation. Ordinary singles/doubles cost Rs 240/500, deluxe rooms are Rs 300/625 and suites cost Rs 750. There's a bar and restaurant (both indoor or garden dining).

Not far from here, the fully air-conditioned *Curzon Court* (☎ 558-2997), 10 Brigade Rd, offers ordinary singles/doubles at Rs 400/500 and deluxe rooms for Rs 425/600 plus there are suites at Rs 600. The nearby *Hotel Nilgiris Nest* (☎ 558-8401), 171 Brigade Rd, on the 3rd floor above a supermarket, has spacious and clean rooms for Rs 300/400, or Rs 375/475 with air-con.

Further west is the popular but shabby *Berrys Hotel* (☎ 558-7211) at 46/1 Church St. It's a large place that's rarely full and the rooms are huge (those ending in eight, eg 308, 408 etc, are the best). Ordinary rooms cost Rs 255/375 or there are deluxe rooms for Rs 400/450. There's a restaurant and the

room staff are amicable but reception can be testy.

Topping this range is *Highgates Hotel* (☎ 559-7172), a brand new, air-con place on Church St. Ordinary singles/doubles cost Rs 650/800 and there are 'Polo Club' rooms (breakfast included) for Rs 850/1000. The rooms are modern and cosy and all have TV, fridge and, wait for it, 'sound absorbing cork finished floors'!

Places to Stay – top end
Bangalore's importance as an industrial and business centre has prompted the construction of a plethora of swanky hotels.

In the M G Rd area, the four-star *Gateway Hotel* (☎ 558-4545; fax 558-4030), 66 Residency Rd, has standard singles/doubles (including breakfast) at Rs 1180/2000 and executive rooms for Rs 1350/2300. Facilities include a coffee shop, restaurant, swimming pool and gymnasium.

Over on Racecourse Rd, there is the recently renovated and very classy *West End Hotel* (☎ 226-9281; fax 220-0010), which has a pleasant eight-hectare garden and a swimming pool (Rs 150 for non-guests). Air-con rooms start at US$100/110.

At the top end of this category are a handful of five-star hotels which all have the usual range of facilities including swimming pools, bars and restaurants.

Ashok Hotel, Kumara Krupa Rd, High Grounds – relatively modern rooms from Rs 1800/2000 plus more expensive suites; the pool costs Rs 80 for non-guests (☎ 226-9462; fax 226-0033)

Holiday Inn, 28 Sankey Rd – rooms from US$50/60 (☎ 226-2233; fax 226-7676)

Oberoi Bangalore, 37 M G Rd – luxurious rooms for US$130/140 which open onto an immense tranquil garden; pool for guests only (☎ 558-5858; fax 558-5960)

Sheraton Windsor Manor, 25 Sankey Rd – beautiful old manor with rooms from US$110/120 and suites for US$375 (☎ 226-9898; fax 226-4941)

Taj Residency, 41/3 M G Rd – rooms range from US$60/70 to US$75/85; pool open to non-guests for Rs 165 a day which includes use of health club facilities such as sauna, jacuzzi etc (☎ 558-4444; fax 558-4748)

KARNATAKA

Places to Eat

Bangalore has some excellent places to eat, with a whole range of different cuisines available. Most of the better restaurants are in the M G Rd area.

A great place to start the day is the *Indian Coffee House* at 78 M G Rd. Breakfasts here typically consist of dosas or fried eggs & chips plus 'strong' coffee. Simple vegetarian meals are available all day (until 8.30 pm) and are served by waiters all done up in shabby white suits replete with cummerbunds and hats. Further along M G Rd, the *Lakeview Milk Bar* has excellent shakes and sundaes. *Ulla's Refreshments*, General Hall (1st floor), also on M G Rd, has a big terrace and is popular for snacks and vegetarian dishes.

A good spot for pure south Indian food is the *Revathi Vegetarian*, around the corner from the KSTDC office. This place is always packed and the food is very cheap (eg three puris for Rs 7.50). If the accompanying sauces torture your taste buds, you can cool off with a curd, lassi or kulfi at the equally popular *Sreeraj Lassi Bar* next door.

Church Street is another diners' hunting ground. Here, at the intersection with St Mark's Rd, is the well-known *K C Das*, a Calcutta-based snack-and-sweet shop famous for ras gullas (little balls of cream cheese flavoured with rose water).

For great Continental cuisine head to *'19 Church St'*, next to Berrys Hotel. Pine furniture and laid-back Western music compliment the delicious food – salads, Italian dishes and seafood – which ranges from Rs 40 to Rs 60. There's a small patio for evening dining or you can just sit here over a pitcher of cold beer. Close by, the *Coconut Grove* is a semi open-air place with a mouthwatering array of exotic dishes, many cooked with coconut milk. Meals here cost about Rs 50 to Rs 70.

Further down Church St, *Mac Fast Food* imitates, as you might expect, a Western food chain of a similar name. It's very popular with young, middle-class Indians and some of the food (eg the pizza) is good, though it's not that cheap.

On Brigade Rd, the very popular and reasonably priced *Rice Bowl* has average Chinese, Tibetan and Continental food and cold beer. It is run by friendly Tibetans eager to play with their sound system (Western music predominates). Further down Brigade Rd is *The Only Place*, in the Mota Royal Arcade, with apple pies (Rs 20) and beef burgers (Rs 30). At the *Nilgiris* supermarket nearby you can get such goodies as wholewheat bread, cheese and Danish pastries as well as delicious samosas.

The *Shanbag Cafe* on Residency Rd does south or north Indian thalis that are fit for a maharaja and cost Rs 43/48 respectively. The steaks and pizzas at *Casa Piccolo*, 131 Residency Rd, justly receive enthusiastic raves from many travellers, plus they do wicked ice cream. It has a good atmosphere and prices are sensible – pizzas Rs 29 to Rs 36, ice cream Rs 10 and sundaes Rs 26 to Rs 34.

For a modest splurge in splendid, shady surroundings, go for a languorous meal at the *Hotel New Victoria*, Residency Rd. The food (Indian and Continental) is reasonably priced plus they have cold beers and, at lunchtime, a Rs 75 buffet. At night the emphasis is on the bar, rather than eating.

For a more expensive act of indulgence, try the sumptuous lunchtime buffet at the *Memories of China* restaurant in the Taj Residency Hotel. You can gorge yourself here on a whole string of Chinese specialities and follow it up with superb desserts and coffee: all-you-can-eat for Rs 229 in a setting of pure luxury.

In the bus stand area, the many restaurants (eating rooms is perhaps a more accurate description) offer typical cheap vegetarian and non-veg Indian food, but the standards of hygiene in some leave much to be desired. The *Sagar Hotel*, Subedar Chatram Rd, has a good veg/non-veg menu while the well-known *Kamat Hotel* next door specialises in pure veg. There's another *Kamat* in the Unity Building near Air India in the City Market area which is just as good.

Entertainment

Bangalore's affluence has bred a kind of pub culture that wouldn't be out of place in any

Western country but which comes as a complete culture shock here in India. Flashy bars, well-lit discos and draught beers are all the rage with well-heeled young people, office workers and businesspeople. Needless to say, you won't feel like a social reprobate for drinking a beer here as you might do in the 'black holes' of Tamil Nadu. In fact, draught beer is about the cheapest drink on order while a fruit juice, for instance, can cost double the price of a beer!

One refreshing aspect of these bars, other than the beverages which they sell, is that they are not male-dominated establishments. Bangalorians are a liberal bunch so women travellers need have no reservations about going into them.

To kick off, try *NASA* on Church St. Its laser light shows, happy hours and megadecibel music will blast you straight out of India. Mugs of beer cost Rs 18 and pitchers are Rs 90. Still on Church St, the *Oasis Bar & Restaurant* is good for winding down when your ears long for a low-decibel conversation.

Around the corner from Berrys Hotel, the *New Night Watchman* is pretty formal and has loud Western music. There are plenty of similar pubs along M G Rd.

The plush *Time Again* cocktail lounge and disco in the Mota Royal Arcade is good for a splurge (Rs 200 cover charge), however, it's restricted to members and (male/female) couples. The *Black Cadillac* is a smooth and popular place on Residency Rd.

Things to Buy

The Cauvery Arts & Crafts Emporium, 23 M G Rd, stocks fine Indian craftwork such as handcrafted statues and tables, jewellery, ceramics, carpets and *agarbathis* (incense). They're good at packing and posting, and also have a smaller branch near the Central bus stand.

Just as good (and slightly cheaper for some items) is the Central Cottage Industries Emporium at 144 M G Rd which also has handicrafts from all over India.

If you prefer smaller shops and haggling, try the little Cottage Arts shop at 52 M G Rd,

close to the junction with Brigade Rd. Also good is Raga of Gifts, next to Casa Piccolo restaurant.

Bangalore's best 'bargain' is silk. Stunning, hand-embroidered saris are designed and made locally and, if bought during one of the sales (such as during Dussehra or Diwali), are quite reasonably priced. Silk emporiums line M G Rd, though fabric is cheaper from the shops in Commercial St further north.

Getting There & Away

Air The Indian Airlines office (☎ 221-1914) is in the Housing Board Buildings, Kempegowda Rd, while NEPC Airlines (☎ 558-7322) is on Church St. For reservations with the other domestic operators, the numbers are: East West ☎ 558-8282, Damania ☎ 558-8736, ModiLuft ☎ 558-2202, Jet ☎ 558-8354 and Sahara ☎ 558-6976.

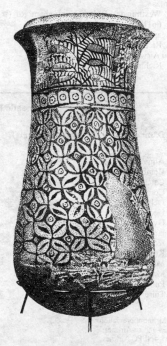

Antique pottery storage jar

See the table below for details of flights from Bangalore.

In addition to the flights listed in the table, East West flies daily to Delhi, Damania twice daily to Calcutta, ModiLuft once daily to Delhi, Jet twice daily to Bombay and Sahara twice weekly to Delhi.

There are no international flights to/from Bangalore, however, it's an indication of the city's growing importance that many airlines maintain offices here. They include:

Air France
    Sunrise Chambers, 22 Ulsoor Rd (☎ 558-9397)
Air India
    Unity Bldgs, Jayachamaraja Rd (☎ 222-4143)
British Airways
    St Mark's Rd (☎ 221 4034)
KLM
    West End Hotel, Racecourse Rd (☎ 226-8703)
Lufthansa
    Dickenson Rd (☎ 558-8791)
Qantas
    Westminster Bldg, Cunningham Rd (☎ 226-6611)
Singapore Airlines
    Richmond Rd (☎ 221-1983)
Thai Airways
    Richmond Rd (☎ 221-9810)

Bus Bangalore's huge and well-organised Central bus stand is directly in front of the City railway station. All the regular buses within the state are operated by the Karnataka State Road Transport Corporation (KSRTC; ☎ 287-3377). Interstate buses are operated by KSRTC as well as the state transport corporation of Andhra Pradesh (APSRTC; ☎ 287-3915; platform 11) and Tamil Nadu's JJTC (☎ 287-6974; platform 12). Computerised advance booking is available for all KSRTC superdeluxe and express buses as well as for the bus companies of neighbouring states. It's advisable to book in advance for long-distance journeys.

KSRTC has departures to Bombay (three times daily, 24 hours), Ernakulam (five times daily), Hospet (10 daily), Jog Falls (twice daily), Kannur (Cannanore, six times daily), Kodaikanal (9.50 pm, 12 hours), Kozhikode (Calicut; six daily), Madras (nine times daily, eight hours), Madurai (twice daily), Udhagamandalam (Ooty, four times daily), Panjim (twice daily), Pondicherry (at 9 pm) and Tirupathi (five times daily). To Mysore (3½ hours) there are buses every 20 minutes from 5.45 am until 9.30 pm.

Domestic Flights from Bangalore

Destination	Duration (hours)	Frequency (d-daily, w-weekly) & Airline*			
		IC	Fare (US$)	D5	Fare (US$)
Ahmedabad	2.05	4w	147	-	-
Bombay	1.30	3d	88	3w	170
Calcutta	2.20	1d	159	-	-
Coimbatore	0.40	4w	32	-	-
Delhi	2.30	2d	182	-	-
Goa	1.15	3w	58	3w	70
Hyderabad	0.50	1-2d	56	-	-
Hubli	1.15	-	-	3w	70
Kochi (Cochin)	0.50	4w	40	3w	50
Kozhikode (Calicut)	0.45	1d	35	-	-
Madras	0.45	3-5d	37	6w	40
Mangalore	0.40	3w	35	3w	45
Pune	1.25	3w	91	3w	90
Thiruvananthapuram	0.50	4w	62	-	-

*Airline abbreviations:
IC – Indian Airlines;
D5 – NEPC Airlines.

The APSRTC has buses to Hyderabad (at 7.45 am and the remainder in the evening) which take 12 hours. JJTC has frequent daily buses to Madras, Madurai and Coimbatore (four times daily, nine hours).

In addition to the various state buses, numerous private companies offer more comfortable and more expensive buses between Bangalore and the other major cities in central and southern India. You'll find them all over the bus stand area. The thing you need to watch out for is the dreaded video coach. Find a non-video bus if you want to retain your sanity, let alone your hearing or any chance of a nap.

Train Train reservations in Bangalore are computerised but there are no tourist quotas on any trains and bookings are heavy on most routes. On the other hand, it's usually possible for travellers to get into the emergency quota – to do so contact the assistant commercial manager (in the Divisional Office to the right before you enter the station building). The booking and enquiry office (☎ 132) is on the left as you're facing the station and is open Monday to Saturday from 8 am to 2 pm and 2.15 to 8 pm; Sunday 8 am to 2 pm. Luggage can be left at the railway station.

Bangalore is usually connected by direct daily express trains with all the main cities in southern and central India. However, at the time of writing services in some areas were cancelled due to the conversion of some of the state's railway lines from metre to broad gauge. (See the boxed section at the beginning of this chapter.) Hopefully, work will have been completed by now – check at the enquiry office.

To get to Hubli, take the *Hyderabad Express* to Dharmavaram at 5.05 pm (arrives at 9.30 pm) and then the *Kittur Express* at 10.30 pm to Hubli (arrives at 6.50 am).

The new, fully air-con *Shatabdi Express* from Bangalore to Madras and to Mysore leaves daily except Tuesday. This train has reclining seats and the fare includes meals and drinks.

See the table below for a selection of major trains from Bangalore.

Caravan Contact Kamplet Caravans (☎ 557-5272), 7 Linden St, Austin Town in Bangalore

Major Trains from Bangalore

Destination	Train number & name	Departure time	Distance (km)	Duration (hours)	Fare (2nd/1st)
Bombay	1014 *Kurla Exp*	9.05 am	1211	22.30	Rs 245/738
	6530 *Udyan Exp*	8.30 pm		24	Rs 245/738
Calcutta	6312 *Howrah Exp*	11.30 pm Fri	2025	38	Rs 308/1062
Ernakulam	6526 *Kanyakumari Exp*	9.00 pm	638	12.45	Rs 155/464
Hospet	6592 *Hampi Exp*	9.55 pm	491	9.30	Rs 120/397
Hyderabad	7086 *Hyderabad Exp*	5.05 pm	790	15.45	Rs 190/567
Madras	2608 *Madras Exp*	6.30 am	356	5.20	Rs 70/253
	2640 *Brindavan Exp*	2.15 pm		6	Rs 70/253
	2008 *Shatabdi Exp* *	4.05 pm		5.10	Rs 310/620
Mysore	6222 *Kaveri Exp*	8.25 am	139	2.30	Rs 41/103
	2007 *Shatabdi Exp* *	11.05 am		2.10	Rs 160/320
	6206 *Tippu Exp*	2.25 pm		2.25	Rs 41/103
	6216 *Chamundi Exp*	6.30 pm		3	Rs 41/103
Delhi	2627 *Karnataka Exp*	6.20 pm	2463	41.50	Rs 349/1162
	2429 *Rajdhani Exp* *	6.45 am Mon		34	Rs 800/1000
Thiruvananthapuram	6526 *Kanyakumari Exp*	9.00 pm	855	15	Rs 179/521

* Air-con only; fare includes meals and drinks

if you're considering 'sightseeing in India from your bedroom window' (as their brochure puts it).

Getting Around

To/From the Airport The airport is 13 km east of the City railway station (but less from the M G Rd area). Since it's outside the city limits, you'll have to haggle over a price for a taxi (around Rs 125) or auto-rickshaw (about Rs 80). There's also a 'pushpack' (No 13) bus for Rs 10 but it's unreliable.

Bus Bangalore has a comprehensive local bus network that includes 'pushpack' buses which ply certain routes and have limited stops. Local buses run from the City bus stand opposite the Central bus stand.

To get from the railway station to the M G Rd area, catch a No 131 or 333 (from platform 18) to the fire station on Residency Rd.

Auto-Rickshaw Any Bangalore resident will be proud to tell you that auto-rickshaw drivers are required by law to use the meters (which are properly calibrated, incidentally) and customers will *insist* on them being used. Do likewise! But don't be surprised if they refuse – after all, you're not a local. If that happens, find another. Flagfall is Rs 4 and less than Rs 1 for each extra km.

AROUND BANGALORE
Whitefields Ashram

About 16 km east of Bangalore, Whitefields is the summer ashram of Sri Sathya Sai Baba. His main ashram, Puttaparthi, is in neighbouring Andhra Pradesh (see that chapter for details).

Transport to both ashrams can be arranged in Bangalore at the Cauvery Continental Hotel (☎ 226-6966), 11 Cunningham Rd. To Whitefields, there are half/full-day tours for Rs 225/350. Puttaparthi, 160 km north-east of Bangalore, is a three-hour drive away and costs Rs 650 one way. Local transport is also available to Whitefields (take the Kadugodi (No 331) bus from the City bus stand) and to Puttaparthi (take a train to Dharmavaram, the nearest main railway station, or ask about buses at the APSRTC counter at the Central bus stand).

Nrityagram

This dance village, 30 km north-west of Bangalore off the Tumkur Rd, was established in the early 1990s to revive Indian classical dance and ancient martial arts. Under the auspices of well-known Orissi dancer, Protima Gauri (formerly Protima Bedi – she changed her name when she set up here as 'bedi' means 'loose motion' in Kannada), it offers the long-term study of classical dance and its allied subjects, such as philosophy, music, mythology and painting, as well as creative choreography. The village, designed by the award-winning Goan architect, Gerard Da Cunha, welcomes and accommodates guests. Tours cost Rs 250 for a day or Rs 1000 overnight – for details, contact Nrityagram's Bangalore office (☎ 558-5400).

Nandi Hills

Telephone Area Code: 08156

This hill station (1615 metres), 68 km north of Bangalore, was a popular summer retreat even in Tipu Sultan's days. **Tipu's Drop**, a 600-metre-high cliff face, provides a good view over the surrounding country. There are two ancient temples here.

Places to Stay The cheapest places to stay are the *cottages* run by the Department of Horticulture. You can make a reservation in Bangalore (☎ 60-2231).

The KSTDC operates the *Hotel Mayura Pine Top* (☎ 8624) in Nandi Hills. Rooms cost Rs 125/150 and it's best to make an advance booking in Bangalore through one of their offices.

Getting There & Away Nandi Hills can be visited on one of KSTDC's one-day tours. For details, see Organised Tours in Bangalore. Alternatively, there are KSRTC buses from the Central bus stand in Bangalore daily at 8, 8.30, 9.30, 10.30 am, 1 and 2.45 pm. The trip takes two hours.

LEANNE LOGAN

LEANNE LOGAN

Karnataka
Top: Tribal women in north-eastern Karnataka.
Bottom: Tribal woman at the bus stand, Bijapur.

PAUL BEINSSEN

PAUL BEINSSEN

PAUL BEINSSEN

Karnataka

Top: Village girls working in the fields, Hampi.
Middle: A shrine to Nandi, Siva's bull, Hampi.
Bottom: A temple at Hampi.

MYSORE

Population: 707,000
Telephone Area Code: 0821

It's easy to see why Mysore, at an altitude of 770 metres, is popular with travellers since it's friendly and easy-going with plenty of shady trees, well-maintained public buildings, clean streets and a good climate. The contrasts with the state capital, Bangalore, couldn't be greater. Mysore has chosen to retain and promote its heritage while Bangalore is hell-bent on confronting the 21st century.

Mysore is also a crafts centre, and there are numerous shops selling a large range of sandalwood, rosewood and teak carvings, and furniture. Probably the most stunning display can be seen at Cauvery Handicrafts in the centre of town.

Until Independence, Mysore was the seat of the maharajas of Mysore, a princely state covering about a third of present-day Karnataka, and their walled Indo-Saracenic palace is a major attraction. Just south of the city is Chamundi Hill, topped by an important Siva temple. North of the city lie the extensive ruins of the fortress of Srirangapatnam, built by Hyder Ali and Tipu Sultan on an island in the middle of the Cauvery River. Tipu Sultan fought the last of his battles with the British here in the closing years of the 18th century. To the east is the beautiful temple of Somnathpur while to the west, below the Krishnaraja Sagar (Dam), are the Brindavan Gardens, a popular attraction with Indian tourists.

Orientation

The railway station and the Central bus terminal are two km apart but both are conveniently close to the city centre and only 10 minutes' walk from all the main hotels and restaurants. The main shopping street is Sayaji Rao Rd, which runs from K R Circle at the north-west corner of the Mysore Palace, across Irwin Rd to the north of the city. Chamundi Hill is an ever present landmark, to the south.

Information

Tourist Office The tourist office (☎ 22-096) is in the Old Exhibition Building on Irwin Rd and is open Monday to Saturday from 10 am to 5.30 pm. There are also counters at the railway station (☎ 30-719), the Central bus terminal (☎ 24-997) and a transport office (☎ 23-652) at the Hotel Mayura Hoysala.

Post & Telecommunications The GPO is on the corner of Irwin and Ashoka Rds, and the poste restante mail is delivered through the window on the right. Make sure you check under all the initials of your name as letters are often filed incorrectly.

The central telegraph office is on the western side of the palace, and is open 24 hours. There are also quite a few private STD/ISD outlets, though not as many as in other large cities.

Bookshops Geetha Book House is on K R Circle across from the City bus stand. The Ashok Book Centre is on Dhanvantri Rd, near the junction with Sayaji Rao Rd.

National Parks Accommodation and trans-

Sandalwood City

Everywhere you go in Mysore you'll find yourself surrounded by the lingering aromas of sandalwood, jasmine, rose, musk, frangipani and many others. Mysore is one of the major centres of incense manufacture in India, and scores of small, family-owned *agarbathi* (incense) factories around town, their products exported all over the world.

The incense sticks are handmade, usually by women and children, and a good worker can turn out at least 10,000 a day! They are made with thin slivers of bamboo, dyed red or green at one end, onto which is rolled a sandalwood putty base. The sticks are then dipped into small piles of powdered perfume and laid out to harden in the shade. You can see them being made at any of the small factories you come across. ∎

KARNATAKA

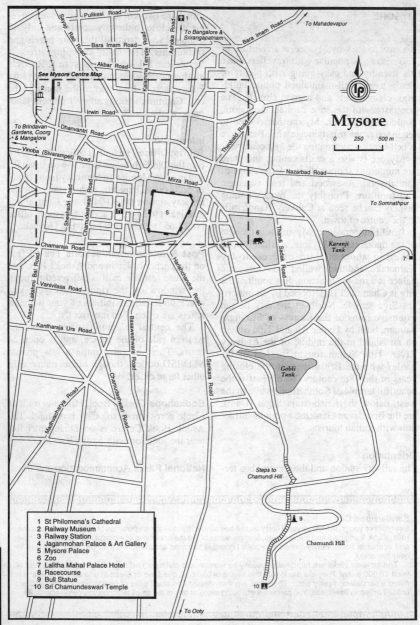

Mysore

0   250   500 m

To Mahadevapur

*To Bangalore &
Srirangapatnam*

See Mysore Centre Map

*To Brindavan
Gardens, Coorg
& Mangalore*

To Somnathpur

To Ooty

*Steps to
Chamundi Hill*

Chamundi Hill

**Karanji
Tank**

**Gobli
Tank**

Pulikesi Road
Sayaji Rao Road
Bara Imam Road
Akbar Road
Kalamma Temple Road
Ashoka Road
Bara Imam Road
Theobald Road
Irwin Road
Dhanvantri Road
Vinoba (Sivarampet) Road
Nazarbad Road
Mirza Road
Sheshadri Road
Chamudeshwari Road
Chamaraja Road
Thand Sadak Road
Vanivilasa Road
Harischandra Road
Jhansi Lakshmi Bai Road
Kantharaja Urs Road
Baswesshwara Road
Sankara Road
Madhvacharya Road
Chamundeshwari Road

1 St Philomena's Cathedral
2 Railway Museum
3 Railway Station
4 Jaganmohan Palace & Art Gallery
5 Mysore Palace
6 Zoo
7 Lalitha Mahal Palace Hotel
8 Racecourse
9 Bull Statue
10 Sri Chamundeswari Temple

port for the national parks of Bandipur (80 km south of Mysore) or Nagarhole (93 km south-west) should be booked with the Forest Officer, Woodyard, Ashokpuram (near the Siddhartha High School in a southern suburb of the city). Take an autorickshaw or a No 61 city bus.

Mysore Palace

Also known as the Amba Vilas Palace, the beautiful profile of this walled Indo-Saracenic palace, the seat of the maharajas of Mysore, graces the city's skyline. An earlier palace burnt down in 1897 and the present one was completed in 1912, at a cost of Rs 4.2 million.

Inside it's a kaleidoscope of stained glass, mirrors, gilt and gaudy colours. Some of it is undoubtedly over the top but there are also beautiful carved wooden doors and mosaic floors, as well as a whole series of mediocre, though historically interesting, paintings depicting life in Mysore during the Edwardian Raj. Note the beautifully carved mahogany ceilings, solid silver doors, white marble floors and superb columned Durbar Hall. The palace even has a selection of Hindu temples within the palace walls including the Varahaswamy Temple with a *gopuram* which set the pattern for the later Sri Chamundeswari Temple on Chamundi Hill. The former maharaja is still in residence at the back of the palace.

The main public rooms of the palace are open to the public although the crowds can sometimes rival the departure lounge of a major international airport. The Rs 5 entry ticket must be paid at the south gate and the ticket retained for the actual palace. Cameras must also be deposited at the gate (free) while shoes must be left at the shoe deposit at the palace entry (Rs 0.25). The palace is open daily from 10.30 am to 5.30 pm. The Residential Museum, incorporating some of the living quarters, is also open, for a further Rs 5 entry charge, but this is rather dull after the magnificence of the palace itself.

On Sunday nights (and on some holidays) 97,000 light bulbs spectacularly illuminate the palace between 7 and 8 pm.

Chamundi Hill

Overlooking Mysore from the 1062-metre summit of Chamundi Hill the **Sri Chamundeswari Temple** makes a pleasant half-day excursion. Pilgrims are supposed to climb the 1000-plus steps to the top but those not needing to improve their kharma will probably find descending more sensible than ascending! There is a road as well as the pathway to the top, and riding up then walking down has the added benefit of avoiding the pilgrim-packed buses which tend to be more crowded coming down than going up. Bus No 101 runs from the City bus stand in Mysore every 40 minutes for Rs 2. A taxi to the top costs about Rs 100.

Before exploring the temple visit the **Godly Museum** by the car park. Here you can ponder the price of various sins and discover some sins you may never have thought of. Aerobics enthusiasts may be distressed to find that 'body-building' is a bad thing since it's a clear case of over-attention to 'body consciousness'.

The temple is dominated by its towering seven-storey, 40-metre-high gopuram. The goddess Chamundi was the family deity of the maharaja, and the statue at the car park is of the demon Mahishasura who was one of Chamundi's victims. The temple is open from 8 am to noon and 5 to 8 pm. Shoes should be left at the *chaapple* stand and if the queues to get in look unmanageable you can jump them by paying Rs 10 at the 'Demand Tickets Special Entrance'. Refreshments, snacks and south Indian vegetarian meals are available at cafes around the temple.

After visiting the temple start back to the car park and look for the top of the stairway, marked by red-and-white striped stone posts and a sign proclaiming 'Way to Bull'. It's a pleasant walk down, there's some shade on the way and the views over the city and surrounding countryside are superb. Two-thirds of the way down you come to the famous **Nandi** (Siva's bull). Standing five metres high and carved out of solid rock in 1659, it's one of the largest in India. It's always garlanded in flowers and constantly visited by bevies of pilgrims offering *prasaad* to the priest in attendance there.

From the bottom of the hill it's still a couple of km back into the centre of Mysore but there are usually auto-rickshaws waiting to ferry pedestrians back to town for Rs 20 to Rs 30. Local tourist literature reports that the summit is 13 km from the city but this is by the winding and switchbacked road; via the steps it's only about four km.

Devaraja Fruit & Vegetable Market

Stretching along Sayaji Rao Rd from Dhanvantri Rd the Devaraja Market is one of the most colourful in India and provides excellent subject material for photographers.

Jaganmohan Palace & Art Gallery

Just west of Mysore Palace the Jayachamarajendra Art Gallery in the Jaganmohan Palace has a collection which includes junk and some weird and wonderful musical machines downstairs, paintings including work by Raja Ravi Varma upstairs and rare musical instruments on the top floor. The palace was built in 1861 and served as a royal auditorium. It's open daily from 8.30 am to 5 pm and entry is Rs 3. Photography is prohibited.

Railway Museum

Across the line from the railway station is a small railway museum with a maharani's saloon carriage, complete with royal toilet, dating from around 1888. It's open daily from 10 am to 1 pm and 2 to 6 pm, entry is Rs 2.

Other Buildings

Mysore is packed with fine buildings in a variety of architectural styles. Dating from 1805 **Government House**, formerly the British Residency, is a fine 'Tuscan Doric' building, owes nothing to its India setting and still has 20 hectares of gardens. Facing Government House is **Wellington Lodge** where the Duke of Wellington lived after the defeat of Tipu Sultan.

In front of the north gate of Mysore Palace, a 1920 **statue** of Maharaja Chama-

rajendar Wodeyar stands in the New Statue Circle, facing the 1927 **Silver Jubilee Clocktower**. If he glanced sideways he'd see the imposing town hall, the **Rangacharlu Memorial Hall** of 1884. The next traffic circle west is the 1950s **Krishnaraja Circle** (K R Circle) with a statue of Maharaja Krishnaraja Wodeyar.

Built between 1933 and 1941 in neo-Gothic style **St Philomena's Cathedral**, originally St Joseph's, is one of the largest churches in India but is not particularly interesting. It stands north of the centre. Converting maharajas' palaces into hotels is a popular activity and the **Lalitha Mahal Palace** of 1921, on the eastern side of town, is a prime example. The **Metropole Hotel** also started life as a guest house of the maharajas. The **Rajendra Vilas Palace** on Chamundi Hill, dating from 1938 but actually a copy of an 1822 building, has been a hotel and there are plans to make it one again. The 1910-11 **Chaluvamba Vilas** on Madikeri Rd was another maharaja's mansion, while the ornate 1891 **Oriental Research Institute** in Gordon Park originally housed the university's Department of Archaeology.

The Royal City by T P Issar (INTACH, Mysore, 1991) is a comprehensive survey of the city's architecture.

Organised Tours

Mysore is one of southern India's major tourist destinations and both the KSTDC and private companies offer a variety of tours in comfortable buses. Prices vary only slightly

Nandi, Siva's bull, Mysore

but private companies will only commence a tour if there's sufficient demand.

Mysore city tours cover the city sights plus Chamundi Hill, Somnathpur temple, Srirangapatnam and the Brindavan Gardens. The tours start daily at 7.30 am, end at 8.30 pm and cost Rs 85 with KSTDC, slightly less with private operators. This isn't a bad tour though some of the sights, particularly Srirangapatnam, are definitely rushed.

KSTDC has a tour to Belur, Halebid and Sravanabelagola every Tuesday, Wednesday, Friday and Sunday (daily in the high season) starting at 7.30 am and ending at 9 pm. The cost is Rs 150. This is an excellent tour if your time is short or you don't want to go to the trouble of independently making your own way to these places. The time you get at each place is probably sufficient for most people.

The KSTDC tour to Ooty leaves every Monday, Thursday and Saturday (daily in the high season) at 7 am and returns at 9 pm. The cost is Rs 150. If you want to sit on a bus all day and see precious little of Ooty then it's ideal. Otherwise, forget it.

KSTDC tours can be booked through the main tourist office, the railway station tourist office branch (☎ 30-719), or at the Hotel Mayura Hoysala (☎ 25-349), 2 Jhansi Lakshmi Bhai Rd. Private companies include Modern Travels (☎ 25-242), Asha Suman Complex, Irwin Rd (near the Central bus terminal), and Seagull Travels (☎ 31-467), Hotel Metropole.

Dussehra Festival

This 10-day festival in the first and second weeks of October is a wonderful time to visit Mysore. The palace is illuminated every night and on the last day the maharaja leads one of India's most colourful processions. Richly caparisoned elephants, liveried retainers, cavalry, and the gaudy and flower-bedecked images of deities make their way through the streets to the sound of jazz and brass bands, and through the inevitable clouds of incense.

Places to Stay

During the 10-day Dussehra Festival in October, accommodation becomes difficult to find, especially in the middle-range places. The real cheapies aren't as badly affected. However, the Indian love of endless paperwork and silly taxes reaches its peak in pricier Mysore establishments where you get hit for a 10% expenditure tax, a 15% sales tax and then a 15% tax on the 15% tax!

Places to Stay – bottom end

Mysore has plenty of budget hotels. The main areas are around Gandhi Square and in the area between Dhanvantri and Vinoba Rds. Starting from the railway station end of Dhanvantri Rd, but in no order of preference, one of the cheapest is the friendly New Gayathri Bhavan (☎ 21-224). It's a large place with a wide variety of rooms starting at Rs 35 for a single with common bathroom; singles/doubles with bathroom are Rs 45/90.

The enthusiastic staff at the modern Hotel Sangeeth (☎ 24-693), 1966 Narayana Shastry Rd, keep it very clean. Rooms with attached bathroom are Rs 95/125; there's hot water 24 hours a day and downstairs there's an excellent vegetarian restaurant. Similar in standard is the Agrawal Lodge (☎ 22-730) just off Dhanvantri Rd and down a side street. It has singles/doubles with attached bathroom for Rs 75/100.

Down the next side street is the Hotel Aashriya (☎ 27-088) which is good value at Rs 60/175 for rooms with attached bathroom. Further down this street is the large Hotel Chalukya (☎ 27-374) which has singles for Rs 60, doubles at Rs 80, deluxe doubles for Rs 165 and larger rooms from Rs 180 to Rs 310. All the rooms have attached bathroom.

Back on Dhanvantri Rd, the Hotel Indra Bhavan (☎ 23-933) is an older place, similar to the Gayathri Bhavan. Ordinary singles/doubles are Rs 80/100, larger doubles Rs 120 and Rs 150, all with attached bathroom.

The Hotel Anugraha (☎ 20-768), in the centre of town near the junction of Sayaji Rao and Sardar Patel Rds is excellent value. It looks like a middle-range hotel but is surprisingly cheap at Rs 90/150 for rooms with attached bathroom.

In the Gandhi Square area are some older places with very reasonable room rates like the *Hotel Srikanth* (☎ 26-111) at Rs 50/95 or the *Hotel Mona* with doubles at Rs 85. The friendly but rather noisy *Hotel Durbar* (☎ 20-029) has rooms at Rs 60/80 or doubles with bathroom for Rs 150. The nearby *Hotel Maurya* (☎ 26-677) is good value at Rs 75/130 for ordinary singles/doubles, Rs 250 for a deluxe double or Rs 190 to Rs 290 for triples. All the rooms have attached bathrooms and there's hot water from 5 to 8 am.

Up in price, but still in the Gandhi Square area, the *Hotel Dasaprakash* (☎ 24-444) is one of a chain of hotels throughout south India. It's a huge place and has a variety of somewhat shabby rooms from Rs 80/165 up to Rs 135/215, although the only difference between the rooms seems to be that you get a few more switches to play with. All rooms have hot and cold water, you get a newspaper under your door in the morning, there's an excellent vegetarian restaurant and for emergencies there's an astro-palmist on call!

Off Gandhi Square towards the Central bus terminal, the modern and spotlessly clean *Hotel Mannars* (☎ 35-060) is an excellent choice. The staff are very friendly and rooms with attached bathroom cost Rs 95/125.

At the top end of this category is the clean and pleasant *Hotel Park Lane* (☎ 30-400), 2720 Sri Harsha Rd, which has rooms with attached bathroom for Rs 70/99 on the ground floor and Rs 90/120 on the upper floor. There's a popular bar and restaurant downstairs.

North of the Central bus terminal the modern *Sri Nandini Hotel* (☎ 31-247) has doubles with attached bathrooms for Rs 120, Rs 150 and Rs 175 and is pleasant enough although the area itself isn't particularly attractive.

Right in the centre of town at 23 K R Circle by the City bus stand, the older *Hotel Calinga* (☎ 31-310) costs Rs 120/150 or Rs 140/180 for the deluxe rooms with colour TV. The staff are friendly and all the rooms have attached bathrooms.

At the railway station there are good *retir-ing rooms* including dormitory beds. There's a *youth hostel* (☎ 36-753) five km from the centre of town to the north-west. The location is inconvenient but if you're keen, take a bus No 27, 41, 51, 53 or 63 from the City bus stand.

Places to Stay – middle

For a touch of class and friendly old-world charm, you can't beat the *Ritz Hotel* (☎ 22-668) next to the Central bus terminal. There are only four rooms; spacious doubles are Rs 191 and four-bed rooms are Rs 329. The rooms are on the upper floor and there's a lounge for residents' use. Downstairs is a pleasant and equally spacious bar and restaurant.

The rather characterless *Mysore Hotel Complex* (☎ 26-217) has doubles at Rs 180 or with air-con at a rather pricey Rs 550. Across the road, the modern *Hotel Roopa* (☎ 33-770) has standard doubles for Rs 160 and a range of deluxe doubles from Rs 200. It's reasonable value but also rather characterless.

The friendly *Hotel Sreekrishna Continental* (☎ 37-042), 73 Nazarbad Main Rd, is good value with doubles at Rs 225 to Rs 250 or deluxe doubles from Rs 350 up to Rs 450 and Rs 550 with air-con.

On the opposite side of the city centre is the KSTDC's *Hotel Mayura Hoysala* (☎ 25-349), 2 Jhansi Lakshmi Bai Rd, which offers spacious, pleasantly decorated singles/doubles with bathroom for Rs 150/225. The hotel has its own quiet gardens as well as a bar and restaurant. Bus tours operated by KSTDC start from this hotel and it's close to the railway station. In the same complex the *Mayura Yathrinivas* (☎ 25-349) has doubles at Rs 140, dorm beds at Rs 40 or dorm beds without a bed at Rs 25!

Also recommended is the new *Hotel Palace Plaza* (☎ 30-875; fax 52-0639), at 2716 Sri Harsha Rd. Standard doubles cost Rs 200, while air-con rooms go for Rs 525.

Places to Stay – top end

Superb value in this range and oozing with character and old-world charm is the *Hotel*

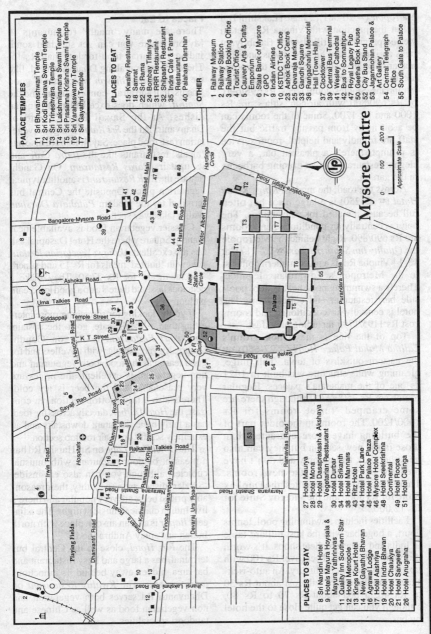

PALACE TEMPLES

- T1 Sri Bhuvaneshwari Temple
- T2 Sri Kodi Bhairava Swami Temple
- T3 Sri Trineshvara Temple
- T4 Sri Lakshmiramana Swami Temple
- T5 Sri Prasanna Krishna Swami Temple
- T6 Sri Varahaswamy Temple
- T7 Sri Gayathri Temple

PLACES TO EAT

- 15 Kwality Restaurant
- 18 Samrat
- 22 Sri Rama
- 24 Bombay Tiffany's
- 31 RRR Restaurant
- 32 Shilpashri Restaurant
- 35 Indra Café & Paras Restaurant
- 40 Palahara Darshan

OTHER

- 1 Railway Museum
- 2 Railway Station
- 3 Railway Booking Office
- 4 Tourist Office
- 5 Cauvery Arts & Crafts Emporium
- 6 State Bank of Mysore
- 7 GPO
- 9 Indian Airlines
- 10 KSTDC Tour Office
- 23 Ashok Book Centre
- 25 Devaraja Market
- 33 Gandhi Square
- 36 Rangacharlu Memorial Hall (Town Hall)
- 37 Clocktower
- 39 Central Bus Terminal
- 41 Wesley Cathedral
- 42 Bus to Somnathpur
- 47 Royal Legacy Pub
- 50 Geetha Book House
- 52 City Bus Stand
- 53 Jaganmohan Palace & Art Gallery
- 54 Central Telegraph Office
- 55 South Gate to Palace

Mysore Centre

0   100   200 m

Approximate Scale

PLACES TO STAY

- 8 Sri Nandini Hotel
- 10 Hotels Mayura Hoysala & Mayura Yathrinivas
- 11 Quality Inn Southern Star
- 12 Hotel Metropole
- 13 Kings Kourt Hotel
- 14 New Gayathri Bhavan
- 16 Agrawal Lodge
- 17 Hotel Aashriya
- 19 Hotel Indra Bhavan
- 20 Hotel Chalukya
- 21 Hotel Sangeeth
- 26 Hotel Anugraha
- 27 Hotel Maurya
- 28 Hotel Mona
- 29 Hotel Dasaprakash & Akshaya Vegetarian Restaurant
- 30 Hotel Durbar
- 34 Hotel Srikanth
- 38 Hotel Mannars
- 43 Ritz Hotel
- 44 Hotel Park Lane
- 45 Hotel Palace Plaza
- 46 Mysore Hotel Complex
- 48 Hotel Sreekrishna Continental
- 49 Hotel Roopa
- 51 Hotel Calinga

KARNATAKA

Metropole (☎ 20-681), 5 Jhansi Lakshmi Bai Rd at the junction with Vinoba Rd. Set in well-kept grounds filled with flamboyant trees and frangipani bushes, it was once the maharaja's guest house. Some of the rooms are enormous and come with wide shady verandahs. Singles/doubles cost Rs 595/690, or Rs 690/800 with air-con, suites are Rs 1000 and Rs 1200. Some of the rooms can be a bit noisy from passing traffic but the staff are friendly and helpful, room service is prompt, there's a pleasant bar, a very elegant restaurant and an evening barbecue in the garden.

Across the road, the modern *Kings Kourt Hotel* (☎ 25-250) is a large place but often full because it's used for conventions. The hotel is centrally air-conditioned and rooms are Rs 690/890. Right behind the Metropole the *Quality Inn Southern Star* (☎ 27-217), at 13-14 Vinoba Rd, is a plush modern contrast to the Metropole's Edwardian elegance. There's a swimming pool, health club, poolside bar, restaurant and coffee shop. The hotel is centrally air-conditioned and rooms cost Rs 1195/1795 including breakfast.

Top of the line is the Ashok group's *Lalitha Mahal Palace Hotel* (☎ 27-650) on the eastern outskirts of town. This huge, gleaming white structure was built in 1921 as one of the maharaja's palaces. Regular rooms are Rs 2500/2700 although there are some cramped 'turret' rooms for Rs 1000/1200. The rooms in the older part of the building have more character than those in the new section but they can also be rather dark and gloomy and don't have pleasant balconies like the new rooms. There are also two huge suites: the Dupleix Suite for Rs 8000 and the Viceroy Suite for Rs 12,000.

Facilities include a swimming pool, tennis court, a huge bar with the best billiard table in India and some excellent shops. It's worth dropping in for a cold beer (over Rs 100 with taxes) just to savour the luxury. An auto-rickshaw from the centre will cost about Rs 30 to Rs 40, a taxi about Rs 70 to Rs 80, although you can get quite close to the hotel by bus.

Places to Eat

There are many 'meals' restaurants in Mysore where you can get standard south Indian vegetarian food for less than Rs 15. There are several along Dhanvantri Rd, like the *Hotel Indra Bhavan* which has a good 'meals' hall and an air-con restaurant, and the *Samrat*, which does excellent north Indian dishes. At the Sayaji Rao Rd end of Dhanvantri Rd the *Sri Rama* is a good vegetarian fast-food place. Sayaji Rao Rd also has 'meals' restaurants like the *Indra Cafe* and its upstairs *Paras Restaurant*. On Gandhi Square the *RRR Restaurant* is another typical vegetarian place. Opposite the Central bus terminal try the modern *Palahara Darshan* with a takeaway section.

Classier vegetarian food is available near Gandhi Square where the Hotel Dasaprakash has the excellent *Akshaya Vegetarian Restaurant* with 'limited' meals for Rs 15 and superb 'special meals' for Rs 27.50. They make a delicious lassi and there's also a good ice-cream parlour.

If you're looking for something more interesting than a 'meals' cafe, go to the upstairs *Shilpashri Restaurant & Bar* on Gandhi Square. It's very popular with travellers and for good reason as the food, both vegetarian and non-vegetarian, is excellent, the prices are very reasonable and the beer is icy cold. There's also a tidy rooftop section. In contrast, the *Hotel Durbar*, directly across the road, has a fairly basic restaurant downstairs and an extremely scruffy open-air rooftop section.

The *Hotel Park Lane* on Sri Harsha Rd has a pleasant outdoor restaurant with unusual cubicles, although you can also eat inside. 'Sizzler' dishes are a speciality, their reasonably priced beers are very popular and there's live Indian classical music at night. The adjacent *Ilapur* is a clean air-con place with north Indian and spicy Andhra food.

The *Ritz Hotel*, close to the Central bus terminal, has a large and busy restaurant and bar area, hidden away behind its innocuous reception area. The *Kwality Restaurant* on Dhanvantri Rd serves both vegetarian and non-vegetarian food as well as Chinese and tandoori specialities.

A number of the hotels have excellent restaurants. At the Hotel Metropole you can start with a drink in the *Planter's Bar* and move on to the elegant *Regency Restaurant* or out into the garden for the evening barbecue. The food is excellent, the service both friendly and efficient, and the prices quite reasonable for a place this good. Count on about Rs 350 for dinner for two with a bottle of beer.

On the other hand, dinner at the *Lalitha Mahal Palace Hotel* is, for India, serious money. Dinner for two could easily set you back Rs 700 to Rs 800, although the food is superb, there's India classical music to accompany the meal and the decor is definitely impressive. Some evenings there's a buffet rather than the à la carte menu. If you come out here from central Mysore it's probably wise to get your auto-rickshaw or taxi to wait for you as it's hard to find transport back.

Entertainment
Bangalore's explosion of classy pubs selling draught beer has spilled over in a small way to Mysore where the *Royal Legacy* on Nazarbad Main Rd, not far from the Central bus terminal, sells draught beer by the mug for Rs 15 or by the pint for Rs 28. It's a popular place with music and dancing upstairs. Other popular places for a beer include the *Hotel Metropole* (Rs 40 to Rs 50), the *Shilpashri* (11 varieties of beer from Rs 27 to Rs 37), *Hotel Park Lane* (Rs 37) or the *Lalitha Mahal Palace Hotel* (Rs 90).

There are many cinemas in the area between the bus terminal and Gandhi Square. The swimming pool at the Lalitha Mahal Palace Hotel is open to non-guests for Rs 100 per day.

Things to Buy
Mysore is famous for carved sandalwood, inlay works, silk saris and incense. The best place to see the whole range is at the Cauvery Arts & Crafts Emporium on Sayaji Rao Rd. It's open daily from 10 am to 1.30 pm and 3 to 7.30 pm. It accepts credit cards, foreign currency or travellers' cheques and will arrange packing and export. Few of the larger things are cheap by Indian standards (the smallest of the inlaid tables costs about US$50), but the place is worth a visit even if you're not going to buy anything.

There are always a number of street hawkers outside the Cauvery Emporium. They sometimes have interesting and cheap bangles, rings and old coins. There are many other craft shops along Dhanvantri Rd with similar prices. Sri Dore at 70 Devaraj Urs Rd has some beautiful items. The best bargains are the carved sandalwood images of Indian deities. They retain their scent for years and come in a huge array of sizes and configurations.

Getting There & Away
Air There are no flights to Mysore but Indian Airlines (☎ 51-6943) has an office in the Hotel Mayura Hoysala. It's open Monday to Saturday from 10 am to 1.30 pm and 2.15 to 5 pm.

Bus The Central bus terminal handles all the KSRTC long-distance buses. There's a timetable in English and you can make reservations three days in advance. The City bus stand, on K R Circle, is for city and Srirangapatnam buses. Other short-distance buses (eg to Somnathpur) leave from opposite the Ritz Hotel.

Buses hurtle off to Bangalore with great frequency and horrifying speed. The trip takes about three hours on the nonstop services which depart every 20 minutes and cost Rs 27. Semi-luxury (Rs 34) and superdeluxe (Rs 41) buses are no faster or less frightening but they are slightly more comfortable.

There are 16 to 20 daily services from Mysore to Hassan and the journey takes three hours. Hassan is the usual base from which to visit Belur, Halebid and Sravanabelagola although you can also use Arsikere. Four times a day buses go direct to Sravanabelagola. Buses to Hospet (for Hampi and the Vijayanagar ruins) are the best ones to take if you're heading there direct rather than taking a bus first to Bellary and then changing.

To Mangalore there are up to 20 buses daily between 5.15 am and 11.30 pm, a journey of about seven hours. To Ooty there are buses 12 times daily (five hours) which pass through Bandipur National Park. There are also some buses which just go to the park. To Ernakulam there are five buses daily (13 hours, Rs 140). There are also a couple of daily buses to Kozhikode (Calicut) and eight to 10 to Kannur (Cannanore).

There are a few direct buses daily to Somnathpur from the corner diagonally opposite the Ritz Hotel. It's more likely that you'll have to catch a bus to T Narisipur or to Bannur first (from the same place), then change to another bus for Somnathpur. These buses leave often and the total journey time is around 1½ hours. If you're standing at the right stop someone will push you on the appropriate bus! There are also buses direct from Bannur to Srirangapatnam.

There are plenty of buses from the City bus stand to Srirangapatnam. The No 125 goes only as far as Srirangapatnam; others pass through on their way to somewhere else. There's no problem getting back to Mysore along the same route. It's also possible to catch a bus from Srirangapatnam on to Somnathpur.

In addition to the KSRTC buses, there are a number of private bus companies which run to such places as Bangalore, Bombay, Goa, Hyderabad, Madras, Mangalore, Ooty and Pune. Their offices are clustered on the street opposite the Hotel Mannars. Fares on these buses are more than the KSRTC buses but they are definitely more comfortable.

Train The booking office at the pretty pink Mysore railway station is computerised and rarely has long queues. The office is open Monday to Saturday from 8 am to 2 pm and 2.15 to 8 pm; Sunday, 8 am to 2 pm. Although the conversion of the Karnataka railway system to broad gauge is underway, Mysore is still predominantly a metre-gauge destination. Getting to other major cities, except Bangalore, usually involves a change of trains at Arsikere, Miraj or Hubli where you can pick up the broad-gauge trunk routes. This can be very time-consuming so in many cases it's quicker to go first to Bangalore and start from there. The broad-gauge conversion process is making connections even worse than usual.

There are five daily express services to Bangalore which take between two and 3¼ hours; the fare for the 139-km journey is Rs 36/140 in 2nd/1st class. The two-hour journey is with the Wednesday to Monday *Shatabdi Express* which is all air-con and costs Rs 160. This train continues to Madras, 7¼ hours from Mysore, for Rs 380. The fare includes 'catering'. Other Madras express services usually involve a change of train in Bangalore. Passenger services between Mysore and Bangalore stop in Srirangapatnam, an alternative to the bus.

The most convenient way of getting to Bombay or to Vasco da Gama in Goa is to take a train to Hassan or Arsikere and transfer to an express but these services have been particularly disrupted by the broad-gauge conversion process. There are three passenger trains daily between Mysore, Hassan and Arsikere. They take 3½ hours to Hassan for Rs 19/126 and four hours to Arsikere for Rs 25/162. Hassan is the nearest place to the Hoysala temple towns of Belur and Halebid. The 1360-km trip to Bombay takes about 40 hours for Rs 198/776, transferring at either Hassan or Arsikere. Getting to Goa, with a transfer for Vasco da Gama at Arsikere, is painfully slow. The 700-km journey takes a full 50 hours for Rs 130/492. An alternative route to Goa is to take a train from Mysore to Talguppa (a few km from Jog Falls) via Arsikere and Birur, and then a bus from there to Goa.

It takes up to 11 hours to Mangalore by train for Rs 39/277. The long journey to Ernakulam costs Rs 141/536.

Getting Around
Bus From the City bus stand No 150 goes to Brindavan Gardens. No 101 goes to Chamundi Hill approximately every 40 minutes at a cost of Rs 2.

Taxi & Auto-Rickshaw There are plenty of

auto-rickshaws, and drivers are usually willing to use the meters. Flagfall is Rs 4.60 for the first km plus Rs 2.30 for subsequent km. Taxis are considerably more expensive and they don't have meters so fares must be negotiated.

AROUND MYSORE
Somnathpur

Telephone Area Code: 08227

The **Sri Channakeshara Temple** stands at the edge of the tranquil village of Somnathpur, 33 km east of Mysore. Built around 1260 AD during the heyday of the Hoysala kings, it's an extremely beautiful and unspoilt building, although not as large as the other Hoysala temples at Belur and Halebid northwest of Mysore. Unlike these, though, it is complete. For more details on Hoysala architecture, see the boxed section under Belur & Halebid later in this chapter.

The walls of the star-shaped temple are literally covered with superb sculptures in stone depicting various scenes from the *Ramayana, Mahabharata, Bhagavad Gita* and the life and times of the Hoysala kings. No two friezes are alike – the carved frieze which goes around the temple has six strips, starting with elephants at the bottom, followed by horses, a floral strip, scenes, crocodiles or lions and finally geese.

The temple is open daily from 9 am to 5.30 pm.

Places to Stay The only place in Somnathpur to find a bed and a meal is the run-down KSTDC's *Hotel Mayura Keshav* (☎ 7017) just outside the temple compound. It has six rooms (used mostly as nesting places for sparrows) with attached bathroom and carpeted floors for Rs 35/60. The restaurant here has little choice.

Getting There & Away Somnathpur is seven km from Bannur and 10 km from T Narsipur. See the earlier Mysore Getting There & Away section for details on public transport.

Srirangapatnam

Sixteen km from Mysore on the Bangalore road stand the ruins of Hyder Ali and Tipu Sultan's capital from which they ruled much of southern India during the 18th century. In 1799, the British, allied with disgruntled local leaders and with the help of a traitor, finally conquered them. Tipu's defeat marked the real beginning of British territorial expansion in southern India.

Srirangapatnam was built on a long island in the Cauvery River. There isn't much left of it as the British did a good job of demolishing the place, but the extensive **ramparts** and battlements and some of the gates still stand. The dungeon where Tipu held a number of British officers has also been preserved. Inside the fortress walls there's a mosque and the **Sri Ranganathaswamy Temple**, a popular place of pilgrimage for Hindus. Non-Hindus can go all the way inside except to the inner sanctum, where there is a black stone image of sleeping Vishnu. The population of the town inside the fort is about 20,000.

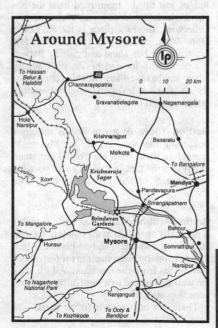

Around Mysore

0   10   20 km

To Hassan Belur & Halebid
Channarayapatna
Sravanabelagola
Nagamangala
Hole Narsipur
Krishnarajpet
Basaralu
Melkote
To Bangalore
Cauvery River
Krishnaraja Sagar
Mandya
Pandavapura
Srirangapatnam
Brindavan Gardens
Bannur
To Mangalore
Hunsur
Mysore
Somnathpur
Narsipur
To Nagarhole National Park
Nanjangud
To Ooty & Bandipur
To Kozhikode

One km east of the fort, across the other side of the main road, stands the **Daria Daulat Bagh** (Tipu's summer palace), set in well-maintained ornamental gardens. It is now a museum housing some of Tipu's belongings as well as many ink drawings of him and his family. It also has 'artists' impressions' of the last battle, drawn by employees of the British East India Company. All around the internal walls of the ground floor are paintings depicting Tipu's campaigns, with the help of French mercenary assistance, against the British. The gardens are open daily; the museum hours are from 9 am to 5 pm daily except Friday; entry is Rs 0.50.

Two km further is the **Gumbaz**, or mausoleum, of Tipu and his father, Hyder Ali. This impressive, cream building with its onion dome and inlaid doors was built by Tipu for his father and his family.

Places to Stay There are a couple of basic lodges just up the main road from the bus stand which would do for an overnight stay. Otherwise, the best place is the KSTDC's *Hotel Mayura River View* (☎ 52-114), a few km from the bus stand and railway station. It's peacefully located beside the Cauvery River and has well-kept double cottages for Rs 300 (no singles) plus an indoor/outdoor restaurant and cold beers.

Getting There & Away Scores of buses (including the No 125) ply the Mysore to Bangalore road; from the Central bus stand in Mysore the fare is Rs 4. It's also possible to take any of the Mysore to Bangalore trains.

Getting Around Walking around the sights is not really an option as the points of interest are well spread out. The best plan is to hire a bicycle on the main street in the fort, about 500 metres from the bus stand. All the sites are well signposted so it's not difficult to find your way around.

There are also *tongas* (horse carts) and auto-rickshaws for hire.

Ranganathittoo Bird Sanctuary

This sanctuary is on one of three islands in the Cauvery River, three km upstream from Srirangapatnam. If you're interested in birds this is a good place to see storks, ibises, egrets, darters, spoon bills and cormorants. It can be visited at any time of year, though it's best between July and August. Access is by a motorable road, open all year, and there are boats available. There is no accommodation.

Brindavan Gardens

Telephone Area Code: 08236

These ornamental gardens are laid out below the immense Krishnaraja Sagar across the Cauvery River, 19 km north-west of Mysore. They're popular for picnics and pleasant enough, but probably not worth a special visit although they are colourfully lit each night – 'cosmic kitsch' is how somebody described the lighting – and there's a musical fountain! The lights are on from 7 to 9 pm, and the fountain from 7.30 to 7.40 pm.

Entry costs Rs 5 plus Rs 10/20 if you have a still/movie camera. Due to fears of sabotage, vehicle access has been restricted to those who have a hotel booking. If you arrive without a booking, you'll have to walk the 1.5 km from the main gate, across the dam, to the gardens and hotels.

Places to Stay The cheapest place to stay is the KSTDC's *Hotel Mayura Cauvery* (☎ 57-282) which costs Rs 95/120 for singles/doubles with attached bathroom.

The *Hotel Krishnaraja Sagar* (☎ 57-222) has rooms with attached bathroom and colour TV for Rs 250/325, or Rs 325/450 with air-con. There's a bar, barbecue and restaurant serving Indian, Chinese and Continental dishes.

Getting There & Away One of the tours operated by the KSTDC will bring you here, or there are buses (No 150) from the Mysore City bus stand every half hour.

Tibetan Settlements

There are many Tibetan refugee settlements

west of Mysore in the area between Hunsur and Madikeri. Scattered over low, rolling hills patterned with green cornfields, the settlements are officially off limits to foreign tourists without the necessary permit, however, it's unlikely you'll be stopped if you do attempt to visit. The Tibetans are extremely friendly and generally very hospitable towards the few travellers who pass here.

Bylakuppe is one of the main settlements and is the site of the monastic university, Sera Gompa. Two smaller monasteries have been established at Camp Nos 1 and 3, and the Tantric college, Gjumed Dratsang, is in Hunsur. Within the region, there are also carpet factories (where you can get Tibetan carpets made to your own design), an incense factory and various social organisations.

As there's no commercial accommodation in any of the settlements, the best place to base yourself is the small market town of **Kushalnagar**, about 90 km west of Mysore. It has a couple of cheap hotels and from here you can get transport (rickshaws and share taxis) to the settlements, most of which have small cafes where you can get *momos* (fried or boiled dumplings with vegetables inside), noodles and delicious curd.

MANDYA DISTRICT

While the Hoysala temples of Somnathpur, Belur and Halebid and the Jain centre of Sravanabelagola are the most famous and visited of the rural sights in southern Karnataka, there are several other beautiful Hoysala temples in the Mandya district which stretches north and east of Mysore.

Some 30 km north of Mysore via the town of Pandavapura, is the Cheluvarayaswami Temple at **Melkote** which was built in the 12th century and later came under the patronage of the Mysore maharajas and even of Tipu Sultan. It's an important religious centre and there's a festival (Vairamudi) each year during March/April when the image is adorned with jewels belonging to the maharajas of Mysore.

North of Melkote is **Nagamangala** which was an important town even in the days of the Hoysalas. Its principal attraction is the Saumyakeshava Temple which was first built in the 12th century and later added to by the Vijayanagar kings.

About 20 km west of Melkote is **Krishnarajpet** and some two km from here is the village of **Hosaholalu**. Here there is a superb example of 13th-century Hoysala temple architecture in the form of the Lakshminarayana Temple which rivals in artistry the temples at Belur and Halebid.

Some 25 km north of Mandya, the district administrative centre on the main Mysore to Bangalore road, stands the village of **Basaralu** where there is the exquisite 12th-century Mallikarjuna Temple executed in early Hoysala style. It's adorned with beautiful sculptures including a 16-armed Siva dancing on Andhakasura's head and Ravana lifting Kailasa.

Getting to any of these towns involves the use of local buses and quite a few changes and you'll have to ask around to find the right ones as all the timetables are in Kannada. Mysore is your best base for all of them except Basaralu for which you might find Mandya town a better base. There's a range of modest accommodation in Mandya.

BANDIPUR NATIONAL PARK

Eighty km south of Mysore on the Mysore to Udhagamandalam (Ooty) road, this wildlife sanctuary covers 865 sq km and is part of a larger national park which also includes the neighbouring wildlife sanctuaries of Mudumalai in Tamil Nadu and Wynad in Kerala. In the days of the Mysore maharajas this was their game reserve.

The sanctuary is one of the 15 selected across the country for Project Tiger, a scheme launched in 1973 by the World Wide Fund for Nature (WWF) to save the tiger and its habitat. The sanctuary is noted for its herds of bison, spotted deer, elephant, sambar, sloth bears and langurs. There are supposed to be two dozen tigers but they are rarely seen. The best time to go is May and June, and again from September to November. If there is a drought, the park may not be worth visiting, as the animals migrate to the adjoining Mudumalai park for water.

KARNATAKA

Visitors must pay a fee of Rs 150 to enter the park (plus Rs 10 for a camera) but this includes a one-hour tour in the Forest Department's bus. This 27-seat bus does one-hour tours each day at 6.30, 7.30 and 8.30 am, and 4 and 5 pm. Elephant rides are the only other means of game viewing and cost Rs 40. Private vehicles are not allowed to tour the park and the Bandipur road is closed from 6.30 pm to 6 am.

Bus tours and Forest Department accommodation must be booked in advance. For reservations, contact either the Chief Wildlife Warden (☎ 334-1993), Aranya Bhavan, 18th Cross, Malleswaram in Bangalore or the Field Director (☎ 52-0901), Project Tiger, Ashokpuram, Mysore.

Places to Stay

The Forest Department's huge deluxe *bungalows* have bathrooms and hot water (if there's no water shortage) and cost Rs 75 per night. The caretaker (or somebody) will fix meals, and you can see chital (spotted deer) right from your windows. These bungalows *must* be booked and paid for in advance – if you turn up without a reservation, it's unlikely you'll be given a room (you may get one late at night when there is no chance of someone with a reservation turning up).

The only private resort is *Bush Betta*, about four km from the Bandipur reception centre off the road to Mudumalai. It's only a few years old and has doubles for Rs 3000 including all meals, an elephant ride and a safari. Bookings must be made in advance at their Bangalore office (☎ 221-0504) at 8 Richmond Rd. A taxi-jeep from the reception centre to the resort costs about Rs 75.

Getting There & Away

All buses between Mysore (2½ hours, Rs 16) and Ooty (three hours) will stop at Bandipur. From Bandipur, they continue via Theppakadu (30 minutes) in Mudumalai to Ooty. The last bus back to Mysore leaves at 5.30 pm.

NAGARHOLE NATIONAL PARK

This 643-sq-km wildlife sanctuary is in an isolated pocket of the Coorg region, 93 km south-west of Mysore. Until a few years ago, it was one of the country's finest deciduous forests and home to the tiger, elephant, panther, sloth bear, bison, barking deer and sambar. Unfortunately, much of the forest was destroyed by fire in 1992 when tensions between officials involved in anti-poaching activities and local graziers and farmers erupted in a frenzy of arson. The destruction is no longer blatantly obvious; however, it will still be many years before the forest has regenerated and the animals have repopulated it.

Not surprisingly, the park has seen few visitors in recent years and facilities are still minimal. Foreigners must pay a Rs 150 per day fee while in the park; the best time to visit is from October to May. In theory, the Forest Department has a minibus available for wildlife viewing but you'd be wise to enquire whether it's operating before going all the way to Nagarhole. Likewise, don't just turn up without reserving Forest Department accommodation in advance. All enquiries and bookings should be directed to either the Chief Wildlife Warden (☎ 334-1993), Aranya Bhavan, 18th Cross, Malleswaram, in Bangalore or the Deputy Conservator of the Forest & Wildlife Division (☎ (08222) 2041) at Hunsur.

Places to Stay & Eat

At the reception centre in the heart of the sanctuary, there are two Forest Department *dormitories* with beds for Rs 20, plus a six-room *lodge* for Rs 75 per person.

The *Kabini River Lodge*, near Karapur on the Mysore to Mananthavadi Rd, is much more expensive at US$110 per person including full board. This place is about 65 km from the sanctuary's reception centre and is run by Jungle Lodges & Resorts Ltd (☎ & fax 558-6163) in Bangalore.

Alternatively, there's an ultra-basic lodge in the one-horse hamlet of Kutta, 10 km from the reception centre.

It may also be worth finding out whether the Taj Group's 16-cottage lodge at Murka, about 15 km north of the reception area, is complete.

BELUR & HALEBID

Telephone Area Code: 08233

The Hoysala temples at Belur and Halebid (Halebeed, Halebidu), along with the one at Somnathpur east of Mysore, are the cream of what remains of one of the most artistically exuberant periods of Hindu cultural development. The sculptural temple decoration even rivals those of Khajuraho (Madhya Pradesh) and Konark (Orissa) or the best of European Gothic art.

The **Hoysaleswara Temple** at Halebid was constructed about 10 years after the temple at Belur, but despite 80 years labour was never completed. Nevertheless, it is easily the most outstanding example of Hoysala art. Every cm of the outside walls and much of the interior are covered with an endless variety of Hindu deities, sages, stylised animals and birds, and friezes depicting the life and times of the Hoysala rulers. No two are alike. Scenes which depict war, hunting, agriculture, music and dance,

and some very sensual sculptures explicitly portraying the après-temple activities of the dancing girls, are all represented here, together with two huge Nandis (Siva's bull) and a monolithic Jain statue of Gomateshvara.

The small museum adjacent to the temple has a collection of temple sculptures and is open from 10 am to 5 pm. There is also a smaller temple, the Kedareswara, at Halebid and, off the road to Hassan, a Jain temple.

At Belur, the **Channekeshava Temple** is the only one at the three Hoysala sites still in daily use. Non-Hindus are allowed inside but not into the inner sanctum. It is very similar to the others in design but here much of the decoration has gone into the internal supporting pillars and lintels, and the larger but still very delicately carved images of deities and guardian beasts. As at Halebid, the external walls are covered in friezes.

The other, lesser, Hoysala temples at Belur are the Channigaraya and the Viranarayana.

The Halebid and Belur temples are open every day for free although there's the usual Rs 0.50 shoe-minder's tip. A spotlight inside

---

Hoysala Architecture

The Hoysalas, who ruled this part of the Deccan between the 11th and 13th centuries, had their origins in the hill tribes of the Western Ghats and were, for a long time, feudatories of the Chalukyans. They did not become fully independent until about 1190 AD, though they first rose to prominence under their leader Tinayaditya (1047-78 AD), who took advantage of the waning power of the Gangas and Rashtrakutas. Under Bittiga (1110-52 AD), better known by his later name of Vishnuvardhana, they began to take off on a course of their own and it was during his reign that the distinctive temples of Belur and Halebid were built.

Typically, these temples are squat, star-shaped structures set on a platform to give them some height. They are more human in scale than the soaring temples found elsewhere in India but what they lack in size they make up in the sheer intricacy of their sculptures.

It's quickly apparent from a study of these sculptures that the arts of music and dancing reached a high point in grace and perfection during the Hoysala period. As with Kathakali dancing in Kerala, the arts were used to express religious fervour, the joy of a victory in battle, or simply to give domestic pleasure. It's obvious that these were times of a relatively high degree of sexual freedom and prominent female participation in public affairs. Most Indian books which describe these temples (and the famous temples at Khajuraho in Madhya Pradesh) bend over backwards to play down the sensuality of these sculptures. Perhaps this embarrassment reflects the repressed attitudes of the average urban Indian today regarding all matters physical. Of course a century ago our Victorian ancestors were also slightly shocked by some Indian temples!

Vishnuvardhana's conversion to Vishnu worship was one of the main factors leading to a decline of Jainism, but it was not the only one. Corruption among the priesthood and the public defeat of the Jain texts by Ramanuja also undermined its influence, but it was by no means extinguished and at least one of Vishnuvardhana's wives and a daughter continued to practise that faith. Later Hoysala rulers also continued to patronise the religion. This normally easy coexistence between Shaivites, Vaishnavaites and Jains explains why you will find images of all these various sects' gods, their consorts and associated companions in Hoysala temples. ■

enables you to see the sculptural work; it costs Rs 5 for the privilege.

Places to Stay & Eat
Halebid The only place to stay here is the peaceful *Tourist Cottages* (☎ 3224) set in a pleasant garden next to the temple. There are just two double rooms – Rs 35/50 for one/two people – which are carpeted and have attached bathrooms and quiet verandahs. There's also one dormitory but it's reserved for groups. The tiny *canteen* here has drinks, toast and omelettes.

Near the temple, the *Hotel Nag* and *Green Restaurant* both have OK food.

Belur The best place to stay is the KSTDC's *Hotel Mayura Velapuri* (☎ 2209) which is only 200 metres from the temple and a five-minute walk from the bus stand. Rooms with attached bathroom cost Rs 100/150 in the old wing, or Rs 150/200 in the new. It also has a new restaurant and bar.

The *Shri Raghavendra Tourist Home* (☎ 2372), to the right of the temple entrance near the massive temple chariot, has basic rooms (mattresses on the floor) for Rs 50. The *Swagath Tourist Home* (☎ 2159), 100 metres before the temple on the left, is cheaper and even more basic.

The *Sri Gayatri Bhavan* (☎ 2255) and the *Sri Vishnu Krupa* (☎ 2263) are both on the main road through town and charge around Rs 35/60 for rooms with common bath. The latter also has rooms with attached bathroom for Rs 75/100. They have veg restaurants and are a two-minute walk from the bus stand.

Cheap non-veg meals and beers are available at the *Hotel Rajatha*, down an alley next to the Sri Gayatri Bhavan lodge.

Getting There & Away
Halebid and Belur are only 16 km apart but buses between the two are infrequent and inevitably crammed full. For details on buses from Hassan or Arsikere, see those sections.

There are no direct buses from these towns to Hospet. You must first take a bus to Shimoga (three hours, Rs 25) from where there are buses to Hospet (five hours, Rs 40).

The KSTDC in Bangalore runs a tour to both towns as well as to Sravanabelagola. See the Bangalore Organised Tours section for details.

SRAVANABELAGOLA
Population: 3800
Telephone Area Code: 08176

This is one of the oldest and most important Jain pilgrimage centres in India, and the site of the huge 17-metre-high naked statue of Bahubali (Gomateshvara), said to be the world's tallest monolithic statue. It overlooks the town of Sravanabelagola from the top of the rocky hill known as Indragiri and is visible from quite a distance. Its simplicity is in complete contrast to the complexity of the sculptural work at the temples of Belur and Halebid. The word Sravanabelagola means the Monk of the White Pond.

Except during Mahamastakabhisheka (for details see the boxed section below), Sravanabelagola is a quiet little country town and a very pleasant place to stay for a few days. The people are friendly, the pace is unhurried and the place is full of cosy little *chai* shops.

Mahamastakabhisheka
Once every 12 years, the Gomateshvara statue is the subject of the spectacular Mahamastakabhisheka ceremony. During this extraordinary event, Sravanabelagola becomes a Mecca for thousands of pilgrims and tourists from all over India and abroad. The climax of Mahamastakabhisheka involves the anointing of Lord Bahubali's head with thousands of pots of coconut milk, yoghurt, ghee, bananas, jaggery, dates, almonds, poppy seeds, milk, gold coins, saffron and sandalwood from the top of a scaffolding erected for the purpose. There must be a lot of work for cleaners after this event! The next one will be in the year 2005. ∎

History

Sravanabelagola has a long historical pedigree going back to the 3rd century BC when Chandragupta Maurya came here with his guru, Bhagwan Bhadrabahu Swami, after renouncing his kingdom. In the course of time Bhadrabahu's disciples spread his teachings all over the region and thus firmly established Jainism in the south. The religion found powerful patrons in the Gangas who ruled the southern part of what is now Karnataka between the 4th and 10th centuries, and it was during this time that Jainism reached the zenith of its influence.

Information

The tourist office is right by the entrance to the hill and is open from 10 am to 5.30 pm, closed Sunday. It's staffed by a friendly and helpful man, and has a few books for sale.

Gomateshvara Statue

The statue of Bahubali was created during the reign of the Ganga king, Rachamalla. It was commissioned by a military commander in the service of Rachamalla and built by the sculptor Aristanemi in 981 AD.

There is no entry fee but you are encouraged to make a donation, and you must leave your shoes at the entrance. This creates a real problem in the summer as you then have to scamper up the 614 rock-cut steps which become scalding hot. Get there before the heat of the day to avoid this small bit of purgatory or, alternatively, have yourself carried up in a wicker chair by the porters waiting at the entrance. It'll cost about Rs 100 for this indulgence. During the hottest days umbrellas may also be available.

Other Temples

In addition to the statue of Bahubali there are several very interesting Jain *bastis* (temples) and *mathas* (monasteries) both in the town and on Chandragiri Hill, the smaller of the two hills between which Sravanabelagola nestles.

Two of these, the **Bhandari Basti** and the **Akkana Basti**, are in the Hoysala style, and a third, the **Chandragupta Basti**, is believed to have been built by Emperor Ashoka. The well-preserved paintings in one of the temples are like a 600-year-old comic strip of Jain stories.

Places to Stay & Eat

Nearly all of Sravanabelagola's accommodation is run by the local Jain organisation (☎ 7223 or 7226) which owns about 10 guest houses in town. One of the best, the new *Yatri Nivas* at the entrance to town, has well-furnished rooms with attached bathroom for Rs 100. The *Shriyans Prasad Guest House* pilgrims' quarters next to the bus stand at the foot of the hill, has double rooms at Rs 50.

The only privately owned place is the *Hotel Raghu* (☎ 7238), 100 metres from the bottom of the stairs to the statue. Singles/doubles with attached bath cost Rs 60/75. It also has a popular restaurant.

There is a very basic refreshment canteen in the bus stand, or you could try the vegetarian restaurants in the street leading up to the hill.

Getting There & Away

There are direct buses from Sravanabelagola to Arsikere, Hassan, Mysore and Bangalore. For details on buses to Sravanabelagola from Hassan and Arsikere, see the transport sections in those towns.

The KSTDC operates tours from Mysore and Bangalore to Sravanabelagola which include Belur and Halebid but they're pretty rushed.

HASSAN

Population: 117,000
Telephone Area Code: 08172

Hassan is probably the most convenient base from which to explore Belur, Halebid and Sravanabelagola. It has little of interest, and is simply a place for accommodation and transport.

Information

The tourist office is a total waste of time, and the staff are not particularly helpful. For foreign exchange, go to the State Bank of Mysore.

KARNATAKA

Places to Stay

A few minutes' walk from the bus stand, the *Vaishnavi Lodging* (☎ 67-413) is excellent value at Rs 60/90 for big, clean singles/doubles with bathroom. The *Sathyaprakash Lodging* (☎ 68-521) next to the bus stand is more basic but it is the cheapest place around. Rooms with bathroom cost Rs 30/50.

In the centre of town the basic *Hotel Lakshmi Prasanna* (☎ 68-391) has good-sized rooms or you could try the *Hotel Sanman* (☎ 68-024) right next door which has rooms for Rs 40/70.

There's just one *retiring room* at the railway station which costs Rs 25.

The *Hotel Amblee Palika* (☎ 66-307), Racecourse Rd, is very clean and well maintained. The rooms are large and comfortable and have mosquito netting on the windows. Ordinary rooms are Rs 150/200, plus there are deluxe rooms for Rs 200/260 if you want carpets and a few more light switches to play with.

The *Hotel Hassan Ashok* (☎ 68-731; fax 67-154) on the Bangalore to Mangalore road is the best hotel in town. Rooms with attached bathrooms and colour TV cost Rs 750/900 or Rs 1000/1250 with air-con. It has a restaurant, bar and souvenir shop.

Places to Eat

The hotels *Sanman* and *Lakshmi Prasanna* have very popular vegetarian restaurants which serve thalis for Rs 9. The former also has excellent dosas and idli.

An old favourite for years has been the restaurant under the Sathyaprakash Lodging. It has undergone a few name changes over the years; in its present incarnation it's known as *Rao Refreshments*. The thalis (Rs 8.50) are still good although the waiters have the annoying habit of hovering for a tip.

For something a bit better, the Hotel Amblee Palika has the *Malanika Restaurant* and a bar. For non-vegetarian food, try the *Hotel New Star*. It is open quite late and does good mutton and beef curries. Good north Indian and Chinese dishes for about Rs 30 are served in the *Abiruchi Restaurant*

although it's a little expensive by local standards.

The *Hotel Hassan Ashok* offers Indian and Continental cuisine in its à la carte restaurant, and dinner here will cost about Rs 75. At lunchtime they do a decent non-veg Indian buffet for Rs 125.

Getting There & Away

Bus If you intend visiting both Belur and Halebid on the same day from Hassan, it's more convenient to go to Halebid first, as there are more buses back from Belur to Hassan and they run until much later at night.

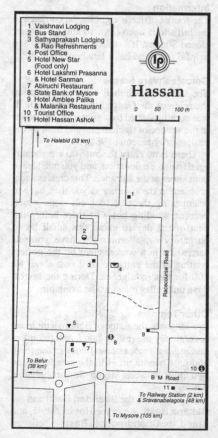

1 Vaishnavi Lodging
2 Bus Stand
3 Sathyaprakash Lodging
   & Rao Refreshments
4 Post Office
5 Hotel New Star
   (Food only)
6 Hotel Lakshmi Prasanna
   & Hotel Sanman
7 Abiruchi Restaurant
8 State Bank of Mysore
9 Hotel Amblee Palika
   & Malanika Restaurant
10 Tourist Office
11 Hotel Hassan Ashok

Hassan

0   50   100 m

To Halebid (33 km)

Racecourse Road

To Belur
(38 km)

B M Road

To Railway Station (2 km)
& Sravanabelagola (48 km)

To Mysore (105 km)

There are 15 buses daily from Hassan to Halebid (33 km, one hour, Rs 9). The first bus departs at 8 am, and the last bus back to Hassan leaves Halebid at 6.15 pm. There are about 20 buses daily from Hassan to Belur (38 km, 1½ hours, Rs 8). The first leaves Hassan at 7 am. Ignore the timetable's claim about some of the buses being 'express'; it's a figment of the imagination.

To Sravanabelagola (48 km, 1½ hours, Rs 13), there are three direct buses daily from Hassan but the first one doesn't leave until 11 am. To get an early start from Hassan, it's better to catch the 7 am bus to Channarayapatna (one hour, Rs 8) and then take the 8.15 am bus from there to Sravanabelagola (30 minutes, Rs 3). Late in the afternoon bus paranoia sets in and the usual chaos results.

From Hassan, there are at least 20 buses daily to Mysore (three hours) and the same number to Bangalore (four hours).

Train The railway station is about two km from the centre of town; Rs 5 by auto-rickshaw.

There are three passenger trains daily to/from Mysore (119 km, 3½ hours) which cost Rs 19/126 in 2nd/1st class. These trains from Mysore also continue on to Arsikere (one hour).

To Mangalore (189 km), there's one daily passenger train (eight hours), as well as a daily express (6½ hours) which costs Rs 26/193 in 2nd/1st class. This line may be closed during the monsoon season from June to September.

ARSIKERE

Like Hassan, this is a convenient base from which to explore the temples of Belur and Halebid and the Jain centre of Sravanabelagola, but unlike Hassan it has a Hoysala temple of its own. Unfortunately, much of the temple has been defaced and vandalised, and many contemporary structures have been added so it's no longer very representative. It's about a 15-minute walk down the road next to the Co-operative Bank on the main road just up from the bus stand.

Arsikere is also a railway junction and (normally) has express trains to Bangalore, Bombay and Goa. The bus stand is in the centre of town, 100 metres from the railway station.

Places to Stay & Eat
Just outside the railway station is the clean, quiet and friendly *Geetha Lodge*. Rooms cost Rs 30/60 and have bucket showers.

The friendly *Hotel Mayura* (☎ 32-358) in the centre has rooms for Rs 40/60. The nearby *Hotel Prashanth* (☎ 32-834) opposite the bus stand has rooms where you stand a sporting chance of surviving for a night without being eaten alive, and it's cheap at Rs 30/50. It has an excellent 'meals' dining hall on the ground floor.

There are also two *retiring rooms* at the railway station – Rs 60 for a room.

In the non-veg food department, the *Elite Hotel*, just up from the bus stand on the main road, is OK.

Getting There & Away
Bus Buses to Halebid or Belur (1½ hours, Rs 8) depart almost hourly throughout the day. For Sravanabelagola, it can be quicker to take a bus to Channarayapatna (Rs 10) and another from there. (See earlier Bus section under Hassan for details.)

Train There are three passenger trains daily to Hassan (one hour, Rs 9) and Mysore (four hours, Rs 25). If you're heading in the direction of Madras or Madurai, take a passenger train first to Bangalore (156 km, Rs 39/170 in 2nd/1st).

Services on the railway line to Hubli and Miraj had been disrupted due to line conversion at the time of updating this book, and trains to Goa and Hospet (via Hubli) had been suspended. If you're heading north, check at the enquiry window at the station for the current state of play. If the line is out of action, you can always get to destinations such as Bombay by taking a train first to Bangalore and then an express from there.

KARNATAKA

Coast & Western Ghats

MADIKERI (Mercara)

Population: 30,000
Telephone Area Code: 08272

The small town of Madikeri, the capital of the Coorg region, is a quiet and unhurried hill station, 124 km west of Mysore. Until 1956, when it was included in Karnataka, Coorg (or Kodagu) was a mini-state in its own right. It is a mountainous area in the south-west of the state where the Western Ghats start to tumble down towards the sea, and is green, scenic and fertile. Traditionally the home of the Kodava tribe, Coorg is now an important coffee-growing area.

The view from **Raja's Seat**, the local scenic lookout close to the KSTDC's hotel, is wonderful. There is a **fort** in Madikeri which has played an important part in Karnataka's tumultuous history. A small museum is housed in an old church within the walls of the fort, while the old palace itself is now used as the local municipal headquarters. There's also the **Omareswara Temple**, one km from the town centre back towards Mysore.

Orientation & Information

The town is well spread out along a series of ridges but the bus stand and the bulk of the hotels and restaurants are together in a compact area.

There is a small tourist bureau in the PWD Bungalow beside the first roundabout on the Mysore road. It is open from 10 am to 5.30 pm, closed Sunday.

Places to Stay

The quiet *Anchorage Guest House* (☎ 26-939) is on a big, bare block of land about three minutes' walk from the bus stand. Double rooms cost Rs 100 with bathroom. Also very close to the bus stand is the *Hotel Sri Venayaka Lodge* with dull but adequate rooms for Rs 30/50. There are a few other rock-bottom places in the main street but they're not very inviting.

The *Hotel Cauvery* (☎ 26-292) is a one-minute walk from the bus stand and next to the cinema. Rooms in this clean and friendly place cost Rs 100/175 with bathroom, and there is hot water in the mornings. The *Chitra Lodge* (☎ 27-311) on the main street is more expensive, with doubles for Rs 310 (Rs 350 with TV).

The KSTDC's *Hotel Mayura Valley View* (☎ 26-387) is one km up behind the town hall, about 20 minutes' walk. It has rooms for Rs 125/150 (Rs 175 for a deluxe room) and great views.

Places to Eat

The *Chitra Lodge* does a good standard 'meal' lunch for Rs 15. Also on the main street is the friendly *Durbar Cafe*.

The *Hotel Capitol*, next to the Hotel Cauvery, is mainly a bar but also serves good food. The menu is limited and the service slow but the vegetable fried rice is worth the wait.

Getting There & Away

The bus stand is right in the centre of town. From here, plenty of buses run via Kushalnagar to Mysore (120 km, three hours, Rs 36) and to Mangalore (136 km, 3½ hours, Rs 41). There are 10 buses daily to Bangalore (256 km, six hours, Rs 76), and at least one bus to Hassan and Arsikere, Belur or Chikmagalur.

MANGALORE

Population: 462,000
Telephone Area Code: 0824

At one time Mangalore was a port of great significance and the major seaport and ship-building centre of Hyder Ali's kingdom. Even today it is a major centre for the export of coffee and cashew nuts, but its attractions are very limited. If Mangalore is on your way it can make a convenient overnight stop, but otherwise you won't miss too much by passing it by.

Orientation

Mangalore is a hilly place so the streets twist and wind all over the place. For this reason navigation can be difficult. Fortunately all the hotels and restaurants are in or around the hectic city centre, as is the railway station. The bus stand is a few km to the north and you'll need to catch an auto-rickshaw (about Rs 10).

Information

There is a tourist office (☎ 21-692) across from the town hall on Dr U P Mallya Rd, but the guy staffing it seems to be permanently out to lunch. It is open from 9 am to 5 pm, closed Sunday.

The GPO is about 15 minutes' walk downhill (south) from the centre, just past Chetty Circle.

On Lighthouse Hill Rd there's a branch of Higginbothams bookshop.

Things to See

The main remnant from the past is the **Sultan's Battery**, four km from the centre on the headland to the old port. It really doesn't rate as one of the not-to-be-missed wonders of India. A No 16 bus from the city centre will get you there; an auto-rickshaw will cost Rs 20 for the round trip.

The **Shreemanthi Bai Memorial Government Museum**, north of the centre just beyond KSRTC bus terminal, is a rather nice

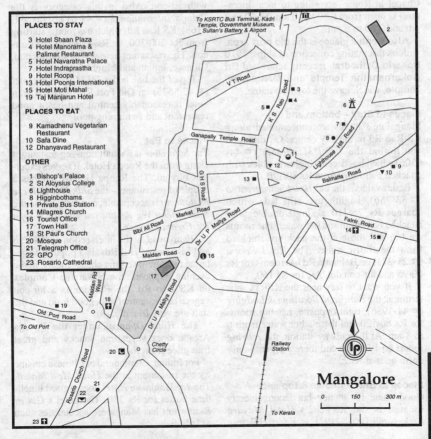

PLACES TO STAY
3 Hotel Shaan Plaza
4 Hotel Manorama & Palimar Restaurant
5 Hotel Navaratna Palace
7 Hotel Indraprastha
9 Hotel Roopa
13 Hotel Poonja International
15 Hotel Moti Mahal
19 Taj Manjarun Hotel

PLACES TO EAT
9 Kamadhenu Vegetarian Restaurant
10 Safa Dine
12 Dhanyavad Restaurant

OTHER
1 Bishop's Palace
2 St Aloysius College
6 Lighthouse
8 Higginbothams
11 Private Bus Station
14 Milagres Church
16 Tourist Office
17 Town Hall
18 St Paul's Church
20 Mosque
21 Telegraph Office
22 GPO
23 Rosario Cathedral

Mangalore

KARNATAKA

building with an interesting collection. It's open Tuesday to Sunday from 9 am to 5 pm, closed second Saturday of the month. Admission is free but you may have to tip the guard. Get there from the centre on bus No 10 or 34.

At the **Kadri Temple**, the Lokeshwara statue is reputed to be one of the best bronzes in India. There are nine tanks around the temple, and nearby is the hilltop lighthouse which gives Lighthouse Hill Rd its name. The lighthouse is reputed to have been built by Hyder Ali and Tipu Sultan.

The **St Aloysius College Chapel** with its painted ceiling ('comparable to the Sistine Chapel in Rome' according to local literature) is open from 8.30 to 10 am, 12.30 to 2 pm and 3.30 to 6 pm.

Also worth a glance is the **old port area**, with its fascinating collection of ships, 1910 **Rosario Cathedral**, recently renovated **Sri Gokarnanatha Temple** and **Mangladevi Temple**, which gave the town its name.

Places to Stay – bottom end

Mangalore's hotels are concentrated along KS Rao Rd in the city centre. On this road you'll find the *Hotel Manorama* (☎ 44-0306) which has decent singles/doubles with attached bathroom from Rs 80/120.

Better value is the old *Hotel Indraprastha* (☎ 33-756), Lighthouse Hill Rd, which charges Rs 75/110 a single/double with attached bathroom and hot water. The rooms are big and those at the back are shielded from the traffic noise. The *Hotel Roopa* (☎ 21-271) on Balmatta Rd has rooms for Rs 60/95 and air-con doubles for Rs 160.

If you want to stay near the KSRTC bus terminal, the *Panchami Boarding & Lodging* (☎ 41-1986), right opposite, has big rooms for Rs 80/120 and there's hot water from 6 to 8 am. At the railway station, the *retiring rooms* cost Rs 100 and there are gents-only dorm beds at Rs 25.

Places to Stay – middle & top end

Good value for money but inconveniently located is the KSTDC's *Hotel Mayura Nethravathi* (☎ 41-1192), at Kedri Hill way

north of the centre. All rooms have phone and hot water, and those at the front have balconies with views out over the city and the ocean. The tariff is Rs 85/105 for singles/doubles.

The *Hotel Navaratna Palace* (☎ 33-781) on KS Rao Rd has well-furnished rooms for Rs 120/170, and more expensive air-con rooms. Almost opposite, the *Shaan Plaza* (☎ 44-0312) has rooms for Rs 150/180, or Rs 250 with air-con.

Up in price, the *Hotel Moti Mahal* (☎ 44-1411), Falnir Rd, has a bar, restaurant, coffee shop and swimming pool, and rooms for Rs 275/325 without air-con and Rs 350/425 with air-con. Also in this category is the *Poonja International* (☎ 44-0171; fax 44-0168), KS Rao Rd, which has rooms starting from Rs 200/300, or Rs 350/450 with air-con. The restaurant here serves Continental, Chinese, Indian and Mughlai dishes.

Top of the line is the *Taj Manjarun Hotel* (☎ 42-5525) on Old Port Rd. This well-run hotel is reasonably central and has a good restaurant and swimming pool.

Places to Eat

The *Safa Dine* is a small non-veg restaurant along from the Roopa Hotel. It serves excellent biryani. The Roopa Hotel itself has a couple of restaurants – the *Shin Min Chinese Restaurant* is acceptable, and there's also the *Kamadhenu Veg Restaurant* and the *Roopa Ice-Cream Parlour*.

Dhanyavad, at the intersection of KS Rao and Lighthouse Hill Rds, is a popular vegetarian restaurant serving cheap 'meals' in the evening. Opposite the Navaratna Complex on KS Rao Rd, the *Palimar* is a air-con vegetarian restaurant with good food and the staff are very friendly.

The *Hotel Dhanraj* under the Poonja Arcade does vegetarian snacks and great fruit juice from Rs 8.

For Indian, Continental or Chinese cuisine try the restaurant at the *Hotel Moti Mahal*. The *Taj Manjarun Hotel* does a good lunchtime buffet for Rs 130. The hotel's *Galley Restaurant* has Mangalore specialities such as lady fish.

Getting There & Away
Air The Indian Airlines and Air India office
(☎ 41-4300) is four km out of town on
Hathill Rd in the Lalbagh area. The office is
open from 9 am to 1 pm and 1.45 to 4 pm
daily. More centrally, Indian Airlines has a
branch office in the Hotel Moti Mahal.

Indian Airlines flies daily to Bombay
(US$75) and three times a week to Madras
(US$52) via Bangalore (US$35).

Jet Airways (☎ 44-0694) and East West
Airlines (☎ 44-0541) both have a daily flight
to Bombay. NEPC Airlines (☎ 45-6659)
flies to Madras (US$80) three times a week
via Bangalore (US$40) and twice a week via
Kochi (US$70) and Coimbatore (US$110).

Bus The main bus stand is about three km
north from the city centre and is fairly quiet
and well organised. There are daily departures to Bangalore (eight hours, Rs 68), Goa
(11 hours, Rs 94), Hassan (four hours, Rs
35), Hospet (10 hours, Rs 90), via Udipi to
Karwar (eight hours, Rs 58), Madikeri (3½
hours, Rs 41), Mysore (seven hours, Rs 52),
Madras and Bombay.

Several private bus companies, serving all
the main destinations, have their offices on
Balmatta and Falnir roads.

Train By now the new west-coast Konkan
Railway should be providing greatly
improved rail links between Mangalore and
Bombay. Ask at the railway station, 400
metres from the city centre, about services
on this line.

Heading east, there are two trains a day to
Hassan (189 km, 6½ hours, Rs 26/193 in
2nd/1st class) and onto Mysore (11 hours, Rs
39/277), from where you have connections
to Bangalore. This line runs through the
Western Ghats and services can be suspended during the monsoon season.

Moving south, trains to Thiruvanantha-
puram (Trivandrum; 921 km, 16 hours) cost
Rs 124/479 in 2nd/1st class, and run via
Kozhikode (Calicut), Ernakulam and Kollam
(Quilon).

Getting Around
To/From the Airport The airport is 20 km
from the city centre. Bus No 48 from the
local bus stand will get you there, or there's
an airport bus (Rs 20) from the Indian Airlines office near the bus terminal. A taxi costs
around Rs 125.

Bus & Auto-Rickshaw The local bus stand
is at the junction of K S Rao and Lighthouse
Hill Rds. There's a confusing array of buses
– the only one you're likely to need is the
'Panambur' bus out to Sultan's Battery or the
airport bus.

As always, there are plenty of auto-
rickshaws.

AROUND MANGALORE
Ullal
Ullal, 13 km south of Mangalore, boasts the
Summer Sands Beach Resort (☎ 46-7690),
one of the few resorts on the Karnatakan
coastline. The beach is passable and the
place makes a pleasantly quiet escape from
the city. Its bungalows each have two double
rooms with attached bathroom, large living
room, kitchen and porch. Doubles without
air-con range from Rs 216 to Rs 282, or from
Rs 360 to Rs 468 with air-con. There's an OK
restaurant and a swimming pool.

Dharmastala
A little south of the Mangalore to Chikmagalur road, about 75 km due east of Mangalore, is Dharmastala. There are a number of
Jain bastis (temples) including the famous
Manjunatha Temple here, as well as a 14-
metre-high statue of Bahubali which was
erected in 1973.

Venur
Midway between Mangalore and Dharmastala, 41 km north-west of the latter, Venur
has eight bastis and the ruins of a Mahadeva
temple. An 11-metre-high **Bahubali statue**
stands on the south bank of the Gurupur
River, where it was installed in 1604.

Mudabidri
At this site, 22 km north-west of Venur, there

are 18 bastis, the oldest of which is the **Chandranatha Temple** with its richly carved 1000-pillar hall.

Karkal

A further 20 km north of Mudabidri, at Karkal, are several important temples and a 13-metre-high **Bahubali statue**, which was completed in 1432.

SRINGERI

In the lush coffee-growing hills of Chikmagalur, north-east of Karkal near Harihar, Sringeri is the southern seat of the orthodox Hindu hierarchy. The other three centres founded by Shankaracharya are Joshimath in the Himalaya (north), Puri (east) and Dwarka (west). The very interesting **Vidyashankar Temple** has zodiac pillars and a huge paved courtyard. A beautifully clean second temple is dedicated to Sharada, the goddess of learning. The Tunga River flows past the old monastery in this charmingly unspoilt town.

Places to Stay & Eat

As this is a major pilgrimage centre, there is a range of pilgrim accommodation available in different buildings around the town. A charge of Rs 25 per person is made for spartan single or double rooms with bathroom. You must report to the small office at the temple entrance to be allocated a room.

There's a vegetarian restaurant in the bus stand, which is in the centre of town.

Getting There & Away

There are plenty of buses from Sringeri to virtually all points in Karnataka, including Mysore, Hassan, Chikmagalur, Sagar and Bangalore.

UDIPI

About 57 km north of Mangalore on the coastal road, Udipi (also known as Udupi) is an important Vaishnavaite town. It was here that the 13th-century religious leader, Madhvacharya, lived and preached, and the town's **Krishna Temple** continues to draw many pilgrims.

Udipi also has another claim to fame – according to local legend, the ubiquitous *masala dosa* was supposedly first created here.

There are a handful of hotels near the central bus stand. Buses to Mangalore, Panaji, Mysore and Bangalore are frequent.

JOG FALLS

Near the coast, about 230 km north of Mangalore, Jog Falls are the highest in India. The Shiravati River drops 253 metres in four separate falls known as the Rani, the Rocket, the Raja and the Roarer.

The best time to see the falls is just after the monsoon, basically December and January. In the wet season they may be totally obscured by mist and fog, and during the dry season the falls almost dry up (though this situation could change if plans go ahead to release water from the Linganamakki Dam upriver on weekends during the dry season).

The most exciting view is from the top of the Raja, where you can see it fall over the Roarer! Even in the dry season the ever-changing fans of rainbows over the falls are superb. The view of the falls from in front of the Inspection Bungalow is also excellent, and there are steps leading down the side of the cliff.

Places to Stay & Eat

Accommodation is heavily booked on Friday and Saturday. The *PWD Inspection Bungalow* commands the best position but is almost always full and has to be booked in Sidapur (20 km north-east of Jog Falls). Alternatively, try the *Tunga Tourist Home* which has dreary singles/doubles for Rs 35/50.

Better is the *Sharagati Tourist Home* with rooms for Rs 50/75 but, again, it is often full. There's a *youth hostel* about two km from the bus stand which has dorm beds for Rs 10.

Food options are even more limited. It's best to order meals in advance at the place you are staying; otherwise there are just the couple of stalls at the bus stand selling chai, bananas and some snacks.

Getting There & Away

Bus There are two buses a day to Karwar (seven hours, Rs 27) which leave at 6 and 11.15 am.

There are more frequent local buses to Sagar, 30 km south-east of Jog Falls, from where you can get connections for destinations further south.

Train The nearest railway station, Talguppa, about 15 km south-east of the falls, is at the end of the line from Birur. However, it was closed for line conversion when we went to press so you'll need to ask at Birur or one of the larger regional junctions such as Hubli or Arsikere to find out if the line has reopened.

KARWAR

Telephone Area Code: 08382

Karwar, only a short distance south of Goa, is a quiet port town stretched out south of the Kali Nadi River. The area around here is very picturesque, with the hills dropping almost straight into the sea, creating small bays and a few calm beaches several km south of the town.

The port is the base for deep sea trawlers, however, the whole nature of the town could change in the future as it has been chosen as the site of a major new naval base to be located a few bays south of Karwar. It's anyone's guess if and when this will actually happen – at last notice, everything was on hold due to financial problems.

You can make trips up the Kali Nadi from Karwar, or take a walk up to the spectacular bridge over the river – it's about a 45-minute walk, or Rs 20 by rickshaw.

Places to Stay & Eat

There's a range of budget hotels close to the bus stand. The *Hotel Ashok* (☎ 6418) is a reasonable place with rooms for Rs 100 plus there's non-veg food. The *Anand Lodge* (☎ 6156), a two-minute walk from the bus stand, is good value at Rs 80 for doubles with

bathroom (hot water in the morning) and balconies.

Three km north of town, just before the Kali Nadi bridge, is the relatively new *Hotel Bhadra* (☎ 25-212). Ordinary double rooms cost Rs 150, or from Rs 275 to Rs 350 with air-con. It has a good veg and non-veg restaurant.

The *Sea View Lodge & Restaurant* on the first corner after the bus stand is supposedly the oldest lodge in Karwar and has a few reasonable rooms and OK food.

A great place for food is *City Dine*, up a side street between the Sea View and Anand lodges. The staff are jovial and there's a decent variety of food, even during the frequent power cuts.

Getting There & Away

The Karwar bus stand, south of the town centre, is total madness at times as hordes of people battle for limited seats.

There are Kadamba buses (eight a day) for the 4½-hour journey to Panaji (Rs 21). Buses for Jog Falls (seven hours) leave at 7.30 am and 3 pm, and cost Rs 27.

There are at least daily departures for Hubli, Bijapur, Belgaum, Mangalore, Bellary, Belur, Sringeri and Chikmagalur.

AROUND KARWAR

Ankola

There's a little-used **beach** at the small village of Ankola, 37 km south of Karwar. Near the main road are the ruined walls of King Sarpamalika's **fort**, and the **Sri Venkatraman Temple** which dates back to the same period, about the 15th century. In an unmarked mud-brick garage near the temple are two giant wooden chariots, large enough to be pulled by elephants and carved all over with scenes from the *Ramayana*.

Gokarna

About 23 km south of Ankola is the village of Gokarna, an important pilgrimage place due to the **Mahabaleshwara Temple** there.

Central Karnataka

HAMPI

Population: 900
Telephone Area Code: 08394

The Vijayanagar city ruins near the village of Hampi are one of the most fascinating historical sites in south India. The superb ruins are set in a strange and beautiful landscape which has an almost magical quality – a hill country that is partly desolate and strewn with enormous, rounded boulders, and partly irrigated and cultivated. The Tungabhadra River runs along the northern edge of this large area.

The best way to soak up the atmosphere here is to spend several days and take your time exploring the area, though it is possible to see all the main sites in one day on foot if you start early. Signposting on the site is somewhat inadequate and the trails sometimes indistinct, but you can't really get lost. It may be best not to wander around the sites alone, especially at dawn or dusk when it's relatively dark, as there have been a couple of muggings here in recent years.

Orientation

There are two main points of entry to the ruins: Hampi Bazaar and the small village of Kamalapuram to the south. Either make a good start for visiting the ruins, though most people prefer to start in Hampi Bazaar. From here it's possible to walk to all the main sites and down to the museum at Kamalapuram, from where there are buses back to Hospet or Hampi Bazaar, or you can walk back to Hampi along the road in 40 minutes. It's at least one full day's outing, and it's a good idea to bring some food and water along, although there are restaurants in both Hampi Bazaar and Kamalapuram as well as a few soft-drink stalls and the occasional chai shop.

Information

A publication entitled *Hampi* (Archaeological Survey) by D Devakunjari is on sale at the museum in Kamalapuram for Rs 12. It gives a history of the Vijayanagar Empire and a description and layout of the ruins. More detailed but still highly readable is *Hampi Ruins* by A H Longhurst, which is on

The Ruins of Vijayanagar

Vijayanagar, or Hampi as it is often called these days, was once the capital of one of the largest Hindu empires in Indian history. Founded by the Telugu princes Harihara and Bukka in 1336, it reached the height of its power under Krishnadevaraya (1509-29), when it controlled the whole of the peninsula south of the Krishna and Tungabhadra rivers, except for a string of commercial principalities along the Malabar coast.

Comparable to Delhi in the 14th century, the city, which covered an area of 33 sq km, was surrounded by seven concentric lines of fortification and was reputed to have had a population of about half a million. It maintained a mercenary army of over one million according to the Persian ambassador, Abdul Razak, and included Muslim mounted archers to defend it from the Muslim states to the north.

Vijayanagar's wealth was based on control of the spice trade to the south and the cotton industry of the south-east. Its busy bazaars, described by European travellers such as the Portuguese Nunez and Paes, were centres of international commerce. The religion was a hybrid of current Hinduism with the gods Vishnu and Siva being lavishly worshipped in the orthodox manner though, as in the Hoysala kingdom, Jainism was also prominent. Brahmins were privileged; *sati* (the burning of widows on the funeral pyres of their husbands) was widely practised and temple prostitution was common. Brahmin inscriptions discovered on the site date the first Vijayanagar settlement back to the 1st century AD and suggest that there was a Buddhist centre nearby.

The empire came to a sudden end in 1565 after the disastrous battle of Talikota when the city was ransacked by the confederacy of Deccan sultans (Bidar, Bijapur, Golconda, Ahmednagar and Berar), thus opening up southern India for conquest by the Muslims.

Excavation at Vijayanagar was started in 1976 by the Archaeological Survey of India in collaboration with the Karnataka state government, and is still continuing.

If anywhere in India is comparable in mystique and romanticism to Macchu Picchu in the Peruvian Andes, then this is the place. ∎

sale (Rs 45) at the Aspiration Stores near the entrance to the Virupaksha Temple at Hampi Bazaar. There are good maps of the area available in Hampi Bazaar – try at the tourist office or better still the Aspiration Stores.

The museum at Kamalapuram (open 10 am to 5 pm) has some very fine sculptures and coins and is worth a visit. For a good overview of Hampi, there's a large-scale model in the courtyard.

It costs Rs 5 to enter Hampi Bazaar in a private car.

Hampi Bazaar

The old Hampi Bazaar is now a bustling village, and the locals (and their animals) have inhabited the old bazaar buildings which line the main street. The village has become something of a travellers' Mecca and it is a superb place to stay if you're not too concerned about minor luxuries or the fact that diluted dung is sprayed on doorsteps every morning to keep the dust down and the *rangolis* (chalk designs) looking fresh!

The western side of Hampi Bazaar is the most bustling area. Here you'll find a number of restaurants catering for Western travellers, the Aspiration Stores which has a variety of books as well as souvenirs such as handmade paper, and plenty of soft-drink and trinket stalls.

The village is dominated by the **Virupaksha Temple** with its 52-metre-high gopuram, those structures which typify temples in Tamil Nadu. The temple dates back to the middle of the 15th century and is popular with Indian tourists. A sign in the temple courtyard reads: 'Please keep off the Plantains from the sight of the Monkies', which translates to something like, 'Watch out or the monkeys will pinch your bananas'.

Vittala Temple

From the far end of Hampi Bazaar an obvious track leads left to the highlight of the ruins, the Vittala Temple, some two km away. This temple is a World Heritage Monument (one of only three in south India, the others being at Thanjavur and Mahabali-puram in Tamil Nadu) and is in a good state of preservation, though purists may well have reservations about the cement-block columns which have been erected to keep the main structure from falling down. Although it was never finished or consecrated, the incredible sculptural work of the Vittala Temple is of the highest standard and is the pinnacle of Vijayanagar art. The outer pillars are known as the musical pillars as they reverberate when tapped, although this practice is being actively discouraged as the pillars are somewhat the worse for wear. The stone chariot or cart in front of the temple is one of the most photographed objects in this part of India; the wheels even used to turn!

Sule Bazaar & Achyutaraya Temple

Halfway from Hampi Bazaar to the Vittala Temple, but off to the right, is the deserted Sule Bazaar, which gives you some idea of what Hampi Bazaar might have looked like if it hadn't been repopulated. At the southern end of this area is the Achyutaraya Temple which, if anything, is even more atmospheric than the Vittala Temple since there's rarely anyone there and the carvings are just as fine.

Royal Enclosure Area

This area of Hampi is quite different from the northern section in that there are nowhere near as many rounded boulders littering the site – most have been used to make a mind-boggling proliferation of beautifully executed stone walls.

It is quite a walk (about two km) from the Achyutaraya Temple to the Royal Enclosure area, and you need to have your wits about you otherwise you could get lost (though not drastically). Leaving the rear (southern end) of Achyutaraya Temple, take the path which passes alongside a small shrine under a huge, old, gnarled tree and then turn right alongside an irrigation ditch and overlooking a field below. Continue along this, crossing over three further irrigation ditches to the valley bottom and then up the far side until you come to the fourth (and largest) irrigation channel (which always has water in it) beside a small, part-ruined Siva temple (there's no Siva image anymore but the Nandi is still there).

Right opposite this temple is a stone bridge across the channel. Cross this and head to the right. This will take you past another (disused) temple after which you need to veer off to the right until you get to the palace walls. The entrance through the walls is off to the right. Once through the walls, turn sharp left and follow the gravel road until you get to the Royal Enclosure area.

Within various stone-walled enclosures here are the rest of Hampi's major attractions. First up are the **Lotus Mahal** and the **Elephant Stables**. The former is a delicately designed pavilion in a walled compound known as the Zanana Enclosure. The building gets its name from the lotus bud carved in the centre of the domed and vaulted ceiling. The Elephant Stables is a grand building with eleven domed chambers for housing the state elephants.

Further south are the Royal Enclosure with its various temples, the **Underground Temple** and the **Queen's Bath**.

Places to Stay

Hampi Bazaar If you came to Hampi for

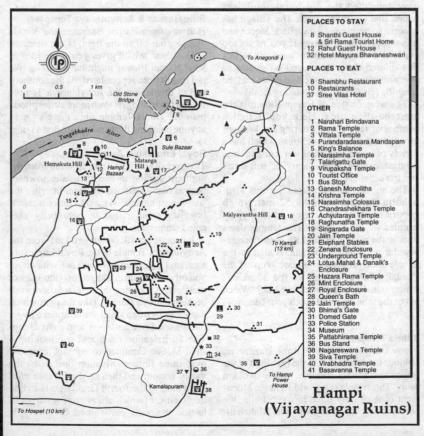

PLACES TO STAY
8 Shanthi Guest House
   & Sri Rama Tourist Home
12 Rahul Guest House
32 Hotel Mayura Bhavaneshwari

PLACES TO EAT
8 Shambhu Restaurant
10 Restaurants
37 Sree Vilas Hotel

OTHER
1 Narahari Brindavana
2 Rama Temple
3 Vittala Temple
4 Purandaradasara Mandapam
5 King's Balance
6 Narasimha Temple
7 Talarigattu Gate
9 Virupaksha Temple
10 Tourist Office
11 Bus Stop
13 Ganesh Monoliths
14 Krishna Temple
15 Narasimha Colossus
16 Chandrashekhara Temple
17 Achyutaraya Temple
18 Raghunatha Temple
19 Singarada Gate
20 Jain Temple
21 Elephant Stables
22 Zenana Enclosure
23 Underground Temple
24 Lotus Mahal & Danaik's
   Enclosure
25 Hazara Rama Temple
26 Mint Enclosure
27 Royal Enclosure
28 Queen's Bath
29 Jain Temple
30 Bhima's Gate
31 Domed Gate
33 Police Station
34 Museum
35 Pattabhirama Temple
36 Bus Stand
38 Nagareswara Temple
39 Siva Temple
40 Virabhadra Temple
41 Basavanna Temple

Hampi
(Vijayanagar Ruins)

romance and atmosphere, then this is the place to be. Accommodation is basic and there's not much choice but it is adequate.

The *Shanthi Guest House* (☎ 51-368) is probably the best and charges Rs 40/50 for basic but very clean singles/doubles with big beds, clean common toilets and cold shower. It's a popular travellers' haunt, and the rooms have a few added extras such as a window and mirror. You can also sleep on the roof for Rs 15 if it's full but, beware, the mosquitoes here are bad. The guest house is well signposted – to get there walk up to the temple entrance, turn right, then the first left and you'll see it up in front of you.

For the same price, the *Rahul Guest House* on the left-hand side just before you enter Hampi Bazaar coming from Hospet has spartan rooms (cement cells is a better description) with mattresses on the ground, communal toilets and bucket showers.

The *Sri Rama Tourist Home*, to the right of the temple, is a big place that's popular with visiting Indians but the dank singles/doubles are overpriced at Rs 40/80.

The *Sri Bhuvaneshvari Guest House* behind the tourist office has miniature 'rooms' for Rs 20/25. Alternatively, they might let you sleep on the roof for free.

Kamalapuram The KSTDC's *Hotel Mayura Bhavaneshwari* (☎ (08394) 5374) at Kamalapuram village is a brand new place that is blossoming under the enthusiasm of its helpful new manager, K T N Murthy. Rooms cost Rs 120/150 and are super clean, have 24-hour hot water, a pot plant or two, mozzie nets and comfortable beds. There's a restaurant (where you can get toast for breakfast) but no bar, although beers can be 'arranged'.

Places to Eat
Hampi Bazaar There are plenty of simple restaurants and soft-drink stalls on the street leading to the Virupaksha Temple. Most of these places are tiny – five or six tables at the most – and serve standard Indian fare as well as standby Western-style dishes – omelettes, chips, spaghetti, etc. There's very little difference between most of them, though they

all can produce extensive menus from which only limited offerings are actually available. Which restaurant you choose on any given day will probably depend simply on whether or not they've got the meal you want to order. Recommended are the *Welcome Restaurant* which does very tasty omelettes and vegetable stews, and the *Gopi* and *Geeta* restaurants. You could also try the *Ramsing Teashop*.

One of the biggest restaurants on this street and the best for Indian food is *Sri Venkateswara*, on the right as you near the temple. It serves tiffin at lunch and thalis (Rs 10) in the evening, and has a long street-level verandah which is ideal for watching the passing parade.

A very popular travellers' hangout is the *Shambhu Restaurant* opposite the Shanthi Guest House. The atmosphere is mellow, the music laid-back and the food is all very much suited to Western tastes.

There's a soft-drink stall (no ice or coolers) outside the Vittala Temple.

Kamalapuram This sleepy village has a few humble eateries, the most notable of which is the *Sree Vilas Hotel* opposite the bus stand. A delightfully rustic place, it claims to make the best pakoras in the whole area. They serve vadai and idli for breakfast, puris for lunch and dosas in the evening (come early as it's closed by 7.30 pm). There are two or three other 'meals' places in the village but they're nothing more than a room in a private house.

The only restaurant is at the KSTDC's *Hotel Mayura Bhavaneshwari*. It serves decent veg and non-veg food.

Getting There & Around
Buses run almost hourly between Hampi Bazaar and Hospet (13 km, 30 minutes, Rs 2.50). The first bus from Hospet is at 6.30 am, and the last one back from Hampi leaves at 8 pm. Buses back to Hospet in the late afternoon are often very crowded. If you want to get on – sharpen your elbows!

There are also hourly buses between Hospet and Kamalapuram, at the southern end of the ruins. The first bus from Kamalapuram to Hospet leaves at 6 am; the last one is at 8.30 pm.

Buses between Hampi Bazaar and Kamalapuram run hourly and cost Rs 1.25; an auto-rickshaw is Rs 20.

Auto-rickshaws are also available from Hospet at the foreigners' rate of Rs 50 to Hampi Bazaar, Rs 40 to the Queen's Bath site close to Kamalapuram, or Rs 35 to Kamalapuram itself.

As an alternative, you could hire a bicycle in Hospet or in Hampi Bazaar, although around the site itself a bike can become something of a liability as the track to the Vittala Temple and many others are only negotiable on foot.

If you're walking around the site, expect to cover at least seven km just to see the main sights. It is possible to see most of the ruins in a day, though you need stamina to do it!

Organised tours of the site start in Hospet – see the following section for details.

HOSPET

Population: 146,000
Telephone Area Code: 08394

Many people who come to see the Vijayanagar ruins at Hampi use Hospet as a base. It's a fairly typical Karnataka country town with dusty roads, plenty of bullock carts, bicycles, dilapidated buses, and an unobtrusive industrial area near Tungabhadra Dam.

Information

The tourist office has absolutely no information and there's no reason to visit it.

The State Bank of Mysore next to the tourist office will exchange American Express travellers' cheques only. The State Bank of India handles cash, but only US dollars and pounds sterling.

Organised Tours

The daily KSTDC tour to the three main sites at Hampi (Hampi Bazaar, Vittala Temple and the Royal Enclosure) and to Tungabhadra Dam departs at 9.30 am and returns at 5.30 pm and costs Rs 60. Bookings can be made at the Hospet tourist office, Malligi Tourist Home or the Hotel Priyardarshini. If possible book a day in advance as this tour is often full. Lunch (not included in the price) is at the KSTDC's hotel in Kamalapuram.

Places to Stay

One of the best places to stay, and an old favourite among travellers, is the friendly *Malligi Tourist Home* (☎ 8101), 6/143 Jambunatha Rd, by the canal. Singles cost Rs 60 and doubles are Rs 95 to Rs 160. There are also family rooms (three beds) at Rs 140 and Rs 160 as well as air-con deluxe rooms at Rs 250 and Rs 300. All the rooms have attached bathrooms with hot water. There's a garden with a bar and restaurant.

Cheaper, and often full, is the small *Hotel Shalini Lodging* (☎ 8910), Station Rd, which has basic rooms with common bathroom for Rs 30/40, or Rs 30/50 with attached bathroom, and triples for Rs 65. The nearby *Hotel Sandarshan* (☎ 8574), Station Rd, is slightly more expensive and looks much better but it isn't.

Also on Station Rd, but better in standard is the *Hotel Vishwa* (☎ 7171), opposite the bus stand. It has large, clean rooms with

---

Muharram Festival

For much of the year Hospet is not a particularly interesting place, but it comes alive during the festival of Muharram which commemorates the martyrdom of Mohammed's grandson, Imam Hussain. If you're here at this time (the date varies from year to year) don't miss the firewalkers, who walk barefoot across the red-hot embers of a fire that's been going all day and night. Virtually the whole town turns out to watch or take part and the excitement reaches fever pitch around midnight. The preliminaries, which go on all day, appear to be a bewildering hybrid of Muslim and Hindu ritual. Those who are scheduled to do the firewalking, for example, have to be physically restrained from going completely berserk just before the event. ■

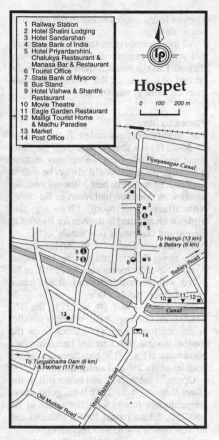

1 Railway Station
2 Hotel Shalini Lodging
3 Hotel Sandarshan
4 State Bank of India
5 Hotel Priyardarshini,
  Chalukya Restaurant &
  Manasa Bar & Restaurant
6 Tourist Office
7 State Bank of Mysore
8 Bus Stand
9 Hotel Vishwa & Shanthi
  Restaurant
10 Movie Theatre
11 Eagle Garden Restaurant
12 Malligi Tourist Home
   & Madhu Paradise
13 Market
14 Post Office

Hospet

0   100   200 m

Vijayanagar Canal

Station Road

To Hampi (13 km)
& Bellary (6 km)

Bellary Road

Canal

To Tungabhadra Dam (6 km)
/ & Hanhar (117 km)

Old Muddar Road

Main Bazaar Road

attached bathroom which are very good value at Rs 60/107, and four-bed rooms at Rs 199. The hotel is set back from the street so the rooms, all with small balconies, are relatively quiet and there's hot water in the morning.

Top of the line is the *Hotel Priyardarshini* (☎ 8838) on Station Rd. Singles cost Rs 70, doubles are Rs 120 to Rs 220, and triples go for Rs 180 to Rs 220. There are also air-con doubles from Rs 300. According to one traveller, this place is an 'oasis of cleanliness'. Indeed, it is comfortable, there's hot water, the rooms have a small balcony and there's an agency for KSTDC tours in the lobby.

There are two *retiring rooms* at the railway station which cost Rs 30 for a double.

Outside Hospet at the Tungabhadra Dam is the KSTDC's *Hotel Mayura Vijayanagar* (☎ 48-270) which has rooms for Rs 75/95 but it's inconvenient for anything other than the dam.

Places to Eat

The *Shanthi Restaurant* in the Hotel Vishwa does excellent vegetarian meals at lunchtime for Rs 12, and snacks the rest of the day. A similar place is the *Madhu Paradise* at the Malligi Tourist Home, which offers good vegetarian food.

Very popular is the outdoor *Eagle Garden Restaurant* behind the Malligi. The food is good and the service prompt, although it's a bit more expensive – count on about Rs 60 to Rs 80 for two. They also have cold beers at normal prices. It's open from 7 am to 11 pm daily.

Another inviting place to eat is the Hotel Priyardarshini which has the enclosed vegetarian *Chalukya Restaurant* and the non-veg open-air garden restaurant called the *Manasa Bar & Restaurant*. The Manasa is a popular drinking and eating spot in the evenings, and is open for lunch and dinner (until 11 pm). The Chalukya is open all day.

Getting There & Away

Bus The bus stand in Hospet is fairly well organised with the bays marked in both English and Kannada. On the other hand, the buses in this part of the state are pretty rough and ready, you must fight to get on, and they're crowded.

More than 10 express buses run daily between 7 am and 11.45 pm to Bangalore (358 km, Rs 70/105 on a normal/express bus) and there are just as many services to Hubli (160 km, 3½ hours, Rs 31).

To Hyderabad (408 km, Rs 85) two express buses depart daily. There's a daily bus to Badami (six hours, Rs 30) and one direct bus to Bijapur (215 km, eight hours, Rs 50).

Buses depart almost hourly to Bellary (65

KARNATAKA

km). Other services include Davanegere, Shimoga, Mangalore, Hassan and Karwar.

Train Hospet railway station is a 20-minute walk or Rs 10 by cycle-rickshaw from the centre of town. There is one direct train daily to Bangalore (on the broad-gauge system) at 8.30 pm (491 km, 10 hours, Rs 120/397 in a 2nd/1st-class sleeper). All other trains to Bangalore (most of which are passenger trains) require a change at Guntakal and cost Rs 101 in 2nd class.

For Badami (152 km, 5½ hours, Rs 24) and Bijapur (eight hours, Rs 35), there's one direct train daily at 12.30 pm which does not involve a change at Gadag.

You'll need to check at the station to find out if trains to Hubli and Goa have resumed and any details about services. In the past, the best train to get to Goa was the *Guntakal-Vasco Express* as it did not involve a change at Hubli or Gadag, however, the situation could be different now due to the upgrading of the line.

Getting Around
Buses run frequently to Hampi from bay No 10 at the bus stand. See the Getting There & Around section in Hampi for more details.

Plenty of buses ply between Hospet and Tungabhadra Dam (15 minutes). However, if you find yourself waiting a while for a bus back to Hospet from the dam, walk down to the junction at the bottom of the road from where there are more frequent buses to Hospet.

HUBLI
Population: 700,000
Telephone Area Code: 0836

Hubli is important to the traveller principally as a major railway junction on the routes from Bombay to Bangalore, Goa and north Karnataka. However, as we updated this book, Hubli's railway station had virtually come to a standstill as regional lines were being converted from metre to broad gauge. The major work should be finished by now, but you'll need to enquire in advance

whether trains are operating in the direction you wish to go.

All the main services (hotels, restaurants, etc) are conveniently close to the railway station. The bus stand is quite central at the far end of Lamington Rd, 15 minutes' walk from the railway station.

Places to Stay
The highly recommended *Hotel Ajanta* (☎ 36-2216) is a short distance off the main street and visible from the railway station. It's a huge place and you'll always be able to find accommodation here. Rooms cost Rs 35/60 with common bathroom or Rs 60/90 with attached bathroom. There are also triples with attached bathroom for Rs 99. On the ground floor there is a 'meals' cafe.

The *Modern Lodge* (☎ 36-2664) is on the main street before you get to the Hotel Ajanta. No-frills rooms cost Rs 25/40, or Rs 40/70 with private bathroom. It too has a ground-floor 'meals' place.

The *Ashok Hotel* (☎ 36-2271; fax 36-8412) is on Lamington Rd, which is parallel to the railway line, 500 metres from the station. Rooms with attached bathrooms are good value at Rs 75/130 plus there are deluxe doubles at Rs 250 and suites for Rs 450.

Opposite the Ashok, and better still, is the *Hotel Kailash* (☎ 52-235). It has good, clean single/double rooms with hot water at Rs 140/250, deluxe rooms for Rs 180/280 and air-con doubles at Rs 415 including tax.

The *retiring rooms* at the railway station are big and cost Rs 60, or Rs 15 for a dorm bed, and are equipped with mosquito nets.

Places to Eat
Kamat's Wasant Bhavan Hotel, opposite the railway station, offers plate meals at lunchtime for Rs 11.50. There's also an air-con dining hall upstairs, and during the rest of the day coffee and tiffin are available. Greater choice is offered at the *Hotel Vaishali*, a couple of doors along from the Modern Lodge. They have excellent biryanis from Rs 18 to Rs 21.

Next to the Modern Lodge is the *Parag*

Bar & Restaurant which has an open-air rooftop restaurant serving veg and non-veg Indian and Chinese cuisine. If there's no moon, it's often too dark to see what you're eating but the food is tasty and they have cold beers.

For dessert or ice cream, try the *Femila Creamball* opposite the Parag.

Getting There & Away

Air The airport is six km from the bus stand. NEPC Airlines (☎ 36-2271) has three flights a week to Bombay (US$100) and to Madras (US$100) via Bangalore (US$70).

Bus Hubli has a large and busy bus stand. The KSRTC has five buses daily to both Panaji in Goa (216 km, six hours, Rs 38) and Bangalore (419 km, nine hours, Rs 81 to Rs 121), three services to Mysore (455 km, 10 hours, Rs 91) and Pune (441 km, 10 hours, Rs 98), twice daily buses to Bombay (596 km, 14 hours, Rs 144) and Bijapur (204 km, six hours, Rs 47) and a daily bus to Mangalore (nine hours, Rs 96). There are also frequent buses to Hospet (3½ hours, Rs 31).

To Panaji there are also blue Goa government Kadamba buses which leave from gate No 10.

Opposite the bus stand are plenty of private companies operating superdeluxe video coaches. These buses run to Bombay and Bangalore, but don't expect any sleep with the confounded video blaring away all day and night.

Train The railway reservation office is open from 9.20 am to 1 pm and 1.50 to 5 pm daily. If you're heading for Hospet (145 km), the *Vijayanagar Express* leaves at 4.14 pm and takes four hours. For Bijapur (258 km, seven hours) there are three trains daily and the fare is Rs 57/209 in 2nd/1st class. Note, however, that it's possible that both these services have been disrupted as conversion of the Hubli to Hospet line was due to start.

Northern Karnataka

BELGAUM

Population: 436,000
Telephone Area Code: 0831

On a rather bald plateau in the north-west corner of the state, Belgaum was a regional capital in the 12th and 13th centuries. Today it's on the Bombay-Pune-Goa bus and train route. There's an old town area, a more modern cantonment on the way to the railway station, and Sunset Point on the old racetrack road which offers fine views.

Fort

The old oval-shaped stone fort near the bus stand is of no real interest unless you like malarial moats. Mahatma Gandhi was locked up here once. Outside the fort gate to the left is the local cattle market, which is colourful and aromatic.

Mosques, Temples & Other Buildings

The **Masjid-Sata** mosque dates from 1519. There are also two interesting **Jain temples**, one with an extremely intricate roof, while the other has some fine carvings of musicians. Belgaum's **watchtower**, on Ganapath Galli in the town centre, gives a nice panorama of the flat countryside and distant hills.

Places to Stay & Eat

The *Hotel Sheetal* (☎ 29-222) is about three minutes' walk from the bus terminal in Khade Bazaar, a mainly pedestrians-only street that starts opposite the bus stand entrance. Rooms here are clean and bright and cost Rs 60/100. There's also a good vegetarian restaurant. The railway *retiring rooms* cost Rs 20/30.

For something a bit better, the KSTDC's brand new *Hotel Mayura* on the NH 4 bypass, just behind the lake, has cottages with double rooms for Rs 150. There's also the tall, white *Hotel Keerthi* (☎ 23-332; fax 23-297), 500 metres to the right as you leave the bus stand. It offers clean, comfortable singles/doubles for Rs 100/150, or Rs

KARNATAKA

150/250 for deluxe rooms. Its restaurant has excellent veg and non-veg food and there's a bar.

The bus stand canteen has inexpensive snack foods. Belgaum also has lots of sweet shops.

Getting There & Away

Belgaum's airport is 11 km from town. From here, East West Airlines (☎ 43-0777) flies three times weekly to Bombay (1½ hours, US$74).

The bus stand is close to the old town area but a fair distance from the railway station; you'll need a rickshaw between the two.

AROUND BELGAUM

About 60 km north of Belgaum, eight km off the railway line from Gokak road, are **Gokak Falls** where the Ghataprabha River takes a notable 52-metre drop.

BADAMI

Population: 17,500
Telephone Area Code: 08357

Set in beautiful countryside amongst red sandstone hills, rock-hewn tanks (artificial lakes) and peaceful farmlands, the small rural village of Badami was once a capital city of the Chalukyan Empire which ruled much of the central Deccan between the 4th and 8th centuries AD. Here, and at nearby Aihole and Pattadakal, you can see some of the earliest and finest examples of Dravidian temples and rock-cut caves. The forms and sculptural work at these sites provided inspiration for the later Hindu empires which rose and fell in the southern part of the peninsula before the arrival of the Muslims.

Though principally promoters of the Vedic culture, the Chalukyans were tolerant of all sects, and elements of Shaivism, Vaishnavism, Jainism and even Buddhism can be found in many of their temples.

Badami was the capital from about 540 until 757 AD when the Chalukyans were overthrown by the Rashtrakutas. It is magnificently settled in a canyon, and all over the sides and tops of the surrounding hills are temples, fortifications, carvings and inscriptions dating not just from the Chalukyan period but from other times when the site was occupied as a fortress. After it fell to the Rashtrakutas, Badami was occupied successively by the Chalukyans of Kalyan (a separate branch of the Western Chalukyans), the Kalachuryas, the Yadavas of Devagiri, the Vijayanagar Empire, the Adil Shahi kings of Bijapur and the Marathas.

All these various rulers have left their mark at Badami, and there's even a Pallava inscription dating back to 642 AD when their king, Narasimha Varman I, briefly overwhelmed the Chalukyans and occupied Badami for 13 years before being driven out again.

Things to See

Badami The town is best known for its **cave temples**, cut into the cliff face of the red sandstone hill and connected by flights of steps. They display the full range of religious sects which have grown up on Indian soil. Two of them are dedicated to Vishnu, one to Siva and the fourth is a Jain temple. There's also one natural cave which is a Buddhist temple.

Between the second and third cave is a stone staircase leading up to the **south fort**. You can climb up here, climb being the operative word as the steps must have been cut by someone with a grudge against anyone less than three metres tall.

The caves overlook the picturesque **Agastyatirtha** (a tank constructed in the 5th century) and are only one of the many things to be seen at Badami. Of the other monuments, some of the most beautiful are the two groups of lakeside temples (known as the **Bhutanatha temples**), near the north fort. The **Archaeological Museum** nearby is also well worth a visit. It houses superb examples of sculpture collected locally, as well as the remarkable Lajja-Gauri images of a fertility cult which flourished in the area. It's open from 10 am to 5 pm, closed Friday.

Badami is a small town and, off the main street, it's full of narrow, winding lanes, old houses, the occasional Chalukyan ruin and tiny squares. It's a pleasant place and people are friendly.

Aihole This village, 43 km from Badami, was the Chalukyan regional capital between the 4th and 6th centuries. Here you can see Hindu temple architecture in its embryonic stage, from the earliest **Ladkhan Temple** to the later and more complex structures like the **Kunligudi** and **Durgigudi** temples. The Durgigudi is particularly interesting, and probably unique in India, being circular in shape and surmounted by a primitive gopuram.

There are over 70 structures in and around this serene village which are monuments to the vigorous experimentation in temple architecture undertaken by the Chalukyans. Most are in a good state of preservation.

Pattadakal This village, 16 km from Badami, was not only the second capital of the Badami Chalukyans, but the place where all coronations took place. It reached the height of its glory during the 7th and 8th centuries, when most of the temples here were built.

The most important monument here, the Lokeshwara or **Virupaksha Temple**, is a huge structure with sculptures that narrate episodes from the Hindu epics, the *Ramayana* and *Mahabharata*, as well as throw light

on the social life of the early Chalukyans. The other main temple, **Mallikarjuna**, has sculptures which tell a different story – this time from the *Bhagavad Gita*, the story of Krishna. The old **Jain temple** with its two stone elephants, about a km from the centre, is also worth visiting.

Places to Stay

There are several basic lodges along the main street of Badami, including the *Mookambika Lodge* (☎ 3267) opposite the bus stand which has clean singles/doubles for Rs 60/100, and the *Shri Laxmi Vilas Hotel*, with noisy rooms for Rs 40/70 with balconies. The sole *retiring room* at the railway station is Rs 50.

The KSTDC's *Hotel Mayura Chalukya* (☎ 3246), Ramdurg Rd, about 400 metres off Station Rd, is in an advanced state of decay but the gardens are quiet and colourful, the beds clean, mosquito nets are provided and the plumbing, though vandalised, still works and there's hot water. Rooms cost Rs 110/135. Don't leave your room open unattended for too long as the resident monkeys are fond of pinching things.

Similar in price is the clean *Hotel Satkar*

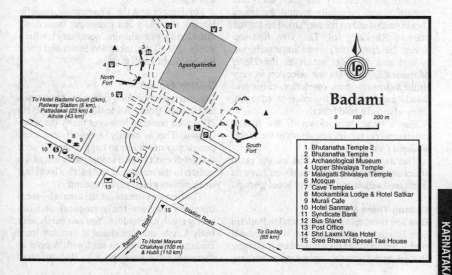

1 Bhutanatha Temple 2
2 Bhutanatha Temple 1
3 Archaeological Museum
4 Upper Shivalaya Temple
5 Malagatti Shivalaya Temple
6 Mosque
7 Cave Temples
8 Mookambika Lodge & Hotel Satkar
9 Murali Cafe
10 Hotel Sanman
11 Syndicate Bank
12 Bus Stand
13 Post Office
14 Shri Laxmi Vilas Hotel
15 Sree Bhavani Spesel Tae House

Badami

0   100   200 m

To Hotel Badami Court (2km),
Railway Station (5 km),
Pattadakal (23 km) &
Aihole (43 km)

North
Fort

Agastyatirtha

South
Fort

Station Road

To Gadag
(65 km)

Ramdurg Road

To Hotel Mayura
Chalukya (100 m)
& Hubli (110 km)

KARNATAKA

next to the Mookambika Lodge. Two sheets, a folded towel and hot water are provided.

The town's top place is the brand new *Hotel Badami Court* (☎ 3430), two km from the centre on the road to the railway station. Doubles cost Rs 350, or Rs 450 with air-con, and have attached bathroom with 24-hour hot water, a bathtub and even a Western loo with a bum squirter. There are no singles.

Accommodation is also available at the quiet KSTDC *Tourist Home* (☎ Amingad 641), one km from the village of Aihole on the Amingad road. It has a row of rooms with communal bath for Rs 35/50 and three spacious rooms with attached bathroom for Rs 60 to Rs 75. It's not as good as the Hotel Mayura Chalukya at Badami. The food is OK but, unless you want to grow old waiting for a meal to arrive, it's wise to order in advance.

Places to Eat

One of the best places for cheap eats is the *Hotel Sanman*. Tasty vegetarian and non-veg food is available, as are cold beers. The lunchtime thalis at the *Murali Cafe* are also recommended but this place doesn't sell beer.

There are plenty of other small cafes and 'meals' places especially around the tonga (horse cart) stand on the main road and at the start of Ramdurg Rd. The *Sree Bhavani Spesel Tae House* (sic) is one that stands out.

You can also get meals at the *Hotel Mayura Chalukya* but the selection is very limited (tomato soup, omelettes, chips and salad) and you need to order in advance. They also have cold beers.

For a treat, head down to the multicuisine, silver service restaurant at the *Hotel Badami Court*.

The *arak* (rice liquor) dens on the main street are worth checking out if you have an iron constitution and a yen for local gossip.

Getting There & Away

Bus The timetable at the bus stand in Badami is in English and Kannada but it's the usual rugby scrum to get on a bus when it arrives. Providing the trains are operating as normal,

you'd be better off using trains for anything other than local travel. There are buses to Bijapur (five times daily, four hours, Rs 28), Bagalkot (hourly), Hospet (three times daily, six hours), Hubli (six times daily), Bangalore (four daily, evening only), Kolhapur (at 8.30 am) and Gadag (six times daily).

Train All the trains passing through Badami station are passenger trains and most are 2nd class only. Some of the services from here could be disrupted during broad-gauge conversion of the Hubli to Hospet line.

There are six daily trains from Badami to Bijapur but two of these are late at night. The most convenient ones are scheduled to come through at 5 am, 12.10, 3.20 and 5.10 pm, though they're often late. The 5.10 pm train terminates at Bijapur (3½ hours, Rs 20) but the earlier three trains continue on to Sholapur (Maharashtra), a major railway junction, where you can change onto the broad-gauge system for cities such as Bombay, Hyderabad and Bangalore.

Heading south, there are passenger trains to the railway junctions of Gadag, Guntakal or Hubli (again, on the broad-gauge system) which leave Badami at 7.30 am, 10.50 am and 3 pm.

For Hospet and the Vijayanagar ruins at Hampi, there is a fast passenger train daily via Gadag (no change necessary) which leaves at 9.30 am, takes 5½ hours and costs Rs 24/150 in 2nd/1st class.

Getting Around

Badami railway station is five km from town and a tonga from outside the station costs Rs 30 shared between however many there are of you. This is clearly a rip-off and local people pay much less so haggle hard. If your budget doesn't stretch to that, walk out of the station to the main road and catch a local bus or minibus (which pass frequently).

The best way to explore the area is by local buses as they are fairly frequent and run pretty much to schedule. You can easily visit both Aihole and Pattadakal in one day from Badami, but it's best to start with Aihole as there are more buses back to Badami from

Pattadakal than from Aihole. There's a bus from Badami to Aihole at 8.15 am which takes two hours. From Aihole, there's a bus at 1 pm to Pattadakal (30 minutes), from where there are frequent buses and minibuses back to Badami. As there's only one place to eat in Aihole (and advance orders are recommended), it's a good idea to bring some food along.

Taxi drivers in Badami quote Rs 500 for a day trip taking in Pattadakal and Aihole.

BIJAPUR

Population: 209,000
Telephone Area Code: 08352

Bijapur is the Agra of the south, full of ruined and still-intact gems of 15th to 17th-century Muslim architecture – mosques, mausoleums, palaces and fortifications. Like Agra, it has its world-famous mausoleum, the Golgumbaz. This enormous structure with its vast hemispherical dome, said to be the world's second largest, dominates the landscape for miles around.

The austere grace of the monuments in this city is in complete contrast to the sculptural extravaganza of the Chalukyan and Hoysala temples further south. The Ibrahim Roza mausoleum, in particular, is one of the most beautiful and finely proportioned Islamic monuments anywhere in India.

Bijapur was the capital of the Adil Shahi kings (1489-1686), one of the five splinter states formed when the Bahmani Muslim kingdom broke up in 1482. The others, formed at roughly the same time, were Bidar, Golconda, Ahmednagar and Gulbarga. Like Bijapur, all these places have their own collection of monuments dating from this period, though the ones at Bijapur are definitely more numerous and generally in a better state of preservation. You will need at least a day to see all the monuments in a leisurely manner since they are spread out across the city.

Bijapur is a pleasant garden town, still strongly Muslim in character. During the day, many tribal people from outlying areas come into town to the market. Most travellers find the town small enough not to be overwhelming, though some solo women travellers have reported being harassed here.

Orientation

The two main attractions, the Golgumbaz and the Ibrahim Roza, are at opposite ends of the town. Between them runs Station Rd (M G Rd) along which are most of the major hotels and restaurants. The bus stand is a five-minute walk from Station Rd; the railway station is two km east of the centre.

Information

The tourist office is on Station Rd near the stadium. The post office, also on Station Rd, is open Monday to Saturday from 8.30 am to 6 pm.

The State Bank of India won't change travellers' cheques; for that you must go to the Canara Bank north of the market.

Power cuts are frequent in Bijapur and often last for hours so have candles handy.

Golgumbaz

The largest and most famous monument is the Golgumbaz. Built in 1659, it is a simple building with four walls that enclose a majestic hall 1704 sq metres in area, buttressed by octagonal seven-storey towers at each of the corners. This basic structure is capped by an enormous dome said to be the world's second largest after St Peter's, Vatican City, Rome. The diameter of St Peter's dome is 42 metres, St Paul's in London is 33 metres, and the Golgumbaz is 38 metres.

Around the base of the dome at the top of the hall is a three-metre-wide gallery known as the 'whispering gallery', since the acoustics here are such that any sound made is repeated 10 times over (some guidebooks claim it's repeated 12 times). Fortunately, you won't have the chance to get embroiled in that controversy as the whispering gallery is permanently full of children and adults running amok and screaming at the top of their voices. 'Bedlam gallery' would be a more appropriate name. Access to the gallery is via a narrow staircase up the south-east tower.

The views over Bijapur from the base of the dome are superb. You can see virtually

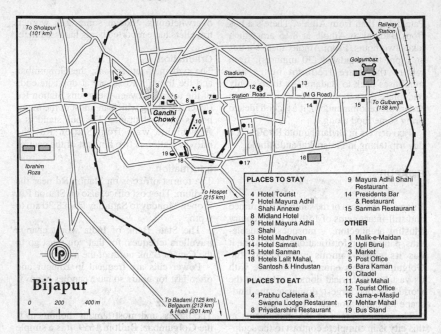

Bijapur

0   200   400 m

To Sholapur
(101 km)

Railway
Station

Stadium

Station Road

(M G Road)

Gandhi
Chowk

Golgumbaz

To Gulbarga
(158 km)

Ibrahim
Roza

To Hospet
(215 km)

To Badami (125 km),
Belgaum (213 km)
& Hubli (201 km)

PLACES TO STAY	
4	Hotel Tourist
7	Hotel Mayura Adhil Shahi Annexe
8	Midland Hotel
9	Hotel Mayura Adhil Shahi
13	Hotel Madhuvan
14	Hotel Samrat
15	Hotel Sanman
18	Hotels Lalit Mahal, Santosh & Hindustan

PLACES TO EAT	
4	Prabhu Cafeteria & Swapna Lodge Restaurant
8	Priyadarshini Restaurant

9	Mayura Adhil Shahi Restaurant
14	Presidents Bar & Restaurant
15	Sanman Restaurant

OTHER	
1	Malik-e-Maidan
2	Upli Buruj
3	Market
5	Post Office
6	Bara Kaman
10	Citadel
11	Asar Mahal
12	Tourist Office
16	Jama-e-Masjid
17	Mehtar Mahal
19	Bus Stand

every other monument and almost the whole of the city walls from here. The views are clearest in the early morning.

The Golgumbaz is the mausoleum of Mohammed Adil Shah (1626-56), his two wives, his mistress (Rambha), one of his daughters and a grandson. Their caskets stand on a raised platform in the centre of the hall, though their actual graves are in the crypt, accessible by a flight of steps under the western doorway.

It is open from 6 am to 6 pm and entrance costs Rs 0.50, except on Friday, when it's free. If you get there before 7 am you may actually be able to test the gallery acoustics too – the school groups don't start to arrive until then. Shoes have to be left at the entrance. An archaeological museum in the front opens at 10 am and is free.

Ibrahim Roza
The beautiful Ibrahim Roza was constructed at the height of Bijapur's prosperity by Ibrahim Adil Shah II (1580-1626) for his queen. Unlike the Golgumbaz, which is impressive only for its immensity, here the emphasis is on elegance and delicacy. Its 24-metre-high minarets are said to have inspired those of the Taj Mahal. It's also one of the few monuments in Bijapur with substantial stone filigree and other sculpturally decorative work.

Buried here are Ibrahim Adil Shah, his queen, Taj Sultana, his daughter, two sons, and his mother Haji Badi Sahiba. There is no entrance charge, and shoes should be left on the steps up to the platform on which the mausoleum stands.

Jama-e-Masjid
This is another finely proportioned building with graceful arches, a fine dome and a large inner courtyard containing fountains and a reservoir. It's quite a large monument covering an area of 10,800 sq metres and has room for 2250 worshippers. Spaces for them are

marked out in black on the polished floor of the mosque.

There's very little ornamentation here, the whole concept being one of simplicity. The flat roof is accessible by several flights of stairs. This mosque was constructed by Ali Adil Shah I (1557-80), who was also responsible for erecting the fortified city walls and Gagan Mahal, and for installing a public water system.

Asar Mahal

To the east of the citadel, the Asar Mahal was built by Mohammed Adil Shah in about 1646 to serve as a Hall of Justice. The rooms on the upper storey are profusely decorated with frescoes, many of them using foliage and flower motifs, some portraying male and female figures in various poses. The latter have all been defaced. The building was also used to house two hairs from the Prophet's beard. The front of the building is graced with a square tank still fed by conduits from Begum Tank.

Women are not allowed inside the main structure.

Citadel

Surrounded by its own fortified walls and wide moat in the city centre, the citadel once contained the palaces, pleasure gardens and Durbar Hall of the Adil Shahi kings. Unfortunately, most of them are now in ruins although some superb fragments remain.

Of the important fragments, the **Gagan Mahal** probably gives the best impression of the scale on which things were built here. This monument was built by Ali Adil Shah I around 1561 to serve the dual purpose of a royal residence and a Durbar Hall. Essentially it's an enormous hall completely open to the north, so that an audience outside the hall had a full and unobstructed view of the proceedings on the raised platform inside. The hall was flanked by small chambers used to house the families of the royal household.

Nearby, the **Sat Manzil**, Mohammed Adil Shah's seven-storey palace, is now substantially in ruins and the remaining parts of it are used for public offices, but just across the

road stands one of the most delicate pieces of architecture in Bijapur. This is the **Jala Manzil** or Jala Mandir, a water pavilion no doubt intended as a cool and pleasant place to relax in the days when it was surrounded by secluded courts and gardens within the palace precincts.

Opposite the citadel on the other side of Station Rd are the graceful arches of **Bara Kaman**, the ruined mausoleum of Ali Roza.

Malik-e-Maidan

This huge cannon must be one of the largest guns ever made in medieval times. It measures over four metres long and almost 1½ metres in diameter, and is estimated to weigh 55 tonnes! It was cast in 1549 by Mohammed-bin-Hasan Rumi, a Turkish officer in the service of the King of Ahmednagar, from an alloy of copper, iron and tin. It was brought to Bijapur as a war trophy and set up here with the might of 10 elephants, 400 oxen and hundreds of men. Its outer surface is polished dark green and adorned with inscriptions in Persian and Arabic. One of them attributed to the Mughal emperor, Aurangzeb, says that he subdued this gun. The name of the cannon, Malik-e-Maidan, means Monarch of the Plains.

Upli Buruj

This watchtower, 24 metres high and on high ground near the western walls of the city, was built by Hyder Khan, a general in the service of Ali Adil Shah I and Ibrahim II, in about 1584. The tower can be climbed by a flight of steps which winds around the outside of the building. The top commands a good view of the city and is well furnished with guns, powder chambers and water cisterns. The guns are much longer than the Malik-e-Maidan (nine metres and 8.5 metres respectively), but of a much narrower bore – only 29 cm.

Other Monuments

There are a number of other monuments worth visiting in Bijapur, the most important being the **Anand Mahal** and the **Mecca Masjid**, both in the citadel, and the **Mehtar**

Mahal. The much-photographed Mehtar Mahal is typical of the architecture of Bijapur and has been richly decorated with sculptural work. It serves as an ornamental gateway leading to a small mosque.

Places to Stay

One of the cheapest habitable places to stay is the *Midland Hotel* (☎ 20-299) which has rooms for Rs 40/60. Much better is the friendly *Hotel Tourist* (☎ 20-655) which has ordinary rooms for Rs 40/70 or Rs 45/85 for the 'special' rooms, although there's nothing special about them. All the rooms have attached bathroom (cold water only).

Cheapest around the bus stand is the *Hotel Lalit Mahal* (☎ 20-761) where the rooms are arranged around a relatively quiet central courtyard. Singles/doubles with common bathroom cost Rs 30/50 or Rs 40/60 with attached bathroom. There's also a restaurant. Close by and equally basic is the *Hotel Hindustan*.

Better appointed rooms can be found at the *Hotel Santosh* (☎ 22-179), right opposite the bus stand. Singles/doubles with a balcony and attached bathroom with bucket shower are Rs 43/75. There are also air-con doubles for Rs 250.

The best place in terms of setting and atmosphere is the KSTDC's *Hotel Mayura Adhil Shahi* (☎ 20-943). The rooms here are set around a quiet, leafy and colourful garden courtyard which doubles as an open-air restaurant in the evening. Clean, airy rooms with attached bathroom and hot water (mornings only) cost Rs 75/95. Mosquito nets are provided.

If the Mayura is full, there's the nearby *Hotel Mayura Adhil Shahi Annexe* (☎ 20-401) which is also shrouded in greenery. The rooms here are bigger and have private terraces, 24-hour hot water, and mosquito nets. Singles/doubles cost Rs 120/140.

Further along Station Rd and down a side lane is the *Hotel Madhuvan* (☎ 25-571). It's the newest hotel in town but the rooms are nothing special and the staff are aloof. Doubles (no singles) start at Rs 80.

The *Hotel Samrat* (☎ 21-620) has good singles/doubles for Rs 55/85. All rooms have attached bathroom, and mosquito nets are provided. The rooms at the front have a balcony.

The *Hotel Sanman* (☎ 21-866) has no-frills doubles for Rs 85 (no singles) and 'tirbuls' (ie triples) for Rs 100. Mosquito nets are provided.

Finally, there is one *retiring room* at the railway station which costs Rs 20/30 for one/two people.

Places to Eat

For a quick bite try *Priyadarshini*, a new, vegetarian, stand-up snack bar next to the Midland Hotel. Also good for a snack is the *Prabhu Cafeteria* on the ground floor next to the Hotel Tourist. It serves excellent dosas, bhelpuri, lassis and other snacks.

On the 2nd floor of the same building, the *Swapna Lodge Restaurant* has good veg and non-veg food as well as cold beers. There's both an air-con section and an open-air terrace which is perfect for evening dining. Don't be put off by the forlorn entry to this place as both the service and food are good – the 'garlic fry' is delicious.

The *Hotel Mayura Adhil Shahi* has a restaurant in the middle of the courtyard, and it's a reasonable place to eat, although the service is slow. Lunch is generally a standard thali but there's more choice in the evening. Of all the bars in town, this one has the most pleasant setting for an evening beer.

The *Hotel Madhuvan* has an air-con vegetarian restaurant with thalis for Rs 12, and an unshaded terrace that's pleasant for an evening drink (non-alcoholic only) but is pretty hot during the day.

In the basement of the Hotel Samrat, the *Presidents Bar & Restaurant* serves tasty vegetarian and non-veg food. The only drawback to eating here is that it's so dark you can hardly see what you're doing. Still, it's air-conditioned (after a fashion) and cold Kingfisher beers are available.

The *Hotel Lalit Mahal* and *Hotel Sanman* also have restaurants.

Getting There & Away

Bus The timetable at the bus stand is entirely

in Kannada. The only place you'll find a timetable in English is in the lobby of the Hotel Tourist. Buses run from Bijapur to Badami (three daily, four hours), Bangalore (630 km, six daily in the evening only), Belgaum (every half hour), Bidar, Hospet (five daily, eight hours), Hubli (hourly, six hours), Hyderabad (three daily), Kolhapur (five daily), Pune (seven daily) and Sholapur (every half hour, three hours).

Train Bijapur station has a healthy quota of sleeping berths allotted to it on all the main trains which pass through Sholapur (Solarpur) and Gadag. These are rarely taken up more than one day in advance.

Going south, there are three daily trains to Hubli at 4.10, 7 and 11.30 am and another only as far as Gadag which leaves at 6 pm. The 258-km trip to Hubli takes seven hours and costs Rs 57/209 in 2nd/1st class.

You can use any of the above trains and the one to Guntakal at 6.15 am to get to either Badami (3½ hours, Rs 20/32 in 2nd-class ordinary/express and Rs 125 in 1st) or Hospet (285 km, about eight hours, Rs 35/57 in 2nd-class ordinary/express and Rs 240 in 1st).

To Bangalore, there's one express daily at 11.35 pm and the fare is Rs 135/507 in 2nd/1st class. This service may be disrupted due to work on the lines south of Bijapur. If so, you can always go to Sholapur and get an express from there.

Going north, there are trains daily to Sholapur at 3.35, 7.15 and 9.50 am and 3.55 and 8.05 pm. Fares are Rs 19/29 in 2nd-class ordinary/express and Rs 122 in 1st. Sholapur is where you connect with the broad-gauge system for trains to Hyderabad and Vijayawada, Bangalore, and Pune and Bombay.

Getting Around
Bus The uncrowded local bus system has only one route: from the railway station, along Station Rd to the gate at the western end of town. Buses run every 15 minutes and the standard fare is Rs 1.

Rickshaw & Tonga Expect to pay Rs 5 for a cycle-rickshaw from the bus stand to the Hotel Mayura Adhil Shahi. Auto-rickshaw drivers charge what they think you will pay – Rs 15 to the railway station after intense haggling is normal.

The tonga drivers are eager for business and will offer to take you around the major sites or to the railway station. From the railway station to the Hotel Mayura Adhil Shahi, they normally charge Rs 10. To make other trips in the vicinity, you'll have to haggle.

THE NORTH-EAST
Bidar
Telephone Area Code: 08482

This little visited, walled town in the extreme north-east corner of the state was the capital of the Bahmani Kingdom from 1428, and later the capital of the Barid Shahi dynasty. It's a pleasant town with a splendid old 15th-century **fort** containing the Ranjeenmahal, Chini Mahal and Turkish Mahal **palaces**.

The impressive **Khwaja Mahmud Gawan Madrasa** in the middle of town has a few colourful remains of typical Islamic mosaics. The huge domed **tombs** of the Bahmani and Barid kings are also worth seeing. These abandoned structures, which dot the countryside to the west and east of town, are seemingly shrouded in a desolate aura and are very enticing.

Bidar also lent its name to the handicraft *bidriware* (for details see the Bidriware of Bidar boxed section on page 938).

Places to Stay & Eat The choice around here is pretty slim. The *Sri New Venkateshwara Lodge* (☎ 6443) on the main street has rooms for Rs 40/60. Across the road, the *Kalpana Hotel* has acceptable food. Just up from the Venkateshwara and similarly priced is the *Hotel Ratna* (☎ 7218).

The *Hotel Prince* (☎ 5747) on the Udgir Rd has singles/doubles for Rs 50/80.

KARNATAKA

The Bidriware of Bidar

During its Islamic heyday, the Persian craftsmen of Bidar came up with a form of damascening now known as *bidriware*. For this craft, imaginative blends of blackened zinc, copper, lead and/or tin were moulded and then embossed, overlaid or inlaid with pure silver. In both design and decoration, the artefacts were heavily influenced by typical Islamic features of the time. Thus you would find finely crafted pieces, many of them for domestic use, such as *hookahs*, goblets, *paan* boxes and bangles, exquisitely embellished with interwoven creepers and flowing floral patterns, and occasionally framed by strict geometric lines. The effect of the delicate silver filigree against the ebony-toned background was scintillating. These days artists still tap away at their craft in the backstreets of Bidar, as well as in the neighbouring city of Hyderabad. ∎

Gulbarga

Population: 336,000
Telephone Area Code: 08472

This town was the Bahmani capital from 1347 until its transfer to Bidar in 1428. Later the kingdom broke up into a number of smaller kingdoms – Bijapur, Bidar, Berar, Ahmednagar and Golconda. The last of these, Golconda, finally fell to Aurangzeb in 1687.

Gulbarga's old moated **fort** is in a much deteriorated state, but it has a number of interesting buildings inside including the **Jama Masjid**, reputed to have been built by a Moorish architect during the late 14th or early 15th century who imitated the great mosque in Cordoba, Spain. The mosque is unique in India, with a huge dome covering the whole area, four smaller ones at the corners, and 75 smaller still all the way around. The fort itself has 15 towers.

Gulbarga also has a number of imposing tombs of Bahmani kings, a shrine to an important Muslim saint and the **Sharana Basaveshwara Temple** .

Places to Stay & Eat The KSTDC's *Hotel Mayura Bahamani* (☎ 20-644) is set back from the road in the public gardens and has rooms for Rs 50/75. This place is very run-down but the staff are genial and the rooms are comfortable and clean enough. Mosquito nets and buckets of hot water are provided. There's a bar and restaurant but neither have much of a clientele.

Immediately opposite on the main road is the new *Hotel Aditya* (☎ 24-040) which has well-appointed rooms (hot water in the mornings only) for Rs 105/180, and deluxe rooms at Rs 125/210. There's a decent vegetarian restaurant.

Andhra Pradesh

Andhra Pradesh was created by combining the old princely state of Hyderabad with the Telugu-speaking portions of the former state of Madras. Most of this large state stands on the high Deccan plateau, sloping down to the low-lying coastal region to the east where the mighty Godavari and Krishna rivers meet the Bay of Bengal in wide deltas.

It is one of the poorest and least developed states in India, although the final nizam (ruler) of Hyderabad was reputed to be one of the richest men in the world! New dams and irrigation projects are improving the barren, scrubby land of the plateau, but much of the state remains economically backward.

Tourism, too, is not well developed in Andhra Pradesh, although not because of the lack of worthwhile sights. The capital, Hyderabad, is naturally a magnet, not only in its own right for its Muslim heritage, famous museum and enormous Buddha statue, but also for the nearby Golconda Fort and Qutab Shahi tombs. Further afield, there are the impressive ruins of the Kakatiya kingdom at Warangal, which was commented on by Marco Polo, and the Buddhist sites of Nagarjunakonda and Amaravathi, as well as the beautiful Kanaka Durga Temple at Vijayawada, and the famous temple complex of Tirumala in the state's extreme south-east.

During the monsoon, the deltas of the Godavari and Krishna rivers may flood, forcing trains between Calcutta and Madras to detour further inland through Raipur, Nagpur and Hyderabad.

History

Andhra Pradesh was once a major Buddhist centre and part of Ashoka's large empire until it broke apart. Traces of that early Buddhist influence still remain in several places, particularly at Amaravathi, the Sanchi of Andhra Pradesh. Later, in the 7th century, the Chalukyas held power, but they in turn fell

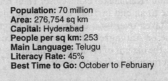

Population: 70 million
Area: 276,754 sq km
Capital: Hyderabad
People per sq km: 253
Main Language: Telugu
Literacy Rate: 45%
Best Time to Go: October to February

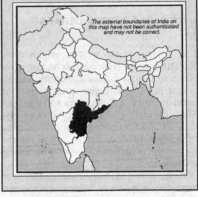

The external boundaries of India on this map have not been authenticated and may not be correct.

to the Chola kingdom of the south around the 10th century.

The 13th century saw the rise of the Kakatiyas who ruled from Warangal, but by this time Muslim power was beginning to assert itself in the form of the sultans of Delhi, who made many raids into the area and established themselves in 1323. However, their hold was tenuous and they were soon displaced by the Hindu Vijayanagar Empire.

There followed two centuries of Hindu-Muslim power struggles until, in the 16th century, the Qutab Shahi dynasty was established at Hyderabad.

It was this dynasty that built the vast and almost impregnable stone fortress of Golconda – surely one of India's most impressive yet seldom visited monuments. Not only that but the nearby tombs of the rulers of this Muslim dynasty rival those of the

Delhi sultans and the early Mughals in size and splendour. None of the other central Deccan Muslim kingdoms ever left monuments quite as grand as these – though Bijapur (Karnataka) came close. Their reign came to an end in 1687 when the kingdom was taken over by a general of the Mughal emperor Aurangzeb. The general's successors, the nizams of Hyderabad, ruled the state right through to Independence.

HYDERABAD & SECUNDERABAD

Population: 4.7 million
Telephone Area Code: 0842

Like Bijapur to the west in neighbouring Karnataka state, Hyderabad is an important centre of Islamic culture and central India's counterpart to the Mughal splendours of the northern cities of Delhi, Agra and Fatehpur Sikri. Consisting of the twin cities of Hyderabad and Secunderabad, it is the capital of Andhra Pradesh and is famous as the former seat of the fabulously wealthy nizams of Hyderabad.

Here, crowded dusty bazaars surround huge and impressive Islamic monuments dating from the 16th and 17th centuries. Unlike cities further south, Hyderabad retains much of its 19th-century atmosphere. It is also unique among southern cities in that Urdu is the major language spoken.

History

Hyderabad, India's fifth-largest city, was founded in 1590 by Muhammad Quli, the fourth of the Qutab Shahi kings. They ruled this part of the Deccan from 1512 until 1687, when the last of their line was defeated by the Mughal emperor, Aurangzeb, following failure to pay the annual tribute to their nominal suzerain in Delhi.

Before the founding of Hyderabad, the Qutab Shahi kings ruled from the fortress city of Golconda, 11 km to the west. The extensive ruins of this fort, together with the nearby tombs of the Qutab Shahi kings, are the city's major attractions.

After Aurangzeb's death in 1707, Mughal control over this part of India rapidly waned and the Asaf Jahi viceroys who had been installed to look after the interests of the Mughal Empire broke away to establish their own independent state, taking first the title of subadar and, later, that of nizam. These new rulers, allied to the French, became embroiled in the Anglo-French rivalry for control of India during the latter half of the 18th century. However, the defeat of the French and subsequent Maratha raids seriously weakened their kingdom and they were forced to conclude a treaty with the British, relinquishing most of their power.

When Indian independence was declared in 1947, the nizam toyed with the idea of

---

Prohibition for Andhra Pradesh

In December 1994, just minutes after a new state government was sworn in, Andhra Pradesh became a 'dry' state. The decision to ban the sale of alcohol follows a remarkable campaign by village women who were fed up with husbands drinking away the housekeeping money. Such was the strength of their movement that the local Telugu Desam party won a resounding victory in the most recent state election by promising to introduce prohibition.

The temperance movement began in 1992 with at times violent anti-booze demonstrations by women against shops selling arak, the potent distilled liquor that is popular in India. Shops were set ablaze, liquor trucks ambushed and, as the movement gained momentum, mobs of women stormed bars or went on cleaning and cooking strikes. A year later the former Congress Party government, which had been responsible for setting up many of the alcohol shops in order to rake in excise revenues, banned the sale of arak. But if the party had expected this measure to carry them through to the state election, then their plan backfired. Within two months of the arak ban, 24 people died after drinking cheap, bootlegged liquor, and Telugu Desam rode to election victory on the wings of this tragedy.

Andhra Pradesh is now one of only two Indian states (the other is Gujarat) which has prohibition. The only places where you'll find a beer these days are the licensed bars in some of the top-end hotels which cater for foreign tourists. ■

declaring an independent state and went so far as to allow an Islamic extremist group to seize control. Eventually, this led to his downfall when the Indian government, mindful of Hyderabad's Hindu majority of around 85% and unwilling to see an independent and possibly hostile state created in the centre of the Deccan, used the insurrection as an excuse to occupy Hyderabad in 1948 and force its accession to the Indian union.

Orientation

The old city of Hyderabad straddles the Musi River while, to the north, the Hussain Sagar effectively separates Hyderabad from its newer twin city Secunderabad. Most of the historical monuments, hotels and restaurants, the city bus terminal and Salar Jung Museum are all in the old city. Budget hotels are mainly found in the area known as Abids, between the GPO and Hyderabad railway station. The state transport company (APSRTC) has its bus stand south-east of Abids, near the river in the Gowliguda area.

The ruins of Golconda Fort and the tombs of the Qutab Shahi kings lie about 11 km west of the city.

Secunderabad lies on the north side of

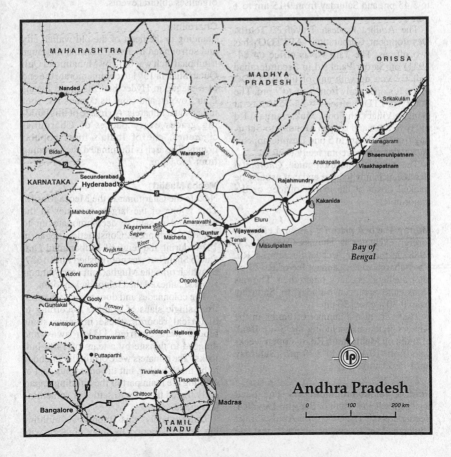

Andhra Pradesh

Hussain Sagar. Many trains terminate at Secunderabad railway station (get off here if you intend staying at the YMCA or YWCA), though quite a few continue on to Hyderabad railway station.

Information

Tourist Offices The tourist information kiosk at Secunderabad railway station is not very good. The Government of India tourist office (☎ 63-0037) is in the Sandozi Building (2nd floor) on Himayatnagar Rd, but they only have the usual range of coloured brochures. It's open weekdays from 9.15 am to 5.45 pm and Saturday from 9.15 am to 1 pm.

The Andhra Pradesh Travel & Tourist Development Corporation (APTTDC) has two offices. The Yatri Nivas office (☎ 84-3931) on Sardar Patel Rd in Secunderabad will fix you up with any of the APTTDC tours. It's open daily from 9 am to 7 pm. The other APTTDC office (☎ 55-7530) is at Gangan Vihar (5th floor), Mukarramjahi Rd in Hyderabad and is open Monday to Saturday from 10.30 am to 5 pm. Despite appearances, this place is completely useless.

The monthly what's-on guide, *Channel 6* (Rs 10), is handy to have and can usually be tracked down at the tourist offices or the major hotels.

Money The best place for fast and efficient foreign exchange is Thomas Cook (☎ 23-1988) in the Nasir Arcade, Secretariat Rd. They charge an encashment fee of Rs 20 on all travellers' cheques other than Thomas Cook, and are open Monday to Saturday from 9.30 am to 5.30 pm.

There are also a number of banks in the Abids Circle area including the State Bank of India on Mahipatram Rd. It's open weekdays from 10.30 am to 2.30 pm (Saturday until 11.30 am).

Post & Telecommunications The head post office is just south of Sarojini Devi Rd, Secunderabad. The GPO is on Abids Circle, Hyderabad, and is open for poste restante collection on weekdays from 10 am to 3 pm (Saturday until 1 pm).

A good place from which to make international calls is Doorshanchar Bhavan, Station Rd. This telecommunications office is open Monday to Saturday from 8 am to 8 pm.

Bookshops & Cultural Centres A good bookshop in Abids is A A Hussain & Co on M G Rd. Gangarams is at 62 Sarojini Devi Rd in Secunderabad.

Alliance Française (☎ 23-6646) is next to the Birla Planetarium on Naubat Pahar. It screens weekly movies in French and also organises cultural events.

Charminar

Standing in the heart of the old walled city and surrounded by lively bazaars, this huge triumphal arch was built by Muhammad Quli Qutab Shah in 1591 to commemorate the end of a plague in Hyderabad. Its name means Four Towers, and from its corners rise four rather squat minarets. An image of this building graces every packet of Charminar cigarettes, one of India's most popular brands. The arch is illuminated each evening from 7 to 9 pm.

Mecca Masjid

Next to the Charminar is the Mecca Masjid. This is one of the largest mosques in the world and is said to accommodate up to 10,000 worshippers. Construction began in 1614, during the reign of Muhammad Quli Qutab Shah, but was not finished until 1687, by which time the Mughal emperor Aurangzeb had annexed the Golconda kingdom.

The colonnades and door arches are made from single slabs of granite. According to historical records, these massive stone blocks were quarried 11 km away and dragged to the site by a team of 1400 bullocks! The minarets were originally intended to be much higher, but the enormous cost of erecting the main part of the building apparently forced the ruler to settle for something less grand.

Unfortunately, this impressive building has been disfigured by huge chicken wire awnings, erected in a vain attempt to stop birds nesting in the ceiling and liming the floor. The steel supports that have been carelessly cemented into the tiled and patterned floor to hold this netting are nothing short of vandalism.

To the left of the mosque is an enclosure containing the tombs of Nizam Ali Khan, who died in 1803, and his successors.

Birla Mandir Temple
This stunningly beautiful modern Hindu temple, built of white marble from Rajas-

than, graces one of the twin rocky hills overlooking the south end of Hussain Sagar. There are excellent views over the city from the summit, especially at sunset. The temple, dedicated to Lord Venkateshwara, is a very popular Hindu pilgrimage centre. It's open to Hindus and non-Hindus alike, from 7 am to noon and 3 to 9 pm. There's no entry fee and the priests do not press you for contributions.

On the other hill, Naubat Pahar, stands the **Birla Planetarium** which has presentations in English several times daily. Admission is Rs 8.

1 Airport
2 APTTDC Tourist Office
   & Yatri Nivas Hotel
3 Paradise Garden Restaurant
4 Head Post Office
5 YMCA - Station Rd
6 Secunderabad Railway Station
7 Hotel Viceroy
8 Buddha Purnima
9 Krishna Holiday Inn
10 Krishna Oberoi
11 Gateway Hotel
12 Tombs of Qutab Shahi Kings
13 Golconda Fort
14 Main Bus Terminal
15 Salar Jung Museum
16 Laad Bazaar
17 Charminar
18 Mecca Masjid
19 Nehru Zoological Park

Pune Road
To NH7 &
Nizamabad
(160 km)
Sanathnagar Road
Sardar Patel Road
Sarojini Devi Road
Subhash Road
M G Rd
Hussain Sagar
Tankbund Road
Secunderabad
To Warangal
(140 km)
Banjara Hills
To NH9 &
Sholapur
(300 km)
Bombay Road
Mahatma Gandhi Road
See Abids Area Map
Goshamahal Road
Nehru Road
Mahatma Gandhi Road
Jhangi Road
Golconda Road
Hyderabad
To Vijayawada
(270 km)
Musi River
Old Town
Golconda Road
Bangalore Road
Sardar Patel Road
Hyderabad
Miralam Cheruvu
0   1   2 km
To NH7 &
Bangalore (585 km)

ANDHRA PRADESH

Buddha Purnima

Hyderabad, in keeping with the state's history as one of the most important Buddhist centres of India, boasts one of the largest stone Buddhas in the world. The brainchild of Telugu Desam's president, N T Rama Rao, work on the project began in 1985 at Raigir, some 50 km from Hyderabad, and was completed in early 1990. From there, the 17.5-metre-high, 350-tonne, monolithic statue was transported to Hyderabad and loaded onto a barge for transportation across Hussain Sagar where it was to be erected on the dam wall.

Unfortunately, disaster struck and the statue sank into the lake taking with it eight people. There it languished for another two years while ways of raising it were discussed. Finally, in mid-1992, a Goan-based salvage company raised it once more – undamaged! – and took it to the dam wall where it was finally erected on the Buddha Purnima complex.

Boats out to the statue leave from the recreational garden just north of Secretariat Rd.

Salar Jung Museum

This is India's answer to the Victoria & Albert Museum in London. The museum's collection was put together by Mir Yusaf Ali Khan (Salar Jung III), the prime minister, or grand-vizier, of the nizam. It contains 35,000 exhibits from all corners of the world and includes sculptures, woodcarvings, religious objects, Persian miniature paintings, illuminated manuscripts, armour and weaponry. In the Jade Room you'll also see the swords, daggers and clothing of the Mughal emperors and of Tipu Sultan, as well as many other objects. All this is housed in 36 rooms of one of the ugliest buildings imaginable.

The museum is open daily, except Friday, from 10 am to 5 pm, but avoid Sundays when it's bedlam. Entry is Rs 5. Bags and cameras must be deposited in the entrance hall. From Abids, bus No 7 will drop you at the Musi River bridge; just cross the river and take the first turn left.

Archaeological Museum

The archaeological museum is in the public gardens to the north of Hyderabad railway station. It has a small collection of archaeological finds from the area, together with copies of paintings from the Ajanta Caves in Maharashtra. Opening hours are 10.30 am to 5 pm daily, except Friday, and entry is Rs 0.50.

The gardens also feature an **aquarium** in the Jawahar Bal Bhavan. It's open daily except Sunday from 10.30 am to 5 pm.

Nehru Zoological Park

One of the largest zoos in India, the Nehru Zoological Park is spread out over 1.2 sq km of landscaped gardens with animals living in large, open enclosures. They don't look any less bored than animals in zoos anywhere else in the world, but at least an effort has been made here, which is more than can be said for most Indian zoos. There's also a prehistoric animal section, a toy train around the zoo (Rs 1, every 15 minutes), and a lion safari trip (Rs 5, every 15 minutes).

The park is across the Musi River, south of the city, and is open daily except Monday from 8.30 am to 5 pm; entry costs Rs 1, or

Avalokitesvara, a Mahayana Buddhist bodhisattva

Rs 20 if you're in a private car. Once again, it's chaos here on Sundays.

Golconda Fort

This is one of the most magnificent fortress complexes in India. The bulk of the ruins date from the time of the Qutab Shahi kings (16th to 17th centuries), though the origins of the fort have been traced to the earlier Hindu periods when the Yadavas and, later, the Kakatiyas ruled this part of India.

In 1512, Sultan Quli Qutab Shah, a Turkoman adventurer from Persia and governor of Telangana under the Bahmani rulers, declared independence and made Golconda his capital.

Golconda remained the capital until 1590, when the court was moved to the new city of Hyderabad. The fort subsequently came into its own again when, on two separate occasions in the 17th century, Mughal armies from Delhi were sent against the kingdom to enforce payment of tribute. Abul Hasan, the last of the Qutab Shahi kings, held out here for seven months against a Mughal army commanded by Emperor Aurangzeb before losing the fort through treachery in 1687. Following Aurangzeb's death early in the next century, his viceroys (later the nizams) made Hyderabad their capital, abandoning Golconda.

The citadel itself is built on a granite hill 120 metres high and is surrounded by crenellated ramparts constructed of large masonry blocks, some of them weighing several tonnes. The massive gates are studded with large pointed iron spikes, intended to prevent elephants from battering them down, and are further protected by a cordon wall to check direct attack. Outside the citadel stands another crenellated rampart with a perimeter of 11 km. All these walls are in an excellent state of preservation.

Unfortunately, many of the structures inside the citadel – the palaces and harem of the Qutab Shahi kings, assembly halls, arsenal, stables and barracks – have suffered a great deal from past sieges and the ravages of time, but enough remains to give a good impression of what the place must once have looked like. Restoration of the buildings around the Balahisar Gate (the main entrance) has been underway for years – even the wrought iron work has been replaced.

One of the most remarkable features of Golconda Fort is its system of acoustics. The sound of hands clapped in the Grand Portico can be heard in the Durbar Hall at the very top of the hill – a fact not lost on tour guides (or their charges), who compete with each other to make as much noise as possible! Another good test of the acoustics may be the sound & light show held (in English) on Sunday and Wednesday at 6.30 pm. Entry to this show costs Rs 15. There is also supposed to be a 'secret' underground tunnel leading from the Durbar Hall to one of the palaces at the foot of the hill.

A small guidebook, *Guide to Golconda Fort & Qutab Shahi Tombs*, may be on sale at the fort, and is a good investment if you intend to spend the day here. Indeed, a full day would not be wasted, so the tourist office bus tours which give you an hour here are ridiculously short.

To get to the fort's main entrance, Balahisar Gate, take city bus No 119 or 142 from Nampally High Rd (Public Gardens Rd), outside the public gardens. The 11-km trip takes an hour and costs about Rs 2. An auto-rickshaw costs Rs 70 return plus waiting time charges of Rs 15 per hour if you retain the driver.

Tombs of Qutab Shahi Kings

These graceful domed tombs stand about 1.5 km north-west of the fort's Balahisar Gate. They are surrounded by landscaped gardens, and a number of them have beautifully carved stonework. The tombs are open daily except Friday from 9.30 am to 4.30 pm and entrance costs Rs 2, plus Rs 5 if you have a camera (Rs 25 for a movie camera). Most people walk from Golconda to the tombs though there are usually a few auto-rickshaws willing to take you for a handsome price.

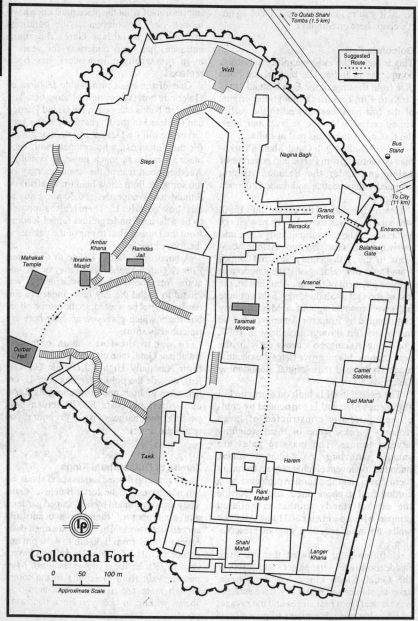

To Qutab Shahi
Tombs (1.5 km)

Suggested
Route

Well

Bus
Stand

To City
(11 km)

Nagina Bagh

Steps

Grand
Portico

Barracks

Entrance

Balahisar
Gate

Ambar
Khana

Ramdas
Jail

Mahakali
Temple

Ibrahim
Masjid

Arsenal

Durbar
Hall

Taramati
Mosque

Camel
Stables

Dad Mahal

Tank

Harem

Rani
Mahal

Golconda Fort

0   50   100 m

Approximate Scale

Shahi
Mahal

Langer
Khana

Organised Tours

The APTTDC offers daily tours of the city which start at 7.30 am from Yatri Nivas and finish at 6 pm at the Birla Mandir. The cost is Rs 75 plus entry charges and includes a vegetarian lunch at Yatri Nivas. The tours visit Buddha Purnima, Qutab Shahi Tombs, Golconda Fort, Salar Jung Museum, Mecca Masjid, Charminar, the zoo, the handicrafts emporium and Birla Mandir/Planetarium.

Unfortunately, five and 10-minute stops are the order of the day except for Golconda Fort (one hour), Salar Jung Museum (90 minutes) and the zoo (one hour).

The APTTDC also runs tours to destinations further afield including Tirupathi and Nagarjunakonda; see those sections for details.

Places to Stay – bottom end

The best of the cheap hotels are all in the Abids area between Abids Circle and Hyderabad railway station. Right opposite the station on Nampally High Rd (Public Gardens Rd) is a whole clutch of lodges including the *Royal Lodge, Royal Home, Royal Hotel, Neo Royal Hotel* and *Gee Royal Lodge.* Good grief! They're all very similar and overpriced for what they are – count on Rs 75/130 for singles/doubles with attached bathroom and fans. Hot water is usually only available in the mornings.

Here too you'll find the *Hotel Rajmata* (☎ 20-1000) which offers budget accommodation in the old wing for Rs 40/60 with common bathroom. The rooms here are quiet but they resemble grotty prison cells. Better are the rooms in the newer block where singles/doubles with attached bathroom are Rs 55/80, and 'deluxe' rooms (no air-con) with colour TV, hot water, towel and soap cost Rs 210/260. There's also an attached restaurant with veg and non-veg food.

Across the road from the above is the *New Asian Lodge* (☎ 20-1275) which is a typical, no-frills Indian boarding house but it's adequate at Rs 70/115 with attached bathroom and fan. Bucket hot water is available.

Somewhat better is the large *Hotel Sri Brindavan* (☎ 20-3970) on Station Rd near

the junction with Abids Circle. It offers singles/doubles with attached bathroom for Rs 125/160. Hot water is available from 4 to 7.30 am. There are vegetarian and very good non-veg restaurants. The rooms are arranged around a quiet courtyard and there's secured parking.

Also reasonable is the *Apsara Hotel* (☎ 50-2663), Station Rd, which has rooms for Rs 90/130 with attached bathroom (with bucket shower), fan, and hot water in the mornings.

The *Hotel Suhail* (☎ 59-0386) is clean, quiet and good value at Rs 110/132, and there are deluxe doubles at Rs 176 and air-con doubles at Rs 220, as well as more expensive suites. All the rooms have attached bathroom with hot water and most have a balcony. The hotel is situated in an alley behind the GPO; the easiest way to find it is to walk through the car park between the Ramakrishna Cinema and the Hotel Aahwaanam and then turn left. The hotel is up a little further, on the left.

In Secunderabad, the *YMCA* (☎ 80-1936) at the northern end of Station Rd takes men and women and has singles/doubles for Rs 50/75. The APTTDC's *Yatri Nivas Hotel* on Sardar Patel Rd has rooms with cold water, mosquitoes and fan for Rs 100/150 but they're bad value and only recommended if you have an early-morning tour to catch.

Only Secunderabad railway station has *retiring rooms.*

Places to Stay – middle

The best value by far in this range is the relatively new and spotlessly clean *Hotel Saptagiri* (☎ 50-3601) just off Station Rd and round the corner from the Annapurna Hotel. The rooms here are small but still good value at Rs 105/155, and Rs 275 a double with air-con, including taxes. All the rooms have a balcony and an attached bathroom with hot water. There's a restaurant of sorts but it only serves snacks.

The huge *Hotel Aahwaanam* (☎ 59-0301), off Nehru Rd and right opposite the Ramakrishna Cinema, has decent rooms for Rs 160/203 or Rs 264/297 with air-con, including tax. All the rooms have attached bathroom (bucket showers) with hot water and a hybrid toilet, and air-con rooms also have a colour TV. There's no restaurant. This place is set back from the road but it can still be noisy when raucous crowds amass outside the cinema to see the latest hit.

Equally good is the *Hotel Jaya International* (☎ 23-2929), in Reddy Hostel Lane off Mahipatram Rd, which has rooms for Rs 140/200 or Rs 300/375 with air-con. There's no restaurant. Nearby, the *Hotel Siddhartha* (☎ 59-0222), Mahipatram Rd, is a quiet place with a grand foyer but lacklustre

rooms. Singles/doubles cost Rs 170/205, or Rs 325/350 with air-con. There are also more expensive suites. The hotel has its own restaurant plus secured parking.

The older and popular *Taj Mahal Hotel* (☎ 23-7988), at the junction of M G and King Kothi Rds, is a huge rambling place set in its own grounds, with car parking facilities and a vegetarian restaurant. Spacious rooms with attached bathroom, hot water and TV cost Rs 200/300, or Rs 275/350 with air-con.

Places to Stay – top end
One of the cheapest in this range is the

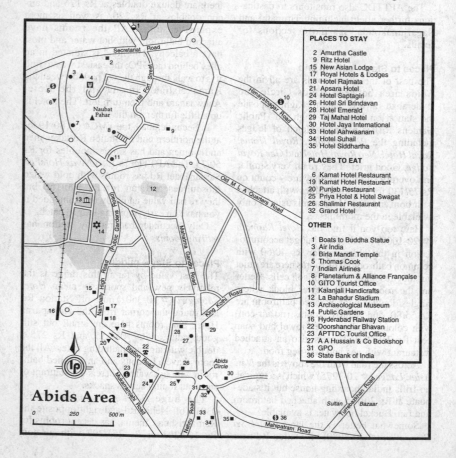

PLACES TO STAY
2 Amurtha Castle
9 Ritz Hotel
15 New Asian Lodge
17 Royal Hotels & Lodges
18 Hotel Rajmata
21 Apsara Hotel
24 Hotel Saptagiri
26 Hotel Sri Brindavan
28 Hotel Emerald
29 Taj Mahal Hotel
30 Hotel Jaya International
33 Hotel Aahwaanam
34 Hotel Suhail
35 Hotel Siddhartha

PLACES TO EAT
6 Kamat Hotel Restaurant
19 Kamat Hotel Restaurant
20 Punjab Restaurant
25 Priya Hotel & Hotel Swagat
26 Shalimar Restaurant
32 Grand Hotel

OTHER
1 Boats to Buddha Statue
3 Air India
4 Birla Mandir Temple
5 Thomas Cook
7 Indian Airlines
8 Planetarium & Alliance Française
10 GiTO Tourist Office
11 Kalanjali Handicrafts
12 La Bahadur Stadium
13 Archaeological Museum
14 Public Gardens
16 Hyderabad Railway Station
22 Doorshanchar Bhavan
23 APTTDC Tourist Office
27 A A Hussain & Co Bookshop
31 GPO
36 State Bank of India

Abids Area

rapidly deteriorating *Hotel Emerald* (☎ 20-2836; fax 20-3902), in Chiragala Lane off M G Rd. The stale rooms start at Rs 425/525 plus there are deluxe rooms for Rs 475/600 and suites for Rs 800.

For a touch of the days of the nizams of Hyderabad, head for the *Ritz Hotel* (☎ 23-3571), Hill Fort St, Basheer Bagh, en route to the Birla Mandir temple. This former palace is rated as a four-star hotel, however it's getting shabby and the musty rooms are overpriced at Rs 750/900. Deluxe doubles cost Rs 1000 and suites are Rs 1500. It has a restaurant (Indian, Continental, Italian and Chinese), swimming pool, tennis court and spacious lawns affording beautiful views over the city and Hussain Sagar.

The brand new *Hotel Viceroy* (☎ 61-8383) on Tankbund Rd also overlooks Hussain Sagar and has modern singles/doubles for Rs 795/995 plus suites for Rs 1795, all including a buffet breakfast. This fully air-con hotel has all the usual facilities including a pool.

If you're into fantasy land, you may want to check whether the *Amurtha Castle*, a brand new five-star Disneyesque hotel on Secretariat Rd, has opened.

There are several other top-end hotels on Road No 1 at Banjara Hill on the western side of Hussain Sagar. They're all centrally air-conditioned and have the full range of facilities. They include:

Gateway Hotel on Banjara Hill – singles/doubles from US$50/60, or US$60/75 in the 'executive' rooms including breakfast; this hotel looks a bit tired (☎ 39-9999; fax 22-2218)

Krishna Holiday Inn – just off Road No 1; brand new and very luxurious with rooms from US$70/80 (☎ 39-3939)

Krishna Oberoi – palatial five-star hotel with rooms costing US$100/110 (☎ 39-2323; fax 22-3079)

Places to Eat

Andhra Pradesh and Hyderabad in particular pride themselves on their local cuisine, but be warned, some of the vegetarian chilli dishes can be real tear-jerkers. A few savoury specialities to look out for include kulcha (charcoal-baked bread), biryani (fragrant steamed rice with meat), haleen (pounded wheat with a lightly spiced mutton sauce) and nihari (spiced tongue and trotters).

The *Grand Hotel*, just around from the Hyderabad GPO, is far from grand but it has cheap non-veg local food such as biryanis and mutton cutlets and is immensely popular at lunchtime.

Good, cheap, south Indian vegetarian meals can be found at any *Kamat Hotel*, where the standard fare costs Rs 15. There's one in Abids on Station Rd and another on Secretariat Rd near Thomas Cook. Almost opposite the former is the small *Punjab Restaurant* which serves north Indian non-veg food that is almost guaranteed to make you break into a sweat.

The air-con *Priya Hotel* on Station Rd has unexciting vegetarian 'meals' for Rs 20 plus non-veg dishes from Rs 20 to Rs 40. 'Meals' at the *Hotel Swagat* almost next door are better and slightly cheaper.

Possibly the best place to eat in Hyderabad without going for a splurge is the *Shalimar Restaurant*, part of the Hotel Sri Brindavan on Station Rd. The food here is excellent and tasty. Soups are Rs 15, curries Rs 25 to Rs 40 and vegetarian dishes Rs 20 to Rs 30. It's open from 11 am to 11 pm daily.

For authentic Hyderabadi cuisine, head to the *Paradise Garden Restaurant* near the corner of Sardar Patel Rd and M G Rd in Secunderabad. Established in 1953, this is *the* place to eat around here and prices are sensible. It features two sections – an open-air patio serving both veg and non-veg fare, and a sidewalk takeaway area where you can get juicy kebabs, freshly baked rotis, oven-fresh biscuits and hot coffee.

For a splurge, try one of the top-end hotels. The Italian cuisine at the Krishna Holiday Inn's *Mama Mia Restaurant* is excellent, though hardly local. The Gateway Hotel's *Dakhni Restaurant* has good non-veg Hyderabadi food.

Things to Buy

Laad Bazaar near Charminar is the real heart of Hyderabad's old town and it's here that you'll find Hyderabadi specialities such as pearls, glass bangles, *bidri* ware (see the boxed section under Bidar in the Karnataka chapter for details) and enamel jewellery. An interesting market closer to Abids is Sultan Bazaar at the end of Mahipatram Rd.

The best place to buy arts & crafts from all over India is Kalanjali on Nampally High Rd. This shop is well laid out, has fixed prices, accepts credit cards, and will reliably send purchases anywhere round the world. It's open daily from 10 am to 8 pm. Also good is the Central Cottage Industries Emporium at 94 Minerva Complex on Sarojini Devi Rd, Secunderabad.

Getting There & Away

Air The Air India office (☎ 23-2747) is in the Samrat Complex (1st floor) on Secretariat Rd. Indian Airlines (☎ 23-6902) is also on Secretariat Rd and is open daily from 10 am to 1 pm and 2 to 5.25 pm.

There are Indian Airlines flights in either direction between Hyderabad and Bangalore (daily, US$56), Bombay (twice daily, US$74), Calcutta (daily except Saturday, US$134), Delhi (twice daily, US$124), Madras (twice daily, US$57) and Bhubaneswar (three times weekly, US$95) via Nagpur (US$61).

Jet Airways (☎ 23-1263) flies daily (except Sunday) to Bombay. ModiLuft (☎ 24-3783) has flights from Monday to Saturday to Madras and Delhi. East West Airlines (☎ 81-3566) flies daily to Bombay and Visakhapatnam (US$58).

Bus Buses leave from the main APSRTC bus terminal, Gowliguda, for all parts of the state. The buses are well organised into separate bays, there's an enquiry counter, a timetable in English, and a computerised advance booking office which is open daily from 8 am to 9 pm.

Some destinations (fares quoted are for superdeluxe buses) are listed in the Bus Services table.

There are also a number of private bus companies offering superdeluxe video buses to such cities as Bangalore, Bombay, Madras, Nagpur and Tirupathi. Most of their offices are on Nampally High Rd close to the

Bus Services from Hyderabad		
Destination	*Frequency* (daily)	*Fare* (*Rs*)
Aurangabad	2	120
Bangalore	9 mainly evening	171
Bidar	19	26
Bombay	10	260
Gulbarga	7	75
Hospet	2	85
Kurnool	20	56
Madras	1 at 4.30 pm	201
Nagpur	2	150
Nizamabad	32	50
Tirupathi	11	171
Vijayawada	30	83

Hyderabad railway station entrance road; try Asian Travels (☎ 20-2128) inside the Asian Lodge. Most have one departure daily, usually in the late afternoon. To Bangalore or Nagpur it's Rs 180 and 12 hours; to Bombay or Madras it's Rs 220 and 14 hours.

Train Secunderabad is the main railway station and this is where you catch through trains (ie, all trains not originating in Hyderabad). However, trains starting in Hyderabad can be boarded here too. Bookings for any train can be made either at Hyderabad Station (☎ 23-1130) or Secunderabad Station (☎ 75-413) Monday to Saturday from 8 am to 2 pm and 2.15 to 8 pm, and on Sunday from 8 am to 4 pm. Both have a tourist quota.

To Calcutta's Howrah station, you must take a train first to Vijayawada and then change to one of the east coast express trains such as the *Coromandel*. The fare to Calcutta is Rs 264/877 in 2nd/1st class and the 1591-km trip takes 32 hours.

See Train Services table for other destinations served from Hyderabad/Secunderabad.

Getting Around

To/From the Airport The airport is about eight km north of Abids at Begampet. There is no airport bus. An auto-rickshaw from Abids should cost about Rs 25 by the meter, though drivers usually refuse to use it for this

Train Services from Hyderabad

Destination	Train number & name	Departure time	Distance (km)	Duration (hours)	Fare (Rs) (2nd/1st)
Aurangabad	1004 *Kacheguda Exp*	6.00 am S*	517	13.00	132/394
Bangalore	7085 *Bangalore Exp*	6.10 pm H**	790	16.30	180/552
Bombay	7032 *Bombay Exp*	8.20 pm S	800	17.15	185/552
Calcutta	8046 *East Coast Exp*	6.45 am H	1591	30.00	264/877
Madras	7054 *Madras Exp*	3.45 pm H	794	14.25	180/552
	6060 *Charminar Exp*	6.40 pm H		14.40	
Delhi	2723 *Andhra Pradesh Exp*	6.05 am H	1397	26.35	250/797
	7021 *H Nizamuddin Exp*	8.00 pm H		33.30	
Tirupathi	7203 *Venkatadri Exp*	3.50 pm S	741	17.40	177/530

Abbreviations for train stations: *S – Secunderabad, **H – Hyderabad

ride so you'll have to haggle. Taxi drivers ask about Rs 85.

Bus Getting on any city bus in Hyderabad, other than at the terminus, is (as one traveller put it) 'like staging a banzai charge on Guadalcanal'. He wasn't exaggerating! Buses you might find useful include:

No 2 – Secunderabad station to Charminar
No 7 – Secunderabad station to Afzalganj and return (this is the one to catch if you're heading for Abids, as it goes down Tankbund Rd and Nehru Rd via the GPO)
No 8 – connects Secunderabad and Hyderabad railway stations
Nos 119 & 142 – Nampally High Rd to Golconda Fort

Auto-Rickshaw & Taxi Flagfall on auto-rickshaws is Rs 4.30 plus Rs 2 for each additional km. Some drivers need no prompting to use the meter but others do. A return trip to Golconda Fort is Rs 70 by the meter plus waiting charges at Rs 15 per hour but they'll expect a tip on top of that.

Taxis tend to be expensive. For a return trip to Golconda, for example, including waiting time, they'll quote you Rs 200.

Car Typical hire rates are Rs 225 for four hours or 40 km, Rs 350 for eight hours or 80 km, and Rs 3.50 per km for journeys longer than a day with a minimum of 300 km per day. These rates include the driver. Try Alpha Motors (☎ 20-1306) in the Abids Shopping

Centre opposite Hotel Emerald or Cosy Cabs (☎ 84-2023).

NAGARJUNAKONDA & NAGARJUNA SAGAR

Nagarjunakonda, about 150 km south-east of Hyderabad on the Krishna River, was one of the largest and most important Buddhist centres in southern India from the 2nd century BC until the 3rd century AD. Known in those days as Vijayapur, Nagarjunakonda takes its present name from Nagarjuna, one of the most revered Buddhist monks, who governed the *sangha* for nearly 60 years around the turn of the 2nd century AD. The Madhyamika school he founded attracted students from as far afield as Sri Lanka and China.

The site was discovered in 1926. Subsequent excavations, particularly in the '50s and '60s, have unearthed the remains of stupas, *viharas, chaityas* and *mandapams*, as well as some outstanding examples of white marble carvings and sculptures depicting the life of the Buddha. These finds were taken to a purpose-built museum on an island which was created following the decision to flood this entire area to build the enormous Nagarjuna Sagar Dam in 1960.

Places to Stay

The choice of accommodation maintained by the APTTDC (☎ (0842) 55-7530) includes the *Vijay Vihar Complex* (☎ 3625)

close to the boat jetty, which has double air-con rooms and cottages, *Project House*, several km away at Hill Colony, and the *Konda Guest House* (☎ (0804883) 2668). There's also a *youth hostel* in Hill Colony.

Getting There & Away
The easiest way to visit Nagarjunakonda and Nagarjuna Sagar is to take the tour organised by the APTTDC. It departs Hyderabad daily (if demand warrants it) at 6.45 am from Yatri Nivas, returns at 10 pm and costs Rs 150. The tour includes visits to the Nagarjunakonda Museum (closed Friday), Pylon (an engraved granite monolith from the Buddhist period), Nagarjuna Sagar, Ethipothala Waterfalls and the working model of the dam.

If you'd prefer to make your own way there, regular buses link Hyderabad, Vijayawada and Guntur with Nagarjuna Sagar. The nearest railway station is at Macherla – a branch line running west from Guntur – and regular buses leave there for Nagarjuna Sagar.

Getting Around
Boat Launches to Nagarjunakonda Museum depart from Nagarjuna Sagar at 9.30 am and 1.30 pm at a cost of Rs 25 per person.

WARANGAL
Population: 512,000
Telephone Area Code: 08712

About 150 km north-east of Hyderabad, Warangal was once the capital of the Kakatiya kingdom which spanned the greater part of present-day Andhra Pradesh from the latter half of the 12th century until it was conquered by the Tughlaqs of Delhi early in the 14th century. The Hindu Kakatiyas were great builders and patrons of the arts, and it was during their reign that the Chalukyan style of temple architecture and decoration reached the pinnacle of its development.

If you have an interest in the various branches of Hindu temple development and have either visited or intend to visit the early Chalukyan sites at Badami, Aihole and

Pattadakal in neighbouring Karnataka state, then an outing to Warangal is worthwhile. Facilities are adequate for an overnight stop, or it can be visited in a long day trip from Hyderabad.

There's a colourful **wool market** a couple of hundred metres past the bus stand.

Fort
Warangal's main attraction is the enormous, abandoned mud-brick fort, which has a terrific atmosphere and many interesting features. Carved stones from wrecked Chalukyan temples are set indiscriminately in the massive stone walls which form a distinct fortification almost a km inside the outer mud walls.

Chalukyan Temples
The most notable remaining Chalukyan temples are the **1000-Pillared Temple** on the slopes of Hanamkonda Hill (one shrine of which is still in use), the **Bhadrakali Temple** on a hillock between Warangal and Hanamkonda, and the Shambu Lingeswara or **Swayambhu Temple** (originally a Siva temple). Built in 1162, the 1000-Pillared Temple is, however, inferior to those found further south. It is in a sad state of disrepair, and looters have removed many of the best pieces and chiselled away the faces of statues.

Places to Stay & Eat
Accommodation facilities are modest. Most of the hotels are on Station Rd, which runs parallel to the railway line; turn left as you leave the station. The *Vijya Lodge* (☎ 25-851) on Station Rd, three minutes from the railway station, is OK value at Rs 50/70. Similar is the *Hotel Shanthi Krishna* (☎ 25-305) which is behind the post office, also on Station Rd.

Up behind the bus stand and near the huge market, the basic *Vikas Lodge* (☎ 24-194) has rooms with bathroom for Rs 35/55.

The *Ashoka* (☎ 78-491) on Main Rd at Hanamkonda, seven km from Warangal railway station, has single/double rooms at Rs 110/180.

There are also a couple of *retiring rooms* at the railway station.

Getting There & Away

Regular buses run between Warangal and Hyderabad, Nizamabad and other major centres. Local buses connect Warangal with Kazipet and Hanamkonda.

Warangal is a major railway junction and there are regular trains to Hyderabad or Secunderabad (three hours, 152 km) and to Vijayawada (Rs 75/204 in 2nd/1st class, four hours, 209 km).

Getting Around

The bus stand is directly opposite the entrance to the railway station. Bus No 28 will take you the five km to the fort at Mantukonda. Otherwise, it would be worth negotiating a fixed price for an auto-rickshaw to take you there and back.

VISAKHAPATNAM

Population: 1.1 million
Telephone Area Code: 0891

This coastal city is the commercial and industrial heart of Andhra Pradesh's isolated north-east corner. Originally it was two separate towns – the northern and more urbane Waltair and the southern port town of Visakhapatnam (known as Vizag). However, as Vizag grew (and continues to rapidly do so), the pair gradually merged.

These days they have little to offer tourists and the pall of industrial smoke that hangs in the air makes them relatively unenticing. The hilly seaside area of Waltair is edged by long beaches affording views across the Bay of Bengal and the busy Calcutta-Madras shipping lane. The best beach is **Rishikonda**, about 10 km north. At Simhachalam Hill, 10 km north of town, there's an 11th-century **Vishnu temple** in fine Orissan style.

Orientation & Information

The railway station and bus stand are about 1.5 km apart. Both are about two km from the city centre, based loosely around the Poorna market area. The beach hotels are located in Waltair.

There is a tourist office in the railway station but it has precious little information.

Places to Stay & Eat

There's no shortage of places to stay to suit all budgets. The *retiring rooms* at the railway station include men-only dorm beds for Rs 10 and very comfortable doubles at Rs 100.

City Centre A good area for cheap hotels is Main Rd near the Poorna Market. Here you'll find the *Hotel Poorna* (☎ 62-344), down an alley off Main Rd, where clean singles/doubles with attached bathroom cost Rs 40/60. Opposite and very similar is the *Hotel Prasanth* (☎ 65-282) with rooms for Rs 59/100. The nearby *Swagath Restaurant* on Main Rd has a small rooftop garden and cheap vegetarian meals and snacks.

The three-star *Hotel Daspalla* (☎ 56-4825) has rooms for Rs 250/280, and Rs 325/360 with air-con. The hotel has several restaurants serving Chinese, Continental and tandoori meals as well as dakshin, the spicy non-veg local cuisine. Up in price but also central, the *Dolphin Hotels Ltd* (☎ 56-7000) is a four-star place with a swimming pool and restaurant. Singles/doubles range from Rs 495/695 to Rs 1195/1395, and breakfast is included in rooms priced above Rs 695/895.

Beach Area The *Palm Beach Hotel* (☎ 55-4026) at the northern end of Beach Rd is old and run-down, but it's OK if you just want to be close to the beach. Rooms are Rs 200/250 or Rs 250/300 with air-con.

The next-door *Park Hotel* (☎ 55-4488; fax 55-4181) looks old and ugly from the outside but the recently renovated rooms are modern and comfortable. Air-con rooms, all with a sea view, cost Rs 1150/1950. There's a swimming pool, bookshop and three restaurants, and the management is very friendly.

Vizag's best hotel is the relatively new *Taj Residency* (☎ 64-371), a luxurious tiered hotel that climbs the hill up from Beach Rd. Singles/doubles start at US$45/70 and it has a swimming pool and a restaurant.

Getting There & Away

Vizag's airport is 13 km west of town; Rs 26 by auto-rickshaw. Indian Airlines (☎ 46-503) has three flights a week to Calcutta (US$81) and Madras (US$70). East West Airlines (☎ 64-119) flies daily to Bombay (US$132) via Hyderabad (US$58). NEPC Airlines (☎ 57-4151) flies Tuesday, Thursday and Saturday to Madras (US$105) via Vijayawada (US$70).

Visakhapatnam Junction railway station is on the main Calcutta to Madras line. To Calcutta (Rs 192/569 in 2nd/1st class, 15 hours, 879 km) the best train is the overnight *Coromandel Express*. Heading south, the same train goes to Vijayawada (5½ hours, 352 km) and Madras Central (Rs 179/541, 17 hours, 784 km).

From the well-organised bus terminal, the APSRTC (☎ 65-038) has services to Puri (Orissa) and state destinations.

AROUND VISAKHAPATNAM

About 25 km north-east of Vizag is **Bheemunipatnam**, one of the safest beaches on this part of the coast. It is also the site of the ruins of the east coast's oldest Dutch settlement (17th century). A little way inland from here is **Hollanders Green**, the Dutch cemetery.

Some 90 km from Vizag are the million-year-old limestone **Borra Caves** which are filled with fascinating stalagmite and stalactite formations.

VIJAYAWADA

Telephone Area Code: 0866

On the banks of the mighty Krishna River, Vijayawada is a major railway junction on the east coast line from Calcutta to Madras. About 265 km east of Hyderabad, it's an important industrial centre and a fairly hectic town. Few travellers stop here but it's the most convenient place from which to visit Amaravathi, the Sanchi of Andhra Pradesh.

In Vijayawada itself, there is a number of important Hindu temples including the **Kanaka Durga Temple** on Indrakila Hill, as well as two 1000-year-old **Jain temples**. About eight km from Vijayawada, across the

river, are the ancient Hindu cave temples of **Undavalil**.

There is a tourist information kiosk at the railway station.

Places to Stay & Eat

The *retiring rooms* at the railway station cost Rs 50/80 but are pretty noisy.

Close to the railway station, the *Modern Cafe Lodging* (☎ 73-171) on Besant Rd has rooms from Rs 40 with the use of a very smelly common toilet. You may find the manager reluctant to allow women to stay here for the simple reason that 'none have ever done so!'

At the new bus terminal, the 200-bed *Hanuman Dormitory* looks more like a hospital ward than somewhere you'd voluntarily spend the night, but it's cheap at Rs 12 for 24 hours. Also on the 1st floor here is the *Deluxe Lodge*, a big room with rows of plastic lounge chairs where you can flake out for Rs 2 an hour.

Best value among the cheapies is the *Hotel Swapna Lodge* (☎ 65-386) on Durgaiah St near the Navrang Theatre, about two km from the railway station. It's on a quiet back-street and is friendly and clean. Rooms cost Rs 50/70, more with air-con. The *Sree Lakshmi Vilas Modern Cafe* (☎ 62-525) on Besant Rd at Governorpet, a bustling shopping district about 1.5 km from the railway station, has rooms with common bathroom for Rs 53/65, or Rs 60/100 with attached bath. The hotel has a good vegetarian restaurant.

Going up in price is the *Hotel Raj Towers* (☎ 61-311), on Congress Office Rd, 1.5 km from the railway station. It has rooms with attached bathroom for Rs 170/235, and Rs 265/315 with air-con, and there's a veg restaurant. A similar place is the *Hotel Manorama* (☎ 77-221), on M G Rd about 500 metres from the new bus terminal, which has rooms with attached bathroom for Rs 200/260, or Rs 250/350 with air-con.

One of the best hotels is the relatively new *Hotel Ilapuram* (☎ 61-282) on Besant Rd. Singles/doubles are Rs 250/300, or Rs 350/400 with air-con and there are more expensive suites. The hotel has both non-veg and veg restaurants.

The *Hotel Nandini* near the bus terminal has veg food. The *Modern Bakery & Ice-Cream Parlour* on Besant Rd is OK for snacks.

Getting There & Away

Air The airport is about 20 km from the city. NEPC Airlines (☎ 47-6493) flies on Tuesday, Thursday and Saturday to Madras (US$70) and Visakhapatnam (US$70).

Bus The enormous new bus terminal on Bandar Rd near the river is about 1.5 km from the railway station. It's very well organised and has good facilities including dormitories, waiting rooms and a restaurant. From here, buses travel to all parts of Andhra Pradesh; every 30 minutes to Hyderabad (Rs 83, six hours, 260 km), eight times daily to Warangal (Rs 60, six hours) and Visakhapatnam seven times daily (Rs 100, 10 hours, 365 km), as well as to Madras twice daily (Rs 120, 10 hours,).

Train Vijayawada is on the main Madras to Calcutta and Madras to Delhi lines and all the express trains stop here. The quickest train from Vijayawada to Madras (Rs 118/352 in 2nd/1st class, seven hours, 432 km) is the Calcutta to Madras *Coromandel Express*. The same train to Calcutta (20 hours, 1236 km) costs Rs 237/737.

There are plenty of trains via Warangal to Hyderabad (Rs 82/303, 6½ hours, 361 km); one of the quickest is the *Godavari Express*. The *Tamil Nadu Express* to New Delhi (27 hours, 1762 km) costs Rs 279/945 in 2nd/1st class.

To Tirupathi (290 km), the daily *Howrah-Tirupathi Express* takes nine hours and costs Rs 83/245 in 2nd/1st class. Heading north to Puri (Orissa), take the *Howrah-Tirupathi Express* to the junction, Khurda Road, then a passenger train or bus for the last 44 km to Puri.

There are also direct weekly trains to Kanyakumari and Bangalore, trains four

times weekly to Varanasi and daily to Thiruvananthapuram (Trivandrum).

AROUND VIJAYAWADA
Amaravathi

Some 30 km due west of Vijayawada, near the bank of the Krishna River, stands the ancient Buddhist centre of Amaravathi, the former capital of the Satvahanas, the successors to the Mauryas in this part of India. Here you can see the 2000-year-old **stupa** with its intricately carved pillars and marble-surfaced dome which itself is equally richly carved. The carvings depict the life of the Buddha as well as scenes from everyday life. It's not as large as that at Sanchi in Madhya Pradesh but it is worth a visit if you're interested in Buddhist relics of the Hinayana era. There's a **museum** on the site containing relics found in the area.

Direct buses from Vijayawada to Amaravathi are few and far between as there is no direct road anyway. It's better to take one of the hourly buses south to Guntur and then another bus from there. All up, the 65-km trip takes two to three hours and costs about Rs 18. The APTTDC also organises bus tours for Rs 45 as well as boat trips for Rs 50 return. Ask at the tourist information kiosk at Vijayawada railway station or at the APTTDC's counter at the Krishnaveni Hotel (☎ 75-382), Sitanagaram, in Vijayawada.

TIRUPATHI & TIRUMALA
Telephone Area Code: 08574

The 'holy hill' of Tirumala, 20 km from its service town of Tirupathi in the extreme south of Andhra Pradesh, is one of the most important pilgrimage centres in all India because of the ancient Vaishnavaite temple of Venkateshwara. This is the god whose picture graces the reception areas of most lodges and restaurants in southern India. He's the one with his eyes covered (since his gaze would scorch the world) and garlanded in so many flowers that only his feet are visible.

Tirumala is an engrossing place where you can easily spend a whole day just wandering around. It's one of the few temples in India which allows non-Hindus into the sanctum sanctorum but, despite this, the place sees very few foreign visitors.

On the flip side, it hosts an army of pilgrims from all over India and, in order to cope with them, everything at Tirumala and at Tirupathi is organised to keep visitors fed, sheltered and moving. Most are housed in special pilgrims' *choultries* in both Tirupathi and Tirumala. However, the private hotels and lodges are in Tirupathi, so a whole fleet of buses constantly ferries pilgrims up and down the hill between Tirupathi and Tirumala from before dawn until well after dark.

Venkateshwara Temple

Among the powers attributed to Venkateshwara by his devotees is the granting of any wish made in front of the idol at Tirumala. It's on the basis of such a legend that pilgrims flock to this temple. There are never less than 5000 here at any one time and, in a day, the total is often as high as 100,000, although the average is a mere 30,000. The temple staff alone number nearly 6000!

Such popularity makes the temple one of the richest in India, with an annual income of a staggering five billion rupees. This is administered by a temple trust which ploughs the bulk of the money back into hundreds of choultries and charities such as homes for the poor, orphanages, craft training centres, schools, colleges and art academies.

It's considered auspicious to have your head shaved when visiting the temple, so if you see people with shaved heads in south India, you can be pretty sure they've recently been to Tirupathi – this applies to men, women and children. This practice is known as tonsuring.

As you face the entrance to the temple, there is a small **museum** at the top of the steps to the left. Among other things, it has a good collection of musical instruments, including a tabla-type drum called a *ubangam*! The museum is open from 8 am to 8 pm and entry is Rs 1.

Organised Tours

The APTTDC runs weekend tours to Tirupathi from Hyderabad. The tours leave at 4 pm on Friday and return at 7 am on Monday and include accommodation and 'special darshan'. The cost is Rs 480. It's also possible to take the bus only; this costs Rs 120 one way.

Daily tours to Tirupathi are also run from Madras (for details see the Organised Tours section in the Madras chapter).

Places to Stay

Tirupathi Tirupathi is the town at the bottom of the hill and the transport hub. It has plenty of hotels and lodges, so there's no problem finding somewhere to stay.

A whole group of hotels is clustered around the main bus terminal, 500 metres from the centre of town. Additionally, there are *retiring rooms* at the railway station.

The friendly *Vasantha Vihar Lodge* (☎ 20-

Special Darshan at Tirumala

After paying Rs 30 for 'special darshan', you'll be allowed to enter Tirumala's Venkateshwara Temple. Special darshan means you can go in ahead of all those who have paid nothing for their ordinary *darshan* (viewing of a god) and who have to queue up – often for 12 hours or more – in the claustrophobic wire cages which ring the outer wall of the temple.

However, although special darshan is supposed to get you to the front of this immense queue in two hours, on weekends when the place is much busier it can take as long as five hours, and you still have to go through the cages. A signboard at the entrance tells you how long you can expect it to take. To find the start of the queue, follow the signs to 'Sarvadarshanam', around to the left of the temple entrance.

Once inside the temple, you'll have to keep shuffling along with everyone else and, before you know it, you'll have viewed Venkateshwara and will be back outside again. ■

460), 141 G Car St, about a one-minute walk from the railway station, has 17 small, basic single/double rooms for Rs 40/60 with fan and attached shower.

A block away, the popular *Bhimas Hotel* (☎ 25-744) at 42 G Car St is OK if you're alone but double rooms here are overpriced. Rooms with bathroom cost Rs 58/180 and doubles with air-con are Rs 375.

Opposite is the *Bhimas Deluxe Hotel* (☎ 25-521), 34-38 G Car St. This is a two-star hotel with good rooms for Rs 175/200, or from Rs 365/390 with air-con. All the rooms have attached bathroom and the air-con rooms have TV.

Going up in price, the *Hotel Mayura* (☎ 25-925; fax 25-911) at 209 T P Area is a three-star hotel close to the main bus terminal which has rooms with attached bathroom for Rs 300, or Rs 450/500 with air-con. There's a restaurant serving Indian and Mughlai cuisine.

Tirumala Most pilgrims stay in the vast *dormitories* which ring the temple – beds here are free and open to anyone. If you want to stay, check in at the accommodation reception and you'll be allocated a bed or a room. It's best to avoid weekends when the place becomes outrageously crowded.

Places to Eat
Tirupathi The *Lakshmi Narayana Bhavan* is a good vegetarian restaurant opposite the main bus terminal. The *Bhimas Hotel* also has a good vegetarian restaurant, including an air-con dining hall. The popular basement restaurant at the *Bhimas Deluxe Hotel* serves north and south Indian food until late at night – the Kashmiri naan here is an extravaganza to behold.

Tirumala Huge dining halls serve thousands of free meals daily to keep the pilgrims happy. Other than that, there are a few no-frills, banana-leaf 'meals' places.

Getting There & Away
Air Tirupathi's airport was closed for upgrading when we updated this guide but

flights from here to Madras, Hyderabad and Bombay should have resumed by now. Check with Indian Airlines (☎ 22-349) in the Hotel Vishnupriya complex, opposite the main bus terminal in Tirupathi.

Bus It is possible to visit Tirupathi on a very long day trip from Madras, but staying overnight makes it far less rushed. Tamil Nadu's state bus company has express buses (route No 802) from the TTC/JJTC bus terminal in Madras at 8.15 am, 3.30 and 8.30 pm. Ordinary buses are more frequent but much slower. The express buses take about four hours to do the 150-km trip, cost Rs 31 and can be booked in advance in Madras.

To Madras, there are express buses from Tirupathi's main bus terminal at 9.45 and 11.15 am, 12.15, 2.45, 3.10 and 8.30 pm.

Most buses to Hyderabad (Rs 171, 12 hours) leave in the late afternoon. There are hourly buses to Vijayawada (Rs 124) as well as plenty of services to Vellore (Rs 19, 2½ hours) in neighbouring Tamil Nadu.

Train Tirupathi is well served by express trains. There are four trains daily to Madras (three hours, 147 km) which cost Rs 38/149 in 2nd/1st class.

The daily *Venkatadri* runs to Hyderabad (17½ hours, 741 km) and there are three daily express trains to Vijayawada (Rs 105/320 in 2nd/1st class, nine hours, 389 km). There's also an express train to Madurai (18 hours, 663 km) via Vellore, Chidambaram and Tiruchirappalli.

Getting Around
Bus Tirumala Link buses operate from two bus stands in Tirupathi: the main bus terminal about 500 metres from the centre of town and the Tirumala bus stand near the railway station. The 20-km trip takes 45 minutes and costs Rs 8/16 one way/return on an ordinary bus, or Rs 10/20 on a so-called 'express' bus.

To get on a bus in either Tirupathi or Tirumala, you usually have to go through a system of crowd-control wire cages which are definitely not for the claustrophobic. At busy times (weekends and festivals), it can take up to two hours to file through the cages and get onto a bus. If you're staying in Tirupathi, it's worth buying a return ticket which saves you some queuing time in the cages at the top of the hill. You can avoid going through the cages at Tirupathi by catching a bus from the main bus terminal (where there are no cages). If you choose to leave from the Tirumala bus stand near Tirupathi railway station, you'll have to go through the cages.

Finding the queue for the buses at the Tirumala bus stand in Tirupathi can also be a task. You must walk through a choultry to reach the cages and ticket office – the choultry is about 200 metres from the entry to Tirupathi railway station (turn to the right as you exit the station) opposite the bottom of the footbridge over the railway line.

The one-way road to Tirumala winds precariously upwards and the bus drivers have perfected the art of maniacal driving. The road they drive down is the old one and is very narrow and winding. It has 57 hairpin bends, which means 57 adrenalin rushes for you as the buses hurtle down – total lunacy.

Taxi If you're in a hurry, or don't like the cages, there are share taxis available all the time. Seats cost around Rs 35, depending on demand. A taxi to yourself costs about Rs 225 one way.

PUTTAPARTHI

Prasanthi Nilayam, the main ashram of Sri Sathya Sai Baba, is in Puttaparthi. Sai Baba's followers are predominantly Indian (and include Prime Minister Narasimha Rao) but he also has many Western devotees. Some 400,000 people inundated his ashram to celebrate his 60th birthday a decade ago – just as many were expected for his 70th celebration in November 1995.

Known as the Abode of Highest Peace, the ashram is spacious and beautiful with good food and accommodation – at least when the numbers aren't overwhelming. Sai Baba generally spends August to February here but moves to Whitefields Ashram near Bangalore in neighbouring Karnataka during the hot, dry season.

Getting There & Away

Puttaparthi is in the south-western corner of Andhra Pradesh, but it is most easily reached from Bangalore (see that section in the Karnataka chapter for details).

Kerala

Kerala, the land of green magic, is a narrow, fertile strip on the south-west coast of India, sandwiched between the Lakshadweep Sea and the Western Ghats. The landscape is dominated by rice fields, mango and cashew-nut trees and coconut palms. The Western Ghats, with their dense tropical forests, misty peaks, extensive ridges and ravines, have sheltered Kerala from mainland invaders but encouraged Keralans to welcome maritime contact with the outside world. In Kochi (Cochin), there is still a small community descended from Jewish settlers who fled Palestine 2000 years ago. Christianity has also been in Kerala for as long as it has been in Europe! When the Portuguese arrived here 500 years ago, they were more than a little surprised to find Christianity already established along the Malabar Coast, and more than a little annoyed that these Christians had never heard of the Pope.

People have been sailing to Kerala for at least 2000 years. They came in search of spices, sandalwood and ivory. Long before Vasco da Gama led the Portuguese to India, the coast had been known to the Phoenicians, then the Romans, and later the Arabs and Chinese. It was the Arabs who initially controlled the shipment of spices to Europe and it was this, in turn, which motivated the Portuguese to find a sea route to India to break the Arab monopoly. In those days, Kerala was not only a spice centre in its own right, but a transshipment point for spices from the Moluccas. It was also through Kerala that Chinese products and ideas found their way to the West. Even today, local fishers still use Chinese fishing nets.

Such long contact with people from overseas has resulted in the blending of various cultures and given Keralans a cosmopolitan outlook. Unlike the Gujaratis and Tamils, who generally followed the fortunes of the British Empire by emigrating to such places as East Africa, South Africa, Malaysia, Fiji and Guyana, Keralans have had a tradition

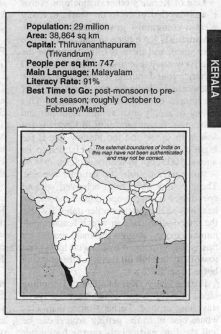

Population: 29 million
Area: 38,864 sq km
Capital: Thiruvananthapuram (Trivandrum)
People per sq km: 747
Main Language: Malayalam
Literacy Rate: 91%
Best Time to Go: post-monsoon to pre-hot season; roughly October to February/March

The external boundaries of India on this map have not been authenticated and may not be correct.

of independently seeking their fortunes overseas or throughout the rest of India. You can generally find a Keralan in any nook and cranny of the world, and they make up 60% of the two-million-strong Indian labour force in the oil fields of the Arabian Gulf.

The present-day state of Kerala was created in 1956 from Travancore, Kochi and Malabar. Malabar was formerly part of Madras State, while both Travancore and Cochin were princely states ruled by maharajas. Unlike some Indian maharajas who exploited their people and squandered the proceeds on high and often frivolous living, the maharajas of Travancore and Cochin paid considerable attention to the provision of basic services and education. It was this early concern for public welfare which gave Keralans a head start and resulted in the post-Independence state being one of the most progressive, literate and highly educated in India.

One of Kerala's other distinctions is that it was the first place in the world to freely elect a communist government (in 1957). Communists have been in and out of office ever since, and there is little doubt that the relatively equitable distribution of land and income, found rarely to the same degree elsewhere in India, is the direct result of successive communist governments. This policy of equity also applies to health and education. Infant mortality in Kerala is the lowest in India, and the literacy rate is the highest. The literacy rate is claimed to be almost 100% but in reality is closer to 90% – still nearly double the national average. These results have been achieved without spending a higher proportion of income on health or education than other states. It's also the only Indian state in which females outnumber males, though the main reason for this is the number of males who have gone to work in the Gulf oil fields before returning home to settle down.

For the visitor, Kerala offers an intriguing blend of cultures and some unusual ways of travelling around. Perhaps more than anywhere else in India, getting around can be half the fun, particularly on the backwater trips along the coastal lagoons. It also offers some of the best and most picturesque beaches in India: Kovalam, a little south of Thiruvananthapuram (Trivandrum), is one of the most popular beaches with travellers. Best of all, Kerala has an easy-going, relaxed atmosphere unlike the bustle you find elsewhere in India. Even the state capital, Thiruvananthapuram, feels like a country town.

Religion

The population of Kerala is roughly 60% Hindu, 20% Muslim and 20% Christian. Christianity was established here earlier than almost anywhere else in the world. In 52 AD, St Thomas the Apostle, or 'Doubting Thomas', is said to have landed on the Malabar Coast near Cranganore (now Kodungallur), where a church with carved Hindu-style columns supposedly dates from the 4th century AD.

Kerala's main Christian area is in the central part of the state, around Kochi and Kottayam. There have been Syrian Christians in Kerala since at least 190 AD, and a visitor at that time reported seeing a Hebrew copy of the gospel of St Matthew. There are 16th-century Syrian churches in Kottayam.

Hindus are mainly concentrated in southern Kerala, around Thiruvananthapuram, though Muslims are also a prominent and vocal component of the population in this area. The main Muslim area is in the northern part of the state, particularly around Kozhikode (Calicut).

The now diminishing Jewish population of Kerala made a very early appearance on the subcontinent. The 'black Jews' are said

No Entry

Despite Kerala's high education standards and its religious diversity, almost every Hindu temple in the state hangs out the 'No Entry' sign for non-Hindus. Don't feel left out – there's at least one temple in the state which bans many Hindus as well. Hindu or not, women between the age of 10 and 50 are not allowed in the Sabarimala Temple in central Kerala. Why? Because women of menstrual age could 'defile' the temple.

In late 1994, the temple and the state government found themselves in a tricky situation when an investigation was launched into complaints, by Sabarimala pilgrims, about the standard of facilities for their use. The Pathanamthitta District Collector was instructed to visit the temple to investigate the complaints until the horrible realisation dawned that the district collector was a 42-year-old woman. The state's high court, which in 1990 had ruled that it was OK to ban women of menstrual age, hurriedly ruled that she could visit the temple, but only on her official duties – worshipping while in the temple was strictly forbidden! Although the case has focussed attention on this clear case of discrimination in a supposedly even-handed state, the rule continues. Lower caste males and females were also banned from temples not so many years ago. ■

Name Changes

A number of towns and districts have been stripped of anglicised names and given new Malayalam names, which can be confusing. In actual fact, the new names are far from universally used. The major places affected include:

Old Name	New Name
Alleppey	Alappuzha
Calicut	Kozhikode
Cannanore	Kannur
Changanacherry	Changanassery
Cochin	Kochi
Palghat	Palakkad
Quilon	Kollam
Sultan's Battery	Suthanbatheri
Tellicherry	Thalasseri
Trichur	Thrissur
Trivandrum	Thiruvananthapuram

railway station is a couple of km south of the town centre. Rooms for around Rs 30/60 can be found in places like the *Enay Tourist Home* (☎ 52-1164), the *Ceeyel Tourist Home* (☎ 52-1177) or, behind the post office, the *Aliya Lodge* (☎ 52-2897). The *City Tower Hotel* (☎ 52-1324) at the bus stand end of M G Rd is a green-and-cream landmark. Singles here cost Rs 100, doubles Rs 170, and air-con rooms Rs 290.

Faster trains do not stop in Bekal, which is a Rs 3 to Rs 5.50 bus ride from Kasaragod, depending on the bus and the route. It's only one to 1½ hours between Kasaragod and

to have fled here in 587 BC when Jerusalem was occupied by Nebuchadnezzar. Their descendants have now intermarried with the Hindu population, but there is still a very small number of later arrivals, known as 'white Jews', in Kochi.

ASARAGOD BEKAL & KASARAGOD

Telephone Area Code: Kasaragod 04995

Bekal, in the far north of the state, has long, palm-fringed beaches and a rocky headland topped by a huge fort built between 1645 and 1660. There are slow-moving plans to build a large resort here, but meanwhile there's hardly a tourist in sight. Limited facilities and the Indian fishing village custom of using the beach as a flushed-twice-a-day outdoor toilet may be a deterrent but, on the positive side, you can stay inside the Bekal Fort walls at the very basic *Tourist Bungalow*. There are just two rooms at Rs 25 for one person or Rs 50 for three. The *Eeyem Lodge* (☎ Udma 343) is three km north of the fort, at the village of Palakunnu, and has rooms for between Rs 55 and Rs 70.

Kasaragod is the nearest town of any size. It's about 20 km north of Bekal and 47 km south of Mangalore (in Karnataka). There are a number of hotels in Kasaragod along M G Rd, near the junction with NH 17. The

Kerala

0   30   60 km

Mangalore by express train (Rs 17) or by the frequent super-fast buses (Rs 10).

THALASSERI (Tellicherry)
Telephone Area Code: 04984

Thalasseri is certainly not worth a special detour but, if you are making your way along the coast, it's a pleasant, unhurried place to stop for a night. The town's fishing fleet returns in the late afternoon, and the beach becomes an animated fish market as people haggle over the catch. Near the waterfront, the East India Company's 1708 fort is neglected but relatively intact, with a fine gateway and a modern lighthouse perched on one corner. It's right behind the fire station; though the town's taxi and auto-rickshaw wallahs don't appear to know of its existence.

Logan's Rd runs from Narangapuram, near the bus and railway stations, to the town's main square.

Places to Stay
Cheap places with rooms at Rs 50 to Rs 70 include the *Brothers Tourist Home* (☎ 21-558) and the *Impala Tourist Home* (☎ 20-484), both at the Narangapuram end of Logan's Rd. Further along is the *Minerva Tourist Home* (☎ 21-731) and, round the corner on Convent Rd, the *Chattanchal Tourist Home* (☎ 22-967).

From the railway station, turn left at Logan's Rd to reach the better class *Hotel Pranam* (☎ 22-0634) in Narangapuram. Rooms cost from Rs 60/80 up to Rs 130/150, or Rs 250/275 with air-con. There's an attached restaurant.

Close to the end of Logan's Rd is the glossy, new *Paris Presidency Hotel* (☎ 20-666), which has rooms for Rs 120/180 or air-con doubles for Rs 270. It's flanked by the cheaper *Paris Lodging House* (☎ 20-666), where rooms are Rs 50/70 up to Rs 250 for an air-con double, and by the *Residency Hotel* (☎ 24-409), which charges Rs 60/90.

Places to Eat
In the busy main square at the end of Logan's Rd, the *Hotel New Westend* has good non-vegetarian food – the fish curry is excellent. A couple of doors away is the *New Surya Restaurant*, which has great chilli chicken. There are a variety of ice-cream parlours and 'cool shops' around the square, including *Kwality Sweets*. There's an *Indian Coffee House* behind the Brothers Tourist Home, and an air-con restaurant in the *Paris Presidency*. The *Parkview Restaurant* is near the railway crossing.

Getting There & Away
Frequent trains and buses head north along the coast to Mangalore and south to Kozhikode and Kochi. An auto-rickshaw to any of the town's hotels should cost Rs 5.

MAHÉ
Telephone Area Code: 04983

Mahé, 60 km north of Kozhikode, was a small French dependency handed over to India at the same time as Pondicherry. It is still part of the Union Territory of Pondicherry. Like Karaikal and Yanam on the east coast of India, there's little French influence left and its main function seems to be supplying passing truck drivers with cheap Pondicherry beer.

The English factory established here in 1683 by the Surat presidency to purchase pepper and cardamom was the first permanent English factory on the Malabar Coast. The East India Company also had a fort here in 1708.

Places to Stay & Eat
It's actually far more pleasant to stay at Thalasseri, eight km north. However, if you want to stay in Mahé, the *Government Tourist Home* near the river mouth, about a km from the bus stand, has singles/doubles for just Rs 12/20 – although it's generally full. The nearby *Hotel Arena* (☎ 33-2421) on Maidan Rd has doubles for Rs 100 or Rs 220 with air-con, and an attached restaurant. Also nearby is the *Premier Tourist Home*, next to the soccer field.

The rather primitive *Shamnas Tourist*

Home, next to the river and the bus stand, has rooms for Rs 60. The quieter rooms overlook the river rather than the road. The restaurant has passable food.

Getting There & Away

Mahé is too small to warrant a bus station, so buses pull up on the northern side of the bridge. There are regular buses to Mangalore and Kozhikode.

KOZHIKODE (Calicut)

Population: 801,000
Telephone Area Code: 0495

Vasco da Gama landed at Calicut in 1498, becoming the first European to reach India via the sea route around the southern cape of Africa. His arrival heralded the period of Portuguese supremacy in India. The history of Calicut after 1498 was certainly dramatic. The Portuguese attempted to conquer the town, a centre of Malabar power under the Zamorins, or Lords of the Sea. The Portu-

guese attacks in 1509 and 1510 were both repulsed, although the town was virtually destroyed in the latter assault. Tipu Sultan laid the whole region to waste in 1789, and British rule was established in 1792.

Despite its colourful past, there is little of interest in the town. The central Ansari Park features musical fountains in the evening, and there's a mediocre beach two km from the town centre. Five km from town, at East Hill, the **Pazhassirajah Museum's** archaeological displays include copies of ancient mural paintings, bronzes, old coins and models of temples and megalithic monuments. Next door, the dusty and musty **Krishnamenon Museum** has memorabilia of the former president of India, while the **Art Gallery** has paintings of Raja Ravi Varma and Raja Raja Varma. The three places are open Tuesday to Sunday from 10 am to 5 pm, except on Wednesday when the Krishnamenon Museum and the Art Gallery don't open until noon.

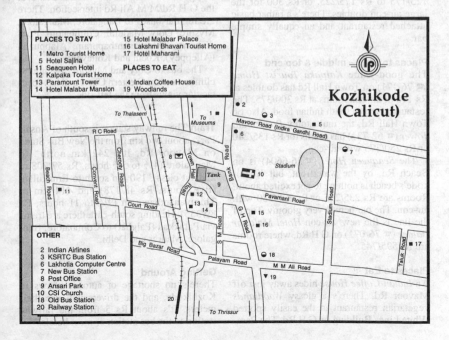

Kozhikode (Calicut)

PLACES TO STAY
1 Metro Tourist Home
5 Hotel Sajina
11 Seaqueen Hotel
12 Kalpaka Tourist Home
13 Paramount Tower
14 Hotel Malabar Mansion
15 Hotel Malabar Palace
16 Lakshmi Bhavan Tourist Home
17 Hotel Maharani

PLACES TO EAT
4 Indian Coffee House
19 Woodlands

OTHER
2 Indian Airlines
3 KSRTC Bus Station
6 Lakhotia Computer Centre
7 New Bus Station
8 Post Office
9 Ansari Park
10 CSI Church
18 Old Bus Station
20 Railway Station

Information

The town's banks won't change travellers' cheques, so go to PL Worldways, Lakhotia Computer Centre, at the junction of Mavoor and Bank Rds. Mavoor Rd is also known as Indira Gandhi Rd.

Places to Stay – bottom end

The *Metro Tourist Home* (☎ 50-029) at the junction of Mavoor and Bank Rds has singles/doubles for Rs 65/100 or air-con doubles for Rs 250. *Hotel Sajina* (☎ 76-146) on Mavoor Rd costs Rs 60/86, while the *Lakshmi Bhavan Tourist Home* (☎ 63-927) on G H Rd is similar at Rs 45/75. Both hotels have air-con rooms and attached restaurants.

The *Hotel Maharani* (☎ 76-161) on Taluk Rd is slightly off the beaten track but quiet. Rooms are Rs 60/100 or Rs 300 for an air-con double. There's a bar and a garden. The KTDC's *Hotel Malabar Mansion* (☎ 76-014) is on Mananchira Square, in the centre of town, near Ansari Park. Rooms are Rs 125/175 to Rs 175/225, or Rs 300 for the large air-con doubles. There's a rather basic attached restaurant and an equally simple bar.

Places to Stay – middle & top end

The good-value *Kalpaka Tourist Home* (☎ 76-171) on Town Hall Rd has doubles at Rs 190 or air-con rooms at Rs 300/375. The restaurant serves south Indian food. Also on Town Hall Rd, the multistorey *Paramount Tower* (☎ 62-731) has rooms for Rs 135/240 or Rs 250/375 with air-con.

The *Seaqueen Hotel* (☎ 36-6604) is on Beach Rd, by the waterfront, but Kozhikode's beach is nothing to get excited about. Rooms are Rs 235/295 or Rs 320/380 with air-con. The bar here is very gloomy. Top of the line is the new, air-con *Hotel Malabar Palace* (☎ 76-071) on G H Rd, where rooms are Rs 595/745.

Places to Eat

An *Indian Coffee House* hides away just off Mavoor Rd. There's a glossy *Woodlands* vegetarian restaurant in the easily spotted White Lines Building on G H Rd. The Para-

mount Tower's *Sunset Point* rooftop barbecue restaurant has great views and will provide beer if you ask discreetly. Stick to the Indian food in the *Malabar Palace's* aircon restaurant. The *Tom 'n Jerry* ice-cream parlour is in the rat-infested garden outside the hotel. The restaurant at the *Seaqueen Hotel* has good seafood.

Getting There & Away

Air The Indian Airlines office (☎ 65-482) is in the Eroth Centre on Bank Rd, close to the Mavoor Rd junction. Indian Airlines flies to Bangalore (Rs 1157), Bombay (Rs 2721) and Madras (Rs 1582). Jet Airways (☎ 35-6052) and East West Airlines (☎ 64-883) also connect to Bombay.

Bus The KSRTC Bus Station is on Mavoor Rd, close to the junction with Bank Rd. There's also the New Bus Stand, further east along Mavoor Rd, and the Old Bus Stand, at the G H Rd/M M Ali Rd intersection. There are regular buses to Bangalore, Mangalore, Mysore, Ooty, Madurai, Coimbatore, Pondicherry, Thiruvananthapuram, Alappuzha (Alleppey), Kochi and Kottayam.

The bus to Ooty and Mysore (5½ hours) climbs over the Western Ghats and has spectacular views from the left side.

Train The railway station is south of Ansari Park, about two km from the New Bus Stand on Mavoor Rd. It's 242 km north to Mangalore (4½ to 5½ hours, Rs 57/208 in 2nd/1st class), 190 km south to Ernakulam (five hours, Rs 48/178) and 414 km to Thiruvananthapuram (9½ to 11 hours, Rs 89/335). Heading south-east, there are trains via Palakkad (Palghat) to Coimbatore, Bangalore, Madras and Delhi.

Getting Around

There's no shortage of auto-rickshaws in Kozhikode, and the drivers will use their meters. It's about Rs 5 from the railway station to the bus station or most hotels.

THRISSUR (Trichur)

Population: 75,000
Telephone Area Code: 0487

Famed for its murals and art work, the Hindus-only **Vadakkunathan Kshetram** sits atop a hill in the centre of Thrissur. There are also two impressively large churches: the **Our Lady of Lourdes Cathedral** and the **Puttanpalli Church**. Skip the **zoo**, a typical Third-World horror story, and the amazingly dusty and decrepit **State Museum** in the zoo grounds. However, the **Archaeological Museum**, further along Museum Road, has temple models, stone reliefs, Gandharan pieces and reproductions of some of the Mattancherry Murals. The zoo and museums are closed on Monday.

The annual **Pooram Festival**, held in April/May, is one of the biggest in the south. It includes fireworks, colourful processions and brightly decorated elephants. This festival was first introduced by Sakthan Thampuram, the maharaja of the former state of Kochi.

The Hindus-only **Sri Krishna Temple** at Guruvayoor, 33 km north of Thrissur, is one of the most famous in Kerala. The temple's 40-plus elephants are kept at nearby **Punnathur Kota**.

Information

Thrissur orbits around Vadakkunathan Kshetram. The encircling roads are named Round North, Round East, Round South and Round West. The Tourist Information Centre, across from the Town Hall, has minimal information.

Places to Stay

If there are rooms available, the *Ramanilayam Government Guest House* (☎ 33-2016) is wonderful for Rs 45 a double. It's at the junction of Palace and Museum Rds. Nearby is the KTDC *Yatri Nivas* (☎ 33-2333) on Stadium Rd, which has rooms for Rs 80/100 or Rs 200/250 with air-con.

Chandy's Tourist Home (☎ 21-167) on Railway Station Rd is close to the bus and railway stations. It has rooms for Rs 50/90. Round the corner, on Kuruppam Rd, the

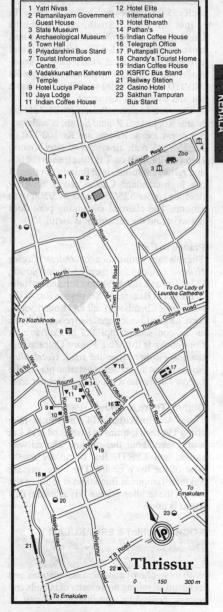

1 Yatri Nivas	12 Hotel Elite
2 Ramanilayam Government	International
Guest House	13 Hotel Bharath
3 State Museum	14 Pathan's
4 Archaeological Museum	15 Indian Coffee House
5 Town Hall	16 Telegraph Office
6 Priyadarshini Bus Stand	17 Puttanpalli Church
7 Tourist Information	18 Chandy's Tourist Home
Centre	19 Indian Coffee House
8 Vadakkunathan Kshetram	20 KSRTC Bus Stand
Temple	21 Railway Station
9 Hotel Luciya Palace	22 Casino Hotel
10 Jaya Lodge	23 Sakthan Tampuran
11 Indian Coffee House	Bus Stand

Thrissur

0   150   300 m

unexciting *Jaya Lodge* (☎ 23-258) has rooms for Rs 35/60; doubles with bathroom are Rs 70.

Just off Round South, on Chembottil Lane, rooms are Rs 70/140 in the large and basic *Pathan's* (☎ 25-623). Across the road is the more upmarket *Hotel Elite International* (☎ 21-033), which has rooms for Rs 140/180 or Rs 350/390 with air-con. It has a bar and an air-con restaurant.

The *Hotel Luciya Palace* (☎ 24-731) on Marar Rd, just off Round South, is undergoing renovations. Rooms are Rs 100/170 or Rs 250/325 with air-con. The tatty *Casino Hotel* (☎ 24-699) on T B Rd, close to the bus and railway stations, is definitely not part of the high-standard Casino chain. Singles/doubles are Rs 325/350 or Rs 475/500 with air-con. The claimed swimming pool does not exist and the restaurant is awful.

Places to Eat

There's an abundance of *Indian Coffee Houses*: you can find them on Round South; PO Rd, near Railway Station Rd; and upstairs in President Bazaar, on Kuruppam Rd. At the junction of Chembottil Lane and Round South, there's a good, basic vegetarian restaurant with an air-con section upstairs in *Pathan's*. A floor above is the *Ming Palace* Chinese restaurant. Further along the road, *Hotel Bharath* is a neat and clean vegetarian place. The *Luciya Palace* has a popular outdoor bar area.

Getting There & Away

Trains to Ernakulam, 74 km south, take about 1½ hours; trains to Kozhikod, 118 km north, take about three hours. The railway station and KSRTC Bus Stand are southwest of the town centre. The large, private Sakthan Tampuran Bus Stand is south of the centre; the smaller, private Priyadarshini Bus Stand is north.

KOCHI (Cochin) & ERNAKULAM

Kochi Population: 582,000
Ernakulam Population: 200,000
Telephone Area Code: 0484

With its wealth of historical associations and its beautiful setting on a cluster of islands and narrow peninsulas, the interesting city of Kochi perfectly reflects the eclecticism of Kerala. Here, you can see the oldest church in India, winding streets crammed with 500-year-old Portuguese houses, cantilevered Chinese fishing nets, a Jewish community whose roots go back to the Diaspora, a 16th-century synagogue, and a palace built by the Portuguese and given to the Raja of Cochin. The palace, which was later renovated by the Dutch, contains some of India's most beautiful murals. Another must-see is a performance of the world-famous Kathakali dance-drama.

The older parts of Fort Cochin and Mattancherry are an unlikely blend of medieval Portugal, Holland and an English country village grafted onto the tropical Malabar Coast – a radical contrast to the bright lights, bustle and big hotels of mainland Ernakulam. The dense population of brightly painted billboards proclaiming the launch of yet another luxury apartment building (some with swimming pools!) confirms what a prosperous town this is.

Kochi is one of India's largest ports and a major naval base. The misty silhouettes of huge merchant ships can be seen anchored off the point of Fort Cochin, waiting for a berth in the docks of Ernakulam or Willingdon Island. This artificial island, created with material dredged up when the harbour was deepened, also provides a site for the airport. All day, ferries scuttle back and forth between the various parts of Kochi. Dolphins can be seen in the harbour.

Orientation

Kochi consists of mainland Ernakulam; the islands of Willingdon, Bolgatty and Gundu in the harbour; Fort Cochin and Mattancherry on the southern peninsula; and Vypeen Island, north of Fort Cochin. All these areas are linked by ferry; bridges also link Ernakulam to Willingdon Island and the Fort Cochin/Mattancherry peninsula. Most hotels and restaurants are in Ernakulam, where you'll also find the main railway and bus stations and the Tourist Reception Centre.

Almost all the historical sites are in Fort Cochin or Mattancherry, but accommodation and restaurant facilities are very limited in these areas. The airport and two of the top hotels are on Willingdon Island.

Information

Tourist Offices The Kerala Tourist Development Corporation's Tourist Reception Centre (☎ 35-3234) on Ernakulam's Shanmugham Rd has limited information but will organise accommodation at the Bolgatty Palace Hotel and arrange conducted harbour cruises. The office is open from 8 am to 7 pm daily. The private enterprise Tourist Desk operates a free service counter at Erna-

kulam's main ferry station, and is open daily from 9 am to 5 pm. The Tourist Desk produces a good map, has tourist literature and books tours. *Hello Cochin* is a handy bimonthly travel information booklet which includes timetables. It's available at bookshops.

The Government of India Tourist Office (ITDC) (☎ 66-8352) is next to the Malabar Hotel on Willingdon Island. The staff here are friendly and helpful, and offer a range of leaflets and maps. There's a Kerala Department of Tourism counter at Kochi Airport during flight hours.

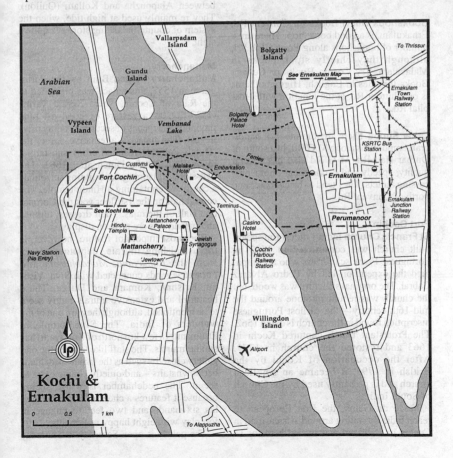

Kochi & Ernakulam

Post & Telecommunications The GPO (including poste restante) is at Fort Cochin, but you can have mail sent to the main post office on Hospital Rd in Ernakulam, as long as it's specifically addressed to that office. STD/ISD phone offices and booths are found all over town.

Visa Extensions Apply at the office of the Commissioner of Police, at the northern end of Shanmugham Rd, Ernakulam. Visa extensions can take up to 10 days to issue and you have to leave your passport at the office during that time.

Bookshops Bhavi Books on Convent Rd, Ernakulam, is a good bookshop. There are a number of bookshops along Press Club Rd, although they chiefly stock books in Malayalam. Try Cosmo Books or Current Books for titles in English. Higginbothams is on Chittoor Rd, at the junction with Hospital Rd.

Other Shops There are a number of handicraft emporiums along M G Rd, just south of Durbar Hall Rd. M G Rd also has several quality, speedy and economical photo processing outlets. They tend to be concentrated north of Convent Rd.

Fort Cochin
St Francis Church India's oldest European-built church was constructed in 1503 by Portuguese Franciscan friars who accompanied the expedition led by Pedro Alvarez Cabral. The original structure was wood, but the church was rebuilt in stone around the mid-16th century – the earliest Portuguese inscription found in the church is dated 1562. The Protestant Dutch captured Kochi in 1663 and restored the church in 1779. After the occupation of Kochi by the British in 1795, it became an Anglican church and is presently used by the Church of South India.

Vasco da Gama, the first European to reach India by sailing around Africa, died in Cochin in 1524 and was buried here for 14 years before his remains were transferred to Lisbon in Portugal. His tombstone can be seen inside the church.

Santa Cruz Basilica This large, impressive church dates from 1902, and has a fantastical pastel-coloured interior.

Chinese Fishing Nets Strung out along the tip of Fort Cochin, opposite Vypeen Island, these cantilevered fishing nets were introduced by traders from the court of Kublai Khan. You can also see them along the backwaters between Kochi and Kottayam, and between Alappuzha and Kollam (Quilon). They're mainly used at high tide, when the system of counterbalancing stones is quite a sight.

Mattancherry
Mattancherry Palace Built by the Portuguese in 1557, this palace was presented to the Raja of Cochin, Veera Kerala Varma (1537-61), as a gesture of goodwill (and probably as a means of securing trading privileges). The palace's alternative name, the 'Dutch Palace', resulted from substantial renovations by the Dutch after 1663. The two-storey, quadrangular building surrounds a courtyard containing a Hindu temple. The central hall on the 1st floor was the Coronation Hall of the rajas. Their dresses, turbans and palanquins are now on display.

The most important feature, however, is the astonishing **murals**, depicting scenes from the *Ramayana, Mahabharata* and Puranic legends connected with Siva, Vishnu, Krishna, Kumara and Durga. These beautiful and extensive murals rarely seem to be mentioned, although they are one of the wonders of India. The Siva temple in Ettumanur (a few km north of Kottayam) has similar murals. The staff like to keep the odd gallery closed – such as the ladies' bedchamber downstairs – and quietly charge extra to see it. The bedchamber is worth seeing because it features a cheerful Krishna using his six hands and two feet to engage in foreplay with eight happy milkmaids.

The palace is open Saturday to Thursday

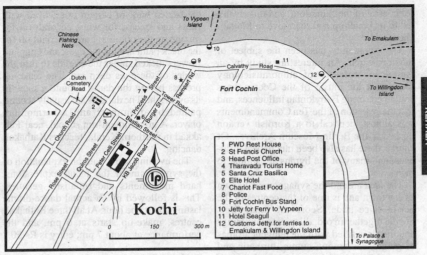

1 PWD Rest House
2 St Francis Church
3 Head Post Office
4 Tharavadu Tourist Home
5 Santa Cruz Basilica
6 Elite Hotel
7 Chariot Fast Food
8 Police
9 Fort Cochin Bus Stand
10 Jetty for Ferry to Vypeen
11 Hotel Seagull
12 Customs Jetty for ferries to
  Ernakulam & Willingdon Island

KERALA

from 10 am to 5 pm; entry is free, but photography is not permitted and there are no postcards or reproductions of the murals on sale. There are B&W photographs of the murals in the Archaeological Survey of India's *Monuments of Kerala* booklet by H Sarkar (1978), and they also appear in *Cochin Murals* by V R Chitra & T N Srinivasan (Cochin, 1940), and *South Indian Paintings* by C Sivaramamurti (New Delhi, 1968).

Jewish Synagogue Constructed in 1568, this is the oldest synagogue in the Commonwealth. The original building was destroyed by shelling during a Portuguese raid in 1662 and was rebuilt two years later when the Dutch took over Kochi. It's an interesting little place, with hand-painted, willow-pattern floor tiles brought from Canton in China in the mid-18th century by one Ezekial Rahabi. He was also responsible for the erection of the clock tower which tops the building.

A synagogue built at Kochangadi in 1344 has since disappeared, although a stone slab from this building, inscribed in Hebrew, can be found on the inner surface of the wall which surrounds the Mattancherry synagogue.

The synagogue is open Sunday to Friday, from 10 am to noon and from 3 to 5 pm. Entry is Rs 1. The synagogue's guardians are friendly and keen to talk about the building and the Jewish community.

This unexpected and isolated Jewish community dates back to the time of St Thomas the Apostle's voyage to India in AD 52. The first Jewish settlement was at Kodungallur (Cranganore), north of Kochi. Like the Syrian Orthodox Christians, the Jews became involved in the trade and commerce of the Malabar Coast. Preserved in the synagogue are a number of copper plates inscribed, in an ancient script, with the grant of the village of Anjuvannam (near Kodungallur) and its revenue to a Jewish merchant, Joseph Rabban, by King Bhaskara Ravi Varman I (962-1020). You may view these plates with the permission of the synagogue guardian.

The concessions given by Ravi Varman I included permission to use a palanquin and parasol – in those days the prerogative of rulers – and so, in effect, sanctioned the creation of a tiny Jewish kingdom. On Rabban's death, his sons fought each other for control of the 'kingdom' and this rivalry led to its break-up and the move to Mattancherry.

The community has been the subject of much research. An interesting study by an American professor of ethnomusicology found that the music of the Cochin Jews contained strong Babylonian influences, and that their version of the Ten Commandments was almost identical to a Kurdish version housed in the Berlin Museum Archives. Of course, there has also been much local influence, and many of the hymns are similar to ragas.

The area around the synagogue is known as Jewtown and is one of the centres of the Kochi spice trade. Scores of small firms huddle together in old, dilapidated buildings and the air is filled with the pungent aromas of ginger, cardamom, cumin, turmeric and cloves. Many Jewish names are visible on business premises and houses, but the community has diminished rapidly since Indian independence and now numbers about 20. There has been no rabbi within living memory, so all the elders are qualified to perform religious ceremonies and marriages. There are many interesting curio shops on the street leading up to the synagogue.

Ernakulam

Kathakali Dancing The origins of India's most spectacular dance-drama go back 500 years to a time when open-air performances were held in temple courtyards or in villages. There are over 100 different arrangements, all of them based on stories from the *Ramayana* and *Mahabharata*. They are designed to continue well into the early hours of the morning. Since most visitors don't have the inclination to stay up all night, the centres which put on the dance in Ernakulam offer shortened versions lasting about 1½ hours.

Kathakali isn't simply another form of dancing – it incorporates elements of yoga and ayurvedic (traditional Indian) medicine. All the props are fashioned from natural materials – powdered minerals and the sap of certain trees for the bright facial make-up;

the beaten bark of certain trees, dyed with fruits and spices, for wigs; coconut oil for mixing up the colours; burnt coconut oil for the black paint around the eyes; and eggplant flowers tucked under the eyelids to turn the whites of the eyes deep red. The make-up process before the dance is quite a show in its own right. The dancers are usually accompanied by drummers and a harmonium player. A government-run school, near Palakkad in northern Kerala, teaches Kathakali dancing.

The evening starts with an explanation of the symbolism of the facial expressions, hand movements and ritualistic gestures. This is followed by an actual dance-drama lasting about one hour. At all three Kathakali centres, make-up starts at 6 pm, and the performance at about 7 pm; entry is Rs 50.

The Indian Performing Arts Centre (☎ 36-6238), in the GCDA shopping centre on the waterfront, has a dull setting, but the performances are competent. There are no signs indicating the centre, so you will have to ask where it is.

Kathakali dancers

The Cochin Cultural Centre (☎ 36-7866), 'Souhardham', Manikath Rd, is south of the centre. The dance is held in a specially constructed air-con theatre designed to resemble a temple courtyard.

The See India Foundation (☎ 36-9471) at Devan Gurukalum, Kalathiparambil Lane, is near the railway station. The rooftop, open-air show features an extraordinary presentation by P K Devan, who explains the dance's history and makes a plucky attempt to simplify Hinduism.

Parishath Thampuram Museum This museum contains 19th-century oil paintings, old coins, sculptures and Moghul paintings, but apart from some interesting temple models, it's nothing special. The museum is housed in an enormous, traditional-style Keralan building (previously Durbar Hall) on Durbar Hall Rd. It's open Tuesday to Sunday from 10 am to 12.30 pm and from 2 to 4.30 pm; entry is free.

Vypeen & Gundu Islands
Ferries shuttle across the narrow strait from Fort Cochin to Vypeen Island. The island boasts a lighthouse at Ochanthuruth (open from 3 to 5 pm daily), good beaches, and the early 16th-century Palliport Fort (open Thursdays). Gundu, the smallest island in the harbour, is close to Vypeen. It has a coir factory where attractive doormats are made out of coconut fibre. Fishers will take you to Gundu from Vypeen.

Around Kochi
The **Hill Palace Museum** is at Tripunithura, 12 km south-east of Ernakulam, en route to Chottanikkara. The hilltop museum houses the collections of the Cochin and Travancore royal families. It's open Tuesday to Sunday from 9 am to 12.30 pm and from 2 to 4.30 pm; entry is Rs 1. Bus No 51 or 58 will take you there.

The **Museum of Kerala History** is at Edapally, 10 km north-east of Ernakulam en route to Aluva (Alwaye). It's open Tuesday to Sunday from 10 am to noon and from 2 to 4 pm; entry is Rs 2. Bus No 22 runs to Edapally.

Organised Tours
The KTDC offers daily conducted boat cruises around Kochi harbour which visit Willingdon Island, Mattancherry Palace, the Jewish Synagogue, Fort Cochin (including St Francis Church), the Chinese fishing nets and Bolgatty Island. The tour departs from the Sealord Boat Jetty, just north of the Tourist Reception Centre, runs from 9 am to 12.30 pm, and costs Rs 40. The KTDC Sunset Cruise from 5.30 to 7 pm costs Rs 25, but is frequently cancelled, so check early in the day to avoid disappointment. Tickets are available from the Tourist Reception Centre and you can board either at the Sealord Boat Jetty, or pick up the tour 20 minutes later at the Malabar Hotel/Tourist Office Jetty on Willingdon Island.

The Tourist Desk by the Ernakulam Jetty operates excellent three-hour village backwater cruises which include bus transport (45 minutes each way) from the jetty car park to the starting point. The trips depart at 9 am and 2 pm and cost Rs 200. They visit coir villages and coconut plantations, and give plenty of opportunity to see how life is lived along the narrow canals. Similar cruises operated by the KTDC depart at 8.30 am and 2.30 pm and cost Rs 300.

Places to Stay
Ernakulam has accommodation in all price brackets. Fort Cochin has a handful of cheap places and one in the mid-range. Bolgatty Island has one unique mid-range place and Willingdon Island has two top-end places.

Places to Stay – bottom end
Fort Cochin The choice is very limited at Fort Cochin, although it's the most romantic place to stay. The peaceful *Tharavadu Tourist Home* (☎ 22-6897) on Quiros St is an airy and spacious traditional house with good views of the surrounding streets from the rooftop area. Doubles with bathroom are Rs 130 or there's an excellent top-floor room for Rs 100, although it involves sharing a bathroom.

On Princess St, the friendly *Elite Hotel* (☎ 22-5733) is a long-term favourite and has rooms for Rs 30/60 or doubles with attached bathroom for Rs 80, 100 and 150. There's an annex to handle overflow, and a popular restaurant downstairs. Nicely situated near the waterfront, the once shabby *PWD Rest House* has reportedly had a change of management and is now better run but still very cheap.

Ernakulam The *Basoto Lodge* (☎ 35-2140) on Press Club Rd is small, simple, friendly and popular, so get there early. Singles cost Rs 30 or Rs 35, while doubles with attached bathroom are Rs 75. Mosquito nets are provided. Turn the corner into Market Rd to find *Deepak Lodge* (☎ 35-3882), which is also good value. Although the rooms are a sickly shade of green, they are large and quiet and cost Rs 25 for singles or Rs 35/70 for singles/doubles with attached bathroom.

Further north on Market Rd, the *Modern Guest House* (☎ 35-2130) has good rooms with attached bathroom for Rs 60/103. Across the road, the *Blue Diamond Hotel* (☎ 35-3221) is at the top of the bottom-end bracket with rooms with attached bathroom from Rs 80/150.

The *Hakoba Hotel* (☎ 35-3933), conveniently located on the busy Shanmughan Rd waterfront, is a good place, although construction has spoilt the views. Rooms with attached bathroom are Rs 65/108, more with air-con, and there's a restaurant, bar and even a (not very reliable) lift.

On Canon Shed Rd, near the ferry jetty, the *Maple Tourist Home* (☎ 35-5156) is good value with ordinary rooms at Rs 75/155, deluxe rooms at Rs 120/161 and air-con doubles at Rs 230. The roof garden overlooks the jetty. The friendly *Bijus Tourist Home* (☎ 36-9881) at the junction of Canon Shed and Market Rds has rooms for Rs 90/160, and air-con doubles for Rs 300. This place is excellent value and even has hot water.

There is a batch of mainly mid-range hotels opposite the Ernakulam Junction Railway Station, but the cheaper *Premier Tourist Home* (☎ 36-8125) has rooms with attached bathroom for only Rs 54/86. Next

to it is the large *Hotel KK International* (☎ 36-6010), which has rooms for Rs 100/160 or Rs 180/250 with air-con. The *Geetha Lodge* (☎ 35-2136) on M G Rd has rooms for Rs 100/120, while the nearby *Anantha Bhavan* (☎ 36-7641) has singles from Rs 52 to Rs 120, doubles from Rs 100 to Rs 170 and air-con doubles for Rs 290.

The KSRTC Bus Stand area is inconvenient for most things in Ernakulam, and the only really cheap place nearby is the dreadful *Ninans Tourist Lodge* (☎ 35-1235) which charges Rs 40/60. The pleasant, friendly *Hotel Luciya* (☎ 35-4433) is not far away and offers much better value at Rs 56/102 or Rs 125/220 with air-con. It has a bar, restaurant, TV lounge and laundry service.

Places to Stay – middle
Fort Cochin The *Hotel Seagull* (☎ 22-8128) on Calvathy Rd is the only mid-range hotel in Fort Cochin. It's right on the waterfront, overlooking the harbour, and was created by converting a number of old houses and warehouses. There are doubles for Rs 165 downstairs, Rs 220 upstairs or Rs 330 with air-con. You can watch ships come and go from the bar and restaurant.

Bolgatty Island Despite being somewhat run-down, the *Bolgatty Palace Hotel* (☎ 35-5003) on Bolgatty Island is spacious and full of character. It was built in 1744 as a Dutch palace, then later became a British Residency. The hotel is now run by the Kerala Tourist Development Corporation. It's set in six hectares of lush, green lawns with a golf course, bar, and a restaurant with enthusiastic staff but very slow service.

The 11 rooms are all different and cost from Rs 300/400 or Rs 500/625 for an air-con cottage. The air-con 'honeymoon' cottages, which are right on the water's edge, cost Rs 750. Considering the harbour views and the pretty gardens, it's ridiculous that some rooms don't have windows. Telephone first or enquire at the Tourist Reception Centre, Shanmugham Rd, otherwise you'll waste a lot of time if the hotel is full. Ferries (Rs 0.40) leave the High Court Jetty in

Ernakulam for Bolgatty Island every 20 minutes from 6 am to 10 pm; at other times, private launches are available.

Ernakulam There are a number of mid-range places opposite the Ernakulam Junction Railway Station, like the glossy new *Metropolitan Hotel* (☎ 36-9931), which is centrally air-conditioned and has rooms for Rs 400/550. Nearby, the atrium-style *Paulson Park Hotel* (☎ 35-4002) has good-value rooms for Rs 110/190 or Rs 240/370 with air-con. The *Hotel Sangeetha* (☎ 36-8736) is a block west on Chittoor Rd. It has singles for between Rs 105 and Rs 135, doubles for between Rs 170 and Rs 200, and air-con rooms for Rs 365. This includes breakfast in the hotel's vegetarian restaurant. Nearby, on Durbar Hall Rd, the well-appointed *Hotel Joyland* (☎ 36-7764) features a rooftop restaurant and has rooms for Rs 300/450 or Rs 375/525 with air-con.

M G Rd has a number of good hotels, like the established *Woodlands Hotel* (☎ 35-1372), a little north of Jos Junction. Rooms here are Rs 175/250 or Rs 300/400 with air-con. All rooms have TV and hot water, and the hotel has a vegetarian restaurant and a roof garden. The three-star *Hotel Excellency* (☎ 37-4001) on Nettipadam Rd, south of Jos Junction, has rooms for Rs 175/225 to Rs 225/250, or Rs 350/400 with air-con. It has good facilities, a restaurant, and even throws in what is described as 'bed tea'.

On Durbar Hall Rd, next to the Indian Airlines office, the *Bharat Tourist Home* (☎ 35-3501) has rooms from Rs 180/230 to Rs 250/300, or from Rs 400/450 to Rs 450/500 with air-con. It has vegetarian and north Indian non-vegetarian restaurants, and a coffee shop.

Places to Stay – top end
Willingdon Island The very well run five-star *Taj Malabar Hotel* (☎ 66-6811) is wonderfully situated at the tip of Willingdon Island, overlooking the harbour. The hotel boasts the full range of facilities, including a swimming pool. Singles/doubles cost from US$70/80, but this is a hotel where the extra

cost of a room with a sea view (from US$80/90) is definitely worth paying. The corner rooms (US$105) offer panoramas of the whole harbour.

The *Casino Hotel* (☎ 66-6821) also has an excellent range of facilities, including a swimming pool. It's much cheaper at US$35/60, but its location is no match for the Taj Malabar.

Ernakulam The centrally air-conditioned *Sealord Hotel* (☎ 35-2682), Shanmugham Rd, is excellent value, although the harbour views have been blocked by the waterfront shopping complex. The pleasantly furnished rooms are Rs 350/450 or Rs 500/700 for deluxe rooms. There's a restaurant with a resident band, a rooftop restaurant (which still has views) and a bar.

The elegant and very spacious *Grand Hotel* (☎ 35-3211) on M G Rd has two restaurants and a 'fully illuminated lawn with fresh air'! The rooms are all air-con and cost Rs 250/300 in the old wing, Rs 350/400 in the new wing. The glossy new *Avenue Regent Hotel* (☎ 37-2660) on M G Rd is centrally air-conditioned and has rooms from US$32/40 to US$37/47.

The *Hotel Abad Plaza* (☎ 36-1636), further north on M G Rd, is a modern, centrally air-conditioned establishment. Rooms here are Rs 500/650 to Rs 600/750. It has restaurants, a coffee shop and a rooftop swimming pool (if it's working). Just off busy M G Rd, the centrally air-conditioned *International Hotel* (☎ 35-3911) has recently been renovated and now has rooms from Rs 490/690 to Rs 650/850. It has restaurants, a bar and a roof garden.

Finally, Ernakulam has a more business-inclined sister hotel to Willingdon Island's Taj Malabar. The *Taj Residency* (☎ 37-1471) is on the waterfront on Marine Drive, offers all mod cons (except a swimming pool), boasts the Harbour View Bar, and charges US$38/65.

Places to Eat
Fort Cochin Eating options in Fort Cochin are severely limited. The *Elite Hotel* on Prin-

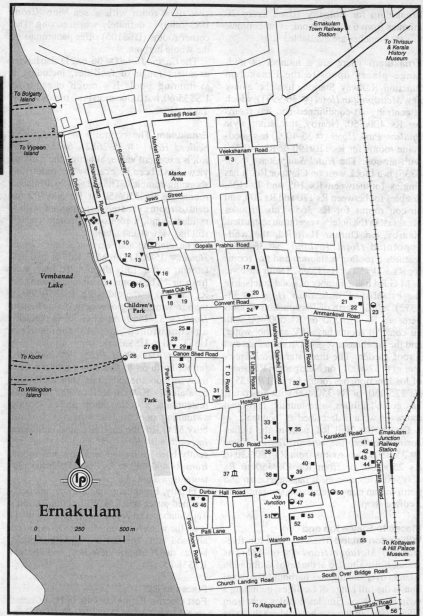

To Bolgatty Island
To Vypeen Island
Marine Drive
Shanmugham Road
Broadway
Banerji Road
Market Road
Veekshanam Road
Market Area
Jews Street
Gopala Prabhu Road
Vembanad Lake
Children's Park
Press Club Rd
Convent Road
Ammankovil Road
Chittoor Road
Canon Shed Road
Park Avenue
P T Usha Road
T D Road
Mahatma Gandhi Road
Hospital Rd
Club Road
Karakkat Road
Durbar Hall Road
Jos Junction
Palli Lane
Warriom Road
Park
Fore Shore Road
Church Landing Road
South Over Bridge Road
Caravara Road
Manikath Road

To Kochi
To Willingdon Island

Emakulam Town Railway Station
To Thrissur & Kerala History Museum

Emakulam Junction Railway Station

To Kottayam & Hill Palace Museum

To Alappuzha

Ernakulam

0   250   500 m

PLACES TO STAY		52	Avenue Regent Hotel	6	GCDA Shopping
		53	Hotel Excellency		Centre (Indian
3	International Hotel				Performing Arts
7	Sealord Hotel	**PLACES TO EAT**			Centre)
8	Blue Diamond Hotel			11	Post Office
9	Modern Guest House	5	Ancient Mariner	15	KTDC Tourist
12	Hakoba Hotel	10	Athul Jyoti		Reception Centre
14	Taj Residency	13	Bharath Coffee House	18	Cosmo Books &
17	Hotel Abad Plaza	16	Caravan Ice Cream		Current Books
19	Basoto Lodge	24	Chariot Restaurant	20	Bhavi Books
21	Hotel Luciya	28	Indian Coffee House	23	KSRTC Bus Station
22	Ninans Tourist Lodge	35	Pandhal	26	Main Jetty
25	Deepak Lodge		Restaurant	27	Tourist Desk
29	Bijus Tourist Home	39	Indian Coffee House	31	Main Post Office
30	Maple Tourist Home	48	Bimbi's & Khyber	32	Higginbothams
33	Grand Hotel		Restaurant	37	Parishath
34	Woodlands	54	Chinese Garden		Thampuram
36	Geetha Lodge		Restaurant		Museum
38	Anantha Bhavan			46	Indian Airlines
40	Hotel Sangeetha	**OTHER**		47	Bus to Fort Cochin
41	Metropolitan			50	Ernakulam South Bus
42	Hotel KK	1	High Court Jetty &		Stand
	International		Ferry to Bolgatty	51	Post Office
43	Paulson Park Hotel		Island	55	See India
44	Premier Tourist Home	2	Vypeen Island Ferry		Foundation
45	Bharat Tourist Home		Jetty	56	Cochin Cultural
49	Hotel Joyland	4	Sealord Boat Jetty		Centre

cess St has fairly basic food, including fish curries for around Rs 20. On the same street, the open-air *Chariot Fast Food* turns out uninspired Indian and Western snacks and light meals, but it's a good place to sip a cold drink and watch the world pass by. The *Hotel Seagull* on Calvetty Rd has a reasonable restaurant and a bar.

Willingdon Island The well-run *Waterfront Cafe* in the Malabar Hotel offers a lunchtime buffet for Rs 170 (plus taxes). The Chinese *Jade Pavilion* and the plush *Rice Boats* restaurants serve excellent seafood. The *Casino Hotel* has a buffet in its gloomy restaurant, but there's a brighter, outdoor seafood restaurant by the pool.

Ernakulam Two *Indian Coffee House* branches, with their quaint waiters in cummerbunds and shabby white uniforms, offer good snacks and breakfasts. One is on Durbar Hall Rd, by Jos Junction; the other is on the corner of Canon Shed Rd and Park Ave, opposite the Main Jetty. They are popular with local people and always busy.

The busy *Bimbi's*, opposite the Jos Junction Indian Coffee House, is a modern, self-serve, fast-food restaurant offering both Indian and Western dishes. An excellent masala dosa costs Rs 9. There's a huge sweet store in the front and the more expensive air-con *Khyber Restaurant* upstairs. *Lotus Cascades/Jaya Cafe,* in the Woodlands Hotel on M G Rd, turns out excellent vegetarian thalis for Rs 24.

The dark, glass front of the relatively expensive *Pandhal Restaurant* on M G Rd hides what could easily be a modern Western chain restaurant. It turns out excellent north Indian food and very competent pizzas and burgers; don't fail to sample a 'sleeping beauty' from the dessert list. The *Chinese Garden Restaurant*, on Warriom Rd, just off M G Rd, is similarly priced. The food is good and the service attentive. There's also a floating restaurant, called the *Ancient Mariner*, on Marine Drive. The *Caravan Ice Cream*, near the Tourist Reception Centre, has good ice cream.

Ernakulam has the usual assortment of 'meals' restaurants. *Athul Jyoti*, on Shanmugham Rd, is a straightforward place with basic vegetarian meals for Rs 11. *The Bharath Coffee House* on Broadway offers similar fare. The *Chariot Restaurant*, with entrances on Convent Rd and Narakathara Rd, has the same menu as the Fort Cochin branch of the same name.

Several hotels have good restaurants, like the 8th-floor *Rooftop Restaurant* in the Sealord Hotel on Shanmugham Rd. It specialises in seafood dishes and has a band playing Western music in the evenings. The classy but reasonably priced *Regency Restaurant* in the Abad Plaza Hotel on M G Rd offers good Indian, Chinese and Western food. The Paulson Park Hotel, near the Ernakulam Junction Railway Station, has the *Moghul Hut* restaurant in its central atrium area. The International Hotel on M G Rd boasts the classy *Restaurant du Coq D'Or*.

Getting There & Away

Hello Cochin and *Jaico Time Table* are handy booklets listing schedules, journey times and air, bus and train fares. They are available from bookshops and newsstands.

Air The Indian Airlines office (☎ 37-0242) is on Durbar Hall Rd, next to the Bharat Tourist Home. Air India (☎ 35-3276) is on M G Rd. East West Airlines (☎ 36-3542), Jet Airways (☎ 36-9423), Modiluft (☎ 37-0015) and NEPC (☎ 36-7720) also fly to Kochi.

Indian Airlines has flights to Bangalore (Rs 1306), Bombay (Rs 2985), Delhi (via Goa, Rs 5694), Goa (Rs 2019), Madras (Rs 1973) and Thiruvananthapuram (Rs 829). Jet and Modiluft also fly to Bombay; East West flies to Bombay direct and via Coimbatore; while NEPC flies to Agatti in the Lakshadweep Islands, Bangalore and Madras via Coimbatore.

Bus The KSRTC Bus Stand (☎ 37-2033) is by the railway line in Ernakulam, between the railway stations. Because the town is in the middle of Kerala, many of the buses leaving Ernakulam started their journey in places north and south of here. Although it's still often possible to get a seat on these buses, you cannot make advance reservations; you simply have to join the scrum when the bus turns up. You can make reservations up to five days in advance for many of the buses which originate in Ernakulam. The timetable is in English as well as Malayalam, and the station staff are usually quite helpful. There are also private bus stands: the Kaloor Stand is north-east of Ernakulam Town Railway Station, and the Ernakulam South Stand is near Ernakulam Junction Railway Station.

The fares and times that follow are for super express buses unless otherwise noted.

Southbound There are two routes to Thiruvananthapuram (221 km): one via Alappuzha and Kollam, and the other via Kottayam. Over 60 KSRTC buses a day take the Alappuzha to Kollam route. Super express buses take 4½ hours to Thiruvananthapuram for Rs 65. It's Rs 54 by superfast or Rs 49 by fast passenger. The intermediate distances, times and fares for super express buses are: Alappuzha (62 km, 1½ hours, Rs 20); Kollam (150 km, three hours, Rs 45), and Kottayam (76 km, 1½ hours, Rs 25). There are also at least two direct buses a day to Kanyakumari (302 km, 8¾ hours, Rs 85).

If you're heading for Fort Cochin rather than Ernakulam, you can get off the bus from Alappuzha just before the bridge which connects Kochi and Willingdon Island. Take a local bus or auto-rickshaw from there into either Mattancherry or Fort Cochin. This saves you a lot of messing about with ferries when you get to Ernakulam.

Eastbound At least four direct buses a day run to Madurai (324 km, 9¼ hours, Rs 85.) For those with phenomenal endurance, there are direct buses to Madras (690 km, 16½ hours, Rs 157).

The Madurai buses pass through Kumily, near the Periyar Wildlife Sanctuary on the Kerala/Tamil Nadu border. In addition, there are three buses direct to Kumily and Thekkady, the centre within the sanctuary (192 km, six hours, Rs 46 by fast passenger bus).

Northbound There are buses every half hour to Thrissur (Trichur) (81 km, two hours, Rs 25) and Kozhikode (219 km, five hours, Rs 50). A couple of buses a day run right up the coast beyond Kozhikode to Kannur (Cannanore), Kasaragod and across the Karnataka state border to Mangalore.

Half a dozen interstate express buses go to Bangalore (565 km, 15 hours, Rs 166) daily. The buses go via Kozhikode, Suthanbatheri (Sultan's Battery) and Mysore.

In addition to the KSRTC state buses, there are a number of private bus companies which have superdeluxe video buses daily to Bangalore, Bombay and Coimbatore. Check out Princy Tours (☎ 35-4712) in the GCDA Complex on Shanmugham Rd, opposite the Sealord Hotel. Others include Indira Travels (☎ 36-0693) and Conti Travels (☎ 35-3080), at the Jos Junction of M G Rd, and Silcon A/C Coach (☎ 36-9596) on Banerji Rd.

Train Ernakulam has two stations, Ernakulam Junction and Ernakulam Town, but the one you're most likely to use is Junction. The booking office at Ernakulam Junction is usually very busy. Note that none of the through trains on the main trunk routes go to the Cochin Harbour Station on Willingdon Island.

Trains run regularly along the coast from Thiruvananthapuram via Kollam and Kottayam to Ernakulam; less frequently on to Thrissur, Kozhikode, Thalasseri and Kasaragod. Two trains daily run right through to Mangalore in Karnataka. The daily *Vanchinad Express* runs between Thiruvananthapuram and Ernakulam in just over four hours, but other services are somewhat slower. Distances, times and fares in 2nd class/1st class on this train include:

Destination	Distance	Time	Fare
Thiruvananthapuram	224 km	4¼ hours	Rs 56/205
Kottayam	63 km	1½ hours	Rs 21/81
Thrissur	72 km	1¾ hours	Rs 23/95
Kozhikode	190 km	4-5 hours	Rs 48/178
Mangalore	411 km	11 hours	Rs 88/330

If you're heading to or from Udhagamandalam (Ooty), there are quite a few expresses which stop at Coimbatore (198 km, six hours, Rs 53/189). There are no direct trains to Goa. The fastest route to Goa is by train to Mangalore and by bus from there – although a railway line to Goa and Bombay is under construction. See the table below for details on major trains departing Ernakulam.

Getting Around

To/From the Airport A bus to the airport costs Rs 1.50. A taxi from Ernakulam to the airport costs Rs 50 to Rs 60; an auto-rickshaw about half that.

Major Trains from Ernakulam

Destination	Train number & name	Departure time	Distance (km)	Duration (hours)	Fare (Rs) (2nd/1st)
Bangalore	6525 *Bangalore Exp*	3.50 pm ET*	637	12.45	155/464
Bombay VT	1082 *Kanyakumari Exp*	12.55 pm EJ	1840	40	284/982
Kozhikode	6349 *Parsuram Exp*	11 am ET	190	4.30	48/178
Madras	6320 *Madras Mail*	6.30 pm ET	697	13	163/492
Mangalore	6029 *Malabar Exp*	11.05 pm ET	414	10.30	113/338
	6349 *Parsuram Exp*	11 am ET		10	
Delhi	2431 *Rajdhani Exp***	12.05 am Sat EJ	2833	40.30	
	2625 *Kerala Exp*	2.40 pm EJ		48	363/1386
Thiruvananthapuram	6303 *Vanchinad Exp*	6 am ET	224	4.15	56/205

* Abbreviation for train station: ET – Ernakulam Town, EJ – Ernakulam Junction
** Air-con only; fare includes meals and drinks

Bus, Auto-Rickshaw & Taxi There are no convenient bus services between Fort Cochin and the Mattancherry Palace/Jewish Synagogue, but it's a pleasant half-hour walk through the busy warehouse area. Auto-rickshaws are available, though the drivers will need persuasion to use the meters – this is tourist territory.

In Ernakulam, auto-rickshaws are the most convenient mode of transport. The trip from the bus or railway stations to the tourist reception centre on Shanmugham Rd should cost about Rs 10 – a bit less on the meter. Flagfall is Rs 4, then Rs 2.60 a km.

Local buses are fairly good and cheap. If you have to get to Fort Cochin after the ferries stop running, catch a bus in Ernakulam on M G Rd, just south of Durbar Hall Rd. The fare is Rs 2.80. Auto-rickshaws will demand at least Rs 50 once the ferries stop.

Taxis charge round-trip fares between the islands, even though you only go in one direction. Ernakulam to Willingdon Island might cost Rs 100 late at night.

Ferry This is the main form of transport between the various parts of Kochi. Nearly all the ferry stops are named, which helps to identify them on the timetable at Main Jetty in Ernakulam. The stop on the east side of Willingdon Island is called Embarkation; the one on the west side, opposite Mattancherry, is Terminus. The main stop at Fort Cochin is known as Customs; the other one (for Vypeen Island) is unnamed.

Getting onto a ferry at Ernakulam can sometimes involve scrambling across several ferries to get to the boat you want. If you have to do this, make sure you get onto the right ferry or you may find yourself going to Vypeen Island instead of Fort Cochin.

Ernakulam to Mattancherry via Willingdon Island (Terminus) and Fort Cochin (Customs). This is the most useful ferry. It runs about 40 times daily from 6.30 am to 10 pm. The fare to Willingdon Island is Rs 1. To Fort Cochin or Mattancherry, the fare is Rs 1.30.

Ernakulam to Vypeen Island via Willingdon Island (Embarkation). Ferries run about 40 times daily from about 6 am to 10 pm. The fare to Vypeen Island is Rs 1. There are also ferries to Vypeen Island (sometimes via Bolgatty Island) from the High Court Jetty on Shanmugham Rd.

Fort Cochin to Willingdon Island Ferries operate between the Customs stop and the Malabar Hotel/Tourist Office Jetty about 30 times daily for Rs 1, but not on Sunday.

Fort Cochin to Vypeen Island Ferries cross this narrow gap virtually nonstop from 6 am until 10 pm; the fare is Rs 0.25. There is also a vehicular ferry every half hour or so.

Hire Boats Motorised boats of various sizes can be hired from the Sealord Jetty or from the small dock adjacent to the Main Jetty in Ernakulam. They're an excellent way of exploring Kochi harbour at your leisure and without the crowds, but you'll need to haggle over the cost of a boat, which starts at around Rs 300 an hour. Rowboats offer to shuttle between Willingdon Island and Fort Cochin or Mattancherry for about Rs 40.

KOTTAYAM

Population: 166,000
Telephone Area Code: 0481

Kottayam was a focus for the Syrian Christians of Kerala. Today, it's a centre for rubber production. There are direct buses from here to Periyar Wildlife Sanctuary, and ferries to Alappuzha, so you may well find yourself passing through. The backwater trip to Alappuzha is a good alternative to the Alappuzha-Kollam trip.

Information

There's a private bus stand in the town centre, but the railway station (two km from the city centre), ferry jetty and KSRTC Bus Stand are all some distance away. The

Tourist Information Centre has no information.

Temples & Churches

The **Thirunakkara Siva Temple** in the centre of town is only open to Hindus. About three km north-west of the centre are two interesting Syrian Christian churches. **Cheriapally**, St Mary's Orthodox Church or the 'small' church, has an elegant façade spoilt by tacked-on entrance porches. The interior is notable for the 400-year-old vegetable dye paintings on the walls and ceiling.

Vallyapally, St Mary's Church or the 'big' church, is only 100 metres away, and is actually smaller than its neighbour. The church was built in 1550 and the altar is flanked by stone crosses, one with a Pahlavi Persian inscription. The cross on the left is thought to be original but the one on the right is a copy. The church's guest book goes back to 1899, and contains a comment from that time worrying that the many tourists were putting a strain on the church. Back then, 'many' seemed to mean half a dozen a year. Now it's one every few days. Haile Selassie of Ethiopia dropped by in 1956.

Places to Stay

Kaycees Lodge (☎ 56-3691) is centrally located on YMCA Rd, and has good rooms with attached bathroom for Rs 60/99. *The KTDC Hotel Aiswarya* (☎ 61-250) is also close to the centre, just off Temple Rd. Rooms are Rs 100/150 or Rs 150/200; Rs 300/350 with air-con. It suffers the usual catalogue of broken fittings and missing light bulbs but the adjacent temple is surprisingly unobtrusive.

The *Hotel Ambassador* (☎ 56-3293) is less conveniently located on K K Rd. Keep a sharp lookout because it's set back from the road and it's easy to miss the driveway. Singles/doubles are Rs 75/125; air-con double are Rs 150. Further east along K K Rd is the pleasant *Homestead Hotel* (☎ 56-

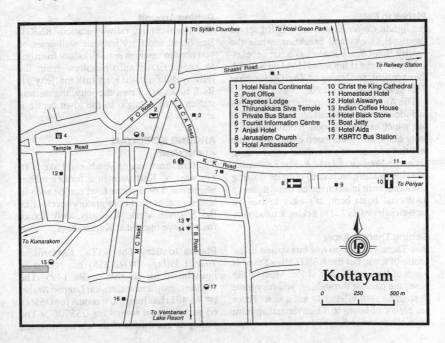

To Syrian Churches / To Hotel Green Park / To Railway Station
Shastri Road
To Kumarakom
To Vembanad Lake Resort
To Periyar

Kottayam

0   250   500 m

1 Hotel Nisha Continental
2 Post Office
3 Kaycees Lodge
4 Thirunakkara Siva Temple
5 Private Bus Stand
6 Tourist Information Centre
7 Anjali Hotel
8 Jerusalem Church
9 Hotel Ambassador
10 Christ the King Cathedral
11 Homestead Hotel
12 Hotel Aiswarya
13 Indian Coffee House
14 Hotel Black Stone
15 Boat Jetty
16 Hotel Aida
17 KSRTC Bus Station

P O Road
YMCA Road
Temple Road
K K Road
M C Road
T B Road

0467) which has rooms for Rs 80/125 or Rs 300 for an air-con double.

The *Hotel Nisha Continental* (☎ 56-3984) on Shastri Rd and the similar standard *Hotel Aida* (☎ 56-8391) on M C Rd have rooms from Rs 150/250. Continuing from the Nisha Continental towards the railway station, the well-kept *Hotel Green Park* (☎ 56-3331), on Kurian Uthup Rd, has a bar and several restaurants – including one outside on the lawn. Singles/doubles are Rs 200/250 or Rs 300/350 with air-con.

Top of the line is the centrally air-conditioned *Anjali Hotel* (☎ 56-3661), part of the excellent local Casino chain. It's near the town centre, on K K Rd. Singles cost between Rs 340 and Rs 570; doubles between Rs 570 and Rs 690. It has a bar, a coffee shop and several restaurants. The *Vembanad Lake Resort* (☎ 56-4866), two km south of the town centre, has cottages in a pleasant lakeside setting for Rs 250 or Rs 375 with air-con.

Places to Eat

An *Indian Coffee House* on T B Rd serves the usual snacks and breakfast, while the nearby *Hotel Black Stone* has basic vegetarian food. At the Homestead Hotel on K K Rd, the excellent, partly air-con *Thali Restaurant* does good thalis for Rs 20.

The Anjali Hotel's selection of restaurants includes the very efficient *Main Street* coffee bar, which has superb food. It makes a pleasantly quiet, air-conditioned escape from the realities of India. It's worth an excursion to eat at the *Vembanad Lake Resort's* romantic lakeside evening barbecue, or in its floating restaurant built in a converted *kettuvallam* (a traditional boat) boat. It's easy to hail an auto-rickshaw (Rs 15) to get back into town.

Getting There & Away

Bus There's a busy private bus station in the centre of town, but the KSRTC Bus Stand is south of the centre, on T B Rd. Most of the buses are passing through, so you may have to sharpen your elbows to get a seat. There are plenty of buses to Thiruvananthapuram via Kollam and to Kochi. It takes about four

hours and costs Rs 22.50 to reach Periyar Wildlife Sanctuary. Seven express buses daily come through from Ernakulam and either terminate at Thekkady, in the sanctuary, or continue to Madurai, a further three hours away.

Train Kottayam is well served by express trains running between Thiruvananthapuram and Ernakulam: Kollam (100 km, Rs 27/124), Thiruvananthapuram (165 km, Rs 43/159) and Ernakulam (65 km, Rs 21/81).

Boat The ferry jetty, on a stretch of canal almost choked with weed, is about a km from the town centre. Eight boats daily make the 2½-hour trip to Alappuzha for about Rs 10. This interesting trip is good if you don't have the time or the inclination for the longer one between Kollam and Alappuzha. You can charter your own boat for Rs 400 to Rs 500, although it's easier to do this from Alappuzha.

Getting Around

The town centre, railway station, KSRTC Bus Stand and ferry jetty are well apart, so you need to catch an auto-rickshaw from one to another. An auto-rickshaw from the railway station to the ferry (ask for 'jetty') is Rs 8 to Rs 10. From the jetty, the railway station or bus station to the town centre is about Rs 5.

AROUND KOTTAYAM
Kumarakom

The bird sanctuary of Vembanad Lake is 16 km west of Kottayam in a former rubber plantation. Local water fowl can be seen in abundance, as well as migratory species like the Siberian stork. Recently, two luxury resorts have opened at Kumarakom.

Places to Stay The KTDC *Kumarakom Tourist Village* (☎ 92-258) has rooms in houseboats for Rs 995 to Rs 1495. The Casino Group's new *Coconut Lagoon Resort* (☎ 92-491) has bungalow rooms for US$60/65 and mansion rooms for US$70/75. The setting is beautiful and there's a swimming pool. The small but luxurious *Taj Garden Retreat* (☎ 92-377) is similarly priced. Buses run to Kumarakom very regularly from Kottayam. The Coconut Lagoon Resort can be reached by boat from near Kottayam, from Thanneermukkom (50 km from Kochi) or all the way from Alappuzha.

Ettumanur

The Siva temple at Ettumanur, 12 km north of Kottayam, is noted for its superb wood carvings and murals. The murals are similar in style to those at Mattancherry Palace in Kochi.

Vijnana Kala Vedi Centre

The Vijnana Kala Vedi Centre at Aranmula, a village 12 km from Changanassery (Changanacherry), offers courses studying Indian arts under expert supervision in a village setting. Main subjects include: Kathakali, Mohiniattam and Bharata Natyam (of Tamil Nadu) dancing, Karnatic vocal music, percussion instruments, wood-carving, mural painting, Keralan cooking, languages (Hindi, Malayalam, Sanskrit), *kaulams* (auspicious decorations), Kalaripayat (Keralan martial art), ayurvedic medicine, mythology, astrology and religion.

You can put your own course together and stay as long as you like, though they prefer people who will stay a minimum of one month. Fees, which include full board and lodging and two subjects of study, start at around US$200 a week – less for longer stays. For further details, contact Louba Schild (Director), Vijnana Kala Vedi Centre, Tarayil Mukku Junction, Aranmula 689533, Kerala. Changanassery is just south of Kottayam and makes an interesting backwater trip from Alappuzha.

PERIYAR WILDLIFE SANCTUARY

Telephone Area Code: 04869

If you go to Periyar hoping to see tigers, you're almost certain to be disappointed. The great cats require an enormous amount of territory on which to lead their solitary lives and it's estimated the 777-sq-km sanctuary has about 35 tigers and leopards. If, on the

other hand, you treat Periyar as a pleasant escape from the rigours of Indian travel, a nice place to cruise on the lake, and an opportunity to see some wildlife and enjoy a jungle walk, then you will probably find a visit well worthwhile. The park encompasses a 26-sq-km artificial lake, created by the British in 1895 to provide water to Madurai, and spreads into Tamil Nadu. It is home to bison, antelopes, sambars, wild boars, monkeys, langurs, a wide variety of birds, and some 750 elephants.

Orientation & Information

Kumily is the junction town straddling the Kerala/Tamil Nadu border just north of the park boundary. It's a busy place, full of spice shops, located about four km from Thekkady. Thekkady is the centre inside the park where the KTDC hotels and the boat jetty are located. When people refer to the sanctuary, they tend to use Kumily, Thekkady and Periyar synonymously, which can be confusing. The name 'Periyar' is used to refer to the whole park.

There's a small tourist office in Kumily and a Wildlife Information Centre near the boat jetty in Thekkady. It's advisable to bring warm clothes and waterproof clothing to Periyar. Entry to the park costs Rs 50 for foreigners and is valid for five days.

Visiting the Park

Boat trips on the lake are the standard way of seeing the sanctuary, but spend one day at Periyar and take a midday boat trip and you're unlikely to see anything. 'As soon as a shy animal sticks its head up', reported one visitor, 'all aboard shout and scream until it goes again'. The standard two-hour boat trips cost Rs 10. The first (7 am) and last (4 pm) departures offer the best wildlife spotting prospects. It's better to get a small group together (the smaller the better) and charter your own boat. They're available in a variety of sizes from Rs 200 for a 12-person boat.

Jungle walks can also be interesting. A daily three-hour walk departs early in the morning and costs Rs 10 per person. Guides can also be arranged from the Wildlife Information Centre for walks further into the park. Curiously, they don't promote this activity, so you must ask insistently about it. Visitors are not allowed to walk in the park without an accompanying guide. Some of the guides are very knowledgeable and they're certainly cautious in areas where animals may be present. Turning a blind corner and stumbling into a wild elephant is not a wise idea.

The third way to see wildlife is to spend a night in one of the observation towers, although these are often booked out weeks in advance. This costs Rs 50 a night plus the boat drop-off charge and you must bring your own food supplies. Elephant rides (Rs 30 for two people for 30 minutes) are for fun, not for serious wildlife viewing.

The best time to visit the sanctuary is between September and May. The hot season (February to May) may be less comfortable but will offer more wildlife sightings because in the hot season other water sources dry up and the wildlife is forced to come down to the lakeside. Weekends are best avoided because of noisy day-trippers. What you see is a matter of luck, but even those elusive tigers do show themselves occasionally. One guide reported that in the three years he had spent at the park, he had seen tigers only twice: on one occasion, he saw a tiger swimming in the lake close to the Lake Palace Hotel.

Mangaladevi Temple
This temple, 13 km from Kumily, is just a jumble of ruins but the views are magnificent. At present, the road to the temple is closed. If it reopens, it's possible to get there by rented jeep or by bicycle – although it's uphill all the way from Kumily. By jeep from

Kumily, count on a three to four-hour round trip, including a lunch stop.

Places to Stay & Eat
Outside the Sanctuary Kumily is a one-street town, but it has accommodation ranging from dirt cheap to luxurious. Although it's four km from the lake, you can catch the semi-regular bus, hire a bicycle or set off on foot – it's a pleasant, shady walk into the park.

The *Mukumkal Tourist Home* (☎ 22-070) is close to the bus station. Avoid the back rooms, which can be noisy if the hotel's generator is switched on. Rooms with attached bathroom are Rs 55/110; aircon doubles are Rs 350. The hotel's *Little Chef Restaurant* is a reasonable place to eat.

The big *Lake Queen Tourist Home* (☎ 22-086), next to the Kottayam road junction, has 54 rooms from Rs 49 to Rs 59 for singles and Rs 97 for doubles. The *Lakeland Restaurant* is downstairs. Along the road to the park is the *Rolex Lodge* (☎ 22-081), which has basic doubles with bathroom for Rs 100. Close by, the *Woodlands Hotel* (☎ 22-077) is a bit gloomy but it's certainly cheap at Rs 50 a double. Continuing towards the park entrance, the *Karthika Tourist Home* (☎ 22-146) has doubles with bath for Rs 100 and a vegetarian restaurant.

Next along the road is the very upmarket *Spice Village* (☎ 22-315), which is part of the Casino Group. This well-designed, new resort has attractive cottages in a pleasant garden with a swimming pool for US$60/65. The *Hotel Ambadi* (☎ 22-192) has cottages for Rs 250 or Rs 300 and rooms for Rs 500. It also has quite a good restaurant. A final

---

Tigers & Trucks
The widely hailed Project Tiger aims to make life safe for the threatened cats by establishing core areas in wildlife sanctuaries where human encroachment is minimised. Just how many teeth this legislation has was revealed in 1994 when the Forest & Wildlife Department decided that timber trucks could take a short cut through the core area of the Periyar Wildlife Sanctuary. ■

possibility is the *Leelapankaj* (☎ 22-299), right by the sanctuary entrance gate, but at Rs 500 for a double it's way overpriced.

Just outside the sanctuary entrance, the outdoor *Coffee Inn* has an interesting selection of music and good travellers' food (including home-made brown bread). In the tradition of travellers' restaurants in India, the food takes a long time to arrive.

Inside the Sanctuary The KTDC has three hotels in the park. It's a good idea to make advance reservations, particularly for weekend visits. This can be done at any KTDC office or hotel. *Periyar House* (☎ 22-026), the cheapest of the three, is very popular. Rooms are Rs 300/350, but they also have rooms for Rs 75/135 without attached bathroom which they seem to keep quiet about. The restaurant serves good vegetarian and non-vegetarian food at reasonable prices.

Aranya Nivas (☎ 22-023) has very pleasant rooms for Rs 895/995 and air-con suites for Rs 1075/1995. These prices drop in the low season. There's a bar, garden area, TV lounge, postal and banking facilities and a small handicrafts shop. Food in the restaurant is excellent, and most nights there's a Rs 150 buffet. Guests at the Aranya Nivas are entitled to a free morning and afternoon boat trip.

The *Lake Palace* (☎ 22-023) is well away from the noise of day-trippers. Guests are transferred to the hotel by boat and should arrive at the Thekkady boat jetty by 4 pm for the final trip of the day back to the hotel. Rooms in the palace, at one time the maharaja's game lodge, cost Rs 1425/2875 a night, including all meals. If you can afford it, this is a delightful place to stay and you can actually see animals from your room. With a guide, it's possible to walk to the Lake Palace from the boat jetty in about an hour.

There are *Rest Houses* in the sanctuary at Manakavala (eight km from Kumily), Mullakkudy (39 km) and Edappalayam (five km). Not all of them may be open for visitors but you can find out and book at the Wildlife Information Centre. The rest houses cost Rs

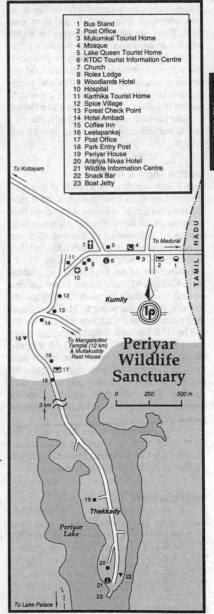

1 Bus Stand
2 Post Office
3 Mukumkal Tourist Home
4 Mosque
5 Lake Queen Tourist Home
6 KTDC Tourist Information Centre
7 Church
8 Rolex Lodge
9 Woodlands Hotel
10 Hospital
11 Karthika Tourist Home
12 Spice Village
13 Forest Check Point
14 Hotel Ambadi
15 Coffee Inn
16 Leelapankaj
17 Post Office
18 Park Entry Post
19 Periyar House
20 Aranya Nivas Hotel
21 Wildlife Information Centre
22 Snack Bar
23 Boat Jetty

Periyar Wildlife Sanctuary

200/300 and have a keeper who will cook for you, although you must bring your own food. There are also watchtowers for Rs 50, which can be booked at the Wildlife Information Centre. Although they're primitive, and you must provide all your own food and bedding, you stand the best chance of seeing animals if you rent one. One of the watchtowers is a short stroll from the Lake Palace.

Near the boat jetty in Thekkady, there's a snack bar offering basic food, snacks and drinks.

Getting There & Away

Bus The bus station in Kumily is just a bit of spare land at the eastern edge of town, near the state border. It's chaotic when more than three buses are there at once. All buses originating or terminating at Periyar start and finish at Aranya Nivas in Thekkady, but they also stop at the Kumily Bus Station.

Buses operate on the Ernakulam, Kottayam, Kumily, Madurai route. There are four express buses daily between Ernakulam and Kumily, three continuing to Madurai. Buses to Ernakulam take six hours and cost Rs 46.

The 110-km trip from Kottayam takes about four hours and costs Rs 22.50. Regular buses go every half hour. The buses pass through rubber plantations and villages with pastel-coloured churches and rocket-like shrines. The road then climbs steadily through a mass of tea, coffee and cardamon plantations.

At least two direct buses daily make the eight-hour trip to Thiruvananthapuram. Another goes to Kovalam (nine hours), and another to Kodaikanal (6½ hours).

Getting Around

A bus operates between Kumily and Thekaddy every 15 minutes for Rs 2 (or at least it's supposed to). An auto-rickshaw costs Rs 25. The KTDC Periyar House and Aranya Nivas both have bicycles for rent costing Rs 25 for half a day – although at one stage, all 10 Aranya Nivas bicycles were out of action waiting for 'a man to come from Kumily to pump up the tyres'!

OTHER SANCTUARIES
Thattekkad Bird Sanctuary

This sanctuary is 20 km from Kothamangalam, on the Ernakulam to Munnar road. It's home to Malabar grey hornbills, woodpeckers, parakeets, and rarer species like the Sri Lankan frogmouth and rose-billed roller. Boat cruises are available from Boothathankettu to Thattekkad. The best time to visit is from 5 to 6 am. There's an *Inspection Bungalow* at Boothathankettu, as well as a few mid-range hotels in Kothamangalam.

Parambikulam Wildlife Sanctuary

The Parambikulam Wildlife Sanctuary, 48 km south of Palakkad, stretches around the Parambikulam, Thunakadavu and Peruvaripallam dams, and covers an area of 285 sq km adjacent to the Anamalai Wildlife Sanctuary in Tamil Nadu. It's home to elephants, bison, gaur, sloth bears, wild boars, sambars, chital, crocodiles and a few tigers and panthers. The sanctuary is open all year, but is best avoided from June to August due to the monsoon.

The sanctuary headquarters are at Thunakadavu, where the Forestry Department has an *Inspection Bungalow* and a tree-top hut (book through the Range Officer). At Parambikulam, there's a *PWD Rest House* and a Tamil Nadu government *Inspection Bungalow* (book through the Junior Engineer, Tamil Nadu PWD, Parambikulam). There are also two watchtowers: one at Anappadi (eight km from Thunakadavu) and another at Zungam (five km from Thunakadavu).

The best access to the sanctuary is by bus from Pollachi (40 km from Coimbatore and 49 km from Palakkad). There are four buses in either direction between Pollachi and Parambikulam daily. The trip takes two hours. Boat cruises operate from Parambikulam and rowboats can be hired at Thunakadavu.

ALAPPUZHA (Alleppey)

Population: 265,000
Telephone Area Code: 0477

Like Kollam, this is a pleasant, easy-going market town surrounded by coconut plantations and built on the canals which service the coir industry of the backwaters. There's precious little to see for most of the year, but the annual Nehru Cup snakeboat race is an event not to be missed. Any other day of the year, the backwater trip to or from Kollam is the only reason to pass through.

Orientation & Information

The bus stand and boat jetty are conveniently close to each other, and within easy walking distance of most of the cheap hotels. Alappuzha's water is notoriously unhealthy. Even if you drink tap water in other places, it's advisable to give Alappuzha's water a miss.

Nehru Cup Snakeboat Race

This famous regatta takes place on the second Saturday of August each year. It's held in the lake to the east of the town. Scores of long, low-slung dugouts with highly decorated sterns and crewed by up to 100 rowers shaded by gleaming silk umbrellas compete for the cup, watched from the banks by thousands of spectators. The annual event celebrates the seafaring and martial traditions of ancient Kerala.

Tickets for the race are available on the day from numerous ticket stands on the way to the lake where the race is held. This entitles you to a seat on the bamboo terraces which are erected for the occasion and which give an excellent view of the lake. The only

KERALA

PLACES TO STAY

1	Sheeba Lodge
2	Komala Hotel
3	Karthika Tourist Home
7	Kuttanad Tourist Home
8	Sree Krishna Bhavan Lodge
11	Kadambari Tourist Home
21	St George's Lodging
24	Hotel Raiban
25	Hotel Annapoorna

PLACES TO EAT

15	Hotel Aryas
16	Indian Coffee House
17	Rajas Hotel
18	Kream Korner
19	Sree Durga Bhavan Restaurant
26	Indian Coffee House

OTHER

4	Boat Jetty
5	Tourist Information Centre
6	Bus Terminal
9	Penguin Tourist Boat Service
10	State Bank of India
12	Temple
13	Post Office
14	Temple
20	Temple
22	Indian Overseas Bank
23	Telegraph Office
27	Hospital

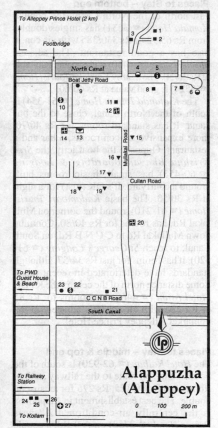

Alappuzha (Alleppey)

drawback is that shortly into the race the terraces are invaded by local (ticketless) youths seeking a better view. So far, the scaffolding has not collapsed, but one day it just might! If you're not keen on testing fate, there are pricier tickets for the Rose Pavilion built in the middle of the lake.

Take food and drink to the race because there's little available on the lake shore. An umbrella is another necessity because the race takes place during the monsoon and the weather can alternate between driving rain and blistering sunshine.

Places to Stay – bottom end

Just north of the North Canal, the popular *Komala Hotel* (☎ 3631) has singles/doubles from Rs 65/92 or Rs 330/385 with air-con. It also has a good restaurant. The adjacent *Sheeba Lodge* (☎ 4460) is cheap and habitable at Rs 30/50. The nearby *Karthika Tourist Home* (☎ 5524) is good value at Rs 40/60.

The *Kuttanad Tourist Home* (☎ 61-354) is south of the North Canal, close to the bus stand. It has standard rooms for Rs 40/70, more expensive air-con rooms, a bar and a restaurant. Opposite the boat jetty, the *Sree Krishna Bhavan Boarding & Lodging* (☎ 60-453) has small, basic rooms built around a courtyard. It's OK (just) for a night at Rs 30/50. The basic *Kadambari Tourist Home* (☎ 61-210), round the corner on Mullakal Rd, has rooms for Rs 40/80. Continue down Mullakal Rd to C C N B Rd, on South Canal, to reach *St George's Lodging* (☎ 61-620). It has rooms for just Rs 34/57, although standards have deteriorated in recent years. Some distance north of the centre, the KTDC *Motel Aram* (☎ 4460) has rooms for Rs 85 or Rs 220 with air-con. It's adjacent to the upmarket Alleppey Prince Hotel.

Places to Stay – middle & top end

The *Hotel Raiban* (☎ 62-930) is south of the South Canal, en route to the railway station. Rooms are Rs 80/125; Rs 275 for an air-con double. The best establishment in Alappuzha is the centrally air-conditioned *Alleppey Prince Hotel* (☎ 3752) on A S Rd, a couple of km north of the centre. It has a bar, an excellent restaurant and a very inviting swimming pool. Rooms in this pleasant hotel cost Rs 400/500. The place is popular, so it's wise to book ahead. An auto-rickshaw from the jetty or town centre should cost Rs 12 to Rs 15; a taxi Rs 50.

Places to Eat

There's an *Indian Coffee House* branch on Mullakal Rd in the town centre, and another, less well kept, branch south of the South Canal, opposite the hospital. The *Hotel Aryas* on Mullakal Rd serves good, straightforward vegetarian meals for Rs 10. *Hotel Komala, Hotel Raiban*, and *Hotel Annapoorna* all have restaurants.

On Cullan Rd, the *Rajas Hotel* is a reasonably priced non-vegetarian restaurant. Across the road, *Sree Durga Bhavan* and the *Kream Korner* are basic, hole-in-the-wall restaurants.

The town's top of the line hotel, the Alleppey Prince, also has the best restaurant – the *Vembanad Restaurant*. It's bright, cheerful and air-conditioned, and serves excellent food.

Getting There & Away

Bus Buses operate frequently on the Thiruvananthapuram, Kollam, Alappuzha, Ernakulam route. From Thiruvananthapuram, it's about 3¼ hours and Rs 45 to Alappuzha by super express bus. It takes 1¾ hours and costs Rs 20 to reach Ernakulam from Alappuzha.

Train The railway station is about four km south of the town centre, close to the seafront. There is a new broad-gauge line which runs up the coast to Ernakulam. The 57-km journey takes one hour at a cost of Rs 20/81 in 2nd/1st class. There are lots of trains to Kayankulam for Rs 16/68.

Boat See the Backwaters section for general information on this fascinating means of travel. Alappuzha is the best starting point to explore the backwaters, and there are options

KERALA

ranging from cheap (public ferries) through middle-range (tourist boats) to expensive (charters).

Although the public ferry service between Alappuzha and Kollam has not been operating for some time, due to a canal blockage at the Kollam end, there are still regular services to Kottayam (about seven a day, 2½ to three hours, Rs 5) and Changanassery (five a day, three hours, Rs 5.50). Changanassery is on the road and railway line, 18 km south of Kottayam, 78 km north of Kollam.

See the Backwaters section for information on the ATDC and DTPC tourist boats to Kollam. The ATDC office (☎ 3462) is at the Karthika Tourist Home, while the DTPC can be found at the Tourist Information Centre.

Boats of various sizes can be privately chartered for short or long trips. The baby-blue tourist boats are moored across the North Canal from the boat jetty. Go directly to the boats if you don't want to deal through an intermediary tout. A one-way trip to Kottayam costs about Rs 450. Alternatively, there are boat operator like the efficient Penguin Tourist Boat Service (☎ 61-522) on Boat Jetty Rd. It has a long list of suggested backwater trips from Alappuzha. Vembanad Tourist Services (☎ 60-395) and the District Tourist Promotion Council (☎ 62-308) also have boats for hire.

THE BACKWATERS

Fringing the coast of Kerala and winding far inland is a complex network of lagoons, lakes, rivers and canals. These backwaters are both the basis of a distinct lifestyle and a fascinating thoroughfare. Travelling by boat along the backwaters is one of the highlights of a visit to Kerala. The boats cross shallow, palm-fringed lakes studded with cantilevered Chinese fishing nets, and travel along narrow, shady canals where coir (coconut fibre), copra (dried coconut meat) and cashews are loaded onto boats.

Stops are made at small settlements where people live on narrow spits of land only a few metres wide. Though practically surrounded by water, they still manage to keep cows,

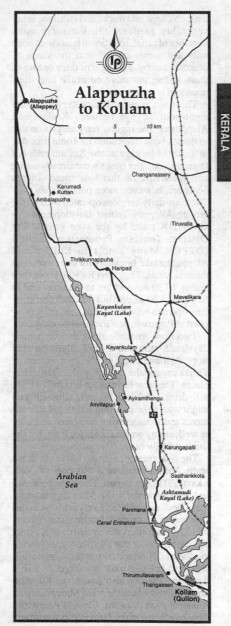

Alappuzha to Kollam

pigs, chickens and ducks and cultivate small vegetable gardens. On the more open stretches of canal, traditional boats with huge sails and prows carved into the shape of dragons drift by. The sight of three or four of these sailing towards you in the late afternoon sun is unforgettable.

The most popular backwater trip is the eight-hour voyage between Kollam and Alappuzha. The regular ferry service on this route has been suspended for some time due to a canal blockage at the Kollam end, but faster and cheaper buses were already eating into the traffic on this long route. Tourist boats are, however, more popular than ever. There are daily services operated by both the private Alleppey Tourist Development Co-Op (ATDC) and by the state government District Tourism Promotion Council (DTPC). Many hotels in Kollam and Alappuzha take bookings for one or other of these services. They cost Rs 100, leave each end at 10.30 am and get to the other end at 6.30 pm. A 30-minute bus ride, included in the fare, operates between Kollam and the starting point at Panmana, past the canal blockage.

Two stops are made along the way, a midday lunch stop and a brief afternoon chai stop. Ayiramthengu or the coir village of Thrikkunnappuha are popular stopping places. The crew have an ice box full of fruit, soft drinks and beer to sell, although you might want to bring along additional refreshments and snacks. Bring sunscreen and a hat as well; sitting on the roof is pleasant, but the sun can really burn.

The boat pauses to drop visitors off at the **Mata Amritanandamayi Mission** (☎ Vallickavu 78) at Amritapuri. This is the residence and headquarters of Sri Sri Mata Amritanandamayi Devi, one of India's very few (but in this case very much revered) female gurus. Visitors should dress conservatively and there is a strict code of behaviour that all visitors are expected to adhere to. Food and accommodation is available here but you must not forget to give a donation. The trip also passes the **Kumarakody Temple** where the noted Malayalam poet Kumaran Asan drowned. Close to Alappuzha, there's a glimpse of the 11th-century **Karumadi**

Kuttan Buddha image close to the canal bank.

Most passengers on the eight-hour Kollam to Alappuzha run will be Western travellers. If you want the local experience, or you simply want a shorter trip, there are still State Water Transport boats from Alappuzha to Kottayam and Changanassery. The two to three-hour trip to Kottayam crosses the Vembanand Lake and then runs along a fascinating canal, making an interesting contrast to the longer trip. See the Alappuzha and Kottayam sections for more information on the public ferries.

An alternative, more expensive option is to charter your own boat. This is easiest from Alappuzha, where there are a great number of boats available. Between a group of people, this can be a quite economical proposition and allows you to make stops and plan your own itinerary – an option not available on the public ferries or tourist boats.

Although the backwaters have become an important tourist attraction, they are also under severe threat from population growth and industrial and agricultural development. Kerala has 29 major lakes on the backwater system, seven of which drain to the sea. It's estimated that the area of these lakes has fallen from 440 sq km in 1968 to less than 350 sq km today due to legal and illegal land reclamation projects and urban development. The vast Vembanad Lake has dropped from 230 to 179 sq km. The modern backwaters only comprise one third their mid-19th century levels. Ecological damage has included pollution, the extinction of mangroves, crocodiles and migratory fish and the destruction of oyster beds. Many migratory birds no longer visit the backwaters and destructive fishing, using dynamite, poison and very fine nets, has also caused great damage. To the casual eye, the most visible danger is the unhindered spread of water hyacinth (African moss or Nile cabbage) which clogs many stretches of canal and causes great difficulties for the boat operators.

KOLLAM (Quilon)

Population: 362,000
Telephone Area Code: 0474

Nestled among coconut palms and cashew tree plantations on the edge of Ashtamudi Lake, Kollam is a typical small Keralan market town, with old wooden houses whose red-tiled roofs overhang winding streets. It's also the southern gateway to the backwaters of Kerala.

The Malayalam era is calculated from the founding of Kollam in the 9th century. The town's later history is interwoven with the Portuguese, Dutch and English rivalry for control of the Indian Ocean trade routes and the commodities grown in this part of the subcontinent.

Information

Kollam is still often referred to as Quilon, pronounced 'koy-lon'. There are tourist office kiosks at the railway station and the KSRTC Bus Stand, open Monday to Saturday from 9 am to 5.30 pm. Chani Books is in the Bishop Jerome Nagar shopping centre.

Things to See

Apart from the extraordinary **Shrine of Our Lady of Velamkanni** near the KSRTC Bus Stand and Chinese fishing nets on **Ashtamudi Lake**, there are no 'sights' in Kollam. The only alternatives are the miserable ruins of a Portuguese/Dutch fort and some 18th-century churches at **Thangasseri**, three km from Kollam's centre. Otherwise, Kollam is just the starting or finishing point for the backwater trip – an overnight halt at the most. Even that can easily be avoided since the burgeoning beach resort of Varkala is only 45 minutes south.

Places to Stay – bottom end

The *Tourist Bungalow*, three km from the centre, is a magnificent, spacious, old British Residency in colourful gardens by the water's edge. Despite its superb potential and 'Lord Curzon slept here' claims, it's rather neglected and sparsely furnished, but at Rs 44/55, it's dirt cheap and the rooms are immense. Getting into town is the biggest

drawback because it can be hard to find an auto-rickshaw.

In the centre of Kollam, the popular *Hotel Karthika* (☎ 76-240) is a large place built around a central courtyard. The sculptures in the courtyard are hideous, but the rooms at Rs 68/111 with attached bathroom are not bad. There are also rooms with air-con. The nearby *Iswarya Lodge* (☎ 75-384) on Main Rd is slightly cheaper at Rs 54/86.

Opposite the KSRTC Bus Stand is the cheap but very basic *Mahalakshmi Lodge* (☎ 79-440) which has rooms with common bathroom for Rs 30/50; you get what you pay for here. Opposite the railway station, the *Hotel Rail View* (☎ 75-361) has rooms for Rs 40/75 and an attached bar and restaurant.

Places to Stay – middle

At a glance, the *Hotel Shah International* (☎ 75-362) on Tourist Bungalow Rd looks as modern as tomorrow but in fact it's as shoddy, tatty and run-down as only a neglected Indian hotel can become. Singles/doubles cost from Rs 100/150 or Rs 240/290 with air-con. The *Hotel Sudarsan* (☎ 75-322) is rather better value at Rs 130/160 or from Rs 255/305 with air-con, although rooms at the front can be noisy from the traffic. All rooms have TV and there are restaurants and a bar.

The large, soulless *Hotel Sea Bee* (☎ 75-371) on Hospital Rd has unkempt rooms for Rs 130/172; Rs 220 for an air-con double.

There are several mid-range alternatives out of town. Just across the inlet from the boat jetty, the KTDC *Yatri Nivas* (☎ 78-638) is large and rather lost looking, although renovations may improve things. Rooms are Rs 80/120 to Rs 125/150; Rs 180 for an air-con double. The riverside location is terrific, there's a pleasant waterfront lawn and the staff will run you across the river to the boat jetty in the hotel's speedboat if you ask nicely.

Hotel Lake View (☎ 20-4669) is a couple of km out of town at Thoppilkadavu. It has pleasant rooms for Rs 60/100 or Rs 250 for an air-con double. The lakeside setting is quite pleasant. Slightly further out at

KERALA

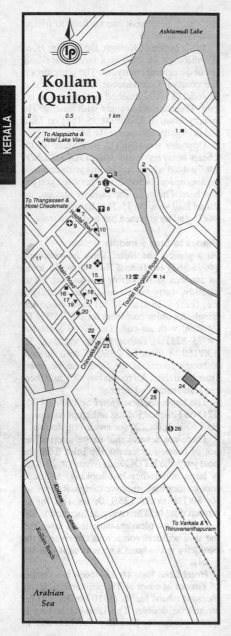

Kollam (Quilon)

Ashtamudi Lake

0   0.5   1 km

To Alappuzha &
Hotel Lake View

To Thangasseri &
Hotel Checkmate

Hospital Road

Main Road

Tourist Bungalow Road

Chinnakkada

Kollam Canal

Kollam Beach

To Varkala &
Thiruvananthapuram

Arabian
Sea

Thirumullavaram, beyond the Thangasseri fort, the seaside *Hotel Checkmate* (☎ 20-4731) has rooms from Rs 200/300. Contrary to their brochure, the beach is most definitely not 'one of the finest in India' and the claimed swimming pool does not exist.

Places to Eat

The *Hotel Guru Prasad* on Main Rd is a fairly ordinary vegetarian place where a 'meal' costs just Rs 7. On the same side of the road is the rather brighter vegetarian and non-vegetarian *Azad Hotel*. Main Rd also has a decent branch of the *Indian Coffee House*. The *Sree Suprabatham Restaurant*, hidden away in a courtyard directly opposite the clock tower, is a typical south Indian vegetarian 'meals' restaurant.

The restaurants in the *Iswarya Lodge* and the *Mahalakshmi Lodge* both have good

PLACES TO STAY	
1	Tourist Bungalow
2	Yatri Nivas
4	Mahalakashmi Lodge
7	Hotel Sea Bee
10	Hotel Sudarsan
14	Hotel Shah International
16	Iswarya Lodge
20	Hotel Karthika
25	Hotel Rail View

PLACES TO EAT	
17	Hotel Guru Prasad
18	Indian Coffee House
19	Hotel Azad
21	Supreme Bakers
22	Sree Suprabatham Restaurant

OTHER	
3	Boat Jetty
5	Tourist Office
6	KSRTC Bus Station
8	Shrine of Our Lady of Velamkanni
9	Hospital
11	Fruit & Vegetable Market
12	Bishop Jerome Nagar Shopping Centre
13	Telegraph Office
15	Post Office
23	Clock Tower
24	Railway Station
26	State Bank of India

vegetarian food. *The Sudarsan Hotel* has a vegetarian 'meals' restaurant and a more expensive non-vegetarian place which has air-con and a TV that tends to distract the staff. It's a good place for breakfast before backwater boat trips depart. The *Shah International* has a reasonable restaurant, but the *Sea Bee's* restaurant is nothing to write home about.

Chef King, in the Bishop Jerome Nagar shopping centre, is a glossy little place offering 'fast food and outdoor catering'. *Snow Field Ice Cream* and *Arum Ice Cream* are in the same complex. *Supreme Bakers* is opposite the post office.

Kollam is a cashew-growing centre and nuts are on sale in many shops and hotels.

Getting There & Away
Bus Many of the buses leaving the Kollam Bus Station are en route from somewhere else, so it's the usual rugby scrum when a bus arrives. Seats in express buses can be reserved in advance, saving much energy and discomfort. Kollam is on the well-serviced Thiruvananthapuram, Kollam, Alappuzha, Ernakulam route. Super express services take 1½ hours for Rs 25 to Thiruvananthapuram; 1¾ hour for Rs 25 to Alappuzha; and 3½ hours for Rs 45 to Ernakulam.

Train Kollam is 159 km south of Ernakulam and the three to four-hour trip costs Rs 42/152 in 2nd/1st class. The *Trivandrum Mail* from Madras goes through Kollam, as does the *Bombay to Kanyakumari Express* and the Mangalore to Thiruvananthapuram coastal service.

The *Quilon Mail* between Kollam and Madras (Egmore) via Madurai covers the 760 km in 20 hours for Rs 141/530. The trip across the Western Ghats is a delight.

Boat See the Backwaters section for information on the popular backwaters trip to Alappuzha. Although the regular ferry is not currently operating due to a canal blockage, there are still public services across the Ashtamudi Lake to Guhanandapuram (one

hour) or Muthiraparam (2½ hours). The daily ATDC and DTPC tourist boats to Alappuzha can be booked at various hotels around town and start by bus from the KSRTC Bus Stand.

Getting Around
The KSRTC Bus Stand and the boat jetty are side by side, but the railway station is on the opposite side of town. Auto-rickshaw drivers are reasonably willing to use their meters. The *Yatri Nivas* speedboat can be hired to explore the waterways around Kollam for Rs 300 an hour.

VARKALA
Varkala is an embryonic beach resort, and the early signs indicate that the Keralan tourist authorities have not learned from their mistakes in Kovalam, which allowed that beach to become a shambles. The garbage is already piling up in Varkala.

The town and the railway station are two km from the beach, which lies beneath towering cliffs and boasts a **mineral-water spring**. The **Janardhana Temple** is at the Beach Rd junction. One of the earliest British East India Company trading posts was established at nearby **Anjengo** in 1684.

Places to Stay
The neat and orderly *Anandan Tourist Home* (☎ 2135), opposite the railway station, has rooms for Rs·40/70 or Rs 235 with air-con. Most places to stay, however, are at the beach: either at the temple junction, on Beach Rd, or half a km north along the cliff tops. As at Kovalam, prices vary seasonally.

The *J A Tourist Home* (☎ 2453) is near the temple. Along Beach Rd, there's the *Akshay Beach Resort* (☎ 2668), which has rooms for Rs 150. It's basically OK, although it would be much better if a little energy went into cleaning and maintenance. Continuing down Beach Rd, there's *Mamma Home* and, overlooking the beach, the *Varkala Marine Palace*, which has rooms for Rs 100. Overlooking the rice paddies, the *Beach Palace* (☎ 2453) is rather primitive but it's cheap at Rs 45/75.

992 Kerala – Varkala

On the cliffs, 10 minutes' walk north, much of the accommodation is with local families who offer rooms for Rs 40 or Rs 50. Some places to stay haven't yet acquired names, so just look for *White House, Green House* or *Red House*, all with rooms at around Rs 100 to Rs 150 in season. Red House is cleverly designed to stay pleasantly cool in the hottest weather. The *Hill Top Resort* has straightforward rooms with attached bathroom for Rs 125 to Rs 150.

Between the two Varkala Beach enclaves, there's an inconveniently situated *Government Guest House*. In 1995, a fancy new hotel, to be part of the Taj Group, was under construction overlooking the rice paddies at the southern end of the beach.

Places to Eat

The *Anandan Tourist Home*, opposite the railway station, has a restaurant downstairs. The popular *Sree Padman Restaurant* is perched right at the edge of the tank at the

temple junction. Apart from the *Kentucky Restaurant* on Beach Rd, most of the eating places are along the cliff top at the northern part of Varkala Beach. *Sky Roof, Oceanus, Tom & Jerry*, the *Sun Set Restaurant*, the *Victoria Restaurant*, the *Cliff Top Restaurant* and *Saipem* all offer similar standards (shaky tables and a diverse collection of rickety chairs), similar food (fresh fish on display out front at night) and similar service (usually incredibly slow).

Getting There & Away

Varkala is 41 km north of Thiruvananthapuram (55 minutes by train, Rs 16/68 in 2nd/1st class) and just 24 km south of Kollam (45 minutes, Rs 13/41). From Varkala, it's easy to get to Kollam in the morning in time to get the backwater boat to Alappuzha. A taxi from Thiruvananthapuram direct to Varkala Beach would cost about Rs 300.

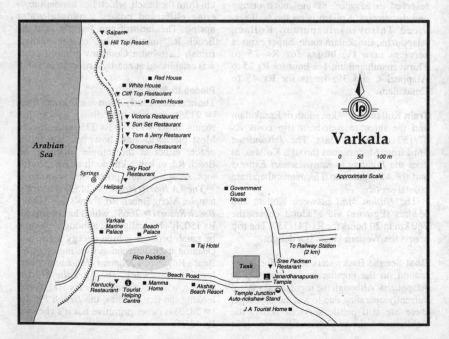

Getting Around

Auto-rickshaws shuttle back and forth between the railway station and the Varkala temple junction for Rs 10 to Rs 12. A taxi to the beach costs about Rs 35.

THIRUVANANTHAPURAM (Trivandrum)

Population: 826,000
Telephone Area Code: 0471

It's hard to believe this friendly, relaxed city, built over seven forested hills, is a state capital. Known as the City of the Sacred Snake, Thiruvananthapuram has managed to retain the magic ambience so characteristic of Kerala – red-tiled roofs, narrow winding lanes, intimate corner cafes, dilapidated municipal buses and necessary business accomplished in a friendly manner with a relatively high degree of efficiency.

When political tensions between the various factions erupt onto the streets, the calm can quickly fade and political slogans, emblems and flags – especially those of the communist and Muslim parties – become a notable feature of the Keralan urban landscape. Politicians parading around in long streams of official cars can also cause delays, but otherwise Keralan politics rarely affects the visitor.

The famous Sri Padmanabhaswamy Temple is only open to Hindus so most Western visitors simply pass through the town. Kovalam Beach is just 16 km south, and there are flight connections to Sri Lanka, the Maldives and the Arabian Gulf.

Orientation

Thiruvananthapuram covers a large area, but most of the services and places of interest are on or very close to Mahatma Gandhi (M G) Rd – the main road from the museum and zoo to the Sri Padmanabhaswamy Temple.

The long-distance bus stand, railway station, tourist reception centre and many of the budget hotels, are all close together, while the municipal bus stand is 10 minutes' walk south, close to the temple. It's three to four km from the southern cluster of hotels and transport facilities to Museum Rd, at the northern end of M G Rd. The large Secretar-

iat Building is a handy landmark halfway along M G Rd.

Information

Tourist Offices The Tourist Reception Centre (☎ 33-0031) in front of the Chaithram Hotel, near the railway station and long-distance bus station, is essentially there to promote KTDC guided tours. There's also a KTDC office by the Mascot Hotel. The Tourist Information Centre (☎ 61-132) on Museum Rd, opposite the museum and zoo, is useless.

Post & Telecommunications The GPO is tucked away down a small side street off M G Rd, about 10 minutes' walk from the Central Station Rd area. Most of the counters, including poste restante, are open Monday to Saturday from 8 am to 8 pm.

The Central Telegraph Office, at the midpoint of M G Rd, is a 20-minute walk from either end. The office is open 24 hours a day. There are numerous STD/ISD counters and kiosks around town.

Visa Extensions The office of the Commissioner of Police (☎ 60-555) on Residency Rd issues visa extensions, but the process takes four days to a week. Fortunately, you don't have to leave your passport. It speeds things up if you give a Thiruvananthapuram hotel address rather than somewhere in Kovalam. The office is open every day except Sunday from 10 am to 5 pm.

Bookshops & Libraries The British Library (☎ 68-716), in the YMCA grounds near the Secretariat building, is supposedly only open to members, but visitors are made to feel welcome. It has three-day-old British newspapers and a variety of magazines. The library is open Tuesday to Saturday from 11 am to 7 pm. Higginbothams bookshop is on M G Rd and the Continental Book Company is nearby.

Museum, Gallery & Zoo

The zoo and a collection of museums are in a park in the north of the city. The museums

KERALA

are open Tuesday to Sunday from 10 am to 4.45 pm, but not until 1 pm on Wednesday. A single Rs 5 entry ticket covers all the museums and is obtainable from the Natural History Museum.

Housed in a bizarrely attractive, decaying, Indo-Saracenic building dating from 1880, the **Napier Museum** has a good collection of bronzes, historical and contemporary ornaments, temple carts, ivory carvings and life-size figures of Kathakali dancers in full regalia.

The **Sri Chitra Art Gallery** has paintings of the Rajput, Mughal and Tanjore schools, together with works from China, Tibet, Japan and Bali. There are also many modern Indian paintings, including works by Ravi Varma, Svetoslav and Nicholas Roerich.

The **Zoological Gardens** are among the best designed in Asia – set among woodland, lakes and very well-maintained lawns – but some of the animal enclosures are miserable. The zoo is open Tuesday to Saturday from 9 am to 5.15 pm; entry is Rs 4.

The separate **Science & Industry Museum** is not that interesting unless you're a high-school science student.

Sri Padmanabhaswamy Temple

This temple, dedicated to Vishnu, was constructed in the Dravidian style by a maharaja of Travancore in 1733. Only Hindus are allowed inside, and even they have to wear a special dhoti. The temple incorporates a tank in which the faithful bathe.

International Centre for Cultural Development

The grandly named ICCD offers up to eight visiting artists the opportunity to study south Indian culture. Food and accommodation is available. For information, contact ICCD, TC 31/1719 Pareeksha Bhavan, Anayara PO, Trivandrum 695029 or fax them on (471) 44-6890. ICCD can be contacted in the Netherlands (☎ +31 30-93-1663 or fax +31 30-31-1337).

Organised Tours

The KTDC operates a variety of tours in the

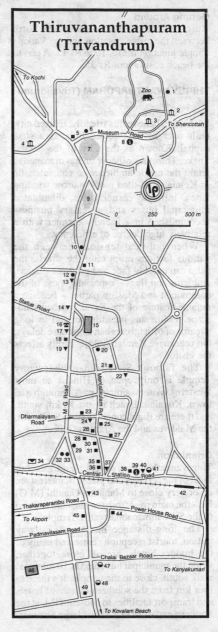

city and further afield. They all depart from the Tourist Reception Centre opposite the railway station.

PLACES TO STAY

5	Mascot Hotel
11	South Park
18	Hotel Pankaj
21	Hotel Residency Tower
23	Bhaskara Bhavan Tourist Paradise
25	Sundar Tourist Home
26	Sivada Tourist Home
27	Hotel Regency
28	Vijai Tourist Home
30	Pravin Tourist Home
31	Manacaud Tourist Paradise
35	Hotel Highland
36	Hotel Ammu
38	Chaithram Hotel
44	Hotel Fort Manor
45	Nalanda Tourist Home
49	Hotel Continental Luciya

PLACES TO EAT

13	Indian Coffee House
14	Ananda Bhavan
17	Athul Jyoti
19	Sri Ram Sweet Stall
22	Snoozzer Ice Cream
24	Vinayak Vegetarian Restaurant
37	Ambika Cafe
40	Indian Coffee House
43	Rangoli

OTHER

1	Sri Chitra Art Gallery
2	Natural History Museum
3	Napier Museum
4	Science & Industry Museum
6	Indian Airlines
7	Stadium
8	Tourist Information Centre
9	Stadium
10	Victoria Jubilee Town Hall
12	Air Maldives
15	Secretariat
16	Central Telegraph Office
20	British Library
29	Higginbothams
32	Continental Book Company
33	East West Airlines
34	GPO
39	Tourist Reception Centre
41	Long-Distance Bus Station
42	Central Railway Station
46	Sri Padmanabhaswamy Temple
47	Local Bus Station
48	Kovalam Buses & Taxis

The daily Thiruvananthapuram city tour departs at 8 am, returns at 7 pm, and costs Rs 60. It visits the Sri Padmanabhaswamy Temple, the museum, art gallery, zoo, Veli Lagoon and Kovalam Beach. This tour is of little interest to Western visitors since the temple is off limits and there's little fascination in gawping at fellow travellers sunbathing on Kovalam Beach.

The daily Kanyakumari (Cape Comorin) tour departs at 7.30 am, returns at 9 pm, and costs Rs 150. It includes visits to Padmanabhapuram Palace (except on Monday) and Kanyakumari, and isn't bad value if you want to avoid the fight to get on public buses and don't want to stay overnight in Kanyakumari. There's also a daily tour to the Ponmudi hill resort which departs at 7.45 am, returns at 7 pm, and costs Rs 100.

The two-day Periyar Wildlife Sanctuary tour leaves most Saturdays at 6.30 am and gets back on Sunday at 9 pm. It costs Rs 250, does not include food or accommodation, and must be one of the silliest tours in India, since there's no time to see any wildlife – even if it were possible in the company of a busload of garrulous honeymooners.

There are other tours to places further afield but they're of little interest.

Places to Stay – bottom end

There are many cheap places around Central Station Rd, near the railway station and long-distance bus stand, but most of them are very basic and the road is busy and noisy. The beach at Kovalam is a far more pleasant place to stay. If you have to stay overnight in Thiruvananthapuram, the best hunting ground is Manjalikulam Rd. Despite its conveniently central location, it's pleasantly quiet and has a collection of cheap to mid-range hotels.

The friendly and cheap *Pravin Tourist Home* (☎ 33-0443) has large rooms for Rs 55/100. The *Bhaskara Bhavan Tourist Paradise* (☎ 79-662) on Dharmalayam Rd, just off Manjalikulam Rd, is a bit gloomy but even cheaper at Rs 35/70. The similar *Vijai Tourist Home* (☎ 79-727) nearby has doubles for Rs 70 but is not particularly welcoming. At the bottom of the scale is the extremely basic *Sundar Tourist Home* (☎ 33-0532) which has singles for Rs 25 to Rs 30 and doubles for Rs 60.

Up the scale a bit, the clean and well-kept *Sivada Tourist Home* (☎ 33-1322) has rooms built around a pleasant courtyard for Rs 60/100 or air-con doubles for Rs 210. At the Central Station Rd end of Manjalikulam Rd, the *Manacaud Tourist Paradise* (☎ 69-5001) has large, clean rooms with attached bathroom for Rs 55/100. Nearby, the *Hotel Ammu* (☎ 33-1937) has rooms for Rs 100/125 or Rs 250/275 with air-con.

The *Nalanda Tourist Home* (☎ 71-864), south of the railway line, is on busy M G Rd, but the rooms at the back are not too noisy and it's cheap at Rs 54/79. There are also *retiring rooms,* including a dormitory, at the railway station.

Places to Stay – middle

The KTDC *Chaithram Hotel* (☎ 33-0977) on Central Station Rd, next to the bus stand, is a popular, modern-looking, atrium hotel that's rarely full. Rooms cost Rs 250/350 or Rs 550/750 with air-con. Facilities include a bookshop, coffee shop, a bright and friendly bar and a mediocre restaurant with tasteless food and slow service.

Back on Manjalikulam Rd, the *Hotel Highland* (☎ 68-200) is one of the tallest buildings in the area and readily visible from Central Station Rd. The staff are friendly and there are a wide variety of rooms from Rs 120/160 or from Rs 220/335 with air-con. The nearby *Hotel Regency* (☎ 33-0377) on Manjalikulam Cross Rd has rooms for Rs 150/250 or Rs 275/375 with air-con. There are two restaurants, one of them on the rooftop. The *Hotel Residency Tower* (☎ 33-1661) on Press Rd, just off Manjalikulam Rd, has rooms for Rs 250/350 or Rs 450/600 with air-con.

The *Hotel Pankaj* (☎ 76-667) on M G Rd, opposite the government Secretariat, has rooms for Rs 360/500 or from Rs 600/850 with air-con. There's a bar and two restaurants, one offering fine views from the top floor.

Places to Stay – top end

Starting on the south side of the city and moving north, the *Hotel Continental Luciya* (☎ 46-3443) is at East Fort, close to the Sri Padmanabhaswamy Temple. It's centrally air-conditioned, has rooms for Rs 895/1095, and boasts a bar, restaurant and bookshop. The *Hotel Fort Manor* (☎ 46-2222) at Power House Junction, just south of the railway line, has air-con rooms from Rs 750/950 and a variety of restaurants, including one on the roof.

Further north on M G Rd, the new, centrally air-conditioned *South Park* (☎ 65-666) has rooms from US$29/36. Finally, the KTDC *Mascot Hotel* (☎ 43-8990) on Museum Rd, north of the centre, is a pleasant hotel with a gloomy design. Rooms are all air-con and start from Rs 695/995. This is the only hotel in town with a swimming pool.

Places to Eat

There's a bizarre, circular *Indian Coffee House* with a spiralling floor next to the long-distance bus stand. If only the waiters wore roller skates! The tiny *Ambika Cafe* at the junction of Central Station Rd and Manjalikulam Rd is a good place for a cheap breakfast.

There are a number of good, cheap vegetarian places opposite the Secretariat, on M G Rd. The *Athul Jyoti* turns out a good thali with a variety of vegetables, dhals and curd. Next to the Pankaj Hotel, the *Sri Ram Sweet Stall* is actually a very good vegetarian restaurant. Continue north to *Ananda Bhavan*, a straightforward south Indian vegetarian restaurant. A little further north again, on M G Rd, is another branch of the *Indian Coffee House.*

Central Station Rd has a number of vegetarian restaurants serving the usual 'meals' thalis. On Dharmalayam Rd, just off Manjalikulam Rd, the *Vinayak Vegetarian Restaurant* prepares excellent food in an attractive, old house. *Rangoli* is south of the railway line, on M G Rd, and has a small entrance leading to a neat and tidy air-conditioned 'family restaurant' upstairs.

There are restaurants in many of the

hotels. On Manjalikulam Rd, the *City Queen Restaurant* in the Highlands Hotel does good Chinese dishes and also serves Indian and Western food. The lunchtime buffets are popular in the *Mascot Hotel*, the *Pankaj Hotel* and particularly in the *South Park*.

Rooftop restaurants are all the go in Trivandrum, and from an elevated position you realise just how green and park-like the city is. The 5th-floor *Sandhya Restaurant* in the Pankaj Hotel has particularly fine views, and the *Fort Manor* and the *Regency* also have top-floor restaurants.

Both KTDC hotels, the *Mascot* and the *Chaithram*, have outdoor ice-cream parlours. Alternatively, try the engagingly named *Snoozzer* on Press Rd.

Getting There & Away

Air Indian Airlines (☎ 43-6870) is on Museum Rd, next to the Mascot Hotel. Air Maldives (☎ 46-1313) and East West (☎ 71-757) are both on M G Rd. Other phone numbers are Air India (☎ 43-4837), Air Lanka (☎ 64-495), Gulf Air (☎ 67-514) and Oman Air (☎ 62-248).

Indian Airlines has direct connections to Bangalore (Rs 1841), Bombay (Rs 3440), Kochi (Rs 829) and Madras (Rs 1922). East West flies to Bombay direct and via Madurai.

There are a number of connections to the Arabian Gulf with Air India, Gulf Air and Oman Air. Air India also connects with Singapore.

Thiruvananthapuram is a popular place from which to fly to Colombo (Sri Lanka) and Malé (Maldives). There's a choice of Air Lanka or Indian Airlines to Colombo, and there are two or more flights a day most days of the week for Rs 1285 one way. Air Maldives and Indian Airlines have regular flights to Malé for Rs 1845 one way.

Bus The long-distance bus station, opposite the railway station, is total chaos. Although there is a timetable in English, it's largely a fiction. Since there are no bays, you have to join the scramble every time a bus arrives just in case it happens to be the one you want. The law of the jungle applies each time a

battered, old bus comes to a screeching halt in a cloud of dust.

Buses operate very regularly north along the coast. Travel times and fares on super express services are Kollam, 1½ hours for Rs 25; Alappuzha, 3¼ hours for Rs 45; Ernakulam, five hours for Rs 65; and Thrissur, 6¾ hours for Rs 85. Buses depart hourly for the two-hour trip to Kanyakumari. There are three buses daily for the eight-hour trip to Thekkady (Periyar Wildlife Sanctuary).

Most of the bus services to places in Tamil Nadu are operated by Thiruvalluvar (the Tamil Nadu state bus service), which has its office at the eastern end of the long-distance bus station. It has services to Madras (four daily, 17 hours), Madurai (10 daily, seven hours), Pondicherry (once daily, 16 hours), Coimbatore (once daily), as well as Nagercoil and Erode. Long-distance buses also operate to Bangalore, but it's better to catch a train if you're going that far.

Train Although the buses are much faster than the trains, Kerala State Road Transport buses, like most others in southern India, make no concessions to comfort and the drivers are pretty reckless. If you prefer to keep your adrenalin levels down, the trains are a pleasant alternative. The reservation office, on the 1st floor of the station building, is efficient and computerised but you should reserve as far in advance as possible because long-distance trains out of Thiruvananthapuram are heavily booked. That doesn't mean you have no chance of getting on, but you must get waitlisted. The booking office is open Monday to Saturday from 8 am to 2 pm and from 2.15 to 8 pm; Sunday from 8 am to 2 pm. If you're just making your way up the coast in short hops from town to town, there's no need to book.

Numerous trains run up the coast via Kollam and Ernakulam to Thrissur. Some trains branch off east and north-east at Kollam and head for Shencottah. Beyond Thrissur, many others branch off east via Palakkad to Tamil Nadu.

Trains which go all the way up the coast

as far as Mangalore in Karnataka include the daily *Parsuram Express* and *Malabar Express*. There's also the daily *Vanchinad Express*, which goes to Ernakulam, and the *Cannanore Express*, which goes to Kannur. It's 65 km from Thiruvananthapuram to Kollam (1½ hours, Rs 21/81 in 2nd/1st class); 224 km to Ernakulam (five hours, Rs 56/200); and 414 km to Kozhikode (10 hours, Rs 89/335).

South of Thiruvananthapuram, it's 87 km to Kanyakumari (Rs 25/104); and 427 km to Coimbatore (nine hours, Rs 91/345). Coimbatore has connections to Mettupalayam and Ooty.

For long-haulers, there's the once-weekly (Friday) *Himsagar Express* to Jammu Tawi which goes via Delhi. See the table below for information on other long-distance train departures from Thiruvananthapuram.

Getting Around

To/From the Airport The small, modern and relaxed airport is six km from the city centre or 15 km from Kovalam Beach. A No 14 local bus will take you there for around Rs 1. Prepaid vouchers for taxis cost Rs 40 to Rs 60 to destinations in the city; Rs 125 to Kovalam Beach.

Local Transport There are very crowded local state government buses, as well as auto-rickshaws and taxis. For transport around the city, auto-rickshaws are your best bet. The drivers are reasonably willing to use their

meters; flagfall is Rs 4. From the railway station to the museum costs about Rs 10.

See the Kovalam Beach section for transport information from Thiruvananthapuram to the beach.

AROUND THIRUVANANTHAPURAM
Padmanabhapuram Palace

Although it's actually in Tamil Nadu, this fine palace is easily visited from Thiruvananthapuram or Kanyakumari. It was once the seat of the rulers of Travancore, a princely state for over 400 years, which included a large part of present-day Kerala and the western littoral of Tamil Nadu. The palace is superbly constructed of local teak and granite, and stands within the massive stone town walls which kept Tipu Sultan at bay in the 18th century. The architecture is exquisite, with ceilings carved in floral patterns, windows laid with jewel-coloured mica, and floors finished to a high polish with a special compound of crushed shells, coconuts, egg-white and the juices of local plants. The 18th-century murals in the puja room on the upper floors have been beautifully preserved, and surpass even those at Mattancherry in Kochi. Ask at the curator's office for special access.

With its banqueting halls, audience chamber, women's quarters, recruiting courtyard and galleries, the palace is a must for anyone visiting this part of the country.

Padmanabhapuram is 65 km south-east of Thiruvananthapuram. To get there, you can either catch a local bus from Thiruvanantha-

Selection of Express Trains from Thiruvananthapuram					
Destination	*Train number & name*	*Departure time*	*Distance (km)*	*Duration (hours)*	*Fare (Rs) (1st/2nd)*
Bangalore	6525 *Bangalore Exp*	10.20 am	851	18	189/553
Bombay	1082 *Kanyakumari Exp*	7.30 am	2062	45	302/1068
Calcutta	6321 *Guwahati Exp*	12.50 pm Thurs	2583	45	340/1282
Coimbatore	2625 *Kerala Exp*	9.45 am	385	9.15	105/320
Ernakulam	2625 *Kerala Exp*	9.45 am	224	4.35	56/205
Madras	6320 *Madras Mail*	1.30 pm	925	18	200/588
Mangalore	6349 *Parsuram Exp*	6.05 am	635	16	155/464
	6029 *Malabar Exp*	5.40 pm			
Delhi	2625 *Kerala Exp*	9.45 am	3033	54	377/1465

puram (or Kovalam Beach) or take one of the Kanyakumari tours organised by the KTDC. The palace is closed on Monday.

KOVALAM

Telephone Area Code: 0471

This beach, 16 km south of Thiruvanantha-puram, is the most popular in southern India. The main part of Kovalam consists of two palm-fringed coves, separated from the beaches on either side by rocky headlands. The southern headland is marked by a prominent lighthouse. The northern headland is topped by the deluxe Ashok Beach Resort. There is good surf but be wary of the rips, which can be dangerously strong. Lifeguards patrol and flags indicate where it's safe to swim. Kovalam has a plethora of places to stay, ranging from cheap concrete boxes to upmarket resorts. There's an equally wide range of restaurants, many tuned in to the standard Asian travellers' menus.

Despite its popularity with Western travellers, Kovalam is still fairly mellow. Back from the beaches, the local people continue to cultivate their crops, fishers still sail their boats out to sea each night (though there's usually an outboard bolted on the stern) and the nets are still pulled in by hand.

The beach's popularity has, however, brought changes. In the November to February high season, the place is awash with bronzed sun, sand and wave worshippers from all over the world. At weekends, it attracts hordes of local tourists, many of them coming solely to stare at the exposed flesh liberally distributed over the sand. Despite this voyeurism, travellers should remember that Hinduism is the predominant religion in Kerala, and bold displays of naked flesh are definitely offensive to local sensibilities.

Not all is well at Kovalam, despite its popularity. Development has been almost totally unplanned and many of the badly maintained hotels and restaurants were ugly even before they started to fall apart. The amount of garbage piled up once you're one step back from the beach is a complete disgrace. Add continual harassment from souvenir sellers and a constant parade of sightseers, and Kovalam Beach is a long way from paradise.

Orientation

It's a 15-minute walk from the bus stand at the Ashok Beach Resort to the lighthouse end of the second cove where most of the hotels and restaurants are located. The maze of paths through the coconut palms and around the back of the paddy fields are hard to negotiate at night without a full moon.

Information
Tourist Information, Banks & Post Office

There's a Tourist Office just inside the entrance to the Ashok Beach Resort. The resort also has a Central Bank of India counter which changes travellers' cheques quickly and without fuss. It's only open Monday to Friday from 10.30 am to 2 pm and on Saturday from 10.30 am to noon. The Wilson Tourist Home has an official money change counter which offers exactly the same rates and is open longer hours. Of course, there are plenty of 'change money' people around.

There's a post office and a telephone centre (open 9 am to 5 pm) in Kovalam Village.

Shops Kovalam Beach has numerous craft and carpet shops (usually of Tibetan, Kashmiri and Rajasthani origin), clothing stores (ready to wear and made to order), book exchanges, general stores selling everything from toilet paper to sunscreen, travel agents, yoga schools and even massage parlours. Just in case you thought you'd left home to immerse yourself in a different culture, Western videos are shown twice a night in a number of restaurants. There are also guys on the beach selling batik lungis, beach mats and leaf paintings. Plenty of others offer cheap Kerala grass.

Warnings Don't drink local well water at Kovalam. There are so many pit toilets adjacent to wells that you're guaranteed to get very sick if you do. Stick to bottled water.

Theft from hotel rooms, particularly

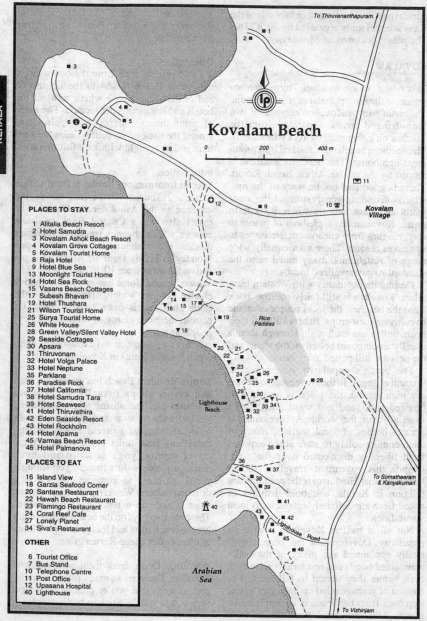

Kovalam Beach

0   200   400 m

Kovalam Village

Rice Paddies

Lighthouse Beach

Arabian Sea

To Thiruvananthapuram

To Somatheeram & Kanyakumari

To Vizhinjam

Lighthouse Road

PLACES TO STAY

1 Alitalia Beach Resort
2 Hotel Samudra
3 Kovalam Ashok Beach Resort
4 Kovalam Grove Cottages
5 Kovalam Tourist Home
8 Raja Hotel
9 Hotel Blue Sea
13 Moonlight Tourist Home
14 Hotel Sea Rock
15 Vasans Beach Cottages
17 Subesh Bhavan
19 Hotel Thushara
21 Wilson Tourist Home
25 Surya Tourist Home
26 White House
28 Green Valley/Silent Valley Hotel
29 Seaside Cottages
30 Apsara
31 Thiruvonam
32 Hotel Volga Palace
33 Hotel Neptune
35 Parklane
36 Paradise Rock
37 Hotel California
38 Hotel Samudra Tara
39 Hotel Seaweed
41 Hotel Thiruvathira
42 Eden Seaside Resort
43 Hotel Rockholm
44 Hotel Aparna
45 Varmas Beach Resort
46 Hotel Palmanova

PLACES TO EAT

16 Island View
18 Garzia Seafood Corner
20 Santana Restaurant
22 Hawah Beach Restaurant
23 Flamingo Restaurant
24 Coral Reef Cafe
27 Lonely Planet
34 Siva's Restaurant

OTHER

6 Tourist Office
7 Bus Stand
10 Telephone Centre
11 Post Office
12 Upasana Hospital
40 Lighthouse

cheap hotels, does occur. The most common trick is to hook stuff out of your room through the bars on the windows – even at night while you're there! Closing the windows isn't much fun on warm nights, so it's more sensible to stash your gear under the bed. Make sure the room has a decent bolt and windows which lock. Make sure you keep an eye on any possessions you take to the beach as well.

Places to Stay

There is no shortage of accommodation at the bottom end of the market – the coconut groves behind the beach are littered with small lodges, houses for rent and blocks of recently constructed rooms. Touts lie in wait for the arrival of buses from Thiruvanantha-puram, but if you let any of these people take you to a hotel or house, you'll pay more. Shop around, but you basically get what you pay for.

Prices climb the closer you get to the beach, and a few minutes' further walk can often mean lower prices or much better rooms for the same price. Prices climb even more dramatically with the season. November to February is the high season but some establishments even have a peak high season over the Christmas-New Year period when prices go even higher.

Places to Stay – bottom end

In the high season, you need to shop around and you need to do this without a pack on your back. If it's obvious you've just arrived, you'll pay whatever they think you can afford. Park your bag and then go looking. Note that most places will offer a substantial discount if you're staying more than just a few days.

Most, though not all, of the cheapest places are along or just back from the beach. There are others along the road from Thiru-vananthapuram and along Lighthouse Rd. Many of the beach restaurants also have a few basic rooms with shared bathroom and toilet facilities, but to get one of these rooms in the high season often involves leaving a

deposit and waiting a few days for people to move on.

The *Eden Seaside Resort* on Lighthouse Rd, opposite the Varmas Beach Resort, is basic but all rooms have attached bathroom, and cost only Rs 150, dropping to half that level in the low season. Almost next door is the *Hotel Thiruvathira* (☎ 48-0787), which has downstairs doubles for Rs 250, and upstairs doubles with balcony and bay views for Rs 400. In the low season, prices drop to Rs 150 and Rs 300. Close to the beach, *Paradise Rock* (☎ 48-0658) climbs all the way to Rs 600 at the Christmas peak. At other times, rooms are Rs 200 to Rs 400, down to Rs 100 in the monsoon.

The *Green Valley/Silent Valley Hotel* (☎ 48-0636) is at the back of the paddy fields, in a wonderfully peaceful location. It has clean, neat and colourful rooms with

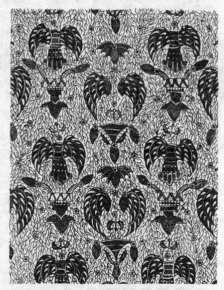

Batik is a relatively recent introduction into India from Indonesia, but it has already become widespread.

attached bathroom for Rs 200 in the peak season, and Rs 100 in the low season. A long walk back from the beach, the *Kovalam Tourist Home* (☎ 48-0441) has pleasant rooms with attached bathroom at Rs 200 in the high season, Rs 150 in the low.

Just back from the beach, the friendly *Surya Tourist Home* is a no-frills place with rooms for Rs 100, Rs 150 or Rs 175 in the high season. Next door is the similarly priced *White House*. There are many other places nearby, like the beachfront *Seaside Cottages* or the pleasant *Apsara* behind them. *Thiruvonam*, on the beach, has pleasant doubles at Rs 300 to Rs 350 in the peak season. Just off the Sea Rock road, *Subesh Bhavan* offers basic accommodation for as low as Rs 50 in the low season. Naturally, you're 'welcome to the *Hotel California*', as the large sign along the wall proclaims. And the *Parklane* suggests you park there and 'experience the art of staying'.

Places to Stay – middle

The best hunting ground for mid-range hotels is Lighthouse Rd. *Hotel Seaweed* (☎ 48-0391) is an excellent, friendly and secure place with sea breezes and bay views. There's a wide variety of rooms from Rs 300 all the way to Rs 700. Prices drop 25% to 30% in the low season.

Just below the Seaweed is the *Hotel Samudra Tara* (☎ 54-653), which has pleasant rooms with attached bathroom and balcony for Rs 500/600. Prices drop to half that level in the low season. Don't confuse this hotel with the KTDC Hotel Samudra, beyond the Ashok Beach Resort.

Another very good choice is *Hotel Rockholm* (☎ 48-0306), further up Lighthouse Rd. It has great views over the small cove beyond the lighthouse. In the high season, rooms cost Rs 750/800; in the low season, there's a 25% discount. Avoid the rooms on the roof if possible because they get very hot during the day.

Next up is the multistorey *Hotel Aparna* (☎ 48-0950), which has rooms for Rs 800 in the peak season, falling to Rs 400 in the low season. Next door is the *Varmas Beach*

Resort (☎ 54-478), which has great balconies overlooking the small cove. Rooms are Rs 850/950 in the high season, dropping to Rs 850/750 in the low season. Across the road, there's a small annexe with rooms for Rs 400 in the high season. This is one of the few mid-range places without its own restaurant.

Although the *Hotel Palmanova* (☎ 54-494) is the furthest up the road, it's actually close to the sandy cove south of the lighthouse headland. This small stretch of beach attracts fewer gawkers and salespeople, so it's a pleasant escape from the frenetic activity on the main beach. The rooms are pleasantly designed, all with attached bathroom and a balcony facing the sea. They cost Rs 1240 for a double (Rs 1540 with air-con) in the peak season. In the low season, they drop as low as Rs 620 (Rs 770 with air-con).

The *Hotel Neptune* (☎ 48-0222) is set back from Lighthouse Beach and has standard rooms for Rs 400, balcony rooms for Rs 480 and air-con rooms for Rs 780 over the Christmas-New Year peak. Prices in the low season fall to less than Rs 200. A few steps closer to the beach is the somewhat similar *Hotel Volga Palace*.

The *Hotel Sea Rock* (☎ 48-0422), on the beach in the northern cove, has been popular for years. The rooms are all doubles and all have attached bathroom. Rooms with a sea view cost Rs 750; back rooms cost Rs 350. These prices tumble to Rs 350 and Rs 250 respectively in the low season. Back in the coconut palms, the small *Hotel Thushara* (☎ 692) has superbly built, beautifully furnished self-contained cottages for Rs 400 (Rs 200 in the low season). There's also a cheaper lodge section.

Right behind the Sea Rock is *Vasans Beach Cottages*, a small cluster of clean and pleasant self-contained cottages for Rs 300 to Rs 500 in the peak season. Further up this road is the popular and squeaky clean *Moonlight Tourist Home* (☎ 48-0375), which has spacious rooms with poster beds and mosquito nets. Doubles, some with small balconies, cost Rs 500 to Rs 600 or Rs 750 with air-con. Prices for the rooms without air-con drop by 30% out of the peak season, and by 50% in the low season.

There are several places along the road to Kovalam Village which don't seem to attract many travellers, perhaps because of the distance from the beach. Overlooking the road, the *Raja Hotel* (☎ 48-0355) has sea-facing rooms with attached bathroom for Rs 430, falling to Rs 250 in the low season. It also has a bar and a restaurant. Other establishments along this road include the pleasant *Hotel Blue Sea* (☎ 54-401), which has a large garden and a swimming pool.

The KTDC *Hotel Samudra* (☎ 48-0089) is rather inconveniently located about two km north of the main beaches but it has its own bar and restaurant. Doubles cost from Rs 720 to Rs 960, or Rs 1700 with air-con. Prices drop as low as Rs 400 in the low season (Rs 750 with air-con). The *Alitalia Beach Resort* is nearby.

Places to Stay – top end

The *Kovalam Ashok Beach Resort* (☎ 48-0101) is superbly located on the headland at the northern end of the second cove. The hotel is centrally air-conditioned and has a bar, restaurants, swimming pool, sports facilities, bank and bookshop. Prices are Rs 2600/2800 from mid-December to mid-February, dropping to Rs 2400/2600 for the other 10 months. The adjacent *Kovalam Grove Cottages* are Rs 200 cheaper.

Places to Eat

Restaurants line Lighthouse Beach and are scattered among the coconut palms behind it. Almost all the restaurants offer the standard Asian travellers' menu: porridge, muesli, eggs, toast, jam and pancakes for breakfast, and seafood with French fries and salad for dinner. At night, you can dine by candlelight on the beach, and select which fish you would like cooked from the restaurant's seafood display. Always check the prices when you order. Costs are high by Indian standards, but not unreasonable. Fish & chips and salad is typically between Rs 70 and Rs 100; tiger prawns will push the price beyond Rs 200.

Many of these restaurants supply music and videos to add to the attraction, but almost without exception you must come prepared for a long wait. The length of time it takes them to grill a fish is quite amazing. The standards of preparation are also mediocre.

If you want to test your luck at one of the places fronting Lighthouse Beach, try the *Coral Reef Café, the Flamingo Restaurant,* the *Hawah Beach Restaurant,* the *Santana Restaurant* and the *Garzia Seafood Corner.* Just beyond the headland is the *Island View.* There are a host of places back from the beach, although seafood is not the number one concern here. Nicely situated in the rice paddies, the *Lonely Planet* vegetarian restaurant turns out some surprisingly good food. No, we have absolutely nothing to do with it and we are not planning to open a franchised chain!

If you get tired of the interminable wait for meals at the beachside places, consider the mid-range hotels back from the beach. These places have better equipped kitchens than the beach shacks and can turn out more consistent food with much greater speed. The Hotel Seaweed runs the popular *Lucky Coral* rooftop restaurant. The *Rockholm's* restaurant includes a garden area overlooking the sea. At the *Palmanova,* you can eat indoors or on the open balcony. The *Sea Rock* has a balcony overlooking the beach.

On the beach, a number of local women sell fruit to sun worshippers. The ring of 'Hello, baba. Mango? Papaya? Banana? Coconut? Pineapple?' will soon become a familiar part of your day. They'll sell you fruit at any price you're willing to pay, but you'll soon establish what the going rate is and, after that, they'll remember your face and you don't have to repeat the performance. The women rarely have any change, but they're reliable about bringing it to you later. Toddy (coconut beer) and feni (spirits made by distilling the fermented mash of either coconuts or cashew nuts) are available from shops in Kovalam Village.

Getting There & Away

Bus The local No 111 bus between Thiruvananthapuram and Kovalam Beach runs every 15 minutes between about 6 am and 10 pm and costs Rs 3.50. The bus leaves Thiruvananthapuram from stand 19 on M G Rd, 100 metres south of the local bus stand, opposite the Hotel Luciya Continental. Although the bus starts out ridiculously over-crowded, it rapidly empties. At Kovalam, the buses start and finish at the entrance to the Ashok Beach Resort.

There are also direct services to Ernaku-lam and Kanyakumari (Cape Comorin), which are a good way of avoiding the crush at Thiruvananthapuram. Kanyakumari is two hours away and there are four departures daily. One bus leaves each morning for The-kkady in the Periyar Wildlife Sanctuary. Direct buses go to Kollam if you want to do the backwater trip.

Taxi & Auto-Rickshaw A taxi between Thiruvananthapuram and Kovalam Beach will cost about Rs 150. The actual cost depends on where you're going to and from: Museum Rd, at the northern end of Thiruvananthapuram, will be more expen-sive than the bus or railway stations at the southern end; Lighthouse Rd, at the southern end of Kovalam, will be more expensive than the Ashok Beach Resort at the northern end. Auto-rickshaws make the trip for Rs 50 to Rs 60. It's best to arrive at the lighthouse end of the beach (Vizhinjam) because this is much closer to the hotels and there usually aren't any touts around. It's easy to get a taxi from Thiruvananthapuram Airport to the beach.

AROUND KOVALAM
Vizhinjam
Vizhinjam is one km south of Kovalam Beach. It has a big artificial harbour domi-nated by a pink and green mosque on the northern side and a huge Catholic church to the south. From Kovalam Beach, you can hear them trading amplified calls to prayer and mass in the early hours. The beach is packed with boats which set out to fish at sunset. From the beach at night, you can see their lights strung like a necklace along the horizon.

Vizhinjam (Vilinjam) was a capital of the 7th to 11th-century Ay kingdom, and a number of rock-cut temples have been found around the village – reminders of the period when the kingdom was under Tamil influ-ence.

Pulinkudi & Somatheeram
At Pulinkudi, eight km south of Kovalam, there are two interesting alternatives to Kovalam's crowded beaches. The *Surya Samudra Beach Garden* (☎ 48-0413) is a small and very select hotel with individual cottages, many of them constructed from transplanted and rebuilt traditional Keralan houses. There are private beaches, a fantastic natural rock swimming pool and music, martial arts or dance performances at night. The food is superb: breakfast costs Rs 120, lunch Rs 240, dinner Rs 360. From Decem-ber to February, most of the rooms are Rs 2900/3200 or Rs 3300/3600. The prices drop from this peak season to high season, regular season and low season rates.

A little further south is Somatheeram Beach, where the *Somatheeram Ayurvedic Beach Resort* (☎ 48-0600) combines beach life with Ayurvedic medical treatment. In the peak season, most rooms are Rs 900 to Rs 1500. Various treatment packages are available.

Pozhikkara Beach
The *Lagoona Beach Resort* (☎ 44-3738) at Pachalloor village, five km north of Kovalam, is a small, basic place with rooms for between Rs 150 and Rs 250. A local ferry shuttles across the narrow lagoon to the beach, and backwater trips are made at 8 am and 4 pm daily.

LAKSHADWEEP
Population: 51,000

The Lakshadweep archipelago consists of 36 islands some 200 to 300 km off the Kerala coast. The islands are a northern extension of the Maldives chain. Ten of the islands are inhabited. They are Andrott, Amini, Agatti, Bitra, Chetlat, Kadmat, Kalpeni, Kavaratti (headquarters), Kiltan and Minicoy. The islands form the smallest of the Union Territories of India and are the country's only coral islands. The population is 93% Muslim (belonging to the Shafi school of the Sunni sect). Malayalam is the language spoken on all the islands except Minicoy, where the populace speaks Mahl – the language spoken in the Maldives. The main occupations of the island people are fishing and the production of copra and coir. Tourism is an emerging industry.

Legend has it that the islands were first settled by sailors from Kodungallur (Cranganore) who were shipwrecked there after going in search of their king, Cheraman Perumal, who had secretly left on a pilgrimage to Mecca. The first historical records date from the 7th century, when a *marabout* (Muslim saint) was shipwrecked on the island of Amini. Despite initial opposition to his efforts to convert the inhabitants to Islam, he eventually succeeded. When he died, he was buried on Andrott. His grave is revered to this day as a sacred site.

Even after the conversion of the entire population to Islam, sovereignty remained in the hands of the Hindu Raja of Chirakkal. It eventually passed to the Muslim rulers of Kannur in the 16th century and, in 1783, to Tipu Sultan. Following the defeat of Tipu Sultan by the British at the battle of Srirangapatnam in 1799, the islands were annexed by the East India Company. The Union Territory was constituted in 1956.

These palm-fringed, coral islands, with their beautiful lagoons, are every bit as inviting as those in the Maldive archipelago but, until very recently, they were effectively off limits. Now there are regular boat cruises and tours to the island for Indian nationals, and the resort on the uninhabited island of Bangaram is open to foreign tourists. Bangaram is in a six-km by 10-km lagoon with three other smaller islands – Thinnakara, Parali-1 and Parali-2.

Information
There are Lakshadweep offices in Kochi and in New Delhi. Foreign tourists are only allowed to visit Bangaram and stay at the Bangaram Island Resort operated by the Casino Hotel group. The Casino Hotel (☎ (0484) 66-6821), Willingdon Island, Kochi, will obtain the necessary free permit in one or two days.

Places to Stay & Eat
Indian tourists on the regular boat cruises to the islands from Kochi usually stay on board their cruise ship. The 30-room *Bangaram Island Resort* is the only option open to foreign visitors. In the peak season, from mid-December to mid-January, accommodation and all meals costs US$220/230 for singles/doubles. Prices drop to US$130/180 for most of the rest of the year, and down to US$80/130 during the low season.

Scuba diving, snorkelling, deep-sea fishing and boat trips are extra, but kayaks, catamarans and sailboats are available without charge. Reservations should be made through the Manager, Bangaram Island Resort, Casino Hotel (☎ (0484) 66-6821), Willingdon Island, Kochi 682003.

Getting There & Away
Air NEPC flies Kochi-Agatti twice a week for US$300 return. It costs US$30 by boat or US$80 by helicopter from Agatti to the resort.

Boat Package tours by luxury ship are arranged through SPORTS (☎ 34-0387), Lakshadweep Office, Indira Gandhi Rd, Willingdon Island, Kochi 682003. At present, these tours are available only to Indian nationals. The ships, MV *Tipu Sultan* and MV *Bharat Seema,* run four and five-day trips to the islands.

Madras

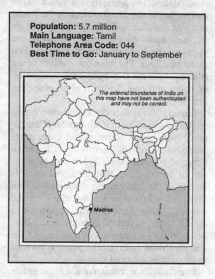

Madras, India's fourth-largest city, is the capital of Tamil Nadu state. It's an enjoyable place because it suffers far less from congestion and overcrowding than other big Indian cities. However, this is rapidly changing and it won't be long before it rivals the others for bustle, noise, fumes and the odours associated with untreated sewage. Catch it while it's still quite pleasant!

Madrassis are zealous guardians of Tamil culture, which they regard as inherently superior to the hybridised cultures further north. They have, for instance, been among the most vociferous opponents of Hindi being made the national language. There is also a deep grass-roots sympathy for the Tamil separatist movement in neighbouring Sri Lanka, though few would have expressed support for the assassination of Rajiv Gandhi at the hands of Tamil extremists.

Although the city has long been important for textile manufacturing, a great deal of industrial expansion, including car-assembly plants, railway coach and truck works, engineering plants, cigarette factories, film studios and educational institutes, has taken place in recent years. Madras is the film centre for Tamil movies – even the State Chief Minister, Jayalalitha Jayaram, is an ex-movie star, as was her predecessor.

The city offers a remarkably efficient range of public services. Here, it's possible to use public buses and urban commuter trains without undue discomfort (except during peak hour). Slums and beggars are less apparent and smaller in number than in other major cities. However, the city suffers from acute water shortages in the summer months, especially if the last monsoon season has been a poor one.

As a tourist attraction, Madras is something of a nonevent compared to the marvels elsewhere in the state. The main reason travellers come here is to transact business or to make a long-distance travel connection.

Population: 5.7 million
Main Language: Tamil
Telephone Area Code: 044
Best Time to Go: January to September

The external boundaries of India on this map have not been authenticated and may not be correct.

Madras

History

Madras was the site of the East India Company's first settlement – founded in 1639 on land given by the Raja of Chandragiri, the last representative of the Vijayanagar rulers of Hampi. A small fort was built at a fishing settlement in 1644 and a town, which subsequently became known as George Town, grew in the area of Fort St George. The settlement became independent of Banten, Java, in 1683 and was granted its first municipal charter in 1688 by James II. It thus has the oldest municipal corporation in India, a fact which Tamil Nadu state governors are only too keen to point out at every available opportunity.

During the 18th and early 19th centuries, when the British and French competed for supremacy in India, the city's fortunes waxed and waned: it was briefly occupied by the French on one occasion. It was used by Clive of India as a base for his military expeditions during the Wars of the Carnatic and, during the 19th century, it was the seat of the Madras presidency, one of the four divisions of British Imperial India.

Orientation

Madras is basically a conglomerate of overgrown villages. However, it can be divided into two main parts. The older section, George Town, is near the dock area northeast of Periyar E V R High Rd (formerly called Poonamallee High Rd). In these narrow, overcrowded streets are the offices of shipping and forwarding agents, some cheaper hotels and restaurants, large office buildings, bazaars and the GPO. The area's focal point is Parry's Corner – the intersection of Prakasam Rd (or Popham's Broadway as it's popularly known) and N S C Bose Rd. Many of the city buses terminate here; the state bus stand and the Thiruvalluvar (TTC) bus stand (the two long-distance bus stands) are close by on Esplanade Rd.

The other main part of the city is south of Periyar E V R High Rd. Through it runs Madras' main road, Anna Salai (also known as Mount Rd), which is home to many of the city's airline offices, theatres, banks, bookshops, craft centres, consulates, tourist offices and top-range hotels and restaurants.

Egmore and Central, Madras' two main railway stations, are close to Periyar E V R High Rd. Egmore is the departure point for most trains to destinations in Tamil Nadu. If you're going interstate, you'll probably leave from Madras Central.

Information

Tourist Offices The Government of India tourist office (☎ 852-4295; fax 852-2193) at 154 Anna Salai is open Monday to Friday from 9.15 am to 5.45 pm, and Saturday and public holidays from 9 am to 2 pm. It's closed Sunday. This office is a good one: the staff are knowledgeable, friendly, and give out heaps of free brochures, including the monthly *Hallo! Madras* guide which lists the city's services (it's also available for Rs 5 from bookstalls around town). Bookings for the India Tourism Development Corporation (ITDC) tours can be made here as well. Bus No 11 or 18 from Parry's Corner or Central station will bring you here.

There are also Government of India information counters at the domestic (☎ 234-0386) and international (☎ 234-5801) airport terminals, but they have limited information.

The ITDC (☎ 827-8884) is at 29 Victoria Crescent, on the corner of Commander-in-Chief (C-in-C) Rd. It's open from 6 am to 6 pm Monday to Saturday and from 6 am to 1 pm Sunday. This is not a tourist office as such, but all the ITDC tours can be booked, and start from, here.

The Tamil Nadu government tourist office (☎ 84-0752; fax 83-0380), 143 Anna Salai, is open daily from 10 am to 5 pm Monday to Friday. You can book all Tamil Nadu Tourism Development Corporation (TTDC) tours from here, as well as make bookings for any of their hotels and lodges. Other branches are at Central station (☎ 56-3351) and the Thiruvalluvar Transport Corporation (TTC) bus stand.

Madras Street Names

Many streets in Madras have recently had official name changes, so there is a confusing melange of names used in the vernacular. Some of them include:

Old Name	New Name
Mount Road	Anna Salai
Poonamallee High Rd	Periyar E V R High Rd
Popham's Broadway	Prakasam Rd
North Beach Rd	Rajaji Salai
South Beach Rd	Kamarajar Salai
Pycroft's Rd	Bharathi Salai
Adam's Rd	Swami Sivananda Salai
Mowbray's Rd	T T K Rd

MADRAS

MADRAS

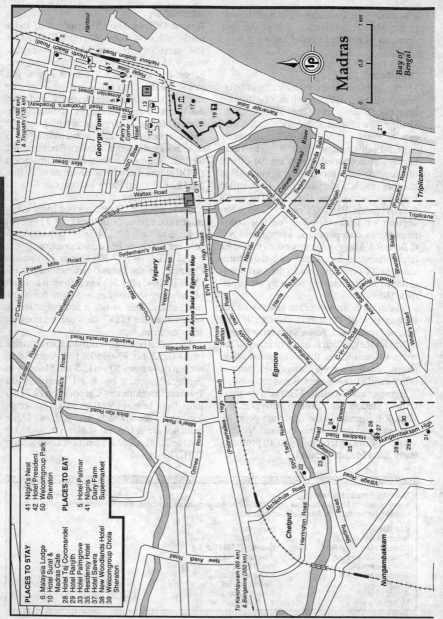

Madras

Bay of Bengal

1 km
0.5
0

PLACES TO STAY
6 Malaysia Lodge
10 Hotel Surat &
   Madras Café
28 Hotel Taj Coromandel
29 Hotel Ranjith
33 Hotel Palmgrove
35 Residency Hotel
37 Hotel Savera
38 New Woodlands Hotel
39 Welcomgroup Chola
   Sheraton
41 Nilgiri's Nest
42 Hotel President
50 Welcomgroup Park
   Sheraton

PLACES TO EAT
5 Hotel Palimar
41 Nilgiris
   Dairy Farm
   Supermarket

MADRAS

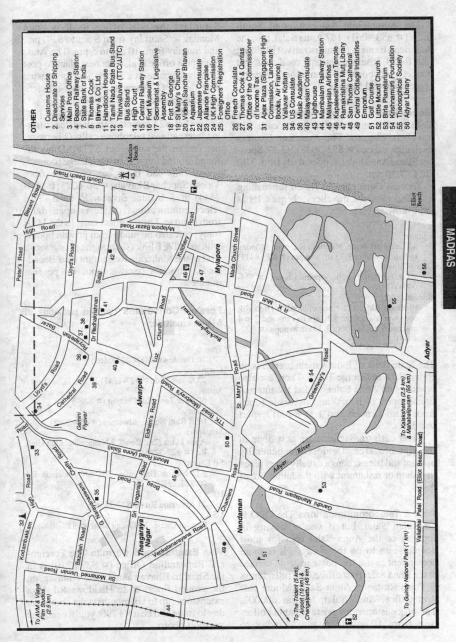

OTHER

1 Customs House
2 Directorate of Shipping
   Services
3 Main Post Office
4 Beach Railway Station
7 State Bank of India
8 Thomas Cook
9 Binny & Co Ltd
11 Handloom House
12 Tamil Nadu State Bus Stand
13 Thiruvalluvar (TTC/JJTC)
   Bus Stand
14 High Court
15 Central Railway Station
16 Fort Museum
17 Secretariat & Legislative
   Assembly
18 Fort St George
19 St Mary's Church
20 Videsh Sanchar Bhavan
21 Aquarium
22 Japanese Consulate
23 Alliance Française
24 UK High Commission
25 Foreigners' Registration
   Office
26 French Consulate
27 Thomas Cook & Qantas
30 Office of the Commissioner
   of Income Tax
31 Apex Plaza (Singapore High
   Commission, Landmark
   Books, Air France)
32 Valluvar Kottam
34 US Consulate
36 Music Academy
40 Malaysian Consulate
43 Lighthouse
44 Mambalam Railway Station
45 Malaysian Airlines
46 Kapaleeshwarar Temple
47 Ramakrishna Mutt Library
48 San Thome Cathedral
49 Central Cottage Industries
   Emporium
51 Golf Course
52 Little Mount Church
53 Birla Planetarium
54 Krishnamurti Foundation
55 Theosophical Society
56 Adyar Library

1010 Madras – Information

The Automobile Association of South India (☎ 852-4061), 187 Anna Salai, is in the American Express (administrative) Building (4th floor). It sells a national road atlas and pocket guidebooks to Bangalore, Mysore, Hyderabad and Madras.

Money Both American Express and Thomas Cook give competitive rates for cash and travellers' cheques. The American Express exchange office (☎ 852-3638), G-17 Spencer Plaza, Anna Salai, is open daily from 9.30 am to 7.30 pm.

Thomas Cook charges Rs 20 for cashing non-Thomas Cook travellers' cheques. It has the following branches:

Egmore
    45 Ceebros Centre, Montieth Rd; open Monday to Saturday from 9.30 am to 6 pm (☎ 825-8417)
George Town
    20 Rajaji Salai; similar opening hours (☎ 534-0994)
Nungambakkam
    Eldorado Bldg, 112 Nungambakkam High Rd; open weekdays from 9.30 am to 1 pm and 2 to 4 pm, and Saturday from 9.30 am to noon (☎ 827-4941)

The State Bank of India's main branch is on Rajaji Salai in George Town. There are also branches on Anna Salai, and at the international (open 24 hours) and domestic (open from 5 am to noon and 1 to 8 pm) airport terminals.

Street cash transactions are best done in the Egmore area. Dealers are generally upfront and the exchange usually takes place in a shop or restaurant with the minimum of fuss.

Post & Telecommunications The GPO is on Rajaji Salai, but if you're staying in Egmore or the Anna Salai area (as most people seem to do these days), it is more convenient to use the poste restante service at the Anna Salai post office. The full address is Poste Restante, Anna Salai (Mount Rd) Post Office, Anna Salai, Madras 600002. The office is open for poste restante collection from 10 am to 6 pm Monday to Saturday; the post office itself is open Monday to Saturday from 8 am to 8.30 pm, and Sunday from 10 am to 5 pm. The Anna Salai post office is also the best place to post parcels because it's much less congested than the GPO. A cheap and super-efficient packing service is available outside.

Both the GPO and the Anna Salai post offices have 24-hour telegraph offices offering international telephone calls. Otherwise, use one of the numerous STD/ISD booths found around town. Reverse-charge (collect) phone calls and faxes can be made from Videsh Sanchar Bhavan (☎ 56-6073; fax 94-4444) at 5 Swami Sivananda Salai. This telecommunications office is open daily from 7 am to 7 pm. Collect calls to the USA (only) can also be made from private booths with an AT&T link (such as the phone kiosk next to the Maharaja Restaurant near Broadlands). This service costs about Rs 4 per five minutes.

Foreign Consulates Foreign missions in Madras include:

France
    16 Haddows Rd (☎ 827-0469)
Germany
    22 C-in-C Rd (☎ 827-1747)
Japan
    60 Spur Tank Rd, Chetput (☎ 826-5594)
Malaysia
    6 Sri Ram Nagar, Alwarpet (☎ 434-3048)
Singapore
    Apex Plaza (2nd floor), 3 Nungambakkam High Rd (☎ 827-3795)
Sri Lanka
    9-D Nawab Habibullah Rd, off Anderson Rd (☎ 827-2270)
UK
    24 Anderson Rd (☎ 827-3136)
USA
    Gemini Circle, 220 Anna Salai (☎ 827-3040)

Visa Extensions & Permits The Foreigners' Registration Office (☎ 827-8210) is in the Shashtri Bhavan annex (rear building, on the ground floor) at 26 Haddows Rd. Visa extensions (up to six months) take about one day to issue and cost Rs 790; you'll need one passport photo.

The office is open weekdays from 9.30 am to 1.30 pm and 2 to 6 pm. Bus Nos 27J and 27RR, from opposite the Connemara Hotel pass by.

If you're planning to visit the Andaman & Nicobar Islands by boat, you'll need to get a permit before buying your boat ticket (air passengers can get the permit on arrival in Port Blair). To get this permit, collect a form from the Directorate of Shipping Services (☎ 522-6873) at 6 Rajaji Salai in George Town. Hand this form, together with two photos, into the Foreigners' Registration Office in the morning, and you should be able to collect the permit the same day between 4 and 5 pm.

Tax Clearance Income tax clearance certificates are available from the Foreign Section, Office of the Commissioner of Income Tax (☎ 827-2011 ext 4004), 121 Nungambakkam High Rd. You need to fill in form No 31 and have a copy of your passport. The procedure takes about 30 minutes.

Libraries & Cultural Centres The British Council Library, 737 Anna Salai, is at the end of a small, bumpy lane next to the building with the big Philips sign on the roof. Casual visitors are not actively encouraged but you can take out temporary membership for Rs 60 a month. It's open Tuesday to Saturday from 11 am to 7 pm.

The American Center Library (☎ 827-3040), attached to the US Consulate, is open daily except Sunday from 9.30 am to 6 pm. The Alliance Française de Madras (☎ 827-1477) at 40 College Rd, Nungambakkam, is open weekdays from 9 am to 1 pm and 3.30 to 6.30 pm, and on Saturday morning.

In Mylapore, the Ramakrishna Mutt Library at 16 Ramakrishna Mutt Rd, not far from the Kapaleeshwarar Temple, specialises in philosophy, mythology and Indian classics. Further south is the Krishnamurti Foundation (☎ 493-7803), 64 Greenways Rd. Across the river, in the Adyar area, is the Adyar Library (☎ 41-3528). It's in the grounds of the Theosophical Society and has a huge collection of books on religion, phi-

losophy and mysticism. It's open Tuesday to Friday from 8 to 11 am and 1.30 to 5 pm. To get to any of these three libraries, take bus No 5 or 19M from Anna Salai.

Bookshops Landmark Books, in the basement of Apex Plaza at 3 Nungambakkam High Rd, has one of the best selections in southern India. Higginbothams at 814 Anna Salai and, to a lesser extent, The Bookshop in Spencer Plaza, have reasonable assortments of novels and coffee-table books. Higginbothams also has kiosks at Central station and the domestic airport.

Bookworms who love inching through mountains of books at close quarters should not miss Giggles Book Shop (☎ 852-0123; fax 852-3361) at the Connemara Hotel. The genial proprietor also runs an extremely efficient and reliable mail-order service.

Travel Agencies The American Express Travel Service (☎ 852-3628) in Spencer Plaza on Anna Salai is efficient.

Medical Services For 24-hour emergency services, head to Apollo Hospital (☎ 827-7447) at 21 Greams Lane.

Fort St George

The fort was built from about 1653 by the British East India Company, but has undergone much alteration since then. It presently houses the Secretariat and the Legislative Assembly. The 46-metre-high flagstaff at the front is actually a mast salvaged from a 17th-century shipwreck.

The **Fort Museum** (☎ 56-1127) has a fascinating collection of memorabilia from the days of the East India Company and the British Raj. Entry is free and it's open from 9 am to 5 pm; closed Friday. Upstairs is the **banqueting hall**, built in 1802, which has paintings of Fort St George's governors and officials of the British regime. Just south of the museum is the **pay accounts office**. It was formerly Robert Clive's house, and one room, known as Clive's Corner, is open to the public.

St Mary's Church, built in 1678-80, was

the first English church in Madras, and is the oldest surviving British church in India. There are reminders in the church of Clive, who was married here in 1753, and of Elihu Yale, the early governor of Madras who went on to found the famous university bearing his name in the USA.

North of the fort, in the High Court Building compound, is the 1844 **lighthouse**, superseded in 1971 by the ugly modern one on the Marina.

If you're coming to Fort St George by auto-rickshaw, ask for 'Secretariat'.

High Court Building

This red Indo-Saracenic monster at Parry's Corner is the main landmark in George Town. Built in 1892, it is said to be the largest judicial building in the world after the Courts of London. You can wander around, and sit in on one of the sessions; court No 13 has the finest furniture and decor.

Government Museum

The government museum is on Pantheon Rd, between Egmore and Anna Salai. The buildings originally belonged to a group of eminent British citizens, known as the Pantheon Committee, who were charged with improving the social life of the British in Madras.

The main building has an excellent **archaeological section** featuring pieces from all the major southern Indian periods including Chola, Vijayanagar, Hoysala and Chalukya. It also houses a good ethnology collection.

The **bronze gallery**, in an adjacent building, has some fine examples of Chola bronze art. Next door is a poorly lit and unimpressive **art gallery**.

The museum complex is open from 9 am to 5 pm; closed Friday and public holidays. Entrance is Rs 3 (Rs 10 for a camera), and the ticket includes entry to the bronze gallery, which the city bus tours omit.

Kapaleeshwarar Temple

This ancient Siva temple, off Kutchery Rd in Mylapore, was constructed in pure Dravid-

ian style and displays the same architectural elements – *gopurams, mandapams*, a tank, etc – that are found in the more famous temple cities of Tamil Nadu. Like most other functioning temples in this state, non-Hindus are only allowed into the outer courtyard. The temple is open for *puja* from 4 am to noon and 4 to 8 pm. There's a camera fee of Rs 10. To get here, catch bus No 21 from Anna Salai or the High Court.

San Thome Cathedral

Built in 1504, then rebuilt in neo-Gothic style in 1893, this Roman Catholic church is said to house the remains of St Thomas the Apostle (Doubting Thomas). It's near Kapaleeshwarar Temple, at the southern end of Kamarajar Salai, close to the seafront.

Sri Parthasarathy Temple

This temple, on Triplicane High Rd, is dedicated to Krishna. Built in the 8th century during the reign of the Pallavas, it was subsequently renovated by the Vijayanagar kings in the 16th century.

Marina & Aquarium

The sandy stretch of beach known as the Marina extends for 13 km. The guides on the city tour insist that this is the longest beach in the world!

The aquarium, on the seafront near the junction of Bharathi Salai and Kamarajar Salai, is open daily between 2 and 8 pm, except on Sunday and holidays when it is open from 8 am. Entrance costs only Rs 0.50, but it's a miserable place, worth missing just to encourage its closure.

South of the aquarium is the **Ice House**. This relic of the Raj era was used to store enormous blocks of ice cut from the Great Lakes in the northern USA and shipped to India for refrigeration purposes.

Guindy National Park

This park (☎ 41-3947), on the southern outskirts of Madras, is so vast that spotting wildlife can be difficult. However, it's the only place in the world where it's still possible to see herds of the fast-dwindling species of Indian antelope (black buck). It also has small numbers of spotted deer, civet cats, jackals, mongoose and various species of monkeys. There's also a separate, uninspiring **snake park**.

Both parks are open between 8.30 am and 5 pm, though the main park is closed on Tuesday; entrance costs Rs 1. Probably the best way to get to Guindy is to take an urban commuter train. There are also regular buses such as Nos 21E, 23C and 18B from Parry's Corner, or Nos 5 and 5A from opposite the Anna Salai post office.

Film Studios

Madras' big film studios, such as Vijaya or AVM, are in the western suburb of Kodambakkam. It's supposedly possible to visit them but you need the manager's permission, which is not readily given.

It's also possible to pick up work as a film extra; the going rate of pay is about Rs 250 for a day. The Maharaja Restaurant, on Triplicane High Rd, is one place where extras are occasionally recruited.

Organised Tours

Tours of Madras and the nearby temple cities are run by the TTDC or ITDC. For details on where to book, see the Tourist Offices section at the start of this chapter. TTDC tours can also be booked at the TTC bus stand on Esplanade Rd (☎ 534-1982) between 6 am and 9 pm, or at Central station (☎ 56-3351).

There are a number of private travel agents around Egmore station which offer similar tours for the same price.

A few examples of tours include:

City Sightseeing Tour
This includes visits to Fort St George, government museum, Valluvar Kottam, Snake Park, Kapaleeshwarar Temple and Marina Beach. The daily tours are fairly good value, although somewhat rushed.
Tours run from 7.30 am to 1.30 pm, and again from 1.30 to 6 pm; the cost is Rs 60. The TTDC tour commentary is a confusion of tautologies and non-English gibberish, but the guides are helpful.

Kanchipuram & Mahabalipuram
This tour includes three of the four ancient temples at Kanchipuram and the 7th-century Pallavan antiquities at Mahabalipuram. A stop is also made at VGP Golden Beach Resort and the Crocodile Bank near Mahabalipuram.
The daily tours go from 6.30 am to 7 pm, and cost Rs 135 or Rs 220 (air-con bus) including breakfast and lunch. It's good value if you're strapped for time, but otherwise it's a breathless dash.

Tirupathi
This all-day tour to the famous Venkateshwara Temple at Tirumala in southern Andhra Pradesh is good value if you don't have the time or inclination to do it yourself. Be warned, however, that at least 12 hours are spent on the bus. The price includes 'special *darshan*' (for details, see the boxed section under Tirupathi in the Andhra Pradesh chapter). This usually takes two hours, but on weekends and holidays it can take five hours, which means the bus doesn't get back to Madras until midnight.
The daily tours officially last from 6 am to 10 pm. The fare is Rs 240 or Rs 325 (air-con), and includes breakfast, lunch and the Rs 30 special darshan fee.

Festivals

From the end of December to the second week of January, Madras is host to a Carnatic classical dance and music festival. Prestigious performances are held at various music academies; contact the Government of India tourist office for details.

Places to Stay

There are four main areas for hotels in Madras. The cheapest hotels are in George Town, between Mint St, N S C Bose Rd and Rajaji Salai. The Egmore area is the main accommodation and travel hub of Madras, but competition for rooms can be fierce. Many of them seem to be permanently full, and getting a bottom or mid-range room after noon requires persistence. Triplicane, a suburb to the south-east of Anna Salai, is less chaotic than Egmore and preferred by many budget travellers. The top-range hotels are mainly along Anna Salai and the roads leading off this principal artery.

If you'd prefer to stay in a private home, contact the Government of India tourist office, which has a list of places in Tamil

MADRAS

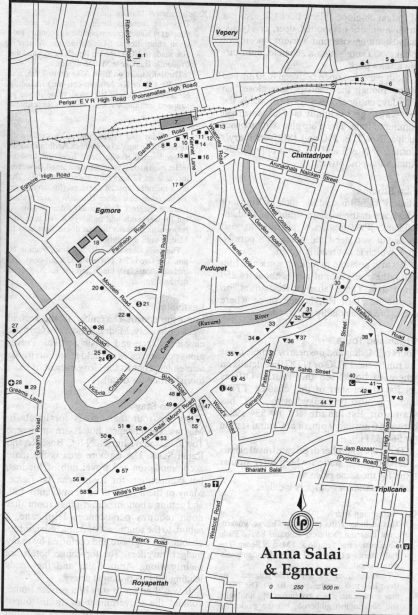

Vepery

Ritherdon Road

1 ■

2 ■

4 ▼
5 ■

Periyar E V R High Road (Poonamallee High Road)

3 ■
6

7

13 ■

Vinayaka Road

Gandhi Irwin Road
Kennet Lane

11 ■ 12 ■
8 ■ 9 ■ 10 ▼
14 ■

15 ■
16 ■

Chintadripet

Arunachala Naicken Street

Egmore High Road

17 ■

Egmore

Pantheon Road

18 ■

19 ■

Marshalls Road

Pudupet

Langs Garden Road

West Cooum Road

Harris Road

Montieth Road

20 ●

21 ●

22 ■

26 ●

23 ●

C-in-C Road

25 ■
24 ■

27 ●

28 ✚
29 ■

Greams Lane

Greams Road

Victoria Crescent

Binny Road

River (Kuvam)

30 ●

31 ■
32 ■

33 ▼

34 ● 36 ▼ 37 ▼

35 ▼

Wallajah Road

Ellis Street

38 ▼

39 ●

40 ◖
41 ■
42 ■

43 ▼

General Patters Road

Thayar Sahib Street

45 ■
46 ■

48 ▼
47 ▼

49 ●

54 ▼
55 ■

50 ●

51 ● 52 ■

Anna Salai (Mount Road)

53 ●

Wood's Road

44 ▼

56 ■

57 ●

58 ■

White's Road

59 ■

Triplicane

Bharathi Salai

Jam Bazaar
(Pycroft's Road)

60 ■

Triplicane High Road

Peter's Road

Westcott Road

61 W

**Anna Salai
& Egmore**

0   250   500 m

Royapettah

MADRAS

	PLACES TO STAY		
1	Salvation Army Red Shield Guest House	11	Rajabhavan, Vasanta Bhavan & Omar Khayyam
2	YWCA International Guest House	16	Shaanti Restaurant
3	TTDC Youth Hostel	32	Mathura Restaurant
8	Hotel Ramprasad & Tourist Home	33	Manasa
9	Alarmel Lodge & Hotel Impala Continental	35	Dasaprakash Restaurant
		36	Buharis Restaurant
11	Hotel Chandra Towers & Hotel Imperial	37	Chungking
		38	Hotel Tirumulai
12	People's Lodge	41	Maharaja Restaurant
13	Hotel Vaigai	43	Hotel Ganga
14	Hotel New Victoria	44	Srinivasa Hotel
15	Lakshmi Lodge	47	Aavin Milk Bar
16	Hotel Sri Durga Prasad & Hotel Pandian	48	Raintree Restaurant
		55	Tom's Place
17	Dayal-De Lodge	56	Yamuna Restaurant
22	Hotel Ambassador Pallava		
25	Hotel Kanchi		**OTHER**
29	Sindoori Hotel	4	U-Rent (Picnic Hotel)
42	Broadlands	5	Train Reservations Office
48	Hotel Connemara & Chola Bar	6	Park Railway Station
56	Hotel Madras International	7	Egmore Railway Station
		11	Sherry's Bar
	PLACES TO EAT	18	Government Museum
		19	Art Gallery
10	Bhoopathy Cafe	20	British Airways
		21	Thomas Cook
		23	Indian Airlines/Air India
		24	India Tourism Development Corporation
		26	German Consulate

27	Sri Lanka High Commission
28	Apollo Hospital
30	India Silk House
31	Anna Salai Post Office
34	Higginbothams
39	NEPC Airlines
40	Big Mosque
45	State Bank of India
46	Tamil Nadu Government Tourist Office
48	Giggles Book Shop
49	Spencer Plaza (American Express, The Bookshop, Cathay Pacific)
50	British Council Library
51	Air Lanka
52	Victoria Technical Institute
53	Lufthansa & Singapore Airlines
54	Government of India Tourist Office
57	Automobile Association of South India
58	Swiss Air
59	Wesley Church
60	Triplicane Post Office
61	Sri Parthasarathy Temple

Nadu (and neighbouring states) which offer **home-stay accommodation** (or paying guest accommodation as it's called here). Some of the participating homes in Tamil Nadu are located on lush tea plantations, and most range in price from about Rs 80 to Rs 300 per person.

Places to Stay – bottom end
George Town If you're in search of crowds and extreme bustle, this is the area to stay. The *Malaysia Lodge* (☎ 522-7053), 44 Armenian St, off Prakasam Rd, was a minor legend among travellers in the 1970s, but few people stay here any longer. It's still very cheap but also very basic, and the dark rooms are anything but spotless. Singles/doubles with common bathroom are Rs 47/70 or Rs

60/80 with attached bathroom. Less basic is the *Hotel Surat* (☎ 58-9236) at 138 Prakasam Rd, above the Madras Cafe. It's not bad value – singles/doubles with attached bathroom cost Rs 126/175 – but the rooms at the front are incredibly noisy.

Egmore A 20-minute walk from Egmore station is the popular *Salvation Army Red Shield Guest House* (☎ 532-1821), 15 Ritherdon Rd, which takes both men and women. It's a clean, quiet place in leafy surroundings. A dorm bed costs Rs 25 and doubles/triples are Rs 90/150. Rooms have clean sheets and fans but bathroom facilities are communal. Checkout is 9 am.

The *TTDC Youth Hostel* (☎ 58-9132) at 3 Periyar E V R High Rd is a couple of minutes' walk from Central station along a horrendously busy road. The dorms don't suffer too badly from the noise, but the double rooms do. Dorm beds are Rs 40, and the ill-kept doubles with attached bathroom are Rs 175. It's not a bad place if you're just in Madras overnight.

There's a string of hotels along Gandhi Irwin Rd, opposite the entrance to Egmore station. The cheapest is *Alarmel Lodge* (☎ 825-1248), at No 17-18, which has singles/doubles with communal bathroom for Rs 50/75. The *Hotel Ramprasad* (☎ 825-4875), at No 22, and the *Tourist Home* (☎ 825-0079), at No 21, are much more expensive and usually full. Overpriced rooms, all with attached bath, start at Rs 150/225 or Rs 175/275 with air-con.

On nearby Kennet Lane, the huge *Lakshmi Lodge* is clean and quiet, and has doubles with attached bathroom for Rs 143 including taxes. The *Hotel Sri Durga Prasad* (☎ 825-3881), at No 10, is similar and has singles/doubles for Rs 80/130. Both these places are often full. At the southern end of Kennet Lane, the quiet *Dayal-De Lodge* (☎ 825-1159), 486 Pantheon Rd, is adequate value at Rs 99/186 for a single/double with attached bathroom and 24-hour hot water. It has lumpy beds, which may account for the fact that it's rarely full.

East of Egmore station, the *People's Lodge* (☎ 83-5938), Whannels Rd, is a relic which has been popular for years. It has doubles with attached bathroom for Rs 150, including taxes, but it too is often full.

There are also *retiring rooms* at Central and Egmore stations.

Triplicane The very popular *Broadlands* (☎ 84-8131/5573) is at 16 Vallabha Agraharam St, off Triplicane High Rd, opposite the Star movie theatre. It's an impressive, pastel-toned, old place with rooms around three interconnected leafy courtyards. The rooms, though simple, are spotless and have wicker easy chairs, a coffee table and fan. There's a good notice board, you can hire bicycles and make collect international phone calls (for a service charge of Rs 30).

No other budget hotel in Madras compares, providing you don't mind their exclusion policy – if you're White, you're all right; if you're Indian, you're not allowed to set foot in the place! Take an Indian friend in with you and see what happens. Dorm beds here cost Rs 45, small single rooms with common bathroom Rs 90, and singles/doubles with attached bathroom are Rs 99/190 including taxes. As a rule, the higher the room number, the better the room (Nos 43 and 44 are the tops). To get there, take an auto-rickshaw – most of the drivers know where it is – or bus No 30, 31 or 32 from Esplanade Rd, outside the TTC bus stand, in George Town. From Egmore station, take bus No 29D, 22 or 27B. It's a 20-minute walk from the GITO.

Places to Stay – middle

Most of the mid-range hotels are in the Egmore area. However, if you're willing to either pay a bit more or explore further afield, you'll find several good options elsewhere.

Egmore The *Hotel Impala Continental* (☎ 825-0484), opposite Egmore station at 12 Gandhi Irwin Rd, is good value. Encircling a quiet courtyard, this hotel offers a range of rooms from singles/doubles at Rs 120/170 to deluxe doubles at Rs 224 and air-con doubles/triples at Rs 324/360. All the rooms have attached bathrooms and there's 24-hour hot water. A TV can be hired for Rs 35 a day. Credit cards are not accepted.

Close by, at No 6, is the *Hotel Imperial* (☎ 825-0376; fax 825-2030). It's fair value, but not if you get one of the older rooms where mosquitoes are a problem. Like the Impala, it's set around a courtyard, containing shops, massage parlours, a newsstand and travel agents. Singles/doubles are Rs 125/250 or Rs 350/375 with air-con. There are also air-con suites for Rs 450/500. The hotel has two restaurants (one open-air), a nightclub and a popular bar.

The *Hotel Vaigai* (☎ 83-4959), at 3 Gandhi Irwin Rd, is a featureless hotel which has doubles at Rs 195 to Rs 250, or Rs 395 to Rs 425 with air-con. The hotel has a vegetarian and non-veg restaurant and a bar.

Somewhat more expensive is the popular *Hotel Pandian* (☎ 825-2901; fax 825-8459), 9 Kennet Lane. Ordinary singles/doubles are Rs 300/350; air-con rooms start at Rs 400/450. The hotel has an excellent restaurant with a veg/non-veg menu, and there's also a bar.

The most expensive option in this area is the refurbished *Hotel Chandra Towers* (☎ 825-8171), 9 Gandhi Irwin Rd. It has modern, but somewhat cramped, singles/doubles for Rs 600/700, and executive rooms for Rs 700/800. There's an impressive permit room (bar; see boxed section later in this chapter) and the staff are welcoming. The *Hotel New Victoria* (☎ 825-3638), 3 Kennet Lane, has similar rates but is overpriced.

Further afield, across the railway lines, is the *YWCA International Guest House* (☎ 532-4234), 1086 Periyar E V R High Rd. Clean and spacious singles/doubles cost Rs 300/350, air-con doubles Rs 450, and family rooms (three beds) Rs 500. It accepts both men and women, but there's a transient membership fee of Rs 10 – valid for one month. Its restaurant serves Indian and Western food.

Elsewhere The *Hotel Kanchi* (☎ 827-1100), 28 C-in-C Rd, looks upmarket but is actually good value. Spacious singles/doubles, all with small balconies, are Rs 275/295 or Rs 365/395 with air-con. There are also more expensive suites. The hotel has an enclosed rooftop restaurant and a cheaper ground-floor dining hall and a bar.

There are a couple of places in Mylapore, south of the centre, which offer excellent value. The *New Woodlands Hotel* (☎ 827-3111), 72/75 Dr Radhakrishnan Salai, has mostly air-con rooms for Rs 250/400. The hotel has a billiard room and two restaurants. On the same road, at No 58, is the newer *Nilgiri's Nest* (☎ 827-5222; fax 826-0214). Bright, modern singles/doubles cost Rs 375/525, and there are deluxe rooms for Rs

575/725. It has a good restaurant and a popular adjoining supermarket.

In Nungambakkam, there are two hotels convenient for consulates, airline offices and the Foreigners' Registration Office. The impersonal *Hotel Ranjith* (☎ 827-0521), 9 Nungambakkam High Rd, has singles/doubles for Rs 400/500, or Rs 500/600 with air-con. The *Hotel Palmgrove* (☎ 827-1881), 5 Kodambakkam High Rd, has rooms for Rs 250/275, or Rs 350/480 with air-con. There's a bar and restaurants but no swimming pool.

Places to Stay – top end

Many of the top-end hotels are situated in an arc which stretches from Nungambakkan High Rd, south-west of Anna Salai, through to Dr Radhakrishnan Salai. There are also a few along or just off Anna Salai itself. Unless otherwise stated, all the following hotels have central air-con, a swimming pool, multi-cuisine restaurants, and a bar.

Just off Anna Salai is perhaps Madras' best-known hotel, the old-fashioned but elegant *Hotel Connemara* (☎ 852-0123; fax 825-7361), Binny Rd. Owned by the Taj Group, it has standard singles/doubles for US$75/85 and deluxe rooms for US$95/105. In the same area is the cheaper and more modern four-star *Hotel Ambassador Pallava* (☎ 826-8584; fax 826-8757), 53 Montieth Rd, which offers smart rooms from Rs 1435/1860.

At No 693 Anna Salai, the *Hotel Madras International* (☎ 852-4111; fax 86-1520) has rooms from Rs 800/950. To the south-west is the *Residency Hotel* (☎ 825-3434; fax 825-0085) at 49 G N Chetty Rd, Theagaraya Nagar. It's one of the cheapest in this range and is popular with middle-class Indian families. Singles/doubles start at Rs 650/800. Neither of these two hotels have a swimming pool.

In Mylapore, Dr Radhakrishnan Salai is a good top-end hunting ground. The *Hotel Savera* (☎ 827-4700; fax 827-3475) at No 69 has well-appointed singles/doubles for Rs 950/1200. The *Hotel President* (☎ 83-2211; fax 83-2299) at No 16 has rooms starting at Rs 590/790. This is a big place with spacious

MADRAS

MADRAS

rooms but the atmosphere is decidedly bland.

Madras has no shortage of five-star hotels where you can indulge in a room for US$90/100 or more. The choice includes:

Hotel Taj Coromandel, 17 Nungambakkam High Rd, is as luxurious as all the Taj Group hotels (☎ 827-2827; fax 825-7104)

The Trident, 1/24 G S T Rd, is the closest luxury hotel to the airport (five km) but it's a long haul from the city centre (☎ 234-4747; fax 234-6699)

Welcomgroup Chola Sheraton, 10 Cathedral Rd (the extension of Dr Radhakrishnan Salai), is closer to the centre and less expensive than the Park Sheraton (☎ 828-0101; fax 827-8779)

Welcomgroup Park Sheraton, 132 T T K Rd, Alwarpet, epitomises executive-class opulence (☎ 499-4101)

Places to Eat

There are thousands of vegetarian restaurants in Madras, ranging from the simple 'meals' restaurants where a *thali* lunch (and sometimes dinner) is served on a banana leaf for around Rs 15 to sumptuous spreads for 10 times that amount in the major hotels. Breakfast at the simpler restaurants, which open shortly after dawn, consists of such staples as *masala dosa, idli,* curd and coffee.

Non-vegetarian restaurants are much thinner on the ground, and Western-style breakfasts are almost impossible to find outside mid-range and top-end hotels. If you're not a vegetarian or simply want a break from south Indian cuisine, it's probably best to go for lunch or dinner at a hotel which has a restaurant specialising in such things as tandoori, Mughlai, Chinese or Continental dishes. Obviously prices vary, but a meat or fish dish in a mid-range hotel should cost between Rs 35 and Rs 60.

George Town In this old part of town, there are many vegetarian restaurants although few stand out. The *Madras Cafe* on Prakasam Rd dishes out excellent and cheap thalis. The *Hotel Palimar* on Armenian St is a good air-con vegetarian restaurant.

Egmore Most of the restaurants here are along Gandhi Irwin Rd, in front of Egmore station. They include the vegetarian *Rajabhavan,* at the entrance to the Hotel Imperial, and the clean, highly recommended *Bhoopathy Cafe,* directly opposite the station. The newly renovated *Vasanta Bhavan,* on the corner of Gandhi Irwin Rd and Kennet Lane, is bustling with waiters and features an upstairs dining hall, from which you can watch the street scene below. The stall at the front sells milk-based sweets.

Non-vegetarian food is good at both the *Omar Khayyam* restaurant in the Hotel Imperial and the restaurant inside the Hotel New Victoria. The *Shaanti* restaurant at the Pandian Hotel is cosy and quiet and serves south Indian, tandoori, Chinese and Continental food. You can expect to pay about Rs 30 to Rs 50 for a meal here.

Triplicane There are several good places for cheap meals along Triplicane High Rd. Most backpackers seem to end up at least once at the *Maharaja Restaurant,* around the corner from Broadlands. The varied vegetarian menu includes toasted sandwiches, lassis, lunchtime thalis, and snacks until midnight. Close by, the little *Hotel Ganga* in the Himalaya Hotel has good vegetarian snacks. Further north, the *Hotel Tirumulai* serves luscious banana-leaf thalis (Rs 15) and produces the biggest dosas you're ever likely to see – ask for the Rs 12 'Tirumulai special dosa.

Another unpretentious locals' haunt is the *Srinivasa Hotel* on Ellis St. This place boasts superb sauces – the korma is particularly divine. There's a partitioned area for women and couples.

If you're after fruit, vegetables or spices, head south along Ellis St to the junction of Bharathi Salai, where you'll find the colourful Jam Bazaar.

Anna Salai Area The *Mathura Restaurant,* on the 2nd floor of the Tarapore Tower on Anna Salai, is an upmarket vegetarian restaurant. Thalis are good value at Rs 40, as is the business lunch (Rs 20), served from 11 am to 3 pm on weekdays.

On the opposite side of the road, the 1st-floor *Buharis Restaurant* has excellent tandoori fare. There's an air-con dining hall and an open-air terrace which is pleasant in the evening. Neighbouring *Chungking* is an excellent and very popular Chinese restaurant. Count on around Rs 50 to Rs 70 per person (closed Thursday).

The *Manasa* restaurant, next to Higginbothams bookshop on Anna Salai, has also been recommended. At No 806 Anna Salai, the *Dasaprakash Restaurant* (also known as AVM Dasa), is an upmarket cafe-style restaurant serving vegetarian fare, including fresh salads (Rs 75). The ice creams here are very good.

Aavin is a stand-up milk bar, a few doors from the Government of India tourist office on Anna Salai. It serves lassis, ice cream and excellent cold milk, plain or flavoured. Round the corner is *Tom's Place*, a small air-con Chinese restaurant catering mainly for businesspeople but it's good for a snack.

The *Hotel Connemara* has a wonderful pastry shop, but for a real treat head for the Connemara's Rs 190 lunchtime buffet (served in the coffee shop). This is a long-running favourite, the food is fantastic and the pianist knows a few good numbers. Also in the Connemara is the *Raintree* restaurant, which is open in the evening. The outdoor setting is superb, the service very attentive and there's live classical dancing and music

every night. It's not difficult to spend Rs 250 on an à la carte meal here. There's also a Rs 190 buffet on Saturday and Sunday nights.

Further south-west along Anna Salai, the air-con *Yamuna Restaurant* at the Madras International Hotel mixes an excellent lassi, and has masala dosas and dahi vadais that are worth trying.

The vegetarian restaurant at the *New Woodlands Hotel* on Dr Radhakrishnan Salai gets rave reviews for its superb, crisp dosas, tandoori fare and milk burfis.

Self-Catering The *Nilgiri Dairy Farm* supermarket, next to the Nilgiri's Nest Hotel on Dr Radhakrishnan Salai, is a good place for dairy products, boxed tea, coffee and other edibles (closed Tuesday).

Entertainment

Outside the top-end hotels, nightlife in Madras is pretty tame. If you don't frequent bars (and let's face it, in most cases why would you want to in Tamil Nadu?), it's early to bed and up at sparrow's fart.

Bars & Discos One bar (sorry, 'permit room') which doesn't resemble purgatory is *Sherry's* at the Hotel Imperial. It's a popular place and attracts a bunch of lively locals who trade jokes and stories all day and night.

MADRAS

Permit Rooms

Until the early 1990s, Tamil Nadu was a 'dry' state and Madras, the capital, was no exception. Anyone who wanted an alcoholic drink had to obtain a liquor permit from the tourist office before being allowed to buy a beer from a 'permit room' (bar). These permits were farcical, since they enabled patrons to purchase enough liquor to get cirrhosis of the liver.

Although prohibition has been abolished, the name 'permit room' survives and drinking alcohol in a bar in Tamil Nadu can still leave you with the feeling that it's only barely tolerated. This is immediately apparent when you enter a hotel (where most permit rooms, except those in the back of wine shops, are located) and ask for the bar. Unless you're in a five-star hotel, the receptionist will inevitably point down – down to the basement where natural light never penetrates, and where the artificial lighting is so dim you could almost believe you're up to no good drinking alcohol.

Thankfully, not all permit rooms are like this. The Hotel Tamil Nadu in Rameswaram, for example, has a permit room at ground level and there's even a view of the sea through its barred windows!

With Tamil Nadu now boasting the highest per capita consumption of alcohol in the country, the prohibition lobby is stronger than ever. For this reason, you'll find health warnings on beer labels, dry days (such as Gandhi's birthday) and draconian government taxes on alcohol which ensure that the price of a beer in Tamil Nadu is one of the highest in India (just over US$1 at the current rate of exchange). ■

If you're looking for one of the city's better permit rooms, head to the *Chola Bar* at the Hotel Connemara. Beers here (Rs 70) are served in gleaming tankards and are presented with a mouthwatering platter of snacks – if you polish all of these off you can forget about dinner.

Maxim's is a nightclub-cum-dance show at the Hotel Imperial which closes at 11 pm.

For discos, there's the choice of *Gatsby* at the Park Sheraton, *Cyclone* at the Hotel President or the *Sindoori Hotel's* Saturday night bash. Expect to pay about Rs 100 per couple to get into these places.

Cinema There are always a few English-language movies being screened around town but they're generally heavy-action macho movies. Check the local papers for details.

Classical Music & Dance The Music Academy (☎ 827-5619), on the corner of T T K Rd and Dr Radhakrishnan Salai, is Madras' most popular public venue for Carnatic classical music and Bharat Natyam dance concerts. Performances are not held daily, so contact the tourist office or check the *Daily Hindu* newspaper to find out what's on. You can expect to pay about Rs 150 for a good seat.

Another concert venue is Kalakshetra, or the Temple of Art, which was founded in 1936 and today is committed to the revival of classical dance and music, together with traditional textile design and weaving. Occupying a huge campus in the southern suburb of Tiruvanmiyur, this place offers students the opportunity to study with a guru in the Indian tradition of *gurukulam*, where education is inseparable from other life experiences.

Things to Buy
For conventional souvenirs, there's a whole range of craft shops and various government emporia along Anna Salai. The emporia, as elsewhere in India, have more-or-less fixed prices. Also on Anna Salai is the Victoria Technical Institute, a rambling old place selling traditional crafts, handmade clothing,

batik greeting cards and other bits and pieces on behalf of development groups.

The best place for quality arts and crafts is the brand new Central Cottage Industries Emporium in Temple Towers, 476 Anna Salai, Nandanam. This place is a visual delight, with superb displays and an excellent range of works from all over India. No 18 bus along Anna Salai will drop you here.

For top-grade silks and cottons, head to either the government-sponsored Handloom House, 7 Rattan Bazaar, George Town, or the more expensive India Silk House on Anna Salai.

The stalls which clutter the footpaths along Anna Salai, around Parry's Corner or in front of Egmore station, are excellent places to pick up cheap 'export reject' clothes. You need to choose carefully, but good shirts for Rs 30 are not hard to find. Unfortunately, most carry logos you'd be embarrassed to sport on your chest, but there are some which might pass muster elsewhere in the world. There are also a lot of stalls selling watches and electronic goods in case you missed the duty free on the way into India.

For musical instruments, try A R Dawood & Sons, 286 Triplicane High Rd, not far from the Broadlands Hotel.

Getting There & Away
Air Madras is an international arrival point and an important domestic airport. The Anna International Airport is well organised and not too heavily used, making Madras a good entry or exit point. There's rarely more than one plane on the ground at any given time. Right next door is the relatively new Kamarajar Domestic Airport.

When leaving India, a departure tax of Rs 150 is payable on flights from Madras to Sri Lanka and the Maldives, and Rs 300 on other international destinations.

Domestic Airlines Addresses of domestic carriers that fly into Madras include:

Damania Airways
    17 K N Khan Rd (☎ 828-0610)
East West Airlines
    9 Kodambakkam High Rd (☎ 827-7007)

Domestic Flights from Madras

Destination	Time (hours)	IC	Fare (US$)	D5	Fare (US$)
Ahmedabad	3.35	4w	143	-	-
Bangalore	0.45	5d	37	6w	40
Bhubaneswar	4.20	-	-	3w	155
Bombay	1.45	2d	110	3w	210
Calcutta	2.10	2d	137	-	-
Coimbatore	2.00	4w	53	1/2d	55
Delhi	2.45	2d	162	-	-
Goa	2.30	3w	100	3w	100
Hubli	2.30	-	-	3w	100
Hyderabad	1.00	2d	57	-	-
Kochi (Cochin)	1.35	3w	70	1d	70
Kozhikode (Calicut)	3.10	-	-	3w	75
Madurai	1.15	3w	50	1/2d	55
Mangalore	2.00	3w	52	5w	80
Port Blair	2.00	3w	136	-	-
Pune	3.00	3w	102	3w	105
Trichy	0.45	3w	34	1d	45
Trivandrum	1.45	1d	65	3w	70
Vijayawada	1.20	-	-	3w	70
Visakhapatnam	2.40	3w	105	3w	105

* Abbreviation code: IC – Indian Airlines
D5 – NEPC Airlines

Indian Airlines
19 Marshalls Rd, Egmore; open Monday to Saturday from 8 am to 8 pm (☎ 825-1677; fax 827-7675)

Jet Airways
14 K N Khan Rd (☎ 825-7914)

Moduluft
Prestige Point (2nd floor), 16 Haddows Rd (☎ 826-0048)

NEPC Airlines
GR Complex, 407/408 Anna Salai (☎ 434-4259; fax 434-4370)

Domestic Flights In addition to the flights from Madras listed in the table above, East West Airlines flies daily to Bombay and Delhi; Moduluft has daily flights to Bombay and six times a week to Hyderabad; Damania Airways flies daily to Bombay and Calcutta; and Jet Airways has services twice daily to Bombay.

International Airlines Addresses of international airlines with offices in Madras include:

Air France
Apex Plaza, 3 Nungambakkam High Rd (☎ 825-0295)

Air India
19 Marshalls Rd, Egmore; open daily from 9.30 am to 1 pm and 1.45 to 5.30 pm (☎ 827-4477)

Air Lanka
Mount Chambers, 758 Anna Salai (☎ 852-2301/4232)

British Airways
Khaleeli Centre, Montieth Rd, Egmore (☎ 827-4272)

Cathay Pacific
Spencer Plaza, 769 Anna Salai (☎ 825-6318)

Kuwait Airways
55 Montieth Rd, Egmore (☎ 826-1331)

Lufthansa
167 Anna Salai (☎ 852-5095)

Malaysian Airlines (MAS)
Karumuttu Centre, 498 Anna Salai (☎ 45-6651)

Maldives Airways
Crossworld Tours, Rosy Towers, 7 Nungambakkam High Rd (☎ 47-1497)

Qantas
112 Nungambakkam High Rd (☎ 827-8680)

Singapore Airlines
167 Anna Salai (☎ 852-1872)

MADRAS

Swiss Air
    191 Anna Salai (☎ 826-1583)

International Flights There are flights
to/from Colombo (Air Lanka and Indian Air-
lines), Dubai (Air India), Frankfurt (Air
India and Lufthansa), Jakarta (Air India),
Kuala Lumpur (Malaysian Airlines, Air
India and Indian Airlines), Malé (Indian Air-
lines), London (British Airways), Penang
(Malaysian Airlines), Riyadh (Saudia), and
Singapore (Singapore Airlines, Malaysian
Airlines, Air India and Indian Airlines).

Bus The Tamil Nadu state bus company,
Thiruvalluvar Transport Corporation (TTC),
and its bus terminal (also known as the
Express bus stand) are on Esplanade Rd in
George Town, around the back of the High
Court building. Interstate buses, which are
run by the affiliated Jayalalitha Jayaram
Transport Corporation (JJTC), also leave
from here.

The TTC/JJTC reservation office (☎ 534-
1835/1408) upstairs is computerised and is
open from 7 am to 9 pm daily. There's a Rs
2 reservation fee, and you have to pay Rs
0.25 for the form!

See the table below for some of the
TTC/JJTC bus services from Madras.

The state bus stand is on the other side of

Prakasam Rd. This terminal is total chaos
and nothing is written in English. However,
this does not present any real difficulties
since an army of young boys attach themselves to every foreigner, and for Rs 1 they'll
find your bus.

The main reason to use this stand is for
buses to Mahabalipuram. There are a number
of services, the most direct being No 188 and
188A/B/D/K. The journey takes two hours
and costs Rs 9.40. There are 20 of these daily.
The other Mahabalipuram services are Nos
19A, 19C, 119A (via Covelong, 21 times
daily) and 108B (via Madras airport and
Chengalpattu, four times daily).

There are also a number of private bus
companies with offices in the Egmore area
which run superdeluxe video buses on a
daily basis to cities such as Bangalore,
Coimbatore, Madurai and Trichy. Prices are
similar to the state buses, although the
private buses tend to be more comfortable.

Train The reservation office at Central
station is on the 2nd floor of the building
adjacent to the station (across the smelly
drain which passes between the two buildings). In this booking hall, you can also make
reservations for trains originating in
Ahmedabad, Bombay, Calcutta, Delhi,
Jaipur, Lucknow, Patna, Pune and many
other places.

Bus Services from Madras					
Destination	**Route No**	**Frequency** **(d-daily)**	**Distance** **(km)**	**Travel time** **(hours)**	**Fare** **(Rs)**
Bangalore	831, 828	20d	351	8	75
Chidambaram	300	3d	233	7	37
Hyderabad	-	1d	717	14	201
Kanyakumari	282	6d	700	16	122
Kodaikanal	461	2d	511	12	79
Madurai	135, 137	30d	447	10	88
Mysore	863	2d	497	11	100
Ooty	468, 860	2d	565	15	108
Rameswaram	166	1d	570	13	85
Thanjavur	323	15d	321	18	50
Tirupathi	802	3d	150	4	31
Trichy	123, 124	35d	319	8	50
Trivandrum	894	3d	752	17	145

Train Services from Madras

Destination	Train number & name	Departure time	Distance (km)	Duration (hours)	Fare (Rs) (2nd/1st)
Bangalore	2007 *Shatabdi Exp***	6 am MC*	356	5.00	310/620
	6007 *Bangalore Mail*	10 pm MC		7.00	99/296
Bombay	6064 *Chennai Exp*	7 am MC	1279	24.00	239/757
	7010 *Bombay Mail*	10.20 pm MC		30.30	
Calcutta	2842 *Coromandel Exp*	8.10 am MC	1669	28.00	273/904
	6004 *Howrah Mail*	10.30 pm MC		32.20	
New Delhi	2621 *Tamil Nadu Exp*	9 pm MC	2194	34.00	308/1122
Hyderabad	6059 *Charminar Exp*	6.10 pm MC	794	14.20	180/552
Kochi (Cochin)	6041 *Alleppey Exp*	7.35 pm MC	700	14.30	163/492
Madurai	6717 *Pandian Exp*	7.10 pm ME	556	11.00	139/415
Mettuppalayam	6005 *Nilgiri Exp*	9.05 pm MC	630	10.00	155/464
Mysore	2007 *Shatabdi Exp***	6 am MC	500	7.15	380/760
Rameswaram	6113 *Sethu Exp*	6.05 pm ME	656	14.30	158/473
Thanjavur	6153 *Cholan Exp*	9.45 am ME	351	9.30	79/296
Tirupathi	6057 *Saptagiri Exp*	6.20 am MC	147	2.45	38/149
Trichy	2637 *Vaigai Exp*	6 am ME	337	5.50	76/282
Trivandrum	6319 *Trivandrum Mail*	6.55 pm MC	921	16.45	200/588
Varanasi	6039 *Ganga Kaveri Exp*	5.30 pm MC	2144	39.00	305/1101

* Abbreviation for train station: MC = Madras Central; ME = Madras Egmore
** Air-con only; fare includes meals and drinks.

Also here is the 'Tourist Cell', which deals with Indrail Pass and tourist-quota bookings. This 'cell' is immensely useful for foreign visitors unfamiliar with the Indian Railways system.

The reservation office (☎ 135, 825-1564/55) is open Monday to Saturday from 8 am to 2 pm and 2.15 to 8 pm; Sunday from 8 am to 2 pm. At Egmore station, the booking office is in the station itself, and is open the same hours as the office at Central station.

See the table above for a selection of trains from Madras.

Boat Services to the Andaman and Nicobar Islands are prone to change, so make enquiries about the latest schedules. There is currently one boat, the *MV Nancowry*, which sails from Madras every 10 or so days to Port Blair, on South Andaman. The trip takes about 52 hours. Once a month, the boat sails via Car Nicobar. This voyage takes an extra two days; foreign nationals are not allowed to disembark at Car Nicobar.

Cabin fares per person are Rs 2000 (two-berth), Rs 1650 (four-berth) and Rs 1300 (six-berth). There's also 'bunk class' (or 'mass accommodation' as it's also described) which costs Rs 550 per person. Meals are available on board for about Rs 160 per day in the cabin classes and Rs 100 per day in the bunk class.

Tickets are issued at the Directorate of Shipping Services (☎ 522-6873) at 6 Rajaji Salai (opposite the Customs House) in George Town. Foreigners must get a permit for the islands before they buy a boat ticket (see the Visa Extensions & Permits section at the start of this chapter for details).

Should you be in need of a shipping agent, try Binny & Co Ltd (☎ 58-6894) at 65 Armenian St, George Town.

Getting Around

To/From the Airport The domestic and international terminals are 16 km south of the city centre. The cheapest way to reach them is by suburban train from Egmore to Tirusulam, which is just across the road from the terminals. The trains run from 4.15 am until 11.45 pm, the journey takes about 30 minutes, and the fare is Rs 4/40 in 2nd/1st class. These trains are not overly crowded, except during peak hours.

Public buses from Anna Salai pass the airport entrance, but trying to board a bus with a rucksack can be fun and games, especially during peak hour. The buses to use are Nos 18J, 52, 52A/B/C/D and 55A. All these buses start and finish at Parry's Corner and go along Anna Salai.

There's also a minibus service for Rs 60 between the airport and the major hotels (it also drops at Broadlands) but it's a slow way to get into town because of the number of stops it makes. The booking counter is adjacent to the taxi counters at the international terminal.

An auto-rickshaw to the airport costs Rs 55 by the meter but, since all drivers refuse to use meters on this journey, you'll need to haggle hard to pay anywhere near this. About Rs 70/100 for a day/night trip is normal. A yellow-and-black taxi costs Rs 150. At the airport itself, you can buy a ticket for a taxi ride into the centre for a fixed price at the prepaid taxi kiosk inside the international terminal. The fares are Rs 125/140/160 to Anna Salai/Egmore/George Town.

Train The suburban Egmore-Beach train costs Rs 2; to Guindy it's Rs 4. Madras' suburban trains have relatively uncrowded ladies' compartments, which can be a blessing (for women travellers only of course!) if you're using the train to get to/from the airport.

Bus The bus system in Madras is less over-burdened than those in the other large Indian cities, although peak hour is still best avoided. The seats on the left-hand side and the rear seat are generally reserved for women.

Some useful routes include:

Nos 23C, 29, 29A, 16 & 27D – Egmore (opposite People's Lodge) to Anna Salai
Nos 31, 32 & 32A – Triplicane High Rd (Broadlands) to Central station and Parry's Corner. The No 31 continues on to Rajaji Salai (for the GPO and the Directorate of Shipping Services)
Nos 22, 27B & 29A – Egmore to Wallajah Rd (for Broadlands)
Nos 9, 10 & 17D – Parry's Corner to Central and Egmore stations
Nos 11, 11A, 11B, 11D, 17A, 18 & 18J – Parry's Corner to Anna Salai

Taxi Up to five people can ride in a taxi. They cost Rs 10 for the first 1.5 km and Rs 2.50 for each subsequent km. Most drivers will attempt to quote you a fixed price rather than use the meter, so negotiate.

Auto-Rickshaw These little yellow monsters cost Rs 5 for the first 1.5 km, and Rs 2.50 for each subsequent km. Again, persuasion may be required before drivers will use the meter.

Moped If you're feeling brave and have an international motorcycle licence, you can hire a moped or scooter. The cost, including a helmet (of sorts), is Rs 100 per day for a Kinetic Honda scooter, or Rs 60 for a TVS moped. Insurance costs a few rupees more. Contact U-Rent (☎ 58-8828) at the Picnic Hotel, 1132 Periyar E V R High Rd.

LEANNE LOGAN

LEANNE LOGAN

LEANNE LOGAN

Madras
Top: The heart of Madras.
Middle: Tika powder vendor, Jam Bazaar.
Bottom: Madras in the monsoon.

LEANNE LOGAN

LEANNE LOGAN

Tamil Nadu
   Top: Krishna Mandapam, Mahabalipuram.
Bottom: Detail of Arjuna's Penance, Mahabalipuram.

Tamil Nadu

The southern state of Tamil Nadu is the most 'Indian' part of India. The Aryans never brought their meat-eating influence to the extreme south, so this is the true home of Indian vegetarianism. The early Muslim invaders and, later, the Mughals made only fleeting incursions into the region. As a result, Hindu architecture here is at its most vigorous while Muslim architecture is virtually nonexistent. Even the British influence was a minor one, despite the fact that Madras was their earliest real foothold on the subcontinent.

There were a number of early Dravidian kingdoms in the south. The Pallavas, with their capital at Kanchipuram, were the earliest and were superseded by the Cholas, centred at Thanjavur (Tanjore). Further south, the Pandyas ruled from Madurai, while in the neighbouring region of Karnataka, the Chalukyans were the main power.

Tamil Nadu is the home of Dravidian art and culture, characterised best by the amazingly ornate temples with their soaring towers known as *gopurams*. A trip through Tamil Nadu is very much a temple hop between such places as Kanchipuram, Chidambaram, Kumbakonam, Tiruchirappalli, Thanjavur, Madurai, Kanyakumari and Rameswaram. There are also earlier temples in Tamil Nadu, most notably the ancient shrines of Mahabalipuram. Sometime in the future, a special tourist train service – similar in concept to Rajasthan's Palace on Wheels – is planned to operate between many of these temple towns.

Population: 61.5 million
Area: 130,069 sq km
Capital: Madras
People per sq km: 472
Main Language: Tamil
Literacy Rate: 64%
Best Time to Go: January to September

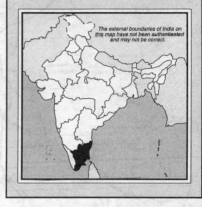

The external boundaries of India on this map have not been authenticated and may not be correct.

Dravidian Temples

The Dravidian temples of the south, found principally in Tamil Nadu, are unlike the classically designed temples located further north. The central shrine of a Dravidian temple is topped by a pyramidal tower of several storeys known as the *vimana*. One or more entrance porches, the *mandapams*, lead to this shrine. Around the central shrine, there is a series of courts, enclosures and even tanks. Many of the larger temples have '1000-pillared halls' although, in fact, there are rarely actually 1000 pillars. At Madurai, there are 985 pillars; the Sri Ranganathaswamy Temple in Tiruchirappalli (Trichy) has 940, while at Tiruvarur there are only 807.

The whole complex, which often covers an enormous area, is surrounded by a high wall with entrances through towering *gopurams*. These rectangular, pyramidal towers are the most notable feature of Dravidian design. They are often over 50 metres high, but their interest lies not only in their size – most are completely covered with sculptures of gods, demons, mortals and animals. The towers positively teem with life, as crowded and busy as any Indian city street. Furthermore, many are painted in such a riot of colours that the whole effect is that of a Hindu Disneyland. This is no recent development – like classical Greek statues, they were all painted at one time. ■

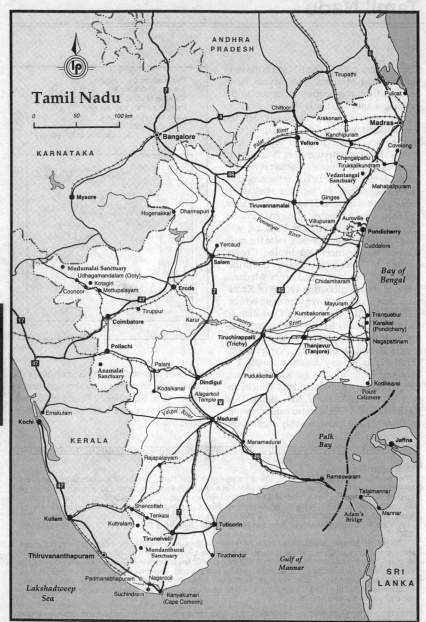

TAMIL NADU

Tamil Nadu

0   50   100 km

ANDHRA
PRADESH

KARNATAKA

Tirupathi

Pulicat

Chittoor

Arakonam

Madras

Bangalore

Vellore

Kanchipuram

Covelong

Chengalpattu

Tirukkalikundram

Mysore

Vedantangal
Sanctuary

Mahabalipuram

Hogenakkal

Dharmapuri

Gingee

Tiruvannamalai

Villupuram

Auroville

Ponnaiyar River

Pondicherry

Yercaud

Cuddalore

Mudumalai Sanctuary

Salem

Udhagamandalam (Ooty)

Kotagiri

Coonoor

Mettupalayam

Erode

Chidambaram

Bay of
Bengal

Mayuram

Tiruppur

Karur

Kumbakonam

Tranquebar

Coimbatore

Cauvery River

Karaikal
(Pondicherry)

Pollachi

Palani

Tiruchirappalli
(Trichy)

Thanjavur
(Tanjore)

Nagapattinam

Anamalai
Sanctuary

Kodaikanal

Dindigul

Pudukkottai

Kodikkarai

Alagarkoil
Temple

Point
Calimere

Ernakulam

Vaigai River

Madurai

Kochi

KERALA

Manamadurai

Palk
Bay

Jaffna

Rajapalaiyam

Talaimannar

Rameswaram

Mannar

Shencottah

Tenkasi

Adam's
Bridge

Kollam

Tuticorin

Kuttralam

Tirunelveli

Thiruvananthapuram

Mundanthurai
Sanctuary

Tiruchendur

Gulf of
Mannar

SRI
LANKA

Padmanabhapuram

Nagercoil

Suchindram

Kanyakumari
(Cape Comorin)

Lakshadweep
Sea

Pilar River

In addition, Tamil Nadu has an important group of wildlife reserves, some fine beaches and a number of pleasant hill stations, including the well-known Udhagamandalam (Ooty).

The people of Tamil Nadu, the Tamils, are familiar faces far from their home state, many having emigrated to Singapore, Malaysia and Sri Lanka. Despite their reputation as hard workers, the state has a relatively easy-going and relaxed feel.

Tamil Nadu offers the traveller excellent value, particularly in accommodation. Hotel prices are generally lower than they are further north and standards are often higher. In addition, the state tourist corporation has created a chain of hotels which offer reasonable mid-range accommodation in most centres of interest. If you'd prefer to stay in a private home, contact the Government of India tourist office which has a list of places in Tamil Nadu (and neighbouring states) which offer home-stay accommodation (or paying guest accommodation as it's called here). Some of the participating homes in Tamil Nadu are located on lush tea plantations, and most range in price from about Rs 80 to Rs 300 per person.

On a culinary level, Tamil Nadu is India's vegetarian state *par excellence*. You may get jaded with endless *thalis* while you're here (you'll never be able to say the same of the Tamils who seem to devour their thalis in acts of physical indulgence), but the food is good and consistently great value. Unfortunately, you'll rarely have the same pleasure drinking alcohol here (to find out why, see the boxed section on Permit Rooms in the Madras chapter) and, if you like a beer with your meal, it's good to remember that most non-vegetarian restaurants will have alcohol while exclusively vegetarian restaurants will not.

Northern Tamil Nadu

VELLORE
Population: 323,000
Telephone Area Code: 0416

Vellore, 145 km from Madras, is a semirural bazaar town. It is noteworthy only for the Vijayanagar fort and its temple, which are in an excellent state of preservation and worth visiting.

The town has a modern church built in an old British cemetery, which contains the tomb of a captain who died in 1799 'of excessive fatigue incurred during the glorious campaign which ended in the defeat of Tipoo Sultaun'. Here, too, is a memorial to the victims of the little known 'Vellore Mutiny' of 1806. The mutiny was instigated by the second son of Tipu Sultan, who was incarcerated in the fort at that time, and was put down by a task force sent from Arcot.

Wildlife Sanctuaries
There are six wildlife sanctuaries in Tamil Nadu, three close to the east coast and the others in the richly forested mountains on the borders of Kerala and Karnataka. The Guindy National Park, within the metropolitan boundaries of Madras, is the smallest.

All the sanctuaries except Guindy offer accommodation in pretty basic Forest Rest Houses. At Mudumalai there are also more comfortable private lodges. It is possible to turn up at the government rest houses without making prior arrangements. However, it's advisable to book in advance as rooms cannot be allocated to unannounced guests until late in the evening when there's no further possibility of anyone arriving with a booking.

On the whole, transport facilities are very limited – some of the parks don't even have a vehicle for animal-viewing. This means getting to the remote parts of the sanctuaries, where you're far more likely to see animals, is all but impossible unless you have your own vehicle. And even with a private vehicle you may not get too far as in some parks (Mudumalai for example) private vehicles have been banned from touring. Some of the sanctuaries offer elephant rides through the forest which should be booked in advance if you don't want to be queuing for hours. Despite all these apparent drawbacks, visiting one of Tamil Nadu's wildlife sanctuaries can be a very rewarding experience. ■

Surprisingly, Vellore also has one of the country's best hospitals, and the people who come here from all over India for medical care give this humble town a cosmopolitan feel.

Vellore Fort

The fort is constructed of granite blocks and surrounded by a moat which is supplied by a subterranean drain fed from a tank. It was built in the 16th century by Sinna Bommi Nayak, a vassal chieftain under the Vijayanagar kings, Sada Sivaraja and Sriranga Maharaja. Later, it became the fortress of Mortaza Ali, the brother-in-law of Chanda Sahib who claimed the Arcot throne, and was taken by the Adil Shahi sultans of Bijapur. In 1676, it passed briefly into the hands of the Marathas until they, in turn, were displaced by the nawab, Daud Khan, of Delhi in 1708. The British occupied the fort in 1760, following the fall of Srirangapatnam and the death of Tipu Sultan. It now houses various public departments and private offices, and is open daily.

The small **museum** inside the fort complex contains sculptures dating back to Pallava and Chola times. Shoes must be taken off before entering.

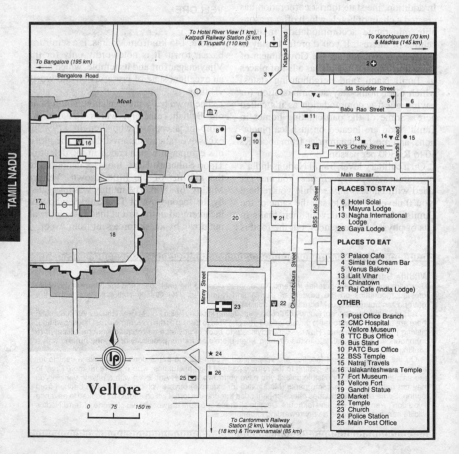

To Hotel River View (1 km),
Katpadi Railway Station (5 km)
& Tirupathi (110 km)

Katpadi Road

To Kanchipuram (70 km)
& Madras (145 km)

To Bangalore (195 km)

Bangalore Road

Moat

Ida Scudder Street

Babu Rao Street

KVS Chetty Street

Gandhi Road

Main Bazaar

Minny Street

BSS Koil Street

Chunambukara Street

Vellore

0   75   150 m

To Cantonment Railway
Station (2 km), Vellamalai
(18 km) & Tiruvannamalai (85 km)

PLACES TO STAY

6   Hotel Solai
11 Mayura Lodge
13 Nagha International
    Lodge
26 Gaya Lodge

PLACES TO EAT

3   Palace Cafe
4   Simla Ice Cream Bar
5   Venus Bakery
13 Lalit Vihar
14 Chinatown
21 Raj Cafe (India Lodge)

OTHER

1   Post Office Branch
2   CMC Hospital
7   Vellore Museum
8   TTC Bus Office
9   Bus Stand
10 PATC Bus Office
12 BSS Temple
15 Natraj Travels
16 Jalakanteshwara Temple
17 Fort Museum
18 Vellore Fort
19 Gandhi Statue
20 Market
23 Temple
22 Temple
23 Church
24 Police Station
25 Main Post Office

TAMIL NADU

Jalakanteshwara Temple

This temple was built about the same time as the fort (around 1550) and, although it doesn't compare with the ruins at Hampi, it is still a gem of late Vijayanagar architecture and has some stunning carvings in the *mandapam*. During the invasions by the Adil Shahis of Bijapur, the Marathas and the Carnatic nawabs, the temple was occupied as a garrison and desecrated. Following this, it ceased to be used. It is open daily from 6 am to 1 pm and 3 to 8 pm, and it costs Rs 0.25 to leave your shoes.

Places to Stay

Vellore's cheap hotels are concentrated along, or close to, Babu Rao St, near the bus stand and hospital. One of the best is the new *Nagha International Lodge* (☎ 26-731) at 13 K V S Chetty St. This modern, five-storey hotel has 60 singles/doubles which, though not as grand as the foyer would imply, are good value at Rs 46/77.

Cheaper is the no-frills *Mayura Lodge* (☎ 25-488) at 85 Babu Rao St. This old favourite has clean and airy rooms for Rs 35/55. On the same street, the *Hotel Solai* (☎ 22-996) is more expensive at Rs 49/80, and the rooms have no windows.

For something a bit better, head one km north on Katpadi Rd to the *Hotel River View* (☎ 25-568). Though modern and clean, this place is definitely misnamed as it's at least 500 metres from the river with views of nothing more exotic than a smelly drain. Rooms cost Rs 210/250 with bathroom, Rs 320/390 with air-con, and there are three restaurants, a bar and a garden.

Places to Eat

Ida Scudder St is dotted with 'meals' restaurants. One of the best is the oddly named *Simla Ice Cream Bar* at No 88. For years, this tiny place has been serving Vellore's best north Indian vegetarian fare – though there's not an ice cream to be seen! Run by the jovial Inder Pal Singh, the restaurant has a tiny tandoori oven which churns out piping-hot naans.

The spacious *Palace Cafe*, near the round-about, does excellent thalis for Rs 10. This place is forever busy and, whether you dine downstairs or on the mezzanine, you'll always feel in the thick of things.

For pseudo-Chinese food, there's *Chinatown*, opposite Natraj Travels on Gandhi Rd, where you can get chicken and rice for Rs 25.

The *Lalit Vihar*, K V S Chetty St, has Gujarati meals for Rs 16 including all-you-can-eat chapatis. In the India Lodge opposite the bazaar, the *Raj Cafe* has vegetarian meals.

The *Venus Bakery*, opposite the CMC Hospital, has freshly baked biscuits and bread.

Getting There & Away

Bus As elsewhere in Tamil Nadu, the area is serviced by the regional bus company, (in this case PATC), and the statewide Thiruvalluvar Transport Corporation (TTC). The dusty bus terminal is chaotic and nothing is in English.

TTC buses run to Tiruchirappalli (No 104, Rs 47), Madras (Nos 139 and 280) and Madurai (Nos 168, 866 and 983, Rs 63). All these buses originate in Vellore and can be booked in advance. Others, which pass through en route (and may be full), go to Madras, Bangalore, Tirupathi (2½ hours, Rs 19), Thanjavur and Ooty.

PATC has 26 buses a day to Kanchipuram (2½ hours, Rs 10) starting at 5 am. They also have buses to Madras (30 daily, Rs 20), Bangalore (14 daily, Rs 34) and Tiruchirappalli (Rs 35).

Train Vellore's main railway station is five km north at Katpadi. This is the junction of the broad-gauge line from Bangalore to Madras, and the metre-gauge Tirupathi to Madurai line (which runs via Tiruvannamalai, Villupuram, Chidambaram, Thanjavur and Tiruchirappalli). The smaller Cantonment station, two km south of town, is on the metre-gauge line only.

The 228-km trip from Katpadi to Bangalore (4½ hours) costs Rs 56/205 in 2nd/1st class. To Madras (130 km, two hours) it's Rs

34/131. The daily train to Madurai (15 hours) leaves at 6.50 pm; to Tirupathi (105 km, three hours) it's at the unsociable hour of 1.50 am.

Buses wait outside Katpadi station for trains to arrive and the journey into Vellore (Rs 1.30) takes anything from 10 to 30 minutes.

AROUND VELLORE
Vellamalai (18 km)
The temple of Vellamalai is dedicated to Siva's son, Kartikaya (Murga in Tamil). There's a temple at the bottom of the hill but the main temple, carved from a massive stone, is at the top. Shoes must be removed at the base of the hill. There's a good view of the bleak countryside around Vellamalai – the ground is stony and strewn with boulders. The cloth knots you will see tied to trees are requests that wishes be granted. The one-hour trip from Vellore on bus No 20 (hourly) costs Rs 4.

KANCHIPURAM
Population: 180,000
Telephone Area Code: 04112

Sometimes known as Siva Vishnu Kanchi, Kanchipuram is one of the seven sacred cities of India and was, successively, capital of the kingdoms of the Pallavas, Cholas and rajas of Vijayanagar. During Pallava times, it was briefly occupied by the Chalukyans of Badami, and by the Rashtrakutas when the battle fortunes of the Pallava kings reached a low ebb.

Kanchipuram is a spectacular temple city and its many gopurams can be seen from a long way away. Of the original 1000 temples, there are still about 125 left spread out across the city. Many of them are the work of the later Cholas and of the Vijaya-nagar kings.

As it's a famous temple city visited by plenty of pilgrims and tourists, there is usually an army of hangers-on. Have plenty of small change handy to meet various demands for baksheesh from 'temple watchmen', 'shoe minders', 'guides' and as-

sorted priests. All the temples are closed between noon and 3.30 or 4 pm.

Kanchi is also famous for its hand-woven silk fabrics. This industry originated in Pallava times, when the weavers were employed to produce clothing and fabrics for the kings. The shops which sell silk fabrics, such as those along the road to the Devarajaswami Temple, are used to busloads of Indian tourists in a hurry and prices are consistently higher than in Madras. To get any sort of bargain you need to know your silk well and have done some legwork on prices in Madras.

Other than the temples, Kanchipuram is a dusty and fairly nondescript town and there's precious little to see or do except when the temple car festivals take place.

Kailasanatha Temple
Dedicated to Siva, Kailasanatha is one of the earliest temples. It was built by the Pallava king, Rayasimha, in the late 7th century, though its front was added later by his son, King Varman III. It is the only temple at Kanchi which isn't cluttered with the more recent additions of the Cholas and Vijaya-nagar rulers, and so reflects the freshness and simplicity of early Dravidian architecture.

Fragments of the 8th-century murals which once graced the alcoves are a visible reminder of how magnificent the temple must have looked when it was first built.

The temple is run by the Archaeology Department and is very interesting. Quite unusually, non-Hindus are allowed into the inner sanctum.

Vaikunta Perumal Temple
Parameshwara and Nandi Varman II built this temple between 674 and 800 AD, shortly after the Kailasanatha Temple. It is dedicated to Vishnu. The cloisters inside the outer wall consist of lion pillars and are representative of the first phase in the architectural evolution of the grand 1000-pillared halls of later temples.

Sri Ekambaranathar Temple
The Sri Ekambaranathar Temple is dedicated

to Siva and is one of the largest temples in Kanchipuram, covering nine hectares. Its 59-metre-high gopuram and massive outer stone wall were constructed in 1509 by Krishna Devaraja of the Vijayanagar Empire, though construction was originally started by the Pallavas and the temple was later extended by the Cholas. Inside are five separate enclosures and a 1000-pillared hall (which actually contains 540 differently decorated pillars).

The temple's name is said to be a modified form of Eka Amra Nathar – the Lord of the Mango Tree – and in one of the enclosures is a very old mango tree, with four branches representing the four Vedas. The fruit of each of the four branches is said to have a different taste, and a plaque nearby claims that the tree is 3500 years old. The tree is revered as a manifestation of the god and is the only 'shrine' that non-Hindus are allowed to walk around. You can also partake of the sacred ash (modest contributions gratefully accep-

ted). As this is still a functioning Hindu temple, non-Hindus cannot enter the sanctum sanctorum. With the permission of the temple priest, it's possible to climb to the top of one of the gopurams.

A 'camera fee' of Rs 3 goes towards the upkeep of the temple. The visit could cost you more, however, as this is undoubtedly one of the worst temples for hustlers.

Kamakshi Amman Temple

Dedicated to the goddess Parvati, this imposing temple is the site of the annual Car Festival, held on the 9th lunar day in February/March. When not in use, the ornately carved wooden car is kept partially covered in corrugated iron halfway up Gandhi Rd. The temple has a golden gopuram in the centre.

Devarajaswami Temple

Like the Sri Ekambaranathar Temple, this is an enormous monument with massive outer

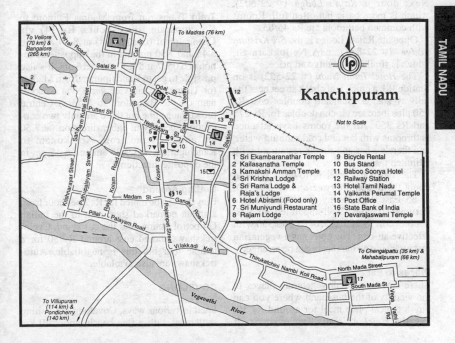

1 Sri Ekambaranathar Temple
2 Kailasanatha Temple
3 Kamakshi Amman Temple
4 Sri Krishna Lodge
5 Sri Rama Lodge & Raja's Lodge
6 Hotel Abirami (Food only)
7 Sri Muniyundi Restaurant
8 Rajam Lodge
9 Bicycle Rental
10 Bus Stand
11 Baboo Soorya Hotel
12 Railway Station
13 Hotel Tamil Nadu
14 Vaikunta Perumal Temple
15 Post Office
16 State Bank of India
17 Devarajaswami Temple

walls and a beautifully sculptured 1000-pillared (actually only 96) hall. One of its most notable features is a huge chain carved from a single piece of stone. The temple is dedicated to Vishnu and was built by the Vijayanagar kings. Entrance is Rs 1 and there is a camera fee of Rs 5.

Places to Stay

Most of the cheap (and noisy) lodges are clustered in the centre of town, just a few minutes' walk from the bus stand. Closest to the bus stand is the friendly *Rajam Lodge* (☎ 22-519), 9 Kamarajar St, which has singles/doubles/triples with attached bathroom for Rs 40/65/100.

At 20 Nellukkara St, the *Sri Rama Lodge* (☎ 22-435) boasts of offering 'gracious living', though the rooms are basic. Singles/doubles start at Rs 80/90, or Rs 250/300 with air-con. All the rooms have attached bathroom with hot and cold running water and the hotel has a good vegetarian restaurant. Next door is *Raja's Lodge* (☎ 22-602), which is more basic but often full. Rooms with common bathroom are Rs 45/65.

Opposite Raja's Lodge is the *Sri Krishna Lodge* (☎ 22-831), 68A Nellukkara St, which is similar in quality and price.

The *Hotel Tamil Nadu* (☎ 22-552) is on Station Rd, a quiet, leafy back street near the railway station. Standard doubles cost Rs 150 plus there are air-con doubles for Rs 275 and 350. All the rooms have attached bathrooms with hot and cold running water, and there's a bar and simple restaurant with a limited menu.

The swankiest hotel in town is without doubt the *Baboo Soorya Hotel* (☎ 22-555), at 85 East Raja Veethy near the Vaikunta Perumal Temple. Well-appointed singles/doubles cost Rs 225/275, or Rs 300/350 with effective air-con. The hotel has a vegetarian restaurant but no bar (beers can be arranged).

Places to Eat

There are many small vegetarian places in the vicinity of the bus stand where you can buy a typical plate meal for around Rs 10. Try the *Hotel Abirami*, Kamarajar St. If you're tired of thalis – and there's not much else – you could try the non-vegetarian *Sri Muniyundi Restaurant* (there's no English sign), also on Kamarajar St.

For a minor splurge, try the restaurant at the *Baboo Soorya Hotel* – but make sure the curd is fresh.

Getting There & Away

Bus As elsewhere, the timetable at the bus stand is in Tamil, but there is no problem finding a bus in the direction you want to go. There are five direct buses daily to Mahabalipuram (No 212A, about two hours, Rs 10). Alternatively, take one of the more frequent buses to Chengalpattu and then catch another one from there to Mahabalipuram.

There are direct TTC buses to Tiruchirappalli (No 122), Madras (No 828, 76 km, two hours) and Bangalore (No 828).

There are also plenty of PATC buses to Madras, Vellore and Tiruvannamalai, as well as private buses to Pondicherry.

Train Trains run from Madras Egmore to Kanchipuram (three hours, Rs 14) via Chengalpattu (Chingleput) at 8.20 am and 5.45 and 7.50 pm and in the opposite direction at 6.05, 7 and 8.30 am and 6 pm. It's also possible to get to Kanchipuram from Madras (or Tirupathi), and vice versa, via Arakkonam on the Bangalore to Madras Central broad-gauge line but there are only two connections per day in either direction (at 7.50 am and 5.20 pm from Arakkonam to Kanchipuram, and 9.25 am and 6.45 pm in the opposite direction).

Getting Around

Bicycles can be rented for Rs 2 per hour from a small, unmarked shop next to the Indian Oil petrol station near the bus stand. Cyclerickshaws should cost around Rs 50 for a temple tour but this is negotiable. Autorickshaws are also available.

COVELONG

Telephone Area Code: 04128

Spelt in various ways, Covelong is a fishing settlement with a fine beach, about 20 km north of Mahabalipuram. The remains of a fort have been converted into the expensive Tamil Nadu Tourist Development Corporation's (TTDC) *Fisherman's Cove Resort* (☎ 2304) where there are rooms from Rs 1700 to Rs 3000, and an excellent restaurant.

MAHABALIPURAM (Mamallapuram)
Population: 13,000
Telephone Area Code: 04113

World famous for its shore temple, Mahabalipuram was the second capital and sea port of the Pallava kings of Kanchipuram, the first Tamil dynasty of any real consequence to emerge after the fall of the Gupta Empire.

Though the dynasty's origins are lost in the mists of legend, it was at the height of its political power and artistic creativity between the 5th and 8th centuries AD, during which time the Pallava kings established themselves as the arbiters and patrons of early Tamil culture. Most of the temples and rock carvings here were completed during the reigns of Narasimha Varman I (630-668 AD) and Narasimha Varman II (700-728 AD). They are notable for the delightful freshness and simplicity of their folk-art origins, in contrast to the more grandiose monuments built by later larger empires such as the Cholas. The shore temple in particular strikes a very romantic theme and is one of the most photographed monuments in India. It and all the other places of interest in Mahabalipuram are floodlit each night.

The wealth of the Pallava Kingdom was based on the encouragement of agriculture, as opposed to pastoralism, and the increased taxation revenue and surplus produce which could be raised through this settled lifestyle. The early Pallava kings were followers of the Jain religion, but the conversion of Mahendra Varman I (600-630 AD) to Shaivism by the saint Appar was to have disastrous effects on the future of Jainism in Tamil Nadu, and explains why most temples at Mahabalipuram (and Kanchipuram) are dedicated to either Siva or Vishnu.

The sculpture here is particularly interest-ing because it shows scenes of day-to-day life – women milking buffaloes, pompous city dignitaries, young girls primping and posing at street corners or swinging their hips in artful come-ons. In contrast, other carvings throughout the state depict gods and goddesses, with images of ordinary folk conspicuous by their absence. Stone carving is still very much a living craft in Mahabalipuram, as a visit to any of the scores of sculpture workshops in and around town testifies.

Positioned at the foot of a low-lying, boulder-strewn hill where most of the temples and rock carvings are to be found, Mahabalipuram is a pleasant little village and very much a travellers' haunt. Here you can find an excellent combination of cheap accommodation, mellow restaurants catering to Western tastes (especially in terms of

Cobra-headed serpent deity, Naga

seafood), a good beach, handicrafts *and* the fascinating remains of an ancient Indian kingdom.

Orientation & Information

The tourist office (☎ 2232) is staffed by helpful and enthusiastic people. They have a range of leaflets as well as a list of bus times and can direct you to an agency which will make bookings for trains out of Madras. It's open daily from 9 am to 5.45 pm.

You can change most travellers' cheques at the Indian Overseas Bank. It is open on weekdays from 10 am to 2 pm and Saturday until noon.

Orient yourself by visiting the lighthouse, from where there are good views. It's open from 2 to 4 pm. Entry costs Rs 1. No photography is allowed for 'security reasons' – there's a nuclear power station visible on the coast, a few km south.

Arjuna's Penance

Carved in relief on the face of a huge rock, Arjuna's Penance is the mythical story of the River Ganges issuing from its source high in the Himalaya. The panel (27 metres by nine metres) depicts animals, deities and other semidivine creatures, fables from the *Panchatantra*, and Arjuna doing a penance to obtain a boon from Siva. It's one of the freshest, most realistic and unpretentious rock carvings in India.

Mandapams

There are eight mandapams (shallow, rock-cut halls) scattered over the main hill, two of which have been left unfinished. They are mainly of interest for their internal figure sculptures.

One of the earliest rock-cut temples is the **Krishna Mandapam**. It features carvings of a pastoral scene showing Krishna lifting up the Govardhana mountain to protect his kinsfolk from the wrath of Indra.

Rathas

These are the architectural prototypes of all Dravidian temples, demonstrating the imposing gopurams and *vimanas*, multi-pillared halls and sculptured walls which dominate the landscape of Tamil Nadu. The *rathas* are named after the Pandavas, the heroes of the *Mahabharata* epic, and are full-size models of different kinds of temples known to the Dravidian builders of the 7th century AD. With one exception, the rathas depict structural types which recall the earlier architecture of the Buddhist temples and monasteries. Though they are popularly known as the Five Rathas, there are actually eight of them.

Shore Temple

This beautiful and romantic temple, ravaged by wind and sea, represents the final phase of Pallava art and was built in the late 7th century during the reign of Rajasimha. The temple's two spires, containing a shrine for Vishnu and one for Siva, were modelled after the Dharmaraja Ratha, but with considerable modification. Such is the significance of the shore temple that it was given World Heritage listing some years ago. Following that, a huge rock wall was constructed on the ocean side to minimise further erosion. It's hardly the most sensitive of structures but at least the temple is no longer in danger of being engulfed by the ocean.

The temple is approached through paved forecourts, with weathered perimeter walls supporting long lines of bulls, and entrances guarded by mythical deities. Although most of the detail of the carvings has disappeared over the centuries, a remarkable amount remains, especially inside the shrines.

On Saturdays there is sometimes a free dance programme at the shore temple. For details, check with the tourist office.

Beach

The village itself is only a couple of hundred metres from the wide beach, north of the shore temple, where local fishers pull in their boats. The local toilet is also here, and a walk along the beach is an exercise in sidestepping the turds. South of the shore temple, or 500 metres or so north, it becomes cleaner.

To Beach Resorts: Temple Bay Ashok (200 m), Hotel Tamil Nadu & Mamalla (1.5 km), Silversands (2 km), Golden Sun (2.5 km) & Ideal Beach (3 km), Tiger Cave (4 km), Crocodile Bank (14 km) & Madras

To Tirukkalikundram (14 km) & Pondicherry (95 km)

Othavadai Street

East Raja Street

Thirukula Street

Kanheri Tank

TAMIL NADU

Mahabalipuram (Mamallapuram)

0   75   150 km

PLACES TO STAY

13 Uma Lodge
17 Tina Blue View Lodge
19 Lakshmi Lodge
20 Surya Hotel
22 Hotel Veeras
23 Mamalla Bhavan Annexe
33 Mamalla Bhavan Hotel
38 Selva Vinayaga
43 Hotel Tamil Nadu Unit II
50 Mrs Rajalaxmi's

PLACES TO EAT

14 Curiosity Restaurant
15 Moonrakers
16 Sea Shore Restaurant
17 Tina Blue View
18 Sea Queen Restaurant
23 Golden Palate Restaurant
24 Village Restaurant
25 Globetrotter
26 Gazebo Restaurant
33 Mamalla Bhavan Restaurant
37 Swamy's Fiesta Restaurant
40 Sun Rise Restaurant
41 New Papillon/Le Bistro
44 La Vie en Rose

OTHER

1 Indian Overseas Bank
2 New Era Travels
3 Tourist Office
4 Post Office
5 Fish Market & Gangai Konda Mandapam
6 Trimurti Cave
7 Mandapam
8 Ratha
9 Ratha
10 Mandapam
11 Krishna's Butter Ball
12 Ratha
21 JRS Travels
27 Dharmaraja Lion Throne
28 Varaha Cave
29 Arjuna's Penance
30 Rayala Gopuram
31 Krishna Mandapam
32 Talasayana Perumai Temple
34 Bus Stand
35 Poompuhar Handicrafts Emporium
36 Cycle Shop
39 Hospital
42 Shore Temple
45 Mandapam
46 Lighthouse
47 Mandapam
48 Shiva & Adivaraha Temples
49 Mandapam
51 Five Rathas

Festival

From January to February there's the month-long **Mamallapuram Dance Festival**. Dances from all over India are staged here including Bharatha Natyam (Tamil Nadu), Kathakali (Kerala), Kuchipudi (Andhra Pradesh) as well as tribal dances, puppet shows and classical/traditional music. Pick up a leaflet of events at the tourist office in Madras.

Places to Stay – bottom end

If you don't mind roughing it a bit, it's possible to stay with families in the area around the Five Rathas, a 15-minute walk from the bus stand. Rooms are generally nothing more than thatched huts, with electricity and fan if you're lucky, and basic washing facilities. Touts who hang around the bus stand will find you accommodation in the village but, of course, you'll pay more if you use them. The usual cost is around Rs 200 per week (more if a tout takes you) and if you stay for less than a week the cost is around Rs 40 to Rs 50 per day.

Competition amongst the locals offering this sort of service is fierce but *Mrs Rajalaxmi's* place is still the best. Her nine rooms have fans and electricity, and there's a communal toilet and bucket shower. Meals are available on request. She also does intricate *rangolis* (white chalk designs put on the doorsteps of many houses) each morning.

Near the beach and very popular with backpackers is the *Lakshmi Lodge* (☎ 2463), a former brothel with light, airy rooms from Rs 125 to Rs 200. Indian and Western food is served on 'private terraces' or, at night, you can dine on the roof under the stars and the sweeping beam of the lighthouse.

A couple of doors down, the *Tina Blue View Lodge & Restaurant* (☎ 2319) is run by the friendly Xavier and has more of a family-style atmosphere. Singles with bathroom cost Rs 60 and doubles are Rs 100 to Rs 150. There's also a new, four-bed cottage. The upstairs restaurant, which catches the sea breeze, is a great place to eat and/or linger over a cold beer. Not too far away is the larger *Uma Lodge* (☎ 2322) which has clean doubles at Rs 60/70 with common/attached bathroom. Larger doubles on the upper floors have Western-style toilets and cost between Rs 90 and Rs 120. There's also one huge quad for Rs 200.

A budget hotel right by the bus stand is the *Mamalla Bhavan* (☎ 2250) which has clean doubles (no singles) with bathroom for Rs 45. This place locks up at 11.30 pm, so if you get back after that time just ring for the night watchman.

The brand new *Selva Vinayaga* (☎ 2445), entered from either East Raja St or Thirukula St, boasts four lovely cottages (all doubles) set in a spacious garden. They're excellent value at Rs 125 for a square cottage, or Rs 150 for a larger round one. All have mosquito nets and private bathroom.

Further along Thirukula St, the *Surya Hotel* (☎ 2292) is situated in shady surroundings overlooking a small lagoon. It offers a number of plain and air-con rooms and cottages with attached bathrooms, but they're overpriced and somewhat airless. Campers can set up (Rs 25 a person) at either the Surya Hotel or the Hotel Tamil Nadu Unit II (see next section).

Places to Stay – middle & top end

In the village itself, there's the spotlessly clean *Mamalla Bhavan Annexe* (☎ 2260) on the main street. This is superb value at Rs 150 for a double with attached bathroom or Rs 250 for an air-con double. There are no singles. The hotel has its own vegetarian restaurant. Next door, the brand new *Hotel Veeras* (☎ 2288) at 116 East Raja St has comfortable doubles (no singles) for Rs 200, or Rs 350 with air-con. There are both vegetarian and non-veg restaurants and the bar should, by now, be up and running.

The TTDC's *Hotel Tamil Nadu Unit II* (☎ 2287), situated in its own shady grounds near the shore temple, has dull double cottages at Rs 150 to Rs 220 depending on position and amenities. All have an attached bathroom and fan but no mosquito nets. Facilities include a bar and restaurant.

The other mid-range and top-end hotels are scattered over several km along the road north to Madras. Each is positioned on its own narrow strip of land, about 300 metres from the road and as close as possible to the beach. All these so-called beach resorts offer a range of facilities which usually include a swimming pool, bar, restaurant(s) catering to both Western and Indian tastes, and most accept credit cards. They vary a lot in price and in the quality and location of the rooms and amenities, but some of them are excellent value for money. Unlike the hotels in the village where checkout time is usually 24 hours, most of these places have noon as their checkout time.

The first up and most expensive is the *Temple Bay Ashok Beach Resort* (☎ 2251; fax 2257), 200 metres from the edge of town. Air-con superdeluxe singles/doubles cost Rs 1190/1500 in either the main block or the detached cottages.

Next, about 1.5 km from town, is the TTDC's *Hotel Tamil Nadu Beach Resort* (☎ 2235; fax 2268). This place has the best setting of all the resort complexes – a forested garden complete with chipmunks and swimming pool. The pleasant rooms are in groups of double-storey cottages facing the sea, all of them with attached bathroom and balcony. Doubles here cost Rs 300, or Rs 400 with air-con.

Further north, but not as close to the sea, are the *Mamalla Beach Cottages* (☎ 2375) with standard doubles from Rs 200 and upstairs air-con doubles at Rs 300. All the rooms have attached bathrooms. Only breakfast is available as the restaurant is still under construction.

Next up is the large *Silversands* (☎ 2228; fax 2280). It has a plethora of inland rooms and cottages, but only the expensive suites and four-bed villas (Rs 2000) are on the beachfront. It's overpriced for what it offers, with seasonal rates ranging from Rs 200/300 to Rs 360/460 for normal singles/doubles, and Rs 400/500 to Rs 500/600 with air-con. The restaurant offers a reasonable buffet for Rs 100.

Further north is the friendly *Golden Sun Beach Resort* (☎ 2245). Singles/doubles here start at Rs 250/275, or Rs 300/350 with

air-con, and go up to Rs 450/550 for sea-facing air-con deluxe rooms. This place is often full on weekends.

The last of the resorts, three km from town, is the *Ideal Beach Resort* (☎ 2240; fax 2243). This place is small enough to retain the owner's intended warm and intimate atmosphere and, as such, is popular with expats and foreigners. Rooms/cottages cost Rs 375/475 or Rs 425/525 with air-con. All have mosquito nets and are well furnished.

Places to Eat

When travellers congregate on a beach, you can be pretty sure that, sooner or later, there will be good seafood restaurants. Mahabalipuram is no exception, with a number of places offering attractively presented seafood in relaxing settings. Most will show you the fresh fish, prawns, crabs and squid before cooking them so you can make your choice. Be sure, however, to ask the price before giving the go-ahead as some items, king prawns for example, can be very expensive. Choosing one of these places over another is really just a matter of personal preference – they're all worth trying.

The only place which offers beachfront dining is the *Sea Shore Restaurant*. It has an open-air terrace with a view of the shore temple (and its ugly protecting wall) and, at night, when the temple is lit up, it's a romantic spot to dine.

The nearby *Tina Blue View* is a good place to eat especially in the heat of the day, as the shady upstairs area catches any breeze that might be around. The service is slow but the mellow atmosphere makes up for that. Cold beers are available. Next door is the *Sea Queen Restaurant* which is reliable for good seafood.

Moonrakers on Othavadai St is one of the newest places in town and, with its bright clean decor and sizeable Western music collection, it attracts travellers like moths to a lamp.

Going south along the back road are the *Globetrotter* and the *Village Restaurant*. The Village is the more popular of the two and also one of the oldest in town. It has an indoor

TAMIL NADU

section plus an intimate garden terrace where you can dine under coconut palms overlooking a small lagoon. Beers are available.

An old favourite and one that is still OK is the *New Papillon/Le Bistro* on the road to the shore temple. This tiny place is run by an enthusiastic crew, and cold beers are available. *Swamy's Fiesta Restaurant*, on the same street, is a bigger place with chairs and tables around a leafy courtyard.

Behind the New Papillon, across the playing field and close to the ocean is the *Sun Rise Restaurant*. Other restaurants worth trying are the *Curiosity Restaurant*, close to the Uma Lodge, and the *Gazebo Restaurant*, on the main street.

For good French cuisine head to *La Vie en Rose*, on the 1st floor of a building at the southern end of East Raja St. This lovely little place offers a different non-vegetarian menu each day and has main course meals for about Rs 70. From some of the tables you can unobtrusively watch sculptors at work across the road.

The place to go for south Indian vegetarian food is *Mamalla Bhavan*, opposite the bus stand. You can eat well at standard Indian 'meals' prices here. Around the back of the main restaurant, the special thali section serves different thalis every day for Rs 17 – it's definitely above average, but at lunchtime only. The dining hall at the front does regular (but still tasty) thalis and other familiar south Indian snacks.

For a vegetarian splurge, try the *Golden Palate Restaurant* in the Mamalla Bhavan Annexe.

Things to Buy
Mahabalipuram has revived the ancient crafts of the Pallava stonemasons and sculptors, and the town wakes every day to the sound of chisels chipping away at pieces of granite. Some excellent work is turned out. The yards have contracts to supply images of deities and restoration pieces to many temples throughout India and Sri Lanka. Some even undertake contract work for the European market. You can buy examples of this work from the Poompuhar Handicrafts

Emporium (fixed prices – in theory) or from the craft shops which line the roads down to the shore temple and to the Five Rathas (prices negotiable).

Exquisite soapstone images of Hindu gods, woodcarvings, jewellery and bangles made from seashells and other similar products are also for sale.

If you're in need of a book exchange service, try Himalaya Handicrafts on the main street.

Getting There & Away
The most direct route to/from Madras (58 km, two hours, Rs 10) is on bus Nos 188 and 188A/B/D/K of which there are 17 daily. Bus Nos 19C and 119A go to Madras via Covelong and there are 21 buses daily. To Madras via the airport you need to take No 108B of which there are nine daily.

To Pondicherry (95 km, 3½ hours, Rs 14) take bus No 188 or 188A of which there are eight daily. Get there early if you want a seat. There are 11 daily buses (Nos 157A/M and 212A/H) to Kanchipuram (65 km, two hours, Rs 10). These buses go via Tirukkalikundram and Chengalpattu (Chingleput). Alternatively, take a bus to Chengalpattu and then another bus (or train) from there to Kanchipuram.

Taxis are also available from the bus stand but long-distance trips require hours of haggling before the price gets anywhere near reasonable.

Getting Around
Bicycles are available for hire if you want to visit some of the places of interest around Mahabalipuram. Bikes (Rs 15 per day) and scooters (Rs 100 a day, petrol extra) can be rented from Lakshmi Lodge, and there's also a bicycle shop next to Merina Lodge opposite the bus stand. No deposit is required – just give your name and passport number.

Auto-rickshaws are also available but, since this is a tourist town, they won't use meters so negotiation is essential.

There are several tour operators such as New Era Travels or JRS Travels, both on the main street, which offer local tours.

AROUND MAHABALIPURAM
Tiger Cave
This shady and peaceful place is four km north of Mahabalipuram and signposted off to the right of the road. It's more a clump of boulders than a cave – its name comes from the shrine (dedicated to Durga) at the entrance which features a crown of carved tiger heads. It's a popular picnic spot on weekends.

Tirukkalikundram
Fourteen km from Mahabalipuram, this pilgrimage centre is also known as Tirukazhukundram, which means Hill of the Holy Eagles. Its hilltop temple is famous as the place where two eagles come each day, just before noon, to be fed by a priest. Legend has it that they come from Varanasi (Benares) and are en route to Rameswaram. (Reality has it that they often don't even turn up.) Five hundred very steep steps lead to the top of the hill; some less-fit visitors get themselves carried up in baskets. The actual village is at the base of the hill and surrounds an amazing temple complex with enormous gopurams. You can get here from Mahabalipuram by bus or by bicycle.

Crocodile Bank
This successful breeding farm was set up to augment the crocodile populations of India's wildlife sanctuaries. Visitors are welcome and you can see crocs (some 5000 of them) of all sizes. The farm is about 15 km from Mahabalipuram on the road to Madras, and is signposted. You can get there by bicycle or on any Madras bus from Mahabalipuram. It's open daily from 8.30 am to 5.30 pm.

VEDANTANGAL BIRD SANCTUARY
About 35 km south of Chengalpattu, this is one of the most spectacular water-bird breeding grounds in India. Cormorants, egrets, herons, storks, ibises, spoonbills, grebes and pelicans come here to breed and nest for about six months from October/November to March, depending on the monsoons. At the height of the breeding season (December and January), you can see up to 30,000 birds at once. Many other species of migratory birds

also visit the sanctuary. The best times to visit are early morning and late afternoon.

The only place to stay is the three-roomed *Forest Department Rest House* at Vedantangal village. Reservations must be made in advance with the Wildlife Warden (☎ (044) 41-3947), 50 4th Main Rd, Adyar, Madras.

Getting to Vedantangal is not all that easy. From Chengalpattu there are occasional buses to Vedantangal village. Another alternative is to get a bus to Madurantakam, the closest town of any size, and then hire transport to take you the last eight km.

TIRUVANNAMALAI
Telephone Area Code: 04175

The temple town of Tiruvannamalai, 85 km south of Vellore, is an important Shaivite town. Of the 100 or more temples, the most outstanding is the Siva-Parvati Temple of Arunachaleswar, which is said to be the largest in India. The main gopuram is 66 metres and 13 storeys high, and there is a 1000-pillared hall.

Places to Stay
The *Udipi Brindavan Lodge* (☎ 22-693) on Anna Salai has simple rooms for Rs 50 and two air-con rooms for Rs 200. Another cheap option is the *Park Lodge* with clean singles/doubles for Rs 30/50.

The friendly *Hotel Trishul* (☎ 22-219), 6 Kanakaraya Mudali St, has rooms for Rs 250/300, or Rs 450/500 with air-con. It's a three-minute walk from the temple.

GINGEE (Senji)
Gingee (pronounced 'shingee') is 37 km east of Tiruvannamalai. There is an interesting complex of forts here, constructed mainly in the 16th century during the Vijayanagar Empire (though some of the structures date back to 1200 AD). The fort is built on three separate hills, joined by three km of fortified walls. The buildings – a granary, audience hall, Siva temple and a mosque in memory of a favourite general – are fairly ordinary, but the boulder-covered mountain landscape is impressive.

Gingee is pleasantly free of postcard

sellers and the like; in fact it's deserted. You can easily spend a whole day here exploring at will. There's an uneven staircase of stone slabs up Krishnagiri Hill, but the route to Rajagiri Fort is much more difficult to follow. A rickshaw from the town to the hills and back, including waiting time at the site while you explore, costs about Rs 20.

PONDICHERRY

Population: 580,000
Telephone Area Code: 0413

Formerly a French colony settled early in the 18th century, Pondicherry became part of the Indian Union in the early '50s when the French voluntarily relinquished control. Together with the other former French enclaves of Karaikal (also in Tamil Nadu), Mahé (Kerala) and Yanam (Andhra Pradesh), it now forms the Union Territory of Pondicherry.

For years, Pondicherry has been promoted as an enduring pocket of French culture on the Indian subcontinent. Up until a few years ago, that image was largely false as the only remaining visible French influences were the French Consulate, the Hôtel de Ville (Town Hall) and the red kepis (caps) and belts worn by the local police. These days, such claims are more realistic due to the extensive restoration work undertaken by the Aurobindo Ashram, the Alliance Française, and other bodies. Many houses and institutions in the streets between the waterfront and the old canal are now very chic and gentrified, their gardens ablaze with flowering trees and bougainvillea, and their entrances adorned with shiny brass plates. The overall impression is one of gleaming whitewashed residences and a concern for maintaining standards rarely encountered elsewhere in India.

Yet, beyond the canal, Pondicherry is as Indian as anywhere else in India, although it is relatively well lit, paved and laid out, and the signs are in English or Tamil, not French.

Most people visit Pondicherry to see the Sri Aurobindo Ashram and its offshoot, Auroville, 10 km outside town.

Orientation

Pondicherry is laid out on a grid plan sur-rounded by a congested semicircular boulevard. A north-south canal divides the eastern side from the larger western part. In colonial days, the canal (now covered) separated Pondicherry's European and Indian sections. The French residential area was near the present-day harbour.

The Aurobindo Ashram, its offices, schools and guest houses, as well as the French institutions and many restaurants, are all on the eastern side while most, but not all, of the hotels are west of the canal. The railway station is at the southern edge of town, while the bus stands are west along the main drag, Lal Bahabhur St.

Information

The tourist office on Goubert Ave is open daily from 8 am to 1 pm and 2 to 6 pm. They have a free town map but little else.

The Indian Overseas Bank, in the courtyard of the Hôtel de Ville (town hall), accepts most travellers' cheques but it won't take Thomas Cook in US dollars. There's also a Canara Bank on Nehru St. Both are open weekdays from 10 am to 2 pm and Saturday until noon.

The GPO, on Rangapillai St, is open from 10 am to 7.30 pm, Monday to Saturday. Next door is the 24-hour telegraph office.

The French Consulate (☎ 34-058), on Compagnie St, is open weekdays from 8 am to noon.

Bookshops The Vak Bookshop, 15 Nehru St, specialises in books on religion and philosophy. Equally good (if you read French) are the Kailash French Bookshop on Lal Bahabhur St and the French Bookshop on Suffren St next to Alliance Française. There's a branch of Higginbothams on Gingy St.

Sri Aurobindo Ashram

Founded by Sri Aurobindo in 1926, this ashram is one of the most popular in India with Westerners, and is also one of the most affluent. Its spiritual tenets represent a synthesis of yoga and modern science. After Aurobindo's death, spiritual authority passed to one of his devotees, a French woman known as The Mother, who herself died in 1973, aged 97. These days, the ashram underwrites and promotes a lot of cultural and educational activities in Pondicherry, though there is a certain tension between it and the local people because it owns virtually everything worth owning in the Union Territory but is reluctant to allow local participation in the running of the society.

The main ashram building is on Marine St and is surrounded by other buildings given over to the various educational and cultural activities of the Aurobindo Society. The ashram is open every day from 8 am to 6 pm and you can be shown around on request. The flower-festooned *samadhi* (tomb) of Aurobindo and The Mother is under the frangipani tree in the central courtyard.

The room in which Aurobindo used to meditate can be viewed daily at 9.30 am. It's open for a short time only and, as you must obtain permission before entering, it's best to arrive by 9 am. The Mother's meditation room is opened to the public on the anniversary of her birth (21 February) and death (17 November).

Opposite the main building is the educational centre where you can sometimes catch a film, slide show, play or lecture (forthcoming events are announced on the ashram's notice board). There's usually no entry charge, but a donation may be collected.

Pondicherry Museum
This museum has an interesting, eclectic and well-displayed variety of exhibits ranging from French furniture to a history of bead making. It is at 1 Romain Roland St and is open from 10 am and 5 pm, Tuesday to Sunday. Entry is free.

Alliance Française
This French cultural centre (☎ 38-146), at 38 Suffren St, runs French, English and Tamil classes as well as a library, computer centre and a nearby French restaurant. Its small monthly newsletter, *Le Petit Journal*, details forthcoming courses and events. The library

(☎ 34-351) is open from 9 am to noon and 4 to 7 pm. Temporary membership (valid for two days) is free.

Places to Stay – bottom end
The cheapest accommodation in Pondicherry is found at the typical Indian hotels west of the canal. The *Amala Lodge* (☎ 33-589), 92 Rangapillai St, and the *Hotel Raj Lodge* (☎ 37-346), opposite at No 55, both offer no-frills singles/doubles with attached shower and toilet for Rs 45/75.

Excellent value in this range is the *Aristo Guest House* (☎ 26-728), 50A Mission St, which is very clean and friendly and has singles/doubles for Rs 70/90 as well as a few air-con doubles for Rs 300. All the rooms have attached bathrooms. Similar in price is the *Victoria Lodge* (☎ 36-366), 79 Nehru St, which is shabby but clean enough, and has rooms for Rs 60/90 with attached bathroom. Also, there's the *G K Lodge* (☎ 33-555) on the very noisy and congested Anna Salai (Pondy's ring road). Self-contained singles/doubles cost Rs 60/100.

At the top end of this range is the *Hotel Kanchi* (☎ 35-540), Mission St, the facade of which would suggest that it was a mid-range hotel – the facilities inside certainly don't match that description. It is, however, clean and quiet and some of the large, tiled rooms have a balcony. Singles/doubles with attached bathroom start at Rs 65/90.

For an old-world atmosphere there's the *Bar Qualithé Hotel* (☎ 34-325) on Labourdonnais St near Government Square. This place is predominantly a pub but it does have six rooms lining the 1st-floor verandah. All are recently renovated but, at Rs 100/200 for a single/double, they're overpriced.

The musty *retiring rooms* at the railway station cost Rs 30/60 and are pretty quiet – the only action around here is cows grazing on the grass that's growing over most of the train tracks.

There's a *youth hostel* on the beach, three km north of town, but its inconvenient location outweighs any fiscal advantage of staying there and the deserted atmosphere is downright depressing. It costs Rs 25 per

Pondicherry

0   100   200 m

TAMIL NADU

To Youth Hostel (3 km),
Auroville (10 km),
Hotel Pondicherry Ashok
(12 km) & Mahabalipuram
(95 km)

Thiyaga Raja Street

P Koil Street

M A Koil Street

I D Koil Street

K A Koil Street

Aurobindo Street

Supraya Chettiar Street

C Koil Street

A H Madam Street

Nehru Street

Rangapillai Street

Nidarajapayer Street

St Theresa Street

Sinna Pappara Street

Lapporth Street

Monthorsier Street

C Mudhaliar Street

To Auroville (11 km),
Kanchipuram (103 km)
& Madras (160 km)

To Hotel Mass (800 m),
Bus Stands, Villupuram
(39 km) & Chidambaram
(70 km)

North Boulevard

B Derichemont Street

L Thollandai Street

Dupuy Street

Marine Street

Rangapillai Street

St Louis Street

Compagnie Street

St Martin Street

Francois Martin Street

Bharathi Street

Anna Salai

S S Pilai Street

Mahatma Gandhi Road

Mission Street

Canteen Street

Capt Xavier Street

Gingy Street

Victor Simonel Street

Suffren Street

Romain Roland Street

Dumas Street

Goubert Avenue

Lal Bahabhur Street

Ellai Amman Koil Street

Labourdonnais Street

Covered Canal

South Boulevard

Botanical
Gardens

To Chidambaram (70 km)

To New
Lighthouse
(700 m)

Harbour

PLACES TO STAY		13	Hotel Dhanalakshmi	15	La Boutique
		27	Le Café (Seafront)		d'Auroville
6	G K Lodge	30	Bar Qualithé Hotel	16	Vak Bookshop
7	Victoria Lodge	31	Hotel Samboorna	17	Canara Bank
10	Aristo Guest House	34	Rendez-vous	18	Higginbothams
12	Amala Lodge	35	Ajantha Restaurant &	20	GPO & Telegraph
14	Hotel Raj Lodge		Bar		Office
19	International Guest	36	Blue Dragon Chinese	21	Cottage Industries
	House		Restaurant	24	Government Square
22	Hotel Kanchi	39	China Town	25	Old Lighthouse
23	Sea Side Guest		Restaurant	26	Gandhi Square
	House	40	Le Club French	28	Indian Overseas
30	Bar Qualithé Hotel		Restaurant		Bank & Hôtel de
35	Ajantha Beach Guest	42	Seagulls		Ville (Town Hall)
	House		Restaurant	29	Pondicherry Museum
41	Park Guest House			32	Tourist Office
				33	Kailash French
		OTHER			Bookshop
PLACES TO EAT				37	French Bookshop &
		1	Vijay Arya Rental		Alliance Française
2	Bliss Restaurant	3	Sri Aurobindo		Library
5	Le Café		Ashram	38	Alliance Française
9	Hotel Aristo	4	French Consulate	43	Railway Station
11	India Coffee House	8	Market		

night, but there's nowhere to eat. To get there, head north along M G Rd and follow the black-and-yellow signs (they're not very obvious).

Places to Stay – middle

The best places to stay by far in Pondy are the guest houses run by the Aurobindo Ashram. They're all immaculately maintained and in the most attractive part of town and, although classified here as mid-range, some offer rooms which are cheaper than those in the budget hotels mentioned above. The only drawback with ashram accommodation is the 10.30 pm curfew, though arrangements can usually be made with the doorkeeper to allow you to come back later. Smoking and alcoholic drinks are banned in all ashram guest houses.

The large *Park Guest House* (☎ 34-412) on Goubert Ave has the best facilities and all the rooms on the front side face the sea and have a balcony. However, unlike the other ashram guest houses, the proprietors here prefer taking devotees rather than visiting tourists. Unless they're full, it's unlikely you'll be turned away, however you may get a slightly cool reception. Singles/doubles

range from Rs 150/200 to Rs 250/300 and all have private bathroom. There's a vegetarian restaurant here.

If the Park Guest House is full (which is rare), try the *International Guest House* (☎ 36-699) on Gingy St. The cheapest rooms here are in the old wing where singles/ doubles start at Rs 50/70. Doubles in the new wing cost Rs 100, and Rs 250 with air-con. All the rooms have attached bathrooms with hot water on request.

More homely than the above is the *Sea Side Guest House* (☎ 26-494) at 14 Goubert Ave. This old house has eight, very spacious rooms all with private bathroom and there's hot water in the showers. Doubles are Rs 120 to Rs 250 depending on size, or Rs 220 to Rs 350 with air-con. Breakfast is available without prior notice but other meals must be ordered in advance.

Apart from the ashram guest houses, there's the shabby *Ajantha Beach Guest House* (☎ 38-898), Goubert Ave, which is part of the Ajantha Restaurant & Bar complex. All the rooms here are on the ground floor so there are no ocean views. There are no singles, and doubles cost Rs 150, or Rs 250 with air-con.

TAMIL NADU

Top of the range in town is the *Hotel Mass* (☎ 37-221; fax 33-654), Maraimalai Adigal Salai (the continuation of Lal Bahabhur St), situated between the TTC and state bus stands, and thus inconvenient for the rest of town. Ordinary singles/doubles are Rs 360/450 and deluxe rooms cost Rs 430/490. All the rooms have air-con, colour TV and hot water. Facilities include veg and non-veg restaurants and a bar. Credit cards are accepted.

Better still is the new *Hotel Pondicherry Ashok* (☎ (85) 24-0468), a Portuguese villa-style hotel some 12 km north of town on the coastal road. Rooms here start at Rs 900/1100.

Places to Eat
Pondicherry has some excellent places to eat Indian, Chinese and French food.

West Side The rooftop restaurant at the *Hotel Aristo* is very popular. It has a 198-item Indian menu with everything made to order, so expect to wait at least 20 minutes for your food to arrive. A great deal of effort is put into preparation and presentation, although the staff are so rushed that the service can be impersonal. Food is cheaper and served faster in the ground-floor restaurant (closed Friday). The rooftop restaurant does not have a licence to sell beer (or any other alcohol) but you can get around this by ordering a pot of 'special tea'.

For Indian snacks or breakfast, the *India Coffee House* on Nehru St is good value. The *Hotel Dhanalakshmi*, 59 Rangapillai St, has mid-priced Indian, Chinese and Continental food. It's dark but cosy and is open from 10 am to 11 pm. Beers are on the menu too.

East Side Close to Aurobindo Ashram, the tiny *Bliss Restaurant* serves straightforward thalis for Rs 10 but is closed on Sundays. Also near the ashram is *Le Café*, Marine St, a former garage turned snack bar which offers good tea and samosas. It's not to be confused with the seafront *Le Café* on Goubert Ave, a crumbly old place frequented by locals after their evening promenade.

Basic south Indian food is available and you can dine with the waves crashing below.

Nearby, overlooking Government Square on Labourdonnais St, is the *Bar Qualithé Hotel*, an old refurbished place with a lot of atmosphere. Though principally a bar, it offers very tasty food including meat, fish and egg dishes (and breakfasts with bacon, sausage, etc) at very reasonable prices (nothing over Rs 30). Just down the road and also cheap is *Hotel Samboorna* at 6 Suffren St.

Rendez-vous, at 30 Suffren St, is a lovely little place with decor straight out of rural France – wicker chairs, chequer tablecloths, and shutters. It's open for dinner only (closed Tuesday) and has meals ranging from Rs 45 for pasta dishes, to Rs 50 for a quiche or Rs 70 for seafood.

Another very popular place, with moderate prices and a big upstairs open-air balcony overlooking the ocean, is *Seagulls Restaurant* at 19 Dumas St. The food (Continental, Chinese and Indian) is tasty and plentiful, and alcoholic drinks are sold.

The *Blue Dragon Chinese Restaurant* at 33 Dumas St serves good Chinese food as does *China Town* on Suffren St.

The rooftop *Ajantha Restaurant*, Goubert Ave, was once popular but it has gone downhill in recent years. A few tables have ocean views but beers are served only in the dull downstairs bar.

For a full-on splurge there's *Le Club*, 33 Dumas St, which has the best food in town. The cuisine is French, the decor peachy and the service immaculate. Wine and beer are available, both French and English are spoken, and it's open for breakfast (7.30 to 9.30 am), lunch (noon to 2 pm) and dinner (7 to 10 pm) every day except Monday. Expect to pay between Rs 40 to Rs 60 for an entree, Rs 110 to Rs 145 for a main course and about Rs 50 for dessert. Drinks are, of course, extra and you'll be looking at a whopping Rs 850 for a cognac.

Entertainment
There's not a great deal to do in Pondy in the evening other than dining out in one of the

TAMIL NADU

restaurants or strolling along the promenade. Beer drinkers, however, are in for a pleasant surprise after the high prices in Tamil Nadu. A bottle of the local Haywards costs merely Rs 20, Kingfisher Rs 21 and Kalyani Black Label Rs 24. The *Bar Qualithé Hotel* and the *Ajantha Bar*, both mentioned previously, stay open until 10.30 pm.

Things to Buy

Pottery, clothing, shoes and a whole range of other Auroville products can be found in La Boutique d'Auroville on Nehru St. Incense and other handicrafts are also sold at Cottage Industries on Rangapillai St.

Getting There & Away

Bus The TTC bus stand, on the road to Villupuram to the west of the centre, is quiet and well organised, in stark contrast to the state bus stand 500 metres further west.

The TTC has buses to Madras at least once an hour, twice daily to Bangalore, Madurai and Tirupathi, and three times daily to Coimbatore and Ooty. All these buses can be booked in advance on the computerised reservation system.

From the chaotic state bus stand, there are regular buses to Bangalore (twice daily), Chidambaram, Kanchipuram (four times daily), Karaikal (half-hourly), Kumbakonam (five times daily), Madras (10 times daily), Mahabalipuram (four times daily), Nagapattinam (three times daily), Tiruchirappalli (five times daily, five hours, Rs 35), Tiruvannamalai (nine times daily), Vellore (five times daily) and Villupuram.

Train Pondicherry's railway station is not very busy as most people go by bus. There are four daily passenger trains to Villupuram (38 km, one hour, Rs 7) on the Madras to Madurai line which leave Pondicherry at 8 and 10.40 am, and 5 and 9 pm. From Villupuram, many expresses go in either direction.

Getting Around

Pondicherry's only public transport is a baffling system of three-wheelers which are a bit like overgrown auto-rickshaws and seem to go all over the place. As there are no signs indicating their destination, they're not much use. It's interesting to watch them on Gingy St – they are often so full that the driver is more out of the vehicle than in and the steering wheel is in front of a passenger. Perhaps it's just as well that it's too complicated to use them.

Although there are plenty of cycle and auto-rickshaws, many people hire a bicycle during their stay. This is also a good idea if you plan to visit Auroville. At many of the bike-hire shops on M G Rd and Mission St, you will be asked for Rs 300 or your passport as a deposit. The only way around this is to have proof of which hotel you are staying in (they may check this, too). The usual rental is Rs 15 per day.

Scooters and Honda Kinetic motorcycles can be rented from Vijay Arya (☎ 36-179), 9 Aurobindo St, for Rs 50/80 a day respectively. Your passport must be left as a deposit, and an international driving licence is needed to rent a motorcycle.

AUROVILLE

Telephone Area Code: 041386

Just over the border in Tamil Nadu, Auroville is the brainchild of The Mother and was designed by French architect Roger Anger. It was conceived as 'an experiment in international living where men and women could live in peace and progressive harmony with each other above all creeds, politics and nationalities'. Its opening ceremony on 28 February 1968 was attended by the President of India and representatives of 121 countries, who poured the soil of their lands into an urn to symbolise universal oneness.

The project has 70 settlements spread over 20 km, and about 900 residents (two thirds of whom are foreigners), including children. The settlements include: Forecomers, involved in alternative technology and agriculture; Certitude, working in sports; Aurelec, devoted to computer research; Discipline, an agricultural project; Fertile, Nine Palms and Meadow, all engaged in tree planting and agriculture; Fraternity, a handicrafts community which works in close cooperation with local Tamil villagers; and

TAMIL NADU

Aspiration, an educational, health care and village industry project.

While most visitors attempt to 'see' Auroville in a day, you will not get the feel of the place unless you spend at least a few days here. In fact, day-trippers and casual tourism are not actively encouraged, although visitors with a genuine interest in Auroville will not be made unwelcome. As the Aurovillians put it: 'Auroville is very much an experiment, that is in its early stages, and it is not at all meant to be a tourist attraction'.

Information

In Pondicherry, La Boutique d'Auroville (☎ 27-264) has information on the community. At Auroville itself, there is a visitor's centre (☎ 2239 or 86-2239 from Pondicherry) near Bharat Nivas. This centre has a permanent exhibition of the community's activities and the helpful staff will address any queries. It's open daily from 9.30 am to 5.30 pm. Next door is an Auroville handicrafts shop.

Matrimandir

The Matrimandir was designed to be the spiritual and physical centre of Auroville. Its construction has been very much a stop-start affair because the flow of funds has been less than steady. However, the meditation chamber and the main structure are now complete leaving only a number of finishing touches (metal discs) to be added to the external skin. Likewise, the extensive landscaping associated with the project is well under way with the help of a small army of local labourers.

The meditation chamber is lined with white marble and houses a huge, solid glass sphere. Sun rays are beamed into this sphere from a tracking mirror located in the roof. On cloudy days, solar lamps do the job.

While the Matrimandir is undoubtedly a remarkable edifice and certainly the focal point of the community, many of the more pragmatic Aurovillians would have preferred the money spent on community infrastructure and on

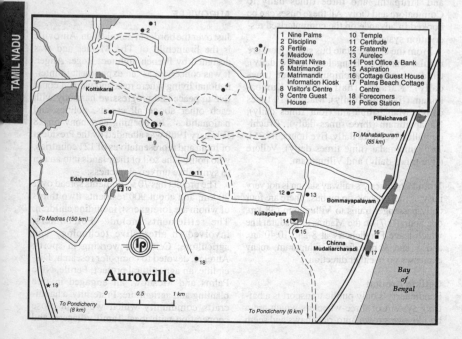

1	Nine Palms	10	Temple
2	Discipline	11	Certitude
3	Fertile	12	Fraternity
4	Meadow	13	Aurelec
5	Bharat Nivas	14	Post Office & Bank
6	Matrimandir	15	Aspiration
7	Matrimandir Information Kiosk	16	Cottage Guest House
8	Visitor's Centre	17	Palms Beach Cottage Centre
9	Centre Guest House	18	Forecomers
		19	Police Station

Auroville

The Battle for Auroville

For a time after Auroville's opening in 1968, idealism ran high and the project attracted many foreigners, particularly from France, Germany, the UK, the Netherlands and Mexico. Construction of living quarters, schools, an enormous meditation hall known as the Matrimandir began, and dams, reafforestation, orchard and other agricultural projects were started. The amount of energy and effort invested in Auroville in those early days – and since – should be immediately obvious to anyone, and the idealism with which the place began is still tangible.

Unfortunately, the death in 1973 of The Mother, undisputed spiritual and administrative head of the Sri Aurobindo Society and Auroville, resulted in an acrimonious power struggle between the Society and the Aurovillians for control of Auroville. On two occasions in 1977 and 1978, violence led to police intervention.

Though the Aurovillians retained the sympathy of the Pondicherry administration, the odds were stacked against them. All funds for the project were channelled through the society which had the benefit of powerful friends in the Indian government. In a demonstration of their hold over Auroville, the society began to hold up funds and construction work, particularly on the Matrimandir, had to be temporarily abandoned.

The Aurovillians reacted resourcefully to this takeover bid, pooling their assets to take care of the food and financial needs of residents and setting up 'Auromitra', a friends-of-Auroville fund-raising organisation. Nevertheless, in early 1976, things became so serious that the ambassadors of France, Germany and the USA were forced to intervene with offers of help from their governments to prevent the residents from starving.

Finally, an Indian government committee recommended that the powers of the Aurobindo Society be transferred to a committee made up of representatives of the various interest groups, including the Aurovillians, with greater local participation. In 1988, under the Auroville Foundation Act, the administration of Auroville was taken over by a body of nine eminent persons who act as intermediaries between the central government and the Aurovillians. The government has actually gone so far as to nationalise Auroville, but the long-term future of the place still seems unclear. ■

projects of a more tangible nature. Others claim that without any such physical manifestation of Auroville's (and, therefore, The Mother's) spiritual ideal, the community may have splintered long ago, particularly in view of the financial and physical hardships endured by many of its less affluent members.

If you want to enter this edifice or wander around its gardens (open daily from 8 am to 4 pm), you must first obtain a pass (free) from the small information kiosk at the entrance to the site. Only 100 people per day are allowed into the meditation chamber which is open daily from 4 to 5 pm (photos are not permitted). It's best to book 24 hours in advance to be sure of a place; however, if you just turn up and there's room, you'll be allowed in.

Places to Stay & Eat

On the road going north from Pondicherry towards Auroville in the village of Chinna Mudaliarchavadi is the *Palms Beach Cottage Centre*. This mellow little place consists of three circular thatched huts as well as smaller rooms in a concrete block. Clean toilets and showers are shared, and there's an open-air gazebo for eating and relaxing in.

Meals are available and the food is good. Singles/doubles cost Rs 45/75.

A little further on, down the lane on the right opposite the turn-off to Auroville, is the *Cottage Guest House*. It offers basic singles/ doubles with mosquito nets in a thatched- roof, semi-concrete block for Rs 40/75 with shared bathroom. Doubles with attached bathroom in the new block are Rs 125. There's a communal dining area and all meals are available.

In Auroville itself, the *Centre Guest House* (☎ 2155), very close to the Matriman- dir, is run by members of the community and offers a range of cottages from Rs 140 to Rs 250 per person per day including three veg- etarian meals and the use of a bicycle.

You can also stay with virtually every one of the 33 community groups here, however, they prefer people who are going to stay at least a week and, although work isn't oblig- atory, it's very much appreciated. You come here, after all, to get to know people involved in Auroville. You should note that none of these community groups will offer free accommodation in exchange for work. For most groups, money is tight. Conditions, facilities and costs vary a great deal. Some places are quite primitive with minimal facilities, others have the lot. Prices range from Rs 35 to Rs 300 though most are in the Rs 80 to Rs 100 range.

The only place in Auroville where casual visitors will find a meal – and it's a good one – is the brightly decorated cafeteria next to the visitor's centre. It's open daily for lunch (Rs 18 for a healthy meal of the day) as well as for dinner on Saturday night. Savoury snacks, cakes, tea and coffee are sold as well.

Getting There & Away

The best way to enter Auroville is from the coast road, at the village of Chinna Mudaliarchavadi. Ask around as it's not well signposted. It's also possible to enter from the main Pondicherry to Madras road at Promesse. The turn-off, one km after the police station, is signposted.

Once at Auroville, you'll need something other than your feet to get around as everything is very spread out. If you rent a bike or scooter in Pondicherry, you can count on cycling at least 30 km there and back. It's mostly tarmac roads or good gravel tracks. Most of the community centres (eg Matrimandir, Bharat Nivas, etc) are signposted but the individual settlements frequently are not.

HOGENAKKAL
Telephone Area Code: 043425

This quiet village, nestled in the forested Melagiri Hills 170 km south of Bangalore, is at the confluence of the Chinnar and Cauvery (Kaveri) rivers. From here the Cauvery enters the plains in a series of impressive waterfalls which, in recent times, have found fame as the backdrop for some of Indian cinema's more tragic love scenes. Sadly, in the last few years, the falls have also attracted dozens of disconsolate real-life lovers who have jumped to their deaths here.

Despite this, Hogenakkal is a popular day trip for families from Bangalore, and can make a peaceful respite for travellers wanting a break from temple hopping through Tamil Nadu. It's most impressive in July/August, when the water is at its peak.

No visit to Hogenakkal is complete without a ride in a coracle. These little round boats, known locally as *parisals*, are made from waterproof hides stretched over lightweight wicker frames. They whisk visitors to the waterfalls and are an effervescent sight, whirling and twirling as they're expertly steered through the rapids. Expect to pay about Rs 15 per person for a one-hour ride, or Rs 250 for the whole day (bring a packed lunch).

Another of Hogenakkal's treats is an oil massage – more than 100 masseurs ply their trade here so you shouldn't have to queue.

Places to Stay & Eat

The *Hotel Tamil Nadu* (☎ 647) has doubles for Rs 200, or Rs 360 with air-con including tax. The large, airy rooms have monkey-proof balconies but they're hardly 'beautifully furnished' as the tariff card claims. Dorm beds (men only) in the attached *youth hostel* are Rs 30. The hotel has an uninspiring restaurant where you can get a thali for Rs 13. Non-vegetarian food should be ordered several hours in advance.

The only other options are the large *Tourist Rest House* and *Tourist Home* next to the bus stand. At both places you'll pay between Rs 60 to Rs 80 for a very basic room. Alternatively, several private homes near the police station (to the right just as you enter the village) have rooms to let.

The stalls at the bus stand all sell tasty fried fish.

Getting There & Away

Hogenakkal straddles the border of Tamil Nadu and Karnataka but can be accessed only from Tamil Nadu. The nearest main town is Dharampuri, 45 km east on the Salem to Bangalore road. From here, there are several daily buses to Hogenakkal (1¼ hours, Rs 80).

YERCAUD
Telephone Area Code: 04281

This quiet hill station (altitude 1500 metres) is 33 km uphill from Salem. Surrounded by coffee plantations in the Servaroyan hills, it's a good place for relaxing, trekking, or boating on the town's artificial lake.

Place to Stay

The *Hotel Tamil Nadu* (☎ 2273) on the Yercaud Ghat Rd near the lake has rooms for Rs 180, and for Rs 225 with air-con. Dorm beds cost Rs 25. Prices go up considerably in the high season. Alternatively you could try the *Hotel Shevarys* (☎ 2288) or the *Township Resthouse* (☎ 2233).

Central Tamil Nadu

THANJAVUR (Tanjore)

Population: 212,000
Telephone Area Code: 04362

Thanjavur was the ancient capital of the Chola kings whose origins, like those of the Pallavas, Pandyas and Cheras with whom they shared the tip of the Indian peninsula, go back to the beginning of the Christian era. Power struggles between these groups were a constant feature of their early history, with one or other gaining the ascendancy at various times. The Cholas' turn for empire building came between 850 and 1270 AD and, at the height of their power, they controlled most of the Indian peninsula south of a line drawn between Bombay and Puri, including parts of Sri Lanka and, for a while, the Srivijaya Kingdom of the Malay peninsula and Sumatra.

Probably the greatest Chola emperors were Raja Raja (985-1014), who was responsible for building the Brihadishwara Temple (Thanjavur's main attraction), and his son Rajendra I (1014-44), whose navies competed with the Arabs for control of the Indian Ocean trade routes and who was responsible for bringing Srivijaya under Chola control.

Thanjavur wasn't the only place to receive Chola patronage. Within easy reach of Thanjavur are numerous enormous Chola temples – the main ones are at Thiruvaiyaru, Dharasuram near Kumbakonam and Gangakondacholapuram (for details see the Around Thanjavur and Around Kumbakonam sections that follow). The Cholas also had a hand in building the enormous temple complex at Srirangam near Tiruchirappalli – probably India's largest.

Orientation

The enormous gopurams of the Brihadishwara Temple dominate Thanjavur. The temple itself, between the Grand Anicut Canal and the old town, is surrounded by fortified walls and a moat. The old town, too, used to be similarly enclosed, but most of the walls have now disappeared. What remains are winding streets and alleys and the extensive ruins of the palace of the Nayaks of Madurai.

Gandhiji Rd, which runs between the railway station and the bus stand at the edge of the old city, has most of the hotels and restaurants, and the Poompuhar Arts & Crafts Emporium.

Information

The tourist office (☎ 23-017), in Jawans Bhavan opposite the GPO, is open from 10 am to 5.45 pm. It has little besides a map of the area (Rs 3).

The Canara Bank on South Main Rd changes travellers' cheques. The Hotel Parisutham does this too, but at a lousy rate.

The GPO, near the railway station, is open daily from 10 am to 4 pm; Sunday from noon. The telegraph office next door is open 24 hours.

Brihadishwara Temple & Fort

Built by Raja Raja, the Brihadishwara Temple is the crowning glory of Chola temple architecture. This superb and fascinating monument is one of only a handful in India with World Heritage listing and is worth a couple of visits. On top of the apex of the 63-metre-high temple, a dome encloses an enormous Siva lingam (Hindus only). Constructed from a single piece of granite weighing an estimated 81 tonnes, the dome was hauled into place along a six-km earthwork ramp in a manner similar to that used for the Egyptian pyramids. It has been worshipped continuously for more than 1000 years.

The gateway to the inner courtyard is guarded by an elephant and one of the largest

Nandis in India measuring six metres long by three metres high, and fashioned from a single piece of rock. The carved stonework of the temple, gopurams and adjoining structures is rich in detail and reflects not only Shaivite influences, but also Vaishnavaite and Buddhist themes. In all, there are 250 lingams in the shrines along the outer walls. The frescoes adorning the walls and ceilings of the inner courtyard have been dated to Chola times and were executed using techniques similar to those used in European fresco work.

Inside the inner courtyard, the well-arranged **Archaeological Museum** has

some interesting exhibits and photographs showing how the temple looked before much of the restoration work was done, as well as charts and maps detailing the history of the Chola Empire. The museum is open daily from 9.30 am to 1 pm and 3 to 5.30 pm. It sells an interesting little booklet titled *Chola Temples* by C Sivaramamurti for Rs 10 (it can also be bought at Madras' Fort St George Museum) which describes the three temples at Thanjavur, Dharasuram and Gangakonda-cholapuram. Also on sale for Rs 4 is a small booklet called *Thanjavur & Big Temple*.

The temple is open daily from 6 am to 1

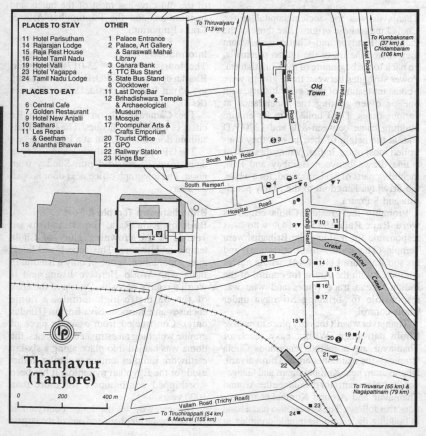

PLACES TO STAY
11 Hotel Parisutham
14 Rajarajan Lodge
15 Raja Rest House
16 Hotel Tamil Nadu
19 Hotel Valli
23 Hotel Yagappa
24 Tamil Nadu Lodge

PLACES TO EAT
6 Central Cafe
7 Golden Restaurant
9 Hotel New Anjalii
10 Sathars
11 Les Repas
   & Geetham
18 Anantha Bhavan

OTHER
1 Palace Entrance
2 Palace, Art Gallery
   & Saraswati Mahal
   Library
3 Canara Bank
4 TTC Bus Stand
5 State Bus Stand
8 Clocktower
11 Last Drop Bar
12 Brihadishwara Temple
   & Archaeological
   Museum
13 Mosque
17 Poompuhar Arts &
   Crafts Emporium
20 Tourist Office
21 GPO
22 Railway Station
23 Kings Bar

To Thiruvaiyaru (13 km)
To Kumbakonam (37 km) & Chidambaram (106 km)
Old Town
East Main Road
Market Road
East Rampart
South Main Road
South Rampart
Hospital Road
Gandhiji Road
Grand Anicut Canal

Thanjavur (Tanjore)

0   200   400 m

Vallam Road (Trichy Road)
To Tiruchirappalli (54 km) & Madurai (155 km)
To Tiruvarur (55 km) & Nagapattinam (79 km)

pm and 3 to 8 pm. There is no admittance charge but, as this is still a functioning Hindu temple, non-Hindus cannot enter the sanctum sanctorum.

Thanjavur Palace

The huge corridors, spacious halls, observation and arsenal towers and shady courtyards of this vast labyrinthine building in the centre of the old town were constructed partly by the Nayaks of Madurai around 1550, and partly by the Marathas. However, due to years of neglect, many sections are in ruins and it was only in 1994 that the Archaeological Survey of India was entrusted with its conservation and renovation. Unfortunately, they'll be hard put to find the estimated Rs 69 *lakh* that is needed to repair the buildings.

The poorly marked entrance is a wide break in the eastern wall, which leads to a large tree on a traffic circle, and a police station. The palace entrance is off to the left, through the arched tunnel.

An **art gallery** occupies the Nayak Durbar Hall, one of two such halls in the palace where audiences were held with the king. It has a superb collection of Chola bronze statues from the 9th to 12th centuries. If the tower on the far side of the courtyard has reopened following renovation, it's worth the climb for the overall view. The gallery is open from 9 am to 1 pm and 3 to 6 pm. Entry costs Rs 2.

The **Saraswati Mahal Library** is next door to the gallery. Established around 1700 AD, the library contains a collection of over 30,000 palm-leaf and paper manuscripts in Indian and European languages, and has a set of prints of prisoners under Chinese torture on the wall! The library itself is closed to the public but the tiny museum here is open daily (except Wednesday) from 10 am to 1 pm and 1.30 to 5.30 pm.

The **Royal Museum,** entered through the archway to the left of the library, has a small collection of artefacts – clothing, headdresses and hunting instruments – from the early 1800s when Serfoji II ruled. The museum is open daily from 9 am to 6 pm. Admission is Rs 1.

Places to Stay – bottom end

Best value in town is the quiet *Raja Rest House* (☎ 20-515) just off Gandhiji Rd. The large rooms are arranged around three sides of a huge courtyard, and cost Rs 35/60 with bathroom and fan. The staff are very friendly. The nearby *Rajarajan Lodge* (☎ 21-730) is similarly priced but very noisy.

Behind the railway station, just off Trichy Rd, is the *Tamil Nadu Lodge* (☎ 22-332) which has singles/doubles with attached bathroom for Rs 60/90. However, it's somewhat inconvenient for the centre of town and the cell-like rooms make you feel like an inmate of Alcatraz. Almost opposite is the renovated *Hotel Yagappa* (☎ 22-421) which has 11 doubles at Rs 140 each. Also here is the Kings Bar, an unusually modern and pleasant permit room.

There are also *retiring rooms* at the railway station.

Places to Stay – middle

The TTDC's *Hotel Tamil Nadu* (☎ 21-421), Gandhiji Rd, offers good value for money. Its spacious and spotless rooms have curtains, desk, wardrobe, fan, comfortable beds and bathrooms with hot water in the mornings. The rooms surround a quiet leafy courtyard, and the staff are helpful. All this costs just Rs 125/150, or Rs 380 for a double with air-con. There is an attached restaurant, and a bar with cold beers. If you want to eat lunch or dinner here then order in advance.

The *Hotel Valli* (☎ 21-584), M K Rd, offers singles/doubles with bathroom but without TV for Rs 90/110, or Rs 130 with TV. Air-con doubles cost Rs 250. There are also triple and four-bed rooms and a restaurant.

Places to Stay – top end

The *Hotel Parisutham* (☎ 21-466; fax 22-318), on the canal at 55 Grand Anicut Canal Rd, is very well appointed and has all the facilities you'd expect of a hotel in this range, including a bar, two restaurants, manicured lawns and a swimming pool. Air-con singles/doubles cost Rs 1078/1478 including breakfast. There are also more expensive deluxe rooms and suites.

Places to Eat

There are plenty of simple vegetarian restaurants with 'leaf meals' (thalis served on a banana leaf) for Rs 10 near the bus stand and on Gandhiji Rd. *Anantha Bhavan* is one that is recommended. The *Central Cafe* on the corner of Hospital and Gandhiji Rds is good for snacks.

The *Golden Restaurant* on Hospital Rd does savoury vegetarian meals in its downstairs hall. The upstairs air-con dining room and rooftop terrace were being renovated when we visited but if you're into cool or open-air dining, check them out.

Sathars is a good non-vegetarian restaurant which has an extensive range of dishes and is open until midnight. Opposite is the brand new *Hotel New Anjalii* which serves non-veg food in brightly lit, modern surroundings. It doesn't have as wide a choice as Sathars but the prices are reasonable.

For a splurge, the Hotel Parisutham has the best restaurants in town – the non-veg *Les Repas* serves Indian and Chinese dishes, and the *Geetham* offers vegetarian food. There's also a basement permit room, called the *Last Drop*, which is a popular place for a late evening beer with complimentary peanuts.

The restaurant at the *Hotel Tamil Nadu* is OK for breakfast but is not the best place to eat lunch or dinner as there's usually only one item on the menu.

Getting There & Away

Bus The TTC bus stand is fairly well organised but, as usual, there is no timetable in English. The computerised reservation office is open from 9 am to 10 pm. Buses, which can be booked in advance, depart for Madras 20 times daily (No 323, 323 km, eight hours, Rs 50), Pondicherry (No 928, twice daily, 177 km) and Tirupathi (No 851, daily). There are also numerous buses passing through on their way to Tiruchirappalli and Madurai.

The state bus stand is chaotic, with no timetable in any language. Buses to Tiruch-

irappalli (54 km, 1½ hours, Rs 9) leave from near the entrance. Kumbakonam buses (37 km, one hour) leave from bays No 7 and 8. There are departures for both every 15 minutes.

Train To Madras (351 km), the overnight *Rameswaram Express* takes nine hours and costs Rs 79/296 in 2nd/1st class. Alternatively, the *Cholan Express* takes eight hours and travels through the day. To Villupuram (for Pondicherry), the 192-km trip takes six hours and costs Rs 48/179. To Tiruchirappalli (50 km, one hour) it costs Rs 17/75. The trip to Kumbakonam takes one hour, and it's 2½ hours to Chidambaram.

AROUND THANJAVUR

Many of the smaller towns in the Thanjavur area are well known for their impressive Chola temples. The distances of each from Thanjavur are in brackets.

Thirukandiyur (10 km)

The temples here, Brahma Sirakandeshwara and Harsaba Vimochana Perumal, are noted for their fine sculptural work.

Thiruvaiyaru (13 km)

The famous temple here is dedicated to Siva and is known as Panchanatheshwara. Accommodation is completely booked out every January, when an eight-day music festival is held in honour of the saint, Thiagaraja.

Tiruvarur (55 km)

The Siva temple at Tiruvarur, between Thanjavur and Nagapattinam, was gradually extended over the years. Its 1000-pillared hall has just 807 pillars, and there's an enormous temple chariot.

KUMBAKONAM

Telephone Area Code: 0435

This bustling south Indian town, nestled along the Cauvery River some 37 km north-east of Thanjavur, is noted for its many temples with their colourful semi-erotic sculpture. The most important are **Sarangapani, Kumbeshwara**

The Tank Festival

Once every 12 years, the waters of the Ganges are said to flow into Kumbakonam's Mahamaham Tank and thousands of devotees flock here to a festival held at that time. According to legend, a *kumbh* (pitcher) came to rest here after a big flood (hence the town name). Siva broke the pot with his arrow, and its spilled contents gathered at what is now the sacred Mahamaham Tank.

The last such festival was held in early 1992 and was attended by Tamil Nadu's Chief Minister Jayalalitha. Unfortunately, things went seriously wrong at one point and there was a stampede in which a number of people were trampled to death and many more seriously injured. Just why this happened isn't clear: some blamed the police for inadequate crowd supervision; others said it was caused by Jayalalitha's appearance on the scene. ■

and **Nageshwara**, the largest of which is second in size only to the Meenakshi Temple at Madurai. They are all closed between noon and 4.30 pm.

Kumbakonam also makes an excellent base from which to visit the very interesting nearby temple towns of Dharasuram and Gangakondacholapuram.

Places to Stay

The *New Diamond Lodge* (☎ 20-870), 93 Ayikulam Rd, has ultra-clean singles/ doubles for Rs 35/49 with attached bathroom. Rooms at the back have a great view over Nageshwara Temple. On the same road and similar in standard is the brand new *Chellam Lodge* (☎ 23-896) at No 57 which offers rooms for Rs 40/75. If these are both full, try the *Pandiyan Hotel* (☎ 20-397), 52 Sarangapani East St or the *PRV Lodge*, 32 Post Office Rd.

Going up in price is the *Hotel Siva/VPR Lodge* (☎ 24-013) at 104-105 T S R Big St in the main bazaar area. This place is actually two hotels sharing one reception. The Siva is the better of the pair, offering huge, spotless doubles with attached bathroom and hot water (5 to 9 am) for Rs 138 (no air-con) and Rs 240 (air-con). The *Hotel ARR* (☎ 21-234) at 21 T S R Big St is slightly more expensive, and also has a bar.

The *Hotel Raya's* (☎ 21-362), 28-29 Post

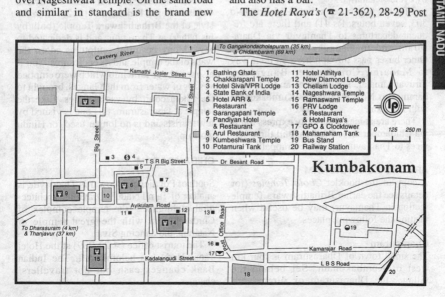

```
To Gangakondacholapuram (35 km)
& Chidambaram (69 km)
```

Cauvery River

Kamathi Josier Street

Mutt Street

To Dharasuram (4 km)
& Thanjavur (37 km)

Big Street

T S R Big Street

Dr Besant Road

Ayikulam Road

Post Office Road

Kadalangudi Street

Kamarajar Road

L B S Road

Kumbakonam

1 Bathing Ghats	11 Hotel Athitya
2 Chakkarapani Temple	12 New Diamond Lodge
3 Hotel Siva/VPR Lodge	13 Chellam Lodge
4 State Bank of India	14 Nageshwara Temple
5 Hotel ARR &	15 Ramaswami Temple
Restaurant	16 PRV Lodge
6 Sarangapani Temple	& Restaurant
7 Pandiyan Hotel	& Hotel Raya's
& Restaurant	17 GPO & Clocktower
8 Arul Restaurant	18 Mahamaham Tank
9 Kumbeshwara Temple	19 Bus Stand
10 Potamurai Tank	20 Railway Station

0   125   250 m

Office Rd, offers well-furnished doubles/ triples (no singles) from Rs 250/325, or Rs 350/450 with air-con. There are separate vegetarian and non-veg restaurants, and a black hole known as the Royal Bar. The attractive *Hotel Athitya* on Ayikulam Rd should, by now, be open and offering mid-range rooms.

There are also *retiring rooms* at the railway station but this is somewhat incon-venient for the town centre.

Places to Eat
The *PRV Lodge* has a good vegetarian res-taurant, though it's hard to find an English-speaking waiter to translate the Tamil menu. The Kashmiri naan here is very good. The non-veg restaurants at the *Hotel ARR* and *Pandiyan Hotel* are two of the few places in town where carnivores can indulge themselves. Also good is the *Arul Restaurant* opposite the Pandiyan.

Getting There & Away
The bus stand and nearby railway station are about two km east of the town centre (Rs 10 by cycle-rickshaw).

TTC has four buses a day to Madras (No 303, seven hours, Rs 41) and there are fre-quent departures to Thanjavur via Dhara-suram and to Gangakondacholapuram. Other buses pass through here on their way to Madurai, Coimbatore, Bangalore, Tiruvannamalai, Pondicherry and Chidam-baram. Bus No 459 connects Kumbakonam with Karaikal.

There are at least four daily express trains via Chidambaram to Madras, and three ser-vices to Thanjavur and Tiruchirappalli.

AROUND KUMBAKONAM
A copy of the booklet *Chola Temples* (for details see the earlier Brihadishwara Temple section in Thanjavur) may be useful when visiting the following places.

Dharasuram
The small town of Dharasuram is four km west of Kumbakonam. Set behind the village, the Dharasuram or **Airatesvara**

Temple is a superb example of 12th-century Chola architecture. This temple was built by Raja Raja II (1146-63) and is in a fine state of preservation.

The temple is fronted by columns with unique miniature sculptures. In the 14th century, the row of large statues around the temple was replaced with brick and concrete statues similar to those found at the Thanjavur temple. Many were taken to the art gallery in the Raja's palace at Thanjavur, but have since been returned to Dharasuram. The remarkable sculptures depict Siva as Kankala-murti (the mendicant) and show a number of sages' wives standing by, dazzled by his beauty. The Archaeological Survey of India has done quite a bit of restoration here.

Although the temple is used very little at present, there is a helpful and knowledgeable priest who is an excellent English-speaking guide as well. He is available (for a small consideration) from 8 am to 8 pm daily.

Gangakondacholapuram
The gopurams of this enormous temple, 35 km north of Kumbakonam, dominate the surrounding landscape. It was built by the Chola emperor, Rajendra I (1012-44), in the style of the Brihadishwara Temple (built by his father) at Thanjavur, and is dedicated to Siva. Many beautiful sculptures adorn the walls of the temple and its enclosures. You'll also see a huge **tank** into which were emptied vessels of water from the Ganges, brought to the Chola court by vassal kings. Like the temple at Dharasuram, this one is visited by few tourists and is no longer used for Hindu worship.

CHIDAMBARAM
Telephone Area Code: 04144
South of Pondicherry, towards Thanjavur, is another of Tamil Nadu's Dravidian architec-tural highlights – the temple complex of Chidambaram with the great temple of Nataraja, the dancing Siva.

The tourist office (☎ 22-739) at the Hotel Tamil Nadu has helpful staff. The Indian Bank changes cash but not travellers' cheques.

TAMIL NADU

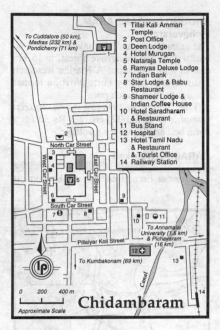

1	Tillai Kali Amman Temple
2	Post Office
3	Deen Lodge
4	Hotel Murugan
5	Nataraja Temple
6	Ramyas Deluxe Lodge
7	Indian Bank
8	Star Lodge & Babu Restaurant
9	Shameer Lodge & Indian Coffee House
10	Hotel Saradharam & Restaurant
11	Bus Stand
12	Hospital
13	Hotel Tamil Nadu & Restaurant & Tourist Office
14	Railway Station

To Cuddalore (50 km), Madras (232 km) & Pondicherry (71 km)

North Car Street
West Car Street
East Car Street
South Car Street
Pillaiyar Koil Street

To Annamalai University (1.5 km) & Pichavaram (16 km)

To Kumbakonam (69 km)

Canal

0   200   400 m
Approximate Scale

Chidambaram

tainly spectacular with fire rituals and the clashing of bells and drums. Every other night at the same time lesser puja ceremonies are conducted. Although non-Hindus are not allowed right into the inner sanctum, there are usually priests around who will take you in – for a fee, of course.

Places to Stay

The best of the cheapies is *Ramyas Deluxe Lodge* (☎ 23-011) at 46 South Car St which has fresh, brightly coloured rooms with modern fittings. Singles/doubles with attached bathroom cost Rs 30/65 and air-con deluxe doubles are Rs 150. The older *Star Lodge* (☎ 22-743) on South Car St has clean and habitable rooms for Rs 35/45, though the windows have grills only – no glass.

The *Shameer Lodge* (☎ 22-983), above the Indian Coffee House on Venugopal Pillai

Nataraja Temple

Chidambaram was a Chola capital from 907 to 1310 and the Nataraja Temple was erected during the reign of Vira Chola Raja (927-997). The complex is said to be the oldest in southern India. It covers 13 hectares and has four gopurams, the north and south ones towering at 49 metres high. Two of the gopurams are carved with the 108 classical postures of Nataraja, Siva in his role as the cosmic dancer.

Other notable features of the temple are the 1000-pillared hall, the Nritta Sabha court carved out like a gigantic chariot, and the image of Nataraja himself in the inner sanctum. There are other lesser temples in the complex, including ones dedicated to Parvati, Subrahmanya and Ganesh, and a newer Vishnu temple.

The Nataraja Temple courtyard with its many shrines is open from 4 am to noon and 4.30 to 9 pm. The special *puja* ceremony, held at 6 pm every Friday evening, is cer-

TAMIL NADU

The well-loved elephant-headed god, Ganesh

St, is good value at Rs 35/49 for singles/
doubles with attached bathroom and clean
sheets. If the above are all full, you could try
the friendly *Deen Lodge* (☎ 22-602) or *Hotel
Murugan* (☎ 20-419), both on West Car St.

The *Hotel Saradharam* (☎ 22-966), 19
V G P St, near the bus stand, has reasonable
singles/doubles for Rs 125/150, or doubles
with air-con for Rs 225, plus a basement bar
and two restaurants.

The *Hotel Tamil Nadu* (☎ 22-323) *may* be
a good place to stay if they've laundered the
sheets recently but they're not keen on doing
this and the staff are apathetic. Singles/
doubles cost Rs 90/145, or Rs 265 for a
double with air-con. Dorm beds are occasionally available for Rs 30.

Places to Eat
The choice of restaurants here is rather
limited. The *Babu Restaurant*, on the ground
floor of the Star Lodge, offers good vegetarian meals in full south-Indian style – banana
leaves, sauce buckets and rock-bottom
prices. For dosas and other tiffin items, try
the *Indian Coffee House* on Venugopal Pillai
St.

One of the most popular places is the
restaurant at the *Hotel Saradharam* – vegetarian at the front and non-veg (air-con) at
the back. Prices are reasonable but get there
early for lunch or dinner as it's very popular.

The *Hotel Tamil Nadu* gets mixed reviews
– some say the food is mediocre while other
travellers have been satisfied by both quality
and quantity.

Getting There & Away
The railway station is a 20-minute walk
south of the Nataraja Temple, or Rs 10 by
cycle-rickshaw. Express and passenger
trains leave for Madras (four times daily),
Kumbakonam, Thanjavur (twice daily),
Tiruchirappalli and Madurai.

The bus stand, used by both TTC and local
buses, is more central. Services leave for
Pondicherry and on to Madras every half
hour (Nos 300, 324 and 326, seven hours, Rs
37) and to Madurai (No 521, eight hours, Rs
45).

AROUND CHIDAMBARAM
Pichavaram
The seaside resort of Pichavaram, with its
backwaters and mangrove forest, is 15 km
east of Chidambaram. A Marine Research
Institute is at nearby Porto Novo, a former
Portuguese and Dutch port.

The TTDC's *Aringar Anna Tourist
Complex* (☎ Killai 32) charges Rs 30 for a
dorm bed and Rs 90 for a cottage.

KARAIKAL (Karikal)
Telephone Area Code: 04368

The former French enclave of Karaikal is

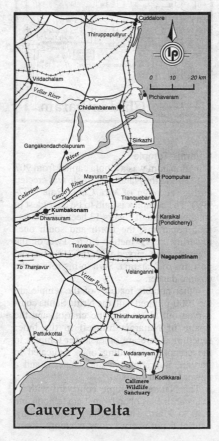

Cauvery Delta

LEANNE LOGAN

LEANNE LOGAN

LEANNE LOGAN

Tamil Nadu
Top: Coconut vendors, Kanchipuram.
Bottom Left: Greetings from a Tamil cycle-rickshaw wallah.
Bottom Right: Welcoming the new day with a freshly drawn rangoli.

Detail of the colourful sculptures on a Hindu temple in Madurai, Tamil Nadu.

part of the Union Territory of Pondicherry but there is little lingering French influence. It is an important Hindu pilgrimage town with its Siva **Darbaranyeswar Temple** and another, the **Ammaiyar Temple**, dedicated to Punithavathi, a female Shaivite saint subsequently elevated to the status of a goddess.

Unless you're a pilgrim, there's little to attract you to Karaikal. However, a deserted, though windy, **beach** lies about 1.5 km from town and boating is possible on the nearby estuary.

The town's main drag is Bharathiar Rd. Along here you'll find the tourist office (☎ 2596) and, 1.25 km further, the bus stand. Also on this road is a number of crowded but discreet bars, tucked away in the back rooms of wine shops.

Places to Stay & Eat
Accommodation is very limited. The *City Plaza Hotel* (☎ 2730) and the nearby *Government Tourist Motel* (☎ 2621), both on Bharathiar Rd near the bus stand, offer singles/doubles for Rs 35/70. Better is the *Presidency Lodge* (☎ 2733), next to City Plaza, which has doubles for Rs 75, or Rs 300 with air-con.

There are a few restaurants on the main street offering south Indian meals. The *Hotel Nala*, next to the City Plaza Hotel, is one of the best. The non-veg *Hotel Nalapreya* at 124 Bharathiar Rd opposite the tourist office has a relatively wide range of Chinese and tandoori dishes.

The tourist corporation operates the *Seagulls Restaurant* at the start of the road which follows the estuary to the beach. It's open from 10 am to 10 pm and serves non-veg meals and beers.

AROUND KARAIKAL
Poompuhar
Only a small village now stands at the mouth of the Cauvery River north of Karaikal but it was here that the rulers of the Chola Empire conducted trade with Rome and with centres to the east. The name of this old Chola seaport has also been given to the TTDC's chain of craft emporia. There's a fine beach,

a *rest house* (☎ via Seerkashi 39) with cottages for Rs 100 and south Indian food.

Tranquebar (Tharangambadi)
Fourteen km north of Karaikal, Tranquebar was a Danish trading post in the 17th and 18th centuries and has a church built by the Lutherans. Later, it came under British rule. **Danesborg Fort** still looks out to sea, impressive and decaying (but being renovated), and there are some fine old colonial houses.

The village has been targeted as a possible beach resort but, although the Tranquebar Sands Hotel has been announced, little has materialised.

Nagore (Nagur)
The Andavar Dargah is an important Muslim pilgrimage centre at the village of Nagore, 12 km south of Karaikal.

Velanganni
Velanganni, 35 km south of Karaikal near the town of Nagapattinam, is the site of the famous Roman Catholic Church of Our Lady of Good Health. People of all religions flock to the church, many donating gold or silver models of cured bodily parts! A major festival is held here at the start of September.

CALIMERE WILDLIFE SANCTUARY
Also known as Kodikkarai, this coastal sanctuary is 90 km south-east of Thanjavur in a wetland which juts out into the Palk Strait separating India and Sri Lanka. It is noted for the vast flocks of migratory water fowl, especially flamingoes, which congregate here every winter. The best time to visit is between November and January when the tidal mud flats and marshes are covered with teals, shovellers, curlews, gulls, terns, plovers, sandpipers, shanks, herons and up to 3000 flamingoes at one time. In the spring, a different set of birds – koels, mynas and barbets – are drawn here by the profusion of wild berries. Black buck, spotted deer and wild pig also congregate here. From April to June there's very little activity; the main

TAMIL NADU

rainy season is between October and December.

The easiest way to get to Calimere is by bus from Vedaranyam, which is the nearest town linked by frequent bus services to Nagapattinam or Thanjavur. There's a *Forest Department Rest House* with cheap, basic but adequate rooms, though all meals will have to be arranged with the staff.

TIRUCHIRAPPALLI (Trichy, Tiruchy)

Population: 754,000
Telephone Area Code: 0431

The most famous landmark of this bustling town is the Rock Fort Temple, a spectacular monument perched on a massive rocky outcrop which rises abruptly from the plain to tower over the old city. It is reached by a flight of steep steps cut into the rock and from its summit you get a fantastic view of the town plus its other main landmark, the Sri Ranganathaswamy Temple (Srirangam). Shrouded in a haze of coconut palms away to the north, Sri Ranganathaswamy is one of the largest and most interesting temple complexes in India, built on an island in the middle of the Cauvery River and covering a staggering 2.5 sq km! There is also another huge temple complex nearby – the Sri Jambukeshwara Temple.

Trichy itself has a long history going back to the centuries before the Christian era when it was a Chola citadel. In the 1st millennium AD, it changed hands between the Pallavas and Pandyas many times before being taken by the Cholas in the 10th century AD. When the Chola Empire finally decayed, Trichy passed into the hands of the Vijayanagar kings of Hampi and remained with them until their defeat, in 1565 AD, by the forces of the Deccan sultans. The town and its fort, as it stands today, was built by the Nayaks of Madurai. It was one of the main centres around which the wars of the Carnatic were fought in the 18th century during the British-French struggle for supremacy in India.

Monuments aside, the city offers a good range of hotels and an excellent local bus system which doesn't demand the strength of an ox and the skin of an elephant to use.

Orientation

Trichy is scattered over a considerable area. Although you will need transport to get from one part to another, most of the hotels and restaurants, the bus stand, railway station, tourist office and GPO are within a few minutes' walk of each other in what is known as the junction (or cantonment) area. The Rock Fort Temple is about 2.5 km north of here, near the Cauvery River.

Information

The tourist office (☎ 40-136), 1 Williams Rd, is open daily, except Sunday and public holidays, between 10 am and 5.30 pm. You can buy (Rs 3) a map of the Trichy area here or pick up the free regional pamphlet. There are also branch offices at the railway station (open daily from 7 am to 9 pm) and the airport but they don't sell the regional map.

The GPO on Dindigul Rd is open Monday to Saturday from 8 am to 7 pm; the poste restante counter is open from 10 am to 5.30 pm.

Rock Fort Temple

The Rock Fort Temple tops an 83-metre-high outcrop. This smooth rock was first hewn by the Pallavas who cut small cave temples into the southern face, but it was the Nayaks who made use of its naturally fortified position.

It's a stiff climb up the 437 steps cut into the stone to the top but well worth it for the views. Non-Hindus are allowed into the Vinayaka Temple at the summit (contributions gratefully accepted), but are not permitted into the bigger Sri Thayumanaswamy Temple dedicated to Siva, halfway up.

The monument is open daily from 6 am until 8 pm. Entry is Rs 0.50, plus Rs 10 if you have a camera. You must leave your shoes at the entrance near the young temple elephant which passes each monotonous day blessing devotees in exchange for money.

Sri Ranganathaswamy Temple (Srirangam)

This superb temple complex at Srirangam,

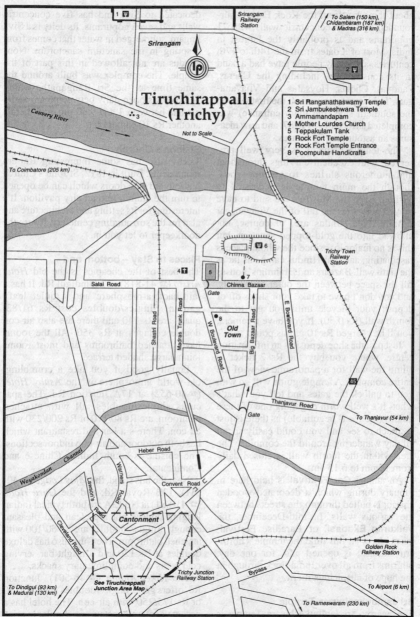

Srirangam Railway Station

To Salem (150 km), Chidambaram (167 km) & Madras (316 km)

Srirangam

Tiruchirappalli (Trichy)

Cauvery River

Not to Scale

1 Sri Ranganathaswamy Temple
2 Sri Jambukeshwara Temple
3 Ammamandapam
4 Mother Lourdes Church
5 Teppakulam Tank
6 Rock Fort Temple
7 Rock Fort Temple Entrance
8 Poompuhar Handicrafts

To Coimbatore (205 km)

Trichy Town Railway Station

Salai Road

Chinna Bazaar

Gate

Shastri Road

Madras Trunk Road

Old Town

W Boulevard Road

Big Bazaar Road

E Boulevard Road

Thanjavur Road

To Thanjavur (54 km)

Gate

Heber Road

Woyakondan Channel

Lawson's Road

Warners Road

Convent Road

Cantonment

Cleveland Road

Golden Rock Railway Station

Trichy Junction Railway Station

To Dindigul (93 km) & Madurai (130 km)

See Tiruchirappalli Junction Area Map

Bypass

To Airport (6 km)

To Rameswaram (230 km)

about three km from the Rock Fort, is surrounded by seven concentric walls with 21 gopurams and is probably the largest in India. Most of it dates from the 14th to 17th centuries, and many people have had a hand in its construction, including the Cheras, Pandyas, Cholas, Hoysalas and Vijayanagars. The largest gopuram in the first wall on the southern side (the main entrance) was completed as recently as 1987, and now measures an astounding 73 metres.

The temple complex is very well preserved, with excellent carvings throughout and numerous shrines to various gods, though the main temple is dedicated to Vishnu. Even the Muslims are said to have prayed here after the fall of the Vijayanagar Empire. Non-Hindus are, of course, not allowed into the gold-topped sanctum, but this is no major loss since the whole place is fascinating, and non-Hindus can go as far as the sixth wall. Bazaars and Brahmins' houses fill the space between the outer four walls, and you don't have to take your shoes off or deposit your bicycle until you get to the fourth wall (Rs 0.50). If you have a camera, you'll be charged Rs 10 at this point.

Just past the shoe deposit is an information centre, where you buy the Rs 2 ticket to climb the wall for a panoramic view of the entire complex. A temple guide will go with you to unlock the gates and tell you what's what. It's well worth engaging one of these guides (the fee is negotiable) as there is just so much to see and you could easily spend all day wandering around the complex. The area within the fourth wall is closed daily from 10 pm to 6.15 am.

An annual **Car Festival** is held here in January during which a decorated wooden chariot is pulled through the streets between the various walls. In mid-December, the **Vaikunta Ekadasi**, or Paradise Festival, takes place. At this time the temple's northern entrance is opened and, for one day, pilgrims from all over India flock through in the hope of auspicious merit.

Sri Jambukeshwara Temple
The nearby Sri Jambukeshwara Temple is dedicated to Siva and has five concentric walls and seven gopurams. Its deity is a Siva lingam, submerged in water that comes from a spring in the sanctum sanctorum. Non-Hindus are not allowed in this part of the temple. The complex was built around the same time as the Sri Ranganathaswamy Temple. It's open daily between 6 am and 1 pm and between 4 and 9.30 pm, and there's another Rs 10 camera fee.

St John's Church
Trichy also has some interesting Raj-era monuments. Built in 1812, St John's Church has louvred side doors which can be opened to turn the church into an airy pavilion. It's interesting for its setting and architecture and also for the surrounding cemetery. Rouse the doorkeeper to let you in.

Places to Stay – bottom end
The best of the cheapies is the old *Hotel Aristo* (☎ 41-818) at 2 Dindigul Rd. It has a laid-back atmosphere and a quiet leafy garden. Singles/doubles cost Rs 61/83, quads are Rs 140 and there are also air-con double cottages at Rs 350. All the rooms have attached bathrooms and most rooms join a large shaded terrace.

Equally good if you like a crumbling, old-world atmosphere is the *Ashby Hotel* (☎ 40-652) at 17A Junction Rd. The spacious singles/doubles, all with attached bathroom, are Rs 80/110 or Rs 200/230 with air-con. There's a bar and restaurant which has both outdoor and air-con indoor sections. The cuisine is south Indian, Chinese and Continental.

Near the bus stand, the *Vijay Lodge* (☎ 40-511), 13B Royal Rd, and the *Guru Hotel* (☎ 41-881) at No 13A are both typical Indian lodging houses but are clean and pleasant enough. Singles/doubles are Rs 60/100 with attached bathroom. The Guru also has deluxe doubles at Rs 120 and a bright bar serving cold beers and complimentary snacks.

The *Hotel Ajanta* (☎ 40-501), Junction Rd, offers good singles/doubles at Rs 90/130 or Rs 175/250 with air-con. The hotel has a decent vegetarian restaurant. Similar in price and facilities is the *Hotel Arun* (☎ 41-421), 24 Dindigul Rd.

The *Hotel Aanand* (☎ 40-545), 1 Racquet Court Lane, is one of the most attractive of the cheaper places, although it's a bit grubby. Rooms cost Rs 90/120, or Rs 250/300 with air-con, all including taxes. All rooms have bathrooms and there is a good garden restaurant.

The *retiring rooms* at the railway station have dorm beds for Rs 30 per person and double rooms without/with air-con for Rs 100/150.

At the Sri Ranganathaswamy Temple, a new 10-room *choultry* at the fourth wall offers rooms with two beds at Rs 35 for 24 hours. It's predominantly for pilgrims and often full.

Places to Stay – middle

Right outside the state bus stand are a whole bunch of relatively new mid-range hotels. At the bottom end of the scale is the *Hotel Tamil*

Nadu (☎ 40-383), McDonald's Rd, which is fairly pleasant and offers singles/doubles for Rs 90/160 or Rs 190/290 with air-con. Towels and toilet paper are provided. There's a bar plus a good non-veg restaurant where a sound Continental breakfast costs Rs 30.

Of the modern hotels, the *Hotel Ramyas* (☎ 41-128), 13 Williams Rd, is excellent value with spotlessly clean rooms (some with a balcony). Singles/doubles cost Rs 125/160, or Rs 290/350 with air-con and colour TV. Room service is good and most credit cards are accepted. The basement bar is open until 11 pm.

Similar to the Ramyas are the *Hotel Mathura* (☎ 43-737) and the *Hotel Mega* (☎ 43-092), both on Rockins Rd. Both have singles/doubles for Rs 125/160, or Rs 240/300 with air-con, and vegetarian restaurants but only the Mathura has a bar.

The equally modern *Hotel Gajapriya* (☎ 41-144), 2 Royal Rd, has rooms at Rs 150/225, or Rs 375 for an air-con double.

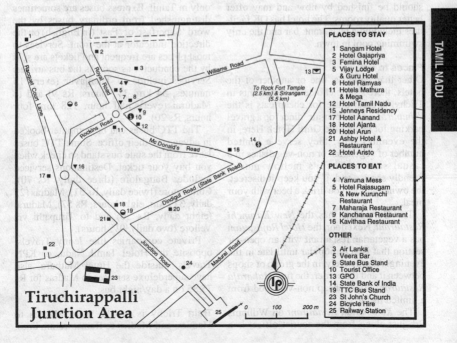

PLACES TO STAY

1 Sangam Hotel
2 Hotel Gajapriya
3 Femina Hotel
5 Vijay Lodge & Guru Hotel
8 Hotel Ramyas
11 Hotels Mathura & Mega
12 Hotel Tamil Nadu
15 Jenneys Residency
17 Hotel Aanand
18 Hotel Ajanta
20 Hotel Arun
21 Ashby Hotel & Restaurant
22 Hotel Aristo

PLACES TO EAT

4 Yamuna Mess
5 Hotel Rajasugam & New Kurunchi Restaurant
7 Maharaja Restaurant
9 Kanchanaa Restaurant
16 Kavithaa Restaurant

OTHER

3 Air Lanka
5 Veera Bar
6 State Bus Stand
10 Tourist Office
13 GPO
14 State Bank of India
19 TTC Bus Stand
23 St John's Church
24 Bicycle Hire
25 Railway Station

To Rock Fort Temple (2.5 km) & Srirangam (5.5 km)

Williams Road
Royal Road
Racquet Court Lane
Rockins Road
McDonald's Road
Dindigul Road (State Bank Road)
Junction Road
Madurai Road

0   100   200 m

Tiruchirappalli Junction Area

TAMIL NADU

There's a bar and restaurant offering both veg and non-veg dishes.

Top of this range is the *Femina Hotel* (☎ 41-551; fax 40-615), 14C Williams Rd, a huge place offering rooms at Rs 190/270, or Rs 350/475 with air-con. There are also more expensive deluxe rooms and suites. The facilities include a restaurant offering south and north Indian, Continental and Chinese cuisine, but there's no bar.

Places to Stay – top end
Neither of Trichy's top-end places are much to rave about. The *Sangam Hotel* (☎ 44-700) on Collector's Office Rd is neither well appointed nor well maintained and so is relatively poor value at Rs 864/1111 for a single/double.

Jenneys Residency (☎ 41-301), 3/14 McDonald's Rd, is an old hotel in the throes of expansion. Air-con singles/doubles on the older floors are pretty shabby and start at Rs 550/700. The newer 4th and 5th levels should be finished by now and may offer better quality rooms. The hotel has OK facilities including a restaurant, bar and the only swimming pool in town.

Places to Eat
Other than eating at one or another of the hotels, there's little choice in restaurants in Trichy. A great place for cheap eats is the *Yamuna Mess*, an open-air 'diner' on a gravel parking lot behind the Guru Hotel. Here, in the evenings only, they serve a limited number of vegetarian or non-veg dishes in a casual setting. There's mellow music, friendly service and, if you keep it discreet, the owner will let you drink a beer with your meal.

The Guru Hotel has the *New Kurunchi Restaurant*. Next door, the *Hotel Rajasugam* has a vegetarian restaurant with an open-air section that is very popular until late in the evening. Alternatively, in the group of shops between it and the corner, the tiny *Maharaja Restaurant* offers cheap non-veg food from a limited menu.

The *Kanchanaa Restaurant* on Williams Rd, just along from the tourist office, is a popular veg and non-veg restaurant which used to have an open-air section; it may be worth enquiring whether it has reopened. Also popular is the vegetarian *Kavithaa Restaurant* which does excellent, highly elaborate thalis (lunchtime only) for Rs 12, and has an air-con room.

Close to the GPO is one of Trichy's few coconut stalls.

Getting There & Away
Air The Indian Airlines office (☎ 42-233) is in the Railway Co-operative Mansion, 4A Dindigul Rd. There are Indian Airlines flights three times a week to Madras (US$34) via Madurai (US$16).

Air Lanka has a flight to Colombo on Tuesday and Sunday. The airline's office (☎ 46-844) is at the Femina Hotel.

Bus The state and TTC bus stands are only a few minutes' walk apart.

As usual, the state bus stand timetables are only in Tamil. Express buses are sometimes distinguished from ordinary buses by the word 'Superfast' or 'Fast' (in English) on the direction indicator at the front. Services to most places are frequent and tickets are sold by the conductor as soon as the bus arrives. Services include to Thanjavur (every 15 minutes, 54 km, 1½ hours, Rs 9) and to Madurai (every half hour, 128 km, four hours, Rs 20).

The TTC buses can be computer-booked in advance at their office. Some TTC buses leave from the state bus stand so check when you buy your ticket. Destinations serviced include: Bangalore (three daily, Rs 70), Coimbatore (twice daily, Rs 31), Madras (23 daily, 319 km, eight hours, Rs 57), Madurai (eight daily, Rs 20) and to Tirupathi via Vellore (two daily, 9½ hours).

Private companies like Jenny Travels, opposite the Hotel Tamil Nadu, or KPN Travels, outside the Hotel Mathura, also have superdeluxe services to Madras for Rs 75/85 on a day/night bus.

Train Trichy is on the main Madras to Madurai and Madras to Rameswaram lines.

Some trains run directly to/from Madras while others go via Chidambaram and Thanjavur. The quickest trains to Madras (337 km, 5¼ hours) are the *Vaigai Express* and the *Pallavan Express* which cost Rs 74/282 in 2nd/1st class. The fastest service to Madurai (155 km) is on the *Vaigai Express* which leaves at 11.56 am and 5.45 pm, takes 2¼ hours and costs Rs 41/151 in 2nd/1st class. The trip to Rameswaram (265 km, seven hours) costs Rs 62/233 in 2nd/1st class.

Getting Around

Bus Trichy's local bus service is excellent. Take a No 7, 59, 58 or 63 bus to the airport (seven km, 30 minutes). The No 1 bus from the state bus stand plies frequently between the railway station, GPO, the Rock Fort Temple, the main entrance to Sri Ranganathaswamy Temple and close to Sri Jambukeshwara Temple.

Bicycle The town lends itself well to cycling as it's dead flat. There are a couple of places on Junction Rd where you can hire bicycles for Rs 15 per day. Note that the incredibly busy Big Bazaar Rd is a one-way road (heading north).

Southern Tamil Nadu

MADURAI

Madurai is an animated city packed with pilgrims, beggars, businesspeople, bullock carts and legions of underemployed rickshaw-wallahs. It is one of southern India's oldest cities, and has been a centre of learning and pilgrimage for centuries. Madurai's main attraction is the famous Sri Meenakshi Temple in the heart of the old town, a riotously baroque example of Dravidian architecture with gopurams covered from top to bottom in a breathless profusion of multi-coloured images of gods, goddesses, animals and mythical figures. The temple seethes with activity from dawn till dusk, its many shrines attracting pilgrims from every part of India and tourists from all over the world. It's been estimated that there are 10,000 visitors here on any one day!

Madurai resembles a huge, continuous bazaar crammed with shops, street markets, temples, pilgrims' choultries, hotels, restaurants and small industries. Although one of the liveliest cities in the south, it's small enough not to be overwhelming and is very popular with travellers.

History

Madurai's history can be divided into roughly four periods, beginning over 2000 years ago when it was the capital of the Pandyan kings. Then, in the 4th century BC, the city was known to the Greeks via Megasthenes, their ambassador to the court of Chandragupta Maurya. In the 10th century AD, Madurai was taken by the Chola emperors. It remained in their hands until the Pandyas briefly regained their independence in the 12th century, only to lose it again in the 14th century to Muslim invaders under Malik Kafur, a general in the service of the Delhi Sultanate. Here, Malik Kafur established his own dynasty which, in turn, was overthrown by the Hindu Vijayanagar kings of Hampi. After the fall of Vijayanagar in 1565, the Nayaks ruled Madurai until 1781 AD. During the reign of Tirumalai Nayak (1623-55), the bulk of the Meenakshi Temple was built, and Madurai became the cultural centre of the Tamil people, playing an important role in the development of the Tamil language.

Madurai then passed into the hands of the British East India Company, which took over the revenues of the area after the wars of the Carnatic in 1781. In 1840, the company razed the fort, which had previously surrounded the city, and filled in the moat. Four broad streets – the Veli streets – were constructed on top of this fill and define the limits of the old city to this day.

Orientation

The old town on the south bank of the Vaigai

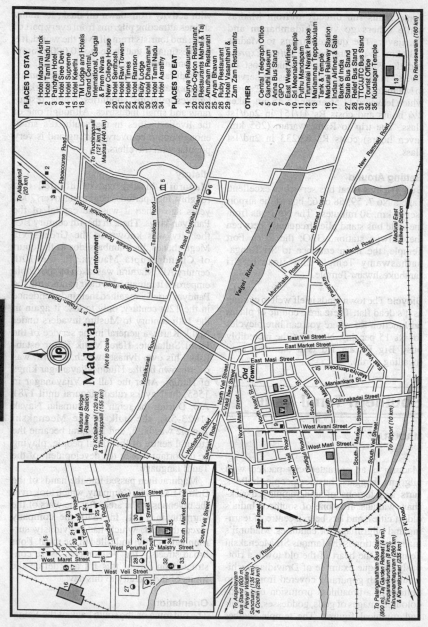

River has most of the main points of interest, some of the transport services, mid-range and budget hotels, restaurants, the tourist office and the GPO.

On the north bank of the river in the cantonment area are top-end hotels, the Gandhi Museum and one bus terminal. The Mariamman Teppakkulam Tank and temple stand on the south bank of the Vaigai, several km east of the old city.

Information

Tourist Offices The tourist office (☎ 34-757), 180 West Veli St, is open weekdays from 10 am to 5.30 pm. The staff are genial and helpful and hand out free maps. There are also branch offices at Madurai railway station and the airport.

Post & Telecommunications The GPO is at the northern end of West Veli St and is open from 7 am to 7.30 pm (Sunday from 10 am to 5 pm). The poste restante counter (No 8) is open daily from 10 am to 5 pm. The central telegraph office is across the river to the north and about two km from the Sri Meenakshi Temple – look for the telecommunications mast.

Sri Meenakshi Temple

Every day, the Meenakshi Temple attracts pilgrims in their thousands from all over India. Its enormous gopurams, covered with gaily coloured statues, dominate the landscape and are visible from many of the rooftops in Madurai. The temple is named after the daughter of a Pandyan king who, according to legend, was born with three breasts. At the time of her birth, the king was told that the extra breast would disappear when she met the man she was to marry, and this duly happened when she met Siva on Mt Kailasa. Siva told her to return to Madurai and, eight days later, arrived there himself in the form of Lord Sundareshwara to marry her.

Designed in 1560 by Vishwanatha Nayak, the present temple was substantially built during the reign of Tirumalai Nayak (1623-55 AD), but its history goes back 2000 years

to the time when Madurai was the capital of the Pandya kings. There are four entrances to the temple, which occupies six hectares. It has 12 towers, ranging in height from 45 to 50 metres, and four outer-rim nine-storey towers, the tallest of which is the 50-metre-high southern tower. The hall of 1000 columns actually has 985.

Depending on the time of day, you can bargain for bangles, spices or saris in the bazaar between the outer and inner eastern walls of the temple, watch pilgrims bathing in the tanks, listen to temple music in front of the Meenakshi Amman Shrine (the music is relayed through the whole complex on a PA system), or wander through the interesting though decidedly dilapidated museum.

This museum, known as the **Temple Art Museum**, is housed in the 1000-pillared hall and contains some beautiful stone and brass images, examples of ancient south Indian scripts, friezes and various attempts to explain the Hindu pantheon and the many legends associated with it, as well as one of the best exhibits on Hindu deities anywhere. Unfortunately, many of the labels are missing. Entrance costs Rs 1, plus Rs 5 for a camera if you intend to use it. It's open from 7 am to 7 pm.

On most evenings at 9 pm, temple music – mantras, fiddle, squeeze box, tabla and bells – is played outside the Meenakshi Amman Shrine.

The temple is usually open between 5 am and 12.30 pm and again between 4 and 9.30 pm. Photography is allowed on payment of Rs 25. Leave your shoes at any of the four entrances, where 'Footwear Safe Custody' stalls will mind them for a small fee.

Many of the priests inside are very friendly and will take the trouble to show you around and explain what's happening. Licensed guides charge negotiable rates.

At 9.30 each evening, there's a closing ceremony in which an image of Siva is carried in procession to Meenakshi's bedroom. (It's taken back at about 6 o'clock the next morning.) The ceremony starts inside the temple, at the Sri Sundareshwara Shrine near the east gopuram.

Tirumalai Nayak Palace

About 1.5 km from the Meenakshi Temple, this Indo-Saracenic palace was built in 1636 by the ruler whose name it bears. Much of it has fallen into ruin, and the pleasure gardens and surrounding defensive wall have disappeared. Today, only the entrance gate, main hall and dance hall remain. The palace was partially restored by Lord Napier, the governor of Madras, in 1866-72, and further restoration was carried out several years ago. The palace entrance is on the far (eastern) side. It is open daily from 9 am to 1 pm and 2 to 5 pm; entry costs Rs 1.

There is a sound & light show (son et lumière) in English, daily at 6.45 pm, telling Madurai's history using sound and coloured lights on the temple carvings. The soundtrack and lighting is quite sophisticated. Tickets cost Rs 2 to Rs 5.

You can get to the palace on a No 11, 11A or 17 bus from the state bus stand, or take the 20-minute walk from the Meenakshi Temple through an interesting bazaar area.

Gandhi Museum

Housed in the old palace of the Rani Mangammal, this oddly moving museum provides some little-known facts about the Mahatma, although the only real piece of Gandhi memorabilia is the blood-stained *dhoti* from the assassination, displayed behind a bulletproof screen. The museum also has an excellent History of India display with some fine old photographs.

The local government museum is in the same grounds, as is a small bookshop stocked with plenty of Gandhi reading matter.

To get there, take a No 1 or 2 bus from the state bus stand to the central telegraph office (look for the telecommunications mast). From there, it's 500 metres along a shady street. The museum is open daily from 10 am to 1 pm and 2 to 5.30 pm. Entry is free but it costs Rs 5 for a camera.

Mariamman Teppakkulam Tank

This tank, five km east of the old city, covers an area almost equal to that of the Meenakshi Temple and is the site of the popular Teppam Festival (see the following section). For most of the year, however, it is empty save for local kids playing cricket in it. The tank was built by Tirumalai Nayak in 1646 and is connected to the Vaigai River by underground channels. The No 4 bus from the state bus stand stops at the tank.

Other Attractions

A couple of temples outside Madurai may also be worth a visit. The **Tiruparankundram** rock-cut temple, eight km south of town, is one of the abodes of Sundareshwara and can be reached by bus Nos 4A, 5 and 32 which leave from the state bus stand. The **Alagarkoil Temple** (also known as Azhagar Koil), 21 km north of Madurai, is a hilltop Vaishnavaite temple. During the festival of Chithirai, a gold icon is carried in procession

---

Mahalakshmi, the Temple Elephant

It was late afternoon when I met Mahalakshmi, one of India's many temple elephants, as she drank water from a metal bucket at the front of the temple. She was having a half-hour break from her work as an incarnation of the elephant-headed god, Ganesh, the most loved of the many Hindu deities.

For 12 hours a day she stands within the thick cement walls of Kudalagar Temple, one of the lesser known places of worship in the famous temple city of Madurai. In the dim light, just inside the main entrance, she stands from early morning until late into the evening, day in, day out. Though unchained, she rarely moves from this small area for she is on duty. Her job: to receive the money donated by incoming devotees and to 'bless' them with a tap of her trunk on their bowed head. In between blessings, she slowly raises one front foot and then the other, as if releasing the pressure of the long, long hours and the monumental tedium. For 26 years she has been doing this. The temple custodians hope she will be doing it for at least 26 more.

Leanne Logan

from this temple to Madurai. Bus No 44, also from the state bus stand, will get you there.

Festivals
Madurai celebrates 11 big annual temple festivals with only the monsoon month, called Ani in Tamil, devoid of festivities. Check with the tourist office for festival dates.

The principal event is **Chithirai** (late April/early May), which celebrates the marriage of Sri Meenakshi to Sundareshwara (Siva) on the festival's 10th day. The next morning, the deities are wheeled around the Masi streets on huge chariots followed by thousands of devotees.

Another festival which attracts pilgrims from all over India is the 12-day **Teppam (Float) Festival** held in January or early February. For this event, images of Sri Meenakshi and Sundareshwara are mounted on floats and taken to the Mariamman Teppakkulam Tank. For several days, they are pulled back and forth across the water to the island temple in the tank's centre, before being taken back to Madurai.

Places to Stay – bottom end
In a pilgrim city of Madurai's size and importance, lots of cheap hotels offer basic accommodation. Many are just flophouses which bear the scars of previous occupants' habits, though a few places are clean and good value. These are mostly along Town Hall and Dindigul Rds.

The *New College House* (☎ 24-311) at 2 Town Hall Rd is a huge place where you'll almost certainly get accommodation at any hour of the day or night. The rooms are clean enough and cost Rs 70/138 for ordinary singles/doubles plus there are more expensive deluxe and air-con rooms.

Close by is the *Hotel Senthosh* (☎ 26-692), 7 Town Hall Rd, which has basic singles/doubles with attached bathroom for Rs 40/65 and deluxe doubles for Rs 80 including taxes. Next door, the *Hotel Ravi Towers* (☎ 36-345) at No 9 is brand new and very clean but otherwise nothing exceptional. Rooms are Rs 90/125, or Rs 150/225 with air-con.

The *Hotel Times* (☎ 36-351) at No 15-16 Town Hall Rd has ordinary/air-con doubles (no singles) for Rs 180/250 and air-con deluxe doubles with TV for Rs 320. The rooms are comfortable but dark and somewhat overpriced. Down a nearby side street is the *Hotel Ramson* (☎ 33-407) which looks expensive but isn't at Rs 40/55 for singles/doubles with attached bathroom. It's often full.

If you want a temple view, you can't beat the friendly *Hotel Sree Devi* (☎ 36-388) at 20 West Avani St. The view of the temple from the roof is the best you'll get in the whole city (of course, this is not news to the owners who are charging an exorbitant Rs 500 for the new air-con rooftop double room). The rooms (no singles) are OK and start at Rs 120 for a double with bathroom, or from Rs 300 with air-con.

The other good hunting ground for both budget and mid-range hotels is West Perumal Maistry St. One of the cheapest is the *Ruby Lodge* (☎ 33-633) at No 92 which has doubles with attached bathrooms (bucket showers only) for Rs 50. The hotel has its own pleasant outdoor restaurant.

Further up this same road going north is another cluster of hotels which, from their outside appearance, would seem to be mid-range yet prices don't reflect this. The *Hotel Grand Central* (☎ 36-311) at No 47-48. Quite big rooms cost Rs 75/110, or Rs 250 for an air-con double. Almost next door is the slightly more expensive *Hotel International* (☎ 31-552) at No 46. Further up, the *Hotel Gangai* (☎ 36-211) has small singles/doubles at Rs 50/90.

The *Hotel Dhanamani* (☎ 24-817) at 20 Sunnambukara St is a brand new hotel with good-value rooms. Singles/doubles with a private bucket shower are Rs 80/120, or Rs 150 for a double with shower. Air-con doubles start at Rs 240.

At the railway station, the *retiring rooms* are noisy and cost Rs 100; dorm beds are Rs 30.

Places to Stay – middle
Very popular in this range is the *Hotel Aarathy* (☎ 31-571), 9 Perumal Koil West Mada St, just a few minutes' walk from the

bus stands. All rooms have bathrooms with (inconsistent) hot water and cost Rs 110/195, or Rs 195/300 for an air-con single/double. Towels, soap and toilet paper are provided, the rooms are comfortable and secure, and most have a small balcony with a great view over the neighbouring temple. Rouse yourself out of bed for sunrise – it's superb! There's a pleasant open-air restaurant (vegetarian) in the courtyard which is frequented daily (6 am and 4 pm) by Mahalakshmi, the temple elephant from next door.

The TTDC's *Hotel Tamil Nadu* (☎ 42-461), West Veli St, has rooms at Rs 100/170 or Rs 175/280 with air-con. It's fairly well run plus there's a restaurant and one of the few bars in town. The *Hotel Tamil Nadu II* (☎ 45-462), across the river on Alagarkoil Rd, is more expensive but less well kept. Ordinary singles/doubles here cost Rs 175/210 or Rs 200/280 with air-con. The bathrooms have hot and cold running water plus the hotel has its own bar and restaurant.

Back in town, the *Hotel Prem Nivas* (☎ 37-531), 102 West Perumal Maistry St, is popular with businesspeople and has singles/doubles for Rs 100/160 and air-con doubles at Rs 260. Facilities are excellent and the hotel has its own air-con vegetarian restaurant. On the same street, the *Hotel Keerthi* (☎ 31-501) at No 40 has amiable staff, constant hot water and fresh towels. The small rooms start at Rs 95/125, or Rs 225 for a double with TV and air-con. The rooms on the top floors get the most breeze. Nearby, but not quite as welcoming, is the *TM Lodge* (☎ 37-481) at No 50. Singles/doubles with attached bathrooms are Rs 90/155 and air-con rooms with TV are Rs 240/250. The upper rooms are lighter and airier.

The *Hotel Supreme* (☎ 36-331), 110 West Perumal Maistry St, has doubles (no singles) at Rs 235, or Rs 355 with air-con, plus more expensive suites. Although the rooms are very dark, the facilities are good and there's an excellent rooftop restaurant.

Places to Stay – top end
Madurai's three best hotels are well out of the town centre. The *Hotel Madurai Ashok*

(☎ 62-531) and the *Pandyan Hotel* (☎ 42-470; fax 42-020) are on Alagarkoil Rd to the north. They both have central air-con, craft shops, restaurants serving Indian, Chinese and Continental food and a bar, but only the Ashok has a swimming pool. They are also both run-down and have rooms which one traveller described as 'dark, humid prison cells'. The Pandyan has singles/doubles from Rs 900/1000 while the Ashok starts at Rs 800/1000. An auto-rickshaw should cost no more than Rs 20, although the price generally doubles when they hear where you want to go! City buses No 2, 16 or 20 (among others) will get you there for about Rs 1.

The *Taj Garden Retreat* (☎ 88-256), four km from town at Pasumalai Hill, ranks as Madurai's best hotel. Rooms come in three varieties: standard (renovated car sheds) at US$60/70 a single/double; old-world (part of the original colonial villa) for US$70/80; and deluxe (new cottages with private terraces and excellent views) at US$85/95. Facilities include a multi-cuisine restaurant, swimming pool (for guests only), a dilapidated tennis court, manicured gardens and a bar. Bus No 5D from the relief bus stand in Madurai stops at the main gate. From here it's still 1.5 km up to the hotel (if you're walking, take the shortcut path leading off to the left about a third of the way up the road). An auto-rickshaw from town costs Rs 40, or Rs 15 from the main gate.

Places to Eat
There are many typical south Indian vegetarian restaurants around the Meenakshi Temple and along Town Hall Rd, Dindigul Rd and West Masi St. The dining hall in *New College House* is popular and the thalis are good value. For the biggest dosa you're ever likely to encounter, head to *Aryan Bhavan* on the corner of West Masi St and Dindigul Rd.

The non-vegetarian *Taj Restaurant* on Town Hall Rd is not bad for breakfast. Even better is the ground-floor restaurant at the *Hotel Supreme* where a pure-veg Indian breakfast of idli, vadai, dosa, two puris and coffee is Rs 24.

Back on Town Hall Rd, there are several

places where you can get decent non-vegetarian food – try the *Indo-Ceylon Restaurant* at No 6, the *Mahal* which is popular with backpackers, or the *Amutham Restaurant*, near the corner of West Masi St.

Better than these is the *Ruby Restaurant* next to the Ruby Lodge on West Perumal Maistry St. Delicious non-veg food is served in a breezy, open-air garden setting and, if you're discreet, they'll serve beer (albeit in metal mugs). Count on paying Rs 80 for two (beers extra). It's open until 1 am and is popular with locals and travellers.

The *Hotel Vasanthani* on West Perumal Maistry St is good for cheap thalis and tiffin and the upstairs section is great for watching the busy street scene. On the corner nearby, *Zam Zam* is a popular shop for sweet or savoury snacks.

For a splurge, you need to go to one of the mid-range hotels on West Perumal Maistry St, or try the superb buffet (Rs 140) held on Saturday and Sunday evenings on the lawn of the *Taj Garden Retreat*. The *Surya* restaurant, on the roof of the Hotel Supreme, has a superb view and catches any breeze. It serves Indian, Chinese and Continental vegetarian food in the evening only (5 pm to midnight) – the cucumber raita and garlic naan here are delicious. Prices are reasonable, the service is friendly and efficient and, if you enquire quietly, they'll organise getting a beer.

Things to Buy
Madurai has long been a textile centre and the streets around the temple still teem with cloth stalls and tailors' shops. A great place to buy locally manufactured cottons as well as the batiks loved by many travellers is Puthu Mandapam, an old, stone-pillared hall just along from the eastern entrance to Sri Meenakshi Temple. Here you'll find lines of textile stalls opposite rows of tailors, each busily treadling away and capable of whipping up a good replica of whatever you're wearing in an hour or two. If you're buying cloth to get garments made up, it's wise to know how much material you'll need as some merchants will talk you into buying way too much only to strike a deal with the

tailor who makes your clothes to keep the leftovers. The owner of the Krishnamoorthy Cloth Store (stall No 108) is reliable and gives fair prices for material. In addition, he refuses to pay the commissions demanded by the many street touts who'll offer to take you to their 'brother's shop' at Puthu Mandapam.

Getting There & Away
Air The Indian Airlines office (☎ 37-234) is on West Veli St. There are three flights weekly to Madras (US$50) and Bombay (US$115). NEPC Airlines (☎ 24-520) has an office in the Supreme Hotel. It flies once or twice daily to Madras (US$55) from where it has connections to Bangalore, Bombay, Kochi, Goa, Hubli, Pune and the Lakshadweep Islands. East West Airlines (☎ 24-995), 119 West Perumal Maistry St, flies daily to Bombay via Trivandrum (US$29).

Bus Madurai has at least five bus stands and three of them are several km from the town centre. You'll need to use either a city bus or a rickshaw to get to these terminals.

The state bus stand is centrally located on West Veli St. It is the principal local bus stand, however, there is also the 'relief' bus stand for some of these services which is situated across the street.

The TTC/JJTC bus stand is also on West Veli St and is for long-distance/interstate buses. Seats on buses originating in Madurai (for details see the Bus Services from Madurai table) can be reserved in advance at the booking office (open daily from 7 am to 10.30 pm) and there's a timetable in English. Plenty of other TTC/JJTC buses stop in Madurai on their way through but these can't be reserved in advance; however, it's not usually a problem to get a seat. TTC does not run buses to Kodaikanal – for that you must go to the Arapalayam bus stand.

The Anna bus stand, across the river to the north, services destinations to the north-east such as Thanjavur and Trichy, as well as Rameswaram. If your bus terminates here, bus No 3 will take you to the state bus stand in town, or you can catch a cycle-rickshaw for Rs 10.

The dusty Arapalayam bus stand (take bus

TTC/JJTC Bus Services from Madurai

Destination	Route number	Frequency (d-daily)	Distance (km)	Duration (hours)	Fare (Rs)
Bangalore	846	14d	550	15	70
Coimbatore	660	2d	227	6	29
Ernakulam	826	2d	324	10	80
Kanyakumari	566	3d	253	6	34
Madras	137, 491	50d	447	10	65 to 77
Pondicherry	847	2d	329	8	50
Thiruvananthapuram	865	2d	305	7	50
Tirupathi	-	4d	595	16	85

No 7A or JJ from the relief bus stand) is for points north-west including Coimbatore, Kodaikanal or Bangalore. There are about eight departures daily to Kodaikanal and the four-hour trip costs Rs 18. During heavy monsoon rain, the road to Kodaikanal sometimes gets washed away and the buses have to go via Palani, adding an hour or two of the journey.

The Palanganatham bus stand to the south-west of town is for buses heading south to destinations such as Kanyakumari and southern Kerala. Bus Nos 7, 7J and JJ7 from the relief bus stand in town will get you there.

There are several private bus companies which offer superdeluxe video buses to such places as Madras and Bangalore. Tickets for these are sold by agencies which operate in the vicinity of the state bus stand. However, beware of buying a ticket for any destination other than the above major cities. All of them will sell you a ticket to virtually anywhere (such as Kodaikanal or Rameswaram) but you'll find yourself dumped on a state bus and they'll have sold you a ticket for it at double the price you could have paid yourself.

Train The railway station is on West Veli St, only a few minutes' walk from the main hotel area.

If you're heading to Kollam (Quilon) in Kerala, the line to Kerala crosses the Western Ghats through some spectacular mountain terrain, and there are some superb gopurams to be seen at Srivilliputur (between Sivakasi and Rajapalaiyam) and Sankarayinarkovil.

Getting Around

To/From the Airport The airport is 11 km south of town and you'll have to haggle like crazy with auto-rickshaw drivers for a reasonable price. Expect to pay around Rs 50.

Indian Airlines runs a bus (Rs 20) to the airport from its office about an hour before each flight. Alternatively, bus No 10A from the state bus stand goes to the airport but don't rely on it being on schedule.

Train Services from Madurai

Destination	Train number & name	Departure	Distance (km)	Duration (hours)	Fare (Rs) (2nd/1st)
Coimbatore	6116 Coimbatore Exp	9.45 pm	229	6.15	56/205
Madras	6718 Pandian Exp	7.35 pm	556	11.10	139/415
	2636 Vaigai Exp	6.45 am		7.35	111/415
Quilon	6161 Quilon Exp	7.20 pm	268	9.40	78/233
Rameswaram	6115 Rameswaram Exp	5.20 am	164	5.10	24/159

Bus Some useful local buses include No 3 to the Anna bus stand, Nos 1 and 2 to near the Gandhi Museum, and Nos 4 and 4A to Mariamman Teppakkulam Tank. All these buses depart from the state bus stand.

Auto-Rickshaw Drivers are extremely reluctant to use the meters and will quote whatever they think you will pay. If you can't agree, they usually won't budge.

RAMESWARAM

Population: 35,000
Telephone Area Code: 04573

Known as the Varanasi of the south, Rameswaram is a major pilgrimage centre for both Shaivites and Vaishnavaites as it was here that Rama (an incarnation of Vishnu in the Indian epic the *Ramayana*) offered thanks to Siva. At the town's core is the Ramanathaswamy Temple, one of the most important temples in southern India.

Rameswaram is on an island in the Gulf of Mannar, connected to the mainland at Mandapam by rail, and by one of India's engineering wonders, the Indira Gandhi Bridge. The bridge took 14 years to build and was opened by Rajiv Gandhi late in 1988.

The town lies on the island's eastern side and used to be the port from which the ferry to Talaimannar (Sri Lanka) departed before passenger services were suspended more than a decade ago. As a result, there are now very few foreign visitors.

Orientation & Information

Most of the hotels and restaurants in this small and dusty town are clustered around the Ramanathaswamy Temple. The bus stand, two km to the west, is connected by frequent shuttle buses to the town centre.

There's a tourist office in the railway station, south-west of the temple, but it opens only when a train arrives. In town, the small tourist office on East Car St has a map of the town and nothing else.

Ramanathaswamy Temple

A fine example of late Dravidian architecture, this temple is most renowned for its magnificent corridors lined with massive sculptured pillars, noted for their elaborate design, style and rich carving. Legend has it that Rama sanctified this place by worshipping Siva here after the battle of Sri Lanka. Construction of the temple began in the 12th century AD and additions were made over the centuries by various rulers, so that today its gopuram is 53 metres high. Only Hindus may enter the inner sanctum. The temple is open from 5 am to noon and 3 to 9 pm.

Like in Kanyakumari, excessively loud and distorted music is blasted out from the temple during festival times from about 4.30 am – just in case you had any ideas about sleeping in.

Kothandaraswamy Temple

This is another famous temple, about 12 km from town. It was the only structure to survive the 1964 cyclone which washed the rest of the village away. Legend states that Vibishana, brother of Sita's kidnapper Ravana, surrendered to Rama at this spot. Buses from the local bus stand opposite the tourist office on East Car St will take you down there.

Adam's Bridge

Adam's Bridge is the name given to the chain of reefs, sandbanks and islets that almost connects Sri Lanka with India. According to legend, this is the series of stepping stones used by Hanuman to follow Ravana, in his bid to rescue Sita.

Other Attractions

The **Gandamadana Parvatham,** on a hill three km north-west of town, is a shrine containing Rama's footprints. Devotees generally visit here at sunrise and sunset (it's closed from 11.30 am to 3.30 pm).

There is a lovely bathing pool at **Dhanushkodi** on the very tip of the peninsula, 18 km from town, but it's difficult to reach. Buses from town stop two km east of Kothandaraswamy, so you have to walk the remaining four km or flag down one of the public carrier vans delivering goods to the villagers.

TAMIL NADU

For a **beach** closer to town, try the one in front of the Hotel Tamil Nadu. Most of the time you'll have it to yourself as the pilgrims prefer to do their auspicious wading at **Agni Theertham**, the seashore closest to the temple.

Places to Stay

Accommodation is tight during festivals especially if you arrive late in the day.

The best of the cheap bunch are the *Santhiya Lodge* and the *Alankar Tourist Home* (☎ 21-216), both on West Car St, or the *Santhana Lodge*, South Car St. At all of these you'll pay about Rs 25/35 for a single/double with common bathroom and Rs 30/50 with attached bath and, without exception, you'll most likely need to ask for clean sheets.

Much better is the *Swami Ramanatha Tourist Home* (☎ 21-217) which has clean doubles with attached shower for Rs 50. There are a number of fairly cheap *retiring rooms* at the railway station, as well as dorm beds.

Going up in price, the best place to stay is the *Hotel Maharaja's* (☎ 21-271) at 7 Middle St. Clean, pleasant doubles/triples with attached bathroom and balcony cost Rs 60/99 and there are air-con doubles with TV for Rs 220.

Not quite as good is the *Hotel Venkatesh* (☎ 21-296), South Car St, which has doubles/triples with attached bathroom for Rs 90/130 and four-bed rooms for Rs 175. There are also a few air-con doubles for Rs 199.

Lastly there's the TTDC's *Hotel Tamil Nadu* (☎ 21-277) facing the sea to the northeast of town. Here you can get a bed in a six-bed dorm for Rs 25 or an ordinary/deluxe double for Rs 125/150. Air-con doubles with TV are Rs 275. The whole place is a bit run-down but it's OK value and all the rooms have a sea view. The restaurant here has vegetarian and non-veg food but it's nothing

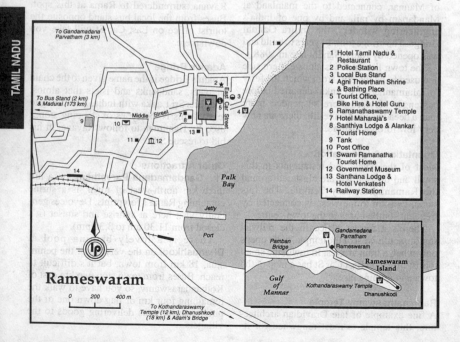

1 Hotel Tamil Nadu & Restaurant
2 Police Station
3 Local Bus Stand
4 Agni Theertham Shrine & Bathing Place
5 Tourist Office, Bike Hire & Hotel Guru
6 Ramanathaswamy Temple
7 Hotel Maharaja's
8 Santhiya Lodge & Alankar Tourist Home
9 Tank
10 Post Office
11 Swami Ramanatha Tourist Home
12 Government Museum
13 Santhana Lodge & Hotel Venkatesh
14 Railway Station

To Gandamadana Parvatham (3 km)

To Bus Stand (2 km) & Madurai (173 km)

Middle   Street

East Car Street

Palk Bay

Jetty

Port

Rameswaram

0   200   400 m

To Kothandaraswamy Temple (12 km), Dhanushkodi (18 km) & Adam's Bridge

Pamban Bridge

Gandamadana Parratham
Rameswaram

Rameswaram Island

Gulf of Mannar

Kothandaraswamy Temple

Dhanushkodi

TAMIL NADU

to rave about. The permit room, however, is worthy of a rave as for once it's not your typical black hole. Instead there are wicker chairs and (barred) windows through which you can see palm trees and turquoise waters.

Places to Eat
A number of vegetarian restaurants along West Car St serve typical south Indian thalis, all of a pretty dismal standard. The *Hotel Guru* on East Car St next to the tourist office is about the best place for a thali. The *Hotel Tamil Nadu* has the only real 'restaurant' in town.

Getting There & Away
Bus TTC buses run four times daily to Madurai (173 km, four hours, Rs 25) and Kanyakumari, and twice daily to Trichy (273 km) and Madras. Local buses run to Madurai more often and take a little longer but are marginally cheaper. There are also buses to Pondicherry and Thanjavur via Madurai.

Train There are two express trains to/from Madras daily – the *Sethu Express* and the *Rameswaram Express*. The 666-km trip takes 15 hours and costs Rs 159/481 in 2nd/1st class. Neither of these trains go through Madurai – they take the direct route through Manamadurai and Trichy.

The only direct way to get from Rameswaram to Madurai by train is on one of the three daily passenger trains that leave at 7.35 am, 4.20 and 9 pm. The 164-km trip takes 5½ hours and costs Rs 24 in 2nd class.

Getting Around
Town buses ply between the temple and the bus stand from early morning until late at night and cost Rs 0.60. In town, the buses stop at the west gopuram and opposite the tourist office on East Car St.

Unmetered auto-rickshaws and cycle-rickshaws are available at all hours; haggle hard if you get one to/from the bus stand.

Cycling is a good way of getting around town and out to Dhanushkodi. You can rent a bike from the shop next to the tourist office on East Car St for Rs 2 an hour.

TIRUCHENDUR
On the coast south of Tuticorin, this impressive shore temple is one of the six abodes of Lord Murugan and is very popular with pilgrims. You may be able to enter the inner sanctums here and watch the enthusiastic proceedings. Be careful if they offer you a gulp of the holy water – pouring it over your hands and rubbing them together joyously is an acceptable substitute for drinking it!

KANYAKUMARI (Cape Comorin)
Population: 18,500
Telephone Area Code: 04653

Kanyakumari is the 'Land's End' of India. Here, the Bay of Bengal meets the Indian Ocean and the Arabian Sea and, at Chaitrapurnima (the Tamil name for the full moon day that generally falls in April), it is possible to enjoy the unique experience of seeing the sun set and the moon rise over the ocean simultaneously.

Kanyakumari is also a popular pilgrimage destination and of great spiritual significance to Hindus. It is dedicated to the goddess Devi Kanya, the Youthful Virgin, who is an incarnation of Devi, Siva's wife. The pilgrims who come here from all over the country represent a good cross section of India.

Otherwise, Kanyakumari is highly overrated, with its trinket stalls, a lousy beach and one of those places with megaphones at the end of each street which, during festival times, rip your eardrums apart between 4 am and 10 pm.

Orientation & Information
The railway station is almost a km to the north of town, while the bus stand is 500 metres to the west. The tourist office is open weekdays from 10 am to 5.45 pm.

Kumari Amman Temple
Picturesquely situated overlooking the shore, this temple and the nearby ghat attract pilgrims from all over India to worship and to bathe. According to legend, Devi did penance here to secure Siva's hand in marriage. When she was unsuccessful, she vowed to remain a virgin *(kanya)*. The temple is open daily from 4.30 to 11.45 am

and from 5.30 to 8.45 pm, but non-Hindus are not allowed into the inner sanctum. Men must remove their shirts, and everyone their shoes, on entering this temple.

Gandhi Memorial

Next to the Kumari Amman Temple, this striking memorial stored the Mahatma's ashes until they were immersed in the sea. It resembles an Orissan temple and was designed so that on Gandhi's birthday (2 October), the sun's rays fall on the place where his ashes were kept. It's open daily from 8.30 am to 12.30 pm and 3 to 6 pm.

Vivekananda Memorial

This memorial is on two rocky islands projecting from the sea about 400 metres offshore. The Indian philosopher Swami Vivekananda came here in 1892 and sat on the rock, meditating, before setting out as one of India's most important religious crusaders. The mandapam which stands here in his memory was built in 1970 and reflects architectural styles from all over India. The ferry to the island (half-hourly) costs Rs 5 per person, plus there's a Rs 3 entry fee to the memorial. The islands are open to visitors from 7 to 11 am and 2 to 5 pm.

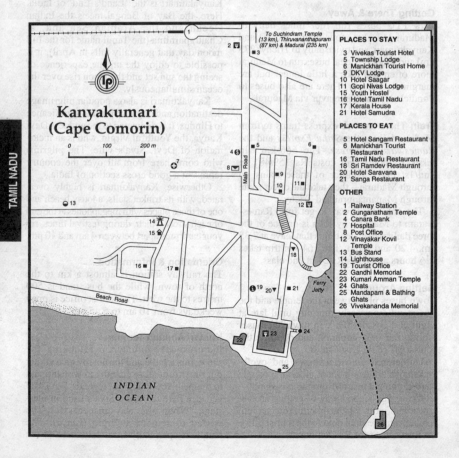

TAMIL NADU

Kanyakumari (Cape Comorin)

0   100   200 m

To Suchindram Temple (13 km), Thiruvananthapuram (87 km) & Madurai (235 km)

Main Road

Beach Road

INDIAN OCEAN

Ferry Jetty

PLACES TO STAY

3 Vivekas Tourist Hotel
5 Township Lodge
6 Manickhan Tourist Home
9 DKV Lodge
10 Hotel Saagar
11 Gopi Nivas Lodge
15 Youth Hostel
16 Hotel Tamil Nadu
17 Kerala House
21 Hotel Samudra

PLACES TO EAT

5 Hotel Sangam Restaurant
6 Manickhan Tourist Restaurant
16 Tamil Nadu Restaurant
18 Sri Ramdev Restaurant
20 Hotel Saravana
21 Sanga Restaurant

OTHER

1 Railway Station
2 Gunganatham Temple
4 Canara Bank
7 Hospital
8 Post Office
12 Vinayakar Kovil Temple
13 Bus Stand
14 Lighthouse
19 Tourist Office
22 Gandhi Memorial
23 Kumari Amman Temple
24 Ghats
25 Mandapam & Bathing Ghats
26 Vivekananda Memorial

Suchindram Temple

This temple, about 13 km north-west of Kanyakumari at Suchindram, is noted for its 'musical' columns and its incredibly tall statue of Hanuman, the monkey god.

Places to Stay

Although hotels are mushrooming in Kanyakumari, demand remains high and everything is heavily booked on weekends and during festivals. Some hotels have seasonal rates so you may find that, during April/May and October to December, room prices are 100% up on what is quoted here.

At the bottom end of the market, there's the *Gopi Nivas Lodge* with basic singles/doubles at Rs 60/80 and the similarly priced *Township Lodge* on Main Rd (no singles).

The comfortable *DKV Lodge* is better than both these, with doubles for Rs 80 with bathroom; there are no singles. At the new and clean *Hotel Saagar* (☎ 71-325), South Car St, doubles (no singles) go for Rs 80 and Rs 100.

For cheap dorm beds, try the deserted *youth hostel* at the northern entrance to the Hotel Tamil Nadu or the gents-only dorm at the *lodge* at the bus stand. This lodge also has good-value doubles for Rs 138. At the railway station there's a six-bed dorm and *retiring rooms*.

Going up in price, the new *Vivekas Tourist Hotel* (☎ 71-192) has colourful, clean rooms all with bath and shower from Rs 100/150 for a double/triple. The *Manickhan Tourist Home* (☎ 71-387) has doubles without/with a sea view for Rs 120/160. The restaurant here is good and does excellent dosas.

The *Hotel Samudra* (☎ 71-162) near the temple has rooms for Rs 250/300 and a decent restaurant.

On the hill just west of the temple, the big, mustard-coloured *Kerala House* (☎ 71-229) has the distinction of being the southernmost house on the subcontinent. It is run by the Kerala Tourism Development Corporation and was opened in 1956. Since then it has seen many prominent visitors, including the Dalai Lama. These days it has the 'slightly decrepit air that characterises most government buildings', according to the apt description in a recent magazine article, and seems to be monopolised by Kerala government officials.

Next door, the *Hotel Tamil Nadu* (☎ 71-257) has doubles for Rs 250, or Rs 380 with air-con. The rooms all have a private balcony affording great views of the Gandhi Memorial.

Places to Eat

The *Hotel Saravana* near the temple has a well-loaded vegetarian menu but many of the items are never available. Still, it offers south Indian and Chinese (of sorts) and is one of the town's most popular eateries. The *Sri Ramdev Restaurant* just up the road offers a mean range of north Indian vegetarian fare on its tiny open-air terrace. The more upmarket *Sanga Restaurant* in Hotel Samudra is also recommended for vegetarians.

Non-vegetarian food is harder to find. The *Manickhan Tourist Home* has perhaps the best non-veg restaurant in town, though the restaurants at *Hotel Sangam* and *Hotel Tamil Nadu* are worth a try too. The latter also has a permit room.

Getting There & Away

Bus The huge, relatively new bus stand is a dusty five-minute walk from the centre. It is well organised, with timetables in English, restaurants and waiting rooms. The reservation office is open from 7 am to 9 pm.

TTC has frequent buses to Madurai (253 km, six hours, Rs 34) and Madras (679 km, 16 hours, Rs 122) as well as buses to Thiruvananthapuram (Trivandrum, three times daily, 87 km, three hours) and Rameswaram (four times daily, 302 km, nine hours).

Local buses go to Nagercoil, Padmanabhapuram (for the palace of the former rulers of Travancore – see the Around Thiruvananthapuram section in the Kerala chapter for details), Thiruvananthapuram and Kovalam, among other places.

Train The one daily passenger train to Thiruvananthapuram leaves Kanyakumari at

5.40 pm and does the 87 km in a dazzling two hours (Rs 14 in 2nd class).

The *Kanyakumari Express* travels to Bombay daily in just under 48 hours, departing Kanyakumari at 5 am. The 2155-km trip costs Rs 308/1107 in 2nd/1st class. This train will also take you to Thiruvananthapuram (2¼ hours, Rs 25/105) and Ernakulam (eight hours, Rs 72/262).

For the real long-haulers, the weekly *Himsagar Express* runs all the way to Jammu Tawi (in Jammu & Kashmir), a distance of 3734 km, taking 74 hours. It's the longest single train ride in India, and leaves from Kanyakumari on Friday at 11.45 am and from Jammu Tawi on Monday at 10.45 pm. This train also passes through Coimbatore (12 hours), Vijayawada (29 hours) and Delhi (60 hours).

MUNDANTHURAI TIGER SANCTUARY

Mundanthurai is in the mountains near the border with Kerala. The closest railway station is at Ambasamudram, about 25 km to the north-east, and buses run from here to Papanasam, the nearest village, from where you can catch another bus to the Forest Department Rest House.

As the name implies, this is principally a tiger sanctuary though it's also noted for chital, sambar and the rare lion-tailed macaque. The best time to visit is between January and March, though it is open any time of the year. The main rainy season is between October and December. Tiger sightings are apparently extremely infrequent and, in addition, the *Forest Rest House* is poorly maintained, food is not available and the staff are unhelpful.

KUTTRALAM (Courtallam)

About 135 km north-west of Kanyakumari at the base of the Western Ghats, the village of Kuttralam is a popular 'health retreat' for Indian families who come to stand and wash under waterfalls believed to be rich in minerals and capable of curing almost anything.

Of the nine waterfalls, the only one in the village itself is the 60-metre-high **Main Falls**, a five-minute walk from the bus stand.

Its sheer rock face is carved with old Hindu insignia that is visible only during the dry months of January and February. Other falls, mostly accessed by shuttle buses, include the picturesque **Five Falls** (five km from town) and the **Old Falls**, eight km away.

The nearest major town is Tenkasi, five km to the north, which is connected to Kuttralam by frequent minibuses.

Places to Stay & Eat

Kuttralam offers only very basic lodging houses which are usually full in 'the season' (June to August). Try the *Parani Lodge* (☎ 22-529) on the lane leading to Main Falls or the better *Pandian Lodge* (☎ 22-139) at 39A Lakshmipuram St, a few minutes' walk from the falls, which has clean singles/doubles at Rs 40/75 and a non-veg restaurant.

For a less humble abode you'll have to stay in Tenkasi. Here the *Krishna Tourist Home* (☎ 23-125), next to the Tenkasi bus stand, has doubles for Rs 150 or Rs 300 with air-con, plus decent non-veg meals. Better is the *Hotel Anandha Classic*, 700 metres from the bus stand on the road to Kuttralam.

Getting There & Away

Tenkasi is the closest railway station to Kuttralam but trains on the main Kollam to Madurai line stop six km east at Shencottah (Sengottai) from where there's one express daily in either direction. Faster and more frequent buses also ply these routes.

The Western Ghats

KODAIKANAL

Population: 30,500
Telephone Area Code: 04542

Of the three main hill stations in the south – Udhagamandalam (Ootacamund, or Ooty), Kodaikanal and Yercaud – Kodaikanal is undoubtedly the most beautiful and, unlike Ooty, the temperature here rarely drops to the point where you need to wear heavy clothing, even in winter.

On the southern crest of the Palani Hills about 120 km north-west of Madurai at an altitude of 2100 metres, Kodaikanal – better known as Kodai – is surrounded by thickly wooded slopes, waterfalls and precipitous rocky outcrops. The journey up and back down again is breathtaking, though there's no toy train and access is by bus or car. In the town, there are lookouts with spectacular views of the south within easy walking distance of the town centre.

Kodai has the distinction of being the only hill station in India to be set up during the Raj by Americans, though it didn't take long before they were joined by the British. American missionaries established a school for European children here in the mid-1840s, the legacy of which is the Kodaikanal International School – one of the most prestigious private schools in the country.

Kodaikanal is not just for those who want to get away from the heat and haze of the dusty plains during the summer months, but also for those seeking a relaxing place to put their feet up for a while and do some occasional hiking in the quiet *sholas* (forests). In the surrounding hills you'll find plantations of Australian blue gums which provide the eucalyptus oil sold in Kodai's many street stalls. Here too is the Kurinji, a shrub with light, purple-blue-coloured blossoms which flowers every 12 years (the next will be in 2004 though there are always a few whose natural clocks seem to be out of time).

April to June or August to October are the best times to visit Kodaikanal. April to June is the main season, whereas the peak of the wet season is November/December. Temperatures here are mild, ranging between 11°C and 20°C in summer and 8°C and 17°C in winter.

Apart from one or two restaurants down Hospital Rd, there's really nowhere for people to gather in the evenings, so it's back to your hotel and early to bed.

Orientation
For a hill station, Kodai is remarkably compact. The main street is Bazaar Rd (Anna Salai), and the bottom-end hotels, restau-

rants and the bus stand are all in this area. Most, though not all, of the better hotels are some distance from the bazaar, but usually not more than about 15 minutes' walk.

Information
The tourist office, close to the bus stand, has precious little information. It's open from 10 am to 1.30 pm and 2 to 5.45 pm, Monday to Saturday. If you want literature about Kodai, try the CLS bookshop more or less opposite.

The banks in town will change some travellers' cheques but they won't touch foreign cash.

Astrophysical Laboratory
Built in 1889, this laboratory stands on the highest point in the area, three km uphill from Kodai's lake. It houses a small **museum** which is open Friday from 10 am to noon and 3 to 5 pm. The buildings with the instruments are off limits. It's a hard 45-minute uphill walk pushing a bicycle, but it only takes five minutes to coast down (you'll need good brakes).

Flora & Fauna Museum
Also worth a visit is the Flora & Fauna Museum at the Sacred Heart College at Shembaganur. It's a six-km hike and all uphill on the way back. The museum is open from 10 am to noon and 3 to 5 pm; closed Sunday. Entry costs Rs 1.

Parks & Falls
Near the start of Coaker's Walk is **Bryant Park**, a botanical park laid out, landscaped and stocked over many years by the British officer after whom it is named. At **Chettiar Park**, about three km uphill from town near the Kurinji Andavar Temple, you may be able to see some Kurinji flowers.

There are numerous waterfalls in the area – the main one, **Silver Cascade** is on the road up to Kodai.

Activities
Walking & Trekking The views from Coaker's Walk which has an observatory with telescope (entry Rs 0.50, camera Rs 1),

and from Pillar Rocks, a seven-km hike (one way), are two of the most spectacular in southern India.

For more serious trekking, head to the District Forest Office, on a windy road down (north) towards Hotel Tamil Nadu. Here you can buy a pamphlet called *Kodaikanal Beauty in Wilderness* which describes 17 local treks ranging from eight-km ambles to 27-km hikes. It costs Rs 10 and includes a rough map plus estimates of the time required to complete each walk and the relative degree of difficulty. This office is open weekdays from 10 am to 1 pm and 2 to 6 pm.

Boating & Riding The lake at Kodai has been wonderfully landscaped, and rowboats are available for half an hour at Rs 20 (four seats) or Rs 30 (six seats) plus a returnable deposit of the same amount. You can also hire pedal boats for Rs 10 to Rs 20 per half hour (plus deposit). The boathouse is below The Carlton Hotel. Down by this same boathouse, you'll be accosted by people who want to rent you horses. They are not cheap, and you'll be quoted as much as they think you're willing to pay. The prevailing rate seems to be Rs 75 per hour and you can ride accompanied or unaccompanied. The saddles are pretty awful, especially if you're used to your own.

Roller Skating The MYH Youth Hostel has a pint-sized skating rink where boot hire plus an hour of skating costs Rs 20. It's likely you'll be dizzy after two rounds of this rink.

Organised Tours
The Hotel Tamil Nadu has tours of Kodai from 8 am to noon and from 2 to 6 pm for Rs 65 a person. Plenty of private operators near the bus stand offer full-day tours taking in 12 to 16 local sights for Rs 65 to Rs 75.

Places to Stay
As with the other hill stations, hotel prices in the high season (1 April to 30 June) jump by up to 300% compared to those during the rest of the year. In some cases, this is nothing but a blatant rip-off, especially at the lower end

of the market. During this season, it's worth considering staying in a mid-range hotel since none of them hike their prices by more than 100% and some considerably less than that.

The other thing to bear in mind is that the majority of hotels here don't have single rooms and they're reluctant to discuss reductions for single occupancy in the high season. Most hotels in Kodai have a 9 or 10 am checkout time in the high season so don't get caught out. During the rest of the year it's usually, but not always, 24 hours.

Places to Stay – bottom end
Most of the ultra-cheap hotels are strung out along the steep Bazaar Rd but many of them (eg *Guru Lodge*) are little more than dosshouses with absolutely minimal facilities. Just make sure that they give you blankets, as it gets pretty chilly here. To get hot water in the morning, you'll have to call for 'bucket service'. The *International Guest House*, halfway up Bazaar Rd, is the pick of these cheapies, with rooms for Rs 100 with attached bathroom.

Better is the amiable *Hotel Sunrise* (☎ 40-358), a few minutes' walk from the bus stand, which has doubles (no singles) with bathroom for Rs 100. The view from the front is excellent, and the rooms have hot-water heaters which work from 6 am to 6 pm.

Further uphill, just off Club Rd, the best value place by far is the friendly *Taj Villa* (☎ 40-940), an old stone-built group of houses in its own small garden with sublime views. Double rooms here (no singles) cost Rs 150 to Rs 300 (low season) and Rs 400 to Rs 600 (high season). Most of the rooms have attached bathrooms and three rooms in the older house have fireplaces. Extra blankets are Rs 10 and hot water is available for two hours each morning and evening.

Close by, the *Zum Zum Lodge* is a dump and exorbitantly overpriced at Rs 150/900 a double in the low/high season. Some rooms have an open fireplace.

Further up Club Rd at the end of Coaker's Walk is the *Greenlands Youth Hostel* (☎ 41-099). This long stone cottage has the best views of any hotel in town and it's where you'll find most of the budget travellers. That said, it can be suffocatingly crowded in the high season, though in the cooler months it's tremendous. A bed in the dorm (six to 15 beds) costs Rs 30/40 in the low/high season. There are also eight double rooms (four have fireplaces – an evening's supply of wood will cost you Rs 25 extra) with attached bathrooms for Rs 80 to Rs 100 in the low season and Rs 130 to Rs 150 in the high season. Breakfast – either Indian or toasted brown bread with jam – and snacks are available.

Dorm beds are also offered at the *youth hostel* at the Hotel Tamil Nadu and at the *MYH Youth Hostel* on Post Office Rd.

Places to Stay – middle

At the bottom end of this category, the *Hotel Anjay* (☎ 41-089), Bazaar Rd, isn't a bad choice though it's often full. Double rooms with attached bathroom and constant hot water start at Rs 250/350 in the low/high season including taxes. Directly behind here, the *Hotel Jaya* (☎ 41-062) is slightly cheaper and also has single rooms. Just down the road, the new *Snooze Inn* (☎ 40-837) has clean rooms with TV and running hot water.

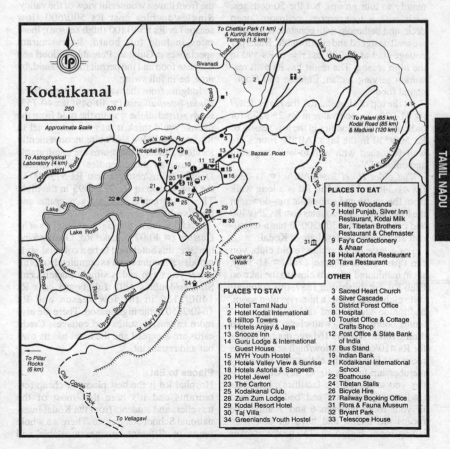

Kodaikanal

0   250   500 m

Approximate Scale

PLACES TO EAT
6 Hilltop Woodlands
7 Hotel Punjab, Silver Inn Restaurant, Kodai Milk Bar, Tibetan Brothers Restaurant & Chefmaster
9 Fay's Confectionery & Ahaar
18 Hotel Astoria Restaurant
20 Tava Restaurant

OTHER
3 Sacred Heart Church
4 Silver Cascade
5 District Forest Office
8 Hospital
10 Tourist Office & Cottage Crafts Shop
12 Post Office & State Bank of India
17 Bus Stand
19 Indian Bank
21 Kodaikanal International School
22 Boathouse
24 Tibetan Stalls
26 Bicycle Hire
27 Railway Booking Office
31 Flora & Fauna Museum
32 Bryant Park
33 Telescope House

PLACES TO STAY
1 Hotel Tamil Nadu
2 Hotel Kodai International
6 Hilltop Towers
11 Hotels Anjay & Jaya
13 Snooze Inn
14 Guru Lodge & International Guest House
15 MYH Youth Hostel
16 Hotels Valley View & Sunrise
18 Hotels Astoria & Sangeeth
20 Hotel Jewel
23 The Carlton
25 Kodaikanal Club
28 Zum Zum Lodge
29 Kodai Resort Hotel
30 Taj Villa
34 Greenlands Youth Hostel

To Chettiar Park (1 km) & Kurinji Andavar Temple (1.5 km)

Sivanadi

Fern Hill Road

Law's Ghat Road

To Palani (65 km), Kodai Road (85 km) & Madurai (120 km)

To Astrophysical Laboratory (4 km)

Hospital Rd

Bazaar Road

Coolie Ghat Rd

Observatory Road

Lake Rd

Lake Road

Coaker's Walk

Club Road

Gymkhana Road

Lower Shola Road

Upper Shola Road

St Mary's Road

To Pillar Rocks (6 km)

Old Coolie Track

To Vellagavi

TAMIL NADU

Doubles (there are no singles) cost Rs 245/450 in low/high season.

Nearby the *Hotel Sangeeth* (☎ 40-456) is good value at Rs 170/250 for a double in the low/high season. All the rooms have attached bathrooms with hot and cold running water. Next door, the *Hotel Astoria* (☎ 40-524) has ordinary/deluxe doubles at Rs 275/300 in the low season and Rs 475/500 in the high. Its restaurant serves north and south Indian dishes.

One of the best places in this range is the *Kodai Resort Hotel* (☎ 41-801) on Noyce Rd near the start of Coaker's Walk. It caters mainly to tour groups, but the 50 cottages, each with a loungeroom, bedroom, open deck, and bathroom with constant hot water, are well designed and comfortable. Rates per cottage start at Rs 290 and rise to Rs 590 in the high season. The resort has its own restaurant serving Indian, Chinese and Continental food.

At the top of Hospital Rd, the *Hotel Jewel* (☎ 41-029) is good value at Rs 250/275 for ordinary/deluxe doubles in the low season or Rs 500/550 in the high. All the rooms are well furnished with wall-to-wall carpeting and colour TV.

The older *Hotel Tamil Nadu* (☎ 41-336; fax 41-340) on Fern Hill Rd is a long walk from the centre and somewhat run-down. In the low/high season doubles cost Rs 250/400 and cottages are Rs 300/500. It has a restaurant and one of the few bars in Kodai.

For a taste of an exclusive old club, you can't pass the *Kodaikanal Club* (☎ 41-341), set in manicured grounds close to the lake on Club Rd. Established in 1887, this colonial-style clubhouse boasts a library, video room, badminton and billiard tables, four 'mud' tennis courts, a bar (with cheap beers) and dining room. It offers 16 large double rooms for Rs 410/600 in the low/high season. This room rate includes the obligatory temporary membership fee (Rs 40 per day which entitles you to use all the facilities), breakfast (Indian or Continental) and 'bed tea' (served in your room between 6 and 7 am). The rooms are quaint and have an adjoining sitting room, bathroom, TV, heater, wicker chairs and 24-hour hot water. Don't expect to get a room here in the high season as it's booked out months ahead.

Places to Stay – top end
The best place to stay at the lower end of this range is the *Hilltop Towers* (☎ 40-413) on Club Rd opposite the Kodai International School. The staff are keen and friendly and double rooms/suites cost Rs 300/400 in the low season and Rs 575/700 in the high.

Also very good is the brand new *Valley View Hotel* (☎ 40-181) on Post Office Rd. The rooms are well appointed and those at the front have a wonderful view of the valley. Singles/doubles cost Rs 500/600 (low season) or Rs 850/1100 (high season); these rates include full board. Its restaurant specialises in Gujarati, Punjabi, tandoori and Chinese food and the permit room should, by now, be in full swing.

Judging from the way in which the *Hotel Kodai International* (☎ 40-649; fax 40-753) is advertised all the way up the road from the plains, you'd think it was the best hotel in Kodai. It isn't. It's also quite inconveniently located, although the rooms are comfortable and have all the amenities you'd expect. Double rooms/cottages cost Rs 575/800 in the low season or Rs 995/1395 in the high. The restaurant is decidedly average and there's a bar.

Kodai's most prestigious hotel is *The Carlton* (☎ 40-071), Lake Rd. Overlooking the lake, this hotel used to be a colonial-style wooden structure but was completely rebuilt a few years ago and is simply magnificent. Singles/doubles with full board cost Rs 1400/2150 in the low season and Rs 1640/2650 in the high season. There are also more expensive suites and cottages. Credit cards are accepted and the hotel has its own bar and restaurant.

Places to Eat
Hospital Rd is the best place for cheap restaurants and it's here that most of the travellers and students from the Kodai International School congregate. There's a whole range of different cuisines available and

which restaurant you choose on any particular day is largely a question of personal choice and who you find yourself with. They're all pretty good.

At the top of the road is the *Tava Restaurant*, below the Hotel Jewel, which offers vegetarian Indian food.

Further down the road are (in order of appearance) the *Hotel Punjab* (excellent tandoori), the tiny *Ahaar* (vegetarian), the *Silver Inn Restaurant* (Continental non-veg food and very popular), the old *Kodai Milk Bar*, the *Tibetan Brothers Restaurant* (Westernised Tibetan food) and the *Chefmaster* (Continental, Chinese and Keralan).

Also on Hospital Rd is *Fay's Confectionery*, a happening little snack bar with the best home-made pastries and cakes in town – the vegetable puffs and banana crunch are divine. It's open daily from 11 am to 8 pm, closed Tuesday. Another recommendation is the *Eco Nut* also on Hospital Rd.

If you're just looking for a cheap Indian vegetarian meal, the restaurant at the *Hotel Astoria* is a good bet. For a classier Indian 'meals' restaurant, head to the *Hilltop Woodlands* next to the Hilltop Towers Hotel. This place is immensely popular at lunchtime.

For a splurge, go to one of the better mid-range hotels or, best of all, to *The Carlton*. Here, they put on an evening buffet from 7.30 to 10 pm which is excellent value for Rs 175. You can relax in the bar after eating though drinks are a little on the expensive side compared with elsewhere in Kodaikanal.

Things to Buy

The Cottage Crafts shop on Bazaar Rd opposite the post office has some excellent bits and pieces for sale. It is run by Corsock, the Co-ordinating Council for Social Concerns in Kodai. This organisation, staffed by volunteers, sells crafts on behalf of development groups, using the commission charged to help the needy. Corsock also runs the Goodwill Centre, Hospital Rd, which sells clothing and rents books, with the proceeds again going to indigent causes.

The road down to the lake (alongside the

Kodaikanal Club) is lined with stalls run by Tibetans selling warm clothing, shawls and other fabrics. Their prices are very reasonable.

Kodai is a lush orchard area and, depending on the season, you'll find various fruits – pears, avocados, guavas, durians and grapefruit – in the street stalls around the bus stand.

Getting There & Away

Bus Kodai's bus stand is basically a patch of dirt opposite the Hotel Astoria and you won't find many timetables nor direction indicators on the buses in English. State buses run eight times a day to Madurai (121 km, 3½ hours, Rs 18), once daily to both Tiruchirappalli (197 km) and Kanyakumari (356 km), and twice a day to both Coimbatore (244 km) and Madras (513 km). As well, there are more frequent buses to Palani (65 km, three hours, Rs 20), Dindigul and Kodai Road (the railway station). There's also a KSRTC semideluxe bus daily to Bangalore for Rs 90 which leaves at 6 pm and takes 12 hours (480 km).

Deluxe minibuses operate in the high season between Kodaikanal and Udhagamandalam (Ooty) but they are suspended in the monsoon. They cost around Rs 130 and take all day to cover the 332 km. Enquire at mid-range hotels for departure times.

Train The nearest railway stations are Palani to the north (on the Coimbatore-Madurai-Rameswaram line), and Kodai Road on the Madurai-Trichy-Madras line to the east. Both are about three hours away by bus.

There's a railway booking office, known as an 'out-agency', up from the bus stand where you can book seats on express trains to Madras. For reservations to other destinations you need to book in Madurai.

Getting Around

The stall outside The Carlton hotel rents mountain bikes for Rs 5/40 per hour/day and small Kinetic Honda motorcycles at Rs 100 for an hour including petrol or Rs 300 a day without petrol. The bicycle stall near the corner of Bazaar and Club Rds has ordinary bikes for Rs 15 per day (negotiable). The hills can present quite a problem but, as you'd be walking up them anyway, it's not that much extra hassle to push a bike and at least you can coast down!

Taxis in Kodaikanal are very expensive compared with elsewhere even though half of them stand idle most of the day. There are no rickshaws of any description.

AROUND KODAI
Palani

There are fine views of the plains and scattered rock outcrops on the bus ride from Kodaikanal to Palani. The town's hill temple, **Malaikovil**, is dedicated to Lord Muruga, and an electric winch takes devotees to the top. Some 200,000 pilgrims gather at this temple for the Thai Pusam Festival in January. See the earlier Getting There & Away section under Kodaikanal for information on getting to Palani.

ANAMALAI WILDLIFE SANCTUARY

This is one of the three wildlife sanctuaries on the slopes of the Western Ghats along the border between Tamil Nadu and Kerala. Though recently renamed the Indira Gandhi Wildlife Sanctuary, most people still refer to it by its original name. It covers almost 1000 sq km and is home to elephant, gaur (Indian bison), tiger, panther, spotted deer, wild boar, bear, porcupine and civet cat. The Nilgiri tahr, commonly known as ibex, can also be spotted, as can many birds.

In the heart of this beautiful forested region is the Parambikulam Dam which has formed an immense plain of water that spreads way into Kerala. The rights to this water, used mainly for irrigation and energy purposes in Tamil Nadu, are the source of one of the area's bitter disputes.

Information

The reception centre and most of the lodges are at Topslip, about 35 km south-west of Pollachi. All accommodation, however, should be booked in advance in Pollachi at the Wildlife Warden's Office (☎ 4345) on Meenkarai Rd. There is no entrance fee at Topslip but if you go on to Parambikulam on the park's Keralan side you must pay Rs 25.

The sanctuary can be visited at any time (it's best from February to June) though without your own transport you're not likely to see much. Tours are rarely run as the Forest Department's sole wildlife-viewing vehicle is perpetually in disrepair, and the public bus that plies daily between Pollachi and Parambikulam scares away everything but monkeys.

Places to Stay & Eat

Accommodation is available at three places. At Topslip, there is a dormitory and four lodges, the best of which is *Ambuli Illam* two km from the reception centre. Topslip, at 740 metres, can get cool at night in winter.

About 24 km east of Topslip near the Varagaliar River and a remote elephant camp is the *Varagaliar Rest House*. It's accessible by 4WD only and you'll need to take your own food. At Parambikulam, the very basic *rest house* has no catering facilities and only a few grungy 'meals' places nearby.

The canteen at Topslip has basic fare – dosas and chapatis – and is the only place in the park where you can get a half decent meal.

Getting There & Away

Anamalai is between Palani and Coimbatore. Regular buses from both these places stop at the nearest large town, Pollachi, which is also on the Coimbatore to Dindigul train line. From Pollachi, there are buses twice daily to the sanctuary via the township of Anamalai. A taxi from Pollachi is Rs 300 one way.

COIMBATORE

Population: 1.2 million
Telephone Area Code: 0422

Coimbatore is a large industrial city known for textile manufacturing and engineering goods, and is full of 'suitings and shirtings' shops. It can make a convenient overnight stop if you're heading up to Ooty or the other Nilgiri hill stations.

TAMIL NADU

Orientation & Information

The two main bus stands are about two km from the railway station. Buses from Kerala and southern Tamil Nadu arrive at a third stand, Ukkadam, south of the railway station. Frequent city buses ply the route from here into town.

There's a tourist office at the railway station, but it's hard to think of a reason to visit it. The GPO is open for poste restante collection from 10 am to 3 pm Monday to Saturday.

Places to Stay – bottom end

Close to the bus stand, the *Hotel Shree Shakti* (☎ 23-4225) at 11/148 Sastri Rd is a large hotel with friendly staff. Rooms have a fan and bathroom and cost Rs 75/120 for singles/doubles. Also on Sastri Rd is the more basic *Zakin Hotel* with rooms for Rs 50/80.

The *Hotel Blue Star* (☎ 23-0635) on Nehru St is good value at Rs 90/150 for rooms with

bathroom (hot water from 7 to 9 am). The rooms out the back are spared the noise from the boisterous movie crowds. There's a basement bar and both a veg and non-veg restaurant.

Opposite the railway station, the small Davey & Co Lane is a solid enclave of relatively quiet hotels. Both the *Hotel Anand Vihar* (☎ 21-2580) and the nearby *Hotel Sivakami* (☎ 21-0271) are friendly and helpful and have singles/doubles with bathroom for Rs 55/100.

The noisy railway *retiring rooms* cost Rs 120, or Rs 175 with air-con. The dorm beds (men only) are Rs 35.

Places to Stay – middle

The *Hotel Tamil Nadu* (☎ 23-6311) on Dr Nanjappa Rd has decent singles/doubles at Rs 150/190, or Rs 250/300 with air-con, and there are deluxe doubles for Rs 400.

The *Hotel City Tower* (☎ 23-0681; fax 23-0103), Sivasamy Rd, has a range of facil-

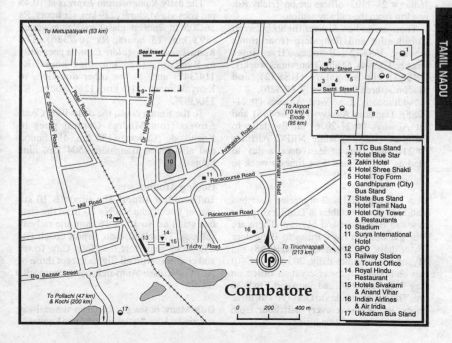

Coimbatore

0   200   400 m

1 TTC Bus Stand
2 Hotel Blue Star
3 Zakin Hotel
4 Hotel Shree Shakti
5 Hotel Top Form
6 Gandhipuram (City) Bus Stand
7 State Bus Stand
8 Hotel Tamil Nadu
9 Hotel City Tower & Restaurants
10 Stadium
11 Surya International Hotel
12 GPO
13 Railway Station & Tourist Office
14 Royal Hindu Restaurant
15 Hotels Sivakami & Anand Vihar
16 Indian Airlines & Air India
17 Ukkadam Bus Stand

To Mettupalayam (53 km)
See Inset
To Airport (10 km) & Erode (95 km)
Sir Shanmugam Road
Patel Road
Dr Nanjappa Road
Avenashi Road
Racecourse Road
Racecourse Road
Mill Road
Trichy Road
Kamarajar Road
Big Bazaar Street
To Pollachi (47 km) & Kochi (200 km)
To Tiruchirappalli (213 km)
Nehru Street
Sastri Street

TAMIL NADU

ities including two restaurants (vegetarian and non-veg). Its rooms are super value at Rs 310/400, or Rs 450/600 with air-con. Credit cards are accepted.

The top-end *Surya International Hotel* (☎ 21-7751; fax 21-6110), 105 Racecourse Rd, has luxurious rooms for Rs 550/700.

Places to Eat

The *Royal Hindu Restaurant*, just north of the railway station, is a huge place offering good vegetarian meals. The *Hotel Top Form* on Nehru St serves savoury non-vegetarian food at reasonable prices. For a splurge, eat at one of the two restaurants at the *Hotel City Towers*.

Bars are not in short supply in Coimbatore and, unlike many other places in Tamil Nadu, they are not even disguised with the name 'permit room'.

Getting There & Away

Air The Indian Airlines (☎ 21-2743) and Air India (☎ 21-3393) offices are on Trichy Rd, one km from the railway station.

There are Indian Airlines flights between Coimbatore and Bangalore (four times weekly, US$32), Bombay (five times weekly, US$94), Madras (four times weekly, US$53) via Bangalore (US$32), and Madurai (three times weekly, US$26).

Additionally, East West Airlines (☎ 21-0285), Damania Airways (☎ 57-6898) and Jet Airways (☎ 21-2036) all fly daily to Bombay (US$94) while NEPC Airlines (☎ 21-6741) flies at least once a day to Madras (US$55) and three times a week to Mangalore (US$110).

Bus The large and well-organised state bus stand only has timetables in Tamil, except for buses to Bangalore and Mysore. There are four lines of bus bays. Buses to Bangalore (twice daily, 312 km, nine hours, Rs 68) and Mysore (three times daily, 205 km, Rs 40) can be booked at the reservation office on Bay 1 between 9 am and noon and 1 to 9.30 pm. The ordinary buses to Ooty (90 km, three hours, Rs 14) leave every half hour from opposite the reservation office.

The TTC/JJTC bus stand is on Cross Cut Rd, five minutes' walk from the state bus stand. The reservations office (☎ 44-969) is open from 7 am to 9 pm. There are services to Mysore via Ooty (20 buses daily between 4 am and midnight), to Madras (No 460, five daily, 492 km, 11½ hours), Madurai (Nos 660 & 626, 227 km, six hours), and Trichy (No 720, 15 daily, 203 km, 5¼ hours).

Train Coimbatore is a major rail junction and has services to most major centres. Catch the daily *Nilgiri Express* at 6.20 am if you're heading for Ooty; it connects with the miniature railway at Mettupalayam. The whole trip takes 4½ hours and costs Rs 28/166 in 2nd/1st class.

There are numerous daily trains between Coimbatore and Madras Central (494 km), the fastest being the *Kovai Express* (departure 2.20 pm) which takes 7½ hours and costs Rs 102/382 in 2nd/1st class. Other trains take up to nine hours.

The daily *Rameswaram Express* at 10.45 pm goes via Madurai (229 km, six hours, Rs 56/205 in 2nd/1st class) to Rameswaram (393 km, 13 hours, Rs 107/326). The *Kanyakumari-Bangalore Express* goes daily to Bangalore (424 km, nine hours, Rs 114/347) and, in the other direction, to Kanyakumari (510 km, 12½ hours, Rs 130/387).

To the Kerala coast, the daily *West Coast Express* from Madras Central goes to Kozhikode (Calicut) (185 km, 4½ hours) and also on to Bangalore (504 km, nine hours).

Getting Around

To/From the Airport The airport is 10 km east of town (take bus No 20 from the state bus stand or No 10 or 16 from the railway station). There's also an airport coach (Rs 25) which runs from the Hotel City Tower and connects with all flights except those of NEPC Airlines. Auto-rickshaws charge Rs 80.

Bus Many buses ply between the railway station and the city bus stand (also known as

Gandhipuram) including bus Nos JJ, 24, 55 and 57. From Gandhipuram to the GPO take bus No 3, 5 or 15.

Auto-Rickshaw The auto-rickshaw drivers here generally need some convincing that the meter should be used. It's about Rs 10 from the railway station to the bus terminals.

COONOOR

Population: 46,000
Telephone Area Code: 04264

At an altitude of 1850 metres, Coonoor is the first of the three Nilgiri hill stations – Udhagamandalam (Ooty), Kotagiri and Coonoor – that you come to when leaving behind the southern plains. Like Ooty, it's on the toy train line from Mettupalayam.

While Kotagiri had the Kotas, and Ooty the Todas, so Coonoor was home to the Coon hill tribe. (The suffix, 'oor', means village.) This now bustling town appears rather squashed between the hills, and it's only after climbing up out of the bustling market area with the bus and train terminals that you'll get a sense of what hill stations were originally all about. For this reason, too, most of the better accommodation is in Upper Coonoor.

Places to Stay & Eat
The *YWCA Guest House* (☎ 20-326) in Upper Coonoor is the best budget option. Open to men and women, it's a handsome old colonial house with two wooden terraces and views over Coonoor. Large clean singles/doubles with bathroom cost Rs 100/250 but they also have dorm beds for Rs 60. There's hot water and basic food is available. To get there, take a town bus to 'Bedford' from where it is a five-minute walk.

The nearby *Vivek Tourist Home* (☎ 20-658) is also worth checking out and is slightly cheaper at Rs 90/150. Alternatively, the *Sri Lakshmi Tourist Home* (☎ 21-022) offers basic singles/doubles for Rs 70/100 (low season) and Rs 150/200 (high season).

The *Taj Garden Retreat* (☎ 20-021) on the hilltop in Upper Coonoor offers top accom-

modation. Standard singles/doubles are US$38/60 and deluxe rooms cost US$39/75. In the high season prices rise by 50%. The restaurant here does a sumptuous buffet.

Next to the Vivek Tourist Home, the *Sankar Restaurant* has basic but good non-veg food and cheap Indian breakfasts. For something a bit more upmarket head to the non-veg *Blue Hill Restaurant* on Mount Rd.

Getting There & Away
Coonoor is on the toy train line between Mettupalayam (28 km) and Ooty (18 km) – for train details see the Ooty section. Buses to Kotagiri (Rs 5) leave every 15 minutes.

KOTAGIRI

Population: 25,000
Telephone Area Code: 04266

Kotagiri (Line of Houses of the Kotas) is a small, quiet village about 28 km east of Ooty, at an altitude of 1950 metres. Though the oldest of the three Nilgiri hill stations – the British started building houses here in 1819 – it is much less touristed than Ooty and calmer than Coonoor. Life is now concentrated around tea production. The road to Ooty winds along hills denuded of their original cover in favour of bright green tea plantations and dotted with Kota settlements.

From Kotagiri you can visit **Catherine Falls** eight km away near the Mettupalayam road (the last three km by foot only), **Elk Falls** (six km) and **Kodanad View Point** (22 km), where there is a fine panoramic view over the Coimbatore plains, the Mysore plateau and the eastern slopes of the Nilgiris.

In town, there's a Women's Cooperative near Ramchand Square which sells local handicrafts.

Places to Stay & Eat
There are a few basic lodges in town such as the *Majestic Lodge*, the *Blue Star* and the *Hotel Ramesh Vihar*. In all, double rooms with attached bathroom start at about Rs 75.

Tempting for its homeliness and wonderful setting is the *Queenshill Christian Guest House*, one km uphill behind the bus stand

TAMIL NADU

and past the Women's Cooperative. Miss Ruth Rose, the friendly, mellow-natured lady who runs the place, offers well-furnished rooms for Rs 85 per person including breakfast (Rs 200 for full board). Meals are served, when possible, with all guests around one table. In the evening you can wind down in front of the open fire with a book from the shelf.

Opposite the Women's Cooperative, the vegetarian *Kasturi Paradise Restaurant* serves all the normal stuff.

Getting There & Away

There are regular buses to Ooty (Rs 5) which cross one of Tamil Nadu's highest passes. Buses to Mettupalayam (Rs 5.50) leave every 30 minutes and to Coonoor (Rs 5) every 15 minutes.

UDHAGAMANDALAM (Ootacamund, Ooty)

Population: 87,000
Telephone Area Code: 0423

This famous hill station near the tri-junction of Tamil Nadu, Kerala and Karnataka in the Nilgiri Hills was founded by the British in the early part of the 19th century to serve as the summer headquarters of the Madras government. Before that time, the area was inhabited by the Todas, the tribal people of which today only 3000 remain. They were polygamists and worshipped buffaloes, and you can see their animist shrines in various places.

Until about two decades ago, Ooty (altitude 2240 metres) resembled an unlikely combination of southern England and Australia: single-storey stone cottages, bijou fenced flower gardens, leafy, winding lanes, and tall eucalypt stands covering the otherwise barren hilltops. Since their introduction back in the 19th century, the eucalypts have spawned a small oil-extraction industry in the area, and bottles of eucalyptus oil are sold in the town's shops.

The other main reminders of the British period are the stone churches, the private schools, the Ooty Club, various maharajas' summer palaces, and the terraced botanical gardens, in which Government House still stands.

But while parts of Ooty still exude a fading atmosphere of leafy seclusion, especially on the lake's western and southern margins, elsewhere hoteliers and real estate developers and the influx of tourist hordes with their city habits have totally transformed it.

These days, at least in the high season, it's a dreadful place full of vacuous yuppies and day-trippers with their ghetto blasters, pushing and shoving their way into and onto everything, and throwing litter everywhere. The sewage system, too, is incapable of dealing with the demand placed on it as a glance at the town's central, open sewer will demonstrate. It's important to remember, should you be thinking of boating, that all this untreated filth flows directly into the lake.

All in all, Ooty is best avoided these days unless you can afford to stay in one of the former palaces. The only things it has going for it are the journey up there on the 'toy' train and the fact that it's cool when the plains down below are unbearably hot. In the winter months and during the monsoon you will need warm clothing as the overnight temperature occasionally drops to 0°C.

Orientation

Ooty is spread over a large area amongst rolling hills and valleys. Between the lake and the racecourse are the railway station and bus stand. From either of these it's a 10-minute walk to the bazaar area and 20 minutes to Ooty's real centre, Charing Cross (the junction of Coonoor, Kelso and Commercial roads).

Information

Tourist Office The tourist office (☎ 3977), on Commercial Rd, is open weekdays from 10 am to 1 pm and 2 to 5.45 pm. The staff give out poor maps of Ooty and will only book visitors on tours.

Money The State Bank of India, Town West Circle, is open weekdays from 10 am to 2 pm and Saturday until noon.

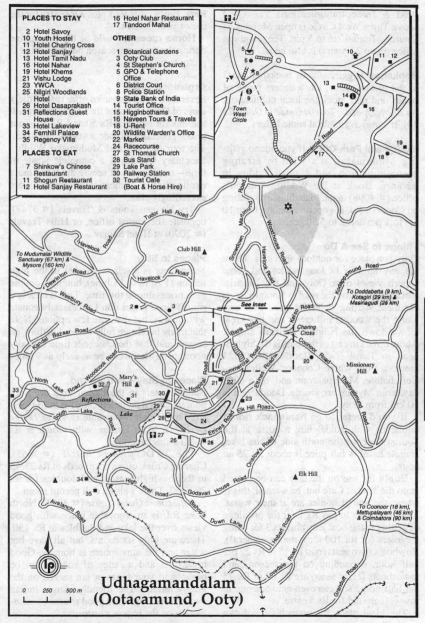

PLACES TO STAY

2   Hotel Savoy
10 Youth Hostel
11 Hotel Charing Cross
12 Hotel Sanjay
13 Hotel Tamil Nadu
16 Hotel Nahar
19 Hotel Khems
21 Vishu Lodge
23 YWCA
25 Nilgiri Woodlands Hotel
26 Hotel Dasaprakash
31 Reflections Guest House
33 Hotel Lakeview
34 Fernhill Palace
35 Regency Villa

PLACES TO EAT

7   Shinkow's Chinese Restaurant
11 Shogun Restaurant
12 Hotel Sanjay Restaurant

16 Hotel Nahar Restaurant
17 Tandoori Mahal

OTHER

1   Botanical Gardens
3   Ooty Club
4   St Stephen's Church
5   GPO & Telephone Office
6   District Court
8   Police Station
9   State Bank of India
14 Tourist Office
15 Higginbothams
16 Naveen Tours & Travels
18 U-Rent
20 Wildlife Warden's Office
22 Market
24 Racecourse
27 St Thomas Church
28 Bus Stand
29 Lake Park
30 Railway Station
32 Tourist Cafe (Boat & Horse Hire)

To Mudumalai Wildlife Sanctuary (67 km) & Mysore (160 km)

To Doddabetta (9 km), Kotagiri (29 km) & Masinagudi (26 km)

To Coonoor (18 km), Mettupalayam (46 km) & Coimbatore (90 km)

TAMIL NADU

0   250   500 m

Udhagamandalam
(Ootacamund, Ooty)

Post & Telecommunications The GPO above Town West Circle is open Monday to Saturday from 9 am to 5 pm. The telegraph office (open 24 hours) is also here.

Bookshop Higginbothams bookshop, next to the tourist office, has a decent range of books and may stock the local publication, *An Encyclopaedic Tourist Guide to Ooty* (Rs 30). It's also available at some lodges.

Mudumalai Park Office If you intend visiting Mudumalai, it's wise to arrange accommodation and elephant rides in advance. Book at the Wildlife Warden's office (☎ 4098) in the Mahalingam Building on Coonoor Rd. It's open weekdays from 10 am to 1 pm and 2 to 5.30 pm.

Things to See & Do
Ooty is a place for outdoor activities. There are any number of long **walks** and some superb views over Ooty and the Nilgiris. **Kotagiri Pass,** on the road to Kotagiri, is an excellent starting point for treks over and along the wooded hill crests and has great views down the Nilgiris' northern slopes. About three km east of this pass is the highest peak in Tamil Nadu, **Doddabetta** (2623 metres), from where Coonoor, Wellington, Coimbatore, Mettupalayam and, on a clear day, even Mysore are visible. Doddabetta is 10 km from Ooty.

If you'd prefer to go **horseback riding** (alone or with guide) hire a horse at the Tourist Cafe on the north side of the lake. Haggle hard! A fair price is about Rs 75 an hour.

Boats for use on the lake can be rented from the Tourist Cafe but, be warned, this is where the tourist hordes are at their worst. You even have to pay Rs 1 for the privilege of getting to the boat jetty plus Rs 3 for using a camera (or Rs 100 for a movie camera!). Rowboats (two seats) cost Rs 15 or Rs 22 per half hour, depending on the season, and motorboats (eight seats) are Rs 65 or Rs 75 per half hour. You can even get someone to row you around for Rs 5 extra.

The ideal place for masochists is **Lake Park.** Entry costs Rs 1 plus a lot extra for the use of your camera.

Horse races are held at the racecourse during the monsoon season but the betting is pretty tame.

Organised Tours
Several private companies offer rushed daily tours of Ooty and/or of the neighbouring hill stations for between Rs 50 and Rs 80. Tour prices generally include a vegetarian lunch. The tour of Ooty and Mudumalai Wildlife Sanctuary (Rs 85) is a complete waste of time – the chances of seeing anything more exotic than a domesticated elephant are exceedingly slim.

Try Naveen Tours & Travels (☎ 3747), opposite the tourist office, or Hills Travels (☎ 2090) at Hotel Sanjay.

Places to Stay
Since Ooty is a sellers' market in the high season (1 April to 15 June), hoteliers double their prices during this time. This is clearly a rip-off since prices don't necessarily equate with quality, but there are few options. Note that many hotels are fully booked in the high season and that the checkout time (usually noon) at any hotel can be as early as 9 am.

Places to Stay – bottom end
Budget hotels in the bazaar area are very poor value and definitely only for the desperate. One which is passable is *Vishu Lodge* (☎ 2971), Main Bazaar, with rooms at Rs 40/60 a single/double.

The TTDC's *youth hostel* (☎ 3665), Charing Cross, offers dorm beds at Rs 25/45 in the low/high season, and doubles for Rs 200/350. There's also a dull permit room.

Reflections Guest House (☎ 3834), North Lake Rd, is an enjoyable place with good views over the lake and doubles at Rs 150. There are only six rooms, but all have hot water and the atmosphere is homely. Good breakfasts and a range of snacks can be brought to your room or are served on the grassy terrace. The friendly, Anglo-Indian owner, Mrs Dique, is a good source of information on the region's history.

TAMIL NADU

The *YWCA* (☎ 2218), Ettines Rd, is also very good value but, because it's cheap, it's often full. A dorm bed costs just Rs 25 and doubles with attached bathrooms are Rs 90 to Rs 175 (low season) and Rs 180 and Rs 250 (high season). There are also double cottages at Rs 175/200 or Rs 300/400 (low/high season) and single cottages for Rs 100/150. Meals are available (Rs 50) and there is a loungeroom with an open fire in winter.

Places to Stay – middle

A good place in this range is the large, pleasant *Hotel Tamil Nadu* (☎ 4370) on the hill above the tourist office. Doubles with attached bathroom cost Rs 215/390 in the low/high season. There's a restaurant but no bar.

Similarly priced is the new *Hotel Charing Cross* (☎ 2387) on Garden Rd. With 105 modern but small rooms, you stand a good chance of getting a room here if all else is full. Nearby and fairly popular is the *Hotel Sanjay* (☎ 3160) at the junction of Coonoor and Commercial Rds. Doubles with attached bathrooms start at Rs 125/200 in the low/high season.

Up in standard, the huge *Hotel Nahar* (☎ 2173; fax 2405) at Charing Cross has reasonable doubles with attached bathroom and TV from Rs 200 to Rs 450 (low season), and Rs 400 to Rs 700 (high season). There are two restaurants and a snack bar.

The relatively new and superbly-appointed *Hotel Khems* (☎ 4188), Shoreham Palace Rd, has a tariff card which claims: 'Nobody gives you Ooty like we do'. It's certainly not your run-of-the-mill hotel but even so, prices are reasonable. Standard/superior doubles are Rs 275/475 (low season) and Rs 450/650 (high season). The hotel has its own restaurant.

The quiet and pleasant *Nilgiri Woodlands Hotel* (☎ 2551; fax 2530), Ettines Rd, is a traditional-style hotel dating from colonial days, with rooms in the main building and a number of detached cottages. In the low season, doubles with attached bathroom cost Rs 200, cottages are Rs 400 and suites Rs

500. Prices in the high season rise by around 75%.

The *Hotel Lakeview* (☎ 3904) at the western end of the lake is popular with affluent Indians. The name is not apt as most of the 'cottages' simply have a view of the back of the 'cottage' in front. Costs range from Rs 190 to Rs 400 (low season), and from Rs 350 to Rs 550 (high). There's a multi-cuisine restaurant and a bar.

The *Hotel Dasaprakash* (☎ 2434) is another long-established hotel and while it's nothing special, it's often full. Doubles with attached bathroom range from Rs 160 to Rs 300 in the low season; prices double in the high season. There's a vegetarian garden restaurant but no bar.

Places to Stay – top end

For a magnificent and palatial touch of the Raj you can't beat the *Fernhill Palace* (☎ 3910). Built in the days when expense was of no concern and master artisans didn't command fortunes, this former retreat of the Maharaja of Mysore is now patronised by the Bombay film set and affluent Westerners. It's in a quiet forest setting and offers a range of doubles from US$30 to US$35 (low season) and US$45 to US$50 (high season). Meals are served in the former ballroom.

Adjacent to the Fernhill Palace, but owned by the same crowd, is *Regency Villa* which is more rustic (cows grazing on the lawns) but just as quiet and cheaper than the Palace itself. The best rooms are ultra spacious and have bay windows, fully tiled Victorian bathrooms (with hot water) and a sitting corner by an open fire. The staff are amiable and simple meals can be arranged in advance. Ordinary/deluxe doubles cost Rs 300/400 and there's a huge triple suite at Rs 500.

For more refined old-world luxury there's the *Hotel Savoy* (☎ 4142; fax 3318) at 77 Sylks Rd. Part of the Taj Group, this place has singles/doubles for US$37/75 in the low season and US$53/105 in the high. High-season prices include full board. It has manicured lawns, clipped hedges, rooms with bathtubs, wooden furnishings and

TAMIL NADU

working fireplaces, a 24-hour bar and multi-cuisine dining room.

Places to Eat

For standard south Indian food, there are good vegetarian restaurants at both the *Hotel Nahar* and *Hotel Sanjay*. The Sanjay is a big, bustling place with large servings and non-veg fare as well. There are plenty of other basic vegetarian 'meals' places further along Commercial Rd and Main Bazaar. A gaggle of street stalls in the vicinity of the bus stand sell snacks and tea. However, before ordering here, just take a look at the open sewer around which they're clustered and the flies which migrate between them.

Back on Commercial Rd, the *Tandoori Mahal* has tasty dishes for around Rs 50 and the service is good.

Up on Town West Circle, *Shinkow's Chinese Restaurant* (also known as the *Zodiac Room)* at 30 Commissioner's Rd has some really good food. It's run by a Chinese family so its dishes (around Rs 40) are fairly authentic. For classier Chinese cuisine, try the *Shogun Restaurant* at the Hotel Charing Cross.

Entertainment

Ooty dies with the sunset. Of the few bars in town, the one at the *Fernhill Palace* is the most enticing, with a range of old hunting photographs and other memorabilia. It's open to non-guests and drinks are not too expensive (Rs 60 for a beer).

Getting There & Away

Bus Local buses leave every 20 minutes for Kotagiri (one hour, Rs 5) and hourly to Coonoor (one hour, Rs 3).

The regional bus company, C & B Transport Corp, has a reservation office at the bus stand open from 9 am to 1 pm and 1.30 to 5.30 pm. It operates buses to Coimbatore every 30 minutes (90 km, three hours, Rs 14) and to Bangalore (seven daily, 300 km, eight hours, Rs 76) via Mysore. To Mysore (160 km, five hours, Rs 43) there are two extra buses daily.

For Mudumalai Wildlife Sanctuary (67 km, 2½ hours, Rs 12), take one of the Mysore buses or one of the small buses which go via the narrow and twisting Sighur Ghat road. Most of these rolling wrecks travel only as far as Masinagudi, from where there are five buses a day to Theppakadu.

The TTC/JJTC reservation office is open from 9 am to 5 pm. It has buses to Bangalore via Mysore four times daily (Rs 56), three times daily to Madras (565 km via Erode and Salem, 15 hours, Rs 108) and daily buses to Kanyakumari (557 km, 14 hours, Rs 88), Thanjavur (10 hours, Rs 57) and Tirupathi (14 hours, Rs 100).

Karnataka's state bus company (KSRTC) has buses at least twice daily to Bangalore, Mysore and Hassan (Rs 63).

Private bus companies offer daily services to Bangalore, Kodaikanal (Rs 200) and Mysore (Rs 65) with superdeluxe buses, often with videos. Seats can be booked (no standing) and there's no hassle with a backpack (they go on the roof). Most of the companies are clustered around Charing Cross. They're a little more expensive than the state buses, but worth it.

Train Like Darjeeling and Matheran, Ooty has a miniature railway connecting it with the lowlands. The trains, with their quaint yellow-and-blue carriages, are not quite as small as the Darjeeling toy train, but they're still tiny. The unique feature of this line is the toothed central rail onto which the locomotives lock on the steeper slopes. Also unusual is the little locomotive, which is at the back pushing rather than pulling from the front. Each of the three or four carriages has its own brakeman, who sits on a little platform of each carriage and, whenever appropriate, waves a red or green flag.

The railway starts at Mettupalayam, north of Coimbatore, and goes via Coonoor to Ooty, en route affording some spectacular views of the precipitous eastern slopes of the rainforest-covered Nilgiris. Views are best from the left on the way up and from the right on the way down.

The departures and arrivals at Mettu-palayam usually connect with those of the

Nilgiri Express which runs between Mettupalayam and Madras. It departs Madras at 9 pm and arrives in Mettupalayam at 7.15 am. From Mettupalayam, it leaves at 7.30 pm. Tickets cost Rs 155/464 in 2nd/1st class. You can catch this train from Coimbatore at 6.20 am.

The miniature train leaves Mettupalayam for Ooty (46 km, Rs 19/136 in 2nd/1st class) at 7.30 am and arrives in Ooty at noon. From Ooty the train leaves at 2.50 pm. The trip down takes about 3½ hours.

During the high season, there's an extra departure in each direction daily, from Mettupalayam at 9.10 am and from Ooty at 2 pm. There are also two extra services between Ooty and Coonoor (Rs 9/68 in 2nd/1st class) at this time – they leave Ooty daily at 9.15 am and 6 pm.

Getting Around

There are plenty of unmetered auto-rickshaws in Ooty, based outside the bus stand. In the high season, the drivers quote outrageous fares, even between the bus stand and Charing Cross. Haggling might get you around 20% off the first price quoted but nothing more, so it's worth walking. In the low season, their fares become more reasonable. Normal taxis are also available – at even higher rates.

Hiring a bicycle is possible at the market but many of the roads are steep so you'll end up pushing them uphill (great on the way down though!). You can also hire scooters from U-Rent (☎ 2128) on Shoreham Palace Rd. It charges Rs 50 for the first hour and Rs 30 for each hour after that.

MUDUMALAI WILDLIFE SANCTUARY

Telephone Area Code: 0423

In the luxuriantly forested foothills of the Nilgiris, this 321-sq-km sanctuary is part of a much larger reserve (3000 sq km) which includes Bandipur and Wynad in neighbouring Karnataka and Kerala. The name Mudumalai means Old Hill in Tamil and, although the park was recently renamed the Jayalalitha Wildlife Sanctuary & National Park, it's still very much known by its original name.

The larger reserve ranges in vegetation from semi-evergreen forests to swamps and grasslands. In Mudumalai, the mostly dense forest is home to chital (spotted deer), gaur (Indian bison), tiger, panther, wild boar and sloth bear. Otters and crocodiles inhabit the Moyar River. The park's wild elephant population, one of the largest in the country, supposedly numbers about 600, however you're more likely to see their domesticated brethren carrying out logging duties or performing in the new farcical puja ceremony (see the boxed section).

The best time to visit Mudumalai is between February and June. Heavy rain is common in October and November and the park may be closed during the dry season (February to March).

Orientation & Information

The main service area in Mudumalai is Theppakadu, on the main road between Udhagamandalam (Ooty) and Mysore, where you'll find the park's reception centre (☎ 235) open daily from 6.30 am to 6 pm. There is some accommodation and an elephant camp here, and sometimes you can see spotted deer, elephant and wild boar. You can also stay in private lodges at Masinagudi or Bokkapuram, both east of Theppakadu, however they're relatively inaccessible if you don't have your own transport.

It's advisable to book sanctuary accommodation in advance with the Wildlife Warden (☎ 4098), Coonoor Rd, Ooty. There are entry fees for visitors (Rs 5/2 for adults/children) and cameras (Rs 5/50 for a still/movie camera).

Wildlife Tours

Tours of the park are limited to the sanctuary's minibuses, a jeep and elephants. Private vehicles are not allowed to make tours. Minibus tours (morning and afternoon) cost Rs 25 per person for one hour. The sanctuary's jeep does night trips for Rs 350. The one-hour elephant rides can be booked in advance at the Wildlife Warden's office in

Ooty or direct at the Theppakadu Reception Centre. They cost Rs 120 for four people and are very popular, however, as the elephants go crashing through the bush you'll be lucky to see anything other than spotted deer, wild boars, gaur and monkeys.

Places to Stay & Eat

The Forest Department maintains three *dormitories* (Rs 5 per bed), five *lodges* (Rs 30/40 for single/double occupancy) and a *watchtower* (Rs 40 for two) throughout the park. The dorms and lodges each have a cook-cum-housekeeper. At the watchtower, deep

within the forest, there's no electricity, water or food.

Theppakadu The best option here is the Forest Department's new *Log House*, on the river about five minutes' walk from the reception centre. The three double rooms have polished timber furnishings and there's a verandah where you can sit and while away a day or two. Unfortunately, the staff do not seem keen to rent this place and will tell you that it is occupied when it's not. Persevere and you might win a night in this lovely, cheap lodge.

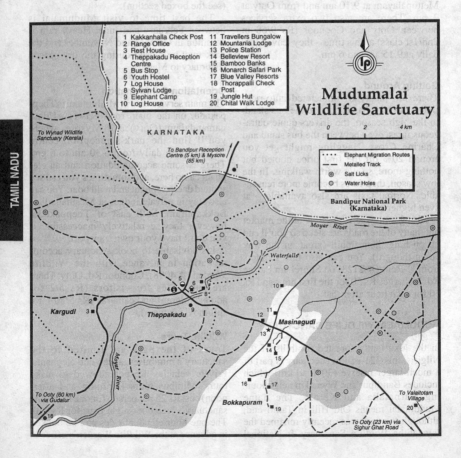

1 Kakkanhalla Check Post
2 Range Office
3 Rest House
4 Theppakadu Reception Centre
5 Bus Stop
6 Youth Hostel
7 Log House
8 Sylvan Lodge
9 Elephant Camp
10 Log House
11 Travellers Bungalow
12 Mountania Lodge
13 Police Station
14 Belleview Resort
15 Bamboo Banks
16 Monarch Safari Park
17 Blue Valley Resorts
18 Thorappalli Check Post
19 Jungle Hut
20 Chital Walk Lodge

Mudumalai Wildlife Sanctuary

0   2   4 km

•••• Elephant Migration Routes
－－－ Metalled Track
⊚ Salt Licks
○ Water Holes

KARNATAKA

To Wynad Wildlife Sanctuary (Kerala)

To Bandipur Reception Centre (5 km) & Mysore (85 km)

Bandipur National Park (Karnataka)

Moyar River

Waterfalls

Kargudi

Theppakadu

Moyar River

Masinagudi

To Ooty (60 km) via Gudalur

Bokkapuram

To Ooty (23 km) via Sighur Ghat Road

To Valaitotam Village

Puja or Penance at Mudumalai?

It was 5 pm and Mudumalai's newest attraction, the Elephant Puja Ceremony, was about to begin. The audience, having each paid the Rs 20 entry fee, had gathered to watch the show on a grassy area across the river from the reception centre. There was an air of excitement as the matriarch, a big old girl whose skin hung loose, lead the troop of 12, predominantly young, elephants into the open-air arena. Each performer, draped in colourful cloth and with ears and trunk brightly painted, was ridden by a turbaned mahout who commanded his charge to line up facing the small gathering.

On cue, the smallest elephant picked up a small brass bell and shook it slowly. The chimes rang out as the elephant bowed onto its two front knees before a tiny statue of Ganesh, the elephant-headed god, that had been placed on the grass. A few seconds passed before it rose and, in doing so, announced the end of the puja and the start of the obscene tricks – balancing acts, walking a plank, and so on – that were to make up the bulk of this so-called ceremony. Circus or wildlife sanctuary? we questioned, trying to reconcile the fact that the authorities of a national park had reduced their charges to objects of jest and ridicule. Boycott this nonsensical show if you will, simply to discourage its continuation.

Leanne Logan & Geert Cole

Right next door and next best is the *Sylvan Lodge*. It also looks out over the river but it's older and not quite as charming. There's a *dormitory* at the reception centre.

The TTDC's *youth hostel* (☎ 249), close to Sylvan Lodge, has dorm beds for Rs 25 but the rooms are musty, and large groups often stay here and party into the night. Basic meals are available.

Masinagudi Area Masinagudi is a small village eight km east of Theppakadu. Accommodation options in the village itself are pretty poor. For example, the *Belleview Resort* (☎ 351), one km from the bus stop, is an old place with no atmosphere; singles/doubles cost Rs 100/250 and there are dorm beds for Rs 25. Right opposite the police station is the basic *Travellers Bungalow*, while further along the road towards Theppakadu is the more expensive *Mountania Lodge* (☎ 237).

South-east of Masinagudi there are several much better options. The first is *Bamboo Banks* (☎ 222), 1.5 km from Masinagudi down a signposted turn-off to the right. It's one of the region's oldest private lodges and is very much a family affair – two of the six rooms are actually inside the family home. Rooms cost Rs 600/840 for a single/double including taxes, and a buffet lunch/dinner is Rs 160/200.

Bokkapuram Next up are three newer resorts set in the Nilgiri foothills in an area

known as Bokkapuram, five km from Masinagudi. The land around here has been worked by tribal communities or cleared by more recent landlords so, unlike at Theppakadu, there is no dense forest.

The *Blue Valley Resorts* (☎ 244), Bokkapuram, is owned by a consortium and currently has eight, well-appointed cottages (seven more are in the pipeline). Ordinary/deluxe cottages start at Rs 475/625 and all have a small terrace with a view of the mountains. The restaurant offers à la carte Indian and Continental food.

About 500 metres further down the same dirt road is the *Jungle Hut* (☎ 240, or 56-3848 in Bangalore). This family-run place has 12 rooms in three bungalows and charges Rs 480/600 for a single/double, including tax. All meals, except breakfast, must be ordered in advance.

Over the hill from here is the *Monarch Safari Park* (☎ 243). Owned by a Bengali movie star, this place has stilt cottages, all with TV, built on a hillock and exudes a very contrived atmosphere. Singles/doubles are Rs 350/500 and à la carte meals are available.

Finally, the *Chital Walk (Jungle Trails) Lodge* (☎ 256), eight km east of Masinagudi, is a good place if you have a keen interest in wildlife. It offers doubles at Rs 300 and good meals are available. The Sighur Ghat buses to/from Ooty can drop you at the Valaitotam turn-off from where it's just a few minutes' walk.

Getting There & Away

The buses from Ooty to Mysore, Bangalore or Hassan stop at Theppakadu, and it's not too difficult to wave them down. (See the earlier Getting There & Away section under Ooty for more details.)

An interesting 'short cut' to/from Ooty (36 km, 1½ hours) involves taking one of the small government buses which make the trip up (or down) the tortuous Sighur Ghat road. The bends are so tight and the gradient so steep that large buses can't use it. In fact, there's a sign on the road leaving Masinagudi warning that 'you will have to strain your vehicle much to reach Ooty'. Therefore most buses take the longer route via Gudalur which is equally interesting but not quite as steep (67 km, 2½ hours).

You can also visit the sanctuary on tours from Ooty, but you're likely to see nothing more than tame elephants.

Getting Around

Five local buses run daily between Theppakadu and Masinagudi. A local jeep taxi charges Rs 40 for the same trip, and an outrageous Rs 60 to go from Masinagudi to Bokkapuram. As there is no bus service to Bokkapuram, the resorts at Blue Valley, Jungle Hut and Monarch Safari Park will generally pick up guests free of charge from Masinagudi – if telephoned in advance.

Andaman & Nicobar Islands

This string of over 300 richly forested tropical islands in the Bay of Bengal lies between India and Myanmar (Burma) and stretches almost to the tip of Sumatra. Ethnically, the islands are not part of India and, until fairly recently, they were inhabited only by indigenous tribal people.

The majority of the Andaman & Nicobar Islands are still uninhabited. Most are surrounded by coral reefs, and have white sandy beaches and incredibly clear water – the perfect tropical paradise. This is an excellent place for snorkelling and scuba diving, and a diving school now offers full courses.

The Maldives must have been something like this before they were 'discovered' and developed. No doubt it's only a matter of time for the Andamans. An extension to the runway at Port Blair Airport has been given the go-ahead and should be completed by 1998. Until then, the place will continue to be protected from mass tourism.

While Indian tourists may roam freely, foreigners are constrained by a 30-day permit allowing only limited travel. The tourist office says this is for our own protection ('some of the tribal people are very aggressive'), but the naval base here may have more to do with it. The government is certainly trying to promote the Andamans as a tourist destination so it's worth checking to see if the permit situation has been relaxed. There's even talk of a new air route between here and Bangkok (only 350 km from Port Blair) but this will not happen until the airport extension is completed.

History

Very little of the early history of the Andaman & Nicobar Islands is known, but Marco Polo was among the first Western visitors. In the early 18th century, the islands were the base of the Maratha admiral, Kanhoji Angre, whose navy harassed and frequently captured British, Dutch and Portuguese merchant vessels. In 1713, Angre

Population: 328,000
Area: 8249 sq km on 319 islands
Capital: Port Blair
Main Languages: Hindi, Bengali, Tamil & tribal languages
Literacy Rate: 73%
Best Time to Go: mid-November to April

The external boundaries of India on this map have not been authenticated and may not be correct.

Andaman & Nicobar

even managed to capture the yacht of the British governor of Bombay, releasing it only after delivery of a ransom of powder and shot. Though attacked by the British and, later, by a combined British/Portuguese naval task force, Angre remained undefeated until his death in 1729.

The islands were finally annexed by the British in the 19th century and used as a penal colony for Indian freedom fighters. Construction of the notorious 'cellular jail' began in the last decade of the 19th century and was finished in 1908. Many of the jail's inmates were executed, either judicially or clandestinely. During WW II, the islands were occupied for a time by the Japanese, but they were not welcomed as liberators and local tribes initiated guerrilla activities against them. The islands were incorporated into the Indian Union when independence came to India in 1947.

ANDAMAN & NICOBAR ISLANDS

The Indian government is fond of eulogising its efforts to bring 'civilisation' to the islands but, reading between the lines, it regards the indigenous tribes as backward, and its attitude towards them is condescending.

In an effort to develop the islands economically, the government has disregarded the needs and land rights of the tribes and has encouraged massive transmigration from the mainland – mainly of Tamils expelled from Sri Lanka. The population has increased from 50,000 to over 300,000 in just 20 years, and the indigenous island cultures are being swamped. It's not only the people who have suffered in the name of 'development': vast tracts of forest were felled in the 1960s and '70s. There has been some replanting of the land with 'economic' timber like teak, but much of it has been turned into rubber plantations.

Climate

There is little seasonal variation in the climate. Continuous sea breezes keep tem-

Tribal People

The indigenous tribal people are victims of the Indian government's continuing policy of colonisation and development. They now constitute less than 10% of the present population and, in most cases, their numbers are falling. The negroid Onge, Sentinelese, Andamanese and Jarawa are all resident in the Andaman Islands. The second group, on the Nicobar Islands, is of Mongoloid descent, and includes the Shompen and Nicobarese.

Onge An anthropological study made in the 1970s suggested that the Onge were declining because they were severely demoralised by loss of territory. Two-thirds of the Onge's island of Little Andaman has been taken over by the Forest Department and 'settled'. The 100 or so remaining members of the Onge tribe are confined to a 100 sq km reserve at Dugong Creek. In spite of the study, the Indian government allowed further development – including the building of roads, jetties and a match factory. The government even built tin huts for these nomadic hunter-gathers to live in.

Sentinelese The Sentinelese, unlike the other tribes in these islands, have consistently repulsed any attempts by outsiders to make contact with them. Every few years, contact parties arrive on the beaches of North Sentinel Island, with gifts of coconuts, bananas, pigs and red plastic buckets, only to be showered with arrows. About 120 Sentinelese remain, and North Sentinel Island is their exclusive territory.

Andamanese Numbering only 30 people, it seems impossible that the Andamanese can escape extinction. There were almost 5000 Andamanese when the British arrived in the mid-19th century. Their friendliness to the colonisers was their undoing and, by the end of the century, most of the population had been swept away by measles, syphilis and influenza epidemics. Their decline continues, although they've now been resettled on tiny Strait Island.

Jarawa The 250 remaining Jarawa occupy the 750 sq km reserve on South and Middle Andaman Islands. Around them, forest clearance continues at a horrific rate and the new Andamans Trunk Road runs through part of their designated territory. Although settlers are encroaching on their reserve, the Jarawa are putting up a fight, killing one or two Indians each year. All buses are now accompanied by an armed guard – though windows are still occasionally shattered by Jarawa arrows.

Shompen Living in the forests on Great Nicobar, only about 200 Shompen remain. They are hunter-gatherers that have resisted integration, tending to shy away from areas occupied by Indian immigrants.

Nicobarese The 29,500 Nicobarese are the only indigenous people whose numbers are not decreasing. They are fair-complexioned horticulturalists who have been partly assimilated into contemporary Indian society. Living in village units led by a headman, they cultivate coconuts, yams and bananas, and farm pigs.

Inhabiting a number of islands in the Nicobar group, centred on Car Nicobar, the majority of the Nicobarese are Christians. ∎

peratures within the 23°C to 31°C range and the humidity at around 80% all year. The south-west monsoons come to the islands between mid-May and October and the north-east monsoons between November and January. The best time to visit is between mid-November and April. December and the early part of January are the high the seasons.

Environment & Tourism

The Indian government continues to destructively mismanage both the tribal people and the unique ecology of the Andaman & Nicobar Islands.

The major issues which need to be addressed are the rights and privacy of the indigenous tribes, and the development of controlled timber farming to halt forest clearing.

Tourism may have a positive role to play in all this. There are over 250 uninhabited islands in this area, most with superb beaches and coral reefs ideal for divers. Looking to the Maldives, where a few uninhabited islands have been developed exclusively for tourism, the Indian government is considering following the same example. This could compensate for the earnings lost from reduced tree-cutting and would place a value-tag on the preservation of the environment. Anything would be preferable to the mass deforestation and decimation of tribes that is happening now.

Permits

Foreigners need a permit to visit the Andaman Islands. (The Nicobar Islands are off limits to non-Indian tourists.) The permit allows foreigners to stay in the Port Blair area of South Andaman, in the villages of Rangat and Mayabunder on Middle Andaman, and in Diglipur on North Andaman. You can also stay on the islands of Neil, Havelock and Long. Day trips are permitted to Mt Harriet, the elephant training camp at Madhuban, Chirya Tapu, Wandoor and the islands of Ross, Viper, Red Skin, Jolly Buoy and Cinque.

The permit is valid for up to 30 days. If you have a good excuse, you might be able

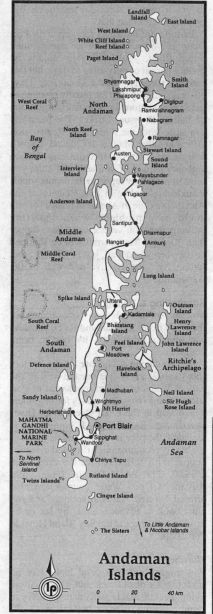

Andaman Islands

0   20   40 km

ANDAMAN & NICOBAR ISLANDS

to get a two or three-day extension but nothing longer than that.

Permits are issued at the airport in Port Blair. If you arrive with an unconfirmed return flight, you'll probably initially be given a permit of only 10 to 15 days, but this can be extended to allow a 30-day stay. Travellers arriving by ship are usually required to get a permit before the Shipping Corporation of India will issue a ticket. The permit is available from the Foreigners' Registration Office in either Madras or Calcutta (allow a couple of hours), or from any Indian embassy abroad. If you arrive by ship, you must immediately report to the deputy superintendent of police in Port Blair (near the Annapurna Cafe in Aberdeen Bazaar) or you could have problems when departing proving that you've not been here longer than 30 days. Your permit will be stamped again when you depart, just to reinforce that Indian red tape is alive and well in the Andamans.

Snorkelling & Diving

You can rent snorkels from tour operators but these are expensive (around Rs 50 per day) and often substandard – it's best to bring your own.

The Andaman & Nicobar Diving Society (fax (03192) 21-389) is one km west of the jetty at Wandoor, 29 km south-west of Port Blair. It runs five-day courses for beginners which lead to the PADI Open Water Diver Certificate (Rs 6500). All equipment is included, the pace is relaxed and the courses are highly recommended. Escorted dives for people with this qualification cost from US$50. The PADI Rescue Diver, and Advanced Open Water courses are also offered. No credit cards are accepted and you must book in advance, either by fax or by leaving a message at the Bay Island Hotel in Port Blair.

Warning

You might think that coral looks like an attractive bit of old rock, but it's actually a living creature that is easily damaged. Try to avoid touching it, never break a piece off,

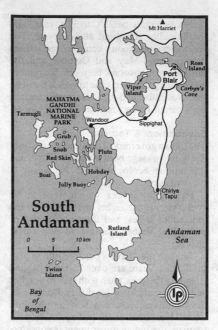

and don't walk on it, even when it's exposed at low tide. Some of the coral off Wandoor Beach has already been damaged by careless tourists.

PORT BLAIR

Telephone Area Code: 03192

The administrative capital, Port Blair, is the only town of any size on the islands. It's pleasantly situated around a harbour on the east coast of South Andaman, and has the lively air of an Indian market town. It's a hilly town, so there are good views from a number of vantage points.

Even though the Andamans are fairly close to mainland Myanmar (Burma), they still run on Indian time. This means that it's dark by 6 pm and light by 4 am.

Orientation

The town is spread over a couple of hills, but most of the hotels, and the bus terminal, passenger dock and Shipping Corporation of

India office are in the main bazaar area, known as Aberdeen Bazaar. The airport is a few km south of town, and the nearest beach is at Corbyn's Cove, 10 km south of Aberdeen Bazaar.

Information

Tourist Offices For up-to-date information on places in the Andamans now open to foreigners, visit the very helpful Government of India tourist office (☎ 21-006). It's above Super Shoppe, a short distance from the centre of town, and is a useful source of information about the islands and other parts of India.

By contrast, the Andaman & Nicobar tourist office (☎ 20-933), which should be the main information centre for the islands, is utterly hopeless. Since few of the staff have been anywhere on the islands other than Port Blair, don't take their word for anything. The office is near the gate to the Secretariat, which is at the top of the hill overlooking the town. Both tourist offices have information counters at the airport.

The library, near the GPO, has a small collection of books on the history, geography, flora & fauna, and tribal people of the islands. The reference section is on the first floor.

Money Travellers' cheques and cash can be exchanged (very slowly) at the State Bank of India. It opens and closes an hour earlier than is usual on the mainland (9 am to 1 pm during the week and 9 to 11 am on Saturday). Most visitors use the efficient service at Island Travels, near Sampat Lodge. You can change money here daily except Sunday between 11 am and 5.30 pm. The larger hotels also have foreign exchange facilities.

Post & Telecommunications The GPO is 750 metres south of Aberdeen Bazaar. The cheapest place to send and receive faxes is at the telegraph office (fax 21-318) next door. The telegraph office is open from 10 am to 5 pm, Monday to Saturday. International telephone calls can be made from here, as well as from a number of places in Aberdeen Bazaar.

Cellular Jail National Memorial
Built by the British at the beginning of this century, the Cellular Jail is now a major tourist attraction, preserved as a shrine to India's freedom fighters. It originally consisted of seven wings radiating out from a central tower, but only three remain today. It still gives a fair impression of the terrible conditions under which the detainees were incarcerated. It's open daily from 9 am to noon and 2 to 5 pm; there's no entry charge.

Don't miss the sound & light show, which is excellent. The English-language show is at 7.15 pm on Wednesday, Saturday and Sunday. Tickets cost Rs 6.

Samudrika Marine Museum
Run by the navy, this interesting museum is divided into five galleries covering the history and geography of the islands, their people, marine life and marine archaeology. There are also good displays of shells and coral, though they may be doing the environment a disservice with their decorative displays of the latter. The museum could do with a few signs informing visitors how slowly coral grows and how easily it is damaged. The museum is open Monday to Saturday from 9 am to 5.30 pm; entry is Rs 3.

Fisheries Museum
Some of the 350 species found in the sea around the islands are displayed here: a few live in tanks, the rest are pickled in glass jars. 'Dreadly poisonous' says the label on the spotted sea snake. Its bite is many times more venomous than that of a cobra, but since its fangs are far back in its mouth it would be difficult for this snake to get a grip on a human. The museum is open every day from 8.30 am to 12.30 pm and 1.30 to 5 pm; entry is Rs 2.

Anthropological Museum
At this small museum, there are displays of tools, dress and photographs of the indigenous tribes. The captions to some of the

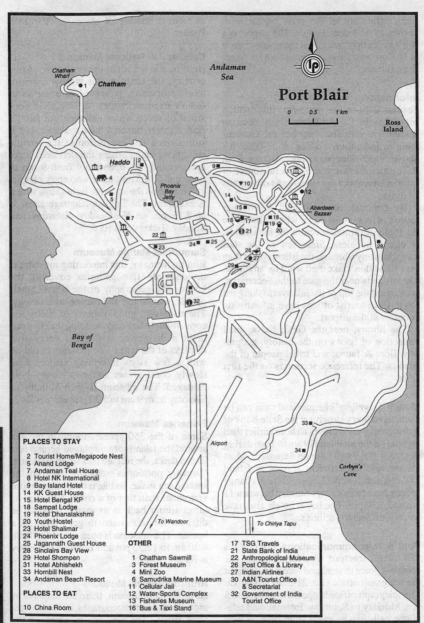

PLACES TO STAY

2 Tourist Home/Megapode Nest
5 Anand Lodge
7 Andaman Teal House
8 Hotel NK International
9 Bay Island Hotel
14 KK Guest House
15 Hotel Bengal KP
18 Sampat Lodge
19 Hotel Dhanalakshmi
20 Youth Hostel
23 Hotel Shalimar
24 Phoenix Lodge
25 Jagannath Guest House
28 Sinclairs Bay View
29 Hotel Shompen
31 Hotel Abhishekh
33 Hornbill Nest
34 Andaman Beach Resort

PLACES TO EAT

10 China Room

OTHER

1 Chatham Sawmill
3 Forest Museum
4 Mini Zoo
6 Samudrika Marine Museum
11 Cellular Jail
12 Water-Sports Complex
13 Fisheries Museum
16 Bus & Taxi Stand
17 TSG Travels
21 State Bank of India
22 Anthropological Museum
26 Post Office & Library
27 Indian Airlines
30 A&N Tourist Office
   & Secretariat
32 Government of India
   Tourist Office

photos are pathetic but telling. 'Why don't you leave us alone?' runs the caption under a photo of some Sentinelese people. It's open from 9 am to noon and 1 to 4 pm daily except Sunday; there's no entry charge.

Mini Zoo & Forest Museum

Over 200 Andaman & Nicobar animal species are found nowhere else in the world. Some can be seen at the mini-zoo, including the Nicobar pigeon and Andaman pig. The zoo's saltwater crocodile breeding programme has been very successful and many have been returned to the wild. Fortunately, their natural habitat is dense mangrove swamps, and there have been no reports locally of crocodiles attacking swimmers. The zoo is open from 8 am to 5 pm but is closed on Monday; entry is Rs 0.50.

Nearby is the small Forest Museum, which has a display of locally-grown woods. These including padauk, which has both light and dark-colours occurring in the same tree. Elephants are still used at some of the lumber camps. The museum is open from 8 am to noon and 2.30 to 5 pm daily except Sunday; entry is free.

Chatham Sawmill

It's possible to visit the sawmill, seasoning chambers and furniture workshop of one of Asia's largest wood processors, situated on the island of Chatham, five km north-west of Aberdeen Bazaar. As the government tourist literature enthuses, you'll see 'some of the rare species of tropical timber like padauk'. If they're acknowledged as rare, you wonder what they're doing in a sawmill. It's open from 6.30 am to 2.30 pm daily except Sunday.

Water-Sports Complex

At the water-sports complex, by the Fisheries Museum, you can rent rowboats, windsurfers and sailing dinghies. Waterskiing costs Rs 50 for 15 minutes; para-sailing Rs 30 per ride. You can rent snorkels here for Rs 15 per hour, but you can't take them anywhere else.

Organised Tours

A range of tours are offered by the A&N tourist office; Shompen Travels (☎ 20-425) in the Hotel Shompen; Island Travels (☎ 21-358) in Aberdeen Bazaar; and the larger hotels. However, apart from visits to Jolly Buoy, Redskin and Cinque islands, sightseeing yourself is easy enough.

Every afternoon at 3 pm, a boat leaves from the Phoenix Bay jetty for a 1½-hour harbour cruise. The trip costs Rs 20 and the main point of interest is the huge, floating dry-dock facility. The tour stops briefly at tiny Viper Island, where the remains of the gallows tower built by the British still stand.

Places to Stay

Accommodation is geared to tourists, but even in the high season it's possible to bargain prices down. Since all the places to stay are quite spread out, it's worth hiring a bicycle or moped to get around.

If you want to be near a beach, the only place to go is Corbyn's Cove, where there's one expensive resort hotel and an overpriced government-run establishment.

Places to Stay – bottom end

The cheapest place to stay is the *Youth Hostel*, which has dorm beds for Rs 10 (Rs 20 for nonmembers) and a few double rooms. There's a good restaurant for guests, which has an extensive veg and non-veg menu.

In Aberdeen Bazaar, the *Sampat Lodge* is basic but friendly with rooms for Rs 35/70. The *KK Guest House* is run down and has tiny rooms for Rs 25/50. The nearby *Hotel Bengal KP* is better. It has clean singles/doubles for Rs 60/100 with attached bathrooms.

The best of the budget places is the excellent *Jagannath Guest House* (☎ 20-148), which has spotless singles/doubles/triples for Rs 75/100/150, all with attached bathroom. Run by a very friendly manager, it's convenient for the bus terminal and Phoenix Bay harbour. Further west along the same road, grubby *Phoenix Lodge* has doubles for Rs 60 with common bathroom; Rs 80 with bath attached. In Haddo, *Anand Lodge* has rooms for Rs 40/60 with common bath, but there are also rooms with bathroom attached.

The *Central Lodge* is a wooden lodge with a verandah near the Hotel Shompen at Middle Point. It has friendly management and rooms from Rs 35/70.

Places to Stay – middle

The *Hotel Abhishekh* (☎ 21-565) is quite good and has clean singles/doubles/triples with attached bathroom for Rs 160/190/230; more for air-con. The place is well run by a friendly manager, and has its own restaurant. Equally good value is the *Hotel Shalimar* (☎ 21-963), which is on the road to Haddo. Rooms are Rs 150/190/250 with attached bathroom; air-con doubles are Rs 300.

The friendly *Hotel Dhanalakshmi* (☎ 21-953) in Aberdeen Bazaar has good rooms with bathroom attached for Rs 160/200 or Rs 240/300 with air-con (the rooms at the back are quietest). It also has a restaurant.

Double rooms (no singles) at the *Hotel Shompen* (☎ 20-360) are overpriced at their quoted rate of Rs 350 or Rs 750 with air-con. However, outside the high season, you should be able to get a discount. The hotel has a restaurant and a travel agency that runs tours to some of the islands.

The *Hotel NK International* (☎ 20-113), near the Phoenix Bay jetty, is a friendly place. Rooms cost Rs 150/200, or Rs 250/300 with air-con. Discounts are sometimes available.

A&N Tourism's *Hornbill Nest Yatri Niwas* is about one km north of Corbyn's Cove and has sea views. It's an excellent location but the place is poorly run. The tourist office's current policy of doubling prices for foreigners makes it overpriced. For foreigners, rooms with two/four/six beds and attached bath are Rs 400/500/600. Mosquito nets are provided. There's a reasonable restaurant but some dishes need to be ordered in advance.

The *Andaman Teal House*, also run by the tourist office, has absolutely nothing going for it. It's poorly located (on the road to Haddo), badly run, and overpriced if you're

a foreigner. Doubles with attached bath cost Rs 400, or Rs 600 with air-con.

The *Tourist Home/Megapode Nest* (☎ 20-207) at Haddo, on the hill above the bay, is much better value at Rs 400 for a large double with attached bath, air-con and Star TV. For upmarket, air-con accommodation, the *Nicobari Cottages*, part of the same complex, are recommended at Rs 700 for a double with attached bath and tub. There's a good restaurant here which has great views of the harbour. Unfortunately, service can be very slow.

Places to Stay – top end

On the road to Corbyn's Cove is the *Sinclairs Bay View* (☎ 21-159). It's currently being renovated and rooms with attached bath will probably cost Rs 700 to Rs 1000 for a double when it reopens. There are good sea views (but no beach), a restaurant, and also a bar in an old Japanese bunker beside the hotel. Tours can be organised from the hotel.

The *Andaman Beach Resort* (☎ 21-462; fax 21-463) at Corbyn's Cove is excellently located in a very quiet part of the island, just across the road from the beach. Rooms in the main block are Rs 1100/1500; rooms in the very pleasant air-con cottages cost Rs 1300/1800; discounts are negotiable outside the peak season. There's a bar, restaurant, foreign exchange facilities and a boat for hire.

The Welcomgroup *Bay Island Hotel* (☎ 20-881; fax 21-389), which has sea views, is the top hotel in Port Blair. Beautifully designed by the well-known Indian architect, Charles Correa, it's partly constructed from local wood. The staff are very friendly, but rooms are a little overpriced at Rs 3500 – although this does include all meals. There's an excellent restaurant and an open-air bar which is good for a quiet beer.

This hotel is to be commended for its attempts at eco-tourism. The swimming-pool is filled with sea water, and guests are reminded not to waste water in bathrooms or damage coral when swimming. At the bottom of the hill, a private pier with a 'human aquarium' extends into the bay. The aquarium enables visitors to climb down into a glass-windowed chamber to view the multicoloured fish that congregate here to be fed.

Places to Eat

Most of the hotels have restaurants, but you may have to order seafood in advance.

There are a number of cheap places in Aberdeen Bazaar. The *Annapurna Cafe*, just south of Hotel Dhanalakshmi, is a recommended restaurant. It's better than it looks, and it serves good lassi, southern Indian food and tasty chicken dishes. In the hotel of the same name, the *Dhanalakshmi* stays open late; main dishes are around Rs 35 and a vegetarian thali costs Rs 16. Nearby is the tiny *Kattappamman Hotel,* serving masala dosas and banana-leaf thalis. You pay extra for meat and have to clear your own leaf away.

The *Delhi Cafeteria*, near the Hotel Shompen, is a basic place that does good tandoori dishes and excellent nans. A half tandoori chicken costs Rs 55.

There are several cheap restaurants at the bottom of the hill in the bazaar, not far from the bus stand. The *Hotel Ashoka* is a good place for breakfast. The *Manila Cafe* and *Anand Lodge* are good for a snack. Near the Cellular Jail, the *Islet* is a new restaurant offering veg and non-veg dishes, and it has views of the bay.

On Corbyn's Cove, *The Waves* is a good place for a drink or a meal. It has tables under the coconut palms. The garlic chicken is excellent and they also do good non-veg dishes. The place is run by the police, which might account for the good supplies of beer (Rs 55).

The *China Room* (☎ 30-759), run by a delightful Burmese couple, is an excellent place to eat. It's really just a small outdoor area and the front room of their house, but the quality of the seafood they serve is superb. Prices range from Rs 25 for basic dishes like veg noodles to Rs 150 for Szechuan-style lobster or Peking duck, though the latter require 24 hours notice. The garlic prawns (Rs 80) are excellent. It's

worth coming here for lunch to discuss the menu for a slap-up dinner the following night.

The open-sided *Mandalay Restaurant* at the Bay Island Hotel is the other place for a splurge. Main dishes are around Rs 80.

Getting There & Away

Air Indian Airlines (☎ 21-108) has flights from Calcutta (US$134) on Wednesday, Friday and Sunday to Port Blair, continuing to Madras (US$136). On Tuesday, Thursday and Saturday, flights run from Madras to Port Blair, then on to Calcutta. The 25% youth discount is applicable on these fares. The flights can also be included on the US$500, three-week flight pass. The two-hour flights leave the mainland soon after dawn.

The Indian Airlines office is round the corner from the post office. The staff here are very friendly and the office has a computer link. Flights can be heavily booked and you need to have a confirmed ticket to be sure of a seat. Passengers on waiting lists usually miss out. The office is open from 9 am to 1 pm, and 2 to 4 pm daily except Sunday.

Train There's a railway out-agency at the Secretariat.

Boat There are usually two to four sailings a month between Port Blair and Madras or Calcutta on vessels operated by the Shipping Corporation of India (SCI). There's also an occasional sailing on the route between Visakhapatnam (Andhra Pradesh) and Port Blair. Contact SCI for the latest information on the erratic schedules. It's better to arrange tickets for the journey from Port Blair back to the mainland in Calcutta or Madras.

The trip takes three to four days on the Madras route, and sometimes one day longer on the Calcutta route. Foreigners usually have to travel 2nd class (four or six-berth), 1st class (two or four-berth) or deluxe (two-berth). Tickets cost Rs 1300/1650/2000 per berth. If you can get a ticket for bunk class, it costs Rs 550. Prices are the same for both the Calcutta and Madras routes. Food costs Rs 240 per day (Rs 150 in bunk class) and is usually thalis for breakfast, lunch and dinner, so you need to bring something (fruit in particular) to supplement this boring diet.

The SCI may insist that you have a permit before selling you a ticket. If they don't, you can get one in Port Blair. However, even if you get your permit in advance, you must still register with the deputy superintendent of police on arrival in Port Blair.

The Port Blair SCI office for the Calcutta boat is in Aberdeen Bazaar (☎ 21-347). For the Madras boat, go to the office at Phoenix Bay. Bookings for the Calcutta boat open only a few days before the boat arrives; for the Madras boat, you can book further in advance.

In Calcutta, the SCI office (☎ 28-4456) is on the 1st floor at 13 Strand Rd. In Madras, the SCI (☎ 522-6873) is at Jawahar Building, Rajaji Salai (opposite the Customs House). In Visakhapatnam, the office where you can find out if this route is operating is A V Bhanoji (☎ 56-266), opposite the main gate at the port. Two photos and a whole lot of form-filling are required, and bookings close four days before sailing.

Getting Around

There are no cycle-rickshaws or auto-rickshaws, just taxis buzzing around Port Blair. They have meters (and charts, since the meters need recalibrating) but drivers need a bit of persuasion to use them. From the airport, the trip to Aberdeen Bazaar should cost Rs 30 to Rs 40; a little less to Corbyn's Cove. A taxi between Corbyn's Cove and Aberdeen Bazaar is around Rs 40. Some of the hotels offer free transport to and from the airport if you stay with them; the tourist office airport bus will take you to any hotel in Port Blair for Rs 15.

From the bus stand in Port Blair, there are regular departures to Wandoor (Rs 4.75, 1½ hours). See the sections below for other bus information.

It's best to have your own transport to explore parts of the island. You can hire bicycles in Aberdeen Bazaar for Rs 20 per day. An even better way to get around is by moped or motorcycle. Roads are not bad and

certainly very quiet. TSG Travels (☎ 20-894) rents motorcycles (Suzuki 100s) and scooters for Rs 120 per day; mopeds for Rs 90. A Rs 500 deposit is required.

Private boats can be hired from the tour operators but charges are high – around Rs 10,000 per day.

AROUND PORT BLAIR
Mt Harriet & Madhuban

Mt Harriet (365 metres) is across the inlet, north of Port Blair. There's a nature trail up to the top and, if regulations are relaxed, it may be possible to stay in the comfortable *Forest Guest House*. To reach Mt Harriet, take the vehicle or passenger ferry from Chatham Wharf to Bamboo Flat (Rs 1, 10 minutes). From there, a road runs seven km along the coast and up to Mt Harriet.

To the north is Mt Harriet National Park and Madhuban, where elephants are trained for the logging camps. Madhuban is only accessible by boat; the tourist office and travel agencies organise occasional trips.

Ross Island

A couple of km east of Port Blair is Ross Island, chosen by the British for their administrative headquarters. In the early part of this century, there would have been manicured lawns leading up to the ballroom, umbrellas round the swimming pool and daily services in the church. Deserted since the British left during WW II, the jungle has taken over and peacocks and spotted deer forage among the ruined buildings. On the top of the hill stand the remains of the church, its tower strangled by roots and vines.

Ross Island is a distinctly eerie and rather sad place, but well worth a visit. There are ferries from Phoenix Bay jetty at 8.30 and 10.30 am, 12.30 and 2 pm daily except on Wednesday. From Ross Island, there are departures at 9 and 11 am, and 1 and 4 pm. The journey takes 20 minutes and a return ticket costs Rs 13. You must sign in on arrival at Ross since the island is in the hands of the navy. Visit the new museum (Rs 2) near the jetty before exploring the island.

Corbyn's Cove

Corbyn's Cove is the nearest beach to Port Blair. It's 10 km south of the town and four km east of the airport. There are a couple of places to stay here and a snack bar by the beach.

Nearby Snake Island is surrounded by a coral reef. You can sometimes catch a ride to the island in a fishing boat: it's inadvisable to swim out to it because of the strong current.

It's a long, though pleasant, clifftop walk to Corbyn's Cove from Port Blair. Taxis cost about Rs 40 each way.

Sippighat Farm

On the road to Wandoor, 15 km from Port Blair, is the government experimental farm, where tour groups often stop. New types of spices, such as cinnamon, pepper, nutmeg and cloves, are being tested here.

Wandoor

The Mahatma Gandhi National Marine Park at Wandoor covers 280 sq km and comprises 15 islands. The diverse scenery includes mangrove creeks, tropical rainforest and reefs supporting 50 types of coral. Boats leave from Wandoor village, which is 29 km south-west of Port Blair, at around 10 am (daily except Monday) for visits to Jolly Buoy or Red Skin Islands. Although it's well worth going along to see the coral (they usually have a few snorkels for hire) only a couple of hours are spent at the islands. It is very frustrating to get to such a stunningly beautiful place only to have to leave so soon.

The trip costs Rs 75 (Rs 50 in the low season when boats go only as far as Red Skin). An entry permit (Rs 2) for the park must first be purchased at the kiosk by the jetty. One km west of the jetty is the Andaman & Nicobar Diving Society (see Snorkelling & Scuba Diving at the start of this chapter).

You can reach Wandoor by bus from Port Blair (Rs 4.75, 1½ hours) or by joining a tour. There are a number of good, sandy beaches at Wandoor, but you should take care not to walk on the coral exposed at low

tide. Part of this reef has, unfortunately, already been damaged.

Chiriya Tapu

Thirty km south of Port Blair is Chiriya Tapu, a tiny fishing village with beaches and mangroves. It's possible to arrange boats from here to Cinque Island. There's a beach a couple of km south of Chiriya Tapu which has some of the best snorkelling in the area. There's a bus to the village every two hours from Port Blair (Rs 4.75, 1½ hours).

OTHER ISLANDS

The A&N Tourism Department has targeted half a dozen beaches for development but the tourist infrastructure is currently very limited and you shouldn't expect too much. Until the tourist complexes in these places are built, the only other accommodation is in PWD or Forest Guest Houses (typically Rs 60 per bed in a double room). These should be reserved in advance in Port Blair, either at the Andaman PWD (near Hotel Shompen) or the Forest Department in Haddo.

Some people bring tents and camp out on the beaches. In Port Blair, you can rent two-person tents for Rs 40 per day from the Andaman Teal House. If you do camp, make sure you burn or bury your rubbish.

Havelock Island

Fifty-four km north-east of Port Blair, Havelock covers 100 sq km and is inhabited by Bengali settlers. There are picture-postcard white-sand beaches, turquoise waters, and good snorkelling. Although there are coral reefs, it's the marine life here – dolphins, turtles and very large fish – that make it interesting.

Only the northern third of the island is settled, and each village is referred to by a number. Boats dock at the jetty at No 1; the main bazaar is a couple of km south at No 3.

Having your own transport is useful – bring a bike from Port Blair or rent one for Rs 30 per day in No 3 village or Rs 40 from the paan shop outside the entrance to the Dolphin Yatri Niwas. There's a local bus which connects the villages on an hourly circuit but it doesn't currently run to No 7 beach, a one-hour walk west over the hill from No 6 village. The tourist bus is a rip-off at Rs 10.

Places to Stay & Eat The *Dolphin Yatri Niwas Complex* offers pleasant accommodation in cottages beside a secluded beach. There's no snorkelling here though. Charges for foreigners are Rs 300 for an ordinary double, Rs 400 for a deluxe room and Rs 800 for an air-con double, all with bath attached. Indians pay half these prices. You need to make a reservation in advance at the A&N tourist office in Port Blair. Good but basic meals are served by the friendly restaurant staff.

A&N tourism's *Tent Resort*, beside No 7 beach, has eight roomy tents (twin beds) set up under the trees. They cost Rs 100 for a double and should be reserved at the tourist office in Port Blair. There's a couple of toilets but no washing facilities other than the well. Basic fish thalis (Rs 25) are available, but no drinks other than tea. Some people bring their own tents, and pots and pans to cook on fires on the beach. You'll need iodine or purification tablets for the water. There's good snorkelling here and the idyllic beach stretches for several km. The only drawback is the sandflies, which make sunbathing an impossibility.

Apart from these two places, there's also the *MS Guest House*. It's half a km west of the jetty and has basic rooms with attached bath for Rs 100. *Gauranga Lodge* is the green wooden building without a sign between villages Nos 1 and 3. It has doubles for Rs 35. The bathroom here contains an Indonesian-style mandi.

Getting There & Away Ferries depart early in the morning on Tuesday, Wednesday, Friday and Saturday from the Phoenix Bay harbour in Port Blair for the four-hour journey to Havelock Island. Tickets cost Rs 7/13 on the lower/upper deck. The ferries return from Havelock to Port Blair one day later.

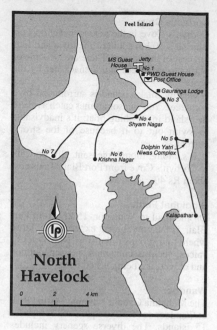

Neil Island

Forty km north-east of Port Blair is Neil Island, which is also populated by Bengali settlers. The Wednesday and Friday ferries from Phoenix Bay visit Neil via Havelock. Until the *Yatri Niwas* is built, accommodation is limited to the two-room PWD *Guest House*. If you bring a tent, camping is possible.

Long Island

This little island off the south-east coast of Middle Andaman has one small village and several sandy beaches that are perfect for camping. The only accommodation is the *Forest Rest House*; though a *Yatri Niwas* is planned for Lalaji Bay.

On Wednesday and Saturday, the ferry from Port Blair and Havelock calls at Long Island before reaching Rangat. Bicycles are the main form of transport on the island.

Middle Andaman

The Andaman Trunk Rd runs from Port Blair

north to Bharatang Island and Middle Andaman, which are linked by frequent ferries. Since this road runs beside Jarawa reserves on the west coasts of South and Middle Andaman, buses carry armed guards. Having lost land to Indian settlers, the Jarawa are hostile to any outsiders and independent travel is inadvisable. If you try to take a motorbike up here you'll probably be stopped at the checkpost about 40 km outside Port Blair. Foreigners are allowed to stay only in Rangat and Mayabunder.

You can get to **Rangat** from Port Blair via the Havelock or Neil and Long Island ferries, or by bus (Rs 33, 5½ hours). There's basic accommodation at the *Hare Krishna Lodge* and in the PWD *Guest House*; a *Yatri Niwas* is planned for Catbird Bay, 25 km east of Rangat.

Mayabunder, 71 km north of Rangat, is linked by the daily bus from Port Blair and also by occasional ferries. There's an 18-bed PWD *Guest House* here. A *Yatri Niwas* is under construction at Karmatang Bay, 10 km north-east of Mayabunder.

North Andaman

Diglipur, on North Andaman, is served by a weekly ferry from Port Blair and daily ferries from Mayabunder. There's a 12-bed PWD *Guest House* and a *Yatri Niwas* is planned for Kalipur Beach, 20 km from Diglipur.

Cinque Island

North and South Cinque are part of the national park south of Wandoor. Surrounded by pristine coral reefs, they are among the most beautiful islands in the Andamans.

Unfortunately, only day visits are allowed and, unless you're going on one of the day trips (Rs 800) occasionally organised by travel agents, you need to get permission from the Forest Department. The islands are two hours by boat from Chiriya Tapu or three hours from Phoenix Bay.

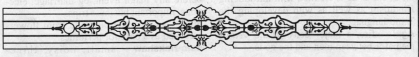

ANDAMAN & NICOBAR ISLANDS

Glossary

Indian English is full of interesting everyday expressions. Whereas in New York you might get robbed by a mugger, in India it will be a *dacoit* who relieves you of your goods. Politicians may employ strong-arm heavies known in India as *goondas*. There is a plethora of Indian terms for general strikes, strikes and lock-ins – Indians can have *bandhs*, *hartaals* and *gheraos*, for example. Then there are all those Indian servants – children get looked after by *ayahs*, your house (and your *godown* or warehouse) is guarded by a *chowkidar*, and when the toilet needs cleaning there is no way your *bearer* is going to do it.

Then there are all the religious terms, the numerous Hindu gods, their attendants, consorts, vehicles and symbols. The multiplicity of religions in India also provides a whole series of terms for temples, shrines, tombs or memorials.

It's surprising how many Indian terms have crept into English usage. We can sit on a *verandah* and drink *chai* (hence 'charlady'), wear *pyjamas* or *sandals* and *dungarees* (which may well be *khaki*), *shampoo* our hair, visit the *jungle*, or worry about protecting our *loot* – they're all Indian words.

The glossary that follows is just a sample of words you may come across during your Indian wanderings. See Food in the Facts for the Visitor chapter for lots more.

abbi – waterfall.
Abhimani – eldest son of Brahma.
Abhimanyu – son of Arjuna.
acha – OK or 'I understand'.
acharya – revered teacher; originally a spiritual guide or preceptor.
adivasi – tribal person.
agarbathi – incense.
Agasti – legendary sage, highly revered in the south as he is credited with introducing Hinduism as well as with developing the Tamil language.
Agni – fire, a major deity in the *Vedas*; mediator between men and the gods.

ahimsa – discipline of non-violence.
AIR – All India Radio, the national broadcaster.
Amir – Muslim nobleman.
amrita – immortality.
ananda – happiness. Ananda was the name of the Buddha's first cousin and favourite disciple.
Andhaka – a 1000-headed demon, killed by Siva.
angrezi – foreigner.
anikut – dam.
anna – a 16th of a rupee; it's no longer legal tender but is occasionally referred to in marketplace parlance. (Eight annas are the equivalent of Rs 0.50.)
Annapurna – form of Durga; worshipped for her power to provide food.
arak – liquor distilled from coconut milk, potatoes or rice.
apsaras – heavenly nymphs who distract the sages.
Aranyani – goddess of forests.
Ardhanari – Siva in half-male, half-female form.
Arishta – A *daitya* (giant) who, having taken the form of a bull, attacked Krishna and was killed by him.
Arjuna – *Mahabharata* hero and military commander who married Krishna's sister (Subhadra), took up arms against and overcame all manner of demons, had the *Bhagavad Gita* related to him by Krishna, led Krishna's funeral ceremony at Dwarka and finally retired to the Himalaya.
Aryan – Sanskrit word for 'noble'; refers to those who migrated from Persia and settled in northern India.
ashram – spiritual community or retreat.
astrology – more than mere entertainment, astrological charts are commonly consulted before any major event, eg marriage, elections, important business trips.
attar – an essential oil made from flowers and used as a base for perfumes.
auto-rickshaw – small, noisy, three-

wheeled, motorised contraption for transporting passengers short distances. Found throughout the country, and cheaper than taxis.

Avalokitesvara – one of the Buddha's most important disciples.

avataar – incarnation of a deity, usually Vishnu.

ayah – children's nurse or nanny.

ayurveda – Indian herbal medicine.

azan – Muslim call to prayer.

baba – religious master, father, and a term of respect.

babu – lower level clerical worker (derogatory).

bagh – garden.

bahadur – brave or chivalrous; honorific title.

baksheesh – tip, bribe or donation.

Balarama – brother of Krishna and viewed by some as the seventh incarnation (avataar) of Vishnu.

bandar – monkey.

bandh – general strike.

banian – T-shirt or undervest.

baniya – moneylender.

banyan – Indian fig tree.

baoli – well, particularly a step-well with landings and galleries, found in Rajasthan and Gujarat.

barra – big, important.

baradari – summer house.

basti – Jain temple.

bazaar – market area. A market town is called a bazaar.

bearer – rather like a butler.

begum – Muslim woman of high rank.

betel – nut of the betel tree; the leaves and nut are mildly intoxicating and are chewed as a stimulant and digestive.

Bhadrakali – another name for Durga.

Bhagavad Gita – Song of the Divine One; Krishna's lessons to Arjuna, the main thrust of which was to emphasise the philosophy of *bhakti* (faith); part of the *Mahabharata*.

bhakti – surrendering to the gods.

Bhairava – the Terrible; refers to the eight incarnations of Siva in his demonic form.

bhang – dried leaves and flowering shoots of the marijuana plant.

bhang lassi – a blend of lassi with bhang (a drink with a kick).

Bharat – Hindi for India.

Bharata – half-brother of Rama; ruled for Rama while the latter was in exile.

bhavan – house, building.

Bhima – another *Mahabharata* hero, brother of Hanuman and renowned for his great strength.

bhisti (bheesti) – water carrier.

bhojnalya – simple eatery.

bidi (beedi) – small, hand-rolled cigarette; really just a rolled-up leaf.

bindi – forehead mark.

black money – undeclared, untaxed money. There's lots of it in India.

bo tree – *ficus religiosa*, the tree under which the Buddha attained enlightenment.

Bodhisattva – one who has almost reached nirvana, but who renounces it in order to help others attain it; literally 'one whose essence is perfected wisdom'.

Brahma – source of all existence and also worshipped as the creator in the Hindu triad. Brahma is depicted as having four heads (a fifth was burnt by Siva's 'central eye' when Brahma spoke disrespectfully). His vehicle is a swan or goose and his consort is Saraswati.

Brahmanism – early form of Hinduism which evolved from Vedism; named after the Brahmin priests and the god Brahma.

Brahmin – a member of the priest caste, the highest Hindu caste.

Buddha – Awakened One; originator of Buddhism who lived in the 5th century BC; regarded by Hindus as the ninth reincarnation of Vishnu.

bugyal – meadow.

bund – embankment or dyke.

burkha – one-piece garment used by Muslim women to cover them from head to toe.

bustee – slum.

cantonment – administrative and military area of a Raj-era town.

caste – one's hereditary station in life.

chai – tea.

chaitya – Buddhist temple. Also prayer room or assembly hall.

chakra – focus of one's spiritual power; disc-like weapon of Vishnu.

chalo, chalo, chalo – 'let's go, let's go, let's go'.

Chamunda – form of the goddess Durga. A real terror, armed with a scimitar, noose and mace, and clothed in elephant hide. Her mission was to kill the demons Chanda and Munda, from whence comes the name.

chance list – waitlist on Indian Airlines flights.

Chanda – another manifestation of the goddess Durga.

Chandra – the moon, or the moon as a god.

Chandragupta – important ruler of India in the 3rd century BC.

chhang – Tibetan rice beer.

chapati – unleavened Indian bread.

chappals – sandals.

charas – resin of the marijuana plant; also referred to as hashish.

charbagh – formal Persian garden, divided into quarters (literally: four gardens).

charpoy – Indian rope bed.

chaat – general term for a snack.

chauri – fly whisk.

chedi – *see* pagoda.

chela – pupil or follower, as George Harrison was to Ravi Shankar.

chhatri – a small, domed Mughal kiosk (literally: umbrella).

chikan – embroidered cloth.

chillum – pipe of a hookah; commonly used to describe the small pipes used for smoking ganja.

chinkara – gazelle.

chital – spotted deer.

choli – sari blouse.

chorten – Tibetan word for stupa.

chota – small, spirit drink measure (as in 'chota peg').

choultry – *dharamsala* (pilgrim accommodation) in southern India.

chowk – a town square, intersection or marketplace.

chowkidar – nightwatchman.

Cong (I) – Congress Party of India.

country liquor – locally produced liquor.

CPI – Communist Party of India.

CPI (M) – Communist Party of India (Marxist).

crore – 10 million.

curd – milk with acid or rennet added to solidify it.

cutcherry/kachairri – office or building for public business.

dacoit – robber, particularly armed robber.

dahin – yoghurt.

dagoba – *see* pagoda.

daityas – demons and giants who fought against the gods.

dak – staging post.

Dalit – preferred term for India's casteless class; *see* Untouchable.

Damodara – another name for Krishna.

dargah – shrine or place of burial of a Muslim saint.

darshan – offering or audience with someone; viewing of a deity.

darwaza – gateway or door.

Dasaratha – father of Rama in the *Ramayana*.

Dattatreya – a Brahmin saint who embodied the Hindu triad.

devadasi – temple dancer.

Devi – Siva's wife. She has a variety of forms.

dhaba – hole-in-the-wall restaurant or snack bar. Boxed lunches delivered to office workers.

dhal – lentil soup; what most of India lives on.

dharma – Hindu-Buddhist moral code of behaviour.

dharna – non-violent protest.

dhobi – person who washes clothes.

dhobi ghat – the place where clothes are washed.

dholi – covered litter or stretcher. You may still see elderly tourists being carried around in a dholi.

dhoti – like a lungi, but the cloth is then pulled up between the legs; worn by Hindu men.

dhurrie – rug.

digambara – sky-clad; a Jain sect whose followers demonstrate their disdain for worldly goods by going naked.

diwan – principal officer in a princely state; royal court or council.

Diwan-i-Am – Hall of Public Audience.

Diwan-i-Khas – Hall of Private Audience.

dosa – paper-thin pancakes made from lentil flour (curried vegetables wrapped inside a dosa make it a *masala dosa*).

dowry – money and goods given by a bride's parents to their son-in-law's family; it's illegal but no arranged marriage – and most marriages are arranged – can be made without it.

Draupadi – wife of the five Pandava princes in the *Mahabharata*.

Dravidian – a member of one of the aboriginal races of India, pushed south by the Indo-Europeans and now mixed with them. The Dravidian languages include Tamil, Malayalam, Telugu and Kannada.

dun – valley.

dupatta – scarf worn by Punjabi women.

durbar – royal court; also used to describe a government.

Durga – the Inaccessible; a form of Siva's wife Devi, a beautiful but fierce woman riding a tiger; major goddess of the Sakti cult.

dwarpal – doorkeeper; sculpture beside the doorways to Hindu or Buddhist shrines.

elatalam – small hand-held cymbals.

election symbols – identifying symbols for the various political parties, used since so many voters are illiterate.

Emergency – the period during which Indira Gandhi suspended many rights. Some observers assumed she intended establishing a dictatorship.

eve-teasing – sexual harassment.

export gurus – gurus whose followers are mainly Westerners.

fakir – a Muslim who has taken a vow of poverty, but also applied to sadhus and other Hindu ascetics.

feni – liquor distilled from coconut milk or cashews; found in Goa.

filmee – music or other aspect of Indian movies

firman – a royal order or grant.

freaks – Westerners wandering India.

gaddi – throne of a Hindu prince.

Ganesh – god of wisdom and prosperity. Elephant-headed son of Siva and Parvati and probably the most popular god in the Hindu pantheon. Also known as Ganapati, his vehicle is a rat. He is depicted as four-handed: in one hand he holds a water lily, in another a club, in a third a shell and the fourth a discus.

Ganga – Ganges River; said to flow from the toe of Vishnu; goddess representing the sacred Ganges River.

ganj – market.

ganja – dried flowering tips of marijuana plant; highly potent form of cannabis.

gaon – village.

garh – fort.

gari – vehicle; motor gari is a car and rail gari is a train.

Garuda – man-bird vehicle of Vishnu.

gaur – Indian bison.

Gayatri – sacred verse of the *Rig-Veda*, repeated mentally by Brahmins twice a day.

ghat – steps or landing on a river; range of hills, or road up hills.

ghazal – Urdu songs derived from poetry; sad love themes.

ghee – clarified butter.

gherao – industrial action where the workers lock-in their employers.

giri – hill.

Gita Govinda – erotic poem by Jayadeva relating Krishna's early life as Govinda the cowherd.

godmen – commercially minded gurus; *see* export gurus.

godown – warehouse.

gompa – Tibetan-Buddhist monastery.

Gonds – aboriginal Indian race, now mainly found in the jungles of central India.

goondas – ruffians or toughs. Political parties often employ gangs of goondas.

gopis – milkmaids. Krishna was very fond of them.

gopuram – soaring pyramidal gateway tower of a Dravidian temple.

Govinda – cowherd.

gram – legumes.

gumbad – a dome on a tomb or mosque.

gurdwara – Sikh temple.

guru – teacher or holy person (in Sanskrit literally, *goe* – 'darkness' and *roe* – 'to dispel').

Haji – a Muslim who has made the pilgrimage *(haj)* to Mecca.

hammam – Turkish bath.

Hanuman – monkey god, prominent in the *Ramayana*, follower of Rama.

Hara – one of Siva's names.

haram – prayer room in mosque.

Hari – another name for Vishnu.

Harijan – name given by Gandhi to India's Untouchables. This term is, however, no longer considered acceptable. *See* Dalit and Untouchable.

hartaal – strike.

hathi – elephant.

haveli – traditional mansions with interior courtyards, particularly in Rajasthan and Gujarat.

havildar – army officer.

hijra – eunuch.

Hinayana – small-vehicle Buddhism.

hindola – swing.

Hiranyakasipu – Daitya king killed by Vishnu in the man-lion (Narasimha) incarnation.

hookah – water pipe.

howdah – seat for carrying people on an elephant's back.

hypothecated – Indian equivalent of leased or mortgaged. You often see small signs on taxis or auto-rickshaws stating that the vehicle is 'hypothecated' to some bank or other.

idgah – open enclosure to the west of a town where prayers are offered during the Muslim festival of Id-ul-Zuhara.

idli – south Indian rice dumpling.

imam – Muslim religious leader.

imambara – tomb of a Shi'ite Muslim holy man.

IMFL – Indian Made Foreign Liquor; beer or spirits produced in India.

Indo-Saracenic – style of colonial architecture that integrated Western designs with Muslim, Hindu and Jain influences.

Indra – the most important and prestigious of the Vedic gods of India. God of rain, thunder, lightning and war. His weapons are the *vajra* (thunderbolt), bow, net and *anka* (hook).

Ishwara – Lord; a name given to Siva.

Jagadhatri – Mother of the World; another name for Siva's wife.

Jagganath – Lord of the World; a form of Krishna. The centre of worship is at Puri (Orissa).

jaggery – hard, brown-sugar-like sweetener made from kitul palm sap.

Jalasayin – literally: sleeping on the waters; a name for Vishnu as he sleeps on his couch over the water during the monsoon.

jali – carved marble lattice screen.

Janaka – father of Sita (Rama's wife in the *Ramayana*).

janata – literally: people. The Janata Party is the People's Party.

Jatakas – tales from the Buddha's various lives.

jauhar – ritual mass suicide by immolation, traditionally performed by Rajput women at times of military defeat to avoid being dishonoured by their captors.

jawan – policeman or soldier.

jheel – swampy area.

jhuggi – shanty settlement. *See* bustee.

ji – honorific that can be added to the end of almost anything; thus Babaji, Gandhiji.

juggernauts – huge, extravagantly decorated temple 'cars' dragged through the streets during Hindu festivals.

jumkahs – earrings.

jyoti lingam – the most important Siva shrines in India, of which there are 12.

kachairri – *see* cutchery.

kachauri – Indian-style breakfast of puris and vegetables.

Kailasa – a mountain in the Himalaya, home of Siva.

Kali – the Black; a terrible form of Siva's wife Devi. Depicted with black skin, dripping with blood, surrounded by snakes and wearing a necklace of skulls.

Kalki – the White Horse. Future (10th) incarnation of Vishnu which will appear at the end of Kali-Yuga, when the world ceases to be. Kalki has been compared to Maitreya in Buddhist cosmology.

Kama – the god of love.

kameez – woman's shirt.

Kanishka – important king of the Kushana Empire who reigned in the early Christian era.

Kanyakumari – the Virgin Maiden; another name for Durga.

karma – principle of retributive justice for past deeds.

karmachario – workers.

Kartlklya – god of war, Siva's son.

kata – Tibetan prayer shawl, traditionally given to a lama when pilgrims are brought into his presence.

Kedarnath – a name of Siva and one of the 12 important lingams.

khadi – homespun cloth; Mahatma Gandhi encouraged people to spin khadi rather than buy English cloth.

Khalistan – Sikh secessionists' name for an independent Punjab.

khan – Muslim honorific title.

khur – Asiatic wild ass.

kibla – direction in which Muslims turn in prayer, often marked with a niche in the mosque wall.

koil – Hindu temple.

kompu – C-shaped, metal trumpet.

kot – fort.

kothi – residence, house or mansion.

kotwali – police station.

Krishna – Vishnu's eighth incarnation, often coloured blue; a popular Hindu deity, he revealed the *Bhagavad Gita* to Arjuna.

kulfi – pistachio-flavoured sweet similar to ice cream.

kumbh – pitcher.

kund – lake.

kurta – shirt.

Kusa – one of Rama's twin sons.

lakh – 100,000. *See* crore.

Lakshmana – half-brother and aide of Rama in the *Ramayana*.

Lakshmi (Laxmi) – Vishnu's consort, goddess of wealth; sprang forth from the ocean holding a lotus. Also referred to as Padma (lotus).

lama – Tibetan-Buddhist priest or monk.

lassi – refreshing yoghurt and iced-water drink.

lathi – large bamboo stick; what Indian police hit you with if you get in the way of a lathi charge.

lenga – long skirt with a waist cord.

lingam – phallic symbol; symbol of Siva.

lok – people.

loka – realm.

Lok Dal – political party; one of the components of the Janata Party.

Lok Sabha – lower house in the Indian parliament, comparable to the House of Representatives or House of Commons.

lungi – like a sarong.

madrasa – Islamic college.

Mahabharata – Great *Vedic* epic of the Bharata Dynasty; an epic poem, containing about 10,000 verses, describing the battle between the Pandavas and the Kauravas.

Mahabodhi Society – founded in 1891 to encourage Buddhist studies in India and abroad.

Mahadeva – the Great God; a name of Siva.

Mahadevi – the Great Goddess; a name of Devi, Siva's wife.

Mahakala – Great Time; a name of Siva the destroyer, and one of the 12 sacred linga (at Ujjain in Madhya Pradesh).

mahal – house or palace.

maharaja, maharana, maharao – king.

maharani – wife of a princely ruler or a ruler in her own right.

mahatma – literally: great soul.

Mahavir – the last tirthankar (Jain teacher).

Mahayana – greater-vehicle Buddhism.

Mahayogi – the Great Ascetic; another name for Siva.

Maheshwara – Great Lord; Siva again.

mahout – elephant rider/master.

maidan – open grassed area in a city.

Makara – mythical sea creature and Varuna's vehicle; also a crocodile.

mali – gardener.

mandala – circle; symbol used in Hindu and Buddhist art to symbolise the universe.

mandapam – pillared pavilion in front of a temple.

mandi – market.

mandir – Hindu or Jain temple.

mani stone – stone carved with the Tibetan-Buddhist mantra 'Om mani padme hum' or 'Hail to the jewel in the lotus'.

mantra – sacred word or syllable used by Buddhists and Hindus to aid concentration; metrical psalms of praise found in the *Vedas*.

Mara – Buddhist god of death; has three eyes and holds the wheel of life.

Maratha (Mahratta) – warlike central Indian people who controlled much of India at various times and who fought the Mughals.

marg – major road.

Maruts – the storm gods.

masjid – mosque. Jama Masjid is the Friday Mosque or main mosque.

mata – mother.

math – monastery.

maund – now largely superseded unit of weight (about 20 kg).

mela – a fair.

memsahib – married European lady (from 'madam-sahib'). More widely used than you'd think.

mendi – henna; ornate henna patterns painted on women's hands and feet for important festivals, particularly in Rajasthan. Beauty parlours and bazaar stalls will do it for you.

Meru – mythical mountain found in the centre of the earth; on it is Swarga, the heaven of Indra.

mihrab – *see* kibla.

mithuna – pairs of men and women; often seen in temple sculpture.

Moghul – alternative spelling for Mughal. The Muslim dynasty of Indian emperors from Babur to Aurangzeb.

Mohini – Vishnu in his female incarnation.

moksha – salvation.

momos – Tibetan fried dumplings with vegetables or meat.

monsoon – rainy season between June and October.

morcha – mob march or protest.

mudra – ritual hand movements used in Hindu religious dancing.

muezzin – one who calls Muslims to prayer from the minaret.

mullah – Muslim scholar, teacher or religious leader.

mund – village (eg Ootacamund).

munshi – writer, secretary or teacher of languages.

nadi – river.

Naga – mythical snake with a human face; a person from Nagaland in north-east India.

namaz – Muslim prayers.

namkin – prepackaged spicy nibbles.

Nanda – the cowherd who raised Krishna.

Nandi – bull, vehicle of Siva. Nandi's images are usually found at Siva temples.

Narasimha (Narsingh) – man-lion incarnation of Vishnu.

Narayan – an incarnation of Vishnu the creator.

Nataraja – Siva as the cosmic dancer.

nautch girls – dancing girls; a nautch is a dance.

nawab – Muslim ruling prince or powerful landowner.

Naxalites – ultra-leftist political movement. Began in Naxal Village, West Bengal, as a peasant rebellion. Characterised by extreme violence. Still exists in Uttar Pradesh, Bihar and Andhra Pradesh.

Nilakantha – form of Siva. His blue throat is a result of swallowing poison that would have destroyed the world.

nilgai – antelope.

nirvana – the ultimate aim of Buddhist existence, final release from the cycle of existence.

niwas – house, building

nizam – hereditary title of the rulers of Hyderabad.

noth – the Lord (Jain).

NRI – Non-Resident Indian, the sub-continent's version of Overseas Chinese and of equal economic importance for modern India.

nullah – ditch or small stream.
numda – Rajasthani rug.

Om – sacred invocation representing the absolute essence of the divine principle. For Buddhists, if repeated often enough with complete concentration, it should lead to a state of emptiness.

pacha – green, pure.
padma – lotus.
padyatra – 'foot journey' made by politicians to raise support at the village level.
pagoda – Buddhist religious monument composed of a solid hemisphere topped by a spire, containing relics of the Buddha; also known as a dagoba, stupa or chedi.
pakoras – bite-size pieces of vegetable dipped in chickpea-flour batter and deep fried.
palanquin – box-like enclosure carried on poles on four men's shoulders; the occupant sits inside on a seat.
Pali – derived from Sanskrit; the original language in which the Buddhist scriptures were recorded. Scholars still refer to the original Pali texts.
palia – memorial stone.
palli – village.
pan – betel nut and leaves plus chewing additives such as lime.
pandit – expert or wise person. Sometimes used to mean a bookworm.
Parasurama – Rama with the Axe; the sixth incarnation of Vishnu.
Parsi – adherent of the Zoroastrian faith.
Parvati – the Mountaineer; another form of Siva's wife.
peepul – fig tree, especially a bo tree.
peon – lowest grade clerical worker.
pice – a quarter of an anna.
pinjrapol – animal hospital maintained by Jains.
POK – Pakistan Occupied Kashmir.
pradesh – state.
pranayama – study of breath control.
prasad – food offering.
puja – literally: respect; offering or prayers.
pukkah – proper; very much a Raj-era term.
punkah – cloth fan, swung by pulling a cord.

Puranas – set of 18 encyclopaedic Sanskrit stories, written in verse, relating to the three gods, dating from the period of the Guptas (5th century AD).
purdah – custom among some Muslims of keeping women in seclusion.
puri – flat pieces of dough that puff up when deep fried.

qila – fort.

Radha – the favourite mistress of Krishna when he lived as Govinda (or Gopala) the cowherd.
raga – any of several conventional patterns of melody and rhythm that form the basis for freely interpreted compositions.
railhead – station or town at the end of a railway line; termination point.
raj – rule or sovereignty.
raja – king.
Rajput – Hindu warrior castes, royal rulers of central India.
rakhi – amulet.
Rama – seventh incarnation of Vishnu. His life story is the central theme of the *Ramayana*.
Ramayana – the story of Rama and Sita and their conflict with Ravana. One of India's most well-known legends, it is retold in various forms throughout almost all South-East Asia.
rangoli – a chalk design.
rani – wife of a king.
ras gullas – sweet little balls of cream cheese flavoured with rose water.
rasta roko – roadblock for protest purposes.
rath – temple chariot or car used in religious festivals.
rathas – rock-cut Dravidian temples at Mahabalipuram.
Ravana – demon king of Lanka (modern-day Sri Lanka). He abducted Sita, and the titanic battle between him and Rama is told in the *Ramayana*.
rawal – nobleman.
rickshaw – small, two-wheeled passenger vehicle. Only in Calcutta and one or two hill stations do the old human-powered rick-

shaws still exist. Bicycle rickshaws are more widely used.

Rig-Veda – the original and longest of the four main *Vedas*, or holy Sanskrit texts.

rishi – originally a sage to whom the hymns of the *Vedas* were revealed; these days any poet, philosopher or sage.

road – railway town which serves as a communication point to a larger town off the line, eg, Mt Abu and Abu Road, Kodaikanal and Kodai Road.

Rukmini – wife of Krishna; died on his funeral pyre.

sabzi – curried vegetables.

sadar – main.

sadhu – ascetic, holy person, one who is trying to achieve enlightenment; usually addressed as 'swamiji' or 'babaji'.

sagar – lake, reservoir.

sahib – 'lord', title applied to any gentleman and most Europeans.

Saivaite (Shaivaite) – follower of Lord Siva.

Saivism – the worship of Siva.

salai – road.

salwar – trousers worn by Punjabi women.

samadhi – an ecstatic state, sometimes defined as 'ecstasy, trance, communion with God'. Also a place where a holy man has been cremated; usually venerated as a shrine.

sambar – deer.

sangam – meeting of two rivers.

Sankara – Siva as the creator.

sanyasin – like a sadhu.

Saraswati – wife of Brahma, goddess of speech and learning; usually seated on a white swan, holding a veena (a stringed instrument).

Sati – wife of Siva. Became a sati ('honourable woman') by immolating herself. Although banned more than a century ago, the act of sati is occasionally performed.

satsang – discourse by a swami or guru.

satyagraha – non-violent protest involving a fast, popularised by Gandhi. From Sanskrit, literally: insistence on truth.

Scheduled Castes – official term for Untouchables or Dalits.

sepoy – formerly an Indian solider in British service.

serai – accommodation for travellers. Caravanserai catered to camel caravans.

shakti – creative energies perceived as female deities; devotees follow the cult of Shaktism.

shikar – hunting expedition.

shikara – gondola-like boat used on Srinagar's lakes in Kashmir.

shirting – the material shirts are made from.

shola – virgin forest.

sikhara – Hindu temple-spire or temple.

singh – literally: lion; name of the Rajput caste and adopted by Sikhs as a surname.

sirdar (sardar) – leader or commander.

Sita – in the *Vedas* the goddess of agriculture. More commonly associated with the *Ramayana*, in which Sita, Rama's wife, is abducted by Ravana and carted off to Lanka.

sitar – Indian stringed instrument.

Siva – (Shiva) the destroyer; also the Creator, in which form he is worshipped as a *lingam* (a phallic symbol).

Skanda – another name for Kartikiya, the god of war.

sonf – aniseed seeds; come with the bill after a meal and used as a digestive.

soma – intoxicating drink derived from the juice of a plant and which features prominently in the *Rig-Veda*. Raised to the status of a deity for its power to heal, provide wealth and impart immortality. In the *Puranas* it symbolises the moon.

sonam – karma built up in successive reincarnations.

sri (sree, shri, shree) – honorific; these days the Indian equivalent of Mr or Mrs.

stupa – *see* pagoda.

Subhadra – Krishna's incestuous sister.

Subrahmanya – another name for Kartikiya, god of war.

sudra – low Hindu caste.

sufi – ascetic Muslim mystic.

suiting – the material suits are made from.

Surya – the sun; a major deity in the *Vedas*.

sutra – string; a list of rules expressed in verse. Many exist, the most famous being the *Kama Sutra*.

swami – title given to initiated monks; means 'lord of the self'. A title of respect.

swaraj – independence.
sweeper – lowest caste servant, who performs the most menial of tasks.
syce – groom.

tabla – a pair of drums.
taluk – district.
tank – reservoir.
Tantric Buddhism – Tibetan-Buddhism with strong sexual and occult overtones.
tatty – woven grass screen which is soaked in water and hung outside windows in the hot season to cool the air.
tempo – noisy three-wheeler public transport vehicle; bigger than an auto-rickshaw.
thakur – Hindu caste.
thali – traditional south Indian and Gujarati 'all-you-can-eat' vegetarian meal.
thanka – rectangular Tibetan painting on cloth.
Theravada – small-vehicle Buddhism.
thiru – holy.
thug – follower of Thuggee; ritual murderers centred in Madhya Pradesh in the last century.
thukpar – Tibetan soup.
tiffin – snack, particularly around lunchtime.
tlka – a mark devout Hindus put on their foreheads with *tika* powder.
tirthankars – the 24 great Jain teachers.
toddy – alcoholic drink, tapped from palm trees.
tola – 11.6 grams.
tonga – two-wheeled horse or pony carriage.
tope – grove of trees, usually mangoes.
topi – pith helmet; widely used during the Raj era.
torana – architrave over a temple entrance.
toy train – narrow-gauge railway, usually for accessing hill stations such as Darjeeling.
Trimurti – Triple Form; the Hindu triad – Brahma, Siva and Vishnu.
Tripitaka – classic Theravada Buddhist scriptures, which are divided into three categories (hence the name the Three Baskets).
tripolia – triple gateway.

Uma – light; Siva's consort.

Untouchable – lowest caste or 'casteless' for whom the most menial tasks are reserved. The name derives from the belief that higher castes risk defilement if they touch one. Formerly known as *Harijan*, now *Dalit*.
Upanishads – Esoteric Doctrine; ancient texts forming part of the *Vedas* (although of a later date), they delve into weighty matters such as the nature of the universe and the soul.

Valmiki – author of the *Ramayana*.
Vamana – the fifth incarnation (avataar) of Vishnu, as the dwarf.
varna – the concept of caste.
Varuna – supreme Vedic god.
Vedas – the Hindu sacred books; a collection of hymns composed in pre-classical Sanskrit during the second millennium BC and divided into four books: *Rig-Veda*, *Yajur-Veda*, *Sama-Veda* and *Atharva-Veda*.
vihara – part of monastery; resting place, garden, cave with cells.
vimana – principal part of a Hindu temple.
Vishnu – the third in the Hindu trinity of gods along with Brahma and Siva. The Preserver and Restorer, who so far has nine avataars: the fish Matsya; the tortoise Kurma; the wild boar Naraha; the man-lion Narasimha; the dwarf Vamana; the Brahmin Parashu-Rama; Rama (of *Ramayana* fame); Krishna; the Buddha.

wallah – man. Can be added onto almost anything, thus dhobi-wallah (clothes washer), taxi-wallah, Delhi-wallah.
wazir – chief minister.

yagna – self-mortification.
yakshi – maiden.
yantra – a geometric plan thought to create energy.
yatra – pilgrimage.
yatri – tourist.
yoni – vagina; female fertility symbol.

zamindar – landowner.
zenana – area in an upper-class Muslim house where the women are secluded.

Index

TEXT

THANKS

Thanks to the following travellers and others (apologies if we've misspelt your name) who took the time to write to us about their experiences of India:

Kimberly Abshoff (C), Nich Abson (UK), Alex Adelaar (C), T Aeschlimann (S), Anil Kumar Agarwal, Bill Aitken, N H Aked (UK), Michael Albers (B), A Alesham (Ind), Ian Alexander (UK), Lynn Allard (UK), Alfred Allen (USA), Kate Allington (UK), Jayme Alpert (USA), Eric Alsruhe (F), Chris Aming (UK), Venci F Anastasov, Helle Andersen (Dk), Jaqueline Anderson (Irl), Lone Anderssen (Nl), Craig Andrews (NZ), Danielle Anna-Villareal (F), H Appleley (NZ), Matti Ariel (Isr), Ann & Paul Ashby (Aus), Ronnie Askey-Doran (Aus), S Aylward (Irl), Dianaen Albert Baas (Nl), Hugh Baertlein (USA), C Baier (D), Tony Bailey (UK), A Bain (UK), Philip Baker (UK), Jeroen Bakker (Nl), Kate Bambury (UK), Sanjai Banerji (Ind), Philip Banks (UK), Monish Bansal (Ind), Sandra Bao (USA), Ness Bar-Nahum (Isr), Barbara & Sarah (UK), S & B Barber (USA), Julie Barlow (UK), Kim Barwick (Aus), Bonnie Baskin (USA), Malcolm Bates (UK), A S Bates (UK), Thomas B Ausch (USA)

Giovanni Bavestrelli (I), Tanya Baxter (UK), Susila Baybars, Blue Bayer (USA), Josselin Beaulicu (C), Angela Beck (UK), P J N M Beehmans (Nl), Mark Behan (USA), Georgina Benison (UK), Richard Bergmans (Nl), Roberto Bergoglio (I), Jill Berlin), Isabelle Bermijn (B), Annette Berther (D), Michael Berube (C), Marlies Beschorner (UK), C N Beucheker (Nl), Dr Naresh Bhandari (Ind), Dr G C Bhandari (Ind), Mrs Rita Bhasin (Ind), Suresh Bhasin (Ind), Amar Bhavan (Ind), A Biedermann (CH), Fay Bien Ent (USA), Belinda Bigold (C), Valerie Birt (UK), Oliver Black (UK), Andrew Black (Aus), David Black (UK), Mark Blackburn (UK), Helen Blackburn (UK), Trevor Blake (C), A Block (B), Prof Abraham Blum (Isr), Sue Bluteau (UK), Brian Bogle (Aus), Robert E Bogner (Aus), Ulla Bogun (D), Denny Bohn (CH), Rosita Boland (Irl), Pierre Bonneau (F), Mrs A Booth (UK), Livio Bortoluzzi (I), Kathy Bortsch (Aus), Tony Bostock (D), Julian Boswell (UK), Jeff Boswell (UK), Mr J M, Boswell), I J Botter (Nl), Helen Bowe (UK), Steve Bowler (UK), Dominic Bowles (UK), Dani Bowles (UK), David Boyall (Aus), Edmond Boyd (C), Julie Brace (UK), Jane Bredna (USA), Todd Breier (USA), Paul Brennan (UK), Kristen Briguglio (Dk), Christopher P Britto (Ind), John Broadbut (UK), Clive Brodier (Aus), Janet Brookes (NZ), Simon Broughton (UK), James Brown (UK), Anne Bruce (UK), Giampadlo Brunazzo (UK), Roberto Bruneri (I), Matt Brunner (Aus), William Buchanan (USA), Birgit Buchel (CH), O Budwilowitz (Nl), R J M Buisman (Nl), Lylies

Bungalow (UK), Nieves Burgos (Sp), Caroline Bushell (UK), Peter Busschers (Nl), Joyce & Len Butcher (UK), Pam Buthwell (UK), Steve Butler (UK), Ashley Butterfield (USA), Pam Buttwell (UK), Mrs Lawrence Buytaert (F), Denise Caignon (USA), Henry Caldwell (USA), J Patrick Caldwell (USA), Stephen Calero (Aus), D I Callaghan (UK), John Cambridge (NZ), Claire Campbell (UK), Janet Campbell (Aus), Fiona Campbell Fraser (UK), P A Carey (Aus), Janet Carlsson (UK), Lisa & Maggie Carpenter (USA), Geoff Carr (USA), John Carr (UK), R Carroll (USA), Cheryl Carruth (USA), Ethan Casey (T), Robin Chakrabarti (UK), Karina Chan (HK), Dr Gerard Chaouat (F), Andy Chaplin (UK), Deirdre Chapman (UK), Rob Chapman (Aus), Gerard Chaquat (F), Martin Charlton (UK), S W Chastain), Jan & Pilu Chauhan (UK), Toby Cheesman (UK), Dr Oby J Cherian (Ind), R R Chisholm (UK), Rosalyn Chissick (UK), Ik Wei Chong (Sin), Gong Yee Choon (Sin), Dr Sushanta Roy Choudhury (Ind) Ashok Chowdhury (UK), Jean Christelow (UK), Peter Christensen (C), David Christian (UK), Schwitzer Christoph (A), Friederike Cichon (D), Netty Clanys (Nl), Ruth Clapp (Aus), Rosemary Clark), Jennifer Clark-Ward (UK), Alan Clarke (UK), Ms C M E Clayton (UK), Leo De Clercq (B), Eugene Clerkin (UK), Rowan Cobelli (UK), Melanie Cochrane (C), Lisa Cole (UK), Sharon Collins (Aus), Stephen Collinson (Aus), Sandra Connan (UK), John Connolly (Aus), David Constable (UK), Paul Cook (Aus), Timothie Cook (UK), Tim Cooper (Aus), Annette & Joe Coppola (Aus), Claire Cornish (UK), Tara Corry (UK), William Cox, Oricina Coyoacan (Mex), Kate Cracknell (UK), Patricia Craig-Jones (UK), Michael Crawshaw (UK), Carlos Cremers (Nl), Thomas Crisman (USA), Lorna Cross (UK), Charles & Keva Crouch (Aus), Jan Currell (UK), Peter Cvjetan, Nicole Cyron

Olivier D'Hose (B), Thais da Rosa Monroy (USA), Sanjay Dabas (Ind), Michael Daffin (UK), A Damasceno (Bra), Carol Darby (Irl), Jane Darling (UK), Peach Darvall (Aus), Subrata Das (Ind), Mr S Davern (UK), Abi Davey (UK), Mark C Davidar, Frank Davidson (Aus), Zubin D Davierwalla (Ind), Greg Davis (C), Hans Davtzenberg (Nl), Rob & Carol Dawkins (Aus), Lydia Dawson (UK), Frederic de Beil (B), Brenda de Boer (Nl), Dorianne de Groot (Nl), Martha De Jong (Nl), L De Wendt (B), David De Wit (Aus), Frank de Zwart (Nl), Terry Deane (UK), Roisin Deane (Ire), Petra Deij (Nl), Jan Deknatel (Nl), Sabrina & Wade Delashmutt (USA) Johan den Drijver (Nl), Dirk Denis (B), Don Derkson (C), Alex Derom (B), Scott Dessain (USA), Walter Deurwaarder (Nl), Bert Karel Deuten (Nl), K Devaraj (Ind), Catherine Devlin (Irl), Mari Devlin (USA), Parvez Dewan, Dr Shymal Dhar (C), Raj Dhoria (Ind), E Didier (B), Keila Diehl (USA), Frank Diehr (D), Wolfgang Dietrich (D), Sandra Dijk (Nl), Iris Dijkstr

(Nl), Spiros Dionysopoulos (Gr), G Divecha (UK), Tim Dixon (UK), Catherine Dobson (UK), Christiane Doering-Saad (UK), Ann Doerschug (USA), Brownie Dog (Aus), Joe Doherty (Aus), Tsering Dolkar (Ind), Anthony Donfurg (UK), Anton van Dongen (Nl), Erborsteria Doram (I), Ivan Doutt, Mr M J Dowling (UK), Miss S J Dowling (UK), A B S Mitchell (UK), Manuel Drees (USA), David Drinkall (Aus), Fiona Druisy (UK), David Drun (Ire), D Dubbin (UK), S P & Sons Dubey (Ind), Emma Duffy (UK), Tony Duffy (UK), Anthony Duffy (UK), Melanie Dugdale (Aus), Jo-anna Duncalf (UK), Lachlan Duncan (Aus), Ms J Dunn (UK), A Dunne, Dianna Dusseault (UK), Raj Kumar Dutt (Ind), Craig Duxbury (USA), Arun Dwarkadas (Ind), Jacob Dyppel (D), Sue Easton (UK), Mr D Eastwood (UK), Stephen Edwards, Mr R Edwards (UK), Martina Ehreche (D), Muna El Naggar (D), Otis Elfert (D), Jost Elliesen (D), Caroline Ellis (UK), Steve Ellison (UK), Ulrich Elsner (D), Derek Emson (UK), David Endicott (UK), Louise Etheridge (UK), Tim Evans (UK), Jonathan Evans (USA), Eric Ezechieli (I), Susan Fairey (NZ), Ursula Fait (I), Lorcan Farrelly (UK), Chris Feierabend (USA), Stefan Fellner (D), Ben Fender (UK), Mark Ferjulian (USA), Lyn Fernandes, Vickie Ficklin (USA), John Filby (HK), Jean-Pierre Filiu (USA), Mark Finlayson (UK), Scott Finneran (USA), Hugh Finsten (C), Vera Fischer (CH), Barry J Fish, Jim Fisher (USA), Patrick Fitz-Gerald (UK), David Fitzgerald (UK), Kirsten Flemming (Dk), Ann Fletcher (UK), Sally Flint (UK), Sue Flynn (Aus), Elizabeth Flynn (Aus), Julie, Fooks (UK), L Foote (USA), Lucy Ford (UK), David Forrest (UK), Alan Fox (UK), Samantha Fox (UK), Ben Fox (USA), Tessa Fox (UK), Peter & Merran Fraenkel (UK), Lucy France (Aus), Samantha Francis (UK), Simone Fraser (Aus), Leslie Freilich (Ind), Nathaniel Frey (USA), Krista Friebel (C), Emma Fung (HK), Paola Furlanetto (I), Catherine Fuss (B), Lorraine Fussey, Jonathan Gabriel (UK), Alec Gagineaux (CH), Jane Galbraith (UK), Mrs E Gardner (CH), Roger Garin-Michaud (Aus), B Garros (Fra), Ian Garson (UK), Ben Garson (USA), Ian Gateley (UK), Surendra Gehlot (Ind), Gina Geiger (D), Gunfried Geiger (D), Marietye Geverinh (Nl), P Ghirga (I), John Gibson (Aus), Lillian & Noel Gibson (Ire), Maria L Gielbert (Nl), Torguet Gilbert (F), Vinai Gillette (USA), Dr Barbieri Giovanni (I), Mark Gipson (UK), Fredenque Girard (F), Nick Gladding (UK), Sabine Gladik (D), N Glaser (USA), Roma Glassl, Mark Gleaves (USA), Ginette Godling (NZ), Ravi Prakesh Goel (Ind), B Gohil (USA), Liz Goodger (UK), Jim Goodson, H J M Goossens (Nl), Mrs S Gopalkrishnan (UK), Guy Gordon (UK), Wolf Gotthilf (D), Lois D Gottlieb (USA), Cor Goudriaan (Nl), Nathalie Gould (UK), Annabel Gouldsworthy (UK), Liza Graae (S), Steffen ___ (D), Sandra Graham (USA), Jim Graham ___, ___her Grange (UK), Dr Travers Grant (UK), ___ves (UK), David Greenfield (UK), Janelle

Gretney (Aus), Jay Griffiths (UK), Divad Griffs (UK), Thomas Grimm (D), Stanley Grossman (UK), Malte Grubitzsch (D), E Gruenwald (UK), W H C Grumitt (UK), Clare Gryce (Aus), Mary Gubser (D), Terje Gudmestad (N), Manuel Guillen (Sp), Mohan Gunatilake (Aus), Jenni Gunn (Aus), A L Gupta (Ind), Govind Gupta (Ind), Ashok Gupta (Ind), Aron Felix Gurski (N), Gote Gustafsson (S), C Gyatso (Ind)

Daniel Hachez (B), Doublas Hadfield (UK), Tom Hadfield (UK), Marcel Hahlweg, Tony Hales (UK), D Hall (Aus), Dr John Hall (UK), Gail & Roger Halpin (USA), Fern Hames (Aus), Douglas Hamilton (USA), Karen Hammink (Nl), Keith Handscombe (Aus), Uwe Robert Hanke (D), S Hanlan (C), Nick Hansen (UK), Max Harcourt (Aus), Anna Harod (UK), Philip Harper (UK), Bridget Harris (UK), Bridget Harris (UK), Nils Harrison (UK), Sarah Harrison (UK), Alan Harrod (UK), Colin Hart (UK), Dr Dennis Harty (USA), William Harvey (UK), Cherise Haslam (Aus), Martina Haslauer (D), Jane Hatfield (Aus), Richard Haycraft (UK), Marilyn Hayward (UK), Stephen Heath (UK), Jorn Heinrichs (D), Torben Heinskou (Dk), Jim Henderson (UK), Mark Henry (UK), Michelle Herbert (Aus), Marianne Herrscher, Ronen Herzig, Jenny Hicks (UK), Stafan Hiemer (D), Mrs K Higgins (Aus), Christopher Hill (Aus), Mr M S Hilton (UK), Neil Hipkiss (UK), Susan Hirst (NZ), Mrs Hobson (UK), Leanne Hodges (Aus), Dick Hoekstra (Nl), Dean Hoge (USA), Elizabeth Hoge (Ind), Martin Hogvall (S), Marc & Michele Holland (UK), Hollie Hollander (Nl), Mal Holliday (Aus), Jonathan Hollow (UK), Clive Holloway (J), Fred & Ann Holmes (USA), Don Holmes (Aus), Shelley Honeychurch (Aus), Marty Hope (Aus), John Hopper (Aus), J Horback (UK), Elizabeth Hore (Aus), Petri Hottola (Fin), Silvie Houben (Nl), Bernadette Howell (UK), Edward Hower (USA), Mike & Caroline Howes (UK), Pat Hubbiday (UK), Pat Hubbleday (UK), Shirley Hudson (USA), Dr G Hughes (UK), David & Greeba Hughes (UK), Anneli Huikkola (Fin), W Lutje Hulsik (Nl), Jeremy Humpage (UK), Dawn Humphries (UK), A Hunse (Nl), D Huskins (UK), Ashfak Hussain (Ind), John Huston (C), Richard Hustwitt (Aus), Suzanne Hutchings (UK), Sinai Ilan (Isr), Richard Ireland (UK), Peter Jack (Aus), Britta Jackle (Aus), Lisa Jackson (UK), Alfred M Jacobsen (Nl), Suraj Jain (Ind), Chris & Janet (NZ), Gareth Jarvis (UK), Michael Jauch (D), David Jay (UK), Nicki Jayne (Aus), Mr Jayshanker (Ind), Zena Jenkins (UK), P J Jethi (Ind), Elizabeth Jogel (UK), Dennis Johnson (UK), Arthur Johnson (USA), Tam Johnson (UK), Penny Johnson (UK), Isabelle Johnson (UK), Rebecca Johnson, Robert Johnson (Aus), Capt Rob Johnson (UK), Samuel Johnson (UK), Penny Johnson (UK), Jemima Johnstone (UK), Frank Jolles (Aus), Aggie Jonas (UK), John Jones (Aus), Barry Jones (Aus), Jennifer Jones (UK), Greg Jones (UK), Lynne Jones (UK),

Jenny Jones, Mr C M Jones (UK), Catrin Jones (UK), John R Jones (USA), Jong Peter (Nl) Hoetjes Joost (Nl), Devin & Mark Jordahl (USA), Vibeke Jorgensen (Dk), Benjamin Kahn (UK), Shabda Kahn (USA), Achal Vir Kakkar (Ind), Shaillandra Karanwal (Ind), Alle Kassen (D), T Kasser (USA), M R Kay, Drys Kazmierczak (UK), Pamela Keefe (UK), Keith (UK), Mary Keller (USA), Daisy Kelly (UK), Will Kemp (Aus), Susanne Kempel (Nl), P Kentie (Nl), Alan Kerr (Irl), Susan Kerry (UK), Helmut Kerschbaumer (USA), Tim Kerton (UK), Petr Kharlson (USA), David King (UK), John King (UK), Janet King (UK), Sandy King (Aus), Malcolm King (UK), S Kitson, Markus Klinkicht (D), Jeanne Knott (USA), Jennifer Knowles (UK), Mrs Penelope Kohli, Kiros Kokkas (G), Susanne Kolb (D), Eva Kondla (UK), Angelique Konyn (Nl), Ger Kraan (Nl), Jessica Krakow (USA), Tine Kratzer (D), Johannes Kremer (D), Jerry Kretsch (USA), Merilyn Kuchel (Aus), Matthias Kuhn (CH), M Kumar (Ind), Ajay Kumar (Ind), Manoj Kumar (Ind), Dilip Kumar (Ind), B Kumari (Ind), Saskia Kunst, Kathleen Kurth (D), Anjali Kwatra (UK), L L Allin (UK), J P Laamanen (Fin), Mr & Mrs Lagden (UK), Laurie Laird (USA), E J Lake (UK), Brian Lambe (Irl), Bryan Lane (Aus), Mike Lane (UK), Melanie Langewort (D), David Langley (Aus), Gwenda Lansbury (Aus), Ms P J Large (UK), Beverly LaRock (USA), Cynthia Lash (C), Douglas Lattey (UK), Jens Lauritsen (Dk), Ben & Emma Law (UK), Sophie Lawes (Aus), Aika & Tom Lawrence (UK), Mrs P A Lea (UK), Josef Lechner (A), K Lee, Damon Lee (UK), Tim Leffel (USA), Stuart Legg (UK), C Lemann (Aus), Jay Lennon (Aus), Ina Lenting (Nl), M Lenzen (D), Marie Leslie (UK), Christiane Levesque (C), Randy Levitch (USA), Marella Levoni (I), Patrick Levy (F), Marc Lewin (C), Chris Lewis (UK), Pericles Lewis (USA), Steph Lewis (Aus), Julie Lewis (Aus), Tim Lewis (UK), Jonas Littorin (S), Robyn & Eric Lloyd (Aus), Rob Lober (UK), M Lobich (D), RA Lock (UK), Asaf Khan Lodhi (Ind), Amy Loewer (J), Bob Longworth (UK), Andrew Lonsdale (UK), Chris Lovell (UK), H & R Lowther (UK), Jonas Ludvigsson (S), Dr A Luft (NZ), Barbara Luksch (USA), John Lumley-Holmes, David Lumsden (UK), Juliet Lunn (UK), V P & Patricia Lyles (UK), Santokh Maan (Nl), Barry MacHale (USA), Warren Macilwain (Aus), Don & Michelle Mackay (Aus), Jo-Anne Macnaughton (Aus), Chris Madden (UK), Sangeetha Madhavan (USA), Jan Magnusson (S), Negin & Amrik Mahal (UK), Ravinder Mahoon (S), Amy Malick (USA), Joan & Rick & Alyss Maloof (USA), Ken Malters (Aus), K L Manchester (SA), Carl Mandabach (USA), Susan Manning (Aus), Diego Marconi (I), U Marie-Jose (B), Jane Marison (Aus), Will Markle (USA), Nilauro Markus (Ind), Jody Marshall (C), Rodney Marr (Aus), David Marriott (USA), Julia May Martin (UK), Nancy Martin-Kershaw (USA), Geoff Martindale (UK), Richard & Emele Max (UK), Brian & Janet Mayes (UK), Ingo Mayz (USA), Sue Mazzetti (UK), James McBride (C), C McCafferty (UK), Basil McCall (T), John McCarthy (Aus), Tsgt Wilfred McCarthy (USA), Barrie McCormick (UK), Ken McDonald (UK), Paul McDonell (UK), Mike McEwan (UK), M & B McGreery (IRE), P L McGregor (NZ), Maggie McIlvaine (USA), Dave McKay (Aus), Eliz McKenzie (USA), Carol McKeown (UK), Beverly McLaughlin (USA), John McMahon (Aus), John McRae (F), Dirk McRobb (C), Eileen & John McSwan (UK), Tuffs Meade (UK), Danny Meadows-Klue (UK), Pawan Mehta (Ind), A P Melgrave (C), Joseph Vincent Menezes, Arvind Kumar Menon (Ind), Gunter H Meyer (USA), Guy Michrowsky (Isr), Derik & Michele Midgley (SA), Marco Miersch (D), Elizabeth Miller (USA), Adrina Moriah Miller (USA), Andrew Miners (UK), Andrew Miners, Jeffrey Minker (USA), Robert Mintzer (J), Prof. V Mishra (Ind), Jenny Mitchell (UK), Klaus Moeller (D), Diana Mogoseanu (UK), S A Jhan Mohamed (Ind), Fida Mohammed (Pak), Col J M Mohan (Ind), Rudolf Mohs (D), Jessica Molligan (USA), Sara Moloney (UK), Monique (UK), Ester Montaner-Colome, Rolando Montecalvo (I), Audrey Mooney (UK), Lynda Moore (Aus), Simon Moore (UK), Catherine Morgan (UK), Nicolas Morin (F), Vicki Morris (UK), Kammie Morrison (USA), Laurence Moser (USA), Dr Aurel Moser (A), Jennifer Moss (C), A A & D Mulcahy (Irl), Gary Mullaley (Aus), Dr Bob Mullan (UK), Claudia Muller (D), Angela Mulligan (UK), John Mullins (UK), S Munme (USA), Brian Murray (Irl), Robert Musker (UK), V Muthuswami (Aus)

Arunkumar Nambiar (Ind), P Nanasi (Hun), Mrs Devika Nanda (Ind), Inge Napfle (D), Chantal Nardu (F), Sara & Shane Nathan (UK), Alfred Nathaniel (Ind), Mark Negus (UK), A K Nehru (Ind), Kay Nellins (UK), Jo Anne New (Aus), Jeffrey Newcomb (USA), Fraser Newham (UK), Mr K R Newman (UK), D I Newman (UK), Katrina Newton (Aus), Jeremy Niblett (UK), Henrik Nielsen (Dk), Dan Niland (J), Tony Nolan (Irl), Christopher Nolan (USA), Udi Nori (Isr), Rebecca Norman, Jennifer North (UK), Sakari Nuottimaki (S), Gilbert O'Brien (UK), Stephen O'Connor (Irl), Leonie & Victor O'Donnell (Aus) Mike O'Neill (Irl), J W O'Sullivan (UK), Louise O'Toole (IR), Isabel Oakeshott (UK), Robert Oettel (J), Wim Offermans (Nl), Mikko Ojala (Fin), Catherine Oldham (UK), Dave Oldman (USA), Kate Olley (UK), Peter van Ooijen (Nl), W Kingsley Ord (Aus), Arlene Orensky, John Osajima (USA), Ciaran, Owen (UK), Fiona Owens (UK), Fabrizio Pacifici (I), Dr Stefan Paganini (D), Bill Page, Antti Pakaslahti (Fin), Gautam Pal (Ind), Diane Palmer (Aus), K P Pandey, Satish Chandra Pareek (Ind), Stephen Parker (UK), Jennifer Parrott (UK), Jean-Claude Pasquier (F), Mrs Almitra Patel (Ind), Mrs A Patel (Ind), Peter Patterson (NZ), Miss Pauline (UK

Chris Pearce (UK), Jess Peck (UK), Jennifer Peck (UK), Andrew Peckover (UK), Brian W Peel (NZ), Andrew & Gill Peet (UK), Tina Peitz (D), Elisabeth Pellicaan (Nl), Maria Penhaner (USA), Leonard Penz, Jonquil Perkins (UK), S G Perry (UK), Brent Peters (USA), Dr K Ulrich Petry, Kjell Pettersson (S), Vadim Petzer (SA), V Peust, Andreas Pfeiffer (D), Thanh Thuy Pham (F), David Philips (Nl), Adam Phillips (UK), Tim Phillips (UK), Racel Philpott (UK), Bette Phimister (UK), Cies Pierrot (Nl), Andrew Pike, Marc Piller (CH), Sharon Pinto (UK), John Platt (Aus), R A Platt (Aus), Katrin Plichta (D), Pete Pluhar (A), Michael Podesciwa (D), Betty Port (UK), Jerome Portelance-Dupe (C), Michelle Porter (UK), Hans Portheine (Nl), Susan Potts (UK), Luke Powell (UK), Lyn & Ian Power (UK), Prem Prakesh (Ind), Brian R Pratt (C), K A Prentice, J M Prescott (UK), Jennifer Pretor-Pinney (UK), Lorna Price (Aus), Nick Price (UK), K J Punnathara (Ind), Richard Pyett (Aus), J D Rabbit (USA), K Radhakrishnan (Ind), Sue Raikes (UK), Sivaram Rajan (USA), P Randell (Aus), Lawrence & Rathnavalu (C), L & M Rathnavalu (C), Michael Read (UK), G. Avanija Reddy (Ind), Mark Redfern (UK), Mrs P Reeves (UK), Fiona Reid (UK), Douglas Reid (UK), Hannah Reid (UK), Peter Reid (UK), Saskia Reijners (NZ), Hielkje ReIndersma (Nl), Mandred Reissner (D), Sanne Reys (NL), Helen Rhodes (UK), Melissa Rich (Aus), Ian Richards (UK), D & M E Ridgway (UK), Speranza Righi (I), Liesbeth Rigtes (Nl), Alistair Ring (UK), Jess River (USA), David Roberts (Aus), Audrey Roberts (USA), Nick Roberts (UK), Peter Roberts (UK), J P Robertson (UK), Judy Robinson (USA), Bradley Robinson (USA), Vernon Robinson (UK), Martha Robson (Aus), John & Glenice Robson (Aus), Suzanne Rodinnar (Aus), Wolfgang Roehler (USA), Thomas Roemer (D), Phillipe Roland (P), Niels Ronnest (Dk), A J Rook (UK), Nicola Roper (UK), Thalia Rose (UK), L Ross (C), M Rossano (UK), Eho Rossi (I), Natalie Rutherford (UK), Juliet Rowland (Aus), Vidya Roy (UK), Olwen Roy-Badziak (UK), Dr Sushanta Roy-Choudhury (Ind), Corianne Roza (Nl), Gilles Rubens (NL), Miss S Ruggi (UK), Marielle Rumph (Nl), Sue Rutherford (USA), Catherine Rutter (UK), Lex Rykels (Nl)

Gerard Sabian (F), D Sabu (Ind), Sara Sallaviita (Fin), Christopher Salt (UK), David Salter (UK), Manoj Saluja (Ind), Katia Sanchez (F), Brian Sandford (UK), Frederic Santschi (CH), Marylen Sapduntz-Parvat, Balmand Sara (F), Nadia Saracini (UK), I Saraswati (NZ), Navin Sarin (Ind), Wiggy Sarsfield (UK), H J du Marchie Sarvaas (Nl), Edwin Sasoon (UK), D W Savage (UK), A W Savage (UK), S S Saxena (Ind), Ad van Schaik (Nl), Martha J Scharpf (USA), John Schattorie (Nl), Max Scheffler (D), Heinz Scheifinger ..., Cornelia Schickerling (USA), Janine W ...nnick (Nl), Christian Schneeweiss (D), ...elzer (D), Ralf Schotte (D), R Todd

Schwebel (USA), Stefano Scoddnibbio (I), Madeleine Scott (Aus), Anne Scruton (UK), Deborah & David Scully-Eggens (C), Sea Green Hotel (Ind), Joyce Seagram (Aus), Doug & Elaine Senior (Aus), A J Severs (NZ), Girish Shah (Ind), Guy Shapira (Isr), H L Sharma (Ind), John Sharman (Aus), Tim Sharp (UK), C Irene Sharp (UK), Michael Sharp (Aus), Mark Sharp (UK), Mark/Annie Jone Sharp (UK), Narelle Sharrock (Aus), David & Chris Shaw (UK), Neal Shegog (UK), Dr Lawrence Sheldon (UK), Sameer Shenoy (Ind), Chewang Sherpa (Ind), Chris Sice (UK), Jens-Peter Sieber (D), Nicole Sierens (B), Hans Sigg-Forycki (CH), Roger & Isobel Sim (NZ), June Simon (USA), Paul Simonite (UK), Sharat Sindhwani (Ind), Kulwant Singh (Ind), Surendra Singh (Ind), C Singh (Ind), Sajjan Singh (Ind), Balwant Singh (UK), Simon Singh (UK), Amitoj Singh (Ind), Chandra Bhanu Singh (Ind), Thakur Nihal Singh (Ind), Suryaveer Singh (Ind), Ram Phool Singh (Ind), Avinash Sinha (Ind), Helen Sirkin (USA), Gota Sjolander (S), Susanne Slangen (D), Valerie Sleneeck (UK), Kelli Sliffe (USA), Peter Slowe (UK), Josh Smaller (UK), Andy Smallman, Rupert Smedley (UK), Gerald Smering (UK), Susan Smiley (USA), Rosalie Smith (Aus), Karyn Smith (USA), Josh Smith (UK), Kenny Smith (UK), J Sommerville, Aktar Somolya (UK), G Souriappan (Ind), Marcel Soyer (Nl), Esther Spanjer (Nl), Rosalind Spencer (UK), Mary & John Spraos (UK), Ian Spurs (UK), Dr N Sriram (Sin), Finn Stahl (G), Kim Stalidzans (Aus), Debbie Stamp (USA), Mark Stanfield (UK), Olivia Stapp (USA), Jorgo Stavokopoulos (B), Derek Stephen (UK), Harriet Stephens (UK), Kay Stevens (UK), David Stevens (UK), Cathy Stewart (Aus), Jan Stiebert (D), Greg Stitt (Aus), Peter & Jill Stone (UK), Agathe Stotz (CH), Sarah Stratton (UK), Mike Street (UK), Mark Strevett (UK), Pamela Strong, Berno Strootman (Nl), Pat Stroud (UK), Marc Stuchy (CH), Philipp Studer (CH), Audreas Sturm (Aus), Dr Michael Stuwe (USA), Brian P Sullivan, Brian Sullivan (Ind), Ralph Susenbeth (D), N A Sutcliffe (UK), Dr David Suttan (UK), David Sutton (UK), Charlott Svensson (Dk), Matthew Swabey (Ind), Sabrina & Alain Tacot-Descombes (CH), J Tafelkruijer (Nl), Stefan Tafvelin (S), Francesca Tanca (I), Simon Tanner (UK), John Tanzosh (USA), Roger Taylor (NZ), Garry Taylor (UK), C Taylor (UK), Paul Taylor (UK), Kim Tewhutu (NZ), Tony Thind (UK), Holly Thoissin (USA), Vincent G Thomas (USA), Ron Thomas (Aus), Grant & Amanda Thomson (Aus), Tali Adini Thorne (USA), Edward Thornton, Chris Thornton (UK), Andrew Thurburn (UK), Hilla Thurow (D), Jane Thurston-Hoskin (UK), V Lafleur- Tighe (C), Jeremy Till (UK), Jon Tilly (SA), Douglas Timms (USA), Thomas Tolk (D), Gustave Tomsich (I), Gilbert Torguet (F), Fabien Torguet (F), Doris Toth (CH), Geoffrey Tozer, Sigrid & Bruno Traverier (F), Chris Trehy (NZ), R M & G F Trevella (NZ), Jan

Tromp (USA), Susan Tschech (D), Conrad Tuerk, Jr (USA), Justin Tuiji (UK), David Turner (UK), Rob Turner (C), Emma & Douglas Tweddle (UK)

Sharda Ugra (Ind), Jean-Philippe Umber (F), Paul Unwin (UK), N Vaithilingam (UK), Sten Valling (D), A van Beech (Nl), Andre van Beeck (Nl), Annette van Citlers (Nl), Jens van den Brink (Nl), Kees van den Broek (Nl), Roel van den Eijnde (Nl), Werner van der Meer (Nl), Maria van Dyik (B), Stephen van Eck, Yvonne van Haaster (Nl), Paul van Horn (USA), Paul van Lersel (B), J J van Oeveren (NZ), Peter van Ooijen (Nl), Angela van Ruijven (Nl), Ad van Schaik (Nl), Jos van Sonderen (Nl), Anneke van Wijchgel (Nl), Dominique van Zuylen (B), Veronica Vanzeller (B), Vatche Varjabedian (USA), Hazel Vdlam (Nl), Tania Velisck (USA), Mark Velthausz (Dk), Kate Verghese (Aus), Dr Frank Verheest (B), Rita Verhoef (Nl), Mohanlal Verhomal (Ind), Brett Verney (NZ), Severine Vezes (F), B J Vincent (UK), Diana Vinding (Dk), Jenny Visser (NZ), De Micheli Vladimiro (I), Cees & ArlInde Vletter (Nl), Christian Vogt (CH), Holger Vormauu (D), Amanda Wade (UK), Mr R C Wadkar (Ind), Ramakant Wadkar (Ind), Mr R C Wadkar (Ind), Carina Wagenaar (Nl), Helen Wall (UK), C M Waller, Anne Walton (Aus), Sarah & Pete Walton (UK), Rob Ward (Aus), P W Warmoltz-Bryne (Nl), N Warren (UK), Polly Watkins (Aus), Adrian Watts (UK), Jill Watts (USA), Nicholas Watts (UK), Daniel Webb (UK), Irene Weber (CH), Victoria & Webster (UK), Werner Weick (S), Anthony Wells (UK), Steve Wells (Aus), David Wells (C), Helen West (UK), Jani West (UK), Laura Weston (Gr), Antonia Wettig (D), Rob Whadcock (UK), Chris Wheeler (Aus), Sara Wheeler (UK), Joanna Whicher (UK), Patricia Whippy (UK), Philip Whiteside (UK), James Whittaker (UK), Rick Wicks (S), Marc Wiebemga (Nl), Almut Wieland (D), Jakob Wiener (Nl), Kathleen Wigan (UK), Jackie Wigh (Aus), Royce Wiles (NZ), Phil Willescroft (UK), Carl & Katie Williams (Aus), Matt Williams (UK), Gaye Williams (UK), Reginald Williams (UK), David Williamson (UK), Cypian Williiowski (Pl), Tom Wilson (USA), Mark Wilson (UK), Kym Wilson (UK), S Winfield (UK), Prof George Winius (USA), Nigel Winspear (UK), Cris & Marion Witt (UK), Mathias Witzens (D), Jens Wohlgemuth (D), Tom Wolff (CH), James Wolford (USA), Willie Wong (HK), David Woodburn (Pak), Rebecca Woodroffe (Aus), Lynette Woods (UK), Jemma & Lucy Wordsworth (UK), James Wormald (UK), Phil & Linda Wotherspoon (Aus), Angela Wright (UK), Anne Wurr, Dirk Wyckmans (B), Paul & Fiona Wynne (Aus), Robin Yates (UK), Prithvi Yoganand (Ind), Japan National Youcka (Ind), Joy Young (Phl), Frank Young (USA), Mark Young (UK), Ronen Youtzis (Isr), Sansad Marg (Ind), Gerard Zavadza (F), Gerard Zawadzki (F), Harold Zuberman (C), Joyce & Harold Zukerman (C), Marina Zwittlingen (A)

A – Austria, Aus – Australia, B – Belgium, Bra – Brazil, C – Canada, CH – Switzerland, D – Germany, Dk – Denmark, F – France, Fin – Finland, Gr – Greece, HK – Hong Kong, Ind – India, I – Italy, Irl – Ireland, Isr – Israel, J – Japan, Mex – Mexico, Nl – Netherlands, NZ – New Zealand, Pak – Pakistan, S – Sweden, Sin – Singapore, Sp – Spain, UK – United Kingdom, USA – United States of America